The New York Times 2000

ALMANAC

—•—

Edited by John W. Wright

WITH EDITORS AND REPORTERS OF

The Times

PENGUIN REFERENCE BOOKS
Published by the Penguin Group
Penguin Putnam Inc., 375 Hudson Street,
New York, New York 10014, U.S.A.
Penguin Books Ltd, 27 Wrights Lane,
London W8 5TZ, England
Penguin Books Australia Ltd,
Ringwood, Victoria, Australia
Penguin Books Canada Ltd,
10 Alcorn Avenue,
Toronto, Ontario, Canada M4V 3B2
Penguin Books (N.Z.) Ltd,
182–190 Wairau Road,
Auckland 10, New Zealand

Penguin Books Ltd, Registered Offices:
Harmondsworth, Middlesex, England

Published in 1999 by
Penguin Reference Books,
a member of Penguin Putnam Inc.

10 9 8 7 6 5 4 3 2 1

ISBN 0 14 05.1457 0
ISSN 1523-7079

Printed in the United States of America
Set in Utopia and Optima

Designed by Virginia Norey

Please direct all comments to:

The New York Times Almanac
122 East 42nd Street
New York, New York 10168

CONTRIBUTORS AND STAFF

General Editor
John W. Wright

Executive Editor
John Rosenthal

Senior Editors and Writers
Bryan Bunch, John Connelly, Jeffrey Hacker,
John Major, Allison Paxton Paine, Lincoln
Paine, Patricia Szczerba, Jenny Tesar

Contributing Editors
Glen Gendzel, Alan Joyce, Deborah Kaple,
Jerold Kappes, Michael Kaufman, Thomas
LaRosa, Steven Lichtman, Lisa Renaud

Researchers and Fact Checkers
Alice Finer, Grant Flowers, Blair Sams,
Robert L. Spring, Victoria Vine

Data Entry
Arlene Jacks, Dorothy Green

Composition
NK Graphics, Keene, N.H.

The New York Times
Mitchel Levitas, Editorial Director, Book
Development, The New York Times

Editors
Laura Chang, Alison Cowan, Henry Fountain,
Rob Fixmer, Rick Gladstone, Winnie O'Kelly,
David Stout, Helen Verongos

Correspondents
Lawrence K. Altman, Edmund L. Andrews,
William J. Broad, Richard L. Berke, Ethan
Bronner, Malcolm W. Browne, Frank Bruni,
Adam Clymer, Suzanne Daley, Celia W.
Dugger, Erik Eckholm, Steven Erlanger, David
Firestone, Ian Fisher, Kevin Flynn, Howard W.
French, Jeff Gerth, Carey Goldberg, Michael R.
Gordon, Linda Greenhouse, Steven
Greenhouse, Saul Hansell, Warren Hoge,
Michael Janofsky, David Johnston, Peter T.
Kilborn, Stephen Kinzer, Stephen Labaton,
Warren E. Leary, Jere Longman, Barry Meier,
Steven Lee Meyers, Alison Mitchell, Gretchen
Morgenson, Seth Mydans, Adam Nagourney,
Timothy L. O'Brien, Norimitsu Onishi, Larry
Rohter, Kevin Sack, David E. Sanger, Eric
Schmitt, Deborah Sontag, William K. Stevens,
Sheryl Gay Stolberg, Don Van Natta Jr.,
Nicholas Wade, Matthew Wald, John Noble
Wilford.

Maps
Steve Hadermeyer, John Papasian

CONTENTS

Golfer Payne Stewart, Five Others Killed In Freak Aviation Accident

A Learjet carrying golfer Payne Stewart and five other people crashed into a South Dakota field on October 25, 1999, killing all aboard. Federal investigators suggested that the plane had lost cabin pressure while in flight, rendering the pilot, copilot, and the four passengers unconscious or dead. With no one at the controls, investigators said, the plane remained on autopilot until it ran out of fuel and crashed.

Stewart, winner of the 1991 and 1999 U.S. Open tournaments, was immediately recognizable in his trademark knickers and tam-o'-shanter. He and the other passengers left Orlando at 9:19 A.M. for Dallas, where Stewart had planned to play in a tournament.

But the twin-engine plane departed from its flight path shortly after passing Gainesville, Fla. Pilots stopped responding to air controllers after 9:44 A.M., and the plane started heading northwest. An Air Force F-16 made visual contact with the plane at 11:09 and reported that the windows had been frosted over, suggesting a lack of oxygen in the cabin.

Buchanan Bolts G.O.P. For Reform Party Bid

Calling the two-party system "a delusion and a fraud upon the nation," conservative commentator Patrick J. Buchanan quit the Republican Party on October 25, 1999, and announced that he would seek the presidential nomination of the Reform Party. Directing his fiery invective on both the Democrats and the party he abandoned, Buchanan said he would "not play our assigned walk-on role in their sham election."

Many political analysts had long anticipated the move, and predicted that it would drain ultra-conservative voters from the campaign of Texas Governor George W. Bush, the frontrunner for the Republican nomination. As expected, Bush criticized Buchanan's decision, saying it reflected little more a failed candidacy. In particular, he derided Buchanan's belief that Hitler presented to threat to the U.S. during World War II. Attempting to paint Buchanan as an extremist rather than a serious conservative alternative, Bush said "Pat sees and America that should have stayed home while Hitler overran Europe and perpetrated the Holocaust."

The leading Democratic candidates for president, Al Gore and Bill Bradley, both of whom stood to benefit by Buchanan's decision, were unsurprisingly mum on the issue.

Gunmen Attack Armenian Parliament, Killing Prime Minister, Seven Others

Five terrorists armed with Kalashnikov rifles stormed into Armenia's Parliament building on Oct. 27, 1999, emptied a magazine of bullets into the body of Prime Minister Vazgen Sarkisian, and then turned their guns onto other senior officials in Parliament. Government guards returned fire, setting off a battle in which the Parliament speaker and six others were killed.

The gunmen held 40 hostages overnight while they negotiated with Pres. Robert Kocharian. The next morning, they released the hostages and lay down their weapons. Prosecutors charged three of the gunmen with terrorism: Nairi Unanian, his brother Karen, and their uncle Vram Galstian. The identities of the two other gunmen were not immediately known, nor was the motivation for the attack.

▶ OBITUARIES

Chafee, John, 77, U.S. liberal Republican politician. As Governor of Rhode Island (1962–68) he pushed for anti-discrimination laws in housing and employment before the Federal Government passed them; as Senator (1977–99) he was a leading voice of bipartisanship and a champion of environmental and health policies. Of heart failure, Bethesda, Md., Oct. 25, 1999.

Sarraute, Nathalie, 99, Russian-born French novelist. Author of more than a dozen books, she first attracted attention with *The Age of Suspicion* (1956), in which she established herself as one of the leading figures of the Nouveau Roman movement. Of old age, Paris, Oct. 19, 1999.

▶ THE NOBEL PRIZES, 1999

PEACE

Doctors Without Borders (Mèdecins Sans Frontieres). Founded in 1970, the organization adheres to the principle that all disaster victims have a right to quick, efficient, professional assistance, without regard to the origin of the disaster, national boundaries, or political circumstances. The organization's high level of independence and its rapid intervention wherever there is suffering have called "public attention to humanitarian catastrophes" and helped " to form bodies of public opinion opposed to violations and abuses of power."

ECONOMIC SCIENCES

Robert A. Mundell, 66, (U.S.,b. Canada), Columbia University, "for his analysis of monetary and fiscal policy under different exchange rate regimes and his analysis of optimum currency areas." Although his work dates back several decades, "Mundell's contributions remain outstanding and constitute the core of teaching in international macroeconomics."

LITERATURE

Günter Grass, 71 (Germany) "whose frolicsome black fables portray the forgotten face of history." His epic 1959 novel, *The Tin Drum* addressed the uncomfortable issue of the German national identity through the Nazi era. In later years, he (and his novels) grew even more political, reflecting the far-left politics of Germany's Social Democrat party.

PHYSIOLOGY OR MEDICINE

Günter Blobel, 63, (Germany) for his discovery that "proteins have intrinsic signals that govern their transport and localization in the cell." Blobel also found that many hereditary diseases are caused by mistakes in these signals and transport mechanisms. His research has also contributed to the use of cells as "protein factories" for the creation of important drugs.

CHEMISTRY

Ahmed H. Zewail, 53, (U.S., b. Egypt), California Institute of Technology, "for showing that it is possible with rapid laser technique to see how atoms in a molecule move during a chemical reaction." His discovery of the field of femtochemistry (a femtosecond is 0.000000000000001 seconds), the scientific equivalent of super slow-motion, has allowed scientists to study chemical reactions in extremely intricate detail, and to theorize why some reactions take place and others don't.

PHYSICS

Gerardus 't Hooft, 53, (Netherlands), University of Utrecht, and **Martinus J.G. Veltman,** 68, (Netherlands) Univ. of Michigan, for placing the theory of particle physics on firm mathematical ground by showing how the theory "may be used for precise calculations of physical quantities." Their research has given scientists the theoretical groundwork which they can use to predict the properties of new particles.

Why the Millennium Counts

The following article is excerpted from a New York Times *Editorial from Jan. 1, 1999.*

Purists claim that New Year's Eve 1999 will not begin a new millennium since mankind will not have actually lived through a second thousand-year cycle until midnight on Dec. 31, 2000. Millennium-phobes argue that the whole event has an air of cultural and religious chauvinism, and that the celebration of the 2,000th anniversary of Jesus Christ's birth might be an event of more interest to Christians than Muslims, Buddhists, or Jews.

But if you want to get technical, we actually passed the 2,000th anniversary of Jesus' nativity around 1995. The gap arises from an error in computation made by Dionysius Exiguus, a sixth-century monk who preferred the more humble name "Dennis the Small." Dennis's real aim was to standardize the liturgical calendar, and in the process he created the system of counting years we use today, starting from the year he calculated Jesus was born. But we know now that Dennis was off by more than four years. Herod, who was ruler of Judea when Christ was born, died in 4 B.C., and Jesus' own unrecorded birth must have happened a year or two earlier.

Dennis was probably distracted by his main concern, which was resolving a complicated, bitter and longstanding dispute about when to celebrate Easter. He lived in a time when people fought about calendric issues with great passion but little information, a combination that remains troublesome to this day.

But his creation, however faulty, has endured and been adopted as a secular measurement of enormous power and utility. It has become the standard measure of time for nations that privately prefer to calculate the years differently. Next year will be 4698 in China, 1421 on the Islamic calendar, 5761 in Israel and 2390 to the Zoroastrians in India. But the people in Shanghai, Bombay, Tel Aviv and Teheran will also know that it will be 2000 for the purposes of business, international relations and worrying about the Y2K computer crisis. In the upcoming year, that fact will be the jumping off point for a big planetary party, commemorated by everything from United Nations documents to the marketing of millennial cheese products.

Historians differ, by the way, on how the Western world celebrated the last millennium, but chances are that the reports of hysteria and anticipation of the end of the world were overstated by later writers who felt that was the way the medieval mind ought to have responded to the sight of all those zeros. The zeros, however, were only being used by people in places like India and the Arab world, who were utterly indifferent to the turnings of a calendar adopted by the Synod of Whitby, which accepted Dennis's recommendation for numbering the years in 664. When the year 1000 rolled around in Christian Europe, the few people who had calendars were counting with Roman numerals, and for them, one thousand just meant the year "M"—a tidy but somehow less threatening concept. The year M was greeted in some places on Dec. 25. But others—following another of Dennis's recommendations—celebrated the turn of the year on March 25, the feast of Jesus' conception. Spain and Portugal did celebrate the New Year on Jan. 1, but they were still counting the years from the date of the Roman conquest of the Iberian peninsula.

Even areas that shared a common calendar often did not have enough common culture to take note of any events that happened more than a few miles down the road. People's lives were for the most part defined by the forests that covered most of the continent, by terrors of the road, and the inability to conceive of a world that stretched beyond their own pastures. Travelers who wandered about without armed escort were regarded as deserving whatever dreadful fate befell them. A monk who got lost on his way to Chartres at the turn of the millennium recalled having to cross a bridge after sundown by crawling over the shield his guard placed to cover the holes in front of him.

From a Western perspective, it was in every way a time of groping in the dark. A scholar could yearn to read a certain book without ever learning that it was available in a nearby monastery. A peasant could pass life without meeting a stranger. People had little sense of belonging to a nation, a culture, or any secular group larger than the men and women they could see around them. In China, Constantinople, Baghdad, and Ghana, the citizens were leading different and often more sophisticated lives. But almost no one in Europe could conceive of their existence, let along bridge the gulfs of ignorance, race, and religious hostility that separated them.

A thousand years later, we understand that there are other folks with widely different histories and viewpoints sharing our planet, and that, like it or not, their needs must be taken into consideration. Cynics, pedants, and otherwise unclassifiable grumps may rightly say that next New Year's Eve, we will be celebrating nothing more than the 2,000th anniversary of the point at which we first began counting—five years too late, thanks to Dennis. But the arbitrariness that some may denigrate makes the occasion more universal in its humanness. The things that bind us, however artificial, are worth noting and making a fuss over.

For if we cannot always see into each other's souls, we have at least agreed on what time it is, down to the last millisecond. We all march forward, from history into the future, and we measure the passage by a common system. That is a beginning worth celebrating, an excuse for us all to look back and consider what our trip over the last thousand years has meant. It is the context in which the hubbub over the millennium makes perfect sense to us.

The Oh Zone: Naming the next decade
By Jack Rosenthal

The word of the '90's is probably millennium. It has not always been spelled correctly (n.b. Maidenform's Millenium undergarments). But the Western world is devoting energetic attention to the event, when three historic zeroes click into place. Meanwhile, a practical problem remains concerning the first word of the next decade: what to call it?

The '90's can be characterized in many ways—a decade of unimaginable American wealth, perhaps, or of Balkan savagery or of China's steady emergence. But whatever the label, the '90's have a name, just like the '80's that came before. The decade that comes after still does not, so here's a formal nomination: the '00's, pronounced the Oh's.

The '00's is, for one thing, numerically logical. For another, the rival possibilities fall short. The Aughties, for example, is how people referred to the first decade of this century. Today, that clanks quaintly, evoking a world of corsets and hot water bottles. The Zeroes? That's disfigured for older Americans: to them, it refers to Japanese fighter planes in World War II. The Oh-Oh's? Too timid, implying a fearful anticipation of danger ahead.

The Oh's, by contrast, conveys a positive expectation of wonder and surprise. In that spirit, let me urge its adoption, if not by acclamation then at least by usage. The new edition of *The New York Times Manual of Style and Usage* is silent on the subject. Allan M. Siegal, *The Times*'s style czar and the manual's co-author, with William G. Connolly, wishes to wait and see how popular usage develops. In other words, all who concur in "the Oh's" would do well to vote early and often. The more people who start using the term, the sooner it will win the respect it is, well, owed.

Jack Rosenthal, an assistant managing editor for the New York Times, *originally wrote this article for the "On Language" column of the* Times *Magazine, Sept. 19, 1999.*

MILLENNIUM CELEBRATIONS

Even though purists insist that the new millennium won't arrive until 2001, most of the world is preparing to party on December 31, 1999 anyway. Major cities around the world are marking the event with fireworks, street fairs, music festivals, and more.

The celebrations begin in Fiji, where the 180° meridian runs through this island nation, allowing it bragging rights as the first place on earth to greet the new millennium (though the Royal Observatory maintains that honor belongs to New Zealand's Pitt Island). There will be five days of music and dancing in the town of Suva, or revelers can head to the Fijian island of Taveuni, to mark the moment while standing right on the International Dateline.

From there, celebrations will erupt around the globe. Among the highlights:

▶**New York City.** Every year, hundreds of thousands gather in Times Square to count down to midnight and watch the ball drop from One Times Square. Record crowds are expected on December 31, 1999, for a multimedia celebration that will last for more than 24 hours, complete with live entertainment and a street carnival. Giant TV monitors will allow the crowds to watch peoples from all around the world greet the New Year every hour; as various time zones strike the midnight hour, New York will salute them with indigenous music and giant colorful puppets. Then, the entire crowd will be showered with confetti and treated to a laser show and special effects at midnight New York time.

▶**Boston.** In addition to its traditional First Night celebrations on New Year's Eve itself, Boston will mark the year 2000 in July with SailBoston 2000, with 200 tall sailing ships arriving in Boston Harbor in a gala procession. The entire waterfront will host a massive street fair.

▶**Walt Disney World (Orlando).** The Mouse will celebrate the millennium every day through January 1, 2001, with the major events centered at Epcot. Disney will unveil a brand-new World Showcase pavilion, highlighting the cultures of 20 nations, with interactive exhibits, working artisans, and live entertainment. The Tapestry of Nations will be a recurring street

festival along the World Showcase Promenade with 120 giant, colorful puppets, pounding drums, and blazing torches. Disney is also updating its Innoventions pavilion to highlight new technology, and inaugurating Illuminations 2000, an updated version of its nightly extravaganza, with fireworks, special effects, and lasers choreographed to accompany a special musical score.

▶**London.** London is preparing to throw one of the biggest New Year's events in the world, with million of participants expected to attend. A giant street party with live music will take place along the Thames riverfront, where revelers will see the water lit in a spectacular 60-meter-tall "river of fire" that will travel up the Thames. The British Airways London Eye, the world's tallest ferris wheel, is scheduled to open; this structure promises to transform the London skyline and allow riders views over 25 miles in all directions. And in nearby Greenwich, New Year's Eve will mark the opening of the much-anticipated Millennium Dome, a massive exhibition of technological innovations and futuristic interactive displays, all under a new 20-acre dome.

▶**Rome.** Pope John Paul II has declared 2000 a holy year, and the city has been frantically sprucing up for the event, restoring monuments, buildings, and art treasures and readying itself to host records numbers of tourists and pilgrims. December 31 will be marked with a huge street party, and there are literally hundreds of special masses and celebrations planned for almost every day throughout 2000, in St. Peter's and in other churches throughout the city.

▶**France.** Aside from greeting the new year with a giant street party in Paris, France will mark 2000 with several special events. The Centre Georges Pompidou will reopen after a long renovation with a major New Year's Eve show featuring multimedia displays and a major exhibition on time. The traditional nationwide Fete de la Musique, held in June, will be a special millennium edition called PeripheRock; the beltway around Paris will be closed to traffic and transformed into a huge stage for rock bands and international groups, creating a 20-mile-long music festival. On July 14, 2000, Bastille Day, there will be a 1,000-km-long picnic along the Paris meridian line, running from Dunkerque in the north through the southern Pyrenees. The line will be planted with thousands of trees and flowers for the occasion, and the 336 towns and villages along its length will offer food, street festivals, an air show, music, and more.

▶**Rio de Janeiro.** Rio will host a blowout New Year's Eve party, with live bands playing along Copacabana and Ipanema beaches. The celebration resumes in March, with the world's first International Samba School parade in the Rio Sambodromo.

▶**Hong Kong.** On New Year's Eve, dragon dancers from 18 districts will converge in a spectacular parade at the Tsim Sha Tsui Clock Tower, kicking off a huge variety show with international artists. Penfold Park will be dramatically lit by a showcase display of thousands of Chinese lanterns. Other events include fireworks over the harborfront, the Millennium Cup Horse Races, and street carnivals all over the city.

▶**Shanghai.** Outside the city, there will be festivities at the Great Wall, with a speech by a 100-year-old citizen, a bell-tolling ceremony, acrobatic shows, fireworks, music, and folk-craft demonstrations.

▶**Sydney.** Sydney plans a spectacular harbor and city show, with fireworks and entertainment all day and night on December 31 and January 1. Some of Australia's top artists will perform at the Sydney Opera House in special shows and outdoor concerts.

▶**New Zealand.** Auckland will host the Millennium's First Sail; skippers and crews enjoy a massive party, then depart Auckland on December 28, 1999, to set out for celebrations three days later

at the International Dateline. They'll then race back to Auckland, in a warm-up for the America's Cup, which will be held in February and March. Nelson welcomes the New Year with an all-night rave dance party called The Gathering.

▶**Egypt.** The World Millennium Celebration at Giza will be marked by a "multimedia opera" and the crowning of the Great Pyramid with a nine-meter cap of gold to restore it to its original height.

Significant Events of the Second Millennium A.D.

▶ THE ELEVENTH CENTURY

1001 Pope Sylvester II grants a royal crown to Stephen of Hungary, part of papal policy to found a chain of states in east-central Europe between Byzantium and the Holy Roman Empire.

1030 Ibn Sina (Avicenna) publishes *Canon of Medicine*, which becomes leading medical encyclopedia for centuries.

1040 Chinese develop gunpowder.

1041 Between 1041 and 1048, Chinese inventor Bi Sheng develops movable type.

1054 Cardinal Humbert, delegate of the already dead pope Leo IX, delivers the bull of excommunication of patriarch Michael Cerularius, sealing the final schism of Christianity's Greek East and Latin West, unhealed to this day.

1055 Baghdad falls to the Seljuk Turks, ending the Abbasid Caliphate (which had been founded in 750) and threatening the Byzantine Empire.

1059 Pope Nicholas II establishes the College of Cardinals as electors of the pope, liberating the Church from both the Roman nobility and the Emperor.

1066 William the Bastard, Duke of Normandy, makes good his claim to the throne of England by defeating the last Anglo-Saxon king, Harold Godwinson, in the Battle of Hastings.

1071 In the Battle of Manzikert, the Seljuk Turks under Alp Arslan defeat the Byzantine Empire, destroy the Byzantine army, and virtually end Byzantine power in Asia Minor.

1073 Vigorous reformer Hildebrand is elected pope, reigning under the name Gregory VII (until 1085), soon to initiate the "Investiture Controversy" with Emperor Henry IV, the great struggle of pope and emperor.

1076 The Almoravids, a Moslem Berber dynasty, pillage Kumbi, the capital of Ghana, initiating the breakup of the great trading empire of Ghana, founded in the fourth century and stretching from the Atlantic to Timbuktu.

1085 Alfonso VI of Castile captures Toledo from the Moors. The Almoravids conquer Spain south of Toledo, integrating it into an African Empire centered in Morocco.

1095 Pope Urban II begins crusading movement with dramatic appeal at the Synod of Clermont to the nobility of France to aid the Byzantine Emperor against the Seljuk Turks and to liberate the Holy Land from Islam.

1099 Jerusalem is besieged, captured and sacked by the crusading army, and Godfrey of Bouillon is elected king of a feudal realm. In Spain, the "crusader" El Cid Compeador, dies and Valencia is soon abandoned to the Almoravids.

▶ THE TWELFTH CENTURY

1115 St. Bernard founds the monastery of Clairvaux with 12 other monks, whose austerity draws thousands of followers until by 1153 there are 160 offshoots from Ireland and Scandinavia to Spain and Hungary of the Cistercian Order of monks.

1122 The Concordat of Worms closes the Investiture Controversy in a compromise arranged by Pope Calixtus II and Emperor Henry V.

1127 The Jurchen Jin dynasty conquers northern China, driving the Song dynasty (founded in 960) south to a new capital Hangzhou, effectively dividing China for over a century.

1146 St. Bernard preaches the Second Crusade (1147-1149). Led by Emperor Conrad III and King Louis VII of France, the crusade accomplishes little except the discrediting of the movement.

1152 Eleanor of Aquitaine marries Henry Plantagenet, Duke of Normandy and Count of Anjou, Maine, and Touraine. (When Henry in 1154 becomes King of England, the "Angevin Empire" includes more than half of France.)

1176 The army of the Lombard League of Italian cities decisively defeats the army of Emperor Frederick Barbarossa, the first great defeat of knights on horseback by infantry, heralding the new role of the bourgeoisie in European life.

1185 At the naval battle of Dan-no-Ura, Minamoto no Yoritomo defeats the Taira clan (which had seized power in Japan in 1160) and takes the heraldic title of *shogun* ("generalissimo"), establishing a military capital at Kamakura, leaving the emperor to reign but not rule in Heian-kyo.

1187 Jerusalem falls to Saladin, precipitating the ineffectual but legendary King's Crusade (1189-1192) led by Richard Lionheart, Frederick Barbarossa, and Philip Augustus.

1198 Averroes, last of the great Moslem philosophers of the Middle Ages, dies. Innocent III unanimously elected pope, whose reign is the zenith of the medieval papacy (to 1216).

▶ THE THIRTEENTH CENTURY

1200 Zhu Xi, systematizer of "neo Confucian" philosophy, dies. By combining Confucian ethics and Buddhist metaphysics neo-Confucianism revitalizes the ideological foundations of the traditional Chinese monarchy.

1202 Leonardo Fibonacci publishes his *Liber Abaci* (The *Book of Calculations*) which popularizes a new numeric approach based on the decimal system developed in India.

1204 Moses ben Maimon (Maimonides), greatest Jewish philosopher of the middle ages, author of *Guide for the Perplexed*, dies. His studies of Aristotle exert great influence on Christian philosophers especially Thomas Aquinas.

1204 The Fourth Crusade captures Constantinople and sacks it with ferocity. The "Latin Empire of the East" is established (until 1261).

1206 A Moslem dynasty is established at Delhi after the conquests of Mohammed of Ghur.

1212 Alfonso VIII of Castile triumphs in the greatest victory of the Christian "reconquista" in Spain, the battle of Las Navas de Tolosa.

The "Children's Crusade" is preached by Stephen of Vendôme and Nicholas of Cologne, leading thousands of little children to leave their homes, confident that God would miraculously assure them passage to the Holy Land. Most are sold into slavery in Marseilles.

1213 The brilliant military leader Genghis Khan begins conquest of northern China and then Turkistan to Afghanistan and rules one of the greatest empires in history.

1215 Pope Innocent III recognizes two new religious orders: the Friars Minor of St. Francis of Assisi and the Order of Preachers of St. Dominic, begging orders of poor men who preach the Christian message to new towns and universities.

At Runnymede, King John of England accepts Magna Carta demanded by his barons, an essentially feudal document primarily concerned with concessions to the nobility but containing also guarantees to towns and the Church collectively establishing the supremacy of law over the king.

1234 Successors of Genghis Khan complete their conquest of northern (Jin) China, adding it to their Mongol Empire. The Song dynasty holds out in southern China until 1260.

1242 The Khanate of the Golden Horde under Batu (grandson of Genghis Khan) organize a Mongol state at Sarai on the lower Volga, ruling all of south Russia and reducing the north Russian princes to vassal status—a dominance that will last until 1480.

1254 With the death of Conrad IV, son and successor to Hohenstaufen emperor Frederick II, there begins the "Great Interregnum" in Germany and the Holy Roman Empire, twenty years of disputed elections and contested kingships signaling the end of the Hohenstaufen dynasty.

1258 The capture and savage sack of Baghdad by the Mongol armies of Hulagu, grandson of Genghis Khan, ends the Abbasid Califate established in 750 and establishes a dynasty that will rule Persia until 1349.

1260 The great victory of the Mamluks of Egypt in the Battle of Goliath's Spring marks the end of Mongol expansion, saving Egypt, the last refuge of Moslem culture.

1261 The Greek army of Michael VIII Paleologus crosses the Bosporus, retakes Constantinople, ends the Latin Empire there, and reestablishes a Greek Byzantine Empire.

1271 The second journey of the Venetian traders, the Polo brothers, this time accompanied by Nicolo's son Marco, sets out for the court of the Great Khan in China. Marco's *Book of Various Experiences* (probably dictated in 1297), colors the whole geographic outlook of Europe.

1273 Imperial electors choose the obscure Swiss prince Rudolph of Habsburg as Holy Roman Emperor, ending the "Great Interregnum" and initiating Europe's greatest dynasty.

The last volume of St. Thomas Aquinas' *Summa Theologica* is published; this vast work (which contains the famous five proofs of God's existence) helps to make Aristotle's thought part of Christian theology for 700 years.

1279 Kublai Khan, Mongol emperor and grandson of Genghis Khan, proclaims Yuan Dynasty in China.

1281 As Kublai Khan's great fleet prepares to invade Japan, it is destroyed at Kyushu by a typhoon (*Kami kaze*, or "divine wind"); 4,000 ships are sunk and tens of thousands of soldiers are drowned.

1288 First-known gun, a small cannon, is made in China

1295 Under King Edward I, England's "Model Parliament" is convened; representation of town burgesses and shire knights proves a precedent for calling their representatives along with the lay lords and church prelates.

▶ THE FOURTEENTH CENTURY

1302 Philip IV of France convenes the first meeting of the Estates General representing the upper clergy, the nobility, and the bourgeoisie, a body that is consultative and not, like the Parliament in England, deliberative.

1309 Pope Clement V moves papacy to Avignon in France to escape the warring factions in Rome and to placate Philip IV of France, commencing the "Avignon Captivity" of the papacy (until 1377).

1312 King Mansa Musa accedes to the throne of the immense Kingdom of Mali, a trading state stretching from the Atlantic east to the Niger River, under whose rule Islam spreads through Africa.

1314 In the Battle Of Bannockburn, Robert the Bruce overwhelmingly defeats Edward II of England, securing Scottish independence and establishing himself on the throne, postponing for centuries a union with England.

1320 Ghiyas-ud-din founds the (Turkish) dynasty of Tughluk at Delhi, the dynasty ruling until 1413. Warangal and Bengal are added to a realm marked by just taxation, improved agriculture.

1325 The Aztecs reach the shores of Lake Tezcuco, erecting on its marshes their impregnable capital Tenochtitlan, whence they extend their control over central and southern Mexico. By 1519, Tenochtitlan is a city of 60,000 households.

1336 General Ashikaga Takauji assists emperor Daido II to end the *shogunate* of the Hojo clan, but Ashikaga proclaims himself *shogun*, establishing a dynasty that reigns until 1568. The Ashikaga exercise only shadowy control over the great lords but patronize Zen Buddhism.

1337 The Hundred Years' War, a series of wars between France and England begins, and lasts until 1453.

1347 The Black Death enters Europe, a disaster lasting in its virulent stage for 30 months, in which one-third of the population was exterminated.

1364 The death of Gaja Mada, the architect of the Majapahit Empire, unites all of the East Indies under one monarchy. Under pressure from the competing Kingdom of Melaka and various newly established Islamic sultanates, the empire dwindles to unimportance by the mid 16th century.

1368 A Chinese rebellion, led by a charismatic ex-Buddhist monk, Zhu Yuanzhang, succeeds in overthrowing the alien Mongol Empire, establishing the Ming Dynasty (to 1644).

1378 The Great Schism begins as 13 cardinals of the Catholic Church repudiate the recently elected pope Urban VI, and claim to elect "Clement VII", thus dividing the Papacy until 1417.

1386 Queen Jadwiga of Poland is wed to Jagiello, Grand Duke of Lithuania, the last pagan ruler of Europe, who becomes a Christian and unites his duchy with the Polish crown. The Polish-Lithuanian Commonwealth is created.

1398 Timur (or Tamerlane) of Samarkand, who had conquered Persia, Mesopotamia and Afghanistan desolates the whole Kingdom of Delhi, massacring 100,000 before sacking the city.

▶ THE FIFTEENTH CENTURY

1415 Excommunication and execution of Czech religious leader Jan Hus, who protested papal abuses, sets off Hussite Wars.

1429 Joan of Arc ends the siege of Orleans, drives the English out of the Loire, and escorts Charles VII to his coronation at Reims Cathedral. The following year she is captured and sold to the English, and is burned at the stake for heresy in 1431.

1433 Criticized by the conservative Confucian bureaucracy as a waste of money and resources, the Ming dynasty's maritime expeditions throughout the South China Sea and the Indian Ocean to the east coast of Africa are abruptly cancelled. China thus fails to "discover" Europe.

1434 The Medici family's dominance of Florence begins, as Cosimo, without holding office, determines who should hold office. Known as Pater Patriae (father of his country), Cosimo establishes a dynasty that lasts until 1494.

1440 Johannes Gutenberg (German) introduces printing with movable type to Europe.

1453 After over 1000 years of existence, the East Roman (Byzantine) Empire ends, as Constantinople falls to Mohammed the Conqueror, his army of over 100,000 triumphing over the 10,000 men at the command of Constantine IX, last Roman emperor.

The English are expelled from France by the forces of King Charles VII in alliance with the Duke of Burgundy, ending the Hundred Years' War.

1454 Johannes Gutenberg prints first Bible with moveable type.

1468 Sonni Ah, ruler of Songhay recaptures Timbuktu from the Saharan Tauregs who had sacked the city in 1433. Islam now dominates not only the northern coast of Africa but almost the entire belt of savanna south of the Sahara as well.

1485 Henry Tudor, earl of Richmond, a Welsh military adventurer triumphs at Bosworth Field over Richard III, ending the 30-year long "Wars of the Roses" and founding the Tudor dynasty that is to rule England until 1603

1488 Following the east coast of Africa, Bartolomeo Diaz rounds the Cape of Good Hope at the southern tip of Africa, establishing the existence of a sea route to the Indies.

1492 The married sovereigns, Queen Isabella of Castile and King Ferdinand of Aragon succeed in conquering Grenada, ending Moorish power in the peninsula; and they fund the discovery of the Americas by Christopher Columbus, opening up endless imperial possibilities; they also expel the Jews from Spain, depriving the towns of an important developing bourgeoisie.

1494 The Treaty of Tordesillas between Portugal and Spain, authorized by Pope Alexander VI, divides the world in half. The Portuguese are to have exclusive rights east of the line, the Spanish exclusive rights west of the line. Brazil thereby falls within the Portuguese hemisphere.

1497 Giovanni Caboto (John Cabot) cruises the southern coast of Newfoundland. Confident he has discovered the country of the Great Khan, he establishes English claims in North America.

1498 Vasco da Gama, having rounded the Cape of Good Hope, reaches Calicut on the coast of India and carries home a cargo of pepper and cinnamon. (Six months later Cabral will initiate sending regular fleets from Portugal.)

▶ **THE SIXTEENTH CENTURY**

1509 Francisco d'Almeida, first Portuguese viceroy in the East, triumphs over Islamic allies of Gujerat, center of the native trading empire, in the battle of Diu so thoroughly that his successor, Albuquerque, can control all Indian Ocean traffic.

1517 Augustinian Friar Martin Luther posts 95 theses on the door of the castle church of Wittenberg, attacking the Church's misuse of indulgences and the worldly lifestyle of the clergy, commencing the Reformation, dividing western Christianity into Protestant and Catholic sectors.

1519 Hernando Cortéz, with 600 men and 10 cannon, and with Totonac allies captures the Aztec capital of Tenochtitlan, nucleus of New Spain.

1521 Ferdinand Magellan, sent out in 1519 by the Spanish crown to find a westward route to the

Moluccas, is killed by Philippine islanders. One of his vessels, under Sebastian del Cano, continues westward to Spain, circumnavigating the globe.

1529 Babur, descendant of 14th century conqueror Tamerlane, wins battle of Gogra, completing conquest of the Kingdom of Delhi. A Turk, his family's long association with the Mongols leads his empire to be styled Moghul (until 1857).

1534 English Parliament proclaims Henry VIII and his successors "the only supreme head on earth of the Church of England", the preliminary step to the Reformation in England.

1535 Francisco Pizarro founds Lima, after conquering the powerful Inca Empire.

1536 John Calvin, a young French scholar, publishes *Institutes of the Christian Religion*, and becomes second major leader of Protestant Christianity; helping to create Presbyterian and other Reformed churches.

1540 Pope Paul III gives formal approval to the Society of Jesus (commonly known as the Jesuit Order) founded by Ignatius Loyola and five associates six years earlier. Later they prove to be the chief agent of Catholic reform.

1541 The magistrates of Geneva invite John Calvin to return to the city from which they expelled him two years earlier. Geneva becomes headquarters for the spread of Calvinism throughout Europe.

1542 Francis Xavier, a founding member of the Jesuits, arrives in Goa, India, and begins decadelong missionary work converting tens of thousands to Christianity in India,Japan, and other parts of the East Indies.

1543 *De Revolutionibus* by Nicholas Copernicus (Polish) postulates that Earth and other planets orbit Sun, initiating the scientific revolution through the stimulus it gives his successors.

1545 Pope Paul III convenes the Council of Trent which undertakes the reform of the Catholic Church. Its work of organizational reform and authoritative restatement of doctrine is completed in 1564.

1555 In the Holy Roman Empire, the Religious Peace of Augsburg halts the wars of religion, granting to Lutheran (but not Calvinist) princes and free cities equal rights with the Catholic states.

1556 Akbar, the third Moghul ruler, ascends to the imperial throne in India. His long rule (to 1605) expands and consolidates the empire.

1565 Spaniards, after destroying the French trading post of Fort Caroline, found the city of St. Augustine in Florida, the first permanent European settlement in North America.

1571 The navy of the Holy League (Spain, Venice and the Holy See), under Don John of Austria, engages the Ottoman navy under Ah Pasha in the greatest naval battle of the century off Lepanto (Gulf of Corinth). The crushing League victory makes Spain dominant in the Mediterranean.

1572 Gaspard de Coligny and 3,000 Calvinists are executed in Paris in the St Bartholomew's Day Massacre (August 24). Within three days perhaps another 20,000 French Calvinists are killed. The fourth French war of religion begins.

1587 Shah Abbas I (the Great) accedes to the throne of Persia, the developer of a new infantry and artillery force for expansion against the Turks and a great patron of the arts. His reign is the high point of the Safavid dynasty of Persia.

1588 Philip II's Spanish Armada, a fleet of 130 ships bent on an invasion of England, meets disaster in the English Channel. English and Dutch ships disperse the Armada, giving heart to European Protestantism.

1591 A Moroccan invasion smashes the great African trading Kingdom of Songhay. The old caravan routes across the Sahara dwindle to a trickle.

1598   Henry IV's Edict of Nantes proclaims a formal settlement to the wars of religion in France. French Calvinists are granted the right to public worship and to assemble within their own towns and territories.

▶ THE SEVENTEENTH CENTURY

1600   William Gilbert (English) suggests that Earth is a giant magnet, which is why magnetic compasses indicate north.

1603   Tokugawa Ieyasu is appointed *shogun* in Japan after defeating a coalition of his rivals in the 1600 battle of Sekigahara. He establishes the military capital at Edo (modern Tokyo) and founds a dynasty that will rule Japan until 1868

1605   Miguel de Cervantes' *Don Quixote de la Mancha* is published; a second part in 1615.

1607   Three ships of the London Company carry 120 settlers to the mouth of the James River. The founding of the Jamestown colony is the first permanent English settlement in the New World.

1608   Samuel de Champlain establishes the French trading-post colony of Quebec.

1609   Henry Hudson, an Englishman in Dutch employ, sails up the river later named for him and establishes the claims of the newly independent United Provinces of the Netherlands in North America. Trading posts follow in 1624 and 1626.

Johannes Kepler in *On the Motion of Mars* publishes his findings that the orbits of the planets are ellipses, giving mathematical order to Tycho Brahe's observations.

1610   Galileo Galilei (Italian) observes Jupiter's moons, phases of Venus, and (although he does not recognize what they are) rings of Saturn.

1611   First publication of the King James Bible, considered the greatest English translation which profoundly affects written prose for 300 years.

1613   The national assembly elects Michael Romanov as czar of Russia, the commencement of the dynasty that would rule until 1917.

1614   John Napier (Scottish) describes his mathematical invention called logarithms.

1618   The fervent Catholic Ferdinand of Styria ascends to the throne of Bohemia and revokes the religious freedoms of the Protestants and Hussites. A revolt of the nobility soon escalates into the devastating Thirty Years' War.

1619   Dutch traders bring their first African slaves to Virginia.

1620   Pilgrims, a small group of English Puritans, establish colony at Plymouth in Massachusetts to escape persecution in England.

1623   First publication of William Shakespeare's plays in one volume, called the First Folio.

1628   William Harvey (English) describes functions of the heart and how blood circulates throughout the body.

1637   Shogun Iemitsu completes the virtual extermination of Christianity in Japan with his victory over the Shimabara uprising.

René Descartes (French) publishes his *Discourse on Method*, the first of several volumes based on a system of universal doubt, the foundation for modern philosophy; his famous first principle is "cogito ergo sum" ("I think therefore I am").

1641   The Dutch East India Company seizes the Malacca fort from the Portuguese (established there since 1511) signaling the end of the Portuguese trade empire in the Indian Ocean and its replacement by the Dutch.

1642   The English Civil Wars begin when Charles I decides to defend militarily his royal authority against Parliament's assertion of independent power.

1643   Evangelista Torricelli (Italian) makes first barometer, thereby producing first vacuum known to science.

1644   The last Ming emperor hangs himself when a bandit leader seizes Beijing. The Manchu army, invited to help expel the rebel band, themselves seize Beijing and establish the Qing (or Manchu) dynasty that will rule China until 1911.

1648   The Peace of Westphalia ends the Thirty Years' War that had devastated the Holy Roman Empire. It affirms the sovereignty of the German princes, recognizes Swiss and Dutch independence, extends religious toleration to Calvinists. France emerges as the dominant European power.

1649   King Charles I of England is executed after a trial arranged by a Puritan army and a rump of the Parliament. The army's great general, Oliver Cromwell, rules as military dictator until 1658.

1649   A series of widespread rebellions (collectively known as the *Fronde*) against the determined policies of royal centralization of Cardinals Richelieu and Mazarin breaks out in Paris and lasts until 1652.

1654   Blaise Pascal and Pierre de Fermat (French) develop the basic laws of probability.

1662   Robert Boyle (Anglo-Irish) announces what becomes known as Boyle's law: For gas kept at constant temperature, pressure and volume vary inversely.

The Royal Society is established in London, providing the first systematic means of disseminating scientific information in Europe.

1665   Robert Hooke (English) observes and names the cell.

1666   Sir Isaac Newton (English) describes his invention of the calculus but does not publish it until 1687, three years after Leibniz.

1671   Giovanni Domenico Cassini (Italian-French) correctly determines distances of the planets from Sun.

1678   Christiaan Huygens (Dutch) develops wave theory of light.

1682   Edmond Halley (English) describes comet now known by his name and in 1705 correctly predicts its return in 1758.

Sieur de La Salle, French explorer, caps his explorations by navigating the Mississippi River to its mouth, claiming the entire valley for Louis XIV and naming it Louisiana.

1683   Muslim Turks are defeated near Vienna, by forces of France and Poland, ending their last attempt to establish a foothold in western Europe.

1685   King Louis XIV revokes the Edict of Nantes, closing all Calvinist churches and schools and exiling their ministers. More than 250,000 emigrate and join the resistance to Louis.

1687   Isaac Newton publishes *Principia Mathematica*, giving mathematical expression to his theory of universal gravitation to explain planetary motion, establishing a basis for physics that endures for over two centuries.

1688   English Whig aristocrats accomplish their "Glorious Revolution" by inviting William of Orange to invade England and overturn the rule of the Catholic King James II. Royal power receives a permanent check by Parliament and the moneyed classes it represents.

1689   The personal rule of Peter the Great begins in Russia. He will proceed to make Russia a major military power, to reorganize its political and economic structures, and to make Russia an active force in European politics.

►THE EIGHTEENTH CENTURY

1701 Jethro Tull (English) invents device for planting seeds called a seed drill.

1713 The Treaty of Utrecht closes the 13-year long War of the Spanish Succession. Louis XIV's grandson becomes king of Spain, the English take Gibraltar, Newfoundland and Acadia, and the Austrians gain the Spanish Netherlands.

1721 The Great Northern War which since 1700 has engulfed northern Europe is brought to and end with the Treaty of Nystadt. Peter the Great gains his "window on the Baltic Sea".

1733 John Kay (English) invents flying-shuttle loom, key to the start of Industrial Revolution.

1739 Persian general Nadir Shah seizes the Moghul capital of Delhi defeating the imperial troops of the now fast-disintegrating Moghul Empire. Nadir leaves the emperor on the throne but exacts a huge indemnity and takes all the territory north and west of the Indus River.

1755 Joseph Black (Scottish) discovers carbon dioxide.

1757 Robert Clive and the English overwhelm the French and their Indian allies in the battle of Plassey. French claims in India are practically destroyed. British ascendancy in India begins.

1759 John Harrison (English) designs a marine chronometer (clock) accurate enough to enable navigators to calculate longitude at sea.

1763 The Treaty of Paris brings the Seven Years' War to an end. Fought on three continents, it was the first world war; in Europe a draw, it was won by England in India and America. France loses almost all of its colonies (including Canada) to England.

1766 Henry Cavendish (English) discovers hydrogen.

1769 James Watt patents the modern steam engine, providing humans with a steady source of power and permitting factories to be located in or near existing urban centers.

Richard Arkwright patents the water frame, which takes cotton textile manufacture out of the home and into the factory.

1772 Joseph Priestley (English-American) notes that burning hydrogen produces water.

Daniel Rutherford (Scottish) and several other chemists discover nitrogen. Karl Wilhelm Scheele (Swedish) discovers oxygen but does not announce discovery until after independent discovery by Joseph Priestly in 1774.

1775 In France, the final volume of the 28-volume *Encyclopédie* appears. Edited by Denis Diderot and Jean D'Alembert (with Rousseau, Voltaire, etc.) and covering all the arts and sciences, it plays an important role in preparing for the French Revolution.

1776 The rebellious American colonies meet in the Continental Congress and issue a "Declaration of Independence" from England, beginning the American Revolution.

Adam Smith publishes his *An Inquiry Into the Nature and Causes of the Wealth of Nations,* advocating a laissez-faire approach to economics.

1778 Antoine-Laurent Lavoisier (French) discovers that air is mostly nitrogen and oxygen.

1781 General George Washington with the Continental army and Admiral de Grasse with the French fleet trap British General Cornwallis at Yorktown, Virginia, securing American independence (which will be legally recognized in the 1783 Treaty of Paris).

1785 William Herschel (German-English) demonstrates that Milky Way is disk-shaped group of many stars, one of which is the Sun.

1788 The Constitution of the United States, hammered out in Philadelphia the year before, is ratified by the ninth state (New Hampshire), placing it into operation, with the first Congress meeting in New York the following year.

1789 In desperate need of money, King Louis XVI of France assembles the Estates General for the first time since 1624. Protesting food shortages, economic depression, and heavy taxes, a Parisian mob storms the Bastille prison and marches on Versailles Palace. Members of the newly established National Assembly abolish all feudal privileges and adopt the *Declaration of the Rights of Man and Citizen.*

1791 The French Royal Family attempts to flee Paris, but are arrested in Varennes. King Louis XVI accepts a constitutional monarchy.

1792 The French Revolutionary Wars begin with France's declaration of war on Austria (April 20). On August 10, crowds storm the Tuileries palace, calling for universal male suffrage and a new constitution. France's new National Convention meets on September 21, abolishes the monarchy, and establishes France as a republic.

Mary Wollestonecraft's *A Vindication of the Rights of Women,* the most famous assertion of women's discontent to this time, is published.

1793 King Louis XVI is executed for treason and the Reign of Terror begins in France. The Committee of Public Safety orders the arrest and guillotining of thousands of "counter-revolutionary" suspects, including the Queen, Marie Antoinette.

Lord McCartney leads mission to Beijing to open normal trade relations between Great Britain and China, but he is rebuffed by the Qianlong Emperor.

Eli Whitney (American) invents the cotton gin, a machine for separating cotton fibers from seeds.

1795 Napoleon Bonaparte defeats an attack on the National Convention by a Royalist-led Parisian mob and he is made commander of the army in Italy. The Directory is established as France's executive body.

The once-powerful state of Poland disappears from the map, partitioned by Russia, Austria and Prussia.

1796 Edward Jenner (English) develops smallpox vaccine from cowpox serum.

1798 Benjamin Thompson, Count von Rumford (American-German) shows that heat is form of motion.

Henry Cavendish (English) determines gravitational constant and mass of Earth.

1799 Napoleon abolishes the Directory and assumes control of France as First Consul.

►THE NINETEENTH CENTURY

1800 Alessandro G.A.A. Volta (Italian) invents first form of chemical battery for producing electric current.

1803 John Dalton (English) establishes atomic theory of matter.

1804 Napoleon is crowned Emperor.

1805 Napoleon crushes the armies of Russia and Austria at Austerlitz, but at Trafalgar the French Navy is destroyed by the English under Lord Nelson.

1806 The Holy Roman Empire is officially dissolved.

1807 Robert Fulton begins steamship service on the Hudson River.

1808 U.S. Congress abolishes the African slave trade.

1812 The Grand Army of Napoleon, one of the largest armies ever assembled, invades Russia, occupying Moscow. Refused a truce and dangerously far from his bases, Napoleon begins his catastrophic retreat which leads to his demise.

The U.S. declares war on Great Britain to reassert its independence and eventually prevails, but Washington D.C. is captured and burned (1814).

1815 The Congress of Vienna concludes its work (interrupted by the return of Napoleon from Elba and his defeat at Waterloo) re-drawing the boundaries of Europe and establishing a general European peace that will last 100 years.

1817 Simón Bolívar establishes independent government in Venezuela.

1818 James Blundel (English) performs first successful human blood transfusion.

1819 The *Savannah* is the first steamship to cross the Atlantic.

1820 André-Marie Ampère (French) formulates first laws of electromagnetism.

1822 Greece proclaims independence from Turkey.

Brazil achieves independence from Portugal.

1823 U.S. President James Monroe announces the Monroe Doctrine, asserting America's interests in its hemisphere in defense of the newly independent Latin American states against the anti-revolutionary European powers.

1830 France's Bourbon monarchy is overturned in an almost bloodless revolution. The July (or Liberal) Monarchy puts Louis Philippe, Duke of Orleans on the throne of a constitutional monarchy.

Sir Charles Lyell (Scottish) begins to publish *Principles of Geology*, the work that convinced geologists that Earth is at least several hundred million years old.

1831 Michael Farraday demonstrates electromagnetic induction, laying the foundations for electrical science.

1832 Great Britain's House of Lords passes the Great Reform Bill. Not a democratic measure, it abolishes "rotten boroughs" and expands the electorate by almost 50 percent to about 200,000

1834 Slavery is abolished throughout the British Empire.

1837 Last of the Hanoverians, Victoria ascends the British throne. Her reign will last until 1901.

1839 The first of two Opium Wars between China and Great Britain breaks out over Britain's trading rights in China, specifically relating to opium, which Chinese leaders sought to ban.

1842 The Treaty of Nanking ends Opium War and Great Britain gains Hong Kong and access to five Chinese ports.

Crawford Long (American) removes tumor from patient inhaling ether—first known operation under general anesthesia.

1844 Samuel F.B. Morse (American) sends first telegraph message.

1845 The United States annexes the independent Republic of Texas, which had won its freedom from Mexico in 1836

Disease blights the Irish potato crop. The resulting famine (1845-1847) will see half a million peasants starve while hundreds of thousands emigrate during the Great Hunger.

1846 The ruin of the Irish potato crop and its consequent threat of famine leads Conservative Sir Robert Peel to back corn law reform, ushering in the era of British free trade.

Elias Howe (American) patents lock-stitch sewing machine.

1847 H.F.L. Helmholtz extends the application of the law of conservation of energy (that energy can neither be created nor destroyed) and formulates it mathematically, the first law of thermodynamics.

1848 A wave of liberal and nationalist revolutions sweeps the capitals of Europe (excluding the most and least industrialized: Britain, Belgium and Russia). The principal beneficiaries are the serfs, liberated by their bourgeois advocates. The European monarchies suppress them all, except in France where the successful Second Republic gives way, in 1852, to the Second Empire of Napoleon III.

Karl Marx and Friedrich Engels publish the *Communist Manifesto*, attacking capitalism, society, and religion, and urging "Workers of the world, unite."

Led by Elizabeth Cady Stanton and Lucretia Mott, a meeting in Seneca Falls, N.Y. issues a declaration of the rights of women urging the nation to give them the right to vote.

1850 The Treaty of Guadalupe Hildalgo ends the war between the U.S. and Mexico, with the U.S. gaining New Mexico and California.

1851 Hung Hsiu-ch'üan leads Taiping Rebellion against the Ch'ing dynasty of China in attempt to create a new dynasty based in part on Christian ideals. The rebel movement captures Nanjing in 1853 and establishes a government that lasts until 1864 when the movement is disbanded by armies funded by Western powers.

1852 Harriet Beecher Stowe's influential anti-slavery novel *Uncle Tom's Cabin* is published to wide acclaim and enormous sales.

1853 Commodore M.C. Perry of the U.S. anchors in Tokyo (Edo) Bay with four ships and presents a letter from Pres. Millard Fillmore to the Emperor. In 1854 Perry returns and secures the Treaty of Kanagawa, opening two ports to American trade.

1856 Henry Bessemer (English) develops way of making inexpensive steel (Bessemer process).

Louis Pasteur (French) discovers that fermentation is caused by micro-organisms.

1857 Indian soldiers in British army revolt for religious and political reasons, but the mutiny is cruelly suppressed. The British depose the Moghul emperor and government authority is transferred to London from the East India Company.

In the Dred Scott Case the U.S. Supreme Court decides that Congress can not limit slavery in the territories and that runaway slaves had no legal rights, further inflaming the sectional crisis.

1859 Charles Darwin (English) publishes *On the Origin of Species by Natural Selection*, outlining the scientific basis for evolution.

Edwin L. Drake (American) drills first oil well, in Titusville, Penn.

1860 Giuseppi Garibaldi leads 1,000 "Red Shirts" in conquest of Sicily and Naples for a new, united Italy.

1861 Abraham Lincoln takes offices as President in March; on April 12, the first guns of the American Civil War are fired by Confederate batteries upon Fort Sumter in Charleston, S.C.

Victor Emmanuel II of Piedmont is proclaimed King of Italy.

Czar Alexander II of Russia proclaims the end of serfdom in his empire: serfs are granted personal freedom, but not free title to their land.

1863 President Abraham Lincoln issues the Emancipation Proclamation, which will provide the basis for the freeing of all slaves in the U.S.

1865 Confederate General Robert E. Lee surrenders to General Ulysses S. Grant at Appomattox Court House in Virginia, ending the American Civil War.

President Lincoln is assassinated by John Wilkes Booth.

The 13th Amendment to the U.S. Constitution abolishes slavery.

Joseph Lister (English) revolutionizes surgery when he introduces use of disinfectants to reduce infection.

Pasteur shows that spoilage of wine can be prevented by heat sterilization; process, called pasteurization, soon applied to milk and other foods.

1866 Cyrus W. Field (U.S.) lays the Trans-Atlantic Cable under the Atlantic Ocean, connecting Europe to America by telegraph wire.

The Augustinian monk and botanist, Gregor Johann Mendel (Austrian), publishes his theory of dominant and recessive genes in obscure local journal, establishing the fundamental principles governing inheritance.

1867 The Austrian Empire, after its crushing defeat by Prussia the previous year, is transformed into the Monarchy of Austria-Hungary.

Karl Marx publishes the first volume of *Das Kapital*, which sees the state as an instrument to support private wealth.

1868 Eager to modernize their country, the nobles of Japan seize control of the Imperial Court from the Tokugawa *shogunate*, abolish the office of the *shogun*, and restore the Meiji emperor, moving the court to Edo.

1869 The Union Pacific and Central Pacific railroads join rails with a golden spike near Great Salt Lake, completing America's first transcontinental railroad.

Europe's sea route to Asia is revolutionized with the opening of the Suez Canal.

1871 France suffers humiliating defeat in brief war with Prussia and is forced to pay a huge indemnity. William I of Prussia is proclaimed German Emperor in the Hall of Mirrors at Versailles. The new Reich, with Otto von Bismarck as Chancellor, includes 25 German states and Alsace-Lorraine (annexed from France).

1876 In their last serious battle against the white man's encroachment, Sitting Bull and Crazy Horse, leaders of the Sioux nation, join forces to defeat the U.S. Army under General George Custer at Battle of Little Big Horn in South Dakota.

Alexander Graham Bell (Scottish-American) invents telephone.

1877 Thomas A. Edison (American) invents phonograph.

1878 The Congress of Berlin meets under Germany's Chancellor Bismarck to revise the excessive Russian gains in her war with Turkey. International recognition is given to the complete independence of Romania, Serbia, and Montenegro.

1879 Edison and Sir Joseph W. Swan (English) independently discover how to make practical electric lights.

1881 Pasteur produces vaccine that prevents anthrax—first disease prevented by vaccine.

1884 A second Congress of Berlin assembles to temper European rivalries in Africa. Its Berlin Act of the following year will regulate further European occupations in Africa. By 1902, all of the continent south of the Moslem Mediterranean states (except Liberia and Ethiopia) will be divided among the European powers.

1885 Six years after founding a company to develop the Congo for profit, King Leopold II of Belgium becomes king of the Congo Free State.

1886 William S. Burroughs (American) develops first commercially successful mechanical adding machine.

1887 Gottlieb Daimler produces the first successful automobile, utilizing the internal combustion engine that he invented the year before.

Thomas Edison invents a motion picture machine in which little pictures, mounted on a cylinder, are viewed in motion under a microscope; two years later he will perfect his "kinetoscope".

1895 Wilhelm Röntgen discovers X rays.

First public showing of a motion picture, *Workers Leaving the Lumiere Factory,* by Auguste and Louis Lumiere in Paris.

1896 Svante A. Arerhenius (Swedish) discovers that global temperatures rise with higher levels of carbon dioxide in atmosphere (greenhouse effect).

Antoine Henri Becquerel, building on William Roentgen's detection of X-rays the year before, discovers the natural radioactivity of uranium.

1897 Sir Joseph Thompson (English) discovers the electron and studies its charge and mass.

1898 United States victory in the Spanish-American War brings to a close Spain's empire, as U.S. annexes Puerto Rico and the Philippines and liberates Cuba.

Imperially sponsored movement for constitutional government in China defeated when Empress Dowager Cixi seizes power.

Pierre and Marie Curie observe the phenomenon of radioactivity and isolate the element of radium.

1899 American Secretary of State, John Hay, gains approval of the European Powers that an "open door" to trade will be maintained in the spheres of influence they have been carving out in China.

The second Boer War breaks out between British and Dutch Afrikaner states of Transvaal and the Orange Free State. British victory (1902) fuels long-term Afrikaner nationalist movement.

▶ THE TWENTIETH CENTURY

1900 Nativist Chinese uprising called the Boxer Rebellion, which opposes both Manchu (Qing) dynasty as well as missionaries and other foreigners; 140,000 occupy Beijing but are smashed by Western troops.

Sigmund Freud (Austrian), founder of psychoanalysis, publishes *The Interpretations of Dreams*.

Max K.E.L. Planck (German) articulates the Quantum Theory of Energy, explaining the behavior of electromagnetic radiation, according to which energy is not a continuous stream but a series of discrete packets which he calls "quanta".

1901 Queen Victoria dies.

1903 Orville and Wilbur Wright (American) fly the first successful airplane at Kitty Hawk, N. C.

1905 Japan defeats Russia in year-long war that exposes weakness of Czar Nicholas II's regime; revolutionaries force him to accept a parliament.

Albert Einstein develops his special theory of relativity and the law $E=mc^2$.

1908 Henry Ford (American) pioneers assembly line technique and introduces Model T, the first affordable automobile.

Oil is discovered in Persia (Iran) opening vast fields for exploration.

1909 Robert E. Peary plants U.S. flag at North Pole.

1912 The British ocean liner *RMS Titanic* hits an iceberg in the mid-Atlantic and sinks with 1,500 passengers on board; 760 others are rescued.

1914 The June 28 assassination of Archduke Francis Ferdinand, heir to the throne of Austria-Hungary, and his wife in Sarajevo starts a chain reaction that brings about World War I, which mainly pits England, France and Russia (the Allies) against Germany, Austria-Hungary and Turkey (the Central Powers).

The Panama Canal opens, drastically reducing the time it takes ships to move between the Atlantic and Pacific Oceans.

1915   Einstein completes his general theory of relativity, a theory of gravity more accurate than that of Sir Isaac Newton (published 1916).

A German submarine torpedoes the British ship *Lusitania*, killing 1,200 (including over 100 Americans) and causing Pres. Woodrow Wilson to demand an end to German submarine warfare.

1917   Czar Nicholas II of Russia is forced to abdicate. The Bolsheviks, led by V.L. Lenin, overthrow the provisional government; Lenin seizes power, establishing Communist Party domination.

The U.S. enters the war on the side of the Allies and dooms Germany to defeat.

1918   The Russians withdraw from the war via the Treaty of Brest-Litovsk.

Germany surrenders and on November 11, the armistice ending World War I is signed.

1919   France, Great Britain, Italy and the U.S. sign the Treaty of Versailles which creates the League of Nations, forces Germany to pay huge reparations for the war, puts limits on its armed forces, adjusts German borders and places the Saar under French administration.

1920   U.S. amends its Constitution to give women the right to vote.

1922   Benito Mussolini becomes premier of Italy and within two years establishes a fascist dictatorship that becomes the model for anti-democratic and anti-communist movements across Europe.

1924   Edwin Hubble (American) shows that galaxies are "island universes"—giant aggregations of stars as large as Milky Way.

Vladimir Kosma Zworykin (Russian-American) develops iconoscope, the beginning of modern television.

1925   Werner Karl Heisenberg (German) develops a mathematical treatment that explains behavior of electrons and protons.

1927   Charles Lindbergh makes the first solo transatlantic flight from New York to Paris in *The Spirit of St. Louis*. He returns to the U.S. as a national hero, and tours the country to promote aviation.

Three years after Lenin's death, Joseph Stalin attains control of the Communist Party in the Soviet Union and soon launches a forced, brutal collectivization of agriculture and rapid industrialization policy. Severe repression and brutal massacres mark his long rule (d. 1953).

Heisenberg develops his uncertainty principle: it is impossible to measure accurately position and momentum of electron or proton at the same time.

1928   After breaking his alliance with the Communists, Chiang Kai-Shek, head of the Kuomintang Party, captures Beijing and seizes power in China.

Sir Alexander Fleming (Scottish) discovers penicillin, a substance in green mold *Penicillum notatum* that destroys certain bacteria.

1929   Robert H. Goddard (American) launches first instrumented, liquid-fueled rocket.

Hubble establishes that the universe is expanding.

U.S. stock market collapses, heralding the start of the Great Depression.

1930   Frank Whittle (British) patents jet engine.

1931   The Japanese army invades Manchuria and extends Japan's power into China and the rest of Southeast Asia. Manchuria and all other territories acquired by force will be stripped from the Empire after Japan's surrender in World War II.

Vannevar Bush (American) completes "differential analyser," first computing machine to use electronic components.

1933   Adolf Hitler, leader of the National Socialist German Workers (Nazi) party, becomes Chancellor of a German coalition cabinet on Jan. 30.

1934   Stalin initiates purges of government, the military the party, etc.; millions are imprisoned, exiled or murdered.

1936   BBC launches first regular television broadcasting service.

1937   Sino-Japanese War begins when Japan invades China and occupies Beijing and other major cities; bloody fighting continues through the end of World War II.

1938   Otto Hahn (German) and Lise Meitner (Austrian-Swedish) split uranium atom, opening way for nuclear bombs and nuclear power.

Konrad Zuse (German) builds "Z1," the first computing machine to use binary, instead of decimal, method of operation.

Germany occupies Austria and annexes it as the province of Ostmark. The "Anschluss" is not reversed until 1945.

In the first public demonstration of Nazi Germany's virulent anti-Semitism, soldiers ransack Jewish businesses and synagogues on *kristallnacht* ("night of crystal," referring to the broken glass left by the night of violence), Nov. 9.

1939   Germany invades Poland without a declaration of war. Britain and France declare war on Germany on Sept. 3.

1940   Almost all of western Europe (including France) is overwhelmed by Nazi forces and Hitler begins bombing England in preparation for invasion. Winston Churchill becomes Prime Minister and vows England will never surrender, helping to inspire the Royal Air Force to win the Battle of Britain.

1941   Japan bombs Pearl Harbor, drawing the U.S. into World War II.

1942   Enrico Fermi (Italian-American) designs first nuclear reactor.

The Battle of Midway (June) marks a turning point in the war in the Pacific: U.S. aircraft destroy four Japanese aircraft carriers, crippling the Japanese navy and forcing a retreat.

The German army is defeated at Stalingrad with 300,000 casualties.

1944   The Allies storm the beach at Normandy (June 6) in history's largest amphibious assault and sweep inland to the Rhine, driving German forces out of France and Belgium, while the Soviets push the Eastern Front back through the Baltic States.

1945   Roosevelt, Churchill and Stalin meet at the Yalta Conference in Ukraine and agree to the formation of the United Nations, a four-power occupation of Germany (France is included), and a guarantee the Soviets would enter war against Japan.

Scientists funded by U.S. government and led by J. Robert Oppenheimer (American) detonate first nuclear-fission explosion (atomic bomb).

Germany agrees to unconditional surrender on May 8. On Aug. 6, the U.S. drops the first atomic bomb on Hiroshima, leveling 90 percent of the city and leaving 130,000 people dead, injured, or missing. On Aug. 9, an atomic bomb is dropped on Nagasaki, destroying one-third of the city and killing or injuring 75,000. Threatened with further mass destruction Japan surrenders on Aug. 14.

The United Nations charter is ratified by world's leading nations in San Francisco.

U.S. and British troops liberate the Nazi death camps at Dachau and elsewhere and the world first learns about the horrors of the Holocaust.

1946 The ENIAC (Electronic Numerical Integrator and Calculator) multiplies five-digit number by itself 5,000 times in half a second.

1947 U.N. approves creation of the new state of Israel in Middle East for settlement by Jews.

India is declared independent by Great Britain and divided into mainly Hindu India and mainly Moslem Pakistan.

Quantum electrodynamics (QED) is born, with many parents.

1948 The U.S. begins airlifting supplies to West Berlin to counter the Soviet land blockade.

John Bardeen, Walter H. Brattain, and William B. Shockley invent the transistor.

George Gamow (Russian-American), Ralph Alpher (American), and Robert Herman (American) develop Big Bang theory of origin of universe.

Mohandas Gandhi, 78-year-old Indian spiritual leader, is assassinated.

The Berlin land blockade is lifted.

New state of Israel is proclaimed in Palestine and is promptly invaded by Egypt.

1949 The Communists in China seize power under Mao Zedong who becomes chairman of the People's Republic. Chiang Kai-Shek flees to the island of Taiwan and establishes a government recognized as the true government of China until 1979.

Led by the U.S., a military alliance called the North Atlantic Treaty Organization (NATO) is established in Europe to defend against Soviet aggression.

1951 UNIVAC (Universal Automatic Computer) is installed at U.S. Bureau of Census. UNIVAC uses magnetic tape for input and becomes first commercially successful machine.

1952 The U.S. conducts first successful test of a hydrogen bomb (a thermonuclear weapon) on the Eniwetok Atoll. The Soviets detonate one the following year, helping to trigger the most dangerous arms race in history. By 1980, over 60,000 nuclear weapons exist.

Jonas Salk (American) develops first vaccine against polio.

1953 James D. Watson (American) and Francis Crick (English) determine structure of DNA, the basis of heredity.

1954 French forces defeated by Vietnamese nationalist forces at Dien Bien Phu.

1956 A popular revolt against communist government in Hungary is cruelly suppressed by Soviets.

The forces of Britain, France, and Israel quickly overrun Egypt after Pres. Gamal Nasser seizes control of the Suez Canal. The U.S. and Soviet Union force them to withdraw.

1957 USSR launches Sputnik 1, the first man-made satellite.

Gordon Gould (American) develops basic idea for the laser, which he succeeds in patenting in 1986 after a long struggle.

The Common Market (European Economic Community or EEC) is formed, the first significant step in the integration of European economies.

1958 Great Leap Forward, an attempt at rapid agricultural and industrial modernization, launched in China; as many as 20 million people die in ensuing famine.

United States opens first experimental nuclear power plant.

The submarine USS Nautilus, the first commissioned nuclear-powered vessel, sails under the North Pole.

First transatlantic jet plane service is established.

1959 First industrial robot is marketed.

1960 The PDP-1, developed by Digital Equipment Corp., is the first commercial computer to use a keyboard and monitor instead of punched cards.

USS Triton circumnavigates the world under water.

1961 Soviets erect wall between East and West Berlin to halt defections.

Soviet cosmonaut Yuri A. Gagarin (Russian) is first human to orbit Earth.

Scientists at Bell Laboratories (Americans) announce first continuously operating laser.

1962 U.S. discovers Soviet missiles in Cuba and demands their removal, causing the first serious standoff between nuclear superpowers. Soviets remove them in exchange for U.S. removal of missiles in Turkey.

First active communications satellite, Telstar, goes into orbit.

Vatican Council II, convened by Pope John XXIII, announces many liberalizing changes in Roman Catholic liturgy and practice; supports cautious involvement with other Christians.

1963 Pres. John F. Kennedy is assassinated in Dallas; two days later, his assassin is shot to death by a local citizen.

1964 Murray Gell-Mann introduces concept of quarks as components of heavy subatomic particles, such as protons and mesons.

The U.S. begins attacking North Vietnamese bases.

The Palestine Liberation Organization is founded for the purpose of destroying Israel, launching guerrilla attacks for decades.

1965 Failed Communist coup in Indonesia leads to nationwide massacre of suspected Communist supporters; President Sukarno gives way to General Suharto, who holds power to 1998.

1966 Great Proletarian Revolution in China; Mao Zedong shakes up Communist Party leadership, organizes youthful Red Guards to root out "counterrevolutionary" tendencies in Party ranks. Ensuing decade of chaos and political repression ends with death of Mao in 1976.

Engineers at ITT demonstrate fiber optics as a method of transmitting data.

1967 Soviet tanks and troops invade Czechoslovakia and remove the government that was introducing democratic reforms.

Israel defeats Egypt in Six-Day War, strengthening its holdings and its chances for survival.

Christiaan Barnard (South African) performs world's first heart transplant.

Rene Favaloro (Argentinian) performs first successful coronary bypass operation.

1968 Civil rights leader Martin Luther King, Jr. is assassinated in Memphis, Tennessee.

The U.S. military buildup in Vietnam reaches 500,000 and by the end of the year more tonnage of bombs will have been dropped on Vietnam than on Germany and Japan in WWII.

Massive student demonstrations in the U.S. and Europe help turn public opinion against the Vietnam War.

1969 Americans Neil Armstrong and Edwin E. ("Buzz") Aldrin walk on Moon.

Jonathan Beckwith (American) and coworkers are first to isolate a single gene.

U.S. and Soviet Union begin Strategic Arms Limitation Talks (SALT).

1970   Boeing 747 jets go into service.
1971   American spacecraft, Mariner 9, is first to orbit another planet, Mars.

First electronic pocket calculator produced by Texas Instruments; it weighs about 2 1/2 pounds and costs about $150.
1972   U.S. Congress passes Clean Water Act, forbidding discharges of pollutants into navigable waters.

The U.S. Environmental Protection Agency bars registration and interstate sales of DDT because of its persistence in the environment and accumulation in the food chain.

The Vietnam Peace Pacts are signed, ending America's longest war.

In a stunning move designed to shift world alliances, President Nixon is first U.S. president to visit China; later he becomes first to visit Moscow.

The CAT scan is invented, revolutionizing medical diagnosis.
1973   Stanley Cohen and Herbert Boyer (Americans) succeed in putting specific gene into bacterium, the first instance of true genetic engineering.
1974   President Nixon resigns over the Watergate scandal but is granted a full pardon by President Gerald Ford.
1975   North Vietnamese forces capture Saigon, ending Vietnam war in communist victory. Khmer Rouge forces occupy Phnom Penh, Cambodia, slaughter opponents in "killing fields." King of Laos abdicates in favor of communists.

Cray Research (founded 1972) announces the Cray-1 supercomputer, capable of 100 million operations per second.
1976   U.S. Viking space probes begin transmitting pictures of surface of Mars.
1977   Apple markets Apple II, the first widely accepted personal computer.

Microsoft Corp. is founded to produce microcomputer operating systems—programs allowing a central processing unit to control and coordinate the elements of a computer's hardware.
1978   Proclamation of Four Modernizations in China inaugurates era of economic and social reform under Deng Xiaoping.

Louise Brown, first so-called "test tube baby," conceived through in vitro fertilization process, is born in England. 300,000 people have been conceived this way by the end of the century.
1979   Egypt and Israel sign treaty ending 30-year-long war.
1980   U.S. Congress passes Comprhensive Environmental Response, Compensation and Liability Act (the "Superfund") to clean up hazardous waste sites.
1981   Scientists identify acquired immune deficiency syndrome (AIDS), a previously unknown disease.

Surgeons at Univ. of California at San Francisco perform first successful operation on a fetus.
1983   Kary B. Mullis (American) invents the use of the polymerase chain reaction, a vital tool in finding specific genes.
1986   Chernobyl nuclear reactor in the Soviet Ukraine explodes and burns, causing 31 deaths shortening the lives of thousands, and forcing the evacuation of hundreds of square miles.

The space shuttle Challenger explodes shortly after liftoff, killing the entire crew.
1989   The Berlin Wall is opened. The following year, East and West Germany reunite after 45 years of separation.

The Soviet military leaves Poland and the Republic of Poland is restored.

Chinese troops attack a major protest in Tienanmen Square, killing several hundred students.

The Human Genome Project is formed to map the complete sequence of DNA in humans.
1990   R. Michael Blaese, W. French Anderson, and Kenneth W. Culver (Americans) develop procedure to infuse genetically engineered blood cells for treatment of immune system disorder—first gene therapy used in a human.

The Hubble Space Telescope is launched.

Tim Berners-Lee writes the program for the World Wide Web to make the Internet easier to use for physicists at CERN in Geneva.

Soviet-backed communist governments throughout Eastern Europe and along the Baltic crumble, and are replaced by democratic ones.
1991   Over 400,000 U.S. troops together with U.N. forces drive Iraq's military from Kuwait.

The Soviet Union is officially dissolved and Russia becomes one of many autonomous states.
1992   U.S. President George Bush and Russian President issue joint statement officially ending the Cold War.

Representatives from 178 countries attend the first-ever Earth Summit in Rio de Janeiro, where they sign treaties pledging to increase the diversity of animal and plant species and to halt global warming.
1993   The Palestinian Liberation Organization and Israel reach a historic peace accord.
1994   Nelson Mandela is elected the first black president of South Africa.
1995   Craig Venter (American) of the Institute for Genomic Research publishes the complete base sequences for all the genes of a free-living organism, the bacterium Haemophilus influenzae.
1996   The Hubble Space Telescope reveals the existence of more than 50 billion galaxies or five times the number previously thought to exist. Later it delivers the first-ever pictures of Pluto.
1997   Ian Wilmut (English) succeeds in cloning a sheep from a cell from an adult ewe, the first mammalian clone using a differentiated cell as the source of the chromosomes; in 1998, the cloned ewe, named Dolly, bears a lamb the natural way.

The Mars Pathfinder arrives on Mars and returns spectacular pictures of the rocky landscape.

After 156 years of British rule, China resumes control of Hong Kong.
1998   Pictures from the Hubble Space Telescope show the first image of a planet outside our solar system.
1999   World population reaches 6 billion, up from 3 billion in 1960, and 5 billion in 1987.

▶**NOVEMBER 1998**

3   Democrats make surprising gains in midterm elections for the House and Senate, a development that seems to derail the drive to impeach Pres. Clinton. (See "Major News Stories of the Year.")

4   For the first time the Russian Government says it will not pay its foreign debts next year and will seek to renegotiate the loans.

5   The Security Council votes unanimously to condemn Iraq and demands that Pres. Saddam Hussein rescind his ban on cooperation with arms inspectors.

The House Judiciary Committee forges ahead with an impeachment inquiry that most Americans say Congress should drop. (See "Major News Stories of the Year.")

6   House Speaker Newt Gingrich announces he will not seek re-election as Speaker and that he will leave Congress in January.

7   After a flight of nine days, the space shuttle *Discovery* returns to the Kennedy Space Center with 77-year old Senator John Glenn declaring he is fit and healthy.

8   Representative Robert L. Livingston (R-La.) declares he will become the next Speaker of the House because he has the votes.

11   Pres. Clinton orders a substantial number of new forces to the Persian Gulf, including B-1 and B-52 bombers.

12   The Clinton Administration signs the international agreement to fight global warming first negotiated in Rio de Janeiro in 1992. Senate approval, however, could be years away.

13   Pres. Clinton agrees to settle the Paula Jones sexual harassment suit for $850,000 and she drops her demand for an apology.

The nation's four largest cigarette makers and officials from eight states announce they have reached a tentative agreement to resolve all remaining state claims over health costs related to smoking. (See "Major News Stories of the Year.")

14   Faced with an imminent American military attack, Pres. Saddam Hussein of Iraq backs down and tells the U.N. that his government will resume full cooperation with arms inspectors.

17   The Federal Reserve again cuts interest rates by a quarter of a point to help keep a gradual economic slowdown from turning into a recession.

18   Special Prosecutor Kenneth Starr's prepared testimony before the House Judiciary Committee is made public and it reveals that he will accuse Pres. Clinton of obstructing his inquiry into the Lewinsky affair. (See "Major News Stories of the Year.")

19   Independent Counsel Kenneth W. Starr testifies before the House Judiciary Committee and accuses Pres. Clinton of obstructing his inquiry.

24   America Online, Inc. announces the details of its agreement to buy Netscape Communications Corp. (See "Major News Stories of the Year.")

Attorney General Janet Reno announces her decision not to seek an independent counsel to investigate Vice Pres. Al Gore's fund-raising role in the 1996 election campaign.

25   A court of the British House of Lords rejects former Chilean dictator Gen. Augusto Pinochet's assertion of immunity from arrest and commits him to remain in custody while Spain seeks his extradition on charges of mass murder and terrorism.

27   In terse, formal responses to 81 written questions submitted by the House Judiciary Committee, Pres. Clinton again denies that he committed perjury in the Monica Lewinsky matter and he acknowledges three times that he misled the American people and had apologized.

29   State elections in India result in humiliating defeats for ruling Hindu nationalist party, creating doubt the Government can stay in power.

▶**DECEMBER**

1   Exxon, the nation's largest oil company, agrees to buy Mobil, the next largest, for $80 bil. in stock thereby forming the world's biggest corporation.

A panel of four expert scientists appointed by a Federal judge issues a report on silicone breast implants that says no scientific evidence can be found linking any disease to the implants.

4   The U.S. Dept. of Labor says that 267,000 jobs were added in November, driving the unemployment rate down to 4.4 percent from 4.6 percent. About 64 percent of all working-age Americans had jobs, the highest percentage on record.

7   Atty. Gen. Janet Reno announces she has found no reasonable grounds to appoint an independent counsel to investigate Pres. Clinton's role in a campaign finance issue regarding Democratic Party advertising in 1996.

8   The White House opens its formal defense of Pres. Clinton as three of his lawyers and 44 anti-impeachment witnesses (including prominent historians and law professors) appear before the House Judiciary Committee and argue that President's behavior does not rise to the level of impeachable offenses.

9   Republicans on the House Judiciary Committee formally propose four articles of impeachment accusing the President of perjury, obstruction of justice, and abuse of power.

10   The House Judiciary Committee begins a rancorous, partisan debate on the four articles of impeachment and the White House tries to mobilize forces for a censure resolution.

11   The House Judiciary Committee votes strictly along party lines to impeach Pres. Clinton and remove him from office for perjury and obstruction of justice. Pres. Clinton publicly apologizes again as the White House continues to press for censure.

12   Republicans on the House Judiciary Committee approve a final article of impeachment and defeat Democrats' censure proposal.

13   At a news conference in Jerusalem, Pres. Clinton states flatly that he did not commit perjury and says he will never resign.

14   In Gaza, Pres. Clinton witnesses the Palestinian Council vote removing the clause from the PLO charter calling for the destruction of Israel.

Results of a *New York Times*/CBS News Poll reveal that 64 percent of Americans, including a majority of independent voters, say they don't want the President impeached.

16   Pres. Clinton announces "strong sustained series of air strikes" against Iraq for its continued refusal to cooperate with U.N. arms inspectors.

17   House Republicans say they will begin impeachment debate on the following day despite continuing U.S. bombing of Iraq.

18   For the first time in over 130 years the House of Representatives debates the impeachment of a President. As bombs rain on Iraq, and a national poll shows the Republicans standing with the public sinking to its lowest levels as an impeachment vote is now seen as inevitable.

19 The House of Representatives votes along strict party lines to impeach Pres. Clinton on two of the four counts presented: perjury and obstruction of justice. Clinton appears outside the White House with his wife and dozens of Democratic House members and vows to serve "until the last hour of the last day of my term."

Speaker-elect Robert Livingston announces in the House that he will not serve as Speaker and that he will quit Congress in the light of the recent allegations that he had extra-marital affairs.

23 With many U.S. Senators indicating they were searching for ways to end the impeachment process quickly, conservative Republicans, insist that the evidence be fully aired to honor the process of impeachment.

The New York Times reports that more than a dozen cities have sued the gun industry, or are preparing to. (See "Major News Stories of the Year.")

24 After several days of sniping and assassinations, Serbian forces in northern Kosovo Province break the two-month cease-fire launching a sustained assault on rebel forces.

27 Rebel forces in Kosovo leave their camps in the hills and attack a large police post on the main road between Belgrade and Pristina, the provincial capital.

30 After Senate Majority Leader Trent Lott says that he doesn't believe witnesses are necessary in the upcoming impeachment trial, he is challenged by the 13 House Republicans in charge of the prosecution indicating how difficult it will be to maintain bipartisanship.

A select House committee unanimously opposes keeping private the contents of a 700-page classified report that over the past 20 years China had acquired a range of American technical secrets, harming national security.

31 Finance ministers from 11 countries celebrate New Year's Eve by launching the euro as Europe's new single currency. (See "Major News Stories of the Year.")

▶ **JANUARY 1999**

1 Clinton Administration officials announce the President's intention to propose an increase in defense spending of $100 bil. over six years, the first real increase since the buildup of the 1980s.

4 The U.S. Agriculture Dept. agrees to pay as much as $300 mil., and possibly more, to settle a lawsuit brought by thousands of black farmers who claim the department discriminated against them by denying loans and other subsidies.

5 A Catholic news agency reports that about 500 people were massacred in the Congo over the Christmas holidays.

6 Ending any hopes held by the White House and the Democrats that the Senate would dispense with impeachment quickly, Senate Majority Leader Trent Lott announces there would be a full trial that could last into February.

Dennis Hastert, a little-known Republican from Illinois, is elected the 51st Speaker of the House for the 106th Congress.

U.S. officials say that American spies had worked undercover on teams of U.N. arms inspectors ferreting out secret Iraqi weapons program.

7 In a hushed Senate chamber under heavy security, Chief Justice William Rehnquist opens the first Presidential impeachment trial in 131 years, swearing in Senators to "do impartial justice" in judging whether Pres. William Jefferson Clinton should be removed from office for perjury and obstruction of justice. (See "Major News Stories of the Year.")

Investigators say they have discovered that payments were made by Salt Lake City officials to members of the International Olympic Committee during the city's bid to be awarded the 2002 Winter Games. (See "Major News Stories of the Year.")

8 The Senate reaches unanimous agreement on rules for proceeding with the impeachment trial; they delay the decision about hearing witnesses.

9 Heavy fighting is reported around Freetown, the capital of Sierra Leone as rebel soldiers continue their battle to depose the restored President. (See "Major News Stories of the Year.")

11 For the first time, Pres. Clinton responds formally to the charges against him; in documents filed with the Senate, he argues that he committed no crimes and that the charges against him are so vague and muddled they are unconstitutional.

13 Brazil's Government devalues the nation's currency, setting off turbulence in many of the world's financial markets.

14 At the opening of their arguments for the removal of Pres. Clinton, the House trial managers say the President repeatedly put himself above the law and they present evidence of obstruction of justice.

15 The Brazilian Government, reeling under a hemorrhage of dollars from its foreign reserves, lifts exchange-rate controls to allow the currency to trade at market value.

Republican prosecutors assert that Pres. Clinton is not telling the truth about his affair with Monica Lewinsky, so they insist that she testify before the Senate.

16 The House managers conclude their opening arguments with Henry Hyde, Chairman of the House Judiciary Committee, saying the Presidency could be "permanently damaged" if the Senate fails to remove Clinton from office.

17 The White House says Pres. Clinton will propose the most aggressive nationwide effort ever to bring greater accountability to state and local school systems, potentially affecting the allocations of billions of dollars in Federal aid.

18 Yugoslav Pres. Slobodan Milosevic defies the allies and threatens the fragile cease-fire as he orders the expulsion of a top U.S. diplomat.

19 Pres. Clinton's lawyers make their first arguments before the Senate and assert unequivocally that he did not commit perjury and he did not obstruct justice. In the evening, the President appears before Congress and presents his annual State of the Union message. He urges Government investment in the stock market to strengthen Social Security, which he says must be the focal point for allocating budget surpluses.

20 White House lawyers accuse the House prosecutors of resorting to "word games" and "legal mumbo jumbo" in their efforts to prove Pres. Clinton guilty of impeachable offenses, and they dismiss the charges as "frivolous."

The Clinton Administration says it is asking Russia to renegotiate the Anti-Ballistic Missile Treaty to permit a limited national system of missile defenses to protect against an attack by a rogue state such as N. Korea.

21 After a tangled four-year trial, Raúl Salinas de Gortari, brother of Mexico's former President, is convicted of ordering the 1994 assassination of a prominent politician. He is sentenced to 50 years in prison.

23 The impeachment trial is thrown into turmoil after a Federal judge orders Monica Lewinsky to submit to questioning from House Republican prosecutors and Senate Republicans say they will query the President in writing.

24 House Republican managers interview Monica Lewinsky for two hours and say she would make an impressive witness who would help Senate "determine the truth" in the trial of Pres. Clinton. Lewinsky tells a friend "I gave them nothing."

25 Senate Republicans reject Democrats' plans

to end the impeachment trial without calling any witnesses, and to have open door debates.

In Armenia, Colombia the worst earthquake in a century levels the city and kills nearly 1,000 people and injures over 3,000.

26 Pope John Paul II ends his trip to Mexico and flies to St. Louis, where he is met by Pres. Clinton and the First Lady. The Pope urges Americans to cherish and celebrate life.

After hearing fervent arguments for both sides about the need to call live witnesses—The House managers prepare only three at the insistence of Senate Republican leaders—the Senate goes behind closed-doors to debate the issue.

27 The Senate votes along party lines to reject a motion to dismiss the charges against Pres. Clinton; minutes later it votes—again along party lines—to summon Monica Lewinsky and two other witnesses for depositions.

28 After defeating the Democrats' proposal to end the trial by going directly to votes on the articles of impeachment, Senate Republicans pass their plan to call Lewinsky and other witnesses.

29 The Federal Government announces that the U.S. gross domestic product surged at 5.6 percent annual rate in the final quarter of 1998 (for all of 1998 the G.D.P. increased 3.9 percent.) Inflation dropped to eight-tenths of a percent, the lowest in more than 40 years.

30 According to *The New York Times*, associates of Kenneth W. Starr say he has concluded that he has the constitutional authority to seek a grand jury indictment of Pres. Clinton.

31 At a meeting in Chicago, virologists announce they have solved the riddle of the origins of H.I.V., the virus that causes AIDS, tracing its roots to a related virus in a subspecies of chimpanzee in Africa.

▶ FEBRUARY

1 House Republican prosecutor Ed Bryant of Tennessee interviews Monica S. Lewinsky under oath and on videotape for nearly four hours.

Pres. Clinton submits a $1.77 trillion budget for the year 2000 and calls it a "progressive but prudent path to our future." Congressional Republicans immediately attack the budget because it calls for new spending and no tax cuts.

2 A *New York Times*/CBS News Poll shows that most Americans now condemn the Senate for its handling of the impeachment trial.

Vernon Jordan, a friend and confidant of the President testifies on videotape but changes little in his previous testimony.

4 The Senate votes overwhelmingly (70 to 30) not to have Monica S. Lewinsky testify in person before the Senate, but they approve using videotape excerpts of her recent deposition.

6 The Senate sees excerpts of the videotaped testimony of Monica S. Lewinsky, Vernon E. Jordan Jr., and Sidney Blumenthal.

7 Senate Democrats close ranks, indicating that they will amass more than enough votes to guarantee Pres. Clinton's acquittal in his impeachment trial. They instead press for a bipartisan censure resolution to rebuke him for his misconduct.

8 The House Republicans and the President's lawyers make closing statements to the Senate and after Majority Leader Trent Lott says he opposes televising the Senate's final deliberations.

9 The Senate votes to keep its impeachment trial deliberations closed to the public and begins to debate the charges.

10 Three Republican Senators announce they will vote against both of the charges against Pres. Clinton, and two others say they will vote against the perjury charge.

A state jury in San Francisco orders the Philip Morris Co. to pay $51.5 mil. to a woman who claims her inoperable lung cancer was caused by 35 years of smoking cigarettes.

11 After a year of heated debate, the Clinton Administration suspends the construction of logging roads in most of the undeveloped back country of the national forests, decisively shifting forest policy toward conservation.

In the first case of its kind, a Federal jury in Brooklyn finds that gun manufacturers are liable for shootings with illegally obtained handguns.

Pilots at American Airlines defy a Federal judge's order to end their protest and return to work, forcing the carrier to cancel more than half of its flights and stranding tens of thousands of travelers.

12 The Senate votes to acquit Pres. Clinton on both articles of impeachment. (See "Major News Stories of the Year.")

13 Pres. Clinton announces he will send nearly 4,000 troops to Kosovo to defend the "national interest" as part of a NATO peacekeeping force.

14 In Rambouillet, France, Sec. of State Madeleine K. Albright brings Serb leaders and ethnic Albanian rebels together for peace talks.

16 After the public announcement that the leader of the Kurdish rebels, Abdullah Ocalan, has been captured, protesters storm diplomatic posts throughout Europe, and elsewhere.

17 In Berlin, Israeli guards open fire on dozens of Kurds trying to occupy the Israeli Consulate, killing three and wounding 16 in the worst violence since Europe-wide protests erupted over the capture of a rebel Kurdish leader.

18 *The New York Times* reports that the Justice Dept. is considering whether to appoint a special investigative prosecutor to conduct its inquiry into charges of misconduct by Kenneth W. Starr.

19 At a news conference in Washington, Pres. Clinton threatens to bomb Serbia if Pres. Slobodan Milosevic of Yugoslavia misses the deadline for an end to peace talks.

20 The Clinton Administration and its NATO partners extend peace talks concerning Kosovo.

For only the third time in fifty years, an Indian Prime Minister—Atal Behari Vajpayee—visits Pakistan to meet with Prime Minister Nawaz Sharif. (See "Major New Stories of the Year.")

22 Scott Ritter, a former U.N. arms inspector in Iraq, says in a new book that the C.I.A. began placing American spies on teams of U.N. weapons inspections in Iraq only a year after the end of the Persian Gulf war of 1991.

24 The Senate overwhelmingly (91-8) approves a sweeping pay and pension increase for the military that is more than the 4.4 percent requested by Pres. Clinton.

25 A truth commission report made public today concludes that the U.S. gave money and training to a Guatemalan military that committed "acts of genocide" against the Mayans during the brutal 36-year civil war.

The Services Employees International Union wins the biggest unionization drive in over half a century when the 74,000 Los Angeles home-care workers vote to have the union represent them.

26 The Clinton Administration issues one of its harshest condemnations of China for the regime's serious human rights violations.

27 In Nigeria, tens of millions of people vote in a presidential election after years of military dictatorship and elect Olusegun Obasanjo. (See "Major New Stories of the Year.")

28 After a week of attacks culminating in the killing of a general and three other Israelis, Israel launches an air bombardment in southern Lebanon where it says Hezbollah guerilla strongholds exist.

▶ MARCH

1   For the third straight day U.S. jets attack strategic targets in Iraq, the most intense bombardment since December.

2   In the Bwindi Impenetrable Forest of Uganda, eight tourists, including an American couple, are killed by a band of rebels said to be remnants of Hutu militias that carried out mass killings in Rwanda in 1994.

In California, Federal officials strike an 11th-hour deal with the Pacific Lumber Co. to turn the largest privately owned grove of ancient redwood trees into a public preserve for $480 mil.

3   As the dispute over bananas and airplanes heat up, the U.S. slaps 100 percent tariffs on $520 mil. in European products and threatens to ban the Concorde from landing here.

In a television interview to promote her new book, Monica S. Lewinsky portrays herself as a romantic who got ensnared in the criminal investigation of Pres. Clinton's misconduct.

4   The Republican leaders of Congress announce agreement on a budget plan for 2000 that they say will wall off Social Security funds so they may not be used to pay for tax cuts or new Government spending.

A court martial jury in Lejeune, N.C. acquits Capt. Richard J. Ashby, the Marine Corp. pilot whose plane severed gondola cables in Italy, sending 20 people to their deaths.

5   *The New York Times* reports that China stole nuclear secrets for bombs from the U.S. during the mid-1980s but it was not detected until 1995. (See "Major News Stories of the Year.")

7   After the F.B.I. questions him, the U.S. fires the Taiwan-born scientist at Los Alamos Laboratory for security breaches in connection with China's suspected theft of nuclear secrets.

China's Foreign Ministry issues a statement calling accusations that spies stole nuclear weapons designs from the U.S. "unfounded."

8   In the face of persistent lawsuits, RJR Nabisco announces it is splitting its food and tobacco businesses and selling its foreign tobacco company to a Japanese buyer.

9   Speaking in Guatemala, Pres. Clinton apologizes for U.S. support of right-wing governments that killed tens of thousands of rebels and Mayan Indians in a 36-year civil war.

11   After a passionate and bitter debate, the House of Representatives votes 219-191 to support Pres. Clinton's plan to send U.S. troops to Kosovo.

12   Poland, Hungary and the Czech Republic formally join NATO, ending the Soviet domination that began after World War II.

13   Three powerful bombs explode in the northern Kosovo town of Pudujevo killing at least six and wounding dozens more, and bringing the war out of the hills for the first time.

14   Pres. Clinton's national security adviser, Sandy Berger, acknowledges that "there's no question" China benefited from obtaining the design of America's most miniaturized nuclear warhead from the Los Alamos Laboratory.

16   The Kosovo peace talks stall as Serbia moves heavy tanks and thousands more troops into the province while Serb negotiators demand extensive changes in the draft peace agreement.

After months of negotiations, North Korea agrees to allow the U.S. to inspect a huge underground site suspected of being an atomic weapons plant.

17   The House of Representatives votes decisively (289-141) to limit steel imports, ignoring opposition from the Republican leadership and a White House warning that the measure would violate world trade agreements.

18   Peace talks about Kosovo end with only the ethnic Albanians signing the agreement on autonomy for the province. The Clinton Administration publicly pushes for air strikes against Serbia.

19   At a White House news conference, Pres. Clinton says that the Serbs have crossed the "threshhold" of acceptable behavior in Kosovo and that force was the answer to prevent further bloodshed. (See "Major News Stories of the Year.")

20   As hundreds of foreign monitors leave Kosovo, Serbian forces launch a heavy offensive against the rebel Kosovo Liberation Army.

22   After three hours of negotiations with Yugoslavia's Pres. Milosevic, special envoy Richard C. Holbrooke says it would be "misleading" to suggest any significant change.

23   NATO allies authorize air strikes against Serbian forces attacking Kosovo. Pres. Clinton warns of dangers to U.S. pilots but says NATO would be discredited if "we didn't keep our word."

24   The forces of NATO open their assault on Serbia with bombs and cruise missiles as Pres. Clinton denounces Pres. Slobodan Milosevic.

A truck fire in a mountain tunnel in Mont Blanc, France engulfs 300 vehicles, causing an inferno that kills at least 35 and injures dozens more.

25   As NATO air assaults continue, the White House vows prolonged and severe attacks, but Serb forces step up their campaign in Kosovo.

A grand jury in the Bronx, N.Y. indicts four white police officers for second-degree murder in the killing of an unarmed African immigrant, on Feb. 4. (See "Major News Stories of the Year.")

The first shipment of nuclear waste leaves Los Alamos, N.M., the birthplace of nuclear weapons, for deep underground burial at a central facility in Carlsbad, N.M.

26   NATO forces step up their air and missile assault on Serbia but Pres. Slobodan Milosevic's, resistance grows stronger and Serbian troops continue to sweep through Albanian villages in Kosovo, forcing thousands of refugees to flee to Macedonia.

A jury in Mich. convicts Dr. Jack Kevorkian of murder for giving a fatal injection to a man with a terminal illness. Kevorkian claims he has helped more than 130 sick people commit suicide.

28   NATO warplanes brave bad weather to step up attacks on Yugoslav troops in Kosovo and allied leaders repeatedly accuse Serbian forces of large-scale atrocities in Kosovo. Tens of thousands of ethnic Albanians from Kosovo are streaming in to Albania, telling stories of being driven from their homes by Serbian police and paramilitary units.

29   For the first time the U.S. State Dept. says there is evidence of "genocide" by Serbian forces as well as assassinations of ethnic Albanian leaders in Kosovo.

The Dow-Jones industrial average closes above 10,000 for the first time, double the 5,000 reached in Nov. 1995, and up tenfold since 1982.

30   The U.S. and NATO agree to escalate the bombing campaign, targeting government buildings in downtown Belgrade.

An Oregon jury orders Philip Morris to pay $81 mil. to the family of a 40-year smoker; it is the largest award of this kind to date.

31   NATO expands its bombing campaign to sites throughout Yugoslavia and says it plans weeks of air attacks.

Three U.S. infantrymen on patrol along Macedonia's Kosovo border are captured by Serb forces.

▶ APRIL

1   Allied forces destroy a bridge over the Danube in northern Serbia, the first air attack on a target that disrupts the lives of ordinary citizens.

2   A barrage of eight NATO cruise missiles strike Belgrade's center, destroying the command centers of the security forces carrying out Pres. Milosevic's offensive against Kosovo. The White House warns that the attack has "barely begun."

At a briefing in Beijing, the U.N. aid coordinator for North Korea predicts that the food scarcity engulfing that nation will worsen significantly over the next two months.

3   NATO announces it will send 6,000-8,000 troops to Albania to provide security and emergency relief for the Kosovo Albanian refugees.

4   NATO announces plans to airlift 100,000 Kosovo refugees to temporary shelter on American and European territory.

5   NATO launches its most ferocious air strikes yet on Yugoslav armored forces operating in Kosovo, and also bombs targets in Serbia's three largest cities including Belgrade.

The two Libyans charged in the 1988 bombing of Pan Am Flight 103 that killed 270 people are brought to the Netherlands for trial. The U.N. immediately removes severe sanctions against the government of Muammar el-Qaddafi.

6   Pres. Slobodan Milosevic announces a unilateral cease-fire by Serbian forces, but NATO dismisses the proposal and takes advantage of clear skies to intensify its aerial bombardment.

The Energy Dept. announces it has suspended all scientific work on computers containing America's most sensitive secrets at its three nuclear weapons laboratories because of fears that security lapses make the computers vulnerable to espionage. (See "Major News Stories of the Year.")

8   The Yugoslav Government asserts that "peace has been restored in Kosovo" and declares an end to its military offensive. NATO dismisses this and says it will continue its bombing campaign.

At a joint news conference in Washington, Pres. Clinton and Chinese Prime Minister Zhu Rongji say that despite significant concessions by China, they fell short of reaching a major trade deal. (See "Major News Stories of the Year.")

10   A senior NATO diplomat says the alliance is prepared to continue air attacks "for many more weeks" but ground troops were not yet an option.

11   *The New York Times* reports that tax returns from Americans earning more than $100,000 a year and from the biggest corporations are escaping scrutiny by the I.R.S.

12   A Federal judge in Little Rock, Ark. holds Pres. Clinton in contempt of court, saying he willfully provided false testimony under oath about his relationship with Monica S. Lewinsky.

A Federal jury in Little Rock, Ark. acquits Susan H. McDougal of charges she obstructed justice when she refused to testify before independent counsel Kenneth Starr's grand jury about the Clintons' financial dealings.

13   After a meeting with over 20 business executives yesterday, the White House announces it has restarted trade negotiations with China after failing to reach an agreement a week earlier.

14   NATO warplanes mistakenly attack a convoy in southern Kosovo that turns out to be ethnic Albanian refugees; at least 64 are killed.

Independent counsel Kenneth W. Starr testifies before a Senate committee and says the independent counsel law "should not be re-authorized" because it has not achieved its main purpose of giving the public a sense that investigations of political figures are free of partisanship.

15   Two teams of astronomers announce the detection of three large planets around a solar-type star, Upsilon Andromedae, 44 light-years away. (See "Major News Stories of the Year.")

17   India's Hindu nationalist-led government loses a vote of confidence by one vote and Prime Minister Atal Behari Vajpayee resigns. (See "Major News Stories of the Year.")

20   In the deadliest school massacre in the nation's history, two young men in Littleton, Colo. kill 12 students and one teacher and wound at least 20 others with guns and explosions. (See "Major News Stories of the Year.")

Government officials say that a comprehensive analysis by U.S. intelligence officials has concluded that China stole design information related to America's most advanced nuclear warhead. (See "Major News Stories of the Year.")

22   Officials in Littleton, Colo. say they have found a large homemade bomb in Columbine High School that lead them to believe the two students who killed 13 people were out to "destroy the school."

23   On the opening day of the NATO summit meeting in Washington, the alliance agrees to impose an oil embargo in Serbia and to enforce it by searching ships in the Adriatic Sea.

25   In a telephone conversation, Pres. Clinton and Pres. Boris Yeltsin of Russia agree to work closely together in the search for a resolution to the conflict in Kosovo.

In Beijing, 10,000 followers of a religious cult called Falun Gong surround China's leadership compound, demanding recognition. It is the biggest protest in China since Tiananmen Square in 1989. (See "Major News Stories of the Year.")

27   U.S. Government officials say a scientist suspected of spying for China improperly transferred huge amounts of secret data from a computer system at the Los Alamos Weapons Laboratory, compromising virtually every nuclear weapon in the U.S. arsenal. (See "Major News Stories of the Year.")

28   In a sharp challenge to Pres. Clinton, the House of Representatives votes (249-180) to bar him from sending ground troops to Yugoslavia without Congressional approval; then on a tie vote it refuses to support NATO air strikes against Serbia.

29   The Clinton Administration says it has decided to sell Taiwan an early warning radar system that will allow it to monitor the launch of Chinese ballistic missiles.

Scientists at NASA announce that the Mars *Global Surveyor* Spacecraft discovers magnetized bands in the Martian crust, adding to evidence of similarities in the geology of Earth and Mars.

30   The Littleton, Colo. sheriff's office acknowledges it had done little to follow up on a complaint that one of the teenage killers at Columbine High School talked "often of making pipe bombs and using them to kill numerous people."

▶ MAY

1   Three U.S. soldiers held captive by Serb forces for more than a month are released and handed over to the Rev. Jesse L. Jackson.

The New York Times reports that a secret report was given to Clinton Administration officials in Nov. 1998 warning that China posed an "acute intelligence threat" to nuclear weapons labs. Yet investigators waited until March to search the computer of a Los Alamos scientist. (See "Major News Stories of the Year.")

3   NATO planes attack Yugoslavia's electrical system knocking out 70 percent of the country's power and disrupting military communications and air defense systems.

A band of vicious tornadoes streaks through Oklahoma and Kansas, killing over 40 people. (See "Major News Stories of the Year.")

Only 24 trading days after the Dow Jones industrial average first closed above 10,000, it surpasses

11,000, the fastest such rise in history. (See "Major News Stories of the Year.")

4   AT&T clears a path to its acquisition of Media One, the number four cable TV company, and makes it clear it seeks a partnership with the Microsoft Corp.

5   For the first time since 1707, voters in Scotland go to the polls to elect their own Parliament; in Wales people vote in their first election.

6   Russia and the West announce that for the first time they agree on the need for an international military presence in Kosovo to keep peace.

7   NATO air strikes against Belgrade mistakenly bomb the Chinese Embassy there. China says two of its citizens were killed and two more are missing. (See "Major News Stories of the Year.")

In Bucharest, Romania, Pope John Paul II meets and prays with Patriarch Teoctist of the Romanian Orthodox Church. He is the first Pope to visit an Orthodox Christian country since the schism of 1054 drove the two churches apart.

8   In Beijing and several other cities in China, large, angry protests erupt around U.S. government offices after news that NATO bombs had hit the Chinese Embassy in Belgrade. In Chengdu the consulate building is set on fire and police use tear gas to disperse the crowd.

9   *The New York Times* reports that a secret Government document reveals that a scientist working on a classified Pentagon project in 1997 provided China with secrets about advanced radar technology to detect submarines.

10   The Chinese Government signals its intent to obstruct the U.S. strategy in Kosovo by demanding NATO halt bombing before the U.N. Security Council can consider any other action.

11   The House Government Reform Committee hears testimony from former Democratic fundraiser, Johnny Chung, who says a high-ranking Chinese intelligence official promised him $300,000 for use in the 1996 Presidential election.

12   Russian Pres. Boris Yeltsin abruptly fires Prime Minister Yevgeny M. Primakov; it is the third government shake-up in 15 months.

13   U.S. intelligence officials say China is close to deploying a nuclear missile warhead whose design draws on stolen American secrets.

14   By a single vote (48-47), the Senate passes a measure to promote background checks at gun shows. Democrats denounce the measure as not strict enough. (See "Major News Stories of the Year.")

15   A Communist-led drive to impeach Russian Pres. Boris Yeltsin fails in Parliament as nearly 100 members unexpectedly stay away.

17   Ehud Barak is overwhelmingly elected Israel's Prime Minister over Benjamin Netanyahu. (See "Major News Stories of the Year.")

The U.S. Supreme Court rules (7-2) that state welfare programs may not restrict new residents to the benefits they have received in their home states. (See "Major News Stories of the Year.")

20   In Conyers, Ga., a 15-year old boy shoots six of his fellow students and then surrenders to an assistant principal. All of the victims survive. Hours later the Senate overwhelmingly passes (73-25) a juvenile-crime bill that contains an array of new gun-control measures. (See "Major News Stories of the Year.")

23   NATO officials report that the Yugoslav military is sending fresh troops to Kosovo to reinforce positions near the border with Albania.

24   The Supreme Court rules (5 to 4) that school districts can be liable for damages under Federal law for failing to stop a student from subjecting another student to severe and pervasive sexual harassment. (See "Major News Stories of the Year.")

25   Congress releases its long-awaited report that describes a pattern of systematic and successful Chinese espionage to learn American nuclear secrets. (See "Major News Stories of the Year.")

NATO approves plans for an armed peacekeeping force of about 50,000 soldiers for Kosovo.

26   India sends combat jets and helicopter gun ships to attack a large guerilla force of Islamic militants dug into the snow-capped mountains of Kashmir and accuses Pakistan of sponsoring them. (See "Major News Stories of the Year.")

27   The international tribunal at The Hague issues an arrest warrant for Slobodan Milosevic, charging him and other Yugoslav officials with crimes against humanity in Kosovo.

31   India agrees to peace talks with Pakistan about the situation in Kashmir even as it continues its bombing.

▶ JUNE

1   The Government of Germany receives a letter from the Yugoslav Government in which Pres. Slobodan Milosevic says he is ready to withdraw forces from Kosovo and accept a "United Nations presence" in the Serbian province.

2   After a marathon negotiating session in Bonn, Germany, Russian envoy, Viktor S. Chernomyrdin, says, "we have found a common approach", to ending the war in Kosovo.

Pres. Clinton announces a NATO plan to dispatch 50,000 troops (7,000 Americans) to the Balkans to escort the 800,000 refugees back to their homes when the conflict ends.

Millions line up in polling places to elect Nelson Mandela's deputy, Thabo Mbeki of the African National Congress by an overwhelming majority. (See "Major News Stories of the Year.")

3   On the 72nd day of NATO's air war against Yugoslavia, Pres. Slobodan Milosevic accepts the NATO peace plan to end the conflict, requiring him to withdraw all military and police forces from Kosovo within seven days.

The leaders of the nations in the European Union announce a plan to make the EU a military power for the first time in its 42-year history.

6   After two days of tense negotiations, NATO commanders fail to get Yugoslav military officials to agree to terms for a Serbian withdrawal from Kosovo, throwing into doubt a peace deal reached last week by political leaders.

7   About 130 million people in Indonesia cast ballots in a parliamentary election that will result in a new President. It is the first free election here in 40 years. (See "Major News Stories of the Year.")

9   The Yugoslav military accepts an agreement that will permit a military force commanded by a NATO general with sweeping powers to occupy Kosovo, clearing the way to an end to the war.

11   Several hours before NATO troops enter Kosovo, Russian forces march through the city of Pristina amid a wild celebration by Serbs. The Russian Foreign Minister says this was a mistake and that the soldiers would be ordered to leave.

12   Thousands of NATO troops with armored vehicles move methodically into Kosovo.

13   Russian soldiers occupying the Pristina airport block the entry of British troops in an embarrassing impasse for NATO's nascent peacekeeping effort in Kosovo.

14   In a unanimous ruling, the Supreme Court strikes down a 65-year-old ban on broadcast advertising of casino gambling.

15   In Kosovo, foreign journalists are allowed to view the areas where the Serbs waged their most brutal campaigns to drive out the Albanian majority. Mass graves, charred farmhouses and smashed shops made it clear just how ferocious the campaign had been.

South Korean naval forces sink a North Korean torpedo boat after a fierce gun battle in the Yellow Sea. (See "Major News Stories of the Year.")

16 More than 12,000 cheering Kosovars leave Albania and begin their journey home, in the first big wave of a reverse exodus of refugees.

17 Clinton Administration officials say that U.S. intelligence agencies have uncovered evidence that North Korea is making initial preparations to test the launch of a ballistic missile later this summer.

18 Leaders from the Group of Seven industrial nations meeting in Cologne, Germany, agree to cut the debt burden of the world's poorest countries, mainly in Africa. The relief could total $65 bil. to $90 bil.

19 NATO commanders in Kosovo say they have reached a tentative agreement with leaders of the Kosovo Liberation Army to disband the rebel force gradually. The European Union announces plans to provide $1.5 bil. over three years for the reconstruction of Kosovo.

20 The last of Serbia's 40,000 troops leave, ending Yugoslavia's control over the center of Serbia's cultural and historical lore.

In a report commissioned by the Institute of Medicine at the request of Congress, an independent panel of 13 scientists conclude that silicone breast implants do not cause any major diseases.

21 Over the objections of doctors groups and consumer advocates, the Federal Government approves the $1 bil. acquisition of Prudential Health Care by Aetna, Inc., which will create the nation's biggest managed health care company.

22 The Supreme Court rules (7-2) that people with physical impairments who can function normally when they wear their glasses or take their medicine cannot be considered disabled, and therefore do not come within the law's protection against employment discrimination.

The Senate kills a bill that would have sharply restricted imports of foreign steel to the U.S., a blow to unions and steel makers and a victory for Pres. Clinton, who had warned that the legislation would revive protectionism.

23 Thrusting the doctrine of state sovereignty well beyond existing boundaries, the Supreme Court places sharp new curbs on the ability of Congress to make Federal law binding on the states. (See "Major News Stories of the Year.")

At its annual meeting, the 152 year-old American Medical Association (A.M.A.) votes to form a union for doctors. (See "Major News Stories of the Year.")

27 Talks on ending 11 months of war in the Congo receive a fresh impetus as the draft of a cease-fire document is completed. If it is approved, a peace summit of African heads of state would be called. (See "Major News Stories of the Year.")

28 Pres. Clinton lays out his proposal to use the fast-growing Federal budget surplus to reduce the national debt while shoring up Social Security.

29 Pres. Clinton proposes fundamental changes to Medicare to make it more like private health insurance and to add coverage of prescription drugs, a benefit long sought by the elderly.

In the first major anti-Government demonstration since NATO stopped bombing Yugoslavia, 10,000 people pack the central square in Cacak, Serbia to demand the resignation of Pres. Milosevic.

30 The Federal Reserve raises its benchmark interest rate by a quarter of a percentage point but says there was no clear case for another rate increase to keep inflation at bay.

▶ **JULY**

1 A major group of health maintenance organizations announces they will increase Medicare premiums or cut benefits for most of their six mil-

lion elderly subscribers because they consider their Federal payments inadequate.

2 Clinton Administration officials say that the U.S. and its NATO allies have blocked Russia from flying hundreds of troops into Kosovo.

5 NATO and Russian military commanders resolve their differences over Russia's role in the Kosovo peacekeeping operation, clearing the way for 3,600 more Russian troops to arrive in the Serbian province.

6 Ehud Barak takes office as Prime Minister of Israel and pledges to pursue a "true, lasting peace", telling the Palestinians he recognizes their "suffering."

7 A Florida jury finds against the nation's biggest tobacco companies in the first class-action case to reach a verdict, holding that the companies conspired to hide the danger and addictiveness of cigarettes.

The warring sides in Sierra Leone's eight-year civil war sign a peace agreement that gives amnesty and a share of power to the rebelling forces. (See "Major News Stories of the Year.")

8 In Los Angeles, Pres. Clinton ends his four-day tour of poverty in America that has received little attention in the media.

9 Russia's Defense Minister says that in June the military carried out a major exercise with 50,000 troops defending against an unnamed Western foe and with nuclear weapons as a key element.

10 *The New York Times* reports that Republicans in Congress will push for the largest and most broadly distributed tax reduction since 1981.

11 India and Pakistan announce that rival forces battling for the last two months in Kashmir would begin a phased withdrawal.

Israeli Prime Minister Ehud Barak meets with Palestinian leader Yasir Arafat, fulfilling his promise to move quickly to carry out the Wye River peace agreement.

Leftist guerillas in Colombia renew their attacks on a score of towns Over 180 people are killed. (See "Major News Stories of the Year.")

12 Taiwan's Government declares it will no longer adhere to the principle that the Chinese mainland and Taiwan are two parts of same country. Beijing responds furiously and threateningly.

In Iran the most widespread and sustained protests in two decades spread throughout the country as students demonstrated in 18 cities. Security forces and their vigilante supporters move to crush demonstrations outside Teheran University. (See "Major News Stories of the Year.")

13 For the first time in U.S. history criminal charges are brought in an airline accident, as a Federal grand jury in Florida charges an aviation maintenance company with 110 counts of murder in the 1996 Valujet crash in the Everglades.

14 The peace process in Northern Ireland comes to a halt as Ulster's main Protestant party says it is unwilling to join Sinn Fein, the I.R.A.'s political wing, in government as scheduled for July 15th. (See "Major News Stories of the Year.")

In Iran, after six days of nationwide pro-democracy protests that deteriorated into violent rioting, huge crowds stage counter-demonstrations in two dozen cities praising the Government and condemning the U.S.

15 After a sharply partisan debate over health care, the Republican-controlled Senate defeats the Democrats' effort to expand the ability of patients to sue managed-care providers and then approves a plan to regulate the companies that provide health insurance for most Americans.

Gov. George W. Bush of Texas declares he will not accept Federal matching funds because his enormous $37 mil. campaign war chest gives him the capacity to far outspend his Republican rivals for the party nomination for President.

16 Leaders of both parties say the House of Representatives will cut off money for the Air Force's $70 bil. F-22 fighter program, stunning the Pentagon and military contractors.

17 Debris from a plane carrying John F. Kennedy Jr., his wife, and her sister is recovered off the Massachusetts coast after the plane, flown by Kennedy, had been reported missing late the night before. (See "Major News Stories of the Year.")

Officials from NATO and from aid agencies in Kosovo report that at least 10,000 people were slaughtered by Serbian forces during their three-month campaign to drive Albanians from Kosovo.

18 After two fruitless days of searching, the Coast Guard tells the Kennedy family there is little hope that any survivors will be found from the plane crash involving John F. Kennedy Jr.

More than a week after the signing of a cease-fire accord, the war in the Congo continues and rebel forces say they have captured more territory. (See "Major News Stories of the Year.")

19 Gov. Gray Davis of California signs into law the nation's toughest and most comprehensive ban on assault-style weapons.

20 A human rights group reports that more than 100 leaders of Falun Gong, the Buddhist spiritual movement that in April had 10,000 adherents silently protest outside the Communist leaders' compound in Beijing, had been arrested. (See "Major News Stories of the Year.")

21 The House Appropriations Committee issues an angry report that says the Pentagon defied the law and the Constitution by spending hundreds of millions of dollars on military projects that lawmakers never approved.

22 China's Government announces it is banning Falun Gong, revealing how seriously it takes the sect as a challenge to its control.

23 A Federal investigation concludes that a scientist in Berkeley, Calif. had faked crucial evidence of a tie between electric power lines and cancer, strengthening the case that electric power is safe.

25 In an attempt to mend relations after the U.S. bombed the Chinese embassy in Belgrade, Sec. of State Madeleine Albright meets with Chinese Foreign Minister in Singapore and they announce that Pres. Clinton will meet with Chinese leader Jiang Zemin in September.

26 The Environmental Protection Agency says it will propose that Congress no longer require oil companies to add M.T.B.E., an ingredient meant to make the air cleaner, because it pollutes water.

27 *The New York Times* reports that the Clinton Administration has developed a plan for an extensive computer monitoring system, overseen by the F.B.I., to protect the nation's crucial data networks from intruders but raising concerns among civil liberties groups.

29 In Atlanta, a securities day trader kills his wife and two children and nine people in two office buildings, then eludes an extensive police manhunt for five hours before killing himself.

30 The Senate approves a tax cut of $792 bil. over the next 10 years, moving the Republican-controlled Congress toward a politically charged showdown with Pres. Clinton.

Linda R. Tripp, whose secretly recorded telephone conversations with Monica Lewinsky exposed an affair that led to Pres. Clinton's impeachment, is indicted on two criminal charges for illegally taping the calls.

▶ AUGUST

1 The nationwide death toll from the heat wave climbs to at least 185, with 80 of them in Illinois

2 The Environmental Protection Agency bans most uses of methyl parathion, a pesticide applied for years on fruits and vegetables, and tightens restrictions on another, in the first regulations intended specifically to protect children.

Federal prosecutors say records from a defunct Cayman Islands bank has resulted in investigations of 1,500 people that could net more than $30 mil. in unpaid taxes and penalties. Federal investigators say the case has helped them penetrate the veil of secrecy of offshore money laundering.

China says it successfully test-launched a new type of long-range missile, and then it excoriates the U.S. for selling military equipment to Taiwan in the middle of a major diplomatic crisis.

3 Republicans reach agreement on a tax plan that would cut taxes by $792 bil. over the next decade as they prepare for a showdown with Pres. Clinton. (See "Major News Stories of the Year.")

4 The U.S. Treasury Dept. announces that for the first time since 1972, it plans to buy back debt and reduce the $3.6 trillion debt it owes to the public in the form of Treasury bonds and other securities.

5 After 14 months of delays caused by Republican objections, the Senate finally confirms Richard C. Holbrooke, architect of the 1995 peace agreement in Bosnia, as U.S. Ambassador to the U.N.

The Federal Communications Commission relaxes rules limiting television ownership and allowing for the first time a single company or network to own two stations in the nation's largest cities.

7 Russian helicopter gun ships fight a fierce battle with hundreds of gunmen who had crossed the border from Chechnya and surrounded three villages in the remote Dagestan region of southern Russia (See "Major News Stories of the Year.")

9 A middle-aged man walks into a Jewish community center in Granada Hills, Calif. and shoots five people, including three young boys.

11 The Kansas Board of Education votes to delete virtually any mention of evolution from the state's science curriculum, in one of the most far reaching efforts by creationists to challenge the teaching of evolution in schools.

Under continued pressure from minority politicians and human rights activists, Pres. Clinton agrees to commute the sentences of 16 Puerto Rican members of F.A.L.N., a nationalist group that was involved in more than 100 bombings in the U.S. over 15 years ago.

Buford O. Furrow Jr., a white supremacist suspected in the shooting of five people at a Jewish community center, surrenders in Nevada.

13 The U.S. military announces its first major revision of guidelines for its policy on homosexuals, including a new requirement that commanders seek approval from civilian officials before opening certain types of investigations. Gay rights activists say the new rules do not go far enough.

14 Gov. George W. Bush of Texas wins the Iowa straw poll of nearly 25,000 voters, a non-binding but high profile test of the Republican Presidential field; Steve Forbes places second.

16 A report by the international agency responsible for carrying out the civilian aspects of the Dayton agreement on Bosnia shows widespread corruption and asserts that as much as $1 bil. has disappeared from public funds or been stolen from international aid projects.

A Federal appeals court upholds the convictions of Sheik Omar Abdel Rahman and nine other Muslim militants for plotting to blow up

New York landmarks, validating the prosecution of terrorists under a Civil War-era sedition law.

17 In northwest Turkey thousands of people are killed when a powerful earthquake strikes before dawn destroying thousands of buildings. (See "Major News Stories of the Year.")

18 Law enforcement officials in New York say that billions of dollars have been channeled through the Bank of New York in the last year in what is believed to be a major money laundering operation by Russian organized crime leaders. (See "Major News Stories of the Year.")

The Metropolitan Life Insurance Co., the nation's second-largest life insurer, agrees to pay hundreds of millions of dollars to settle lawsuits that accused it of cheating customers through deceptive sales practices.

19 In Belgrade tens of thousands of people gather outside the Federal Parliament demanding the resignation of Pres. Slobodan Milosevic.

20 In Turkey, as the death toll from the recent earthquake rises above 10,000 with 34,000 injured, relief workers say they now face the problem of disease. (See "Major News Stories of the Year.")

22 With winds reaching 125 m.p.h. and a tidal surge as high as 12 feet, Hurricane Bret rumbles ashore on the south Texas coast just hours after tens of thousands of residents evacuated inland along clogged highways.

23 The Dow Jones industrial average closes at a record high of 11,299.76, up 199.15 points.

24 Chinese authorities announce that they are preparing to prosecute senior members of Falun Gong, the spiritual movement that was banned last month after it startled China's leaders with its ability to organize potent anti-Government protests.

The Federal Reserve, as expected, raises interest rates by a quarter of a percentage point, the second increase in two months, saying the action should help avert inflation while allowing the nation's long economic expansion to continue.

25 After six years of denials the F.B.I. concedes that it used "pyrotechnic" tear-gas canisters on the final day of the 1993 standoff with the Branch Davidian cult near Waco, Texas and orders a full inquiry. (See "Major News Stories of the Year.")

The Clinton Administration announces plans to withdraw the last American troops stationed in Haiti, even though peace there remains tenuous.

26 Government officials say that a wide range of Federal law-enforcement agencies were asked to review a clemency petition by imprisoned members of a Puerto Rican nationalist group and unanimously opposed any leniency.

Chandra X-ray Observatory, the world's largest telescope, transmits its first image showing in striking detail, Cassiopeia A, the 320-year old remnant of an exploding star.

27 Over the objections of civil liberties groups and privacy advocates, the Federal Government announces new technical standards for cellular phones that will broadly expand the ability of law-enforcement agents to monitor conversations and locate criminal suspects.

The last full-time crew of *Mir*, the 13-year old Russian space station, departs; in less than a year the station will be abandoned.

30 In East Timor, huge numbers of people turn out to vote in a referendum on whether they want autonomy within Indonesia or independence. (See "Major News Stories of the Year.")

31 The day after 98.6 percent of eligible voters cast their ballots in East Timor's referendum, anti-independence militias set up roadblocks through the region near the capital of Dili. (See "Major News Stories of the Year.")

SEPTEMBER

1 Atty. Gen. Janet Reno orders U.S. marshals to F.B.I. headquarters to seize a previously undisclosed tape recording of voice communications between F.B.I. commanders and field agents during the assault on the Branch Davidian compound.

4 Israeli Prime Minister Ehud Barak and Palestinian leader Yasir Arafat sign a broad agreement that could lead to a new era of peace. (See "Major News Stories of the Year.")

First Lady, Hillary Rodham Clinton calls on Pres. Clinton to immediately withdraw his offer to commute the prison sentences of 16 Puerto Rican nationalists.

5 In a major setback for the Russian military, Islamic militants mount a ferocious assault in the Caucasus region of Dagestan, a powerful bomb demolishes an apartment building housing Russian officials.

6 *The New York Times* reports that armed thugs have taken over East Timor, killing and terrorizing residents and trapping U.N. workers in their compound. (See "Major News Stories of the Year.")

7 Viacom Inc. announces it will acquire the CBS Corp. for $37.3 bil.. If approved, this would be the biggest media merger ever, and would create the second-largest media company after Time Warner Inc.

The U.N. says that as many as 200,000 people, a quarter of East Timor's population, have been driven from their homes by militias opposed to independence.

9 Pres. Clinton demands that Indonesia permit an international peacekeeping force to try to restore order in East Timor if the Indonesian military is unable to end "this madness."

Gov. George W. Bush of Texas, the front-runner for the Republican Presidential nomination, begins posting on his Internet site a detailed list of the size and source of every contribution to his campaign, an unprecedented gesture of voluntary disclosure.

10 Militias in East Timor menace the 1,000 refugees still taking shelter in the U.N. compound.

After three decades of busing for desegregation, a Federal judge in Charlotte, N.C. rules that forced integration of the Charlotte-Mecklenburg School District was no longer necessary, ending the court-ordered busing first approved by the Supreme Court in 1971.

11 At the annual Asian economic summit in Auckland, New Zealand, Pres. Clinton and China's leader, Jiang Zemin, declare an end to months of frozen relations following the U.S. bombing of the Chinese Embassy in Belgrade.

12 Pres. B.J. Habibie of Indonesia capitulates to international pressure and invites the U.N. to send a peacekeeping force to East Timor. (See "Major News Stories of the Year.")

13 For the third time in two weeks, a huge bomb explodes in Moscow. This one, in an apartment building, kills at least 95 people. Russian authorities say the bombs are the work of Islamic militants. (See "Major News Stories of the Year.")

14 Residents of Florida, Georgia, and the Carolinas brace for an encounter with Hurricane Floyd, a huge Category 4 storm with winds of 140 to 150 miles an hour. Over two million people are ordered to evacuate coastal areas.

Defying the wishes of the Republican leadership, the House votes 252 to 177 in favor of campaign finance reform, as 54 Republicans split from their party.

15 At a Baptist church in Fort Worth, Tex., a 47-year old man with a handgun shoots and kills eight people and wounds several others and then shoots himself.

William H. Gates 3d, co-founder and chairman of the Microsoft Corp., pledges $1 bil. to pay for full scholarships over the next 20 years for minority students.

17   Hurricane Floyd wreaks havoc on the East Coast, especially in North Carolina, where 20 inches of rain cause rivers to overflow and inundate entire towns. (See "Major News Stories of the Year.")

19   Led by Australia, the first unit of an international peacekeeping force lands in East Timor to crush the campaign of terror launched by anti-independence militias.

21   A powerful earthquake measuring 7.6 on the Richter Scale rocks Taiwan, killing more than 2,000 people, toppling buildings, and trapping hundreds in the wreckage.

22   The Justice Dept. closes the book on a criminal investigation of the tobacco industry and files a far-reaching civil lawsuit that accuses the largest cigarette company of conspiring since the 1950's to defraud and mislead the public about the health effects of smoking.

Atty. Gen. Janet Reno and F.B.I. Director Louis J. Freeh order Federal agents to broaden their investigation into evidence of Chinese nuclear espionage. (See "Major News Stories of the Year.")

23   The House of Representatives proposes legislation that would make it almost impossible to bring large class-action lawsuits against tobacco companies, gun makers and a wide variety of other businesses.

Russian warplanes bomb the Grozny airport in Chechnya and set an oil refinery ablaze, a major step-up in its struggle against Islamic militants.

24   A Federal appeals court in St. Louis rules that laws in Nebraska, Iowa and Arkansas banning late-term, so-called partial- birth abortions are unconstitutional.

26   After days of intensive air bombardment by Russian planes, tens of thousands of desperate refugees clog the roads of Chechnya causing a crisis. (See "Major News Stories of the Year.")

27   With only four days left in the fiscal year, Republican leaders in Congress concede publicly that they will not meet the deadline for passing the annual spending bills. The White House lays down a new deadline, three weeks away.

Prosecutors in Italy say they have concrete evidence that suspected organized crime operators from Russia have funneled millions of dollars through the Bank of New York whose accounts are under investigation by the F.B.I. (See "Major News Stories of the Year.")

28   Opposition parties in Mexico say they are unable to forge a coalition that would back a single presidential candidate, greatly increasing chances that the PRI will win power again next year.

29   Vice Pres. Al Gore, acknowledging that his lagging Presidential campaign needs a jolt, announces that he is moving his headquarters from Washington to his home state of Tennessee. The move is designed to pare down a top-heavy operation and to symbolize a break from the Beltway—and from the Clinton Administration.

30   At a nuclear fuel plant 87 miles from Tokyo, an out-of-control chain reaction spews high levels of radiation into the air. This is the worst accident in Japan's troubled history with nuclear power, as 35 people are exposed and 300,000 residents are ordered to stay indoors.

OCTOBER

2   Russian troops continue to move into Chechnya and the breakaway republic's President vows to repulse them.

3   The Census Bureau reports that the number of Americans without health coverage rose last year by 833,000, despite a strong economy and a new law intended to provide coverage for children. The ranks of the uninsured have grown by 4.5 million people since Pres. Clinton took office.

4   MCI Worldcom Inc., the nation's second-largest long-distance phone company, announces it has agreed to acquire the Sprint Corp. in a stock swap valued at $108 bil. If approved by Government regulators, the deal would be the largest acquisition in corporate history.

5   U.N. Sec. Gen. Kofi Annan presents a sweeping plan for the U.N. to take full control of East Timor and guide the territory to statehood.

Two commuter trains collide and burst into flames in West London, killing at least 70 people but with 100 more missing.

7   In defiance of the Republican leadership, the House passes a bill (275-151) to give patients a wide range of new rights, including the right to sue health insurance plans that cause injury by denying care or providing substandard treatment.

In India the results of national elections are announced and the Hindu nationalist party, Bharatiya Janata, wins a clear victory, and returns to power after losing a vote of confidence in April.

8   Pres. Clinton pleads with Republican Senate leaders to delay voting on the Comprehensive Test Ban Treaty (already signed by 150 nations) because it will be defeated without any meaningful hearings.

The Federal Communications Commission decides to loosen substantially the rules that keep one company from controlling too much of the cable industry. The new rules clear the way for AT&T to own more than a third of the nation's franchises offering TV, phone, and high-speed Internet service.

10   The president of the A.F.L.-C.I.O., John J. Sweeney, says that Vice-Pres. Al Gore will receive the powerful labor federation's endorsement at its convention this week.

11   Gov. Gray Davis of California signs a bill that will make his state the first to require hospitals to meet fixed nurse-to-patient ratios, in an effort to force higher quality care.

12   On its new Internet site, the Philip Morris Corp. acknowledges that scientific evidence shows that smoking causes lung cancer and other deadly diseases.

13   Pres. Clinton says that he will permanently protect at least 40 million acres of Federal forest land from road building, logging, and mining, by using administrative actions that bypass powerful opponents in Congress.

Just hours after the Prime Minister of Pakistan fires the powerful chief of the army, the army strikes back with a swift, bloodless coup. (See "Major News Stories of the Year.")

The Senate rejects a treaty banning all underground nuclear testing in a 51-48 vote, dealing Pres. Clinton a humiliating defeat on one of his key policy aims. (See "Major News Stories of the Year.")

14   Pres. Clinton delivers a blistering attack on the Republicans who defeated the nuclear test ban treaty, saying they were retreating into a "new isolationism" that threatened national security.

Biologists at Princeton Univ. challenge the longstanding belief that adults never generate new brain cells. (See "Major News Stories of the Year.")

15   A jittery stock market plunges by 2.59 percent (266.9 points), ending the worst week on the New York Stock Exchange since Oct. 1989. (See "Major News Stories of the Year.")

Obituaries October. 16, 1998–October. 15, 1999

Ally, Carl, 74, U.S. advertising executive whose aggressive campaigns broke genteel rules and named rivals, bringing recognition to unknown companies like Federal Express and MCI. Of a heart attack, Rowayton, Conn., Feb. 15, 1999.

Bird, Vere, 89, Caribbean political leader who led the independence movement in Antigua and became Prime Minister (1981-94), establishing a ruling family dynasty recently accused of shady dealings in international finance. After a long illness, St. John's, Antigua, June 28, 1999.

Blackmun, Harry A., 90, associate justice of the Supreme Court 1970-94. A moderate Republican appointed by Pres. Nixon, he was the author of the 1973 *Roe v. Wade* decision affirming a constitutional right to choose abortion, forever linking his name to a divisive national issue. Of surgery complications after a fall, Washington, March 5, 1999.

Bogarde, Dirk, 78, British actor who first achieved popularity in the comic "Doctor" films, then critical acclaim for his wily portrayals in such films as *The Servant, Darling,* and *Death in Venice.* Knighted in 1992. Of a heart attack after an earlier stroke, London, May 8, 1999.

Calhoun, Rory, 76, U.S. film actor in many western movies, usually as the rugged cowboy. Through the late 1950's and '60's, he appeared on TV, notably in *The Texan* series and on the soap opera *Capitol.* Of diabetes and emphysema, Burbank, Calif., April 28, 1999.

Callahan, Harry, 86, U.S. photographer best known for his experimental treatments of ordinary objects and the striking portraits of his wife, Eleanor. He was a highly influential teacher whose work has been widely exhibited. Cause undisclosed, Atlanta, March 15, 1999.

Carmichael, Stokely, 57, Trinidad-born U.S. civil rights activist and self-proclaimed revolutionary who changed his name to Kwame Ture in honor of two African socialists. He was a commanding orator whose cry for "Black Power" in 1966 electrified young blacks, alarmed whites and older integrationists, and made him a dominant figure in the civil rights struggle. Of prostate cancer, Conakry, Guinea (where he moved in 1969 after breaking with the Black Panthers), Nov. 15, 1998.

Castelli, Leo, 91, leading U.S. art dealer who brought attention to such artists as Jasper Johns, Robert Rauschenberg, and Roy Lichtenstein, as well as Andy Warhol; promoted Pop, Minimalism, Conceptualism, and other movements of the 60's and 70's. Of old age, New York, August 21, 1999.

Chamberlain, Wilt (the Stilt), 63, U.S. Hall of Fame basketball player whose size (7'-1" and 275 pounds) and agility transformed the game, forcing rule changes to make him less dominant. He scored 100 points in a game on March 2, 1962, a record that will likely never be broken. Of an apparent heart attack, Los Angeles, Oct. 12, 1999.

Chiles, Lawton, 68, U.S. Senator (D-Fla.) 1970-88 and Governor of Florida, 1990-98. A supporter of the environment and fiscal accountability in government; leader of legislation by states against tobacco interests. Of a heart attack, Tallahassee, Dec. 12, 1998.

Cockerell, Christopher, 88, British inventor of the hovercraft (1959), a boat that travels over water supported on a cushion of air, paring commercial timetables. Of complications after a fall, Hythe, Hampshire, England, June 1, 1999.

Conrad, Pete (Charles), 69, U.S astronaut. As commander of Apollo 12, he became the third man to walk on the Moon in November 1969. Of motorcycle accident injuries, Ojai, Calif., July 8, 1999.

Crichton, Charles, 89, British film director, master of whimsy in the 1950's, most notably *The Lavender Hill Mob,* and later *A Fish Called Wanda* (1986). Cause undisclosed, London, Sept. 14, 1999.

Delany, Sadie (Sarah), 109, the more amiable of the celebrated Delany sisters, whose memoir, *Having Our Say,* was a best seller and the source of a Broadway play. Of old age, Mount Vernon, N.Y., Jan. 25, 1999.

DiMaggio, Joseph ("Joltin' Joe"), 84, U.S. baseball legend and American icon. The Yankee Clipper was New York's center fielder 1936-51; his 56-game hitting streak in 1941 has never since been equaled. More widely famous for his short-lived marriage to Marilyn Monroe and Simon and Garfunkel's lyric "Where have you gone, Joe DiMaggio?" Of lung cancer, Hollywood, Fla., March 8, 1999.

Dmytryk, Edward, 90, Canadian-born U.S. film director, one of the Hollywood Ten jailed for refusing to cooperate with the House Un-American Activities Committee. His early movies include *Crossfire,* which hit hard against anti-Semitism. Cause undisclosed, Encino, Calif., July 1, 1999.

Ehrlichman, John D., 73, U.S. political adviser and aide to Pres. Nixon, who went to prison for his involvement in the Watergate scandal. He fiercely defended Nixon but later expressed remorse and went on to become a writer and business executive. Of diabetes, Atlanta, Feb. 14, 1999.

Elion, Gertrude, 81, U.S. scientist, co-winner of 1988 Nobel Prize in Physiology or Medicine for development of drugs that combat such conditions as herpes, transplant rejection, rheumatoid arthritis, gout, and AIDS. Cause undisclosed, Chapel Hill, N.C., Feb. 22, 1999.

Ewbank, Weeb, 91, U.S. football coach of the championship 1958 Baltimore Colts and the 1968 New York Jets. Voted to the Pro Football Hall of Fame in 1978. Of old age, Oxford, Ohio, Nov. 17, 1998.

Exner, Judith, 65, alleged inamorata of Pres. Kennedy. She claimed to have carried money and messages between Kennedy and Mafia don Sam Giancana, another of her lovers. Of breast cancer, Duarte, Calif., Sept. 24, 1999.

Fadiman, Clifton, 95, U.S. man of letters—writer, editor, anthologist—widely known as the moderator of the popular 1938-48 radio program *Information Please,* and a founder of the Book-of-the-Month Club. Of old age, Sanibel Island, Fla., June 20, 1999.

Farmer, James, 79, U.S. civil rights activist. A co-founder of the Congress of Racial Equality (CORE), he was at the forefront of the civil rights movement of the 1950's and '60's, risking his life several times opposing police. Of diabetes complications, Fredericksburg, Va., July 9, 1999.

Forrest, Helen, 82, U.S. pop singer with the big bands of the late 30's and 40's, most notably, Harry James, with whom she recorded "I Had the Craziest Dream," a No. 1 wartime hit. Of congestive heart failure, Los Angeles, July 11, 1999.

Funt, Allen, 84, U.S. TV personality who made people laugh when he caught them unawares as the creator and host of one of TV's longest-running programs: *Candid Camera* (1949-92). Of stroke complications, Pebble Beach, Calif. Sept. 5, 1999.

Gaddis, William, 75, reclusive U.S. author of four novels highly regarded by critics as experimental and ingenious (notably *The Recognitions* and *JR*) though not widely read by the public. Of prostate cancer, East Hampton, N.Y., Dec. 16, 1998.

Garrity, W. Arthur Jr., 79, U.S. Federal judge whose 1974 ruling brought desegregation to Boston's schools and a controversial system of enforced busing that roiled the city until a 1999 decision to drop it. Of cancer, Wellesley, Mass., Sept. 16, 1999.

Goldwater, John L., 83, U.S. writer who created the internationally popular *Archie* comic strip that featured the lovable teenager and his friends. At its peak, the strip appeared in 750 newspapers, and comic book sales hit 50 million a year. Of a heart attack, New York, Feb. 26, 1999.

Gorbachev, Raisa, 67, wife of former Soviet President Mikhail Gorbachev, whose hectoring attitude and stylish wardrobe raised eyebrows at home and abroad as the Soviet Union opened to the West after 1985 in its passage to collapse. Of leukemia, Münster, Germany, Sept. 20, 1999.

Gore, Albert Sr., 90, U.S. Senator (D-Tenn.), 1953-70. A Southern liberal who supported civil rights and opposed the Vietnam war, positions that cost him his seat. Father of Vice President Al Gore. Of old age, Carthage, Tenn., Dec. 5, 1998.

Greenfield, Meg, 68, U.S. journalist. As editor of the highly regarded editorial page of the *Washington Post* for 20 years, she was an astute and witty observer of the capital scene and a strong influence on other writers. Of lung cancer, Washington, May 13, 1999.

Hall, Huntz, 78, U.S. actor, one of the original "Dead End Kids" and "Bowery Boys." He made more than 80 movies, always playing a dim-witted teenager. Of cardiac disease, Los Angeles, Jan. 30, 1999.

Hassan II, 70, King of Morocco. He ruled his country from 1961 with a deft ability to balance the interests of the elite, the middle class, and the rural peasantry (even surviving several assassination attempts), while maintaining close ties with the U.S. and brokering talks with Israel. Of a lung infection leading to a heart attack, Rabat, July 23, 1999.

Herlihy, Ed, 89, longtime U.S. radio and TV announcer. A familiar, friendly voice for Kraft Foods and the *Horn and Hardart Children's Hour* as well as many soap operas and variety shows. Cause undisclosed, New York, Jan. 30, 1999.

Herzberg, Gerhard, 94, German-born Canadian scientist, 1971 winner of the Nobel Prize in Chemistry for the development of modern molecular spectroscopy for the measurement of light from atoms and molecules, leading to investigative tools for many fields of research. Of old age, Ottawa, March 3, 1999.

Hess, Leon, 85, U.S. businessman, longtime head of Amerada Hess oil company, but better known as the long-suffering owner of the hapless New York Jets football team. Of a blood disease, New York, May 7, 1999.

Higginbotham, A. Leon, 70, U.S. jurist, one of three black judges to become Chief Judge of a federal appeals court, serving 1990-93 for the Third Circuit. Originally named to the federal bench in 1964 by Pres. Johnson, he was a strong voice for social justice and author of several influential books. After a stroke, Boston, Dec. 14, 1998.

Hirt, Al, 76, U.S. musician whose trumpet-playing epitomized New Orleans Dixieland jazz. A bandleader and composer, he toured with the big bands of the 1940's before starting his own group. Of liver disease, New Orleans, April 27, 1999.

Hodgkin, Alan Lloyd, 84, British scientist. Co-winner of 1963 Nobel Prize in Physiology or Medicine for experiments with squids showing how nerves pass data to the brain, resulting in physical action. After a long illness, Cambridge, England, Dec. 20, 1998.

Holzman, Red (William) 78, U.S. basketball coach who led legendary New York Knick teams of 1970 and 1973 to the franchise's only championships. Voted to the Basketball Hall of Fame in 1991. Of leukemia, Long Island, N.Y., Nov. 15, 1998.

Hunter, Jim (Catfish), 53, U.S. Hall of Fame pitcher for the Oakland Athletics and New York Yankees (1965-79). A member of five World Championship teams, he pitched a perfect game in 1968. A technicality in his contract enabled him to become baseball's first free agent in 1975. Of amyotrophic lateral sclerosis (Lou Gehrig's disease), Hertford, N.C., Sept. 9, 1999.

Hussein, King of Jordan, 63. Proclaimed king in 1952 at age 16, he ruled with craft and wisdom through numerous political crises, wars, and assassination attempts to become an advocate for peace in the Middle East, notably in accords with Israel. Of cancer, Amman, Jordan, Feb. 7, 1999.

Johnson, Frank M. Jr., 80, influential Federal judge from Alabama in the vanguard of desegregation in the South by ruling Montgomery's bus-segregation law unconstitutional in 1955. Other significant decisions included open voter registration, and poll tax elimination. Of pneumonia after a fall, Montgomery, Ala., July 23, 1999.

Kane, Bob, 83, U.S. cartoonist who in 1939 created *Batman, the Caped Crusader* and his sidekick "Robin, the Wonder Boy," both of whom became the central characters in comics, TV shows, and movies that attained worldwide popularity. Of undisclosed causes, Los Angeles, Nov. 3, 1998.

Kanin, Garson, 86, U.S. stage and film writer and director who with his wife, actress Ruth Gordon, wrote the screenplays for *Adam's Rib* and *Pat and Mike* for Tracy and Hepburn; wrote and directed *Born Yesterday* with Judy Holliday. Cause undisclosed, New York, March 13, 1999.

Kelley, DeForest, 79, U.S. actor in more than 150 movies and TV shows, best remembered as *Star Trek*'s Dr. Leonard "Bones" McCoy, who always asserted he was "just a country doctor." Cause undisclosed, Los Angeles, June 11, 1999.

Kendall, Henry, 72, U.S. scientist, co-winner of 1990 Nobel Prize in Physics for confirming the existence of "quarks," earlier theorized as the basic building blocks of matter. In a diving accident, Wakulla Springs State Park, Fla., Feb. 15, 1999.

Kennedy, John F. Jr., 38, much-photographed son of Pres. Kennedy and Jacqueline Onassis, from his memorable salute to his slain father to the celebrity coverage of his love life. Founding editor of *George*, a magazine of politics as entertainment. In a plane crash, off Martha's Vineyard, July 16, 1999. (See "Major News Stories of the Year.")

Kiley, Richard, 76, versatile U.S. actor in musicals and dramas. He won two Tony Awards, most notably as Don Quixote in *Man of La Mancha*. Of a blood disorder, Middletown, N.Y., March 5, 1999.

Kirkland, Lane, 77, U.S. labor leader. He was president of the A.F.L.-C.I.O. from 1979-95, a difficult period of shrinking importance for organized labor. Criticized by some for his interest in international affairs, he was a crucial supporter of Poland's Solidarity movement. Of lung cancer, Washington, D.C., Aug. 14, 1999.

Kubrick, Stanley, 70, U.S. film director whose quirky perfectionism created such works as *Paths of Glory, Spartacus, Lolita, Dr. Strangelove, 2001: A Space Odyssey,* and *A Clockwork Orange.* His early success allowed him to be one of the few directors who received total control over his films. Cause undisclosed, outside London, March, 7, 1999.

Leontief, Wassily, 93, Russian-born economist and longtime U.S. academic. Winner of 1973 Nobel Prize in Economics for development of analytic methods of interconnected industrial production planning. Of old age, New York, Feb. 5, 1999.

Lini, Walter, 57, political leader of the Melanesian islands of Vanuatu. An Anglican priest, he led his people to independence in 1980 and served as Prime Minister until 1991. Of undisclosed causes, Vanuatu, Feb. 21, 1999.

Lortel, Lucille, 98, U.S. theatrical producer whose pioneering efforts Off-Broadway brought attention to numerous actors and playwrights as well as directors starting with Threepenny Opera at the Greenwich Village theater now bearing her name. Of old age, New York, April 4, 1999.

Marasco, Robert, 62, U.S. playwright and novelist whose first Broadway success, *Child's Play* (1970), won three Tony awards. His best-selling novel *Burnt Offerings* (1973) was turned into a highly successful film starring Bette Davis. Of lung cancer, Manhasset, N.Y., Dec. 6, 1998.

Mature Victor, mid-80's, U.S. film actor, perhaps the first "beefcake" star, best known for *Samson and Delilah, The Robe*, and other muscular biblical epics. He received critical kudos for *My Darling Clementine* and *Kiss of Death*. Of cancer, San Diego County, Calif., August 4, 1999.

McCann, Donal, 56, leading Irish actor warmly praised on both sides of the Atlantic for his low-key, highly emotional style. His most notable roles came in plays by Brian Friel and in John Huston's film of Joyce's *The Dead*. Of pancreatic cancer, Dublin, July 17, 1999.

Mellon, Paul, 91, U.S. philanthropist and banking heir who supported numerous cultural causes at a price tag of nearly a billion dollars. His legacy includes Washington's National Gallery, envisioned by his father, banker Andrew Mellon, and the Bollingen Prize in poetry. Of old age, Upperville, Va., Feb. 1, 1999.

Menuhin, Yehudi, 82, U.S.-born violinist, later a British subject, whose long career began as a famous child prodigy, continued as a worldwide virtuoso of a range of standard and contemporary works, and ended as a conductor and organizer of music festivals and benefactor of charities. Cause undisclosed, Berlin, March 12, 1999.

Mitchell, Guy, 72, U.S. pop singer known for his string of hit recordings of novelties and folk tunes in the early 1950's—"Singing the Blues," "My Heart Cries for You," and "The Roving Kind." Of surgery complications, Las Vegas, July 1, 1999.

Moore Archie, 84, U.S. prizefighter. He was light heavyweight champion from 1952-60, scoring 141 knockouts, the most ever by a professional. Cause undisclosed, San Diego, Dec. 9, 1998.

Moore, Brian, 77, Irish writer of 19 novels, many depicting introverts caught in a web of parochialism, notably *The Lonely Passion of Judith Hearne*. Of pulmonary fibrosis, Malibu, Calif., Jan 11, 1999.

Morita, Akio, 78, Japanese executive and co-founder of the Sony Corporation. His marketing expertise brought his company worldwide recognition as one of the most reliable brand names and helped bring postwar prosperity to Japan. Of pneumonia after a stroke, Tokyo, Oct. 3, 1999.

Morris, Willie, 64, U.S. journalist. As editor of *Harper's Magazine* (1967-71), he helped create a new kind of journalism. *North Toward Home* is his memoir of the changes in the South as he grew up there. Of heart failure, Jackson, Miss., August 2, 1999.

Motley, Marion, 79, U.S. football star considered by many the best fullback of all time. He was one of the first blacks in the N.F.L. with the Cleveland Browns, (1946-53). Of prostate cancer, Cleveland, June 27, 1999.

Murdoch, Iris, 79, British writer whose 26 novels display an unusual blend of dramatic storytelling and philosphical inquiry, notably *The Sea, the Sea*, and *A Severed Head*. Of Alzheimer's disease, Oxford, England, Feb. 8, 1999.

Murray, Kathryn, 92, U.S. ballroom dancing entrepreneur who with her husband, Arthur, developed a nationwide franchise of dance schools and the 1950's *TV Arthur Murray Party*, in which she blithely danced with celebrities and bears. Cause undisclosed, Honolulu, August 6, 1999.

Newley, Anthony, 67, British entertainer. He was a singer, writer, and director best remembered for his Broadway successes such as *Stop the World—I Want to Get Off*. His hit songs include "What Kind of Fool Am I?" Of cancer, Jensen Beach, Fla., April 14, 1999.

Nkomo, Joshua, 62, African leader in the struggle for independence for Zimbabwe from Britain and then Rhodesia; overshadowed by his rival, Pres. Robert Mugabe. Of prostate cancer, Harare, Zimbabwe, July 1, 1999.

Norvo, Red (Kenneth Norville), 91, U.S. jazz musician who played the xylophone and vibraphone, making them part of the mainstream; an influential leader of bands and small groups. Of old age, Santa Monica, Calif., April 6, 1999.

Nyerere, Julius, ca. 77, socialist founder of Tanzania, one of the early leaders of African nationalism and statehood. As Prime Minister and later as President (1961-85), he promoted literacy and paternalistic economic policies. After a stroke and leukemia treatment, London, Oct. 14, 1999.

Ogilvy, David, 88, British-born advertising executive. He created the "Man in the Hathaway Shirt" and many other eye-catching commercial ads for such products as Schweppes and Rolls-Royce that appealed to consumers' intelligence and sense of humor. Of old age, Bonnes, France, July 21, 1999.

Pakula, Alan, 70, U.S. movie director of 16 films, including *The Sterile Cuckoo, Klute, All the President's Men*, and *Sophie's Choice*, all of which won Academy Awards, though not for the director. Of auto accident injuries on New York's Long Island Expressway, Nov. 19, 1998.

Papadopoulos, George, 80, Greek colonel who led a military coup that took power from 1967 until 1973. His dictatorial regime was accused of torture and other repressive measures, for which he was found guilty of treason and imprisoned for life. Of a heart attack, Athens, June 27, 1999.

Paterson, Jennifer, 71, eccentric British chef. She was one of the *Two Fat Ladies* TV cooking show that gleefully hyped red meat and butter to the consternation of the "health police" and thereby quickly gained a cult following. Of lung cancer, London, Aug. 10, 1999.

Powers, J.(ames) F.(arl), 81, U. S. writer of novels and short stories, many about the difficulties of religious life. His works were critically acclaimed though not best sellers; notable is his 1963 National Book Award winner, *Morte d'Urban*. Cause undisclosed, Collegeville, Minn., June 12, 1999.

Puzo, Mario, 78, best-selling U.S. author of *The Godfather*, the hugely popular novel and series of movies chronicling the saga of the Corleone Mafia family. Winner of two Academy Awards. Of heart failure, Bay Shore, N.Y., July 2, 1999.

Quintero, José, 74, Panamanian-born theater director best known for his productions of the plays of Eugene O'Neill, particularly the American premiere of *Long Day's Journey Into Night* on Broadway in 1956; helped establish the Off Broadway movement with the Circle in the Square theater. Of cancer, New York, Feb. 26, 1999.

Reed, Oliver, 61, robust British actor best known for film work in *Women in Love* and the cold-blooded Bill Sikes in *Oliver!* Cause undisclosed after collapsing in Malta while filming, May 2, 1999.

Reese, Pee Wee (Harold), 81, Hall of Fame baseball shortstop and leader of the Brooklyn Dodgers teams of the 1950's. His acceptance of Jackie Robinson helped defuse the tension of integrating America's pastime. Of lung cancer, Louisville, Ky., Aug. 14, 1999.

Rockefeller, Mary C., 91, U.S. socialite whose 1962 divorce from New York Governor Nelson Rockefeller after a 31-year marriage helped to cause his failure to win Republican presidential nominations. Of old age, New York, April 22, 1999.

Rodbell, Martin, 73, U.S. scientist, co-winner of 1994 Nobel Prize in Medicine and Physiology for work on "G-proteins," regulators of basic cellular activity, further pointing to some causes of cancer. Of cardiovascular disease, Chapel Hill, N.C., Dec. 7, 1999.

Rogers, Buddy (Charles), 94, early U.S. movie star of *Wings* (1927), the first Oscar winner. He appeared in 35 films and married Mary Pickford. Of old age, Rancho Mirage, Calif., April 21, 1999.

Roman, Ruth, 75, versatile U.S. movie actress who could play the steady wife or the sultry girlfriend; made more than 30 films, including *Champion* and *Strangers on a Train*. Cause undisclosed, Laguna Beach, Calif., Sept. 9, 1999.

Roventini, Johnny, 86, Brooklyn bellhop who became the icon for a tobacco company with his "Call for Philip Morris" heard on radio and seen in magazines from the 1930's, to the '50's. Of a facial infection, Suffern, N.Y., Nov. 30, 1998.

Sarazen, Gene, 97, U.S. golf legend of the 1920's and '30's. He was the first player to win all four major tournaments (Masters, British Open, U.S. Open, and P.G.A.). Invented the sand wedge. Of pneumonia complications, Naples. Fla., May 13, 1999.

Schawlow, Arthur, 77, U.S. scientist, co-winner of 1981 Nobel Prize in Physics for work contributing to the development of lasers. Of leukemia, Palo Alto, Calif., April 28, 1999.

Scott, George C., 71, U.S. actor of fiery intensity and gravelly voice, at home on stage and screen. Best-known for his portrayal of *Patton* (for which he won an Academy Award he refused to accept), and earlier for Gen. Buck Turgidson in Stanley Kubrick's *Dr. Strangelove*. Of a ruptured aneurysm, Westlake Village, Calif., Sept. 22, 1999.

Seaborg, Glenn, 86, U.S. scientist, co-winner of 1951 Nobel Prize in Chemistry for experiments that produced several artificial elements, including plutonium, used in the 1945 atomic bomb that destroyed Nagasaki. The radioactive element Seaborgium is named for him. Of stroke complications, Lafayette, Calif., Feb. 26, 1999.

Semon, Waldo, 100, U.S. inventor who created vinyl in 1928; one of his nonstarters was synthetic rubber bubble gum. Of old age, Hudson, Ohio, May 26, 1999.

Señor Wences (Wenceslao Moreno), 103, Spanish-born ventriloquist who became enormously popular on TV's *Ed Sullivan Show* in the 1950's and '60's; he simply manipulated his hand to become the mischievous Johnny ("Difficult for you, easy for me.") or the grouchy Pedro ("S'all right"). Of old age, New York, April 20, 1999.

Shaw, Robert, 82, U.S. musician, famous as a conductor of choral groups, notably the professional Robert Shaw Chorale; longtime conductor of the Atlanta Symphony; winner of 14 Grammys. Of a stroke, New Haven, Conn., Jan. 25, 1999.

Sidney, Sylvia, 88, U.S. actress best remembered as the plucky heroine of gritty melodramas of the 1930's such as *Street Scene* and *Dead End*. Of old age, New York July 1, 1999.

Silverstein, Shel, 67, U.S. writer whose goofy, macabre poems and cartoons for children— *Where the Sidewalk Ends* and *A Light in the Attic* most notably—were enormous best sellers. Cause undisclosed, Key West, Fla., May 10, 1999.

Siskel, Gene, 53, U.S. film critic who became popular and influential as part of a TV team with Roger Ebert with their signature "thumbs up" or "thumbs down" reviews. After brain surgery, Chicago, Feb. 20, 1999.

Springfield, Dusty, 59, British pop singer, best known for her 60's hits "I Only Want to Be With You", "The Look of Love", and "The Windmills of Your Mind." Of breast cancer, Henley-on-Thames, England, March 2, 1999.

St. Cyr, Lili, 80, U.S. burlesque queen known for her bubble bath routine and choreographed impersonations of fabled temptresses. Cause undisclosed, Hollywood, Calif., Jan 29, 1999.

Strasberg, Susan, 60, U.S. stage and film actress who achieved sudden stardom at 17 as Anne Frank in the 1955 Tony-award-winning play. Her films include *Picnic* and *The Cobweb*. Of cancer, New York, Jan. 21, 1999.

Talbert, Bill, 80, U.S. tennis champion, winner of 33 national titles, he served as captain of 1950's U.S. Davis Cup teams and director of the U.S. Open 1971-75 and 1978-87. After surgery complications, New York, Feb. 28, 1999.

Torme, Mel, 73, peerless U.S. vocalist of wide-ranging styles (pop, jazz, scat). Dubbed the "Velvet Fog" for his smooth style and flawless pitch, he was also a composer ("The Christmas Song") and arranger. Of stroke complications, Los Angeles, June 5, 1999.

Udall, Morris K., 76, U.S. Representative (D-Ariz.) 1961-91. He was an outspoken liberal from a conservative district that approved of his support of environmental causes and campaign reform. A presidential hopeful in 1976 and 1980. Of Parkinson's disease, Washington, Dec. 12, 1998.

West, Morris, 83, Australian writer of popular novels, several of which deal with Vatican affairs, notably *The Devil's Advocate* and *The Shoes of the Fisherman*, both made into successful 1960's films. Cause undisclosed, Sydney, Oct. 9, 1999.

Whittingham, Charlie, 86, U.S. Hall of Fame horse trainer. His horses won the Kentucky Derby in 1986 (Ferdinand) and 1989 (Sunday Silence). Of leukemia, Sierra Madre, Calif., April 20, 1999.

Whyte, William H., 81, U.S. writer and observer of the American urban scene, best remembered for *The Organization Man* (1956), a best-selling critique of white-collar conformity and a lifestyle of suburban security. Cause undisclosed, New York, Jan. 12, 1999.

Williams, Joe, 80, U. S. singer known for his mellow, impeccably articulated style in jazz, blues, and ballads. Notable for appearances with the Count Basie Orchestra in the 1950's, then as solo performer and recording artist into the '90's. Of respiratory failure, Las Vegas, March 29, 1999.

Wilson, Flip (Clerow), 64, U.S. comedian and TV personality, the first black star to host a hit network variety show. His many personas, notably Geraldine ("The devil made me do it."), conveyed street-wise, non-confrontational humor nationwide. Of liver cancer, Malibu, Calif., Nov. 25, 1998.

Wisdom, John Minor, 93, Federal judge who rendered the 1962 decision ordering the University of Mississippi to admit James Meredith, its first black student, as well as numerous other bans on segregation in the 1950's and '60's. Winner of the Presidential Medal of Freedom 1993. Of old age, New Orleans, May 15, 1995.

Wynn, Early, 79, U.S. Hall of Fame pitcher, primarily with the Cleveland Indians, who won 313 games over 23 seasons. He won the Cy Young Award in 1959 at the age of 39. Of stroke complications, Venice, Fla., April 4, 1999.

Young, Freddie, 96, British cinematographer whose long career included Hitchcock's *Blackmail*, the first British talkie, and David Lean's *Lawrence of Arabia, Dr. Zhivago*, and *Ryan's Daughter*, all three of which earned Oscars for Young. Of old age, London, Dec. 1, 1998.

Major News Stories of 1999

By Correspondents of The New York Times

NATIONAL NEWS

Midterm Election Setbacks Force Gingrich to Resign

Democrats scored unexpected successes in the 1998 Congressional campaigns. The outcome demonstrated how Republicans had fundamentally misread the electorate in refusing to heed months of polls showing that voters were not particularly exercised by the White House scandal.

In crucial Senate and Gubernatorial races around the country, Democrats won impressive victories. The outcome left Republicans controlling the House with the slimmest majority in about half a century. And Republicans made no net gain in Senate seats; their publicly-stated goal was to win a magic 60 Senate seats, the number needed to cut off filibusters by Democrats blocking Republican legislation. Instead, the Republicans wound up with 55 seats.

The biggest casualty was Speaker Newt Gingrich, who was driven from office. Only four days after winning re-election to his Georgia congressional seat, he announced that he would not seek re-election as Speaker and would leave Congress when his existing term expired in January. (Representative J. Dennis Hastert of Illinois, a low-key former high school wrestling coach, was elected Speaker after the first choice, Representative Robert Livingston of Louisiana, quit the House amid allegations about his private life.)

While Republicans maintained control of the House, the Democrats gained five seats in 1998, bucking a historic trend that the President's party usually loses seats in the mid-term elections. On July 16, 1999, Representative George Brown, a California Democrat, died. The next day, Representative Michael Forbes of Long Island announced he was switching from the Republican to the Democratic Party. Pending a special election to fill the California vacancy, the Republicans had 222 seats to 211 for the Democrats, with one independent.

In the most coveted single prize, Gray Davis, the Lieutenant Governor of California, defeated Dan Lungren, the Republican Attorney General. Mr. Davis because the first Democrat elected governor of the state in 16 years. Another major upset was the ouster of Senator Alfonse M. D'Amato, the New York Republican, by Representative Charles E. Schumer.

Despite Davis's victory in California, Republicans also maintained their domination of governorships. Gov. George W. Bush of Texas won re-election by a huge margin, solidifying his position as the early favorite among many in his party for the Republican Presidential nomination in 2000.

Strategists in both parties said that rather than provoke mass defections from the Republicans—or drive independents to the Democratic column—the decision by Republicans to put their hopes in the impeachment controversy simply gave the Democrats room to galvanize their supporters by focusing on issues. Acknowledging the miscalculation, Mr. Gingrich said a day after the election, "We probably should have almost maniacally focused on cutting taxes, reforming Government, working on saving Social Security."

Another big surprise was the election of Jesse Ventura as Governor of Minnesota on the Reform Party ticket. Mr. Ventura, who was best known as a professional wrestler, captured 37 percent of the vote, triumphing over established Republican and Democratic contenders. His election underscored a dissatisfaction with traditional politicians; many of his supporters were young people who had never before voted.

—Richard L. Berke

The Impeachment and Trial Of William Jefferson Clinton

It was just after noon on Feb. 12, 1999 when a political confrontation with little precedent reached its climax: the Senate stood poised for only the second time in the history of the Republic to vote on whether to remove a President from office.

"Is respondent William Jefferson Clinton guilty or not guilty?" asked Chief Justice William H. Rehnquist, who had presided over a 37-day trial of the nation's 42nd President on two impeachment counts stemming from his efforts to hide his affair with Monica S. Lewinsky, a young White House intern.

One after another, the Senators delivered their verdict. By a vote of 55-45, they rejected a charge of perjury against Mr. Clinton. The Senate then split 50-50 on a second charge accusing Mr. Clinton of obstruction of justice—far short of the two thirds majority of 67 Senators the Constitution requires to remove the nation's chief executive from office.

Every Democrat stood with the leader of their party. Ten Republicans broke ranks to oppose Mr. Clinton's removal from office on the first count; five bolted from the party on the second count. At the White House, a subdued Mr. Clinton called on Americans to "rededicate ourselves to the work of serving our nation and building our future together."

And for a time, America simply seemed relieved to put behind it an 18-month preoccupation with the President's sex life, an issue that had paralyzed official Washington, defined the final year of the 105th Congress, helped bring down a Republican Speaker, and made the President a figure of ridicule.

But there were signs as a new Presidential campaign dawned that the scandal was yet having repercussions. Vice President Al Gore was consistently running 15 percent or more behind Texas's Republican Governor, George W. Bush, in public opinion polls. Strategists said he was being hurt by his association with Mr. Clinton. The fresh crop of Presidential candidates themselves were putting a heavy emphasis on religion, morality, and character.

The last time the nation faced a Constitutional crisis akin to President Clinton's trial was in 1974, when Richard M. Nixon resigned rather than face impeachment by the full House. But if Mr. Nixon's fall grew out of a break-in at Democratic headquarters, Mr. Clinton's case had to do with sex—a distinction that bedeviled prosecutors from the start.

The case had its origins in a lawsuit brought by Paula Corbin Jones, a former Arkansas state employee who accused Mr. Clinton of making an unwanted sexual advance to her in 1991 when he was governor. To bolster her case, her lawyers set out to show a pattern of behavior, asking Mr. Clinton about other women. Questioned under oath on Jan. 17, 1998, Mr. Clinton denied that he had had sexual relations with Ms. Lewinsky. He sat silently as his lawyer brandished a false affidavit from Ms. Lewinsky to buttress the President's denial.

Within days, the White House was shaken by news that Kenneth W. Starr, the independent prosecutor who had been investigating an Arkansas real estate deal known as Whitewater, had broadened his inquiry as to whether Mr. Clinton had induced Ms. Lewinsky to lie. For seven months Mr. Clinton publicly denied the affair. Only on Aug. 17, 1998, as he appeared before a grand jury did he acknowledge "inappropriate intimate contact." If the investigation was sparked by Mr. Clinton's sexual behavior, the impeachment saga also seemed to be the culmination of a long-running public debate over morality and over what line should be drawn between the personal and political behavior of the nation's highest officeholders.

To the surprise of both parties, voters made a judgment that this was not the public's business: they seemed to emphasize the point by denying the Republicans the off-year election gains that by tradition they should have expected. Instead, the President's party gained House sets in a midterm election for the first time since 1934 (see the related story, above).

The election result led to the resignation of Speaker Newt Gingrich. But it did not stop the impeachment drive. On Dec. 11 and 12, 1998, the House Judiciary Committee approved four articles of impeachment against Mr. Clinton.

An effort by some Republican moderates to avert impeachment through some kind of censure deal quickly collapsed, as House leaders led by Representative Tom DeLay, the majority whip from Texas, pushed for impeachment and called censure an unconstitutional role for the House. On Dec. 19, 1998, on a day of extraordinary partisan bitterness, the House voted virtually along party lines to impeach Mr. Clinton on two counts of perjury and obstruction of justice.

Showcasing sharply different views, Mr. DeLay said the impeachment struggle was about "relativism versus absolute truth." Representative Richard A. Gephardt, the House Minority leader made a plea for tolerance for personal failings. "Our founding fathers created a system of government of men, not of angels," he said. The debate also cost the Republicans one of their own. Representative Robert L. Livingston of Louisiana who had been poised to become the next Speaker in the new Congress, instead resigned because of revelations of adultery.

On Jan. 7, 1999, the Senate opened the trial of the President under rules from another century. But from the start, the trial was shaped by the knowledge that unless the unexpected occurred, there would not be sufficient votes to convict.

So the Senate's quandary became how to conduct a trial that could be seen as credible and yet not paralyze the government for months on end. Toward that goal, the Senate relied on a good deal of improvisation. On Jan. 8, all 100 Senators held an extraordinary bipartisan caucus in the ceremonial Old Senate Chamber for three hours and hammered out a bipartisan trial plan. The plan allowed for several weeks of opening arguments from the President's legal team and from the 13 House managers prosecuting the case against him. It deferred a decision on whether to call witnesses before the Senate.

Across the 37-day trial the prosecutors argued that President Clinton should be removed from office not for his sexual escapades but for his efforts in legal forums to hide the truth about his relationship with Ms. Lewinsky. "No man is above the law and no man is below it," said Representative F. James Sensenbrenner Jr. (R-Wisc.).

The President's lawyers did not defend Mr. Clinton's conduct. Instead they accused the House of building a circumstantial case made of, as Charles F.C. Ruff, the White House counsel, put it, "sealing wax and strings and spiders' webs."

After weeks of such arguments, Senate Republicans forced the House managers to whittle their witness list to only three people: Ms. Lewinsky, Vernon Jordan, the President's confidant, and Sidney Blumenthal, a White House aide. And while those three were deposed, they were never called before the Senate. The world and the Senate instead watched the image of Ms. Lewinsky, 25, in a demure dark suit, answer questions on videotape.

—Alison Mitchell

House Committee Says China Stole Nuclear Secrets

On Sept. 25, 1992, China tested a nuclear bomb. It took U.S. Government officials three years to realize its significance: Beijing had learned the miniaturization secret of building a modern nuclear arsenal. China could now fit many H-bombs atop a single missile or fire them from trucks, submarines and other mobile platforms.

By 1995 U.S. intelligence officials had also learned that China had stolen design secrets for several advanced U.S. warheads, including the W-88, a miniature hydrogen bomb. The officials concluded that espionage had occurred and that it had likely helped China make significant advances in its development of nuclear weapons.

The issue became public in 1999 after a select House committee, chaired by Christopher Cox, a California Republican, came across the Federal inquiry into nuclear espionage and lax security at the Department of Energy's nuclear weapons laboratories.

The Federal Bureau of Investigation focused its criminal inquiry on a scientist at Los Alamos National Laboratory, Wen Ho Lee, based on circumstantial evidence such as Mr. Lee's acknowledgement that he had shared unclassified data with Chinese scientists. Mr. Lee was not charged and two Senators later found fault with investigators for not pursuing other suspects in the case. Mr. Lee complained he had been unfairly singled out because of his ethnic background—he was born in Taiwan.

Mr. Lee was fired from Los Alamos in March 1999 for security violations. A few weeks later investigators discovered he had downloaded into an unprotected computer system a secret coded history of U.S. weapons tests. Bill Richardson, the Secretary of Energy, ordered dramatic changes in security at the weapons labs. Congress sought to beef up security by proposing a semi-autonomous agency to oversee the labs.

The proposal came after a Presidential intelligence advisory board had sharply criticized the department and recommended a drastic reorganization and cultural change. The board, chaired by Warren Rudman, a former Republican Senator, also criticized the Administration for responding too slowly to the issue.

President Clinton was first briefed in the summer of 1997. In February 1998 he signed a secret order to tighten security at the labs. It became public with the completion of the Cox committee. After the release of the committee's report in May 1999, it came under criticism from some nuclear scientists who said it went too far in saying it would have been "virtually impossible" for China to have made the nuclear weapon design leap without the espionage.

The critics said China was right when it insisted that it had succeeded in advancing its program all on its own. But by last September, a new intelligence report prepared by the entire U.S. intelligence community, concluded that within 15 years China would likely be aiming missiles at the United States that will be fitted with small nuclear warheads "in part influenced by U.S. technology gained through espionage."

The debate remained unresolved as the year came to an end.

—Jeff Gerth

Senate Rejects Test Ban Treaty But Clinton Vows to Fight On

On October 13, 1999, the United States Senate rejected a treaty banning all underground nuclear weapons tests in a 51 to 48 vote that crushed one of President Clinton's top foreign policy goals.

The vote on the Comprehensive Test Ban Treaty was largely along party lines. The accord fell far short of the two-thirds majority that the Constitution requires for ratification of international treaties, and gave conservatives a ringing triumph after a weeklong power play in which Democrats, the White House and some moderate Republicans tried to postpone action until after President Clinton left office.

The treaty's defeat marked the first time the Senate had rejected a major international security pact since the Treaty of Versailles, creating the League of Nations, failed to win Senate approval in 1920.

Mr. Clinton, speaking after the vote on the White House lawn, denounced the rejection as a "reckless" and "partisan" act, and vowed that the United States would continue its seven-year moratorium on testing and seek a permanent ban on all such test explosions. "When all is said and done, the United States will ratify the treaty," Mr. Clinton said.

The Senate's rejection raised serious doubts about the treaty's survival. Supporters abroad argued that if it was not adopted by the United States, other nuclear powers including Pakistan, India, Russia and China would follow suit, denying the 1996 accord the 44 ratifications it needs to go into force.

Supporters argued that the treaty would lock in the United States' nuclear superiority gained from more than 1,000 tests between 1945 and 1992, while banning all militarily significant testing.

But critics contended that the pact would permanently bind an accord-abiding United States in place while rogue nations, like North Korea and Iran, cheated and conducted tests and eroded the American deterrent. Opponents also feared that the safety and reliability of the nation's aging nuclear arsenal would be imperiled if all testing were banned.

Senator Trent Lott, the Republican leader, insisted after the vote was taken that the Senate had defeated a "dangerous" treaty, and said the vote illustrated the Senate's equal role with the President in the treaty-making process. "The Founding Fathers never envisioned that the Senate would be a rubber stamp for a flawed treaty."

But the Democratic leader, Thomas A. Daschle, said, "No constitutional obligation has been treated so cavalierly, so casually, as this treaty."

President Clinton signed the treaty in September 1996, and a year later sent it to the Senate for ratification. But the pact remained bottled up in the Senate Foreign Relations Committee until August 1999, when Senate Democrats threatened to tie up the Senate floor unless Republicans allowed hearings and a vote on the bill.

On September 30, Mr. Lott abruptly called the Democrats bluff. After hearings in three committees, 16 hours of floor debate started on October 8. Only four Republicans—Gordon H. Smith of Oregon, Arlen Specter of Pennsylvania, James M. Jeffords of Vermont and John H. Chafee of Rhode Island—voted with 44 Democrats in favor of the treaty. Senator Robert C. Byrd, a West Virginia Democrat, voted present.

—Eric Schmitt

States to Receive $20 Billion From Big Tobacco Companies

One of the most contentious chapters in the tobacco industry's recent history was brought to a close on November 20, 1998, when 46 states accepted $206 billion from cigarette makers to settle all remaining state lawsuits that were filed to recover Medicaid money spent treating diseases related to smoking.

Under the plan, the nation's four biggest tobacco producers agreed to pay the states the money over 25 years to settle claims that they had misled the public about the health risks of smoking and the addictive nature of nicotine. The cigarette makers involved were the Philip Morris Companies, R.J. Reynolds Tobacco, a subsidiary of RJR Nabisco Holdings Corporation; Lorillard Tobacco, a subsidiary of Loews Corporation and Brown & Williamson Tobacco, a subsidiary of B.A.T. Industries P.L.C.

The state attack on the industry had begun in 1994 and four states—Florida, Mississippi, Minnesota and Texas—had previously settled their lawsuits for a total of $40 billion to be paid over 25 years. Cigarette makers had found themselves under constant scrutiny as secret documents showed that they suppressed health data and had sought to attract teenagers as "replacement smokers".

But while the states got their money, few would dedicate the bulk of it to anti-smoking efforts, spending the funds instead on projects like hospital constructions, schools, and tax cuts. The tobacco industry also did not get the peace it had sought; with public sentiment stirred against it, producers would soon be hit by large damage awards in lawsuits brought by individual smokers.

On Sept. 22, 1999, the Justice Department filed a far-reaching Federal lawsuit that accused cigarette makers of conspiring for five decades to defraud and mislead the public about the health effects of smoking.

—Barry Meier

Billions in Campaign Cash Overshadow Reform Bill

In 1999, Washington engorged itself on a feast of campaign cash. Although the 2000 Presidential and Congressional elections were more than a year away, the candidates and the major political parties established mind-boggling fund-raising records. Some predicted that a total of $3 billion would be raised for the 2000 elections.

George W. Bush, the Texas governor and Republican hopeful, raised a mind-boggling $50 million in just six months. No candidate for public office had ever raised so much money so fast.

And the Republican National Committee began soliciting $250,000 donations each year for a special program dubbed "season pass holders." Fund-raisers said the name of the club meant that donors would receive "passes" to everything, from passes to skyboxes at the convention to private meals with Congressional leaders.

At the same time, the perpetual campaign to change the nation's campaign finance laws continued. With public outrage increasing over past fund-raising abuses and the ravenous appetites for cash of the major parties, the advocates said they were as hopeful as ever that Congress would finally pass a meaningful bill, that would produce real reforms.

On Sept. 14, the House of Representatives voted for a significant campaign finance reform bill that would dramatically limit the influence of money in politics. By a 252-to-177 vote, the House passed a bill that bans the limitless "soft money" donations to the political parties. The bill's prospects in the Senate were doubtful.

Many legislators, both Republican and Democrat, agreed that the public had become increasingly cynical by the parties continued dependence on larger and larger donations.

"The reach and influence of special interests have grown out of control," said Representative Marge Roukema, a New Jersey Republican. "As a consequence, people believe their elected officials are bought and paid for."

But as it did the year before, the Senate killed the campaign finance reform bill in the Fall of 1999.

—Don Van Natta

Fiscal Bliss Stirs Political Debate About Surplus

President Clinton's main point in his State of the Union Address on Jan. 19, 1999, was to call on Congress to use the surprising budget surplus for 1999 and coming years "to save Social Security," and, once that was accomplished, to use more surplus funds to extend the solvency of Medicare, the health plan for the elderly.

There was an obvious logic behind his call. With the first surpluses in three decades coming before the wave of baby-boomer retirements early in the next century, a fix now could be accomplished with less pain—higher premiums or lowered benefits—than could be managed if Congress waited a few years.

But there was also a clear political point: by devoting most of the trillion dollars or so expected in surplus funds over the next decade, Clinton could block Republican efforts to use it for a large tax cut—one of the few issues that unified the fractured Republican majorities in Congress.

At first, there were some signs that Congress would take up the challenge, with Republicans pushing to let taxpayers invest Social Security funds in the stock market, and both sides battling out different approaches to the issue. And when midyear economic figures showed the surplus much larger than expected even six months before, the opportunity grew.

But just as Mr. Clinton's State of the Union address itself was all but overshadowed by the impeachment proceedings that surrounded it, the strategic politics of the surplus—tax cuts versus spending on the elderly—came to overwhelm even such poll-tested concepts as preserving Social Security and Medicare, especially since the same booming economy that produced the surpluses pushed off the years of reckoning over their solvency.

And while 1999 was the best year imaginable, fiscally, to deal with long-term issues, it was an awful year, politically. This was especially true in the House, where tax, Medicare, and Social Security legislation originates.

Not only did the impeachment bitterness linger, but the House had a new, obscure speaker, J. Dennis Hastert, and a partisan division so narrow as to make it ungovernable. For most of the year, the House had 222 Republicans, 211 Democrats, and one independent whose vote Democrats could count on. That meant that Hastert only had to lose a net of five votes before he could not pass a bill, and with the deep ideological divisions in the Republican caucus, that was a real risk on all but the simplest measures.

The stalemate over what to do with all that money did provide one benefit, however. With funds going to neither Republican tax cuts nor Clinton Administration spending proposals, the budget surplus automatically went to paying down the most important component of the national debt: the $3.6 trillion in Treasury bonds. The effect of this, not unlike an individual paying off credit card debt, is an increase in the government's ability to borrow in the future.

—Adam Clymer

Two Students Shoot 13 in Colorado High School Massacre

The ordinariness of Littleton, Colo., a quiet Denver suburb, was shattered on April 20, 1999 when two students at Columbine High School brought weapons into the school and opened fire at random, killing 12 students and a teacher and injuring almost two dozen other students before killing themselves.

It was the worst episode of student-on-student killings in American history and another reminder of the inexplicable forces driving young people in recent years to vent rage and frustration through the use of deadly weapons.

The Columbine killers were identified as Eric Harris, 18, and Dylan Klebold, 17, who were known by others at the school to have felt alienated from most of the other students. Both came from stable, middle-class families and were regarded as above-average students.

While the killings stirred a long-simmering national debate about access to guns, it was left largely to state and local governments, rather than the Federal Government, to do anything. Many jurisdictions used Columbine as a reason to change laws, making it harder for people with mental illness or criminal backgrounds, as well as young people, to obtain guns. In addition, school districts around the country took new measures to tighten security, through the use of metal detectors, surveillance cameras, armed security patrols or restrictions on dress to make it difficult to conceal weapons. Other schools, including those in Jefferson County, where Columbine is located, brought in counselors to help students deal with fears.

How much any of these efforts helped remained an open question. Just a month after the Columbine shootings, a 15-year-old gunman wounded six students at Heritage High School in Conyers, Ga., and on the day Columbine opened for the fall term, students found swastikas scratched into the school's exterior brick walls and inside a girls' bathroom. And several weeks after classes began, five Jefferson County high schools received threatening letters that said "Columbine is just the beginning."

—*Michael Janofsky*

Recurring Episodes of Gun Violence Lead to New Laws and New Lawsuits

In a single day, with a single spasm of violence, the atmosphere surrounding gun control changed in America, yielding an array of significant movements toward greater restrictions of firearms and putting gun manufacturers on the defensive. That was the legacy of April 20th at Columbine High School in Littleton, Colo., where two students brandishing several guns fatally shot 12 classmates and a teacher, and then killed themselves.

The massacre belonged to a string of multiple shootings at schools, but its dimensions galvanized advocates of gun control and, according to opinion polls, rendered many Americans more receptive to the advocates' cause, which they pursued on several fronts. More than two dozen counties and cities across America, including Chicago and Los Angeles, filed lawsuits against gun makers, accusing them of failing to include safety devices on firearms and of marketing those weapons in ways that helped criminals and children purchase them. The move was reminiscent of, and seemed to be modeled after, the legal action previously taken by 40 state attorneys general against the tobacco industry.

What the cities and counties sought, specifically, was reimbursement for the costs of dealing with the damage wrought by guns, but there was clearly a larger aim, too: to put a chill into gun manufacturers and to disrupt the easy, steady flow of guns onto city streets. In June, one manufacturer, Davis Industries, filed for bankruptcy as a result.

In Congress, gun control received more extensive debate than it had since 1994, when Democrats had successfully pushed through several significant new restrictions on firearms. Many Democrats had subsequently come to believe that this legislation—and the National Rifle Association's subsequent efforts to defeat Democrats who had passed it—led to Democrats' loss of their majority in the House of Representatives in Congressional elections later that year.

But in the aftermath of Columbine, many Democrats were newly emboldened, and they promoted a series of new Federal restrictions, including a ban on the import of high-capacity ammunition devices, a requirement that new handguns be sold with child safety devices, and, most controversially, a mandate that a thorough background check be performed on anyone and everyone buying a firearm at a gun show. The debate over these proposals raged well into the fall, but the fact that it was occurring at all, and receiving so much attention, was an indisputable sign of change.

So was the feverish activity surrounding gun control in statehouses throughout the country. In Illinois, for example, Gov. George Ryan, a Republican, signed into law provisions that required safety devices for handguns, that held parents' legally accountable if their guns ended up in the hands of children and were used in acts of violence, and that automatically stiffened the penalty for a felony if a gun was brandished during its commission.

In California, the nation's most populous state and a bellwether for political trends, Gov. Gray Davis, a Democrat, signed into law the nation's toughest and most comprehensive ban on the manufacture, import or distribution of assault-style weapons, a measure that went dramatically further than an existing Federal ban. Mr. Davis also signed into law a measure that barred any individual from purchasing more than one handgun a month.

—*Frank Bruni*

F.B.I. Admits It Lied About Waco Assault Six Years Ago

Six years after the Federal Bureau of Investigation's disastrous tear-gas assault on the Branch Davidian religious compound near Waco, Tex., Federal authorities found themselves once again caught up in a raging debate over the deadly conflagration that burned the cultists' prairie bunker to the ground.

The controversy over the Government's tear-gas operation revived after a documentary filmmaker in Texas uncovered evidence that the F.B.I. had fired flammable tear gas canisters on the day of the April 19, 1993, assault. The disclosure contradicted Attorney General Janet Reno and F.B.I. officials who had long said that Federal agents did nothing during the tear-gas operation —or the 51-day stand-off that preceded it —that could have started the deadly fire.

The disclosure prompted the F.B.I. to review its files, a search that quickly led to the discovery of infrared videotapes which showed that Federal agents received authorization from their superiors on the morning of the assault to fire the flammable rounds into a concrete bunker near the compound. Hours later, the building erupted in a blaze that Attorney General Janet Reno had blamed on David Koresh, the Branch Davidian leader.

Investigators who searched the charred rubble counted the bodies of about 80 people, including a number of children. Ms. Reno, who said she had been unaware that the flammable rounds were used, acknowledged that the disclosure badly undermined her credibility, but said it did not change her mind that Mr. Koresh was responsible for the fire. Nevertheless, under heavy criticism from law enforcement critics and Republicans in Congress, Ms. Reno, on Sept. 9, 1999, named former Republican Senator John C. Danforth of Missouri as a special counsel to investigate what Mr. Danforth described as the "dark questions," including whether there was a Government cover-up of the F.B.I.'s actions.

—*David Johnston*

The Supreme Court Rules On Federal vs. State Power

The Supreme Court term that began Oct. 4, 1998 and concluded on June 23, 1999 was light in cases but weighty in consequences. In 75 decisions—half the number the Court typically issued in the mid-1980's—the Justices asserted their authority by reconfiguring the balance of state and Federal power, invalidating acts of Congress on subjects ranging from broadcast advertising to welfare law, and frustrating the Clinton Administration's plans to conduct the 2000 Census by means of statistical sampling.

Three federalism cases decided by 5-to-4 votes on the term's final day demonstrated both the conservative majority's resolve to shift the balance in favor of the states, as well as that same majority's tenuous hold. Indeed, federalism appeared to represent the major fault line on the current Court, with several other important rulings on the subject slated for the 1999-2000 term.

In the three cases, the Court invoked a broad principle of sovereign immunity to shield states from suit for violations of Federal law. The majority, made up of Chief Justice William H. Rehnquist and Justices Sandra Day O'Connor, Antonin Scalia, Anthony M. Kennedy, and Clarence Thomas, held in *Alden v. Maine* that states cannot be sued in their own courts by state employees for violations of Federal labor law.

In *Florida Prepaid v. College Savings Bank*, the same majority ruled that states cannot be sued for infringing patents, despite the determination of Congress in a 1992 law providing for such suits that patent violations by states represented a growing problem. The third case (involving the same parties), *College Savings Bank v. Florida Prepaid*, also immunized states from trademark suits.

The dissenters in all three cases were Justices John Paul Stevens, David H. Souter, Ruth Bader Ginsburg, and Stephen G. Breyer.

In another important case, the Court ruled by a 5-to-4 vote on Jan. 25 that Federal law required the 2000 Census to be conducted by the traditional headcount rather than through the use of statistical sampling, as the Administration had proposed (*Department of Commerce v. U.S. House of Representatives*).

The Justices were unanimous in striking down, on June 14, a 65-year-old Federal ban on the broadcast advertising of casino gambling (*Greater New Orleans Broadcasting Assoc. v. U.S.*). By a 7-to-2 vote on May 14, the Court ruled that states may not pay lower welfare benefits to new residents, as Congress had authorized the states to do under a 1996 welfare law (*Saenz v. Roe*).

In addition to these constitutional rulings, the Court also issued important statutory decisions. Interpreting the Federal law that bars sex discrimination in schools, the Justices ruled by a 5-to-4 vote on May 24 that school districts can be liable for failing to stop a student from subjecting another to severe sexual harassment. (*Davis v. Monroe County*).

Three 7-to-2 rulings issued on June 22 interpreted the Americans With Disabilities Act, taking a restrictive view of the 1990 law's definition of disability and holding that people whose impairments can be corrected or controlled, such as by wearing glasses or taking medication, are generally not disabled and so do not come within the act's protection (*Sutton v. United Airlines, Albertson's v. Kirkingburg*, and *Murphy v. United Parcel Service*).

—*Linda Greenhouse*

School Vouchers Debate Widens

In 1999, the question of how to fix public education became one of the nation's top political concerns. Despite noisy debates, liberals and conservatives actually agreed more than they disagreed on the issue, with both calling for higher standards and greater accountability for teachers and schools. But on one subject they were nearly always divided: vouchers.

The idea behind vouchers is that tax money used to send youngsters to public schools is made available to parents to help send their children to private schools. Conservatives say that by creating competition—building a market in education—the public school system will be forced to improve and children in the worst schools will get an opportunity to learn. Liberals, backed by teachers unions, say that vouchers will drain the ambitious students and accompanying funds away from public schools and lead not to their improvement but to their complete demise.

The nation's oldest voucher program began in Milwaukee in 1990. Nine years later, more than 6,000 poor children, 6 percent of the city's students, received publicly financed vouchers of nearly $5,000 a year to attend private or parochial schools. Researchers and educators remained divided on the program's success.

But whether or not the Milwaukee plan was working, another question concerned its legality. Opponents contended that allowing parents to use public money to send children to parochial schools violated the Constitution's separation of state and religion. The Wisconsin Supreme Court disagreed and upheld the program. Other courts have indicated that vouchers may not be used in church-sponsored schools. The United States Supreme Court is expected ultimately to rule on the question, although in late 1998 it declined to take an appeal on the Wisconsin case, letting that state's high court decision stand.

Meanwhile, voucher programs continued to proliferate. Cleveland's two-year-old voucher system was first invalidated by a Federal judge and then, under a storm of protest, permitted to continue with no new students until final judgment on its constitutionality. Florida adopted the nation's first statewide voucher plan in which students at the worst schools are able to get a private or parochial education at taxpayer expense. That program too was under court challenge.

—*Ethan Bronner*

John F. Kennedy Jr. Dies in Crash of Plane He Was Piloting

Three people died in an unfortunate plane crash. And Americans re-affirmed, through their intense vicarious grief and their rapt attention to a week of unrelenting news coverage, that for them, the Kennedys were, are, and long will be the closest thing to royalty.

That, in a nutshell, is what happened the week of July 17, 1999, beginning on a quiet summer Saturday when word suddenly flashed across TV screens that John F. Kennedy Jr.'s plane was missing.

Mr. Kennedy, 38, the only son of the 35th president of the United States, had been flying his single-engine Piper Saratoga on Friday night with his wife, Carolyn Bessette Kennedy, and her sister, Lauren G. Bessette, from New Jersey to the Massachusetts island of Martha's Vineyard. He had planned to drop off his sister-in-law on the Vineyard, then fly on with his wife to the wedding of his cousin, Rory Elizabeth Kennedy, at the Kennedy compound in Hyannisport, Mass. But the plane never reached Martha's Vineyard. By Saturday morning a search was launched, and the disconcerting news had leaked. By Saturday afternoon, there was a very bad sign: some bathers on a Martha's Vineyard beach had found luggage bobbing in the surf, including a garment bag bearing Ms. Bessette's business card.

That was enough to launch a torrent of all-but-obituaries: nonstop retrospectives on the Kennedy legacy of tragedy; on the romance of the 1996 Kennedy-Bessette marriage; and on "John-John" Kennedy's visible growth from the son of an assassinated president, to a pretty face crowned "the sexiest man in the world," to a public person in his own right, editor of the flashy political magazine *George*.

On the fifth day of the search, officials announced that they had found the underwater fuse-lage and all three bodies. The ashes of the three were promptly consigned to the sea from a Navy destroyer in a private family ceremony on July 22.

Along with all the grief, there were some whispers of blame: that Mr. Kennedy, a relatively new pilot, had gotten out of his depth on a hazy night. But whatever the factors in the crash, the majority of Americans seemed cast back to the trauma inflicted by the assassination of his father: Once again, a dashing, promising young Kennedy had been killed, and tears tinged by past sorrows flowed anew.

—Carey Goldberg

New York Police Shoot Unarmed Man 19 Times

Like most American cities at the end of the decade, New York City continued to enjoy a declining crime rate. But in 1999, two events shifted the spotlight away from the New York Police Department successes. The fatal police shooting on Feb. 4 of Amadou Diallo, an unarmed street peddler, and the trial of officers accused in the stationhouse torture of Abner Louima, fed criticism that the police had grown so aggressive they were too often trampling civil rights, especially those of minorities.

Mr. Diallo, a West African immigrant, died in the vestibule of his Bronx apartment building when he was hit by 19 of 41 bullets fired at him by four members of the N.Y.P.D.'s elite Street Crime Unit. The officers said they mistakenly believed he had been reaching for a gun.

The shooting triggered a debate over the city's crime-fighting tactics: the predominantly white, plainclothes unit had been tremendously successful at seizing illegal guns, but also widely criticized for searching blacks and Hispanics without cause. The debate evolved into two months of protests in which more than 1,200 people, including a former mayor and several congressmen, were arrested outside police headquarters. The protests (and arrests) continued until March, when all four of the officers were indicted on second-degree murder charges.

Police officials characterized the shooting as a tragedy, not an incident of brutality, but they made adjustments nonetheless, putting the unit back into uniform for a period, and transferring in more black and Hispanic officers.

The Diallo demonstrations had barely ended when four officers went on trial in May on charges of brutalizing Abner Louima, who had been assaulted by police two years earlier. Federal prosecutors said, first inside a police car and later in a bathroom of the 70th Precinct stationhouse in Brooklyn.

After several days of damaging testimony from fellow officers, the lead defendant, Justin A. Volpe, pleaded guilty, acknowledging that he had thrust a stick into Mr. Louima's rectum. A second officer

was found guilty at the conclusion of the jury trial. Three others were acquitted.

Police officials denounced the brutality but pointed to the fact that officers had testified for the prosecution as evidence that the so-called "blue wall" of silence, in which police refuse to report misconduct by their colleagues, was crumbling.

—Kevin Flynn

Vicious Hate Crimes Stun the Nation

Nearly a century had gone by since lynchings were a routine racist hobby, and falling crime rates gave the impression that society was finally growing more civil. But a series of breathtakingly savage hate crimes reminded the nation that on its darkened back roads, simple differences in skin color or sexuality remained an invitation to the most extreme brutality.

On June 7, 1998, James Byrd Jr., a 49-year-old black man known for his amiable meanderings around Jasper, Tex., was beaten, chained to the back of a pickup truck, and dragged for two miles until his body was shredded and his head severed. The authorities arrested three men known for their racist beliefs and support of the local Ku Klux Klan, one of whom was sentenced to death as the others awaited trial.

Four months later, a passing bicyclist in Laramie, Wyo., found Matthew Shepard, 22, beaten, burned, and tied to a fence. Mr. Shepard, a student at the University of Wyoming, died five days later, and the police quickly determined that he had been selected as a victim because he was openly gay. More than any similar death in recent years, the attack on Mr. Shepard reminded gay people across the country that their existence was often precarious, particularly outside of large cities.

That sense was only heightened when Billy Jack Gaither's body was found on Feb. 20, 1999, along a creek near the small town of Sylacauga, Ala. Neither his parents nor most of the town knew that Mr. Gaither, 39, was gay, but his two assailants did, and it made them angry enough that they smashed in his head and threw his body on a pyre of burning tires.

These crimes, and others that were less prominent, led to calls for stronger hate-crime laws. But in fact, arrests were quickly made in each case, and those who have been sentenced received severe punishments. Many of the victims' relatives made it clear that they considered understanding and mercy more precious than the exacting retribution of justice. "I can't see taking another human being's life, no matter what," said Marion Gaither, urging that his son's killer not be executed.

—David Firestone

Bribes Brought Olympic Games to Salt Lake City

Three years after Salt Lake City was awarded the 2002 Winter Olympics, the city became the focus of the biggest bidding scandal in the history of the games. Six members of the International Olympic Committee were expelled on Jan. 24, and another four resigned, over accusations that they and their families had received cash, tuition aid, medical treatment, and lavish gifts as Salt Lake City's organizing committee attempted to sway votes in favor of its bid.

All told, Salt Lake City doled out more than $1 million in payments and gifts as it tried to win the Olympics after having failed four times previously. The city was allowed to keep the 2002 games, although many viewed the event as now tarnished, and the controversy made it more difficult for the city to obtain corporate sponsorships.

The standing of the International Olympic Committee, based in Lausanne, Switzerland, was even more damaged. An organization that purported to uphold the highest standards of ethical behavior, the I.O.C. was exposed as one whose members had their hands out for their own personal interest. Although the committee voted to expel six of their members, they stood by their longtime president, Juan Antonio Samaranch, who had been under pressure to resign.

In Utah, government and Olympic officials tried to assign most of the blame to Tom Welch and Dave Johnson, the city's two principal organizers, but as the scandal unfolded it became clear that many people had had knowledge of the excessive efforts to land the games. Mr. Johnson said that Anita DeFrantz, an American and a high-ranking member of the I.O.C., knew about scholarship payments to members' families but did nothing to halt them. She has denied the accusation.

It also became clear that such excessive efforts to sway committee votes did not begin with Salt Lake City. More than 30 of the committee's 114 members were implicated in reports of bribes related to bids for previous winter and summer Olympics, including Sydney's successful bid to hold the 2000 summer games.

—Jere Longman

Clinton Fails to Bring China Into World Trade Organization

October 1, 1999 was the 50th anniversary of the creation of the People's Republic of China, and the country's leaders hoped that—in addition to a huge military parade—they would celebrate with entry into the organization that sets the rules and arbitrates commerce around the globe: the World Trade Organization. But the deal proved elusive, and became a major issue between Beijing and Washington.

For entry, China needed to make a vast number of concessions that would allow foreigners to compete in markets that China has long kept closed, from telecommunications to agriculture. In April, Prime Minister Zhu Rongji came to Washington with a long list of those concessions: Not everything Washington asked for, but close. But President Clinton, after listening to conflicting opinions from his economic team, decided it wasn't enough to get through Congress, which was already in an anti-China mood after spying charges and new crackdowns on dissidents and the budding religious group called Falun Gong.

The American business community was outraged, and urged the Administration to take the deal as soon as possible. But then a United States B-2 bomber mistakenly destroyed the Chinese embassy in Belgrade during the NATO action in Kosovo, deeply angering the Chinese, who believed it was a deliberate act. And Mr. Zhu, under fire at home for offering to give away too much at a time that China's economy is suffering from deflation and unemployment, had to retreat.

Presidents Clinton and Jiang Zemin met in September at the Asian summit in New Zealand to get relations back on track, but their negotiators had a difficult time working out the remaining differences. While they agreed in principle to get China into the WTO by the end of the year, it was unclear that there was enough time left for Congress to pass its part of the bargain: Permanent trading rights for China, and an end to the annual debate over whether to renew those rights. Unions and Democrats worried about China's human rights policy, and conservatives worried about its growing military power, do not want to give up the leverage of that annual Congressional review. So it is unclear whether domestic politics in China and in the United States will provide room for one of the world's great trading powers to enter the WTO soon.

—David Sanger

Russian Crime Money Laundered In New York Bank

Russians have their own term for money laundering. They call it "prokrutki," which translates as "spinning around" in English. And in 1999, the Bank of New York was at the vortex. Federal investigators were looking into the venerable bank, one of the country's oldest, in connection with what they described as the biggest money laundering investigation in history. Suspect funds from Russia—at least $4.2 billion—passed through Bank of New York accounts in 1998 and 1999.

As much as $10 billion may be involved and investigators believe a big chunk of that money comes from corporate embezzlement, political graft, and organized crime activities in Russia. The Bank of New York, a conservative institution unaccustomed to center stage in major financial scandals, has been cooperating with the federal investigation since September of 1998. But before then a great deal of money already had passed through the bank.

The investigation has also revived international concerns about endemic corruption in Russia, including renewed scrutiny of whether International Monetary Fund aid to Russia has been misappropriated. At the same time news reports offered fresh evidence that members of Russian Pres. Boris N. Yeltsin's administration and family may have accepted bribes to help steer Kremlin construction contracts to a Swiss firm called Mabetex. Mr. Yeltsin and the Kremlin have repeatedly denied any wrongdoing.

Mr. Yeltsin was not the only one criticized since the Bank of New York investigation became public on Aug. 19. Vice President Al Gore, a longtime proponent of deeper financial connections with Russia, has been criticized by his political opponents for ignoring corruption in Russia in favor of broader policy goals.

—Timothy L. O'Brien

Pilot Who Cut Ski Cable in Italy Found Not Guilty

When a Marine Corps jet on a low-altitude training mission hit the cables supporting a gondola in the Italian alps on Feb. 3, 1998, killing all 20 people aboard, many people, including Italian officials, assumed that the crew was guilty of negligence at the very least. But a Court Martial at Camp Lejeune, N.C. ruled that the pilot, Capt. Richard Ashby, of Mission Viejo, Calif., who was 30 years old at the time of the accident, had not committed any crime in the conduct of the flight, and the Corps dropped similar charges against his navigator, Capt. Joseph P. Schweitzer, of Westbury, N.Y.

Testimony at the trial concentrated on the fact that the cableway, although in place for three decades, was not on the navigation chart supplied by the Pentagon, and that the Marine squadron, which was rotating through for duty over Bosnia, was not properly briefed by the resident Air Force squadron on local procedures.

But Capt. Schweitzer pleaded guilty on March 1, 1999 to obstruction and conspiracy for his role in destroying a videotape that he had shot during the mission, and Capt. Ashby, who tucked the tape into a flight suit pocket as he left the crippled jet after landing at a base in Aviano, was convicted on May 7 of the same crimes. He was sentenced to six months in jail and dismissal from the Corps, but was appealing the sentence.

—Matthew Wald

Massive Tornadoes Maul Oklahoma and Kansas

The wind did far more than just whistle down the plain in Oklahoma on May 4, 1999. With little warning, a series of immensely powerful tornadoes skipped across the Oklahoma City metropolitan area early that evening, flattening entire suburbs and etching miles-long skid marks in the earth.

In Oklahoma, the twisters killed 44 people, injured 795, and destroyed or damaged 8,079 houses. State officials estimated the damage at $150 million. The storm system also wreaked havoc in southern Kansas, where tornadoes killed 6 people, injured 150, and destroyed or damaged 3,347 houses, one manufacturing plant, and 44 retail and commercial firms. Kansas officials estimated the damage at $22 million.

Even by the standards of the Midwestern tornado belt, the May storms were massive and merciless. Videotape of the roiling cyclones showed swirling gray clouds that seemed to fill the entire horizon. The tornadoes' track stretched more than 100 miles in Oklahoma, an unusually long distance. They were classified, for the most part, at a level of F4, with wind speeds ranging from 207 to 260 miles per hour. Some experts believed the storms may have reached F5 level, with winds as strong as 318 miles per hour, a nearly unprecedented velocity.

In Bridge Creek, Okla., a rural community where the death count was high because of the large number of mobile homes, Jeannette L. Ralston emerged from her storm cellar and synthesized her impressions of the wasteland into one word: "Hiroshima." In the Oklahoma City suburb of Moore, whole neighborhoods were reduced to rubble.

Many Oklahoma City residents could not help but compare the disaster to the bombing of the Federal Building in their downtown in April 1995. "This is like eight or nine Murrah Buildings scattered around the city," said Representative J.C. Watts Jr., a Republican from the area.

—Kevin Sack

Record Floods from Hurricane Floyd Devastate North Carolina

Hurricane Floyd, which was spotted off the Bahamas on Sept. 12, 1999, and ravaged the eastern United States through Sept. 16, fulfilled its billing as one of the biggest and fiercest storms ever. Winds near its eye initially exceeded 150 miles per hour, and it covered an area larger than the state of Florida as it started moving north.

But in defiance of forecasts, the storm mostly sideswiped hurricanes' usual targets along shorelines. Floyd did its heaviest damage along low-lying, river-laced regions just inland, in Virginia and in northern and central New Jersey and especially in heavily agricultural eastern North Carolina. And its big weapon was water, not wind.

In North Carolina, Floyd created what state officials called a major environmental disaster. Tens of thousands of hogs and more than a million turkeys and chickens were killed in the flooding. Lagoons of livestock waste overflowed. Agricultural and industrial chemicals leached from flooded farms and factories. Farming losses alone were estimated to be at least $1 billion.

Floyd's rain lifted rivers like the Tar and the Neuse to more than 20 feet above flood stage, leaving lakes of stagnant brown swill in downtown Tarboro and in parts of Goldsboro, Rocky Mount, and Wilson. At least 48 deaths in North Carolina and about 20 in other states were attributed to the storm.

Princeville, N.C., population 1,900, the nation's first community founded by freed slaves, was left with just some rooftops showing. Coffins floated from Princeville graves. Throughout the state, 300 roads were closed for days, including long stretches of two important arteries, Interstates 40 and 95.

Floyd may have a political toll, too, in South Carolina. To move shoreline residents to safety, states organized the largest mass evacuation in the nation's history. But anger and a 10-hour traffic jam ensued for people fleeing Charleston because state officials put off opening the empty westbound lanes of Interstate 26 until 10 P.M. on the eve of the storm.

—Peter T. Kilborn

The First Lady Ponders New York Senate Race

It seemed, at first, like a throwaway line: Senator Robert Torricelli of New Jersey, the head of the Senate Democratic campaign committee, went on television in January and suggested that Hillary Rodham Clinton might run for the Senate seat that was becoming vacant with the retirement of Daniel Patrick Moynihan of New York. The notion appeared to catch everyone by surprise —New York State Democratic leaders, who described the idea as fanciful, the White House, friends of Mrs. Clinton and even, it seemed, the First Lady herself.

At least at first.

But by the 10th time Mrs. Clinton made a trip to New York on "official business," it seemed undeniable that, for the first time in the nation's history, the wife of a sitting President was about to embark on a race for political office. What is more, her Republican opponent was probably going to be Rudolph W. Giuliani, the Mayor of New York. A race for the White House in 2000? Who cared? This was shaping up as one of the most compelling political contests anywhere in years.

Before long, it was hard to believe that the election was not until November 2000. Almost every day, Mr. Giuliani was attacking Mrs. Clinton for being a carpetbagger; he went so far as to stage a quick trip to Arkansas, where Mrs. Clinton lived when the President was Governor, to remind people that she had never lived a day in New York.

Mrs. Clinton formally created an exploratory committee in July and began a "listening tour" of New York, meetings with small groups of voters in which she was shown nodding her head and scribbling notes. She also began to try to distinguish her prospective candidacy from her husband's administration, taking different positions on everything from Mideast peace policy to milk price supports. And with an eye to even busier times ahead, the Clintons bought a $1.67 million house in the Westchester County suburb of Chappaqua. No more trips back to Washington or spending the night with friends: The First Lady will have her own place in New York to call home where she can retire at the end of the campaign day.

—Adam Nagourney

U.S. BUSINESS

The Bulls Turn Skittish on Wall Street

The nation's economy steamed ahead in 1999, and United States corporations surprised many with double-digit profit growth, but this was not enough to keep the stock market engine racing all year long. Stock market milestones toppled fast in the first half of the year. By fall, though, the broad market averages had pulled well back from their peaks.

Technology stocks continued to reward investors as they had in previous years. But in 1999, well-known technology companies such as Microsoft, Cisco Systems, and Intel shared the spotlight with more obscure Internet companies, many of which came public in wildly popular offerings of stock. The preferred method for trading Internet shares became—what else—the Internet, and online trading boomed.

Other market sectors that had produced great gains in recent years lost their luster. Shares of major drug companies such as Merck and Pfizer, soft drink maker Coca-Cola, and banking giants like Citigroup and Bank of America, all contributors to the market's rise in the mid- to late-1990s, fell sharply in 1999.

The Dow Jones industrial average hit 10,000 in late March. On May 3, it closed above 11,000 for the first time. In just four months, it had risen 2,000 points or 22 percent. By August, the average had tacked on 300 more points.

Then it started to sink. A month and a half later, the Dow industrials had fallen almost 10 percent, a decline known in Wall Street parlance as a correction. The Dow's performance in the early months of the year kept the average in positive territory. But for most investors, the Dow's double-digit gains were more to envy than to enjoy. Few investors own all 30 stocks that make up the Dow; most instead own mutual funds that mirror the action in the broader Standard & Poor's 500 stock index. This made much of 1999 a tough year for investors, as the S.&P.'s gain remained in the low single digits, one-half or one-third of the appreciation in the Dow.

Several factors weighed heavily on the market in the second half. Most significant was the Federal Reserve Board's moves to raise short-term interest rates by one-quarter of a percentage point in June and again in September. The Fed clearly hoped that the rate increases would help ensure that inflation would remain low even in a hot economy. But rising rates hurt stocks because they cut into profits at companies forced to pay more to borrow funds for their operations.

Higher interest rates also make bonds more attractive to investors as the payouts rise from these instruments. As a result, stocks struggled. The weakening of the U.S. dollar against the Japanese yen acted as an additional depressant on stocks in the latter part of the year. A strong dollar had been the linchpin of the stock market from the mid-1990s and was responsible for much of the market's strength in the period. A powerful dollar induced overseas investors to buy U.S. financial assets, made imported goods more affordable for Americans and helped keep inflation in check.

But after peaking in May, the dollar started a slide that had taken it down approximately 17 percent against the yen by September. The sharp decline lessened the appeal of U.S. stocks to Japanese investors, who had been eager buyers, because returns in their own currency were diminished after any gains in dollars were converted to yen.

The currency's drop also contributed to fears that inflation, dormant for more than a decade in America, might be on its way back. A sharp increase in the price of gold, oil, and other commodities in the latter part of the year contributed to inflation worries.

The recovery of some stock markets abroad—most notably in Japan—gave U.S. stocks some competition. For the previous two years, as the global economic crisis crept from the Pacific Rim to Russia and then to South America, U.S. equities had been the only port in the storm. As several of these foreign markets began making their comebacks and as investors gained confidence in their growth potential, American shares lost some of their allure.

Even though higher interest rates and a falling dollar contributed to stock market angst, Americans' love affair with stocks continued in 1999. Investors borrowed more money than ever to buy stocks—$177 billion from brokerage firms alone—and some Americans even quit their jobs to sit and trade stocks in so-called day-trading salons operated by brokerage firms.

Day-trading, in which an investor makes lightning-fast purchases and sales of stocks many times during the day but does not hold shares overnight, took an ugly turn in late July, when a disgruntled day trader with big losses, opened fire on fellow traders at two brokerage firm offices in Atlanta and then killed himself.

Technology played an increasingly important role in the markets in 1999. Trading stocks via computer surged in popularity: The number of investors using online brokerage accounts to buy and sell shares soared to 7.1 million, and 35 percent of trades initiated by individual investors was done online.

In addition, the development of electronic networks on which investors meet to buy and sell Nasdaq stocks without a middleman provided alternatives to established exchanges. Some of these networks also allowed investors to trade shares after the regular market close of 4 P.M., the first step toward 24-hour trading of stocks.

Watching warily as these upstart networks gained acceptance among investors, the nation's major stock markets announced plans to offer shares in their operations to the investing public to raise money for technology improvements and acquisitions. The New York Stock Exchange and the Nasdaq Stock Market stated they intended to offer stock to the public, though their initial plans were pushed back from late 1999 until the millennium. Numerous regulatory issues, among others, had to be resolved first.

Although shares in technology companies proved the most profitable for investors over the year, the mania for Internet stocks subsided a bit. Many Internet favorites that peaked in the first half of the year were trading at half those levels by September.

Nevertheless, Internet stocks took on an increased role in the broad market indexes during the year, accounting for 26 percent of the value of the S.&P. 500 and almost half of the Nasdaq Composite's worth.

—*Gretchen Morgenson*

Thriving On The Internet: Mergers, Acquisitions (and Don't Forget Shopping)

The rising popularity of the World Wide Web created one of those rare environments in which evolution of business was unusually rapid. Thousands of new companies emerged from the primordial stew of capital, talent, and opportunity, especially in Silicon Valley south of San Francisco. And some of them grew so rapidly, in sales and stock market value, that the existing giants that dominated business began to move to adapt to the new way of the Internet, out of fear of extinction.

The lightning bolt that accelerated the transformation was the 1998 Christmas selling season, during which consumers bought $3.1 billion worth of goods and services on the Internet. And millions more people bought personal computers for the first time, attracted by prices that were below $1,000 for the first time, and by the lure of the Internet. Overall, the pace of Internet commerce continued to rise briskly. Consumers spent an estimated $14.9 billion online in 1999, according to Jupiter Communications, nearly double the $7.8 billion spent in 1998.

The new behemoth in electronic commerce was Amazon.com, the Seattle company that was founded as an online bookstore by Jeff Bezos, a former investment banker. Just before Christmas 1998, Amazon started selling music and videos. And in 1999, it began to offer videos, toys, electronics, and thousands of other items; it then started a vast auction service to compete with the highly successful Ebay. Amazon also invested in other companies that sold drugs, pet supplies, groceries, and wedding gifts. With 1999 sales estimated to exceed $1.5 billion, Amazon was poised to become the Web's first true department store.

As Amazon expanded, its competitors scrambled to stay afloat in its wake. In October, 1998, CDNow and N2K, two of the older online music vendors, agreed to merge; then only 10 months later (July 1999), the combined company, still trailing Amazon, sold a controlling interest to Time Warner and Sony. Meanwhile, among booksellers, the giant German publisher Bertelsmann decided to abort its own plan for an Internet bookstore in the United States and join forces with the category's distant No.2, Barnes&Noble. com

In industry after industry, the leaders felt compelled to respond to challenges from online upstarts. Most notably, Merrill Lynch, the number one retail broker, after years of dismissing cheaper online brokers like E-Trade, reversed itself in July, 1999, and said that it would let investors trade through the Internet for $29.95, compared to the $80 to $100 its brokers usually charge.

Throughout the Internet, strong companies continued to buy the weak. Most notably, in November 1998, America Online, by far the most popular service for connecting to the Internet, agreed to buy Netscape Communications for $4 billion. Netscape, which developed the most popular browser software to surf the Web, was the first company to set off Internet mania on Wall Street. But in the face of relentless—and in the view of the Justice Department, illegal—competition from Microsoft, Netscape's market share and stock price had been plummeting.

America Online, meanwhile, continued to rise, despite competition from Microsoft, AT&T, and a valley full of well-financed startups. By October, 1999, it had 18 million subscribers, up some 5 million in a year, proving that consumers still prefer its easy software and broad community of members to more technologically sophisticated services.

Much of the merger activity was among the companies, like Yahoo and Excite, born as Internet search engines and then became known as portals because they expanded to offer a gateway to a range of online services, from electronic mail to shopping. These sites had become the most popular on the Internet. In January, 1999, Excite was bought by the At Home Corporation, which offers high speed Internet access through cable television systems. Lycos, another portal, agreed to merge with the Home Shopping Network unit of USA Networks, but that deal was aborted because of shareholder resistance to combining a high-flying Internet company like Lycos with a company that is growing much more slowly.

All of the major television networks affiliated with portals, which many see as the networks of the Internet. Disney linked its ABC and ESPN to Infoseek. NBC bought a controlling interest in Snap. And CBS started a portal called Iwon.com, that offered people prizes for surfing.

Yahoo, the leading portal, resisted many suitors, and decided to remain independent. It did buy Geocities, a collection of 3 million personal home pages, and Broadcast.com, which offers audio and video programming over the Internet, in deals that allowed it to maintain its audience lead, even as its competitors grew.

As much drama came from companies that debuted with initial public offerings. For example, in March, shares started trading in Priceline, a service that offers a new way to buy discounted airline tickets and other products. With a stock market value in excess of $10 billion, the money-losing Priceline was worth more than any airline.

—Saul Hansell

Congress Repeals Depression-Era Law Separating Banking, Insurance, and Securities Industries

After decades of failed attempts, Congress and the White House were poised to overhaul the nation's financial system, repealing Depression-era laws that had restricted banks, insurers and securities firms from expanding into each other's businesses.

The landmark legislation came together in the early morning hours of Oct. 22, when negotiators from the Clinton Administration struck a deal with Senator Phil Gramm, Republican of Texas, to repeal major sections of the Glass-Steagall Act of 1933.

The agreement followed months of partisan wrangling between the Clinton Administration and Mr. Gramm, who heads the banking committee, over the measure's impact on lending rules for the disadvantaged. It also came a week after Alan Greenspan, chairman of the Federal Reserve, reached an agreement with Treasury Secretary Lawrence H. Summers over a new regulatory regime in which both agencies would share oversight over the banks that become part of the new financial conglomerates created as a result of the new law.

The Glass-Steagall Act, named for the two lawmakers who wrote it, broke up the House of Morgan and separated the world of Wall Street into investment bankers and commercial bankers. The idea behind the law was that speculative trading could be reduced and America's financial house could best be kept in order by keeping bankers and brokers in separate rooms.

Although conglomerates had found some ways around the old rules restricting the cross-ownership of banks, securities underwriters, and insurers, those rules had made it difficult, and at times impossible, to expand into new lines of financial services.

Wall Street and many of the nation's largest banks have spent years lobbying Congress to repeal Glass-Steagall, but competing industries and regulatory turf fights had stalemated the lawmakers until this year. Senator Gramm had also killed the measure last year because he said it did not go far enough to curb the abuses of the Community Reinvestment Act, a 1977 law aimed at eradicating discrimination in lending.

Still, critics of the Financial Services Act of 1999 said it did not go far enough to protect the privacy interests of consumers, particularly since it permits financial companies in many circumstances to share private information.

Mr. Clinton had vowed to veto the measure if it diluted the Community Reinvestment Act. The deal struck by the Administration and Senator Gramm requires that banks have satisfactory lending records before expanding into the insurance or securities businesses. It also gives a break to small banks with satisfactory lending records. They will undergo Federal reviews less frequently.

The deal struck by the Republican lawmakers and President Clinton marked one of the few significant legislative achievements of the 106th Congress. But it also marked the end of one of the greatest gravy trains for politicians in Congressional history. The legislation was the product of more than $300 million in campaign contributions and lobbying costs by the three industries in the last two years.

—*Stephen Labaton*

INTERNATIONAL NEWS

NATO Bombs Serbia to Halt Atrocities in Kosovo

For the first time in its history, the North Atlantic Treaty Organization, designed to deter a Soviet invasion of Western Europe, went to war, forcing the Yugoslav President, Slobodan Milosevic, to pull his forces out of the Serbian province of Kosovo.

NATO had bombed the Bosnian Serbs briefly in 1995, accelerating the negotiation of the Dayton Accords that marked the formal end of the fighting in Bosnia, but this time the war was in earnest, with the introduction of ground troops becoming a growing possibility as Belgrade remained defiant despite NATO's air strikes. The Alliance barely held together under the strain of the campaign against a European country that had committed no international aggression, but rather abuses against its own citizens.

The bombing began on March 24, 1995 after the failure of Western-sponsored negotiations over Kosovo in France—in Rambouillet and then

Paris—and lasted 78 days, until the first week of June, after Mr. Milosevic accepted a settlement offer on June 3.

Some 750,000 of Kosovo's nearly two million ethnic Albanian residents were expelled from Kosovo or fled to neighboring countries; less than two months after the war ended, nearly all had returned to face burned houses and scorched villages. And within a few weeks, most of the Serbs of Kosovo had themselves fled the province.

The Serbs are estimated to have killed about 11,000 Kosovar Albanians in their war against the separatist Kosovo Liberation Army and during their "ethnic cleansing"; NATO is estimated to have killed about 1,200 Yugoslav civilians through bombing accidents and about the same number of Yugoslav Army troops, though Mr. Milosevic asserted the military death toll was less than 600 and NATO 5,000.

From a legal standpoint, the war was controversial, justified under the doctrine of "humanitarian intervention," with no recourse to a United Nations Security Council Resolution to authorize the use of force. But Mr. Milosevic's continued abuse of the ethnic Albanian majority in Kosovo, under the pretext of a counter-insurgency war against the Kosovo Liberation Army, was so vivid—and so humiliating to the Clinton Administration and the new leftish Governments of Tony Blair in the United Kingdom and Gerhard Schröder in Germany—that bombing became essentially inevitable.

The previous October, after a brutal Serbian offensive against the KLA, the American envoy, Richard C. Holbrooke, had negotiated a cease-fire with Mr. Milosevic and the introduction of 1,800 unarmed international observers under the Organization for Security and Cooperation in Europe. But the observers, under an American, William Walker, failed to prevent the re-infiltration of the KLA, which came to hold nearly 40 percent of the province, and on Jan. 15, a Serbian army and police offensive against the KLA at the little village of Racak resulted in the deaths of 45 ethnic Albanians and charges of a massacre.

Racak was the catalyst to a new Western effort to negotiate a Kosovo settlement, with wide autonomy for the province and the introduction of foreign forces. These were terms that Mr. Milosevic—who built his political career on an appeal to Serbian nationalism over Kosovo—could not accept.

Mr. Holbrooke made a final appeal in Belgrade to Mr. Milosevic to come to terms on March 22 and 23, but Mr. Milosevic refused to even acknowledge the Serbian offensive in Kosovo. The bombing began the next day. But it was clear that NATO was making up the war as it went along. Early expectations in Washington that Mr. Milosevic would return to the negotiating table after a few symbolic days of bombing—expectations widely derided in Belgrade—proved empty.

After lingering in Budapest for nearly a week, hoping to return to Belgrade for further talks, Mr. Holbrooke (and American diplomats evacuated from Belgrade) returned to the United States. And NATO Secretary-General Javier Solana's assertion that the war would be over by the time of NATO's 50th anniversary summit meeting in Washington on April 23-25 was also badly mistaken.

Holding together the 19-nation alliance—the Czech Republic,Hungary and Poland had just joined—took much diplomatic skill and internal argument. It meant that the military plans of Gen. Wesley Clark, the American who was the Supreme

Commander of NATO, were modified and sometimes delayed by political misgivings among the southern tier of NATO, especially by the Italians, Greeks and even the Germans. It also meant, as General Clark admitted later, sometimes overruling political objections—including the controversial decision to bomb Belgrade's state television center at 2:10 A.M. on April 23, an attack that killed at least 16 civilians.

Another important factor was President Clinton's unwillingness to risk American lives in combat, which meant that even the threat of ground troops was off the table throughout almost the entire conflict, arguably prolonging it. For the same reason, Mr. Clinton kept Army Apache helicopters from going into combat over Kosovo after two men died in a training accident.

The war also caused deep strains with Moscow and with Beijing, after the Chinese Embassy in Belgrade was bombed in early May, apparently by mistake.

One result of NATO's internal political-military squabbling was General Clark's own early retirement. But it seemed clear, afterwards, that NATO's efforts to destroy the Yugoslav Army and its armor in Kosovo were not especially successful, and that NATO wartime propaganda had been exaggerated. And it was only when NATO attacked essentially civilian targets in Serbia—bridges, electrical power plants, heating plants and water supplies—that the political pressure on Mr. Milosevic became great enough that he chose to end the war on what were largely NATO's terms.

In another racheting up of pressure, Mr. Milosevic and four other Serbian officials were also indicted on war-crimes charges for their actions or policies in Kosovo by the International War Crimes Tribunal for the Former Yugoslavia in the Hague. But with the negotiating help of Moscow, Mr. Milosevic succeeded in getting a Kosovo settlement passed through the U.N. Security Council (as opposed to simply accepted from NATO), in confirming Yugoslavia's sovereignty over Kosovo and in eliminating all reference to any sort of referendum in Kosovo over its future status.

But Mr. Milosevic's defeat—his acceptance of 50,000 armed NATO-led troops in Kosovo, the administration of the province by the United Nations and the withdrawal of all Yugoslav troops and police from the province—undermined his political position in Serbia. By late August, as the United Nations and the peacekeeping forces proved slow to assert their authority over Kosovo, Serbs fled by the thousands. Their exodus called into question Western commitments to a democratic and multiethnic province with security for all its inhabitants and gave Mr. Milosevic more political justification for waging the war in the first place.

Serbia's democratic opposition to Mr. Milosevic, though badly divided, took on new enthusiasm and held a series of anti-Milosevic rallies through much of the summer and the fall, aided by growing moves toward independence by Serbia's sister republic, Montenegro, and continued international isolation of Mr. Milosevic and his regime. Toward year's end, however, Mr. Milosevic, a master at coalition politics, was still hanging on to power.

—Steven Erlanger

Military Coup in Pakistan Ends Tumultuous Year on Subcontinent

Relations between India and Pakistan, subcontinental neighbors who both became declared nuclear powers in 1998, have been turbulent and unpredictable in 1999, with giddy highs followed by frightening lows.

India's prime minister, Atal Behari Vajpayee, made a much-publicized journey to Pakistan in February to meet with Pakistan's Prime Minister, Nawaz Sharif. With great pomp and bonhomie, the two men embraced and signed a joint declaration promising that they would work to settle their differences through negotiation.

The visit gave rise to hopes that these two nations, home to more than a billion people, could finally set aside the enmities that have soured relations since 1947 when they were created from the British Indian empire. The diplomacy also eased the world's fears that tensions between the two newest nuclear powers could spin out of control.

But within months, the visions of progress dissolved. Mr. Vajpayee's fragile coalition government came apart in April when his most mercurial and flamboyant ally, Jayalalitha Jayaram of Tamil Nadu, pulled out. No other party was able to put together a majority in Parliament, so with new elections coming in the fall, Mr. Vajpayee continued as a caretaker. As Mr. Vajpayee's government was losing its grip on power, Mr. Sharif in Pakistan was tightening his hold. His chief rival, Benazir Bhutto of the Pakistan People's Party, was convicted in April on charges of having taken kickbacks while she was prime minister in the mid-1990s. She was sentenced to 5 years in prison and barred from holding office.

Also in April, both India and Pakistan test fired ballistic missiles capable of carrying nuclear warheads. And American hopes that India would sign the comprehensive test ban treaty by an informal September deadline faded.

The events that put India and Pakistan on the verge of all-out war unfolded in May. Infiltrators backed by Pakistan occupied peaks in Indian-held portions of Kashmir, and India's military went into combat to win back control of its own territory. They succeeded after two months of bloody fighting. But damage to the trust between the two nations was incalculable. Mr. Vajpayee said that Pakistan must have been plotting the military incursion even as its leaders talked peace with him in February.

October brought new tumult to both countries. When the votes were counted on Oct. 7, after India's lengthy elections, the Hindu nationalist Bharatiya Janata Party had won a clear victory as the leader of a centrist coalition of 24 parties, dealing the once-dominant Congress Party its most bitter defeat ever.

Before India's new Government was even sworn in, the Pakistani Government was overthrown by a military coup on Oct. 12. On Oct. 15, General Pervez Musharraf imposed martial law, declared himself the country's chief executive, suspended the Constitution and dismissed Parliament.

—Celia W. Dugger

Russia's Economy Stabilizes as War Heats Up in Chechnya

Russian troops were fighting in Chechnya. Members of the nation's political elite were tarred by allegations of corruption. And President Boris N. Yeltsin fired his prime ministers so often that sometimes it was difficult to remember who was in charge.

All in all, however, many Russians, inured to

hardship, seem to have concluded that things might well have turned out worse.

Certainly, 1999 began on a rather inauspicious note. Reeling from the August 1998 collapse of its currency, Russia started the year mired in an economic crisis. The capital's fledging financial sector was hit by layoffs. The purchasing power of consumers shrank. The ranks of the poor swelled. And there were fears that many Russians would be compelled do without electricity and adequate food.

Not only did the economy pull out of its nose dive, but some Russian enterprises even prospered and most people managed to adapt to their circumstances and get by. The weakening ruble raised the price of imported goods, protecting domestic producers of food, cars and building supplies from foreign competition. It also made Russian commodities more attractive to foreign buyers, boosting revenues from exports like oil, steel and timber.

And while Russia's economic reformers were largely discredited by the devaluation, the government resisted the temptation to lurch back toward socialism. Major companies were not nationalized, and the government was careful to avoid the scourge of hyper-inflation by limiting the money supply. Some economists even predicted economic growth in 2000.

"The gloomy forecasts have not come true," Prime Minister Vladimir V. Putin said. The economy, however, was only part of the story. The battle to succeed Mr. Yeltsin in the 2000 presidential election kept political circles preoccupied. The Russian president was determined to have a hand in the decision and regularly fired prime ministers for being either too independent or too weak.

Yevgeny M. Primakov was dispatched from the prime minister's post on May 12, 1999. Mr. Yeltsin complained that the former Soviet official was too much a man of the past and not the sort of leader Russia needed in the next century. Mr. Primakov's efforts to position himself as Mr. Yeltsin's successor, however, were also a factor.

Mr. Primakov was replaced by Sergei Stepashin, who was himself fired on Aug. 10. Mr. Yeltsin apparently believed Mr. Stepashin was not dealing sternly enough with the Kremlin's opponents.

Mr. Putin, a former intelligence chief, took Mr. Stepashin's place and guided the nation while Mr. Yeltsin was troubled by health problems. The political struggle took place amid broad allegations of corruption.

The Kremlin and its opponents were involved in mudslinging over allegations of kickbacks, insider deals and capital flight, and the flames were fanned by investigations into money laundering in Switzerland and the United States.

Mr. Putin avoided the taint of corruption. Nor did anybody accuse him of being weak. Rather, the question was whether he was too quick to demonstrate his firmness, particularly after fighting erupted in the northern Caucasus.

The breakaway republic of Chechnya was a quagmire for Russian troops during the Chechen war of 1994 to 1996. And Chechnya again became a burning political, as well as military, concern in 1999 after Islamic militants left their sanctuaries there and crossed into neighboring Dagestan in August.

Russia's anxiety grew as a series of mysterious terrorist explosions at apartment houses in Moscow and other parts of Russia killed several hundred people, many while they slept. The Russ-

ian government blamed the blasts on the Islamic rebels. But the leaders of the militants, Shamil Basayev, a Chechen warlord, and a man known as Khattab, an ethnic Chechen who was born in the Middle East, denied any responsibility.

Taking the fight to the rebels, Mr. Putin decided on a punishing series of air and ground attacks. Russian warplanes attacked industrial centers throughout Chechnya and Russian troops seized the northern third of the republic. The firm riposte boosted Mr. Putin's ratings in the polls. But it left many analysts wondering whether Russia had struck a decisive blow against the rebels or merely set the stage for a new and more brutal round of fighting.

—*Michael R. Gordon*

Democracy Takes Root in Indonesia, But Violence Mars East Timor Vote

Democracy came to Indonesia this year with two historic elections, both of them remarkably free and fair but both producing turbulent and disputed outcomes.

In the first, on June 6, the nation's first truly democratic vote in more than 40 years resulted in a plurality for the opposition leader, Megawati Sukarnoputri, daughter of first independence leader Sukarno, but was only the first step in a five-month process of hard bargaining over the presidency.

In the second, on Aug. 30, the 800,000 people of East Timor voted overwhelmingly to break free of 24 years of Indonesian rule, only to find themselves terrorized by an organized backlash that left the remote territory in ruins.

The general election in June was designed to produce a successor to former President Suharto, who was forced to resign in May 1998 and was replaced by his handpicked vice president, B.J. Habibie. Voting day was largely free of violence, intimidation and fraud but the counting process was slowed by incompetence and political bickering. Mrs. Megawati's party, the Indonesian Democratic Party of Struggle, won 34 percent of the vote, followed by Mr. Habibie's party, Golkar, with 22 percent.

The presidential contest then moved in October to a 700-seat assembly that included 462 members elected in June. Back-room dealing involved both power and payoffs but also amounted to a showdown between Mr. Habibie's old order and the fresh start symbolized by Mrs. Megawati. The Assembly produced a surprise. On Oct. 13 it elected a respected Muslim leader, Abdurram Wahid, who overcame the challenges of both Mrs. Megawati and Mr. Habibie. The following day Mrs. Megawati was chosen as vice president.

In East Timor, the referendum proposed by Mr. Habibie and supervised by the United Nations faced violent opposition from irregular militias armed, supported and sometimes led by the Indonesian military, which had invaded the former Portuguese colony in 1975. The moment the result was announced, on Aug. 4, the militias launched a campaign of vengeance in which almost every town and city was emptied of its population and most buildings were burned or vandalized. An international peacekeeping force, organized by the United Nations and led by Australian troops, landed on Sept. 21 and began the process of pacifying the territory and bringing food, medicine and shelter to its people. It met little initial resistance but as it moved through the territory in the following weeks, it engaged in small firefights with groups of armed men. Slowly and cautiously, the people of East Timor emerged from the hills to try to rebuild their lives.

—*Seth Mydans*

Chinese Ban Spiritual Group After 10,000 Exercise At Government Compound

They seemed to appear from nowhere: in April, 1999, some 10,000 followers of a fast-growing spiritual movement held a surprise, unapproved vigil around the national leaders' compound in Beijing, asking for official recognition. By summer, an embarrassed and apparently threatened Government responded by banning the movement, known as Falun Gong, leading to one of China's strangest social rifts in years.

In 1992 an obscure man named Li Hongzhi had revealed his new synthesis of traditional *qigong*, in which breathing and other exercises are said to harness cosmic forces, with elements of Buddhism and Taoism. Those who practiced his exercises precisely and faithfully could achieve better health and, his writings suggested, tap supernatural powers. Followers were urged to give up smoking and drinking and lead honest lives.

His teachings immediately became popular, especially with retirees and middle-aged women, as well as with enough Government and Party cadres to incense the leaders. By 1999, Falun Gong had millions of followers in China and local groups were performing its strict exercises in many urban parks.

The followers were not stereotypical rebels. But China's rulers were shocked by the evidence of a mass movement outside Party control. They outlawed the group in July, arresting many organizers and staging an all-out media campaign of invective, describing Li as a liar out to destroy the state. Li himself had moved to New York in 1998, where he continued to dispense his wisdom over the Internet and insisted his movement was not political. Millions of Chinese were left perplexed, never imagining that their morning exercise groups would be declared a sinister plot.

—*Erik Eckholm*

Saddam Still Standing, But Bombing of Iraq Quietly Continues

While most of the world's attention focused on NATO's air war against Yugoslavia, the United States and Britain waged a smaller, less intense but no less hostile war against Iraq. Throughout late 1998 and all through 1999, American and British fighter pilots patrolling "no-flight" zones over northern and southern Iraq repeatedly attacked military targets inside Iraq, including antiaircraft artillery batteries, missile launchers, radar stations, and other parts of Iraq's air defenses. The strikes, which came every few days on average, followed repeated attempts by Iraq's military to challenge the patrols overhead.

The strikes began shortly after the United States and Britain launched a concentrated barrage of air and missile strikes against Iraq over four days in December 1998. The aim then was to deliver a sharp, but short military blow against Pres. Saddam Hussein to punish him for refusing to cooperate with United Nations weapons inspections.

It was low-level conflict, and enormously one-sided. By the fall of 1999, no American or British aircraft had been struck by Iraqi fire, let alone shot down, despite flying nearly as many combat and combat-support missions as the NATO allies flew against Yugoslavia. The Iraqis, however, endured strike after strike.

After eight months of skirmishes, the Pentagon estimated that the cumulative attacks had weakened Iraq's air-defense system within the zones by 40 to 50 percent, though the strikes did little to quash Iraq's defiance. In a few instances, the Pentagon acknowledged that bombs and missiles had gone astray, killing civilians, though they said Iraq's claims of casualties were almost always exaggerated.

When the smoke cleared, however, Pres. Hussein was anything but cowed. Instead, he declared that Iraq would no longer tolerate the "no-flight" zones, which the United States and its allies created after the Persian Gulf war ended in 1991 to protect ethnic populations long repressed by the Iraqi regime. He even offered a $14,000 bounty to any Iraqi soldier who could shoot down an American or British jet.

—*Steven Lee Myers*

New Prime Minister Brings Israel to the Peace Table

The overwhelming victory of Ehud Barak as Prime Minister on May 17, 1999, was widely seen as a resounding call for a revival of Israel's languishing efforts to make peace with its Arab neighbors.

Barak, a former top general, presented himself as a dovish hawk in the model of his mentor, the late Yitzhak Rabin who was assassinated by a Jewish extremist in 1995. Picking up where Rabin left off, Barak immediately sought to restore a relationship with the Palestinians and to reopen negotiations with Syria. Sworn in on July 6, he promised to pull Israel's troops out of southern Lebanon within a year. And he set a daunting deadline of 15 months for forging a framework of peace in the region.

Having studied and learned from Rabin's mistakes, Barak moved forward swiftly but cautiously and quietly. With his eye on garnering broad public support for his peacemaking, Barak cobbled together a large and unusual coalition government. He included the Jewish settlers and the ultra-Orthodox and left some secular moderates and the Israeli-Arabs outside, technically in the opposition, but really behind him on the issue of peace.

He also kept an unusually low public profile, rarely appearing on television or making high-wattage public appearances. Barak said it would take him two months to reach a breakthrough with the Palestinians and it did.

On Sept. 4, in a ceremony in Sharm al-Sheikh, Egypt, he signed a new peace deal with the Palestinians. It really was a reiteration and slight modification of a previous agreement, an American-brokered land-for-security deal that had been signed and frozen by Benjamin Netanyahu, his predecessor. The new deal called for immediate steps, which were taken. The Israelis quickly turned over an additional 7 percent of the West Bank—about 160 square miles—to the Palestinians and released 200 Palestinian prisoners. The Palestinians handed over a detailed list of who was serving in all their security forces.

At the same time, negotiations for a permanent peace began, the talks that aim to move the Israelis and the Palestinians beyond interim steps toward a final status arrangement. Wrenching and difficult issues were placed on the table: the status of Jerusalem, the fate of the Jewish settlements in the West Bank, and Palestinian statehood.

Meanwhile, despite many public overtures to Hafez al-Assad, the Syrian President, Barak did not succeed in restarting negotiations with Syria during his first few months. It was unclear just what was taking place behind the scenes, however.

—*Deborah Sontag*

Stalemate in Irish Peace Plan

The year began with the greatest hope in generations of a lasting peace in Northern Ireland, the British province with a sectarian conflict that has cost more than 3,330 lives over the last three decades. It became instead a frustrating year of missed deadlines and lost opportunities as a belligerent stalemate between Ulster's polarized politicians stalled progress in putting in place a new government structured to distribute power equally between the majority (55 percent) Protestants and minority (45 percent) Catholics.

The proposed new government was a product of the Northern Ireland peace agreement of April 1998 that created a new legislature in Belfast and set an Oct. 31, 1998 goal for the crucial last step—the creation of a 10-person executive of Catholic and Protestant political leaders to run the assembly and become, in effect, the cabinet of the new government. More than a year later, that step remained to be taken.

Standing in the way was the refusal by the Ulster Unionists, the province's largest Protestant party, to let members of Sinn Fein, the political wing of the Irish Republican Army, take up their two cabinet seats before the I.R.A. had begun to disarm.

The British Prime Minister, Tony Blair, and his Irish counterpart Bertie Ahern, sponsors of the talks that produced the original agreement, returned to the province in April to spend four days with Ulster's politicians trying to break the deadlock. When on July 15 the Ulster Unionists boycotted the session of the assembly at which the new cabinet was to be installed, the legislature was shut down, and the peace settlement appeared to be in danger of collapsing.

Former U.S. Sen. George J. Mitchell, the chairman of the talks, came back to Belfast in September to begin a formal rescue operation to try to salvage the accord, and in October, Mr. Blair signaled his continuing commitment to finding a way out of the impasse by naming his closest confidant, Peter Mandelson, to succeed Mo Mowlam as Britain's Northern Ireland Secretary.

During the year there were isolated incidents of sectarian violence and continued brutal episodes of the paramilitary policing practice of punishment beatings of petty criminals in working-class neighborhoods. But the I.R.A. and Protestant guerrilla groups maintained their formal ceasefires, leaving the province free of the organized violence that had plagued it for decades. That kept alive the hope that, whatever the outcome of the current peace effort, Ulster might have become accustomed to fighting with words instead of weapons.

—*Warren Hoge*

Hurricane Mitch Devastates Central America

The hurricane season seemed to be winding down to an uneventful finish in October of 1998 when a routine, late-forming tropical wave developed off the coast of Africa and began to move across the Atlantic. Before it disintegrated over Mexico more than three weeks later, though, Hurricane Mitch would become Central America's worst natural disaster of modern times, killing as many as 11,000 people in six countries and inflicting billions of dollars in damage.

Much of that havoc derived from the storm's unusual, even freakish, course and behavior. Though Mitch at its peak had winds that exceeded 180 miles per hour, it was the rains accompanying the storm that accounted for most of the death and destruction. Even as the hurricane was losing force while stalled for four days off the northern coast of Honduras, it was dumping as much as two feet of water on some areas in a single 24-hour period.

The resulting torrent quickly became almost Biblical in proportion and was soon engulfing towns and cities, as rivers overflowed their banks and mountains already stripped of trees proved unable to hold or even slow the flow. In Honduras, the country which bore the brunt of the destruction, entire neighborhoods of the capital, Tegucigalpa, were swept away, while out in the countryside, crops and livestock were devastated. No single place suffered more, however, than the area around Posoltega, a small town at the foot of the Casita Volcano in northwestern Nicaragua.

Nearly a week of rain filled the volcano's crater until it could withstand no more, and it finally broke apart, sending a gigantic wall of mud down the slope that buried 14 nearby villages. At least 1,500 people are known to have died in the avalanche, but the exact death toll probably will never be known.

Once the full dimensions of the tragedy were known, international assistance from governments and private sources was swift to arrive. But the destruction of roads, bridges, airports and harbors and the factories, churches, hospitals and schools that could have served as shelters and distribution points made it difficult to get the aid to the millions clamoring for it, and political discontent followed.

It also became clear as the relief effort gained momentum and the toll of human suffering abated that the storm had inflicted enormous long-term damage that would take decades to repair. Honduras, the second-poorest country in the Western Hemisphere even before Mitch, estimated that 70 percent of its infrastructure was destroyed, and though Central America obtained some debt relief from its international creditors in 1999, the scars, both physical and psychological, largely remain unhealed.

"I have experienced earthquakes, droughts, two wars, cyclones and tidal waves," said Miguel Cardinal Obando y Bravo, who as the Roman Catholic archbishop of Managua is the senior religious figure in Central America. "But this is undoubtedly the worst thing that I have ever seen."

—*Larry Rohter*

South Africa's Election Confirms Mandela's Legacy

On the eve of South Africa's first all-race elections in 1994, the country was fraught with excitement and in the grip of opposing forces: exhilaration and violence, unity and intolerance, anticipation and fear. But this year, South Africa's second elections after the end of apartheid took place in the sort of ho-hum atmosphere that might be expected of a long-established democracy.

President Nelson Mandela, 81 years old, held to

his promise to retire after one term. His party, the African National Congress, was re-elected in a landslide victory, winning more than 66 percent of the vote and surpassing even the 62 percent victory of 1994. As expected, Parliament then elected Mr. Mandela's bookish deputy, Thabo Mbeki, 56, to succeed him as the country's second black president. Mr. Mbeki, a British-educated economist, made clear he would concentrate on trying to deliver a better life to the millions of impoverished South Africans, most of whom are black.

Indeed, the elections highlighted the country's deep racial divisions, as most of the country's blacks, about 77 percent of the population, voted for the ANC while most of the country's whites, mixed-race and citizens of Indian extraction supported white-led parties.

As Mr. Mbeki took over from Mr. Mandela, who spent 27 years in jail for his belief that the black majority should have the vote, he called on South Africans of all races to work together for a rebirth of the country.

In the last five years, the ANC has achieved a great deal, bringing electricity and clean water to millions who did not have them before. The government also revamped a legal system that had systematically discriminated against non-whites, restricting them in myriad ways including dictating where they could live and go to school. However, the country has been plagued by unemployment, as high as 40 percent among blacks, and a soaring crime rate.

During the campaign black South Africans registered deep dissatisfaction with the government, complaining that they still lacked housing, good schools and most of all jobs. But as the June 2, 1999 election date drew nearer, polls showed that black voters believed that the ANC would need more than five years to undo the damage of 40 years of repression under apartheid.

—Suzanne Daley

Democracy Restored in Nigeria

On May 29, 1999, Nigeria's military rulers turned over power to elected politicians, ushering in an era of civilian government and renewed hope in the West African nation of 110 million people. The handover ended nearly 16 years of uninterrupted military rule, a period that was marked by economic, political and social decline in a country that is the world's sixth-largest crude oil producer and Africa's most populous nation.

Nigerians chose as their president a familiar face, Olusegun Obasanjo, a retired general who was the head of state from 1976 and 1979. At that time, General Obasanjo had earned the international community's lasting esteem by becoming Nigeria's first military ruler to give up power voluntarily to a civilian regime. Many inside and outside Nigeria thus urged him to run in the presidential elections that took place on Feb. 27, 1999. The results of the elections, though marred by fraud on the part of both rival parties, were considered sufficiently fair by international observers to prevent doubt from being cast on Obasanjo's overwhelming victory.

The handover was the culmination of a tumultuous year that began on June 8, 1998, with the sudden death by heart attack of the dictator Gen. Sani Abacha, whose repressive and brutal five-year rule had made Nigeria into an international pariah. A month later, Nigerians were again stunned by the equally unexpected death in prison of Moshood K.O. Abiola, a tycoon and popular politician who was widely believed to have won presidential elections in 1993. The military annulled those elections and, when Mr. Abiola insisted on claiming the presidency, put him in jail. An autopsy performed by American and Western doctors concluded that Mr. Abiola had died of heart disease.

—Norimitsu Onishi

Africa's Bloody Wars Rage On

Barely a year after optimists proclaimed an "African renaissance," much of the continent was again embroiled in war as 1999 began. The conflicts, in fact, involved some of the nations that seemed to hold the greatest promise for economic development.

The war in Congo, ignited in August 1998, flared into what many experts called the continent's "First World War." Six nations stationed troops in Congo: Uganda and Rwanda backing the rebels; Zimbabwe, Angola, Namibia and Chad (which withdrew its troops early in the year) backing the Government.

The war pitted Congo's President, Laurent Kabila, against an unlikely alliance of rebels. The rebels accused him of having become as much of a dictator as the man he overthrew in 1997, Mobutu Sese Seko. But the war was also spurred by Rwanda's concerns over its border with Congo, and specifically Mr. Kabila's failure to control Hutu rebels in the borderlands who had carried out the genocide of at least 500,000 Tutsi in Rwanda in 1994.

The rebels quickly took control of nearly half the nation to the east. It soon became clear the war was as much a scramble among the combatants for Congo's vast riches in diamonds, gold, timber and copper. Politically, Mr. Kabila's main allies, Zimbabwe and Angola, lost their appetite for war because of troubles at home. The rebels and their allies had their own problems. In May, the main rebel faction split into two camps, one backed by Rwanda, the other by Uganda. Tensions rose to a peak in August when troops from Uganda and Rwanda, once close allies, battled for three days in the northeast city of Kisangani.

On Aug. 31, the last holdouts signed a peace accord in Lusaka, Zambia, which called for a ceasefire, a foreign peacekeeping mission and a "national dialogue" for the Congolese to decide their own fate. But it was far from clear the fighting was over.

If the Congo war was unique for the number of combatants, the war between Ethiopia and Eritrea produced singularly high casualties. In August, President Clinton said 70,000 people had died since fighting broke out in May 1998. More conservative estimates ran between 40,000 and 50,000 dead.

After an eight month lull, fighting erupted along their disputed border in February, 1999, in the form of a full-blown conventional war, with trenches, tank battles and air bombings. On one level, the war seemed another example of how old colonial borders caused conflict in Africa: the colonial maps are ambiguous and both Ethiopia and Eritrea claim the Badme region as their own. But the war was also the result of tensions over trade and other economic issues. In August, Eritrea accepted a peace plan brokered by the Organization of African Unity. Ethiopia accepted the plan's outlines but was noncommittal on its details.

In Angola, fighting continued after a peace agreement that held for four years dissolved in December 1998. President Jose Eduardo dos Santos had predicted a swift victory over the UNITA rebels, led by Jonas Savimbi. But Mr. Savimbi, a veteran of 30 years of fighting and enriched by the trade in diamonds, began capturing towns and shelling Government strongholds of Huambo and Malanje. The fighting became so intense by February that the United Nations ended its four-year peacekeeping mission there.

In Sudan, even as the famine of 1998 receded, there was no sign of a let-up in 16-year civil war between the northern Islamic Government and the divided rebels, mostly Christian and animist, in the south. The Government in Khartoum issued several conciliatory statements saying it was willing to let the south succeed. In August, as oil began to flow north from oilfields in the south, Khartoum announced a nationwide ceasefire. But the rebels, claiming that the Government had kept up its bombing campaign, rejected the offer.

The President of Niger, Ibrahim Bare Mainassara, was assassinated in April, 1999, by members of the presidential guard and was succeeded by their commander, Maj. Daouda Malam Wanke.

In Guinea Bissau, along West Africa's coast, President Joao Bernardo Vieira, was ousted in May, 1999, after months of heavy fighting and replaced by Malan Bacai Sanha, the former head of Parliament. New elections were called for November.

—*Ian Fisher*

Earthquake Kills 17,000 in Turkey

A devastating earthquake hit the heavily populated industrial region of northwest Turkey before dawn on Aug. 17, killing more than 17,000 people and leaving a quarter of a million homeless. Thousands more are still missing. The quake spared Istanbul's historic monuments.

Many victims were killed as they slept when walls and roofs collapsed on them, especially in apartment buildings built with substandard materials and shoddy construction techniques. Survivors bitterly accused architects, contractors and municipal officials of inexcusable failures. Several contractors were arrested, and at least one needed heavy police protection to protect him from lynch mobs.

Much public anger was also directed against the Government and army, which some survivors said had been slow to respond to the crisis. One television station was ordered closed for a week as punishment for broadcasting reports that portrayed the relief effort as chaotic.

More than 80 countries sent relief aid. Most prominent among them was Greece, Turkey's traditional rival. The outpouring of Greek aid set off a wave of friendship between the two countries, leading to hopes that they might be able to bury their long hostility. Greece said it would no longer block Turkey's application for membership in the European Union.

Israel was also quick to send aid, including rescue teams and a field hospital. This sealed the friendship between the two countries, which has already reshaped the political map of the Middle East.

Debate over failures in the relief effort led to new calls for political reform in Turkey. A senior judge called for scrapping the constitution and writing a new one that would guarantee freedom of expression and political organization. Civic organizations, many of which gained new prestige for their work in the relief effort, supported the judge's call and said that they would support a campaign for lasting political change.

—*Stephen Kinzer*

Turks Seize Leader of Rebel Kurds

Since the mid-1980s, Turkey's war with Kurdish nationalists has taken the lives of more than 30,000 people, forced many more from their homes, cost Turkey tens of billions of dollars and blackened the country's name abroad. So the arrest of the Kurdish insurgent leader, Abdullah Ocalan, in February, 1999, naturally set off a wave of emotion.

Ocalan was seized in Kenya, where he had been living clandestinely under the protection of Greek diplomats. It was the last stop on a zigzagging flight that had taken him to several countries in search of refuge. The authorities in Syria, where he had lived for years, forced him out after demands by Turkish generals.

Within Turkey, where Ocalan is blamed for the Kurdish uprising, many people were overjoyed to see pictures of him blindfolded and handcuffed in the custody of Turkish commandos. But in the mostly Kurdish provinces in the southeast, many people were saddened and even grief-stricken at the capture of the man some call "our leader." Reactions were violent within the Kurdish diaspora, which is concentrated in Western Europe. Kurds who support Ocalan rioted, protested at embassies in several cities and some protesters set themselves ablaze.

Ocalan was found guilty of treason and sentenced to hang for his role in organizing and waging the war against the Government, but the Government seemed in no hurry to carry out the sentence. At his trial, Ocalan said the grievances of most Kurds could be addressed by loosening restrictions on the use of the Kurdish language in Turkey. Later he ordered an end to the armed uprising, and his organization, the Kurdistan Workers Party, said it would obey.

—*Stephen Kinzer*

Rebel Guerillas in Colombia Challenge New President

A civil conflict three decades old took a turn for the worse in Colombia in 1999, as the nation's principal left-wing guerrilla group, the Revolutionary Armed Forces of Colombia, or FARC, made significant political and military advances. Right-wing paramilitary death squads also strengthened their hold over sections of the country, eroding the authority of Colombia's embattled president, Andres Pastrana.

Mr. Pastrana, a Conservative, won election handily in mid-1998 on a peace platform, and in order to coax FARC leaders into peace talks in November 1998, he granted them control of a region the size of Switzerland. But in January the principal rebel leader, Manuel Marulanda, failed to appear at the beginning of discussions between the two sides, and the formal start of the negotiations was twice postponed, first from May to July and then indefinitely after the FARC refused to allow government or international observers in its territory. After the second delay, the FARC launched an offensive that briefly brought its troops within 25 miles of the outskirts of Bogota, the capital, and Mr. Pastrana responded by decreeing a limited curfew in one-third of the country. Army troops eventually pushed FARC units back, but the group's firepower continued to grow, thanks largely to weapons acquired with millions of dollars brought in through kidnappings and drug trafficking.

Another guerrilla group, the National Liberation Army, or ELN, was also active. Resentful of the privileged treatment the FARC was receiving, it carried out a wave of mass kidnappings, hijacking a passenger plane in April and abducting more than 150 people from a Sunday Mass in May. But the ELN appeared to be losing ground in the north, where attacks on its forces by right-wing paramilitary forces were becoming more frequent and fierce, leading to a sharp increase in deaths and displacement among the local civilian population.

—*Larry Rohter*

Chile's Former Dictator Arrested For Crimes Against Humanity

The arrest and year-long detention of the former Chilean dictator Gen. Augusto Pinochet in London and the passage of the case through Britain's highest courts transformed international law and galvanized human rights and exile groups.

Gen. Pinochet was taken into custody in Britain on Oct. 16, 1998, at the request of a Spanish judge, Baltasar Garzón, who had been investigating atrocities committed in Latin America during the so-called "dirty wars "of the 1970's. Mr. Garzón asked that Gen. Pinochet be extradited to Madrid to stand trial for crimes against humanity in connection with the deaths or disappearances of more than 3,000 people between 1973 and 1990, the period that he ruled Chile.

Gen. Pinochet appealed to Britain's High Court, which ruled that he enjoyed immunity from arrest as a former head of state. The court, however, said he could not be freed until the ruling had been reviewed by Britain's highest court, the law Lords of the House of Lords. On the General's 83rd birthday, Nov. 25, 1998, the Lords overturned the High Court's decision and, setting a stunning legal precedent, upheld the legality of his arrest.

On Dec. 17, the Lords said they would reconsider their verdict after discovering that one of them, Lord Hoffmann, was associated with Amnesty International, a party to the case. On March 24, however, they upheld their first finding, while drastically reducing the number of counts and limiting the scope of the case from torture and conspiracy charges to torture alone.

With the legality of General Pinochet's arrest settled, Britain's Home Secretary, Jack Straw, allowed the Spanish request to go forward, and on Oct. 8 the Bow Street Magistrates Court approved it, ruling that the General could be extradited to Spain to stand trial on 35 torture charges. His lawyers indicated they would appeal. The Chilean Government asked Britain later that month to free him on compassionate grounds of age and failing health, citing his doctor's report that he had suffered two small strokes in September. Britain said it could not act on the case until all appeals had been exhausted.

In an interview with The Daily Telegraph in July from the rented house in the London suburbs where he was living under police guard, Gen. Pinochet said that he bore no direct responsibility for atrocities in Chile and he considered himself the victim of a kidnapping. "At this very precise moment," he said. "Let's say the only political prisoner in England is me."

—*Warren Hoge*

The Euro Makes a Grand Entrance, Followed by Quick Fade

After years of arduous diplomacy and preparations, 11 European nations finally achieved the dream of adopting a common currency. Shortly after European finance ministers popped open bottles of champagne in Brussels on New Year's Eve, the euro officially came into existence and began trading in world markets on Jan. 4.

The new "euro zone" now includes Germany, France, Italy, Spain, Finland, Austria, Belgium, the Netherlands, Luxembourg, Ireland and Portugal. Of the remaining countries in the European Union, Britain, Denmark and Sweden qualified for membership but chose to stay out of the currency union. Greece did not qualify, because its budget deficit and inflation were too high, but it hopes to join within two or three years.

For the moment, the euro exists only in the ephemeral form of electronic trade. European stock exchanges and banks transact business in euros. A growing number of stores and businesses accept credit card and check payments in euros. And currency traders trade euros in foreign exchange markets. But the actual bills and coins will not enter circulation until the year 2002. Indeed, about the only euros to be found on New Year's Day were chocolate coins wrapped in gold foil.

Still, in a fundamental sense the euro is entirely real. In the months leading up to its birth, the 11 countries essentially locked their individual monetary policies together and gave up individual sovereignty over their exchange rates.

Since its start, the euro has had a bumpy ride. Largely because of slow growth in Germany and Italy, the euro sank drastically against the dollar from about $1.17 to nearly $1.01 in July. Although it recovered a bit after that, by autumn it remained well below its opening value. The volatile start marked a baptism of fire for the new European Central Bank, based in Frankfurt, which now decides monetary policy for all 11 countries. The bank came under intense criticism from Germany's left-wing finance minister, Oskar Lafontaine, who pushed for an easier monetary policy. Others complained that the bank seemed to speak with multiple voices, sewing confusion.

But the real issue for the euro will be Europe's own economic strength. That in turn is likely to depend on whether countries like Germany can push through plans to reduce taxes and give companies more flexibility.

—*Edmund L. Andrews*

SCIENCE AND MEDICINE

Goodbye El Niño, Hello La Niña

In 1999, heat and drought once again focused the attention of Americans on weather, climate and the question of whether the atmosphere was changing in some basic way.

The year began with a run of extreme weather:

record snows in Buffalo and Chicago, record numbers of tornadoes in the country's midsection, all-time low temperatures in the Midwest and Maine. One big factor, climatologists said, was a weather pattern associated with La Niña, an abnormally cold pool of water stretching across the equatorial Pacific that sets off far-flung changes in atmospheric circulation. These large-scale circulation patterns determine where it is warmer or colder, wetter or drier at any given time.

La Niña is the flip side of El Niño, in which abnormally warm equatorial waters in the Pacific bring about an entirely different global circulation pattern. One effect of La Niña in early 1999 was to shift the jet stream, the main bearer of storms and moisture, from the East to the Midwest, giving the Atlantic coast a drier than normal later winter and spring. Then, in the summer, the jet stream shifted to the north, and the Middle Atlantic region was further deprived of rain, ruining crops and turning lawns brown across the region.

Abnormal heat also plagued much of the East in early July, and then spread westward, setting record after record. With many days on which the temperature hit 95 or higher, it was never so hot so often in any one month in New York City. The heat wave appeared to extend what Federal scientists said was a national trend toward more extreme summer temperatures since World War II. The trend, in turn, accompanied a warming of the American climate that in some places, particularly the nation's northern tier and parts of the Middle Atlantic region and the Northeast, has amounted to 2 to 5 degrees over the last century, on an annual average, according to Federal climatologists.

The temperature trends were consistent with a broader pattern. Scientists in 1999 reported that the Northern Hemisphere was warmer in the 20th century than in any other century of the last thousand years.

Are humans responsible? Researchers reported during the year that a variety of natural and human factors combined to produce temperature changes in the first part of the century. But the dominant influence in the last part of the century was found to be the warming effect of rising concentrations of heat-trapping atmospheric gases—chiefly carbon dioxide, which is produced by the burning of fossil fuels like coal and oil.

In other evidence of a warming, scientists also reported that the southern half of the Greenland ice sheet, the second-largest expanse of land-bound ice on earth, had shrunk substantially in the preceding five years. And a number of studies confirmed earlier findings that as the atmosphere has warmed, spring warmth was arriving earlier and autumn coolness was coming later in the Northern Hemisphere.

Adding its voice to a long list of other prestigious scientific groups that have made declarations about global warming, the American Geophysical Union, the nation's most broadly based professional organization in earth and space science, said there was "no known geologic precedent" for the conversion of carbon from the Earth's crust into atmospheric carbon dioxide, in the amounts being burned as fossil fuels, without changing the climate.

—*William K. Stevens*

Astronomers Find a New Family of Planets

Astronomers in 1999 discovered the first family of planets known to be around another star far from the Sun. Laying to rest any lingering notion of the solar system being a singular phenomenon in the universe, the astronomers detected three large planets orbiting Upsilon Andromedae, a solar-type star 44 light-years away.

Solitary planets had been observed around several other stars in recent years, but this was the first clear evidence showing another star accompanied by multiple planets in a stable system bearing some resemblance to the Sun's.

These are giant worlds. Two of the planets have several times the mass of Jupiter, the solar system's colossus, which is 318 times heftier than Earth. The third planet, with at least three-quarters the Jovian mass, is so close to the star that it completes a full orbit (its year) every 4.6 Earth days.

Though Upsilon Andromedae is visible to the unaided eye, the three planets cannot be seen even with the most powerful telescopes. Astronomers infer their existence, orbits and minimum masses from years of careful study of their gravitational effects on the host star.

Astronomers would not be surprised if they eventually find other, more distant objects around the same star. But their detection would require more prolonged observations and may be beyond current technology. Finding Earth-size planets may not be possible until a spacecraft called Terrestrial Planet Finder is put in orbit, perhaps in 2010.

The new discovery was made by teams led by Dr. Geoffrey W. Marcy of San Francisco State University and Dr. Robert Noyes of the Harvard-Smithsonian Center for Astrophysics. "The single planets we found around other stars was a glorious discovery, but the architecture of other planetary systems had been missing," Dr. Marcy said. "Here for the first time, we can see a kinship between these planets and our own solar system."

Further study of the Upsilon Andromedae planetary system will probably challenge some theories of planet formation and evolution and hatch new ones. It had been thought that such giant gas bodies could only form at great distances from a star, not in as close as Venus and Earth are from the Sun. Nature apparently has many ways of making planetary systems, and the solar system may not be a common configuration.

Astronomers were less surprised by the discovery than relieved. There had been centuries of speculation, often more fanciful than scientific, about families of worlds elsewhere. It seemed only a matter of time, after the first discoveries of single extra-solar planets, that other planetary systems would be found. After all, the Sun is a common type of star, one of 200 billion in the Milky Way alone, and beyond lie more than 80 billion other galaxies. So it seemed unlikely that the Sun's planets were unique, and now the discovery at Upsilon Andromedae suggests that planetary systems may be ubiquitous and the existence of habitable planets more probable.

—*John Noble Wilford*

16 Nations Begin Work On Huge Space Station

It appears to be a new star in the sky, but it is the International Space Station, and it is set to grow brighter as it gets bigger over the next four years.

Construction of what is to become a million-pound orbital outpost with solar panels expanding to an area as large as a football field began in November 1998 when Russia launched its Zarya utility module. The following month, an American space shuttle attached a docking module called Unity to begin assembly of a $60 billion research complex with an internal volume equal to that of a 747 jumbo jet.

Supported by 16 nations led by the United States, the completed base with its six laboratories is to become home for an international crew of up to seven astronauts at a time. It is expected to take at least 40 more flights of space shuttles and Russian rockets, coupled with an expected 1,700 hours of spacewalks, to complete the ambitious undertaking.

Progress has been slower than expected. The shuttle *Discovery* visited the budding station in June 1999, carrying tons of supplies for future crews and adding tools and cranes to the exterior for upcoming spacewalks. But expanding the station has been slowed because of repeated delays in finishing the critical third section, a Russian-made service module that is to provide laboratory and living space for early crews. Hampered by a lack of money as well as technical and political problems, Russia pledged finally to launch the module, called *Zvezda*, in November of 1999.

To concentrate their diminished resources on the international project, the Russians on Aug. 28 pulled the last full-time crew from their Mir space station. This ended what had been almost constant occupancy of the 13-year-old post, the pride of the former Soviet manned space program. If construction of the international station gets back on schedule, the first crew to begin permanent human presence there—two Russians and an American—should arrive in the spring of 2000.
—*Warren E. Leary*

Scientists Slow Down The Speed of Light

Ordinarily, light zips along at about 186,000 miles per second, and a moonbeam takes only a little over one second to reach the earth. But a team of physicists at the Rowland Institute for Science in Cambridge, Mass., disclosed on Feb. 18, 1999 that they had devised a system for slowing light down almost to a walk—38 miles an hour.

The laser light they used was not slowed by such conventional means as passing it through glass or water or some other translucent substance. Instead, it was passed through a bizarre medium called a "Bose-Einstein condensate," in which an assemblage of atoms was chilled to such a low temperature (50 one-billionths of a degree above absolute zero) that the atoms slowed down, synchronized their motion, expanded, overlapped each other and merged into a kind of superatom.

Since 1995 when the first Bose-Einstein condensate was created at the Joint Institute for Laboratory Astrophysics in Boulder, Colo., this strange form of matter has been the object of intense study by many physicists. The main reason is that a Bose-Einstein condensate provides a window through which the strange world of quantum mechanics can be directly viewed from the everyday world. (The condensate is named for Satyendra Nath Bose and Albert Einstein, who predicted that such a state of matter was theoretically possible.)

Quantum mechanics is a set of probabilistic rules describing the behavior of atoms, the components of nuclei, and other quantum particles. One of its governing rules, the Heisenberg Uncertainty Principle, dictates that the more precisely a particle's momentum is known, the less precisely is it possible to know the particle's position, and vice versa.

If an ultracold particle slows to almost a standstill, its momentum also approaches zero: a very precise number. Because of the uncertainty principle, the particle's position therefore becomes very uncertain, and the region of space where the particle could be found expands enormously, and overlapping atoms merge.

Dr. Lene Vestergaard Hau and her team at the Rowland Institute, reporting in the journal *Nature*, succeeded in "entangling" such a superatom with a resonating laser beam and then firing another laser into the entangled condensate. Some of the light from the second laser passed through, but at only one 20-millionth of the normal speed of light.

"We're getting the speed of light so low we can almost send a beam into the system, go for a coffee, and return in time to see the light come out," Dr. Hau said.

Practical uses might include computer chips with switches so sensitive they could be turned on or off by a single photon of light, but for the time being, scientists are content to explore the subtle nature of their astonishing quantum plaything.
—*Malcolm W. Browne*

Scientists Create a Smarter Mouse

Providing a deep insight into the nature of intelligence, scientists led by Dr. Joe Z. Tsien of Princeton University genetically engineered a smarter strain of mouse.

The experiment, announced in the Sept. 2, 1999 issue of the journal *Nature*, was designed as an attempt to prove that a certain brain cell component, known as the NMDA receptor, was indeed part of the basic mechanism of memory, as long suspected. But the mice whose NMDA receptors were genetically enhanced turned out to have improved all-round intelligence, as measured by their performance on standard tests of mouse learning ability.

The finding is relevant to human memory and intelligence because people also have NMDA receptors whose function is encoded by genes of very similar DNA sequence to those of the mouse.

Dr. Tsien took advantage of recent findings by other biologists that the NMDA receptor is made of two kinds of subunit, a main one known as NR1 which works with a variety of partners including two known as NR2A and NR2B.

In young animals, the NR2B subunit predominates, but with age the NR2B is replaced by NR2A. This changeover of subunits, deliberately engineered by nature by turning down activity of the NR2B gene, is apparently the basic reason that underlies the fading of memory with age. The reason is perhaps that young animals need to learn ferociously in order to survive, but the learning rate must be tamped down later in life to avoid running out of storage space or causing memory access problems.

Dr. Tsien took copies of the mouse's NR2B gene, the one that makes the youthful form of the receptor subunit, and linked it to a special sequence of DNA that is known to cause the adjacent gene to be switched on just in cells of the mouse's forebrain. He then injected this combined DNA fragment into fertilized mouse eggs, where it integrated itself into the mouse's other genes.

Because of the extra activity of the NR2B gene, the genetically engineered mice had more of the NR2B units in the NMDA receptors of their brain cells. At the peak of their learning power, the mice were tested and compared with normal mice of the same age. They did better on a range of tests, involving several different areas of the brain, from which Dr. Tsien concluded he had improved not only their memory but also their problem-solving ability and general intelligence.

Dr. Tsien said his finding raised the question of whether memory and intelligence could be enhanced in humans. Drugs might be found to influence the NMDA receptor in the same way genetic engineering influenced the mouse receptor. Or, when methods of gene therapy are developed, genetically engineered cells could perhaps be introduced into the human brain. Brain cells involved in memory are one of the few types that are renewed during a person's lifetime.

Other experts generally agreed on the importance of Dr. Tsien's mice but noted that his approach might well fail in the human brain because of its far greater complexity.

—*Nicholas Wade*

Biologists Discover Brain Adds New Cells in Adult Monkeys

Biologists at Princeton University discovered that new cells are continually being added to the cerebral cortex of adult monkeys, a finding that is expected to prove true of people as well.

The role of the cells is not yet known but they could be involved in memory and learning. Discovery of the new brain cells, together with other recent findings, is a strong challenge to the conventional view that no new cells are formed in the adult brain.

The Princeton scientists injected monkeys with a chemical that tags new cells because it is incorporated into DNA when a cell divides. They found new cells were being generated in a zone toward the center of the brain, then migrating upward to the cortex, the outermost part of the brain, and sending out axons to connect with other cells.

The new cells were found in the pre-frontal area of the cortex, which handles short-term memory and decision-making, and in cortical areas to the side of the head, which handle visual representations. But no new cells were seen in the striate cortex, a region to the back of the head that merely processes information from the eyes and forwards it to other cortical regions.

This is a strong hint that the new cells are needed in cortical regions that lay down memory. A longstanding mystery is how the brain associates most memories with times and dates. The stream of new cells that arrive each day in the cortex suggests a possible mechanism. The cells could load up with memories as they mature and then join the archives. The date of origin of each cell could be the time tag placed on the memories it contains.

The Princeton biologists now intend to explore what the new cells do, firstly by blocking their generation and seeing what deficits develop in the monkeys' behavior.

—*Nicholas Wade*

Two Labs Decode an Animal's DNA

Scientists for the first time decoded the DNA of an animal, a small roundworm much studied by geneticists and known as Caenorhabditis elegans. Members of a rival team then said they would sequence the genome of another much studied laboratory organism, the Drosophila fruitfly. The two teams are racing to decode the human genome,

and the worm and fruitfly serve as useful pilot projects in both cases.

The sequencing of the worm genome, by a joint team at the Sanger Centre, near Cambridge, England, and Washington University, St. Louis, gives biologists their first look at the genetic programming of an animal. The DNA in each cell of the tiny worm has some 97 million chemical units, containing 19,099 genes, the scientists announced in the journal *Science* on Dec. 11, 1998.

The two laboratories involved in sequencing the full DNA, or genome, of the worm are also leaders in the project to sequence the human genome. They undertook the much smaller worm genome in part as a pilot project to prepare for decoding the human genome, thought to be three billion DNA units in length.

The laboratories are members of an international consortium which has said it will produce a "first draft" of the human genome by the spring of 2000 and the complete sequence by 2003, two years earlier than originally planned. By September of 1999, the consortium had completed 13 percent of the genome.

The stepped-up pace occurred after the Celera Corporation, headed by Dr. J. Craig Venter, leaped into the race, saying it would complete the human genome by the end of 2001. Dr. Venter, for his pilot project, chose the laboratory fruitfly, saying he would start sequencing in June and finish the genome by the end of the year.

Experience with C. elegans has shown how difficult it is to decode every last bit of DNA. The worm genome, although substantially complete, contains many small gaps consisting of pieces of DNA that for technical reasons have proved very hard to decode. The gaps are probably of little or no biological importance. Still, they are a warning that similar or greater difficulties may face both teams as they race to complete the human genome.

The *C. elegans* genome has already proved of high value to biologists working in human genetics. Many human genes have a counterpart gene in the roundworm, sufficiently similar in its DNA sequence that it can be recognized by a computer program. A researcher studying an unknown human gene can search the genetic data bases for its worm counterpart, about which much may already have been discovered.

The sequencing of the worm genome also gave biologists their first insight into the overall arrangement of genes on the chromosomes, the giant DNA molecules into which the genes are packaged. The regular, housekeeping genes needed by all forms of life, tend to lie in the center of the chromosomes. The faster-evolving genes, which are special to the roundworm, lie further out at the ends of the chromosomes. The reason for this unexpected pattern remains to be understood

—*Nicholas Wade*

Stem Cell Breakthrough Leads to Abortion Uproar

The promise of creating an all-purpose repair kit for the body's tissues became brighter as scientists reported advances involving human embryonic stem cells.

Biologists at the University of Wisconsin and Johns Hopkins University announced in November 1998 that they had independently succeeded in the long sought goal of isolating human embryonic stem cells, a special kind of all-purpose cell that is formed from the fertilized egg and can give rise to all the different tissues of the body.

The achievement set off an intense public debate this year. Because the stem cells are derived principally from the surplus human embryos created in fertility clinics, abortion opponents lobbied Congress not to allow federally funded researchers to use the cells. Because most university biologists depend on Federal grants, any such ban would put a major crimp on research.

But most scientists, together with many patient advocacy groups, emphasized to Congress the enormous medical benefits that might be gained. The National Institutes of Health, backed by the Administration and in most respects by the National Bioethical Advisory Commission, resolved to support the research unless Congress specifically vetoed it. The cells can be grown in profusion in laboratory glassware, and biologists believe they will learn in time how to nudge the cells down their natural developmental pathways into becoming primitive heart or skin or brain cells.

These primitive cells could then be injected into the appropriate organ of patient. Obeying local signals in the patient's body, the cells would then develop into adult heart cells, say, complementing or replacing the damaged tissue.

No one knows for sure whether such a scheme would work—problems of immune rejection would need to be addressed—but the chance of repairing the body's tissues by its own methods, instead of the crude assaults of drugs or surgery, seemed to many scientists too good to pass up. The phrase "regenerative medicine" has been coined to denote the futuristic concept of treating the body only with its own cells and chemical signals.

Besides embryonic stem cells, interest also intensified this year in a subclass of stem cells, ones that are specific to each of the body's tissues. These tissue stem cells are descended from embryonic stem cells, but are committed to forming only the cells of their own tissue type.

Scientists at Osiris Pharmaceuticals announced in April that they had isolated human mesenchymal stem cells, the stem cells from which all bone and connective tissues are derived, including those of muscle, tendon and cartilage. The company had also learned how to make the cells develop in the laboratory into each of these main tissue types.

Because mesenchymal cells can be isolated from a patient's own bone marrow, they should present no problem of immune rejection. It is too early to say whether embryonic stem cells or tissue-specific cells will have the greater practical importance. Biologists say they need to explore both possibilities in order to develop the best therapies.

—*Nicholas Wade*

Stockpiles of Smallpox Virus to Remain Intact

A turning point in the history of public health came April 22 when the United States—one of two official repositories of the smallpox virus around the globe, along with Russia—announced it would delay its intended destruction of the germ, reversing years of planning and Washington's previous stance.

Over the ages, the deadly virus has killed more people than any other infectious disease. In the 20th century alone, experts estimate, it took up to a half billion lives, more than all the wars and epidemics put together. After a successful effort to

eradicate the bane from human populations, the last laboratory stocks were to have been destroyed in June 1999, making it the first species driven to extinction by design rather than accident. But the Clinton Administration, after careful study, concluded that clandestine supplies of the germ probably exist around the globe and could cause the disease to emerge suddenly in war. And it reasoned that living samples might aid the development of new treatments and antidotes.

Officially, destruction of the virus has been put off three years, until at least June 2002, as world health authorities debate the stay. But few analysts expect momentum to be regained for the destruction of the last samples of the virus. Instead, new studies of them are picking up.

In March, the National Academy of Sciences released a 108-page report listing new research frontiers, many of which American and Russian scientists are already pursuing, such as trying to understand the genetic secrets that make the virus so deadly. The academy report, combined with a secret intelligence report warning that other countries are harboring smallpox for military use, are said to have influenced the Clinton Administration's decision to forgo destruction of the virus.

—*William J. Broad*

Deaths from AIDS Fall in U.S., But Explode in Africa

AIDS continued its deadly progression in 1999, showing worrisome strength on some fronts in the United States and asserting itself as the leading killer in Africa.

Figures released in August by the Centers for Disease Control and Prevention showed that deaths from AIDS in the United States fell 20 percent from 1997 to 1998, a far smaller decline than the sharp drops seen just after powerful combination drug therapies were introduced in 1995. And the annual rate of new infections with H.I.V., the AIDS virus, continued as it has for several years at a steady 40,000. The rates are much lower than they were at their peak in the 1980's. Nevertheless, the slowing of progress worries health officials. They urged renewed efforts at prevention, particularly in groups with dangerously high rates of new infections: young gay men, heterosexual women, blacks and members of other minorities.

The highest rates of H.I.V. infection, as shown through a new method of testing blood, are found among men and women who are also infected with other sexually transmitted diseases, like syphilis, gonorrhea and chlamydia. These other infections cause inflammation and sores that allow more H.I.V. to concentrate in genital secretions and thus greatly increase the risk of acquiring and transmitting H.I.V.

The first comprehensive study of AIDS and sexually transmitted diseases among prisoners in the United States found the prevalence of AIDS to be five times that of the general population. The rates for some other sexually transmitted diseases were even higher.

The AIDS virus continued to devastate underdeveloped countries, statistics by the United Nations AIDS Program showed. In 1999, AIDS became the leading killer in Africa. That development came only 18 years after the infection was first recognized, in the United States. In sub-Saharan Africa, H.I.V. has infected 34 million people and killed 11.5 million, dwarfing malaria and tuberculosis. In 1998, AIDS accounted for

1.8 million deaths in sub-Saharan Africa, nearly double the 1 million deaths from malaria and about nine times the 209,000 deaths from tuberculosis. But hundreds of thousands of AIDS deaths might have been prevented if political and religious leaders had responded with effective public health programs earlier.

In July, American and Ugandan scientists announced that they had come up with a simpler way to reduce significantly the incidence of AIDS in children in developing countries. The more practical and less costly therapy—$4 rather than more than $250—comes from substituting one marketed drug, nevirapine, for the standard drug, AZT. In the new therapy, both the infected mother and her infant take nevirapine just one time. A mother takes a pill once during labor and her baby is fed the drug as a syrup once during the first three days of life. Monitoring in the study will continue for another 18 months to determine whether adverse effects show up later in infancy. Virus detectives offered an answer for the many who have wondered about the origins of H.I.V. The source appears to have been an endangered subspecies of chimpanzee, Pan troglodytes, which lives in West Africa. Because the chimpanzees apparently can live with a related simian immunodeficiency virus, S.I.V.cpz, without falling ill, a hope is to use it to eventually improve therapies and develop a vaccine for humans.

—*Lawrence K. Altman*

10,000 Mummies Found in 2,000-Year-Old Cemetery

The ruins of ancient Egypt have by no means exhausted their power to astonish.

Years may go by without an eye-popping discovery, but then archeologists stumble on something like the 2,000-year-old cemetery at Bahariya Oasis 230 miles southwest of Cairo—one of the most spectacular Egyptian discoveries in decades. In the buried tombs were rows of mummies lavishly prepared for the afterlife with masks and waistcoats covered in gold. The find should provide insights into the art, religion and funerary practices of an affluent wine-producing community in the Roman period of Egypt, in the first two centuries A.D.

"Never before have such a number of mummies been found in a single site in Egypt," said Dr. Zahi Hawass, director of excavations at what is being called the Valley of the Golden Mummies.

The sheer size and pristine condition of the cemetery, as much as the gilded mummies, impressed scholars. It may be the largest ancient Egyptian burial ground to have escaped looters. Archeologists estimate that the entire cemetery, extending over two square miles, might yield 10,000 mummies. In the first four tombs explored in 1999, archeologists counted 105 mummies—men, women and children. Entire families appeared to be together in repose. No two mummy decorations were alike. Looking at the painted masks, Dr. Hawass said, "The eyes of some gazed at me as if they were alive."

The mummy excavations were a highlight of the year marking the 200th anniversary of the 1799 discovery of the Rosetta Stone by Napoleon's army in Egypt. A dark gray basalt fragment of an inscribed commemorative slab, the stone bore writing in both Greek and Egyptian and thus became the key to deciphering hieroglyphics—and the foundation for the scholarly field of Egyptology.

—*John Noble Wilford*

The A.M.A. Fights Back And Forms a Union

The American Medical Association, which has long been viewed as an elite professional organization, voted on June 23 to form a union for doctors in an effort to give them a stronger voice in their dealings with hospitals and managed-care organizations.

The 290,000-member association, which represents about a third of the nation's doctors, decided at its annual meeting in Chicago to put aside its longtime stance against unions because so many doctors complained about feeling powerless when dealing with health-maintenance organizations. The association also feared growing competition from traditional labor unions, which had unionized about 40,000 doctors by promising to represent them vigorously.

Under the plan, the A.M.A. did not transform itself into a union, but rather voted to set up a branch, named Physicians for Responsible Negotiations, that would seek to set up dozens of union locals representing two groups of doctors: salaried employees and medical residents. Anti-trust laws prohibit physicians in private practice from bargaining with managed-care organizations.

Eager to reassure the public that it was not forsaking the Hippocratic oath, the A.M.A. insisted that its union would never go on strike.

—*Steven Greenhouse*

Regulators Act to Curb the Wild West of Internet Pharmacies

The Internet, which has turned American homes into virtual shopping malls, this year gave rise to a new—and, Federal and state regulators say, worrisome—commercial trend, the electronic sale of prescription drugs and other medical treatments.

As more people began using the World Wide Web to purchase medicine, state and Federal regulators struggled to impose restrictions on the practice, with little success. In June, the Federal Trade Commission said it had identified hundreds of Web sites promoting phony cures for more than 30 ailments, but took legal action against only four, including one that advertised shark cartilage as a cure for cancer. The following month, Congress convened a hearing to examine the illegal sale of foreign drugs on-line, as well as domestic sales that experts say are not illegal, but unethical.

The domestic market is closely tied to another recent development: the emergence of so-called "life-style drugs," like Viagra, the impotence pill, and Xenical, a drug for obesity approved this year by the Food and Drug Administration. Amid consumer demand for such medications, some doctors set up shop on the Internet to write prescriptions for patients they had not physically examined. And virtual pharmacies began shipping pills across state lines, without the required licenses. "It is strictly the Wild West of drug dealing via the Internet," said Representative Ron Klink, Democrat of Pennsylvania, who is sponsoring legislation that would require virtual drugstores to post detailed information about their licenses, and the licenses of the doctors who write their prescriptions.

—*Sheryl Gay Stolberg*

Calendar of the Year

UNDERSTANDING CALENDARS

The day Earth turns at a fairly steady pace about the imaginary line that defines the North and South Poles. This line through the poles is called Earth's *axis*. Each turn about the axis, called a *rotation*, takes slightly less than 24 hours. Since Earth is also traveling around the Sun, however, the time from noon to noon is longer than the time it takes for one rotation—about 3 minutes and 56 seconds longer, or almost exactly 24 hours. The time from noon to noon changes slightly during the year, depending on where Earth is in its path. If you average all the days in a year, the mean time from noon to noon is exactly 24 hours.

The year All the nine planets of the solar system travel in nearly circular paths, called *orbits*, around the Sun. Each trip around the Sun is called a *revolution*. The planets all revolve in the same direction, which can be observed from Earth by noting the position the Sun has among the background stars, which are traditionally grouped into constellations. (Since you can't see the Sun and stars at the same time, you can observe where the Sun rises or sets each day and then note the stars that appear in the same region.) Over the course of a year, the Sun appears to pass through the 12 constellations that make up the zodiac.

Earth's trip around the Sun, reflected in the Sun's trip through the zodiac, takes about 365.25 days. This varies slightly from time to time, so astronomers add or delete a second in some years to keep their records in tune with Earth's motion. (see also "Precession of the *equinoxes*" below).

Seasons The seasons mark the change in the pattern of daylight over the course of the year. Because the Earth is tilted with respect to its path around the Sun, different parts receive different amounts of sunlight during Earth's annual orbit, the time we know as a year. Between late September (around the 21st) and late March, Earth's Northern Hemisphere is tilted away from the Sun. This period constitutes the fall and winter seasons for the Northern Hemisphere, during which there are fewer than 12 hours of daylight each day. For the rest of the year, spring and summer, the Northern Hemisphere is tilted toward the Sun, and daylight hours constitute more than half of each day. In the Southern Hemisphere, this situation is reversed: spring and summer last from late September to late March, while fall and winter make up the other half of the year.

At the points of transition from long days and short nights to short days and long nights and vice versa, the *equinoxes* occur—the two days of the year when periods of daylight and darkness are equal. The *vernal equinox*, marking the first day of spring, takes place on or around March 21 in the Northern Hemisphere, while the *autumnal equinox*, marking the beginning of fall, is on or around September 21. Officially, summer begins on the day of the longest daytime during the year, about June 21 in the Northern Hemisphere, called the *summer solstice*. The *winter solstice*, about December 21 in the Northern Hemisphere, has the shortest amount of daylight and the longest night of the year. The word *solstice* means "standing still Sun." These two days are so called because the apparent movement of where the Sun rises or sets reaches its extreme positions on the solstices and then reverses direction.

Precession of the equinoxes Ancient Greek astronomers determined that the direction of Earth's axis is constantly, but very slowly, changing in a regular pattern. The kind of change is similar to the way a spinning top slowly leans one way then another as its axis changes direction. This movement of the Earth is caused by several factors, the most dominant being one called *precession*. The precession of the Earth results from its not being a perfect sphere. Earth's diameter is about 27 miles greater from one side of the equator to the other than it is from one pole to the other. (Earth is oblate, or fat around the middle, as a result of its rotation.)

Picture Earth without considering its revolution. Keep Earth's center in the same place mentally, and think about how the axis changes position during precession. Any point on Earth's axis (except the center of the planet) moves in a slow circle as a result of precession. This movement is so slow that it takes 26,000 years for a point to return to its original spot. In the meantime, the axis gradually changes its position in relation to the stars. While what we call the North Star (officially known as Polaris) is currently positioned above the North Pole about one degree off center, over time the axis will shift, so that about A.D. 15,000 the star Vega will be above the North Pole within about four degrees of that axis. By about A.D. 28,000, Polaris will have returned to its present position.

As the precession continues, one of its effects is to change the times of the year that seasons occur. Our calendar is corrected for this; if it were not, the vernal equinox would, over 13,000 years, shift from around March 21 to about September 21, the date at which the autumnal equinox is now. For this reason, the precession of the Earth is generally known as the precession of the equinoxes.

Although the precession of the equinoxes is slow, it can be easily observed. The year of about 365.25 days is the time it takes from one vernal

Solar Phenomena: The Seasons, 2000

Solar phenomenon	Month	Day	Hour	Min
Perigee[1]	Jan.	3	05	—
Vernal equinox	Mar.	20	07	35
Summer solstice	June	21	01	48
Apogee[2]	July	4	00	—
Autumnal equinox	Sept.	22	17	27
Winter solstice	Dec.	21	13	37

Note: Shown in Universal time (UT). To convert to local time, see "Timing Planetary Phenomena." 1. Sun closest to the Earth (91.4 million miles). 2. Sun farthest from the Earth (94.5 million miles). **Source:** U.S. Naval Observatory, *Astronomical Phenomena for the Year 2000* (1998)

equinox to the next. Because of the precession of the equinoxes, however, the time it takes the Sun to appear in the same position with respect to the stars is 20 minutes, 24 seconds longer than the period from one equinox to the next. For this reason, accurate star maps have to specify both the date and the year for which they are intended.

Lunar Calendar

There is some evidence that very early humans (c. 25,000 B.C.) used marks on bone to indicate the passage of time, which they may have measured by the Moon's phases. A calendar for the year can be based upon the Moon's phases, which gives a year of 12 periods from new moon to new moon (hence the word *month*) lasting about 354 days. This is about 11 days shorter than the time it takes Earth to revolve around the Sun. The Chinese, who still use a version of this calendar, resolve the discrepancy by inserting extra months at fixed intervals to bring the lunar and solar years into alignment. The Chinese year is divided into months that are either 29 or 30 days long, since the time from new moon to new moon is approximately 29.5 days. The New Year begins at the first new moon over China between Jan. 21 and Feb. 19, and is celebrated for a four-day period. Each year has both a number and a name. The year 1999, or 4636 in the Chinese era, is the Year of the Rabbit.

Solar Calendar

The ancient Egyptians were the first people known to have instituted a solar calendar. In actuality, their calendar might be called a stellar calendar, since the year began with the rising of Sirius (the brightest star in the sky) at the same place the Sun rises, which generally happened at the same time the Nile flooded. The Egyptians determined that a year was 365 days, about one-quarter of a day short of the true solar year, so gradually the Egyptian calendar no longer coincided with the seasons. Historical records reveal when the Egyptian calendar and the rising of Sirius coincided, from which astronomers inferred that the Egyptian calendar must have been instituted in either 4241 B.C. or 2773 B.C. The Egyptian calendar had 12 months of 30 days and five days of festival, a system adopted by various early cultures, although some continued to use lunar calendars.

Julian Calendar

In 46 B.C., Julius Caesar realized that various parts of the land controlled by Rome used different calendars, so he asked the astronomer Sosigenes to develop a uniform calendar. Sosigenes proposed that since the year was 365.25 days long (though not exactly), a 365-day calendar be kept with one day added (a leap day) every fourth year. When Caesar introduced the new system, he also added days to the year 46 B.C. to bring the seasons in line with the calendar. With a total of 445 days, 46 B.C. is the longest calendar year on record. A year at that time began in what we call March, and the months were numbered. *September, October, November, and December* derive from this system and mean "seventh," "eighth," "ninth," and "tenth" months respectively.

There was a little further adjustment of the calendar, however, by Augustus Caesar, the first Roman emperor. The name of the fifth month (our July) was changed from Quintilis to honor Julius Caesar, and Augustus named the sixth month August after himself. So that August would not be shorter than 31-day July, Augustus borrowed a day from February.

Because of the Roman Empire's great sphere of influence, the Julian calendar became the ordinary calendar of Western nations.

Gregorian Calendar

From at least A.D. 730, it was known that the solar year—measured from vernal equinox to vernal equinox—was somewhat short of 365.25 days. Each century the solar year gets about half a second shorter. In 1990 the solar year is calculated at 365 days, 5 hours, 48 minutes, and 45.5 seconds long, not 365¼ days, which is what the Julian calendar assumes. Because the date of Easter (the Sunday following the first full Moon after the vernal equinox) was slipping, Pope Gregory XIII instituted calendar reform in 1582. He proclaimed that the day following Oct. 4 would be Oct. 15, which dropped 10 days from the year. Furthermore, on the advice of astronomer Christoph Clavius, the new calendar would be kept in line by omitting the leap year in century years unless they were divisible by 400. Thus 1900 was not a leap year in the Gregorian calendar, as it came to be, but 2000 would be.

Most Roman Catholic countries and some other Western countries adopted the new system, but England did not. Finally, in 1752, England and its colonies adopted the Gregorian calendar, but they had to drop 11 days to fit common Western practice. It was at this time that New Year's Day in England was moved from Mar. 25 to Jan. 1, changing the number of the year for the almost three months affected. Thus George Washington was born according to the Julian calendar on Feb. 11, 1731, but he came to celebrate his birthday on Feb. 22, 1732 according to the Gregorian calendar.

Because the solar year is shortening, astronomers today keep the Gregorian calendar in line by making a one-second adjustment, as needed, usually on Dec. 31 at midnight, whenever the error's accumulation nears one second.

The Millennium

Some time in the last week of 1999, at least half a dozen smart alecks on television will attempt to remind viewers in the Western Hemisphere that the millennium does not actually end on Dec. 31 1999, but a year later, on Dec. 31, 2000. This claim is based on the fact that our calendar began in the year 1, rather than the year 0. Consequently, a thousand years did not pass until the end of the year 1000, and the second millennium will not end until the end of year 2000.

This information is technically correct, but by the same token, the 1980s began in 1981 and ended in 1990, and the 1990s won't end until January 1, 2001. Yet we routinely consider years ending in 0 to be the first year of a decade or a century rather than the last, so why should it be any different for millennia? Also, remember that calendars are an inexact science (the concept of negative numbers, for example, didn't exist in Europe until the 16th century) and plenty of shifting of days, months, and years, has been perpetrated over the years by kings, emperors, and popes.

The Jewish calendar counted more than 3,700 years before Western calendars counted their first, while the Chinese celebrated the beginning of the third millennium more than 1,600 years ago. The numbers on the Western calendar are just that: counting revolutions around the Sun since the day Christ was born, and even that date isn't universally agreed upon. Most scholars now believe Christ was born a few years before A.D. 1, (in which case the third millennium already began several years ago) but records are too sketchy to prove it. The third millennium could also be said to begin on Dec. 25, 2001, exactly two thousand years and one second after the agreed-upon day of Christ's birth.

Of course, none of this information will cause anybody to postpone their end of the millennium parties until 2000. Everybody just wants to see all the nines turn to zeros; it's the same reason they drive around the block a few times when the car odometer reaches 99,999 miles. Everybody will call Jan. 1, 2000 the beginning of the third millennium and the start of the 21st century, and attempts to stop the practice will be dismissed as pedantic. See also the special section on the millennium at the beginning of the book. For an even more detailed explanation, see the U.S. Naval Observatory's Web site: **http://aa.usno.navy.mil/AA/faq/docs/faq2.html**

Perpetual Calendar, 1775–2050

A perpetual calendar lets you find the day of the week for any date in any year. Since January 1 may fall on any of the seven days of the week, and may be a leap or non-leap year, 14 different calendars are possible. The number next to each year corresponds to one of the 14 calendars. For example, in 1776, calendar 9 (a leap year in which Jan. 1 fell on a Monday) was used; July 4 of that year was a Thursday. Calendar 6 was used in 1999; Calendar 14 will be used in 2000.

Year	No.	Year	No.	Year	No.	Year	No.	Year	No.	Year	No.	Year	No.
1775	1	1815	1	1855	2	1895	3	1935	3	1975	4	2015	5
1776	9	1816	9	1856	10	1896	11	1936	11	1976	12	2016	13
1777	4	1817	4	1857	5	1897	6	1937	6	1977	7	2017	1
1778	5	1818	5	1858	6	1898	7	1938	7	1978	1	2018	2
1779	6	1819	6	1859	7	1899	1	1939	1	1979	2	2019	3
1780	14	1820	14	1860	8	1900	2	1940	9	1980	10	2020	11
1781	2	1821	2	1861	3	1901	3	1941	4	1981	5	2021	6
1782	3	1822	3	1862	4	1902	4	1942	5	1982	6	2022	7
1783	4	1823	4	1863	5	1903	5	1943	6	1983	7	2023	1
1784	12	1824	12	1864	13	1904	13	1944	14	1984	8	2024	9
1785	7	1825	7	1865	1	1905	1	1945	2	1985	3	2025	4
1786	1	1826	1	1866	2	1906	2	1946	3	1986	4	2026	5
1787	2	1827	2	1867	3	1907	3	1947	4	1987	5	2027	6
1788	10	1828	10	1868	11	1908	11	1948	12	1988	13	2028	14
1789	5	1829	5	1869	6	1909	6	1949	7	1989	1	2029	2
1790	6	1830	6	1870	7	1910	7	1950	1	1990	2	2030	3
1791	7	1831	7	1871	1	1911	1	1951	2	1991	3	2031	4
1792	8	1832	8	1872	9	1912	9	1952	10	1992	11	2032	12
1793	3	1833	3	1873	4	1913	4	1953	5	1993	6	2033	7
1794	4	1834	4	1874	5	1914	5	1954	6	1994	7	2034	1
1795	5	1835	5	1875	6	1915	6	1955	7	1995	1	2035	2
1796	13	1836	13	1876	14	1916	14	1956	8	1996	9	2036	10
1797	1	1837	1	1877	2	1917	2	1957	3	1997	4	2037	5
1798	2	1838	2	1878	3	1918	3	1958	4	1998	5	2038	6
1799	3	1839	3	1879	4	1919	4	1959	5	1999	6	2039	7
1800	4	1840	11	1880	12	1920	12	1960	13	2000	14	2040	8
1801	5	1841	6	1881	7	1921	7	1961	1	2001	2	2041	3
1802	6	1842	7	1882	1	1922	1	1962	2	2002	3	2042	4
1803	7	1843	1	1883	2	1923	2	1963	3	2003	4	2043	5
1804	8	1844	9	1884	10	1924	10	1964	11	2004	12	2044	13
1805	3	1845	4	1885	5	1925	5	1965	6	2005	7	2045	1
1806	4	1846	5	1886	6	1926	6	1966	7	2006	1	2046	2
1807	5	1847	6	1887	7	1927	7	1967	1	2007	2	2047	3
1808	13	1848	14	1888	8	1928	8	1968	9	2008	10	2048	11
1809	1	1849	2	1889	3	1929	3	1969	4	2009	5	2049	6
1810	2	1850	3	1890	4	1930	4	1970	5	2010	6	2050	7
1811	3	1851	4	1891	5	1931	5	1971	6	2011	7		
1812	11	1852	12	1892	13	1932	13	1972	14	2012	8		
1813	6	1853	7	1893	1	1933	1	1973	2	2013	3		
1814	7	1854	1	1894	2	1934	2	1974	3	2014	4		

1

JANUARY
S	M	T	W	T	F	S
1	2	3	4	5	6	7
8	9	10	11	12	13	14
15	16	17	18	19	20	21
22	23	24	25	26	27	28
29	30	31				

FEBRUARY
S	M	T	W	T	F	S
			1	2	3	4
5	6	7	8	9	10	11
12	13	14	15	16	17	18
19	20	21	22	23	24	25
26	27	28				

MARCH
S	M	T	W	T	F	S
			1	2	3	4
5	6	7	8	9	10	11
12	13	14	15	16	17	18
19	20	21	22	23	24	25
26	27	28	29	30	31	

APRIL
S	M	T	W	T	F	S
						1
2	3	4	5	6	7	8
9	10	11	12	13	14	15
16	17	18	19	20	21	22
23	24	25	26	27	28	29
30						

MAY
S	M	T	W	T	F	S
	1	2	3	4	5	6
7	8	9	10	11	12	13
14	15	16	17	18	19	20
21	22	23	24	25	26	27
28	29	30	31			

JUNE
S	M	T	W	T	F	S
				1	2	3
4	5	6	7	8	9	10
11	12	13	14	15	16	17
18	19	20	21	22	23	24
25	26	27	28	29	30	

JULY
S	M	T	W	T	F	S
						1
2	3	4	5	6	7	8
9	10	11	12	13	14	15
16	17	18	19	20	21	22
23	24	25	26	27	28	29
30	31					

AUGUST
S	M	T	W	T	F	S
		1	2	3	4	5
6	7	8	9	10	11	12
13	14	15	16	17	18	19
20	21	22	23	24	25	26
27	28	29	30	31		

SEPTEMBER
S	M	T	W	T	F	S
					1	2
3	4	5	6	7	8	9
10	11	12	13	14	15	16
17	18	19	20	21	22	23
24	25	26	27	28	29	30

OCTOBER
S	M	T	W	T	F	S
1	2	3	4	5	6	7
8	9	10	11	12	13	14
15	16	17	18	19	20	21
22	23	24	25	26	27	28
29	30	31				

NOVEMBER
S	M	T	W	T	F	S
			1	2	3	4
5	6	7	8	9	10	11
12	13	14	15	16	17	18
19	20	21	22	23	24	25
26	27	28	29	30		

DECEMBER
S	M	T	W	T	F	S
					1	2
3	4	5	6	7	8	9
10	11	12	13	14	15	16
17	18	19	20	21	22	23
24	25	26	27	28	29	30
31						

2

JANUARY
S	M	T	W	T	F	S
	1	2	3	4	5	6
7	8	9	10	11	12	13
14	15	16	17	18	19	20
21	22	23	24	25	26	27
28	29	30	31			

FEBRUARY
S	M	T	W	T	F	S
				1	2	3
4	5	6	7	8	9	10
11	12	13	14	15	16	17
18	19	20	21	22	23	24
25	26	27	28			

MARCH
S	M	T	W	T	F	S
				1	2	3
4	5	6	7	8	9	10
11	12	13	14	15	16	17
18	19	20	21	22	23	24
25	26	27	28	29	30	31

APRIL
S	M	T	W	T	F	S
1	2	3	4	5	6	7
8	9	10	11	12	13	14
15	16	17	18	19	20	21
22	23	24	25	26	27	28
29	30					

MAY
S	M	T	W	T	F	S
		1	2	3	4	5
6	7	8	9	10	11	12
13	14	15	16	17	18	19
20	21	22	23	24	25	26
27	28	29	30	31		

JUNE
S	M	T	W	T	F	S
					1	2
3	4	5	6	7	8	9
10	11	12	13	14	15	16
17	18	19	20	21	22	23
24	25	26	27	28	29	30

JULY
S	M	T	W	T	F	S
1	2	3	4	5	6	7
8	9	10	11	12	13	14
15	16	17	18	19	20	21
22	23	24	25	26	27	28
29	30	31				

AUGUST
S	M	T	W	T	F	S
			1	2	3	4
5	6	7	8	9	10	11
12	13	14	15	16	17	18
19	20	21	22	23	24	25
26	27	28	29	30	31	

SEPTEMBER
S	M	T	W	T	F	S
						1
2	3	4	5	6	7	8
9	10	11	12	13	14	15
16	17	18	19	20	21	22
23	24	25	26	27	28	29
30						

OCTOBER
S	M	T	W	T	F	S
	1	2	3	4	5	6
7	8	9	10	11	12	13
14	15	16	17	18	19	20
21	22	23	24	25	26	27
28	29	30	31			

NOVEMBER
S	M	T	W	T	F	S
				1	2	3
4	5	6	7	8	9	10
11	12	13	14	15	16	17
18	19	20	21	22	23	24
25	26	27	28	29	30	

DECEMBER
S	M	T	W	T	F	S
						1
2	3	4	5	6	7	8
9	10	11	12	13	14	15
16	17	18	19	20	21	22
23	24	25	26	27	28	29
30	31					

3

JANUARY
S	M	T	W	T	F	S
		1	2	3	4	5
6	7	8	9	10	11	12
13	14	15	16	17	18	19
20	21	22	23	24	25	26
27	28	29	30	31		

FEBRUARY
S	M	T	W	T	F	S
					1	2
3	4	5	6	7	8	9
10	11	12	13	14	15	16
17	18	19	20	21	22	23
24	25	26	27	28		

MARCH
S	M	T	W	T	F	S
					1	2
3	4	5	6	7	8	9
10	11	12	13	14	15	16
17	18	19	20	21	22	23
24	25	26	27	28	29	30
31						

APRIL
S	M	T	W	T	F	S
	1	2	3	4	5	6
7	8	9	10	11	12	13
14	15	16	17	18	19	20
21	22	23	24	25	26	27
28	29	30				

MAY
S	M	T	W	T	F	S
			1	2	3	4
5	6	7	8	9	10	11
12	13	14	15	16	17	18
19	20	21	22	23	24	25
26	27	28	29	30	31	

JUNE
S	M	T	W	T	F	S
						1
2	3	4	5	6	7	8
9	10	11	12	13	14	15
16	17	18	19	20	21	22
23	24	25	26	27	28	29
30						

JULY
S	M	T	W	T	F	S
	1	2	3	4	5	6
7	8	9	10	11	12	13
14	15	16	17	18	19	20
21	22	23	24	25	26	27
28	29	30	31			

AUGUST
S	M	T	W	T	F	S
				1	2	3
4	5	6	7	8	9	10
11	12	13	14	15	16	17
18	19	20	21	22	23	24
25	26	27	28	29	30	31

SEPTEMBER
S	M	T	W	T	F	S
1	2	3	4	5	6	7
8	9	10	11	12	13	14
15	16	17	18	19	20	21
22	23	24	25	26	27	28
29	30					

OCTOBER
S	M	T	W	T	F	S
		1	2	3	4	5
6	7	8	9	10	11	12
13	14	15	16	17	18	19
20	21	22	23	24	25	26
27	28	29	30	31		

NOVEMBER
S	M	T	W	T	F	S
					1	2
3	4	5	6	7	8	9
10	11	12	13	14	15	16
17	18	19	20	21	22	23
24	25	26	27	28	29	30

DECEMBER
S	M	T	W	T	F	S
1	2	3	4	5	6	7
8	9	10	11	12	13	14
15	16	17	18	19	20	21
22	23	24	25	26	27	28
29	30	31				

4

JANUARY
S	M	T	W	T	F	S
			1	2	3	4
5	6	7	8	9	10	11
12	13	14	15	16	17	18
19	20	21	22	23	24	25
26	27	28	29	30	31	

FEBRUARY
S	M	T	W	T	F	S
						1
2	3	4	5	6	7	8
9	10	11	12	13	14	15
16	17	18	19	20	21	22
23	24	25	26	27	28	

MARCH
S	M	T	W	T	F	S
						1
2	3	4	5	6	7	8
9	10	11	12	13	14	15
16	17	18	19	20	21	22
23	24	25	26	27	28	29
30	31					

APRIL
S	M	T	W	T	F	S
		1	2	3	4	5
6	7	8	9	10	11	12
13	14	15	16	17	18	19
20	21	22	23	24	25	26
27	28	29	30			

MAY
S	M	T	W	T	F	S
				1	2	3
4	5	6	7	8	9	10
11	12	13	14	15	16	17
18	19	20	21	22	23	24
25	26	27	28	29	30	31

JUNE
S	M	T	W	T	F	S
1	2	3	4	5	6	7
8	9	10	11	12	13	14
15	16	17	18	19	20	21
22	23	24	25	26	27	28
29	30					

JULY
S	M	T	W	T	F	S
		1	2	3	4	5
6	7	8	9	10	11	12
13	14	15	16	17	18	19
20	21	22	23	24	25	26
27	28	29	30	31		

AUGUST
S	M	T	W	T	F	S
					1	2
3	4	5	6	7	8	9
10	11	12	13	14	15	16
17	18	19	20	21	22	23
24	25	26	27	28	29	30
31						

SEPTEMBER
S	M	T	W	T	F	S
	1	2	3	4	5	6
7	8	9	10	11	12	13
14	15	16	17	18	19	20
21	22	23	24	25	26	27
28	29	30				

OCTOBER
S	M	T	W	T	F	S
			1	2	3	4
5	6	7	8	9	10	11
12	13	14	15	16	17	18
19	20	21	22	23	24	25
26	27	28	29	30	31	

NOVEMBER
S	M	T	W	T	F	S
						1
2	3	4	5	6	7	8
9	10	11	12	13	14	15
16	17	18	19	20	21	22
23	24	25	26	27	28	29
30						

DECEMBER
S	M	T	W	T	F	S
	1	2	3	4	5	6
7	8	9	10	11	12	13
14	15	16	17	18	19	20
21	22	23	24	25	26	27
28	29	30	31			

5

JANUARY
S	M	T	W	T	F	S
				1	2	3
4	5	6	7	8	9	10
11	12	13	14	15	16	17
18	19	20	21	22	23	24
25	26	27	28	29	30	31

FEBRUARY
S	M	T	W	T	F	S
1	2	3	4	5	6	7
8	9	10	11	12	13	14
15	16	17	18	19	20	21
22	23	24	25	26	27	28

MARCH
S	M	T	W	T	F	S
1	2	3	4	5	6	7
8	9	10	11	12	13	14
15	16	17	18	19	20	21
22	23	24	25	26	27	28
29	30	31				

APRIL
S	M	T	W	T	F	S
			1	2	3	4
5	6	7	8	9	10	11
12	13	14	15	16	17	18
19	20	21	22	23	24	25
26	27	28	29	30		

MAY
S	M	T	W	T	F	S
					1	2
3	4	5	6	7	8	9
10	11	12	13	14	15	16
17	18	19	20	21	22	23
24	25	26	27	28	29	30
31						

JUNE
S	M	T	W	T	F	S
	1	2	3	4	5	6
7	8	9	10	11	12	13
14	15	16	17	18	19	20
21	22	23	24	25	26	27
28	29	30				

JULY
S	M	T	W	T	F	S
			1	2	3	4
5	6	7	8	9	10	11
12	13	14	15	16	17	18
19	20	21	22	23	24	25
26	27	28	29	30	31	

AUGUST
S	M	T	W	T	F	S
						1
2	3	4	5	6	7	8
9	10	11	12	13	14	15
16	17	18	19	20	21	22
23	24	25	26	27	28	29
30	31					

SEPTEMBER
S	M	T	W	T	F	S
		1	2	3	4	5
6	7	8	9	10	11	12
13	14	15	16	17	18	19
20	21	22	23	24	25	26
27	28	29	30			

OCTOBER
S	M	T	W	T	F	S
				1	2	3
4	5	6	7	8	9	10
11	12	13	14	15	16	17
18	19	20	21	22	23	24
25	26	27	28	29	30	31

NOVEMBER
S	M	T	W	T	F	S
1	2	3	4	5	6	7
8	9	10	11	12	13	14
15	16	17	18	19	20	21
22	23	24	25	26	27	28
29	30					

DECEMBER
S	M	T	W	T	F	S
		1	2	3	4	5
6	7	8	9	10	11	12
13	14	15	16	17	18	19
20	21	22	23	24	25	26
27	28	29	30	31		

6

JANUARY
S	M	T	W	T	F	S
					1	2
3	4	5	6	7	8	9
10	11	12	13	14	15	16
17	18	19	20	21	22	23
24	25	26	27	28	29	30
31						

FEBRUARY
S	M	T	W	T	F	S
	1	2	3	4	5	6
7	8	9	10	11	12	13
14	15	16	17	18	19	20
21	22	23	24	25	26	27
28						

MARCH
S	M	T	W	T	F	S
	1	2	3	4	5	6
7	8	9	10	11	12	13
14	15	16	17	18	19	20
21	22	23	24	25	26	27
28	29	30	31			

APRIL
S	M	T	W	T	F	S
				1	2	3
4	5	6	7	8	9	10
11	12	13	14	15	16	17
18	19	20	21	22	23	24
25	26	27	28	29	30	

MAY
S	M	T	W	T	F	S
						1
2	3	4	5	6	7	8
9	10	11	12	13	14	15
16	17	18	19	20	21	22
23	24	25	26	27	28	29
30	31					

JUNE
S	M	T	W	T	F	S
		1	2	3	4	5
6	7	8	9	10	11	12
13	14	15	16	17	18	19
20	21	22	23	24	25	26
27	28	29	30			

JULY
S	M	T	W	T	F	S
				1	2	3
4	5	6	7	8	9	10
11	12	13	14	15	16	17
18	19	20	21	22	23	24
25	26	27	28	29	30	31

AUGUST
S	M	T	W	T	F	S
1	2	3	4	5	6	7
8	9	10	11	12	13	14
15	16	17	18	19	20	21
22	23	24	25	26	27	28
29	30	31				

SEPTEMBER
S	M	T	W	T	F	S
			1	2	3	4
5	6	7	8	9	10	11
12	13	14	15	16	17	18
19	20	21	22	23	24	25
26	27	28	29	30		

OCTOBER
S	M	T	W	T	F	S
					1	2
3	4	5	6	7	8	9
10	11	12	13	14	15	16
17	18	19	20	21	22	23
24	25	26	27	28	29	30
31						

NOVEMBER
S	M	T	W	T	F	S
	1	2	3	4	5	6
7	8	9	10	11	12	13
14	15	16	17	18	19	20
21	22	23	24	25	26	27
28	29	30				

DECEMBER
S	M	T	W	T	F	S
			1	2	3	4
5	6	7	8	9	10	11
12	13	14	15	16	17	18
19	20	21	22	23	24	25
26	27	28	29	30	31	

7

JANUARY
S	M	T	W	T	F	S
						1
2	3	4	5	6	7	8
9	10	11	12	13	14	15
16	17	18	19	20	21	22
23	24	25	26	27	28	29
30	31					

FEBRUARY
S	M	T	W	T	F	S
		1	2	3	4	5
6	7	8	9	10	11	12
13	14	15	16	17	18	19
20	21	22	23	24	25	26
27	28					

MARCH
S	M	T	W	T	F	S
		1	2	3	4	5
6	7	8	9	10	11	12
13	14	15	16	17	18	19
20	21	22	23	24	25	26
27	28	29	30	31		

APRIL
S	M	T	W	T	F	S
					1	2
3	4	5	6	7	8	9
10	11	12	13	14	15	16
17	18	19	20	21	22	23
24	25	26	27	28	29	30

MAY
S	M	T	W	T	F	S
1	2	3	4	5	6	7
8	9	10	11	12	13	14
15	16	17	18	19	20	21
22	23	24	25	26	27	28
29	30	31				

JUNE
S	M	T	W	T	F	S
			1	2	3	4
5	6	7	8	9	10	11
12	13	14	15	16	17	18
19	20	21	22	23	24	25
26	27	28	29	30		

JULY
S	M	T	W	T	F	S
					1	2
3	4	5	6	7	8	9
10	11	12	13	14	15	16
17	18	19	20	21	22	23
24	25	26	27	28	29	30
31						

AUGUST
S	M	T	W	T	F	S
	1	2	3	4	5	6
7	8	9	10	11	12	13
14	15	16	17	18	19	20
21	22	23	24	25	26	27
28	29	30	31			

SEPTEMBER
S	M	T	W	T	F	S
				1	2	3
4	5	6	7	8	9	10
11	12	13	14	15	16	17
18	19	20	21	22	23	24
25	26	27	28	29	30	

OCTOBER
S	M	T	W	T	F	S
						1
2	3	4	5	6	7	8
9	10	11	12	13	14	15
16	17	18	19	20	21	22
23	24	25	26	27	28	29
30	31					

NOVEMBER
S	M	T	W	T	F	S
		1	2	3	4	5
6	7	8	9	10	11	12
13	14	15	16	17	18	19
20	21	22	23	24	25	26
27	28	29	30			

DECEMBER
S	M	T	W	T	F	S
				1	2	3
4	5	6	7	8	9	10
11	12	13	14	15	16	17
18	19	20	21	22	23	24
25	26	27	28	29	30	31

8

JANUARY
S	M	T	W	T	F	S
1	2	3	4	5	6	7
8	9	10	11	12	13	14
15	16	17	18	19	20	21
22	23	24	25	26	27	28
29	30	31				

FEBRUARY
S	M	T	W	T	F	S
			1	2	3	4
5	6	7	8	9	10	11
12	13	14	15	16	17	18
19	20	21	22	23	24	25
26	27	28	29			

MARCH
S	M	T	W	T	F	S
				1	2	3
4	5	6	7	8	9	10
11	12	13	14	15	16	17
18	19	20	21	22	23	24
25	26	27	28	29	30	31

APRIL
S	M	T	W	T	F	S
1	2	3	4	5	6	7
8	9	10	11	12	13	14
15	16	17	18	19	20	21
22	23	24	25	26	27	28
29	30					

MAY
S	M	T	W	T	F	S
		1	2	3	4	5
6	7	8	9	10	11	12
13	14	15	16	17	18	19
20	21	22	23	24	25	26
27	28	29	30	31		

JUNE
S	M	T	W	T	F	S
					1	2
3	4	5	6	7	8	9
10	11	12	13	14	15	16
17	18	19	20	21	22	23
24	25	26	27	28	29	30

JULY
S	M	T	W	T	F	S
1	2	3	4	5	6	7
8	9	10	11	12	13	14
15	16	17	18	19	20	21
22	23	24	25	26	27	28
29	30	31				

AUGUST
S	M	T	W	T	F	S
			1	2	3	4
5	6	7	8	9	10	11
12	13	14	15	16	17	18
19	20	21	22	23	24	25
26	27	28	29	30	31	

SEPTEMBER
S	M	T	W	T	F	S
						1
2	3	4	5	6	7	8
9	10	11	12	13	14	15
16	17	18	19	20	21	22
23	24	25	26	27	28	29
30						

OCTOBER
S	M	T	W	T	F	S
	1	2	3	4	5	6
7	8	9	10	11	12	13
14	15	16	17	18	19	20
21	22	23	24	25	26	27
28	29	30	31			

NOVEMBER
S	M	T	W	T	F	S
				1	2	3
4	5	6	7	8	9	10
11	12	13	14	15	16	17
18	19	20	21	22	23	24
25	26	27	28	29	30	

DECEMBER
S	M	T	W	T	F	S
						1
2	3	4	5	6	7	8
9	10	11	12	13	14	15
16	17	18	19	20	21	22
23	24	25	26	27	28	29
30	31					

9

JANUARY
S	M	T	W	T	F	S
	1	2	3	4	5	6
7	8	9	10	11	12	13
14	15	16	17	18	19	20
21	22	23	24	25	26	27
28	29	30	31			

FEBRUARY
S	M	T	W	T	F	S
				1	2	3
4	5	6	7	8	9	10
11	12	13	14	15	16	17
18	19	20	21	22	23	24
25	26	27	28	29		

MARCH
S	M	T	W	T	F	S
					1	2
3	4	5	6	7	8	9
10	11	12	13	14	15	16
17	18	19	20	21	22	23
24	25	26	27	28	29	30
31						

APRIL
S	M	T	W	T	F	S
	1	2	3	4	5	6
7	8	9	10	11	12	13
14	15	16	17	18	19	20
21	22	23	24	25	26	27
28	29	30				

MAY
S	M	T	W	T	F	S
			1	2	3	4
5	6	7	8	9	10	11
12	13	14	15	16	17	18
19	20	21	22	23	24	25
26	27	28	29	30	31	

JUNE
S	M	T	W	T	F	S
						1
2	3	4	5	6	7	8
9	10	11	12	13	14	15
16	17	18	19	20	21	22
23	24	25	26	27	28	29
30						

JULY
S	M	T	W	T	F	S
	1	2	3	4	5	6
7	8	9	10	11	12	13
14	15	16	17	18	19	20
21	22	23	24	25	26	27
28	29	30	31			

AUGUST
S	M	T	W	T	F	S
				1	2	3
4	5	6	7	8	9	10
11	12	13	14	15	16	17
18	19	20	21	22	23	24
25	26	27	28	29	30	31

SEPTEMBER
S	M	T	W	T	F	S
1	2	3	4	5	6	7
8	9	10	11	12	13	14
15	16	17	18	19	20	21
22	23	24	25	26	27	28
29	30					

OCTOBER
S	M	T	W	T	F	S
		1	2	3	4	5
6	7	8	9	10	11	12
13	14	15	16	17	18	19
20	21	22	23	24	25	26
27	28	29	30	31		

NOVEMBER
S	M	T	W	T	F	S
					1	2
3	4	5	6	7	8	9
10	11	12	13	14	15	16
17	18	19	20	21	22	23
24	25	26	27	28	29	30

DECEMBER
S	M	T	W	T	F	S
1	2	3	4	5	6	7
8	9	10	11	12	13	14
15	16	17	18	19	20	21
22	23	24	25	26	27	28
29	30	31				

10

JANUARY
S	M	T	W	T	F	S
		1	2	3	4	5
6	7	8	9	10	11	12
13	14	15	16	17	18	19
20	21	22	23	24	25	26
27	28	29	30	31		

FEBRUARY
S	M	T	W	T	F	S
					1	2
3	4	5	6	7	8	9
10	11	12	13	14	15	16
17	18	19	20	21	22	23
24	25	26	27	28	29	

MARCH
S	M	T	W	T	F	S
						1
2	3	4	5	6	7	8
9	10	11	12	13	14	15
16	17	18	19	20	21	22
23	24	25	26	27	28	29
30	31					

APRIL
S	M	T	W	T	F	S
		1	2	3	4	5
6	7	8	9	10	11	12
13	14	15	16	17	18	19
20	21	22	23	24	25	26
27	28	29	30			

MAY
S	M	T	W	T	F	S
				1	2	3
4	5	6	7	8	9	10
11	12	13	14	15	16	17
18	19	20	21	22	23	24
25	26	27	28	29	30	31

JUNE
S	M	T	W	T	F	S
1	2	3	4	5	6	7
8	9	10	11	12	13	14
15	16	17	18	19	20	21
22	23	24	25	26	27	28
29	30					

JULY
S	M	T	W	T	F	S
		1	2	3	4	5
6	7	8	9	10	11	12
13	14	15	16	17	18	19
20	21	22	23	24	25	26
27	28	29	30	31		

AUGUST
S	M	T	W	T	F	S
					1	2
3	4	5	6	7	8	9
10	11	12	13	14	15	16
17	18	19	20	21	22	23
24	25	26	27	28	29	30
31						

SEPTEMBER
S	M	T	W	T	F	S
	1	2	3	4	5	6
7	8	9	10	11	12	13
14	15	16	17	18	19	20
21	22	23	24	25	26	27
28	29	30				

OCTOBER
S	M	T	W	T	F	S
			1	2	3	4
5	6	7	8	9	10	11
12	13	14	15	16	17	18
19	20	21	22	23	24	25
26	27	28	29	30	31	

NOVEMBER
S	M	T	W	T	F	S
						1
2	3	4	5	6	7	8
9	10	11	12	13	14	15
16	17	18	19	20	21	22
23	24	25	26	27	28	29
30						

DECEMBER
S	M	T	W	T	F	S
	1	2	3	4	5	6
7	8	9	10	11	12	13
14	15	16	17	18	19	20
21	22	23	24	25	26	27
28	29	30	31			

11

JANUARY
S	M	T	W	T	F	S
			1	2	3	4
5	6	7	8	9	10	11
12	13	14	15	16	17	18
19	20	21	22	23	24	25
26	27	28	29	30	31	

FEBRUARY
S	M	T	W	T	F	S
						1
2	3	4	5	6	7	8
9	10	11	12	13	14	15
16	17	18	19	20	21	22
23	24	25	26	27	28	29

MARCH
S	M	T	W	T	F	S
1	2	3	4	5	6	7
8	9	10	11	12	13	14
15	16	17	18	19	20	21
22	23	24	25	26	27	28
29	30	31				

APRIL
S	M	T	W	T	F	S
			1	2	3	4
5	6	7	8	9	10	11
12	13	14	15	16	17	18
19	20	21	22	23	24	25
26	27	28	29	30		

MAY
S	M	T	W	T	F	S
					1	2
3	4	5	6	7	8	9
10	11	12	13	14	15	16
17	18	19	20	21	22	23
24	25	26	27	28	29	30
31						

JUNE
S	M	T	W	T	F	S
	1	2	3	4	5	6
7	8	9	10	11	12	13
14	15	16	17	18	19	20
21	22	23	24	25	26	27
28	29	30				

JULY
S	M	T	W	T	F	S
			1	2	3	4
5	6	7	8	9	10	11
12	13	14	15	16	17	18
19	20	21	22	23	24	25
26	27	28	29	30	31	

AUGUST
S	M	T	W	T	F	S
						1
2	3	4	5	6	7	8
9	10	11	12	13	14	15
16	17	18	19	20	21	22
23	24	25	26	27	28	29
30	31					

SEPTEMBER
S	M	T	W	T	F	S
		1	2	3	4	5
6	7	8	9	10	11	12
13	14	15	16	17	18	19
20	21	22	23	24	25	26
27	28	29	30			

OCTOBER
S	M	T	W	T	F	S
				1	2	3
4	5	6	7	8	9	10
11	12	13	14	15	16	17
18	19	20	21	22	23	24
25	26	27	28	29	30	31

NOVEMBER
S	M	T	W	T	F	S
1	2	3	4	5	6	7
8	9	10	11	12	13	14
15	16	17	18	19	20	21
22	23	24	25	26	27	28
29	30					

DECEMBER
S	M	T	W	T	F	S
		1	2	3	4	5
6	7	8	9	10	11	12
13	14	15	16	17	18	19
20	21	22	23	24	25	26
27	28	29	30	31		

12

JANUARY
S	M	T	W	T	F	S
				1	2	3
4	5	6	7	8	9	10
11	12	13	14	15	16	17
18	19	20	21	22	23	24
25	26	27	28	29	30	31

FEBRUARY
S	M	T	W	T	F	S
1	2	3	4	5	6	7
8	9	10	11	12	13	14
15	16	17	18	19	20	21
22	23	24	25	26	27	28
29						

MARCH
S	M	T	W	T	F	S
	1	2	3	4	5	6
7	8	9	10	11	12	13
14	15	16	17	18	19	20
21	22	23	24	25	26	27
28	29	30	31			

APRIL
S	M	T	W	T	F	S
				1	2	3
4	5	6	7	8	9	10
11	12	13	14	15	16	17
18	19	20	21	22	23	24
25	26	27	28	29	30	

MAY
S	M	T	W	T	F	S
						1
2	3	4	5	6	7	8
9	10	11	12	13	14	15
16	17	18	19	20	21	22
23	24	25	26	27	28	29
30	31					

JUNE
S	M	T	W	T	F	S
		1	2	3	4	5
6	7	8	9	10	11	12
13	14	15	16	17	18	19
20	21	22	23	24	25	26
27	28	29	30			

JULY
S	M	T	W	T	F	S
				1	2	3
4	5	6	7	8	9	10
11	12	13	14	15	16	17
18	19	20	21	22	23	24
25	26	27	28	29	30	31

AUGUST
S	M	T	W	T	F	S
1	2	3	4	5	6	7
8	9	10	11	12	13	14
15	16	17	18	19	20	21
22	23	24	25	26	27	28
29	30	31				

SEPTEMBER
S	M	T	W	T	F	S
			1	2	3	4
5	6	7	8	9	10	11
12	13	14	15	16	17	18
19	20	21	22	23	24	25
26	27	28	29	30		

OCTOBER
S	M	T	W	T	F	S
					1	2
3	4	5	6	7	8	9
10	11	12	13	14	15	16
17	18	19	20	21	22	23
24	25	26	27	28	29	30
31						

NOVEMBER
S	M	T	W	T	F	S
	1	2	3	4	5	6
7	8	9	10	11	12	13
14	15	16	17	18	19	20
21	22	23	24	25	26	27
28	29	30				

DECEMBER
S	M	T	W	T	F	S
			1	2	3	4
5	6	7	8	9	10	11
12	13	14	15	16	17	18
19	20	21	22	23	24	25
26	27	28	29	30	31	

13

JANUARY
S	M	T	W	T	F	S
					1	2
3	4	5	6	7	8	9
10	11	12	13	14	15	16
17	18	19	20	21	22	23
24	25	26	27	28	29	30
31						

FEBRUARY
S	M	T	W	T	F	S
	1	2	3	4	5	6
7	8	9	10	11	12	13
14	15	16	17	18	19	20
21	22	23	24	25	26	27
28	29					

MARCH
S	M	T	W	T	F	S
		1	2	3	4	5
6	7	8	9	10	11	12
13	14	15	16	17	18	19
20	21	22	23	24	25	26
27	28	29	30	31		

APRIL
S	M	T	W	T	F	S
					1	2
3	4	5	6	7	8	9
10	11	12	13	14	15	16
17	18	19	20	21	22	23
24	25	26	27	28	29	30

MAY
S	M	T	W	T	F	S
1	2	3	4	5	6	7
8	9	10	11	12	13	14
15	16	17	18	19	20	21
22	23	24	25	26	27	28
29	30	31				

JUNE
S	M	T	W	T	F	S
			1	2	3	4
5	6	7	8	9	10	11
12	13	14	15	16	17	18
19	20	21	22	23	24	25
26	27	28	29	30		

JULY
S	M	T	W	T	F	S
					1	2
3	4	5	6	7	8	9
10	11	12	13	14	15	16
17	18	19	20	21	22	23
24	25	26	27	28	29	30
31						

AUGUST
S	M	T	W	T	F	S
	1	2	3	4	5	6
7	8	9	10	11	12	13
14	15	16	17	18	19	20
21	22	23	24	25	26	27
28	29	30	31			

SEPTEMBER
S	M	T	W	T	F	S
				1	2	3
4	5	6	7	8	9	10
11	12	13	14	15	16	17
18	19	20	21	22	23	24
25	26	27	28	29	30	

OCTOBER
S	M	T	W	T	F	S
						1
2	3	4	5	6	7	8
9	10	11	12	13	14	15
16	17	18	19	20	21	22
23	24	25	26	27	28	29
30	31					

NOVEMBER
S	M	T	W	T	F	S
		1	2	3	4	5
6	7	8	9	10	11	12
13	14	15	16	17	18	19
20	21	22	23	24	25	26
27	28	29	30			

DECEMBER
S	M	T	W	T	F	S
				1	2	3
4	5	6	7	8	9	10
11	12	13	14	15	16	17
18	19	20	21	22	23	24
25	26	27	28	29	30	31

14

JANUARY
S	M	T	W	T	F	S
						1
2	3	4	5	6	7	8
9	10	11	12	13	14	15
16	17	18	19	20	21	22
23	24	25	26	27	28	29
30	31					

FEBRUARY
S	M	T	W	T	F	S
		1	2	3	4	5
6	7	8	9	10	11	12
13	14	15	16	17	18	19
20	21	22	23	24	25	26
27	28					

MARCH
S	M	T	W	T	F	S
		1	2	3	4	
5	6	7	8	9	10	11
12	13	14	15	16	17	18
19	20	21	22	23	24	25
26	27	28	29	30	31	

APRIL
S	M	T	W	T	F	S
						1
2	3	4	5	6	7	8
9	10	11	12	13	14	15
16	17	18	19	20	21	22
23	24	25	26	27	28	29
30						

MAY
S	M	T	W	T	F	S
	1	2	3	4	5	6
7	8	9	10	11	12	13
14	15	16	17	18	19	20
21	22	23	24	25	26	27
28	29	30	31			

JUNE
S	M	T	W	T	F	S
				1	2	3
4	5	6	7	8	9	10
11	12	13	14	15	16	17
18	19	20	21	22	23	24
25	26	27	28	29	30	

JULY
S	M	T	W	T	F	S
						1
2	3	4	5	6	7	8
9	10	11	12	13	14	15
16	17	18	19	20	21	22
23	24	25	26	27	28	29
30	31					

AUGUST
S	M	T	W	T	F	S
		1	2	3	4	5
6	7	8	9	10	11	12
13	14	15	16	17	18	19
20	21	22	23	24	25	26
27	28	29	30	31		

SEPTEMBER
S	M	T	W	T	F	S
					1	2
3	4	5	6	7	8	9
10	11	12	13	14	15	16
17	18	19	20	21	22	23
24	25	26	27	28	29	30

OCTOBER
S	M	T	W	T	F	S
1	2	3	4	5	6	7
8	9	10	11	12	13	14
15	16	17	18	19	20	21
22	23	24	25	26	27	28
29	30	31				

NOVEMBER
S	M	T	W	T	F	S
			1	2	3	4
5	6	7	8	9	10	11
12	13	14	15	16	17	18
19	20	21	22	23	24	25
26	27	28	29	30		

DECEMBER
S	M	T	W	T	F	S
					1	2
3	4	5	6	7	8	9
10	11	12	13	14	15	16
17	18	19	20	21	22	23
24	25	26	27	28	29	30
31						

HOLIDAYS AND HOLY DAYS

▶ FEDERAL HOLIDAYS IN THE UNITED STATES

Congress and the president have designated 10 days as federal holidays. Although these are so widely observed as to be considered "national" holidays, they technically apply only to federal employees and the District of Columbia. It is up to the individual states to designate their own holidays. When a federal holiday falls on a Saturday or a Sunday, it is observed on the preceding Friday or the following Monday.

New Year's Day (January 1) The observance of the New Year dates back to pre-Christian times when rites were performed to ensure the return of spring.

Martin Luther King, Jr., Day (Third Monday in January) Before his assassination in 1968, Martin Luther King, Jr., was the foremost civil rights leader of the 1950s and 1960s, and in 1964 he won the Nobel Peace Prize. In 1983, Congress set aside this day to celebrate his life and accomplishments.

Washington's Birthday (Third Monday in February) Originally celebrated on the actual birthday of America's first president (February 22), this holiday was officially moved in 1971 to the third Monday in February to create a three-day weekend. It is sometimes known as Presidents' Day, because the birthday of Abraham Lincoln (Feb. 12) is so close.

Memorial Day (Last Monday in May) Memorial Day (also known as Decoration Day) honors soldiers fallen in battle. Dating from the Civil War, it is traditionally marked with parades and memorial services.

Independence Day (Fourth of July) The most important U.S. holiday, Independence Day commemorates the signing of the Declaration of Independence on July 4, 1776, an event that marked America's birth as a free nation. The holiday was first observed in 1777 and is celebrated with fireworks, parades, and oratory.

Labor Day (First Monday in September) The idea of Peter J. McGuire, president of the United Brotherhood of Carpenters and Joiners of America, the official observance of a day celebrating the American worker was signed into law on June 28, 1894.

Columbus Day (Second Monday in October) On Oct. 12, 1492, Christopher Columbus and his crew landed in the Bahama Islands after sailing across the Atlantic. First celebrated in 1792, Columbus Day was not officially recognized until 1909. Its observance is of special national pride to Italian-Americans who claim the Genoese Columbus for their own.

Veterans' Day (Nov. 11) Armistice Day, which marked the end of World War I on Nov. 11, 1918, was made a legal holiday in 1938. The name was changed to Veterans' Day in 1954 to honor all of America's veterans.

Thanksgiving (Fourth Thursday in November) Thanksgiving Day was first observed in Plymouth Colony (Massachusetts) in 1621, the year in which the Pilgrims landed in the New World and gave thanks for their first harvest and for the new land they had colonized. President Lincoln proclaimed Thanksgiving a national holiday in 1863.

Christmas is celebrated December 25. (See also "Christian Holy Days.")

▶ U.S. MINOR HOLIDAYS AND OCCASIONS

April Fool's Day (April 1) A day for practical jokes, the origins of April Fool's Day are obscure, but it bears some resemblance to an ancient Roman festival honoring the goddess of nature.

Arbor Day (Last Friday in April) Dedicated to trees and their preservation, and its observance is meant to encourage preservation of the environment. Internationally it is observed on December 22.

Important Dates in the U.S. and Canada, 1999–2004

Event	1999	2000	2001	2002	2003	2004
New Year's Day[2]	Jan. 1	Jan. 1	Jan. 1	Jan. 1	Jan. 1	Jan. 1
Martin Luther King Day[2]	Jan. 18	Jan. 17	Jan. 15	Jan. 21	Jan. 20	Jan. 19
Groundhog Day	Feb. 2	Feb. 2	Feb. 2	Feb. 2	Feb. 2	Feb. 2
St. Valentine's Day	Feb. 14	Feb. 14	Feb. 14	Feb. 14	Feb. 14	Feb. 14
Susan B. Anthony Day	Feb. 15	Feb. 15	Feb. 15	Feb. 15	Feb. 15	Feb. 15
Washington's Birthday[2]	Feb. 15	Feb. 21	Feb. 19	Feb. 18	Feb. 17	Feb. 16
Mardi Gras	Feb. 16	Mar. 7	Feb. 27	Feb. 12	Feb. 11	Feb. 24
St. Patrick's Day	Mar. 17	Mar. 17	Mar. 17	Mar. 17	Mar. 17	Mar. 17
April Fool's Day	Apr. 1	Apr. 1	Apr. 1	Apr. 1	Apr. 1	Apr. 1
Daylight Saving begins	Apr. 4	Apr. 2	Apr. 1	Apr. 7	Apr. 6	Apr. 4
Arbor Day	Apr. 30	Apr. 28	Apr. 27	Apr. 26	Apr. 25	Apr. 30
National Teacher Day	May 4	May 9	May 8	May 7	May 6	May 4
Mother's Day[2]	May 9	May 14	May 13	May 12	May 11	May 9
Armed Forces Day	May 15	May 20	May 19	May 18	May 17	May 15
Victoria Day[3]	May 24	May 22	May 21	May 20	May 19	May 24
National Maritime Day	May 22	May 22	May 22	May 22	May 22	May 22
Memorial Day[2]	May 31	May 29	May 28	May 27	May 26	May 31
Flag Day	June 14	June 14	June 14	June 14	June 14	June 14
Father's Day	June 20	June 18	June 17	June 16	June 15	June 20
Canada Day[3]	July 1	July 1	July 1	July 1	July 1	July 1
Independence Day[2]	July 4	July 4	July 4	July 4	July 4	July 4
Labor Day[2, 3]	Sept. 6	Sept. 4	Sept. 3	Sept. 2	Sept. 1	Sept. 6
Citizenship Day	Sept. 17	Sept. 17	Sept. 17	Sept. 17	Sept. 17	Sept. 17
Columbus Day[2]	Oct. 11	Oct. 9	Oct. 8	Oct. 14	Oct. 13	Oct. 11
Thanksgiving Day[3] (Can.)	Oct. 11	Oct. 9	Oct. 8	Oct. 14	Oct. 13	Oct. 11
United Nations Day	Oct. 24	Oct. 24	Oct. 24	Oct. 24	Oct. 24	Oct. 24
Daylight Saving ends	Oct. 31	Oct. 29	Oct. 28	Oct. 27	Oct. 26	Oct. 31
Halloween	Oct. 31	Oct. 31	Oct. 31	Oct. 31	Oct. 31	Oct. 31
Election Day (U.S.)	Nov. 2	Nov. 7	Nov. 6	Nov. 5	Nov. 4	Nov. 2
Veterans'(Armistice) Day[2]	Nov. 11	Nov. 11	Nov. 11	Nov. 11	Nov. 11	Nov. 11
Remembrance Day[3]	Nov. 11	Nov. 11	Nov. 11	Nov. 11	Nov. 11	Nov. 11
Thanksgiving Day[2] (U.S.)	Nov. 25	Nov. 23	Nov. 22	Nov. 28	Nov. 27	Nov. 25
Christmas Day[2,3]	Dec. 25	Dec. 25	Dec. 25	Dec. 25	Dec. 25	Dec. 25
Boxing Day[3]	Dec. 26	Dec. 26	Dec. 26	Dec. 26	Dec. 26	Dec. 26
Kwanzaa[4]	Dec. 26	Dec. 26	Dec. 26	Dec. 26	Dec. 26	Dec. 26
New Year's Eve	Dec. 31	Dec. 31	Dec. 31	Dec. 31	Dec. 31	Dec. 31

1. Leap year; February has 29 days. 2. Federal holiday in U.S. 3. Federal holiday in Canada. 4. First day of seven-day holiday.

Armed Forces Day (Third Saturday in May) A day to honor of the members of the United States Armed Forces.

Citizenship Day (September 17) First observed by presidential proclamation in 1952, Citizenship Day falls on the same day as the old Constitution Day, which it replaces, but the name of which is still in use.

Daylight Saving Time The idea of moving clocks ahead one hour to capture more daylight on summer evenings dates back to colonial times—Benjamin Franklin first suggested it in a 1784 essay—but it did not become a nationwide practice until the Uniform Time Act of 1966 (effective April of 1967). During World War I, World War II, and the energy crisis of 1973–74, the U.S. adopted daylight saving time all year round to save money on fuel. Daylight saving time is not observed in Hawaii, the Eastern time zone portion of Indiana, most of Arizona (except on the Navajo Indian Reservation) or in the territories of American Samoa, Guam, Puerto Rico, and the Virgin Islands. By law, daylight saving time begins at 2 A.M. on the first Sunday in April and ends at 2 A.M. on the last Sunday in October, when clocks are turned back one hour. Remember to "Spring ahead, Fall back."

Election Day (Tuesday after first Monday in November) In years evenly divisible by four, presidential elections are held; in years evenly divisible by two, elections for all members of the House of Representatives and for one-third of the members of the Senate are held.

Father's Day (Third Sunday in June) Father's Day was first observed in West Virginia in 1908, but it was not until 1972 that the president signed a Congressional resolution designating its official observance. Father's Day is a uniquely American institution.

Flag Day (June 14) The first observance of Flag Day was in 1877, the centenary of the adoption of the Flag Resolution, which adopted the design of the American flag flown today. President Truman signed the Flag Day Bill in 1949.

Groundhog Day (February 2) On this day the groundhog peeks out of his burrow to look for his shadow. If he sees his shadow, six weeks of winter will follow; if he doesn't, spring is just around the corner.

Halloween (October 31) All Hallow's Eve (the day before the feast of All Saints in the Christian calendar) began as a pagan custom honoring the dead and a celebration of autumn. The wearing of costumes can be traced back to Medieval religious practice in which parishioners dressed as saints and angels and paraded through the churchyard. The modern practice of "trick or treating" is of American origin with no apparent historical basis.

Kwanzaa (or Kwanza) This secular celebration by African-Americans commemorates their African heritage and emphasizes the role of family and community. It begins on Dec. 26 and lasts for seven days; on each day one candle of a candelabrum is lighted. Kwanzaa was developed by Maulana Karenga and was first observed in 1966.

Mother's Day (Second Sunday in May)   Conceived by Anne M. Jarvis of Philadelphia, where it was first observed, as a day for children to pay tribute to their mothers, this was declared a national holiday by presidential proclamation in 1914.

National Maritime Day (May 22)   Designated by presidential proclamation in 1935, this commemorates the anniversary of the departure of the SS *Savannah* on the first successful transoceanic voyage of a steam-powered vessel, in 1819. It is also a day of remembrance of merchant mariners who died in defense of their country.

National Teacher Day (Tuesday of first full week in May)   This is a day when students and communities around the country honor their teachers and the teaching profession.

St. Patrick's Day (March 17)   A day in honor of Ireland's patron saint, St. Patrick's Day is a religious, political, and social event rolled into one. In Ireland, St. Patrick is honored by church ceremonies and a three-day period of devotion. In the United States, March 17 is celebrated with parades and the "wearing of the green."

St. Valentine's Day (February 14)   Originally an occasion to honor two Christian saints martyred by the Roman Emperor Claudius (214-270), since the Middle Ages St. Valentine's Day has been dedicated to lovers, probably because it is believed to be the day that birds choose their mates.

Susan B. Anthony Day (February 15)   Anthony (1820–1906) was one of the first women's rights advocates, working especially for equal suffrage—that is, the right to vote. She was a co-founder and later president of the National Woman Suffrage Association.

United Nations Day (October 24)   This commemorates the ratification of the United Nations Charter on this date in 1945 by the five permanent members of the Security Council and a majority of the other Charter signatories.

▶**CHRISTIAN HOLY DAYS**

Christmas   is the celebration of Christ's birth. The exact date of his birth is unknown, but the date of December 25 was probably chosen because it coincided with the ancient mid-winter celebrations honoring pagan deities. The 12 days of Christmas fall between Christmas and Epiphany (January 6), the day the Wise Men visited the Christ child.

Easter   is the most important holy day in the Christian religion. It is the celebration of Christ's Resurrection from the dead, which gave Christians the hope of salvation and eternal life. Although Easter is only one day, the full observance of the holy day spans from Septuagesima Sunday (70 days before Easter Sunday), which may fall as early as January, to Pentecost, which can occur as late as June.

Easter always falls on the first Sunday after the first full moon after the vernal equinox on March 21. Thus, Easter can fall no earlier than March 23 (if the first full moon is a Saturday March 22) and no later than April 24 (if the first full moon is a Sunday, April 17).

Mardi Gras (Shrove Tuesday; Fat Tuesday) Originally a day of penance, the last day before the beginning of Lent is now celebrated with feasting and merrymaking.

Ash Wednesday derives its name from the rite of burning the palms carried on the Palm Sunday of the year before and using the ashes to mark worshippers' foreheads with a cross.

Lent, a 40-day period of fasting and penitence beginning on Ash Wednesday and ending on Easter Sunday, Lent is traditionally observed by fasting, performing acts of charity, and by giving up certain pleasures and amusements.

Palm Sunday, the Sunday before Easter, celebrates Jesus's triumphant entry into Jerusalem where palm branches were spread before Him to honor His path.

Holy (Maundy) Thursday, is the anniversary of the Last Supper. The traditional services mark three events that occurred during the week before Jesus was crucified: He washed the feet of his 12 disciples; He instituted the Eucharist (the sacrament of Holy Communion); and He was arrested and imprisoned.

Good Friday marks the day of Christ's Crucifixion. The holy day is observed with fasting, mourning, and penitence.

Holy Saturday is the day that anticipates the Resurrection. In the Catholic church, special vigils are held on Holy Saturday evening.

Calendar of Christian Holy Days

Year A.D.	Ash Wednesday	Good Friday	Easter Sunday	Pentecost	Trinity Sunday	Advent
1998	Feb. 25	Apr. 10	Apr. 12	May 31	June 7	Nov. 29
1999	Feb. 17	Apr. 2	Apr. 4	May 23	May 30	Nov. 28
2000	Mar. 8	Apr. 21	Apr. 23	June 11	June 18	Dec. 3
2001	Feb. 28	Apr. 13	Apr. 15	June 3	June 10	Dec. 2
2002	Feb. 13	Mar. 29	Mar. 31	May 19	May 26	Dec. 1
2003	Mar. 5	Apr. 18	Apr. 20	June 8	June 15	Nov. 30
2004	Feb. 25	Apr. 9	Apr. 11	May 30	June 6	Nov. 28
2005	Feb. 10	Mar. 25	Mar. 27	May 15	May 22	Nov. 27

Easter Sunday marks the day of Christ's Resurrection. Many worshippers celebrate the holy day with sunrise services, a custom believed to be inspired by the example of Mary Magdalene, who went to Christ's tomb "early, while it was yet dark."

Pentecost (literally, "fiftieth day") is the end of the full ecclesiastical observance of Easter. It takes place on the seventh Sunday after Easter Sunday and commemorates the descent of the Holy Spirit upon the Apostles.

The Annunciation This holy day marks the archangel Gabriel's announcement to Mary that she would conceive and give birth to Jesus. It is celebrated by Roman Catholics on March 25; it is not observed by Protestant denominations.

Trinity Sunday The Sunday after Pentecost, this occasion honors the Father, Son, and Holy Spirit. It was declared a part of the church calendar in 1334 by Pope John XXII and is observed by Roman Catholics and by some Protestant denominations.

Corpus Christi This feast celebrates the presence of the body (*corpus*) of Christ in the Eucharist. At one time this was the principal feast of the church year, but today it is observed only by Catholic churches. Corpus Christi is celebrated on the Thursday following Trinity Sunday.

All Saints' Day, celebrated on November 1, honors all of the Christian saints. In America, many churches mark the Sunday nearest November 1 as a day to pay tribute to those who have died during the year. All Saints' Day is observed primarily by Roman Catholics.

Advent, a religious season that begins on the Sunday nearest Nov. 30 and lasts until Christmas, both celebrates the birth of Jesus and anticipates His second coming. At one time Advent was a solemn season observed by fasting, but this is no longer the case.

Holy Days of Obligation are feast days in the Catholic calendar observed by attendance at Mass and rest from unnecessary work. Six holy days of obligation are observed in the United States:

1. Solemnity of Mary, Jan. 1 (formerly, Christ's circumcision, the first shedding of his blood, was commemorated on this day).
2. Ascension (of Jesus to Heaven), 40 days after Easter
3. Assumption of the Blessed Virgin into Heaven, Aug. 15
4. All Saints Day, Nov. 1
5. Mary's Immaculate Conception (honoring the Mother of God as the only person conceived without original sin), Dec. 8
6. Christmas, Dec. 25

▶ THE JEWISH CALENDAR

The months of the Jewish year are Tishri, Heshvan, Kislev, Tebet, Shebat, Adar, Nisan, Iyar, Sivan, Tammuz, Ab, and Elul. The Jewish era dates from the year of the creation (*anno mundii* or A.M.), which is equal to 3761 B.C.), thus 5758 began in 1997 and ends in 1998 of the Gregorian calendar. (Tishri, the first month of the Jewish year, falls in either September or October of the Gregorian calendar.)

Because the Jewish calendar is a blend of solar and lunar calendars, there are intercalated months to keep the lunar and solar years in alignment. (Intercalation is the insertion of an extra day, month, or other unit—February 29 in a leap year, for example—into a calendar). The intercalated month is called Adar Sheni or Veadar—Second Adar.

▶ JEWISH HOLY DAYS

Sabbath is the first and most important Jewish holy day, occurring each week from sundown Friday to sundown Saturday. It is a day of rest and spiritual growth, given to men and women so they will remember the sweetness of freedom and keep it. Sabbath takes precedence over all other observances.

Rosh Hashanah (New Year) held to be the birthday of the world, is also called the Day of Judgment and Remembrance, and the day of the shofar—a ram's horn—which is blown to remind Jews of Abraham's willingness to sacrifice his son Isaac. The holiday takes place on the first and second days of Tishri (in September or October).

Yom Kippur (Day of Atonement) concludes the 10 days of repentance that Rosh Hashanah begins and takes place from sundown on the ninth day of Tishri until sundown on the 10th. The observance begins with the recitation of the most famous passage in the Jewish liturgy—*Kol Nidre*—which nullifies unfulfilled vows made in the past year. The entire day is spent praying and fasting.

Sukkoth (Tabernacles) is a harvest festival celebrated from the 15th through the 22nd of Tishri. Sukkoth also commemorates the journey of the Jewish people through the wilderness to the land of Israel. Jewish families take their meals this week in a roughly constructed *sukkah* (booth)—a reminder of an agricultural society, of the Exodus, and of how precarious and fragile life can be. On the Simchat Torah, the 23rd of Tishri, a congregation finishes reading the last book of the Torah and immediately starts again with the first.

Calendar of Jewish Holy Days, 5759–66

Year AM	Rosh Hashanah[1]	Yom Kippur	Sukkoth[1]	Hanukkah[1]	Purim	Pesach[1]	Shabuoth[1]
5759	Sept. 21, 1998	Sept. 30, 1998	Oct. 5, 1998	Dec. 14, 1998	Mar. 2, 1999	Apr. 1, 1999	May 21, 1999
5760	Sept. 11, 1999	Sept. 20, 1999	Sept. 25, 1999	Dec. 4, 1999	Mar. 21, 2000	Apr. 20, 2000	June 9, 2000
5761	Sept. 30, 2000	Oct. 9, 2000	Oct. 14, 2000	Dec. 22, 2000	Mar. 9, 2001	Apr. 8, 2001	May 28, 2001
5762	Sept. 18, 2001	Sept. 27, 2001	Oct. 2, 2001	Dec. 10, 2001	Feb. 26, 2002	Mar. 28, 2002	May 17, 2002
5763	Sept. 7, 2002	Sept. 16, 2002	Sept. 21, 2002	Nov. 30, 2002	Mar. 18, 2003	Apr. 17, 2003	June 6, 2003
5764	Sept. 27, 2003	Oct. 6, 2003	Oct. 11, 2003	Dec. 20, 2003	Mar. 7, 2004	Apr. 6, 2004	May 26, 2004
5765	Sept. 16, 2004	Sept. 25, 2004	Sept. 30, 2004	Dec. 9, 2004	Mar. 25, 2005	Apr. 24, 2005	June 13, 2005
5766	Oct. 4, 2005	Oct. 13, 2005	Oct. 18, 2005	Dec. 26, 2005	Mar. 14, 2006	Apr. 13, 2006	June 2, 2006

Note: The Jewish day begins and ends at sundown. Thus, all holidays begin at sundown of the day preceding the date shown.
1. Multi-day holiday; first day of holiday shown. **Source:** B'nai B'rith.

Hanukkah (Chanukah, Feast of Dedication; Festival of Lights)

The importance of the eight-day feast, which begins on the 25th day of Kislev, is its commemoration of the first war in human history fought in the cause of religious freedom. The Maccabees vanquished not just the military threat to Judaism, but the internal forces for assimilation into the Hellenistic culture of Israel's rulers. Jews light candles for eight nights to mark a miracle: a day's supply of oil, found in the recaptured Temple, which according to religious myth, burned for eight days.

Purim (Feast of Lots)

set on the 14th day of Adar, is another celebration of survival, noting the events described in the Book of Esther. At Purim, Jews rejoice at Queen Esther's and her cousin Mordecai's defeat of Haman, the Persian King Ahaseurus's advisor who plotted to slaughter all the Persian Jews around 400 B.C.

Pesach (Passover)

beginning on the 15th day of Nisan and lasting seven days, commemorates the exodus of the Hebrews from Egypt in about 1300 B.C. The name, Passover, also recalls God's sparing (passing over) the Jewish first-born during the plagues upon the land brought by God through Moses. The holiday is marked by eating only unleavened foods, participating in a *seder*, or special meal, and reading the *Haggadah*, the story of the Hebrews' deliverance from Egypt.

Shabuoth (Feast of Weeks)

is observed on the sixth or seventh day of Sivan. Originally an agricultural festival, Shabuoth is a celebration of the revelation of the Torah at Mt. Sinai, by which God established his covenant with the Jewish people.

▶ THE ISLAMIC CALENDAR

The 12 months of the Islamic year are: Muharram, Safar, Rab'i I, Rab'i II, Jomada I, Jomada II, Rajab, Sha'ban, Ramadan, Shawwal, Dhu al-Qa'dah, Dhu al-Hijja. The Islamic calendar is based on a lunar year of 12 months of 30 and 29 days (alternating every month) and the year is equal to 354 days. It runs in cycles of 30 years, of which the 2nd, 5th, 7th, 10th, 13th, 16th, 18th, 21st, 24th, 26th, and 29th are leap years. Leap years have 355 days, the extra day being added to the last month, Dhu al-Hijja. There are no intercalated months or leap years, so the Islamic year does not keep a constant relationship to the solar year—which dictates the seasons—and months occur about 10 or 11 days earlier than in the year before.

The caliph Abu Bakr adopted 622 A.D., the year of the *hejira* (Mohammed's migration from Mecca to Medina), as the first year of Islam. However, dating of the Muslim era varies throughout the Islamic world. In some countries, the year of the Muslim era is obtained by subtracting 622 from the Gregorian year; 2000 A.D. equals 1378 A.H. (anno hegirae, in the year of the *hejira*).

Other countries (Saudi Arabia, Yemen, and the principalities of the Persian Gulf) continue to use a purely lunar year. To approximate the Muslim era equivalent of the Gregorian year, subtract 622 (the year of *hejira* in the Gregorian calendar) from the current year, and multiply the result by 1.031 (days in the year of the Gregorian calendar divided by days in the lunar year): 2000 A.D. = (2000-622) x 1.031 = 1421 A.H.

▶ MUSLIM HOLY DAYS

Ramadan

the ninth month of the Islamic calendar, is the Islamic faith's holiest period. To honor the month in which the Koran was revealed, all adult Muslims of sound body and mind fast, eschewing food, water, or even a kiss between the hours of sunrise and sunset. Exempted from the fast are women in menstruation or childbirth bleeding, the chronically ill, or people on a journey, all of whom must make up the fast days at a later date.

Id al-Fitr

This day of feasting is celebrated at the end of Ramadan. To mark the fast's break, worshippers also attend an early morning service, Salat-ul-'Id, at which they give alms in staple foodstuffs or their monetary value.

Id al-Adha

The Feast of Sacrifice takes place on the 10th day of Dhu al-Hijja, the last month of the year and the season of the haj, or pilgrimage. The day begins with a service in the mosques or other places of gathering, and for those who are not pilgrims, continues with the ritual slaughter of a sheep in commemoration of God's ransom of Abraham's son from sacrifice. At least a third of the meat of the animal is to be given in charity.

Fridays

At noontime, Muslims attend mosque or comparable gathering places to say the congregational Friday prayer that ends the week. While Friday is the holy day of the weekly Muslim calendar, it is not a Sabbath comparable to Christian Sundays or Jewish Saturdays, and there are no restrictions on work or other worldly enterprises.

▶ THE HINDU YEAR

The Hindu year consists of 12 months: Caitra, Vaisakha, Jyaistha, Asadha, Sravana, Bhadrapada, Asvina, Karttika, Margasivsa, Pansa, Magha, and Phalguna. Calendrically, holidays are of two types, lunar and solar. Solar holidays in the Hindu calendar include:

Mesasamkranti

The beginning of the new astrological year, when the Sun enters the constellation Aries.

Calendar of Muslim Holy Days

Year A.H. (A.D.)	New Year's Day 1 Muharram	1 Ramadan	Id al-Fitr, 1 Shawwal	Id al-Adha, 10 Dhu al-Hijja
1419 (1998-99)	April 28, 1998	Dec. 20, 1998	Jan. 19, 1999	Mar. 28, 1999
1420 (1999-2000)	April 18, 1999	Dec. 9, 1999	Jan. 8, 2000	Mar. 17, 2000
1421 (2000-01)	April 6, 2000	Nov. 27, 2000	Dec. 27, 2000	Mar. 10, 2001
1422 (2001-02)	March 26, 2001	Nov. 17, 2001	Dec. 16, 2001	Feb. 23, 2002
1423 (2002-03)	March 15, 2002	Nov. 6, 2002	Dec. 6, 2002	Feb. 12, 2003
1424 (2003-04)	March 4, 2003	Oct. 27, 2003	Nov. 25, 2003	Feb. 1, 2004
1425 (2004-05)	Feb. 22, 2004	Oct. 15, 2004	Nov. 14, 2004	Jan. 21, 2005

Note: The Islamic calendar is based on calculation and depends on actual sighting of the moon. Therefore the dates above are estimates. For exact dates, contact your local masjid, organization, or scholar.   **Source:** *Islamic Calendar* (www.assirat.org/Hcal). Copyright © 1999 Dar Assirat. All rights reserved.

Chinese Years, 1900–2014

Rat	Ox	Tiger	Hare (Rabbit)	Dragon	Snake	Horse	Sheep (Goat)	Monkey	Rooster	Dog	Pig
1900	1901	1902	1903	1904	1905	1906	1907	1908	1909	1910	1911
1912	1913	1914	1915	1916	1917	1918	1919	1920	1921	1922	1923
1924	1925	1926	1927	1928	1929	1930	1931	1932	1933	1934	1935
1936	1937	1938	1939	1940	1941	1942	1943	1944	1945	1946	1947
1948	1949	1950	1951	1952	1953	1954	1955	1956	1957	1958	1959
1960	1961	1962	1963	1964	1965	1966	1967	1968	1969	1970	1971
1972	1973	1974	1975	1976	1977	1978	1979	1980	1981	1982	1983
1984	1985	1986	1987	1988	1989	1990	1991	1992	1993	1994	1995
1996	1997	1998	1999	2000	2001	2002	2003	2004	2005	2006	2007
2008	2009	2010	2011	2012	2013	2014	2015	2016	2017	2018	2019

Makaraj-Samkranti The winter solstice, when the sun enters the constellation Capricorn.

Mahavisuva Day is New Year's Eve.

Principal holidays determined by the lunar year are:

Ramanavami (Caitra 9), celebrates the birth of Rama, in Hindu folklore, the epitome of chivalry, courage, and obedience to sacred law. Considered an incarnation of Vishnu, his name is synonymous with God.

Rathayatra (Asadha 2), the pilgrimage of the chariot festival of Orissa.

Janmastami (Sravana 8), The birthday of Krishna, an incarnation of the supreme deity, Vishnu, celebrated as a philosopher-king and hero.

Dasahra (Asvina 7-10), commemorates Rama's victory over the demon Ravana.

Laksmipuja (Asvina 15), honors Laksmi, goddess of good fortune.

Dipavali (Karttika 15), festival of lights and exchanging of presents.

Mahasivaratri (Magha 13), which honors the god Shiva, one of the three supreme Hindu gods. Shiva, whose name means "Auspicious One," is a god of both reproduction and destruction.

Months of the Year

Gregorian	Hebrew	Hindu	Muslim
January	Shebat	Magha	*Muharram*
February	Adar	Phalguna	Safar
March	Nisan	*Caitra*	Rab'i I
April	Iyar	Vaisakha	Rab'i II
May	Sivan	Jyaistha	Jomada I
June	Tammuz	Asadha	Jomada II
July	Ab	Sravana	Rajab
August	Elul	Bhadrapada	Sha'ban
September	*Tishri*	Asvina	Ramadan
October	Heshvan	Karttika	Shawwal
November	Kislev	Margasivsa	Dhu al-Qa'dah
December	Tebet	Pansa	Dhu al-Hijja

Note: The months of the Gregorian, Hebrew, Hindu, and reformed Muslim calendars occur at roughly the same time of year, while those of the traditional (lunar) Muslim calendar occur at different times every year. Months in italics indicate the first month of the year in the respective calendars.

Wedding Anniversaries

Anniversary	Type of gift	Anniversary	Type of gift
1st	Paper	14th	Ivory
2nd	Cotton	15th	Crystal
3rd	Leather	20th	China
4th	Fruit, flowers	25th	Silver
5th	Wood	30th	Pearl
6th	Sugar	35th	Coral
7th	Copper, wool	40th	Ruby
8th	Bronze, pottery	45th	Sapphire
9th	Pottery, willow	50th	Gold
10th	Tin	55th	Emerald
11th	Steel	60th	Diamond
12th	Silk, linen	70th	Platinum
13th	Lace		

Birthstones

Month	Stone
January	Garnet
February	Amethyst
March	Aquamarine, Bloodstone
April	Diamond
May	Emerald
June	Alexandrite, Moonstone, Pearl
July	Ruby
August	Peridot, Sardonyx
September	Sapphire
October	Opal, Tourmaline
November	Topaz
December	Turquoise, Lapis Lazuli

Astrological Calendar

Dates	Sign
January 20 - February 18	Aquarius, the water bearer
February 19-March 20	Pisces, the fishes
March 21-April 19	Aries, the ram
April 20-May 20	Taurus, the bull
May 21-June 20	Gemini, the twins
June 21-July 22	Cancer, the crab
July 23-August 22	Leo, the lion
August 23-September 22	Virgo, the virgin
September 23-October 22	Libra, the scales
October 23-November 21	Scorpio, the scorpion
November 22-December 21	Sagitarrius, the archer
December 22-January 19	Capricorn, the goat

ASTRONOMICAL EVENTS, 2000

The main astronomical events included in this section are the phases of the Moon, the Moon's perigee (when it is closest to the Earth) and apogee (when it is farthest away), lunar and solar eclipses, and the visibility of the planets.

▶ PHASES OF THE MOON

The relative position of the Earth, Moon, and Sun affect what, if any, part of the Moon we can see illuminated by the Sun during our night. A *new moon* is when the Moon is precisely aligned between the Earth and the Sun, making the Moon invisible from the Earth. When the Moon is at *first quarter* (90° from the Sun relative to the Earth), its sunlit part appears in the shape of a D (in the Southern Hemisphere, a backward D). A *full moon*, when the Moon shows an almost fully illuminated face, occurs when the Moon is 180° around the sky from the Sun. The *last quarter* (or third quarter) is when the Moon is again moving toward a position between the Earth and the Sun, and it appears as a backward D (a normal D in the Southern Hemisphere). Intermediate phases are the *crescent moon*—between the new Moon and first quarter, and between the last quarter and new Moon; and the *gibbous moon*, occurring between the half and the full Moon. The full cycle from one phase through all the other phases takes about 29.53 days and is called a *lunation*.

▶ VISIBILITY OF THE PLANETS, 2000

Mercury   can only be seen low in the east before sunrise, or low in the west after sunset (about the time of the beginning or end of twilight). It is visible in the mornings between the following approximate dates: March 8–May 1, July 15–Aug. 14, and Nov. 5–Dec. 8. The planet is brighter at the end of each period, (the best conditions in northern latitudes occur in mid-November, and in southern latitudes from late March to early April). It is visible in the evenings between the following approximate dates: Jan. 29–Feb. 24, May 17–June 27, and Sept. 1–Oct. 24. The planet is brighter at the beginning of each period, (the best conditions in northern latitudes occur during mid-February and early June and in southern latitudes from late September to mid-October.

Venus   is a brilliant object in the morning sky from the beginning of the year until early May, when it becomes too close to the Sun for observation. It reappears the third week in July in the evening sky, where it stays until the end of the year. Venus is in conjunction with Mercury on March 15 and April 28.

Mars   can be seen in the evening sky in Aquarius at the beginning of the year. It moves into Pisces in early February, briefly into Cetus in the last week of February, Aries during the second half of March, and into Taurus from late April. It becomes too close to the Sun for observation after the first week of May, reappearing in the morning sky from the second half of August in into Cancer. It then continues into Leo after late August (passing 0.8° N of *Regulus* on Sept. 16) and into Virgo from late October (passing 4° N of *Spica* on Dec. 11). Mars is in conjunction with Jupiter on April 6, with Saturn on April 16, and with Mercury on May 19 and Aug. 10.

Jupiter   is in Pisces at the beginning of the year. For the first half of January, it can be seen for more than half the night, after which it can only be seen in the evening sky as it moves through Pisces and into Aries from mid-February. Its eastward elongation gradually decreases and during the second half of April it becomes too close to the Sun for observation. It reappears in the morning sky in Aries in the second half of May, and at the end of this month it moves into Taurus, where it remains for the rest of the year (passing 5° N of *Aldebaran* on Sept. 7 and on Oct. 21). Its westward elongation gradually increases, until it is at opposition on Nov. 28, when it is visible throughout the night. Jupiter is in conjunction with Mars on April 6 and with Saturn on May 31.

Saturn   is in Aries at the beginning of the year. Until late January, it can be seen for more than half the night, after which it can be seen only in the evening sky. Its eastward elongation gradually decreases and during the second half of April it becomes too close to the Sun for observation. It reappears in the morning sky in late May, passing from Aries into Taurus, where it remains for the rest of the year. Its westward elongation gradually increases and is at opposition on Nov. 19, when it can be seen throughout the night. Saturn is in conjunction with Mars on April 16, and with Jupiter on May 31.

Uranus   is visible in the evening sky at the beginning of January in Capricornus and remains in this constellation throughout the year. It then becomes too close to the Sun for observation until late February, when it reappears in the morning sky. It is at opposition on August 11, when it can be seen throughout the night. From early November on, it can only be seen in the evening sky.

Neptune   is visible as an evening star at the beginning of January in Capricornus, and remains in this constellation throughout the year. It then becomes too close to the Sun for observation until mid-February, when it reappears in the morning sky. It is at opposition on July 27, and after late October, it can only be seen in the evening sky.

Do not confuse

(1) Mercury with Venus in mid-March and again from mid-April to early May. On both occasions, Venus is the brighter object. (2) Jupiter with Mars from late March to mid-April, and with Saturn in mid-April and again from late May to mid-July. On all occasions Jupiter is the brighter object. (3) Saturn with Mars in mid-April. Saturn is the brighter object; Mars' reddish tint should assist in its identification.

▶ TIMING PLANETARY PHENOMENA

The times for astronomical data shown here are expressed in Universal Time (UT) which is the standard time of the Greenwich meridian (0° of

Visibility of the Planets, 2000

Planet	Morning Twilight	Evening Twilight
Venus	Jan. 1–May 5	July 18–Dec. 31
Mars	Aug. 20–Dec. 31	Jan. 1–May 8
Jupiter	May 22–Nov. 28	Jan. 1–April 24; Nov. 28–Dec. 31
Saturn	May 29–Nov. 19	Jan. 1–April 23; Nov. 19–Dec. 31

Source: U.S. Naval Observatory, *Astronomical Phenomena for the Year 2000* (1998).

Phases of the Moon, 2000

New moon				First quarter				Full moon				Last quarter			
Month	d	h	m	Month	d	h	m	Month	d	h	m	Month	d	h	m
Jan.	6	18	14	Jan.	14	13	34	Jan.	21	04	40	Jan.	28	07	57
Feb.	5	13	03	Feb.	12	23	21	Feb.	19	16	27	Feb.	27	03	53
Mar.	6	05	17	Mar.	13	06	59	Mar.	20	04	44	Mar.	28	00	21
Apr.	4	18	12	Apr.	11	13	30	Apr.	18	17	41	Apr.	26	19	30
May	4	04	12	May	10	20	00	May	18	07	34	May	26	11	55
June	2	12	14	June	9	03	29	June	16	22	27	June	25	01	00
July	1	19	20	July	8	12	53	July	16	13	55	July	24	11	02
July	31	02	25	Aug.	7	01	02	Aug.	15	05	13	Aug.	22	18	51
Aug.	29	10	19	Sept.	5	16	27	Sept.	13	19	37	Sept.	21	01	28
Sept.	27	19	53	Oct.	5	10	59	Oct.	13	08	53	Oct.	20	07	59
Oct.	27	07	58	Nov.	4	07	27	Nov.	11	21	15	Nov.	18	15	24
Nov.	25	23	11	Dec.	4	03	55	Dec.	11	09	03	Dec.	18	00	41
Dec.	25	17	22												

Note: Shown in Universal Time (UT). To convert to local time, see "Timing Planetary Phenomena." **Source:** U.S. Naval Observatory, *Astronomical Phenomena for the Year 2000* (1998).

longitude) also known as Greenwich mean time (GMT). To convert to local time, determine your longitude and subtract 1 hour for every 15° of longitude west of 0°; or add 1 hour for every 15° of longitude east of 0°.

The first new moon of 2000 occurs Jan. 6 at 1814 hours in UT. The equivalent time in New York (74°W) is 5 hours earlier, or Jan. 6 at 1314 hours (1:14 P.M.); in Chicago (87°W), 6 hours earlier, or Jan. 6 at 12:14 P.M.; in Denver (105°W), 7 hours earlier, or Jan. 6 at 11:14 A.M.; and in San Francisco (122°W), 8 hours earlier, or Jan 6 at 10:14 A.M. (To obtain the P.M. equivalent of UT times later than 1200, subtract 12: 1827 = 6:27 P.M.) Note that local clock times may differ from these standard times, especially in summer when clocks are often advanced by 1 hour.

▶ECLIPSES
Eclipses of the Moon
A lunar eclipse occurs when the Sun, Earth, and Moon are in a straight line and the shadow of the Earth falls on the Moon. There are three kinds of lunar eclipse. A *total eclipse* occurs when the Moon passes completely into the Earth's total umbra, or shadow, so the Sun cannot be seen from the Moon. A *partial eclipse* occurs when only part of the Earth's umbra falls across the Moon and the Sun is partially visible from some places on the Moon. A *penumbral eclipse* occurs when only the Earth's penumbra (partial shadow) shades the Moon; and from the Moon one's view of the Sun would be only partially blocked by the Earth. It is usually difficult to detect a penumbral eclipse from the Earth.

During 2000, there will be two total eclipses of the Moon. (All times shown in universal time (UT). To convert to local time, see *Timing Planetary Phenomena*.)

January 21, 2000-Total eclipse. *Moon enters penumbra* 2:02.9, *Moon enters umbra* 3:01.4, *Moon enters totality* 4:04.6, *Middle of eclipse* 4:43.5, *Moon leaves totality* 5:22.3, *Moon leaves umbra* 6:25.4, *Moon leaves penumbra* 7:24.1. The beginning of the penumbral phase will be visible in North and South America, most of Africa, Europe, western Asia, Greenland, the arctic region, the Atlantic Ocean, and the eastern Pacific Ocean. The end will be visible in North and South America, extreme western Africa, Europe except the extreme southeastern portion, Greenland, the

arctic region, and portions of the Pacific and Atlantic oceans.

July 16, 2000-Total Eclipse. *Moon enters penumbra* 10:46.6, *Moon enters umbra* 11:57.2, *Moon enters totality* 13:02.0, *Middle of eclipse* 13:55.5, *Moon leaves totality* 14:49.0, *Moon leaves umbra* 15:53.8, *Moon leaves penumbra* 17:04.5. The beginning of the umbral phase will be visible in the western United States and Canada, Hawaii, the southern half of Alaska, most of Mexico, extreme southern South America, Australia, New Zealand, the east coast of Asia, Antarctica, the Pacific Ocean, and the southeastern Indian Ocean. The end will be visible in most of Asia, Australia, New Zealand, Hawaii, the east coast of Africa, Antarctica, the Indian Ocean, and the western Pacific Ocean.

Eclipses of the Sun
A solar eclipse occurs when the Moon passes between the Earth and the Sun; there are three types. A *total eclipse* occurs when the Moon's shadow completely covers the Sun and the sky turns dark. Total eclipses occur along a narrow path (typically 100–200 miles wide) called the track of totality and last only a few minutes at any point on the track. During the 1990s, no total eclipse will be visible from the continental United States, though a Mar. 8-9, 1997 eclipse was visible from parts of Alaska. A *partial eclipse* occurs when the Moon covers only a portion of the Sun. Whether an eclipse is total or partial depends on where one is standing; the July 11, 1991 eclipse that was total over a narrow strip of Mexico was partial over much of North and Central America. An *annular* (ring-shaped) *eclipse* occurs when the Moon is too far from the Earth to completely cover the Sun, so that at the height of the eclipse a ring of light surrounds the Moon. The most prominent annular eclipse in the United States during the 1990s took place May 10, 1994, and was visible from Texas to Maine.

In 2000, there will be four partial eclipses of the Sun. The first one, on Feb. 5, will be visible only over Antarctica and the Southern Indian Ocean. The one on July 1 will be visible in the South Pacific Ocean and the Patagonian peninsula of South America. A July 31 partial eclipse will be visible over the Arctic Circle, northern Asia, and northwest Canada and Alaska. A Dec. 25 partial eclipse will be visible over most of North and Central America.

Part II

THE UNITED STATES
U.S. Geography

The United States of America shares the North American continent with Canada, Mexico, and the Central American nations. The 48 conterminous states lie in a broad land mass from approximately 24°N to 49°N from south to north, and 67°W to 124°W from east to west. It is bordered on the north by Canada, on the south by Mexico and the Gulf of Mexico, on the east by the Atlantic Ocean, and on the west by the Pacific Ocean. The two nonconterminous states of Alaska and Hawaii are located to the northwest on the North American continent, and in the Pacific Ocean Basin approximately 2,400 miles southwest of the state of California, respectively.

▶ POLITICAL-GEOGRAPHIC DIVISIONS
The Bureau of the Census groups the states in a number of divisions and sub-divisions.

Northeast
New England Maine, New Hampshire, Vermont, Massachusetts, Rhode Island, Connecticut.
Middle Atlantic New York, New Jersey, Pennsylvania.

Midwest
East North Central Ohio, Indiana, Illinois, Michigan, Wisconsin.
West North Central Minnesota, Iowa, Missouri, North Dakota, South Dakota, Nebraska, Kansas.

South
South Atlantic Delaware, Maryland, District of Columbia, Virginia, West Virginia, North Carolina, South Carolina, Georgia, Florida.
East South Central Kentucky, Tennessee, Alabama, Mississippi.
West South Central Arkansas, Louisiana, Oklahoma, Texas.

Pacific
Mountain Montana, Idaho, Wyoming, Colorado, New Mexico, Arizona, Utah, Nevada.
Pacific Washington, Oregon, California, Alaska, Hawaii.

▶ PHYSIOGRAPHIC REGIONS
The physiographic regions, or the primary geological features and landforms, of the United States are:

Atlantic and Gulf Coast Plains
These run from the islands of southern New England, Cape Cod, and Long Island, through New Jersey, Delaware, Maryland, Virginia, North Carolina, South Carolina, Georgia, Florida, Alabama, Mississippi, Louisiana, Texas; includes lower Mississippi Valley in Arkansas, Missouri, Tennessee.

Appalachian System
The Appalachian System is divided into five parts:
New England White Mountains (New Hampshire), Green Mountains (Vermont), Champlain Lowland and Hudson Valley (Vermont, New York), Catskill Mountains (New York).
The Piedmont Pennsylvania, Virginia, North Carolina, South Carolina, Georgia, Alabama.
Great Smoky and Blue Ridge Mountains Pennsylvania (Poconos), [discontinuous], Virginia, North Carolina, Georgia.
Ridge and Valley Pennsylvania, West Virginia, Virginia, Kentucky, Tennessee, Alabama.
Appalachian Plateau Pennsylvania, Ohio, West Virginia, Kentucky, Tennessee, Alabama.

Canadian (or Laurentian) Shield
This region covers much of eastern Canada and extends into the U.S. in two places:
Adirondack Mountains New York.
Superior Upland Upper Michigan, Wisconsin, Minnesota.

Central Lowland
The Central Lowland includes most of the U.S. interior, and is divided into four parts:
Interior Lowlands Ohio, Kentucky, Tennessee.
Mississippi Great Lakes Basin Ohio, Indiana, Illinois, Michigan, Wisconsin, Iowa, North Dakota, South Dakota.
Interior Highlands Ozark Mountains: Missouri, Arkansas, Oklahoma; Ouachita Mountains: Arkansas, Oklahoma.
Great Plains North Dakota, South Dakota, Nebraska, Kansas, Oklahoma, Texas, Montana, Wyoming, Colorado, New Mexico.

Cordilleran Province
Rocky Mountains New Mexico, Colorado, Wyoming, Montana.

Intermontane Range
This range is divided into four sections:
Colorado Plateau Colorado, Utah, New Mexico, Arizona (including Grand Canyon).
Basin and Range Plateau Nevada, Utah (including Wasatch Range).
Desert Basin and Range California (including Death Valley), Arizona.
Snake and Columbia River Basins Idaho, Washington, Oregon.

U.S. Geographic Extremes

Because the Aleutian Islands wrap around the Greenwich Meridian, Alaska technically contains both the easternmost and westernmost point in the United States.

Extreme	Contiguous 48 states (Long. or Lat.)	U.S. (Long. or Lat.)[1]
North	Northwest Angle Inlet, Minn. 49° 23' N	Point Barrow, Alaska, 71° 23' N
South	Key West, Fla. 24° 33' N	Ka Lae, Hawaii 18° 55' N
East	West Quoddy Head, Maine, 66° 57' W	Pochnoi Point, Alaska, 179° 46' E
West	Capa Alava, Wash. 124° 44' W	Amatignak Island, Alaska 179° 06' W

1. U.S. states only; does not include U.S. territories and possessions. **Source:** U.S. Geological Survey, *Elevations and Distances in the United States,* online edition. **http://mapping.usgs.gov/mac/isb/pubs/booklets/elvadist/elvadist.html**

Pacific Coastlands

This region is divided into four sections, three oriented north-south, the other east-west.

Cascade Mountains and Sierra Nevada Washington, Oregon, California.

Puget Sound, Willamette Valley, and Central Valley Washington, Oregon, California.

Coast Ranges Washington, Oregon, California.

Los Angeles Extension Tehachapi Mountains (east-west), San Gabriel Mountains, and San Bernardino Mountains.

▶ NATIONAL PARK SYSTEM

The National Park System of the U.S. began in March 1872 with the establishment of the Yellowstone National Park in the Territories of Montana and Wyoming, "as a public park or pleasuring ground for the benefit and enjoyment of the people" and placed it "under exclusive control of the Secretary of the Interior." The founding of Yellowstone began a worldwide national park movement and today more than 100 countries contain some 1,200 national parks or equivalent preserves.

President Woodrow Wilson created the National Park Service as a bureau within the Department of the Interior in 1916, and charged it with protecting the 35 national parks and monuments then in existence. Today, the U.S. National Park System comprises 378 areas covering more than 83 million acres (3 percent of total U.S. area) in 49 states (there are no areas in Delaware), the District of Columbia, Guam, Puerto Rico, Saipan, and the Virgin Islands. Additions to the National Park System are generally made through acts of Congress, and national parks can be created only through such acts. But under the Antiquities Act of 1906, the President has authority to proclaim national monuments on lands already under Federal jurisdiction.

The diversity of the parks managed by the National Park Service (NPS) is reflected in the variety of titles given to them. Although the system is best known for its scenic National Parks, more than half the areas of the National Park System preserve places, and commemorate persons, events, and activities important in the nation's history. Brief definitions of each type of park follow, together with the number of areas and total Federal acreage. An additional 11 areas such as the White House, the National Mall, etc., totaling 38,947 acres of Federal land were without designation.

National battlefields/battlefield parks/ battlefield site/military parks

cover a variety of areas associated with U.S. military history (Antietam National Battlefield, Maryland). (1 battlefield site, 1 acre; 9 military parks, 35,099 acres; 11 battlefields, 11,803 acres; 3 battlefield parks, 8,173 acres)

National Capital Parks

include more than 346 sites (The Ellipse; Lafayette Park) throughout the Washington, D.C., area. (6,482 acres)

National historical parks

are areas of greater physical extent and complexity than historic sites (Nez Perce, Idaho). (38; 114,463 acres)

National historic sites

include areas of prehistoric and modern historical interest (Tuskegee Institute, Mississippi), archaeological sites, historic structures and the like. Because it is of importance to both the U.S. and Canada, St. Croix Island (22 acres) is designated an International Historic Site. (76; 19,386 acres)

National lakeshores/seashores

(Cape Cod NS, Massachusetts; Pictured Rocks NL, Michigan) preserve shoreline areas and offshore islands while providing water-oriented recreation. (10 seashores, 477,561 acres; 4 lakeshores, 145,463 acres)

National memorial

designates an area or structure that is commemorative in nature (Mt. Rushmore, South Dakota). (28; 7,979 acres)

National monuments

are intended to preserve at least one nationally significant resource (Rainbow Bridge, Utah). They are usually smaller than national parks and lack the diversity of attractions. (73; 1,898,607 acres)

National parks

contain a variety of resources and encompass large land and water areas (Grand Canyon, Arizona) to help provide adequate protection of resources. (54; 49,415,510 acres)

National parkways

are ribbons of land flanking roadways (Natchez Trace, Mississippi, Alabama and Tennessee) that offer an opportunity for leisurely driving through areas of scenic interest. (4; 163,729 acres)

National preserves

serve primarily to protect certain resources (Big Thicket, Texas). Activities like hunting and fishing or mineral extraction may be permitted. (16; 21,406,176 acres)

National recreation areas

were originally areas surrounding reservoirs (Lake Mead, Nevada and Arizona), but now include other lands and waters set aside for recreational use. (19; 3,360,952 acres)

National reserves

are similar to the preserves, but are administered by state or local authorities (City of Rocks, Idaho). (2; 10,830 acres)

National rivers/wild and scenic riverways

preserve ribbons of land bordering free-flowing streams that have not been dammed, channelized, or otherwise altered (Delaware River, Pennsylvania and New Jersey). Activities such as hiking, boating and hunting may be permitted. (16; 312,172 acres)

National scenic trails

are usually long-distance footpaths winding through areas of natural beauty (Appalachian Trail, Maine to Georgia). (3; 155,916 acres)

National wilderness areas

are designated under the Wilderness Act of 1964, which provides that "there shall be no commercial enterprise and no permanent road within any wilderness area . . . and (except for emergency uses) no temporary road, no use of motor vehicles, motorized equipment or motorboats, no landing of aircraft, no other form of mechanical transport, and no structure or installation." Wilderness areas are usually part of other larger entities.

In addition to the National Park System, there are three groups of areas that are closely linked in importance and purpose to areas managed by the NPS.

Affiliated areas

(designated by Act of Congress, 1970) are areas in the U.S. and Canada that preserve significant areas outside the National Park System but that rely on NPS assistance.

U.S. National Parks: Acreage, Visits, and Overnight Stays, 1990-98

National Park, State	Acres under Federal protection 1998	Visits ('000s) 1990	1997	1998	Overnight stays ('000s) 1990	1997	1998
Acadia, Maine	45,813	2,413	2,760	2,595	223	155	170
Arches, Utah	66,344	621	859	837	58	48	50
Badlands, South Dakota	232,822	1,326	971	1,021	35	44	38
Big Bend, Texas	775,279	257	306	338	215	225	218
Biscayne, Florida	170,811	573	392	403	29	N.A.	N.A.
Bryce Canyon , Utah	35,833	863	1,175	1,166	144	160	150
Canyonlands, Utah	337,570	277	434	437	78	108	112
Capitol Reef, Utah	222,753	562	626	656	48	42	42
Carlsbad Caverns, New Mexico	46,427	747	541	522	N.A.	N.A.	1
Channel Islands, California	70,519	144	489	574	32	128	129
Crater Lake, Oregon	183,224	385	452	472	45	34	69
Death Valley, California-Nevada	3,348,929	(¹)	1,188	1,178	(¹)	188	223
Denali, Alaska	4,724,735	547	354	373	118	129	122
Dry Tortugas, Florida[2]	61,480	19	47	60	25	100	66
Everglades, Florida	1,398,617	958	990	1,118	128	83	96
Gates of the Arctic, Alaska	7,076,081	1	7	8	5	6	14
Glacier Bay, Alaska	3,222,378	204	347	404	36	51	53
Glacier, Montana	1,013,154	1,987	1,709	1,831	330	325	339
Grand Canyon, Arizona[2]	1,180,863	3,777	4,792	4,240	908	1,119	973
Grand Teton, Wyoming	307,620	1,588	2,659	2,757	597	552	575
Great Basin, Nevada	77,180	65	91	80	44	36	25
Great Smoky Mountain, Tennessee-North Carolina	520,977	8,152	9,965	9,989	463	488	470
Guadalupe Mountains, Texas	86,190	193	232	228	18	24	22
Haleakala, Hawaii	27,619	1,261	1,674	1,477	19	29	25
Hawaii Volcanoes, Hawaii	207,643	1,097	1,832	1,352	112	115	121
Hot Springs, Arkansas	4,880	1,123	1,510	1,496	8	8	7
Isle Royale, Michigan	539,282	23	21	24	56	62	64
Joshua Tree, California	548,822	(¹)	1,226	1,410	(¹)	229	246
Katmai, Alaska[2]	3,611,495	41	19	45	12	15	15
Kenai Fjords, Alaska[2]	599,944	66	306	264	1	2	4
Kings Canyon, California	461,845	1,063	485	540	302	223	220
Kobuk Valley, Alaska[2]	1,669,729	3	3	6	N.A.	N.A.	N.A.
Lake Clark, Alaska	2,226,570	10	9	11	1	3	3
Lassen Volcanic, California[2]	106,367	461	392	318	113	92	76
Mammoth Cave, Kentucky	52,003	1,925	1,998	2,114	98	97	94
Mesa Verde, Colorado[2]	51,891	611	628	604	159	138	115
Mount Rainier, Washington	235,613	1,327	1,316	1,354	184	179	191
North Cascades, Washington	504,575	456	27	33	97	17	18
Olympic, Washington	913,339	2,795	3,847	3,577	404	435	443
Petrified Forest, Arizona	93,533	845	823	817	1	2	3
Redwood, California[2]	77,646	348	382	383	16	87	66
Rocky Mountain, Colorado	265,316	2,647	2,965	3,035	209	226	235
Saguaro, Arizona	86,365	(¹)	739	716	(¹)	2	2
Sequoia, California[2]	402,335	1,064	1,009	861	345	248	230
Shenandoah, Virginia[2]	197,039	1,772	1,588	1,473	323	296	288
Theodore Roosevelt, North Dakota	69,702	461	393	448	26	29	27
Virgin Island, US Virgin Islands	12,910	665	593	557	173	162	255
Voyageurs, Minnesota	132,460	224	223	232	47	18	18
Wind Cave, South Dakota[2]	28,295	586	832	850	11	3	12
Wrangell-St. Elias, Alaska[2]	7,661,519	36	32	28	3	28	5
Yellowstone, Montana-Wyoming	2,219,789	2,824	2,890	3,121	1,345	1,221	1251
Yosemite, California	759,530	3,125	3,670	3,657	2,220	1,635	1589
Zion, Utah	143,035	2,102	2,446	2,370	292	272	234
Total National Parks	49,116,690	54,619	65,259	64,462	10,156	9,916	9,814
Total National Parks System[3]	77,415,474	255,655	275,236	286,739	17,625	16,376	16,171

1. Area was not a National Park in 1990. 2. Data are not directly comparable with previous years due to changes in the counting methods or because of special events such as anniversaries and natural disasters. 3. Includes National Historic Sites, National Memorials, National Seashores, National Parkways, and other areas under the jurisdiction of the National Park Service.
Source: *U.S. National Park Service Statistical Abstract 1998.*

Wild and Scenic Rivers System (designated by Act of Congress, 1968) preserves undeveloped rivers as free-flowing streams accessible for public use. Wild rivers are free of dams and generally accessible only by trails; scenic rivers have relatively primitive shorelines and are largely undeveloped but may be accessible by road.

National Trails System (designated by National Trails System Act of 1968) includes trails in both urban and rural settings for persons of all ages, interests, skills, and physical abilities. The Appalachian Trail and the Pacific Crest were the first two trails designated under the National Trails System. Today, there are more than 800 trails, in every state, Puerto Rico, and the District of Columbia, totaling more than 9,000 miles in length.

Source: National Park Service, *The National Parks: Index 1997-99.*

▶**RIVERS AND LAKES**
Major Navigable Waterways of the United States
The U.S inland and intracoastal waterway system handles over 500 million tons of traffic each year, carried by a fleet of more than 5,000 towboats and 31,000 barges on over 11,000 miles of primary channels. Ninety percent of these channels have depths of between 9 and 14 feet. Maintenance and improvement of the waterways—including channel dredging, bridge and levee maintenance, and the construction of canals and locks—are in large measure the responsibility of the U.S. Army Corps of Engineers. The 522-mile New York State Barge Canal System is the only major nonFederal waterway in the country.

Mississippi River System The major inland river transportation network is the Mississippi River and its tributaries. This north-south-oriented system includes the Mississippi River, the Ohio River System, the Illinois Waterway, and the Arkansas and Missouri rivers, among others. In this system there are about 7,000 miles of heavily used, improved navigable channels, 85 percent of which have at least nine-foot navigable channel depths.

Intracoastal Waterways At its mouth, the Mississippi River is intersected by the Gulf Intracoastal Waterway (GIWW), which parallels the Gulf Coast for 1,180 miles from St. Marks River, Florida, to Brownsville, Texas, at the Mexican border. The GIWW is intersected by a number of river systems in addition to the Mississippi, including the Mobile River, the Apalachicola, and the Houston Ship Channel.

This network of major inland and coastal waterways connects some of the largest Gulf Coast ports—New Orleans, La.; Houston, Beaumont and Corpus Christi, Tex.; and Mobile, Ala.—with some of the largest inland ports—St. Louis, Mo.; Pittsburgh, Pa.; Huntington, W. Va.; Cincinnati, Ohio; Memphis, Tenn; and Chicago, Ill. The 40-foot controlling depth of the Mississippi River between the Gulf of Mexico and Baton Rouge allows ocean shipping to join the barge traffic, making this segment especially vital to both the domestic and foreign commerce of the United States.

The Atlantic Intracoastal Waterway provides 1,329 miles of protected channels for commercial and recreational navigation along the Atlantic Coast from Key West, Fla., to Norfolk, Va. Partially protected segments of the waterway continue north from Norfolk along the Delmarva Peninsula, the New Jersey coast, and Long Island. Among the major Atlantic Coast ports located along this waterway are Miami, Fla.; Savannah, Ga.; Baltimore, Md.; Philadelphia, Pa.; and the Port of New York and New Jersey.

Pacific Coast In comparison with the Mississippi River system and the intracoastal waterways of the Atlantic and Gulf coasts, the inland and coastal waterways of the Pacific are few. Shallow draft waterways include the Columbia-Snake Waterway and the Willamette River above Portland, Oreg.; the Sacramento River above Sacramento, Calif.; the San Joaquin River above Stockton, Calif.; and a few short navigable rivers stretching along the Washington and Oregon coasts.

The accompanying table shows the major navigable rivers in the United States, their total length, the distance commercially navigable, the body of water they flow into, and the head of navigation—the upriver point beyond which commercial ships cannot pass—and the states through or by which the rivers pass, from source to mouth.

Great Lakes and St. Lawrence Seaway The Great Lakes have been crucial to the development of the United States. They were the highways along which people and finished goods moved west, and along which raw materials such as lumber, minerals, and grains were transported to eastern markets. Later, the cities of the Great Lakes, such as Chicago, Duluth, Detroit, and Buffalo, became important centers of finance, industry, and trade in their own right. So important was the maritime trade of the Lakes that in the 1890s, Chicago was the fourth-largest port in the world, despite being closed by ice for as many as five months a year.

An early obstacle to Great Lakes navigation was the fact that the lakes are not all at the same elevation: there is a difference of 354 feet between the level of the westernmost Lake Superior and easternmost Lake Ontario, and there is another 246 feet descent from Lake Ontario down the St. Lawrence River where it empties into the Atlantic Ocean. (It is 2,342 miles from Duluth, Minnesota, at the western end of Lake Superior, to the mouth of the St. Lawrence.)

The first canal (1799) was built on the St. Mary's River between Lake Superior and Lake Huron. (Today, there are two Sault Sainte Marie [or Soo] Canals—along the 70-mile river.) In 1825, the United States opened the way between the upper Lakes (all but Lake Ontario) and the Atlantic via

The Great Lakes					
Characteristic	Ontario	Erie	Michigan	Huron	Superior
Area (sq.mi.)	7,540	9,940	22,400	23,010	31,820
(sq. km.)	19,529	25,745	58,016	59,596	82,414
Depth (feet)	002	210	923	750	1,333
(meters)	244	64	281	229	406
Height above sea level (feet)	246	571	577	577	600
(meters)	75	174	176	176	183

Source: U.S. Environmental Protection Agency and Environment Canada, *The Great Lakes: An Environmental Atlas and Resource Book* (1987).

the 175-mile Erie Canal between Buffalo, on Lake Erie, and Albany, on the Hudson River north of New York City. Canada followed with the 27-mile Welland Canal (1833) connecting Welland on Lake Erie and St. Catharine's on Lake Ontario.

The most ambitious undertaking was the construction of the St. Lawrence Seaway, a joint Canadian-American effort to open the entire length of the St. Lawrence and the Great Lakes to oceangoing navigation. Started in 1955 and opened to navigation in 1959, the seaway's system of canals and locks allows ships of up to 730 feet in length and 27 feet draft to sail the entire 2,342 miles from the mouth of the St. Lawrence to Duluth, Minn., at the western end of Lake Superior. The seaway also provides hydroelectric power for Canada and the United States.

The Panama Canal One of the great engineering feats of the world, the 44-mile Panama Canal bisects the continents of North and South America, making it possible for ships to sail between the Atlantic and Pacific oceans without rounding the treacherous Cape Horn at the tip of South America. The U.S. government began construction of the canal in 1904, and it was opened

State Parks and Recreation Areas by State, 1998

State	Areas	Total Acreage	Visitors ('000s) Day	Total[1]	Expenditures ('000s)	Revenues ('000s)
Total U.S.	5,870	12,653,569	701,492	780,830	$1,378,192	$614,822
Alabama	23	49,710	4,669	5,740	27,867	23,066
Alaska	139	3,290,070	2,743	3,459	5,379	1,938
Arizona	27	46,356	1,659	2,276	8,690	4,506
Arkansas	66	51,407	6,547	7,208	25,526	13,451
California	263	1,372,040	79,319	85,522	186,932	61,936
Colorado	259	335,359	10,711	11,551	21,745	11,684
Connecticut	124	175,860	8,047	8,406	9,197	3,428
Delaware	25	18,189	2,369	2,571	11,084	5,679
Florida	149	525,809	12,859	14,140	48,788	24,135
Georgia	63	71,150	14,368	15,095	43,151	17,182
Hawaii	67	24,589	14,000	14,071	5,621	275
Idaho	24	41,039	1,938	2,242	7,483	2,880
Illinois	384	411,156	39,580	40,169	41,230	4,744
Indiana	33	178,507	15,279	17,949	23,524	28,747
Iowa	173	63,071	12,882	13,547	9,600	2,026
Kansas	24	32,300	5,334	6,856	6,330	3,447
Kentucky	49	43,310	7,589	8,720	65,599	44,732
Louisiana	56	39,136	933	1,442	11,420	2,902
Maine	328	587,558	1,755	1,959	6,268	1,730
Maryland	97	292,279	9,381	9,974	30,129	11,979
Massachusetts	235	285,264	11,773	12,686	33,028	3,587
Michigan	92	266,251	21,145	26,389	33,600	29,557
Minnesota	79	241,137	7,456	8,358	22,827	10,611
Mississippi	29	24,327	4,200	4,801	18,200	10,297
Missouri	85	135,738	16,142	17,332	28,463	7,621
Montana	367	51,115	1,136	1,394	5,301	1,416
Nebraska	86	133,024	7,953	9,491	16,377	12,190
Nevada	24	131,831	3,159	3,347	8,070	1,707
New Hampshire	84	74,471	3,463	3,681	4,037	4,037
New Jersey	115	341,301	14,261	14,658	26,234	7,509
New Mexico	31	90,693	2,018	5,045	13,134	3,442
New York	727	485,045	62,934	67,062	125,444	59,363
North Carolina	56	147,693	12,253	12,653	20,494	3,299
North Dakota	31	20,046	952	1,105	1,815	808
Ohio	73	204,852	45,370	47,719	58,748	24,597
Oklahoma	52	71,931	15,137	16,514	37,871	20,250
Oregon	227	92,606	37,281	39,274	27,867	13,491
Pennsylvania	116	283,001	33,032	34,697	62,301	10,904
Rhode Island	74	8,748	4,592	4,949	6,030	2,252
South Carolina	56	81,798	8,686	9,927	22,638	15,104
South Dakota	86	96,099	6,141	6,725	8,942	6,876
Tennessee	84	142,847	29,961	31,217	44,967	23,842
Texas	123	628,227	19,201	20,821	33,649	15,480
Utah	54	113,799	6,378	7,687	19,941	6,559
Vermont	66	77,631	392	775	5,227	5,585
Virginia	56	72,610	4,443	4,844	14,385	5,134
Washington	246	258,506	48,645	50,786	34,892	10,668
West Virginia	47	195,565	7,447	8,018	26,630	16,436
Wisconsin	65	127,811	12,219	13,774	16,898	11,036
Wyoming	31	120,707	1,761	2,200	4,620	698

1. Includes overnight visitors.   **Source:** National Association of State Park Directors (Tucson, Ariz.), *1998 Annual Information Exchange.*

to commercial navigation Aug. 15, 1914. For inter-ocean shippers, the savings in distance and time afforded by the canal are enormous. A ship sailing from New York to San Francisco via the Panama Canal travels a distance of 5,264 miles, a savings of more than 7,800 miles—or about 20 days— over the 13,100-mile route around Cape Horn. The minimum depth of the canal is 41 feet, the minimum width 300 feet, and the highest elevation above sea level 85 feet.

The Canal Zone, a 10-mile-wide strip of land around the canal in the Republic of Panama was acquired in 1903 by the United States, who governed it until 1979. The Panama Canal Treaty of 1977 abolished the Canal Zone as an independent political entity, but the canal's maintenance and operation remain the responsibility of the U.S. Panama Canal Commission until 1999, when the Republic of Panama assumes full responsibility.

Land Cover and Use, by State, 1992 (thousands of acres)

State	Total surface area[1]	Federal land area	Developed[2]	Non-Federal land areas Rural cropland	Rural pasture land	Rural rangeland	Rural forestland
United States	1,937,678	407,899	91,946	381,950	125,215	389,803	394,437
Alabama	33,091	921	2,046	3,147	3,760	67	20,968
Arizona	72,960	30,280	1,404	1,198	76	32,227	4,718
Arkansas	34,040	3,207	1,322	7,730	5,727	159	14,267
California	101,572	46,792	5,001	10,052	1,161	17,140	14,794
Colorado	66,618	23,923	1,694	8,940	1,256	23,537	3,755
Connecticut	3,212	15	816	229	110	—	1,760
Delaware	1,309	33	205	499	26	—	353
Florida	37,545	3,791	4,645	2,997	4,373	3,476	12,378
Georgia	37,702	2,087	3,077	5,173	3,075	—	21,714
Hawaii	4,093	432	170	274	88	925	1,483
Idaho	53,481	33,298	587	5,600	1,243	6,668	4,024
Illinois	36,061	521	3,094	24,100	2,764	—	3,419
Indiana	23,159	487	2,095	13,513	1,866	—	3,626
Iowa	36,016	184	1,779	24,988	3,712	—	1,931
Kansas	52,658	606	1,997	26,565	2,306	15,723	1,331
Kentucky	25,862	1,201	1,653	5,092	5,859	—	10,312
Louisiana	30,561	1,264	1,764	5,972	2,269	227	12,961
Maine	21,290	164	697	448	111	—	17,557
Maryland	6,695	167	1,095	1,673	545	—	2,364
Massachusetts	5,302	89	1,309	272	170	—	2,778
Michigan	37,457	3,166	3,686	8,985	2,353	—	15,608
Minnesota	54,017	3,383	2,418	21,356	3,282	—	13,815
Mississippi	30,521	1,726	1,337	5,726	4,047	—	15,765
Missouri	44,606	2,017	2,336	13,347	11,911	126	11,656
Montana	94,109	27,122	1,096	15,035	3,370	36,835	5,156
Nebraska	49,507	739	1,252	19,239	2,066	22,669	777
Nevada	70,759	60,290	394	762	297	7,854	353
New Hampshire	5,938	747	563	142	98	—	3,932
New Jersey	4,984	159	1,588	650	159	—	1,766
New Mexico	77,819	27,394	866	1,892	212	39,792	4,600
New York	31,429	231	3,005	5,616	3,001	—	17,178
North Carolina	33,708	2,448	3,542	5,960	2,019	—	15,979
North Dakota	45,250	1,951	1,344	24,743	1,168	10,325	426
Ohio	26,451	375	3,558	11,929	2,269	—	6,624
Oklahoma	44,772	1,202	1,875	10,081	7,720	14,061	6,988
Oregon	62,127	32,291	1,125	3,776	1,900	9,375	11,839
Pennsylvania	28,997	682	3,432	5,596	2,326	—	15,316
Rhode Island	776	4	190	25	24	—	393
South Carolina	19,912	1,156	1,856	2,983	1,190	—	10,922
South Dakota	49,354	2,907	1,135	16,436	2,158	21,933	540
Tennessee	26,972	1,379	2,161	4,857	5,165	—	11,580
Texas	170,756	3,203	8,231	28,261	16,710	94,155	9,960
Utah	54,336	35,582	561	1,815	665	10,050	1,626
Vermont	6,153	368	324	635	349	—	4,138
Virginia	26,091	2,389	2,183	2,901	3,444	—	13,539
Washington	43,608	12,479	1,851	6,745	1,352	5,476	12,547
West Virginia	15,508	1,201	689	915	1,609	—	10,534
Wisconsin	35,938	1,829	2,357	10,813	2,954	—	13,410
Wyoming	62,598	30,020	541	2,272	901	26,015	975

Note: U.S. Totals exclude Alaska and the District of Columbia. 1. Includes 107.9 million acres of water area and minor land cover and uses not shown separately. 2. Includes urban and built-up areas in units of 10 acres or greater, and rural transportation areas.
Source: U.S. Department of Agriculture, Soil Conservation Service and Iowa State University, Statistical Laboratory, *Summary Report, 1992 National Resources Inventory,* December, 1995.

Major Navigable Rivers in the U.S.

Ultimate outflow/river	Length (miles)	Navigable length (miles)	Mouth to head of navigation	States/provinces (from source to mouth)
ATLANTIC OCEAN				
St. Lawrence	760	760	Gulf of St. Lawrence to Lake Ontario	N.Y.; Ontario, Quebec (Canada)
Cape Cod Canal	17	17	Sandwich to Buzzards Bay, Mass.	Mass.
Connecticut	407	52	Long Island Sound to Hartford, Conn.	N.H., Vt., Mass., Conn.
Hudson	306	134	New York Bay to Troy Lock, N.Y. New York State Barge Canal links to Lake Erie (353 mi. Troy to Buffalo), and to Lakes Champlain, Ontario, Cayuga, Seneca.	N.Y.
Delaware	367	77	Delaware Bay to Trenton, N.J.	N.Y., Pa., N.J., Del.
Chesapeake and Delaware Canal	14	14	Delaware Bay to Chesapeake Bay	Del., Md.
Potomac	287	101	Chesapeake Bay to Washington, D.C.	Va., Md., D.C.
James	340	87	Chesapeake Bay to Richmond, Va.	Va.
Roanoke	410	112	Atlantic Ocean to Altavista, N.C.	Va., N.C.
Cape Fear	202	111	Atlantic Ocean to Fayetteville, N.C.	N.C.
Savannah	314	181	Atlantic Ocean to Augusta, Ga.	S.C., Ga.
Saint Johns	285	160	Atlantic Ocean to Lake Harney	Fla.
GULF OF MEXICO				
Chattahoochee	436	194	Apalachicola River to Columbus, Ga.	Ga., Ala.
Apalachicola	90	90	Gulf of Mexico to Chattahoochee, Fla.	Fla.
Mobile	45	45	Mobile Bay to confluence of Alabama and Tombigbee rivers	Ala.
Alabama	318	305	Mobile River to Montgomery, Ala.	Ala.
Tombigbee	362	362	Mobile River to Amory, Miss. Linked to Tennessee River by Tennessee-Tombigbee Waterway (253 mi.)	Miss., Ala.
Black Warrior	217	217	Tombigbee River to Birmingham, Ala.	Ala.
Houston Ship Channel	57	57	Galveston Bay to Houston, Tex.	Tex.
Rio Grande[1]	1,885	13	Gulf of Mexico to Brownsville, Tex.	Colo., N.Mex., Tex., Mexico
MISSISSIPPI RIVER SYSTEM				
Mississippi	2,348	1,807	Gulf of Mexico to Minneapolis, Minn.,	Minn., Wis., Iowa, Ill., Mo., Ky., Tenn., Ark., Miss., La
EASTERN TRIBUTARIES				
Illinois	273	273	Mississippi River to Joliet. Also linked to Mississippi by Illinois and Mississippi Canal (La Salle to Rockport); and to Lake Michigan (at Chicago, Calumet, East Chicago Gary) by Illinois Waterway	Ill.
Ohio	981	981	Mississippi River to Pittsburgh, Pa.	Pa., Ohio, W.Va., Ind., Ky., Ill.
Monongahela	129	129	Ohio River to Fairmont, W.Va.	W.Va., Pa.
Allegheny	325	72	Ohio River to East Brady, Pa.	N.Y., Pa.
Kanawha	97	91	Ohio River to Charleston, W.Va.	W.Va.
Kentucky	259	82	Ohio River to Beattyville, Ky.	Ky.
Green	360	103	Ohio River to Bowling Green, Ky.	Ky.
Cumberland	694	387	Ohio River to Burnside, Ky.	Ky., Tenn.
Tennessee	652	648	Ohio River to Knoxville, Tenn.	Tenn., Ala., Miss., Ky.
Yazoo	169	165	Mississippi River to Greenwood, Miss.	Miss.
WESTERN TRIBUTARIES				
Missouri	2,315	735	Mississippi River to Ponca, Nebr.	Mont., N.Dak., S.Dak., Nebr., Iowa, Kans., Mo.
Arkansas	1,396	448	McClellan-Kerr Arkansas River System from Mississippi River to Catoosa, Okla., incorporates sections of White, Arkansas, Verdigris rivers.	Colo., Kans., Okla., Ark.,
Ouachita[2]	605	351	Mississippi River to Camden, Ark.	Ark., La.
Red	1,018	236	Mississippi River to Shreveport, La.	N.Mex., Tex., Okla., Ark., La.
Atchafalaya[3]	220	220	Atchafalaya Bay to Mississippi River	La.
PACIFIC OCEAN AND ARCTIC OCEAN				
San Joaquin	340	103	Sacramento River to Hills Ferry, Calif.	Calif.
Sacramento	374	163	San Francisco Bay to Chico Landing, Calif.	Calif.
Columbia	1,210	285	Pacific Ocean to Pasco, Wash.	British Col. (Can.), Wash., Oreg.
Snake	1,083	192	Columbia River to Johnson Bar Landing.	Wyo., Idaho, Oreg., Wash.
Willamette	294	133	Columbia River to Harrisburg, Oreg.	Oreg.
Yukon	1,979	1,699	Arctic Ocean to Whitehorse, Yukon	Yukon (Can.), Alaska

Note: All distances given in nautical miles except for the Mississippi River and its tributaries: 1 nautical mile = 1.151 statute miles. 1. In Mexico known as the Río Bravo or Río Bravo del Norte. 2. Lower 57 miles known as the Black River. 3. Flows from the Mississippi River to the Gulf of Mexico.
Source: National Oceanic and Atmospheric Administration, *Distances Between United States Ports, 1987* (1987).

Extreme Elevations of States and Outlying Areas

State	Highest Point Name	Elevation Feet	Elevation Meters	Lowest Point Name	Elevation Feet	Elevation Meters
United States	Mount McKinley, Alaska	20,320	6,198	Death Valley, Calif.	-282	-86
Alabama	Cheaha Mountain	2,405	733	Gulf of Mexico	Sea level	
Alaska	Mount McKinley	20,320	6,198	Pacific Ocean	Sea level	
Arizona	Humphreys Peak	12,633	3,853	Colorado River	70	21
Arkansas	Magazine Mountain	2,753	840	Ouachita River	55	17
California	Mount Whitney	14,494	4,419	Death Valley	-282	-86
Colorado	Mount Elbert	14,433	4,402	Arkansas River	3,350	1,022
Connecticut	Mount Frissell, South slope	2,380	726	Long Island Sound	Sea level	
Delaware	Elbright Rd., New Castle Co.	442	135	Atlantic Ocean	Sea level	
Dist of Columbia	Tenleytown	410	125	Potomac River	1	0.3
Florida	Sec.30,T6N,R20W, Walton Co.	345	105	Atlantic Ocean	Sea level	
Georgia	Brasstown Bald	4,784	1,459	Atlantic Ocean	Sea level	
Hawaii	Puu Wekiu	13,796	4,208	Pacific Ocean	Sea level	
Idaho	Borah Peak	12,662	3,862	Snake River	710	217
Illinois	Charles Mound	1,235	377	Mississippi River	279	85
Indiana	Franklin Township, Wayne Co.	1,257	383	Ohio River	320	98
Iowa	Sec. 29, T100N, R41W Osceola Co.	1,257	509	Mississippi River	480	146
Kansas	Mount Sunflower	4,039	1,232	Verdigris River	679	207
Kentucky	Black Mountain	4,139	1,262	Mississippi River	257	78
Louisiana	Driskill Mountain	535	163	New Orleans	-8	-2
Maine	Mount Katahdin	5,267	1,606	Atlantic Ocean	Sea level	
Maryland	Backbone Mountain	3,360	1,025	Atlantic Ocean	Sea level	
Massachusetts	Mount Greylock	3,487	1,064	Atlantic Ocean	Sea level	
Michigan	Mount Arvon	1,979	604	Lake Erie	571	174
Minnesota	Eagle Mountain, Cook Co.	2,301	702	Lake Superior	600	183
Mississippi	Woodall Mountain	806	246	Gulf of Mexico	Sea level	
Missouri	Taum Sauk Mountain	1,772	540	St. Francis River	230	70
Montana	Granite Peak	12,799	3,904	Kootenai River	1,800	549
Nebraska	Johnson Township, Kimball Co.	5,426	1,654	Missouri River	840	256
Nevada	Boundary Peak	13,140	4,007	Colorado River	479	146
New Hampshire	Mount Washington	6,288	1,918	Atlantic Ocean	Sea level	
New Jersey	High Point	1,803	550	Atlantic Ocean	Sea level	
New Mexico	Wheeler Peak	13,161	4,014	Red Bluff Reservoir	2,842	867
New York	Mount Marcy	5,344	1,630	Atlantic Ocean	Sea level	
North Carolina	Mount Mitchell	6,684	2,039	Atlantic Ocean	Sea level	
North Dakota	White Butte, Slope Co.	3,506	1,069	Red River	750	229
Ohio	Campbell Hilll	1,549	472	Ohio River	455	139
Oklahoma	Black Mesa	4,973	1,517	Little River	289	88
Oregon	Mount Hood	11,239	3,428	Pacific Ocean	Sea level	
Pennsylvania	Mount Davis	3,213	980	Delaware River	Sea level	
Rhode Island	Jerimoth Hill	812	248	Atlantic Ocean	Sea level	
South Carolina	Sassafras Mountain	3,560	1,086	Atlantic Ocean	Sea level	
South Dakota	Harney Peak	7,242	2,209	Big Stone Lake	966	295
Tennessee	Clingmans Dome	6,643	2,026	Mississippi River	178	54
Texas	Guadalupe Peak	8,749	2,668	Gulf of Mexico	Sea level	
Utah	Kings Peak	13,528	4,126	Beaverdam Creek	2,000	610
Vermont	Mount Mansfield	4,393	1,340	Lake Champlain	95	29
Virginia	Mount Rogers	5,729	1,747	Atlantic Ocean	Sea level	
Washington	Mount Rainier	14,410	4,395	Pacific Ocean	Sea level	
West Virginia	Spruce Knob	4,861	1,483	Potomac River	240	73
Wisconsin	Timms Hill	1,951	595	Lake Michigan	579	177
Wyoming	Gannett Peak	13,804	4,210	Belle Fourche River	3,099	945
Puerto Rico	Cerro de Punta	4,390	1,339	Atlantic Ocean	Sea level	
Amer. Samoa	Lata Mountain	3,160	964	Pacific Ocean	Sea level	
Guam	Mount Lamlam	1,332	405	Pacific Ocean	Sea level	
Virgin Islands	Crown Mountain	1,556	475	Atlantic Ocean	Sea level	

Note: Sec. denotes section; T, township; R, range; N, north; W, west.
Source: U.S. Geological Survey, *Elevations and Distances in the United States* (1990).

U.S. History

DOCUMENTS OF U.S. HISTORY

▶**THE DECLARATION OF INDEPENDENCE**
After a year of war with Britain, American patriots were driven to make the final break in 1776. On June 7, before the Continental Congress in Philadelphia, Richard Henry Lee of Virginia proposed a declaration that the colonies "are, and of right ought to be, free and independent States." A committee of five, headed by Thomas Jefferson, was appointed to draw up the formal Declaration of Independence on June 10. The committee brought its version, mainly the work of Jefferson, back to Congress on June 28. Congress voted unanimously to declare independence on July 2, and after making several changes in the Jefferson committee's draft, they unanimously adopted the Declaration of Independence on July 4. Copies of the Declaration were dispatched to the states for approval. Charles Carroll of Maryland was the last surviving signer of the Declaration when he died on November 14, 1832. The original document is on display today at the National Archives in Washington, D.C.

In Congress, July 4, 1776,
THE UNANIMOUS DECLARATION
OF THE
THIRTEEN UNITED STATES
OF AMERICA,
When in the Course of human events, it becomes necessary for one people to dissolve the political bands which have connected them with another, and to assume among the Powers of the earth, the separate and equal station to which the Laws of Nature and of Nature's God entitle them, a decent respect to the opinions of mankind requires that they should declare the causes which impel them to the separation.

We hold these truths to be self-evident, that all men are created equal, that they are endowed by their Creator with certain unalienable Rights, that among these are Life, Liberty and the pursuit of Happiness. That to secure these rights, Governments are instituted among Men, deriving their just powers from the consent of the governed. That whenever any Form of Government becomes destructive of these ends, it is the Right of the People to alter or to abolish it, and to institute new Government, laying its foundation on such principles and organizing its powers in such form, as to them shall seem most likely to effect their Safety and Happiness. Prudence, indeed, will dictate that governments long established should not be changed for light and transient causes; and accordingly all experience hath shown, that mankind are more disposed to suffer, while evils are sufferable, than to right themselves by abolishing the forms to which they are accustomed. But when a long train of abuses and usurpations, pursuing invariably the same Object evinces a design to reduce them under absolute Despotism, it is their right, it is their duty, to throw off such Government, and to provide new Guards for their future security. Such has been the patient sufferance of these Colonies; and such is now the ne-

cessity which constrains them to alter their former Systems of Government. The history of the present King of Great Britain is a history of repeated injuries and usurpations, all having in direct object the establishment of an absolute Tyranny over these States. To prove this, let Facts be submitted to a candid world.

He has refused his Assent to Laws, the most wholesome and necessary for the public good.

He has forbidden his Governors to pass Laws of immediate and pressing importance, unless suspended in their operation till his Assent should be obtained; and when so suspended, he has utterly neglected to attend to them.

He has refused to pass other Laws for the accommodation of large districts of people, unless those people would relinquish the right of Representation in the Legislature, a right inestimable to them and formidable to tyrants only.

He has called together legislative bodies at places unusual, uncomfortable, and distant from the depository of their Public Records, for the sole purpose of fatiguing them into compliance with his measures.

He has dissolved Representative Houses repeatedly, for opposing with manly firmness his invasions on the rights of the people.

He has refused for a long time, after such dissolutions, to cause others to be elected; whereby the Legislative Powers, incapable of Annihilation, have returned to the People at large for their exercise; the State remaining in the mean time exposed to all the dangers of invasion from without, and convulsions within.

He has endeavoured to prevent the population of these States; for that purpose obstructing the Laws of Naturalization of Foreigners; refusing to pass others to encourage their migration hither, and raising the conditions of new Appropriations of Lands.

He has obstructed the Administration of Justice, by refusing his Assent to Laws for establishing Judiciary Powers.

He has made Judges dependent on his Will alone, for the tenure of their offices, and the amount and payment of their salaries.

He has erected a multitude of New Offices, and sent hither swarms of Officers to harass our People, and eat out their substance.

He has kept among us, in times of peace, Standing Armies without the Consent of our legislature.

He has affected to render the Military independent of and superior to the Civil Power.

He has combined with others to subject us to a jurisdiction foreign to our constitution, and unacknowledged by our laws; giving his Assent to their acts of pretended legislation:

For quartering large bodies of armed troops among us:

For protecting them, by a mock Trial, from Punishment for any Murders which they should commit on the Inhabitants of these States:

For cutting off our Trade with all parts of the world:

For imposing taxes on us without our consent:

For depriving us in many cases, of the benefits of Trial by Jury:

For transporting us beyond Seas to be tried for pretended offences:

For abolishing the free System of English Laws in a neighbouring Province, establishing therein an Arbitrary government, and enlarging its Boundaries so as to render it at once an example and fit instrument for introducing the same absolute rule into these Colonies:

For taking away our Charters, abolishing our most valuable Laws, and altering fundamentally the forms of our Government:

For suspending our own legislature, and declaring themselves invested with Power to legislate for us in all cases whatsoever.

He has abdicated Government here, by declaring us out of his Protection and waging War against us.

He has plundered our seas, ravaged our Coasts, burnt our towns, and destroyed the lives of our people.

He is at this time transporting large armies of foreign mercenaries to compleat the works of death, desolation and tyranny, already begun with circumstances of Cruelty & perfidy scarcely paralleled in the most barbarous ages, and totally unworthy of the Head of a civilized nation.

He has constrained our fellow Citizens taken Captive on the high Seas to bear Arms against their Country, to become the executioners of their friends and Brethren, or to fall themselves by their Hands.

He has excited domestic insurrections amongst us, and has endeavoured to bring on the inhabitants of our frontiers, the merciless Indian Savages, whose known rule of warfare, is an undistinguished destruction of all ages, sexes and conditions.

In every stage of these Oppressions We have Petitioned for Redress in the most humble terms: Our repeated Petitions have been answered only by repeated injury. A prince, whose character is thus marked by every act which may define a Tyrant, is unfit to be the ruler of a free People.

Nor have We been wanting in attention to our British brethren. We have warned them from time to time of attempts by their legislature to extend an unwarrantable jurisdiction over us. We have reminded them of the circumstances of our emigration and settlement here. We have appealed to their native justice and magnanimity, and we have conjured them by the ties of our common kindred to disavow these usurpations, which would inevitably interrupt our connections and correspondence. They too have been deaf to the voice of justice and of consanguinity. We must, therefore, acquiesce in the necessity, which denounces our Separation and hold them, as we hold the rest of mankind, Enemies in War, in Peace Friends.

We, therefore, the Representatives of the United States of America, in General Congress, Assembled, appealing to the Supreme Judge of the world for the rectitude of our intentions, do, in the Name, and by Authority of the good People of these Colonies, solemnly publish and declare, That these United Colonies are, and of Right ought to be Free and Independent States; that they are Absolved from all Allegiance to the British Crown, and that all political connection between them and the State of Great Britain, is and ought to be totally dissolved; and that as Free and Independent States, they have full Power to levy War, conclude Peace, contract Alliances, establish Commerce, and to do all other Acts and Things which Independent States may of right do. And for the support of this Declaration, with a firm reliance on the Protection of Divine Providence, we mutually pledge to each other our Lives, our Fortunes and our sacred Honor.

▶ THE U.S. CONSTITUTION

During and after the Revolution, the United States was governed by the Continental Congress under the Articles of Confederation, which delegated very limited powers to the national government and reserved the rest to the states. Economic chaos, political confusion, and widespread dissatisfaction with the lack of central authority peaked after Shays' Rebellion in 1786. George Washington lent his prestige to the call for a convention to consider a new form of government. Congress endorsed the plan on February 21, 1787, "for the sole and express purpose of revising the Articles of Confederation." All states but Rhode Island sent delegates to the convention, which opened in Philadelphia on May 14. The delegates moved at once to discard the Articles, draw up a new Constitution, and conduct their meetings in secrecy, while Washington presided and James Madison took notes. A long summer of debate and compromise finally produced the document that most of the delegates signed on September 17. Congress ordered the Constitution sent to the states for ratification on September 28, requiring approval by at least nine of them to validate the new charter. Whether the Constitution would be adopted was in doubt until June 21, 1788, when New Hampshire became the ninth state to ratify it. The Constitution went into effect on March 4, 1789. All of the original thirteen states eventually ratified the Constitution, ending with Rhode Island on May 29, 1790. The U.S. Constitution remains the world's oldest written constitution.

Preamble

We, the people of the united states, in order to form a more perfect union, establish justice, insure domestic tranquillity, provide for the common defense, promote the general welfare, and secure the blessing of liberty to ourselves and our posterity, do ordain and establish this Constitution for the United States of America.

Article I

Section 1 All legislative powers herein granted shall be vested in a Congress of the United States, which shall consist of a Senate and House of Representatives.

Section 2 [1] The House of Representatives shall be composed of members chosen every second year by the people of the several States, and the electors in each State shall have the qualifications requisite for electors of the most numerous branch of the State legislature.

[2] No person shall be a Representative who shall not have attained to the age of twenty-five years, and been seven years a citizen of the United States, and who shall not, when elected, be an inhabitant of that State in which he shall be chosen.

[3] Representatives and direct taxes shall be apportioned among the several States which may be included within this Union, according to their respective numbers, which shall be determined by adding to the whole number of free persons, including those bound to service for a term of years, and excluding Indians not taxed, three-fifths of all other persons. The actual enumeration shall be made within three years after the first meeting of the Congress of the United States, and within every subsequent term of ten years, in such manner as they shall by law direct. The number of Representatives shall not exceed one for every thirty thousand, but each State shall have at least one Representative; and until such enumeration

Signers of the Declaration of Independence

Delegate	State	Born/Died	Delegate	State	Born/Died
Adams, John	Massachusetts	1735–1826	Lynch, Thomas, Jr.	South Carolina	1749–1779
Adams, Samuel	Massachusetts	1722–1803	McKean, Thomas	Delaware	1734–1817
Bartlett, Josiah	New Hampshire	1729–1795	Middleton, Arthur	South Carolina	1742–1787
Braxton, Carter	Virginia	1736–1797	Morris, Lewis	New York	1726–1798
Carroll, Charles	Maryland	1737–1832	Morris, Robert	Pennsylvania	1734–1806
Chase, Samuel	Maryland	1741–1811	Morton, John	Pennsylvania	1724–1777
Clark, Abraham	New Jersey	1726–1794	Nelson, Thomas Jr.	Virginia	1738–1789
Clymer, George	Pennsylvania	1739–1813	Paca, William	Maryland	1740–1799
Ellery, William	Rhode Island	1727–1820	Paine, Robert Treat	Massachusetts	1731–1814
Floyd, William	New York	1734–1821	Penn, John	North Carolina	1741–1788
Franklin, Benjamin	Pennsylvania	1706–1790	Read, George	Delaware	1733–1798
Gerry, Elbridge	Massachusetts	1744–1814	Rodney, Caesar	Delaware	1728–1784
Gwinnett, Button	Georgia	1732–1777	Ross, George	Pennsylvania	1730–1779
Hall, Lyman	Georgia	1724–1790	Rush, Benjamin	Pennsylvania	1745–1813
Hancock, John	Massachusetts	1737–1793	Rutledge, Edward	South Carolina	1749–1800
Harrison, Benjamin	Virginia	1726–1791	Sherman, Roger	Connecticut	1721–1793
Hart, John	New Jersey	?–1779	Smith, James	Pennsylvania	1713–1806
Hewes, Joseph	North Carolina	1730–1779	Stockton, Richard	New Jersey	1730–1781
Heyward, Thomas, Jr.	South Carolina	1746–1809	Stone, Thomas	Maryland	1743–1787
Hooper, William	North Carolina	1742–1790	Taylor, George	Pennsylvania	1716–1781
Hopkins, Stephen	Rhode Island	1707–1785	Thornton, Matthew	New Hampshire	1714–1803
Hopkinson, Francis	New Jersey	1737–1791	Walton, George	Georgia	1741–1804
Huntington, Samuel	Connecticut	1731–1796	Whipple, William	New Hampshire	1730–1785
Jefferson, Thomas	Virginia	1743–1826	Williams, William	Connecticut	1731–1811
Lee, Richard Henry	Virginia	1732–1794	Wilson, James	Pennsylvania	1742–1798
Lee, Francis Lightfoot	Virginia	1734–1797	Witherspoon, John	New Jersey	1723–1794
Lewis, Francis	New York	1713–1803	Wolcott, Oliver	Connecticut	1726–1797
Livingston, Philip	New York	1716–1778	Wythe, George	Virginia	1726–1806

shall be made, the State of New Hampshire shall be entitled to choose three; Massachusetts, eight; Rhode Island and Providence Plantations, one; Connecticut, five; New York, six; New Jersey, four; Pennsylvania, eight; Delaware, one; Maryland, six; Virginia, ten; North Carolina, five; South Carolina, five; and Georgia, three.

[4] When vacancies happen in the representation from any State, the executive authority thereof shall issue writs of election to fill such vacancies.

[5] The House of Representatives shall choose their Speaker and other officers, and shall have the sole power of impeachment.

Section 3 [1] The Senate of the United States shall be composed of two Senators from each State, chosen by the legislature thereof for six years; and each Senator shall have one vote.

[2] Immediately after they shall be assembled in consequence of the first election, they shall be divided as equally as may be into three classes. The seats of the Senators of the first class shall be vacated at the expiration of the second year, of the second class at the expiration of the fourth year, and of the third class at the expiration of the sixth year, so that one-third may be chosen every second year; and if vacancies happen by resignation or otherwise during the recess of the legislature of any State, the executive thereof may make temporary appointments until the next meeting of the legislature, which shall then fill such vacancies.

[3] No person shall be a Senator who shall not have attained to the age of thirty years, and been nine years a citizen of the United States, and who shall not, when elected, be an inhabitant of that State for which he shall be chosen.

[4] The Vice-President of the United States shall be President of the Senate, but shall have no vote, unless they be equally divided.

[5] The Senate shall choose their other officers and also a President pro tempore in the absence of the Vice-President, or when he shall exercise the office of President of the United States.

[6] The Senate shall have the sole power to try all impeachments. When sitting for that purpose, they shall be on oath or affirmation. When the President of the United States is tried, the Chief Justice shall preside; and no person shall be convicted without the concurrence of two-thirds of the members present.

[7] Judgment in cases of impeachment shall not extend further than to removal from office, and disqualification to hold and enjoy any office of honor, trust, or profit under the United States; but the party convicted shall, nevertheless, be liable and subject to indictment, trial, judgment, and punishment, according to law.

Section 4 [1] The times, places, and manner of holding elections for Senators and Representatives shall be prescribed in each State by the legislature thereof; but the Congress may at any time by law make or alter such regulations, except as to the places of choosing Senators.

[2] The Congress shall assemble at least once in every year, and such meeting shall be on the first Monday in December, unless they shall by law appoint a different day.

Section 5 [1] Each House shall be the judge of the elections, returns, and qualification of its own members, and a majority of each shall constitute a quorum to do business; but a smaller number may adjourn from day to day, and may be authorized to compel the attendance of absent members, in such manner, and under such penalties, as each House may provide.

[2] Each House may determine the rules of its proceedings, punish its members for disorderly behavior, and with the concurrence of two-thirds, expel a member.

[3] Each House shall keep a journal of its

proceedings, and from time to time publish the same, excepting such parts as may in their judgment require secrecy, and the yeas and nays of the members of either House on any question shall, at the desire of one-fifth of those present, be entered on the journal.

[4] Neither House, during the session of Congress, shall, without the consent of the other, adjourn for more than three days, nor to any other place than that in which the two Houses shall be sitting.

Section 6 [1] The Senators and Representatives shall receive a compensation for their services, to be ascertained by law and paid out of the Treasury of the United States. They shall, in all cases except treason, felony, and breach of the peace, be privileged from arrest during their attendance at the session of their respective Houses, and in going to and returning from the same; and for any speech or debate in either House they shall not be questioned in any other place.

[2] No Senator or Representative shall, during the time for which he was elected, be appointed to any civil office under the authority of the United States, which shall have been created, or the emoluments whereof shall have been increased during such time; and no person holding any office under the United States shall be a member of either House during his continuance in office.

Section 7 [1] All bills for raising revenue shall originate in the House of Representatives; but the Senate may propose or concur with amendments as on other bills.

[2] Every bill which shall have passed the House of Representatives and the Senate shall, before it becomes a law, be presented to the President of the United States; if he approves he shall sign it, but if not he shall return it, with his objections, to that House in which it shall have originated, who shall enter the objections at large on their journal and proceed to reconsider it. If after such reconsideration two-thirds of that House shall agree to pass the bill, it shall be sent, together with the objections, to the other House, by which it shall likewise be reconsidered, and if approved by two-thirds of that House it shall become a law. But in all such cases the vote of both Houses shall be determined by yeas and nays, and the names of the persons voting for and against the bill shall be entered on the journal of each House respectively. If any bill shall not be returned by the President within ten days (Sundays excepted) after it shall have been presented to him, the same shall be a law, in like manner as if he had signed it, unless the Congress by their adjournment prevent its return, in which case it shall not be a law.

[3] Every order, resolution or vote to which the concurrence of the Senate and House of Representatives may be necessary (except on a question of adjournment) shall be presented to the President of the United States; and before the same shall take effect shall be approved by him, or being disapproved by him, shall be repassed by two-thirds of the Senate and House of Representatives, according to the rules and limitations prescribed in the case of a bill.

Section 8 [1] The Congress shall have power to lay and collect taxes, duties, imposts and excises, to pay the debts and provide for the common defense and general welfare of the United States; but all duties, imposts and excises shall be uniform throughout the United States;

[2] To borrow money on the credit of the United States;

[3] To regulate commerce with foreign nations, and among the several States, and with the Indian tribes;

[4] To establish an uniform rule of naturalization, and uniform laws on the subject of bankruptcies throughout the United States;

[5] To coin money, regulate the value thereof, and of foreign coin, and fix the standard of weights and measures;

[6] To provide for the punishment of counterfeiting the securities and current coin of the United States;

[7] To establish post offices and post roads;

[8] To promote the progress of science and useful arts by securing for limited times to authors and inventors the exclusive right to their respective writings and discoveries;

[9] To constitute tribunals inferior to the Supreme Court;

[10] To define and punish piracies and felonies committed on the high seas and offenses against the law of nations.

[11] To declare war, grant letters of marque and reprisal, and make rules concerning captures on land and water;

[12] To raise and support armies, but no appropriation of money to that use shall be for a longer term than two years;

[13] To provide and maintain a navy;

[14] To make rules for the government and regulation of the land and naval forces;

[15] To provide for calling forth the militia to execute the laws of the Union, suppress insurrections, and repel invasions;

[16] To provide for organizing, arming and disciplining the militia, and for governing such part of them as may be employed in the service of the United States, reserving to the States respectively the appointment of the officers, and the authority of training the militia according to the discipline prescribed by Congress;

[17] To exercise exclusive legislation in all cases whatsoever over such district (not exceeding ten miles square) as may, by cession of particular States and the acceptance of Congress, become the seat of the Government of the United States, and to exercise like authority over all places purchased by the consent of the legislature of the State in which the same shall be, for the erection of forts, magazines, arsenals, dockyards, and other needful buildings;

[18] To make all laws which shall be necessary and proper for carrying into execution the foregoing powers, and all other powers vested by this Constitution in the Government of the United States, or in any department or officer thereof.

Section 9 [1] The migration or importation of such persons as any of the States now existing shall think proper to admit shall not be prohibited by the Congress prior to the year one thousand eight hundred and eight, but a tax or duty may be imposed on such importation, not exceeding ten dollars for each person.

[2] The privilege of the writ of habeas corpus shall not be suspended, unless when in cases of rebellion or invasion the public safety may require it.

[3] No bill of attainder or ex post facto law shall be passed.

[4] No capitation or other direct tax shall be laid, unless in proportion to the census or enumeration hereinbefore directed to be taken.

[5] No tax or duty shall be laid on articles exported from any State.

[6] No preference shall be given by any regulation

of commerce or revenue to the ports of one State over those of another; nor shall vessels bound to or from one State be obliged to enter, clear or pay duties in another.

[7] No money shall be drawn from the Treasury but in consequence of appropriations made by law; and a regular statement and account of the receipts and expenditures of all public money shall be published from time to time.

[8] No title of nobility shall be granted by the United States; and no person holding any office of profit or trust under them shall, without the consent of the Congress, accept of any present, emolument, office, or title of any kind whatever from any king, prince, or foreign state.

Section 10 [1] No State shall enter into any treaty, alliance, or confederation; grant letters of marque and reprisal; coin money, emit bills of credit, make anything but gold and silver coin a tender in payment of debts; pass any bill of attainder, ex post facto law or law impairing the obligation of contracts, or grant any title of nobility.

[2] No State shall, without the consent of the Congress, lay any imposts or duties on imports or exports, except what may be absolutely necessary for executing its inspection laws; and the net produce of all duties and imposts, laid by any State on imports or exports, shall be for the use of the Treasury of the United States; and all such laws shall be subject to the revision and control of the Congress.

[3] No State shall, without the consent of Congress, lay any duty of tonnage, keep troops and ships of war in time of peace, enter into any agreement or compact with another State or with a foreign power, or engage in war, unless actually invaded or in such imminent danger as will not admit of delay.

Article II

Section 1 [1] The executive power shall be vested in a President of the United States of America. He shall hold his office during the term of four years, and together with the Vice-President, chosen for the same term, be elected as follows:

[2] Each State shall appoint, in such manner as the legislature thereof may direct, a number of Electors, equal to the whole number of Senators and Representatives to which the State may be entitled in the Congress; but no Senator or Representative, or person holding an office of trust or profit under the United States shall be appointed an Elector.

[3] The Electors shall meet in their respective States and vote by ballot for two persons, of whom one at least shall not be an inhabitant of the same State with themselves. And they shall make a list of all the persons voted for, and of the number of votes for each; which list they shall sign and certify, and transmit sealed to the seat of government of the United States, directed to the President of the Senate. The President of the Senate shall, in the presence of the Senate and House of Representatives, open all the certificates, and the votes shall then be counted. The person having the greatest number of votes shall be the President, if such number be a majority of the whole number of Electors appointed; and if there be more than one who have such majority, and have an equal number of votes, then the House of Representatives shall immediately choose by ballot one of them for President; and if no person have a majority, then from the five highest on the list the said House shall in like manner choose the President.

But in choosing the President the votes shall be taken by States, the representation from each State having one vote; a quorum for this purpose shall consist of a member or members from two-thirds of the States, and a majority of all the States shall be necessary to a choice. In every case, after the choice of the President, the person having the greatest number of votes of the Electors shall be the Vice-President. But if there should remain two or more who have equal votes, the Senate shall choose from them by ballot the Vice-President.

[4] The Congress may determine the time of choosing the Electors and the day on which they shall give their votes, which day shall be the same throughout the United States.

[5] No person except a natural-born citizen, or citizen of the United States at the time of the adoption of this Constitution, shall be eligible to the office of President; neither shall any person be eligible to that office who shall not have attained to the age of thirty-five years, and been fourteen years a resident within the United States.

[6] In case of the removal of the President from office, or of his death, resignation, or inability to discharge the powers and duties of the said office, the same shall devolve on the Vice-President, and the Congress may by law provide for the case of removal, death, resignation, or inability, both of the President and Vice-President, declaring what officer shall then act as President, and such officer shall act accordingly until the disability be removed or a President shall be elected.

[7] The President shall, at stated times, receive for his services a compensation, which shall neither be increased nor diminished during the period for which he shall have been elected, and he shall not receive within that period any other emolument from the United States or any of them.

[8] Before he enter on the execution of his office he shall take the following oath or affirmation:

"I do solemnly swear (or affirm) that I will faithfully execute the office of President of the United States, and will to the best of my ability preserve, protect, and defend the Constitution of the United States."

Section 2 [1] The President shall be Commander-in-Chief of the Army and Navy of the United States, and of the militia of the several States when called into the actual service of the United States; he may require the opinion, in writing, of the principal officer in each of the executive departments, upon any subject relating to the duties of their respective offices, and he shall have power to grant reprieves and pardons for offenses against the United States, except in cases of impeachment.

[2] He shall have power, by and with the advice and consent of the Senate, to make treaties, provided two-thirds of the Senators present concur; and he shall nominate, and, by and with the advice and consent of the Senate, shall appoint ambassadors, other public ministers and consuls, judges of the Supreme Court, and all other officers of the United States whose appointments are not herein otherwise provided for, and which shall be established by law; but the Congress may by law vest the appointment of such inferior officers, as they think proper, in the President alone, in the courts of law, or in the heads of departments.

[3] The President shall have power to fill up all vacancies that may happen during the recess of the Senate, by granting commissions which shall expire at the end of their next session.

Section 3 He shall from time to time give to the Congress information of the state of the Union, and recommend to their consideration such measures as he shall judge necessary and expedient; he may, on extraordinary occasions, convene both Houses, or either of them, and in case of disagreement between them with respect to the time of adjournment, he may adjourn them to such time as he shall think proper; he shall receive ambassadors and other public ministers; he shall take care that the laws be faithfully executed, and shall commission all the officers of the United States.

Section 4 The President, Vice-President and all civil officers of the United States shall be removed from office on impeachment for and conviction of treason, bribery, or other high crimes and misdemeanors.

Article III

Section 1 The judicial power of the United States shall be vested in one Supreme Court, and in such inferior courts as the Congress may from time to time ordain and establish. The judges, both of the Supreme and inferior courts, shall hold their offices during good behavior, and shall, at stated times, receive for their services a compensation which shall not be diminished during their continuance in office.

Section 2 [1] The judicial power shall extend to all cases, in law and equity, arising under this Constitution, the laws of the United States, and treaties made, or which shall be made, under their authority; to all cases affecting ambassadors, other public ministers, and consuls; to all cases of admiralty and maritime jurisdiction; to controversies to which the United States shall be a party; to controversies between two or more States; between a State and citizens of another State; between citizens of different States; between citizens of the same State claiming lands under grants of different States, and between a State, or the citizens thereof, and foreign states, citizens, or subjects.

[2] In all cases affecting ambassadors, other public ministers and consuls, and those in which a State shall be party, the Supreme Court shall have original jurisdiction. In all the other cases before mentioned the Supreme Court shall have appellate jurisdiction, both as to law and fact, with such exceptions and under such regulations as the Congress shall make.

[3] The trial of all crimes, except in cases of impeachment, shall be by jury; and such trial shall be held in the State where the said crimes shall have been committed; but when not committed within any State, the trial shall be at such place or places as the Congress may by law have directed.

Section 3 [1] Treason against the United States shall consist only in levying war against them, or in adhering to their enemies, giving them aid and comfort. No person shall be convicted of treason unless on the testimony of two witnesses to the same overt act, or on confession in open court.

[2] The Congress shall have power to declare the punishment of treason, but no attainder of treason shall work corruption of blood or forfeiture except during the life of the person attained.

Article IV

Section 1 Full faith and credit shall be given in each State to the public acts, records, and judicial proceedings of every other State. And the Congress may by general laws prescribe the manner in which such acts, records, and proceedings shall be proved, and the effect thereof.

Section 2 [1] The citizens of each State shall be entitled to all privileges and immunities of citizens in the several States.

[2] A person charged in any State with treason, felony, or other crime, who shall flee from justice, and be found in another State, shall, on demand of the executive authority of the State from which he fled, be delivered up, to be removed to the State having jurisdiction of the crime.

[3] No person held to service or labor in one State, under the laws thereof, escaping into another, shall, in consequence of any law or regulation therein, be discharged from such service or labor, but shall be delivered up on claim to the party to whom such service or labor may be due.

Section 3 [1] New States may be admitted by the Congress into this Union; but no new State shall be formed or erected within the jurisdiction of any other State; nor any State be formed by the junction of two or more States or parts of States, without the consent of the legislatures of the States concerned as well as of the Congress.

[2] The Congress shall have power to dispose of and make all needful rules and regulations respecting the territory or other property belonging to the United States; and nothing in this Constitution shall be so construed as to prejudice any claims of the United States or of any particular State.

Section 4 The United States shall guarantee to every State in this Union a republican form of government, and shall protect each of them against invasion, and on application of the legislature, or of the executive (when the legislature cannot be convened), against domestic violence.

Article V

The Congress, whenever two-thirds of both Houses shall deem it necessary, shall propose amendments to this Constitution, or, on the application of the legislatures of two-thirds of the several States, shall call a convention for proposing amendments, which in either case shall be valid to all intents and purposes as part of this Constitution, when ratified by the legislatures of three-fourths of the several States, or by conventions in three-fourths thereof, as the one or the other mode of ratification may be proposed by the Congress; provided that no amendment which may be made prior to the year one thousand eight hundred and eight shall in any manner affect the first and fourth clauses in the Ninth Section of the First Article; and that no State, without its consent shall be deprived of its equal suffrage in the Senate.

Article VI

[1] All debts contracted and engagements entered into, before the adoption of this Constitution, shall be as valid against the United States under this Constitution as under the Confederation.

[2] This Constitution, and the laws of the United States which shall be made in pursuance thereof, and all treaties made, or which shall be made, under the authority of the United States, shall be the supreme law of the land; and the judges in every State shall be bound thereby, anything in the Constitution or laws of any State to the contrary notwithstanding.

[3] The Senators and Representatives before mentioned, and the members of the several State legislatures, and all executive and judicial officers both of the United States and of the several States,

shall be bound by oath or affirmation to support this Constitution; but no religious test shall ever be required as a qualification to any office or public trust under the United States.

Article VII
The ratification of the conventions of nine States shall be sufficient for the establishment of this Constitution between the States so ratifying the same.

Amendments to the Constitution
[The first 10 amendments, known collectively as The Bill of Rights, were adopted in 1791.]

Amendment I
Congress shall make no law respecting an establishment of religion, or prohibiting the free exercise thereof; or abridging the freedom of speech or of the press; or the right of the people peaceably to assemble, and to petition the government for a redress of grievances.

Amendment II
A well-regulated militia being necessary to the security of a free State, the right of the people to keep and bear arms shall not be infringed.

Amendment III
No soldier shall, in time of peace, be quartered in any house without the consent of the owner, nor in time of war, but in a manner to be prescribed by law.

Amendment IV
The right of the people to be secure in their persons, houses, papers, and effects, against unreasonable searches and seizures, shall not be violated, and no warrants shall issue but upon probable cause, supported by oath or affirmation, and particularly describing the place to be searched, and the persons or things to be seized.

Amendment V
No person shall be held to answer for a capital, or otherwise infamous crime, unless on a presentment or indictment of a grand jury, except in cases arising in the land or naval forces, or in the militia, when in actual service in time of war or public danger; nor shall any person be subject for the same offense to be twice put in jeopardy of life or limb; nor shall be compelled in any criminal case to be a witness against himself, nor be deprived of life, liberty or property, without due process of law; nor shall private property be taken for public use without just compensation.

Amendment VI
In all criminal prosecutions, the accused shall enjoy the right to a speedy and public trial, by an impartial jury of the State and district wherein the crime shall have been committed, which district shall have been previously ascertained by law, and to be informed of the nature and cause of the accusation; to be confronted with the witnesses against him; to have compulsory process for obtaining witnesses in his favor, and to have the assistance of counsel for his defense.

Amendment VII
In suits at common law, where the value in controversy shall exceed twenty dollars, the right of trial by jury shall be preserved, and no fact tried by a jury shall be otherwise re-examined in any court of the United States, than according to the rules of the common law.

Amendment VIII
Excessive bail shall not be required, nor excessive fines imposed, nor cruel and unusual punishments inflicted.

Amendment IX
The enumeration in the Constitution of certain rights shall not be construed to deny or disparage others retained by the people.

Amendment X
The powers not delegated to the United States by the Constitution, nor prohibited by it to the States, are reserved to the States respectively, or to the people.

Amendment XI   [Adopted Jan. 8, 1798]
The judicial power of the United States shall not be construed to extend to any suit in law or equity, commenced or prosecuted against one of the United States by citizens of another State, or by citizens or subjects of any foreign state.

Amendment XII   [Adopted Sept. 25, 1804]
[1] The Electors shall meet in their respective States and vote by ballot for President and Vice-President, one of whom, at least, shall not be an inhabitant of the same State with themselves; they shall name in their ballots the person voted for as President, and in distinct ballots the person voted for as Vice-President, and they shall make distinct lists of all persons voted for as President and of all persons voted for as Vice-President, and of the number of votes for each; which lists they shall sign and certify, and transmit sealed to the seat of the government of the United States, directed to the President of the Senate. The President of the Senate shall, in the presence of the Senate and House of Representatives, open all the certificates and the votes shall then be counted. The person having the greatest number of votes for President shall be the President, if such number be a majority of the whole number of Electors appointed; and if no person have such majority, then from the persons having the highest numbers not exceeding three on the list of those voted for as President, the House of Representatives shall choose immediately, by ballot, the President. But in choosing the President the votes shall be taken by States, the representation from each State having one vote; a quorum for this purpose shall consist of a member or members from two-thirds of the States, and a majority of all the States shall be necessary to a choice. And if the House of Representatives shall not choose a President whenever the right of choice shall devolve upon them, before the fourth day of March next following, then the Vice-President shall act as President, as in the case of the death or other constitutional disability of the President.

[2] The person having the greatest number of votes as Vice-President shall be the Vice-President, if such number be a majority of the whole number of Electors appointed; and if no person have a majority, then from the two highest numbers on the list the Senate shall choose the Vice-President; a quorum for the purpose shall consist of two-thirds of the whole number of Senators, and a majority of the whole number shall be

necessary to a choice. But no person constitutionally ineligible to the office of President shall be eligible to that of Vice-President of the United States.

Amendment XIII [Adopted Dec. 18, 1865]

Section 1 Neither slavery nor involuntary servitude, except as a punishment for crime whereof the party shall have been duly convicted, shall exist within the United States, or any place subject to their jurisdiction.

Section 2 Congress shall have power to enforce this article by appropriate legislation.

Amendment XIV [Adopted July 28, 1868]

Section 1 All persons born or naturalized in the United States, and subject to the jurisdiction thereof, are citizens of the United States and of the State wherein they reside. No State shall make or enforce any law which shall abridge the privileges or immunities of citizens of the United States; nor shall any State deprive any person of life, liberty or property, without due process of law; nor deny to any person within its jurisdiction the equal protection of the laws.

Section 2 Representatives shall be apportioned among the several States according to their respective numbers, counting the whole number of persons in each State, excluding Indians not taxed. But when the right to vote at any election for the choice of Electors for President and Vice-President of the United States, Representatives in Congress, the executive and judicial officers of a State, or the members of the legislature thereof, is denied to any of the male inhabitants of such State, being twenty-one years of age, and citizens of the United States, or in any way abridged except for participation in rebellion or other crime, the basis of representation therein shall be reduced in the proportion which the number of such male citizens shall bear to the whole number of male citizens twenty-one years of age in such State.

Section 3 No person shall be a Senator or Representative in Congress, or elector of President and Vice-President, or hold any office, civil or military, under the United States or under any State, who, having previously taken an oath as a member of Congress, or as an officer of the United States, or as a member of any State legislature, or as an executive or judicial officer of any State, to support the Constitution of the United States, shall have engaged in insurrection or rebellion against the same, or given aid or comfort to the enemies thereof. But Congress may, by a vote of two-thirds of each House, remove such disability.

Section 4 The validity of the public debt of the United States, authorized by law, including debts incurred for payment of pensions and bounties for services in suppressing insurrection or rebellion, shall not be questioned. But neither the United States nor any State shall assume or pay any debt or obligation incurred in aid of insurrection or rebellion against the United States, or any claim for the loss or emancipation of any slave; but all such debts, obligations, and claims shall be held illegal and void.

Section 5 The Congress shall have power to enforce, by appropriate legislation, the provisions of this article.

Amendment XV [Adopted Mar. 30, 1870]

Section 1 The right of citizens of the United States to vote shall not be denied or abridged by the United States or by any State on account of race, color, or previous condition of servitude.

Section 2 The Congress shall have power to enforce this article by appropriate legislation.

Amendment XVI [Adopted Feb. 25, 1913]

The Congress shall have power to lay and collect taxes on incomes, from whatever source derived, without apportionment among the several States, and without regard to any census or enumeration.

Amendment XVII [Adopted May 31, 1913]

Section 1 The Senate of the United States shall be composed of two Senators from each State, elected by the people thereof, for six years; and each Senator shall have one vote. The electors in each State shall have the qualifications requisite for electors of the most numerous branch of the State legislatures.

Section 2 When vacancies happen in the representation of any State in the Senate, the executive authority of such State shall issue writs of election to fill such vacancies: Provided, that the legislature of any State may empower the executive thereof to make temporary appointments until the people fill the vacancies by election as the legislature may direct.

Section 3 This amendment shall not be so construed as to affect the election or term of any Senator chosen before it becomes valid as part of the Constitution.

Amendment XVIII [Adopted Jan. 29, 1919]

Section 1 After one year from the ratification of this article the manufacture, sale or transportation of intoxicating liquors within, the importation thereof into, or the exportation thereof from the United States and all territory subject to the jurisdiction thereof, for beverage purposes, is hereby prohibited.

Section 2 The Congress and the several States shall have concurrent power to enforce this article by appropriate legislation.

Section 3 This article shall be inoperative unless it shall have been ratified as an amendment to the Constitution by the legislatures of the several States, as provided in the Constitution, within seven years from the date of the submission hereof to the States by the Congress.

Amendment XIX [Adopted Aug. 26, 1920]

Section 1 The right of citizens of the United States to vote shall not be denied or abridged by the United States or by any State on account of sex.

Section 2 Congress shall have power to enforce this article by appropriate legislation.

Amendment XX [Adopted Feb. 6, 1933]

Section 1 The terms of the President and Vice-President shall end at noon on the 20th day of January, and the terms of Senators and Representatives at noon on the 3d day of January, of the years in which such terms would have ended if this article had not been ratified; and the terms of their successors shall then begin.

Section 2 The Congress shall assemble at least once in every year, and such meeting shall begin at noon on the 3d day of January, unless they shall by law appoint a different day.

Section 3 If, at the time fixed for the beginning of the term of the President, the President-elect shall have died, the Vice-President-elect shall become President. If a President shall not have been chosen before the time fixed for the beginning of his term or if the President-elect shall have failed to qualify, then the Vice-President-elect shall act as President until a President shall have qualified; and the Congress may by law provide for the case wherein neither a President-elect nor a Vice-President-elect shall have qualified, declaring who shall then act as President, or the manner in which one who is to act shall be selected, and such person shall act accordingly until a President or Vice-President shall have qualified.

Section 4 The Congress may by law provide for the case of the death of any of the persons from whom the House of Representatives may choose a President whenever the right of choice shall have devolved upon them, and for the case of death of any of the persons from whom the Senate may choose a Vice-President whenever the right of choice shall have devolved upon them.

Section 5 Sections 1 and 2 shall take effect on the 15th day of October following the ratification of this article.

Section 6 This article shall be inoperative unless it shall have been ratified as an amendment to the Constitution by the legislatures of three-fourths of the several States within seven years from the date of its submission.

Amendment XXI [Adopted Dec. 5, 1933]

Section 1 The eighteenth article of amendment to the Constitution of the United States is hereby repealed.

Section 2 The transportation or importation into any State, territory, or possession of the United States for delivery or use therein of intoxicating liquors, in violation of the laws thereof, is hereby prohibited.

Section 3 This article shall be inoperative unless it shall have been ratified as an amendment to the Constitution by conventions in the several States, as provided in the Constitution, within seven years from the date of the submission hereof to the States by the Congress.

Amendment XXII [Adopted Feb. 26, 1951]

Section 1 No person shall be elected to the office of President more than twice, and no person who has held the office of President, or acted as President, for more than two years of a term to which some other person was elected President shall be elected to the office of President more than once. But this Article shall not apply to any person holding the office of President when this Article was proposed by the Congress, and shall not prevent any person who may be holding the office of President, or acting as President, during the term within which this Article becomes operative from holding the office of President or acting as President during the remainder of such term.

Section 2 This article shall be inoperative unless it shall have been ratified as an amendment to the Constitution by the legislatures of three-fourths of the several States within seven years from the date of its submission to the States by the Congress.

Amendment XXIII [Adopted Apr. 3, 1961]

Section 1 The District constituting the seat of Government of the United States shall appoint in such manner as the Congress may direct:

A number of electors of President and Vice President equal to the whole number of Senators and Representatives in Congress to which the District would be entitled if it were a State, but in no event more than the least populous State; they shall be in addition to those appointed by the States, but they shall be considered, for the purposes of the election of President and Vice-President, to be electors appointed by a State; and they shall meet in the District and perform such duties as provided by the twelfth article of amendment.

Section 2 The Congress shall have power to enforce this article by appropriate legislation.

Amendment XXIV [Adopted Jan. 23, 1964]

Section 1 The right of citizens of the United States to vote in any primary or other election for President or Vice-President, for electors for President or Vice-President, or for Senator or Representative in Congress, shall not be denied or abridged by the United States or any State by reason of failure to pay any poll tax or other tax.

Section 2 The Congress shall have power to enforce this article by appropriate legislation.

Amendment XXV [Adopted Feb. 10, 1967]

Section 1 In case of the removal of the President from office or of his death or resignation, the Vice-President shall become President.

Section 2 Whenever there is a vacancy in the office of the Vice-President, the President shall nominate a Vice-President who shall take office upon confirmation by a majority vote of both Houses of Congress.

Section 3 Whenever the President transmits to the President pro tempore of the Senate and the Speaker of the House of Representatives his written declaration that he is unable to discharge the powers and duties of his office, and until he transmits to them a written declaration to the contrary, such powers and duties shall be discharged by the Vice-President as Acting President.

Section 4 Whenever the Vice-President and a majority of either the principal officers of the executive departments or of such other body as Congress may by law provide, transmit to the President pro tempore of the Senate and the Speaker of the House of Representatives their written declaration that the President is unable to discharge the powers and duties of his office, the Vice-President shall immediately assume the powers and duties of the office as Acting President.

Thereafter, when the President transmits to the President pro tempore of the Senate and the Speaker of the House of Representatives his written declaration that no inability exists, he shall resume the powers and duties of his office unless the Vice-President and a majority of either the principal officers of the executive department or of such other body as Congress may by law provide, transmit within four days to the President pro tempore of the Senate and the Speaker of the House of Representatives their written declaration that the President is unable to discharge the powers and duties of his office. Thereupon Congress shall decide the issue, assembling within forty-eight hours for that purpose if not in session. If the Congress, within twenty-one days after receipt of the latter written declaration, or, if Congress is not in session, within twenty-one days after Congress is required to assemble, determines by two-thirds vote of both Houses that the President is unable to discharge the powers and duties of his office, the Vice-President shall continue to discharge the same as Acting President; otherwise the President shall resume the powers and duties of his office.

Amendment XXVI [Adopted June 30, 1971]

Section 1 The right of citizens of the United States, who are eighteen years of age or older, to vote shall not be denied or abridged by the United States or by any State on account of age.

Section 2 The Congress shall have power to enforce this article by appropriate legislation.

Amendment XXVII [Adopted May 18, 1992]
No law, varying the compensation for the services of the Senators and Representatives, shall take effect until an election of Representatives shall have intervened.

▶ THE EMANCIPATION PROCLAMATION

On July 22, 1862, Abraham Lincoln read to his cabinet a preliminary draft of an emancipation proclamation. Secretary of State William Seward suggested that the proclamation not be issued until a military victory had been won. The battle of Antietam gave Lincoln his desired opportunity, and on Sept. 22, he read to his cabinet a second draft of the proclamation. After some changes this was issued as a preliminary proclamation; the formal and definite proclamation came Jan. 1, 1863.

A Proclamation.

Whereas on the 22nd day of September, A.D. 1862, a proclamation was issued by the President of the United States, containing among other things, the following, to wit:

"That on the 1st day of January, A.D. 1863, all persons held as slaves within any State or designated part of a State the people whereof shall then be in rebellion against the United States shall be then, thenceforward, and forever free; and the executive government of the United States, including the military and naval authority thereof, will recognize and maintain the freedom of such persons and will do no act or acts to repress such persons, or any of them, in any efforts they may make for their actual freedom.

"That the executive will on the 1st day of January aforesaid, by proclamation, designate the States and parts of States, if any, in which the people thereof, respectively, shall then be in rebellion against the United States; and the fact that any State or the people thereof shall on that day be in good faith represented in the Congress of the United States by members chosen thereto at elections wherein a majority of the qualified voters of such States shall have participated shall, in the absence of strong countervailing testimony, be deemed conclusive evidence that such State and the people thereof are not then in rebellion against the United States."

Now, therefore, I, Abraham Lincoln, President of the United States, by virtue of the power in me vested as Commander-in-Chief of the Army and Navy of the United States in time of actual armed rebellion against the authority and government of the United States, and as a fit and necessary war measure for suppressing said rebellion, do, on this 1st day of January, A.D. 1863, and in accordance with my purpose so to do, publicly proclaimed for the full period of one hundred days from the first day above mentioned, order and designate as the States and parts of States wherein the people thereof, respectively, are this day in rebellion against the United States the following, to wit:

Arkansas, Texas, Louisiana (except the parishes of St. Bernard, Plaquemines, Jefferson, St. John, St. Charles, St. James, Ascension, Assumption, Terrebonne, Lafourche, St. Mary, St. Martin, and Orleans, including the city of New Orleans), Mississippi, Alabama, Florida, Georgia, South Carolina, North Carolina, and Virginia (except the forty-eight counties designated as West Virginia, and also the counties of Berkeley, Accomac, Northhampton, Elizabeth City, York, Princess Anne, and Norfolk, including the cities of Norfolk and Portsmouth), and which excepted parts are for the present left precisely as if this proclamation were not issued.

And by virtue of the power and for the purpose aforesaid, I do order and declare that all persons held as slaves within said designated States and parts of States are, and henceforward shall be, free; and that the Executive Government of the United States, including the military and naval authorities thereof, will recognize and maintain the freedom of said persons.

And I hereby enjoin upon the people so declared to be free to abstain from all violence, unless in necessary self-defense; and I recommend to them that, in all cases when allowed, they labor faithfully for reasonable wages.

And I further declare and make known that such persons of suitable condition will be received into the armed service of the United States to garrison forts, positions, stations, and other places, and to man vessels of all sorts in said service.

And upon this act, sincerely believed to be an act of justice, warranted by the Constitution upon military necessity, I invoke the considerate judgment of mankind and the gracious favor of Almighty God.

▶ THE GETTYSBURG ADDRESS

Abraham Lincoln's most famous and most eloquent words were delivered on Nov. 19, 1863, at the dedication of the cemetery that held the remains of the 45,000 soldiers who fell at the Battle of Gettysburg, a significant Union victory.

"Fourscore and seven years ago our fathers brought forth on this continent, a new nation, conceived in Liberty, and dedicated to the proposition that all men are created equal.

"Now we are engaged in a great civil war, testing whether that nation or any nation so conceived and so dedicated, can long endure. We are met on a great battle-field of that war. We have come to dedicate a portion of that field, as a final resting place for those who here gave their lives that that nation might live. It is altogether fitting and proper that we should do this.

"But, in a larger sense, we can not dedicate—we can not consecrate—we can not hallow—this ground. The brave men, living and dead, who struggled here, have consecrated it, far above our poor power to add or detract. The world will little note, nor long remember what we say here, but it can never forget what they did here. It is for us the living, rather, to be dedicated here to the unfinished work which they who fought here have thus far so nobly advanced. It is rather for us to be here dedicated to the great task remaining before us—that from these honored dead we take increased devotion to that cause for which they gave the last full measure of devotion—that we here highly resolve that these dead shall not have died in vain—that this nation, under God, shall have a new birth of freedom—and that government of the people, by the people, for the people, shall not perish from the earth."

▶ PLEDGE OF ALLEGIANCE

The original version of the Pledge of Allegiance appeared in the September 8, 1892, issue of *Youth's Companion* magazine. Authorship was in dispute between magazine staffers Francis Bellamy and James B. Upham until 1939, when the United States Flag Association declared Bellamy the author, and the Library of Congress concurred in 1957. Congress mandated two wording changes in the original version by substituting "the flag of the United States of America" for "my flag" in 1923, and adding "under God" in 1954. Public schools throughout the United States made the daily Pledge of Allegiance obligatory, and students who refused were expelled until the Supreme Court ruled in *West Virginia Board of Education v. Barnette* (1943) that the First Amendment protected the "right of silence" as well as freedom of speech.

"I pledge allegiance to the flag of the United States of America, and to the Republic, for which it stands, one nation, under God, indivisible, with liberty and justice for all."

CHRONOLOGY OF U.S. HISTORY

c. 1000 Viking explorer Leif Ericson explores North American coast and founds temporary colony called Vinland.

1492 On first voyage to America, Christopher Columbus lands at San Salvador island in Bahamas.

1493 Pope Alexander VI divides New World between Spain and Portugal.

1497 John Cabot claims Newfoundland for King Henry VII of England.

1499 Florentine merchant Amerigo Vespucci visits New World and begins writing popular accounts of his voyages.

1506 Columbus dies poor and embittered, convinced he found a new route to Asia and refusing to believe he discovered new continent.

1507 German mapmaker Martin Waldseemüller, after reading Vespucci's descriptions of the New World, names it "America" after him.

1513 Juan Ponce de León discovers Florida. Vasco Nuñez de Balboa crosses Panama and sights Pacific Ocean.

1519 Hernán Cortés lands in Mexico.

1520 Ferdinand Magellan, leader of the first expedition to circumnavigate the globe, discovers the South American straits that bear his name. In 1521, he is killed in the Philippines by natives.

1522 Cortés captures Mexico City and conquers Aztec empire.

1524 Giovanni de Verrazano, commissioned by King Francis I of France, discovers New York harbor and Hudson River.

1534 Jacques Cartier of France explores coast of Newfoundland and Gulf of St. Lawrence.

1536 Traveling overland from Gulf of Mexico, Alvar Núñez Cabeza de Vaca reaches Gulf of California.

1539 Fernando de Soto conquers Florida and begins three-year trek across Southeast.

1540 Francisco Vásquez de Coronado explores Southwest, discovering Grand Canyon and introducing horses to North America.

1541 Coronado discovers Mississippi River.

1542 João Rodrígues Cabrilho explores coast of California, missing San Francisco Bay.

1565 Don Pedro Menéndez de Aviles founds first permanent European settlement in North America at St. Augustine, Florida.

1572 Sir Francis Drake of England makes first voyage to America, landing in Panama.

1576 English explorer Martin Frobisher searches for Northwest Passage.

1577 Drake begins voyage of plunder around the world.

1579 Drake lands north of San Francisco Bay and claims region for Queen Elizabeth I.

1584 Sir Walter Raleigh discovers Roanoke Island. He names land Virginia, after Queen Elizabeth.

1585 Raleigh establishes England's first American colony at Roanoke.

1586 Drake evacuates surviving Roanoke settlers.

1587 Raleigh resettles Roanoke with 150 new colonists. Virginia Dare first child of English parents born in America.

1591 Relief expedition returns to the Roanoke colony; all settlers disappeared without trace.

1602 Captain Bartholomew Gosnold, first Englishman to set foot in New England, explores Cape Cod and Martha's Vineyard.

1603 Samuel de Champlain of France explores St. Lawrence Seaway, later founds Quebec.

1607 First permanent English settlement in America established at Jamestown, Virginia. Only 32 of original 105 colonists survive first winter.

1608 Captain John Smith imprisoned by Indians and saved by Pocahontas, daughter of Chief Powhatan.

1609 Henry Hudson sets out in search of Northwest Passage. Champlain sails into Great Lakes.

1611 Hudson cast adrift by mutinous crewmen to die in bay named after him.

1612 First Dutch trading post appears on Manhattan Island.

1616 Smallpox epidemic decimates Indian tribes from Maine to Rhode Island.

1619 Dutch traders bring first African slaves to Virginia for sale. Americans hold first election when Virginia planters vote for House of Burgesses.

1620 Pilgrims and others arrive in Plymouth, Massachusetts, aboard *Mayflower.* They draw up the Mayflower Compact.

1622 Most of Virginia colony wiped out in an Indian attack.

1624 King James I revokes Virginia's charter and makes it royal colony.

1626 The Dutch colony of New Amsterdam founded on Manhattan Island, bought from Indians for about $24.

1630 John Winthrop sets sail for Massachusetts with 900 Puritans and others, beginning Great Migration to New England.

1632 King Charles I of England grants Lord Baltimore charter to establish colony in Maryland.

1634 Massachusetts adopts representative government. Jean Nicolet of France begins trading with Indians in Wisconsin.

1635 Roger Williams, banished from Massachusetts, founds dissident colony of Rhode Island.

1636 New Englanders massacre hundreds of Indians in Pequot War. Harvard College established.

1638 First Swedish colony founded in Delaware.

1639 "Oath of a Free Man" the first English document printed in America. First public school appears in Dorchester, first post office in Boston, and Connecticut writes first colonial constitution.

1644 Indians make last unsuccessful attempt to expel English settlers from Virginia. First American ship built in Boston.

1647 Margaret Brent of Maryland first American woman to demand right to vote. Massachusetts passes first compulsory education law. First witchcraft execution occurs in Hartford, Conn.

1648 Boston shoemakers and coopers establish first American labor unions.

1651 Parliament passes first Navigation Act regulating colonial trade.

1652 Rhode Island first colony to outlaw slavery. First American coins minted in Boston.

1654 Jacob Barsimon, first American Jew, arrives in New Amsterdam, followed by 23 more Jews from Brazil.
1655 Dutch colonists capture Swedish colony in Delaware. Lady Deborah Moody of Long Island first American woman to vote.
1656 First Quakers arrive in America; imprisoned in Boston, beaten, and deported.
1659 Massachusetts hangs two Quakers on Boston Common.
1660 Parliament forbids Americans to export goods to countries other than England. Massachusetts outlaws celebration of Christmas.
1661 Virginia becomes the first colony to recognize slavery as legal.
1662 Connecticut granted royal charter. Massachusetts appoints official press censors and institutes half-way covenant.
1663 Parliament requires colonial imports from Europe to pass first through England. King Charles II grants charters to Carolina and Rhode Island
1664 New Amsterdam captured by Richard Nicolls, who renames it New York. New Jersey established.
1670 Charles Town, later called Charleston, first permanent settlement in Carolina.
1672 Parliament tightens trade restrictions on colonies and appoints American customs collectors.
1673 French explorers Jacques Marquette and Louis Joliet paddle down Mississippi River to Arkansas. Regular mail service begins between Boston and New York. Dutch forces recapture New York.
1674 Treaty of Westminster restores New York to England. King Louis XIV of France sends Sieur de La Salle to explore Mississippi River.
1675 Thousands die in King Philip's War between New Englanders and five Indian tribes.
1676 Bacon's Rebellion overthrows government of Virginia and burns down Jamestown.
1680 New Hampshire separated from Massachusetts and made royal colony.
1681 King Charles II names William Penn proprietor of Pennsylvania.
1682 Penn founds Philadelphia. Sieur de La Salle claims North American interior for France, naming it Louisiana.
1683 First German-Americans, group of Mennonites, arrive in Philadelphia.
1684 King Charles II revokes Massachusetts charter.
1686 King James II appoints Sir Edmund Andros governor-general of Dominion of New England, dissolving colonial governments.
1688 Quakers publish first anti-slavery tracts in Pennsylvania.
1689 Andros surrenders to Boston mobs and colonial self-government is reestablished. Jacob Leisler seizes power in New York uprising. King William's War begins in America.
1690 Massachusetts issues first colonial paper money. American campaigns against French Canada fail. French and Indians burn Schenectady, N.Y.
1691 Jacob Leisler surrenders and is hanged. Massachusetts rechartered with religious freedom.
1692 Witchcraft hysteria breaks out in Salem, Mass., leading to 20 executions.
1693 College of William and Mary chartered, the second college in America.
1695 New York City organizes public relief for poor and homeless.

1696 Parliament places more commercial restrictions on colonies. American merchants join slave trade.
1697 Treaty of Ryswick ends King William's War.
1701 Antoine de la Mothe Cadillac establishes French outpost at Detroit, Michigan. Yale College founded. Delaware separated from Pennsylvania.
1702 Queen Anne's War breaks out.
1704 *Boston News-Letter* first regularly published newspaper in America.
1710 German Migration to America begins. British and American forces capture Port Royal, Nova Scotia.
1711 Anglo-American attack on Quebec fails. Tuscarora Indian War breaks out in North Carolina.
1712 Militia quell slave rebellion in New York City. Pennsylvania prohibits importing slaves.
1713 Treaty of Utrecht ends Queen Anne's War.
1716 First American theater built in Williamsburg, Va. Slavery introduced to French Louisiana.
1718 Jean Baptiste le Moyne founds French city of New Orleans.
1721 Sir Robert Walpole loosens colonial trade restrictions with policy of "salutary neglect."
1722 France declares New Orleans capital of Louisiana.
1723 America's first business corporation chartered in Connecticut.
1724 France expels all Jews from Louisiana.
1728 First American synagogue built in New York City.
1729 North and South Carolina receive royal charters.
1731 Benjamin Franklin founds first American library in Philadelphia.
1732 King George II grants charter to Georgia. Only Catholic church in colonial America opens in Philadelphia. Benjamin Franklin begins publishing *Poor Richard's Almanac*. George Washington born in Virginia.
1733 Parliament passes the Molasses Act, taxing imports from non-British sugar islands.
1734 Beginning of Great Awakening, widespread religious revival.
1735 French begin settling in Illinois.
1737 Boston holds its first public celebration of St. Patrick's Day.
1739 War of Jenkin's Ear begins. South Carolina slaves mount Stono Rebellion. French explorers Pierre and Paul Mallet discover Rocky Mountains.
1741 Danish navigator Vitus Bering, hired by Peter the Great of Russia, explores coast of Alaska. *American Magazine*, first in colonies, begins publishing in Philadelphia. Slave insurrection panic sweeps New York City.
1742 First sugar cane planted in Louisiana.
1744 King George's War breaks out.
1745 British and Americans capture Fort Louisbourg on Cape Breton Island. French and Indians raid Maine.
1748 Treaty of Aix-la-Chapelle ends King George's War and returns Fort Louisbourg to France.
1751 Parliament forbids New England colonies to issue paper money.
1752 Benjamin Franklin conducts famous kite experiment. Liberty bell is cracked in Philadelphia.
1753 Governor Dinwiddie of Virginia sends George Washington into Ohio country to demand withdrawal of French. First steam engine arrives in America.
1754 Washington skirmishes with French patrol, touching off French and Indian War. Franklin presents Albany Plan of Union for colonies.

1755 Quakers withdraw from Pennsylvania assembly rather than vote for military spending. Washington leads retreat from Battle of the Wilderness.

1758 British and American forces lose Battle of Ticonderoga, but capture Louisbourg and Fort Duquesne. New Jersey sets aside first Indian reservation for Onami tribe.

1759 General Wolfe defeats General Montcalm as British capture Quebec. Both generals fall in battle.

1760 After fall of Montreal, all of New France surrenders to Britain. King George III crowned in England.

1762 King Louis XV of France secretly cedes Louisiana to Spain.

1763 Treaty of Paris ends French and Indian War. France cedes Canada to Britain. King George III prohibits Americans to settle in West. Conspiracy of Pontiac threatens frontier.

1764 Parliament passes Sugar Act and forbids all colonies to issue paper money. French settlers found St. Louis. "Paxton Boys" march on Philadelphia. In Boston, James Otis protests, "no taxation without representation."

1765 Parliament passes Stamp Act (tax on newspapers, legal documents, etc.) and Quartering Act (requiring housing of British soldiers in homes). Sons of Liberty organize resistance and non-importation throughout colonies. Stamp Act Congress meets in New York.

1766 Parliament repeals the Stamp Act, but passes Declaratory Act affirming its right to pass laws binding on colonies. Chief Pontiac makes peace.

1767 Parliament enacts Townshend Duties and suspends New York assembly for resisting Quartering Act.

1768 "Regulators" rebel in North Carolina. Boston riots against Townshend Duties.

1769 Daniel Boone explores Kentucky. Father Junipero Serra founds San Diego, first Spanish mission in California. Gaspar de Portola sails into San Francisco Bay.

1770 Five Americans perish in Boston Massacre (Mar. 5). Parliament repeals Townshend Duties, except tax on tea.

1772 Rhode Island mob burns British revenue ship *Gaspee*. Boston appoints first Committee of Correspondence.

1773 Parliament passes Tea Act, leading to Boston Tea Party (Dec. 16).

1774 Parliament passes "Intolerable Acts" punishing colonists for Tea Party. Boston is occupied by British forces. First Continental Congress meets in Philadelphia.

1775 American Revolution begins with Battle of Lexington and Concord (Apr. 19). Second Continental Congress appoints George Washington as commander of Continental Army. British win Battle of Bunker Hill. First abolition society organized in Pennsylvania.

1776 Tom Paine's *Common Sense* published. Declaration of Independence signed. Congress adopts name, "United States of America." British occupy New York City. Washington crosses Delaware to win Battle of Trenton, N.J.

1777 Americans win battles at Princeton and Saratoga. British occupy Philadelphia. Congress adopts Stars and Stripes flag and endorses Articles of Confederation. Washington's army spends winter at Valley Forge, Pa.

1778 France makes alliance with U.S. and declares war on Britain. When French fleet arrives, British evacuate Philadelphia.

1779 Congress offers to make peace in exchange for independence. British withdraw from New York City.

1780 Pennsylvania first state to abolish slavery. British occupy Charleston, S.C. Washington quells Continental Army mutiny. Benedict Arnold defects to British.

1781 French and American victory at Battle of Yorktown ends the American Revolution. Articles of Confederation take effect. Los Angeles founded by Spanish missionaries.

1782 Parliament votes for peace with U.S. Negotiations in Paris lead to provisional Anglo-American peace treaty. Virginia permits owners to free their slaves. First English Bible printed in America.

1783 Massachusetts, Connecticut, and Rhode Island abolish slavery. Treaty of Paris signed (Sept. 3), officially ending American Revolution . Washington retires to Mount Vernon, Va.

1784 Congress ratifies Treaty of Paris. Spain closes Mississippi River to American trade. First bale of American cotton shipped to Britain.

1785 First state university chartered in Georgia.

1786 Virginia proclaims religious freedom. Shays's Rebellion put down in Massachusetts. Annapolis Convention calls for revising Articles of Confederation. New Jersey abolishes slavery.

1787 Convention in Philadelphia writes Constitution. Congress passes Northwest Ordinance and submits Constitution for state approval.

1788 Constitution ratified by New Hampshire (June 21), the ninth state to do so thereby marking its final approval.

1789 Constitution takes effect (March 4). George Washington wins first presidential election unopposed. Federal government begins meeting in New York City. Congress enacts first Federal tariff.

1790 First antislavery petitions are submitted to Congress. Temporary capital moved to Philadelphia. Pope Pius VI appoints John Carroll first Catholic bishop in U.S. First U.S. census lists population at 3,929,625.

1791 Congress sets up First Bank of the United States and first internal revenue law, a tax on whiskey. Vermont enters union as 14th state. Bill of Rights takes effect. Pres. Washington selects site of new U.S. capital on the Potomac River.

1792 New York stock traders begin meeting under a tree on Wall Street. President Washington is unanimously reelected. Construction begins on White House.

1793 Eli Whitney invents cotton gin. Congress passes first Fugitive Slave Act. President Washington holds first official cabinet meeting and lays cornerstone for Capitol. Britain begins confiscating American ships trading with France.

1794 President Washington defeats Whiskey Rebellion in Pennsylvania. U.S. and Britain sign Jay's Treaty. Ohio Indians defeated at Battle of Fallen Timbers.

1795 Georgia stung by scandal of Yazoo land frauds. Senate ratifies Jay's Treaty with Britain.

1796 President Washington delivers "Farewell Address." France begins to confiscate ships trading with Britain.

1797 France insults American diplomats in XYZ Affair. Spanish begin building Mission San Juan Capistrano in California.

1798 Georgia last state to abolish slave trade. Congress passes Alien and Sedition Acts. U.S. renounces alliance with France as unofficial naval war breaks out.

1799 Russian-American trading company set up in Alaska. New York abolishes slavery.

1800 Library of Congress founded. Convention of 1800 signed, ending quasi-war between U.S. and France. Spain secretly cedes Louisiana to France. Congress begins meeting in Washington.
1801 Election of Thomas Jefferson results in first transfer of executive power between rival parties. Congress takes jurisdiction over District of Columbia. Tripoli pirates declare war on U.S.
1802 U.S. Military Academy established at West Point, N.Y.
1803 Louisiana Purchase from France doubles size of the U.S. Federal outpost founded at Fort Dearborn, Illinois, future site of Chicago.
1804 Lewis and Clark expedition sets out from St. Louis. Alexander Hamilton killed in duel with Aaron Burr.
1805 Barbary War with Tripoli ends.
1806 Congress authorizes construction of Cumberland Road. Noah Webster's first dictionary published.
1807 Britain and France enact blockades in Europe, confiscating American trading ships. British attack USS *Chesapeake*. Embargo Act forbids all American exports.
1808 Congress declares end to African slave trade.
1809 Embargo Act replaced with Non-Intercourse Act, outlawing exports to Britain and France. First steamboat sea voyage made from New York City to Philadelphia.
1810 President Madison annexes West Florida.
1811 Worst earthquake in U.S. history rocks Ohio-Mississippi valleys. Russians settle at Ft. Ross, California. First Bank of the United States fails to obtain recharter. Gen. William Henry Harrison defeats Indians at Battle of Tippecanoe.
1812 War of 1812 begins by close vote in Congress. New England resists war. British clamp blockade on U.S. ports, capture Detroit, and repel American attack on Canada at Queenstown.
1813 Americans regain Detroit, attack Toronto and Ft. George in Canada, but surrender to British at Beaver Dams, Ontario. Captain Oliver H. Perry wins control of the Great Lakes. British and Indians burn Buffalo, N.Y.
1814 British destroy Fort Oswego, N.Y., and set fire to Washington, D.C. Francis Scott Key writes "The Star Spangled Banner." New Englanders opposed to war meet secretly at Hartford Convention. First textile mill established at Waltham, Mass. Treaty of Ghent ends War of 1812.
1815 General Andrew Jackson routs British at Battle of New Orleans, before news arrives that War of 1812 is over.
1816 Congress charters Second Bank of the U.S.
1817 Rush-Bagot Treaty between Britain and U.S. demilitarizes Great Lakes. New York Stock and Exchange Board organized. Work begins on Erie Canal. Indian attack starts Seminole War in Florida.
1818 Cumberland Road opened. Congress adopts present format for American flag. Canadian boundary dispute with Britain settled.
1819 Panic of 1819 plunges South and West into depression. U.S. obtains Florida from Spain in Adams-Onís Treaty, settling border of Louisiana. *Savannah* makes first successful trans-Atlantic crossing under steam power.
1820 Missouri Compromise solves crisis over admission of Missouri as slave state. Abolitionists begin colonizing freed slaves to Africa.
1821 First Catholic cathedral in U.S. built in Baltimore.

1822 Denmark Vesey and 36 others executed for organizing rebel slave conspiracy in Charleston, S.C.
1823 Monroe Doctrine, masterminded by Secy. of State John Quincy Adams, announced by Pres. Monroe.
1824 Russia and U.S. settle territorial disputes in Pacific Northwest. First presidential nominating convention held in Utica, N.Y.
1825 John Quincy Adams chosen President in infamous "Corrupt Bargain" with Henry Clay, who becomes Secy. of State. Erie Canal opened. Mexico invites Americans to settle in Texas.
1826 Anti-Mason party organized. John Adams and Thomas Jefferson die on 50th anniversary of Declaration of Independence. Jedediah Smith leads first overland expedition to California.
1827 U.S. and Britain agree to joint occupation of Pacific Northwest.
1828 Congress passes protectionist "Tariff of Abominations" over Southern protests.
1829 Mexico refuses President Jackson's offer to buy Texas.
1830 Webster-Hayne Debate in U.S. Senate reveals sectional tension. Church of Latter-Day Saints (the Mormons) founded by Joseph Smith in Fayette, N.Y. Mexico forbids further American immigration to Texas.
1831 Nat Turner leads bloodiest of all slave rebellions, killing 57 whites in Virginia.
1832 Black Hawk War fought in Illinois and Wisconsin. First nationwide Democratic Party convention held in Baltimore. President Jackson vetoes bill to recharter national bank. South Carolina nullifies "Tariff of Abominations."
1833 Massachusetts last state to end tax support for churches. Congress lowers tariff and passes "Force Bill" to pressure South Carolina, which rescinds nullification. American Anti-Slavery Society organized.
1834 Whig party organized by Senators Henry Clay and Daniel Webster in opposition to President Jackson. Anti-abolitionist riots break out in New York and Philadelphia.
1835 Samuel Morse invents telegraph. National debt completely paid off. President Jackson survives first attempt to assassinate a president. Second Seminole War begins in Florida.
1836 Samuel Colt invents revolver. Texas declares independence from Mexico and requests U.S. annexation. Mexican army captures Alamo, but Texans are victorious at San Jacinto.
1837 Panic of 1837 begins lengthy depression.
1838 Joshua Giddings of Ohio is first abolitionist elected to Congress. Trans-Atlantic steamship service established. Congress blocks abolitionist petitions with "Gag Rule."
1839 Abner Doubleday of Cooperstown, N.Y., codifies rules of baseball. Congress outlaws dueling in Washington, D.C.
1840 "Log Cabin Campaign" between William Henry Harrison and Martin Van Buren begins era of mass political participation. Liberty Party founded by abolitionists in Albany, N.Y.
1841 First emigrant train of 48 covered wagons arrives in California. President Harrison dies after month in office. First Japanese immigrant arrives in New Bedford, Mass.
1842 Webster-Ashburton Treaty settles Canada boundary disputes between U.S. and Britain. U.S. accidentally seizes California, then returns it with apology to Mexico.
1843 End of Second Seminole War. B'Nai B'rith founded in New York. Mormons begin practicing polygamy.

1844   Baptists first church to split North and South over slavery. Samuel Morse sends first telegraph message. James K. Polk, first "Dark horse" candidate, elected President.

1845   "Potato Famine" begins massive Irish immigration. U.S. annexes Texas, over Mexican protests. U.S. Naval Academy opens at Annapolis, Md.

1846   Mexican War begins when U.S. troops are attacked in disputed Texas territory. American settlers in California stage Bear Flag Revolt. Oregon Treaty gives U.S. sole possession of Pacific Northwest up to 49th parallel. First recorded baseball game played in Hoboken, N.J.

1847   Wilmot Proviso, forbidding slavery expansion, passes House and sets off wave of panic in South. General Winfield Scott conquers Mexico City. Brigham Young leads Mormons to Utah. Abraham Lincoln of Illinois arrives in Congress.

1848   Treaty of Guadalupe-Hidalgo ends Mexican War, ceding Southwest to U.S. Revolution of 1848 begins wave of German immigration. New York-Chicago telegraph line completed. Chicago Board of Trade established. Free Soil party organized. Gold discovered in California. First Chinese immigrants arrive in San Francisco. Lucretia Mott and Elizabeth Cady Stanton hold first Women's Rights Convention in Seneca Falls, N.Y.

1849   Gold Rush brings hundreds of thousands to California. Elizabeth Blackwell first American woman to receive medical degree.

1850   Sen. Henry Clay's Compromise of 1850 solves crisis over slavery expansion. Clayton-Bulwer Treaty pledges Anglo-American cooperation in building any Central American canal. John C. Calhoun of South Carolina delivers last address to Senate.

1851   Y.M.C.A. established. Northern mobs resist Fugitive Slave Act. Maine is first state to pass prohibition laws. *New York Times* founded. Herman Melville's *Moby Dick* published.

1852   Harriet Beecher Stowe's *Uncle Tom's Cabin* published.

1853   U.S. buys Gila River valley from Mexico in Gadsden Purchase. Native American, or "Know-Nothing," party founded. Commodore Matthew C. Perry opens trade with Japan.

1854   Congress passes Kansas-Nebraska Act, setting off mass protests across North. Republican Party founded. U.S. threatens to seize Cuba from Spain in Ostend Manifesto.

1855   "Bleeding Kansas" fighting begins as proslavery and anti-slavery settlers hold rival state conventions. First railroad train crosses Mississippi River at Rock Island, Ill., into Davenport, Iowa.

1856   Cong. Preston Brooks of South Carolina beats Sen. Charles Sumner of Massachusetts unconscious on Senate floor. John Brown leads Pottawatomie massacre in Kansas. First Republican national convention nominates John C. Frémont for president in Pittsburgh, Pa.

1857   New York-St. Louis railroad completed. Supreme Court hands down controversial *Dred Scott* decision protecting slavery. Panic of 1857 sends North into depression.

1858   Lincoln-Douglas Debates dramatize issue of slavery expansion in Illinois race for Senate. First trans-Atlantic telegraph cable laid.

1859   John Brown's raid on Harper's Ferry arsenal to launch abolitionist war against slavery ends in his capture and execution. Slave insurrection panic sweeps South. Comstock Silver Lode discovered in Nevada. First producing oil well in U.S. flows in Titusville, Pa.

1860   Democratic Party splits into Northern and Southern wings. South Carolina is first state to secede from Union after victory of Abraham Lincoln. Crittenden Compromise fails to preserve Union. Pony Express begins mail delivery between California and Missouri.

1861   Civil War begins with attack on Ft. Sumter in South Carolina (Apr. 12). Pres. Lincoln calls for 75,000 volunteers to put down rebellion. Jefferson Davis of Mississippi elected Pres. of Confederate States of America. New York-San Francisco telegraph link completed. Yale awards first American Ph.D. Congress enacts first Federal income tax.

1862   Congress issues "greenbacks," subsidizes transcontinental railroad, abolishes slavery in District of Columbia, and passes Homestead Act. President Lincoln issues Emancipation Proclamation after Battle of Antietam, bloodiest of Civil War.

1863   Emancipation Proclamation takes effect (Jan. 1). Union victories at Vicksburg, Miss., and Gettysburg, Pa., signal turning point of Civil War. West Virginia secedes from Virginia and rejoins Union. Hundreds killed in New York City draft riot. Pres. Lincoln proclaims Thanksgiving national holiday.

1864   President Lincoln names General Ulysses S. Grant as commander of Union armies. General William T. Sherman destroys Atlanta and conducts "March to the Sea." Confederate army of General Robert E. Lee crippled in Wilderness Campaign. Cheyenne and Arapaho Indians slaughtered in Sand Creek Massacre in Colorado.

1865   General Lee surrenders to General Grant at Appomattox Court House, Virginia (Apr. 9). President Lincoln assassinated by John Wilkes Booth in Washington, D.C. (Apr. 14). Confederacy dissolved, ending Civil War. President Johnson proclaims amnesty for most rebels. Slavery outlawed by adoption of Thirteenth Amendment. Ku Klux Klan founded in Pulaski, Tenn.

1866   In the struggle over Reconstruction policy, Congress overrides Pres. Johnson's vetoes of Civil Rights Act and New Freedmen's Bureau Bill. Whites riot in New Orleans to protest black suffrage. Grand Army of the Republic organized by Union veterans.

1867   Congress takes control of Reconstruction in the South by passing First Reconstruction Act over Pres. Johnson's veto and Tenure of Office Act. U.S. purchases Alaska from Russia for $7.2 million (2¢ an acre). Farmers organize Patrons of Husbandry, beginning Granger movement.

1868   For violating Tenure of Office Act of 1867, Pres. Johnson is impeached in the House (Feb. 24), but acquitted in the Senate by a single vote (May 16). U.S. and China sign Burlingame Treaty to allow immigration. Fourteenth Amendment grants equal citizenship and protection to freedmen (July 28). Half a million black votes help elect Gen. Ulysses S. Grant to the presidency. The typewriter invented.

1869   "Hard Money" prevails when Congress passes Public Credit Act, promising repayment of government debts in gold. Transcontinental railroad completed when Union Pacific and Central Pacific lines meet at Promontory Point, Utah (May 10). Jay Gould and James Fisk cause financial panic by trying to corner gold market on "Black Friday" (Sept. 24). Knights of Labor national union organized. National Women's Suffrage Association formed in New York. Wyoming Territory grants first U.S. women's suffrage.

1870   Fifteenth Amendment guarantees right to vote for all U.S. citizens, though only Wyoming and Utah territories allow women's suffrage (Mar. 30). Congress passes first Ku Klux Act to enforce

Fifteenth Amendment. First black senator and black congressman are elected.

1871 Congress passes second Ku Klux Act to enforce Fourteenth Amendment in the South. Tammany Hall ring overthrown in New York City when *New York Times* begins publishing exposé of Boss William Marcy Tweed. Most of Chicago destroyed in the Great Fire (Oct. 8-11). Anti-Chinese race riots in Los Angeles. Illinois enacts first railroad regulations.

1872 Liberal Republicans bolt from Pres. Grant and nominate newspaperman Horace Greeley for president. Crédit Mobilier scandal implicates Vice President Schuyler Colfax and embarrasses Grant administration. Yellowstone National Park created. Susan B. Anthony arrested for leading suffragists to the polls. Montgomery Ward opens for business in Chicago.

1873 Silver withdrawn from money supply in the "Crime of '73." Congressmen raise their own salaries 50%, retroactive for two years, and double president's pay in "Salary Grab" Act. Panic of 1873, triggered by failure of Jay Cooke's banking house, begins depression of 1870s. New York Stock Exchange forced to close for ten days. Great Bonanza silver lode discovered in Nevada. San Francisco installs first cable cars.

1874 Granger movement begins passing railroad regulations in Midwestern states. Women's Christian Temperance Union founded in Cleveland, Ohio. Democrats recapture Congress for first time since Civil War. Greenback Party formed in Indianapolis. Black rioters attack courthouse in Vicksburg, Miss. Chautauqua movement begins bringing educational speakers to rural communities across the country.

1875 Congress passes Specie Resumption Act to reduce money supply by redeeming greenbacks for gold, and Civil Rights Act to guarantee equal rights for freedmen. Whiskey Ring scandal casts further pall on Grant administration. Archbishop John McCloskey of New York first American bishop. *Aristides* wins first Kentucky Derby at Churchill Downs, Ky.

1876 U.S. awards patent to Alexander Graham Bell for the telephone. Gen. George A. Custer and 265 men are massacred by Sioux Indians at Little Big Horn, Montana (June 25). Centennial of the United States celebrated. Democrat Samuel Tilden outpolls Republican candidate Rutherford B. Hayes as presidential election is thrown into the House (Nov. 7). Professional baseball's National League established. Kappa Alpha opens first college fraternity house at Williams College. Central Park in New York completed.

1877 Congress appoints Electoral Commission to solve impasse over disputed 1876 election (Jan. 29). House votes 185 to 184 to declare Rutherford B. Hayes president-elect, three days before his inauguration (Mar. 2). Reconstruction officially ends with withdrawal of Federal troops from the South (Apr. 24). Pres. Hayes sends in troops as Great Railroad Strike paralyzes much of the country (July 17). Anti-Chinese riots break out in San Francisco. Colorado silver rush begins.

1878 Sen. A. A. Sargent introduces Women's Suffrage Amendment in Congress. Greenback-Labor Party formed in Toledo, Ohio. Limited coinage of silver resumes with Bland-Allison Act. Democrats win control of both houses of Congress for first time since 1858. American Bar Association organized in Saratoga, N.Y. Edison Electric begins operating in New York City. New Haven, Conn., sets up first commercial telephone network.

1879 U.S. resumes specie payments for greenbacks. Pres. Hayes battles with Congress over use of Federal troops in elections. F.W. Woolworth opens his first store in Utica, N.Y. First Church of Christ, Scientist, founded in Boston. Thomas Edison invents light bulb. California adopts state constitution forbidding employment of Chinese labor. Henry George's radical social critique, *Progress and Poverty*, becomes best-seller.

1880 Pres. Hayes declares U.S. must control any Isthmian canal. U.S. and China agree to Chinese Exclusion Treaty (Nov. 17). National Farmers' Alliance organized in Chicago. American branch of Salvation Army founded in Philadelphia, Pa. Census lists U.S. population over 50 million for first time (50,155,783).

1881 Pres. Garfield assassinated by Charles Guiteau in Washington, D.C. (July 2—dies Sept. 19). Chester Alan Arthur becomes president (Sept. 20). Clara Barton creates American Red Cross. Booker T. Washington founds Tuskegee Institute for black education in Alabama. Russian Jews begin immigrating to U.S. to escape pogroms.

1882 John D. Rockefeller organizes Standard Oil trust, first such combination. Congress passes first Chinese Exclusion Act (May 10), and legislates first immigration restrictions: no paupers, convicts, or mental defectives (Aug. 3). Knights of Columbus founded with permission from Roman Catholic Church.

1883 Congress passes Pendleton Act, requiring civil service competition for Federal jobs. Brooklyn Bridge opened in New York. Supreme Court strikes down Civil Rights Act of 1875. New York-Chicago telephone service begins. Ohio River floods devastate Cincinnati. U.S. Navy builds its first steel ships. Railroads agree on Standard Time zones for North America.

1884 "Mugwumps" bolt Republican Party. Statue of Liberty cornerstone laid (Aug. 5). Belva A. Lockwood of Equal Rights Party first woman candidate for president. Grover Cleveland of New York first Democrat elected president since Civil War. Home Insurance Building of Chicago first skyscraper in the world. Moses Fleetwood Walker first black professional baseball player.

1885 Washington Monument completed after 36 years of construction. U.S. Marines land in Panama (Apr. 24). Senate refuses to ratify treaty for building a canal across Nicaragua. Congress outlaws building fences on public lands in the West. Josiah Strong's best-seller *Our Country* argues for American imperialism.

1886 Knights of Labor rail strike sets off national wave of strikes for eight-hour day. Haymarket Riot in Chicago leads to execution of seven anarchists. Statue of Liberty in New York Harbor dedicated (Oct. 28). American Federation of Labor (AFL) founded in Columbus, Ohio. Indian wars end with capture of Geronimo.

1887 Congress creates Interstate Commerce Commission, first Federal regulatory agency, but with weak enforcement powers. Congress distributes reservation land to Indians, also bans opium imports. First electric trolley line built in Richmond, Va. U.S. Navy leases base at Pearl Harbor, Hawaii. First American golf club founded in Foxburg, Pa.

1888 Snow falls for 36 hours in New York, killing 400 people in "Great Blizzard of '88" (Mar. 12). First secret ballot election in Louisville, Ky. George Eastman brings first Kodak camera to the market. National Geographic Society founded in Washington, D.C. Edward Bellamy's utopian novel, *Looking Backward*, a sensational best-seller.

1889   Four new states—N.D., S.D., Mont., Wash.—all admitted in one day (Feb. 22). Oklahoma Land Rush results when former Indian territory opened for settlement (Apr. 22). Johnstown Flood claims thousands of lives in Pennsylvania (May 31). Kansas passes first antitrust law. Jane Addams founds Hull House in Chicago. First "All-American" college football players chosen. Tower Building, first New York skyscraper, completed.
1890   Congress passes Sherman Antitrust Act (July 2) and Sherman Silver Purchase Act. Wyoming admitted as first state with women's suffrage (July 10). Sioux uprising ends at Battle of Wounded Knee (Dec. 29). Yosemite National Park created. Mississippi leads South in disfranchising black voters. Jacob Riis's *How the Other Half Lives* awakens Americans to urban poverty. First Army-Navy football game played—Navy 24, Army 0.
1891   Pres. Cleveland denounces "dangerous and reckless experiment" of silver coinage. New Orleans mob lynches 11 Italian immigrants. People's, or Populist, Party organized in Cincinnati. U.S. and Chile nearly go to war over death of two American sailors in Valparaiso (Oct. 16). Dr. James A. Naismith invents basketball in Springfield, Mass. Thomas Edison patents first American-made motion picture camera.
1892   Populist candidate James B. Weaver of Iowa receives over a million votes for president. Violent strikes break out among steel workers in Homestead, Pa., and silver miners in Coeur d'Alene, Idaho. Chinese immigrants forced to register with Federal government. First gasoline-powered American automobile built in Chicopee, Mass. Boll weevil first appears in Texas.
1893   U.S. gold reserve falls below $100 million (Apr. 21). Panic of 1893, touched off by New York stock market crash (June 27), begins second-worst depression in U.S. history. Congress repeals Sherman Silver Purchase Act (Oct. 30). Hawaii requests U.S. annexation. Mormon Temple dedicated in Salt Lake City, Utah. Thousands perish in Louisiana cyclone. Frank Lloyd Wright completes first solo project, the Winslow home in Chicago.
1894   Coxey's Army of unemployed march on Washington, D.C. (Apr. 30). U.S. Treasury issues two $50 million bond offerings to shore up dwindling gold reserves. Congress enacts first peacetime Federal income tax, denounced as "socialism, communism, devilism" (Aug. 27). Pullman strike paralyzes railroads across the country. Thomas Edison exhibits his kinetoscope.
1895   Billionaire banker J.P. Morgan bails out U.S. Treasury, faced with a gold drain. "Silver Democrats" appeal for unlimited silver coinage as way out of depression. Supreme Court rules income tax unconstitutional (May 20). Venezuelan boundary dispute brings U.S. and Britain close to war. Cuban insurrection against Spanish rule begins, winning American sympathy. National Association of Manufacturers formed in Cincinnati. First professional football game played in Latrobe, Pa.
1896   Supreme Court approves segregation (Plessy vs. Ferguson). William Jennings Bryan, "Silver Democrat" of Nebraska, wins nomination with "Cross of Gold" speech (July 7). Gold discovered in Klondike, Alaska, defusing the money question (Aug. 16). American athletes sweep nine of 12 events at first International Olympics. Henry Ford builds his first automobile. First American motion pictures appear in theaters. "The Yellow Kid," first comic strip, begins running in *New York World.*

1897   U.S. and Britain consent to arbitration of boundary disputes in Olney-Paunceforte Convention (Jan. 11). Venezuelan boundary dispute ends with Britain accepting arbitration. Klondike gold rush to Alaska moves into full swing. U.S. offers to mediate Cuban rebellion, lodges official complaint against Spanish brutality. "Yellow press" newspapers keep up constant assault on Spain. First American subway completed in Boston.
1898   After mysterious explosion of battleship *Maine* in Havana harbor (Feb. 15), Spanish-American War breaks out (Apr. 21). Commodore George Dewey destroys Spanish fleet at Manila Bay (May 1) and U.S. takes Manila (Aug. 13). After Battle of San Juan Hill (July 1), Spanish garrison at Santiago, Cuba, surrenders (July 17). U.S. takes Cuba, Puerto Rico, Guam, Wake Island, and Philippines from Spain in Treaty of Paris (Dec. 10). Senate agrees to annex Hawaii.
1899   Philippine Revolt against U.S. rule erupts. Secy. of State John Hay issues Open Door notes to European powers and Japan, requesting no spheres of influence in China (Sept. 6). U.S. and Germany agree to partition Samoan Islands (Dec. 2). Congress investigates incompetence in War Department, revealed during Spanish-American War.
1900   "Hard Money" triumphs as U.S. returns to single gold standard (Mar. 14). Puerto Rico and Hawaii become U.S. territories by acts of Congress (Apr. 12 & Apr. 30). U.S. troops relieve foreign legations under siege in Peking, China, during Boxer Rebellion (Aug. 14). Olds Company opens first Detroit auto factory. Carrie Nation leads hatchet-wielding women into Kansas saloons to smash liquor barrels.
1901   J.P. Morgan creates U.S. Steel, first billion-dollar corporation. U.S. retains control over Cuba with Platt Amendment. Pres. McKinley shot by anarchist Leon Czolgosz in Buffalo, N.Y. (Sept. 6—dies Sept. 14). Hay-Pauncefote Treaty secures British approval for a U.S.-built canal in Panama (Nov. 18). First great Texas oil strike made near Beaumont, Tex. Pres. Roosevelt promises to "speak softly and carry a big stick."
1902   End of Philippine Insurrection. Reclamation Act initiates Federal policy of conservation of natural resources (June 17). Congress declares Philippines an unorganized territory and its inhabitants are not U.S. citizens (July 1). First Rose Bowl football game played. Pres. Roosevelt helps mediate Pennsylvania coal strike.
1903   U.S. prevails over Canada in Alaskan boundary dispute. Pres. Roosevelt helps Panama gain independence from Colombia, then negotiates treaty to build Panama Canal. Orville and Wilbur Wright conduct first powered flight near Kitty Hawk, N.C. (Dec. 17). *The Great Train Robbery,* first feature-length motion picture, released. Wisconsin holds first primary elections. Ford Motor Company formed. Boston defeats Pittsburgh in first baseball World Series.
1904   Supreme Court upholds antitrust dissolution of Northern Securities company (Mar. 14). Pres. Roosevelt wins reelection and says he will not run again (Nov. 8). "Roosevelt Corollary" to Monroe Doctrine justifies U.S. intervention to keep other powers out of Western hemisphere. First New York City subway opened. New York state enacts first speed limit: 20 mph on open roads. Deaf, dumb, and blind, Helen Keller graduates from Radcliffe College.
1905   Supreme Court disallows limits on length of working day. Industrial Workers of the World, a radical labor union, formed in Chicago. Pres.

Roosevelt mediates Treaty of Portsmouth, ending Russo-Japanese War. U.S. takes control of Santo Domingo trade. Black leaders hold Niagara Falls Conference, calling for equal rights.

1906 San Francisco destroyed by earthquake and fire (Apr. 18-19). Responding to consumer pressure, Congress passes Pure Food and Drug Act and Meat Inspection Act. Race riot breaks out in Atlanta (Sept. 22). Japan protests segregation of Asian students in California schools (Oct. 25). Pres. Roosevelt first American to win the Nobel Peace Prize, and first sitting president to leave U.S. on visit to Panama.

1907 Panic of 1907 triggers crash on Wall Street (Mar. 13) and run on banks across the country. Pres. Roosevelt orders exclusion of Japanese laborers (Mar. 14). U.S. Navy's "Great White Fleet" embarks on tour around the world. Congress outlaws corporate contributions to political campaigns. Hundreds killed in coal mine explosions in Monongah, W. Va., and Jacobs Creek, Pa. All-time record 1,285,349 immigrants arrive in one year.

1908 U.S. and Japan conclude "Gentleman's Agreement" limiting immigration. Ford Model T appears on the market (Oct. 1). Root-Takahira Agreement promises U.S. and Japan will respect each other's interests in Pacific. Pres. Roosevelt appoints National Conservation Commission. Federal Bureau of Investigation established. New York City outlaws women smoking in public.

1909 Robert E. Peary plants American flag at North Pole (Apr. 6). Pres. Taft opens 700,000 acres for settlement in the West. W.E.B. DuBois founds National Association for the Advancement of Colored People (NAACP), advocating racial equality. U.S. troops land in Nicaragua.

1910 Theodore Roosevelt calls for "New Nationalism" in a speech at Ossawatomie, Kans. *Los Angeles Times* building destroyed by terrorist bomb (Oct. 1). Glacier National Park created. Mann Act cracks down on "white slave" trade. Boy Scouts of America chartered. Ballinger-Pinchot controversy reveals major differences over conservation policy in Taft administration.

1911 Sen. Robert M. LaFollette of Wisconsin founds National Progressive Republican League to promote reform (Jan. 21). Pres. Taft orders U.S. troops to border during Mexican Revolution. Supreme Court upholds antitrust breakups of Standard Oil and American Tobacco. Calbraith P. Rodgers makes first transcontinental airplane flight. U.S. bankers take control of Nicaragua's finances. Steel magnate Andrew Carnegie donates $125 million for philanthropic purposes.

1912 *Titanic* sinks on maiden voyage from England (Apr. 15). Progressive, or "Bull Moose," Party founded by Theodore Roosevelt, who survives an assassination attempt by John Schrank in Milwaukee (Oct. 14). Massachusetts adopts first minimum wage law. U.S. Marines land in Honduras, Cuba, Nicaragua, and Santo Domingo. Textile strike in Lawrence, Mass.

1913 Sixteenth Amendment empowers Federal government to collect income taxes (Feb. 25), and Seventeenth Amendment allows for popular election of U.S. senators (May 31). Congress creates Federal Reserve system. Ford Motor Company introduces assembly line. John D. Rockefeller donates $100 million to philanthropic Rockefeller Foundation. Grand Central Station opens in New York City.

1914 Pres. Wilson nearly goes to war with Mexico over arrests of American sailors in Tampico. U.S. Navy shells Vera Cruz and lands Marines in retaliation (Apr. 21). U.S. declares neutrality in World War I (Aug. 4). Congress passes Clayton Act, toughening antitrust standards. Congress proclaims Mother's Day.

1915 *Birth of a Nation,* first movie blockbuster. Pres. Wilson strongly protests German sinking of *Lusitania* with 128 Americans aboard (May 7). U.S. Marines land in Haiti (July 28). Ku Klux Klan revived in Atlanta, Ga. Coast-to-coast long distance telephone service begins.

1916 House-Grey Memorandum warns Germany that refusal to negotiate may bring U.S. into World War I. Gen. John Pershing chases Pancho Villa into Mexico after border raid on Columbus, N.Mex. (Mar. 15). Britain blacklists U.S. firms doing business with Germany. U.S. acquires Virgin Islands from Denmark for $25 million. Pres. Wilson wins reelection with slogan, "He Kept Us Out of War" (Nov. 7). Jeanette Rankin of Montana first woman elected to Congress. Louis D. Brandeis first Jewish member of Supreme Court. Margaret Sanger opens first birth control clinic in Brooklyn, N.Y. National Park Service created.

1917 Germany resumes unrestricted submarine warfare, leading U.S. to sever diplomatic relations (Feb. 3). Gen. John Pershing withdraws from Mexico. Zimmerman Telegram, intercepted by British intelligence and made public, reveals German overtures to Mexico in case of war (Feb. 24). U.S. merchant ships armed for self-defense against German submarines (Mar. 13). After Pres. Wilson proclaims "the world must be made safe for democracy," Congress declares war on Germany (Apr. 6) and Austria-Hungary (Dec. 7). Prohibition begins as wartime conservation measure. Race riot breaks out in East St. Louis.

1918 Pres. Wilson announces U.S. war aims in "Fourteen Points" speech (Jan. 8). U.S. troops join Allied intervention in Russian Revolution (Aug. 2). Congress passes Sedition Act. Over a million U.S. troops participate in month-long Meuse-Argonne campaign (Sept. 26-Nov. 11). Republicans win control of Congress, a rebuke to Pres. Wilson . Armistice Day ends World War I (Nov. 11) as mass celebrations break out across the country. Pres. Wilson goes to Europe for peace conference. Supreme Court approves draft laws and strikes down child labor laws. Influenza epidemic takes hundreds of thousands American lives.

1919 Eighteenth Amendment establishes Prohibition (Jan. 29). Strike wave sweeps country, triggering "Red Scare." American Communist Party organized in Chicago. Race riots in Washington, D.C., and Chicago. Pres. Wilson suffers incapacitating stroke during nationwide speaking tour (Sept. 26). Volstead Act implements national Prohibition enforcement. Versailles Treaty, including League of Nations, rejected by Senate (Nov. 19). Grand Canyon National Park created. New York-Chicago daily airmail service begins.

1920 Attorney General A. Mitchell Palmer stages "Palmer Raids," arresting and deporting thousands of radicals and immigrants. Sacco and Vanzetti are arrested for murder in Braintree, Mass. Supreme Court upholds Prohibition. Nineteenth Amendment establishes women's suffrage (Aug. 26). National League of Women Voters organized. Wall Street rocked by a terrorist bomb, killing 30 bystanders (Sept. 16). First regular radio broadcasts begin in East Pittsburgh, Pa. Pres. Wilson receives Nobel Peace Prize. U.S. population, more urban than rural for first time, tops 100 million (105,710,620).

1921 Pres. Harding, promising a "return to normalcy," takes office. U.S. negotiates separate peace with Germany, Austria, and Hungary.

Ku Klux Klan spreads terror in the South. International disarmament conference meets in Washington, D.C. Jack Dempsey defeats Georges Carpentier first million-dollar prize fight.

1922 Washington Conference concludes with nine international treaties to limit naval arms race, relax tensions in the Pacific, and protect China. Supreme Court upholds women's suffrage. Lincoln Memorial dedicated in Washington, D.C. (May 30). Pres. Harding vetoes "Bonus Bill" for World War I veterans. Congress passes joint resolution in favor of Jewish homeland in Palestine (Sept. 21). First commercial radio show broadcast in New York.

1923 Last U.S. occupation troops leave Germany (Jan. 10). Senate begins investigating corruption in Veterans Bureau and Teapot Dome oil leases (Oct. 25). Pres. Harding dies mysteriously of "apoplexy" in San Francisco (Aug. 2). Pres. Coolidge's address to Congress, calling for economy in government, first radio broadcast of a presidential speech (Dec. 6). Oklahoma declares martial law to crack down on Ku Klux Klan. Yankee Stadium opens.

1924 Congress provides bonuses for World War I veterans over Pres. Coolidge's veto. Congress passes Immigration Act, imposing strict national quota system. European powers accept Dawes Plan for repayment of war debts and reparations. U.S. Marines withdraw from Santo Domingo. Coast-to-coast air mail service begins. Tornados wreak havoc in Midwest.

1925 Tennessee outlaws teaching evolution in school, leading to the Scopes Trial in Dayton, Tenn. (July 10-21). Ku Klux Klan marches on Washington, D.C. (Aug. 8) Nellie Tayloe Ross of Wyoming first woman governor. Florida land boom draws hordes of speculators. Colonel Billy Mitchell suspended from U.S. Army for advocating stronger air force. Chicago gang wars break out as Al Capone consolidates bootlegging operations.

1926 Secy. Treasury of Andrew Mellon's drastic tax cuts approved. Admiral Richard E. Byrd and Floyd Bennett first to fly over North Pole (May 9). Henry Ford institutes 8-hour day and 5-day work week at Ford Motor Company factories. Hurricane sweeps Florida, killing 372 people. Book of the Month Club founded. U.S. Marines return to Nicaragua.

1927 Charles Lindbergh completes non-stop solo flight from New York to Paris (May 20-21), returns home to huge welcoming crowds. Sacco and Vanzetti executed in Massachusetts, despite international protests. *The Jazz Singer* with Al Jolson becomes first "talkie" motion picture (Oct. 6). Holland Tunnel in New York opened. Mississippi River floods causes $300 million damage. Ford Model A unveiled. Mechanical cotton picker invented. New York-London commercial telephone service begins.

1928 U.S. joins fourteen countries in signing Kellogg-Briand Pact for the "outlawry of war" (Aug. 27). Clark Memorandum disavows future U.S. interventions in Latin America. Pres. Coolidge refuses to aid American farmers mired in agricultural depression. Walt Disney creates "Steamboat Willie," first Mickey Mouse cartoon. George Eastman demonstrates color motion picture technology. Republicans promise "a chicken in every pot, a car in every garage."

1929 St. Valentine's Day Massacre claims six lives in Chicago gang wars. Young Plan replaces Dawes Plan for payment of war debts and reparations. Albert B. Fall, former secretary of the Inte-

rior, found guilty in Teapot Dome scandal. Stock market crash on "Black Friday" (Oct. 29) ushers in Great Depression.

1930 Wave of bank failures sweeps U.S., wiping out millions of savings accounts and leading to private hoarding of gold. U.S., Britain, and Japan sign London Naval Treaty limiting naval arms race (Apr. 22). Hawley-Smoot Tariff raises barriers to world trade, worsening Depression. Congress creates Veteran's Administration (July 3).

1931 World War I veterans are offered "Bonus Loans" to combat Depression. "Star Spangled Banner" becomes national anthem. "Scottsboro Boys" arrested for rape in Alabama. Empire State Building, tallest building in the world, opens in New York City. Pres. Hoover declares moratorium on international debt and reparations payments.

1932 Stimson Doctrine announces U.S. disapproval of Japanese invasion of China. Congress approves Reconstruction Finance Corporation to help recovery. Norris-LaGuardia act restricts use of injunctions against labor strikes. Franklin D. Roosevelt, promising a "New Deal" for Americans, elected president in Democratic landslide. Stock market drops to 10% of its 1929 value; national income cut in half. "Bonus Army" of poor veterans marches on Washington, D.C. Amelia Earhart first woman to fly solo across the Atlantic.

1933 Giuseppe Zangara kills Chicago Mayor Anton J. Cermak in a Miami, Fla., motorcade, narrowly missing president-elect Franklin D. Roosevelt (Feb. 15). Banks are closed for four days by presidential order (Mar. 5). During "Hundred Days" (Mar. 9-June 16), Pres. Roosevelt pushes New Deal through Congress, conducts first "Fireside Chat" on radio, and takes U.S. off gold standard. Beer and wine made legal again (Mar. 22). Congress passes National Industrial Recovery Act (June 16). U.S. recognizes Soviet Union (Nov. 16). U.S. Marines withdraw from Nicaragua. Frances Perkins, Sec. of Labor, becomes first woman cabinet member.

1934 Dust storms inundate Southwest, driving "Okies" and "Arkies" to California. General strike paralyzes San Francisco (July 16). John Dillinger, public enemy number one, killed by FBI agents (July 22). Sen. Gerald P. Nye of North Dakota begins investigating role of U.S. munitions manufacturers in World War I. U.S. releases Cuba from Platt Amendment. U.S. troops withdrawn from Haiti.

1935 Supreme Court invalidates National Industrial Recovery Act. Pres. Roosevelt pushes more "Second New Deal" legislation through Congress, notably the Wagner Act protecting unions, Social Security Act, and "Soak the Rich" Wealth Tax Act. Sen. Huey P. Long of Louisiana assassinated (Sept. 8). Congress of Industrial Organization (CIO) formed (Nov. 9). Congress passes first Neutrality Act. Alcoholics Anonymous founded.

1936 Congress passes second Neutrality Act. France, Britain, and U.S. sign New London Naval Treaty (Mar. 25). U.S. declares neutrality in Spanish Civil War (Aug. 7). CIO auto workers begin sit-down strikes in Flint, Mich. (Dec. 30). *Life* magazine begins publishing. Jesse Owens wins four gold medals at "Nazi Olympics" in Berlin.

1937 Congress passes third Neutrality Act. Pres. Roosevelt proposes controversial "court-packing" plan. German dirigible *Hindenburg* explodes and burns in Lakehurst, N.J. (May 6). Pres. Roosevelt angers isolationists with "Quarantine Speech" (Oct. 5). Japanese planes sink U.S. Navy gunboat *Panay* in China (Dec. 12). Slow recovery ends abruptly as Depression worsens.

1938 Republican gains in Congress signal end of New Deal. Pres. Roosevelt calls for military buildup (Jan. 28). Mexico seizes U.S.-owned oil wells (Mar. 18). Rep. Martin Dies of Texas begins House Un-American Activities Committee (HUAC) investigations of Communists and Fascists. Howard Hughes sets record for around-the-world flight in less than four days (July 14). "Invasion from Mars" radio broadcast by Orson Welles causes widespread panic (Oct. 30). Hurricane devastates Atlantic coast, killing 700 people.

1939 Supreme Court upholds Tennessee Valley Authority. Pan Am begins first regular trans-Atlantic passenger service. U.S. declares neutrality in World War II (Sept. 5). Congress passes fourth Neutrality Act, approving Pres. Roosevelt's request for "cash-and-carry" arms sales to belligerents. Nylon stockings appear on the market.

1940 As World War II engulfs Europe, Pres. Roosevelt announces U.S. has moved from "neutrality" to "non-belligerency" (June 10). U.S. and Britain conclude Destroyers-for-Bases deal. Congress enacts a peacetime draft (Sept. 16) and massive increases in military spending. Over 16 million men register for draft as Pres. Roosevelt's embargo on strategic exports takes effect. Roosevelt, reelected to an unprecedented third term, calls for U.S. to become "the arsenal of democracy" (Dec. 20).

1941 Congress appropriates $7 billion in Lend-Lease aid to Britain. German submarine sinks merchant ship *Robin Moor*, first U.S. casualty of war (May 21). Roosevelt responds by declaring "unlimited national emergency" (May 27), freezing German and Italian assets in U.S. (June 14), and promising aid to Soviet Union (June 24). Roosevelt freezes Japanese assets in retaliation for invasion of Indochina (July 25). Pres. Roosevelt and Prime Minister Winston Churchill issue Atlantic Charter (Aug. 12). U.S. Navy is ordered to "shoot on sight" at German warships (Sept. 11). "America has been attacked, the shooting has started," Pres. Roosevelt informs the country (Oct. 27). Japanese planes attack Pearl Harbor, Hawaii, killing 2,400 U.S. servicemen and civilians (Dec. 7). U.S. declares war on Japan (Dec. 10) and on Germany and Italy (Dec. 11).

1942 Roosevelt creates War Production Board, calls for mass mobilization, and puts New Deal on hold. U.S. troops land in North Ireland, first to arrive in Europe (Jan. 26). Pres. Roosevelt approves internment of Japanese-Americans for duration of war (Feb. 20). Japanese submarine shells an oil refinery in Santa Barbara, Calif. (Feb. 23). Maj. James H. Doolittle stages carrier-launched bombing raid on Tokyo (Apr. 18). U.S. forces surrender in Philippines (May 6), but win major naval victories over Japan in Coral Sea (May 4-8) and at Midway (June 3-6). U.S. offensive begins in Pacific with invasion of Guadalcanal Island (Aug. 7). First all-U.S. bombing attack launched against German forces at Rouen, France (Aug. 17). Congress approves "Victory Tax" on wartime incomes. Allies land 400,000 men in North Africa (Nov. 7-8). Eight German saboteurs apprehended in New York; six executed. Cocoanut Grove nightclub fire in Boston kills 492.

1943 Congress appropriates $100 billion for war effort. Roosevelt and Churchill demand "unconditional surrender" at Casablanca conference in Morocco (Jan. 24). U.S. Marines drive last Japanese from Guadalcanal (Feb. 9). U.S. troops defeated in first battle with Germans at Kasserine Pass, Tunisia (Feb. 20). Pres. Roosevelt declares wage-and-price freeze to stem inflation. U.S. and Britain invade Sicily (July 10) and Italy proper (Sept. 3). Roosevelt and Churchill meet with Chiang Kai-Shek of China in Cairo, Egypt (Nov. 22), and with Josef Stalin of Soviet Union in Teheran, Iran (Dec. 4-6). Gen. Dwight D. Eisenhower named Supreme Commander of Allied forces in Europe. Congress approves Federal income tax withholding. Race riots in Detroit and Harlem kill 40.

1944 U.S. and British planes begin around-the-clock bombing of Berlin. Allied forces land at Anzio, Italy (Jan. 22). Congress approves $1.35 billion for United Nations Relief and Reconstruction Agency, first U.S. foreign aid (Mar. 29). Allied forces enter Rome (June 5) as reconquest of Europe begins with D-Day invasion of Normandy (June 6). Allied breakout from Normandy sends German forces reeling across France (July 25). Postwar financial arrangements made at an international conference in Bretton Woods, N.H. (July 1-22). Plans for United Nations made at Dumbarton Oaks conference (Aug. 21-Oct. 7). Gen. Douglas MacArthur begins reconquest of Philippines with landings at Leyte Gulf (Oct. 20). Congress passes Servicemen's Readjustment Act, known as "GI Bill of Rights." Roosevelt wins fourth term.

1945 Roosevelt, Churchill, and Stalin meet for last time at Yalta in Soviet Crimea to begin postwar planning (Feb. 4-11). Allied forces cross Rhine River and drive into heart of Germany (Mar. 7). U.S. air raids destroy Tokyo (Mar. 10-11). Pres. Roosevelt dies suddenly of cerebral hemorrhage in Warm Springs, Ga. (Apr. 12). United Nations Conference begins meeting in San Francisco (Apr. 24). Germany surrenders, ending war in Europe (May 7). Fifty nations sign U.N. Charter (June 26). First atomic explosion occurs in test at Alamagordo, N.Mex. (July 16). Pres. Truman meets with Churchill and Stalin at Potsdam, Germany (July 17-Aug. 2). Atomic bombs dropped on Hiroshima (Aug. 6) and Nagasaki (Aug. 9); Japan surrenders (Aug. 14), ending World War II. Council of Allied Foreign Ministers meets in London, unable to agree on peace treaty (Dec. 16-27). Television channels are allotted for commercial use. Empire State Building hit by B-25 bomber in heavy fog.

1946 Strike wave sweeps U.S., idling 4.6 million U.S. workers. Congress passes Employment Act, committing Federal government to postwar economic management. Winston Churchill warns Americans about Communist expansion with "Iron Curtain" speech at Westminster College in Fulton, Mo. (Mar. 5). Pres. Truman seizes control of railroads and coal mines during strikes. Paris Peace Conference ends in failure (July 29-Oct. 15). U.S. presents Baruch Plan for international control of atomic energy, grants independence to Philippines (July 4), and agrees to loan Britain $3.5 billion for postwar reconstruction. Congress creates Atomic Energy Commission. U.N. General Assembly begins meeting in New York.

1947 Council of Foreign Ministers meets in Moscow, again unable to agree on peace treaty (Mar. 10-Apr. 24). Pres. Truman announces Truman Doctrine, promising aid to countries threatened by subversion (May 12). Secy. of State George C. Marshall announces Marshall Plan for postwar reconstruction of Europe (June 5). Republican-dominated Congress restricts union organizing with Taft-Hartley Act. House Committee on Un-American Activities (HUAC) begins investigating Communism in Hollywood (Oct. 20). Texas City, Tex., wiped out when a munitions ship explodes, killing over 500 people. Jackie Robinson of Brooklyn Dodgers breaks color line in baseball.

1948 Postwar inflation keeps prices rising fast. Congress approves $5.3 billion for Marshall Plan aid to Europe with Foreign Assistance Act. U.S. recognizes new state of Israel (May 14) and admits 205,000 war refugees from Europe. Britain and U.S. begin airlifting supplies into West Berlin after Soviets cut off all traffic into city (June 26). Pres. Truman orders peacetime draft and desegregation of U.S. armed forces. HUAC charges Alger Hiss with spying for Soviet Union. Pres. Truman wins upset reelection victory over Republican candidate Thomas E. Dewey of New York. Idlewild International Airport, largest in the world, opens in New York.

1949 Pres. Truman calls for "Fair Deal" domestic programs and "Point Four" foreign aid programs. U.S., Canada, and 10 Western European nations sign treaty that will lead to North Atlantic Treaty Organization (NATO). Berlin Airlift ends when Soviets finally lift blockade (May 12). Pres. Truman announces Soviet atomic bomb test (Sept. 23). Eleven U.S. Communist leaders convicted of conspiring to overthrow government. Steel strike idles half a million workers nationwide (Oct. 1-Nov. 11). *Lucky Lady II* of U.S. Air Force completes first non-stop around-the-world flight.

1950 Sen. Joseph R. McCarthy of Wisconsin issues his first accusations of Communists in government at a speech in Wheeling, W. Va. North Korea invades South Korea, beginning Korean War (June 25). Pres. Truman orders U.S. intervention (June 27), obtains U.N. support (July 7), asks Congress for a $10 billion rearmament program (July 20), and calls up reserves (Aug. 4). Inchon landing begins rout of North Korean invaders (Sept. 15). U.N. troops recapture Seoul (Sept. 26) and invade North Korea (Oct. 7). Congress passes Internal Security Act, requiring registration of Communist organizations, over Pres. Truman's veto (Sept. 23). Puerto Rican nationalists nearly assassinate Pres. Truman in Washington (Nov. 11). After China intervenes in the Korean War, Pres. Truman proclaims a national emergency (Dec. 16).

1951 Gen. Dwight D. Eisenhower comes out of retirement to accept command of Allied forces in Europe (Apr. 4). Julius and Ethel Rosenberg sentenced to death for atom spying (Apr. 5). Pres. Truman removes Gen. Douglas MacArthur from command in Korea for insubordination (Apr. 11). MacArthur returns to the U.S., greeted by exultant crowds, to deliver address to Congress. Missouri River floods devastate Kansas City, causing over $1 billion in damages (July 11–25). U.S. concludes a mutual defense pact with Australia and New Zealand, and signs a peace treaty with Japan (Sept. 8). Congress passes the Mutual Security Act, providing $7 billion for foreign aid and military cooperation with pro-U.S. nations. CBS transmits first color television broadcast from New York.

1952 Pres. Truman seizes steel mills paralyzed by strikes (Apr. 8). U.S., Britain, and France sign a peace treaty with West Germany (May 26). Construction begins on USS *Nautilus*, first atomic submarine. Supreme Court upholds barring subversives from teaching in schools. Sen. Richard M. Nixon of California, Republican candidate for Vice President, delivers "Checkers Speech" on national television to explain his "secret slush fund." Republicans win control of White House and both houses of Congress for first time since 1928. U.S. announces first successful hydrogen bomb test at Eniwetok Atoll in Marshall Islands (Nov. 16).

1953 Thirteen more Communist leaders are convicted of conspiring to overthrow the government. Julius and Ethel Rosenberg are executed in Ossining, N.Y. (June 19). Pres. Eisenhower lifts

wage and price controls, increases U.S. support for French war' effort in Indochina, negotiates armistice ending Korean War (June 27). Congress creates Department of Health, Education, and Welfare (Apr. 1). U.S. pledges aid to Spain in exchange for military bases (Sept. 26). Major Chuck Yeager of the U.S. Air Force sets new air speed record in rocket-powered X-1 jet plane.

1954 Secy. of State John Foster Dulles vows "massive retaliation" against Soviet aggression (Jan. 12). Foreign Ministers Conference in Berlin fails to achieve reunification of Germany (Jan. 25-Feb. 18). Puerto Rican nationalists shoot five Congressmen on the floor of the House of Representatives (Mar. 1). U.S. negotiates the Southeast Asia Treaty Organization (SEATO) security pact (Sept. 8). Supreme Court orders school desegregation in the *Brown* decision (May 17). CIA helps overthrow the Arbenz government in Guatemala (June 29). Congress passes Communist Control Act. Senate censures Sen. Joseph McCarthy. France announces that U.S. has paid for most of the Indochina war. New York Stock Exchange prices finally reattain 1929 levels.

1955 Pres. Eisenhower promises to use atomic weapons in case of war and conducts first televised press conference. U.S., Soviet Union, and Allies agree on Austrian peace treaty to end occupation. Summit conference of U.S., British, French, and Soviet leaders in Switzerland produces "Spirit of Geneva." Supreme Court orders school desegregation to proceed "with all deliberate speed." Pres. Eisenhower hospitalized for three weeks following heart attack. Interstate Commerce Commission orders desegregation on interstate trains and buses. AFL and CIO labor federations merge to form the AFL-CIO, with 15 million members. Dr. Jonas Salk perfects polio vaccine. Dr. Martin Luther King, Jr., leads bus boycott in Montgomery, Ala.

1956 Pres. Eisenhower refuses to intervene against Soviet invasion of Hungary and exerts pressure on Allies to withdraw from Suez. Congressmen signing Southern Manifesto promise "massive resistance" to school desegregation. Atomic Energy Commission approves commercial nuclear power plants. Congress passes Highway Act, appropriating $32 billion for construction of a vast nationwide road system. TWA and United airliners collide in midair and crash into Grand Canyon, killing 128 people (June 30). First transAtlantic telephone cable begins operating. Grace Kelly marries Prince Rainier III of Monaco.

1957 Pres. Eisenhower announces Eisenhower Doctrine, promising aid to any Middle Eastern country threatened by Communism. McClellan Committee begins investigating corruption and racketeering in International Brotherhood of Teamsters union. Sen. J. Strom Thurmond of South Carolina sets all-time filibuster record (24 hours, 27 minutes) with speech against civil rights (Aug. 30). Congress eventually approves the first Civil Rights Act since Reconstruction (Sept. 9). Pres. Eisenhower sends troops to Little Rock, Ark., to enforce Federal desegregation order (Sept. 24). First underground atomic test conducted in Nevada (Sept. 19).

1958 In response to Soviet launch of Sputnik, U.S. launches Explorer I, first American satellite; Congress creates National Aeronautics and Space Administration (NASA) and passes National Defense Education Act. Vice President Nixon nearly killed by angry mob in Caracas, Venezuela. At request of weak government in Beirut, Pres.

Eisenhower orders U.S. Marines to land in Lebanon (July 15). Nuclear submarine *Nautilus* performs first undersea crossing of North Pole (Aug. 5). 6). Presidential assistant Sherman Adams forced to resign in scandal over accepting favors (Sept. 22). **1959** Fidel Castro's takeover of Cuba begins rapid deterioration of U.S.-Cuba relations (Jan. 1). Alaska becomes 49th state (Jan. 3), and Hawaii becomes 50th state (Aug. 21). Joint U.S.-Canada St. Lawrence Seaway project completed. Congress passes the Landrum-Griffin Act to suppress racketeering in labor unions. Vice Pres. Richard M. Nixon holds impromptu "kitchen debate" in Moscow with Soviet Premier Nikita Khrushchev. Charles Van Doren testifies that his victory on the "$64,000 Question" TV game show was fixed.
1960 U.S. and Japan conclude new security treaty (Jan. 19). Black students stage first sit-in at a Woolworth's lunch counter in Greensboro, N.C. (Feb. 1). U-2 spy plane, with American pilot Francis Gary Powers, is shot down over the Soviet Union (May 1). Congress passes second Civil Rights Act since Reconstruction. Congress investigates "payola" in the radio industry, leading to the arrest of Alan Freed, "father of rock 'n roll." After Cuba rejects American protests over confiscated property, Pres. Eisenhower imposes trade embargo. John F. Kennedy and Richard M. Nixon hold first televised presidential campaign debates. Kennedy wins election by 0.3% of popular vote, closest presidential election since 1884 (Nov. 8).
1961 Pres. Eisenhower breaks diplomatic relations with Cuba, warns Americans to beware of "military-industrial complex." CIA-backed Bay of Pigs invasion fails to overthrow Castro regime in Cuba (Apr. 17). Commander Alan B. Shephard, Jr., U.S. Navy, first American in space on Mercury rocket (May 5). Soviet construction of Berlin Wall creates temporary crisis (Aug. 13). Pres. Kennedy creates Peace Corps and Alliance for Progress. American families advised to build nuclear fallout shelters. "Freedom Rides" civil rights protests broken up by riots in Anniston and Birmingham, Ala. American Medical Association reports link between smoking and heart disease. National Council of Churches endorses birth control for families.
1962 Lt. Col. John H. Glenn, Jr., first American to orbit Earth. Stock market has worst day since 1929 (May 28). Pres. Kennedy convinces steel companies to rescind price increases. U.S. conducts first successful test of sea-launched long-range ballistic missile with nuclear warhead. Pres. Kennedy sends U.S. marshals to protect James H. Meredith, a black student at University of Mississippi. U.S. extends a $100 million emergency loan to the United Nations. Threat of nuclear war during Cuban Missile Crisis averted when Soviet Union agrees to withdraw missiles from Cuba (Oct. 22-28). Rachel Carson's *Silent Spring* draws attention to environmental crisis. U.S. Military Assistance Command set up in South Vietnam.
1963 Pres. Kennedy proposes the Medicare program. U.S., Great Britain, and the Soviet Union conclude the Nuclear Test-Ban Treaty outlawing atmospheric testing (July 25). "Hot line" between Washington and Moscow put in place. Civil rights movement reaches a climax with mass demonstrations in Birmingham, Ala., and epic March on Washington, where Martin Luther King delivers his "I Have a Dream" speech (Aug. 28). Pres. Kennedy is assassinated in Dallas, Tex., by Lee Harvey Oswald (Nov. 22), who is murdered by Jack Ruby (Nov. 24). Joseph Valachi testifies before Congress about the extent of organized crime in the U.S.

1964 Pres. Johnson, taking up Pres. Kennedy's cause, calls for a "War on Poverty." Supreme Court orders states to redraw Congressional boundaries to ensure fair representation. Alaska declared disaster area after major earthquake rocks Anchorage (Mar. 28). Mississippi "Freedom Summer" begins with murder of three civil rights workers (June 22). Pres. Johnson pushes landmark Civil Rights and Economic Opportunity acts through Congress. After alleged North Vietnamese attack on U.S. Navy destroyers, Congress passes Tonkin Gulf Resolution giving Pres. Johnson free hand in Vietnam (Aug. 7). Warren Commission reports there was no conspiracy to assassinate Pres. Kennedy (Sept. 27). Martin Luther King wins Nobel Peace Prize.
1965 Pres. Johnson calls for the "Great Society." Black nationalist Malcolm X is assassinated in New York City (Feb. 21). Pres. Johnson orders U.S. Marines into South Vietnam (Mar. 8) and into Santo Domingo (Apr. 38). U.S. troops authorized to undertake offensive operations in South Vietnam (June 8). Martin Luther King leads civil rights marches from Selma to Montgomery, Ala., and in white neighborhoods of Chicago. Congress approves Medicare (July 30) and Voting Rights Act (Aug. 6). The Watts Riot in Los Angeles leaves 34 dead and over $200 million in damage (Aug. 11-16), accelerating wave of ghetto riots. Tornadoes sweep Midwest, killing 271 and injuring 5,000. East Coast power blackout affects over 30 million Americans and Canadians (Nov. 9-10).
1966 Pres. Johnson orders first B-52 strategic bombing raids on North Vietnam (Apr. 12). Supreme Court rules police must advise suspects of their rights. Cesar Chavez leads United Farm Workers strike and boycott against California grape growers. Stokeley Carmichael of Student Non-Violent Coordinating Committee demands "Black Power." Congress enacts safety standards for automobiles. Edward W. Brooke of Massachusetts is first black Senator since Reconstruction. National Football League and American Football League agree to play Super Bowl championship game. Number of blacks voting in the South nearly doubles in one year. U.S. troops in Vietnam increases from 215,000 to over 400,000.
1967 The 500th U.S. plane shot down over North Vietnam (Apr. 4). Hundreds of thousands of antiwar protestors march on Washington (Apr. 15 & Oct. 21-22). Pres. Johnson announces U.S. troop level will reach 525,000 by end of 1968. Worst race riot in U.S. history erupts in Detroit (July 23), leaving 43 dead, while riot in Newark, N.J., (July 12) kills another 26. Sen. Eugene McCarthy (D-Minn.) announces antiwar candidacy for president (Nov. 30). U.S. agrees to refrain from placing nuclear weapons in space and joins General Agreement on Tariffs and Trade (GATT). Albert DeSalvo, the "Boston Strangler," sentenced to life in prison. Stalin's daughter Svetlana Aliluyeva defects to U.S. Thurgood Marshall becomes first black justice on Supreme Court.
1968 North Korea seizes USS *Pueblo*, holding 82 crewmen hostage (Jan. 23). North Vietnam and Viet Cong launch massive Tet Offensive (Jan. 30). Pres. Johnson makes surprise announcement that he will not seek re-election (Mar. 31). Martin Luther King assassinated by James Earl Ray in Memphis, Tenn. (Apr. 4). Student protestors take over Columbia University (Apr. 23). Washington-Hanoi peace talks begin in Paris (May 10). After winning California primary, Sen. Robert F. Kennedy of New York murdered by Sirhan Sirhan

in Los Angeles (June 5). U.S. signs Nuclear Non-Proliferation Treaty. Democratic Convention in Chicago marred by riots and police violence against antiwar demonstrators. Shirley Chisholm of New York is the first black woman elected to Congress. Apollo VIII completes first moon orbit. **1969**   Oil spill off Santa Barbara, Calif., draws attention to need for environmental protection (Feb. 5). Pres. Nixon asks Congress to fund Anti-Ballistic Missile program (ABM) as "safeguard" for strategic defense. U.S. losses in Vietnam exceed losses in Korean War. U.S. troop withdrawals from Vietnam begin (July 8). Sen. Edward M. Kennedy (D-Mass.) drives off a bridge at Chappaquiddick, Mass., killing Mary Jo Kopechne (July 18). Neil Armstrong and Buzz Aldrin of Apollo XI are first men to walk on the moon (July 20). Hurricane Camille claims over 300 victims in the South. Trial of Chicago Eight (later Chicago Seven, after Bobby Seale tried separately) begins. Woodstock music festival near Bethel, N.Y., draws 400,000 young fans (Aug. 15–18). Vietnam Moratorium and "March Against Death" antiwar demonstrations draw hundreds of thousands to Washington. U.S. and the Soviet Union begin Strategic Arms Limitation Talks (SALT) in Helsinki, Finland.
1970   Pres. Nixon calls for "Vietnamization" to decrease U.S. involvement in war. U.S. bombing of North Vietnam escalates dramatically; nationwide protests break out when U.S. invades Cambodia (Apr. 29). Four students are killed and nine wounded by National Guard units at Kent State University in Ohio (May 4). SALT negotiations reopen in Vienna, Austria. Lt. William L. Calley court martialed for massacre of 102 civilians in My Lai South Vietnam (Nov. 12). Supreme Court upholds new 18-year-old voting age (Dec. 21). Congress passes Water Quality Improvement Act, Air Quality Control Act, and Occupational Safety and Health Act. U.S. troops in Vietnam down to 340,000 at year end.
1971   Pres. Nixon proposes Federal revenue sharing with states. Charles Manson and three women followers convicted for Tate-LaBianca murders in Los Angeles (Jan. 25). Major earthquake rocks Southern California, killing 64 and injuring over 1,000 (Feb. 9). U.S. ping-pong team visits China, relaxing Cold War tensions. Supreme Court approves busing to achieve school integration. Indian occupation of Alcatraz Island in San Francisco Bay comes to an end. Prison riot in Attica, N.Y., kills 43 inmates and guards. *New York Times* begins publishing "Pentagon Papers," top-secret history of Vietnam War (June 13). U.S. devalues dollar (Dec. 18). U.S. troops in Vietnam reach 139,000; U.S. air attacks are heaviest since 1968.
1972   Nixon first president to visit China (Feb. 21–28) and the Soviet Union (May 22–30). Airlines begin screening passengers to prevent hijackings. Congress passes Equal Rights Amendment and submits it to states for ratification. Gov. George Wallace of Alabama shot and seriously wounded by Arthur Bremer while campaigning for president in Laurel, Md. (May 15). Five men arrested for breaking into Democratic National Committee headquarters at the Watergate complex in Washington (June 17). Federal grand jury indicts five burglars and two former White House aides in Watergate trial (Sept. 15). Pres. Nixon angers farmers with the "Great Grain Robbery," a secret deal to sell wheat at discount to Soviet Union. National Security Advisor Henry Kissinger announces "peace is at hand" in Vietnam in time for Pres. Nixon to carry 49 states in election. U.S. troops in

Vietnam fall to 69,000 as Nixon orders resumption of heavy bombing of North Vietnam (Dec. 18).
1973   Supreme Court disallows state restrictions on abortions (*Roe vs. Wade*). U.S. signs Paris peace accords ending Vietnam War (Jan. 27). Trial of Watergate burglars reveals conspiracy to conceal White House involvement. Top presidential aides H.R. Haldeman, John Ehrlichman, John Dean, and Attorney General Richard Kleindienst resign amid charges of White House cover-up (Apr. 30). Sen. Sam Ervin of North Carolina chairs Senate investigation of Watergate scandal on national television (May 17–Nov. 15). Pres. Nixon fires Watergate Special Prosecutor Archibald Cox and others in "Saturday Night Massacre" (Oct. 20). Vice President Spiro Agnew resigns after threat of for tax evasion (Oct. 10). Gasoline prices skyrocket after Arab nations embargo oil exports to U.S. in retaliation for U.S. aid to Israel in Yom Kippur War (Oct. 17). Pres. Nixon turns over first White House tapes, which include mysterious 18 1/2 minute gap (Nov. 26). Gerald R. Ford of Michigan sworn in as first vice president chosen under 25th Amendment (Dec. 6). Indians defy Federal authority in Wounded Knee, S.D.
1974   Arab oil embargo of U.S. lifted (Mar. 18). Supreme Court rules that Pres. Nixon must submit all White House tapes to Special Prosecutor Leon Jaworski (July 24). House Judiciary Committee votes three articles of impeachment (July 24–30). Pres. Nixon releases transcripts of tapes that show he ordered cover-up (Aug. 5). Citing "political" difficulties, Pres. Nixon resigns (Aug. 8), elevating Vice President Ford to presidency (Aug. 9). Pres. Ford shocks nation by pardoning Nixon for all crimes (Sept. 8). Pres. Ford meets with Soviet Premier Leonid Brezhnev in Vladivostock to approve SALT treaty (Nov. 23 –24). Newspaper heiress Patty Hearst kidnapped in Berkeley, Calif., by radical Symbionese Liberation Army.
1975   Nixon aides convicted of obstructing justice in Watergate investigation (Jan. 1). Last Americans evacuate Saigon as South Vietnam falls to North Vietnamese invasion (Apr. 30). Cambodia seizes USS *Mayaguez* (May 12), and Pres. Ford orders rescue operation (May 14). Apollo-Soyuz, joint Soviet-American space mission, achieves link-up in space (July 17). Lynette "Squeaky" Fromme and Sarah Jane Moore attempt to assassinate Pres. Ford in separate California incidents (Sept. 5 & Sept. 22). Congress votes to admit women to Army, Navy, and Air Force academies. President's Commission on Civil Rights reports Southern schools more integrated than Northern schools. House Democrats dismantle seniority system. Church Committee discovers CIA helped overthrow Salvador Allende of Chile and plotted to assassinate Fidel Castro of Cuba.
1976   Congress repeatedly overrides Pres. Ford's vetoes of bills providing for jobs, health, education, and welfare programs. Senate investigators find Lockheed Corp. paid $22 million in bribes to foreign officials. Supreme Court upholds death penalty (July 3). Bicentennial of U.S. celebrated coast to coast. Pres. Ford, in campaign debate with Democratic candidate Jimmy Carter, insists there is "no Soviet domination of Eastern Europe" (Oct. 7). Justice Department begins probing South Korean bribery of Congressmen and other officials. NASA's Viking I and Viking II space probes land on Mars and transmit scientific data, along with color photographs, back to Earth. "Legionnaire's Disease" breaks out at American Legion convention in Philadelphia, eventually claiming

29 victims. Patty Hearst convicted of armed robbery in California. Hundreds of West Point cadets found to have cheated on exams.

1977 Cold winter and heavy snows hit Eastern states. Pres. Carter pardons Vietnam War draft evaders, threatens to reduce foreign aid for countries violating human rights, calls for "moral equivalent of war" in energy conservation, and signs Panama Canal treaty (Sept. 7). U.S. declares 200-mile sovereignty zone in Atlantic and Pacific oceans to exclude foreign fishing vessels. Power blackout sets off arson and looting spree in New York City (July 13–14). Oil begins flowing through the Alaska pipeline. Pres. Carter accuses oil industry of "the biggest rip-off in history" (Oct. 13). Severe drought leads to water rationing on West Coast. ABC mini-series *Roots*, draws 130 million viewers.

1978 Pres. Carter postpones production of neutron bomb. California voters approve Proposition 13, reducing property taxes and setting off a nationwide "taxpayers' revolt." Supreme Court gives limited approval to affirmative action programs, but disallows quotas for college admissions (June 28). In private talks with Anwar Sadat and Menachem Begin, Pres. Carter mediates peace between Egypt and Israel with landmark Camp David Accords (Sept. 17). Nearly one thousand American followers of the Rev. Jim Jones commit mass suicide in Jonestown, Guiana, after cult members murder Rep. Leo Ryan of California and others (Nov. 18). House investigations of John F. Kennedy and Martin Luther King assassinations conclude that conspiracies were probable in both cases (Dec. 30). Congress extends deadline for ratifying Equal Rights Amendment. Federal loan guarantees rescue New York City from financial crisis.

1979 U.S. resumes diplomatic relations with China (Jan 1). Pres. Carter commutes Patty Hearst's sentence, releasing her from jail. Farmers drive thousands of tractors into Washington to dramatize grievances. Worst nuclear accident in U.S. history takes place at Three Mile Island power plant near Harrisburg, Pa. Pres. Carter and Premier Brezhnev sign SALT II treaty in Vienna (June 18). The Shah of Iran and Anastasio Somoza of Nicaragua, both U.S.-supported dictators, flee revolutions in their countries. Iranian militants seize U.S. Embassy in Teheran, taking 66 American hostages and demanding return of the Shah from U.S. (Nov. 4). Iranians release 13 American hostages, all blacks or women. Pres. Carter deports illegal Iranian students, freezes Iranian assets, and bars oil imports from Iran. Pope John Paul II visits U.S. Inflation reaches highest level in 33 years as Organization of Petroleum Exporting Countries (OPEC) doubles price of oil.

1980 Canadian embassy officials help six Americans escape from Iran (Jan. 29). In response to Soviet invasion of Afghanistan, Pres. Carter embargoes grain and high technology exports to Soviet Union, approves arms sales to China, and secures U.S. boycott of Olympics in Moscow. Congress grants Pres. Carter's request for Crude Oil Windfall Profits Tax and for resumption of Selective Service draft registration. Pres. Carter's secret rescue mission for American hostages in Iran fails when a U.S. Navy hellcopter crashes in desert, killing eight servicemen (Apr. 24). Mt. St. Helens erupts in Washington state, killing 26 people and causing $2.7 billion in damage (May 18). Banking and trucking industries deregulated. FBI's "Abscam" operation implicates over 30 public officials, including a Senator and seven Congressmen, for accepting bribes.

1981 Minutes after Pres. Reagan is sworn in, Iran releases 52 American hostages after 444 days in captivity. Pres. Reagan shot by John Hinckley in Washington (Mar. 30), but undergoes surgery and makes full recovery. *Columbia* completes first successful space shuttle mission (Apr. 12–14). Gov. Jerry Brown of California orders aerial spraying to combat Mediterranean fruit fly. Federal air traffic controllers go on strike and lose jobs when Pres. Reagan fires all 13,000 of them. Sandra Day O'Connor unanimously confirmed as first woman justice of Supreme Court. Pres. Reagan lifts grain embargo against Soviet Union, but imposes new sanctions after Poland declares martial law. Congress accepts Pres. Reagan's plans for tax cuts, lower domestic spending, and major defense buildup. U.S. sends military advisors and aid to El Salvador. Professional baseball players stage two-month strike.

1982 Ending 13-year antitrust suit, AT&T agrees to surrender control of local Bell System phone companies in return for expansion into new business pursuits (Jan. 8). Pres. Reagan calls for "New Federalism," transferring programs to state and local control. Congress rejects nuclear freeze (Aug. 5). Unemployment exceeds 10% for first time since Great Depression, and Federal budget deficit exceeds $100 billion a year for first time ever. After a decade, Equal Rights Amendment fails falling three states short of ratification.

1983 Inflation slows as oil prices decline sharply. Congress admits internment of Japanese-Americans during World War II was unjust, and agrees to bail out the Social Security system. National Commission on Excellence in Education reports U.S. is a "nation at risk" because of inferior elementary and secondary schools. Sally Ride is first American woman astronaut, aboard space shuttle *Challenger*. Klaus Barbie, Nazi war criminal, revealed to be living in U.S. with government protection. Pres. Reagan strongly condemns Soviet Union for shooting down Korean airliner with 269 people aboard (Sept. 1). U.S. Marines join multinational peacekeeping force in Beirut, Lebanon, where Muslim terrorists kill 240 of them in suicide bombing (Oct. 23). U.S. invades Grenada to overthrow Cuban-backed regime (Oct. 25). Pres. Reagan calls for large-scale funding of Strategic Defense Initiative, or "Star Wars."

1984 Reagan recovery underway as unemployment falls, inflation rate declines, economic growth accelerates, and U.S. dollar soars on international markets. Lt. Robert C. Goodman, Jr., U.S. Navy pilot downed over Lebanon during air raid against Muslim positions, freed by Syrian intercession (Jan. 3). Pres. Reagan orders U.S. Marines out of Lebanon (Feb. 7). Congress censures Pres. Reagan for misusing funds to mine Nicaraguan harbors, later condemned by World Court. Pres. Reagan visits China (Apr. 26–May 1). Rep. Geraldine Ferraro, Democrat of New York, first woman to receive major party nomination for vice president. Soviet bloc countries boycott Olympics in Los Angeles. Jesse Jackson, Democrat of Illinois, mounts first major challenge by black candidate for major party nomination. Pres. Reagan wins landslide re-election over Democratic challenger Walter Mondale.

1985 Pres. Reagan calls for more tax and budget cuts to sustain economic growth (Feb. 4–6). Despite worldwide protests from Jewish organizations, Pres. Reagan visits West Germany to deliver address at Bitburg cemetery, where Nazi SS troops are buried (May 5). Muslim terrorists hijack TWA airliner (June 14), kill one American hostage, then release rest in Beirut (June 30). Palestinian terrorists kill an American hostage aboard hijacked Italian cruise ship *Achille Lauro* (Oct. 9). Pres. Reagan and Soviet Premier Mikhail Gorbachev hold their first summit meeting in Geneva (Nov. 19–21). Pres. Reagan signs Gramm-Rudman Act, requiring automatic spending cuts if Congress cannot reduce burgeoning Federal deficit.

1986 Space shuttle *Challenger* explodes in midair over Florida, killing six astronauts and a civilian passenger (Jan. 28). Investigations reveal NASA relaxed safety regulations to speed up launch date. U.S. Navy repels attack by Libyan forces during maneuvers in Gulf of Sidra (Mar. 24). Pres. Reagan blames Libya for death of two Americans in terrorist bombing of West Berlin disco, then orders retaliatory air raids on Tripoli and Benghazi (Apr. 14). Second Reagan-Gorbachev summit in Reykjavik, Iceland, reaches impasse over arms control and "Star Wars" (Oct. 12). Congress approves sweeping revision of U.S. tax structure. Democrats regain control of Senate. Pres. Reagan denies trading arms for hostages as Iran-Contra scandal breaks (Nov. 19). Wall Street financier Ivan Boesky fined $100 million for illegal insider trading on stock market.

1987 Pres. Reagan submits first trillion-dollar U.S. budget to Congress as national debt mounts steadily. Stock market closes above 2000 for first time in U.S. history. Tower Commission inquiry into Iran-Contra affair criticizes White House staff and Pres. Reagan's "management style." TV evangelist Jim Bakker resigns after admitting his affair with Jessica Hahn. U.S.-Japan trade war erupts. After Pres. Reagan orders U.S. Navy into Persian Gulf to escort Kuwaiti oil tankers, an Iraqi warplane accidentally attacks USS *Stark*, killing 37 sailors (May 27). Bernhard Goetz acquitted of major charges in New York City "Subway Vigilante" shootings. Stock market crashes 508 points in one day, an all-time record, jolting markets around the world (Oct. 16). Third Reagan-Gorbachev summit in Washington produces agreement to dismantle medium-range missiles in Europe (Dec. 8).

1988 U.S. pressure on ruler Mañuel Noriega to step down plunges Panama into economic turmoil. After Iran lays mines in Persian Gulf, U.S. Navy warships and planes destroy two Iranian oil platforms and repel Iranian counterattacks (Apr. 18–19). USS *Vincennes* accidentally shoots down Iranian passenger plane, killing 290 people (July 3). Pres. Reagan visits Moscow to meet with Premier Gorbachev. George Bush becomes first sitting vice president elected president since 1836. PLO Chairman Yasser Arafat is denied U.S. visa to address United Nations. Terrorist bomb aboard Pan Am Flight 103 kills all 259 aboard, mostly Americans, and 11 on the ground in Lockerbie, Scotland (Dec. 21). Drexel Burnham Lambert agrees to pay all-time record $650 million penalty for securities fraud (Dec. 21).

1989 *Exxon Valdez* supertanker spills over 11 million gallons of oil off Alaska coast (Mar. 24). HUD scandal reveals fraud, mismanagement, and influence-peddling under Reagan administration. Top Democrats Jim Wright—Speaker of the House—and Tony Coelho—majority whip—resign from House over ethics violations. Supreme Court upholds the right to burn U.S. flag and approves state limits on abortion. President Bush signs $300 billion savings-and-loan bailout (Aug. 9). Severe earthquake, second worst in U.S. history, inflicts $6 billion damage and leaves 62 dead in San Francisco Bay area (Oct. 17). L. Douglas Wilder of Virginia is the first black elected gover-

nor (Nov. 7). After Panama declares a "state of war" with the U.S., Pres. Bush sends 24,000 U.S. troops to overthrow the Noriega regime and install a popularly elected government (Dec. 20).

1990 After Iraq invades Kuwait (Aug.2), U.S. launches Operation Desert Shield: more than 200,000 U.S. troops move into Saudi Arabia and the navy blockades all oil exports from Iraq and all imports except food. Pres. Bush refuses any compromise with Iraq's dictator, Saddam Hussein, and works with UN Security Council to obtain condemnation of invasion and imposition of stringent economic sanctions. Bush and Gorbachev meet twice: U.S. agrees to some economic aid, grants USSR most favored nation trade status, also secures some arms reductions and agreement that Iraq must withdraw from Kuwait. Pres. Bush breaks campaign pledge of "no new taxes." A major flaw in the $1.5 bil. Hubble Space Telescope is discovered shortly after its deployment. Drexel Burnham Lambert defaults on $100 mil. in loans, and Michael Milken, head of "junk bond" department, is fined $600 mil. and sentenced to jail.

1991 U.S. Operation Desert Storm quickly and decisively drives Iraq's armed forces out of Kuwait. The ground war lasts only 100 hours and involves only 144 American casualties. Bush and Gorbachev sign first nuclear arms reduction treaty (July 31) but Soviet Union's government and economy continue to crumble. U.S. establishes diplomatic relations with former Soviet republics, Estonia, Latvia, and Lithuania. Unemployment rate rises to highest level in a decade. Interest rates are cut to lowest levels in 20 years. Senate's confirmation of Clarence Thomas's nomination to Supreme Court is delayed by Anita Hill's luridly detailed charges (Oct. 6) of sexual harassment 10 years earlier. U.S. regulators seize Bank of Credit and Commerce International (BCCI) on charges of fraud and money-laundering world-wide. Oliver North and John Poindexter are exonerated in connection with the Iran-contra scandal. Four white Los Angeles policemen indicted for videotaped beating of black motorist Rodney King.

1992 The Americans with Disabilities Act, the most sweeping anti-discrimination legislation since the Civil Rights Act of 1964 guarantees equal access for the disabled (Jan. 26). Pres. Bush and Russian Pres. Boris Yeltsin issue joint statement officially ending the Cold War (Feb.1). Riots erupt in Los Angeles minutes after an all-white jury acquits four L.A. police officers on charges of beating Rodney King (April 29–May 4). More than 50 people are killed, 2,000 injured, and over 7,000 arrested in the week-long turmoil. At first-ever Earth summit (June 3–17), U.S. is lone industrial nation not to sign biodiversity treaty on preservation of plant, animal and microbial species. Billionaire-populist Ross Perot enters the presidential race as a third-party candidate. Federal Reserve cuts discount rate to 3%, its lowest rate since 1963, after unemployment skyrockets to 7.8%, its highest level since 1983 (July 2). Bill Clinton defeats George Bush and Ross Perot to become the 42nd President of the United States (Nov. 3). Pres. Bush commits at least 28,000 U.S. troops to protect the delivery of relief supplies to war- and famine-torn Somalia (Dec. 3). IBM announces it will cut 25,000 more jobs in 1993 in the wake of $6 billion losses, the biggest loss ever for an American corporation. Pres. Bush pardons six Reagan Administration officials for their involvement in the Iran-Contra scandal (Dec. 24).

1993 In the first attempt ever to eliminate an entire category of weapons, more than 120 nations, including the U.S. and Russia, sign an agreement to ban production, stockpiling, and use of all chemical weapons and to destroy them all within 10 years (Jan. 13). Hillary Rodham Clinton becomes the first First Lady to have an office in the White House. She chairs a committee to overhaul the nation's health care system. Sears Roebuck and Co. announces it will close 113 stores, eliminate 50,000 jobs, and cease publication of the Sears Catalog after 97 years (Jan. 25). Congress passes the family leave bill guaranteeing workers up to 12 weeks of unpaid leave for medical emergencies. Pres. Clinton signs this bill that Bush had twice vetoed (Feb. 4). A powerful car bomb rips through the underground parking garage at New York's World Trade Center, killing 7, injuring about 1,000, and causing the evacuation of more than 50,000 workers. (Feb. 26). Four agents from the Federal Bureau of Alcohol, Tobacco and Firearms are killed in a bloody gunfight at the Waco, Texas compound of religious cult leader David Koresh, beginning a 51-day standoff that ends when Koresh sets the buildings on fire, resulting in a conflagration that kills him and 86 of his followers, including 17 children (April 19). "The worst storm of the century" according to the National Weather Service pelts the mid-Atlantic and Northeast regions with as much as 40 inches of snow, killing at least 104 people. The Supreme Court rules (9-0) that public school systems must permit religious groups to use their buildings after hours if they allow community groups to do so (June 7). Law enforcement officials raid a suspected bomb factory in New York City, uncovering a highly organized terrorist group plotting to bomb the UN, Federal office buildings, and the Lincoln and Holland tunnels, and to assassinate several prominent politicians. Eight suspects are arrested, all said to be Muslim extremists (June 24). The Supreme Court rules (5-4) that legislative districts drawn to increase black representation can violate the constitutional rights of white voters. At least 12 U.S. soldiers are killed and 78 wounded by Somali gunmen during UN military operations in Mogadishu. Pres. Clinton signs the Brady bill, requiring gun purchasers to wait five days before taking possession to give sellers and law enforcement officials time to check the buyers' backgrounds for criminal records or mental instability. The United States and Europe agree on new terms for the General Agreement of Tariffs and Trade (GATT), reducing tariffs substantially on trade in more industries in more countries than any other pact in history. The Pentagon rules that gays and lesbians may now serve in the military, but may not openly engage in homosexual behavior or proclaim their sexual orientation. Astronauts succeed in restoring full vision to the Hubble Space Telescope.

1994 Federated Department Stores acquires rival R.H. Macy & Company, creating the largest department store chain in America. Iran-contra prosecutor, Lawrence E. Walsh, releases his final report on the incident, finding no credible evidence that President Ronald Reagan or Vice President George Bush broke the law. (Jan. 18). Federal prosecutors accuse former CIA agent Aldrich H. Ames of being a double-agent for the KGB and compromising some of the most closely guarded U.S. intelligence secrets (Feb. 22). All four of the men on trial for the World Trade Center bombing are found guilty of all 38 charges against them and are each sentenced to 240 years in prison. The Dow Corning Corporation, Bristol-Myers Squibb Company, and the Baxter-Healthcare Corporation agree to pay $3.7 billion over 30 years to up to 25,000 women injured by silicone breast implants. Rodney King wins $3.8 mil. in damages in compensation for his 1991 beating by the L.A. police. L.A. police charge former football star O.J. Simpson with murdering his ex-wife Nicole Brown and Ron Goldman. Simpson leads police on a bizarre 60-mile low-speed car chase (televised live on all major networks) before surrendering to police (June 17). The dollar dips below 100 Japanese yen, a post-World War II low (June 21). Major league baseball players begin the longest strike in professional sports history, resulting in the cancellation of the World Series for the first time ever (Aug. 11). Pres. Clinton signs the crime bill, outlawing semiautomatic weapons and increasing police. The Bureau of Justice Statistics announces that the number of inmates in state and Federal prisons topped one million, giving the U.S. the highest incarceration rate in the world. In midterm elections, Republicans take control of both Houses of Congress for the first time in 40 years (Nov. 8).

1995 Pres. Clinton signs the Congressional Accountability Act, ending Congress's exemption from laws against workplace harassment and discrimination. The Dow Jones industrial average tops the 4,000 mark for the first time (Feb. 23). A Federal judge issues an injunction aganst major league baseball owners for unfair labor practices, restoring the arbitration and free agency of the previous collective bargaining agreement, and persuading players to end the longest strike in sports history. In the deadliest bombing in the U.S. in 75 years, a massive car bomb blows up a Federal building in Oklahoma City, killing 169 people, including 15 children in a day-care center in the building (April 19). Authorities apprehend Timothy McVeigh (April 21) as a prime suspect. The Supreme Court votes 5-4 that neither the states nor Congress may impose term limits on Congressional office without a constitutional amendment, wiping out term-limit legislation in 23 states. The Supreme Court (5-4) rules that affirmative action programs can only survive constitutional scrutiny if they are "narrowly tailored" to accomplish a "compelling governmental interest," but stops short of dismantling affirmative action completely. Pres. Clinton announces full diplomatic recognition of Vietnam (July 11). The Walt Disney Company acquires Capital Cities/ABC for $19 bil. A Federal grand jury indicts Timothy J. McVeigh and Terry L. Nichols on charges of blowing up the Oklahoma City Federal Building. A Federal grand jury indicts Pres. Clinton's Whitewater business partners for fraud, conspiracy, and making false statements to obtain federally secured loans for Madison Guarantee Savings and Loan (Aug. 17). The Chase Manhattan Corporation merges with the Chemical Banking Corporation, creating the largest bank in the nation. The League of Women Voters reports that more than five million Americans have registered to vote—the greatest expansion of voter rolls in history—in the eight months since "The Motor Voter Law." Sen. Bob Packwood (R-Oreg.) resigns from the Senate as the Ethics Committee releases over 10,000 pages of evidence documenting his salacious behavior. Sheik Omar Abdel Rahman and nine of his militant Muslim followers are convicted of conspiring to blowup the United Nations and assassinate political leaders from Egypt and the U.S. A mostly black Los Angeles jury finds O.J. Simpson not guilty of murdering his ex-wife Nicole Brown Simpson and her friend Ronald Goldman. Much of the nine-month-long trial had been broadcast live by many television networks.

The verdict divides the country largely along racial lines. (Oct. 3). At the urging of Nation of Islam leader Louis Farrakhan, an estimated 400,000 black men gather in Washington, D.C. for the "Million Man March," where they pledge to protect their communities against violence. Nonessential offices of the Federal government shut down while Pres. Clinton and the Republican-controlled Congress spar over the budget, putting 800,000 employees out of work for six days. Pres. Clinton dispatches 20,000 U.S. troops to Bosnia as part of an international deployment to enforce the Dayton peace agreements to end the four-year civil war in the Balkans.

1996 Congress votes to return hundreds of thousands of workers to their jobs and to reopen nonessential government offices that had been shut down for three weeks in the budget impasse. Pres. Clinton offers a plan to balance the budget within seven years, as Republicans had demanded, but promising smaller tax cuts (Jan. 5–6). The Hubble Space Telescope returns pictures showing the existence of more than 50 billion galaxies, or five times the number previously thought to exist. According to the new information, the Sun is one of 100 billion stars in the Milky Way. Hillary Rodham Clinton becomes the first First Lady to testify before a grand jury when she is subpoenaed to testify about whether White House personnel obstructed the Whitewater investigation. Congress approves a vast bill rewriting laws governing the telecommunications industries, deregulating cable television, increasing competition among local phone companies, and requiring a v-chip in new televisions to screen out violence (Feb. 1). Conservative columnist Pat Buchanan shocks Bob Dole and the Republican party with a narrow victory in the New Hampshire primary (Feb. 20). Bob Dole captures eight primaries in delegate-rich states across the country, re-establishing himself as the front-runner for the Republican presidential nomination (Mar. 5). The Hubble Space Telescope returns the first-ever pictures of Pluto (Mar. 7). The Liggett Group becomes the first U.S. cigarette manufacturer to break ranks and agree to a settlement in a giant classs action suit against the tobacco industry (Mar. 13). FBI agents raid a cabin in rural Montana and capture former university professor Theodore J. Kaczynski, allegedly the Unabomber, a terrorist mail bomber who has killed three people and injured 23 others over a 17-year period (April 2). Pres. Clinton signs the line-item veto, which allows the president to invalidate certain bills without negating entire packages of legislation. (Apr. 9). Former House Ways and Means Chairman Dan Rostenkowski pleads guilty to mail fraud and begins a 17-month prison sentence, making him the most prominent official ever to go to prison for official corruption. Pres. Clinton signs legislation allowing workers to take their health insurance with them when they change or leave jobs and to restrict insurers' ability to deny policies to workers with preexisting medical conditions. The worst drought since the Dust Bowl era of the 1930s plagues the southwest, bankrupting 10,000 farmers in Oklahoma alone. The Supreme Court overturns an amendment to Colorado's state constitution that would have prevented local communities from enacting gay rights legislation (May 20). Ark. Gov. Jim Guy Tucker and James and Susan McDougal , three former business partners of Pres. Clinton, are convicted of felonies in connection with the failed Madison Guaranty Savings and Loan. The Freemen, a right-wing anti-govern-

ment militia group, surrender to Federal agents after an 81-day standoff at their compound in Jordan, Montana (June 13). The Census Bureau reports that the gap between the richest 20 percent of Americans and everybody else has reached postwar high (June 18). A truck bomb blows up a housing complex in Saudi Arabia, killing 19 U.S. soldiers and wounding 300 others (June 25). TWA Flight 800 explodes in midair and crashes into the Atlantic Ocean, killing all 230 aboard (July 17). The FTC approves a merger between Time Warner and Turner Broadcasting, creating the world's largest media company. A pipe bomb blows up in Atlanta's Centennial Olympic Park, killing one woman and injuring more than 100; Olympic officials pledge to continue the games (July 27). Pres. Clinton signs welfare reform legislation, ending more than 60 years of Federal cash assistance and replacing it with a system of block grants to the states (July 31). Republicans nominate Bob Dole and Jack Kemp for president and vice president (Aug. 15). The Reform Party nominates Ross Perot for President (Aug. 17). Democrats renominate Bill Clinton and Al Gore for president and vice president (Aug. 28). Hurricane Fran batters the southeast coast, killing 22 people and causing $1 billion worth of damage (Sept. 4–7). Pres. Clinton signs the Defense of Marriage Act, denying Federal recognition to same-sex marriages, (Sept. 21). Pres. Clinton defeats Bob Dole and Ross Perot to win re-election (Nov. 5).

1997 The U.S. economy continues to grow, driving unemployment below 5 percent for the first time in 24 years. The stock market soars (the Dow Jones Industrial Average breaks 7,000 in Feb., and 8,000 in July) and mergers and acquisitions of major corporations in all fields reach record levels: notably Dean Witter and Morgan Stanley, Lockheed Martin and Northrup Grumman, World Com and MCI. Two bombs explode at an Atlanta abortion clinic injuring six people (Jan. 16). A House subcommittee cites a pattern of ethics flaws in Speaker Newt Gingrich's behavior and the House votes 395-28 to fine him $300,000. (Jan. 21). Madeleine Albright is confirmed by the Senate to be the first woman Sec. of State. A civil jury finds O.J. Simpson liable in the killings of his ex-wife and her friend and orders Simpson to pay $33.5 million in damages to their families. The Senate unanimously approves a very broad investigation into White House and Congressional campaign fund-raising (March 11). Pres. Clinton and Boris Yeltsin meet in Helsinki (March 20-21) and report agreements regarding arms control and a partnership role in NATO for Russia. Comet Hale-Bopp, with its brilliant 31-million-mile tail, makes continuous appearances from March to May. Police in San Diego County find the bodies of 39 members of a cult called Heaven's Gate who committed suicide together when Comet Hale-Bopp appeared (March 26). Atty. General Janet Reno rejects Republican demands for a special prosecutor to investigate President Clinton's re-election campaign. The Senate approves (74-26) the Chemical Weapons Convention prohibiting the production and storage of poison gas. President Clinton and Republican leaders reach agreement on a plan to balance the budget by 2002. (May 2). The Army charges Sergeant Major Gene C. McKinney, its highest-ranking enlisted man, with sexual misconduct and indecent assault. The first U.S. Ambassador to Vietnam in 22 years arrives in Hanoi. (May 9). The Supreme Court rules unanimously that a sitting president can be sued for actions outside the scope of his official duties thereby allowing the Paula Jones sexual harassment suit to proceed. After a trial lasting five weeks, Timothy J. McVeigh is found guilty on all 11 counts of murder and conspiracy in the 1995 bombing of the Federal building in Oklahoma City that killed 168 (June 2); he is sentenced to death. The tobacco industry agrees to pay $368.5 bil. over 25 years to compensate states for the cost of smoking-related illnesses. The Supreme Court rules (5-4) that the Constitution allows public school teachers to work in parochial schools that need remedial or supplemental classes. Pres. Clinton approves EPA's tighter pollution limits on deadly soot and smog. The Federal deficit is expected to drop to $37 bil., its lowest level in 23 years. The Teamsters union conducts a 15-day strike against United Parcel Service, the nation's largest shipping company, winning a five-year contract that includes more full-time jobs and a raise for part-timers. *Mars Pathfinder*, a robotic spacecraft, arrives on Mars (July 4), and sends back panoramic pictures of the landscape. Federal officials say 95,000 children will lose their disability benefits under the 1996 welfare law. IBM Computer, Deep Blue, defeats world chess champion Garry Kasparov. Pres. Clinton uses the new line item veto for the first time to strike two tax breaks for New York State. (Aug. 11). Ted Turner, founder of CNN, pledges $1 bil. to the UN, one of the largest single donations ever. Atty. General Janet Reno absolves Pres. Clinton of criminal wrongdoing because the Justice Department found no credible evidence he broke any campaign finance laws. The Hubble Space Telescope returns pictures of a star as bright as 10 million suns. Republican-led Congress holds hearings about abuses committed by the I.R.S. and calls for a tax payer bill of rights. An Iowa woman gives birth to seven babies, the most ever born alive in the U.S. (Nov. 19). The Dept. of Agriculture issues sweeping regulations covering organically grown foods, including what can legally be labeled as organic. A jury in Denver convicts Terry L. Nichols of conspiring to bomb the Oklahoma City Federal Building and of involuntary manslaughter (but not murder) in the explosion that killed 168 people. (The judge later sentences him to life in prison). Thirty of Wall Street's largest brokerage firms agree to pay $900 million to end a civil suit contending they conspired for years to fix prices on the Nasdaq stock market.

1998 Pres. Clinton becomes the first sitting President ever to submit as a defendant in a civil court challenge when he defends himself against charges that he sexually harassed Paula Jones when he was Governor of Arkansas (Jan. 17). Clinton denies that he had an affair with White House intern Monica S. Lewinsky. Lewinsky's friend Linda Tripp had secretly recorded her conversations with Lewinsky in which Lewinsky admitted having an affair with the President and said he told her to lie about it. Pres. Clinton addresses the nation on television and emphatically denies having sexual relations with Monica Lewinsky (Jan. 26). Theodore J. Kaczynski admits he was the Unabomber and pleads guilty to all Federal charges against him in exchange for a life sentence rather than the death penalty. Texas executes Karla Faye Tucker, a convicted murderer, the first woman put to death there since the Civil War. Students at schools in Jonesboro, Ark. (March 24) and Springfield, Ore. (May 21) open fire on students and teachers killing four in Arkansas and three in Oregon, and injuring dozens of others. The F.D.A. approves the pill known as Viagra for male impotence. Merger mania sweeps the country. In April, Citicorp and Travelers Group agree to a $70 bil. union creating the world's largest financial services business, Nationsbank merges with Bank America, and Banc One merges with First Chicago; in May, SBC Communications acquires Ameritech Corp. for $62 bil., creating the nation's largest local phone company; and in June, AT&T announces it will acquire Tele-Communications Inc. for $31.8 bil. The Senate votes overwhelmingly to expand NATO to include Poland, Hungary, and the Czech Republic (April 30). Astronomers detect a titanic explosion in the outer reaches of the cosmos rivaled only by the Big Bang (May 6). The Senate overwhelmingly approves (and Pres. Clinton immediately signs) legislation to overhaul the I.R.S. and make it more friendly to citizens. The Federal Government and 20 state Attorneys General file two broad, aggressive antitrust lawsuits against Microsoft, accusing it of attempting to control the Internet. A Federal district judge rejects Pres. Clinton's invocation of special privilege to prevent his Secret Service agents from testifying in the Monica Lewinsky matter. Pictures from the Hubble Space Telescope show the first image of a planet outside our solar system (May 28). Scientists break the code of the tuberculosis bacterium, a germ that kills more people in the world than any other infectious agent. Pres. Clinton extends the moratorium on oil drilling off most of U.S. ocean coastlines for 10 more years. The Supreme Court rules (6-3) that the Line Item Veto Act is unconstitutional. Wild fires sweep through northeast Florida, forcing thousands of people to evacuate their homes. Dow Corning Corp. agrees to pay $3.2 billion to thousands of women claiming injury from silicone breast implants, ending 10 years of litigation. Whitewater independent counsel Kenneth W. Starr subpoenas Pres. Clinton (the first time this has ever happened to a sitting President), requiring him to testify before the grand jury investigating the Monica Lewinsky matter. Starr later withdraws the subpoena, and Clinton agrees to submit to Starr's questions at the White House with his own lawyers present. In exchange for immunity from Federal prosecution, Monica Lewinsky testifies that she and Pres. Clinton had a sexual affair in the White House. Two powerful bombs explode minutes apart outside the U.S. Embassies in Kenya and Tanzania, killing at least 190 people and wounding nearly 5,000, mostly in Nairobi (Aug. 7). Pres. Clinton testifies that he had an "inappropriate" relationship with former White House intern Monica Lewinsky. Later he goes on nationwide TV to confess he had lied in January. (Aug. 17). The U.S. retaliates for the bombings of two of its Embassies, by deploying about 75 U.S. cruise missiles on targets near Kabul in Afghanistan and in Khartoum, the capital of Sudan. Administration officials say these countries harbored terrorist activities financed by Osama bin Laden, believed to be the mastermind of the embassy bombings. In Wall Street's worst day of the year, the Dow Jones industrial average falls 4.19 percent or 357.36 points to close at 8,165.99, and beginning several months of global economic uncertainty. St. Louis Cardinals slugger Mark McGwire (Sept. 8) and Chicago Cubs outfielder Sammy Sosa (Sept. 13) both shatter Roger Maris's single-season home run record with their 62nd roundtrippers of the year. McGwire finishes with 70 homers; Sosa hits 66. Kenneth Starr sends his Whitewater report to Congress, claiming it contains "substantial and credible information that may constitute grounds for impeachment" of Pres. Clinton. The Republican-controlled House Judiciary Committee releases videotape of Pres. Clinton's grand jury testimony. Surprisingly, it improves the President's standing in the polls, which also reveal that a majority of Americans disapprove of the Judiciary Committee's handling of the matter. The Committee nevertheless votes along party lines (21 to 16) to recommend a formal impeachment investigation. Pres. Clinton announces a budget surplus of about $70 bil., the first since 1969 and the largest on record. The National Center for Health Statistics reports that AIDS deaths in the U.S. decreased by 46 percent in 1997, the steepest one-year drop ever. Congressional Republicans and the White House announce a $1.7 trillion budget agreement, the first in 30 years that projects a surplus and the biggest peacetime increase in military spending since Pres. Reagan's 1985 build-up. A Buffalo obstetrician who had fought with anti-abortion groups for years is shot to death in his home by a gunman with a high-powered rifle. Democrats surprisingly pick up five seats in mid-term elections for the House, a development that would seem to indicate distaste for the drive to impeach Pres. Clinton (Nov. 3). Nevertheless, the Republican-controlled House Judiciary Committee forges ahead with impeachment proceedings. Despite winning re-election three days earlier, House Speaker Newt Gingrich says he will resign from Congress in January when his term expires. Sen. John Glenn, 77, successfully completes a nine-day mission on the space shuttle *Discovery*, becoming the oldest person ever to do so. Pres. Clinton agrees to settle the Paula Jones sexual harassment suit for $850,000 and she drops her demand for an apology (Nov. 13). The nation's four largest cigarette makers agree to pay $206 billion to resolve all remaining state claims over health costs related to smoking. The settlement is less costly to the tobacco companies than earlier versions, but does not shield them from punitive damages and class action suits (Nov. 23). Atty. Gen. Janet Reno finds no reason to seek an independent counsel to investigate the fundraising roles of Bill Clinton or Al Gore during the 1996 election. Eight days after the House Judiciary Committee recommends four articles of impeachment against Pres. Clinton, the full House, strictly along party lines, approves two of the articles: perjury and obstruction of justice (Dec. 19). That same day, House-Speaker-elect Robert Livingston announces he will quit Congress in light of allegations that he had had extramarital affairs. He urges Pres. Clinton to follow his lead.

BIOGRAPHIES OF U.S. PRESIDENTS

1. George Washington (1789–97)

Born in Westmoreland County, Virginia, on Feb. 22, 1732, the first president, with a love for the land, trained as a surveyor in his teens. At age 16 he went to live with his brother Lawrence, who built Mount Vernon. Lawrence died only four years later, leaving his property to George, who went on to become one of Virginia's foremost landowners, ultimately acquiring more than 100,000 acres in Virginia and what is now West Virginia. In 1753 Washington joined the French and Indian War as an officer in the Virginia militia and fought bravely if poorly. The war provided Washington with the beginnings of his anti-British sentiments, exposing him to the arrogance of his British commanders. Upon returning to plantation life, and marrying Martha Custis, in 1759, Washington's resentment of the British was further fueled by their commercial restrictions. With the passage of the Stamp Act of 1765, Washington joined opposition to imperial rule in the Virginia House of Burgesses, becoming ever more active in resisting the British. He went as a delegate to the Continental Congress, which chose him to command the Continental Army when war with Britain broke out in 1775. Washington proved an uncommonly resourceful general, keeping his ragtag army together through years of defeat, retreat, and hard winters to outlast the British and finally prevail at Yorktown in 1781. Here, as in all his life, Washington earned respect for his judgment, dignity, and bearing. Retiring to Mount Vernon after the war, the general quashed suggestions that he assume military dictatorship of the fledgling republic, not wanting to subvert the very principles for which the Americans had fought. But because of his belief in a strong central government, Washington felt compelled to return to public life to salvage his country from the chaotic Articles of Confederation. In 1787 he presided over the Constitutional Convention in Philadelphia, which framed the presidency with him in mind, the only president ever elected unanimously in the electoral college (twice).

Washington's renowned judgment equaled the task of setting presidential precedent, for, as he wrote, "It is devoutly wished on my part, that these precedents may be fixed on true principles." His first act as president was to urge adoption of the Bill of Rights. Other notable achievements included national unity, quelling the Whiskey Rebellion, bolstering the treasury with a national bank, settling Jay's Treaty of commerce with Britain, and maintaining neutrality in the French Revolution. Washington successfully implemented executive power and quieted fears and suspicions of executive tyranny. But he regretted the rivalry between Thomas Jefferson and Alexander Hamilton, which led to the birth of political parties in his own cabinet; Washington feared that allegiance to "factions" would someday eclipse the guiding light of patriotism. After refusing a third term in 1796, Washington in his Farewell Address warned against party spirit, sectionalism, and "entangling alliances" with other nations. He died on Dec. 14, 1799, "first in war, first in peace, and first in the hearts of his countrymen," as his friend Henry Lee eulogized him.

2. John Adams (1797–1801)

A fifth-generation American directly descended from a Mayflower passenger, John Adams was born on Oct. 30, 1735, in Braintree, Massachusetts. At Harvard Adams considered the ministry but turned to law. He joined his cousin Sam Adams as an early opponent of the Stamp Act of 1765, organizing the Sons of Liberty and defending Americans accused of smuggling. Yet he also defended the British soldiers brought to trial for the Boston Massacre in 1770. In the Revolution, Adams persuaded the Continental Congress to commission George Washington as commander in chief, declare independence, and put stars and stripes on the flag. He wrote the Massachusetts state constitution in 1779 and negotiated peace with Britain in 1782. The first vice president, Adams called that position the "most insignificant office that ever the invention of man contrived or his imagination conceived."

Elected president as a Federalist in 1796, Adams retained Washington's cabinet, but Alexander Hamilton turned the party against him for refusing to make war on France. Adams built up the navy and kept the peace, but disaffecting the Federalists and signing the Alien and Sedition Acts (1798) politically weakened "His Rotundity." Adams lost the 1800 election to the increasingly popular Thomas Jefferson. The first president to reside in the White House, Adams lived to be 90, able to see his son John Quincy Adams elected the sixth president in 1824. John Adams died on the same day that Thomas Jefferson did: July 4, 1826, the 50th anniversary of the Declaration of Independence they both signed.

3. Thomas Jefferson (1801–09)

Thomas Jefferson was born on Apr. 13, 1743, in Albemarle County, Virginia, son of a self-made Virginian who died when Jefferson was 14. Jefferson graduated from William and Mary in 1762, began practicing law in 1767, and joined the Virginia House of Burgesses in 1769. With his pen Jefferson sharply criticized British rule, winning a place on Virginia's Committee of Correspondence to keep in touch with patriots in other colonies. His writings amassed great respect, earning him the right, as a delegate to the Continental Congress in 1776, to draft the Declaration of Independence. He then returned to Virginia as wartime governor, narrowly escaping capture when British troops destroyed his home. Congress sent Jefferson to Europe in 1784; he was minister to France during the Constitutional Convention and the early French Revolution, an event that affected him profoundly. As secretary of state under Washington, Jefferson's faith in democracy and states' rights clashed repeatedly with Alexander Hamilton's pursuit of central executive power. Jefferson resigned in 1793 and led opposition to the Federalists, whom Jefferson called "monarchists in principle." As vice president after 1796, Jefferson speeded the Federalists' downfall by secretly authoring the Kentucky Resolutions, critical of the Alien and Sedition Acts.

The House of Representatives chose Jefferson (ironically, with Hamilton's support) over Aaron Burr, whose electoral votes for president equaled his in 1800. "We are all Republicans—we are all Federalists," appealed Jefferson in his inaugural address, easing the transfer of power. In his first term, Jefferson slashed the budget, lowered taxes, reduced the national debt, and sent marines to fight Barbary pirates. Despite some concern over his constitutional authority to make the acquisition, Jefferson's greatest feat was the Louisiana Purchase from France in 1803, which doubled the size of the United States. "The less said about the constitutional difficulties, the better," wrote Jefferson, sending Lewis and Clark to explore the new lands. In his second term, Jefferson's unpopular Embargo Act (1807) was an attempt to avoid war with Britain or France, but it ruined American merchants. Retiring to Monticello in 1809, Jefferson busied himself with inventions and designing the University of Virginia. He died on the 50th anniversary of the Declaration of Independence, July 4, 1826. His broad interests spanned music, science, architecture, agronomy, and the classics, as well as politics and government.

4. James Madison (1809–17)

James Madison was born to a wealthy family on Mar. 16, 1751, in Port Conway, Virginia. A Princeton graduate, Madison attended the first Virginia state convention in 1776, drafting a bill that guaranteed religious liberty. As the youngest member of the Continental Congress in 1780, he led the movement to revise the Articles of Confederation. At the Constitutional Convention in Philadelphia in 1787, Madison's Virginia Plan became the pivot of discussion. Madison, dubbed the Father of the Constitution, t&irelessly directed debate and applied his political wisdom. His voluminous notes provide the best record of the convention. Madison helped ratify the Constitution by coauthoring The Federalist (1787–88) with John Jay and Alexander Hamilton. A four-term congressman, Madison drafted the Bill of Rights and cofounded the Democratic-Republican party. In 1794 he married a young and ebullient widow, Dolley Payne Todd, an especially popular first lady. Madison led the opposition to the Federalists' Alien and Sedition Acts with the Virginia Resolutions, arguing the acts were unconstitutional attacks on liberty. Jefferson chose Madison as his secretary of state and later as his successor. Madison easily won the election of 1808. Britain and France preyed on American shipping throughout Madison's first term. Pushed by war hawks in Congress, Madison asked for a declaration of war to defend American rights against British outrages. Reelected despite numerous American defeats in the War of 1812, Madison barely escaped Washington as the British burned the White House. Yet he persisted in "Mr. Madison's War" until the Peace of Ghent (1814) and belated victory at New Orleans (1815) vindicated him. War expenses forced Madison to recharter the national bank and raise the tariff, contrary to his Jeffersonian principles. But by 1817 Madison could retire confident of secure independence, surging nationalism, and the total collapse of his Federalist opponents who had opposed the war. He died on June 28, 1836, having outlived all the founding fathers. Madison's presidency pales beside his greatest contributions—the Constitution and the Bill of Rights.

5. James Monroe (1817–25)

The last Revolutionary hero and member of the "Virginia Dynasty" to become president, James Monroe was born on Apr. 28, 1758, in Westmoreland County, Virginia. He left the College of William and Mary to answer the call to arms in 1775. Wounded at Trenton, Monroe fought courageously and rose to lieutenant colonel under Gen. Washington. He learned law as an aide to Thomas Jefferson, who helped Monroe into Congress and the Senate. Much diplomatic experience followed Monroe's appointment as minister to France in 1794. Governor of Virginia from 1799 to 1802, Monroe returned to Europe to negotiate the Louisiana Purchase and later served in Britain and Spain. James Madison appointed him secretary of state in 1811 and secretary of war in 1814. Chosen to succeed Madison, Monroe won the 1816 election and presided over the Era of Good Feeling, a period marked by minimal sectional or partisan discord. Monroe bought Florida from Spain in 1819, and his popularity survived the Panic of 1819 as well as rancorous debates over the admission of Missouri as a slave state. Monroe toured the nation to jubilant crowds, winning reelection with all but one electoral vote in 1820. John Quincy Adams, his secretary of state, suggested Monroe proclaim American opposition to European encroachment in the Western Hemisphere, which he did in 1823; decades later this became known as the Monroe Doctrine. After retiring, Monroe became a regent of the University of Virginia (1826) and a member of the Virginia constitutional convention of 1829. Because of lack of attention over the years, his private affairs had suffered greatly, and Monroe discovered he was lapsing into bankruptcy. He sold his plantation and died all but penniless on Independence Day, July 4, 1831.

6. John Quincy Adams (1825–29)

The only president's son to become president, John Quincy Adams was born on July 11, 1767, in Braintree, Massachusetts. A true child of the Revolution, Adams watched the Battle of Bunker Hill while holding his mother's hand, and he spent his teens in Europe with his father, John Adams, on diplomatic missions for the new nation. He entered Harvard in 1785, already an experienced diplomat fluent in seven languages. After a brief career as a Boston lawyer, Adams was minister to Holland in 1794 and to Prussia in 1797. As a Federalist, Adams was elected to the Senate in 1803, but after supporting Thomas Jefferson, he had to resign. James Madison made Adams minister to Russia in 1809, in time to witness Napoleon's invasion. Then Adams helped negotiate the Peace of Ghent (1814) before serving as ambassador to England, the second of three Adams generations to hold that post. James Monroe recalled Adams from Europe—where he had spent most of his life—to appoint him secretary of state in 1817, and in that post, Adams purchased Florida from Spain, patched relations with Britain, and conceived the Monroe Doctrine.

Running for president in 1824, Adams was beaten by Andrew Jackson in both popular and electoral votes; but with Henry Clay's support, the House of Representatives made Adams president. No one ever became president with less than Adams's 31 percent of the vote, yet he refused to conciliate his foes or even act like a politician. Adams posed above politics and made no effort to deal with Congress or use patronage. Consequently, elaborate plans for internal improvements and national academies came to naught. Adams, like his father, could not win a second term, as Jackson gained revenge at the polls in 1828. Massachusetts rescued Adams from despair by sending him to Congress in 1830, and "Old Man Eloquent" remained a powerful antislavery leader until he collapsed on the floor of the House at age 80; he died in the Speaker's Room on Feb. 23, 1848. John Quincy Adams, who considered himself a failure as president, worked for the first 11 presidents and numbers among the most important architects of early American foreign policy.

7. Andrew Jackson (1829–37)

Born to Scotch-Irish immigrants in Waxhaw, South Carolina, on Mar. 15, 1767, Andrew Jackson was the first first-generation American to become president, as well as the first president from the western frontier and the first of seven to be born in a log cabin. Orphaned at 15, he was by then already a Revolutionary veteran, a former prisoner of war, and scarred by the saber of a British officer whose boots he refused to clean. Jackson read law and made his way to the Tennessee frontier, marrying Rachel Donelson Robards in 1791. She neglected to divorce her first husband, but Jackson challenged to a duel anyone who questioned his marriage, once even killing a man on the field of honor. Jackson's frontier law practice prospered, and Tennessee elected him its first congressman in 1796. He served only briefly in the Senate; Washington so disgusted the rough-hewn Jackson

that he resigned. Back in Tennessee, Jackson became a respected judge and honorary major general of the militia. In the War of 1812, Jackson led troops to victory at the Battle of New Orleans (1815), his men routing British invaders twice their number.

"Old Hickory" was now a national icon, reentering the Senate in 1823 and running for president as a hero above party. Jackson won more popular and electoral votes than anyone in 1824 but lost when the election was thrown into the House and Henry Clay supported John Quincy Adams. Vowing revenge against the politicians, Jackson swept to victory in 1828 as the "people's choice" reform candidate. Jackson's wife died on the eve of his inauguration. As president, Jackson aggrandized the power of his office on behalf of the common man by expanding suffrage, rotating officeholders (the "spoils system"), and economizing in government. Under Jackson the Federal government completely paid off the national debt. Jackson vetoed Federal roadbuilding and banking—yet he asserted Federal authority by ordering troops to South Carolina in the Nullification Crisis of 1832–33. The Whig party arose in opposition to "King Andrew I," especially to his high-handed veto of the national bank, but voters endorsed Jackson's war on privilege by reelecting him in 1832. In his second term, Jackson seized land from the Native Americans, ignoring the Supreme Court, and he recognized Texas in hopes of taking more land from Mexico. He became the first president to ride a train (1833) and to survive an assassination attempt (1835). After placing his friend Martin Van Buren in the White House, Jackson retired to the Hermitage, his plantation in Tennessee. He remained quite influential behind the scenes, persuading the Democrats to discard Van Buren and nominate James K. Polk in 1844. Andrew Jackson finally succumbed to dropsy and old wounds on June 8, 1845.

8. Martin Van Buren (1837–41)

The first president to have played no part in the Revolution, Martin Van Buren was born to a Dutch family in Kinderhook, New York, on Dec. 5, 1782. Apprenticed to a lawyer at 14, Van Buren took to law and politics—so well, in fact, that he came to be called the Little Magician. By 1821 staunch party loyalty elevated him to the Senate, where Van Buren led northern supporters of Andrew Jackson and guided his victory in 1828. Brief service as New York governor ended when Jackson appointed him secretary of state in 1829. Van Buren helped build the Democratic party, and Jackson made him vice president in 1832. As Jackson's heir apparent, Van Buren won the 1836 election, but two months after he took office, the Panic of 1837 launched a severe depression that spoiled his presidency. "Martin Van Ruin" responded by creating the independent treasury system, but his lack of popularity was beyond repair. He made enemies in the North by protecting slavery and in the South by refusing to annex Texas. Though the self-made son of an innkeeper, Van Buren was cast by his opponents as an aristocrat; William Henry Harrison's "Hard Cider" campaign of 1840 (touting that Van Buren sipped champagne while Harrison preferred hard cider) washed him out of office. In 1844 Van Buren lost the Democratic nomination when Jackson abandoned him over the Texas issue. But in 1848 Van Buren guaranteed a Democratic defeat by founding the Free Soil party and running for president, which split the decisive New York vote. Van Buren died a Unionist on July 24, 1862, the only president whose life touched both the Revolution and the Civil War.

9. William Henry Harrison (1841)

Son of a signatory of the Declaration of Independence and grandfather of a president, William Henry Harrison was born in Charles City County, Virginia, on Feb. 9, 1773. Campaign legend held that his birthplace was a log cabin, but in fact it was a plantation mansion. Harrison left medical school to join the army and fight Native Americans in the Northwest in 1791. After an illustrious military career, he served in Congress (1816–19), the U.S. Senate (1825–28), and as ambassador to Colombia (1828–29) before falling victim to Andrew Jackson's spoils system. Harrison fit Whig designs of defeating Jacksonians with a war hero of their own and received the Whig nomination to face Martin Van Buren in 1840. Harrison's campaign sidestepped issues to cast him as a plain frontiersman who guzzled hard cider while Van Buren sipped champagne. In the first modern election full of hoopla and hype, "Tippecanoe and Tyler Too"—the Whig slogan—linked Harrison's most famous victory with his obscure running mate. A huge turnout gave Harrison the victory at age 67, the oldest president before Ronald Reagan. Harrison delivered a record 8,500-word inaugural address hatless and coatless on a drizzly winter day. He caught a cold that never left and succumbed to pneumonia on Apr. 4, 1841, the first president to die in the White House—where he lived for only 31 days. His grandson, Benjamin Harrison, was the 23rd president.

10. John Tyler (1841–45)

The first vice president to become president by succession, the first president to see impeachment proposed against him, and the only president to change parties in office, John Tyler was born on Mar. 29, 1790, in Charles City County, Virginia. He was a Virginia legislator, congressman, senator, and governor before the Whigs chose him as William Henry Harrison's running mate in 1840. Though a strict constructionist and states' rights advocate, Tyler earned the Whigs' favor by opposing Andrew Jackson. But as president after Harrison's death, "His Accidency" earned their ire by vetoing, in mid-1842, two tariff bills vital to the Whig party. Eventually, his cabinet resigned and his party expelled him. Outraged members of Congress called for his impeachment. On July 10, 1842, John Minor Botts, a Whig representative from Richmond, Va., proposed the appointment of a special committee to investigate Tyler's conduct in office with an eye toward impeachment. The proposal was defeated on Jan. 10, 1843, by a vote of 127 to 83. This was the first time presidential impeachment proceedings were introduced in Congress. Tyler concluded the Webster-Ashburton Treaty (1842), which adjusted the northeastern boundary of the United States, and the Texas annexation (1845), but without popular or partisan support, he was powerless and decided against running for reelection. A veto on his last day in office became the first ever to be overridden. Tyler died on Jan. 18, 1862, awaiting his seat in the Confederate Congress.

11. James Knox Polk (1845–49)

The first dark-horse president, James Knox Polk was born in Mecklenburg County, North Carolina, on Nov. 2, 1795. A star orator in Tennessee politics,

Polk idolized Andrew Jackson. "Young Hickory" took Jackson's old seat in Congress in 1825 and was reelected seven times. Polk was Speaker of the House from 1835 to 1839 and governor of Tennessee until 1841. He lost two bids for reelection, and his political career seemed over when the Democrats nominated him for president in 1844. Polk's name had not even appeared on the first seven ballots, but the deadlocked convention latched onto Polk as a proexpansion dark horse. In the election he defeated Henry Clay by 1.5 percent of the vote on a platform that ignored slavery. From his inaugural address onward, Polk pursued expansion in the West. In 1846, he bluffed the British into believing the United States would go to war over Oregon, extracting a treaty for it. When Mexico attacked U.S. troops in disputed Texas territory, Polk called it an invasion and got a declaration of war. The ensuing Mexican War (1846–48) won California and the Southwest for the United States in the Treaty of Guadalupe-Hidalgo. Polk declined a second term, having fulfilled the nation's "Manifest Destiny" to span the continent. The last strong president before Abraham Lincoln, Polk added a million square miles to the United States. But the issue of slavery in the new territories split the Democrats and soon the whole country. "The presidency is not a bed of roses," complained Polk, who left the White House totally exhausted and died three months later, on June 15, 1849.

12. Zachary Taylor (1849–50)

Zachary Taylor, the first president to have no previous political experience, was born on Nov. 24, 1784, in Montebello, Virginia. His father was a colonel in the Revolutionary War, and Taylor—along with four brothers—served as a professional soldier for nearly 40 years. After distinguished service against the British and Native Americans, Gen. Taylor's finest hour came during the Mexican War, when he captured Monterrey and smashed Gen. Santa Ana's much larger army at the Battle of Buena Vista (1847). Though Taylor had never held office or even voted, the Whigs eagerly nominated "Old Rough and Ready" for president in 1848; Taylor, like William Henry Harrison, was an apolitical war hero above the slavery controversy. He won the election when the new Free Soil party siphoned off Democratic votes, but Taylor took office with Congress in chaos over the admission of California as a free state. Taylor opposed the Compromise of 1850 and probably would have vetoed it, but he died suddenly of acute indigestion on July 9, 1850. (A long, hot Fourth of July at Washington Monument ceremonies had no doubt contributed to his weakened state.) Backers of the compromise rejoiced that Taylor's death saved the Union. Taylor was both the last of eight slave owners and the last Whig to be elected president.

13. Millard Fillmore (1850–53)

Born in a log cabin on Jan. 7, 1800, Millard Fillmore was the son of a poor farmer in Locke Township, New York. Apprenticed to a cloth maker in his youth, Fillmore struggled for an education and got a job teaching even though he never attended college. Clerking for a judge taught Fillmore enough law to join the bar at age 23, and he became a prosperous New York attorney. Fillmore entered politics as an Anti-Mason and was a four-term congressman when the Whigs made him Zachary Taylor's vice president in 1848. Dignified good looks were Fillmore's main political asset; he was quite unprepared for the presidency when Taylor died suddenly in 1850. Fillmore delayed civil war another decade by signing the Compromise of 1850, but he lost the nomination in 1852 when the Whigs turned to Gen. Winfield Scott, yet another genial war hero and their last candidate. In 1856 Fillmore ran again for president as candidate of the American, or "KnowNothing," party. Fillmore hoped to unite the country behind anti-Catholicism and nativism, submerging the slavery issue, but he carried only Maryland. Though a Unionist in the Civil War, Fillmore denounced Abraham Lincoln and remained sharply critical of Republicans until his death on Mar. 8, 1874.

14. Franklin Pierce (1853–57)

Son of a Revolutionary War hero, Franklin Pierce was born in Hillsboro, New Hampshire, on Nov. 23, 1804—the first president born in the 19th century. A leader of Jacksonian Democrats in Congress in the 1830s, Pierce had been absent from national politics for a decade when the deadlocked Democratic convention nominated him for president on the 49th ballot in 1852. A dark horse candidate, Pierce won enough southern votes to defeat Gen. Winfield Scott, his Mexican War commander, becoming the youngest president as of that date. Pierce greatly hastened the coming of the Civil War by signing the Kansas-Nebraska Act (1854), which repealed the Missouri Compromise and reopened the dangerous issue of slavery expansion. He continually appeased the South by backing proslavery ruffians in "Bleeding Kansas," encouraging slavery expansionists who coveted Cuba, and buying the land known as the Gadsden Purchase from Mexico for a southern railroad. As a result Pierce's party lost elections to Republicans who charged that "slave power" controlled the White House. In 1856 Pierce became the only elected president to be denied his own party's renomination. During the Civil War, Pierce criticized the Emancipation Proclamation and was nearly lynched by angry New Englanders. He died a forgotten, depressed alcoholic, in Concord, New Hampshire, on Oct. 8, 1869, the only president from New Hampshire.

15. James Buchanan (1857–61)

Considered one of the worst presidents because of his lack of good judgment and moral courage, and also the only bachelor president, James Buchanan was born in Mercersburg, Pennsylvania, on Apr. 23, 1791. A lawyer and veteran of the War of 1812, Buchanan compiled more than 40 years of public service as legislator and diplomat. The Democrats nominated Buchanan in 1856 largely because he was in England during the Kansas-Nebraska debate and thus remained untainted by either side of the issue. Millard Fillmore's "Know-Nothing" candidacy helped Buchanan defeat John C. Frémont, the first Republican candidate for president. Buchanan favored "popular sovereignty" over slavery in the territories and was the last of the Doughfaces, or northern politicians submissive to the South. Few Americans shared Buchanan's faith that the Supreme Court's Dred Scott decision (1857) would end conflict over slavery expansion "speedily and finally." When it did not, Buchanan tried to close the issue himself by urging that Kansas be admitted as a slave state—an even worse miscalculation. Democrats deserted him, and Republicans won the House in 1858, but Buchanan's vetoes and southern votes in the Senate stalemated the government. He inadvertently helped

Abraham Lincoln win in 1860 by refusing to conciliate his own party. The secession crisis paralyzed Buchanan, who denied both the southern right to secede and the Federal government's right to do anything about it; he was relieved to hand Lincoln the reins. Buchanan died on June 1, 1868. On the day before, he predicted that "history will vindicate my memory," but historians continue mainly to denigrate him.

16. Abraham Lincoln (1861–65)

A largely unpopular president until he was assassinated (the first assassinated president), Abraham Lincoln was born in a log cabin in Hodgenville, Kentucky, on Feb. 12, 1809. He accumulated barely a year's total education while growing up, though he did learn to write and developed a fondness for reading. Family moves took him to Indiana and then to Illinois by the time he was 21. At age 19 Lincoln had worked his way down the Mississippi and came away appalled at slavery. He served in the Black Hawk War (1832) before losing an election for the state legislature. A failed storekeeper, Lincoln worked odd jobs while he taught himself law, sometimes walking 20 miles to borrow books. He finally made the state legislature in 1834 as a Whig, and in 1842 married Mary Todd, having canceled their engagement once before.

Elected to Congress in 1846, Lincoln denounced James K. Polk for precipitating the Mexican War. He returned to his Springfield, Ill., law practice after only one term. But the repeal of the Missouri Compromise shocked Lincoln back into politics, and he helped organize the Illinois Republicans. An unsuccessful candidate for the Senate in 1858, Lincoln drew national attention in debates with Stephen A. Douglas, the nation's leading Democrat. Lincoln was rewarded with his party's nomination for president in 1860, the least objectionable candidate among several more prominent Republicans. He defeated three opponents in the election, though his name did not even appear on the ballot in the South. As southern states left the Union, Lincoln preached conciliation and promised no harm to slavery—but he vowed to crush secession and forced the issue at Ft. Sumter. After early reverses in the Civil War, Lincoln decided slavery had to be abolished altogether to restore the Union, and he issued the Emancipation Proclamation (1862). Lincoln's management of the war was thwarted by incompetent generals, feuding politicians, and his own inexperience, which matched that of his troops. Yet, like them, Lincoln learned on the job, settling on Ulysses S. Grant as his top general by 1864. The powers of the presidency expanded dramatically under Lincoln, who stretched the Constitution on behalf of the war effort. Lincoln defeated Gen. George McClellan for reelection in 1864, vowing to "bind up the nation's wounds." Before he had the chance, Lincoln was shot on Good Friday, five days after the war's end, by John Wilkes Booth, an arch-Confederate. Lincoln died the next morning, on Apr. 15, 1865. His martyrdom spurred the vengefulness of Reconstruction, ironically against Lincoln's own wishes. Millions of Americans lined the 1,700-mile route of Lincoln's funeral train, their mournful cries resounding all the way back to Illinois. Lincoln's prestige has grown with time, until many have come to regard him as the greatest president.

17. Andrew Johnson (1865–69)

The first president to be impeached, Andrew Johnson was born in Raleigh, North Carolina, on

Dec. 29, 1808, the son of a poor laborer. No president could claim humbler origins: Johnson's father died when he was three, his mother worked as a washerwoman, and he never attended a day of school in his life. As a teenager he ran away to Tennessee, opened a successful tailor's shop, and got elected mayor of Greeneville by age 21. A fiery Democratic stump speaker, Johnson's attacks on Whigs and rich planters won him a seat in the state legislature in 1835 and in Congress in 1843, made him governor in 1853, and took him to the Senate in 1857. Alone among 22 southern senators, Johnson stayed loyal to the Union in 1861, though a mob of Virginians nearly lynched him for it. Lincoln appointed Johnson military governor of Tennessee, and he was nominated for vice president on the "National Union" ticket in 1864. Suddenly made president by Lincoln's assassination, Johnson vowed to carry on Lincoln's policy of leniency toward the South, but radical Republican opposition and his own coarse ineptitude led to serious clashes with Congress. Johnson vetoed 29 bills and was overridden 15 times, more than any other president to that time. A former slave owner, Johnson resisted Republican efforts to aid the freedmen. His only victory was the unpopular purchase of Alaska in 1867. Congress systematically stripped him of power until Johnson fought back by removing his disloyal secretary of war, Edwin M. Stanton. Impeached in the House for defying the Tenure of Office Act, Johnson was tried in the Senate and acquitted by a single vote on May 26, 1868. Few presidents were so stymied in office. Tennessee helped vindicate Johnson by making him the only former president elected to the Senate, he died a few months later, on July 31, 1875.

18. Ulysses S. Grant (1869–77)

A better general than president, Ulysses Simpson Grant was born in Point Pleasant, Ohio, on Apr. 27, 1822. Having barely passed West Point's height requirement for entrance, Grant attended the academy and graduated in the middle of his class in 1843. Fifty of Grant's classmates fought with or against him as Civil War generals. He served under Gen. Zachary Taylor in the Mexican War before marrying his sweetheart, Julia Dent, in 1848. Assigned to isolated posts after 1852, Grant grew bored away from his family and reportedly turned to heavy drinking. Finally resigning from the army in 1854, he went to Missouri, only to fail in farming and real estate. When the Civil War began, Grant was working in his younger brother's leather shop in Galena, Ill. He received a commission and rose rapidly to brigadier general. U.S. Grant acquired the nickname Unconditional Surrender for his string of western victories, notably at Vicksburg and Chattanooga in 1863. Once Abraham Lincoln made him supreme commander in 1864, Grant opened a relentless offensive that quickly ended the war. He personally accepted Gen. Robert E. Lee's surrender at Appomattox in 1865. After feuding with Andrew Johnson, Grant joined the Republicans and was elected president in 1868. Grant pressed radical Reconstruction in the South with mixed results. Corruption—notably the Jay Gould (1869), Cr\aedit Mobilier (1872), and Whiskey Ring (1875) scandals—marred Grant's presidency; nevertheless, he easily won reelection in 1872. The Panic of 1873 triggered a deep economic depression that dissuaded Grant from a third term in 1876. Reconsidering in 1880, he sought the Republican nomination again and nearly succeeded. Afterward Grant retired and went bankrupt. To provide for his family, he began

writing his memoirs. Developing cancer, Grant valiantly hung on to finish the project, which would earn him some literary fame and his family half a million dollars. He died on July 23, 1885, just four days after completing his autobiography.

19. Rutherford B. Hayes (1877–81)

Rutherford Birchard Hayes was born a frail child on Oct. 4, 1822, in Delaware, Ohio, where he was raised by his mother. After attending Harvard Law School, he set up a successful Cincinnati law practice in 1849. Hayes defended fugitive slaves and helped found the Ohio Republicans. In 1852 he married Lucy Ware Webb, the first college graduate first lady. A decorated Civil War veteran, Hayes was wounded five times and promoted to general. From 1868 to 1876 he served as governor of Ohio. Republicans turned to Hayes as a scandal-free hero in 1876 and nominated him for president. He lost the election to Samuel Tilden of the Democrats, but Republicans in Congress disputed enough state vote totals to connive "Rutherfraud" into office with the support of southern Democrats. Hayes's first acts were to appoint an ex-Confederate to his cabinet and to withdraw Federal troops from the South. He never overcame the resulting stigma of political bargain, and facing a Democratic Congress, Hayes seemed destined for a weak presidency. Yet he put the nation back on the gold standard, put down railroad strikes, reformed the civil service, and banished liquor from the White House before keeping his promise to serve only one term. Hayes viewed the return of prosperity and Republican majorities in Congress as personal triumphs. He worked quietly for charitable causes until his death on Jan. 17, 1893.

20. James A. Garfield (1881)

The last log cabin president, James Abram Garfield was born near Orange, Ohio, on Nov. 19, 1831, and like Rutherford B. Hayes, Garfield was raised by his mother. Garfield graduated from Williams College in 1856, became a classics professor, president of Hiram College, a lawyer, and at age 30 the youngest Union general in the Civil War. Garfield left the battlefield in 1864 to enter Congress, where he remained until the Republicans nominated him for president in 1880, a dark-horse compromise between Grant and James G. Blaine. Garfield defeated Gen. Winfield Scott Hancock of the Democrats by 0.1 percent of the vote in a campaign stressing tariffs. Republicans immediately swarmed to Garfield, demanding patronage for their rival "Stalwart" and "Half-Breed" factions. After only four months in office, Garfield was shot in a train station by Charles J. Guiteau, a disappointed Stalwart office-seeker. Garfield died 80 days later, on Sept. 19, 1881, the second presidential assassination ending the second-shortest presidency. When hordes of Republican hopefuls had besieged the White House begging for jobs, Garfield had exclaimed: "My God! What is there in this place that a man should ever want to get in it?"

21. Chester A. Arthur (1881–85)

Chester Alan Arthur was born a preacher's son on Oct. 5, 1829, in Fairfield, Vermont. He grew up in Vermont and in New York to become an ardent abolitionist like his father. A true machine politician, Arthur worked for Republican candidates in New York and enjoyed several patronage jobs during the Civil War. Ulysses S. Grant appointed him collector of the port of New York in 1871, and Arthur prospered there until 1879, when Rutherford B. Hayes removed him in the name of reform.

In 1880 "Half-Breed" Republicans nominated Arthur for vice president in a conciliatory gesture to his "Stalwart" faction. "The office of Vice President is a greater honor than I ever dreamed of attaining," he said. But Arthur acceded to the presidency on Sept. 19, 1881, when another Stalwart assassinated James A. Garfield. Perhaps shamed into supporting civil service reform, Arthur signed the Pendleton Act (1883) and rooted out post office graft. Democrats in Congress thwarted the rest of Arthur's initiatives; Republicans, whose calls for spoils Arthur ignored, denied him renomination in 1884. He lost a Senate race in New York and died two years later, on Nov. 18, 1886. Arthur was the last of three presidents in the single year 1881.

22, 24. Grover Cleveland (1885–89; 1893–97)

The only president to serve two nonconsecutive terms, Stephen Grover Cleveland was a minister's son, born in Caldwell, New Jersey, on Mar. 18, 1837. The family moved to New York, where Cleveland's uncle made him a lawyer. He showed scant interest in politics until Buffalo elected him mayor in 1881, and the next year Cleveland became governor. His war on corrupt Tammany Hall made Cleveland the perfect Democratic reform candidate for president in 1884. During the election campaign, backers of James G. Blaine, the Republican candidate, accused Cleveland of fathering an illegitimate child. He admitted it and won anyway—by 0.3 percent of the vote—but not before the Republicans came up with the immortal campaign chant "Ma! Ma! Where's my Pa?/Gone to the White House,/Ha! Ha! Ha!" The first Democratic president after the Civil War, Cleveland pushed for civil service reform and lower tariffs. In the first White House wedding, Cleveland married Frances Folsom in 1886. Cleveland cast over 300 vetoes—more than twice the combined total of all previous presidents. He cut Civil War pensions, seized 81 million acres of unused land from railroads, and signed the Interstate Commerce Act (1887). Defeated in the 1888 election, Cleveland claimed there was "no happier man in the United States"; yet four years later he won a rematch with Benjamin Harrison. Back in the White House, Cleveland underwent a secret operation to remove his cancerous upper jaw. His tight-money policies did nothing to help the depression after the Panic of 1893. Cleveland sent Federal troops to break up the Pullman strike (1894) and supported William McKinley, a Republican, for president in 1896. "I have tried so hard to do right," Cleveland said on his deathbed on June 24, 1908.

23. Benjamin Harrison (1889–93)

Benjamin Harrison was born on Aug. 20, 1833, at the North Bend, Ohio, farm of his grandfather William Henry Harrison, the ninth president. He took up the law in Indiana before joining the Union Army in 1862. Harrison finished the Civil War a brigadier general and returned to Indiana, where he was a prominent Republican, defeated for governor in 1876 but elected senator in 1881. A colorless compromise candidate for president, Harrison won the 1888 election despite receiving fewer popular votes than Grover Cleveland. Harrison bowed to the "Billion Dollar Congress" of free-spending Republicans who escalated Civil War pensions, transportation subsidies, naval construction, and spoils patronage. The McKinley Tariff, the Sherman Anti-Trust Act, the Sherman Silver Purchase Act (all 1890), and Secretary of State James G. Blaine's vigorous foreign policy were hallmarks of Harrison's administration, which oversaw the admission of six new states. Democrats won back Congress in 1890 and the White House in 1892, when Harrison lost to Cleveland in their rematch. A legal expert, Harrison taught at Stanford University and defended Venezuela in a boundary dispute with Britain before his death, on Mar. 13, 1901. Harrison referred to the White House as "my jail."

25. William McKinley (1897–1901)

The last Civil War veteran to become president, William McKinley was born in Niles, Ohio, on Jan. 29, 1843, son of an iron founder. A college dropout, McKinley was a post office clerk when the Civil War began. He volunteered as a private and mustered out as a 22-year-old major. McKinley studied law and was elected to Congress in 1876. A longtime Republican floor leader, he authored the record-high McKinley Tariff of 1890, before losing his seat that same year. Ohio millionaire Marcus Hanna, McKinley's political manager, engineered two governor's terms for him and funded McKinley's run for the presidency in 1896. William Jennings Bryan opposed him on a free-silver platform, but McKinley's dignified front porch campaign stressed sound money, tariffs, and the "full dinner pail." He won the election with the first popular majority since Grant's reelection. Strongly probusiness, McKinley raised the tariff still higher and reluctantly led the country into the Spanish-American War (1898). By acquiring the Philippines and other islands, the country became a world power under McKinley, who went on to proclaim the open-door policy in China. McKinley defeated Bryan by an even larger margin in 1900 and was enjoying great popularity when anarchist Leon Czolgosz shot him in Buffalo, N.Y. McKinley died two weeks later, on Sept. 14, 1901.

26. Theodore Roosevelt (1901–09)

Theodore Roosevelt was born in New York City on Oct. 27, 1858, the only president born there. A small, sickly child plagued by asthma, Roosevelt overcame a pampered youth to live the "strenuous life:" he boxed, hiked, hunted, rode horses, and climbed the Matterhorn. After graduating Phi Beta Kappa from Harvard in 1880, he attended Columbia Law School and became the youngest member of New York's legislature. Rich men of his day did not consider politics a suitable avocation, but Roosevelt desperately wanted "to be of the governing class." His first wife, Alice Hathaway Lee, died on the same day his mother died in 1884. Roosevelt wrote books and ran a cattle ranch in North Dakota until he married Edith Kermit Carow in 1886 and they moved to Oyster Bay, N.Y. During the Spanish-American War, Roosevelt left a job at the Navy Department in 1898 to lead the Rough Riders volunteer regiment in Cuba, achieving glory in the Battle of San Juan Hill. Elected governor of New York immediately upon returning home, Roosevelt was named William McKinley's running mate, in 1900. Roosevelt learned of McKinley's death while on a mountain-climbing expedition.

The youngest president at 42, "T.R." promised a Square Deal to close the gap between capital and labor. He mounted well-publicized campaigns against big business and successfully arbitrated major strikes. "Teddy's" popularity soared when he humbled billionaire J.P. Morgan in the Northern Securities case, and a record plurality reelected him in 1904. Roosevelt signed progressive laws to regulate railroads, inspect food and drugs, and create more than 150 million acres of national parks and forests. No less vigorous in foreign policy, Roosevelt's corollary to the Monroe Doctrine asserted the country would intervene to prevent European involvement in Latin America. For helping to end the RussoJapanese War, Roosevelt became the first American to win the Nobel Prize, but he considered the Panama Canal his greatest achievement. Roosevelt kept his pledge not to seek a third term in 1908—but in 1912 he ran against his chosen successor, William Howard Taft. Denied his party's nomination, Roosevelt survived an assassination attempt and won more than four million votes as the Progressive, or Bull Moose, candidate. During World War I, Roosevelt bitterly denounced the neutrality policy of Woodrow Wilson, who then denied Roosevelt's request to lead troops in France. While laying plans for another run at the White House, Roosevelt died suddenly of a cardiac embolism on Jan. 6, 1919. "No president has ever enjoyed himself as much as I have," he said.

27. William Howard Taft (1909–13)

By far the largest president at over 330 pounds, William Howard Taft was born in Cincinnati, Ohio, on Sept. 15, 1857. He graduated from Yale in 1878, then followed his father into law and Republican politics: "I always had my plate right side up when offices were falling," Taft wrote. William McKinley sent him to govern the Philippines in 1900, and Theodore Roosevelt appointed him secretary of war in 1904. Taft traveled around the world as Roosevelt's personal emissary, becoming T.R.'s chosen successor in 1908. As president, Taft tried to carry on Roosevelt's policies, but he wrecked the Republican party by alienating progressives from conservative "Stand-Patters" over tariff and conservation issues. Taft initiated the income tax and pursued antitrust suits against big business—but generally he sided with wealthy interests. An infuriated Roosevelt challenged Taft unsuccessfully for the Republican nomination in 1912, then outpolled him in the election, giving Woodrow Wilson the victory. With eight electoral votes, Taft suffered the worst-ever defeat for an incumbent president. But the better part of his career lay ahead: Taft, always more comfortable as a jurist, taught law at Yale until he was appointed chief justice of the United States in 1921. He served with distinction, alternating a liberal nationalism in economic affairs with political and social conservatism. Taft died on Mar. 8, 1930. Never nostalgic for the White House, Taft once said, "I don't remember that I ever was president."

28. Woodrow Wilson (1913–21)

Born on Dec. 28, 1856, in Staunton, Virginia, the son of a Presbyterian minister, Thomas Woodrow Wilson grew up in Virginia, Georgia, South Carolina, and North Carolina—the first southern president since Andrew Jackson. Probably dyslexic, Wilson was slow to read; yet he became the most highly educated president. Graduated from Princeton in 1879, Wilson studied law before taking a Ph.D. in political science at Johns Hopkins in 1886. He taught at Bryn Mawr and Wesleyan University before Princeton appointed him professor in 1890. Wilson attracted the attention of Democratic bosses after he was elected Princeton's president in 1902, and they persuaded him to run for New Jersey governor in 1910. A strong progressive, Wilson won easily—and then turned

on party bosses by sponsoring anti-machine reforms. In 1912 the Democrats nominated Wilson for president on the 46th ballot, and he won, with Theodore Roosevelt and William Howard Taft splitting the Republican vote.

Wilson's expert knowledge of government and strong party leadership pushed the Underwood Tariff, the Federal Reserve Act, the Federal Trade Commission, and the Clayton Antitrust Act through Congress by 1914. Restoring competition to the monopoly-plagued economy was the goal of Wilson's "New Freedom," until war in Europe made neutrality his top priority. German attacks on Allied ships carrying Americans strained Wilson's commitment, but he was narrowly reelected in 1916 on the slogan "He Kept Us Out of the War." After Germany spurned Wilson's mediation and resumed attacks on Allied shipping, Congress declared war at Wilson's behest in April 1917. World War I would "make the world safe for democracy," Wilson vowed, and he issued "Fourteen Points" for a just peace. After the armistice in November 1918, Wilson became the first president to visit Europe, when he attended the Paris peace conference that produced the Versailles Treaty. Wilson's dream of "peace without vengeance" was frustrated at Versailles, where he compromised away his Fourteen Points to obtain the League of Nations for collective security. In July 1919, Wilson returned home to face hostile Republicans in the Senate, where his treaty languished. On a nationwide speaking tour, Wilson collapsed from exhaustion in Colorado and suffered a paralytic stroke in October 1919. Wilson, all but incapacitated, refused to compromise as the Senate rejected the Versailles Treaty. Wilson's second wife, Edith Bolling Galt, whom he married in 1915, shielded the disabled president from the press and politicians until the end of his term in 1921. Woodrow Wilson died in his sleep on Feb. 3, 1924, frustrated by his own country's refusal to join the League of Nations.

29. Warren G. Harding (1921–23)

The first president born after the Civil War, Warren Gamaliel Harding was born in Blooming Grove, Ohio, which earlier had been named Corsica, on Nov. 2, 1865. He taught, studied law, and sold insurance before following his father into the newspaper business. Marriage to Florence DeWolfe, a wealthy widow, in 1891 helped finance Harding's paper, the Marion Star. A staunch Republican, Harding's probusiness editorials got him elected state senator and lieutenant governor. Although defeated for governor in 1910, Harding was elected senator four years later. Republicans turned to him in 1920 as a compromise candidate for president, the "best of the second-raters"; his good looks were expected to win over women first-time voters. Elected by an unprecedented 61 percent majority, Harding promised a return to "normalcy" for Americans tired of war and Woodrow Wilson. Harding's administration featured higher tariffs, lower taxes, and immigration restriction—but perhaps most notably, pervasive corruption and incompetence by Harding's crooked appointees. Harding was disturbed by the dishonesty of "my God-damn friends," two of whom committed suicide to avoid prosecution. While visiting San Francisco, Harding died suddenly of an embolism on Aug. 2, 1923. Scandals involving secret love affairs, official graft, and the vast Teapot Dome swindle erupted soon thereafter. Mrs. Harding zealously tracked down Harding's letters and destroyed them, leaving him the most enigmatic president, and certainly one of the worst.

30. Calvin Coolidge (1923–29)

The only president to share the nation's birthday, John Calvin Coolidge was born in Plymouth, Vermont, on July 4, 1872. Descended from a long line of New Englanders, he graduated from Amherst in 1895, practiced law in Massachusetts, and entered Republican politics in 1899. Coolidge rose slowly through a succession of state offices until he was elected governor of Massachusetts in 1918. Acclaimed for crushing the Boston police strike in 1919, Coolidge became the unexpected Republican vice-presidential nominee in 1920. After Warren G. Harding's death while still in office, Coolidge's own father swore him in as the new president. "Silent Cal" was the butt of jokes for his laconic utterances, but his minimalist approach to government fit the public mood, and he restored respectability to the White House, tainted by Harding's corrupt appointees and all-night poker parties. Instead of the whiskey that once flowed freely there, ice water in paper cups was served to visitors. Coolidge, untouched by leftover scandals, won the election in his own right in 1924. Pronouncing that the "business of America is business," he ushered in the heady years of Coolidge Prosperity, as the stock market soared higher and higher. Coolidge ignored foreign affairs and made frugality his trademark, slashing the budget at the expense of farmers and veterans, even driving out a White House cook who could not abide Coolidge's cost cutting. "It's a pretty good idea to get out when they still want you," Coolidge said, surprising the nation at the peak of his success by declining to run again in 1928. A popular president, Coolidge was safely out of politics when the Great Depression arrived. He died on Jan. 5, 1933, on the eve of the New Deal.

31. Herbert Hoover (1929–33)

Born in West Branch, Iowa, on Aug. 10, 1874, Herbert Clark Hoover was the first president from west of the Mississippi. Orphaned at eight and raised by Quaker relatives in Iowa and Oregon, Hoover joined the first graduating class of Stanford University in 1895. He became a world-famous mining engineer and a multimillionaire by age 40. In World War I, Hoover helped rescue Americans stranded in Europe, distributed food supplies to occupied Belgium, and convinced the nation to save food ("Hooverize") for the war effort. Hoover advised Woodrow Wilson's economic adviser at Versailles, and he organized relief for famine-struck Russia during the revolution. Joining the Republicans in 1919, Hoover earned prominence as the secretary of commerce in the 1920s and was elected president in 1928—the only electoral victory of his life. He promised a "chicken in every pot," but a few months later, the Wall Street crash brought on the Great Depression. Paralyzed by his conservative instincts, Hoover could not halt the spread of bank failures, bankruptcy, unemployment, and despair. Government should not get involved, he believed, and public relief would ruin American morals—so Hoover called for a balanced budget while promising the return of prosperity. He sent tanks to disperse veterans begging for pensions, and shantytowns across the country were dubbed Hoovervilles. Massively defeated by Franklin D. Roosevelt in 1932, Hoover called the New Deal "socialistic, collectivistic, fascistic and commu-

nistic." For decades Americans blamed Hoover for the depression and criticized his hard-hearted refusal to help the needy. Hoover lived another 31 years, the longest postpresidential lifespan, and he salvaged his reputation with more relief work after World War II. In retirement Hoover chaired two bipartisan commissions on government reorganization, issuing many important recommendations for Federal reform. Boulder Dam on the Colorado River was renamed to honor Hoover before he died, at age 90, on Oct. 20, 1964.

32. Franklin D. Roosevelt (1933–45)

The only president elected more than twice, Franklin Delano Roosevelt was born to a wealthy Hyde Park, New York, family on Jan. 30, 1882. He followed his cousin, Theodore Roosevelt, into Harvard and Columbia Law School—but not into the Republican party. F.D.R. was a Democratic state senator, assistant secretary of the navy, and nominee for vice president in 1920. Paralyzed by polio in 1921, Roosevelt learned to walk with braces and canes. As governor of New York after 1928, he pioneered unemployment relief in the Great Depression, earning him the Democratic nomination for president in 1932. Herbert Hoover, brooding and baffled by the depression, posed little challenge to the beaming, magnetic Roosevelt, who won the election by 23 million to 16 million votes. F.D.R. promised vague but bold experimentation ("above all, try something"), and as he took office in the worst inaugural crisis since Abraham Lincoln's, he assured Americans they had "nothing to fear but fear itself." F.D.R.'s first 100 days set a breakneck pace as compliant congressmen approved his New Deal for relief and recovery. Major landmarks were the National Industrial Recovery Act, the Agricultural Adjustment Act, the Tennessee Valley Authority, the Works Progress Administration, the National Labor Relations Act (Wagner Act), and the Social Security Act (1933–35). Though often contradictory and ineffective, the New Deal established the Federal government's responsibility for protecting farmers, workers, and the unemployed while actively regulating the economy to prevent another crash. F.D.R.'s high-profile "fireside chats," public works projects, and Social Security programs overcame despair and restored public confidence in the economy and government.

Reelected by a huge margin in 1936, Roosevelt proved incapable of ending the depression, as he ran afoul of the "nine old men" on the Supreme Court. Almost as many Americans called Roosevelt a Communist as praised him for rescuing the common man. Despite alienating many voters with his court-packing plan and "soak the rich" taxes, F.D.R. won an unprecedented third term in 1940. As war loomed in Europe, F.D.R. used his mastery of public opinion to lead Americans away from isolation, helping Britain with the destroyers-for-bases deal (1940) and Lend-Lease Act (1941) even before Pearl Harbor. World War II then occupied F.D.R.'s full attention as he shelved the New Deal and orchestrated the mammoth war effort. Roosevelt crisscrossed the globe to meet with Allied leaders and kept close personal control of diplomacy and grand strategy. He rallied a powerful sense of national purpose in the war, winning his fourth election in 1944. Together with Winston Churchill and Josef Stalin, F.D.R. planned a postwar peace of UN cooperation. Just after the Yalta Conference, Roosevelt died suddenly of a cerebral hemorrhage on Apr. 12, 1945, days before the war's end. His wife of 40 years, Eleanor Roosevelt, easily the most influential first lady, led her husband's campaign on behalf of disadvantaged Americans and continued it long after his death.

33. Harry S Truman (1945–53)

A plain midwestern farmer and World War I artilleryman, Harry S Truman (the S does not stand for a middle name) was born on May 8, 1884, in Lamar, Missouri. After his Kansas City haberdashery failed, Truman entered politics as a Democrat in the 1920s, and the local Pendergast machine arranged his election to the Senate as a New Dealer in 1934. National attention came to Truman when he headed a congressional committee investigating government waste during World War II. When Franklin D. Roosevelt needed a new vice president in 1944, he chose Truman. After only a few weeks in office, Truman had the presidency thrust upon him by Roosevelt's sudden death in April 1945. "Pray for me boys," he told his first press conference. Utterly unprepared, Truman did not even know about the atomic bomb project, but he vowed to carry on Roosevelt's policies. Truman proved a remarkably capable chief executive, educating himself in foreign affairs and dispatching crucial decisions rapidly. In his first four months, Truman approved the United Nations, accepted the German surrender, met with Allied leaders at Potsdam, and ordered atomic bombs dropped on Japan. As the Cold War commenced, Truman talked tough with the Soviets, accusing them of breaking agreements and intimidating helpless neighbors. In 1947 he proclaimed the Truman Doctrine, promising U.S. aid to threatened countries, and the Marshall Plan to aid European recovery and contain communism. The next year Truman ordered the Berlin airlift when the Soviets cut off West Berlin, and he promised to help Third World countries with the Point Four program. No less assertive at home, Truman made progress on civil rights, subdued restive unions, and prevented the Republican-controlled Congress from dismantling the New Deal—a specter that he effectively raised to win surprise reelection in 1948. Truman committed the country to the NATO alliance in 1949 and sent troops to South Korea when Communist armies invaded in 1950. But as Congress rejected Truman's ambitious Fair Deal domestic program and the Korean War bogged down, Truman's last years were barren. He had more vetoes overridden than all presidents but Andrew Johnson, and his poll ratings were lower than all but Jimmy Carter's. Truman, who initially raised fears of subversion with his loyalty program, could not quell the Red Scare that swept his party from power in 1952, as Republicans hammered away on the theme that Democrats were "soft on communism." Truman was convinced that he saved the world from communism, prevented World War III, and could have won another term if he chose to run in 1952. "He did his damndest" was the only eulogy Harry Truman desired on his death, on Dec. 26, 1972. Out of favor when he left office, Truman has gained rising respect since his death.

34. Dwight D. Eisenhower (1953–61)

The last war hero president, Dwight David Eisenhower was born in Denison, Texas, on Oct. 14, 1890, and grew up poor in Kansas. A military history buff, Eisenhower graduated with the 1915 class of West Point that produced 59 generals. He married Mamie Doud, his wife of 52 years, and spent World War I as a tank-training instructor. Eisenhower, only a major at age 40, rose rapidly during World War II, promoted past 350 senior officers to become commander of U.S. forces in Europe in 1942. By the end of 1944, he was the first U.S. five-star general and Supreme Allied Commander, taking the German surrender in May 1945. By that point a global celebrity, Eisenhower was army chief of staff until 1948, when he resigned to become president of Columbia University. Harry S Truman named him to command NATO forces in 1950, but two years later Eisenhower retired again to take the Republican nomination and run for president against Adlai E. Stevenson.

"Ike" became perhaps the most popular president in U.S. history, though many questioned his lax work habits, detached management style, and baffling speeches. Prominent millionaires in Eisenhower's cabinet and archconservatives such as Sec. of State John Foster Dulles seemed to have free rein, and Eisenhower acquiesced in Sen. Joe McCarthy's wild charges of subversion. His administration stockpiled atomic weapons and promised "massive retaliation" against Soviet aggression—yet did nothing when the Red Army rolled into Hungary in 1956. Eisenhower did end the Korean War, concluded several alliance agreements, and cut the defense budget. The "Eisenhower Doctrine" promised U.S. aid to Middle Eastern countries fighting communism. When Britain, France, and Israel invaded the Suez Canal in 1956, Eisenhower led UN condemnation and forced them to withdraw, though he sent U.S. Marines into Lebanon two years later. He began heavy U.S. involvement in Vietnam by backing the French and then the puppet Diem regime. At home Eisenhower promised to scale back the government—yet he expanded Social Security; created the Department of Health, Education, and Welfare; and spent billions on public housing and freeways. He pointedly stressed religious devotion. The Supreme Court's *Brown* decision, which Eisenhower deeply regretted, inaugurated the civil rights movement. Eisenhower defeated Stevenson again in 1956, but Soviet domination of space, revolution in Cuba, embarrassment over the Soviets' shooting down of a U.S. spy plane, and his own ill health marred his second term. Eisenhower reluctantly sent paratroopers to enforce desegregation in Little Rock, Ark., in 1957. Democrats controlled Congress for all but two years of Eisenhower's presidency. In retirement Eisenhower approved of U.S. intervention in Vietnam and counseled presidents until his death, on Mar. 28, 1969.

35. John F. Kennedy (1961–63)

The youngest man elected president, the only Roman Catholic, and the first born in the 20th century, John Fitzgerald Kennedy was born in Brookline, Massachusetts, on May 29, 1917, to a family of Irish politicos. His father, Joseph P. Kennedy, was ambassador to England and one of the richest men in America. Kennedy attended Dexter and Choate Academies, the London School of Economics, and Princeton before graduating from Harvard in 1940. A patrol boat commander in World War II, Kennedy was decorated for bravery in saving the lives of wounded crew members. Kennedy's father arranged his election to Congress, where he served three undistinguished terms before entering the Senate in 1952. In 1953, he married wealthy socialite Jacqueline Bouvier, and in 1957, he won the Pulitzer Prize for *Profiles in Courage*, a study of principled politicians. In 1960, running on a platform that lambasted Republicans for insufficient anticommunism and "vigor," Kennedy became the first candidate to utilize the presidential primary system to defeat three prominent opponents for the Democratic nomination. In the general election, Kennedy edged sitting vice president Richard M. Nixon by the narrowest of margins: 118,000 votes out of 69 million cast. The campaign was the first to feature televised presidential debates, in which Kennedy's poise, polish, and charisma were an invaluable asset.

During the campaign, Kennedy had pledged a New Frontier, but his social programs languished in Congress. Undaunted, he plunged into foreign affairs, his primary interest. Just after taking office, he approved the disastrous Bay of Pigs invasion, and a year later, he terrified the world by confronting the Soviets over the presence of their missiles in Cuba. He visited the Berlin Wall and expressed solidarity with Germans under the Russian gun. But he also set up the Washington-Moscow hotline, and signed the Nuclear Test Ban Treaty (1963).

Thousands of U.S. troops went to Vietnam as Kennedy escalated the commitment to containing communism. Kennedy vastly increased spending for defense and space programs, vowing to put a man on the Moon. He also engineered a $10 billion tax cut that eventually brought prosperity and increased revenues. As racial unrest spread, Kennedy cautiously supported the civil rights movement, introducing sweeping legislation that would not pass in his lifetime—nor would his plans for aid to education and medical care for the elderly reach fruition before his death. In a Dallas, Tex., motorcade on Nov. 22, 1963, he was fatally shot. Kennedy's alleged assassin, Lee Harvey Oswald, a left-wing ex-marine, was in turn murdered by Jack Ruby two days later. While doubts persisted that Oswald acted alone, Kennedy's martyrdom helped realize his legislative legacy, and subsequent revelation of his many peccadilloes have not tarnished the "Kennedy myth."

36. Lyndon B. Johnson (1963–69)

The eighth vice president to succeed by death of a president, Lyndon Baines Johnson was born on his father's Texas ranch near Stonewall on Aug. 27, 1908. He worked his way through Southwest Texas State Teachers College, taught briefly, then took a job in Washington—where he would live for all but two years until he left the White House. Government fascinated Johnson, and he reveled in making connections, marrying heiress Claudia Alta "Lady Bird" Taylor after a two-month courtship in 1934. An ardent New Dealer, Johnson won election to Congress as a Democrat in 1937. Reelected three times without opposition, Johnson became the first congressman to volunteer for combat in World War II, winning a Silver Star before returning to Washington. In 1948, on his second try, "Landslide Lyndon" was elected to the Senate by just 87 votes. Hard work and Texas oil money made Johnson the youngest Senate majority leader by 1955. A huge man, Johnson's powers of persuasion were legendary, but he failed in his bid for the Democratic nomination for president in 1960. Johnson accepted John F. Kennedy's offer of the vice presidency and campaigned hard in the South to aid their narrow victory. Made president a thousand days later by the tragedy in Dallas, Johnson vowed to continue Kennedy's programs, pushing them through Congress with surprising ease. Notable were the Civil Rights Act outlawing segregation and the Equal Opportunity Act, which declared "war on poverty." After less

than a year in office, Johnson defeated Barry Goldwater by the biggest plurality in history.

Now president in his own right, Johnson unveiled plans for a Great Society free from poverty and discrimination and passed the Education Act, Medical Care Act, and the Voting Rights Act in 1965. But Johnson came to grief in Vietnam, where he broke his 1964 campaign promise not to send "American boys to fight Asian wars." Earlier administrations committed the U.S. to defending South Vietnam, but Johnson intervened massively to prove American credibility to allies and enemies alike. No doubt he also feared resurgent McCarthyism if another nation were "lost" to communism. Following the Tonkin Gulf incident (1964), Johnson steadily expended American power and lives in Vietnam, but victory, or a means to achieve it, never came within reach—despite the presence of over half a million U.S. troops by 1968. Johnson's presidency unraveled as American losses mounted, antiwar protests grew strident, race riots exploded in inner cities across the nation, and the government developed a credibility gap. Virtually a prisoner of the White House, Johnson faced a war he could neither win nor leave behind and a nation more deeply divided than at any time since the Civil War. In March 1968 Johnson effectively resigned by announcing he would not seek another term. He retired to his sprawling Texas ranch and stayed out of politics until his death, on Jan. 22, 1973.

37. Richard M. Nixon (1969–74)

The only president to resign from office, Richard Milhous Nixon was born in Yorba Linda, California, to a poor Quaker family on Jan. 9, 1913. A graduate of Whittier College and Duke University Law School, Nixon married Thelma "Pat" Ryan in 1940, saw noncombat service in World War II, and rode into Congress on the Republican wave of 1946. He gained fame in the anti-Communist trial of Alger Hiss before entering the Senate in 1950. Dwight D. Eisenhower made Nixon his running mate in 1952, but Nixon was nearly forced to resign for accepting questionable contributions. He appealed for national exoneration in the televised "Checkers" speech. A well-traveled vice president, Nixon almost lost his life to hostile Latin American mobs in 1958, and he waged an impromptu debate in Moscow with Soviet premier Nikita Khrushchev in 1959. Eisenhower's obvious successor in 1960, Nixon narrowly lost the election to John F. Kennedy, and when he lost a California gubernatorial race in 1962, Nixon's career seemed over. Yet he practiced law in New York until the Republicans nominated him again in 1968. To a nation riven by the Vietnam War, Nixon promised "law and order," appealing to calm and unity against a background of riots, assassinations, and protest. Nixon defeated Hubert H. Humphrey with the smallest victor's share of the vote since 1912.

Vowing to "bring us together," Nixon tried to thwart the bureaucracy and Democrats in Congress by centralizing executive power. To control inflation, he ordered wage-price controls and devalued the dollar for the first time since the depression. Seeking "peace with honor" in Vietnam, Nixon built up the South Vietnamese army and withdrew U.S. troops—while massively escalating bombing of North Vietnam. Antiwar protests reached fever pitch when the United States invaded Cambodia in 1970. Nixon responded with appeals to the "silent majority," attacks on press freedom, and clandestine harassment of administration critics. High points of his first administration were the Apollo moon landing in 1969, Nixon's pathbreaking visit to China in 1972, and the first Strategic Arms Limitation Treaty with the Soviet Union. Twelve days after announcing "peace is at hand" in Vietnam, Nixon was reelected by a landslide, carrying an unprecedented 49 states. During the campaign five burglars were arrested in the Democratic party headquarters, and by early 1973, they were linked to the White House. The ensuing "Watergate" scandal exposed the Nixon administration's rampant corruption, illegality, and deceit. Nixon himself downplayed the scandal as mere politics, but when his aides resigned in disgrace, Nixon's role in ordering an illegal cover-up came to light in the press, courts, and congressional investigations. Nixon evaded taxes, accepted illicit campaign contributions, ordered secret bombings, and harassed opponents with executive agencies, wiretaps, and break-ins. Vice Pres. Spiro T. Agnew resigned in October 1973 for accepting bribes, but Nixon hung on to power, claiming, "I am not a crook," as the House began impeachment proceedings. Subpoenas and Supreme Court orders forced Nixon to release tapes of his White House conversations authorizing the Watergate cover-up. Ultimately, he resigned to avoid impeachment for obstruction of justice, abuse of power, and contempt of Congress. Claiming to have lost his "political base," Nixon announced his resignation on national television on Aug. 9, 1974. He never admitted wrongdoing, though he later conceded errors of judgment. Saved by a blanket pardon from Gerald R. Ford, his second vice president, Nixon retired to California, later moving to New York and then New Jersey. He dedicated the remainder of his life to unsullying his name, while becoming a foreign policy adviser to presidents until his death at the age of 81 in 1994.

38. Gerald R. Ford (1974–77)

The only vice president and president never elected to either office, Gerald Rudolph Ford was born in Omaha, Nebraska, on July 14, 1913. An Eagle Scout, he grew up in Michigan and attended the University of Michigan on a football scholarship, playing on the national championship teams of 1932 and 1933. After graduating in 1935, Ford coached football and boxing at Yale while attending law school. In the navy he earned 10 battle stars in the Pacific during World War II. Ford ran for Congress in 1948 as a Republican, marrying divorcée Betty Bloomer during the campaign, which he won. Thereafter he would be reelected 12 times, never by less than 60 percent of the vote. In Congress Ford's solid conservative record elevated him to House Republican minority leader by 1965. For supporting Richard M. Nixon in Congress, Ford was rewarded with the vice presidency in December 1973, replacing Spiro T. Agnew under the 25th Amendment. "I do not think the public would stand for it," Ford said at his confirmation hearings, when asked if he would ever pardon Nixon. For eight months Ford stayed loyal to Nixon, until his resignation made Ford the new president on Aug. 9, 1974. Ford announced "our long national nightmare is over," but a month later he shocked the nation by giving Nixon a blanket pardon. Ford denied any deal had been made, but his public standing never recovered. He struggled with huge Democratic majorities in Congress to stem soaring inflation and unemployment, casting 66 vetoes in all. Congress refused Ford's request for aid to South Vietnam and intervention in the Angolan civil war. In the Mayaguez incident, Ford sent the marines to rescue 39 Americans captured by Cambodia.

Breaking a 1973 pledge, Ford decided to seek reelection, and while campaigning, he survived two assassination attempts by California women. Ford was far behind Jimmy Carter in the polls, but he carried four more states than Carter in the election—which Ford lost by 57 electoral votes. It was the first defeat of an incumbent president since Herbert Hoover's.

39. Jimmy Carter (1977–81)

James Earl Carter, the first deep-southerner elected president in 128 years, was born in Plains, Georgia, on Oct. 1, 1924. He grew up on a farm with no plumbing or electricity but realized his dream of attending the U.S. Naval Academy. Carter graduated in 1946 and married Rosalynn Smith. He joined the submarine fleet and studied nuclear physics, leaving the navy in 1953 to run the family peanut business. He was elected to the Georgia state senate in 1962. Defeated for governor in 1966, Carter campaigned constantly for the next four years, winning on his second try in 1970. Carter reorganized the government and hired more blacks, declaring that the "time for racial discrimination is over." A month before leaving office in 1974, Carter was the first Democrat to announce his candidacy for president in 1976, again campaigning constantly. "Jimmy Who?" burst into headlines by winning narrow pluralities over nine rivals in early primaries. Carter's grinning, homespun style and earnest vows of honesty ("I will never lie to you") struck a chord with voters after Watergate. Carter won the nomination and defeated incumbent Gerald R. Ford by 2 percent of the vote. Lack of Washington connections helped his candidacy but not his presidency, for Carter never shook his image as the provincial amateur. Democratic majorities in Congress ignored Carter's pleas for tax reform and a long-range energy policy. Transportation deregulation, environmental protection, and new departments of energy and education were Carter's main domestic achievements.

But as Federal spending mounted and oil prices doubled, most Americans blamed Carter for runaway inflation. His 20 percent approval rating in August 1979 was the lowest ever recorded in opinion polls. In foreign affairs Carter obtained a Panama Canal treaty, normalized relations with China, and mediated the Camp David peace accords between Israel and Egypt. He moved toward closer relations with the Soviet Union, signing the SALT II treaty in 1979, but the Soviet invasion of Afghanistan led Carter to embargo grain sales to the USSR and to order a boycott of the 1980 Moscow Olympics. The Carter Doctrine announced the United States would defend the Persian Gulf, where ironically, Carter soon met his downfall in the Iran hostage crisis. Early public support for Carter's restraint gradually withered under the glare of relentless media coverage. Carter himself became a hostage of Iran, trapped in the White House as Edward Kennedy nearly deprived him of the Democratic nomination. In April 1980, Carter approved a military rescue mission, its tragic failure reinforcing his image of incompetence and weakness, which Republican candidate Ronald Reagan flayed. Reagan won the election in a landslide. Carter left the White House discredited, his informal style ridiculed as inappropriate, his appeals for support seen as poor leadership. Yet Carter was a hard-working president wrecked by a hostile press, extortionate oil exporters, and forces beyond his control. In later years he won recognition as a trustworthy international negotiator.

40. Ronald Reagan (1981–89)

Ronald Wilson Reagan was born in Tampico, Illinois, on Feb. 6, 1911. He excelled at acting and campus politics in high school and at Eureka College. Reagan was a radio sports announcer when he made his first movie in 1937. Over 50 more films would follow in Reagan's prolific Hollywood career. In 1940 he married actress Jane Wyman, who divorced him in 1948. During World War II, Reagan made training films, and after the war he was president of the Screen Actors Guild. Then a Democrat, Reagan assailed Communists in Hollywood. He married Nancy Davis, another actress, in 1952. As his movie career waned, Reagan hosted television shows and espoused conservative causes, switching to the Republican party in 1960. Reagan made a dramatic speech at the end of the 1964 campaign, and despite his total lack of experience he was elected governor of California in 1966 by a million votes. As governor, Reagan broke all promises by raising taxes, increasing spending, and expanding the state government—yet he easily won reelection in 1970. He made unsuccessful runs for the Republican presidential nomination in 1968 and 1976 before winning it in 1980. He swept past Jimmy Carter in the crushing "Reagan Revolution" of 1980, carrying 44 states and making huge Republican gains in Congress.

"Reaganomics" promised to cut taxes and social spending while vastly increasing the defense budget and somehow balancing the budget. Congress was unmoved until Mar. 20, 1981, when a crazed youth named John Hinckley shot Reagan twice in the chest. Reagan's good humor and rapid recovery charmed Americans—especially the press, which had questioned his age and health. Reagan then prevailed over Congress to pass mammoth tax cuts. The national debt began its meteoric rise under Reagan as defense spending outweighed cuts in social programs. By 1986 the U.S. had become a net borrower for the first time since World War I, but falling oil prices slowed inflation and rekindled economic growth, for which Reagan took credit. Calling the Soviet Union an "evil empire," Reagan built up the armed forces, deployed U.S. nuclear missiles in Europe, and began the Strategic Defense Initiative. He sent U.S. Marines to Lebanon, where 240 of them died in a terrorist attack. To halt the spread of communism, Reagan ordered the invasion of Grenada and isolated the Sandinista government of Nicaragua. Reelected by another landslide in 1984, with the economy booming and his public esteem high, Reagan seemed headed for an even more successful second term. He ordered bombing raids on Libya and met with Soviet leader Mikhail Gorbachev, eventually producing historic arms control agreements. But in 1987 Reagan's invincible popularity finally succumbed to the Iran-Contra scandal: White House staff secretly sold arms to Iran in hopes of freeing American hostages held in Lebanon, using the profits illegally to fund Contra fighters in Nicaragua. Many top Reagan aides had to resign, but more damaging was the president's apparent loss of control over his own administration.

By 1988 Reagan was reduced to "lame duck" status, and bestowed his mantle on Vice Pres. George Bush. He left office with the highest approval rating of any departing president since Franklin Roosevelt. In retirement Reagan was knighted by Queen Elizabeth and traveled around the globe, accepting $2 million from a Japanese media company for a pair of 20-minute speeches.

As the Iran-Contra trials continued in 1990, Reagan was ordered to testify under oath on videotape. Questioned at length about his role in the scandal, Reagan responded 130 times with "I don't recall" or "I don't remember." In 1995, he revealed he was suffering from Alzheimer's disease.

41. George Bush (1989–93)

The first sitting vice president elected president in over 150 years, George Herbert Walker Bush was born in Milton, Massachusetts, on June 12, 1924. His father was Prescott Sheldon Bush, Wall Street banker and U.S. senator from Connecticut from 1952 to 1963. As a navy pilot during World War II, Bush was shot down over the Pacific and rescued at sea. After the war, he married Barbara Pierce, a Smith College student, on Jan. 6, 1945, and graduated Phi Beta Kappa in economics from Yale in 1948. Bush spurned an offer from his father's Wall Street firm in order to pursue a career in the Texas oil fields that eventually made him a millionaire in his own right. He entered politics in the early 1960s.

Running on a conservative anti-Communist and anti-civil rights platform, Bush won the Republican nomination for Senate in 1964 and again in 1970, but lost the general election both times. In between, he was elected to Congress from a wealthy suburban Houston district, the only elected office he had held until he won the vice-presidency in 1980. Presidents Richard Nixon and Gerald Ford rewarded the Republican party loyalist with appointed offices, including U.S. ambassador to the United Nations (1971), chairman of the Republican National Committee (1973), chief of the U.S. Liaison Office in China (1974), and director of the CIA (1976). After losing the Republican presidential nomination to Ronald Reagan in 1980, Bush accepted Reagan's offer to join him on the winning ticket.

One of the few members of Reagan's staff to emerge unscathed by the Iran-Contra affair, Bush bested Robert Dole for the Republican nomination in 1988. With Reagan's endorsement, Bush defeated Massachusetts governor Michael S. Dukakis, renewing the Reagan pledge of "no new taxes" and vowing to uphold the Reagan legacy of less government, strong defense, and family values. He declared war on "this scourge" of drugs by creating an office of National Drug Control Policy within the White House. Bush's first official act was to proclaim January 20 as the "National Day of Prayer."

Bush suffered early criticism for lack of leadership. For months, many key administration posts went unfilled, and the Senate rejected John Tower as Bush's nominee for defense secretary. But Bush struck back with major initiatives, including major arms control proposals and two summit meetings with Soviet premier Mikhail Gorbachev. In December 1989, Bush ordered the invasion of Panama to protect U.S. citizens and overthrow the regime of Gen. Manuel Noriega.

As one eastern bloc country after another opted for democracy in 1989 and 1990, Bush enjoyed the highest public approval rating of any postwar president. This popularity gave him the political leverage to renege on his campaign pledge of "no new taxes." His popularity rose to record levels when he ordered Operation Desert Storm to liberate Kuwait from Iraqi occupation. As time passed, however, it became apparent that Bush had given the cease-fire order much too early, allowing Saddam Hussein to retain power in Iraq.

Throughout 1991, as the Soviet Union was crumbling, Bush acted quickly and decisively to support those republics seeking independence, and to provide food and medical supplies where needed. He and Gorbachev declared an end to the arms race by signing the first nuclear arms reduction pact in July. He also won high praise for his administration's determination to launch serious Mideast peace talks, which began in October of 1991. He was seriously criticized, however, for granting China most-favored-nation trade status in the wake of the Tiananmen Square massacre and continued repressive government action.

Bush had less success on the domestic front. By the spring of 1992, his approval rating had dipped below 40 percent, reflecting the deepening economic recession that drove unemployment levels to their highest level in a decade. Bush was challenged first in the primaries and then in the general election by opponents who made the economy the central issue of their campaigns. Bush survived a vicious attack from the right wing of his party to win the Republican nomination. But unable to get the economy on course, Bush lost to Bill Clinton in a three-way race that saw independent candidate Ross Perot capture nearly 20 percent of the vote. It marked only the 10th time in history that an incumbent president had been unseated.

42. Bill Clinton (1993–)

William Jefferson Clinton was born in tiny Hope, Arkansas, on Aug. 19, 1946. His father, William Jefferson Blythe 3d, was killed before his son was born, leaving his wife, Virginia, to raise their son alone. Four years later, she married Roger Clinton, who legally adopted Bill, and moved the family to Hot Springs, Ark. After graduating from Georgetown University, Clinton went to Oxford University on a Rhodes scholarship and then to Yale Law School, where he met Hillary Rodham, whom he married two years after they both graduated in 1973.

Clinton was elected Arkansas attorney general in 1976, and two years later became the nation's youngest governor in 40 years. In 1980 he became the nation's youngest ex-governor, a victim of the nationwide Republican landslide that ushered Ronald Reagan into the White House. But in 1982, Clinton won his old job back, and kept it until his 1992 election as president.

In 1992, he emerged as a shaky frontrunner among six Democratic hopefuls for the presidential nomination. Allegations that he had extramarital affairs, dodged the draft during the Vietnam War, and smoked marijuana threatened to derail his campaign early. But as the candidate with the most money, the most flattering press coverage, and the only one with a clearly articulated campaign strategy—creating more jobs—Clinton was able to stay in the race the longest, fending off all his rivals long before the Democratic convention.

In a three-way race that saw billionaire populist Ross Perot enter, withdraw, and then re-enter the field as an independent candidate, Clinton garnered 366 of the 538 electoral votes, despite winning only 43 percent of the popular vote. Incumbent George Bush captured 37 percent, and Perot 19 percent, of the record 104 million votes cast in 1992.

Clinton entered office hoping that a Democratic president and a Democratic Congress could untangle the gridlock that had paralyzed Washington for the previous 12 years. But his first act as President, a pledge to end the ban on lesbians and gay men in the armed forces, met with heavy resistance from top military leaders. And his economic stimulus package fell to defeat in the face of a remarkable Republican filibuster in the Senate.

His second 100 days proved more fruitful. He signed the family leave bill, lifted the restrictions on abortion counseling at federally funded clinics, and laid the groundwork for the North American Free Trade Agreement. And after some last-minute arm-twisting, he got his budget through Congress.

Clinton had even greater success on the foreign policy front, assuring the stability of Russia's government through a coup attempt, and negotiating a historic peace treaty between Israel and the PLO that recognized Palestinian self-rule in Gaza and part of the West Bank. Clinton's handling of the escalating conflict in Bosnia (placing the issue in the hands of the UN) allowed him to avoid engagement while placing the responsibility for inaction squarely on the European nations. And his brinksmanship with North Korea resulted in Pyongyang's agreement to dismantle nuclear reactors that could be used to produce ammunition for nuclear weapons.

On the domestic front, however, Clinton still found little support for his programs. A complex, poorly presented plan (devised by a committee headed by First Lady Hillary Rodham Clinton) called for guaranteed health coverage to all Americans, regardless of pre-existing conditions or ability to pay. But its health purchasing cooperatives promised a huge government bureaucracy that opponents claimed would be less efficient than the post office. Politicians of all stripes responded with half a dozen alternate plans, with the end result that no reform at all took place.

Throughout 1993, Clinton's approval ratings sagged, and in the 1994 midterm elections, the GOP won control of both Houses of Congress for the first time in more than 40 years. New House Speaker Newt Gingrich moved to center stage, proclaiming a Republican revolution, and Clinton barely raised a contrary voice or a veto threat as the House raced through the provisions of the Contract with America. Republicans in Congress also flexed their new muscles in 1995 by opening hearings on the Clintons' controversial investment in a land deal known as Whitewater.

As he prepared to run for a second term, Clinton's approval ratings started to rebound in mid-1995. He took centrist positions on most of the important issues, including abortion rights, welfare reform, and affirmative action. He took pains to avoid being branded "liberal," signing the Republican welfare bill that ended 60-year-old guarantees for poor people. He also stood up to the aggressive Republican majority on the contentious issue of how quickly to reduce the $4.5 trillion Federal deficit. This stalemate forced brief shutdowns of the Federal government in November 1995 and January 1996, for which Clinton managed to put the blame on Gingrich.

Clinton's successes in foreign policy also buoyed him in 1995 and 1996 as he oversaw the peaceful election of a new President in Haiti, secured $20 billion in emergency loans to rescue Mexico from economic disaster, and established full diplomatic relations with Vietnam.

With the stock market soaring, unemployment falling, and inflation firmly in check, Clinton again relied on the prosperous economy to propel his candidacy. He won re-election almost effortlessly against an aged Bob Dole, whose campaign lacked both vigor and focus.

Clinton's second term began with modest goals. He remained on the defensive against a Republican-controlled Congress determined to pass tax cuts for high income families while cutting social programs. The Whitewater scandal, however, came back to haunt him in an unexpected way. Failing to uncover anything directly implicating the President or Mrs. Clinton in connection with the land deal, independent counsel Kenneth Starr expanded his inquiry far beyond its original scope and unearthed evidence of an affair between Clinton and White House intern Monica Lewinsky. At first, Clinton emphatically denied the allegation, saying "I did not have sex with that woman." But after becoming the first sitting president ever subpoenaed to testify before a Federal grand jury, Clinton later admitted that he had had an "inappropriate" relationship with Monica Lewinsky, and that he had lied about it earlier.

Clinton's admission did little to hurt his approval ratings, which remained high, some said, because of the strong economy. In the mid-term elections, Democrats actually gained five seats in the House and didn't lose any strength in the Senate. Despite polls indicating that an overwhelming majority of Americans wanted Congress to drop the Lewinsky matter, the House Judiciary Committee (still controlled by Republicans) voted along party lines to recommend four articles of impeachment against the President. The full House, also along party lines, approved two of the impeachment articles—perjury and obstruction of justice—making Clinton the first president to be impeached since Andrew Johnson. The month-long trial in the Senate was filled with legal wrangling on all sides, but in the end, not even a simple majority could be mustered to support either impeachment article, far short of the two-thirds necessary for conviction.

Clinton appeared chastened but not humbled by the whole affair. He pursued a predictable domestic agenda in 1999, but focused most of his attention on foreign policy. The day after his acquittal, Clinton announced plans to send 4,000 troops to Kosovo to defend the "national interest" as part of a NATO peacekeeping force, which the House approved after a month of bitter and passionate debate. NATO forces began their assault on Serbia in late March and continued through the spring. Congress approved more than $12 billion in emergency spending for an air war, but refused to authorize funds for use of ground troops. This proved unimportant, however, since other members of NATO were totally opposed to a ground war.

Many doubted that NATO could win such a war without sending ground troops, but the alliance continued air strikes for 72 days until Serbian Pres. Slobodan Milosevic finally agreed to accept the peace plan offered by NATO. Under the terms of the agreement, Milosevic was forced to withdraw all military and police forces from Kosovo within a week; an international peacekeeping force of 50,000 troops began policing the province under the U.N. flag. This victory was the most important foreign policy achievement of Clinton's presidency. *(For further details of the Clinton presidency in 1999, see Part I: Major News Stories of the Year.)*

Presidential Elections, 1796–1996

George Washington of Virginia ran unopposed for president in 1789 and 1792. He received 69 and 132 electoral votes in those years, respectively. John Adams of Massachusetts was elected vice-president in both years, receiving 34 and 77 electoral votes.

1796

Party	Candidate	Popular vote	Percent	Electoral vote
Federalist	John Adams (Mass.)	N.A.	N.A.	71
	and Thomas Pinckney (S.C.)	N.A.	N.A.	59
Democratic-	Thomas Jefferson (Va.)	N.A.	N.A.	68
Republican	and Aaron Burr (N.Y.)	N.A.	N.A.	30

Key Issues Washington set a precedent by refusing to run for a third term. Though the Founders hoped to avoid parties, factions developed around Hamilton and Jefferson during Washington's first term. Hamilton's Federalists supported a strong central government that would play a major role in the national economy and represent the commercial interests of the north. Jefferson's Republicans advocated states' rights and the agrarian interests of the south. **Regional Influences** Though led by Hamilton, the Federalists nominated the more moderate Adams. Jefferson's strength in the south was balanced by Adams's power in the north. Eleven Federalist electors in New Hampshire failed to vote for Pinckney, their party's vice-presidential nominee, giving the position to Jefferson.

1800

Party	Candidate	Popular vote	Percent	Electoral vote
Democratic-	Thomas Jefferson (Va.)	N.A.	N.A.	73
Republican	and Aaron Burr (N.Y.)	N.A.	N.A.	73
Federalist	John Adams (Mass.)	N.A.	N.A.	65
	and Charles C. Pinckney (S.C.)	N.A.	N.A.	64
Federalist	John Jay (N.Y.)	N.A.	N.A.	1

Key Issues Adams divided the Federalists by keeping the U.S. out of war with France over seizures of American ships by the French. In the meantime the Republicans under Jefferson organized nationally. They accused the Federalists of aristocratic and monarchical leanings, citing large taxes levied to maintain a standing army and navy, the Alien and Sedition Acts seeking to silence the administration's critics, and suppression of the Whiskey Rebellion. **Regional Influences** The Republicans again carried the South, but also won New York through the efforts of vice-presidential nominee Burr. The election was thrown into the House when Jefferson and Burr received an equal number of electoral votes. With Hamilton's support, Jefferson won the election in the Federalist-dominated House.

1804

Party	Candidate	Popular vote	Percent	Electoral vote
Democratic-	Thomas Jefferson (Va.)	N.A.	N.A.	162
Republican	and George Clinton (N.Y.)	N.A.	N.A.	162
Federalist	Charles C. Pinckney (S.C.)	N.A.	N.A.	14
	and Rufus King (N.Y.)	N.A.	N.A.	14

Key Issues In 1804 Vice-President Burr, a northern Republican, joined with a group of northeastern Federalists in a plot to unite New York and New England in a separate nation. The plot was exposed, discrediting the Federalists. Jefferson, already popular for his personal qualities as well as the Louisiana Purchase, swept to an easy victory. **Regional Influences** Jefferson lost only three states, and even swept all of New England with the exception of Connecticut.

1808

Party	Candidate	Popular vote	Percent	Electoral vote[1]
Democratic-	James Madison (Va.)	N.A.	N.A.	122
Republican	and George Clinton (N.Y.)	N.A.	N.A.	113
Federalist	Charles C. Pinckney (S.C.)	N.A.	N.A.	47
	and Rufus King (N.Y.)	N.A.	N.A.	47

Key Issues Jefferson reinforced the two-term precedent by refusing to run for a third term. Madison, his chosen successor, easily won the Republican nomination and the presidency. **Regional Influences** Pinckney and the Federalists regained most of the New England votes lost four years earlier and increased their strength in Congress due to commercial opposition to the embargo imposed by Jefferson on the export of American goods to warring European nations.

[1]Clinton received six electoral votes for president. Madison and James Monroe of Virginia both received three electoral votes for vice-president.

1812

Party	Candidate	Popular vote	Per cent	Electoral vote
Democratic-	James Madison (Va.)	N.A.	N.A.	128
Republican	and Elbridge Gerry (Mass.)	N.A.	N.A.	131
Federalist	DeWitt Clinton (N.Y.)	N.A.	N.A.	89
	and Jared Ingersoll (Pa.)	N.A.	N.A.	86

Key Issues The election was a referendum on Madison's bid for a declaration of war against Great Britain in response to Britain's attempts to block the sale of southern raw materials in European markets. A vote for Madison was a vote for war, a vote for Clinton a vote for peace. **Regional Influences** Commercial interests in the northeast opposed war with Great Britain. The original 13 states were evenly split in the election, favoring Madison 90-89. New England, except Vermont, voted for Clinton, as did a majority of the Middle Atlantic states. The South voted unanimously for Madison. But all of the western states voted for Madison and thus for war.

1816

Party	Candidate	Popular vote	Per cent	Electoral vote
Democratic-	James Monroe (Va.)	N.A.	N.A.	183
Republican	and D. D. Tompkins (N.Y.)	N.A.	N.A.	183
Federalist	Rufus King (N.Y.)	N.A.	N.A.	34
	and John E. Howard (Md.)	N.A.	N.A.	22

Key Issues Nationalism triumphed after the war with Britain, a time of national and economic growth that saw establishment of an expanded standing army, central bank, Federal tariff and large internal improvements despite opposition from northeastern Federalists. **Regional Influences** Monroe, Madison's chosen successor, won a landslide victory that seemed to validate Madison's nationalistic program, which called for a stronger standing army, a protective tariff, uniform currency and a nationwide system of roads and canals, including the Cumberland Road. The Federalists won only three states, all in New England.

1820

Party	Candidate	Popular vote	Per cent	Electoral vote
Democratic-	James Monroe (Va.)	N.A.	N.A.	231
Republican	and D.D. Tompkins (N.Y.)	N.A.	N.A.	218
Democratic- Republican	John Q. Adams (Mass.)	N.A.	N.A.	1

Key Issues The election was held at the height of the "Era of Good Feelings," though sectional differences over slavery earlier in the year led to the Missouri Compromise, which in its final version resulted in the admittance of Missouri as a slave state with the provision that it allow free Negroes of other states to retain their freedom while in Missouri. The Federalists ceased to exist as a functioning party by the time of the election and failed to run a candidate against Monroe. **Regional Influences** Monroe ran unopposed for reelection. One elector from New Hampshire voted for Adams so that only Washington would hold the honor of being elected to the presidency by a unanimous vote.

1824

Party	Candidate	Popular vote	Per cent	Electoral vote
Democratic- Republican	John Q. Adams (Mass.)	113,122	30.92	84
Democratic- Republican	Andrew Jackson (Tenn.)	151,271	41.34	99
Democratic- Republican	William H. Crawford (Ga.)	40,876	11.17	41
Democratic- Republican	Henry Clay (Ky.)	47,531	12.99	37
Other		13,053	3.57	—
	Total Vote	365,833		
	Jackson Plurality	38,149		

Key Issues Personalities dominated an election in which all four candidates ran as Democratic-Republicans. Crawford, Monroe's treasury secretary, won the nomination of the party's

congressional caucus. But few attended the caucus and most electors were chosen by state legislatures. Crawford later suffered a stroke and was not a serious candidate. John C. Calhoun of South Carolina ran unopposed for vice-president. **Regional Influences** Each candidate represented his region Adams the commercial northeast, Crawford the cotton south, Clay and Jackson the agrarian west. Jackson, a hero of the War of 1812 and battles against Indians, won a clear plurality of the popular vote and was the only candidate with support outside his home region. But no candidate won a majority of the electoral vote and the election was decided in the House, where Speaker Clay's support gave the victory to Adams.

1828

Party	Candidate	Popular vote	Per cent	Electoral vote
Democratic- Republican	Andrew Jackson (Tenn.)	642,553	55.97	178
	and John C. Calhoun (S.C.)			171
National- Republican	John Q. Adams (Mass.)	500,987	43.63	83
	and Richard Rush (Pa.)			83
Other		4,568	0.40	—
	Total Vote	1,148,018		
	Jackson Plurality	141,656		

Key Issues Personalities again overshadowed issues. The Jackson campaign catered to popular prejudices, portraying the contest as one between democracy and aristocracy. The Jackson coalition was a forerunner of the modern Democratic Party and reestablished two-party politics in the U.S. **Regional Influences** Jackson won the south and west easily, and appealed to discontented laborers in the north. Adams carried only New England, New Jersey, Maryland and Delaware.

1832

Party	Candidate	Popular vote	Per cent	Electoral vote
Democrat	Andrew Jackson (Tenn.)	701,780	54.23	219
	and Martin Van Buren (N.Y.)			189
National- Republican	Henry Clay (Ky.)	484,205	37.42	49
	and John Sergeant (Pa.)			49
Anti- Masonic	William Wirt (Md.)	100,715	7.78	7
	and Amos Ellmaker (Pa.)			7
Independent	John Floyd (Va.)	—	—	11
	and Henry Lee (Mass.)			11
Other		7,273	0.56	—
	Total Vote	1,293,973		
	Jackson Plurality	217,575		

Key Issues The Anti-Masons, the first third-party in American politics, began in opposition to secret societies in particular and privileged groups in general, but were at heart an anti-Jackson party. The two established parties followed the Anti-Masons lead by holding national nominating conventions to select a presidential nominee. While Jackson's opposition to the Bank of the United States was made an issue by the two major parties, the election was more a referendum on Jackson himself. **Regional Influences** Anti-Masonic strength was concentrated in rural sections of New England and the Middle Atlantic states. In those states National-Republicans and Anti-Masons supported the same ticket. With the forces against him divided, Jackson won easily. Clay won only half of the New England states, Wirt won only Vermont. Jackson captured Maine and New Hampshire. In South Carolina, where electors still were chosen by the legislature, nullificationists cast their ballots for Floyd.

1836

Party	Candidate	Popular vote	Per cent	Electoral vote
Democrat	Martin Van Buren (N.Y.)	764,716	50.83	170
	and Richard M. Johnson (Ky.)	147		
Whig	William Henry Harrison (Ohio)	550,816	36.63	73
Whig	Hugh L. White (Tenn.)	146,107	9.72	26
Whig	Daniel Webster (Mass.)	41,201	2.74	14
	Willie P. Mangum (N.C.)	—	—	11
Other		1,234	0.08	—
	Total Vote	1,503,534		
	Van Buren Plurality	213,360		

Key Issues Jackson's heavy-handed tactics, especially in his successful battle against the national bank, led the National-Republicans to rename themselves Whigs, after the 18th Century British party that tried to lessen the power of the crown. But lacking effective national leadership and divided along sectional lines, the anti-Jackson forces could not agree on a single candidate or platform and instead ran three regional candidates. **Regional Influences** Whig strategy was to throw the election into the House, where they could unite around a single candidate. Webster was to win New England, Harrison the west and Lawson the south. Van Buren, forced on the Democrats by Jackson, foiled the plan by picking up enough states throughout the nation to win by a slim majority. Johnson fell one electoral vote short of a majority for vice-president and was selected by the Senate. The South Carolina legislature cast its votes for Mangum.

1840

Party	Candidate	Popular vote	Per-cent	Electoral vote
Whig	William Henry Harrison (Ohio) and John Tyler (Va.)	1,275,390	52.88	234
Democrat	Martin Van Buren (N.Y.)	1,128,854	46.81	60
Liberty	James G. Birney (N.Y.)	6,797	0.28	—
Other		767	0.03	—
	Total Vote	2,411,808		
	Harrison Plurality	146,536		

Key Issues With the country still reeling from the Panic of 1837, the Democrats were on the defensive. Though differences prevented them from writing a platform, the Whigs rallied around Harrison. In a campaign notable for its absence of issues, the Whigs turned the tables on Jackson's party. Harrison, despite his wealthy origins, was portrayed as the "log-cabin, hard-cider candidate" opposing the allegedly aristocratic Van Buren. The Democrats left the selection of a vice-presidential candidate to each state. **Regional Influences** Van Buren won only seven states, just one outside of the south or west. Harrison was long associated with the west and Tyler was a conservative Southerner and friend of Henry Clay. For the first time, active two-party politics was established across the nation. The 68-year-old Harrison caught a severe cold after delivering a lengthy Inaugural Address in the rain and died one month into his term.

1844

Party	Candidate	Popular vote	Per-cent	Electoral vote
Democrat	James K. Polk (Tenn.) and George M. Dallas (Pa.)	1,339,494	49.54	170
Whig	Henry Clay (Ky.) and Theodore Frelinghuysen (N.J.)	1,300,004	48.08	
Abolitionist	James G. Birney (N.Y.)	62,103	2.30	—
Other		2,058	0.08	—
	Total Vote	2,703,659		
	Polk Plurality	39,490		

Key Issues Manifest Destiny, the goal of a U.S. stretching from the Atlantic to the Pacific, was the central issue because of the question of the annexation of Texas. With the election approaching, opponents of slavery lead the Senate to reject a treaty between Texas and the Tyler Administration that would have preserved Texan slavery and made it a U.S. territory. The two leading presidential candidates, Clay and Van Buren, sought to smother the Texas issue by ignoring it. But Polk snatched the Democratic nomination with his clear and vocal advocacy of annexation of Texas and general territorial expansion. **Regional Influences** Expansionism was immensely popular, especially in the south and west, where memories of the depression following 1837 added to the attraction of new, vast, and open public lands. Support for manifest destiny more than made up for anti-slavery sentiment elsewhere and Polk won a narrow plurality but a clear victory.

1848

Party	Candidate	Popular vote	Per-cent	Electoral vote
Whig	Zachary Taylor (La.) and Millard Fillmore (N.Y.)	1,361,393	47.28	163
Democrat	Lewis Cass (Mich.) and William O. Butler (Ky.)	1,223,460	42.49	127
Free Soil	Martin Van Buren (N.Y.) and Charles Francis Adams (Mass.)	291,501	10.12	—
Other		2,830	0.10	—
	Total Vote	2,879,184		
	Taylor Plurality	137,933		

Key Issues The Wilmot Proviso, calling for a ban on extension of slavery into territories acquired in the Mexican War, dominated the election. But both major parties evaded the issue. Slavery foes banded together to form the Free Soil Party, which won no electoral votes but drew enough popular support away from the Democrats to throw the election to "Old Rough and Ready," Zachary Taylor, a slave-holder. Taylor died in July 1850. **Regional Influences** Both major parties balanced their tickets with a Northerner and Southerner. Free Soilers were mostly Northern Democrats, anti-slavery Whigs and abolitionists. There was no distinct pattern in the Electoral College following a lackluster campaign. Free Soil strength in New York gave the state and the election to the Whigs.

1852

Party	Candidate	Popular vote	Per-cent	Electoral vote
Democrat	Franklin Pierce (N.H.) and William R. D. King (Ala.)	1,607,510	50.84	254
Whig	Winfield Scott (Va.) and William A. Graham (N.C.)	1,386,942	43.87	42
Free Soil	John P. Hale (N.H.) and George Washington Julian (Ind.)	155,210	4.91	—
Other		12,168	0.38	—
	Total Vote	3,161,830		
	Pierce Plurality	220,568		

Key Issues The election was a referendum on the Compromise of 1850, in which Congress voted to admit California as a free state, create the territories of New Mexico and Utah with no restriction on slavery, abolish the slave trade in the District of Columbia, purchase disputed land from Texas on behalf of New Mexico, and toughen the Fugitive Slave Act. The Democrats strongly endorsed the Compromise, but the bitterly divided Whigs only vaguely accepted it. **Regional Influences** The Democrats won a resounding electoral victory, capturing 27 states to the four taken by the Whigs Massachusetts, Vermont, Kentucky and Tennessee. Free Soilers returned to the Democrats and the Whigs never again were a political force in a nation which believed the slave question was behind it.

1856

Party	Candidate	Popular vote	Per-cent	Electoral vote
Democrat	James Buchanan (Pa.) and John C. Breckinridge (Ky.)	1,836,072	45.28	174
Republican	John C. Fremont (Calif.) and William L. Dayton (N.J.)	1,342,345	33.11	114
Whig	Millard Fillmore (N.Y.) and Andrew J. Donelson (Tenn.)	873,053	21.53	8
Other		3,177	0.08	—
	Total Vote	4,054,647		
	Buchanan Plurality	493,727		

Key Issues The Democrats firmly endorsed "popular sovereignty" even though it led to great turmoil in the territory of Kansas. But they chose as their nominee Buchanan, largely because he had been out of the country and was untainted by "Bleeding Kansas" battle, which pitted supporters and foes of slavery trying to organize the territory into a slave or free state. The Republicans, a new party of northern Whigs and Democrats committed to the containment of slavery ran Fremont, a popular general and explorer. **Regional Influences** Fremont carried all but five of the free states. But Buchanan won all of the south in addition to the five northern states and was elected. Fillmore, supported by the Know-Nothings and Whig remnants, only won Maryland but strongly challenged the Democrats in the south.

1860

Party	Candidate	Popular vote	Per-cent	Electoral vote
Republican	Abraham Lincoln (Ill.) and Hannibal Hamlin (Maine)	1,865,908	39.82	180
Democrat	Stephen A. Douglas (Ill.) and Herschel V. Johnson (Ga.)	1,380,202	29.46	12
Democrat	John C. Breckinridge (Ky.) and Joseph Lane (Oreg.)	848,019	18.09	72
Constitutional	John Bell (Tenn.)	590,901	12.61	39
Union and Other	Edward Everett (Mass.)	531	0.01	—
	Total Vote	4,685,561		
	Lincoln Plurality	485,706		

Key Issues Sectional differences over slavery came to a head in 1860. The Democrats could not agree on a candidate and split into northern and southern factions. The Northerners backed Douglas and popular sovereignty, the Southerners Breckinridge and Federal protection of slavery in the territories. The Republicans, virtually all Northerners, were a pro-tariff, nationalistic party that opposed the extension of slavery but did not seek to overturn it where it already existed. Bell, the candidate of Whigs and Know-Nothings who backed Fillmore in 1856, were a compromise party expressing support for preservation of the Union. **Regional Influences** In effect there were two separate contests in 1860 Lincoln versus Douglas in the north, Breckinridge versus Bell in the south. Free states outnumbered slave states and cast half again as many electoral votes. Lincoln won every northern state except New Jersey and, though not even on the ballot in 10 southern states, was elected president. Breckinridge captured 11 of the 15 southern states. The four southern states won by Douglas and Bell were in the upper south.

1864

Party	Candidate	Popular vote	Per-cent	Electoral vote
Republican	Abraham Lincoln (Ill.) and Andrew Johnson (Tenn.)	2,218,388	55.02	212
Democrat	George B. McClellan (N.Y.) and George H. Pendleton (Ohio)	1,812,807	44.96	21
	Total Vote	4,031,887		
	Lincoln Plurality	405,581		

Key Issues Lincoln's renomination was not assured. Radical Republicans thought he was not aggressive enough in his conduct of the war or plans for the eventual peace, but moderation ultimately prevailed. The Republicans ran as the Union Party and nominated Johnson, a pro-Union Democrat, for vice-president. The Democrats ran a peace campaign, calling the war a failure. But McClellan, a popular general, broke with his party's platform and denied the war was a failure, denouncing members of his party who seemed to advocate peace at any price. He opposed emancipation as a goal of the war. **Regional Influences** Military victories around election time helped the embattled incumbent. Lincoln won a convincing popular and electoral victory with the support of middle-class professionals, farmers, laborers and the strongly pro-Union voters who voted for Bell four years earlier. McClellan was strongest in areas carried by Breckinridge four years before. Eleven Confederate states did not participate in the election.

1868

Party	Candidate	Popular vote	Per-cent	Electoral vote
Republican	Ulysses S. Grant (Ohio) and Schuyler Colfax (Ind.)	3,013,650	52.66	214
Democrat	Horatio S. Seymour (N.Y.) and Francis P. Blair (Mo.)	2,708,744	47.34	80
Other		46	—	—
	Total Vote	5,722,440		
	Grant Plurality	304,906		

Key Issues The Republicans waved the "bloody shirt" of the war and ran on their program of Radical Reconstruction. While calling for Negro suffrage in the south, the Republicans asserted it was a matter for individual northern states to decide for themselves. Democrats ran against Reconstruction, declaring that the question of Negro suffrage should be decided by individual southern states as well. **Regional Influences** Despite Grant's popularity, the Republicans were just able to win the election. Seymour carried only eight states, though he did well in the states won by Grant. Without black votes in the South, Grant would not have received a majority of the popular vote. The votes of the "unreconstructed" states of Mississippi, Texas and Virginia were not counted.

1872

Party	Candidate	Popular vote	Per-cent	Electoral vote
Republican	Ulysses S. Grant (Ohio) and Henry Wilson (Mass.)	3,598,235	55.63	286
Liberal Republican/ Democrat	Horace Greeley (N.Y.) and Benjamin Gratz Brown (Mo.)	2,834,761	43.83	—
Straight Democrat	Charles O'Conor (N.Y.)	18,602	—	—
	Other	16,081	0.25	—
	Total Vote	6,467,679		
	Grant Plurality	763,474		

Key Issues Liberal Republicans broke with Grant over corruption in his administration, high tariffs and continued Radical Reconstruction. They nominated Greeley, editor of the *New York Tribune.* The Democrats endorsed Greeley and the Liberal platform. But the great scandals of the Grant administration were not yet revealed and the Republicans again waved the bloody shirt to victory. **Regional Influences** Greeley carried only two states in the lower South and four border states. He died shortly after the election (Nov. 29, 1872) and his electoral votes went to other candidates: Thomas Hendricks, Indiana, 42; Benjamin Gratz Brown, Missouri, 18; Charles J. Jenkins, Georgia, 2; and David Davis, Illinois, 1.

1876

Party	Candidate	Popular vote	Per-cent	Electoral vote
Republican	Rutherford B. Hayes (Ohio) and William A. Wheeler (N.Y.)	4,034,311	47.95	185
Democrat	Samuel J. Tilden (N.Y.) and Thomas A. Hendricks (Ind.)	4,288,546	50.97	184
Greenback	Peter Cooper (N.Y.)	75,973	0.90	—
Other		14,271	0.17	
	Total Vote	8,413,101		
	Tilden Plurality	254,235		

Key Issues The Republicans were in trouble as 1876 approached due to rampant corruption in the Grant administration and the economic depression that followed the Panic of 1873. Hayes, a three-term Ohio governor known for his unassailable integrity, was nominated to run against the favored Democrat, Tilden, a New York reform governor whose reputation was made in opposition to the Tweed political machine. Both men espoused conservative economics. Cooper and the Greenbacks advocated currency expansion. **Regional Influences** As

Election Day approached, Tilden could count on winning all of the south except for the three states still controlled by Republican carpetbaggers: South Carolina, Louisiana, and Florida. He seemed assured of victory when those states appeared to vote for him along with several northern states, including New York and New Jersey. But Republicans claimed South Carolina, Louisiana and Florida for Hayes, arguing that thousands of blacks who would have voted for Hayes were barred from voting there. Election boards in those Republican-controlled states gave Hayes the needed majority, and thus the election. In the uproar that followed Congress set up an Election Commission to validate the returns. The commission voted strictly along party lines, eight to seven, to give the election to Hayes. Despite charges that Republicans stole the election, Hayes later was inaugurated peaceably after he let it be known that as president he would end military reconstruction by withdrawing Federal troops from the south and that he would restore "efficient local government" to the south.

1880

Party	Candidate	Popular vote	Per-cent	Electoral vote
Republican	James A. Garfield (Ohio) and Chester A. Arthur (N.Y.)	4,461,158	48.27	214
Democrat	Winfield S. Hancock (Pa.) and William H. English (Ind.)	4,444,260	48.25	155
Greenback	James B. Weaver (Iowa) and Benjamin J. Chambers (Tex.)	305,997	3.32	—
Other		14,005	0.15	—
	Total Vote	9,210,420		
	Garfield Plurality	1,898		

Key Issues With the war and Reconstruction behind, no major issues arose over which the major parties disagreed. The Democrats, the party of secession 20 year earlier, nominated General Hancock to help combat the stigma of treason. Garfield made a protectionist tariff central to his campaign. **Regional Influences** The balance between Republican strength in the Midwest and west and Democratic strength in the south resulted in a plurality of less than 2,000 for Garfield out of more than 9 million votes cast. Four months into his term Garfield was shot by a disappointed office-seeker.

1884

Party	Candidate	Popular vote	Per-cent	Electoral vote
Democrat	Grover Cleveland (N.Y.) and Thomas A. Hendricks (Ind.)	4,874,621	48.50	219
Republican	James G. Blaine (Maine) and John A. Logan (Ill.)	4,848,936	48.25	182
Greenback	Benjamin F. Butler (Mass.)	175,096	1.74	—
Prohibition	John P. St. John (Kans.)	147,482	1.47	—
Other		3,619	0.04	—
	Total Votes	10,049,754		
	Cleveland Plurality	25,685		

Key Issues The private lives and morals of the candidates were the focus of a campaign notable for mudslinging. Blaine was accused of accepting bribes from a railroad company for whom he obtained a Federal grant and Republicans taunted Cleveland for fathering a son out of wedlock. Still, Cleveland, known for his independence and integrity in public life, attracted the votes of many liberal Republicans and reformers unable to stomach Blaine, a Radical Republican leader. **Regional Influences** Cleveland carried all of the southern states as well as the key swing states of Indiana, New Jersey, Connecticut and New York, becoming the first Democrat elected president since the Civil War. Cleveland carried his home state of New York and its 36 electoral votes by less than 1,200 votes.

1888

Party	Candidate	Popular vote	Per-cent	Electoral vote
Republican	Benjamin Harrison (Ind.) and Levi P. Morton (N.Y.)	5,443,892	47.82	233
Democrat	Grover Cleveland (N.Y.) and Allen G. Thurman (Ohio)	5,534,488	48.62	168
Prohibition	Clinton B. Fisk (N.J.)	249,813	2.19	—
Union Labor	Alson J. Streeter (Ill.)	146,602	1.29	—
Other		8,519	0.07	—
	Total Votes	11,383,320		
	Cleveland Plurality	90,596		

Key Issues Cleveland made tariff reform central to his administration, seeking to lower existing high tariffs. The Republicans campaigned on the need to maintain high wages by keeping a high tariff on imported goods. **Regional Influences** Despite the emphasis on the tariff, Cleveland still carried such manufacturing states as New Jersey and Connecticut as well as most of the south. But though Cleveland won 90,000 more popular votes than Harrison, the Republican carried the pro-tariff swing states of Indiana and New York by slight margins to win the election in the electoral college in one of the most corrupt campaigns in history.

1892

Party	Candidate	Popular vote	Per-cent	Electoral vote
Democrat	Grover Cleveland (N.Y.) and Adlai E. Stevenson (Illinois)	5,551,883	46.05	277
Republican	Benjamin Harrison (Indiana) and Whitelaw Reid (N.Y.)	5,179,244	42.96	145
Populist	James B. Weaver (Iowa) and James G. Field (Virginia)	1,024,280	8.50	22
Prohibition	John Bidwell (California)	270,770	2.25	—
Other		29,920	0.25	
	Total Votes	12,056,097		
	Cleveland Plurality	372,639		

Key Issues Cleveland and Harrison again fought a battle over the tariff, which the Republicans drastically raised in 1890. Both men were out of touch with the growing agrarian and populist discontent. Weaver, campaigning for free silver, became the first third-party candidate to gain electoral votes since the war. **Regional Influences** Cleveland improved upon his 1884 and 1888 showings to win the most decisive presidential victory in 20 years. This time he carried the swing states of New York, New Jersey, Connecticut and Indiana as well as the traditionally Republican states of Illinois, California and Wisconsin.

1896

Party	Candidate	Popular vote	Per-cent	Electoral vote
Republican	William McKinley (Ohio) and Garret A. Hobart (N.J.)	7,108,480	51.01	271
Democrat/ Populist	William J. Bryan (Nebr.) and Democrat Arthur Sewall (Me.) and Populist Thomas E. Watson (Ga.)	6,511,495	46.73	176 / 149
National Democrat	John M. Palmer (Ill.)	133,435	0.96	—
Prohibition	Joshua Levering (Md.)	125,072	0.90	—
Other		57,256	0.41	—
	Total Votes	13,935,738		
	McKinley Plurality	596,985		

Key Issues The Democrats absorbed Populist energies and abandoned the conservatism of Cleveland by nominating Bryan and adopting key elements of the Populist program, especially the call for free silver. The pro-tariff and pro-gold Republicans led by McKinley and Mark Hanna outspent the

Democrats by almost 12 to 1. In losing, Bryan amassed more votes than any victorious candidate before him. **Regional Influences** Bryan did not carry a single state north of Virginia or east of Missouri. His hold on the agricultural south and west was broken by Republican victories in Maryland, Delaware, West Virginia, Kentucky, California and Oregon. Bryan, failing to appeal to labor, carried no industrial or urban states.

1900

Party	Candidate	Popular vote	Per-cent	Electoral vote
Republican	William McKinley (Ohio) and Theodore Roosevelt (N.Y.)	7,218,039	51.67	292
Democrat	William J. Bryan (Nebr.) and Adlai E. Stevenson (Ill.)	6,358,345	45.51	155
Prohibition	John C. Woolley (Ill.)	209,004	1.50	—
Social Democrat	Eugene V. Debs (Ind.)	86,935	0.62	—
Other		98,147	0.70	—
	Total Vote	13,970,470		
	McKinley Plurality	859,694		

Key Issues Imperialism in the Philippines joined free silver and the tariff as the key issues in a replay of the 1896 election. Bryan tried to unite the silver interests in the west and south with supporters of the gold standard in a coalition against imperialism, which the Democratic platform called the "paramount issue" of the campaign. But voters did not desert McKinley in a time of prosperity. **Regional Influences** Bryan carried only the Solid South and four silver states in the west, and was defeated in the silver states of Kansas, South Dakota, Utah and Wyoming as well as his home state of Nebraska. Both houses of Congress were led by significant Republican majorities.

1904

Party	Candidate	Popular vote	Per-cent	Electoral vote
Republican	Theodore Roosevelt (N.Y.) and Charles W. Fairbanks (Ind.)	7,626,593	56.41	336
Democrat	Alton B. Parker (N.Y.) and Henry G. Davis (W. Va.)	5,082,898	37.60	140
Socialist	Eugene V. Debs (Ind.)	402,489	2.98	—
Prohibition	Silas C. Swallow (Pa.)	258,596	1.91	—
Other		148,388	1.10	—
	Total Votes	13,518,964		
	Roosevelt Plurality	2,543,695		

Key Issues Roosevelt stole the mantle of reform from the Democrats with his campaigns against the "malefactors of great wealth." The Democrats turned to the right by nominating the lackluster Parker, a judge with close ties to Wall Street. Parker turned his back on Bryan Democrats by renouncing free silver. **Regional Influences** Roosevelt won a landslide victory based largely on his own personality and popularity. The Democrats won only 13 states, none outside the south.

1908

Party	Candidate	Popular vote	Per-cent	Electoral vote
Republican	William H. Taft (Ohio) and James S. Sherman (N.Y.)	7,662,258	51.58	321
Democrat	William J. Bryan (Nebr.) and John W. Kern (Ind.)	6,406,801	43.05	162
Socialist	Eugene V. Debs (Ind.)	420,380	2.82	—
Prohibition	Eugene W. Chafin (Ill.)	252,821	1.70	—
Other		126,474	0.85	—
	Total Vote	14,882,734		
	Taft Plurality	1,269,457		

Key Issues The immensely popular Roosevelt declined to run. Taft, his secretary of war and handpicked successor, debated Bryan over who was better qualified to complete TR's progressive program. Bryan abandoned silver and courted labor but ran a lackluster losing campaign. **Regional Influences** Bryan again carried the South. But the appeal of Roosevelt's reform programs helped the Republicans to do well in the west and Taft's background as a Yale graduate and Federal jurist enabled him to carry the east as well.

1912

Party	Candidate	Popular vote	Per-cent	Electoral vote
Democrat	Woodrow Wilson (N.J.) and Thomas Marshall (Ind.)	6,293,152	41.84	435
Progressive	Theodore Roosevelt (N.Y.) and Hiram Johnson (Calif.)	4,119,207	27.39	88
Republican	William H. Taft (Ohio) and James S. Sherman (N.Y.)	3,486,333	23.18	8
Socialist	Eugene V. Debs (Ind.)	900,369	5.99	—
Other		241,902	1.61	—
	Total Vote	15,040,963		
	Wilson Plurality	2,173,945		

Key Issues Taft's conservatism and political ineptitude led Roosevelt to challenge him within the party from the left. Unable to wrest the nomination from Taft, Roosevelt ran a third-party campaign. The election boiled down to a contest between Roosevelt and Wilson and their respective conceptions of progressivism. Roosevelt's "New Nationalism" called for strong Federal regulations to control the trusts and big businesses. Wilson's "New Freedom" sought instead to revive competition through vigorous application of anti-trust laws. The Progressives advocated a broad array of social reforms to be implemented by the Federal government while the Democrats emphasized the primacy of the states in such matters. **Regional Influences** Though he amassed fewer votes than did Bryan in 1908, Wilson took advantage of the split in the Republican ranks to win a decisive plurality of the vote. He did best in traditional Democratic states, but was able to win most traditionally Republican states as well. Roosevelt won only 6 states, including California, which he carried by fewer than 200 votes. Taft carried Utah and Vermont. The Democrats also won control of both houses of Congress, their best overall performance since the Civil War.

1916

Party	Candidate	Popular vote	Per-cent	Electoral vote
Democrat	Woodrow Wilson (Va.) and Thomas Marshall (Ind.)	9,126,300	49.24	277
Republican	Charles Evans Hughes (N.Y.) and Charles W. Fairbanks (Ind.)	8,546,789	46.11	254
Socialist	Allen L. Benson (N.Y.)	589,924	3.18	—
Prohibition	James F. Hanly (Ind.)	221,030	1.19	—
Other		50,979	0.28	—
	Total Vote	18,535,022		
	Wilson Plurality	579,511		

Key Issues The campaign was a referendum on Wilson's first term, his program of domestic reform, and his policy toward the war in Europe. He ran a peace campaign with the slogan "He kept us out of war" and attracted the votes of many Bull Moosers. Voters who felt Wilson was either too harsh or too lenient toward Germany tended to vote Republican. Irish-American and German-American extremists, virulently opposed to aiding Great Britain, embarrassed Hughes with their vocal support. A coalition of labor, farmers, reformers, and intellectuals won the election for Wilson. **Regional Influences** Hughes, a former reform governor of New York who left the Supreme Court to challenge Wilson, carried all of the east except New Hampshire and all of the Old Northwest except Ohio. But the South was again solid for the Democrats and so was every state west of the Mississippi except Minnesota, Iowa, South Dakota and Oregon, which Wilson lost by close margins. The electoral vote was the closest since 1876.

1920

Party	Candidate	Popular vote	Per- cent	Elec- toral vote
Republican	Warren G. Harding (Ohio) and Calvin Coolidge (Mass.)	16,133,314	60.30	404
Democrat	James M. Cox (Ohio) and Franklin D. Roosevelt (N.Y.)	9,140,884	34.17	127
Socialist	Eugene V. Debs (Ind.)	913,664	3.42	—
Farmer-Labor	Parley P. Christensen (Utah)	264,540	0.99	—
Other		301,384	1.13	—
	Total Vote	26,753,786		
	Harding Plurality	6,992,430		

Key Issues The voters turned against Wilsonian progressivism and internationalism by electing Harding, a vacuous party hack who promised a "return to normalcy" after the turbulent years of domestic reform and world war. The undistinguished Cox ran in support of the League of Nations and little else. **Regional Influences** Harding carried every state outside of the south, except Tennessee. The Republicans added to their majorities in both houses of Congress, regained in 1918.

1924

Party	Candidate	Popular vote	Per- cent	Elec- toral vote
Republican	Calvin Coolidge (Mass.) and Charles G. Dawes (Ohio)	15,717,553	54.00	382
Democrat	John W. Davis (N.Y.) and Charles W. Bryan (Nebr.)	8,386,169	28.84	136
Progressive Socialist	Robert M. LaFollette (Wis.) and Burton K. Wheeler (Mont.)	4,814,050	16.56	13
Other		158,187	0.55	—
	Total Vote	29,075,959		
	Coolidge Plurality	7,331,384		

Key Issues The country "kept cool with Coolidge" as the Democrats could not overcome prosperity or themselves. Davis, a conservative Wall Street lawyer, was a compromise nominee selected by a bitterly divided party after 103 ballots. Reformers, labor and farmers flocked to the LaFollette candidacy. **Regional Influences** All 12 of the Democratic states were from the south. LaFollette's 13 electoral votes came from his home of Wisconsin.

1928

Party	Candidate	Popular vote	Per- cent	Elec- toral vote
Republican	Herbert C. Hoover (Calif.) and Charles E. Curtis (Kans.)	21,411,911	58.20	444
Democrat	Alfred E. Smith (N.Y.) and Joseph T. Robinson (Ark.)	15,000,185	40.77	87
Socialist	Norman Thomas (N.Y.)	266,453	0.72	—
Worker's	William Z. Foster (Ill.)	48,170	0.13	—
Other		63,565	0.17	—
	Total Vote	36,790,364		
	Hoover Plurality	6,411,806		

Key Issues Booze, bigotry, Tammany, and prosperity did in the Democrats. Rural America would not vote for an anti-Prohibition, big-city, Catholic machine politician, despite Smith's success as governor of New York, especially while the Republicans could convincingly cite the success of their economic leadership. **Regional Influences** The solid south was shattered as Hoover Democrats gave Republicans the states of Virginia, North Carolina, Tennessee, Florida and Texas for the first time since Reconstruction. Smith lost his own state and every western and border state. But Smith set the stage for the New Deal coalition with the votes of urban ethnics, he carried the nation's 12 largest cities, all of which had been won by the Republicans four years earlier. The Democrats also won votes in the traditionally Republican west among farmers unsure about prosperity.

1932

Party	Candidate	Popular vote	Per- cent	Elec- toral vote
Democrat	Franklin D. Roosevelt (N.Y.) and John Nance Garner (Tex.)	22,825,016	57.42	472
Republican	Herbert C. Hoover (Calif.) and Charles E. Curtis (Kans.)	15,758,397	39.64	59
Socialist	Norman Thomas (N.Y.)	883,990	2.22	—
Communist	William Z. Foster (Ill.)	102,221	0.26	—
Other		179,758	0.45	—
	Total Vote	39,749,382		
	Roosevelt Plurality	7,066,619		

Key Issues The Democrats won by blaming the Republicans for the Great Depression. Roosevelt was the first presidential nominee of a major party to address his nominating convention, pledging to help "the forgotten man at the bottom of the economic pyramid." In a vague and contradictory platform, the Democrats promised to balance the Federal budget by drastically reducing expenses and vowed to spend Federal dollars to attack the nation's economic woes. **Regional Influences** Roosevelt lost only six states, Maine, New Hampshire, Vermont, Connecticut, Delaware, and Pennsylvania, carrying all of the agricultural West and South. He put the finishing touches on the New Deal coalition by also improving upon Smith's margins of victory in the nation's big cities.

1936

Party	Candidate	Popular vote	Per- cent	Elec- toral vote
Democrat	Franklin D. Roosevelt (N.Y.) and John Nance Garner (Tex.)	27,747,636	60.79	523
Republican	Alfred M. Landon (Kans.) and Frank Knox (Ill.)	16,679,543	36.54	8
Union	William Lemke (N.Dak.)	892,492	1.96	—
Socialist	Norman Thomas (N.Y.)	187,785	0.41	—
Other		134,847	0.30	—
	Total Vote	45,642,303		
	Roosevelt Plurality	11,068,093		

Key Issues Despite intense opposition to the New Deal, its great public appeal was confirmed in the most one-sided election since 1820 and sweeping victories for the Democrats in Congress. The populist forces of the late Huey Long coalesced around Lemke but failed to gather widespread support. **Regional Influences** Roosevelt carried every state except Maine and Vermont. The New Deal coalition was at its height as every large city voted overwhelmingly for FDR. The middle-class, farmers in the west and south, big-city ethnics, labor and reform intellectuals flocked to the Democrats. Northern Blacks also began to vote heavily Democratic for the first time.

1940

Party	Candidate	Popular vote	Per- cent	Elec- toral vote
Democrat	Franklin D. Roosevelt (N.Y.) and Henry A. Wallace (Iowa)	27,263,448	54.70	449
Republican	Wendell L. Willkie (Ind.) and Charles L. McNary (Oreg.)	22,336,260	44.82	82
Socialist	Norman Thomas (N.Y.)	116,827	0.23	—
Prohibition	Roger W. Babson (Mass.)	58,685	0.12	—
Other		65,223	0.13	—
	Total Vote	49,840,443		
	Roosevelt Plurality	4,927,188		

Key Issues With war raging in Europe the electorate turned its attention from domestic to foreign affairs. The international scene led the Democrats to break with tradition and renominate FDR for a third term. The Republicans turned to businessman and political neophyte Willkie, a charismatic former

Democrat. Willkie's internationalism and the pledge of both candidates to keep the U.S. out of the war minimized the role of foreign policy in the campaign. **Regional Influences** Willkie carried only 10 states, mostly in the Midwest. But Roosevelt's percentage of the popular vote was markedly down from 1936.

1944

Party	Candidate	Popular vote	Per cent	Electoral vote
Democrat	Franklin D. Roosevelt (N.Y.) and Harry S Truman (Mo.)	25,611,936	53.39	432
Republican	Thomas E. Dewey (N.Y.) and John W. Bricker (Ohio)	22,013,372	45.89	99
Socialist	Norman Thomas (N.Y.)	79,100	0.16	—
Prohibition	Claude A. Watson (Calif.)	74,733	0.16	—
Other		195,778	0.41	—
	Total Vote	47,974,819		
	Roosevelt Plurality	3,598,564		

Key Issues With both candidates supporting New Deal social legislation and an international organization to maintain the peace after the war, the nation chose to let FDR lead America into the post-war era. Big-city bosses and southern conservatives, with FDR's private support, ousted Wallace from the ticket in favor of Truman. **Regional Influences** Roosevelt won 36 states and the Democrats improved their control over Congress and the nation's statehouses. The Republicans only won a handful of western and New England states.

1948

Party	Candidate	Popular vote	Per cent	Electoral vote
Democrat	Harry S Truman (Mo.) and Alben W. Barkley (Ky.)	24,105,587	49.51	303
Republican	Thomas E. Dewey (N.Y.) and Earl Warren (Calif.)	21,970,017	45.12	189
States' Rights	Strom Thurmond (S.C.) and Fielding L. Wright (Miss.)	1,169,134	2.40	39
Progressive	Henry A. Wallace (Iowa) and Glen H. Taylor (Idaho)	1,157,057	2.38	—
Other		290,647	0.60	—
	Total Vote	48,692,442		
	Truman Plurality	2,135,570		

Key Issues The Republicans were sure of victory after 16 years of Democratic rule and the desertion of the Democrats by conservative Southern Dixiecrats and the ultra-liberal Wallace faction. But Dewey's dour personality and Truman's intense whistle-stop campaign against the "do-nothing, good-for-nothing" Republican Eightieth Congress resulted in one of the biggest upsets in presidential history. **Regional Influences** Dewey captured all of the Middle Atlantic and New England states, except Massachusetts and Connecticut, along with the Dakotas, Nebraska and Kansas in the Midwest and Oregon in the northwest. Thurmond won South Carolina, Mississippi, Alabama and Louisiana in the Deep South.

1952

Party	Candidate	Popular vote	Per cent	Electoral vote
Republican	Dwight D. Eisenhower (Kans.) and Richard M. Nixon (Calif.)	33,936,137	55.13	442
Democrat	Adlai E. Stevenson (Ill.) and John J. Sparkman (Ala.)	27,314,649	44.38	89
Progressive	Vincent W. Hallinan (Calif.)	140,416	0.23	—
Prohibition	Stuart Hamblen (Calif.)	73,413	0.12	—
Other		86,503	0.14	—
	Total Vote	61,551,118		
	Eisenhower Plurality	6,621,485		

Key Issues Popular war hero Eisenhower swept to victory after uniting the internationalist and isolationist factions of the Republican party. He routed the Democrats by promising to kick out alleged crooks and communists in Washington, wage a more aggressive fight against communists worldwide and "go to Korea," implying that he had a plan to end the war there. **Regional Influences** Stevenson, who appealed to northern liberals as well as southern states' rights Democrats, carried only nine states in the south. The Republicans also won slight majorities in both houses of Congress and were in control of the national government for the first time in 20 years.

1956

Party	Candidate	Popular vote	Per cent	Electoral vote
Republican	Dwight D. Eisenhower (Kans.) Richard M. Nixon (Calif.)	35,585,247	57.37	457
Democrat	Adlai E. Stevenson (Ill.) and Estes Kefauver (Tenn.)	26,030,172	41.97	73
Constitution/ States' Rights	T. Coleman Andrews (Va.)	108,055	0.17	—
Socialist-Labor	Eric Hass (New York)	44,300	0.07	—
Other		257,600	0.42	—
	Total Vote	62,025,372		
	Eisenhower Plurality	9,555,073		

Key Issues Eisenhower won an easy victory in a rematch of the 1952 election. His popularity did not translate into victories for his party elsewhere, as Democrats increased their control of Congress, regained in 1954, and their hold on the nation's governorships. **Regional Influences** Winning even more handsomely than he did in 1952, Eisenhower lost only seven southern states.

1960

Party	Candidate	Popular vote	Per cent	Electoral vote
Democrat	John F. Kennedy (Mass.) and Lyndon B. Johnson (Tex.)	34,221,344	49.72	303
Republican	Richard M. Nixon (Calif.) and Henry Cabot Lodge (Mass.)	34,106,671	49.55	219
Socialist-Labor	Eric Hass (N.Y.)	47,522	0.07	—
Other		337,175	0.48	15
Unpledged		116,248	0.17	—
	Total Vote	68,828,960		
	Kennedy Plurality	114,673		

Key Issues Kennedy called for the government to play a larger role in stimulating the national economy in order to fund domestic social programs as well as to sustain a defense build-up and keep ahead militarily of the Soviet Union. The election was the first in which there were nationally televised debates between the two candidates. Kennedy's slick television performance played a role in his narrow triumph. **Regional Influences** The Democrats won a thin victory by narrowly defeating the Republicans in the Middle Atlantic states, the Deep South, Illinois and Texas. Nixon carried most of the Midwest, border and western states. Conservative Democratic Senator Harry F. Byrd of Virginia received 15 electoral votes: all eight of Mississippi's, six of Alabama's 11, and one of Oklahoma's eight.

> "When I was a boy, I was told that anybody could become President; I'm beginning to believe it."
> —**Clarence Darrow**

1964

Party	Candidate	Popular vote	Per cent	Electoral vote
Democrat	Lyndon B. Johnson (Tex.) and Hubert H. Humphrey (Minn.)	43,126,584	61.05	486
Republican	Barry M. Goldwater (Ariz.) and William E. Miller (N.Y.)	27,177,838	38.47	52
Socialist-Labor	Eric Hass (N.Y.)	45,187	0.06	—
Socialist Workers	Clifton DeBerry (N.Y.)	32,701	0.05	—
Other		258,794	0.37	—
	Total Vote	70,641,104		
	Johnson Plurality	15,948,746		

Key Issues Johnson ran for election in his own right on the basis of his Great Society domestic programs. The reactionary Goldwater campaigned against the New Deal and for the bombing of North Vietnam. **Regional Influences** Johnson won all but six states—Goldwater's home state of Arizona and five states in the Deep South—in the biggest popular and electoral landslide since 1936. Forty new Northern Democrats were elected to the House on LBJ's coattails.

1968

Party	Candidate	Popular vote	Per cent	Electoral vote
Republican	Richard M. Nixon (Calif.) and Spiro T. Agnew (Md.)	31,785,148	43.42	301
Democrat	Hubert H. Humphrey (Minn.) and Edmund S. Muskie (Maine)	31,274,503	42.72	191
American Independent	George C. Wallace (Ala.) and Curtis LeMay (Ohio)	901,151	13.53	46
Socialist-Labor	Henning A. Blomen (Mass.)	52,591	0.07	—
Other		189,977	0.20	—
	Total Vote	73,203,370		
	Nixon Plurality	510,645		

Key Issues With the country divided over Vietnam, Humphrey failed to emerge from the shadow of the unpopular Johnson, while the previously hawkish Nixon pledged to end the war and hinted that he had a secret plan to do so. Wallace attacked Federal encroachment on states' rights, desegregation, "pointy-headed" intellectuals and the Administration's timidity in Vietnam, in an effort to capture blue-collar votes. **Regional Influences** Barely more than 500,000 votes separated Nixon and Humphrey, but the Republican edge in the Electoral College was comfortable and the combined anti-Democratic vote amounted to a repudiation of the Johnson-Humphrey Administration. Humphrey's strength was in the eastern seaboard states. Wallace won five states in the Deep South.

1972

Party	Candidate	Popular vote	Per cent	Electoral vote
Republican	Richard M. Nixon (Calif.) and Spiro T. Agnew (Md.)	47,170,179	60.69	520
Democrat	George S. McGovern (S.Dak.) and R. Sargent Shriver (Md.)	29,171,791	37.53	17
American Independent	John G. Schmitz (Calif.)	1,090,673	1.40	—
People's	Benjamin Spock	78,751	0.10	—
Other		216,196	0.28	(1)
	Total Vote	77,727,590		
	Nixon Plurality	17,998,388		

Key Issues Seeking to create a Republican majority by converting Wallace Democrats, Nixon pursued a "Southern strategy" of denouncing busing, the welfare state, the media and intellectuals. McGovern was unable to overcome an image of radicalism

furthered by Republican charges that he was the candidate of "acid, abortion, and amnesty." **Regional Influences** The GOP's Southern strategy was aided by an assassination attempt on Wallace that knocked him out of the race. Nixon lost only Massachusetts and the District of Columbia, but Democrats added to their majority in the Senate and maintained control of the House.

[1] The Libertarian slate of John Hospers and Theodora Nathan received 1 electoral vote from a Republican elector in Virginia.

1976

Party	Candidate	Popular vote	Per cent	Electoral vote
Democrat	Jimmy Carter (Ga.) and Walter F. Mondale (Minn.)	40,830,763	50.06	297
Republican	Gerald R. Ford (Mich.) and Robert Dole (Kans.)	39,147,793	48.00	240[1]
Independent	Eugene J. McCarthy (Minn.)	756,691	0.93	—
Libertarian	Roger MacBride (Va.)	173,011	0.21	—
Other		647,631	0.79	—
	Total Vote	81,555,889		
	Carter Plurality	1,682,970		

Key Issues In the wake of Watergate, Carter ran a moralistic campaign as a political outsider. Vague on issues, he railed against the Washington bureaucracy and vowed to lead "a government that is as good and honest and decent . . . as filled with love as are the American people." He also promised Americans that he would never lie to them. **Regional Influences** Ford nearly overcame a huge early deficit in the polls. But Carter's background as a southern moderate enabled him to eke out a victory through wins in northern, southern and border states.

[1] Ronald Reagan received one electoral vote from an elector in Washington.

1980

Party	Candidate	Popular vote	Per cent	Electoral vote
Republican	Ronald Reagan (Calif.) and George Bush (Tex.)	43,901,812	50.75	489
Democrat	Jimmy Carter (Ga.) and Walter F. Mondale (Minn.)	35,483,820	41.02	49
Independent	John B. Anderson (Ill.) and Patrick J. Lucey (Wis.)	5,719,722	6.61	—
Libertarian	Edward E. Clark (Calif.)	921,188	1.06	—
Other		486,754	0.56	—
	Total Vote	86,513,296		
	Reagan Plurality	8,417,992		

Key Issues Inflation, an energy shortage, the taking of American hostages by Iran and a strong primary challenge from Edward Kennedy of Massachusetts weakened Carter. Reagan, promising to get government "off the backs fo the American people," pledged to cut taxes, increase defense spending, and balance the Federal budget. Anderson, a Republican, ran as an independent to the left of both Carter and Reagan. **Regional Influences** Reagan swept to a landslide win in the Electoral College as Carter carried only six states and the Washington, D.C.

1984

Party	Candidate	Popular vote	Per cent	Electoral vote
Republican	Ronald Reagan (Calif.) and George Bush (Tex.)	54,450,603	58.78	525
Democrat	Walter F. Mondale (Minn.) and Geraldine Ferraro (N.Y.)	37,573,671	40.56	13
Libertarian	David Bergland (Calif.)	227,949	0.25	—
Other		570,343	0.61	
	Total Vote	92,628,458		
	Reagan Plurality	16,876,932		

Key Issues The economy was flying after emerging in late 1983 from the worst economic downturn since the Great Depression. Reagan, whose commercials proclaimed it was "morning in America," ridiculed Mondale as an old-fashioned "tax-and-spend, gloom-and-doom" Democrat. Controversy over her husband's finances blunted Ferraro's appeal as the first woman on a major party ticket. **Regional Influences** Mondale carried only his home state of Minnesota and the District of Columbia as Reagan won the greatest electoral victory in American history and the fifth highest share of the popular vote.

1988

Party	Candidate	Popular vote	Per- cent	Elec- toral vote
Republican	George Bush (Tex.) and J. Danforth Quayle (Ind.)	48,881,011	53.37	426
Democrat	Michael S. Dukakis (Mass.) and Lloyd Bentsen (Tex.)	41,828,350	45.67	111[1]
Libertarian	Ron Paul (Texas)	431,499	0.47	—
New Alliance	Lenora Fulani (New York)	218,159	0.24	—
Other		226,852	0.25	—
	Total Vote	91,585,871		
	Bush Plurality	7,052,661		

Key Issues Trailing Dukakis by 17 points in early summer, Bush made an issue of his opponent's "liberalism," depicting the Massachusetts governor as soft on crime. Bush made a household name out of Willie Horton, a black Massachusetts prison inmate who raped a woman while on a prison furlough. Bush also called Dukakis a card-carrying member of the American Civil Liberties Union and said that he didn't share the same values as the American people. Dukakis' failure to respond to those charges and to shed the "liberal" label until late in the campaign ultimately doomed his candidacy, despite Bush's links to the Iran-Contra scandal and to Panama's drug-running leader, Gen. Manuel Noriega. **Regional Influences** Dukakis won the District of Columbia and only 10 states: Washington, Oregon, Hawaii, New York, Minnesota, Wisconsin, Iowa, New York, West Virginia, Rhode Island, and his home state of Massachusettts. Bush easily captured the formerly Democratic "solid South."

[1] Bentsen received one electoral vote for President.

1992

Party	Candidate	Popular vote	Per- cent	Elec- toral vote
Democrat	Bill Clinton (Ark.) and Al Gore (Tenn.)	44,908,233	42.95	370
Republican	George Bush (Tex.) and J. Danforth Quayle (Ind.)	39,102,282	37.40	168
Indepen- dent	Ross H. Perot (Tex.) and James H. Stockdale (Calif.)	19,721,433	18.86	—
Other		820,788	0.79	
	Total Vote	104,552,736		
	Clinton Plurality	5,805,951		

Key Issues Bush's approval ratings were sky high as little as 13 months before the election, but a flagging economy and a national debt that wouldn't go away spelled his downfall in a three-way race that saw billionaire Ross Perot capture more votes than any third-party candidate since Theodore Roosevelt in 1912. Excitement for Perot, who entered the race in March, quit in July, and re-entered the campaign in October, brought a record 102 million people to the polls. Clinton ran especially strong among women, who supported his stances in favor of abortion rights and a strong defense of the environment. **Regional Influences** Perot's presence prevented either major party candidate from capturing an outright majority in every state except New York, Maryland, Arkansas (all of which went for Clinton) and Mississippi (which supported Bush). But Clinton won pluralities in California, Georgia, Illinois, Massachusetts, Michigan, Minnesota, Missouri, New Jersey, Ohio, Pennsylvania, Tennessee, Washington, and Wisconsin. The only states with double-digit electoral votes in Bush's column were Florida, Indiana, North Carolina, Texas, and Virginia.

1996

Party	Candidate	Popular vote	Per- cent	Elec- toral vote
Democrat	Bill Clinton (Ark.) and Al Gore (Tenn.)	47,402,357	49.24	379
Republican	Bob Dole (Kans.) and Jack Kemp (N.Y.)	39,198,755	40.71	159
Reform	Ross H. Perot and Patrick Choate	8,085,402	8.40	—
Green	Ralph Nader	684,902	0.71	
Libertarian	Harry Browne	485,798	0.50	
U.S. Taxpayers	Howard Phillips	184,658	0.19	
Natural Law	John Hagelin	113,668	0.12	
Workers World	Monica Moorehead	29,083	0.03	
Peace & Freedom	Marsha Feinland	25,332	0.03	
Independent	Charles Collins	8,941	0.01	
Socialist Workers	James Harris	8,476	0.01	
Other[1]		49,851	0.05	
	Total Vote	96,277,223		
	Clinton Plurality	8,203,602		

[1] Other includes write-ins and "none of the above."

▶ THE 1996 PRESIDENTIAL ELECTION

President Bill Clinton easily won re-election on November 5, 1996, convincingly defeating former Republican Senate Majority Leader Bob Dole and Reform-party candidate Ross Perot. Clinton captured 49 percent of the popular vote, compared to 41 percent for Dole and 8 percent for Perot. Other candidates received a total of 2 percent of the vote. The president carried 31 states, including New York, California, Florida, Illinois, and Pennsylvania, for a total of 379 electoral votes, far more than the 270 required for re-election. Dole won 19 states, including Texas, Virginia, North Carolina, Georgia, and Indiana, as well as his home state of Kansas, for a total of 159 electoral votes. Perot failed to carry a state.

As in almost every presidential election, people voted their pocketbooks, despite reservations about Clinton's character. And there were plenty of reasons for doubt. The Whitewater and Filegate scandals, dubious political contributions to the president by foreign investors, and a House and Senate solidly opposed to the incumbent might have derailed a re-election bid in less prosperous times. But the strong economy and declining crime rate coupled with Dole's inability to present a coherent vision of how he would change the country for the better, insured four more years of Democratic leadership in the White House.

Less than half of the voting age population went to the polls, the lowest number since 1924. Among those who did vote, Clinton ran strong with women, Asian-Americans, and Hispanics, and captured about half of the voters who described themselves as Independents. Dole's refusal to contravene his own party's strict stand against abortion hurt him dearly among women, who overwhelmingly chose Clinton. But male voters, who had been largely responsible for the Republican recapture of Congress in 1994, also opted for Clinton, though by a much smaller margin. Dole's 96-hour campaign closing marathon, in which he stressed his plan to cut taxes 15 percent, helped him narrow the gap—people who waited until the last minute to decide chose Dole by a 2-1 margin—but not enough to win a majority.

Dole was severely hampered by the Republican leaders in the House of Representatives. Dole was a highly respected leader in the Senate but as the

1996 Election Results by State

State	(Democrat) Bill Clinton/ Al Gore Popular vote	Percent	Electoral votes	(Republican) Bob Dole/ Jack Kemp Popular vote	Percent	Electoral votes	(Reform) Ross Perot/ Pat Choate Popular vote	Percent
Alabama	662,165	43.2%	—	769,044	50.1%	9	92,149	6.0%
Alaska	80,380	33.3	—	122,746	50.8	3	26,333	10.9
Arizona	653,288	46.5	8	622,073	44.3	—	112,072	8.0
Arkansas	475,171	53.7	6	325,416	36.8	—	69,884	7.9
California	5,119,835	51.1	54	3,828,380	38.2	—	697,847	7.0
Colorado	671,152	44.4	—	691,848	45.8	8	99,629	6.6
Connecticut	735,740	52.8	8	483,109	34.7	—	139,523	10.0
Delaware	140,355	51.8	3	99,062	36.6	—	28,719	10.6
District of Columbia	158,220	85.2	3	17,339	9.3	—	3,611	2.6
Florida	2,546,870	48.0	25	2,244,536	42.3	—	483,870	9.1
Georgia	1,053,849	45.8	—	1,080,843	47.0	13	146,337	6.4
Hawaii	205,012	56.9	4	113,943	31.6	—	27,358	7.6
Idaho	165,443	33.6	—	256,595	52.2	4	62,518	12.8
Illinois	2,341,744	54.3	22	1,587,021	36.8	—	346,408	8.0
Indiana	887,424	41.6	—	1,006,693	47.1	12	224,299	10.5
Iowa	620,258	50.3	7	492,644	39.9	—	105,159	8.5
Kansas	387,659	36.1	—	583,245	54.3	6	92,639	8.6
Kentucky	636,614	45.8	8	623,283	44.9	—	120,396	8.7
Louisiana	927,837	52.0	9	712,586	39.9	—	123,293	6.9
Maine	312,788	51.6	4	186,378	30.8	—	85,970	14.1
Maryland	966,207	54.2	10	681,530	38.3	—	115,812	6.5
Massachusetts	1,571,763	61.5	12	718,107	28.1	—	227,217	8.9
Michigan	1,989,653	51.7	18	1,481,212	38.5	—	336,670	8.87
Minnesota	1,120,438	51.1	10	766,476	35.0	—	257,704	11.8
Mississippi	394,022	44.1	—	439,838	49.2	7	52,222	5.8
Missouri	1,025,935	47.5	11	890,016	41.2	—	217,188	10.1
Montana	167,922	41.1	—	179,652	44.1	3	55,229	13.6
Nebraska	236,761	35.0	—	363,467	53.7	5	71,278	10.5
Nevada	203,974	43.9	4	199,244	42.9	—	43,986	9.5
New Hampshire	246,214	49.3	4	196,532	39.4	—	48,390	9.7
New Jersey	1,652,329	53.7	15	1,103,078	35.9	—	262,134	8.5
New Mexico	273,495	49.2	5	232,751	41.9	—	32,257	5.8
New York	3,756,177	59.5	33	1,933,492	30.6	—	503,458	8.0
North Carolina	1,107,849	44.0	—	1,225,938	48.7	14	168,059	6.7
North Dakota	106,905	40.1	—	125,050	46.9	3	32,515	12.2
Ohio	2,148,222	47.4	21	1,859,883	41.0	—	483,207	10.7
Oklahoma	488,105	40.4	—	582,315	48.3	8	130,788	10.8
Oregon	649,641	47.2	7	538,152	39.1	—	121,221	8.8
Pennsylvania	2,215,819	49.2	23	1,801,169	40.0	—	430,984	9.6
Rhode Island	233,050	59.7	4	104,683	26.8	—	43,723	11.2
South Carolina	506,283	44.0	—	573,458	49.8	8	64,386	5.6
South Dakota	139,333	43.0	—	150,543	46.5	3	31,250	9.6
Tennessee	909,146	48.0	11	863,530	45.6	—	105,918	5.6
Texas	2,459,683	43.8	—	2,736,167	48.8	32	378,537	6.7
Utah	221,633	33.3	—	361,911	54.4	5	66,461	10.0
Vermont	137,894	53.4	3	80,352	31.1	—	31,024	12.0
Virginia	1,091,060	45.2	—	1,138,350	47.1	13	159,861	6.6
Washington	1,123,323	49.8	11	840,712	37.3	—	201,003	8.9
West Virginia	327,812	51.5	5	233,946	36.8	—	71,639	11.3
Wisconsin	1,071,971	48.8	11	845,029	38.5	—	227,339	10.4
Wyoming	77,934	36.8	—	105,388	49.8	3	25,928	12.3
Total	**47,402,357**	**49.2%**	**379**	**39,198,755**	**40.7%**	**159**	**8,085,402**	**8.4%**

Republican Congress tried to push through its plan for balancing the budget, Dole became associated with the radical agenda of Newt Gingrich and Dick Armey, whom Clinton outmaneuvered by refusing to sign their spending bills thereby allowing the Federal government to shut down at the end of 1995. The American people blamed this foolish act on the Republicans and Dole was grad-ually forced to distance himself from Gingrich who became the least popular U.S. politician in recent history.

▶ THE ELECTORAL COLLEGE

The Electoral College is the body of electors chosen by all of the states that ultimately is responsi-

Voter Turnout in Presidential Elections, 1928–96

Year	Total Vote	Voting Age Population		Registered Voters	
		Number	Percent Voting	Number[1]	Percent Voting
1928	36,879,414	71,185,000	51.8%	N/A	N/A
1932	39,816,522	75,768,000	52.6	N/A	N/A
1936	45,646,817	80,354,000	56.8	N/A	N/A
1940	49,815,312	84,728,000	58.8	N/A	N/A
1944	48,025,684	95,573,000	56.1	N/A	N/A
1948	48,833,680	95,573,000	51.1	N/A	N/A
1952	61,551,919	99,929,000	61.6	N/A	N/A
1956	62,033,908	104,515,000	59.4	N/A	N/A
1960	68,838,204	109,159,000	63.06	N/A	N/A
1964	70,644,592	114,090,000	61.92	73,715,818	95.83%
1968	73,211,875	120,328,186	60.84	81,658,180	89.65
1972	77,718,554	140,776,000	55.21	97,328,541	79.85
1976	81,555,789	152,309,190	53.55	105,037,986	77.64
1980	86,515,221	164,597,000	52.56	113,043,734	76.53
1984	92,652,680	174,466,000	53.11	124,150,614	74.63
1988	91,594,693	182,778,000	50.11	126,379,628	72.48
1992	104,405,155	189,529,000	55.09	133,821,178	78.01
1996	96,456,345	196,511,000	49.08	146,211,960	65.85

Source: Federal Election Commission

ble for selecting the president of the United States. The Framers did not want the nation's Chief Executive chosen by either the national legislature or the people directly. Instead they set up what came to be known as the Electoral College, under Article II, sections 2 and 3 of the Constitution to provide for indirect election of the president: "Each State shall appoint, in such manner as the legislature thereof may direct, a number of Electors, equal to the whole number of Senators and Representatives to which the State may be entitled in the Congress; but no Senator or Representative, or person holding an office of trust or profit under the United States, shall be appointed an Elector."

Electors were supposed to be distinguished, enlightened citizens who would cast a disinterested vote for president. From the start, however, electors have been instruments of partisan passions. At first, most state legislatures were responsible for choosing electors. By 1828, however, all states except South Carolina allowed electors to be chosen by direct popular election. (In South Carolina, the legislature continued to select electors until the Civil War.) When electors began to be selected by popular vote, parties presented slates of candidates for presidential electors who were tacitly pledged to support the party's nominees for president and vice president. This is how the practice began of states voting as a unit. Subsequently, many states passed laws requiring their electors to vote as a bloc. Where it is not required by law, it is customary for all of a state's electors to vote for the candidate receiving a plurality of the popular vote in that state. The names of the candidates for electors may or may not appear on the ballot alongside the names of the candidates to whom they are pledged. Voters really vote for presidential electors, though, even when they seem to be casting a ballot for a presidential candidate.

The presidential electors chosen by the voters in November meet in their state capitals on the first Monday after the second Wednesday in December to cast their vote for president and vice president. The results of this balloting are sent to the president of the U.S. Senate, the directors of the U.S. General Services Administration, the

state's secretary of state, and to the judge of the Federal District Court of the district in which the electors gathered. Sealed state ballots are opened and counted at a joint session of Congress on January 6 following the election year.

Originally electors voted for two individuals for president on a single ballot. The winner of a majority of the vote was elected president, the runner-up vice-president. The Framers fully expected there to be many elections in which no candidate would gain a majority of the vote and the president would have to be selected by the House of Representatives, where each state delegation would cast a single vote. But in 1789 and 1792 every elector voted for George Washington. In both years John Adams was the runner-up and, thus, vice president.

Problems inherent in this system became apparent once Washington no longer was a candidate. In 1796, Adams and Thomas Jefferson finished first and second in the balloting and were elected president and vice president, respectively, despite being fierce foes. By 1800, two formal parties had evolved which nominated a single candidate for both president and vice president. A Federalist elector purposely failed to vote for the party's vice presidential nominee, Thomas Pinckney, in order to assure a potential majority for Adams. But overzealous Republican electors all voted for both Jefferson and the party's vice presidential nominee, Aaron Burr. Both men received the same majority of the electoral vote and the election had to be decided by the House, where Jefferson won. This led to adoption of the Twelfth Amendment to the Constitution, implemented in 1804, which required that electors cast separate ballots for president and vice president. If no candidate achieves a majority of the electoral vote for vice president, the position is filled by the Senate with each senator casting a single ballot. This has happened only once, when the Senate selected Richard M. Johnson after he fell one electoral vote short of a majority for vice president in 1836.

Currently 270 votes are needed to reach a majority in the Electoral College. There have been two elections in which no candidate received a ma-

Campaign Contribution Limits for Individuals and PACs

Recipient	Individual contributor	Multi-candidate committee	Other political committee
Each candidate or candidate committee	$1,000	$5,000	$1,000
National party committee	20,000	15,000	20,000
Other political committee	5,000	5,000	5,000
Total per calendar year	**$25,000**	**no limit**	**no limit**

jority of the electoral vote. In 1824 no candidate achieved a majority of the vote and in 1876 disputed results in several states prevented either Rutherford B. Hayes or Samuel J. Tilden from achieving a majority. (John Quincy Adams and Hayes won those contests, respectively.) A candidate also can be elected president despite losing the popular vote. This occurred, again in 1824 and 1876, when the House selected Adams and Hayes, though they lost the popular vote to Andrew Jackson and Tilden, respectively, and in 1888 when Benjamin Harrison was elected over Grover Cleveland despite receiving a minority of the popular vote.

▶THE FEDERAL ELECTION CAMPAIGN ACT

In 1971 Congress passed the Federal Election Campaign Act to deal with various aspects of campaign financing. The law was amended and strengthened in 1974 and 1976, and the Federal Election Commission (FEC) was established to administer the law, which affects candidates for the U.S. House of Representatives, the U.S. Senate, and the presidency, as well as the political committees that support them. The act requires disclosure of sources and uses of funds for Federal elections, provides public financing for presidential elections, and sets limits on campaign contributions. The specific requirements of each of these three parts of the act are detailed below.

Public disclosure   Candidates for Federal office and the political committees that support them must register and file periodic disclosures of their campaign finance activities with the clerk of the House, the secretary of the Senate, or the FEC. These reports are available to the public within 48 hours of their disclosure. A candidate is defined as one who has raised or spent more than $5,000 in any given year in campaigning for Federal office. A political committee is defined as a club, committee, association, or organization that receives contributions or makes expenditures of more than $1,000 to a Federal candidate in any calendar year. In recent years they have come to be called PACs, for Political Action Committee.

Public financing   Public financing is provided for eligible presidential candidates in primary and general elections, and for national party committees for the nominating conventions. Financing is given in the form of matching payments to primary candidates, public grants to nominees in the general election, and public grants to the national party committees for the conventions. The money for public financing is raised by the Presidential Election Campaign Fund, which collects three dollars from the tax payment of every taxpayer who checks off this box on his or her Federal income tax return.

Contribution limits and prohibitions   In Federal elections the act prohibits contributions from the treasuries of national banks, corporations, and labor organizations; contributions from government contractors; contributions from foreign nationals (green card holders); cash contributions in excess of $100 per person; contributions supplied by one person in the name of another person.

Additionally, the act sets contribution limits as shown in the accompanying table.

POLITICAL OFFICE HOLDERS

▶THE VICE PRESIDENCY

Unlike the office of the president, that of the vice president has sometimes been left vacant after the death of the vice president, or his assumption of higher office on the death of the president. Until adoption of the 25th Amendment to the Constitution in 1967, there was no provision to fill a vacancy in the vice presidency. Under the amendment, the president must name a vice president when the office is vacant, and the nominee must pass a majority vote of approval in both houses of Congress. Gerald Ford, Richard Nixon's choice to replace Spiro Agnew after the latter's resignation in 1973, was the first vice president to gain the office under the amendment. The second was Nelson Rockefeller, whom Ford nominated to the position after he became president upon Nixon's resignation the following year. While the 25th Amendment does not supersede the presidential order of succession, it decreases the likelihood of the office's ever falling to the Speaker of the House or a sitting cabinet member.

▶PRESIDENTIAL ORDER OF SUCCESSION

Article II of the Constitution gives to Congress the power to determine the presidential order of succession should both the president and vice president die, become incapacitated or be disqualified from office. The present law, passed in 1947, puts the Speaker of the House first in line to the presidency, followed by the president pro tempore of the Senate. The order of succession then goes through the members of the Cabinet, in the order in which the executive departments were established:

(1) Secretary of State, (2) Secretary of the Treasury, (3) Secretary of Defense, (4) Attorney General, (5) Secretary of the Interior, (6) Secretary of Agriculture, (7) Secretary of Commerce, (8) Secretary of Labor, (9) Secretary of Health and Human Services, (10) Secretary of Housing and Urban Development, (11) Secretary of Transportation, (12) Secretary of Energy, (13) Secretary of Education, (14) Secretary of Veterans' Affairs. The following

sentence, composed of words using the first letter (or letters) of each cabinet department, is often used as a mnemonic device to remember the order: See The Dog Jump In A Circle; Leave HEr HOme To ENtertain EDucated Veterans. (State, Treasury, Defense, Justice, Interior, Agriculture, Commerce, Labor, HEalth and Human Services, HOusing and Urban Development, Transportation, ENergy, EDucation, Veterans Affairs. Until the 1970 legislation removing the Postmaster General from the Cabinet and establishing

an independent Postal Service, the Postmaster General was fifth in line to the presidency. The heads of new departments are automatically added to the line of succession as the new departments are created.

A Cabinet member must be a natural-born U.S. citizen and at least 35 years old in order to become acting president. If a Cabinet member next-in-line to fill a presidential vacancy were not yet 35, the presidency would pass to the next Cabinet member in the order of succession who had attained that age.

Vice Presidents of the United States

Name	Party	Tenure	State, birth-death
1. John Adams	Fed.	1789–97	Mass., 1735–1826
2. Thomas Jefferson	D-R	1797–1801	Va., 1743–1826
3. Aaron Burr	D-R	1801–05	N.Y., 1756–1836
4. George Clinton	D-R	1805–13†	N.Y., 1739–1812
5. Elbridge Gerry	D-R	1813–17†	Mass., 1744–1814
6. Daniel D. Tompkins	D-R	1817–25	N.Y., 1774–1825
7. John C. Calhoun	D-R	1825–33[1]	S.C., 1782–1850
8. Martin Van Buren	D	1833–37	N.Y., 1782–1862
9. Richard M. Johnson	D	1837–41[2]	Ky., 1780–1850
10. John Tyler	Whig	1841[3]	Va., 1790–1862
11. George M. Dallas	D	1845–49	Pa., 1792–1864
12. Millard Fillmore	Whig	1849–50[4]	N.Y., 1800–74
13. William R. King	D	1853–57†	Ala., 1786–1853
14. John C. Breckenridge	D	1857–61	Ky., 1821–75
15. Hannibal Hamlin	R	1861–65	Maine, 1809–91
16. Andrew Johnson	D	1865[5]	Tenn., 1808–75
17. Schuyler Colfax	R	1869–73	Ind., 1823–85
18. Henry Wilson	R	1873–77†	Mass., 1812–75
19. William A. Wheeler	R	1877–81	N.Y., 1819–87
20. Chester A. Arthur	R	1881[6]	N.Y., 1829–86
21. Thomas A. Hendricks	D	1885†	Ind., 1819–85
22. Levi P. Morton	R	1889–93	N.Y., 1824–1920
23. Adlai E. Stevenson	D	1893–97	Ill., 1835–1914
24. Garret A. Hobart	R	1897–1901†	N.J., 1844–99
25. Theodore Roosevelt	R	1901[7]	N.Y., 1858–1919
26. Charles W. Fairbanks	R	1905–09	Ind., 1852–1918
27. James S. Sherman	R	1909–13†	N.Y., 1855–1912
28. Thomas R. Marshall	D	1913–21	Ind., 1854–1925
29. Calvin Coolidge	R	1921–23[8]	Mass., 1872–1933
30. Charles G. Dawes	R	1925–29	Ill., 1865–1951
31. Charles Curtis	R	1929–33	Kans., 1860–1936
32. John Nance Garner	D	1933–41	Tex., 1868–1967
33. Henry A. Wallace	D	1941–45	Iowa, 1888–1965
34. Harry S Truman	D	1945[9]	Mo., 1884–1972
35. Alben W. Barkley	D	1949–53	Ky., 1877–1956
36. Richard M. Nixon	R	1953–61	Calif., 1913–95
37. Lyndon B. Johnson	D	1961–63[10]	Tex., 1908–73
38. Hubert H. Humphrey	D	1965–69	Minn., 1911–78
39. Spiro T. Agnew	R	1969–73[11]	Md., 1918–96
40. Gerald R. Ford	R	1973–74[12]	Mich., 1913–
41. Nelson A. Rockefeller	R	1974–77[13]	N.Y., 1908–79
42. Walter F. Mondale	D	1977–81	Minn., 1928–
43. George Bush	R	1981–89	Tex., 1924–
44. J. Danforth Quayle	R	1989–93	Ind., 1947–
45. Albert Gore	D	1993–	Tenn., 1948–

Notes: Fed. = Federalist. D = Democrat. D-R = Democratic-Republican. R = Republican. † = Died in office. 1. Resigned to become senator from South Carolina (1832-43). 2. Voted in by senate after no candidate for vice president gained a majority in the electoral college. 3. Became president after Benjamin Harrison's death. 4. Became president after Zachary Taylor's death. 5. Nominated by Republicans to run with Abraham Lincoln on the Union ticket; became president after Lincoln's assassination. 6. Became president after James Garfield's assassination. 7. Became president after William McKinley's assassination. 8. Became president after Warren Harding's death. 9. Became president after Franklin D. Roosevelt's death. 10. Became president after John F. Kennedy's assassination. 11. Resigned while under investigation for receiving kickbacks as governor of Maryland. 12. First vice president named under terms of the 25th amendment; assumed presidency after Richard Nixon resigned. 13. Named vice president by Ford.

Speakers of the U.S. House of Representatives

Name	Party	State	Dates in Office
1. Frederick A.C. Muhlenberg	D-R	Pa.	1789–91
2. Jonathan Trumbull	Fed.	Conn.	1791–93
3. Frederick A. C. Muhlenberg	D-R	Pa.	1793–95
4. Jonathan Dayton	Fed.	N.J.	1795–97
5. George Dent	Fed.	Md.	1797–99
6. Theodore Sedgwick	Fed.	Mass.	1799–1801
7. Nathaniel Macon	D-R	N.C.	1801–07
8. Joseph B. Varnum	D-R	Mass.	1807–11
9. Henry Clay	D-R	Ky.	1811–14
10. Langdon Cheves	D-R	S.C.	1814–15
11. Henry Clay	D-R	Ky.	1815–20
12. John W. Taylor	D-R	N.Y.	1820–21
13. Philip Barbour	D-R	Va.	1821–23
14. Henry Clay	D-R	Ky.	1822–23
15. John W. Taylor	D-R	N.Y.	1825–27
16. Andrew Stevenson	D	Va.	1827–34
17. John Bell	D	Tenn.	1834–35
18. James K. Polk	D	Tenn.	1835–39
19. Robert M.T. Hunter	NP	Va.	1839–41
20. John White	Whig	Ky.	1841–43
21. John W. Jones	D	Va.	1843–45
22. John W. Davis	D	Ind.	1845–47
23. Robert C. Winthrop	Whig	Mass.	1847–49
24. Howell Cobb	D	Ga.	1849–51
25. Linn Boyd	D	Ky.	1851–55
26. Nathaniel Banks	R	Mass.	1855–57
27. James L. Orr	D	S.C.	1857–59
28. William Pennington	Whig	N.J.	1859–61
29. Galusha A. Grow	R	Pa.	1861–63
30. Schuyler Colfax	R	Ind.	1863–69
31. James G. Blaine	R	Maine	1869–75
32. Michael C. Kerr	D	Ind.	1875–76
33. Samuel J. Randall	D	Pa.	1876–81
34. J. Warren Keifer	R	Ohio	1881–83
35. John G. Carlisle	D	Ky.	1883–89
36. Thomas B. Reed	R	Maine	1889–91
37. Charles F. Crisp	D	Ga.	1891–95
38. Thomas B. Reed	R	Maine	1895–99
39. David B. Henderson	R	Iowa	1899–1903
40. Joseph G. Cannon	R	Ill.	1903–11
41. Champ Clark	D	Mo.	1911–19
42. Frederick H. Gillett	R	Mass.	1919–25
43. Nicholas Longworth	R	Ohio	1925–31
44. John N. Garner	D	Tex.	1931–33
45. Henry T. Rainey	D	Ill.	1933–34
46. Joseph W. Byrns	D	Tenn.	1935–36
47. William B. Bankhead	D	Ala.	1936–39
48. Sam Rayburn	D	Tex.	1940–46
49. Joseph W. Martin Jr.	R	Mass.	1947–49
50. Sam Rayburn	D	Tex.	1949–52
51. Joseph W. Martin Jr.	R	Mass.	1953–54
52. Sam Rayburn	D	Tex.	1955–61
53. John W. McCormack	D	Mass.	1962–71
54. Carl B. Albert	D	Okla.	1971–76
55. Thomas P. O'Neill Jr.	D	Mass.	1977–87
56. James C. Wright Jr.	D	Tex.	1987–89
57. Thomas S. Foley	D	Wash.	1989–95
58. Newt Gingrich	R	Ga.	1995–99
59. J. Dennis Hastert	R	Ill.	1999–

Notes: D = Democrat. Fed. = Federalist. R = Republican.

Cabinet Members

Washington Administration (1789-97)

Secretary of State	Thomas Jefferson	1789–93
	Edmund Randolph	1794–95
	Timothy Pickering	1795–97
Secretary of Treasury	Alexander Hamilton	1789–95
	Oliver Wolcott	1795–97
Secretary of War	Henry Knox	1789–94
	Timothy Pickering	1795–96
	James McHenry	1796–97
Attorney General	Edmund Randolph	1789–93
	William Bradford	1794–95
	Charles Lee	1795–97
Postmaster General	Samuel Osgood	1789–91
	Timothy Pickering	1791–94
	Joseph Habersham	1795–97

John Adams Administration (1797–1801)

Secretary of State	Timothy Pickering	1797–1800
	John Marshall	1800–1801
Secretary of Treasury	Oliver Wolcott	1797–1800
	Samuel Dexter	1800–1801
Secretary of War	James McHenry	1797–1800
	Samuel Dexter	1800–1801
Attorney General	Charles Lee	1797–1801
Postmaster General	Joseph Habersham	1797–1801
Secretary of Navy	Benjamin Stoddert	1798–1801

Jefferson Administration (1801–09)

Secretary of State	James Madison	1801–09
Secretary of Treasury	Samuel Dexter	1801
	Albert Gallatin	1801–09
Secretary of War	Henry Dearborn	1801–09
Attorney General	Levi Lincoln	1801–05
	Robert Smith	1805
	John Breckinridge	1805–06
	Caesar Rodney	1807–09
Postmaster General	Joseph Habersham	1801
	Gideon Granger	1801–09
Secretary of Navy	Robert Smith	1801–09

Madison Administration (1809–17)

Secretary of State	Robert Smith	1809–11
	James Monroe	1811–17
Secretary of Treasury	Albert Gallatin	1809–13
	George Campbell	1814
	Alexander Dallas	1814–16
	William Crawford	1816–17
Secretary of War	William Eustis	1809–17
	John Armstrong	1813–14
	James Monroe	1814–15
	William Crawford	1815–17
Attorney General	Caesar Rodney	1809–11
	William Pinkney	1811–14
	Richard Rush	1814–17
Postmaster General	Gideon Granger	1809–14
	Return Meigs	1814–17
Secretary of Navy	Paul Hamilton	1809–13
	William Jones	1813–14
	Benjamin Crowninshield	1814–17

Monroe Administration (1817–25)

Secretary of State	John Quincy Adams	1817–25
Secretary of Treasury	William Crawford	1817–25
Secretary of War	George Graham	1817
	John C. Calhoun	1817–25
Attorney General	Richard Rush	1817
	William Wirt	1817–25
Postmaster General	Return Meigs	1817–23
	John McLean	1823–25
Secretary of Navy	Benjamin Crowninshield	1817–18
	Smith Thompson	1818–23
	Samuel Southard	1823–25

John Quincy Adams Administration (1825–29)

Secretary of State	Henry Clay	1825–25
Secretary of Treasury	Richard Rush	1825–25
Secretary of War	James Barbour	1825–29
	Peter Porter	1828–29
Attorney General	William Wirt	1825–29
Postmaster General	John McLean	1825–29
Secretary of Navy	Samuel Southard	1825–29

Jackson Administration (1829–37)

Secretary of State	Martin Van Buren	1829–33
	Edward Livingston	1831–33
	Louis McLane	1833–34
	John Forsyth	1834–37
Secretary of Treasury	Samuel Ingham	1829–31
	Louis McLane	1831–33
	William Duane	1833
	Roger B. Taney	1833–34
	Levi Woodbury	1834–37
Secretary of War	John H. Eaton	1829–31
	Lewis Cass	1831–37
	Benjamin Butler	1837
Attorney General	John M. Berrien	1829–31
	Roger B. Taney	1831–33
	Benjamin Butler	1833–37
Postmaster General	William Barry	1829–35
	Amos Kendall	1835–37
Secretary of Navy	John Branch	1829–31
	Levi Woodbury	1831–34
	Mahlon Dickerson	1834–37

Van Buren Administration (1837–41)

Secretary of State	John Forsyth	1837–41
Secretary of Treasury	Levi Woodbury	1837–41
Secretary of War	Joel Poinsett	1837–41
Attorney General	Benjamin Butler	1837–38
	Felix Grundy	1838–40
	Henry D. Gilpin	1840–41
Postmaster General	Amos Kendall	1837–40
	John M. Niles	1840–41
Secretary of Navy	Mahlon Dickerson	1837–38
	James Paulding	1838–41

William Harrison Administration (1841)

Secretary of State	Daniel Webster	1841
Secretary of Treasury	Thomas Ewing	1841
Secretary of War	John Bell	1841
Attorney General	John J. Crittenden	1841
Postmaster General	Francis Granger	1841
Secretary of Navy	George Badger	1841

Tyler Administration (1841–45)

Secretary of State	Daniel Webster	1841–43
	Hugh S. Legaré	1843
	Abel P. Upshur	1843–44
	John C. Calhoun	1844–45
Secretary of Treasury	Thomas Ewing	1841
	Walter Forward	1841–43
	John C. Spencer	1843–44
	George Bibb	1844–45
Secretary of War	John Bell	1841
	John C. Spencer	1841–43
	James M. Porter	1843–44
	William Wilkins	1844–45
Attorney General	John J. Crittenden	1841
	Hugh S. Legaré	1841–43
	John Nelson	1843–45
Postmaster General	Francis Granger	1841
	Charles Wickliffe	1841
Secretary of Navy	George Badger	1841
	Abel P. Upshur	1841
	David Henshaw	1843–44
	Thomas Gilmer	1844
	John Y. Mason	1844–45

Polk Administration (1845–49)

Secretary of State	James Buchanan	1845–49
Secretary of Treasury	Robert J. Walker	1845–49
Secretary of War	William L. Marcy	1845–49
Attorney General	John Y. Mason	1845–46
	Nathan Clifford	1846–48
	Isaac Toucey	1848–49
Postmaster General	Cave Johnson	1845–49
Secretary of Navy	George Bancroft	1845–46
	John Y. Mason	1846–49

Taylor Administration (1849–50)

Secretary of State	John M. Clayton	1849–50
Secretary of Treasury	William Meredith	1849–50
Secretary of War	George Crawford	1849–50
Attorney General	Reverdy Johnson	1849–50
Postmaster General	Jacob Collamer	1849–50
Secretary of Navy	William Preston	1849–50
Secretary of Interior	Thomas Ewing	1849–50

Fillmore Administration (1850–53)

Secretary of State	Daniel Webster	1850–52
	Edward Everett	1852–53
Secretary of Treasury	Thomas Corwin	1850–53
Secretary of War	Charles Conrad	1850–53
Attorney General	John J. Crittenden	1850–53
Postmaster General	Nathan Hall	1850–52
	Sam D. Hubbard	1852–53
Secretary of Navy	William A. Graham	1852–53
	John P. Kennedy	1852–53
Secretary of Interior	Thomas McKennan	1850
	Alexander Stuart	1850–53

Pierce Administration (1853–57)

Secretary of State	William L. Marcy	1853–57
Secretary of Treasury	James Guthrie	1853–57
Secretary of War	Jefferson Davis	1853–57
Attorney General	Caleb Cushing	1853–57
Postmaster General	James Campbell	1853–57
Secretary of Navy	James C. Dobbin	1853–57
Secretary of Interior	Robert McClelland	1853–57

Buchanan Administration (1857–61)

Secretary of State	Lewis Cass	1857–60
	Jeremiah S. Black	1860–61
Secretary of Treasury	Howell Cobb	1857–60
	Philip Thomas	1860–61
	John A. Dix	1861
Secretary of War	John B. Floyd	1857–61
	Joseph Holt	1861
Attorney General	Jeremiah S. Black	1857–60
	Edwin M. Stanton	1860–61
Postmaster General	Aaron W. Brown	1857–59
	Joseph Holt	1859–61
	Horatio King	1861
Secretary of Navy	Isaac Toucey	1857–61
Secretary of Interior	Jacob Thompson	1857–61

Lincoln Administration (1861–65)

Secretary of State	William H. Seward	1861–65
Secretary of Treasury	Salmon P. Chase	1861–65
	William P. Fessenden	1864–65
	Hugh McCulloch	1865
Secretary of War	Simon Cameron	1861–62
	Edwin M. Stanton	1862–65
Attorney General	Edward Bates	1861–64
	James Speed	1864–65
Postmaster General	Horatio King	1861
	Montgomery Blair	1861–64
	William Dennison	1864–65
Secretary of Navy	Gideon Welles	1861–65
Secretary of Interior	Caleb B. Smith	1861–63
	John P. Usher	1863–65

Andrew Johnson Administration (1865–69)

Secretary of State	William H. Seward	1865–69
Secretary of Treasury	Hugh McCulloch	1865–69
Secretary of War	Edwin M. Stanton	1865–67
	Ulysses S. Grant	1867–68
	Lorenzo Thomas	1868
	John M. Schofield	1868–69
Attorney General	James Speed	1865–66
	Henry Stanbery	1866–68
	William M. Evarts	1868–69
Postmaster General	William Dennison	1865–66
	Alexander Randall	1866–69
Secretary of Navy	Gideon Welles	1865–69
Secretary of Interior	John P. Usher	1865
	James Harlan	1865–66
	Orville H. Browning	1866–69

Grant Administration (1869–77)

Secretary of State	Elihu B. Washburne	1869
	Hamilton Fish	1869–77
Secretary of Treasury	George S. Boutwell	1869–73
	William Richardson	1873–74
	Benjamin Bristow	1874–76
	Lot M. Morrill	1876–77
Secretary of War	John A. Rawlins	1869
	William T. Sherman	1869
	William W. Belknap	1869–76
	Alphonso Taft	1876
	James D. Cameron	1876–77
Attorney General	Ebenezer Hoar	1869–70
	Amos T. Ackerman	1870–71
	G. H. Williams	1871–75
	Edwards Pierrepont	1875–76
	Alphonso Taft	1876–77

Postmaster General	John A. J. Creswell	1869–74
	James W. Marshall	1874
	Marshall Jewell	1874–76
	James N. Tyner	1876–77
Secretary of Navy	Adolph E. Borie	1869
	George M. Robeson	1869–77
Secretary of Interior	Jacob D. Cox	1869–70
	Columbus Delano	1870–75
	Zachariah Chandler	1875–77

Hayes Administration (1877–81)

Secretary of State	William M. Evarts	1877–81
Secretary of Treasury	John Sherman	1877–81
Secretary of War	George W. McCrary	1877–79
	Alex Ramsey	1879–81
Attorney General	Charles Devens	1877–81
Postmaster General	David M. Key	1877–80
	Horace Maynard	1880–81
Secretary of Navy	Richard W. Thompson	1877–80
	Nathan Goff, Jr.	1881
Secretary of Interior	Carl Schurz	1877–81

Garfield Administration (1881)

Secretary of State	James G. Blaine	1881
Secretary of Treasury	William Windom	1881
Secretary of War	Robert T. Lincoln	1881
Attorney General	Wayne MacVeagh	1881
Postmaster General	Thomas L. James	1881
Secretary of Navy	William H. Hunt	1881
Secretary of Interior	Samuel J. Kirkwood	1881

Arthur Administration (1881–85)

Secretary of State	F. T. Frelinghuysen	1881–85
Secretary of Treasury	Charles J. Folger	1881–84
	Walter Q. Gresham	1884
	Hugh McCulloch	1884–85
Secretary of War	Robert T. Lincoln	1881–85
Attorney General	Benjamin H. Brewster	1881–85
Postmaster General	Timothy O. Howe	1881–83
	Walter Q. Gresham	1883–84
	Frank Hatton	1884–85
Secretary of Navy	William H. Hunt	1881–82
	William E. Chandler	1882–85
Secretary of Interior	Samuel J. Kirkwood	1881–82
	Henry M. Teller	1882–85

Cleveland Administration (1885–89)

Secretary of State	Thomas F. Bayard	1885–89
Secretary of Treasury	Daniel Manning	1885–87
	Charles S. Fairchild	1887–89
Secretary of War	William C. Endicott	1885–89
Attorney General	Augustus H. Garland	1885–89
Postmaster General	William F. Vilas	1885–88
	Don M. Dickinson	1888–89
Secretary of Navy	William C. Whitney	1885–89
Secretary of Interior	Lucius Q. C. Lamar	1885–88
	William F. Vilas	1888–89
Secretary of Agriculture	Norman J. Colman	1889

Benjamin Harrison Administration (1889–93)

Secretary of State	James G. Blaine	1889–92
	John W. Foster	1892–93
Secretary of Treasury	William Windom	1889–91
	Charles Foster	1891–93
Secretary of War	Redfield Proctor	1889–91
	Stephen B. Elkins	1891–93

Attorney General	William H. H. Miller	1889–91
Postmaster General	John Wanamaker	1889–93
Secretary of Navy	Benjamin F. Tracy	1889–93
Secretary of Interior	John W. Noble	1889–93
Secretary of Agriculture	Jeremiah M. Rusk	1889–93

Cleveland Administration (1893–97)

Secretary of State	Walter Q. Gresham	1893–95
	Richard Olney	1895–97
Secretary of Treasury	John G. Carlisle	1893–97
Secretary of War	Daniel S. Lamont	1893–97
Attorney General	Richard Olney	1893–95
	James Harmon	1895–97
Postmaster General	Wilson S. Bissell	1893–95
	William L. Wilson	1895–95
Secretary of Navy	Hilary A. Herbert	1893–97
Secretary of Interior	Hoke Smith	1893–96
	David R. Francis	1896–97
Secretary of Agriculture	Julius S. Morton	1893–97

McKinley Administration (1897–1901)

Secretary of State	John Sherman	1897–98
	William R. Day	1898
	John Hay	1898–1901
Secretary of Treasury	Lyman J. Gage	1897–1901
Secretary of War	Russell A. Alger	1897–99
	Elihu Root	1899–1901
Attorney General	Joseph McKenna	1897–98
	John W. Griggs	1898–1901
	Philander C. Knox	1901
Postmaster General	James A. Gary	1897–98
	Charles E. Smith	1898–1901
Secretary of Navy	John D. Long	1897–1901
Secretary of Interior	Cornelius N. Bliss	1897–99
	Ethan A. Hitchcock	1899–1901
Secretary of Agriculture	James Wilson	1897–1901

Theodore Roosevelt Administration (1901–09)

Secretary of State	John Hay	1901–05
	Elihu Root	1905–09
	Robert Bacon	1909
Secretary of Treasury	Lyman J. Gage	1901–02
	Leslie M. Shaw	1902–07
	George B. Cortelyou	1907–09
Secretary of War	Elihu Root	1901–04
	William H. Taft	1904–08
	Luke E. Wright	1908–09
Attorney General	Philander C. Knox	1901–04
	William H. Moody	1904–06
	Charles J. Bonaparte	1906–09
Postmaster General	Charles E. Smith	1901–02
	Henry C. Payne	1902–04
	Robert J. Wynne	1904–05
	George B. Cortelyou	1905–07
	George von L. Meyer	1907–09
Secretary of Navy	John D. Long	1901–02
	William H. Moody	1902–04
	Paul Morton	1904–05
	Charles J. Bonaparte	1905–06
	Victor H. Metcalf	1906–08
	Truman H. Newberry	1908–09
Secretary of Interior	Ethan A. Hitchcock	1901–07
	James R. Garfield	1907–09
Secretary of Agriculture	James Wilson	1901–09
Secretary of Labor and Commerce	George B. Cortelyou	1903–04
	Victor H. Metcalf	1904–06
	Oscar S. Straus	1906–09
	Charles Nagel	1909

Taft Administration (1909–13)

Secretary of State	Philander C. Knox	1909–13
Secretary of Treasury	Franklin MacVeagh	1909–13
Secretary of War	Jacob M. Dickinson	1909–11
	Henry L. Stimson	1911–13
Attorney General	George W. Wickersham	1909–13
Postmaster General	Frank H. Hitchcock	1909–13
Secretary of Navy	George von L. Meyer	1909–13
Secretary of Interior	Richard A. Ballinger	1909–11
	Walter Fisher	1911–13
Secretary of Agriculture	James Wilson	1909–13
Secretary of Labor and Commerce	Charles Nagel	1909–13

Wilson Administration (1913–21)

Secretary of State	William J. Bryan	1913–15
	Robert Lansing	1915–20
	Bainbridge Colby	1920–21
Secretary of Treasury	William G. McAdoo	1913–18
	Carter Glass	1918–20
	David F. Houston	1920–21
Secretary of War	Lindley M. Garrison	1913–16
	Newton D. Baker	1916–21
Attorney General	James C. McReynolds	1913–14
	Thomas W. Gregory	1914–19
	A. Mitchell Palmer	1919–21
Postmaster General	Albert S. Burleson	1913–21
Secretary of Navy	Josephus Daniels	1913–21
Secretary of Interior	Franklin K. Lane	1913–20
	John B. Payne	1920–21
Secretary of Agriculture	David F. Houston	1913–20
	Edwin T. Meredith	1920–21
Secretary of Commerce	William C. Redfield	1913–19
Secretary of Labor	William B. Wilson	1913–21

Harding Administration (1921–23)

Secretary of State	Charles E. Hughes	1921–23
Secretary of Treasury	Andrew Mellon	1921–23
Secretary of War	John W. Weeks	1921–23
Attorney General	Harry M. Daugherty	1921–23
Postmaster General	Will H. Hays	1921–22
	Hubert Work	1922–23
	Harry S. New	1923
Secretary of Navy	Edwin Denby	1921–23
Secretary of Interior	Albert B. Fall	1921–23
	Hubert Work	1923
Secretary of Agriculture	Henry C. Wallace	1921–23
Secretary of Commerce	Herbert C. Hoover	1921–23
Secretary of Labor	James J. Davis	1921–23

Coolidge Administration (1923–29)

Secretary of State	Charles E. Hughes	1923–25
	Frank B. Kellogg	1925–29
Secretary of Treasury	John W. Weeks	1923–25
	Dwight F. Davis	1925–29
Attorney General	Henry M. Daugherty	1923–24
	Harlan F. Stone	1923–25
	John G. Sargent	1925–29
Postmaster General	Harry S. New	1923–29
Secretary of Navy	Edwin Denby	1923–24
	Curtis D. Wilbur	1924–29
Secretary of Interior	Hubert Work	1923–28
	Roy O. West	1928–29
Secretary of Agriculture	Henry C. Wallace	1923–24
	Howard M. Gore	1924–25
	William M. Jardine	1925–29

Secretary of Commerce	Herbert C. Hoover	1923–28
	William F. Whiting	1928–29
Secretary of Labor	James J. Davis	1923–29

Hoover Administration (1929–33)

Secretary of State	Henry L. Stimson	1929–33
Secretary of Treasury	Andrew Mellon	1929–32
	Ogden L. Mills	1932–33
Secretary of War	James W. Good	1929
	Patrick J. Hurley	1929–33
Attorney General	William D. Mitchell	1929–33
Postmaster General	Walter F. Brown	1929–33
Secretary of Navy	Charles F. Adams	1929–33
Secretary of Interior	Ray L. Wilbur	1929–33
Secretary of Agriculture	Arthur M. Hyde	1929–33
Secretary of Commerce	Robert P. Lamont	1929–32
	Roy D. Chapin	1932–33
Secretary of Labor	James J. Davis	1929–30
	William N. Doak	1930–33

Franklin D. Roosevelt Administration (1933–45)

Secretary of State	Cordell Hull	1933–44
	Edward R. Stettinius, Jr.	1944–45
Secretary of Treasury	William H. Woodin	1933–34
	Henry Morgenthau, Jr.	1934–45
Secretary of War	George H. Dern	1933–36
	Henry A. Woodring	1936–40
	Henry L. Stimson	1940–45
Attorney General	Homer S. Cummings	1933–39
	Frank Murphy	1939–40
	Robert H. Jackson	1940–41
	Francis Biddle	1941–45
Postmaster General	James A. Farley	1933–40
	Frank C. Walker	1940–45
Secretary of Navy	Claude A. Swanson	1933–40
	Charles Edison	1940
	Frank Knox	1940–44
	James V. Forrestal	1944–45
Secretary of Interior	Harold L. Ickes	1933–45
Secretary of Agriculture	Henry A. Wallace	1933–40
	Claude R. Wickard	1940–45
Secretary of Commerce	Daniel C. Roper	1933–39
	Harry L. Hopkins	1939–40
	Jesse Jones	1940–45
	Henry A. Wallace	1945
Secretary of Labor	Frances Perkins	1933–45

Truman Administration (1945–53)

Secretary of State	Edward R. Stettinius, Jr.	1945
	James F. Byrnes	1945–47
	George C. Marshall	1947–49
	Dean G. Acheson	1949–53
Secretary of Treasury	Fred M. Vinson	1945–46
	John W. Snyder	1946–53
Secretary of War	Robert P. Patterson	1945–47
	Kenneth C. Royall	1947
Attorney General	Tom C. Clark	1945–49
	J. Howard McGrath	1949–52
	James P. McGranery	1952–53
Postmaster General	Frank C. Walker	1945
	Robert E. Hannegan	1945–47
	Jesse M. Donaldson	1947–53
Secretary of Navy	James V. Forrestal	1945–47
Secretary of Interior	Harold L. Ickes	1945–46
	Julius A. Krug	1946–49
	Oscar L. Chapman	1949–53
Secretary of Agriculture	Clinton P. Anderson	1945–48
	Charles F. Brannan	1948–53

Secretary of Commerce	Henry A. Wallace	1945–46
	W. Averell Harriman	1946–48
	Charles W. Sawyer	1948–53
Secretary of Labor	Lewis B. Schwellenbach	1945–48
	Maurice J. Tobin	1948–53
Secretary of Defense	James V. Forrestal	1947–49
	Louis A. Johnson	1949–50
	George C. Marshall	1950–51
	Robert A. Lovett	1951–53

Eisenhower Administration (1953–61)

Secretary of State	John Foster Dulles	1953–59
	Christian A. Herter	1959–61
Secretary of Treasury	George M. Humphrey	1953–57
	Robert B. Anderson	1957–61
Attorney General	Herbert Brownell, Jr.	1953–58
	William P. Rogers	1958–61
Postmaster General	Arthur E. Summerfield	1953–61
Secretary of Interior	Douglas McKay	1953–56
	Fred A. Seaton	1956–61
Secretary of Agriculture	Ezra T. Benson	1953–61
Secretary of Commerce	Sinclair Weeks	1953–58
	Lewis L. Strauss	1958–59
	Frederick H. Mueller	1959–61
Secretary of Labor	Martin P. Durkin	1953
	James P. Mitchell	1953–61
Secretary of Defense	Charles E. Wilson	1953–57
	Neil H. McElroy	1957–59
	Thomas S. Gates, Jr.	1959–61
Secretary of Health, Education, and Welfare	Oveta Culp Hobby	1953–55
	Marion B. Folsom	1955–58
	Arthur S. Flemming	1958–61

Kennedy Administration (1961–63)

Secretary of State	Dean Rusk	1961–63
Secretary of Treasury	C. Douglas Dillon	1961–63
Attorney General	Robert F. Kennedy	1961–63
Postmaster General	J. Edward Day	1961–63
	John A. Gronouski	1963
Secretary of Interior	Stewart L. Udall	1961–63
Secretary of Agriculture	Orville L. Freeman	1961–63
Secretary of Commerce	Luther H. Hodges	1961–63
Secretary of Labor	Arthur J. Goldberg	1961–62
	W. Willard Wirtz	1962–63
Secretary of Defense	Robert S. McNamara	1961–63
Secretary of Health, Education, and Welfare	Abraham A. Ribicoff	1961–62
	Anthony J. Celebrezze	1962–63

Lyndon Johnson Administration (1963–69)

Secretary of State	Dean Rusk	1963–69
Secretary of Treasury	C. Douglas Dillon	1963–65
	Henry H. Fowler	1965–69
Attorney General	Robert F. Kennedy	1963–64
	Nicholas Katzenbach	1965–66
	Ramsey Clark	1967–69
Postmaster General	John A. Gronouski	1963–65
	Lawrence F. O'Brien	1965–68
	Marvin Watson	1968–69
Secretary of Interior	Stewart L. Udall	1963–69
Secretary of Agriculture	Orville L. Freeman	1963–69
Secretary of Commerce	Luther H. Hodges	1963–64
	John T. Connor	1964–67
	Alexander B. Trowbridge	1967–68
	Cyrus R. Smith	1968–69
Secretary of Labor	W. Willard Wirtz	1963–69
Secretary of Defense	Robert F. McNamara	1963–68
	Clark Clifford	1968–69

Secretary of Health, Education, and Welfare	Anthony J. Celebrezze	1963–65
	John W. Gardner	1965–68
	Wilbur J. Cohen	1968–69
Secretary of Housing and Urban Development	Robert C. Weaver	1966–69
	Robert C. Wood	1969
Secretary of Transportation	Alan S. Boyd	1967–69

Nixon Administration (1969–74)

Secretary of State	William P. Rogers	1969–73
	Henry A. Kissinger	1973–74
Secretary of Treasury	David M. Kennedy	1969–70
	John B. Connally	1971–72
	George P. Shultz	1972–74
	William E. Simon	1974
Attorney General	John N. Mitchell	1969–72
	Richard G. Kleindienst	1973–73
	Elliot L. Richardson	1973
	William B. Saxbe	1973–74
Postmaster General	Winton M. Blount	1969–71
Secretary of Interior	Walter J. Hickel	1969–70
	Rogers Morton	1971–74
Secretary of Agriculture	Clifford M. Hardin	1969–71
	Earl L. Butz	1971–74
Secretary of Commerce	Maurice H. Stans	1969–72
	Peter G. Peterson	1972–73
	Frederick B. Dent	1973–74
Secretary of Labor	George P. Shultz	1969–70
	James D. Hodgson	1970–73
	Peter J. Brennan	1973–74
Secretary of Defense	Melvin R. Laird	1969–73
	Elliot L. Richardson	1973
	James R. Schlesinger	1973–74
Secretary of Health, Education, and Welfare	Robert H. Finch	1969–70
	Elliot L. Richardson	1970–73
	Caspar W. Weinberger	1973–74
Secretary of Housing and Urban Development	George Romney	1969–73
	James T. Lyon	1973–74
Secretary of Transportation	John A. Volpe	1969–73
	Claude S. Brinegar	1973–74

Ford Administration (1974–77)

Secretary of State	Henry A. Kissinger	1974–77
Secretary of Treasury	William E. Simon	1974–77
Attorney General	William Saxbe	1974–75
	Edward Levi	1975–77
Secretary of Interior	Rogers Morton	1974–75
	Stanley K. Hathaway	1975
	Thomas Kleppe	1975–77
Secretary of Agriculture	Earl L. Butz	1974–76
	John A. Knebel	1976–77
Secretary of Commerce	Frederick B. Dent	1974–75
	Rogers Morton	1975–76
	Elliot L. Richardson	1976–77
Secretary of Labor	Peter J. Brennan	1974–75
	John T. Dunlop	1975–76
	W. J. Usery	1976–77
Secretary of Defense	James R. Schlesinger	1974–75
	Donald Rumsfeld	1975–77
Secretary of Health, Education, and Welfare	Caspar Weinberger	1974–75
	Forrest D. Mathews	1975–77
Secretary of Housing and Urban Development	James T. Lynn	1974–75
	Carla A. Hills	1975–77
Secretary of Transportation	William T. Coleman	1975–77

Carter Administration (1977–81)

Secretary of State	Cyrus R. Vance	1977–80
	Edmund Muskie	1980–81
Secretary of Treasury	W. Michael Blumenthal	1977–79
	G. William Miller	1979–81
Attorney General	Griffin Bell	1977–79
	Benjamin R. Civiletti	1979–81
Secretary of Interior	Cecil D. Andrus	1977–81
Secretary of Agriculture	Robert Bergland	1977–81
Secretary of Commerce	Juanita M. Kreps	1977–79
	Philip M. Klutznick	1979–81
Secretary of Labor	F. Ray Marshall	1977–81
Secretary of Defense	Harold Brown	1977–81
Secretary of Health, Education, and Welfare	Joseph A. Califano	1977–79
	Patricia R. Harris	1979–80
Secretary of Health and Human Services[1]	Patricia R. Harris	1980–81
Secretary of Housing and Urban Development	Patricia R. Harris	1977–79
	Moon Landrieu	1979–81
Secretary of Transportation	Brock Adam	1977–79
	Neil E. Goldschmidt	1979–81
Secretary of Energy	James R. Schlesinger	1977–79
	Charles W. Duncan	1979–81
Secretary of Education[1]	Shirley M. Hufstedler	1980–81

1. The Dept. of Health, Education, and Welfare was split into the Dept. of Education and the Dept. of Health and Human Services on May 4, 1980.

Reagan Administration (1981–89)

Secretary of State	Alexander M. Haig	1981–82
	George P. Shultz	1982–89
Secretary of Treasury	Donald Regan	1981–85
	James A. Baker, III	1985–89
Secretary of Defense	Caspar Weinberger	1981–87
	Frank Carlucci	1987–89
Attorney General	William F. Smith	1981–85
	Edwin A. Meese, III	1985–88
	Richard L. Thornburgh	1988–89
Secretary of Interior	James Watt	1981–83
	William P. Clark, Jr.	1983–85
	Donald P. Hodel	1985–89
Secretary of Agriculture	John Block	1981–86
	Richard E. Lyng	1986–89
Secretary of Commerce	Malcolm Baldrige	1981–89
Secretary of Labor	Raymond Donovan	1981–85
	William E. Brock	1985–89
Secretary of Health and Human Services	Richard Schweiker	1981–83
	Margaret Heckler	1983–85
	Otis R. Bowen	1985–89
Secretary of Housing and Urban Development	Samuel Pierce	1981–89
Secretary of Transportation	Drew Lewis	1981–83
	Elizabeth Dole	1983–89
Secretary of Energy	James Edwards	1981–82
	Donald P. Hodel	1982–85
	John S. Herrington	1985–89
Secretary of Education	Terrel H. Bell	1981–85
	William J. Bennett	1985–89

Bush Administration (1989–93)

Secretary of State	James A. Baker III	1989–92
	Lawrence Eagleburger	1992–93
Secretary of Treasury	Nicholas F. Brady	1989–93
Secretary of Defense	Dick Cheney	1989–93
Attorney General	Richard L. Thornburgh	1989–91
	William P. Barr	1991–93
Secretary of Interior	Manuel Lujan	1989–93
Secretary of Agriculture	Clayton K. Yeutter	1989–91
	Edward Madigan	1991–93
Secretary of Commerce	Robert A. Mosbacher	1989–91
	Barbara Franklin	1991–93
Secretary of Labor	Elizabeth Hanford Dole	1989–90
	Lynn Martin	1990–93
Secretary of Health and Human Services	Louis Sullivan	1989–93
Secretary of Housing and Urban Development	Jack F. Kemp	1989–93
Secretary of Transportation	Samuel K. Skinner	1989–91
	Andrew Card	1991–93
Secretary of Energy	James D. Watkins	1989–93
Secretary of Education	Lauro D. Cavazos	1989–90
	Lamar Alexander	1990–93
Secretary of Veterans' Affairs	Edward J. Derwinski	1989–92
	Anthony J. Principi	1992–93

Clinton Administration (1993–)

Secretary of State	Warren M. Christopher	1993–97
	Madeleine K. Albright	1997–
Secretary of Treasury	Lloyd Bentsen	1993–94
	Robert E. Rubin	1994–99
	Lawrence H. Summers	1999–
Secretary of Defense	Les Aspin	1993–94
	William Perry	1994–97
	William S. Cohen	1997–
Attorney General	Janet Reno	1993–
Secretary of Interior	Bruce Babbitt	1993–
Secretary of Agriculture	Mike Espy	1993–94
	Dan Glickman	1995–
Secretary of Commerce	Ronald H. Brown	1993–96
	Mickey Kantor	1996–97
	William M. Daley	1997–
Secretary of Labor	Robert B. Reich	1993–97
	Alexis M. Herman	1997–
Secretary of Health and Human Services	Donna E. Shalala	1993–
Secretary of Housing and Urban Development	Henry G. Cisneros	1993–97
	Andrew M. Cuomo	1997–
Secretary of Transportation	Federico F. Peña	1993–97
	Rodney E. Slater	1997–
Secretary of Energy	Hazel O'Leary	1993–97
	Federico F. Peña	1997–98
	Bill Richardson	1998–
Secretary of Education	Richard W. Riley	1993–98
Secretary of Veterans' Affairs	Jesse Brown	1993–97
	Hershel Gober, acting	1997–98
	Togo D. West Jr.	1998–

THE U.S. SUPREME COURT

▶IMPORTANT SUPREME COURT DECISIONS

Marbury v. Madison (1803) The Court struck down a law "repugnant to the constitution" for the first time and set the precedent for judicial review of acts of Congress. In a politically ingenious ruling on the Judiciary Act of 1789, Chief Justice John Marshall asserted the Supreme Court's power "to say what the law is," while avoiding a confrontation with President Thomas Jefferson. Not until the *Dred Scott* case of 1857 would another Federal law be ruled unconstitutional.

Fletcher v. Peck (1810) The Court ruled that Georgia could not deprive land speculators of their title, even though the previous owners had obtained the land from the state through fraud and bribery. Arising from the infamous Yazoo land frauds of 1795, this decision followed the Constitution's obligation of contracts clause and was the first time the Court invalidated a state law.

Dartmouth College v. Woodward (1819) The Court encouraged business investment with this decision by treating corporate charters as fully protected contracts. Not even the state legislatures that originally granted them could tamper with charters to private corporations, unless they retained the power to do so. Dartmouth College remained a private institution despite New Hampshire's attempt to take it over. This decision, which opened the way for abuse of corporate privileges, would later be modified in the *Charles River Bridge* (1837) and *Munn v. Illinois* (1877) cases.

Chief Justices of the United States, 1789–1999

Chief Justice	Tenure[1]	Appointed by
John Jay	1789–1795	George Washington
John Rutledge[3]	1795	George Washington
Oliver Ellsworth	1796–1800	George Washington
John Marshall[4]	1801–35	John Adams
Roger B. Taney	1836–64	Andrew Jackson
Salmon P. Chase	1864–73	Abraham Lincoln
Morrison R. Waite	1874–88	Ulysses S. Grant
Melville W. Fuller	1888–1910	Grover Cleveland
Edward D. White	1910–21	William Howard Taft
William Howard Taft[5]	1921–30	Warren G. Harding
Charles Evans Hughes[2]	1930–41	Herbert Hoover
Harlan F. Stone[2]	1941–46	Franklin D. Roosevelt
Fred M. Vinson	1946–53	Harry S Truman
Earl Warren	1953–69	Dwight D. Eisenhower
Warren E. Burger	1969–87	Richard M. Nixon
William H. Rehnquist[2]	1987–	Ronald Reagan

1. Dates are for tenure as Chief Justice. For complete tenure on Supreme Court, see "Supreme Court Justices." 2. Served as Associate Justice prior to appointment as Chief Justice. 3. Served one term, but appointment not confirmed by Senate. 4. Longest tenure as Chief Justice. 5. Formerly served as 27th president of the United States.

McCulloch v. Maryland (1819) "Broad," as opposed to "strict," construction of the Constitution received high court approval in Chief Justice John Marshall's opinion upholding the constitutionality of the national bank against a Maryland challenge. This ruling enhanced Federal governmental authority by liberally interpreting the power of Congress to make laws "necessary and proper" for its specified powers. At a time when states were trying to tax the Bank of the United States out of existence, this decision also forbade such state interference with the Federal government. "The power to tax," Marshall wrote, "involves the power to destroy."

Cohens v. Virginia (1821) With this ruling, the Court reiterated its power to hear appeals from state courts, and affirmed the national supremacy of Federal judicial power. Virginia's conviction of the Cohens for selling lottery tickets in violation of state law was upheld, but so too was the Cohens' right to appeal to the Court, which Virginia had challenged. Critics of judicial "consolidationalism" were reminded of the Court's comprehensive powers as the ultimate appellate court for all Americans.

Gibbons v. Ogden (1824) In a dispute arising from a New York ferry monopoly, the Court ruled that states could not restrain interstate commerce in any way, and that congressional power to regulate interstate commerce "does not stop at the jurisdictional lines of the several states." The decision helped prevent interstate trade wars, quite common under the Articles of Confederation, from breaking out under the Constitution. Chief Justice Marshall's opinion also confirmed the broad potential power of the Constitution's commerce clause.

Charles River Bridge v. Warren Bridge (1837) A key decision for economic development, this case arose when state-chartered proprietors of a Boston toll bridge objected that a new state-chartered bridge across the Charles River would put them out of business. Chief Justice Roger B. Taney, in his first constitutional ruling, held that state charters implied no vested rights and that ambiguities must be construed in favor of the public, which would benefit from the new toll-free bridge. This decision balanced private property rights against the public welfare.

Dred Scott v. Sanford (1857) Dred Scott, a Missouri slave, sued for his liberty after his owner took him into free territory. The Court ruled that Congress could not bar slavery in the territories. Scott remained a slave because the Missouri Compromise of 1820, prohibiting slavery from part of the Louisiana Purchase, violated the Fifth Amendment by depriving slave owners of their right to enjoy property without due process of law. Scott himself could not even sue, for he was held to be property, not a citizen. This decision sharpened sectional conflict by sweeping away legal barriers to the expansion of slavery.

Ex Parte Milligan (1866) President Abraham Lincoln's suspension of some civil liberties during the Civil War was attacked in this decision, which upheld the right of *habeas corpus*. The Court ruled that the president could not hold military tribunals in areas remote from battle and where civil courts were open and functioning. Milligan's conviction by such a Civil War tribunal in Indianapolis, Indiana, was overturned. The Constitution, admonished the Court, applies "at all times, and under all circumstances."

Slaughter-House Cases (1873)   In its first ruling on the Fourteenth Amendment, the Court held that Louisiana's grant of a butcher monopoly did not violate the privileges and immunities of competitors, nor deny them equal protection of the laws, nor deprive them of property without

Justices of the Supreme Court of the United States, 1789–1999

Name	Tenure	Appointed by	Name	Tenure	Appointed by
Baldwin, Henry	1830–44	Andrew Jackson	Livingston, H. Brockholst	1806–23	Thomas Jefferson
Barbour, Philip P.	1836–41	Andrew Jackson	Lurton, Horace H.	1910–14	William Howard Taft
Black, Hugo L.	1937–71	Franklin D. Roosevelt	Marshall, John[1]	1801–35	John Adams
Blackmun, Harry A.	1970–1994	Richard M. Nixon	Marshall, Thurgood	1967–92	Lyndon B. Johnson
Blair, John	1789–96	George Washington	Matthews, Stanley	1881–89	James A. Garfield
Blatchford, Samuel	1882–93	Chester A. Arthur	McKenna, Joseph	1898–1925	William McKinley
Bradley, Joseph P.	1870–92	Ulysses S. Grant	McKinley, John	1837–52	Martin Van Buren
Brandeis, Louis D.	1916–39	Woodrow Wilson	McLean, John	1829–61	Andrew Jackson
Brennan, William J., Jr.	1956–90	Dwight D. Eisenhower	McReynolds, James C.	1914–41	Woodrow Wilson
Brewer, David J.	1889–1910	Benjamin Harrison	Miller, Samuel F.	1862–90	Abraham Lincoln
Breyer, Stephen G.	1994–	Bill Clinton	Minton, Sherman	1949–56	Harry S Truman
Brown, Henry B.	1890–1906	Benjamin Harrison	Moody, William H.	1906–10	Theodore Roosevelt
Burger, Warren E.[1]	1969–87	Richard M. Nixon	Moore, Alfred	1799–1804	John Adams
Burton, Harold H.	1945–58	Harry S Truman	Murphy, Frank	1940–49	Franklin D. Roosevelt
Butler, Pierce	1922–39	Warren G. Harding	Nelson, Samuel	1845–72	John Tyler
Byrnes, James F.	1941–42	Franklin D. Roosevelt	O'Connor, Sandra Day	1981–	Ronald Reagan
Campbell, John A.	1853–61	Franklin Pierce	Paterson, William	1793–1806	George Washington
Cardozo, Benjamin N.	1932–38	Herbert Hoover	Peckham, Rufus W.	1895–1910	Grover Cleveland
Catron, John	1837–65	Martin Van Buren	Pitney, Mahlon	1912–22	William Howard Taft
Chase, Salmon P.[1]	1864–73	Abraham Lincoln	Powell, Lewis F., Jr.	1972–87	Richard M. Nixon
Chase, Samuel	1796–1811	George Washington	Reed, Stanley F.	1938–57	Franklin D. Roosevelt
Clark, Tom C.	1949–67	Harry S Truman	Rehnquist, William H.[1]	1972–	Richard M. Nixon
Clarke, John H.	1916–22	Woodrow Wilson	Roberts, Owen J.	1930–45	Herbert Hoover
Clifford, Nathan	1858–81	James J. Buchanan	Rutledge, John[1]	1789–91	George Washington
Curtis, Benjamin R.	1851–57	Millard Fillmore		1795	George Washington
Cushing, William	1789–1810	George Washington	Rutledge, Wiley B.	1943–49	Franklin D. Roosevelt
Daniel, Peter V.	1841–60	Martin Van Buren	Sanford, Edward T.	1923–30	Warren G. Harding
Davis, David	1862–77	Abraham Lincoln	Scalia, Antonin	1986–	Ronald Reagan
Day, William R.	1903–22	Theodore Roosevelt	Shiras, George	1892–1903	Benjamin Harrison
Douglas, William O.[2]	1939–75	Franklin D. Roosevelt	Souter, David H.	1990–	George Bush
Duval, Gabriel	1811–36	James Madison	Stevens, John Paul	1975–	Gerald R. Ford
Ellsworth, Oliver[1]	1796–1800	George Washington	Stewart, Potter	1959–81	Dwight D. Eisenhower
Field, Stephen J.	1863–97	Abraham Lincoln	Stone, Harlan F.[1]	1925–46	Calvin Coolidge
Fortas, Abe	1965–69	Lyndon B. Johnson	Story, Joseph	1811–45	James Madison
Frankfurter, Felix	1939–62	Franklin D. Roosevelt	Strong, William	1870–80	Ulysses S. Grant
Fuller, Melville W.[1]	1888–1910	Grover Cleveland	Sutherland, George	1922–38	Warren G. Harding
Ginsburg, Ruth Bader	1993–	Bill Clinton	Swayne, Noah H.	1862–81	Abraham Lincoln
Goldberg, Arthur J.	1962–65	John F. Kennedy	Taft, William Howard[1,5]	1921–30	Warren Harding
Gray, Horace	1881–1902	Chester A. Arthur	Taney, Roger B.[1]	1836–64	Andrew Jackson
Grier, Robert C.	1846–70	James K. Polk	Thomas, Clarence	1991–	George Bush
Harlan, John Marshall	1877–1911	Rutherford B. Hayes	Thompson, Smith	1823–43	James Monroe
Harlan, John Marshall[3]	1955–71	Dwight D. Eisenhower	Todd, Thomas	1807–26	Thomas Jefferson
Harrison, Robert H.	1789–90	George Washington	Trimble, Robert	1826–28	John Quincy Adams
Holmes, Oliver Wendell	1902–32	Theodore Roosevelt	Van Devanter, Willis	1910–37	William Howard Taft
Hughes, Charles Evans[1,4]	1910–16	William Howard Taft	Vinson, Fred M.[1]	1946–53	Harry S Truman
	1930–41	Herbert Hoover	Waite, Morrison R.[1]	1874–88	Ulysses S. Grant
Hunt, Ward	1872–82	Ulysses S. Grant	Warren, Earl[1]	1953–69	Dwight D. Eisenhower
Iredell, James	1790–99	George Washington	Washington, Bushrod	1798–1829	John Adams
Jackson, Howell E.	1893–95	Benjamin Harrison	Wayne, James M.	1835–67	Andrew Jackson
Jackson, Robert H.	1941–54	Franklin D. Roosevelt	White, Byron R.	1962–93	John F. Kennedy
Jay, John[1]	1789–95	George Washington	White, Edward D.[1]	1894–1921	Grover Cleveland
Johnson, Thomas	1791–93	George Washington	Whittaker, Charles E.	1957–62	Dwight D. Eisenhower
Johnson, William	1804–34	Thomas Jefferson	Wilson, James	1789–98	George Washington
Kennedy, Anthony M.	1987–	Ronald Reagan	Woodbury, Levi	1845–51	James K. Polk
Lamar, Joseph R.	1911–16	William Howard Taft	Woods, William B.	1880–87	Rutherford B. Hayes
Lamar, Lucius Q. C.	1888–93	Grover Cleveland			

Note: Dates reflect complete tenure on the Supreme Court, including tenure as Chief Justice. 1. See "Chief Justices of the United States" for dates of tenure and appointment as Chief Justice. 2. Longest-serving justice. 3. The two Harlans were grandfather and grandson. 4. Stepped down as Associate Justice to run for president in 1916; later appointed Chief Justice. 5. Formerly served as 27th president of the United States.

due process. Only a few rights deriving from "Federal citizenship" were subject to Federal protection, while states still protected most civil and property rights. Federal protection of civil rights, even for former slaves, was very narrowly interpreted in this ruling. But this decision broadly upheld business regulation by states until *Santa Clara Co. v. Southern Pacific Railroad Co.* (1886) applied the Fourteenth Amendment to defense of corporate property rights.

Munn v. Illinois (1877) This decision, in one of the "Granger Cases," enabled states to regulate private property in the public interest when the public had an interest in that property. The Court held that Illinois laws setting maximum rates for grain storage did not violate the Fourteenth Amendment's ban on deprivation of property without due process of law, and did not restrain interstate commerce. But for the next half century, the Court imposed the burden of proof on the states for their regulatory laws.

Civil Rights Cases (1883) Racial equality was postponed eighty years by this decision, which struck down the Civil Rights Act of 1875 and allowed for private segregation. The Fourteenth Amendment's guarantee of equal protection, the Court ruled, applied against state action—but not against private individuals, whose discrimination unaided by the states was beyond Federal control. Segregation of public facilities was approved soon afterward in *Plessy v. Ferguson* (1896).

United States v. E.C. Knight Co. (1895) The first ruling on the Sherman Antitrust Act of 1890, this decision curtailed Federal regulation of monopolies by placing national manufacturers beyond the reach of the Constitution's commerce clause. Only the actual interstate commerce of monopolies, not their production activities, was subject to Federal control. The Court's distinction between production and commerce impeded Federal regulation of manufacturing until *National Labor Relations Board v. Jones & Laughlin Steel Corp.* (1937).

Plessy v. Ferguson (1896) The "separate but equal" doctrine supporting public segregation by law received the Court's approval in this ruling, which originated with segregated railroad cars in Louisiana. The Court held that as long as equal accommodations were provided, segregation was not discrimination and did not deprive blacks of equal protection of the laws under the Fourteenth Amendment. This decision was overturned in *Brown v. Board of Education* (1954).

Lochner v. New York (1905) This decision struck down a New York law placing limits on maximum working hours for bakers. The law violated the Fourteenth Amendment by restricting individual "freedom of contract" to buy and sell labor, and was an excessive use of state police power, the Court held. The ruling was soon modified in *Muller v. Oregon* (1908), which approved state-regulated limits on women's labor after the Court utilized sociological and economic data to consider the health and morals of women workers.

Standard Oil Co. of New Jersey v. United States (1911) Federal efforts to break up monopolies under the Sherman Antitrust Act had to follow the "rule of reason," according to this ruling. Only those combinations in restraint of trade which were contrary to the public interest, and therefore unreasonable, were illegal. Although the Taft administration's prosecution of Standard Oil was upheld, breaking up one of the nation's leading monopolies, further antitrust suits were impaired by this decision, which facilitated the 1920s merger movement.

Schenk v. United States (1919) The Court unanimously held that World War I limits on freedom of speech did not violate the First Amendment—if the speech in question represented a "clear and present danger." That famous doctrine of Justice Oliver Wendell Holmes, which approved the arrest of a draft resister for handing out pamphlets to soldiers in wartime, became an important standard for interpreting the First Amendment. But in subsequent cases of this period, the Court added that the mere "bad tendency" of speech to cause danger could be grounds for censorship.

Schechter Poultry Corp. v. United States (1935) At the height of its assault on the New Deal, the Court struck down the National Industrial Recovery Act in the famous "Sick Chicken Case." The NIRA was found to delegate excessive legislative regulatory powers to the executive without constitutional authority, and to regulate commerce within states in violation of the commerce clause. Schechter's kosher chicken supply house in New York did not have to abide by the NIRA's rigid industry codes, the Court ruled.

National Labor Relations Board v. Jones & Laughlin Steel Corp. (1937) Under pressure from public opinion and President Franklin D. Roosevelt, the Court made an abrupt about-face and began approving New Deal legislation. In this case, laws protecting unions and barring "unfair labor practices" were upheld by the "stream of commerce" doctrine that employers who sold their goods and obtained their raw materials through interstate commerce were subject to Federal regulation. This ruling overturned *United States v. E.C. Knight Co.* (1895) and became the basis for the modern, expansive understanding of the commerce power.

West Virginia Board of Education v. Barnette (1943) The Court reversed its earlier ruling in *Minersville School District v. Gobitis* (1940), which had required Jehovah's Witnesses to salute the flag in school. In this case, also brought against a Jehovah's Witness, the Court recognized that refusing to salute the flag did not violate anyone's rights, and that the First Amendment protected the "right of silence" as well as freedom of speech.

Korematsu v. United States (1944) President Franklin D. Roosevelt's Executive Order No. 9066, which approved the West Coast evacuation and internment of 120,000 Japanese-Americans during World War II, was upheld on the grounds of "military necessity" in this ruling. The Court was reluctant to interfere with executive authority in time of national emergency. But in *Ex parte Endo* (1944), the Court held that persons of proven loyalty should not be interned. In August 1988, Congress made a formal apology to former internees and appropriated $1.25 billion in compensation for the 60,000 survivors.

Dennis v. United States (1951)

At the height of the postwar "Red Scare," the Court upheld the conviction of eleven American Communist leaders under the Smith Act of 1940, which made it a crime to belong to organizations teaching or advocating the violent overthrow of the government. The "clear and present danger" doctrine could be disregarded, the Court held, if "the gravity of the 'evil,' discounted by its improbability, justifies such invasion of free speech as is necessary to avoid the evil." Over one hundred Communists were indicted as a result, effectively destroying the Communist Party as a political force.

Youngstown Sheet and Tube Co. v. Sawyer (1952)

During the Korean War, when President Harry S Truman seized steel plants to keep them operating despite a strike, the Court held that his action was an unconstitutional usurpation of legislative authority. Only an act of Congress, not the president's inherent executive powers or military powers as commander-in-chief, could justify such a sizeable confiscation of property, despite the wartime emergency.

Brown v. Board of Education of Topeka (1954)

Chief Justice Earl Warren led the Court unanimously to decide that segregated schools violated the equal protection clause of the Fourteenth Amendment. The "separate but equal" doctrine of Plessy v. Ferguson (1896) was overruled after a series of cases dating back to Missouri ex. rel. Gaines v. Canada (1938) had already limited it. "Separate educational facilities are inherently unequal," held the Court. Efforts to desegregate southern schools after the Brown decision met with massive resistance for many years.

Baker v. Carr (1962)

Overrepresentation of rural districts in state legislatures, which effectively disfranchised millions of voters, led the Court to abandon its traditional non-interference in drawing legislative boundaries. Tennessee citizens deprived of full representation by "arbitrary and capricious" malapportionment were denied equal protection under the Fourteenth Amendment, ruled the Court. All states eventually reapportioned their legislatures in conformance with the "one man, one vote" doctrine of Reynolds v. Sims (1964).

Gideon v. Wainwright (1963)

Reversing an earlier ruling in Betts v. Brady (1942), the Court held that the Sixth Amendment guaranteed access to qualified counsel, which was "fundamental to a fair trial." Gideon was entitled to a retrial because Florida failed to provide him with an attorney. After this decision, states were required to furnish public defenders for indigent defendants in felony cases. In Argersinger v. Hamlin (1972), the ruling was extended to all cases that might result in imprisonment.

Heart of Atlanta Motel, Inc. v. United States (1964)

The Court upheld Title II of the Civil Rights Act of 1964, outlawing private discrimination in public accommodations, as a legitimate exertion of Federal power over interstate commerce. Congress had "ample power" to forbid racial discrimination in facilities that affected commerce by serving interstate travelers. The Heart of Atlanta Motel was located on two interstate highways, so the Court could sidestep the Civil Rights Cases (1883) protection of private discrimination to overrule it.

Griswold v. Connecticut (1965)

In striking down an 1879 Connecticut law against the use of contraceptives, the Court established a "right to privacy" that was implied by, though not specifically enumerated in the First, Third, Fourth, Fifth, Ninth, and Fourteenth Amendments. The case is most notable for laying the groundwork for other legal challenges invoking this newfound right to privacy. Foremost among them is the 1973 Roe v. Wade decision allowing women to choose abortion.

South Carolina v. Katzenbach (1966)

Federal intervention on behalf of voting rights was upheld in this decision. South Carolina sued the Attorney General, contending that the 1965 Voting Rights Act encroached on the reserved powers of the states, treated the states unequally, and violated separation of powers. Chief Justice Warren ruled that the Fifteenth Amendment gave Congress broad powers to "use any rational means to effectuate the constitutional prohibition of racial discrimination in voting." After this decision, blacks registered and voted in massive numbers in the South.

Miranda v. Arizona (1966)

Expanding upon Gideon v. Wainwright (1963) and Escobedo v. Illinois (1964), the Court set forth stringent interrogation procedures for criminal suspects to protect their Fifth Amendment freedom from self-incrimination. Miranda's confession to kidnapping and rape was obtained without counsel and without his having been advised of his right to silence, so it was ruled inadmissable as evidence. This decision obliged police to advise suspects of their rights upon taking them into custody.

New York Times Co. v. United States (1971)

When the New York Times and the Washington Post published the top-secret "Pentagon Papers" in 1971, revealing government duplicity in the Vietnam War, the Nixon administration obtained an injunction against the Times on grounds of national security. But in a brief per curiam opinion, the Court observed that in this case, the government had not met the "heavy burden of showing justification" for "prior restraint" on freedom of the press.

Roe v. Wade (1973)

In a controversial ruling, the Court held that state laws restricting abortion were an unconstitutional invasion of a woman's right to privacy. Only in the last trimester of pregnancy, when the fetus achieved viability outside the womb, might states regulate abortion—except when the life or health of the mother was at stake. Feelings ran high on both sides in the aftermath of this decision. In Planned Parenthood of Central Missouri v. Danforth (1976), the Court added further that wives did not need their husbands' consent to obtain abortions.

United States v. Nixon (1974)

In a unanimous ruling, the Court held that the secret White House recordings of President Richard M. Nixon's conversations with aides were subject to subpoena in the Watergate coverup trial. Nixon's claim to "executive privilege" was rejected as invalid because military and national security issues were not at stake, and Chief Justice Warren Burger cited Marbury v. Madison (1803) to assert the Court's primacy in constitutional issues. Once the tapes were released, documenting Nixon's obstruction of justice, the president resigned to avoid impeachment.

University of California Regents v. Bakke (1978)
Twice refused admission to medical school, Bakke sued the University of California for giving "affirmative action" preference to less-qualified black applicants. In an ambiguous 5-4 ruling, the Court agreed that Bakke's right to equal protection was denied, that he should be admitted, and that affirmative action quotas should be discarded. But at the same time, the Court recognized race as "a factor" in admissions and hiring decisions. Affirmative action could continue as long as rigid quotas did not constitute, in effect, "reverse discrimination."

Immigration and Naturalization Service v. Chadha (1983)
The legislative veto, contained in hundreds of Federal statutes since 1932, was disallowed in this decision. Congress exceeded its constitutional powers when it blocked the Attorney General's suspension of a deportation order for Jagdish Rai Chadha, a Kenyan student who overstayed his visa. The Court held that the Immigration and Nationality Act's legislative veto provision violated the constitutional separation of powers. Chief Justice Burger recognized that Congress would prefer to delegate authority to the executive branch and reserve the right to veto administrative regulations, but "we have not found a better way to preserve freedom" than the separation of powers.

Bowers v. Hardwick (1986)
In a controversial 5-4 decision applauded by fundamentalists but protested by gay activists, the Court ruled that the constitutional right to privacy does not protect homosexual relations, even between consenting adults in their own homes. Georgia's law against oral and anal sex, passed in 1816, could be applied to homosexuals—though the Court declined to rule on whether heterosexuals might also be prosecuted. The decision raised fears of bedroom patrols and sexual surveillance, despite the constitutional right to privacy in intimate personal matters established in cases dating back to the 1920s. Justice Byron White ruled that "none of the rights announced in those cases bears any resemblance to the claimed constitutional right of homosexuals to engage in acts of sodomy."

The Federal Government

In their desire to create a government based on an elaborate system of "checks and balances," the Founding Fathers divided the sources of power into three separate and distinct branches of government—the legislative, the judicial, and the executive. The fundamental purpose, organization, and workings of these three branches are set down in the first three articles of the Constitution. Despite the passing of more than two centuries, the creation of dozens of departments, agencies, and commissions, the ongoing employment of almost 2.5 million civilian workers, and the presence of a standing peacetime military force of some 1.5 million, this structure remains essentially unchanged.

Below is a list of every major body within the Federal Government. Wherever possible, a Web home page is included. Every entry mentions the date each entity was founded and summarizes its official function. (The primary source of this information is the National Archives and Records Administration, Office of the Federal Register, *United States Government Manual*.)

THE LEGISLATIVE BRANCH

Architect of the Capitol U.S. Capitol Building, Washington, D.C. 20515. (202) 228-1793. www.aoc.gov. First Architect appointed in 1793 by President. Permanent authority for care of Capitol established by Act of August 15, 1876. Responsible for care and maintenance of Capitol building and grounds, Library of Congress buildings, and U.S. Supreme Court building. Operates Senate and House restaurants. Maintains, operates, and cares for House and Senate office buildings. Plans future construction, renovation, reconstruction, and alterations to existing buildings.

U.S. Botanic Garden Director's Office: 245 First Street SW, Washington, D.C. 20024. (202) 225-8333. www.aoc.gov. Conservatory: Maryland Avenue-First to Second Streets SW; Washington, D.C. 20024. (202) 225-6646. Created in 1820. Collects, cultivates, and grows vegetable and plant matter of this and other countries for exhibition and display. Provides study materials on vegetable and plant matter for students, botanists, horticulturists, floriculturists, and garden clubs.

How A Bill Becomes Law
Usually bills are raised in any of the various committees of the Senate or House of Representatives. If the bill is supported by a majority of the committee, it is brought to the floor of the house in which it originated, and voted upon. If it gains majority support in the full Senate or House, the other house of Congress votes on it. If the bill is passed in both the Senate and House, it is sent to the President, who may either sign it, veto it, or not act on it.

If the president signs it or refuses to act within 10 days and the Congress is still in session, the bill becomes law. If the president vetoes it, it is returned to the Senate and the House for another vote; a two-thirds majority in each house is then required to overturn the presidential veto. However, if the president refuses to act on a bill and Congress adjourns before the end of the 10-day period, the legislation is dead. This is known as a pocket veto.

Occasionally, bills are raised on the floor of the Senate or the House, in which case the first step of committee voting is avoided and the legislation process begins with the full Senate or House Vote. All other processes remain the same.

How to Contact Your Senator or Representative

To contact any Senator, call (202)-224-3121. More information about the Senate is available on the Internet at **www.senate.gov**. To reach a Representative, call (202)-225-3121. More information about the House is available on the Internet at **www.house.gov**

The 106th Congress of the United States

The upper house of the U.S. Congress, the Senate, is composed of 100 members: two from each state. Members are elected to six-year terms. One-third of the Senate faces re-election every two years. Senators must have been U.S. citizens for at least 9 years and must be at least 30 years old.

The lower house of government is known as the House of Representatives, and is composed of 435 members. The number of representatives from each state is determined by population every 10 years; every state is entitled to at least one representative. Members face re-election every two years. Representatives must have been U.S. citizens for at least 7 years and must be at least 25 years old.

In addition to state representatives, there are delegates from the District of Columbia, American Samoa, Guam, and the Virgin Islands, and a resident commissioner from Puerto Rico. They may take part in floor debates, but may not vote.

Senate Offices

President	Albert Gore Jr. (D)
Majority Leader	Trent Lott (R)
Majority Whip	Don Nickles (R)
Minority Leader	Thomas A. Daschle (D)
Minority Whip	Harry Reid (D)

House Offices

Speaker	Dennis Hastert (R)
Majority Leader	Dick Armey (R)
Majority Whip	Tom DeLay (R)
Minority Leader	Richard Gephardt (D)
Minority Whip	David Bonior (D)

THE SENATE

State	Senator	State	Senator
Alabama	Richard C. Shelby (R) Jeff Sessions (R)	Montana	Max Baucus (D) Conrad R. Burns (R)
Alaska	Ted Stevens (R) Frank H. Murkowski (R)	Nebraska	Robert J. Kerrey (D) Charles Hagel (R)
Arizona	John McCain (R) Jon Kyl (R)	Nevada	Harry Reid (D) Richard H. Bryan (D)
Arkansas	Tim Hutchinson (R) Blanche Lincoln (D)	New Hampshire	Bob Smith (R) Judd Gregg (R)
California	Dianne Feinstein (D) Barbara Boxer (D)	New Jersey	Frank R. Lautenberg (D) Robert Torricelli (D)
Colorado	Ben Nighthorse Campbell (R) Wayne A. Allard (R)	New Mexico	Pete V. Domenici (R) Jeff Bingaman (D)
Connecticut	Christopher J. Dodd (D) Joseph I. Lieberman (D)	New York	Daniel Patrick Moynihan (D) Charles Schumer (D)
Delaware	William V. Roth Jr. (R) Joseph R. Biden Jr. (D)	North Carolina	Jesse Helms (R) John Edwards (D)
Florida	Bob Graham (D) Connie Mack (R)	North Dakota	Kent Conrad (D) Byron L. Dorgan (D)
Georgia	Paul Coverdell (R) Max Cleland (D)	Ohio	Mike DeWine (R) George Voinovich (R)
Hawaii	Daniel K. Inouye (D) Daniel K. Akaka (D)	Oklahoma	Don Nickles (R) James Inhofe (R)
Idaho	Larry E. Craig (R) Mike Crapo (R)	Oregon	Ron Wyden (D) Gordon Smith (R)
Illinois	Peter Fitzgerald (R) Richard J. Durbin (D)	Pennsylvania	Arlen Specter (R) Rick Santorum (R)
Indiana	Richard G. Lugar (R) Evan Bayh (D)	Rhode Island	John H. Chafee (R) Jack Reed (D)
Iowa	Chuck Grassley (R) Tom Harkin (D)	South Carolina	Strom Thurmond (R) Ernest F. Hollings (D)
Kansas	Pat Roberts (R) Sam Brownback (R)	South Dakota	Thomas A. Daschle (D) Tim Johnson (D)
Kentucky	Mitch McConnell (R) Jim Bunning (R)	Tennessee	Fred Thompson (R) William H. Frist (R)
Louisiana	John B. Breaux (D) Mary Landrieu (D)	Texas	Phil Gramm (R) Kay Bailey Hutchison (R)
Maine	Olympia J. Snowe (R) Susan Collins (R)	Utah	Orrin G. Hatch (R) Robert F. Bennett (R)
Maryland	Paul S. Sarbanes (D) Barbara A. Mikulski (D)	Vermont	Patrick J. Leahy (D) James M. Jeffords (R)
Massachusetts	Edward M. Kennedy (D) John F. Kerry (D)	Virginia	John W. Warner (R) Charles S. Robb (D)
Michigan	Carl Levin (D) Spencer Abraham (R)	Washington	Slade Gorton (R) Patty Murray (D)
Minnesota	Paul Wellstone (DFL) Rod Grams (IR)	West Virginia	Robert C. Byrd (D) John D. Rockefeller IV (D)
Mississippi	Thad Cochran (R) Trent Lott (R)	Wisconsin	Herb Kohl (D) Russell D. Feingold (D)
Missouri	Christopher S. Bond (R) John Ashcroft (R)	Wyoming	Craig Thomas (R) Mike Enzi (R)

Note: The senior senator is listed first.

THE HOUSE OF REPRESENTATIVES

State/Dist.	City	Representative
Alabama		
1st	Mobile	Sonny Callahan (R)
2nd	Montgomery	Terry Everett (R)
3rd	Anniston	Bob Riley (R)
4th	Jasper	Robert B. Aderholt (R)
5th	Huntsville	Robert E. (Bud) Cramer Jr. (D)
6th	Birmingham	Spencer Bachus (R)
7th	Tuscaloosa	Earl F. Hilliard (D)
Alaska		
1st	At-Large	Don Young (R)
Arizona		
1st	Tempe	Matt Salmon (R)
2nd	Phoenix	Ed Pastor (D)
3rd	Flagstaff	Bob Stump (R)
4th	Scottsdale	John Shadegg (R)
5th	Tucson	Jim Kolbe (R)
6th	Mesa	J.D. Hayworth (R)
Arkansas		
1st	Jonesboro	Marion Berry (D)
2nd	Little Rock	Vic Snyder (D)
3rd	Fort Smith	Asa Hutchinson (R)
4th	Pine Bluff	Jay Dickey (R)
California		
1st	Fairfield	Mike Thompson (D)
2nd	Chico	Wally Herger (R)
3rd	Sacramento	Doug Ose (R)
4th	Roseville	John T. Doolittle (R)
5th	Sacramento	Robert T. Matsui (D)
6th	Marin County	Lynn C. Woolsey (D)
7th	Richmond	George Miller (D)
8th	San Francisco	Nancy Pelosi (D)
9th	Oakland	Barbara Lee (D)
10th	Walnut Creek	Ellen O. Tauscher (D)
11th	Stockton	Richard W. Pombo (R)
12th	San Mateo	Tom Lantos (D)
13th	Hayward	Fortney Pete Stark (D)
14th	Palo Alto	Anna G. Eshoo (D)
15th	Sunnyvale	Tom Campbell (R)
16th	San Jose	Zoe Lofgren (D)
17th	Monterey	Sam Farr (D)
18th	Modesto	Gary A.Condit (D)
19th	Fresno	George P. Radanovich (R)
20th	Fresno	Calvin M. Dooley (D)
21st	Bakersfield	William M. Thomas (R)
22nd	Santa Barbara	Lois Capps (D)
23rd	Simi Valley	Elton Gallegly (R)
24th	Thousand Oaks	Brad Sherman (D)
25th	Santa Clarita	Howard "Buck" McKeon (R)
26th	Van Nuys	Howard L. Berman (D)
27th	Pasadena	James E. Rogan (R)
28th	Claremont	David Dreier (R)
29th	Hollywood	Henry A. Waxman (D)
30th	Boyle Heights	Xavier Becerra (D)
31st	Alhambra	Matthew G. Martinez (D)
32nd	Culver City	Julian C. Dixon (D)
33rd	East Los Angeles	Lucille Roybal-Allard (D)
34th	La Puente	Grace F. Napolitano (D)
35th	Watts	Maxine Waters (D)
36th	Rolling Hills	Steven T. Kuykendall (R)
37th	Compton	Juanita Millender-McDonald (D)
38th	Long Beach	Stephen Horn (R)
39th	Fullerton	Edward R. Royce (R)
40th	Redlands	Jerry Lewis (R)
41st	Ontario	Gary G. Miller (R)
42nd	San Bernardino	vacancy
43rd	Riverside	Ken Calvert (R)
44th	Moreno Valley	Mary Bono (R)
45th	Huntington Beach	Dana Rohrabacher (R)
46th	Anaheim	Loretta Sanchez (D)
47th	Irvine	Christopher Cox (R)
48th	San Clemente	Ron Packard (R)
49th	San Diego	Brian P. Bilbray (R)
50th	Chula Vista	Bob Filner (D)
51st	Escondido	Randy "Duke" Cunningham (R)
52nd	El Cajon	Duncan Hunter (R)

State/Dist.	City	Representative
Colorado		
1st	Denver	Diana DeGette (D)
2nd	Boulder	Mark Udall (D)
3rd	Pueblo	Scott McInnis (R)
4th	Greeley	Bob Schaffer (R)
5th	Colorado Springs	Joel Hefley (R)
6th	Lakewood	Thomas G. Tancredo (R)
Connecticut		
1st	Hartford	John B. Larson (D)
2nd	New London	Samuel Gejdenson (D)
3rd	New Haven	Rosa L. DeLauro (D)
4th	Stamford	Christopher Shays (R)
5th	Waterbury	James H. Maloney (D)
6th	New Britain	Nancy L. Johnson (R)
Delaware		
1st	At-Large	Michael N.Castle (R)
Florida		
1st	Pensacola	Joe Scarborough (R)
2nd	Tallahassee	Allen Boyd (D)
3rd	Jacksonville	Corrine Brown (D)
4th	Jacksonville	Tillie K. Fowler (R)
5th	Gainesville	Karen L.Thurman (D)
6th	Ocala	Cliff Stearns (R)
7th	New Smyrna Bch	John L.Mica (R)
8th	Orlando	Bill McCollum (R)
9th	Clearwater	Michael Bilirakis (R)
10th	St. Petersburg	C.W. Bill Young (R)
11th	Tampa	Jim Davis (D)
12th	Lakeland	Charles T. Canady (R)
13th	Sarasota	Dan Miller (R)
14th	Fort Myers	Porter J. Goss (R)
15th	Melbourne	Dave Weldon (R)
16th	West Palm Beach	Mark Foley (R)
17th	Miami	Carrie P.Meek (D)
18th	Miami Beach	Ileana Ros-Lehtinen (R)
19th	Boca Raton	Robert Wexler (D)
20th	Pembroke Pines	Peter Deutsch (D)
21st	Hialeah	Lincoln Diaz-Balart (R)
22nd	Fort Lauderdale	E. Clay Shaw Jr. (R)
23rd	Fort Lauderdale	Alcee L.Hastings (D)
Georgia		
1st	Savannah	Jack Kingston (R)
2nd	Albany	Sanford D. Bishop (D)
3rd	Columbus	Mac Collins (R)
4th	DeKalb County	Cynthia A. McKinney (D)
5th	Atlanta	John Lewis (D)
6th	Alfaretta-Roswell	Johnny Isakson (R)
7th	Rome	Bob Barr (R)
8th	Macon	Saxby Chambliss (R)
9th	LaFayette	Nathan Deal (R)
10th	Augusta	Charlie Norwood (R)
11th	Athens	John Linder (R)
Hawaii		
1st	Honolulu	Neil Abercrombie (D)
2nd	Outer Islands	Patsy T. Mink (D)
Idaho		
1st	Boise	Helen Chenoweth (R)
2nd	Pocatello	Michael K. Simpson (R)
Illinois		
1st	Chicago, south	Bobby L. Rush (D)
2nd	Lake Calumet	Jesse L. Jackson Jr. (D)
3rd	Oak Lawn	William O. Lipinski (D)
4th	Chicago	Luis Gutierrez (D)
5th	Chicago, north	Rod R. Blagojevich (D)
6th	Des Plaines	Henry J. Hyde (R)
7th	Chicago, loop	Danny K. Davis (D)
8th	Schaumburg	Philip M. Crane (R)
9th	Evanston	Janice D. Schakowsky (D)
10th	Waukegan	John Edward Porter (R)
11th	Joliet	Jerry Weller (R)
12th	Belleville	Jerry F. Costello (D)
13th	Oak Brook	Judy Biggert (R)
14th	Batavia	J. Dennis Hastert (R)
15th	Bloomington	Thomas W. Ewing (R)
16th	Rockford	Donald A. Manzullo (R)

THE HOUSE OF REPRESENTATIVES

State/Dist.	City	Representative	State/Dist.	City	Representative
Illinois			11th	Bloomfield Hills	Joe Knollenberg (R)
17th	Moline	Lane Evans (D)	12th	Sterling Heights	Sander M. Levin (D)
18th	Peoria	Ray LaHood (R)	13th	Ann Arbor	Lynn N. Rivers (D)
19th	Decatur	David D. Phelps (D)	14th	Detroit	John Conyers Jr. (D)
20th	Springfield	John Shimkus (R)	15th	Detroit	Carolyn C. Kilpatrick (D)
Indiana			16th	Dearborn	John D. Dingell (D)
1st	Gary	Peter J. Visclosky (D)	**Minnesota**		
2nd	Muncie	David McIntosh (R)	1st	Rochester	Gil Gutknecht (IR)
3rd	South Bend	Tim Roemer (D)	2nd	Willmar	David Minge (DFL)
4th	Fort Wayne	Mark E. Souder (R)	3rd	Bloomington	Jim Ramstad (R)
5th	Kokomo	Steve E. Buyer (R)	4th	St. Paul	Bruce F. Vento (DFL)
6th	Indianapolis	Dan Burton (R)	5th	Minneapolis	Martin Olav Sabo (DFL)
7th	Terre Haute	Edward A. Pease (R)	6th	Stillwater	Bill Luther (DFL)
8th	Evansville	John N. Hostettler (R)	7th	St. Cloud	Colin C. Peterson (DFL)
9th	Bloomington	Baron P. Hill (D)	8th	Duluth	James L. Oberstar (DFL)
10th	Indianapolis	Julia Carson (D)	**Mississippi**		
Iowa			1st	Oxford	Roger F. Wicker (R)
1st	Cedar Rapids	Jim Leach (R)	2nd	Vicksburg	Bennie G. Thompson (D)
2nd	Waterloo	Jim Nussle (R)	3rd	Meridian	Charles W. "Chip" Pickering (R)
3rd	Ames	Leonard L. Boswell (D)	4th	Jackson	Ronnie Shows (D)
4th	Des Moines	Greg Ganske (R)	5th	Pascagoula	Gene Taylor (D)
5th	Sioux City	Tom Latham (R)	**Missouri**		
Kansas			1st	St. Louis	William (Bill) Clay (D)
1st	Dodge City	Jerry Moran (R)	2nd	Kirkwood	James M. Talent (R)
2nd	Topeka	Jim Ryun (R)	3rd	St. Louis	Richard A. Gephardt (D)
3rd	Kansas City	Dennis Moore (D)	4th	Jefferson City	Ike Skelton (D)
4th	Wichita	Todd Tiahrt (R)	5th	Kansas City	Karen McCarthy (D)
Kentucky			6th	St. Joseph	Pat Danner (D)
1st	Paducah	Edward Whitfield (R)	7th	Springfield	Roy Blunt (R)
2nd	Owensboro	Ron Lewis (R)	8th	Cape Girardeau	Jo Ann Emerson (R)
3rd	Louisville	Anne M. Northrup (R)	9th	Hannibal	Kenny C. Hulshof (R)
4th	Covington	Ken Lucas (D)	**Montana**		
5th	Somerset	Harold Rogers (R)	1st	At-Large	Rick Hill (R)
6th	Lexington	Ernie Fletcher (R)	**Nebraska**		
Louisiana			1st	Lincoln	Doug Bereuter (R)
1st	Metairie	David Vitter (R)	2nd	Omaha	Lee Terry (R)
2nd	New Orleans	William J. Jefferson (D)	3rd	Grand Island	Bill Barrett (R)
3rd	Houma	W.J. (Billy) Tauzin (D)	**Nevada**		
4th	Shreveport	Jim McCrery (R)	1st	Las Vegas	Shelley Berkley (D)
5th	Alexandria	John Cooksey (R)	2nd	Reno	Jim Gibbons (R)
6th	Baton Rouge	Richard H. Baker (R)	**New Hampshire**		
7th	Lake Charles	Christopher John (D)	1st	Manchester	John E. Sununu (R)
Maine			2nd	Concord	Charles Bass (R)
1st	Portland	Thomas H. Allen (D)	**New Jersey**		
2nd	Bangor	John Elias Baldacci (D)	1st	Camden	Robert E. Andrews (D)
Maryland			2nd	Atlantic City	Frank A. LoBiondo (R)
1st	Annapolis	Wayne T. Gilchrest (R)	3rd	Cherry Hill	Jim Saxton (R)
2nd	Towson	Robert L. Ehrlich Jr. (R)	4th	Trenton	Christopher H. Smith (R)
3rd	Baltimore	Benjamin L. Cardin (D)	5th	Ridgewood	Marge Roukema (R)
4th	Landover	Albert Russell Wynn (D)	6th	New Brunswick	Frank Pallone Jr. (D)
5th	Bowie	Steny H. Hoyer (D)	7th	Union	Bob Franks (R)
6th	Hagerstown	Roscoe G. Bartlett (R)	8th	Paterson	Bill Pascrell Jr. (D)
7th	Baltimore	Elijah E. Cummings (D)	9th	Hackensack	Steven R. Rothman (D)
8th	Rockville	Constance A. Morella (R)	10th	Newark	Donald M. Payne (D)
Massachusetts			11th	Morristown	Rodney P. Frelinghuysen (R)
1st	Pittsfield	John W. Olver (D)	12th	Princeton	Rush D. Holt (D)
2nd	Springfield	Richard E. Neal (D)	13th	Jersey City	Robert Menendez (D)
3rd	Worcester	James P. McGovern (D)	**New Mexico**		
4th	Brookline	Barney Frank (D)	1st	Albuquerque	Heather Wilson (R)
5th	Lowell	Martin T. Meehan (D)	2nd	Picacho	Joseph R. Skeen (R)
6th	Salem	John F. Tierney (D)	3rd	Santa Fe	Tom Udall (D)
7th	Lexington	Edward J. Markey (D)	**New York**		
8th	Cambridge	Michael E. Capuano (D)	1st	Centereach	Michael P. Forbes (R)
9th	Boston	John Joseph Moakley (D)	2nd	Babylon	Rick Lazio (R)
10th	Quincy	William D. Delahunt (D)	3rd	Westbury	Peter T. King (R)
Michigan			4th	Garden City	Carolyn McCarthy (D)
1st	Upper Peninsula	Bart Stupak (D)	5th	Queens	Gary L. Ackerman (D)
2nd	Muskegon	Peter Hoekstra (R)	6th	Jamaica	Gregory W. Meeks (D)
3rd	Grand Rapids	Vernon J. Ehlers (R)	7th	Flushing	Joseph Crowley (D)
4th	Houghton Lake	Dave Camp (R)	8th	Manhattan, West	Jerrold Nadler (D)
5th	Saginaw	James A. Barcia (D)	9th	Brooklyn	Anthony D. Weiner (D)
6th	Kalamazoo	Fred Upton (R)	10th	Brooklyn Heights	Edolphus Towns (D)
7th	Jackson	Nick Smith (R)	11th	Flatbush	Major R. Owens (D)
8th	Lansing	Debbie Stabenow (D)	12th	Brooklyn	Nydia M. Velázquez (D)
9th	Flint	Dale E. Kildee (D)	13th	Staten Island	Vito Fossella (R)
10th	Port Huron	David E. Bonior (D)	14th	Manhattan, East	Carolyn B. Maloney (D)

THE HOUSE OF REPRESENTATIVES

State/Dist.	City	Representative
New York		
15th	Harlem	Charles B. Rangel (D)
16th	Bronx	José E. Serrano (D)
17th	Yonkers	Eliot L. Engel (D)
18th	White Plains	Nita M. Lowey (D)
19th	Poughkeepsie	Sue W. Kelly (R)
20th	Newburgh	Benjamin A. Gilman (R)
21st	Albany	Michael R. McNulty (D)
22nd	Saratoga Springs	John E. Sweeney (R)
23rd	Utica	Sherwood L. Boehlert (R)
24th	Watertown	John M. McHugh (R)
25th	Syracuse	James T. Walsh (R)
26th	Kingston	Maurice D. Hinchey (D)
27th	Seneca Falls	Thomas M. Reynolds (R)
28th	Rochester	Louise McIntosh Slaughter (D)
29th	Niagara Falls	John J. LaFalce (D)
30th	Buffalo	Jack Quinn (R)
31st	Corning	Amo Houghton (R)
North Carolina		
1st	Greenville	Eva M. Clayton (D)
2nd	Raleigh	Bob Etheridge (D)
3rd	Outer Banks	Walter B. Jones (R)
4th	Raleigh-Durham	David E. Price (D)
5th	Winston-Salem	Richard Burr (R)
6th	Greensboro	Howard Coble (R)
7th	Wilmington	Mike McIntyre (D)
8th	Fayetteville	Robin Hayes (R)
9th	Charlotte	Sue Wilkins Myrick (R)
10th	Hickory	Cass Ballenger (R)
11th	Asheville	Charles H. Taylor (R)
12th	Charlotte	Melvin L. Watt (D)
North Dakota		
1st	At-Large	Earl Pomeroy (D)
Ohio		
1st	Cincinnati	Steve Chabot (R)
2nd	Indian Hill	Rob Portman (R)
3rd	Dayton	Tony P. Hall (D)
4th	Lima	Michael G. Oxley (R)
5th	Sandusky	Paul E. Gillmor (R)
6th	Portsmouth	Ted Strickland (D)
7th	Marysville	David L. Hobson (R)
8th	Hamilton	John A. Boehner (R)
9th	Toledo	Marcy Kaptur (D)
10th	Cleveland	Dennis Kucinich (D)
11th	Shaker Heights	Stephanie Tubbs Jones (D)
12th	Columbus	John R. Kasich (R)
13th	Oberlin	Sherrod Brown (D)
14th	Akron	Thomas C. Sawyer (D)
15th	Columbus	Debra Pryce (R)
16th	Canton	Ralph Regula (R)
17th	Youngstown	James A. Traficant Jr. (D)
18th	Steubenville	Robert W. Ney (R)
19th	Ashtabula	Steven C. LaTourette (R)
Oklahoma		
1st	Tulsa	Steve Largent (R)
2nd	Muskogee	Tom A. Coburn (R)
3rd	Marietta	Wes Watkins (R)
4th	Norman	J.C. Watts Jr. (R)
5th	Oklahoma City	Ernest J. Istook (R)
6th	Cheyenne	Frank D. Lucas (R)
Oregon		
1st	Portland	David Wu (D)
2nd	Medford	Greg Walden (R)
3rd	Portland	Earl Blumenauer (D)
4th	Eugene	Peter A. DeFazio (D)
5th	Salem	Darlene Hooley (D)
Pennsylvania		
1st	Philadelphia	Robert A. Brady (D)
2nd	West Philadelphia	Chaka Fattah (D)
3rd	NE Philadelphia	Robert A. Borski (D)
4th	Beaver	Ron Klink (D)
5th	State College	John Peterson (R)
6th	Reading	Tim Holden (D)
7th	Swarthmore	Curt Weldon (R)
8th	Bucks County	James C. Greenwood (R)
9th	Altoona	Bud Shuster (R)

State/Dist.	City	Representative
10th	Scranton	Don Sherwood (R)
11th	Wilkes-Barre	Paul E. Kanjorski (D)
12th	Johnstown	John P. Murtha (D)
13th	Villanova	Joseph M. Hoeffel (D)
14th	Pittsburgh	William J. Coyne (D)
15th	Allentown	Patrick J. Toomey (R)
16th	Lancaster	Joseph R. Pitts (R)
17th	Harrisburg	George W. Gekas (R)
18th	McKeesport	Michael F. Doyle (D)
19th	York	William F. Goodling (R)
20th	Washington	Frank Mascara (D)
21st	Erie	Phil English (R)
Rhode Island		
1st	Providence	Patrick J. Kennedy (D)
2nd	Warwick	Robert A. Weygand (D)
South Carolina		
1st	Charleston	Marshall "Mark" Sanford (R)
2nd	Columbia	Floyd Spence (R)
3rd	Anderson	Lindsey O. Graham (R)
4th	Spartanburg	Jim DeMint (R)
5th	Rock Hill	John M. Spratt Jr. (D)
6th	Florence	James E. Clyburn (D)
South Dakota		
1st	At-Large	John R. Thune (R)
Tennessee		
1st	Kingsport	William L. Jenkins (R)
2nd	Knoxville	John J. Duncan Jr. (R)
3rd	Chattanooga	Zach Wamp (R)
4th	Shelbyville	Van Hilleary (R)
5th	Nashville	Bob Clement (D)
6th	Murfreesboro	Bart Gordon (D)
7th	Memphis	Ed Bryant (R)
8th	Jackson	John S. Tanner (D)
9th	Memphis	Harold E. Ford Jr. (D)
Texas		
1st	Texarkana	Max Sandlin (D)
2nd	Lufkin	Jim Turner (D)
3rd	North Dalllas	Sam Johnson (R)
4th	Tyler	Ralph M. Hall (D)
5th	Dallas	Pete Sessions (R)
6th	Waxahachie	Joe Barton (R)
7th	Houston	Bill Archer (R)
8th	College Station	Kevin Brady (R)
9th	Beaumont	Nick Lampson (D)
10th	Austin	Lloyd Doggett (D)
11th	Waco	Chet Edwards (D)
12th	Fort Worth	Kay Granger (R)
13th	Amarillo	Mac Thornberry (R)
14th	Victoria	Ron Paul (R)
15th	McAllen	Rubén Hinojosa (D)
16th	El Paso	Silvestre Reyes (D)
17th	Abilene	Charles W. Stenholm (D)
18th	Houston	Sheila Jackson-Lee (D)
19th	Lubbock	Larry Combest (R)
20th	San Antonio	Charles A. Gonzalez (D)
21st	Midland	Lamar S. Smith (R)
22nd	Brazoria	Tom DeLay (R)
23rd	Laredo	Henry Bonilla (R)
24th	Arlington	Martin Frost (D)
25th	Pasadena	Ken Bentsen (D)
26th	Irving	Richard K. Armey (R)
27th	Corpus Christi	Solomon P. Ortiz (D)
28th	San Antonio	Ciro D. Rodriguez (D)
29th	Houston	Gene Green (D)
30th	Dallas	Eddie Bernice Johnson (D)
Utah		
1st	Ogden	James Hansen (R)
2nd	Salt Lake City	Merrill Cook (R)
3rd	Provo	Christopher Cannon (R)
Vermont		
1st	At-Large	Bernard Sanders (I)
Virginia		
1st	Newport News	Herbert H. Bateman (R)
2nd	Virginia Beach	Owen B. Pickett (D)
3rd	Norfolk	Robert C. Scott (D)
4th	Portsmouth	Norman Sisisky (D)

THE HOUSE OF REPRESENTATIVES

State/Dist.	City	Representative
Virginia		
5th	Charlottesville	Virgil H. Goode Jr. (D)
6th	Roanoke	Bob Goodlatte (R)
7th	Richmond	Tom Bliley (R)
8th	Alexandria	James P. Moran (D)
9th	Blacksburg	Rick Boucher (D)
10th	Arlington	Frank R. Wolf (R)
11th	Fairfax	Thomas M. Davis (R)
Washington		
1st	Redmond	Jay Inslee (D)
2nd	Everett	Jack Metcalf (R)
3rd	Olympia	Brian Baird (D)
4th	Yakima	Doc Hastings (R)
5th	Spokane	George R. Nethercutt Jr. (R)
6th	Tacoma	Norman D. Dicks (D)
7th	Seattle	Jim McDermott (D)
8th	Bellevue	Jennifer Dunn (R)
9th	Renton	Adam Smith (D)
West Virginia		
1st	Wheeling	Alan B. Mollohan (D)
2nd	Charleston	Robert E. Wise Jr. (D)
3rd	Huntington	Nick J. Rahall, II (D)
Wisconsin		
1st	Kenosha	Paul Ryan (R)

State/Dist.	City	Representative
2nd	Madison	Tammy Baldwin (D)
3rd	Eau Claire	Ron Kind (D)
4th	Milwaukee	Gerald D. Kleczka (D)
5th	Wauwatosa	Thomas M. Barrett (D)
6th	Oshkosh	Thomas Petri (R)
7th	Wausau	David R. Obey (D)
8th	Green Bay	Mark Green (R)
9th	Sheboygan	F. James Sensenbrenner Jr. (R)
Wyoming		
1st	At Large	Barbara Cubin (R)

NON-VOTING REPRESENTATIVES

American Samoa		Delegate Eni F. H. Faleomavaega (D)
Dist. of Columbia		Delegate Eleanor Holmes Norton (D)
Guam		Delegate Robert A. Underwood (D)
Puerto Rico		Resident Commissioner Carlos A. Romero-Barceló (D)
Virgin Island		Delegate Donna M. Christian-Green (D)

Note: D = Democrat; DFL = Democratic-Farmer-Labor (Minn.); I= Independent; IR = Independent Republican (Minn.); R = Republican. **Source:** Clerk of the U.S. House of Representatives.

General Accounting Office (GAO) 441 G Street NW Washington, D.C. 20548. (202) 512-3000. www.gao.gov. Created in 1921 by Budget and Accounting Act. Provides legal, accounting, auditing, and claims settlement services for Congress. Facilitates more efficient and effective government operations.

Government Printing Office (GPO) 732 North Capitol Street NW, Washington, D.C. 20401. (202) 512-0000. www.access.gpo.gov. Created June 23, 1860 by Congressional Joint Resolution 25. Provides printing and binding services for Congress and the departments and establishments of the Federal Government. Furnishes blank paper, ink, and supplies to all agencies. Prepares and distributes catalogs and Government publications.

Library of Congress 101 Independence Ave. SE Washington, D.C. 20540. (202) 707-5000. www.loc.gov. Created by law of April 24, 1800. Librarian appointed by the President. Buys books necessary for use by Congress and/or other governmental agencies. National library of the United States. Develops and maintains national book classification systems such as the Library of Congress and Dewey Decimal systems. Maintains and publishes The National Union Catalogs.

Congressional Budget Office (CBO) Second and D Streets SW Washington, D.C. 20515. (202) 226-2600. www.cbo.gov. Created by Congressional Budget Act of 1974. Provides Congress with basic budget data. Analyzes and evaluates alternative fiscal and budgetary policy options and programs and makes recommendations to Congress. Publishes annual report on the budget.

THE JUDICIAL BRANCH

▶ SUPREME COURT OF THE UNITED STATES

United States Supreme Court Building; 1 First St. NE, Washington, D.C. 20543. (202) 479-3000. Created by Judiciary Act of September 24, 1789 in accordance with Article III, Section 1 of the Constitution. Comprised of the chief justice and a number of associate justices to be fixed by Congress. Justices (including the chief justice) are chosen by the president with the advice and consent of the Senate and have lifetime tenure. Court terms begin the first Monday of October and usually last until the end of June. In recent years, the Court has seen the size of its docket nearly double (from 4,212 in 1970 to close to 8,000 in 1997), but it has heard fewer and fewer of these cases (see the accompanying table).

The Supreme Court, 1999

Name	Appointed by	Born	Law school
William H. Rehnquist (chief justice)	Nixon, 1972 Reagan, 1986	1924	Stanford
John Paul Stevens	Ford, 1975	1920	Northwestern
Sandra Day O'Connor	Reagan, 1981	1930	Stanford
Antonin Scalia	Reagan, 1986	1936	Harvard
Anthony M. Kennedy	Reagan, 1987	1936	Harvard
David H. Souter	Bush, 1990	1939	Harvard
Clarence Thomas	Bush, 1991	1948	Yale
Ruth Bader Ginsburg	Clinton, 1993	1933	Columbia
Stephen G. Breyer	Clinton, 1994	1945	Yale

►LOWER COURTS
U.S. Courts of Appeals

These intermediate appellate courts were created by act of March 3, 1891, to relieve the Supreme Court of having to reconsider all trials originally decided by Federal courts. Decisions of these courts are final except when law provides for direct review by the Supreme Court. Each of the 50 states is assigned to one of the following judicial circuits that compose the Court of Appeals system.

District of Columbia Circuit: Washington, D.C.
First Circuit: Maine, Massachusetts, New Hampshire, Rhode Island, Puerto Rico.
Second Circuit: Connecticut, New York, Vermont
Third Circuit: Delaware, New Jersey, Pennsylvania, Virgin Islands
Fourth Circuit: Maryland, North Carolina, South Carolina, Virginia, West Virginia
Fifth Circuit: Louisiana, Missisippi, Texas
Sixth Circuit: Kentucky, Michigan, Ohio, Tennessee
Seventh Circuit: Illinois, Indiana, Wisconsin
Eighth Circuit: Arkansas, Iowa, Minnesota, Missouri, Nebraska, North Dakota, South Dakota
Ninth Circuit: Alaska, Arizona, California, Guam, Hawaii, Idaho, Montana, Nevada, Northern Mariana Islands, Oregon, Washington
Tenth Circuit: Colorado, Kansas, New Mexico, Oklahoma, Utah, Wyoming
Eleventh Circuit: Alabama, Florida, Georgia
Federal Circuit

U.S. District Courts These are trial courts of general Federal jurisdiction. There are 89 courts in the 50 states, including at least one in each state and the District of Columbia. Each court has from 2 to 28 federal district judgeships, depending on the amount of work within the territory. Overall, there are 610 permanent district judges in the 50 states, 15 in the District of Columbia and 7 in Puerto Rico. Usually one judge is required to decide a case, but in some limited cases it is required that three judges be called together to comprise the court.

Administrative Office of the U.S. Courts

Thurgood Marshall Federal Judiciary Building, One Columbus Circle NE, Washington, D.C. 20544. (202)-273-0107. www.uscourts.gov Created by act of Aug. 7, 1939. Its areas of primary concern are administering courts, supervising probation office, and overseeing administration of bankruptcy courts, magistrate offices, and public defender's offices.

Federal Judicial Center
Thurgood Marshall Federal Judiciary Building, One Columbus Circle NE, Washington, D.C. 20002-8003. (202)-273-4000. www.fjc.gov. Created by act of Dec. 20, 1967. Its mission is to further the development and adoption of improved judicial administration in U.S. courts. The Chief Justice of the Supreme Court is the permanent chairman of the center's Board of Directors.

United States Sentencing Commission.
Suite 2-500, South Lobby, One Columbus Circle NE, Washington, D.C. 20002-8002. (202)-273-4500. wwww.ussc.gov. Created by the Sentencing Reform Act of 1984. Establishes sentencing guidelines (including forms and severity of punishment) for federal offenses.

Cases Before U.S. Supreme Court, U.S. Courts of Appeals, and U.S. District Courts, 1970–97

Status	1970	1980	1985	1990	1995	1996	1997
U.S. Supreme Court[1]							
Total cases on docket	4,212	5,144	5,158	6,316	7,565	7,602	7,692
Cases argued	151	154	171	125	90	90	96
Number of signed opinions	109	123	146	112	75	80	91
U.S. Courts of Appeals[2]							
Cases commenced	11,662	23,200	33,360	40,898	49,671	51,524	52,571
Cases terminated	10,699	20,887	31,387	38,520	50,085	49,359	51,295
Cases disposed of[3]	6,139	10,607	16,369	21,006	28,187	26,988	26,287
Median months to final disposition[4]	8.2	8.9	10.3	10.1	10.5	10.3	11.1
U.S. District Courts[2]							
Civil cases commenced[5]	87,300	168,800	273,700	217,900	239,013	272,661	265,200
Trials[5, 6]	8,000	10,100	12,300	9,200	7,700	7,500	7,400
Percent reaching trial	10.0%	6.5%	4.7%	4.3%	3.4%	3.1%	3.0%
Criminal cases commenced[5,7]	38,100	28,000	38,500	46,500	44,200	47,100	48,700
Defendants disposed of	36,400	36,600	47,400	56,500	55,300	59,500	62,100
Not convicted	8,200	8,000	8,800	9,800	9,000	8,500	7,500
Convicted	28,200	28,600	38,500	46,700	46,300	51,000	54,500

1. Statutory term of court begins first Monday in October. 2. For year ending June 30. 3. Terminated on the merits after hearing or submission. Beginning 1980, data not comparable with earlier years due to changes in criteria. 4. Prior to 1985, the figure is from filing of complete record to final disposition; beginning 1985, figure is from filing notice of appeal to final disposition. 5. Figures rounded in source. 6. A trial is defined as a contested proceeding (other than a hearing on a motion) before either court or jury in which evidence is introduced and final judgment sought. 7. Excludes transfers. **Source:** Office of the Clerk, Supreme Court of the United States, unpublished data; Administrative Office of the U.S. Courts, *Annual Report of the Director.*

THE EXECUTIVE BRANCH

▶EXECUTIVE OFFICE OF THE PRESIDENT

White House Office 1600 Pennsylvania Ave. NW, Washington, DC 20500 (202) 456-1414. www.whitehouse.gov. Serves president in performance of duties incident to his office. Maintains communication with Congress, individual members of Congress, heads of executive agencies, media, and public.

Office of the Vice President of the United States

Old Executive Office Building, Washington, DC 20501. (202) 456-2326. www.whitehouse.gov. Vice president participates in cabinet meetings and is, by statute, a member of National Security Council and board of regents of the Smithsonian Institution; serves as president of Senate; empowered to succeed to presidency pursuant to Article II and the 20th and 25th amendments to the Constitution.

Council of Economic Advisers

Old Executive Office Building; Washington, DC 20502. (202) 395-5084. www.whitehouse.gov/WH/EOP/CEA/html. Created by Employment Act of 1946. Council's three members—appointed by president—analyze the various segments of the economy, appraise and assess existing economic programs, recommend new economic programs, and assist in preparation President's economic reports to Congress.

Council on Environmental Quality

722 Jackson Place NW, Washington DC 20503. (202) 395-5750. www.whitehouse.gov/ceq/. Old Executive Office Building, Room 360, Washington DC 20501. (202) 456-6224. Created by National Environmental Policy Act of 1969. Recommends national policies to improve quality of environment. Analyzes environmental changes and trends. Assesses and evaluates existing environmental programs. Assists president in compiling annual environmental quality report to Congress.

National Security Council (NSC)

Old Executive Office Building, Washington DC 20506. (202) 456-1414. Created by National Security Act of 1947. Chaired by president. Members include vice president and secretaries of state and defense. Chairman of Joint Chiefs of Staff is statutory military adviser; CIA director is intelligence adviser. Advises president on integration of domestic, foreign, and military policies relating to national security.

Office of Administration

Old Executive Office Building, 725 17th St. NW, Washington, DC 20503. (202) 395-6963. Created December 12, 1977. Provides administrative services to all units within executive office except those in direct support of president.

Office of Management and Budget (OMB)

Executive Office Building, Washington, DC 20503. (202 -395-3080. www.whitehouse.gov/OMB/. Created July 1, 1970. Assists president in reviewing and assessing efficiency of structure and management of executive branch. Expands interagency cooperation. Assists president in preparing Government's budget and fiscal program. Supervises, controls, and administers the budget. Coordinates departmental advice and makes recommendations to president based on this advice. Plans, conducts, and promotes evaluation efforts to help president assess program objectives, performance, and efficiency. Keeps president informed of work planned and performed by the various Government agencies.

Office of National Drug Control Policy

Executive Office of the President, Washington, DC 20500. (202) 395-6700. www.whitehousedrugpolicy.gov. Created by National Narcotics Leadership Act of 1988. Coordinates Federal, state and local ef-

The Cabinet

The president is the administrative head of the executive branch of the Federal government. A creation of custom and tradition dating back to George Washington's administration, the Cabinet functions at the pleasure of the president. Its purpose is to advise the president on any subject on which he requests information. The Cabinet is composed of the heads of the 14 executive departments. In the Clinton Administration, Cabinet-level rank has been accorded to the officials listed below. (**Note:** As of Oct. 11, 1999)

President Bill Clinton
Vice President Albert Gore Jr.

Office	Officer
Secretary of State	Madeleine K. Albright
Secretary of the Treasury	Lawrence H. Summers
Secretary of Defense	William S. Cohen
Attorney General (Dept. of Justice)	Janet Reno
Secretary of the Interior	Bruce Babbitt
Secretary of Agriculture	Dan Glickman
Secretary of Commerce	William M. Daley
Secretary of Labor	Alexis M. Herman
Secretary of Health and Human Services	Donna E. Shalala
Secretary of Housing and Urban Development	Andrew M. Cuomo
Secretary of Transportation	Rodney E. Slater
Secretary of Energy	Bill Richardson
Secretary of Education	Richard W. Riley
Secretary of Veterans Affairs	Togo West Jr.
Chief of Staff	John Podesta
Director, Central Intelligence Agency	George Tenet
Chairman, Council of Economic Advisors	Janet Yellen
Administrator, Environmental Protection Agency	Carol Browner
Director, Federal Emergency Management Agency	James Lee Witt
Director, Office of Management and Budget	Jacob J. Lew
Director, Office of National Drug Control Policy	Barry McCaffrey
Administrator, Small Business Administration	Aida Alvarez
Ambassador to the United Nations	Richard C. Holbrooke
U.S. Trade Representative	Charlene Barshefsky

forts to control illegal drug abuse and devises national strategies to ensure that national anti-drug activities are carried out effectively.

Office of Policy Development
Old Executive Office Building, Washington, D.C. 20502. Comprised of the *Domestic Policy Council* (202-456-2216) and *National Economic Council* (202-456-6630), which are responsible for advising and assisting the president in the formulation, coordination, and implementation of domestic and economic policy.

Office of Science and Technology Policy
Old Executive Office Building, Washington, DC 20500. (202) 395-7347. www.whitehouse.gov/ostp.html. Created May 11, 1976. Serves as source of scientific, engineering, and technological analysis and expertise for president with respect to public policy in areas of economy, national security, health, foreign relations, and environment. Appraises sale, quality, and effectiveness of U.S. efforts in science and technology.

Office of the U.S. Trade Representative
600 17th St. NW, Washington, DC 20508. (202)-395-3230. Created as Office of the Special Representative for Trade Negotiations, Jan. 15, 1963. Congress made it agency of executive office under Trade Act of 1974. Sets and administers overall trade policy. Representative is chief U.S. representative for all activities of the General Agreement on Tariffs and Trade (GATT) and at discussions, meetings, and negotiations in most conferences in which trade and commodity are issues.

▶DEPARTMENT OF AGRICULTURE (USDA)
14th St. and Independence Ave. SW, Washington, DC 20250. (202) 720-2791. www.usda.gov. Created May 15, 1862; incorporated into Cabinet, Feb. 8, 1889. Improves and maintains farm income, develops agricultural markets abroad, curbs poverty, hunger, and malnutrition. Through inspection and grading services, safeguard standards of quality in the nation's food supply. The dept. was reorganized in 1994 into eight program or mission areas: *Rural Development, Alternative Agricultural Research & Commercialization Center, Marketing & Regulatory Programs, Food Safety, Food Nutrition & Consumer Services, Farm & Foreign Agriculture Services, Research Education & Economics,* and *Natural Resources & Environment.* Each program area is headed by an undersecretary of agriculture, and may be further divided into more specific agencies, such as the Rural Housing Service or the Food Safety and Inspection Service.

▶DEPARTMENT OF COMMERCE
14th St. between Constitution and Pennsylvania Avenues NW, Washington, DC 20230. (202) 482-2000. www.doc.gov. Created Feb. 14, 1903 as part of Dept. of Commerce and Labor. Redesignated Dept. of Commerce Mar. 4, 1913. Promotes international trade, economic growth, and technological advancement through encouragement of competitive free-enterprise system, prevention of unfair trade, granting of patents, promotion of tourism, and assistance in the growth of minority businesses. The department is divided into 12 operating units; only the major agencies are described in detail below.

Bureau of the Census
www.census.gov. Created Mar. 6, 1902 by act of Congress. Collects, tabulates, and publishes census statistics about America, its people, and its economy. Statistics are used by Congress, president, and public to aid development and evaluation of public policy. Population and housing censuses are performed every 10 years. Censuses of agriculture, state and local governments, manufacturers, mineral industries, distributive trades, and construction and transportation industries are performed every five years. Special censuses are performed on demand from state and local governments.

Economic Development Administration (EDA)
Created by Public Works and Economic Development Act of 1965. Promotes new jobs, protects existing jobs, and stimulates job growth in areas where unemployment is high or incomes are low.

International Trade Administration (ITA)
www.ita.gov. Created Jan. 2, 1980. Promotes world trade and strengthens U.S. position in relation to world trade and investment.

Minority Business Development Agency (MBDA)
www.mbda.gov. Created Nov. 1, 1979. Promotes minority business. Ensures effective, equitable, and competitive participation by minority business in free enterprise system.

National Oceanic and Atmospheric Administration (NOAA)
www.noaa.gov. Created Oct. 3, 1970. Investigates and maps oceans of world. Discovers, utilizes, and conserves living resources of oceans. Monitors and predicts conditions of atmosphere, sun, and oceans; warns against deterioration of these conditions arising from natural and man-made events and circumstances. Provides weather reports and forecasts. Forecasts floods, hurricanes, and other weather-related natural disasters.

Technology Administration
Created by Congress in 1988 and includes the Office of Technology, National Technical Information Service, and the National Institute of Standards and Technology. Works with U.S. industries to promote competitiveness and to maximize the impact of technology on economic growth.

▶DEPARTMENT OF DEFENSE (DOD)
The Pentagon, Washington, DC 20301-1155. (703) 545-6700. www.defenselink.mil. Created by National Security Act Amendments of 1949. Provides necessary military forces to deter war and protect security of the country. The three armed forces departments and the Organization of the Joint Chiefs of Staff comprise the military side of the Defense Dept. (Additional information can be found later in "National Defense.")

Organization of the Joint Chiefs of Staff
Consists of Chairman of Joint Chiefs of Staff, the chiefs of staff of the three armed forces departments, and the Commandant of the Marine Corps. Advises and assists president and secretary of defense on most military issues. Assists president and secretary of defense in planning, direction, and allocation of strategic resources.

Compares strengths and capabilities of American forces with those of potential adversaries.

Department of the Air Force   www.af.mil.
Created Sept. 18, 1947 by National Security Act of 1947. Works in conjunction with other armed forces to protect peace and security of the U.S. Focuses on air missions and protecting American interests from invasion by air.

Department of the Army   www2.army.mil.
U.S. Army created June 14, 1775 by Continental Congress. Dept. of the Army created 1947 by National Security Act of 1947. Organizes, trains, and equips active and reserve forces to protect peace, security, welfare, and defense of the U.S. Its mission focuses on land operations and maneuvers.

Department of the Navy   www.navy. mil.
U.S. Navy created Oct. 13, 1775, by Continental Congress. Dept. of the Navy created Apr. 30, 1798. Protects U.S. from attack by sea. Encompasses Marine Corps. Maintains freedom of the seas.

▶DEPARTMENT OF EDUCATION
600 Independence Ave. SW, Washington, DC 20202. (800) USA-LEARN. www. ed.gov. Created Oct. 17, 1979, by Dept. of Education Organization Act. Establishes policy for, administers, and coordinates almost all Federal assistance to education.

▶DEPARTMENT OF ENERGY (DOE)
1000 Independence Ave. SW, Washington, DC 20585. (202) 586-5000. www.doe.gov. Created Oct. 1, 1977, by Dept. of Energy Organization Act. Coordinates and administrates energy functions of Federal Government, including research and development of energy technology, marketing Federal power, energy conservation, nuclear weapons, and energy regulation.

▶DEPARTMENT OF HEALTH AND HUMAN SERVICES (HHS)
200 Independence Ave. SW, Washington, DC 20201. (202) 619-0257. www.dhhs.gov. Created Apr. 11, 1953, as Dept. of Health, Education, and Welfare. Re-designated Dept. of Health and Human Services Oct. 17, 1979, by Dept. of Education Organization Act. Advises president in formulation of public policy regarding health, welfare, and income and security programs. The department is divided into 12 major administrations and agencies; only the major agencies are described in detail below

Administration for Children and Families (ACF)   www.acf.gov. Created April 15, 1991. Administers child welfare services, foster care and child care programs, the Head Start Program, and other family preservation and support services.

Centers for Disease Control and Prevention (CDC)   www.cdc.gov. Reorganized, Nov. 9, 1995. Responsible for protecting the public health by preventing and controlling diseases.

Food and Drug Administration (FDA)
www.fda.gov. Created by Agriculture Appropriation Act of 1931; reorganized into HHS Dept. Nov. 9, 1995. It protects the health of the nation against impure and unsafe foods, drugs, cosmetics, and other hazards.

Health Care Financing Administration (HCFA)   www.hcfa.gov. Created Mar. 8, 1977. Oversees Medicare and Medicaid Health Insurance and grant programs. (See the section on "Social Insurance Programs" for additional information about these programs).

National Institutes of Health (NIH)
www.nih.gov. Reorganized, Nov. 1995. The principal biomedical research agency of the Federal Government, its mission is to employ science in the pursuit of knowledge to improve human health conditions.

Substance Abuse and Mental Health Services Administration   www.samhsa.gov. Disseminates accurate and up-to-date information on and provides leadership in the prevention and treatment of addictive and mental disorders.

▶DEPARTMENT OF HOUSING AND URBAN DEVELOPMENT (HUD)
451 Seventh St. SW, Washington, DC 20410. (202) 708-1422. www.hud.gov. Created Nov. 9, 1965, by Dept. of Housing and Urban Development Act. Administers mortgage programs to help families become homeowners. Fosters construction of new housing and renovation of existing rental housing. Provides aid for low-income families who cannot afford their rent. Enacts programs to prevent housing discrimination. Encourages strong private sector housing industry.

▶DEPARTMENT OF THE INTERIOR
1849 C St. NW, Washington, DC 20240. (202) 208-3171. www.doi.gov. Created Mar. 3, 1849. Principal U.S. conservation agency. Directs use and conservation of public lands and natural resources; administers over 500 million acres of Federal land and has trust responsibilities for approximately 50 million acres, mostly Indian reservations. Prescribes use of land and water resources, fish and wildlife, national parks and historic places, and mineral resources; aids in preservation of American Indian reservation communities.

United States Fish and Wildlife Service
www.fws.gov. Conserves and protects fish and wildlife and their habitats. Assesses environmental impact of pesticides, thermal pollution, hydroelectric dams, and nuclear power sites.

National Park Service   www.nps.gov. Created Aug. 25, 1916. Administers, protects, and maintains diverse system of national parks, monuments, historic areas, and recreation areas and encourages understanding of the historic value of these sites through lectures, tours, exhibits, and films.

U.S. Geological Survey   www.usgs.gov. Created Mar. 3, 1879. Identifies and classifies land, water, energy, and mineral resources. Investigates potential hazards such as earthquakes and volcanoes. Conducts topographic mapping.

Bureau of Indian Affairs   www.usgs.gov/ doi/bureau-indian-affairs.html. Created 1824 as part of Dept. of War. Transferred to Dept. of Interior in 1849. Trains American Indian and Alaska native peoples to manage their own affairs under trust relationship to Federal Government.

Facilitates public and private aid to advancement of these peoples.

Bureau of Land Management (BLM)
www.blm.gov. Created July 16, 1946, by consolidation of the General Land Office and the Grazing Service. Manages 270 million acres of public lands primarily in Far West and in Alaska. Resources in these lands include timber, oil, gas, hard minerals, and wildlife habitats.

▶ DEPARTMENT OF JUSTICE
Constitution Avenue and 10th St. NW, Washington, DC 20530. (202) 514-2000. www.usdoj.gov. Created June 22, 1870. Enforces the law in the public interest. Ensures fair competition in free enterprise system; enforces drug, immigration, and naturalization laws; Conducts all Supreme Court suits in which U.S. is party or is concerned. Advises president on legal matters.

Federal Bureau of Investigation (FBI)
www.fbi.gov. Created 1908. Principal investigative bureau of Justice Dept. Investigates violations of Federal law. Areas of primary concern are organized crime (including drug trafficking), terrorism, white-collar crime, and foreign counter-intelligence.

Bureau of Prisons
Imprisons and rehabilitates criminals convicted of Federal crimes and sentenced to serve time in Federal prison.

United States Marshals Service
Provides security and support to Federal court system. Apprehends Federal fugitives. Ensures safety of Federal witnesses. Executes court orders and arrest warrants. Maintains custody, manages, and sells property seized from criminals.

Immigration and Naturalization Service (INS)
Created Mar. 3, 1891. Controls immigration into U.S. by facilitating entry to qualified persons and denying admission to unqualified aliens. Deports illegal aliens already in U.S. Encourages and facilitates naturalization and citizenship.

Drug Enforcement Administration (DEA)
Created July 1973. Investigates interstate drug-trafficking. Enforces Government regulations regarding manufacture, distribution, sale, and dispensing of controlled substances;

▶ DEPARTMENT OF LABOR
200 Constitution Ave NW, Washington, DC 20210. (202) 219-5000. www.dol.gov. Created Mar. 4, 1913. Improves welfare and working conditions of wage earners. Guarantees minimum wages and overtime pay as well as unemployment insurance and workers' compensation. Prevents employment discrimination. Protects pension rights. Provides for job training programs. Pays special attention to labor-related needs of minority workers, old and young, women, and disabled people.

Employment and Training Administration (ETA)
www.doleta.gov. Provides employment security through unemployment insurance, worker dislocation programs, and Federal-state employment service system. Trains or retrains and finds employment for disadvantaged workers through Job Training Partnership Act (JTPA).

Pension and Welfare Benefits Administration (PWBA)
www.dol.gov/dol/pwba/. Created Sept. 2, 1974, by Employment Retirement Income Security Act of 1974 (ERISA). Requires private pension and welfare plan administrators to give participants summaries of pension and welfare plans. Keeps summaries on file. Regulates financial operations of pension and welfare plans.

Occupational Safety and Health Administration (OSHA)
www.osha.gov. Created 1970 by Occupational Safety and Health Act. Promotes safety and health standards in workplace. Issues regulations, conducts investigations, issues citations, and proposes penalties for violations of health standards and regulations.

Bureau of Labor Statistics (BLS)
www.bls.gov. Data-gathering agency. Collects, processes, interprets, and distributes data involving employment, unemployment, wages, family income and expenditures, worker's compensation, industrial relations, productivity, and technological change.

Veteran's Employment and Training Service (VETS)
Maximizes training and employment opportunities for veterans and disabled. Ensures that legislation involving veterans is carried out by local public employment services and by private enterprise.

▶ DEPARTMENT OF STATE
2201 C Street NW; Washington, D.C. 20520. (202) 647-4000. www.state.gov. Created July 27, 1789, as Dept. of Foreign Affairs. Renamed Dept. of State Sept. 15, 1789. Advises president on foreign policy. Formulates and executes policy to protect and defend American interests overseas. Negotiates treaties and agreements with foreign countries.

United States Mission to the United Nations
Represents U.S. at UN. Carries out U.S. foreign policy as it relates to UN.

Foreign Service
Maintains relations with more than 140 nations around world. Reports to State Dept. on developments relating to safety and welfare of U.S., its citizens, and their interests. Ambassadors to each country are personal representatives of the president and have full responsibility for carrying out U.S. foreign policy within the country. Ambassadors negotiate agreements between host country and U.S., explain and administer U.S. foreign policy, and maintain relations with government and public of host country.

▶ DEPARTMENT OF TRANSPORTATION (DOT)
400 Seventh St. SW, Washington, DC 20590. (202) 366-4000. www.dot.gov. Created Oct. 15, 1966. Establishes nation's comprehensive transportation policy. Several umbrella administrations are responsible for highway planning, development, and construction; urban mass transit; railroads; aviation; and the safety of waterways, ports, highways, and oil and gas pipelines.

United States Coast Guard
www.uscg. mil. Created Jan. 28, 1915. Included in Dept. of Transportation Apr. 1, 1967. Coast Guard is at all

times a branch of armed forces and a service with Dept. of Transportation except when operating as part of Navy during war. Primary maritime law enforcement agency for U.S. Suppresses drug smuggling and trafficking. Licenses marine vessels. Administers and inspects violations of safety standards for design, construction, equipment and maintenance of commercial marine vessels and offshore structures in U.S. waters. Provides search and rescue functions for saving lives and property in U.S. waters. Operates ice-breaking vessels to facilitate marine transportation.

Federal Aviation Administration (FAA)

www.faa.gov. Created 1958 by Federal Aviation Act. Included in Dept. of Transportation in 1967. Regulates air commerce in effort to promote safety and secure national defense interests. Directs use of navigable U.S. airspace. Develops and operates system of air traffic control for both civil and military aircraft. Regulates aircraft noise.

Federal Highway Administration (FHWA)

www.fhwa.dot.gov. Included in Dept. of Transportation in 1967 by Dept. of Transportation Act. Promotes highway safety. Provides aid for construction and maintenance of state and Federal highway systems.

Federal Railroad Administration (FRA)

www.fra.dot.gov. Created by Dept. of Transportation Act of 1966. Administers and enforces railroad safety regulations such as track maintenance, inspection and equipment standards, and operating practices.

National Highway Traffic Safety Administration

www.nhtsa.dot.gov. Created by Highway Safety Act of 1970. Research and development programs are aimed at reducing number of highway collisions, reducing severity of injuries and economic loss involved in highway accidents, and reducing fatalities resulting from highway crashes.

Federal Transit Administration

www.fta.dot.gov. Created July 1, 1968. Improves equipment and methods used in urban mass transit. Encourages planning of cost-effective mass transit systems. Provides economic and technical assistance for mass transit programs.

Maritime Administration (MARAD)

www.marad.dot.gov. Created May 24, 1950. Included in Dept. of Transportation Aug. 6, 1981, by Maritime Act of 1981. Constructs or supervises construction of U.S. flag merchant ships for Federal government. Generates business for U.S. ships. Develops ports and facilities for maritime transport.

Saint Lawrence Seaway Development Corporation

www.dot.gov/slsdc/. Created May 13, 1954. Owns, develops, maintains, and operates St. Lawrence Seaway between Montreal and Lake Erie within territorial limits of U.S. Provides safe and efficient waterway for maritime commerce.

Research and Special Programs Administration

www.rspa.dot.gov. Created Sept. 23, 1977. Responsible for transportation of hazardous materials and pipeline safety. Oversees Office of Hazardous Materials Safety.

Bureau of Transportation Statistics

www.bts.gov. Created by Transportation Efficiency Act of 1991. Compiles, analyzes, and disseminates statistics and other information on the nation's transportation systems.

Surface Transportation Board

www.stb.dot.gov. Created by ICC Termination Act of 1995. A bipartisan adjudicatory body whose three members are appointed by the President with the Senate's consent. It judges disputes over the various laws pertaining to interstate surface transportation.

▶DEPARTMENT OF THE TREASURY

1500 Pennsylvania Ave. NW, Washington, DC 20220. (202) 622-2000. www.treas.gov. Created Sept. 2, 1789. Formulates and recommends economic, financial, and fiscal policies. Acts as financial agent for U.S. Government. Manufactures coins and currency.

Bureau of Alcohol, Tobacco and Firearms

www.atf.treas.gov/. Created July 1, 1972. Enforces and administers laws regulating production, use, distribution, and sale of alcohol and tobacco products, firearms, and explosives. Bureau's objectives are to eliminate illegal trafficking, possession and use of firearms and explosives, to suppress illegal alcohol and tobacco trafficking, and to ensure safety of storage facilities for explosives.

United States Customs Service

www.customs.treas.gov/. Created Mar. 3, 1927 as Bureau of Customs. Re-designated Customs Service Apr. 4, 1973. Collects revenue from imports. Enforces customs treaties. Assesses and collects customs duties, excise taxes, fees, and penalties on imported merchandise. Seizes contraband including narcotics and illegal drugs. Processes people, mail, carriers, and cargo in and out of U.S. Apprehends violators of U.S. customs regulations and related laws including copyright, patent, and trademark, and import quotas. Suppresses traffic of illegal narcotics, pornography, counterfeit monetary instruments; quarantines animals, plants, and foods.

Bureau of Engraving and Printing

www.bep.treas.gov/. Created July 11, 1862. Designs, prints, and finishes Federal Reserve notes, U.S. postage stamps, identification cards, and Treasury securities. Inhibits counterfeiting of these documents.

Internal Revenue Service (IRS)

www.irs.gov. Created July 1, 1862. Administers and enforces internal revenue laws except those relating to alcohol, tobacco, firearms, and explosives. Determines, assesses, and collects Federal tax revenues from public. Encourages, assesses, and enforces compliance with tax laws.

United States Mint

www.usmint.treas.gov/. Mint of the United States created Apr. 2, 1792. Bureau of the Mint created Feb. 12, 1873. Renamed United States Mint Jan. 9, 1984. Manufactures and distributes coins for circulation through Federal Reserve Banks. Mints foreign coins. Processes gold and silver bullion. Manufactures national medals, proof coin sets, and commemorative coins for sale to public.

Bureau of the Public Debt   www.publicdebt.
treas.gov/. Created June 30, 1940. Manages public
debt. Offers public debt securities. Audits retired
securities and interest coupons. Maintains accounting control over public debt receipts and
expenditures, securities, and interest costs. Adju-
dicates claims of lost, stolen, or destroyed securities.

United States Secret Service   www.treas.
gov.usss/. Protects president and vice president
(and president-elect and vice president-elect) of
U.S. and their families. Protects former presidents
and their wives until their death. Protects distinguished foreign visitors and U.S. officials abroad
at direction of president. Detects and apprehends
counterfeiters. Suppresses forgery of government
securities and documents.

Office of Thrift Supervision (OTS)   1700
G St., NW, Washington, DC 20552. (202) 906-6913.
www.ots.treas.gov. Created by the Financial Institutions Reform, Recovery and Enforcement Act,
Aug. 9, 1989. Established by Congress as part of a
reorganization of the thrift regulatory structure,
the OTS has authority to charter Federal thrift institutions, and to serve as the primary regulator of
Federal and state chartered thrifts belonging to
the Savings Association Insurance Fund (SAIF).

▶**DEPARTMENT OF VETERANS
AFFAIRS**
810 Vermont Ave. NW, Washington, DC 20420.
(202) 273-4900. www.va.gov. Created by Dept. of
Veterans Affairs Act of 1988; predecessor Veterans
Administration created 1930. Administers benefit
programs for veterans and their families, including military-related death or disability compensation, pensions, education and rehabilitation,
home loan guaranty, medical care programs, and
the National Cemetery System.

Veterans Health Administration   Provides hospital, nursing home, and outpatient care
to eligible veterans. Operates over 100 medical
centers, nearly 400 outpatient clinics, over 100
nursing home care units and many Vietnam Veteran Outreach Centers.

Veterans Benefit Administration   Has responsibility for claims for disability compensation
and pension, specially adapted housing and automobiles, special clothing allowances, and emergency officers' retirement pay, survivors' claims
for death compensation, dependency and indemnity compensation, burial and plot allowance
claims, and reimbursement for headstones.

▶**INDEPENDENT ESTABLISHMENTS,
   CORPORATIONS, AND QUASI-
   OFFICIAL AGENCIES**
African Development Foundation   1400
Eye St. NW, Washington, DC 20005. (202) 673-
3916. www.adf.gov. Created in 1984 by African
Development Foundation Act. Nonprofit Govern-
ment corporation. Through grants, loans, and
loan guarantees, aids self-help efforts by poor
people in African countries.

**AMTRAK (National Railroad Passenger
Corporation)**   60 Massachusetts Ave. NE,
Washington, DC 20002. (202) 906-3000. www.
amtrak.com. Created by Rail Passenger Service
Act of 1970. Develops, operates, and improves

inter-city rail passenger service to create national
rail transportation system.

Central Intelligence Agency (CIA)
Washington, DC 20505. (703) 482-1100. www.
odci.gov/cia. Created by National Security Act of
1947. Under direction of president and National
Security Council. Advises NSC on intelligence
matters of national security. Collects, evaluates,
and disseminates intelligence information relating to national security and to drug production
and trafficking. Collects, produces, and disseminates counterintelligence and foreign intelligence
here (in conjunction with FBI) and abroad. Conducts special activities as directed by president.
Protects security of its activities, information, and
personnel by necessary and appropriate means.

**Commodity Futures Trading Commis-
sion (CFTC)**   1155 21st St. NW, Washington,
DC 20581. (202) 418-5000. www.cftc.gov/. Created
May 14, 1973 by Commodity Futures Act of 1973.
Regulates trading on the 11 U.S. futures exchanges. Regulates activities of commodity exchange members, public brokerage houses,
commodity trading advisers, and other related
employees.

**Consumer Product Safety Commission
(CPSC)**   East-West Towers, 4330 East-West
Highway, Bethesda, Md. 20814. www.cpsc.gov.
(301) 504-0580. Created May 14, 1973 by Consumer Product Safety Act. Protects public from
unreasonable risk of injury from consumer products. Develops, enforces, and evaluates safety
standards for consumer products.

**Corporation for National Community
Service**   1201 New York Ave. NW, Washington,
DC 20525. (202) 606-5000. www.nationalservice.
gov. Created by National and Community Service
Act of 1993. Incorporates programs previously administered by ACTION. Administers agencies
such as AmeriCorps and AmeriCorps VISTA,
which encourage and provide national and community service by volunteers, schools, and retired
and senior volunteers.

Defense Nuclear Facilities Safety Board
625 Indiana Ave. NW, Suite 700, Washington, D.C.
20004. (202) 208-6400. www.dnfsb.gov. Created
by Atomic Energy Act of 1954; established as independent agency Sept. 29, 1988. Reviews and evaluates standards for defense nuclear facilities of
the Department of Energy. Investigates practices
that may imperil public health and safety.

Environmental Protection Agency (EPA)
401 M St. SW, Washington, DC 20460. (202) 260-
2090. www.epa.gov. Created Dec. 2, 1970. Protects
and enhances environment. Controls and reduces pollution of air and water. Regulates solid-
waste disposal and use of pesticides, radiation,
and toxic substances.

**Equal Employment Opportunity Com-
mission (EEOC)**   1801 L St. NW, Washington,
DC 20507. (202) 663-4900. www.eeoc.gov. Created
July 2, 1965, by Title VII of Civil Rights Act of 1964.
Protects against discrimination based on race,
color, handicap, religion, sex, age, and national
origin in hiring, promoting, firing, wages, testing,
training, apprenticeship, and all other terms and
conditions of employment.

Export-Import Bank of the United States 811 Vermont Ave. NW, Washington, DC 20571. (800) 565-EXIM. www.exim.gov. Created Feb. 2, 1934. Facilitates and aids exports of U.S. goods and services through loans, loan guarantees, and insurance to exporters and private banks.

Farm Credit Administration 1501 Farm Credit Drive, McLean, Va. 22102-5090. (703) 883-4056. www.fca.gov. Created by Farm Credit Act of 1971. Regulates and examines programs, banks, associations, and organizations of the Farm Credit System, which provides credit to farmers, ranchers, producers of farm products, rural home owners, and associations and organizations of farmers, ranchers, and farm-equipment producers.

Federal Communications Commission (FCC) 1919 M Street NW, Washington, DC 20554. (888) 225-5322. www.fcc.gov. Created by Communications Act of 1934. Regulates interstate and foreign communications by radio, television, wire, and cable. Oversees development of broadcast services and the rapid and efficient provision of telephone and telegraph services nationwide.

Federal Deposit Insurance Corporation (FDIC) 550 17th St. NW, Washington, DC 20429. (202) 393-8400. www.fdic.gov. Created June 16, 1933, by Federal Reserve Act. Protects money supply by insuring deposits in and reviewing operations of state-chartered banks that are not members of the Federal Reserve System. Assumed responsibility for insuring savings and loan institutions formerly insured by defunct Federal Savings and Loan Insurance Corp. (FSLIC) in 1989.

Federal Election Commission (FEC) 999 E St. NW, Washington, DC 20463. (800) 424-9530. www.fec.gov. Created by Federal Election Campaign Act of 1971. Provides public funding for presidential elections. Ensures public disclosure of campaign finance activities. Administers and enforces contribution and spending limits for Federal elections. (See also "U.S. Presidential Elections.")

Federal Emergency Management Agency (FEMA) 500 C St. SW, Washington, DC 20472. (202) 646-4600. www.fema.gov Created Mar. 31, 1979. Provides single point of accountability for all Federal emergency preparedness, mitigation, and response activities. Facilitates most efficient use of resources in cases of natural or man-made emergencies.

Federal Labor Relations Authority (FLRA) 607 14th St. NW, Washington, DC 20424 (202) 482-6550. www.flra.gov. Created Jan. 1, 1979. Protects rights of Federal employees to organize, bargain collectively, and participate in labor organizations. Oversees rights and obligations of Federal employees and the labor organizations that represent them.

Federal Maritime Commission 800 North Capitol St. NW, Washington, D.C. 20573-0001. (202) 523-5707. www.fmc.gov. Created August 12, 1961. Regulates waterborne foreign commerce, insures that U.S. international trade is open to all nations on fair and equitable terms, and protects against unauthorized, concerted activity in U.S. waterborne commerce.

Federal Reserve System Board of Governors of Federal Reserve System. 20th St. and Constitution Ave. NW, Washington, DC 20551. (202) 452-3000. www.federalreserve.gov. Created Dec. 23, 1913, by Federal Reserve Act. Central Bank of U.S. Administers and creates national credit and monetary policy. Regulates money supply. Maintains soundness of banking industry. (See also the section on "The U.S. Economy").

Federal Trade Commission (FTC) Pennsylvania Ave. at Sixth St. NW, Washington, DC 20580. (202) 326-2222. www.ftc.gov. Created in 1914 by Federal Trade Commission Act and Clayton Act. Maintains free and fair competition in free enterprise system. Breaks up monopolies. Seeks to prevent corruption, restraints on trade, and unfair trade practices.

General Services Administration (GSA) General Service Building, 18th and F Sts. NW, Washington, DC 20405. (202) 708-5082. www.gsa.gov. Created July 1, 1949, by Federal Property and Administrative Services Act of 1949. Establishes policy for and manages Government property and records, construction of buildings, distribution of supplies, and other Government services. Its services are divided among four service agencies: the *Information Resources Management Services,* the *Federal Supply Service,* the *Public Buildings Service (PBS),* and the *Federal Property Resources Service (FPRS).*

Inter-American Foundation 901 North Stuart St., Arlington, Va. 22203. (703) 841-3800. Created by Congress in 1969. Supports social and economic development in Latin America and Caribbean. Makes grants to self-help organizations for the poor.

National Aeronautics and Space Administration (NASA) 300 E. Street SW, Washington, DC 20546. (202) 358-0000. www.nasa.gov. Created by National Aeronautics and Space Act of 1958. Develops, constructs, tests, and operates vehicles for in-flight research within and outside Earth's atmosphere. Disseminates information about space exploration and agency's activities.

National Archives and Records Administration (NARA) 8601 Adelphi Rd., College Park, Md. 20740-6001. (301) 713-6800. www.nara.gov. Created Oct. 19, 1984. Establishes policy for managing records of U.S. Government and making them available to public. Maintains 11 regional archives and 14 Federal records centers, as well as 11 presidential libraries or collections.

National Capital Planning Commission 801 Pennsylvania Ave. NW, Suite 301, Washington, D.C. 20576. www.ncpc.gov. Created as a park planning agency by act of June 6, 1924. Serves as the central planning agency for development activities for Federal lands in the National Capital region in and around Washington.

National Credit Union Administration (NCUA) 1775 Duke St., Alexandria, Va. 22314-3428. (703) 518-6300. www.ncua.gov. Created Mar. 10, 1970. Charters, insures, supervises, and examines Federal credit unions. Administers National Credit Union Share Insurance Fund. Supplies emergency loans to credit unions through Central Liquidity Facility.

National Foundation on the Arts and the Humanities
1100 Pennsylvania Ave. NW, Washington, DC 20506. Created by National Foundation on the Arts and the Humanities Act of 1965. Its three divisions encourage and support national progress in humanities and arts. The *National Endowment for the Arts (NEA)* (202-682-5400) fosters professional excellence in arts. The *National Endowment for the Humanities (NEH)* (202-606-8400; www.neh.gov) is an independent grant-making agency that supports research, education, and public programs in humanities. The *Institute of Museum and Library Services (IMS)* (202-606-8536; www.imls.fed.gov) assists museums in maintaining, increasing, and improving services to public.

National Labor Relations Board (NLRB)
1099 14th Street NW, Washington, DC 20570. (202) 273-1000. www.nlrb.gov. Created by National Labor Relations Act of 1935 (also known as Wagner Act). Administers Federal labor law. Safeguards employees' rights to organize, conducts elections to determine whether workers want unions as their bargaining representative, and prevents or remedies unfair labor practices.

National Mediation Board
1301 K Street NW, Suite 250 East, Washington, DC 20572. (202) 523-5920. www.nmb.gov. Created June 21, 1934, by amendment to Railway Labor Act. Resolves and investigates representation disputes in railroad and airline industries that could interrupt flow of commerce and endanger national economy.

National Railroad Passenger Corporation
See "AMTRAK"

National Science Foundation (NSF)
4201 Wilson Blvd., Arlington, Va. 22230. (703) 306-1234. www.nsf.gov. Created by National Science Foundation Act of 1950. Promotes progress of science and engineering through support of research and education programs.

National Transportation Safety Board (NTSB)
490 L'Enfant Plaza SW, Washington, DC 20594. (202) 314-6000. www.ntsb.gov. Created Apr. 1, 1975, by Independent Safety Board Act of 1974. Ensures safe operation of all types of transportation in U.S. Investigates accidents, conducts studies, and makes policy recommendations to government agencies, transportation industry, and others.

Nuclear Regulatory Commission (NRC)
Washington, DC 20555. (301) 415-7000. www.nrc.gov. Created by Energy Reorganization Act of 1974. Licenses and regulates uses of civilian nuclear energy to protect public health and environment. Sets licensing regulations, issues licenses for, and inspects construction, ownership, and operation of nuclear reactors and other nuclear materials.

Office of Personnel Management (OPM)
1900 E St. NW, Washington, DC 20415. (202) 606-1800. www.opm.gov. Created Jan. 1, 1979. Recruits, examines, trains, and promotes people for Government jobs, regardless of race, religion, sex, political influence, and other nonmerit factors.

Provides direct benefits, including health and life insurance, to employees and to retired employees and their survivors.

Panama Canal Commission
1825 Eye St. NW, Suite 1050, Washington, DC 20006. (202) 634-6441. www.pancanal.gov. Created by Panama Canal Act of 1979. Operates, maintains, and improves the Panama Canal to provide safe and economical transit for world shipping. Will perform these functions until expiration of Panama Canal Treaty of 1979 on Dec. 31, 1999, when Republic of Panama will assume full responsibility for canal.

Peace Corps
1111 20th St. NW, Washington, DC 20526. (202) 692-2000. www.peacecorps.gov. Created by Peace Corps Act of 1961. Promotes world peace and friendship. Helps people of other countries develop manpower by bringing U.S. volunteers abroad to participate in public works programs. Special emphasis placed on helping the poorest areas of countries served by the Peace Corps.

Pension Benefit Guaranty Corporation (PBGC)
1200 K St. NW, Washington, DC 20005. (202) 326-4000. www.pbgc.gov. Created Sept. 2, 1974, by Title IV of Employee Retirement Income Security Act of 1974. Guarantees payment of nonforfeitable pension benefits in covered private sector defined benefit pension plans.

Postal Rate Commission
1333 H St. NW, Washington, DC 20268-0001. (202) 789-6800. www.prc.gov. Created Aug. 12, 1970, by Postal Reorganization Act. Recommends changes in postal rates, fees, services, programs, studies, and mail classification schedules. Hears complaints about postal rates, services, and fees.

Securities and Exchange Commission (SEC)
450 Fifth St. NW, Washington, DC 20549. (202) 942-4150. www.sec.gov. Created July 2, 1934 by Securities Exchange Act of 1934. Provides fullest possible disclosure to the public of securities sales, operations, and registrations. Protects public against malpractice in securities and financial markets.

Selective Service System
National Headquarters, Arlington, Va. 22209-2425. (703) 605-4000. www.sss.gov. Created June 24, 1948, by Military Selective Service Act. Requires registration, and maintains list of males age 18-26 eligible to serve in armed forces in case of national security emergency.

Small Business Administration (SBA)
409 Third St. SW, Washington, DC 20416. (202) 205-6600. www.sba.gov. Created by Small Business Act of 1953. Aids, counsels, makes loans to, and protects interests of small businesses; ensures that they receive a fair amount of Government purchases and contracts.

Social Security Administration
6401 Security Blvd., Baltimore, Md. 21235. (410) 965-1234. www.ssa.gov. Created July 16, 1946; made independent agency by Social Security Independence Act of 1994. Manages the nation's social insurance program, consisting of retirement, survivors, and disability insurance programs, commonly known as Social Security. Also administers the Supplemental Security Income program for

the aged, blind, and disabled. Studies poverty and recommends solutions. Assigns Social Security numbers to all U.S. workers.

Tennessee Valley Authority (TVA) 400 West Summit Hill Dr., Knoxville, Tenn. 37902. (615) 632-2101. 1 Massachusetts Ave. NW, Washington, DC 20444-0001. (202)-898-2999. www.tva. gov. Created May 18, 1933. Government-owned corporation. Conducts resource development programs for advancement of growth in Tennessee Valley region. Controls floods, develops navigation, produces electric power, develops fertilizer, improves recreation, and develops forestry and wildlife.

United States Commission on Civil Rights 624 Ninth St. NW, Washington, DC 20425. (202) 376-8177. www.usccr.gov. Created by Civil Rights Act of 1957. Collects and studies information on discrimination based on race, color, religion, age, sex, handicap, or national origin. Assures equal protection in voting rights and enforcement of civil rights laws. Promotes equal opportunity in education, employment, and housing.

United States Information Agency (USIA) 301 Fourth St. SW, Washington, DC 20547. (202) 619-4700. www.usia.gov. Created by United States Information and Educational Exchange Act of 1948 and Mutual Educational and Cultural Exchange Act of 1961. Oversees and administers overseas information and cultural programs, including Voice of America and Fulbright scholarship program. Strengthens foreign understanding of American society and tries to obtain support abroad for U.S. foreign policies. Advises president and National Security Council on worldwide opinion of U.S. policies.

United States International Development Cooperation Agency (IDCA) 1300 Pennsylvania Ave. NW, Washington, DC 20523-0001. (202) 712-0000. Created Oct. 1, 1979. Plans, sets, and coordinates policy relevant to international economic issues affecting developing countries. It is divided into two umbrella agencies. The *Agency for International Development (AID)* (www.infousaid.gov) carries out economic assistance and self-help programs for people in developing countries. The *Overseas Private Investment Corporation (OPIC)* (www.opic.gov) facilitates, fosters, and encourages U.S. investments in more than 100 foreign countries that both reap profits for investors and help the social and economic development of the countries.

United States International Trade Commission 500 E St. SW, Washington, DC 20436. (202) 205-2000. www.usitc.gov. Created Sept. 8, 1916. Furnishes studies, reports, and recommendations regarding international trade and tariffs to president, Congress, and other government agencies.

United States Postal Service 475 L'Enfant Plaza SW, Washington, DC 20260-0010. (202) 268-2000. www.usps.gov. Created Aug. 12, 1970, by Postal Reorganization Act. Provides mail processing and delivery service to individuals and businesses in U.S. Protects mail from loss or theft and apprehends violators of postal laws.

FEDERAL EMPLOYEES AND BUDGET

▶FEDERAL JOBS AND SALARIES

As of March 31, 1998, there were 1,698,587 full-time non-postal Federal civilian employees. Nearly 97 percent of the Federal civilian workforce was employed in the United States; 12,318 (0.7 percent) worked in U.S. territories, and 40,658 (2.4 percent) worked in foreign countries. The majority of government employees worked in metropolitan statistical areas, led by the Washington, D.C., MSA, with 265,833, or 15.7 percent of the total.

Four executive departments accounted for nearly 70 percent of the Federal civilian workforce. The Department of Defense employed 691,644 civilians (40.7 percent of the total), Veterans Affairs employed 195,208 (11.5 percent), the Treasury 147,714 (8.7 percent), and Justice 115,894 or 6.8 percent).

Federal Government civilian employees are paid according to a number of different systems: the General Schedule (GS), Federal Wage Systems, and other acts and administratively determined systems. Overall, the average salary for full-time civilian government employees was $45,546. Employees under the General Schedule on average earned more than those on Federal Wage Systems ($44,824 to $35,126), but not as much as employees covered by other acts and administrative determinations, who averaged $60,682. Average General Schedule salaries by major geographic areas were: United States, $45,674; Washington,

The Federal Government: Employees and Budget, 1901–99

		Budget (millions)		
Year	Number of employees[1]	Receipts	Outlays	Surplus or deficit (-)
1901	239,476	$588	$525	$63
1910	388,708	676	694	-18
1920	655,265	6,649	6,358	291
1930	601,319	4,058	3,320	738
1940	1,042,420	6,548	9,468	-2,920
1945	3,816,310	45,159	92,712	-47,553
1950	1,960,708	39,443	42,562	-3,119
1960	2,398,704	92,492	92,191	301
1970	2,984,574	192,807	195,649	-2,842
1980	2,875,866	517,112	590,947	-73,835
1985	3,001,000	734,165	946,499	-212,334
1990	3,128,267	1,031,969	1,253,163	-221,194
1991	3,112,145	1,055,041	1,324,400	-269,359
1992	3,085,323	1,091,279	1,381,681	-290,402
1993	3,013,508	1,154,401	1,409,414	-255,013
1994	2,971,584	1,258,627	1,461,731	-203,104
1995	2,920,277	1,351,830	1,515,729	-163,899
1996	2,847,392	1,453,062	1,560,512	-107,450
1997	2,787,137	1,579,292	1,601,232	-21,940
1998	2,789,541	1,721,798	1,652,552	69,246
1999[2]	N.A.	1,806,334	1,727,071	79,263

1. Paid civilians only. 2. Projected.
Source: Office of Management and Budget, *Budget of the United States Government, FY 2000* (1999).

D.C. area, $57,582; foreign countries, $43,264; and U.S. territories, $35,977.

White-Collar Employees
General Schedule   The number of white-collar employees has been declining for four years. General schedule employment totaled 1,257,800 in 1998, a drop of nearly 2.5 percent over the previous year. There are 15 grades broadly defined in terms of responsibility, difficulty, and qualifications; within each grade there are 10 steps. Within-grade advancement occurs on a fixed schedule, though employees demonstrating "high-quality performance" can receive "quality step increases." In all, General Schedule employees make up more than three-quarters of all civilians employed by the Government.

Federal Government Pay Systems, 1998

Grade	Employees	Mean Salary
General Schedule		
GS-1	798	$14,107
GS-2	2,023	16,618
GS-3	17,560	18,964
GS-4	60,723	22,152
GS-5	127,384	25,004
GS-6	92,564	28,040
GS-7	132,550	30,876
GS-8	40,905	35,059
GS-9	124,207	37,236
GS-10	15,864	41,997
GS-11	178,727	45,263
GS-12	206,931	54,418
GS-13	154,806	65,391
GS-14	67,013	78,164
GS-15	35,745	93,621
Total	**1,257,800**	**$44,824**
Senior Level (SL)	445	$87,030-118,400[1]
Executive Schedule (EX)		
Level I	17	$151,800
Level II	37	136,700
Level III	84	125,900
Level IV	253	118,400
Level V	20	110,700
Total	**411**	**$122,587**
Senior Executive Service (ES)		
ES-1	716	$99,200
ES-2	768	103,900
ES-3	1,024	108,600
ES-4	2,629	114,500
ES-5	1,208	118,400
ES-6	566	118,400
Total	**6,911**	**$111,864**

Note: As of March 31. 1. Mean salary not available. Salary range shown.   Source: U.S. Office of Personnel Management, *Pay Structure of the Federal Civil Service 1998,* (1999).

Foreign Service Personnel and Veterans Affairs
There were 4,381 Foreign Service Officers in 1998, with an average salary of $74,399. Non-officers in the foreign service numbered 6,275 and averaged $51,951 in salary. The pay system of the Department of Veterans Affairs covered 7,262 physicians and dentists with an average salary of $93,622; 212 podiatrists and optometrists ($82,754); 31,291 nurses ($49,775); and 1,066 physicians' assistants ($59,961).

Executive Schedule (EX) and Senior Executive Service (ES)
The very top executives in the executive branch are paid under a system known as the Executive Schedule (EX).

Salaries of Federal Officials

In 1999, Congress voted to double the next president's salary from $200,000 to $400,000. Less noticed was the fact that legislators were due for their own 3.4 percent cost of living raise. The other salaries below will be in effect on January 1, 2000, unless Congress votes to rescind the raise before then.

Branch/Official	Salary
Executive branch	
President	$200,000
Expense allowance	50,000
Travel allowance	100,000
Vice President	181,400
Expense allowance	10,000
Legislative branch	
Senate:[1]	
President pro tempore, Majority and Minority Leaders	$157,000
Expense allowance	10,000
Senators	141,300
Expense allowance for the majority and minority leaders, each	10,000
Expense allowance for majority and minority whips, each	5,000
Expense allowance for chairmen of majority and minority conference committees, each	3,000
House of Representatives:[1]	
Speaker of the House	$181,400
Expense allowance	25,000
Minority and majority leaders	157,000
Expense allowance, each	10,000
Representatives	141,300
Expense allowance for majority and minority whips, each	5,000
Judicial branch	
Chief Justice	$181,400
Associate justices	173,6000
Circuit judges	149,900
District and other judges	141,300

1. Expenses listed are over and above personnel, expense, and transportation allowances given to all members of Congress, the amount of which is based on the population of the senator or representative's district and the distance between his or her home state and Washington D.C.
Source: Office of Personnel Management, 1999.

Broadly speaking, the five Executive Schedule levels include the following job titles: level I, cabinet members; level II, deputy secretaries of major departments; level III, presidential advisors, chief administrators of major independent agencies, and under secretaries; level IV, assistant secretaries, deputy under secretaries, and general counsels in executive departments; and level V, deputy assistant secretaries, administrators, commissioners, and directors. Executive Schedule employment was 411 in 1998, with an average salary of $122,771. The Senior Executive Service (ES) covers most managerial and policy positions in the executive branch that do not require Senate confirmation. In 1998 there were 6,911 employees covered by ES; salaries averaged $119,656.

Special rates The Government has difficulty recruiting and retaining qualified personnel in certain occupations and for certain locations with higher competitive salaries. To alleviate this problem, the Office of Personnel Management has the authority to establish special rates for certain white-collar positions. The number of white-collar employees receiving special-rate salaries varies from year to year; in 1998, it was 156,010.

Blue-Collar Employees

As of March 31, 1997, the federal government employed 222,308 workers (13.1 percent of the civilian Government workforce) in blue-collar (trades and labor) occupations. Most of these (217,567 or 97.9 percent) were employed in the United States; 12,504, or 5.6 percent, worked in and around the Washington, D.C. metro area. The Department of Defense employed 166,300 or 74.8 percent of all blue-collar government workers.

Blue-collar pay rates are governed by federal Wage Systems and determined on a prevailing rate basis by pay locality. The worldwide average salary for the blue-collar workforce in 1997 was $34,763. Salaries were highest in the United States (where they averaged $34,891) and lowest in foreign countries, (where they averaged just $27,991). Blue-collar salaries averaged $34,974 in the Washington D.C. metropolitan area, but only $28,768 in U.S. territories and possessions.

▶ GLOSSARY OF FEDERAL BUDGET TERMS

Budget authority The term budget authority means the authority provided by law to incur financial obligations that result in immediate or

U.S. Federal Employment, 1992–98

Description	1992	1996	1997	1998
Executive branch civilian employment[1]	2,226,778	1,933,931	1,871,791	1,855,796
U.S. Postal Service[2]	792,049	852,333	853,350	871,520
Military personnel on active duty[3]	1,847,600	1,506,965	1,473,699	1,442,520
Department of Defense	1,808,131	1,471,722	1,438,562	1,406,830
Department of Transportation (Coast Guard)	39,469	35,243	35,137	35,459
Total executive branch employment	**4,866,427**	**4,293,229**	**4,198,840**	**4,169,605**
Legislative branch	38,509	31,547	31,355	30,474
Judicial branch	27,987	29,581	30,641	31,742
Total Federal employment	**4,932,923**	**4,354,357**	**4,260,836**	**4,231,821**

1. Excludes Postal Service employees. 2. Includes Postal Rate Commission. 3. Excludes reserve components.
Source: Office of Management and Budget, *Budget of the United States Government, FY 2000 (1999).*

Government Employment and Population, 1961–98

Fiscal year	Federal executive branch[1] ('000s)	Government employment Total Federal personnel ('000s)	State and local governments ('000s)	All governmental units ('000s)	Executive branch employment as a percent of all governmental units[1]	Executive branch employment per 1,000 population[1]
1962	2,485	5,354	6,549	11,903	20.9%	13.3%
1965	2,496	5,215	7,696	12,911	19.3	12.8
1970[2]	2,944	6,085	9,822	15,907	18.5	14.4
1975	2,848	5,061	11,937	16,998	16.8	13.2
1980[2]	2,821	4,965	13,375	18,340	15.4	12.4
1985	3,008	5,256	13,519	18,775	16.0	12.6
1990[2]	3,067	5,234	15,219	20,453	15.0	12.3
1991[2]	3,048	5,152	15,436	20,588	14.8	12.1
1992	3,017	4,931	15,675	20,606	14.6	11.8
1993	2,947	4,758	15,926	20,684	14.2	11.4
1994	2,908	4,620	16,258	20,878	13.9	11.2
1995	2,858	4,475	16,484	20,959	13.6	10.9
1996	2,786	4,354	16,662	21,016	13.3	10.5
1997	2,725	4,261	16,870	21,131	12.9	10.2
1998	2,727	4,232	15,969	20,201	13.5	10.1

1. Civilian employment only, including full-time permanent, temporary, part-time, and intermittent employees in the executive branch, including the Postal Service, and beginning in 1970, includes various disadvantaged worker-trainee programs. 2. Includes temporary employees in the decennial census.   **Source:** Office of Management and Budget, *Budget of the United States Government, FY 2000* (1999).

future outlays involving government funds or to collect offsetting receipts.

Budget deficit/surplus A budget deficit occurs when government outlays exceed government receipts; a surplus occurs when receipts exceed outlays. The budget deficit in 1997 was $21.9 billion; the record deficit was $290.4 billion in 1992. The last year in which a budget surplus was recorded was 1969 ($3.2 bil.).

Fiscal year The Federal Government's fiscal year begins Oct. 1 and ends Sept. 30 of the next calendar year; so, FY 2000 began Oct. 1, 1999, and ends Sept. 30, 2000.

Intergovernmental expenditure/revenue Amounts paid to or received from other governments either in the form of shared revenues and grants-in-aid, as reimbursements for performance of general government activities or for specific services such as care of prisoners for the paying government, or in lieu of taxes.

Off-budget/on-budget Some presentations in the Federal budget distinguish on-budget totals from off-budget totals. On-budget totals reflect the transactions of all Federal Government entities except those excluded from the budget totals by law, the two Social Security trust funds (old-age and survivors insurance and the Federal disability insurance trust funds), and the Postal Service fund. Off-budget totals reflect the transactions of government entities excluded from the on-budget totals by law.

Offsetting collections Offsetting collections are collections from the public that result from business-type or market-oriented activities and collections; examples include proceeds from the sale of electric power by the Tennessee Valley Authority, voluntary medical insurance premiums paid to the supplementary medical insurance trust fund, and the sale of postage stamps.

Outlays Budget outlays are expenditures and net lending of funds under budget authority during the fiscal year. They constitute the spending side of the budget and are compared to receipts in calculating the budget surplus or deficit.

Receipts Budget receipts constitute the income side of the budget and are composed almost entirely of taxes or other compulsory payments to the government. They are compared to outlays in calculating the budget surplus or deficit.

Federal Government Employment and Outlays, by Branch and Agency, 1998–2000

| Agency | Employment 1998[1] | Outlays (millions of dollars) | | | |
| | | Actual | | Estimated | |
		1997	1998	1999	2000
Legislative branch	30,474	$2,363	$2,600	$2,850	$3,210
Judicial branch	31,742	3,259	3,467	3,913	4,133
Executive branch[2]:	1,790,200				
Executive Office of the President	N.A.	221	237	374	263
Department of Agriculture	96,400	52,547	53,947	63,412	55,167
Department of Commerce	35,700	3,783	4,046	4,767	6,647
Department of Defense[3] (military functions)	707,200	258,322	256,122	265,556	260,834
Department of Defense (civil functions)	N.A.	30,282	31,216	32,311	33,220
Department of Education	4,500	30,009	31,463	34,360	34,971
Department of Energy	16,300	14,467	14,438	15,544	15,756
Department of Health and Human Services	57,900	339,535	350,568	375,532	400,327
Dept. of Housing and Urban Development	9,800	27,527	30,227	32,324	32,533
Department of the Interior	64,000	6,720	7,218	8,426	8,470
Department of Justice	117,300	14,310	16,168	16,458	19,794
Department of Labor	16,300	30,458	30,007	34,923	38,652
Department of State	26,400	6,033	5,382	6,791	6,959
Department of Transportation	63,400	39,832	39,463	41,873	45,503
Department of the Treasury	142,100	379,342	390,140	385,976	377,916
Department of Veterans Affairs	207,100	39,280	41,773	43,474	49,953
Environmental Protection Agency	17,700	6,164	6,284	6,667	7,346
General Services Administration	14,100	1,084	1,091	328	429
National Aeronautics & Space Administration (NASA)	19,100	14,360	14,206	14,043	13,357
Office of Personnel Management	2,800	45,404	46,305	48,266	50,531
Small Business Administration	4,400	333	-77	-866	287
Social Security Administration (off-budget)	N.A.	358,372	370,069	381,316	398,221
Totals[4, 5]	1,852,416	$1,601,232	$1,652,552	$1,727,071	$1,765,687

Note: Outlays are the measure of Government spending—payments to liquidate obligations (other than the repayment of debt), net of cash, and offsetting collections. Outlays are generally recorded on a cash basis, but also include many cash-equivalent transactions and interest accrued on public issues of the public debt. 1. Employment figures exclude developmental positions under the Worker-Trainee Opportunity Program; participants in the Cooperative Education Program; disadvantaged summer and part-time workers under such Office of Personnel Management programs as Summer Aides, stay-in-school, and junior fellowship; and certain statutory exemptions. Figures for executive branch rounded at source. 2. Civilian employment. 3. By law (10 U.S.C. Chapter 4, section 140b) the Department of Defense is exempt from full-time equivalent employment controls. Data shown are estimated. 4. Employment totals do not include FDIC or U.S. Postal Service. 5. Outlay totals do not account for undistributed offsetting receipts.
Source: Office of Management and Budget, *Budget of the United States Government, FY 2000* (1999).

Trust fund In the Federal budget, a trust fund means only that the law requires that funds must be accounted for separately and used only for specified purposes. The largest trust funds are those for civil service and military retirement, Social Security, Medicare, and unemployment insurance. These are financed largely by Social Security taxes and contributions and payments from the general fund. There are also major trust funds for transportation and bank deposit insurance which are financed by user charges.

User charges These are charges for services rendered, collected in the form of taxes, such as highway excise taxes to fund the highway trust fund.

The Congressional Budget Process

On or before	Action to be completed
First Monday in February	President submits his budget. Congressional committees have six weeks to submit views and estimates to Budget Committees.
February 15	Congressional Budget Office submits report to budget committees.
April 1	Senate budget committee reports concurrent resolution on the budget.
April 15	Congress completes action on concurrent resolution on the budget.
May 15	Annual appropriation bills may be considered in the House.
June 10	House Appropriations Committee reports last annual appropriations bill.
June 15	Congress completes action on reconciliation legislation.
June 30	House completes action on annual appropriation bills.
October 1	Fiscal year begins.

1. A concurrent resolution sets levels for new budget authority and outlays, direct loan obligations, primary loan guarantee commitments, the amount by which Federal revenues should be increased or decreased, the budget surplus or deficit, the public debt, and so on. **Source:** Committee on Ways and Means, U.S. House of Representatives, *Overview of Entitlement Programs*, (annual).

Federal Government Receipts By Source, 1934–99
(billions of dollars)

Year	Individual income taxes	Corporation income taxes[1]	Social insurance & retirement receipts	Excise taxes	Other[2]	Total
1934	$0.4	$0.3	([3])	$1.4	$0.8	**$3.0**
1940	0.9	1.2	1.8	2.0	0.7	**6.5**
1950	15.8	10.4	4.3	7.6	1.4	**39.4**
1960	40.7	21.5	14.7	11.7	3.9	**92.5**
1970	90.4	32.8	44.3	15.7	9.5	**192.8**
1980	244.1	64.6	157.8	24.3	26.3	**517.1**
1990	466.9	93.5	380.0	35.3	56.2	**1,032.0**
1995	590.2	157.0	484.5	57.5	62.6	**1,351.8**
1996	656.4	171.8	509.4	54.0	61.4	**1,453.1**
1997	737.5	182.3	539.4	56.9	63.2	**1,579.3**
1998	828.6	188.7	571.8	57.7	75.0	**1,721.8**
1999[4]	868.9	182.2	608.8	68.1	78.3	**1,806.3**

1. Beginning in 1990 includes trust fund receipts for the hazardous substance Superfund. 2. Includes estate and gift taxes, customs duties and fees, federal reserve deposits, and other. 3. Less than $100 million. 4. Estimate. **Source:** Office of Management and Budget, *Budget of the United States Government, FY 2000* (1999).

Outlays by Budget Enforcement Act Category, 1970–99 (billions)

Category	1970	1980	1990	1995	1997	1998	1999[1]
Total Outlays	$195.6	$590.9	$1,253.2	$1,515.7	$1,601.2	$1,652.6	$1,727.1
Discretionary outlays	120.2	276.1	500.3	545.4	548.6	554.7	581.2
National defense	81.9	134.6	300.1	273.6	271.7	270.2	277.5
International	4.0	12.8	19.1	20.1	19.0	18.1	19.8
Domestic	34.3	128.7	181.1	251.7	257.9	266.3	283.8
Mandatory outlays	61.1	262.3	568.7	738.2	808.6	854.5	918.6
Social Security	29.6	117.1	246.5	333.3	362.3	376.1	389.2
Deposit Insurance	-0.5	-0.4	57.9	-17.9	-14.4	-4.4	-5.0
Means-tested entitlements[2]	10.1	45.0	94.1	181.6	194.0	200.3	215.1
Other	30.5	120.6	206.8	285.6	316.7	329.6	359.5
Undistributed offsetting receipts[3]	-8.6	-19.9	-36.7	-44.5	-50.0	-47.2	-40.0
Net interest	14.4	52.5	184.2	232.2	244.0	243.4	227.2

1. Estimate. 2. Includes Medicaid, food stamps, family support assistance (AFDC), supplemental security income (SSI), child nutrition programs, earned income tax credits, and veterans' pensions. 3. Includes asset sales. **Source:** Office of Management and Budget, *Budget of the United States Government, FY 2000* (1999).

Federal Government Dollar, Fiscal Year 2000

Revenues: $1,806 billion

Outlays $1,727 billion

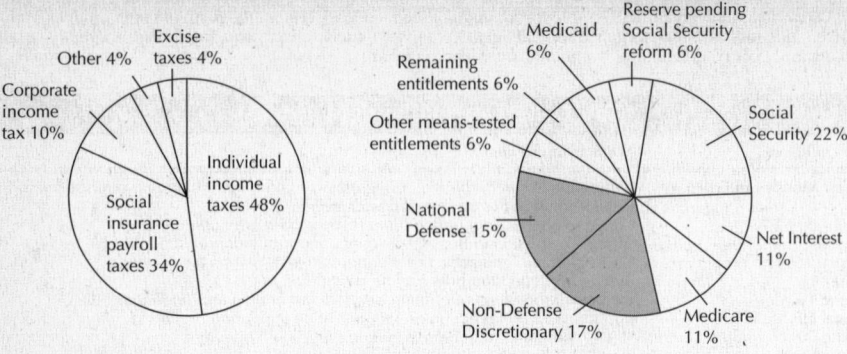

Note: Gray-shaded areas are discretionary outlays. All other outlays are mandatory.
Source: Office of Management and Budget, *Budget of the United States Government, FY 2000* (1999).

Budget Outlays and Percent Distribution, by Function, 1970–98 (millions of dollars)

Function	1970	1980	1990	1995	1997	1998
National defense	**$81,692**	**$133,995**	**$299,331**	**$272,066**	**$270,505**	**$268,456**
As percentage of total	41.8%	22.7%	23.9%	17.9%	16.9%	16.2%
Human resources	**$75,349**	**$313,374**	**$619,329**	**$923,765**	**$1,002,336**	**$1,033,389**
As percentage of total	38.5%	53.0%	49.4%	60.9%	62.6%	62.5%
Education, training, employment and social services	$ 8,634	$31,843	$38,755	$54,263	$53,008	$54,919
Health	5,907	23,169	57,716	115,418	123,843	131,440
Medicare	6,213	32,090	98,102	159,855	190,016	192,822
Income Security	15,655	86,540	147,076	220,493	230,889	233,202
Social Security	30,270	118,547	248,623	335,846	365,257	379,225
Veterans benefits & services	8,669	21,185	29,058	37,890	39,313	41,781
Physical resources	**$15,574**	**$65,985**	**$126,004**	**$59,197**	**$59,992**	**$74,732**
As percentage of total	8.0%	11.2%	10.1%	3.9%	3.7%	4.5%
Energy	$ 997	$10,156	$3,341	$4,936	$1,475	$1,270
Natural resources and environment	3,065	13,858	17,080	22,078	21,369	22,396
Commerce and housing credit	2,112	9,390	66,952	-17,808	-14,624	1,014
Transportation	7,008	21,329	29,485	39,350	40,767	40,332
Community and regional development	2,392	11,252	8,498	10,641	11,005	9,720
Net interest	**$14,380**	**$52,538**	**$184,221**	**$232,169**	**$244,016**	**$243,359**
As percentage of total	7.4%	8.9%	14.7%	15.3%	15.2%	14.7%
Other functions	**$17,286**	**$44,996**	**$60,893**	**$72,987**	**$74,356**	**$79,810**
As percentage of total	8.8%	7.6%	4.9%	4.8%	4.6%	4.8%
International affairs	$4,330	$12,714	$13,764	$16,434	$15,228	13,109
General science, space, & technology	4,511	5,832	14,444	16,724	17,174	18,219
Agriculture	5,166	8,839	11,958	9,778	9,032	12,206
Administration of justice	959	4,584	9,993	16,216	20,173	22,832
General govenment	2,320	13,028	10,734	13,835	12,749	13,444
Total[1]	**$195,649**	**$590,947**	**$1,252,163**	**$1,515,729**	**$1,601,232**	**$1,652,552**

1. Includes undistributed offsetting receipts not shown separately.   **Source:** Office of Management and Budget, *Budget of the United States Government, FY 2000* (1999).

Summary of Federal Government Finances, 1991–94 (millions)

Item	1991	1993	1994
REVENUES			
Revenue, total	**$1,200,682**	**$1,306,395**	**$1,400,664**
General revenue	812,339	888,440	948,857
General revenue from own sources	809,105	887,096	945,638
Taxes	641,982	712,912	780,269
Income	565,913	627,200	683,440
Individual	467,827	509,680	543,055
Corporation	98,086	117,520	140,385
Sales, gross receipts, and customs	58,495	67,447	74,648
Customs duties	16,034	18,931	20,264
Motor fuel	16,917	20,223	26,441
Alcoholic beverages	7,227	7,704	7,600
Public utilities	7,253	7,835	8,924
Air transportation	4,300	4,662	5,253
Telephone	2,953	3,173	3,671
Tobacco products	4,782	5,700	5,744
Other sales and gross receipts taxes	6,282	7,054	5,675
Motor fuel vehicles, chassis, and body	928	1,211	1,558
Tires, inner tubes, and tread rubber	284	311	346
Other categories not shown	5,070	5,532	3,771
Other taxes	17,574	18,265	22,181
Death and gift	11,138	12,577	15,225
All other	6,436	5,688	6,956
Charges and miscellaneous general revenue	167,123	174,184	165,369
Current charges	86,292	94,613	96,670
Postal receipts	42,592	46,502	48,412
National defense and international relations	9,206	12,014	10,075
Natural resources	15,528	13,149	13,150
Commodity Credit Corporation—sale of	937	769	454
agricultural products Tennessee Valley Authority	5,565	5,538	5,770
Department of Interior—energy sales	1,021	919	876
Mineral ore and product sales	573	4	406
Timber sales	861	665	380
All other resource charges	6,571	5,254	5,264
Other current charges	18,966	22,948	25,033
Sale of property	3,663	3,602	3,670
Interest earnings	11,159	10,897	10,482
Other miscellaneous general revenue	66,009	65,072	54,547
Federal Reserve System—earnings	19,158	14,908	18,023
Continental shelf lands—lease and			
royalty revenues	3,150	2,785	3,001
Other	43,701	47,379	33,523
Insurance trust revenue	388,343	417,955	451,807
Social Security and Medicare insurance (OASDHI)	378,510	407,860	441,983
Employee retirement	4,446	4,684	4,540
Railroad retirement	4,461	4,451	4,386
Veterans' life insurance	742	896	871
Unemployment compensation	184	64	27
EXPENDITURES			
Expenditure, total	**$1,480,408**	**$1,569,505**	**$1,630,283**
Expenditure, by function			
General expenditure	1,060,407	1,083,257	1,107,501
Intergovernmental expenditure	160,145	204,632	217,919
Education[2]	24,537	29,190	26,752
Elementary and secondary education	4,985	6,301	6,566
School breakfast and lunch	4,246	5,030	5,310
Federally affected area assistance	743	467	744
Public welfare[2]	78,419	105,521	114,908
Medical assistance	54,464	77,821	84,090
Maintenance assistance	11,929	13,639	14,256
Low-income energy assistance	3,556	4,114	5,481
Health and hospitals[2]	6,500	8,336	9,257
Special supplemental food programs—WIC	2,387	3,034	3,342
National Institutes of Health	986	1,228	1,308
Highways	14,611	16,860	19,199
Natural Resources, parks, and recreations	2,253	2,581	2,777
Housing and community development	13,501	18,739	21,099
Other[2]	20,324	23,405	23,927

Item	1991	1993	1994
Urban mass transportation	$ 3,855	$ 3,543	$ 3,970
Contribution to District of Columbia	671	699	700
Direct expenditure	900,262	878,625	889,582
Selected Federal programs:			
National defense and international relations[2]	366,112	344,008	333,380
Military functions	335,849	311,006	300,578
Economic assistance	7,996	8,110	7,037
Atomic energy	10,970	12,422	13,151
Foreign affairs, n.e.c.	4,808	6,059	6,361
Food for freedom	1,553	1,559	1,903
Military assistance	4,725	4,646	4,116
Postal service	43,102	44,528	46,110
Space research and technology	13,514	13,873	13,553
Education service:			
Education	21,091	25,878	23,239
Veterans' education benefits	1,277	1,548	1,827
Other	19,814	24,330	21,412
Libraries	397	297	511
Social service and income maintenance:			
Public welfare	40,716	51,609	56,204
Hospitals	9,425	10,875	11,351
Public hospitals	9,140	10,524	10,966
Veterans	7,966	8,859	9,333
Other public hospitals	1,174	1,665	1,633
Other hospitals	285	351	385
Health	12,282	13,443	13,816
Social insurance administration	4,943	5,642	5,790
Veterans' services	19,006	21,198	21,878
Transportation:			
Highways	665	619	691
Air transportation	5,157	6,214	6,482
Water transport and terminals	2,817	2,953	2,848
Public safety:			
Police protection	6,170	7,356	7,328
Correction	1,941	2,422	2,587
Environment and housing:			
Natural resources, parks and recreation	46,162	51,278	52,791
Soil, water, mineral, and electric energy resources[2]	15,059	18,361	20,117
Energy programs	5,216	6,534	5,745
Tennessee Valley Authority	3,857	5,144	4,929
Army Corps of Engineers	452	513	547
Soil Conservation Service	811	925	975
Stabilization of farm prices and income[2]	14,954	16,708	15,620
Commodity Credit Corporation	12,227	14,261	12,228
Farm credit programs	6,463	5,139	4,369
Forestry	2,291	2,486	2,696
Other agricultural resources	2,088	2,384	2,476
Other natural resources[2]	3,519	4,065	5,359
National Oceanographic and Atmospheric Administration (NOAA)	1,412	1,686	1,881
Housing and community development	16,698	12,582	15,817
Government administration:			
Financial administration	10,209	11,647	11,788
Judicial and legal	3,995	4,680	4,766
Other government administration	1,516	1,677	1,704
Interest on general debt	195,142	198,795	202,663
General expenditure, not shown elsewhere	79,202	47,051	54,285
Insurance trust expenditure	420,001	486,248	522,782
Social Security and Medicare Insurance (OASDHI)	376,933	440,994	472,461
Employee retirement	33,624	35,232	36,723
Railroad retirement	7,168	7,592	10,958
Veterans' life insurance	2,189	2,360	2,557
Unemployment compensation	87	70	83

DEBT

Gross debt outstanding at end of fiscal year	$3,683,054	$4,436,171	$4,721,292
Public debt	3,665,303	4,411,489	4,692,750
Federal agency debt	17,751	24,682	28,542
Held by Federal government	919,713	1,116,713	1,213,115
Other debt outstanding	2,763,341	3,319,458	3,508,178

NATIONAL DEFENSE

In 1998, the United States spent over $250 billion to keep 1.4 million people in active military service and to build and maintain the greatest arsenal of weapons ever known.

Since the end of World War II, a large percentage of people and material have been committed to regions around the world that the Government has determined are vital to U.S. interests. Between 1961 and 1980, the defense budget averaged around $200 billion annually (in 1982 constant dollars)—even during the Vietnam War. In 1981, however, the Reagan administration began a massive defense buildup which swelled successive defense budgets to unprecedented peacetime levels and in the process helped to quadruple the annual federal deficit in less than five years.

Since the end of the Cold War, the defense budget has gradually declined from approximately $300 billion to a projected $262.6 billion for 1999, still an extraordinary sum in peacetime (and up $4 billion over 1998). But the U.S. remains committed to maintaining active duty and reserve forces sufficient for quick and effective response to crises around the world, and is equipped to fight significant wars on two fronts should such a situation arise.

The defense establishment The earliest precursor to the Department of Defense was the War Department, established by Congress in 1789; a separate Navy Department was created in 1798. These were merged under the National Security Act of 1947 and subsequent amendments. By 1949 the secretary of defense was established as the principal assistant to the president on defense matters in charge of the Defense Department.

The Department of Defense (DoD) is a cabinet-level organization responsible for providing the military forces needed to deter war and protect the security of the United States. The major elements of these forces are the Army, Navy, Air Force, and Marine Corps. Under the president, who is also the commander-in-chief, the secretary of defense exercises direction, authority and control over the Department of Defense, which includes the three military departments, the Joint Chiefs of Staff and Joint Staff, 10 unified and specified commands, the DoD inspector general, 13 defense agencies, and seven DoD field activities.

The four armed services are subordinate to the military departments, which are responsible for recruiting, training and equipping their forces. The Marine Corps is the second armed service in the Department of the Navy. (A fifth armed service, the U.S. Coast Guard, reports to the Department of Transportation in peacetime and to the Department of the Navy in wartime.)

Chain of command Operational command of U.S. combat forces is assigned to the nation's unified and specified commands. The chain of command runs from the president to the secretary of defense, through the Joint Chiefs of Staff to the commanders-in-chief of the unified and specified commands. (The four service secretaries are not part of this chain of command.) A *unified command* is composed of forces from two or more services, has a broad and continuing mission and is normally organized on a geographical basis. A *specified command* also has a broad and continuing mission but is organized on a functional basis and is normally made up of forces from a single service.

U.S. Service Academies

U.S. Military Academy, West Point, N.Y. 10996; (Founded, 1802).

U.S. Naval Academy, Annapolis, Md. 21402; (1845).

U.S. Air Force Academy, Colorado Springs, Colo. 80840; (1954).

U.S. Coast Guard Academy, New London, Conn. 06320; (1876).

U.S. Merchant Marine Academy, Kings Point, N.Y. 11024; (1943).

Chairmen of the Joint Chiefs of Staff, 1949–98

General of the Army Omar N. Bradley, USA	1949–53
Adm. Arthur W. Radford, USN	1953–57
Gen. Nathan F. Twining, USAF	1957–60
Gen. Lyman L. Lemnitzer, USA	1960–62
Gen. Maxwell D. Taylor, USA	1962–64
Gen. Earle G. Wheeler, USA	1964–70
Adm. Thomas H. Moorer, USN	1970–74
Gen. George S. Brown, USAF	1974–78
Gen. David C. Jones, USAF	1978–82
Gen. John W. Vessey Jr., USA	1982–85
Adm. William J. Crowe, USN	1985–89
Gen. Colin L. Powell, USA	1989–93
Gen. John Shalikashvili, USA	1993–Oct. 9, 1997
Gen. H. Hugh Shelton, USA	1997–present

Federal Budget Outlays for National Defense Functions, 1970–99 (billions of dollars)

Function	1970	1980	1990	1995	1997	1998	1999[1]
Military personnel	$29.0	$40.9	$78.9	$71.6	$70.3	$69.8	$70.9
Percent of defense budget	35.5%	30.5%	26.9%	28.0%	27.2%	27.0%	27.0%
Operations & maintenance	$21.6	$44.9	$88.3	$93.8	$92.4	$97.2	$98.1
Procurement	21.6	29.0	81.3	43.6	42.9	44.8	49.0
Research, development, test and evaluation	7.2	13.1	36.4	34.5	36.4	37.1	36.6
Military construction	1.2	2.5	5.1	5.4	5.7	5.5	5.1
Family housing	0.6	1.7	3.1	3.4	4.1	3.8	3.6
Other[2]	-1.1	-1.1	-0.3	3.4	6.1	0.3	-0.7
Total outlays	**$81.7**	**$134.0**	**$293.6**	**$255.7**	**$258.0**	**$258.5**	**$262.6**

1. Estimate. 2. Includes revolving and management funds, contingency funds, trust funds, special foreign currency programs, allowances and offsetting receipts. **Source:** U.S. Dept. of Management and Budget, *Budget of the United States Government, FY 2000.*

▶ U.S. ARMY

In peacetime, the primary mission of the continental U.S. armies is to train reserves and national guard, plan for mobilization, and coordinate domestic emergency relief efforts. The largest unit is a numbered *army*, such as the Fifth Army. (In time of war, two or three armies may be brought under a single command in an *army group*.) An *army* is made up of 2 or more corps plus a headquarters (HQ) unit; a *corps* is made up of 2 to 5 divisions and an HQ.

There are 18 active and 10 reserve divisions in the U.S. Army combat forces. The *division* is a self-sufficient force, typically consisting of 3 *brigades* (each comprising 3 to 5 battalions) and various combat support elements. A *brigade* is made up of 2 or more regiments or battalions; a *regiment*, of subordinate units such as battalions, companies or squadrons; a *battalion*, of 4 or more companies; a *company* of several platoons; and a *platoon* of 4 squads. A *squad* consists of about 10 soldiers.

▶ U.S. MARINE CORPS

Marine Corps organization emphasizes the close integration of air-ground operations for service with the U.S. fleet and for the conduct of land operations essential to the prosecution of a naval campaign. All Marines serve "at the pleasure of the president," and the Corps's mission includes "performing such other duties as the President may direct."

The smallest tactical unit of Marine Corps infantry is the *fire team*, which consists of 4 Marines. A *squad* is made up of three fire teams, and there are three squads to a *platoon*, three platoons to a *company*, three companies to a *battalion*, three battalions to a *regiment*, three regiments to a *brigade*, and three squads to a *division*.

These components are organized into three basic organizational structures called *Marine air-ground task forces*, or MAGTFs. The largest—about 47,500 personnel—is the *Marine Expeditionary Force* (MEF), which consists of a Marine air wing (330 planes), a Marine division, and a force service support group. The *Marine Expeditionary Brigade* (MEB) consists of a Marine air group (150 planes), a regimental landing group and a brigade service support group—about 15,000 personnel. The smallest and most responsive Marine force, the *Marine Expeditionary Unit* (MEU), consists of about 2,500 personnel and is made up of a helicopter squadron, a battalion landing team, and a unit service support group. MEUs are sea-based, can be airlifted and they are equipped and trained to be self-sustaining in the field for up to 15 days.

▶ U.S. NAVY

The ships of the U.S. Navy are organized into the Pacific Fleet, the Atlantic Fleet, and U.S. Naval Forces Europe. These are composed of numbered fleets which consist of *carrier battle groups, battleship surface action groups* and one or more *underway replenishment groups*. Smaller subdivisions of naval forces are the *flotilla* consisting of two or more squadrons; a *squadron*, of two or more divisions; and a *division*, normally made up of four ships.

A naval *task force* designates a collection of ships under a single command designed to accomplish a particular tactical or strategic purpose. An *amphibious squadron* consists of amphibious assault ships, amphibious transport docks, dock landing ships and tank landing ships, and transports troops and equipment necessary for an assault landing from the sea.

Major U.S. Army Forces

Unit	Headquarters
Forces Command	**Ft. McPherson, Ga.**
Central Command/Third U.S. Army	Ft. McPherson, Ga.
First U.S. Army	Ft. Gillem, Ga.
Fifth U.S. Army	Ft. Sam Houston, Tex.
I Corps	Ft. Lewis, Wash.
III Corps, "Phantom Corps"	Ft. Hood, Tex.
4th Infantry Division (mech.), "The Ivy Division"	Ft. Hood, Tex.
1st Cavalry Division	Ft. Hood, Tex.
III Corps Artillery	Ft. Sill, Okla.
13th Corps. Support Command	Ft. Hood, Tex.
XVIII Airborne Corps	Ft. Bragg, N.C.
10th Mountain Division (Light Infantry)	Ft. Drum, N.Y.
3rd Infantry Division (mech.)	Ft. Stewart, Ga.
82nd Airborne Division, "All American"	Ft. Bragg, N.C.
101st Airborne Division (air assault), "Screaming Eagles"	Ft. Campbell, Ky.
XVIII Airborne Corps Artillery	Ft. Bragg, N.C.
1st Corps Support Command	Ft. Bragg, N.C.
National Training Center	Ft. Irwin, Calif.
U.S. Army Europe (7th Army)	**Heidelberg, Germany**
V Corps	Heidelberg, Germany
3rd Infantry Division (mech.), "Marine"	Würzburg, Germany
1st Armored Division, "Old Ironsides"	Bad Kreuznach, Germany
1st Personnel Command	Schwetzingen, Germany
3rd Corps Support Command	Wiesbaden, Germany
21st Theater Army Area Command	Kaiserslautern, Germany
Seventh Army Training Command	Grafenwöhr, Germany
U.S. Army Pacific	**Ft. Shafter, Hawaii**
U.S. Army, Japan/ 9th Theater Army Area Command	Camp Zama, Japan
U.S. Army, Alaska	Ft. Wainwright, Alaska
25th Infantry Division (light)/ U.S. Army Hawaii	Schofield Barracks, Hawaii
8th Army	**Seoul, South Korea**
2nd Infantry Division, "Indianhead"	Uijonbu, South Korea
19th Theater Army Area Command	Taegu, South Korea
U.S. Army South	**Ft. Clayton, Panama**
Military Police Command	Ft. Clayton, Panama
Army Materiel Command	**Alexandria, Va.**
Army Special Operations Command	**Ft. Bragg, N.C.**
Army Training and Doctrine Command	**Ft. Monroe, Va.**
Army Intelligence and Security Command	**Ft. Belvoir, Va.**
Information Systems Command	**Ft. Huachuca, Ariz.**
Criminal Investigation Command	**Ft. Belvoir, Va.**
Corps of Engineers	**Washington, D.C.**
Medical Command	**Ft. Sam Houston, Tex.**
National Guard divisions:	
28th Infantry Division, "Keystone"	Harrisburg, Pa.
29th Infantry Division (light), "Blue and Grey"	Ft. Belvoir, Va.
34th Infantry Division	St. Paul, Minn.
35th Infantry Division (mech.), "Santa Fe"	Ft. Leavenworth, Kans.
38th Infantry Division, "Cyclone"	Indianapolis, Ind.
40th Infantry Division (mech.), "Sunshine"	Los Alamitos, Calif.
42nd Infantry Division, "Rainbow"	Troy, N.Y.
49th Armored Division, "Lone Star"	Austin, Tex.

Source: U.S. Army Force Command.

▶U.S. COAST GUARD

The Coast Guard is a branch of the armed forces of the United States at all times. What distinguishes it from the other services is that it is part of the Department of Transportation—not Defense—except during wartime, or at the direction of the president, when it operates as part of the Navy. A successor to the Revenue Marine established in 1790, its primary function is to enforce federal maritime law.

▶U.S. AIR FORCE

The Air Force is organized into a number of commands. Within commands concerned with the strategic or tactical operation of aircraft, the primary subdivisions are indicated by the term air force prefaced by a number, as the Eighth Air Force. Such an *air force* is comprised of wings; a *wing* consists of two or more groups or squadrons; a *group* consists of two or more squadrons; and a *squadron* is made up of two or more flights. A *flight* is the basic tactical unit and consists of four or more planes.

▶SPECIAL OPERATIONS FORCES (SOF)

A unified command whose elements are drawn from the four major services, the special operations forces are designated to achieve military objectives of a limited and specific nature. Among the various elements of the SOF are: *Army* special forces; Rangers; psychological operations, civil affairs, and special operations aviation units; *Navy* SEAL and SEAL delivery vehicle teams; and *Air Force* Twenty-third Air Force special operations force.

Defense Establishment Employees, 1998

| Branch | Active Duty[1] | | | Civilian |
	Officers	Enlisted	Total	employees
Army	78,498	401,188	483,880	257,886
Navy[2]	54,999	323,120	382,338	207,601
Marine Corps	17,892	155,250	173,142	N.A.
Air Force	71,892	291,590	367,470	172,845
Total DoD	**223,281**	**1,171,148**	**1,406,830**	**756,290**

Note: As of September 30, 1998. 1. Includes Academy Cadets and Midshipmen, not shown separately. 2. Includes Marine Corps civilian personnel.   **Source:** U.S. Dept. of Defense, *Defense '99.* www.defenselink.mil.

Major Naval Operating Forces

Name	Headquarters
Pacific Fleet	Pearl Harbor, Hawaii
Third Fleet	San Diego, Calif.
Seventh Fleet	Yokosuka, Japan
Atlantic Fleet	Norfolk, Va.
Second Fleet	Norfolk, Va.
U.S. Naval Forces Europe	London, England
Sixth Fleet	Gaeta, Italy
Military Sealift Command	Washington, D.C.
Naval Reserve Force	New Orleans, La.
Mine Warfare Command	Ingleside, Texas
Operational and Test Evaluation Force	Norfolk, Va.
Naval Forces Southern Command	Rodman, Panama
Naval Forces Central Command	Manama, Bahrain
Fifth Fleet	Manama, Bahrain
Naval Special Warfare Command	Coronado, Calif.

Source: U.S. Dept. of Defense, *Defense '99.* www.defenselink.mil

Major Marine Corps Commands

Name	Headquarters
Fleet Marine Force, Atlantic	Camp Lejeune, N.C.
Fleet Marine Force, Pacific	Camp H.M. Smith, Hawaii
Marine Corps Combat Development Command	Quantico, Va.
Marine Corps Systems Command	Quantico, Va.
I Marine Expeditionary Force	Camp Pendleton, Calif.
II Marine Expeditionary Force	Camp Lejeune, N.C.
III Marine Expeditionary Force	Camp Butler, Okinawa, Japan
Marine Corps Air Ground Combat Center	Twentynine Palms, Calif.
Marine Reserve Forces	New Orleans, La.

Source: U.S. Dept. of Defense, *Defense '99.* www.defenselink.mil

Major Coast Guard Commands

Name	Headquarters
Coast Guard Headquarters	Washington, D.C.
Atlantic Area	Portsmouth, Va.
1st District	Boston, Mass.
5th District	Portsmouth, Va.
7th District	Miami, Fla.
8th District	New Orleans, La.
9th District	Cleveland, Ohio
Pacific Area	Alameda, Calif.
13th District	Seattle, Wash.
14th District	Honolulu, Hawaii
17th District	Juneau, Alaska

Source: U.S. Coast Guard.

Major Air Force Units

Name	Headquarters/Location
Air Combat Command	Langley AFB, Hampton, Va.
Air Force Materiel Command	Wright-Patterson AFB, Dayton, Ohio
Air Force Space Command	Peterson AFB, Colorado Spring, Colo.
Air Force Special Operations Command	Hurlburt Field, Fort Walton Beach, Fla.
Air Mobility Command	Scott AFB, Belleville, Ill.
Air Education and Training Command	Randolph AFB, San Antonio, Texas
Pacific Air Forces	Hickam AFB, Honolulu, Hawaii
U.S. Air Forces, Europe	Ramstein AB, Ramstein, Germany

Note: AB = air base; AFB = air force base; RAF = Royal Air Force (UK).   **Source:** Air Force Association, *USAF Almanac 1999.*

Top 10 Defense Contractors, 1998

Company	Awards (billions)
1. Lockheed Martin Corporation	$12.34
2. Boeing Company	10.87
3. Raytheon Company	5.67
4. General Dynamics Corp.	3.68
5. Northrop Grumman Corporation	2.69
6. United Technologies Corporation	1.98
7. Textron Inc.	1.84
8. Litton Industries	1.64
9. Newport News Shipbuilding Inc.	1.55
10. TRW Inc.	1.35

Source: U.S. Dept. of Defense, *Defense '99.* www.defenselink.mil

U.S. Armed Forces Worldwide, 1998

Region/Area	Army	Navy	Marine Corps	Air Force	Total
U.S., total[1]	**374,433**	**323,374**	**144,220**	**304,932**	**1,146,959**
Continental U.S.	344,724	202,085	131,040	282,968	960,817
Alaska	6,676	71	128	9,476	16,351
Hawaii	15,133	7,882	7,081	4,547	34,643
Guam	30	1,865	7	2,033	3,935
Johnston Atoll	205	2	0	13	220
Puerto Rico	142	1,763	22	43	1,970
Transients	7,519	11,695	5,303	5,851	30,368
Afloat	0	98,011	639	0	98,650
Europe, total[1]	**69,397**	**12,356**	**3,324**	**31,367**	**116,444**
Belgium[2]	994	99	34	518	1,645
Bosnia and Herzegovina	6,900	0	9	3	6,912
Croatia	101	3	4	11	119
Germany[2]	55,720	289	181	13,473	69,663
Greece[2]	10	252	10	169	441
Greenland[2]	0	0	0	130	130
Hungary	1,357	0	17	5	1,379
Iceland[2]	3	945	94	609	1,651
Italy[2]	2,696	4,423	152	4,248	11,519
Macedonia, Former Yugoslav Republic	441	0	0	1	442
Netherlands[2]	368	12	14	291	685
Portugal[2]	19	56	23	935	1,033
Spain[2]	5	2,878	98	238	3,219
Sweden	1	1	98	6	106
Turkey[2]	312	15	19	2,172	2,518
United Kingdom[2]	378	1,177	178	8,423	10,156
Afloat	0	2,161	2,153	0	4,314
NATO, Total	(60,531)	(10,177)	(851)	(31,301)	(102,860)
East Asia and Pacific, total[1]	**29,840**	**21,612**	**21,530**	**22,698**	**95,680**
Australia	10	39	15	258	322
Japan	1,799	5,626	19,184	13,755	40,364
Korea	27,918	287	105	8,580	36,890
Singapore	6	89	17	40	152
Thailand	40	8	42	34	124
Afloat	0	15,525	2,102	0	17,627
North Africa, Near East and South Asia, total[1]	**3,688**	**17,220**	**545**	**6,416**	**27,869**
Bahrain	15	667	216	18	916
Diego Garcia	10	685	0	20	715
Egypt	918	32	26	65	1,041
Kuwait	1,933	12	146	1,830	3,921
Saudi Arabia	737	24	44	4,068	4,873
United Arab Emirates	4	6	6	297	313
Afloat	0	15,781	0	0	15,781
Sub-Saharan Africa, total	**279**	**4**	**218**	**14**	**515**
Somalia	231	0	0	0	231
Western Hemisphere, total[1]	**3,922**	**3,548**	**1,280**	**2,036**	**10,786**
Canada	17	57	0	82	156
Cuba (Guantanamo)	145	671	531	1	1,348
Ecuador	355	1	6	5	367
Haiti	300	0	56	0	356
Honduras	402	1	11	180	594
Panama	2,622	102	258	1,712	4,694
Afloat	0	2,669	251	0	2,920
Worldwide, total[1]	**483,880**	**382,338**	**173,142**	**367,470**	**1,406,830**
Ashore	483,880	247,919	167,997	367,470	1,267,266
Afloat	0	134,419	5,145	0	139,564

Note: As of Sept. 30, 1998. 1. Includes other countries not shown separately. 2. Member of NATO Europe. **Source:** U.S. Dept. of Defense. **www.defenselink.mil.**

▶RESERVE FORCES

The United States has always relied on reserve forces that can be called to active duty or mobilized to deal with emergencies beyond the capacities of active forces. The reserve forces constitute the initial and primary augmentation of active forces in any emergency requiring rapid expansion of those forces.

There are seven reserve components: Army National Guard, Army Reserve, Naval Reserve, Marine Corps Reserve, Air National Guard, Air Force Reserve, and Coast Guard Reserve. All National Guard and Reserve personnel are assigned to one of three categories: the Ready Reserve, the Standby Reserve, or the Retired Reserve. All National Guard members are in the Ready Reserve.

U.S. Service and Casualties in Major Wars and Conflicts

War or conflict	Number serving	Battle deaths	Other deaths	Wounds not mortal
Revolutionary War (1775–83)				
Army	N.A.	4,044[1]	N.A.	6,004
Navy	N.A.	342	N.A.	114
Marines	N.A.	49	N.A.	70
Total	N.A.	4,435	N.A.	6,188
War of 1812 (1812–15)				
Army	N.A.	1,950	N.A.	4,000
Navy	N.A.	265	N.A.	439
Marines	N.A.	45	N.A.	66
Total	286,730	2,260	N.A.	4,505
Mexican War (1846–48)				
Army	N.A.	1,721	11,550	4,102
Navy	N.A.	1	N.A.	3
Marines	N.A.	11	N.A.	47
Total	78,718	1,733	11,550	4,152
Civil War (1861–65)[1]				
Army	2,128,948	138,154	221,374	280,040
Navy	84,415[2]	2,112	2,411	1,710
Marines	—	148	312	131
Total	2,213,363	140,414	224,097	281,881
Spanish-American War (1898)				
Army	280,564	369	2,061	1,594
Navy	22,875	10	0	47
Marines	3,321	6	0	21
Total	306,760	385	2,061	1,662
World War I (1917–1918)				
Army	4,057,101	50,510	55,868	193,663
Navy	599,051	431	6,856	819
World War I (1917–1918) (continued)				
Marines	78,839	2,461	390	9,520
Total	4,734,991	53,402	63,114	204,002
World War II (1941–46)				
Army	11,260,000	234,874	83,400	565,861
Navy	4,183,466	36,950	25,664	37,778
Marines	669,100	19,733	4,778	67,207
Total	16,112,566	291,557	113,842	670,846
Korean Conflict (1950–53)				
Army	2,834,000	27,709	806	77,596
Navy	1,177,000	468	939	1,576
Marines	424,000	4,267	1,261	23,744
Air Force	1,285,000	1,302	243	368
Total	5,720,000	33,746	3,249	103,284
Vietnam Conflict (1964–73)				
Army	4,368,000	30,905	7,275	96,802
Navy	1,842,000	1,631	925	4,178
Marines	794,000	13,081	1,754	51,392
Air Force	1,740,000	1,738	842	931
Total	8,744,000	47,355	10,796	153,303
Operation Desert Storm (1990–91)[3]				
Army	246,682	98	105	N.A.
Navy	98,652	6	14	N.A.
Marines	71,254	24	26	N.A.
Air Force	50,571	20	6	N.A.
Total	467,159	148	151	467

Note: N.A. = not available. Prior to World War I, dates are approximate. Actual period covered for World War I: Apr. 6, 1917-Nov. 11, 1918; World War II: Dec. 7, 1941-Dec. 31, 1946; Korea: June 25, 1950-July 27, 1953; Vietnam: Aug. 4, 1964-Jan. 27, 1973. 1. Union Forces only; authoritative statistics for Confederate forces not available. Estimates of the number who served range from 600,000 to 1.5 million. *The Final Report of the Provost Marshal General, 1863-1866* indicated 133,821 Confederate deaths (74,524 battle and 59,297 other) based upon incomplete returns. In addition, an estimated 26,000-31,000 Confederate prisoners died in prisons. 2. Includes Navy and Marines. 3. DMDC, Sept. 9, 1991. Deployment figures changed continuously throughout the operation and have since, and have depended on, among other things, the timely reporting and posting of data.
Source: U.S. Dept. of Defense, *Defense '97.* www.defenselink.mil

Military Personnel on Active Duty, 1801–1997

Year/War	Total[1]	Year/War	Total[1]	Year/War	Total[1]
1789	718	**1870**	50,348	**Korean Conflict (1950–53)**	
1795	5,296	**1880**	37,894	*1950*	*1,460,261*
1801	7,108	**1890**	38,666	*1951*	*3,249,455*
1810	11,554			*1952*	*3,635,912*
		Spanish-American War (1898)		*1953*	*3,555,067*
War of 1812 (1812-15)		*1898*	*235,785*		
1812	*12,631*			**1960**	2,476,435
1813	*25,152*	**1900**	139,344		
1814	*46,858*	**1915**	174,112	**Vietnam Conflict (1964-73)**	
1815	*40,885*			*1964*	*2,687,409*
		World War I (1917-18)		*1965*	*2,655,389*
1820	15,113	*1917*	*643,833*	*1966*	*3,094,058*
1830	11,942	*1918*	*2,897,167*	*1967*	*3,376,880*
1840	21,616			*1968*	*3,547,902*
		1919	1,172,602	*1969*	*3,460,162*
Mexican War (1846–48)		**1920**	343,302	*1970*	*3,066,294*
1846	*39,165*	**1930**	255,648		
1847	*57,761*	**1940**	458,365	**1975**	2,128,120[2]
1848	*60,308*			**1980**	2,050,627
		World War II (1941–46)		**1985**	2,151,032
1850	20,824	*1941*	*1,801,101*		
1860	27,958	*1942*	*3,858,791*	**Operation Desert Storm (1990–91)**	
		1943	*9,044,745*	*1990*	*2,043,705*
Civil War (1861–65)		*1944*	*11,451,719*	*1991*	*1,985,555*
1861	*217,112*	*1945*	*12,123,455*		
1862	*673,124*	*1946*	*3,030,088*	**1992**	1,807,180
1863	*960,061*			**1993**	1,705,103
1864	*1,031,724*			**1994**	1,610,490
1865	*1,062,848*			**1995**	1,514,224
				1996	1,471,722
				1997	1,438,562

Note: Figures in italics are wartime years. 1. Excludes the Coast Guard.
Source: Bureau of the Census, *Statistical History of the U.S.* (1976) and U.S. Dept. of Defense, unpublished statistics.

Women in Uniform: Female Active Duty Military Personnel 1945-98

Year	Total DoD	Army Officers	Army Enlisted	Navy Officers	Navy Enlisted	Marine Corps. Officers	Marine Corps. Enlisted	Air Force Officers	Air Force Enlisted
1945	266,256	62,775	93,095	19,188	72,833	809	17,556	N.A.	N.A.
1950	22,069	4,431	6,551	2,447	2,746	45	535	1,532	3,782
1960	31,550	4,263	8,279	2,711	5,360	123	1,488	3,675	5,651
1970	41,479	5,248	11,476	2,888	5,795	299	2,119	4,667	8,987
1975	96,868	4,594	37,701	3,676	17,498	345	2,841	4,981	25,232
1980	171,418	7,609	61,729	4,877	30,103	487	6,219	8,493	51,901
1985	211,606	10,828	68,419	6,913	45,690	654	9,041	11,927	58,134
1990	227,018	12,404	71,217	7,808	52,099	677	8,679	13,331	60,803
1995	196,116	10,786	57,260	7,899	47,931	690	7,403	12,068	52,079
1996	197,693	10,584	59,039	7,825	46,867	750	7,814	12,047	52,767
1997	192,404	10,293	58,876	7,805	41,381	765	8,133	12,092	53,059
1998	198,420	10,367	60,787	7,777	42,261	854	8,928	11,971	53,542

Source: U.S. Dept. of Defense, *Defense '99*. www.defenselink.mil

Minorities in Uniform, 1998

Service	Black Americans Number	Black Americans Percent	Hispanic Americans Number	Hispanic Americans Percent	Other[1] Number	Other[1] Percent	Total Number	Total Percent
Officers								
Army	9,205	11.8%	2,965	3.8%	4,007	5.1%	16,177	20.8%
Navy	3,464	6.4	2,154	4.0	2,323	4.3	7,941	14.8
Marines	1,280	7.2	848	4.7	561	3.1	2,689	15.1
Air Force	4,302	6.1	1,538	2.2	3,470	4.9	9,310	13.2
Total	**18,251**	**8.3%**	**7,505**	**3.4%**	**10,361**	**4.7%**	**36,117**	**16.4%**
Enlisted								
Army	117,302	29.5%	30,791	7.7%	26,429	6.6%	174,522	43.9%
Navy	62,756	20.0	28,530	9.1	25,303	8.1	116,589	37.2
Marines	25,548	16.7	19,049	12.4	6,961	4.5	51,558	33.6
Air Force	51,632	17.9	14,838	5.1	12,232	4.2	78,702	27.2
Total	**257,238**	**22.3%**	**93,208**	**8.1%**	**70,925**	**6.1%**	**421,371**	**36.5%**
DoD Total	**275,489**	**20.1%**	**100,713**	**7.3%**	**81,286**	**5.9%**	**457,488**	**33.3%**

Note: As of December 31, 1998. 1. Includes Native Americans, Alaskan Natives, and Pacific Islanders.
Source: U.S. Dept. of Defense, *Defense '99*. www.defenselink.mil.

Guard and Reserve Forces, 1998

Status	Army National Guard	Army Reserve	Naval Reserve	Marine Corps Reserve	Air National Guard	Air Force Reserve	Total DoD	Coast Guard Reserve
Selected Reserve								
Officers	31,305	40,665	19,405	3,760	13,235	15,938	124,308	1,059
Warrant Officers	7,988	3,017	276	462	—	—	11,743	216
Enlisted	323,150	161,286	73,381	36,619	94,861	56,032	745,329	6,312
Total	362,443	204,968	93,062	40,841	108,096	71,970	881,380	7,587
Individual Ready Reserve/Inactive National Guard								
Officers	437	46,450	15,454	3,218	—	9,849	75,408	171
Warrant Officers	77	3,120	36	94	—	—	3,327	14
Enlisted	4,200	176,909	97,615	54,964	—	46,610	380,298	5,099
Total	4,714	226,479	113,105	58,276	—	56,459	459,033	5,284
Total Ready Reserve								
Officers	31,742	87,115	34,859	6,978	13,235	25,787	199,716	1,230
Warrant Officers	8,065	6,137	312	556	—	—	15,070	230
Enlisted	327,350	338,195	170,996	91,583	94,861	102,642	1,125,627	11,411
Total	**367,157**	**431,447**	**206,167**	**99,117**	**108,096**	**128,429**	**1,340,413**	**12,871**

Note: As of September 30, 1998.   Source: U.S. Dept. of Defense, *Defense '99*. www.defenselink.mil.

The Ready Reserve consists of the Selected Reserve, the Individual Ready Reserve, and the Inactive National Guard. Some reservists are organized in units, others train as individuals. All are subject to orders for active duty in time of war or national emergency.

In addition, members of the Selected Reserve may be ordered to active duty under implementation of the presidential call-up authority, under which the president can activate up to 200,000 members of the Selected Reserve involuntarily, for operational missions, for not more than 90 days, without declaring a national emergency.

▶NUCLEAR FORCES

Nuclear forces are classified as either strategic or nonstrategic. The strategic triad—a cornerstone of post-World War II U.S. defense—is composed of land-based missile forces, including intercontinental ballistic missiles (ICBMs); submarine-launched ballistic missiles (SLBMs); and manned aircraft of the strategic bomber force. Nonstrategic nuclear weapons are shorter-range weapons that can be deployed on the battlefield and include sea-launched cruise missiles, artillery-fired atomic projectiles, and dual-capable (conventional and nuclear) aircraft.

Major Weapon Systems and Combat Forces, 1980–99

Weapon or force	1980	1984	1990	1998	1999
STRATEGIC (NUCLEAR) FORCES					
Land-based ICBMs					
Minuteman	1,000	1,000	950	500	500
Peacekeeper	0	0	50	50	50
Heavy bombers[1]					
B-52	241	241	154	56	56
B-1	0	0	90	70	74
B-2 (stealth bomber)	0	0	0	12	13
Submarine-Launched Ballistic Missiles[2]					
Poseidon (C-3 and C-4)[3]	336	384	368	0	0
Trident (C-4 and D-5)	0	72	216	432	432
GENERAL PURPOSE FORCES					
Active land forces					
Army divisions	16	16	18	10	10
Marine Corps divisions	3	3	3	3	3
Army Separate brigades[4]	8	8	8	3	3
Army Special Forces groups	2	4	5	5	5
Army Ranger regiment	0	0	1	1	1
Active tactical air forces (PAA/squadrons)					
Air Force attack and fighter aircraft	1,608/74	1,734/77	1,722/76	936/52	906/49
Navy attack and fighter aircraft	696/60	616/63	622/57	456/36	432/36
Marine Corps attack and fighter aircraft	329/25	256/24	334/24	308/21	208/21
Naval forces					
Strategic forces ships	48	41	39	18	18
Battle forces ships	384	425	412	271	256
Support forces ships	41	46	65	26	23
Reserve forces ships	6	12	31	18	18
Total battle forces deployable	479	524	547	333	315
Coastal defense, mine warfare, and other	52	33	19	21	22
AIRLIFT AND SEALIFT FORCES					
Intertheater airlift (PMAI)[5]					
C-5	70	70	109	104	104
C-141	234	234	234	143	136
KC-10	0	25	57	54	54
C-17	0	0	0	30	37
Intratheater airlift					
C-130[6]	482	520	460	425	425
Sealift ships[7]					
Tankers, active	21	21	28	10	10
Cargo, active	23	30	40	43	49
Ready Reserve Force (RRF)	24	51	96	88	87

Note: PMAI = primary mission aircraft inventory. 1. Excludes backup and attrition reserve aircraft. 2. Number operational. 3. C-3 missiles were removed from Poseidon submarines in September of 1992. 4. Includes the Eskimo scout group and the armored cavalry regiments. 5. Excludes development/test and training aircraft. 6. Excludes Dept. of Navy aircraft. 7. Includes fast sealift ships, afloat prepositioned force ships, and common user (charter) ships.
Source: U.S. Dept. of Defense, *Defense '99.* www.defenselink.mil.

Department of Defense Contract Awards, Payroll, and Civilian and Military Personnel by State, 1998

State	Payroll[1] ('000s)	Contract awards[2] ('000s)	Personnel[3] Military	Personnel[3] Civilian
Alabama	$2,450,246	$2,201,526	14,708	22,100
Alaska	850,010	617,134	16,351	4,017
Arizona	1,842,276	3,003,486	20,825	8,300
Arkansas	721,455	216,750	4,812	3,694
California	11,478,877	17,401,098	116,206	71,774
Colorado	2,300,955	2,380,692	29,040	11,205
Connecticut	533,262	3,408,719	4,257	2,724
Delaware	282,251	88,249	3,760	1,399
District of Columbia	1,131,403	1,365,594	13,632	12,598
Florida	6,715,734	5,463,717	53,692	27,726
Georgia	4,565,207	3,689,655	62,316	31,268
Hawaii	2,484,584	889,607	34,643	16,028
Idaho	357,912	171,609	4,315	1,357
Illinois	2,059,349	1,284,629	31,508	13,848
Indiana	774,972	1,649,500	923	6,404
Iowa	249,194	459,195	395	1,411
Kansas	1,075,337	1,007,244	16,024	5,616
Kentucky	1,717,882	1,637,070	34,169	6,942
Louisiana	1,198,080	1,241,305	15,274	7,756
Maine	536,876	895,009	1,680	5,430
Maryland	3,466,270	5,220,476	29,497	33,291
Massachusetts	815,642	4,245,094	2,746	7,513
Michigan	811,549	1,064,877	956	7,892
Minnesota	407,886	1,215,345	689	2,490
Mississippi	1,213,888	1,352,241	12,121	9,817
Missouri	1,399,997	4,653,388	13,506	9,198
Montana	262,698	106,805	3,574	1,085
Nebraska	649,481	232,891	8,360	3,365
Nevada	737,235	231,157	7,683	2,069
New Hampshire	245,453	425,910	284	1,041
New Jersey	1,450,514	2,661,459	7,077	15,202
New Mexico	1,074,253	632,990	12,211	7,225
New York	1,703,444	3,061,543	19,647	11,801
North Carolina	4,078,326	1,003,716	87,445	16,965
North Dakota	344,527	139,599	7,769	1,667
Ohio	2,130,679	2,471,715	7,376	24,501
Oklahoma	2,189,552	920,536	25,553	19,810
Oregon	522,688	289,073	616	2,830
Pennsylvania	2,145,726	3,318,098	3,071	27,762
Rhode Island	469,031	216,632	3,093	4,532
South Carolina	2,267,027	969,159	37,661	9,808
South Dakota	223,280	88,015	3,090	1,261
Tennessee	1,049,580	1,216,017	2,157	5,529
Texas	8,343,053	7,980,196	106,892	45,743
Utah	914,547	470,140	4,619	11,809
Vermont	91,441	92,380	50	527
Virginia	10,441,395	12,670,561	80,295	79,978
Washington	3,766,848	2,631,335	32,967	23,323
West Virginia	248,786	107,451	520	1,689
Wisconsin	379,441	557,267	546	1,851
Wyoming	207,881	67,994	3,379	947
Undistributed	N.A.	12,989,329	26,389	0
Total U.S.	$97,377,980	$122,375,179	1,030,369	654,118

Note: For year ending Sept. 30. 1. Payroll estimates cover active duty military and direct hire civilian personnel, including Army Corps of Engineers. 2. Military awards for supplies, services and construction; expenditures relating to awards may extend over several years. Net value of contracts of over $25,000 for work in each state; the state in which the prime contractor is located is not necessarily the state in which the subcontracted work is done. 3. Personnel figures are as of Sept. 30, 1998.
Source: U.S. Dept. of Defense, *Defense '99*. www.defenselink.mil

Active Duty, Monthly Basic Pay Table

Pay Grade	Army Rank	Years of Service			
		2	10	20	26
	Commissioned Officers				
O-10	General, Admiral	$8,114	$8,426	$10,167	$10,800
O-9	Lieut. General, Vice-Admiral	7,129	7,466	8,893	9,529
O-8	Maj. General, Rear Admiral	6,481	7,129	8,426	8,634
O-7	Brig. General, Commodore	5,584	6,172	7,619	7,619
O-6	Colonel, Captain	4,257	4,537	5,834	6,694
O-5	Lt. Colonel, Commander	3,639	4,008	5,278	5,462
O-4	Major, Lt. Commander	3,181	3,855	4,567	4,567
O-3	Captain, Lieutenant	2,714	3,674	3,950	3,950
O-2	1st Lieutenant, Lieut. (J.G.)	2,312	2,930	2,930	2,930
O-1	2nd Lieutenant, Ensign	1,913	2,312	2,312	2,312
	Warrant Officers				
W-5	Chief Warrant Officer	N.A.	N.A.	$4,221	4,698
W-4	Chief Warrant Officer	$2,654	$3,087	3,792	4,224
W-3	Chief Warrant Officer	2,438	2,838	3,336	3,578
W-2	Chief Warrant Officer	2,130	2,531	2,993	3,114
W-1	Warrant Officer	1,881	2,312	2,778	2,778
	Enlisted Personnel				
E-9	Sgt. Major, Master C.P.O.	N.A.	$2,877	$3,208	$3,705
E-8	Master Sgt., Senior C.P.O.	N.A.	2,482	2,811	3,308
E-7	Sgt.1st Class, Chief Petty Officer	$1,819	2,150	2,480	2,977
E-6	Staff Sgt., Petty Officer 1st Class	1,580	1,912	2,173	2,173
E-5	Sergeant, Petty Officer 2d Class	1,384	1,746	1,844	1,844
E-4	Corporal, Petty Officer 3d Class	1,253	1,485	1,485	1,485
E-3	Pvt. 1st Class, Seaman	1,179	1,275	1,275	1,275
E-2	Private, Seaman	1,076	1,076	1,076	1,076
E-1	Recruit, Seaman Recruit	959	959	959	959

Note: Effective Jan. 1, 1999. Numbers rounded to nearest dollar. N.A.: Not Applicable   **Source:** U.S. Department of Defense.

SOCIAL INSURANCE PROGRAMS

In order to provide a "safety net" for the disadvantaged, the elderly, and the disabled, the Federal Government administers a range of social insurance and social assistance programs. Many of these programs are administered by the Social Security Administration, which became an independent Government agency in 1995. But many cabinet-level departments, other independent Government agencies, and state government human services agencies also run programs such as food stamps (Dept. of Agriculture), public housing (Dept. of Housing and Urban Development), and programs for veterans (Dept. of Veterans Affairs).

Social insurance programs were not developed all at once to fulfill a specific agenda of national need. Rather they are a hodgepodge of legislation passed (and often altered) over the years to meet the needs of particular groups of citizens at particular times. In what the Government calls "social insurance programs," certain risks—injury, disability, unemployment, old age, and death—are lumped together. "Premiums," usually in the form of a payroll tax, are paid by employees and/or their employers. The benefit is paid, regardless of other financial resources (other than earnings), when one of those "risks" occurs.

▶ SOCIAL SECURITY

The Depression proved that the traditional support systems—the family, private charities, and local government—failed in nationwide economic hard times. Many old people had exhausted their savings and were destitute; in fact, during the Depression less than 10 percent of the aged left estates large enough to be probated. This led to the enactment of one of the most comprehensive pieces of legislation ever passed by Congress, the Social Security Act.

Signed into law by Franklin Roosevelt on August 14, 1935, the Social Security Act established two social insurance programs: a Federal system of old-age benefits for retired workers in commerce and industry and a federal-state system of unemployment insurance. The law also provided for Federal matching grants-in-aid to states to help them assist the needy aged, the blind, and children. Today, in the words of former Social Security Commissioner Dorcas R. Hardy, it is "the most complex Government program that God and Congress ever created."

The first payments of monthly benefits were made in 1940. Major changes in the scope of Social Security were made in 1956, when the program was broadened through the addition of disability insurance; in 1965, through the addition of Medicare and Medicaid; in 1970, when the black lung program was developed to provide benefits to coal miners (and their survivors) who suffer from pneumoconiosis (black lung disease); in 1974, when social security insurance was taken over by the Social Security Administration; and in 1972 Congress authorized provisions for cost-of-living increases. In 1983, amendments provided for the taxing of up to one-half of benefits for certain upper-income beneficiaries.

Workers and their employers each contribute an equal amount to the Social Security program to pay for retirement, disability, and Medicare benefits. The amount deducted from paychecks in-

SOCIAL SERVICE PROGRAMS INFORMATION

Information about social service programs can be obtained from the following government agencies:

Aid to Families with Dependent Children (AFDC) This program was abolished under the Welfare Reform Act of 1996. It was replaced with the Temporary Assistance to Needy Families (TANF) program. Information is available from the Administration for Children and Families, U.S. Dept. of Health and Human Services. (202)-401-9200. **www.acf.dhhs.gov**

Black lung program Office of Workers Compensation Programs, U.S. Dept. of Labor. (202)-693-0046. **www.dol.gov/dol/esa/public/owcp-org.htm**

Food Stamps Food and Consumer Service, U.S. Dept. of Agriculture. (703) 305-2276. **www.usda.gov/fcs/fcs.htm**

Head Start Administration for Children and Families, U.S. Dept. of Health and Human Services. (202)-401-9200. **www.acf.dhhs.gov**

Medicaid Health Care Financing Administration, U.S. Dept. of Health and Human Services. (410) 786-3151. **www.ssa.gov/hcfa/hcfahp2.html**

Medicare (HI) Health Care Financing Administration, U.S. Dept. of Health and Human Services. (410) 786-3151. **www.ssa.gov/hcfa/hcfahp2.html**

Social Security (OASDI) Social Security Administration. (410) 965-7700. **www.ssa.gov/**

Special nutrition programs Food and Consumer Service, U.S. Dept. of Agriculture. (703) 305-2276. **www.usda.gov/fcs/fcs.htm**

Supplemental Security Income (SSI) Social Security Administration. (410) 965-7700. **www.ssa.gov/.**

Temporary disability insurance Office of Workers Compensation Programs, U.S. Dept. of Labor. (202)-219-7503. **www.dol.gov/dol/esa/public/owcp-org.htm**

Unemployment insurance Office of Workers Compensation Programs, U.S. Dept. of Labor. (202)-219-7503. **www.dol.gov/dol/esa/public/owcp-org.htm**

Veterans' benefits U.S. Dept. of Veterans Affairs. (202) 273-5700. **www.va.gov.**

creased steadily from 1983 before levelling off in 1990 at 7.65 percent. Employers must contribute the same amount. Self-employed workers, who are both employee and employer, pay both shares, or a total of 15.3 percent. Contributions are limited to the first $72,600 of earnings although Medicare taxes continue at a rate of 1.45 percent each for employer and employee (twice that amount for the self-employed) for all earnings above that amount.

Old Age, Survivors and Disability Insurance (OASDI)

This program's basic principles are that benefits are related to earnings in covered work, benefits are paid regardless of income from savings, pensions, etc. and universal compulsory coverage is to assure a base of economic security. Monthly benefits are payable at age 65 to workers who are eligible, and lump sum payments are made to the estates of workers who die before reaching 65. The addition of disability insurance in 1956 and hospital insurance in 1965 broadened the program's scope, and in 1972 Congress authorized provisions for cost-of-living increases. The 1983 amendments improved the program's financial footing with tax rate increases in self-employment tax rates, and taxing up to one-half of benefits for certain upper-income beneficiaries.

To receive Social Security benefits, generally you must have worked for 10 years in a job in which you contributed to the Social Security fund. Your social Security benefit is not directly dependent on the number of years you worked. Rather it is based on your average earnings over your working lifetime. The average recipient receives benefits equivalent to 42 percent of an average working year's earnings. Because Social Security is designed to benefit low-income workers, people in upper-income brackets generally receive a lower percentage of their working year's earnings when they collect their benefits. However, you can still earn money while collecting Social Security. Recipients under age 65 may earn up to $9,600 before their benefits are reduced; after that amount, $1 is withheld for every $2 earned. Recipients between 65 and 69 may earn up to $15,500, after which $1 is withheld for every $3 earned. Recipients over age 70 may earn any amount of money while collecting Social Security benefits.

Social Insurance Programs: Beneficiaries and Payments, 1998

Program	Beneficiaries ('000s)	Benefits (billions)
OASDI	44,246	$375.6
Medicare	38,574	207.1[1]
Medicaid[1]	33,579	123.6
Food Stamps	19,787	16.9
TANF (Welfare)	8,770	16.6
SSI[1]	6,564	29.1

Note: OASDI = Old Age, Survivors, and Disability Insurance; AFDC = Aid to Families with Dependent Children; SSI = Social Security Insurance. 1. Figure for 1997. **Source:** Social Security Administration; Administration on Children and Families; Health Care Financing Administration.

OASDI Beneficiaries and Benefit Payments, 1998

Type of Beneficiaries	Number ('000s)	Average monthly benefit
Retired workers	27,511	$780
Spouses of retired workers	2,864	400
Children of retired workers	439	358
Survivors of deceased workers	7,097	N.A
Surviving children	1,884	960
Widowed mothers and fathers	221	545
Aged widows and widowers	4,799	749
Disabled widows and widowers	194	487
Disabled workers	4,698	733
Spouses of disabled workers	190	182
Children of disabled workers	1,446	208
Total monthly beneficiaries	**44,246**	**N.A**

Note: OASDI = old-age, survivors and disability insurance. **Source:** Social Security Administration, *Fact Sheet on OASDI*

Approximate Monthly Retirement, Disability, and Survivor Benefits

Worker's age, 1999	Worker's family	Insured worker's earnings, 1998				
		$20,000	$30,000	$40,000	$50,000	$68,400 or more
Retirement Benefits[1]						
45	Retired worker only	$826	$1,092	$1,310	$1,435	$1,687
	Worker and spouse[2]	1,239	1,638	1,965	2,152	2,530
55	Retired worker only	826	1,092	1,310	1,428	1,622
	Worker and spouse[2]	1,239	1,638	1,965	2,142	2,433
65	Retired worker only	767	1,016	1,197	1,269	1,373
	Worker and spouse[2]	1,150	1,524	1,795	1,911	2,059
Disability Benefits[3]						
25	Disabled worker only	$826	$1,092	$1,310	$1,435	$1,644
	Disabled, with dependents[4]	1,239	1,639	1,965	2,152	2,466
35	Disabled worker only	826	1,092	1,310	1,435	1,649
	Disabled, with dependents[4]	1,239	1,639	1,965	2,152	2,474
45	Disabled worker only	826	1,092	1,310	1,409	1,624
	Disabled, with dependents[4]	1,239	1,639	1,965	2,113	2,436
55	Disabled worker only	826	1,092	1,307	1,435	1,539
	Disabled, with dependents[4]	1,239	1,639	1,961	2,152	2,309
64	Disabled worker only	773	1,023	1,208	1,285	1,384
	Disabled, with dependents[4]	1,159	1,535	1,813	1,928	2,076
Survivor benefits[5]						
35	Spouse and 1 child[6]	$1,239	$1,639	$1,965	$2,132	$2,484
	Spouse and 2 children[7]	1,459	1,962	2,292	2,511	2,898
	1 child only	619	819	982	1,076	1,242
	Spouse at age 608	590	781	936	1,026	1,184
45	Spouse and 1 child[6]	1,239	1,639	1,965	2,152	2,445
	Spouse and 2 children[7]	1,459	1,962	2,292	2,511	2,853
	1 child only	619	819	982	1,076	1,222
	Spouse at age 60	590	781	936	1,026	1,165
55	Spouse and 1 child[6]	1,239	1,639	1,961	2,113	2,309
	Spouse and 2 children[7]	1,459	1,962	2,288	2,466	2,694
	1 child only	619	819	980	1,056	1,154
	Spouse at age 60	590	781	934	1,007	1,100

Note: Assumes steady earnings; actual benefits depend on the pattern of past and future earnings. 1. If worker retires at normal retirement age with steady lifetime earnings. 2. Spouse is assumed to be the same age as the worker. Spouse may qualify for a higher retirement benefit based on his or her own work record. 3. For workers with steady earnings and disabled in 1999. 4. Includes spouse and child, the maximum family benefit. 5. For workers with steady earnings who died in 1999. 6. Benefits are the same for two children if no parent survives or if the surviving parent has substantial earnings. 7. Equals maximum family benefit. 8. Figures for 1997 only. Spouses turning 60 in the future would receive higher benefits.
Source: Social Security Administration, *Social Security: Understanding the Benefits* (1999).

Medicare: Recipients and Benefits, 1975–99

Category	1975	1980	1985	1990	1995	1998	1999[1]
Hospital Insurance (HI)							
Total enrolled ('000s)	23,842	27,540	30,065	33,363	37,015	38,574	36,639
Aged	21,795	24,572	27,121	30,050	32,649	33,447	32,252
Disabled	2,047	2,968	2,944	3,313	4,366	5,127	4,387
Total Beneficiaries ('000s)	5,362	6,664	6,840	6,989	8,000	7,520[2]	7,220[2]
Aged	4,906	5,943	6,168	6,314	7,080	6,650[2]	6,390[2]
Disabled	456	721	672	675	920	870[2]	830[2]
Average annual benefit	$434	$863	$1,587	$1,970	$3,063	$3,482	$3,362
Aged	432	853	1,563	1,947	3,078	3,541	3,414
Disabled	460	948	1,808	2,176	2,955	3,098	3,029
Supplementary Medical Insurance (SMI)							
Total enrolled	23,339	27,120	29,721	32,333	35,496	36,841	36,866
Aged	21,504	24,422	27,049	29,426	31,622	32,361	32,404
Disabled	1,835	2,698	2,672	2,907	3,874	4,480	4,462
Total Beneficiaries	12,108	17,703	22,132	26,004	29,774	32,540[2]	26,367[2]
Aged	11,311	16,034	20,199	23,820	26,681	28,777[2]	23,033[2]
Disabled	797	1,669	1,933	2,184	3,093	3,763[2]	3,334[2]
Average annual benefit	$161	$374	$734	$1,282	$1,788	$2,259	$2,469
Aged	153	348	705	1,250	1,728	2,208	2,409
Disabled	259	610	1,022	1,603	2,282	2,623	2,904

1. Estimate. 2. Beneficiary numbers for 1998 and 1999 include only those receiving care under Fee For Service programs. A small number of beneficiaries who received benefits under managed care programs are not included in this figure. **Source:** Health Care Financing Administration, Division of Budget, unpublished data, 1999.

You may start collecting Social Security as early as age 62, but you will receive only 80 percent of the amount you would have received if you retired at age 65. The normal retirement age will be increased gradually from 65 to 67, beginning in the year 2000. See the accompanying table for approximate monthly retired, disabled, and survivor benefits.

If you become disabled—defined as having a physical or mental impairment that permanently prevents you from doing any substantial work (i.e. worth more than $500 a month)—you are eligible for additional benefits after six months. See the accompanying table for examples of disability benefits.

Additional benefits are also paid to the survivors of workers eligible for Social Security. Widows and widowers over the age of 60, children under the age of 18, and certain other survivors each generally receive amounts equivalent to 75 percent to 100 percent of the worker's Social Security benefit. There is, however, a per-family benefit limit, usually equal to 150-180 percent of the worker's benefit rate.

The OASDI programs are financed from taxes collected on earnings in covered jobs from employees and employers, which are deposited in two separate trust funds. The money received by the trust funds can be used only to pay OASDI benefits and operating expenses.

Medicare

The Social Security Amendments of 1965 established two contributory health insurance programs designed to provide assistance for medical expenses for the aged and disabled. The first is a compulsory program of hospital insurance (HI) which provides basic protection against the costs of inpatient hospital services and related post-hospital care, including home health services, part-time nursing care, and physical therapy. This is commonly referred to as Part B. Persons reaching age 65 without qualifying for HI may voluntarily enroll by paying a monthly premium. In 1999, HI paid all hospital bills for the first 60 days after the patient paid a deductible of $768. After day 60, the patient was responsible for a co-payment of $192 per day. For nursing homes, the first 20 days have no deductible, but $96 a day thereafter, up to 100 days.

The second health program, called Part B, is supplementary medical insurance (SMI) coverage, a voluntary program in which enrolled individuals pay a monthly premium. The program's coverage includes physician's and surgeon's services, outpatient services, laboratory tests, ambulance services, surgical dressings, home health services, and comprehensive outpatient services. In 1999, the premium was $45.50 per month after the patient has paid the deductible ($100); Part B pays for 80 percent of covered services.

As with OASDI, hospital insurance is financed by a tax on earnings: of the 7.65 percent tax on earnings (FICA) deducted from employee paychecks, 1.65 percent is for hospital insurance and 6 percent is for OASDI.

(Medicaid, a separate program that helps the financially needy of all ages pay for health care, is

Supplemental Security Insurance Beneficiaries and Benefits, 1975–97

| | Beneficiaries | | | | Benefits (millions) | | | |
| | | | State Supplement | | | | | State Supplement |
Year	Total[1]	Federal SSI	Federally admin- istered	State admin- istered	Total	Federal SSI	Federally admin- istered	State admin- istered
Total								
1975	4,359,625	3,893,419	1,684,018	303,391	$5,878.2	$4,313.5	$1,402.5	$162.2
1980	4,194,100	3,682,411	1,684,765	249,474	7,941.7	5,866.4	1,848.3	226.1
1990	4,888,180	4,412,131	2,058,273	285,530	16,598.7	12,893.8	3,239.2	465.7
1995	6,515,753	6,194,493	2,517,805	299,603	27,627.7	23,919.4	3,117.9	590.4
1996	6,676,729	6,325,531	2,421,470	310,211	28,791.9	25,264.9	2,987.6	539.5
1997	6,564,613	6,211,867	2,372,479	656,970	29,052.1	25,457.4	2,913.2	681.5
Aged								
1975	2,333,685	2,024,765	843,917	184,679	$2,604.8	$1,843.0	$ 673.5	$ 88.3
1980	1,838,381	1,533,366	702,763	134,555	2,734.3	1,860.2	756.8	117.2
1990	1,484,160	1,256,623	649,530	115,890	3,736.1	2,521.4	1,038.0	176.7
1995	1,479,415	1,314,720	663,390	114,451	4,467.1	3,374.8	864.5	227.9
1996	1,446,321	1,296,462	638,173	114,587	4,507.2	3,449.4	833.1	224.7
1997	1,395,845	1,251,374	619,516	130,652	4,532.0	3,479.9	823.6	228.4
Blind								
1975	75,315	68,375	31,376	4,933	$130.9	$ 92.4	$34.8	$3.7
1980	79,139	68,945	36,214	3,649	190.1	131.5	54.3	4.2
1990	84,109	74,781	40,334	3,042	334.1	238.4	90.5	5.2
1995	84,273	77,064	38,695	3,577	375.3	298.2	69.2	8.0
1996	82,815	76,180	36,759	3,414	371.9	298.9	65.9	7.1
1997	81,449	74,926	36,050	4,543	374.9	302.7	65.2	7.0
Disabled								
1975	1,950,625	1,800,279	808,725	113,504	$3,142.5	$2,378.1	$ 694.2	$ 70.2
1980	2,276,130	2,080,100	945,788	104,367	5,013.9	3,874.7	1,037.1	102.2
1990	3,319,911	3,080,727	1,368,409	166,598	12,520.6	10,134.0	2,110.6	275.9
1995	5,010,326	4,802,709	1,815,720	179,542	22,782.1	20,246.4	2,184.2	347.9
1996	5,145,850	4,952,889	1,746,538	186,955	23,905.6	21,516.6	2,088.6	300.4
1997	5,078,995	4,885,567	1,716,913	281,274	24,006.3	21,685.4	2,024.4	296.6

1. Total beneficiaries includes some people who receive both Federal SSI and a state supplement.
Source: Social Security Administration, *Social Security Bulletin, Annual Statistical Supplement.*

not a part of Social Security. It is discussed in "Other Income Support Programs," below).

Supplemental Security Income (SSI)
In 1974, Congress replaced the federal-state programs for needy aged (over 65 years old), blind, and disabled people with a single Federal Supplementary Security Income program. SSI eligibility depends on whether you work and in what state you live. In addition, SSI recipients may have no more than $2,000 in assets ($3,000 for married couples), though houses and cars are not usually counted as assets in this equation. The qualifying standards for disability benefits are the same as those used for the Social Security disability insurance program. Nearly 6.6 million people received SSI benefits in 1997; the basic monthly Federal benefit is the same in all states: $458 for one person and $687 for a couple. States have the option of supplementing Federal SSI under their own programs administered. Nearly 2.4 million persons received state supplements in 1997; the average payment was about $100.

Black Lung Program
Established by the Federal Coal Mine Health and Safety Act of 1969, this provides monthly cash benefits to coal miners who are totally disabled because of "black lung" disease (pneumoconiosis) and to survivors of miners who die from this disease. Benefits are paid mostly out of a trust fund financed by an excise tax on coal. The number of beneficiaries continues to decline as older beneficiaries are dying in greater numbers than new claimants are entering the program. A total of 94,488 miners, widows, and their dependents received a total of $459.06 million in 1998, down from $1.0 billion in 1985, when 294,846 people were receiving benefits.

Social Security And You
While Social Security benefits are automatic for all people who hold a Social Security card and who are eligible for programs, the Social Security Administration (SSA) recommends that workers check the agency's records of their earnings every three to five years. If their records are not accurate—the SSA says that 1 percent of eligible wages are not credited to workers' records—your benefits could be lower than you deserve.

To find out what your earnings are, pick up a Personal Earnings and Benefit Estimate Statement (PEBES). This, as well as free booklets detailing eligibility requirements and benefit payments, is available at any of the more than 1,300 local SSA offices nationwide. They are also available by calling 1-800-234-5SSA, 1-800-772-1212, or on the Internet at www.ssa.gov.

▶ OTHER INCOME SUPPORT PROGRAMS
Welfare
The Social Security Act of 1935 included a provision authorizing Aid to Families with Dependent Children (AFDC), commonly known as "welfare." Benefits were limited to families with children under 18. But in the much-ballyhooed 1996 welfare reform effort, the Federal Government ended more than 60 years of guaranteed assistance to the needy, and replaced it with a system of block grants to the states, who could use the money to enact their own welfare programs. The Temporary Assistance to Needy Families (TANF) Block Grant replaced AFDC on July 1, 1997. TANF gives states broad discretion to determine eligibility and benefit levels. However, families may not receive benefits for longer than 60 months, unwed teenage parents must stay in school and live at home, and people convicted of drug-related felonies are banned from receiving TANF or Food Stamp benefits. In addition, non-working adults must participate in community service within two months of receiving benefits, and must find work within two years. Parents with children under age 1 are exempt from the work requirements (under age 6 if child care is not available).

Welfare reform has succeeded in reducing the number of people receiving Government assistance. In April, 1999, President Clinton announced that the total number of people receiving welfare benefits had dropped to 7.6 million, its lowest level in 30 years. That's a 38 percent decrease in the three years since welfare reform went into effect, and nearly a 50 percent drop from the all-time high of 14.4 million reached in March, 1994.

The President's Council of Economic Advisers said that nearly half of the decline in the welfare rolls can be attributed to the growth of the economy. Another 30 percent, the Council said, resulted from welfare reform.

Medicaid
Enacted jointly with Medicare in 1965, Medicaid provides Federal matching funds to states to help pay the cost of medical care and services for low-income persons. Payments are made to suppliers of the care and service. To be eligible for matching funds, a state Medicaid program must cover all persons who receive assistance under TANF. (Most SSI recipients are also covered.) In 1997, 33.6 million aged, blind, disabled, or poor persons with families received Medicaid benefits at a total cost to state and Federal governments of $124 billion. Medicaid may also pay the premiums for supplementary medical insurance and the deductible and co-insurance cost of hospital insurance. Medicaid also covers some medical services that Medicare does not.

Welfare Beneficiaries and Benefits, 1970–98

| | Average monthly beneficiaries ('000s) | | | Benefits | |
Year	Recipients	Families	Children	Total (millions)	Average monthly benefit
1970	7,429	1,909	5,494	$ 4,082	$178
1975	11,067	3,269	7,821	8,153	208
1980	10,597	3,574	7,220	11,540	269
1985	10,813	3,692	7,165	14,580	329
1990	11,460	3,974	7,755	18,539	389
1991	12,595	4,375	8,515	20,356	388
1992	13,625	4,769	9,225	22,240	389
1993	14,144	4,981	9,539	22,286	373
1994	14,226	5,046	9,590	22,796	376
1995	13,652	4,876	9,274	22,032	377
1996	12,649	4,553	8,673	20,295	371
1997	10,936	3,946	N.A.	13,360	N.A.
1998	8,770	3,179	N.A.	16,562	N.A.

Note: "Welfare" refers to the Aid to Families with Dependent Children (AFDC) program through 1996; in 1997, AFDC was renamed Temporary Assistance to Needy Families (TANF), and many more restrictions were added. Source: Administration for Children and Families, unpublished data.

Food Stamps

By providing eligible applicants with coupons to buy food, this program enables families in need to purchase a nutritionally adequate diet. In general, a household is considered eligible if it has less than $2,000 in liquid assets, or if 30 percent of its countable cash income is insufficient to purchase an adequate low-cost diet as defined by the U.S. Department of Agriculture (USDA) "Thrifty Food Plan." The Food Stamp Act of 1964 set eligibility requirements for food stamp program participants and provides coupons through state and local agencies that are used to buy food in approved retail stores. States delegate varying degrees of authority to counties and cities, but the Federal Government finances 100 percent of the state-issued food benefits and part of the state's administrative costs. The Omnibus Budget Reconciliation Act of 1982 tightened eligibility and authorized pilot projects in which recipients lose their stamps if they don't work at least 20 hours a week.

Special nutrition programs

The USDA administers a number of programs designed to help safeguard the health and well-being of the nation's children by assisting the states

Federal Food Assistance Programs, 1970–98

Program	1970	1980	1990	1995	1997	1998
Participants (millions)						
Food stamps	4.3	21.1	20.1	26.6	22.9	19.8
National school lunch program[1]	22.4	26.6	24.1	25.7	26.3	26.6
School breakfast[1]	0.5	3.6	4.1	6.3	6.9	7.1
Women-infants-children[2]	—	1.9	4.5	6.9	7.4	7.4
Child and adult care[3]	0.1	0.7	1.5	2.4	2.5	2.6
Summer feeding[4]	0.2	1.9	1.7	2.1	2.3	N.A.
Federal cost (millions)						
Food stamps	$4,624	$8,721	$14,187	$22,765	$19,548	$16,879
National school lunch program[1]	300	2,279	3,214	4,467	4,934	5,084
School breakfast[2]	11	288	596	1,048	1,214	1,264
Women-infants-children	—	584	1,637	2,516	2,815	2,811
Child and adult care[3]	6	207	720	1,296	1,392	1,373
Summer feeding[4]	2	104	145	212	213	N.A.

1. Average monthly participation during school year. Covers public and private elementary and secondary schools and residential child care institutions. Costs do not include the value of USDA donated commodities. 2. WIC serves pregnant and postpartum women, infants, and children up to age five. 3. Provides year-round subsidies to feed preschool children in child care centers and family day care programs. Certain care centers serving disabled or elderly adults also receive meal subsidies. 4. Provides free meals to poor children in summer months. Number of participants is July average daily attendance at participating institutions.
Source: U.S. Dept. of Agriculture, *Annual Historical Review of Food and Nutrition Service Programs*, annual, and unpublished data.

Medicaid Recipients and Vendor Payments, 1975–97

Year	Aged	Blind	Disabled	Dependent children under 21	Adults in families with dependent children	Other/ Unknown	Total
Recipients ('000s)							
1975	3,615	109	2,355	9,598	4,529	1,800	22,207
1981	3,367	86	2,993	9,581	5,187	1,364	21,980
1985	3,061	80	2,937	9,757	5,518	1,239	21,814
1990	3,202	83	3,635	11,220	6,010	1,105	25,255
1995	4,119	92	5,767	17,164	7,604	1,536	36,282
1996	4,285	95	6,126	16,739	7,127	1,745	36,118
1997	3,954	(1)	6,129	15,269	6,797	1,429	33,579
Medical Vendor Payments (millions of dollars)							
1975	$4,358	$93	$3,052	$2,186	$2,062	$492	$12,242
1981	9,926	154	9,301	3,508	3,763	552	27,204
1985	14,096	249	13,203	4,414	4,746	798	37,508
1990	21,508	434	23,969	9,100	8,590	1,258	64,859
1995	36,527	848	48,570	17,976	13,511	2,709	120,141
1996	36,947	869	51,196	17,544	12,275	2,853	121,685
1997	37,721	(1)	54,129	15,666	12,298	3,737	123,551
Payments Per Capita							
1975	$1,205	$850	$1,296	$228	$455	$273	$556
1981	2,948	1,784	3,108	366	725	405	1,238
1985	4,605	3,104	4,496	452	860	658	1,719
1990	6,717	5,212	6,595	811	1,429	1,062	2,568
1995	8,868	9,256	8,422	1,047	1,777	1,762	3,311
1996	8,622	9,143	8,357	1,048	1,722	2,152	3,369
1997	9,539	(1)	8,832	1,026	1,809	2,615	3,679

Note: Figures are in current dollars A small number of recipients are in more than one category.   1. Figures for blind were combined with those for the disabled in 1997.   **Source:** Health Care Financing Administration, *2082 Report* (1999).

in providing adequate meals to all children at a moderate cost. The programs include the National School Lunch Program, the School Breakfast Program, the Summer Food Service Program, the Child Care Food Program, the Special Milk Program, and the Special Supplemental Food Program for Women, Infants, and Children (WIC) Program. The nutrition program for the elderly requires no income test, but preference is given to those with the greatest need.

Housing subsidies

The Federal Government has traditionally provided housing aid directly to lower-income households in the form of rental and mortgage-interest subsidies. The primary purposes are to improve housing quality and to reduce housing costs for lower-income households. Other goals include promoting residential construction, expanding housing opportunities for disadvantaged groups and groups with special housing needs, promoting neighborhood preservation and revitalization, increasing homeownership, and empowering the poor to become homeowners.

Most housing aid is targeted to very-low-income renters through two basic types of rental assistance programs. Project-based aid is typically tied to projects specifically produced for lower-income households through new construction or substantial renovation. Almost all project-based aid is provided through production-oriented programs, including the public-housing program, the section 8 new construction and substantial rehabilitation program, and the section 236 mortgage-interest-subsidy program (administered by the Department of Housing and Urban Development), and the section 515 mortgage-interest-subsidy program administered by the Farmers Home Administration.

Household-based subsidies that permit renters to choose from standard housing units in the existing private housing stock. Rental assistance programs generally reduce tenants' rent payments to 30 percent of their income, with the Government paying the balance of the contract rents.

The Federal Government also assists some lower- and moderate-income households in becoming homeowners by making long-term commitments to reduce their mortgage interest. These generally reduce mortgage payments, property taxes, and insurance costs to a fixed percentage of income, ranging from 20 percent to 28 percent.

The total number of households receiving assistance has increased substantially, from 3.2 million in 1977 to 5.7 million in 1995. Total outlays for housing aid rose from $2.9 billion in 1977 to an estimated 26.0 billion in 1996; outlays per unit rose from $1,160 to $5,480 over the same period.

Housing for the homeless

HUD funding for homeless programs is made available to state and local governments, Indian tribes, and non-profit organizations. The specific programs are the Emergency Shelter Grants (ESG) Program, the Supportive Housing Demonstration Program, the Shelter-Plus-Care Homeless Rental Housing Assistance, and the HUD-Owned Single Property Disposition Program.

Head Start

Head Start provides a wide range of services to children of low-income families (and their families) up to the age of five. Its goals are to improve the social competence, learning skills, and health and nutrition status of low-income children so that they can begin school on an equal footing with their more advantaged peers. The services include cognitive and language development, medical, dental, and mental health services (including screening and immunizations), and nutritional and social services. Parental involvement is extensive, through both volunteer participation and employment of parents as Head Start staff.

At least 90 percent of Head Start children come from families with incomes at or below the poverty line, and at least 10 percent of enrollment slots in each state must be available to disabled children. In 1998, more than 830,000 children were served in Head Start programs, at a total Federal cost of $4.4 billion, or an average cost of $5,301 per child. More than 60 percent of Head Start families have incomes of less than $9,000 per year, and 77.7 percent have yearly incomes of less than $12,000. Since 1980, the children served by

Head Start Participation and Funding, 1966–98

Year	Enrollment	Appropriations
1966	733,000	$198.9
1970	477,400	325.7
1980	376,300	735.0
1990	540,930	1,552.0
1994	740,493	3,325.7
1995	750,696	3,534.1
1996	752,077	3,569.3
1997	793,809	3,980.5
1998	830,000[1]	4,355.0

1. Estimate. **Source:** U.S. Dept of Health and Human Services, Administration for Children and Families. **www.acf.hhs.gov**

U.S. Weighted Average Poverty Thresholds by Family Size, 1960–98

Year	Maximum yearly family income						
	1 person	2 people	3 people	4 people	5 people	6 people	7 people
1960	$1,490	$1,924	$2,359	$3,022	$3,560	$4,002	$4,921[1]
1970	1,954	2,525	3,099	3,968	4,680	5,260	6,468[1]
1980	4,190	5,363	6,565	8,414	9,966	11,269	12,761
1990	6,652	8,509	10,419	13,359	15,792	17,839	20,241
1993	7,363	9,414	11,522	14,763	17,449	19,718	22,383
1994	7,547	9,661	11,821	15,141	17,900	20,235	22,923
1995	7,763	9,933	12,158	15,569	18,408	20,804	23,552
1996	7,995	10,233	12,516	16,036	18,952	21,389	24,268
1997[2]	8,183	10,473	12,802	16,400	19,380	21,886	24,802
1998	8,480[2]	10,915[2]	12,750	16,813	20,275	23,320	26,833

1. Seven or more people. 2. Householder under 65 years. **Source:** U.S. Bureau of the Census, *Current Population Survey* (1999).

Head Start have grown younger, less black, and more Hispanic. Five-year-olds made up 21 percent of the Head Start population in 1980; in 1997 they constituted only 6 percent. Meanwhile, four-year-olds increased from 55 to 60 percent. In 1980, 19 percent of Head Start children were Hispanic; in 1998, 26 percent were Hispanic, while black Head Start children declined from 42 to 36 percent over the same period.

Poverty income guidelines

The poverty income guidelines are used to determine whether a person or family is eligible for assistance under a particular federal program. The poverty threshold is established each year by increasing the previous year's threshold by the change in the Consumer Price Index. The original poverty threshold was devised in 1960 and was equal to three times the amount of money to buy the cheapest "nutritionally adequate" diet as dictated by the Department of Agriculture.

Unemployment Compensation

The Social Security Act provided an inducement to states to enact unemployment insurance laws, and by 1937 all 48 states, the territories of Alaska and Hawaii, and the District of Columbia had passed such laws. All contributions collected under state laws are deposited in the unemployment trust fund of the U.S. Treasury. A state may withdraw money from its account only to pay benefits. Each state has major responsibility for the content and development of its unemployment insurance law. Nationwide, about 120 million workers were covered in 1998.

Workers must be ready, able and willing to work and must be registered for work at a state public employment office. A worker's benefit is based on his or her employment in covered work over a prior performance period. No state can deny benefit to a claimant if he or she refuses to accept a new job under substandard labor conditions or where he or she would be required to join a company union.

In any given week in 1998, between 289,000 and 387,000 people filed for unemployment compensation for the first time, and a total of between 2.0 and 2.4 million were receiving benefits. In all, 10.4 million people filed for unemployment during 1998 (of those, only 7.3 million actually received benefits). That's down from 12.2 million in 1990, 16.2 million in 1982, and 15.4 million in 1975. The average weekly benefit in 1998 was $199, and the average duration of benefit was 13.9 weeks, making the average total benefit $2,767. The weekly benefit varies from state to state, but the general formula is designed to compensate for between 50 percent and 70 percent of average weekly pre-tax wage, up to a state-determined minimum. Average weekly benefits ranged from $145 in Maine to $269 in Hawaii.

Workers' compensation

Social insurance began in the United States with worker's compensation. A law covering Federal civilian employees was passed in 1908; the first state compensation law to be held constitutional was enacted in 1911. These laws made industry responsible for the compensation of workers (or their survivors) injured or killed while on the job. A worker incurring an occupational injury is compensated regardless of fault or blame in the accident. A separate Federal program enacted in 1969 protects coal miners (see "Black lung program" below).

Workers' compensation is almost exclusively financed by employers on the principle that the cost of work-related accidents is part of the expense of production. Every state except Texas mandates coverage under workers' compensation for private employees. Certain categories of workers, usually domestic, agricultural, and casual laborers, are often exempted from this requirement. Employers can use private insurance companies or can qualify as self-insurers. Workers' compensation covered 115 million workers in 1996, or 86 percent of the civilian labor force. The cash benefit for temporary total disability, permanent, total or partial disability, or death of a breadwinner is usually about 66.7 percent of weekly earnings at the time of the accident. Most state laws pay temporary disability benefits for as long as the disability lasts and the condition has not been stabilized to the point where no further improvement can result from medical treatment. Total benefit payments under workers' compensation programs in 1996 topped $42 billion, an increase of 10.8 percent over 1990.

Permanent partial disability compensation

for specific, or "schedule" injuries (for clearly measurable matters) is generally subject to different (usually lower) dollar maximums and is determined without regard to loss of earning power. Compensation for "nonschedule" injuries (injuries to head, back, nervous system) is the difference between wages before and after impairment. Death benefits are related to earnings and graduated by the number of dependents. Medical benefits are furnished without limit as to time or amount for accidental injuries. Temporary Disability Insurance provides coverage against the risk of lost wages due to short-term nonoccupational disability. The Federal Unemployment Tax Act permits states where employees make contributions under the unemployment insurance program to use some or all of those contributions for disability benefits. It is estimated that about two-thirds of the nation's wage and salary earners in private employment have some protection through various voluntary and governmental group arrangements. In general the benefit amount for a week is intended to replace at least half the weekly wage loss for a maximum of 26 to 39 weeks per year.

▶VETERANS' BENEFITS

The tradition of veterans' benefits dates to the 18th century when the Continental Congress provided disability pensions for veterans of the Revolutionary War. Today, the Department of Veterans Affairs (DVA) offers a wide range of services and benefits to eligible veterans, their dependents, and their survivors.

While the veteran population as a whole is decreasing in numbers (from about 29.5 million in 1975 to 25.5 million in 1997), the number of veterans age 65 or older is increasing rapidly, (from about 2.2 million in 1975 to more than 9 million in 1997.) The use and cost of medical care are expected to grow more rapidly over the next several years than those of other veterans' benefits and services. Compensation and pension caseloads are decreasing steadily due to beneficiary deaths, terminations for excess incomes, and age limitation for dependents. The number of trainees under the Montgomery GI bill will increase as more veterans become eligible.

Veterans who have incurred injuries or illness while in service are entitled to service-connected compensation. The amounts are determined by disability ratings. Death compensation or dependency and indemnity compensation is paid to survivors of veterans who died as a result of service-connected causes.

War veterans who have become permanently and totally disabled from non-service-connected causes, and to survivors of war veterans may receive means-tested veterans' pensions. Benefits are based on family size, and the pensions provide a floor of income. About 418,000 persons received $3.8 billion in veterans pension payments in 1996.

Veterans Benefits and Services: Outlays and Recipients, 1975–97

Fiscal year	Compensation and pensions	Readjustment, education, job training	Medical programs	Housing loans
		Outlays (millions)		
1975	$ 7,860	$4,593	$3,665	(1)
1980	11,688	2,342	6,515	(1)
1985	14,714	1,059	9,547	(1)
1990	15,241	278	12,134	(1)
1995	18,966	1,124	16,428	(1)
1996	17,170	1,106	16,572	(1)
1997	19,389	1,167	17,122	(1)
		Recipients ('000s)		
1975	4,855	2,804	1,985	290
1980	4,646	1,232	2,671	297
1985	4,005	491	2,963	179
1990	3,614	329	3,018	196
1995	3,332	476	2,696	263
1996	2,253	297	1,509	321
1997	2,200	N.A.	N.A.	259

1. No dollar figures for housing loans are provided because these are revolving funds and are not comparable to program expenditures in the other columns.   **Source:** U.S. Dept. of Veterans Affairs, *Annual Report of the Secretary of Veterans Affairs.*

Medical programs   The DVA operates 173 hospital centers, 133 nursing homes, 40 domiciliaries, and 398 outpatient clinics. In 1996 the DVA's nationwide health system received 1.6 million applications for care, almost all of whom received outpatient care. In 1997, DVA medical programs cost the Federal Government $17.1 billion.

The DVA extends free priority care to service-connected disabled veterans, to veterans in special categories, and to needy nonservice-connected veterans. As facilities and other resources permit, the DVA provides care to non-service-connected veterans with incomes that exceed the mandatory care income limits.

Housing and loan programs   The DVA made 258,775 guaranteed loans for housing for veterans in 1997. The maximum guaranty is as follows: 50 percent of the loan amount for loans of $45,000 or less; $22,500 for loans between $45,001 and $56,250; the lesser of $36,000 or 40 percent of the loan for loans between $56,251 and $144,000; and the lesser of $46,000 or 25 percent of the loan for loans in excess of $144,000.

Other veterans' programs   In 1996, the DVA spent $1.4 billion for a variety of education and training programs for eligible veterans and military personnel. The largest program is the Montgomery GI bill, which provides educational assistance. Contributions are required, and veterans can receive a basic educational benefit of up to $400 per month for 36 months while in an educational program.

The Veterans Job Training Act program provides payments to defray training costs of employers who hire certain veterans of the Korean conflict or Vietnam era who have been unemployed for long periods of time.

THE INTERNAL REVENUE SERVICE

Founded in 1862, the Internal Revenue Service (I.R.S.) is the office of the Department of the Treasury charged with collecting Federal taxes. The Constitution empowers Congress to levy excise taxes and—in emergencies—to raise direct taxes. Congress's right to levy taxes on the income of individuals and corporations was contested throughout the 19th century, but that authority was written into the Constitution with the passage of the 16th Amendment in 1913. Today, the source of most of the Federal Government's revenues are the individual income tax, corporate income tax, excise taxes, estate taxes, and gift taxes. The I.R.S. is responsible for these taxes as well as for collecting employee and employer payments for social insurance and retirement insurance (see "Social Insurance Programs").

In 1998, Congress enacted a major overhaul of the I.R.S. in hopes of transforming the agency from a menacing symbol of Government authority into a resource for taxpayers trying to cope with the increasingly bewildering tax code. The legislation established an outside board with broad authority to supervise the I.R.S.'s operations, and

perhaps more important, shifted the burden of proof in tax dispute cases to the I.R.S. (previously, taxpayers had to prove their innocence).

Initial reaction to the legislation was overwhelmingly favorable. But tax experts correctly predicted the law would give scofflaws greater incentive to cheat on their taxes. Property seizures dropped by 98 percent between 1997 and 1999, garnishments of bank accounts and paychecks were a quarter of their level two years earlier, and tax liens, which insure that back taxes are paid when properties are sold, were down by 67 percent.

But the most damaging change was the anti-harassment section of the legislation, which tax collectors say is thwarting them from collecting taxes from delinquent filers. Several I.R.S. agents said they no longer pursued outstanding tax bills vigorously because they feared losing their jobs under the anti-harassment policy.

"If you don't want to pay your taxes today all you have to do is say two magic words: installment agreement," said one I.R.S. collection officer in Washington state who spoke on condition of anonymity because he feared retaliation by supervisors.

"You just say you want one, and even if the terms you propose are ridiculous—like $10 a week when you owe tens of thousands—collection stops while your proposal goes up and down the chain of managers, until 90 days later you are told no," the I.R.S. employee said. "Then you just need to say another magic word—harassment—and because of this new law, the collection process stops while your complaint gets reviewed."

"Basically there is no enforcement going on right now, and that undermines the whole tax system," said Montie Day, a former I.R.S. criminal investigator and Federal prosecutor who now regularly sues the I.R.S. on behalf of taxpayers. "As word about this gets out, people who are inclined to cheat will say to themselves that since they aren't going to be made to pay up, they should cheat."

The decline in aggressive pursuit of tax cheats actually began even before the new law went into effect. In 1996, the I.R.S. audited 2.13 million of the 155 million tax returns filed, a rate of 1.38 percent. In 1997, the agency examined only 1.73 million returns, or 1.09 percent of the 158 million returns filed. Almost all of the decrease in audits came in individual returns. The I.R.S. audited just under 2 million individual returns in 1996; in 1997, that number was down to 1.5 million. Meanwhile, the agency stepped up its vigilance of corporate

tax filings. It audited 69,650 corporate returns (2.67 percent of the 2.6 million filed) in 1997, compared with 59,832 (2.34 percent) the year before.

The shift can also be seen in the number and distribution of I.R.S. employees. Total I.R.S. employment dropped from 102,082 in 1996 to 97,404 in 1997, but that's only half the story. The number of tax collectors dropped 38 percent from 17,610 to 10,856, and the number of auditors and tax examiners fell from 27,433 to 25,724. Meanwhile, the I.R.S.'s customer service staff skyrocketed from 1,777 employees in 1996 to a whopping 12,216 in 1997. That's a 587 percent increase in just one year.

For now, the shift in emphasis hasn't hurt the Federal coffers. The I.R.S. collected more total tax dollars ($1.62 billion) and more taxes per capita ($6,046) in 1997 than ever before. The cost of collecting $100, meanwhile, dropped from an all-time high of 60 cents in 1993 to 44 cents in 1997, about the same as it was in 1967. One example of the I.R.S.'s economical use of resources: it examined close to half of the 20,500 returns filed by corporations with total revenues of $250 million or

Average Itemized Deductions By Income Level, 1998

Adjusted gross income ranges	Percent itemizing deductions	Average deduction for:			
		Taxes	Gifts	Interest	Total[1]
0- $15,000	3.41%	$1,928	$1,172	$5,751	$10,279
$15,000- $30,000	14.93	2,225	1,506	5,496	10,446
$30,000- $50,000	38.84	3,013	1,600	6,028	11,237
$50,000- $100,000	70.67	4,956	2,113	7,336	14,781
$100,000-$200,000	90.52	9,449	3,573	11,065	23,547
$200,000 or more	92.90	35,231	19,032	22,003	63,349

Note: 1998 data based on tax returns for the 1997 tax year. 1. Does not include deductions for medical expenses not shown separately. Very few medical expenses are deductible. Source: Research Institute of America, *Federal Taxes Weekly Alert,* July, 1999.

Tax Rate Schedules, 2000

Taxable income	What you pay
Single Individual	
$ 0-$ 22,100	15.0% of sum over $0.00
$ 22,100-$ 53,500	$ 3,315 + 28.0% of sum over $ 22,100
$ 53,500-$115,000	$12,107 + 31.0% of sum over $ 53,500
$115,000-$250,000	$31,172 + 36.0% of sum over $115,000
over $250,000	$79,772 + 39.6% of sum over $250,000
Heads of Households	
$ 0-$ 28,750	15.0% of sum over $0.00
$ 28,750-$ 76,400	$ 4,312.50 + 28.0% of sum over $ 28,750
$ 76,400-$127,500	$17,024.50 + 31.0% of sum over $ 76,400
$127,500-$250,000	$33,385.00 + 36.0% of sum over $127,500
over $250,000	$77,485.00 + 39.6% of sum over $250,000
Married individuals filing jointly, or qualifying widow(er)	
$ 0-$ 36,900	15.0% of sum over $0.00
$ 36,900-$ 89,150	$ 5,535.00 + 28.0% of sum over $ 36,900
$ 89,150-$140,000	$20,165.00 + 31.0% of sum over $ 89,150
$140,000-$250,000	$35,928.50 + 36.0% of sum over $140,000
over $250,000	$75,528.50 + 39.6% of sum over $250,000
Married, Filing Separate Return	
$ 0-$ 18,450	15.0% of sum over $0.00
$18,450-$ 44,575	$ 2,767.50 + 28.0% of sum over $ 18,450
$44,575-$ 70,000	$10,082.50 + 31.0% of sum over $ 44,575
$70,000-$125,000	$17,964.25 + 36.0% of sum over $ 70,000
over $125,000	$37,764.25 + 39.6% of sum over $125,000

Source: Internal Revenue Service

Returns Filed and Examined, and Additional Taxes and Penalties, 1996–97

Type of return	Total returns filed, 1996[1]	Total returns examined, 1997	Percent examined	Additional taxes and penalties (thousands)[2]	Average tax and penalty per return[3]
All returns, total	158,014,000	1,728,122	1.09%	$28,805,090	—
Individual, total	118,362,600	1,519,243	1.28	8,363,918	$19,337
1040A, TPI under $25,000	45,699,300	659,094	1.44	2,398,274	16,794
Non 1040A, TPI under $25,000	13,091,400	157,978	1.21	489,342	9,544
TPI $25,000-$50,000	27,931,600	196,489	0.70	681,746	15,861
TPI $50,000-$100,000	18,274,200	140,330	0.77	502,802	11,156
TPI $100,000 and over	5,260,500	119,575	2.27	1,780,844	29,005
Schedule C—TGR under $25,000	2,464,700	78,553	3.19	460,824	18,762
Schedule C—TGR $25,000-$100,000	3,140,300	80,861	2.57	506,469	10,750
Schedule C—TGR $100,000 and over	1,770,700	73,049	4.13	1,422,196	23,846
Schedule F—TGR under $100,000	459,200	5,868	1.28	13,601	6,183
Schedule F—TGR $100,000 and over	270,700	7,446	2.75	107,822	26,826
Corporation, total	2,608,600	69,650	2.67	16,568,203	58,634
No balance sheet	304,700	3,552	1.17	136,438	27,159
Under $250,000	1,587,000	18,846	1.19	202,033	10,658
$250,000-$1 mil.	431,500	15,202	3.52	273,209	17,975
$1 mil-$ 5 mil.	183,900	14,302	7.78	417,274	29,185
$5 mil-$10 mil.	27,600	4,421	16.02	150,405	34,084
$10 mil-$50 mil.	30,500	6,129	20.10	687,152	111,227
$50 mil-$100 mil.	7,900	1,548	19.59	672,170	296,857
$100 mil-$250 mil.	7,200	1,647	22.88	543,441	301,511
$250 mil. and over	7,800	3,648	46.77	13,115,760	716,419
Form 1120F	20,500	355	1.73	370,319	826,859
Fiduciary	3,266,800	5,753	0.18	56,729	26,337
Estate, total	90,600	11,686	12.90	1,400,907	122,775
Gross estate under $1 mil.	52,100	3,560	6.83	94,394	27,467
Gross estate $1 mil.-$5 mil.	35,500	6,703	18.88	351,037	53,069
Gross estate $5 mil. and over	3,000	1,423	47.43	955,476	680,054
Gift	232,000	2,085	0.90	375,004	129,708
Employment	28,723,000	51,208	0.18	933,057	10,767
Excise	786,400	24,701	3.14	973,327	31,297
Miscellaneous taxable[4]	—	410	—	77,779	29,622
Partnerships	1,653,100	9,811	0.59	—	—
S-Corporations	2,290,900	23,898	1.04	—	—
Miscellaneous nontaxable	—	16	—	—	—

Note: TPI = total personal income. TGR = total gross receipts. Totals may not add due to rounding. 1. Calendar year. 2. Recommended. 3. Includes only returns reviewed by revenue agents. Additional taxes and penalties were recovered through reviews of individual returns by tax auditors and service centers. 4. Includes taxable small business corporations (1120S).
Source: Internal Revenue Service, *1997 Data Book* (1998).

Tax Returns Processed, 1990–97

Type of return	Number of returns ('000s)				
	1990	1993	1995	1996	1997
Individual income tax (Form 1040 series)	112,492	114,155	116,298	118,833	120,745
Individual estimated tax (Form 1040ES)	38,188	41,201	35,475	36,044	38,634
Fiduciary (Form 1041 series)	2,702	2,970	3,187	3,259	3,310
Fiduciary estimated tax (Form 1041ES)	651	706	583	664	814
Partnership (Form 1065)	1,741	1,583	1,572	1,623	1,770
Corporation (Forms 1120 series, 1066)	4,311	4,593	4,781	4,874	5,158
Estate tax (Forms 706, 706NA)	59	73	83	86	97
Gift tax (Form 709)	146	211	215	226	251
Employment taxes (Forms 94X series, CT-1, 1042)	28,914	28,879	29,006	28,562	28,918
Exempt organizations (Forms 990 series, 4720, 5227)	484	543	560	573	607
Employee plans (Form 5500 series)	1,016	1,206	1,262	855	1,337
Excise taxes (Forms 720, 730, 2290, 11C)	840	860	787	765	821
Supplemental documents (1040X, 2688, 4868, 7004, 1041A)	10,170	10,443	11,937	12,573	14,048
Total tax returns	**201,715**	**207,423**	**205,747**	**208,938**	**216,510**

Source: Internal Revenue Service, *1997 Data Book* (1998).

Internal Revenue Collections by Principal Sources, 1961–97 (thousands of dollars)

Year	Total Internal Revenue collections	Corporate income & profits tax	Individual income tax	Employment taxes	Estate and gift taxes	Excise taxes
1961	$94,401,086	$21,764,940	$46,153,001	$12,502,451	$ 1,916,392	$12,064,302
1970	195,722,096	35,036,983	103,651,585	37,449,188	3,680,076	15,904,264
1980	519,375,273	72,379,610	287,547,782	128,330,480	6,498,381	24,619,021
1990	1,056,365,652	110,016,539	540,228,408	367,219,321	11,761,939	27,139,445
1995	1,375,731,835	174,422,173	675,779,337	465,405,305	15,144,394	44,980,627
1996	1,486,546,674	189,054,791	745,313,276	492,365,178	17,591,817	42,221,611
1997	1,623,272,071	204,492,336	825,020,880	528,596,833	20,356,401	44,805,621

Source: Internal Revenue Service, *1997 Data Book* (1998).

Internal Revenue Collections, Costs, and Tax Per Capita, 1960–97

Fiscal year	Collections	Cost of collecting $100	Tax per capita
1960	$ 91,774,802,823	$ 0.40	$ 507.97
1965	114,434,633,721	0.52	588.95
1970	195,722,096,497	0.45	955.31
1975	293,822,725,772	0.54	1,375.84
1980	519,375,273,361	0.44	2,275.66[1]
1985	742,871,541,283	0.48	3,098.99[1]
1990	1,056,365,651,631	0.52	4,222.00[1]
1995	1,375,731,835,498	0.55	5,216.44
1996	1,486,546,674,000	0.49	5,586.23
1997	1,623,272,071,000	0.44	6,045.82

Note: In current dollars. 1. Tax Per Capita figures have been revised to agree with the Census Bureau's adjusted data on population.
Source: Internal Revenue Service, *1997 Data Book* (1998).

Internal Revenue Collections, 1997 (millions of dollars)

Type of return	Gross collections	Refunds[1]	Net collections Amount	Percent of total
Corporation income taxes	$204,492	$22,199	$182,293	12.3%
Individual income taxes[2]	825,021	113,6083	711,413	48.0
Employment taxes, total	528,597	3,030	525,567	35.4
Estate and gift taxes	20,356	512	19,845	1.4
Excise taxes	44,806	1,760	43,045	2.9
Grand total	$1,623,272	$141,109	$1,482,163	100.0%

1. Does not include interest paid on refunds. 2. Includes Presidential Election Campaign Fund contributions of $66,935,288 in fiscal year 1997. 3. Does not include amounts for Earned Income Tax Credits of $21.78 billion.
Source: Internal Revenue Service, *1997 Data Book* (1998).

more, resulting in $13 billion in additional taxes and penalties, or more than $700,000 per audit. The other closely monitored group of tax returns is from estates valued at $5 million or more. There were 3,000 such returns filed in 1997; the I.R.S. examined 47.4 percent of them, resulting in $955 million in additional taxes and penalties ($680,000 per examination).

▶ PRINCIPAL DEDUCTIONS

Taxes: Taxpayers who pay a state and/or local tax may deduct this amount from their Federal tax payment. In addition, in Alabama, Iowa, Louisiana, Missouri, Oklahoma, Oregon, and Utah, taxpayers may deduct their Federal income tax before calculating their state tax payments.

Personal exemptions: Taxpayers are allowed to claim personal exemptions for the taxpayer and each dependent claimed in filing income tax. Congress determines the amount (since 1990, pegged to the inflation rate) allowable for deductions on personal and other exemptions. Because the personal exemption is the same for a single person as for a married couple, the tax schedule effectively dissuades people from getting married. For several years, politicians have discussed eliminating the so-called marriage tax penalty, but to date have not remedied this situation.

Interest expenses: The most common interest deduction is on home mortgages, thus making the cost of owning a home more affordable to most Americans. Although politically very popular, the mortgage deduction is what experts call an

"upside-down" subsidy because the more a taxpayer earns, the greater the tax cut yielded. In recent years, 20 percent of the tax savings from home mortgage interest has gone to taxpayers earning more than $200,000.

Medical expenses: Although almost all medical expenses are deductible, it is difficult to take a deduction because your combined expenses for the year must total 7.5 percent of your adjusted gross income. So, for someone with an adjusted gross income of $25,000, medical expenses would have to exceed $1,875 not covered by any medical insurance.

▶ ELECTRONIC FILING

The number of people filing their tax returns electronically has jumped dramatically in the 1990s. Just over 4 million individuals filed electronically in 1990; by 1993, that number had tripled to 12.3 million. In 1996, 15.0 million people filed electronically, and 19.2 million did so in 1997.

▶ CHECK BOXES

In 1997, just under 15 million people checked the little box authorizing the IRS to send a portion of their tax to the Presidential Election Campaign Fund. That meant $66.9 million went to that fund. Since 1972, a total of just under $1 billion has gone to public financing of presidential elections.

THE U.S. POSTAL SERVICE

With more than 800,000 employees moving more than 190 billion pieces of mail annually, or more than 41 percent of the world total, the Postal Service provides one of the most vital Government services to business and the citizenry alike. What most people don't realize is that it's done at a cost to the consumer significantly less than in any other industrial nation, and that for first-class mail, the on-time delivery rate is still over 95 percent for local mail and 90 percent for cross-country.

First established by the Continental Congress in 1775, the Postal Service was made part of the Federal system in the Constitution and the office of postmaster general established in George Washington's very first cabinet. In 1969, however, in response to vociferous complaints of mismanagement, waste, unreliable service, and staggering financial losses, the Nixon administration reorganized the service as an independent establishment within the executive branch. The Postal Service Act of 1969 removed the postmaster general from the cabinet and created a self-supporting postal corporation owned by the Federal Government and vested power in an 11-member Board of Governors, nine of whom are appointed by the president with the consent of the Senate; these in turn appoint the postmaster general who serves as the CEO of the postal service; the 11th member of the board is chosen by the other ten and serves as deputy postmaster general.

Finally, the 1969 law established an independent Postal Rate Commission of five members, appointed by the president, to recommend postal rates and classifications for adoption by the Board of Governors. Under this agreement, the Postal Service turned a profit five times in the early 1980s. But between 1989 and 1994, the Postal Service lost money every year. A 1995 hike in the price of stamps helped create record-level profits in 1995, 1996, and 1997, more than wiping out the $2.6 billion lost between 1993 and 1994. But this didn't stop the Board of Governors from approving a one-cent hike in the price of stamps in 1999. Measured in constant dollars, the real cost of a stamp in 1999 was 8 cents, the same amount it was in 1971. But most of the public's complaints about stamp price increases result not from the amount of the increase, but from the hassle of obtaining stamps in the new denominations.

Despite the advent of overnight delivery services, couriers, messengers, and fax machines, the Postal Service has remained on relatively stable footing because the total volume of mail is growing faster than the agency is losing market share. In 1988, the Postal Service delivered 77 percent of all business and personal correspondence, which was then a $25.9 billion business. In 1996, the Postal Service's share of that market had slipped to 59 percent, with e-mail and faxes making up the difference. But the total amount of correspondence had nearly doubled, to $48 billion, meaning that the Postal Service lost millions of potential customers but nevertheless increased its revenues from $19.9 billion to $28.3 billion. In 1998, the Postal Service delivered a record 198 billion pieces of mail, and delivers more mail each day than Federal Express delivers all year. If the Postal Service were privately held, its $58.0 billion in revenues would rank it 8th on the list of *Fortune* 500 companies.

Domestic Postage Rates 1999

Weight not over	Rate	Weight not over	Rate	Weight not over	Rate
1 oz.	$0.33	5 oz.	$1.21	9 oz.	$2.09
2 oz.	0.55	6 oz.	1.43	10 oz.	2.31
3 oz.	0.77	7 oz.	1.65	11 oz.	2.53
4 oz.	0.99	8 oz.	1.87		

Post cards 20 cents. Post cards cannot exceed 4.25" x 6", nor be smaller than 3.5" x 5".

Priority mail Priority mail is a zone-based domestic service providing two-day delivery between all major business centers in the U.S. The rates for packages up to 5 pounds are as follows, regardless of the zone to which they are going:

Weight not over	Rate	Weight not over	Rate
2 lbs.	$3.20	4 lbs.	$5.40
3 lbs.	4.30	5 lbs.	6.50

For packages weighing more than five pounds, different rates apply depending on weight and the zone, from $6.60 for a six-pound package to Zone 1 to a maximum of $88.80 for a 70-lb package to zone 8.

Express mail is an overnight delivery service available every day of the year for items up to 70 lbs. in weight and 108 in. in combined length and girth. The post office will pick up packages to be sent by express mail for a $8.95 fee. Call 1-800-222-1811.

Weight not over	Rate
8 oz.	$11.75
2 lbs.	15.75
3-70 lbs.	18.50-113.80

Standard Mail (A) Formerly known as third-class mail, this service was eliminated when the rates changed in January, 1999. Use priority mail or first-class mail instead.

Standard Mail B (parcels) Formerly known as parcel post, Standard Mail B is a zone-based class of mail for sending merchandise; written communications having the nature of current and personal correspondence are not permitted. A regular package up to two pounds is $3.15; the maximum rate is $37.07 for a 70-pound package sent to zone 8.

Source: U.S. Postal Service.

International Postage Rates

Type/Weight	Canada	Mexico	All other countries
First-class letters			
0.5 oz.	$0.46	$0.40	$0.60
1 oz.	0.52	0.46	1.00
1.5 oz.	0.64	0.66	1.40
2 oz.	0.72	0.86	1.80
Postcards	0.40	0.35	0.50
Aerogrammes	0.50	0.50	0.50

Source: U.S. Postal Service

The price of a first-class letter is 27 cents in Australia, 59 cents in Japan, 66 cents in Germany, 55 cents in Switzerland, 53 cents in France, 44 cents in Great Britain, 48 cents in Italy, and 33 cents in the U.S.

Volume and Revenue of Mail by Type, 1990–98

Type of Service	Millions of pieces				Revenues, 1998 (millions)
	1990	1996	1997	1998	
First-class	89,269	98,216	99,660	101,172	$33,983
Priority mail	518	937	1,068	1,164	4,150
Express mail	59	58	64	66	854
Mailgrams	14	4	5	4	2
Periodicals	10,682	10,126	10,411	10,317	2,072
Third-class	63,725	71,686	77,254	82,875	13,753
Fourth-class	663	949	988	971	1,626
International surface	166	104	97	96	184
International air	632	949	910	848	1,416
U.S. Postal Service	538	360	377	377	N.A.
Free for the blind	35	50	53	53	N.A.
Total mail	**166,301**	**183,440**	**190,888**	**198,945**	**$58,039**

Source: U.S. Postal Service, 1998 Annual Report.

Postal Service Employees and Offices, 1990–98

Category	1990	1998
Employees		
Headquarters (Washington, D.C.)	2,291	2,231
Field support units	5,691	4,307
Inspection services (field)	4,259	4,280
Area offices	N.A.	1,703
Postmasters	26,995	26,156
Supervisors, managers	43,458	36,508
Professional, administrative, and technical personnel	9,793	11,703
Clerks	290,380	293,829
Nurses	286	189
Mailhandlers	51,123	62,247
City delivery carriers	236,081	240,813
Motor vehicle operators	7,308	9,026
Rural delivery carriers (full-time)	42,252	52,241
Special delivery messengers	2,012	7
Building and equipment maintenance personnel	33,323	41,054
Vehicle maintenance personnel	4,874	5,524
Total career employees	**760,668**	**792,041**
Non-career employees	26,829	17,222
Offices, stations and branches		
Post offices	28,959	27,952
Stations and branches	11,108	10,207
Classified stations and branches	5,008	5,661
Contract stations and branches	4,397	2,974
Community post offices	1,703	1,572
Total offices, stations, and branches	**40,067**	**38,159**

Source: U.S. Postal Service, 1998 Annual Report.

Postal Abbreviations for States and Territories

State	Abb.	State	Abb.
Alabama	AL	Nevada	NV
Alaska	AK	New Hampshire	NH
Arizona	AZ	New Jersey	NJ
Arkansas	AR	New Mexico	NM
California	CA	New York	NY
Colorado	CO	North Carolina	NC
Connecticut	CT	North Dakota	ND
Delaware	DE	Ohio	OH
District of Columbia	DC	Oklahoma	OK
Florida	FL	Oregon	OR
Georgia	GA	Pennsylvania	PA
Hawaii	HI	Rhode Island	RI
Idaho	ID	South Carolina	SC
Illinois	IL	South Dakota	SD
Indiana	IN	Tennessee	TN
Iowa	IA	Texas	TX
Kansas	KS	Utah	UT
Kentucky	KY	Vermont	VT
Louisiana	LA	Virginia	VA
Maine	ME	Washington	WA
Maryland	MD	West Virginia	WV
Massachusetts	MA	Wisconsin	WI
Michigan	MI	Wyoming	WY
Minnesota	MN	American Samoa	AS
Mississippi	MS	Guam	GU
Missouri	MO	Northern Mariana Islands	CM
Montana	MT	Puerto Rico	PR
Nebraska	NE	Virgin Islands	VI

Zip Codes

There are about 42,000 separate ZIP codes designated by the U.S. Postal Service; the number is constantly changing. There is a national ZIP code directory available in every post office. Recently, directory assistance telephone operators have begun providing ZIP codes as well as phone numbers and addresses. You can also find ZIP codes at the Postal Service's Website (www.usps.gov/ncsc). A Website run by the State University of New York at Buffalo (www.cedar.buffalo.edu/adserv.html.) provides the same service, and also shows maps of the surrounding area.

States, Territories, and Possessions

This section, a compilation of history and statistics about the 50 United States, the District of Columbia, and U.S. territories and possessions, includes a brief history of each state and territory; its official motto and other emblems; a summary of geographic, demographic, and economic facts; and a list of prominent natives, places, and dates.

Statistical sources include the U.S. Census Bureau's 1990 decennial census and *The Statistical Abstract* (annual); the Council of State Government's *Book of the States* and *State Elective Officials and the Legislatures*; and the Bureau of Economic Analysis's *Survey of Current Business.*

The headings for demographic statistics in the paragraphs on People and Language conform to U.S. Census Bureau usage, except "Indian" is used as a short form for American Indian, Eskimo, and Aleut, and "Asian" is used for Asian and Pacific Islander. Note that Hispanics may be of any race.

Estimates of the Resident Population, April, 1990–July, 1998

State	Population ('000s) 1990 census	July 1, 1998	Change 1990 to 1998 Number	Percent
U.S. Total	248,718	270,299	21,533	8.7%
Alabama	4,040	4,352	312	7.7
Alaska	550	614	64	11.6
Arizona	3,665	4,669	1,003	27.4
Arkansas	2,351	2,538	188	8.0
California	29,758	32,667	2,881	9.7
Colorado	3,294	3,971	677	20.5
Connecticut	3,287	3,274	–13	–0.4
Delaware	666	744	77	11.6
District of Columbia	607	523	–84	–13.8
Florida	12,938	14,916	1,978	15.3
Georgia	6,478	7,642	1,164	18.0
Hawaii	1,108	1,193	85	7.6
Idaho	1,007	1,229	222	22.0
Illinois	11,431	12,045	615	5.4
Indiana	5,544	5,899	355	6.4
Iowa	2,777	2,862	86	3.1
Kansas	2,478	2,629	151	6.1
Kentucky	3,687	3,936	250	6.8
Louisiana	4,220	4,369	147	3.5
Maine	1,228	1,244	16	1.3
Maryland	4,781	5,135	354	7.4
Massachusetts	6,016	6,147	131	2.2
Michigan	9,295	9,817	522	5.6
Minnesota	4,376	4,725	350	8.0
Mississippi	2,575	2,752	177	6.9
Missouri	5,117	5,439	322	6.3
Montana	799	880	81	10.2
Nebraska	1,578	1,663	84	5.3
Nevada	1,202	1,747	545	45.4
New Hampshire	1,109	1,185	76	6.8
New Jersey	7,730	8,115	367	4.7
New Mexico	1,515	1,737	222	14.6
New York	17,991	18,175	185	1.0
North Carolina	6,632	7,546	914	13.8
North Dakota	639	638	–1	–0.1
Ohio	10,847	11,209	362	3.3
Oklahoma	3,146	3,347	201	6.4
Oregon	2,842	3,282	440	15.5
Pennsylvania	11,883	12,001	119	1.0
Rhode Island	1,003	988	–15	–1.5
South Carolina	3,486	3,836	350	10.0
South Dakota	696	738	42	6.1
Tennessee	4,877	5,431	553	11.3
Texas	16,986	19,760	2,773	16.3
Utah	1,723	2,100	377	21.9
Vermont	563	591	28	5.0
Virginia	6,189	6,791	602	9.7
Washington	4,867	5,689	823	16.9
West Virginia	1,793	1,811	18	1.0
Wisconsin	4,892	5,224	332	6.8
Wyoming	454	481	27	6.0

Note: Includes armed forces residing in each state. **Source:** Population Estimates Program, Population Division, U.S. Bureau of the Census, Washington, DC 20233

▶ ALABAMA

The memory of the Native American presence is particularly strong in Alabama. Trade with the Northeast via the Ohio River valley began during the Burial Mound Period (1000 B.C.–A.D. 700) and continued until European contact. Meso-American influence is evident in the agrarian Mississippian culture that followed. Pressured by white settlers in the early 19th century, the Creeks warred against the U.S. government until defeated by General Andrew Jackson.

The cradle of the Confederacy during the Civil War, Alabama was at stage center in the civil rights movement of the 1950s and 1960s. Although cotton is still a major crop, the northern part of the state around Birmingham is a major industrial area with abundant coal, iron ore, limestone, and electricity from the TVA. Increasingly urban—70 percent of the population lived in rural areas 50 years ago, compared with less than 40 percent today—Alabama's economy is progressing slowly, although it still ranks near last in taxes and in money spent on education.

Name Probably after Alabama tribe. **Nickname** Yellowhammer State, Heart of Dixie. **Capital** Montgomery. **Entered union** Dec. 14, 1819 (22nd). **Motto** "We dare defend our rights."
Emblems **Bird** Yellowhammer. **Dance** Square dance. **Game bird** Wild turkey. **Fish** Tarpon. **Fossil** *Basilosaurus oetoides.* **Mineral** Hematite. **Nut** Pecan. **Song** "Alabama." **Stone** Marble. **Tree** Southern (longleaf) pine.
Land **Total area** 51,705 sq. mi. (29th), incl. 938 sq. mi. inland water. **Borders** Tenn., Ga., Fla., Gulf of Mexico, Miss. **Rivers** Alabama, Chattahoochee, Mobile, Tennessee, Tennessee-Tombigbee Waterway, Tensaw, Tombigbee. **Lakes** Guntersville, Pickwick, Wheeler, Wilson (all formed by Tennessee Valley Authority [TVA]); Dannelly Res., Martin, Lewis Smith, Weiss. **Mountains** Cumberland, Lookout, Raccoon, Sand.
Elected officials Gov. Don Siegelman (D, term exp. 2003) Lt. Gov. Steve Windom (R). Sec. State Jim Bennett (R). Atty. Gen. William Pryor (R).
People (1998) 4,351,999 (23rd). **Race/national origin** (1990): White 73.6%. Black 25.3%. Indian 0.4%. Asian 0.5%. Other 0.1%. Hispanic 0.6%.
Cities (1996 estimate) Birmingham 258,543. Mobile 202,581. Montgomery 196,363. Huntsville 170,424. Tuscaloosa 82,379. Dothan 55,944. Hoover 55,464. Decatur 53,797. Gadsden 41,155. Florence 38,999.
Business **Gross State Product,** 1997: $103.11 bil. (25th). **Leading Sectors of GSP** (1997): Manufacturing 21.45%; Services 16.64%; Government 15.26%. *Fortune* **500 Companies** (1998): 7:

Population Density of U.S. States, 1980–97

State	Population per square mile		
	1980	1990	1997
U.S. Total	64.1	70.3	75.7
Alabama	76.7	79.6	85.1
Alaska	0.7	1.0	1.1
Arizona	23.9	32.3	40.1
Arkansas	43.9	45.1	48.4
California	151.7	191.0	206.9
Colorado	27.9	31.8	37.5
Connecticut	641.4	678.5	674.9
Delaware	304.0	340.8	374.2
District of Columbia	10,397.9	9,884.4	8,615.0
Florida	180.7	239.9	271.7
Georgia	94.3	111.8	129.3
Hawaii	150.2	172.5	184.7
Idaho	11.4	12.2	14.6
Illinois	205.6	205.6	214.0
Indiana	153.1	154.6	163.5
Iowa	52.1	49.7	51.1
Kansas	28.9	30.3	31.7
Kentucky	92.1	92.8	98.4
Louisiana	96.5	96.9	99.9
Maine	36.5	39.8	40.2
Maryland	431.4	489.1	521.2
Massachusetts	732.0	767.6	780.5
Michigan	163.0	163.6	172.0
Minnesota	51.2	55.0	58.9
Mississippi	53.7	54.9	58.2
Missouri	71.4	74.3	78.4
Montana	5.4	5.5	6.0
Nebraska	20.4	20.5	21.6
Nevada	7.3	10.9	15.3
New Hampshire	102.6	123.7	130.8
New Jersey	992.7	1,044.3	1,085.4
New Mexico	10.7	12.5	14.3
New York	371.8	381.0	384.1
North Carolina	120.7	136.1	152.4
North Dakota	9.5	9.3	9.3
Ohio	263.7	264.9	273.2
Oklahoma	44.1	45.8	48.3
Oregon	27.4	29.6	33.8
Pennsylvania	264.7	265.1	268.2
Rhode Island	906.4	960.3	944.9
South Carolina	103.6	115.8	124.9
South Dakota	9.1	9.2	9.7
Tennessee	111.4	118.3	130.2
Texas	54.3	64.9	74.2
Utah	17.8	21.0	25.1
Vermont	55.3	60.8	63.7
Virginia	135.0	156.3	170.1
Washington	62.1	73.1	84.3
West Virginia	81.0	74.5	75.4
Wisconsin	86.6	90.1	95.2
Wyoming	4.8	4.7	4.9

Note: Persons per square mile were calculated on the basis of land area data from the 1990 census. Source: U.S. Bureau of the Census, 1990 Census of Population and Housing, (CPH–2); and ST–97–1 Estimates of the Population of States: Annual Time Series, July 1, 1990, to July 1, 1997. www.census.gov/population/estimates/state/ST9097T1.txt>.

Medpartners, SCI Systems, Saks, Healthsouth, Sonat, Regions Financial, Southtrust Corp.
Famous natives Hank Aaron, baseball player. Tallulah Bankhead, actress. William B. Bankhead, politician. Hugo L. Black, jurist. Wernher von Braun (b. Germany), rocket scientist. Nat "King" Cole, singer. Red Eagle (William Weatherfield), Creek leader. W.C. Handy, musician. Frank M. Johnson, Jr., jurist. Helen Keller, author. Coretta Scott (Mrs. Martin Luther) King, reformer. Harper Lee, author. Joe Louis, boxer. Jesse Owens, runner. Leroy Robert "Satchell" Paige, baseball player. Walker Percy, author. George Wallace, politician. Hank Williams, singer.

Noteworthy places Alabama Deep Sea Fishing Rodeo, Dauphin Island. Alabama Space and Rocket Center, U.S. Space Camp, Huntsville. Battleship USS *Alabama*, Mobile. Birmingham Museum of Art. First White House of the Confederacy, Montgomery. Horseshoe Bend Natl. Military Park. Mound State Monument Archaeological Museum, Moundville. Museum of Natural History, Univ. Alabama, Tuscaloosa. Point Clear (resort). Russell Cave Natl. Monument. Tuskegee Institute.

Memorable events Humans first inhabit Russell Cave c. 6000 B.C. Temple Mound culture flourishes around Moundville, A.D. 1200–1500. First Europeans in Mobile Bay 1519. Hernando de Soto's battle with Tuscaloosa possibly bloodiest encounter ever between Europeans and Native Americans in U.S. 1540. Spanish at Mobile Bay 1599. Pierre Le Moyne, sieur d'Iberville, establishes first permanent colony at Mobile 1711. Treaty of Paris gives Mobile to Britain 1763. U.S. control recognized 1783. Chickasaws, Choctaws, and Cherokees cede lands to U.S. 1805. First Baptist Church established 1808. Gen. Andrew Jackson defeats Creek Indian Confederacy at Horseshoe Bend 1814. Cotton principal cash crop 1820s. Beginning of coal and iron mining and steel manufacturing 1850s. Alabama secedes from Union; first capital of Confederate States of America at Montgomery 1861. Battle of Mobile Bay 1864. Readmitted to Union 1868. Booker T. Washington founds Tuskegee Institute 1881. Destruction of cotton crops by boll weevils leads to diversification of rural economy 1915. Tennessee Valley Authority enacted by Congress 1933. Montgomery bus boycott 1955. Freedom march from Selma to Montgomery 1965.

Tourist information 1-800-ALABAMA. www.state.al.us.

▶ALASKA

One-fifth the size of the entire lower 48 states, Alaska is a vast, geographically varied wilderness. The coast from the Bering Sea to the Arctic was originally inhabited by Eskimos and Aleuts, while inland and to the south were Athapascans and people of the Northwest Indian culture. Russian fur traders in the 1740s were the first Europeans to recognize the region's commercial potential, and the Russian Orthodox faith is still found in the old territorial capital of Sitka (New Archangel).

Russia sold Alaska to the United States in 1867 for $7.2 million—2 cents an acre—and Alaska experienced successive booms in furs, fishing and whaling, and gold. Discovery of oil on the North Slope near Prudhoe Bay in 1968 and completion of an 800-mile trans-Alaska pipeline a decade later made oil production the centerpiece of the state's economy in the 1980s. Although the population has grown by more than 10 percent during the 1990s, the number of people per square mile remains below 1.5. In recent years, tourism based on the state's extraordinary beauty, has grown substantially and now many Alaskans oppose proposed oil exploration at the Arctic National Wildlife Refuge. The memory of the *Exxon Valdez* oil spill into Prince William Sound in 1989 has had a powerful effect.

Name From Aleut *alaska* and Eskimo *alakshak*, both meaning "mainland." **Nickname** None. **Capital** Juneau. **Entered union** Jan. 3, 1959 (49th). **Motto** "North to the future."

Emblems **Bird** Willow ptarmigan. **Fish** King salmon. **Flower** Forget-me-not. **Gem** Jade. **Marine mammal** Bowhead whale. **Mineral** Gold. **Song** "Alaska's Flag." **Sport** Mushing (dog-team racing). **Tree** Sitka spruce.

Land Total area 591,004 sq. mi. (1st), incl. 20,171 sq. mi. inland water. **Borders** Arctic Ocean (Chukchi Sea, Beaufort Sea), Yukon, British Columbia, Pacific Ocean, Bering Strait. **Rivers** Colville, Porcupine, Noatak, Yukon, Susitna, Copper, Kobuk, Koyukuk, Kuskokwim, Tanana. **Mountains** Alaska Range (Mt. McKinley 20,320 ft., highest in North America), Aleutian Range, Brooks Range, Kuskokwim, St. Elias. **Other notable features** Aleutian Islands, Alexander Archipelago, Kodiak Island, Nunivak Island, Point Barrow (71°23'N), Pribilof Islands, Seward Peninsula, St. Lawrence Island.

Elected officials Gov. Tony Knowles (D, term exp. 2003). Lt. Gov. Fran Ulmer (D). Atty. Gen. Atty. Gen. Bruce M. Botelho (D).

People (1998) 614,010 (48th). **Race/national origin** (1990): White 75.5%. Black 4.1%. Indian 15.6%. Asian 3.6%. Other 1.2%. Hispanic 3.2%.

Cities (1996 estimate) Anchorage 250,505. Fairbanks 32,960. Juneau 29,756. Sitka 8,510. Ketchikan 8,274. Kenai 7,706. Kodiak 7,677. Bethel 5,952. Wasilla 5,350. Homer 4,608.

Business Gross State Product, 1997: $24.49 bil. (45th). **Leading Sectors of GSP** (1997): Mining 21.10%; Government 19.75%; Transportation & public utilities 15.60%. *Fortune* 500 Companies (1998): 0.

Famous natives Aleksandr Baranov (b. Russia), first governor of Russian America. Vitus Bering (b. Denmark), explorer. Ernest Gruening (b. N.Y.), governor. Carl Ben Eielson, bush pilot. Walter Hickel (b. Kans.), governor.

Noteworthy places Aniakchak Natl. Monument. Cape Krusenstern Natl. Monument. Denali Natl. Park (formerly Mt. McKinley Natl. Park). Gates of the Arctic Natl. Park. Glacier Bay Natl. Park. Katmai Natl. Park (Valley of Ten Thousand Smokes). Kenai Fjords Natl. Park. Klondike Gold Rush Natl. Hist. Park. Kobuk Valley Natl. Park. Lake Clark Natl. Park. Little Diomede Island—2.5 mi. from Big Diomede Island (Russia). Sitka Natl. Hist. Park. St. Michael's Cathedral, Sitka. Wrangell–St. Elias Natl. Park.

Memorable events Earliest migration from Asia to Americas across Bering Sea land bridge, c. 15,000 years ago. Alaska inhabited by Tlingits, Tinnehs, Aleuts, and Eskimos. Peter the Great sponsors expedition to find land opposite Siberia 1728. Bering expedition lands near Mt. Elias; begins Pacific Northwest fur trade with Europe and Asia 1741. Russians establish first European settlement at Three Saints Bay 1784. Russian-American Company chartered 1799. Baranov's massacre of Tlingits at Sitka 1802. Gold discovered at Stikine Creek (1861), Juneau (1880), Fortymile Creek (1886), Nome (1898), Fairbanks (1903). Russians sell Alaska to U.S. for $7.2 million 1867. First salmon cannery established 1878. Japanese occupy Agattu, Attu, and Kiska islands 1942–43. Alaskans vote for statehood 1946. Statehood 1959. Earthquake destroys Anchorage, Northwest Panhandle, and Cook Inlet; tsunami wipes out Valdez; coast sinks 32 ft. at Kodiak and Seward and rises 16 ft. at Cordova 1964. Oil discovered on North Slope 1968. Alaska Native Claims Settlement Act gives Alaska's Native Americans 44 million acres for native landholdings 1971. Completion of 789-mi. pipeline to Valdez 1977. Population growth of 32.8% highest in U.S. 1980–86. *Exxon Valdez* spills 10 million gallons of oil into Prince William Sound off Valdez — worst oil spill in U.S. history 1989. **Tourist information** 1-907-465-2010. **www.state.ak.us.**

▶ARIZONA

The Hopi village of Oraibi is the oldest continuously inhabited town in the United States, and today vast tracts of Arizona are reserved for Apaches, Hopis, Navajos, Papagos and other Native Americans. Last of the 48 conterminous states admitted to the union, Arizona was sparsely settled until the advent of airconditioning in the postwar years made it habitable and a popular destination for retirees. More recently, there has been a boom in manufacturing and light industry, and in the last decade, population growth has been among the highest in the nation. Mexican-Americans are an important political force.

As in most southwestern states, water scarcity is a major problem. Arizona draws 2.8 million acre-feet of water from the Colorado River, whose water it shares with 5 other states and Mexico.

Name Probably from the Pima or Papago for "place of small springs." **Nickname** Grand Canyon State. **Capital** Phoenix. **Entered union** Feb. 14, 1912 (48th). **Motto** *Ditat deus* (God enriches).

Emblems **Bird** Cactus wren. **Flower** Blossom of the saguaro cactus. **Gemstone** Turquoise. **Official neck wear** Bola tie. **Songs** "Arizona March Song," "Arizona." **Tree** Palo verde.

Land Total area 114,000 sq. mi. (6th), incl. 492 sq. mi. inland water. **Borders** Utah, Colo., N.Mex., Sonora, Baja California Norte, Calif., Nev. **Rivers** Colorado, Gila, Little Colorado, Salt, Zuni. **Lakes** Havasu, Mead, Mohave, Powell, Roosevelt, San Carlos. **Mountains** Black, Gila, Hualpai, Mohawk, San Francisco Peaks (Humphreys Peak 12,633 ft.). **Other notable features** Grand Canyon, Kaibab Plateau, Painted Desert, Petrified Forest, Sonoran Desert.

Elected officials Gov. Jane Dee Hull (R, term exp. 2003). Atty. Gen. Janet Napolitano (D). Sec. State Betsy Bayless (R).

People (1998) 4,668,631 (21st). **Race/national origin** (1990): White 80.8%. Black 3.0%. Indian 5.6%. Asian 1.5%. Other 9.1%. Hispanic 18.8%.

Cities (1996 estimate) Phoenix 1,159,014. Tucson 449,002. Mesa 344,764. Glendale 182,219. Scottsdale 179,012. Tempe 162,701. Chandler 142,918. Peoria 76,045. Gilbert 64,326. Yuma 60,519.

Business Gross State Product, 1997: $121.24 bil. (24th). **Leading Sectors of GSP** (1997): Services 20.60%; Finance, insurance, and real estate 19.41%; Manufacturing 14.69%. *Fortune* 500 Companies (1998): 3: Avnet, Microage, Phelps Dodge.

Famous natives Bruce Babbitt, politician. Cesar Chavez, labor leader. Cochise, Apache chief. Andrew Ellicott Douglass (b. Vt.), dendrochronologist. Wyatt Earp (b. Ill.), lawman. Barry Goldwater, politician. Goyathlay (Geronimo), Apache chieftain. Carl T. Hayden, congressman. Eusebio Kino (b. Italy), missionary. Sandra Day O'Connor, jurist. William H. Rehnquist, jurist. Linda Ronstadt, singer. Morris Udall, politician.

Noteworthy Places Canyon de Chelly Natl. Monument. Casa Grande Ruins Natl. Monument. Chiricahua Natl. Monument. Ft. Bowie. Grand Canyon Natl. Park. Heard Museum, Phoenix. London Bridge, Lake Havasu City. Montezuma Castle Natl. Monument. Navajo Natl. Monument. Organ Pipe Cactus Natl. Monument. Painted Desert. Petrified Forest Natl. Park. Pipe Spring Natl. Monument. Saguaro Natl. Monument. Sunset Crater Natl. Monument. Taliesin West, near Scottsdale. Tonto Natl. Monument. Tumacacori Natl. Monument. Tuzigoot Natl. Monument. Walnut Canyon Natl. Monument. Wupatki Natl. Monument.

Memorable Events Apaches and Navajos absorb Pueblos c. A.D. 1000. Alvar Núñez Cabeza de Vaca, first Spanish explorer 1536. Marcos de Niza 1539. Ruled as part of New Spain 1598–1821. First missionaries among Hopis 1638. Tubac first European settlement 1752. Tucson founded 1776. Apaches wipe out settlements under Mexican control, except Tucson 1821. Northern part ceded to U.S. following Mexican War 1848. Area south of Gila River to U.S. after Gadsden Purchase 1853. Territory 1863. Southern Pacific Railroad reaches Tucson 1880. Apaches subjugated 1886. Congress refuses to grant statehood 1906. Roosevelt Dam and Reservoir built on Salt River 1911. Native Americans given right to vote 1948. Glen Canyon Dam built on Colorado River 1964. Population growth of 24.3 percent is second highest in U.S., 1990–97.

Tourist information 1-602-230-7733.
www.state.az.us.

►ARKANSAS

First inhabited by bluff dwellers 10,000 years ago, the Boston and Ouachita mountains of western Arkansas are the only mountains between the Appalachians and the Rockies. By the time of the Hernando De Soto expedition of 1541, Arkansas was inhabited by a variety of peoples: the agrarian Quapaws to the south, the Caddo to the west and south, the Osage to the north, and the Chickasaw and Choctaw in the northeast. The Arkansas Post, the first permanent settlement in the Mississippi Valley, became the pillar of the French claim to the region of what became the Louisiana Purchase.

Not fully part of the deep south, and cut off geographically from the Midwest, Arkansas has developed slowly. Although cotton was a mainstay of the economy and Arkansas joined the Confederacy during the Civil War, it was the first southern state to have integrated public colleges after World War II, a fact overshadowed by Gov. Orville Faubus's resistance to the integration of the Little Rock public schools. In recent years, Arkansas has attracted manufacturing and industry, but has one of the highest rural populations and ranks low in services, income, and education attainment.

Name For term for Quapaw tribe given by other Indians. **Nickname** Land of Opportunity. **Capital** Little Rock. **Entered union** June 15, 1836 (25th). **Motto** *Regnat populus* (Let the people rule).

Emblems **Bird** Mockingbird. **Flower** Apple blossom. **Gem** Diamond. **Song** "Arkansas." **Tree** Pine.

Land **Total area** 53,187 sq. mi. (27th), incl. 1,109 sq. mi. inland water. **Borders** Mo., Tenn, Miss., La., Tex., Okla. **Rivers** Arkansas, Mississippi, Ouachita, Red, St. Francis, White. **Lakes** Beaver, Bull Shoals, Chicot, Dardanelle, Greers Ferry, Greeson, Norfolk, Ouachita. **Other notable features** Ozark Mts.

Elected officials Gov. Mike Huckabee (R, term exp. 2003). Lt. Gov. Winthrop P. Rockefeller (R). Sec. State Sharon Priest (D). Atty. Gen. Mark Pryor (D).

People (1998) 2,538,303 (33rd). **Race/national origin** (1990): White 82.7%. Black 15.9%. Indian 0.5%. Asian 0.5%. Other 0.3%. Hispanic 0.8%.

Cities (1996 estimate) Little Rock 175,752. Fort Smith 75,776. North Little Rock 60,468. Pine Bluff 54,165. Jonesboro 52,656. Fayetteville 52,360. Springdale 38,572. Hot Springs 36,255. Conway 35,827. Rogers 35,355.

Business **Gross State Product,** 1997: $58.48 bil. (32nd). **Leading Sectors of GSP** (1997): Manufacturing 23.95%; Services 15.15%; Government 11.94%. *Fortune* **500 Companies** (1998): 4: Wal-Mart Stores, Dillard's, Tyson Foods, Alltel.

Famous natives Maya Angelou, author. Linda Bloodworth-Thomason, television producer/director. Glen Campbell, singer. Hattie W. Caraway, first woman senator. Johnny Cash, singer. Eldridge Cleaver, author. Bill Clinton, U.S. president. William Fulbright (b. Mo.), politician. Alan Ladd, actor. Douglas MacArthur, general. Dick Powell, actor. Brooks Robinson, baseball player. Winthrop Rockefeller (b. N.Y.), politician/philanthropist. Edward Durrell Stone, architect. C. Vann Woodward, historian.

Noteworthy places Arkansas Post Natl. Monument (first permanent French settlement in lower Mississippi Valley). Buffalo Natl. River. Crater of Diamonds State Park, Murfreesboro. Eureka Springs. Ft. Smith Natl. Hist. Site. Hot Springs Natl. Park. Pea Ridge Natl. Military Park.

Memorable Events Bluff-dwellers present c. A.D. 500, followed by mound-building cultures. Hernando de Soto explores for Spain 1541. Jacques Marquette and Louis Jolliet explore for France 1673. René-Robert de La Salle meets Quapaws 1682. Henri de Tonti founds Arkansas Post on Arkansas River 1686. Ceded from France to Spain 1782; to France 1800; to U.S. 1803. Territory 1819. Admitted to Union as slave state, under terms of 1820 Missouri Compromise, 1836. Secedes from Union 1861. Fall of Little Rock to Union army 1863. Readmitted to Union 1868. Bauxite discovered 1887. Oil production begins 1920s. Federal troops called to Little Rock to ensure high school desegregation 1957. Winthrop Rockefeller (b. N.Y.) first Republican governor since Reconstruction 1966. McClellan-Kerr Arkansas River Navigation System links Arkansas and Oklahoma to Mississippi River system 1971. Governor Bill Clinton Elected U.S. President 1992.

Tourist information 1-800-NATURAL or 1-800-482-8999.
www.state.ar.us.

►CALIFORNIA

Before the arrival of Europeans, no area of comparable size in North America was home to a greater variety of languages and cultures than what is now California, and today the state's population is more diverse than that of any other. Some demographers expect that within 50 years more than 40 percent of California's population will be of Hispanic origin, a larger proportion than at any time since before the Gold Rush of 1849. But the trend toward a two-tiered society is also increasing, with Caucasians and Asians on top and African-Americans and Hispanics on the bottom.

The largest state by population since the 1960s, California gained seven additional representatives in Congress as a result of the 1990 census, for a total of 52. By some estimates, California is the sixth largest economic power in the world.

Despite these attractions, and the state's rugged terrain and dramatic vistas, California has problems. The state's position as a leader in agriculture masks an alarming lack of water. It already draws off 4.4 million acre-feet from the Colorado River, mostly for irrigating the Imperial Valley—a desert when settlers crossed it 150 years ago. Almost the entire flow of the San Joaquin River is similarly diverted for the Central Valley. This inefficient use of water leaves less and less for consumption by people, whose numbers have leaped from 15 million in 1960 to over 32 million today.

Of more immediate concern is the threat of earthquakes. California has already suffered eight major earthquakes in this century. The 1906 quake destroyed San Francisco, and the Loma Prieta earthquake on October 17, 1989—one of the most powerful quakes in U.S. history—killed 67 people, left 48,000 people homeless and resulted in $10 billion of property damage. Like surfers waiting for the perfect wave, scientists are still bracing for "the big one."

Name Probably from mythical island in García Ordoñez de Montalvo's 16th-century romance, *The Deeds of Esplandián*. **Nickname** Golden State. **Capital** Sacramento. **Entered union** Sept. 9, 1850 (31st). **Motto** "Eureka" (I have found it). **Emblems Animal** California grizzly bear (extinct). **Bird** California valley quail. **Fish** California golden trout. **Flower** Golden poppy. **Fossil** California saber-toothed cat. **Gemstone** Benitoite. **Insect** California dog-face butterfly. **Marine mammal** California gray whale. **Mineral** Gold. **Reptile** California desert tortoise. **Rock** Serpentine. **Song** "I Love You, California." **Tree** California redwood. **Land Total area** 158,706 sq. mi. (3rd), incl. **2,407** sq. mi. inland water. **Borders** Oreg., Nev., Ariz., Baja California Norte, Pacific Ocean. **Rivers** American, Colorado, Colorado River Aqueduct, Eel, Friant-Kern Canal, Klamath, Russian, Sacramento, Salinas, San Joaquin. **Lakes** Clear, Goose, Honey, Mono, Owens, Salton Sea, Shasta, Tahoe. **Mountains** Coast Ranges, Klamath, Lassen Peak, Sierra Nevada (Mt. Whitney 14,494 ft.). **Other notable features** Catalina Islands, Death Valley (282 ft. below sea level), San Francisco Bay, San Joaquin Valley.
Elected officials Gov. Gray Davis (D term exp. 2003). Lt. Gov. Cruz Bustamante (D) Sec. State Bill Jones (R). Atty. Gen. Bill Lockyer (D).
People (1998) 32,666,550 (1st). **Race/national origin** (1990): White 69.0%. Black 7.4%. Indian 0.8%. Asian 9.6%. Other 13.2%. Hispanic 25.8%. **Cities** (1996 estimate) Los Angeles 3,553,638. San Diego 1,171,121. San Jose 838,744. San Francisco 735,315. Long Beach 421,904. Fresno 396,011. Sacramento 376,243. Oakland 367,230. Santa Ana 302,419. Anaheim 288,945.
Business Gross State Product, 1997: $133.02 bil. (1st). **Leading Sectors of GSP** (1997): Finance, insurance, and real estate 22.97%; Services 22.94%; Manufacturing 14.15%. *Fortune 500* **Companies** (1998): 56: including Hewlett-Packard, Chevron, Intel, Safeway, Walt Disney, Ingram Micro, McKesson HBOC, Wells Fargo, PG&E Corp., Bergen Brunswig, Atlantic Richfield, Sun Microsystems, Gap, Northrop Grumman, Cisco Systems, Rockwell International, Gateway 2000, Oracle, Occidental Petroleum, Apple Computer, 3Com, Unocal, Mattel, Dole Food, Hilton Hotels, Times Mirror, Longs Drug Stores.

Famous natives Ansel Adams, photographer. Dave Brubeck, musician. Luther Burbank (b. Mass.), horticulturist. John Cage, composer. Joe DiMaggio, baseball player. Robert Frost, poet. Ernest and Julio Gallo (b. Italy), vintners. Pancho Gonzales, tennis player. Samuel Ichiye Hayakawa, politician/educator. William Randolph Hearst, publisher. Steve Jobs, computer scientist. Billie Jean King, tennis player. Allen Lockheed, aviator. Jack London, author. Paul Masson (b. France), vintner. Marilyn Monroe, actress. John Muir (b. Scotland), naturalist. Richard M. Nixon, U.S. president. John Northrop, aviator. Adlai Stevenson, politician. John Steinbeck, author. Levi Strauss (b. Germany), clothier. Edward Teller (b. Hungary), nuclear physicist. Shirley Temple, actress. Earl Warren, politician/jurist.
Noteworthy places Big Sur, Monterey. Cabrillo Natl. Monument. California Academy of Sciences, San Francisco. California Palace of the Legion of Honor, San Francisco. Channel Islands Natl. Park. Devils Postpile Natl. Monument. Death Valley Natl. Monument. Disneyland. Fine Arts Museum of San Francisco. Fishermen's Wharf, San Francisco. Hollywood. Huntington Library and Botanical Gardens, San Marino. J. Paul Getty Museum, Malibu. Joshua Tree Natl. Monument. Kings Canyon Natl. Park. Lassen Volcanic Natl. Park. Lava Beds Natl. Monument. Los Angeles Co. Museum of Art. Muir Woods Natl. Monument. Mt. Palomar Observatory. Natl. Maritime Museum, San Francisco. Natural History Museum, Los Angeles. Natural History Museum of San Diego. Norton Simon Museum of Art at Pasadena. Pinnacles Natl. Monument. Redwood Natl. Park. Rosicrucian Egyptian Museum, San José. San Diego Museum of Art. San Diego Museum of Man. San Diego Zoo. San Francisco Museum of Modern Art. Sequoia Natl. Park. Southwest Museum (Casa de Adobe), Los Angeles. Yosemite Natl. Park.
Memorable events João Rodrigues Cabrilho lands at San Diego Bay 1542. Francis Drake lands north of San Francisco Bay 1579. Junípero Serra founds missions at San Diego (1769), Monterey (1770), San Luis Obispo (1772), and San Juan Capistrano (1776). California declares allegiance to independent Mexico 1821. First wagon train from Missouri 1841. Gold discovered north of Los Angeles 1842. California declares itself independent republic 1846. Gold found at John Sutter's mill; nine days later, by Treaty of Guadalupe Hidalgo, Mexico cedes California to U.S. 1848. Announcement of gold discovery brings 80,000 'Forty-niners. Gold rush peaks 1852. Transcontinental telegraph completed 1861. Transcontinental railway completed 1869. U.S. Congress enacts Chinese Exclusion Act, prohibiting immigration of Chinese laborers 1882, 1892, and 1902; Act repealed 1943. San Francisco earthquake kills 452, destroys 28,000 buildings 1906. Webb Alien Land Law prohibits Japanese from holding land 1913. Los Angeles has one car for every three people, twice national average, 1925. Dust Bowl immigrants 1930. Hollywood produces bulk of movies for U.S. theaters, which number more than banks 1940. Most populous state 1963. Proposition 13 limits property tax 1978. Loma Prieta earthquake registers 7.1 on Richter scale — second most powerful in U.S. history; 67 dead, 48,000 homeless, and $10 billion in property damage 1989. Riots in Los Angeles kill 60 and cause $1 billion in damage 1992.
Tourist information 1-800-TO-CALIF. www.state.ca.us.

▶COLORADO

The native peoples of Colorado were the Plains Indians (Arapahoe and Cheyenne) to the east and Great Basin Indians (Utes) to the west. This pre-Columbian division of the land is reflected today in Colorado's economy, which is a mix of agriculture and technology in the east and mining and ski tourism in the mountains. During the oil price shocks of the 1970s, shale-oil production on the Western Slope created a boom comparable to Colorado's silver and lead boom in the late 19th century. During the 1990s, strong job growth has attracted many young people: the population has increased by more than 18 percent, while the percentage of people over 65 has fallen to 10 percent, one of the lowest in the nation. While a state of great natural beauty, it must cope with a high altitude that almost doubles the effect of auto emissions. Economic development means in large part resource extraction and requires more and more water, whose limited supply poses a great question for the future.

Name For Spanish for the color red. **Nickname** Centennial State. **Capital** Denver. **Entered union** Aug. 1, 1876 (38th). **Motto** *Nil sine numine* (Nothing without providence).

Emblems **Animal** Rocky Mountain bighorn sheep. **Bird** Lark bunting. **Flower** Rocky Mountain Columbine. **Gem** Aquamarine. **Song** "Where the Columbines Grow." **Tree** Colorado blue spruce.

Land Total area 104,091 sq. mi. (8th), incl. **496** sq. mi. inland water. **Borders** Wyo., Nebr., Kans., N.Mex., Ariz., Utah. **Rivers** Arkansas, Colorado, Green, Platte, Rio Grande. **Lakes** Blue Mesa, Dillon, Granby. **Mountains** Front Range, Laramie, Sangre de Cristo, San Juan, Sawatch Range (Mt. Elbert 14,443 ft.).

Elected officials Gov. Bill Owens (R, term exp. 2003). Lt. Gov. Joe Rogers (R). Sec. State Victoria Buckley (R). Atty. Gen. Ken Salazar (D).

People (1998) 3,970,971 (24th). **Race/national origin** (1990): White 88.2%. Black 4.0%. Indian 0.8%. Asian 1.8%. Other 5.1%. Hispanic 12.9%.

Cities (1996 estimate) Denver 497,840. Colorado Springs 345,127. Aurora 252,341. Lakewood 134,999. Fort Collins 104,196. Pueblo 99,406. Arvada 96,340. Westminster 93,115. Boulder 90,928. Greeley 68,593.

Business **Gross State Product,** 1997: $126.08 bil. (22nd). **Leading Sectors of GSP** (1997): Services 22.09%; Finance, insurance, and real estate 17.36%; Government 12.60%. *Fortune* 500 Companies (1998): 6: US West, Tele-Communications, Corporate Express, KN Energy, New Century Energies, Ball.

Famous natives Charlie Bent (b. Va.), trapper. "Unsinkable" Molly Brown, *Titanic* survivor. Scott Carpenter, astronaut. Lon Chaney, actor. Jack Dempsey, boxer. Mamie Eisenhower, first lady. Douglas Fairbanks, actor. Scott Hamilton, ice skater. Anne Parrish, novelist. Lowell Thomas, journalist. Byron R. White, jurist. Paul Whiteman, conductor.

Noteworthy Places Black Canyon of the Gunnison Natl. Monument. Buffalo Bill grave site, Evergreen. Central City Opera House. Colorado Springs Fine Arts Center. Denver Art Museum. Denver Mint. Denver Museum of Natural History. Dinosaur Natl. Monument. Florissant Fossil Beds Natl. Monument. Garden of the Gods, Colorado Springs. Great Sand Dunes Natl. Monument. Hovenweep Natl. Monument. Mesa Verde Natl. Park. Molly Brown House, Denver. Pikes Peak. Red Rocks Amphitheater. Rocky Mountain Natl. Park, Aspen. U.S. Air Force Academy, Colorado Springs. U.S. Olympic Headquarters, Colorado Springs. Yucca House Natl. Monument.

Memorable events Pueblos build cliff dwellings near Mesa Verde through 1200s. Arapahos and Cheyennes settle area after 13th century. France abandons claims 1763. Juan de Uribarri explores area 1786. Spain restores area to France 1801. To United States as part of Louisiana Purchase 1803. Zebulon Pike explores for United States 1806. Kit Carson and other scouts explore and trade with Native Americans 1810s–20s. Native Americans form alliance at Brent's Fork 1840. John Frémont's explorations 1842–53. Present territorial limits after Mexican War 1848. First permanent settlement at San Luis 1851. Gold found west of Denver—"Pike's Peak or Bust"—1858. Mineral springs bring first tourists 1861. Homestead Act encourages farming 1862. U.S. Army kills 400 Cheyenne at Sand Creek Massacre 1864. Utes and Cheyennes fight white settlement through 1870s. John Wesley Powell and nine others navigate Colorado River from the Green River branch in Wyoming to the end of Grand Canyon in Arizona 1869. Railroad link to Denver 1870. Silver and lead discoveries 1875. Uranium discovered near Grand Junction 1946. U.S. Air Force Academy founded Denver 1954; to Colorado Springs 1958. Shale oil boom on Western Slope 1974 and 1979. Accumulation of nuclear waste threatens suspension of operations at Rocky Flats 1988.

Tourist information 1-800-COLORADO. www.state.co.us.

▶CONNECTICUT

Called the "arsenal of the nation" during the Revolution, Connecticut remained in modern times the leader among the 50 states in defense-contract dollars per capita. In recent years, this has caused a serious dislocation in the economy as the nation downsizes its military capabilities. Still, as home to over a dozen *Fortune* 500 companies (including several major insurance companies), and with easy access to New York City, Connecticut remains the state with the highest per capita income in the country.

Severe budget deficits in 1991 forced passage of a state income tax and helped to reveal the disparities in wealth between the very rich suburbs and the decaying industrial cities such as Bridgeport. As the economy is being retooled, population has actually declined slightly.

Name From Mahican word meaning "beside the long tidal river." **Nicknames** Constitution State, Nutmeg State. **Capital** Hartford. **Entered union** Jan. 9, 1788 (5th). **Motto** *Qui transtulit sustinet* (He who transplanted still sustains).

Emblems **Animal** Sperm whale. **Bird** American robin. **Flower** Mountain laurel. **Hero** Nathan Hale. **Insect** European praying mantis. **Mineral** Garnet. **Ship** USS *Nautilus.* **Song** "Yankee Doodle." **Tree** White oak.

Land Total area 5,018 sq. mi. (48th), incl. **146** sq. mi. inland water. **Borders** Mass., R.I., Long Island Sound, N.Y. **Rivers** Connecticut, Housatonic, Mianus, Naugatuck, Thames. **Lakes** Bantam, Barkhamstead, Candlewood, Waramaug. **Other notable features** Berkshire Hills, Long Island Sound.

Elected officials Gov. John G. Rowland (R, term exp. 2003). Lt. Gov. Jodi Rell (R). Sec. State Susan Bysiewicz (D). Atty. Gen. Richard Blumenthal (D).

People   (1998) 3,274,069 (29th). **Race/national origin** (1990): White 87.0%. Black 8.3%. Indian 0.2%. Asian 1.5%. Other 2.9%. Hispanic 6.5%.
Cities   (1996 estimate) Bridgeport 137,990. Hartford 133,086. New Haven 124,665. Stamford 110,056. Waterbury 106,412. Norwalk 77,977. New Britain 71,512. Danbury 65,506. Bristol 59,619. Meriden 57,189.
Business   Gross State Product, 1997: $134.57 bil. (21st). **Leading Sectors of GSP** (1997): Finance, insurance, and real estate 28.97%; Services 21.69%; Manufacturing 16.73%. *Fortune* **500 Companies** (1998): 16: General Electric, United Technologies, Aetna, Xerox, Hartford Financial Services, Tosco, Tenneco, Nebco Evans, Union Carbide, Champion International, Praxair, Fortune Brands, Oxford Health Plans, Pitney Bowes, Northeast Mutual Life, Phoenix Home Life Mutual.
Famous natives   Benedict Arnold, traitor. P.T. Barnum, showman. Lyman Beecher, theologian. John Brown, abolitionist. Samuel Colt, inventor. Jonathan Edwards, theologian. Charles Goodyear, inventor. Nathan Hale, patriot. Katharine Hepburn, actress. Charles Ives, composer. J.P. Morgan, financier. Ralph Nader, consumer advocate. Frederick Law Olmsted, landscape architect. Harriet Beecher Stowe, author. John Trumbell, artist. Noah Webster, lexicographer. Eli Whitney, inventor.
Noteworthy places   Charles Ives Center, Danbury. Eugene O'Neill Memorial Theater Center, Waterford. Gilette Castle. Housatonic State Park. Mark Twain House, Hartford. Mystic Marinelife Aquarium. Mystic Seaport. Norwalk Maritime Center. U.S. Coast Guard Academy. USS *Nautilus,* New London. Wadsworth Atheneum, Hartford. Whitney Museum of Modern Art, Stamford. Yale Center for British Art, New Haven. Yale University, New Haven.
Memorable events   Adriaen Block claims for Dutch 1614. First English settlement in Windsor 1633. Royal charter of 1662 hidden in Charter Oak 1687. *Hartford Courant,* oldest continuously published newspaper in U.S., first published 1764. Samuel Colt develops six-shooter 1835. Horace Wells uses first anesthesia 1844. Elias Howe invents sewing machine 1845. U.S. Coast Guard Academy founded New London 1876. First woman governor elected in her own right, Ella T. Grasso, 1974.
Tourist information   1-800-CT-BOUND. www.state.ct.us.

▶**DELAWARE**
The du Pont family has enjoyed a political and economic prominence in Delaware unmatched in the history of the other 49 states. Seven generations ago E.I. du Pont de Nemours and Co. was founded as a gunpowder mill, then grew into a monopoly, and in the wake of World War I, diversified into today's giant, with interests in banking, media, and real estate. Only half the size of Los Angeles County, Delaware was called the corporate state by Ralph Nader's "raiders" in 1973. Its liberal incorporation laws have led more than half the *Fortune* 500 companies to incorporate there. (A total of more than 170,000 corporations are incorporated in Delaware). It was one of the few states to prosper even during the recessions of the early 1980s and early 1990s.
   Name For Thomas West, Lord De La Warre, colonial governor of Virginia. **Nicknames** First State, Diamond State. **Capital** Dover. **Entered**

union Dec. 7, 1787 (1st). **Motto** "Liberty and Independence."
Emblems   Bird Blue hen chicken. **Fish** Weakfish. **Flower** Peach blossom. **Insect** Ladybug. **Rock** Sillimanite. **Song** "Our Delaware." **Tree** American holly.
Land   Total area 2,044 sq. mi. (49th), incl. **112** sq. mi. inland water. **Borders** Pa., N.J., Atlantic Ocean, Md. **Rivers** Chesapeake & Delaware Canal, Delaware, Nanticoke.
Elected officials   Gov. Thomas R. Carper (D, term exp. 2001). Lt. Gov. Ruth Ann Minner (D). Sec. State Edward Freel (D). Atty. Gen. M. Jane Brady (R).
People   (1998) 743,603 (45th). **Race/national origin** (1990): White 80.3%. Black 16.9%. Indian 0.3%. Asian 1.4%. Other 1.1%. Hispanic 2.4%.
Cities   (1996 estimate) Wilmington 69,490. Dover 30,414. Newark 27,870. Milford 6,557. Seaford 6,400. Elsmere 5,787. Smyrna 5,502. New Castle 4,912. Middletown 4,291. Georgetown 4,092.
Business   Gross State Product, 1997: $31.59 bil. (41st). **Leading Sectors of GSP** (1997): Finance, insurance, and real estate 39.09%; Manufacturing 19.34%; Services 14.19%. *Fortune* **500 Companies** (1998): 3: E.I. DuPont Nemours, MBNA, Conectiv.
Famous natives   Valerie Bertinelli, actress. John Dickinson (b. Md.), Penman of the Revolution. Eleuthère I. du Pont, manufacturer. Pierre S. ("Pete") du Pont, politician. Morgan Edwards, founder of Brown University (R.I.). Thomas Macdonough, navy officer. Howard Pyle, illustrator. Edward R. Squibb, physician/manufacturer. Christopher Ward, historian.
Noteworthy places   Brandywine Zoo, Wilmington. Delaware Art Museum, Wilmington. Delaware State Museum, Dover. Dover Downs International Speedway. Grand Opera House, Wilmington. Hagley Museum, Wilmington. Rehoboth Beach.
Memorable events   Dutch arrive 1631. Swedes establish first permanent settlement at Wilmington 1638. Captured by Dutch 1655. To England 1664. Part of territory granted to William Penn 1682. Breaks off from Pennsylvania; first to ratify Constitution 1787. E.I. du Pont de Nemours Co. founded 1802. Railroad connects Wilmington to Philadelphia and Baltimore 1838. Though slave state, sides with Union during Civil War 1861–65. Delaware last state to abolish whipping post (last used 1952) 1972.
Tourist information   1-800-441-8846. www.state.de.us.

▶**DISTRICT OF COLUMBIA**
Chosen as the site for the nation's capital by George Washington, Washington, D.C., was carved out of land ceded by Maryland and Virginia. Although under Federal jurisdiction, the District has petitioned for statehood as New Columbia. In 1961 Congress enacted the 23rd Amendment granting citizens of D.C. the right to vote in Presidential elections for the first time, and 10 years later gave the District a nonvoting delegate to the House of Representatives. The District's largest employer is the federal government, and printing is the largest industry. Pres. John F. Kennedy called it a city of "Southern efficiency and Northern charm," but since his time, the city has become a leading patron of the arts. The problems of any large city are made worse by the city's largely transient population of government

workers. The city, as the seat of the U.S. Government is a mecca for tourists from around the world, and more than 17 million people visit it each year.

Name After Christopher Columbus; Columbia was commonly used for the United States before 1800. **Nickname** None. **Capital** Washington. **Became capital** Dec. 1, 1800. **Motto** *Justitia omnibus* (Justice for all).
Emblems   Bird Wood thrush. **Flower** American beauty rose. **Tree** Scarlet oak.
Land   Total area 69 sq. mi., incl. 6 sq. mi. inland water. **Borders** Md., Va. **Rivers** Anacostia, Potomac.
Elected officials   Mayor Anthony A. Williams (D, term exp. 2003).
People   (1998) 523,124 (N.A.). **Race/national origin** (1990): White 29.6%. Black 65.8%. Indian 0.2%. Asian 1.8%. Other 2.5%. Hispanic 5.4%.
Business   Gross State Product, 1997: $52.37 bil. (N.A.). **Leading Sectors of GSP** (1997): Government 37.12%; Services 32.40%; Finance, insurance, and real estate 18.20%. *Fortune* **500 Companies** (1998): 3: Fannie Mae, U.S. Office Products, Danaher.
Famous natives   Edward Albee, playwright. Carl Bernstein, journalist. John Foster Dulles, politician. Duke Ellington, composer. J. Edgar Hoover, FBI director. Marjorie Kinnan Rawlings, novelist. John Philip Sousa, composer.
Noteworthy places   The Capitol. Chesapeake & Ohio Canal Natl. Hist. Park. Corcoran Gallery of Art. Dumbarton Oaks. FDR Memorial. Folger Shakespeare Library. Freer Gallery of Art. Hirshhorn Museum. Jefferson Memorial. Kennedy Center. Korean War Veterans Memorial. Library of Congress. Lincoln Memorial. Natl. Air and Space Museum. Natl. Gallery of Art. Natl. Museum of African Art. Natl. Museum of American Art. Natl. Museum of American History. Natl. Museum of Natural History. Natl. Portrait Gallery. Naval Observatory. Navy Memorial Museum. Renwick Gallery. Smithsonian Institution. Vietnam Veterans Memorial. Washington Monument. Washington Zoo. White House. Woodrow Wilson House.
Memorable events   Originally part of Maryland. Congress approves plan to secure land for seat of Federal Government, no more than 10 miles square, on land in Virginia and Maryland 1787. George Washington commissions Pierre Charles l'Enfant to lay out city 1791. Government moves 1800. British sail up the Potomac and burn capital 1814. Virginia reclaims its half of District 1846. President Abraham Lincoln assassinated 1865. Coxey's Army marches on Washington 1894. The Bonus Army—17,000 veterans—marches on Washington 1932. Led by Martin Luther King, Jr., 200,000 march for Civil Rights 1963. One hundred thousand protest Vietnam War 1971. Democratic party headquarters at Watergate burglarized by men linked to President Richard M. Nixon's reelection effort 1972. Congress grants limited self-rule; mayor and city council elected 1975.
Tourist information   1-202-789-7000.
www.ci.washington.dc.us.

▶ **FLORIDA**
A vast network of swamps, rivers, and lakes, much of Florida is barely above sea level. Florida is home to Disney World, Cypress Gardens, the wealth-laden resort of Palm Beach, the *National Enquirer*, and the Okefenokee Swamp. The pleasant climate and proximity to the Caribbean and Latin America have attracted large populations of

the elderly (almost 19 percent of the population is over 65) and immigrants, as well as millions of tourists. Over the last two decades, it has been one of the fastest-growing states. The growth has brought with it, however, attendant increases in drug trafficking, racial disturbances, and environmental damage to such wildlife as the crocodile, alligator, and the Florida panther.

Name By Juan Ponce de León for Pascua Florida (Easter festival of the flowers). **Nickname** Sunshine State. **Capital** Tallahassee. **Entered union** Mar. 3, 1845 (27th). **Motto** "In God We Trust." **Poet laureate** Dr. Edmund Skellings.
Emblems   Animal Florida panther. **Beverage** Orange juice. **Bird** Mockingbird. **Flower** Orange blossom. **Freshwater fish** Florida largemouth bass. **Gem** Moonstone. **Marine mammals** Dolphin, manatee. **Saltwater fish** Atlantic sailfish. **Shell** Horse conch. **Song** "Old Folks at Home" ("Swanee River"). **Stone** Agatized coral. **Tree** Sabal palmetto palm.
Land   Total area 58,664 sq. mi. (22nd), incl. 4,511 sq. mi. inland water. **Borders** Ga., Atlantic Ocean, Gulf of Mexico, Ala. **Rivers** Apalachicola, Caloosahatchee, Indian, Kissimmee, Perdido, St. Johns, St. Mary's, Suwanee, Withlacoochee. **Lakes** Apopka, George, Okeechobee, Seminole. **Other notable features** Everglades, Florida Keys, Okefenokee Swamp.
Elected officials   Gov. John Ellis "Jeb" Bush (D, term exp. 2003). Lt. Gov. Frank Brogan (R). Sec. State Katherine Harris (R). Atty. Gen. Robert A. Butterworth (D).
People   (1998) 14,915,980 (4th). **Race/national origin** (1990): White 83.1%. Black 13.6%. Indian 0.3%. Asian 1.2%. Other 1.8%. Hispanic 12.2%.
Cities   (1996 estimate) Jacksonville 679,792. Miami 365,127. Tampa 285,206. St. Petersburg 235,988. Hialeah 204,684. Orlando 173,902. Ft. Lauderdale 151,805. Tallahassee 136,812. Hollywood 127,894. Coral Springs 105,275.
Business   Gross State Product, 1997: $380.61 bil. (5th). **Leading Sectors of GSP** (1997): Services 23.96%; Finance, insurance, and real estate 22.01%; Government 12.23%. *Fortune* **500 Companies** (1998): 11: Republic Industries, Winn-Dixie Stores, Publix, Tech Data, Office Depot, CHS Electronics, FPL Group, Ryder System, Harris, Florida Progress, Darden Restaurants.
Famous natives   Mary Bethune, educator/reformer. Faye Dunaway, actress. Chris Evert, tennis player. Zora Neale Hurston, writer. James Weldon Johnson, lawyer/novelist. Osceola, Seminole chief. Sidney Poitier, actor. A. Philip Randolph, labor leader. Edmund Kirby Smith, Confederate general. Joseph Warren "Vinegar Joe" Stillwell, army officer. Ben Vereen, actor/singer.
Noteworthy places   Biscayne Natl. Park. Castillo de San Marcos, St. Augustine. Everglades Natl. Park. Florida State Museum, Gainesville. Ft. Jefferson Natl. Monument. Ft. Matanzas Natl. Monument. Kennedy Space Center, Cape Canaveral. Ringling Museum, Sarasota. St. Augustine. Walt Disney World/EPCOT Center, Orlando.
Memorable events   Juan Ponce de León claims Florida for Spain 1513. French stake claim for Florida 1562; build Ft. Caroline 1564. Pedro Menéndez de Avilés founds St. Augustine, first permanent European settlement in U.S. 1565. Spain cedes Florida to United States 1819. Seminole War 1835–42. State secedes from Union 1861. Readmitted 1868. Carl Fisher begins to develop Miami Beach as resort 1912. Florida's first paper mill opens expanding forest industry 1931. More than 100,000 Cuban refugees enter United States,

most through Florida, during Mariel boat lift 1980. Army Corps of Engineers announce plans to let Kissimmee River, canalized in 1971, return to natural course to Lake Okeechobee; the largest back-to-nature project ever undertaken in U.S. 1990. Hurricane Andrew causes $10 billion in damage to South Florida 1992.
Tourist information   1-888-735-2872.
www.state.fl.us.

▶ GEORGIA

The largest state east of the Mississippi River, Georgia is diverse in its terrain, embracing the woods of the Blue Ridge Mountains to the north and the alligators of the Okefenokee Swamp in the south. Though two-thirds of the population are urban dwellers, Georgia's farms rank at or near the top in poultry production and are leading producers of pecans, cattle, hogs, and peanuts. Up from a past of slavery and separate-but-equal facilities, in the early 1970s Atlanta elected Andrew Young the first black member of the U.S. Congress and Maynard Jackson the first black mayor from the South since Reconstruction. Today divisions linger in Georgia, the cities favoring a progressive stance and the rural areas clinging to some of the ways of the Old South.

Name For King George II of England 1732. **Nicknames** Empire State of the South, Peach State. **Capital** Atlanta. **Entered union** Jan. 2, 1788 (4th). **Motto** "Wisdom, justice, moderation."
Emblems **Bird** Brown thrasher. **Fish** Largemouth bass. **Flower** Cherokee rose. **Fossil** Shark tooth. **Gem** Quartz. **Insect** Honeybee. **Songs** "Georgia," "Georgia on My Mind." **Tree** Live oak. **Wildflower** Azalea.
Land **Total area** 58,910 sq. mi. (21st), incl. 854 sq. mi. inland water. **Borders** Tenn., N.C., S.C., Atlantic Ocean, Fla., Ala. **Rivers** Altamaha, Apalachicola, Chattahoochee, Flint, Ocmulgee, Oconee, Savannah, Suwanee. **Lakes** Clark Hill, Harding, Hartwell, Seminole, Sidney Lanier, Sinclair, Walter F. George, West Point Lake. **Other notable features** Blue Ridge Mountains (Mount Enotah 4,784 ft.), Okefenokee Swamp.
Elected officials Gov. Roy Barnes (D, term exp. 2003). Lt. Gov. Mark Taylor (D). Sec. State Cathy Cox (D). Atty. Gen. Thurbert Baker (D).
People (1998) 7,642,207 (10th). **Race/national origin** (1990): White 71.0%. Black 27.0%. Indian 0.2%. Asian 1.2%. Other 0.7%. Hispanic 1.7%.
Cities (1996 estimate) Atlanta 401,907. Columbus 182,828. Savannah 136,262. Macon 113,352. Athens-Clarke County 89,405. Albany 78,591. Roswell 55,462. Marietta 50,937. Warner Robins 45,559. Valdosta 41,816.
Business **Gross State Product,** 1997: $229.47 bil. (10th). **Leading Sectors of GSP** (1997): Services 18.49%; Manufacturing 17.45%; Finance, insurance, and real estate 16.46%. *Fortune* **500 Companies** (1998): 15: Home Depot, United Parcel Service, Bellsouth, Coca-Cola, Delta Air Lines, Coca-Cola Enterprises, Georgia-Pacific, Southern, Suntrust Banks, AFLAC, Genuine Parts, First Data, Shaw Industries, Flowers Industries, AGCO.
Famous natives James Brown, singer. Erskine Caldwell, author. James Earl ("Jimmy") Carter, U.S. president. Ray Charles, musician. Ty Cobb, baseball player. James Dickey, poet. Martin Luther King, Jr., minister/reformer. Sidney Lanier, author. Little Richard, musician. Carson McCullers, author. Alexander McGillivray, Creek chief. Margaret Mitchell, author. Elijah Muhammad, religious leader. Flannery O'Connor, author. Burt Reynolds, actor. Jackie Robinson, baseball player.

Tomochichi, Yamacraw chief. Ted Turner (b. Ohio), businessman. Joanne Woodward, actress.
Noteworthy places Chickamauga and Chattanooga Natl. Military Park. Confederate Memorial, Stone Mountain. Ft. Frederica Natl. Monument. Ft. Pulaski Natl. Monument. High Museum of Art, Atlanta. Martin Luther King Natl. Hist. Site., Atlanta. Ocmulgee Natl. Monument. Okefenokee Swamp. Savannah Historic District.
Memorable events Hernando de Soto explores region 1540. Cotton gin invented 1793. Georgia expels Cherokee Indian tribes on Trail of Tears 1832–38. Secedes from Union 1860. Gen. William T. Sherman's 60,000 troops cut 60-mi. swathe in their "march to the sea" 1864. Formula for Coca-Cola developed by chemist in search of cure for hangover 1886. Cyclone kills 1,000 in Charleston, S.C., and Savannah 1893. Franklin D. Roosevelt dies at the Little White House, Warm Springs 1945. First state to give vote to 18-year-olds 1948. Emory University designated to receive $100-million philanthropic gift from Robert W. Woodruff 1979. Dept. of Justice rules that state's process for electing superior court judges violates 1965 Voting Rights Act 1990. Summer Olympics held in Atlanta 1996.
Tourist information 1-800-VISIT-GA.
www.state.ga.us.

▶ HAWAII

What the air conditioner did for the Sunbelt, the jetliner has done for Hawaii, the last state to enter the Union. Because of the jet, Hawaii is a possible vacation spot for millions and welcomes 20 times the air travelers of 25 years ago. Tourism is Hawaii's key industry, attracting more than 6.5 million visitors to the state each year. Recent economic problems in Japan have had a negative effect on Hawaii's tourism numbers, and the state economy has suffered greatly as a result. Thousands of miles from both California and mainland Asia, Hawaii was originally peopled by Polynesian seafarers around A.D. 500 and has the richest ethnic mix of any state, with the lowest percentage of whites and highest percentages of Asians. It was partly fear of this diversity that stalled its statehood. A link between the United States and Asia, Hawaii is the center of U.S. defense in the Pacific and is home to 100,000 veterans, three-quarters of them veterans of Vietnam. Hawaii produces large quantities of pineapples and sugar cane, and efforts are under way to harness thermal electric power from Mauna Loa volcano.

Name Of unknown origin, perhaps from Hawaii Loa, traditional discoverer of islands, or from Hawaiki, the traditional Polynesian homeland. **Nicknames** Aloha State, Paradise of the Pacific. **Capital** Honolulu. **Entered union** Aug. 21, 1959 (50th). **Motto** *Ua mau ke ea o ka aina i ke pono* (The life of the land is perpetuated in righteousness).
Emblems **Bird** Nene (Hawaiian goose). **Fish** Humuhumunukunukuapuaa. **Flower** Pua aloalo (hibiscus). **Song** "Hawaii Ponoi." **Tree** Kukui (candlenut).
Land **Total area** 6,470 sq. mi. (47th), incl. 45 sq. mi. inland water. Surrounded by Pacific Ocean. **Rivers** Kaukonahua Stream, Wailuku Stream. **Lakes** Halulu, Kolekole, Salt Lake, Waiia Res. **Other notable features** Pearl Harbor. Hualalai, Kilauea, Mauna Kea (13,796 ft.), and Mauna Loa volcanoes. **Main islands** Hawaii, Kauai, Maui, Molokai, Oahu.
Elected officials Gov. Benjamin J. Cayetano (D, term exp. 2003). Lt. Gov/Sec. State, Mazie K. Hirono (D). Atty. Gen. Thomas K. Keller (D, acting).

People   (1998) 1,193,001 (41st). **Race/national origin** (1990): White 33.4%. Black 2.5%. Indian 0.5%. Asian 61.8%. Other 1.9%. Hispanic 7.3%.
Cities   (1990 Census) Honolulu 423,475 (1996 estimate). Hilo 37,808. Kailua 36,818. Kaneohe 35,448. Waipahu 31,435. Pearl City 30,993. Waimalu 29,967. Mililani Town 29,359. Schofield Barracks 19,597. Wahiawa 17,386.
Business   Gross State Product, 1997: $38.02 bil. (40th). **Leading Sectors of GSP** (1997): Finance, insurance, and real estate 22.36%; Services 22.13%; Government 21.13%. *Fortune* **500 Companies** (1998): 0.
Famous natives   Bernice P. Bishop, philanthropist. Sanford B. Dole, statehood advocate. Charlotte (b. Ohio) and Luther Halsey Gulick, Camp Fire Girls founders. Don Ho, singer. Daniel J. Inouye, politician. Duke Kahanamoku, swimmer. Victoria Kaiulani, last heiress presumptive to Hawaiian throne. Kamehameha I, king. Kamehameha III, king. Liliuokalani, queen. Bette Midler, singer.
Noteworthy places   Bernice P. Bishop Museum, Honolulu. Diamond Head. Haleakala Natl. Park, Maui. Hawaii Volcanoes Natl. Park (Kilauea and Mauna Loa), Hawaii. Iolani Palace, Honolulu. Kaloko-Honokohau Natl. Hist. Park, Molokai. Natl. Cemetery of the Pacific and USS *Arizona* Memorial. Polynesian Cultural Center, Laiea. Pu'uhonua o Honaunau Natl. Hist. Park, Hawaii.
Memorable events   Polynesians first arrive 6th century. Second wave of Polynesians arrive 10th century. Captain James Cook first European to visit islands 1778; killed on Hawaii 1779. Sugar production begins 1835. Land reform ends feudal system 1848. Monarchy rule ends in revolution 1893. Becomes U.S. Territory 1900. Japanese attack Pearl Harbor 1941. Statehood 1959.
Tourist information   1-800-464-2924. www.state.hi.us.

▶**IDAHO**
Home to some of the most isolated and rugged country in the United States, Idaho's diversified economy has traditionally been based on lumber and potatoes (more than 13 billion pounds in 1993). In the 1980s these were augmented by a number of small high-tech industries fleeing the high cost of business in California. During the 1990s the population has grown rapidly (20 percent by 1997).
   Name Means "gem of the mountains." **Nickname** Gem State. **Capital** Boise. **Entered union** July 3, 1890 (43rd). **Motto** *Esto perpetua* (May it last forever).
Emblems   **Bird** Mountain bluebird. **Flower** Syringa. **Gem** Star garnet. **Horse** Appaloosa. **Song** "Here We Have Idaho." **Tree** Western white pine.
Land   Total area 83,564 sq. mi. (13th), incl. 1,152 sq. mi. inland water. **Borders** British Columbia, Mont., Wyo., Utah, Nev., Oreg., Wash. **Rivers** Bear, Clearwater, Payette, Salmon, Snake. **Lakes** American Falls Res., Coeur d'Alene, Pend Oreille. **Mountains** Bitterroot Range, Centennial, Clearwater, Salmon River, Sawtooth Range (Castle Peak 11,820 ft.), Wasatch Range. **Other notable features** Grand Canyon of the Snake River.
Elected officials   Gov. Dirk Kempthorne (R, term exp. 2003). Lt. Gov. C.L. "Butch" Otter (R). Sec. State Pete T. Cenarrusa (R). Atty. Gen. Alan G. Lance (R).
People   (1998) 1,228,684 (40th). **Race/national origin** (1990): White 94.4%. Black 0.3%. Indian 1.4%. Asian 0.9%. Other 3.0%. Hispanic 5.3%.

Cities   (1996 estimate) Boise 152,737. Pocatello 51,344. Idaho Falls 48,079. Nampa 37,558. Twin Falls 31,989. Coeur d'Alene 31,076. Lewiston 30,271. Caldwell 21,089. Meridian 20,627. Moscow 20,101.
Business   Gross State Product, 1997: $29.15 bil. (43rd). **Leading Sectors of GSP** (1997): Manufacturing 19.93%; Services 16.67%; Government 13.29%. *Fortune* **500 Companies** (1998): 3: Albertson's, Boise Cascade, Micron Technology.
Famous natives   Joseph, Nez Percé chief. Ezra Taft Benson, politician. Gutzon Borglum, sculptor. Frank Church, politician. Ezra Pound, poet. Harmon Killebrew, baseball player. Jerry Kramer, football player. Sacagawea (Bird Woman), Shoshone interpreter. Lana Turner, actress.
Noteworthy places   Craters of the Moons Natl. Monument. Hell's Canyon Natl. Recreation Area. Nez Percé Natl. Hist. Park. Sawtooth Natl. Recreation Area. Sun Valley ski resort. Yellowstone Natl. Park.
Memorable events   Lewis and Clark expedition 1805. Becomes part of United States when Idaho Treaty concluded with Britain 1846. Gold Rush 1860. Nez Percé War 1877. Statehood 1890. World's first breeder reactor built at Idaho Falls, 1951. Snake River opened to navigation, linking Lewiston to Pacific Ocean at Astoria, Oregon, 1975. New Teton River Dam collapses as it is being filled for first time; 10 dead, $400 million in damage 1976.
Tourist information   1-800-635-7820. www.state.id.us.

▶**ILLINOIS**
The Illinois economy is enormously productive and diverse. While Chicago is a leader in world finance and trade, the southern part of the state has rich farmlands (the state is second to Iowa in corn and soybean exports) and mineral deposits (both coal and gas — there are especially rich coal deposits in the southeast region around Cairo, known as Little Egypt). Manufacturing centers on Chicago, Rockford—the state's second-largest city—and Springfield, the capital. Chicago is also a major transportation hub with extensive rail networks, an international port serving ships from both the Atlantic and Gulf of Mexico, and the largest airport in the country.
   Name Corruption of *iliniwek* ("tribe of the superior men"), natives at time of earliest French explorations. **Nickname** Prairie State. **Capital** Springfield. **Entered union** Dec. 3, 1818 (21st). **Motto** "State sovereignty—national unity." **Slogan** "Land of Lincoln."
Emblems   **Animal** White-tailed deer. **Bird** Cardinal. **Flower** Violet. **Insect** Monarch butterfly. **Mineral** Fluorite. **Song** "Illinois." **Tree** White oak.
Land   Total area 56,345 sq. mi. (24th), incl. 700 sq. mi. inland water. **Borders** Wis., Lake Michigan, Ind., Ky., Mo., Iowa. **Rivers** Fox, Illinois, Illinois Waterway, Kankakee, Kaskaskia, Mississippi, Ohio, Rock, Vermillion, Wabash. **Lakes** Carlyle, Crab Orchard. **Other notable features** Charles Mound (1,235 ft.), Little Egypt.
Elected officials   Gov. George H. Ryan (R, term exp. 2003). Lt. Gov. Corinne G. Wood (R). Sec. State Jesse white (D). Atty. Gen. Jim Ryan (R).
People   (1998) 12,045,326 (5th). **Race/national origin** (1990): White 78.3%. Black 14.8%. Indian 0.2%. Asian 2.5%. Other 4.2%. Hispanic 7.9%.
Cities   (1996 estimate) Chicago 2,721,547. Rockford 143,531. Aurora 116,405. Springfield 112,921. Peoria 112,306. Naperville 107,001. Joliet 86,749.

Elgin 86,034. Decatur 81,369. Arlington Heights Village 76,740.
Business **Gross State Product,** 1997: $393.53 bil. (4th). **Leading Sectors of GSP** (1997): Services 20.93%; Finance, insurance, and real estate 20.19%; Manufacturing 18.21%. *Fortune* **500 Companies** (1998): 39: including State Farm Insurance, Sears Roebuck, Motorola, Allstate, Bank One Corp., Caterpillar, Sara Lee, UAL, Ameritech, Archer Daniels Midland, Walgreen, Deere, McDonald's, Navistar International, R.R. Donnelley & Sons, Quaker Oats, Brunswick, Smurfit-Stone Container, Ace Hardware, Tribune.
Famous natives Jane Addams, reformer (Nobel Peace Prize, 1930). Ernie Banks, baseball player. Saul Bellow, author (Nobel Prize, 1976). Harry A. Blackmun, jurist. Ray Bradbury, author. Gwendolyn Brooks, poet. William Jennings Bryan, politician. Edgar Rice Burroughs, novelist. St. Frances Xavier Cabrini (b. Italy). Clarence Darrow, lawyer. Miles Davis, musician. John Dos Passos, novelist. Enrico Fermi (b. Italy), nuclear physicist (Nobel Prize, 1938). Robert Louis ("Bob") Fosse, choreographer. Milton Friedman, economist (Nobel Prize, 1976). Benny Goodman, musician. Ernest Hemingway, novelist. Charlton Heston, actor. William Holden, actor. Vachel Lindsay, poet. Archibald MacLeish, poet. Ludwig Mies van der Rohe (b. Germany), architect. Charles W. Post, cereal manufacturer. Ronald Reagan, U.S. president. Carl Sandburg, poet. Albert G. Spalding, merchant. John Paul Stevens, jurist. Gloria Swanson, actress.
Noteworthy places Art Institute of Chicago. Crab Orchard Wildlife Refuge. Dickson Mounds Museum, Lewistown. Field Museum of Natural History, Chicago. Ft. Chartres. Ft. Kaskaskia. Ft. Massac. Frank Lloyd Wright Historic District, Oak Park. Illinois State Museum, Springfield. Lincoln Home Natl. Hist. Park, Springfield. Mormon Settlement, Nauvoo. Morton Arboretum, Lisle. Museum of Science and Industry, Chicago. Shawnee Natl. Forest. Starved Rock State Park.
Memorable events French missionary explorers Jacques Marquette and Louis Jolliet in Illinois 1673. Cahokia first European settlement 1699. Territory to England after French and Indian War 1763. Chicago founded by Jean-Baptiste Point du Sable 1779. Illinois and Michigan Canal links Lake Michigan and Mississippi River 1848. Lincoln-Douglas Debates at Springfield 1860. Half of Chicago destroyed by great fire 1871. Terrorist bombing leaves nine dead and 130 wounded in Haymarket affair, Chicago 1886. Columbia Exposition, Chicago 1893. First successful nuclear chain reaction created at University of Chicago 1942. Riots at Democratic National Convention in Chicago 1968. Sears Tower, world's tallest building (1,454 ft.), completed in Chicago 1973. Mississippi and Illinois rivers flood and cause $1.5 billion in damage 1993.
Tourist information 1-800-2-CONNECT or 1-800-223-0121.
www.state.il.us.

▶ INDIANA

Indiana is strong in both farms and manufacturing. Its southern half has large coal deposits and produces most of the limestone quarried in the United States. To the north the fertile land helps make Indiana one of the primary farm-belt states. Indiana is also very much a part of the industrial Midwest, where unemployment is always a threat, especially in the heavily industrial areas of Gary and Indianapolis (the latter of which has devel-
oped into a center for high-tech industries through the 1980s and 1990s). These geographic divisions have parallels in the political history of the state, which during the Civil War was Union in the north and Confederate in the south.
Name For the land of Indians by early settlers, who found many distinct tribes living in region. **Nickname** Hoosier State. **Capital** Indianapolis. **Entered union** Dec. 11, 1816 (19th). **Motto** "The Crossroads of America."
Emblems **Bird** Cardinal. **Flower** Peony. **Poem** "Indiana." **Song** "On the Banks of the Wabash, Far Away." **Stone** Indiana limestone. **Tree** Tulip tree.
Land **Total area** 36,185 sq. mi. (38th), incl. 253 sq. mi. inland water. **Borders** Lake Michigan, Mich., Ohio, Ky., Ill. **Rivers** Kankakee, Ohio, Tippecanoe, Wabash, White, Whitewater. **Lakes** Freeman, Shafer.
Elected officials Gov. Frank O'Bannon (D, term exp. 2001). Lt. Gov. Joseph Kernan (D). Sec. State Sue Ann Gilroy (R). Atty. Gen. Jeffrey A. Modisett (D).
People (1998) 5,899,195 (14th). **Race/national origin** (1990): White 90.6%. Black 7.8% Indian 0.2%. Asian 0.7%. Other 0.7%. Hispanic 1.8%.
Cities (1996 estimate) Indianapolis 746,737. Fort Wayne 184,783. Evansville 123,456. Gary 110,975. South Bend 102,100. Hammond 80,081. Muncie 69,058. Bloomington 66,479. Anderson 59,131. Terre Haute 54,585.
Business **Gross State Product,** 1997: $161.70 bil. (15th). **Leading Sectors of GSP** (1997): Manufacturing 31.02%; Services 15.88%; Finance, insurance, and real estate 13.2%. *Fortune* **500 Companies** (1998): 7: Eli Lilly, Conseco, Bindley Western, Cummins Engine, Lincoln National, Anthem Insurance, Nipsco Industries.
Famous natives Larry Bird, basketball player. Hoagy Carmichael, composer. Eugene V. Debs, politician/organizer. Theodore Dreiser, author. Benjamin Harrison, U.S. president. Jimmy Hoffa, union leader. Michael Jackson, singer. David Letterman, comedian. Carole Lombard, actress. Cole Porter, composer. Ernie Pyle, journalist. Knute Rockne (b. Norway), football coach. Paul Samuelson, economist (Nobel Prize, 1960). Booth Tarkington, author. Kurt Vonnegut, author. Wendell L. Willkie, politician. Wilbur Wright, aviation pioneer.
Noteworthy places Ernie Pyle birthplace, Dana. George Rogers Clark Natl. Hist. Park, Vincennes. Benjamin Harrison home, Indianapolis. Hoosier Natl. Forest. Indiana Dunes Natl. Lakeshore. Indianapolis Motor Speedway and Museum. Indianapolis Museum of Art. New Harmony village. Notre Dame Univ., South Bend. Old state capital, Corydon. Wilbur Wright State Memorial, Millville. Wyandotte Cave. Tippecanoe sites.
Memorable events Mound Builders present c. A.D. 1000. René-Robert Cavelier de La Salle explores for French 1679–87. French near Vincennes from c. 1700. French cede territory to British 1763. Gen. Ambrose Clark captures Ft. Vincennes 1779. Territory ceded to U.S. 1783; included in Northwest Territory 1787. Miamis defeat U.S. twice in 1790. Gen. Anthony Wayne defeats Miamis at Battle of Fallen Timbers 1794. Territory included in Indiana Territory 1800. Gen. William Henry Harrison defeats Tecumseh's Indian Confederation at Tippecanoe 1811. Statehood 1816. Studebaker wagon company founded in South Bend 1852. U.S. Steel establishes mill at company-built town of Gary 1906. First Indianapolis 500 run 1911.

Only a dozen car companies producing cars, down from a pre-World War I peak of 375, 1920. Studebaker, last Indiana-based car manufacturer, closes 1963.
Tourist information   1-800-289-6646.
www.state.in.us.

▶**IOWA**
Iowa lies between the two great rivers of the central United States, the Mississippi and the Missouri, with a quarter of the nation's richest and deepest topsoil. Iowa's farmers lead the country in the production of corn, and Iowa is also a big producer of hogs, cattle, and other livestock. With about 75 percent of Iowans employed in agriculture-related industries and 90 percent of the land farmed, Iowa can be deeply affected by natural disasters such as droughts and floods. Yet more than 100 *Fortune* 500 companies have production facilities in this farm state. Industrial production has risen since World War II. Iowans send abroad a quarter of the food they produce. As a result, this traditionally Republican state is better attuned to world developments than one might initially suspect.

Name For Iowa tribe. **Nickname** Hawkeye State. **Capital** Des Moines. **Entered union** Dec. 28, 1846 (29th). **Motto** "Our liberties we prize and our rights we will maintain."
Emblems   **Bird** Eastern goldfinch. **Flower** Wild rose. **Song** "The Song of Iowa." **Stone** Geode. **Tree** Oak.
Land   **Total area** 56,275 sq. mi. (25th), incl. 310 sq. mi. inland water. **Borders** Minn., Wis., Ill., Mo., Nebr., S.Dak. **Rivers** Big Sioux, Des Moines, Mississippi, Missouri. **Lakes** Okoboji, Rathbun Res., Red Rock, Saylorville Res., Spirit, Storm. **Other notable features** Ocheyedan Mound (1,675 ft.).
Elected officials   Gov. Tom Vilsack (D, term exp. 2003). Lt. Gov. Sally Pederson (D). Sec. State Chet Culver (D). Atty. Gen. Thomas J. Miller (D).
People   (1998) 2,862,447 (30th). **Race/national origin** (1990): White 96.6%. Black 1.7%. Indian 0.3%. Asian 0.9%. Other 0.5%. Hispanic 1.2%.
Cities   (1996 estimate) Des Moines 193,422. Cedar Rapids 113,482. Davenport 97,010. Sioux City 83,791. Waterloo 65,022. Iowa City 60,923. Dubuque 57,312. Council Bluffs 55,569. Ames 47,698. West Des Moines 40,380.
Business   **Gross State Product,** 1997: $80.48 bil. (29th). **Leading Sectors of GSP** (1997): Manufacturing 24.38%; Services 15.32%; Finance, insurance, and real estate 14.77%. *Fortune* 500 **Companies** (1998): 2: Principal Financial, Maytag.
Famous natives   Norman E. Borlaug, agronomist (Nobel Peace Prize, 1970). William F. ("Buffalo Bill") Cody, scout/showman. George Gallup, pollster. Josiah B. Grinnell (b. Vt.), abolitionist. Herbert Hoover, U.S. president. Harry L. Hopkins, politician. John L. Lewis, labor leader. John R. Mott, religious leader. Billy Sunday, baseball player/evangelist. John Wayne, actor. Meredith Wilson, composer. Grant Wood, painter.
Noteworthy places   Amana Colonies. Davenport Art Gallery. Des Moines Art Center. Effigy Mounds Natl. Monument, Marquette. Ft. Dodge Hist. Museum. Herbert Hoover birthplace and library, West Branch. Natl. Rivers Hall of Fame, Dubuque. Putnam Museum, Davenport.
Memorable events   Mound Builders present c. A.D. 1000. Jacques Marquette and Louis Jolliet claim land for France 1673. Part of Louisiana Purchase 1803. Part of Missouri Territory 1812–21. Black Hawk Wars 1832, 1834–37. First permanent settlement at Dubuque 1833. Organized as Iowa

Territory (incl. parts of Minnesota, North Dakota, and South Dakota) 1838. Statehood 1846. Capital moved from Iowa City to Des Moines 1857. Fifty percent of Iowa's farms foreclosed during depression 1929–35. Urban population exceeds rural for first time 1960. Population loss of 7.9 percent in the 1980s. Floods cause $2.2 billion in damage 1993.
Tourist information   1-800-345-IOWA.
www.state.ia.us.

▶**KANSAS**
Kansas burst on the American scene as the territory called Bleeding Kansas, seething with conflict over the spread of slavery. Victorious New England abolitionists imprinted the state with the Puritan ethic. They were early supporters of prohibition, partly to discourage foreign newcomers. Kansas suffered enormously during the Great Depression and "Dust Bowl" days of the 1930s but rebounded strongly during the war. Wichita's aircraft industries, vital to the war effort, helped the Kansas economy to remain strong in the postwar years as family farming declined dramatically. Today Kansas remains a primary producer of wheat, cattle, and other agricultural products. Its manufacturing base still includes extensive aircraft industries, and it leads the states in the production of helium. The geographic center of the continental United States is near Lebanon.

Name For Kansa or Kaw, "people of the south wind." **Nickname** Sunflower State. **Capital** Topeka. **Entered union** Jan. 29, 1861 (34th). **Motto** *Ad astra per aspera* (To the stars through adversity).
Emblems   **Animal** American buffalo. **Bird** Western meadowlark. **Flower** Wild native sunflower. **March** "The Kansas March." **Song** "Home on the Range." **Tree** Cottonwood.
Land   **Total area** 82,277 sq. mi. (14th), incl. 499 sq. mi. inland water. **Borders** Nebr., Mo., Okla., Colo. **Rivers** Arkansas, Kansas, Missouri, Republican, Saline, Smoky Hill, Solomon. **Lakes** Kanapolis, Malvern, Perry, Pomona, Tuttle Creek, Waconda. **Other notable features** Flint Hills.
Elected officials   Gov. Bill Graves (R, term exp. 2003). Lt. Gov. Gary Sherrer (R). Sec. State Ron Thornburgh (R). Atty. Gen. Carla J. Stovall (R).
People   (1998) 2,629,067 (32nd). **Race/national origin** (1980): White 90.1%. Black 5.8%. Indian 0.9%. Asian 1.3%. Other 2.0%. Hispanic 3.8%.
Cities   (1996 estimate) Wichita 320,395. Kansas City 142,654. Overland Park 131,053. Topeka 119,658. Olathe 78,666. Lawrence 71,887. Salina 44,176. Shawnee 43,006. Manhattan 42,117. Leavenworth 39,431.
Business   **Gross State Product,** 1997: $71.74 bil. (31st). **Leading Sectors of GSP** (1997): Manufacturing 17.82%; Services 17.14%; Government 13.60%. *Fortune* 500 **Companies** (1998): 2: Sprint, Yellow.
Famous natives   "Buffalo Bill" Cody. Walter Chrysler, carmaker. Robert Dole, politician. Amelia Earhart, aviator. Dwight David Eisenhower (b. Tex.), general/U.S. president. Dennis Hopper, actor. William Inge, playwright. Nancy Landon Kassebaum, politician. Alf Landon, politician. Edgar Lee Masters, poet. James Naismith, inventor of basketball. Carry Nation (b. Ky.), prohibitionist. Charlie ("Bird") Parker, musician. Damon Runyon, writer. Gale Sayers, football player. William Allen White, the Sage of Emporia, editor.
Noteworthy places   Agricultural Hall of Fame, Kansas City. Dodge City. Eisenhower Center,

Abilene. Ft. Larned. Ft. Leavenworth. Ft. Riley. Ft. Scott. John Brown's Cabin, Osawatomie. Kansas Cosmosphere and Space Discovery Center, Hutchinson. Kansas State Historical Society Museum, Topeka. Wichita Art Museum.

Memorable events   First major expedition to region under Francisco Vásquez de Coronado 1540–41. La Salle claims territory including Kansas for France 1682. Part of Louisiana Purchase 1803. Area visited by Meriwether Lewis and George Rogers Clark (1803), Zebulon Pike (1806), and Stephen H. Long (1819). Santa Fe Trail crosses Kansas 1821. Fts. Leavenworth (1827), Scott (1842), and Riley (1853) established to protect pioneers on Santa Fe and Oregon trails. Organized as Territory by Kansas-Nebraska Act 1854, which repealed Missouri Compromise of 1820. "Bleeding Kansas" scene of free vs. slave rivalry 1854–56. Statehood 1861. Introduction of winter wheat makes Kansas leading U.S. wheat producer 1870. Airplane manufacturing starts in Wichita 1919. World-famous Menninger Foundation for mental health founded 1919. "Dust Bowl" drought drives thousands of farmers off the land, especially in western Kansas, 1934–35. Murder of Clutter family by Richard E. Hickock and Perry E. Smith at Holcomb (later the subject of Truman Capote's *In Cold Blood*, 1959).

Tourist information   1-800-252-6727. **www.state.ks.us.**

▶KENTUCKY, COMMONWEALTH OF

First pioneered by English immigrants in the mid-17th century, Kentucky's golden age as a choice frontier destination in the early 1800s was brought to an end by the Civil War. During the Civil War, the Bluegrass gentry supported the Confederacy, while the Appalachian backwoods men enlisted in the Union Army. Many took advantage of their uniforms to settle old accounts, and the social order was often threatened before the turn of the century. Though the state is known today for its bourbon and horse breeding, many Kentuckians make their living from the land as tobacco farmers or coal miners. The Appalachian part of the state in the east delivers about 20 percent of the nation's coal, but its economic problems remain acute, despite vast expenditures during the "war on poverty."

Name   Corruption of the Iroquois *kenta-ke* (meadow land) or Wyandot *kah-ten-tah-teh* (land of tomorrow). **Nickname** Bluegrass State. **Capital** Frankfort. **Entered union** June 1, 1792 (15th). **Motto** "United we stand, divided we fall."

Emblems   **Bird** Cardinal. **Colors** Blue and gold. **Fish** Bass. **Flower** Goldenrod. **Song** "My Old Kentucky Home." **Tree** Tulip poplar. **Wild animal** Gray squirrel.

Land   **Total area** 40,409 sq. mi. (37th), incl. 740 sq. mi. inland water. **Borders** Ind., Ohio, W.Va., Va., Tenn., Mo., Ill. **Rivers** Cumberland, Kentucky, Licking, Ohio, Tennessee. **Lakes** Barkley, Barren River Res., Dewey, Grayson Res., Laurel Res., Nolin Res., Rough Res. **Mountains** Appalachian (Black Mt. 4,145 ft.), Cumberland. **Other notable features** Tennessee Valley.

Elected officials   Gov. Paul E. Patton (D, term exp. 2002). Lt. Gov. Stephen L. Henry, M.D. (D). Sec. Commonwealth John Y. Brown III (D). Atty. Gen. A.B. Chandler (D).

People   (1998) 3,936,499 (25th). **Race/national origin** (1990): White 92.0%. Black 7.1%. Indian 0.2%. Asian 0.5%. Other 0.2%. Hispanic 0.6%.

Cities   (1996 estimate) Louisville 260,689. Lexington-Fayette 239,942. Owensboro 54,350. Bowl-ing Green 44,208. Covington 40,971. Hopkinsville 28,317. Frankfort 26,695. Paducah 26,601. Henderson 26,456. Richmond 26,227.

Business   **Gross State Product,** 1997: $100.08 bil. (26th). **Leading Sectors of GSP** (1997): Manufacturing 27.34%; Services 15.21%; Government 13.23%. *Fortune* **500 Companies** (1998): 6: Humana, Tricon Global Restaurants, Ashland, LG & E Energy, Vencor, Lexmark International.

Famous natives   Muhammad Ali, boxer. Alben W. Barkley, politician. Daniel Boone (b. Pa.), frontiersman. Louis D. Brandeis, jurist. Kit Carson, frontiersman. Henry Clay, politician. Jefferson Davis, president of Confederate States of America. D.W. Griffith, director. John Marshall Harlan, jurist. Abraham Lincoln, U.S. president. Col. Harland Sanders, entrepreneur. Frederick M. Vinson, jurist. Robert Penn Warren, author.

Noteworthy places   Abraham Lincoln birthplace, Hodgenville. Churchill Downs, Louisville. George S. Patton, Jr. Military Museum, Fort Knox. J.B. Speed Art Museum, Louisville. Land Between the Lakes Natl. Rec. Area. Mammoth Cave Natl. Park. My Old Kentucky Home, Bardstown. Old Ft. Harrod State Park.

Memorable events   English enter territory through Cumberland Gap 1750. Territory included in area ceded by French 1763. Daniel Boone leads expeditions into region 1769. First settlement Harrodsburg 1774. Daniel Boone blazes Wilderness Trail through Cumberland Gap, establishes Ft. Boonesborough 1775. Organized as a county of Virginia 1776. British support Indian resistance ("Dark and Bloody Wars") until George Rogers Clark captures British forts in Indiana and Illinois 1778. Included as part of United States after Revolution 1783. Virginia approves separate statehood, achieved 1792. First steamboat reaches Louisville from New Orleans 1815. Invaded by Confederate armies 1862. Kentucky Derby first run at Louisville 1875. State has highest per capita income of southern states 1900; ranks last among all 48 states in per capita income 1940. Farm population decreases by 76%, and total number of farms by 53%, 1945–80.

Tourist information   1-800-225-TRIP or 1-800-255-PARK. **www.state.ky.us.**

▶LOUISIANA

European influences and ethnic diversity distinguish Louisiana from the rest of the nation. When Louisiana entered the Union in 1812, it brought with it a French legal system and a bilingualism that still survive. African-Americans, Cajuns and Creoles have contributed to its distinctive music and cuisine. The state has rich farmland, more oil and gas reserves than any other state but Texas, and in New Orleans an international port that serves the most extensive river system in North America.

The "devil's bargain" with the petrochemical industry struck by charismatic populist governor Huey Long (assassinated in 1935) brought needed jobs to the state. But the environmental impact of 100 loosely regulated petrochemical plants on the Mississippi River between New Orleans and Baton Rouge is being assessed only now. The state's reliance on the petroleum industry was felt when a downturn in oil prices in the 1980s led to massive unemployment. Economic diversification is under way, especially in the field of tourism.

Name   For King Louis XIV. **Nickname** Pelican State. **Capital** Baton Rouge. **Entered union** Apr.

30, 1812 (18th). **Motto** "Union, justice, confidence."

Emblems   Bird Eastern brown pelican. **Colors** Gold, white, and blue. **Crustacean** Crawfish. **Dog** Catahoula leopard. **Flower** Magnolia. **Fossil** Petrified palmwood. **Gem** Agate. **Insect** Honeybee. **Songs** "Give Me Louisiana," "You Are My Sunshine." **Tree** Bald cypress.

Land   Total area 47,751 sq. mi. (31st), incl. 3,230 sq. mi. inland water. **Borders** Ark., Miss., Gulf of Mexico, Tex. **Rivers** Atchafalaya, Mississippi, Ouachita, Pearl, Red, Sabine. **Lakes** Bistineau, Borgne, Caddo, Catahoula, Grand, Maurepas, Pontchartrain, Salvador, White. **Other notable features** Bayou Barataria, Bayou Bodcau, Bayou D'Arbonne, Driskill Mt. (535 ft.).

Elected officials   Gov. Mike Foster Jr. (D, term exp. 2000). Lt. Gov. Kathleen B. Blanco (D). Sec. State W. Fox McKeithen (R). Atty. Gen. Richard Ieuyob (D).

People   (1998) 4,368,967 (22nd). **Race/national origin** (1990): White 67.3%. Black 30.8%. Indian 0.4%. Asian 1.0%. Other 0.5%. Hispanic 2.2%.

Cities   (1996 estimate) New Orleans 476,625. Baton Rouge 215,882. Shreveport 191,558. Lafayette 104,899. Kenner 72,345. Lake Charles 71,445. Bossier City 55,686. Monroe 54,588. Alexandria 46,051. New Iberia 32,513.

Business   Gross State Product, 1997: $124.35 bil. (23rd). **Leading Sectors of GSP** (1997): Services 16.19%; Mining 15.92%; Manufacturing 15.73%. *Fortune* **500 Companies** (1998): 1: Entergy.

Famous natives   Louis "Satchmo" Armstrong, jazz musician. Pierre Beauregard, Confederate general. Terry Bradshaw, football player. Braxton Bragg, Confederate general. Truman Capote, author. Clyde Cessna, aviator. Michael DeBakey, surgeon. Fats Domino, singer. Lillian Hellman, author. Mahalia Jackson, singer. Jean Baptiste Le Moyne, sieur de Bienville (b. Canada), founded New Orleans. Jerry Lee Lewis, singer. Huey P. Long, senator. Ferdinand Joseph La Menthe "Jelly Roll" Morton, musician. Leonidas K. Polk, clergyman/Confederate general. Henry Miller Shreve (b. NJ), riverboat captain. Edward D. White, Jr., jurist.

Noteworthy places   Avery Island. Cabildo, New Orleans. French Quarter, New Orleans. Garden District, New Orleans. Hodges Gardens, Natchitoches. Jean Lafitte Natl. Hist. Park, Chalmette. Kent House Museum, Alexandria. Longfellow-Evangeline State Commemorative Area, St. Martinsville. Louisiana Maritime Museum, Baton Rouge. New Orleans Museum of Art.

Memorable events   Area first visited by Alonso Alvarez de Piñeda 1519. Claimed by René-Robert Cavelier de La Salle for France 1682. New Orleans founded 1718. French crown colony 1731. Four thousand Acadians (Cajuns) from Nova Scotia forcibly transported by British to Louisiana and settled in Bayou Teche 1755. Lands west of Mississippi given to Spain for help in French and Indian War 1763. Lands east of Mississippi ceded to Britain 1763. Same lands retroceded to France 1800. Jefferson negotiates Louisiana Purchase; U.S. acquires 885,000 sq. mi. for $15 million 1803. Statehood 1812. Andrew Jackson beats British at Battle of New Orleans 1815. State secedes 1861. Surrenders to Union forces 1862. Readmitted to Union 1868. Petroleum discovered 1901. Huey "The Kingfish" Long elected to Senate 1928; assassinated 1935. Racial designation law of 1970 repealed 1983.

Tourist information   1-800-964-7321 or 1-800-33-GUMBO.
www.state.la.us.

▶MAINE

Down-Easters—the original Puritans as well as the later French Canadians—are distinct from the New Englanders of Maine's economically more vital sister states. Their land, especially the coast, is rugged, and the living everywhere is hard. Maine touches only one other state, and it has an end-of-the-line feel to it. Lumbering, fishing, and potato farming were the traditional industries. More than half of the state is still unorganized territory largely owned by paper companies. In the 18th century, canneries, textiles, and shoe factories developed. Recently Maine's economy has combined light industry and tourism that is moving it into the mainstream. The modern Maine entrepreneur, often an out-of-stater, seeks an economy based on small industries and more in keeping with Maine's independent temperament.

Name   Either for Maine in France or to distinguish mainland from islands in the Gulf of Maine. **Nickname** Pine Tree State. **Capital** Augusta. **Entered union** Mar. 15, 1820 (23rd). **Motto** *Dirigo* (I direct).

Emblems   Animal Moose. **Bird** Chickadee. **Fish** Landlocked salmon. **Flower** White pinecone and tassel. **Insect** Honeybee. **Mineral** Tourmaline. **Song** "State of Maine Song." **Tree** Eastern white pine.

Land   Total area 33,265 sq. mi. (39th), incl. 2,270 sq. mi. inland water. **Borders** Quebec, New Brunswick, Atlantic Ocean, N.H. **Rivers** Alagash, Androscoggin, Aroostock, Kennebec, Machias, Penobscot, Piscataqua, Salmon Falls, St. John. **Lakes** Chamberlain, Chesuncook, Grand, Moosehead, Rangeley, Sebago. **Other notable features** Longfellow Mts. (Mt. Katahdin 5,268 ft.), Mt. Desert Island, Penobscot Bay.

Elected officials   Gov. Angus S. King, Jr. (I, term exp. 2003). Sec. State Dan A. Gwadowsky (D). Atty. Gen. Drew Ketterer (D).

People   (1998) 1,244,250 (39th). **Race/national origin** (1990): White 98.4%. Black 0.4%. Indian 0.5%. Asian 0.5%. Other 0.1%. Hispanic 0.6%.

Cities   (1996 estimate) Portland 63,123. Lewiston 36,830. Bangor 31,649. Auburn 22,997. South Portland 22,985. Biddeford 20,788. Augusta 20,441. Westbrook 16,459. Waterville 16,400. Saco 15,681.

Business   Gross State Product, 1997: $30.16 bil. (42nd). **Leading Sectors of GSP** (1997): Services 19.23%; Finance, insurance, and real estate 19.16%; Manufacturing 17.09%. *Fortune* **500 Companies** (1998): 2: Unum, Hannaford Brothers.

Famous natives   Cyrus H.K. Curtis, publisher. Hannibal Hamlin, politician. Sarah Orne Jewett, novelist. Henry Wadsworth Longfellow, poet. Sir Hiram and Hudson Maxim, inventors. Edna St. Vincent Millay, poet. Edmund S. Muskie, politician. John Knowles Paine, composer. Kenneth Roberts, novelist. Edward Arlington Robinson, poet. Nelson Rockefeller, politician. Marguerite Yourcenar (b. France), author.

Noteworthy places   Acadia Natl. Park, Mt. Desert Island. Allagash Natl. Wilderness Waterway. Boothbay Railway Museum Campobello-Longfellow House, Portland. Maine Maritime Museum, Bath. Portland Art Museum Roosevelt-Campobello Intl. Park, Campobello Island. St. Croix Island Natl. Monument.

Memorable events Vikings explore coast c. A.D.1000. Bartholomew Gosnold sails along coast 1602. French settlers at St. Croix River 1604. Included in grant to Plymouth Company 1606. Monhegan Island and Saco settled 1622. Annexed to Massachusetts Colony 1652. French attack northern territory intermittently through 1713. Statehood 1820. Border with Canada settled 1842. First state prohibition law enacted 1851. Penobscot and Passamaquoddy tribes file claim against state for $300 million compensation for land seized in violation of 1790 Indian Non-Intercourse Act, 1972; settled for $81.5 million 1980. First state to allow inheritance taxes to be paid with works of art 1979.
Tourist information   1-800-533-9595.
www.state.me.us.

▶**MARYLAND**
Maryland wraps like a fishhook from the Atlantic Ocean around the fish-rich Chesapeake Bay and into the Cumberland Mountains in the northwest. Baltimore—full of urban problems but newly redeveloped with urban homesteading and shopsteading—holds the center. The suburbs of Baltimore and Washington seem far removed from the Delmarva (**de**laware, **mary**land, **virg**inia) peninsula with its watermen hanging on to an older way of life. Terrain, cultures, and history are a border state's mix of North and South. Founded as a haven for Catholics, Maryland's population is still 20 percent Catholic.
Name For Henrietta Maria, queen consort of Charles I. **Nicknames** Old Line State, Free State. **Capital** Annapolis. **Entered union** Apr. 28, 1788 (7th). **Motto** *Fatti maschii, parole femine* (Manly deeds, womanly words).
Emblems   **Bird** Baltimore oriole. **Dog** Chesapeake Bay retriever. **Fish** Rockfish. **Flower** Black-eyed Susan. **Fossil** *Ecphora quadricostata* (extinct snail). **Insect** Baltimore checkerspot butterfly. **Song** "Maryland, My Maryland." **Sport** Jousting. **Tree** White oak.
Land   **Total area** 10,460 sq. mi. (42nd), incl. 623 sq. mi. inland water. **Borders** Pa., Del., Atlantic Ocean, Va., D.C., W.Va. **Rivers** Chester, Choptank, Nanticoke, Patapsco, Patuxent, Pocomoke, Potomac, Susquehanna. **Other notable features** Allegheny Mts., Blue Ridge Mts., Chesapeake Bay.
Elected officials Gov. Parris N. Glendening (D, term exp. 2003). Lt. Gov. Kathleen Kennedy Townsend (D). Sec. State John T. Willis (D). Atty. Gen. J. Joseph Curran, Jr. (D).
People   (1998) 5,134,808 (19th). **Race/national origin** (1990): White 71.0%. Black 24.9%. Indian 0.3%. Asian 2.9%. Other 0.9%. Hispanic 2.6%.
Cities   (1996 estimate) Baltimore 675,401. Frederick 46,227. Rockville 46,019. Gaithersburg 45,361. Bowie 40,181. Hagerstown 34,633. Annapolis 33,234. College Park 24,987. Cumberland 22,341. Greenbelt 21,840.
Business   **Gross State Product**, 1997: $153.80 bil. (16th). **Leading Sectors of GSP** (1997): Services 23.58%; Finance, insurance, and real estate 22.20%; Government 17.22%. ***Fortune* 500 Companies** (1998): 10: Lockheed Martin, Marriott Intl., Sodexho Marriott Services, U.S. Foodservice, Black & Decker, Giant Food, Host Marriott, Hechinger, BG & E, Integrated Health Services.
Famous natives   Russell Baker, journalist. Benjamin Banneker, surveyor. Eubie Blake, pianist. Rachel Carson, biologist/author. Stephen Decatur, navy officer. Frederick Douglass, abolitionist. Billie Holiday, singer. Johns Hopkins,

financier/philanthropist. Francis Scott Key, lawyer/poet. Thurgood Marshall, jurist. H.L. Mencken, writer. Charles Willson Peale, artist. William Pinckney, statesman. James Rouse, urban planner. Babe Ruth, baseball player. Upton Sinclair, author. Roger B. Taney, jurist. Harriet Tubman, abolitionist. John Waters, filmmaker.
Noteworthy places Aberdeen Proving Ground. Antietam Natl. Battlefield, Sharpsburg. Assateague Island Natl. Seashore. Natl. Aquarium in Baltimore. Baltimore Museum of Art. Baltimore Museum of Industry. Calvert Marine Museum, Solomons. Chesapeake & Ohio Canal Natl. Hist. Park. Chesapeake Bay Maritime Museum, St. Michaels. Ft. McHenry Natl. Monument, Baltimore. Harpers Ferry Natl. Hist. Park. Liberty ship *John W. Brown*, Baltimore. St. Marys City. State House, Annapolis. U.S. Naval Academy, Annapolis. USS *Constellation*, Baltimore. Walters Art Gallery, Baltimore.
Memorable events   John Smith explores area 1608. William Claiborne sets up trading post on Kent Island 1631. Land granted to Cecilius Calvert, Lord Baltimore, 1632. Leonard Calvert and 200 Roman Catholic settlers land on Blakistone Island 1634. Mason Dixon Line establishes northern boundary of state 1763–67; later identified as boundary between slave and nonslave states. Francis Scott Key composes "The Star Spangled Banner" after British fail to take Ft. McHenry 1814. U.S. Naval Academy founded Annapolis 1845. State under federal military control during Civil War 1861–65. First state to adopt income tax 1938. Alabama Gov. George C. Wallace shot while campaigning in Democratic presidential primary 1972.
Tourist Information   1-800-MD-IS-FUN.
www.state.md.us.

▶**MASSACHUSETTS, COMMONWEALTH OF** .
Massachusetts is rich in the history of the early American republic. The Boston Tea Party, the "shot heard 'round the world" from Lexington and Concord, and the Battle of Bunker Hill are American folklore. So is the feast of Thanksgiving, first celebrated by the Puritans at Plymouth. Fishing, trade, textiles, and leather industries were the backbone of Massachusetts's 19th-century economy. In the 1980s, Boston's Route 128 became the East Coast's counterpart to California's Silicon Valley, with some of the nation's most advanced computer and electronic research and manufacturing. The state's "economic miracle" of the 1980s ended abruptly, and Massachusetts endured a severe downturn in the recession of the early 1990s. It has recently rebounded, together with most of the nation.
A staple of the Massachusetts scene is education, in which the state is a national leader. Boston alone boasts such institutions as Harvard University (founded 1636), M.I.T., Northeastern, Brandeis, Boston University, Boston College, Wellesley, and Tufts. To the west are the University of Massachusetts, Amherst, Williams, Smith, and Mt. Holyoke.
Name For Massachuset tribe, whose name means "at or about the great hill." **Nickname** Bay State. **Capital** Boston. **Entered union** Feb. 6, 1788 (6th). **Motto** *Ense petit placidam sub libertate quietem* (By the sword we seek peace, but peace only under liberty).
Emblems   **Beverage** Cranberry juice. **Bird** Chickadee. **Building & monument stone** Granite. **Dog** Boston terrier. **Explorer rock** Dighton

Rock. **Fish** Cod. **Flower** Mayflower. **Folk song** "Massachusetts." **Gem** Rhodonite. **Heroine** Deborah Samson. **Historical rock** Plymouth Rock. **Horse** Morgan. **Insect** Ladybug. **Marine mammal** Right whale. **Mineral** Babingtonite. **Poem** "Blue Hills of Massachusetts." **Rock** Roxbury pudding stone. **Song** "All Hail to Massachusetts." **Stone** Granite. **Tree** American elm.

Land **Total area** 8,284 sq. mi. (45th), incl. 460 sq. mi. inland water. **Borders** Vt., N.H., Atlantic Ocean, R.I., Conn., N.Y. **Rivers** Cape Cod Canal, Connecticut, Merrimack, Taunton. **Other notable features** Buzzard's Bay, Cape Ann, Cape Cod, Cape Cod Bay, Connecticut Valley, Elizabeth Islands, Martha's Vineyard, Monomoy Island, Nantucket Island.

Elected officials Gov. A. Paul Cellucci (R, term exp. 2003). Lt. Gov. Jane M. Swift (R). Sec. of Commonwealth William Francis Galvin (D). Atty. Gen. Thomas Reilly (D).

People (1998) 6,147,132 (13th). **Race/national origin** (1990): White 89.8%. Black 5.0%. Indian 0.2%. Asian 2.4%. Other 2.6%. Hispanic 4.8%.

Cities (1996 estimate) Boston 558,394. Worcester 166,350. Springfield 149,948. Lowell 100,973. New Bedford 96,903. Cambridge 93,707. Brockton 92,324. Fall River 90,865. Quincy 85,532. Lynn 80,563.

Business **Gross State Product, 1997:** $221.01 bil. (11th). **Leading Sectors of GSP** (1997): Services 26.45%; Finance, insurance, and real estate 24.30%; Manufacturing 14.66%. ***Fortune* 500 Companies** (1998): 16: Raytheon, Liberty Mutual Group, Massachusetts Mutual Life Insurance, Gillette, Fleet Financial Group, John Hancock Mutual Life, TJX, BankBoston Corp., Staples, Harcourt General, State Street Corp., EMC, Thermo Electron, BJ's Wholesale Club, Allmerica Financial, Reebok International.

Famous natives John Adams, U.S. president. John Quincy Adams, U.S. president. Samuel Adams, patriot. Horatio Alger, clergyman/author. Susan B. Anthony, suffragette. Clara Barton, nurse. Leonard Bernstein, composer. George Herbert Walker Bush, U.S. president. John ("Johnny Appleseed") Chapman, pioneer. Richard Cardinal Cushing, prelate. Bette Davis, actress. Emily Dickinson, poet. Ralph Waldo Emerson, author. Marshall Field, merchant. R. Buckminster Fuller, inventor/engineer. John Hancock, patriot. Oliver Wendell Holmes, jurist. Winslow Homer, painter. John F. Kennedy, U.S. president. Jack Kerouac, author. Cotton Mather, theologian. Samuel Eliot Morison, historian. Samuel Morse, inventor. Thomas P. "Tip" O'Neill, congressman. Edgar Allan Poe, poet/author. Paul Revere patriot/silversmith. Louis Sullivan, architect. Henry David Thoreau, author.

Noteworthy places Addison Gallery of American Art, Andover. Arnold Arboretum, Boston. Arthur M. Sackler Museum, Cambridge. Berkshires Museum, Pittsfield. Boston Museum of Fine Arts. Boston Natl. Hist. Park (incl. Bunker Hill, Charlestown Navy Yard, Old North Church). Busch-Reisinger Museum, Cambridge. Cape Cod Natl. Seashore. Clark Art Institute, Williamsburg. Fogg Art Museum, Boston. Gardner Art Museum, Boston. Lowell Natl. Hist. Park. Minute Man Natl. Hist. Park, Lexington and Concord. Nantucket Hist. Society. Old Sturbridge. Peabody Museum, Salem. Plimoth Plantation, Plymouth. Shaker Village. Tanglewood Music Festival, Lenox. USS *Constitution* ("Old Ironsides"), Charlestown. Walden Pond. Woods Hole Oceanographic Institute. Worcester Art Museum.

Memorable events Pilgrims land at Plymouth 1620. First Thanksgiving celebrated 1621. Harvard College founded 1636. Region acquires province of Maine 1652. Colonists battle Wampanoags in King Philip's War 1655–56. Boston Massacre 1770. Boston Tea Party protests taxation 1773. Battles at Lexington, Concord, and Bunker Hill 1775. Shays's Rebellion 1785–86. Maine becomes a separate state 1820. Massachusetts receives influx of Irish immigrants fleeing famine 1845. Textile workers' strike at Lawrence brings International Workers of the World (IWW) to prominence in East 1912. Cape Cod Canal completed 1914. International protest follows trial and execution of anarchists Nicola Sacco and Bartolomeo Vanzetti for robbery and murder 1920; names cleared by governor's proclamation 1970. Eleven robbers steal $2.7 million from Brink's North Terminal Garage 1950. Martha's Vineyard and Nantucket symbolically vote to secede from state 1973.

Tourist information 1-800-227-MASS. **www.state.ma.us.**

▶MICHIGAN

The automobile is the single commodity with which Michigan is most identified, and it is the home of the big three automakers, General Motors, Ford, and Chrysler. More than 50 percent of Michiganders live in the southeastern corner of the state, where the car industry flourishes. In the Upper Peninsula, across the Straits of Mackinac, lumber and copper have been the principal commodities from the 19th century, and the northern part of the Lower Peninsula boasts rich farmland. Michigan's boundaries include parts of four of the five Great Lakes, and it has more coastline than any state except Alaska. Michigan has had an outstanding reputation in higher education, and the University of Michigan at Ann Arbor and Michigan State are helping to foster the state's high-tech industries. But the state's heavy reliance on auto manufacturing makes the state vulnerable to economic downturns, as well as the general contraction of the American industry.

Name From the Fox *mesikami*, "large lake." **Nicknames** Wolverine State, Lake State. **Capital** Lansing. **Entered union** Jan. 26, 1837 (26th). **Motto** *Si quaeris peninsulam amoenam circumspice* (If you are looking for a beautiful peninsula, look around you).

Emblems **Bird** Robin. **Fish** Trout. **Flower** Apple blossom. **Gem** Chlorastrolite. **Insect** Dragonfly. **Song** "Michigan, My Michigan." **Stone** Petoskey stone. **Tree** White pine.

Land **Total area** 58,527 sq. mi. (23rd), incl. 1,573 sq. mi. inland water. **Borders** Lake Superior, Ontario, Lake Huron, Lake Erie, Ohio, Ind., Lake Michigan, Wisc. **Rivers** Brule, Detroit, Kalamazoo, Menominee, Montreal, Muskegon, St. Joseph, St. Mary's. **Lakes** Burt, Higgins, Houghton, Huron, Manistique, Michigan, Mullett, St. Clair, Superior. **Other notable features** Isle Royale, Mt. Curwood (1,980 ft.), Saginaw Bay, Traverse Bay, Whitefish Bay.

Elected officials Gov. John R. Engler (R, term exp. 2003). Lt. Gov. Dick Posthumus (R). Sec. State Candice S. Miller (R). Atty. Gen. Jennifer Granholm (D).

People (1998) 9,817,242 (8th). **Race/national origin** (1990): White 83.4%. Black 13.9%. Indian 0.6%. Asian 1.1%. Other 0.9%. Hispanic 2.2%.

Cities (1996 estimate) Detroit 1,000,272. Grand Rapids 188,242. Warren 138,078. Flint 134,881. Lansing 125,736. Sterling Heights 118,698. Ann

Arbor 108,758. Livonia 105,099. Dearborn 91,418. Westland 90,798.

Business   Gross State Product, 1997: $272.61 bil. (9th). **Leading Sectors of GSP** (1997): Manufacturing 25.76%; Services 18.94%; Finance, insurance, and real estate 15.35%. *Fortune 500* **Companies** (1998): 14: General Motors, Ford Motor, Kmart, Dow Chemical, Whirlpool, Lear, Kellogg, CMS Energy, Federal-Mogul, Masco, DTE Energy, Kelly Services, Meritor Automotive, Comerica.

Famous natives   Ralph J. Bunche, statesman (Nobel Peace Prize, 1950). Paul de Kruif, bacteriologist. Thomas Dewey, politician. Herbert H. Dow (b. Canada), chemical manufacturer. Edna Ferber, author. Gerald Ford (b. Neb.) U.S. president. Henry Ford, industrialist. Edgar Guest, journalist/poet. Robert Ingersoll, industrialist. Will Kellogg, businessman/philanthopist. Charles A. Lindbergh, aviator. Madonna, singer. Antoine de La Mothe, sieur de Cadillac (b. France), founded Detroit. Pontiac, Ottawa chief. William Upjohn, drug manufacturer.

Noteworthy places   Detroit Historical Society. Detroit Institute of Arts. Dossin Great Lakes Museum, Detroit. Great Lakes Indian Interpretive Museum, Detroit. Greenfield Village, Dearborn. Historic Ft. Wayne, Detroit. Isle Royale Natl. Park. Mackinac Island. Pictured Rocks Natl. Lakeshore, Lake Superior. Sleeping Bear Dunes Natl. Lakeshore, Lake Superior.

Memorable events   French explorers in region 1634. Jacques Marquette settles Sault Ste. Marie 1668. Detroit founded as French military post 1701. Region ceded to England 1763; to United States 1783. Included in Northwest Territory but British maintain control until 1796. Michigan Territory 1805. First steamboat on Great Lakes reaches Detroit 1818. Statehood 1837. First state to outlaw capital punishment 1846. Republican party organized at Jackson 1854. Canals at Sault Ste. Marie link Lakes Superior and Huron 1855. Ransom E. Olds and Henry Ford, working independently, develop gasoline-powered car 1896. United Auto Workers first to use sit-down strike successfully in contract negotiations 1935. Race riot, one of the worst in U.S. history, leaves 43 dead and $200 million in damages in Detroit 1967. Congress authorizes $1.5 billion in federal loan guarantees to bail out Chrysler Corporation 1979. **Tourist information**   1-800-543-2YES. www.state.mi.us.

▶MINNESOTA

A land of at least 10,000 lakes, Minnesota is a magnet for those who love the outdoors. It is also home to the largest Scandinavian populations in the United States. Originally exploited for its wealth of lumber and iron—the Mesabi Range still produces much of the nation's iron ore—Minnesota also has highly developed agribusinesses (especially dairy products), manufacturing, and transportation industries. Minneapolis and St. Paul are at the north end of the Mississippi River system, and Duluth at the westernmost point of Lake Superior is the largest U.S. inland port. Both self-sufficient and politically liberal, Minnesota has one of the best state school systems.

Name From the Sioux *minisota*, "sky-tinted waters." **Nicknames** North Star State, Gopher State. **Capital** St. Paul. **Entered union** May 11, 1858 (32rd). **Motto** *L'étoile du nord* (Star of the north). **Emblems Bird** Common loon. **Beverage** Milk. **Fish** Walleye. **Flower** Pink and white lady's-slipper. **Gem** Lake Superior agate. **Grain** Wild rice.

Mushroom Morel, or sponge mushroom. **Song** "Hail, Minnesota!." **Tree** Red pine.

Land   Total area 84,402 sq. mi. (12th), incl. 4,854 sq. mi. inland water. **Borders** Manitoba, Ontario, Lake Superior, Wisc., Iowa, S.Dak., N.Dak. **Rivers** Minnesota, Mississippi, Red River of the North, St. Croix. **Lakes** Itasca, Lake of the Woods, Leech, Mille Lacs, Red, Winnibigoshish. **Other notable features** Mesabi Range.

Elected officials   Gov. Jesse Ventura (Reform party, term exp. 2003). Lt. Gov. Mac Schunk (Reform) Sec. State Mary Kiffmeyer (R). Atty. Gen. Mike Hatch (D).

People   (1998) 4,725,419 (20th). **Race/national origin** (1990): White 94.4%. Black 2.2%. Indian 1.1%. Asian 1.8%. Other 0.5%. Hispanic 1.2%. **Cities**   (1996 estimate) Minneapolis 358,785. St. Paul 259,606. Bloomington 86,664. Duluth 83,699. Rochester 75,638. Coon Rapids 62,790. Brooklyn Park 61,335. Plymouth 60,103. Eagan 57,294. Burnsville 57,087.

Business   Gross State Product, 1997: $149.39 bil. (18th). **Leading Sectors of GSP** (1997): Services 19.97%; Manufacturing 18.92%; Finance, insurance, and real estate 18.42%. *Fortune 500* **Companies** (1998): 13: Dayton Hudson, United Healthcare, Supervalu, Minnesota Mining & Manufacturing (3M), St. Paul Cos., NWA, Honeywell, Best Buy, US Bancorp, General Mills, Nash Finch, Hormel Foods, Lutheran Brotherhood.

Famous natives   Warren Burger, jurist. Bob Dylan, musician. F. Scott Fitzgerald, novelist. Judy Garland, actress. J. Paul Getty, businessman. Garrison Keillor, humorist. Sinclair Lewis, author (Nobel Prize, 1930). Paul Manship, sculptor. William and Charles Mayo, surgeons. Eugene McCarthy, politician. Walter F. Mondale, politician. Charles Schulz, cartoonist. Richard W. Sears, merchant.

Noteworthy places   Boundary Waters Canoe Area. Grand Portage Natl. Monument. International Falls. Lake Itasca State Park (headwaters of Mississippi). Mayo Clinic, Rochester. Minneapolis Institute of Arts. Minnehaha Falls, Minneapolis. Minnesota Zoo, Apple Valley. Pipestone Natl. Monument. Tyrone Guthrie Theater, Minneapolis. Voyageurs Natl. Park. Walker Art Center, Minneapolis.

Memorable events

Pierre Esprit Radisson and Médard Chouart des Grosselliers visit area 1654–60. René-Robert de La Salle and Louis Hennepin explore upper Mississippi 1680. Daniel Greysolon, sieur de Duluth, claims region for France 1679. Area east of Mississippi to Britain 1763; to United States 1783. Western region of state as part of Louisiana Purchase 1803. Britain cedes northern strip to United States 1818. Ft. Snelling built 1820. Northern border settled by Ashburton Treaty 1842. Minnesota Territory created 1849. Statehood 1858. Sioux driven from state after uprising led by Chief Little Crow 1862. Iron ore deposits discovered in Mesabi Range 1890. Democratic party merges with Farmer-Labor party 1944. **Tourist information**   1-800-657-3700. www.state.mn.us.

▶MISSISSIPPI

Mississippi's rank as the poorest state in the nation can be traced to the Civil War. Before the Civil War, Mississippi was the fifth-wealthiest state in the nation. The war cost the state 30,000 men. Plantation owners who survived the war were virtually bankrupted by the emancipation of the slaves, and Union troops under Sherman and others left widespread destruction in their wake. The increasingly harsh race-laws passed around 1900 also cost the state in the emigration of almost half a million (75 percent blacks, 25 percent whites) in the 1940s. Compounding all this was the fact that until World War II, Mississippi had virtually no urban center such as Jackson to attract or sustain major industry. In race relations particularly, Mississippi has made vast improvements, and there have been substantial gains in education and the attraction of out-of-state companies, especially light industry.

Name From the Ojibwa *misi sipi*, "great river." **Nickname** Magnolia State. **Capital** Jackson. **Entered union** Dec. 10, 1817 (20th). **Motto** *Virtute et armis* (By virtue and arms).

Emblems   Beverage Milk. **Bird** Mockingbird. **Fish** Largemouth or black bass. **Flower** Magnolia. **Fossil** Prehistoric whale. **Insect** Honeybee. **Mammal** White-tailed deer. **Song** "Go, Mississippi." **Stone** Petrified wood. **Tree** Magnolia. **Waterfowl** Wood duck. **Water mammal** Porpoise.

Land   Total area 47,689 sq. mi. (32nd), incl. 456 sq. mi. inland water. **Borders** Tenn., Ala., Gulf of Mexico, La., Ark. **Rivers** Big Black, Mississippi, Pearl, Tennessee, Yazoo. **Lakes** Arkabutla, Grenada, Ross Barnett Res., Sardis. **Other notable features** Pontotoc Ridge.

Elected officials   Gov. Kirk Fordice (R, term exp. 2000). Lt. Gov. Ronnie Musgrove (D). Sec. State Eric Clark (D). Atty. Gen. Mike Moore (D).

People   (1998) 2,752,092 (31st). **Race/national origin** (1990): White 63.5%. Black 35.6%. Indian 0.3%. Asian 0.5%. Other 0.1%. Hispanic 0.6%.

Cities   (1996 estimate) Jackson 192,923. Gulfport 64,829. Biloxi 48,414. Hattiesburg 44,803. Greenville 42,933. Meridian 40,835. Tupelo 35,194. Vicksburg 27,056. Pascagoula 27,026. Columbus 22,724.

Business   Gross State Product, 1997: $58.31 bil. (33rd). **Leading Sectors of GSP** (1997): Manufacturing 22.63%; Services 16.68%; Government 14.93%. ***Fortune* 500 Companies** (1998): 1: MCI Worldcom.

Famous natives   Medgar Evers, civil rights leader. William Faulkner, novelist. Shelby Foote, historian. Jim Henson, puppeteer. B.B. King, musician. Elvis Presley, singer. Leontyne Price, opera singer. Jerry Rice, football player. John C. Stennis, politician. Conway Twitty, singer. Muddy Waters, musician. Eudora Welty, novelist. Ben Ames Williams, novelist. Tennessee Williams, playwright. Richard Wright, author.

Noteworthy places   Delta Blues Museum, Clarksdale. Natchez Trace Natl. Parkway. Seafood Industry Museum, Biloxi. Tupelo Natl. Battlefield. Vicksburg Natl. Military Park.

Memorable events   Hernando de Soto's expedition travels through Mississippi 1540–41. René-Robert Cavelier de La Salle claims Mississippi valley for France 1682. Pierre Le Moyne, sieur d'Iberville builds Ft. Maurepas on Biloxi Bay 1699. Natchez (Ft. Rosalie) established 1716. France cedes territory to Britain 1763. Mississippi Territory (including present day Alabama) created 1798. Statehood (Natchez first capital) 1817. Secedes from Union; Jefferson Davis becomes president of Confederacy 1861. Siege of Vicksburg 1863. Petroleum discovered 1939. Gov. Ross R. Barnett found guilty of contempt in preventing desegregation of University of Mississippi; James H. Meredith first black enrolled at University of Mississippi 1962. Civil rights leader Medgar Evers assassinated in Jackson and buried in Arlington National Cemetery 1963. White civil rights workers James Cheney, Andrew Goodman, and Michael Schwener killed 1964.

Tourist information   1-800-WARMEST. **www.state.ms.us.**

▶MISSOURI

Missouri is remarkable for the number and variety of its neighbors—southern states (Arkansas, Kentucky, and Tennessee), midwestern states (Illinois and Iowa), and Plains states (Oklahoma, Nebraska, and Kansas). For Missouri, geography was destiny. Still one of the country's most important inland ports, St. Louis was founded at the confluence of the Missouri and Mississippi rivers and became the gateway to the West; and Independence (now part of metropolitan Kansas City) got its start provisioning wagons for the Oregon and Santa Fe trails. The Pony Express from St. Joseph to Sacramento began in 1860, and the first attempt at airmail service was tried in St. Louis in 1911. While farming and livestock are still important to the state's economy, manufacturing and services are now the biggest sectors.

Name From the Iliniwek *missouri*, "owner of big canoes." **Nickname** Show Me State. **Capital** Jefferson City. **Entered union** Aug. 10, 1821 (24th). **Motto** *Salus populi suprema lex esto* (The welfare of the people shall be the supreme law).

Emblems   Bird Bluebird. **Flower** Hawthorne. **Insect** Honeybee. **Mineral** Galena. **Rock** Mozarkite. **Song** "Missouri Waltz." **Tree** Dogwood.

Land   Total area 69,697 sq. mi. (19th), incl. 752 sq. mi. inland water. **Borders** Iowa, Ill., Ky., Tenn., Ark., Okla., Kans., Nebr. **Rivers** Des Moines, Mississippi, Missouri, Osage, St. Francis. **Lakes** Bull Shoals, Clearwater, Lake of the Ozarks, Lake of the Woods, Table, Wappapella. **Other notable features** Ozark Mts. (Taum Sauk Mt. 1,772 ft.).

Elected officials   Gov. Mel Carnahan (D, term exp. 2000). Lt. Gov. Roger B. Wilson (D). Sec. State Rebecca McDowell Cook (D). Atty. Gen. Jeremiah W. Nixon (D).

People   (1998) 5,438,559 (16th). **Race/national origin** (1990): White 87.7%. Black 10.7%. Indian 0.4%. Asian 0.8%. Other 0.4%. Hispanic 1.2%.

Cities   (1996 estimate) Kansas City 441,259. St. Louis 351,565. Springfield 143,407. Independence 110,303. Columbia 76,756. St. Joseph 70,208. Lee's Summit 61,861. St. Charles 56,525. Florissant 50,491. St. Peters 48,493.

Business   Gross State Product, 1997: $152.10 bil. (17th). **Leading Sectors of GSP** (1997): Manufacturing 20.51%; Services 19.61%; Finance, insurance, and real estate 14.87%. ***Fortune* 500 Companies** (1998): 15: Emerson Electric, May Department Stores, Utilicorp United, Anheuser-Busch, Farmland Industries, Monsanto, Ralston Purina, GenAmerica, Graybar Electric, Clark USA, Leggett & Platt, Ameren, Interstate Bakeries, TWA, Mercantile Bancorp.

Famous natives   Thomas Hart Benton, painter. Yogi Berra, baseball player. George Caleb Bingham (b. Va.), painter. Omar Bradley, general. Adophus Busch (b. Germany), brewer. George Washington Carver, botanist. Walter Cronkite, journalist. Walt Disney, film producer. T.S. Eliot, poet. Walker Evans, photographer. Langston Hughes, poet. Jesse James, outlaw. Marianne Moore, poet. Reinhold Niebuhr, theologian. J.C. Penny, businessman. John J. "Black Jack" Pershing, soldier. Joseph Pulitzer (b. Hungary), publisher. Ginger Rogers, dancer. Casey Stengel, baseball player. Virgil Thompson, composer. Harry S Truman, U.S.

president. Mark Twain, writer. Tom Watson, golfer. Shelley Winters, actress.

Noteworthy places Churchill Memorial, St. Aldermanbury Church, Fulton. Gateway Arch, St. Louis. George Washington Carver Natl. Monument, Diamond. Harry S Truman Library, Independence. Mark Twain Area, Hannibal. Nelson-Atkins Museum of Art, Kansas City. Pony Express Museum, St. Joseph. St. Louis Art Museum. Wilson's Creek Natl. Battlefield.

Memorable events French miners and hunters settle at Ste. Genevieve 1735. Pierre Laclade settles St. Louis 1765. New Madrid earthquakes (8.6 on Richter scale) rock buildings as far away as Baltimore 1811-12. Statehood 1821. Missouri legislature split over secesssion: minority party adopts secession ordinance; Missouri admitted to Confederacy; majority party remains loyal to Union 1861. Jesse James killed by fellow gang member at St. Joseph 1882. Lake of the Ozarks formed after completion of Bagnell Dam on Missouri River 1931. Winston Churchill delivers "iron curtain" speech at Fulton 1952. Gateway Arch, 630 ft. high, opened at St. Louis 1964. St. Louis population declines 47 percent 1950–80. Floods cause $3 billion in damage 1993.

Tourist information 1-800-877-1234.
www.state.mo.us.

▶ MONTANA

Mountains account for only the western two-fifths of "Big Sky Country," where copper mining, lumber, and tourism are the chief industries. The eastern portion of the state is part of the Great Plains, devoted to agriculture and ranching. For many years Montana was in the grip of the Anaconda Copper Mining Company, which virtually owned the state government and took most its profits out of the state. After Anaconda's demise in the 1970s, Montana developed some of the most stringent environmental laws in the West. In recent years, many famous Hollywood stars, as well as media mogul Ted Turner, have bought large tracts of land in Western Montana.

Name From Spanish *montaña*, "mountainous."
Nicknames Treasure State, Big Sky Country. **Capital** Helena. **Entered union** Nov. 8, 1889 (41st). **Motto** *Oro y plata* (Gold and silver).
Emblems Bird Western meadowlark. **Fish** Blackspotted cutthroat trout. **Flower** Bitterroot. **Gems** Yogo sapphire, Montana agate. **Grass** Bluebunch wheatgrass. **Song** "Montana." **State ballad** "Montana Melody." **Tree** Ponderosa pine.
Land Total area 147,046 sq. mi. (4th), incl. 1,658 sq. mi. inland water. **Borders** British Columbia, Alberta, Saskatchewan, N.Dak., S.Dak., Wyo., Idaho. **Rivers** Kootenai, Milk, Missouri, Musselshell, Powder, Yellowstone. **Lakes** Bighorn, Canyon Ferry, Elwell, Flathead, Ft. Peck. **Mountains** Absaroka Range, Beartooth Range (Granite Peak 12,799 ft.), Big Belt, Bitterroot Range, Centennial, Crazy, Lewis Range, Little Belt. **Other notable features** Continental Divide, Missoula Valley.
Elected officials Gov. Marc Racicot (R, term exp. 2000). Lt. Gov. Judy Martz (R). Sec. State Mike Cooney (D). Atty. Gen. Joseph Mazurek (D).
People (1998) 880,453 (44th). **Race/national origin** (1990): White 92.7%. Black 0.3%. Indian 6.0%. Asian 0.5%. Other 0.5%. Hispanic 1.5%.
Cities (1996 estimate) Billings 91,195. Great Falls 57,758. Missoula 51,204. Butte-Silver Bow 34,051. Bozeman 28,522. Helena 27,982. Kalispell 15,678. Havre 10,232. Anaconda-Deer Lodge Co. 10,093. Miles City 8,882.
Business Gross State Product, 1997: $19.16 bil. (47th). **Leading Sectors of GSP** (1997): Services 19.69%; Government 15.68%; Finance, insurance, and real estate 13.53%. *Fortune* **500 Companies** (1998): 0.

Famous natives Gary Cooper, actor. Marcus Daly (b. Ireland), mine owner. Chet Huntley, journalist. Myrna Loy, actress. Mike Mansfield (b. N.Y.), politician/diplomat. Jeanette Rankin, politician/reformer. Charles M. Russell, artist.
Noteworthy places Big Hole Natl. Battlefield. Bob Marshall Wilderness. Charles M. Russell Museum, Great Falls. Custer Battlefield Natl. Monument. Ft. Union Trading Post Natl. Hist. Site. Lewis and Clark Caverns State Park. Museum of the Plains Indian, Browning. Natl. Bison Range. Waterton-Glacier International Peace Park. World Museum of Mining, Butte. Yellowstone Natl. Park.
Memorable events French explorers and trappers visit region 1740s. Large part of state in Louisiana Purchase 1803. Lewis and Clark expedition 1805–6. Ft. Benton first permanent settlement 1846. Western part of state included in Washington Territory 1853 and 1859; eastern part in Nebraska (1854) and Dakota (1861) territories. Gold discovered at Bannack (1862) and Alder Gulch (1863). Organized as Montana Territory 1864. Dakota and Cheyenne defeat U.S. troops under Gen. William Armstrong Custer at Battle of Little Bighorn 1876. Under Chief Joseph, Nez Percé beat U.S. Army at Big Hole Basin 1877. Marcus Daly discovers copper near Butte 1880s. Statehood 1889. Homesteaders enter state 1909. Ft. Peck Dam completed 1940. Anaconda Copper Mining, dominant in Montana industry and politics since 1915, closes mining operations at Butte 1983. Elizabeth Prophet (Guru Ma) convinces 3,000 disciples of the Church Universal and Triumphant to await nuclear cataclysm in underground shelters in Paradise Valley while state bureaucrats worried over sewage facilities 1990.
Tourist information 1-800-VISIT-MT, 1-800-548-3390.
www.state.mt.us.

▶ NEBRASKA

Although set aside as Indian territory in 1834 and made off-limits to white settlement, thousands of whites crossed the region along the Independence, Mormon, and Oregon trails. Eventually Congress opened the land to settlement, which accelerated after the Homestead Act of 1862 and the coming of the railroads. The newcomers took up ranching and farming under hard conditions. The winter of 1886–87 killed thousands of cattle and drove many large-scale ranchers into bankruptcy, while the dust bowl of the 1930s spurred a mass exodus. Significant industry did not develop until World War II, when many war-related industries and army airfields moved to the center of the country. Nebraska is among the leading agricultural states, especially in the production of corn for grain and livestock. A state constitutional amendment passed in 1982 prevents the sale of farmlands and ranch lands from being sold to anyone other than a Nebraska family farm corporation.

Name From the Oto *nebrathka*, "flat water." **Nickname** Cornhusker State. **Capital** Lincoln. **Entered union** Mar. 1, 1867 (37th). **Motto** "Equality before the law."
Emblems Bird Western meadowlark. **Flower** Goldenrod. **Fossil** Mammoth. **Gem** Blue agate. **Grass** Little blue stem. **Insect** Honeybee. **Mammal** White-tailed deer. **Rock** Prairie agate. **Soil** Soils of the Holdrege series. **Song** "Beautiful Nebraska." **Tree** Western cottonwood.

Land   Total area 77,355 sq. mi. (15th), incl. 711 sq. mi. inland water. **Borders** S.Dak., Iowa, Mo., Kans., Colo., Wyo. **Rivers** Missouri, North Platte, Republican, South Platte. **Lakes** Harlan Co. Res., Lewis and Clark Lake. **Other notable features** Pine Ridge, Sand Hills.

Elected officials   Gov. Mike Johanns (R, term exp. 2003). Lt. Gov. Dave Maurstad (R). Sec. State Scott Moore (R). Atty. Gen. Don Steinberg (R).

People   (1998) 1,662,719 (38th). **Race/national origin** (1990): White 93.8%. Black 3.6%. Indian 0.8%. Asian 0.8%. Other 1.0%. Hispanic 2.3%.

Cities   (1996 estimate) Omaha 364,253. Lincoln 209,192. Bellevue 42,807. Grand Island 41,177. Kearney 27,314. Fremont 24,223. Norfolk 23,423. North Platte 23,369. Hastings 22,008. Columbus 20,848.

Business   **Gross State Product,** 1997: $48.81 bil. (36th). **Leading Sectors of GSP** (1997): Services 17.75%; Finance, insurance, and real estate 15.22%; Government 14.22%. *Fortune* **500 Companies** (1998): 6: Conagra, Berkshire Hathaway, IBP, Inacom, Mutual of Omaha Insurance, Peter Kiewit Sons.

Famous natives   Fred Astaire, dancer. Marlon Brando, actor. William Jennings Bryan, politician. Johnny Carson (b. Iowa), comedian. Willa Cather (b. Va.), author. Loren Eiseley, anthropologist. The Rev. Edward J. Flanagan (b. Ireland), reformer. Henry Fonda, actor. Rollin Kirby, cartoonist. Melvin Laird, politician. Harold Lloyd, actor. Mahpiua Luta (Red Cloud), Oglala Sioux chief. Malcolm X, religious leader. Roscoe Pound, educator.

Noteworthy places   Agate Fossil Beds Natl. Monument. Arbor Lodge State Park, Nebraska City. Boys Town, Omaha. Buffalo Bill Ranch State Hist. Park. Chimney Rock Hist. Site. Homestead Natl. Monument, Beatrice. Oregon Trail. Pioneer Village, Minden. Scotts Bluff Natl. Monument. Stuhr Museum of the Prairie Pioneer, Grand Island.

Memorable events   Acquired as part of Louisiana Purchase 1803. Separate territory created by Kansas-Nebraska Act 1854. Size reduced after creation of Colorado and Dakota territories 1861. Statehood 1867. To encourage tree planting, becomes first state to observe Arbor Day 1872. Adopts unicameral legislature 1937. Oil discovered 1939. Population peaks at 1,605,000 1984–85.

Tourist information   1-800-228-4307.
www.state.ne.us.

▶**NEVADA**
Set in the Great Basin desert, Nevada is one of the most barren places in North America, and the state receives less rainfall than any other. First explored by Europeans in 1776, it was 75 years before anyone thought of establishing a town in the area, and it did not last a decade. Miners came to Nevada early, but the discovery of the Comstock Lode in 1859 brought thousands. To add free-state congressional votes, Nevada was hustled into the Union in 1864, three years before its boundaries were settled. That boom was over by the 1870s, and it took more gold and silver strikes in the early 1900s, as well as the discovery of copper, to get the economy rolling again. The mainstay of the economy since World War II has been the gambling industry, which generates virtually half of all tax revenues. During the 1990s, Nevada has been the fastest growing state in the union, with skyrocketing tourism fueling much of the growth.

Name   From Spanish, meaning "snow-covered sierra." **Nicknames** Sagebrush State, Silver State. **Capital** Carson City. **Entered union** Oct. 31, 1864 (36th). **Motto** "All for our country."

Emblems   **Animal** Desert bighorn sheep. **Bird** Mountain bluebird. **Flower** Sagebrush. **Fossil** Icthyosaur. **Grass** Indian ricegrass. **Metal** Silver. **Song** "Home Means Nevada." **Tree** Single-leaf piñon.

Land   Total area 110,561 sq. mi. (7th), incl. 667 sq. mi. inland water. **Borders** Oreg., Idaho, Utah, Ariz., Calif. **Rivers** Colorado, Humboldt. **Lakes** Pyramid, Walker, Winnemucca. **Other notable features** Black Rock Desert, Carson Sink, Humboldt Salt Marsh, Mojave Desert.

Elected officials   Gov. Kenny Guinn (R, term exp. 2003). Lt. Gov. Lorraine Hunt (R). Sec. State Dean Heller (R). Atty. Gen. Frankie Sue Del Papa (D).

People   (1998) 1,746,898 (36th). **Race/national origin** (1990): White 84.3%. Black 6.6%. Indian 1.6%. Asian 3.2%. Other 4.4%. Hispanic 10.4%.

Cities   (1996 estimate) Las Vegas 376,906. Reno 155,499. Henderson 122,339. North Las Vegas 78,659. Sparks 59,496. Carson City 47,237. Elko 19,371. Boulder City 14,249. Winnemucca 8,004. Fallon 7,940.

Business   **Gross State Product,** 1997: $57.41 bil. (34th). **Leading Sectors of GSP** (1997): Services 32.52%; Finance, insurance, and real estate 18.77%; Government 9.91%. *Fortune* **500 Companies** (1998): 0.

Famous natives   Andre Agassi, tennis player. Walter Van Tilburg Clark (b. Me.), author. Sarah Winnemucca Hopkins, interpeter/teacher. John William MacKay, miner. William Morris Stewart (b. N.Y.), lawyer/senator.

Noteworthy places   Death Valley Natl. Monument. Lehman Caves Natl. Monument. Valley of the Fire State Park, Overton.

Memorable events   Francisco Tomás Garcés explores area 1775–76. Jedediah Smith, trader, crosses region 1826–27. Old Spanish Trail (1830) and California Trail (1833) cross region. John Frémont explores area 1843–45. To United States after Mexican War 1846. Genoa, first settlement in Nevada, founded as Mormon Station 1849. Gold of Comstock Lode discovered 1859. Organized as separate territory 1861. Statehood 1864. Nevada legalizes gambling 1931. Hoover Dam built on Colorado River 1935. Nuclear tests begun at Yucca Flats 1951. Population grows more than 550 percent 1950–88, and 25 percent in 1990s.

Tourist information   1-800-NEVADA8.
www.state.nv.us.

▶**NEW HAMPSHIRE**
New Hampshire has a disproportionate influence on presidential elections because by state law its primary must fall at least one week before any other state's (though Iowa's caucuses can come earlier). Through independence the mainstays of the economy were fishing, trade, and farming. Boston proved more suitable for trade, and New Hampshire's stubborn land was outproduced by the more fertile valleys to the south and west. The state's economy receded until the beginning of the Industrial Revolution, when there was tremendous growth in textile-producing mill towns in the Merrimack River Valley. The mills began to close after World War I, and the economy faltered again. Improvement came as high-tech firms from Boston sought refuge in New Hampshire's favorable tax climate. The

state's economy was pummeled by the severe New England recession in the early 1990s, but has rebounded since.

Name For English county of Hampshire. **Nickname** Granite State. **Capital** Concord. **Entered union** June 21, 1788 (9th). **Motto** "Live free or die." **Emblems** **Amphibian** Spotted newt. **Bird** Purple finch. **Flower** Purple lilac. **Gem** Smoke quartz. **Insect** Ladybug. **Mineral** Beryl. **Song** "Old New Hampshire." **Tree** White birch.

Land Total area 9,279 sq. mi. (44th), incl. 286 sq. mi. inland water. **Borders** Quebec, Maine, Atlantic Ocean, Mass., Vt. **Rivers** Connecticut, Merrimack, Piscataqua, Saco, Salmon Falls. **Lakes** First Connecticut, Francis, Newfound, Ossipee, Sunapee, Winnipesaukee. **Other notable features** Isles of Shoals, White Mts. (Mt. Washington 6,288 ft., highest peak in Northeast).

Elected officials Gov. Jeanne Shaheen (D, term exp. 2003). Sec. State William Gardner (D). Atty. Gen. Philip McLaughlin (D).

People (1998) 1,185,048 (42nd). **Race/national origin** (1990): White 98.0%. Black 0.6%. Indian 0.2%. Asian 0.8%. Other 0.3%. Hispanic 1.0%.

Cities (1996 estimate) Manchester 100,967. Nashua 81,094. Concord 37,021. Rochester 27,704. Dover 25,766. Portsmouth 25,034. Keene 22,325. Laconia 16,264. Claremont 13,970. Lebanon 12,571.

Business Gross State Product, 1997: $38.11 bil. (39th). **Leading Sectors of GSP** (1997): Manufacturing 24.99%; Finance, insurance, and real estate 21.98%; Services 18.38%. **Fortune 500 Companies** (1998): 0.

Famous natives Salmon P. Chase, jurist. Ralph Adams Cram, architect. Mary Baker Eddy, founder, Church of Christ, Scientist. Daniel Chester French, sculptor. Horace Greeley, journalist. Sarah Buell Hale, author. Franklin Pierce, U.S. president. Augustus Saint-Gaudens (b. Ireland), sculptor. Alan Shepard, astronaut. Daniel Webster, politician. Eleazar Wheelock (b. Conn.), Dartmouth founder.

Noteworthy places Currier Gallery of Art, Manchester. The Flume (gorge). Franconia Notch. Isles of Shoals. Lake Winnipesaukee. Mt. Washington. Shaker Village, Canterbury. St. Gaudens Natl. Hist. Site. Strawberry Bank. White Mountains Natl. Forest.

Memorable events Martin Pring sails along coast 1603. Champlain explores area 1604. John Smith visits Isles of Shoals 1614. Included in king's grant to John Mason and Sir Ferdinando Gorges 1622. First settlers at Little Harbor, near Portsmouth 1623. Made separate royal province 1679, though under Massachusetts governor 1699–1741. Rogers's Rangers halt Indian raids 1759. New Hampshire patriots seize British fort at Portsmouth and drive out Royal governor 1775. Province relinquishes claims to New Connecticut (Vermont) 1782. First textile mill built 1803. Treaty of Portsmouth ends Russo-Japanese War 1905. Bretton Woods conference leads to establishment of International Monetary Fund 1944. First state to adopt lottery to support public education 1963.

Tourist information 1-800-FUN-IN-NH, ext. 159.

www.state.nh.us.

▶ **NEW JERSEY**

With the entire state population classified as living in metro areas, New Jersey is the most densely populated state, 15 times the national average. The image survives of New Jersey as a chemical-industrial wasteland south of New York Harbor. Pharmaceuticals and chemicals are in fact New Jersey's leading products, but the next most important industry is tourism, because of the money tourists spend at the gaming tables of Atlantic City. What earns New Jersey its nickname, the Garden State, is its extensive small-scale agriculture, which produces tomatoes, dairy products, asparagus, blueberries, corn, and poultry.

New Jersey lies on a plain between Philadelphia and New York City, two larger neighbors that have overshadowed New Jersey on the national scene since colonial days. Yet during the Revolution, more than 100 battles were fought on New Jersey soil, and today the overwhelming majority of containerized shipping in the Port of New York and New Jersey is shipped from New Jersey terminals. Per capita income is always among the top five in the nation.

Name After English Channel Island of Jersey. **Nickname** Garden State. **Capital** Trenton. **Entered union** Dec. 18, 1787 (3rd). **Motto** "Liberty and prosperity."

Emblems **Animal** Horse. **Bird** Eastern goldfinch. **Flower** Violet. **Insect** Honeybee. **Memorial tree** Dogwood. **Tree** Red oak.

Land Total area 7,787 sq. mi. (46th), incl. 319 sq. mi. inland water. **Borders** N.Y., Atlantic Ocean, Del., Pa. **Rivers** Delaware, Hackensack, Hudson, Passaic. **Lakes** Greenwood, Hopatcong, Round Valley Res., Spruce Run. **Other notable features** Delaware Water Gap, Kittatinny Mts., Palisades, Pine Barrens, Ramapo Mts.

Elected officials Gov. Christine Todd Whitman (R, term exp. 2002). Sec. State Lonna R. Hooks (R). Atty. Gen. Peter Verniero (R).

People (1998) 8,115,011 (9th). **Race/national origin** (1990): White 79.3%. Black 13,4%. Indian 0.2%. Asian 3.5%. Other 3.6%. Hispanic 9.6%.

Cities (1996 estimate) Newark 268,510. Jersey City 229,039. Paterson 150,270. Elizabeth 110,149. Trenton 85,437. Camden 84,844. Clifton 71,305. East Orange 70,534. Bayonne 60,499. Union City 57,126.

Business Gross State Product, 1997: $294.06 bil. (8th). **Leading Sectors of GSP** (1997): Finance, insurance, and real estate 23.41%; Services 21.89%; Manufacturing 13.96%. **Fortune 500 Companies** (1998): 24: including Prudential of America, Lucent Technologies, Merck, Johnson & Johnson, AlliedSignal, American Home Products, Toys "R" Us, Warner-Lambert, Best Foods, Ingersoll-Rand, Schering-Plough, Campbell Soup, Pharmacia & Upjohn, American Standard, Chubb, Public Service Enterprise Group, Union Camp, Becton Dickinson.

Famous natives Count Basie, jazz musician. William J. Brennan, jurist. Aaron Burr, politician. Grover Cleveland, U.S. president. James Fenimore Cooper, novelist/historian. Stephen Crane, author. Thomas Edison, inventor. Albert Einstein (b. Germany), nuclear physicist. Waldo Frank, author. Joyce Kilmer, poet. Jerry Lewis, actor. Jack Nicholson, actor. Zebulon Pike, explorer. Molly Pitcher, Revolutionary War heroine. Paul Robeson, actor/singer. Walter Schirra, astronaut. Frank Sinatra, singer. Alfred Stieglitz, photographer. Meryl Streep, actress. Aaron Montgomery Ward, merchant. William Carlos Williams, poet.

Noteworthy places Cape May Historic District. Edison Natl. Hist. Site, West Orange. Lakehurst Naval Air Station. Liberty State Park, Jersey City. Morristown Natl. Hist. Park. Newark Museum.

Palisades Interstate Park. Pine Barrens wilderness area. Princeton University. Walt Whitman House, Camden.

Memorable events Giovanni de Verrazano explores 1524. Hudson explores up Hudson River 1609. Dutch settlers establish Ft. Nassau 1623. New Jersey taken over by British and organized as colony under Sir George Carteret 1665. Major battles of Revolution at Trenton (1776), Princeton (1777), and Monmouth (1778). Women given vote at Elizabethtown 1800. Voting rights restricted to men 1807. Adopts state constitution 1844. Passenger ship *Morro Castle* burns off Asbury Park; 134 die 1934. Dirigible *Hindenburg* explodes while mooring at Lakehurst; 36 die 1937. New Jersey Turnpike linking New York City and Philadelphia opens 1952. Five days of race riots in Newark leave 26 dead 1967. Gambling legalized in Atlantic City 1978. State enacts strictest gun legislation in United States 1990.

Tourist information 1-800-JERSEY7, ext. 7963. **www.state.nj.us.**

▶NEW MEXICO

The development problem of the western states is shared by New Mexico, which of all states has the smallest percentage of its area covered by water. Rich in other resources, it is the uranium capital of the world. The state mineral tax brings in a large percentage of state revenues, some of which goes into permanent endowments. Distribution of wealth in New Mexico remains uneven, but Hispanics, who tend to register as Democrats, vote in roughly the same ways as Anglos. A higher percentage of Native Americans live in New Mexico than in any other state.

Today, mining's influence on the state economy has waned in favor of service industry jobs. Despite the enormous governmental investment in research at Los Alamos, where the atom bomb was born, the highly classified nature of this work limits the development of related industry.

Name By Spanish explorers after Mexico. **Nickname** Land of Enchantment. **Capital** Santa Fe. **Entered union** Jan. 6, 1912 (47th). **Motto** *Crescit eundo* (It grows as it goes).

Emblems **Animal** Black bear. **Bird** Roadrunner (chaparral bird). **Fish** Cutthroat trout. **Flower** Yucca. **Fossil** *Coelphysis* dinosaur. **Gem** Turquoise. **Songs** "O, Fair New Mexico," "Así es Nuevo Mejico." **Tree** Piñon. **Vegetables** Frijole, chili.

Land Total area 121,593 sq. mi. (5th), incl. 258 sq. mi. inland water. **Borders** Colo., Okla., Tex., Chihuahua, Ariz. **Rivers** Gila, Pecos, Rio Grande, Zuni. **Lakes** Conchas Res., Eagle Nest, Elephant Butte Res., Navajo Res., Ute Res. **Mountains** Chuska, Guadalupe, Sacramento, San Andres, Sangre de Cristo. **Other notable features** Carlsbad Caverns, Continental Divide, Staked Plain. **Elected officials** Gov. Gary E. Johnson (R, term exp. 2003). Lt. Gov. Walter D. Bradley (R). Sec. State Rebecca Vigil-Giron (D). Atty. Gen. Patricia Madrid (D).

People (1998) 1,736,931 (37th). **Race/national origin** (1990): White 75.6%. Black 2.0%. Indian 8.9%. Asian 0.9%. Other 12.6%. Hispanic 38.2%. **Cities** (1996 estimate) Albuquerque 419,681. Las Cruces 74,779. Santa Fe 66,522. Roswell 47,559. Rio Rancho 46,565. Farmington 37,936. Clovis 34,663. Alamogordo 29,036. Hobbs 27,986. Carlsbad 26,535.

Business **Gross State Product,** 1997: $45.24 bil. (37th). **Leading Sectors of GSP** (1997): Manu-facturing 17.43%; Services 17.22%; Government 17.12%. *Fortune* **500 Companies** (1998): 1: Sun Healthcare Group.

Famous natives William "Billy the Kid" Bonney (b. N.Y.), outlaw. Peter Hurd, artist. Archbishop Jean Baptiste Lamy (b. France), missionary. Georgia O'Keeffe (b. Wis.), artist. Popé, Tewa Pueblo chief. Harrison Schmitt, astronaut.

Noteworthy places Aztec Ruins Natl. Monument. Bandelier Natl. Monument. Capulin Mt. Natl. Monument. Carlsbad Caverns Natl. Park. Chaco Culture Natl. Hist. Park. El Morro Natl. Monument. Ft. Union Natl. Monument. Gila Cliff Dwellings Natl. Monument. Museum of New Mexico, Santa Fe. Pecos Mission. Salinas Mission. Santa Fe Opera. Wheelwright Museum of the American Indian, Santa Fe. White Sands Natl. Monument.

Memorable events Marcos de Niza enters Zuni country 1539. Juan de Oñate establishes first Spanish settlement on Rio Grande near Espanola 1598. Santa Fe founded; becomes capital of New Mexico 1710. Santa Fe Trail from Independence, Missouri, completed; Mexico secedes from Spain 1821. Manuel Armijo suppresses revolt against Mexican rule (1837); defeats invasion from Republic of Texas (1841). Land annexed by United States after Mexican-American War 1848. Organized as territory with Arizona and part of Colorado 1850. Lincoln County War pits cattlemen against merchants 1878–81. Statehood; 17 killed in raid by Pancho Villa 1912. Los Alamos selected as first research and development facility for nuclear weapons 1942. First atom bomb exploded at Alamagordo Air Base 1945.

Tourist information 1-800-545-2040. **www.state.nm.us.**

▶NEW YORK

New York's greatest and most inviting asset has always been its strategic location and long arteries into the hinterland. New York Bay is one of the great natural harbors of the world, and the broad Hudson River is one of the most fortunately placed. After the opening of the Erie Canal between the Hudson and Lake Erie in 1825, New York City became the trading center for the Midwest as well as the Hudson Valley and the Atlantic Coast. Buffalo also experienced a boom, becoming a major Great Lakes industrial port. New York is still the first state in number of manufacturing establishments and employees. Wall Street alone employs half a million people.

Although New York's population grew by nearly half a million people between 1980 and 1990, its relatively slow rate of growth resulted in a loss of three congressional seats—an indication of the change in the state's political clout. As its place among the 50 states has fallen by some measures, New York City's worldwide importance in business, culture, and communications has risen.

Name For Duke of York, later James II, of England. **Nickname** Empire State. **Capital** Albany. **Entered union** July 26, 1788 (11th). **Motto** *Excelsior* (Higher).

Emblems **Animal** Beaver. **Beverage** Milk. **Bird** Bluebird. **Fish** Brook or speckled trout. **Flower** Rose. **Fossil** Prehistoric crab (*Eurypterus remipes*). **Fruit** Apple. **Gem** Garnet. **Song** "I Love New York." **Tree** Sugar maple.

Land Total area 49,108 sq. mi. (30th), incl. 1,731 sq. mi. inland water. Borders Lake Ontario, Ontario, Quebec, Vt., Mass., Conn., Atlantic Ocean, N.J., Pa., Lake Erie. Rivers Allegheny,

Delaware, Genesee, Hudson, Mohawk, New York State Barge Canal, Niagara, St. Lawrence, Susquehanna. **Lakes** Cayuga, Champlain, Chautauqua, Erie, George, Oneida, Ontario, Seneca. **Mountains** Adirondack (Mt. Marcy 5,344 ft.), Allegheny, Berkshire Hills, Catskill, Kittatinny, Ramapo. **Other notable features** Hudson Valley, Mohawk Valley, Niagara Falls, Palisades, Thousand Islands.

Elected officials Gov. George E. Pataki (R, term exp. 2003). Lt. Gov. Mary Donohue (R). Sec. State Alexander F. Treadwell (R). Atty. Gen. Eliot Spitzer (D).

People (1998) 18,175,301 (3rd). **Race/national origin** (1990): White 74.4%. Black 15.9%. Indian 0.3%. Asian 3.9%. Other 5.5%. Hispanic 12.3%. **Cities** (1996 estimate) New York 7,380,906. Buffalo 310,548. Rochester 221,594. Yonkers 190,316. Syracuse 155,865. Albany 103,564. New Rochelle 67,369. Mount Vernon 67,112. Schenectady 62,893. Utica 61,368.

Business Gross State Product, 1997: $651.65 bil. (2nd). **Leading Sectors of GSP** (1997): Finance, insurance, and real estate 31.19%; Services 22.75%; Manufacturing 11.42%. *Fortune* **500 Companies** (1998): 59: including International Business Machines, Citigroup, Philip Morris, AT&T, TIAA-CREF, Merrill Lynch, American International Group, Chase Manhattan Corp., Texaco, Bell Atlantic, Morgan Stanley Dean Witter, Metropolitan Life, Pepsico, Loews, American Express, Time Warner, Eastman Kodak, Viacom, CBS, Colgate-Palmolive, McGraw Hill, Corning, Barnes & Noble, New York Times.

Famous natives Woody Allen, director. John Jacob Astor (b. Germany), merchant. Humphrey Bogart, actor. George Burns, actor. Aaron Copland, composer. Agnes De Mille, choreographer. George Eastman, camera inventor. Millard Fillmore, U.S. president. Lou Gehrig, baseball player. George Gershwin, composer. Julia Ward Howe, reformer. Washington Irving, author. Henry James, author. Vince Lombardi, football coach. Groucho Marx, comedian. Herman Melville, author. Ogden Nash, poet/humorist. Eugene O'Neill, playwright. Otetiani "Red Jacket", Seneca chief. Channing E. Phillips, minister/reformer. John D. Rockefeller, industrialist. Norman Rockwell, illustrator. Richard Rodgers, composer. Franklin Delano Roosevelt, U.S. president. Theodore Roosevelt, U.S. president. Jonas Salk, physician. Elizabeth Ann Seton, first American saint. Elizabeth Cady Stanton, suffragette. James Johnson Sweeney, art critic. Martin Van Buren, U.S. president. Mae West, actress. E.B. White, author. Walt Whitman, poet.

Noteworthy places Albright-Knox Gallery of American Art, Buffalo. American Merchant Marine Museum, Kings Point. Baseball Hall of Fame, Cooperstown. Bear Mt. State Park. Buffalo Museum of Science. Corning Glass Center, Corning. Erie Canal Museum, Syracuse. Farmers' Museum, Cooperstown. Fenimore House, Cooperstown. Franklin D. Roosevelt Natl. Hist. Site, Hyde Park. Ft. Stanwix Natl. Monument, Rome. Ft. Ticonderoga. Hudson Valley. Mohawk Valley. Niagara Falls. Palisades Interstate Park. Saratoga Natl. Hist. Park. Vanderbilt Museum, Hyde Park. U.S. Military Academy, West Point. Women's Rights Natl. Hist. Park, Seneca Falls. **New York City** American Academy of Arts & Sciences. American Museum of Natural History. Bronx Zoo. Brooklyn Botanical Garden. Brooklyn Museum. Cathedral of St. John the Divine. Cooper-Hewitt Museum. Federal Hall. Fraunces Tavern. Frick Collection. Guggenheim Museum. Hispanic Society of America. Jewish Museum. Lincoln Center for the Performing Arts. Metropolitan Museum of Art. Museum of Modern Art. Museum of the American Indian. N.Y. Public Library. N.Y. Stock Exchange. Rockefeller Center. South Street Seaport Museum. Statue of Liberty. United Nations.

Memorable events Giovanni de Verrazano sails into New York Bay 1524. Samuel de Champlain sails down the St. Lawrence River 1603. Henry Hudson sails up Hudson River 1609. Dutch establish Ft. Orange (Albany) 1614. Peter Minuit buys Manhattan Island and founds colony of New Amsterdam 1625. British take New Amsterdam and name it New York 1664. Ethan Allen takes Ft. Ticonderoga 1775. George Washington inaugurated president New York City 1789. U.S. Military Academy founded West Point 1802. Erie Canal opened 1825. Statue of Liberty dedicated 1886. New York City includes Manhattan, Bronx, Queens, Brooklyn, and Staten Island 1898. President William McKinley assassinated in Buffalo 1901. UN headquarters established at New York City 1945. St. Lawrence Seaway opened 1959. One-fourth of New York City below poverty level 1984.

Tourist information 1-800-CALL-NYS. **www.state.ny.us.**

▶ NORTH CAROLINA

At the time of the Revolution, tobacco and rice plantations dominated the economy of the eastern part of the state, which in turn dominated the legislature. Next to last to ratify the Constitution, North Carolina was the last Southern state to secede from the Union. The Civil War cost North Carolina dearly; reconstruction was short-lived, and blacks were effectively disenfranchised again by the turn of the century. Since World War II, the state has grown increasingly prosperous, especially in the "academic triangle" that encloses the University of North Carolina at Chapel Hill, Duke, and North Carolina State. The traditional industries of textiles, furniture, and tobacco still lead, partly because of diversification within them. North Carolina benefits from the general Sunbelt boom and from an influx of foreign capital; it maintains a healthy manufacturing sector, and has enjoyed steady economic growth in the 1990s.

Name For King Charles I (Carolus is Latin for Charles). **Nicknames** Tarheel State, Old North State. **Capital** Raleigh. **Entered union** Nov. 21, 1789 (12th). **Motto** *Esse quam videri* (To be rather than to seem).

Emblems Bird Cardinal. **Fish** Channel bass. **Flower** Dogwood. **Insect** Honeybee. **Precious stone** Emerald. **Reptile** Eastern box turtle. **Rock** Granite. **Shell** Scotch bonnet. **Song** "The Old North State." **Tree** Pine.

Land Total area 52, 669 sq. mi. (28th), incl. 3,826 sq. mi. inland water. **Borders** Va., Atlantic Ocean, S.C., Tenn. **Rivers** Pee Dee, Roanoke, Yadkin. **Lakes** Buggs Island, High Rock, Mattamuskeet, Norman, Waccamaw. **Mountains** Black, Blue Ridge, Great Smoky, Unaka. **Other notable features** Great Dismal Swamp, Mount Mitchell, Outer Banks, Pamlico Sound.

Elected officials Gov. James B. Hunt (D, term exp. 2000). Lt. Gov. Dennis A. Wicker (D). Sec. State Elaine Marshall (D). Atty. Gen. Mike Easley (D).

People (1998) 7,546,493 (11th). **Race/national origin** (1990): White 75.6%. Black 22.0%. Indian 1.2%. Asian 0.8%. Other 0.5%. Hispanic 1.2%.

Cities (1996 estimate) Charlotte 441,297. Raleigh 243,835. Greensboro 195,426. Winston-Salem 153,541. Durham 149,799. Fayetteville 79,631. Cary 75,676. High Point 74,417. Jacksonville 69,889. Asheville 64,067.

Business Gross State Product, 1997: $218.89 bil. (12th). **Leading Sectors of GSP** (1997): Manufacturing 26.48%; Services 15.69%; Finance, insurance, and real estate 15.10%. *Fortune* 500 **Companies** (1998): 9: BankAmerica Corp., First Union Corp., Duke Energy, Lowe's, Wachovia Corp., VF, Nucor, Carolina Power & Light, BB&T Corp.

Famous natives Benjamin Newton Duke and James Buchanan Duke, industrialists/philanthropists. Richard J. Gatling, inventor. Billy Graham, minister. Andy Griffith, actor. O. Henry, writer. Andrew Johnson, U.S. president. William Rufus King, politician. Charles Kuralt, journalist. Meadowlark Lemon, athlete. Dolley Madison, First Lady. Thelonius Monk, musician. Edward R. Murrow, journalist. James Knox Polk, U.S. president. Moses Waddell, Confederate general. Thomas Wolfe, author.

Noteworthy places Bennett Place. Blue Ridge Natl. Parkway. Cape Hatteras and Cape Lookout Natl. Seashore. Carl Sandburg Home, Hendersonville. Ft. Raleigh. Great Smoky Mountains Natl. Hist. Park. Guilford Courthouse Natl. Military Park. Mint Museum, Charlotte. Moores Creek Natl. Battlefield. North Carolina Maritime Museum, Beaufort. North Carolina Museum of Art, Raleigh. Roanoke Island. Wright Brothers Natl. Memorial, Kitty Hawk.

Memorable events Part of Carolina grant given to eight noblemen by Charles II 1663. Culpepper's Rebellion in reaction to unfair tax collection policies 1677. Tuscarora lose war against European immigrants 1713. Proprietors sell rights to Crown; becomes royal province 1729. Mecklenburg Declaration (1775), forerunner of Declaration of Independence. Becomes first colony to sanction explicitly declaration of independence from Britain in Apr. 1776. Gen. Charles Cornwallis wins Battle of Guilford Courthouse, but British lose control of colony 1781. Ratifies Constitution 1789. Gives up claims to western territories, now part of Tennessee 1790. Establishes first state university system in United States 1829. Cherokees driven out of North Carolina to Oklahoma 1838. Secedes 1861. Readmitted to Union 1868. American Tobacco Company founded 1890. Wright brothers launch first successful airplane at Kitty Hawk 1903. Confrontation between Ku Klux Klan and anti-Klan demonstrators leaves five dead; 12 Klansmen charged with first-degree murder 1979.

Tourist information 1-800-VISIT-NC.
www.state.nc.us.

▶NORTH DAKOTA

The first permanent settlers in North Dakota were Scots-Canadians who settled at Pembina on the Red River near the Canadian border, and who traded primarily with Winnipeg and St. Paul. The arrival of the Northern Pacific Railway in 1872 created a surge of huge farms, many of which were wiped out by drought and harsh winters in the 1880s. There followed a huge influx of Norwegians and Germans whose influence is still very apparent today. North Dakota's economy is heavily agricultural and leads the nation in production of wheat. Farming is centered in the fertile Red River of the North Valley, with livestock throughout the rest of the state.

Name For northern section of Dakota territory; *dakota* is Sioux word for "allies." **Nicknames** Sioux State, Peace Garden State, Flickertail State. **Capital** Bismarck. **Entered union** Nov. 2, 1889 (39th). **Motto** "Liberty and union, now and forever, one and inseparable."

Emblems **Beverage** Milk. **Bird** Western meadowlark. **Fish** Northern pike. **Flower** Wild prairie rose. **Fossil** Teredo petrified wood. **Grass** Western wheatgrass. **March** "Spirit of North Dakota." **Song** "North Dakota Hymn." **Tree** American elm.

Land Total area 70,703 sq. mi. (17th), incl. 1,403 sq. mi. inland water. **Borders** Saskatchewan, Manitoba, Minn., S.Dak., Mont. **Rivers** Missouri, Red River of the North. **Lakes** Ashtabula, Devils, Oahe, Sakakawea. **Other notable features** Geographical center of North America, Missouri Plateau, Red River Valley, Rolling Drift Prairie.

Elected officials Gov. Edward T. Schafer (R, term exp. 2000). Lt. Gov. Rosemarie Myrdal (R). Sec. State Alvin A. Jaegar (R). Atty. Gen. Heidi Heitkamp (D).

People (1998) 638,244 (47th). **Race/national origin** (1990): White 94.6%. Black 0.6%. Indian 4.1%. Asian 0.5%. Other 0.3%. Hispanic 0.7%.

Cities (1996 estimate) Fargo 83,778. Bismarck 53,514. Grand Forks 50,675. Minot 35,926. Dickinson 16,094. Mandan 15,648. Jamestown 14,983. West Fargo 13,566. Williston 12,718. Wahpeton 9,039.

Business Gross State Product, 1997: $15.79 bil. (49th). **Leading Sectors of GSP** (1997): Services 18.42%; Government 15.44%; Finance, insurance, and real estate 13.48%. *Fortune* 500 **Companies** (1998): 0.

Famous natives Angie Dickinson, actress. John Bernard Flannagan, sculptor. Louis L'Amour, novelist. Peggy Lee, singer. Roger Maris, baseball player. Eric Sevareid, broadcaster. Vihjalmur Stefansson (b. Canada), ethnologist. Lawrence Welk, entertainer.

Noteworthy places Ft. Abraham Lincoln State Park. Ft. Union Trading Post Natl. Hist. Site. International Peace Garden. Knife River Indian Villages Natl. Hist. Site. Theodore Roosevelt Natl. Park, the Badlands.

Memorable events Pierre Gaultier de Varennes, sieur de Vérendrye first European to visit area 1738. United States acquires half of territory in Louisiana Purchase 1803. Meriwether Lewis and George Rogers Clark expedition builds Ft. Mandan 1804–5. First permanent settlement at Pembina 1812. Britain cedes western half of state to United States 1818. Missouri River steamboats reach territory 1838. First railroad arrives 1873. Statehood 1889. First state to hold presidential primary 1912. Garrison Dam completed forming Lake Sakakawea; gambling (blackjack) legalized 1981. Red River floods, devastating agriculture, 1997.

Tourist information 1-800-437-2077.
www.state.nd.us.

▶OHIO

The first settlements in Ohio were Marietta, in 1788, and Cincinnati in 1789, on the Ohio River, but significant migration into the state didn't occur until after the War of 1812. Shipping flourished in the 1820s and 1830s thanks to a network of canals connecting the Ohio and Lake Erie. Since 1959 the St. Lawrence Seaway has helped keep Ohio among the top five exporting states. Heavy industry also flourished in the northern cities that had access to coal and iron ore from the

Lake Superior region. The 1870s saw the development of a manufacturing base that later became an integral part of the automotive industry. Although Ohio's economy has traditionally been well balanced between agriculture, industry, mining, and trade, the recession of the early 1980s weakened manufacturing, triggered flight from the industrial cities, and saw a dramatic shift to a service economy and to high-tech industry.

Name From the Iroquois *oheo*, "beautiful." **Nickname** Buckeye State. **Capital** Columbus. **Entered union** Mar. 1, 1803 (17th). **Motto** "With God, all things are possible."

Emblems **Beverage** Tomato juice. **Bird** Cardinal. **Flower** Scarlet carnation. **Gem** Ohio flint. **Insect** Ladybug. **Song** "Beautiful Ohio." **Tree** Buckeye.

Land Total area 41,330 sq. mi. (35th), incl. 326 sq. mi. inland water. **Borders** Mich., Lake Erie, Pa., W.Va., Ky., Ind. **Rivers** Cuyahoga, Maumee, Miami, Muskingum, Ohio, Sandusky, Scioto. **Lakes** Berlin Res., Dillon Res., Erie, Mosquito Res., St. Mary's.

Elected officials Gov. Bob Taft (R, term exp. 2003). Lt. Gov. Maureen O'Connor (R). Sec. State. Kenneth Blackwell (R) Atty. Gen. Betty D. Montgomery. (R).

People (1998) 11,209,493 (7th). **Race/national origin** (1990): White 87.8%. Black 10.6%. Indian 0.2%. Asian 0.8%. Other 0.5%. Hispanic 1.3%.

Cities (1996 estimate) Columbus 657,053. Cleveland 498,246. Cincinnati 345,818. Toledo 317,606. Akron 216,882. Dayton 172,947. Youngstown 87,405. Parma 85,006. Canton 81,079. Lorain 69,800.

Business **Gross State Product,** 1997: $320.51 bil. (7th). **Leading Sectors of GSP** (1997): Manufacturing 26.16%; Services 18.03%; Finance, insurance, and real estate 15.90%. *Fortune* **500 Companies** (1998): 27: including Procter & Gamble, Kroger, Cardinal Health, Federated Department Stores, Nationwide Insurance Enterprise, Dana, Goodyear Tire, TRW, Limited, National City Corp. Keycorp, Eaton, NCR, Owens Corning, Sherwin-Williams, Mead, OfficeMax, B.F. Goodrich.

Famous natives Sherwood Anderson, writer. Neil Armstrong, astronaut. George Bellows, artist. Ambrose Bierce, author. George Armstrong Custer, army officer. Paul Laurence Dunbar, poet. Thomas A. Edison, inventor. James A. Garfield, U.S. president. John Glenn, astronaut/politician. Ulysses S. Grant, U.S. president/general. Zane Grey, author. Warren G. Harding, U.S. president. Benjamin Harrison, U.S. president. Rutherford B. Hayes, U.S. president. Bob Hope, entertainer. William McKinley, U.S. president. Annie Oakley, markswoman. Ransom Eli Olds, carmaker. Eddie Rickenbacker, pilot. William Sherman, army officer. William Howard Taft, U.S. president/chief justice. Art Tatum, pianist. Tecumseh, Shawnee chief. James Thurber, humorist. Orville Wright, airplane inventor.

Noteworthy places Air Force Museum, Dayton. Cleveland Museum of Art. Cleveland Museum of Natural History. Columbus Museum of Art. Great Lakes Historical Society Museum, Vermilion. Mound City Group Natl. Monument, Chillicothe. Neil Armstrong Air and Space Museum, Wapakoneta. Ohio River Museum, Marietta. Pro Football Hall of Fame, Canton. Toledo Museum of Art.

Memorable events Hopewell Mound-Builders present throughout state prior to arrival of Miamis, Shawnees, Wyandots, and Delawares. Conflicting claims by France, Virginia, Connecticut, and New York 1609–1786. René-Roger Cave-

lier de La Salle visits region 1669–70. To Britain 1763. To United States after 1783. Becomes part of Northwest Territory 1787. First settlement at Marietta 1788. Gen. "Mad" Anthony Wayne beats Tecumseh at Battle of Fallen Timbers 1794. Enters Union 1803. Harrison beats Tecumseh at Battle of Tippecanoe 1811. Oliver Hazard Perry beats British fleet at Battle of Put-in-Bay 1813. Ohio and Erie Canal completed 1832. Dayton flood kills 400 in Miami River Valley; damage put at $100 million 1913. Carl B. Stokes elected mayor of Cleveland, first black mayor of major U.S. city 1967. Four students protesting Vietnam War killed by National Guard at Kent State University 1970.

Tourist information 1-800-BUCKEYE. www.state.oh.us.

▶ OKLAHOMA

French trappers entered the region of Oklahoma in the 1700s. In 1830 the land was designated the Indian Country, set aside for members of the Cherokees, Chickasaw, Choctaw, Creek, and Seminole deported from the southeast by the Indian Removal Act of 1830. These "Five Civilized Tribes," among others, fared well until the Civil War. They supported the Confederacy (some were actually slave-holders), and in 1868 Col. George Armstrong Custer led a massacre of Cheyenne at the Battle of the Washita. Twenty years later the government abrogated its treaty commitments and opened the territory to settlement. Today the state has a distinctly southern character. The region bordering the Red River is known as "Little Dixie," and as many as two-thirds of all Oklahomans consider themselves born-again Christians.

Oklahoma has a diversified economy. The state led the country in oil and gas production through the 1920s. Agriculture was hit heavily by the dust bowl of the 1930s, and thousands of "Okies" fled west. While agriculture and petroleum are still vital to the economy, manufacturing is increasingly important. The state is crossed by two of the country's longest rivers. The Arkansas links Catoosa (near Tulsa) to the Gulf of Mexico and the Mississippi River system; but the Red River is not navigable in Oklahoma, and dissolved salts make it useless for agriculture, industry or residential purposes.

Name From the Choctaw *okla humma,* "land of the red people." **Nickname** Sooner State. **Capital** Oklahoma City. **Entered union** Nov. 16, 1907 (46th). **Motto** *Labor omnia vincit* (Work overcomes all obstacles).

Emblems **Animal** American buffalo. **Bird** Scissor-tailed flycatcher. **Colors** Green and white. **Fish** White bass. **Floral emblem** Mistletoe. **Grass** Indian grass. **Poem** "Howdy Folks." **Reptile** Collared lizard (mountain boomer). **Song** "Oklahoma!" **Stone** Barite rose (rose rock). **Tree** Redbud. **Waltz** "Oklahoma Wind."

Land Total area 69,956 sq. mi. (18th), incl. 1,301 sq. mi. inland water. **Borders** Kans., Mo., Ark., Tex., N.Mex., Colo. **Rivers** Arkansas, Canadian, Cimarron, Red. **Lakes** Canton, Lake o' the Cherokees, Oologah, Texoma. **Other notable features** Ouachita Mts., Ozark Plateau, Staked Plain, Wichita Mts.

Elected officials Gov. Frank Keating (R, term exp. 2003). Lt. Gov. Mary Fallin (R). Sec. State Mike Hunter (R). Atty. Gen. Drew Edmondson (R).

People (1998) 3,346,713 (27th). **Race/national origin** (1990): White 82.1%. Black 7.4%. Indian 8.0%. Asian 1.1%. Other 1.3%. Hispanic 2.7%.

Cities (1996 estimate) Oklahoma City 469,852. Tulsa 378,491. Norman 90,228. Lawton 82,582. Broken Arrow 69,175. Edmond 63,475. Midwest City 54,252. Enid 45,724. Moore 44,472. Stillwater 38,487.

Business **Gross State Product,** 1997: $76.64 bil. (30th). **Leading Sectors of GSP** (1997): Services 17.63%; Manufacturing 16.98%; Government 15.77%. *Fortune* **500 Companies** (1998): 3: Fleming, Phillips Petroleum, Williams.

Famous natives Ralph Ellison, author. Woody Guthrie, reformer/musician. Patrick J. Hurley, diplomat. Karl Jansky, electrical engineer. Mickey Mantle, baseball player. Wiley Post, aviator. Tony Randall, actor. Oral Roberts, evangelist. Will Rogers, humorist. Maria Tallchief, ballerina. Jim Thorpe, athlete.

Noteworthy places American Indian Hall of Fame, Anadarko. Chisholm Trail Museum, Kingfisher. Ft. Gibson Stockade, Muskogee. Natl. Cowboy Hall of Fame, Oklahoma City. Ouachita Natl. Forest. Pioneer Woman Museum, Ponca City. Will Rogers Memorial, Claremore.

Memorable events Francisco Vásquez de Coronado expedition in territory 1541. Except for panhandle, becomes part of Louisiana purchase 1803. Region made Indian Territory (not organized) in 1830 and becomes home of "Five Civilized Tribes"—Cherokee, Choctaw, Chickasaw, Creek, and Seminole—after they left the southeast on Trail of Tears 1828–46. United States acquires panhandle with annexation of Texas 1845. Territory opened to homesteaders 1889. Commercial oil well at Bartlesville 1897. Indian Territory and Oklahoma Territory merged and granted statehood 1907. Gov. John C. Walton impeached after declaring martial law to quell violence 1923. McClellan-Kerr Arkansas River Navigation system links Oklahoma to Mississippi, making Catoosa (Tulsa) major inland port 1971. Timothy McVeigh blows up Federal Building in Oklahoma City, killing 168 people 1995.
Tourist information 1-800-652-6552.
www.state.ok.us.

▶OREGON

Although the Lewis and Clark expedition reached the mouth of the Columbia River in 1805, interest in the area was kindled by the Hudson's Bay Company and later by Jason Lee, a Methodist minister who settled near Salem in 1834. After the decline of the fur trade, lumbering became the most important industry in Oregon. Though lumbering and related industries are still leading employers—the state is the leading grower of Christmas trees—Oregon has benefited from the arrival of smaller computer and electronics firms leaving California in search of a more favorable business climate. Traditionally progressive, it is one of most active states in the environmental protection movement. Only one-third of the population is affiliated with an organized religion.

Name Unknown origin, first applied to Columbia River. **Nickname** Beaver State. **Capital** Salem. **Entered union** Feb. 14, 1859 (33rd). **Motto** "She flies with her own wings." **Poet laureate** William E. Stafford.

Emblems **Animal** Beaver. **Bird** Western meadowlark. **Dance** Square dance. **Fish** Chinook salmon. **Flower** Oregon grape. **Insect** Swallowtail butterfly. **Song** "Oregon, My Oregon." **Stone** Thunderegg. **Tree** Douglas fir.

Land **Total area** 97,073 sq. mi. (10th), incl. 889 sq. mi. inland water. **Borders** Wash., Idaho, Nev., Calif., Pacific Ocean. **Rivers** Columbia, Snake,

Willamette. **Mountains** Cascade Range, Coast Range, Klamath. **Other notable features** Willamette Valley.

Elected officials Gov. John A. Kitzhaber (D, term exp. 2003). Sec. State Phil Keisling (D). Atty. Gen. Hardy Myers (D).

People (1998) 3,281,974 (28th). **Race/national origin** (1990): White 92.8%. Black 1.6%. Indian 1.4%. Asian 2.4%. Other 1.8%. Hispanic 4.0%.

Cities (1996 estimate) Portland 480,824. Eugene 123,718. Salem 122,566. Gresham 81,583. Beaverton 63,224. Medford 56,067. Hillsboro 52,479. Springfield 49,430. Corvallis 47,518. Albany 37,919.

Business **Gross State Product,** 1997: $98.37 bil. (27th). **Leading Sectors of GSP** (1997): Manufacturing 25.08%; Services 17.31%; Finance, insurance, and real estate 15.15%. *Fortune* **500 Companies** (1998): 4: Fred Meyer, Nike, Pacificorp, Willamette Industries.

Famous natives In-mut-too-yah-lat-lat (Joseph), Nez Percé chief. Ursula LeGuin (b. Calif.), author. Edwin Markham, poet. Dr. John McLoughlin, fur trader, "Father of Oregon". Linus Pauling, chemist. John Reed, author. William Simon U'Ren (b. Wis.), lawyer/reformer.

Noteworthy places Bonneville Dam, Columbia River. Columbia River Gorge. Columbia River Museum, Astoria. Crater Lakes Natl. Park. Ft. Clatsop Natl. Monument. Hells Canyon. High Desert Museum, Bend. John Day Fossil Beds Natl. Monument. Mt. Hood. Oregon Caves Natl. Monument. Oregon Dunes Natl. Recreation Area. Point Perpetua. Timberline Lodge.

Memorable events Sir Francis Drake turns away from fogbound coast of Pacific Northwest 1578. Capt. James Cook visits 1778. Mouth of Columbia River explored by Capt. Robert Gray, who claims region for U.S. 1792. Meriwether Lewis and George Rogers Clark expedition arrives at mouth of Columbia 1805. Claims to Oregon Territory, from California border to Alaska and east to Montana and Wyoming, relinquished by Spain (1819), Russia (1825), and Britain (1846). First settlers arrive Willamette Valley 1843. Organized as territory 1848. Statehood 1859. Railroad arrives 1883. Bonneville Dam completed 1937. Following severe rain and snow that claim 40 lives, Oregon declared disaster area 1964. First state to enact "bottle law" 1972. Snake River opened to navigation, linking Astoria to Lewiston, Idaho, 1975.
Tourist information 1-800-547-7842.
www.state.or.us.

▶PENNSYLVANIA, COMMONWEALTH OF

William Penn and his Quakers encouraged settlement and religious tolerance, and Pennsylvania was the first state to abolish slavery. In the late colonial period, Philadelphia was the cultural capital of the colonies. The first Continental Congress convened there in 1774, and it was for a decade the U.S. capital. With access to both the Great Lakes and to the Atlantic, Pennsylvanians took a lead in opening up the Midwest. Its resources include large coal deposits—which contribute to its iron-making capabilities—lumber, textiles, and leather. Leadership in these sectors lasted well into the 20th century, when Pennsylvania lost ground to Sunbelt states. As in many states, there has been growth in tourist and service industries, though machinery production and trade continue to expand significantly.

Name For Adm. William Penn, father of William Penn, founder of commonwealth. **Nickname** Keystone State. **Capital** Harrisburg. **Entered union** Dec. 12, 1787 (2nd). **Motto** "Virtue, liberty and independence."

Emblems **Animal** White-tailed deer. **Beautification and conservation plant** Penngift crown vetch. **Beverage** Milk. **Bird** Ruffed grouse. **Dog** Great Dane. **Fish** Brook trout. **Flower** Mountain laurel. **Insect** Firefly. **Tree** Hemlock.

Land Total area 45,308 sq. mi. (33rd), incl. 420 sq. mi. inland water. **Borders** N.Y., N.J., Del., Md., W.Va., Ohio, Lake Erie. **Rivers** Allegheny, Delaware, Juniata, Monongahela, Ohio, Schuylkill, Susquehanna. **Lakes** Allegheny Res., Erie, Pymatuning Res., Shenango Res. **Mountains** Allegheny, Kittatinny, Laurel Hills, Pocono.

Elected officials Gov. Tom Ridge (R, term exp. 2003). Lt. Gov. Mark Schweiker (R). Sec. Commonwealth Yvette Kane (D). Atty. Gen. D. Michael Fisher (R).

People (1998) 12,001,451 (6th). **Race/national origin** (1990): White 88.5%. Black 9.2%. Indian 0.1%. Asian 1.2%. Other 1.0%. Hispanic 2.0%.

Cities (1996 estimate) Philadelphia 1,478,002. Pittsburgh 350,363. Erie 105,270. Allentown 102,211. Scranton 77,189. Reading 75,723. Bethlehem 70,245. Lancaster 53,597. Harrisburg 50,886. Altoona 50,101.

Business **Gross State Product, 1997:** $339.94 bil. (6th). **Leading Sectors of GSP** (1997): Services 21.85%; Manufacturing 20.04%; Finance, insurance, and real estate 18.99%. **Fortune 500 Companies** (1998): 27: Including USX, Cigna, ALCOA, Rite Aid, H.J. Heinz, Amerisource Health, Crown Cork & Seal, PNC Bank, PPG Industries, Unisource, UNISYS, Mellon Bank Corp., IKON Office Solutions, Bethlehem Steel, Hershey Foods, York International, Wesco International.

Famous natives Louisa May Alcott, author. Maxwell Anderson, playwright. James Buchanan, U.S. president. Alexander Calder, sculptor. Andrew Carnegie (b. Scotland), industrialist/philanthropist. Mary Cassatt, painter. Wilt Chamberlain, basketball player. Bill Cosby, comedian/philanthropist. Stephen Foster, songwriter. Benjamin Franklin (b. Mass.), inventor/statesman. Robert Fulton, inventor. Milton S. Hershey, chocolatier. George C. Marshall, statesman. Andrew W. Mellon, financier/philanthropist. Robert E. Peary, explorer. Betsy Ross, patriot. Andy Warhol, artist. Johnny Weismuller, swimmer/actor. Benjamin West, painter.

Noteworthy places Academy of Natural Sciences, Philadelphia. Carnegie Institute, Pittsburgh. Delaware Water Gap Natl. Recreation Area. Ft. Necessity Natl. Battlefield. Franklin Institute, Philadelphia. Gettysburg Battlefield. Hugh Moore Hist. Park and Museums, Easton. Independence Natl. Hist. Park, Philadelphia. Liberty Bell, Carpenters Hall, Philadelphia. Pennsylvania Academy of Fine Arts, Philadelphia. Pennsylvania Dutch Country. Philadelphia Museum of Art. Pine Creek Gorge. Valley Forge Natl. Hist. Park.

Memorable events Cornelis Jacobssen sails into Delaware Bay 1614. Swedes settle at Tinicum Island 1643. Charles II grants proprietary charter to William Penn 1681. First U.S. hospital established, in Philadelphia, 1751. Mason-Dixon Line establishes southern boundary of state 1763–67—later boundary between slave and nonslave states. Declaration of Independence (1776) and Constitution (1787) signed in Philadelphia. Becomes first state to abolish slavery 1780. Bank of North America becomes first bank chartered in United States 1781. Philadelphia capital of United States 1790–1800. First iron furnace in United States 1792. First oil well in the world driven near Titusville 1859. Battle of Gettysburg turning point in Civil War; Lincoln's Gettysburg Address 1863. Centennial Exhibition at Philadelphia 1876. Johnstown flood—worst in U.S. history—kills 2,200 people 1889. Pinkerton detectives kill 12 strikers at Homestead steel works near Pittsburgh 1892. Twenty coal miners killed during strike for eight-hour day and other concessions 1897. More than 500 injured during three-day race riot in Philadelphia 1964. Partial meltdown at Three Mile Island forces closure of nuclear reactor 1979. Storage tank spills 713,000 gallons diesel fuel into Monongahela River, disrupting water supplies in Pennsylvania, West Virginia, and Ohio 1988.

Tourist information 1-800-VISIT-PA, ext. 109. **www.state.pa.us.**

▶ RHODE ISLAND AND PROVIDENCE PLANTATIONS

Giovanni de Verrazano was the first European to record visiting the area of Narragansett Bay, the prominent inlet that almost splits the eastern third of the state from the rest. The first settlers were followers of Roger Williams, who left the restrictive religious atmosphere of the Puritan Massachusetts Bay Colony to found Providence in 1636. Rhode Island is the site of the first U.S. Baptist church, at Providence, and at Newport the first Quaker meetinghouse and the first synagogue. It was the last of the 13 original colonies to ratify the Constitution, the centralized federalism of which many Rhode Islanders objected to. The development of 19th-century Rhode Island was influenced by immigration and the Industrial Revolution; the state's leading manufacturers are still silver, jewelry and textiles. Although it ranks 43rd in population, Rhode Island is second in population density (behind New Jersey) at 947.6 people per square mile.

Name For Rhode Island in Narragansett Bay, named in turn for Mediterranean island of Rhodes. **Nicknames** Ocean State, Little Rhody. **Capital** Providence. **Entered union** May 29, 1790 (13th). **Motto** "Hope."

Emblems **Bird** Rhode Island red. **Flower** Violet. **Mineral** Bowenite. **Rock** Cumberlandite. **Song** "Rhode Island." **Tree** Red maple.

Land Total area 1,212 sq. mi. (50th), incl. 157 sq. mi. inland water. **Borders** Mass., Atlantic Ocean, Conn. **Rivers** Blackstone, Pawcatuck, Providence, Sakonnet. **Other notable features** Block Island, Narragansett Bay, Rhode Island (Aquidneck Island).

Elected officials Gov. Lincoln Almond (R, term exp. 2003). Lt. Gov. Charles Fogarty (R). Sec. State James R. Langevin (D). Atty. Gen. Sheldon Whitehouse (D).

People (1998) 988,480 (43rd). **Race/national origin** (1990): White 91.4%. Black 3.9%. Indian 0.4%. Asian 1.8%. Other 2.5%. Hispanic 4.6%.

Cities (1996 estimate) Providence 152,558. Warwick 84,514. Cranston 74,324. Pawtucket 69,068. East Providence 48,389. Woonsocket 41,817. Newport 24,295. Central Falls 16,620.

Business **Gross State Product, 1997:** $27.81 bil. (44th). **Leading Sectors of GSP** (1997): Finance, insurance, and real estate 24.96%; Services 21.91%; Manufacturing 15.63%. **Fortune 500 Companies** (1998): 3: CVS, Textron, Hasbro.

Famous natives George M. Cohan, actor/producer. Nathanael Greene, army officer. Galway

Kinell, poet. Metacomet (King Philip), Wampanoag chief. Oliver H. Perry and Matthew C. Perry, naval officers. Gilbert Stuart, portraitist.
Noteworthy places John Carter Brown Library, Providence. First Baptist Church in North America (1638), Providence. Nathanael Greene homestead, Coventry. Hoffenreffer Museum of Anthropology, Bristol. Museum of Art of the Rhode Island School of Design, Providence. Newport mansions. Museum of Yachting, Newport. Tennis Hall of Fame, Newport. Touro Synagogue (1763, oldest extant in North America), Newport. Brown University, Providence.
Memorable events Roger Williams, expelled from Massachusetts Bay Colony, settles in Providence 1636. Other religious exiles settle in Portsmouth (1638), Newport (1639), and Warwick (1642). King Philip's War 1675–76. First Quaker meetinghouse in North America founded 1699. First colony to renounce allegiance to Britain 1776. Last colony to ratify Constitution 1790. Dorr's Rebellion achieves liberalization of state constitution, which had remained unchanged since 1663, 1842. America's Cup Race held in Newport for first time 1930. Newport Bridge across Narragansett Bay completed 1969. *Australia II* first non-United States boat to win America's Cup in 132 years 1983.
Tourist information 1-800-556-2484. **www.state.ri.us.**

▶**SOUTH CAROLINA**
South Carolina's early economy was based on rice—its plantations worked by slaves—though tobacco later played a major role. As was true in North Carolina, many settlers made their way into the back country where they eked out a living as tenant farmers. During the Revolution, Ft. Charlotte was the first British installation to fall to Colonial troops, and at the outbreak of the Civil War, Ft. Sumter was the first Union installation to fall to Confederate forces. While agriculture remained a staple of the state's economy through the close of the 19th century, textile manufacture took over in the early 20th century. The postwar era has seen the rapid expansion of the chemical and paper industries, as well as large-scale development of the Atlantic Coast ports of Charleston, Georgetown, and Port Royal.
  Name For King Charles II (Carolus is Latin for Charles). **Nickname** Palmetto State. **Capital** Columbia. **Entered union** May 23, 1788 (8th). **Motto** *Animis opibusque parati* (Prepared in mind and deed); *Dum spiro spero* (While I breathe I hope). **Poet laureate** Helen von Kolnitz Hyer.
Emblems **Animal** White-tailed deer. **Beverage** Milk. **Bird** Carolina wren. **Dance** Shag. **Dog** Boykin spaniel. **Fish** Striped bass. **Flower** Yellow jessamine. **Fruit** Peach. **Shell** Lettered olive. **Song** "Carolina." **Stone** Blue granite. **Tree** Palmetto. **Wild game Bird** Wild turkey.
Land Total area 31,113 sq. mi. (40th), incl. 910 sq. mi. inland water. **Borders** N.C., Atlantic Ocean, Ga. **Rivers** Congaree, Edisto, Pee Dee, Savannah, Tugalos, Wateree. **Lakes** Greenwood, Hartwell, Keowee, Marion, Murray, Santee Res., Wylie. **Other notable features** Blue Ridge Mts., Congaree Swamp, Sea Islands.
Elected officials Gov. Jim Hodges (D, term exp. 2003). Lt. Gov. Bob Peeler (R). Sec. State Jim Miles (R). Atty. Gen. Charles Condon (R).
People (1998) 3,835,962 (26th). **Race/national origin** (1990): White 69.0%. Black 29.8%. Indian 0.2%. Asian 0.6%. Other 0.3%. Hispanic 0.9%.

Cities (1996 estimate) Columbia 112,773. Charleston 71,052. North Charleston 59,923. Greenville 57,064. Rock Hill 44,061. Spartanburg 42,136. Sumter 38,565. Mount Pleasant Town 34,262. Florence 30,168. Hilton Head Island 29,088.
Business Gross State Product, 1997: $93.26 bil. (28th). **Leading Sectors of GSP** (1997): Manufacturing 24.97%; Services 15.68%; Government 14.82%. *Fortune* **500 Companies** (1998): 0:
Famous natives James F. Byrnes, politician/jurist. John C. Calhoun, politician. Dizzy Gillespie, musician. Althea Gibson, athlete. DuBose Heyward, author. Andrew Jackson, U.S. president. Eartha Kitt, singer. James Longstreet, army officer. Francis Marion, army officer/politician. Charles C. Pinckney and Thomas Pinckney, diplomats. Edward Rutledge and John Rutledge, politicians. Strom Thurmond, politician.
Noteworthy places Charleston Museum (1773, oldest in United States). Congaree Swamp Natl. Monument. Cowpens Natl. Battlefield. Ft. Moultrie, Ft. Johnson, and Ft. Sumter Natl. Monument, Charleston. Hilton Head Island. Kings Mountain Natl. Military Park. Ninety-Six Natl. Hist. Site, Greenwood. Patriots Point Maritime Museum, Charleston. Sea Islands. Spoleto Music Festival, Charleston.
Memorable events Spanish visit 1521. French Huguenots at Port Royal 1562. Included in Carolina grant by Charles II 1663. Charleston founded 1680. Becomes royal province 1729. Ratifies Constitution 1787. *Best Friend of Charleston,* first American steam locomotive built for passenger use 1833. First state to secede from Union Dec. 20, 1860. Confederate forces attack Ft. Sumter Apr. 12, 1861. Secession repealed 1865. Readmitted to Union 1868. Cyclone kills 1,000 in Savannah, Georgia, and Charleston 1893. Savannah River nuclear plant begins production near Aiken 1951; closed for safety reasons 1988. Hurricane Hugo kills 24 and causes $700 million in property damage 1989. BMW opens plant in Spartanburg 1994.
Tourist information 1-803-734-0122. **www.state.sc.us.**

▶**SOUTH DAKOTA**
The United States did not organize the Dakota Territory until 1861, and even then interest in the region was scant until gold was discovered in 1874. The majority of those who remained after the gold rush turned to cattle ranching, which was a mainstay of the economy through the first half of the 20th century. The manufacturing base was developed after four major dams were built on the Missouri River in the 1930s. They provided hydroelectric power and increased irrigation along the Missouri, which cuts the state in half. Concerned especially over the abrogation of 19th-century treaties, the American Indian Movement (AIM) took over the courthouse at Wounded Knee for 10 weeks in 1973. While U.S. courts have found in favor of the Sioux in several cases concerning the earlier treaties, many maintain that the settlements were insufficient.
  Name For southern section of Dakota territory; *dakota* is Sioux word for "allies." **Nicknames** Coyote State, Sunshine State. **Capital** Pierre. **Entered union** Nov. 2, 1889 (40th). **Motto** "Under God the people rule."
Emblems **Animal** Coyote. **Bird** Chinese ringnecked pheasant. **Fish** Walleye. **Flower** Pasque flower. **Gem** Fairburn agate. **Grass** Western wheatgrass. **Insect** Honeybee. **Mineral** Rose

quartz. **Song** "Hail, South Dakota." **Tree** Black Hills spruce.

Land Total area 77,116 sq. mi. (16th), incl. 1,164 sq. mi. inland water. **Borders** N.Dak., Minn., Iowa, Nebr., Wyo., Mont. **Rivers** Cheyenne, James, Missouri, Moreau, White. **Lakes** Belle Fourche Res., Big Stone, Traverse. **Other notable features** Badlands, Black Hills (Harney Peak 7,242 ft.).

Elected officials Gov. Bill Janklow (R, term exp. 2003). Lt. Gov. Carole Hillard (R). Sec. State Joyce Hazeltine (R). Atty. Gen. Mark Barnett (R).

People (1998) 738,171 (46th). **Race/national origin** (1990): White 91.6%. Black 0.5%. Indian 7.3%. Asian 0.4%. Other 0.2%. Hispanic 0.8%.

Cities (1996 estimate) Sioux Falls 113,223. Rapid City 57,642. Aberdeen 25,088. Watertown 19,619. Brookings 17,413. Mitchell 14,191. Yankton 13,969. Pierre 13,422. Huron 12,428. Vermillion 10,521.

Business Gross State Product, 1997: $20.19 bil. (46th). **Leading Sectors of GSP** (1997): Finance, insurance, and real estate 20.51%; Services 16.51%; Manufacturing 13.34%. *Fortune* 500 Companies (1998): 0.

Famous natives Tom Brokaw, journalist. Martha "Calamity" Jane Burk (b. Mo.), frontierswoman. Alvin Hansen, economist. Hubert H. Humphrey, politician. Ernest O. Lawrence, physicist (Nobel Prize, 1939). George McGovern, politician. Ta-sunko-witko (Crazy Horse), Oglala Sioux chief. Tatanka Iyotake (Sitting Bull), Sioux chief.

Noteworthy places Badlands Natl. Park. Crazy Horse State Memorial, Custer. Custer State Park. Ft. Sisseton. Geographical center of the United States. Jewel Cave Natl. Monument. Mount Rushmore. Natl. Memorial. Wind Cave Natl. Park.

Memorable events French visit region 1742–43. To United States in Louisiana Purchase 1803. Ft. Pierre first permanent settlement 1817. Part of Dakota Territory 1861. Gold discovered in Black Hills 1874. Divided from North Dakota; statehood 1889. U.S. troops massacre Sioux at Battle of Wounded Knee 1890.

Tourist information 1-800-SDAKOTA. www.state.sd.us.

▶**TENNESSEE**

At first claimed by Virginia and later by North Carolina, Tennessee had its first great pioneer in Daniel Boone, who traversed the region in the 1760s. Political attitudes in the 18th century were shaped by the land, with the cotton and tobacco growers in the fertile western part of the state favoring slavery and the backwoods people of the eastern hills opposed to it. The Cherokees were removed to Oklahoma by the federal government in the 1830s. The state was captured by Union troops in 1862 and put under the governorship of Andrew Johnson, later a U.S. president.

Its economy was radically altered in the 1930s and 1940s by the creation of the Tennessee Valley Authority, which provided abundant energy for industry, and to a lesser extent by the location of the government's first uranium enrichment facility at Oak Ridge during World War II. The state's leading industries are textiles, food processing, and chemicals, and there is considerable lead and coal mining in the east.

Name For Tenase, principal village of Cherokees. **Nickname** Volunteer State. **Capital** Nashville. **Entered union** June 1, 1796 (16th). **Motto** "Agriculture and commerce." **Slogan** "Tennessee—America at its best." **Poet laureate** Richard M. ("Pek") Gunn.

Emblems Animal Raccoon. **Bird** Mockingbird. **Folk dance** Square dance. **Cultivated flower** Iris. **Gem** Tennessee pearl. **Insects** Ladybug, firefly. **Poem** "Oh Tennessee, My Tennessee." **Public school song** "My Tennessee." **Rock** Limestone agate. **Songs** "When It's Iris Time in Tennessee," "The Tennessee Waltz," My Homeland, Tennessee," "Rocky Top." **Tree** Tulip poplar. **Wildflower** Passion flower.

Land Total area 42,144 sq. mi. (34th), incl. 989 sq. mi. inland water. **Borders** Ky., Va., N.C., Ga., Ala., Miss., Ark., Mo. **Rivers** Clinch, Cumberland, Mississippi, Tennessee. **Lakes** Boone, Center Hill, Cherokee, Dale Hollow, Douglass, J. Percy Priest, Watauga. **Other notable features** Cumberland Mts., Great Smoky Mts., Tennessee Valley, Unaka Mts.

Elected officials Gov. Don Sundquist (R, term exp. 2003). Lt. Gov. John S. Wilder (D). Sec. State Riley C. Darnell (D). Atty. Gen. Paul Summers (D).

People (1998) 5,430,621 (17th). **Race/national origin** (1990): White 83.0%. Black 16.0%. Indian 0.2%. Asian 0.7%. Other 0.2%. Hispanic 0.7%.

Cities (1996 estimate) Memphis 596,725. Nashville-Davidson (CC) 511,263. Knoxville 167,535. Chattanooga 150,425. Clarksville 94,879. Johnson City 55,542. Murfreesboro 53,966. Jackson 50,406. Kingsport 41,335. Hendersonville 37,261.

Business Gross State Product, 1997: $147.00 bil. (20th). **Leading Sectors of GSP** (1997): Manufacturing 21.28%; Services 20.31%; Finance, insurance, and real estate 14.44%. *Fortune* 500 Companies (1998): 7: Columbia/HCA Healthcare, FDX, Eastman Chemical, Provident Cos, Service Merchandise, Autozone, Dollar General.

Famous natives James Agee, author. Davy Crockett, frontiersman. David Farragut, naval officer. Aretha Franklin, singer. Morgan Freeman, actor. Al Gore, (b. Washington, D.C.), politician. Cordell Hull, statesman (Nobel Peace Prize, 1945). Dolly Parton, singer. Sikawyi (Sequoya), Cherokee scholar. Alvin York, soldier.

Noteworthy places American Museum of Science and Energy, Oak Ridge. Andrew Johnson Natl. Hist. Site, Greenville. Chickamauga and Chattanooga Natl. Military Park. Cumberland Natl. Hist. Park. Ft. Donelson Natl. Military Park. Grand Old Opry, Nashville. Great Smoky Mountains Natl. Park. The Hermitage (Andrew Jackson home), Nashville. Lookout Mountain, Chattanooga. The Parthenon, Nashville. Shiloh Natl. Military Park, Pittsburgh Landing. Stones River Natl. Battlefield, Murfreesboro.

Memorable events De Soto expedition passes through region 1540. French claim territory as part of Louisiana; English claim territory as part of Carolina grant 1663. French claim given up after French and Indian War 1763. State of Franklin established in what is now eastern Tennessee 1784–87. Organized as Territory South of the Ohio 1790. Statehood 1796. Secedes from Union 1861. Battles of Shiloh (1862), Chattanooga (1863), Stones River (1863), and Nashville (1864). Readmitted to Union 1866. Clarence Darrow defends John T. Scopes for violating ban on teaching evolution in public schools; loses case 1925. Congress creates Tennessee Valley Authority 1933. First operational nuclear reactor at Oak Ridge 1943. Martin Luther King assassinated at Memphis 1968. World's Fair held in Knoxville 1982.

Tourist information 1-800-836-6200. www.state.tn.us.

▶ TEXAS

The land that is Texas today was originally part of Spain's holdings in Mexico. After Mexico won independence, the new government invited U.S. citizens to settle there. After many clashes between the Mexican and Anglo cultures, Texas broke away and for 10 years was an independent country before becoming a state in 1845. Modern Texas was made by oil, discovered at Spindletop in 1901, and the state's economy has been tied to the oil market ever since. After World War II, the Texas economy soared, bringing both prosperity and an unprecedented population boom. With the oil glut of the early 1980s, growth came to a halt, causing a drastic realignment of economic priorities. Unemployment jumped more than 20 percent during the 1980s, and remained higher than the national average in 1990, a year that saw many bank failures. The economy has been forced to diversify; currently the petroleum industry accounts for only 7 percent of state revenues, down from 25 percent a decade before. Texas has enormous resources ranging from cotton, cattle, and timber to aerospace, computers, and electronics. The largest of the 48 conterminous states, Texas's image as a state of wide-open spaces is understandable, but fully 80 percent of its people live in metropolitan areas, and Dallas, Houston, and San Antonio are among the nation's 10 largest cities. Twenty-five percent of the population is Hispanic, and the majority of those are Mexican-American.

Name From the Caddo *tavshas*, "friends." **Nickname** Lone Star State. **Capital** Austin. **Entered union** Dec. 29, 1845 (28th). **Motto** "Friendship." **Emblems Bird** Mockingbird. **Dish** Chili. **Flower** Bluebonnet. **Gem** Topaz. **Grass** Sideoats grama. **Songs** "Texas, Our Texas," "The Eyes of Texas." **Stone** Palmwood. **Tree** Pecan.

Land Total area 266,807 sq. mi. (2nd), incl. 4,790 sq. mi. inland water. **Borders** Okla., Ark., La., Gulf of Mexico, Tamaulipas, Coahuila, Chihuahua, N.Mex. **Rivers** Brazos, Colorado, Natchez, Red, Rio Grande, Sabine, Trinity. **Lakes** Sam Rayburn Res., Texoma, Toledo Bend Res. **Other notable features** Balcones Escarpment, Diablo Sierra, Edwards Plateau, Guadalupe Mts., Staked Plain, Stockton Plateau.

Elected officials Gov. George Walker Bush (R, term exp. 2003). Lt. Gov. Rick Perry (R). Sec. State Elton Bomer (R). Atty. Gen. John Cornyn (R).

People (1998) 19,759,614 (2nd). **Race/national origin** (1990): White 75.2%. Black 11.9%. Indian 0.4%. Asian 1.9%. Other 10.6%. Hispanic 25.5%.

Cities (1996 estimate) Houston 1,744,058. San Antonio 1,067,816. Dallas 1,053,292. El Paso 599,865. Austin 541,278. Ft. Worth 479,716. Arlington 294,816. Corpus Christi 280,260. Lubbock 193,565. Plano 192,280.

Business Gross State Product, 1997: $601.64 bil. (3rd). **Leading Sectors of GSP** (1997): Services 18.49%; Manufacturing 15.78%; Finance, insurance, and real estate 14.54%. *Fortune* **500 Companies** (1998): 36: Including Exxon, Enron, Compaq Computer, JC Penney, SBC Communications, GTE, AMR, Dell Computer, Halliburton, Electronic Data Systems, Sysco, Texas Utilities, Kimberly-Clark, Union Pacific, Texas Instruments, Continental Airlines, Coastal, CompUSA, Tandy, Browning-Ferris Industries, Southwest Airlines, Centex.

Famous natives Stephen Austin (b. Va.), pioneer. James "Jim" Bowie (b. Ky.), army officer. Carol Burnett, comedian. J. Frank Dobie, folklorist. Dwight D. Eisenhower, U.S. president/general. Samuel Houston (b. Va.), president Republic of Texas/governor State of Texas. Howard Hughes, industrialist/aviator. Lyndon Baines Johnson, U.S. president. Janis Joplin, singer. Barbara Jordan, politician. Audie Murphy, soldier/actor. Chester Nimitz, navy officer. Katherine Anne Porter, author. Samuel T. Rayburn, politician. Mildred "Babe" Didrikson Zaharias, athlete.

Noteworthy places The Alamo, San Antonio. Alibates Flint Quarries Natl. Monument. Big Bend Natl. Park. Ft. Davis. Galveston Historical Foundation. Guadalupe Mountains Natl. Park. Houston Museum of Fine Arts. Lyndon B. Johnson Natl. Hist. Park, Johnson City. Lyndon B. Johnson Space Center, Houston. Old Stone Ft., Nacogdoches. Padre Island Natl. Seashore. San Antonio Missions Natl. Hist. Park. Texas Ranger Museum, Waco.

Memorable events Alonzo Alvarez de Piñeda sails along coast 1519. Estevanico blazes trail through West Texas 1539. Spanish establish settlement at Ysleta near El Paso 1682. René-Robert Cavelier de La Salle attempts to found colony on Matagorda Bay, establishing claim to region for France 1685. Effective Spanish occupation 1715. United States acquires French claim to region with Louisiana Purchase 1803. United States relinquishes claim to Spain 1819. Americans move into region in early 19th century. Mexico, of which Texas is a province, wins independence from Spain 1821. Declaration of Independence from Mexico; Santa Anna victor at Battle of the Alamo; Sam Houston victor at Battle of San Jacinto; founding of Republic of Texas 1836. Texas granted statehood by United States 1845. Secedes from Union 1861; readmitted 1870. Hurricane kills 6,000 at Galveston 1900. NASA Space Center opens at Houston 1962. Pres. Kennedy assassinated at Dallas 1963. Price of oil plunges during 1980s, crippling state economy

Tourist information 1-800-888-8TEX, ext. 728. **www.state.tx.us.**

▶ UTAH

In the middle of the Great Basin between the Rocky Mountains and the Sierra Nevada, Utah was an arid and uninviting region. After Joseph Smith, the founder of the Church of Jesus Christ of Latter-day Saints (Mormons), was shot in Illinois, Brigham Young led his people west, ultimately to the Salt Lake Valley in 1847. The chief obstacle to statehood was polygamy, which the church eventually renounced. There was an influx of non-Mormons after the discovery of silver in 1863, but Mormons still comprise two-thirds of the state's population, and the state remains conservative in outlook. Although the federal government is a major employer, government policy has lately been challenged by increased concern over the issues of chemical weapons testing, the MX missile, and disposal of nuclear waste from the Rocky Mountain Arsenal in neighborhing Colorado.

Name For Ute Indians. **Nicknames** Beehive State, Mormon State. **Capital** Salt Lake City. **Entered Union** Jan. 4, 1896 (45th). **Motto:** "Industry."

Emblems Animal Elk. **Bird** California Gull. **Emblem** Beehive **Fish** Rainbow Trout **Flower** Sego lily. **Gem** Topaz. **Song** "Utah, We Love Thee." **Tree** Blue spruce.

Land Total area 84,899 sq. mi. (11th), incl. 2,826 sq. mi. inland water. **Borders** Idaho, Wyo., Colo., Ariz., Nev. **Rivers** Bear, Colorado, Green, Sevier. **Lakes** Bear, Great Salt, Utah. **Mountains** La Sal, Uinta (Kings Peak 13,528 ft.) Wasatch Range.

Other notable features Great Salt Lake Desert (Bonneville Salt Flats) Kaibab Plateau.
Elected officials Gov. Michael O. Leavitt (R, term exp. 2000). Lt. Gov./Sec. State Olene Walker (R). Atty. Gen. Jan Graham (D).
People (1998) 2,099,758 (34th). **Race/national origin** (1990): White 93.8%. Black 0.7%. Indian 1.4%. Asian 1.9%. Other 2.2%. Hispanic 4.9%.
Cities (1996 estimate) Salt Lake City 172,575. Provo 99,606. West Valley City 99,136. Sandy 94,593. Orem 79,736. Ogden 65,720. West Jordan 57,600. Layton 50,906. St. George 42,763. Bountiful 39,595.
Business   Gross State Product, 1997: $55.42 bil. (35th). **Leading Sectors of GSP** (1997): Services 19.37%; Finance, insurance, and real estate 16.46%; Manufacturing 15.52%. *Fortune* **500 Companies** (1998): 2: American Stores, Autoliv.
Famous natives Maude Adams, actress. John Moses Browning, inventor. Philo Farnsworth, engineer. Merlin Olsen, football player/actor. Ivy Baker Priest, U.S. treasurer. Brigham Young (b. Vt.), religious leader. Loretta Young, actress.
Noteworthy places Arches Natl. Park. Bryce Canyon Natl. Park. Canyonlands Natl. park. Capitol Reef Natl. Park. Cedar Breaks Natl. Monument. Dinosaur Natl. Monument. Flaming Gorge Dam Natl. Monument. Great Salt Lake. Lake Powell Natl. Monument. Monument Valley. Mormon Tabernacle, Salt Lake City. Natural Bridges Natl. Monument. Promontory Point. Rainbow Bridge Natl. Monument. Temple Square, Salt Lke City. Timpanogos Cave Natl. Monument. Zion Natl. Park.
Memorable events First visted probably by explorers from Coronado expedition 1540. Silvestre Vélez de Escalante and Francisco Atanasio Dominguez explore for Spain 1776. James Bridger discovers Great Salt Lake 1824. Led by Brigham Young, Mormons reach Great Salt Lake 1847. United States acquires Utah region from Mexico 1848. Mormons organize state of Deseret 1849; Congress refuses to recognize and instead organizes Territory of Utah 1850. Silver discovered at Little Cottonwood Canyon 1868. First transcontinental railroad completed with driving of golden spike at Promontory Point 1869. Mormon church renounces polygamy 1890, paving way to statehood 1896. Uranium discovered near Moab 1952. Winter Olympics to be held in Salt Lake City 2002.
Tourist Information   1-800-200-1160.
www.state.ut.us.

▶**VERMONT**
Originally claimed by both New Hampshire and New York, Vermont's independence was asserted by Ethan Allen. His Green Mountain Boys rid the state of New Yorkers in 1770, fought well against the British in the Revolution, and declared the independent republic of New Connecticut in 1777. Allen was eventually overthrown, and Vermont joined the Union in 1791.

Vermont traditionally has strong ties to Canada, and there was an influx of French-Canadians as Vermont began to develop its manufacturing base in the mid-19th century. Vermont's politics have always been characterized by tolerance and progressivism. As New Connecticut, it abolished slavery and allowed universal male suffrage. Vermont's environmental concerns focus on acid rain and the degree to which development (especially by the tourist industry) should infringe on the state's remaining unspoiled land.

Name From French *vert mont,* "green mountain." **Nickname** Green Mountain State. **Capital** Montpelier. **Entered Union** Mar. 4, 1791 (14th). **Motto** "Freedom and unity."
Emblems Animal Morgan horse. **Beverage** Milk. **Bird** Hermit thrush. **Cold-Water Fish** Brook trout. **Flower** Red Clover. **Insect** Honeybee. Song "Hail, Vermont!" **Tree** Sugar Maple. **Warm-Water Fish** Walleye pike.
Land   Total Area 9,614 sq. mi. (43rd), incl. 341 sq. mi. inland water. **Borders** Quebec, N.H., Mass., N.Y. **Rivers** Connecticut, Lamoille, Otter Creek, Poultney, White, Winooski. **Lakes** Bomoseen, Champlain, Memphremagog, Willoughby. **Other Notable Features** Grand Isle, Green Mts. (Mt. Mansfield 4,393 ft.), Taconic Mts.
Elected officials   Gov. Howard Dean (D, term exp. 2003). Lt. Gov. Douglas Racine (D). Sec. State Deborah Markowitz (D). Atty. Gen. William H. Sorrell (D).
People (1998) 590,883 (49th). **Race/national origin** (1990): White 98.6%. Black 0.2%. Indian 0.1%. Asian 0.2%. Other 0.2%. Hispanic 0.5%.
Cities (1996 estimate) Burlington 39,004. Rutland 17,605. South Burlington 13,860. Barre 9,206. Essex Junction 8,546. Montpelier 7,856. St. Albans 7,370. Winooski 6,651. Newport 4,384. Bellows Falls 3,195.
Business   Gross State Product, 1997: $15.21 bil. (50th). **Leading Sectors of GSP** (1997): Services 21.05%; Finance, insurance, and real estate 18.07%; Manufacturing 17.95%. *Fortune* **500 Companies** (1998): 0.
Famous natives Ethan Allen (b. Conn.), army officer. Chester A. Arthur, U.S. President. Calvin Coolidge, U.S. president. John Deere, industrialist. George Dewey, naval officer. John Dewey, philosopher. Stephen Douglas, politician. James Fisk, financier. Robert Frost (b. Calif.), poet. Rudy Vallee, singer.
Noteworthy places Bennington Battleground/ Monument. Calvin Coolidge Homestead, Plymouth. Maple Grove Maple Museum, Rock of Ages Tourist Center, Graniteville. Shelburne Museum. St. Johnsbury. Vermont Marble Exhibit, Proctor.
Memorable events Samuel de Champlain explores for France 1609. First French settlement at Ste. Anne 1666. First English settlers build Ft. Drummer near Brattleboro 1724. Bennington settled 1761. Ethan Allen organizes Green Mountain Boys 1764. Green Mountain Boys capture Ft. Ticonderoga and Ft. Crown Point 1775. Gen. John Stark defeats British general John Burgoyne near Bennington; constitution abolishes slavery and grants universal male suffrage 1777. Claims to area relinquished by Massachusetts (1781), New Hampshire (1782), and New York (1790). First state admitted after original 13 1791. MacDonough defeats British Lake Champlain fleet 1814. Canal between Hudson River and Lake Champlain gives Vermont direct access to port of New York 1823. Confederate soldiers steal $400,000 from St. Albans bank 1864. Blue law repealed, allowing stores to open on Sundays 1982.
Tourist Information   1-800-VERMONT
www.state.vt.us.

▶**VIRGINIA, COMMONWEALTH OF**
The first successful English settlement in America was at Jamestown in 1607. The differences between the Virginia colonists and those of Massachusetts were pronounced, and the commercial southern planter class shared little of their New England counterparts' religious zeal. Virginia bred its own strain of independence, and it was the fiery Patrick Henry who heralded the

American Revolution with the cry "Give me liberty or give me death." Seven of the first 12 presidents were from Virginia. With an economy very dependent on labor-intensive tobacco in the mid-19th century, Virginia seceded from the Union over the slavery issue, despite the misgivings of many, including Robert E. Lee. After the war Virginia developed an increasingly diversified industrial and manufacturing base that survives today, with food products, tobacco, and chemicals leading the way. Despite the dramatic decline of the American merchant marine, Virginia's shipbuilding industry in Newport News flourished in the 1980s, thanks to the Pentagon's commitment to a 600-ship navy. Norfolk is also one of the country's leading commercial ports.

Name For Elizabeth I, called Virgin Queen. **Nicknames** Old Dominion, Mother of Presidents, Mother of States. **Capital** Richmond. **Entered union** June 25, 1788 (10th). **Motto** *Sic semper tyrannis* (Thus always to tyrants).
Emblems **Beverage** Milk. **Bird** Cardinal. **Dog** Foxhound. **Flower** Dogwood. **Shell** Oyster. **Song** "Carry Me Back to Old Virginia." **Tree** Dogwood.
Land Total area 40,767 sq. mi. (36th), incl. 1,063 sq. mi. inland water. **Borders** Md., D.C., Atlantic Ocean, N.C., Tenn., Ky., W.Va. **Rivers** James, Potomac, Rappahannock, Roanoke, Shenandoah, York. **Lakes** Buggs Island, Claytor, Gaston, Leesville. **Mountains** Allegheny, Blue Ridge, Cumberland, Unaka. **Other notable features** Great Dismal Swamp, Shenandoah Valley.
Elected officials Gov. Jim Gilmore (R, term exp. 2002). Lt. Gov. John H. Hager (R). Sec. Commonwealth Anne P. Petera (R). Atty. Gen. Mark L. Earley (R).
People (1998) 6,791,345 (12th). **Race/national origin** (1990): White 77.4%. Black 18.8%. Indian 0.2%. Asian 2.6%. Other 0.9%. Hispanic 2.6%.
Cities (1996 estimate) Virginia Beach 430,385. Norfolk 233,430. Richmond 198,267. Chesapeake 192,342. Newport News 176,122. Arlington 175,334. Hampton 138,757. Alexandria 117,586. Portsmouth 101,308. Roanoke 95,548.
Business Gross State Product, 1997: $211.33 bil. (13th). **Leading Sectors of GSP** (1997): Services 20.54%; Finance, insurance, and real estate 18.24%; Government 18.18%. *Fortune* **500 Companies** (1998): 18: Mobil, Freddie Mac, CSX, Circuit City Group, USAirways Group, Fort James, Columbia Energy Group, Dominion Resources, Reynolds Metals, Gannett, General Dynamics, Norfolk Southern, Universal, Smithfield Foods, Pittston, Richfood Holdings, Owens & Minor, SLM Holding.
Famous natives Richard E. Byrd, explorer/aviator. William Clark, explorer. Jerry Falwell, evangelist. William Henry Harrison, U.S. president. Patrick Henry, Revolutionary patriot. Thomas Jefferson, U.S. president. Joseph E. Johnston, Confederate general. John Paul Jones (b. Scotland), navy officer. Robert E. Lee, Confederate general. Meriwether Lewis, explorer. James Madison, U.S. president. John Marshall, jurist. Cyrus Hall McCormick, inventor. James Monroe, U.S. president. Walter Reed, doctor. Pat Robertson, evangelist/politician. Bill "Bojangles" Robinson, dancer. George C. Scott, actor. Thomas Sumter, army officer. Zachary Taylor, U.S. president. John Tyler, U.S. president. Booker T. Washington, educator. George Washington, U.S. president. Woodrow Wilson, U.S. president.
Noteworthy places Appomattox Courthouse Natl. Hist Park. Arlington Natl. Cemetery. Booker T. Washington Natl. Monument, Roanoke. Colonial Natl. Hist. Park (incl. Jamestown, Yorktown & Williamsburg). Fredericksburg and Spotsylvania Natl. Military Park. George Washington birthplace, Frederick Co. Harpers Ferry Natl. Hist. Site. The Mariners' Museum, Newport News. Monticello, Charlottesville. Mount Vernon. Petersburg Natl. Battlefield. Robert E. Lee Memorial, Lexington. Shenandoah Natl. Park. Virginia Beach. Virginia Museum of Fine Arts. Wolf Trap Farm for the Performing Arts, Reston.
Memorable events John Smith founds Jamestown, first permanent settlement in North America, 1607. John Rolfe marries Pocahontas, daughter of Powhatan, leader of so-called Powhatan Confederacy 1614. First English women arrive at Jamestown; House of Burgesses established 1619. Northampton Declaration first resistance to taxation without representation 1653. College of William and Mary founded 1693. First state to establish Committee of Correspondence 1773. American Revolution ends with Charles Cornwallis's surrender to George Washington at Yorktown 1781. Nat Turner's slave revolt 1831. State secedes from Union 1861. Civil War ends with Robert E. Lee's surrender to Ulysses S. Grant at Appomattox Courthouse 1865. Readmitted to Union 1870. Norfolk Naval Base founded 1917. John D. Rockefeller, Jr. undertakes restoration of Colonial Williamsburg 1926. E. Claiborne Robins donates $50 million to University of Richmond 1969. Douglas Wilder becomes nation's first black governor in 1989.
Tourist information 1-800-VISIT-VA. **www.state.va.us.**

▶ WASHINGTON

The northwest corner of the continental United States was originally the locus of a rich Native American culture noted today primarily for its ornately carved canoes and totem poles. In 1792, Boston merchant Capt. Robert Gray began a trade in sea otter pelts; but the first permanent settlers in the region did not establish themselves for almost 50 years. Agriculture and lumbering were, and remain, mainstays of the state's economy—the farming regions in the east, rich in dairy products, fruit and wheat, and the lumber industry in the western part of the state rely heavily on exports to the Far East. This geographic split reflects the weather patterns: eastern Washington rarely gets more than 10 inches of rain in a year, while on the Pacific coast almost 40 inches is the average.

Since World War I, Puget Sound has been a center of heavy industry and shipbuilding, and 60 percent of the population is concentrated in the region. Boeing maintains one of the country's largest airplane-manufacturing plants in the Seattle-Tacoma area, and Microsoft, the world's leading software company, is located in Redmond. The industrial work force was open to progressive and sometimes radical unionism, and the International Workers of the World (Wobblies) had their national headquarters at Seattle. Before statehood the territorial government pioneered women's suffrage, but Congress declared the women's right to vote unconstitutional.

Name For George Washington. **Nickname** Evergreen State. **Capital** Olympia. **Entered union** Nov. 11, 1889 (42nd). **Motto** *Alki* (By and by).
Emblems **Bird** Willow goldfinch. **Fish** Steelhead trout. **Flower** Western rhododendron. **Gem** Petrified wood. **Song** "Washington, My Home." **Tree** Western hemlock.
Land Total area 68,138 sq. mi. (20th), incl. 1,627 sq. mi. inland water. **Borders** British Columbia,

Idaho, Oreg., Pacific Ocean. **Rivers** Chehalis, Columbia, Pend Oreille, Snake, Yakima. **Lakes** Baker, Bank, Chelan, Franklin D. Roosevelt, Ross, Rufus Woods. **Mountains** Cascade Range, Coast Range, Kettle River Range, Olympic. **Other notable features** Puget Sound, San Juan Islands, Strait of Juan de Fuca.

Elected officials Gov. Gary Locke (D, term exp. 2001). Lt. Gov. Brad Owen (D). Sec. State Ralph Munro (R). Atty. Gen. Christine Gregoire (D).

People (1998) 5,689,263 (15th). **Race/national origin** (1990): White 88.5%. Black 3.1%. Indian 1.7%. Asian 4.3%. Other 2.4%. Hispanic 4.4%.

Cities (1996 estimate) Seattle 524,704. Spokane 186,562. Tacoma 179,114. Bellevue 92,267. Everett 81,028. Federal Way 68,088. Yakima 65,110. Bellingham 61,043. Vancouver 59,982. Kennewick 51,184.

Business Gross State Product, 1997: $172.25 bil. (14th). **Leading Sectors of GSP** (1997): Services 21.61%; Finance, insurance, and real estate 18.20%; Government 14.25%. *Fortune* **500 Companies** (1998): 10: Boeing, Costco, Microsoft, Washington Mutual, Weyerhaeuser, Paccar, Safeco, Nordstrom, Avista Corp. Airborne Freight.

Famous natives Harry L. "Bing" Crosby, singer. Merce Cunningham, choreographer. Jimi Hendrix, guitarist. Henry M. "Scoop" Jackson, politician. Robert Joffrey, choreographer. Theodore Roethke (b. Mich.), poet. Marcus Whitman (b. N.Y.), missionary/pioneer.

Noteworthy places Klondike Gold Rush Natl. Hist. Park, Seattle. Mount Rainier Natl. Park. Mount Saint Helens Natl. Monument. North Cascades Natl. Park. Olympic Natl. Park. San Juan Islands Natl. Hist. Park. Seattle Art Museum.

Memorable events Sir Francis Drake skirts coast of Pacific Northwest 1579. Juan de Fuca sails into straits now bearing his name. Bruno de Heceta lands at Hoh River 1775. Capt. James Cook arrives 1778. Capt. Robert Gray discovers mouth of Columbia River, which he names for his ship; George Vancouver explores Puget Sound 1792. Lewis and Clark expedition winters at Columbia River 1805. Marcus Whitman, Protestant Mission Board, settles near Walla Walla 1836. Territorial status 1853. Northern Pacific railroad reaches Puget Sound 1883. Alaska-Yukon-Pacific Exposition at Seattle 1909. Grand Coulee Dam, largest concrete hydroelectric dam in United States, completed 1941. Hanford works atomic energy plant opens 1943. Upholding treaty provisions from Washington's days as a territory, a decision awards Native Americans half the catch of Northwest salmon and steelhead 1974. Mt. Saint Helens erupts, killing 26, 1980. Washington Public Power Supply System (known as "whoops") defaults on $8.25 billion bond issue 1983. Reports linking growth-enhancing chemical Alar to cancer generate $140 million loss for Washington's apple growers 1988.

Tourist information 1-800-544-1800. **www.state.wa.us.**

▶ WEST VIRGINIA

When Virginia seceded in 1861, its western counties reorganized and in 1863 were admitted to the Union as a separate state. Despite the rugged terrain, through which transportation has always been difficult, farming remained the backbone of the economy until the close of the 19th century, when coal mining and other extractive industries developed. After World War II, the manufacturing base developed to include steel and chemical manufacturing. Even with vast natural resources,

West Virginia has long been one of the poorest states in the union. Population losses since the 1950s have been pronounced, and the 8 percent loss between 1980 and 1990 was the highest in the country. There is low participation in the workforce by women and educational achievement is well below the national average.

Name for western part of Virginia. **Nickname** Mountain State. **Capital** Charleston. **Entered union** June 20, 1863 (35th). **Motto** *Montani semper liberi* (Mountaineers are always free).

Emblems Animal Black bear. **Bird** Cardinal. **Colors** Old gold and blue. **Fish** Brook trout. **Flower** *Rhododendron maximum* (big laurel). **Fruit** Apple. **Songs** "The West Virginia Hills," "West Virginia, My Home Sweet Home," "This Is My West Virginia." **Tree** Sugar maple.

Land Total area 24,231 sq. mi. (41st), incl. 112 sq. mi. inland water. **Borders** Ohio, Pa., Md., Va., Ky. **Rivers** Big Sandy, Guayandotte, Kanawha, Little Kanawha, Monongahela, Ohio, Potomac. **Lakes** Summersville Dam. **Mountains** Allegheny, Blue Ridge, Cumberland.

Elected officials Gov. Cecil H. Underwood (R, term exp. 2000). Sec. State Ken Hechler (D). Atty. Gen. Darrell V. McGraw (D).

People (1998) 1,811,156 (35th).**Race/national origin** (1990): White 96.2%. Black 3.1%. Indian 0.1%. Asian 0.4%. Other 0.1%. Hispanic 0.5%.

Cities (1996 estimate) Charleston 56,098. Huntington 53,941. Wheeling 33,311. Parkersburg 32,766. Morgantown 26,919. Weirton 21,731. Fairmont 19,731. Beckley 18,353. Clarksburg 17,410. Martinsburg 14,541.

Business Gross State Product, 1997: $38.23 bil. (38th). **Leading Sectors of GSP** (1997): Manufacturing 17.48%; Services 16.83%; Government 14.05%. *Fortune* **500 Companies** (1998): 0.

Famous natives Newton D. Baker, politician. Pearl Buck, novelist (Nobel Prize, 1938). John W. Davis, politician. Dwight Whitney Morrow, lawyer/diplomat. Michael Owens, manufacturer. Walter Reuther, labor leader. Cyrus Vance, statesman. Jerry West, basketball player. Charles "Chuck" Yeager, pilot.

Noteworthy places Cass Scenic Railroad. Harpers Ferry Natl. Hist. Park. Monongahela Natl. Forest. New River Gorge Bridge. Science and Cultural Center, Charleston.

Memorable events First permanent settlement by Morgan Morgan at Mill Creek 1731. Coal discovered on Coal River 1742. Wheeling Convention repudiates act of secession; forms new state of Kanahwa 1861. Enters Union as West Virginia 1863. Population peaks at 2.5 million 1950. Unemployment jumps 8.6% to 18.0%, highest in nation, 1980–83.

Tourist information 1-800-CALL-WVA. **www.state.wv.us.**

▶ WISCONSIN

The indigenous people of the region had a largely agricultural economy, but the fur trade drew Europeans into the region. Native resistance to white settlement was strong and not overcome until the Black Hawk Wars of 1832. In the early 19th century, German, Scandinavian, and Dutch farmers migrated to the region in large numbers. Many social welfare policies now common to the nation as a whole—including aid to dependent children, workmen's compensation, and old-age assistance—were pioneered in Wisconsin. Although manufacturing accounts for the lion's share of Wisconsin's profits, agriculture is extremely important, and the state is the nation's leading producer of dairy products. There are major shipping facilities at Superior, Green Bay, and Milwaukee.

Name From the Ojibwa *wishkonsing,* "place of the bearer." **Nickname** Badger State. **Capital** Madison. **Entered union** May 29, 1848 (30th). **Motto** "Forward."

Emblems **Animal** Badger. **Bird** Robin. **Domestic animal** Dairy cow. **Fish** Muskellunge. **Flower** Wood violet. **Insect** Honeybee. **Mineral** Galena. **Rock** Red granite. **Soil** Antigo silt loam. **Song** "Oh, Wisconsin!" **Symbol of peace** Mourning dove. **Tree** Sugar maple. **Wildlife animal** White-tailed deer. **Land** Total area 56,153 sq. mi. (26th), incl. 1,727 sq. mi. inland water. **Borders** Minn., Lake Superior, Mich., Lake Michigan, Ill., Iowa. **Rivers** Black, Chippewa, Menominee, Mississippi, St. Croix, Wisconsin. **Lakes** Chippewa, Du Bay, Mendota, Michigan, Superior, Winnebago. **Other notable features** Apostle Islands, Door Peninsula, Green Bay.

Elected officials Gov. Tommy G. Thompson (R, term exp. 2003). Lt. Gov. Scott McCallum (R). Sec. State Douglas La Follette (D). Atty. Gen. James Doyle (D).

People (1998) 5,223,500 (18th). **Race/national origin** (1990): White 92.2%. Black 5.0%. Indian 0.8%. Asian 1.1%. Other 0.9%. Hispanic 1.9%.

Cities (1996 estimate) Milwaukee 590,503. Madison 197,630. Green Bay 102,076. Kenosha 86,888. Racine 82,572. Appleton 65,862. West Allis 60,550. Waukesha 60,197. Janesville 58,960. Eau Claire 58,872.

Business **Gross State Product,** 1997: $147.33 bil. (19th). **Leading Sectors of GSP** (1997): Manufacturing 27.75%; Services 16.76%; Finance, insurance, and real estate 16.24%. *Fortune* **500 Companies** (1998): 9: Northwestern Mutual Life Insurance, Johnson Controls, Manpower, Case, American Family Insurance Group, Kohl's, Firstar, Aid Association for Lutherans, Shopko Stores.

Famous natives King Camp Gillette, inventor/businessman. Eric Heiden, speed skater. Harry Houdini (b. Hungary), magician. Robert La Follette, politician. Liberace (Wladziu Valentino), pianist. Alfred Lunt, actor. Joseph R. McCarthy, politician. Spencer Tracy, actor. Thorstein Veblen, economist. Orson Welles, director. Laura Ingalls Wilder, novelist. Thornton Wilder, author. Frank Lloyd Wright, architect.

Noteworthy places Apostle Island Natl. Lakeshore. Chequamegon Natl. Forest. Circus World Museum, Baraboo. Door County Peninsula. Ice Age Natl. Scientific Reserve. Manitowoc Maritime Museum. Milwaukee Art Museum. Milwaukee Public Museum. Nicolet Natl. Forest. Old Wade House and Carriage Museum, Greenbush. Old World Wisconsin, Eagle. Villa Louis, Prairie du Chien. Wisconsin Dells.

Memorable events Jean Nicolet lands at Green Bay 1634. French establish mission and trading post near Ashland 1634. British take control of region 1763. Land ceded to United States 1787, but U.S. control not established until after War of 1812. Becomes independent Territory 1836. Statehood 1848. More than 800 die in forest fire near Peshtigo 1871. First hydroelectric plant completed at Appleton 1882. Ringling Brothers circus formed at Baraboo 1884. First state to enact income tax 1911. Milwaukee transfers more than 11,000 students between city and suburban schools 1986. **Tourist information** 1-800-432-TRIP or 1-800-372-2737. **www.state.wi.us.**

▶ WYOMING

Tens of thousands of migrants traveled through the region along the Oregon Trail, but few settled the land until Ft. Laramie was built in 1834. Territorial status came in 1869. Wyoming was the first state to give the vote to women, and in 1925 Nellie Tayloe Ross became the first woman governor following the death of her husband. Cattle ranching is the traditional mainstay of the economy. The state ranks second in uranium output, petroleum and coal production have become increasingly important. Wyoming is best known for its natural wonders. Yellowstone National Park—the site of Old Faithful—is the oldest and largest national park in the country. Following a decade-long mining boom in the 1970s and 1980s, Wyoming's population declined, and it has fallen behind even Alaska in total population. Although the population has increased in the 1990s, there are still no more than five people per square mile.

Name From the Delaware *maugh-wau-wa-ma,* "large plains" or "mountains and valleys alternating." **Nickname** Equality State. **Capital** Cheyenne. **Entered union** July 10, 1890 (44th). **Motto** "Equal rights."

Emblems **Bird** Meadowlark. **Flower** Indian paintbrush. **Gem** Jade. **Song** "Wyoming." **Tree** Cottonwood.

Land Total area 97,809 sq. mi. (9th), incl. 820 sq. mi. inland water. **Borders** Mont., S.Dak., Nebr., Colo., Utah, Idaho. **Rivers** Bighorn, Green, North Platte, Powder, Snake, Yellowstone. **Lakes** Bighorn, Yellowstone. **Mountains** Absaroka, Bighorn, Black Hills, Laramie, Owl Creek, Teton Range, Wind River Range, Wyoming Range.

Elected officials Gov. Jim Geringer (R, term exp. 2003). Sec. State Joe Meyer (R). Atty. Gen. Gay Woodhouse (R).

People (1998) 480,907 (50th). **Race/national origin** (1990): White 94.2%. Black 0.8%. Indian 2.1%. Asian 0.6%. Other 2.3%. Hispanic 5.7%.

Cities (1996 estimate) Cheyenne 53,729. Casper 48,800. Laramie 26,583. Rock Springs 19,742. Gillette 19,202. Sheridan 14,730. Green River 13,289. Evanston 11,514. Riverton 10,050. Rawlins 8,947.

Business **Gross State Product,** 1997: $17.56 bil. (48th). **Leading Sectors of GSP** (1997): Mining 31.39%; Transportation & public utilities 13.17%; Government 12.56%. *Fortune* **500 Companies** (1998): 0.

Famous natives James Bridger (b. Va.), pioneer. J.C. Penney, businessman. Jackson Pollock, painter. Nellie Tayloe Ross (b. Mo.), politician.

Noteworthy places Buffalo Bill Museum, Cody. Devil's Tower Natl. Monument. Ft. Bridger State Park. Ft. Laramie Natl. Hist. Site. Fossil Butte Natl. Monument. Grand Teton Natl. Park. Natl. Elk Refuge. Yellowstone Natl. Park (Old Faithful).

Memorable events Part of Louisiana Territory claimed for France 1682. Pierre Gaultier de Varennes, sieur de Vérendrye explores region for France 1743. Region to United States with Louisiana Purchase 1803. John Colter crosses area of Yellowstone 1807–08. Indian Wars follow massacre of army detachments 1854 and 1866. Wyoming Territory organized 1868. Women's suffrage adopted permanently (first instance in United States); Union Pacific railroad crosses state 1869. Yellowstone, world's first national park, opens 1872. White mob kills 28 Chinese miners and burns Chinatown in Rock Springs 1885. Statehood 1890. Nellie Tayloe Ross first woman governor 1925. First Intercontinental Ballistic

Missile (ICBM) base opens near Cheyenne 1951. Fires consume 1.6 million acres of land in and around Yellowstone Park 1988.

Tourist information   1-800-CALL-WYO.
www.state.wy.us.

STATE GOVERNMENT FINANCES

▶REVENUES AND EXPENDITURES

Revenues

Revenue of state governments from all sources in 1997 was $1.04 trillion, a 7 percent increase over the year before. Taxes accounted for 42.6 percent, or $443.3 billion of the total state general revenue. Another 22 percent of state revenues came from the federal government. Sales taxes and gross receipts accounted for about another 23 percent, while individual income taxes made up 13.9 percent of general revenue. Charges were responsible for 7.0 percent of state revenues.

Expenditures
State government expenditures in 1997 totaled $893.8 billion, an increase of 3.9 percent from the amount spent in 1996. State general expenditures amounted to $788.2 billion, 4.4 percent more than in 1996. The leading expenditure categories, by function, were education services (31 percent), public welfare programs (23 percent), highways (7 percent) and health and hospitals (7 percent).

State Tax Collections Per Capita, By Type, 1998

State	Total taxes[1]	Property taxes	Sales taxes	Licenses	Income taxes Individual	Corporate
U.S. Total	$1,760.69	$39.52	$842.94	$110.03	$597.72	$115.31
Alabama	1,317.58	32.13	687.86	99.82	412.12	56.02
Alaska	1,931.95	79.01	190.23	153.64	0.00	449.11
Arizona	1,488.50	54.01	858.54	49.94	399.09	113.11
Arkansas	1,598.15	3.58	828.04	93.52	547.73	99.62
California	2,072.87	118.49	811.58	95.99	850.55	171.05
Colorado	1,485.37	2.05	583.85	69.96	725.65	68.28
Connecticut	2,869.09	0.00	1,441.79	109.96	1,040.27	163.39
Delaware	2,664.69	0.00	342.82	872.91	1,023.99	276.05
Florida	1,509.33	66.02	1,134.85	96.80	0.00	85.23
Georgia	1,516.51	4.95	653.22	51.92	695.79	96.80
Hawaii	2,662.40	0.00	1,602.47	77.66	908.12	51.76
Idaho	1,674.46	0.00	775.39	159.56	633.94	95.79
Illinois	1,641.41	17.11	756.44	100.26	580.06	162.85
Indiana	1,652.33	0.57	747.36	36.72	689.09	157.35
Iowa	1,677.77	0.00	773.59	158.21	642.28	68.77
Kansas	1,767.90	17.53	827.86	81.33	663.35	116.36
Kentucky	1,807.48	92.47	827.52	113.48	614.29	84.76
Louisiana	1,392.10	5.22	732.22	104.54	332.07	82.29
Maine	1,904.62	34.60	916.78	95.27	728.45	86.10
Maryland	1,789.84	47.03	748.38	68.33	806.10	73.75
Massachusetts	2,356.95	0.02	711.01	73.30	1,306.62	220.41
Michigan	2,209.66	159.84	967.83	112.56	691.96	239.86
Minnesota	2,434.48	2.07	1,043.93	185.18	1,005.16	159.39
Mississippi	1,578.23	8.41	1,046.69	108.12	307.79	88.77
Missouri	1,511.86	3.08	698.65	105.72	619.97	65.81
Montana	1,512.74	237.97	307.64	173.37	534.51	102.74
Nebraska	1,583.68	2.99	792.38	101.66	585.73	85.49
Nevada	1,847.96	41.20	1,569.41	192.34	0.00	0.00
New Hampshire	851.04	0.49	420.20	105.25	52.15	199.31
New Jersey	1,922.98	0.31	942.74	92.82	688.92	145.17
New Mexico	2,057.96	21.32	1,123.10	108.22	460.01	103.64
New York	1,989.21	0.00	683.51	53.19	1,006.26	172.08
North Carolina	1,837.86	0.03	759.98	111.54	811.60	132.48
North Dakota	1,689.60	3.60	955.76	124.96	278.69	129.33
Ohio	1,573.92	1.52	741.44	129.97	621.60	68.32
Oklahoma	1,583.89	0.00	600.47	223.11	563.31	66.52
Oregon	1,523.20	0.02	204.55	154.14	1,047.72	85.07
Pennsylvania	1,718.92	12.46	807.21	181.71	502.01	130.22
Rhode Island	1,804.70	1.52	872.87	88.67	744.21	70.53
South Carolina	1,481.54	3.02	754.51	105.56	544.18	55.69
South Dakota	1,129.36	0.00	895.95	142.12	0.00	51.84
Tennessee	1,288.27	0.00	979.75	120.85	29.62	111.85
Texas	1,246.43	0.00	1,006.27	178.85	0.00	0.00
Utah	1,646.70	0.00	806.40	71.16	654.61	91.47
Vermont	1,620.72	16.91	717.59	110.95	618.76	77.66
Virginia	1,552.41	3.13	575.92	67.06	795.93	65.62
Washington	2,075.17	359.86	1,526.17	92.95	0.00	0.00
West Virginia	1,663.02	1.50	860.14	87.79	478.21	122.31
Wisconsin	2,134.54	14.48	878.14	122.04	966.31	130.30
Wyoming	1,779.38	205.83	837.45	164.58	0.00	0.00

1. Includes other taxes not shown separately.   **Source:** U.S. Bureau of the Census, *State Government Tax Collections, 1998.*

Summary of State Government Finances, 1995–97

Item	Amount (millions) 1995	Amount (millions) 1997	Per Capita 1997	Item	Amount (millions) 1995	Amount (millions) 1997	Per Capita 1997
TOTAL REVENUES	**$903,756**	**$1,039,423**	**$3,891.41**	General expenditure	$733,503	$788,176	$ 2,950.79
General Revenue	739,016	814,382	3,048.90	Intergovernmental	240,978	264,207	989.14
Intergovernmental revenue	215,558	230,592	863.30	expenditure			
Taxes	399,148	443,335	1,659.77	Direct expenditure	492,525	523,969	1,961.64
Sales and gross receipts	222,934	243,954	913.32	General expenditure, by function:			
				Education	249,670	275,821	1,032.62
Individual income	125,610	144,668	541.61	Public Welfare	194,854	203,204	760.76
Corporation net income	29,075	30,662	114.79	Hospitals	29,139	29,313	109.74
				Health	30,865	33,880	126.84
Other Taxes	21,528	24,052	90.05	Highways	57,374	60,204	225.39
Current charges	64,774	72,303	270.69	Police protection	6,451	7,501	28.08
Miscellaneous general revenue	59,536	68,151	255.15	Correction	26,069	29,043	108.73
				Natural resources	12,534	12,909	48.33
Utility revenue	3,845	4,046	15.15	Parks and recreation	3,403	3,900	14.60
Liquor stores revenue	3,073	3,292	12.32	Governmental administration	26,078	28,656	107.28
Insurance trust revenue	157,821	217,703	815.04	Interest on general debt	24,485	26,310	98.50
				Other and unallocable	72,648	77,434	289.90
TOTAL EXPENDITURES	**$836,894**	**$893,827**	**$3,346.32**	Utility expenditure	7,586	7,783	29.14
Intergovernmental expenditure	240,978	264,207	989.14	Liquor stores expenditure	2,522	2,697	10.10
Direct expenditure	595,916	629,620	2,357.18	Insurance trust expenditure	93,282	95,172	356.31
Current operation	396,035	425,899	1,594.49				
Capital outlay	57,829	59,658	223.35	**Debt at end**	**$427,239**	**$455,697**	**$1,706.05**
Insurance benefits and repayments	93,282	95,172	356.31	**of fiscal year**			
Assistance and subsidies	23,511	21,867	81.87	**Cash and Security**	**$1,388,527**	**$1,784,947**	**$6,682.52**
Interest on debt	25,259	27,025	101.18	**holdings**			
Exhibit: Salaries and wages	125,432	135,598	507.65				

Source: U.S. Bureau of the Census, *State Government Finances in 1997* (1998).

State Government Individual Income Taxes, 1998

State	Taxable income rate range	Taxable income brackets Lowest: amount under	Taxable income brackets Highest: amount over	State	Taxable income rate range	Taxable income brackets Lowest: amount under	Taxable income brackets Highest: amount over
Alabama[1,2]	2.0–5.0%	$ 500	$ 3,000	**Missouri**[1,2]	1.5–6.0%	$ 1,000	$ 9,000
Arizona	2.9–5.17	10,000	150,000	**Montana**	2.0–11.0	1,900	67,900
Arkansas	1.0–7.0	3,000	25,000	**Nebraska**	2.51–6.68	2,400	26,500
California	1.0–9.3	4,908	32,207	**New Hampshire**	5.0% on dividend and interest		
Colorado	5.0% on modified federal taxable income				income over $1,200		
Connecticut	4.5% on income over $12,000			**New Jersey**	1.4–6.37	20,000	75,001
Delaware	3.1–6.9	5,000	30,000	**New Mexico**	1.7–8.5	5,500	65,000
District of Columbia	6.0–9.5	10,000	20,000	**New York**[2]	4.0–6.85	8,000	20,000
Georgia	1.0–6.0	750	7,000	**North Carolina**	6.0–7.75	12,750	60,000
Hawaii	2.0–10.0	1,500	20,500	**North Dakota**	14% of federal income tax liability		
Idaho[2]	2.0–8.2	1,000	20,000	**Ohio**[2]	0.71–7.2	5,000	200,000
Illinois	3.0% on income over $1,000			**Oklahoma**[1]	0.5–7.0	1,000	10,000
Indiana[2]	3.4% of federal adjusted gross income			**Oregon**[1,2,3]	5.0–9.0	2,250	5,700
Iowa[1]	0.4–9.98	1,112	50,000	**Pennsylvania**[2]	2.8% on taxable income		
Kansas	4.1–7.75	20,000	30,000	**Rhode Island**	27.5% of modified federal income		
Kentucky	2.0–6.0	3,000	8,000		tax liability		
Louisiana[1]	2.0–6.0	10,000	50,000	**South Carolina**	2.5–7.0	2,280	11,400
Maine	2.0–8.5	4,150	16,500	**Tennessee**	6.0% on interest and dividend income		
Maryland[2]	2.0–4.875	1,000	3,000	**Utah**[1,4]	2.55–7.2	750	3,750
Massachusetts	5.95% on earned income; 12.0%			**Vermont**	25% of federal income tax liability		
	on unearned income			**Virginia**	2.0–5.75	3,000	17,000
Michigan[2]	4.4% of federal adjusted gross income			**West Virginia**	3.0–6.5	10,000	60,000
Minnesota	6.0–8.5	14,780	48,550	**Wisconsin**	4.85–6.87	7,500	15,000
Mississippi	3.0–5.0	5,000	10,000				

Note: Rates and brackets shown are for single taxpayers. Brackets for married taxpayers filing jointly are double those shown, except in Maryland, where they are the same. Alaska, Florida, Nevada, South Dakota, Texas, Washington, and Wyoming have no state income tax. 1. State with a provision that allows the taxpayer to deduct fully the federal income tax payment. 2. States in which one or more local governments levy a local income tax. 3. Federal tax deduction limited to $3,000. 4. Only half of the federal income tax payment is deductible. **Source:** Government of the District of Columbia, Dept. of Finance and Revenue, *Tax Rates and Tax Burdens in the District of Columbia: A Nationwide Comparison* (July, 1998)

Revenues and Expenditures of State Governments, 1997

State	Revenues		Expenditures	
	Total ('000s)	Per capita (rank)	Total ('000s)	Per capita (rank)
Alabama	$14,007,883	$3,243.32 (41)	$12,944,867	$2,997.19 (35)
Alaska	9,438,512	15,498.38 (1)	5,722,455	9,396.48 (1)
Arizona	13,692,375	3,006.01 (47)	12,418,681	2,726.38 (46)
Arkansas	8,843,946	3,505.33 (32)	7,684,652	3,045.84 (33)
California	131,099,489	4,062.83 (20)	117,209,422	3,632.37 (18)
Colorado	12,779,639	3,282.72 (39)	10,861,228	2,789.94 (45)
Connecticut	14,519,780	4,440.30 (13)	13,826,021	4,228.14 (6)
Delaware	4,210,673	5,752.29 (2)	3,403,619	4,649.75 (3)
Florida	41,432,077	2,827.36 (50)	37,463,858	2,556.56 (49)
Georgia	24,028,450	3,209.78 (42)	21,975,372	2,935.53 (37)
Hawaii	6,700,545	5,644.94 (3)	6,093,375	5,133.42 (2)
Idaho	4,289,173	3,544.77 (31)	3,674,210	3,036.54 (34)
Illinois	39,038,066	3,281.61 (40)	35,301,874	2,967.54 (36)
Indiana	17,536,856	2,990.60 (48)	16,370,436	2,791.68 (44)
Iowa	9,509,064	3,334.17 (37)	9,347,768	3,277.62 (28)
Kansas	7,949,762	3,063.49 (45)	7,496,081	2,888.66 (40)
Kentucky	15,032,508	3,846.60 (26)	12,949,018	3,313.46 (24)
Louisiana	15,928,979	3,660.15 (29)	14,258,704	3,282.56 (27)
Maine	5,215,004	4,198.88 (17)	4,441,284	3,575.91 (20)
Maryland	20,128,472	3,951.41 (24)	16,199,545	3,180.12 (30)
Massachusetts	26,537,977	4,337.69 (15)	25,790,660	5,326.65 (7)
Michigan	45,509,221	4,656.15 (9)	36,092,175	3,692.67 (15)
Minnesota	22,881,630	4,882.98 (6)	18,443,264	3,935.82 (11)
Mississippi	9,400,400	3,442.11 (33)	9,005,740	3,297.60 (26)
Missouri	16,600,626	3,073.05 (44)	14,229,714	2,634.16 (48)
Montana	3,523,812	4,008.89 (23)	3,203,897	3,644.93 (17)
Nebraska	5,537,331	3,341.78 (36)	4,801,745	2,897.85 (38)
Nevada	6,494,347	3,872.60 (25)	5,129,625	3,058.81 (32)
New Hampshire	3,560,750	3,035.59 (46)	3,323,538	2,833.37 (42)
New Jersey	36,086,757	4,481.16 (12)	29,429,586	3,654.49 (16)
New Mexico	8,188,172	4,733.05 (8)	7,058,693	4,080.17 (8)
New York	95,442,410	5,262.30 (5)	83,243,290	4,589.69 (4)
North Carolina	25,526,697	3,437.94 (34)	22,864,451	3,079.39 (31)
North Dakota	2,817,603	4,395.64 (14)	2,425,660	3,784.18 (14)
Ohio	45,249,896	4,045.23 (21)	37,406,884	3,344.08 (23)
Oklahoma	11,327,842	3,415.09 (35)	9,592,711	2,891.98 (39)
Oregon	15,004,426	4,626.71 (10)	12,388,248	3,820.00 (13)
Pennsylvania	49,317,529	4,102.96 (19)	39,296,244	3,269.24 (29)
Rhode Island	4,229,308	4,285.01 (16)	4,001,776	4,054.48 (9)
South Carolina	13,804,751	3,671.48 (28)	12,847,221	3,416.81 (22)
South Dakota	2,315,652	3,137.74 (43)	2,070,482	2,805.53 (43)
Tennessee	15,696,299	2,924.05 (49)	14,284,301	2,661.01 (47)
Texas	63,864,034	3,285.36 (38)	48,887,370	2,514.91 (50)
Utah	7,723,664	3,751.17 (27)	6,817,750	3,311.19 (25)
Vermont	2,369,972	4,023.72 (22)	2,123,269	3,604.87 (19)
Virginia	24,322,031	3,611.83 (30)	19,286,506	2,864.05 (41)
Washington	26,841,468	4,784.58 (7)	22,206,885	3,958.45 (10)
West Virginia	7,466,718	4,111.63 (18)	7,145,479	3,934.74 (12)
Wisconsin	23,858,753	4,614.85 (11)	18,199,533	3,520.22 (21)
Wyoming	2,559,063	5,331.38 (4)	2,126,805	4,430.84 (5)

Source: U.S. Bureau of the Census, *1997 Survey of State Government Finances.*

Composition of State Legislatures, 1998–99

State or other jurisdiction	Senate Demo-crats	Repub-licans	Total	House Demo-crats	Repub-icans	Total	State or other jurisdiction	Senate Demo-crats	Repub-licans	Total	House Demo-crats	Repub-icans	Total
Alabama	**22**	13	35	**71**	34	105	New Jersey	16	**24**	40	32	**48**	80
Alaska	6	**14**	20	15	**25**	40	New Mexico	**25**	17	42	**42**	28	70
Arizona	12	**18**	30	22	**38**	60	New York	26	**35**	61	**95**	52	150[2]
Arkansas	**28**	7	35	**86**	14	100	North Carolina	**30**	20	50	59	**61**	120
California	**23**	16	40[1]	**42**	37	80[2]	North Dakota	18	**29**	49[2]	26	**71**	98[2]
Colorado	15	**20**	35	24	**41**	65	Ohio	12	**20**	33[1]	39	**60**	99
Connecticut	**19**	17	36	**96**	55	151	Oklahoma	**33**	15	48	**65**	36	101
Delaware	**13**	8	21	13	**28**	41	Oregon	10	**20**	30	29	**31**	60
Florida	17	**23**	40	57	**63**	120	Pennsylvania	20	**30**	50	99	**104**	203
Georgia	**34**	22	56	**102**	78	180	Rhode Island	**42**	8	50	**84**	16	100
Hawaii	**23**	2	25	**39**	12	51	South Carolina	**25**	21	46	52	**71**	124[1]
Idaho	5	**30**	35	11	**59**	70	South Dakota	13	**22**	35	22	**48**	70
Illinois	28	**31**	59	**60**	58	118	Tennessee	**18**	15	33	**61**	38	99
Indiana	19	**31**	50	50	50	100	Texas	14	**17**	31	**82**	68	150
Iowa	22	**28**	50	46	**54**	100	Utah	9	**20**	29	21	**54**	75
Kansas	13	**27**	40	48	**77**	125	Vermont	**17**	13	30	**89**	57	150[1]
Kentucky	**20**	18	38	**64**	36	100	Virginia	19	**21**	40	51	48	100[1]
Louisiana	**25**	14	39	**78**	27	105	Washington	23	**26**	49	41	**57**	98
Maine	**19**	15	35[1]	**81**	69	151[1]	West Virginia	**25**	9	34	**74**	26	100
Maryland	**32**	15	47	**99**	41	141[2]	Wisconsin	**17**	16	33	46	**51**	99[2]
Massachusetts	**31**	8	40[2]	**130**	29	160[1]	Wyoming	9	**21**	30	17	**43**	60
Michigan	16	**22**	38	**58**	51	110[2]	Dist./Columbia[3]	**11**	1	13[1]	Unicameral		
Minnesota	**42**	24	67[1]	70	**64**	134	American Samoa	Nonpartisan		18	Nonpartisan		20
Mississippi	**34**	18	52	**84**	36	122[1]	Guam	**10**	**11**	21	Unicameral		
Missouri	**19**	15	34	**85**	76	163[1,2]	No. Mariana Isl.	3	**6**	9	2	**14**	18[1]
Montana	16	**33**	50[2]	35	**65**	100	Puerto Rico	**19**	8	28[1]	**37**	16	54[1]
Nebraska	Nonpartisan		49	Unicameral			U.S. Virgin Isl.	**5**	2	15[1]	Unicameral		
Nevada	9	**12**	21	25	17	42	Total	**1,041**	963	2,089[4]	**2,903**	2,550	5,532[5]
New Hampshire	9	**15**	24	147	**248**	400[1,2]							

Note: As of April, 1998. Numbers in bold indicates the party in the majority. 1. Includes one or more Independent or other third-party legislator . 2. Includes one or more vacancy. 3. Council of the District of Columbia. 4. Includes 67 nonpartisans (from Nebraska and American Samoa), 13 Independent or other third-party legislators, and five vacancies. 5. Includes 20 nonpartisans (from American Samoa), 16 Independent or other third-party legislators, and 14 vacancies.
Source: Council of State Governments, State Elective Officials and the Legislatures, 1998-99.

Salaries of Major State Administrative Officials, 1998–99

State	Governor	Lieutenant governor	Secretary of state	Attorney general	State	Governor	Lieutenant governor	Secretary of state	Attorney general
Alabama	$87,643	$90,720[1]	$61,780	$115,695	Montana	$78,246	$53,407	$62,848	$66,756
Alaska	81,648	76,176	(2)	83,292	Nebraska	65,000	47,000	52,000	64,500
Arizona	75,000	(3)	54,600	76,440	Nevada	90,000	20,000	62,500	85,000
Arkansas	65,182	31,505	40,739	54,318	New Hampshire	86,235	(5)	53,375[6]	76,983
California	114,286	94,500	94,500	107,100	New Jersey	85,000	(5)	100,225	100,225
Colorado	70,000	48,500	48,500	60,000	New Mexico	90,000	65,500	65,000	72,500
Connecticut	78,000	55,000	50,000	60,000	New York	130,000	110,000	90,832	110,000
Delaware	107,000	44,600	89,900	99,100	North Carolina	107,132	94,552	94,552	94,552
Florida	107,961	103,415	106,870	106,461	North Dakota	73,176	60,132	55,464	65,592
Georgia	111,480	78,812	89,538	102,211	Ohio	111,467	57,637	82,347	85,509
Hawaii	94,780	90,041	(2)	85,302	Oklahoma	70,000	62,500	42,500	75,000
Idaho	85,000	22,500	67,500	75,000	Oregon	88,300	(3)	67,900	72,800
Illinois	126,590	89,357	111,697	111,697	Pennsylvania	105,035	83,027	72,024	107,016
Indiana	77,199[4]	64,000	45,999	59,202	Rhode Island	69,900	52,000	52,000	55,000
Iowa	101,313	70,919	80,524	94,485	South Carolina	106,078	46,545	92,007	92,007
Kansas	85,225	96,661	66,206	76,144	South Dakota	84,740	30,766[7]	57,576	71,973
Kentucky	93,905	79,832	79,832	79,832	Tennessee	85,000	(5)	86,484	107,820
Louisiana	95,000	85,000	85,000	85,000	Texas	99,122	99,122	76,966	79,247
Maine	70,000	(5)	60,154	69,347	Utah	87,600	68,100	(2)	73,700
Maryland	120,000	100,000	70,000	100,000	Vermont	80,725	40,289	60,825	61,027
Massachusetts	75,000	60,000	85,000	62,500	Virginia	110,000	32,000	76,346	97,500
Michigan	124,195	91,686	112,439	112,439	Washington	121,000[4]	62,700	64,300	92,000
Minnesota	114,506	62,980	62,980	89,454	West Virginia	99,000	(5)	65,000	75,000
Mississippi	83,160	40,800	75,000	90,800	Wisconsin	101,861	54,795	49,719	97,756
Missouri	107,268	64,823	86,046	93,120	Wyoming	95,000	(3)	77,000	80,000

1. Receives $50 per session day, and $3,780 per month in expenses. 2. Lieutenant governor also serves as secretary of state. 3. Secretary of state also serves as lieutenant governor. 4. Official salary; governor accepts less or returns part of salary. 5. No lieutenant governor. Speaker or President of the Senate next in line of succession to the governorship. 6. Minimum salary. Maximum salary is $68,768. 7. Annual salary for duties as presiding officer of the Senate. Source: Council of State Governments, The Book of the States, 1998-99.

U.S. TERRITORIES AND POSSESSIONS

The United States administers a number of overseas territories and commonwealth states under a variety of circumstances. The provisions of the Northwest Ordinance of 1787 established the system under which territories of the United States can achieve statehood. In order to elect a territorial legislature and send a nonvoting delegate to Congress, a territory must contain 5,000 inhabitants of voting age; it is eligible for statehood when the population numbers 60,000.

▶ AMERICAN SAMOA
Territory of American Samoa
Geography Location: seven islands (Tutuila, Ta'u, Olosega, Ofu, Aunun, Rose, Swain's) in southern central Pacific Ocean. **Boundaries:** Hawaii about 2,300 mi. (3,700 km) to NNE, Cook Islands to E, Tonga to SW, Western Samoa to W. **Total area:** 76.1 sq. mi. (199 sq km). **Coastline:** 72 mi. (116 km). **Comparative area:** slightly larger than Washington, DC. **Land use:** 5% arable land; 10% permanent crops; 0% meadows and pastures; 70% forest and woodland; 15% other. **Major cities:** (1980 census) Pago Pago (capital) 3,075.
People Population: 62,093 (July, 1998 est.). **Nationality:** noun—American Samoan(s); adjective—American Samoan. **Ethnic groups:** 89% Samoan (Polynesian), 2% Caucasian, 4% Tongan, 5% other. **Languages:** Samoan (closely related to Hawaiian and other Polynesian languages) and English; most people are bilingual. **Religions:** 50% Christian Congregationalist, 20% Roman Catholic, 30% mostly Protestant denominations and other.
Government Type: unincorporated and unorganized territory of U.S. **Constitution:** ratified 1966, in effect 1967. **National holiday:** Flag Day, Apr. 17 (1900). **Heads of Government:** Tauese P. Sunia, Governor (since Jan. 1997). **Structure:** executive—governor is popularly elected to four-year term and exercises authority under direction of U.S. Secretary of Interior; legislative—bicameral legislature (Fono) with 18 member Senate chosen by county councils to serve four-year terms and House of Representatives with 20 members popularly elected to serve two-year terms, plus a nonvoting delegate from Swain's Island; judicial—High Court with chief justice and associate justices appointed by U.S. Secretary of Interior.
Economy Monetary unit: U.S. dollar. **Budget:** (1990 est.) *income:* $97 mil.; *expend.:* N.A.. **GDP:** $128 mil.; $2,600 per capita (1995 est.). **Chief crops:** bananas, coconuts, vegetables, taro, breadfruit, yams, copra, pineapples, papayas. **Natural resources:** pumice and pumicite. **Major industries:** tuna canneries, handicrafts. **Labor force:** 14,400 (1990) 33% government, 34% tuna canneries, 33% other. **Exports:** $318 mil. (f.o.b., 1992); 93% canned tuna. **Imports:** $418 mil. (c.i.f., 1992); 56% material for canneries, 8% food, 7% petroleum products, 6% machinery and parts. **Major trading partners:** (1992) *exports:* 99.6% U.S.; *imports:* 62% U.S., 9% Japan, 11% Australia, 7% New Zealand, 4% Fiji, 7% other.
American Samoa consists of seven islands between 14° and 15°S, and 168° and 171°W. It was first peopled by Polynesians in the first millennium B.C. The first European to visit the islands was Louis Antoine de Bougainville, who came in 1768 and called them "The Islands of the Navigators," in recognition of the islanders' seamanship. American whalers and missionaries began visiting the islands in the 1830s, and the United States secured trading privileges by treaty in 1878. In 1889, the United States, Britain, and Germany established tripartite control of the islands. The High Chiefs of Tutuila ceded the islands of Tutuila and Aunun to the United States in 1900, and the High Chiefs of the Manu'a islands ceded those of Tau, Ofu, Olosega, and Rose in 1904. Swain's Island became part of American Samoa in 1925.
The islands have been administered by Department of Interior since 1904. American Samoa is an unincorporated and unorganized territory of the United States, with its own government but under the plenary authority of the Department of the Interior.

▶ BAKER AND HOWLAND ISLANDS
About 1,600 mi. (2,575 km) southwest of Hawaii and 1,000 miles west of Jarvis Island are Baker Island (0°14'N, 176°28'W) and Howland Island (0°48'N, 176°38'W, 40 miles north of Baker). Discovered in 1842, the two coral atolls were worked for guano until about 1890. Great Britain claimed them in 1889, but the U.S. made them territories in 1935 and sent colonists to them. With an area about of about 1 sq. mi. each, neither is inhabited today. Both are unincorporated territories administered by the U.S. Fish and Wildlife Service as part of the National Wildlife Refuge.

▶ GUAM
Territory of Guam
Geography Location: southernmost and largest of Mariana Islands in western North Pacific Ocean; Agaña 13°28'N, 144°45'E. **Boundaries:** Tokyo, Japan about 1,350 mi. (2,170 km) to N, Honolulu, Hawaii 3,300 mi. (5,955 km) to ENE; Federated States of Micronesia to S, Philippines to W across Philippine Sea. **Total area:** 209 sq. mi. (541 sq km). **Coastline:** 78 mi. (125.5 km). **Comparative area:** Three times size of Washington, D.C. **Land use:** 18% forest and woodland; 15% meadows and pastures; 11% arable land; 11% permanent crops; 45% other. **Major cities:** Agaña (capital).
People Population: 148,060 (July 1998 est.). **Nationality:** noun—Guamanian(s); adjective—Guamanian. **Ethnic groups:** 47% Chamorro, 25% Filipino, 10% Caucasian, 18% Chinese, Japanese, Korean, other. **Languages:** English, Chamorro, and Japanese. **Religions:** 98% Roman Catholic, 2% other.
Government Type: organized, unincorporated territory of U.S. **Constitution:** Organic Act of Aug. 1, 1950. **National holiday:** Guam Discovery Day, first Monday in Mar. **Heads of Government:** Carl Gutierrez, governor (since Nov. 8, 1994); election scheduled for Nov., 1998. **Structure:** executive—governor elected to 4-year term; legislative—unicameral; Senate has 21 members elected for 2-year terms; judicial—U.S. District Court, Guam Superior Court.
Economy Monetary unit: U.S. dollar. **Budget:** (1995) *income:* $524.3 mil.; *expend.:* $361.4 mil. **GDP:** $3.0 bil., $19,000 per capita (1996 est.). **Chief crops:** fruits, copra, vegetables, eggs; relatively undeveloped with most food imported. **Livestock:** poultry, pigs, cows. **Natural resources:**

fishing (largely undeveloped), tourism (especially from Japan). **Major industries:** U.S. military, tourism, construction, transshipment services, concrete products, printing and publishing, food processing, textiles. **Labor force:** 65,660 (1995) ; 33% services, 31% government, 21% trade, 12% construction, 3% other. **Exports:** $86.1 mil. (f.o.b., 1992); mostly transshipments of refined petroleum products, construction materials, fish, food and beverage products. **Imports:** $202.4 mil. (c.i.f., 1992); petroleum and petroleum products; food, manufactured goods. **Major trading partners:** *exports:* 25% U.S., 63% Trust Territory of the Pacific Islands, 12% other; *imports:* 23% U.S., 19% Japan, 58% other.

Guam was inhabited by Chamorros from the Malay Peninsula as early as 1500 B.C. The first European to stop at Guam was Ferdinand Magellan in 1521. Spanish colonization began with the arrival of Jesuit missionaries in 1668. By 1700 pestilence and insurrection had reduced the Chamorro population from 50,000 to about 2,000. Guam was ceded to the United States in 1899. In 1941 it was occupied by Japan—the only inhabited territory of the U.S. to be seized by enemy forces during World War II. It was retaken by the Americans in 1944. Though unincorporated, the Congressionally approved Guam Organic Act provides for a republican form of government with executive, legislative, and judicial branches.

More than one million tourists visit Guam annually, but the impact of military downsizing will nevertheless cause new economic problems.

▶JARVIS ISLAND, KINGMAN REEF, AND PALMYRA ATOLL

Jarvis Island (0°23'S, 160°02'W, about 1,510 mi. S of Hawaii), Kingman Reef (6°24'N, 162°22'W, about 1,070 mi. SSW of Hawaii), and Palmyra Atoll (5°52'N, 162°05'W, about 1,100 mi. SSW of Hawaii) in the Line Island group.

Discovered in 1798, Kingman Reef (0.4 sq. mi.; 1 sq km) was annexed by the U.S. in 1922, and used as an aviation station during the 1930s. Discovered in 1802, Palmyra Atoll consists of about 50 islets with a combined area of four square miles. It was annexed by the Kingdom of Hawaii in 1862, by Great Britain in 1889, and claimed by the U.S. in 1912. Privately owned, it is administered by the Department of the Navy, as is Kingman Reef. Jarvis Island was claimed by the U.S. in 1857, annexed by Great Britain in 1889, and reclaimed by the U.S. in 1935. Its rich guano deposits were worked by U.S. and British companies in the late 19th century.

▶JOHNSTON ATOLL

Geography Location: Johnston Island and Sand Island (uninhabited) in central Pacific Ocean. **Boundaries:** Honolulu, Hawaii about 825 mi. (1,330 km) to ENE, Marshall Islands to SW. **Total area:** 1.1 sq. mi. (2.8 sq km). **Coastline:** 6.21 mi. (10 km). **Comparative area:** about 4.7 times size of The Mall in Washington, DC. **Land use:** 0% arable land; 0% permanent crops; 0% meadows and pastures; 0% forest and woodland; 100% other. **Major cities:** none.
People Population: 1,200 (Jan. 1997), all U.S. government personnel and contractors.
Government Type: unincorporated territory of U.S.

Johnston Atoll (16°45'N, 169°32'W) , 820 miles SW of Hawaii) includes Johnston, Hikina, and Akan Islands, with a total area of 1.1 square miles. Claimed by the U.S. in 1858, Johnston Atoll is manned and administered by the U.S. Defense Special Weapons Agency and managed jointly as a National Wildlife Refuge by the DSWA and the Fish and Wildlife Service.

▶MIDWAY ISLANDS

Geography Location: Sand Island and Eastern Island in northern Pacific Ocean; 28°15'N, 177°25'W. **Boundaries:** Honolulu, Hawaii about 1,460 mi. (2,350 km) to SE, Marshall Islands to SW. **Total area:** 2.0 sq. mi. (5.2 sq km). **Coastline:** 9.3 mi. (15.0 km). **Comparative area:** about nine times size of The Mall in Washington, DC. **Land use:** 0% arable land; 0% permanent crops; 0% meadows and pastures; 0% forest and woodland; 100% other. **Major cities:** none.
People Population: 453 U.S. military personnel (July, 1995 est.). No indigenous population. **Nationality:** noun—Midway Islander(s); adjective—Midway Island. **Languages:** English. **Religions:** Christianity.
Government Type: unincorporated territory of U.S.
Economy Monetary unit: U.S. dollar. **Major industries:** support of U.S. naval air facility.

Midway Atoll consists of Eastern Island and Sand Island. Although they are part of the Leeward Islands—the westernmost islands of the Hawaiian chain—they are not part of the state of Hawaii. They were the site of the Battle of Midway, June 1942, a turning point in the Pacific theater of World War II. Today they are administered by the Department of the Navy, which maintains a naval air station there. The Navy and the Fish and Wildlife Service jointly manage the islands as a National Wildlife Refuge.

▶NAVASSA

Located in the Caribbean between the islands of Jamaica and Haiti and 100 mi (160km) south of the U.S. Naval Base at Guantánamo, Cuba, Navassa was claimed by the U.S. in 1856. It is uninhabited except for a lighthouse under U.S. Coast Guard administration. The island is about 2 sq. mi. (5.2 sq km).

▶NORTHERN MARIANA ISLANDS
Commonwealth of the Northern Mariana Islands (CNMI)

Geography Location: Fourteen major islands (including Saipan, Rota, and Tinian) in western central Pacific Ocean. Saipan 15°13'N, 145°44'E. **Boundaries:** Japan to N; Honolulu, Hawaii about 3,500 mi. (5,635 km) to E; Guam to SW; Philippines to W across Philippine Sea. **Total area:** 293 sq. mi. (759 sq km). **Coastline:** undetermined. **Comparative area:** slightly more than 2.5 times size of Washington, D.C. **Land use:** 19% meadows and pastures, 21% arable land, 60% other. **Major cities:** (1990 census) Saipan (capital) 38,896.
People Population: 66,561 (July 1998 est.) **Nationality:** undetermined. **Ethnic groups:** Chamorro majority; Carolinians, other Micronesians; Caucasian, Japanese, Chinese, Korean. **Languages:** English, Chamorro, Carolinian; 86 percent speak a language other than English at home. **Religions:** Christian (Roman Catholic majority); some traditional beliefs.
Government Type: commonwealth associated with U.S. **Constitution:** Covenant Agreement effective Nov. 3, 1986. **National holiday:**

Commonwealth Day, Jan. 8. **Heads of Government:** Pedro P. Tenorio, governor (since January, 1998). **Structure:** executive—governor elected by popular vote; legislative—bicameral legislature (nine-member Senate elected for four-year term, 15-member House of Representatives elected for two-year term; judiciary—U.S. District Court, Commonwealth Trial Court, Commonwealth Appeals Court.

Economy Monetary unit: U.S. dollar. **Budget:** (1994/5) *income:* $190.4 mil. *expend:* 190.4 mil. **GDP:** $524 mil., $10,500 per capita (1994). **Chief crops:** coconuts, fruits, vegetables. **Livestock:** cattle. **Natural resources:** arable land, fish. **Major industries:** tourism, construction, light industry, handicrafts. **Labor force:** 7,476 total indigenous labor force, 2,699 unemployed, 22,560 foreign workers (1995). **Exports:** $263.4 mil. (f.o.b. 1991 est.) garments. **Imports:** $392.4 million (c.i.f. 1991 est.) food, construction equipment and materials, petroleum products. **Major trading partners:** U.S., Japan.

Running north from the island of Guam across a 600-mile-long archipelago in the Pacific Island group known as Micronesia, the islands of the Northern Marianas (CNMI) were originally settled by Pacific argonauts as early as 1500 B.C. Ferdinand Magellan landed at Saipan in 1521, introducing Western culture to the region. The Spanish took control of the archipelago in 1565 and ruled until 1898, when Germany took over the islands. After World War I, the League of Nations mandated the Marianas to Japan, who developed extensive sugar processing works on Saipan. Allied forces took the Marianas in 1944.

In 1947, the islands were included in the United Nations Trust Territory of the Pacific and placed under U.S. administration. In 1976, the CNMI adopted its own constitution. A mutually approved Covenant to Establish a Commonwealth was implemented by the Marianas and the United States in 1986. The Northern Marianas are subject to provisions of U.S. law, except regarding customs, minimum wages, immigration, and taxation. The people are, as a rule, U.S. citizens. The CNMI benefits from substantially from United States assistance.

▶ PUERTO RICO
Commonwealth of Puerto Rico

Geography Location: large island of Puerto Rico, together with Vieques, Culebra, and many smaller islands, in northeastern Caribbean Sea. San Juan 18° 29′N, 66° 08′W **Boundaries:** Atlantic Ocean to N, Virgin Islands to E, Caribbean Sea to S, Dominican Republic 50 mi. (80 km) to W. **Total land area:** 3,459 sq. mi. (8,959 sq km). **Coastline:** 311 mi. (501 km). **Comparative area:** slightly less than three times size of Rhode Island. **Land use:** 26% pastures; 16% forest and woodland; 5% permanent crops; 4% arable land; 49% other; **Major cities:** (1990 census) San Juan (capital) 437,745; Bayamón 220,262; Ponce 187,749; Carolina 177,806; Caguas 133,447.

People Population: 3,857,070 (July 1998 est.). **Nationality:** noun—Puerto Rican(s); adjective—Puerto Rican. **Ethnic groups:** almost entirely Hispanic. **Languages:** Spanish (official), English. **Religions:** mostly Christian, 85% Roman Catholic, 15% Protestant denominations and other.

Government Type: commonwealth associated with U.S. **Constitution:** effective July 25, 1952. **National holiday:** U.S. Independence Day, July 4. **Heads of Government:** Pedro Rossello, governor, since Jan. 1993. **Structure:** executive—governor elected by direct vote to four-year term; legislative—bicameral legislature (Senate with 28 members, House of Representatives with 54 members, all elected by popular vote to four-year terms); judiciary—Supreme Court appointed by governor.

Economy Monetary unit: U.S. dollar. **Budget:** (1994/5) *income:* $5.1 bil.; *expend.:* $5.1 bil. **GDP:** $31.6 bil., $8,200 per capita (1996 est.). **Chief crops:** sugarcane, coffee, pineapples, plantains, bananas (imports a large share of food needs). **Livestock:** cattle, chickens. **Natural resources:** copper, nickel; potential for crude oil. **Major industries:** manufacturing of pharmaceuticals, electronics, apparel, food products, instruments, tourism. **Labor force:** 1.3 mil. (1996); 19% government, 17% trade, 13% manufacturing, 5% construction, 32% other; 13% unemployed. **Exports:** $22.9 bil. (f.o.b 1996); pharmaceuticals, electronics, apparel, canned tuna, rum, beverage concentrates, medical equipment, tourism. **Imports:** $19.1 bil. (c.i.f 1996); chemicals, clothing, food, fish, petroleum products. **Major trading partners:** (1996 est.) *exports:* 88% U.S; *imports:* 62% U.S.

Puerto Rico was initially peopled by the Igneri and Taíno tribes. The island's first European visitor was Christopher Columbus, who landed on the island in 1493. In 1508, Juan Ponce de Léon led the first settlers to San Juan, and by 1514 the Taíno population had dropped from an estimated 30,000 to 4,000. In the 17th and 18th centuries, Puerto Rico was invaded by both English and Danish forces, and though San Juan was captured or burned several times, the Spanish maintained control.

The Spanish constitution granted Puerto Ricans citizenship in 1812, but a revolution was put down in 1868. Spain granted Puerto Rico self-government in 1897 but this was repealed when sovereignty was transferred to the U.S. after the Spanish-American War. Despite early attempts to Americanize Puerto Rico, including an effort to make English the official language and granting citizenship in 1917, the Popular Democratic Party, founded in 1938, brought about a change in political status from that of a U.S. colony to an autonomous commonwealth in 1952.

Governed under the Puerto Rican Federal Relations Act and a constitution modeled on that of the U.S., Puerto Rico is nonetheless an autonomous political entity in voluntary association with the U.S. Despite dramatic increases in industrial development since the 1950s, Puerto Rico suffered from net outward migration until 1988.

Puerto Ricans remain almost equally divided between those who favor statehood and those who favor maintaining commonwealth status, with those seeking independence constituting a vocal but small minority. The statehood-minded argue that limited citizenship is disadvantageous since it allows them to be drafted into the U.S. military but they cannot vote in national elections. The other side fears the burden of full U.S. taxes. In the most recent balloting on the issue, held December 13, 1998, 50.2 percent of Puerto Ricans voted for "none of the above," an option that maintained Puerto Rico's commonwealth status; 46.5 percent voted for statehood, while 2.5 percent preferred independence.

▶VIRGIN ISLANDS
Virgin Islands of the United States
Geography Location: three main inhabited islands (St. Croix, St. Thomas and St. John) and about 50 smaller islands, mostly uninhabited, in northeastern Caribbean Sea. Charlotte Amalie 18°22'N, 64°56'W. **Boundaries:** British Virgin Islands to N, Netherlands Antilles to E, Caribbean Sea to S, Puerto Rico about 40 mi. (64 km) to W. **Total area:** 136 sq. mi. (352 sq km). **Coastline:** 117 mi. (188 km). **Comparative area:** twice the size of Washington, DC. **Land use:** 26% meadows and pastures; 15% arable land; 6% permanent crops; 6% forest and woodland; 47% other. **Major cities:** (1990 census) Charlotte Amalie (capital) 12,331; Christiansted 2,555; Frederiksted 1,064.

People Population: 118,211 (July 1998) **Nationality:** noun—Virgin Islander(s); adjective—Virgin Islander. **Ethnic groups:** 74% West Indian (45% born in Virgin Islands, 29% born elsewhere in West Indies), 13% U.S. mainland, 5% Puerto Rican, 8% other; 80% black, 15% white, 5% other; 14% of Hispanic origin. **Languages:** English (official), Spanish, Creole. **Religions:** 42% Baptist, 34% Roman Catholic, 17% Episcopalian, 7% other.

Government Type: organized, unincorporated territory of U.S. **Constitution:** Revised Organic Act of July 22, 1954 serves as constitution. **National holiday:** Transfer Day (from Denmark to U.S.), Mar. 31. **Heads of Government:** Dr. Roy L. Schneider, governor (since Jan. 1995). **Structure:** executive—governor elected to four-year term; unicameral legislature—senate with 15 members elected to two-year terms; judiciary—two U.S. district courts.

Economy Monetary unit: U.S. dollar. **Budget:** (1992) *income:* $364.4 mil.; *expend.:* $364.4 mil. **GDP:** $1.2 bil., $11,000 per capita (1987). **Chief crops:** truck gardens, fruit, sorghum. **Livestock:** chickens, cattle, goats, sheep, pigs. **Natural resources:** sun, sand, sea, surf. **Major industries:** tourism, government service, petroleum refining. **Labor force:** 47,443 (1990); 62% services, 20% industry, 18% other; 6.2% unemployment. **Exports:** $1.8 bil. (f.o.b., 1992); 94% refined petroleum products to U.S. **Imports:** $2.2 bil. (c.i.f., 1992); 82% crude petroleum for refining. **Major trading partners:** *exports:* U.S., Puerto Rico; imports: U.S., Puerto Rico.

The Virgin Islands of the United States (USVI) consists of more than 50 islands located about 40 miles east of Puerto Rico, and about 1,730 east-

southeast of Miami. Excavations have revealed evidence of human habitation in the Virgin Islands from as early as A.D. 100. By 1493, when Christopher Columbus landed in the islands—which he named for the virgin martyr St. Ursula—they were inhabited by Carib Indians who were driven out by the Spanish in 1555.

In 1672, St. Thomas was settled by the Danish West India Company. The Danes laid claim to St. John in 1683 and purchased St. Croix from the French in 1773. The United States purchased the Virgin Islands from Denmark for $25 million in 1917, and they were made a territory under the jurisdiction of the Navy. U.S. citizenship was granted in 1927, and the Department of the Interior assumed administration of the islands in 1931. The first governor elected by popular vote was installed in 1970, and an independent constitution was voted down by the electorate 1979.

The primary industry is tourism, which accounts for 70 percent of GDP and employs 70 percent of the work force. Inernational business and financial services are increasingly important.

▶WAKE ISLANDS
Geography Location: three islands (Wake, Wilkes, and Peale) in North Pacific Ocean; Wake 19°18'N, 166°36'E. **Boundaries:** Honolulu, Hawaii 2,3000 mi. (3,700 km) to E, Marshall Islands to S, Guam about 1,280 mi. (2,060 km) to W. **Total area:** 2.5 sq. mi. (6.5 sq km). **Coastline:** 12 mi. (19.3 km) **Comparative area:** about 11 times size of the Mall in Washington, D.C. **Land use:** 0% arable land; 0% permanent crops; 0% meadows and pastures; 0% forest and woodland; 100% other. **Major cities:** none.

People Population: 302 (July, 1995); no indigenous inhabitants; temporary population consists of U.S. Air Force personnel and about 225 U.S. and Thai contractors.

Government Type: unincorporated territory of U.S., administered by U.S. Air Force.

The Wake Island group was first discovered by British captain William Wake in 1796. It was chartered by Capt. Charles Wilkes's surveying expedition, which was accompanied by a naturalist named Peale. Annexed by the United States in 1898, Wake became a civil aviation station in the 1930s, and was captured by the Japanese shortly after Pearl Harbor. It was retaken in 1944. Formerly an important commercial aviation base, it is now used only by some commercial cargo planes and for emergency landings.

Resident Population of U.S. Territories, 1960–2020 (in thousands)

Territory	1960	1970	1980	1990	1998	2020[1]
Puerto Rico	2,358	2,716	3,206	3,605	3,857	4,227
Guam	67	86	107	134	149	230
Virgin Islands	33	63	98	101	118	111
American Samoa	20	27	32	47	62	86
Northern Mariana Islands	9	12	17	44	67	86

1. Estimated. **Source:** U.S. Census Bureau, International Data Base.

Cities and Counties in the U.S.

Included here is basic information about population change, cost of living, and government finances in major U.S. cities, metropolitan statistical areas, and counties. In addition, there are brief descriptions of the 50 largest cities—from Albuquerque to Washington, D.C. Statistical sources include the U.S. Census Bureau's decennial census, *City Government Finances*, *County Government Finances*, and the *Statistical Abstract of the United States* (all annual publications).

▶FORMS OF LOCAL GOVERNMENT

In addition to the one federal and 50 state governments, the Bureau of the Census recognizes five basic types of organized local government. In addition to these, which are authorized in state constitutions and statutes, some local governments operate under a "home-rule charter" the form and organization of which are specified by locally approved charters rather than by general or special state law. The number of local governments and officials continues to skyrocket even as the size of the federal bureaucracy shrinks. In 1992, there were a total of 85,006 state and local governments and 510,497 elected officials, compared with 83,236 and 497,155 five years earlier.

Counties

County governments are established to provide general government; and include those governments designated as boroughs in Alaska, parishes in Louisiana, and counties in the other states. In 1992, there were 3,043 county governments; the most common forms are:

Council-commission A county government without a chief executive but with an elected governing body that shares administrative responsibility with officials elected or appointed to specific positions.

Council-administrator A county government with an elected governing body responsible for overall policy, and an appointed administrator (sometimes called a county manager, county commissioner, or county judge) responsible for administration. The powers of the administrator under this form of government may vary widely.

Council-elected executive A county government with an elected governing body and an elected chief executive—sometimes called a president or a chairperson of the board. The powers of the executive under this form of government may vary widely.

Municipalities

Municipal governments are established to provide general government for a specific concentration of population in a defined area and include those governments designated as cities, villages, boroughs (except in Alaska), and towns (except in the six New England states, Minnesota, New York and Wisconsin). In 1992, there were 19,279 municipal governments; the most common forms are:

Mayor-council A municipal government with an elected mayor and an elected council or other governing body. In some mayor-council munici-palities, the mayor is the chief executive, with broad powers. In some other mayor-council cities, the mayor has limited powers.

Council-manager A municipal government with an elected council or other governing body responsible for overall policy, and an appointed manager responsible for administration. The council may select a chairperson from among their own number who may be designated as the mayor.

Commission A municipal government with an elected board of commissioners responsible for overall policy. Each commissioner is responsible for administration of one or more departments of the municipal government. The board may select a chairperson from among their own number who may be designated as the mayor.

Towns

Township governments are established to provide general government for areas defined without regard to population concentration and include those governments designated as towns in Connecticut, Maine (including organized plantations), Massachusetts, Minnesota, New Hampshire (including organized locations), New York, Rhode Island, Vermont, and Wisconsin, and townships in other states. In 1992, there were 16,656 township governments; the most common forms are:

Town meeting A township government in which an annual town meeting of resident voters makes basic policy. An elected board (often called "a board of selectmen" or "township supervisors") is responsible for day-to-day administration of the township.

Representative town meeting A township government in which a town meeting composed of elected representatives of the resident voters makes basic policy. This form of government is usually found in more populous towns or townships. An elected board (often called "a board of selectmen" or "township supervisors") is responsible for day-to-day administration of the township.

School districts

School district governments are organized local entities providing public elementary, secondary and/or higher education which, under state law, have sufficient administrative and fiscal autonomy to qualify as separate governments. Excludes "dependent public school systems" of county, township or state governments. In 1992, there were 14,422 school district governments.

Special district governments

All organized local entities other than the four categories listed above, authorized by state law to provide only one or a limited number of designated functions, and with sufficient administrative and fiscal autonomy to qualify as separate governments; known by a variety of titles, including districts, authorities, boards, commissions, etc., as specified in the state legislation. In 1992, there were 31,355 special district governments.

Source: U.S. Bureau of the Census.

THE 50 LARGEST CITIES, 1990–96

Between 1990 and 1996, the westward movement of the U.S. population again revealed its strength as two cities in the east (Buffalo and Toledo) fell from the list of the 50 largest cities in the U.S. They were replaced by Colorado Springs and Las Vegas, two of the fastest growing cities in the country. Colorado Springs, located at the eastern boundary of the Rocky Mountains in the shadow of Pikes Peak, is the home of the Air Force Academy and the North American Aerospace Defense Command. In 1990, it was the 54th largest city in the country, with 280,430 people, but by 1996, it had mushroomed to 345,127 people, ranking it 50th.

Among the largest cities in the U.S., however, no city came close to Las Vegas in terms of population growth. Between 1990 and 1996, its population increased by 46 percent, from 258,204 to 376,906. It leapfrogged more than 20 cities in going from the 63rd largest city to the 41st.

Following are brief descriptions of the 50 largest cities in the U.S. according to 1996 Census Bureau population estimates. They are set forth in alphabetical order. Several tables showing the growth of major cities in America follow this section. See also the section on Metropolitan Statistical Areas (MSAs) later in this chapter.

Note: According to Census Bureau estimates from 1999, Mesa, Ariz. joined the list of the top 50 cities in 1998, replacing Cincinnati.

▶ ALBUQUERQUE, NEW MEXICO

Seventy million years ago, earthquakes and volcanoes pushed the land that is now Albuquerque above the sea, forming the Rio Grande Valley and a ring of mountain ranges. Even today, the 10,000 foot-high Sandia Mountains are rising slowly and the Rio Grande Valley continues gradually to deepen. During the Ice Age, Sandia Man roamed the area hunting mastodon and buffalo, and some 3,000 years ago, the Anasazi built stone and adobe cities which still stand. The 1530s marked the arrival of Spanish conquistadors and missionaries.

Founded as a Spanish Villa in 1706, when 35 families moved to the land along the Rio Grande, Albuquerque was named by Don Francisco Cuervo y Valdez in honor of the Duke of Albuquerque, King Phillip's Viceroy of New Spain. Indian raids arrested the villa's expansion, and one hundred years after its founding, its population numbered a mere 2,200. Benefitting from their proximity to the Santa Fe trail, the people farmed, raised cattle, marketed wool and adobe for building, and ran trading posts, military supply depots, saloons, hotels, and mercantile businesses. The introduction of the railroad in 1880 spurred Albuquerque's growth, and the 1940 population of 35,000 has since grown more than tenfold.

Today, Albuquerque occupies a central position along the Rio Grande Research Corridor, which stretches from Los Alamos to Las Cruces, and is home to the University of New Mexico and such major high-tech installments as GTE Communications, UNISYS, GE, and Sandia National Laboratories. Albuquerque's cultural and historical attractions include the Albuquerque Museum, the Indian Pueblo Culture Center, the Maxwell Museum of Anthropology, the National Atomic Museum, and Petroglyph National Monument.

Population 419,681 (1996). Rank: 37th. Race/national origin (1990): Black 3.0%; Hispanic 34.5%; Asian 1.7%; American Indian 3.0%.
Location: 35°05'N, 106°47'W. County: Bernalillo.
Terrain and climate Elev.: 5,300 ft. Area: 127.2 sq. mi. (329.4 sq km). Avg. daily min. temp.: Jan.: 22.3°F/-5.3°C; avg. daily max. July: 92.8°F/33.7°C. Avg. annual: rainfall, 8.12"; snowfall, 11"; clear days, 71; precipitation days, 135.
Government Form: mayor and council. Mayor Jim Baca. Election: Oct. 2001 Municipal tel. number: (505) 768-3000.
Visitor info: (505) 842-9918 or 1-800-284-2282. www.abqcvb.org

▶ ATLANTA, GEORGIA

Atlanta, the capital and largest city of Georgia, lies at the base of the Blue Ridge Mountains, near the Chattahoochee River. First settled in 1836, the area became the terminus for the Georgia Railroad in 1845 and took the name Atlanta. The population grew to 15,000 by 1861, and during the Civil War, Atlanta became a strategic Confederate depot and collection point for recruits, establishing it as one of the most important cities of the Confederacy and making it a vital objective during Gen. William Tecumseh Sherman's infamous "March to the Sea" in 1864. After two months of bitter battle, Sherman took the city on Sept. 1 and burned most of it to the ground. After the war, the ravaged city was rebuilt; it became the state capital in 1868.

The leading city of the so-called "New South," Atlanta is a the chief commercial hub of the southeastern United States. Atlanta is nicknamed the "City Without Limits" because there are no major rivers, mountains, or coastlines to retard its burgeoning growth into the ever-expanding suburbs. Several *Fortune* 500 Companies have their headquarters in Atlanta (including Coca-Cola and United Parcel Service) as do CNN and the U.S. Centers for Disease Control. Hartsfield Atlanta International (the major hub for Delta Airlines) is the world's second busiest airport, giving rise to the saying, "whether you're going to heaven or hell, you still have to change planes in Atlanta."

The city is also an important educational and cultural center, home to more than 30 institutions of higher learning, including Georgia Tech, Emory University, and Morehouse and Spelman Colleges. The Jimmy Carter Presidential Library is here, as is the grave of the Rev. Martin Luther King Jr.

The 1996 Summer Olympics thrust Atlanta into the international spotlight, and helped fuel the city's economic future. The Olympiad was responsible for adding hundreds of thousands of jobs (most of them permanent) and an estimated $500 million in construction to Atlanta's economy. It also brought Centennial Olympic Park and Turner Field to the downtown landscape.

Population 401,907 (1996). Rank: 38th. Race/national origin (1990): Black 67.1%; Hispanic 1.9%; Asian 0.9%; American Indian 0.1%.
Location: 33°50'N, 84°24'W. County: Fulton.
Terrain and climate Elev.: 1,034 ft. Area: 131.2 sq. mi. (339.80 sq km). Avg. daily min. temp.: Jan.: 32.6°F/0.3°C; avg. daily max. July: 87.9°F/31°C. Avg. annual: rainfall, 48.61"; snowfall, 2"; clear days, 108; precipitation days, 116.
Government Form: mayor and council. Mayor William Craig Campbell. Election: Nov. 2001. Municipal tel. number: (404) 330-6100.
Visitor info: (404) 222-6688. www.ci.atlanta.ga.us

◄AUSTIN, TEXAS

Austin, the capital of Texas, lies about 80 miles northeast of San Antonio on the banks of the Colorado River. First inhabited by nomadic Indian tribes, the area had as its first permanent European settler Jacob Harrell, in 1835, who established the town of Waterloo. In 1839, it was chosen as the site of the Texas Republic's capital and was renamed after Stephen F. Austin, who brought the first Anglo settlers to Texas in the 1820s. After 1845, when Texas gained admission into the Union, Austin began to flourish, and by 1930 it had grown into a major regional center with a population of 75,000.

Originally a business and distribution center serving the farmers of the Blackland Prairies to the east, Austin's farmers produce cotton, maize, corn, livestock and poultry. Traditional industries such as meat packing, canning, and furniture manufacturing have been outstripped by the high-tech companies that have helped to nearly double the population since 1970. The city's economic landscape has for decades been defined by the state government (responsible for 131,000 jobs, or one-fourth of Austin's workforce) The University of Texas, founded in 1881 in Austin, boasts the highest endowment of any U.S. university—a legacy of the Texas oil fields. As the University developed into a first-class institution (with 50,000 students) feeding the city's cultural and economic life, and with the influx of electronics and computer companies, Austin has prospered into a metropolis of national, even worldwide, scope.

In recent years, the university's academic excellence and Austin's reputation for liberalism and progressivism (coffeehouses are more common here than cowboy hats) have attracted both the arts and high tech companies such as Dell Computer, Motorola, 3M, IBM, and Texas Instruments.

Population   541,278 (1996). Rank: 22nd. Race/national origin (1990): Black 12.4%; Hispanic 23.0%; Asian 3.0%; American Indian 0.4%.
Location: 30°20'N, 97°45'W. Counties: Travis, Williamson
Terrain and climate   Elev.: 570 ft. Area: 232 sq. mi. (600.9 sq km). Avg. daily min. temp.: Jan.: 38.8°F/3.8°C; avg. daily max. July: 95.4°F/35.2°C. Avg. annual: rainfall, 31.50"; snowfall, 1"; clear days, 115; precipitation days, 82.
Government   Form: council and manager. Mayor Kirk Watson. Election: May 2000. Municipal tel. number: (512) 499-2000.
Visitor info: 1-800-888-8287 or (512) 478-0098 www.ci.austin.tx.us

►BALTIMORE, MARYLAND

One of America's most active seaports since Colonial days and chartered in 1729 as a major conduit of tobacco exportation, Baltimore was named after the founder of the colony of Maryland, George Calvert, Lord Baltimore. By the time of the Revolutionary War, it earned fame as an important commercial and maritime center, and ships sailing from Baltimore plied their trade with northern Europe, the Mediterranean, and the Caribbean. Chartered as a city in 1797, Baltimore's commercial activity began to surge, spurred by its burgeoning iron and copper industries, its proximity to the nation's capital, and the arrival of the Baltimore and Ohio Railroad, which developed links to the Midwest. However, the deep, divisive passions of the Civil War stunted growth and it would take years before the city recovered.

A fire in 1904 destroyed almost every building in the downtown area, providing impetus for needed revitalization. The two world wars renewed demands for Baltimore's port facilities and fostered development of a solid heavy industrial base. After World War II, however, the city's infrastructure aged and decayed. Today, Baltimore remains a large port and industrial city with one of the largest steel plants in the world (Bethlehem Steel's Sparrow Point works). Much of the city has been rebuilt through urban renewal efforts, including the nationally acclaimed Inner Harbor Project, and Oriole Park at Camden Yards. The population seems to have stabilized after a loss of almost 20 percent since 1960.

Among the city's historic sites is Fort McHenry, where Francis Scott Key wrote "The Star-Spangled Banner." Baltimore is home to St. Mary's Seminary and University (1791), Johns Hopkins University (1876), and the University of Baltimore (1925), among other noted institutions of higher learning.

Population   675,401 (1996). Rank: 15th. Race/national origin (1990): Black 59.2%; Hispanic 1.0%; Asian 1.1%; American Indian 0.3%.
Location: 39°18'N, 76°37'W. County: independent city within Baltimore County.
Terrain and climate   Elev.: 155 ft. Area: 80.3 sq. mi. (208 sq km). Avg. daily min. temp.: Jan.: 24.3°F/-4.2°C; avg. daily max. July: 87.1°F/30.6°C. Avg. annual: rainfall, 43.39"; snowfall, 22"; clear days, 106; precipitation days, 112.
Government   Form: mayor and council. Mayor Kurt L. Schmoke. Election: Nov. 1999. Municipal tel. number: (410) 396-3100.
Visitor info: (410) 837-4636 or 1-800-282-6632. www.ci.baltimore.md.us

►BOSTON, MASSACHUSETTS

Named for the English port from which many Puritan immigrants to America came, Boston was first settled in 1630 under the leadership of John Winthrop. As the capital of the Massachusetts Bay Colony, it quickly became the cultural and mercantile capital of the New England colonies. Bostonians never wholly embraced British authority, and they provided the earliest challenges to British rule in their reaction to the Stamp Act (1765) and the Boston Tea Party (1783). The colonists killed in the Boston Massacre (1770) were the first to fall in the years immediately preceding the American Revolution.

With the end of the Revolution, Boston merchants found themselves shut out of English ports by prohibitive tariffs, and in their quest for new markets for American goods opened American trade to the Orient and India. In the 19th century, Boston benefitted early from the industrial revolution, and from several waves of immigration, particularly blacks from the southern states, and Irish and Italians from Europe.

Although Boston's preeminence in trade and industry did not survive the 19th century, it continues to be a major center for banking and financial services. Since World War II its suburbs have flourished as a center of research and development and of the computer industry—Route 128 was the East Coast's answer to California's Silicon Valley during the 1980s—spurring investment in downtown Boston. As the gateway to New England and the birthplace of the Revolution, Boston is also a center for tourism.

Perhaps most important to its identity is Boston's wealth of educational, cultural, and religious tolerance. Harvard University (across the Charles River in Cambridge, 1636) is the country's oldest, and Roxbury Latin (1645) the country's oldest privately endowed secondary school. Today Boston is home to more than 30 colleges and universities, as well as to some of the finest cultural institutions in the country, including the American Academy of Arts and Sciences (1780), the Massachusetts Historical Society (1791), the Boston Athenaeum (1807), the Boston Public Library (the nation's first, 1854), the Boston Museum of Fine Arts (1870), and the Boston Symphony (1881). Boston is also home to three major medical schools and 27 hospitals including the world famous Massachusetts General and Brigham and Women's.

Population   558,394 (1996). Rank: 20th. Race/national origin (1990): Black 25.6%; Hispanic 10.8%; Asian 5.3%; American Indian 0.3%.

Location: 42°20'N, 71°05'W. County: Suffolk.

Terrain and climate Elev.: 10 ft. Area: 47.2 sq. mi. (122.2 sq km). Avg. daily min. temp.: Jan.: 22.8°F/-5.1°C; avg. daily max. July: 81.8°F/27.6°C. Avg. annual: rainfall, 43.81"; snowfall, 42"; clear days, 99; precipitation days, 128.

Government   Form: mayor and council. Mayor Thomas M. Menino. Election: Nov. 2001. Municipal tel. number: (617) 635-4000.

Visitor info: (617) 536-4100.

www.ci.boston.ma.us

▶ CHARLOTTE, NORTH CAROLINA

An area of lush green foothills lying at the southernmost tip of the Carolina Piedmont, Charlotte has long been a crossroads city and an important distribution point for the surrounding farmlands. About 250 years ago, Scottish and Irish settlers retracing old Catawba Indian trading routes established a settlement where the paths crossed and in 1762, it was named Charlotte, after the new bride of King George III. Remembering Gen. Cornwallis's reference to Charlotte as a "hornet's nest" while his army briefly occupied it during the American Revolution, the city adopted the symbol as its emblem.

The discovery of a 17-pound gold nugget in 1799 triggered a gold rush, and although the mines dotting the landscape boosted business, the California gold rush in the mid-1800s lured away prospectors, putting Charlotte on its future course as a top cotton producer. A leading city of the Confederacy in the Civil War, Charlotte hosted the last full meeting of the Confederate cabinet in 1865. The Queen City's second population surge has occurred over the past 20 years, as Charlotte has become an international banking center, with two of the country's top 25 banks making their headquarters there.

Recently, the city's economic base has diversified beyond the production of chemicals, foodstuffs, machinery, metals, and textiles, and matured into a major center of world trade and technology, with more than 160 multinational companies engaging in such businesses as microelectronics, insurance, machining, and biomedical supplies. Located equidistant from the northwestern, Midwestern, and southern Florida markets, Charlotte remains a key distribution conduit. A mid-sized city at the heart of a rapidly expanding metropolitan region, Charlotte ranks as the nation's fifth largest urban area with a population of over five million living within a 100-mile radius of the city. The Charlotte Hornets, the Carolina Panthers, and the Charlotte Motor Speedway are all sources of the city's legendary civic pride and boosterism.

Population   441,297 (1996). Rank: 32nd. Race/national origin (1990): Black 31.8%; Hispanic 1.4%; Asian 1.8%; American Indian 0.4%.

Location: 35°16'N, 80°46'W. County: Mecklenburg.

Terrain and climate Elev.: 665 ft. Area: 152.1 sq. mi. (393.9 sq km). Avg. daily min. temp.: Jan.: 30.7°F/-0.7°C; avg. daily max. July: 88.3°F/31.2°C. Avg. annual: rainfall, 43.16"; snowfall, 6"; clear days, 111; precipitation days, 111.

Government   Form: council and manager. Mayor Patrick McCrory. Election: Nov. 1999. Municipal tel. number: (704) 336-2241.

Visitor Info: (704) 331-2700 or 1-800-231-4636.

www.ci.charlotte.nc.us.

◀ CHICAGO, ILLINOIS

Chicago extends roughly 26 miles along the southwestern shoreline of Lake Michigan. The city has historically been a major transportation hub and gateway to the Great Plains, and continues to be one today with major air, rail, and highway hubs. Nineteen trunk-line railroad routes converge at Chicago, linking it with every major U.S. and Canadian city. The city has three major airports, including O'Hare, the busiest in the nation. It is also the terminus for major interstate highways running east-west and north-south.

Historically, Chicago's rise parallels the growth of the American republic to the west. Chicago was first settled in 1779, when Jean Baptiste Point de Sable built a house on the site. In 1803, federal troops built a stockade named Fort Dearborn, but by 1830 only 12 families had settled in the area. In the 1830s, however, the population grew rapidly as Americans spread westward, and the city of Chicago was incorporated in 1837 with a population of 4,170. Chicago then began to grow into a bustling Great Lakes port, connected to the Mississippi via a system of rivers and canals.

Chicago has maintained its strategic importance despite changes in transportation technology and remains today a prosperous city. Over the years, Chicago has been noted as a hotbed of labor reform, the center of violent organized crime gang wars during the prohibition era, and a prime example of the good and the bad of American city machine politics. But despite its checkered past, it has grown into the wealthiest and most vibrant city in the Midwest with hardly a sign of the rust belt malaise plaguing many of its sister cities. Chicago has grown into a financial center with three of the nation's four largest futures exchanges and the world's largest listed stock options exchange.

Chicago also far outstrips other Midwestern cities in cultural, entertainment, recreational and commercial facilities. Major attractions include the Museum of Science and Industry, the Field Museum of Natural History, the Chicago Historical Society, the Lincoln Park Zoo, the Chicago Lyric Opera Company, the Chicago Symphony Orchestra, and the Chicago Art Institute. Downtown Chicago currently has three of the five tallest man-made structures in the world—the Sears Tower (110 stories, 1,454 ft. high), the John Hancock Building (1,127 ft.), and the Amoco Building (1,136 ft.). It is also home to the world's tallest apartment complex, the 70-story Lake Point Tower, and the world's largest commercial building, the Merchandise Mart.

Population   2,721,547 (1996). Rank: 3rd. Race/national origin (1990): Black 39.1%; Hispanic 19.6%; Asian 3.7%; American Indian 0.3%.

Location: 41°53'N, 87°40'W. County: Cook.

Terrain and climate Elev.: 623 ft. Area: 228.1 sq. mi. (590.8 sq km). Avg. daily min. temp.: Jan.: 13.6°F/-10.2°C; avg. daily max. July: 83.3°F/28.5°C. Avg. annual: rainfall, 33.34"; snowfall, 40"; clear days, 94; precipitation days, 123.

Government   Form: mayor and council. Mayor Richard M. Daley. Election: March 2003. Municipal tel. number: (312) 744-4000.
Visitor info: (312) 744-2400 or 1-800-226-6632.
www.ci.chi.il.us

▶ CINCINNATI, OHIO

Cincinnati's origins can be traced to 1789, when the U.S. government set up Fort Washington in the town Losantiville to quell Indian attacks. A year later, the burgeoning city was renamed Cincinnati after the Society of Cincinnati, a group of Revolutionary War veterans. Settlement of the city increased after the Battle of Fallen Timbers (1794) put down the Miami Indian tribe's resistance to European settler control of the region.

In 1811, the *New Orleans*, the first steamboat on the western rivers, arrived from Pittsburgh, and thereafter Cincinnati became a major inland port. The city's commercial status was consolidated in the 1840s after the opening of the Miami and Erie Canal, which joined the Ohio River at Cincinnati with Lake Erie at Toledo, and the arrival of the first railroads in 1843. Large numbers of German immigrants gave the city a European flavor. By mid-century, Cincinnati had reached its zenith as a commercial and manufacturing center and well deserved Longfellow's epithet, "Queen City of the West." Cincinnati continued to prosper after the Civil War, though it was beset by problems which ranged from perennial flooding to extensive government. By 1910, its population had reached 360,000, about what it is today.

Cincinnati continues to be a hub of transportation and industry, particularly strong in the manufacture of transportation equipment and industrial machinery, food and beverage products, steel, and in printing. It is one of the nation's largest inland coal ports and a regional center for wholesaling, retailing, insurance, and finance.

Among its many colleges and universities are the University of Cincinnati, Cincinnati Technical College, The Athenaeum of Ohio , Hebrew Union College-Jewish Institute of Religion (founded in 1875 and the oldest rabbinic college in the US), and Cincinnati Bible Seminary. It is the home of the William Howard Taft birthplace, the Harriet Beecher Stowe House State Memorial, Tyler-Davidson Fountain, and the Cincinnati Zoo, the second oldest in the U.S.
Population   345,818 (1996). Rank: 49th. Race/ national origin (1990): Black 37.9%; Hispanic 0.7%; Asian 1.1%; American Indian 0.2%.
Location: 39°10'N, 84°26'W. County: Hamilton.
Terrain and climate   Elev.: 540 ft. Area: 78 sq. mi. (202 sq km). Avg. daily min. temp.: Jan.: 20.4°F/-6.4°C; avg. daily max. July: 85.8°F/29.8°C. Avg. annual: rainfall, 40.10"; snowfall, 19"; clear days, 80; precipitation days, 131.
Government   Form: council and manager. Mayor Roxanne Qualls. Election: Nov. 1999. Municipal tel. number: (513) 352-3000.
Visitor info: 1-800-CINCYUSA or (513) 621-2142
www.ci.cincinnati.oh.us

▶ CLEVELAND, OHIO

The heart of the largest metropolitan area in Ohio, Cleveland was founded in 1796 and named after Moses Cleaveland, a surveyor with the Connecticut Land Company, which administered the state of Connecticut's lingering claim on 3.5 million acres of what is now Ohio (the Western Reserve). A frontier village at the mouth of the Cuyahoga River on Lake Erie, Cleveland was transformed into the business and manufacturing center of northern Ohio by the opening of the Erie Canal in 1825, and the Ohio and Erie Canal, which linked Cleveland with Portsmouth on the Ohio River. When the Soo Locks opened Lake Superior to trade with the Lower Lakes in 1855, Cleveland became a major shipping center for ore, lumber, copper, coal, and farm produce.

During the Civil War, the city's iron ore and coal deposits were mined for steel production and commercial activity increased to meet the Union's increased demands for heavy machinery, railroad equipment, and ships. In the postwar years, Cleveland's mills and factories expanded even further to satisfy the increased needs of the new cities and farms springing up in the wake of westward migration.

Although heavy manufacturing still employs about 20 percent of the city's workforce, the national trend toward a service economy had a severe impact on the local economy, and the population of the Cleveland metropolitan area declined from a high of 2.8 million in 1970 to only 1.8 million today. Nonetheless, Cleveland is still home to many large industrial companies. In addition, there are many medical and industrial research firms, most notably the world-famous Cleveland Clinic and NASA's Lewis Research Center.

Cleveland's industrial strength manifests itself in its flourishing cultural institutions, including the Cleveland Play House, the oldest repertory house in the nation, the world-famous Cleveland Orchestra, the Cleveland Institute of Art, the Cleveland Museum of Natural History, Western Reserve Historical Society, the Cleveland Health Museum, the Allen Memorial Medical Library, and the Cleveland Zoo.
Population   498,246 (1996). Rank: 25th. Race/ national origin (1990): Black 46.6%; Hispanic 4.6%; Asian 1.0%; American Indian 0.3%.
Location: 41°28'N, 81°43'W. County: Cuyahoga.
Terrain and climate   Elev.: 805 ft. Area: 79 sq. mi. (204.6 sq km). Avg. daily min. temp.: Jan.: 18.5°F/-7.5°C; avg. daily max. July: 81.7°F/27.6°C. Avg. annual: rainfall, 35.40"; snowfall, 52"; clear days, 70; precipitation days, 156.
Government   Form: mayor and council. Mayor Michael R. White. Election: Nov. 2001. Municipal tel. number: (216) 664-2000.
Visitor Info: 1-800-321-1004 or (216) 621-4110.
www.travelcleveland.com

▶ COLORADO SPRINGS, COLORADO

Colorado's second-largest city lies on the eastern edge of the Rocky Mountains, some 60 miles south of Denver. Most of the city is nestled among rolling hills with views of the 14,110–foot Pikes Peak to the west. General William Jackson Palmer was the first to recognize the area's natural beauty when he founded the city in 1871. In its early years, it was popular with Europeans, especially Britons, and the city acquired the nickname Little London.

The city's first big boom came during the 1890s, when gold was discovered in nearby Cripple Creek in 1891. The gold rush ended in 1917, when the U.S. began coining money with silver. Since the beginning of World War II, the military has been a major presence in Colorado Springs, beginning with the establishment of Fort Carson in 1942 and continuing with the location of the Air Force Academy, several Air Force bases, and the North American Aerospace Defense Command (NORAD) over the years since then.

The city's manufacturing base experienced record growth during the 1960s and '70s due to Colorado Springs' low cost of living and sunny weather patterns (the city has hundreds of clear days and receives less snow than Denver or Minneapolis). Semiconductors, electronic equipment, computers, and plastics are among the major manufacturing industries.

Leading an expansion of the service industry in the Pikes Peak region, the United States Olympic Committee has its headquarters in Colorado Springs, as well as its Olympic Training Center, the world's premier multi-sport training facility.

Colorado Springs also prides itself on its extremely clean air. According to local officials, the city's pollen counts are among the lowest in the country, providing relief to people suffering from asthma, nasal allergies, and other respiratory ailments.

Population   345,127 (1996). Rank: 50th. Race/national origin (1990): Black 7.0%; Hispanic 9.1%; Asian 2.4%; American Indian 0.8%.
Location: 38°48'N, 104°42'W. County: El Paso.
Terrain and climate   Elev. 6,145 ft. Area 183.2 sq. mi. (474.5 sq km). Avg. daily min. temp.: Jan.: 16.1°F/–8.8°C; avg. daily max. July: 86.5°F/30.3°C. Avg. annual: rainfall, 16.24"; snowfall, 51"; clear days, 129; precipitation days, 98.
Government   Form: council and manager. Mayor Lou Makepeace. Election: April 2003.
Visitor info: www.colorado-springs.com/

▶COLUMBUS, OHIO

The Ohio legislature designated a site along the banks of the Scioto River in the center of the state as the capital in 1812, and named it Columbus in honor of the famous explorer of the New World. From the first, the city exploited its status as the seat of government and its prime location in the middle of the nation's growing network of roads, canals and highways. Incorporated in 1834, Columbus became a thriving hub of agricultural trade.

Between 1850 and 1900, its population grew from 17,800 to over 100,000. Because of the many carriage factories, in the 19th century Columbus was known as the "Buggy Capital of the World." Five railroads passed through the city, so banks soon began to spring up, making Columbus a financial center for the surrounding farm counties.

As in the 19th century, Columbus's modern economy is built on government, agriculture, local finance, and education. In 1950, to counter the trend of suburbanization, the city developed a policy of annexation of surrounding communities. Because it is less reliant on heavy industry than other midwestern cities, it has weathered the decline of the rust belt better than most and it remains a bustling metropolis. In the 1980s, the city realized the creation of more than $780 million in new development and about 100,000 new jobs.

Ohio State University, one of the nation's largest universities, opened as the Ohio Agricultural and Mechanical College in 1870, and the city today has a rich academic community that includes the Ohio Dominican College (whose origins date to 1868), the Columbus College of Art and Design and the Ohio Institute of Technology. Business leaders and politicians have joined in an effort to make the city a center for the arts, refurbishing three theaters and building a complex of three more.

Population   657,053 (1996). Rank: 16th. Race/national origin (1990): Black 22.6%; Hispanic 1.1%; Asian 2.4%; American Indian 0.2%.

Location: 39°57'N, 83°01'W. Counties: Fairfield, Franklin.
Terrain and climate   Elev.: 833 ft. Area: 186.8 sq. mi. (483.8 sq km). Avg. daily min. temp.: Jan.: 19.4°F/-7°C; avg. daily max. July: 84.4°F/29.1°C. Avg. annual: rainfall, 36.97"; snowfall, 28"; clear days, 75; precipitation days, 136.
Government   Form: mayor and city council. Mayor Gregory S. Lashutka. Election: Nov. 1999. Municipal tel. number: (614) 645-7671.
Visitor info: 1-800-354-2657 or (614) 221-6623. www.ci.columbus.oh.us

▶DALLAS, TEXAS

First settled in 1841 by John Neely Bryan, a Tennessee trader and lawyer, Dallas stretches about 30 miles east of Forth Worth on the Trinity River. Named in 1846 after James K. Polk's vice president, George Mifflin Dallas, it was chartered as a city in 1871. Though it grew substantially with the arrival of railroads in 1872, the population numbered a mere 92,000 in 1910.

Located in the heart of the northern Texas oil belt, Dallas today thrives on a diverse economic base, which, in addition to oil and natural gas, includes production of brick clay and the raw materials for Portland cement, and cotton, grains, fruits, beef, dairy cattle, hogs, sheep and poultry from the farms that surround the city. One of the largest inland cotton markets, and a leading distributor of farm goods and machinery, Dallas also serves as the southwest's banking center with major banks, insurance companies, and the Federal Reserve Bank for the Eleventh District. Key manufacturing industries include aerospace, electronics, transportation equipment, machinery, food and related products, and apparel. Among its leading high-tech employers are Texas Instruments, Electronic Data Systems, and E Systems Inc.

Some of Dallas's distinguished universities are Southern Methodist, Southwestern Medical School of the University of Texas, the Dallas Theological Seminary and Graduate School of Theology, and the Baylor University Schools of Dentistry and Nursing. The Dallas Symphony Orchestra, the Dallas Theater Center, the Dallas Civic Opera, the Dallas Historical Society Museum in the Texas Hall of State, and the Dallas Garden Center, contribute to the city's rich cultural life. Fair Park, the site of the annual State Fair of Texas, remains the most widely attended state fair in the country.

Population   1,053,292 (1996). Rank: 9th. Race/national origin (1990): Black 29.5%; Hispanic 20.9%; Asian 2.2%; American Indian 0.5%.
Location: 32°50'N, 96°50'W. Counties: Collin, Dallas, Denton, Kaufman, Rockwall.
Terrain and climate   Elev.: 596 ft. Area: 331.4 sq. mi. (858.3 sq km). Avg. daily min. temp.: Jan.: 33.9°F/1°C; avg. daily max. July: 97.8°F/36.5°C. Avg. annual: rainfall, 34.16"; snowfall, 3"; clear days, 138; precipitation days, 79.
Government   Form: council and manager. Mayor Ronald Kirk. Election: May 2003. Municipal tel. number: (214) 670-4054.
Visitor info: 1-800-CDALLAS or (214) 746-6677. www.ci.dallas.tx.us

▶DENVER, COLORADO

Denver was born during the great "Pikes Peak or Bust" gold rush of 1859 when small flakes of placer gold were found where the South Platte River meets Cherry Creek. In its first few years, the city survived a flood, several major fires, Indian attacks, and an invasion by Confederate soldiers during the Civil War. With the discovery of more gold in the Rocky Mountains, Denver became a boom town. Saloons, gambling halls, and wagon trains lined the mud-filled streets and just about every outlaw, desperado, and lawman in the West made at least one visit to the city. The turn of the century brought respectability and the wealth of the mountains was poured into parks, fountains, tree-lined streets, and elaborate mansions.

During the oil crisis of the late 1970s and early '80s, Denver experienced a second boom when it became a corporate center for oil-from-shale companies working the Western Slope of the Rockies. Then one of the fastest-growing cities in the United States, in 1983, it doubled its office space as part of a five-year building campaign that added 16 skyscrapers, a $76 million pedestrian mall, and an $80 million performing arts center. Expansion was slowed by the energy glut of the mid-1980s, but it has rebounded dramatically in the 1990s and the population grew by close to 10,000 per year in the first few years of the 1990s.

In 1993, the Colorado Rockies baseball team drew more than four million fans to a converted football stadium. And in 1995, after countless setbacks stemming from problems with its automated baggage system, the much-heralded Denver International Airport finally opened its doors, thus completing the final chapter of a vastly overbudget boondoggle.

Denver's population is among the youngest in the nation, and the youthful flavor of the city is very evident. Denver leads the nation in movie attendance and has more sporting goods stores per resident than any city in the world. The city's 205 parks are so active that a speed limit was recently instituted—for bicycles.

Population 497,840 (1996). Rank: 26th. Race/national origin (1990): Black 12.8%; Hispanic 23.0%; Asian 2.4%; American Indian 1.2%.
Location: 39°45'N, 105°00'W. County: Denver.
Terrain and climate Elev.: 5,280 ft. Area: 106.8 sq. mi. (276.6 sq km). Avg. daily min. temp.: Jan.: 15.9°F/-8.9°C; avg. daily max. July: 88°F/31°C. Avg. annual: rainfall, 15.31"; snowfall, 60"; clear days, 115; precipitation days, 88.
Government Form: mayor and council. Mayor Wellington E. Webb. Election: June 2003. Municipal tel. number: (303) 640-2721.
Visitor info: 1-800-645-3446 or (303) 892-1112 www.denvergov.org

▶ **DETROIT, MICHIGAN**
Founded in 1701 by Antoine de La Mothe, sieur de Cadillac, Detroit lies on the Detroit River between Lake Erie and Lake Huron. Named Fort Pontchartrain-du-Détroit (of the strait), the oldest permanent settlement on the Great Lakes flourished as a trading post for trappers, under French control (to 1760), then British (to 1796) and then American.

The first steamboat reached Detroit from Buffalo in 1818, but it was the easy access to eastern markets via the Erie Canal in 1825 that allowed Detroit to exploit the abundant natural resources in the Michigan peninsula and fostered its emergence as a modern industrial giant in the post-Civil War years. Tenth among cities in the value of its manufactures by 1899, Detroit's main exports included iron ore, copper, lead, salt, and fish. The development of the automotive industry, which eventually became centered in Detroit, propelled Detroit to number three by the 1920s. While Detroit is the home of General Motors, Chrysler, and Ford, recently the automotive industry has been as much a curse as a blessing, for every setback to

any of the "Big Three" is felt throughout the Motor City.

Despite the fact that it remains third in industrial manufacturing in the U.S., Detroit has been plagued by urban decline. The relatively low standard of living among the predominantly black inhabitants ignited riots in the 1940s and 1960s, and the city's crime rate is today among the highest in the nation. However, it was Detroit blacks who gave rise to one of the most sensational expressions of popular culture in the 1960s. Founded in 1960, the Tamla Motown label propelled the Jackson 5, the Supremes, and Stevie Wonder—among others—to world renown, and in the process created one of the largest black-owned businesses in the country.

The city's rich and diverse cultural institutions include the Detroit Institute of Arts, which includes one of the largest collections of American art in the world in addition to extensive European holdings, the Detroit Symphony, the Cranbrook Academy of Art, and the 1,000-acre Belle Isle Park, situated on an island in the Detroit River and includes beaches, a yacht basin, a zoo, an aquarium, and a botanical gardens.

Population 1,000,2724 (1996). Rank: 10th. Race/national origin (1990): Black 75.7%; Hispanic 2.8%; Asian 0.8%; American Indian 0.4%.
Location: 42°23'N, 83°05'W. County: Wayne.
Terrain and climate Elev.: 581 ft. Area: 135.6 sq. mi. (351.2 sq km). Avg. daily min. temp.: Jan.: 16.1°F/-8.8°C; avg. daily max. July: 83.1°F/28.3°C. Avg. annual: rainfall, 30.97"; snowfall, 39"; clear days, 75; precipitation days, 133.
Government Form: mayor and council. Mayor Dennis Archer. Election: Nov. 2001. Municipal tel. number: (313) 224-3270.
Visitor info: 1-800-DETROIT or (313) 202-1800. www.ci.detroit.mi.us

▶ **EL PASO, TEXAS**
The largest Texas city bordering Mexico, El Paso sits in the western part of the state on the northern bank of the Rio Grande across from Juarez. A major port of entry, with the biggest commercial and manufacturing base in the area, the city encompasses a region of mines, oil fields, livestock ranches, and farms (principal crops: pecans, fruit, cotton, alfalfa, onions, lettuce, chiles). Important industries include metals smelting and refining, oil and gas refining, textiles, meat packing, and food processing. The city is also home to the University of Texas, at El Paso.

In 1536, Alvar Núñez Cabeza de Vaca crossed the Rio Grande, becoming the first European to set foot in the area, but settlement did not follow until 1659, with the establishment of both El Paso del Norte on the southern bank of the Rio Grande, and the Mission of Guadalupe. In 1682, settlers from New Mexico founded Ysleta, an area within the current city limits of El Paso, but permanent settlement did not begin until the arrival of Juan Maria Ponce de Leon in 1827. Incorporated as a city in 1873, El Paso grew into a major industrial center with the introduction of the railroads in 1881.

El Paso's access to sources of cheap labor complemented its mining, refining, and agricultural activities and helped build the city's manufacturing base. In recent years, however, the movement of manufacturing back to Mexico, where labor costs are far less, has created some concern for that portion of the economy. El Paso's proximity to Juarez, Mexico, makes it a vibrant tourist haven, and its pleasant climate, combined with its position on the immigration route from Latin America, have made El Paso one of the fastest growing

cities in the U.S. El Paso also has the highest percentage of citizens with Hispanic ancestry of any American city.
Population 599,865 (1996). Rank: 17th. Race/national origin (1990): Black 3.4%; Hispanic 69.0%; Asian 1.2%; American Indian 0.4%.
Location: 31°50'N, 106°30'W. County: El Paso.
Terrain and climate Elev.: 3,700 ft. Area: 239.7 sq. mi. (620.8 sq km). Avg. daily min. temp.: Jan.: 30.4°F/-0.8°C; avg. daily max. July: 95.3°F/35.1°C. Avg. annual: rainfall, 7.82"; snowfall, 5"; clear days, 194; precipitation days, 45.
Government Form: mayor and council. Mayor Carlos Ramirez. Election: May 2003. Municipal tel. number: (915) 541-4145.
Visitor info: 1-800-351-6024 or (915) 534-0653
www.ci.el-paso.tx.us

►FORT WORTH, TEXAS
Named in 1849 after Gen. William J. Worth, commander of the U.S. Army in Texas, Forth Worth originally served to protect settlers from Indian attacks. It grew slowly mainly as a stopover on the cattle drives along the Chisholm Trail until the Texas and Pacific Railroad reached the city in 1871. Stockyards sprang up, making Fort Worth a conduit of cattle shipping, and with the building of a grain elevator, it developed into a milling center as well. By the turn of the century, it had also emerged as a flourishing meat packing market. Oil was discovered in 1917, bringing prosperity and transforming the city into a major refining center with a dozen operating facilities. The two world wars introduced military installations (particularly airfields) to the area. Fort Worth is the sixth largest city in Texas, boasting the state's three finest art museums and a network of parks with total acreage second only to Chicago's.
Population 479,716 (1996). Rank: 28th. Race/national origin (1990): Black 22.0%; Hispanic 19.5%; Asian 2.0%; American Indian 0.4%.
Location 32°45'N, 97°25'W. County: Tarrant.
Terrain and climate Elev.: 670 ft. Area: 258.5 sq. mi. (670.3 sq km). Avg. daily min. temp.: Jan.: 33.9°F/1°C; avg. daily max. July: 97.8°F/36.5°C. Avg. annual: rainfall, 29.45"; snowfall, 1.4"; clear days, 137; precipitation days, 78.
Government Form: council and manager. Mayor Kenneth Barr. Election: May 2001. Municipal tel. number: (817) 871-8900.
Visitor info: 1-800-433-5747 or (817) 336-8791.
www.ci.fort-worth.tx.us

►FRESNO, CALIFORNIA
Fresno grew up around a train station established in 1872 for what became the Southern Pacific Railway. The city was incorporated in 1874. With the introduction of irrigation to the fertile San Joaquin Valley in the 1880s, the small city thrived at the center of a healthy agricultural economy. Today Fresno County is the number one producer of agricultural products in the nation—and the world—and averages more than $2 billion a year in the production and processing of 200 commercial crops, including grapes (for wine and raisins), melon, cotton, alfalfa, barley, grains, cattle, sheep, and poultry.

Fresno's population grew 63 percent between 1980 and 1990, and in the 1980s it was the ninth fastest growing city in the United States and by far the fastest growing of the nation's 50 largest cities.

Located in central California, Fresno—the name is Spanish for ash tree—is a gateway to the Sierra Nevadas, and it is less than 90 minutes from three national parks—Kings Canyon (55 miles),

Sequoia (85 miles) and Yosemite (92 miles). Among the attractions to be found within the city limits are the Fresno Art Museum, the Fresno Zoo, the Kearney Mansion Museum (restored home of Theo Kearney, "Raisin King of California"), the Fresno Metropolitan Museum, and the Discovery Center. There are also 10 colleges and universities including a campus of California State University and Fresno City College.
Population 396,011 (1996). Rank: 39th. Race/national origin (1990): Black 8.3%; Hispanic 29.9%; Asian 12.5%; American Indian 1.1%.
Location 36°47'N, 119°50'W. County: Fresno.
Terrain and climate Elev. 328 ft.; Area: 99.4 sq. mi. (257 sq km). Avg. daily min. temp. Jan.: 37.4°/3°C; avg. daily max. July: 98°.7F/37°C. Avg. annual rainfall: 10"; snowfall 0"; clear days: 200; precipitation days: 44.
Government Form: council manager. Mayor: Jim Patterson. Election: May 2000. Municipal tel.: (209) 498-1560.
Visitor info: (209) 233-0836 or 1-800-788-0836.
www.ci.fresno.ca.us

►HONOLULU, HAWAII
First visited by Europeans in 1794, Honolulu, meaning "sheltered harbor," has attracted droves of visitors ever since. Situated on Oahu Island, it benefits from a large bay fully protected by coral reefs and its large port facilities. Because of its hospitable climate, the beaches of Waikiki, its majestic mountains, and exotic locale, tourism is Honolulu's major industry; several million visitors come annually, mainly from the U.S. mainland and the Far East, particularly from Japan.

The defense industry is the second mainstay of Honolulu's economy, as the U.S. has long maintained major installations around the island, including the naval base at Pearl Harbor, Hickam Air Force Base, and the U.S. Army's Schofield Barracks and Fort Shafter. Honolulu also serves as the center for Hawaii's export crops—sugar, pineapple, and molasses—and is the principal port for the import of much of the island state's necessities.
Population 423,475 (1996). Rank: 35th. Race/national origin (1990): Black 1.3%; Hispanic 4.6%; Asian 70.5%; American Indian 0.3%.
Location: 21°19'N, 157°52'W. County: Honolulu.
Terrain and climate Elev.: 15 ft. Area: 25.3 sq. mi. (65.52 sq km). Avg. daily min. temp.: Jan.: 65.3°F/18.5°C; avg. daily max. July: 87.1°F/30.6°C. Avg. annual rainfall: 23.47"; snowfall: 0"; clear days: 90; precipitation days: 102.
Government Form: mayor and council. Mayor Jeremy Harris. Election: Nov. 2000. Municipal tel. number: (808) 523-4141.
Visitor info: (808) 923-1811.
www.gohawaii.com

►HOUSTON, TEXAS
On August 30, 1836, brothers August C. and John K. Allen founded this city and named it after Sam Houston, the first president of the Republic of Texas. The Allens paid just over $1.40 per share for 6,642 acres of land near the headwaters of Buffalo Bayou about 50 miles inland from the Gulf of Mexico. Houston's proximity to Stephen Austin's central Texas colonies gave it great potential as a marketing and distribution site. Incorporated in 1837, the city served as capital of the Republic of Texas until 1840. When the first railroad in Texas began operating out of Houston in 1853, the city developed into a major agricultural center while

the discovery of oil in southeast Texas at Spindletop in 1901, and the opening of the man-made Houston Ship Channel in 1914, stimulated petroleum refining and metal fabricating. During World War II, petrochemical production began on a large scale, and with the building of NASA's $761 million complex in the early 1960s (now known as the Johnson Space Center), Houston took center stage as the main player in manned spacecraft.

A major corporate and international business center—15 *Fortune* 500 companies are based here—present-day Houston has successfully limited its dependence on the energy economy. The Port of Houston is the eighth-largest in the world in terms of tonnage handled; the city is also home to four of the nation's 10 major liquid gas pipelines. The presence of the Texas Medical Center also makes Houston a vital U.S. center for the practice and progress of modern high-tech medicine. The Center's 39 institutions occupy in excess of 550 acres and employ more than 50,000 workers. Houston's total health employment exceeds 100,000.

Population 1,744,058 (1996). Rank: 4th. Race/national origin (1990): Black 28.1%; Hispanic 27.6%; Asian 4.1%; American Indian 0.3%.
Location: 29°50'N, 95°20'W. Counties: Fort Bend, Harris, Montgomery.
Terrain and climate Elev.: 49 ft. Area: 572.7 sq. mi. (1,483.3 sq km). Avg. daily min. temp.: Jan.: 40.8°F/4.8°C; avg. daily max. July: 93.6°F/34.2°C. Avg. annual rainfall: 44.77"; snowfall: 0"; clear days: 94; precipitation days: 107.
Government Form: mayor and council. Mayor Lee P. Brown. Election: Nov. 1999. Municipal tel. number: (713) 247-1000.
Visitor info: (713) 227-3100 or 1-800-365-7575. www.ci.houston.tx.us

▶ **INDIANAPOLIS, INDIANA**
Indianapolis, the capital of Indiana and a major commercial center in the country's heartland, is intersected by more highways than any other in the nation, earning it the name, the "Crossroads of America." Fifty percent of America's population is within a day's drive of the city, a geographic asset that makes it a focal point of transportation and manufacturing.

The first European-American settlement, established in 1820 where Fall Creek meets the White River, was chosen as the location of Indiana's capital in 1825. The state government created jobs triggering an expanding population that further swelled with the routing of the National Road (US 40) in 1830. Development mushroomed in 1839 with the building of the Central Canal on the White River, providing a vital transportation link and the necessary water power to run factories, sawmills, and paper mills. Maintenance of the canal, however, proved impossible, and the town declined until the introduction of the railroad. By 1853, railroad lines fed into Indianapolis from every corner of the nation and at one point, nearly 200 trains passed through daily. At the turn of the century, Indianapolis had emerged as a sophisticated city with sidewalks and streetcars. The city's economy prospered during the early stages of the automotive industry, producing more than 50 types of car—including the Duesenberg, the Marmon, and the Stutz—before Detroit gained ascendancy.

Having survived the decline in heavy industry and the flight of the affluent to the suburbs, Indianapolis remains a hub of manufacturing and transportation, with a bustling wheat, soybean, and livestock market. Key industries include electronics, metal fabrication, pharmaceuticals, and trans-

portation equipment. Downtown Indianapolis has enjoyed a renaissance with the construction of a convention center, the Hoosier Dome, Market Square Arena, and the refurbishment of Union Station. But the city's premier attraction remains the Indianapolis 500, the annual Memorial Day weekend auto race, first held in 1911.

Population 746,737 (1996). Rank: 12th. Race/national origin (1990): Black 22.6%; Hispanic 1.1%; Asian 0.9%; American Indian 0.2%.
Location 39°42'N, 86°10'W. County: Marion.
Terrain and climate Elev.: 808 ft. Area: 352 sq. mi. (911.7 sq km). Avg. daily min. temp.: Jan.: 17.8°F/-7.8°C; avg. daily max. July: 85.2°F/29.5°C. Avg. annual rainfall: 39.12"; snowfall: 21"; clear days: 90; precipitation days: 122.
Government Form: mayor and council. Mayor: Stephen Goldsmith. Election: May 2000. Municipal tel. number: (317) 327-3200.
Visitor info: (317) 237-5200 or 1-800-323-4639. www.ci.indianapolis.in.us

▶ **JACKSONVILLE, FLORIDA**
The first Europeans to visit the area were French Huguenots who in 1564 established a colony at Fort Caroline on the Saint Johns River in northeast Florida. The Spanish destroyed the fort in the following year. Permanent settlement began in 1816, and in 1822 Jacksonville was laid out and named for then Maj. Gen. Andrew Jackson, who had led the U.S. campaign to take Florida from the Spanish. Growth was slow until after the Civil War. After World War II, several large naval bases were located here and by 1960 the population was over 200,000. In 1968, the population jumped to more than 500,000 when it was consolidated with Duval County, and Jacksonville became one of the largest cities by area in the U.S.

Florida's largest city, Jacksonville is a major regional center for commerce, industry, finance, and medicine. After years of improvements on its harbor, 25 miles west from the mouth of the Saint Johns, it has grown into a major port of entry and it is the primary distribution center for the region. Jacksonville has also emerged as a leading resort with extensive recreational and convention facilities. Among its amenities are the Haydon Burns Library, the Cummer Gallery of Art, the Jacksonville Art Museum, the Jacksonville Zoological Park, the Saint Johns River Park, and Fort Caroline National Memorial, site of the first European colony in Florida. Among its leading educational institutions are Jacksonville University and the University of Northern Florida.

Population 679,792 (1996). Rank: 14th. Race/national origin (1990): Black 25.2%; Hispanic 2.6%; Asian 1.9%; American Indian 0.3%.
Location: 30°15'N, 81°38'W. County: Duval.
Terrain and climate Elev.: 31 ft. Area: 840 sq. mi. (1,967.6 sq km). Avg. daily min. temp.: Jan.: 41.7°F/ °C; avg. daily max. July: 90.7°F/29.5°C. Avg. annual rainfall: 52.77"; snowfall: 0"; clear days: 98; precipitation days: 116.
Government Form: mayor and council. Mayor John A. Delaney. Election: May 2003. Municipal tel. number: (904) 630-1776.
Visitor info: 1-800-733-2668 or (904) 798-9111. www.ci.jax.fl.us

▶ **KANSAS CITY, MISSOURI**
Kansas City was begun as a trading outpost by the French fur trader François Chouteau in 1821. In 1833, the town of Westport was founded nearby, and in 1850 the City of Kansas received its first charter. (Its name was changed to Kansas City in 1889.)

Situated at the confluence of the Kansas and Missouri rivers, Kansas City prospered early on as a river port and as the terminus of the Santa Fe and Oregon trails. With the arrival of the railroad in 1866, Kansas City's status as a major commercial hub was assured, Thanks to its central location and the development of excellent and diversified transportation and storage facilities, Kansas City is one of the nation's key markets for agricultural and livestock products, as well as for the distribution of heavy agricultural machinery. The Kansas City Board of Trade is one of the largest grain and commodities trading markets in the world. Other major industries are greeting card publishing, telecommunications, and high-tech manufacturing, especially instrument landing systems for airplanes. Kansas City is also home to the 10th Federal Reserve Bank.

An early oasis of culture in the midst of an un-settled, untamed prairie (the city once boasted two opera houses), Kansas City remains a mecca of the arts, with such cultural offerings as the Kansas City Art Institute, the Nelson Atkins Museum of Art, the Kansas City Symphony, the Lyric Opera, and the Missouri Repertory Theatre. The city's beginnings are preserved in the Lone Jack Civil War Museum and Missouri Town 1855, and it is the site of the annual American Royal Livestock, Horse Show, and Rodeo, held as part of the annual convention of the Future Farmers of America. Among its institutes of higher learning are Rockhurst College (1916), the University of Missouri-Kansas City, and the DeVry Institute of Technology.

Population   441,259 (1996). Rank: 33rd. Race/national origin (1990): Black 29.6%; Hispanic 3.9%; Asian 1.2%; American Indian 0.5%.
Location: 39°07'N, 94°38'W. Counties: Cass, Clay, Jackson, and Platte.
Terrain and climate   Elev.: 744 ft. Area: 316.4 sq. mi. (819.5 sq km). Avg. daily min. temp.: Jan.: 17.2°F/-8.2°C; avg. daily max. July: 88.5°F/31.3°C. Avg. annual rainfall: 29.27"; snowfall: 5.9"; clear days: 132; precipitation days: 97.
Government   Form: council and manager. Mayor Kay Barnes. Election April 2003. Municipal tel. number: (816) 274-2000.
Visitor info: 1-800-767-7700 or (816) 221-5242.
www.kcmo.org

▶LAS VEGAS, NEVADA

Las Vegas was originally settled by Mormons in 1855, but its modern history began in 1931, when Nevada legalized gambling and liberalized marriage and divorce laws. From then until 1978 (when Atlantic City re-opened its casinos), Las Vegas prospered while it enjoyed a monopoly on casino gambling in the U.S. Since 1980, it has been one of America's fastest-growing cities, more than doubling in size between 1980 and 1996. There were 164,674 people living in Las Vegas in 1980; by 1996 the city's population had climbed to 376,906. City government officials estimate the population in 1999 to be well over 400,000. Las Vegas is growing so fast, it prints phone books twice a year.

To be sure, gambling has fueled this growth—gaming revenues topped $6 billion in 1997—but the city's expansion has come even as dozens of other cities across the country have legalized casino gambling on riverboats, at Native American reservations, or even in the French Quarter of New Orleans. Las Vegas has thrived because of a mix of gambling, nightlife, shopping, and an un-equivocal commitment to excess. Since 1993, five major resorts have been torn down, only to make way for newer, bigger properties. The nation's 10 biggest hotels (including the 5000–room MGM Grand) are all here. Over the past decade, the city has built hotels replicating New York City, Paris, Venice (complete with canals through the desert landscape), and the pyramids of Egypt.

More than 30 million visitors (including 3 million conventioneers) travel to Las Vegas each year. With all this tourism has come tens of thousands of new jobs and new housing (an average of 578 new homes per month). Because the city is laid out in a desert, there are few geographical barriers to limit urban expansion, except the availability of drinking water. The city is beginning to confront problems of urban sprawl such as traffic, air pollution, and distribution of resources such as schools and water.

Population   376,906 (1996). Rank: 41st. Race/national origin (1990): Black 11.4%; Hispanic 12.5%, Asian 3.6%, American Indian 0.9%.
Location: 36° 05'N, 115°10'W. County: Clark.
Terrain and climate   Elev.: 2,162 ft. Area: 83.3 sq. mi. (215.7 sq km). Avg. daily min. temp.: Jan.: 33.6°F/0.9°C; avg. daily max. July: 105.9°F/41.1°C. Avg. annual rainfall: 4"; snowfall: 1"; clear days: 211; precipitation days: 26.
Government   Form: Council and manager. Mayor Oscar B. Goodman. Election: June, 2003. Municipal tel. number (702) 229-6501.
Visitor info: (702) 892-7575.
www.ci.las-vegas.nv.us

▶LONG BEACH, CALIFORNIA

Originally the site of an Indian trading camp, by the end of the 18th century the area of what is now Long Beach was part of the Spanish Ranchos Los Alamitos and Cerritos. In 1881, William E. Willmore began development of the land as a resort (which he named for himself). When first incorporated in 1888, it was named Long Beach after its 8.5 miles of Pacific beachfront. Content to remain a resort community, Long Beach's fortunes were rewritten in 1921 when extensive petroleum deposits were first discovered at Signal Hill. Today, industry is a major presence in Long Beach—especially ship repair, transportation, oil refining, and marine research; in addition, the Navy maintains a large base with dry dock facilities.

Among the cultural and recreational attractions Long Beach boasts are its own Museum of Art, the Terrace Theater, home of the Long Beach Symphony Orchestra, and the Long Beach Community Playhouse. Popular tourist attractions include Los Cerritos, a Spanish adobe house which dates to 1844, the magnificent ocean liner *Queen Mary* which today serves as a floating maritime museum, convention center, and hotel. Long Beach is also the site of a Formula 1 Grand Prix every spring. Disneyland is in nearby Anaheim.

Population   421,904 (1996). Rank: 36th. Race/national origin (1990): Black 13.7%; Hispanic 23.6%; Asian 13.6%; American Indian 0.6%.
Location: 33°46'N, 118°10'W. County: Los Angeles.
Terrain and climate   Elev.: 35 ft. Area: 49.8 sq. mi. (129 sq km). Avg. daily min. temp.: Jan.: 44.3°F/6.8°C; avg. daily max. July: 83°F/28.3°C. Avg. annual rainfall: 12"; snowfall: 0"; clear days: 143; precipitation days: 35.
Government   Form: council and manager. Mayor Beverly O'Neill. Election: April 2002. Municipal tel. number: (562) 570-6801.
Visitor info: 1-800-4LB-STAY or (562) 436-3645.
www.ci.long-beach.ca.us

▶ LOS ANGELES, CALIFORNIA

In pre-Spanish days, the area of Los Angeles was inhabited by approximately 4,000 Indians representing some 30 tribes. The village of Yang-na, with a population of 300, was located in what is now downtown Los Angeles, in the vicinity of Alameda and Commercial Streets. In October of 1542, João Rodrigues Cabrilho, a Portuguese explorer in the employ of Spain, became the first European to set foot on Los Angeles soil, but 200 years passed before a land expedition under the command of Gaspar de Portola crossed the territory on the way from Monterey to San Diego, in 1769.

The establishment of the Mission of San Gabriel (destined to become the largest of the Franciscan Missions) followed and in 1781, the Spanish Governor Felipe Neve founded the city of El Pueblo de Nuestra Señora de los Angeles de Porciuncula ("The Village of Our Lady of the Angels") as part of a plan to colonize California. Spanish rule continued until 1822 when she relinquished her holdings in western America, prompting California to pledge her allegiance to the Mexican empire. With the Treaty of Guadalupe Hidalgo (1848) the U.S. acquired all of California from Mexico and in 1850 Los Angeles was incorporated as a city. Introduction of the Southern Pacific Railroad in 1876 sparked a 12-year land boom, promoting the city's growth. By 1892, Los Angeles thrived as a center of oil production and in 1899 work began on the largest man-made deep-water facility in the world. Emerging as the motion picture capital of the world by 1910, industry accelerated in the 1920s and today L.A. ranks as one of the three great industrial cities in the country.

A thriving metropolis, Los Angeles boasts one of the finest highway systems in the world, handling about 6 million cars registered in its five-county area—a car for every two people, the highest ratio in the world. Three transcontinental railway systems terminate in L.A., about 40 certified air carriers fly to all parts of the world, its harbors have 46 miles of waterfront, and the city has the largest trucking center in the west. L.A. remains the world's movie mecca, teeming with studios, stars, and the starstruck.

Los Angelenos live with daily problems of smog, traffic jams, spectacular traffic accidents, and the ever-present threats of mud slides, fires, floods, high winds, and earthquakes. But the year-round sunshine, and the number of beaches and mountain areas, all within an easy drive, tend to ameliorate one's anxiety.

Population   3,553,638 (1996). Rank: 2nd. Race/national origin (1990): Black 14.0%; Hispanic 39.9%; Asian 9.8%; American Indian 0.5%.
Location: 34°00'N, 118°10'W. County: Los Angeles.
Terrain and climate   Elev.: 104 ft. Area: 465.9 sq. mi. (1206.7 sq km). Avg. daily min. temp.: Jan.: 47.3°F/8.5°C; avg. daily max. July: 75.3°F/24°C. Avg. annual rainfall: 14.85"; snowfall: 0"; clear days: 143; precipitation days: 35.
Government   Form: mayor and council. Mayor: Richard Riordan. Election: June 2001. Municipal tel. number: (213) 485-2121.
Visitor Info: (213) 624-7300.
www.ci.la.ca.us

▶ MEMPHIS, TENNESSEE

The first settlers in the area of Memphis arrived on the bluffs overlooking the Mississippi River more than a thousand years ago. The Chickasaw forcibly displaced these people and then lived there for eight centuries until 1838, when the U.S. government scattered the entire tribe to Oklahoma and parts further west so its citizens could develop the land. The Spanish explorer Hernando de Soto first set eyes on the bluffs in 1541. Other explorers passed through over the next century and in 1739 the French built Fort Assumption. The French, Spanish, and the Chickasaw fought over the land for the balance of the 18th century until it became a part of the U.S. in 1797. The area's original American owners, Gen. James Winchester, Judge John Overton, and Gen. Andrew Jackson (who later sold his share and went on to become President), established the town in 1819, and named it Memphis, after the ancient Egyptian city on the Nile.

Riverboatmen gave young Memphis a reputation for brawls and bawdiness, while mosquitoes gave it a history of yellow fever epidemics, which in the 1880s claimed more than half the city's population and jeopardized its charter. A sewage system, the first of its kind, helped finally conquer the epidemic. Between the river traffic and cotton crops, the city prospered, attracting Irish and German immigrants, and by the 20th century was on its way to becoming the unofficial capital of the mid-south. Elvis Presley, who expanded the city's rhythm and blues tradition to become the world's first rock and roll idol, remains the city's most enduring contribution to popular culture. In 1991, the Lorraine Motel, where civil rights leader Dr. Martin Luther King Jr. was assassinated in 1968, was opened as the National Civil Rights Museum. In recent years the city's central location has helped it to attract major corporations, most notably FedEx and Northwest Airlines.

Population   596,725 (1996). Rank: 18th. Race/national origin (1990): Black 54.8%; Hispanic 0.7%; Asian 0.8%; American Indian 0.2%.
Location: 35°07'N, 90°00'W. County: Shelby.
Terrain and climate   Elev.: 307 ft. Area: 264.1 sq. mi. (684 sq km). Avg. daily min. temp.: Jan.: 30.9°F/-0.6°C; avg. daily max. July: 91.5°F/33°C. Avg. annual rainfall: 51.57"; snowfall: 6"; clear days: 118; precipitation days: 106.
Government   Form: mayor and council. Mayor: Willie Herenton. Election: Oct. 2003. Municipal tel. number: (901) 576-6000.
Visitor info: (901) 543-5300.
www.ci.memphis.tn.us

▶ MIAMI, FLORIDA

Miami, the most southerly major city in the continental U.S., sits about two degrees north of the Tropic of Cancer, a location that has made it a long-standing resort haven. Miami in the 1980s also thrived as a major hub of commerce and as a population center for Latin American immigrants, particularly those arriving from Cuba, whose ambition and business acumen contributed to the city's prosperity. While tourists still generate over 60 percent of the area's economic activity, many other areas of enterprise, such as construction, light industry, and agriculture (limes, tomatoes, avocados, mangoes and beans) have flourished.

Miami (whose name is thought to derive from the Indian *mayami*, meaning "big water"), dates back to the 16th century when Native Americans occupied the southern part of Florida. Fort Dallas, built near the mouth of the Miami River in 1836 as a base of war against the Seminoles, became the first permanent European-American settlement. The building of the Florida East Coast Railroad, coinciding with Miami's incorporation as a city in 1896 (population 343), offered ready access to the area. Resort hotels quickly cropped up and Miami, along with the rest of Florida, enjoyed great success. In 1926, a severe hurricane submerged much of its land under water, abruptly ending Miami's prosperity, but the city managed to steadily grow by draining and developing swampland. After World War II, new resorts rose up, and Miami thrived both as a haven for older retirees and a refuge for a substantial number of Cubans fleeing Castro's repressive regime.

Today Miami bills itself as the "Gateway of the Americas," where the value of exports and imports has increased by over 20 percent a year for the last decade and foreign banking has expanded rapidly.

Population 365,127 (1996). Rank: 44th. Race/national origin (1990): Black 27.4%; Hispanic 62.5%; Asian 0.6%; American Indian 0.2%.
Location: 25°45'N, 80°15'W. County: Dade.
Terrain and climate Elev.: 12 ft. Area: 34.3 sq. mi. (88.8 sq km). Avg. daily min. temp.: Jan.: 59.2°F/15.1°C; avg. daily max. July: 88.7°F/31.5°C. Avg. annual rainfall: 57.55"; snowfall: 0"; clear days: 76; precipitation days: 129.
Government Form: council and manager. Mayor: Joe Carollo. Election: Nov. 2001. Municipal tel. number: (305) 250-5400.
Visitor info: 1-800-933-8448 or (305) 539-3000.
www.ci.miami.fl.us

▶ MILWAUKEE, WISCONSIN

During the 1670s the French explorers Jacques Marquette and Louis Joliet were the first Europeans to visit the site of present-day Milwaukee, an area on the western shore of Lake Michigan at the confluence of the Menomonee and Kinnickinnic Rivers. In 1795, Jacques Vicau of the North West Company established a trading post and in 1818, Solomon Laurent Juneau, the first permanent settler, founded Milwaukee (from the Indian term millioke, meaning "beautiful land"). From the 1840s on, large numbers of German immigrants came to the city, making up over 60 percent of the 1850 population; today, an estimated one-third of the city's residents are of German descent.

A flourishing agricultural center, Milwaukee had by the Civil War become the largest wheat market in the world. Its industrial base expanded after the war and by 1940 the city ranked fourth in manufacturing among U.S. cities. Still one of the most vigorous producers of durable goods, especially automotive parts, construction and road building equipment, diesel and gasoline engines, tractors, and outboard motors, Milwaukee also emerged as a major meat packing center. Reflecting its German heritage, the city developed a thriving brewing industry with several of the largest beer-producing companies in the U.S. (Though by 1996, almost all had disappeared). A major Great Lakes and international port, Milwaukee handles several international steamship lines.

Population 590,503 (1996). Rank: 19th. Race/national origin (1990): Black 30.5%; Hispanic 6.3%; Asian 1.9%; American Indian 0.9%.
Location: 43°09'N, 87°58'W. County: Milwaukee.
Terrain and climate Elev.: 581 ft. Area: 95.8 sq. mi. (248.1 sq km). Avg. daily min. temp.: Jan.: 11.3°F/-11.5°C; avg. daily max. July: 79.8°F/26.5°C. Avg. annual rainfall: 30.94"; snowfall: 45"; clear days: 96; precipitation days: 122.
Government Form: mayor and council. Mayor: John O. Norquist. Election: Apr. 2000. Municipal tel. number: (414) 286-3200.
Visitor info: 1-800-231-0903 or (414) 273-3950.
www.milwaukee.org

▶ MINNEAPOLIS, MINNESOTA

With an average annual temperature of 45° F, Minneapolis is the second coldest city in the U.S. But despite its arctic winters, it is one of the most desirable cities in the U.S. It sits astride the Mississippi River, near the headwaters of the Minnesota River, about 350 miles northwest of Chicago. While it is the largest commercial metropolis in the north between Milwaukee and Seattle, no single industry dominates, although many large computer and electronics companies make Minneapolis their home. A regional banking center and the site of the Federal Reserve Bank for the Ninth District, Minneapolis has the world's largest cash grain exchange, the world's four largest wheat-flour-milling companies, and provides the upper Midwest with truck, barge, and air transport.

In 1682 Father Louis Hennepin, the French priest who explored the Mississippi, was the first European to set eyes on the Falls of St. Anthony, the future site of Minneapolis. Unsettled until Fort Snelling was built in 1819 to protect the fur traders from the Sioux and Chippewa, the town of St. Anthony began growing up on one side of the Mississippi and a second settlement sprung up on the other. The two were consolidated in 1872; the new name was a hybrid of the Indian word minne, meaning "water," and the Greek word for "city," polis. Minneapolis blossomed on the basis of its flour and lumber milling. By century's end, the forests to the north had been depleted, but flour milling continues as a thriving industry to this day.

Long considered a center of progressive political and social thinking, it is a mecca of education and culture. Minneapolis contains the main campus of the University of Minnesota, and boasts the Minnesota Orchestra, and the Minneapolis Institute of the Arts. A haven for outdoor enthusiasts, the park system numbers 153 parks encompassing 6,000 acres, and with 10 percent of its surface covered by water, Minneapolis has 12 lakes within its city limits. Despite all this, the city has been steadily losing population (160,000 since 1950) to suburban areas.

Population 358,785 (1996). Rank: 46th. origin (1990): Black 13.0%; Hispanic 2.1%; Asian 4.3%; American Indian 3.3%.
Location: 44°58'N, 93°20'W. County: Hennepin.
Terrain and climate Elev.: 828 ft. Area: 55.1 sq. mi. (142.7 sq km). Avg. daily min. temp.: Jan.: 2.4°F/-16.4°C; avg. daily max. July: 83.4°F/28.5°C. Avg. annual rainfall: 26.36"; snowfall: 46"; clear days: 100; precipitation days: 113.
Government Form: mayor and council. Mayor: Sharon Sayles Belton. Election: Nov. 2001. Municipal tel. number: (612) 673-2100.
Visitor info: 1-800-445-7412 or (612) 661-4700.
www.ci.minneapolis.mn.us

▶ NASHVILLE, TENNESSEE

In the winter of 1779–80, settlers from North Carolina, led by James Robertson, arrived at a place on the Cumberland River called Big Salt Lick, and built forts on both sides of the river, one of which they named Nashborough, after Gen. Francis Nash of the Revolutionary Army. Adopting the name Nashville in 1784, the settlement was chartered as a city in 1806, became state capital in 1843, and prospered until the Civil War as the northern terminus of the Natchez Trace, a 500-mile road to Natchez, Mississippi. The site of one of the war's last major battles in December 1864, the city underwent a long period of rebuilding and by the end of the century, the population reached

81,000. The city continued to grow, doubling in population by World War II, and has experienced even greater expansion since that time.

While best known as a major center of both the recording and music-publishing industries, Nashville enjoys a widely diversified economic foundation and serves as a distribution and marketing point for the upper southern region of the U.S. Several religious organizations and their publishing operations are headquartered here, and the city is home to more than a dozen institutions of higher learning, including Vanderbilt University, Fisk University, and Tennessee State University. With a growing base of manufacturing, especially in the automotive sector, and with the insurance and banking industries firmly entrenched, Nashville leaders project a prosperous future. As home of the Grand Ole Opry, Nashville has also developed into a regional tourist and convention attraction. A full-scale replica of the Greek temple the Parthenon is a noted site.

Population   511,263 (1996). Rank: 24th. Race/national origin (1990): Black 24.3%; Hispanic 0.9%; Asian 1.4%; American Indian 0.2%.

Location: 36°12'N, 86°46'W. County: Davidson.

Terrain and climate   Elev.: 605 ft. Area: 479.5 sq. mi. (1241.9 sq km). Avg. daily min. temp.: Jan.: 27.8°F/-2.3°C; avg. daily max. July: 89.8°F/32.1°C. Avg. annual rainfall: 48.49"; snowfall: 10.7"; clear days: 103; precipitation days: 119.

Government   Form: mayor and council. Mayor: Bill Purcell. Election: Aug. 2001. Municipal tel. number: (615) 862-6000.

Visitor info: (615) 259-4755.
www.nashville.org

▶ NEW ORLEANS, LOUISIANA

Founded in 1718 by Jean Baptiste le Moyne and named Ville d'Orléans after the regent of France, the city of New Orleans is one of the nation's most distinctive cities. Situated only 110 miles from the mouth of the Mississippi River, it has long been a major international port (it ranks second in the nation today), and thanks to overlapping waves of French, Spanish, African-American, and Anglo-American immigrants, it has one of the most richly textured cultures of any city in North America. It is geographically distinct, too, in that much of it is below sea level; the almost constant threat of flooding is mitigated by an intricate network of canals and levees.

After half a century under French rule, New Orleans became the capital of Spanish Louisiana in 1763. It was briefly under French rule again (1800–1803) before being acquired by the United States as part of the Louisiana Purchase. Although Louisiana was admitted as a state in 1815, New Orleans continues to reflect its Spanish and French heritage in its architecture, cuisine, and its flamboyant Mardi Gras celebration in the days leading up to the beginning of Lent. African-American traditions are strong here, too, and Dixieland jazz—long heralded as a uniquely American music—is a fusion of African and European styles.

In addition to being a major port for the export of cotton, rice, petroleum products, iron, steel, and corn, and and the import of sugar, bananas, coffee, bauxite, and molasses, New Orleans is a major center for offshore drilling in the Gulf of Mexico. In recent years its industrial sector, with an emphasis on aerospace research and technology, petroleum refinement, and shipbuilding, has been strong.

A major tourist attraction in its own right, the city includes among its special points of interest St. Louis Cathedral, the French Market, Preservation Hall and Dixieland Hall, and the Presbytère—all in the French Quarter—as well as the celebrated residential architecture of the Garden District, the New Orleans Museum of Art, the Confederate Museum, and Audubon Park Zoo. Among its educational institutions are Tulane University, Sophie Newcomb College, and Dillard University.

Population   476,625 (1996). Rank: 29th. Race/national origin (1990): Black 61.9%; Hispanic 3.5%; Asian 1.9%; American Indian 0.2%.

Location: 30°00'W., 90°05'W. Parish: Orleans.

Terrain and climate   Elev.: 30 ft. Area: 199.4 sq. mi. (516.4 sq km). Avg. daily min. temp.: Jan.: 43°F/6.1°C; avg. daily max.: July: 90.7°F/32.6°C. Avg. annual rainfall: 59.74"; snowfall: 0.2"; clear days: 109; precipitation days: 113.

Government   Form: mayor and council. Mayor: Marc H. Morial. Election: Jan. 2002. Municipal tel. number: (504) 565-6000.

Visitor info: (504) 566-5011.
www.neworleanscvb.com

▶ NEW YORK CITY, NEW YORK

Even before the arrival of Europeans in North America, the waters that today make New York one of the world's foremost ports—and the foremost city in the United States—were the scene of lively trade between the predominant Algonquian tribes in the region. The city's modern history dates to 1524 when the Florentine explorer, Giovanni de Verrazano, sailed into New York Bay. In 1609, Henry Hudson, an English navigator sailing for the Dutch East India Company, explored the river that bears his name today. In 1625, the Dutch West India Company purchased Manhattan and established Nieuw Amsterdam, which quickly became a profitable trading post. Dutch settlers soon expanded beyond the original colony settling Breukelen, Nieuw Harlem, Bronx, and Staaten Eylandt. Taken by the British in 1664 (the Dutch briefly regained control in 1673-74), and renamed for the Duke of York, the town continued to prosper.

As resentment of British authority grew, New York became a seat of colonial discontent, participating in actions against the Stamp Act (1765) and tea tax (1773). But after the Battle of Long Island and Washington's retreat in August 1776, the British held New York through the end of the war. Yet Washington was inaugurated President at Federal Hall (today the site of the second Federal Reserve Bank) on Wall Street, and from 1789-90 New York was the nation's capital.

Industry and trade expanded dramatically after the opening of the Erie Canal from Troy (150 miles up the Hudson River) and Buffalo (350 miles west of Troy) gave New York direct access to the raw materials and the markets of the Great Lakes states. In the mid-19th century, New York became the primary port of immigration to the U.S. and many of the millions of immigrants who came to America carved out distinctly ethnic neighborhoods throughout the city in a patchwork that survives to the present.

In 1898, an act of the state legislature created "Greater New York," and today New York's population is greater than that of Los Angeles and Chicago (the second and third largest cities in the country) combined. Even if they were separate cities, four of New York's boroughs would rank in the top 10—Brooklyn fourth (2.3 million), Queens fifth (1.9 million), Manhattan eighth (1.5 million), and the Bronx ninth (1.2 million).

New York's attractions are seemingly innumerable—enough to draw over 17 million visitors

annually—but they include 150 museums, 400 art galleries, dozens of Broadway theaters, and scores of concert halls, clubs, and dance halls. In addition, there are close to 1,000 landmark buildings, more than 50 landmark interiors, and more than 50 historic districts. (A list of attractions can be found under "New York State.") The city leads the nation in the arts, fashion, advertising, banking and financial services, publishing, broadcasting, and certain service industries; it is also the home of the General Assembly of the United Nations. There are 87 colleges and universities here, including Columbia University, New York University, Long Island University, Brooklyn College, Fordham University, the Pratt Institute of Technology, the Juilliard School, and the School of Visual Arts. Manufactured goods include apparel, chemicals, metal products, and printing.
Population   7,380,906 (1996). Rank: 1st. Race/national origin (1990): Black 28.7%; Hispanic 24.4%; Asian 7.0%; American Indian 0.4%.
Location: 40°45'N, 74°00'W. Counties: Bronx, Kings, New York, Queens, and Richmond.
Terrain and climate   Elev.: 87 ft. Area: 301.5 sq. mi. (780.9 sq km). Avg. daily min. temp.: Jan.: 25.6°F/-3.5°C; avg. daily max. July: 85.3°F/29.6°C. Avg. annual rainfall: 44.12"; snowfall: 29"; clear days: 107; precipitation days: 121.
Government   Form: mayor and council. Mayor: Rudolph Giuliani. Election: Nov. 2001. Municipal tel. number: (212) 788-3000.
Visitor info: (212) 397-8222 or 1-800-692-8474. www.ci.nyc.ny.us

▶ OAKLAND, CALIFORNIA

The first European-American to settle present-day Oakland was Dom Luis Maria Peralta, who established the 44,000-acre settlement called Rancho San Antonio in 1820. Its first real growth began with the establishment of ferry service to San Francisco in 1852, though the ferry's importance was overshadowed by Oakland's selection as the western terminus of the first transcontinental railroad in 1869. The city remained in the economic shadow of its more sophisticated neighbor across the Bay until the San Francisco earthquake of 1906 drove 100,000–150,000 people to Oakland for shelter. An estimated 65,000 of these are thought to have settled there permanently, providing an impetus for a long period of growth as an international port and industrial center.

A major commercial and cultural center with a container port ranked 10th in the world, Oakland is also the major northern hub of the California freeway system, which is integrated into the Bay Area Rapid Transit (BART) system. It has also become the premier biotechnology center in the region, and it is home to regional and international headquarters for firms in finance, medicine, telecommunications, international trade, and heavy industry.

Long a primarily industrial urban center, Oakland has pumped hundreds of millions of dollars into development of its downtown area and the Jack London waterfront—named for the author who spent his youth on the Oakland docks. Oakland embraces a racially and culturally diverse populace. Oakland sustained heavy damage in the 1989 Loma Prieta earthquake. Two years later, almost to the day, the worst fire in California history leveled more than 1,000 buildings in the Oakland Hills neighborhood, killing 14 people and inflicting more than $1.5 billion in damage.
Population   367,230 (1996). Rank: 43rd. Race/national origin (1990): Black 43.9%; Hispanic 13.9%; Asian 14.8%; American Indian 0.6%.
Location: 37°50'N, 122°18'W. County: Alameda.

Terrain and climate   Elev.: 42 ft. Area: 53.9 sq. mi. (139.6 sq km). Avg. daily min. temp.: Jan.: 43.4°F/6.3°C; avg. daily max. July: 70.6°F/29.6°C. Avg. annual rainfall: 18.03"; snowfall: N.A.; clear days: N.A; precipitation days: N.A.
Government   Form: council and manager. Mayor: Jerry Brown. Election: Nov. 2002. Municipal tel. number: (510) 238-3611.
Visitor info: 1-800-262-5526 or (510) 839-9000. www.oaklandnet.com

▶ OKLAHOMA CITY, OKLAHOMA

Oklahoma City quite literally sprang up during the Great Land Rush of 1889 and, by presidential proclamation, opened for European-American settlement officially on April 22 of that year. At day's end, approximately 10,000 settlers had moved in—the greatest one-day non-annexation population increase in the history of cities. Oklahoma became a state in 1907 and Oklahoma City its capital in 1910, by which time the population had swelled to about 64,000. Since then, it has become Oklahoma's largest city, its leading commercial center, and home to the National Cowboy Hall of Fame.

Oklahoma City's economy, based on oil and livestock, thrives on petroleum production, meat processing, and the breeding of stocker and feeder cattle. The city hosts a flourishing printing and publishing industry and manufactures a diversity of products including automobiles, electronic equipment, computers, communications switches, and oil well supplies. As a vital banking center serving the central and western regions of the state, Oklahoma City boasts a Federal Reserve branch bank. On a somewhat less positive note, Oklahoma City reportedly sparked the "go-go" banking syndrome that characterized the 1970s oil boom, when Penn Square Bank's ill-advised oil patch loans nearly devastated the U.S. banking system.

Oklahoma City was the site of the deadliest terrorist bombing in U.S. history on April 19, 1995, when a 5,000-pound car bomb ripped a huge hole in the Alfred Murrah Federal Building, killing 169 people, including 15 children in a day care center within the building.
Population   469,852 (1996). Rank: 30th. Race/national origin (1990): Black 16.0%; Hispanic 5.0%; Asian 2.4%; American Indian 4.2%.
Location: 35°25'N, 97°30'W. Counties: Canadian, Cleveland, McClain, Oklahoma.
Terrain and climate   Elev.: 1,304 ft. Area: 604 sq. mi. (1,564.4 sq km). Avg. daily min. temp.: Jan.: 25.2°F/-3.7°C; avg. daily max. July: 93.5°F/34.1°C. Avg. annual: rainfall, 30.89"; snowfall, 9"; clear days, 141; precipitation days, 81.
Government   Form: council and manager. Mayor: Kirk Humphries. Election: Apr. 2002. Municipal tel. number: (405) 297-2424.
Visitor info: 1-800-225-5652 or (405) 297-8910. www.okccvb.org

▶ OMAHA, NEBRASKA

Permanent settlement in what is now Omaha began with a fur-trading post established shortly after the Lewis and Clark expedition passed through the area in 1804. In 1820, the government built Ft. Atkinson, and the surrounding community became a major stop on both the Mormon and the Lewis and Clark trails, and was incorporated as a city in 1854. After strong lobbying by citizens of Council Bluffs, Iowa, just across the Missouri River to the east, Omaha (the name means "above all others on the stream") became the eastern terminus of the Union-Pacific transcontinental railroad, the country's first, in

1869. Within six years, the population grew to 39,000 and by the turn of the century, it had passed the 100,000 mark.

As a major transportation hub of the Midwest—Omaha today boasts seven major railroads and the recently expanded Port of Omaha services a dozen barge lines—the city became a major distribution center for meat and grain, living up to its motto "We feed the world" (ConAgra is based here). Its major food products include pasta, potato chips, coffee, pancake mixes, frozen dinners, and Omaha steaks. With dozens of *Fortune* 500 manufacturing operations, and a healthy publishing industry (roughly one out of every four manufacturers is either a publisher or printer), Omaha's diversified economy also has strong roots in insurance (Mutual of Omaha), communications, direct mail/telemarketing, and sophisticated medical facilities are centered at the medical schools of Creighton University and the University of Nebraska. Since 1989 employment in the metro area has grown by 15 percent, while the unemployment rate, one of the lowest in the nation, has been less than 3 percent for several years.

Among its performing arts institutions are the Omaha Symphony, Opera/Omaha, and the Omaha Ballet, the Orpheum Theater, and the Omaha Community Playhouse. Museums and historic sites include the Boys Town Hall of Fame, the Henry Doorly Zoo and Aquarium, the Great Plains Black Museum, the historic ships USS *Hazard* and USS *Marlin*, and the Old Market, a mixed-use National Historic District on the Missouri River.
Population   364,253 (1996). Rank: 45th. Race/national origin (1990): Black 13.1%; Hispanic 3.1%; Asian 1.0%; American Indian 0.7%.
Location: 41°15'N, 95°55'W. County: Douglas.
Terrain and climate   Elev.: 982 ft. Area: 99.3 sq. mi. (257.2 sq km). Avg. daily min. temp.: Jan.: 10.2°F/-12.1°C; avg. daily max: July: 88.5°F/31.3°C. Avg. annual rainfall: 30.34"; snowfall: 32"; clear days: 113; precipitation days: 99.
Government   Form: mayor and council. Mayor: Hal Daub. Election: May 2001. Municipal tel. number: (402) 444-5000.
Visitor info: 1-800-332-1819 or (402) 444-4660. www.ci.omaha.ne.us

▶ **PHILADELPHIA, PENNSYLVANIA**
In 1632, a small contingent of Swedes and Finns came to the land where the Schuylkill River meets the Delaware and founded New Sweden. In 1655, Peter Stuyvesant seized New Sweden for the Dutch, inciting conflict with the British until the Dutch relinquished their rights to the territory in 1673. Nine years later, William Penn established a town between the Schuylkill and the Delaware Rivers, named it Philadelphia, "the city of brotherly love," and in two years it evolved into an active settlement of about 2,500 people, most of them Quakers.

In the mid-1700s, Benjamin Franklin began shaping the destiny of Philadelphia by presiding over the founding of the University of Pennsylvania, the Pennsylvania Hospital, and a fire insurance company (both firsts for the young nation). Under his guidance, Philadelphia became the premier colonial city for the arts and the home of many famous educators, scientists, mathematicians, authors, and painters. In addition, a total of 17 libraries were founded at this time. The meeting place of the Continental Congress and the site of the signing of the Declaration of Independence, Philadelphia was the nation's capital from 1790 to 1800, when the federal government moved permanently to Washington, D.C.

Throughout the 19th century, the influx first of Irish and German, then Jewish, Italian, Polish, and Slavic immigrants from Europe, and blacks from the South, helped build the city's industrial base. Today, Philadelphia ranks high among U.S. cities in oil refining; other principal industries are electrical machinery, automobile and truck bodies, petrochemicals, metalworking, and scientific instruments. But many other businesses have left the city and unemployment and poverty have taken a heavy toll in recent years. Between 1990–96 the city lost almost 7 percent of its population.
Population   1,478,002 (1996). Rank: 5th. Race/national origin (1990): Black 39.9%; Hispanic 5.6%; Asian 2.7%; American Indian 0.2%.
Location: 40°00'N, 75°10'W. County: Philadelphia.
Terrain and climate   Elev.: 28 ft. Area: 136 sq. mi. (352.2 sq km). Avg. daily min. temp.: Jan.: 23.8°F/-4.5°C; avg. daily max. July: 86.1°F/30°C. Avg. annual rainfall: 41.42"; snowfall: 20"; clear days: 92; precipitation days: 116.
Government   Form: mayor and council. Mayor: Edward G. Rendell. Election: Nov. 1999. Municipal tel. number: (215) 686-1776.
Visitor info: (215) 636-1666. www.phila.gov

▶ **PHOENIX, ARIZONA**
Arizona's capital and its largest city sits in the Salt River Valley in a former desert that has become a prosperous agricultural area because of a network of irrigated dams located northeast of the city. Long a resort area owing to its mild climate, Phoenix has recently emerged as a lively commercial and agricultural center as well. A flourishing high-tech haven attracting businesses engaged in electronics, communications, and research and development, the city also has a strong manufacturing base that includes airplane parts, electronic equipment, agricultural chemicals, radios, air conditioners, and leather goods. Among its agricultural products are lettuce, melons, vegetables, grapefruit, oranges, lemons, and olives.

While Phoenix benefits from modern irrigation efforts, the Hohokam Indian people dug the area's first irrigation ditches in the 3rd century, B.C. and developed an extensive network of canals that lasted until their culture's decline in A.D. 1400. The area was not resettled until 1864, when a hay camp was established to supply Camp McDowell 30 miles away. Jack Weilling and "Lord Darrell" Dupa rebuilt the old Indian irrigation ditches in 1867, and named the site Phoenix, after the mythical bird that rose from its own ashes. The settlement grew as a trading post, was incorporated as a city in 1881, became capital of the territory in 1889 and the state capital when Arizona was admitted to the Union in 1912.

With the westward exodus from the snowbelt states, and the perfecting of air conditioning to make the summer heat bearable, the small 1950s resort city of 106,818 people has since swelled almost nine-fold. In the 1980s alone, Phoenix's population grew 24.5 percent from 789,704 to just under a million. Between 1990 and 1996, it grew another 17.7 percent.
Population   1,159,014 (1996). Rank: 7th. Race/national origin (1990): Black 5.2%; Hispanic 20.0%; Asian 1.7%; American Indian 1.9%.
Location: 33°30'N, 112°04'W. County: Maricopa.
Terrain and climate   Elev.: 1,117 ft. Area: 375 sq. mi. (971.3 sq km). Avg. daily min. temp.: Jan.: 44.4°F/6.8°C; avg. daily max. July: 107.5°F/41°C. Avg. annual rainfall: 7.11"; snowfall: 0"; clear days: 214; precipitation days: 34.

Government Form: Mayor and council. Mayor: Skip Rimsza. Election: Nov. 1999. Municipal tel. number: (602) 262-6011.
Visitor info: (602) 254-6500.
www.ci.phoenix.az.us

▶ PITTSBURGH, PENNSYLVANIA

Long one of the leading urban industrial areas in the country, Pittsburgh sits at the confluence of the Allegheny and Monongahela rivers, which join to form the Ohio River. In 1754 the British chose the site for its access to this extensive river network (which today reaches to the Gulf of Mexico, the Great Lakes, and up the Missouri River) and began building Fort Pitt, named for Prime Minister William Pitt. Pittsburgh is also situated in the midst of extensive deposits of oil, coal, and, natural gas; the production of steel and iron began in the 1790s. In the 19th century, Pittsburgh was one of the largest producers of steel and iron in the country, and in 1881 its industrial workers formed the American Federation of Labor.

After the boom years of the 1940s and '50s, the city's fortunes began to shrivel with the decline of heavy industry, a dwindling population, and high unemployment in the 1980s. Yet with 40 miles of riverfront, Pittsburgh remains the nation's largest inland port, and is still a leader in the manufacture of petrochemicals and glass products. Pittsburgh is home to more than 150 industrial research companies.

Moreover, Pittsburgh's industrial past has left a rich cultural legacy, which contributed to its ranking in the mid-1980s as the number one city in the country by *Places Rated Almanac*. Its cultural institutions include the Phipps Conservatory, the Buhl Planetarium, the Carnegie Institute, Carnegie Music Hall, and Carnegie Museum of Natural History (the latter three named for the Scots-born industrialist and philanthropist Andrew Carnegie), as well as the Pittsburgh Symphony Orchestra, the Pittsburgh Public Theater, and Pittsburgh Dance Theater. Its universities include the University of Pittsburgh, Pittsburgh Theological Seminary, Duquesne University, and Carnegie-Mellon University.

Population 350,363 (1996). Rank: 48th. Race/national origin (1990): Black 25.8%; Hispanic 0.9%; Asian 1.6%; American Indian 0.2%.
Location: 40°25'N, 79°55'W. County: Allegheny.
Terrain and climate Elev.: 1,223 ft. Area: 55.4 sq. mi. (143.5 sq km). Avg. daily min. temp.: Jan.: 19.2°F/-7.1°C; avg. daily max. July: 86.1°F/30°C. Avg. annual rainfall: 36.29"; snowfall: 45"; clear days: 59; precipitation days: 152.
Government Form: mayor and council. Mayor: Tom Murphy. Election: Nov. 2001. Municipal tel. number: (412) 255-2626.
Visitor info: 1-800-366-0093 or (412) 281-7711.
www.city.pittsburgh.pa.us

▶ PORTLAND, OREGON

Portland's renowned beauty is a result of its unique natural setting, which offers a view of the Cascade Mountains and Mt. Hood to the east, Mt. Adams to the northeast, and Mt. St. Helens and Mt. Rainier to the north. Eleven bridges span the Willamette River, which divides the city into east and west sections.

Indian traders traveling between Oregon City and Vancouver carved out an acre of land by the Willamette River 12 miles north of Oregon City, which became known as The Clearing. In 1884 William Overton claimed the 640 acres surrounding the area, which he then sold to Asa Lovejoy and Francis W. Pettygrove, who set out to build a city. Winning a coin toss, Pettygrove named the city-to-be after his hometown in Maine.

As a vital port of entry (the coast's only freshwater port) with a large inland harbor, Portland is a leader in the shipping of lumber, flour, and grain, and has blossomed into Oregon's largest city. Main industries also include paper and pulp, mining, high technology equipment, and aerospace. Portland enjoys a flourishing arts community and its residents partake of the beaches and ski slopes within easy driving distance.

Population 480,824 (1996). Rank: 27th. Race/national origin (1990): Black 7.7%; Hispanic 3.2%; Asian 5.3%; American Indian 1.2%.
Location: 45°35'N, 122°40'W. Counties: Clackamas, Multnomah, Washington.
Terrain and climate Elev.: 39 ft. Area: 113.9 sq. mi. (295 sq km). Avg. daily min. temp.: Jan.: 33.5°F/0.8°C; avg. daily max. July: 79.5°F/26.3°C. Avg. annual rainfall: 37.39"; snowfall: 7"; clear days: 69; precipitation days: 152.
Government Form: commission. Mayor: Vera Katz. Election: Sept. 2000. Municipal tel. number: (503) 823-4000.
Visitor info: 1-800-345-3214 or (503) 222-2223.
www.ci.portland.or.us

▶ SACRAMENTO, CALIFORNIA

The capital of California and its seventh largest city, Sacramento sits 75 miles northwest of San Francisco at the confluence of the American and Sacramento rivers. A wholesale and retail center for the surrounding rich farmland, the city includes among its main commercial enterprises food processing and canning, and one of the world's largest almond-shelling plants.

Receiving a land grant from the Mexican government in 1839, Swiss-American John Augustus Sutter founded a colony called New Helvetia, and when Fort Sutter was constructed in 1844, it became one of California's chief trading posts. Established soon after the discovery of gold in 1848, Sacramento grew to 7,000 residents by 1850, became state capital in 1854, and in 1863 was incorporated as a city.

The "Gateway to the Goldfields," "Old Sacramento" became a pivotal point of commerce in the 1860s, connected to the mining towns by the American River, and transporting produce from the farms and orchards lining the banks of the Sacramento River. Sailors stopping in San Francisco visited Sacramento to replenish their stocks of fresh produce and to entertain themselves in the saloons and gambling halls. The wealthy lived in great mansions by the river and the cobblestone streets, gaslights, and wood sidewalks imbued the town with a touch of civility. Today's Sacramento, appreciated for its subtle, quiet charms, boasts 120 parks, hiking and biking trails along the American River Parkway, a large collection of art galleries, two symphony orchestras, ballet, theater and opera companies, and a number of jazz clubs and coffee houses.

Population 376,243 (1996). Rank: 42nd. Race/national origin (1990): Black 15.3%; Hispanic 16.2%; Asian 15.0%; American Indian 1.2%.
Location: 38°33'N, 121°30'W. County: Sacramento.
Terrain and climate Elev.: 25 ft. Area: 97.3 sq. mi. (252 sq km). Avg. daily min. temp.: Jan.: 37.9°F/3.2°C; avg. daily max. July: 93.3°F/34°C. Avg. annual rainfall: 17.87"; snowfall: 0.1"; clear days: 193; precipitation days: 57.
Government Form: council and manager. Mayor: Joe Serna, Jr. Election: June 2000. Municipal tel. number: (916) 264-5704.

Visitor info: (916) 264-7777.
www.sacto.org

▶SAINT LOUIS, MISSOURI

St. Louis is one of the nation's major centers of transportation, manufacturing, commerce, and education. With abundant water and electric power, a workforce of over a million people in the metropolitan area, and a location in an area rich in mineral resources, St. Louis ranks as one of the top 10 industrial areas in the country. It is also one of the nation's busiest river ports, the third-largest rail center, the eighth-largest trucking center, and has the sixth-busiest airport. Aircraft, automobiles, printing, beer, and chemicals are among the principal products. The metropolitan area boasts five universities, 23 colleges, and seven junior colleges. St. Louis University, oldest west of the Mississippi, founded in 1818, and Washington University are world famous for their medical schools and research programs and their Nobel Prize winners.

For the 40 years after its founding in 1764 by Pierre Laclade, St. Louis was a French settlement and trading post, outfitting fur trading expeditions up the Missouri River. With the Louisiana Purchase in 1803, St. Louis came under American control. The city was incorporated in 1823 with a population of almost 5,000 people. The first steamboat docked at St. Louis in 1817 and steamboats then became a vital part of the city's growth. Fueled by settlers from the East and by waves of Irish and German immigrants attracted by the prosperity of the river trade, the city's population grew rapidly. In 1870, St. Louis had a population of 311,000, and it was the country's third largest city after New York and Philadelphia. The population continued to grow to a peak of 856,800 in 1950, but the post-World War II flight to the suburbs hit St. Louis hard, reducing its population by almost half.

The downtown St. Louis area has many landmarks and historic buildings. The Old Cathedral, completed in 1834, and the Old Courthouse, where the Dred Scott case was first tried, have been preserved as part of the Jefferson National Expansion Memorial. Atop the famous Gateway Arch, the observation room provides a panoramic view of the city. Kiel Auditorium contains a 3,500-seat opera house and a 10,000-seat convention hall. Forest Park, site of the 1904 Louisiana Purchase Exposition (also known as the St. Louis World's Fair), contains the St. Louis Zoo, McDonnell Planetarium, and the Jewel Box, an all-glass floral display house. St. Louis is also the home of the Missouri Botanical Gardens, which features the Climatron—a geodesic dome with rare orchids and other tropical plants—and the largest Japanese garden in the United States. The St. Louis Symphony (founded in 1880) is the country's second oldest and is housed in the Powell Symphony Hall.

Population   351,565 (1996). Rank: 47th. Race/national origin (1990): Black 47.5%; Hispanic 1.3%; Asian 0.9%; American Indian 0.2%.
Location: 38°40'N, 90°12'W. County: independent city.
Terrain and climate   Elev.: 564 ft. Area: 61.4 sq. mi. (159 sq km). Avg. daily min. temp.: Jan.: 19.9°F/-6.7°C; avg. daily max. July: 89°F/31°C. Avg. annual rainfall: 33.91"; snowfall: 18"; clear days: 105; precipitation days: 108.
Government   Form: mayor   and   council. Mayor: Clarence Harmon. Election: Apr. 2001. Municipal tel. number: (314) 622-3201.
Visitor info: 1-800-888-3861 or (314) 421-1023.
http://stlouis.missouri.org

▶SAN ANTONIO, TEXAS

San Antonio, the third largest city in Texas, lies in the state's south-central region at the edge of the Gulf Coastal Plain 140 miles from the Gulf of Mexico. Its economy thrives on agriculture, livestock, and the activity of the wholesale traders who dominate the commerce of southwestern Texas and northern Mexico. It is also a regional leader in biotechnology. Adding further stimulus to the economy are five major military installations—Fort Sam Houston, Randolph Air Force Base, Kelly Air Force Base, Lackland Air Force Base, and Brooks Air Force Base. The military contributes approximately $3 billion annually to the area economy.

The founding of the mission of San Antonio de Valero (later known as the Alamo) and the Presidio of San Antonio in 1718 represented the area's first permanent settlement. When 56 settlers from the Canary Islands joined the original coterie of ranchmen, missionaries, and soldiers, they formed the first municipal organization in Texas, called the villa of San Fernando de Bexar, which became a city in 1809, and suffered under Mexican rule until the battle of San Jacinto in 1836. With the influx of American pioneers and German immigrants (following Texas's statehood in 1845), the population grew to over 96,000 by 1910, and has since increased nearly tenfold. By 1998 it had reached 1.1 million, up 22 percent since 1990.

Today San Antonio is a popular haven for vacationers, with over 10 million visitors per year. San Antonio's attractions include the Alamo and its four sister missions, the Riverwalk along the San Antonio River, Breckenridge Park (home of one of America's largest zoos), Sea World of Texas; La Villita, the Tower of the Americas, and the Spanish Governor's Palace.

Population   1,067,816 (1996). Rank: 8th. Race/national origin (1990): Black 7.0%; Hispanic 55.6%; Asian 1.1%; American Indian 0.4%.
Location: 29°30'N, 98°30'W. County: Bexar.
Terrain and climate   Elev.: 701 ft. Area: 304.5 sq. mi. (788.7 sq km). Avg. daily min. temp.: Jan.: 39°F/3.8°C; avg. daily max. July: 96.3°F/35.7°C. Avg. annual rainfall: 29.13"; snowfall: 0.5"; clear days: 110; precipitation days: 81.
Government   Form: council and manager. Mayor: Howard W. Peak. Election: June 2001. Municipal tel. number: (210) 207-7060.
Visitor info: 1-800-447-3372 or (210) 270-8700.
www.ci.sat.tx.us

▶SAN DIEGO, CALIFORNIA

Sixty years after João Rodrigues Cabrilho first sailed into San Diego Bay, Sebastian Vizcaino embarked from Spain with three ships to explore the coast of California, and in November 1602 anchored on the lee of what is now known as Point Loma. When he finished charting the bay two days later, he changed its original name, San Miguel, to San Diego, in honor of the saint San Diego de Alcalal de Henares, In 1769, Father Junipero Serra established California's first mission, the Mission San Diego de Alcala.

Compared to its sister cities to the north—Los Angeles and San Francisco—San Diego developed slowly, despite its large and hospitable harbor. In 1887, the city became the southern terminus for the Santa Fe Railroad, but floods soon washed out the tracks and trackbeds, and the railroad was rebuilt to terminate in L.A. which had a new manmade harbor. This put San Diego at an almost insurmountable disadvantage. With its industrial development stunted, San Diego welcomed the establishment of a U.S. Navy base during World War I; since then, about a quarter of the Navy's seagoing vessels and roughly 20 percent of the Marine Corps' forces have located there. Jonas Salk's work on polio and the emergence of the University of California at San Diego have earned the city the reputation as a premier biomedical research center, luring billions of dollars in development and research grants.

San Diego, a picturesque city with many tourist attractions, enjoys an average of 350 days of sunshine, enticing both residents and visitors to its 70 beaches and the parks, resorts, and health spas lining its great bay. Coronado Island is a popular attraction. Balboa Park, host to international expositions in 1915 and 1935, contains the San Diego Zoo, one of the finest in the nation. The pleasure boats berthed at the city's numerous yacht clubs offer a curious contrast to the naval warships moored nearby. San Diego was the site of the 1992 America's Cup yacht races.

Population   1,171,121 (1996). Rank: 6th. Race/ national origin (1990): Black 9.4%; Hispanic 20.7%; Asian 11.8%; American Indian 0.6%.
Location: 32°43'N, 117°10'W. County: San Diego.
Terrain and climate   Elev.: 13 ft. Area: 329 sq. mi. (852.1 sq km). Avg. daily min. temp.: Jan.: 48.4°F/9.1°C; avg. daily max. July: 75.6°F/24.2°C. Avg. annual rainfall: 9.32"; snowfall: 0"; clear days: 150; precipitation days: 41.
Government   Form: council and manager. Mayor: Susan Golding. Election: Nov. 2000. Municipal tel. number: (619) 236-5555.
Visitor info: (619) 236-1212.
www.ci.san-diego.ca.us

▶ SAN FRANCISCO, CALIFORNIA

Located near the Golden Gate, the strait between San Francisco Bay and the Pacific Ocean, fogbound San Francisco hid from some of the greatest European navigators to explore the West Coast. João Rodrigues Cabrilho discovered the Farrallon Islands just off the coast in 1542 and Sir Francis Drake landed a few miles north of the Golden Gate in 1579. Yet it was another 200 years before Don Gasper de Portola sailed into the Bay, followed six years later by Don Juan Manuel Ayala who established a town and mission.

Neither the Spanish nor (after 1821) the Mexican governments was very keen on capitalizing on San Francisco's temperate and strategic location, and when Captain John Montgomery raised the American flag there on July 9, 1846, the community consisted of only 840 people. The discovery of gold at Sutter's mill in 1848, and the gold rush of 1849—which brought 40,000 of the hopeful to California, most by ship—catapulted San Francisco onto the world map, and the following year it was incorporated as a city.

San Francisco continued to prosper as a major transportation and industrial center, but in 1906 an earthquake registering 8.6 on the Richter scale claimed 452 lives, 28,000 buildings, and losses totalling approximately $350 million. San Francisco rose from the ashes to become a thriving, multifaceted, cosmopolitan city and one of the country's leaders in world trade. Another major earthquake, measuring 7.1 on the Richter scale, struck on Oct. 17, 1989, causing extensive damage and 67 deaths in the region, but did not devastate the city as thoroughly as the 1906 tremor.

San Francisco today is a port of call for more than 40 steamship lines which import approximately $25 billion worth of goods from more than 300 ports around the world. A major international financial center, it is the headquarters of three of the nation's largest banks, the 12th Federal Reserve District, and the Pacific Stock Exchange. There are also more than 650 insurance companies, and the city is a haven for venture capitalists and entrepreneurs: more than 90 percent of its businesses have fewer than 25 employees. There are also several U.S. military installations in the area.

Well known for its spirit of individualism, San Francisco was a haven for the beat movement of the 1950s, and the capital of the hippie movement of the 1960s was the Haight-Ashbury district. Its more traditional arts institutions include the San Francisco Ballet, the San Francisco Opera, the San Francisco Symphony, and the American Conservatory Theater. Among its leading educational institutions are the University of San Francisco, the Heald Institute of Technology , the University of California, the San Francisco Art Institute, the San Francisco Conservatory of Music, and the San Francisco College of Mortuary Science. Among its many museums are the National Maritime Historic Park, the Fine Arts Museum, and the California Palace of the Legion of Honor. Other attractions include its historic cable cars (first used in 1873), Chinatown, and Fisherman's Wharf.

Population   735,315 (1996). Rank: 13th. Race/ national origin (1990): Black 10.9%; Hispanic 13.9%; Asian 29.1%; American Indian 0.5%.
Location: 37°47'N, 122°30'W. County: San Francisco.
Terrain and climate   Elev.: 155 ft. Area: 46.4 sq. mi. (120.2 sq km). Avg. daily min. temp.: Jan.: 41.5°F/5.2°C; avg. daily max. July: 71°F/21°C. Avg. annual rainfall: 19.71"; snowfall: 0"; clear days: 162; precipitation days: 67.
Government   Form: mayor and council. Mayor: Willie L. Brown Jr. Election: Nov. 2000. Municipal tel. number: (415) 554-6141.
Visitor info: (415) 974-6900.
www.ci.sf.ca.us

▶ SAN JOSE, CALIFORNIA

Located at the southern end of San Francisco Bay, about 45 miles south of San Francisco, San Jose was the first nonreligious European community founded in California. Pueblo de San Jose de Guadalupe was settled in 1777 by enterprising farmers who sought to make themselves and the region independent of Mexico and the Spanish mission network for their supplies. Fruit and olive trees, hides, tallow, livestock, grain, and lively retail activity all contributed to San Jose's early prosperity, and it was the first state capital (1849–52).

San Jose remained an agricultural center until World War II, when industry and technology began to expand. The rapid growth of innovative industry over the last 20 years, taking its lead from research and development begun at nearby Stanford University in the 1930s, changed the area dramatically. With the revolution in high technology, Santa Clara County became known as Silicon Valley, excelling in the production of information systems, personal computers, peripherals, and fostering a burgeoning semi-conductor industry. At the same time, financial services, real estate, construction, and retail industries all flourished.

More than 2,600 high tech companies employing 250,000 people are located in San Jose, and one-third of the labor force works in manufacturing, a very high proportion in post-industrial America. Santa Clara County has the highest median family income in California, and median housing prices in San Jose are perennially among the highest in the nation.

Population   838,744 (1996). Rank: 11th. Race/ national origin (1990): Black 4.7%; Hispanic 26.6%; Asian 19.5%; American Indian 0.7%.
Location: 37°20'N, 121°53'W. County: Santa Clara.

Terrain and climate   Elev.: 65 ft. Area: 169.2 sq. mi. (438.2 sq km). Avg. daily min. temp.: Jan.: 41.1°F/5°C; avg. daily max.: July: 81.5°F/27.5°C. Avg. annual rainfall: 13.86"; snowfall: 0"; clear days: N.A.; precipitation days: N.A.
Government   Form: council and manager. Mayor: Ron Gonzales. Election: Nov. 2002. Municipal tel. number: (408) 277-4237.
Visitor info: 1-800-SAN JOSE or (408) 295-9600. www.ci.san-jose.ca.us

▶ SEATTLE, WASHINGTON

Located on the protected waters of Puget Sound, Seattle was the first European-American settlement established in the Pacific Northwest north of the Columbia River. Starting out at Alki Point in 1851, the settlers moved to what is now known as Pioneer Square. Befriended by the Suquamish Chief Sealth (Seattle is a loose approximation of his name), the people turned to lumber harvesting and log milling, which formed the backbone of the city's economy.

With the completion of the Great Northern Railway in 1893 and the Alaska gold rush of 1897, when Seattle became "the Gateway to the Klondike," the city was transformed into a metropolis of merchants and entrepreneurs. Even as gold fever abated, and despite a devastating fire in 1899, the city prospered as a major port to the Orient and as an industrial center. In 1909 Seattle was the site of the Alaska-Yukon-Pacific Exposition. The completion of the Panama Canal in 1914 brought even more business to the already bustling port. Two years later, a small company began building two-seater biplanes, marking the start of Seattle's enduring link with the aerospace industry. In time the little company became Boeing, the world's largest producer of commercial planes, which employs more than 100,000 people in the Seattle area.

Endowed with spectacular natural beauty, with the broad expanse of Puget Sound before it, and the snow-capped peaks of the Cascade Mountains and Mt. Rainier visible to the south and east, the Seattle area offers a wide variety of outdoor activities, from skiing and hiking, to fishing and boating. A second international exposition, the Seattle World's Fair in 1962, helped establish the city's reputation as a center of technology, trade, industry, and tourism. The leading cultural programs are put on by the Seattle Symphony Orchestra, the Seattle Opera Association, and the Seattle Repertory Theater. Other attractions include the Seattle Art Museum, Pioneer Square, Pike Place Market, the historic ships on Lake Union, and Woodland Park and Zoo, as well as the many events at the 74-acre Seattle Convention Center, whose buildings, and park-like grounds and fountains are legacies of the World's Fair. Among the 20 universities and colleges in the area are the University of Washington and Seattle Pacific University.

Population   524,704 (1996). Rank: 23rd. Race/ national origin (1990): Black 10.1%; Hispanic 3.6%; Asian 11.8%; American Indian 1.4%.
Location: 47°41'N, 122°15'W. County: King.
Terrain and climate   Elev.: 450 ft. Area: 83.6 sq. mi. (216.5 sq km). Avg. daily min. temp.: Jan.: 34.3°F/1.2°C; avg. daily max.: July: 75.2°F/24°C. Avg. annual rainfall: 38.85"; snowfall: 15"; clear days: 57; precipitation days: 160.
Government   Form: mayor and council. Mayor: Paul Schell. Election: Nov. 2001. Municipal tel. number: (206) 684-4000.
Visitor info: (206) 461-5840. www.ci.seattle.wa.us

▶ TUCSON, ARIZONA

The first European to travel through the area that is now Tucson was the Jesuit missionary Eusebio Kino, in 1692. In 1700 the mission of San Xavier del Bac was established among the Papago Indians nearby. It was not until 1776, however, that the Spanish established a permanent settlement, taking its name from the Papago *Stjukshon* (or *Chuk Shon*), meaning "village of the dark spring at the foot of the mountain." Tucson remained under Spanish and Mexican control until acquired by the U.S. government as part of the Gadsden Purchase in 1853. During the Civil War it was under Confederate control, but from 1867 to 1877 it was the territorial capital.

Despite the arrival of the Southern Pacific railroad in 1880 and the discovery of extensive copper deposits in southern Arizona, neither its location nor Tucson's natural resources much stimulated its economy. It was best known as a winter and health resort, and as a commercial hub for the surrounding agricultural and mining industries. In 1950, the population was only 45,500.

The last half-century has seen a dramatic change. One of the many beneficiaries of the exodus from the industrial states to the Sunbelt, Tucson's population has grown almost tenfold in that period, and in the last decade Tucson added 20,000 manufacturing jobs. Surrounded by a wealth of natural beauty, the city is still appealing to retirees and tourists, as is reflected in the many golf courses, ranches, and resorts in and around Tucson. It is ringed by four mountain ranges: the Rincon, Santa Catalina, Tucson, and Santa Rita. Other natural wonders include Sabino Canyon (which has the only year-round stream in the region), the Saguaro National Monument (a preserve for Saguaro cacti), and Tucson Mountain Park, home of the Arizona-Sonora Desert Museum. The University of Arizona is located in Tucson, and the Davis-Mothan Air Force Base and Kitts Peak Observatory are nearby.

Population   449,002 (1996). Rank: 31st. Race/ national origin (1990): Black 4.3%; Hispanic 29.3%; Asian 2.2%; American Indian 1.6%.
Location: 32°14'N, 110°59'W. County: Pima.
Terrain and climate   Elev.: 2,584 ft. Area: 125 sq. mi. (324.8 sq km). Avg. daily min. temp.: Jan.: 38.1°F/3.3°C; avg. daily max. July: 98.5°F/3.3°C. Avg. annual rainfall: 11.14"; snowfall: 2"; clear days: 198; precipitation days: 50.
Government   Form: council and manager. Mayor: George Miller. Election: Nov. 1999. Municipal tel. number: (520) 791-4201.
Visitor info: (520) 624-1817 or 1-800-638-8350. www.ci.tucson.az.us

▶ TULSA, OKLAHOMA

Tulsa was first settled by Indian nations forced out of the South Atlantic States by the Indian Removal Act of 1830. The name they chose for their new home was Tulsey Town, a corruption of *Tullahassee*, meaning "old town." The name Tulsa was made official with the establishment of a post office in 1879. In 1900, Tulsa's population numbered less than 2,000, but the discovery of extensive oil fields at the turn of the century, beginning with the Glenn Pool and Red Fork strikes, started Tulsa on the way from a small Indian settlement to a sizable metropolis. By 1907, its population had increased to 7,298, and by 1920 it was 10 times that. Soon Tulsa was "the Oil Capital of the World."

While still heavily involved in the oil and gas industry—it remains the home of about 500 oil-related companies—modern Tulsa is a far more diverse city than its oil patch origins. Among Tulsa's top employers are regional, national and international firms involved in aviation and aerospace, energy, computer technology, insurance, telecommunications, health care, and electronic equipment. The Port of Catoosa, which opened in 1971 after the completion of the 445-mile Arkansas-Mississippi Waterway, is a major inland port that provides Tulsa with a direct link to the Mississippi River system and the Gulf of Mexico.

While growing in business, Tulsa has preserved the cultural heritage of its early oil barons and workers as well as that of its original Indian settlers. Thomas Gilcrease, a Creek Indian, became a millionaire with the Glenn Pool oil strike, and founded the Thomas Gilcrease Institute of American History and Art, devoted to the American Indian. The Tulsa Opera Company was founded in the early 1900s, and along with the city's philharmonic, ballet, and theaters, it gives Tulsa just cause to lay claim to being the cultural capital of Oklahoma. Tulsans also honor their roots through rodeos and regional music festivals. In addition, representatives of the state's 65 Indian tribes gather in Tulsa each summer for their annual powwow. Among Tulsa's colleges and universities are the University of Tulsa and Oral Roberts University.

Population 378,491 (1996). Rank: 40th. Race/national origin (1990): Black 13.6%; Hispanic 2.6%; Asian 1.4%; American Indian 4.7%.
Location: 36°10'N, 96°00'W. Counties: Osage, Tulsa.
Terrain and climate Elev.: 676 ft. Area: 186.1 sq. mi. (482 sq km). Avg. daily min. temp.: Jan.: 24.8°F/-4°C; avg. daily max. July: 93.9°F/34.3°C. Avg. annual rainfall: 38.77"; snowfall: 9"; clear days: 127; precipitation days: 90.
Government Form: commission. Mayor: M. Susan Savage. Election: April 2002. Municipal tel. number: (918) 596-7411.
Visitor info: (918) 585-1201 or 1-800-558-3311. www.tulsachamber.com

▶VIRGINIA BEACH, VIRGINIA

Throughout much of its history—which dates to the the the landing of the Jamestown colonists at Point Henry in 1607—Virginia Beach was overshadowed by its northern neighbor, Norfolk, which with its magnificent harbor was long the home of many shipping and naval enterprises at the mouth of Chesapeake Bay. But Virginia Beach has seen remarkable change in the last two decades.

In 1970, Virginia Beach's population was 172,000, only slightly more than half that of Norfolk. By 1990, it had grown 128 percent, to 393,000, and it is still one of the fastest-growing of the country's 50 largest cities. Local initiative accounts for most of this growth: in the same period Norfolk's population fell 11 percent. A dominant presence is the U.S. Navy, which has three bases— Oceana Naval Air Station, Little Creek Naval Amphibious Base, and the Dam Neck Fleet Training Center—and which together with the U.S. Army's Fort Story employ 36,000 military and civilian personnel.

With 38 miles of Atlantic shoreline, 28 miles of public beaches, and the Seashore State Park— 2,700 acres of shady upland woods, cypress swamps, and Spanish moss—the city continues to depend on tourism as a major factor in its economy, attracting 2.5 million visitors a year. The city's main industries, which include marine and

engineering services, construction, communications, and electronics, occupy 10 industrial/business parks, including four built by the Virginia Beach Development Authority.

Among Virginia Beach's outstanding historic and recreational attractions are the Virginia Marine Science Museum, the Adam Thoroughgood House (c. 1680, one of the oldest brick houses in North America), the Old Cape Henry Lighthouse, authorized by the first Congress in 1790, and the statue of Admiral Compte de Grasse whose defeat of the British at the Battle of the Virginia Capes brought about the defeat of Gen. Cornwallis at Yorktown and the end of the American Revolution in 1781.

Population 430,385 (1996). Rank: 34rd. Race/national origin (1990): Black 13.9%; Hispanic 3.1%; Asian 4.3%; American Indian 0.4%.
Location: 36°54'N, 75°58'W. County: independent city.
Terrain and climate Elev.: 12 ft. Area: 225.9 sq. mi. (585.1 sq km). Avg. daily min. temp.: Jan.: 31.7°F/-0.1°C; avg. daily max. July: 86.9°F/30.5°C. Avg. annual rainfall: 45.22"; snowfall: 7"; clear days: 110; precipitation days: 115.
Government Form: council and manager. Mayor: Meyera E. Oberndorf. Election: May 2000. Municipal tel. number: (757) 427-4581.
Visitor info: 1-800-VA-BEACH (822-3224). www.virginia-beach.va.us

▶WASHINGTON, D.C.

[*For description, see District of Columbia entry in "States, Territories, and Possessions."*]
Population 543,213 (1996). Rank: 21st. Race/national origin (1990): Black 65.8%; Hispanic 5.4%; Asian 1.8%; American Indian 0.2%.
Location: 38°52'N, 77°00'W. County: independent city.
Terrain and climate Elev.: 30 ft. Area: 62.7 sq. mi. (162.4 sq km). Avg. daily min. temp.: Jan.: 27.5°F/-2.5°C; avg. daily max. July: 87.9°F/31°C. Avg. annual rainfall: 39"; snowfall: 16"; clear days: 101; precipitation days: 111.
Government Form: mayor and council. Mayor: Anthony A. Williams. Election: Nov. 2002. Municipal tel. number: (202) 727-2980.
Visitor info: (202) 789-7000. www.ci.washington.dc.us

CITIES IN AMERICA

The number of large U.S. cities continues to grow. There were 218 cities with populations over 100,000 in July 1998, an increase of 19 from April, 1990. However, 55 of these 218 cities (25 percent) lost population since 1990. There were eight cities with populations over a million in 1990; Phoenix and San Antonio joined that list by 1998, but Detroit fell from it, to 970,196.

New York, the nation's largest city, grew by just over 97,000 from 1990 to 1998, according to the Census Bureau, an increase of just 1.3 percent. Meanwhile, Los Angeles, which actually declined in population early in the decade, grew by an overall 112,000 people (3.2 percent) between 1990 and 1998.

Major U.S. Cities: Population, Population Change, Population Density, and Land Area, 1970–90

City	Pop. ('000s) 1970	1980	1990	Rank 1990	Population Percent change 1980–90	Per sq. mi. 1990	Land area (sq.mi.) 1990
Abilene, Tex	90	98	107	180	8.5%	1,035	103.1
Akron, Ohio	275	237	223	71	-6.0	3,586	62.2
Albany, N.Y.	116	102	100	196	-1.7	4,674	21.4
Albuquerque, N.Mex.	245	332	385	38	15.5	2,909	132.2
Alexandria, Va.	111	103	111	164	7.7	7,267	15.3
Allentown, Pa.	110	104	105	183	1.5	5,949	17.7
Amarillo, Tex.	127	149	158	110	5.6	1,793	87.9
Anaheim, Calif.	166	219	266	59	21.4	6,014	44.3
Anchorage, Alaska	48	174	226	69	29.8	133	1,697.7
Ann Arbor, Mich.	100	108	110	170	1.5	4,231	25.9
Arlington, Tex.	90	160	262	61	63.5	2,814	93.0
Atlanta, Ga.	495	425	394	36	-7.3	2,990	131.8
Aurora, Colo.	75	159	222	72	40.1	1,676	132.5
Austin, Tex.	254	346	466	27	34.6	2,138	217.8
Bakersfield, Calif.	70	106	175	97	65.5	1,904	91.8
Baltimore, Md.	905	787	736	12	-6.4	9,108	80.8
Baton Rouge, La.	166	220	220	73	-0.4	2,969	74.0
Beaumont, Tex.	118	118	114	155	-3.2	1,427	80.1
Berkeley, Calif.	114	103	103	190	-0.6	9,783	10.5
Birmingham, Ala.	301	284	266	60	-6.5	1,791	148.5
Boise City, Idaho	75	102	126	145	23.0	2,726	46.1
Boston, Mass.	641	563	574	20	2.0	11,860	48.4
Bridgeport, Conn.	157	143	142	123	-0.6	8,855	16.0
Buffalo, N.Y.	463	358	328	50	-8.3	8,083	40.6
Cedar Rapids, Iowa	111	110	109	173	-1.3	2,033	53.5
Charlotte, N.C.	241	315	396	35	25.5	2,272	174.3
Chattanooga, Tenn.	120	170	152	113	-10.0	1,288	118.4
Chesapeake, Va.	90	114	152	114	32.8	446	340.7
Chicago, Ill.	3,369	3,005	2,784	3	-7.4	12,251	227.2
Chula Vista, Calif.	68	84	135	131	61.0	4,661	29.0
Cincinnati, Ohio	454	385	364	45	-5.5	4,717	77.2
Cleveland, Ohio	751	574	506	23	-11.9	6,565	77.0
Colorado Springs, Colo.	136	215	281	54	30.7	1,535	183.2
Columbia, S.C.	114	101	103	188	2.2	884	117.1
Columbus, Ga.[1]	155	169	179	93	5.5	827	216.1
Columbus, Ohio	540	565	633	16	12.0	3,315	190.9
Concord, Calif.	85	104	111	163	7.3	3,773	29.5
Corpus Christi, Tex.	205	232	257	64	10.9	1,907	135.0
Dallas, Tex.	844	905	1,008	8	11.4	2,943	342.4
Dayton, Ohio	243	194	182	89	-5.9	3,310	55.0
Denver, Colo.	515	493	468	26	-5.1	3,051	153.3
Des Moines, Iowa	201	191	193	80	1.1	2,567	75.3
Detroit, Mich.	1,514	1,203	1,028	7	-14.6	7,410	138.7
Durham, N.C.	95	101	137	130	35.1	1,972	69.3
Elizabeth, N.J.	113	106	110	168	3.6	8,929	12.3
El Monte, Calif.	70	79	106	181	33.5	11,175	9.5
El Paso, Tex.	322	425	515	22	21.2	2,100	245.4
Erie, Pa.	129	119	109	175	-8.7	4,944	22.0
Escondido, Calif.	37	64	109	176	68.8	3,048	35.6
Eugene, Oreg.	79	106	113	159	6.6	2,962	38.0
Evansville, Ind.	139	130	126	144	-3.2	3,102	40.7
Flint, Mich.	193	160	141	125	-11.8	4,161	33.8
Fort Lauderdale, Fla.	140	153	149	116	-2.6	4,753	31.4
Fort Wayne, Ind.	178	172	173	99	0.4	2,762	62.7
Fort Worth, Tex.	393	385	448	28	16.2	1,592	281.1
Fremont, Calif.	101	132	173	98	31.4	2,250	77.0
Fresno, Calif.	166	217	354	47	62.9	3,573	99.1
Fullerton, Calif.	86	102	114	156	11.6	5,160	22.1
Garden Grove, Calif.	121	123	143	120	16.0	7,974	17.9
Garland, Tex.	81	139	181	91	30.1	3,150	57.4
Gary, Ind.	175	152	117	154	-23.2	2,322	50.2
Glendale, Ariz.	36	97	148	117	52.4	2,837	52.2
Glendale, Calif.	133	139	180	92	29.5	5,882	30.6
Grand Rapids, Mich.	198	182	189	83	4.0	4,273	44.3
Greensboro, N.C.	144	156	184	88	18.2	2,304	79.8
Hampton, Va.	121	123	134	133	9.1	2,583	51.8
Hartford, Conn.	158	136	140	128	2.5	8,077	17.3
Hayward, Calif.	93	94	111	162	19.0	2,560	43.5

City	Pop. ('000s) 1970	Pop. ('000s) 1980	Pop. ('000s) 1990	Rank 1990	Population Percent change 1980–90	Population Per sq. mi. 1990	Land area (sq.mi.) 1990
Hialeah, Fla.	102	145	188	85	29.4%	9,772	19.2
Hollywood, Fla.	107	121	122	148	0.3	4,464	27.3
Honolulu, Hawaii[2]	325	365	377	39	3.3	4,400	85.7
Houston, Tex.	1,234	1,595	1,631	4	2.2	3,021	539.9
Huntington Beach, Calif.	116	171	182	90	6.5	6,871	26.4
Huntsville, Ala.	139	143	160	109	12.2	973	164.4
Independence, Mo.	112	112	112	160	0.5	1,436	78.2
Indianapolis, Ind.[1]	737	701	731	13	4.3	2,022	361.7
Inglewood, Calif.	90	94	110	169	16.4	11,952	9.2
Irvine, Calif.	[3]	62	110	167	77.6	2,607	42.3
Irving, Tex.	97	110	155	112	41.0	2,293	67.6
Jackson, Miss.	154	203	197	78	-3.1	1,804	109.0
Jacksonville, Fla.[1]	504	541	635	15	17.9	837	758.7
Jersey City, N.J.	260	224	229	67	2.2	15,337	14.9
Kansas City, Kans.	168	161	150	115	-7.1	1,390	107.8
Kansas City, Mo.	507	448	435	31	-2.9	1,397	311.5
Knoxville, Tenn.	175	175	165	102	-5.7	2,135	77.2
Lakewood, Colo.	93	114	126	143	11.1	3,100	40.8
Lansing, Mich.	131	130	127	142	-2.4	3,755	33.9
Laredo, Tex.	69	91	123	147	34.4	3,739	32.9
Las Vegas, Nev.	126	165	258	63	56.8	3,100	83.3
Lexington-Fayette, Ky.[1]	108	204	225	70	10.4	792	284.5
Lincoln, Nebr.	150	172	192	81	11.7	3,033	63.3
Little Rock, Ark.	132	159	176	96	10.5	1,709	102.9
Livonia, Mich.	110	105	101	193	-3.8	2,823	35.7
Long Beach, Calif.	359	361	429	32	18.8	8,586	50.0
Los Angeles, Calif.	2,812	2,969	3,485	2	17.4	7,426	469.3
Louisville, Ky.	362	299	270	58	-9.8	4,341	62.1
Lowell, Mass.	94	92	103	189	11.9	7,506	13.8
Lubbock, Tex.	149	174	186	87	6.8	1,789	104.1
Macon, Ga.	122	117	107	179	-8.2	2,241	47.9
Madison, Wis.	172	171	191	82	11.8	3,300	57.8
Memphis, Tenn.	624	646	610	18	-5.5	2,384	256.0
Mesa, Ariz.	63	152	288	53	89.0	2,653	108.6
Mesquite, Tex.	55	67	101	191	51.3	2,369	42.8
Miami, Fla.	335	347	359	46	3.5	10,074	35.6
Milwaukee, Wis.	717	636	628	17	-1.3	6,537	96.1
Minneapolis, Minn.	434	371	368	43	-0.7	6,706	54.9
Mobile, Ala.	190	200	196	79	-2.1	1,663	118.0
Modesto, Calif.	62	107	165	103	54.0	5,458	30.2
Montgomery, Ala.	133	178	188	86	5.4	1,389	135.0
Moreno Valley, Calif.	[3]	[3]	119	151	N.A.	2,418	49.1
Nashville-Davidson, Tenn.[1]	426	456	488	25	6.9	1,032	473.3
Newark, N.J.	382	329	275	56	-16.4	11,554	23.8
New Haven, Conn.	138	126	130	138	3.5	6,922	18.9
New Orleans, La.	593	558	497	24	-10.9	2,751	180.7
Newport News, Va.	138	145	171	100	18.3	2,510	68.3
New York, N.Y.	7,896	7,072	7,323	1	3.5	23,701	309.0
Norfolk, Va.	308	267	261	62	-2.2	4,856	53.8
Oakland, Calif.	362	339	372	40	9.7	6,640	56.1
Oceanside, Calif.	40	77	128	140	67.1	3,164	40.5
Oklahoma City, Okla.	368	404	445	29	10.1	731	608.2
Omaha, Nebr.	347	314	336	48	7.0	3,336	100.7
Ontario, Calif.	64	89	133	134	49.9	3,624	36.8
Orange, Calif.	77	91	111	166	21.0	4,741	23.3
Orlando, Fla.	99	128	165	104	28.4	2,448	67.3
Overland Park, Kans.	78	82	112	161	36.7	2,007	55.7
Oxnard, Calif.	71	108	143	121	31.8	5,843	24.4
Pasadena, Calif.	113	118	132	137	11.4	5,724	23.0
Pasadena, Tex.	90	113	119	150	6.1	2,726	43.8
Paterson, N.J.	145	138	141	124	2.1	16,693	8.4
Peoria, Ill.	127	124	114	157	-8.6	2,776	40.9
Philadelphia, Pa.	1,949	1,688	1,586	5	-6.1	11,734	135.1
Phoenix, Ariz.	584	790	983	9	24.5	2,342	419.9
Pittsburgh, Pa.	520	424	370	41	-12.8	6,649	55.6
Plano, Tex.	18	72	128	141	76.8	1,929	66.3
Pomona, Calif.	87	93	132	136	42.0	5,770	22.8
Portland, Oreg.	380	368	437	30	18.8	3,508	124.7
Portsmouth, Va.	111	105	104	186	-0.6	3,139	33.1
Providence, R.I.	179	157	161	107	2.5	8,707	18.5
Raleigh, N.C.	123	150	211	74	40.4	2,395	88.1
Rancho Cucamonga, Calif.	[3]	55	101	192	83.5	2,682	37.8

City	Pop. ('000s) 1970	1980	1990	Rank 1990	Population Percent change 1980–90	Per sq. mi. 1990	Land area (sq.mi.) 1990
Reno, Nev.	73	101	134	132	32.8%	2,328	57.5
Richmond, Va.	249	219	203	76	-7.5	3,374	60.1
Riverside, Calif.	140	171	227	68	32.8	2,916	77.7
Rochester, N.Y.	295	242	230	66	-4.7	6,435	35.8
Rockford, Ill.	147	140	140	127	0.2	3,110	45.0
Sacramento, Calif.	257	276	369	42	34.0	3,836	96.3
Salem, Oreg.	69	89	108	178	21.0	2,595	41.5
St. Louis, Mo.	622	453	397	34	-12.4	6,405	61.9
St. Paul, Minn.	310	270	272	57	0.7	5,157	52.8
St. Petersburg, Fla.	216	239	240	65	0.7	4,059	59.2
Salinas, Calif.	59	80	109	174	35.2	5,839	18.6
Salt Lake City, Utah	176	163	160	108	-1.9	1,467	109.0
San Antonio, Tex.	654	786	936	10	19.1	2,810	333.0
San Bernardino, Calif.	107	119	164	105	38.2	2,980	55.1
San Diego, Calif.	697	876	1,111	6	26.8	3,428	324.0
San Francisco, Calif.	716	679	724	14	6.6	15,502	46.7
San Jose, Calif.	460	629	782	11	24.3	4,568	171.3
Santa Ana, Calif.	156	204	294	52	44.0	10,842	27.1
Santa Clarita, Calif.	(³)	(³)	111	165	N.A.	2,733	40.5
Santa Rosa, Calif.	50	83	113	158	37.1	3,362	33.7
Savannah, Ga.	118	142	138	129	-2.6	2,204	62.6
Scottsdale, Ariz.	68	89	130	139	46.8	706	184.4
Seattle, Wash.	531	494	516	21	4.5	6,154	83.9
Shreveport, La.	182	206	199	77	-4.1	2,013	98.6
Simi Valley, Calif.	60	78	100	195	29.3	3,034	33.0
Sioux Falls, S.Dak.	72	81	101	194	24.0	2,236	45.1
South Bend, Ind.	126	110	106	182	-3.8	2,897	36.4
Spokane, Wash.	171	171	177	94	3.4	3,169	55.9
Springfield, Ill.	92	100	105	184	5.2	2,474	42.5
Springfield, Mass.	164	152	157	111	3.1	4,890	32.1
Springfield, Mo.	120	133	140	126	5.5	2,068	68.0
Stamford, Conn.	109	102	108	177	5.5	2,865	37.7
Sterling Heights, Mich.	61	109	118	152	8.1	3,215	36.6
Stockton, Calif.	110	150	211	75	42.3	4,013	52.6
Sunnyvale, Calif.	96	107	117	153	10.0	5,353	21.9
Syracuse, N.Y.	197	170	164	106	-3.7	6,528	25.1
Tacoma, Wash.	154	159	177	95	11.5	3,677	48.1
Tallahassee, Fla.	73	82	125	146	53.0	1,972	63.3
Tampa, Fla.	278	272	280	55	3.1	2,577	108.7
Tempe, Ariz.	64	107	142	122	32.7	3,590	39.5
Thousand Oaks, Calif.	36	77	104	185	35.4	2,104	49.6
Toledo, Ohio	383	355	333	49	-6.1	4,132	80.6
Topeka, Kans.	125	119	120	149	1.0	2,173	55.2
Torrance, Calif.	135	130	133	135	2.5	6,487	20.5
Tucson, Ariz.	263	331	405	33	22.6	2,594	156.3
Tulsa, Okla.	330	361	367	44	1.8	2,001	183.5
Vallejo, Calif.	72	80	109	171	36.0	3,613	30.2
Virginia Beach, Va.	172	262	393	37	49.9	1,583	248.3
Waco, Tex.	95	101	104	187	2.3	1,367	75.8
Warren, Mich.	179	161	145	118	-10.1	4,226	34.3
Washington, D.C.	757	638	607	19	-4.9	9,883	61.4
Waterbury, Conn.	108	103	109	172	5.5	3,815	28.6
Wichita, Kans.	277	280	304	51	8.6	2,640	115.1
Winston-Salem, N.C.	134	132	143	119	8.8	2,018	71.1
Worcester, Mass.	177	162	170	101	4.9	4,520	37.6
Yonkers, N.Y.	204	195	188	84	-3.7	10,403	18.1

Note: Cities over 100,000 population. 1. Represents the portion of a consolidated city not within one or more separately incorporated areas. 2. Data represent the census designated place of Honolulu, as delineated by the State of Hawaii. 3. Not incorporated **Source:** U.S. Bureau of the Census, *Statistical Abstract of the United States 1990* (1990), and Release (1991).

Resident Population of Major U.S Cities by Race and Hispanic Origin, 1990

City	Total Population	Black	Hispanic[1]	Asian or Pacific Islander	American Indian
Abilene, Tex.	106,707	7.0%	15.5%	1.3%	0.4%
Akron, Ohio	223,019	24.5	0.7	1.2	0.3
Albuquerque, N.Mex.	384,915	3.0	34.5	1.7	3.0
Alexandria, Va.	111,182	21.9	9.7	4.2	0.3
Allentown, Pa.	105,301	5.0	11.7	1.3	0.2
Amarillo, Tex.	157,571	6.0	14.7	1.9	0.8
Anaheim, Calif.	266,406	2.5	31.4	9.4	0.5
Anchorage, Alaska	226,338	6.4	4.1	4.8	6.4
Ann Arbor, Mich.	109,608	9.0	2.6	7.7	0.4
Arlington, Va	261,717	10.5	13.5	6.8	0.3
Arlington, Tex.	170,897	8.4	8.9	3.9	0.5
Atlanta, Ga	393,929	67.1	1.9	0.9	0.1
Aurora, Colo.	222,103	11.4	6.6	3.8	0.6
Austin, Tex.	472,020	12.4	23.0	3.0	0.4
Bakersfield, Calif.	176,264	9.4	20.5	3.6	1.1
Baltimore, Md.	736,014	59.2	1.0	1.1	0.3
Baton Rouge, La.	219,531	43.9	1.6	1.7	0.1
Beaumont, Tex.	114,323	41.3	4.3	1.7	0.2
Birmingham, Ala.	265,347	63.3	(Z)	0.6	0.1
Boise City, Idaho	126,685	0.6	2.7	1.6	0.6
Boston, Mass.	574,283	25.6	10.8	5.3	0.3
Bridgeport, Conn.	141,686	26.6	26.5	2.3	0.3
Brownsville, Texas	107,027	0.2	90.1	0.3	0.1
Buffalo, N.Y.	328,175	30.7	4.9	1.0	0.8
Cedar Rapids, Iowa	108,772	2.9	1.1	1.0	0.2
Charlotte, N.C.	419,539	31.8	1.4	1.8	0.4
Chattanooga, Tenn.	152,393	33.7	0.6	1.0	0.2
Chesapeake, Va.	151,982	27.4	1.3	1.2	0.3
Chicago, Ill.	2,783,726	39.1	19.6	3.7	0.3
Chula Vista, Calif.	135,160	4.6	37.3	8.9	0.6
Cincinnati, Ohio	364,114	37.9	0.7	1.1	0.2
Citrus Heights, Calif.	505,616	2.3	6.9	3.3	1.1
Cleveland, Ohio	280,430	46.6	4.6	1.0	0.3
Colorado Springs, Colo.	110,734	7.0	9.1	2.4	0.8
Columbus, Ga.	178,683	38.1	3.0	1.4	0.3
Columbus, Ohio	632,945	22.6	1.1	2.4	0.2
Concord, Calif.	111,308	2.4	11.5	8.7	0.7
Corpus Christi, Tex.	257,453	4.8	50.4	0.9	0.4
Dallas, Tex.	1,007,618	29.5	20.9	2.2	0.5
Dayton, Ohio	182,005	40.4	0.7	0.6	0.2
Denver, Colo.	467,610	12.8	23.0	2.4	1.2
Des Moines, Iowa	193,189	7.1	2.4	2.4	0.4
Detroit, Mich.	1,027,974	75.7	2.8	0.8	0.4
Durham, N.C.	138,894	45.7	1.2	2.0	0.2
El Monte, Calif.	106,162	1.0	72.5	11.8	0.6
El Paso, Tex.	515,342	3.4	69.0	1.2	0.4
Elizabeth, N.J.	110,002	19.8	39.1	2.7	0.3
Erie, Pa.	108,718	12.0	2.4	0.5	0.2
Escondido, Calif.	108,648	1.5	23.4	3.7	0.8
Eugene, Oreg.	112,733	1.3	2.7	3.5	0.9
Evansville, Ind.	126272	9.5	0.6	0.6	0.2
Flint, Mich.	140,925	47.9	2.9	0.5	0.7
Fort Lauderdale, Fla.	149,238	28.1	7.2	0.9	0.2
Fort Wayne, Ind.	191,839	16.7	2.7	1.0	0.3
Fort Worth, Tex.	447,619	22.0	19.5	2.0	0.4
Fremont, Calif.	173,339	3.8	13.3	19.4	0.7
Fresno, Calif.	354,091	8.3	29.9	12.5	1.1
Fullerton, Calif.	114,144	2.2	21.3	12.2	0.5
Garden Grove, Calif.	142,965	1.5	23.5	20.5	0.6
Garland, Tex.	180,635	8.9	11.6	4.5	0.5
Gary, Ind.	116,646	80.6	5.7	0.2	0.2
Glendale, Ariz.	147,864	3.0	15.5	2.1	0.9
Glendale, Calif.	180,038	1.3	21.0	14.1	0.3
Grand Rapids, Mich.	189,126	18.5	5.0	1.1	0.8
Greensboro, N.C.	183,894	33.9	1.0	1.4	0.5
Hampton, Va.	133,811	38.9	2.0	1.7	0.3
Hartford, Conn.	139,739	38.9	31.6	1.4	0.3
Hayward, Calif.	114,705	9.8	23.9	15.5	1.0
Hialeah, Fla.	188,008	1.9	87.6	0.5	0.1

City	Total Population	Black	Hispanic[1]	Asian or Pacific Islander	American Indian
Hollywood, Fla.	121,720	8.5%	11.9%	1.3%	0.2%
Honolulu, Hawaii	377,059	1.3	4.6	70.5	0.3
Houston, Tex.	1,637,859	28.1	27.6	4.1	0.3
Huntington Beach, Calif.	181,519	0.9	11.2	8.3	0.6
Huntsville, Ala.	159,880	24.4	1.2	2.1	0.5
Independence, Mo.	112,301	1.4	2.0	1.0	0.6
Indianapolis, Ind.	731,278	22.6	1.1	0.9	0.2
Inglewood, Calif.	109,602	51.9	38.5	2.5	0.4
Irvine, Calif.	110,330	1.8	6.3	18.1	0.2
Irving, Tex.	155,037	7.5	16.3	4.6	0.6
Jackson, Miss.	202,062	55.7	0.4	0.5	0.1
Jacksonville, Fla.	635,230	25.2	2.6	1.9	0.3
Jersey City, N.J.	228,517	29.7	24.2	11.4	0.3
Kansas City, Kans.	151,521	29.3	7.1	1.2	0.7
Kansas City, Mo.	434,829	29.6	3.9	1.2	0.5
Knoxville, Tenn.	169,761	15.8	0.7	1.0	0.2
Lakewood, Colo.	126,475	1.0	9.1	1.9	0.7
Lansing, Mich.	127,321	18.6	7.9	1.8	1.0
Laredo, Tex.	122,899	0.1	93.9	0.4	0.2
Las Vegas, Nev.	258,204	11.4	12.5	3.6	0.9
Lexington-Fayette, Ky.	225,366	13.4	1.1	1.6	0.2
Lincoln, Nebr.	191,972	2.4	2.0	1.7	0.6
Little Rock, Ark.	175,727	34.0	0.8	0.9	0.3
Long Beach, Calif.	429,321	13.7	23.6	13.6	0.6
Los Angeles, Calif.	3,485,557	14.0	39.9	9.8	0.5
Louisville, Ky.	269,555	29.7	0.7	0.7	0.2
Lubbock, Tex.	186,206	8.6	22.5	1.4	0.3
Macon, Ga.	107,365	52.2	0.6	0.4	0.1
Madison, Wis.	190,766	4.2	2.0	3.9	0.4
Memphis, Tenn.	618,652	54.8	0.7	0.8	0.2
Mesa, Ariz.	289,199	1.9	10.9	1.5	1.0
Miami, Fla.	358,648	27.4	62.5	0.6	0.2
Milwaukee, Wis.	628,088	30.5	6.3	1.9	0.9
Minneapolis, Minn.	368,383	13.0	2.1	4.3	3.3
Mobile, Ala.	196,263	38.9	1.0	1.0	0.2
Modesto, Calif.	164,746	2.7	16.3	7.9	1.0
Montgomery, Ala.	190,350	42.3	0.8	0.7	0.2
Moreno Valley, Calif.	118,779	13.8	22.9	6.6	0.7
Nashville-Davidson, Tenn.	488,366	24.3	0.9	1.4	0.2
New Haven, Conn.	130,474	36.1	13.2	2.4	0.3
New Orleans, La.	496,938	61.9	3.5	1.9	0.2
New York, N.Y	7,322,564	28.7	24.4	7.0	0.4
Bronx Borough	1,204,000[2]	37.3	43.5	3.0	0.5
Brooklyn Borough	2,301,000[2]	37.9	20.1	4.8	0.3
Manhattan Borough	1,488,000[2]	22.0	26.0	7.4	0.4
Queens Borough	1,952,000[2]	21.7	19.5	12.2	0.4
Staten Island Borough	379,000[2]	8.1	8.0	4.5	0.2
Newark, N.J.	275,221	58.5	26.1	1.2	0.2
Newport News, Va.	171,439	33.6	2.8	2.3	0.3
Norfolk, Va.	261,250	39.1	2.9	2.6	0.4
Oakland, Calif.	372,242	43.9	13.9	14.8	0.6
Oceanside, Calif.	128,090	7.9	22.6	6.1	0.7
Oklahoma City, Okla.	444,724	16.0	5.0	2.4	4.2
Omaha, Nebr.	342,862	13.1	3.1	1.0	0.7
Ontario, Calif.	133,179	7.3	41.7	3.9	0.7
Orange, Calif	110,658	1.4	22.8	7.9	0.5
Orlando, Fla.	164,674	26.9	8.7	1.6	0.3
Overland Park, Kans.	111,790	1.8	2.0	1.9	0.3
Oxnard, Calif.	142,560	5.2	54.4	8.6	0.8
Pasadena, Calif.	131,586	19.0	27.3	8.1	0.4
Pasadena, Tex.	119,604	1.0	28.8	1.6	0.5
Paterson, N.J.	140,891	36.0	41.0	1.4	0.3
Peoria, Ill.	113,513	20.9	1.6	1.7	0.2
Philadelphia, Pa.	1,585,577	39.9	5.6	2.7	0.2
Phoenix, Ariz.	984,310	5.2	20.0	1.7	1.9
Pittsburgh, Pa.	369,879	25.8	0.9	1.6	0.2
Plano, Tex.	127,885	4.1	6.2	4.0	0.3
Pomona, Calif.	131,700	14.4	51.3	6.7	0.6
Portland, Oreg.	463,634	7.7	3.2	5.3	1.2
Providence, R.I.	160,728	14.8	15.5	5.9	0.9
Raleigh, N.C.	212,092	27.6	1.4	2.5	0.3
Reno, Nev.	133,850	2.9	11.1	4.9	1.4
Richmond, Va.	202,798	55.2	0.9	0.9	0.2

City	Total Population	Black	Hispanic[1]	Asian or Pacific Islander	American Indian
Riverside, Calif.	226,546	7.4%	26.0%	5.2%	0.8%
Rochester, N.Y.	230,356	31.5	8.7	1.8	0.5
Rockford, Ill.	141,787	15.0	4.2	1.5	0.3
Sacramento, Calif.	369,365	15.3	16.2	15.0	1.2
St. Louis, Mo.	396,685	47.5	1.3	0.9	0.2
St. Paul, Minn.	272,235	7.4	4.2	7.1	1.4
St. Petersburg, Fla.	240,318	19.6	2.6	1.7	0.2
Salem, Oreg.	107,793	1.5	6.1	2.4	1.6
Salinas, Calif.	108,777	3.0	50.6	8.1	0.9
Salt Lake City, Utah	159,928	1.7	9.7	4.7	1.6
San Antonio, Tex.	959,295	7.0	55.6	1.1	0.4
San Bernardino, Calif.	170,036	16.0	34.6	4.0	1.0
San Diego, Calif.	1,110,623	9.4	20.7	11.8	0.6
San Francisco, Calif.	723,959	10.9	13.9	29.1	0.5
San Jose, Calif.	782,224	4.7	26.6	19.5	0.7
Santa Ana, Calif.	293,827	2.6	65.2	9.7	0.5
Santa Clarita, Calif.	120,050	1.5	13.4	4.2	0.6
Santa Rosa, Calif.	113,261	1.8	9.5	3.4	1.2
Savannah, Ga.	137,812	51.3	1.4	1.1	0.2
Scottsdale, Ariz.	130,075	0.8	4.8	1.2	0.6
Seattle, Wash.	516,259	10.1	3.6	11.8	1.4
Shreveport, La.	198,525	44.8	1.1	0.5	0.2
South Bend, Ind.	105,511	20.9	3.4	0.9	0.4
Spokane, Wash.	177,165	1.9	2.1	2.1	2.0
Springfield, Ill.	105,417	13.0	0.8	1.0	0.2
Springfield, Mass.	156,983	19.2	16.9	1.0	0.2
Springfield, Mo.	140,494	2.5	1.0	0.9	0.7
Stamford, Conn.	108,056	17.8	9.8	2.6	0.1
Sterling Heights, Mich.	117,810	0.4	1.1	2.9	0.2
Stockton, Calif.	210,943	9.6	25.0	22.8	1.0
Sunnyvale, Calif.	117,324	3.4	13.2	19.3	0.5
Syracuse, N.Y.	163,860	20.3	2.9	2.2	1.3
Tacoma, Wash.	176,664	11.4	3.8	6.9	2.0
Tallahassee, Fla.	124,773	29.1	3.0	1.8	0.2
Tampa, Fla.	280,015	25.0	15.0	1.4	0.3
Tempe, Ariz.	141,993	3.2	10.9	4.1	1.3
Toledo, Ohio	332,943	19.7	4.0	1.0	0.3
Topeka, Kans.	119,883	10.6	5.8	0.8	1.3
Torrance, Calif.	133,107	1.5	10.1	21.9	0.4
Tucson, Ariz.	411,480	4.3	29.3	2.2	1.6
Tulsa, Okla.	367,302	13.6	2.6	1.4	4.7
Vallejo, Calif.	109,199	21.2	10.8	23.0	0.7
Virginia Beach, Va.	393,089	13.9	3.1	4.3	0.4
Warren, Mich.	144,864	0.7	1.1	1.3	0.5
Washington, D.C.	606,900	65.8	5.4	1.8	0.2
Waterbury, Conn.	108,961	13.0	13.4	0.7	0.3
Wichita, Kans.	304,017	11.3	5.0	2.6	1.2
Winston-Salem, N.C.	150,958	39.3	0.9	0.8	0.2
Worcester, Mass.	169,759	4.5	9.6	2.8	0.3
Yonkers, N.Y.	188,082	14.1	16.7	3.0	0.2

Note: Cities with populations over 105,000 as of April 1, 1990. Z=Less than .05 percent. 1. Hispanic persons may be of any race. 2. Figure rounded in source. **Source:** U.S. Bureau of the Census, Press Release, 1992.

Cities, by Population Size, 1960–90

Population size	Number of Cities				Population (mil.)				Percent of Total			
	1960	1970	1980	1990	1960	1970	1980	1990	1960	1970	1980	1990
Total	18,088	18,666	19,097	19,262	115.9	131.9	140.3	152.9	100%	100%	100%	100%
1 million +	5	6	6	8	17.5	18.8	17.5	20.0	15.1	14.2	12.5	13.0
500,000–1 million	16	20	16	15	11.1	13.0	10.9	10.1	9.6	9.8	7.8	6.6
250,000–500,000	30	30	33	41	10.8	10.5	11.8	14.2	9.3	7.9	8.4	9.3
100,000–250,000	79	97	114	131	11.4	13.9	16.6	19.1	9.8	10.5	11.8	12.5
50,000–100,000	180	232	250	309	12.5	16.2	17.6	21.2	10.8	12.2	12.3	13.9
25,000–50,000	366	455	526	567	12.7	15.7	18.4	20.0	11.0	11.9	13.1	13.0
10,000–25,000	978	1,127	1,260	1,290	15.1	17.6	19.8	20.3	13.1	13.3	14.1	13.3
<10,000	16,434	16,699	16,892	16,901	24.9	26.4	28.0	28.2	21.5	20.0	20.0	18.4

Source: U.S. Bureau of the Census, *Statistical Abstract of the United States* (annual).

25 Fastest-Growing Major Cities in the U.S., 1980–90

City	Population		Change, 1980–90		Overall rank	
	1980	1990	Number	Percent	1980	1990
1. Mesa, Ariz.	152,404	289,199	136,795	89.8%	102	53
2. Rancho Cucamonga, Calif.	55,250	101,409	46,159	83.5	N.A.	191
3. Plano, Texas	72,331	127,885	55,554	76.8	N.A.	143
4. Irvine, Calif.	62,134	110,330	48,196	77.6	N.A.	167
5. Escondido, Calif.	64,355	108,635	44,280	68.8	N.A.	176
6. Oceanside, Calif.	76,698	128,398	51,700	67.4	N.A.	141
7. Bakersfield, Calif.	105,611	174,820	69,209	65.5	152	97
8. Arlington, Texas	160,113	261,721	101,608	63.5	94	61
9. Fresno, Calif.	217,491	354,202	136,711	62.9	65	47
10. Chula Vista, Calif.	83,927	135,163	51,236	61.8	N.A.	131
11. Las Vegas, Nev.	164,674	258,877	94,203	57.2	89	63
12. Modesto, Calif.	106,963	164,730	57,767	54.0	147	103
13. Tallahassee, Fla.	81,548	124,773	43,225	53.0	N.A.	146
14. Glendale, Ariz.	97,172	147,070	49,898	51.4	N.A.	120
15. Mesquite, Texas	67,053	101,484	34,431	51.3	N.A.	190
16. Ontario, Calif.	88,820	133,179	44,359	49.9	N.A.	134
17. Virginia Beach, Va.	262,199	393,069	130,870	49.9	56	37
18. Scottsdale, Ariz.	88,622	127,885	39,263	44.3	N.A.	141
19. Santa Ana, Calif.	204,023	293,742	89,719	44.0	69	52
20. Stockton, Calif.	148,283	210,943	62,660	42.3	107	74
21. Pomona, Calif.	92,742	131,723	38,981	42.0	N.A.	136
22. Irving, Texas	109,943	155,037	45,094	41.0	142	112
23. Aurora, Colo.	158,588	222,103	63,515	40.1	97	72
24. Raleigh, N.C.	150,255	207,951	57,696	38.4	105	75
25. San Bernardino, Calif.	118,794	164,164	45,370	38.2	131	105

Note: Cities over 100,000 population.   Source: U.S. Bureau of the Census release (1991).

25 Fastest-Growing Major Cities in the U.S., 1990–98

City	Population		Change, 1990–98		Overall rank	
	1990	1998	Number	Percent	1990	1998
1. Henderson, Nevada	64,948	152,717	87,769	135.1%	218	126
2. Chandler, Ariz.	89,862	160,329	70,467	78.4	207	121
3. Pembroke Pines, Fla.	65,566	115,361	49,795	75.9	217	180
4. Plano, Texas	127,885	219,486	91,601	71.6	143	72
5. Las Vegas, Nevada	258,877	404,288	145,411	56.2	63	37
6. Scottsdale, Ariz.	130,099	195,394	65,295	50.2	141	86
7. Corona, Calif.	75,943	112,815	36,872	48.6	215	186
8. Laredo, Texas	122,893	175,783	52,890	43.0	149	110
9. Coral Springs, Fla.	78,864	111,744	32,880	41.7	214	187
10. Palmdale, Calif.	73,314	100,157	26,843	36.6	216	218
11. Naperville, Ill.	85,806	117,091	31,285	36.5	211	177
12. Glendale, Ariz.	147,070	193,482	46,412	31.6	120	89
13. Chesapeake, Va.	151,982	199,564	47,582	31.3	117	83
14. Brownsville, Texas	107,027	137,883	30,856	28.8	183	141
15. Provo, Utah	86,835	110,419	23,584	27.2	210	196
16. McAllen, Texas	84,021	106,822	22,801	27.1	212	206
17. Fontana, Calif.	87,535	109,777	22,242	25.4	208	199
18. Aurora, Ill.	99,672	124,736	25,064	25.1	198	162
19. Overland Park, Kans.	111,790	139,685	27,895	25.0	165	140
20. Mesa, Ariz.	289,199	360,076	70,877	24.5	53	46
21. Fort Collins, Colo.	87,491	108,905	21,414	24.5	209	200
22. Boise City, Idaho	126,685	157,452	30,767	24.3	145	122
23. Irvine, Calif.	110,330	136,446	26,116	23.7	170	147
24. Colorado Springs, Colo.	280,430	344,987	64,557	23.0	54	48
25. Carrollton, Texas	82,169	100,463	18,294	22.3	213	216

Note: Cities over 100,000 population.   Source: U.S. Bureau of the Census release, 1999.
www.census.gov/population/estimates/metro-city/SC100K98-T2-DR.txt

25 Fastest-Declining Major U.S. Cities, 1980-90

City	Population		Change, 1980-90		Overall rank	
	1980	1990	Number	Percent	1980	1990
1. Gary, Ind.	151,968	116,646	-35,322	-23.2%	104	157
2. Newark, N.J.	329,248	275,221	-54,027	-16.4	46	56
3. Detroit, Mich.	1,203,368	1,027,974	-175,394	-14.6	6	7
4. Pittsburgh, Pa.	423,959	369,879	-54,080	-12.8	30	41
5. St. Louis, Mo.	452,801	396,685	-56,116	-12.4	26	35
6. Cleveland, Ohio	573,822	505,616	-68,206	-11.9	18	23
7. Flint, Mich.	159,611	140,925	-18,686	-11.7	95	127
8. New Orleans, La.	557,927	496,938	-60,989	-10.9	22	24
9. Warren, Mich.	161,134	144,864	-16,270	-10.1	93	118
10. Chattanooga, Tenn.	169,514	152,466	-17,048	-10.1	88	113
11. Louisville, Ky.	298,694	269,063	-29,631	-9.9	49	58
12. Macon, Ga.	116,896	106,612	-10,284	-8.8	135	180
13. Erie, Pa.	119,123	108,718	-10,405	-8.7	130	178
14. Peoria, Ill.	124,160	113,504	-10,656	-8.6	126	157
15. Buffalo, N.Y.	357,870	328,175	-29,695	-8.3	39	50
16. Richmond, Va.	219,214	203,056	-16,158	-7.4	64	76
17. Chicago, Ill.	3,005,072	2,783,726	-221,346	-7.4	2	3
18. Atlanta, Ga.	425,022	394,017	-31,005	-7.3	29	36
19. Kansas City, Kans.	161,148	151,521	-9,627	-6.0	92	118
20. Birmingham, Ala.	284,413	265,968	-18,445	-6.5	50	60
21. Baltimore, Md.	786,741	736,014	-50,727	-6.4	10	12
22. Toledo, Ohio	354,635	332,943	-21,692	-6.1	40	49
23. Philadelphia, Pa.	1,688,210	1,585,577	-102,633	-6.1	4	5
24. Akron, Ohio	237,177	223,019	-14,158	-6.0	59	71
25. Dayton, Ohio	193,536	182,011	-11,459	-5.9	73	91

Note: Cities over 100,000 population.   **Source:** U.S. Bureau of the Census release (1991).

25 Fastest-Declining Major U.S. Cities, 1990-98

City	Population		Change, 1990-98		Overall rank	
	1990	1998	Number	Percent	1990	1998
1. Norfolk, Va.	261,250	215,215	-46,035	-17.6	62	75
2. St. Louis, Mo.	396,685	339,316	-57,369	-14.5	35	50
3. Washington, D.C.	606,900	523,124	-83,776	-13.8	19	23
4. Baltimore, Md.	736,014	645,593	-90,421	-12.3	12	16
5. Philadelphia, Pa.	1,585,577	1,436,287	-149,290	-9.4	5	5
6. Buffalo, N.Y.	328,175	300,717	-27,458	-8.4	50	56
7. Dayton, Ohio	182,011	167,475	-14,536	-8.0	91	115
8. Pittsburgh, Pa.	369,879	340,520	-29,359	-7.9	41	49
9. Milwaukee, Wisc.	628,088	578,364	-49,724	-7.9	17	19
10. Cincinnati, Ohio	364,114	336,400	-27,714	-7.6	45	51
11. Syracuse, N.Y.	163,860	152,215	-11,645	-7.1	108	128
12. Gary, Ind.	116,646	108,469	-8,177	-7.0	157	201
13. Jackson, Miss.	202,062	188,419	-13,643	-6.8	77	94
14. Kansas City, Kans.	151,521	141,297	-10,224	-6.7	118	139
15. Flint, Mich.	140,925	131,668	-9,257	-6.6	127	152
16. New Orleans, La.	496,938	465,538	-31,400	-6.3	24	31
17. Toledo, Ohio	332,943	312,174	-20,769	-6.2	49	53
18. Providence, R.I.	160,728	150,890	-9,838	-6.1	110	130
19. Hartford, Conn.	139,739	131,523	-8,216	-5.9	130	153
20. Rochester, N.Y.	230,356	216,887	-13,469	-5.8	66	73
21. Springfield, Mass.	156,983	148,144	-8,839	-5.6	114	132
22. Detroit, Mich.	1,027,974	970,196	-57,778	-5.6	7	10
23. Erie, Pa.	108,718	102,640	-6,078	-5.6	178	209
24. New Haven, Conn.	130,474	123,189	-7,285	-5.6	140	165
25. St. Paul, Minn.	272,235	257,284	-14,951	-5.5	57	63

Note: Cities over 100,000 population.   **Source:** U.S. Bureau of the Census release, 1999.
www.census.gov/population/estimates/metro-city/SC100K98-T2-DR.txt

Population Change in the 75 Largest U.S. Cities, 1980–98

City (1990 Rank)	Population 1980	Population 1990	Population 1998	Percent change, 1980–90	Change, 1990–98 Number	Change, 1990–98 Percent
Akron, Ohio (71)	237,177	223,019	215,712	-6.0%	-7,307	-3.3%
Albuquerque, N.Mex (38)	332,920	384,915	419,311	15.6	34,396	8.9
Anaheim, Calif. (59)	219,494	266,406	295,153	21.4	28,747	10.8
Anchorage, Alaska (69)	174,731	226,338	254,982	29.5	28,644	12.7
Arlington, Texas (61)	160,113	261,717	306,497	63.5	44,780	17.1
Atlanta, Ga. (36)	425,022	393,929	403,819	-7.3	9,890	2.5
Aurora, Colo. (72)	158,588	222,103	250,604	40.1	28,501	12.8
Austin, Texas (26)	345,890	472,020	552,434	34.6	80,414	17.0
Baltimore, Md. (12)	786,741	736,014	645,593	-6.4	-90,421	-12.3
Baton Rouge, La. (73)	220,394	219,531	211,551	-0.4	-7,980	-3.6
Birmingham, Ala. (60)	284,413	265,347	252,997	-6.5	-12,350	-4.7
Boston, Mass. (20)	562,994	574,283	555,447	2.0	-18,836	-3.3
Buffalo, N.Y (50)	357,870	328,175	300,717	-8.3	-27,458	-8.4
Charlotte, N.C (33)	315,474	419,539	504,637	25.5	85,079	20.3
Chicago, Ill. (3)	3,005,072	2,783,726	2,802,079	-7.4	18,353	0.7
Cincinnati, Ohio (45)	385,409	364,114	336,400	-5.5	-27,714	-7.6
Cleveland, Ohio (23)	573,822	505,616	495,817	-11.9	-9,799	-1.9
Colorado Springs, Colo. (54)	215,105	280,430	344,987	30.7	64,557	23.0
Columbus, Ohio (16)	565,021	632,945	670,234	12.0	37,289	5.9
Corpus Christi, Texas (64)	232,134	257,453	281,453	10.9	24,025	9.3
Dallas, Texas (8)	904,599	1,007,618	1,075,894	11.3	68,276	6.8
Denver, Colo. (27)	492,686	467,610	499,055	-5.1	31,445	6.7
Detroit, Mich. (7)	1,203,368	1,027,974	970,196	-14.6	-57,778	-5.6
El Paso, Texas (22)	425,259	515,342	615,032	21.2	99,690	19.3
Fort Worth, Texas (29)	385,164	447,619	491,801	16.2	44,182	9.9
Fresno, Calif. (47)	217,491	354,091	398,133	62.9	44,042	12.4
Honolulu, Hawaii. (39)	365,048	377,059	395,789	0.1	18,730	5.0
Houston, Texas (4)	1,595,138	1,637,859	1,786,691	2.2	132,343	8.0
Indianapolis, Ind. (13)	711,539	731,278	741,304	4.3	10,026	1.4
Jacksonville, Fla. (15)	571,003	635,230	693,630	17.9	58,400	9.2
Jersey City, N.J. (67)	223,532	228,517	232,429	2.2	3,912	1.7
Kansas City, Mo. (31)	448,028	434,829	441,574	-2.9	6,745	1.6
Las Vegas, Nev. (63)	164,674	258,204	404,288	56.9	145,411	56.2
Lexington-Fayette, Ky. (70)	204,165	225,366	241,749	10.4	16,383	7.3
Long Beach, Calif. (32)	361,498	429,321	430,905	18.8	1,584	0.4
Los Angeles, Calif. (2)	2,968,528	3,485,557	3,597,556	17.4	111,999	3.2
Louisville, Ky. (58)	298,694	269,555	255,045	-9.9	-14,510	-5.4
Memphis, Tenn. (18)	646,174	618,652	603,507	-5.5	-15,145	-2.4
Mesa, Ariz. (53)	152,404	289,199	360,076	89.0	70,877	24.5
Miami, Fla. (46)	346,681	358,648	368,624	3.4	9,976	2.8
Milwaukee, Wis. (17)	636,297	628,088	578,364	-1.3	-49,724	-7.9
Minneapolis, Minn. (43)	370,951	368,383	351,731	-0.7	-16,652	-4.5
Nashville, Tenn. (25)	477,811	488,366	510,274	6.9	21,908	4.5
New Orleans, La. (24)	557,927	496,938	465,538	-10.9	-31,400	-6.3
New York, N.Y. (1)	7,071,639	7,322,564	7,420,166	3.5	97,602	1.3
Newark, N.J. (56)	329,248	275,221	267,823	-16.4	-7,398	-2.7
Norfolk, Va. (62)	266,979	261,250	215,215	-2.2	-46,035	-17.6
Oakland, Calif. (40)	339,337	372,242	365,874	9.7	-6,368	-1.7
Oklahoma City, Okla. (30)	404,014	444,724	472,221	10.1	27,497	6.2
Omaha, Nebr. (48)	313,939	342,862	371,291	7.0	26,828	7.8
Philadelphia, Pa. (5)	1,688,210	1,585,577	1,436,287	-6.1	-149,290	-9.4
Phoenix, Ariz. (9)	789,704	984,310	1,198,064	24.5	210,049	21.3
Pittsburgh, Pa. (41)	423,959	369,879	340,520	-12.8	-29,359	-7.9
Portland, Oreg. (28)	368,148	463,634	503,891	18.8	17,916	3.7
Raleigh, N.C. (74)	150,255	212,092	259,423	38.4	40,564	18.5
Riverside, Calif. (68)	170,591	226,546	262,140	32.8	35,594	15.7
Rochester, N.Y. (66)	241,741	230,356	216,887	-4.2	-13,469	-5.8
Sacramento, Calif. (42)	275,741	369,365	404,168	34.0	34,803	9.4
San Antonio, Texas (10)	785,940	959,295	1,114,130	19.1	137,616	14.1
San Diego, Calif. (6)	875,538	1,110,623	1,220,666	26.8	110,043	9.9
San Francisco, Calif. (14)	678,974	723,959	745,774	6.6	21,815	3.0
San Jose, Calif. (11)	629,400	782,224	861,284	24.3	79,060	10.1
Santa Ana, Calif. (52)	204,023	293,827	305,955	44.0	12,128	4.1
Seattle, Wash. (21)	493,846	516,259	536,978	4.5	20,719	4.0
St. Louis, Mo. (35)	452,801	396,685	339,316	-12.4	-57,369	-14.5
St. Paul, Minn. (57)	270,320	272,235	257,284	0.7	-14,951	-5.5
St. Petersburg, Fla. (65)	238,647	240,318	236,029	-0.0	-4,289	-1.8
Stockton, Calif. (75)	148,283	210,943	240,143	42.3	29,200	13.8

City (1990 Rank)	Population			Percent change,	Change, 1990–98	
	1980	1990	1998	1980–90	Number	Percent
Tampa, Fla. (55)	271,577	280,015	289,156	3.1	9,141	3.3
Toledo, Ohio (49)	354,635	332,943	312,174	-6.1	-20,769	-6.2
Tucson, Ariz. (34)	330,537	411,480	460,466	22.6	45,022	10.8
Tulsa, Okla. (44)	360,919	367,302	381,393	1.8	14,091	3.8
Virginia Beach, Va. (37)	262,199	393,089	432,380	49.9	39,291	10.0
Washington, D.C (19)	638,432	606,900	523,124	-4.9	-83,776	-13.8
Wichita, Kans. (51)	279,838	304,017	329,211	8.6	25,194	8.3

Source: U.S. Bureau of the Census, 1999. www.census.gov/population/estimates/metro-city/SC100K98-T1-DR.txt

Population of the 50 Largest Cities, 1950–1998

1990 Rank, City	1950	1960	1970[1]	1980[1]	1990	1998	Population change, 1990–98	Rank 1998
1. New York, N.Y.	7,891,957	7,781,984	7,896,000	7,072,000	7,322,564	7,420,166	97,602	1
2. Los Angeles, Calif.	1,970,358	2,479,015	2,812,000	2,969,000	3,485,557	3,597,556	111,999	2
3. Chicago, Ill.	3,620,962	3,550,404	3,369,000	3,005,000	2,783,726	2,802,079	18,353	3
4. Houston, Texas	596,163	938,219	1,234,000	1,595,000	1,630,864	1,786,691	132,343	4
5. Philadelphia, Pa.	2,071,605	2,002,512	1,949,000	1,688,000	1,585,577	1,436,287	-149,290	5
6. San Diego, Calif.	334,387	573,224	697,000	876,000	1,110,623	1,220,666	110,043	6
7. Detroit, Mich.	1,849,568	1,670,144	1,514,000	1,203,000	1,027,974	970,196	-57,778	10
8. Dallas, Texas	434,462	679,684	844,000	905,000	1,007,618	1,075,894	68,276	9
9. Phoenix, Ariz.	(2)	439,170	584,000	790,000	984,309	1,198,064	210,049	7
10. San Antonio, Texas	408,442	587,718	654,000	786,000	935,393	1,114,130	137,616	8
11. San Jose, Calif.	(2)	(2)	460,000	629,000	782,224	861,284	79,060	11
12. Baltimore, Md.	949,708	939,024	905,000	787,000	736,014	645,593	-90,421	16
13. Indianapolis, Ind.[3]	427,173	476,258	737,000	701,000	731,311	741,304	10,026	13
14. San Francisco, Calif.	775,357	742,855	716,000	679,000	723,959	745,774	21,815	12
15. Jacksonville, Fla.[3]	204,517	(2)	504,000	541,000	635,230	693,630	58,400	14
16. Columbus, Ohio	375,901	471,316	540,000	565,000	632,945	670,234	37,289	15
17. Milwaukee, Wisc.	637,392	741,324	717,000	636,000	628,088	578,364	-49,724	19
18. Memphis, Tenn.	396,000	497,524	624,000	646,000	618,652	603,507	-15,145	18
19. Washington, D.C.	802,178	763,956	757,000	638,000	606,900	523,124	-83,776	23
20. Boston, Mass.	801,444	697,197	641,000	563,000	574,283	555,447	-18,836	20
21. Seattle, Wash.	467,591	557,087	531,000	494,000	516,259	536,978	20,719	22
22. El Paso, Texas	(2)	276,687	322,000	425,000	515,342	615,032	99,690	17
23. Cleveland, Ohio	914,808	876,050	751,000	574,000	505,616	495,817	-9,799	28
24. New Orleans, La.	570,445	627,525	593,000	558,000	496,938	465,538	-31,400	31
25. Nashville, Tenn.[3]	(2)	(2)	426,000	456,000	488,366	510,274	21,908	24
26. Denver, Colo.	415,786	493,887	515,000	493,000	467,610	503,891	17,916	26
27. Austin, Texas	(2)	(2)	254,000	346,000	465,648	552,434	80,414	21
28. Fort Worth, Texas	278,778	356,268	393,000	385,000	447,619	499,055.	31,445	27
29. Oklahoma City, Okla.	243,504	324,253	368,000	404,000	444,724	491,801	44,182	29
30. Portland, Oreg.	373,628	372,676	380,000	368,000	438,802	472,221	27,497	30
31. Kansas City, Mo.	456,622	475,539	507,000	448,000	434,829	441,574	6,745	33
32. Long Beach, Calif.	250,767	344,168	359,000	361,000	429,321	430,905	1,584	35
33. Tucson, Ariz.	(2)	(2)	263,000	331,000	408,754	504,637	85,079	25
34. St. Louis, Mo.	856,796	750,026	622,000	453,000	396,685	460,466	45,022	32
35. Charlotte, N.C.	(2)	(2)	241,000	315,000	395,934	339,316	-57,369	50
36. Atlanta, Ga.	332,314	487,455	495,000	425,000	393,929	403,819	9,890	39
37. Virginia Beach, Va.	(2)	(2)	172,000	262,000	393,089	432,380	39,291	34
38. Albuquerque, N.Mex.	(2)	(2)	245,000	332,000	384,619	419,311	34,396	36
39. Honolulu, Hawaii[4]	248,034	294,194	325,000	365,000	377,059	395,789	18,730	41
40. Oakland, Calif.	384,575	367,548	362,000	339,000	372,242	365,874	-6,368	45
41. Pittsburgh, Pa.	676,806	604,332	520,000	424,000	369,879	340,520	-29,359	49
42. Sacramento, Calif.	(2)	(2)	257,000	276,000	369,365	404,168	34,803	38
43. Minneapolis, Minn.	521,718	482,872	434,000	371,000	368,383	351,731	-16,652	47
44. Tulsa, Okla.	(2)	261,685	330,000	361,000	367,302	381,393	14,091	42
45. Cincinnati, Ohio	503,998	502,550	454,000	385,000	364,114	336,400	-27,714	51
46. Miami, Fla.	249,276	291,688	335,000	347,000	358,648	368,624	9,976	44
47. Fresno, Calif.	(2)	(2)	166,000	217,000	354,091	398,133	44,042	40
48. Omaha, Neb.	251,117	301,598	347,000	314,000	335,719	371,291	26,828	43
49. Toledo, Ohio	303,616	318,003	383,000	355,000	332,943	312,174	-20,769	53
50. Buffalo, N.Y.	580,132	532,759	463,000	358,000	328,175	300,717	-27,458	56

Note: The 4/1/90 census counts include count resolution corrections and boundary changes processed through December 1993, and do not include adjustments for census coverage errors. 1. Figure rounded in source. 2. City was not one of the 50 largest that year. 3. City is part of a consolidated city-county government; populations of the other incorporated places in the county have been excluded from the population totals shown here. 4. Not incorporated as a city, but recognized for census purposes as large urban places. Honolulu CDP is coextensive with Honolulu Judicial District within the City and County of Honolulu.
Source: U.S. Bureau of the Census, Current Population Reports, 1999. www.census.gov/population/estimates/metro-city/SC100K98-T1-DR.txt

CITY FINANCES

►TAX BURDENS AND PROGRESSIVITY IN MAJOR U.S. CITIES

Tax rates differ widely not only from state to state and city to city, but also from one income level to another. Any tax system in which the percentage of taxes paid rises with the income level is said to be *progressive*. A system where the percentage tax burden is the same at all income levels is said to be *proportional*. And a system in which the percentage of taxes paid decreases as income rises is said to be *regressive*. Because progressivity is mea-

sured as the ratio of one tax rate to another, progressivity does not necessarily reflect the actual tax burden.

Several factors contribute to the progressivity of a tax system. A graduated individual income tax rate combined with exemptions and credits to lessen the regressiveness of the property tax will increase the progressivity of a tax system. Progressivity can be lessened by a lack of an individual income tas as well as by reliance on regressive taxes such as the sales tax and certain automobile taxes. The upper and lower income levels chosen for comparison also affect progressiveness. The accompanying tables show the percentage tax burden at various income levels and the five most and least progressive cities.

The Cost of Living Index in Selected U.S. Cities, 1999

Urban area	Composite index (100%)	Grocery items (16%)	Housing (28%)	Utilities (8%)	Transportation (10%)	Health care (5%)	Misc. goods & services (33%)
New York (Manhattan), N.Y.	232.1	150.2	455.6	163.2	125.4	187.0	137.9
Oakland (Pleasanton), Calif.	159.2	124.2	257.4	107.8	130.1	152.5	115.0
Nassau-Suffolk, N.Y.	142.9	125.5	173.1	167.6	117.2	148.2	126.6
Boston, Mass.	136.6	112.9	182.3	141.6	116.5	134.0	114.7
Los Angeles-Long Beach, Calif.	126.2	113.6	157.7	120.0	122.0	115.7	110.1
San Diego, Calif.	125.6	122.8	157.2	104.3	128.7	120.9	115.5
Washington, D.C.	123.7	111.2	146.4	95.5	129.9	123.6	115.5
Philadelphia, Pa.	120.5	109.2	139.3	144.2	120.4	99.2	107.6
Sacramento, Calif.	112.8	122.0	101.9	115.9	131.9	159.3	104.1
Cleveland, Ohio	112.6	108.8	117.7	135.0	115.0	122.4	102.6
Riverside, Calif.	112.4	112.7	108.5	134.4	115.3	132.1	106.3
Portland, Oreg.	111.7	107.0	123.3	80.9	120.4	120.5	107.7
Detroit, Mich.	110.9	104.7	133.9	110.5	101.7	112.4	97.2
Denver, Colo.	107.9	110.8	121.4	86.1	110.6	114.2	98.7
Tampa-St. Petersburg, Fla.	103.8	102.2	108.5	88.2	102.9	113.4	103.3
Minneapolis, Minn.	103.4	98.2	95.6	104.1	117.4	116.4	106.0
Atlanta, Ga.	103.3	103.3	102.9	102.3	101.5	118.5	102.0
Phoenix-Mesa, Ariz.	101.9	102.0	99.0	103.1	112.2	112.6	99.2
Orlando, Fla.	100.5	98.6	95.4	102.3	96.6	112.5	104.6
Dallas, Texas	100.4	98.5	95.2	101.8	105.1	109.6	102.5
Cincinnati, Ohio	98.7	94.4	98.1	109.3	102.1	92.1	98.6
Kansas City, Mo.	98.2	95.5	90.4	102.0	94.3	107.0	105.0
St. Louis, Mo.	96.9	100.7	96.0	101.2	93.0	106.8	94.5
Norfolk-Va. Beach-Newport News Va.	96.5	97.5	85.1	123.7	105.4	100.6	95.9
Indianapolis, Ind.	96.0	100.7	88.8	98.7	93.8	95.4	100.0
Baltimore, Md.	95.3	94.8	93.5	118.6	102.2	91.9	89.9
Houston, Texas	94.9	90.6	84.3	101.0	106.7	110.2	98.5
Fort Worth, Texas	93.9	99.4	80.3	100.9	100.4	99.6	98.2
San Antonio, Texas	89.9	93.7	84.0	77.1	98.7	89.0	98.5

Note: Metropolitan areas with more than 1.5 million population. Percentage figures in parentheses show relative weight of component indexes used in calculating composite cost of living index. Figures are for first quarter, 1999.   Source: American Chamber of Commerce Researchers Association, ACCRA Cost of Living Index (1999).

Tax Progressivity in Selected Cities, 1997

Most progressive		Least progressive	
City	Index	City	Index
Boise City, Idaho	0.554	Anchorage, Alaska	1.243
Minneapolis, Minn.	0.570	Seattle, Wash.	1.283
New York, N.Y.	0.579	Sioux Falls, S.D.	1.333
Billings, Mont.	0.608	Cheyenne, Wyo.	1.359
Columbia, S.C.	0.643	Las Vegas, Nevada	1.387
Average progressivity[1]	0.860		

Note: An index coefficient of less than 1.000 indicates a progressive tax system; an index coefficient of greater than one indicates a regressive tax system. A proportional system is indicated by a coefficient of 1.000. 1. The average of the largest city in each state plus the District of Columbia.   Source: Government of the District of Columbia, Dept. of Finance and Revenues, *Tax Rates and Tax Burdens in the District of Columbia: A Nationwide Comparison* (1999).

State and Local Taxes for Families by Income Level in Selected Cities, 1997

City	$25,000 Percent[1]	$25,000 Amount	$50,000 Percent[1]	$50,000 Amount	$75,000 Percent[1]	$75,000 Amount	$100,000 Percent[1]	$100,000 Amount
Albuquerque, N.Mex.	6.7%	$1,684	7.6%	$3,794	8.7%	$6,529	9.2%	$9,171
Anchorage, Alaska	3.8	957	3.5	1,739	3.5	2,636	3.3	3,298
Atlanta, Ga.	7.8	1,951	8.9	4,444	10.0	7,466	10.3	10,253
Baltimore, Md.	8.1	2,037	11.0	5,490	11.5	8,597	11.4	11,381
Billings, Mont.	5.9	1,474	6.8	3,422	8.1	6,106	8.9	8,903
Birmingham, Ala.	8.7	2,170	8.3	4,165	8.7	6,550	8.8	8,830
Boise City, Idaho	5.7	1,426	8.0	3,990	9.3	6,986	9.8	9,812
Boston, Mass.	8.7	2,181	10.0	5,004	10.8	8,075	10.8	10,816
Bridgeport, Conn.	19.0	4,738	18.0	9,013	20.3	15,254	20.0	20,045
Burlington, Vt.	8.2	2,060	8.7	4,337	9.4	7,066	9.8	9,791
Charleston, W.Va.	7.7	1,921	7.5	3,738	8.5	6,368	8.9	8,885
Charlotte, N.C.	7.5	1,869	8.4	4,180	9.2	6,930	9.7	9,704
Cheyenne, Wyo.	5.0	1,253	3.9	1,942	4.1	3,087	3.9	3,903
Chicago, Ill.	8.5	2,124	8.4	4,177	8.8	6,565	8.6	8,625
Columbia, S.C.	6.3	1,577	7.8	3,921	9.1	6,818	9.5	9,494
Columbus, Ohio	8.6	2,154	9.1	4,571	10.0	7,472	10.3	10,333
Denver, Colo.	6.6	1,647	7.2	3,591	7.6	5,698	7.7	7,675
Des Moines, Iowa	8.6	2,154	8.9	4,438	9.7	7,296	9.7	9,749
Detroit, Mich.	10.2	2,551	10.6	5,278	11.0	8,215	10.9	10,907
Fargo, N. Dak.	6.9	1,731	6.7	3,346	7.1	5,325	7.2	7,227
Honolulu, Hawaii	8.7	2,168	9.6	4,778	10.5	7,905	10.8	10,805
Houston, Tex.	5.3	1,325	4.9	2,433	5.1	3,808	4.9	4,869
Indianapolis, Ind.	7.8	1,945	7.4	3,716	7.6	5,717	7.5	7,528
Jackson, Miss.	6.4	1,595	6.9	3,462	7.8	5,840	8.0	8,019
Jacksonville, Fla.	3.9	982	3.5	1,769	3.8	2,841	3.7	3,664
Kansas City, Mo.	8.7	2,175	8.5	4,231	8.9	6,704	9.2	9,160
Las Vegas, Nev.	5.8	1,450	4.6	2,296	4.7	3,520	4.5	4,461
Little Rock, Ark.	8.3	2,083	8.3	4,132	9.0	6,774	9.3	9,262
Los Angeles, Calif.	7.9	1,970	8.4	4,222	10.0	7,526	11.0	11,004
Louisville, Ky.	10.1	2,520	10.2	5,089	10.5	7,891	10.6	10,593
Manchester, N.H.	11.5	2,869	10.4	5,198	10.5	7,858	9.9	9,938
Memphis, Tenn.	6.1	1,519	4.9	2,467	5.3	3,999	5.2	5,208
Milwaukee, Wis.	9.5	2,371	10.8	5,421	11.4	8,574	11.4	11,420
Minneapolis, Minn.	6.7	1,679	9.2	4,584	10.9	8,167	11.3	11,349
New Orleans, La.	5.8	1,449	6.7	3,335	7.7	5,747	7.8	7,798
New York, N.Y.	8.5	2,123	11.4	5,707	13.2	9,872	13.9	13,878
Newark, N.J.	15.2	3,792	14.3	7,160	14.8	11,070	14.7	14,660
Oklahoma City, Okla.	8.4	2,095	8.3	4,167	9.1	6,855	9.3	9,318
Omaha, Nebr.	8.3	2,081	8.6	4,321	9.7	7,284	10.0	10,050
Philadelphia, Pa.	13.0	3,241	12.2	6,098	12.2	9,136	11.9	11,882
Phoenix, Ariz.	8.2	2,051	7.8	3,889	8.2	6,123	8.3	8,292
Portland, Maine	10.8	2,705	12.2	6,094	13.5	10,139	13.8	13,752
Portland, Oreg.	7.7	1,923	8.8	4,405	9.7	7,259	9.8	9,843
Providence, R.I.	9.6	2,411	10.8	5,407	11.6	8,686	12.0	11,988
Salt Lake City, Utah	7.4	1,858	8.5	4,241	9.2	6,870	9.2	9,217
Seattle, Wash.	7.5	1,871	6.4	3,188	6.4	4,823	6.1	6,135
Sioux Falls, S.Dak.	6.7	1,669	5.4	2,713	5.5	4,107	5.2	5,245
Virginia Beach, Va.	8.9	2,214	8.6	4,297	9.2	6,892	9.3	9,296
Washington, D.C.	8.8	2,203	9.3	4,660	10.6	7,933	11.0	10,984
Wichita, Kans.	7.6	1,894	7.3	3,661	8.3	6,251	8.7	8,697
Wilmington, Del.	6.0	1,497	7.1	3,545	7.9	5,905	8.1	8,082
51 city average[2]	8.1%	$2,027	8.4%	$4,221	9.2%	$6,885	9.3%	$9,318

Note: Tax burdens computed for a family of four. The four major taxes compared are the individual income tax, real property taxes on residential property, general sales and use taxes, and various automobile taxes, including the gasoline tax, registration fees, excise taxes, and personal property taxes. 1. Percentage of income. 2. Average of the largest city in each state plus the District of Columbia. Source: Government of the District of Columbia, Dept. of Finance and Revenue, *Tax Rates and Tax Burdens in the District of Columbia: A Nationwide Comparison* (1999).

20 Best-Paid U.S. Mayors, 1998

Rank, Mayor	City	Salary	Rank, Mayor	City	Salary
1. Richard M. Daley	Chicago	$170,000	11. Michael A. Guido	Dearborn, Mich.	$119,000
2. Rudolph Giuliani	New York	165,000	12. John O. Norquist	Milwaukee	115,851
3. Lee P. Brown	Houston	160,500	13. John Spencer	Yonkers, N.Y.	115,000
4. Dennis Archer	Detroit	157,300	14. Paul Schell	Seattle	112,731
5. Richard Riordan[1]	Los Angeles	147,390	15. Willie W. Herenton	Memphis	110,000
6. Sharpe James	Newark, N.J.	147,000	15. Edward Rendell	Philadelphia	110,000
7. Willie Brown	San Francisco	146,891	15. Dick A. Greco	Tampa, Fla.	110,000
8. John A. Delaney	Jacksonville	127,230	18. Joseph P. Riley Jr.	Charleston, S.C.	108,815
9. Thomas Menino	Boston	125,000	19. Gregory Lashutka	Columbus, Ohio	107,087
10. Joseph Delfino	White Plains, N.Y.	121,000	20. Wellington E. Webb	Denver	103,056

1. Official salary. Riordan accepts only $1 of the mayoral salary.   Source: U.S. Conference of Mayors.

METROPOLITAN STATISTICAL AREAS (MSAs)

Because population patterns don't conform strictly to city boundaries, statisticians have devised a way of measuring city populations to include people who live around an urban area but whose address is outside the city limits. Known as Metropolitan Statistical Areas (or MSAs), these measures give a much more accurate reflection of how many people actually live in the area than do city population figures. For example, the city of Boston is relatively small: just 558,934 people lived in Boston proper in 1996, making it the 20th-largest city in America. But the Boston metropolitan area, which includes suburbs ranging from Rhode Island to New Hampshire, is the seventh-largest in the country, with a total population of 5.6 million within an hour's commute of the Hub. Likewise San Francisco, which ranked 14th among U.S. cities in 1996 with a population of 731,315, but placed fifth among MSAs (6.2 million) when the populations of nearby Oakland, Silicon Valley, and Marin County were included.

The United States Office of Management and Budget (OMB) first defined metropolitan areas (MAs) in 1949, subsequently changed the designation to "standard metropolitan area," "standard metropolitan statistical area," and finally "metropolitan statistical area" in 1983.

Defining MSAS, CMSAs, and PMSAs

Currently, the OMB distinguishes between MSAs, consolidated metropolitan statistical areas (CMSAs), and primary metropolitan statistical areas (PMSAs).

Metropolitan Statistical Areas (MSAs) are defined as an area that includes at least one city with 50,000 or more inhabitants, or a Census Bureau-defined urbanized area (of at least 50,000 inhabitants) and a total metropolitan population of at least 100,000. An MSA includes the county in which the central city is located plus any adjacent counties in which at least 50 percent of the population lives in the urbanized area. Additional "outlying counties" are included in the MSA if they meet specified requirements of commuting to the central counties and other selected requirements of metropolitan character (such as population density and percent urban). In New England, MSAs are defined in terms of cities and towns rather than counties.

Consolidated Metropolitan Statistical Areas (PMSAs) are defined as MSAs with populations of one million or more that also contain separate component areas that can each be identified as smaller urban areas, or *Primary Metropolitan Statistical Areas (PMSAs)*. For example, the New York CMSA includes the Primary MSAs of Nassau and Suffolk Counties on Long Island, Bergen and Passaic Counties in Northern New Jersey, and Bridgeport and Milford Counties in Connecticut. PMSAs, like the CMSAs that contain them, are composed of entire counties, except in New England where they are composed of cities and towns.

The 1990 Census counted 284 MSAs in the U.S., including 20 CMSAs. As of June 30, 1998, there were 274 MSAs, including 18 CMSAs comprising 73 PMSAs. Although MSAs take up only about 16 percent of the country's land area, they are home to more than 75 percent of all Americans.

According to the 1990 Census, the U.S. population living in all metropolitan areas totaled 192,725,741, an increase of just over 20 million (11.6 percent) since 1980. The same areas grew a mere 10.6 percent in the 1970s. The population living outside metropolitan areas totaled only 55,984,132 people, increasing by only about 2.1 million (3.9 percent) between 1980 and 1990.

The 1950 Census indicated that there were 14 metropolitan areas of at least one million population; these areas had a combined population of about 45 million people, or less than 30 percent of the national total. By the 1990 Census, the number of MSAs with a million people had grown to 39, with a combined population of 124.8 million people, or 50.2 percent of the U.S. total. By 1996, eight more metro areas had joined that list, bringing the total population of the 47 largest MSAs to 148.7 million, or 56.1 percent of the national total.

Population of Metropolitan Statistical Areas, 1980–90

Metropolitan Statistical Area	1980	1990	Change 1980–90 Number	Percent	CMSA/MSA rank 1980	1990
Abilene, Tex. MSA	110,932	119,655	8,723	7.9%	235	235
Albany, Ga. MSA	112,394	112,561	167	0.1	232	248
Albany-Schenectady-Troy, N.Y. MSA	824,729	861,424	36,695	4.4	46	48
Albuquerque, N.Mex. MSA	485,429	589,131	103,702	21.4	80	77
Alexandria, La. MSA	135,282	131,556	-3,726	-2.8	196	210
Allentown-Bethlehem, Pa.-N.J. MSA	551,052	595,081	44,029	8.0	54	58
Altoona, Pa. MSA	136,621	130,542	-6,079	-4.4	195	219
Amarillo, Tex. MSA	173,699	187,547	13,848	8.0	157	164
Anchorage, Alaska MSA	174,431	226,338	51,907	29.8	156	143
Anderson, Ind. MSA	139,336	130,669	-8,667	-6.2	189	217
Anderson, S.C. MSA	133,235	145,196	11,961	9.0	199	197
Anniston, Ala. MSA	119,761	116,034	-3,727	-3.1	218	241
Appleton-Oshkosh-Neenah, Wis. MSA	291,369	315,121	23,752	8.2	107	114
Asheville, N.C. MSA	177,761	191,774	14,013	7.9	171	171
Athens, Ga. MSA	104,672	126,262	21,590	20.6	204	182
Atlanta, Ga. MSA	2,233,229	2,959,950	726,721	32.5	16	12
Atlantic City, N.J. MSA	276,385	319,416	43,031	15.6	113	112
Augusta, Ga.-S.C. MSA	344,905	395,065	50,160	14.5	95	91
Austin, Tex. MSA	585,051	846,227	261,176	44.6	63	52
Bakersfield, Calif. MSA	403,089	543,477	140,388	34.8	84	68

Metropolitan Statistical Area	1980	1990	Change 1980–90 Number	Percent	CMSA/MSA rank 1980	1990
Baltimore, Md. MSA	2,199,497	2,382,172	182,675	8.3%	15	18
Bangor, Maine MSA	86,079	91,629	5,550	6.4	270	268
Baton Rouge, La. MSA	444,083	470,050	25,967	5.8	69	71
Battle Creek, Mich. MSA	141,579	135,982	-5,597	-4.0	186	205
Beaumont-Port Arthur, Tex. MSA	373,211	361,226	-11,985	-3.2	88	102
Bellingham, Wash. MSA	106,701	127,780	21,079	19.8	242	221
Benton Harbor, Mich. MSA	171,276	161,378	-9,898	-5.8	161	177
Billings, Mont. MSA	108,035	113,419	5,384	5.0	240	246
Biloxi-Gulfport-Pascagoula, Miss. MSA	300,176	312,368	12,192	4.1	153	156
Binghamton, N.Y. MSA	263,460	264,497	1,037	0.4	123	127
Birmingham, Ala. MSA	815,333	840,140	24,807	3.0	42	46
Bismarck, N.Dak. MSA	79,988	83,831	3,843	4.8	275	273
Bloomington, Ind. MSA	98,787	108,978	10,191	10.3	253	251
Bloomington-Normal, Ill. MSA	119,149	129,180	10,031	8.4	219	220
Boise City, Idaho MSA	256,881	295,851	38,970	15.2	158	154
Boston-Brockton-Nashua, Mass.-N.H.-Maine-Conn. CMSA	5,121,673	5,455,403	333,730	6.5	7	7
Boston, Mass.-N.H.-Maine-Conn. PMSA	4,762,629	5,050,761	288,132	6.0	N.A.	N.A.
Brockton, Mass. PMSA	224,902	236,409	11,507	5.1	N.A.	N.A.
Lawrence-Haverhill, Mass.-N.H. PMSA	339,090	393,516	54,426	16.1	N.A.	N.A.
Lowell, Mass.-N.H. PMSA	243,142	273,067	29,925	12.3	N.A.	N.A.
Nashua, N.H. PMSA	134,142	168,233	34,091	25.4	N.A.	N.A.
Salem-Gloucester, Mass. PMSA	258,231	264,356	6,125	2.4	N.A.	N.A.
Bradenton, Fla. MSA	148,445	211,707	63,262	42.6	181	152
Bremerton, Wash. MSA	147,152	189,731	42,579	28.9	182	160
Brownsville-Harlingen, Tex. MSA	209,727	260,120	50,393	24.0	138	129
Bryan-College Station, Tex. MSA	93,588	121,862	28,274	30.2	259	229
Buffalo-Niagara Falls, N.Y. CMSA	1,242,826	1,189,288	-53,538	-4.3	29	33
Buffalo, N.Y. PMSA	1,015,472	968,532	-46,940	-4.6	N.A.	N.A.
Niagara Falls, N.Y. PMSA	227,354	220,756	-6,598	-2.9	N.A.	N.A.
Burlington, N.C. MSA	99,319	108,213	8,894	9.0	251	253
Burlington, Vt. MSA	133,117	151,506	18,389	13.8	225	212
Canton, Ohio MSA	404,421	394,106	-10,315	-2.6	83	93
Casper, Wyo. MSA	71,856	61,226	-10,630	-14.8	278	283
Cedar Rapids, Iowa MSA	169,775	168,767	-1,008	-0.6	163	174
Champaign-Urbana-Rantoul, Ill. MSA	168,392	173,025	4,633	2.8	164	172
Charleston, S.C. MSA	430,346	506,875	76,529	17.8	77	73
Charleston, W.Va. MSA	269,595	250,454	-19,141	-7.1	118	134
Charlotte-Gastonia-Rock Hill, N.C.-S.C. MSA	971,447	1,162,093	190,646	19.6	36	34
Charlottesville, Va. MSA	113,568	131,107	17,539	15.4	226	214
Chattanooga, Tenn.-Ga. MSA	393,422	399,487	6,065	1.5	78	82
Cheyenne, Wyo. MSA	68,649	73,142	4,493	6.5	281	281
Chicago-Gary-Kenosha, Ill.-Ind.-Wis. CMSA	8,114,844	8,239,820	124,976	1.5	3	3
Aurora-Elgin, Ill. PMSA	315,607	356,884	41,277	13.1	N.A.	N.A.
Chicago, Ill. PMSA	7,246,048	7,410,858	164,810	2.3	N.A.	N.A.
Gary-Hammond, Ind. PMSA	642,733	604,526	-38,207	-5.9	N.A.	N.A.
Joliet, Ill. PMSA	355,042	389,650	34,608	9.7	N.A.	N.A.
Kenosha, Wis. PMSA	123,137	128,181	5,044	4.1	N.A.	N.A.
Lake County, Ill. PMSA	440,388	516,418	76,030	17.3	N.A.	N.A.
Chico, Calif. MSA	143,851	182,120	38,269	26.6	185	167
Cincinnati-Hamilton, Ohio-Ky.-Ind. CMSA	1,726,430	1,817,571	91,141	5.3	20	23
Cincinnati, Ohio-Ky.-Ind. PMSA	1,467,643	1,526,092	58,449	4.0	N.A.	N.A.
Hamilton-Middletown, Ohio PMSA	258,787	291,479	32,692	12.6	N.A.	N.A.
Clarksville-Hopkinsville, Tenn.-Ky. MSA	150,220	169,439	19,219	12.8	179	173
Cleveland-Akron, Ohio CMSA	2,938,277	2,859,644	-78,633	-2.7	11	13
Akron, Ohio PMSA	660,328	657,575	-2,753	-0.4	N.A.	N.A.
Cleveland-Lorain-Elyria, Ohio PMSA	2,277,949	2,202,069	-75,880	-3.3	N.A.	N.A.
Colorado Springs, Colo. MSA	309,424	397,014	87,590	28.3	105	90
Columbia, Mo. MSA	100,376	112,379	12,003	12.0	250	249
Columbia, S.C. MSA	409,953	453,331	43,478	10.6	82	79
Columbus, Ga.-Ala. MSA	254,660	260,860	6,200	2.4	131	136
Columbus, Ohio MSA	1,214,291	1,345,450	131,159	10.8	28	29
Corpus Christi, Tex.	326,228	349,894	23,666	7.3	99	105
Cumberland, Md.-W.Va.	107,782	101,643	-6,139	-5.7	241	259
Dallas-Fort Worth, Tex. CMSA	3,046,136	4,037,282	991,146	32.5	10	9
Dallas, Tex. PMSA	2,055,284	2,676,248	620,964	30.2	N.A.	N.A.
Fort Worth-Arlington, Tex. PMSA	990,852	1,361,034	370,182	37.4	N.A.	N.A.
Danville, Va. MSA	111,789	108,711	-3,078	-2.8	233	252
Davenport-Rock Island-Moline, Iowa-Ill. MSA	384,749	350,861	-33,888	-8.8	86	104

Metropolitan Statistical Area	1980	1990	Change 1980–90 Number	Change 1980–90 Percent	CMSA/MSA rank 1980	CMSA/MSA rank 1990
Dayton-Springfield, Ohio MSA	942,083	951,270	9,187	1.0%	39	44
Daytona Beach, Fla. MSA	269,675	399,413	129,738	48.1	124	96
Decatur, Ala. MSA	120,401	131,556	11,155	9.3	217	211
Decatur, Ill. MSA	131,375	117,206	-14,169	-10.8	210	239
Denver-Boulder-Greeley, Colo. CMSA	1,741,899	1,980,140	238,241	13.7	21	22
Boulder-Longmont, Colo. PMSA	189,625	225,339	35,714	18.8	N.A.	N.A.
Denver, Colo. PMSA	1,428,836	1,622,980	194,144	13.6	N.A.	N.A.
Des Moines, Iowa MSA	367,561	392,928	25,367	6.9	89	94
Detroit-Ann Arbor-Flint, Mich. CMSA	5,293,161	5,187,171	-105,990	-2.0	6	6
Ann Arbor, Mich. PMSA	454,977	490,058	35,081	7.7	N.A.	N.A.
Detroit, Mich. PMSA	4,387,735	4,266,654	-121,081	-2.8	N.A.	N.A.
Dothan, Ala. MSA	122,453	130,964	8,511	7.0	214	215
Dubuque, Iowa MSA	93,745	86,403	-7,342	-7.8	258	271
Duluth-Superior, Minn.-Wis. MSA	266,650	239,971	-26,679	-10.0	119	140
Eau Claire, Wis. MSA	130,932	137,543	6,611	5.0	203	204
El Paso, Tex. MSA	479,899	591,610	111,711	23.3	70	66
Elkhart-Goshen, Ind. MSA	137,330	156,198	18,868	13.7	193	183
Elmira, N.Y. MSA	97,656	95,195	-2,461	-2.5	255	266
Enid, Okla. MSA	62,820	56,735	-6,085	-9.7	284	284
Erie, Pa. MSA	279,780	275,572	-4,208	-1.5	111	124
Eugene-Springfield, Oreg. MSA	275,226	282,912	7,686	2.8	115	119
Evansville-Henderson, Ind.-Ky. MSA	276,252	278,990	2,738	1.0	114	121
Fargo-Moorhead, N.Dak.-Minn. MSA	137,574	153,296	15,722	11.4	191	185
Fayetteville, N.C. MSA	247,160	274,566	27,406	11.1	127	125
Fayetteville-Springdale-Rogers, Ark. MSA	178,609	210,908	32,299	18.1	249	247
Fitchburg-Leominster, Mass. MSA	94,018	102,797	8,779	9.3	257	258
Flint, Mich. MSA	450,449	430,459	-19,990	-4.4	73	84
Florence, Ala. MSA	135,065	131,327	-3,738	-2.8	197	213
Florence, S.C. MSA	110,163	114,344	4,181	3.8	236	245
Fort Collins-Loveland, Colo. MSA	149,184	186,136	36,952	24.8	180	165
Fort Myers-Cape Coral, Fla. MSA	205,266	335,113	129,847	63.3	140	110
Fort Pierce-Port St. Lucie, Fla. MSA	151,196	251,071	99,875	66.1	178	133
Fort Smith, Ark.-Okla. MSA	162,813	175,911	13,098	8.0	169	169
Fort Walton Beach, Fla. MSA	109,920	143,776	33,856	30.8	237	198
Fort Wayne, Ind. MSA	444,772	456,281	11,509	2.6	93	100
Fresno, Calif. MSA	577,737	755,580	177,843	30.8	67	59
Gadsden, Ala. MSA	103,057	99,840	-3,217	-3.1	245	260
Gainesville, Fla. MSA	151,369	181,596	30,227	20.0	160	155
Glens Falls, N.Y. MSA	109,649	118,539	8,890	8.1	238	238
Grand Forks, N.Dak.-Minn. MSA	100,944	103,181	2,237	2.2	283	282
Grand Rapids-Muskegon-Holland, Mich. MSA	840,824	937,891	97,067	11.5	56	57
Great Falls, Mont. MSA	80,696	77,691	-3,005	-3.7	274	279
Greeley, Colo. MSA	123,438	131,821	8,383	6.8	212	209
Green Bay, Wis. MSA	175,280	194,594	19,314	11.0	155	158
Greensboro—Winston-Salem—High Point, N.C. MSA	950,763	1,050,304	99,541	10.5	44	45
Greenville-Spartanburg-Anderson, S.C. MSA	744,428	830,563	86,135	11.6	59	62
Hagerstown, Md. MSA	113,086	121,393	8,307	7.3	227	230
Harrisburg-Lebanon-Carlisle, Pa. MSA	556,242	587,986	31,744	5.7	62	67
Hartford, Conn. MSA	1,080,710	1,157,585	76,875	7.1	35	36
Bristol, Conn. PMSA	73,762	79,488	5,726	7.8	N.A.	N.A.
Hartford, Conn. PMSA	715,923	767,841	51,918	7.3	N.A.	N.A.
Middletown, Conn. PMSA	81,582	90,320	8,738	10.7	N.A.	N.A.
New Britain, Conn. PMSA	142,241	148,188	5,947	4.2	N.A.	N.A.
Hickory-Morganton, N.C. MSA	270,457	292,409	21,952	8.1	142	148
Honolulu, Hawaii MSA	762,565	836,231	73,666	9.7	47	51
Houma-Thibodaux, La. MSA	176,876	182,842	5,966	3.4	154	166
Houston-Galveston-Brazoria, Tex. CMSA	3,118,480	3,731,131	612,651	19.6	9	10
Brazoria, Tex. PMSA	169,587	191,707	22,120	13.0	N.A.	N.A.
Galveston-Texas City, Tex. PMSA	195,738	217,399	21,661	11.1	N.A.	N.A.
Houston, Tex. PMSA	2,753,155	3,322,025	568,870	20.7	N.A.	N.A.
Huntington-Ashland, W.Va.-Ky.-Ohio MSA	311,350	288,189	-23,161	-7.4	97	115
Huntsville, Ala. MSA	242,971	293,047	50,076	20.6	144	141
Indianapolis, Ind. MSA	1,305,911	1,380,491	74,580	5.7	30	31
Iowa City, Iowa MSA	81,717	96,119	14,402	17.6	273	265
Jackson, Mich. MSA	151,495	149,756	-1,739	-1.1	177	191
Jackson, Miss. MSA	362,038	395,396	33,358	9.2	92	92
Jackson, Tenn. MSA	74,548	77,982	3,436	4.6	277	278
Jacksonville, Fla. MSA	722,252	906,727	184,475	25.5	50	47

Metropolitan Statistical Area	1980	1990	Change 1980–90 Number	Change 1980–90 Percent	CMSA/MSA rank 1980	CMSA/MSA rank 1990
Jacksonville, N.C. MSA	112,784	149,838	37,054	32.9%	229	190
Jamestown-Dunkirk, N.Y. MSA	146,925	141,895	-5,030	-3.4	183	202
Janesville-Beloit, Wis. MSA	139,420	139,510	90	0.1	188	203
Johnson City-Kingsport-Bristol, Tenn.-Va. MSA	433,638	436,047	2,409	0.6	76	81
Johnstown, Pa. MSA	264,506	241,247	-23,259	-8.8	121	138
Joplin, Mo. MSA	127,513	134,910	7,397	5.8	209	207
Kalamazoo-Battle Creek, Mich. MSA	420,771	429,453	8,682	2.1	136	146
Kankakee, Ill. MSA	102,926	96,255	-6,671	-6.5	246	264
Kansas City, Mo.-Kans. MSA	1,449,380	1,582,875	133,495	9.2	25	25
Killeen-Temple, Tex. MSA	214,587	255,301	40,714	19.0	135	131
Knoxville, Tenn. MSA	546,488	585,960	39,472	7.2	60	65
Kokomo, Ind. MSA	103,715	96,946	-6,769	-6.5	243	263
La Crosse, Wis.-Minn. MSA	109,438	116,401	6,963	6.4	262	262
Lafayette, La. MSA	330,786	344,953	14,167	4.3	150	153
Lafayette, Ind. MSA	153,247	161,572	8,325	5.4	215	218
Lake Charles, La. MSA	167,223	168,134	911	0.5	165	175
Lakeland-Winter Haven, Fla. MSA	321,652	405,382	83,730	26.0	101	87
Lancaster, Pa. MSA	362,346	422,822	60,476	16.7	91	85
Lansing-East Lansing, Mich. MSA	419,750	432,674	12,924	3.1	81	83
Laredo, Tex. MSA	99,258	133,239	33,981	34.2	252	208
Las Cruces, N.Mex. MSA	96,340	135,510	39,170	40.7	256	206
Las Vegas, Nev.-Ariz. MSA	528,000	852,737	324,737	61.5	72	53
Lawrence, Kans. MSA	67,640	81,798	14,158	20.9	282	275
Lawton, Okla. MSA	112,456	111,486	-970	-0.9	231	250
Lewiston-Auburn, Maine MSA	89,265	93,679	4,414	4.9	268	269
Lexington, Ky. MSA	370,900	405,936	35,036	9.4	103	106
Lima, Ohio MSA	154,795	154,340	-455	-0.3	175	184
Lincoln, Nebr. MSA	192,884	213,641	20,757	10.8	147	151
Little Rock-North Little Rock, Ark. MSA	474,463	513,117	38,654	8.1	71	72
Longview-Marshall, Tex. MSA	180,355	193,801	13,446	7.5	176	176
Los Angeles-Riverside-Orange County, Calif. CMSA	11,497,548	14,531,529	3,033,981	26.4	2	2
Anaheim-Santa Ana, Calif. PMSA	1,932,921	2,410,556	477,635	24.7	N.A.	N.A.
Los Angeles-Long Beach, Calif. PMSA	7,477,238	8,863,164	1,385,926	18.5	N.A.	N.A.
Riverside-San Bernardino, Calif. PMSA	1,558,215	2,588,793	1,030,578	66.1	N.A.	N.A.
Ventura, Calif. PMSA	529,174	669,016	139,842	26.4	N.A.	N.A.
Louisville, Ky.-Ind. MSA	953,520	948,829	-4,691	-0.5	38	43
Lubbock, Tex. MSA	211,651	222,636	10,985	5.2	137	147
Lynchburg, Va. MSA	182,207	193,928	11,721	6.4	187	200
Macon, Ga. MSA	272,945	290,909	17,964	6.6	122	120
Madison, Wis. MSA	323,545	367,085	43,540	13.5	100	99
Manchester, N.H. MSA	129,305	147,809	18,504	14.3	205	193
Mansfield, Ohio MSA	181,280	174,007	-7,273	-4.0	202	223
McAllen-Edinburg-Mission, Tex. MSA	283,323	383,545	100,222	35.4	110	95
Medford-Ashland, Oreg. MSA	132,456	146,389	13,933	10.5	200	196
Melbourne-Titusville-Palm Bay, Fla. MSA	272,959	398,978	126,019	46.2	116	89
Memphis, Tenn.-Ark.-Miss. MSA	938,777	1,007,306	68,529	7.3	40	41
Merced, Calif. MSA	134,558	178,403	43,845	32.6	198	168
Miami-Fort Lauderdale, Fla. CMSA	2,643,766	3,192,582	548,816	20.8	12	11
Fort Lauderdale-Hollywood-Pompano Beach, Fla. PMSA	1,018,257	1,255,488	237,231	23.3	N.A.	N.A.
Miami, Fla. PMSA	1,625,509	1,937,094	311,585	19.2	N.A.	N.A.
Midland, Tex. MSA	82,636	106,611	23,975	29.0	272	255
Milwaukee-Racine, Wis. CMSA	1,570,152	1,607,183	37,031	2.4	23	24
Milwaukee-Waukesha, Wis. PMSA	1,397,020	1,432,149	35,129	2.5	N.A.	N.A.
Racine, Wis. PMSA	173,132	175,034	1,902	1.1	N.A.	N.A.
Minneapolis-St. Paul, Minn.-Wis. MSA	2,198,190	2,538,834	340,644	15.5	17	16
Mobile, Ala. MSA	443,536	476,923	33,387	7.5	74	78
Modesto, Calif. MSA	265,900	370,522	104,622	39.3	120	97
Monroe, La. MSA	139,241	142,191	2,950	2.1	190	201
Montgomery, Ala. MSA	272,687	292,517	19,830	7.3	117	117
Muncie, Ind. MSA	128,587	119,659	-8,928	-6.9	206	234
Muskegon, Mich. MSA	157,589	158,983	1,394	0.9	173	181
Naples, Fla. MSA	85,971	152,099	66,128	76.9	266	186
Nashville, Tenn. MSA	850,505	985,026	134,521	15.8	45	40
New Bedford, Mass. MSA	166,699	175,641	8,942	5.4	166	170
New Haven-Meriden, Conn. MSA	500,642	530,180	29,718	5.9	68	69
New London-Norwich, Conn.-R.I. MSA	272,900	290,734	17,834	6.5	125	126
New Orleans, La. MSA	1,304,212	1,285,270	-18,942	-1.5	27	32
New York-Newark, N.Y.-N.J.-Pa. PMSA	16,448,157	16,937,653	489,496	3.0	1	1
Bergen-Passaic, N.J. PMSA	1,292,970	1,278,440	-14,530	-1.1	N.A.	N.A.
Bridgeport-Milford, Conn. PMSA	438,557	443,722	5,165	1.2	N.A.	N.A.

Metropolitan Statistical Area	1980	1990	Change 1980–90 Number	Change 1980–90 Percent	CMSA/MSA rank 1980	CMSA/MSA rank 1990
Danbury, Conn. PMSA	170,369	187,867	17,498	10.3%	N.A.	N.A.
Jersey City, N.J. PMSA	556,972	553,099	-3,873	-0.7	N.A.	N.A.
Middlesex-Somerset-Hunterdon, N.J. PMSA	886,383	1,019,835	133,452	15.1	N.A.	N.A.
Monmouth-Ocean, N.J. PMSA	849,211	986,327	137,116	16.1	N.A.	N.A.
Nassau-Suffolk, N.Y. PMSA	2,605,813	2,609,212	3,399	0.1	N.A.	N.A.
New York, N.Y. PMSA	8,274,961	8,546,846	271,885	3.3	N.A.	N.A.
Newark, N.J. PMSA	1,879,147	1,824,321	-54,826	-2.9	N.A.	N.A.
Norwalk, Conn. PMSA	126,692	127,378	686	0.5	N.A.	N.A.
Orange County, N.Y. PMSA	259,603	307,647	48,044	18.5	N.A.	N.A.
Stamford-Norwalk, Conn. PMSA	325,546	329,935	4,389	1.3	N.A.	N.A.
Norfolk-Virginia Beach-Newport News, Va.-N.C. MSA	1,200,998	1,443,244	242,246	20.2	31	28
Ocala, Fla. MSA	122,488	194,833	72,345	59.1	213	157
Odessa-Midland, Tex. MSA	198,010	225,545	27,535	13.9	224	236
Oklahoma City, Okla. MSA	860,969	958,839	97,870	11.4	43	42
Olympia, Wash. MSA	124,264	161,238	36,974	29.8	211	178
Omaha, Nebr.-Iowa MSA	605,419	639,580	34,161	5.6	57	63
Orlando, Fla. MSA	804,774	1,224,852	420,078	52.2	51	37
Owensboro, Ky. MSA	85,949	87,189	1,240	1.4	267	270
Panama City, Fla. MSA	97,740	126,994	29,254	29.9	254	222
Parkersburg-Marietta, W.Va.-Ohio MSA	157,893	149,169	-8,724	-5.5	172	192
Pascagoula, Miss. MSA	118,015	115,243	-2,772	-2.3	221	243
Pensacola, Fla. MSA	289,782	344,406	54,624	18.9	109	107
Peoria-Pekin, Ill. MSA	365,864	339,172	-26,692	-7.3	90	108
Philadelphia-Wilmington-Atlantic City, Pa.-N.J.-Del.-Md. CMSA	5,649,031	5,892,937	243,906	4.3	4	5
Philadelphia, Pa.-N.J. PMSA	4,781,235	4,922,175	140,940	2.9	N.A.	N.A.
Trenton, N.J. PMSA	307,863	325,824	17,961	5.8	N.A.	N.A.
Vineland-Millville-Bridgeton, N.J. PMSA	132,866	138,053	5,187	3.9	N.A.	N.A.
Wilmington-Newark, Del.-Md. PMSA	458,545	513,293	54,748	11.9	N.A.	N.A.
Phoenix-Mesa, Ariz. MSA	1,600,093	2,238,480	638,387	39.9	24	20
Pine Bluff, Ark. MSA	90,718	85,487	-5,231	-5.8	263	272
Pittsburgh, Pa. MSA	2,571,223	2,394,811	-176,412	-6.9	13	19
Beaver County, Pa. PMSA	204,441	186,093	-18,348	-9.0	N.A.	N.A.
Pittsburgh, Pa. PMSA	2,218,870	2,056,705	-162,165	-7.3	N.A.	N.A.
Pittsfield, Mass. MSA	93,871	88,695	-5,176	-5.5	271	277
Portland, Maine MSA	198,277	221,095	22,818	11.5	145	150
Portland-Salem, Oreg.-Wash. CMSA	1,583,518	1,793,476	209,958	13.3	26	27
Portland-Vancouver, Oreg.-Wash. PMSA	1,333,623	1,515,452	181,829	13.6	N.A.	N.A.
Portland, Oreg. PMSA	1,105,750	1,239,842	134,092	12.1	N.A.	N.A.
Vancouver, Wash. PMSA	192,227	238,053	45,826	23.8	N.A.	N.A.
Portsmouth-Dover-Rochester, N.H.-Maine MSA	190,938	223,578	32,640	17.1	148	145
Poughkeepsie, N.Y MSA	245,055	259,462	14,407	5.9	129	130
Providence-Fall River-Warwick, R.I.-Mass. MSA	1,076,557	1,134,350	57,793	5.4	33	35
Fall River, Mass.-R.I. PMSA	157,222	157,272	50	0.0	N.A.	N.A.
Pawtucket-Woonsocket-Attleboro, R.I.-Mass. PMSA	307,403	329,384	21,981	7.2	N.A.	N.A.
Providence, R.I. PMSA	618,514	654,854	36,340	5.9	N.A.	N.A.
Provo-Orem, Utah MSA	218,106	263,590	45,484	20.9	134	128
Pueblo, Colo. MSA	125,972	123,051	-2,921	-2.3	210	226
Raleigh-Durham-Chapel Hill, N.C. MSA	664,788	855,545	190,757	28.7	61	54
Rapid City, S.Dak. MSA	70,361	81,343	10,982	15.6	279	276
Reading, Pa. MSA	312,509	336,523	24,014	7.7	104	109
Redding, Calif. MSA	115,613	147,036	31,423	27.2	223	194
Reno, Nev. MSA	193,623	254,667	61,044	31.5	146	132
Richland-Kennewick-Pasco, Wash. MSA	144,469	150,033	5,564	3.9	184	189
Richmond-Petersburg, Va. MSA	761,311	865,640	104,329	13.7	48	49
Roanoke, Va. MSA	220,393	224,477	4,084	1.9	133	144
Rochester, Minn. MSA	92,006	106,470	14,464	15.7	261	256
Rochester, N.Y. MSA	1,030,630	1,062,470	31,840	3.1	37	39
Rockford, Ill. MSA	325,852	329,676	3,824	1.2	112	118
Sacramento-Yolo, Calif. CMSA	1,099,814	1,481,102	381,288	34.7	32	26
Saginaw-Bay City-Midland, Mich. MSA	421,518	399,320	-22,198	-5.3	79	88
Salem, Oreg. PMSA	249,895	278,024	28,129	11.3	126	122
Salinas, Calif. MSA	290,444	355,660	65,216	22.5	108	103
Salt Lake City-Ogden, Utah MSA	910,222	1,072,227	162,005	17.8	41	38
San Angelo, Tex. MSA	84,784	98,458	13,674	16.1	269	261
San Antonio, Tex. MSA	1,088,881	1,324,749	235,868	21.7	34	30
San Diego, Calif. MSA	1,861,846	2,498,016	636,170	34.2	19	15
San Francisco-Oakland-San Jose,	5,367,900	6,253,311	885,411	16.5	5	4

Metropolitan Statistical Area	1980	1990	Change 1980–90		CMSA/MSA rank	
			Number	Percent	1980	1990
Calif. CMSA						
Oakland, Calif. PMSA	1,761,710	2,082,914	321,204	18.2%	N.A.	N.A.
San Francisco, Calif. PMSA	1,488,895	1,603,678	114,783	7.7	N.A.	N.A.
San Jose, Calif. PMSA	1,295,071	1,497,577	202,506	15.6	N.A.	N.A.
Santa Cruz-Watsonville, Calif. PMSA	188,141	229,734	41,593	22.1	N.A.	N.A.
Santa Rosa, Calif. PMSA	299,681	388,222	88,541	29.5	N.A.	N.A.
Vallejo-Fairfield-Napa, Calif. PMSA	334,402	451,186	116,784	34.9	N.A.	N.A
Santa Barbara-Santa Maria-Lompoc,						
Calif. PMSA	298,694	369,608	70,914	23.7	106	98
Santa Fe, N.Mex. MSA	93,118	117,043	23,925	25.7	260	240
Sarasota-Bradenton, Fla. MSA	350,696	489,483	138,787	39.6	143	123
Savannah, Ga. MSA	230,728	258,060	27,332	11.8	132	137
Scranton-Wilkes-Barre-Hazleton,	659,387	638,466	-20,921	-3.2	49	55
Pa. MSA						
Seattle-Tacoma-Bremerton, Wash. CMSA	2,408,749	2,970,328	561,579	23.3	18	14
Seattle-Bellevue-Everett, Wash. PMSA	1,651,666	2,033,156	381,490	23.1	N.A.	N.A.
Tacoma, Wash. PMSA	485,667	586,203	100,536	20.7	N.A.	N.A.
Sharon, Pa. MSA	128,299	121,003	-7,296	-5.7	208	231
Sheboygan, Wis. MSA	100,935	103,877	2,942	2.9	248	257
Sherman-Denison, Tex. MSA	89,796	95,021	5,225	5.8	264	267
Shreveport-Bossier City, La. MSA	376,789	376,330	-459	—	98	111
Sioux City, Iowa-Nebr. MSA	117,457	115,018	-2,439	-2.1	222	244
Sioux Falls, S.Dak. MSA	123,377	139,236	15,859	12.9	239	224
South Bend, Ind. MSA	241,617	247,052	5,435	2.2	130	135
Spokane, Wash. MSA	341,835	361,364	19,529	5.7	96	101
Springfield, Ill. MSA	187,770	189,550	1,780	0.9	151	161
Springfield, Mass. MSA	569,777	587,884	18,107	3.2	66	70
Springfield, Mo. MSA	228,118	264,346	36,228	15.9	139	139
St. Cloud, Minn. MSA	133,348	148,976	15,628	11.7	168	159
St. Joseph, Mo. MSA	101,868	97,715	-4,153	-4.1	265	274
St. Louis, Mo.-Ill. MSA	2,414,061	2,492,525	78,464	3.3	14	17
State College, Pa. MSA	112,760	123,786	11,026	9.8	230	225
Steubenville-Weirton, Ohio-W.Va. MSA	163,734	142,523	-21,211	-13.0	167	199
Stockton-Lodi, Calif. MSA	347,342	480,628	133,286	38.4	94	76
Syracuse, N.Y. MSA	722,865	742,177	19,312	2.7	53	61
Tallahassee, Fla. MSA	190,329	233,598	43,269	22.7	149	142
Tampa-St. Petersburg-Clearwater,	1,613,600	2,067,959	454,359	28.2	22	21
Fla. MSA						
Terre Haute, Ind. MSA	155,476	147,585	-7,891	-5.1	194	216
Texarkana, Tex.-Texarkana, Ark. MSA	113,067	120,132	7,065	6.2	228	233
Toledo, Ohio MSA	616,864	614,128	-2,736	-0.4	55	64
Topeka, Kans. MSA	154,916	160,976	6,060	3.9	174	179
Tucson, Ariz. MSA	531,443	666,880	135,437	25.5	64	60
Tulsa, Okla. MSA	657,173	708,954	51,781	7.9	52	56
Tuscaloosa, Ala. MSA	137,541	150,522	12,981	9.4	192	188
Tyler, Tex. MSA	128,366	151,309	22,943	17.9	207	187
Utica-Rome, N.Y. MSA	320,180	316,633	-3,547	-1.1	102	113
Victoria, Tex. MSA	68,807	74,361	5,554	8.1	280	280
Visalia-Tulare-Porterville, Calif. MSA	245,738	311,921	66,183	26.9	128	116
Waco, Tex. MSA	170,755	189,123	18,368	10.8	162	162
Washington, D.C.-Md.-Va.-W.Va. PMSA	3,477,972	4,223,485	745,513	21.4	8	8
Waterbury, Conn. MSA	190,812	205,811	14,999	7.9	141	149
Waterloo-Cedar Falls, Iowa MSA	137,961	123,798	-14,163	-10.3	170	195
Wausau, Wis. MSA	111,270	115,400	4,130	3.7	234	242
West Palm Beach-Boca Raton, Fla. MSA	576,758	863,518	286,760	49.7	58	50
Wheeling, W.Va.-Ohio MSA	185,566	159,301	-26,265	-14.2	152	180
Wichita Falls, Tex. MSA	128,348	130,351	2,003	1.6	216	228
Wichita, Kans. MSA	442,401	485,270	42,869	9.7	75	75
Williamsport, Pa. MSA	118,416	118,710	294	0.2	220	237
Wilmington, N.C. MSA	103,471	120,284	16,813	16.2	244	232
Worcester, Mass. MSA	402,918	436,905	33,987	8.4	85	80
Yakima, Wash. MSA	172,508	188,823	16,315	9.5	159	163
York, Pa. MSA	312,963	339,574	26,611	8.5	87	86
Youngstown-Warren, Ohio MSA	644,922	600,895	-44,027	-6.8	65	74
Yuba City, Calif. MSA	101,979	122,643	20,664	20.3	247	227
Yuma, Ariz. MSA	76,205	106,895	30,690	40.3	276	254

Note: CMSA = consolidated metropolitan statistical area; MSA = metropolitan statistical area; PMSA = primary metropolitan statistical area; N.A. = not applicable.   Source: U.S. Bureau of the Census release, 1991.

Population of U.S. Metropolitan Areas by Race and Hispanic Origin, 1990

Rank/Metropolitan area	Total	White	Black	American Indian	Asian or Pacific Islander	Other race	Hispanic origin[1]
1. New York-Northern New Jersey-Long Island, N.Y.-N.J.-Conn. CMSA	18,087,251	12,699,119	3,289,465	46,191	873,213	1,179,263	2,777,951
New York, N.Y. PMSA	8,546,846	4,826,081	2,250,026	29,711	556,399	884,629	1,889,662
Nassau-Suffolk, N.Y. PMSA	2,609,212	2,305,434	193,967	4,636	62,399	42,776	165,238
Newark, N.J. PMSA	1,824,321	1,279,952	422,802	3,144	52,898	65,525	188,299
Bergen-Passaic, N.J. PMSA	1,278,440	1,043,437	106,108	2,221	66,743	59,931	147,868
Middlesex-Somerset-Hunterdon, N.J. PMSA	1,019,835	865,158	70,670	1,420	56,804	25,783	71,695
Monmouth-Ocean, N.J. PMSA	986,327	895,986	59,264	1,327	19,098	10,652	36,357
Jersey City, N.J. PMSA	553,099	380,612	79,770	1,460	36,777	54,480	183,465
Bridgeport-Milford, Conn. PMSA	443,722	371,493	45,826	806	6,577	19,020	44,741
Orange County, N.Y. PMSA	307,647	273,600	22,223	824	3,549	7,451	21,535
Stanford, Conn. PMSA	202,557	171,834	20,767	203	5,570	4,183	13,732
Danbury, Conn. PMSA	187,867	175,780	5,398	301	4,355	2,033	7,136
Norwalk, Conn. PMSA	127,378	109,752	12,644	138	2,044	2,800	8,223
2. Los Angeles-Anaheim-Riverside, Calif. CMSA	14,531,529	9,388,957	1,229,809	87,487	1,339,048	2,486,228	4,779,118
Los Angeles-Long Beach, Calif. PMSA	8,863,164	5,035,103	992,974	45,508	954,485	1,835,094	3,351,242
Riverside-San Bernardino, Calif. PMSA	2,588,793	1,930,095	178,525	24,905	100,792	354,476	686,096
Anaheim-Santa Ana, Calif. PMSA	2,410,556	1,894,593	42,681	12,165	249,192	211,925	564,828
Oxnard-Ventura, Calif. PMSA	669,016	529,166	15,629	4,909	34,579	84,733	176,952
3. Chicago-Gary-Lake County Ill.-Ind-Wis. CMSA	8,065,633	5,772,110	1,547,725	15,758	256,050	473,990	893,422
Chicago, Ill. PMSA	6,069,974	4,098,747	1,332,919	11,550	229,492	397,266	734,827
Gary-Hammond, Ind. PMSA	604,526	460,532	117,142	1,108	3,716	22,028	48,384
Lake County, Ill. PMSA	516,418	450,666	34,771	1,198	12,588	17,195	38,570
Joliet, Ill. PMSA	389,650	335,284	38,382	737	4,887	10,360	20,721
Aurora-Elgin, Ill. PMSA	356,884	307,694	19,216	693	4,698	24,583	45,340
Kenosha, Wis. PMSA	128,181	119,187	5,295	472	669	2,558	5,580
4. San Francisco-Oakland-San Jose, Calif. CMSA	6,253,311	4,334,064	537,753	40,847	926,961	413,686	970,403
Oakland, Calif. PMSA	2,082,914	1,372,818	303,826	14,230	269,566	122,474	273,087
San Francisco, Calif. PMSA	1,603,678	1,058,796	122,494	7,232	329,599	85,557	233,274
San Jose, Calif. PMSA	1,497,577	1,032,190	56,211	9,269	261,466	138,441	314,564
Vallejo-Fairfield-Napa, Calif. PMSA	451,186	325,761	47,043	3,898	47,044	27,440	61,458
Santa Rosa-Petaluma, Calif. PMSA	388,222	351,650	5,547	4,397	10,774	15,854	41,223
Santa Cruz, Calif. PMSA	229,734	192,849	2,632	1,821	8,512	23,920	46,797
5. Philadelphia-Wilmington-Trenton Pa.-N.J.-Del.-Md. CMSA	5,899,345	4,540,541	1,100,347	11,307	123,458	123,692	225,868
Philadelphia, Pa.-N.J. PMSA	4,856,881	3,717,175	929,907	8,335	104,595	96,869	173,980
Wilmington, Del.-N.J.-Md. PMSA	578,587	477,243	85,641	1,128	7,737	6,838	13,875
Trenton, N.J. PMSA	325,824	244,656	61,481	533	9,992	9,162	19,665
Vineland-Millville-Bridgeton, N.J. PMSA	138,053	101,467	23,318	1,311	1,134	10,823	18,348
6. Detroit-Ann Arbor, Mich. CMSA	4,665,236	3,569,087	975,199	17,961	69,454	33,535	90,947
Detroit, Mich. PMSA	4,382,299	3,332,697	943,479	16,885	57,730	31,508	85,216
Ann Arbor, Mich. PMSA	282,937	236,390	31,720	1,076	11,724	2,027	5,731
7. Boston-Lawrence-Salem, Mass.-N.H. CMSA	4,171,643	3,708,228	239,059	7,542	121,405	95,409	193,199
Boston, Mass. PMSA	2,870,669	2,499,859	209,970	5,250	95,044	60,546	128,883
Lawrence-Haverhill, Mass.-N.H. PMSA	393,516	359,052	7,363	857	5,146	21,098	36,300
Lowell, Mass.-N.H. PMSA	273,067	248,937	3,598	388	14,251	5,893	12,193
Salem-Gloucester, Mass. PMSA	264,356	257,396	2,448	305	2,347	1,860	5,506

Rank/Metropolitan area	Total	White	Black	American Indian	Asian or Pacific Islander	Other race	Hispanic origin[1]
Brockton, Mass. PMSA	189,478	168,133	13,770	445	2,158	4,972	7,044
Nashua, N.H. PMSA	180,557	174,851	1,910	297	2,459	1,040	3,273
8. Washington, D.C.-Md.-Va. MSA	3,923,574	2,577,933	1,041,934	11,036	202,437	90,234	224,786
9. Dallas-Fort Worth, Tex. CMSA	3,885,415	2,924,673	554,616	18,972	97,578	289,576	518,917
Dallas, Tex. PMSA	2,553,362	1,854,577	410,766	12,635	67,195	208,189	368,884
Fort Worth-Arlington, Tex. PMSA	1,332,053	1,070,096	143,850	6,337	30,383	81,387	150,033
10. Houston-Galveston-Brazoria, Tex. CMSA	3,711,043	2,507,455	665,378	11,029	132,131	395,050	772,295
Houston, Tex. PMSA	3,301,937	2,188,370	611,243	9,465	126,601	366,258	707,536
Galveston-Texas City, Tex. PMSA	217,399	164,210	38,154	752	3,569	10,714	30,962
Brazoria, Tex. PMSA	191,707	154,875	15,981	812	1,961	18,078	33,797
11. Miami-Fort Lauderdale, Fla. CMSA	3,192,582	2,438,598	591,440	5,700	43,437	113,407	1,061,846
Miami-Hialeah, Fla. PMSA	1,937,094	1,413,015	397,993	3,066	26,307	96,713	953,407
Fort Lauderdale-Hollywood-Pompano Beach, Fla. PMSA	1,255,488	1,025,583	193,447	2,634	17,130	16,694	108,439
12. Atlanta, Ga. MSA	2,833,511	2,020,017	736,153	5,532	51,486	20,323	57,169
13. Cleveland-Akron-Lorain, Ohio CMSA	2,759,823	2,261,217	441,940	5,133	28,187	23,346	52,997
Cleveland, Ohio PMSA	1,831,122	1,435,768	355,619	3,038	20,528	16,169	33,921
Akron, Ohio PMSA	657,575	583,900	65,091	1,357	6,180	1,047	3,815
Lorain-Elyria, Ohio PMSA	271,126	241,549	21,230	738	1,479	6,130	15,261
14. Seattle-Tacoma, Wash. CMSA	2,559,164	2,211,710	123,266	32,071	164,286	27,831	75,555
Seattle, Wash. PMSA	1,972,961	1,713,068	81,056	23,727	135,251	19,859	54,993
Tacoma, Wash. PMSA	586,203	498,642	42,210	8,344	29,035	7,972	20,562
15. San Diego, Calif. MSA	2,498,016	1,672,256	159,306	20,066	198,311	248,077	510,781
16. Minneapolis-St. Paul, Minn.-Wis. MSA	2,464,124	2,270,360	89,710	23,956	65,204	14,894	37,448
17. St. Louis, Mo.-Ill. MSA	2,444,099	1,985,500	423,182	4,947	23,686	6,784	26,014
18. Baltimore, Md. MSA	2,382,172	1,709,309	616,065	6,444	42,634	7,720	30,160
19. Pittsburgh-Beaver Valley, Pa.CMSA	2,242,798	2,041,897	178,857	2,257	16,174	3,613	12,852
Pittsburgh, Pa. PMSA	2,056,705	1,867,138	168,382	2,054	15,797	3,334	11,728
Beaver County, Pa. PMSA	186,093	174,759	10,475	203	377	279	1,124
20. Phoenix, Ariz. MSA	2,122,101	1,799,420	74,257	38,017	36,294	174,113	345,498
21. Tampa-St. Petersburg-Clearwater, Fla. MSA	2,067,959	1,827,492	185,503	5,467	23,055	26,442	139,248
22. Denver-Boulder, Colo. CMSA	1,848,319	1,599,734	97,755	13,884	42,642	94,304	226,200
Denver, Colo. PMSA	1,622,980	1,389,544	95,796	12,571	37,134	87,935	211,005
Boulder-Longmont, Colo. PMSA	225,339	210,190	1,959	1,313	5,508	6,369	15,195
23. Cincinnati-Hamilton, Ohio-Ky.-Ind. CMSA	1,744,124	1,521,061	203,607	2,457	14,260	2,739	9,376
Cincinnati, Ohio-Ky.-Ind. PMSA	1,452,645	1,246,169	190,473	2,078	11,601	2,324	7,909
Hamilton-Middleton, Ohio, PMSA	291,479	274,892	13,134	379	2,659	415	1,467
24. Milwaukee-Racine, Wis. CMSA	1,607,183	1,335,470	214,182	8,522	19,786	29,223	60,340
Milwaukee, Wis. PMSA	1,432,149	1,183,372	197,183	8,001	18,782	24,811	51,306
Racine, Wis. PMSA	175,034	152,098	16,999	521	1,004	4,412	9,034
25. Kansas City, Mo.-Kans. MSA	1,566,280	1,320,564	200,508	7,631	17,444	20,133	45,227
26. Sacramento, Calif. MSA	1,481,102	1,170,505	101,940	17,021	114,520	77,116	172,374
27. Portland-Vancouver, Oreg.-Wash. CMSA	1,477,895	1,350,155	41,671	13,603	52,030	20,436	49,921
Portland, Oreg. PMSA	1,239,842	1,124,963	38,695	11,307	46,360	18,517	44,049
Vancouver, Wash. PMSA	238,053	225,192	2,976	2,296	5,670	1,919	5,872
28. Norfolk-Virginia Beach-Newport News, Va. MSA	1,396,107	947,160	398,093	4,679	35,205	10,970	32,329
29. Columbus, Ohio MSA	1,377,419	1,184,770	164,602	2,880	21,059	4,108	11,363
30. San Antonio, Tex. MSA	1,302,099	978,505	88,778	4,648	16,058	214,110	620,290
31. Indianapolis, Ind. MSA	1,249,822	1,061,142	172,326	2,510	10,081	3,763	11,084
32. New Orleans, La. Msa	1,238,816	770,406	430,470	3,615	21,380	12,945	53,226
33. Buffalo-Niagara Falls, N.Y. CMSA	1,189,288	1,037,211	121,956	7,611	11,026	11,484	24,347

Rank/Metropolitan area	Total	White	Black	American Indian	Asian or Pacific Islander	Other race	Hispanic origin[1]
Buffalo, N.Y. PMSA	968,532	831,903	109,852	5,600	10,220	10,957	22,249
Niagara Falls, N.Y. PMSA	220,756	205,308	12,104	2,011	806	527	2,098
34. Charlotte-Gastonia-Rock Hill, N.C.-S.C. PMSA	1,162,093	911,904	231,654	4,107	11,304	3,124	10,671
35. Providence-Pawtucket-Fall River, R.I.-Mass. CMSA	1,141,510	1,055,370	37,106	3,782	20,050	25,202	47,467
Providence, R.I. PMSA	654,854	590,671	30,526	3,079	14,522	16,056	31,453
Pawtucket-Woonsocket-Attleboro, R.I.-Mass. PMSA	329,384	310,677	5,494	535	3,987	8,691	13,949
Fall River, Mass.-R.I. PMSA	157,272	154,022	1,086	168	1,541	455	2,065
36. Hartford-New Britain-Middletown, Conn. CMSA	1,085,837	933,568	94,925	1,826	15,845	39,673	75,627
Hartford, Conn. PMSA	767,841	641,345	81,550	1,365	12,201	31,380	58,362
New Britain, Conn. PMSA	148,188	132,519	6,574	190	1,937	6,968	13,387
Middletown, Conn. PMSA	90,320	82,829	5,454	143	1,163	731	2,059
Bristol, Conn. PMSA	79,488	76,875	1,347	128	544	594	1,819
37. Orlando, Fla. MSA	1,072,748	888,913	133,308	3,199	20,474	26,854	96,418
38. Salt Lake City-Ogden, Utah MSA	1,072,227	1,000,082	10,464	8,337	25,598	27,746	61,964
39. Rochester, N.Y. MSA	1,002,410	875,886	93,819	2,870	13,978	15,857	31,238
40. Nashville, Tenn. MSA	985,026	818,424	152,349	2,121	10,012	2,120	7,665
41. Memphis, Tenn.-Ariz.-Miss.-MSA	981,747	570,511	399,011	1,791	8,178	2,256	7,986
42. Oklahoma City, Okla. MSA	958,839	777,589	101,082	45,720	17,742	16,706	34,152
43. Louisville, Ky.-Ind. MSA	953,662	818,898	124,761	1,576	5,640	1,787	5,765
44. Dayton-Springfield, Ohio MSA	951,270	811,393	126,238	1,915	9,278	2,446	7,254
45. Greensboro-Winston-Salem-High Point, N.C. MSA	942,091	747,835	182,284	3,196	6,381	2,395	7,096
46. Birmingham, Ala. MSA	907,810	655,609	245,726	1,506	4,014	955	3,989
47. Jacksonville, Fla. MSA	906,727	701,911	181,265	2,587	15,362	5,602	22,479
48. Albany-Schenectady-Troy N.Y. MSA	874,304	815,315	41,112	1,560	10,789	5,528	15,840
49. Richmond-Petersburg, Va. MSA	865,640	595,714	252,340	2,705	11,864	3,017	9,327
50. West Palm Beach-Boca Raton-Delray Beach, Fla. MSA	863,518	732,231	107,705	1,211	9,020	13,351	66,613
51. Honolulu, Hawaii MSA	836,231	264,372	25,875	3,532	526,459	15,993	56,884
52. Austin, Tex. MSA	781,572	600,023	72,254	2,827	18,770	87,698	159,942
53. Las Vegas, Nev. MSA	741,459	602,658	70,738	6,416	26,043	35,604	82,904
54. Raleigh-Durham, N.C. MSA	735,480	533,056	183,447	1,933	13,834	3,210	9,019
55. Scranton-Wilkes-Barre, Pa. MSA	734,175	720,692	7,660	580	3,827	1,416	5,640
56. Tulsa, Okla. MSA	708,954	590,612	58,186	48,196	6,563	5,397	14,534
57. Grand Rapids, Mich. MSA	688,399	623,787	41,311	3,394	7,831	12,076	22,631
58. Allentown-Bethehem-Easton, Pa.-N.J. MSA	686,688	649,890	13,466	688	7,293	15,351	28,885
59. Fresno, Calif. MSA	667,490	422,839	33,423	7,119	57,239	146,870	236,634
60. Tucson, Ariz. MSA	666,880	524,976	20,795	20,330	11,964	88,815	163,262
61. Syracuse, N.Y. MSA	659,864	605,924	39,095	3,948	7,740	3,157	8,926
62. Greenville-Spartanburg, S.C. MSA	640,861	522,632	111,334	959	4,617	1,319	5,120
63. Omaha, Nebr.-Iowa MSA	618,262	550,758	51,426	3,159	6,374	6,545	16,371
64. Toledo, Ohio MSA	614,128	526,555	69,717	1,423	6,146	10,287	20,382
65. Knoxville, Tenn. MSA	604,816	561,535	36,400	1,505	4,540	836	3,232
66. El Paso, Tex. MSA	591,610	452,512	22,110	2,590	6,485	107,913	411,619
67. Harrisburg-Lebanon-Carlisle, Pa. MSA	587,986	536,738	39,472	737	6,251	4,788	10,239
68. Bakersfield, Calif. MSA	543,477	378,479	30,131	7,026	16,541	111,300	151,995
69. New Haven-Meriden, Conn. MSA	530,180	441,831	64,220	947	8,430	14,752	32,907
70. Springfield, Mass. MSA	529,519	457,749	35,081	864	5,397	30,428	47,635
71. Baton Rouge, La. MSA	528,264	363,692	156,509	902	5,657	1,504	7,532
72. Little Rock-North Little Rock, Ark. MSA	513,117	404,808	101,862	1,870	3,347	1,230	4,164
73. Charleston, S.C. MSA	506,875	343,776	153,227	1,613	6,113	2,146	7,512
74. Youngstown-Warren, Ohio MSA	492,619	432,024	54,902	785	1,958	2,950	7,400
75. Wichita, Kans. MSA	485,270	423,784	36,979	5,160	9,109	10,238	19,793
76. Stockton, Calif. MSA	480,628	353,169	27,094	5,085	59,690	35,590	112,673
77. Alburquerque, N. Mex. MSA	480,577	369,445	13,199	16,296	7,386	74,251	178,310
78. Mobile, Ala. MSA	476,923	339,418	130,512	2,570	3,619	804	4,186

Rank/Metropolitan area	Total	White	Black	American Indian	Asian or Pacific Islander	Other race	Hispanic origin[1]
79. Columbia, S.C. MSA	453,331	307,454	137,906	1,013	4,820	2,138	5,949
80. Worcester, Mass. MSA	436,905	408,123	9,553	891	7,967	10,371	20,009
81. Johnson City-Kinsport-Bristol, Tenn.-Va. MSA	436,047	424,751	8,925	766	1,247	358	1,690
82. Chattanooga, Tenn.-Ga. MSA	433,210	370,586	58,218	891	2,825	690	2,539
83. Lansing-East Lansing, Mich. MSA	432,674	381,371	31,365	2,655	8,320	8,963	16,963
84. Flint, Mich. MSA	430,459	336,651	84,257	3,132	2,902	3,517	8,877
85. Lancaster, Pa. MSA	422,822	397,815	10,038	484	4,652	9,833	15,639
86. York, Pa. MSA	417,848	399,694	11,911	501	2,471	3,271	6,381
87. Lakeland-Winter Haven, Fla. MSA	405,382	341,952	54,385	1,158	2,486	5,401	16,600
88. Saginaw-Bay City-Midland, Mich. MSA	399,320	346,643	38,810	1,975	2,504	9,388	17,715
89. Melbourne-Titusville-Palm Bay, Fla. MSA	398,978	358,391	31,417	1,369	5,379	2,422	12,261
90. Colorado Springs, Colo. MSA	397,014	341,400	28,593	3,242	9,841	13,938	34,473
91. Augusta, Ga.-S.C. MSA	396,809	264,801	123,482	941	5,438	2,147	5,620
92. Jackson, Miss. MSA	395,396	224,999	167,899	346	1,754	398	1,944
93. Canton, Ohio MSA	394,106	365,675	25,187	1,015	1,558	671	2,854
94. Des Moines, Iowa MSA	392,928	368,386	14,952	1,015	6,218	2,357	6,614
95. McAllen-Edinburg-Mission, Tex. MSA	383,545	286,858	806	668	1,088	94,125	326,972
96. Daytona Beach, Fla. MSA	370,712	328,530	33,455	915	2,739	5,073	14,840
97. Modesto, Calif. MSA	370,522	297,315	6,450	4,039	19,223	43,495	80,897
98. Santa Barbara-Santa Maria-Lompoc, Calif. MSA	369,608	285,461	10,402	3,351	16,429	53,965	98,199
99. Madison, Wis. MSA	367,085	344,617	10,511	1,201	8,666	2,090	5,744
100. Fort Wayne, Ind. MSA	363,811	326,568	30,380	1,056	2,769	3,038	6,628
101. Spokane, Wash. MSA	361,364	341,874	5,105	5,539	6,569	2,277	6,994
102. Beaumont-Port Arthur, Tex. MSA	361,226	264,365	84,665	890	5,687	5,619	15,241
103. Salinas-Seaside-Monterey, Calif. MSA	355,660	227,008	22,849	3,017	27,856	74,930	119,570
104. Davenport-Rock Island-Mcline, Iowa-Ill. MSA	350,861	322,805	19,115	902	2,502	5,537	13,134
105. Corpus Christi, Tex. MSA	349,894	265,002	13,659	1,394	2,646	67,193	181,860
106. Lexington-Fayette, Ky. MSA	348,428	305,725	37,212	561	4,037	893	3,117
107. Pensacola, Fla. MSA	344,406	277,620	55,893	3,347	6,021	1,525	6,236
108. Peoria, Ill. MSA	339,172	309,325	25,142	587	2,759	1,359	3,642
109. Reading, Pa. MSA	336,523	314,561	10,003	333	2,746	8,880	17,174
110. Fort Myers-Cape Coral, Fla. MSA	335,113	306,200	22,184	672	1,894	4,163	15,094
111. Shreveport, La. MSA	334,341	213,610	116,892	863	2,023	951	4,394
112. Atlantic City, N.J. MSA	319,416	260,185	44,398	778	5,389	8,666	17,972
113. Utica-Rome, N.Y. MSA	316,633	297,746	13,849	613	2,314	2,111	6,174
114. Appleton-Oshkosh-Neenah, Wis. MSA	315,121	306,775	932	2,796	3,805	813	2,280
115. Huntington-Ashland, W.Va.-Ky.-Ohio MSA	312,529	304,244	6,751	372	937	225	1,274
116. Visalia-Tulare-Porterville, Calif. MSA	311,921	204,835	4,618	3,992	13,319	85,157	120,893
117. Montgomery, Ala. MSA	292,517	184,414	105,196	622	1,782	503	2,124
118. Rockford, Ill. MSA	283,719	251,783	23,383	697	3,136	4,720	9,836
119. Eugene-Springfield, Oreg. MSA	282,912	269,798	2,107	3,207	5,557	2,243	6,852
120. Macon-Warner-Robins, Ga. MSA	281,103	180,383	97,294	571	1,941	914	2,832
121. Evansville, Ind.-Ky. MSA	278,990	260,832	16,115	477	1,237	329	1,321
122. Salem, Oreg. MSA	278,024	255,212	2,332	4,041	4,746	11,693	21,027
123. Sarasota, Fla. MSA	277,776	262,836	12,073	483	1,430	954	5,882
124. Erie, Pa. MSA	275,572	257,879	14,304	438	1,411	1,540	3,364
125. Fayetteville, N.C. MSA	274,566	170,069	87,496	4,425	5,769	6,807	13,298
126. New London-Norwich, Conn.-R.I. MSA	266,819	245,933	12,077	1,433	3,549	3,827	8,517
127. Binghamton, N.Y. MSA	264,497	254,447	4,647	450	3,990	963	2,845
128. Provo-Orem, Utah MSA	263,590	253,596	374	1,913	3,958	3,749	8,488
129. Brownsville-Harlington, Tex. MSA	260,120	214,424	825	413	750	43,708	212,995
130. Poughkeepsie, N.Y. MSA	259,462	229,194	21,788	374	5,826	2,280	9,765
131. Killeen-Temple, Tex. MSA	255,301	181,144	49,687	1,405	7,201	15,864	31,238

Rank/Metropolitan area	Total	White	Black	American Indian	Asian or Pacific Islander	Other race	Hispanic origin[1]
132. Reno, Nev. MSA	254,667	225,095	5,680	4,921	9,824	9,147	22,959
133. Fort Pierce, Fla. MSA	251,071	214,278	30,709	526	1,565	3,993	10,680
134. Charleston, W.Va. MSA	250,454	234,518	13,919	292	1,450	275	1,042
135. South Bend-Mishawaka, Ind. MSA	247,052	216,984	24,190	846	2,507	2,525	5,201
136. Columbus, Ga.-Ala. MSA	243,072	144,326	91,484	765	3,107	3,390	7,388
137. Savannah, Ga. MSA	242,622	152,513	86,228	515	2,412	954	2,951
138. Johnstown, Pa. MSA	241,247	236,459	3,836	152	527	273	1,216
139. Springfield, Mo. MSA	240,593	233,186	3,784	1,471	1,600	552	1,991
140. Duluth, Minn.-Wis. MSA	239,971	232,507	1,276	4,487	1,342	359	1,153
141. Huntsville, Ala. MSA	238,912	184,197	48,116	1,601	4,232	766	2,984
142. Tallahassee, Fla. MSA	233,598	158,398	70,227	568	2,788	1,617	5,679
143. Anchorage, Alaska MSA	226,338	182,736	14,544	14,569	10,910	3,579	9,258
144. Roanoke, Va. MSA	224,477	194,645	27,602	281	1,602	347	1,359
145. Portsmouth-Dover-Rochester, N.H.-Maine MSA	223,578	218,216	2,285	414	2,136	527	1,994
146. Kalamazoo, Mich. MSA	223,411	197,427	19,879	1,017	3,168	1,920	3,950
147. Lubbock, Tex. MSA	222,636	176,037	17,154	686	2,722	26,037	51,011
148. Hickory-Morganton, N.C. MSA	221,700	201,558	17,540	417	1,673	512	1,449
149. Waterbury, Conn. MSA	221,629	196,680	15,414	538	1,576	7,421	16,384
150. Portland, Maine MSA	215,281	211,376	1,188	562	1,867	208	1,257
151. Lincoln, Nebr. MSA	213,641	202,663	4,659	1,207	3,367	1,745	3,938
152. Bradenton, Fla. MSA	211,707	190,328	16,400	501	1,227	3,251	9,424
153. Lafayette, La. MSA	208,740	154,146	51,378	440	1,915	861	3,115
154. Boise City, Idaho MSA	205,775	198,888	958	1,382	2,887	1,660	5,556
155. Gainesville, Fla. MSA	204,111	158,479	38,982	443	4,656	1,551	7,205
156. Biloxi-Gulfport, Miss. MSA	197,125	156,255	35,055	595	4,495	725	3,488
157. Ocala, Fla. MSA	194,833	167,094	24,844	638	945	1,312	5,860
158. Green Bay, Wis. MSA	194,594	186,621	1,012	3,869	2,522	570	1,525
159. St. Cloud, Minn. MSA	190,921	188,080	738	637	1,171	295	910
160. Bremerton, Wash. MSA	189,731	171,063	5,107	3,211	8,282	2,068	6,169
161. Springfield, Ill. MSA	189,550	173,114	14,373	319	1,391	353	1,311
162. Waco, Tex. MSA	189,123	146,100	29,520	563	1,384	11,556	23,643
163. Yakima, Wash. MSA	188,823	139,514	1,938	8,405	1,922	37,044	45,114
164. Amarillo, Tex. MSA	187,547	158,517	9,788	1,355	3,216	14,671	25,390
165. Fort Collins-Loveland, Colo. MSA	186,136	175,971	1,114	1,063	2,777	5,211	12,227
166. Houma-Thibodaux, La. MSA	182,842	147,453	26,735	6,814	1,370	470	2,625
167. Chico, Calif. MSA	182,120	165,200	2,361	3,241	5,170	6,148	13,606
168. Merced, Calif. MSA	178,403	120,280	8,523	1,516	15,128	32,956	58,107
169. Fort Smith, Ark.-Okla. MSA	175,911	155,580	6,831	9,054	3,755	691	2,120
170. New Bedford, Mass. MSA	175,641	161,018	4,623	504	841	8,655	7,347
171. Asheville, N.C. MSA	174,821	158,979	14,336	486	765	255	1,173
172. Champaign-Urbana-Rantoul, Ill. MSA	173,025	146,506	16,559	331	8,033	1,596	3,485
173. Clarksville-Hopkinsville, Tenn.-Ky. MSA	169,439	128,583	34,801	688	2,712	2,655	5,567
174. Cedar Rapids, Iowa MSA	168,767	163,164	3,334	363	1,401	505	1,591
175. Lake Charles, La. MSA	168,134	128,181	38,445	387	590	531	1,847
176. Longview-Marshall, Tex. MSA	162,431	122,270	35,975	670	635	2,881	3,053
177. Benton Harbor, Mich. MSA	161,378	133,259	24,872	685	1,487	1,075	2,683
178. Olympia, Wash. MSA	161,238	148,221	2,864	2,498	6,101	1,554	4,873
179. Topeka, Kans. MSA	160,976	141,189	13,365	1,836	1,179	3,407	7,785
180. Wheeling, W.Va.-Ohio MSA	159,301	155,313	3,196	145	546	101	569
181. Muskegon, Mich. MSA	158,983	133,931	21,617	1,338	555	1,542	3,623
182. Athens, Ga. MSA	156,267	124,076	29,003	257	2,352	579	2,011
183. Elkhart-Goshen, Ind. MSA	156,198	146,505	7,106	453	997	1,137	2,932
184. Lima, Ohio MSA	154,340	140,402	12,379	252	749	558	1,483
185. Fargo-Moorhead, N.Dak.-Minn. MSA	153,296	149,004	446	1,497	1,396	953	1,879
186. Naples, Fla. MSA	152,099	139,073	6,986	428	584	5,028	20,734
187. Tyler, Tex. MSA	151,309	113,676	31,572	520	638	4,903	8,986
188. Tuscaloosa, Ala. MSA	150,522	109,398	39,377	253	1,264	230	948
189. Richland-Kennewick-Pasco, Wash. MSA	150,033	129,749	2,395	1,124	3,115	13,650	19,940
190. Jacksonville, N.C. MSA	149,838	111,939	29,808	939	2,994	4,158	8,035
191. Jackson, Mich. MSA	149,756	135,557	11,983	655	653	908	2,303
192. Parkersburg-Marietta, W.Va.-Ohio MSA	149,169	146,698	1,567	242	520	142	479
193. Manchester, N.H. MSA	147,809	144,159	1,133	278	1,442	797	2,415
194. Redding, Calif. MSA	147,036	137,977	1,081	3,954	2,684	1,340	5,652

Rank/Metropolitan area	Total	White	Black	American Indian	Asian or Pacific Islander	Other race	Hispanic origin[1]
195. Waterloo-Cedar Falls, Iowa MSA	146,611	136,236	8,584	237	1,137	417	984
196. Medford, Oreg. MSA	146,389	140,188	340	1,863	1,429	2,569	5,949
197. Anderson, S.C. MSA	145,196	120,384	24,151	173	340	148	559
198. Fort Walton Beach, Fla. MSA	143,776	125,191	13,007	776	3,658	1,144	4,427
199. Steubenville-Weirton, Ohio-W. Va. MSA	142,523	136,078	5,591	237	439	178	710
200. Lynchburg, Va. MSA	142,199	110,847	30,079	277	743	253	923
201. Monroe, La. MSA	142,191	96,870	44,096	239	740	246	1,194
202. Jamestown-Dunkirk, N.Y. MSA	141,895	136,311	2,405	558	545	2,076	4,055
203. Janesville-Beloit, Wis. MSA	139,510	130,803	6,638	369	985	715	1,754
204. Eau Claire, Wis. MSA	137,543	134,056	269	617	2,400	204	611
205. Battle Creek, Mich. MSA	135,982	118,737	14,383	696	1,068	1,098	2,583
206. Las Cruces, N. Mex. MSA	135,510	123,434	2,172	1,009	1,164	7,731	76,448
207. Joplin, Mo. MSA	134,910	130,093	1,327	2,452	751	287	1,150
208. Laredo, Tex. MSA	133,239	93,657	156	201	484	38,741	125,069
209. Greeley, Colo. MSA	131,821	117,247	567	785	1,133	12,089	27,502
210. Decatur, Ala. MSA	131,556	113,685	14,879	2,434	389	169	686
211. Alexandria, La. MSA	131,556	92,989	36,805	564	908	290	1,526
212. Burlington, Vt. MSA	131,439	128,580	814	299	1,465	281	1,171
213. Florence, Ala. MSA	131,327	114,380	16,263	302	289	93	500
214. Charlottesville, Va. MSA	131,107	109,049	18,895	148	2,623	392	1,384
215. Dothan, Ala. MSA	130,964	100,878	27,801	526	1,201	558	1,679
216. Terre Haute, Ind. MSA	130,812	122,933	6,029	338	1,176	336	1,063
217. Anderson, Ind. MSA	130,669	119,734	9,870	299	415	351	885
218. Lafayette-West Lafayette, Ind. MSA	130,598	122,013	2,660	320	4,821	784	2,078
219. Altoona, Pa. MSA	130,542	128,840	1,073	118	380	131	431
220. Bloomington-Normal, Ill. MSA	129,180	121,057	5,563	203	1,624	733	1,671
221. Bellingham, Wash. MSA	127,780	119,229	650	4,014	2,363	1,524	3,718
222. Panama City, Fla. MSA	126,994	109,570	13,713	949	2,229	533	2,256
223. Mansfield, Ohio MSA	126,137	115,078	9,981	223	578	277	903
224. Sioux Falls, S. Dak. MSA	123,809	120,454	754	1,680	714	207	648
225. State College, Pa. MSA	123,786	116,552	2,801	179	3,841	413	1,350
226. Pueblo, Colo. MSA	123,051	104,304	2,253	991	729	14,774	44,090
227. Yuba City, Calif. MSA	122,643	95,062	3,478	2,616	10,996	10,491	17,320
228. Wichita Falls, Tex. MSA	122,378	102,427	11,221	903	1,851	5,976	10,555
229. Bryan-College Station, Tex. MSA	121,862	94,866	13,672	274	4,313	8,737	16,713
230. Hagerstown, Md. MSA	121,393	112,828	7,245	241	793	286	905
231. Sharon, Pa. MSA	121,003	114,479	5,882	115	393	134	506
232. Wilmington, N.C. MSA	120,284	94,895	24,097	435	616	241	924
233. Texarkana, Tex.-Texarkana, Ark. MSA	120,132	92,342	26,423	560	405	402	1,644
234. Muncie, Ind. MSA	119,659	111,232	7,167	274	641	345	853
235. Abilene, Tex. MSA	119,655	100,237	7,547	450	1,449	9,972	17,511
236. Odessa, Tex. MSA	118,934	91,309	5,557	647	662	20,759	37,315
237. Williamsport, Pa. MSA	118,710	115,040	2,816	219	469	166	641
238. Glens Falls, N.Y. MSA	118,539	115,157	2,352	214	392	424	1,789
239. Decatur, Ill. MSA	117,206	102,197	14,135	157	506	211	540
240. Santa Fe, N. Mex. MSA	117,043	96,454	711	2,948	941	15,989	50,947
241. Anniston, Ala. MSA	116,034	92,873	21,578	296	869	418	1,282
242. Wausau, Wis. MSA	115,400	112,189	89	490	2,499	133	470
243. Pascagoula, Miss. MSA	155,243	90,114	23,581	254	1,115	179	1,060
244. Sioux City, Iowa-Nebr. MSA	115,018	107,579	1,953	1,999	1,624	1,863	3,728
245. Florence, S.C. MSA	114,344	69,501	44,276	145	307	115	508
246. Billings, Mont. MSA	113,419	107,921	511	3,235	612	1,140	3,158
247. Fayetteville-Springdale, Ariz. MSA	113,409	108,743	1,676	1,486	1,043	461	1,526
248. Albany, Ga. MSA	112,561	60,041	51,522	281	498	219	928
249. Columbia, Mo. MSA	112,379	100,055	8,377	394	3,129	424	1,226
250. Lawton, Okla. MSA	111,486	79,666	19,908	5,153	3,065	3,694	6,923
251. Bloomington, Ind. MSA	108,978	102,752	2,835	216	2,713	462	1,367
252. Danville, Va. MSA	108,711	73,817	34,350	117	325	102	515
253. Burlington, N.C. MSA	108,213	86,373	20,822	303	487	228	736
254. Yuma, Ariz. MSA	106,895	80,702	3,056	1,429	1,393	20,315	43,388
255. Midland, Tex. MSA	106,611	86,977	8,281	414	888	10,051	22,780
256. Rochester, Minn. MSA	106,470	101,880	788	295	3,237	270	970
257. Sheboygan, Wis. MSA	103,877	100,389	430	357	2,061	640	1,688

Rank/Metropolitan area	Total	White	Black	American Indian	Asian or Pacific Islander	Other race	Hispanic origin[1]
258. Fitchburg-Leominster, Mass. MSA	102,797	95,540	2,356	196	1,789	2,916	7,312
259. Cumberland, Md.-W.Va. MSA	101,643	98,821	2,270	71	391	90	420
260. Gadsden, Ala. MSA	99,840	85,274	13,799	250	419	98	331
261. San Angelo, Tex. MSA	98,458	79,533	4,136	373	998	13,418	25,501
262. La Crosse, Wis. MSA	97,904	94,319	438	340	2,667	140	640
263. Kokomo, Ind. MSA	96,946	91,410	4,408	246	508	374	1,178
264. Kankakee, Ill. MSA	96,255	80,194	14,399	150	644	868	1,946
265. Iowa City, Iowa MSA	96,119	89,649	1,979	176	3,837	478	1,435
266. Elmira, N.Y. MSA	95,195	88,370	5,245	211	690	679	1,441
267. Sherman-Denison, Tex. MSA	95,021	85,553	6,565	1,046	412	1,445	2,795
268. Bangor, Maine MSA	88,745	86,328	467	1,008	798	144	509
269. Lewiston-Auburn, Maine MSA	88,141	86,799	443	197	514	188	559
270. Owensboro, Ky. MSA	87,189	83,168	3,619	101	229	72	312
271. Dubuque, Iowa MSA	86,403	85,367	354	77	437	168	437
272. Pine Bluff, Ark. MSA	85,487	47,878	36,877	227	352	153	427
273. Bismarck, N.Dak. MSA	83,831	81,306	79	2,016	286	144	435
274. St. Joseph, Mo. MSA	83,083	79,378	2,635	273	266	531	1,709
275. Lawrence, Kans. MSA	81,798	72,885	3,324	2,161	2,581	847	2,138
276. Rapid City, S.Dak. MSA	81,343	72,769	1,288	5,835	933	518	1,777
277. Pittsfield, Mass. MSA	79,250	76,597	1,702	142	548	261	770
278. Jackson, Tenn. MSA	77,982	53,423	24,170	66	253	70	376
279. Great Falls, Mont. MSA	77,691	72,345	1,061	3,072	792	421	1,398
280. Victoria, Tex. MSA	74,361	59,251	4,906	208	257	9,739	25,372
281. Cheyenne, Wyo. MSA	73,142	66,280	2,218	528	821	3,295	7,310
282. Grand Forks, N.Dak. MSA	70,683	66,766	1,446	1,244	881	346	1,053
283. Casper, Wyo. MSA	61,226	59,323	458	404	280	761	2,252
284. Enid, Okla. MSA	56,735	52,403	2,020	1,234	587	491	1,086

1. Hispanic persons may be of any race.   **Source:** U.S Bureau of the Census, Press Release CB91-229

Population Change in the Top 100 Metropolitan Statistical Areas, 1990–96

Note that since the 1990 Census, the Census Bureau has changed the boundaries of several dozen metropolitan statistical areas, merging some areas within others and separating some areas out of larger MSAs. For example, Washington D.C. and Baltimore, Md. are now considered one consolidated metropolitan statistical area rather than two. As a result, population statistics before and after 1990 are not directly comparable for more than 75 MSAs.

Metropolitan Statistical Area	Population 1990	Population 1996	Change, 1990–96 Number	Change, 1990–96 Percent
1. New York-Northern New Jersey-Long Island, N.Y.-N.J.-Conn.-Pa. CMSA	19,549,649	19,938,492	388,843	2.0%
2. Los Angeles-Riverside-Orange County, Calif. CMSA	14,531,529	15,495,155	963,626	6.6
3. Chicago-Gary-Kenosha, Ill.-Ind.-Wis. CMSA	8,239,820	8,599,774	359,954	4.4
4. Washington-Baltimore, D.C.-Md.-Va.-W.Va. CMSA	6,726,395	7,164,519	438,124	6.5
5. San Francisco-Oakland-San Jose, Calif. CMSA	6,249,881	6,605,428	355,547	5.7
6. Philadelphia-Wilmington-Atlantic City, Pa.-N.J.-Del.-Md. CMSA	5,893,019	5,973,463	80,444	1.4
7. Boston-Worcester-Lawrence, Mass.-N.H.-Maine-Conn. CMSA	5,455,403	5,563,475	108,072	2.0
8. Detroit-Ann Arbor-Flint, Mich. CMSA	5,187,171	5,284,171	97,000	1.9
9. Dallas-Fort Worth, Texas CMSA	4,037,282	4,574,561	537,279	13.3
10. Houston-Galveston-Brazoria, Texas CMSA	3,731,029	4,253,428	522,399	14.0
11. Atlanta, Ga. MSA	2,959,500	3,541,230	581,730	19.7
12. Miami-Fort Lauderdale, Fla. CMSA	3,192,725	3,514,403	321,678	10.1
13. Seattle-Tacoma-Bremerton, Wash. CMSA	2,970,300	3,320,829	350,529	11.8
14. Cleveland-Akron, Ohio CMSA	2,859,644	2,913,430	53,786	1.9
15. Minneapolis-St. Paul, Minn.-Wis. MSA	2,538,776	2,765,116	226,340	8.9
16. Phoenix-Mesa, Ariz. MSA	2,238,498	2,746,703	508,205	22.7
17. San Diego, Calif. MSA	2,498,016	2,655,463	157,447	6.3
18. St. Louis, Mo.-Ill. MSA	2,492,348	2,548,238	55,890	2.2
19. Pittsburgh, Pa. MSA	2,394,811	2,379,411	-15,400	-0.6
20. Denver-Boulder-Greeley, Colo. CMSA	1,980,140	2,277,401	297,261	15.0
21. Tampa-St. Petersburg-Clearwater, Fla. MSA	2,067,959	2,199,231	131,272	6.3
22. Portland-Salem, Oreg.-Wash. CMSA	1,793,476	2,078,357	284,881	15.9
23. Cincinnati-Hamilton, Ohio-Ky.-Ind. CMSA	1,817,569	1,920,931	103,362	5.7
24. Kansas City, Mo.-Kans. MSA	1,582,874	1,690,343	107,469	6.8
25. Milwaukee-Racine, Wis. CMSA	1,607,183	1,642,658	35,475	2.2
26. Sacramento-Yolo, Calif. CMSA	1,481,220	1,632,133	150,913	10.2

Metropolitan Statistical Area	Population 1990	Population 1996	Change, 1990–96 Number	Change, 1990–96 Percent
27. Norfolk-Virginia Beach-Newport News, Va.-N.C. MSA	1,444,710	1,540,252	95,542	6.6%
28. Indianapolis, Ind. MSA	1,380,491	1,492,297	111,806	8.1
29. San Antonio, Texas MSA	1,324,749	1,490,111	165,362	12.5
30. Columbus, Ohio MSA	1,345,450	1,447,646	102,196	7.6
31. Orlando, Fla. MSA	1,224,844	1,417,291	192,447	15.7
32. Charlotte-Gastonia-Rock Hill, N.C.-S.C. MSA	1,162,140	1,321,068	158,928	13.7
33. New Orleans, La. MSA	1,285,262	1,312,890	27,628	2.1
34. Salt Lake City-Ogden, Utah MSA	1,072,227	1,217,842	145,615	13.6
35. Las Vegas, Nev.-Ariz. MSA	852,646	1,201,073	348,427	40.9
36. Buffalo-Niagara Falls, N.Y. MSA	1,189,340	1,175,240	-14,100	-1.2
37. Hartford, Conn. MSA	1,157,585	1,144,574	-13,011	-1.1
38. Greensboro–Winston-Salem–High Point, N.C. MSA	1,050,304	1,141,238	90,934	8.7
39. Providence-Fall River-Warwick, R.I.-Mass. MSA	1,134,350	1,124,044	-10,306	-0.9
40. Nashville, Tenn. MSA	985,026	1,117,178	132,152	13.4
41. Rochester, N.Y. MSA	1,062,470	1,088,037	25,567	2.4
42. Memphis, Tenn.-Ark.-MS MSA	1,007,306	1,078,151	70,845	7.0
43. Austin-San Marcos, Texas MSA	846,221	1,041,330	195,103	23.1
44. Oklahoma City, Okla. MSA	958,839	1,026,657	67,818	7.1
45. Raleigh-Durham-Chapel Hill, N.C. MSA	858,485	1,025,253	166,768	19.4
46. Grand Rapids-Muskegon-Holland, Mich. MSA	937,891	1,015,099	77,208	8.2
47. Jacksonville, Fla. MSA	906,727	1,008,633	101,906	11.2
48. West Palm Beach-Boca Raton, Fla. MSA	863,503	992,840	129,337	15.0
49. Louisville, Ky.-Ind. MSA	949,012	991,765	42,753	4.5
50. Dayton-Springfield, Ohio MSA	951,270	950,661	-609	-0.1
51. Richmond-Petersburg, Va. MSA	865,640	935,174	69,534	8.0
52. Greenville-Spartanburg-Anderson, S.C. MSA	830,539	896,679	66,140	8.0
53. Birmingham, Ala. MSA	839,942	894,702	547,60	6.5
54. Albany-Schenectady-Troy, N.Y. MSA	861,623	878,527	16,904	2.0
55. Honolulu, Hawaii MSA	836,231	871,766	35,535	4.2
56. Fresno, Calif. MSA	755,580	861,753	106,173	14.1
57. Tucson, Ariz. MSA	666,957	767,873	100,916	15.1
58. Tulsa, Okla. MSA	708,954	756,493	47,539	6.7
59. Syracuse, N.Y. MSA	742,237	745,691	3,454	0.5
60. El Paso, Texas MSA	591,610	684,446	92,836	15.7
61. Omaha, Neb.-Iowa MSA	639,580	681,698	42,118	6.6
62. Albuquerque, N.Mex. MSA	589,131	670,092	80,961	13.7
63. Knoxville, Tenn. MSA	585,960	649,277	63,317	10.8
64. Scranton–Wilkes-Barre–Hazleton, Pa. MSA	638,524	628,073	-10,451	-1.6
65. Bakersfield, Calif. MSA	544,981	622,729	77,748	14.3
66. Harrisburg-Lebanon-Carlisle, Pa. MSA	587,986	614,755	26,769	4.6
67. Allentown-Bethlehem-Easton, Pa. MSA	595,081	614,304	19,223	3.2
68. Toledo, Ohio MSA	614,128	611,417	-2,711	-0.4
69. Youngstown-Warren, Ohio MSA	600,895	598,582	-2,313	-0.4
70. Springfield, Mass. MSA	587,884	576,561	-11,323	-1.9
71. Baton Rouge, La. MSA	528,261	567,388	39,127	7.4
72. Little Rock-North Little Rock, Ark. MSA	513,026	548,352	35,326	6.9
73. Stockton-Lodi, Calif. MSA	480,628	533,392	52,764	11.0
74. Sarasota-Bradenton, Fla. MSA	489,483	528,803	39,320	8.0
75. Mobile, Ala. MSA	476,923	518,975	42,052	8.8
76. Wichita, Kans. MSA	485,270	512,965	27,695	5.7
77. McAllen-Edinburg-Mission, Texas MSA	383,545	495,594	112,049	29.2
78. Charleston-North Charleston, S.C. MSA	506,877	495,143	-11,734	-2.3
79. Columbia, S.C. MSA	453,932	488,207	34,275	7.6
80. Fort Wayne, Ind. MSA	456,281	475,299	19,018	4.2
81. Colorado Springs, Colo. MSA	397,014	472,924	75,910	19.1
82. Johnson City-Kingsport-Bristol, Tenn.-Va. MSA	436,047	458,229	22,182	5.1
83. Daytona Beach, Fla. MSA	399,438	456,464	57,026	14.3
84. Melbourne-Titusville-Palm Bay, Fla. MSA	398,978	453,998	55,020	13.8
85. Augusta-Aiken, Ga.-S.C. MSA	415,220	453,612	38,392	9.2
86. Lancaster, Pa. MSA	422,822	450,834	28,012	6.6
87. Lansing-East Lansing, Mich. MSA	432,684	447,538	14,854	3.4
88. Chattanooga, Tenn.-Ga. MSA	424,347	446,096	21,749	5.1
89. Kalamazoo-Battle Creek, Mich. MSA	429,453	444,428	14,975	3.5
90. Lexington, Ky. MSA	405,936	441,073	35,137	8.7
91. Lakeland-Winter Haven, Fla. MSA	405,382	440,954	35,572	8.8
92. Des Moines, Iowa MSA	392,928	427,436	34,508	8.8
93. Jackson, Miss. MSA	395,396	421,068	25,672	6.5
94. Modesto, Calif. MSA	370,522	415,786	45,264	12.2
95. Spokane, Wash. MSA	361,333	404,920	43,587	12.1
96. Saginaw-Bay City-Midland, Mich. MSA	399,320	403,301	3,981	1.0
97. Canton-Massillon, Ohio MSA	394,106	402,928	8,822	2.2
98. Madison, Wis. MSA	367,085	395,366	28,281	7.7
99. Pensacola, Fla. MSA	344,406	385,820	41,414	12.0
100. Santa Barbara-Santa Maria-Lompoc, Calif. MSA	369,608	385,573	15,965	4.3

Note: CMSA = consolidated metropolitan statistical area; MSA = metropolitan statistical area. For component areas see "Population of Metropolitan Statistical Areas, 1980-90." **Source:** U.S. Bureau of the Census, 1998.

25 Fastest-Growing Metropolitan Statistical Areas, 1980–90

Metropolitan Statistical Area	Population 1980	Population 1990	Change, 1980–90 Number	Change, 1980–90 Percent
1. Naples, Fla. MSA	85,971	152,099	66,128	76.9%
2. Fort Pierce, Fla. MSA	151,196	251,071	99,875	66.1
3. Fort Myers-Cape Coral, Fla. MSA	205,266	335,113	129,847	63.3
4. Las Vegas, Nev. MSA	463,087	741,459	278,372	60.1
5. Ocala, Fla. MSA	122,488	194,833	72,345	59.1
6. Orlando, Fla. MSA	699,904	1,072,748	372,844	53.3
7. West Palm Beach-Boca Raton-Delray Beach, Fla. MSA	576,758	863,518	286,760	49.7
8. Melbourne-Titusville-Palm Bay, Fla. MSA	272,959	398,978	126,019	46.2
9. Austin, Texas MSA	536,688	781,572	244,884	45.6
10. Daytona Beach, Fla. MSA	258,762	370,712	111,950	43.3
11. Bradenton, Fla. MSA	148,445	211,707	63,262	42.6
12. Las Cruces, N. Mex.MSA	96,340	135,510	39,170	40.7
13. Phoenix, Ariz. MSA	1,509,175	2,122,101	612,926	40.6
14. Yuma, Ariz. MSA	76,205	106,895	30,690	40.3
15. Modesto, Calif. MSA	265,900	370,522	104,622	39.3
16. Stockton, Calif. MSA	347,342	480,628	133,286	38.4
17. Sarasota, Fla. MSA	202,251	277,776	75,525	37.3
18. McAllen-Edinburg-Mission, Texas MSA	283,323	383,545	100,222	35.4
19. Bakersfield, Calif. MSA	403,089	543,477	140,388	34.8
20. Sacramento, Calif. MSA	1,099,814	1,481,102	381,288	34.7
21. San Diego, Calif. MSA	1,861,846	2,498,016	636,170	34.2
22. Laredo, Texas MSA	99,258	133,239	33,981	34.2
23. Jacksonville, N.C. MSA	112,784	149,838	37,054	32.9
24. Dallas-Fort Worth, Texas CMSA	2,930,568	3,885,415	954,847	32.6
25. Merced, Calif. MSA	134,558	178,403	43,845	32.6

Note: CMSA = consolidated metropolitan statistical area; MSA = metropolitan statistical area. For component areas see "Population of Metropolitan Statistical Areas, 1980-90."   **Source:** U.S. Bureau of the Census release, 1991.

25 Fastest-Declining Metropolitan Statistical Areas, 1980-90

Metropolitan Statistical Area	Population 1980	Population 1990	Change, 1980-90 Number	Change, 1980-90 Percent
1. Casper, Wyo. MSA	71,856	61,226	-10,630	-14.8%
2. Wheeling, W.Va.-Ohio MSA	185,566	159,031	-26,265	-14.2
3. Steubenville-Weirton, Ohio-W.Va. MSA	163,734	142,523	-21,211	-13.0
4. Decatur, Ill. MSA	131,375	117,206	-14,169	-10.8
5. Duluth, Minn.-Wis. MSA	266,650	239,971	-26,679	-10.0
6. Waterloo-Cedar Falls, Iowa MSA	162,781	146,611	-16,170	-9.9
7. Enid, Okla. MSA	62,820	56,735	-6,085	-9.7
8. Davenport-Rock Island-Moline, Iowa-Ill. MSA	384,749	350,861	-33,888	-8.8
9. Johnstown, Pa. MSA	264,506	241,247	-23,259	-8.8
10. Dubuque, Iowa MSA	93,745	86,403	-7,342	-7.8
11. Pittsburgh-Beaver Valley, Pa. CMSA	2,423,311	2,242,798	-180,513	-7.4
12. Youngstown-Warren, Ohio MSA	531,350	492,619	-38,731	-7.3
13. Peoria, Ill. MSA	365,864	339,172	-26,692	-7.3
14. Huntington-Ashland, W.Va.-Ky.-Ohio MSA	336,410	312,529	-23,881	-7.1
15. Charleston, W.Va. MSA	269,595	250,454	-19,141	-7.1
16. Muncie, Ind. MSA	128,587	119,659	-8,928	-6.9
17. Kokomo, Ind. MSA	103,715	96,946	-6,769	-6.5
18. Kankakee, Ill. MSA	102,926	96,255	-6,671	-6.5
19. Anderson, Ind. MSA	139,336	130,669	-8,667	-6.2
20. Benton Harbor, Mich. MSA	171,276	161,378	-9,898	-5.8
21. Pine Bluff, Ark. MSA	90,718	85,487	-5,231	-5.8
22. Sharon, Pa. MSA	128,299	121,003	-7,296	-5.7
23. Cumberland, Md.-W.Va.	107,782	101,643	-6,139	-5.7
24. Parkersburg-Marietta, W.Va.-Ohio MSA	157,893	149,169	-8,724	-5.5
25. St. Joseph, Mo. MSA	87,888	83,803	-4,805	-5.5

Note: CMSA = consolidated metropolitan statistical area; MSA = metropolitan statistical area. For component areas see "Population of Metropolitan Statistical Areas, 1980-90."   **Source:** U.S. Bureau of the Census release, 1991.

25 Fastest-Growing Metropolitan Statistical Areas, 1990–96

Metropolitan Statistical Area	Population		Change, 1990–96	
	1990	1996	Number	Percent
1. Las Vegas, Nev.-Ariz. MSA	852,646	1,201,073	348,427	40.9%
2. Laredo, Texas MSA	133,239	176,792	43,553	32.7
3. McAllen-Edinburg-Mission, Texas MSA	383,545	495,594	112,049	29.2
4. Boise City, Idaho MSA	295,851	372,587	767,36	25.9
5. Fayetteville-Springdale-Rogers, Ark. MSA	210,908	260,940	50,032	23.7
6. Naples, Fla. MSA	152,099	188,187	36,088	23.7
7. Austin-San Marcos, Texas MSA	846,227	1,041,330	195,103	23.1
8. Phoenix-Mesa, Ariz. MSA	2,238,498	2,746,703	508,205	22.7
9. Provo-Orem, Utah MSA	263,590	319,694	56,104	21.3
10. Brownsville-Harlingen-San Benito, Texas MSA	260,120	315,015	54,895	21.1
11. Las Cruces, N. Mex. MSA	135,510	163,849	28,339	20.9
12. Wilmington, N.C. MSA	171,269	206,738	35,469	20.7
13. Richland-Kennewick-Pasco, Wash. MSA	150,033	179,949	29,916	19.9
14. Atlanta, Ga. MSA	2,959,500	3,541,230	581,730	19.7
15. Raleigh-Durham-Chapel Hill, N.C. MSA	858,485	1,025,253	166,768	19.4
16. Bellingham, Wash. MSA	127,780	152,512	24,732	19.4
17. Colorado Springs, Colo. MSA	397,014	472,924	75,910	19.1
18. Fort Collins-Loveland, Colo. MSA	186,136	221,725	35,589	19.1
19. Ocala, Fla. MSA	194,835	230,068	35,233	18.1
20. Punta Gorda, Fla. MSA	110,975	130,426	19,451	17.5
21. Reno, Nev. MSA	254,667	298,787	44,120	17.3
22. Santa Fe, N. Mex. MSA	117,043	137,223	20,180	17.2
23. Yuma, Ariz. MSA	106,895	125142	18,247	17.1
24. Killeen-Temple, Texas MSA	255,299	296,896	41,597.	16.3
25. Grand Junction, Colo. MSA	93,145	108,371	15,226	16.3

Note: MSA = metropolitan statistical area. For component areas see "Population of Metropolitan Statistical Areas, 1980-90."
Source: U.S. Bureau of the Census.

25 Fastest-Declining Metropolitan Statistical Areas, 1990–96

Metropolitan Statistical Area	Population		Change, 1990–96	
	1990	1996	Number	Percent
1. Salinas, Calif. MSA	355,660	339,047	-16,613	-4.7%
2. Utica-Rome, N.Y. MSA	316,645	302,405	-14,240	-4.5
3. Alexandria, La. MSA	131,556	126,290	-5,266	-4.0
4. Lewiston-Auburn, Maine MSA	93,679	89,893	-3,786	-4.0
5. Binghamton, N.Y. MSA	264,497	254,053	-104,44	-3.9
6. Pittsfield, Mass. MSA	88,695	85,342	-3,353	-3.8
7. Jacksonville, N.C. MSA	149,838	144,533	-5,305	-3.5
8. Champaign-Urbana, Ill. MSA	173,025	167,392	-5,633	-3.3
9. Steubenville-Weirton, Ohio-W.Va. MSA	142,523	138,315	-4,208	-3.0
10. Pine Bluff, Ark. MSA	85,487	83,007	-2,480	-2.9
11. Bangor, Maine MSA	91,629	89,364	-2,265	-2.5
12. Charleston-North Charleston, S.C. MSA	506,877	495,143	-11,734	-2.3
13. Wheeling, W.Va.-Ohio MSA	159,301	155,808	-3,493	-2.2
14. Anniston, Ala. MSA	116,032	113,511	-2,521	-2.2
15. Elmira, N.Y. MSA	95,195	93,282	-1,913	-2.0
16. Springfield, Mass. MSA	587,884	576,561	-11,323	-1.9
17. Scranton–Wilkes-Barre–Hazleton, Pa. MSA	638,524	628,073	-10,451	-1.6
18. Decatur, Ill. MSA	117,206	115,416	-1,790	-1.5
19. New London-Norwich, Conn.-RI MSA	290,734	286,719	-4,015	-1.4
20. Buffalo-Niagara Falls, N.Y. MSA	1,189,340	1,175,240	-14,100	-1.2
21. Hartford, Conn. MSA	1,157,585	1,144,574	-13,011	-1.1
22. Cumberland, Md.-W.Va. MSA	101,643	100,600	-1,043	-1.0
23. Providence-Fall River-Warwick, R.I.-Mass. MSA	1,134,350	1,124,044	-10,306	-0.9
24. Johnstown, Pa. MSA	241,280	239,017	-2,263	-0.9
25. Muncie, Ind. MSA	119,659	118,600	-1,059	-0.9

Note: CMSA = consolidated metropolitan statistical area; MSA = metropolitan statistical area. For component areas see "Population of Metropolitan Statistical Areas, 1980-90." Source: U.S. Bureau of the Census.

COUNTIES IN AMERICA

In 1998 there were 3,142 counties in the United States. While 50 percent of Americans live in cities, almost every American lives in a county. Counties were originally the creation of state governments, which saw them as the local arm of state authority, with special responsibility for rural areas. Counties were intended more for the administrative convenience of the state than to meet the immediate needs of county residents and were not designed to have the intimate relationship with, or understanding of, the needs of localities theoretically characteristic of municipalities. But most states have loosened the reins on county governments in recent years, giving them more authority to meet the needs of population centers that have pushed beyond municipal limits. (Note that in Louisiana, counties are called parishes, and in Alaska and New York City, they are known as boroughs.)

Like cities and metropolitan areas, the fastest-growing counties are in the southern and western United States. Of the nation's 2,426 counties with at least 10,000 people in 1998, four of the 10 fastest-growing were in Georgia, two each were in Colorado and Texas, and one each were in Nevada and Virginia. The counties with the largest numerical increase in population 1997-98 are all in the western U.S.: Los Angeles (97,027), Maricopa County, Ariz. (84,977), Orange County, Calif. (58,140), and San Diego (56,881).

In addition, the counties with greatest growth are those in or around major metropolitan areas. All of the 10 fastest-growing counties between 1997 and 1998 were in or near metropolitan areas. Forsyth County, Ga. (within the Atlanta metropolitan area) was the fastest-growing county, increasing by 13.0 percent, while Douglas County, Colo. (a part of the Denver metropolitan area) was second, increasing by 11.2 percent. Between 1990 and 1998, Douglas County grew by more than 133 percent. The Atlanta area also had the fourth, sixth, and seventh-fastest growing counties between 1997 and 1998.

The 50 Largest Counties, 1980–90

| Rank, 1990/County | Population | | Change 1980–90 | | Rank |
	1990	1980	Number	Percent	1980
1. Los Angeles County, Calif.	8,863,164	7,477,238	1,385,926	18.5%	1
2. Cook County, Ill.	5,105,067	5,253,628	-148,561	-2.8	2
3. Harris County, Texas	2,818,199	2,409,547	408,652	17.0	3
4. San Diego County, Calif.	2,498,016	1,861,846	636,170	34.2	8
5. Orange County, Calif.	2,410,556	1,932,921	477,635	24.7	6
6. Kings County, N.Y.	2,300,664	2,231,028	69,636	3.1	5
7. Maricopa County, Ariz.	2,122,101	1,509,175	612,926	40.6	12
8. Wayne County, Mich.	2,111,687	2,337,843	-226,156	-9.7	4
9. Queens County, N.Y.	1,951,598	1,891,325	60,273	3.2	7
10. Dade County, Fla.	1,937,094	1,625,509	311,585	19.2	10
11. Dallas County, Texas	1,852,810	1,556,419	296,391	19.0	11
12. Philadelphia County, Pa.	1,585,577	1,688,210	-102,633	-6.1	9
13. King County, Wash.	1,507,319	1,269,898	237,421	18.7	20
14. Santa Clara County, Calif.	1,497,577	1,295,071	202,506	15.6	18
15. New York County, N.Y.	1,487,536	1,428,285	59,251	4.1	15
16. San Bernardino County, Calif.	1,418,380	895,016	523,364	58.5	30
17. Cuyahoga County, Ohio	1,412,140	1,498,400	-86,260	-5.8	13
18. Middlesex County, Mass.	1,398,468	1,367,034	31,434	2.3	16
19. Allegheny County, Pa.	1,336,449	1,450,195	-113,746	-7.8	14
20. Suffolk County, N.Y.	1,321,864	1,284,231	37,633	2.9	19
21. Nassau County, N.Y.	1,287,348	1,321,582	-34,234	-2.6	17
22. Alameda County, Calif.	1,279,182	1,105,379	173,803	15.7	22
23. Broward County, Fla.	1,255,488	1,018,257	237,231	23.3	23
24. Bronx County, N.Y.	1,203,789	1,168,972	34,817	3.0	21
25. Bexar County, Texas	1,185,394	988,971	196,423	19.9	26
26. Riverside County, Calif.	1,170,413	663,199	507,214	76.5	52
27. Tarrant County, Texas	1,170,103	860,880	309,223	35.9	34
28. Oakland County, Mich.	1,083,592	1,011,793	71,799	7.1	25
29. Sacramento County, Calif.	1,041,219	783,381	257,838	32.9	40
30. Hennepin County, Minn.	1,032,431	941,411	91,020	9.7	29
31. St. Louis County, Mo.	993,529	974,180	19,349	2.0	27
32. Erie County, N.Y.	968,532	1,015,472	-46,940	-4.6	24
33. Franklin County, Ohio	961,437	869,126	92,311	10.6	32
34. Milwaukee County, Wis.	959,275	964,988	-5,713	-0.6	28
35. Westchester County, N.Y.	874,866	866,599	8,267	1.0	33
36. Hamilton County, Ohio	866,228	873,203	-6,975	-0.8	31
37. Palm Beach County, Fla.	863,518	576,758	286,760	49.7	70
38. Hartford County, Conn.	851,783	807,766	44,017	5.4	37
39. Pinellas County, Fla.	851,659	728,531	123,128	16.9	45
40. Honolulu County, Hawaii	836,231	762,565	73,666	9.7	43
41. Hillsborough County, Fla.	834,054	646,939	187,115	28.9	57
42. Fairfield County, Conn.	827,645	807,143	20,502	2.5	38
43. Shelby County, Tenn	826,330	777,113	49,217	6.3	41
44. Bergen County, N.J.	825,380	845,385	-20,005	-2.4	36
45. Fairfax County, Va.	818,584	595,754	222,830	37.4	66
46. New Haven County, Conn.	804,219	761,325	42,894	5.6	44
47. Contra Costa County, Calif.	803,732	656,331	147,401	22.5	54
48. Marion County, Tenn.	797,159	765,233	31,926	4.2	42
49. DuPage County, Ill.	781,666	658,858	122,808	18.6	53
50. Essex County, N.J.	778,206	851,304	-73,098	-8.6	35

Source: U.S. Bureau of the Census release, 1991.

The 75 Largest Counties, 1990–98

Rank, 1998/Country	Population		Population change, 1990–98	
	July 1, 1998	1990 census	Number	Percent
1. Los Angeles County, Calif.	9,213,533	8,863,052	350,481	4.0%
2. Cook County, Ill.	5,189,689	5,105,044	84,645	1.7
3. Harris County, Texas	3,206,063	2,818,101	387,962	13.8
4. Maricopa County, Ariz.	2,784,075	2,122,101	661,974	31.2
5. San Diego County, Calif.	2,780,592	2,498,016	282,576	11.3
6. Orange County, Calif.	2,721,701	2,410,668	311,033	12.9
7. Kings County, N.Y.	2,267,942	2,300,664	−32,722	−1.4
8. Dade County, Fla.	2,152,437	1,937,194	215,243	11.1
9. Wayne County, Mich.	2,118,129	2,111,687	6,442	0.3
10. Dallas County, Texas	2,050,865	1,852,810	198,055	10.7
11. Queens County, N.Y.	1,998,853	1,951,598	47,255	2.4
12. King County, Wash.	1,654,876	1,507,305	147,571	9.8
13. Santa Clara County, Calif.	1,641,215	1,497,577	143,638	9.6
14. San Bernardino County, Calif.	1,635,234	1,418,380	216,854	15.3
15. New York County, N.Y.	1,550,649	1,487,536	63,113	4.2
16. Broward County, Fla.	1,503,407	1,255,531	247,876	19.7
17. Riverside County, Calif.	1,478,838	1,170,413	308,425	26.4
18. Philadelphia County, Pa.	1,436,287	1,585,577	−149,290	−9.4
19. Middlesex County, Mass.	1,424,116	1,398,468	25,648	1.8
20. Alameda County, Calif.	1,400,322	1,304,346	95,976	7.4
21. Cuyahoga County, Ohio	1,380,696	1,412,140	−31,444	−2.2
22. Suffolk County, N.Y.	1,371,269	1,321,768	49,501	3.7
23. Tarrant County, Texas	1,355,273	1,170,103	185,170	15.8
24. Bexar County, Texas	1,353,052	1,185,394	167,658	14.1
25. Nassau County, N.Y.	1,302,623	1,287,444	14,776	1.1
26. Allegheny County, Pa.	1,268,446	1,336,449	−68,003	−5.1
27. Bronx County, N.Y.	1,195,599	1,203,789	−8,190	−0.7
28. Oakland County, Mich.	1,176,488	1,083,592	92,896	8.6
29. Clark County, Nev.	1,162,129	741,368	420,761	56.8
30. Sacramento County, Calif.	1,144,202	1,041,219	102,983	9.9
31. Hennepin County, Minn.	1,059,669	1,032,431	27,238	2.6
32. Palm Beach County, Fla.	1,032,625	863,503	169,122	19.6
33. Franklin County, Ohio	1,021,194	961,437	59,757	6.2
34. St. Louis County, Mo.	998,696	993,508	5,188	0.5
35. Erie County, N.Y.	934,471	968,584	−34,113	−3.5
36. Fairfax County, Va.	929,239	818,358	110,881	13.5
37. Hillsborough County, Fla.	925,277	834,054	91,223	10.9
38. Contra Costa County, Calif.	918,200	803,732	114,468	14.2
39. Milwaukee County, Wisc.	911,713	959,275	−47,562	−5.0
40. Westchester County, N.Y.	897,920	874,866	23,054	2.6
41. DuPage County, Ill.	880,491	781,689	98,802	12.6
42. Pinellas County, Fla.	878,231	851,659	26,572	3.1
43. Honolulu County, Hawaii	872,478	836,231	36,247	4.3
44. Shelby County, Tenn.	868,825	826,330	42,495	5.1
45. Bergen County, N.J.	858,529	825,380	33,149	4.0
46. Salt Lake County, Utah	850,667	725,956	124,711	17.2
47. Hamilton County, Ohio	847,403	866,228	−18,825	−2.2
48. Montgomery County, Md.	840,879	762,207	78,672	10.3
49. Fairfield County, Conn.	838,362	827,645	10,717	1.3
50. Hartford County, Conn.	828,200	851,783	−23,583	−2.8
51. Marion County, Ind.	813,405	797,159	16,246	2.0
52. Orange County, Fla.	805,837	677,491	128,346	18.9
53. New Haven County, Conn.	793,504	804,219	−10,715	−1.3
54. Pima County, Ariz.	790,755	666,957	123,798	18.6
55. Macomb County, Mich.	787,698	717,400	70,298	9.8
56. Prince George's County, Md.	777,811	723,373	54,438	7.5
57. Fresno County, Calif.	755,730	667,490	88,240	13.2
58. Essex County, N.J.	750,273	777,964	−27,691	−3.6
59. San Francisco County, Calif.	745,774	723,959	21,815	3.0
60. Fulton County, Ga.	739,367	648,779	90,588	14.0
61. Duval County, Fla.	735,733	672,971	62,762	9.3
62. Ventura County, Calif.	731,967	669,016	62,951	9.4
63. Worcester County, Mass.	731,881	709,705	22,176	3.1
64. Baltimore County, Md.	721,874	692,134	29,740	4.3
65. Montgomery County, Pa.	719,718	678,193	41,525	6.1
66. Middlesex County, N.J.	716,176	671,811	44,365	6.6
67. Monroe County, N.Y.	716,072	713,968	2,104	0.3
68. Travis County, Texas	710,626	576,407	134,219	23.3
69. El Paso County, Texas	703,127	591,610	111,517	18.8
70. San Mateo County, Calif.	700,765	649,623	51,142	7.9
71. Essex County, Mass.	698,806	670,080	28,726	4.3
72. Pierce County, Wash.	676,505	586,203	90,302	15.4
73. Jefferson County, Ky.	672,104	665,123	6,981	1.0
74. Jefferson County, Ala.	659,524	651,520	8,004	1.2
75. Jackson County, Mo.	654,986	633,234	21,752	3.4

Source: U.S. Bureau of the Census, 1999

The American People Today

The United States is the third most populous nation in the world, ranking behind only China and India. According to the U.S. Census Bureau, on March 6, 1990, the resident population of the U.S. reached the 250 million mark, more than three times the 1900 figure of 76 million, about double what it was in 1930, and almost 100 million more than the 1950 total. As of July 1, 1998, the population stood at 270.3 million. The Census Bureau predicts that this kind of rapid growth, based as it was mainly on high birth rates and, during the first two decades of the century, extraordinarily high immigration rates, cannot occur during the next century. In fact the underlying shifts in social behavior that will cause dramatic changes in the nature of the population have been in place for 20 years or so, just at the end of a most extraordinary period of population expansion.

Between 1946 and 1964 just over 75 million babies were born in the U.S., a demographic achievement so noteworthy that those born during this time have their own collective designation, "The Baby Boom Generation." During these years the crude birth date soared to as high as 24 live births (per 1,000 population) in some years, compared to 20 or so in the years before the war; fertility rates, too, reached exceptional levels ranging from 101 to 121 (per 1,000 women aged 15-44) as compared to an average of about 75 in earlier years. As a result the population grew at an annual rate of between 1.4 percent and 1.8 percent.

Quite remarkably, however, this festival of fecundity came to a sudden unexpected halt, so sudden that by 1968 the population growth rate had sunk to 1.0 percent; the birth rate to under 18, and fertility rates to about 85, levels that have sunk much further since. As a result projected population growth over the next few decades is extremely low: 7.1 percent for 1990s, and 5.3 percent for the first decade of the new century. By way of comparison between 1950 and 1960 the population grew 19 percent.

It is that period of unparalleled growth that has affected so many aspects of daily life and will continue to do so for another fifty years. Demographers sometimes refer to the Baby Boomers, somewhat inelegantly perhaps, as the "Pig in the Python" in order to explain how this group has continued to distort the normal contours of the general body of the population. During the fifties their numbers required great capital outlays for new schools, and later for expanding colleges and universities. In the seventies they jammed the labor market causing higher unemployment rates, but helped the economy by increasing consumption and expanding the housing market. After the turn of the century the Baby Boom generation will begin to enter the retirement years and even here they will cause a strain on the existing structures. What will happen is that the ratio of people working—those born during the '70s and '80s, now being called the Baby Bust—to those retired will shrink dramatically. Today that ratio is 5-1, but by 2020 or so it will be 2.5-1.

If the Baby Boomers and those in much smaller numbers who followed them represent, demographically speaking, the most significant group among the American people, it is the immigrant group that has caused the most interest in recent years. Because their numbers have increased greatly since the 1960s, many see them as the key

to preventing future population decline as birth rates and fertility rates in the U.S. seem to be stabilizing at a very low level. In recent years, immigration has accounted for over 25 percent of the nation's growth. Over the last 20 years the origins of most immigrants have been Asian and Latin American nations, so the ethnic composition of the American people is clearly going to change and become even more diverse than today.

In the pages that follow, all of these matters are taken up—fertility, race, immigration—to create a statistical portrait of the population both past and present, with a glimpse at the future as well. Note that the Census Bureau updates some information more often than every 10 years with annual population estimates. In the subsequent portions of this chapter, we have tried, wherever possible, to furnish data that is more recent than 1990 census figures.

THE 1990 CENSUS

Article I, section 2 of the U.S. Constitution requires Congress to undertake a census of the population every 10 years for the purpose of apportioning seats in the House of Representatives. Today the decennial census is also used to apportion federal and state funds totalling as much as $100 billion a year, so it is vitally important to local governments and individuals throughout the country. City and county planners, health care administrators, as well as the entire marketing and advertising industries are all strongly dependent on census data for their day-to-day operations. So it's not surprising that the 1990 census, officially taken on April 1, was the largest undertaking of its kind in our history. The first results—state population figures—were released in December 1990, as required by law.

▶ HIGHLIGHTS OF THE 1990 CENSUS

Population growth   Between the 1980 census and the 1990 census, the resident population of the United States increased by 22,164,873—from 226,545,805 to 248,709,873—a growth rate of 9.8 percent, the second lowest in census history. Only the Depression decade of the 1930s was lower (7.3 percent) while by contrast the Baby Boom era of the 1950s reached a growth rate of 18.5 percent. (Between 1790 and 1910 the rate was never less than 21 percent.)

Regional growth   During the 1980s the South and the West together accounted for 89 percent of national population growth, about the same as they did in the 1970s. As of 1990 their combined share of the U.S. population reached 55.6 percent, up from 52.3 percent in 1980, and 48.0 percent in 1970.

The West had the highest growth rate (22.3 percent) in the eighties, a slight decline from the seventies (23.9 percent) but still more than twice the national rate. The South's growth rate fell sharply to 13.4 percent from 20.0 percent, but was still significantly higher than the national rate. Growth rates rose in the Northeast (from 0.2 percent to 3.4 percent), but fell in the Midwest (4.0 percent to 1.4 percent).

U.S. Resident Population and Population Change by State, 1980–90

State	1980 Population	Rank	1990 Population	Rank	Change, 1980–90 Number	Percent
United States	226,545,805	—	248,709,873	—	22,165,068	9.8%
Alabama	3,893,888	(22)	4,040,587	(22)	146,699	3.8
Alaska	401,851	(50)	550,043	(49)	148,192	36.9
Arizona	2,718,215	(29)	3,665,228	(24)	947,013	34.8
Arkansas	2,286,435	(33)	2,350,725	(33)	64,290	2.8
California	23,667,902	(1)	29,760,021	(1)	6,092,119	25.7
Colorado	2,889,964	(28)	3,294,394	(26)	404,430	14.0
Connecticut	3,107,576	(25)	3,287,116	(27)	179,540	5.8
Delaware	594,338	(47)	666,168	(46)	71,830	12.1
District of Columbia[1]	638,333	—	606,900	—	-31,433	-4.9
Florida	9,746,324	(7)	12,937,926	(4)	3,191,602	32.7
Georgia	5,463,105	(13)	6,478,216	(11)	1,015,111	18.6
Hawaii	964,691	(39)	1,108,229	(41)	143,538	14.9
Idaho	943,935	(41)	1,006,749	(42)	62,814	6.7
Illinois	11,426,518	(5)	11,430,602	(6)	4,084	0.0
Indiana	5,490,224	(12)	5,544,159	(14)	53,935	1.0
Iowa	2,913,808	(27)	2,776,755	(30)	-137,053	-4.7
Kansas	2,363,679	(32)	2,477,574	(32)	113,895	4.8
Kentucky	3,660,777	(23)	3,685,296	(23)	24,519	0.7
Louisiana	4,205,900	(19)	4,219,973	(21)	14,073	0.3
Maine	1,124,660	(38)	1,227,928	(38)	103,268	9.2
Maryland	4,216,975	(18)	4,781,468	(19)	564,493	13.4
Massachusetts	5,737,037	(11)	6,016,425	(13)	279,388	4.9
Michigan	9,262,078	(8)	9,295,297	(8)	33,219	0.4
Minnesota	4,075,970	(21)	4,375,099	(20)	299,129	7.3
Mississippi	2,520,638	(31)	2,573,216	(31)	52,578	2.1
Missouri	4,916,686	(15)	5,117,073	(15)	200,387	4.1
Montana	786,690	(44)	799,065	(44)	12,375	1.6
Nebraska	1,569,825	(35)	1,578,385	(36)	8,560	0.5
Nevada	800,493	(43)	1,201,833	(39)	401,340	50.1
New Hampshire	920,610	(42)	1,109,252	(40)	188,642	20.5
New Jersey	7,364,823	(9)	7,730,188	(9)	365,365	5.0
New Mexico	1,302,894	(37)	1,515,069	(37)	212,175	16.3
New York	17,558,072	(2)	17,990,455	(2)	432,383	2.5
North Carolina	5,881,766	(10)	6,628,637	(10)	746,871	12.7
North Dakota	652,717	(46)	638,800	(47)	-13,917	-2.1
Ohio	10,797,630	(6)	10,847,115	(7)	49,485	0.5
Oklahoma	3,025,290	(26)	3,145,585	(28)	120,295	4.0
Oregon	2,633,105	(30)	2,842,321	(29)	209,216	7.9
Pennsylvania	11,863,895	(4)	11,881,643	(5)	17,748	0.1
Rhode Island	947,154	(40)	1,003,464	(43)	56,310	5.9
South Carolina	3,121,820	(24)	3,486,703	(25)	364,883	11.7
South Dakota	690,768	(45)	696,004	(45)	5,236	0.8
Tennessee	4,591,120	(17)	4,877,185	(17)	286,065	6.2
Texas	14,229,191	(3)	16,986,510	(3)	2,757,319	19.4
Utah	1,461,037	(36)	1,722,850	(35)	261,813	17.9
Vermont	511,456	(48)	562,758	(48)	51,302	10.0
Virginia	5,346,818	(14)	6,187,358	(12)	840,540	15.7
Washington	4,132,156	(20)	4,866,692	(18)	734,536	17.8
West Virginia	1,949,644	(34)	1,793,477	(34)	-156,167	-8.0
Wisconsin	4,705,767	(16)	4,891,769	(16)	186,002	4.0
Wyoming	469,557	(49)	453,588	(50)	-15,969	-3.4

1. If the District of Columbia were included with the states, it would have ranked 47th in 1980 and 48th in 1990.
Source: U.S. Bureau of the Census, 1991.

State population growth For the first time in census history, three states accounted for over half the national population growth. The combined increases in California (6.1 million), Florida (3.2 million), and Texas (2.8 million) totalled 12.0 million or 54 percent of the 22.2 million national population increase.

California continued to grow at record levels during the 1980s, so that by 1990, 12.0 percent of all Americans lived there. In addition its numerical growth of 6.1 million and its 26 percent share of national population growth are unprecedented.

The five fastest-growing states during the 1980s were Nevada (50.1 percent), Alaska (36.9 percent), Arizona (34.8 percent), Florida (32.7 percent), and California (25.7 percent). Over the last 50 years Arizona, Florida, and Nevada have been on every such list while Alaska and California missed only once.

Only two states in the Northeast had growth rates higher than the national average: New Hampshire (20.5 percent) and Vermont (10.0 percent); none of the Midwest states did. Four states lost population during the 1980s: West Virginia (down 8.0 percent), Iowa (-4.7 percent), Wyoming (-3.4 percent), and North Dakota (-2.1 percent).

Urban and rural population growth Since the 1920 census, more than one half of all Americans have lived in an urban area, which can be loosely defined as a place of 2,500 or more

State Urban and Rural Percentage of Land Area and Population, 1980–90

State	Sq. miles	Land area, 1990 Urban	Rural	Population 1980 Urban	Rural	1990 Urban	Rural
U.S. total	3,536,278	2.5%	97.5%	73.7%	26.3%	75.2%	24.8%
Alabama	50,750.2	5.3	94.7	60.0	40.0	60.4	39.6
Alaska	570,373.5	0.1	99.9	64.5	35.5	67.5	32.5
Arizona	113,642.2	1.8	98.2	83.8	16.2	87.5	12.5
Arkansas	52,075.3	2.3	97.7	51.6	48.4	53.5	46.5
California	155,973.2	5.2	94.8	91.3	8.7	92.6	7.4
Colorado	103,728.8	1.3	98.7	80.6	19.4	82.4	17.6
Connecticut	4,845.4	25.9	74.1	78.8	21.2	79.1	20.9
Delaware	1,954.6	10.7	89.3	70.7	29.3	73.0	27.0
Dist. of Columbia	61.4	100.0	0.0	100.0	0.0	100.0	0.0
Florida	55,937.2	9.5	90.5	84.3	15.7	84.8	15.2
Georgia	57,918.7	4.9	95.1	62.3	37.7	63.2	36.8
Hawaii	6,423.4	10.0	90.0	86.5	13.5	89.0	11.0
Idaho	82,751.0	0.4	99.6	54.0	46.0	57.4	42.6
Illinois	55,593.3	5.5	94.5	83.0	17.0	84.6	15.4
Indiana	35,870.1	5.0	95.0	64.2	35.8	64.9	35.1
Iowa	55,874.9	2.0	98.0	58.6	41.4	60.6	39.4
Kansas	81,823.0	1.1	98.9	66.7	33.3	69.1	30.9
Kentucky	39,732.3	2.7	97.3	50.8	49.2	51.8	48.2
Louisiana	43,566.1	3.7	96.3	68.6	31.4	68.1	31.9
Maine	30,864.5	2.3	97.7	47.5	52.5	44.6	55.4
Maryland	9,774.6	16.1	83.9	80.3	19.7	81.3	18.7
Massachusetts	7,838.0	27.4	72.6	83.8	16.2	84.3	15.7
Michigan	56,809.2	4.7	95.3	70.7	29.3	70.5	29.5
Minnesota	79,616.5	2.3	97.7	66.8	33.2	69.9	30.1
Mississippi	46,913.7	2.4	97.6	47.3	52.7	47.1	52.9
Missouri	68,898.1	2.74	97.3	68.1	31.9	68.7	31.3
Montana	145,556.3	0.2	99.8	52.9	47.1	52.5	47.5
Nebraska	76,877.7	0.5	99.5	62.7	37.3	66.1	33.9
Nevada	109,805.5	0.9	99.1	85.3	14.7	88.3	11.7
New Hampshire	8,969.4	5.7	94.3	52.2	47.8	51.0	49.0
New Jersey	7,418.8	32.7	67.3	89.0	11.0	89.4	10.6
New Mexico	121,364.5	0.7	99.3	72.2	27.8	73.0	27.0
New York	47,223.8	7.2	92.8	84.6	15.4	84.3	15.7
North Carolina	48,718.1	4.6	95.4	48.0	52.0	50.4	49.6
North Dakota	68,994.3	0.2	99.8	48.8	51.2	53.3	46.7
Ohio	40,952.6	8.8	91.2	73.3	26.7	74.1	25.9
Oklahoma	68,678.5	2.7	97.3	67.3	32.7	67.7	32.3
Oregon	96,002.5	0.9	99.1	67.9	32.1	70.5	29.5
Pennsylvania	44,819.6	6.7	93.3	69.3	30.7	68.9	31.1
Rhode Island	1,045.0	28.5	71.5	87.0	13.0	86.0	14.0
South Carolina	30,111.1	4.7	95.3	54.1	45.9	54.6	45.4
South Dakota	75,896.0	0.3	99.7	46.4	53.6	50.0	50.0
Tennessee	41,219.5	5.7	94.3	60.4	39.6	60.9	39.1
Texas	261,914.3	2.9	97.1	79.6	20.4	80.3	19.7
Utah	82,168.1	0.9	99.1	84.4	15.6	87.0	13.0
Vermont	9,249.3	1.5	98.5	33.8	66.2	32.2	67.8
Virginia	39,597.8	5.5	94.5	66.0	34.0	69.4	30.6
Washington	66,658.1	2.7	97.3	73.6	26.4	76.4	23.6
West Virginia	24,086.6	1.6	98.4	36.2	63.8	36.1	63.9
Wisconsin	54,313.7	2.9	97.1	64.2	35.8	65.7	34.3
Wyoming	97,104.6	0.2	99.8	62.8	37.2	65.0	35.0

Source: U.S. Bureau of the Census, 1991.

inhabitants. During the 1980s, the population of urban areas grew by 20 million people, from 167.1 to 187.1 people, an increase of 12 percent. By 1990, the proportion of the U.S. population living in urban areas reached 75.2 percent, up from 73.7 percent in 1980. California had the higest proportion of urban population, at 92.6 percent. In comparison, the country's rural population grew by 3.6 percent, from 59.5 million in 1980 to 61.7 million in 1990. Only 11 states, however, had increased percentages of rural population in the 1980s (see the accompanying table) even though 32 states recorded an increase in the number of rural residents. Vermont had the highest rural percentage of population: 67.8 percent.

Population growth in metropolitan areas

The 1990 census revealed that 77.5 percent of all U.S. residents (192,725,741) lived in one of the 284 metropolitan areas in the U.S., an increase of 11.6 percent or more than 20 million. The number of 1 million-plus metropolitan areas rose from 35 to 39 and the population in these rose to 124.8 million or 50.2 percent of the total U.S. population. About 90 percent of population growth in the 1980s took place in metropolitan areas.

A total of 46 metropolitan areas grew by more than 25 percent (Florida dominated the list with nine of the 11 top areas). The Los Angeles-Anaheim-Riverside metropolitan area gained about 3 278million people in the eighties, by far the largest

U.S. Population by State, 1790–1990

State	1790	1800	1810	1820	1830	1840	1850
Total U.S.	3,929,214	5,308,483	7,239,881	9,638,453	12,860,702	17,063,353	23,191,876
Alabama	—	1,250	9,046	127,901	309,527	590,756	771,623
Alaska	—	—	—	—	—	—	—
Arizona	—	—	—	—	—	—	—
Arkansas	—	—	1,062	14,273	30,388	97,574	209,897
California	—	—	—	—	—	—	92,597
Colorado	—	—	—	—	—	—	—
Connecticut	237,946	251,002	261,942	275,248	297,675	309,978	370,792
Delaware	59,096	64,273	72,674	72,749	76,748	78,085	91,532
District of Columbia	—	8,144	15,471	23,336	30,261	33,745	51,687
Florida	—	—	—	—	34,730	54,477	87,445
Georgia	82,548	162,686	252,433	340,989	516,823	691,392	906,185
Hawaii	—	—	—	—	—	—	—
Idaho	—	—	—	—	—	—	—
Illinois	—	—	12,282	55,211	157,445	476,183	851,470
Indiana	—	5,641	24,520	147,178	343,031	685,866	988,416
Iowa	—	—	—	—	—	43,112	192,214
Kansas	—	—	—	—	—	—	—
Kentucky	73,677	220,955	406,511	564,317	687,917	779,828	982,405
Louisiana	—	—	76,556	153,407	215,739	352,411	517,762
Maine	96,540	151,719	228,705	298,335	399,455	501,793	583,169
Maryland	319,728	341,548	380,546	407,350	447,040	470,019	583,034
Massachusetts	378,787	422,845	472,040	523,287	610,408	737,699	994,514
Michigan	—	—	4,762	8,896	31,369	212,267	397,654
Minnesota	—	—	—	—	—	—	6,077
Mississippi	—	7,600	31,306	75,448	136,621	375,651	606,526
Missouri	—	—	19,783	66,586	140,455	383,702	682,044
Montana	—	—	—	—	—	—	—
Nebraska	—	—	—	—	—	—	—
Nevada	—	—	—	—	—	—	—
New Hampshire	141,885	183,858	214,460	244,161	269,328	284,574	317,976
New Jersey	184,139	211,149	245,562	277,575	320,823	373,306	489,555
New Mexico	—	—	—	—	—	—	61,547
New York	340,120	589,051	959,049	1,372,812	1,918,608	2,428,921	3,097,394
North Carolina	393,751	478,103	555,500	638,829	737,987	753,419	869,039
North Dakota	—	—	—	—	—	—	—
Ohio	—	45,365	230,760	581,434	937,903	1,519,467	1,980,329
Oklahoma	—	—	—	—	—	—	—
Oregon	—	—	—	—	—	—	12,093
Pennsylvania	434,373	602,365	810,091	1,049,458	1,348,233	1,724,033	2,311,786
Rhode Island	68,825	69,122	76,931	83,059	97,199	108,830	147,545
South Carolina	249,073	345,591	415,115	502,741	581,185	594,398	668,507
South Dakota	—	—	—	—	—	—	—
Tennessee	35,691	105,602	261,727	422,832	681,904	829,210	1,002,717
Texas	—	—	—	—	—	—	212,592
Utah	—	—	—	—	—	—	11,380
Vermont	85,425	154,465	217,895	235,981	280,652	291,948	314,120
Virginia[2]	747,610	880,200	974,600	1,065,366	1,211,405	1,239,797	1,421,661
Washington	—	—	—	—	—	—	1,201
West Virginia	—	—	—	—	—	—	—
Wisconsin	—	—	—	—	—	30,945	305,391
Wyoming	—	—	—	—	—	—	—

numerical increase of any area (in fact the increase alone was greater than the total population of 272 metropolitan areas).

The population living outside metropolitan areas totalled 55,984,132, an increase of only 2.1 million (3.9 percent) over the decade.

Race and Hispanic origin Between 1980 and 1990 the number of whites in the U.S. population increased from 188.4 million to 199.7 million, a growth rate of 6.0 percent, significantly below the 9.8 percent national rate. Since 1970, the white population of the U.S. has de-

creased from 87.5 percent of the total to 80.3 percent.

The black population increased by 13.2 percent during the 1980s, from 26.5 million to 29.09 million, and now makes up 12.1 percent of the total population, up from 11.1 percent in 1970.

The Hispanic population continued its dramatic growth—53 percent—during the last census decade, as their numbers increased from 14.6 million in 1980 to 22.4 million in 1990. Hispanics now make up 9.0 percent of the U.S. population, up from an estimated 4.5 percent in 1970, and 6.4 percent in 1980.

State	1860	1870	1880	1890	1900	1910	1920
Total U.S.	31,443,321	38,558,371	50,189,209	62,979,766	76,212,168	92,228,496	106,021,537
Alabama	964,201	996,992	1,262,505	1,513,401	1,828,697	2,138,093	2,348,174
Alaska	—	—	33,426	32,052	63,592	64,356	55,036
Arizona	—	9,658	40,440	88,243	122,931	204,354	334,162
Arkansas	435,450	484,471	802,525	1,128,211	1,311,564	1,574,449	1,752,204
California	379,994	560,247	864,694	1,213,396	1,485,053	2,377,549	3,426,861
Colorado	34,277	39,864	194,327	413,249	539,700	799,024	939,629
Connecticut	460,147	537,454	622,700	746,258	908,420	1,114,756	1,380,631
Delaware	112,216	125,015	146,608	168,493	184,735	202,322	223,003
District of Columbia	75,080	131,700	177,624	230,392	278,718	331,069	437,571
Florida	140,424	187,748	269,493	391,422	528,542	752,619	968,470
Georgia	1,057,286	1,184,109	1,542,180	1,837,353	2,216,331	2,609,121	2,895,832
Hawaii	—	—	—	—	154,001	191,874	255,881
Idaho	—	14,999	32,610	88,548	161,772	325,594	431,866
Illinois	1,711,951	2,539,891	3,077,871	3,826,352	4,821,550	5,638,591	6,485,280
Indiana	1,350,428	1,680,637	1,978,301	2,192,404	2,516,462	2,700,876	2,930,390
Iowa	674,913	1,194,020	1,624,615	1,912,297	2,231,853	2,224,771	2,404,021
Kansas	107,206	364,399	996,096	1,428,108	1,470,495	1,690,949	1,769,257
Kentucky	1,155,684	1,321,011	1,648,690	1,858,635	2,147,174	2,289,905	2,416,630
Louisiana	708,002	726,915	939,946	1,118,588	1,381,625	1,656,388	1,798,509
Maine	628,279	626,915	648,936	661,086	694,466	742,371	768,014
Maryland	687,049	780,894	934,943	1,042,390	1,188,044	1,295,346	1,449,661
Massachusetts	1,231,066	1,457,351	1,783,085	2,238,947	2,805,346	3,366,416	3,852,356
Michigan	749,113	1,184,059	1,636,937	2,093,890	2,420,982	2,810,173	3,668,412
Minnesota	172,023	439,706	780,773	1,310,283	1,751,394	2,075,708	2,387,125
Mississippi	791,305	827,922	1,131,597	1,289,600	1,551,270	1,797,114	1,790,618
Missouri	1,182,012	1,721,295	2,168,380	2,679,185	3,106,665	3,293,335	3,404,055
Montana	—	20,595	39,159	142,924	243,329	376,053	548,889
Nebraska	28,841	122,993	452,402	1,062,656	1,066,300	1,192,214	1,296,372
Nevada	6,857	42,491	62,266	47,355	42,335	81,875	77,407
New Hampshire	326,073	318,300	346,991	376,530	411,588	430,572	443,083
New Jersey	672,035	906,096	1,131,116	1,444,933	1,883,669	2,537,167	3,155,900
New Mexico	93,516	91,874	119,565	160,282	195,310	327,301	360,350
New York	3,880,735	4,382,759	5,082,871	6,003,174	7,268,894	9,113,614	10,385,227
North Carolina	992,622	1,071,361	1,399,750	1,617,949	1,893,810	2,206,287	2,559,123
North Dakota	—	2,405	36,909	190,983	319,146	577,056	646,872
Ohio	2,339,511	2,665,260	3,198,062	3,672,329	4,157,545	4,767,121	5,759,394
Oklahoma	—	—	—	258,657	790,371	1,657,155	2,028,283
Oregon	52,465	90,923	174,768	317,704	413,536	672,765	783,389
Pennsylvania	2,906,215	3,521,951	4,282,891	5,258,113	6,302,115	7,665,111	8,720,017
Rhode Island	174,620	217,353	276,531	345,506	428,556	542,610	604,397
South Carolina	703,708	705,606	995,577	1,151,149	1,340,316	1,515,400	1,683,724
South Dakota	4,837	11,776	98,268	348,600	401,570	583,888	636,547
Tennessee	1,109,801	1,258,520	1,542,359	1,767,518	2,020,616	2,184,789	2,337,885
Texas	604,215	818,579	1,591,749	2,235,527	3,048,710	3,896,542	4,663,228
Utah	40,273	86,786	143,963	210,779	276,749	373,351	449,396
Vermont	315,098	330,551	332,286	332,422	343,641	355,956	352,428
Virginia[2]	1,596,318	1,225,163	1,512,565	1,655,980	1,854,184	2,061,612	2,309,187
Washington	11,594	23,955	75,116	357,232	518,103	1,141,990	1,356,621
West Virginia	—	442,014	618,457	762,794	958,800	1,221,119	1,463,701
Wisconsin	775,881	1,054,670	1,315,497	1,693,330	2,069,042	2,333,860	2,632,067
Wyoming	—	9,118	20,789	62,555	92,531	145,965	194,402

The fastest-growing population group in the U.S. is the Census Bureau category Asian or Pacific Islander. With literally millions of Asian immigrants coming to the U.S., the number in this category has grown by an extraordinary 108 percent in only one decade, from 3.5 million to 7.3 million. While the Asian or Pacific Islander group made up just under 3 percent of the total U.S. population in 1990, this was about twice what it was in 1980 (1.5 percent).

Population Growth and Change, 1990–98

Several significant changes in the composition of the U.S. population have occurred since the 1990 census. Primary among them is the continuing migration of Americans away from the Northeastern states and into the South and West. California (population 32.3 million) remained the most populous state, while Texas (19.8 million) supplanted New York (18.2 million) as the second biggest state. The population of the entire northeastern United States grew by fewer than 1 million people—less than 2 percent—between 1990 and 1998. Meanwhile, the South grew by nearly 10 million people (11.6 percent) over the same period, and the West experienced a population increase of 7.4 million.(14.1 percent).

Another startling development is the growth of the minority population. Between 1990 and 1997, the black population increased by 4.0 million, more

State	1930	1940	1950	1960	1970	1980[1]	1990
Total U.S.	123,202,624	132,164,569	151,325,798	179,323,175	203,302,031	226,542,203	248,709,873
Alabama	2,646,248	2,832,961	3,061,743	3,266,740	3,444,354	3,894,025	4,040,587
Alaska	59,278	72,524	128,643	226,167	302,583	401,851	550,043
Arizona	435,573	499.261	749,587	1,302,161	1,775,399	2,716,546	3,665,228
Arkansas	1,854,482	1,949,387	1,909,511	1,786,272	1,923,322	2,286,357	2,350,725
California	5,677,251	6,907,387	10,586,223	15,717,204	19,971,069	23,667,764	29,760,021
Colorado	1,035,791	1,123,296	1,325,089	1,753,947	2,209,596	2,889,735	3,294,394
Connecticut	1,606,903	1,709,242	2,007,280	2,535,234	3,032,217	3,107,564	3,287,116
Delaware	238,380	266,505	318,085	446,292	548,104	594,338	666,168
District of Columbia	486,869	663,091	802,178	763,956	756,668	638,432	606,900
Florida	1,468,211	1,897,414	2,771,305	4,951,560	6,791,418	9,746,961	12,937,926
Georgia	2,908,506	3,123,723	3,444,578	3,943,116	4,587,930	5,462,982	6,478,216
Hawaii	368,300	422,770	499,794	632,772	769,913	964,691	1,108,229
Idaho	445,032	524,873	588,637	667,191	713,015	944,127	1,006,749
Illinois	7,630,654	7,897,241	8,712,176	10,081,158	11,110,285	11,427,409	11,430,602
Indiana	3,238,503	3,427,796	3,934,224	4,662,498	5,195,392	5,490,214	5,544,159
Iowa	2,470,939	2,538,268	2,621,073	2,757,537	2,825,368	2,913,808	2,776,755
Kansas	1,880,999	1,801,028	1,905,299	2,178,611	2,249,071	2,364,236	2,477,574
Kentucky	2,614,589	2,845,627	2,944,806	3,038,156	3,220,711	3,660,324	3,685,296
Louisiana	2,101,593	2,363,880	2,683,516	3,257,022	3,644,637	4,206,116	4,219,973
Maine	797,423	847,226	913,774	969,265	993,722	1,125,043	1,227,928
Maryland	1,631,526	1,821,244	2,343,001	3,100,689	3,923,897	4,216,933	4,781,468
Massachusetts	4,249,614	4,316,721	4,690,514	5,148,578	5,689,170	5,737,093	6,016,425
Michigan	4,842,325	5,256,106	6,371,766	7,823,194	8,881,826	9,262,044	9,295,297
Minnesota	2,563,953	2,792,300	2,982,483	3,413,864	3,806,103	4,075,970	4,375,099
Mississippi	2,009,821	2,183,796	2,178,914	2,178,141	2,216,994	2,520,770	2,573,216
Missouri	3,629,367	3,784,664	3,954,653	4,319,813	4,677,623	4,916,762	5,117,073
Montana	537,606	559,456	591,024	674,767	694,409	786,690	799,065
Nebraska	1,377,963	1,315,834	1,325,510	1,411,330	1,485,333	1,569,825	1,578,385
Nevada	91,058	110,247	160,083	285,278	488,738	800,508	1,201,833
New Hampshire	465,293	491,524	533,242	606,921	737,681	920,610	1,109,252
New Jersey	4,041,334	4,160,165	4,835,329	6,066,782	7,171,112	7,365,011	7,730,188
New Mexico	423,317	531,818	681,187	951,023	1,017,055	1,303,302	1,515,069
New York	12,588,066	13,479,142	14,830,192	16,782,304	18,241,391	17,558,165	17,990,455
North Carolina	3,170,276	3,571,623	4,061,929	4,556,155	5,084,411	5,880,095	6,628,637
North Dakota	680,845	641,935	619,636	632,446	617,792	652,717	638,800
Ohio	6,646,697	6,907,612	7,946,627	9,706,397	10,657,423	10,797,603	10,847,115
Oklahoma	2,396,040	2,336,434	2,233,351	2,328,284	2,559,463	3,025,487	3,145,585
Oregon	953,786	1,089,684	1,521,341	1,768,687	2,091,533	2,633,156	2,842,321
Pennsylvania	9,631,350	9,900,180	10,498,012	11,319,366	11,800,766	11,864,720	11,881,643
Rhode Island	687,497	713,346	791,896	859,488	949,723	947,154	1,003,464
South Carolina	1,738,765	1,899,804	2,117,027	2,382,594	2,590,713	3,120,729	3,486,703
South Dakota	692,849	642,961	652,740	680,514	666,257	690,768	696,004
Tennessee	2,616,556	2,915,841	3,291,718	3,567,089	3,926,018	4,591,023	4,877,185
Texas	5,824,715	6,414,824	7,711,194	9,579,677	11,198,655	14,225,513	16,986,510
Utah	507,847	550,310	688,862	890,627	1,059,273	1,461,037	1,722,850
Vermont	359,611	359,231	377,747	389,881	444,732	511,456	562,758
Virginia	2,421,851	2,677,773	3,318,680	3,966,949	4,651,448	5,346,797	6,187,358
Washington	1,563,396	1,736,191	2,378,963	2,853,214	3,413,244	4,132,353	4,866,692
West Virginia	1,729,205	1,901,974	2,005,552	1,860,421	1,744,237	1,950,186	1,793,477
Wisconsin	2,939,006	3,137,587	3,434,575	3,951,777	4,417,821	4,705,642	4,891,769
Wyoming	225,565	250,742	290,529	330,066	332,416	469,557	453,588

Note: Excludes military and overseas population. Wherever possible, 1980 state boundaries are used in calculating populations of regions, areas, and territories prior to their statehoods. 1. 1980 figures are revised estimates issued by the Census Bureau in 1987. 2. The figures for Virginia through 1860 are from the 1960 census; in the 1980 summary, the Census Bureau gave separate figures for West Virginia between 1790 and 1860, even though it did not become a state until 1863. Since the result diminishes Virginia's population by over 300,000 in 1850 and 1860, a crucial period, we decided to keep the earlier breakdowns. Sources: U.S. Bureau of the Census, 1980 Census of Population: U.S. Summary, Number of Inhabitants (1981), and Release (1990).

than during the entire previous decade. Asian and Pacific Islanders remain the fastest-growing minority group, increasing by 37.9 percent, or 2.8 million, between 1990 and 1997. Hispanics experienced the largest numerical growth: 7.0 million, a 31.3 percent increase between 1990 and 1997. The white population, meanwhile, increased by 21.6 million over the same period, an increase of just 10.8 percent.

The 2000 Census In an attempt to improve the accuracy of the census—the 1990 census failed to count 8.4 million people and counted 4.4 million people twice or in the wrong place— the Census Bureau sought to use statistical sampling methods to enumerate the hardest-to-count 10 percent of the population. The Bureau had also planned to compare its head count with a follow-up survey of 750,000 households, which would point out any inaccuracies.

But because Census numbers are used to apportion Congressional districts and because blacks and Hispanics (who tend to vote Democratic) made up a significant portion of the 1990 undercount, Republicans in Congress challenged the plan, fearing that an accurate count of the country's minority population would erode GOP numbers. In August, 1998, a Federal court struck down the use of sampling, saying it violated 1957

and 1976 Federal laws governing the Census, and in July 1999, the Supreme Court rejected the Clinton Administration's appeal of the decision.

As a result, the 2000 Census Bureau will have to spend an additional $1.7 billion (over the $5 billion budgeted) to count each and every person, even those who don't want to cooperate with Census pollsters. Because of the additional cost involved in doing this, the Census Bureau said it would have to cut the size of its follow-up survey to 300,000 households. Because children made up more than half of the 1990 undercount, the Bureau also launched a "Census in the Schools" program to alert children and their parents about the importance of participating in the Census. The program will target approximately 43,000 schools in areas with low Census response rates, especially those with large numbers of American Indian students and children of migrant farm workers.

Population Growth by Region, 1790–2000 (in thousands)

Year	Northeast	Midwest[1]	South[2]	West
1790	1,968	N.A.	1,961	N.A.
1800	2,636	51	2,622	N.A.
1810	3,487	292	3,461	N.A.
1820	4,360	859	4,419	N.A.
1830	5,542	1,610	5,708	N.A.
1840	6,761	3,352	6,951	N.A.
1850	8,627	5,404	8,983	179
1860	10,594	9,097	11,133	619
1870	12,299	12,981	12,288	991
1880	14,507	17,364	16,517	1,801
1890	17,407	22,410	20,028	3,134
1900	21,047	26,333	24,524	4,309
1910	25,869	29,889	29,389	7,082
1920	29,662	34,020	33,126	9,214
1930	34,427	38,594	37,858	12,324
1940	35,977	40,143	41,666	14,379
1950	39,478	44,461	47,197	20,190
1960	44,678	51,619	54,973	28,053
1970	49,041	56,572	62,795	34,804
1980	49,135	58,866	75,372	43,172
1990	50,809	59,669	85,446	52,786
2000[3]	51,800	59,600	96,900	59,400

1. Called North Central prior to 1980. 2. Includes black slave population through 1860. 3. Projections. **Source:** U.S. Bureau of Census, *The Statistical History of the U.S.* (1976); *The Statistical Abstract of the United States* (annual).

U.S. Population by Region, 1990–98

Region	1990 Census	July 1, 1998
United States	**248,765,170**	**270,298,524**
Northeast	**50,828,313**	**51,721,625**
New England	13,206,943	13,429,862
Middle Atlantic	37,621,370	38,291,763
Midwest	**59,669,135**	**62,889,382**
East North Central	42,008,929	44,194,756
West North Central	17,660,206	18,694,626
South	**85,455,793**	**95,429,486**
South Atlantic	43,571,473	48,944,678
East South Central	15,179,959	16,471,211
West South Central	26,704,361	30,013,597
West	**52,811,929**	**60,258,031**
Mountain	13,658,794	16,813,233
Pacific	39,153,135	43,444,798

Source: U.S. Census Bureau.

U.S. Population, Population Density, and Area of Residence, 1790–1990

Year	Total population	Percent increase	Population per square mile	Percent urban	Percent rural
1790	3,929,214	N.A.	4.5	5.1%	94.9%
1800	5,308,483	35.1%	6.1	6.1	93.9
1810	7,239,881	36.4	4.3	7.3	92.7
1820	9,638,453	33.1	5.5	7.2	92.8
1830	12,866,020	33.5	7.4	8.8	91.2
1840	17,069,453	32.7	9.8	10.8	89.2
1850	23,191,876	35.9	7.9	15.3	84.7
1860	31,443,321	35.6	10.6	19.8	80.2
1870	39,818,449	26.6	13.4	25.7	74.3
1880	50,155,783	26.0	16.9	28.2	71.8
1890	62,947,714	25.5	21.2	35.1	64.9
1900	75,994,575	20.7	25.6	39.6	60.4
1910	91,972,266	21.0	31.0	45.6	54.4
1920	105,710,620	14.9	35.6	51.2	48.8
1930	122,775,046	16.1	41.2	56.1	43.9
1940	131,669,275	7.2	44.2	56.5	43.5
1950	150,697,361	14.5	50.7	64.0	36.0
1960	179,323,175	18.5	50.6	69.9	30.1
1970	203,302,031	13.4	57.4	73.5	26.5
1980	226,545,805	11.4	64.0	73.7	26.3
1990	248,709,873	9.8	70.3	75.2	24.8

Source: U.S. Bureau of Census, *The Statistical History of the U.S.* (1976); *The Statistical Abstract of the United States* (annual).

POPULATION BY RACE AND HISPANIC ORIGIN

It is important to note that the Census Bureau's classification of the population by race, in its words, "reflects common usage not an attempt to define biological stock." Only since 1960, however, have the Census Bureau's race figures been based on self-identification.

The people of the United States are predominantly white, accounting for an estimated 84.1 percent of the total population in 1990. This dominance has been true since colonial days although even then the indigenous peoples and the African slaves were significant racial minorities. In fact as slave labor became essential to the Southern economy so many slaves were brought here that just before the Civil War blacks constituted 15 percent of the U.S. population.

After the war, the proportion of whites rapidly increased as millions of immigrants from northern Europe settled throughout the country. The relentless movement of the population westward deprived the Native Americans of their lands and—with the assistance of several bloody wars—helped to reduce their numbers to a small fraction (less than 100,000 perhaps) of what they were estimated to have been only a century before.

The black population, with 9-10 percent of the total, remained the only significant minority group until the 1960s, when a surge of new immigrants from Puerto Rico, Mexico, and Cuba made the Hispanic presence felt. So rapid and strong an impression did these groups make that the Census Bureau created a new population category,

"Hispanic Origin." Since some Hispanics are black, some white, and still others Indian, this designation has nothing to do with race.

During the 1970s and 1980s, the arrival of several million Asians again caused a noticeable change in the composition of the population. The 1990 census was the first one to include a separate category for Asians and Pacific Islanders; in previous years, they had been included together with American Indians, Aleuts, and Eskimos in the "other races" grouping.

In 1997, persons of more than one ethnicity lobbied the Census Bureau to create a "mixed race" grouping so they would not have to choose between their ethnicities when identifying themselves. But the Census Bureau refused to add the category.

▶ THE BLACK POPULATION

Ever since the Founding Fathers reached their famous "compromise" declaring a slave the equivalent of three-fifths of a person, the black population has had a less-than-equal standing in relation to the majority of Americans. Over the last two centuries, the struggle for equality, even in a nation pledged to that ideal, has proven long, hard, and in many cases, intractable, as so many contemporary facts and figures in this book make all too evident. From higher infant mortality rates and poverty rates to lower life expectancy and family income levels, the black population continues to suffer the effects of two centuries of slavery and one of institutionalized segregation.

In May, 1999, the black population numbered 34.8 million, an estimated 12.8 percent of all Americans, by far the nation's largest minority group. The black population has grown by more than 30 percent since 1980 and 14 percent since 1990. By contrast, the non-Hispanic white population has increased only 4.1 percent since 1990.

Resident Population of the U.S., by Race and Hispanic Origin, 1980-98

Race/Hispanic origin[1]	1980		1990		1998[2]	
	Number	Percent	Number	Percent	Number	Percent
Total population	226,545,805	100.0%	248,709,873	100.0%	270,299,000	100.0%
White	188,371,622	83.1	199,686,070	80.3	223,001,000	82.5
Black	26,495,025	11.7	29,986,060	12.1	34,431,000	12.7
American Indian, Eskimo, or Aleut	1,420,400	0.6	1,959,234	0.8	2,360,000	0.9
Asian or Pacific Islander	3,500,439	1.5	7,273,662	2.9	10,507,000	3.9
Other Race	6,758,319	3.0	9,804,847	3.9	N.A.	N.A.
Hispanic origin[1]	14,608,673	6.4	22,354,059	9.0	30,250,000	11.2

Note: 1980 and 1990 figures are from the decennial censuses; 1998 figures are estimated by the U.S. Census Bureau. 1. Persons of Hispanic origin may be of any race. 2. Numbers rounded at source. **Source:** U.S. Bureau of the Census.

Change in the Resident Population, by Race and Hispanic Origin, 1980-98

Race/Hispanic origin[1]	Change, 1980-90		Change, 1990-98	
	Number	Percent	Number	Percent
Total population	22,164,068	9.8%	21,589,127	7.99%
White	11,314,448	6.0	23,314,930	10.46
Black	3,491,035	13.2	4,444,940	12.91
American Indian, Eskimo, or Aleut	538,834	37.9	400,766	16.98
Asian or Pacific Islander	3,773,223	107.8	3,233,338	30.77
Other Race	3,046,528	45.1	N.A.	N.A.
Hispanic origin	7,745,386	53.0	7,895,941	26.10

Note: 1980 and 1990 figures are from the decennial censuses; 1998 figures are estimated by the U.S. Census Bureau. 1. Persons of Hispanic origin may be of any race. **Source:** U.S. Bureau of the Census.

Resident Population of States by Race and Hispanic Origin: July 1, 1997

State	Total	White	Black	American Indian, Eskimo, or Aleut	Asian or Pacific Islander	Hispanic origin
United States	267,636,061	221,334,048	33,947,084	2,322,044	10,032,885	29,347,865
Alabama	4,319,154	3,155,849	1,120,315	15,238	27,752	39,304
Alaska	609,311	461,688	23,792	97,098	26,733	23,325
Arizona	4,554,966	4,045,974	160,858	255,463	92,671	998,623
Arkansas	2,522,819	2,085,753	405,799	13,421	17,846	45,134
California	32,268,301	25,788,064	2,396,532	306,690	3,777,015	9,941,014
Colorado	3,892,644	3,598,367	168,411	36,012	89,854	556,074
Connecticut	3,269,858	2,885,863	299,760	7,940	76,295	259,159
Delaware	731,581	574,708	140,155	2,445	14,273	24,069
District of Columbia	528,964	178,837	332,897	1,648	15,582	37,898
Florida	14,653,945	12,093,507	2,252,679	54,641	253,118	2,105,689
Georgia	7,486,242	5,205,515	2,126,126	17,493	137,108	207,053
Hawaii	1,186,602	395,846	35,401	6,607	748,748	94,918
Idaho	1,210,232	1,174,044	6,628	16,320	13,240	85,997
Illinois	11,895,849	9,671,367	1,815,051	26,625	382,806	1,182,964
Indiana	5,864,108	5,312,849	483,558	14,340	53,361	136,568
Iowa	2,852,423	2,752,500	55,634	8,511	35,778	53,092
Kansas	2,594,840	2,374,843	152,781	23,188	44,028	132,623
Kentucky	3,908,124	3,593,455	283,152	5,970	25,547	30,123
Louisiana	4,351,769	2,882,333	1,396,453	19,487	53,496	113,193
Maine	1,242,051	1,221,801	6,064	5,653	8,533	8,533
Maryland	5,094,289	3,487,378	1,396,830	15,435	194,646	179,379
Massachusetts	6,117,520	5,509,638	383,601	14,410	209,871	358,521
Michigan	9,773,892	8,171,565	1,391,812	59,678	150,837	253,834
Minnesota	4,685,549	4,377,363	133,143	57,130	117,913	80,707
Mississippi	2,730,501	1,708,765	993,372	9,907	18,457	21,654
Missouri	5,402,058	4,717,216	606,604	20,522	57,716	82,167
Montana	878,810	815,779	3,210	54,695	5,126	15,137
Nebraska	1,656,870	1,554,800	66,193	14,841	21,036	67,850
Nevada	1,676,809	1,448,210	125,346	29,642	73,611	253,329
New Hampshire	1,172,709	1,148,802	8,373	2,243	13,291	16,864
New Jersey	8,052,849	6,437,573	1,170,042	21,496	423,738	958,885
New Mexico	1,729,751	1,503,406	44,491	158,036	23,818	692,570
New York	18,137,226	13,901,663	3,208,344	74,483	952,736	2,570,382
North Carolina	7,425,183	5,594,769	1,642,980	95,398	92,036	149,390
North Dakota	640,883	602,165	4,029	29,529	5,160	6,810
Ohio	11,186,331	9,762,897	1,277,566	22,467	123,401	172,744
Oklahoma	3,317,091	2,757,290	257,007	260,029	42,765	122,066
Oregon	3,243,487	3,040,327	58,202	44,451	100,507	189,809
Pennsylvania	12,019,661	10,647,834	1,164,128	17,158	190,541	302,317
Rhode Island	987,429	913,240	47,459	4,811	21,919	61,483
South Carolina	3,760,181	2,588,237	1,130,354	9,157	32,433	46,273
South Dakota	737,973	670,128	5,009	58,218	4,618	7,951
Tennessee	5,368,198	4,422,259	884,477	12,005	49,457	56,614
Texas	19,439,337	16,447,858	2,374,164	93,343	523,972	5,722,535
Utah	2,059,148	1,961,673	17,543	29,069	50,863	133,360
Vermont	588,978	579,486	3,102	1,536	4,854	5,151
Virginia	6,733,996	5,138,839	1,343,941	18,286	232,930	238,863
Washington	5,610,362	5,002,696	196,047	100,309	311,310	339,618
West Virginia	1,815,787	1,747,164	57,599	2,493	8,531	10,147
Wisconsin	5,169,677	4,760,505	286,115	45,967	77,090	127,702
Wyoming	479,743	461,360	3,955	10,510	3,918	28,400

1. Persons of Hispanic origin may be of any race. **Source:** U.S. Bureau of the Census.

The black population is also significantly younger than the white population. In 1999, the median age for blacks was 30.1, eight years younger than the non-Hispanic white population's median age of 38.0. Other indications of the youthful nature of the black population are the proportion over 65 (only 8 percent in 1990, compared with 14 percent for whites) and the percentage under 18 (32 percent to 25 percent).

Most black people (55.2 percent) continue to live in the South, where they made up 20.2 percent of the population in 1998. Blacks constituted 12.2 percent of the population in the Northeast, 10.0 percent in the Midwest, and just 4.9 percent in the West in 1998. The majority of blacks (54.5 percent) lived in central cities of metropolitan areas, more than twice the population for non-Hispanic whites (22.0 percent). The ratios for the suburbs were just the opposite: 55.4 percent of non-Hispanic whites live in suburban areas, compared to just 31.0 percent of blacks.

Significant differences between the races also exist in other demographic categories, most notably in the high rates of both divorce and single-motherhood for blacks. In 1998, more black families were headed by a single woman than by a married couple. Between 1970 and 1998, the percentage of black families headed by a female with no husband present jumped from 33.0 percent to 46.7 percent. Meanwhile, the percentage of black married-couple families declined from 64.3 percent in 1970 to 46.6 percent in 1998. A mere 562,000 black families (6.7 percent) were headed by a man with no wife present. (See also "The U.S. Economy" for information about black employment, income, wealth and poverty.)

Black Population of the U.S., 1790–1999

Year	Number ('000s)	Percent of total population
1790	757	19.3%
1800	1,002	18.9
1850	3,639	15.7
1960	4,442	14.1
1870	4,880	12.7
1880	6,581	13.1
1890	7,489	11.9
1900	8,834	11.6
1910	9,828	10.7
1920	10,463	9.9
1930	11,891	9.7
1940	12,866	9.8
1950	15,042	10.0
1960[1]	18,872	10.5
1970	22,581	11.1
1980	26,683	11.8
1985	28,994	12.1
1990	30,486	12.3
1995	33,098	12.6
1996	33,518	12.6
1997	33,973	12.7
1998	34,431	12.7
1999	34,817	12.8

Note: Decennial census figures are as of April 1. Figures for 1995-98 are as of July 1. Figure for 1999 is for May 1. 1. Includes Alaska and Hawaii for first time. Source: U.S. Bureau of the Census, Population Estimates Program. www.census.gov.

Ten States With Largest Black Populations, 1997

Rank, State	Black population	Percent of total population
1. New York	3,208,344	17.69%
2. California	2,396,532	7.43
3. Texas	2,374,164	12.21
4. Florida	2,252,679	15.37
5. Georgia	2,126,126	28.40
6. Illinois	1,815,051	15.26
7. North Carolina	1,642,980	22.13
8. Maryland	1,396,830	27.42
9. Louisiana	1,396,453	32.09
10. Michigan	1,391,812	14.24

Source: U.S. Bureau of the Census.

Twenty U.S. Cities with Largest Black Populations, 1990

Black rank	Overall rank	City, State	Total population (000s)	Black population (000s)	Percent black
1	1	New York, N.Y.	7,322.6	2,102.5	29%
2	3	Chicago, Ill.	2,783.7	1,087.7	39
3	7	Detroit, Mich.	1,028.0	777.9	76
4	5	Philadelphia, Pa.	1,585.6	631.9	40
5	2	Los Angeles, Calif.	3,485.4	487.7	14
6	4	Houston, Tex.	1,630.6	458.0	28
7	13	Baltimore, Md.	736.0	435.8	59
8	19	Washington, D.C.	606.9	399.6	66
9	18	Memphis, Tenn.	610.3	334.7	55
10	25	New Orleans, La.	496.9	307.7	62
11	8	Dallas, Tex.	1,006.9	297.0	30
12	36	Atlanta, Ga.	394.0	264.3	67
13	24	Cleveland, Ohio	505.6	235.4	47
14	17	Milwaukee, Wis.	628.1	191.3	31
15	34	St. Louis, Mo.	396.7	188.4	48
16	60	Birmingham, Ala.	266.0	168.3	63
17	12	Indianapolis, Ind.	742.0	165.6	22
18	15	Jacksonville, Fla.	673.0	163.9	24
19	39	Oakland, Calif.	372.2	163.3	44
20	56	Newark, N.J.	275.2	160.9	59

Source: Populations Reference Bureau, "African Americans in the 1990s" (1991), based on unpublished data from 1990 census.

Black Population of Metropolitan Areas, 1980–90

Rank/Metropolitan area	1980	1990	Population change, 1980–90 Number	Percent
1. New York-Northern New Jersey-Long Island, N.Y.-N.J.-Conn. CMSA	2,825,102	3,289,465	464,363	16.4%
2. Chicago-Gary-Lake County, Ill.-Ind.-Wis. CMSA	1,557,287	1,547,725	-9,562	-0.6
3. Los Angeles-Anaheim-Riverside, Calif. CMSA	1,059,124	1,229,809	170,685	16.1
4. Philadelphia-Wilmington-Trenton, Pa.-N.J.-Del.-Md. CMSA	1,032,882	1,100,347	67,465	6.5
5. Washington, D.C.-Md.-Va. MSA	870,657	1,041,934	171,277	19.7
6. Detroit-Ann Arbor, Mich. CMSA	921,168	975,199	54,031	5.9
7. Atlanta, Ga. MSA	525,676	736,153	210,477	40.0
8. Houston-Galveston-Brazoria, Tex. CMSA	564,838	665,378	100,540	17.8
9. Baltimore, Md. MSA	560,952	616,065	55,113	9.8
10. Miami-Fort Lauderdale, Fla. CMSA	394,042	591,440	197,398	50.1
11. Dallas-Fort Worth, Tex. CMSA	419,030	554,616	135,586	32.4
12. San Francisco-Oakland,San Jose, Calif. CMSA	468,477	537,753	69,276	14.8
13. Cleveland-Akron-Lorain, Ohio CMSA	425,861	441,940	16,079	3.8
14. New Orleans, La. MSA	409,076	430,470	21,394	5.2
15. St. Louis, Mo.-Ill. MSA	407,918	423,182	15,264	3.7
16. Memphis, Tenn.-Ark.-Miss. MSA	364,253	399,011	34,758	9.5
17. Norfolk-Virginia Beach-Newport News, Va. MSA	326,102	398,093	71,991	22.1
18. Richmond-Petersburg, Va. MSA	221,456	252,340	30,884	13.9
19. Birmingham, Ala. MSA	240,271	245,726	5,455	2.3
20. Boston-Lawrence-Salem, Mass.-N.H. MSA	176,265	239,059	62,794	35.6
21. Charlotte-Gastonia-Rock Hill, N.C.-S.C. MSA	194,056	231,654	37,598	19.4
22. Milwaukee-Racine, Wis. CMSA	164,571	214,182	49,611	30.1
23. Cincinnati-Hamilton, Ohio-Ky.-Ind. CMSA	185,728	203,607	17,879	9.6
24. Kansas City, Mo.-Kans. MSA	180,161	200,508	20,347	11.3
25. Tampa-St. Petersburg-Clearwater, Fla. MSA	148,465	185,503	37,038	24.9
26. Raleigh-Durham, N.C. MSA	146,624	183,447	36,823	25.1
27. Greensboro-Winston-Salem-High Point, N.C. MSA	162,134	182,284	20,150	12.4
28. Jacksonville, Fla. MSA	156,025	181,265	25,240	16.2
29. Pittsburgh-Beaver Valley, Pa. CMSA	181,644	178,857	-2,787	-1.5
30. Indianapolis, Ind. MSA	157,254	172,326	15,072	9.6
31. Jackson, Miss. MSA	149,457	167,899	18,442	12.3
32. Columbus, Ohio MSA	137,287	164,602	27,315	19.9
33. San Diego, Calif. MSA	104,452	159,306	54,854	52.5
34. Baton Rouge, La. MSA	137,581	156,509	18,928	13.8
35. Charleston, S.C. MSA	133,478	153,227	19,749	14.8
36. Nashville, Tenn. MSA	137,348	152,349	15,001	10.9
37. Columbia, S.C. MSA	117,906	137,906	20,000	17.0
38. Orlando, Fla. MSA	90,595	133,308	42,713	47.1
39. Mobile, Ala. MSA	126,835	130,512	3,677	2.9
40. Dayton-Springfield, Ohio MSA	118,294	126,238	7,944	6.7
41. Louisville, Ky.-Ind. MSA	120,610	124,761	4,151	3.4
42. Augusta, Ga.-S.C. MSA	106,729	123,482	16,753	15.7
43. Seattle-Tacoma, Wash. CMSA	87,976	123,266	35,290	40.1
44. Buffalo-Niagara Falls, N.Y. CMSA	113,975	121,956	7,981	7.0
45. Shreveport, La. MSA	110,478	116,892	6,414	5.8
46. Greenville-Spartanburg, S.C. MSA	97,561	111,334	13,773	14.1
47. West Palm Beach-Boca Raton-Delray Beach, Fla. MSA	77,576	107,705	30,129	38.8
48. Montgomery, Ala. MSA	94,494	105,196	10,702	11.3
49. Sacramento, Calif. MSA	61,594	101,940	40,346	65.5
50. Little Rock-North Little Rock, Ark. MSA	90,783	101,862	11,079	12.2

Source: U.S. Bureau of the Census.

Ten States With Highest Percentage of Black Population, 1997

Rank, State	Black population	Total population	Percentage black
1. Mississippi	993,372	2,730,501	36.38%
2. Louisiana	1,396,453	4,351,769	32.09
3. South Carolina	1,130,354	3,760,181	30.06
4. Georgia	2,126,126	7,486,242	28.40
5. Maryland	1,396,830	5,094,289	27.42
6. Alabama	1,120,315	4,319,154	25.94
7. North Carolina	1,642,980	7,425,183	22.13
8. Virginia	1,343,941	6,733,996	19.96
9. Delaware	140,155	731,581	19.16
10. New York	3,208,344	18,137,226	17.69
United States	33,947,084	267,636,061	12.68%

Source: U.S. Bureau of the Census.

►THE HISPANIC POPULATION

The Hispanic population is one of the fastest-growing segments of the U.S. population. Between 1980 and 1999, the number of Hispanics more than doubled, from 14.6 million to 31.2 million, according to the Census Bureau. The rapid growth of the Hispanic population is due to immigration and a higher fertility rate than that of the non-Hispanic population. For example, the fertility rate per 100,000 women ages 15-44 was 65.0 in 1998, but for Hispanic women, it was 102.8. Mexican-American women had the highest fertility rates of all: 116.6 births per 100,000 women aged 15-44, or approximately double the rate for Cuban-American women.

Within the next 10 years, the Census Bureau projects that the Hispanic population will become the largest minority in the U.S., surpassing blacks, who in 1990 outnumbered Hispanics by about eight million. But by 2010, Hispanics are projected to total 39 million, according to Census Bureau projections, compared to 38 million blacks.

Geographical distribution   Over half of all U.S. Hispanics (53.5 percent) live in California or Texas. In 1996, 9.6 million (30.2 percent, up from 25.8 percent in 1990) of the residents of California and 5.5 million (28.7 percent) of the residents of Texas were Hispanic. The great majority of the Hispanics in these two states are of Mexican origin. New York, with 2.5 million (14.0 percent), is the state with the third largest number of Hispanics, the majority of whom are Puerto Rican. Another 2.0 million Hispanics (14.0 percent) live in Florida, giving it the fourth-largest Hispanic population; the majority are of Cuban background.

Who is Hispanic?   Broadly understood, the term Hispanic refers to people of Spanish or Spanish-American origin. American Hispanics are of diverse backgrounds. The majority trace their roots to Mexico, Puerto Rico or Cuba; however, every Spanish-speaking country is represented in the U.S. Hispanic population. (People of Brazilian origin are not included because Brazil is a Portuguese-speaking country.) In recent years extreme poverty and political upheaval have led Salvadorans and other Central Americans to migrate to the U.S. in increasing numbers.

Contrary to popular opinion Spanish-speaking countries are not culturally homogeneous, but varied and complex. They incorporate Spanish and other European influences, as well as Indian and African traits. In the Caribbean area, Panama, and the coasts of Venezuela, Colombia, Ecuador, and sections of Peru, African culture has left a strong legacy. In Mexico, most of Central America, and the Andean countries, diverse Indian cultures have had a major impact. Latin-American society varies greatly according to social class and vast differences exist between urban and rural areas. Since American Hispanics come from different countries and social backgrounds, they do not compose a uniform, cohesive population group.

U.S. Hispanics are of many races. In some areas, intermingling has made it impossible to distinguish one race from another, but in others, races are clearly defined. In Argentina, for example, there is a white majority of 85 percent—mostly of Italian, German, or English extraction. Cuba, the Dominican Republic, Panama, Venezuela, and the coastal areas of Colombia, Ecuador, and Peru all have significant black populations. In Bolivia, about one-half of the population is Indian and a third is mestizo (of mixed white and Indian ancestry). Both Peru and Cuba have concentrations of persons of Chinese ancestry and Peru has a growing Japanese population. About 63 percent of U.S. Hispanics trace their roots to Mexico, where about 55 percent of the population is mestizo, 30 percent Indian, and 15 percent white.

Despite their diversity, the Hispanic peoples are united by many factors, among them language, religion, customs, and attitudes toward self, family, and society. In the United States, these factors vary in importance according to the degree to which an individual has assimilated into the mainstream. For example, although language has traditionally been an important unifying factor, large numbers of second-generation Hispanics are English-dominant. About 85 percent of U.S. Hispanics speak English. Although the Spanish language continues to exert a strong emotional pull among U.S. Hispanics, it is difficult to assess to what extent Spanish will remain a unifying force among future generations.

Origins of U.S. Hispanics   The majority of U.S. Hispanics are of Mexican origin. Mexicans and Mexican-Americans comprise 63.3 percent (19 million people) of the total U.S. Hispanic population. The number of people of Mexican background living in the U.S. more than doubled between 1980 and 1990, and increased another 39 percent between 1990 and 1997. The Immigration and Reform Control Act of 1986, which allowed

Resident Hispanic Population by Region, 1990

	Total	Northeast	Midwest	South	West
			Number of Hispanics		
All Hispanics	22,354	3,754	1,727	6,767	10,106
Mexican	13,496	175	1,153	4,344	7,824
Puerto Rican	2,728	1,872	258	406	192
Cuban	1,044	184	37	735	88
Other Hispanic	5,086	1,524	279	1,282	2,002
			Percent Distribution		
All Hispanics	100%	16.8%	7.7%	30.3%	45.2%
Mexican	100	1.3	8.5	32.2	58.0
Puerto Rican	100	68.6	9.4	14.9	7.0
Cuban	100	17.6	3.5	70.5	8.5
Other Hispanic	100	30.0	5.5	25.2	39.4

Source: U.S. Bureau of Census.

Hispanic Population of Metropolitan Areas, 1980–90

			Population change, 1980–90	
Rank/Metropolitan area	1980	1990	Number	Percent
1. Los Angeles-Anaheim-Riverside, Calif. CMSA	2,755,914	4,779,118	2,023,204	73.4%
2. New York-Northern New Jersey-Long Island, N.Y.-N.J.-Conn. CMSA	2,050,998	2,777,951	726,953	35.4
3. Miami-Fort Lauderdale, Fla. CMSA	621,309	1,061,846	440,537	70.9
4. San Francisco-Oakland, San Jose, Calif. CMSA	660,190	970,403	310,213	47.0
5. Chicago-Gary-Lake County, Ill.-Ind.-Wis. CMSA	632,443	893,422	260,979	41.3
6. Houston-Galveston-Brazoria, Tex. CMSA	448,460	772,295	323,835	72.2
7. San Antonio, Tex. MSA	481,511	620,290	138,779	28.8
8. Dallas-Fort Worth, Tex. CMSA	247,823	518,917	271,094	109.4
9. San Diego, Calif. MSA	275,177	510,781	235,604	85.6
10. El Paso, Tex. MSA	297,001	411,619	114,618	38.6
11. Phoenix, Ariz. MSA	199,003	345,498	146,495	73.6
12. McAllen-Edinburg-Mission, Tex. MSA	230,212	326,972	96,760	42.0
13. Fresno, Calif. MSA	150,790	236,634	85,844	56.9
14. Denver-Boulder, Colo. CMSA	173,687	226,200	52,513	30.2
15. Philadelphia-Wilmington-Trenton, Pa.-N.J.-Del.-Md. CMSA	147,902	225,868	77,966	52.7
16. Washington, D.C.-Md.-Va. MSA	94,968	224,786	129,818	136.7
17. Brownsville-Harlingen, Tex. MSA	161,654	212,995	51,341	31.8
18. Boston-Lawrence-Salem, Mass.-N.H. CMSA	92,463	193,199	100,736	108.9
19. Corpus Christi, Tex. MSA	158,119	181,860	23,741	15.0
20. Albuquerque, N.Mex. MSA	154,620	178,310	23,690	15.3
21. Sacramento, Calif. MSA	105,665	172,374	66,709	63.1
22. Tucson, Ariz. MSA	111,418	163,262	51,844	46.5
23. Austin, Tex. MSA	94,367	159,942	65,575	69.5
24. Bakersfield, Calif. MSA	87,026	151,995	64,969	74.7
25. Tampa-St. Petersburg-Clearwater, Fla. MSA	80,265	139,248	58,983	73.5

Source: U.S. Bureau of the Census.

Mexicans and other immigrants living illegally in the United States to obtain legal U.S. citizenship, has played a large role in that growth (See the section on immigration later in this chapter).

About 3.2 million, or 10.6 percent of U.S. Hispanics are Puerto Rican. These figures do not include 3.9 million Puerto Ricans living in Puerto Rico, which is a U.S. territory, but for which a separate census is issued. In recent years, the flow of Puerto Ricans to U.S. cities has been reversed, with more Puerto Ricans emigrating from the mainland to the island than the other way around.

As recently as 1981, the numbers of Central Americans living in the United States were so small that the Census Bureau lumped them together with "other" Hispanics, rather than breaking them out as a separate category. But beginning in 1982, the U.S. Central American population had increased so significantly that the Census Bureau created a new category: Central and South American. Today, this is still one of the fastest-growing segments of the Hispanic (and the U.S.) population, nearly doubling in number since it was first counted in 1982. The Census Bureau's 1990 figures counted more than 2.8 million Americans of Central or South American origin. In 1997, they numbered 4.3 million, or 14.4 percent of the total U.S. Hispanic population.

Most Central American immigrants are from

Nicaragua and El Salvador, although a significant number are from Guatemala. Statistical data on Salvadorans is uncertain, since the 1980 census did not break the Central American category down according to country of origin and since many Salvadorans arrived here illegally after 1980 and do not figure in any subsequent census update. During the latter part of the 1980s, large numbers of Nicaraguans entered the country as political refugees. In Miami, where hundreds of Central American immigrants arrive every week, Central Americans comprised nearly 17 percent of the entire Hispanic population in 1990; in 1970,

by contrast, they comprised less than 1 percent. There are an estimated 250,000 Nicaraguans presently living in the U.S.

Cubans and Cuban-Americans (1.3 million people) make up 4.2 percent of the total number of Hispanics in the United States. The largest increase in the number of Cuban-Americans in the U.S. came in 1961 during the Cuban airlift and again in 1980 during the Mariel boat lift. The number of Americans of Cuban origin increased again between 1980 and 1991, when it went from 800,000 to over a million. Between 1990 and 1997, the number of Cubans has increased by just over 200,000.

The remaining 7.4 percent of the U.S. Hispanic population is of "Other Spanish" origin.

▶ THE ASIAN AND PACIFIC ISLANDER POPULATION

In 1970 the Census Bureau counted about 1.5 million Asians and Pacific Islanders living in the U.S. By the 1980 census that figure had more than doubled to 3.4 million, thanks in large part to the more than 400,000 Southeast Asian refugees who came to America between 1975-80 under the Refugee Resettlement Program. By the 1990 Census, their numbers had doubled yet again, with Koreans and Vietnamese responsible for the majority of the increase. Chinese are still the largest group of Asians in the U.S., followed closely by Filipinos and Japanese. In 1999, the Asian population of the U.S. totaled 10.8 million.

Ten States With Largest Hispanic Populations, 1997

State	Hispanic population	Total population	Percentage Hispanics
California	9,941,014	32,268,301	30.81%
Texas	5,722,535	19,439,337	29.44
New York	2,570,382	18,137,226	14.14
Florida	2,105,689	14,653,945	14.37
Illinois	1,182,964	11,895,849	9.94
Arizona	998,623	4,554,966	21.92
New Jersey	958,885	8,052,849	11.91
New Mexico	692,570	1,729,751	40.04
Colorado	556,074	3,892,644	14.29
Massachusetts	358,521	6,117,520	5.86
United States	29,347,865	267,636,061	10.97%

Source: U.S. Bureau of the Census.

Asian and Pacific Islander Population of Metropolitan Areas, 1980–90

Rank/Metropolitan area	1980	1990	Population change, 1980–90 Number	Percent
1. Los Angeles-Anaheim-Riverside, Calif. CMSA	561,876	1,339,048	777,172	138.3%
2. San Francisco-Oakland-San Jose, Calif. CMSA	454,647	926,961	472,314	103.9
3. New York-Northern New Jersey-Long Island, N.Y.-N.J.-Conn. CMSA	370,731	873,213	502,482	135.5
4. Honolulu, Hawaii MSA	456,465	526,459	69,994	15.3
5. Chicago-Gary-Lake County, Ill.-Ind.-Wis. CMSA	144,626	256,050	111,424	77.0
6. Washington, D.C.-Md.-Va. MSA	83,008	202,437	119,429	143.9
7. San Diego, Calif. MSA	89,861	198,311	108,450	120.7
8. Seattle-Tacoma, Wash. CMSA	78,255	164,286	86,031	109.9
9. Houston-Galveston-Brazoria, Tex. CMSA	53,056	132,131	79,075	149.0
10. Philadelphia-Wilmington-Trenton, Penn.-N.J.-Del.-Md. CMSA	53,291	123,458	70,167	131.7

Source: U.S. Bureau of the Census.

Asian Population of the U.S., 1980–90

Group	1980 Census Number	Percent	1990 Census Number	Percent	Population change, 1980–90 Number	Percent
Asian Indian	361,531	0.2%	815,447	0.3%	453,916	125.6%
Chinese	806,040	0.4	1,645,472	0.7	839,432	104.1
Filipino	774,652	0.3	1,406,770	0.6	632,118	81.6
Guamanian	32,158	0.0	49,345	0.0	17,187	53.4
Hawaiian	166,814	0.1	211,014	0.1	44,200	26.5
Japanese	700,974	0.3	847,562	0.3	146,588	20.9
Korean	354,593	0.2	798,849	0.3	444,256	125.3
Samoan	41,948	0.0	62,964	0.0	21,016	50.1
Vietnamese	261,729	0.1	614,547	0.2	352,818	134.8
Other Asian or Pacific Islander	N.A.	N.A.	821,692	0.3	N.A.	N.A.
Total Asian or Pacific Islander	3,500,439[1]	1.5%	7,273,662	2.9%	3,773,223	107.8%

Note: N.A. = Not available from 1980 tabulations. 1. Figures for 1980 are not strictly comparable with those for 1990. The total for 1980 includes only the nine specific groups listed. Source: U.S. Bureau of the Census.

10 States With Largest Asian Populations, 1997

State	Asian population	Total population	Percentage Asian
California	3,777,015	32,268,301	11.71%
New York	952,736	18,137,226	5.25
Hawaii	748,748	1,186,602	63.10
Texas	523,972	19,439,337	2.70
New Jersey	423,738	8,052,849	5.26
Illinois	382,806	11,895,849	3.22
Washington	311,310	5,610,362	5.55
Florida	253,118	14,653,945	1.73
Virginia	232,930	6,733,996	3.46
Massachusetts	209,871	6,117,520	3.43

Source: U.S. Bureau of the Census.

10 States with Largest Percentage of Asian Population, 1997

State	Asian population	Total population	Percentage Asian
Hawaii	748,748	1,186,602	63.10%
California	3,777,015	32,268,301	11.71
Washington	311,310	5,610,362	5.55
New Jersey	423,738	8,052,849	5.26
New York	952,736	18,137,226	5.25
Alaska	26,733	609,311	4.39
Nevada	73,611	1,676,809	4.39
Maryland	194,646	5,094,289	3.82
Virginia	232,930	6,733,996	3.46
Massachusetts	209,871	6,117,520	3.43
United States	10,032,885	267,636,061	3.75%

Source: U.S. Bureau of the Census.

▶THE AMERICAN INDIAN, ESKIMO, AND ALEUT POPULATION

Revised figures from the 1990 census report 1,959,234 American Indians, including 85,698 Alaska Natives (Eskimos and Aleuts), living in the United States. This represents a significant increase since the 1960 census, when only 524,000 (42,500 Alaska Natives) were counted. About 46 percent of American Indians live in the West, 29.7 percent in the South, 17.8 percent in the Midwest, and only 6.5 percent in the Northeast. According to the 1990 census, four states had over 100,000 Native Americans: Oklahoma (252,089), California (236,078), Arizona (203,009), and New Mexico (134,097).

The 1990 census reported that only 437,431 members of the American Indian, Eskimo, and Aleut populations lived inside federally "identified areas." There were 554 such areas in 1997, according to the federal government's Bureau of Indian Affairs. These areas include reservations that the federal government recognizes as territory in which American Indian tribes have jurisdiction (state governments are lands held in trust by state governments for the use and benefit of a given tribe), and "trust lands" that are held in trust by the federal government but that consist of property associated with a particular tribe or reservation. The Bureau of Indian Affairs counted 314 reservations in 1997.

In July 1997, the Native American population was 2.3 million, according to Census Bureau estimates. The greatest number of American Indians lived in California (306,690), Oklahoma (260,029), Arizona (255,463), New Mexico (158,036), and Washington (100,309). By percentage, the greatest concentrations of Native Americans were in Alaska (15.94 percent), New Mexico (9.14 percent), South Dakota (7.89 percent), and Oklahoma (7.84 percent).

Population of Selected Reservations and Trust Lands, 1990

Rank/Reservation or Trust Land	Total population	American Indian, Eskimo or Aleut Population	Percent of total
1. Navajo and Trust Lands, Ariz., N.Mex., Utah	148,451	143,405	96.6%
2. Pine Ridge and Trust Lands, Nebr.-S.Dak.	12,215	11,182	91.5
3. Fort Apache, Ariz.	10,394	9,825	94.5
4. Gila River, Ariz.	9,540	9,116	95.6
5. Papago, Ariz.	8,730	8,480	97.1
6. Rosebud and Trust Lands, S.Dak.	9,696	8,043	83.0
7. San Carlos, Ariz.	7,294	7,110	97.5
8. Zuni Pueblo, Ariz.-N.Mex.	7,412	7,073	95.4
9. Hopi and Trust Lands, Ariz.	7,360	7,061	95.9
10. Blackfeet, Mont.	8,549	7,025	82.2
11. Turtle Mountain and Trust Lands, N.Dak.-S.Dak.	7,106	6,772	95.3
12. Yakima and Trust Lands, Wash.	27,668	6,307	22.8
13. Osage, Okla.[1]	41,645	6,161	14.8
14. Fort Peck, Mont.	10,595	5,782	54.6
15. Wind River, Wyo.	21,851	5,676	26.0
16. Eastern Cherokee, N.C.	6,527	5,388	82.5
17. Flathead, Mont.	21,259	5,130	24.1
18. Cheyenne River, S.Dak.	7,743	5,100	65.9
19. Standing Rock, N.Dak.-S.Dak.	7,956	4,870	61.2
20. Crow and Trust Lands, Mont.	6,370	4,724	74.2
21. Mississippi Choctaw and Trust Lands, Miss.	4,073	3,932	96.5
22. Colville, Wash.	6,957	3,788	54.4
23. Laguna Pueblo and Trust Lands, N.Mex.	3,731	3,634	97.4
24. Red Lake, Minn.	3,699	3,602	97.4
25. Northern Cheyenne and Trust Lands, Mont.-S.Dak.	3,923	3,542	90.3

Note: Ranked by total American Indian, Eskimo, or Aleut population. 1. The Osage Reservation is coextensive with Osage County.
Source: U.S. Bureau of the Census.

THE U.S. POPULATION BY AGE AND SEX

▶ **THE POPULATION BY AGE**

With birth rates and fertility rates declining rapidly since 1965 it should come as no surprise that the average age of the U.S. population has been increasing almost as quickly. It will continue to rise for the foreseeable future in part be-

cause of the aging members of the Baby Boom generation.

During the Baby Boom years of the 1950s and 1960s, the median age of the population actually declined, the only time it has done so. Since then, however, the steady decline in the percentage of young people, especially those under 18 years of age (from 34.1 percent in 1970, to 25.6 percent in 1990), combined with the increase of those between 25 and 44 (they were 23.6 percent of the population in 1970, but 32.6 percent in 1990) has driven the median age from 28.0 in 1970 to 33.0 in 1990. A five-year increase in 20 years is unprecedented in U.S. history, but what's more revealing is that we will most likely duplicate that feat over the

Number of Persons and Percent of Total Population, by Age Group, 1960–2050 (numbers in thousands)

Age in Years	1960	1970	1980	1990	2000	2010	2050
Under 5	20,341	17,166	16,458	18,849	18,987	20,012	27,106
Percent	11.3%	8.4%	7.2%	7.6%	6.9%	6.7%	6.9%
5-13	32,965	36,672	31,095	31,996	36,043	35,605	47,804
Percent	18.2	17.9	13.7	12.8	13.1	12.0	12.1
14-17	11,219	15,924	16,142	13,311	15,752	16,894	21,207
Percent	6.2	7.8	7.1	5.3	5.7	5.7	5.4
18-24	16,128	24,712	30,350	26,826	26,258	30,138	36,333
Percent	8.9	12.1	13.3	10.8	9.6	10.1	9.2
25-34	22,919	25,323	37,626	43,139	37,233	38,292	49,365
Percent	12.7	12.3	16.5	17.3	13.6	12.9	12.5
35-44	24,221	23,150	25,868	37,766	44,659	38,521	47,393
Percent	13.4	11.3	11.4	15.1	16.3	12.9	12.0
45-64	36,203	41,999	44,515	46,280	60,992	78,848	85,862
Percent	20.0	20.5	19.5	18.6	22.2	26.5	21.8
65 & over	16,675	20,107	25,704	31,235	34,709	39,408	78,859
Percent	9.2	9.8	11.3	12.5	12.6	13.2	20.0
85 & over	940	1,430	2,269	3,057	4,259	5,671	18,223
Percent	0.5	0.7	1.0	1.2	1.6	1.9	4.6
100 & over	3	5	15	37	72	131	834
Percent	-	-	-	-	-	-	0.2
Total U.S. population	**180,671**	**205,052**	**227,757**	**249,402**	**274,634**	**297,716**	**393,931**
Median age	**29.4**	**27.9**	**30.0**	**33.0**	**35.7**	**37.2**	**38.1**

1. Figures for 1990 are estimated. Figures for 2000 and after are the projections the Census Bureau calls the "middle" or "most likely" series.　**Source:** U. S. Bureau of the Census, *Projections of the Population of the U.S., by Age, Sex, and Race: 1995 to 2050* (1996).

Growth of the Over-65 Population, 1900–2050

Year	Population 65 and over		Population 85 and over	
	Number ('000s)	Percent of total population	Number ('000s)	Percent of total population
1900	3,099	4.1%	N.A.	N.A.
1910	3,986	4.3	N.A.	N.A.
1920	4,929	4.7	N.A.	N.A.
1930	6,705	5.5	N.A.	N.A.
1940	9,031	6.9	N.A.	N.A.
1950	12,397	8.1	N.A.	N.A.
1960	16,675	9.2	940	0.5%
1970	20,107	9.8	1,430	0.7
1980	25,549	11.3	2,269	1.0
1990	31,235	12.5	3,057	1.2
1996	33,861	12.8	3,761	1.4
2000	34,709	12.6	4,259	1.6
2010	39,408	13.2	5,671	1.9
2020	53,220	16.5	6,460	2.0
2030	69,379	20.0	8,455	2.4
2040	75,233	20.3	13,552	3.7
2050	78,859	20.0	18,223	4.6

Note: Prior to 1960, the Census Bureau did not count persons over 85 separately. Figures for 2000 through 2050 are Census Bureau projections based on their "most likely" series of estimates. Figure from 1996 is based on annual population projections.
Source: U.S. Bureau of the Census, *Population Projections of the U.S by Age, Sex, Race, and Hispanic Origin, 1995-2050* (1996).

Resident Population of States, by Age, 1998 (numbers in thousands)

State	Resident population	Under 5 years	5-17 years	18-24 years	25-44 years	45-64 years	65 years and over	Median age
United States	270,298	18,966	50,906	25,470	83,294	57,261	34,401	35.2
Alabama	4,352	295	789	436	1,307	957	568	35.5
Alaska	614	49	143	69	186	133	34	31.5
Arizona	4,669	368	895	449	1,381	958	618	34.6
Arkansas	2,538	175	479	251	711	559	363	35.8
California	32,667	2,564	6,347	3,167	10,695	6,279	3,615	33.3
Colorado	3,971	279	762	377	1,234	917	402	35.5
Connecticut	3,274	211	579	258	1,043	713	469	37.0
Delaware	744	49	130	67	245	156	96	35.7
District of Columbia	523	31	72	43	188	117	73	36.7
Florida	14,916	953	2,587	1,206	4,243	3,192	2,734	38.3
Georgia	7,642	568	1,454	755	2,522	1,588	755	33.8
Hawaii	1,193	84	214	119	355	261	158	36.2
Idaho	1,229	91	260	139	338	261	139	33.3
Illinois	12,045	891	2,297	1,121	3,722	2,519	1,496	34.9
Indiana	5,899	411	1,107	572	1,780	1,271	740	35.2
Iowa	2,862	182	540	277	808	624	431	36.6
Kansas	2,629	182	515	262	773	542	354	35.2
Kentucky	3,936	264	725	398	1,178	879	493	35.6
Louisiana	4,369	313	878	475	1,272	927	504	33.9
Maine	1,244	67	224	110	387	282	175	37.4
Maryland	5,135	344	943	434	1,722	1,100	592	35.6
Massachusetts	6,147	393	1,064	505	2,024	1,299	861	36.2
Michigan	9,817	657	1,895	921	3,025	2,096	1,223	35.3
Minnesota	4,725	317	942	439	1,459	985	583	35.2
Mississippi	2,752	202	555	300	795	564	336	33.4
Missouri	5,439	364	1,043	509	1,620	1,158	745	35.8
Montana	880	53	172	89	237	213	117	37.5
Nebraska	1,663	115	331	167	475	347	229	35.3
Nevada	1,747	136	331	148	542	389	200	35.2
New Hampshire	1,185	73	225	96	404	245	142	35.7
New Jersey	8,115	547	1,443	672	2,559	1,788	1,106	36.7
New Mexico	1,737	133	371	174	494	366	198	34.0
New York	18,175	1,253	3,249	1,598	5,690	3,960	2,424	35.9
North Carolina	7,546	527	1,393	700	2,348	1,632	947	35.2
North Dakota	638	40	122	68	181	134	92	35.8
Ohio	11,209	742	2,102	1,053	3,390	2,422	1,501	35.8
Oklahoma	3,347	228	651	338	941	740	448	35.6
Oregon	3,282	217	608	303	962	759	433	36.7
Pennsylvania	12,001	720	2,140	1,022	3,574	2,641	1,904	37.6
Rhode Island	988	62	176	83	315	199	154	36.4
South Carolina	3,836	253	706	384	1,183	841	468	35.2
South Dakota	738	50	151	77	204	150	106	35.2
Tennessee	5,431	362	969	515	1,676	1,229	679	35.9
Texas	19,760	1615	4,014	2,049	6,071	4,011	2,000	33.0
Utah	2,100	204	498	290	574	350	184	26.7
Vermont	591	33	109	52	190	135	73	36.7
Virginia	6,791	447	1,198	657	2,250	1,472	767	35.2
Washington	5,689	387	1,086	540	1,792	1,233	652	35.3
West Virginia	1,811	99	305	183	505	445	275	38.6
Wisconsin	5,224	333	1,018	498	1,574	1,110	691	35.7
Wyoming	481	31	99	53	131	112	56	35.7

Note: Includes armed forces residing in each state. Figures as of July 1, 1998. Source: U.S. Bureau of the Census, Population Division, *Current Population Reports*. www.census.gov/population.

next 20 years. By 1999, the median age of the U.S. population had already increased to 35.5.

The other major factor in the so-called "graying of America" is the increased life expectancy for older people. In 1950, the over-65 population totalled 7 percent of all Americans and numbered nine million. In 1990, 31.7 million Americans (12.3 percent of the population) were over 65; this represents a 24.1 percent increase since 1980 and a 1,000 percent increase since 1900. In 1999, there were 34.5 million people over 65.

As the population ages, 65 no longer seems old to most people. Especially when millions more people are living past the age of 80. There were 7 million people 80 or older in 1990, 3 million age 85 or older, nearly a million 90 years or older, and 36,000 people over the age of 100. By 1999, there were 16.5 million people over the age of 75, 9.0 million age 80 or older, and 4.2 million age 85 or more.

Over the first decade of the 21st century, the over-65 population will grow another 10-12 percent—but between 2010 and 2030 the projected increases jump to 31.2 percent and 25.6 percent as the Baby Boom generation finally become senior citizens. In the year 2030, an estimated 21 percent of the population, or 65 million Americans, will be 65 years old or older.

Characteristics of Persons 65 or Older, 1998

Characteristic	Total	Male	Female
Total (millions)	**32.1**	**13.5**	**18.6**
Percent distribution	**100.0%**	**42.1%**	**57.9%**
Marital status:			
Single	4.3%	3.8%	4.7%
Married	56.6	75.1	42.9
Spouse absent	2.4	2.5	2.2
Widowed	32.5	14.9	45.2
Divorced	6.7	6.1	7.1
Family status:			
In families[1]	66.8	79.6	57.5
Nonfamily householders	31.9	18.4	41.7
Secondary individuals	1.3	2.0	0.7
Living arrangements:			
Spouse present	54.2	72.6	40.7
Living alone	30.9	17.3	40.8
Living with someone else	14.9	10.0	18.4
Labor force participation:			
Employed	11.6	15.9	8.3
Unemployed	0.4	0.5	0.3
Not in labor force	88.1	83.5	91.4
Percent below poverty level	10.5	7.0	13.1

1. Excludes those living in unrelated subfamilies.
Source: U.S. Bureau of the Census, *Statistical Abstract of the United States* (annual)

▶ THE POPULATION BY SEX

In 1998, according to the Census Bureau, there were 36.4 million men and 43.1 million women 18 years and over who had never married or who were currently widowed or divorced, a ratio of 84 unmarried men per 100 unmarried women. The popular interpretation of these figures—that there is a shortage of eligible men—fails to consider that women are more likely to live longer (and so be counted among the widowed) and less likely to remarry after a divorce. In fact, the surplus of women can be entirely attributed to the fact that there are seven million more widows than widowers over the age of 65. But during the peak marrying ages, unmarried men actually outnumber unmarried women: among persons between the ages of 18 and 24 there were 112 unmarried men for every 100 unmarried women; in the 25-to-34 age group, there were 120 men for every 100 women; and men 35-44 outnumber women 109 to 100. It's not until the 45-to-64 group that the reversal begins (68 unmarried men for every 100 available women), and among the 65-and-over there is a dramatic change, with only 32 unmarried men for every 100 unmarried women.

VITAL STATISTICS

The National Center for Health Statistics does a month-by-month tracking of four sets of numbers which both it and the Census Bureau refer to as "vital": births, deaths, marriages, and divorces.

Births An estimated 3.94 million babies were born in the U.S. in 1998, up from 3.88 million the year before. Meanwhile, the *crude birth rate* (the number of live births per 1,000 total population) rebounded slightly to 14.6, after dropping to 14.5 in 1997, its lowest level since 1976. The fertility rate (the number of births per 1,000 women aged 15-44) also bounced back to 66.0 after a 20-year low of 65.0 the previous year.

Deaths An estimated 2.33 million people died in 1998, but the death rate of 8.6 per 1,000 population (down slightly from 1995 and 1996) confirmed that people are living longer. In 1910, for example, the death rate was 14.7. (For infant mortality figures and for more specific information about death rates by cause see the section, "Health and Medicine.")

In 1998 there were 1,615,000 more births than deaths; this figure is called the *natural increase*, meaning the growth in population without immigration (which has accounted for close to 700,000 people per year in recent years).

Marriages An estimated 2.24 million couples married during 1998, a slight decrease from 1997 levels; the marriage rate of 8.6 per 1,000 people (unchanged from the year before) matched the lowest level since the 1960s. In addition to getting married in fewer numbers, people are getting married at a later age. In 1960, for example, about 40 percent of all 19-year-old women were married, but by 1990 only 11 percent were. Also in 1960, about 92 percent of all women were married before they reached age 30, but by 1990 only 81 percent were. Moreover, between 1970 and 1990, the proportion of 30-to-34-year-olds who had never married almost tripled, rising from 6 percent to 16 percent for women, and from 9 percent to 27 percent for men; for those age 35 to 39, the proportion of never married doubled over the two decades, from 5 percent to 10 percent for women and from 7 percent to 15 percent for men.

U.S. Population by Sex: Totals and Ratio of Males to Females, 1920–98

Year	Male ('000s)	Female ('000s)	Males per 100 females			
			All ages	14-24	25-44	65+
1920	53,900	51,810	104.0	97.3	105.1	101.3
1930	62,137	60,638	102.5	98.4	101.8	100.5
1940	66,062	65,608	100.7	98.9	98.5	95.5
1950	74,833	75,864	98.6	98.2	96.4	89.6
1960	88,331	90,992	97.1	98.7	95.7	82.8
1970	98,926	104,309	94.8	98.7	95.5	72.1
1980	110,053	116,493	94.5	101.9	97.4	67.6
1990	122,049	127,875	95.1	104.6	98.9	67.2
1995	128,314	134,441	95.4	104.7	98.8	69.1
1996	129,810	135,474	95.8	105.7	99.4	69.4
1997	131,018	136,618	95.5	104.8	98.7	69.9
1998	132,046	138,252	95.5	104.8	98.6	70.3

Source: U.S. Bureau of the Census, *Statistical Abstract of the United States* (annual)

Divorces An estimated 1.13 million divorces were granted in 1998, down slightly from the previous year. The divorce rate per 1,000 population was 4.2, its lowest rate in more than 20 years. The divorce rate peaked in 1979 at 5.3 per 1,000 population. (In that year there were 22.8 divorced women for every 1,000 married women, up from 9.2 in 1960. While the divorce rate has stabilized, the ratio of divorced persons to married persons (with spouse present) has skyrocketed. Between 1970 and 1998, the proportion nearly quadrupled, from 47 divorced per 1,000 married to 175 per 1,000. For blacks, the rise was even greater, going from 83 per 1,000 to 336 per 1,000 in the same period.

In 1998, there were 19.4 million currently divorced persons in the U.S., 9.8 percent of the total adult population over 18. There are more divorced women (11.1 million) than men (8.3 million) because women are less likely to remarry.

Divorced Persons per 1,000 Married Persons by Sex and Race 1960–98

Sex/race	All races	White	Black	Hispanic[1]
Both sexes:				
1960	35	33	62	N.A.
1970	47	44	83	61
1980	100	92	203	98
1990	142	133	282	129
1995	161	152	303	152
1996	167	156	344	151
1997	177	167	331	149
1998	175	168	336	150
Male:				
1960	28	27	45	N.A.
1970	35	32	62	40
1980	79	74	149	64
1990	118	112	208	103
1995	134	130	212	130
1996	142	134	266	127
1997	150	142	254	118
1998	150	144	253	127
Female:				
1960	42	38	78	N.A.
1970	60	56	104	81
1980	120	110	258	132
1990	166	153	358	155
1995	187	173	397	174
1996	192	178	425	173
1997	203	191	411	179
1998	200	187	422	172

Note: Persons 18 years and over. Per 1,000 married persons with spouse present. 1. Persons of Hispanic origin may be of any race.
Source: U.S. Bureau of the Census, *Marital Status and Living Arrangements: March 1998* (1999). **www.census.gov**

Black-White Married Couples in the U.S., 1960–98 (thousands)

Year	Total married couples	Total black-white couples	Husband black, wife white	Wife black, husband white
1960	40,491	51	25	26
1970	44,598	65	41	24
1980	49,714	167	122	45
1990	53,256	211	150	61
1992	53,512	246	163	83
1993	54,199	242	182	60
1994	54,251	296	196	100
1995	54,937	328	206	122
1997	54,666	311	201	110
1998	55,305	330	210	120

Source: U.S. Bureau of the Census, *Current Population Reports.*

Percent of Population Never Married, by Age and Sex, 1960–98

Age	1960	1970	1980	1990	1995	1998
MEN						
Total: 15 and over	**23.2%**	**28.1%**	**29.6%**	**29.9%**	**31.0%**	**31.2%**
15-17	98.8	99.4	99.4	99.8	99.3	99.3
18	94.6	95.1	97.4	98.5	97.7[1]	97.3[1]
19	87.1	89.9	90.9	95.3	(1)	(1)
20-24	53.1	54.7	68.8	79.3	80.7	83.4
25-29	20.8	19.1	33.1	45.2	51.0	51.0
30-34	11.9	9.4	15.9	27.0	28.2	29.2
35-39	8.8	7.2	7.8	14.7	20.3	21.6
40-44	7.3	6.3	7.1	10.5	14.0	15.6
45-54	7.4	7.5	6.1	6.3	8.1	8.9
55-64	8.0	7.8	5.3	5.8	5.0	5.4
65 and over	7.7	7.5	4.9	4.2	4.2	3.8
WOMEN						
Total: 15 and over	**17.3%**	**22.1%**	**22.5%**	**22.8%**	**23.5%**	**24.7%**
15-17	93.2	97.3	97.0	98.5	98.9	98.4
18	75.6	82.0	88.0	92.0	91.7[1]	94.3[1]
19	59.7	68.8	77.6	88.7	(1)	(1)
20-24	28.4	35.8	50.2	62.8	66.7	70.3
25-29	10.5	10.5	20.9	31.1	35.3	38.6
30-34	6.9	6.2	9.5	16.4	19.0	21.6
35-39	6.1	5.4	6.2	10.4	12.6	14.3
40-44	6.1	4.9	4.8	8.0	8.7	9.9
45-54	7.0	4.9	4.7	5.0	6.1	7.2
55-64	8.0	6.8	4.5	3.9	4.3	4.6
65 and over	8.5	7.7	5.9	4.9	4.2	4.7

1. Population aged 18-19 included under 18.
Source: U.S. Bureau of the Census, *Marital Status and Living Arrangements: March 1998* (1999). **www.census.gov**

Marital Status, by Race and Hispanic Origin, 1970–98

Race and marital status	1970 Number ('000s)	1970 Per-cent	1980 Number ('000s)	1980 Per-cent	1990 Number ('000s)	1990 Per-cent	1998 Number ('000s)	1998 Per-cent
All races	132,507	100.0%	159,528	100.0%	181,849	100.0%	197,412	100.0%
Married	94,999	71.7	104,564	65.5	112,552	61.9	117,856	59.7
Unmarried	37,508	28.3	54,964	34.5	69,297	38.1	79,555	40.3
Never married	21,443	16.2	32,342	20.3	40,361	22.2	44,561	23.6
Widowed	11,784	8.9	12,734	8.0	13,810	7.6	13,594	6.9
Divorced	4,282	3.2	9,886	6.2	15,125	8.3	19,400	9.8
White	118,179	100.0%	139,480	100.0%	155,454	100.0%	165,337	100.0%
Married	85,784	72.6	93,800	67.2	99,450	64.0	102,618	62.1
Unmarried	32,395	27.4	45,681	32.8	56,004	36.0	62,718	37.9
Never married	18,444	15.6	26,405	18.9	31,633	20.3	35,132	21.2
Widowed	10,280	8.7	10,938	7.8	11,730	7.5	11,452	6.9
Divorced	3,671	3.1	8,338	6.0	12,640	8.1	16,134	9.8
Black	12,972	100.0%	16,638	100.0%	20,320	100.0%	23,091	100.0%
Married	8,310	64.1	8,545	51.4	9,302	45.8	9,643	41.7
Unmarried	4,662	35.9	8,093	48.6	11,017	54.2	13,447	58.2
Never married	2,668	20.6	5,070	30.5	7,141	35.1	8,989	38.9
Widowed	1,427	11.0	1,627	9.8	1,730	8.5	1,752	7.6
Divorced	567	4.4	1,396	8.4	2,146	10.6	2,706	11.7
Hispanic[1]	5,066	100.0%	7,888	100.0%	13,560	100.0%	19,835	100.0%
Married	3,637	71.8	5,176	65.6	8,365	61.7	11,677	58.8
Unmarried	1,429	28.2	2,711	34.4	5,195	38.3	8,158	41.2
Never married	943	18.6	1,901	24.1	3,694	27.2	5,883	29.7
Widowed	286	5.6	350	4.4	548	4.0	747	3.8
Divorced	200	3.9	460	5.8	952	7.0	1,528	7.7

Note: Only those people 18 years old and over are included. 1. Hispanic persons may be of any race.
Source: U.S. Bureau of the Census, *Marital Status and Living Arrangements: March 1998* (1999). **www.census.gov.**

Marital Status of the Population by Sex and Age, 1998 (numbers in thousands)

Age	Total	Single	Married	Widowed	Divorced
MALE					
18-19	3,807	3,706	91	—	10
20-24	8,826	7,360	1,332	—	133
25-29	9,450	4,822	4,219	10	398
30-34	10,076	2,939	6,345	20	773
35-39	11,299	2,444	7,598	44	1,213
40-44	10,756	1,676	7,633	50	1,397
45-54	16,598	1,481	12,665	150	2,303
55-64	10,673	572	8,559	275	1,266
65-74	7,992	328	6,331	707	626
75-84	4,527	145	3,327	888	166
85+	1,006	45	502	423	36
Total 18+	**95,009**	**25,518**	**58,601**	**2,567**	**8,322**
FEMALE					
18-19	3,780	3,565	211	—	5
20-24	8,788	6,178	2372	17	222
25-29	9,546	3,689	5298	35	525
30-34	10,282	2,219	7044	55	964
35-39	11,392	1,626	8145	138	1,484
40-44	11,015	1,095	8016	166	1,738
45-54	17,459	1,263	12345	697	3,154
55-64	11,582	538	7847	1,526	1,671
65-74	9,882	425	5420	3,155	882
75-84	6,754	340	2300	3,752	362
85+	1,923	106	258	1,487	71
Total 18+	**102,403**	**21,043**	**59,255**	**11,027**	**11,078**

Note: Totals may not add up due to independent rounding.
Source: U.S. Bureau of the Census, *Marital Status and Living Arrangements: March 1998* (1999). **www.census.gov.**

Marriages and Divorces in the U.S., 1920–98

Year	Marriages ('000s)	Rate per 1,000 population	Divorces ('000s)	Rate per 1,000 population
1920	1,274	12.0	171	1.6
1925	1,188	10.3	175	1.5
1930	1,127	9.2	19.6	1.6
1935	1,327	10.4	218	1.7
1940	1,596	12.1	264	2.0
1945	1,613	12.2	485	3.5
1950	1,667	11.1	385	2.6
1955	1,531	9.3	377	2.3
1960	1,523	8.5	393	2.2
1965	1,800	9.3	479	2.5
1970	2,163	10.6	708	3.5
1975	2,153	10.0	1,036	4.8
1980	2,390	10.0	1,036	4.8
1985	2,413	10.1	1,190	5.0
1990	2,448	9.8	1,175	4.7
1995	2,336	8.9	1,169	4.4
1996	2,344	8.8	1,150	4.3
1997	2,384	8.9	1,163	4.3
1998	2,244	8.3	1,135	4.2

Source: U.S. National Center for Health Statistics, *Vital Statistics of the United States* (annual) and *Monthly Vital Statistics Report,* July 6, 1999.

Births and Deaths in the U.S., 1910–98

Year	Live births (000s)	Birth rate[1]	Deaths[2] (000s)	Death rate[1]
1910	2,777	30.1	N.A.	14.7
1920	2,950	27.7	N.A.	13.0
1930	2,618	21.3	N.A.	11.3
1935	2,377	18.7	1,393	10.9
1940	2,559	19.4	1,417	10.8
1945	2,858	20.4	1,402	10.6
1950	3,632	24.1	1,452	9.6
1955	4,097	25.0	1,529	9.3
1960	4,258	23.7	1,712	9.5
1965	3,760	19.5	1,828	9.4
1970	3,731	18.4	1,921	9.5
1975	3,144	14.6	1,893	8.8
1980	3,612	15.9	1,990	8.8
1985	3,761	15.8	2,086	8.8
1990	4,158	16.7	2,148	8.6
1995	3,892	14.8	2,309	8.8
1996	3,899	14.7	2,311	8.7
1997	3,882	14.5	2,294	8.6
1998	3,946	14.6	2,333	8.6

1. Per 1,000 total population. 2. Excludes fetal deaths.
Source: U.S. National Center for Health Statistics, *Vital Statistics of the United States,* (annual) and *Monthly Vital Statistics Report,* July 6, 1999.

Births, Deaths, and Marriages in the U.S., By Month, 1998

Month	Births Number	Births Rate per 1,000 population	Deaths Number	Deaths Rate per 1,000 population	Marriages Number	Marriages Rate per 1,000 population
January	290,000	12.7	225,000	9.8	104,000	4.8
February	309,000	15.0	209,000	10.1	141,000	7.2
March	325,000	14.2	219,000	9.6	144,000	6.6
April	342,000	15.4	191,000	8.6	164,000	7.8
May	324,000	14.1	188,000	8.2	209,000	9.1
June	343,000	15.5	184,000	8.3	241,000	10.9
July	359,000	15.6	187,000	8.2	230,000	10.0
August	329,000	14.3	191,000	8.3	237,000	10.3
September	337,000	15.2	175,000	7.9	215,000	9.6
October	342,000	14.9	189,000	8.2	213,000	9.3
November	315,000	14.2	178,000	8.0	177,000	7.9
December	332,000	14.4	194,000	8.4	170,000	7.4

Note: Figures are provisional. Source: U.S. National Center for Health Statistics, *Monthly Vital Statistics Report,* (July 6, 1999).

Median Age at First Marriage, By Sex, 1890–1998

Year	Male	Female	Year	Male	Female
1890	26.1	22.0	1990	26.1	23.9
1900	25.9	21.9	1991	26.3	24.1
1910	25.1	21.6	1992	26.5	24.4
1920	24.6	21.2	1993	26.5	24.5
1930	24.3	21.3	1994	26.7	24.5
1940	24.3	21.5	1995	26.9	24.5
1950	22.8	20.3	1994	26.7	24.5
1960	22.8	20.3	1995	26.9	24.5
1970	23.2	20.8	1996	27.1	24.8
1980	24.7	22.0	1997	26.8	25.0
1985	25.5	23.3	1998	26.7	25.0

Source: U.S. Bureau of the Census, *The Statistical History of the U.S.* (1976), *Marital Status and Living Arrangements, March 1998* (1999).

▶FERTILITY RATES OF AMERICAN WOMEN

Population experts predict future trends by studying many factors including the crude birth rate (see "Vital Statistics") and the all-important fertility rates. The *general fertility rate* measures the ratio of live births to the total number of women aged 15 to 44. (Until 1990, the Census Bureau had reported based on the number of women 18 to 44, thus projecting a higher fertility rate but discounting the high number of teenage pregnancies.)

The *total fertility rate* is the number of births 1,000 women aged 10 to 50 would have in their lifetimes if, at each year of age, they experienced the birth rates occurring to women of that age in the specified calendar year. The total fertility rate is sometimes defined in the popular media as the number of *likely* births one woman will have in her lifetime; they do this by dividing by 1,000.

The total fertility rate is most helpful in measuring long term trends, especially in determining whether or not the nation is sustaining a level of reproduction necessary for maintaining current population levels. That level, generally regarded as 2,100 per 1,000 women, has not been achieved in the U.S. since 1971. But since 1990, the figure has hovered just below that number.

▶WOMEN AND CHILDBEARING: CURRENT TRENDS

According to the Census Bureau's Current Population Survey there were 59.7 million women in the U.S. between the ages of 15 and 44 in 1997, the latest year for which statistics are available. Some 3.9 million of them reported having a birth in the preceding 12 months, resulting in an estimated fertility rate of 65.0 births per 1,000 women ages 15 to 44. That's a slight drop from the year before, when the fertility rate was 65.3, but a dramatic drop from 1990, when it was 70.9

Minorities   Significantly higher fertility rates were reported among minorities: 70.7 for black women, 69.1 for American Indian women, and 66.3 for Asian women, compared with 63.9 for white women. For women of Hispanic origin, the rate was 102.8, down from 107.7 in 1990. Mexican women had the highest fertility rates: 116.6 per 1,000 women, nearly double the rate for non-Hispanic women (60.1).

Older women   Although the overall birth rate continues to decline each year, the birth rate for women over 30 has increased every year since 1991, and the rate for women over 45 has doubled (From 0.2 per 1,000 women to 0.4) over the same period. Birth rates for women aged 20-30 are up from 1995 levels, but still below 1990 figures.

Unmarried women   The U.S. Department of Health and Human Services reported that the number of children born to unmarried women declined in 1997 to 44.0 births per 1,000 unmarried women aged 15-44. That's 2 percent lower than 1996, when the rate was 44.8, and 6 percent below the all-time high of 46.9 recorded in 1994. The total of 1,257,444 children born to unmarried women in 1997 was down from 1,260,306 the year before, but still represented 32.4 percent of all births. The rates for black and Hispanic women were even higher. Four out of every 10 births to Hispanic women were to unmarried women, and 69.2 percent of black children were born to unwed mothers. Among white women, 25.8 percent of births were to unmarried women.

Fertility Rates of U.S. Women, 1930–97

Year	General fertility rate	Total fertility rate	Year	General fertility rate	Total fertility rate
1930	89.2	2,600	1980	68.4	1,840
1935	77.2	2,250	1985	66.2	1,843
1940	79.9	2,301	1990	70.9	2,081
1945	85.9	2,491	1991	69.6	2,073
1950	106.2	3,091	1992	68.9	2,065
1955	118.3	3,574	1993	67.6	2,046
1960	118.0	3,654	1994	66.7	2,036
1965	96.6	2,928	1995	65.6	2,019
1970	87.9	2,480	1996	65.3	2,027
1975	66.0	1,774	1997	65.0	2,032

Source: U.S. Bureau of the Census, Population Division, *The Fertility of American Women* and U.S. National Center for Health Statistics, *Vital Statistics* (annual).

Women and Childbearing in the U.S, by Age, 1976–97

Characteristic	1976	1980	1990	1995	1997
Total number of women, 18-44 years old ('000s)[1]	41,618	45,652	58,381	60,225	59,688
Births per 1,000 women					
All women 15-44 years old[1]	67.2	71.1	67.0	64.7	61.4
15-19 years	N.A.	53.0	59.9	56.8	52.3
20-24 years	93.2[2]	115.1	116.5	109.8	110.4
25-29 years	104.8	112.9	120.2	112.2	113.8
30-34 years	56.4	61.9	80.8	82.5	85.3
35-39 years	22.6	19.8	31.7	34.3	36.1
40-44 years	6.5	3.9	5.5	6.6	7.1

1. Figures for 1976 and later includes women 18-44 years old. 2. Women 18-19 included with women 20-24 years old.
Source: National Center for Health Statistics, *National Vital Statistics Report*, April 29, 1999.

Births to teenagers Every year in the U.S., almost 500,000 teenagers give birth. Most of these women are unmarried. In 1997, some 385,802 unmarried teenagers gave birth, up dramatically from 288,000 in 1994. The *rate* of teenage births, however, is beginning to decline. The birth rate for women aged 15-19 hit a 20-year high of 62.1 in 1991, but has declined every year since then, to 52.3. For women under 15, the rate was 1.1 in 1997, down from the all-time high reached every year between 1989 and 1994. According to the National Center for Health Statistics, the sharpest declines were among black teenagers, whose rate fell 24 percent between 1991 and 1997, from 115.5 to 88.2 births per 1,000 black women 15-19. This rate is still much higher, however, than the 46.3 births per 1,000 white teenagers. The rate in 1997 for Hispanics, who tend to marry younger than non-Hispanics, was 102.8, down from 108.6 in 1991.

Multiple births According to the Centers for Disease Control, the use of fertility drugs has greatly increased the number of multiple births. There were 104,137 babies born as twins in 1997 (not all twin births are live deliveries), up from 68,339 in 1980, an increase of 52 percent. In 1980, 18.9 births out of every 1,000 resulted in twins; in 1997, the rate was 26.8 per 1,000, an increase of 42 percent. In 1997 there were 6,148 children born as triplets, 510 quadruplets, and 79 babies born as quintuplets, sextuplets, septuplets, and octuplets.

▶**ADOPTION**
Between 1973 and 1994, the percent of ever-married women who have ever adopted a child declined from 2.1 percent to 1.3 percent, according to National Surveys of Family Growth from those years. The National Center for Health Statistics attributed the drop to several factors, including the legalization of abortion in 1973 and the development of new reproductive technologies that have reduced the number of unwanted pregnancies. Almost all of the decrease since 1973 has come in unrelated children; the percent of women adopting their nieces, nephews, stepchildren, boyfriend's children, or other related (blood or otherwise) children has held steady.

Perhaps the greatest shift has come in the number of children available for adoption. Before 1973, never-married women under the age of 45 relinquished 8.7 percent of their children for adoption. In 1995, they gave up less than 1 percent. Almost all of this decrease has come among never-married white women, who relinquished nearly 20 percent of their children before 1973. Never-married black women have consistently kept their babies: Only 1.5 percent relinquished their children before 1973, and only 1.1 percent did between 1982 and 1988 (1995 figures were unavailable).

In 1995, there were 37.4 million ever-married women between the ages of 18 and 44. Of these, 9.9 million, or 26.4 percent, had considered adoption, 1.6 million had taken steps toward adoption, and 472,000 were currently looking to adopt a child. According to the Survey, steps toward adoption include contacting an adoption agency or lawyer, placing a newspaper ad, or having previously adopted a child.

HOUSEHOLDS AND FAMILIES

Since the very first census in 1790, the Federal Government has not only attempted to count every individual, it has also tried to determine where those individuals live and with whom. While the definition of *household* has changed somewhat over the years, it has remained a central element in understanding the basic structure of American society. Since 1970, changes in the size and composition of the household unit have revealed the extent of social change more clearly than any other measure.

▶**HOUSEHOLDS**
Virtually all Americans are part of a household. As of March 1998, the Census Bureau determined that 269 million persons belonged to a household, even if that household consisted of only one person. A small number of people in institutions or in unique group living arrangements do not belong to households. According to the official Census Bureau definition, a household consists of all persons who occupy a housing unit. A house, an apartment or

U.S. Households, Number and Size, 1940-98

Year	Number of households ('000s)	Average number per household All ages	Under 18 years	18 years and older
1940	34,949	3.67	1.14	2.53
1950	43,544	3.37	1.06	2.31
1955	47,874	3.33	1.14	2.19
1960[1]	52,799	3.33	1.21	2.12
1965	57,436	3.29	1.21	2.09
1970	63,401	3.14	1.09	2.05
1975	71,120	2.94	0.93	2.01
1980	80,776	2.76	0.79	1.97
1985	86,789	2.69	0.72	1.97
1990	93,347	2.63	0.69	1.94
1995	98,990	2.65	0.71	1.93
1996	99,627	2.65	0.71	1.94
1997	101,018	2.64	0.71	1.93
1998	102,528	2.62	0.70	1.92

1. Alaska and Hawaii included for first time. **Source:** U.S. Bureau of the Census, *The Statistical History of the U.S.* (1976); *Household and Family Characteristics: March 1998* (1999). www.census.gov.

Unmarried Couple Households, 1960-98

Year	Total	Without children under 15	With children under 15
1960	439,000	242,000	197,000
1970	523,000	327,000	196,000
1980	1,589,000	1,159,000	431,000
1985	1,983,000	1,380,000	603,000
1990	2,856,000	1,966,000	891,000
1991	3,039,000	2,077,000	962,000
1992	3,308,000	2,187,000	1,121,000
1993	3,510,000	2,274,000	1,236,000
1994	3,661,000	2,391,000	1,270,000
1995	3,668,000	2,349,000	1,319,000
1996	3,958,000	2,516,000	1,442,000
1997	4,130,000	2,660,000	1,470,000
1998	4,236,000	2,716,000	1,520,000

Note: Figures may not add to total due to rounding. **Source:** *Marital Status and Living Arrangements: March 1998* (1999).

other group of rooms, or a single room, is regarded as a housing unit when it is occupied or intended for occupancy as separate living quarters; that is when the occupants do not live and eat with any other persons in the structure and there is direct access from the outside or through a common hall.

There are two major categories of households identified by the Census Bureau: family and nonfamily. A family or family household requires the presence of at least two persons, the householder (i.e. the person in whose name the housing unit is owned or rented) and one or more additional family members related to the householder through birth, adoption or marriage. A nonfamily household consists of a householder who either lives alone or exclusively with persons who are not related to the householder. Since 1970 the rapid growth of nonfamily households has led to a continuous increase in the number of households and a fall in the average number of persons in each.

As of March 1998 there were 102.5 million households in the U.S., the largest number ever, with an average of 2.62 persons in each. This continues a trend begun during the 1970s when the number of households increased by more than 20 percent and over 17.3 million units, nearly double the growth of the 1940s and 1950s and over 60 percent more than the relatively explosive 1960s. The most significant change helping to ignite this surge was the un-

precedented increase in the number of nonfamily households, which grew by 77.7 percent in the 1970s and 28.4 percent during the 1980s.

Several factors help to account for this change, including the rapid rise in the divorce rate, as well as an increase in the number of young single people living on their own and deciding to postpone marriage. In 1998, more than 26 million people, or nearly one in 10, lived alone. The most recent Census Bureau figures indicate that the trend is abating, however. The number of people living alone grew 59 percent during the 1970s, 21 percent during the 1980s, but only 10 percent from 1990 to 1998.

An additional 4.2 million unmarried-couple households were another large segment of the nonfamily population. Unmarried couples made up only a small percentage of all U.S. couples, but their numbers have continued to skyrocket since their sudden appearance on the American social landscape during the 1970s. There were only 523,000 unmarried couples living together in 1970, but their numbers had tripled to 1.6 million in 1980. A growing number of unmarried couples (1.5 million in 1998) have children under 15 years old in their households. This doesn't necessarily mean more children are being born out of wedlock, however, since this category includes children from previous marriages living with an unremarried parent. As currently defined by the

Living Arrangements of Children Under 18, by Race, 1970–98 (thousands)

Arrangement	1970 Number	1970 Percent	1980 Number	1980 Percent	1990 Number	1990 Percent	1998 Number	1998 Percent
All children								
Children under 18	69,162	100.0%	63,427	100.0%	64,137	100.0%	71,377	100.0%
Living with:								
Two parents	58,939	85.2	48,624	76.7	46,503	72.5	48,642	68.2
One Parent	8,199	11.9	12,466	19.7	15,867	24.7	19,777	27.7
Mother only	7,452	10.8	11,406	18.0	13,874	21.6	16,634	23.3
Father only	748	1.1	1,060	1.7	1,993	3.1	3,143	4.4
Other relatives	1,547	2.2	1,949	3.1	1,421	2.2	2,126	3.0
Nonrelatives only	477	0.7	388	0.6	346	0.5	833	1.2
White children								
Children under 18	58,791	100.0%	52,242	100.0%	51,390	100.0%	56,124	100.0%
Living with:								
Two parents	52,624	89.5	43,200	82.7	40,593	79.0	41,547	74.0
One Parent	5,110	8.7	7,901	15.1	9,869	19.2	12,772	22.8
Mother only	4,581	7.8	7,059	13.5	8,321	16.2	10,210	18.2
Father only	528	0.9	842	1.6	1,549	3.0	2,562	4.6
Other relatives	695	1.2	887	1.7	708	1.4	1,164	2.1
Nonrelatives only	362	0.6	254	0.5	220	0.4	635	1.1
Black children								
Children under 18	9,422	100.0%	9,375	100.0%	10,018	100.0%	11,414	100.0%
Living with:								
Two parents	5,508	58.5	3,956	42.2	3,781	37.7	4,137	36.2
One Parent	2,995	31.8	4,297	45.8	5,484	54.7	6,254	54.8
Mother only	2,783	29.5	4,117	43.9	5,132	51.2	5,830	51.1
Father only	213	2.3	180	1.9	353	3.5	424	3.7
Other relatives	822	8.7	999	10.7	655	6.5	843	7.4
Nonrelatives only	97	1.0	123	1.3	98	1.0	172	1.5
Hispanic children								
Children under 18	4,006	100.0%	5,459	100.0%	7,174	100.0%	10,863	100.0%
Living with:								
Two parents	3,111	77.7	4,116	75.4	4,789	66.8	6,909	63.6
One Parent	NA	NA	1,152	21.1	2,154	30.0	3,397	31.3
Mother only	NA	NA	1,069	19.6	1,943	27.1	2,915	26.8
Father only	NA	NA	83	1.5	211	2.9	482	4.4
Other relatives	NA	NA	183	3.4	177	2.5	380	3.5
Nonrelatives only	NA	NA	8	0.1	54	0.8	171	1.6

Note: NA= Not available. Hispanic children may be of any race. Excludes persons under 18 years who were maintaining households or family groups and spouses. **Source:** U.S. Bureau of the Census, *Marital Status and Living Arrangements: March 1999* (1999).

Census Bureau, an unmarried-couple household is two persons of the opposite sex who share living quarters; although a close personal relationship is implied, other types—including tenancy—are included. But no more than two unrelated adults are present in an unmarried-couple household although children under age 15 may be present.

Despite all the attention given to the growth of nonfamily households, the fact remains that the overwhelming majority of Americans—225 million in 1998—live in some kind of family situation. This is not to say that the size and structure of the family hasn't undergone major revamping in recent decades but rather to emphasize its inherent strength as the basic social unit despite the presence of powerful forces for change.

▶ FAMILIES

In 1998 there were 70.8 million families in the U.S., up from 51.6 million in 1970. But the typical American family of the 1990s bears less and less resemblance to the family of 1970. Market researchers who once assumed the family consisted of four members now base their assumptions on families of three, reflecting a steady, dramatic decline in the average family size, from 3.58 in 1970 to 3.18 in 1998. These numbers indicate a growing number of families opting not to have children. They constituted 44.1 percent of all families in 1970, but since 1990, they have outnumbered families with children. In 1998, 34.8 million families had children under 18, compared to 36.1 million without children.

More important, perhaps, the proportion of married-couple families declined from 86.9 percent of all family households in 1970 to 76.6 percent in 1998, while the number of family households headed by females with no husbands present soared from 5.5 million, or 10.7 percent of all family households in 1970, to 12.7 million, or 17.8 percent in 1998. (A startling 46.7 percent of black families were headed by single women in 1998, up from 28.0 percent in 1970.)

A related development, recently turned into a political issue by those advocating "family values," has been the rising number of single-parent situations. More than 27 percent of families with children were headed by a single parent in 1998, up from only 13 percent in 1970. The vast majority (81.1 percent) of these single-parent families were

Households and Families: Growth and Change, 1960–98 (in thousands)

Type of unit	1960	1970	1980	1990	1998	Percent change 1970–80	Percent change 1980–90
All Households	**52,799**	**63,401**	**80,776**	**93,347**	**102,528**	**27.4%**	**15.5%**
Average size	3.33	3.14	2.76	2.63	2.62	—	—
Families	**45,111**	**51,586**	**59,550**	**66,090**	**70,880**	**15.4%**	**11.0%**
Average size	3.67	3.58	3.29	3.17	3.18	—	—
Married couple	39,329	44,755	49,112	52,317	54,317	9.7	6.5
Male householder[1]	1,275	1,239	1,733	2,884	3,911	39.9	66.4
Female householder[1]	4,507	5,591	8,705	10,890	12,652	55.7	25.1
Unrelated subfamilies	**207**	**130**	**360**	**534**	**575**	**176.9%**	**48.3%**
Married couple	75	27	20	68	41	N.A.[2]	N.A.[2]
Father-child[1]	47	11	36	45	72	N.A.[2]	N.A.[2]
Mother-child[1]	85	91	304	421	463	234.1	38.5
Related subfamilies	**1,514**	**1,150**	**1,150**	**2,403**	**2,870**	**0%**	**109.0%**
Married couple	871	617	582	871	947	-5.7	49.7
Father-child[1]	115	48	54	153	250	N.A.[2]	183.0
Mother-child[1]	528	484	512	1,378	1,673	5.8	169.1
Nonfamily households	**7,895**	**11,945**	**21,226**	**27,257**	**31,648**	**77.7%**	**28.4%**
Male householder	2,716	4,063	8,807	11,606	14,133	116.8	31.8
Female householder	5,179	7,882	12,419	15,651	17,516	57.6	26.0
One person	6,896	10,851	18,296	22,999	26,327	68.6	25.7

1. No spouse present. 2. Not shown; base less than 75,000.
Source: U.S. Bureau of the Census, *Household and Family Characteristics: March 1998* (1999). **www.census.gov**

Families: Number, Average Size and Percent Distribution by Number of Children, 1970–98

Year	Number of families ('000s)	Average size of family	Percent distribution by number of own children under 18 None	1	2	3	4 or more
1970	51,586	3.58	44.1%	18.2%	17.4%	10.6%	9.8%
1975	55,712	3.42	46.0	19.7	18.0	9.3	6.9
1980	59,550	3.29	47.9	20.9	19.3	7.8	4.1
1985	62,706	3.23	50.4	20.9	18.6	7.2	3.0
1990	66,090	3.17	51.1	20.5	18.5	7.0	2.8
1995	69,305	3.19	50.5	20.3	19.1	7.3	2.8
1996	69,594	3.20	50.9	20.2	19.0	7.1	2.9
1997	70,241	3.19	50.6	20.4	18.9	7.3	2.8
1998	70,880	3.18	51.0	20.3	18.5	10.3[1]	([1])

1. In 1998, the Census Bureau changed the "4 or more" category to "3 or more."
Source: U.S. Bureau of the Census, *Household and Family Characteristics: March 1998* (1999). **www.census.gov**

headed by women. The number of households headed by never-married women with children continues to grow. There were 248,000 such households in 1970; in 1998, there were 4.1 million of them, more even than the 3.4 million households headed by divorced women with children.

According to the Census Bureau, the period between 1990 and 1998 has seen a general stabilizing of these trends as the percentage of married couple families and single-parent families remained constant. The one startling change has been the growth rate of single-parent homes headed by fathers. In 1998, they numbered 1.8 million, or 5 percent of all families.

Another important though less vital sign of change is the growth in the number of so-called *subfamilies*. These are families who live in a household and are either related or not to the householder; the Census Bureau describes a *related subfamily* as a married couple with or without children, or one parent with one or more own single (never married) children under 18, living in a household and related to the person who maintains the household. They are not counted in the total number of families. Related subfamilies have nearly tripled since 1980 and now stand at 2.9 million.

An *unrelated subfamily* is a group of two persons or more who are related to one another by birth, marriage, or adoption, but who are not related to the householder. Unrelated subfamilies numbered 575,000 in 1998.

▶ **SINGLE PARENTS AND GROWN CHILDREN LIVING AT HOME**
Among the social changes that have taken place over the last 20 years, two of the most revealing are with whom children live and how soon young people get to live on their own. Since 1970, the percentage of children under 18 living with only one parent has more than doubled. In 1998, 28 percent lived with only one parent, as compared to just under 12 percent in 1970. This increase reflects not only a soaring divorce rate, but a startling increase in the number of children born to unwed mothers, especially among blacks. The numbers of households headed by unmarried black women and divorced black women were equal in 1970. In 1997, unwed black mother households outnumbered divorced-mother black households by nearly four to one. Since 1990, more than half of all black children, one-fifth of white children, and 31 percent of Hispanic chilren under the age of 18 have lived with one parent only, usually the mother.

Inflation, soaring housing costs, stagnant wage rates, and postponement of marriage have helped to keep young adults of both sexes living at home with their parents for an increasingly long period. In 1970, 8.0 percent of 25-to-34-year-olds lived with their parents. By 1987, that number had increased to close to 12 percent, where it has remained ever since. Because they marry younger, women aged 25-34 were only half as likely (9 percent in 1997) as men (15 percent) to live with their parents.

▶ **LIVING WITH GRANDPARENTS**
In 1998, the Census Bureau found that 5.6 percent of the nation's 71 million children under age 18 lived in the home of their grandparents. This is up from 3.2 percent in 1970 and 3.6 percent in 1980, but down slightly from the all-time high of 5.7 percent in 1996. A total of 4.0 million children under 18 lived with grandparents in 1998, down from 4.1 million in 1996. Of those children, nearly half lived there with their mothers. Some 6.0 percent (247,000) lived there with their fathers, up from 5.4 percent in 1996. An additional 12.6 percent (503,000) lived with both parents in a grandparent's home, down from 14.2 percent the year before. The remaining 35.5 percent (1,415,000) lived with their grandparents with neither parent present, down from 35.2 percent in 1996.

Source: U.S. Bureau of the Census, *Marital Status and Living Arrangements: March 1998* (1999).

HOUSING

According to the Census Bureau's biannual American Housing Survey, there were 99.4 million occupied housing units in the U.S. in 1997, the latest year for which data are available. Of these units, 65.5 million (65.8 percent) were occupied by homeowners, while the remaining 34.0 million (34.1 percent) were occupied by renters.

Housing units The American ideal of the intact nuclear family may be somewhat tarnished in these days of high divorce rates and growing single-parent households, but U.S. housing patterns still reflect traditional values. Nearly two of every three homes (62.1 million) were detached single unit structures. Mobile homes or trailers, numbering 6.5 million, are not included in those totals. Another 5.8 million were attached single-unit structures such as a brownstone or row house. Cooperatives and condominiums, totaling more than 5.9 million, are counted separately since they may include any number of dwellings.

Size of housing units The median number of rooms per house in 1997 was 5.9, up from 5.5 only two years earlier, and the vast majority of homes (73.7 million, or 74.2 percent) had between four and seven rooms. Most houses had two (29.0 percent) or three (40.8 percent) bedrooms and one full bathroom (44.5 percent). The median size of all single, detached one-family houses (including mobile homes) was 1,750 square feet, up from 1,732 in 1995; for owner-occupied houses, the figure was 1,825 square feet. About 20 percent of single houses (13.9 million) had more than 2,500 square feet, and 12.5 percent (8.6 million) had less than 1,000 square feet. The biggest houses are the newest ones: homes built in the past four years had a median area of 1,876 square feet.

Growth of housing In 1997, the median age of all housing structures in the U.S. was only 30 years (i.e. built in 1967). Only 8.8 million units built before 1919 were still in use. This reflects the extraordinary growth of the housing industry during the 1970s and 80s, when 35.3 million of the 99.5 million extant units were built. By comparison, only 18.0 million of the housing units still in use were built between 1920 and 1950.

Home ownership Extremely low mortgage rates, a strong economy, and low unemployment combined in 1998 to create the highest rate of homeownership in U.S. history: 66.3 percent. Rates are up among all groups, even young people and minorities, who typically have lower homeownership rates. Some 45.6 percent of blacks owned their own homes in 1998, up from 42.3 percent in 1994; Hispanic homeownership was 44.7 percent, up from 41.2 in 1994. The rate for homeowners under 25 was 18.2 percent, up from 15.7 in 1990.

Homeownership rates were lower for all age groups in 1998 than in 1982 except householders 55-64, which was about the same, and the 65 and over category, which has been creeping up every year (see the accompanying table). This pronounced change reflects the growing independence of the nation's elderly population.

The increase in homeownership follows a decade—the 1980s—in which skyrocketing home prices and high interest rates prevented many people from buying homes. The decline in home-

ownership rates in the 1980s was the first in 50 years.

Married couple families own most of the homes in the U.S. In 1997, 52.3 million homes (79.8 percent of all owner-occupied units) belonged to such families. Just over 25 million homes were owned by single householders. The majority of single homeowners (14.6 million) were women, half of whom (7.2 million) were 65 or over.

Housing costs According to an annual survey by the Chicago Title Insurance Company, the median price of a single-family home in 1998 was $167,900, up more than 5 percent from $159,700 in 1997. First-time buyers paid a median price of

Characteristics of Occupied Housing Units 1993–97

Characteristic	1993 Units ('000)	1993 Percent of units	1995 Units ('000)	1995 Percent of units	1997 Units ('000)	1997 Percent of units
Total occupied units	**94,724**	**100.0%**	**97,693**	**100.0%**	**99,487**	**100.0%**
Owner occupied	61,252	64.7	63,544	65.0	65,487	65.8
Renter occupied	33,472	35.3	34,150	35.0	34,000	34.1
Units in structure						
Single, detached	58,918	62.2%	60,826	62.3%	62,111	62.4%
Single, attached	5,375	5.7	5,545	5.7	5,840	5.9
2 to 4	9,279	9.8	9,299	9.5	8,973	9.0
5 to 9	4,724	5.0	4,803	4.9	4,852	4.9
10 to 19	4,190	4.4	4,342	4.4	4,264	4.3
20 to 49	3,154	3.3	3,244	3.3	6,903	6.9
50 or more	3,429	3.6	3,470	3.6	N.A.	N.A.
Mobile home or trailer	5,655	5.9	6,164	6.3	6,544	6.6
Size						
Size of unit (sq. ft.)	1,725	N.A.	1,732	N.A.	1,750	N.A.
Size of lot (acres)	4.3	N.A.	4.3	N.A.	3.5	N.A.
Median number of rooms	5.5	N.A.	5.5	N.A.	5.9	N.A.
Median number of bedrooms	2.7	N.A.	2.7	N.A.	3.2	N.A.
Number of bathrooms						
None	526	0.6%	465	0.5%	750	0.8%
One	43,944	46.4	43,777	44.8	44,223	44.4
One and a half	14,740	15.6	14,780	15.1	14,987	15.1
Two or more	35,515	37.5	38,671	39.6	39,527	39.7
Median age (years)	28	N.A.	28	N.A.	30	N.A.
Mortgage status						
None, owned free and clear	24,068	39.3[1]%	24,518	38.6[1]%	25,453	38.9[1]%
One mortgage	32,302	52.7[1]	34,730	54.7[1]	29,210	44.6[1]
Two mortgages	3,975	6.5[1]	4,244	6.7[1]	6,345	9.7[1]
Three or more mortgages	71	0.1[1]	52	0.1[1]	444	0.7[1]
Median years remaining	19	N.A.	20	N.A.	21	N.A.
Median amount outstanding	$48,357	N.A.	$48,466	N.A.	$52,543	N.A.

1. As a percentage of all owner-occupied units. Not all homeowners reported their mortgage status.
Source: U.S. Bureau of the Census, *1997 American Housing Survey* (1999).

Average Sales Prices of New One-Family Houses, by Region, 1965–98

Year	United States	Northeast	Midwest	South	West
1965	$21,500	$22,900	$22,800	$18,900	$23,200
1970	26,600	32,800	28,000	24,000	26,900
1975	42,600	47,000	43,400	39,600	44,300
1900	76,400	80,300	74,400	69,100	89,400
1985	100,800	121,900	95,400	88,900	111,800
1990	149,800	190,500	133,000	123,500	180,600
1995	158,700	216,600	157,200	142,000	169,800
1996	166,400	226,100	158,900	144,200	186,200
1997	176,200	234,100	173,000	151,400	198,200
1998	181,900	240,100	179,000	159,700	200,500

Note: Figures are in current dollars. **Source:** U.S. Bureau of the Census, *New One-Family Houses Sold* (March 1999).

Fair Market Monthly Rents for Existing Housing for Selected Metropolitan Areas, 1999

Metropolitan area	Studio	1 Bedroom	2 Bedrooms	3 Bedrooms	4 Bedrooms
Albuquerque, N.M	$392	$467	$584	$805	$950
Atlanta, Ga.	530	590	688	916	1,109
Austin-San Marcos, Tex.	434	525	699	970	1,147
Baltimore, Md.	421	515	628	831	951
Boston, Mass.	643	723	906	1,132	1,329
Charlotte, N.C.	434	489	551	726	870
Chicago, Ill.	516	619	737	922	1,031
Cincinnati, Ohio	309	397	531	712	769
Cleveland-Lorain-Elyria, Ohio	382	480	594	755	851
Colorado Springs, Colo.	435	467	623	868	1,025
Columbus, Ohio	364	431	553	702	807
Dallas, Tex.	487	560	718	994	1,175
Denver, Colo.	418	499	664	922	1,088
Detroit, Mich.	386	525	634	793	889
El Paso, Tex.	397	445	527	730	865
Fort Lauderdale, Fla.	479	564	698	971	1,143
Fort Worth-Arlington, Tex.	417	453	588	820	967
Fresno, Calif.	374	419	500	695	802
Honolulu, Hawaii	613	733	863	1,167	1,262
Houston, Tex.	413	464	601	837	986
Indianapolis, Ind.	361	453	545	682	765
Jacksonville, Fla.	422	472	569	752	836
Kansas City, Mo.	353	444	534	739	819
Las Vegas, Nev.	491	582	693	965	1,139
Los Angeles-Long Beach, Calif.	494	592	749	1,011	1,206
Memphis, Tenn.	387	451	530	736	774
Miami, Fla.	449	563	702	965	1,118
Milwaukee-Waukeshau, Wis.	368	482	605	758	847
Minneapolis-St. Paul, Minn.	405	521	666	901	1,020
Nashville, Tenn.	425	508	626	853	958
New Orleans, La.	364	417	520	708	856
New York, N.Y[1]	704	785	891	1,114	1,249
Oakland, Calif.	567	686	861	1,180	1,410
Oklahoma City, Okla.	331	361	468	651	728
Orange County, Calif.	645	704	871	1,212	1,349
Philadelphia, Pa	475	584	722	903	1,132
Phoenix-Mesa, Ariz.	417	505	634	882	1,039
Pittsburgh, Pa.	335	411	495	620	693
Portland-Vancouver, Oreg.-Wash.	425	523	645	897	974
Sacramento, Calif.	434	490	613	850	1,002
Saint Louis, Mo.	317	386	501	652	721
Salt Lake City, Utah	432	501	635	884	1,036
San Antonio, Tex.	371	428	554	771	911
San Diego, Calif.	495	566	708	984	1,161
San Francisco, Calif.	713	923	1,167	1,601	1,693
San Jose, Calif.	808	922	1,139	1,561	1,753
Seattle-Bellevue-Everett, Wash.	478	582	736	1,022	1,208
Tampa-St. Petersburg, Fla.	396	472	584	776	940
Tucson, Ariz.	365	438	582	810	956
Tulsa, Okla.	332	397	520	724	853
Washington, D.C.-Md.-Va.	615	699	820	1,118	1,347
West Palm Beach-Boca Raton, Fla.	495	578	715	950	1,175

Note: Except where indicated figures are projections for 1999 made in 1998. 1. Figures include areas outside Manhattan. **Source:** U.S. Dept. of Housing and Urban Development, Office of the Federal Housing Commissioner, *Fair Market Rents*, Sept. 25, 1998

$142,200; they constituted 46.2 percent of all home buyers. Buyers who previously owned a home paid a median price of $189,900, up 6.3 percent from the previous year. San Francisco was by far the most expensive place to buy a house: the median price was $315,300 for all homes in the Bay area. That's more than double the median price in Atlanta ($145,400), Philadelphia ($143,900), and Denver ($151,300) and more than $100,000 over and above the medians in Chicago ($169,600) and even New York City ($183,800). Surprisingly, median sales prices in Washington D.C. ($198,400) and in Boston ($196,200) were both higher than in New York City. Housing prices in Orlando, Fla. were cheapest of the 20 metropolitan areas surveyed; the median sales price was $107,100.

Average monthly mortgage payments for all homeowners rose from $1,114 in 1997 to $1,212 in 1998. These payments represented 32.3 percent of owners's incomes, down slightly from the year before, but way up from 1976, when only 24.0 percent went to mortgage payments. Payments were higher among repeat buyers, but first-time buyers paid a larger percentage of their incomes toward

Existing One-Family Houses Sold and Median Sales Price, by Region, 1970–98

Year	United States	Northeast	Midwest	South	West
			Houses sold		
1970	1,612,000	251,000	501,000	568,000	292,000
1975	2,476,000	370,000	701,000	862,000	543,000
1980	2,973,000	403,000	806,000	1,092,000	672,000
1985	3,134,000	561,000	806,000	1,063,000	704,000
1990	3,211,000	469,000	831,000	1,202,000	709,000
1995	3,812,000	577,000	992,000	1,431,000	813,000
1996	4,196,000	584000	986,000	1,511,000	1,116,000
1997	4,381,000	606,000	1,005,000	1,596,000	1,117,400
1998	4,970,000	662,000	1,130,000	1,868,000	1,309,000
			Median sales price (current dollars)		
1970	$23,000	$25,200	$20,100	$22,200	$24,300
1975	35,300	39,300	30,100	34,800	39,600
1980	62,200	60,800	51,900	58,300	89,300
1985	75,500	88,900	58,900	75,200	95,400
1990	95,500	141,200	74,000	85,900	139,600
1995	113,100	136,900	93,600	97,800	148,300
1996	118,200	140,900	99,800	102,800	152,900
1997	124,100	145,100	106,100	109,000	160,300
1998	130,600	149,700	113,700	115,400	172,000

Source: National Association of Realtors, *Home Sales* (May 1999).

Median Sales Prices of Existing Single-Family Homes for Selected Metropolitan Areas, 1985–99

Metropolitan area	1985	1990	1995	1998	1999[1]
Atlanta, Ga.	$66,200[2]	$86,400	$ 97,500	$115,400	N.A.
Baltimore, Md.	72,600	105,900	111,300	120,600	$121,300
Boston, Mass.	134,200	174,100	179,000	212,600	216,000
Chicago, Ill.	81,100	116,800	147,900	166,800	166,100
Cincinnati, Ohio-Ky.-Tenn.	60,200	79,800	100,400	116,300	117,500
Cleveland, Ohio	64,400	80,600	104,700	121,800	119,200
Dallas, Tex.	94,000	89,500	96,400	120,400	N.A.
Denver, Colo.	84,300	86,400	127,300	152,200	159,000
Detroit, Mich.	51,700	76,700	98,200	132,600	136,400
Houston, Tex.	78,600	70,700	79,200	97,500	98,400
Kansas City, Mo.-Kans.	61,400	74,100	91,700	114,000	118,000
Los Angeles area, Calif.	125,200	212,100	179,900	192,600	185,000
Miami-Hialeah, Fla.	80,500	89,300	107,100	121,500	133,000
Milwaukee, Wis.	67,500	84,400	114,700	132,900	130,000
Minneapolis-St. Paul, Minn.-Wis.	75,200	88,700	106,800	128,000	131,700
New York City area, N.Y.	134,000	174,900	169,700	188,100	193,600
Philadelphia, Pa-N.J.	74,000	108,700	118,700	N.A.	126,600
Phoenix, Ariz.	74,800	84,000	96,800	120,200	123,100
Pittsburgh, Pa.	N.A.	70,100	82,100	89,000	88,100
St. Louis, Mo.-Ill.	65,700	76,700	87,700	101,700	100,300
San Diego, Calif.	107,400	183,200	171,600	207,100	214,700
San Francisco Bay Area, Calif.	145,100	259,300	254,400	321,700	331,100
Seattle, Wash.	N.A.	142,000	159,000	175,300	182,900
Tampa-St. Petersburg-Clearwater, Fla.	58,400	71,400	78,300	89,300	89,800
Washington, D.C.-Md.-Va.	97,100	150,500	156,500	172,100	168,100
U.S. average	N.A.	N.A.	$112,900	$130,600	$131,600

1. First quarter only. 2. Figure is for 1984.   Source: National Association of Realtors, *Home Sales* (May 1999).

their mortgages. Low interest rates were responsible for the resurgent popularity of fixed-rate mortgages, in which the consumer locks into a monthly payment for the life of the loan. Fixed-rate mortgages were the choice of 79 percent of mortgage buyers in 1998, up from 69 percent the year before, and 55 percent in 1995.

Adjustable, or variable rate mortgages, in which the monthly payment rises and falls based on the prevailing national interest rates, usually feature lower interest rates (as much as 3 percentage points) for the first several years, and higher rates toward the end of the loan. They were responsible for 13.5 percent of all mortgages in 1998, down from 23.4 percent the year before, and the all-time high of 36.2 percent in 1995.

The average mortgage length was 28.9 years for first-time home buyers and 27.9 years for repeat

Homeownership Rates in the U.S. by Age, Race, and Hispanic Origin, 1982–98

Characteristic	1982	1985	1990	1995	1996	1997	1998
U.S., total	**64.8%**	**63.9%**	**63.9%**	**64.7%**	**65.4%**	**65.7%**	**66.3%**
By age							
Under 25	19.3%	17.2%	15.7%	15.9%	18.0%	17.7%	18.2%
Under 35	41.2	39.9	38.5	38.6	39.1	38.7	39.3
35 to 44	70.0	68.1	66.3	65.2	65.5	66.1	66.9
45 to 54	77.4	75.9	75.2	75.2	75.6	75.8	75.7
55 to 64	80.0	79.5	79.3	79.5	80.0	80.1	80.9
65 and over	74.4	74.8	76.3	78.1	78.9	79.1	79.3
By race							
White	N.A.	N.A.	N.A.	68.7%	69.1%	69.3%	70.0%
Black	N.A.	N.A.	N.A.	42.7	44.1	44.8	45.6
Hispanic	N.A.	N.A.	N.A.	42.0	42.8	43.3	44.7

Source: U.S. Bureau of the Census, *1998 Housing Vacancy Survey,* 1999.

Characteristics of Recent Home Buyers, 1976–98

Item	1976	1980	1990	1995	1997	1998
Median purchase price	$43,340	$68,714	$131,200	$147,700	$159,700	$167,900
First-time buyers	37,670	61,450	106,000	128,300	135,400	142,200
Repeat buyers	50,090	75,750	149,400	164,300	178,700	189,800
Average monthly mortgage payment	$329	$599	$1,127	$1,062	$1,114	$1,212
First-time buyers	313	N.A.	N.A.	988	1,020	1,069
Repeat buyers	342	N.A.	N.A.	1,125	1,197	1,343
As percent of income	24.0%	32.4%	33.8%	32.6%	32.8%	32.3%
Percent buying:						
New houses	15.1%	22.4%	21.2%	21.5%	20.9%	21.2%
Existing houses	84.9	77.6	78.8	78.5	79.1	78.8
Single-family houses	88.8	82.4	83.8	83.1	81.6	82.3
Condominiums	11.2	17.6	13.1	14.0	15.5	14.7
For the first time	44.8	32.9	41.9	46.2	46.8	46.2
Down payment as percentage of sales price	25.2%	28.0%	23.3%	20.4%	20.3%	19.3%
First-time buyers	18.0	20.5	15.7	13.3	13.7	12.8
Repeat buyers	30.8	32.7	28.9	26.8	26.1	24.9
Average age (in years)						
First-time buyers	28.1	28.3	30.5	32.1	32.1	32.2
Repeat buyers	35.9	36.4	39.1	40.7	41.1	41.1

Source: Chicago Title and Trust Company, *Who's Buying Homes in America* (annual).

Homeownership Rates, 1890–1998

Year	Homeownership rate	Year	Homeownership rate
1890	47.8%	1970	62.9%
1900	46.7	1980	64.4
1910	45.9	1990	64.2
1920	45.6	1995[1]	64.7
1930	47.8	1996[1]	65.4
1940	43.6	1997[1]	65.7
1950	55.0	1998[1]	66.3
1960	61.9		

1. Figures from 1890–1990 are from the decennial census, which counts every home. Figures from 1995–98 are from the Census Bureau's annual *Housing Vacancy Survey,* which uses statistical samples. **Source:** U.S. Census Bureau.

buyers. Both numbers are up slightly from the year before, reflecting an increased popularity in 30-year mortgages. Meanwhile, the average down payment as a percentage of the purchase price continues to decline. In 1976, 26.9 percent of buyers put 10 percent or less down on a home purchase. In 1998, that number had more than doubled to 54.5 percent.

The average down payment was 19.3 percent, down from 25.2 percent in 1976.

Housing and the poor Two studies published in 1998, one by the Dept. of Housing and Urban Development, and one by the Center on Budget and Policy Priorities, revealed that despite the strong economic growth of the recent years, the housing problems of the poor have grown worse. A severe shortage of affordable apartments has existed all around the nation for several years, forcing 4.4 million poor families to pay more than half their income on rent, usually 60 percent or more than double what the government calls affordable rent.

The major reasons for this development are stagnating wages for the unskilled, rising real estate values, and the government's failure to supply enough subsidized housing. The number of new subsidized units fell to 70,000 a year during the Reagan-Bush years, down from 260,000 during the Carter Administration. In 1995, when the Republicans took over Congress, the government actually stopped expanding the pool of subsidized housing for the first time in modern history.

About 15 million households currently qualify for federal housing assistance, but only 4.5 million families get it. Of those, about one-third live

Funding for Federal Homeless Assistance Programs, 1995-98

Agency and Program	Budget (millions)			
	1995	1996	1997	1998
Dept. of Agriculture				
Homeless Children Nutrition Program	$1.7	$1.7	$2.1	$1.9
Dept. of Education				
Education for Homeless Children and Youth	28.8	23.0	25.0	28.8
Federal Emergency Management Agency				
Emergency Food and Shelter Program	130.0	100.0	100.0	100.0
Dept. of Health and Human Services				
Health Care for the Homeless	65.4	65.5	69.3	71.3
Projects for Assistance in Transition from Homelessness	29.5	20.0	20.0	23.0
Runaway and Homeless Youth Programs	54.1	64.2	66.6	73.5
Dept. of Housing and Urban Development				
Emergency Shelter Grants	155.0	115.0	115.0	165.0
Single-Room Occupancy Moderate Rehabilitation	N.A.	N.A.	10.1	23.5
Shelter Plus Care	162.0	89.0	61.0	116.9
Supportive Housing Program	602.0	577.0	620.0	574.2
Dept. of Labor				
Homeless Veterans Reintegration Project	N.A.	N.A.	N.A.	3.0
Dept. of Veterans' Affairs				
Domiciliary Care for Homeless Veterans	38.9	41.1	37.2	38.5
Homeless Chronically Mentally Ill Veterans	32.3	32.1	32.0	36.4
Homeless Providers Grant and Per Diem Program	6.3	6.3	6.1	5.9
Total	**$1,306.0**	**$1,134.9**	**$1,164.4**	**$1,261.9**

Source: General Accounting Office: *Report to Congressional Committee: Homelessness,* February, 1999.

in conventional housing projects, while the rest receive subsidies that allow them to live in private housing. In each case, the tenants contribute 30 percent of their income toward the rent and the government provides the rest.

▶ THE HOMELESS

Although homeless people have become a common sight in almost every community, their plight is always surrounded by some kind of controversy, one that is fueled by a wide range of opinions, some based on fact and others on stereotypes. The often shrill debate about just who the homeless are and what can or should be done for them has been hampered by a lack of reliable information on everything from the causes of homelessness to the actual number of people living on the streets or in shelters.

The number of homeless Because homelessness is a temporary circumstance, it is nearly impossible to measure the number of homeless.

The first comprehensive federal effort to count the homeless was done as part of the 1990 census count. The Census Bureau hired approximately 22,000 people, armed with flashlights and survey questionnaires, who attempted to locate every homeless person they could find between 6 p.m. and 4 a.m. on March 20-21. They visited 11,000 shelters and 24,000 street sites and reported a total of 228,621 homeless persons—178,828 in emergency shelters and 49,793 at "pre-identified street locations." Among the states, California (48,887) and New York (43,204) ranked first and second, the next two, Florida and Pennsylvania were far behind with 10,299 and 9,549 respectively. Among the major cities none came remotely close to New York's 33,830.

No one, not even the Census Bureau, believes that nearly all the homeless were counted. In fact, census officials claim they never believed they could count all the homeless but that a strong effort was needed to help estimate the total homeless population of the country. Despite this disclaimer, every advocacy group for the homeless feared the low count would be used to lower the amount of federal funding currently allocated.

Homeless families Families with children account for more than half the homeless population in Chicago, Kansas City, New York City, Norfolk, San Antonio, and Trenton. They account for 20 percent or less in Boston, Hartford, Nashville, Portland, Saint Paul, San Francisco and San Juan. Among homeless families, 28 percent were headed by two parents; the rest by single parents, usually a woman with two to three children under the age of five. A 1988 U.S. Education Department survey estimated that there were 220,000 homeless school-age children. Of those children, more than 65,000 do not attend school regularly.

Federal funding The various federal government programs to assist the homeless are grouped under the Stewart B. McKinney Homeless Assistance Act, which became law in July 1987. The act includes 16 different provisions for emergency shelter, food, health care, mental health care, housing, educational programs, job training, and other community services. Federal agencies providing services specifically for the homeless include the Federal Emergency Management Agency, and Departments of Agriculture, Education, Health and Human Services, Housing and Urban Development, Labor, and Veterans' Affairs. An additional 34 programs, ranging from Medicaid and the Supplemental Security Income program to the Public and Indian housing program and the Ryan White CARE Act, provide general assistance to low-income people, including the homeless. The number of homeless people that these non-homeless-specific programs serve, however, is impossible to determine.

Since 1994, the federal government has budgeted more than $1 billion in funding for the McKinney program. Nevertheless, states and cities still foot the major part of the bill for caring for the homeless.

IMMIGRATION

Over the last four centuries the mingling of peoples from all parts of the world has been a vital element in the formation of the United States both as a land of opportunity and in its emergence as a world power. In one relatively brief period between 1880 and 1920 the massive influx of more than 20 million European immigrants provided the continuous labor supply necessary to transform the nation from an agricultural society to an industrialized one with extraordinary rapidity.

Over the next 40 years, however, the flow of immigration slowed dramatically as the government decided to close the doors to most foreign groups. Motivated at first by a disconcerting kind of nativism, the nation's anti-immigration sentiments were later bolstered by the Great Depression and the need to provide work for those already living here. World War II and the subsequent national readjustment limited immigration for several decades.

Since 1960 a steadily increasing number of immigrants—both legal and illegal—has had a very noticeable impact on both the size and ethnic composition of the American population. The startling upsurge in the number of Asians and Hispanic immigrants during the 1970s, '80s, and '90s has been caused by a variety of factors from wars and political upheaval to the mundane fact of geographical proximity in the case of Mexico.

The Statue of Liberty

The Statue of Liberty was conceived and designed by Frederic Auguste Bartholdi (with Gustave Eiffel's help) and given to the U.S. by the French government in honor of the centennial of American independence in 1876. Funded by subscriptions from the French people it was dedicated by President Grover Cleveland in 1886 and became a national monument in 1924.

Measuring 151 feet (46 m) to the top of her torch, Miss Liberty still stands guard over the entrance to New York harbor, the inscription on its base a poignant reminder of the vision Americans once had of their country:

Give me your tired, your poor
Your huddled masses yearning to breathe free,
The wretched refuse of your teeming shore,
Send these, the homeless, tempest-tost to me:
I lift my lamp beside the golden door.

U.S. Immigration Rate by Decade, 1820–1997

Period	Total immigrants	Rate per 1,000 U.S. population
1820-30	151,824	1.2
1831-40	599,125	3.9
1841-50	1,713,251	8.4
1851-60	2,598,214	9.3
1861-70	2,314,824	6.4
1871-80	2,812,191	6.2
1881-90	5,246,613	9.2
1891-1900	3,687,564	5.3
1901-10	8,795,386	10.4
1911-20	5,735,811	5.7
1921-30	4,107,209	3.5
1931-40	528,431	0.4
1941-50	1,035,039	0.7
1951-60	2,515,479	1.5
1961-70	3,321,677	1.7
1971-80	4,493,314	2.1
1981-90	7,338,062	2.9
1991-97[1]	6,944,591	2.6
Total 1820-1997	63,938,605	N.A.

1. Includes more than 2 million aliens adjusting under the legalization provisions of the Immigration and Control Act (IRCA) of 1986. **Source:** U.S. Dept. of Justice, *1997 Statistical Yearbook of the Immigration and Naturalization Service* (1998).

Immigration as a Percentage of Total Population Growth, 1901–97

Period	Percent	Period	Percent
1901-10	39.6%	1950-54	10.6%
1911-20	17.7	1955-59	10.7
1921-30	15.0	1960-64	12.5
1931-34	-0.1	1965-69	19.7
1935-39	3.2	1970-80	19.4
1940-44	7.4	1981-90	32.8
1945-49	10.2	1991-97	45.5

Source: U.S. Dept. of Justice, U.S. Census Bureau.

Percent of Immigrants Admitted by Region, 1955–97

Region	Total, 1955-96	1955-64	1965-74	1975-84	1985-94	1995	1997
Europe	49.0%	50.2%	29.8%	13.4%	11.0%	17.8%	15.0%
Asia	8.6	7.7	22.4	43.3	32.2	37.2	33.3
Africa	0.9	0.7	1.5	2.4	2.6	5.9	6.0
Oceania	0.4	0.4	0.7	0.8	0.5	0.7	0.5
North America[1]	36.0	35.9	39.6	33.6	48.0	32.1	38.5
Caribbean	7.2	7.0	18.0	15.1	11.0	13.4	13.2
Central America	2.5	2.4	2.5	3.7	6.6	4.4	5.5
Other North America[1]	26.2	26.4	19.0	14.8	30.5	14.3	19.9
South America	5.2	5.1	6.0	6.6	6.6	6.3	6.6

Note: Data are for fiscal years. 1. Includes more than 2 million illegal immigrants from Mexico granted permanent legal residence under the 1986 Immigration Reform & Control Act. **Source:** U.S. Dept. of Justice, *Legal Immigration, FY 97* (1999).

Immigration to the U.S. by Country of Last Residence, 1820-1997

Since 1820, Germany has sent more immigrants to the U.S. than has any other country, but Mexico is gaining fast. Nearly 5.7 million people migrated to the U.S. from Mexico between 1820 and 1997, 60 percent of them since 1981. The vast majority of Mexican immigrants in 1989-91 were already living illegally in the U.S. and granted permanent legal residence under the 1986 Immigration Reform and Control Act. But the tide of Mexican immigration shows few signs of abating. More immigrants to the United States came from Mexico than from the next three countries combined in 1997. The following table ranks the top 10 nations by the total number of U.S. immigrants since 1820.

| | 1820–1997 | | 1981–90 | | 1991–97 | |
| | | Percent of | | Percent of | | Percent of |
Country	Number	total	Number	total	Number	total
All Countries	63,938,603	100.0%	7,338,062	100.0%	6,944,589	100.0%
Germany	7,149,334	11.2	91,961	1.2	65,869	0.9
Mexico	5,689,305	8.9	1,655,843	22.6	1,800,576	25.9
Italy	5,429,488	8.5	67,254	1.0	56,380	0.8
United Kingdom	5,237,651	8.2	14,667	0.2	115,501	1.7
Ireland	4,779,091	7.5	31,969	0.4	53,958	0.8
Canada	4,438,854	6.9	156,938	2.1	143,269	2.1
Austria-Hungary[1]	4,362,687	6.9	24,885	0.3	19,905	0.3
Former USSR	3,801,049	5.9	57,677	0.8	357,343	5.2
Norway-Sweden[2]	2,159,242	3.4	15,182	0.2	13,288	0.2
Philippines	1,427,245	2.2	548,764	7.5	400,592	5.8

1. Austria and Hungary not counted separately for all years. 2. Norway and Sweden not counted separately for all years.
Source: U.S. Dept. of Justice, *Legal Immigration FY97* (1999).

Estimated Number of U.S. Immigrants, by Region and Selected Country of Last Residence, 1820-1997

Region/country	Total 1820–1997	1997	Region/country	Total 1820–1997	1997
Europe	**38,140,151**	**122,358**	Philippines	1,427,245	47,842
Austria[1]	1,842,112	1,044	Turkey	441,338	4,596
Belgium	215,740	633	Vietnam	683,384	37,121
Czechoslovakia[2]	152,376	1,169	Other Asia	1,608,898	62,902
Denmark	375,101	507			
France	813,689	3,007	**North America**	**16,494,073**	**307,019**
Germany	7,149,334	6,941	Canada	4,438,854	15,788
Greece	720,281	1,483	Mexico	5,689,305	146,680
Hungary[1]	1,674,499	920	Caribbean	3,452,755	101,095
Ireland	4,779,091	932	Cuba	870,006	29,913
Italy	5,429,488	2,190	Dominican Republic	789,934	24,966
Netherlands	384,157	1,197	Haiti	362,622	14,941
Norway[3]	805,204	391	Jamaica	553,805	17,585
Poland	743,621	11,729	Other Caribbean	876,388	13,690
Portugal	520,174	1,690	Central America	1,207,026	43,451
Romania	239,273	5,276	El Salvador	439,388	17,741
Soviet Union	3,801,049	48,238	Other Central America	767,638	25,710
Spain	298,640	1,607			
Sweden[3]	1,293,783	1,126	**South America**	**1,648,571**	**52,600**
Switzerland	367,956	1,302	Argentina	152,050	2,055
United Kingdom	5,237,651	11,950	Colombia	388,274	12,795
Yugoslavia[4]	176,274	9,913	Ecuador	208,958	7,763
Other Europe	214,327	9,113	Other South America	899,289	29,987
Asia	**8,153,132**	**258,561**	**Other America**	**110,157**	**N.A.**
China[5]	1,210,186	33,526			
Hong Kong	390,898	7,974	**Africa**	**576,881**	**44,668**
India	717,061	36,092			
Iran	228,915	6,291	**Oceania**	**245,803**	**4,855**
Israel	167,960	2,951			
Japan	512,039	5,640	**Not specified**	**275,965**	**8,317**
Korea	765,208	13,626	**All countries**	**63,938,605**	**798,378**

Note: Because of changes in boundaries and government, figures for many countries, especially those in Asia, are not available for all years or were not reported separately for all years, and are therefore not strictly comparable throughout. Data for many countries are included with countries to which they belonged prior to World War I. 1. Data for Austria and Hungary not reported separately for all years. Total does not include 846,076 immigrants whose country of last residence is listed as Austria-Hungary. 2. Data for 1995 includes both Czech and Slovak Republics. 3. Data for Norway and Sweden not reported separately for all years. Total does not include 60,255 immigrants whose country of last residence is listed as Norway-Sweden. 4. Since 1922, includes immigrants from the Serb, Croat, and Slovene Kingdom. 5. Beginning in 1957, China includes Taiwan.
Source: U.S. Dept. of Justice, *1997 Statistical Yearbook of the Immigration and Naturalization Service* (1999).

Top 20 Metropolitan Areas of Intended Residence for U.S. Immigrants, 1995–97

	Immigrants					
	1995		1996		1997	
Rank, 1997 and Metropolitan area	Number	Percent of total	Number	Percent of total	Number	Percent of total
1. New York, N.Y.	111,687	15.5%	133,168	14.5%	107,434	13.5%
2. Los Angeles-Long Beach, Calif.	54,669	7.6	64,285	7.0	62,314	7.8
3. Miami, Fla.	30,935	4.3	41,527	4.5	45,707	5.7
4. Chicago, Ill.	31,730	4.4	39,989	4.4	35,386	4.4
5. Washington D.C.-Md-Va.	25,717	3.6	34,327	3.7	31,444	3.9
6. Orange County, Calif.	18,187	2.5	17,580	1.9	18,190	2.3
7. Houston, Tex.	14,379	2.0	21,387	2.3	17,439	2.2
8. San Jose, Calif.	12,855	1.8	13,854	1.5	17,374	2.2
9. San Francisco, Calif.	15,773	2.2	18,171	2.0	16,892	2.1
10. Oakland, Calif.	12,011	1.7	15,759	1.7	15,723	2.0
11. San Diego, Calif.	12,077	1.7	18,226	2.0	14,758	1.8
12. Boston-Lawrence-Lowell Mass.	16,750	2.3	18,726	2.0	13,937	1.7
13. Dallas, Tex.	9,843	1.4	15,915	1.7	11,061	1.4
14. Philadelphia, Pa.-N.J.	11,440	1.6	13,034	1.4	10,858	1.4
15. Newark, N.J.	11,162	1.5	17,939	2.0	10,801	1.4
16. Seattle-Bellevue-Everett, Wash.	9,652	1.3	10,429	1.1	10,692	1.3
17. Fort Lauderdale, Fla.	8,373	1.2	10,290	1.1	10,646	1.3
18. Detroit, Mich.	9,899	1.4	11,929	1.3	10,019	1.3
19. Atlanta, Ga.	9,494	1.3	9,870	1.1	9,823	1.2
20. Bergen-Passaic, N.J.	9,385	1.3	15,682	1.7	9,788	1.2
Total, all metropolitan areas[1]	720,461	100.0%	915,900	100.0%	798,378	100.0%

1. Includes other MSAs not shown separately.
Source: U.S. Dept. of Justice, *1997 Statistical Yearbook of the Immigration and Naturalization Service* (1998).

Top 20 Countries of Birth for U.S. Immigrants, and Major Categories of Admission, 1997

			Category of admission				
Country of birth	Total immigrants[1]	Percent of total	Relative prefer-ences	Occu-pational prefer-ences	Immediate relatives	Refugees and asylees	IRCA legal-ization[2]
All countries	798,378	100.0%	213,331	90,607	321,008	112,158	2,548
1. Mexico	146,865	18.4	68,996	3,081	71,293	60	2,039
2. Philippines	49,117	6.2	16,196	7,075	25,506	68	23
3. China, mainland	41,147	5.2	10,643	13,939	15,781	692	0
4. Vietnam	38,519	4.8	8,171	98	6,834	22,297	0
5. India	38,071	4.8	14,229	9,204	13,926	462	10
6. Cuba	33,587	4.2	1,134	54	1,063	30,377	3
7. Dominican Republic	27,053	3.4	11,581	238	15,098	23	14
8. El Salvador	17,969	2.2	6,501	2,774	8,220	198	97
9. Jamaica	17,840	2.2	7,512	962	9,294	0	13
10. Russia	16,632	2.1	92	1,749	5,780	6,985	0
11. Ukraine	15,696	2.0	69	487	1,107	12,137	0
12. Haiti	15,057	1.9	7,522	297	6,009	1,074	17
13. Korea	14,239	1.8	4,086	4,710	5,381	3	3
14. Colombia	13,004	1.6	2,956	881	8,882	154	22
15. Pakistan	12,967	1.6	4,392	1,576	5,326	280	7
16. Poland	12,038	1.5	3,573	1,649	3,103	143	6
17. Canada	11,609	1.4	931	5,516	4,677	12	5
18. Peru	10,853	1.4	2,494	880	6,590	489	7
19. Yugoslavia, former	10,750	1.4	443	397	1,494	7,597	3
20. United Kingdom	10,708	1.3	865	4,208	5,176	12	7

1. Total includes Amerasians, Soviet and Indochinese parolees, foreign government officials, special immigrants, and admissions from nonpreference "underrepresented countries," suspension of deportation, and private law not shown separately. 2. Under the Immigration Reform and Control Act (IRCA) of 1986, illegal aliens with temporary resident status became eligible for permanent legal residence.
Source: U.S. Dept. of Justice, *1997 Statistical Yearbook of the Immigration and Naturalization Service* (1999).

Approximately 750,000 new legal immigrants are arriving annually and well over half are from those two ethnic backgrounds.

While immigration is higher today than in the recent past, it is hard to predict what the future holds. Many demographers argue that if the immigration rate falls much below current levels the effect on American population growth could be severe. With the dramatic decline in its birth rates and fertility rates, the U.S. might very well

Naturalization Rates for U.S. Immigrants by Nation, 1977–95

Almost half of the people who immigrated to the U.S. in 1977 had become a naturalized U.S. citizen by 1995. The following table shows immigrants by country from 1977 and the number and percentage that had been naturalized by 1995.

Region and country of birth	Immigrants admitted, 1977	Naturalizations through 1995 Number	Naturalizations through 1995 Rate	Region and country of birth	Immigrants admitted, 1977	Naturalizations through 1995 Number	Naturalizations through 1995 Rate
All countries	**352,070**	**161,438**	**45.9%**	Ghana	392	238	60.7%
				Kenya	418	257	61.5
Europe	**54,867**	**17,591**	**32.1%**	Morocco	366	182	49.7
Austria	342	61	17.8	Nigeria	570	231	40.5
Belgium	300	67	22.3	South Africa	1,331	856	64.3
Czechoslovakia	504	263	52.2	Tanzania	256	175	68.4
Denmark	362	55	15.2	Uganda	200	119	59.5
Finland	231	40	17.3	Other Africa	1,275	701	55.0
France	1,283	391	30.5				
Germany	4,899	824	16.8	**Oceania**	**2,927**	**735**	**25.1%**
Greece	6,577	2,208	33.6	Australia	1,016	90	8.9
Hungary	771	405	52.5	Fiji	551	274	49.7
Ireland	1,076	297	27.6	New Zealand	449	97	21.6
Italy	5,843	1,131	19.4	Tonga	349	98	28.1
Netherlands	828	152	18.4	Western Samoa	369	136	36.9
Norway	283	32	11.3	Other Oceania	193	40	20.7
Poland	3,468	1,656	47.8				
Portugal	6,964	2,051	29.5	**North America**	**142,313**	**54,068**	**38.0%**
Romania	1,620	1,097	67.7	Canada	9,000	1,626	18.1
Soviet Union	4,535	2,965	65.4	Mexico	30,967	6,869	22.2
Spain	2,086	427	20.5	Caribbean, total	89,885	39,662	44.1%
Sweden	485	66	13.6	Anguilla	354	136	38.4
Switzerland	485	161	33.2	Antigua-Barbuda	614	307	50.0
United Kingdom	8,981	2,032	22.6	Bahamas, The	238	61	25.6
Yugoslavia	2,256	959	42.5	Barbados	2,134	1,037	48.6
Other Europe	688	251	36.5	British Virgin Islands	367	78	21.3
				Cuba	57,023	26,668	46.8
Asia	**119,226**	**72,318**	**60.7%**	Dominica	392	194	49.5
Bangladesh	460	317	68.9	Dominican Republic	8,955	2,561	28.6
Burma (Myanmar)	776	528	68.0	Grenada	1,023	529	51.7
China, People's Republic	14,421	9,444	65.5	Haiti	4,268	1,841	43.1
Cyprus	410	210	51.2	Jamaica	7,896	3,587	45.4
Hong Kong	3,146	2,404	76.4	St. Kitts & Nevis	699	349	49.9
India	15,033	8,877	59.1	St. Lucia	408	202	49.5
Indonesia	658	330	50.2	St. Vincent & Grenadines	456	224	49.1
Iran	3,404	1,855	54.5	Trinidad & Tobago	4,516	1,722	38.1
Iraq	1,996	1,260	63.1	Other Caribbean	542	166	30.6
Israel	2,078	1,332	64.1	Central America	**12,381**	**5,890**	**47.6%**
Japan	3,602	601	16.7	Belize	660	285	43.2
Jordan	2,187	1,379	63.1	Costa Rica	1,221	471	38.6
Korea	19,824	11,745	59.2	El Salvador	3,402	1,688	49.6
Lebanon	3,900	2,551	65.4	Guatemala	2,825	1,291	45.7
Macau	248	182	73.4	Honduras	1,228	640	52.1
Malaysia	387	231	59.7	Nicaragua	1,351	679	50.3
Pakistan	2,563	1,655	64.6	Panama	1,694	836	49.4
Philippines	31,686	20,094	63.4	Other North America	80	21	26.3
Singapore	226	119	52.7				
Sri Lanka	314	194	61.8	**South America**	**25,024**	**12,198**	**48.7%**
Syria	1,342	857	63.9	Argentina	2,136	995	46.6
Taiwan	2,460	1,922	78.1	Bolivia	576	344	59.7
Thailand	3,009	1,202	39.9	Brazil	1,128	299	26.5
Turkey	1,546	623	40.3	Chile	2,047	958	46.8
Vietnam	2,724	1,911	70.2	Colombia	6,138	3,126	50.9
Yemen	284	159	56.0	Ecuador	4,063	1,319	32.5
Other Asia	542	336	62.0	Guyana	4,115	2,439	59.3
				Peru	3,158	1,902	60.2
Africa	**7,713**	**4,528**	**58.7%**	Uruguay	947	529	55.9
Cape Verde	647	263	40.6	Venezuela	485	175	36.1
Egypt	1,964	1,319	67.2	Other South America	231	112	48.5
Ethiopia	294	187	63.6				

Source: U.S. Dept. of Justice, *1996 Statistical Yearbook of the Immigration and Naturalization Service* (1997).

Foreign-Born Population by State, 1980–90

	1980			1990		
	Total population	Foreign-born population	Percent foreign-born	Total population	Foreign-born population	Percent foreign-born
United States	226,545,805	14,079,906	6.2%	248,709,873	19,767,316	7.9%
Alabama	3,893,888	39,002	1.0	4,040,587	43,533	1.1
Alaska	401,851	16,216	4.0	550,043	24,814	4.5
Arizona	2,718,215	162,806	6.0	3,665,228	278,205	7.6
Arkansas	2,286,435	22,371	1.0	2,350,725	24,867	1.1
California	23,667,902	3,580,033	15.1	29,760,021	6,458,825	21.7
Colorado	2,889,964	114,130	3.9	3,294,394	142,434	4.3
Connecticut	3,107,576	267,806	8.6	3,287,116	279,383	8.5
Delaware	594,338	18,829	3.2	666,168	22,275	3.3
District of Columbia	638,333	40,559	6.4	606,900	58,887	9.7
Florida	9,746,324	1,058,732	10.9	12,937,926	1,662,601	12.9
Georgia	5,463,105	91,480	1.7	6,478,216	173,126	2.7
Hawaii	964,691	137,016	14.2	1,108,229	162,704	14.7
Idaho	943,935	23,404	2.5	1,006,749	28,905	2.9
Illinois	11,426,518	823,696	7.2	11,430,602	952,272	8.3
Indiana	5,490,224	101,802	1.9	5,544,159	94,263	1.7
Iowa	2,913,808	47,659	1.6	2,776,755	43,316	1.6
Kansas	2,363,679	47,891	2.0	2,477,574	62,840	2.5
Kentucky	3,660,777	34,562	0.9	3,685,296	34,119	0.9
Louisiana	4,205,900	85,502	2.0	4,219,973	87,407	2.1
Maine	1,124,660	43,402	3.9	1,227,928	36,296	3.0
Maryland	4,216,975	195,581	4.6	4,781,468	313,494	6.6
Massachusetts	5,737,037	500,982	8.7	6,016,425	573,733	9.5
Michigan	9,262,078	417,152	4.5	9,295,297	355,393	3.8
Minnesota	4,075,970	107,474	2.6	4,375,099	113,039	2.6
Mississippi	2,520,638	23,527	0.9	2,573,216	20,383	0.8
Missouri	4,916,686	85,616	1.7	5,117,073	83,633	1.6
Montana	786,690	18,319	2.3	799,065	13,779	1.7
Nebraska	1,569,825	31,000	2.0	1,578,385	28,198	1.8
Nevada	800,493	53,784	6.7	1,201,833	104,828	8.7
New Hampshire	920,610	40,961	4.4	1,109,252	41,193	3.7
New Jersey	7,364,823	757,822	10.3	7,730,188	966,610	12.5
New Mexico	1,302,894	52,405	4.0	1,515,069	80,514	5.3
New York	17,558,072	2,388,938	13.6	17,990,455	2,851,861	15.9
North Carolina	5,881,766	78,358	1.3	6,628,637	115,077	1.7
North Dakota	652,717	14,818	2.3	638,800	9,388	1.5
Ohio	10,797,630	302,185	2.8	10,847,115	259,673	2.4
Oklahoma	3,025,290	56,294	1.9	3,145,585	65,489	2.1
Oregon	2,633,105	107,805	4.1	2,842,321	139,307	4.9
Pennsylvania	11,863,895	401,016	3.4	11,881,643	369,316	3.1
Rhode Island	947,154	84,001	8.9	1,003,464	95,088	9.5
South Carolina	3,121,820	46,080	1.5	3,486,703	49,964	1.4
South Dakota	690,768	9,599	1.4	696,004	7,731	1.1
Tennessee	4,591,120	48,369	1.1	4,877,185	59,114	1.2
Texas	14,229,191	856,213	6.0	16,986,510	1,524,436	9.0
Utah	1,461,037	50,451	3.5	1,722,850	58,600	3.4
Vermont	511,456	20,995	4.1	562,758	17,544	3.1
Virginia	5,346,818	177,318	3.3	6,187,358	311,809	5.0
Washington	4,132,156	239,050	5.8	4,866,692	322,144	6.6
West Virginia	1,949,644	21,980	1.1	1,793,477	15,712	0.9
Wisconsin	4,705,767	125,297	2.7	4,891,769	121,547	2.5
Wyoming	469,557	9,607	2.0	453,588	7,647	1.7

Source: U.S. Bureau of the Census, 1999.

begin to experience negative population growth by the year 2030; by 2020 immigration will add more population than natural increase will. According to the Office of Population Research at Princeton University, the U.S. will need 464,000 immigrants each year over the next century just to keep total population in 2100 at the same size as in 1980.

▶ELIGIBILITY

Prior to 1875 anyone from any foreign country could enter the U.S. freely and take up permanent residence here. Over the next 60 years, however, Congress passed laws restricting immigration on the basis of morality (no prostitutes or convicts), race (the Chinese Exclusion Act of 1882 was the first), and national origin (immigrants from Southern and Central Europe as well as Asia were severely limited during the 1920s). In 1952 Congress passed the Immigration and Nationality Act which reaffirmed national origin as the central criterion for eligibility and in 1965, the Hart-Cellar Immigration Act established a preferential system for skilled workers and relatives of U.S. citizens, but restricted the total number of immigrants to 270,000 each year. However, the number of exceptions to this limit was far greater even than the 270,000 limit. An average of more than 700,000 immigrants legally entered the U.S. each year during the 1980s (not counting illegal aliens naturalized under provisions of the 1986 Immigration Reform and Control Act).

In 1992, the 270,000 limit was replaced with a sliding cap that is even less restrictive than previous immigration laws. The 1990 Immigration Act limited the total number of immigrants to 700,000 from 1992 to 1995, and to 675,000 thereafter. The Act increased the number of openings for immigrants with valuable employment skills from 54,000 to 140,000 each year, and reserved 55,000 openings each year for immigrants from underrepresented countries. In addition, the new law introduced a sliding scale for admitting family-sponsored immigrants. As in previous years, there is no limit to the number of immediate family members admitted each year. However, beginning in 1995, the number of immediate family members admitted in the previous year is subtracted from 480,000 to determine the number of family-sponsored immigrants eligible for admission. The family-sponsored limit may not go below 226,000 in any year, however.

▶ THE FOREIGN-BORN POPULATION

The strong increase in the number of immigrants since the 1970s has helped to reshape the makeup of American society. According to the Census Bureau, as of 1997, some 25.8 million U.S. residents (9.7 percent of the total) were foreign-born. The last time the figure was higher was in 1930, when 11.6 percent of the population was born in another country.

In 1997, about half of the foreign-born population (13.1 million) were natives of Central America, South America, and the Caribbean. Of these, more than half (7 million) listed Mexico as their birthplace. The five states with the highest percentage of foreign-born residents were California (24.7 percent, or nearly three times the national average), New York (19.6 percent), Florida (1.4 percent), New Jersey (15.4 percent), and Texas (11.3 percent).

Foreign Born Population by Sex and Race, 1990-98

Characteristic	1990[1]	1995	1997	1998
Total	19,840,000	22,958,000	24,418,000	25,208,000
Percent of U.S. population	8.0%	8.7%	9.1%	9.3%
By sex				
Male	9,734,000	11,161,000	11,825,000	12,182,000
Female	10,106,000	11,796,000	12,592,000	13,026,000
By race				
White	13,426,000	14,928,000	14,755,000	16,201,000
Black	1,705,000	2,104,000	2,317,000	2,428,000
American Indian, Eskimo, Aleut	86,000	120,000	135,000	143,000
Asian and Pacific Islander	4,624,000	5,807,000	6,222,000	6,436,000
Hispanic Origin[2]	7,995,000	9,528,000	10,302,000	10,718,000

1. Figures are from the April 1990 Census. All other figures are as of July 1 of the year shown. 2. People of Hispanic origin may be of any race. **Source:** U.S. Bureau of the Census, *Foreign-Born Resident Population Estimates of the U.S., 1990-98*, (1999). www.census.gov.

Foreign-Born Population by Region of Birth, 1850-1990

Year	Total population	Foreign-born population	Percent foreign-born	Europe	Asia	Africa	Oceania	Latin America	North America
1850[1]	23,191,876	2,244,602	9.7%	2,031,867	1,135	551	588	20,773	147,711
1860[1]	31,443,321	4,138,697	13.2	3,807,062	36,796	526	2,140	38,315	249,970
1870	38,558,371	5,567,229	14.4	4,941,049	64,565	2,657	4,028	57,871	493,467
1880	50,155,783	6,679,943	13.3	5,751,823	107,630	2,204	6,859	90,073	717,286
1890	62,622,250	9,249,547	14.8	8,030,347	113,383	2,207	9,353	107,307	980,938
1900	75,994,575	10,341,276	13.6	8,881,548	120,248	2,538	8,820	137,458	1,179,922
1910	91,972,266	13,515,886	14.7	11,810,115	191,484	3,992	11,450	279,514	1,209,717
1920	105,710,620	13,920,692	13.2	11,916,048	237,950	16,126	14,626	588,843	1,138,174
1930	122,775,046	14,204,149	11.6	11,784,010	275,665	18,326	17,343	791,840	1,310,369
1940	131,669,275	11,594,896	8.8	N.A.	N.A.	N.A.	N.A.	N.A.	N.A.
1950	150,216,110	10,347,395	6.9	N.A.	N.A.	N.A.	N.A.	N.A.	N.A.
1960	179,325,671	9,738,091	5.4	7,256,311	490,996	35,355	34,730	908,309	952,500
1970	203,210,158	9,619,302	4.7	5,740,891	824,887	80,143	41,258	1,803,970	812,421
1980	226,545,805	14,079,906	6.2	5,149,572	2,539,777	199,723	77,577	4,372,487	853,427
1990	248,709,873	19,767,316	7.9	4,350,403	4,979,037	363,819	104,145	8,407,837	753,917

1. In 1850 and 1860, information on nativity was not collected for slaves. The data in the table assume, as was done in 1870 Census reports, that all slaves in 1850 and 1860 were native, even though 0.2 percent were foreign-born.
Source: U.S. Bureau of the Census.

Foreign-Born Population by Place of Birth, 1990

Place of Birth	Number	Percent	Place of Birth	Number	Percent
All Foreign-born persons	21,631,601	100.0%	**North America**	8,524,594	39.4%
			Canada	870,850	4.0
Europe	4,812,117	22.2%	Caribbean, total	1,986,835	9.2
Austria	94,398	0.4	Antigua-Barbuda	12,452	0.1
Belgium	41,111	0.2	Bahamas	24,341	0.1
Czechoslovakia	90,042	0.4	Barbados	44,311	0.2
Denmark	37,657	0.2	Cuba	750,609	3.5
Estonia	9,251	0.0	Dominican Republic	356,971	1.7
Finland	23,547	0.1	Grenada	18,183	0.1
France	162,934	0.8	Haiti	229,108	1.1
Germany	1,163,004	5.4	Jamaica	343,458	1.6
Greece	189,267	0.9	Trinidad/Tobago	119,221	0.6
Hungary	112,419	0.5	Other Caribbean	88,181	0.4
Ireland	177,420	0.8	Central America, total	5,650,374	26.1
Italy	639,518	3.0	Belize	31,222	0.1
Latvia	26,380	0.1	Costa Rica	48,264	0.2
Lithuania	30,344	0.1	El Salvador	472,885	2.2
Netherlands	104,216	0.5	Guatemala	232,977	1.1
Norway	46,240	0.2	Honduras	114,603	0.5
Poland	397,014	1.8	Mexico	4,447,439	20.6
Portugal	218,525	1.0	Nicaragua	171,950	0.8
Romania	92,627	0.4	Panama	124,695	0.6
Spain	103,518	0.5	Other Central America	6,339	0.0
Sweden	57,166	0.3	Other North America	16,535	0.1
Switzerland	43,991	0.2			
United Kingdom	764,627	3.5	**South America**	1,107,000	5.1%
Yugoslavia	144,563	0.7	Argentina	97,422	0.5
Other Europe	42,338	0.2	Bolivia	33,637	0.2
			Brazil	94,023	0.4
Soviet Union	336,889	1.6%	Chile	61,212	0.3
			Colombia	303,918	1.4
Asia	5,412,127	25.0%	Ecuador	147,867	0.7
Afghanistan	28,988	0.1	Guyana	122,554	0.6
Cambodia	119,581	0.6	Peru	152,315	0.7
China	543,208	2.5	Uruguay	21,628	0.1
Hong Kong	152,263	0.7	Venezuela	51,571	0.2
India	463,132	2.1	Other South America	20,853	0.1
Indonesia	50,388	0.2			
Iran	216,963	1.0	**Africa**	400,691	1.9%
Iraq	45,936	0.2	Cape Verde	14,821	0.1
Israel	97,006	0.4	Egypt	68,662	0.3
Japan	421,921	2.0	Ethiopia	37,422	0.2
Jordan	33,019	0.2	Ghana	21,714	0.1
Korea (South)	663,465	3.1	Kenya	15,871	0.1
Laos	172,925	0.8	Morocco	21,529	0.1
Lebanon	91,037	0.4	Nigeria	58,052	0.3
Malaysia	34,906	0.2	Senegal	2,369	0.0
Myanmar	20,441	0.1	South Africa	38,163	0.2
Pakistan	93,663	0.4	Other Africa	122,088	0.6
Philippines	997,745	4.6			
Saudi Arabia	17,312	0.1	**Oceania**	122,137	0.6%
Syria	37,654	0.2	Australia	52,469	0.2
Taiwan	253,719	1.2	Fiji	16,269	0.1
Thailand	119,862	0.6	New Zealand	18,039	0.1
Turkey	65,244	0.3	Tonga	11,040	0.1
Vietnam	556,311	2.6	Western Samoa	12,638	0.1
Other Asia	115,438	0.5	Other Oceania	11,682	0.1
			Not reported	916,046	4.2%

Note: The foreign-born population includes 1,864,285 persons who were born abroad of American parents.
Source: U.S. Bureau of the Census, 1990 Census Special Tabulations (1992).

Selected Characteristics of Foreign-Born Population, 1997

The foreign-born population of the United States consists of naturalized citizens and more recent immigrants who have not obtained citizenship. As the following table illustrates, the foreign-born population is heavily represented in the West (17.6 percent of the population was not born here) and the Northeast (11.9 percent) and lowest in the Midwest (4.3 percent). Also note that more than 60 percent of Asian and Pacific Islanders and nearly 40 percent of Hispanics in the U.S. are first generation immigrants.

Characteristic	Total U.S. population ('000s)	Foreign-born population			
		Total number ('000s)	As percent of U.S. population	Naturalized citizens ('000s)	Not citizens ('000s)
Total Population	266,792	25,779	9.7%	9,043	16,736
Age					
Under 5 years	19,781	299	1.5	37	262
5 to 15 years	43,630	1,832	4.2	223	1,609
16 or 17 years	7,813	487	6.2	73	414
18 to 24 years	24,987	2,940	11.8	485	2,455
25 to 29 years	19,260	2,771	14.4	614	2,157
30 to 34 years	20,996	3,154	15.0	777	2,377
35 to 44 years	43,960	5,297	12.0	1,929	3,368
45 to 64 years	54,488	6,211	11.4	3,132	3,079
65 years or more	31,877	2,789	8.7	1,772	1,017
Sex					
Male	130,636	12,946	9.9%	4,391	8,555
Female	136,156	12,832	9.4	4,651	8,181
Race and Hispanic Origin					
White	220,070	17,504	8.0%	5,610	11,894
Black	34,218	2,028	5.9	716	1,312
American Indian/Eskimo/Aleut	2,433	142	5.8	23	119
Asian/Pacific Islander	10,071	6,105	60.6	2,694	3,411
Hispanic Origin	29,703	11,392	38.4	2,456	8,936
Educational Attainment					
Not a high school graduate	30,524	7,009	23.0%	1,789	5,220
High School graduate or some college	99,360	8,261	8.3	3,858	4,403
Bachelor's degree	27,357	3,172	11.6	1,635	1,537
Graduate/Professional degree	13,341	1,778	13.3	942	836
Economic Status					
Employed	127,680	14,523	11.4%	5,542	8,981
Unemployed	7,547	1,069	14.2	250	819
Not in labor force	67,288	8,013	11.9	2,954	5,059
Received public assistance	9,268	1,269	13.6	387	882
Below poverty	36,529	5,412	14.8	936	4476
Region of Residence					
Northeast	51,541	6,129	11.9%	2,434	3,695
Midwest	62,092	2,672	4.3	1,109	1,563
South	93,327	6,467	6.9	2,261	4,206
West	59,833	10,509	17.6	3,238	7,271

Source: U.S. Bureau of the Census, *Current Population Survey*, March, 1997

SEX IN AMERICA

Pollsters scrutinize every angle of American life, including what goes on beyond closed bedroom doors. The research ranges from the statistical—like the survey done by the National Center for Health Statistics—to the anecdotal, such as reader polls taken by popular magazines. Here's a summary of the two most serious studies, one conducted by the federal government, the other by a leading university.

▶WOMEN AND SEX

The National Survey of Family Growth is conducted periodically by the National Center for Health Statistics, with a national sample of women aged 15 to 44 years old. The most recent report, issued in May, 1997, used data compiled in 1995. Questions concerned marriage and sexual activity. Some findings from the report:

- 75 percent of all married women had pre-marital intercourse; only 12 percent of women waited until marriage to have sex for the first time.
- 52 percent of women aged 20-44 had their first intercourse by age 18, and 75 percent were sexually experienced by age 20, up from 40 percent and 60 percent respectively in 1988.

Methods of Contraception, by Age, Race and Marital Status of U.S. Women, 1995

Age, race and marital status	Women ('000s)	Percent using any method	As percentage of all women using contraceptives				
			Sterilization		Pill	Condom	Other
			Female	Male			
All women	60,201	64.2%	27.7%	10.9%	26.9%	20.4%	14.0%
By age							
15–19	8,961	29.8%	0.3%	—	43.8%	36.7%	19.2%
20–24	9,041	63.5	4.0	1.1%	52.1	26.4	16.4
25–29	9,693	69.2	17.1	4.5	39.1	24.2	15.1
30–34	11,065	72.8	29.4	10.4	28.4	18.4	13.3
35–39	11,211	73.1	40.7	18.6	11.1	16.8	12.8
40–44	10,230	71.4	49.8	20.3	5.9	12.4	11.5
By marital status							
Never married	22,679	46.6%	9.4%	0.9%	43.8%	29.9%	16.1
Currently married	29,673	76.4	31.2	17.3	20.4	17.4	13.7
Formerly married	7,849	69.2	49.2	3.8	21.1	14.6	11.2
By race and Hispanic origin							
White[1]	45,522	66.1	24.6%	13.6%	23.8%	20.1%	13.7%
Black[1]	8,210	62.1	40.1	1.7	28.5	19.6	14.2
Hispanic[2]	6,702	59.0	36.6	4.0	23.0	20.5	15.8

Source: U.S. Dept. of Health and Human Services, National Center for Health Statistics, *1995 National Survey of Family Growth*, (1997). 1. Non-Hispanic. 2. People of Hispanic origin may be of any race.

- Nearly 14 percent of women aged 20-24 had sex before age 15.; the median age at first intercourse for these women was 16.6 years old.
- 28 percent of women had an unintended birth; poor women and non-Hispanic black women were most likely to have had an unplanned birth.
- 20.4 percent of women reported having involuntary intercourse at some time in their lives; more than one-fourth of these women were under 15 when they were forced to have sex.
- 47 percent of unmarried women reported having just one sexual partner in the past year; 11.2 percent had two partners, and 34.5 percent said they had no partners. But over their lifetimes, women of all marital statuses reported many more sexual partners. More than half of all women had three or more sexual partners in their lifetimes.
- 64.2 percent of women currently use contraceptives; the remaining 35.8 percent are divided among women who are pregnant, seeking to have children, or abstinent. Only 5.2 percent of women admitted having unprotected sex. Among women using contraceptives, sterilization (27.7 percent) was the most popular method, followed by the pill (26.9 percent) and the condom (20.4). Women under the age of 30 were most likely to use the pill.

▶ SEX PARTNERS AND FREQUENCY OF INTERCOURSE

The National Opinion Research Center at the University of Chicago (NORC) periodically conducts a study of the sexual behavior of adults. The Center interviews a nationwide representative sample of about 1,500 adults to collect accurate data on a wide range of topics dealing with sex. Here are some of the survey's primary findings.

Cohabitation As premarital sex becomes more commonplace and the average age at first marriage grows older, the number of couples living together out of wedlock continues to spiral. Just over 1.1 percent of all couples were living together in 1960; in 1997 (the latest year for which data are available), the rate was 7.0 percent. In 1988, 23.4 percent of married couples had lived together before marrying; by 1994, 28.0 percent had. Cohabiting was most popular among younger

Homosexuality in the U.S., 1998

Category	Men	Women
Total	3.3%	2.3%
By race		
Whites	2.7	2.1
Blacks	5.3	1.8
By age		
18-29	3.5	2.6
30-39	3.6	2.1
40-49	2.8	2.5
50-59	2.4	0.8
60-69	1.9	1.4
70 and over	1.7	0.5
By education		
Postgraduate degree	3.2	3.3
College graduate	3.6	1.7
Some college	2.4	2.7
High school graduate	2.6	1.8
Less than high school	3.1	2.5
By household income		
Less than $10,000	6.1	3.2
$10,000-19,999	4.6	2.5
$20,000-29,999	4.0	2.8
$30,000-39,999	2.2	1.8
$40,000-59,999	2.7	1.4
$60,000 or more	1.1	1.6
Refused	2.7	1.7
By church attendance		
Rarely	2.7	3.4
Occasionally	2.5	1.3
Regularly	3.0	1.3

Note: Refers to individuals reporting a same-gender sexual experience within the last 12 months as a percentage of sexually active adults.   Source: National Opinion Research Center (NORC) General Social Survey, 1998.

couples: 9.4 percent of people 18-29 were cohabiting in 1998, and 43.7 percent had cohabited with their current spouse before marriage. The exact same percentage of 30-39-year-olds cohabited before marriage, but only 7.6 percent of the people in this age group were currently cohabiting in 1998.

Extramarital sex Numbers regarding sex out of wedlock are usually unreliable, since most people are reluctant to admit their affairs to interviewers. The percentage of currently married people admitting to extramarital sex within the last year (3.6 percent in 1998) has fluctuated very little since 1988. More people were willing to admit having an affair at one point in their lives. In 1991, 14.6 percent of people who had ever been married admitted having at least one affair while married; in 1998, 16.5 percent said they had had extramarital sex. These figures are much higher than the one-year numbers because they include married people as well as those who are separated and divorced, perhaps as a result of one of these affairs. Men (4.9 percent in the last year, and 20.8 percent ever) were more likely than women (2.5 percent 13.4 respectively) to admit extramarital activity.

Gender of sex partners   For the same reasons, many people are also reluctant to admit homosexual behavior. The percentage of sexually active adults admitting to homosexual behavior within the last year has remained steady at between 2 and 3.5 percent from 1988-98, but the actual number is probably somewhat higher. A smaller percentage (never more than 1 percent) of people claim to have had sex with partners of both genders. Men who attend church regularly (3.0 percent) were more likely to have had a same sex partner than those who attended church occasionally (2.5 percent) or rarely (2.7 percent).

Frequency of sexual intercourse   Americans had intercourse an average of 59.1 times a year in 1998. That's down from 65.3 times a year in 1996, but about the same as in most other surveys from 1989 to 1994, suggesting that the 1996 number

was an aberration. Not surprisingly, married people aged 18-29 had the most sex—111.6 times a year (or more than twice a week); women 70 and over had the least sex: an average of 5.4 times annually. Just over 17 percent of adults had no sex at all in 1998, and 11 percent have not had sex for the past five years.

Number of sex partners   The average number of sex partners per person has remained fairly constant over the past few years. A majority of adults have had only one sexual partner in the past five years, and more than two-thirds had only one partner in the past year. Adults had an average of 1.24 partners in the last 12 months, and 2.5 partners in the past five years. In 1998, the average adult had 7.65 partners since the age of 18, about the same as in 1991. That number was slightly lower in 1989 and 1990, but slightly higher in 1994 and 1996. Men had an average of 12.4 sex partners since age 18, while women had an average of 4.0.

Sex for money   Since the NORC began asking men whether they had ever paid for sex, approximately 17 percent admitted to doing so, though less than 1 percent said they had done so in the past 12 months. In 1998, 14.2 percent of men admitted having paid for sex; 0.7 percent admitted to doing it within the last year. Black men (22.7 percent) were more likely than white men (15.5 percent) to have paid for sex, and men over the age of 60 (24.3 percent) were more likely than younger men. Veterans (37.1 percent) were three times as likely as those who did not serve in the military to have paid for sex.

Frequency of Sexual Intercourse by Age, Race, and Marital Status 1996-98

	Mean number of times per year, 1996			Mean number of times per year, 1998		
Category	All adults	Married	Unmarried	All adults	Married	Unmarried
All Adults	65.3	N.A.	N.A.	59.1	66.1	N.A.
By race						
Whites	61.2	N.A.	N.A.	60.2	N.A.	N.A.
Blacks	64.7	N.A.	N.A.	62.7	N.A.	N.A.
By age						
18-29	83.7	111.4	71.8	82.6	111.6	69.1
30-39	79.7	82.4	76.9	78.6	85.7	65.6
40-49	63.4	63.4	63.4	63.6	69.2	49.8
50-59	47.4	51.5	43.5	47.4	53.8	31.2
60-69	28.1	32.0	23.7	27.4	32.5	15.7
70+	9.8	14.9	6.4	9.8	16.2	2.6

Source: National Opinion Research Center (NORC) General Social Survey, 1998.

Number of Sexual Partners by Adults, 1991-98

	Number of sexual partners							
Year	None	1	2	3	4	5–9	10+	Mean
	Last 12 months							
1991	18.4	71.2	5.9	1.9	0.8	1.4	0.4	1.12
1994	18.4	70.6	6.0	2.4	1.1	1.2	0.3	1.09
1996	15.1	72.2	6.1	3.2	1.6	1.3	0.5	1.36
1998	17.4	70.7	6.0	2.2	1.5	1.4	0.4	1.24
	Last five years							
1991	11.3	60.3	8.3	6.7	3.3	6.0	4.2	2.70
1994	11.1	59.4	8.6	7.2	4.1	6.4	3.2	2.79
1996	10.0	57.8	10.2	7.2	4.7	6.4	3.4	2.83
1998	11.2	59.0	9.2	6.0	4.7	5.7	2.9	2.50

Source: National Opinion Research Center (NORC) General Social Survey, 1998.

Agriculture

In recent years, U.S. agriculture has become an integral part of the global economy. American farmers currently produce over 40 percent of the world's corn, 45 percent of its soybeans, and 10 percent of its wheat. Much of this they export to all parts of the world, but especially to Asia and Latin America. In 1990, U.S. agricultural exports totaled $39.4 billion, but by 1998, they surpassed $51 billion. About 30 percent of that total was in grains and feeds; 20 percent was in animals and animal products.

This is a far cry from the small nation of "embattled farmers" who launched the American Revolution. In the early years of the Republic, agriculture, while vital (involving 95 percent of the population), remained relatively small-scale and in economic terms primitive, with the exception of large plantations in the South devoted to cotton, tobacco, and rice. The Civil War brought higher food prices and increased mechanization throughout the farming industry. It also led to federal legislation aimed at encouraging farming; the Homestead Act of 1862 and the Morrill Land Grant College Act were especially important. The decision to build a transcontinental rail system—undertaken by private enterprise abetted by government grants—opened up large areas of the Great Plains to farming, and the railroad companies recruited immigrants to buy and farm the land the government had given the companies.

In the early 20th century, machinery gradually replaced animal power. In 1910, for example, U.S. farms used 24.2 million horses and mules and only about a thousand tractors; by 1959 the figures had changed to 4.7 million tractors and only 3.2 million draft animals. World War I stimulated agriculture, but the stimulus led to overproduction, which, with the coming of peace, depressed prices and land values. This decline both contributed to and was intensified by the Great Depression, one of the most paralyzing aspects of which was a near total cessation of world agricultural trade. The plight of farmers during the 1930s prompted considerable government remedies, including various forms of credit, price supports, rural electrifica-

tion, and serious efforts at soil conservation. World War II again gave impetus to agriculture.

After the war, new machinery, new chemicals, and hybrid crops, more resistant to weather and biological enemies significantly increased crop yields. By the end of the 1940s, the United States had become the world's largest single producer of wheat, corn, and soybeans. One byproduct of this success was the creation of huge surpluses. U.S. agriculture proved a potent force in the world economy and in foreign policy, and in 1954, Public Law 480 provided for the export of surplus grains to poorer nations both to prevent starvation and stimulate economic development, and to alleviate the pressures on the domestic agriculture sector caused by the surpluses.

Since 1960, the number of American farms has declined as small units lose out to huge agribusinesses owned by corporations. Between 1980 and

Percent of U.S. Agricultural Exports by Region and Selected Nation, 1980–98

Category	1980	1990	1998
Total agricultural exports (billions)	$41.2	$39.5	$51.8
Percent by region and nation			
Asia	36.5%	44.8%	40.3%
Japan	14.9	20.6	17.5
Korea, South	4.4	6.7	4.3
Taiwan	2.7	4.2	3.5
China	5.6	2.1	2.6
Hong Kong	1.1	1.8	2.9
Western Europe	31.4	18.7	15.8
European Union	29.6	17.4	15.2
Latin America	15.0	13.0	22.0
Mexico	6.0	6.5	11.9
Canada	4.7	10.7	13.5
Africa	5.5	4.9	4.0

Source: U.S. Dept. of Agriculture, *Agricultural Statistics, 1998.*

U.S. Farms, Acreage and Population, 1850–1998

Year	Farms ('000s)	Acreage Total ('000s)	Acreage Per farm	Acreage Percent of US	Farm Population Total ('000s)	Farm Population Percent of US
1850	1,449	293,561	203	15.6%	—	—
1860	2,044	407,213	199	21.4	—	—
1870	2,660	407,735	153	21.4	—	—
1880	4,009	536,082	134	28.2	21,973	43.8%
1890	4,565	623,219	137	32.7	24,771	42.3
1900	5,740	841,202	147	37.0	29,835	41.9
1910	6,366	881,431	139	38.8	32,077	34.9
1920	6,454	958,677	149	42.2	31,974	30.1
1930	6,295	990,112	157	43.6	30,529	24.9
1940	6,102	1,065,114	175	46.8	30,547	23.2
1950	5,388	1,161,420	216	51.1	23,048	15.3
1960	3,962	1,176,946	297	49.5[1]	15,635	8.7
1970	2,954	1,102,769	373	47.0[2]	9,712	4.8
1980	2,440	1,039,000	426	44.8	6,051	2.7
1990	2,146	987,000	460	42.7	4,801	1.9
1995	2,196	963,000	438	N.A.	N.A.	N.A.
1996	2,191	959,000	438	N.A.	N.A.	N.A.
1997	2,191	956,000	436	N.A.	N.A.	N.A.
1998	2,192	954,000	435	N.A.	N.A.	N.A.

Note: Acreage figures after 1980 rounded in source. 1. Figure for 1959. 2. Figure for 1969.   **Source:** U.S. Bureau of the Census, *Statistical History of the United States* (1970); *Statistical Abstract of the United States 1999*

1998, the number of farms fell from 2.44 million to 2.19 million, (a decline of 11 percent) while average acreage per farm rose from 426 to 435. Overall, the total land area devoted to farming dropped from 1,039,000 acres to 954,000 a decline of 11 percent. Meanwhile, improved technology has made farming less labor intensive, so the total farm population has also declined precipitously, and is now less than 2 percent of the total population, down from 42 percent at the turn of the century, and 15 percent in 1950. The surpluses created by expanded and more efficient production required governments to prop up prices, often at the consumer's expense. Complaints that these programs, initiated in the country during the 1930s to help farmers, have become wasteful

and counterproductive, have led to some cuts by recent congressional actions. In 1996, Congress repealed price guarantees on most major crops, fully effective by 2002.

The worldwide nature of agricultural progress—the "green revolution"—has increased competition for markets, in some cases hurting farmers who depend upon exporting a large share of their crop. Nevertheless, the U.S. continues to export agricultural products worth close to $60 billion a year, almost half of the total to Asia. The 1997-98 financial crisis there drove down the price of all major commodities, and led to a decline in farm exports. In all likelihood, today's farmers face a difficult future. Record crops from 1996 to 1998 have also pushed prices down, in some cases as

Farms—Number and Acreage, by State, 1980–98

State	Number of Farms (000's)		Acreage (millions)		Acreage per farm	
	1980	1998	1980	1998	1980	1998
U.S. total	2,440	2,192	1,039	954	426	435
Alabama	59	49	12	10	207	194
Alaska	(z)	1	2	1	3,378	1,625
Arizona	8	8	38	28	5,080	3,582
Arkansas	59	50	17	15	280	298
California	81	89	34	29	417	320
Colorado	27	30	36	32	1,358	1,092
Connecticut	4	4	(z)	(z)	117	93
Delaware	4	3	1	1	186	215
Florida	39	45	11	11	344	236
Georgia	59	50	15	11	254	226
Hawaii	4	6	2	1	458	262
Idaho	24	25	15	12	623	490
Illinois	107	79	29	28	269	352
Indiana	87	66	17	16	193	236
Iowa	119	97	34	33	284	340
Kansas	75	65	48	48	644	731
Kentucky	102	90	15	14	143	154
Louisiana	37	30	10	8	273	273
Maine	8	7	2	1	195	186
Maryland	18	13	3	2	157	168
Massachusetts	6	6	1	1	116	95
Michigan	65	52	11	10	175	200
Minnesota	104	80	30	29	291	361
Mississippi	55	42	15	12	265	276
Missouri	120	110	31	30	261	274
Montana	24	28	62	58	2,601	2,091
Nebraska	65	55	48	46	734	844
Nevada	3	3	9	7	3,100	2,300
New Hampshire	3	3	1	(z)	160	135
New Jersey	9	10	1	1	109	86
New Mexico	14	16	47	45	3,467	2,831
New York	47	38	9	8	200	205
North Carolina	93	58	12	9	126	162
North Dakota	40	31	42	40	1,043	1,274
Ohio	95	80	16	15	171	186
Oklahoma	72	83	35	34	481	410
Oregon	35	40	18	17	517	435
Pennsylvania	62	60	9	8	145	128
Rhode Island	1	1	(z)	(z)	87	87
South Carolina	34	25	6	5	188	196
South Dakota	39	33	45	44	1,169	1,354
Tennessee	96	91	14	12	142	131
Texas	196	226	138	132	705	582
Utah	14	15	12	12	919	773
Vermont	8	7	2	1	226	200
Virginia	58	49	10	9	169	180
Washington	38	40	16	16	429	393
West Virginia	22	21	4	4	191	176
Wisconsin	93	78	19	16	200	210
Wyoming	9	9	35	35	3,846	3,761

Note: z= Fewer than 500,000 acres. **Source:** U.S. Dept. of Agriculture, *Farm Numbers and Land in Farms,* (July, 1999).

low as during the Depression. Further consolidation in the industry threatened to force even more family farmers from the business, and continue the trend of agribusinesses swallowing up land once individually owned and farmed.

U.S. Agricultural Exports: Principal Commodities by Value and Percentage of Agriculture Exports, 1990–98

Category	1980 Value (billions)	Percent	1990 Value (billions)	Percent	1998 Value (billions)	Percent
Total agricultural exports	$41.2	100.0%	$39.5	100.0%	$51.8	100.0%
Commodities						
Grains and feeds	$19.1	46.4%	$14.4	36.5%	$14.0	27.0%
Oilseeds and products	9.4	22.8	5.7	14.4	9.5	18.3
Animals and animal products	3.8	9.2	6.7	16.9	10.7	20.6
Cotton	2.9	7.0	2.8	7.0	2.5	4.9
Tobacco, unmanufactured	1.3	3.3	1.4	3.6	1.5	2.8
Fruits and preparations	1.3	3.3	2.4	6.0	3.2	6.2
Vegetables and preparations	1.2	2.9	2.2	5.6	4.2	8.1
Nuts and preparations	0.8	1.9	1.0	2.5	1.4	2.6
Other	1.5	3.6	2.9	7.3	4.9	9.5

Source: U.S. Dept. of Agriculture, *Agricultural Statistics, 1998.*

U.S. Production of Leading Farm Products as Percent of World Total, 1995–98

Product	U.S. production (millions of metric tons) 1995	1997	1998	As percent of world total 1995	1997	1998
Total production						
Corn	187.0	234.0	248.0	36.3%	40.8%	41.5%
Soybeans	59.0	73.0	75.0	47.4	46.8	48.1
Wheat	59.0	68.0	69.0	11.0	11.2	11.8
Cotton[1]	19.7	18.9	18.8	23.0	21.0	20.5
Rice, milled	5.6	6.0	6.1	1.5	1.6	1.6
Amount exported						
Corn	52.7	37.7	44.0	72.3%	59.5%	69.6%
Wheat	33.1	28.1	28.5	33.5	28.0	29.7
Soybeans	23.2	23.7	22.0	72.5	58.7	56.8
Cotton[1]	9.4	6.9	7.5	33.0	25.7	28.2
Rice, milled	3.1	2.3	3.1	14.8	12.1	11.4

1. Millions of bales.   **Source:** U.S. Dept. of Agriculture, Foreign Agricultural Service, *Foreign Agricultural Commodity Circular Series.*

Top Agricultural States by Farm Marketings, 1997

Rank, State	Farm marketings (millions)	Crops	Livestock and products	Principal commodities
1. California	$25,289	$18,995	$6,294	Dairy products, grapes, greenhouse, cattle
2. Texas	13,461	5,277	8,184	Cattle, cotton, greenhouse, dairy products
3. Iowa	12,841	7,311	5,530	Corn, soybeans, hogs, cattle
4. Nebraska	10,092	4,550	5,542	Cattle, corn, soybeans, hogs
5. Illinois	9,276	7,339	1,937	Corn, soybeans, hogs, cattle
6. Kansas	9,001	3,985	5,017	Cattle, wheat, corn, sorghum, grain
7. North Carolina	8,302	3,608	4,694	Hogs, broilers, tobacco, greenhouse
8. Minnesota	8,155	4,101	4,054	Soybeans, corn, dairy products, hogs
9. Florida	6,243	4,978	1,265	Greenhouse, oranges, tomatoes, sugar
10. Georgia	5,887	2,445	3,442	Broilers, cotton, peanuts, chicken eggs

Source: U.S. Dept. of Agriculture, Economic Research Service, *Farm Business Economic Report, 1997.*

Crime and Punishment

►SERIOUS CRIME

Serious crime is the Justice Department's measure of the total number of violent crimes (murder, rape, robbery, and assault) plus property crimes (burglary, larceny/theft, motor vehicle theft, and arson). The number of serious crimes in the U.S., has decreased every year for the past six years, from an all-time high of close to 15 million in 1991 to just over 13 million in 1997.

The number of violent crimes peaked at 1.93 million in 1992, and has declined every year since then, to 1.63 million in 1997. That's still significantly higher, however, than the 1.09 million violent crimes recorded in 1978 or even the 1.56 million in 1988. There were 18,210 murders reported to police in the U.S. in 1997, down 7.3 percent from the year before, but about the same as the number in 1984. Guns were the weapon of choice, accounting for more than two-thirds of all homicides; handguns alone accounted for more than half of all murders.

Property crime reached its all-time high in 1991, at 12.96 million total offenses reported to police. It too has decreased every year, and totaled 11.54 million in 1997. That's about the same number as in 1982. The number of burglaries has dropped 23.5 percent, from 3.22 million in 1988 to 2.46 million in 1997.

The surging economy and thriving job market are major reasons for the steadily declining number of serious crimes, especially the crimes of robbery, burglary, and motor vehicle theft, which have experienced some of the biggest drops. But it does not necessarily explain the equally impressive drop in the number of murders, which experts say is due to the aging of the population, and more police and better policing techniques. In addition, tougher sentencing laws have increased the number of people in prison. Note, however, that these explanations do not account for the nearly 80 percent increase in the number of aggravated assaults since 1978. Assaults have declined slightly from the all-time high of 1.14 million reached in 1994, but were still higher in 1997 (1.02 million) than they were in 1989 (951,710).

The number of forcible rapes has increased 42 percent since 1978, but a portion of this significant jump is most likely the result of more women reporting this crime to police, rather than an increase in the number of incidents. Since 1992, the number of rapes reported dropped from 109,060 to 96,120.

The crime rate   Raw numbers of crime do not necessarily tell the whole story. To account for population growth, criminologists use the crime rate per 100,000 population to compare crime statistics from different years. Because the population continues to grow, the rate of crime is dropping even more precipitously than the raw number of crimes. The total number of serious crimes fell 6.9 percent between 1993 and 1997, but the rate dropped 10.2 percent. In other words, the likelihood that you will become a victim of crime is dropping even more quickly.

The biggest declines in crime rates have come in property crime. There were 610.8 violent crimes for every 100,000 people in 1997, down 4.0 percent from the year before, but about the same as in 1988 Meanwhile, property crimes per 100,000 inhabitants fell from 5,088.5 in 1988 to 4,311.9 in 1997, a drop of 14.2 percent.

The largest states, of course, had the most numbers of crimes. But the rate of crime was by far the greatest in Florida (7,271.8 serious crimes per 100,000 residents) and Arizona (7,195.0). Both states have the reputation of being tough on crime, and both have the death penalty—Florida

Serious Crime in the U.S., 1975-97

Crime	1975	1980	1990	1995	1996	1997	Percent change, 1988-97
Number of Offenses Reported to Police							
Violent crime	1,039,710	1,344,520	1,820,130	1,798,790	1,688,540	1,634,770	4.4%
Murder	20,510	23,040	23,440	21,610	19,650	18,210	-11.9
Forcible rape	56,090	82,990	102,560	97,470	96,250	96,120	3.9
Robbery	470,500	565,840	639,270	580,510	535,590	497,950	-8.3
Aggravated assault	492,620	672,650	1,054,860	1,099,210	1,037,050	1,022,490	12.4
Property crime	10,252,700	12,063,700	12,655,500	12,063,900	11,805,300	11,540,300	-6.6%
Burglary	3,265,300	3,795,200	3,073,900	2,593,000	2,506,400	2,461,100	-23.5
Larceny/theft	5,977,700	7,136,900	7,945,700	7997700	7,904,700	7,725,500	0.3
Motor vehicle theft	1,009,600	1,131,700	1,635,900	1,472,400	1,394,200	1,353,700	-5.5
Total serious crimes	11,292,400	13,408,300	14,475,600	13,867,100	13,493,900	13,175,100	-5.4%
Rate per 100,000 inhabitants							
Violent crime	487.8	596.6	731.8	684.6	636.5	610.8	-4.1%
Murder	9.6	10.2	9.4	8.2	7.4	6.8	-19.0
Forcible rape	26.3	36.8	41.2	37.1	36.3	35.9	-4.5
Robbery	220.8	251.1	257.0	220.9	201.9	186.1	15.8
Aggravated assault	231.1	298.5	424.1	418.3	390.9	382.0	3.2
Property crime	4,810.7	5,353.3	5,088.5	4,951.3	4,450.1	4,311.9	-14.2%
Burglary	1,532.1	1,684.1	1,235.9	987.1	944.8	919.6	-29.8
Larceny/theft	2,804.8	3,167.0	3,194.8	3,043.8	2,979.7	2,886.5	-7.9
Motor vehicle theft	473.7	502.2	657.8	560.4	525.6	505.8	-13.2
Total serious crimes	5,298.5	5,950.0	5,820.3	5,275.9	5,086.6	4,922.7	-13.1%

Note: Totals may not add up due to independent rounding. **Source:** Federal Bureau of Investigation, *Uniform Crime Reports: Crime in the United States 1997*

Serious Crime per 100,000 Population, by State, 1997

| State | All serious crime | Violent crime | | | | Property crime | | |
		Murder	Forcible rape	Robbery	Aggravated assault	Burglary	Larceny/ theft	Motor vehicle theft
U.S.	4,922.7	6.8	35.9	186.1	382.0	919.6	2,886.5	505.8
Alabama	4,889.7	9.9	32.3	160.5	361.8	1,013.8	2,954.8	356.7
Alaska	5,272.6	8.9	66.2	106.4	519.7	702.1	3,412.2	457.1
Arizona	7,195.0	8.2	32.8	165.7	417.1	1,318.9	4,282.0	970.4
Arkansas	4,718.7	9.9	43.5	111.5	361.9	1,013.4	2,863.8	314.6
California	4,865.3	8.0	31.6	252.5	506.2	927.4	2,430.9	708.8
Colorado	4,650.4	4.0	43.1	83.3	232.8	796.1	3,077.3	413.7
Connecticut	3,984.3	3.8	22.6	152.9	211.6	738.3	2,410.4	444.7
District of Columbia	9,839.1	56.9	41.2	850.9	1,075.2	1,316.3	5,067.9	1,430.8
Delaware	5,138.3	2.5	65.0	179.5	430.9	767.8	3,184.7	507.9
Florida	7,271.8	6.9	51.9	276.1	688.7	1,459.8	4,056.9	731.5
Georgia	5,791.7	7.5	31.1	206.7	361.3	1,086.3	3,503.4	595.4
Hawaii	6,022.9	4.0	31.3	118.2	124.5	1073.4	4,126.7	544.9
Idaho	3,925.2	3.2	28.9	19.6	205.0	758.3	2,709.4	200.7
Illinois[1]	5,141.1	9.2	37.1	278.4	536.7	870.5	2,943.3	465.9
Indiana	4,466.3	7.3	32.9	132.4	342.1	821.7	2,701.9	428.0
Iowa	3,815.8	1.8	20.3	55.9	232.0	771.5	2,500.0	234.3
Kansas[1]	4,563.5	6.0	42.4	93.3	267.6	970.6	2,933.5	250.1
Kentucky[1]	3,127.0	5.8	33.4	90.7	187.0	681.6	1,880.4	248.1
Louisiana	6,449.2	15.7	41.3	239.1	559.7	1,239.3	3,748.0	606.0
Maine	3,131.7	2.0	20.5	20.7	77.6	663.5	2,215.2	132.2
Maryland	5,653.1	9.9	35.6	336.8	464.4	940.7	3,263.8	602.0
Massachusetts	3,675.2	1.9	26.9	109.1	506.2	661.8	1,887.8	481.4
Michigan	4,916.9	7.8	51.9	152.8	377.5	825.9	2,832.6	668.4
Minnesota	4,413.8	2.8	52.2	114.7	168.1	752.6	2,942.2	381.3
Mississippi	4,630.2	13.1	39.0	137.0	279.9	1,187.4	2,632.3	341.6
Missouri	4,814.5	7.9	28.2	156.1	385.2	868.2	2,878.0	490.9
Montana[1]	4,408.8	4.8	19.5	20.4	87.5	569.1	3,459.7	247.9
Nebraska	4,283.8	3.0	24.5	66.2	344.7	592.2	2,918.7	334.4
Nevada	6,064.5	11.2	59.9	302.4	425.3	1,310.4	3,167.1	788.3
New Hampshire[1]	2,639.6	1.4	33.7	23.4	54.8	393.2	1,997.4	135.8
New Jersey	4,057.0	4.2	21.5	210.6	256.4	756.2	2,297.0	511.2
New Mexico	6,906.5	7.7	50.4	171.4	623.7	1,452.4	3,883.7	717.2
New York	3,910.9	6.0	22.5	309.3	350.8	652.3	2,130.6	439.4
North Carolina	5,491.5	8.3	31.6	172.6	394.5	1,346.8	3,208.5	329.2
North Dakota	2,711.4	.9	24.8	6.4	55.1	358.8	2,085.3	180.0
Ohio	4,514.6	4.7	40.8	158.7	231.2	849.0	2,824.1	406.0
Oklahoma	5,494.7	6.9	45.7	103.9	403.0	1,206.4	3,287.3	441.5
Oregon	6,269.8	2.9	40.3	117.5	283.7	1,033.2	4,197.6	594.5
Pennsylvania	3,431.5	5.9	27.4	156.3	252.6	567.5	2,054.0	367.8
Rhode Island	3,654.4	2.5	36.8	71.6	222.6	717.6	2,178.2	425.0
South Carolina	6,134.0	8.4	48.9	176.2	756.9	1,232.0	3,492.7	419.0
South Dakota	3,245.0	1.4	48.4	23.3	124.4	553.9	2,377.4	116.3
Tennessee	5,511.8	9.5	56.9	214.0	509.2	1,171.7	2,921.8	628.6
Texas	5,480.5	6.8	41.2	157.0	397.5	1,034.3	3,320.4	523.3
Utah	5,995.5	2.4	47.5	68.4	215.8	890.5	4,326.9	444.1
Vermont[1]	2,828.2	1.5	26.5	13.4	78.3	613.1	1,959.6	135.8
Virginia	3,876.2	7.2	27.0	124.5	186.5	571.4	2,679.0	280.5
Washington	5,926.3	4.3	51.4	120.0	265.0	1,106.3	3,811.5	567.8
West Virginia	2,469.1	4.1	19.5	43.1	151.9	586.3	1,483.1	181.0
Wisconsin	3,677.6	4.0	20.3	100.9	145.5	570.7	2,533.9	302.5
Wyoming	4,180.8	3.5	28.5	17.7	205.4	624.6	3,166.3	134.8

Note: Offense totals are based on reporting agencies and estimated for unreported areas. 1. Complete data not available for the states of Illinois, Kansas, Kentucky, Montana, New Hampshire, and Vermont. Some data are estimated.
Source: Federal Bureau of Investigation, *Uniform Crime Reports: Crime in the United States 1997.*

does so with zeal—yet these measures have apparently had little impact on crime. Meanwhile, New York, supposedly one of the most dangerous states, was at 3,910.9 crimes per 100,000 residents, significantly below the national average. The most dangerous place to live, however, was the nation's capital, with 9,839.1 serious crimes per 100,000 residents, double the national average. By metropolitan area, Miami (10,792.3) Albuquerque (8,875.7), West Palm Beach (8,373.2) and Tucson

(7,914.4) topped the list of dangerous cities, followed by Oklahoma City and Phoenix.

New Orleans, with 25.9 homicides per 100,000 residents, was the murder capital of the United States for the third straight year in 1997 (though down significantly from the 31.9 recorded in 1996). Richmond, Va. was second, with 20.1 per 100,000 residents, and Birmingham, Ala., had only 16.3 murders per 100,000 people. The rate in New York City was 9.3.

Serious Crime Per 100,000 Population, by Metropolitan Area, 1997

| Metropolitan area | All serious crime | Violent crime | | | | Total violent crime[1] | Total property crime[2] |
		Murder	Forcible rape	Robbery	Aggravated assault		
Albuquerque	8,875.7	9.0	58.2	303.0	718.4	1,742.9	7,787.1
Atlanta	6,711.5	8.6	35.5	296.2	411.9	752.2	5,959.3
Austin, Texas	5,905.2	5.8	45.7	144.3	295.1	490.9	5,414.3
Baltimore	6,609.0	14.2	38.1	486.2	602.5	1,140.9	5,468.1
Bergen-Passaic, N.J.	3,069.4	2.4	12.9	124.1	155.0	294.4	2,775.0
Birmingham, Ala.	5,639.6	16.3	41.3	241.2	405.9	704.7	4,934.9
Boston	3,445.9	2.3	24.1	127.6	386.1	540.1	2,905.8
Charlotte, N.C.	6,847.8	9.3	42.5	274.9	706.2	1,032.9	5,814.8
Columbus, Ohio	6,478.2	7.0	66.2	257.7	243.6	574.5	5,903.7
Dallas	6,188.3	9.2	44.1	232.0	432.4	717.6	5,470.6
Denver	5,014.6	5.4	48.2	124.6	243.6	421.8	4,592.8
Detroit	5,931.5	12.5	45.9	245.1	481.2	784.7	5,146.8
El Paso	6,491.4	4.6	40.0	157.4	554.0	756.0	5,735.4
Fort Lauderdale, Fla.	7,294.7	4.6	34.8	288.4	455.2	783.0	6,511.7
Fort Worth	5,461.3	6.8	43.8	145.6	424.2	620.4	4,840.9
Fresno	6,973.8	10.5	42.1	266.4	659.1	978.2	5,995.6
Grand Rapids, Mich.	4,459.9	3.8	37.5	92.8	327.3	461.4	3,998.4
Greensboro, N.C.	5,941.6	7.6	36.6	188.1	379.1	611.4	5,330.1
Greenville, S.C.	6,004.2	5.9	46.7	173.8	753.3	979.7	5,024.5
Hartford, Conn.	3,930.6	3.4	17.2	148.8	175.6	345.1	3,585.5
Honolulu	6,067.4	3.9	29.2	137.9	128.5	299.5	5,768.0
Houston	5,518.3	9.1	36.8	268.9	503.6	818.3	4,700.0
Indianapolis	5,260.6	11.4	47.7	256.8	411.5	727.4	4,533.2
Jacksonville, Fla.	7,107.3	8.6	76.4	263.9	784.9	1,133.8	5,973.5
Los Angeles-Long Beach	4,744.7	12.5	30.3	410.9	681.8	1,135.5	3,609.2
Memphis	7,839.1	15.9	107.4	542.2	640.7	1,306.2	6,532.9
Miami, Fla.	10,792.3	14.7	59.9	602.2	1,015.1	1,691.8	9,100.5
Middlesex, N.J.	2,956.6	1.6	9.9	84.5	130.9	226.8	2,729.7
Milwaukee	4,966.5	8.8	24.7	266.0	221.5	521.1	4,445.5
Minneapolis	5,364.5	3.8	54.4	179.9	220.0	458.1	4,906.4
Monmouth-Ocean, N.J.	3,107.9	1.7	15.7	77.3	151.8	246.6	2,861.3
Nashville	7,510.3	12.1	68.9	266.9	737.1	1,085.0	6,425.2
Nassau-Suffolk, N.Y.	2,701.7	2.1	6.5	78.3	93.9	180.7	2,521.0
Newark, N.J.	4,721.7	6.0	25.7	358.1	359.0	748.7	3,973.0
New Orleans	7,408.7	25.1	49.8	417.9	600.2	1,092.9	6,315.8
New York City	4,606.7	9.3	26.8	540.8	552.6	1,129.5	3,477.2
Norfolk, Va.	5,232.1	9.2	36.3	227.3	238.7	511.5	4,720.6
Oakland, Calif.	6,184.3	9.1	34.2	317.5	489.9	850.8	5,333.5
Oklahoma City	7,910.7	7.6	60.7	173.6	435.0	676.9	7,233.8
Orange County, Calif.	3,542.6	3.9	21.2	142.0	262.0	429.1	3,113.5
Orlando, Fla.	7,658.0	4.1	53.4	267.5	742.4	1,067.3	6,590.7
Phoenix	7,907.1	9.7	32.7	194.8	419.3	656.5	7,250.7
Pittsburgh	2,783.4	4.0	22.9	103.7	179.5	310.0	2,473.3
Portland, Oreg.	6,408.2	4.1	41.9	162.8	428.5	637.3	5,770.8
Providence, R.I.	3,686.1	2.2	34.9	72.6	232.1	341.8	3,344.3
Raleigh, N.C.	6,295.1	8.4	31.7	246.9	350.5	637.5	5,657.6
Richmond, Va.	5,463.4	20.1	32.9	243.9	309.8	606.7	4,856.6
Riverside, Calif.	5,193.9	8.7	33.5	213.8	501.3	757.2	4,436.7
Rochester, N.Y.	4,187.6	5.8	24.2	173.8	115.4	319.2	3,868.4
Sacramento	6,474.3	6.4	36.1	245.3	401.4	689.1	5,785.2
Salt Lake City	7,008.9	3.2	50.5	97.9	261.5	413.1	6,595.9
San Antonio	6,661.5	7.4	48.3	149.6	185.6	390.9	6,270.6
San Diego	4,417.1	4.6	32.6	177.2	451.9	666.4	3,750.8
San Francisco	4,929.2	5.2	24.6	327.0	331.4	688.2	4,240.0
San Jose, Calif.	3,777.7	3.9	33.7	89.0	452.3	578.9	3,198.8
Seattle	6,286.9	4.5	49.2	162.7	223.0	439.4	5,847.5
Syracuse, N.Y.	3,515.6	3.2	17.5	97.5	174.4	292.6	3,222.9
Tampa, Fla.	6,453.4	5.5	47.8	253.1	717.3	1,023.6	5,429.7
Tucson	7,914.4	7.8	50.0	213.4	514.9	786.1	7,128.3
Tulsa	5,299.0	7.1	50.6	134.8	557.8	750.4	4,548.6
Washington, D.C.	4,879.2	10.3	26.9	231.7	307.6	576.5	4,302.7
West Palm Beach, Fla.	8,373.2	7.6	45.3	289.8	642.5	985.2	7,388.0

1. Violent crimes are offenses of murder, forcible rape, robbery, and aggravated assault. 2. Property crimes are offenses of burglary, larceny-theft, and motor vehicle theft. Data are not included for the property crime of arson.
Source: Federal Bureau of Investigation, *Uniform Crime Reports: Crime in the United States 1997.*

Crimes per 100,000 Population in Metropolitan Areas, 1993-97

Metropolitan area	All serious crimes[2]			Violent crimes[1]		
	1993	1996	1997	1993	1996	1997
Albuquerque	7,547.8	8,301.1	8,875.7	1,273.6	1,082.0	1,742.9
Atlanta	7,594.5	7,647.7	6,711.5	923.8	781.3	752.2
Austin	7,584.5	5,960.0	5,905.2	528.2	520.9	490.9
Baltimore	7,275.4	7,026.9	6,609.0	1,356.1	1,237.3	1,140.9
Bergen-Passaic, N.J.	N.A.	3,305.0	3,069.4	N.A.	322.4	294.4
Birmingham, Ala.	N.A.	5,932.0	5,639.6	N.A.	780.8	704.7
Boston	4,844.6	3,768.2	3,445.9	777.1	580.9	540.1
Buffalo	5,283.8	4,563.7	N.A.	754.7	538.8	N.A.
Charlotte	7,277.0	6,841.0	6,847.8	1,204.5	979.2	1,032.9
Columbus	6,012.8	6,332.5	6,478.2	682.2	579.6	574.5
Dallas	7,290.9	6,350.2	6,188.3	946.3	784.4	717.6
Denver	6,090.8	5,415.9	5,014.6	731.7	460.4	421.8
Detroit	N.A.	6,081.7	5,931.5	N.A.	828.9	784.7
El Paso	7,827.7	6,980.8	6,491.4	1,031.1	811.3	756.0
Fort Lauderdale	8,904.1	N.A.	7,294.7	1,005.4	N.A.	783.0
Fort Worth	6,880.9	5,865.4	5,461.3	824.6	661.9	620.4
Fresno	8,099.6	7,620.3	6,973.8	1,084.6	1,043.2	978.2
Grand Rapids, Mich.	N.A.	4,602.2	4,459.9	N.A.	489.9	461.4
Greensboro, N.C.	N.A.	6,157.5	5,941.6	N.A.	659.1	611.4
Greenville, S.C.	N.A.	6,361.9	6,004.2	N.A.	1,083.9	979.7
Hartford, Conn.	N.A.	4,224.2	3,930.6	N.A.	420.1	345.1
Honolulu	6,442.9	6,840.1	6,067.4	285.6	313.0	299.5
Houston	N.A.	5,761.0	5,518.3	N.A.	859.0	818.3
Indianapolis	N.A.	5,400.0	5,260.6	N.A.	726.5	727.4
Jacksonville, Fla.	8,598.0	N.A.	7,107.3	1,419.9	N.A.	1,133.8
Los Angeles-Long Beach, Calif.	7,049.6	5,442.4	4,744.7	1,682.5	1,278.0	1,135.5
Memphis, Tenn.	7,408.6	7,862.4	7,839.1	1,109.3	1,316.3	1,306.2
Miami, Fla.	13,500.4	N.A.	10,792.3	2,136.2	N.A.	1,691.8
Middlesex, N.J.	N.A	2,9287.2	2,956.6	N.A	229.1	226.8
Milwaukee	5,355.8	5,206.8	4,966.5	482.1	474.6	521.1
Minneapolis	N.A.	5,346.1	5,364.5	N.A.	468.5	458.1
Monmouth-Ocean, N.J.	N.A.	3,280.8	3,107.9	N.A.	242.6	246.6
Nashville	7,331.8	7,593.9	7,510.3	1,098.6	1,149.4	1,085.0
Nassau-Suffolk, N.Y.	N.A.	2,898.5	2,701.7	N.A.	213.0	180.7
Newark, N.J.	N.A.	5,216.3	4,721.7	N.A.	869.5	748.7
New Orleans	8,511.7	8,267.7	7,408.7	1,312.7	1,326.0	1,092.9
New York City	7,532.9	4,896.6	4,606.7	1,865.6	1,191.9	1,129.5
Norfolk, Va.	N.A.	5,338.2	5,232.1	N.A.	507.2	511.5
Oakland, Calif.	7,329.6	6,250.3	6,184.3	1,137.5	871.2	850.8
Oklahoma City	7,692.7	8,252.3	7,910.7	828.2	707.8	676.9
Orange County, Calif.	N.A.	3,983.5	3,542.6	N.A.	465.3	429.1
Philadelphia	4,355.3	4,630.8	N.A.	662.2	733.2	N.A.
Phoenix	7,787.9	7,730.2	7,907.1	806.8	668.0	656.5
Pittsburgh	3,111.2	2,665.1	2,783.4	393.4	303.2	310.0
Portland, Oreg.	6,244.5	6,154.7	6,408.2	711.8	644.5	637.3
Providence, R.I.	N.A	4,014.0	3,686.1	N.A	353.8	341.8
Raleigh, N.C.	N.A.	6,076.4	6,295.1	N.A.	570.9	637.5
Richmond, Va.	N.A.	5,455.2	5,463.4	N.A.	596.6	606.7
Riverside, Calif.	N.A.	5,560.6	5,193.9	N.A.	814.6	757.2
Rochester, N.Y.	N.A.	4,275.3	4,187.6	N.A.	310.8	319.2
Sacramento	7,038.4	6,279.1	6,474.3	815.6	700.8	689.1
Salt Lake City	N.A.	7,037.6	7,008.9	N.A.	421.5	413.1
San Antonio	8,450.9	7,080.7	6,661.5	629.7	428.2	390.9
San Diego	6,160.5	4,623.8	4,417.1	873.8	710.0	666.4
San Francisco	6,697.5	5,381.6	4,929.2	1,088.1	801.3	688.2
San Jose, Calif.	4,640.3	4,020.3	3,777.7	524.7	562.1	578.9
Seattle	6,588.1	N.A.	6,286.9	569.8	N.A.	439.4
Syracuse, N.Y.	N.A.	3,551.3	3,515.6	N.A.	288.0	292.6
Tucson, Ariz.	9,219.9	7,853.6	7,914.4	754.2	809.2	786.1
Tulsa, Okla.	5,484.1	5,272.9	5,299.0	801.0	740.6	750.4
Washington, D.C.	5,462.4	5,450.7	4,879.2	771.4	679.7	576.5

1. Violent crimes are offenses of murder, forcible rape, robbery, and aggravated assault. 2. Property crimes are offenses of burglary, larceny-theft, and motor vehicle theft. Data are not included for the property crime of arson. **Source:** Federal Bureau of Investigation, *Uniform Crime Reports: Crime in the United States 1997.*

Violent crime in other nations   Although every recent official report and news story about crime has emphasized the continuing decline of serious crime, it is helpful to keep in mind that the U.S. remains far and away the most violent industrialized nation. Over the past 20 years, about 20,000 murders have been committed here each year (or 8 to 10 murders a year per 100,000 population). By comparison, the murder rate is about 0.5 per 100,000 in Japan, 1.1 per 100,000 in France, and 3.4 per 100,000 in Germany.

In 1999, the Bureau of Justice Statistics released a detailed comparison of crime rates in the U.S and England. Although violent crime is increasing in England while it is decreasing in the U.S., the rates of murder, rape, and robbery are still significantly higher in this country than in the U.K. The U.S. murder rate is six times as high as England's, the number of rapes per 100,000 population is three times as high, and the robbery rate is 40 percent higher. It is interesting to note, however, that the rate of assault is 13 percent higher in England, while the rates for burglary and motor vehicle theft are about double U.S. rates.

Homicide, Guns, and Young People
Murders by youthful offenders have followed the same downward trend evidenced in the population at large, but still remain alarmingly high. The rate of homicides by 14-17-year-olds dropped from an all-time high of 30 per 100,000 in 1993 to about 16 murders per 100,000 population in 1997. But that's still almost double the rate in 1984, when the rate was 9 per 100,000. Similarly, the homicide rate for 18-24-year-olds was 34 per 100,000 in 1997, down from highs of more than 40 in 1991 and 1993, but still considerably higher

than the 22 in 1985. Over the period 1976-97, the number of nongun homicides by offenders aged 14-24 has remained largely unchanged, while the number of murders involving guns has more than tripled. By comparison, the number of gun homicides by offenders over the age of 25 has actually declined by more than 2,500 since 1976.

▶ CRIME VICTIMS
Crime victimization statistics are a second measure of the so-called crime rate. Unlike reported crime statistics (above), which are based on reports to law enforcement authorities, crime victimization statistics are based on Bureau of Justice Statistics interviews with a sampling of people about their personal experience with crime. (The BJS does not ask about or keep statistics on homicides because it is impossible to question the victim.)

In 1997, the rate of criminal victimization dropped to its lowest level since the BJS began keeping statistics in 1973. Violent crime was down 21 percent since 1993, while property crime declined 22 percent over the same period.

As the accompanying table shows, the victims of most kinds of crime are most likely to be black, young, poor, urban, and except for rape and domestic violence, male. People with family incomes of less than $7,500 were the most likely be victimized by crime, especially violent crime. In general, the poorer a person is, the more likely he or she is to be the victim of a crime. And while senior citizens often feel most vulnerable to crime, it is teenagers who are most likely to be victimized by all kinds of crime. Children 12-19 years old are 20 times as likely to be the victims of violent crime as people over the age of 65.

Crime Rates in the U.S. and England, 1981-96

Year	Murder U.S.	England	Rape U.S.	England	Robbery U.S.	England	Assault U.S.	England	Burglary U.S.	England	Motor Vehicle Theft U.S.	England
1981	9.83	1.13	70.59	4.19	258.75	40.86	289.73	197.49	1,649.47	1,447.36	474.72	670.09
1985	7.95	1.24	72.83	7.19	208.54	54.94	302.94	237.62	1,287.30	1,733.71	461.97	734.98
1990	9.42	1.32	80.86	12.04	257.03	71.15	424.13	351.26	1,235.94	1,979.19	657.75	971.51
1995	8.22	1.44	72.73	18.90	220.95	131.37	418.33	392.63	987.61	2,391.90	560.48	981.18
1996	7.41	1.31	70.79	21.77	202.44	142.35	388.19	439.60	942.95	2,239.15	525.93	948.83

Note: Statistics for England include Wales. Rates are crimes per 100,000 residents.
Source: U.S. Bureau of Justice Statistics, *Crime and Justice in the U.S. and England and Wales, 1981-96.*

Criminal Victimization Rates, 1992-97

Crime	Victimizations ('000s) 1992	1996	1997	Victimization rate per 1,000 persons 1992	1996	1997
All crimes[1]	42,834	36,796	34,788	N.A.	N.A.	N.A.
Violent crimes[1]	10,249	9,125	8,614	49.0	42.0	39.2
Simple assault	6,053	5,773	5,476	28.9	26.6	24.9
Aggravated assault	2,317	1,910	1,883	11.1	8.8	8.6
Robbery	1,272	1,134	944	6.1	5.2	4.3
Rape/sexual assault	607	307	311	2.9	1.4	1.4
Personal theft	369	318	357	1.8	1.5	1.6
Property crime	32,217	27,353	25,817	325.3	266.3	248.3
Property thefts	24,579	21,120	19,749	248.2	205.7	189.9
Household burglary	5,803	4,845	4,635	58.6	47.2	44.6
Motor vehicle theft	1,835	1,387	1,443	18.5	13.5	13.8

Note: Rates per 1,000 people ages 12 or older. 1. The National Crime Victimization Survey cannot measure murder because it is impossible to question the victim.   Source: Bureau of Justice Statistics Bulletin, *Criminal Victimization 1997.*

Victimization Rates, by Sex, Age, Race, Income, Residence and Marital Status, 1997

| Characteristic | Total | Crimes of violence[1] | | | Theft |
		Rape/Sexual assault	Robbery	Assault	
By sex					
Male	45.8	0.3	6.1	39.4	1.6
Female	33.0	2.5	2.6	27.9	1.7
By age					
12-15	87.9	2.5	8.2	77.1	2.8
16-19	96.2	5.6	10.2	80.4	3.5
20-24	67.8	2.4	7.4	57.9	1.8
25-34	46.9	2.3	4.7	39.9	1.1
35-49	32.2	0.6	3.7	27.9	1.6
50-64	14.6	0.2	2.2	12.2	1.1
65+	4.4	0.2	0.9	3.4	1.2
By race					
White	38.3	1.4	3.8	33.1	1.4
Black	49.0	1.6	7.4	39.9	3.3
Hispanic[2]	43.1	1.5	7.3	34.3	2.4
Family Income					
Less than $7,500	71.0	5.2	10.1	55.6	2.7
$ 7,500-$14,999	51.2	2.2	7.0	42.0	2.0
$15,000-$24,999	40.1	1.5	4.6	34.0	1.7
$25,000-$34,999	40.2	1.5	4.2	34.6	1.5
$35,000-$49,999	38.7	0.6	2.9	35.2	1.4
$50,000-$74,999	33.9	0.7	3.1	30.1	1.6
$75,000 or more	30.7	1.1	3.7	26.0	1.4
By Residence					
Urban	51.2	2.0	7.4	41.8	2.8
Suburban	36.3	1.2	3.4	31.7	1.3
Rural	29.2	1.1	2.1	26.0	0.7
By Marital Status					
Never married	71.5	3.0	8.3	60.1	2.4
Married	19.0	0.3	1.7	17.0	1.0
Divorced/separated	62.8	2.8	7.3	52.7	2.5
Widowed	8.0	0.3	1.0	6.6	1.5

Note: Rates per 1,000 people ages 12 or older. 1. The National Crime Victimization Survey cannot measure murder because it is impossible to question the victim. 2. Persons of Hispanic Origin may be of any race.   **Source:** Bureau of Justice Statistics Bulletin, *Criminal Victimization 1997.*

Arrests in the U.S., 1984–97

| Crime | Total Arrests | | | | | Rate per 100,000, 1997 |
	1984	1989	1995	1996	1997	
Violent crime	400,877	487,673	619,230	548,146	501,353	273.6
Murder	15,126	16,146	16,701	14,447	12,764	7.0
Forcible rape	28,565	27,461	26,561	24,347	22,133	12.1
Robbery	115,522	123,317	137,811	121,781	94,034	51.3
Aggravated assault	241,664	320,749	438,157	387,571	372,422	203.2
Property crime	1,431,812	1,600,947	1,620,704	1,506,549	1,409,600	769.3
Burglary	338,737	320,470	292,315	264,193	245,816	134.2
Larceny/theft	981,812	1,102,112	1,164,371	1,096,488	1,033,901	564.2
Motor vehicle theft	96,975	165,317	149,053	132,023	116,052	63.3
Arson	14,288	13,048	14,965	13,755	13,831	7.5
All serious crimes	1,832,689	2,088,620	2,239,934	2,054,605	1,910,953	1,042.9
Other crimes	6,995,758	7,902,737	9,167,354	9,033,747	8,629,262	N.A.
Total arrests	8,828,447	9,991,357	11,407,288	11,088,352	10,540,215	5,752.1

Note: Based on a survey of approximately 10,000 law enforcement agencies representing approximately 200,000,000 inhabitants. The number of agencies surveyed and the populations they represent changes from year to year.
Source: Federal Bureau of Investigation, *Uniform Crime Reports: Crime in the United States 1997.*

▶ LAW ENFORCEMENT

The nation's collective response to perceptions of increasing crime continues to be building more prisons and hiring more police. As of October 1997, there were 618,127 sworn police officers in the United States (up from 595,170 the year before) and an additional 240,405 civilians employed in police departments. This translates into 2.5 full-time po-lice officers for every 1,000 residents. Including full-time civilian employees, the ratio was 3.4 per 1,000. In cities with more than 250,000 residents, the ratio was even higher, averaging 4.0 law enforcement employees per 1,000 residents. The ratio was 4.4 and 4.0 in rural and suburban counties, but that was due primarily to a large number of civilian employees in those police departments.

Arrests by Race, 1997

Offense charged	Total	White		Black		Other[1]	
		Number	Percent	Number	Percent	Number	Percent
All arrests	**10,516,707**	**7,061,803**	**67.1%**	**3,201,014**	**30.4%**	**253,890**	**2.5%**
Violent crime	**500,621**	**284,523**	**56.8%**	**205,823**	**41.1%**	**10,275**	**2.0%**
Murder	12,759	5,345	41.9	7,194	56.4	220	1.7
Forcible rape	22,115	12,867	58.2	8,788	39.7	460	2.1
Robbery	93,979	38,679	41.2	53,657	57.1	1,643	1.8
Aggravated assault	371,768	227,632	61.2	136,184	36.6	7,952	2.1
Property crime	**1,407,793**	**912,058**	**64.8%**	**455,469**	**32.4%**	**40,266**	**2.9%**
Burglary	245,564	167,100	68.0	72,780	29.6	5,684	2.3
Larceny/theft	1,032,467	667,528	64.7	334,046	32.4	30,893	2.9
Motor vehicle theft	115,948	67,316	58.1	45,203	39.0	3,429	2.9
Arson	13,814	10,114	73.2	3,440	24.9	260	1.9
All serious crimes	**1,908,414**	**1,196,581**	**62.7%**	**661,292**	**34.7%**	**50,541**	**2.6%**

Note: Based on a survey of 9,271 law enforcement agencies representing 183 million inhabitants. 1. Includes American Indian, Alaskan Native, Asian, and Pacific Islander. **Source:** Federal Bureau of Investigation, *Uniform Crime Reports: Crime in the United States 1997.*

Arrests and Convictions for Crimes Committed in the U.S., 1996

As the following table demonstrates, the number of police and the number of prisons have very little effect on the number of crimes committed because people who commit crimes have very little expectation of getting caught. Except for murder, most felonies rarely even result in an arrest, and result in a conviction even more infrequently. These statistics indicate neither a shortage of police nor leniency by judges, but simply the difficulty of solving a crime after it has been committed and proving who did it.

Offense	Number of crimes reported to police	Number of adults arrested	Arrests as percent of number of crimes	Number of felony convictions	Convictions as percent of number arrested	Convictions as percent of number of crimes
Murder[1]	19,650	16,161	82.2%	11,430	70.7%	58.1%
Robbery	537,050	106,178	19.8	42,831	40.3	8.0
Aggravated assault	1,029,810	445,005	43.2	69,522	15.6	6.7
Burglary	2,501,500	229,745	9.2	93,197	40.6	3.7
Motor vehicle theft	1,395,200	102,578	7.4	17,794	17.3	1.3
Drug trafficking	N.A.	322,393	N.A.	212,504	65.9	N.A.

1. Includes non-negligent manslaughter.
Source: Bureau of Justice Statistics Bulletin, *Felony Sentences in State Courts, 1996,* January, 1999.

Overall, civilians made up 28 percent of the law enforcement workforce in 1997. Suburban and rural police departments employed roughly two civilians for every three sworn officers, while big cities employed close to four officers for each civilian. Northeastern states have the greatest number of sworn officers (2.8 officers per 1,000 inhabitants); the West has the fewest (1.8). By sex, nine out of every ten sworn officers in almost every police department is male, but civilian police employees are overwhelmingly female (63 percent on average, and as much as 75 percent in some departments).

Arrests Nationwide, law enforcement agencies made an estimated 10.5 million arrests in 1997 (down from 11.1 million the year before) for all criminal infractions except traffic violations. This represents a rate of 5,752 arrests per 100,000 population. In cities with populations of 250,000 or more, the arrest rate was 7,491 per 100,000; it was 4,301 per 100,000 for suburban counties, and 4,358 per 100,000 for rural counties. The greatest number of arrests were for drug abuse (1.1 million), larceny or theft (1.0 million) and driving under the influence of drugs or alcohol (986,339).

By age, 6 percent of all people arrested nationwide in 1997 were under 15; 19 percent were under 18; 32 percent were under 21; and 45 percent were under 25. By sex, 78 percent of all those arrested were males. Females were most often arrested for larceny/theft. These crimes alone accounted for 16 percent of all arrests of women, and for 73 percent of all serious crime arrests of women. By race, 67 percent of all those arrested were white, 30 percent were black, and 3 percent were of other races.

▶ CORRECTIONS

The United States has more people in prison (as well as more people in prison per capita) than any other western industrialized nation. In 1998 the Bureau of Justice Statistics reported a record 1.3 million inmates in federal and state prisons. The prison population has increased 68.4 percent since 1990, and 295 percent since 1980. Federal and state governments continue to build more and more prisons and to impose mandatory sentences for many drug-related crimes. Since 1980 the number of sentenced inmates per 100,000 residents has risen from 139 to 461.

During 1998, seven states experienced double-digit growth in their prison populations. Mississippi reported the largest increase (16.7 percent), followed by North Dakota (14.8 percent) Wisconsin (13.4 percent), Vermont (12.3 percent), Oregon (11.6 percent), West Virginia (10.5 percent) and Louisiana (10.1). Overall, the prison population nationwide grew by 4.8 percent.

The states with the highest incarceration rates (number of prisoners sentenced to more than one year per 100,000 residents) were all in the South. Louisiana led the way with 736 prisoners per 100,000 residents, followed by Texas (724), Oklahoma (622), Mississippi (574), and South Carolina (550). The lowest rates were found in four of the coldest states: Minnesota (117), Maine (125), North Dakota (128), and New Hampshire (182). The national average was 461, and the highest incarceration rate in the country was in the nation's capital, where 1,913 of every 100,000 residents were in prison.

Prison and race Blacks have made up the majority of the increase in the prison population. Between 1990 (the last year in which white prisoners outnumbered blacks) and 1997, the number of blacks behind bars jumped from 360,000 to 584,400, an increase of 62 percent. Meanwhile, the white prison population grew 46 percent, from 370,900 in 1990 to 578,000 in 1997. Black males have the highest incarceration rates (3,253 per 100,000 residents in 1997) while white females have the lowest (32 per 100,000 residents). Put another way, 3.3 percent of all black males are in prison. In the 25-29 age group, 8.6 percent of black males are in prison.

Jails and prisons Although the terms tend to be used synonymously, "jails" and "prisons" differ in the types of inmates they house, their locations, their physical size and their programs. Jails are locally administered facilities which house inmates after arraignment, prisoners serving terms of less than one year, and prisoners who cannot be housed in state prisons due to overcrowding.

Prisons are administered by either state or federal government authority. Typically they hold convicted offenders sentenced to terms of confinement for more than one year. They tend to be located away from dense population centers, and they are usually larger than jails and have more rehabilitation programs.

Costs of prisons According to the Criminal Justice Institute, total U.S. expenditures for adult correctional facilities was $28.9 billion in 1997. In

Prisoners in the U.S. by System, Sex, and Race, 1980-98

Year	By system			By sex and race[1]			
	Total	Federal	State	White male	Black male	White female	Black female
Number							
1980	329,821	24,363	305,458	159,500	140,600	5,900	6,300
1985	502,507	40,223	462,284	242,700	210,500	10,800	10,200
1990	773,919	65,526	708,393	350,700	340,300	20,200	19,700
1995	1,125,874	100,250	1,025,624	487,400	509,800	30,500	31,900
1996	1,183,368	105,544	1,077,824	511,300	528,600	33,800	34,000
1997	1,242,153	112,973	1,129,180	541,700	548,900	36,300	35,500
1998	1,302,019	123,041	1,178,978	N.A.	N.A.	N.A.	N.A.
Rate (Prisoners per 100,000 resident population)							
1980	139	9	130	168	1,111	6	45
1985	201	14	187	246	1,559	10	68
1990	292	20	272	338	2,234	19	117
1995	411	32	379	449	3,095	27	176
1996	427	33	394	468	3,164	30	185
1997	445	35	410	491	3,253	32	192
1998	461	38	423	N.A.	N.A.	N.A.	N.A.

Note: Prisoners sentenced to more than one year. N/A = not available. 1. Prisoners of other races not shown.
Source: Bureau of Justice Statistics Bulletin, *Prisoners in 1998* (1999).

Jail Population, 1985–98

Age and sex	1985	1990	1995	1997	1998
Number of inmates at midyear	**256,615**	**405,320**	**507,044**	**567,079**	**592,462**
Adults	254,986	403,019	499,300	557,974	584,372
Male	235,909	365,821	448,000	498,678	520,581
Female	19,077	37,198	51,300	59,296	63,791
Juveniles	1,629	2,301	7,800	9,105	8,090
Held as adults	—	—	5,900	7,007	6,542
Held as juveniles	1,629	2,301	1,800	2,098	1,548
Average daily population	**265,010**	**408,075**	**509,828**	**556,586**	**593,808**

Note: As of June 30 of each year. The average daily population is the sum of the number of inmates in a jail each day for a year, divided by 365. Juveniles are persons defined by state statute as being under a certain age, usually 18, and subject initially to juvenile court authority even if tried as adults. In 1994, the definition was changed to include all persons under age 18.
Source: Bureau of Justice Statistics, *Prison and Jail Inmates at Midyear 1998* (1999).

state prisons, the average cost per inmate was $54.25 per day in 1996. In a state like California, this comes to $34,000 a year.

Total U.S. prison capital costs increased from $538 million in 1980 to $2.3 billion in 1994, an increase of 141 percent (in constant dollars). Operating costs surged from $3.1 billion in 1980. to $17.7 billion in 1994. In California, where 20 new prisons were built during this period, expenditures on prisons rose from $336 million to $3 billion, with capital expenditures increasing by

1,327 percent (in constant dollars). In Texas, capital expenditures rose over 1,500 percent.

Probation and Parole   When an offender is convicted, the primary sentencing alternatives are incarceration or probation. Once imprisoned, the offender may become eligible for parole, a form of conditional release. The explosion in the prison population has understandably led to a corresponding increase in the number of prisoners released on probation or parole. In 1997,

Number of Prisoners and Incarceration Rates by State, 1997–98

Region and jurisdiction	Total prisoners		Percent change, 1997–98	Total sentenced to more than one year		Incarceration rate, 1998
	1997	1998[1]		1997	1998	
U.S. total	1,242,153	1,302,019	4.8%	1,195,498	1,252,830	461
Federal	112,973	123,041	8.9	94,987	103,682	38
State	1,129,180	1,178,978	4.4	1,100,511	1,149,148	423
Alabama	22,290	23,326	4.6	21,680	22,655	519
Alaska[2]	4,165	4,097	-1.6	2,571	2,541	413
Arizona	23,484	25,311	7.8	22,353	23,955	507
Arkansas	10,021	10,638	6.2	9,936	10,561	415
California	155,790	161,904	3.9	152,739	159,109	483
Colorado	13,461	14,312	6.3	13,461	14,312	357
Connecticut[2]	17,241	17,605	2.1	11,920	12,193	372
Delaware[2]	5,435	5,558	2.3	3,264	3,211	429
District of Columbia[2]	9,353	9,949	6.4	9,353	9,949	1,913
Florida	64,626	67,224	4.0	64,574	67,193	447
Georgia	36,505	39,262	7.6	35,787	38,758	502
Hawaii[2]	4,978	4,924	-1.1	3,448	3,670	307
Idaho	3,911	4,083	4.4	3,911	4,083	330
Illinois[3]	40,788	43,051	5.5	40,788	43,051	357
Indiana	17,903	19,197	7.2	17,730	19,016	321
Iowa[3]	6,938	7,394	6.6	6,938	7,394	258
Kansas[3]	7,911	8,183	3.4	7,911	8,183	310
Kentucky	14,600	14,987	2.7	14,600	14,987	379
Louisiana	29,265	32,227	10.1	29,265	32,227	736
Maine	1,620	1,612	-0.5	1,542	1,562	125
Maryland	22,232	22,572	1.5	21,088	21,540	418
Massachusetts	11,947	11,832	-1.0	10,847	10,739	275
Michigan	44,771	45,879	2.5	44,771	45,879	466
Minnesota	5,326	5,572	4.6	5,306	5,557	117
Mississippi	14,296	16,678	16.7	13,676	15,855	574
Missouri	23,998	24,974	4.1	23,998	24,949	457
Montana	2,517	2,734	8.6	2,517	2,734	310
Nebraska	3,402	3,676	8.1	3,329	3,588	215
Nevada	9,024	9,651	6.9	9,024	9,651	542
New Hampshire	2,168	2,169	0.0	2,168	2,169	182
New Jersey[3]	28,361	31,121	9.7	28,361	31,121	382
New Mexico	4,688	4,985	6.3	4,450	4,732	271
New York	70,295	72,638	3.3	70,021	72,289	397
North Carolina	31,612	31,811	0.6	27,567	27,193	358
North Dakota	797	915	14.8	715	814	128
Ohio[3]	48,016	48,450	0.9	48,016	48,450	432
Oklahoma[3]	20,542	20,892	1.7	20,542	20,892	622
Oregon	7,999	8,927	11.6	7,589	8,596	260
Pennsylvania	34,964	36,377	4.0	34,957	36,373	303
Rhode Island[2]	3,371	3,445	2.2	2,100	2,175	220
South Carolina	21,173	22,115	4.4	20,264	21,236	550
South Dakota	2,242	2,435	8.6	2,242	2,430	329
Tennessee[3]	16,659	17,738	6.5	16,659	17,738	325
Texas[3]	140,351	144,510	3.0	140,351	144,510	724
Utah	4,301	4,391	2.1	4,280	4,337	205
Vermont[2]	1,270	1,426	12.3	828	1,110	188
Virginia	28,385	28,560	0.6	27,524	27,191	399
Washington	13,214	14,161	7.2	13,214	14,154	247
West Virginia	3,148	3,478	10.5	3,148	3,478	192
Wisconsin	16,277	18,451	13.4	15,639	17,477	334
Wyoming	1,549	1,571	1.4	1,549	1,571	327

Note: The incarceration rate is equal to the number of prisoners sentenced to more than 1 year per 100,000 residents. 1. Estimated. 2. Includes jail population. 3. Includes some inmates sentenced to one year or less.
Source: Bureau of Justice Statistics Bulletin, *Prisoners in 1998* (1999).

Lifetime Likelihood of Going to Prison by Age, Sex, Race, and Hispanic Origin

One of every 20 people in the U.S. (5.1 percent) will serve time in a prison during their lifetime, according to a March, 1997, BJS report, if 1991 incarceration rates do not change dramatically. Men (9.0 percent) are much more likely than women (1.1 percent) to be incarcerated in prison at least once during their life, and black men (28.5 percent) are six times as likely as white men (4.4 percent) to be imprisoned. Sixteen percent of Hispanic men are likely to be imprisoned.

Category	Percent expected to go to prison at some time, by age[1]						
	Birth	20	25	30	35	40	45
Total	5.1%	4.5%	3.1%	2.1%	1.4%	0.9%	0.6%
By Sex							
Male	9.0	7.9	5.5	3.7	2.5	1.6	1.0
Female	1.1	1.0	0.8	0.6	0.3	0.2	0.1
By Race/Hispanic origin							
White (non-Hispanic)	2.5%	2.3%	1.7%	1.2%	0.9%	0.6%	0.4%
Male	4.4	4.1	3.0	2.1	1.5	1.1	0.8
Female	0.5	0.5	0.4	0.3	0.2	0.1	0.1
Black (non-Hispanic)	16.2	14.1	9.6	6.0	3.6	2.0	1.2
Male	28.5	25.3	17.3	10.8	6.5	3.6	2.1
Female	3.6	3.5	2.8	1.9	1.1	0.6	0.4
Hispanic	9.4	8.7	6.4	4.9	3.8	2.3	1.6
Male	16.0	14.8	11.1	8.6	6.8	4.3	3.0
Female	1.5	1.5	1.2	0.9	0.6	0.4	0.2

1. Among those not previously incarcerated. **Source:** Bureau of Justice Statistics *Lifetime Likelihood of Going to State or Federal Prison,* March, 1997.

according to the Bureau of Justice Statistics, a record 5.7 million people were under "correctional supervision" in the United States: in jail, in prison, on probation, or on parole. More than half this population (3.3 million or 1,647 people per 100,000 adult residents) were on probation; another 700,000 were on parole.

▶**CAPITAL PUNISHMENT**
The United States is the only western industrialized nation that allows capital punishment. In the period 1930–97, 4,291 executions were carried out under state or federal authority. The majority of those (3,859) occurred in the years before the Supreme Court ruled capital punishment unconstitutional in 1972. The Court reinstated the death penalty in 1976; since then, an additional 432 executions have been carried out; all but one were males. Another 3,335 prisoners were on death row at the end of 1997 (all of whom had been convicted of murder) where they had been waiting for an average of more than seven years while they exhausted their legal appeals. (In Tennessee and Nebraska, death row prisoners waited an average of more than 10 years; in Oregon, they waited less than three years). Prisoners actually executed in 1997 had been on death row for an average of just under 11 years since their most recent conviction. That's nearly twice as long as death row prisoners spent awaiting their executions in 1985 (5 years and 11 months).

A positive aspect of this long delay is that it allows some death row prisoners to prove their innocence before they face the death chamber. According to the Death Penalty Information Center in Washington, D.C., 82 prisoners were released from death row between 1972 and 1999 because they were improperly convicted or because evidence of their innocence was discovered after they were sentenced to death. Put another way, for every seven executions since 1976, one wrongly condemned inmate has been set free.

Sixteen states have carried out 100 or more executions since 1930; as of 1996, 12 states and the District of Columbia did not authorize the death penalty for any crime. In Maine, Minnesota, and Wisconsin, there has been no death penalty statute in force since 1930, and Alaska and Hawaii have never had death penalty statutes. The death penalty was either abolished or declared unconstitutional in Michigan (1963), Iowa and West Virginia (1965), the District of Columbia (1973), Rhode Island (1979), Oregon (1981), and Massachusetts (1984). Kansas abolished the death penalty in 1973, but restored it in July, 1994. New York abolished it in 1984, but restored it in 1995. And South Dakota abolished the death penalty in 1915, restored it in 1939, abolished it again 1977, and restored it again 1979.

Prisoners Executed by Race, 1930–97

Year	Total	White	Black	Other
1930-39	1,667	827	816	24
1940-49	1,284	490	781	13
1950-59	717	336	376	5
1960-67	191	98	93	0
Total, 1930-67	**3,859**	**1,751**	**2,066**	**42**
1977-79	3	3	0	0
1980-89	117	68	49	0
1990	23	16	7	0
1991	14	7	7	0
1992	31	19	11	1
1993	38	23	14	1
1994	31	20	11	0
1995	56	33	22	1
1996	45	31	14	0
1997	74	45	27	2
Total, 1977-97	**432**	**265**	**162**	**5**
Total, 1930-97	**4,291**	**2,016**	**2,228**	**47**

Note: Executions under civil authority only. Does not include 160 executions carried out under military authority since 1930. There were no executions carried out between 1968 and 1977.
Source: Bureau of Justice Statistics, *Sourcebook of Criminal Justice Statistics* and *Capital Punishment 1997* (1998).

Prisoners Executed by System, 1930–97

System	Number executed			On death row, 1997[1]	Method of execution	Minimum age authorized for execution
	Since 1930	Since 1977	In 1997			
Alabama	151	16	3	159	Electrocution	16
Alaska	0	0	0	0	No death penalty statute	
Arizona	46	8	2	120	Gas; injection	none
Arkansas	134	16	4	38	Electrocution; injection	14
California[2]	296	4	0	486	Gas; injection	18
Colorado	48	1	1	4	Injection	18
Connecticut	21	0	0	4	Electrocution	18
Delaware	20	8	0	15	Injection; hanging	16
District of Columbia	40	0	0	0	No death penalty statute	
Federal system	33	0	0	15	Injection	18
Florida	209	39	1	370	Electrocution	16
Georgia	388	22	0	115	Electrocution	17
Hawaii	0	0	0	0	No death penalty statute	
Idaho[2]	4	1	0	19	Injection	none
Illinois	100	10	2	159	Injection	18
Indiana	46	5	1	44	Electrocution	16
Iowa	18	0	0	0	No death penalty statute	
Kansas[3]	15	0	0	0	Injection	18
Kentucky[2]	104	1	1	30	Electrocution	16
Louisiana[2]	157	24	1	70	Injection	none
Maine	0	0	0	0	No death penalty statute	
Maryland	70	2	1	17	Gas; injection	18
Massachusetts	27	0	0	0	No death penalty statute	
Michigan	0	0	0	0	No death penalty statute	
Minnesota	0	0	0	0	No death penalty statute	
Mississippi[2]	158	4	0	64	Gas; injection	16
Missouri[2]	91	29	6	88	Gas; injection	16
Montana[2]	7	1	0	7	Hanging; injection	none
Nebraska	7	3	1	11	Electrocution	18
Nevada	35	6	0	87	Injection	16
New Hampshire	1	0	0	0	Hanging; injection	17
New Jersey	74	0	0	14	Injection	18
New Mexico	8	0	0	4	Injection	18
New York[4]	329	0	0	0	Injection	18
North Carolina	271	8	0	176	Gas; injection	17
North Dakota	0	0	0	0	No death penalty statute	
Ohio	172	0	0	177	Electrocution; injection	18
Oklahoma	69	9	1	137	Injection	16
Oregon	21	2	1	20	Injection	18
Pennsylvania	154	2	0	214	Injection	none
Rhode Island	0	0	0	0	No death penalty statute	
South Carolina	175	13	2	68	Electrocution	none
South Dakota[2]	1	0	0	2	Injection	none
Tennessee	93	0	0	98	Electrocution	18
Texas	441	144	37	438	Injection	17
Utah[2]	18	5	0	10	Firing squad; injection	none
Vermont	4	0	0	0	No death penalty statute	
Virginia	138	46	9	43	Electrocution	16
Washington	49	2	0	12	Hanging; injection	18
West Virginia	40	0	0	0	No death penalty statute	
Wisconsin	0	0	0	0	No death penalty statute	
Wyoming	8	1	0	0	Gas; injection	16
Total U.S.	4,291	432	74	3,335		

Note: 1. As of December 31. 2. State authorizes capital punishment for selected crimes other than murder. 3. Death penalty restored in 1994; no executions yet carried out. 4. Death penalty restored in 1995; no executions yet carried out. Source: Bureau of Justice Statistics Bulletin, Capital Punishment 1997 (1999).

Race and capital punishment Apart from the broad question of whether it is right for the state to take the life of an individual, the three major issues of concern to those opposed to capital punishment are whether it is a deterrent to crime, whether it violates the Eighth Amendment to the Constitution, prohibiting "cruel and unusual punishment" (the U.S. is the only industrialized democracy in the world that hasn't abolished it), and whether it is used fairly with respect to race.

Historically, blacks have been more likely to be executed than whites in proportion both to the general population and to the prison population. In the 1940s, for example, blacks made up less than 10 percent of the population, but more than 60 percent of prisoners executed were black. That's beginning to change, however. Since 1930, 52 percent of prisoners executed have been black, and since 1977, blacks constituted only 38 percent of executions (although they made up 48 percent of the prison population).

Economy and Business

THE U.S. ECONOMY

▶ **GROSS NATIONAL PRODUCT AND GROSS DOMESTIC PRODUCT**

The goal of an economic system is to transform resources into final products by business enterprises for consumption by society. This includes manufacturing goods such as cars, bread, furniture, and so on, and providing services such as health care, education, and motion pictures. The most commonly used measures associated with this goal are Gross National Product (GNP) and Gross Domestic Product (GDP). GNP is the total national output of goods and services valued at market prices. GNP in this broad context measures the output attributable to the factors of production—labor and property—supplied by a country's residents. GNP differs from "national income" mainly in that GNP includes allowances for depreciation and for indirect business taxes (sales and property taxes). GDP is the measure of the output of production attributable to all factors of production (labor and property) physically located within a country. GDP, therefore, excludes net property income from abroad (such as the earnings of U.S. nationals working overseas), which is included in the GNP.

The word *final* serves to exclude intermediate goods sold to producers and used to make finished products eventually sold to consumers in the market. Auto parts such as batteries and tires are examples of intermediate goods and are included in GNP or GDP only through the price of a car when it is sold. GNP and GDP, in terms of expenditure categories, comprise purchases of goods and services by consumers and government, gross private domestic investment (or business purchases), and net exports.

The assessment of GNP and GDP in current dollars is referred to as a nominal measure. Nominal measures may be misleading because GNP and GDP can appear to rise as average prices rise with inflation. An alternative method is to evaluate GNP and GDP by measuring the value of goods and services using constant prices for a given year; the government currently uses 1992 as

GDP in Current and Constant (1992) Dollars, 1960–98 (billions)

Item	1960	1970	1980	1990	1995	1997	1998
CURRENT DOLLARS							
Gross domestic product (GDP)	$526.6	$1,035.6	$2,784.2	$5,743.8	$7,269.6	$8,110.9	$8,511.0
Personal consumption expenditures	332.2	648.1	1,760.4	3,839.3	4,957.7	5,485.8	5,807.9
Durable goods	43.3	85.0	213.5	476.5	608.5	659.3	754.7
Nondurable goods	152.9	272.0	695.5	1,245.3	1,475.8	1,592.0	1,662.4
Services	136.0	291.1	851.4	2,117.5	2,873.4	3,234.5	3,420.8
Gross private domestic investment	78.8	150.2	465.9	799.7	1,038.2	1,242.5	1,367.4
Fixed investment	75.5	148.1	473.5	791.6	1,008.1	1,174.1	1,307.8
Change in business inventories	3.2	2.2	-7.6	8.0	30.1	68.4	59.3
Net exports of goods and services	2.4	1.2	-14.9	-71.3	-86.0	-101.1	-151.2
Exports	25.3	57.0	278.9	557.3	818.4	957.1	959.0
Imports	22.8	55.8	293.8	628.6	904.5	1,058.1	1,110.2
Government consumption	113.2	236.1	572.8	1,176.1	1,355.5	1,452.7	1,487.1
Federal	65.6	115.9	248.4	503.6	509.6	523.8	520.6
National defense	54.9	90.6	174.2	373.1	344.6	350.3	340.3
State and local	47.6	120.2	324.4	672.6	846.0	928.9	966.5
CONSTANT (1992) DOLLARS							
Gross domestic product (GDP)	$2,262.9	$3,397.6	$4,615.0	$6,136.3	$6,761.7	$7,269.8	$7,551.9
Personal consumption expenditures	1,432.6	2,197.8	3,009.7	4,132.2	4,595.3	4,867.5	5,153.3
Gross private domestic investment	270.5	426.1	528.3	815.0	991.5	1,197.0	1,330.1
Net exports of goods and services	-21.3	-65.0	10.1	-61.9	-98.8	-146.5	-238.2
Exports	86.8	158.1	331.4	564.4	791.2	962.7	984.7
Imports	108.1	223.1	321.3	626.3	890.1	1,109.2	1,222.9
Government consumption	617.2	866.8	941.4	1,250.4	1,251.9	1,269.6	1,296.9

Source: U.S. Bureau of Economic Analysis, *National Income and Product Accounts of the United States* (1996) and *Survey of Current Business,* May 1999.

the base year. Assessments based on constant prices are referred to as real measures because they indicate the change in quantity of output produced by the economy.

▶DEFINITIONS OF OUTPUT, INCOME, AND EXPENDITURE TERMS

Capital consumption adjustment Used for corporations, nonfarm sole proprietorships, and partnerships, this is the difference between capital consumption claimed on income tax returns and capital consumption allowances measured at straight-line depreciation, consistent service lives, and replacement cost. The tax return data are valued at historical costs and reflect changes over time in service lives and depreciation patterns as permitted by tax regulations.

Consumer expenditure Consumer expenditure statistics presented in the accompanying tables are arrived at from the findings of the Consumer Expenditure Survey program, designed to provide a continuous flow of data on the buying habits of American consumers, necessary for future revisions of the Consumer Price Index. One group of 5,000 consumers in 85 urban areas around the country keeps diaries of expenditures on small, frequently purchased items, such as food and beverages, tobacco, housekeeping supplies, nonprescription drugs, and personal care products and services. Another 5,000 consumers are interviewed quarterly for information about large expenditures, such as those for property, automobiles and major appliances, or expenditures occurring on a fairly regular basis, such as rent, utilities, and insurance premiums.

Gross Domestic Product (GDP), by Industry, in Current and Constant (1992) Dollars, 1987–97 (billions)

Industry	Current dollars			Constant (1992) dollars		
	1987	1990	1997	1987	1990	1997
Gross Domestic Product (GDP)	**$4,692.3**	**$5,743.8**	**$8,110.9**	**$5,649.5**	**$6,136.3**	**$7,269.8**
All Private industries	4,039.1	4,951.4	7,083.3	4,784.9	5,246.0	6,395.3
Agriculture, forestry, and fisheries	**88.6**	**108.7**	**131.7**	**93.6**	**99.3**	**127.6**
Farms	65.1	79.6	90.2	65.2	70.7	90.3
Agricultural services	23.5	29.1	41.5	23.8	28.6	38.0
Mining	88.3	112.3	120.5	86.4	96.9	109.9
Construction	217.0	245.2	328.8	239.6	247.5	274.4
Manufacturing	**889.0**	**1,031.4**	**1,378.9**	**1,041.7**	**1,090.0**	**1,369.9**
Durable goods	513.3	572.8	784.0	565.0	600.4	838.6
Nondurable goods	375.7	458.5	594.9	477.9	489.4	537.6
Transportation and public utilities	**420.7**	**482.3**	**676.3**	**453.9**	**491.7**	**644.3**
Transportation	157.9	176.4	255.5	175.3	176.7	241.5
Communications	124.9	146.6	211.6	132.9	149.2	196.4
Electric, gas, and sanitary services	137.9	159.3	209.2	149.2	168.4	206.3
Wholesale trade	**301.0**	**367.3**	**562.8**	**322.8**	**360.5**	**532.0**
Retail trade	**435.8**	**503.5**	**712.9**	**509.2**	**546.4**	**713.5**
Finance, insurance, and real estate	**830.7**	**1,025.2**	**1,570.3**	**1,015.7**	**1,109.0**	**1,286.0**
Depository institutions	145.0	169.2	266.4	215.7	214.9	191.9
Nondepository institutions	13.7	21.5	56.3	25.3	25.6	39.3
Security and commodity brokers	38.5	39.7	106.6	39.6	41.2	120.5
Insurance carriers	50.7	69.3	146.0	56.3	70.2	93.5
Insurance agents, brokers, and service	29.4	37.1	50.7	38.3	40.8	43.1
Real estate	535.3	673.0	935.0	637.5	706.8	814.8
Services	**784.6**	**1,059.4**	**1,656.8**	**1,041.4**	**1,181.7**	**1,398.6**
Hotels and other lodging places	36.5	46.1	69.0	42.7	49.2	56.8
Personal services	31.2	38.2	51.5	39.6	41.7	44.1
Business services	142.4	199.0	364.7	179.7	216.5	323.1
Auto repair, services, and parking	39.8	48.9	73.3	50.0	54.0	64.4
Motion pictures	14.6	20.4	30.5	18.9	22.1	26.6
Amusement and recreation services	27.3	39.1	66.7	34.7	42.8	56.2
Health services	229.4	307.9	460.1	337.5	356.9	379.0
Legal services	61.1	80.7	106.6	83.3	91.5	87.0
Educational services	31.2	39.8	61.5	41.7	44.3	50.4
Social services and membership organizations	20.6	29.6	52.2	26.5	32.5	46.3
Other services	103.1	147.8	234.6	130.7	160.4	201.3
Government	**653.2**	**792.5**	**1,027.6**	**810.0**	**867.0**	**884.0**
Federal	255.2	293.5	338.1	315.8	327.7	286.9
State and local	398.1	499.0	689.6	494.3	539.4	597.4

Source: U.S. Bureau of Economic Analysis, *National Income and Product Accounts of the United States* (1998) and *Survey of Current Business,* August 1998.

National Income, by Type of Income, 1970-98 (billions of current dollars)

Type of Income	1970	1980	1990	1995	1996	1997	1998
National income	$833.5	$2,216.1	$4,652.1	$5,828.9	$6,254.5	$6,646.5	$6,694.7
Compensation of employees	618.3	1,653.9	3,352.8	422.7	4,426.9	4,687.2	4,981.0
Wages and salaries	551.5	1,377.6	2,757.5	3,433.2	3,633.6	3,893.6	4,153.9
Government	117.1	261.2	517.2	621.7	642.6	664.2	689.3
Other	434.3	1,116.4	2,240.3	2,811.5	2,991.0	3,229.4	3,464.6
Supplements to wages, salaries	66.8	276.3	595.2	789.5	793.3	793.7	827.1
Employer contributions for social insurance	34.3	136.4	294.6	365.5	385.7	400.7	420.1
Other labor income	32.5	139.8	300.6	424.0	407.6	392.9	406.9
Proprietors' income[1,2]	79.9	167.9	374.0	486.1	520.3	551.2	577.2
Farm	14.6	13.8	35.4	27.9	37.2	35.5	28.7
Nonfarm	65.3	154.1	338.6	458.2	483.1	515.8	548.5
Rental income of persons[1]	17.8	35.3	61.0	111.7	146.3	158.2	162.6
Corporate profits[1,2]	77.5	167.1	397.1	604.8	735.9	817.9	824.6
Corporate profits[2]	71.8	198.3	358.2	570.8	674.1	741.2	732.3
Profits before tax	78.4	241.4	371.7	598.9	676.6	734.4	717.8
Profits tax liability	34.4	84.8	140.5	218.7	229.0	246.1	240.1
Profits after tax	44.0	156.6	231.2	380.2	447.6	488.3	477.7
Dividends	23.7	59.3	151.9	227.4	304.8	275.1	279.2
Undistributed profits	20.3	97.3	79.4	152.8	142.8	213.2	198.5
Inventory valuation adjustment	-6.6	-43.0	-13.5	-28.1	-2.5	6.9	14.5
Capital consumption adjustment	5.6	-31.2	38.9	34.0	61.8	76.6	92.3
Net interest	40.0	191.9	467.3	403.6	425.1	432.0	449.3

1. With capital consumption adjustment. 2. With inventory valuation adjustment. **Source:** U.S. Bureau of Economic Analysis, *National Income and Product Accounts of the United States*, and *Survey of Current Business*, July, 1999.

Percent Distribution of National Income, by Type, 1970-98

Type of income	1970	1980	1990	1995	1996	1997	1998
National income, total	100.0%	100.0%	100.0%	100.0%	100.0%	100.0%	100.0%
Compensation of employees	74.2	74.9	73.7	72.6	70.8	70.7	74.4
Wages and salaries	66.2	62.7	61.4	59.0	58.1	58.3	62.0
Supplements to wages, salaries	8.0	12.2	12.2	13.6	12.7	12.4	12.4
Proprietors' income[1]	9.6	7.8	8.2	8.2	8.3	8.2	8.6
Farm	1.8	0.5	0.9	0.5	0.6	0.6	0.4
Nonfarm	7.8	7.3	7.3	7.7	7.7	7.6	8.2
Rental income of persons[2]	2.1	0.6	-0.2	2.1	2.3	2.2	2.4
Corporate profits[1]	9.2	8.1	8.1	9.9	11.8	12.1	12.3
Profits before tax	9.4	11.0	8.0	10.3	10.8	11.0	10.7
Profits after tax	5.3	7.1	4.9	6.6	7.2	7.2	7.1
Net interest	4.8	8.7	10.3	6.9	6.8	6.8	6.7

1. With inventory valuation and capital consumption adjustments (not shown separately). 2. With capital consumption adjustment (not shown separately). **Source:** U.S. Bureau of the Census, based on data from U.S. Bureau of Economic Analysis, *The National Income and Product Accounts of the United States, 1929-82*, and *Survey of Current Business*, annual.

Disposable personal income is that income after personal tax and nontax payments; this is the income available to persons for spending and saving. Personal tax and nontax payments are tax payments (except personal contributions for social insurance, net of refunds) by persons that are not chargeable to business expense, and also include certain personal payments to general government that are treated like taxes. Personal taxes include income, estate, gift, and personal property taxes and motor vehicle licenses. Nontax payments include passport fees, fines and penalties, donations, and tuitions and fees paid to schools and hospitals operated mainly by government.

Family income The term *family* refers to a group of two or more persons related by birth, marriage, or adoption who reside together; all such persons are considered as members of one family. Family income refers to the sum of all income of the family members.

Gross domestic product (GDP) see "Gross National Product and Gross Domestic Product," above.

Gross national product (GNP) see "Gross National Product and Gross Domestic Product," above.

Gross state product (GSP) is the gross market value of the goods and services attributable to labor and property located in a state. It is the state counterpart of the nation's GDP.

Household income A household includes related family members and all unrelated persons, if any—such as lodgers, foster children, wards, or employees—who share a house, an apartment, or a single room when it is occupied or intended for occupancy as separate living quarters by that household; that is, when the members of the household do not live and eat with any other persons in the structure and there is direct access from the outside or through a common hall. Household income, therefore, is the sum of all income of household members. The *householder* (which replaced the term *head of household* beginning with the 1980 Current Population Survey) is the person in whose name the home is owned or rented. In the case of joint ownership, one person in each household is designated as the householder for statistical purposes.

Inventory valuation adjustment This represents the difference between the book value of inventories used in production and the cost of replacing them.

Mean vs. median income Mean (or average) income refers to the sum of all incomes of a group divided by the number of incomes in that group. Median income is the middle income when they are arranged in order of size—that is, there are the same number of incomes above and below the median. For example, consider incomes of $2,000, $3,000, $4,000, $15,000 and $95,000: the mean income is the sum of these divided by five, or $23,800; the median income is $4,000.

Money income This refers to income received (exclusive of certain money receipts such as capital gains) before payments for such things as personal income taxes, Social Security, union dues, and Medicare deductions. Money income does not include income in the form of noncash benefits such as food stamps, health benefits, and subsidized housing; rent-free housing and goods produced and consumed on farms; or the use of business transportation and facilities, full or partial payments by business for retirement programs, medical and educational expenses, and so on. These elements should be considered when comparing income levels. None of the aggregate income concepts (GNP, national income, or personal income) is exactly comparable with money income, although personal income is the closest.

National income, the aggregate of labor and property earnings derived from the current production of goods and services, is the sum of employee compensation, proprietors' income, rental income, corporate profits, and net interest. It measures the total factor costs of the goods and services produced by the economy. Income is measured before deduction of taxes.

Personal income is the current income received by persons from all sources minus their personal contributions for social insurance. *Persons* include individuals (including owners of unincorporated firms), nonprofit institutions serving

Per Capita Money Income, by Race and Hispanic Origin, 1970-97

	Current dollars				Constant (1997) dollars			
Year	All races	White	Black	Hispanic[1]	All races	White	Black	Hispanic[1]
1970	$3,177	$3,354	$1,869	N.A.	$12,346	$13,034	$7,263	N.A.
1975	4,818	5,072	2,972	$2,847	13,760	14,485	8,488	$8,131
1980	7,787	8,233	4,804	4,865	15,186	16,056	9,369	9,488
1985	11,013	11,671	6,840	6,613	16,427	17,409	10,203	9,864
1990	14,387	15,265	9,017	8,424	17,667	18,745	11,073	10,345
1995	17,227	18,304	10,982	9,300	18,143	19,277	11,566	9,794
1996	18,136	19,181	11,899	10,048	18,552	19,621	12,172	10,279
1997	19,241	20,425	12,351	10,773	19,241	20,425	12,351	10,773

Note: N.A. = Not available. 1. Hispanic persons may be of any race.
Source: U.S. Bureau of the Census, *Current Population Reports* (series).

Median Income of Families by Race and Hispanic Origin, 1997

	Number of families ('000s)				Median family income			
Characteristic	All families[1]	White	Black	Hispanic[2]	All families[1]	White	Black	Hispanic[2]
All families	70,884	59,515	8,408	6,961	$44,568	$46,754	$28,602	$28,142
Type of family								
Married-couple families	54,321	48,070	3,921	4,804	$51,591	$52,098	$45,372	$33,914
Wife in paid labor force	33,535	29,334	2,716	2,650	60,669	61,441	51,702	42,280
Wife not in paid labor force	20,786	18,726	1,205	2,153	36,027	36,343	28,757	23,749
Male Householder[3]	3,911	3,137	562	545	32,960	34,802	25,654	25,543
Female Householder[3]	12,652	8,308	3,926	1,612	21,023	22,999	16,879	14,994
Number of earners								
No earners	9,835	8,367	1,202	815	$19,731	$21,516	$9,012	$8,870
One earner	20,494	16,293	3,396	2,434	30,204	32,811	19,597	19,662
Two earners	31,752	27,467	2,973	2,761	55,443	56,624	45,780	37,425
Three earners	6,638	5,618	676	669	68,028	69,239	57,701	47,549
Four or more earners	2,165	1,824	160	282	85,978	87,747	75,641	59,456

Note: 1. Includes other races not shown separately. 2. Hispanic persons may be of any race. 3. Spouse absent.
Source: U.S. Bureau of the Census, *Current Population Reports: Money Income in the United States, 1997.*

individuals, private trust funds, and private non-insured welfare funds. Personal income includes transfers (payments not resulting from current production) from government and business, such as Social Security benefits and public assistance, but excludes transfers among persons. Also included are certain nonmonetary types of income: estimated net rental value to owner-occupants of

their homes, the value of services furnished without payment by financial intermediaries, and food and fuel produced and consumed on farms. **Poverty level** is an estimate of the income necessary to purchase what society defines as a minimally acceptable standard of living. Families and unrelated individuals are classified as being above or below the poverty level according to their

Number and Percent of Persons Below Poverty Level, by State, 1990–97

| | | Percent | | | | | Percent | |
| | Number | | 1996 | | Number | | 1996 |
State	1990	1990	-97[1]	State	1990	1990	-97[1]
Alabama	723,614	18.3%	14.9%	Montana	124,853	16.1%	16.3%
Alaska	47,906	9.0	8.5	Nebraska	170,616	11.1	10.0
Arizona	564,362	15.7	18.9	Nevada	119,660	10.2	9.6
Arkansas	437,089	19.1	18.5	New Hampshire	69,104	6.4	7.8
California	3,627,585	12.5	16.8	New Jersey	573,152	7.6	9.3
Colorado	375,214	11.7	9.4	New Mexico	305,934	20.6	23.4
Connecticut	217,347	6.8	10.2	New York	2,277,296	13.0	16.6
Delaware	56,223	8.7	9.1	North Carolina	829,858	13.0	11.8
District of Columbia	96,278	16.9	23.0	North Dakota	88,276	14.4	12.3
Florida	1,604,186	12.7	14.3	Ohio	1,325,768	12.5	11.9
Georgia	923,085	14.7	14.7	Oklahoma	509,854	16.7	15.2
Hawaii	88,408	8.3	13.0	Oregon	344,867	12.4	11.7
Idaho	130,588	13.3	13.3	Pennsylvania	1,283,629	11.1	11.4
Illinois	1,326,731	11.9	11.7	Rhode Island	92,670	9.6	11.9
Indiana	573,632	10.7	8.2	South Carolina	517,793	15.4	13.1
Iowa	307,420	11.5	9.6	South Dakota	106,305	15.9	14.2
Kansas	274,623	11.5	10.5	Tennessee	744,941	15.7	15.1
Kentucky	681,827	19.0	16.5	Texas	3,000,515	18.1	16.7
Louisiana	967,002	23.6	18.4	Utah	192,415	11.4	8.3
Maine	128,466	10.8	10.7	Vermont	53,369	9.9	11.0
Maryland	385,296	8.3	9.4	Virginia	611,611	10.2	12.5
Massachusetts	519,339	8.9	11.2	Washington	517,933	10.9	10.6
Michigan	1,190,698	13.1	10.8	West Virginia	345,093	19.7	17.5
Minnesota	435,331	10.2	9.7	Wisconsin	508,545	10.7	8.5
Mississippi	631,029	25.2	18.7	Wyoming	52,453	11.9	12.7
Missouri	663,075	13.3	10.7	U.S. Total	33,600,000	12.6	11.0[2]

1. Average percent below poverty between 1996 and 1997. 2. Figure for 1997.   **Source:** U.S. Bureau of the Census, 1990 Census and *Current Population Survey*, (1999).

Persons Below Poverty Level, by Race, 1960–97

| | Number below poverty level (millions) | | | | Percent below poverty level | | | | Average income cutoffs for family of four |
Year	All races[1]	White	Black	His-panic[2]	All races[1]	White	Black	His-panic[2]	at poverty level[3]
1960	39.9	28.3	N.A.	N.A.	22.2%	17.8%	N.A.	N.A.	$ 3,022
1970	25.4	17.5	7.5	N.A.	12.6	9.9	33.5%	N.A.	3,968
1975	25.9	17.8	7.5	3.0	12.3	9.7	31.3	26.9%	5,500
1980	29.3	19.7	8.6	3.5	13.0	10.2	32.5	25.7	8,414
1985	33.1	22.9	8.9	5.2	14.0	11.4	31.3	29.0	10,989
1990	33.6	22.3	9.8	6.0	13.5	10.7	31.9	28.1	13,359
1991	35.7	23.7	10.2	6.3	14.2	11.3	32.7	28.7	13,924
1992	38.0	25.3	10.8	7.6	14.8	11.9	33.4	28.7	14,335
1993	39.3	26.2	10.9	8.1	15.1	12.2	33.1	29.6	14,763
1994[4]	38.0	25.4	10.2	8.4	14.5	11.7	30.6	30.7	15,141
1995[4]	36.4	24.4	9.9	8.6	13.8	11.2	29.3	30.3	15,569
1996[4]	36.5	24.6	9.7	8.7	13.7	11.2	28.4	29.4	16,036
1997[4]	35.5	24.4	9.1	8.3	13.3	11.0	26.5	27.1	16,400

1. Includes other races not shown separately. 2. Hispanic races may be of any race. 3. Beginning 1981, income cutoffs for nonfarm families are applied to all families, both farm and nonfarm. 4. Beginning in 1994, the Census Bureau changed its definition of the poverty level, so data are not directly comparable with previous years.   **Source:** U.S. Bureau of the Census, *Current Population Reports* (series).

money income as a group and the number of people in the group (e.g. in 1990, a family of four with total money income below $13,359 lived below the poverty level). Classification is based on the poverty index originated by the Social Security Administration in 1964 and revised in 1969 and 1980. The poverty index is based solely on money income and does not reflect the fact that many low-income persons receive non-cash benefits such as food stamps, Medicaid, and public hous-

ing. The poverty thresholds are updated every year to reflect changes in the Consumer Price Index. **Private domestic investment** This consists of (1) non-residential fixed investment, i.e., firms' purchases of capital goods such as plants and equipment; (2) residential fixed investment (the building of single- and multi-family housing units); and (3) the change in business inventories, which are stocks on hand of raw materials and finished goods.

Per Capita Personal Income by State, 1970–98

State	Personal income (rank)				
	1970	1980	1990	1997	1998[1]
Alabama	$2,960 (49)	$7,720 (48)	$15,225 (43)	$20,672 (39)	$21,442 (41)
Alaska	5,071 (2)	13,863 (1)	21,047 (10)	24,969 (19)	25,675 (21)
Arizona	3,810 (27)	9,328 (31)	16,542 (36)	21,998 (36)	23,060 (36)
Arkansas	2,841 (50)	7,457 (50)	14,032 (50)	19,595 (48)	20,346 (47)
California	4,777 (8)	11,792 (4)	21,287 (9)	26,314 (13)	27,503 (13)
Colorado	4,058 (17)	10,710 (14)	19,224 (19)	27,015 (10)	28,657 (10)
Connecticut	5,077 (1)	12,246 (3)	26,375 (1)	35,863 (1)	37,598 (1)
Delaware	4,611 (9)	10,614 (15)	21,696 (7)	28,493 (7)	29,814 (7)
District of Columbia	5,013 (3)	12,487 (2)	25,628 (2)	35,704 (2)	37,278 (2)
Florida	3,980 (20)	9,894 (22)	19,106 (20)	24,799 (21)	25,852 (20)
Georgia	3,395 (38)	8,395 (38)	17,378 (29)	23,882 (26)	25,020 (24)
Hawaii	4,995 (4)	10,860 (11)	21,333 (8)	25,598 (18)	26,137 (18)
Idaho	3,503 (35)	8,569 (37)	15,317 (42)	20,392 (43)	21,081 (44)
Illinois	4,587 (10)	10,986 (9)	20,494 (12)	27,688 (9)	28,873 (9)
Indiana	3,789 (30)	9,307 (32)	17,174 (31)	23,202 (30)	24,219 (30)
Iowa	3,839 (25)	9,505 (28)	16,959 (34)	23,120 (32)	23,925 (33)
Kansas	3,794 (29)	9,877 (23)	17,988 (23)	23,972 (24)	24,981 (25)
Kentucky	3,150 (44)	8,079 (42)	15,088 (44)	20,570 (40)	21,506 (40)
Louisiana	3,090 (47)	8,761 (35)	14,761 (46)	20,458 (42)	21,346 (42)
Maine	3,409 (37)	8,259 (39)	17,167 (32)	21,937 (37)	22,952 (37)
Maryland	4,519 (12)	10,889 (10)	22,483 (6)	28,674 (6)	29,943 (6)
Massachusetts	4,547 (11)	10,745 (13)	23,203 (4)	31,239 (4)	32,797 (4)
Michigan	4,145 (14)	10,273 (16)	18,710 (21)	24,956 (20)	25,857 (19)
Minnesota	4,012 (19)	10,149 (17)	19,374 (17)	26,243 (14)	27,510 (12)
Mississippi	2,608 (51)	6,915 (51)	12,710 (51)	18,098 (51)	18,958 (51)
Missouri	3,825 (26)	9,341 (30)	17,656 (26)	23,629 (28)	24,427 (29)
Montana	3,554 (34)	8,825 (34)	15,042 (45)	19,660 (47)	20,172 (48)
Nebraska	3,799 (28)	9,096 (33)	17,624 (27)	23,618 (29)	24,754 (28)
Nevada	4,889 (5)	11,577 (6)	20,124 (13)	26,514 (11)	27,200 (15)
New Hampshire	3,910 (23)	9,854 (26)	20,671 (11)	27,766 (8)	29,022 (8)
New Jersey	4,835 (7)	11,703 (5)	24,925 (3)	32,356 (3)	33,937 (3)
New Mexico	3,163 (43)	8,222 (40)	14,441 (47)	19,298 (49)	19,936 (49)
New York	4,866 (6)	11,003 (8)	23,132 (5)	30,250 (5)	31,734 (5)
North Carolina	3,255 (40)	8,067 (43)	16,664 (35)	23,168 (31)	24,036 (32)
North Dakota	3,145 (45)	7,825 (47)	15,324 (41)	20,103 (46)	21,675 (39)
Ohio	4,052 (18)	9,872 (25)	18,125 (22)	24,163 (22)	25,134 (22)
Oklahoma	3,456 (36)	9,444 (29)	15,584 (38)	20,305 (44)	21,072 (45)
Oregon	3,913 (21)	9,938 (19)	17,437 (28)	23,920 (25)	24,766 (27)
Pennsylvania	4,061 (16)	9,989 (18)	19,365 (18)	25,670 (16)	26,792 (17)
Rhode Island	4,086 (15)	9,646 (27)	19,691 (15)	25,667 (17)	26,797 (16)
South Carolina	3,027 (48)	7,624 (49)	15,421 (40)	20,508 (41)	21,309 (43)
South Dakota	3,215 (41)	7,866 (46)	15,538 (39)	21,076 (38)	22,114 (38)
Tennessee	3,168 (42)	8,123 (41)	16,295 (37)	22,699 (34)	23,559 (34)
Texas	3,651 (32)	9,922 (20)	17,219 (30)	23,707 (27)	24,957 (26)
Utah	3,324 (39)	8,003 (45)	14,204 (48)	20,185 (45)	21,019 (46)
Vermont	3,616 (33)	8,583 (36)	17,691 (25)	23,017 (33)	24,175 (31)
Virginia	3,771 (31)	9,918 (21)	19,996 (14)	26,109 (15)	27,385 (14)
Washington	4,188 (13)	10,755 (12)	19,583 (16)	26,451 (12)	27,961 (11)
West Virginia	3,098 (46)	8,041 (44)	14,177 (49)	18,724 (50)	19,362 (50)
Wisconsin	3,912 (22)	9,874 (24)	17,720 (24)	24,048 (23)	25,079 (23)
Wyoming	3,841 (24)	11,414 (7)	17,061 (33)	22,596 (35)	23,167 (35)
U.S. average	**$4,072**	**$10,029**	**$19,142**	**$25,288**	**$26,412**

Note: in current dollars. 1. Preliminary.   Source: Bureau of Economic Analysis, *Survey of Current Business,* (monthly). www.bea.doc.gov.

Per Capita Personal Income by Metropolitan Area, 1970–97

Metropolitan Statistical Area (ranked by 1997 income)	1970	1980	1990	1995	1997
United States	$4,047	$9,940	$18,666	$23,059	$25,288
Metropolitan portion	4,302	10,540	19,788	24,470	26,840
Nonmetropolitan portion	3,109	7,782	14,270	17,449	19,089
Highest per capita income, 1997					
1. San Francisco, Calif.[1]	$6,105	$15,226	$29,672	$36,668	$41,128
2. New Haven-Bridgeport-Stamford-Danbury-Waterbury, Conn.[1]	5,384	12,945	27,791	36,233	40,928
3. West Palm Beach-Boca Raton, Fla.	4,851	12,820	29,103	35,078	38,772
4. San Jose, Calif.[1]	4,869	13,084	24,547	32,289	37,856
5. Bergen-Passaic, N.J.	5,424	13,136	28,174	33,425	36,769
6. Trenton, N.J.[1]	4,843	11,965	25,877	32,483	36,598
7. Naples, Fla.	5,403	12,298	27,296	32,836	36,210
8. Middlesex-Somerset-Hunterdon, N.J	4,855	12,583	26,106	32,461	35,734
9. Newark, N.J.	5,121	12,028	25,433	31,906	35,038
10. Nassau-Suffolk, N.Y.	5,224	12,615	26,733	31,890	34,902
11. New York, N.Y.	5,383	11,721	24,664	31,189	34,459
12. Washington, D.C.-Md.-Va.-W.Va.[1]	5,089	12,487	25,132	30,761	33,433
13. Seattle-Bellevue-Everett, Wash.	4,616	12,369	22,962	29,088	33,373
14. Hartford, Conn.[1]	4,875	11,773	24,091	28,899	32,035
15. Boston-Worcester-Lawrence-Lowell, Mass.	4,539	10,766	22,589	28,612	31,808
16. Sarasota-Bradenton, Fla.	4,393	11,501	23,233	28,918	31,792
17. Boulder-Longmont, Colo.	4,241	11,325	21,125	28,269	31,393
18. Oakland, Calif.	4,906	12,414	23,359	28,061	31,338
19. Wilmington-Newark, Del.-Md.[1]	4,863	11,518	23,335	27,582	30,851
20. Denver, Colo.	4,577	12,041	21,694	27,553	30,743
21. Chicago, Ill.	4,985	11,829	22,156	27,978	30,717
22. Dallas, Texas[1]	4,423	11,703	21,535	27,081	30,481
23. Monmouth-Ocean, N.J.	4,409	11,254	23,154	28,000	30,275
24. Reno, Nev.	5,272	13,228	23,114	27,761	30,214
25. Barnstable-Yarmouth, Mass.	4,846	11,557	23,453	27,199	30,199
Lowest per capita income, 1997					
1. McAllen-Edinburg-Mission, Tex.	$1,930	$5,244	$9,012	$11,044	$12,005
2. Brownsville-Harlingen, Tex.	2,163	5,693	9,592	11,967	12,857
3. Laredo, Tex.	2,204	5,371	8,977	11,696	12,999
4. Las Cruces, N.M.	2,897	6,632	12,281	14,194	14,923
5. El Paso, Tex.	2,962	6,377	11,510	14,037	15,216
6. Yuma, Ariz.	3,034	7,920	12,096	16,889	15,629
7. Provo-Orem, Utah	2,657	6,244	11,395	14,821	16,567
8. Sumter, S.C.	2,574	6,356	12,249	15,225	16,883
9. Jacksonville, N.C.	3,088	5,977	10,202	15,113	16,900
10. Visalia-Tulare-Porterville, Calif.	3,549	9,176	14,393	15,985	17,116
11. Clarksville-Hopkinsville, Tenn.-Ky.	3,012	7,210	12,088	16,351	17,248
12. Merced, Calif.	3,736	9,246	14,264	15,546	17,485
13. Lawton, Okla.	3,093	7,231	13,181	16,323	17,487
14. Killeen-Temple, Tex.	3,343	7,575	12,894	16,563	17,861
15. Hattiesburg, Miss.	2,753	7,143	12,749	16,523	17,889
16. Bryan-College Station, Tex.	2,879	7,001	12,480	15,749	17,963
17. Pine Bluff, Ark.	2,781	7,465	13,135	16,538	18,109
18. Yuba City, Calif.	3,838	9,426	14,916	17,217	18,183
19. Flagstaff, Ariz.-Utah	3,010	7,306	12,913	16,663	18,184
20. Bakersfield, Calif.	3,833	10,674	15,641	17,201	18,319
21. Pocatello, Idaho	3,287	8,563	13,735	17,063	18,596
22. Goldsboro, N.C.	3,022	6,976	13,150	16,877	18,611
23. Huntington-Ashland, W. Va.	3,145	8,207	14,405	17,272	18,652
24. Steubenville-Weirton, Ohio-W.Va.	3,593	9,504	15,245	17,887	18,794
25. Anniston, Ala.	2,771	7,234	13,815	17,350	18,855

Note: in current dollars. 1. Primary Metropolitan Statistical Area.
Source: U.S. Bureau of Economic Analysis, *Survey of Current Business,* May, 1999. www.bea.doc.gov.

▶ECONOMIC INDICATORS

All market economies regularly go through cycles of recession—when output declines and unemployment rises—and expansion—when output and employment rise. These "business cycles" are one of the most important factors determining the socioeconomic conditions in any society.

Although economists still have very little idea what actually causes recessions and what leads the economy to begin expanding again, they have had some success in predicting business cycles. Economic forecasting is the science of making these predictions. It is especially useful to be able to predict recessions sufficiently far in advance so

Per Capita Personal Income by County, 1997

Rank/County	Per capita income 1997	Percent of national average
Highest per capita income		
1. New York, New York	$68,686	271.6%
2. Fairfield, Connecticut	50,423	199.4
3. Pitkin, Colorado	49,266	194.8
4. Marin, California	46,936	185.6
5. Somerset, New Jersey	46,392	183.5
6. Westchester, New York	45,595	180.3
7. Alexandria City, Virginia	43,676	172.7
8. Bergen, New Jersey	43,123	170.5
9. Morris, New Jersey	42,913	169.7
10. Teton, Wyoming	42,311	167.3
11. Arlington, Virginia	41,708	164.9
12. Montgomery, Maryland	41,539	164.3
13. Nantucket, Massachusetts	41,240	163.1
14. San Francisco, California	40,357	159.6
15. Lake, Illinois	40,260	159.2
16. Montgomery, Pennsylvania	40,249	159.2
17. San Mateo, California	39,989	158.1
18. Fairfax-Fairfax City-Falls Church, Virginia	39,951	158.0
19. Hunterdon, New Jersey	39,830	157.5
20. Nassau, New York	39,691	157.0
21. Oakland, Michigan	38,913	153.9
22. DuPage, Illinois	38,826	153.5
23. Palm Beach, Florida	38,772	153.3
24. Chester, Pennsylvania	38,708	153.1
25. Santa Clara, California	37,856	149.7
Lowest per capita income		
1. McPherson, Nebraska	$3,961	15.7%
2. Keya Paha, Nebraska	5,666	22.4
3. Loup, Nebraska	6,163	24.4
4. Slope, North Dakota	6,619	26.2
5. Billings, North Dakota	7,340	29.0
6. Starr, Texas	7,550	29.9
7. Ziebach, South Dakota	8,646	34.2
8. Zavala, Texas	8,855	35.0
9. Sioux, North Dakota	8,993	35.6
10. Todd, South Dakota	9,263	36.6
11. Maverick, Texas	9,327	36.9
12. Presidio, Texas	9,391	37.1
13. Hudspeth, Texas	9,655	38.2
14. Shannon, South Dakota	9,753	38.6
15. Arthur, Nebraska	9,958	39.4
16. Grant, Nebraska	9,977	39.5
17. Jefferson, Mississippi	10,729	42.4
18. Corson, South Dakota	10,784	42.6
19. Elliott, Kentucky	10,799	42.7
20. Grant, North Dakota	10,803	42.7
21. Blaine, Nebraska	10,915	43.2
22. Apache, Arizona	11,044	43.7
23. Kinney, Texas	11,056	43.7
24. Banner, Nebraska	11,075	43.8
25. Union, Florida	11,077	43.8

Source: U.S. Bureau of Economic Analysis, *Survey of Current Business* (May, 1999).

Composite Index of Economic Indicators, 1950–99 (1992=100)

Year	Leading indicators	Coincident indicators	Lagging indicators
1960	74.5	42.9	87.5
1965	82.6	50.0	92.5
1970	85.2	61.1	102.4
1975	83.9	66.8	104.0
1980	90.1	80.8	104.9
1985	96.8	87.6	102.7
1990	100.0	99.6	106.7
1991	97.8	98.5	106.5
1992	99.4	99.0	101.3
1993	100.7	101.4	99.2
1994	101.2	103.6	99.8
1995	101.5	108.5	102.2
1996	100.5	110.3	104.6
1997	102.9	114.3	104.8
1998	104.6	119.0	105.3
1999	106.9	122.9	108.0

Note: As of January of each year.
Source: U.S. Dept. of Commerce, unpublished data.

but suffered a setback when the early forecasters failed to predict the Great Depression in 1929. During the depression the government asked a private research group, the National Bureau of Economic Research, to develop a set of measures that would help predict changes in business cycles. The group devised a list of measures based on analyses of previous business cycles. Since then, the list has been revised several times to reflect changes in the way the economy is structured.

Leading Indicators

There are currently 10 leading economic indicators, representing a broad spectrum of economic activity. These indicators are said to "lead" because their numbers change months in advance of a change in the general level of economic activity. They are as follows:

1. Average length of workweek of production workers in manufacturing.

2. Average weekly state unemployment insurance claims.

3. New orders for consumer goods and materials (in constant dollars).

4. Vendor performance (percent of companies receiving slower deliveries from suppliers).

5. Contracts and orders for plant and equipment (in constant dollars).

6. Index of new private housing units authorized by local building permits.

7. Index of stock prices, i.e., of 500 common stocks (Standard and Poor's 500).

8. Money supply-M2 in 1992 dollars. (See "Money and Banking" section.)

9. Interest rate spread.

10. Index of consumer expectations. (See "Note" below.)

This composite of leading economic indicators is published by the U.S. Department of Commerce, Bureau of Economic Analysis. The composite has a noteworthy record: since 1948 it has accurately predicted every downturn and upswing in the economy. One major reason for this success is that many of the indicators represent commitments to economic activity in the coming months. The average lead for the index is 9.5 months at business cycle peaks (indicating the

that governments can take actions to stimulate the economy and reduce the severity of these downturns.

Economic indicators track developments in areas of the economy that are thought to be crucial to the future health of the economy, just as a barometer measures changes in air pressure that are crucial to changes in the weather. The development of economic indicators began around World War I end of a business cycle expansion and the beginning of a recession) and 4.5 months at business cycle troughs (indicating the end of a business cycle recession and the beginning of an expansion).

Coincident and Lagging Indicators

In addition to the leading economic indicators, two other sets of measures are used to track business cycles and the state of the economy. One set includes the coincident indicators, which measure how well the economy is doing at that moment (roughly, within three months of the business cycle turning points). These include the number of employees on nonagricultural payrolls; manufacturing and trade sales (in constant dollars); index of industrial production; and personal income less transfer payments (in constant dollars). The second set includes lagging economic indicators. These are the ratio of consumer installment credit outstanding to personal income; commercial and industrial loans outstanding (in constant dollars); the average prime interest rate charged by banks; the ratio of manufacturing and trade inventories to sales (in constant dollars); the average duration of unemployment in weeks (inverted); the change in index of labor cost per unit of output in manufacturing; and the change in the Consumer Price Index for services per unit labor costs. At business cycle peaks, the average lag of the index is 4.5 months, and at business cycle troughs 8.5 months. It seems reasonable to wonder what use there is for an indicator that tells you where you have already been. But in fact that is exactly their

use: they provide another way of measuring whether turning points in the business cycle truly have occurred.

The government produces a wide variety of economic indicators in addition to those discussed here for use in tracking more specific aspects of the economy, such as labor or capital markets.

The Employment Cost Index (ECI)

The ECI measures the *rate of change* in total employee compensation (wages, salaries, employer cost for employee benefits) in nonfarm private industry and in state and local governments. Provided quarterly by the Bureau of Labor Statistics, the ECI has become one of the most closely watched indices because any significant rise could signal an inflationary trend. During the late 1980s, the ECI grew annually by 4 to 5 percent, but in the 1990s, it has been 3 percent and less.

▶ PRICES AND INFLATION
Inflation

Inflation is a sustained rise in the general price level in the economy. It affects the level and timing of spending in the economy since it indicates the extent to which income will cover the purchase of a consumer's basket of goods (food, clothes, entertainment, medical services, housing, gasoline, and so on). For example, if a consumer is considering purchasing a television and inflation is high (that is, prices are rising rapidly), he or she will buy the television as soon as possible

Employment Cost Index (ECI) 1985-98 (1989 = 100)

Group	Index				Percent Change		
	1985	1990	1997	1998	1984-85	1989-90	1997-98
Civilian workers	86.8	107.6	135.2	139.8	4.3%	4.9%	3.4%
White collar	85.8	108.3	136.9	141.4	4.9	5.2	3.6
Blue collar	88.4	106.5	132.4	136.1	3.3	4.4	2.8
Service occupations	87.2	108.0	135.6	140.0	3.9	5.1	3.2
Manufacturing	87.8	107.2	135.3	138.9	3.3	5.1	2.7
Non-manufacturing	86.4	107.8	135.1	139.9	4.7	4.9	3.6
Private Industry Workers	87.3	107.0	135.1	139.8	3.9	4.6	3.5
State & Local Government	84.6	110.4	135.7	139.8	5.6	5.8	3.0

Note: Figures are as of December of each year and are not seasonally adjusted. 1. Excludes farm, household, and federal government workers. **Source:** U.S. Bureau of Labor Statistics, *News, Employment Cost Index,* (quarterly)

Purchasing Power of the Dollar, 1950-98

Year	Annual average as measured by:		Year	Annual average as measured by:	
	Producer prices	Consumer Prices		Producer prices	Consumer Prices
1950	$3.546	$4.151	1991	$0.822	$0.734
1955	3.279	3.732	1992	0.812	0.713
1960	2.994	3.373	1993	0.802	0.692
1965	2.933	3.166	1994	0.797	0.675
1970	2.545	2.574	1995	0.782	0.656
1975	1.718	1.859	1996	0.762	0.638
1980	1.136	1.215	1997	0.759	0.623
1985	0.955	0.928	1998	0.766	0.600
1990	0.839	0.766			

Source: U.S. Bureau of Economic Analysis, *Survey of Current Business* (monthly).

Consumer Price Indexes for Selected Metropolitan Statistical Areas, 1998 (1982–84 = 100)

Area	All items	Food and bever-ages	Food	Housing	Apparel and upkeep	Transpor-tation	Medical care	Fuel and Utilities
U.S. city average	163.0	161.1	160.7	160.4	133.0	141.6	242.1	128.5
Anchorage, Alaska	146.9	147.3	147.5	131.0	125.6	144.9	255.7	148.4
Atlanta, Ga.	161.2	164.7	169.1	161.1	137.6	127.8	245.0	142.1
Boston-Lawrence-Salem, Mass.-N.H.	171.7	165.8	166.3	165.8	147.0	139.5	313.9	119.1
Chicago-Gary-Lake County, Ill.-Ind.-Wis.	165.0	164.8	164.3	164.2	121.6	138.0	244.3	120.1
Cincinnati-Hamilton, Ohio-Ky.-Ind.	155.1	148.4	146.8	149.9	129.0	136.6	224.5	126.6
Cleveland-Akron-Lorain, Ohio	159.8	163.3	165.0	158.4	129.9	141.8	214.7	130.1
Dallas-Ft. Worth, Tex.	153.6	160.1	157.8	143.2	136.6	138.5	229.0	128.4
Denver-Boulder, Colo.	161.9	151.6	153.6	154.4	100.6	166.5	275.0	128.6
Detroit-Ann Arbor, Mich.	159.8	154.6	153.7	153.6	133.7	148.9	230.6	124.3
Honolulu, Hawaii	171.5	159.1	159.1	176.0	112.2	162.5	226.1	131.0
Houston-Galveston-Brazoria, Tex.	146.8	150.9	150.3	129.6	140.9	135.7	235.4	107.8
Kansas City, Mo.-Kans.	157.8	159.7	160.8	151.8	129.1	137.2	217.7	134.5
Los Angeles-Anaheim-Riverside, Calif.	162.3	167.3	165.5	160.1	123.1	142.6	236.7	146.1
Miami-Ft. Lauderdale, Fla.	160.5	169.0	169.4	153.5	152.1	144.2	227.3	118.0
Milwaukee, Wis.	160.3	157.5	158.6	159.9	118.7	140.8	239.8	112.6
Minneapolis-St. Paul, Minn.-Wis.	158.3	166.6	163.6	145.0	144.2	141.9	229.6	119.2
New York-Northern New Jersey-Long Island, N.Y.-N.J.-Conn.	173.6	166.1	165.3	175.9	127.9	151.1	255.0	116.5
Philadelphia-Wilmington-Trenton, Pa.-N.J.-Del.-Md.	168.2	155.1	154.1	170.1	106.2	149.3	254.8	132.2
Pittsburgh-Beaver Valley, Pa.	159.2	153.6	152.4	160.1	142.5	130.3	235.0	143.6
Portland-Vancouver, Oreg.-Wash.	167.1	153.7	154.1	168.4	132.4	146.9	223.1	138.0
San Diego, Calif.	166.9	165.0	163.0	170.1	125.1	149.4	240.9	117.7
San Francisco-Oakland-San Jose, Calif.	165.5	166.3	167.1	174.4	115.9	132.0	228.0	140.7
Seattle-Tacoma, Wash.	167.7	165.2	165.7	170.9	126.5	145.4	232.7	121.4
St. Louis-East St. Louis, Mo.-Ill.	154.5	158.4	156.8	147.0	126.2	138.4	233.9	123.5
Tampa-St. Petersburg-Clearwater, Fla.[1]	137.5	132.7	132.6	132.2	144.1	124.2	192.1	119.8
Washington, D.C.-Md.-Va.	102.1	101.6	101.5	103.1	99.3	98.4	104.4	105.6

1. 1987=100.   **Source:** U.S. Bureau of Labor Statistics, *Monthly Labor Review* and *CPI Detailed Report* (Jan. issues).

Consumer Price Index (CPI-U) 1947–98 (1982–84=100)

Year	CPI-U	Year	CPI-U	Year	CPI-U
1947	22.3	1982	96.5	1991	136.2
1950	24.1	1983	99.6	1992	140.3
1955	26.8	1984	103.9	1993	144.5
1960	29.6	1985	107.6	1994	148.2
1965	31.5	1986	109.6	1995	152.4
1970	38.8	1987	113.6	1996	156.9
1975	53.8	1988	118.3	1997	160.5
1980	82.4	1989	124.0	1998	163.0
1981	90.9	1990	130.7		

Source: U.S. Bureau of the Census, *Current Population Reports* (series).

since savings may not cover the cost a month or a year from now. Inflation is closely watched to determine wage contracts and Social Security benefits that contain cost-of-living adjustment clauses. If wage contracts cover a long period of time and inflation is rapid, consumers' standard of living will fall in the interim before new contracts can be negotiated. Savings will tend to fall as consumers store their wealth in the form of commodities.

The cause of inflation is often described as "too much money chasing too few goods," brought about by the money supply rising rapidly or production of goods falling behind demand for them. Inflation may be due to (1) cost-push factors—that is, if the cost of inputs such as labor, raw materials, or other intermediate goods rises, the cost of the final product also rises; or (2) demand-pull factors—that is, if the demand for goods and services rises above the full employment level, wages rise as employers compete for labor, and the general price level of goods and services rises.

Consumer Price Index

Often referred to as the "cost of living index," the Consumer Price Index is the most commonly used measure of inflation. The index measures the average change in prices relative to an arbitrary base year of a common bundle of goods and services bought by the average consumer on a regular basis. The Bureau of Labor Statistics publishes two CPI's: (1) CPI-U for All Urban Consumers, which includes wage earners and clerical workers; professional, managerial, and technical workers; the self-employed; short-term workers; the unemployed; retirees and others not in the labor force—altogether covering 80 percent of the population—and (2) CPI-W for Urban Wage Earners and Clerical Workers, covering 32 percent of the population. Prices (including direct taxes) are collected from over 57,000 housing units and 19,000 establishments in 85 areas across the country. In calculating the index number, based

on 100,000 price quotes a month, larger weights are assigned to goods that represent larger proportions of consumer expenditure. The index costs $26 million a year to produce and requires 40 economists and analysts tracking price changes in 365 categories.

Producer Price Index

The Producer Price Index measures average changes in prices received by producers of all commodities, at all stages of processing, produced in the United States. Prices used in constructing the index are collected from sellers and generally apply to the first significant large-volume commercial transaction for each commodity—i.e., the manufacturer's or other producer's selling price or the selling price on an organized exchange or at a central market. The weights used in the index represent the total net selling value of commodities produced or processed in the country. Values are f.o.b. (free on board) at the production point and are exclusive of excise taxes.

Implicit Price Deflator

The implicit price deflator (also called the GDP deflator) is derived from the ratio of current-to-constant dollar GDP (multiplied by 100) and measures the value of current production in current prices relative to the value of the same goods and services in prices for the base year. For example, in 1998, GDP in current dollars was $8,511.0 billion and GDP in constant (1992) dollars was $7,551.9 billion. Therefore, the GDP deflator for 1998 was (8,511.0 ÷ 7,551.9) x 100, or 112.7, which is simply a comparison between 1992 and 1998 prices. It is a weighted average of the detailed price indexes used in the deflation of GDP, but the indexes are combined using weights that reflect the composition of GDP in each period. Thus changes in the implicit price deflator reflect not only changes in prices, but also changes in the composition of GDP.

Producer Price Indexes for Selected Commodities, 1970–98 (1982=100)

Commodity group	1970	1975	1980	1985	1990	1995	1997	1998
All commodities	38.1	58.4	89.8	103.2	116.3	124.7	127.6	124.4
Farm products & processed foods & feeds	44.9	74.0	98.3	100.7	118.6	120.5	127.0	122.7
Farm products	45.8	77.0	102.9	95.1	95.1	107.4	112.9	104.6
Processed foods and feeds	44.6	72.6	95.9	103.5	103.5	127.0	134.0	131.6
Industrial commodities	35.2	54.9	88.0	103.7	115.8	125.5	127.7	124.8
Textile products and apparel	52.4	67.4	89.7	102.9	114.9	120.8	122.6	122.9
Hides, skins, leather related products	42.0	56.5	94.7	108.9	141.7	153.7	154.2	148.0
Fuels, related products, power	15.3	35.4	82.8	91.4	82.2	78.0	86.1	75.3
Chemicals and allied products	35.0	62.0	89.0	103.7	123.6	142.5	143.6	143.9
Rubber and plastic products	44.9	62.2	90.1	101.9	113.6	124.3	123.2	122.6
Lumber and wood products	39.9	62.1	101.5	106.6	129.7	178.1	183.8	179.1
Pulp, paper, and allied products	37.5	59.0	86.3	113.3	141.3	172.2	167.9	171.7
Metals and metal products	38.7	61.5	95.0	104.4	123.0	134.5	131.8	127.8
Machinery and equipment	40.0	57.9	86.0	107.2	120.7	126.6	125.9	124.9
Furniture and household durables	51.9	67.5	90.7	107.1	119.1	128.2	130.8	131.3
Nonmetallic mineral products	35.3	54.4	88.4	108.6	114.7	129.0	133.2	135.4
Transportation equipment	41.9	56.7	82.9	107.9	121.5	139.7	141.6	141.2

Source: U.S. Bureau of Labor Statistics, *Producer Price Indexes*, monthly and annual.

▶MONEY AND BANKING
Federal Reserve System

The government's interest in monitoring and controlling the banking industry and managing the money supply led to the Federal Reserve Act of 1913. The act created the Federal Reserve System (or the "Fed," as it is popularly known), the nation's central bank. There are 12 regional Fed banks located in major cities throughout the country (Boston, New York, Philadelphia, Cleveland, Richmond, Atlanta, Chicago, St. Louis, Minneapolis, Kansas City, Dallas, and San Francisco). Commercial banks within each region select a majority of the directors who run each regional Fed bank. The president of the United States appoints a board of governors for the whole system, and the board is responsible for coordinating policies across the system. But the regional Feds play an important role in shaping those policies by representing regional interests and decentralizing the decision-making process.

The Fed has three main policy tools for managing the overall economy. First, it controls the *reserve requirements* at all depository institutions. These requirements determine what percentage of a bank's deposits must be held in reserve in the form of either deposits with Federal Reserve banks or vault cash. Raising the reserve requirements reduces the amount of loans available to borrowers and helps slow down the economy.

A more frequently used instrument is *the discount rate*, the interest rate the Federal Reserve banks charge their commercial bank customers to borrow money. The Fed is known as the lender of last resort because of its responsibility to lend to banks in need, and it thus maintains the stability of the banking system. Raising the discount rate generally leads the commercial banks to raise the interest rates they charge their customers. This raises the costs of borrowing in the private sector and slows the economy. (Cutting the discount rate does the reverse and stimulates the economy.)

Most important, the Fed can also control the level of bank reserves through *open market operations*; that is, the direct sale on purchase of Treasury securities and other government debt instruments. When the Fed sells securities, it takes money from the buyer and holds it in its reserves, reducing the money supply; when it buys these instruments, it pays for them by taking money from its reserves, which then goes into circulation, increasing the money supply.

Controlling the money supply through open market operations is certainly the most common and, many would argue, the most important function of the Fed. The money supply shapes interest rates, through the supply and demand of money. Because the Fed is constantly involved in these open market operations (in order to keep the size of the money supply in proportion with a growing economy, for example), adjustments can be made subtly.

In addition, the Federal Reserve regulates banks through the Federal Deposit Insurance Corporation, influences foreign-currency exchange rates through the sale or purchase of foreign currencies, and coordinates international financial policy.

The money supply   Money provides a medium of exchange as well as a way to store value. Traditionally, currency (paper money and coins) served that role exclusively. But over time, new financial instruments have developed that serve at least some of the functions of money. Checking accounts serve exactly the same role as currency, and to an extent, so do money market funds and other instruments.

The Fed uses four different measures of the money supply, which include different monetary instruments:

M1 is the original and most commonly reported measure of the money supply, which embraces currency and coins, demand deposits, traveler's checks, and other checkable deposits.

M2 is M1 plus money-market accounts, and savings and small time-deposits.

M3 is M2 plus money-market mutual-fund balances held by financial institutions, term repurchase agreements and term Eurodollars, and large time-deposits.

The U.S. Banking System

Commercial banks are the largest financial institutions in the country and are the principal vehicles for exchanging money. The nation's first commercial bank was the Bank of America (now First Pennsylvania Bank), established in Philadelphia in 1782. Commercial banks hold about two-thirds of the nation's money deposits. Savings and loans, the next-largest source of deposits, hold about half as much.

Federal Reserve Bank Discount Rates, 1976–99

Effective Date	Rate per year	Effective Date	Rate per year
Jan. 19, 1976	5.50%	Oct. 12, 1982	9.50%
Nov. 22, 1976	5.25	Nov. 22, 1982	9.00
Aug. 31, 1977	5.75	Dec. 15, 1982	8.50
Oct. 26, 1977	6.00	April 9, 1984	9.00
Jan. 9, 1978	6.50	Nov. 21, 1984	8.50
May 11, 1978	7.00	Dec. 24, 1984	8.00
July 3, 1978	7.25	May 20, 1985	7.50
Aug. 21, 1978	7.75	March 7, 1986	7.00
Sept., 22, 1978	8.00	April 21, 1986	6.50
Oct. 16, 1978	8.50	July 11, 1986	6.00
Nov. 1, 1978	9.50	Aug. 21, 1986	5.50
July 20, 1979	10.00	Sept. 4, 1987	6.00
Aug. 17, 1979	10.50	Aug. 9, 1988	6.50
Sept. 19, 1979	11.00	Feb. 24, 1989	7.00
Oct. 8, 1979	12.00	Dec. 19, 1990	6.50
Feb. 15, 1980[1]	13.00	Feb. 1, 1991	6.00
May 30, 1980	12.00	April 30, 1991	5.50
June 13, 1980	11.00	Sept. 13, 1991	5.00
July 28, 1980	10.00	Nov. 6, 1991	4.50
Sept. 26, 1980	11.00	Dec. 20, 1991	3.50
Nov. 17, 1980	12.00	July 2, 1992	3.00
Dec. 5, 1980	13.00	May 17, 1994	3.50
May 5, 1981	14.00	Aug. 16, 1994	4.00
Nov. 2, 1981	13.00	Nov. 15, 1994	4.75
Dec. 4, 1981	12.00	Feb. 1, 1995	5.25
July 20, 1982	11.50	Jan. 31, 1996	5.00
Aug. 2, 1982	11.00	Oct. 15, 1998	4.75
Aug. 16, 1982	10.50	Nov. 17, 1998[2]	4.50
Aug. 27, 1982	10.00		

Note: The Discount Rate is for short-term adjustment credit. 1. The discount rates for 1980 and 1981 do not include the surcharge applied to frequent borrowings by large institutions. The surcharge reached 3% in 1980 and 4% in 1981, and was eliminated in November 1981. 2. Rate in effect as of August 25, 1999.   **Source:** Board of Governors of the Federal Reserve System, *Federal Reserve Bulletin*, monthly, and *Annual Statistical Digest.*

There are approximately 10,000 commercial banks in the country. They may be chartered either by the federal government or by individual states. While banks themselves may not operate across states, they may be owned by holding companies that can operate interstate, if state laws permit.

Commercial banks can make loans to individuals and to commercial operations, establish checking or demand deposits, maintain "trust" departments that make investments for customers, and perform a variety of other functions such as issuing credit cards. Until the deregulation of the 1980s, commercial banks were the only ones permitted to issue checking accounts. Regulations that developed after bank failures in the Great Depression still keep these banks out of the investment business — largely to protect depositors and the solvency of banks from potential effects of bad investments. But deregulation of the banking industry in the 1980s is blurring many of these distinctions. In particular, investment companies are now permitted to issue demand deposits and to compete with banks in other areas as well. (As a result these companies are sometimes referred to as nonbanks.)

Bank failures are especially serious problems because of the domino effect they may have on other financial institutions and businesses. Banks, and indeed all depository institutions, ultimately fail when many of their loans go bad and cannot be repaid. But even before that happens, depositors may get nervous about the security of their accounts and withdraw them all at once—a "run on the bank." Because banks loan out deposits and hold in reserve only a small percentage of the value of those deposits, banks experiencing a run would have to call in some of their loans (mainly those already due), putting sudden pressure on many commercial borrowers and causing some to fail. In addition the withdrawal of deposits and of loans reduces the money supply sharply. This process was an important cause of the Great Depression. Following the banking failures during the depression (2,293 banks failed in 1931, and 4,000 banks failed in 1933), the Federal Deposit Insurance Corporation (FDIC) was created in 1933 to protect the accounts of depositors and, more important, to help prevent bank failures. The FDIC charges banks a premium to pay for this coverage. The corporation is designed to prevent runs on banks by insuring deposits and lending to banks to prevent the need to call in loans.

But banks still fail because of bad loans. Between 1945 and 1980, U.S. banks failed at the rate of about six per year. Since then, hundreds of banks have failed each year. Most of these failures occurred in agricultural states where the failure of farms led to defaults on loans; more than half of all bank failures can be attributed to agriculture loans. Fraud also played an important role, especially in Tennessee, where more than 30 banks

The Money Supply, 1970–98 (billions of dollars)

Item	1970	1980	1985	1990	1995	1997	1998
M1, total	$214	$408	$619	$825	$1,127	$1,075	$1,093
Currency[1]	49	115	168	247	372	424	459
Travelers' checks[2]	1	3	5	7	8	8	8
Demand deposits[3]	165	261	267	277	389	396	377
Other checkable deposits[4]	(z)	28	180	294	357	246	249
M2, total	$628	$1,600	$2,497	$3,279	$3,649	$4,047	$4,413
M1	214	408	619	825	1,127	1,075	1,093
Non-M1 components in M2	414	1,192	1,878	2,455	2,522	2,972	3,320
Money market funds, retail	(z)	64	177	358	456	602	763
Savings deposits (including money market deposit accounts)	261	400	815	923	1,135	1,400	1,605
Commercial banks	99	186	457	582	775	1,023	1,190
Thrift institutions	162	215	359	342	360	377	415
Small time deposits[5]	151	729	886	1,173	932	969	952
Commercial banks	79	286	386	611	575	626	626
Thrift institutions	72	442	499	563	357	343	326
M3, total	$677	$1,996	$3,210	$4,156	$4,619	$5,405	$6,016
M2	628	1,600	2,497	3,279	3,649	4,047	4,413
Non-M1 components in M3	49	396	712	876	969	1,358	1,604
Large time deposits[6]	45	260	422	482	421	576	638
Commercial banks[7]	44	215	271	361	347	490	549
Thrift institutions	1	45	152	121	74	86	89
Repurchase agreements[8]	4	58	121	151	199	253	298
Eurodollars[8]	(z)	61	104	103	94	149	152
Money market funds, institution only	(z)	16	65	140	256	380	516

Note: As of December of year shown. Adjusted seasonally. Figures may not add up because of independent rounding. Z = less than $500 million. 1. Currency outside U.S. Treasury, Federal Reserve Banks, and the vaults of depository institutions. 2. Outstanding amount of nonbank issuers. 3. At commercial banks and foreign-related institutions. 4. Consists of negotiable order of withdrawal (NOW) and automatic transfer service (ATS) accounts at all depository institutions, credit union share draft balances and demand deposits at thrift institutions. 5. Issued in amounts of less than $100,000. Includes retail repurchase agreements. Excludes individual retirement accounts (IRAs) and Keogh accounts. 6. Issued in amounts of $100,000 or more. Excludes those booked at international banking facilities. 7. Excludes those held by money market mutual funds, depository institutions, U.S. Government, foreign banks, and official institutions. 8. Excludes those held by depository institutions and money market mutual funds. **Source:** Board of Governors of the Federal Reserve System, *Federal Reserve Bulletin*, monthly, and *Money Stock, Liquid Assets, and Debt Measures, Federal Reserve Statistical Release H.6*, weekly.

have failed since 1982. When a bank fails, the FDIC pays off each depositor and then sells the bank's assets. Sometimes the FDIC arranges for another bank's acquisition of the failed bank by subsidizing the sale.

Thrifts are depository institutions including savings and loans (S&Ls), savings banks, and credit unions. The largest and most important thrifts are the S&Ls, which were created to provide home mortgages for borrowers and long-term savings deposits for individual investors. Until recently, thrifts were prohibited from engaging in riskier loans—including most commercial loans—and issuing checking deposits, and a ceiling was placed on the rate of interest they could pay depositors. Congress lifted the ceiling on interest payments to depositors in 1980 and in 1982 allowed the S&Ls to issue commercial loans and to invest directly in real estate developments. Unwise investment in these areas by many thrifts was a major cause of the savings and loan debacle of the late 1980s and early 1990s.

The Federal Home Loan Bank System was established in 1932 to serve some of the same functions for S&Ls that the Federal Reserve provides for banks. It has now been succeeded by the Office of Thrift Supervision (OTS), which identifies institutions that may be financially distressed or likely to fail. All federally chartered S&Ls are regulated by the system (and must have the word *Federal* in their name). Less than half the thrifts are federally chartered, however; the rest are chartered by states, although most of these have joined the system as well. The FSLIC (Federal Savings and Loan Insurance Corporation) insured deposits at member S&Ls until 1989, when it became insolvent and was dismantled.

Savings and loan crisis The S&Ls came under enormous economic pressure during the 1970s, when interest rates paid by banks and other financial institutions rose well above the rate ceiling for thrifts, and they started losing depositors. Further, they were in a financial bind because their outstanding loans were all in mortgages—long-term, 30-year loans issued at low interest. In part because of this, the thrifts were deregulated, released from many of the restrictions on their activities and allowed to pursue a

Consumer Credit Outstanding, 1980-98 (billions of dollars)

Type of Credit	1980	1985	1990	1995	1996	1997	1998
Total	**$350.1**	**$584.7**	**$796.4**	**$1,095.7**	**$1,181.9**	**$1,233.1**	**$1,308.4**
Automobile	112.0	210.9	282.4	364.2	392.3	413.4	447.2
Revolving[1]	55.1	122.1	223.3	443.2	499.5	531.1	558.6
Other[2]	183.0	251.7	290.7	288.3	290.1	288.6	302.6

1. Consists mainly of outstanding balances on credit card accounts, but also includes borrowing under check credit and overdraft plans, and unsecured personal lines of credit. 2. Includes noninstallment credit.
Source: Board of Governors of the Federal Reserve System, *Federal Reserve Bulletin* (monthly).

Assets and Deposits of FDIC/BIF-Insured Banks, 1997-98

Charter class	1997			1998		
	Banks	Assets (millions)	Deposits (millions)	Banks	Assets (millions)	Deposits (millions)
All banks	**10,922**	**$6,041,103**	**$5,553,811**	**10,461**	**$6,528,628**	**$5,971,975**
Commercial banks	9,143	5,014,884	4,596,989	8,774	5,440,943	4,978,718
National banks	2,597	2,893,910	2,648,918	2,458	3,183,032	2,908,849
State banks (Fed members)	992	1,231,209	1,144,378	994	1,310,353	1,213,499
State banks (Fed nonmembers)	5,554	889,765	803,692	5,322	947,559	856,370
Savings banks	1,779	1,026,219	936,826	1,687	1,087,684	993,257
Federal charter	1,007	744,873	683,478	952	783,208	719,624
State charter	772	281,346	253,348	735	304,476	273,633

Note: As of Dec. 31 of each year. **Source:** Federal Deposit Insurance Corp., *Statistics on Banking, 1998* (1999).

Assets and Deposits of Deposit-Taking Institutions, 1998

Type of institution	Number of institutions	Percent share	Assets (millions)	Percent share	Deposits (millions)	Percent share
Commercial banks	8,774	38.8%	$5,440,943	70.3%	$4,978,718	73.1%
Savings banks[1]	1,687	7.5	1,087,684	14.1	993,257	14.6
Savings & Loans (thrifts)	1,145	5.1	817,200	10.6	498,492	7.3
Credit unions[2]	10,995	48.6	388,700	5.0	340,300	5.0
Total	**22,601**	**100.0%**	**$7,734,527**	**100.0%**	**$6,810,767**	**100.0%**

1. Includes Federal and State-chartered Savings institutions. 2. Federally insured credit unions only. 3. Credit union shares.
Sources: Federal Deposit Insurance Corp., *Statistics on Banking, 1997* (1998), Office of Thrift Supervision; National Credit Union Association, *1997 Year-end Statistics*.

Top 25 U.S. Bank Holding Companies Ranked by Assets and by Deposits, 1998

Rank by assets/Name, city	Assets (millions)	Deposits (millions)	Rank by deposits
1. Citigroup Inc., New York	$667,400	$228,649	2
2. BankAmerica Corp., San Francisco	617,679	357,260	1
3. Chase Manhattan Corp., New York	365,875	212,437	3
4. Bank One Corp., Chicago	261,496	161,542	4
5. J.P. Morgan & Co. Inc., New York	261,067	55,028	10
6. First Union Corp., Charlotte, N.C.	237,363	142,467	5
7. Wells Fargo & Co., San Francisco	202,475	137,065	6
8. Bankers Trust Corp., New York	133,115	37,334	17
9. Fleet Financial Group Inc., Boston	104,382	69,678	7
10. SunTrust Banks Inc., Atlanta	93,170	59,033	8
11. National City Corp., Cleveland	88,246	58,247	9
12. KeyCorp, Cleveland	80,020	42,583	15
13. PNC Bank Corp., Pittsburgh	77,207	47,496	13
14. U.S. Bancorp Inc., Minneapolis	76,438	50,034	11
15. BankBoston Corp.	73,513	48,500	12
16. Wachovia Corp., Winston-Salem, N.C.	64,123	40,995	16
17. Bank of New York Co.	63,579	44,672	14
18. Mellon Bank Corp., Pittsburgh	50,777	34,383	18
19. Republic New York Corp.	50,424	33,220	19
20. State Street Corp., Boston	47,082	27,539	22
21. Firstar Corp., Milwaukee	38,476	28,851	20
22. SouthTrust Corp., Birmingham, Ala.	38,134	24,840	23
23. Regions Financial Corp., Birmingham, Ala.	36,832	28,350	21
24. Comerica Inc., Detroit	36,601	24,313	25
25. Mercantile Bancorp. Inc., St. Louis, Mo.	34,571	24,781	24

Source: *American Banker* (March 25, 1999).

Top 25 U.S. Thrift Holding Companies Ranked by Assets and by Deposits, 1998

Rank by assets/Name, city	Assets (millions)	Deposits (millions)	Rank by deposits
1. Washington Mutual Inc., Seattle[1]	$165,493.3	$85,492.1	1
2. Golden State Bancorp, San Francisco	54,580.2	25,246.0	3
3. Golden West Financial Corp., Oakland, Calif.	38,468.7	26,219.1	2
4. Charter One Financial, Cleveland[2]	24,467.3	15,165.1	4
5. Dime Bancorp, New York	22,320.9	13,651.5	5
6. Sovereign Bancorp, Wyomissing, Pa.	21,913.9	12,322.7	6
7. Astoria Financial Corp., New York	20,587.7	9,668.3	8
8. Bank United, Houston	14,791.5	6,917.9	11
9. GreenPoint Financial Corp., New York	13,970.3	11,173.1	7
10. Commercial Federal Corp., Omaha, Neb.	12,178.3	7,394.0	9
11. Peoples Heritage Financial Group, Portland, Maine	10,102.5	6,981.2	10
12. Webster Financial Corp., Waterbury, Conn.	9,033.9	5,651.3	13
13. Hudson City Savings, Paramus, N.J.	7,752.3	6,807.3	12
14. Ohio Savings Financial Corp., Cleveland	6,595.8	5,331.0	15
15. Downey Financial Corp., Newport Beach, Calif.	6,270.4	5,039.7	16
16. Emigrant Savings Bank, New York	6,260.9	5,340.9	14
17. St. Paul Bancorp, Chicago[2]	6,034.1	3,895.0	21
18. Third Federal Savings, Cleveland	5,741.0	4,837.6	18
19. Washington Federal Inc., Seattle	5,723.1	3,260.5	23
20. Capitol Federal Savings, Topeka, Kan.	5,406.8	3,994.8	20
21. Apple Bank for Savings, New York	5,344.0	4,847.8	17
22. Independence Community Bank, New York	5,138.0	3,513.0	22
23. First Midwest Bancorp., McHenry, Ill.	5,053.0	4,055.5	19
24. MAF Bancorp Inc., Clarendon Hills, Ill.	4,121.1	2,656.9	24
25. TR Financial Corp., Garden City, N.Y.	4,079.9	2,195.5	25

Note: FSB = federal savings bank; FA = federal association. 1. Consolidated to include thrift subsidiaries. 2. Owned by a commercial banking company. 3. Mutual institution.   **Source:** *American Banker* (May 27, 1999).

more diverse market for loans. With this new freedom, however, many S&Ls took on loans at a higher level of risk in order to earn a higher rate of return. Some argue that the insurance on deposits provided by the Federal Home Loan Bank encouraged the S&Ls to make loans that were too risky.

Lending institutions fail mainly if a large percentage of their loans go bad and cannot be collected. And mortgage loans fail, not just because buyers cannot make their payments, but also because the collateral (the buildings) may decline in price so that it is less than the value of the loan. Especially in the Southwest, many of the loans for real estate development failed when the oil industry declined in the 1980s, taking local economies with it. S&Ls started to collapse at an alarming rate—517 thrifts closed between 1980 and 1988. With liabilities of $100 billion in excess of assets, the FSLIC ran out of money. Its insurance obligations passed to the FDIC, and the Resolution Trust Corporation (RTC) was formed to dispose of (sell) approximately $400 billion of insolvent thrifts' assets. The government dealt with 205 insolvent S&Ls in 1988 alone by subsidizing their sale to more secure institutions.

Credit unions are employer-sponsored cooperative organizations that provide consumer and mortgage credit to their members. Employers often arrange for payroll-deduction savings plans through the credit union. Perhaps in response to the high rates charged by commercial banks for maintaining checking accounts, the number of people joining credit unions has jumped dramatically in recent years, from 61.4 million members in 1992 to 73.5 million in 1998.

Mortgage loans Mortgages are loans backed by buildings—either private dwellings or commercial buildings. Until the 1970s, virtually all mortgages had fixed-interest payments and 30-year terms. With the escalation of interest rates beginning in the late 1970s, however, several alternative arrangements have developed. For example, in order to reduce the interest payments, many borrowers repay their loans in 15 years. Others use a *variable* or *adjustable rate mortgage* in which the interest rate varies with market rates. Some mortgages that hold payments down in the first few years and then increase them rapidly for the remaining term of the mortgage are known as balloon mortgages.

Money Instruments
Treasury bills, also called T-bills, are securities sold by the U.S. Treasury in denominations of $10,000 that mature at various dates, but all in less than one year. Treasury bills pay an interest rate that is adjusted by the Treasury according to supply and demand. The Treasury bill rate is thought to have the highest risk-free rate of return among all investments.

Federal funds are the reserves the Fed requires depository institutions such as commercial banks to hold on deposit at their regional Federal Reserve Bank as protection against withdrawals. Banks and other depository institutions can loan reserves in excess of those required by the Fed to each other. These Fed Fund loans can provide institutions with large amounts of liquid assets on very short notice, and most loans are for no more than one day.

Certificates of deposit (CDs) Customers who make these deposits at commercial banks or thrift institutions receive a certificate describing the maturity date of the deposit (e.g., a five-year CD). CDs guarantee a rate of return for as long as 10 years into the future. In addition, the fact that

Money Market Interest Rates and Mortgage Rates, 1970–98						
Type	1970	1980	1985	1990	1997	1998
Federal funds, effective rate	7.18%	13.35%	8.10%	8.10%	5.46%	5.35%
Commercial paper, 3-month[1, 2]	N.A.	12.61	7.95	8.06	5.58	N.A.
Prime rate charged by banks	7.91	15.26	9.93	10.01	8.44	8.35
Eurodollar deposits, 3-month	8.52	14.00	8.27	8.16	5.61	5.45
Finance paper, 3-month[2, 3]	7.18	11.49	7.77	7.87	5.48	N.A.
Bankers acceptances, 90-day[2, 4]	7.31	12.67	7.91	7.93	5.54	5.39
Large negotiable certificates of deposit, 3-month, secondary market	7.56	13.07	8.05	8.15	5.62	5.47
Federal Reserve discount rate[5]	5.50–6.00	10.00–13.00	7.50–8.00	6.50–7.00	5.00	4.50–5.00
U.S. Government securities:[6]						
3-month Treasury bill	6.39	11.39	7.47	7.50	5.06	4.78
6-month Treasury bill	6.51	11.32	7.65	7.46	5.18	4.83
1-year Treasury bill	6.48	10.85	7.81	7.35	5.36	4.80
Home mortgages (HUD series[7]):						
FHA insured, secondary market[8]	9.03	13.44	12.24	10.17	7.89	7.04
Conventional, new-home[9, 10]	8.52	13.95	12.28	10.08	7.76	7.00
Conventional, existing-home[9]	8.56	13.95	12.29	10.08	7.76	7.01

N.A. = Not available. 1. Based on daily offering rates of dealers. 2. Yields are quoted on a bank-discount basis, rather than an investment yield basis (which would give a higher figure). 3. Placed directly; averages of daily offering rates quoted by finance companies. 4. Based on representative closing yields. From Jan. 1, 1981, rates of top-rated banks only. 5. Federal Reserve Bank of New York, low and high. The discount rates for 1980 and 1981 do not include the surcharge applied to frequent borrowings by large institutions. The surcharge reached 3% in 1980 and 4% in 1981. Surcharge was eliminated in November 1981. 6. Averages based on daily closing bid yields in secondary market, bank discount basis. 7. HUD = Housing and Urban Development. 8. Averages based on quotations for 1 day each month as compiled by FHA. 9. Primary market. 10. Average contract rates on new commitments. **Source:** Except as noted, Board of Governors of the Federal Reserve System, *Federal Reserve Bulletin*, monthly, and *Annual Statistical Digest*.

they can be purchased at local banks also makes them easy to secure. These factors make them appealing to the general public. The interest paid on CDs is set by the market and is generally the same across large institutions. Smaller institutions often offer higher rates to attract depositors.

Money-market accounts Customers pool their money into a fund that then purchases short-term debt such as Treasury bills and commercial paper in order to earn a high rate of return while maintaining liquidity (i.e., being able to convert assets quickly into cash). Customers typically can write checks on their money-market accounts, which are processed through cooperating banks, but checks generally have to be in large denominations—greater than $250—to prevent customers from using them as demand deposit accounts.

Capital Instruments
Stock, or equity, the most important source of capital for firms, represents a claim on the assets or equity of a business as well as on its earnings. See the chapter on U.S. Business later in this section.

Treasury bonds, or notes, have longer-term dates of maturity, from one to 10 years, than do Treasury bills. They are sold by the Treasury in denominations of $1,000 and are the principal means of funding government borrowing and the national debt. The interest on these bonds is paid out regularly. *Thirty-year Treasury Bonds,* commonly called the Long Bond, are also sold by the Treasury; their yield is watched closely because it forms the basis for all other interest rates, including mortgage-backed securities and fixed rates. Bond prices are determined by the relative number of investors willing to buy and sell them on the open market. Their decisions are in turn based on expectations about inflation. When the Federal Reserve announces that it will not change interest rates, indicating its belief that inflation will remain steady, more investors are willing to buy long-term investments, so bond prices rise, but

result in a lower yield. When the economy heats up, however—that is, with increased business activity employing more workers—inflation is expected to rise, resulting in fewer investors willing to buy long-term instruments, and bond prices will fall as yields and other interest rates rise.

Other government securities Some agencies of the government that are involved in lending are permitted to sell securities in order to raise funds. The most important of these is the Federal National Mortgage Association—FNMA, or "Fanny Mae." It buys and sells mortgages insured by the federal government and stabilizes the market for those mortgages in the process.

Municipal bonds are issued by state and local governments to raise funds, usually to provide public works and other facilities. The federal government is prohibited by the Constitution from interfering in the ability of state and local governments to raise revenue, so income from municipal bonds is not subject to federal taxes. So-called revenue bonds are paid for by user fees—for example, tolls collected on a parkway are used to pay for the bonds used to build it. General-obligation bonds are paid for through general taxes. Municipal bonds tend to be very safe, although there have been occasions on which some state and local governments have had to take extraordinary actions to avoid default—most notably, New York City in 1975, which received a federal loan and sold new bonds to its municipal employee unions in order to avoid default.

▶ GOVERNMENT DEBT
One of the most debated economic issues since the 1980s has been the importance of the government's budget deficit. The government raises most of its resources through taxes, but it can also raise money by borrowing. The government borrows by selling bonds (treasury bonds, savings bonds, for example) which have increasingly been purchased by investors outside the U.S. The

Bonds and Stock Yields, 1970-98

Type	1970	1980	1990	1995	1997	1998
U.S. Treasury, constant maturities:[1,2]						
3-year	7.29%	11.51%	8.26%	6.25%	6.10%	5.14%
5-year	7.38	11.45	8.37	6.38	6.22	5.15
10-year	7.35	11.43	8.55	6.57	6.35	5.26
U.S. Govt., long-term bonds [2,3]	6.58	10.81	8.74	6.93	6.67	5.69
State and local govt. bonds, Aaa[4]	6.12	7.86	6.96	5.80	5.32	4.93
State and local govt. bonds, Baa[4]	6.75	9.02	7.29	6.10	5.50	5.14
High-graded municipal bonds (Standard & Poor's)[5]	6.51	8.51	7.25	N.A.	N.A.	N.A.
Municipal (Bond Buyer, 20 bonds)	6.35	8.59	7.27	5.95	5.52	5.09
Corporate Aaa seasoned[4]	8.04	11.94	9.32	7.59	7.27	6.53
Corporate Baa seasoned[4]	9.11	13.67	10.36	8.20	7.87	7.22
Corporate (Moody's) [4,6]	8.51	12.75	9.77	7.83	7.54	6.87
Industrials (49 bonds)[7]	8.26	12.35	9.77	7.76	7.47	6.79
Public utilities (51 bonds)[8]	8.68	13.15	9.76	7.76	7.63	7.00

1. Yields on the more actively traded issues adjusted to constant maturities by the U.S. Treasury. 2. Yields are based on closing bid prices quoted by at least five dealers. 3. Averages (to maturity or call) for all outstanding bonds neither due nor callable in less than 10 years, including several very low yielding "flower" bonds. 4. **Source:** Moody's Investors Service, New York, NY. 5. **Source:** U.S. Bureau of Economic Analysis, Survey of Current Business, monthly. Annual averages of weekly figures. 6. For 1970-85, includes railroad bonds, which were discontinued as part of composite in 1989. 7. Covers 40 bonds for 1970-1983, 38 bonds for 1984-86, and 37 bonds for 1987 and 1988. 8. Covers 40 bonds for 1970-88. **Source:** Except as noted, Board of Governors of the Federal Reserve System, *Federal Reserve Bulletin,* monthly.

bonds raise money now but must be repaid in the future through revenues from taxes. The *budget deficit* in any year indicates the difference between what the government takes in through taxes and other forms of revenues, and the expenditures it makes. The deficit therefore suggests how much the government needed to borrow to fill that gap. The total amount of present and past borrowing, plus interest, constitutes the total *national debt*.

Governments routinely borrow to pay for long-term projects that will give benefits to the community into the future. It can be argued that because much of the benefit from projects such as highways and other public works will be enjoyed by the next generation of tax payers, they should also bear much of the cost. And they can do that by paying off the government debt (paying the premiums on the government bonds) through taxes in the future. Controversy arises when the government borrows to pay for its more routine expenditures. One justification for such borrowing is that it can be used to manage business cycles in the economy: in other words, during recessions, the government can borrow in order to increase expenditures and expand the economy without raising taxes, which would slow it down.

When the total amount of government debt becomes large, some economists believe that it damages the economy in the following ways. First the fact that the government is selling large amounts of debt means that it is competing for limited investor dollars with private borrowers, driving up the cost of borrowing, and making it harder for private sector businesses to make investments for future growth. Second, the future taxes needed to pay off large amounts of government debt may place a serious drain on the future

economy, again diverting resources from investment in the private sector. Politicians are concerned because debt payments must be funded from tax revenues so they must either raise taxes or reduce government spending in other areas (e.g. in defense, entitlement programs).

The debate over debt really turns on how much is "too much." Between 1935 and 1981 the only two significant increases in the deficit occurred during World War II and certain years of the Vietnam War, when deficits were about $25 billion. Between 1981 an 1989, however, the Reagan Administration consistently ran annual deficits averaging $167 billion and increased the nation's total outstanding gross debt from just over $1 trillion to over $2.6 trillion.

The strong economy and prudent government accounting allowed the Clinton Administration to wipe out the annual deficit in 1998, posting a one-year surplus of $69.2 billion. But the total national debt still topped $5.4 trillion in 1998, and the interest on that debt remains burdensome. The interest alone on the huge debt created during the 1980s is still close to 14 percent of the entire federal budget.

▶ THE LABOR FORCE
Labor Force Participation Rate

The Labor Force Participation Rate (LFPR), often referred to simply as the labor force, is that proportion of the population that is either employed or actively seeking employment. It represents the supply of labor available to the economy. The LFPR is lower for young people because many are in school, and for older people because many have retired. It is highest for married men and for women who are heads of households.

Deficits and the Debt, 1940–98
(billions of dollars)

Year	Total receipts	Total outlays	Surplus or Deficit	Gross Federal Debt	Debt held by the public	Net interest paid[1] Total	Net interest paid[1] As percent of federal outlays
1940	$ 6.5	$ 9.5	$ -2.9	$ 50.7	$ 42.7	$ 1.0	9.5%
1945	45.2	92.7	-47.6	260.1	235.2	3.1	3.4
1950	39.4	42.6	-3.1	256.9	219.0	4.8	11.3
1955	65.5	68.4	-3.0	274.4	226.6	4.9	7.1
1960	92.5	92.2	0.3	290.5	236.8	6.9	7.5
1965	116.8	118.2	-1.4	322.3	260.8	8.6	7.3
1970	192.8	195.6	-2.8	380.9	283.2	14.4	7.4
1975	279.1	332.3	-53.2	541.9	394.7	23.2	7.0
1980	517.1	590.9	-73.8	909.1	709.8	52.5	8.9
1985	734.2	946.5	-212.3	1,817.5	1,499.9	129.5	13.7
1990	1,032.0	1,253.2	-221.2	3,206.6	2,410.7	184.2	14.7
1991	1,055.0	1,324.4	-269.4	3,598.5	2,688.1	194.5	14.7
1992	1,091.3	1,381.7	-290.4	4,002.1	2,998.8	199.4	14.4
1993	1,154.4	1,409.4	-255.0	4,351.4	3,247.5	198.8	14.1
1994	1,258.6	1,461.7	-203.1	4,643.7	3,432.1	203.0	13.9
1995	1,351.8	1,515.7	-163.9	4,921.0	3,603.4	232.2	15.3
1996	1,453.1	1,560.5	-107.4	5,181.9	3,733.0	241.1	15.5
1997	1,579.3	1,601.2	-21.9	5,369.7	3,771.1	244.0	15.2
1998	1,721.8	1,652.6	69.2	5,478.7	3,719.9	243.4	14.7
1999[2]	1,806.3	1,727.1	79.2	5,614.9	3,669.7	227.2	13.2

Note: For fiscal years ending in year shown.[1] Public debt excludes debt held by Federal Government accounts. 1. Net interest is interest paid on debt held by the public. 2. Estimate. **Source:** *Budget of the United States Government, Fiscal Year 2000* (1999).

Women in the work force One of the most important developments in the labor force has been the sharp increase in the LFPR of women, which has virtually doubled since the early 1960s. With higher levels of education than ever before, most women now opt for careers in the labor force rather than homemaking. Women are having fewer children, and are having them later in life, after they have started to establish their careers, and are returning to work sooner after childbirth. Furthermore, women are continuing to make inroads into professions like law and medicine that have previously been dominated by men.

Women have joined the labor force at an astounding rate since 1960. In 1998, 59.8 percent of women were in the labor force, up from 37.7 percent in 1960. Over the same period, the percentage of men in the labor force has actually dropped, from 83.3 percent to 75.0 percent. Women constituted 52 percent of the entire civilian population in 1998, about the same as in 1960, but only 33 percent of the labor force was female in 1960; in 1998, it was 46 percent.

Unemployment rate One of the most closely watched labor force statistics is the unemployment rate, which surged to 7.4 percent in 1992. But in early 1997, it fell below 5 percent for the first time in 30 years (It dropped even further, to 4.5 percent in 1998 and 4.3 percent in 1999.) Contrary to popular opinion, the unemployment rate is only an indirect measure of the people without jobs, since it only measures the number of active (within the last four weeks) job seekers as a proportion of the total labor force. So the unemployment rate may rise as new job seekers enter the labor force. Every spring, for example, it rises slightly as school graduates enter the labor force and look for jobs. It may also fall as workers retire or otherwise leave the labor force. And when the economy is in a prolonged recession, the unemployment rate may actually drop slightly because some of the job seekers may give up trying to find a job and withdraw from the labor force.

The unemployment rate over time for the United States is a measure associated with identifying periods of expansion and recession. It reached a peak of 9.6 percent during the 1982-83 recession. The relatively high periods of unemployment beginning in the mid-1970s are in part due to the expansion of the labor force as the Baby Boom generation left school and began looking for work. Unemployment rates for women have paralleled those for men since 1990.

Hispanics People of Hispanic origin constitute the fastest-growing population group in the labor force, in large part due to immigration, with Mexicans making up the largest share. The proportion of Hispanic women working—historically, these women were more likely to stay at home—has boosted Hispanic participation in the labor force. But a doubling of the Hispanic population in the U.S. since 1980 has been responsible for most of the growth. By the year 2000, the number of Hispanic workers in the labor force will account for 10 percent of the total labor force. Overall, however, Hispanic workers earn only 74 percent as much as the average for all workers. They also have a significantly higher unemployment rate.

Percent of Female Workers in Selected Occupations, 1975–98

Occupation	Women as percent of total employed				
	1975	1985	1996	1997	1998
Airline pilot	—	2.6%	1.4%	1.2%	3.4%
Auto mechanic	0.5%	0.6	1.2	1.5	0.8
Bartender	35.2	47.9	53.8	57.2	54.6
Bus driver	37.7	49.2	46.8	47.8	50.4
Cab driver, chauffeur	8.7	10.9	10.7	8.3	10.5
Carpenter	0.6	1.2	1.3	1.6	1.2
Child care worker	98.4	96.1	97.1	96.8	96.5
Computer programmer	25.6	34.3	30.8	30.0	28.5
Computer systems analyst	14.8	28.0	28.1	28.6	26.9
Data entry keyer	92.8	90.7	84.5	81.9	81.8
Data processing equipment repairer	1.8	10.4	18.3	13.3	16.9
Dentist	1.8	6.5	13.7	17.3	19.8
Dental assistant	100.0	99.0	79.8	96.7	98.1
Economist	13.1	34.5	54.4	52.2	46.3
Editor, reporter	44.6	51.7	55.7	51.2	51.0
Garage, gas station attendant	4.7	6.8	5.8	9.6	4.1
Lawyer, judge	7.1	18.2	29.0	26.7	28.6
Librarian	81.1	87.0	82.7	80.5	83.4
Mail carrier (Postal Service)	8.7	17.2	28.3	30.7	29.7
Office machine repairer	1.7	5.7	3.7	4.6	2.1
Physician	13.0	17.2	26.4	26.2	26.6
Registered nurse	97.0	95.1	93.3	93.5	92.5
Social worker	60.8	66.7	68.5	69.3	68.4
Teacher, college & university	31.1	35.2	43.5	42.7	42.3
Teacher, elementary school	85.4	84.0	83.3	73.9	84.0
Telephone installer, repairer	4.8	12.8	13.9	13.1	12.0
Telephone operator	93.3	88.8	90.5	83.5	85.8
Waiter/waitress	91.1	84.0	77.9	77.8	78.3
Welder	4.4	4.8	5.0	5.6	5.1

N.A. = Not available. **Source:** U.S. Department of Labor, Bureau of Labor Statistics, *Employment and Earnings* January issues.

Employment Status of the Population by Sex, Race, and Hispanic Origin 1960-98 (numbers in thousands)

Year	Civilian noninstitutional population[1]	Civilian labor force		Number employed	Employment/ population ratio[2]	Percent unemployed
		Total	Percent of population			
Total						
1960	117,245	69,628	59.4%	65,778	56.1%	5.5%
1970	137,085	82,771	60.4	78,678	57.4	4.9
1980	167,745	106,940	63.8	99,303	59.2	7.1
1985	178,206	115461	64.8	107150	60.1	7.2
1990	188,049	124,787	66.4	117,914	62.7	5.5
1995[3]	198,584	132,304	66.6	124,900	62.9	5.6
1996[3]	200,591	133,934	66.8	126,708	63.2	5.4
1997[3]	203,133	136,297	67.1	129,558	63.8	4.9
1998[3]	205,220	137,673	67.1	131,463	64.1	4.5
Male						
1960	55,662	46,388	83.3%	43,904	78.9%	5.4%
1970	64,304	51,228	79.7	48,990	76.2	4.4
1980	79,398	61,453	77.4	57,186	72.0	6.9
1985	84,469	64,411	76.3	59,891	70.9	7.0
1990	89,650	68,234	76.1	64,435	71.9	5.6
1995[3]	95,178	71,360	75.0	67,377	70.8	5.6
1996[3]	96,206	72,087	74.9	68,207	70.9	5.4
1997[3]	97,715	73,261	75.0	69,685	71.3	4.9
1998[3]	98,758	73,959	74.9	70,693	71.6	4.4
Female						
1960	61,582	23,240	37.7%	21,874	35.5%	5.9%
1970	72,782	31,543	43.3	29,688	40.8	5.9
1980	88,348	45,487	51.5	42,117	47.7	7.4
1985	93,736	51,050	54.5	47,259	50.4	7.4
1990	98,399	56,554	57.5	53,479	54.3	5.4
1995[3]	103,406	60,944	58.9	57,523	55.6	5.6
1996[3]	104,385	61,857	59.3	58,501	56.0	5.4
1997[3]	105,418	63,036	59.8	59,873	56.8	5.0
1998[3]	106,462	63,715	59.8	60,771	57.1	4.6
White						
1975	134,790	82,831	61.5%	76,411	56.7%	7.8%
1980	146,122	93,600	64.1	87,715	60.0	6.3
1985	153,679	99,926	65.0	93,736	61.0	6.2
1990	160,415	107,177	66.8	102,087	63.6	4.7
1995[3]	166,914	111,950	67.1	106,490	63.8	4.9
1996[3]	168,317	113,108	67.2	107,808	64.1	4.7
1997[3]	169,993	114,693	67.5	109,856	64.6	4.2
1998[3]	171,478	115,415	67.3	110,931	64.7	3.9
Black						
1975	15,751	9,263	58.8%	7,894	50.1%	14.8%
1980	17,824	10,865	61.0	9,313	52.2	14.3
1985	19,664	12,364	62.9	10,501	53.4	15.1
1990	21,300	13,493	63.3	11,966	56.2	11.3
1995[3]	23,246	14,817	63.7	13,279	57.1	10.4
1996[3]	23,604	15,134	64.1	13,542	57.4	10.5
1997[3]	24,003	15,529	64.7	13,969	58.2	10.0
1998[3]	24,373	15,982	65.6	14,556	59.7	8.9
Hispanic[4]						
1975	N.A.	N.A.	N.A.	N.A.	N.A.	N.A.
1980	9,598	6,146	64.0%	5,527	57.6%	10.1%
1985	11,915	7,698	64.6	6,888	57.8	10.5
1990	14,297	9,576	67.0	8,808	61.6	8.0
1995[3]	18,629	12,267	65.8	11,127	59.7	9.3
1996[3]	19,213	12,774	66.5	11,642	60.6	8.9
1997[3]	20,321	13,796	67.9	12,726	62.6	7.7
1998[3]	21,070	14,317	67.9	13,291	63.1	7.2

Note: N.A.=Not Available. 1. Age 16 and over. 2. Civilians employed as a percent of the civilian noninstitutional population. 3. Data for 1995-98 are not directly comparable with data for previous years because of a major redesign of the Current Population Survey questionnaire and collection methodology and the introduction of 1990 census-based population controls, adjusted for the estimated undercount. 4. Hispanic persons may be of any race. **Source:** U.S. Bureau of Labor Statistics, *Employment and Earnings,* January issues.

Productivity measures how much output an economy or organization can generate from a given amount of input. Higher levels of productivity suggest greater efficiency—doing more with the same amount of resources, just as an efficient or economical car goes farther on a gallon of gasoline. Increases in productivity, as the result of better tools or improved methods, provide the main mechanism for increasing output in an economy and ultimately for raising standards of living. Productivity is usually measured in terms of labor—output per worker or per hour of labor—not only because labor is the most important resource but also because it is one of the easiest to measure.

Wages vary not only among the different professions but also between sexes and regions of the country. For example, women in year-round, full-time executive, administrative, and managerial positions have a median yearly income of only 61 percent of the median income for men in the same occupation group. This percentage is higher in the field of laborers, precision production, craft, and repair; but for all major occupation groups reported by the U.S. Bureau of the Census, women receive only a fraction of that received by their male counterparts. This may be due, in part, to the fact that women enter and leave the work force more times throughout their lives than do

U.S. Membership in AFL-CIO Affiliated Unions, 1979–97

Labor organization	1979	1985	1995	1997
Total[1]	N.A.	N.A.	12,986,453	12,955,696
Actors and Artists	75,000	100,000	75,893	69,000
Automobile, Aerospace and Agriculture (UAW)	N.A.	974,000	760,038	766,032
Bakery, Confectionery and Tobacco	131,000	115,000	95,186	94,871
Boilermakers	129,000	110,000	42,802	41,775
Bricklayers	106,000	95,000	84,000	62,275
Carpenters and Joiners	626,000	609,000	354,306	323,929
Communications Workers (CWA)	485,000	524,000	490,482	503,558
Electrical Workers (IBEW)	825,000	791,000	673,117	653,946
Electronic, Electrical, and Salaried[2, 4]	243,000	198,000	136,502	128,441
Firefighters	150,000	142,000	151,000	156,000
Flight Attendants	N.A.	N.A.	31,776	34,609
Food and Commercial Workers (UFCW)[2]	1,123,000	989,000	1,009,523	989,340
Garment Workers (ILGWU)	314,000	210,000	N.A.	N.A.
Glass, Molders, Pottery, and Plastics[2]	50,000	72,000	69,000	65,000
Government Employees (AFGE)	236,000	199,000	157,100	169,500
Graphic Communications[2]	171,000	141,000	95,580	90,493
Hotel and Restaurant Employees	373,000	327,000	232,160	224,937
Ironworkers	146,000	140,000	80,485	79,342
Laborers	475,000	383,000	330,694	297,618
Letter Carriers (NALC)	151,000	186,000	210,000	210,000
Longshoreman's Association	63,000	65,000	60,595	63,343
Machinists and Aerospace (IAM)[2]	688,000	520,000	431,619	431,058
Mine Workers	N.A.	N.A.	75,021	75,250
Needletrades, Industrial and Textile Employees	308,000	228,000	244,783	225,000
Office and Professional Employees	83,000	90,000	82,987	83,295
Operating Engineers	313,000	330,000	295,833	294,500
Oil, Chemical, Atomic Workers (OCAW)	146,000	108,000	82,080	80,228
Painters	160,000	133,000	90,000	80,000
Paperworkers International	262,000	232,000	235,302	225,741
Plumbing and Pipefitting	228,000	226,000	219,800	219,800
Postal Workers	245,000	232,000	265,757	279,313
Retail, Wholesale, Department Store	122,000	106,000	73,133	71,480
Rubber, Cork, Linoleum, Plastic	158,000	106,000	N.A.	N.A.
Seafarers	84,000	80,000	80,250	80,250
Service Employees (SEIU)[2, 5]	537,000	688,000	1,077,854	1,080,572
Sheet Metal Workers	120,000	108,000	103,042	93,000
Stage Employees, Moving Picture Machine Operators	50,000	50,000	50,900	47,100
State, County, Municipal (AFSCME)[5]	889,000	997,000	1,210,949	1236,042
Steelworkers	964,000	572,000	516,880	499,090
Teachers (AFT)	423,000	470,000	631,529	694,402
Teamsters[6]	N.A.	N.A.	1,286,371	1271,039
Transit Union	94,000	94,000	96,340	97,607
Transport Workers	85,000	85,000	75,000	75,000
Transportation Union, United	121,000	52,000	59,575	59,575

Note: Figures represent the labor organizations as constituted in 1989 and reflect past merger activity. Membership figures based on average per capita paid membership to the AFL-CIO for the 2-year period ending in June of the year shown and reflect only actively-employed members. Not all unions shown. 1. Includes other AFL-CIO affiliated unions, not shown separately. 2. Figures reflect mergers with one or more unions since 1979. 3. Includes Blacksmiths, Forgers and Helpers. 4. Includes Machine and Furniture Workers. 5. Excludes Hospital and Health Care Employees which merged into both unions on June 1, 1989 (membership of 23,000 in 1985, and 58,000 in 1989). 6. Includes Chauffeurs, Warehousemen and Helpers.   **Source:** American Federation of Labor and Congress of Industrial Organizations, *Report of the AFL-CIO Executive Council* (annual).

men and spend a smaller percentage of their lives economically active.

Another factor influencing the discrepancy between men's and women's wages is the concentration of women in occupations that pay less. Women made up 97 percent of child care workers, 86 percent of telephone operators, and 82 percent of data entry keyers, three poorly paid positions.

Minimum wage in the nation was first enacted by the state of Massachusetts in 1912, covered only women, and was designed to shorten hours and raise pay in the covered industries. The nationwide minimum wage was established in 1938, and has grown in both dollar value and the types of employees it covers since then (see the accompanying table). Some states may establish minimum wages higher than the federal minimum.

Unions are organizations of workers who engage in collective bargaining with employers for higher wages, better working conditions, and in-

creased benefits. In the United States, unions are organized at three levels: (1) labor federations or voluntary associations of national unions, which settle disputes between national unions, lobby for favorable labor legislation, and engage in public relations. There is only one labor foundation in the country—the American Federation of Labor and Congress of Industrial Organizations, or AFL-CIO—to which virtually all union members belong; (2) national unions, which coordinate agreements across local unions and conduct collective bargaining negotiations with industry employers; and (3) local unions, which administer labor contracts, serving individual members, employers, and in some cases, establishments directly. Unions can be divided into two groups: (1) industrial unions, representing workers of a particular firm or industry, such as autoworkers and steelworkers, and (2) craft unions, representing employees with a specific skill, such as pilots and musicians.

Many workers choose not to unionize because of the potential costs involved in membership, such as dues, lost pay during strikes, and possible retribution by employers. Union membership in the nation has held steady at around 16 million since 1990, but that's down significantly from 1954, when 25.4 percent of the total labor force was unionized. Notable examples of membership decline are among steelworkers, garment workers, and oil, chemical, and atomic workers, which each fell by about 50 percent during 1979-90. Virtually all of these losses are due to the loss of jobs in unionized firms. Several factors may have contributed to this decline, such as changes in technology that displace workers, increased factor costs and international competition, and "downsizing," in which firms lay off large numbers of employees to keep the company's stock prices high.

Federal Minimum Wage Rates, 1938–99

The Fair Labor Standards Act of 1938 set a minimum wage of 25 cents per hour for employees engaged in interstate commerce or in the production of goods for interstate commerce. Over the years, the government has expanded the numbers of workers covered by the federal minimums (waiters and workers under age 20 in their first three months of work, for example, may be paid less than minimum wage) and has increased the minimum amount. But, as the following table shows, the increases have not always kept up with inflation.

Effective date	Hourly minimum (current dollars)	Purchasing power in constant (=1996) dollars
Oct. 24, 1938	$0.25	$2.78
Oct. 24, 1939	0.30	3.39
Oct. 24, 1945	0.40	3.49
Jan. 25, 1950	0.75	4.88
Mar. 1, 1956	1.00	5.77
Sept. 3, 1961	1.15[1]	6.03
Sept. 3, 1961	1.25	6.41
Feb. 1, 1967	1.40[2]	6.58
Feb. 1, 1968	1.60	7.21
May 1, 1974	2.00	6.37
Jan. 1, 1975	2.10	6.12
Jan. 1, 1976	2.30	6.34
Jan. 1, 1978	2.65	6.38
Jan. 1, 1979	2.90	6.27
Jan. 1, 1980	3.10	5.90
Jan. 1, 1981	3.35	5.78
Apr. 1, 1990	3.50	4.56
Apr. 1, 1991	4.25	4.90
Oct. 1, 1996	4.75	4.75
Sept. 1, 1997[3]	5.15	N.A.

Note: Purchasing power is based on the CPI-U Consumer Price Index. 1. A lower rate of $1.00 per hour was extended to employees in large retail and service enterprises as well as to local transit, construction, and gas service station employees. This rate was increased to $1.15 in 1964, and put on par with the higher rate on Sept. 3, 1965. 2. A lower rate of $1.00 was extended to state and local government employees of hospitals, nursing homes, and schools, and to laundries, dry cleaners, and large hotels, motels, restaurants, and farms. This rate continued to lag behind the rate guaranteed other workers until 1977 (1978 for farm workers). 3. Rate in effect as of Nov. 1, 1999.
Source: U.S. Department of Labor.

Work Stoppages, 1960–98

			Days idle	
	Number of work stoppages[1]	Workers involved[2] ('000s)	Number[3] ('000s)	Percent estimated working time[4]
1960	222	896	13,260	0.09%
1965	268	999	15,140	0.10
1970	381	2,468	52,761	0.29
1975	235	965	17,563	0.09
1980	187	795	20,844	0.09
1985	54	324	7,079	0.03
1989	51	452	16,996	0.07
1990	44	185	5,926	0.02
1991	40	392	4,584	0.02
1992	35	364	3,989	0.01
1993	35	182	3,981	0.01
1994	45	322	5,021	0.02
1995	31	192	5,771	0.02
1996	37	273	4,887	0.02
1997	29	339	4,497	0.01
1998	34	387	5,116	0.02

Note: Excludes work stoppages involving fewer than 1,000 workers and lasting less than 1 day. 1. Beginning in year indicated. 2. Workers counted more than once if involved in more than one stoppage during the year. 3. Resulting from all stoppages in effect in a year, including those that began in an earlier year. 4. Agricultural and government employees are included in the total working time; private household, forestry and fishery employees are excluded. **Source:** U.S. Bureau of Labor Statistics, *Compensation and Conditions*, monthly.

Average Earnings of Year-Round Full-Time Workers by Age and Educational Attainment, 1997

Age and Sex	All workers	Less than 9th grade	Some high school	High school graduate	Some college	Associate degree	Bachelor's degree or more
Male, total	**$43,709**	**$22,748**	**$27,638**	**$32,611**	**$39,367**	**$40,465**	**$66,393**
18 - 24 years old	20,294	13,377	16,576	19,470	21,945	23,297	28,498
25 - 34 years old	34,807	17,714	24,517	28,772	32,354	34,670	48,688
35 - 44 years old	45,780	24,304	26,285	34,790	40,919	42,968	67,652
45 - 54 years old	52,429	23,261	35,163	38,340	45,588	44,431	74,985
55 - 64 years old	55,702	28,510	36,561	38,179	55,987	44,129	86,818
65 years and over	51,148	33,425	32,911	30,549	54,905	N.A.	68,470
Female, total	**$29,261**	**$14,957**	**$18,594**	**$22,656**	**$26,562**	**$29,776**	**$41,626**
18 - 24 years old	17,510	N.A.	13,915	15,727	15,506	19,894	26,297
25 - 34 years old	27,805	13,526	18,814	21,289	24,127	25,431	37,321
35 - 44 years old	31,273	13,820	19,409	23,011	28,561	31,090	46,154
45 - 54 years old	32,524	15,419	18,430	24,624	31,350	35,932	45,105
55 - 64 years old	28,876	16,826	19,317	25,243	29,535	30,773	40,203
65 years and over	27,567	N.A.	N.A.	22,523	27,596	N.A.	36,825

Note: High school graduate category includes equivalency. **Source:** U.S. Bureau of the Census, *Current Population Reports.*

Average Hourly and Weekly Earnings in Current and Constant (1982) Dollars, By Private Industry Group, 1970-98

While average hourly and weekly wages (in current dollars) have more than tripled since 1970, the following table illustrates that when inflation is accounted for, real earnings (in constant dollars) have decreased steadily over the past two decades. Hourly earnings have fallen 4% since 1970, while weekly earnings have dropped 10%. Thus, even though 1998 paychecks have more zeroes on the end, they don't go as far as a 1970 paycheck to cover living expenses.

Private industry group	Current dollars					Constant (1982)[1] dollars				
	1970	1980	1990	1995	1998	1970	1980	1990	1995	1998
Average hourly earnings	**$3.23**	**$6.66**	**$10.01**	**$11.43**	**$12.77**	**$8.03**	**$7.78**	**$7.52**	**$7.39**	**$7.75**
Mining	3.85	9.17	13.68	15.30	16.95	9.58	10.71	10.28	9.90	10.29
Construction	5.24	9.94	13.77	15.09	16.56	13.03	11.61	10.35	9.76	10.05
Manufacturing	3.35	7.27	10.83	12.37	13.49	8.33	8.49	8.14	8.00	8.19
Transportation, public utilities	3.85	8.87	12.92	14.13	15.34	9.58	10.36	9.71	9.14	9.31
Wholesale trade	3.43	6.95	10.79	12.43	14.01	8.53	8.12	8.11	8.04	8.50
Retail trade	2.44	4.88	6.75	7.69	8.75	6.07	5.70	5.07	4.97	5.31
Finance, insurance, real estate	3.07	5.79	9.97	12.32	14.06	7.64	6.76	7.49	7.97	8.53
Services	2.81	5.85	9.83	11.39	12.84	6.99	6.83	7.39	7.37	7.79
Average weekly earnings	**$120**	**$235**	**$345**	**$394**	**$442**	**$296**	**$275**	**$259**	**$255**	**$268**
Mining	164	397	603	684	744	409	464	453	442	452
Construction	195	368	526	587	643	486	430	395	380	390
Manufacturing	133	289	442	515	563	332	337	332	333	341
Transportation, public utilities	156	351	496	557	606	388	410	373	360	368
Wholesale trade	137	267	411	476	538	341	312	309	308	326
Retail trade	82	147	194	221	255	205	172	146	143	155
Finance, insurance, real estate	113	210	357	442	512	281	245	268	286	311
Services	97	191	319	369	420	240	223	240	239	255

1. Earnings in current dollars divided by the Consumer Price Index on a 1982 base.
Source: U.S. Bureau of Labor Statistics, *Employment and Earnings,* monthly. http://stats.bls.gov/ceshome.htm>

25 Metropolitan Areas with Fastest Job Growth, 1999-2025

Rank Metropolitan statistical area	Number of jobs 1999	2025	Annual percent increase 1999-2025
1. Punta Gorda, Fla.	49,500	107,100	3.0%
2. Orlando, Fla.	1,022,900	2,087,300	2.8
3. Naples, Fla.	125,200	253,900	2.8
4. Myrtle Beach, S.C.	121,900	237,500	2.6
5. Las Vegas, Nev.	843,400	1,622,600	2.5
6. Provo-Orem, Utah	185,800	355,900	2.5
7. Austin-San Marcos, Tex.	790,500	1,514,400	2.5
8. Phoenix-Mesa, Ariz.	1,837,300	3,497,800	2.5
9. Fort Collins-Loveland, Colo.	152,200	287,600	2.5
10. Sarasota-Bradenton, Fla.	334,300	626,900	2.4
11. Olympia, Wash.	109,800	205,300	2.4
12. Fort Myers-Cape Coral, Fla.	208,400	388,500	2.4
13. Fort Pierce-Port St. Lucie, Fla.	133,200	248,100	2.4
14. McAllen-Edinburg-Mission, Tex.	186,800	347,200	2.4
15. Boulder-Longmont, Colo.	220,000	408,000	2.4
16. Laredo, Tex.	80,400	148,700	2.4
17. Bryan-College Station, Tex.	94,500	174,800	2.4
18. Ocala, Fla.	105,900	195,700	2.4
19. Sacramento, Calif.	914,300	1,679,700	2.4
20. Yolo, Calif.	112,500	206,300	2.4
21. Fort Walton Beach, Fla.	109,700	200,200	2.3
22. Tucson, Ariz.	425,600	774,000	2.3
23. Salt Lake City, Utah	877,800	1,595,400	2.3
24. Santa Fe, N.Mex.	99,600	180,800	2.3
25. Atlanta, Ga.	2,570,000	4,657,500	2.3

Source: NPA Data Services, Inc., *Regional Economic Growth in the U.S.: Projections for 1999-2025* (1999).

25 Metropolitan Areas with Highest Job Growth, 1999-2025

Rank Metropolitan statistical area	Number of jobs 1999	2025	Jobs added 1999-2025
1. Atlanta, Ga.	2,570,000	4,657,500	2,087,500
2. Houston, Tex.	2,495,100	4,161,600	1,666,500
3. Phoenix, Ariz.	1,837,300	3,497,800	1,660,500
4. Dallas, Tex.	2,353,600	3,938,100	1,584,400
5. Washington, D.C.-Md.-Va.-W.Va.	3,294,600	4,786,500	1,491,900
6. Los Angeles-Long Beach, Calif.	5,352,800	6,802,100	1,449,300
7. San Diego, Calif.	1,625,900	2,885,900	1,259,900
8. Seattle, Wash.	1,727,500	2,950,700	1,223,200
9. Orange County, Calif.	1,786,600	3,005,400	1,218,900
10. Tampa- St. Petersburg- Clearwater, Fla.	1,403,700	2,523,600	1,119,900
11. Chicago, Ill.	5,025,100	6,144,500	1,119,400
12. Denver, Colo.	1,426,300	2,520,000	1,093,700
13. Orlando, Fla.	1,022,900	2,087,300	1,064,400
14. Boston, Mass[1]	3,866,200	4,891,100	1,024,900
15. Minneapolis-St. Paul, Minn.	2,094,400	3,107,800	1,013,400
16. Riverside-San Bernardino, Calif.	1,263,600	2,088,500	824,900
17. Las Vegas, Nev.-Ariz.	843,400	1,622,600	779,300
18. Sacramento, Calif.	914,300	1,679,700	765,500
19. Portland-Vancouver, Oreg.-Wash.	1,203,000	1,937,700	734,700
20. Austin-San Marcos, Tex.	790,500	1,514,400	724,000
21. Salt Lake City-Ogden, Utah	877,800	1,595,400	717,600
22. Fort Worth-Arlington, Tex.	959,000	1,647,700	688,600
23. San Jose, Calif.	1,214,800	1,901,600	686,900
24. San Francisco, Calif.	1,605,800	2,247,900	642,100
25. Raleigh-Durham-Chapel Hill, N.C.	822,300	1,426,800	604,500

1. Includes Worcester, Lawrence, Lowell, Brockton, and portions of New Hampshire.   **Source:** NPA Data Services, Inc., *Regional Economic Growth in the U.S. Projections for 1999-2025* (1998).

U.S. BUSINESS

The Office of Management and Budget (OMB) classifies the entire national economy into industries, based on principal product or activity. There are nine industrial divisions, which are further classified into groups and subgroups. For example, under "manufacturing" would fall "food and kindred products," and beneath that, "meat-packing plants." The nine industrial divisions listed in the OMB's Standard Industry Classification (SIC) are agriculture, forestry, and fishing; mining; construction; manufacturing; transportation and public utilities; finance, insurance and real estate; wholesale trade; retail trade; and services. In 1996, 6.7 million establishments employed 102 million workers with payrolls totaling $2.8 trillion.

Services and Manufacturing

Another way to view the economy is to divide it into manufacturing industries, producing tangible goods such as cars, shoes and furniture, and services industries, whose products are intangible, such as entertainment, tourism and banking. The manufacturing industries are further broken down into those that produce durable goods—that is, goods that are consumed over time, such as cars and houses—and nondurable goods that are consumed in the short run (food and soap). Services have played an increasingly important role in the economy, partly because companies in the manufacturing sector increasingly contract out services such as transportation, accounting, marketing and communications, previously performed in-house.

The service sector, which includes government, is responsible for approximately three-quarters of U.S. employment, and is expected to account for four of every five jobs by the year 2005. Seven of the 10 fastest-growing industries over the next 10 years are service industries. They include health services, computer and data processing services, and child day care services.

Financing Business

When an individual or a group of individuals decides to start a new company, they need money to rent or buy offfice space and equipment and to pay workers. Since there is a time lag between the day a business opens and the day a business sells its first good or service, funds must be borrowed from a bank or other financial institution or from individual investors to meet costs before revenues are generated. Additional funds may be needed throughout the life of the business to finance research and development of a new product or service or for the construction of new factories. Financing can take many forms, from short-term bank loans, commercial paper, or trade credit to long-term stocks and bonds.

Short-term Financing   *Trade credit*, the largest category of short-term financing, is an arrangement between a company and its suppliers, whereby materials and supplies are delivered to the company with a promise to pay the invoice, plus interest, usually within a specified number of weeks. Commercial bank lending may take the form of a single loan with repayment in a lump sum or in installments over the life of the loan, or it may be a line of credit up to a maximum the bank will allow the company to overdraw on its account. *Commercial paper* is a promissory note of a well-established firm sold primarily to other business firms, with repayments made in two to six months. The only problem with commercial paper is that its resources are limited to the liquidity that corporations have at any given time for lending to other firms.

Intermediate-term financing,   with a time frame of one to 15 years, may take the form of *lease financing*, whereby a company rents, rather than buys, the assets it uses; conditional sales contracts, by which equipment is bought over a period of time (the seller continues to have title of ownership until payment is completed); or term loans or business credit supplied by commercial banks and life insurance companies, repaid by amortization payments over the life of the loan (one to 15 years).

Number of Business Establishments with Employees and Payroll, by Major Group, 1996

Major group	Number of establishments	Number of employees	Annual payroll ('000s)
Total	**6,738,541**	**102,198,864**	**$2,848,955,378**
Agricultural services, forestry, and fishing	**113,000**	**664,281**	**13,288,710**
Agricultural services	107,986	628,436	12,324,498
Forestry	2,567	21,372	504,461
Fishing, hunting, and trapping	2,382	11,965	371,759
Administrative and auxiliary	65	2,508	87,992
Mining	**26,857**	**574,310**	**26,489,393**
Metal mining	866	48,291	2,207,504
Coal mining	2,024	94,460	4,333,869
Oil and gas extraction	17,300	256,859	10,848,279
Nonmetallic minerals, except fuels	5,637	100,843	3,692,988
Administrative and auxiliary	1,030	73,857	5,406,753
Construction	**657,718**	**5,206,925**	**160,877,060**
General contractors and operative builders	198,127	1,249,835	38,213,266
Heavy construction contractors	35,083	709,903	26,974,939
Special trade contractors	424,071	3,230,543	94,651,797
Administrative and auxiliary	437	16,644	1,037,058
Manufacturing	**393,060**	**18,558,100**	**659,644,221**
Food and kindred products	21,256	1,541,700	41,789,551

Major group	Number of establishments	Number of employees	Annual payroll ('000s)
Tobacco products	135	31,115	1,568,899
Textile mill products	6,401	582,188	13,569,665
Apparel and other textile products	24,278	843,140	14,858,739
Lumber and wood products	37,663	732,400	17,805,610
Furniture and fixtures	11,939	498,464	12,260,743
Paper and allied products	6,580	625,764	23,288,234
Printing and publishing	63,779	1,490,400	46,990,172
Chemicals and allied products	12,377	833,230	37,963,629
Petroleum and coal products	2,123	108,378	5,415,300
Rubber and misc. plastics products	16,532	997,421	28,727,216
Leather and leather products	1,938	86,480	1,738,479
Stone, clay, and glass products	16,615	495,480	16,013,465
Primary metal industries	6,728	683,433	26,153,600
Fabricated metal products	36,686	1,462,001	47,034,194
Industrial machinery and equipment	56,891	1,920,533	71,280,615
Electric and electronic equipment	17,159	1,545,179	56,959,096
Transportation equipment	11,908	1,521,541	66,497,044
Instruments and related products	11,430	813,682	34,736,812
Miscellaneous manufacturing industries	18,397	391,657	10,245,593
Administrative and auxiliary	12,245	1,353,914	84,747,565
Transportation and other public utilities	**295,205**	**6,057,058**	**211,880,187**
Local and interurban passenger transit	19,454	419,286	6,976,042
Trucking and warehousing	129,387	1,849,642	51,329,343
Water transportation	9,368	168,081	5,812,699
Transportation by air	12,649	755,746	26,314,927
Pipelines, except natural gas	975	15,120	826,265
Transportation services	52,417	412,267	11,730,503
Communication	45,586	1,375,879	57,947,581
Electric, gas, and sanitary services	22,860	878,411	42,635,814
Administrative and auxiliary	2,509	182,626	8,307,013
Wholesale trade	**531,220**	**6,664,654**	**240,313,774**
Wholesale trade—durable goods	335,559	3,733,757	138,854,271
Wholesale trade—nondurable goods	189,881	2,592,286	83,120,095
Administrative and auxiliary	5,780	338,611	18,339,408
Retail trade	**1,579,264**	**21,487,322**	**317,659,785**
Building materials and garden supplies	64,741	768,469	15,438,783
General merchandise stores	36,903	2,261,324	28,621,400
Food stores	179,345	3,300,025	44,093,437
Automotive dealers and service stations	201,997	2,266,634	55,535,790
Apparel and accessory stores	132,678	1,087,482	13,163,208
Furniture and home furnishings stores	115,697	877,750	16,742,178
Eating and drinking places	466,386	7,416,595	69,145,730
Miscellaneous retail	365,360	2,639,546	43,192,605
Administrative and auxiliary	16,157	869,497	31,726,654
Finance, insurance, and real estate	**650,161**	**7,194,274**	**285,031,578**
Depository institutions	105,114	2,061,206	65,815,403
Nondepository institutions	48,217	539,822	21,681,123
Security and commodity brokers	45,550	567,909	57,740,282
Insurance carriers	41,758	1,536,984	59,296,277
Insurance agents, brokers and service	127,278	695,139	24,685,419
Real estate	252,572	1,421,648	35,399,708
Holding and other investment offices	28,348	303,496	16,568,861
Administrative and auxiliary	1,324	68,070	3,844,505
Services	**2,461,235**	**35,749,974**	**933,003,163**
Hotels and other lodging places	57,344	1,600,846	25,650,791
Personal services	207,875	1,289,301	17,504,564
Business services	376,873	7,224,569	179,750,257
Auto repair, services, and garages	188,512	1,045,436	21,643,375
Miscellaneous repair services	69,703	443,888	12,164,452
Motion pictures	43,977	512,308	12,647,369
Amusement and recreation services	97,585	1,383,859	28,005,601
Health services	482,617	10,990,227	328,578,123
Legal services	168,276	959,809	45,245,116
Educational services	47,782	2,101,429	44,257,538
Social services	161,186	2,304,056	34,053,685
Museums, botanical, zoological gardens	5,119	79,896	1,625,247
Membership organizations	249,534	2,213,936	32,877,510
Engineering and management services	277,656	2,994,928	120,111,351
Miscellaneous services	17,221	105,803	5,135,921
Administrative and auxiliary	9,975	499,683	23,752,263
Unclassified establishments	**30,821**	**41,966**	**767,507**

Note: Excludes most government employees, railroad employees, and self-employed persons.   **Source:** U.S. Bureau of the Census, *County Business Patterns 1995* (1997).

Long-term financing The issuance of stocks and bonds constitute the long-term source of finance for firms. *Bonds* are debt instruments (IOUs issued by a company to the bondholder) that obligate the firm to pay interest at specific times. Alternatively firms can raise money by issuing preferred and common stocks. Unlike bonds, *stocks* entitle the holder to share in ownership and profits made by the firm through dividends paid out for the entire period the investor owns the stock. However, if the business has low profits or limited funds, bondholders are paid first, preferred stockholders next, and common stockholders last.

▶ WALL STREET

The U.S. stock market, commonly known as Wall Street, began in the late 19th century as a merchant-organized public auction in stocks and government bonds for the purpose of financing the government and expanding business and trade. At that time, brokers handed over securities to auctioneers who sold securities to the highest bidder. Today, while the form of the stock exchange has changed dramatically, the purpose remains the same.

The most commonly cited index of Wall Street's performance is the Dow Jones Industrial average (see "Glossary of Financial Terms"). From the Dow's inception in 1896 until the early 1980s, the 1,000 mark was considered the benchmark of a bull market. During that period, the Dow passed the 1,000 mark for the first time in 1972 and hovered around it in 1976 before eventually falling back below 1,000. But beginning in 1982, the Dow began an unparalleled stretch in which the average soared past both the 1,000 mark and the 2,000 mark before coming back down to earth on "Black Monday," the October, 19, 1987 crash that saw the Dow Jones average plummet more than 500 points in a single day. The 22 percent loss in value was nearly 10 pecentage points greater even than the Great Crash of 1929.

The Bull Market of the 1990s has made Black Monday a distant memory. The Dow passed the 3,000 mark in 1991, 4,000 and 5,000 in 1995, 6,000 in 1996, 7,000 and 8,000 in 1997, 9,000 in 1998, and 10,000 and 11,000 in 1999. This unprecedented growth, combined with easier access to trading due to on-line brokerages, has attracted hundreds of thousands of new investors to the stock market. By 1997, more than 42 percent of all American families owned stocks, either directly or through pension plans or mutual funds. That's up from 31.7 percent in 1989 and 19 percent in 1983.

Even more alarming is the percentage of the average American's wealth invested in the market. In 1998, stock investments made up a record 34 percent of Americans' household wealth, more even than the value of their homes. As recently as 1990, Americans had only 16 percent of their wealth invested in the stock market. Even during the bull market of the 1980s, the percentage of income invested in securities never topped 19 percent.

There are three major stock and bond markets in the U.S., all located in New York City. The growth of all three markets has been staggering. A total of 19.7 billion shares were traded on all three exchanges in 1980; in 1998, 379.1 billion shares were traded in the three markets.

NYSE Listed Stocks, 1924–98 (in millions)

Year	Number of Shares	Market Value	Average Price[1]
1924	43	$27,072	$62.45
1945	1,592	73,765	46.33
1950	2,353	93,807	39.86
1960	6,458	306,967	47.53
1970	16,065	636,380	39.61
1975	22,478	85,110	30.48
1980	33,709	1,242,803	36.87
1985	52,427	1,950,332	37.20
1990	90,732	2,819,778	31.08
1995	154,719	6,012,971	38.86
1996	176,944	7,300,351	41.26
1997	207,089	9,413,109	45.45
1998	239,302	10,864,472	45.40

1. This average cannot be used as an index of price trend owing to changes in shares listed caused by new listing, suspensions, stock splits, and stock dividends. **Source:** New York Stock Exchange, *Fact Book, 1998*

NYSE: Daily Shares Traded, 1900–98 (in thousands)

Year	Daily Average	Record High	Record Low
1900	505	1,627	89
1910	601	1,656	111
1920	828	2,008	227
1930	2,959	8,279	1,090
1940	751	3,940	130
1950	1,980	4,859	1,061
1960	2,578	7,717	1,230
1965	3,042	5,303	1,894
1970	6,176	11,434	3,028
1975	18,551	35,158	8,670
1980	44,871	84,297	16,132
1985	109,169	181,027	62,055
1990	156,777	292,364	56,853
1995	346,101	652,829	117,723
1996	411,953	680,913	130,303
1997	526,925	1,201,347	154,787
1998	673,590	1,216,326	246,928

Source: New York Stock Exchange, *Fact Book, 1998*

NYSE Membership Prices, 1875–98

Year	High	Low
1875	$6,800	$4,300
1895	20,000	17,000
1905	85,000	72,000
1915	74,000	38,000
1925	150,000	99,000
1935	140,000	65,000
1945	95,000	49,000
1955	90,000	80,000
1965	250,000	190,000
1970	320,000	130,000
1975	138,000	55,000
1980	275,000	175,000
1985	480,000	310,000
1990	430,000	250,000
1995	1,050,000	785,000
1996	1,450,000	1,225,000
1997	1,750,000	1,175,000
1998	2,000,000	1,225,000

Source: New York Stock Exchange, *Fact Book, 1998*

In July, 1999, the New York Stock Exchange and the NASDAQ both announced plans to become public companies, meaning it will be possible to buy and sell stock *in* these exchanges, on these exchanges.

New York Stock Exchange (NYSE)

The oldest exchange in the country was formally founded in 1817, when less than 100 shares were traded each day. In 1998, more than 169.7 billion shares were traded on the New York Stock Exchange. The growth in the value of those stocks has been equally impressive. The market value of all stocks traded on the NYSE doubled between 1987 and 1993, and then more than doubled again between 1993 and 1998, when it reached a staggering $10.9 trillion.

The American Stock Exchange (AMEX)

The American Stock Exchange, located a few blocks from the New York Stock Exchange in New York's financial district, is known as the stock market for the small investor and small companies. The stock issues of organizations that do not meet the listing and size requirements of the NYSE are typically traded there. For years, the Amex was known as the "New York Curb Exchange" because its trading was conducted on the street outside the office buildings of many brokers. The exchange moved indoors in 1921.

Trading on the Amex reached new all-time highs for the third straight year in 1998. Average daily trading volume was a record 29.0 million shares, up dramatically from the previous high of 24.4 set just a year earlier. The number of companies listed dropped by one, to 770. More than 7.3 billion shares changed hands on the Amex in 1998, up from 6.1 billion in 1997.

In 1998, the American Stock Exchange joined the parent organization of the NASDAQ stock market. The merger brought the NASDAQ's advanced technology to the Amex's trading floor, but the two exchanges will continue to operate as separate entities. Experts speculated that smaller-harder-to-trade companies will most likely switch to the Amex.

NASDAQ

The National Association of Securities Dealers Automated Quotations was founded in 1971 and was the first to use computers and high-technology telecommunications to trade—and to monitor the trading of—millions of securities daily. Today, all the major stock markets have followed suit. In terms of the number of shares traded, the NASDAQ is the largest stock exchange in the world, with a record 202 billion shares trading hands in 1998, more even than the 169.7 billion traded on the New York Stock Exchange. However, the NASDAQ's total market value ($2.6 trillion in 1998, more than double its 1995 level), still significantly trailed the NYSE's.

Online trading

Internet, or online brokerages allow people to trade stocks directly without a broker for commissions as low as $5 per trade. The number of households with such accounts increased from 2.2 million in December, 1997, to more than 6.3 million in April, 1999, according to numbers compiled by NFO Worldwide. An estimated total of eight million accounts managed approximately $400 billion in assets in 1999. The popularity of online accounts has encouraged investors to make more trades, and to buy and sell more quickly to take advantage of short-term changes in market prices. Online trading has also sparked the creation of the day trader: an investor who buys and sells thousands of shares in hundreds of different stocks each day.

Mutual funds,

in which investors pool their funds to purchase a variety of securities rather than investing in a single stock or bond, date back to 1924 in the U.S., but few Americans were aware of them until their popularity surged in the 1980s. In 1998, according to the Investment Company Institute, an estimated 77 million Americans in 44 million households owned some kind of mutual funds. Total assets of all mutual funds was $5.53 trillion in 1998, up nearly 25 percent from 1997, and more than five times the amount invested in 1990 ($1.1 trillion). More money is invested in mutual funds today than in any other financial institution—more even than in commercial banks, which held a total of $5.4 trillion in assets in 1998, according to the Federal Deposit Insurance Corporation (FDIC).

There are four kinds of mutual funds: stock (or equity), bond, hybrid, and money market. Funds

Performances of the Three Major Stock Exchanges, 1986–98

Year	NYSE	AMEX	NASDAQ
Companies listed			
1986	1,575	796	4,417
1988	1,681	896	4,451
1990	1,771	859	4,132
1995	2,675	791	5,122
1996	2,907	751	5,556
1997	3,047	771	5,487
1998	3,114	770	5,068
Shares traded (billions)			
1986	35,680	2,979	28,737
1988	40,801	2,515	31,070
1990	39,665	3,329	33,380
1995	87,217	5,072	101,158
1996	104,636	5,627	138,112
1997	133,312	6,170	163,900
1998	169,745	7,310	202,000
Dollar volume of shares traded (billions)			
1986	$1,388.8	$45.4	$378.2
1988	1,365.9	30.9	347.1
1990	1,336.2	37.7	452.4
1995	3,110.2	72.7	2,398.2
1996	4,102.1	91.3	3,301.8
1997	5,778.7	143.2	4,481.7
1998	7,395.4	283.7	5,758.6

Source: New York Stock Exchange, *Fact Book, 1998*, American Stock Exchange, *1998 Annual Report,* unpublished data, NASDAQ *Fact Book 1998.*

Milestones in the Dow Jones Industrial Average, 1906–99

Date	Average	Date	Average
Jan. 12, 1906	100	Nov. 21, 1995	5,000
Sept. 1, 1929	381	Oct. 14, 1996	6,000
June 8, 1932	41	Feb. 13, 1997	7,000
Mar. 12, 1956	500	July 16, 1997	8,000
Nov. 14, 1972	1,000	April 6, 1998	9,000
Jan. 8, 1987	2,000	Mar. 16, 1999	10,000
April 17, 1991	3,000	May 3, 1999	11,000
Feb. 23, 1995	4,000		

Source: Dow Jones.

Top U.S. Mutual Fund Managers, 1999, by Assets

Rank	Fund Manager	Assets
1.	Fidelity Investments	$738,312,907
2.	Vanguard Group	484,860,645
3.	Capital Research & Management	316,332,513
4.	Putnam Funds	228,897,476
5.	Merrill Lynch Asset Management	214,820,627
6.	Franklin Templeton Group	168,950,202
7.	TIAA-CREF	154,445,862
8.	SSB Citi Asset Management	136,836,206
9.	Federated Investors	129,700,245
10.	Morgan Stanley Dean Witter	117,582,174
11.	Oppenheimer Funds/MassMutual	115,169,016
12.	AIM Group	111,463,932
13.	American Express Funds	110,810,617
14.	Janus	108,531,120
15.	Dreyfus Corporation	108,466,691
16.	Scudder Kemper Investments	106,675,787
17.	Alliance Capital Management	102,752,305
18.	SEI Investments	100,689,682
19.	T. Rowe Price	100,198,433
20.	Prudential Mutual Funds	92,759,596
21.	Schwab Funds	90,149,681
22.	Massachusetts Financial Services	88,324,163
23.	American Century Investments	85,087,179
24.	Evergreen Funds	71,437,826
25.	NationsBanc Advisors Inc.	66,498,283

Note: As of May 31, 1999.   **Source:** Investment Company Institute.

can consist of stocks, bonds, gold, government securities, or other assets. The share price of a mutual fund, called the *net asset value (NAV)*, is the market value of all the fund's securities, minus expenses, divided by the total number of shares outstanding, and rises or falls based on the performance of the securities in which the fund is invested. Each fund employs a professional fund manager, who chooses a diverse range of securities, so that a drop in the value of one security will not cause a shock to the entire portfolio. As securities prices rise or fall, the fund manager may seek to change the composition of the fund's portfolio. Like securities, but unlike investments offered by banks, mutual funds are not insured by the FDIC or any other government agency.

There were 7,314 mutual funds in 1998, nearly double the number in 1992, representing the full spectrum of investment objectives. *Aggressive growth funds* seek the maximum capital growth but also carry the greatest risk, because the stocks they invest in are very volatile. *Income-equity funds* forgo high growth rates in favor of a constant stream of income from stocks with a history of steady dividends. *Bond funds*, which invest in corporate bonds and government-issued securities, are generally more conservative than stock funds. *Hybrid funds* invest in both stocks and bonds. *Money market funds* are called short-term funds because they invest in securities that mature in a year or less, such as Treasury bills, CDs, and commercial paper. Many money market funds offer

Number of Funds, Accounts, and Total Assets of Mutual Funds, 1970–98

Year	Total	Equity	Hybrid	Bond & Income	Money market Taxable	Money market Tax exempt
Number of Funds						
1978	505	294	N.A.	150	61	—
1980	564	288	N.A.	170	96	10
1985	1,528	579	87	404	346	111
1990	3,105	1,116	203	1,024	508	235
1995	5,761	2,193	460	2,079	672	325
1996	6,293	2,572	470	2,224	666	322
1997	6,778	2,951	501	2,219	682	331
1998	7,314	3,513	525	2,250	685	341
Number of Accounts (millions)						
1978	8.7	6.8	N.A.	1.4	0.5	—
1980	12.1	5.8	N.A.	1.5	4.8	—
1985	34.8	11.5	1.5	6.9	14.4	0.5
1990	62.0	22.4	3.2	13.4	21.6	1.4
1995	131.3	70.5	9.7	20.8	27.9	2.3
1996	150.2	85.4	12.1	20.5	29.9	2.3
1997	170.5	101.8	12.9	20.2	33.0	2.7
1998	193.9	119.8	13.8	21.3	36.4	2.4
Total Net Assets (billions)						
1970	$47.6	$45.1	N.A.	$2.5	—	—
1975	45.9	37.5	N.A.	4.7	$3.7	—
1978	55.9	32.7	N.A.	12.3	10.9	—
1980	134.8	44.4	N.A.	14.0	74.5	$1.9
1985	495.5	116.9	12.0	122.6	207.5	36.3
1990	1,065.5	245.6	37.2	284.3	414.7	83.6
1995	2,811.5	1,266.8	204.8	587.0	629.7	123.3
1996	3,526.3	1,726.1	252.9	645.4	762.0	139.8
1997	4,468.2	2,368.0	317.1	724.2	898.1	160.8
1998	5,525.2	2,978.2	364.7	830.6	1,163.2	188.5

1. Bond and Income Funds were divided into Bond Funds and Hybrid Funds beginning in 1984. Data from before 1984 in all categories is not directly comparable to later years.   **Source:** Investment Company Institute, *Mutual Fund Fact Book* (1999).

Assets of IRA Plans by Type of Investment, 1990–98

Year	Total (billions)	Bank and thrift deposits[1]		Life insurance companies		Mutual funds		Securities[2]	
		Amount (billions)	Percent of total	Amount (billions)	Percent of total	Amount (billions)	Percent of total	Amount (billions)	Percent of total
1990	$ 636	$266	41.8%	$ 53	8.3%	$140	22.0%	$177	27.8%
1995	1,289	261	20.2	94	7.3	472	36.6	461	36.2
1996	1,467	258	17.6	110	7.5	593	40.4	505	34.4
1997	1,804	254	14.1	168	9.3	761	42.2	621	34.4
1998	2,102	249	11.9	196	9.3	934	44.4	724	34.4

1. Includes Keogh deposits. 2. Stocks, bonds, CDs sold by brokers, and other investments held in brokerage accounts. **Source:** Investment Company Institute, *Mutual Fund Fact Book* (1998).

World's 25 Largest Mergers and Acquisitions

Acquiring Company	Acquired company	Date effective	Value (millions)
1. Exxon Corp.	Mobil Corp.	Dec. 1, 1998[1]	$86,355.1
2. Travelers Group	Citicorp	Oct. 8, 1998[1]	72,558.2
3. SBC Communications Inc.	Ameritech Corp.	May 11, 1998	72,356.5
4. Bell Atlantic Corp.	GTE Corp.	July 28, 1998[1]	71,323.6
5. AT&T Corp.	Tele-Communications Inc.	Aug. 9, 1999	69,896.5
6. Vodafone Group Plc.	AirTouch Communications	June 30, 1999	65,901.9
7. AT&T Corp.	MediaOne Group Inc.	Apr. 22, 1999[1]	63,115.3
8. NationsBank Corp.	BankAmerica Corp	Sept. 30, 1998	61,633.4
9. Elf Aquitaine	Total Fina SA	July 19, 1999[1]	56,209.9
10. British Petroleum Co. Plc.	Amoco Corp.	Dec. 31, 1998	55,040.1
11. Qwest Communications Intl.	US West Inc.	June 14, 1999[1]	48,439.8
12. WorldCom Inc.	MCI Communications Corp.	Sept. 14, 1998	43,351.9
13. Daimler-Benz-AG	Chrysler Corp.	Nov. 12, 1998	40,466.5
14. Viacom Inc.	CBS Corporation	Sept. 7, 1999[1]	37,300.0
15. Olivetti	Telecom Italia	May 21, 1999	34,757.9
16. Norwest Corp.	Wells Fargo & Co.	Nov. 2, 1998	34,352.6
17. Mitsubishi Bank Ltd.	Bank of Tokyo Ltd.	Apr. 1, 1996	33,787.7
18. BP Amoco Plc.	ARCO	Apr. 1, 1999[1]	33,701.9
19. SENECA Group Plc.	Astra AB	Dec. 9, 1998[1]	31,787.0
20. Shareholders	US West Media Group	June 12, 1998	31,710.9
21. Bell Atlantic Corp.	NYNEX Corp.	Aug. 15, 1997	30,786.1
22. Shareholders	Electronic Data Systems Corp.	June 10, 1996	29,687.7
23. Banc One Corp.	First Chicago NBD Corp.	Oct. 2, 1998	29,616.0
24. Kohlberg, Kravis, Roberts	RJR Nabisco Inc.	April 28, 1989	29,406.8
25. Rhone-Poulenc SA	Hoechst AG	May 17, 1999[1]	28,526.0

Note: As of Sept. 15, 1999.   1. Date merger was announced. Deal still pending final approval.   **Source:** Securities Data Company.

tax-exempt income (though their rate of return is often lower than taxable money market funds). *Special funds* meet the needs of specific investors by investing only in certain segments of financial markets (e.g. biotechnology, telecommunications, small-companies) or by pegging the fund's net asset value to one of several economic indexes (hence the name index fund). *Global equity funds* invest in the stock markets of other countries (see "The International Economy").

By far the largest segment of the mutual fund industry has been stock or equity funds. Assets of all equity funds in 1998 totaled $2.98 trillion, or 54 percent of all fund assets. The next biggest segment was taxable money market funds, which held $1.16 trillion in assets (21.1 percent of the total). Bond and income funds had assets of $830.6 billion, or 15.0 percent of the total).

Mergers and Acquisitions
Throughout the boom years of the 1980s, and then again in the '90s, an ever-increasing number of companies have sought to increase their power in the new global marketplace by buying rival companies or by merging with one. Because fierce competition tends to drive down prices, making profitability more difficult, and because one company needs fewer employees than two—not to mention the financial windfalls to the CEOs who broker the deals—the reasons for the current merger mania are very compelling.

For three consecutive years (1995-97), the value of mergers and acquisitions in the U.S. increased to record levels. More than 27,600 companies joined hands during that time, more than in the entire decade of the '80s. And the trend continues: in 1999, even more companies rushed to join forces with each other rather than be trampled by the behemoth corporations created by megamergers. In 1998, the biggest merger on record was Travelers Group's $72.6 billion acquisition of Citicrop, while the 25th-largest deal was worth $18.3 billion. A year later, a planned $86.4 billion merger between Exxon and Mobil threatened to dwarf the Travelers deal, while the 25th-largest deal was valued at $28.5 billion, or 56 percent higher than a year earlier. With more mergers announced every day, the accompanying table should be viewed only as a snapshot of this everburgeoning playing field.

▶GLOSSARY OF FINANCIAL TERMS

Arbitrage Simultaneous purchase and sale of a commodity or currency in at least two markets where price discrepancies exist. The arbitrageur makes a profit by buying an asset with a low price in one market and selling it in another market where the asset carries a higher price.

Bear/bull A bear is a speculator who expects prices to fall and sells stocks or bonds in order to buy them later at a lower price. A bull expects prices to rise and therefore buys now for resale later. Thus, a bearish (bullish) market is one in which prices are generally falling (rising).

Blue chip stock A stock that is considered a safe investment, with a low yield and a high price per share, issued by companies that are well known and have a history of good management and increasing profit levels.

Bond A debt obligation that requires the issuer to pay a fixed sum of money annually until maturity (interest payments) and then, at maturity, a fixed sum of money to repay the initial amount borrowed (principal). (See CORPORATE BONDS.)

Capital gain An increase in the market value of an asset above the price originally paid for it, realized when the asset is sold.

Capital loss A decrease in the market value of an asset below the price originally paid for it, realized when the asset is sold.

Common stock/equity A piece of paper that entitles the owner to a share of the firm's profits and a share of the voting power in shareholder elections. In other words, a shareholder is part owner of the firm. If he owns 50 percent of the issued shares of common stock (when no preferred stock is issued), he owns 50 percent of the company, and will receive 50 percent of profits paid out in dividends. Over 40 million Americans invest in common stocks.

Convertible bond A debt instrument which carries an option for the holder to convert it into a specified amount of company stock.

Corporate bonds Debt obligations that require the corporation to pay a fixed sum of money annually until maturity (interest payments) and then, at maturity, a fixed sum of money to repay the initial amount borrowed (principal). Bonds carry no claim to ownership and therefore pay no dividends, but payments to bondholders take priority over payments to stockholders.

Debentures Debt securities issued by a company, that pay a fixed interest rate, in order to raise finance for commercial or industrial operations.

Divestiture The sales by a company of a product line, subsidiary or division. The number of divestitures sold peaked in 1986, with a total of 1,316, for a record total price of $65.2 billion.

Dividends Payments made to common and preferred stockholders out of a firm's profits either in the form of cash or additional shares.

Dow Jones Industrial Average Dating back to 1893, this index of 30 blue-chip stocks in industry traded on the New York Stock Exchange (and determined by the editors of the *Wall Street Journal*) is the most widely cited indicator of how the stock market is doing.

Establishment A physical place of business activity such as a factory, assembly plant, retail store, warehouse, etc. where goods are made, stored or processed, or where services are performed.

Eurocurrency Currency of the major industrial and financial countries held in the banks of major financial and industrial countries for the purpose of lending and borrowing. Most loans are for up to one year and are used for payments of deficits. Eurodollars are U.S. dollars held in foreign banks.

Firm A business organization that owns and/or operates one or more establishments. Also called a company, enterprise or business venture. Firms can be of three types: 1) sole proprietorships—firms owned directly by one person; 2) partnerships—firms whose ownership is shared by a fixed number of proprietors; and 3) corporations—firms created by a government charter, granting them greater accessibility to financial capital through the selling of common or preferred stock, greater accessibility to debt capital through the selling of bonds, and limited liability in the event of bankruptcy.

Futures market/forward market A market in which commodities or securities are bought and sold at prices fixed now, for delivery at specified future date. Futures are traded on the American Stock Exchange; the Chicago Board of Trade; Chicago Board Options Exchange; Chicago Mercantile Exchange; Chicago Rice and Cotton Exchange; Commodity Exchange, New York (COMEX); Kansas City Board of Trade; MidAmerica Commodity Exchange, Chicago; Minneapolis Grain Exchange; New York Coffee, Sugar, and Coca Exchange (including the Citrus Associates); New York Cotton Exchange; New York Futures Exchange; and New York Mercantile Exchange; New York Stock Exchange; Pacific Stock Exchange, Los Angeles and San Francisco; and Philadelphia Stock Exchange.

Greenmail Analogous to blackmail, greenmail is the practice of purchasing enough shares in a firm or trading company to threaten a takeover, thereby forcing the owners to buy them back at a higher rate in order to retain control of the business.

Individual Retirement Account (IRA) An account set up by individual investors to hold and invest funds until retirement. Under a traditional IRA, which was established as an alternative for people not eligible for employee-sponsored pension plans, individuals may contribute up to $2,000 pre-tax per year to a tax-deferred retirement account. In 1997, Congress established the Roth IRA, which allows individuals to contribute $2,000 post-tax to a retirement account on which earnings are tax free forever in most cases.

Insider trading Trading in the stock market based on information that has not been made public, and which is intended to remain confidential—for example, information that a small company is about to become part of a national corporation. The penalties paid by individuals and corporations for such activities in recent years have reached into the hundreds of millions of dollars. Drexel Burnham Lambert, Inc., was fined $650 million to settle six charges of securities law violations; and investor Ivan Boesky was fined $100 million and imprisoned for his insider trading activities.

Junk bond/high-yield bond Bonds with a rating below investment grade (at or below Ba1 (Moody's Investors Service), at or below BB+ (Standard & Poor's), or unrated. Issuers of junk bonds are usually small companies who in the past have been limited to borrowing from banks to raise capital for corporate growth. Despite the fact that the major ratings services consider junk bonds risky (hence their name), they have a historically low default rate—only 1.5 percent between the mid 1970s and mid-1980s. The junk market grew considerably in the 1980s, and by 1987 accounted for over 25 percent of the value of all corporate bonds outstanding.

Leveraged buyout   The purchase of a company by one of its employee groups (usually upper management) or a large shareholder with borrowed funds, usually using the company's assets as security for the loans. Leveraged buy-outs have been used to combat hostile takeover bids.

Mutual fund   A pool of financial assets in which investors may buy shares and get the benefits (or share the losses) depending on the performance of the collective securities. Shares are sold publicly and can be redeemed at any time. Funds can consist of stocks, bonds, gold, government securities, or other assets, and their names are descriptive of their primary purpose; for example, bonds funds, equity-fund portfolios, income funds, money market-mutual funds, and municipal funds. (See the section on mutual funds earlier in this chapter; see also MONEY MARKET ACCOUNTS in "Money and Banking.")

Option   A contract to buy or sell commodities or securities within a given time period at a fixed price. For stocks, this period is usually three months. A contract to sell is a *put option* (or put); to buy, a *call option* (or call) and one to buy or sell is a *double option*. A buyer (seller) will gain if the trading price rises (falls) by more than the cost of entering into the contract. Options are traded on the same exchanges as futures contracts (see FUTURES MARKET).

Over-the-counter (OTC) stock   A security not listed on an exchange that is traded between two individuals. The name stems from the eighteenth century practice of merchants selling stocks over the counter in their own shops directly to investors without the use of stockbrokers or auctioneers.

Pension fund   An arrangement whereby private or public-sector employers, unions, and—as in the case of individual retirement accounts (IRAs) and Keogh plans—individuals contribute to a fund from which money is paid out to the employees, union members, or contributors (or their dependents) upon death, disability or retirement. Contributions can be based on a percentage of salary or corporate profits; in some cases employees may make voluntary or mandatory contributions to the fund. Pension fund assets are usually held in the form of securities or property with a preference for long-term assets.

Preferred stock   Similar to COMMON STOCK, except that owners of preferred stock have no voting rights, and preferred stock holders are paid their dividends at a fixed rate, before common stockholders receive any dividends.

Rating   An agency evaluation of the quality of a debt instrument or a company issuing debt. Standard & Poor's and Moody's Investment Service are the two major credit ratings agencies in the U.S. The ratings measure the safety of interest and principal payments of bonds. S&P bond ratings are, from most to least secure: AAA, AA, A, BBB, BB, B, CCC, CC, C. Moody's ratings are: Aaa, Aa, A, Baa, Ba, B, Caa, Ca, C.

Russell Indexes   These measure the performance of the largest U.S.-headquartered companies, based on total market capitalization. The Russell 3,000 Index measures the 3,000 largest U.S.-based companies (their total market capitalization represents approximately 98 percent of the investable U.S. equity market). The Russell 1,000 measures the largest 1,000 of these companies. The Russell 2,000 measures the smallest 2,000 companies in the Russell 3,000.

Securities   Financial assets (usually long-term), such as equities/stocks and debentures/bonds; may also refer to shorter-term assets such as U.S. Treasury bills.

Securities and Exchange Commission (SEC)   U.S. government agency that regulates the securities industry by requiring registration of brokers, dealers, and stock exchanges. The SEC also reviews the financial position of companies issuing securities for public sale, and investigates illegal activities such as insider trading.

Standard & Poor's 500 Composite Stock Price Index (S&P 500)   A widely used measure of the movement of the U.S. stock market. The S&P 500 was introduced in 1957 and is one of 12 leading economic indicators used by the U.S. Commerce Department. The 500 issues include 400 industrial, 40 utility, 20 transportation and 40 financial companies—primarily those listed on the New York Stock Exchange (NYSE). The index is considered to be value-weighted because each stock is weighted according to its market value. As of December 31, 1987, the market value of issues tracked by the S&P 500 was equal to approximately 70 percent of the value of all publicly traded U.S. equities. Its value is calculated on a total return basis with dividends reinvested.

Stock exchange   A market in which securities (other than bills and similar short-term instruments) issued by central and local government bodies, and public companies are traded (e.g., the New York Stock Exchange, the American Stock Exchange, the London Stock Exchange). Only members of a stock exchange may deal on it, and membership and arrangements for trading are strictly regulated. Stock exchanges in the United States are the American Stock Exchange (New York); Boston Stock Exchange; Cincinnati Stock Exchange; Intermountain Stock Exchange (Salt Lake City); Midwest Stock Exchange (Chicago); New York Stock Exchange; Pacific Stock Exchange (Los Angeles, San Francisco); Philadelphia Stock Exchange; and Spokane Stock Exchange.

Stock market   An institution where stocks and shares are traded, existing in all advanced Western countries. Stock markets enable companies to more easily raise equity or loan capital from the public since investors can quickly realize their holdings because of the stock exchange share quotation. In other words, there is a ready market. The principal overseas stock markets are located in Amsterdam, Brussels, Frankfurt, Hong Kong, Johannesburg, London, Milan, Paris, Singapore, Stockholm, Sydney, Tokyo, Toronto, and Zurich.

Stockbroker   An individual who acts as an adviser and an agent (working on commission), to buy and sell stocks on behalf of a client on a particular stock exchange where the stockbroker is a member.

Wilshire 5000 Index   The broadest measure of the U.S. stock market, containing some 5,000 issues including all publicly traded U.S. stocks for which daily pricing is available (i.e., includes all Amex, NYSE, and OTC stocks).

Yield   The annual return on a security, as a percentage of its current market price. A stock's dividend yield is the annual dividend divided by its current stock price.

▶BIG BUSINESS: THE *FORTUNE* 500

The ultimate measure of success in the business world is inclusion on *Fortune* magazine's annual list of the 500 biggest companies in America. In recent years, the inclusion of service companies (for many years, Fortune had ranked service corporations and industrial corporations in separate lists) and the global trend toward mega-mergers creating monolithic organizations have raised the bar for admission to this select circle. As recently as 1995, the 500th-ranked corporation had revenues of $2.43 billion, whereas in 1998, the 500th-ranked company's revenues topped $2.90 billion. At the very top, the change has been even more pronounced. Although GM's revenues have actually dropped from $168.8 billion to just over $161 billion over that same time period, the revenues of the 50th-ranked corporation grew from $17.7 billion (Sara Lee) in 1995 to $23.8 billion (ConAgra) in 1998.

The accompanying tables list the top 100 companies of the Fortune 500 by revenues, the top 3 companies in several performance categories, and the top companies by industry.

The Top U.S. Companies, by Industry and *Fortune* 1,000 Rank, 1998

Industry, Company (*Fortune* 1,000 Rank)

Aerospace
Boeing (9)
Lockheed Martin (41)
United Technologies (43)
AlliedSignal (100)
Airlines
AMR (American) (71)
UAL (United) (82)
Delta Air Lines (111)
Apparel
Nike (166)
VF (301)
Reebok International (458)
Beverages
Pepsico (54)
Coca-Cola (73)
Coca-Cola Enterprises (119)
Chemicals
E.I. Du Pont Nemours (16)
Dow Chemical (75)
Monsanto (187)
Commercial Banks
BankAmerica Corp. (11)
Chase Manhattan Corp. (23)
Bank One Corp. (44)
First Union Corp. (56)
Wells Fargo (62)
J.P. Morgan & Co. (76)
Computer/Data Services
Electronic Data Service (90)
Unisys (232)
Computer Sciences (253)
Computer Software
Microsoft (109)
Oracle (234)
Computer Assoc. Intl. (335)
Computers, Office Equipment
IBM (6)
Hewlett-Packard (14)
Compaq Computer (28)
Xerox (63)
Dell Computer (78)
Electronics, Electrical Equipment
General Electric (5)
Lucent Technologies (33)
Motorola (34)
Raytheon (69)
Engineering, Construction
Halliburton (85)
Fluor (116)
Foster Wheeler (339)
Entertainment
Walt Disney (53)
Time Warner (108)
Viacom (138)
Food
ConAgra (50)
Sara Lee (64)
RJR Nabisco Holdings (89)
Archer Daniels Midland (91)

Food & Drug Stores
Kroger (36)
Safeway (48)
American Stores (67)
Albertson's (92)
Walgreen (98)
CVS (99)
Forest & Paper Products
International Paper (70)
Georgia-Pacific (122)
Kimberly-Clark (136)
General Merchandisers
Wal-Mart Stores (3)
Sears Roebuck (15)
Kmart (21)
Dayton Hudson (30)
JCPenney (31)
Federated Dept. Stores (95)
Health Care
Cigna (57)
Aetna (61)
Columbia/HCA Healthcare (74)
United Healthcare (84)
Industrial & Farm Equipment
Caterpillar (58)
Deere (113)
Ingersoll-Rand (199)
Insurance
State Farm Insurance (12)
TIAA-CREF (18)
Prudential of America (20)
American Int'l Group (22)
Metropolitan Life (39)
Allstate (42)
Loews (60)
New York Life (68)
Mail, Package Freight Delivery
United Parcel Service (46)
FDX (94)
Pittston (403)
Metal Products
Gillette (159)
Crown Cork & Seal (198)
ITW (290)
Metals
Alcoa (96)
Reynolds Metals (281)
Bethlehem Steel (346)
Motor Vehicles & Parts
General Motors (1)
Ford Motor (2)
Dana (127)
Network Communications
Cisco Systems (192)
3Com (303)
Bay Networks (573)
Petroleum Refining
Exxon (4)
Mobil (13)
Texaco (24)
Chevron (38)
USX (47)

Pharmaceuticals
Merck (37)
Johnson & Johnson (51)
Bristol-Myers Squibb (7)
Pipelines
Enron (27)
Dynegy (110)
Williams (216)
Publishing & Printing
R.R. Donnelley & Sons (277)
Gannett (315)
McGraw-Hill (406)
Railroads
Union Pacific (154)
CSX (162)
Burlington No. Santa Fe (178)
Savings Institutions
Washington Mutual (128)
Golden West Financial (471)
Golden State Bancorp. (484)
Securities
Merrill Lynch (19)
Morgan Stanley (29)
Lehman Brothers Hldgs. (66)
Semiconductors
Intel (40)
Texas Instruments (191)
Advanced Micro Devices. (550)
Soaps & Cosmetics
Procter & Gamble (17)
Colgate-Palmolive (177)
Avon Products (308)
Telecommunications
AT&T (10)
Bell Atlantic (25)
SBC Communications (35)
GTE (45)
BellSouth (52)
MCI Worldcom (80)
Ameritech (87)
Sprint (90)
Temporary Help
Manpower (183)
Olsten (338)
Kelly Services (377)
Tobacco
Philip Morris (8)
Universal (361)
Dimon (546)
Toys & Sporting Goods
Mattel (331)
Hasbro (445)
Trucking
CNF Transportation (321)
Yellow (449)
Roadway Express (524)
Utilities, Gas & Electric
PG&E Corp. (68)
Duke Energy (81)
Texas Utilities (105)

Source: *Fortune* (April 28, 1999)

Fortune 500 Performance Leaders, 1998

Profits	(millions)
1. Ford Motor (2)	$22,071
2. General Electric (5)	9,296
3. AT&T (10)	6,398

Market Value	(millions)
1. Microsoft (109)	$418,579
2. General Electric (5)	360,251
3. Wal-Mart Stores (3)	212,850

Return to Investors (1 year)	(percent)
1. Dell Computer (78)	248.5%
2. Best Buy (195)	232.9
3. Apple Computer (273)	211.9

Return on Revenues	(percent)
1. Times Mirror (446)	43.1%
2. Microsoft (109)	31.0
3. Tele-Communications (228)	26.4

Return on Assets	(percent)
1. Limited (169)	45.1%
2. Ryerson Tull (376)	41.0
3. Times Mirror (446)	33.6

Return to Investors (10 years)	(percent)
1. Dell Computer (78)	79.7%
2. EMC (386)	69.0
3. Charles Schwab (435)	63.4

Note: Numbers in parentheses reflect overall Fortune 500 rank.

Fortune 100 Largest U.S. Corporations, 1998

Rank	Company (1997 Rank)	Revenues (millions)	Rank	Company (1997 Rank)	Revenues (millions)
1.	General Motors (1)	$161,315.0	50.	ConAgra (45)	$23,840.5
2.	Ford Motor Company (2)	144,416.0	51.	Johnson & Johnson (49)	23,657.0
3.	Wal-Mart Stores (4)	139,208.0	52.	BellSouth (56)	23,123.0
4.	Exxon (3)	100,697.0	53.	Walt Disney (51)	22,976.0
5.	General Electric (5)	100,469.0	54.	Pepsico (31)	22,348.0
6.	International Business Machines (6)	81,667.0	55.	Ingram Micro (79)	22,034.0
7.	Citigroup (17)	76,431.0	56.	First Union Corp. (96)	21,543.0
8.	Philip Morris (9)	57,813.0	57.	Cigna (59)	21,437.0
9.	Boeing (11)	56,154.0	58.	Caterpillar (66)	20,977.0
10.	AT&T (10)	53,588.0	59.	McKesson HBOC (105)	20,857.3
11.	Bank of America (54)	50,777.0	60.	Loews (63)	20,713.0
12.	Mobil (8)	47,678.0	61.	Aetna (71)	20,604.1
13.	Hewlett-Packard (14)	47,061.0	62.	Wells Fargo (157)	20,482.0
14.	State Farm Insurance Cos. (13)	44,620.9	63.	Xerox (72)	20,019.0
15.	Sears Roebuck (16)	41,322.0	64.	Sara Lee (61)	20,011.0
16.	E.I.du Pont de Nemours (15)	39,130.0	65.	PG&E Corp. (85)	19,942.0
17.	Procter & Gamble (20)	37,154.0	66.	Lehman Brothers Holdings (77)	19,894.0
18.	TIAA-CREF (30)	35,889.1	67.	American Stores (65)	19,866.7
19.	Merrill Lynch (24)	35,853.0	68.	New York Life Insurance (67)	19,848.9
20.	Prudential Insurance Company of America (18)	34,427.0	69.	Raytheon (100)	19,530.0
			70.	International Paper (58)	19,500.0
21.	Kmart (23)	33,674.0	71.	AMR (70)	19,205.0
22.	American International Group (26)	33,296.0	72.	American Express (73)	19,132.0
23.	Chase Manhattan Corp. (27)	32,379.0	73.	Coca-Cola (68)	18,813.0
24.	Texaco (12)	31,707.0	74.	Columbia/HCAHealthcare (69)	18,681.0
25.	Bell Atlantic (28)	31,565.9	75.	Dow Chemical (60)	18,441.0
26.	Fannie Mae (33)	31,498.8	76.	J.P. Morgan and Co. (74)	18,425.0
27.	Enron (57)	31,260.0	77.	Bristol-Myers Squibb (78)	18,283.6
28.	Compaq Computer (42)	31,169.0	78.	Dell Computer (125)	18,243.0
29.	Morgan Stanley Dean Witter Discover (35)	31,131.0	79.	Freddie Mac (95)	18,048.0
30.	Dayton Hudson (34)	30,951.0	80.	MCI WorldCom (62)	17,678.0
31.	JCPenney (25)	30,678.0	81.	Duke Energy (81)	17,610.0
32.	Home Depot (44)	30,219.0	82.	UAL (75)	17,561.0
33.	Lucent Technologies (37)	30,147.0	83.	Republic Industries (151)	17,487.3
34.	Motorola (29)	29,398.0	84.	United Healthcare (130)	17,355.0
35.	SBC Communications (40)	28,777.0	85.	Halliburton (177)	17,353.1
36.	Kroger (36)	28,203.3	86.	Supervalu (80)	17,201.4
37.	Merck (46)	26,898.2	87.	Ameritech (82)	17,154.0
38.	Chevron (19)	26,801.0	88.	Sprint (90)	17,134.3
39.	Metropolitan Life Insurance (43)	26,735.0	89.	RJR Nabisco Holdings (76)	17,037.0
40.	Intel (38)	26,273.0	90.	Electronic Data Systems (88)	16,891.0
41.	Lockheed Martin (32)	26,266.0	91.	Archer Daniels Midland (99)	16,108.6
42.	Allstate (39)	25,879.0	92.	Albertson's (92)	16,005.1
43.	United Technologies (41)	25,715.0	93.	Cardinal Health (145)	15,918.1
44.	Bank One Corp. (113)	25,595.0	94.	FDX (134)	15,872.8
45.	GTE (48)	25,473.0	95.	Federated Department Stores (83)	15,833.0
46.	United Parcel Service (52)	24,788.0	96.	ALCOA (104)	15,489.4
47.	USX (55)	24,754.0	97.	Sysco (94)	15,327.5
48.	Safeway (50)	24,484.2	98.	Walgreen (108)	15,307.0
49.	Costco (53)	24,269.9	99.	CVS (117)	15,273.6
			100.	Allied-Signal (93)	15,128.0

Source: *Fortune* (April 26, 1999).

▶ SMALL BUSINESS

Small businesses account for 99 percent of the 23.3 million nonfarm businesses in the United States today, according to the Small Business Administration. Sole proprietorships make up 16.7 million of these small businesses, while 1.6 million are partnerships, and 5 million are corporations (these figures are based on tax returns, so the number of sole proprietorships may be inflated by artists, freelance writers, and other self-employed people who are not technically businesses). As of 1996, small businesses employed 53 percent of the private work force, made 47 of percent of all sales in America, and accounted for 51 percent of all private sector output. According to the Department of Labor, about 750,000 new small businesses are created every year; about 10 percent of them fail.

Franchising Franchising, a century-old tradition, has never been more popular in the United States than it is now. There were 540,000 franchised businesses in 1995, employing more than 8 million people, and doing more than $758 billion in sales. Franchised business represents nearly 40 percent of all U.S. retail sales. The Department of Commerce estimates that by the year 2000, franchising will account for more than half of all sales.

Top 50 Franchises, by Number of Franchises, 1998

Rank Franchise	Business	Franchise fees	Number of franchises
1. Kumon Math & Reading Centers	Supplemental education	$500	19,667
2. McDonald's	Hamburgers, chicken, salads	45,000	16,319
3. 7-Eleven Convenience Stores	Convenience stores	12,500+ (varies)	14,549
4. Subway	Submarine sandwiches	10,000	13,395
5. Jani-King	Commercial cleaning services	6,500-33,000	7,038
6. KFC	Chicken	25,000	6,635
7. Dairy Queen	Soft-serve dairy products/sandwiches	20,000/35,000	5,800
8. Jazzercise Inc.	Dance/exercise classes	325/650	4,909
9. Dunkin' Donuts	Donuts & baked goods	40,000	4,813
10. Yogen Fruz Worldwide	Frozen yogurt & ice cream	25,000	4,722
11. Coverall Cleaning Concepts	Commercial office cleaning	5,000-32,200	4,419
12. ServiceMaster	Commercial/residential contract cleaning	14,700-26,500	4,210
13. Snap-on Tools	Professional tools & equipment	5,000	4,157
14. Baskin-Robbins USA Co	Ice cream & yogurt	30,000	4,111
15. Wendy's Int'l. Inc.	Quick-service restaurant	25,000	4,032
16. Chem-Dry	Carpet, drapery & upholstery cleaning	18,950	3,912
17. Mail Boxes Etc.	Postal/business/communications services	29,9500	3,655
18. Re/Max Int'l. Inc.	Real estate services	7,500-25,000	3,109
19. Arby's Inc.	Roast beef sandwiches, chicken, subs	25,000/37,5000	3,105
20. Coldwell Banker Real Estate	Real estate brokerage	12,500-27,500	2,954
21. Taco Bell Corp	Mexican fast-food restaurant	45,000	2,927
22. TCBY Treats	Frozen yogurt, ice cream,	5,000-20,000	2,913
23. Novus Windshield Repair	Windshield repair	16,500	2,519
24. Budget Rent A Car	Auto and truck rentals	20,000+	2,490
25. Merle Norman Cosmetics	Cosmetics studios	19,46000	2,029
26. CleanNet USA Inc.	Commercial office cleaning	29,500-32,000	2,019
27. Blimpie Int'l. Inc.	Submarine sandwiches	18,000	1,982
28. RadioShack	Consumer electronics	7,500	1,963
29. Jackson Hewitt Tax Service	Computerized tax prep./electronic filing services	25,000	1,836
30. Super 8 Motels Inc.	Economy motels	20,000+	1,715
31. Tim Hortons	Donuts & baked goods	35,000	1,529
32. Sonic Drive In Restaurants	Drive-in restaurant	30,000	1,512
33. The Prudential Real Estate Affiliates Inc.	Real estate brokerage	25,000	1,450
34. Miracle Ear Hearing Systems	Hearing aids	30,000+	1,374
35. A & W Restaurants Inc	Burgers, hot dogs, root beer	20,000	1,347
36. Fantastic Sams	Hair salons	10,000-30,000	1,313
37. Carlson Wagonlit Travel	Travel agency	39,500/34,500	1,302
38. GNC Franchising Inc.	Vitamin & nutrition stores	30,000	1,290
39. The Medicine Shoppe	Pharmacy	10,000-18,000	1,249
40. Papa John's Pizza	Pizza	20,000	1,247
41. Thrifty Rent-A-Car System	Vehicle rentals and leasing	10,500	1,140
42. Merry Maids	Residential cleaning	13,500-21,500	1,128
43. Matco Tools	Automotive/professional tools & equipment	50,300-127,600	1,106
44. Great Clips Inc	Family hair salons	17,500	1,098
45. Popeyes Chicken & Biscuits	Fried chicken & biscuits	15,000/17,500	1,065
46. Blockbuster Video	Videotape sales & rentals	10,000-55,000	1,010
47. Futurekids Inc.	Children's computer learning	35,000	996
48. Ramada Franchise Systems Inc.	Limiteds/inns/plaza hotels	Varies	965
49. Jiffy Lube International Inc.	Fast oil change	35,000	963
50. Church's Chicken	Southern fried chicken & biscuits	5,000/15,000	904

Note: Includes only companies that have a U.S. disclosure document verified by *Entrepreneur* magazine. Does not include franchises owned by the company.   **Source:** *Entrepreneur* (Jan. 1999). Reprinted by permission.

ADVERTISING

Few facts and figures reveal the extraordinary growth of the mass-consumption society as vividly as those dealing with the advertising business. In 1950, as the postwar economy began to heat up, American business spent $5.7 billion to advertise its goods and services; by 1960 that figure would double, and then almost double again by 1970. Between 1970 and 1990, as the Baby Boom generation entered the marketplace and the economy expanded, advertising expenditures grew at a spiraling rate, topping $100 billion in 1986. That rate of growth has not been sustained, but advertising spending continues to reach new highs every year, nevertheless. Total expenditures on all forms of advertising in 1997 were more than $201 billion.

Nearly 60 percent of all advertising dollars are spent to place ads in newspapers or magazines or to run commercials on radio and television. The biggest advertisers are the nation's largest manufacturers of automobiles, food, soft drinks, tobacco, and beer. Most advertising dollars are filtered through about 13,000 advertising agencies who mainly create the ads and buy the space or time from the media. The agency business has undergone a dramatic restructuring recently, as the corporate raider mentality invaded Madison Avenue with a vengeance. Many of the largest agencies, most of them with worldwide connections, have merged to form enormous corporations. In 1997, the New York-based Omnicom Group acquired the GGT Group to become the world's largest advertising organization. Omnicom had a worldwide income of more than $4.8 billion in 1998; Interpublic Group of Companies, also based in New York, was second, with a worldwide income of $4.3 billion. American advertising agencies within the Omnicom Group include BBDO Worldwide, DDB Needham, and TBWA International (Chiat/Day). Interpublic's agencies include Ammirati Puris Lintas, Lowe Group, and Draft Worldwide.

Advertising Expenditures in the U.S., 1776–1998 (in millions)

Year	Amount[1]	Year	Amount[1]
1776	$0.2	1940	$2,110
1800	1	1950	5,700
1820	3	1960	11,960
1840	7	1970	19,550
1850	12	1975	28,160
1860	22	1980	54,780
1867	40	1985	94,750
1880	175	1990	128,640
1890	300	1995	160,930
1900	450	1996	175,230
1909	1,000	1997	187,529
1915	1,100	1998	201,594

1. These are estimated figures of the monies spent on placing advertising in all media; the costs of producing the advertising are not included.   **Source:** *Advertising Age.*

Total U.S. Advertising Volume by Medium, 1997–98

Medium	1997 Expenditures (millions)	1997 Percent share	1998 Expenditures (millions)	1998 Percent share	Percent change 1997–98
Newspapers, total	$41,670	22.2%	$44,292	22.0%	6.4%
National	5,016	2.7	5,402	2.7	7.7
Local	36,654	19.5	38,890	19.3	6.1
Broadcast TV, total	44,519	23.8	39,173	19.4	6.1
Four TV networks	13,020	7.0	13,736	6.8	5.5
Cable TV networks	5,454	2.9	12,105	6.0	6.9
Syndication[1]	2,438	1.3	2,609	1.3	7.0
Spot (national)	9,999	5.3	10,659	5.3	6.6
Spot (local)	11,436	6.1	12,169	6.0	6.4
Cable TV, total	7,237	3.9	8,301	4.1	14.7
Cable networks	5,067	2.7	5,827	2.9	15.0
Spot (local)	2,172	1.2	2,474	1.2	14.0
Radio, total	13,491	7.1	15,073	7.5	11.7
Network	560	0.3	622	0.3	11.0
Spot (national)	2,455	1.3	2,823	1.4	15.0
Spot (local)	10,476	5.5	11,628	5.8	11.0
Yellow pages, total	11,423	6.1	11,990	5.9	5.0
National	1,711	0.9	1,870	0.9	9.3
Local	9,712	5.2	10,120	5.0	4.2
Direct mail	36,890	19.7	39,620	19.7	7.4
Business papers	4,109	2.2	4,232	2.1	3.0
Billboards, total	1,455	0.8	1,576	0.8	8.3
National	795	0.4	845	0.4	6.3
Local	660	0.4	731	0.4	10.8
Internet. total	600	0.3	1,050	0.5	75.0
Miscellaneous, total	23,827	12.7	25,769	12.8	7.6
National	17,640	9.4	19,153	9.5	7.9
Local	6,187	3.3	6,616	3.3	6.9
Total national	110,232	58.8	118,966	59.0	7.9
Total local	77,297	41.2	82,628	41.0	6.9
Grand total	$187,529	100.0%	$201,594	100.0%	7.5%

1. Includes UPN and WB. **Source:** *Advertising Age*, May 17, 1999. Reprinted by permission.

Top 25 U.S.-Based Consolidated Ad Agencies, by Gross Domestic Income, 1998 (Millions Of Dollars)

U.S. rank/Agency, headquarters	U.S. gross income	U.S. gross billings	U.S. employees	World-wide gross income	Rank by world-wide gross income
1. DDB Needham Worldwide, New York	$732.0	$6,673.0	6,461	$1,605.0	3
2. McCann-Erickson Worldwide, New York	690.3	6,418.5	3,468	1,952.0	1
3. BBDO Worldwide, New York	585.4	3,904.6	4,806	1,655.7	2
4. Young & Rubicam, New York	582.8	6,287.7	2,069	1,354.2	4
5. Grey Advertising, New York	555.2	3,731.5	3,161	1,160.7	6
6. Ammirati Puris Lintas, New York	514.8	4,149.3	2,945	1,014.9	9
7. J. Walter Thompson, New York	478.8	3,347.0	2,401	1,240.7	5
8. Leo Burnett Co., Chicago	396.3	2,703.5	2,342	949.8	10
9. Ogilvy & Mather Worldwide, New York	380.8	3,456.3	1,972	1,117.9	8
10. Euro RSCG Worldwide, New York	366.3	4,161.5	1,477	1,129.8	7
11. Foote, Cone & Belding, Chicago	320.4	3,725.1	2,098	532.3	15
12. D'Arcy Masius Benton & Bowles, N.Y.	311.8	3,214.5	2,297	736.9	13
13. Lowe Group Worldwide, New York	292.2	2,084.6	1,655	553.7	14
14. Brann Worldwide, Deerfield, Ill.	287.6	1,918.2	N.A.	435.7	17
15. Carlson Marketing Group, Minneapolis	254.1	1,844.7	2,457	326.8	21
16. Saatchi & Saatchi, New York	244.1	3,137.2	1,295	495.7	16
17. TMP Worldwide, New York	239.2	2,641.7	N.A.	349.3	20
18. Bozell Worldwide, New York	234.7	2,140.0	1,661	371.9	19
19. TBWA International, New York	231.8	1,739.8	1,945	818.8	12
20. US Web/CKS, Santa Clara, Calif.	208.6	N.A.	N.A	228.6	23
21. Draft Worldwide, Chicago	180.6	1,337.5	1,700	238.9	22
22. Publicis Worldwide, New York	172.5	1,432.8	1,057	860.4	11
23. CommonHealth USA, Parsippany, N.J.	141.8	797.8	820	141.8	24
24. Nelson Communications, New York	130.8	1,027.4	1459	N.A.	N.A.
25. Bronner Slosberg Humphrey, Boston	124.2	1,402.4	N.A	N.A.	N.A.

Note: N.A.= not available. Includes income from advertising-related subsidiaries and international networks.
Source: *Advertising Age* (April 19, 1999); reprinted by permission of Crain Communications, Inc.

The 100 Leading U.S. Advertisers, 1991—98

1998 Rank, Company (1997 rank)	Total spending (millions of dollars)			
	1991	1995	1997	1998
1. General Motors Corp. (1)	$1,056.5	$1,499.6	$2,226.9	$2,121.0
2. Procter and Gamble Co. (2)	1,166.4	1,507.4	1,703.1	1,724.3
3. Chrysler Corp. (4)	414.8	954.7	1,311.8	1,410.7
4. Philip Morris Cos. Inc. (3)	1,110.4	1,397.7	1,319.0	1,264.4
5. Ford Motor Co. (5)	517.7	891.8	973.1	1,147.6
6. Time Warner Inc. (7)	311.3	543.0	779.1	829.2
7. Walt Disney Co. (8)	257.3	777.8	746.3	809.9
8. Sears Roebuck & Co. (10)	462.3	557.8	734.1	720.5
9. Unilever PLC (12)	371.4	442.7	619.0	691.2
10. Diageo PLC(11)	N.A	N.A	685.0	659.1
11. Johnson & Johnson (9)	371.1	601.3	738.7	658.8
12. MCI Communications Corp. (22)	94.1	322.6	455.4	658.8
13. Toyota Motor Corp. (15)	442.5	513.4	592.3	652.0
14. Ford Motor Co. Local Dealers (14)	87.4	586.4	609.5	633.2
15. News Corp. Ltd. (13)	358.6	275.9	613.8	611.4
16. McDonald's Corp. (16)	387.4	490.6	580.8	571.7
17. Sony Corp. (19)	262.8	431.0	493.3	567.1
18. Federated Dept. Stores Inc. (17)	111.4	407.6	532.5	563.9
19. AT&T Corp. (20)	391.7	675.2	475.9	556.8
20. National Amusements Inc. (24)	N.A.	404.2	450.6	497.7
21. Tricon Global Restaurants Inc. (N.A.)	N.A.	N.A.	N.A.	496.6
22. May Department Stores Co. (25)	194.0	339.4	446.0	488.2
23. Honda Motor Co. Ltd. (26)	242.5	388.8	436.5	484.9
24. General Motor.- Local Dealers (21)	123.6	460.7	469.0	473.9
25. General Motors Dealers Assn. (18)	198.0	503.7	512.1	473.2
26. Circuit City Stores Inc. (27)	128.2	291.6	433.1	472.7
27. Ford Motor Co. Dealers Assn. (31)	126.1	315.6	372.3	468.3
28. Political Adv. (N.A.)	N.A.	N.A.	N.A.	467.3
29. Nissan Motor Co. Ltd. (23)	212.0	367.7	452.7	461.3
30. General Mills Inc. (28)	419.1	367.7	416.9	430.5
31. L'Oreal SA (37)	N.A.	N.A.	325.4	403.1

1998 Rank, Company (1997 rank)	Total spending (millions of dollars)			
	1991	1995	1997	1998
32. Warner-Lambert Co. (32)	$224.5	$308.2	$371.6	$391.8
33. Chrysler Corp. Local Dealers (36)	43.0	231.8	330.5	385.9
34. Dayton Hudson Corp. (34)	108.7	259.3	334.0	377.6
35. JC Penney Co. Inc. (33)	105.2	273.9	362.5	372.0
36. Sprint Corp. (45)	N.A.	213.9	290.5	359.1
37. Toyota Motor Co. Ltd. Local Dealers (43)	68.7	280.9	302.6	350.8
38. U.S. Government (38)	123.4	219.9	323.9	348.1
39. Anheuser-Busch Cos. Inc. (49)	327.9	320.5	264.2	340.7
40. PepsiCo Inc. (6)	542.0	730.2	797.4	339.4
41. RJR Nabisco Holdings Corp. (44)	N.A.	243.2	295.0	325.7
42. Seagram Co. Ltd. (41)	N.A.	333.1	311.3	325.1
43. Kellogg Co. (29)	381.3	488.2	403.6	324.3
44. Bristol-Myers Squibb Co. (30)	184.0	219.4	398.3	323.3
45. American Home Products Corp. (35)	290.6	355.5	333.7	321.5
46. Coca-Cola Co. (39)	218.8	238.2	316.3	315.8
47. K Mart Corp. (46)	186.5	241.2	268.9	314.3
48. IBM Corp. (47)	49.5	289.8	265.7	306.5
49. American Express Co. (40)	156.2	210.4	314.6	296.0
50. Schering-Plough Corp. (90)	95.9	104.0	139.4	295.4
51. Valassis Communications Inc. (48)	239.6	229.2	264.7	287.2
52. Mars Inc. (42)	128.2	210.1	310.6	276.5
53. Nestlé S.A. (54)	307.6	490.1	236.1	273.8
54. Chrysler Corp. Dealer Assoc. (67)	90.8	175.4	191.3	265.8
55. Hasbro Inc. (64)	161.1	201.7	194.8	264.2
56. Volkswagen A.G. (82)	N.A.	N.A.	157.8	254.4
57. Mattel Inc. (52)	63.8	184.5	245.6	245.2
58. Campbell Soup Co. (51)	109.5	169.0	250.8	244.8
59. Wal-Mart Stores Inc. (77)	76.7	143.2	172.7	240.7
60. SmithKline Beecham PLC (50)	83.3	173.2	261.8	239.0
61. Clorox Co. (60)	127.8	157.8	203.0	237.4
62. Microsoft Corp. (66)	N.A.	147.7	193.2	236.1
63. Bayer Group (70)	55.8	160.5	183.1	235.1
64. Pfizer Inc. (63)	N.A.	N.A.	197.7	234.3
65. Visa USA Inc. (53)	52.1	154.6	242.0	226.1
66. Bell Atlantic Corp. (59)	N.A.	N.A.	210.3	225.3
67. Novartis AG (56)	N.A.	N.A.	227.1	220.8
68. Home Depot Inc. (68)	N.A.	96.6	189.5	217.9
69. Toyota Motor Corp. Dealers Assn. (71)	73.4	109.9	180.9	217.3
70. S.C. Johnson & Sons Inc (72)	93.1	115.6	177.9	217.0
71. Dillard Department Stores Inc. (84)	26.2	113.2	154.5	211.2
72. SBC Communications Inc. (65)	N.A.	N.A.	194.5	211.2
73. Gap Inc. (N.A.)	N.A.	N.A.	N.A.	206.9
74. Best Buy Co. (79)	N.A.	94.0	169.2	206.7
75. First Union Corp. (N.A.)	N.A.	N.A.	N.A.	203.9
76. Mazda Motor Corp. (55)	157.2	241.3	232.2	199.6
77. Nike Inc. (58)	109.5	146.3	211.2	198.1
78. Nissan Motor Co. Ltd. Local Dealers (61)	61.1	179.4	202.9	196.7
79. Wendy's International Inc. (76)	94.4	161.3	173.1	190.3
80. Ralston Purina Co. (78)	141.6	150.0	169.7	189.3
81. Hershey Foods Corp. (73)	74.0	111.7	177.7	186.2
82. Glaxo Wellcome PLC (62)	N.A.	N.A.	200.8	183.8
83. Gateway Inc. (N.A.)	N.A.	N.A.	N.A.	183.2
84. Quaker Oats Co. (74)	111.7	133.1	177.0	180.0
85. Kimberly-Clark Corp. (99)	85.4	124.8	125.8	175.6
86. Mitsubishi Motors Corp. (95)	77.0	133.6	131.2	174.7
87. MacAndrews & Forbes Holdings Inc. (83)	N.A.	N.A.	155.9	172.6
88. Honda Motor Co. Ltd. Local Dealers (85)	37.1	132.7	151.8	167.1
89. Gillette Co. (80)	93.1	122.6	167.7	163.7
90. Morgan Stanley Dean Witter Discover (86)	N.A.	119.7	148.0	160.5
91. Credit Lyonnais S.A. (N.A.)	N.A.	N.A.	N.A.	160.5
92. Mastercard International Inc. (N.A.)	N.A.	N.A.	N.A.	157.5
93. Philips Electronics NV (57)	N.A.	N.A.	226.1	156.3
94. Montgomery Ward & Co. Inc. (75)	63.6	115.2	174.1	155.0
95. Cendant Corp. (N.A.)	N.A.	N.A.	N.A.	153.3
96. Eastman Kodak Co. (97)	N.A.	N.A.	128.8	151.1
97. Sara Lee Corp. (92)	129.5	199.0	138.8	150.1
98. Merck & Co. Inc.(81)	N.A.	N.A.	158.5	147.6
99. Compaq Computer Corp. (N.A.)	N.A.	N.A.	N.A.	144.7
100. Darden Restaurants (93)	N.A.	133.5	138.5	139.6
Total Top 100 companies	N.A.	N.A.	$36,389.1	$39,018.5

Note: The top 100 companies in previous years are not the same as in 1997.
Source: Competitive Media Reporting, *Top 100 Companies by 11-Media Advertising 1998* (1999).

Education

The American people's unwavering commitment to public education dates back more than 150 years. Fueled by a demand for literacy from two different creeds, one described in the Bible, the other in the Declaration of Independence, the American system of education grew to be an essential element in our faith that this nation was uniquely the land of opportunity.

Today that belief has evolved into what is called equality of opportunity, and this vital idea has helped to create a school system whose size, scope, and ambitions are unrivalled by any Western democracy. Over 65 million students and nearly 4 million teachers, administrators, and support staff are directly involved in education. The cost of this undertaking is, of course, staggering: more than half a trillion dollars annually—close to $7,000 per student—or 7.2 percent of the gross domestic product, virtually all of it for public education. The portion of GDP spent on education rose rapidly between 1959 to 1969, declined in the 1970s as enrollment in elementary and secondary schools fell, and began rising steadily again in 1984. Since 1990, it has remained relatively stable. And while some complain bitterly about the quality of the results, or about overt waste, mismanagement, and even fraud, no one any longer questions the essential role of education in American life today.

▶ PUBLIC ELEMENTARY AND SECONDARY SCHOOLS

Expenditures on public elementary and secondary schools have been increasing faster than inflation in almost every year since figures were first kept in 1900. The exception was the period between 1978 and 1982, when inflation outpaced increases in expenditures. Total expenditures for public elementary and secondary schools topped $300 billion in 1997-98; and expenditures per student were $6,943. The accompanying table shows that even after adjusting for inflation, the amount spent to educate each student at public elementary and secondary schools continues to skyrocket.

In 1979, a historic shift occurred in the source of money to operate the American public school system. That was the year the state share of revenues rose above the local share for the first time. The federal share for elementary and secondary schools has always been relatively small.

Enrollment in public elementary schools declined dramatically from 1970 to 1985 (from 32.6 million to 27.0 million) as the number of young

Revenues For Public Elementary and Secondary Schools, 1920–96

School year	Total revenues (millions)	Percentage Federal	State	Local[1]
1919–20	$970	0.3%	16.5%	83.2%
1929–30	2,089	0.4	16.9	82.7
1939–40	2,261	1.8	30.3	68.0
1949–50	5,437	2.9	39.8	57.3
1959–60	14,747	4.4	39.1	56.5
1969–70	40,267	8.0	39.9	52.1
1974–75	64,445	9.0	42.0	49.0
1979–80	96,881	9.8	46.8	43.4
1984–85	137,295	6.6	48.9	44.4
1989–90	208,548	6.1	47.3	46.6
1990–91	223,341	6.2	47.2	46.7
1991–92	234,581	6.6	46.4	47.0
1992–93	247,626	7.0	45.8	47.2
1993–94	260,159	7.1	45.2	47.8
1994–95	273,149	6.8	46.8	46.4
1995–96	287,703	6.6	47.5	45.9

1. Includes a relatively small amount from nongovernmental sources (gifts and tuition and transportation fees from patrons). These sources accounted for 2.6 percent of total revenues in 1995–96. **Source:** U.S. Dept. of Education, National Center for Education Statistics, *Digest of Education Statistics, 1998.*

Education Expenditures, 1950–98

School year	All educational institutions Total expenditures (millions)	As percentage of GDP	Elementary and Secondary schools Public Total (millions)	Per pupil (constant dollars)[1]	Private (millions)	Colleges and Universities Public (millions)	Private (millions)
1949–50	$ 8,911	N.A.	$ 5,838	$1,578	$ 411	$ 1,430	$ 1,233
1959–60	23,860	4.7%	15,613	2,422	1,100	3,904	3,244
1969–70	68,459	7.0	40,683	3,764	2,500	16,234	9,041
1979–80	165,627	6.5	95,962	4,770	7,200	41,434	21,031
1984–85	247,657	6.3	137,000	5,285[2]	12,400	63,705	34,553
1989–90	381,525	7.0	212,770	6,591	18,200	96,387	54,169
1990–91	412,652	7.2	229,430	6,626	19,500	104,433	59,288
1991–92	432,987	7.3	241,055	6,587	20,200	108,667	63,065
1992–93	456,070	7.3	252,935	6,587	21,400	115,169	66,566
1993–94	477,237	7.3	265,307	6,633	22,200	119,573	70,157
1994–95	503,925	7.3	279,000	6,676	23,400	127,594	73,930
1995–96[3]	529,561	7.3	293,611	6,745	24,600	132,752	78,597
1996–97[2]	559,500	7.3	310,200	6,814	25,800	140,000	83,500
1997–98[2]	583,800	7.2	324,300	6,943	27,000	145,500	87,000

1. Expenditure per pupil in fall enrollment, as measured in constant (1997–98) dollars, based on the Consumer Price Index. 2. Estimated. 3. Preliminary. **Source:** U.S. Dept. of Education, National Center for Education Statistics, *Digest of Education Statistics, 1998.*

Number of Schools and Teachers in the U.S., Fall, 1996

School type	Schools			Teachers		
	Total	Public	Private	Total	Public	Private
Elementary and secondary	**115,909**	**88,223**	**27,686**[1]	**3,053,000**	**2,666,000**	**387,000**[2]
Elementary	78,549	61,805	16,744[1]	1,856,000	1,582,000	274,000[2]
Secondary	23,840	21,307	2,533[1]	1,197,000	1,084,000	113,000[2]
Combined	11,389	2,980	8,409[1]	N.A.	N.A.	N.A.
Other schools	2,131	2,131	N.A	N.A.	N.A.	N.A.
Colleges and universities	**4,009**	**1,702**	**2,307**	**677,736**[1]	**475,209**[1]	**202,527**[1]
4-year colleges	2,267	614	1,653	515,853[1]	321,664[1]	194,189[1]
2-year colleges	1,742	1,088	654	161,883[1]	153,545[1]	8,338[1]

1. Data is from Fall, 1995 2. Estimates. **Source:** U.S. Dept. of Education, National Center for Education Statistics, *Digest of Education Statistics, 1998.*

School Enrollment, Kindergarten Through University Level, 1970–98 (millions of students)

Year	Type of school						
	Elementary (K-8)		Secondary (9-12)		Higher education		
	Public	Private	Public	Private	Public	Private	Total
1970	32.6	4.1	13.3	1.3	6.4	2.2	**59.9**
1975	30.5	3.7	14.3	1.3	8.8	2.4	**61.0**
1980	27.6	4.0	13.2	1.3	9.5	2.6	**58.3**
1985	27.0	4.2	12.4	1.4	9.5	2.8	**57.2**
1990	29.9	4.1	11.3	1.1	10.8	3.0	**60.3**
1994	31.9	4.4[1]	12.2	1.2[1]	11.1	3.1	**64.0**
1995	32.3	4.4[1]	12.5	1.3[1]	11.1	3.2	**64.8**
1996	32.8	4.5[1]	12.9	1.3[1]	11.0[2]	3.2[2]	**65.7**
1997[2]	33.0	4.5	13.0	1.3	11.2	3.1	**66.2**
1998[2]	33.5	4.6	13.3	1.4	11.4	3.2	**67.3**

Note: Totals may not add up due to independent rounding. 1. Estimated. 2. Projected. **Source:** U.S. Dept. of Education, National Center for Education Statistics, *Digest of Education Statistics, 1998.*

people decreased. That trend evidenced itself in secondary school populations between 1980 and 1990. Since 1990, however, populations of both elementary and secondary school populations are again on the rise, increasing slightly each year. In 1998, the public elementary school population reached a projected new high of 33.5 million, while public secondary school enrollment topped 13 million. These numbers suggest that baby boomers started a baby boom of their own, the fruits of which are now starting to reach high school.

Teachers have more than kept pace with the growth in the number of students. There were 1.6 million elementary school teachers and 1.1 million secondary school teachers in 1996-97, more than double the number in 1955. The number of secondary school teachers has remained at about one million since 1975, while the number of public elementary school teachers has risen consistently every year since 1982, when teachers numbered 1.2 million. A more telling statistic, though, is pupil-teacher ratios. Despite constant complaints about overcrowded inner-city classrooms, the average number of pupils supervised by each teacher has declined dramatically in the past 30 years. Each elementary school teacher was responsible for 18.8 students in 1996-97, down from 24.3 in 1970, while secondary schools had a pupil-teacher ratio of 14.6 to 1, down from 19.8 to 1 in 1970.

Nursery schools have increased dramatically in popularity since 1965, when 27.1 percent of 3-to-5-year-olds were enrolled in a kindergarten or pre-kindergarten program. That percentage has increased gradually ever since, reaching a high of 64.9 percent in 1997. The percentage of youngsters attending full-time nursery school has also been on the rise. Only 17 percent of pre-primary students were in full-time programs in 1970; in 1997, 49.9 percent were full-time enrollees. Most nursery school students were in private schools, while most kindergarten students were enrolled in public schools.

School districts declined drastically between 1930, when there were 119,000 of them, and 1984, when there were a mere 15,747. Numbers since 1985 are not directly comparable with earlier years, but school districts have remained constant at about 15,000. There were 14,883 school districts in 1996. The greatest number of school districts had between 1,000 and 2,499 students in them, but school districts with 25,000 students or more were responsible for educating the lion's share (30.5 percent) of public school students.

▶PRIVATE SCHOOLS
The U.S. Department of Education updates its data on private schools less frequently than it does for public institutions. The 1995–96 school year is the latest year for which data is available for private elementary and secondary schools. (Data for tuitions and teachers are from 1993–94, the latest year available).

How the States Rank in Public Education, 1996–97

State	Enrollment	Rank	Expenditures per pupil	Rank	Average teacher salary	Rank
U.S.	45,351,937	—	$5,889	—	$38,611	—
Alabama	741,110	23	5,255	34	32,549	38
Alaska	129,919	46	8,900[1]	2	50,647[1]	1
Arizona	789,668[1]	21	4,048[1]	50	33,350[1]	32
Arkansas	456,468	34	4,172[1]	49	30,319[1]	45
California	5,612,965	1	5,284	33	43,474[1]	9
Colorado	673,438	24	5,147[1]	36	36,271	22
Connecticut	527,920	29	8,376[1]	4	50,426	2
D.C.	79,861	51	7,175[1]	6	45,012[1]	7
Delaware	110,549	48	7,086	7	41,436	12
Florida	2,241,411	4	5,427	29	33,889	29
Georgia	1,321,239	9	5,585	25	35,596	27
Hawaii	188,486	42	5,720	23	35,842[1]	24
Idaho	245,252	39	4,500[1]	46	31,818	39
Illinois	1,973,040	5	5,423[1]	30	42,125	11
Indiana	982,757	13	5,886	21	38,876	16
Iowa	502,941	31	5,720	23	33,272	33
Kansas	466,367	33	5,493	28	35,802	26
Kentucky	635,718	26	5,346	32	33,797	30
Louisiana	786,375	22	4,527[1]	45	28,347	48
Maine	213,866	40	6,385	15	33,676	31
Maryland	818,583	20	6,547	11	41,148	13
Massachusetts	929,773	15	7,069[1]	8	43,806	8
Michigan	1,684,294	8	6,654[1]	10	48,238[1]	4
Minnesota	845,804	19	6,041	16	38,281	18
Mississippi	503,967	30	4,269[1]	47	27,720	49
Missouri	883,327	17	4,949[1]	40	33,143	35
Montana	164,627	43	5,380	31	29,958	46
Nebraska	290,890	37	5,250	35	31,768	40
Nevada	282,131	38	4,998	39	37,340	20
New Hampshire	196,753	41	6,014[1]	18	36,029	23
New Jersey	1,214,797	10	9,455[1]	1	49,349[1]	3
New Mexico	330,522	35	4,927	41	29,685	47
New York	2,812,031	3	8,658	3	48,000	5
North Carolina	1,199,962	11	5,028	38	31,286	43
North Dakota	118,433	47	4,667	44	27,711	50
Ohio	1,843,311	6	5,527	27	38,831	17
Oklahoma	621,000	27	4,187	48	30,369	44
Oregon	537,000	28	5,988	19	40,960	14
Pennsylvania	1,804,256	7	6,967[1]	9	47,147	6
Rhode Island	151,324	44	7,665	5	43,019[1]	10
South Carolina	644,007	25	5,105	37	32,830	37
South Dakota	135,126	45	4,680	43	26,764	51
Tennessee	891,535	16	4,898	42	34,222	28
Texas	3,828,975	2	5,551	26	33,038	36
Utah	478,028	32	3,837	51	31,750	41
Vermont	107,922	49	6,503[1]	13	37,200[1]	21
Virginia	1,096,093	12	5,920[1]	20	35,837	25
Washington	976,639	14	5,805	22	37,860	19
West Virginia	303,441	36	6,406	14	33,257	34
Wisconsin	879,259	18	6,521	12	39,057	15
Wyoming	98,777	50	6,036	17	31,721	42

1. Data estimated by NEA   **Source:** National Education Association, *Rankings of the States 1997.*

Schools and enrollment There were 27,686 private schools engaged in educating 5,032,200 students. Of these schools, 16,744 were elementary schools (responsible for educating 2,835,247 students), 2,533 were secondary schools (811,422 students), and 8,409 offered instruction in all 12 grades (1,385,531 students). Most private schools were religiously affiliated. One third, or 8,248 schools, were affiliated with the Catholic Church; 13,081 were affiliated with other religious groups. Only 6,357 private schools were nonsectarian.

Tuitions Average tuition for private school students was $3,116 per year. But that average is kept so low by the large number of parochial schools offering free or low-cost private education. The average cost of all nonsectarian private schools (elementary and secondary) was $6,631, and more than half of such schools charge at least $5,000 per year in tuition. Average tuition for nonsectarian secondary schools was over $9,000 per year.

Teachers There were 378,365 full-time private school teachers; almost all of them were under the age of 50. The vast majority of these teachers (285,235) were women, and an even greater number (347,811) were white. The average teacher salary in private schools was $23,395, a fraction of the $35,924 earned by public school teachers. Male teachers earned substantially more than their female counterparts in both public and private schools, but the difference was most pronounced in private schools, where male compensation ($28,948) was 34 percent greater than female salaries ($21,657).

Race and ethnicity   Private schools remain almost entirely white enclaves. More than half (13,875) of all private schools had minority enrollments of under 9 percent, and another quarter (6,517) had minority populations below 29 percent, even though the majority of private school students came from central cities.

Student-teacher ratios   Students in private schools continue to get more teacher attention than do students in public schools. Pupil-teacher ratios were 16.5–1 in private elementary schools, compared with 19.3–1 in public elementary schools. The difference was even more pronounced on the secondary school level, where private school teachers averaged 11.4 students, while each public school teacher was responsible for 14.4 pupils.

▶COLLEGE ENTRANCE EXAMINATION SCORES

SATs (Scholastic Assessment Tests) purportedly measure verbal and mathematical reasoning abilities. These tests are developed and administered by

Catholic Schools, Pupils & Teachers, 1960–99

				Teachers	
Year	Schools	Pupils	Total	Religious	Lay
Elementary schools					
1960	10,501	4,373,000	108,000	79,000	29,000
1970	9,362	3,355,000	112,000	52,000	60,000
1980	8,043	2,269,000	97,000	25,000	72,000
1990	7,291	1,883,906	91,039	10,837	80,202
1995	6,979	1,990,784	116,494	10,564	105,930
1996	7,022	2,014,156	118,753	10,002	108,751
1997	7,005	2,014,272	107,548	8,113	99,435
1998	7,004	2,015,041	105,767	7,539	98,408
1999	6,990	2,013,112	105,943	7,609	98,334
Secondary schools					
1960	2,392	880,000	44,000	33,000	11,000
1970	1,981	1,008,000	55,000	29,000	26,000
1980	1,516	837,000	49,000	14,000	35,000
1990	1,296	591,533	40,159	6,579	33,580
1995	1,238	614,571	46,599	6,193	40,406
1996	1,228	624,062	48,006	5,667	42,339
1997	1,226	631,190	45,728	4,812	40,916
1998	1,219	633,818	46,541	4,590	41,951
1999	1,227	635,742	47,138	4,391	42,747

Source: National Catholic Education Association.

Average SAT and ACT Scores by Group

	Composite scores				Total test-takers,
Group	1987	1990	1997	1998	class of 1998
SAT Scores					
American Indian, Alaskan Native	934	934	950	963	10,159
Asian American, Pacific Islander	1,020	1,029	1,056	1,060	94,066
Black	839	847	857	860	114,912
Mexican-American	912	917	909	913	41,028
Puerto Rican	868	872	901	899	13,635
Other Hispanic	926	923	934	927	35,749
White	1,038	1,034	1,052	1,054	704,462
Men	1,035	1,026	1,037	1,040	473,651
Women	983	989	997	998	576,122
National average[1]	**1,008**	**1,001**	**1,016**	**1,017**	**1,049,773**
ACT Scores					
American Indian, Alaskan Native	17.5	18.0	19.0	19.0	11,132
Asian American, Pacific Islander	21.9	21.7	21.7	21.8	30,988
Black	16.6	17.0	17.1	17.1	100,537
Mexican-American	18.1	18.3	18.8	18.5	34,617
Other Hispanic	19.3	19.3	19.0	19.6	17,500
White	21.3	21.2	21.7	21.7	707,496
Men	21.2	21.0	21.1	21.2	430,742
Women	20.1	20.3	20.8	20.9	564,315
National average[1]	**20.6**	**20.6**	**21.0**	**21.0**	**995,057**

Note: The Educational Testing Service changed the Scholastic Assessment Test in 1994; numbers from years before then have been recalibrated for comparison with statistics after 1994. 1. Includes students of other ethnicities and students who did not identify their ethnicities.   Source: The College Board, American College Testing Program.

the Educational Testing Service of Princeton, N.J., for the College Board, which is headquartered in New York City. The College Board is a nonprofit organization that provides tests and many other educational services for students, schools, and colleges. The test is scored on a range from 400 to 1600, with average scores usually around 900. Male students consistently outscore females on the SAT, and whites and Asians typically score at least 100 points higher than all other ethnic groups, and nearly 200 points higher than blacks. In response to criticisms of racial and gender bias, the College Board rewrote the SAT in 1994 to make it a test of aptitude, rather than of knowledge or test-taking techniques. The new test (called the SAT1) has fewer multiple choice questions and more open-ended questions, which the College Board claims makes the test uncoachable. But while scores for almost all ethnic and gender groups have gone up gradually every year since 1994, the gender and ethnicity gaps have not changed, suggesting that the new test may be just as biased as the old one.

ACTs are administered by the American College Testing Program, a nonprofit educational organization headquartered in Iowa City, Iowa. Its use is more popular than the SAT in states west of the Mississippi River. The ACT composite score is the average of four tests that measure academic abilities in English, mathematics, social studies, and natural sciences. Although similar numbers of students take each test, the ACT draws less criticism than the SAT, even though both tests evidence similar racial and gender biases.

► HIGHER EDUCATION

The accompanying figures give a startling picture of just how the coming of age of the Baby Boom generation transformed U.S. higher education. In just one decade (the 1960s) the number of undergraduate degrees conferred more than doubled, while the number of doctorates actually tripled. These extraordinary changes were matched in kind by dramatic shifts in what students wanted to study: during the late 1960s, for example, the number of degrees in sociology and psychology jumped by more than 15,000 each in just a few years (1966-1970), while interest in business soared during the 1980s. That trend has begun to reverse in the 1990s, as the need for social workers and other health and human service professionals has expanded.

College enrollment Between 1980 and 1992, college enrollment increased about 20 percent, from just over 12 million to a record 14.5 million. Since then, enrollment has not fluctuated much, even though the traditional college age-population has dropped. Much of the growth in college enrollment was fueled by increases in older students (students 25 and over numbered 6.1 million in 1994), women, and minorities on

Average Cost Of 4-Year Colleges in Current and Constant Dollars, 1971–99 (tuition and fees, per year)

Despite low rates of inflation, the cost of a college education continues to skyrocket. Tuition and fees in 1998–99 were nearly three times what they were as recently as 1984–85. For many years, the rule of thumb was that a year of college should cost about the same as a new Chevrolet. But in recent years, college costs have increased far faster than new car prices. In current dollars—not adjusted for inflation—the cost of a four-year private college has increased 800 percent between 1971 and 1999; for public colleges, costs have increased 862 percent.

In constant dollars (which negate the effect of inflation), the cost of college has more than doubled since 1981–82. That's a departure from the trend during the 1970s, when the real cost of college actually decreased several times, and never rose above $7,200.

Parents of undergraduates bear most of this burden, but increasingly, students themselves are taking on heavy debt loads to finance their own educations. Since 1993, the percentage of college graduates who owed more than $20,000 has more than doubled to 19 percent. And since education debt is no longer tax-deductible, the impact is even more pronounced.

Year	Current dollars Private	Current dollars Public	Constant dollars Private	Constant dollars Public
1971–72	$1,820	$376	$7,218	$1,491
1975–76	2,272	433	6,686	1,274
1980–81	3,617	804	6,814	1,515
1984–85	5,556	1,228	8,573	1,895
1985–86	6,121	1,318	9,180	1,977
1986–87	6,658	1,414	9,769	2,075
1987–88	7,048	1,485	9,929	2,092
1988–89	8,004	1,578	10,778	2,125
1989–90	8,663	1,696	11,134	2,180
1990–91	9,340	1,908	11,382	2,325
1991–92	9,812	2,107	11,586	2,488
1992–93	10,449	2,334	11,965	2,673
1993–94	11,007	2,535	12,285	2,829
1994–95	11,719	2,705	12,716	2,935
1995–96	12,216	2,811	12,904	2,969
1996–97	12,994	2,975	13,345	3,055
1997–98	13,785	3,111	13,909	3,139
1998–99	14,508	3,243	14,508	3,243

Source: The College Board.

Most Popular Majors Among Incoming Freshmen, 1990–98

Major	Percentage 1990	1997	1998
Elementary education	5.1%	5.1%	5.8%
Business administration	5.5	4.5	4.5
Psychology	4.2	3.8	4.1
Premedicine, predental, preveterinary	3.2	3.9	4.0
Computer science	1.7	3.1	3.5
Nursing	4.2	3.5	3.5
Therapy	2.3	3.6	3.5
Accounting	5.3	3.0	3.2
General biology	1.8	3.0	2.8
Management	4.0	2.7	2.8
Arts	2.0	2.0	2.2
Law enforcement	1.7	2.2	2.2
Marketing	2.5	2.0	2.2
Secondary education	1.9	2.0	2.1
Electrical engineering	2.5	2.4	2.0
Political science	3.0	2.0	2.0
Mechanical engineering	2.0	2.0	1.9
Communications	2.3	1.9	1.8
Data processing	N.A.	1.5	1.5
English	1.0	1.5	1.4

Source: Higher Education Research Institute, University of California, Los Angeles, The American Freshman: National Norms for Fall, 1998.

campus. Women have outnumbered men on college campuses since 1979, when there were just under 6 million of each in institutions of higher education. Since then, male enrollment has increased only 13 percent, to 6.3 million, while female enrollment has leapt 34 percent to 8.0 million. Minorities, especially Hispanics and Asians, have increased from 15.7 percent of the campus population in 1976 to 26.1 percent in 1996. The percentage of blacks on campus fluctuated for

Number Of Degrees Conferred in U.S. by Type, 1950–99

Year	All degrees[1]	Bachelor's	First professional[2]	Master's	Doctorate
1949–50	496,661		432,058[3]	58,183	6,420
1959–60	476,704		392,440[3]	74,435	9,829
1969–70	1,065,098	792,317	34,578	208,291	29,912
1979–80	1,330,244	929,417	70,131	298,081	32,615
1984–85	1,373,734	979,477	75,063	286,251	32,943
1989–90	1,485,004	1,051,344	70,988	324,301	38,371
1994–95	1,678,009	1,160,134	75,800	397,629	44,446
1995–96	1,692,479	1,164,792	76,734	406,301	44,652
1996–97[4]	1,692,400	1,166,000	79,700	402,000	44,700
1997–98[4]	1,701,600	1,172,000	78,400	406,000	45,200
1998–99[4]	1,697,600	1,166,000	75,800	410,000	45,800

1. Does not include associate of arts (A.A.) or associate of science (A.S.) degrees; more than 400,000 of these have been given each year since 1980. 2. Degrees are: medical doctor, law, dentistry, optometry, podiatry, pharmacy, theology, chiropractic, and veterinary medicine. 3. Prior to 1961, bachelor's and first professional degrees were listed together. 4. Projected.
Source: U.S. Dept. of Education, National Center for Education Statistics, *Digest of Education Statistics, 1998.*

Educational Attainment of the Population 25+ Years, 1940–98

Year	Completed 4 years of high school or more			Completed 4 years of college or more		
	Both Sexes	Male	Female	Both Sexes	Male	Female
1940	24.5%	22.7%	26.3%	4.6%	5.5%	3.8%
1950	34.3	32.6	36.0	6.2	7.3	5.2
1959	43.7	42.2	45.2	8.1	10.3	6.0
1970	55.2	55.0	55.4	11.0	14.1	8.2
1980	68.6	69.1	68.1	17.0	20.8	13.5
1991	78.4	78.5	78.3	21.4	24.3	18.8
1992	79.4	79.7	79.2	21.4	24.3	18.6
1993	80.2	80.5	80.0	21.9	24.8	19.2
1994	80.9	81.0	80.7	22.2	25.1	19.6
1995	81.7	81.7	81.6	23.0	26.0	20.2
1996	81.7	81.9	81.6	23.6	26.0	21.4
1997	82.1	82.0	82.2	23.9	26.2	21.7
1998	82.8	82.8	82.9	24.4	26.5	22.4

Source: Bureau of the Census, *Current Population Survey: Educational Attainment in the United States, March, 1998.*

Educational Attainment of the Population, Ages 25 and Over, 1998

Characteristic	Number of people ('000s)	4 years high school or more	Some college or more	4 years college or more
All persons	**172,211**	**82.8%**	**49.1%**	**24.4%**
Sex:				
Male	82,376	82.8	50.5	26.5
Female	89,835	82.9	47.7	22.4
Race:				
White	145,078	83.7	49.8	25.0
Black	19,376	76.0	40.0	14.7
Hispanic origin[1]	16,044	55.5	28.6	11.0
Age groups:				
25 to 29 years	18,996	88.1	57.8	27.3
30 to 34 years	20,358	87.7	54.3	27.6
35 to 39 years	22,691	87.3	52.5	25.7
40 to 44 years	21,771	88.7	55.5	27.0
45 to 49 years	18,634	88.6	56.9	29.0
50 to 54 years	15,424	85.6	52.9	28.5
55 to 59 years	12,190	82.1	45.3	23.9
60 to 64 years	10,065	76.4	38.3	19.7
65 to 69 years	9,361	73.2	36.3	18.1
70 to 74 years	8,512	68.7	33.0	15.1
75 years or older	14,209	62.0	28.8	12.5
Residence				
Metropolitan area	137,382	83.4	58.0	26.0
Nonmetropolitan area	33,199	76.8	35.3	14.8

1. People of Hispanic origin may be of any race.
Source: Bureau of the Census, *Current Population Survey: Educational Attainment in the United States, March, 1998* (1999).

many years, but began increasing again in 1990. Nearly 11 percent of college students were black in 1996, up from 9.3 percent in 1990.

▶ EDUCATIONAL ATTAINMENT

Despite complaints about the state of education in America, there can be no doubt that the general population continues to grow more educated every year. In 1998, almost 83 percent of all adults over the age of 25 had completed high school, and more than 24 percent of American adults had a bachelor's degree or more. It's not surprising that those numbers were both a lot lower in 1940, when only 24 percent of adults had graduated

from high school and college degrees belonged to fewer than 5 percent of the population. But even as recently as 1980, only 69 percent of adults over 25 had a high school diploma and only 17 percent had graduated from college. (See the accompanying table).

The greatest proof of the importance of education is the correlation between years of schooling and higher salaries. In 1997, adults with bachelor's degrees earned an average of $40,478 per year, compared with $22,895 for those with only high school diplomas. Those with post-graduate educations made more than $63,000 while those who failed to graduate from high school averaged only $16,124.

Educational Attainment by State, 1998

State	Persons over 25 ('000s)	4 years high school or more	Rank	4 years college or more	Rank
U.S. Total	172,211	82.8%	—	24.4%	—
Alabama	2,857	78.8	43	20.6	39
Alaska	389	90.6	2	24.2	20
Arizona	2,824	81.9	35	21.9	32
Arkansas	1,606	76.8	50	16.2	51
California	20,401	80.1	40	26.4	17
Colorado	2,522	89.6	4	34.0	2
Connecticut	2,181	83.7	30	31.4	4
Delaware	474	85.2	21	25.1	19
District of Columbia	350	83.8	29	36.5	1
Florida	9,990	81.9	36	22.5	27
Georgia	4,699	80.0	41	20.7	37
Hawaii	773	84.6	23	24.0	21
Idaho	757	82.7	33	20.3	42
Illinois	7,517	84.2	26	25.8	18
Indiana	3,642	83.5	31	17.7	48
Iowa	1,793	87.7	11	20.3	41
Kansas	1,609	89.2	7	28.5	9
Kentucky	2,501	77.9	47	20.1	43
Louisiana	2,781	78.6	44	19.5	45
Maine	862	86.7	13	19.2	47
Maryland	3,398	84.7	22	31.8	3
Massachusetts	4,043	85.6	18	31.0	6
Michigan	6,136	85.4	20	22.1	30
Minnesota	2,981	89.4	5	31.0	5
Mississippi	1,689	77.3	48	19.5	46
Missouri	3,438	82.9	32	22.4	28
Montana	565	89.1	8	23.9	22
Nebraska	1,022	87.7	12	20.9	36
Nevada	1,141	89.1	9	20.6	38
New Hampshire	760	84.0	28	26.6	16
New Jersey	5,239	86.5	15	30.1	8
New Mexico	1,075	79.6	42	23.1	25
New York	11,775	81.5	37	26.8	15
North Carolina	4,843	81.4	38	23.3	23
North Dakota	394	84.3	25	22.5	26
Ohio	7,235	86.2	17	21.5	34
Oklahoma	2,127	84.6	24	20.5	40
Oregon	2,173	85.5	19	27.7	12
Pennsylvania	8,002	84.1	27	22.1	31
Rhode Island	653	80.7	39	27.8	11
South Carolina	2,403	78.6	45	21.3	35
South Dakota	426	86.3	16	21.8	33
Tennessee	3,561	76.9	49	16.9	49
Texas	11,906	78.3	46	23.3	24
Utah	1,141	89.3	6	27.6	13
Vermont	384	86.7	14	27.1	14
Virginia	4,482	82.6	34	30.3	7
Washington	3,740	92.0	1	28.1	10
West Virginia	1,243	76.4	51	16.3	50
Wisconsin	3,405	88.0	10	22.3	29
Wyoming	301	90.0	3	19.8	44

Source: U.S. Bureau of the Census, *Current Population Survey, March 1998* (1999).

U.S. Energy

Energy is usually measured in millions or larger quantities of British thermal units (Btu). One Btu is approximately equal to the energy released in burning a wooden match. An engine burning eight gallons of gasoline releases 1 million (10^6) Btu. One quadrillion (10^{15}) Btu is the equivalent of the energy released from an engine burning eight billion gallons of gasoline.

Total U.S. energy production was a record 72.3 quadrillion Btu in 1997. Natural gas and coal each accounted for more than one-quarter of domestic energy production. Fossil fuels, which also include crude oil, accounted for 80 percent of all energy production, down from 95.3 percent as recently as 1970. Nuclear energy (9.2 percent) and renewable energy forms like solar energy and wind power (9.6 percent) have made up the difference.

U.S. energy consumption also hit a record high in 1997, of 94.21 quadrillion Btu. With prices low, American consumers have been lavish in their use of energy, opting for convenience over energy efficiency at nearly every turn. The average home size increased by more than 500 square feet between 1973 and 1997 (bringing with it an attendant increase in heating costs), and is now packed with many more energy-sucking appliances than ever before, including whirlpool tubs, microwave ovens, toaster-ovens, washer-dryers, and central air-conditioning. In addition, Americans are driving bigger, less-efficient cars and trucks, and are driving them more total miles each year (16.9 percent more in 1996 than in 1973), meaning they are consuming more gas than ever before.

Petroleum continues to be the energy of choice among U.S. consumers. It accounted for 39 percent of all U.S. energy consumption in 1997, compared to 23 percent for coal and 24 percent for natural gas. Since the U.S. consumes more petroleum than it produces (and consumes more total energy than it produces), it must import the difference. Consumption of nuclear energy has grown steadily from nearly zero in 1960 to 6.69 quadrillion Btu in 1997. Renewable energy consumption has grown similarly, from 1.66 quadrillion Btu, in 1960, to 7.14 quadrillion Btu in 1997.

The relationship between total energy consumption and real gross domestic product (GDP) is a primary indicator of the energy intensity of the economy. In 1949, the country used 20,580 Btu of energy per dollar of GDP (measured in constant 1992 dollars). From 1949 to 1972, energy consumption more than doubled (from 30 quadrillion to 74 quadrillion Btu), increasing at approximately the same rate as GDP. Since then, consumption has continued to record levels every year, but increases in energy efficiency, conservation, and the expansion of the service sector of the economy have kept energy consumption to 13,100 Btu per dollar of GDP, or 32 percent less than in 1972. In other words, the country is using much more energy but not paying much77 more for it.

A second indicator is per capita consumption, which rose from 204 million Btu per capita in 1949 to 352 million Btu in 1978. Efforts at conservation persuaded people to decrease their consumption

U.S. Energy Overview, 1960–97

Activity and energy source	(Quadrillion Btu)							As percent of total, 1997
	1960	1970	1980	1990	1995	1996	1997[1]	
Production, Total	**41.49**	**62.07**	**64.76**	**70.78**	**71.04**	**72.32**	**72.32**	**100.0%**
Coal	10.82	14.61	18.60	22.46	21.98	22.65	23.17	32.0
Natural gas (dry)	12.66	21.67	19.91	18.36	19.10	19.30	19.47	26.9
Crude oil[2]	14.93	20.40	18.25	15.57	13.89	13.72	13.57	18.8
Natural gas plant liquids	1.46	2.51	2.25	2.17	2.44	2.53	2.54	3.5
Nuclear electric power	0.01	0.24	2.74	6.16	7.18	7.17	6.69	9.2
Renewable energy[3]	1.61	2.65	3.01	6.09	6.48	6.98	6.92	9.6
Imports, Total	**4.23**	**8.39**	**15.97**	**18.99**	**22.48**	**23.97**	**24.96**	**100.0%**
Natural gas	0.16	0.85	1.01	1.55	2.90	3.00	3.04	12.2
Petroleum[4]	4.00	7.47	14.66	17.12	18.86	20.27	21.22	85.0
Other[5]	0.06	0.07	0.28	0.26	0.72	0.70	0.71	2.8
Exports, Total	**1.48**	**2.66**	**3.72**	**4.91**	**4.58**	**4.71**	**4.57**	**100.0%**
Coal	1.02	1.94	2.42	2.77	2.32	2.37	2.19	47.9
Petroleum	0.43	0.55	1.16	1.82	1.99	2.06	2.10	46.0
Other[6]	0.03	0.18	0.14	0.32	0.27	0.28	0.29	6.3
Consumption, Total	**43.80**	**66.43**	**75.96**	**84.12**	**90.86**	**93.87**	**94.21**	**100.0%**
Coal	9.84	12.26	15.42	19.10	20.09	21.01	21.44	22.8
Natural gas	12.39	21.79	20.39	19.30	22.16	22.56	22.59	24.0
Petroleum products[7]	19.92	29.52	34.20	33.55	34.66	35.86	36.31	38.5
Nuclear electric power	0.01	0.24	2.74	6.16	7.18	7.17	6.69	7.1
Renewable energy[3]	1.66	2.67	3.23	6.17	6.76	7.32	7.14	7.6

Note: Sum of components may not equal due to independent rounding. 1. Preliminary. 2. Includes lease condensate. 3. Includes hydroelectric power, geothermal energy, solar energy, wind energy, and biofuels such as wood waste, landfill gases, fish oils, and other waste. The marked increase in 1990 is due to expanded coverage of such forms of energy, not a dramatic increase in their use. 4. Includes imports of crude oil for the Strategic Petroleum Reserve, which began in 1977. 5. Includes coal, coal coke, and electricity. 6. Includes natural gas, coal coke, and petroleum products. 7. Petroleum products supplied include natural gas plant liquids and crude oil burned as fuel.   **Source:** U.S. Dept. of Energy, *Annual Energy Review (1997)* 1998.

to 308 million Btu in 1986, but per capita use has increased steadily since then, to 352 million Btu in 1997. Not surprisingly, Alaska and Texas, two of the sparsest states, were the biggest per capita consumers of energy. New York and Hawaii used the least energy per capita—Hawaii because so few houses need to be heated, and New York because so many people live in apartments, which require much less energy to heat and insulate.

(For facts and figures about energy consumption and production worldwide, see the section on World Energy in Part III).

▶ FOSSIL FUELS
Petroleum

Since 1958 the United States has consumed more energy than it produces; the difference has been met with energy imports. Net imports of energy (primarily petroleum) grew rapidly through 1973, when they totaled 13 quadrillion Btu, or 20 percent of consumption.

Despite the Arab oil embargo of 1973–74 and increases in the price of crude oil, petroleum net imports continued to grow, reaching a peak of nearly 19 quadrillion Btu in 1977. That year, U.S. dependence on petroleum net imports peaked at 47 percent of consumption. In 1985, petroleum net imports dropped to 9 quadrillion Btu and U.S. dependence on foreign oil fell to 27 percent of consumption, its lowest level since 1972.

But a drop in the worldwide price of oil inhibited domestic production and caused U.S. reliance on imports to jump back up in the late 1980s. Oil prices rebounded briefly during the Gulf War, but by 1994, the price was back down to $12.55 a barrel (measured in constant dollars), its lowest annual average in 21 years. The price per barrel in 1997 was up to $15.34, only slightly higher than it was in 1949 ($14.03). Dependence on exports in 1997 were a record high 48 percent of consumption, primarily because of the low price of foreign oil. Saudi Arabia, Venezuela, Canada and Mexico are the U.S.'s primary suppliers of foreign oil; each exports more than 1.3 million barrels of oil per day to the U.S.

U.S. Energy Consumption, Total and Per Capita, 1950–97

Year	Total energy consumption (quadrillion Btu)		Per capita consumption (million Btu)	
	Total	End-use[1]	Total	End-use[1]
1950	33.08	29.37	219	194
1955	38.82	34.02	235	206
1960	43.80	37.96	244	212
1965	52.68	44.93	272	232
1970	66.43	54.91	327	270
1975	70.55	56.16	327	261
1980	75.96	58.60	335	259
1985	73.98	55.39	310	232
1990[2]	84.12	63.78	338	256
1995	90.86	69.05	346	263
1996	93.87	71.41	354	269
1997[3]	94.21	71.48	352	267

1. Total energy consumption less losses from generation, transmission and distribution of electricity, power plant use and unaccounted for losses. 2. There is a discontinuity in this series between 1989 and 1990 due to expanded coverage of non-electric utility use of renewable energy beginning in 1990. 3. Preliminary. **Source:** U.S. Dept. of Energy, *Annual Energy Review (1997)* 1998.

U.S. Fuel Consumption by Type and End-Use Sector, 1950–97

Year	Residential and commercial	Industrial	Transportation	Electric utilities	Total
Petroleum (million barrels/day)					
1950	1.07	1.82	3.36	0.21	6.46
1960	1.71	2.71	5.14	0.24	9.80
1970	2.18	3.81	7.78	0.93	14.70
1980	1.52	4.84	9.55	1.15	17.06
1990	1.14	4.32	10.97	0.55	16.99
1995	1.11	4.60	11.73	0.29	17.72
1996[1]	1.18	4.84	11.98	0.32	18.31
1997[1]	1.17	4.94	12.10	0.37	18.58
Natural gas (trillion cubic feet/year)					
1950	1.59	3.43	0.13	0.63	5.77
1960	4.12	5.77	0.35	1.72	11.97
1970	7.24	9.25	0.72	3.93	21.14
1980	7.36	8.20	0.63	3.68	19.88
1990	7.01	8.25	0.66	2.79	18.72
1995	7.88	9.80	0.70	3.20	21.58
1996	8.40	10.12	0.71	2.73	21.97
1997[1]	8.28	10.05	0.71	2.96	21.99
Coal (million short tons/year)					
1950	114.6	224.6	63.0	91.9	494.1
1960	40.9	177.4	3.0	176.7	398.1
1970	16.1	186.6	0.3	320.2	523.2
1980	6.5	127.0	(2)	569.3	702.7
1985	7.8	116.4	(2)	693.8	818.0
1990	6.7	115.2	(2)	773.5	895.5
1995	5.8	106.1	(2)	850.2	962.0
1996	6.0	102.6	(2)	869.6	1,005.6
1997[1]	6.0	99.8	(2)	921.3	1,027.1

1. Preliminary. 2. Small quantities consumed by transportation sector are included in industrial column. **Source:** U.S. Dept. of Energy, *Annual Energy Review (1997)* 1998.

In 1998, a worldwide glut of oil pushed petroleum prices down below $15 per barrel, a downward trend that continued into 1999 and had some OPEC countries talking about reducing production.

Natural gas

Once considered a useless byproduct of oil well drilling (it was simply burned off at the site), natural gas is today the primary source of energy for space heating in 50 million U.S. households. U.S. natural gas trade was limited to the border countries of Mexico and Canada until shipping natural gas in liquefied form emerged as an alternative to pipelines. In 1969, the first shipments of liquefied natural gas (LNG) were sent to Japan, and U.S. imports from Algeria began the following year. In 1997, U.S. net imports of natural gas by all routes totaled 2.97 trillion cubic feet (the vast majority from Canada).

Coal

Since World War II coal has been the major U.S. energy export. Throughout most of the 1960s and 1970s, U.S. exports of coal increased, peaking at 113 million short tons in 1981. Exports dropped to just under 80 million short tons in 1987, rebounded to 109 million in 1991, fell again to 71 million short tons in 1994, before recovering again in 1997 to 83.5 million short tons. Canada and Japan were the largest markets for U.S. coal; together, they accounted for 28 percent of total coal exports in 1997. Brazil, Italy, and the United Kingdom all imported more than 7 million short tons of U.S. coal in 1997.

Electric utilities are the primary domestic consumers of coal. Their consumption grew from a 17 percent share in 1949 to an 87 percent share in 1997. Over the same period, consumption in all other sectors declined, most dramatically in the transportation sector, due primarily to railroads switching from coal to petroleum-driven trains.

Gasoline and Heating Oil Retail Prices, 1950–97 (cents per gallon)

Year	Motor gasoline (including taxes)[1]		Residential heating oil[2]	
	Current	Constant[3]	Current	Constant[3]
1950	26.8¢	146.4¢	N.A.	N.A.
1955	29.1	140.6	N.A.	N.A.
1960	31.1	133.5	15.0¢	64.4¢
1965	31.2	124.8	16.0	64.0
1970	35.7	117.0	18.5	60.5
1975	56.7	134.7	37.7	89.3
1980[4]	122.1	202.5	97.4	161.3
1985	119.6	152.4	105.3	134.3
1990	121.7	130.0	106.3	113.6
1991	119.6	122.9	101.9	104.7
1992	119.0	119.0	93.4	93.4
1993	117.3	114.3	91.1	88.8
1994	117.4	111.7	88.4	84.3
1995	120.5	111.8	86.7	80.6
1996	128.8	116.9	98.8[5]	90.1[5]
1997	129.1	114.9	N.A.	N.A.

Note: NA= Not available. 1. Prices are calculated from a sample of stations providing all types of services (i.e., full-, mini-, and self-serve). Geographic coverage: 1949–73, 55 representative cities; 1974–77, 56 urban areas; 1978 on, 85 urban areas. 2. Prices derived by dividing sum of estimated national retail sales for residential heating oil (No. 2 fuel oil) by the estimated volume of retail sales for residential heating. 3. In 1992 dollars, calculated using implicit GDP price deflators. 4. Prices are for leaded regular gasoline only from 1950–75. Prices after 1975 are an average of all grades of gasoline. 5. Preliminary.
Source: U.S. Dept. of Energy, *Annual Energy Review (1997)* 1998.

Transportation sector consumption, which topped 70 million short tons in 1949, has totaled fewer than 50,000 short tons every year since 1975. Consumption by the residential and commercial sector has also declined steadily, from a high of 117 million short tons in 1949 to 6.0 million short tons in 1997.

►ELECTRICITY

Net generation of electricity by electric utilities topped 3 trillion kilowatthours (kWh) in 1997. Coal continued to fuel most of the generation, accounting for 1.8 trillion kWh, while natural gas contributed 284 billion kWh. Despite lower petroleum prices, petroleum-fired generation decreased from 91 billion kWh in 1994 to 79 billion kWh in 1997. Meanwhile, nuclear-based generation declined from 673 billion kWh in 1995 to 629 billion kWh in 1997. Hydroelectric generation was a record high 341 billion kWh, up from just 247 kWh in 1994.

The weighted average real price (based on 1992 dollars) of electricity to all sectors in 1996 was 6.1 cents per kWh, 30 percent below the price in 1982, but about the same as in 1967. But although prices of other major energy sources increased significantly during the same period, electricity remained by far the most expensive source of energy on a Btu basis.

►NUCLEAR POWER

The number of nuclear power plants in operation in the U.S. skyrocketed from 18 in 1970 to 112 in 1990, and net nuclear generation of electricity jumped from 21.8 to 577 kWh. Since 1990, two new plants have opened, and seven have closed, but generation nonetheless increased to 629 kWh in 1997 (down from a high of 675 the previous year). More than three-quarters of the 110 nuclear power plants in the U.S. are located east of the Mississippi River. The U.S. has the highest number of reactors of any country in the world, but far fewer than the 236 that were in the stages of planning, construction or operation as recently as 1975.

Several factors have contributed to the decline in the number of planned nuclear units. Growth in electricity demand has been slower than expected; longer lead times for licensing and construction coupled during the 1980s with higher financing expenses increased costs; and rising interest rates and an uncertain economic environment eroded electric utilities' willingness to commission new plants. Furthermore, nuclear plant operators have been able to increase their generation of electricity without increasing the number of reactors. Nuclear plants ran at 70.8 percent of capacity in 1997, up from 58.0 percent 10 years earlier.

A further deterrent has been the increased public opposition to nuclear power plants because of uncertainties concerning their safety and the disposal of spent nuclear fuel. These concerns were heightened in the wake of the accident at Three Mile Island near Harrisburg, Pennsylvania, in 1979, and the far more devastating one at Chernobyl in Ukraine in 1986.

►THE STRATEGIC PETROLEUM RESERVE

In an attempt to minimize the wild fluctuations in prices caused by the Arab oil embargoes of the 1970s, the U.S. in 1977 created the Strategic Petroleum Reserve, which permitted the storage of 580 million barrels of oil. The reserve proved useful in preventing additional oil price hikes during the Iraqi invasion of Kuwait in 1990.

The reserve can also be used as an emergency supply of oil in case of a complete oil embargo. In 1985, the reserve held enough oil to provide a nor-mal level of petroleum to the U.S. for 115 days in the absence of any other petroleum imports. Since then, the measure has declined to 63 days, because U.S. energy consumption as well as its reliance on foreign imports have both increased.

U.S. Net Generation of Electricity by Utilities, by Energy Source, 1950–97 (billion kilowatthours)

Year	Coal	Natural gas	Petroleum[1]	Nuclear Power	Hydroelectric power	Geothermal and other[2]	Total
1950	155	45	34	0	96	[3]	329
1955	301	95	37	0	113	[3]	547
1960	403	158	48	1	146	[3]	756
1965	571	222	65	4	194	[3]	1,055
1970	704	373	184	22	248	1	1,532
1975	853	300	289	173	300	3	1,918
1980	1,162	346	246	251	276	6	2,286
1985	1,402	292	100	384	281	11	2,470
1990	1,560	264	117	577	283	11	2,808
1991	1,551	264	111	613	280	10	2,825
1992	1,576	264	89	619	244	10	2,797
1993	1,639	259	100	610	269	10	2,883
1994	1,635	291	91	640	247	9	2,911
1995	1,653	307	61	673	296	6	2,995
1996	1,738	263	67	675	331	7	3,077
1997[4]	1,789	284	79	629	341	7	3,126

1. Includes distillate fuel oil, residual fuel oil (including crude oil burned as fuel), jet fuel and petroleum coke. 2. Other is wood, waste, photovoltaic and solar thermal energy used to generate electricity for distribution. 3. Less than 0.5 billion kilowatthours. 4. Preliminary. Source: U.S. Dept. of Energy, Annual Energy Review (1997) 1998.

U.S. Commercial Nuclear Plants, 1998

There are 107 operable nuclear reactors in 31 states. The following table lists the states, with the total number of reactors in each, the names of the individual units and their location.

Alabama = 5
Browns Ferry 1, 2 & 3, Decatur
Joseph M. Farley 1 & 2, Dothan
Arizona = 3
Palo Verde 1, 2 & 3, Wintersburg
Arkansas = 2
Arkansas Nuclear 1 & 2, Russellville
California = 4
Diablo Canyon 1 & 2, Avila Beach
San Onofre 2 & 3, San Clemente
Conecticticut = 3
Millstone 1, 2 & 3, Waterford
Florida = 5
Crystal River 3, Red Level
St. Lucie 1 & 2, Ft. Pierce
Turkey Point 3 & 4, Florida City
Georgia = 4
Hatch 1 & 2, Baxley
Vogtle 1 & 2, Waynesboro
Illinois = 13
Braidwood 1 & 2, Braidwood
Byron 1 & 2, Byron
Clinton 1, Clinton
Dresden 2 & 3, Morris
La Salle 1 & 2, Seneca
Quad Cities 1 & 2, Cordova
Zion 1 & 2, Zion
Iowa = 1
Duane Arnold, Palo
Kansas = 1
Wolf Creek, Burlington
Louisiana = 2
River Bend 1, St. Francisville
Waterford 3, Taft

Maryland = 2
Calvert Cliffs 1 & 2, Lusby
Massachusetts = 1
Pilgrim 1, Plymouth
Michigan = 4
Donald C. Cook 1 & 2, Bridgman
Fermi 2, Newport
Palisades, South Haven
Minnesota = 3
Monticello, Monticello
Prairie Island 1 & 2, Red Wing
Mississippi = 1
Grand Gulf 1, Port Gibson
Missouri = 1
Callaway 1, Fulton
Nebraska = 2
Cooper, Brownville
Fort Calhoun 1, Fort Calhoun
New Hampshire = 1
Seabrook 1, Seabrook
New Jersey = 4
Hope Creek 1, Salem
Oyster Creek 1, Forked River
Salem 1 & 2, Salem
New York = 6
Indian Point 2 & 3, Buchanan
James Fitzpatrick 1, Scriba
Nine Mile Point 1 & 2, Oswego
Robert E. Ginna, Rochester
North Carolina = 5
Brunswick 1 & 2, Southport

McGuire 1 & 2, Cowens Ford Dam
Shearon Harris 1, New Hill
Ohio = 2
Davis-Besse 1, Oak Harbor
Perry 1, North Perry
Pennsylvania = 9
Beaver Valley 1 & 2, Shippingport
Limerick 1 & 2, Pottstown
Peach Bottom 2 & 3, Lancaster
Susquehanna 1 & 2, Berwick
Three Mile Island 1, Middletown
South Carolina =7
Catawba 1 & 2, Clover
H.B. Robinson 2, Hartsville
Oconee 1, 2 & 3, Seneca
Summer 1, Jenkinsville
Tennessee = 2
Sequoyah 1 & 2, Daisy
Watts Bar 1, Spring City
Texas = 4
Comanche Peak 1&2, Glen Rose
South Texas 1 & 2, Bay City
Vermont = 1
Vermont Yankee 1, Vernon
Virginia = 4
North Anna 1 & 2, Mineral
Surry 1 & 2, Surry
Washington = 1
Washington Nuclear 2, Richland
Wisconsin = 3
Kewaunee, Carlton
Point Beach 1 & 2, Two Creeks

Source: U.S. Dept. of Energy, Nuclear Power Generation and Fuel Cycle Report 1998.

U.S. Health and Medicine

►QUALITY OF HEALTH

Americans are living longer, healthier lives than ever before, yet many of the health problems they face could be avoided or alleviated with appropriate prevention or treatment. With this in mind, government health officials have three broad goals: increasing the span of healthy life, reducing health disparities, and achieving access to preventive services for everyone.

Health quality varies significantly by economic level, age group, and geographic region. Among the most persistent disparities are sickness and mortality rates for various racial and ethnic groups. These disparities are especially stark for white and black Americans. For example:

- A white baby can expect to live 77.1 years; a black baby, 71.2 years (1997 data)
- Whites can expect 63.8 years of healthy life; blacks, 55.6 years (1994).
- Whites experience 8.7 tuberculosis cases per 100,000 people; blacks, 23.9 (1995).
- Whites have 22.5 diabetes-related deaths per 100,000 people; blacks, 32.2 (1996).
- Blacks are 34 percent more likely to die of cancer than whites (1990-95).
- The age-adjusted death rate for stroke for blacks is 80 percent higher than for whites. (1996).
- The HIV infection rate is 5.8 times higher for blacks than whites (1996).
- The age-adjusted homicide rate for blacks is six times the rate for whites (1996).
- The maternal mortality rate is 19.6 deaths per 100,000 for black pregnant women, 5.3 deaths for white pregnant women. (1987-96).
- The infant mortality rate is 6.0 per 1,000 live births for whites, 13.7 for blacks (1997).
- Overall mortality for blacks is 52 percent higher than for whites (1997).

A growing body of evidence indicates that race, discrimination, and social and cultural factors influence the care that people receive and, consequently, their health.

►HEALTH CARE EXPENDITURES

The years 1993-97 saw a halt in the steady upward path of health spending as a share of gross domestic product (GDP) observed over past decades. Even though total national health care spending topped the $1 trillion mark for the first time ever in 1996 and rose to almost $1.1 trillion in 1997, as a share of GDP health care spending fell slightly to 13.5 percent in 1997, the lowest in five years.

A variety of factors contribute to the high cost of health care, including:

1. Use of sophisticated, expensive medical equipment.
2. New, higher priced prescription drugs and increased consumer demand induced by advertising.
3. Excessive and arguably unnecessary procedures, including duplication of tests and use of technologies that yield similar results.
4. Increasing elderly population, which use medical care more intensely than younger people.
5. Increasing number of accidents and crimes that require emergency medical services.
6. Labor intensiveness and earnings growth for health care professionals and executives.
7. Malpractice insurance.
8. Administrative waste.
9. Fraud.

The United States spends more than any other developed nation on health care relative to its economy. The nation's 1997 health expenditures amounted to almost $4,000 per person, up from $2,683 in 1990—and only $141 in 1960. Close to 90 percent of this money went for personal health care; the remainder went to research, construction, program administration, the net cost of private health insurance, and public health activities.

National Expenditures for Health Care, 1960–97

Category	1960	1970	1980	1985	1990	1995	1996	1997
Amount (billions)								
Total expenditures	$26.9	$73.2	$247.3	$428.7	$699.4	$993.7	$1,035.1	$1,092.4
Private	20.2	45.5	142.5	254.5	416.2	538.5	552.0	585.3
Public	6.6	27.7	104.8	174.2	283.2	455.2	483.1	507.1
Federal	2.9	17.8	72.0	123.2	195.2	326.0	350.9	367.0
State and local	3.7	9.9	32.8	51.0	88.0	129.2	132.2	140.0
Per capita amount								
Total expenditures	$141	$341	$1,052	$1,735	$2,690	$3,637	$3,759	$3,925
Private	106	212	606	1,030	1,601	1,971	2,005	2,103
Public	35	129	446	705	1,089	1,666	1,754	1,822
Federal	15	83	306	498	751	1,193	1,274	1,319
State and local	20	46	140	206	338	473	480	503
Percent distribution								
Total expenditures	100.0%	100.0%	100.0%	100.0%	100.0%	100.0%	100.0%	100.0%
Private	75.2	62.2	57.6	59.4	59.5	54.2	53.3	53.6
Public	24.8	37.8	42.4	40.6	40.5	45.8	46.7	46.4
Federal	10.9	24.3	29.1	28.7	27.9	32.8	33.9	33.6
State and local	13.9	13.5	13.3	11.9	12.6	13.0	12.8	12.8
Health care expenditures as percent of GDP	5.1%	7.1%	8.9%	10.3%	12.2%	13.7%	13.6	13.5%

Note: Figures may not add to totals because of rounding.   **Source:** U.S. Dept. of Health and Human Services, Health Care Financing Administration, Office of National Health Statistics.

Health Care Quality, by State, 1999

To measure the quality of health care across state lines, statisticians at Health Risk Management Inc. use a weighted average of 46 individual measures relating to population health, health care systems, and consumer health status, based on data contained in reports from various medical associations and U.S. government agencies. Examples of measures include drinking water quality, alcohol-related traffic deaths, public health expenditures, physician and dentist shortages, immunizations, infant mortality rate, and heart disease deaths. The average score is 100

Rank	State	Score	Rank	State	Score	Rank	State	Score
1.	Minnesota	118.2	18.	Kansas	107.0	35.	Florida	96.6
2.	Hawaii	115.7	19.	Virginia	106.7	36.	Georgia	95.8
3.	Wisconsin	114.6	20.	Wyoming	106.6	37.	North Carolina	95.7
4.	New Hampshire	113.9	21.	South Dakota	105.3	38.	Nevada	93.9
5.	Vermont	113.1	22.	Oregon	105.0	39.	Arizona	93.6
6.	Massachusetts	112.8	23.	Ohio	103.7	40.	West Virginia	93.2
7.	Connecticut	111.9	24.	Pennsylvania	104.5	41.	Kentucky	92.5
8.	Washington	110.2	25t.	California	103.2	42.	Texas	92.1
9.	Maine	110.0	25t.	Montana	103.2	43.	Alabama	91.0
10.	Iowa	109.3	27.	Illinois	102.8	44.	New Mexico	90.4
11.	Utah	108.8	28.	Michigan	101.9	45.	South Carolina	90.0
12.	Colorado	108.4	29.	Maryland	101.6	46.	Oklahoma	88.9
13.	Alaska	108.3	30.	New York	100.6	47.	Tennessee	87.1
14.	Nebraska	108.1	31.	Indiana	99.8	48.	Arkansas	86.6
15.	North Dakota	107.7	32.	Delaware	98.8	49t.	Mississippi	83.1
16.	Rhode Island	107.2	33.	Idaho	98.1	49t.	Louisiana	83.1
17.	New Jersey	107.0	34.	Missouri	98.0			

Source: Health Risk Management Inc., QualityFIRST Index, 1999.

Hospital Care

Hospital care has long claimed the biggest share of health care dollars. In 1950 hospital care accounted for 30.4 percent of personal health care costs. By 1980, the percentage had zoomed to 47.3 percent. More recently it declined—to 39.5 percent in 1996—as hospitals contained costs with shorter hospital stays and increased treatment on an outpatient basis.

In 1996, the average stay in community hospitals (excluding federal hospitals, psychiatric institutions, and long-term hospitals) was 6.2 days. The average costs to the hospital were $1,005 per day and $6,226 per stay. In contrast, the average stay in 1980 was 7.6 days; average costs were $244 per day and $1,844 per stay.

Costs vary markedly depending on the care required and the locale. For example, according to the Health Insurance Association of America, surgical costs of an abdominal hysterectomy averaged $4,854 in New York City in 1993, as compared to $1,884 in Denver; a triple coronary bypass averaged $6,610 in Philadelphia versus $5,727 in Dallas.

Nursing-Home Care

In mid-1998 approximately 1.6 million elderly and disabled people were receiving care in some 16,800 nursing homes across the United States. The number of nursing home residents (of all ages) per 1,000 resident population 85 and older varied significantly, from lows in 1996 for Oregon (231.4), Florida (236.2), and Arizona (243.2) to highs for Louisiana (608.7), Indiana (549.0), and Minnesota (547.5).

Because of the dramatic growth in the number of Americans over age 75, the nursing home population is frailer than ever before and requires more specialized care. Almost half of all nursing home residents have some form of dementia. In 1995 the average monthly charge in a nursing home was $3,135 per resident. This charge varied widely by geographic region from about $2,700 in the Midwest and South to $3,700 and $3,900 in the West and Northeast. Medicare payments to nursing facilities reached $9.1 billion in 1995; in addition, Medicare spent $1.9 billion on hospice care.

Americans spent $800 million on nursing-home care in 1960, $4.2 billion in 1970, $17.6 billion in 1980, and $50.9 billion in 1990. By 1996, the figure had reached $78.5 billion. Out-of-pocket payments, including personal savings and social security benefits, covered 31.4 percent of this cost; Medicare and Medicaid covered most of the remaining costs.

Paying for Health Care

Medical care is generally paid for in one of three ways:

1. By patients; according to the U.S. Dept. of Health and Human Services, an estimated 18.9 percent of the nation's personal health care costs in 1996 were paid directly by patients.

2. By an insurance plan; employers, employees and individuals paid $337.3 billion for private health insurance premiums in 1996, funding almost one-third of all health care spending. Managed care plans enrolled 85 percent of employees in 1997-up from 48 percent in 1992, according to a survey by a unit of the William M. Mercer benefits consulting firm. Costs for active employees, typically shared by employers and workers, ranged from an average of $3,165 in health maintenance organizations (HMOs) to $3,521 in fee-for-service plans; for early retirees under age 65 the average cost was $4,985.

3. As a public charge, which means that the government—and, ultimately, the taxpayer—pays the bill. An estimated 47 percent of personal health care costs in 1996 were paid

Health Care Spending by Category, 1997

Category	Amount (billions)	Change 1996–97
Hospital care	$371.1	2.9%
Physicians' services	217.6	4.4
Drugs, other non-durables	108.9	10.7
Nursing-home care	82.8	4.3
Other professional services	61.9	7.7
Dental services	50.6	6.5
Administration and net cost of private health insurance	50.0	-4.8
Government public health activities	38.5	13.1
Home health care	32.3	3.7
Research	18.0	4.7
Construction	16.9	14.3
Vision products, other durables	13.9	3.6
Other personal health care	29.9	9.0
Total	**$1,092.4**	**4.8%**

Source: U.S. Dept. of Health and Human Services, Health Care Financing Administration, Office of the Actuary.

Health Expenditures as a Percent of GNP for Selected Countries, 1960–96

Nation	1960	1970	1980	1996
United States	5.1%	7.1%	8.9%	14.0%
Germany	4.8	5.9	8.4	10.5
Switzerland	3.3	5.2	7.3	10.2
France	4.2	5.8	7.6	9.7
Canada	5.5	7.1	7.4	9.6
Netherlands	3.8	5.9	7.9	8.6
Sweden	4.7	7.1	9.4	8.6
Australia	4.9	5.7	7.3	8.5
Italy	3.6	5.2	6.9	7.8
Spain	1.5	3.7	5.7	7.4
New Zealand	4.3	5.2	7.2	7.3
Japan	3.0	4.6	6.6	7.2
United Kingdom	3.9	4.5	5.6	6.9
Greece	2.9	4.0	4.3	6.8

Source: U.S. Dept. of Health and Human Services, National Center for Health Statistics, *Health United States, 1995* (1996) and *OECD Health Data 98* (1998).

Hospital Facilities and Their Use, 1946–96

Year	Number of hospitals	Number of beds ('000s)	Admissions ('000s)	Average stay (days)	Outpatient visits ('000s)
1946	6,125	1,436	15,675	9.1	N.A.
1950	6,788	1,456	18,483	8.1	N.A.
1960	6,876	1,658	25,027	7.6	N.A.
1965	7,123	1,704	28,812	7.8	125,793
1970	7,123	1,616	31,759	8.2	181,370
1975	7,156	1,466	36,157	7.7	254,844
1980	6,965	1,365	38,892	7.6	262,951
1985	6,872	1,318	36,304	7.1	282,140
1990	6,649	1,213	33,774	7.3	368,184
1995	6,291	1,081	33,282	6.5	483,195
1996	6,201	1,062	33,307	6.2	505,455

Note: N.A.= Not Available.   Source: American Hospital Association, *Hospital Statistics* (annual).

for by federal, state, and local governments—the highest level ever recorded. In some instances the percentage is even greater. For example, injuries caused by firearms cost an estimated $429 million annually in hospital expenses alone. According to a University of California study published in 1988, 85.6 percent of this is borne by taxpayers. The cost would top $1 billion if expenses such as ambulance services, doctors' fees, follow-up care, and rehabilitation were included.

Health insurance Americans spend more than 3 percent of their disposable income for health insurance premiums. There are five basic types of insurance:
1. Hospital expense insurance—pays costs of hospital room, X-rays, medicines, etc.
2. Surgical expense insurance—pays costs of an operation.
3. Medical expense insurance—pays for visits to a physician's office.
4. Major medical expense insurance—pays costs associated with extended sickness or injury.
5. Disability income insurance—pays a benefit when the person is unable to work because of illness or injury.

Federal insurance plans Two government health programs, Medicare and Medicaid, financed $374.5 billion in health care services in

1997, more than one-third of the nation's total health care bill. These programs were responsible for almost three-quarters of all public spending on health care. (The remaining federal health spending covers military and veterans' health care.)

Medicare is a federal health insurance plan for people age 65 and older and for severely disabled people under age 65. Medicaid is a health care program for poor people. It is funded jointly by federal and state agencies. (See also Part II: "Social Insurance Programs.")

Medicare reimburses about one-half of the health care goods and services used by the eligible population. About 80 percent of this population have supplementary insurance. In 1996, 87 percent of those covered by Medicare received their care in the fee-for-service sector and 13 percent were enrolled in managed care plans.

Managed care (HMOs, PPOs) A managed health care plan provides comprehensive health care coverage to enrolled members on a prepaid basis; that is, insurance and health care delivery are integrated within one system. The objective is to control costs, assure access to effective treatments, and eliminate inappropriate and duplicative services.

The oldest managed care providers are health maintenance organizations (HMOs), which started in the 1940s. They either employ physicians in

Uninsured Americans, 1997

Category	Number ('000s)	Percent uninsured	Category	Number ('000s)	Percent uninsured
Total	**43,448**	**16.1%**	**Education level[2]**		
			No high school diploma	9,189	26.1%
Sex			High school grad only	12,204	18.5
Male	23,130	17.6	Some college	5,974	15.6
Female	20,319	14.8	Associate degree	1,726	12.3
Age			Bachelor's degree (or more)	3,611	8.2
Under 18	10,743	15.0	**Citizenship**		
18-24	7,582	30.1	Native-born	34,444	14.2
25-34	9,162	23.3	Foreign-born	9,003	34.3
35-44	7,699	17.3	Naturalized citizen	1,798	18.5
45-64	7,928	14.1	Non-citizen	7,206	43.6
65 and older	333	1.0	**Annual household income**		
Race/Ethnicity			Under $25,000	18,361	25.4
White[1]	23,135	12.0	$25,000-$49,999	14,527	18.1
Black[1]	7,432	21.5	$50,000-$74,999	5,678	10.1
Hispanic	10,534	34.2	$75,000 or more	4,882	8.1

1. Non-Hispanic. 2. Persons age 18 and older. **Source:** U.S. Bureau of the Census, *Current Population Survey,* March 1998.

People With and Without Health Insurance Coverage, by State, 1997

State	People with coverage ('000s)	People without coverage ('000s)	Percent of people without coverage	State	People with coverage ('000s)	People without coverage ('000s)	Percent of people without coverage
United States	**225,646**	**43,448**	**16.1%**	Missouri	4,653	669	12.6%
Alabama	3,588	659	15.5	Montana	720	174	19.5
Alaska	525	116	18.1	Nebraska	1,482	180	10.8
Arizona	3,514	1,141	24.5	Nevada	1,423	301	17.5
Arkansas	1,983	639	24.4	New Hampshire	1,059	141	11.8
California	25,892	7,095	21.5	New Jersey	6,657	1,320	16.5
Colorado	3,337	592	15.1	New Mexico	1,435	412	22.3
Connecticut	2,904	395	12.0	New York	14,969	3,174	17.5
Delaware	652	98	13.1	North Carolina	6,211	1,141	15.5
District of Columbia	434	84	16.2	North Dakota	542	97	15.2
				Ohio	9,934	1,297	11.5
Florida	11,582	2,817	19.6	Oklahoma	2,745	593	17.8
Georgia	6,303	1,344	17.6	Oregon	2,858	440	13.3
Hawaii	1,094	89	7.5	Pennsylvania	10,713	1,209	10.1
Idaho	1,034	223	17.7	Rhode Island	848	96	10.2
Illinois	10,592	1,506	12.4	South Carolina	3,175	640	16.8
Indiana	5,196	669	11.4	South Dakota	628	84	11.8
Iowa	2,490	340	12.0	Tennessee	4,786	756	13.6
Kansas	2,286	304	11.7	Texas	14,915	4,836	24.5
Kentucky	3,335	587	15.0	Utah	1,805	280	13.4
Louisiana	3,423	827	19.5	Vermont	526	55	9.5
Maine	1,043	182	14.9	Virginia	5,898	854	12.6
Maryland	4,380	677	13.4	Washington	5,093	655	11.4
Massachusetts	5,249	755	12.6	West Virginia	1,447	300	17.2
Michigan	8,661	1,133	11.6	Wisconsin	4,717	409	8.0
Minnesota	4,329	438	9.2	Wyoming	415	76	15.5
Mississippi	2,187	550	20.1				

Source: U.S. Census Bureau, *Current Population Survey,* March 1998.

clinics or hospital-like buildings, or contract with hundreds or even thousands of physicians who practice in their private offices.

HMO patients generally must use their HMO's physicians in order to be reimbursed. Preferred provider organizations (PPOs), a modified version of HMOs, permit enrollees to use non-plan providers (physicians and hospitals). However, patients who use services outside their PPO must pay a financial penalty.

By mid-1998, according to InterStudy Publications, there were 652 HMOs, with an enrollment of 78.8 million people. The Association of Managed Healthcare Organizations reported that the number of PPO plans grew to 1,020 in 1998 and that more than 80 million people were members of PPOs and other network-based plans.

The uninsured An ever-growing number of Americans have no health insurance. According to the Census Bureau, approximately 43.4 million people—16.1 percent of the population—were without health insurance during all of 1997, an increase of 1.7 million from the previous year. The number of uninsured children under 18 was 10.7 million (15.0 percent).

The probability of being uninsured varied by the place of residence, earnings, and the size of the company for which a person worked. The Census Bureau, using three-year averages from 1995-97, found that uninsured rates ranged from 7.5 percent in Hawaii to 24.5 percent in Texas and Arizona. High incomes and employment in large companies increase the likelihood that a person has health insurance.

Milestones In the History of Medicine

B.C.

c. 2700   Chinese emperor Shen Nung develops principles of herbal medicine and acupuncture.
c. 1700   The Code of Hammurabi, king of Babylon, comprises regulations concerning physicians, including what they may treat and what their fees should be.
c. 1500   The Ebers Papyrus describes many remedies used in Ancient Egypt to treat dental ailments.
c. 400   Hippocrates of Cos (Greek: c. 460–c. 377), teacher and medical practitioner known as Father of Medicine, writes Hippocratic Oath, which sets ethical standards still followed by physicians throughout the world.
c. 300   Herophilus (Greek: c. 355–280) pioneers dissection of human body and founds first school of anatomy.

A.D.

c. 20   Aulus Cornelius Celsus (Roman: first cent.) writes first-known medical textbook.
c. 100   Romans develop a public medical service and appoint physicians to provide medical help to poor.
c. 180   Galen (Greek: c. 130–c. 201) writes *Methodus Medando*, which summarizes medical knowledge of ancient times. Galen's views on human physiology and disease would influence medical thought for more than 1,500 years.
c. 450   Susruta (Indian) notes relationship of malaria to mosquitoes and of bubonic plague to rats.
c. 900   Rhazes (Persian: c. 865–923/35) is first to describe smallpox and establish criteria for diagnosing and treating it.
1030   Ibn Sina (Avicenna; Persian: 980–1037) publishes *Canon of Medicine*, which becomes leading medical encyclopedia for centuries.
c. 1270–80   Spectacles are introduced by Venetian glassmakers.
1403   Venice imposes world's first quarantine of infected areas as safeguard against Black Death (bubonic plague).
1543   Andreas Vesalius (Flemish: 1514–64) publishes first accurate anatomy text and establishes foundations of modern anatomy.
1597   Gaspare Tagliacozzi (Italian) publishes first textbook of plastic surgery and revives operation of rhinoplasty (nose surgery).
1601   Sir James Lancaster (English: c. 1554–1618) writes that lemon juice helps prevent scurvy.
1628   William Harvey (English: 1578–1657) describes functions of the heart and how blood circulates throughout the body.
1658   Jan Swammerdam (Dutch: 1637–80) discerns red blood cells.
1670   Thomas Willis (English: 1621–75) rediscovers connection between sugar in urine and diabetes (known in antiquity by Greeks, Chinese, and Indians).
1751   Pennsylvania Hospital, first general hospital in U.S., founded in Philadelphia by Quakers.
1761   Leopold Auenbrugger von Auenbrugg (Australian: 1722–1809) discovers that fluid in chest cavity and other health problems can be detected by tapping gently on the chest.
   Giovanni B. Morgagni (Italian: 1682–1771) establishes modern pathological anatomy with publication of *On the Seats and Causes of Disease*.

1796   Edward Jenner (English: 1749–1823) develops smallpox vaccine from cowpox serum.
1816   René T.H. Laënnec (French: 1781–1826) invents stethoscope and introduces practice of auscultation (monitoring sounds made by internal organs).
1818   James Blundel (English) performs first successful human blood transfusion.
1831   Samuel Guthrie (American: 1782–1848) discovers chloroform.
1833   William Beaumont (American: 1785–1853) provides first clear insight into nature of gastric digestion.
1839   Horace Hayden (American: 1769–1844) and Chapin Harris (1806–60) found world's first dental school, Baltimore College of Dental Surgery.
1842   Crawford Long (American: 1815–78) removes tumor from patient inhaling ether—first known operation under general anesthesia; publishes his findings in 1849, three years after William Morton (American: 1819–68) demonstrates effectiveness of ether as anesthetic.
1850   Hermann Helmholtz (German: 1821–94) invents ophthalmoscope, instrument used to examine interior of the eye.
1855   Manuel Garcia (Spanish: 1805–1906) invents modern laryngoscope, device used to inspect the throat, especially the larynx and vocal cords.
1863   International Red Cross established at Geneva, Switzerland.
1865   Joseph Lister (English: 1827–1912) revolutionizes surgery when he introduces use of disinfectants to reduce infection.
   Louis Pasteur (French: 1822–95) shows that spoilage of wine can be prevented by partial heat-sterilization; process, called pasteurization, soon applied to milk and other foods.
1866   Sir Thomas C. Allbutt (English: 1836–1925) invents clinical thermometer.
1868   Carl Wunderlich (German: 1815–77) establishes that fever is a symptom, not a disease, and introduces use of thermometer for taking body temperature.
1881   Pasteur produces vaccine that successfully prevents anthrax—first disease prevented by vaccine.
1890   Emil von Behring (German: 1854–1917) and Shibasaburo Kitasato (Japanese: 1852–1931) independently discover antitoxins.
1892   Dmitri Ivanovski (Russian: 1864–1920) discovers filterable viruses (viruses tiny enough to pass through fine filters previously believed to trap all living organisms).
1893   Felix Hofmann (German) develops a process for production of acetylsalicylic acid, the form of aspirin used today.
1895   Wilhelm Röntgen (German: 1845–1923) discovers X rays.
1900   Sigmund Freud (Austrian: 1856–1955), founder of psychoanalysis, publishes *The Interpretations of Dreams*.
   Karl Landsteiner (Austrian-American: 1868–1943) discovers three blood groups, later named A, B, and O; fourth group, to be named AB, discovered in 1902.
   Walter Reed (American: 1851–1902) establishes that yellow fever virus is transmitted by mosquitoes.

1901 Jokichi Takamine (Japanese-American: 1854–1922) isolates adrenaline, first hormone to be isolated.

1902 Eugene Opie (American) establishes that diabetes results from destruction of specific portions of pancreatic tissue—the islets of Langerhans.

1905 Albert Einhorn (American) synthesizes procaine (novocaine), which becomes the most widely used dental anesthetic.

1906 August von Wassermann (German: 1866–1925) develops blood test for syphilis.

1910 Marie Curie (French: 1867–1934) isolates pure radium metal, which came to be used to treat cancer.

1913 Béla Schick (Hungarian-American: 1877–1967) perfects test for determining susceptibility to diphtheria.

1915 Death certificates come into general use in U.S.

Margaret Sanger (American: 1883–1966) founds the National Birth Control League, which in 1942 becomes Planned Parenthood.

1918 Francis Benedict (American: 1870–1957) devises basal metabolism test for measuring rate at which metabolism (total of all chemical reactions) occurs in the body.

1921 Sir Frederick G. Banting (Canadian: 1891–1941) and Charles H. Best (1899–1978) extract insulin from the pancreas.

1928 Sir Alexander Fleming (Scottish: 1881–1955) discovers penicillin, a substance in green mold *Penicillium notatum* that destroys certain bacteria.

1929 Hans Berger (German: 1873–1941) publishes his results of the first electroencephalograms (EEGs) of humans.

1935 Gerhard Domagk (German: 1895–1964) announces discovery of Prontosil (sulfonamidecrysoidin), the first useful sulfa drug.

1937 First blood bank is established, at Cook County Hospital in Chicago.

Alton Ochsner (American: 1896–1981) and Michael De Bakey (1908–) suggest that cigarette smoking is cause of lung cancer.

1944 Willem Kolff (Dutch-American: 1911–) develops first kidney dialysis machine.

Oswald Avery (Canadian: 1877–1955), Colin MacLeod, and Maclyn McCarty prove that DNA (deoxyribonucleic acid) is blueprint of heredity that determines how an organism develops.

First eye bank, Eye-Bank for Sight Restoration, founded in New York.

Albert Schatz (American: 1921–) and Selman Waksman (American: 1888–1973) isolate streptomycin, an antibiotic effective against bacterium that causes tuberculosis.

1945 Alfred Blalock (American: 1899–1964) introduces first operation to enable blue, or cyanotic, babies to survive (cyanosis, caused by poor circulatory flow or other problems, results in diminished oxygen in blood, causing bluish discoloration of the skin).

1947 Eugene Payne (American) uses chloromycetin, developed by Parke-Davis researchers, to treat typhus patients; first use of "broadspectrum" antibiotic.

1948 Philip S. Hench (American: 1896–1965) and Edward C. Kendall (1886–1972) synthesize cortisone and use it to treat arthritis victims.

1952 Jonas Salk (American: 1914–95) develops first vaccine against polio.

1953 John H. Gibbon, Jr. (American: 1903–) uses heart-lung machine he invented in successful open-heart operation.

1954 Surgeons led by Joseph Murray (American) perform first successful kidney transplant.

E. Cuyler Hammond (American: 1912–86) and Daniel Horn (American) present dramatic evidence of dangers in smoking.

1957 Alick Isaacs (Scottish: 1921–67) and Jean Lindenmann (Swiss) discover interferon, a protein that interferes with viral reproduction.

1958 Wilson Greatbatch (American) invents the implantable artificial pacemaker.

1961 Scientists at Bell Laboratories (Americans) announce first continuously operating laser, a tool having many surgical uses.

1963 Thomas Starzl (American: 1926–) performs first human liver transplant operation.

1964 James Hardy (American: 1918–) performs first human lung transplant.

1965 Medicare and Medicaid are established, guaranteeing medical insurance coverage for the aged and the poor.

1966 Paul Parkman and Harry Myer (Americans) develop vaccine for rubella (German measles).

Insulin synthesized independently by Michael Katsoyannis (American) and scientists in the People's Republic of China—first hormone to be synthesized.

1967 Christiaan Barnard (South African: 1922–) performs world's first heart transplant.

Rene Favaloro (Argentinian) performs first successful coronary bypass operation.

First modern hospice founded in London.

1969 Denton Cooley (American: 1920–) implants first temporary artificial heart in human being.

1972 Computerized axial tomography (CAT scan) is introduced in Great Britain.

1977 Scientists at Genentech Corporation (Americans) induce bacteria to make humanbrain hormone somatostatin—first human chemical produced by recombinant-DNA techniques.

The first known human cases of cyclospora infection are diagnosed.

1978 First "test tube baby" (person conceived outside human body) is born, in England.

1981 Scientists identify acquired immune deficiency syndrome (AIDS), a previously unknown disease.

Surgeons at University of California at San Francisco perform first successful operation on a fetus.

1982 William DeVries (American) performs first complete replacement of human heart with artificial heart at University of Utah.

1984 First baby produced from frozen embryo is born, in Melbourne, Australia.

Luc Montagnier (French) discovers virus believed to cause AIDS.

1990 R. Michael Blaese, W. French Anderson, and Kenneth W. Culver (Americans) develop procedure to infuse genetically engineered blood cells for treatment of immune system disorder—first gene therapy used in a human.

1993 The U.S. Environmental Protection Agency concludes that environmental tobacco smoke ("secondhand smoke") is a lung carcinogen and causes respiratory problems for infants and young children.

1996 British scientists announce the possibility that a new form of Creutzfeldt-Jakob disease is transmitted to humans through the meat of cattle infected with bovine spongiform encephalopathy ("mad cow disease").

1999 Surgeons at Vanderbilt University Medical Center perform first successful brain surgery on a fetus.

▶SURGERY

Increases in the number of surgical operations during recent years have been accompanied by dramatic changes in the rates of some procedures. An example is the incidence of cesarean sections—surgical incisions through the abdomen and uterus for removal of a baby, performed when normal vaginal delivery is deemed hazardous for the mother or child. Cesareans accounted for 20.7 percent of all live births in 1996—a significant decline from 24.4 percent in 1988, but almost four times the rate in 1970 (5.5 percent) and among the highest rates for developed nations.

The frequency of certain procedures varies according to age, but, surprisingly, there may also be variations from one geographical region to another. For example, the 1996 Cesarean rate ranged from 15.1 percent in Colorado to 26.6 percent in Mississippi. A survey by Dartmouth Medical Schools researchers released in 1996 also noted disparities in the treatment of choice. For example, they found that a person in Kingsport, Tennessee, with a herniated disk was seven times as likely to have back surgery as one in Provo, Utah.

Organ Transplantation

Transplant surgery is more successful than ever, thanks to improved surgical techniques, a better understanding of the body's immune system, and

Number and Survival Rates of Transplant Operations, 1998

Organ	Year first performed	Number (1998)[1]	Survival rates[2]
Heart	1967	2,340	79%
Heart-lung	1982	45	65
Intestine	1990	69	56
Kidney	1954	11,990	—
Cadaver	—	7,974	89
Living donor	—	4,016	94
Liver	1963	4,450	79
Lung	1963	849	61
Pancreas	1966	215	91

1. In addition, 965 kidney-pancreas operations were performed. 2. Three-year patient survival rates for operations performed in 1995 (except intestines, for which data is based on operations performed in 1992).   **Source:** United Network for Organ Sharing.

Cardiovascular Operations in the U.S., 1996

Operation	Sex		Age			
	Male	Female	Under 15	15–44	45–64	65 plus
Total procedures	**3,231,000**	**2,213,000**	**164,000**	**544,000**	**1,882,000**	**2,853,000**
Cardiac catheterization	754,000	488,000	16,000	105,000	524,000	596,000
Bypass	452,000	214,000	—	37,000	307,000	322,000
Angioplasty	424,000	175,000	—	20,000	242,000	335,000
Pacemaker	77,000	78,000	—	—	19,000	132,000
Endarterectomy	77,000	54,000	—	—	27,000	102,000
Valve replacement	41,000	33,000	—	8,000	19,000	41,000
Defibrillator implants	15,000	—	—	—	8,000	9,000
Open heart surgery[1]	515,000	239,000	25,000	40,000	280,000	397,000

Note: Estimated figures. Breakdowns not available for some procedures, causing entries for some categories not to add up to the total. Does not include outpatient and other nonhospitalized procedures. 1. Includes valves, bypass, and "other" open heart procedures. **Source:** American Heart Association, *1999 Heart and Stroke Statistical Update.*

Common Operations, 1995

Type of Operation	Total	Males	Females
All operations[1]	**22,530,000**	**8,388,000**	**14,142,000**
Cardiac catheterization	1,068,000	660,000	408,000
Repair of lacerations due to giving birth	964,000	—	964,000
Cesarean section	785,000	—	785,000
Coronary artery bypass	573,000	423,000	150,000
Hysterectomy	583,000	—	583,000
Gall bladder removal	470,000	142,000	328,000
Removal of one or both ovaries	447,000	—	447,000
Coronary artery obstruction, removal	434,000	285,000	149,000
Reduction of fracture (excluding skull, nose and jaw)	414,000	177,000	238,000
Destruction or closing off of fallopian tubes	327,000	—	327,000
Pacemaker insertion or replacement	314,000	157,000	156,000
Spinal disc operation	273,000	162,000	111,000
Prostatectomy	239,000	239,000	—
Appendectomy	237,000	135,000	102,000
Knee replacement (total)	216,000	75,000	141,000

1. Includes operations not shown separately.   **Source:** U.S. Dept. of Health and Human Services, National Center for Health Statistics, National Hospital Discharge Survey: Annual Summary, 1995 (Jan. 1998).

the development of drugs that combat rejection of implanted organs. Kidney transplants, for instance, enjoy a high rate of success and are much less expensive—and much more convenient—than maintaining a patient on dialysis. Unfortunately, a scarcity of donor organs keeps thousands of patients waiting, sometimes in vain. An estimated 62,000 Americans are currently waiting for a heart, lung, liver, kidney, or pancreas. In 1998 about 4000 people died before they could get one. The good news was that the number of donors increased 5.6 percent in 1998, resulting in about 600 more transplants than in 1997.

In addition to organs, tissues—cornea, bone, and skin—can be transplanted. In fact, corneal transplants are the most frequently performed transplant surgery. According to the Eye Bank Association, there were 35,861 such operations in 1998, with a success rate averaging better than 90 percent. As with organs, the need for tissues frequently exceeds the supply.

There are 53 independent and 9 hospital organ procurement programs in the United States. Many have toll-free telephone numbers. The United Network for Organ Sharing (UNOS) operates the national waiting list (1-888-TX-INFO1).

To perform transplants, hospitals must be licensed. According to UNOS, 272 medical institutions operated organ transplant programs as of late 1997. These can be separated into organ-specific programs, including:

252—kidney transplants
153—heart transplants
125—liver transplants
125—pancreas transplants
94—heart-lung transplants
89—lung transplants
32—intestine transplants

Abortion

The deliberate termination of a pregnancy before the fetus is capable of living outside the womb has generally been legal in the United States since 1973, when the Supreme Court ruled (in *Roe v. Wade*) that abortion cannot be prohibited during the first three months of pregnancy. From 1973 through 1980, the ratio of abortions to live births increased significantly, to 359 per 1,000 live births. Since then, the ratio has declined, to 314 per 1,000 live births in 1996.

According to a 1998 report from the Centers for Disease Control and Prevention (CDC), women who obtained abortions in 1996 were predominantly 24 years of age or younger, white, unmarried, and had no live-born children. More than half of the abortions were performed during the first eight weeks of gestation; approximately 88 percent were performed in the first 12 weeks. Curettage was the primary abortion procedure, accounting for 99 percent of all abortions.

▶DISEASE

Five of the most common categories of disease are:
1. Hereditary diseases—transferred from parent to child by genes. Examples: hemophilia, Down's syndrome, cystic fibrosis, sickle cell anemia.
2. Deficiency diseases—caused by lack of vitamins or other essential nutrients. Examples: scurvy, pellagra.
3. Infectious diseases—caused by viruses, bacteria, fungi, and other organisms and transferred from person to person. Examples: common cold, influenza, chicken pox, measles, tuberculosis, AIDS.
4. Diseases caused by chemical and physical agents such as radiation, smoke, drugs, and poisons. Examples: allergies, asbestosis, bysinosis, lead poisoning.
5. Degenerative diseases—resulting from natural aging processes. In some cases, cancer and high blood pressure are degenerative diseases.

Heart Disease

Cardiovascular diseases (diseases of the heart and blood vessels) are America's number one killer.

Reported Abortions, 1972–96					
Category	1972	1980	1990	1995[1]	1996[1]
NUMBER OF ABORTIONS					
Reported abortions	586,760	1,297,606	1,429,577	1,210,883	1,221,585
Number per 1,000 live births	180	359	345	311	314
PERCENT OF TOTAL					
Race					
White	77.0%	69.9%	64.8%	59.5%	59.1%
Black[2]	23.0	30.1	31.8	35.0	35.2
Marital Status					
Married	29.7%	23.1%	21.7%	20.3%	16.1%
Unmarried	70.3	76.9	78.3	79.7	83.9
Age					
Under 20	32.6%	29.2%	22.4%	20.1%	20.3%
20–24	32.5	35.5	33.2	32.5	31.9
25 or older	34.9	35.3	44.4	47.4	47.8
Weeks of gestation					
Up to 8	34.0%	51.7%	51.6%	54.0%	54.6%
9–10	30.7	26.2	25.3	23.1	22.6
11–12	17.5	12.2	11.8	10.9	11.0
13–15	8.4	5.1	6.4	6.3	6.0
16–20	8.2	3.9	4.0	4.3	4.3
21 or more	1.2	0.9	1.0	1.4	1.5

1. Preliminary. 2. Data for 1972 and 1980 include other nonwhite groups. **Source:** U.S. Dept of Health and Human Services, Centers for Disease Control and Prevention, *Morbidity and Mortality Weekly Report* (Dec. 4, 1998).

Almost one in four Americans—more than 58 million people—suffer some form of cardiovascular disease. During 1996 these diseases claimed 959,227 lives. This represented 41.4 percent of all deaths—an average of a death every 33 seconds.

Death rates vary according to age, sex, race, even geographical location. Rates increase with age and are higher among men than among women. For both sexes, death rates are significantly higher among blacks than among whites, though the disparity has narrowed in the past 25 years.

In 1995, Utah had the lowest death rate from cardiovascular disease (141.4 per 100,000 population) followed by Colorado, Hawaii, New Mexico, and Alaska. Mississippi had the highest death rate (255.8) followed by South Carolina, Tennessee, the District of Columbia, and Lousiana.

The good news is that the death rates from cardiovascular disease have declined dramatically. In 1950 the death rate was 424.2 per 100,000 population; by 1995 it had dropped to 177.7. This is due in part to improved drug treatments and other medical advancements. Another factor has been improved personal health habits: people have stopped smoking, lowered the fat content of their diets, and taken other steps that reduce the risks of cardiovascular disease.

Heart attacks   A heart attack occurs when the blood supply to the heart muscles is blocked. An uncomfortable pressure, fullness, squeezing, or pain in the center of the chest that lasts for two minutes or more may be a sign of a heart attack. Sweating, dizziness, nausea, fainting, or shortness of breath may also occur. Some 1.1 million people suffer heart attacks annually. One-third of these people do not survive. Of the survivors, 42 percent of the women and 24 percent of the men will die within one year. Many survivors develop congestive heart failure, which can leave the heart unable to pump blood effectively; it is the only form of heart disease on the rise in the United States.

Strokes and bypass surgery   Each year, approximately 600,000 Americans—72 percent of them age 65 or older—suffer a stroke; of these, more than 155,000 die. A stroke occurs when the blood supply to the brain is blocked, usually by a clot. The primary signal of a stroke is a sudden, temporary weakness or numbness of the face, arm, or leg on one side of the body. Other signals include temporary loss of speech, difficulty in speaking or understanding speech, temporary vision problems (particularly in one eye), unsteadiness, or unexplained dizziness.

The American Heart Association estimates that 598,000 bypass operations were performed on 367,000 patients in 1996, more than triple the number performed in 1980. In this operation a blood vessel from elsewhere in the body is used to reroute blood around a blocked coronary artery. The purpose: to reduce the person's risk of a stroke. While bypass operations have resulted in improved survival rates and better quality of life for many people, some research has found that a large percentage of these operations are unnecessary or inappropriate; in such cases, patients treated nonsurgically do equally well.

Cancer
The nation's second leading cause of death is a group of diseases characterized by the unrestrained growth of cells. It afflicts people of all ages and races, and it varies greatly in cause, symptoms, response to treatment, and possibility of cure.

A U.S. male has a 1 in 2 probability of developing invasive cancer at some time during his life;

Reported Cases of Common Infectious Diseases, 1950–98

Disease	1950	1960	1970	1980	1990	1997	1998[1]
Brucellosis (undulant fever)	3,510	751	213	183	85	76	62
Cholera	N.A.	N.A.	N.A.	9	6	10	12
Legionnellosis	N.A.	N.A.	N.A.	N.A.	1,370	1,054	1,327
Leprosy (Hansen's disease)	44	54	129	223	198	109	105
Malaria	2,184	72	3,051	2,062	1,292	1,772	1,381
Meningococcal infections	3,788	2,259	2,505	2,840	2,451	3,017	2,633
Mumps	N.A.	N.A.	104,953	8,576	5,292	612	606
Pertussis (whooping cough)	120,718	14,809	4,249	1,730	4,570	5,519	6,279
Plague[2]	N.A.	N.A.	13	18	2	4	8
Poliomyelitis	33,300	3,190	33	9	7	1	1
Psittacosis	26	113	35	124	113	37	49
Rabies, in animals	7,901	3,567	3,224	6,421	4,826	7,853	7,084
Rabies, in humans	18	2	3	0	1	2	0
Rubella (German measles)	N.A.	N.A.	56,552	3,904	1,125	161	345
Tetanus	486	368	148	95	64	43	34
Toxic shock syndrome	N.A.	N.A.	N.A.	N.A.	322	134	132
Trichinosis	327	160	100	131	129	9	24
Tuberculosis	N.A.	55,494	37,137	27,749	25,701	19,855	14,756
Typhoid fever	2,484	816	346	510	552	346	327
Venereal disease							
Gonorrhea	286,746	258,933	600,072	1,004,029	690,169	289,870	345,087
Syphilis[3]	23,939	16,145	21,982	27,204	50,223	7,917	7,183

1. Incomplete due to late reporting. 2. Plague: disease caused by the bite of fleas infected with the bacterium *Yersinia pestis*. 3. Primary and secondary syphilis cases.   **Source:** U.S. Dept of Health and Human Services, Centers for Disease Control and Prevention, *Morbidity and Mortality Weekly Report,* Oct. 6, 1995, Jan. 9, 1998, and Jan. 8, 1999.

a female, 1 in 3. The incidence of cancer varies from state to state. The American Cancer Society predicted that the highest cancer death rates in 1998 would occur in the District of Columbia (218 cancer deaths per 100,000 population), Delaware (196), Louisiana (194), and Kentucky (192). The states with the lowest cancer death rates were expected to be Utah (126), Hawaii (137), New Mexico (146), and Colorado (147).

Cancer survival rates   The National Cancer Institute estimates that approximately 8.2 million Americans alive today have a history of cancer. Chances of surviving cancer have steadily improved. In the 1930s, about one in four American cancer patients survived at least five years after diagnosis. In contrast, six out of 10 who get cancer this year will be alive five years after diagnosis.

Heart Disease Death Rates, 1960–96 (per 100,000 population)

Age	1960[1]	1970	1980	1990	1995	1996
All ages						
Age adjusted	286.2	253.6	202.2	152.0	138.3	134.5
Crude	369.0	362.0	336.0	289.5	280.7	276.4
Under 1 year	6.6	13.1	22.8	20.1	17.1	16.6
1–4 years	1.3	1.7	2.6	1.9	1.6	1.4
5–14 years	1.3	0.8	0.9	0.9	0.8	0.9
15–24 years	4.0	3.0	2.9	2.5	2.9	2.7
25–34 years	15.6	11.4	8.3	7.6	8.5	8.3
35–44 years	74.6	66.7	44.6	31.4	32.0	30.5
45–54 years	271.8	238.4	180.2	120.5	111.0	108.2
55–64 years	737.9	652.3	494.1	367.3	322.9	315.2
65–74 years	1,740.5	1,558.2	1,218.6	894.3	799.9	776.2
75–84 years	4,089.4	3,683.8	2,993.1	2,295.7	2,064.7	2,010.2
85 and older	9,317.8	7,891.3	7,777.1	6,739.9	6,484.1	6,314.5

1. Includes deaths of nonresidents of the U.S.
Source: U.S. Dept. of Health and Human Services, *Health, United States, 1998* (1998).

Estimated New Cancer Cases and Deaths by Site and Sex, 1999

Site	New cases			Deaths		
	Total	Male	Female	Total	Male	Female
All Sites	**1,221,800**	**623,800**	**598,000**	**563,100**	**291,100**	**272,000**
Skin[1]	54,000	33,400	20,600	9,200	5,800	3,400
Oral	29,800	20,000	9,800	8,100	5,400	2,700
Lung, bronchus, and other respiratory	187,600	106,800	80,800	164,200	94,900	69,300
Breast	176,300	1,300	175,000	43,700	400	43,300
Esophagus	12,500	9,400	3,100	12,200	9,400	2,800
Stomach	21,900	13,700	8,200	13,500	7,900	5,600
Small intestine	4,800	2,500	2,300	1,200	600	600
Colon, rectum, and anus	132,700	63,800	68,900	57,100	28,000	29,100
Liver and bile passages	21,700	12,600	9,100	17,200	9,700	7,500
Pancreas	28,600	14,000	14,600	28,600	13,900	14,700
Other digestive organs	4,100	1,200	2,900	1,200	400	800
Urinary (bladder, kidney, etc.)	86,500	58,400	28,100	24,500	15,600	8,900
Leukemia	30,200	16,800	13,400	22,100	12,400	9,700
Lymphoma	64,000	36,400	27,600	27,000	14,100	12,900
Multiple myeloma	13,700	7,300	6,400	11,400	5,800	5,600
Bone and joints	2,600	1,400	1,200	1,400	800	600
Endocrine system	19,800	5,400	14,400	2,000	900	1,100
Eye	2,200	1,200	1,000	200	100	100
Brain, other nervous system	16,800	9,500	7,300	13,100	7,200	5,900
Ovary	25,200	—	25,200	14,500	—	14,500
Uterus	50,200	—	50,200	11,200	—	11,200
Other genital, female	5,600	—	5,600	1,500	—	1,500
Prostate	179,300	179,300	—	37,000	37,000	—
Testis	7,400	7,400	—	300	300	—
Other genital, male	1,400	1,400	—	200	200	—
All other plus unspecified sites	42,900	20,600	22,300	40,500	20,300	20,200

Note: Except for bladder, figures for invasive cancer only. Carcinoma in situ of the breast accounts for about 39,900 new cases annually and melanoma carcinoma in situ accounts for about 23,200 new cases annually. 1. Melanoma and other nonepithelial skin cancers only; highly curable basal cell and squamous cell skin cancers account for approximately 1 million new cases annually.
Source: American Cancer Society, *Cancer Facts & Figures 1999.*

5-Year Survival Rates for Cancer, by Race and Site, 1960-94

Cancer Site	1960-63	1970-73	1980-82	1989-94	1960-63	1970-73	1980-82	1989-94
	Whites				Blacks			
All sites	39%	43%	52%	62%	27%	31%	40%	47%
Brain	18	20	25	30	19	19	31	38
Breast (females)	63	68	77	87	46	51	66	71
Cervix	58	64	68	72	47	61	61	59
Colon	43	49	56	64	34	37	49	52
Leukemia	14	22	39	44	N.C.	N.C.	33	31
Liver	N.C.	N.C.	4	6	N.C.	N.C.	2	2
Lung	8	10	14	15	5	7	12	11
Ovary	32	36	39	50	32	32	39	46
Pancreas	1	2	3	4	1	2	5	4
Prostate	50	63	75	95	25	55	65	81
Rectum	38	45	53	61	27	30	38	53
Stomach	11	13	16	19	8	13	19	21
Testis	63	72	92	96	N.C.	N.C.	90	90
Thyroid	83	86	94	96	N.C.	N.C.	94	88
Urinary bladder	53	61	79	84	24	36	58	62
Uterus	73	81	83	87	31	44	54	54

Note: Rates are an average of cases diagnosed in years shown. N.C.: valid rate could not be calculated. **Source:** U.S. Dept. of Health and Human Services, National Cancer Institute; published in American Cancer Society, *Cancer Facts and Figures, 1999.*

Survival depends on many factors. Two of the most important are the site of the tumor and how much the cancer has spread before treatment is begun. Lifestyle choices are also important. The American Cancer Society estimated that 173,000 lives would be lost in 1999 to cancer because of tobacco use, and evidence suggests that up to one-third of the cancer deaths in 1999 were related to nutrition.

Cancer death incidence and rates After increasing steadily for most of the century, cancer incidence and death rates for all cancers combined and for most of the top ten cancer sites declined from 1990 and 1995. Incidence rates decreased an average of 0.7 percent per year, with the greatest decrease occurring after 1992. The overall cancer death rate declined on average by about 0.5 percent per year during 1990-95. The decline in mortality was greatest among persons younger than age 65 and greater for males (0.9 percent per year) than for females (0.1 percent per year). Almost all racial and ethnic groups are included in this downturn, except for Asian and Pacific Islander females. Improved detection and treatment, coupled with healthier lifestyles, are believed to account for the declining rates.

The American Cancer Society estimated that about 563,100 Americans would die of cancer in 1999—more than 1,500 people a day. Lung cancer is the leading cause of cancer deaths, killing an estimated 90,900 men and 68,000 women in 1999. Among women, breast cancer is the second most common killer, though if detected early and treated properly, it has a very high cure rate. Among men, prostate cancer causes the second greatest number of deaths. It, too, has a high survival rate if discovered while still localized within the general region of the prostate.

Cancer warning signs
Early detection is the key in fighting cancer. See your doctor if one of the following symptoms lasts longer than two weeks.
1. Unusual bleeding or discharge.
2. A sore that does not heal.
3. A change in a wart or mole
4. A lump or thickening in the breast or elsewhere.
5. A change in bowel or bladder habits.
6. Nagging cough or hoarseness.
7. Indigestion or difficulty in swallowing.

AIDS
The world faces a "runaway epidemic" of acquired immune deficiency syndrome (AIDS) said Dr. Peter Piot, head of the United Nations HIV/AIDS program, in mid-1998. In the United States, however, there was some cause for optimism, as new treatments slowed the onset of AIDS and the progression of AIDS to death in people infected with human immunodeficiency virus (HIV), the cause of the disease. In 1997, an estimated 270,841 people were living with AIDS, a 12 percent increase from 1996. Nonetheless, the Centers for Disease Control and Prevention (CDC) reported that the disease—unknown until 1981—had been diagnosed in 688,200 people in the United States and its territories by the end of 1998; of these, 410,800 had died.

HIV is spread through contact with infected body fluids such as blood and semen. Infected people may harbor the virus within their bodies for several years or even longer before developing symptoms of AIDS. Though symptomless, they can still infect others. The CDC estimates that 650,000 to 900,000 Americans are now living with HIV, and at least 40,000 new infections occur each year.

A small group of people seem to be immune to HIV, and in 1996 scientists discovered a genetic mutation that prevents HIV from gaining a foothold in the body. There also have been reports of HIV-positive infants who fought off the infection. No cure for the disease has yet been developed, and vaccine trials have been disappointing. Therapies that involve two types of drugs—protease inhibitors and nucleoside analogs—have been extremely effective for some patients, but the high cost of the drugs put them beyond the reach of the vast majority of the world's HIV-positive people. In addition, by 1998 there were reports of drug-resistant HIV strains. AIDS experts stressed that preventive measures, including sex education, condom distribution, and needle-exchange programs for drug addicts, need to be emphasized. (See also "World Health" for information about AIDS worldwide.)

AIDS patients In the United States, homosexual and bisexual males make up almost 50 percent of all adult and adolescent AIDS patients. The other major group afflicted with AIDS is intravenous drug abusers—both men and women—who constitute 26 percent of the total. An additional 6 percent of the cases are men who both have sex with men and inject drugs.

Cases are not limited to these high-risk groups. Anyone may become infected by having sex with someone who is infected with the HIV virus. Babies of infected women may be born with the disease because it can be transmitted from the

mother to the baby before or during birth. Also, prior to blood screening that began in 1985, some hemophiliacs and other people were infected when they received blood contaminated with the HIV virus.

By 1998, due at least in part to a significant decrease in cases among whites, AIDS was becoming largely an epidemic among blacks. Blacks were 13 percent of the U.S. population, but they accounted for 57 percent of new HIV infections. The overwhelming majority of AIDS cases are found in large cities and metropolitan areas. Through 1998, metropolitan areas with 500,000 or more population accounted for 578,010 of the 688,200 reported AIDS cases (84.0 percent).

Heterosexuals and AIDS Cases of AIDS attributed to heterosexual contacts represent 10 percent of the total number of U.S. cases. Despite the comparatively low percentage, the disease is spreading faster among heterosexuals than among any other group. Heterosexuals most at risk are those with venereal disease and multiple sex partners. Evidence suggests that sexually transmitted diseases that cause genital ulcers, such as herpes and syphilis, are especially dangerous because they cause breaks in the skin through which HIV can enter. People with these diseases are three to five times more likely than usual to get HIV if they have sex with an HIV-infected person.

Of the adult and adolescent AIDS cases reported during 1998, only 4 percent of all AIDS cases in men were attributed to heterosexual contact. In contrast, 39 percent of all AIDS cases in women were attributed to heterosexual contact. Many women infected with the AIDS virus give birth to babies that are also infected. By the end of 1998, there were 7,687 reported cases of AIDS transmission from mothers to newborns.

Sexually Transmitted Diseases

Sexually transmitted diseases (STDs) have been around since the beginning of recorded history, and while the prevalence of some have declined, rates for others have exploded. Today, millions of Americans suffer from STDs, in large part because they engage in unprotected sex and have more than one sexual partner. According to a 1996 Institute of Medicine report, the United States has the highest rate of STDs of any developed country in the world.

An estimated 15.3 million new cases of STDs occur annually in the United States, and at least one

AIDS Cases and Deaths in the U.S., 1981–97

Year	Cases diagnosed	Cases diagnosed to date	Known deaths	Known deaths to date
Pre-1981	93	93	31	31
1981	332	425	128	159
1982	1,201	1,626	463	622
1983	3,145	4,771	1,508	2,130
1984	6,335	11,106	3,505	5,635
1985	11,990	23,096	6,972	12,607
1986	19,319	42,415	12,110	24,717
1987	28,999	71,414	16,412	41,129
1988	35,957	107,371	21,119	62,248
1989	43,168	150,539	27,791	90,039
1990	49,069	199,608	31,538	121,577
1991	60,124	259,732	36,616	158,193
1992	79,054	338,786	41,094	199,287
1993	79,049	417,835	44,636	243,923
1994	71,209	489,044	48,663	292,586
1995	66,233	555,277	48,371	340,957
1996	54,656	609,933	34,947	375,904
1997	31,153	641,086	14,338	390,242

Note: Delays in reporting cases and deaths substantially impact data, particularly for recent years. In addition, through 1997 there were 450 people known to have died but whose dates of death are unknown. **Source:** U.S. Dept. of Health and Human Services, Centers for Disease Control and Prevention, *HIV/AIDS Surveillance Report*, Vol. 9, No. 2 (1998).

Adults and Adolescents With AIDS, 1981–98

Exposure category	Males Cases	Males Percent	Females Cases	Females Percent	Total Cases	Total Percent
Homosexual/Bisexual males	326,051	57%	—	—	326,051	48%
Intravenous (IV) drug abusers	126,889	22	46,804	43%	173,693	26
Homosexual male and IV drug abusers	43,640	8	—	—	43,640	6
Hemophilia/Coagulation disorder	4,663	1	248	0	4,911	1
Heterosexual contact	23,361	4	43,128	39	66,490	10
Blood transfusion, blood components, or tissue	4,784	1	3,598	3	8,382	1
Other/Undetermined[1]	41,037	7	15,533	14	56,572	8
Total[2]	570,425	100%	109,311	100%	679,739	100%

Note: Provisional data. Cases with more than one risk factor other than the combinations listed are tabulated only in the category listed first. 1. Includes patients whose mode of exposure to HIV is unknown; also includes 113 persons who acquired HIV infection perinatally but were diagnosed with AIDS after age 13. 2. Due to rounding, category totals may not total 100%. **Source:** U.S. Dept. of Health and Human Services, Centers for Disease Control and Prevention, *HIV/AIDS Surveillance Report*, Vol. 10, No. 2 (1999).

AIDS in the Cities, 1998

City	Number of cases
New York, N.Y.	109,050
Los Angeles, Calif.	38,670
San Francisco, Calif.	26,332
Miami, Fla.	21,502
Washington, D.C.	20,121
Chicago, Ill.	18,776
Houston, Texas	17,585
Philadelphia, Pa.	16,123
Newark, N.J.	15,426
Atlanta, Ga.	14,217
Baltimore, Md.	12,533
Boston, Mass.	12,231
Ft. Lauderdale, Fla.	11,190
Dallas, Texas	11,153
San Diego, Calif.	9,643
Tampa-St. Petersburg, Fla.	7,454
Oakland, Calif.	7,447
Detroit, Mich.	6,882
West Palm Beach, Fla.	6,682
New Orleans, La.	6,219
Riverside-San Bernardino, Calif.	6,199
Seattle, Wash.	6,159
Jersey City, N.J.	6,136
Nassau-Suffolk, N.Y.	6,121
New Haven, Conn.	5,933
Orlando, Fla.	5,240
Denver, Colo.	5,156
Orange County, Calif.	5,116

Note: Provisional data.   Source: U.S. Dept. of Health and Human Services, Centers for Disease Control and Prevention, HIV/AIDS Surveillance Report, Vol. 10, No. 2 (1999).

in every three sexually active people will contract an STD by age 24, reported the American Social Health Association in 1998. The most prevalent STDs are the human papilloma virus, which causes warts and genital cancers (5.5 million new cases annually); trichomoniasis, caused by a protozoan (5.0 million); chlamydia, caused by a bacterium (3.0 million); genital herpes, caused by a virus (1.0 million); and gonorrhea, caused by a bacterium (650,000). Public health officials note that people with STDs have a significantly increased risk of becoming infected with HIV, in part because they may have open sores that provide the virus with an easy route of entry to the body.

Viral Hepatitis: A Major Cause of Liver Disease
Several viruses are responsible for viral hepatitis, a sometimes-fatal disease that attacks the liver. In the United States 97 percent of acute cases and 83 percent of chronic cases are accounted for by hepatitis viruses A, B, C, D, and E—particularly the first three.

Hepatitis A is spread primarily by fecal contamination of food and water and through person-to-person contact. The Centers for Disease Control and Prevention (CDC) estimates that the virus infects 150,000 Americans each year. In 1995, the United States licensed the first vaccine to prevent this disease.

Hepatitis B is generally transmitted via contact with the blood of an infected person during sex, during birth, or through contaminated needles and syringes. People at high risk are intravenous drug users who share needles, homosexual men, and heterosexuals with multiple partners.

According to the CDC, an estimated 200,000 new infections of hepatitis B are diagnosed annually. Some of those infected become chronic carriers. An estimated one million Americans are believed to be chronic carriers, capable of transmitting the virus to other people. Furthermore, chronic carriers are at high risk of developing cirrhosis or liver cancer; each year in the United States, about 4,000 to 5,000 hepatitis B patients die of these illnesses. The CDC and medical associations recommend that all newborns be vaccinated against hepatitis B.

Hepatitis C is the leading reason for liver transplants in the United States and is believed to be responsible for much of the increase in liver cancer in recent years. An estimated 4 million Americans carry the virus, which is most commonly spread by needle sharing among intravenous blood users. Therapies often are ineffective or cause serious side effects, and no vaccine is available.

Alzheimer's disease
Alzheimer's disease is a progressive degenerative condition characterized by forgetfulness in early stages and, as the disease progresses, increasingly severe debilitating symptoms that create demanding care-giving needs. An estimated 4 million Americans, most of them elderly, have Alzheimer's disease It causes approximately 20,000 deaths annually, and contributes to the deaths of 20,000 others, making it the eighth-leading cause for persons 65 and older. Many more women than men die from Alzheimer's, but this mainly reflects the larger number of women alive at older ages. Death rates are much higher for whites than blacks, but the risk of acquiring Alzheimer's is higher for blacks than whites.

▶DEATH
In 1997, an estimated 2,314,729 deaths occurred in the United States, down from the all-time high of 2,322,265 recorded the year before. The death rate of 864.9 was down from the record of 872.5, also in 1996.

Males experience greater numbers of deaths and higher death rates than females, with black males having significantly higher numbers and rates than white males. Age-adjusted death rates (which take into account changes and variations in the age composition of the population) for 1997 were: white females, 358.2 deaths per 100,000 population; black females, 538.5; white males, 573.8; and black males, 900.3

Socioeconomic disparities in death rates also exist. A 1998 report from University of Michigan researchers said that adults in the lowest income group (less than $10,000 annual income) were 3.2 times more likely to die compared with those in the highest income bracket ($30,000 or more). Middle income adults ($10,000-$29,999) were 2.3 times as likely to die as those in the high-income group. Possible factors for higher death rates among the poor include depression, social isolation, a lack of optimism, low self-esteem, and chronic stress.

Causes of Death
For the purposes of national mortality statistics, every death is attributed to one underlying condition. The 15 leading causes of death in 1997 accounted for approximately 85 percent of all deaths in the United States. The leading causes of death from 1980 through 1997 generally were the same, but the order sometimes varied. The excep-

Leading Causes of Death, 1970–97

Cause of death	Deaths in 1997	Death rate per 100,000				
		1970	1980	1990	1996	1997
All causes	**2,314,729**	**945.3**	**878.3**	**861.9**	**875.4**	**864.9**
Heart diseases	725,790	362.0	336.0	289.0	276.6	271.2
Cancer	537,390	162.8	183.9	201.7	205.2	200.8
Cerebrovascular diseases	159,877	101.9	75.1	57.9	60.5	59.7
Pulmonary diseases	110,637	15.2	24.7	35.5	40.0	41.3
Accidents	92,191	56.4	46.7	37.3	35.4	34.4
Pneumonia and influenza	88,383	30.9	24.1	31.3	31.1	33.0
Diabetes mellitus	62,332	18.9	15.4	19.5	23.2	23.3
AIDS	29,725	11.6	11.9	12.3	12.3	11.1
Suicide	25,570	4.4	7.4	8.3	11.6	9.6
Liver disease and cirrhosis	24,765	15.5	13.5	10.2	9.5	9.3
Kidney diseases	22,604	1.7	4.2	7.9	9.2	8.4
Septicemia	22,527	N.A.	N.A.	N.A.	8.1	8.4
Alzheimer's disease	18,774	8.3	10.7	10.2	8.0	7.0
Homicide and legal intervention	16,685	—	—	9.6	7.8	6.2
Atherosclerosis	15,844	15.6	13.0	6.6	6.3	5.9

Note: Provisional data, estimated from a 10 percent sample of deaths. **Source:** U.S. Dept. of Health and Human Services, National Center for Health Statistics, *National Vital Statistics Report* (Oct. 7, 1998).

Deaths and Death Rates, 1997

Age	Total deaths	Rate per 100,000 population		
		Both sexes	Male	Female
All ages	2,314,738	864.9	880.8	849.6
Under 1 year	27,691	729.4	807.4	647.7
1–4 years	5,480	35.7	39.4	31.8
5–14 years	8,044	20.7	23.8	17.5
15–24 years	30,962	84.6	121.6	45.5
25–34 years	44,931	113.4	157.8	69.1
35–44 years	88,827	201.9	264.1	140.4
45–54 years	144,093	428.4	546.1	315.6
55–64 years	231,253	1,060.2	1,332.0	812.9
65–74 years	464,577	2,511.4	3,195.2	1,958.7
75–84 years	672,221	5,742.7	7,140.5	4,828.4
85 and older	596,193	15,400.1	17,558.7	14,530.4
Not stated	467	—	—	—

Note: Preliminary data.
Source: U.S. Dept. of Health and Human Services, National Center for Health Statistics. *National Vital Statistics Report* (Oct. 7, 1998).

Death Rates (per 100,000 population) by Sex and Race, 1940–97

Year	Total	All races		Whites		Black	
		Male	Female	Male	Female	Male	Female
1940	1,076.4	1,197.4	954.6	1,162.2	919.4	N.A.	N.A.
1950	963.8	1,106.1	823.5	1,089.5	803.3	N.A.	N.A.
1960	954.7	1,104.5	809.2	1,098.5	800.9	1,181.7	905.0
1970	945.3	1,090.3	807.8	1,086.7	812.6	1,186.6	829.2
1980	878.3	976.9	785.3	983.3	806.1	1,034.1	733.3
1985	873.9	945.0	806.6	960.0	837.1	976.8	727.7
1990	863.8	918.4	812.0	930.9	846.9	1,008.0	747.9
1995	880.0	914.1	847.3	932.1	891.3	980.7	759.0
1996	875.4	900.2	851.6	922.6	898.7	939.5	752.2
1997	864.9	880.8	849.6	908.0	900.0	882.6	733.1

Note: Death rates are based on population estimates prepared by the U.S. Bureau of the Census.
Source: U.S. Dept. of Health and Human Services, National Center for Health Statistics.

Changes in Leading Causes of Death, 1900–97

Cause of death	Death rate (per 100,000 population)
1900: All causes	**1,719.1**
Pneumonia and influenza	202.2
Tuberculosis	194.4
Diarrhea, enteritis, and ulceration of the intestines	142.7
1920: All causes	**1,298.9**
Pneumonia and influenza	207.3
Heart disease	159.6
Tuberculosis	113.1
1940: All causes	**1,074.1**
Heart disease	291.3
Cancer	120.0
Cerebrovascular disease	90.8
1960: All causes	**954.7**
Heart disease	369.0
Cancer	149.2
Cerebrovascular disease	108.0
1980: All causes	**878.3**
Heart disease	336.0
Cancer	183.9
Cerebrovascular disease	75.1
1990: All causes	**863.8**
Heart disease	289.5
Cancer	203.3
Cerebrovascular disease	57.9
1997: All causes	**864.9**
Heart disease	271.2
Cancer	200.8
Cerebrovascular disease	59.7

Source: U.S. Dept. of Health and Human Services, National Center for Health Statistics.

Suicide in the U.S., 1950–96

Age	Total 1996	Rate per 100,000 population 1950	Rate per 100,000 population 1996
All ages	**30,903[1]**	**11.4**	**11.6**
0–4 years	—	—	—
5–14 years	302	0.2	0.8
15–24 years	4,358	4.5	12.0
25–34 years	5,861	9.1	14.5
35–44 years	6,741	14.3	15.5
45–54 years	4,837	20.9	14.9
55–64 years	2,925	27.0	13.7
65–74 years	2,806	29.3	15.0
75–84 years	2,290	31.1	20.0
85 and older	759	28.8	20.2

Note: Provisional data. 1. Includes 12 people of unknown age.
Source: U.S. Dept. of Health and Human Services, National Center for Health Statistics, *National Vital Statistics Report,* Nov. 10, 1998.

cated by drug abuse. Having a parent who committed suicide also seems to increase a person's vulnerability.

Significant differences in suicide rates exist among the states. For 1996, the highest rates were reported for Nevada (20.9 per 100,000 population), Alaska (19.8), Montana (19.8), New Mexico (18.6), and Wyoming (18.3). The lowest were for the District of Columbia (6.4), New York (7.3), New Jersey (7.3), Massachusetts (8.0), and Rhode Island (8.4).

Almost two-thirds of the Americans who commit suicide shoot themselves, usually with handguns. Other common methods, in decreasing order of frequency, include drug overdose (primarily drugs prescribed by physicians), cutting and stabbing, jumping from high places, inhaling poisonous gas, hanging, and drowning.

Many experts believe that suicide statistics are grimmer than reported. They contend that numerous suicides are categorized as accidents or other deaths to spare families.

▶ ACCIDENTS

Every 10 minutes, two people are killed and about 370 suffer a disabling injury in accidents in the United States. Accidents are the nation's fifth most common cause of death. But for people between the ages of 1 and 44, accidents are the leading cause of death.

The accident death rate has declined significantly from the 1912 rate of 82.5 deaths per 100,000 population. In 1992 it reached a record low of 34.0, before increasing again to 35.4 in 1996. It dropped slightly to 35.0 in 1997, or a total of 93,800 accidental deaths, according to National Safety Council estimates. Accident rates vary significantly from one place to another. National Safety Council estimates indicate that the highest accidental death rates in 1996 were in Alaska (62.4), Wyoming (60.7), and Mississippi (58.5), the lowest were in Massachusetts (19.8), New York (20.7), and Rhode Island (21.3).

Approximately 19.3 million disabling injuries occurred in 1997—injuries that disabled people for one or more days.

The costs incurred from accidents totaled an estimated $478.3 billion in 1997—for medical

tions were AIDS, which ranked as a cause of death for the first time in 1987, and Alzheimer's disease, for which increased mortality is believed to reflect improved diagnosis and reporting rather than an increase in prevalence.

During the 20th century the leading causes of death have changed significantly. In 1900, infectious diseases took many lives, a fact reflected in the five leading causes of death: (1) pneumonia and influenza, (2) tuberculosis, (3) gastritis, (4) heart disease, and (5) cerebrovascular diseases. Today none of the top five causes of death is an infectious disease.

Suicide

Each year, approximately 30,000 Americans kill themselves—about one person every 20 minutes. In addition, about 500,000 people are treated in emergency rooms each year after attempting suicide. Although women make more attempts, men succeed in killing themselves far more often. In 1996, 24,998 men, but only 5,905 women committed suicide.

Particularly troublesome is the suicide rate for teens and young adults, which has soared since 1950. The causes of youth suicide are not fully known, although some evidence suggests that suicide is not as frequently associated with depression in young people as it is in adults. Many young suicide victims had a history of impulsive, aggressive, or antisocial behavior, often complicare, wage loss, insurance administration, property damage, fire loss, and so on.

Motor Vehicle Deaths, 1997

Since the nation's first motor vehicle death (reportedly in New York City on September 13, 1899) some 2.9 million people have died in motor vehicle accidents. Over the years, however, the numbers of deaths per 100,000 population and per 100,000 registered vehicles have declined drastically. For example, noted the National Safety Council, there were 3,100 motor vehicle deaths in 1912, when the number of registered vehicles totaled only 950,000. In 1997, there were 43,200 fatalities, but registered vehicles had risen to more than 214 million. Here's how people died in motor vehicle accidents in 1997:

- 21,300 died in collisions between two or more motor vehicles
- 10,800 died in collisions with guardrails and other fixed objects
- 5,700 pedestrians were struck by motor vehicles
- 4,200 died in non-collision accidents
- 700 died in collisions with cyclists
- 400 died in collisions with railroad trains
- 100 died in other types of collisions, usually involving animals or animal-drawn vehicles.

Data suggest that safety belts, air bags, bicycle and motorcycle helmets, child safety seats, strict drunk-driving laws, and speed limits save thousands of lives each year. In 1997, for example, safety belts saved an estimated 10,414 lives. However, if all passenger vehicle occupants over age four had worn safety belts, an additional 9,754 lives could have been saved.

By the end of 1996, in response to passage by Congress of the National Highway System Designation Act of 1995, 32 states had raised speed limits on their interstate highways, and saw interstate fatalities increase by an average of more than 10 percent. Total interstate fatalities for states that

Estimated Number of Injuries in U.S. From Selected Products, 1997

Product group	Estimated injuries
Stairs, ramps, landings, floors	928,393
Basketball	644,921
Bicycles and accessories	567,002
Beds, mattresses, pillows	413,276
Football	334,420
Baseball, softball	326,569
Nails, screws, tacks, bolts	165,623
Bathtubs, showers	164,749
Ladders, stools	157,758
Soccer	148,913
Fences, fence posts	110,731
Power, hand saws	109,538
Drinking glasses	104,858
Carpets, rugs	98,693
Trampolines	82,722
Footwear	75,804
Swings, swingsets	73,923
Fishing	72,598
Wheelchairs	70,112
Swimming pools	62,812
Lawn mowers	60,804
Weightlifting	56,724
Jewelry	54,720
Crutches, canes, walkers	49,526
Skateboards	48,186
Golf, golf carts	47,777
Clothing	47,263
Toilets	44,335
Television sets, stands	42,909
Hammers	41,518
Razors, shavers	40,773
Scissors	30,290

Notes: These national estimates are based on injuries treated in hospital emergency rooms participating in the National Electronic Injury Surveillance System. Patients said their injuries were related to the products; this does not necessarily mean the injuries were caused by the products.
Source: Consumer Product Safety Commission, National Electronic Injury Surveillance System.

Accidental Deaths in the U.S., 1910–97 (per 100,000 population)

Year	Death rate	Year	Death rate
1910	84.4	1970	56.2
1920	71.2	1980	46.5
1930	80.5	1990	36.9
1940	73.4	1995	35.5
1950	60.3	1996	35.2
1960	52.1	1997	35.0

Source: U.S. Dept. of Health and Human Services, National Center for Health Statistics.

Types of Accidental Deaths in U.S., 1997

Type	Number of deaths	Age group (years)						
		0–4	5–14	15–24	25–44	45–64	65–74	75+
All accidents	93,800	3,000	3,500	12,700	26,200	16,400	8,800	23,200
Motor vehicle	43,200	1,100	2,000	9,900	14,000	7,900	3,200	5,100
Falls	14,900	70	80	250	1,000	1,500	1,900	10,100
Poisoning by solids and liquids[1]	8,600	30	20	450	5,500	2,100	200	300
Drowning	4,000	600	450	600	1,200	550	300	300
Fires and burns	3,700	450	250	250	700	700	500	850
Suffocation	3,300	140	60	50	250	550	450	1,800
Firearms	1,500	40	180	450	450	240	80	60
Poisoning by gases	700	20	60	100	200	160	70	90
All other[2]	13,900	550	400	650	2,900	2,700	2,100	4,600

1. Deaths from poisons, drugs, medicines, mushrooms, and shellfish. Excludes poisonings from spoiled foods, salmonella, etc., which are classified as disease deaths. 2. Medical complications, air and water transport, machinery, excessive cold, etc.
Source: National Safety Council, Accident Facts (1998).

Average Remaining Life Expectancy in U.S. (in years)

Age in 1996	All races M	F	White M	F	Black M	F	Age in 1996	All races M	F	White M	F	Black M	F
At birth	73.1	79.1	73.9	79.7	66.1	74.2	43	33.3	37.9	33.7	38.2	28.6	34.5
1	72.6	78.6	73.4	79.1	66.2	74.2	44	32.4	37.0	32.8	37.3	27.8	33.6
2	71.7	77.6	72.4	78.1	65.2	73.2	45	31.5	36.1	31.9	36.4	27.1	32.8
3	70.7	76.7	71.4	77.1	64.3	72.3	46	30.6	35.1	31.0	35.4	26.3	31.9
4	69.7	75.7	70.5	76.2	63.3	71.3	47	29.8	34.2	30.1	34.5	25.6	31.0
5	68.8	74.7	69.5	75.2	62.4	70.3	48	28.9	33.3	29.2	33.6	24.8	30.2
6	67.8	73.7	68.5	74.2	61.4	69.4	49	28.0	32.4	28.4	32.7	24.1	29.4
7	66.8	72.7	67.5	73.2	60.4	68.4	50	27.2	31.5	27.5	31.7	23.4	28.5
8	65.8	71.7	66.5	72.2	59.4	67.4	51	26.3	30.6	26.6	30.8	22.7	27.7
9	64.8	70.8	65.5	71.2	58.4	66.4	52	25.5	29.7	25.8	29.9	21.9	26.9
10	63.8	69.8	64.5	70.2	57.5	65.4	53	24.7	28.8	25.0	29.1	21.3	26.1
11	62.9	68.8	63.5	69.2	56.5	64.4	54	23.9	28.0	24.1	28.2	20.6	25.3
12	61.9	67.8	62.6	68.3	55.5	63.4	55	23.1	27.1	23.3	27.3	19.9	24.5
13	60.9	66.8	61.6	67.3	54.5	62.5	56	22.3	26.2	22.5	26.4	19.2	23.7
14	59.9	65.8	60.6	66.3	53.5	61.5	57	21.5	25.4	21.7	25.6	18.6	23.0
15	58.9	64.8	59.6	65.3	52.6	60.5	58	20.7	24.5	20.9	24.7	17.9	22.2
16	58.0	63.8	58.7	64.3	51.6	59.5	59	20.0	23.7	20.1	23.9	17.3	21.4
17	57.0	62.9	57.7	63.3	50.7	58.6	60	19.2	22.9	19.4	23.0	16.7	20.7
18	56.1	61.9	56.8	62.4	49.8	57.6	61	18.5	22.1	18.6	22.2	16.1	20.0
19	55.2	60.9	55.8	61.4	48.9	56.6	62	17.8	21.3	17.9	21.4	15.6	19.3
20	54.2	60.0	54.9	60.4	48.0	55.7	63	17.1	20.5	17.2	20.6	15.0	18.6
21	53.3	59.0	54.0	59.5	47.2	54.7	64	16.4	19.7	16.5	19.8	14.5	17.9
22	52.4	58.0	53.0	58.5	46.3	53.7	65	15.7	19.0	15.8	19.1	13.9	17.2
23	51.5	57.0	52.1	57.5	45.4	52.8	66	15.1	18.2	15.2	18.3	13.4	16.6
24	50.6	56.1	51.2	56.5	44.6	51.8	67	14.4	17.5	14.5	17.5	12.8	15.9
25	49.6	55.1	50.2	55.6	43.7	50.9	68	13.8	16.7	13.9	16.8	12.2	15.2
26	48.7	54.1	49.3	54.6	42.8	49.9	69	13.2	16.0	13.2	16.1	11.7	14.6
27	47.8	53.2	48.4	53.6	42.0	49.0	70	12.6	15.3	12.6	15.4	11.2	13.9
28	46.9	52.2	47.4	52.6	41.1	48.0	71	12.0	14.6	12.0	14.6	10.7	13.4
29	45.9	51.2	46.5	51.7	40.2	47.1	72	11.4	13.9	11.4	14.0	10.2	12.8
30	45.0	50.3	45.6	50.7	39.4	46.2	73	10.9	13.2	10.9	13.3	9.8	12.2
31	44.1	49.3	44.6	49.7	38.5	45.2	74	10.3	12.6	10.3	12.6	9.4	11.7
32	43.2	48.3	43.7	48.8	37.6	44.3	75	9.8	12.0	9.8	12.0	9.0	11.2
33	42.2	47.4	42.8	47.8	36.8	43.4	76	9.3	11.3	9.3	11.3	8.6	10.6
34	41.3	46.4	41.9	46.8	36.0	42.5	77	8.8	10.7	8.8	10.7	8.2	10.1
35	40.4	45.5	40.9	45.9	35.1	41.6	78	8.3	10.1	8.3	10.1	7.7	9.5
36	39.5	44.5	40.0	44.9	34.3	40.7	79	7.8	9.5	7.8	9.5	7.3	9.0
37	38.6	43.6	39.1	43.9	33.4	39.8	80	7.3	8.9	7.3	8.9	7.0	8.5
38	37.7	42.6	38.2	43.0	32.6	38.9	81	6.9	8.4	6.9	8.4	6.6	8.0
39	36.8	41.7	37.3	42.0	31.8	38.0	82	6.5	7.8	6.5	7.8	6.2	7.5
40	35.9	40.7	36.4	41.1	31.0	37.1	83	6.1	7.3	6.0	7.3	5.9	7.1
41	35.0	39.8	35.5	40.1	30.2	36.2	84	5.7	6.8	5.7	6.8	5.6	6.6
42	34.1	38.9	34.6	39.2	29.4	35.3	85 and over	5.4	6.4	5.3	6.3	5.3	6.2

Note: Based on an individual's age in 1996. For example, a black female age 28 in 1996 would be expected to live 48 more years, or to about 76 years old. A white male born in 1996 would be expected to live to almost 74 years of age.   **Source:** U.S. Dept. Health and Human Services, National Center for Health Statistics, *National Vital Statistics Report,* December 24, 1998.

did not increase speed limits in 1996 remained unchanged.

▶ LIFE EXPECTANCY

Life expectancy figures represent the average number of years that infants are expected to live. Life expectancy has improved steadily over the years, due largely to a decline in deaths during childhood. The development of drugs to combat infectious diseases, plus improved nutrition and better environmental sanitation, have all played major roles in combating early deaths.

In 1997, the average length of life in the U.S. was a record high 76.5 years. For whites, life expectancy was 77.1 years; for blacks it was 71.2 years, or 5.9 fewer years. Homicides, killings in police confrontations, auto accidents, AIDS, tuberculosis, and several other diseases have had a disproportionate impact on black people's life expectancy rates in recent years.

▶ INFANT MORTALITY

In 1997, there were 27,962 reported deaths of infants age one year or younger. The most commonly used index for measuring the risk of dying during the first year of life are infant mortality rates, which are calculated by dividing the number of infant deaths by the number of live births registered for the same period. The 1997 rate of 7.1 infant deaths per 1,000 live births was the lowest ever recorded for the United States.

The rate among white infants was less than half that of black infants: 6.0 infant deaths per 1,000 live births for whites in 1997, versus 13.7 per 1,000 for blacks. The reasons for this discrepancy are not clear, although an important factor is believed to be the quality of medical care received by people of different socioeconomic groups. For example, several studies of infant deaths have shown that adequate prenatal care is strongly associated with higher infant birth weight and survival.

Many black mothers, who are far more likely to be poor than white mothers, do not have access to proper prenatal care. Poor nutrition, alcohol and drug abuse, ant other social factors also play significant roles.

Disproportionate poverty among minority groups is not the whole story, however. Studies have shown that even black infants born to college-educated mothers had nearly twice the mortality rate of comparable white infants.

The four leading causes of infant deaths in 1997 were congenital anomalies (155.7 deaths per 100,000 live births), disorders relating to short gestation and low birthweight (95.7), sudden infant death syndrome (69.4), and respiratory distress syndrome (32.4).

(See also "World Health" for infant mortality rates in other nations.)

▶SUBSTANCE ABUSE
Illicit Drugs

A significant portion of the American public uses illegal drugs. The 1997 National Household Survey on Drug Abuse estimated that 13.9 million Americans age 12 and older (over 6 percent of the

Life Expectancy in U.S., 1950–97

Year	All races Male	All races Female	Whites Male	Whites Female	Blacks Male	Blacks Female
At birth						
1950[1]	65.6	71.1	66.5	72.2	58.9	62.7
1960[1]	66.6	73.1	67.4	74.1	60.7	65.9
1970	67.1	74.7	68.0	75.6	60.0	68.3
1980	70.0	77.4	70.7	78.1	63.8	72.5
1990	71.8	78.8	72.7	79.4	64.5	73.6
1996	73.0	79.0	73.8	79.6	66.1	74.2
1997	73.6	79.2	74.3	79.8	67.3	74.7
At age 65 (years remaining)						
1950[1]	12.8	15.0	12.8	15.1	12.9	14.9
1960[1]	12.8	15.8	12.9	15.9	12.7	15.1
1970	13.1	17.0	13.1	17.1	12.5	15.7
1980	14.1	18.3	14.2	18.4	13.0	16.8
1990	15.1	18.9	15.2	19.1	13.2	17.2
1996	15.7	18.9	15.8	19.0	13.9	17.2
1997	15.8	19.0	15.9	19.1	14.2	17.4

1. Includes deaths of persons who were not residents of the 50 states and the District of Columbia. **Source:** U.S. Dept. of Health and Human Services, National Center for Health Statistics, *Health United States 1996-97* and *Monthly Vital Statistics Report* (Oct. 7, 1998).

U.S. Infant Mortality Rate, 1940–97 (per 1,000 live births)

Year	All races	White	Black
1940	47.0	43.2	72.9
1950	29.2	26.8	43.9
1960	26.0	22.9	44.3
1970	20.0	17.8	32.6
1980	12.6	11.0	21.4
1990	9.2	7.6	18.0
1996	7.2	6.0	14.2
1997	7.1	6.0	13.7

Source: U.S. Dept. Health and Human Services, National Center for Health Statistics, *National Vital Statistics Report*, Oct. 7, 1998.

Childhood Vaccines: Recommended Immunization Schedule

Age	Vaccines
Birth	Hepatitis B
2 months	Hepatitis B; polio; diphtheria, tetanus, pertussis (DTP); Haemophilus B (Hib)
4 months	Polio, DTP, Hib
6 months	Hepatitis B, DTP, Hib
6-18 months	Polio
12-15 months	Hib; measles, mumps, rubella (MMR); chicken pox
15-18 months	DTP
4-6 years	Polio, DTP, MMR
11-16 years	Tetanus, diphtheria

Note: It generally takes several doses of each vaccine for full protection. In some cases, there is a range of acceptable ages for vaccination. For example, the third dose of hepatitis B vaccine may be given between 6 and 18 months of age. Children who have not been vaccinated against Hepatitis B in infancy may begin the series during any childhood visit. For additional information, contact your physician. **Sources:** American Academy of Pediatrics; American Academy of Family Physicians; and U.S. Dept. of Health and Human Services, Centers for Disease Control and Prevention.

Commonly Abused Drugs

Drug	Primary Effect	Popular names
Alcohol	Depressant	Drink, booze
Amphetamines	Stimulant	Pep pills, uppers; *metamphetamines*: speed, crystal, crank, ice
Amyl or butyl nitrites	Stimulant	Poppers, snappers rush, locker room
Barbiturates	Depressant	Sleeping pills, dolls
Cocaine	Stimulant	Coke, snow, lady; smokable form: crack
Ephedra	Stimulant	Ma huang; *brand names* Herbal Ecstasy, Euphoria, Buzz Tablets, Brain Wash
Heroin	Depressant	Snow, smack, P-dope; *synthetic heroin*: China white, Persian heroin, gasoline dope; *combined heroin and cocaine*: speedball
D-lysergic acid diethylamide	Hallucinogen	LSD, acid
Marijuana	Hallucinogen/depressant	Pot grass, joint dope, reefer, herb, weed, skunk
MDMA (combination of synthetic mescaline and an amphetamine	Stimulant/ hallucinogen	Ecstasy, love potion
Mescaline	Hallucinogen	Peyote, cactus
Morphine	Depressant	
PCP (phencyclidine)	Hallucinogen	Angel dust
Tranquilizers	Depressant	Downers

Drug Use by U.S. High School Seniors, 1975–98

Drug	1975	1980	1985	1990	1995	1997	1998
Alcohol	68.2%	72.0%	65.9%	57.1%	51.3%	52.7%	52.0%
Cigarettes	36.7	30.5	30.1	29.4	33.5	36.5	35.1
Marijuana	27.1	33.7	25.7	14.0	21.2	23.7	22.8
LSD	2.3	2.3	1.6	1.9	4.0	3.1	3.2
Cocaine	1.9	5.2	6.7	1.9	1.8	2.3	2.4
Heroin	0.4	0.2	0.3	0.2	0.6	0.5	0.5

Note: Drug use during the 30 days preceding the survey. Source: U.S. Dept. of Health and Human Services, National Institute on Drug Abuse, *Monitoring the Future Study*, 1998.

Lifetime Experience With Illicit Drugs, 1997

Age	Used in lifetime	Used in past year	Used in past month
All ages[1]	35.0%	11.2%	6.4%
12-17	23.7	18.8	11.4
18-25	45.4	25.3	14.7
26-34	50.8	14.3	8.4
35 and older	31.5	6.1	3.6

Note: Includes marijuana, cocaine, heroin, hallucinogens, inhalants, or prescription-type psychotherapeutic drugs (stimulants, sedatives, tranquilizers, and analgesics) for nonmedical purposes. 1. Age 12 and older. Source: U.S. Dept. of Health and Human Services, Substance Abuse and Mental Health Services Administration, *National Household Survey on Drug Abuse 1997* (August 1998).

population) were current users, meaning they had used an illicit drug in the month prior to interview. Although most illicit drug users were white, the percentage of blacks who use drugs (7.5 percent) was somewhat higher than for whites (6.4 percent) and Hispanics (5.9 percent). Rates of drug use generally decline with age. The highest rates were among young people age 16-17 (19.2 percent) and 18-20 (17.3 percent); only 1.0 percent of persons 50 and older reported current use.

A measure of the health consequences of drug use is the Drug Abuse Warning Network (DAWN), which collects information on patients seeking hospital emergency room treatment related to their abuse of legal and illicit drugs. In 1996 the most commonly reported motive for taking a substance was attempted suicide (181,600), followed by dependence (159,700). Whites accounted for 54 percent of the episodes, blacks for 27 percent, and Hispanics for 10 percent. The proportion of episodes among men and women was approximately equal.

Marijuana is the most commonly used illegal drug, used by 77 percent of current U.S. drug users. It is made from the leaves and flowering tops of the hemp plant, *Cannabis sativa*, which contains psychoactive substances called cannabinoids. The primary psychoactive ingredient in marijuana and hashish (a resin exuded from the flowering tops) is tetrahydrocannabinol, or THC. The amount of each cannabinoid varies markedly from one plant to another depending on climate, soil, and other factors.

Marijuana is typically prepared as a tobacco-like mixture that is smoked in hand-rolled cigarettes or in pipes. It typically produces a "high"— a feeling of well-being, relaxation, and sleepiness. It also interferes with coordination and mental abilities. For instance, it distorts judgment and reaction time, which can be particularly dangerous when a user drives a car.

Possession or sale of marijuana has been illegal in the United States since 1937. Nonetheless, marijuana has legitimate medical uses. A significant body of evidence shows that marijuana combats nausea and weight loss in cancer and AIDS patients. It also helps reduce pressure within the eyes of glaucoma patients. But because the drug is illegal, most patients find it difficult or impossible to obtain. By late 1998 voters in six states (Alaska, Arizona, California, Nevada, Oregon, and Washington) had approved initiatives to legalize medical use of marijuana. And in 1999 a study commissioned by the federal government confirmed that marijuana had medical uses, and that there was no evidence that giving the drug to sick people would increase illicit use in the general population.

Cocaine is made from the leaves of the coca plant, a shrub native to South America. In the late 1800s and early 1900s, before its dangers were recognized, cocaine was used by doctors as an anesthetic because of its effectiveness in depressing nerve endings. It has since been replaced by less toxic, non-addictive anesthetics.

Cocaine causes a short-lived euphoria. It also suppresses appetite, interferes with sleep, and increases heart rate and blood pressure. Even small doses have been linked to heart attacks and cerebral hemorrhages. Repeated usage is required to maintain a "high." Abusers who try to abstain often experience a tremendous craving for the drug—a hallmark of addiction.

Crack is a highly addictive, smokable form of cocaine, sold in small beige chunks called pellets or rocks. Its effects on the brain are almost immediate, producing a brief but intense high. Within minutes, however, depression sets in, combined with a craving for another "hit." People can become addicted to crack in weeks or even days.

Heroin is a synthetic compound derived from morphine, which is made from opium poppies (Papaver somniferum). Highly addictive, heroin fell out of favor in the United States during the 1970s but there has been an increasing trend in new use since 1992. A large portion of new users smoked, snorted, or sniffed heroin, and most were under age 26; an estimated 171,000 teenagers used heroin for the first time in 1996. One concern is that young heroin snorters may shift to needle injecting, which would place them at increased risk for HIV/AIDS.

Alcohol

Consumption of alcohol constitutes the nation's most common drug abuse problem. Almost 20,000 alcohol-induced deaths occur each year. In addi-

Alcohol Use in U.S. 1997

Characteristic	Total[1]	By Age			
		12-17	18-25	26-34	35 and older
Total	51.4%	20.5%	58.4%	60.2%	52.8%
Race/Ethnicity					
White	55.1	22.0	63.5	64.8	56.1
Black	40.4	16.3	46.6	51.0	40.9
Hispanic	42.4	18.8	48.5	51.6	42.8
Sex					
Male	58.2	21.0	65.9	67.9	60.6
Female	45.1	19.9	50.8	52.6	46.0
Population Density					
Large Metro	54.3	21.4	58.5	62.4	56.6
Small Metro	52.0	20.4	58.7	62.3	53.5
Non-Metro	44.9	19.0	58.0	51.0	45.4
Region					
Northeast	54.0	19.3	59.9	60.3	56.7
North Central	55.6	23.4	68.0	66.6	55.3
South	47.4	19.3	55.1	57.9	47.7
West	51.7	20.3	53.3	56.8	55.7
Adult Education					
Less than high school	38.0	N.A.	52.4	48.7	32.7
High school graduate	54.0	N.A.	56.7	56.9	52.7
Some college	58.2	N.A.	61.3	61.6	56.0
College graduate	66.6	N.A.	67.4	68.9	65.9
Current Employment					
Full-time	61.9	N.A.	65.3	64.0	60.4
Part-time	56.6	N.A.	51.5	59.9	58.4
Unemployed	58.8	N.A.	55.8	55.7	61.7
Other[2]	42.1	N.A.	51.3	44.6	40.8

Notes: Percentages reporting use of alcohol in the previous month. N.A. = Not Applicable. 1. Age 12 and older. 2. Includes retired, disabled, homemaker, student, etc. **Source:** U.S. Dept. of Health and Human Services, Substance Abuse and Mental Health Services Administration, *National Household Survey on Drug Abuse,* 1997 (August 1998).

tion, alcohol is involved in some 16,000 traffic deaths (about 38 percent of all traffic deaths) annually.

The 1997 National Household Survey on Drug Abuse reported that approximately 111 million people age 12 and older currently used alcohol (defined as any use in the previous month); 31.9 million engaged in binge drinking (defined as five or more drinks on at least one occasion in the past month), and 11.2 million were heavy drinkers (five or more drinks on the same occasion on at least five different days in the past month). About 11 million current drinkers were under age 21; of these, 4.8 million were binge drinkers, including 2.0 million heavy drinkers. As in prior years, the level of alcohol use was strongly associated with illicit drug use. Of the 11.2 million heavy drinkers, 30 percent (3.3 million) were current illicit drug users.

Consumption According to the National Institute of Alcohol Abuse and Alcoholism (NIAAA), per capita consumption of beer, spirits, and wine grew slightly (1.0 percent) during the 1950s, rose rapidly (21.3 percent) during the 1960s, rose moderately (9.1 percent) in the 1970s, and decreased (12.0 percent) during the 1980s. The decline continued in the 1990s as annual per capita consumption from all alcoholic beverages dropped from 2.45 gallons in 1990 to 2.19 gallons in 1996. Studies show that men are heavier drinkers than women, and much more likely to be binge drinkers. Younger people drink more than older people. Consumption was highest in New Hampshire (4.41 gallons of ethanol per capita), Nevada (4.19), and the District of Columbia (3.90). It was lowest in Utah (1.32), West Virginia (1.67), and Oklahoma (1.72).

Several factors have contributed to consump-

U.S. Alcohol Consumption, 1940–96 (gallons of ethanol, per capita)

Year	Beer	Wine	Spirits	All beverages
1940	0.73	0.16	0.67	1.56
1950	1.04	0.23	0.77	2.04
1960	0.99	0.22	0.86	2.07
1970	1.14	0.27	1.11	2.52
1980	1.38	0.34	1.04	2.76
1990	1.34	0.33	0.78	2.46
1995	1.25	0.29	0.64	2.17
1996	1.25	0.30	0.64	2.19

Note: Based on population age 15 and older prior to 1970 and on population age 14 and older thereafter. **Source:** U.S. Dept. of Health and Human Services, National Institute on Alcohol Abuse and Alcoholism, *Surveillance Report #47,* (December, 1998).

tion declines, including the general aging of the population, increased state and federal taxes on alcoholic beverages, stricter penalties for drinking and driving, and the formation of minority advocacy groups to counter industry efforts to target minority populations.

Tobacco

Smoking is the single most preventable cause of death in our society. Each year, an estimated 430,700 people die in the United States as a result of smoking. Government agencies and independent economists estimate that smoking costs the nation more than $100 billion a year—for lost productivity, medical bills, insurance premiums, heating and cooling expenses, maintenance, and cleaning costs. For medical care alone, smoking-attributable costs in 1993 totaled $72.7 billion.

The percentage of adults who smoke decreased dramatically after 1964, the year the U.S. surgeon general first warned about the link between smoking and health problems such as cancer and heart disease. At that time, 40 percent of the adult population were smokers; in 1998 less than 25 percent (47 million adults) smoked. The increased cost of cigarettes, a growing number of smoking restrictions in public places, and decreasing social acceptability of smoking also played roles in the decline. Cigarette smoking among adults was highest in Kentucky, where 30.8 percent of the population age 18 and older were smokers in 1997. It was lowest in Utah (13.7 percent).

The adult smoking population has been relatively stable since 1990, but teenage smoking has increased, and is a primary barrier to reducing smoking prevalence. Surveys indicate that more than 90 percent of adults who are regular smokers began smoking while they were teenagers and that 32 percent of young people who become regular smokers will die of a smoking-related disorder. Both sexes are equally likely to smoke, but male adolescents are significantly more likely than females to use smokeless tobacco.

Health effects The major effects of smoking include:

- Shortened life span. Each year, some 430,000 Americans—and over 3 million people worldwide—die prematurely as a result of smoking.
- Cancer of the lungs, mouth, esophagus, stomach, bladder, kidney, pancreas, and cervix. Smoking accounts for at least 30 percent of all cancer deaths in the United States each year, including 87 percent of lung cancer deaths.
- Cardiovascular disease, including heart attack, stroke, aneurysm, and the peripheral vascular disease. Smoking weakens the heart's ability to pump blood, promotes clot formation, and damages the inner lining of blood vessels.
- Pulmonary illness, including emphysema, pneumonia, and chronic bronchitis. Annually, more than 80,000 Americans die from non-cancerous chronic lung diseases linked to smoking.
- Spontaneous abortions. Women who smoke during pregnancy are 10 times more likely to miscarry than are nonsmokers.
- Underweight, sickly babies. Each year, the deaths of more than 2,000 children under a year old are attributed to the mothers' smoking while pregnant. Infants of smokers have a 50 percent higher risk of developing Sudden Infant Death Syndrome (SIDS) and are 74 percent more likely to be of low birth weight than are infants born to mothers who do not smoke. An infant exposed to *any* cigarette smoke is 3.5 times more likely to die of SIDS than an infant not exposed to smoke.
- Environmental smoking risks. Nonsmokers who are exposed to the tobacco smoke of other people are at increased risk for various diseases. Exposure to secondhand smoke is responsible for approximately 3,000 lung cancer deaths annually among nonsmokers and 150,000 to 300,000 cases of lower respiratory tract infections such as bronchitis and pneumonia in children up to 18 months old. It also doubles a person's risk of heart disease.

U.S. Cigarette Consumption, 1900–98

	Consumption	
Year	billions of cigarettes	Per capita[1]
1900	2.5	54
1910	8.6	151
1920	44.6	665
1930	119.3	1,485
1940	181.9	1,976
1950	369.8	3,552
1960	484.4	4,171
1970	536.5	3,985
1980	631.5	3,849
1990	525.0	2,817
1997	480.0	2,423
1998	470.0	2,261

1. Among persons age 18 and older. **Source:** U.S. Dept. of Health and Human Services, Centers for Disease Control and Prevention; USDA, Economic Research Service.

Adult Cigarette Smokers in the U.S., 1995

Year	Men	Women	Total
Total	27%	22.6%	24.7%
Age			
18–24	27.8	21.8	24.8
25–44	30.5	26.8	28.6
45–64	27.1	24.0	25.5
65 and older	14.3	11.5	13.0
Race			
White[1]	27.1	24.1	25.6
Black[1]	28.8	23.5	25.8
Hispanic	21.7	14.9	18.3
Education[2]			
9 to 11 years	41.9	33.7	37.5
12 years	33.7	26.2	29.5
13 to 15 years	25.0	22.5	23.6
16 years or more	14.3	13.7	14.0

1. Non-Hispanic. 2. Among those age 25 and older. **Source:** U.S. Dept. of Health and Human Services, Centers for Disease Control and Prevention, *Morbidity and Mortality Weekly Report,* (Dec. 26, 1997).

Teenage Tobacco Users, 1997

Category	Cigarettes	Cigars	Smokeless Tobacco
Total	36.4%	22.0%	9.3%
Sex			
Male	37.7	31.2	15.8
Female	34.7	10.8	1.5
Race/Ethnicity			
White[1]	39.7	22.5	12.2
Black[1]	22.7	19.4	2.2
Hispanic	34.0	20.3	5.1
High school grade			
9	33.4	17.3	9.7
10	35.3	22.3	6.8
11	36.6	24.2	10.0
12	39.6	23.8	10.5

Note: Used at least once during the 30 days preceding the survey. 1. Non-Hispanic. **Source:** U.S. Dept. of Health and Human Services, Centers for Disease Control and Prevention, *Morbidity and Morality Weekly Report,* April 3, 1998.

The Media

THE PRINT MEDIA

▶NEWSPAPERS

The mutual distrust between government and the media dates back to the very first American newspaper in 1690, when a three-page publication called *Publick Occurrences, Both Foreign and Domestick* was suppressed by the government after one issue. A number of newspapers sprang up during the pre-Revolutionary period and by 1775, the colonies, with a population of 2.5 million people, were served by 48 weekly newspapers, small in both size and circulation.

The first daily, the *Pennsylvania Evening Post and Daily Advertiser,* was not published until 1783. By 1800 there were 20 daily newspapers and more than 1,000 small town and frontier weeklies. Most of the dailies, filled with political and business news, were expensive and aimed at educated, affluent readers. The first of the mass-circulation dailies, known as the penny press, was the *New York Sun,* started in 1833 and sold for the bargain price of one cent. The *Sun,* with its crime stories and soft features, marked a dramatic change in newspaper coverage.

The next major change in newspapers came in the era during and after the Civil War. Dramatic technological improvements like the transatlantic cable, the telephone, the electric light bulb, typewriters, web-fed, presses, and typesetting machine made possible cheap, mass circulation newspapers. By 1900 the number of daily newspapers had jumped to 2,326. Over the next half century, the number of newspapers steadily declined while readership increased, due in part to the popularity in Sunday editions.

Newspapers today

In 1998, 1,489 daily newspapers were published in the United States—781 afternoon publications and 721 morning papers. (There were 12 papers printed all day in 1998; they are counted as both morning and evening papers, but are counted only once in the total). The number of news-papers has been declining for decades, in part because of radio, television and the Internet, but also because in the fight for readers and advertising, competing papers have battled until a single winner emerged. Fewer than 50 cities have competing newspapers today, a major change from the turn of the century when most major cities had more than two newspapers. By contrast, 14 cities have competing newspapers only by virtue of a joint operating agreement that combines all of the two papers' operations except for their editorial staffs, which remain independent (in some cases fiercely) of each other.

The number of weekly newspapers has remained fairly constant at around 7,000-8,000 ever since 1960 (it was 8,193 in 1998). But circulation of these papers has increased dramatically. The average circulation of weekly papers doubled from 2,566 papers in 1960 to 5,324 in 1980. In 1998, it was 9,067.

The vast majority of newspapers have circulations of less than 50,000; 128 have circulations between 50,000 and 100,000; and 103 have a daily circulation of more than 100,000. The top six newspaper companies—Gannett, Knight-Ridder, Newhouse, Dow Jones & Co., Times Mirror, and The New York Times Co.—account for more than a third of all newspaper circulation. The newspapers with the greatest circulations in the world are all published in Japan and in Europe. The world's most widely read newspapers are Japan's *Yomiuri Shimbun,* with a circulation of over 14 million, and its rival, the *Asahi Shimbun,* read by more than 12 million people. By comparison, The *Wall Street Journal,* tops in the U.S. in circulation, reaches just 1.7 million people.

Daily circulation for all newspapers dropped for the 11th consecutive year in 1998, to 56.2 million, according to the American Newspaper Association. Evening newspapers were responsible for all of the drop-off, even counteracting a 211,000 increase in circulation by morning papers. Circulation of Sunday editions dropped slightly to 60.1 million. The percentage of people who read a newspaper continues to drop ever so slightly from year to year: 58.6 percent of people read a daily paper, down from 59.7 in 1997, 58.8 in 1996, and 62.4 in 1990. Sunday edition readership was 68.2 per-

	Total		Morning		Evening		Sunday	
Year	Number of Daily papers	Daily circulation ('000s)	Number of papers	Daily circulation ('000s)	Number of papers	Daily circulation ('000s)	Number of papers	Daily circulation ('000s)
1900	2,226	15,102	—	—	—	—	—	—
1920	2,042	27,791	437	—	1,605	—	522	17,084
1930	1,942	39,589	388	—	1,554	—	521	26,413
1940	1,878	41,132	380	16,114	1,498	25,008	525	32,371
1950	1,772	53,829	322	21,266	1,450	32,563	549	46,582
1960	1,763	58,882	312	24,029	1,459	34,853	563	47,699
1970	1,748	62,108	334	25,934	1,429	36,174	586	49,217
1980	1,745	62,202	387	29,414	1,388	32,787	735	54,672
1990	1,611	62,324	559	41,308	1,084	21,015	863	62,634
1995	1,533	58,193	656	44,310	891	13,883	888	61,529
1996	1,520	56,990	686	44,789	846	12,200	890	60,798
1997	1,509	56,728	705	45,434	816	11,294	903	60,486
1998[1]	1,489	56,182	721	45,643	781	10,539	897	60,061

Daily Newspapers, Number and Circulation, 1900–98

Note: All-day newspapers are listed in both morning and evening columns, but are counted only once in the total. There were 12 such papers in 1998. 1.Preliminary.   **Source:** Newspaper Association of America, *Facts About Newspapers, 1999.*

Top 100 U.S. Daily Newspapers by Circulation, 1998

Rank	Newspaper	Average daily paid circulation	Rank	Newspaper	Average daily paid circulation
1.	The Wall Street Journal (m)	1,740,450	53.	Richmond Times-Dispatch (m)	207,175
2.	USA Today (m)	1,653,428	54.	Daily Oklahoman (m)	204,963
3.	The Los Angeles Times (m)	1,067,540	55.	Los Angeles Daily News (m)	201,107
4.	The New York Times (m)	1,066,658	56.	St. Paul Pioneer Press (m)	199,119
5.	The Washington Post (m)	759,122	57.	Norfolk Virginian-Pilot (m)	197,773
6.	New York Daily News (m)	723,143	58.	Seattle Post-Intelligencer (m)	196,271
7.	Chicago Tribune (m)	673,508	59.	Cincinnati Enquirer (m)	196,181
8.	Newsday (N.Y.) (m)	572,444	60.	Nashville Tennessean (m)	184,979
9.	Houston Chronicle (m)	550,763	61.	Austin American-Statesman (m)	183,319
10.	Chicago Sun-Times (m)	485,666	62.	Philadelphia Daily News (m)	175,448
11.	Dallas Morning News (m)	479,863	63.	Rochester Democrat and Chronicle (m)	174,579
12.	San Francisco Chronicle (m)	475,324			
13.	Boston Globe (m)	470,825	64.	Little Rock Democrat-Gazette (m)	173,316
14.	New York Post (m)	437,467	65.	West Palm Beach Post (m)	173,074
15.	Phoenix Arizona Republic (m)	435,330	66.	Jacksonville Times-Union (m)	172,511
16.	Philadelphia Inquirer (m)	428,895	67.	Providence Journal (m)	167,381
17.	Newark Star-Ledger (m)	407,026	68.	Memphis Commercial Appeal (m)	163,603
18.	Cleveland Plain Dealer (m)	382,933	69.	Des Moines Register (m)	163,292
19.	Detroit Free Press (m)	378,256	70.	Tulsa World (m)	162,186
20.	San Diego Union-Tribune (all day)	378,112	71.	Riverside Press-Enterprise (m)	161,612
21.	Orange County Register (m)	356,953	72.	Asbury Park (N.J.) Press (all day)	159,472
22.	Miami Herald (m)	349,114	73.	Raleigh News & Observer (m)	157,634
23.	Portland Oregonian (all day)	346,593	74.	Fresno Bee (m)	155,931
24.	St. Petersburg Times (m)	344,784	75.	Dayton Daily News (m)	152,308
25.	Denver Post (m)	341,554	76.	White Plains Journal News (m)	151,695
26.	Minneapolis Star Tribune (m)	334,751	77.	Las Vegas Review-Journal (m)	151,162
27.	Rocky Mountain News (Denver) (m)	331,978	78.	Birmingham News (m)	148,835
28.	St. Louis Post-Dispatch (m)	329,582	79.	Toledo Blade (m)	146,138
29.	Baltimore Sun (m)	314,033	80.	Akron Beacon Journal (m)	143,199
30.	Atlanta Constitution (m)	303,698	81.	Bergen (N.J.) Record (m)	141,368
31.	San Jose Mercury News (m)	290,885	82.	Arlington Heights (Ill.) Daily Herald (m)	141,703
32.	Milwaukee Journal Sentinel (m)	285,776			
33.	Sacramento Bee (m)	283,589	83.	Grand Rapids Press (e)	139,703
34.	Kansas City Star (m)	281,596	84.	Salt Lake City Tribune (m)	129,612
35.	Boston Herald (m)	271,425	85.	Allentown (Pa.) Morning Call (m)	129,522
36.	New Orleans Times-Picayune (m)	259,317	86.	Tacoma News Tribune (m)	129,247
37.	Fort Lauderdale Sun-Sentinel (m)	258,726	87.	Wilmington (Del.) News Journal (all day)	125,401
38.	Orlando Sentinel (all day)	258,726			
39.	Los Angeles Investor's Business Daily (m)	251,172	88.	Columbia (S.C.) State (m)	120,433
			89.	Knoxville News-Sentinel (m)	115,248
40.	Columbus Dispatch (m)	246,528	90.	Spokane Spokesman-Review (m)	114,475
41.	Detroit News (e)	245,351	91.	San Francisco Examiner (e)	113,198
42.	Charlotte Observer (m)	243,818	92.	Lexington (Ky.) Herald-Leader (m)	113,036
43.	Pittsburgh Post-Gazette (m)	243,453	93.	Albuquerque Journal (m)	112,751
44.	Buffalo News (all day)	237,229	94.	Sarasota Herald-Tribune (m)	109,438
45.	Tampa Tribune (m)	235,786	95.	Charleston Post & Courier (m)	109,272
46.	Fort Worth Star-Telegram (m)	232,112	96.	Atlanta Journal (e)	106,896
47.	Indianapolis Star (m)	230,223	97.	Worcester (Mass.) Telegram & Gazette (m)	105,896
48.	Louisville Courier-Journal (m)	228,144			
49.	Seattle Times (e)	227,715	98.	Jackson (Miss.) Clarion-Ledger (m)	105,382
50.	Omaha World-Herald (all day)	219,891	99.	Long Beach (Calif.) Press-Telegram (m)	105,167
51.	San Antonio Express-News (m)	218,661			
52.	Hartford Courant (m)	211,041	100.	Honolulu Advertiser (m)	102,358

Note: (m) = morning paper; (e) = evening paper; (all day) = paper published all day.
Source: Editor and Publisher Yearbook, 1999. © The Editor & Publisher Co. 1999 All Rights Reserved. www.mediainfo.com

cent in 1998, just below the 68.5 percent recorded in 1996 and 1997. Newspaper readership is highest among those with the most education, the highest income, and the greatest job responsibilities. And the audience for newspapers continues to grow older: 73 percent of people over 65 read a daily paper, compared with only 44 percent of 18-24-year-olds, a percentage that continues to decline.

Newspapers tomorrow

The future heralds even greater drops in readership, as more and more people turn to the Internet for their news, rather than wait for the paper to come out the next day. In 1999, America Online reported that it had more than 20 million sub-scribers, or more than the readership of the top 20 newspapers in America *combined.* Newspapers have rushed to create a presence on the Web in an effort to capture this audience, with varying degrees of success. Approximately 1,000 newspapers in North America (including the top 100 in circulation) now have online products of some kind, ranging from classified ads to complete reproductions of the entire newspaper. According to the Newspaper Association of America, an online presence doesn't significantly cut into readership of the printed product. Some 82 percent of online readers say they read the printed paper with the same or increased frequency.

Weekly Newspapers in the U.S., 1960–98

Year	Number of newspapers[1]	Average circulation	Total weekly circulation	Year	Number of newspapers[1]	Average circulation	Total weekly circulation
1960	8,174	2,566	20,974,338	1992	7,417	7,358	54,577,034
1965	8,061	3,106	25,036,031	1993	7,437	7,629	56,734,526
1970	7,612	3,660	27,857,332	1994[2]	7,176	10,975	78,763,120
1975	7,612	4,715	35,892,409	1995[2]	8,453	9,425	79,668,266
1980	7,954	5,324	42,347,512	1996[2]	7,915	10,307	81,582,295
1985	7,704	6,359	48,988,801	1997[2]	7,214	9,763	70,434,299
1990	7,606	6,958	52,919,846	1998[2]	8,193	9,067	74,284,112
1991	7,476	7,323	54,746,332				

1. Includes paid and free-circulation newspapers. 2. 1994–98 not comparable to prior years due to change in information collection procedures.   **Source:** Newspaper Association of America, *Facts About Newspapers, 1999.*

Top 100 U.S. Magazines by Circulation, 1998

Rank	Magazine	Average paid circulation per issue	Percent change 1997-98	Rank	Magazine	Average paid circulation per issue	Percent change 1997-98
1.	Modern Maturity	20,468,227	0.22%	52.	Outdoor Life	1,362,418	-0.68%
2.	NRTA/AARP Bulletin	20,359,318	-0.32	53.	Boy's Life	1,330,814	-0.37
3.	Reader's Digest	14,221,558	-5.58	54.	American Rifleman	1,276,633	-9.90
4.	TV Guide	12,832,942	-2.32	55.	Consumers Digest	1,272,381	-0.19
5.	National Geographic	8,697,927	-3.49	56.	Rolling Stone	1,251,646	-0.15
6.	Better Homes and Gardens	7,614,682	0.06	57.	Scholastic Parent & Child	1,246,791	4.90
7.	Family Circle	5,004,998	-1.46	58.	Parenting Magazine	1,239,152	10.96
8.	Good Housekeeping	4,551,296	-2.99	59.	Car and Driver	1,234,824	7.64
9.	Ladies' Home Journal	4,548,983	-0.06	60.	Discover	1,224,117	1.21
10.	McCall's	4,221,216	-0.35	61.	In Style	1,207,777	20.19
11.	Woman's Day	4,156,126	-3.42	62.	Motor Trend	1,192,991	12.76
12.	Time	4,091,631	-1.48	63.	The Elks Magazine	1,192,468	N.A.
13.	People Weekly	3,676,704	3.31	64.	New Woman	1,180,898	-0.28
14.	Sports Illustrated	3,267,131	0.46	65.	PC Magazine	1,179,186	1.29
15.	Playboy	3,243,854	2.30	66.	Mademoiselle	1,174,997	1.89
16.	Newsweek	3,189,775	-1.12	67.	Vogue	1,168,678	4.99
17.	Prevention	3,148,299	-4.04	68.	PC World	1,147,925	1.21
18.	Home & Away	3,038,968	10.02	69.	Weight Watchers	1,146,216	9.26
19.	Redbook	2,861,200	0.05	70.	Self	1,145,326	2.07
20.	The American Legion Magazine	2,701,377	-1.55	71.	Endless Vacation	1,136,093	0.71
				72.	Shape	1,125,097	18.26
21.	Cosmopolitan	2,675,123	2.35	73.	The Family Handyman	1,117,911	1.73
22.	Avenues	2,613,967	2.22	74.	Us	1,103,232	-1.20
23.	Via Magazine	2,498,973	N.A.	75.	Soap Opera Digest	1,101,146	-5.29
24.	Southern Living	2,494,467	0.42	76.	Vanity Fair	1,097,523	0.15
25.	Seventeen	2,426,461	-3.71	77.	Sesame Street Magazine	1,085,703	6.51
26.	Martha Stewart Living	2,295,004	-1.41	78.	Bon Appétit	1,073,013	-1.17
27.	National Enquirer	2,225,480	-11.45	79.	Scouting	1,072,575	-1.13
28.	U.S. News & World Report	2,191,377	-1.38	80.	Health	1,071,808	3.31
				81.	Family Fun	1,071,248	10.58
29.	Glamour	2,186,283	4.55	82.	Country Home	1,058,145	-0.20
30.	YM	2,178,697	-0.24	83.	Kiplinger's Personal Finance	1,046,924	-3.48
31.	Smithsonian	2,064,717	-0.17				
32.	'Teen	1,964,045	12.13	84.	PC/Computing	1,026,712	1.91
33.	AAA Going Places	1,961,032	87.73	85.	Home	1,018,690	-0.92
34.	Money	1,918,938	-1.00	86.	Michigan Living	1,013,828	-0.15
35.	Star	1,860,912	-10.47	87.	American Health-For Women	1,006,139	9.72
36.	V.F.W. Magazine	1,824,943	-2.34				
37.	Ebony	1,798,900	-1.56	88.	American Homestyle & Gardening	1,003,046	-3.17
38.	Field & Stream	1,760,642	0.45				
39.	Parents	1,742,226	-0.01	89.	Travel & Leisure	1,001,998	-0.11
40.	Country Living	1,676,007	1.17	90.	Essence	1,000,608	0.04
41.	Men's Health	1,605,908	6.44	91.	Penthouse	996,323	10.31
42.	First For Women	1,591,198	12.05	92.	Fitness	980,131	14.21
43.	Woman's World	1,572,020	5.05	93.	Victoria	967,122	4.50
44.	Popular Science	1,563,066	0.24	94.	Elle	958,295	2.78
45.	Life	1,558,823	-0.86	95.	Today's Homeowner	954,525	3.89
46.	Golf Digest	1,548,161	0.88	96.	Jet	934,260	-1.44
47.	Sunset	1,461,631	0.11	97.	The American Hunter	933,323	-7.32
48.	Entertainment Weekly	1,442,430	10.27	98.	Business Week	911,156	0.29
49.	Golf Magazine	1,435,375	8.01	99.	Country America	904,675	0.11
50.	Popular Mechanics	1,428,849	0.24	100.	Gourmet	885,564	1.04
51.	Cooking Light	1,424,254	1.86		**Total, Top 100**	**248,718,172**	**1.86%**

Note: Leading Audit Bureau of Circulation (ABC) magazines by average paid combined circulation per issue.
Source: Magazine Publishers of America, 1999.

Top 50 U.S. Magazines by Advertising Revenues, 1998

Rank	Magazine	Advertising revenues (millions)	Percent change 1997–98	Rank	Magazine	Advertising revenues (millions)	Percent change 1997–98
1.	People Weekly	$626.60	6.5%	26.	McCall's	$122.19	3.3%
2.	Time	561.66	5.3	27.	Redbook	121.14	7.0
3.	Sports Illustrated	554.93	1.2	28.	Car And Driver	110.03	1.8
4.	TV Guide	453.52	-3.4	29.	Vanity Fair	109.37	14.5
5.	Better Homes & Gardens	410.10	8.6	30.	Parents	107.92	10.5
6.	Newsweek	399.96	-2.1	31.	Elle	105.88	5.5
7.	Business Week	361.61	9.7	32.	PC Computing	102.27	-7.4
8.	PC Magazine	314.19	-5.8	33.	Inc.	94.92	5.1
9.	Forbes	265.33	8.8	34.	In Style	90.64	70.9
10.	Fortune	253.57	12.3	35.	Golf Magazine	90.33	14.7
11.	Good Housekeeping	242.31	10.5	36.	Country Living	90.28	1.4
12.	Reader's Digest	237.60	11.9	37.	Seventeen	89.73	19.1
13.	Woman's Day	229.23	0.4	38.	The New Yorker	88.95	-5.4
14.	U. S. News & World Report	226.77	-5.2	39.	GQ	88.63	16.8
15.	Family Circle	218.81	6.3	40.	Travel & Leisure	88.06	14.8
16.	Cosmopolitan	214.09	13.6	41.	W	87.56	13.9
17.	Ladies' Home Journal	213.31	16.0	42.	Bride's	83.52	0.2
18.	Entertainment Weekly	166.04	13.7	43.	Parenting	81.05	16.1
19.	Glamour	150.18	9.3	44.	Modern Bride	80.90	7.8
20.	Vogue	149.99	0.7	45.	Harper's Bazaar	78.25	6.4
21.	Money	136.99	3.3	46.	Road & Track	72.88	-1.3
22.	Rolling Stone	135.79	11.7	47.	Motor Trend	72.03	15.3
23.	Martha Stewart Living	133.59	20.4	48.	Self	71.26	2.7
24.	Golf Digest	129.26	7.5	49.	Sunset	68.92	12.7
25.	Southern Living	128.84	6.7	50.	Architectural Digest	67.72	22.4

Source: Magazine Publishers of America, *Publishers Information Bureau Publications Ranked by Revenue, January-December 1998* (1999).

►MAGAZINES

Consumer magazines range from the very specialized (*Fly Fisherman*) to the general interest (*People*) and are sold either by subscription or through retail outlets (supermarkets, newsstands, etc.) The Audit Bureau of Circulations (ABC) monitors the sales of about 500 of the most popular consumer magazines. Trade publications are magazines with a narrow focus in a particular area of business (e.g. trucking, restaurants, computers). There are about 2,700 trade publications; they are sold either by subscription or distributed free.

Almost all magazines make money through revenues from both circulation and advertising. The most financially successful magazines are not necessarily the largest sellers, the difference being in the advertising fees they are able to obtain. *Fortune*, for example, is among the top 15 of all magazines in revenues, but does not even make the top-100 list in circulation.

►BOOKS

Sales of books in the United States increased in 1998 for the eighth straight year, according to figures released by the Book Industry Study Group, which monitors the reading habits of American households. Sales of hardcover books grew by 6 percent, while paperback sales increased 5 percent. The dollar volume of book sales increased faster than the number of books sold, indicating that the average price of books is also going up. The price of paperbacks increased even faster than inflation, from an average of $4.12 in 1994 to $4.56 in 1998.

The increase in sales came even as the total number of titles published declined. After hitting an all-time high of 68,175 titles in 1996, production dropped slightly in 1997 (to 65,796) and dramatically in 1998, to 56,129. While this is a significant decline (almost 15 percent), the number of titles produced is still higher than it was in 1990 (46,748). Ironically, it is the computer, predicted by many to be the book industry's death knell, which has been responsible for the increase in book production since 1990. Computers not only reduce publishers' production costs, enabling the publication of many more titles. They have also made possible the "superstore" where

Number of Libraries in U.S. and Canada by Type, 1980–97

Type of Library	1980	1990	1997	1998
Public	8,717	9,060	9,767	9,815
Branches of public libraries	5,936	5,833	6,332	6,435
Special	7,649	9,051	9,983	9,898
Medicine	1,674	1,861	1,924	1,900
Religious	913	946	1,019	1,010
Law	417	647	1,123	1,153
Academic	4,591	4,593	4,707	4,700
Junior college	1,191	1,233	1,265	1,270
Colleges, universities	3,400	3,360	3,442	3,430
Departmental	1,489	1,454	1,466	1,452
Law, medicine, religious	269	501	489	491
Government	1,260	1,735	1,837	1,897
Armed forces	485	489	378	363
Total, U.S.	28,638	30,761	33,004	33,108
Total, U.S. and Canada	31,564	34,613	36,923	37,039

Source: R.R. Bowker Co., *The Bowker Annual: Library and Book Trade Almanac.* (1999). Used with the permission of R.R. Bowker ® a Unit of Cahners Business Information.

computer indexes, rather than humans, keep track of so many titles.

Steadily rising levels of educational attainment over two decades—nearly 83 percent of the population had finished high school in 1998, compared with 68.1 percent in 1980, while 24.4 percent had finished college, compared with 17.0 percent in 1980—has created a growing audience for the printed word. It has also fueled a corresponding increase in the number of libraries in the U.S. Since 1980, the number of libraries has grown by more than 15 percent.

New Books and Editions Published, by Subject, 1980-98

Production of American books reached an all-time high of 68,175 titles in 1996, before dropping to 65,796 in 1997. Preliminary figures for 1998 indicate a more dramatic decrease, to 56,129, a decline of nearly 15 percent.

Subject	1980	1990	1997	1998[1]	Subject	1980	1990	1997	1998[1]
Agriculture	461	514	871	801	Medicine	3,292	3,014	4,136	3,676
Art	1,691	1,262	1,912	1,685	Music	357	289	433	408
Biography	1,891	1,957	3,069	2,657	Philosophy,				
Business	1,185	1,191	1,657	1,456	psychology	1,429	1,688	2,321	2,104
Education	1,011	1,039	1,438	1,224	Poetry, drama	1,179	874	1,545	1,125
Fiction	2,835	5,764	7,963	7,096	Religion	2,055	2,285	3,857	3,153
General works	1,643	1,760	3,159	2,237	Science	3,109	2,742	3,942	3,432
History	2,220	2,248	3,713	3,108	Sociology,				
Home economics	879	758	1,593	1,200	economics	7,152	7,042	10,064	8,970
Juvenile	2,859	5,172	3,683	3,381	Sports, recreation	971	978	1,691	1,367
Language	529	649	1,056	840	Technology	2,337	2,092	2,765	1,999
Law	1,102	896	1,390	1,189	Travel	504	495	809	652
Literature	1,686	2,049	2,729	2,369	**Total**	**42,377**	**46,748**	**65,796**	**56,129**

Note: Comprises new books (published for the first time), and new editions (with changes in text or format). Includes mass-market paperbacks. Excludes government publications, books sold only by subscription, dissertations, periodicals, quarterlies, and pamphlets under 49 pages. 1. Preliminary. **Source:** R.R. Bowker Co., *The Bowker Annual: Library and Book Trade Almanac.* (1999). Used with the permission of R.R. Bowker ® a Unit of Cahners Business Information.

Best-Sellers in America, 1917-98

Year	Fiction	Nonfiction
1917	*Mr. Britling Sees It Through,* H.G. Wells	*Rhymes of A Red Cross Man,* Robert W. Service
1918	*The U.P. Trail,* Zane Grey	*Rhymes of A Red Cross Man,* Robert W. Service
1919	*The Four Horsemen of the Apocalypse,* V. Blasco Iañez	*The Education of Henry Adams,* Henry Adams
1920	*The Man of the Forest,* Zane Grey	*Now It Can Be Told,* Philip Gibbs
1921	*Main Street,* Sinclair Lewis	*The Outline of History,* H.G. Wells
1922	*If Winter Comes,* A.S.M. Hitchinson	*The Outline of History,* H.G. Wells
1923	*Black Oxen,* Gertrude Atherton	*Etiquette,* Emily Post
1924	*So Big,* Edna Ferber	*Diet and Health,* Lulu Hunt Peters
1925	*Soundings,* A. Hamilton Gibbs	*Diet and Health,* Lulu Hunt Peters
1926	*The Private Life of Helen of Troy,* John Erskine	*The Man Nobody Knows,* Bruce Barton
1927	*Elmer Gantry,* Sinclair Lewis	*The Story of Philosophy,* Will Durant
1928	*The Bridge on San Luis Rey,* Thornton Wilder	*Disraeli,* Andre Maurois
1929	*All Quiet on the Western Front,* Erich Maria Remarque	*The Art of Thinking,* Ernest Dimmet
1930	*Cimarron,* Edna Ferber	*The Story of San Michele,* Axel Munthe
1931	*The Good Earth,* Pearl S. Buck	*Education of a Princess,* Grand Duchess Marie
1932	*The Good Earth,* Pearl S. Buck	*The Epic of America,* James Truslow Adams
1933	*Anthony Adverse,* Hervey Allen	*Life Begins at Forty,* Walter Pitkin
1934	*Anthony Adverse,* Hervey Allen	*While Rome Burns,* Alexander Woollcott
1935	*Green Light,* Lloyd C. Douglas	*North to the Orient,* Anne Morrow Lindbergh
1936	*Gone With the Wind,* Margaret Mitchell	*Man the Unknown,* Alexis Carrel
1937	*Gone With the Wind,* Margaret Mitchell	*How to Win Friends and Influence People,* Dale Carnegie
1938	*The Yearling,* Marjorie Kinnan Rawlings	*The Importance of Living,* Lin Yutang
1939	*The Grapes of Wrath,* John Steinbeck	*Days of Our Years,* Piere von Paaseen
1940	*How Green Was My Valley,* Richard Llewellyn	*I Married Adventure,* Osa Johnson
1941	*The Keys of the Kingdom,* A.J. Cronin	*Berlin Diary,* William C. Shirer
1942	*The Song of Bernadette,* Franz Werfel	*See Here, Private Hargrove,* Marion Hargrove

Year	Fiction	Nonfiction
1943	*The Robe,* Lloyd C. Douglas	*Under Cover,* John Roy Carlson
1944	*Strange Fruit,* Lillian Smith	*I Never Left Home ,* Bob Hope
1945	*Forever Amber,* Kathleen Winsor	*Brave Men,* Ernie Pyle
1946	*The King's General,* Daphne du Maurier	*The Egg and I,* Betty MacDonald
1947	*The Miracle of the Bells,* Russell Janney	*Peace of Mind,* Joshua L. Liebman
1948	*The Big Fisherman,* Lloyd C. Douglas	*Crusade in Europe,* Dwight D. Eisenhower
1949	*The Egyptian,* Mika Waltari	*White Collar Zoo,* Clare Barnes, Jr.
1950	*The Cardinal,* Henry Morton Robinson	*Betty Crocker's Picture Cookbook*
1951	*From Here to Eternity,* James Jones	*Look Younger, Live Longer,* Gayelord Hauser
1952	*The Silver Chalice,* Thomas B.Costain	*The Holy Bible: Revised Standard Version*
1953	*The Robe,* Lloyd C. Douglas	*The Holy Bible: Revised Standard Version*
1954	*Not As A Stranger,* Morton Thompson	*The Holy Bible: Revised Standard Version*
1955	*Marjorie Morningstar,* Herman Wouk	*Gift from the Sea,* Anne Morrow Lindbergh
1956	*Don't Go Near the Water,* William Brinkley	*Arthritis and Common Sense,* Dan Dale Alexander
1957	*By Love Possessed,* James Gould Cozzens	*Kids Say the Darndest Things!,* Art Linkletter
1958	*Doctor Zhivago,* Boris Pasternak	*Kids Say the Darndest Things!,* Art Linkletter
1959	*Exodus,* Leon Uris	*'Twixt Twelve and Twenty,* Pat Boone
1960	*Advise and Consent,* Allen Drury	*Folk Medicine,* D.C. Jarvis
1961	*The Agony and the Ecstasy,* Irving Stone	*The New English Bible: The New Testament*
1962	*Ship of Fools,* Katherine Anne Porter	*Calories Don't Count,* Dr. Herman Taller
1963	*The Shoes of the Fisherman,* Morris L. West	*Happiness Is a Warm Puppy,* Charles M. Schulz
1964	*The Spy Who Came in From the Cold,* John le Carré	*Four Days,* American Heritage
1965	*The Source,* James A. Michener	*How To Be a Jewish Mother,* Dan Greenburg
1966	*Valley of the Dolls,* Jacqueline Susann	*How to Avoid Probate,* Norman F. Dacey
1967	*The Arrangement,* Elia Kazan	*Death of a President,* William Manchester
1968	*Airport,* Arthur Hailey	*Better Homes & Gardens New Cook Book*
1969	*Portnoy's Complaint,* Philip Roth	*American Heritage Dictionary of the English Language,* ed. William Morris
1970	*Love Story,* Erich Segal	*Everything You Wanted to Know About Sex but Were Afraid to Ask,* David Reuben, M.D.
1971	*Wheels,* Arthur Hailey	*The Sensuous Man,* "M."
1972	*Jonathan Livingston Seagull,* Richard Bach	*The Living Bible,* Kenneth Taylor
1973	*Jonathan Livingston Seagull,* Richard Bach	*The Living Bible,* Kenneth Taylor
1974	*Centennial,* James A. Michener	*The Total Woman,* Marabel Morgan
1975	*Ragtime,* E. L. Doctorow	*Angels: God's Secret Agents,* Billy Graham
1976	*Trinity,* Leon Uris	*The Final Days,* Bob Woodward, Carl Bernstein
1977	*The Silmarillion,* J.R.R. Tolkien	*Roots,* Alex Haley
1978	*Chesapeake,* James A. Michener	*If Life is a Bowl of Cherries—What Am I Doing in the Pits?* Erma Bombeck
1979	*The Matarese Circle,* Robert Ludlum	*Aunt Erma's Cope Book,* Erma Bombeck
1980	*The Covenant,* James Michener	*Crisis Investing,* Douglas R. Casey
1981	*Noble House,* James Clavell	*The Beverly Hills Diet,* Judy Mazel
1982	*E.T. The Extra-Terrestrial Storybook,* William Kotzwinkle	*Jane Fonda's Workout Book,* Jane Fonda
1983	*Return of the Jedi Storybook,* Joan D. Vinge	*In Search of Excellence,* Thomas J. Peters, Robert H. Waterman Jr.
1984	*The Talisman,* Stephen King, Peter Straub	*Iacocca: An Autobiography,* Lee Iacocca with William Novak
1985	*The Mammoth Hunters,* Jean M.Auel	*Iacocca: An Autobiography,* Lee Iacocca with William Novak
1986	*It,* Stephen King	*Fatherhood,* Bill Cosby
1987	*The Tommyknockers,* Stephen King	*Time Flies,* Bill Cosby
1988	*The Cardinal of the Kremlin,* Tom Clancy	*The Eight-Week Cholesterol Diet,* Robert Kowalski
1989	*Clear and Present Danger,* Tom Clancy	*All I Really Need to Know I Learned in Kindergarten,* Robert Fulghum
1990	*The Plains of Passage,* Jean Auel	*A Life on the Road,* Charles Kuralt
1991	*Scarlett,* Alexandra Ripley	*Me: The Stories of My Life ,* Katharine Hepburn
1992	*Dolores Claiborne,* Stephen King	*The Way Things Ought to Be,* Rush Limbaugh
1993	*The Bridges of Madison County,* Robert James Walker	*See, I Told You So,* Rush Limbaugh
1994	*The Chamber,* John Grisham	*In the Kitchen with Rosie,* Rosie Daley
1995	*The Rainmaker,* John Grisham	*Men are From Mars, Women are From Venus,* John Gray
1996	*The Runaway Jury,* John Grisham	*Make the Connection,* Oprah Winfrey & Bob Greene
1997	*The Partner,* John Grisham	*Angela's Ashes,* Frank McCourt
1998	*The Street Lawyer,* John Grisham	*The Nine Steps to Financial Freedom,* Suze Orman

Sources: Alice Payne Hackett, *70 Years of Best Sellers;* Publishers Weekly.

Number and Value of U.S. Books Sold, 1990-98 (in millions)

Type of publication and market area	Publishers' units			Domestic consumer expenditures		
	1990	1997	1998[1]	1990	1997	1998[1]
TYPE OF PUBLICATION						
Trade	730.7	785.6	860.3	$6,497.8	$9,172.7	$10,349.5
Adult trade	420.4	441.8	496.6	4,776.8	6,831.7	7,791.3
Juvenile trade	310.3	343.8	363.7	1,721.0	2,341.0	2,558.2
Religious	137.7	166.6	170.5	1,361.9	1,958.3	2,037.0
Professional	148.6	165.2	170.3	2,956.8	4,464.7	4,750.9
Book clubs	110.6	137.7	141.3	704.7	1,113.6	1,176.0
Mail order publications	142.6	85.7	78.1	751.7	538.7	486.5
Mass market paperback	488.8	473.2	483.7	1,775.4	2,220.4	2,348.0
University press	15.8	17.8	18.5	284.1	426.6	454.6
Elementary and high school	218.7	286.5	302.2	1,947.9	2,866.4	3,215.6
College	149.7	168.2	175.9	2,319.0	3,110.2	3,365.0
Subscription reference	1.1	1.2	1.2	443.6	578.6	602.8
All books	**2,144.3**	**2,287.7**	**2,402.3**	**$19,042.9**	**$26,540.2**	**$28,785.9**
Hardbound total[2]	721.9	766.5	816.0	10,593.9	14,694.8	15,926.7
Paperbound total[2]	1,278.7	1,434.3	1,507.0	7,253.7	10,638.1	11,769.9
MARKET AREA						
Domestic (total)	2,005.0	2,144.1	2,253.6	$19,042.9	$26,540.2	$28,785.9
General retailers	1,009.8	1,078.4	1,142.6	8,465.4	11,957.6	13,102.4
Colleges	254.6	274.4	290.8	3,403.2	4,697.7	5,121.5
Libraries and institutions	88.4	95.5	102.0	1,591.8	2,209.6	2,393.8
Schools and school libraries	244.1	308.6	326.3	2,365.0	3,387.8	3,779.6
Direct to consumers	304.1	290.9	292.5	2,901.0	3,820.0	3,989.3
Other	104.1	96.2	99.4	316.5	377.5	399.3
Export	139.4	143.6	148.7	—	—	—
Total	**2,144.3**	**2,287.7**	**2,402.3**			

Note: Includes all titles released by publishers in the United States, and imports that appear under the imprint of American publishers. Multi-volume sets such as encyclopedias are counted as one unit. School libraries included with school, not libraries. 1. Excludes standardized tests. 2. Does not include mail order or subscription reference publications.
Source: Book Industry Study Group, Inc., *Book Industry Trends*, annual (1999), reprinted by permission.

THE ELECTRONIC MEDIA

▶ TELEVISION

Few people today doubt the pervasiveness of television's influence on America. Once a symbol of luxury, the color television has found its way into almost every home in America, and a great majority of American households have two or more televisions. According to the A.C. Nielsen Company, which monitors television viewership, at least one of these televisions was on in each household for seven hours and 37 minutes during the 1998–99 television season. That's an hour and 18 minutes more than in 1971, when the average was just over 6 hours and 19 minutes, but three minutes less than in 1997–98. Average daily viewing per person is still much higher than 1970s levels, but down slightly from the year before. Women over the age of 18 watched longest: they averaged four hours and 51 minutes per day, (down two minutes from the year before), while men over 18 watched for four hours and 16 minutes (down from 4:16 in 1997–98). Children aged 12–17 watched an average of 2 hours and 54 minutes, down dramatically from 3:07 in 1997–98 and a half hour less than in 1984–85. Viewing by children 2–11 has dropped from 3 hours and 49 minutes in 1984–85 to three hours and 3 minutes in 1997–98. Primetime viewership is highest on Sunday nights (106 million people) and lowest on Friday and Saturday nights (89.7 million).

Top 20 TV Shows of the 1998-99 Season

Rank, Program (Network)	Avg. rating	Avg. share
1. *E.R.* (NBC)	17.8	29
2. *Friends* (NBC)	15.7	26
3. *Frasier* (NBC)	15.6	24
4. *NFL Monday Night Football* (ABC)	13.9	22
5. *Jesse* (NBC)	13.7	22
5. *Veronica's Closet* (NBC)	13.7	21
7. *60 Minutes* (CBS)	13.2	22
8. *Touched by an Angel* (CBS)	13.1	20
9. *CBS Sunday Movie*	12.1	19
10. *20/20, Wednesday* (ABC)	11.2	19
11. *Home Improvement* (ABC)	11.0	18
12. *Everybody Loves Raymond* (CBS)	10.6	16
13. *NYPD Blue* (ABC)	10.5	18
14. *Law and Order* (NBC)	10.1	17
15. *The Drew Carey Show* (ABC)	9.9	16
15. *20/20, Friday* (ABC)	9.9	18
17. *JAG* (NBC)	9.8	16
17. *NFL Monday Showcase* (ABC)	9.8	16
17. *Providence* (NBC)	9.8	18
17. *Dateline, Friday* (NBC)	9.8	17

Note: For the period from Sept. 4, 1998, to May 26, 1999. Does not include movies of the week programs or programs broadcast for fewer than 10 weeks. **Rating** is the percentage of all television owners watching that program. **Share** is the percentage of TVs that are on at the time of the program. For example, on a given Thursday night, 29 percent of the people watching TV at 10 P.M. were tuned to *E.R.*, but because not every TV owner was watching television that night, only 17.8 percent of all TV owners were tuned in to *E.R.* **Source:** Nielsen Media Research.

Top 50 Single Shows in TV History, by Rating

Rank/Program	Date	Network	Rating	Share
1. *M*A*S*H* Special (Last episode)	2/28/83	CBS	60.2%	77%
2. *Dallas* (Who shot J.R.?)	11/21/80	CBS	53.3	76
3. *Roots*, part 8	1/30/77	ABC	51.1	71
4. Super Bowl XVI (San Francisco/Cincinnati)	1/24/82	CBS	49.1	73
5. Super Bowl XVII (Washington/Miami)	1/30/83	NBC	48.6	69
6. XVII Winter Olympics (Figure skating round 1)	2/23/94	CBS	48.5	64
7. Super Bowl XX (Chicago/New England)	1/26/86	NBC	48.3	70
8. *Gone With the Wind*, part 1	11/7/76	NBC	47.7	65
9. *Gone With the Wind*, part 2	11/8/76	NBC	47.4	64
10. Super Bowl XII (Dallas/Denver)	1/15/78	CBS	47.2	67
11. Super Bowl XIII (Pittsburgh/Dallas)	1/21/79	NBC	47.1	74
12. *Bob Hope Christmas Show*	1/15/70	NBC	46.6	64
13. Super Bowl XVIII (L.A. Raiders/Washington)	1/22/84	CBS	46.4	71
13. Super Bowl XIX (San Francisco/Miami)	1/20/85	ABC	46.4	63
15. Super Bowl XIV (Pittsburgh/L.A. Rams)	1/20/80	CBS	46.3	67
16. Super Bowl XXX (Dallas/Pittsburgh)	1/28/96	NBC	46.0	68
16. *ABC Theater "The Day After"*	1/20/83	ABC	46.0	62
18. *Roots*, part 6	1/28/77	ABC	45.9	66
18. *The Fugitive*	8/29/67	ABC	45.9	72
20. Super Bowl XXI (N.Y. Giants/Denver)	1/25/87	CBS	45.8	66
21. *Roots*, part 5	1/27/77	ABC	45.7	71
22. *Cheers* (Last episode)	5/20/93	NBC	45.5	66
22. Super Bowl XXVIII (Dallas/Buffalo)	1/29/94	NBC	45.5	64
24. *The Ed Sullivan Show*	2/9/64	CBS	45.3	60
25. Super Bowl XXVII (Dallas/Buffalo)	1/31/93	NBC	45.1	66
26. *Bob Hope Christmas Show*	1/14/71	NBC	45.0	61
27. *Roots*, part 3	1/25/77	ABC	44.8	68
28. Super Bowl XXXII (Denver/Green Bay)	1/25/98	NBC	44.5	67
29. Super Bowl XI (Oakland/Minnesota)	1/9/77	NBC	44.4	73
29. Super Bowl XV (Oakland/Philadelphia)	1/25/81	NBC	44.4	63
31. Super Bowl VI (Dallas/Miami)	1/16/72	CBS	44.2	74
32. *Roots*, part 2	1/24/77	ABC	44.1	64
32. XVII Winter Olympics (Figure skating finals)	2/25/94	CBS	44.1	62
34. *The Beverly Hillbillies*	1/8/64	CBS	44.0	65
35. *Roots*, part 4	1/26/77	ABC	43.8	66
35. *The Ed Sullivan Show* (w/ the Beatles)	2/16/64	CBS	43.8	60
37. Super Bowl XXIII (San Francisco/Cincinnati)	1/22/89	NBC	43.5	68
38. Academy Awards	4/7/70	ABC	43.4	78
39. Super Bowl XXXI (Green Bay/New England)	1/26/97	FOX	43.3	65
40. *The Thorn Birds*, part 3	3/29/83	ABC	43.2	62
41. *The Thorn Birds*, part 4	3/30/83	ABC	43.1	62
42. NFC Championship game (San Francisco/Dallas)	1/10/82	CBS	42.9	62
43. *The Beverly Hillbillies*	1/15/64	CBS	42.8	62
44. Super Bowl VII (Miami/Washington)	1/14/73	NBC	42.7	72
45. *The Thorn Birds*, part 2	3/28/83	ABC	42.5	59
46. Super Bowl IX (Pittsburgh/Minnesota)	1/12/75	NBC	42.4	72
46. *The Beverly Hillbillies*	2/26/64	CBS	42.4	60
48. Super Bowl X (Pittsburgh/Dallas)	1/18/76	CBS	42.3	78
48. *Roots*, part 7	1/29/77	ABC	42.3	65
48. *Love Story* (Sunday night movie)	10/1/72	ABC	42.3	62
48. *Cinderella*	2/22/65	CBS	42.3	59
48. *Airport* (Movie Special)	11/11/73	ABC	42.3	63

Note: As of Sept. 1, 1999. Does not include programs broadcast on more than one network, e.g. the Apollo moon landing or programs under 30 minutes scheduled duration. Rating is the number of people watching as a percentage of all television owners. Share is the number watching as a percentage of people with their TVs on at that particular time.   **Source:** Nielsen Media Research.

▶CABLE TELEVISION

Cable television was originally designed as a means of improving TV reception in some rural areas. In the 1960s, operators realized that viewers were willing to pay for commercial-free programming, but their efforts to capitalize on the idea were hampered by stringent Federal Communications Commission restrictions. Not until 1975, when RCA put its first communications satellite into operation, did the industry really bloom. Under the name Home Box Office, the company started to transmit programming that could be received by independent operators around the country and then relayed to subscribers at minimal cost. With the dismissal of most of the FCC's regulations by a federal court in 1977, the door was opened for the development of what is now a multibillion-dollar industry.

As the accompanying table demonstrates, cable has changed the television broadcasting landscape, drawing away more than one-third of the total television viewing audiences. As a result, the fractured total television audience means that no

Longest Running National Network Series of All Time

Program	Seasons	Years[1]
Walt Disney	33	1954-90
60 Minutes	32	1968-
The Ed Sullivan Show	24	1948-71
Gunsmoke	20	1955-75
The Red Skelton Show	20	1951-71
Meet the Press	18	1947-65[2]
What's My Line	18	1950-67
I've Got a Secret	17	1952-76
Lassie	17	1954-71
The Lawrence Welk Show	17	1955-71

Note: Includes prime-time (6-11 p.m.) shows only; sports broadcasts and movie series are not included. 1. Dates reflect the first and last broadcasts of each show. Programs did not necessarily run continuously throughout this period. 2. Ceased broadcasting in prime-time in 1965, though still on the air.

Primetime Viewing Shares of Free and Cable TV Networks, 1985-98

Year	Network affiliates	Ad-supported basic cable	All other television[1]
1985-86	69.3%	7.5%	23.2%
1989-90	58.1	16.4	25.5
1990-91	55.1	19.3	25.6
1991-92	54.9	19.8	25.3
1992-93	52.9	21.1	26.0
1993-94	52.4	21.3	26.3
1994-95	48.7	24.3	27.0
1995-96	46.0	26.7	27.3
1996-97	42.1	29.7	28.2
1997-98	39.6	32.5	27.9

Note: For all television viewing Monday-Sunday, 8-11 p.m. EST. Due to multiset use and independent roundings, totals add up to more than 100. 1. Includes the FOX network, UPN, WB, other independent stations, pay cable, and public television.
Source: Cable Advertising Bureau, *Cable TV Facts* (1999).

Basic and Pay Cable TV Systems and Subscribers, 1952-99

Year	Number of of systems	Basic cable		Pay cable	
		Subscribers	Percent of U.S. TV households	Subscribers	Percent of households with cable
1952	70	14,000	0.1%	N.A.	N.A.
1955	400	150,000	0.5	N.A.	N.A.
1960	640	650,000	1.4	N.A.	N.A.
1970	2,490	3,900,000	6.7	N.A.	N.A.
1975	3,506	9,196,690	13.2	469,000	23.6%
1980	4,225	17,671,490	22.6	9,144,000	50.6
1985	6,600	39,872,520	46.2	30,596,000	83.5
1990	9,575	54,871,330	59.0	39,900,000	77.1
1995	11,218	62,956,470	65.7	46,100,000	74.2
1996	11,119	64,654,160	66.7	47,700,000	75.1
1997	10,950	65,929,420	67.3	48,000,000	73.9
1998	10,845	67,011,180	67.4	47,700,000	72.2
1999	10,700[1]	67,607,910	68.0	N.A	N.A.

1. Estimate. **Sources:** National Cable Television Association, *Cable TV Developments* (Spring, 1999); Nielsen Media Research.

Video and Audio: Sales & Penetration in U.S. Homes, 1990-99

Product	Sales (thousands of units)				Percent of U.S. homes			
	1990	1997	1998[1]	1999[1]	1990	1997	1998	1999
Video								
Color television set	20,384	21,293	21,185	22,500	96%	98%	98%	98%
Color TV with stereo	6,655	11,096	12,100	12,400	19	55	59	63
Projection television	351	917	1,060	1,050	6	11	12	13
TV/VCR combination	424	2,311	3,100	3,555	N.A.	8	10	10
VCR[2]	11,986	24,282	25,620	25,740	68	89	90	91
Laserdisc player	168	49	20	10	N.A.	2	2	2
Camcorder	2,962	3,650	3,700	3,780	10	26	30	33
Satellite dish	330	2,200	2,830	3,100	3	11	11	13
Audio								
Radio	21,585	17,664	18,700	19,650	99%	98%	98%	98%
Rack audio system	1,557	501	380	375	92	54	55	55
Compact disc player	9,155	33,095	40,900	42,500	19	49	52	55
Compact audio system	2,447	7,275	9,000	9,930	N.A.	36	38	40

N.A.= Not available. 1. Estimate. 2. Includes mono and stereo decks, but not machines that play but do not record. Does not include TV/VCR combinations. **Source:** Consumer Electronics U.S. Sales, © 1999 Electronic Industries Association. Reprinted by permission.

single program will likely ever reach the kind of viewership numbers achieved during the 1960s and '70s, when viewers had only three or four choices. A case in point: the final episode of *Seinfeld*, broadcast in the spring of 1998, was the most talked-about program in a decade, but it didn't attract as many viewers as regular episodes of *The Beverly Hillbillies*.

The number of cable subscribers is currently increasing by about a half million per year. But despite deregulation and increased competition from direct satellite providers, the average cable

Top 15 Cable Television Networks, 1998

Rank/Network	Subscribers (millions)	Number of systems	Launch date	Content
1. The Discovery Channel	75.3	10,882	1985	Nonfiction, nature, science
2. TBS	75.0	11,668	1976	Movies, sports, original & syndicated shows
3. C-SPAN	74.1	6,404	1979	Public affairs, live Congressional coverage.
4. Fox Family Channel	73.0	10,880	1998	Original and syndicated family programming.
5. ESPN	73.0	27,600	1979	Sports events and sports news
6. Cable News Network (CNN)	73.0	11,528	1980	24–hour news, special interest reports
7. Lifetime Television	72.5	11,000	1984	Programming aimed at women
8. The Nashville Network (TNN)	72.4	N/A	1983	Country music and lifestyle programming
9. A&E Television	72.0	12,000	1984	Original programming, biographies, documentaries.
10. The Weather Channel	71.6	7,000	1982	Weather updates
12. USA Network	69.7	12,500	1980	Sports, family entertainment
11. CNN Headline News	69.8	6,917	1982	Half-hour news updates
13. MTV: Music Television	69.4	9,176	1981	Music videos
14. AMC (American Movie Classics)	69.0	N/A	1984	Classic Hollywood movies
15. The Learning Channel (TLC)	67.5	6,608	1980	Educational programming

Source: National Cable Television Association, *Cable TV Developments* (Spring, 1999).

Top 5 Pay-Cable Services, 1998

Rank/Network	Subscribers	Content
1. HBO	20,800,000	Movies, variety, sports, documentaries
2. The Disney Channel	16,100,100	Movies, cartoons
3. Spice	15,400,000	Adult movies
4. Showtime/The Movie Channel	14,800,000	Movies, variety, comedy, sports
5. Sundance Channel	12,000,000	Independent films, shorts, and animation

Sources: National Cable Television Association, *Cable TV Developments* (Spring, 1999).

U.S. Radio Stations and Radio Sales, 1946–98

Year	Radio stations on air[1]	Unit sales to dealers[2]
1946	961	N.A.
1950	2,773	N.A.
1955	3,211	7,327
1960	4,133	18,031
1965	5,249	31,689
1970	6,760	34,049
1975	7,744	25,276
1980	8,566	27,104
1985	10,359	21,575
1990	10,788	21,585
1991	10,989	18,530
1992	11,118	21,553
1993	11,371	19,697
1994	11,565	18,323
1995	11,834	17,051
1996	12,295	17,581
1997	12,482	17,664
1998	12,641	18,700[3]

1. Includes AM and FM, commercial and noncommercial.
2. Includes table, clock, and portable—but not car— radios.
3. Estimate **Source:** M Street Corporation, 1999; Electronic Industries Association, *Consumer Electronics, U.S. Sales*, (1999).

Radio Stations by Primary Format, 1990–98

Format	1990	1997	1998
Total commercial stations	9,444	10,350	10,394
Country	2,452	2,491	2,368
Adult contemporary	2,135	1,508	1,493
News, Talk, Business, Sports	405	1,331	1,382
Religion (teaching & music)	745	1,063	1,076
Oldies & Classic hits	659	927	991
Rock (Album, Modern, Classic)	419	803	868
Spanish & other ethnic	342	549	570
Adult standards	383	551	561
Top 40	824	358	379
Urban, Black, Urban adult contemporary	294	349	354
Jazz and new age	68	92	88
Variety	97	50	43
Classical, Fine arts	52	44	40
Easy listening	240	49	39
Pre-teen	3	40	37
Comedy	1	0	0
Off Air	210	143	102
Changing formats or not available	115	2	3
Total non-commercial stations	1,636	2,132	2,247
Total all stations	11,080	12,482	12,641

Note: As of November of each year.
Source: M Street Corporation, 1999.

bill continues to increase. It was $7.69 in 1980; in 1998, it was $27.81, an increase of 262 percent over 18 years. The nation's biggest cable providers are Tele-Communications (TCI), with 13,059,000 basic subscribers, Time Warner Cable (12,600,000), and MediaOne (4,933,000).

▶ RADIO
According to statistics compiled by the Radio Advertising Bureau, 98 percent of all U.S. households own at least one radio. Of Americans over age 12, 95.3 percent listen to radio for an average of 3 hours and 20 minutes each workday. There are a total of 576.5 million radios in the U.S., 26 percent more than in 1980, distributed as follows: 367.4 million are in homes, 142.8 million in cars, 43.7 million in trucks, vans, and RVs, and 22.6 million in the workplace.

▶ THE RECORDING INDUSTRY
In fewer than 10 years, the compact disc has gone from technological breakthrough to the music format of choice among most consumers. Along the way, it resuscitated an industry that many feared was sagging at the hands of video games, computers, and movies.

Fewer than 100,000 CDs were sold in 1983, the first year they were available, but the format quickly overtook LPs by 1988, and topped cassette sales in 1992. More than two-thirds of all music sold is now produced on CDs. The recording industry's willingness to support the new technology, by releasing a large amount of music on disc, has no doubt played a large part in the CD's growth. And why shouldn't it? Discs cost no more than albums or cassettes to produce, yet consumers are still willing to pay about twice as much for the digital format. The CD has also revived the entire music industry, which in the late 1970s and early '80s was worried about losing young consumers to movies and videogames. The industry was also concerned that home taping was cutting into sales of records. With the CD's superior sound quality, that's no longer a serious issue. The total U.S. dollar value of all music sold was $13.7 billion in 1998, more than double the amount as recently as 1989 ($6.6 billion).

Sales by Category
The sales of different types of music are in almost as constant a flux as the music types themselves. The category defined as rock accounted for nearly half of all music sales in 1987; in 1998, it was only a quarter. Country, Rhythm & Blues, and Rap have made up the difference. For many years, the single largest group of recorded music consumers (as a percentage of total dollar value) was teenagers (buyers aged 15–19). But in 1998, the over-45 crowd elbowed them aside. The 15–19-year-olds were responsible for 15.8 percent of all dollars spent, while the 45 and over crowd contributed 18.1 percent. The greatest decline has come

Top-Selling Albums of 1998

Title	Artist	Copies sold (millions)
Titanic	Soundtrack	9.2
Let's Talk About Love	Celine Dion	5.6
Backstreet Boys	Backstreet Boys	4.9
Come on Over	Shania Twain	4.2
City of Angels	Soundtrack	3.8
'N Sync	'N Sync	3.2
Big Willie Style	Will Smith	3.2
Savage Garden	Savage Garden	3.1
Yourself or Someone Like You	Matchbox 20	3.0
Hello Nasty	Beastie Boys	2.9

Source: *Soundscan*, 1998.

Recorded Music Sales by Genre, Format, and Age Group, 1987–98

Characteristic	1987	1990	1994	1995	1996	1997	1998
Genre							
Rock	45.5%	36.1%	35.1%	33.5%	32.6%	32.5%	25.7%
Country	10.6	9.6	16.3	16.7	14.7	14.4	14.1
R&B	9.0	11.6	9.6	11.3	12.1	11.2	12.8
Pop	13.5	13.7	10.3	10.1	9.3	9.4	10.0
Rap	3.8	8.5	7.9	6.7	8.9	10.1	9.7
Gospel	2.9	2.5	3.3	3.1	4.3	4.5	6.3
Classical	3.9	3.1	3.7	2.9	3.4	2.8	3.3
Jazz	3.8	4.8	3.0	3.0	3.3	2.8	1.9
Other[1]	6.2	8.8	8.5	10.1	8.2	9.4	11.3
Format							
CDs	11.5%	31.1%	58.4%	65.0%	68.4%	70.2%	74.8%
Cassettes	62.5	54.7	32.1	25.1	19.3	18.2	14.8
LPs	20.1	4.7	0.8	0.5	0.6	0.7	0.7
Singles (all types)	5.7	8.7	7.4	7.5	9.3	9.3	6.8
Music videos	N.A.	N.A.	0.8	0.9	1.0	0.6	1.0
Age group							
10–14	7.3%	7.6%	7.9%	8.0%	7.9%	8.9%	9.1%
15–19	24.2	18.3	16.8	17.1	17.2	16.8	15.8
20–24	19.1	16.5	15.4	15.3	15.0	13.8	12.2
25–29	14.5	14.6	12.6	12.3	12.5	11.7	11.4
30–34	10.8	13.2	11.8	12.1	11.4	11.0	11.4
35–39	8.2	10.2	11.5	10.8	11.1	11.6	12.6
40–44	4.8	7.8	7.9	7.5	9.1	8.8	8.3
45+	10.7	11.1	15.4	16.1	15.1	16.5	18.1

Note: Figures represent a percentage of that year's total U.S. dollar sales. 1. Includes soundtracks, children's music, and other categories not shown separately. Totals may not add to 100 percent due to "Don't Know/No Answer" Responses.
Source: Recording Industry Association of America, *1998 Consumer Profile* (1998).

among adults 20–24 and 25–29. They accounted for 32.9 of every 100 dollars spent on music in 1989; by 1998, they were responsible for only 23.6 percent. For the second straight year, women made more than half of the music purchases in the U.S. in 1998. That's a significant change from 1987, when women constituted only 44.8 percent of the market.

A decision in 1996 by Wal-Mart stores to restrict music sales of albums with controversial lyrics caused understandable consternation among record executives because of discount stores' increasing influence on the industry's bottom line. In 1989, 71.7 percent of all recorded music was sold in record stores, while 15.6 percent was sold in "other stores," which includes discount and consumer electronic stores. In 1998, record stores accounted for only 50.8 percent of music purchases, while the Wal-Marts, Kmarts, and Targets of America made up 34.4 percent of music sales. In many remote areas, the local Wal-Mart is the only place to buy recorded music of any kind, forcing many top musical acts to release special Wal-Mart versions of their albums, with bowdlerized lyrics.

Individual Record Sales

Up until 1958, the term **gold** album simply meant a hit album. But in that year, the Recording Industry Association of America codified the term to mean a record that had reached $1 million in sales. (Separate levels were established for singles, which have since been amended). The cast album from *Oklahoma!* was the first gold album. By 1975, inflation had diluted the importance of the award, so the RIAA also required gold records to sell at least 500,000 copies. The following year, it introduced the **platinum** record, awarded to albums that sell at least one million copies. The Eagles' *Their Greatest Hits 1971–1975* was the first platinum album. **Multi-platinum** awards go to albums selling more than two million copies. Michael Jackson's *Thriller* was one of the first albums to go multi-Platinum, and with 25 million copies sold, remains the top-selling album of all time. In 1999, the RIAA introduced the **Diamond** award, for singles or records with U.S. sales of 10 million or more. As of March 1999, 62 titles had qualified for the award, in genres ranging from pop, R&B, and rock to rap, country, and instrumental.

Top Selling and Renting Videos

Rank by sales	Rank by rentals	Rank by sales	Rank by rentals
1998		**ALL-TIME**	
1. *Titanic*	1. *Titanic*	1. *The Lion King*	1. *Top Gun*
2. *Hercules*	2. *Air Force One*	2. *Titanic*	2. *Pretty Woman*
3. *The Little Mermaid*	3. *Con Air*	3. *Toy Story*	3. *The Little Mermaid*
4. *Lion King 2: Simba's Pride*	4. *Face/Off*	4. *Forrest Gump*	4. *Home Alone*
5. *Peter Pan*	5. *As Good as it Gets*	5. *Snow White and the Seven Dwarfs*	5. *Ghost*
6. *Lady and the Tramp*	6. *My Best Friend's Wedding*	6. *Beauty and the Beast*	6. *Beauty and the Beast*
7. *Flubber*	7. *Men in Black*	7. *Independence Day*	7. *The Lion King*
8. *Men in Black*	8. *The Devil's Advocate*	8. *Jurassic Park*	8. *Terminator II: Judgment Day*
9. *Anastasia*	9. *Armageddon*	9. *Cinderella*	9. *Forrest Gump*
10. *Air Force One*	10. *G.I. Jane*	10. *E.T.: The Extra-Terrestrial*	10. *Dances with Wolves*

Note: Rental figures are based on number of transactions; sales figures are based on number of purchases, not dollar value. All-time sales figures are for February 16, 1988-December 31, 1998; all-time rental figures are for March 1, 1987-December 31, 1998.
Source: Alexander & Associates, Inc.

U.S. Film Box-Office Receipts, Theaters, Admission, and Admission Charges, 1926–98

Year	Box office receipts (millions)	Theaters Indoor	Theaters Drive-in	Annual admissions Total (millions)	Annual admissions Per person	Average admission charge	Number of $20 million hits
1926	$ 720.0	N.A.	N.A.	2,600	N.A.	N.A.	N.A.
1930	732.0	N.A.	N.A.	4,680	N.A.	N.A.	N.A.
1935	566.0	N.A.	N.A.	3,900	N.A.	$0.24	N.A.
1940	735.0	N.A.	N.A.	4,160	N.A.	0.24	N.A.
1950	1,376.0	N.A.	N.A.	3,120	N.A.	0.53	N.A.
1960	951.0	N.A.	N.A.	2,080	N.A.	0.69	N.A.
1970[1]	1,162.0	10,335	3,720	920	N.A.	1.55	N.A.
1980	2,748.5	14,029	3,561	1,022	4.5	2.69	17
1990[2]	5,021.8	22,774	915	1,189	4.8	4.23	30
1991	4,803.2	23,662	908	1,141	4.5	4.21	30
1992	4,871.0	24,233	872	1,173	4.6	4.15	36
1993	5,154.2	24,887	850	1,244	4.8	4.14	28
1994	5,396.2	25,701	885	1,292	5.0	4.18	33
1995	5,493.5	26,958	847	1,263	4.8	4.35	36
1996	5,911.5	28,864	826	1,339	5.0	4.42	31
1997	6,365.9	30,825	815	1,388	5.2	4.59	39
1998	6,949.0	33,440	746	1,481	5.5	4.69	37

1. Theater figures are for 1971. 2. Beginning in 1990, admission totals and average prices are supplied by the National Association of Theater Owners and are not strictly comparable with data from previous years, which are based on the U.S. Department of Commerce's Consumer Price Index. **Source:** U.S. Dept. of Commerce; *Film Daily Yearbook;* Motion Picture Association of America, *1998 U.S. Economic Review.*

▶ VIDEO

In 20 years, the video cassette recorder (VCR) has gone from a curiosity to a luxury to an appliance found in close to 90 percent of American homes. The vast majority of people continue to use their VCRs simply to watch pre-recorded videos from their local rental store. More than 700 million pre-recorded videos were sold to dealers in 1998. But a sizable number of owners have figured out how to program their VCRs and were responsible for the sale of 420 million blank cassettes in 1998.

▶ FILM

The motion picture industry does close to $7 billion in business each year. A relatively small number of people are involved in this endeavor: only 564,800 in 1998. The various studios release an average of about 500 films per year, about half of which they submit to the Motion Picture Association of America for ratings and wide release in theaters. Close to two-thirds of these movies (65 percent in 1998) receive an R rating. The rest receive a PG or PG-13 rating. Only 6 percent of 1998 movies were G-rated, and even fewer (1 percent) received an NC-17 or X-rating. Because many theaters simply refuse to show NC-17 movies, producers are loath to release a film with an NC-17 label.

Movie Budgets

The cost of making movies has escalated dramatically in recent years. In 1988, the average price tag of a motion picture was $18.1 million according to the MPAA. Today, that's less than the average marketing budget for a feature film. Rising actors' salaries, increased demand for special effects, and other spiraling costs drove the average cost of making a movie to a whopping $52.7 million in 1998, up a staggering 32.2 percent over 1996 ($39.8 million), but surprisingly down 1.4 percent over 1997. Still, the cost of making a movie has more than doubled just since 1991 ($26.1 million), when the special effects of *Terminator* 2 were cutting edge. The megabudget films *Titanic* and *The Lost World* no doubt fueled this rise in costs. And because both movies were big money makers (*Titanic*, with a worldwide gross of more than $1 billion and counting, is one of the most successful movies ever made, despite its $200 million-plus price tag), Hollywood is sure to embrace the big-budget trend in years to come. In addition to these production costs, studios spent an average of $25.3 million on advertising and publicity in 1998, or more than double what they spent in 1991 ($12.1 million).

Most Popular Films, By Decade

Title (Year)	Director	Rental (millions)	Title (Year)	Director	Rental (millions)
Pre-1930			**1970–79**		
The Birth of a Nation (1915)	D.W. Griffith	$10.0	Star Wars (1977)	G. Lucas	$193.77
The Big Parade (1925)	K. Vidor	5.5	Jaws (1975)	S. Spielberg	129.55
The Singing Fool (1928)	L. Bacon	4.0	Grease (1978)	R. Kleiser	96.30
			The Exorcist (1973)	W. Friedkin	89.00
1930–39			The Godfather (1972)	F. F. Coppola	86.30
Gone With the Wind (1939)	V. Fleming	$77.6			
Snow White and the Seven Dwarfs (1937)	(Animated)	62.8	**1980–89**		
King Kong (1933)	M. Cooper	5.0	E.T.—The Extra-Terrestrial (1982)	S. Spielberg	$228.17
The Wizard of Oz (1939)	V. Fleming	4.5	Return of the Jedi (1983)	R. Marquand	168.19
San Francisco (1936)	W.S. Van Dyke	4.0	Batman (1989)	T. Burton	150.50
			The Empire Strikes Back (1980)	J. Kershner	141.67
1940–49[1]			Ghostbusters (1984)	I. Reitman	132.72
Cinderella (1949)	(Animated)	$38.5	Raiders of the Lost Ark (1981)	S. Spielberg	115.60
Pinocchio (1940)	(Animated)	32.9	Indiana Jones and the Last Crusade (1989)	S. Spielberg	115.50
Song of the South (1946)	H. Foster/ W. Jackson	29.2	Indiana Jones and the Temple of Doom (1984)	S. Spielberg	109.00
Fantasia (1940)	(Animated)	28.5	Beverly Hills Cop (1984)	M. Brest	108.00
Bambi (1942)	(Animated)	28.4	Back to the Future (1985)	R. Zemeckis	105.50
1950–59			**1990–98**		
The Ten Commandments (1956)	C.B. DeMille	$43.0	Titanic (1997)	J. Cameron	$600.8
Lady and the Tramp (1955)	(Animated)	40.2	Jurassic Park (1993)	S. Spielberg	357.1
Ben-Hur (1959)	W. Wyler	36.7	Forrest Gump (1994)	R. Zemeckis	329.7
Around the World in 80 Days (1956)	M. Anderson	23.1	The Lion King (1993)	R. Allers/R. Minkoff	312.9
Sleeping Beauty (1959)	(Animated)	21.5	Star Wars, The Phantom Menace (1999)[2]	G. Lucas	309.2
			Independence Day (1996)	R. Emmerich	306.2
1960–69			Home Alone (1990)	C. Columbus	285.0
The Sound of Music (1965)	R. Wise	$79.98	Men in Black (1997)	B. Sonnenfeld	250.7
Doctor Zhivago (1965)	D. Lean	60.96	Twister (1996)	J. DeBont	241.7
Butch Cassidy and the Sundance Kid (1969)	G.R. Hill	45.95	The Lost World (1997)	S. Spielberg	229.1
Mary Poppins (1964)	R. Stevenson	45.00			
The Graduate (1968)	M. Nichols	44.09			

Note: Films from the 1990s are ranked according to their gross box office receipts. Films for previous decades are ranked according to film rentals, the portion of a film's box-office receipts paid by theater owners to the film's distribution company for renting the film. Figures include the U.S. and Canada. 1. All films listed for this decade were made by Disney studios and have been rereleased on a regular basis ever since. Their dominance on this chart is partly due to the fact that they are continually generating revenue. 2. Still in active release when table was calculated, June 17, 1998. **Sources:** *Variety,* Exhibitor Relations Co., Inc.

20 Top-Grossing Feature Films, 1998

Rank, Film	Distributor	Director	Gross (millions)
1. *Saving Private Ryan*	Dreamworks	Steven Spielberg	$216.12
2. *Armageddon*	Buena Vista	Michael Bay	201.58
3. *There's Something About Mary*	Fox	Bobby and Peter Farrelly	176.47
4. *A Bug's Life*	Buena Vista	John Lasseter, Andrew Stanton	162.79
5. *The Waterboy*	Buena Vista	Frank Coraci	161.49
6. *Doctor Dolittle*	Fox	Betty Thomas	144.16
7. *Rush Hour*	New Line	Brett Ratner	141.15
8. *Deep Impact*	Paramount	Mimi Leder	140.46
9. *Godzilla*	Sony/Tri-Star	Roland Emmerich	136.31
10. *Patch Adams*	Universal	Tom Shadyac	135.01
11. *Lethal Weapon 4*	Warner Bros.	Richard Donner	129.73
12. *The Truman Show*	Paramount	Peter Weir	125.62
13. *Mulan*	Buena Vista	Tony Bancroft, Barry Cook	120.62
14. *You've Got Mail*	Warner Bros.	Nora Ephron	115.73
15. *Enemy of the State*	Buena Vista	Tony Scott	111.54
16. *The Prince of Egypt*	Dreamworks	Brenda Chapman, Steve Hickner	101.22
17. *The Rugrats Movie*	Paramount	Igor Kovalyov, Norton Virgien	100.49
18. *Shakespeare in Love*	Miramax	John Madden	97.70[1]
19. *The Mask of Zorro*	Sony	Martin Campbell	93.77
20. *Stepmom*	Sony	Chris Columbus	91.03

Note: Domestic grosses as of June 20, 1999. 1.Still in active release as of June 20, 1999. **Source:** Exhibitor Relations Co., Inc.

Top-Grossing Movies of All-Time

Because of inflation and periodic re-releases, it is nearly impossible to compare the successes of films from different eras. What is simpler to compare is the number of people who went to see a film, regardless of when it was released, and regardless of how much they paid for their ticket. To arrive at this number, the Exhibitor Relations Co. divided domestic gross receipts by the average ticket prices for the year(s) in which the film was released. The estimated number of admissions is then multiplied by the average ticket price in 1998 ($4.69) to give an idea of what each film's domestic gross would be if it were released today. It is admittedly an imperfect measure, but it makes it quite clear that despite its $600 million gross, *Titanic* will have to be re-released several times to match the success of *Gone With the Wind*, which has made only $173 million over the years, but has been seen by 70 million more people.

Rank, Film, (Year of Release)	Estimated admissions	Inflation-adjusted domestic gross (millions)
1. *Gone With the Wind* (1939)	200,605,313[1]	$940.8
2. *Star Wars* (1977)	178,119,595[1]	835.4
3. *The Sound of Music* (1965)	142,415,376[1]	667.9
4. *E.T. The Extra-Terrestrial* (1982)	135,987,938[1]	637.8
5. *The Ten Commandments* (1956)	131,000,000	614.4
6. *Titanic* (1997)	130,860,448	613.7
7. *Jaws* (1975)	128,078,818[1]	600.7
8. *Snow White and the Seven Dwarfs* (1937)	109,000,000[1]	511.2
9. *101 Dalmatians* (1961)	105,207,663[1]	493.4
10. *The Empire Strikes Back* (1980)	98,106,044[1]	460.1
11. *Ben-Hur* (1959)	98,000,000[1]	459.6
12. *The Exorcist* (1973)	94,285,714	442.2
13. *Return of the Jedi* (1983)	94,026,245[1]	441.0
14. *The Sting* (1973)	91,209,330	427.8
15. *Raiders of the Lost Ark* (1981)	87,185,055[1]	408.9
16. *Jurassic Park* (1993)	86,193,170	404.2
17. *Fantasia* (1940)	83,043,478[1]	389.5
18. *The Godfather* (1972)	79,353,089	372.2
19. *Forrest Gump* (1994)	78,873,439	369.9
20. *Mary Poppins* (1964)	78,181,818	366.7

Note: As of June 18, 1999. 1. Includes re-issues. Grosses for all films prior to 1980 are estimated from the film rental, which is approximately 50 percent of the gross. **Source:** Exhibitor Relations Co., Inc.

Religion in America

▶RELIGIOUS AFFILIATION

As of 1998, approximately 169 million Americans claimed affiliation with a religious group. The vast majority of these, 159 million, claimed membership in a Christian church. The rest were Jews (5.8 million), Muslims (3 million), Buddhist, or members of other religions.

Because the U.S. Census Bureau does not ask questions about religious affiliation, all of these numbers can be regarded as educated approximations at best. Each year, the *Yearbook of American and Canadian Churches* asks more than 200 Christian religious bodies "How many members does your organization have?" The answers to these questions, which necessarily vary from denomination to denomination, are reflected in the accompanying table, which arranges Christian churches by their size and family. Denominations listed in the same family nearly always share common historical roots and some principal doctrines, but they should not be assumed to be similar in belief or practice. Denominations with 80,000 or more members are shown separately within their families

The following are brief descriptions of each of the Christian denominational families and of major non-Christian faiths in the U.S. For information about religion internationally, see Part III: "World Religions."

▶CHRISTIANITY
Roman Catholic Church

The Roman Catholic Church is the largest single Christian denomination in the United States. It claims nearly 37 percent of all religiously affiliated people—23 percent of the total population. Worldwide, there are nearly 900 million Roman Catholics (see "World Religions").

Many U.S. Catholics—descendants of immigrants from Ireland, Germany, Poland, Italy, and France—are concentrated in the Northeast and the industrial Midwest. Hispanic-Americans in Florida and the Southwest are also predominantly Catholic.

The church is hierarchically organized. Bishops, who administer church affairs in a given region, are appointed by higher authority. The world leader of the Roman church is the pope, who directs the church from Vatican City in Rome.

Priests are male and in most parts of the church must be and remain unmarried. Orders of nuns and monks provide many educational and charitable services. Many local churches operate parochial elementary schools. Regional bodies and religious orders operate high schools and help administer many seminaries and church-related colleges. In recent years the number of applicants for the priesthood and for religious orders has sharply decreased, even as membership in the church has continued to increase.

Catholic leaders have taken strong stands on many contemporary issues. The National Conference of Catholic Bishops has taken relatively liberal positions on efforts to bring about world peace and economic justice. In areas of personal conduct, the church is more conservative. It leads the campaign to outlaw abortion and opposes artificial means of birth control.

Baptist Churches

The Baptist family of churches is the largest Protestant family in the United States. Baptists trace their theological roots back to radical reformers in Europe in the 1500s, but the number of Baptists in the world was tiny until the 1800s, when Baptist faith and practice became predominant in the American South (both for whites and for blacks). Baptists are still most heavily represented in the southern and border states.

Local Baptist congregations have great independence, determining many of their own policies. At the same time, these churches share many practices. They agree that the rite of baptism should be administered only to those who have reached an age of independent judgment. Consequently, children are baptized no earlier than the age of six or seven, often by total immersion in the baptismal water. A Baptist child is not counted as a member until after baptism, which means that small children are not included in the membership totals reported above.

Most Baptists take a strong stand on the authority of the Bible, and many (though not all) believe that it should be interpreted literally. Baptists have traditionally been strong supporters of separation of church and state. Many Baptist denominations have mounted energetic missionary campaigns to bring the Christian message to people around the world.

The Southern Baptist Convention, a predominantly white church, is the largest Protestant denomination in the United States. The National Baptist Convention U.S.A. and the Progressive National Baptist Convention are predominantly black churches. Together they account for the religious affiliation of more blacks than any other family of churches.

Methodist Churches

Methodist churches trace their origins to John Wesley (1703-91), a minister in the Church of England who sought to bring a new sense of warmth and commitment to individuals' religious life. He urged his followers to set aside regular times to study the Bible and pray together. Wesley's opponents laughingly called his followers Methodists because of their discipline and seriousness. Wesley himself remained in the Church of England his whole life, but his followers began to develop independent organizations, both in England and the United States.

On the American frontier, Methodist "circuit riders" traveled from settlement to settlement, preaching and marrying, baptizing and burying members of pioneer families. Methodism grew with astonishing swiftness. By 1820 it was the largest religious family in the United States, and it remained the largest Protestant family until the 1920s.

The United Methodist Church accounts for more than two-thirds of the Methodist family's total membership. This denomination is made up of not only traditional Methodists but also several churches of German origin whose beliefs and spirit accorded well with Methodism. The two "African" churches and the Christian Methodist Church are predominantly black churches, and they account for nearly all of the remaining third of the Methodist group.

Lutheran Churches

Lutherans trace their churches back to the German reformer Martin Luther (1483-1546). Luther sought to reform the doctrine and practice of the Roman Christian Church in Europe. He complained about corruption among the clergy and advocated worship in the language of the people rather than in Latin. He also came to favor a married, rather than a celibate, clergy. The Church of Rome considered Luther disloyal and eventually drove him out. He then helped establish independent churches in northern Germany.

Immigrants from Germany and Scandinavia brought the Lutheran faith to North America, concentrating first in Pennsylvania. Later immigrants settled in the upper Midwest. By 1900 scores of small Lutheran church bodies were divided from one another by language, theology, and degree of assimilation into American society. The Evangelical Lutheran Church in America represents a uniting of many of those earlier churches. The Lutheran Church-Missouri Synod, a national church despite its name, is more conservative theologically.

Pentecostal Churches

The Pentecostal churches share a belief that God grants believers special spiritual gifts—especially the experience called "speaking in tongues," a common feature of Pentecostal services.

Pentecostal churches trace their origin to the day of Pentecost, described in the biblical book of Acts, when early Christians received ecstatic or mystical powers. Modern Pentecostalism began in the early 1900s, when members of some Holiness churches received the gift of tongues (see "Holiness Churches").

Pentecostal congregations tend to be small. They may meet in storefronts or in rented quarters on upper floors. Yet the Pentecostal faith, with its immediacy and emotional power, is perhaps the fastest-growing in the nation, attracting thousands of new adherents each year. In addition, Pentecostal beliefs have had an impact on Roman Catholic, Lutheran, Episcopal, and other denominations. These denominations report a growth among adherents of "charismatic renewal," a movement based on spiritual gifts.

The two Churches of God in Christ and the United Pentecostal Church are predominantly black denominations. The Assemblies of God is the largest predominantly white denomination. Many Pentecostal organizations are regional or purely local. Because of this loose organization, there are likely to be thousands of Pentecostal believers not counted here because their local congregations are not affiliated with a regional or national group.

Reformed Churches

The Reformed churches are those that trace their descent to the French-Swiss reformer John Calvin (1509-64). These churches were especially significant in the early settlement of the present-day United States. The Pilgrims and Puritans who settled in New England established the Congregational church, which is a main component of today's United Church of Christ. New York was settled by the Dutch, who established the present-day Reformed Church in America. Later, immigrants of Scottish and Scotch-Irish descent established a strong Presbyterian church. Presbyterians differed from Congregationalists in matters of church governance but shared many points of theology and practice.

Reformed church buildings are generally simple and sparsely adorned. Similarly, worship in these churches is austere and simple. Reformed churches generally value a well-educated clergy. In the past they helped found Harvard, Yale, and Princeton. Direct ties to these universities have ended, but Reformed organizations still support many colleges.

The Presbyterian Church (USA) is the result of several mergers between smaller Presbyterian churches that had been separated by regional and doctrinal differences. The United Church of Christ includes, in addition to Congregational churches, descendants of German Reformed churches and of the Evangelical and Reformed Church (also of German descent). The Reformed Church in America and the Christian Reformed Church are both of Dutch descent.

Orthodox Churches

The first great schism in the Christian church occurred in A.D. 1054 between the Western church, centered at Rome, and the Eastern church, centered at Constantinople (present-day Istanbul). In 1054 Eastern Christianity was predominant in Greece and the Middle East, and missionaries had already introduced the faith in Russia. The Russian church celebrated its 1,000th anniversary in 1988. Immigrants from these countries brought Orthodox churches to the United States.

The two largest Orthodox churches in the U.S. today are Greek and Russian, respectively. The next largest represent Armenians and Syrians. Together these four churches have more than 80 percent of the Orthodox membership.

Orthodox churches are organized hierarchically. Archbishops and bishops possess special spiritual authority and administer church affairs. Religious observances tend to be solemn and elaborate. Ancient liturgies in the ancient languages have been carefully preserved. Orthodox clergy are male, and in most churches they are allowed to marry. Because of differences in calculating feast days, Easter and other movable feasts may occur on different dates in the Orthodox Church than in the Western churches.

In the U.S., many Orthodox churches have served as cultural centers for immigrants seeking to preserve their own ethnic heritage. At the same time, however, many denominations are active members of ecumenical groups such as the National Council of Churches.

Latter-day Saints (Mormons)

The Church of Jesus Christ of Latter-day Saints, known popularly as the Mormon church, was "established anew," according to Mormon doctrine, on Apr. 6, 1830, by a 19th-century American prophet named Joseph Smith (1805-44). Smith, who grew up in western New York State, reported direct revelations from God. The Book of Mormon, which Smith said he translated, tells of a visit by the resurrected Jesus Christ to pre-Columbian America.

Smith assembled a community of believers that settled first in western New York and later in Ohio, Missouri, and Illinois. Wherever they went, the Mormons aroused the antagonism of neighboring non-Mormons, in part because Mormons allowed men to take more than one wife. Persecution peaked with the murder of Smith himself in 1844.

The next great leader of the church was Brigham Young (1801-77), who led the majority of Mormons westward to settle in the then-uninhabited basin by the Great Salt Lake. There the church grew and prospered. To this day, the majority of religiously affiliated people in Utah are Mormons. There are also many adherents in surrounding states, especially western Colorado and Idaho.

Most of the church's ten million-plus members live in the United States, but the Mormons' legendary missionary work goes on around the globe. Since about 1900, the church has encouraged converts to stay in their own countries and organize congregations there.

The Reorganized Church is the largest of the groups that did not make the trek to the Great Salt Lake. Its headquarters are in Independence, Missouri, which Smith had designated as the site of a great future temple. Members of the Reorganized Church do not consider themselves Mormons.

Christian Churches and Churches of Christ

This family of churches traces its origins to a great religious awakening in 1800 on the Pennsylvania and Kentucky frontiers. Discouraged by sectarian competition among Methodists, Presbyterians, and others, leaders of the revival did not seek to form a denomination but to reestablish a single nondenominational Christian church. In time they became a denomination themselves.

In the 1870s the Churches of Christ and the Christian Church (Disciples) split over questions of using musical instruments in worship and over the issue of centralizing some church functions. The Churches of Christ opposed both instrumental music and national organization. The Disciples allowed instrumental music and established a central missionary board to coordinate mission work. They are ecumenically minded and have a long history of cooperation and discussion with other denominations.

The third group, the Christian churches and Churches of Christ, split from the Disciples in the 1920s and 1930s. They do allow instrumental music but are theologically more conservative than the Disciples.

Episcopal Family of Churches

The Episcopal churches are descendants of the Church of England, which was established as a separate church by King Henry VIII in 1534. Churches descending from the English church make up the worldwide Anglican Communion. The American church takes its name from the word *bishop*, which suggests its hierarchical organization.

In colonial times the Church of England was established in the southern colonies and had some influence in the middle colonies, but it was not welcome in New England, where Reformed churches were predominant. During the American Revolution, most Church of England members and clergy remained loyal to England. Thousands migrated to Canada. Those who remained were under suspicion, and some were persecuted. The church almost ceased to function.

After the Revolution, a small group of Anglicans loyal to the United States gradually revived the church. It never grew as rapidly as the Methodist and Baptist families, but it did gain considerable influence. Especially in eastern cities, many families of wealth and power were Episcopalian.

The Episcopal Church accommodates a wide spectrum of belief and practice. It is usually considered Protestant and shares much with other Protestant denominations, yet its worship services retain much of pre-Reformation Catholic tradition. One wing of the church retains a strong emphasis on the church's Catholic heritage.

Holiness Churches

The Holiness churches grew from a religious revival in the late 1800s, primarily in Methodist congregations. The originators of the movement objected to the excessive bureaucracy of established denominations and sought to refocus attention on the need for deep personal change. They placed great emphasis on the teachings of Methodism's founder, John Wesley, that those who

are saved may aspire to the gift of complete sanctification, or holiness.

Around 1900, groups of especially intense Holiness worshipers began experiencing further "gifts of the Spirit." From these experiences grew the first Pentecostal churches with their emphasis on speaking in tongues. Many who began as adherents of Holiness churches became Pentecostalists. The Holiness churches rejected what they considered the extremism of Pentecostal worship.

Jehovah's Witnesses

Jehovah's Witnesses are a remarkably active and dynamic sect, visible to most from street-corner or door-to-door encounters. They were founded by Charles Taze Russell (1852-1916) in western Pennsylvania in the 1870s. The Witnesses preach a slightly unorthodox form of the Christian message and look intently for the end of the present world. They claim three million members worldwide, of whom about a quarter live in the United States.

Church of Christ, Scientist

Christian Scientists, as adherents are often known, follow the teaching of Mary Baker Eddy (1821-1910), who founded the church in 1879 in Boston and wrote *Science and Health with a Key to the Scriptures*, which remains a major sourcebook for the church. Christian Science asserts that sickness and other adversities exist only in the mind and that disciplined spiritual thinking can correct them. Thus, Christian Scientists refuse most or all medical treatment. Christian Science practitioners help adherents deal with illness but do not serve as clergy. The church operates many reading rooms open to the public.

The Adventist Family of Churches

Adventist churches sprang up in the U.S. in the 1840s with a wave of concern about prophecies of the end of the world. Adventists anticipate and prepare for the world's end and the second coming of Jesus Christ. The largest Adventist group, the Seventh-day Adventists, is one of the most dynamic religious groups in the world today, claiming a worldwide membership of five million and a growth rate of more than 7 percent annually. As their name suggests, they worship on Saturday rather than Sunday. They operate parochial schools, colleges, medical schools, and hospitals.

The Salvation Army

The Salvation Army is familiar to outsiders through its work among the homeless and the poor and its fund-raising on the streets, especially before Christmas. The church, which originated in England in 1865, is organized in quasi-military style, and many of its members devote their lives to its service.

Roman Rite Churches

The Roman Rite churches are those that have split from the Roman Catholic Church in recent times but have maintained many of its rituals and doctrines. The Polish church was established in Scranton, Pennsylvania, in the 1890s by church leaders of Polish descent. The Old Catholic churches had their origin in Europe after 1870.

Mennonite Churches

Mennonites trace their roots to a small group of Christians after 1530 who sought a reformation even more radical than those advocated by Lutherans and Calvinists. They were called Mennonites after Menno Simons (1469-1561), one of their early leaders. Their most distinctive practice is adult baptism, offered only to those who have made a decision to follow Christ's teachings.

Because they would not swear oaths and would not bear arms in the service of their temporal leaders, Mennonites were severely persecuted. Small bands were scattered to many corners of the world. Some settled in Pennsylvania beginning in the late 1600s. In the 1870s other groups arrived from Russia. Today more that 40 percent of the world's Mennonites live in the U.S.. The next-largest group (estimated to be 150,000) lives in the nations of the former Soviet Union. In recent times Mennonites have become well known for their world relief work.

The Amish are groups with Mennonite beliefs who seek to remain quite aloof from the surrounding culture. The Old Order Amish, centered in Pennsylvania, wear "plain" clothing and still drive horses and buggies rather than automobiles.

Churches of the Brethren

The Brethren, founded as a dissenting group in Germany in the early 1700s, immigrated to Pennsylvania in the 1720s to escape persecution. There they have remained. Brethren share many doctrinal points with their neighbors, the Mennonites. They practice adult baptism, refuse to swear oaths, and will not serve as combatants in war. The various Brethren denominations agree in basic theology but differ on less significant matters of interpretation.

Unitarian Universalist Association

Unitarianism was an outgrowth of New England Congregationalism in the late 1700s and early 1800s. Unitarians asserted God's unity and repudiated the doctrine of the Trinity. They also interpreted other Christian beliefs in a liberal, figurative manner. Universalism was a separate movement emphasizing the availability of God's care to all people, not only to a small chosen group. In 1961 Unitarian and Universalist organizations merged.

Friends (Quaker) Churches

Known popularly as Quakers, the Friends were established by the English religious mystic George Fox (1624-91) in the mid-1600s. They were persecuted in England for refusing to take oaths or to serve as combatants in war. Under the protection of William Penn (1644-1718), many settled in Pennsylvania. According to Fox, they were called Quakers because they were admonished to "tremble at the word of the Lord." In Pennsylvania the Quakers set themselves apart, dressing plainly and avoiding worldly amusements. In Philadelphia they became influential business people.

The most distinctive doctrine of the Friends is that of the Inner Light, the spark of God in each individual. Friends have avoided setting up formal church structures, and many groups have no clergy. Friends have organized remarkable world relief and peace organizations, by which they are perhaps best known to outsiders.

Other Christian Churches

Among the other denominations reported by the *Yearbook of American and Canadian Churches*, there is a wide variety of religious belief and practice. Many of the groups are radically congregational, making generalizations risky. Other groups are heterodox offshoots from the Pentecostal family. In many cases they depend on a single strong leader. The smallest denominations listed may actually be a single local congregation that reports as a separate church body.

Among the miscellaneous groups are spiritualist and other "New Age" groups. Some of these mix spiritualism with Christianity; others may not consider themselves Christian in any sense.

▶OTHER RELIGIONS

Judaism

Judaism is the largest non-Christian religious family in the United States. Jewish organizations report that there are 5.8 million American Jews. Of these, perhaps 3.8 million are religiously affiliated or observant. The remaining two million consider their Judaism to be more ethnic or cultural than religious.

As descendants of the Jews of biblical times, Jews worship one God and follow the religious precepts in the Hebrew scriptures, the writings called the Old Testament by Christians. Jews recognize Jesus as a religious teacher but do not acknowledge him as the Messiah or Son of God. Jews still await the coming of the Messiah as foretold by the prophets.

A handful of Jews arrived in North America in the 1600s. In the 1800s, Jews from Germany arrived with other immigrants. Then between 1890 and 1920, several million Jews arrived from eastern Europe, fleeing persecution and hard times in Russia and Poland. In the 1930s and 1940s, Jews reached America as refugees from the Nazi extermination campaigns. The slaughter of some six million Jews by the Germans, called the Holocaust, is one of two central facts of modern Jewish experience. The second is the establishment of Israel as an independent state in 1948. Today more Jews live in Israel than in any other country except the U.S.

There are three main branches of religious Judaism in the U.S. today: Orthodox, Reform, and Conservative.

Orthodox Judaism is by far the most rigorous and by far the smallest of the three branches, with an estimated 400,000 adherents. Orthodox Jews may keep entirely separate kitchens for milk and meat, refuse to operate electric and mechanical devices on the Sabbath, and often attend temple services or hold prayer sessions every day. Orthodox services are conducted in Hebrew, and require men and women to pray separately, even when not in temple. Many orthodox communities, especially self-contained communities such as the Hasidic Jews (located mainly in New York), impose strict dress codes, dictating not only the clothes, but also the hairstyles of their members.

Reform Judaism is the least strict branch. It flowered in the U.S. in the late 1800s, especially among immigrants from Germany. Reform Jews do not generally wear yarmulkes, don't usually observe the kosher dietary laws, and conduct their religious services primarily in English (though most of the prayers are recited in Hebrew). About 1.4 million Jews are affiliated with Reform temples.

Conservative Judaism rose in response to the Reform movement. It sought to preserve more of the ancient observances of the old orthodoxy, but without losing touch with American culture and behavior. As a middle road between Reform and Orthodox Judaism, Conservative Judaism has gained many adherents. About two million Jews are affiliated with Conservative institutions.

Islam

The Islamic faith, whose followers are called Muslims, is the third of the great theistic world religions, along with Judaism and Christianity. The first sizable group of Muslims arrived in the U.S. from Lebanon in the early 1900s. Later waves of immigration have brought Pakistanis, Indians, Arabs, and Iranians, among others.

There are about 600 Islamic centers in the U.S., many of which include a mosque for worship. An estimated 3,000,000 Muslims are in the U.S., most in cities in the Northeast and industrial Midwest. Observances may vary from one center to another, depending on the nationality of its adherents and their length of residence in the United States. In general, recent immigrants are more conservative and follow Islamic ritual and custom more closely.

Buddhist Churches of America

The Buddhist Churches of America is the oldest and largest U.S. Buddhist group. It represents the Judo Shinshu sect of Buddhism, and many of its members are of Japanese descent. There are many other Buddhist organizations in the U.S., and there may be as many as 500,000 additional Americans who subscribe to Buddhist tenets. (See also "World Religions.")

Christian Churches in the United States by Size and Family

Family/Denomination	Local congregations	Total clergy	Total membership
TOTAL CHRISTIAN CHURCHES	**344,754**	**476,825**	**159,118,442**
Roman Catholic Church	**22,728**	**49,071**	**61,207,914**
Baptist Churches	**96,284**	**120,662**	**36,412,484**
Southern Baptist Convention	40,565	71,257	15,691,964
National Baptist Convention, USA Inc.	33,000	32,832	8,200,000
National Baptist Convention of America	2,500	N.A.	3,500,000
Progressive National Baptist Convention Inc.	2,000	N.A.	2,500,000
National Missionary Baptist Convention of America	N.A.	N.A.	2,500,000
American Baptist Churches in the USA	5,807	7,929	1,503,267
Baptist Bible Fellowship International	3,600	N.A.	1,500,000
Baptist Missionary Association of America	1,349	2,598	232,069
National Association of Free Will Baptists	2,491	2,900	210,305
Conservative Baptist Association of America	1,084	N.A.	200,000
Baptist General Conference	875	N.A.	136,120
General Association of Regular Baptist Churches	1,440	N.A.	115,950
Other (5 denominations)	1,573	3,146	122,809
Methodist Churches	**52,891**	**58,447**	**14,185,952**
United Methodist Church	36,361	38,455	8,495,378
African Methodist Episcopal Church	8,000	N.A.	3,500,000
African Methodist Episcopal Zion Church	3,098	2,767	1,252,369
Christian Methodist Episcopal Church	2,340	N.A.	718,922
Wesleyan Church	1,580	2,639	118,021
Other (6 denominations)	1,512	493	101,262
Pentecostal Churches	**43,945**	**90,614**	**10,659,966**
Church of God in Christ	15,300	33,593	5,499,875
Assemblies of God	11,884	32,314	2,467,855
Pentecostal Assemblies of the World	1,760	4,262	1,000,000
Church of God (Cleveland, Tenn.)	6,060	5,556	753,230
International Church of the Foursquare Gospel	1,773	2,869	229,643
Full Gospel Fellowship of Churches and Ministers Intl.	650	N.A.	195,000
International Pentecostal Holiness Church	1,658	1,909	164,132
Pentecostal Church of God	1230	1,818	111,900
Other (14 denominations)	3,630	8,293	238,331
Lutheran Churches	**19,077**	**28,193**	**8,319,348**
Evangelical Lutheran Church in America	10,936	17,402	5,180,910
Lutheran Church-Missouri Synod	6,099	8,215	2,601,144
Wisconsin Evangelical Lutheran Synod	1,235	1,604	412,942
Other (9 denominations)	807	972	124,352
Latter-day Saints Churches	**12,223**	**16,933**	**4,980,486**
Church of Jesus Christ of Latter-day Saints	11,000	N.A.	4,800,000
Reorganized Church of Jesus Christ of Latter-day Saints	1,160	16,671	177,779
Church of Jesus Christ (Bickertonites)	63	262	2,707
Orthodox (Eastern) Churches	**1,571**	**1,437**	**4,959,116**
Orthodox Church in America	600	792	2,000,000
Greek Orthodox Archdiocese of North & South America	532	N.A.	1,950,000
Diocese of the Armenian Church of America	72	70	414,000
Coptic Orthodox Church	85	68	180,000
Armenian Apostolic Church of America	28	58	180,000
Other (8 denominations)	254	449	235,116
Churches of Christ	**23,419**	**20,100**	**4,231,913**
Churches of Christ	14,000	13,000	2,250,000
Christian Churches and Churches of Christ	5,579	N.A.	1,071,616
Christian Church (Disciples of Christ)	3,840	7,100	910,297
Presbyterian Churches	**14,213**	**25,468**	**4,133,166**
Presbyterian Church (USA)	11,328	20,783	3,637,375
Presbyterian Church in America	1,299	2,476	267,764
Cumberland Presbyterian Church	774	826	88,066
Other (14 denominations)	812	1,383	139,961
Episcopal Church	**7,415**	**15,073**	**2,536,550**
Reformed Churches	**7,866**	**13,467**	**1,983,359**
United Church of Christ	6,110	10,311	1,452,565
Reformed Church in America	909	1,865	304,113
Christian Reformed Church in North America	737	1,175	201,795
Other (4 denominations)	110	116	24,886

Family/Denomination	Local congregations	Total clergy	Total membership
Jehovah's Witnesses	**10,671**	**n.a.**	**975,829**
Adventist Churches	**4,780**	**5,762**	**841,122**
Seventh-Day Adventists	4,363	5,184	809,159
Other (3 denominations)	417	578	31,963
Church of the Nazarene	**5,135**	**9,741**	**608,008**
Salvation Army	**1,264**	**5,242**	**453,150**
Mennonite Churches	**3,303**	**8,293**	**366,392**
Mennonite Church	1,004	2,817	90,959
General Conference of Mennonite Brethren Churches	368	n.a.	82,130
Old Order Amish Church	898	3,617	80,820
Other (8 denominations)	1,033	2,985	112,483
Christian and Missionary Alliance	**1,850**	**2,832**	**311,612**
Churches of God	**2,992**	**5,364**	**275,533**
Church of God (Anderson, Ind.)	2,327	4,630	229,240
Other (3 denominations)	665	734	46,293
International Council of Community Churches	**517**	**501**	**250,000**
Evangelical Free Church of America	**1,224**	**2,436**	**242,619**
Brethren Churches	**1,802**	**3,234**	**218,476**
Church of the Brethren	1,106	1,946	141,811
Other (7 denominations	696	1,378	76,665
Friends (Quaker) Churches	**2,472**	**192**	**189,466**
Religious Society of Friends (Conservative)	1,200	n.a.	104,000
Other (3 denominations)	1,272	192	85,466
Christian Congregation	**1,437**	**1,435**	**114,685**
Christian Brethren	**1,150**	**500**	**100,000**
Evangelical Covenant Church	**615**	**1,110**	**93,136**
Moravian Churches (2 denominations)	**150**	**268**	**48,831**
Church of Christ, Scientist	**N.A.**	**N.A.**	**N.A.**
Other Christian Churches (21 denominations)	**3,580**	**4,543**	**419,329**

Source: *1998 Yearbook of American and Canadian Churches.* ©National Council of the Churches of Christ in the U.S.A. Editor Eileen W. Lindner. www.ncccusa.org. Reprinted by permission.

Christian Denominations in the U.S., 1998

The 31 largest churches in the United states (as ranked by membership) comprise more than 95 percent of all Christian church membership. However, because not all churches report membership figures to the Yearbook of American and Canadian Churches every year, these figures must be considered an approximation at best.

Denomination	Membership, 1998	Percent of total
Roman Catholic Church	61,207,914	38.38%
Southern Baptist Convention	15,691,964	9.84
The United Methodist Church	8,495,378	5.33
National Baptist Convention, USA, Inc.	8,200,000	5.14
Church of God in Christ	5,499,875	3.45
Evangelical Lutheran Church in America	5,180,910	3.25
Church of Jesus Christ of Latter-day Saints	4,800,000	3.01
Presbyterian Church (U.S.A.)	3,637,375	2.28
African Methodist Episcopal Church	3,500,000	2.19
National Baptist Convention of America, Inc.	3,500,000	2.19
The Lutheran Church—Missouri Synod	2,601,144	1.63
Episcopal Church	2,536,550	1.59
National Missionary Baptist Convention of America	2,500,000	1.57
Progressive National Baptist Convention, Inc.	2,500,000	1.57
Assemblies of God	2,467,588	1.55
Churches of Christ	2,250,000	1.41
Orthodox Church in America	2,000,000	1.25
Greek Orthodox Archdiocese of North and South America	1,950,000	1.22
American Baptist Churches in the U.S.A.	1,503,267	0.94
Baptist Bible Fellowship International	1,500,000	0.94
United Church of Christ	1,452,565	0.91
African Methodist Episcopal Zion Church	1,252,369	0.79
Christian Churches and Churches of Christ	1,071,616	0.67
Pentecostal Assemblies of the World	1,000,000	0.63
Jehovah's Witnesses	975,829	0.61
Christian Church (Disciples of Christ)	910,297	0.57
Seventh-day Adventists	809,159	0.51
Church of God (Cleveland, Tenn.)	753,230	0.47
Christian Methodist Episcopal Church	718,922	0.45
Church of the Nazarene	608,008	0.38
The Salvation Army	453,150	0.28

Source: *1998 Yearbook of American and Canadian Churches.* ©National Council of the Churches of Christ in the U.S.A. Editor Eileen W. Lindner. www.ncccusa.org. Reprinted by permission.

Transportation

Americans spend nearly $600 billion for transportation products and services annually. Transportation expenditures accounted for 10.7 percent of disposable personal income in 1996, the largest single expense after food, housing, and medical care. In 1996, the United States recorded 4.4 trillion passenger miles of travel and 3.7 trillion revenue ton-miles of freight traffic. More than 223 million vehicles were involved in domestic transportation, using more than 174 billion gallons of fuel, and causing 44,505 fatalities.

The government has traditionally played a leading role in the development of the nation's transportation infrastructure. Technological, economic, and demographic changes all shape the government's priorities. In the 19th and early 20th

Number of Vehicles in the U.S., 1970–96

Mode of Transport	1970	1980	1990	1995	1996[1]
Air, total	128,308	205,305	201,527	188,172	193,273
Air carrier, certificated, all services	2,690	2,818	4,727	5,567	5,961
General aviation	125,618	202,487	196,800	182,605	187,312
Highway, total[1]	111,242,295	161,490,159	193,057,376	205,427,212	210,236,393
Passenger car & motorcycle	92,067,655	127,294,783	137,959,958	132,283,966	133,599,578
Other 2-axle 4-tired vehicle	14,210,591	27,875,934	48,274,555	65,738,322	68,933,798
Truck, total	4,586,487	5,790,473	6,195,876	6,719,421	7,006,408
Intercity bus	377,562	528,789	626,987	685,503	696,909
Local transit, total[2]	61,298	75,388	92,961	115,874	119,556
Motor bus	49,700	59,411	58,714	67,107	67,874
Light rail	1,262	1,013	913	999	1,140
Heavy rail	9,286	9,641	10,419	10,157	10,201
Trolley bus	1,050	823	832	885	871
Commuter rail	—	4,500	4,415	4,565	4,665
Demand response	—	—	16,471	29,352	31,853
Other	—	—	1,197	2,809	2,952
Rail, total[3]	1,450,998	1,198,755	679,918	604,333	592,163
Class I Freight cars	1,423,921	1,168,114	658,902	583,486	570,865
Class I Locomotives	27,077	28,094	18,835	18,812	19,269
Amtrak[4]	—	2,547	2,181	2,035	2,029
Water transport, total	7,427,371	8,639,652	11,036,334	11,775,150	11,919,537
Non self-propelled vessels	19,337	31,662	31,209	31,360	32,811
Self-propelled vessels	6,455	7,126	8,236	8,281	8,293
Oceangoing ships[5]	1,579	864	636	509	495
Recreational boats	7,400,000	8,600,000	10,996,253	11,735,000	11,877,938

1. Registered vehicles. 2. Prior to 1984, excludes most rural and smaller transit systems. 3. Does not includes non-Class I freight cars or shippers' freight cars. 4. Includes passenger cars and locomotives. 5. Vessels 1,000 gross tons and over.
Source: U.S. Dept. of Transportation, *National Transportation Statistics 1998*.

Passenger Miles and Ton-Miles of Freight, By Mode of Transportation, 1970–96 (numbers in millions)

Mode of transport	1970	1980	1990	1995	1996[1]
Passenger miles, total[2]	2,220,000	2,803,000	3,689,000	4,308,000	4,412,000
Air carrier[3]	108,40	204,400	345,900	414,400	445,200
General aviation, intercity	9,100	14,700	13,000	10,500	10,600
Highway:					
Passenger car and motorcycle	1,837,000	2,014,000	2,141,000	2,298,000	2,345,000
Truck	62,200	108,500	146,200	178,200	182,800
Transit	4,600	39,900	41,100	39,800	41,300
Amtrak	6,200	4,500	6,000	5,500	5,100
Ton-miles of freight, total	2,206,000	2,989,000	3,196,000	3,648,000	3,739,000
Air carrier[4]	2,189	4,528	9,064	12,520	12,861
Intercity trucks	412,000	555,000	735,000	921,000	986,000
Class I rail	764,809	918,958	1,033,969	1,305,688	1,355,975
Water transport	596,195	921,835	833,544	807,728	764,687
Oil pipeline	431,000	588,200	584,100	601,100	619,200

1. Preliminary. 2. Includes mileage not shown separately. 3. Domestic, all services. 4. Includes revenue ton-miles, U.S. and foreign mail, and express, as reported on AIM Form 41.   Source: U.S. Dept. of Transportation, *National Transportation Statistics 1998*.

centuries, for instance, the government made enormous direct and indirect contributions to the development of the nation's railroads. Today, the government spends vastly more on highways ($20.1 billion) and aviation ($10.4 billion) than on railroad transportation ($1.0 billion). The government contributes $4.5 billion toward mass transit and $3.7 billion toward water transportation out of a total of $40 billion in transportation outlays.

World Motor Vehicle Production 1997 (numbers in thousands)

Country	Passenger cars	Commercial vehicles	Total
Argentina	366,466	79,579	446,045
Australia	320,000	29,000	349,000
Austria	97,774	10,215	107,989
Belgium	355,779	73,902	429,681
Brazil	1,679,644	387,808	2,067,452
Canada	1,373,561	1,197,561	2,571,122
China	481,611	1,096,287	1,577,898
Czech Republic	321,498	47,200	368,698
France	2,258,782	322,360	2,581,142
Germany	4,678,022	344,906	5,022,928
India	409,896	336,255	746,151
Italy	1,562,865	253,645	1,816,510
Japan	8,491,440	2,483,647	10,975,087
Korea, South	2,308,476	509,799	2,818,275
Malaysia	280,000	0	280,000
Mexico	854,809	503,304	1,358,113
Netherlands	197,225	20,428	217,653
Poland	294,767	27,050	321,817
Portugal	186,010	81,153	267,163
Romania	107,711	20,530	128,241
Russia	981,887	191,890	1,173,777
Spain	2,342,248	219,829	2,562,077
Sweden	375,705	104,034	479,739
Taiwan	268,060	113,043	381,103
Turkey	242,780	101,572	344,352
Ukraine	1,085	1,401	2,486
U.K.	1,698,015	237,703	1,935,718
U.S.	5,927,281	6,191,888	12,119,169
Yugoslavia	11,124	2,379	13,503
Total	38,474,521	14,988,368	53,462,889

Source: American Automobile Manufacturers Association, *AAMA Motor Vehicle Facts & Figures 1997.*

▶ PASSENGER TRAVEL

In order to compare the costs of different modes of transportation, statisticians calculate the cost of carrying one passenger one mile. For modes of transportation that carry large numbers of passengers at once, these numbers are remarkably similar. In 1996, it cost 13.7 cents to carry a passenger one mile by plane, 12.9 cents by commuter rail, 16.6 cents by Amtrak, and 12.4 by intercity bus. By comparison, the average cost of operating a car in 1997 (including variable costs for gas and oil, maintenance and tires, and fixed costs for insurance, registration, depreciation and finance charges) was 53 cents per mile. The average fare was $110 for an airline seat, $43 for a ride on Amtrak, $23 for an intercity bus ticket, and $3.24 for a commuter rail trip. Fares are double what they were in 1980 for all modes of transportation except flying. Airfares have risen only 30 percent since 1980, a sure sign that despite all its flaws, airline deregulation has succeeded in making air travel more accessible to all Americans. The average trip was 838 miles by air (up dramatically from 791 in 1995), 257 miles on Amtrak, 143 miles by intercity bus, and 24 miles by commuter rail.

▶ TRANSPORTATION SAFETY

Because they kill large numbers of people at once, plane crashes attract much more attention than do automobile accidents. But only 1,088 people died in air crashes in 1996, and of those, only 380 died on commercial carriers. (The others died on smaller commuter or private planes). That means that more people died in boating accidents (709) than on the nation's major airlines. Meanwhile, 41,907 people died in auto accidents (94 percent of all transportation fatalities), and another 3.5 million were injured (a staggering 99 percent of all transportation injuries). Despite safety improvements to the production of automobiles, wider highway lanes, better lighting, and lower speed limits, the annual number of automobile accidents, injures, and fatalities have not changed much since 1970. But over the same period, the number of miles traveled has more than doubled (from one trillion miles in 1970 to 2.5 trillion miles in 1997), indicating that Americans are driving more miles without having any more accidents. What has changed, though, is the number of car accidents involving light trucks. Fewer than 4,000

World Motor Vehicle Production, 1950–97 (in thousands)

Year	United States	Canada	Europe	Japan	Other	World total	U.S. share of total
1950	8,006	388	1,991	32	160	10,577	75.7%
1960	7,905	398	6,837	482	866	16,488	47.9
1970	8,284	1,160	13,049	5,289	1,637	29,419	28.2
1980	8,010	1,324	15,496	11,043	2,692	38,565	20.8
1985	11,653	1,933	16,113	12,271	2,939	44,909	25.9
1990	9,783	1,928	18,866	13,487	4,496	48,554	20.1
1991	8,811	1,888	17,804	13,245	5,180	46,928	18.8
1992	9,729	1,961	17,628	12,499	6,269	48,088	20.2
1993	10,898	2,246	15,208	11,228	7,205	46,785	23.3
1994	12,263	2,321	16,195	10,554	8,167	49,500	24.8
1995	11,985	2,408	17,045	10,196	8,349	49,983	24.0
1996	11,799	2,397	17,550	10,346	9,241	51,332	23.0
1997	12,119	2,571	17,773	10,975	10,024	53,463	22.7

Source: American Automobile Manufacturers Association, *AAMA Motor Vehicle Facts & Figures 1998.*

U.S. Roads and Streets, 1904–97

Year	State control	County & local control[1]	Total	Percent paved
		Mileage ('000s)		
1904	—	—	2,351	N.A.
1921	203	2,957	3,160	N.A.
1930	324	2,935	3,259	N.A.
1940	551	2,666	3,287	N.A.
1950	609	2,623	3,313	23.5%
1960	694	2,725	3,546	34.7
1970	755	2,762	3,731	44.5
1980	848	2,764	3,860	53.7
1990	798	2,889	3,867	58.4
1991	798	2,908	3,884	58.7
1992	800	2,918	3,901	59.0
1993	800	2,924	3,905	58.3
1994	800	2,931	3,907	60.0
1995	803	2,937	3,912	60.8
1996	803	2,946	3,919	60.5
1997	697	2,971	3,945	60.9

Note: Some years contain estimates by the Federal Highway Administration. 1. Reflects State highway agency roadways prior to 1980. Includes state park, state toll, and other state agency roadways beginning in 1980. 2. After 1930, includes mileage in federal parks, forests, and reservations not part of the state and local highway system and not shown separately.
Source: U.S. Department of Transportation, *Highway Statistics Summary to 1995* and *Highway Statistics 1997*.

crashes occurred between cars and light trucks in 1987; in 1995, there were 5,426. When someone is killed in such a crash, four out of five times it's the person in the car. And the increasing weight gap between light trucks (4,000+ pounds in 1997, up from 3,500 in 1984) and cars (just over 3,000 pounds in 1995) means those odds will continue to grow even more lopsided.

Comprehensive statistics for 1997 and 1998 were not available for all modes of transportation, but the National Transportation Safety Board reported that 1998 was the first year in which not a single person was killed in an accident involving a scheduled U.S. commercial airplane anywhere in the world. There have been other years in which the major commercial airlines were accident-free, most recently 1993, but never one in which there were also no fatal propellor or commuter plane crashes. The only air travel-related death in 1998 occurred on November 4, when a Northwest Airlines baggage handler walked into the turning propellors of a commuter plane in Memphis.

▶ MOTOR VEHICLES

Although the accompanying table would suggest that the average fuel efficiency of U.S. cars is on the rise, the statistics mask the explosion in the number of light trucks, minivans, and sport-utility vehicles favored by so many American drivers of the 1990s. These vehicles get much poorer gas mileage than most cars, but because they are classified as trucks, they are not included with average fuel

U.S. Retail Sales of Passenger Cars by Size and Country of Origin, 1983–97

Category	1983	1990	1996	1997
By size				
Small	38.8%	32.8%	27.3%	26.8%
Middle	40.6	44.8	49.4	49.0
Large	10.7	9.4	9.9	9.5
Luxury	9.9	13.0	13.5	14.8
By origin				
U.S.	74.0%	74.2	85.1%	83.6%
Imports	26.0	25.8	14.9	16.4
Japan	20.9	18.5	8.5	8.8
Germany	3.0	2.9	2.8	3.6
Other Countries	2.0	4.4	3.6	4.0

Source: American Automobile Manufacturers Association, *AAMA Motor Vehicle Facts & Figures 1998.*

World Motor Vehicle Registrations, 1960–96

Year	Cars	Trucks and buses	Total vehicles	Per car	Per vehicle
	Registrations ('000s)			Population	
1960	98,317	28,637	126,955	29	23
1970	193,516	52,852	246,368	18	14
1980	320,539	90,573	411,113	14	11
1985	374,727	112,816	487,544	13	10
1990	444,900	138,082	582,982	12	9
1991	456,033	139,274	595,307	11	9
1992	469,943	143,587	613,530	11	9
1993	469,460	147,627	617,087	12	9
1994	479,533	149,545	629,077	11	9
1995	477,010	169,749	646,759	12	9
1996	485,954	185,404	671,358	12	9

Source: American Automobile Manufacturers Association, *AAMA Motor Vehicle Facts & Figures 1997.*

Traffic Deaths by Selected Country, 1994-96

Country	1994	1995	1996	Country	1994	1995	1996
	Fatalities per 100,000 registered vehicles				Fatalities per 100,000 registered vehicles		
Austria	31.6	27.7	22.9	Korea, South	136.2	121.9	132.4
Belgium	36.2	30.5	28.0	Netherlands	19.8	21.2	18.4
Brazil	44.1	N.A.	N.A.	Norway	14.0	14.8	12.4
Canada	N.A.	20.1	18.3	Poland	173.2	175.3	70.2
Denmark	N.A.	28.9	24.6	Portugal	59.0	61.1	57.1
Finland	22.3	20.2	18.1	Romania	188.5	119.0	97.9
France	28.4	27.8	26.3	Sweden	15.1	13.1	12.3
Germany	22.9	21.7	19.8	Switzerland	19.6	19.6	17.3
Hong Kong	63.0	52.0	51.9	Turkey	160.6	148.6	125.4
Italy	20.2	19.8	18.5	U.K.	13.3	13.5	13.1
Japan	16.4	16.0	14.5	U.S.	21.6	21.5	21.0

Source: American Automobile Manufacturers Association, *AAMA Motor Vehicle Facts & Figures 1998.*

U.S. Motor Vehicle Registrations by State, 1997

State	Automobiles[1]	Buses	Trucks	Total motor vehicles	Automobiles per capita
Alabama	1,905,811	8,576	1,755,052	3,669,439	0.44
Alaska	224,770	2,078	315,550	542,398	0.37
Arizona	1,852,690	4,486	1,285,967	3,143,143	0.40
Arkansas	857,314	5,814	770,702	1,633,830	0.34
California	15,705,806	44,469	9,194,701	24,944,976	0.48
Colorado	1,919,850	5,721	1,597,019	3,522,590	0.49
Connecticut	1,963,185	9,486	686,847	2,659,518	0.60
Delaware	403,797	2,045	207,859	613,701	0.54
District of Columbia	196,077	2,622	34,971	233,670	0.36
Florida	7,374,840	42,076	3,457,115	10,874,031	0.50
Georgia	3,688,005	16,499	2,537,703	6,242,207	0.49
Hawaii	442,889	3,959	245,956	692,804	0.37
Idaho	494,486	3,643	582,923	1,081,052	0.40
Illinois	5,853,560	16,817	2,572,445	8,442,822	0.49
Indiana	3,247,725	25,408	2,072,643	5,345,776	0.55
Iowa	1,636,347	8,035	1,207,001	2,851,383	0.57
Kansas	1,137,271	3,813	1,011,023	2,152,107	0.44
Kentucky	1,633,671	11,812	1,135,323	2,780,806	0.41
Louisiana	1,930,142	20,585	1,460,296	3,411,023	0.44
Maine	637,418	2,824	418,357	1,058,599	0.51
Maryland	2,628,171	11,567	1,146,316	3,786,054	0.51
Massachusetts	3,832,386	11,363	1,226,683	5,070,432	0.62
Michigan	5,110,851	24,771	2,888,109	8,023,731	0.52
Minnesota	2,317,021	13,817	1,596,411	3,927,249	0.49
Mississippi	1,262,969	10,081	960,747	2,233,797	0.46
Missouri	2,549,791	12,745	1,788,008	4,350,544	0.47
Montana	455,140	2,820	521,740	979,700	0.51
Nebraska	811,678	5,497	689,821	1,506,996	0.48
Nevada	659,079	1,748	484,829	1,145,656	0.39
New Hampshire	739,132	1,789	386,466	1,127,387	0.63
New Jersey	4,268,888	19,327	1,528,365	5,816,580	0.52
New Mexico	779,596	3,542	731,361	1,514,499	0.44
New York	8,063,496	46,192	2,763,560	10,873,248	0.44
North Carolina	3,479,993	29,861	2,275,679	5,785,533	0.46
North Dakota	336,610	2,283	356,213	695,106	0.52
Ohio	6,700,396	34,444	3,372,811	10,107,651	0.60
Oklahoma	1,528,947	15,538	1,339,234	2,883,719	0.46
Oregon	1,578,081	12,596	1,300,275	2,890,952	0.48
Pennsylvania	6,050,365	33,912	2,740,670	8,824,947	0.50
Rhode Island	515,446	1,745	192,489	709,680	0.52
South Carolina	1,765,458	15,203	1,069,700	2,850,361	0.47
South Dakota	377,737	2,699	337,967	718,403	0.51
Tennessee	2,755,950	17,400	1,761,492	4,534,842	0.51
Texas	7,085,404	77,864	5,759,985	12,923,253	0.35
Utah	850,812	1,223	677,474	1,529,509	0.41
Vermont	290,593	1,916	203,207	495,716	0.49
Virginia	3,630,241	17,477	2,061,273	5,708,991	0.53
Washington	2,690,616	8,476	2,003,060	4,702,152	0.48
West Virginia	754,685	3,306	597,001	1,354,992	0.41
Wisconsin	2,551,207	12,972	1,668,552	4,232,731	0.49
Wyoming	222,311	2,606	328,457	553,374	0.45
Total	129,748,704	697,548	77,307,408	207,753,660	0.48

Note: Includes privately owned vehicles and federal, state, and municipal vehicles; does not include vehicles owned by the military services. Farm trucks, registered at a nominal fee and restricted to use on farms, are not included. 1. Includes taxicabs.
Source: U.S. Dept. of Transportation, *Highway Statistics 1997* (1998).

efficiency standards for cars. In 1980, over 80 percent of all new vehicles were cars (9.1 million), with an average fuel efficiency of 23 miles per gallon. In comparison, there were only 2.2 million new trucks, which got 18 miles per gallon. But 1996 sales figures told a different story. The number of cars sold had dropped to 8.5 million, while the number of pickups, minivans, and sport utility vehicles had tripled, to 6.9 million. Thus nearly one of every two new vehicles (45 percent) was a gas-guzzling truck averaging 20 miles per gallon (compared with the 28 mpg attained by new cars).

The popularity of larger vehicles, which up until 1999 were allowed to produce up to three times as much pollution per mile as standard cars, has also had implications for the environment. To remedy that situation, the Clinton Administration in 1999 announced that minivans, pickup trucks, and sport utility vehicles would be subject to the same pollution standards as ordinary cars. The Administration also issued regulations requiring oil companies to reduce the amount of sulfur in gasoline sold in the U.S. by 90 percent, beginning in 2004.

U.S. Motor Vehicle Sales and Registrations, 1900–96

| Year | Factory sales | | | Motor vehicle registrations[1] |
	Passenger cars	Trucks and buses	Total	
1900	4,192	—	4,192	8,000
1910	181,000	6,000	187,000	468,500
1920	1,905,560	321,789	2,227,349	9,239,161
1930	2,787,456	575,364	3,362,820	26,749,853
1940	3,717,385	754,901	4,472,286	32,453,233
1950	6,665,863	1,337,193	8,003,056	49,161,691
1960	6,674,796	1,194,475	7,869,271	73,857,768
1970	6,546,817	1,692,440	8,239,257	108,418,197
1980	6,400,026	1,667,283	8,067,309	155,796,219
1985	8,002,259	3,464,327	11,466,586	171,653,675
1990	6,049,749	3,725,205	9,774,954	188,655,462
1991	5,407,120	3,387,503	8,794,623	188,371,935
1992	5,685,299	4,062,002	9,747,301	190,362,228
1993	5,961,754	4,895,224	10,856,978	194,063,482
1994	6,548,562	5,640,275	12,188,837	198,045,365
1995	6,309,836	5,713,469	12,023,305	201,530,021
1996	6,140,454	5,775,730	11,915,184	206,365,156

1. Data exclude military vehicles as well as farm trucks registered at a nominal fee in certain states and restricted to use in the vicinity of owners' farms; in 1995, there were 60,490 such trucks.
Source: American Automobile Manufacturers Association, *AAMA Motor Vehicle Facts & Figures 1998.*

Top-Selling Passenger Cars and Trucks in the U.S., 1996–97

CARS	Units sold, 1996	Units sold, 1997
1. Toyota Camry	359,433	397,156
2. Honda Accord	382,298	384,609
3. Ford Taurus	401,049	357,162
4. Honda Civic	286,350	315,546
5. Chevrolet Cavalier	277,222	302,161
6. Ford Escort	284,644	283,898
7. Saturn	278,574	250,810
8. Chevrolet Lumina	237,973	228,451
9. Toyota Corolla	209,048	218,461
10. Pontiac Grand Am	222,477	204,078
11. Chevrolet Malibu	N.A.	164,654
12. Ford Contour	174,187	151,060
13. Buick LeSabre	131,316	150,744
14. Nissan Altima	147,910	144,483
15. Pontiac Grand Prix	N.A.	142,018
16. Nissan Maxima	128,395	123,215
17. Nissan Sentra	129,596	122,468
18. Dodge Neon	139,831	121,854
19. Dodge Intrepid	145,502	118,537
20. Ford Mustang	122,674	116,610

LIGHT TRUCKS	Units sold, 1996	Units sold, 1997
1. Ford F-Pickups	780,838	746,111
2. Chevrolet C/K	549,167	553,729
3. Ford Explorer	402,663	383,852
4. Dodge Ram Pickup	383,960	350,257
5. Ford Ranger	288,393	298,796
6. Dodge Caravan	300,117	285,736
7. Jeep Grand Cherokee	279,195	260,875
8. Chevrolet S/10 Blazer	246,307	221,400
9. Ford Expedition	190,178	214,524
10. Ford Windstar	209,033	205,356

Source: American Automobile Manufacturers Association, *AAMA Motor Vehicle Facts & Figures 1998.*

Fuel Efficiency of U.S. Passenger Cars and Trucks, 1955–97

Since 1980, car manufacturers have been required to maintain a corporate average fuel efficiency (CAFE) established by the federal government. The CAFE standard for cars was 20 miles per gallon (mpg) in 1980, but has been 27.5 mpg since 1985. But because light trucks, minivans, and sport utility vehicles are exempted from the CAFE standards (they are subject to a much lower standard of 20.7 mpg) the overall average for all vehicles is much lower than the federally mandated standard for cars.

| | | New vehicles[1] (model year) | |
Year	Average U.S. passenger car	Passenger cars	Light trucks
1955	14.5 mpg	16.0 mpg	—
1960	14.3	15.5	—
1965	14.3	15.4	—
1970	13.5	14.1	—
1975	13.5	15.1	—
1980	15.9	22.6	16.8 mpg
1985	17.4	26.3	19.6
1990	20.2	26.9	20.3
1994	20.7	27.5	20.5
1995	21.1	27.7	20.3
1996	21.3	28.3	20.5
1997	—	27.9	20.1

Note: Calculated on the basis of 55% city and 45% highway miles sales weighted average. 1. Domestic vehicles only. Imported vehicles average 2-3 mpg better fuel efficiency in most years shown. **Source:** U.S. Dept. of Transportation, *National Transportation Statistics 1998.*

Traffic

According to the Census Bureau, almost 90 percent of Americans have access to a motor vehicle, and half of the nation's households have two or more vehicles. Approximately 88 percent of all U.S. workers drove to work in 1990: 76 percent drove alone; only 12 percent were in car pools. (Of the remaining 12 percent, only 5 percent used mass transportation, while 6 percent walked or worked at home and one percent used bicycles, motorcycles, boats, etc.

It's no wonder, then, that traffic jams are routine. In 1975, peak travel times were about an hour in the morning and evenings, and the urban Interstate System was congested 41 percent of these times. By 1993, the peak travel times had grown much longer than an hour, and the congestion rate had skyrocketed to 69 percent. In short, more people are sitting in traffic more often, regardless of when they start their commute. Nearly 70 percent of all U.S. workers began their commutes between 6 and 9 A.M.; 17 percent started for work between 7:30 and 8:00 A.M.

The average commute was 36 minutes in New York City, where more than half of commuters

Commuter and Rapid Rail Systems in the U.S., 1997

System	Passenger trips ('000s)	Passenger miles ('000s)	Stations	Route miles	Vehicles operated
Commuter Rail					
New York, Long Island RR	96,535.0	2,115,830.2	134	638.2	982
Chicago RTA-Metra	66,217.4	1,434,360.1	226	939.4	951
New York, Metro North	64,057.5	1,700,280.1	106	535.4	739
Newark, New Jersey Transit	49,513.3	1,101,596.1	163	1,192.8	726
Boston MBTA	27,813.1	517,434.8	102	575.0	308
Philadelphia SEPTA	25,464.7	356,505.9	177	419.2	282
Los Angeles, SCRRA	5,534.6	199,683.0	45	758.8	118
Indiana, NICTD	3,384.4	92,056.7	18	151.0	53
Rapid or Heavy Rail					
New York City TA	1,579,782.5	7,101,712.0	468	492.9	4,837
Washington Metro Area TA	198,003.4	1,078,247.3	75	184.9	618
Chicago RTA-CTA	151,010.4	902,389.0	141	206.3	938
Boston, MBTA	113,714.9	393,908.4	53	75.8	325
Atlanta, MARTA	90,991.0	547,885.7	36	92.2	182
Philadelphia, SEPTA	86,244.6	386,667.7	76	76.1	279
San Francisco, BART	80,489.7	967,427.6	39	190.1	480
New York, PATH	67,998.1	296,974.3	13	28.6	260
Miami/Dade Co. TA	14,019.9	108,155.9	21	42.2	86
Baltimore MTA	12,599.8	66,046.1	14	29.4	54
Los Angeles MTA-Metro	11,628.3	22,487.4	8	10.0	24
Philadelphia, PATCO	10,659.6	93,996.3	13	31.5	96
Cleveland RTA	7,694.8	56,561.1	18	38.2	30
New York, Staten Island MTA	4,617.6	33,609.0	22	28.6	36

Note: Rapid rail includes subways, elevated trains, and metros. BART = Bay Area Rapid Transit Authority; MBTA = Metropolitan Boston Transit Authority; PATH = Port Authority Trans Hudson; SCRRA = Southern California Railroad Authority; SEPTA = Southeastern Pennsylvania Transit Authority.
Source: Federal Transit Administration, *1997 National Transit Database, Transit Summaries and Trends.*

U.S. Railroads: Mileage and Accident Rates, 1997–98

Railroad	1997			1998		
	Train-miles operated	Accidents		Train-miles operated	Accidents	
		Total	Per million train miles		Total	Per million train miles
Amtrak (National Railroad Passenger Corp.)	3,7063,760	84	2.27	35,414,704	89	2.51
Burlington Northern Santa Fe	154,612,101	439	2.84	162,701,393	435	2.67
Consolidated Rail Corp. (Conrail)	45,356,069	187	4.12	46,565,355	236	5.07
CSX Transportation	83,733,024	257	3.07	83,447,524	310	3.71
Grand Trunk Western Railroad Inc.	5,657,394	25	4.42	5,376,050	21	3.91
Illinois Central Railroad Co.	9,107,722	58	6.37	9,337,411	73	7.82
Kansas City Southern Railway Co.	8,261,015	71	8.59	8,658,390	66	7.62
Norfolk Southern Corp.	64,344,218	170	2.64	68,179,879	149	2.19
Soo Line Railroad Co.	8,384,726	54	6.44	8,309,227	42	5.05
Union Pacific Railroad Co.	165,453,043	581	3.51	157,382,443	727	4.62

Source: U.S. Dept. of Transportation, Federal Railroad Administration, Office of Safety, *Accident/Incident Bulletin Calendar Year 1998.*
www.fra.dot.gov.

Amtrak Operating Statistics, 1985–98

Category	1985	1990	1995	1997	1998
Ridership					
Passengers (millions)	20.8	22.2	20.7	20.2	21.1
Passenger miles (millions)	4,582	6,057	5,545	5,166	5,304
Passenger-Train Cars					
Operating fleet (active units)	1,854	1,863	1,722	1,728	1,962
Average age (years)	14.2	20.0	21.8	19.8	21.1
Train-miles operated (millions)	30	33	32	32	33
On-time performance	81%	76%	76%	71%	74%
Short Distance (<400 miles)	82	82	81	79%	81%
Long Distance (400+ miles)	78	53	57	53%	59%
Financial					
Revenues (millions)	$ 825	$1,308	$1,497	$1,674	$2,285
Expenses (millions)	1,600	2,012	2,305	2,436	2,638

Source: *Statistical Appendix to Amtrak FY98 Annual Report.*

took public transportation to work. In Los Angeles, 65 percent of workers drove; average travel time was 26 minutes. Workers in Tulsa and Toledo both had average commutes of under 18 minutes. In both cities, more than 80 percent of people drove to work. Measured another way, drivers in Los Angeles lost a total 1.9 million hours per day in 1992 due to traffic delays, New York drivers lost 1.7 million, and Chicago drivers lost 624,000 hours.

▶ **AVIATION**

An obvious effect of the deregulation of the airline industry has been the growth of the biggest airlines and the winnowing of smaller carriers from the market. The three largest airlines (Delta, United, and American) flew almost as many passengers as all other carriers combined. A second tier of national and regional airlines (Southwest, US Airways, Northwest, Continental, TWA, America West, Alaska, and American Eagle) compete for passengers not well served by the bigger carriers. None of the rest of the top 25 airlines—primarily commuter and short hop companies—carried more than 6 million passengers in 1998.

Despite the reduction in competition, plane ticket prices have remained low throughout the 1990s. Airline prices kept pace with the Consumer Price Index from 1986-90, but since 1991, they have increased at a much slower rate. Using

Top 25 U.S. Airlines, 1998

Rank by passengers/Airline	Passengers ('000s)	Revenue passenger miles (millions)[1]	Rank by miles
1. Delta	105,213	103,245	3
2. United	86,799	124,540	1
3. American	81,431	108,873	2
4. Southwest	59,053	31,423	7
5. US Airways	57,990	41,252	6
6. Northwest	50,490	66,706	4
7. Continental	41,613	50,943	5
8. Trans World	23,893	24,422	8
9. America West	17,769	16,357	9
10. Alaska	13,029	11,266	10
11. American Eagle	10,284	2,259	17
12. Continental Express	5,683	1,564	19
13. AirTran	5,464	3,025	15
14. Aloha	5,144	N.A.	N.A.
15. Reno	5,099	2,752	16
16. Hawaiian	5,000	3,619	14
17. Horizon Air	4,389	1,144	22
18. American Trans Air	4,274	5,803	11
19. Mesaba	4,120	1,050	23
20. Atlantic Southeast	4,027	1,032	24
21. Air Wisconsin	2,757	N.A.	N.A.
22. Trans States	2,450	N.A.	N.A.
23. Continental Micronesia	2,282	4,040	12
24. Midwest Express	1,881	1,623	18
25. Midway	1,875	996	25

Note: Carriers certificated under section 401, Federal Aviation Act. 1. One paying passenger traveling 1 mile generates 1 revenue passenger mile. **Source:** Air Transport Association of America, *Air Transport 1999: The Annual Report of the U.S. Scheduled Airline Industry* (1999).

Top 25 U.S. Cargo Airlines, 1998

Rank/Airline	Freight ton-miles (millions)[1]
1. Federal Express	6,586.9
2. United Parcel Service	3,816.2
3. United	2,343.8
4. Northwest	1,698.5
5. American	1,607.0
6. Delta	1,316.5
7. Emery	963.5
8. Polar Air	911.5
9. Evergreen International	871.9
10. Continental	602.1
11. Airborne Express	578.1
12. DHL Airways	364.7
13. Challenge	222.5
14. US Airways	200.5
15. Trans World	147.9
16. Continental Micronesia	100.7
17. Amerijet	96.6
18. Southwest	67.8
19. Alaska	65.8
20. Florida West	59.9
21. Arrow	59.5
22. Hawaiian	56.5
23. America West	44.0
24. Atlas Air	36.7
25. American International	23.7

Note: Carriers certificated under Section 401, Federal Aviation Act. 1. One ton of freight traveling 1 mile generates 1 freight-ton mile. **Source:** Air Transport Association of America, *Air Transport 1999: The Annual Report of the U.S. Scheduled Airline Industry* (1999).

World's 50 Busiest Airports, 1998

Rank, Airport (code)		Rank, Airport (code)	
TOTAL PASSENGERS		**TOTAL CARGO (metric tons)**	
1. Hartsfield Atlanta Intl. (ATL)	73,474,298	1. Memphis Intl., Tennessee (MEM)	2,368,975
2. Chicago O'Hare Intl. (ORD)	72,485,228	2. Los Angeles Intl. (LAX)	1,861,050
3. Los Angeles Intl. (LAX)	61,215,712	3. Miami Intl., Florida (MIA)	1,793,009
4. Heathrow Intl., London (LHR)	60,659,593	4. Hong Kong Intl. (HKG)	1,654,356
5. Dallas/Fort Worth Intl. (DFW)	60,482,700	5. Tokyo Intl.-Narita (NRT)	1,637,521
6. Tokyo-Haneda Intl. (HND)	51,240,704	6. Kennedy Intl., New York (JFK)	1,604,422
7. Frankfurt/Main, Germany (FRA)	42,716,270	7. Frankfurt/Main, Germany (FRA)	1,464,955
8. San Francisco Intl. (SFO)	40,060,326	8. Chicago O'Hare Intl. (ORD)	1,441,829
9. Charles de Gaulle, Paris (CDG)	38,628,926	9. Kimpo Intl., Seoul (SEL)	1,425,009
10. Denver Intl., Colo. (DEN)	36,831,400	10. Standiford, Louisville, Ky. (SDF)	1,394,999
11. Schiphol, Amsterdam (AMS)	34,420,143	11. Changi, Singapore (SIN)	1,305,592
12. Miami Intl., Florida (MIA)	33,935,491	12. Heathrow Intl., London (LHR)	1,301,251
13. Newark Intl., N.J. (EWR)	32,512,106	13. Anchorage Intl., Alaska (ANC)	1,289,266
14. Sky Harbor Intl., Phoenix (PHX)	31,769,113	14. Schiphol, Amsterdam (AMS)	1,218,746
15. Detroit Metropolitan (DTW)	31,544,426	15. Newark Intl., N.J. (EWR)	1,094,383
16. Kennedy Intl., New York (JFK)	31,436,478	16. Charles de Gaulle, Paris (CDG)	1,067,255
17. Houston Intercontinental (IAH)	31,026,369	17. Chiang Kai Shek Intl., Taiwan (TPE)	916,881
18. Minneapolis-St. Paul Intl. (MSP)	30,347,920	18. Hartsfield Atlanta Intl. (ATL)	907,208
19. McCarran Intl., Las Vegas (LAS)	30,227,287	19. Dayton Intl., Ohio (DAY)	893,239
20. Kimpo Intl., Seoul (SEL)	29,429,044	20. Indianapolis Intl., (IND)	812,664
21. Gatwick Intl., London (LGW)	29,173,196	21. Dallas/Fort Worth Intl. (DFW)	801,968
22. Lambert-St. Louis Intl. (STL)	28,700,622	22. San Francisco Intl. (SFO)	771,931
23. Hong Kong Intl. (HKG)	27,919,935	23. Osaka Intl., Osaka (KIX)	766,607
24. Orlando Intl., Fla. (MCO)	27,748,571	24. Bangkok Intl. (BKK)	719,255
25. Pearson Intl., Toronto (YYZ)	26,744,530	25. Oakland Intl., Calif. (OAK)	698,771
26. Logan Intl., Boston (BOS)	26,526,708	26. Tokyo-Haneda Intl. (HND)	693,191
27. Sea-Tac Intl., Seattle (SEA)	25,863,132	27. Brussels Natl., Belgium (BRU)	596,915
28. Bangkok Intl. (BKK)	25,623,901	28. Toledo Express, Ohio (TOL)	537,188
29. Barajas, Madrid (MAD)	25,466,612	29. Sharjah Intl., United Arab Emirates (SHJ)	534,899
30. Fiumicino, Rome (FCO)	25,337,365	30. Kingsford Smith, Sydney (SYD)	524,835
31. Orly Intl., Paris (ORY)	24,951,984	31. Philadelphia Intl. (PHI)	512,256
32. Tokyo Intl.-Narita (NRT)	24,441,365	32. Shanghai Intl. (SHA)	451,757
33. Philadelphia Intl. (PHI)	24,230,374	33. Denver Intl., Colo. (DEN)	447,266
34. Changi, Singapore (SIN)	23,803,180	34. Honolulu Intl., Hawaii (HNL)	443,963
35. Charlotte/Douglas Intl. (CLT)	22,951,636	35. Dubai Intl. (DXB)	442,493
36. LaGuardia Intl. New York (LGA)	22,846,488	36. Logan Intl., Boston (BOS)	440,241
37. Honolulu Intl., Hawaii (HNL)	22,636,354	37. Sea-Tac Intl., Seattle (SEA)	428,272
38. Hebron Intl., Cincinnati (CVG)	21,179,209	38. Ontario Intl., Canada (ONT)	411,986
39. Kingsford Smith, Sydney (SYD)	21,152,001	39. Luxembourg Intl. (LUX)	382,658
40. Pittsburgh Intl. (PIT)	20,556,075	40. Johannesburg Intl., S. Africa (JNB)	377,352
41. Salt Lake City Intl. (SLC)	20,297,371	41. B. Aquino Intl., Manila (MNL)	377,222
42. Munich, Germany (MUC)	19,321,355	42. Cologne Bonn, Germany (CGN)	375,324
43. Zurich, Switzerland (ZRH)	19,276,782	43. Copenhagen Intl., Denmark (CPH)	374,141
44. Osaka Intl., Osaka (KIX)	19,161,035	44. Guarulhos Intl., Sao Paulo (GRU)	366,922
45. Mexico City Intl. (MEX)	18,946,440	45. Minneapolis-St. Paul Intl. (MSP)	365,417
46. Brussels Natl., Belgium (BRU)	18,481,897	46. Hebron Intl., Cincinnati (CVG)	364,368
47. Palma de Mallorca, Spain (PMI)	17,660,402	47. Beijing Capital Intl., China (PEK)	361,468
48. Fukuoka Intl., Japan (FUK)	17,574,001	48. Houston Intercontinental (IAH)	354,961
49. Manchester, England (MAN)	17,556,839	49. Dulles Intl., Washington D.C. (IAD)	354,482
50. Beijing Capital Intl., China (PEK)	17,318,999	50. Tullamarine Intl., Melbourne (MEL)	352,948

Source: Airports Association Council International, *Worldwide Airport Traffic Report—Calendar Year 1998* (1999).

constant dollars to account for inflation, the average plane ticket was 18 percent cheaper in 1996 than in 1986.

The airline industry posted profits of $4.9 billion in 1998, down from the record $5.2 billion in 1997, but still way up from 1996 ($2.8 billion). More than 600 million passengers flew on U.S. airlines in 1998, most of them on domestic flights. The average flight length was 1009 miles. Some 8.3 million planes took off and landed in 1998, up

slightly from the year before. The average airplane was 70.9 percent full, up from 69.3 in 1996.

With more than 70 million people passing through its security detectors each year, Chicago's O'Hare International is the busiest airport in the world. But the airport that handles the most cargo (2.2 million tons) each year is Tennessee's Memphis International, thanks to the fact that it is the primary hub for Federal Express, which logged more than 6.2 billion freight ton miles of cargo in 1998.

Top 30 Domestic Airline Routes, 1998

Rank	Cities		Passengers
1.	New York	Los Angeles	3,625,000
2.	New York	Chicago	3,069,000
3.	New York	Miami	2,834,000
4.	New York	San Francisco	2,683,000
5.	New York	Boston	2,651,000
6.	Honolulu	Kahului, Maui	2,541,000
7.	New York	Orlando	2,521,000
8.	New York	Atlanta	2,377,000
9.	New York	Washington, D.C.	2,372,000
10.	Dallas/Fort Worth	Houston	2,213,000
11.	Los Angeles	Las Vegas	2,055,000
12.	Los Angeles	San Francisco	2,020,000
13.	New York	Fort Lauderdale	1,808,000
14.	New York	San Juan, Puerto Rico	1,798,000
15.	Chicago	Los Angeles	1,680,000
16.	Honolulu	Lihue, Kauai	1,637,000
17.	New York	West Palm Beach, Fla.	1,560,000
18.	Honolulu	Kona, Hawaii	1,467,000
19.	Chicago	Atlanta	1,467,000
20.	Los Angeles	Oakland	1,459,000
21.	Chicago	Detroit	1,458,000
22.	New York	Dallas/Fort Worth	1,457,000
23.	Los Angeles	Phoenix	1,344,000
24.	Boston	Washington, D.C.	1,340,000
25.	Los Angeles	Honolulu	1,335,000
26.	Chicago	Dallas/Fort Worth	1,329,000
27.	Chicago	Minneapolis/St. Paul	1,278,000
28.	Los Angeles	Seattle	1,246,000
29.	New York	Detroit	1,229,000
30.	Chicago	San Francisco	1,193,000

Source: Air Transport Association of America, *Air Transport 1999: The Annual Report of the U.S. Scheduled Airline Industry* (1999).

World's Top 30 Tourist Destinations 1998

1998 Rank/Destination	International arrivals[1]	1985 rank	1990 rank
1. France	70,000,000	1	1
2. Spain	47,749,000	2	3
3. United States	46,395,000	4	2
4. Italy	34,829,000	3	4
5. United Kingdom	25,750,000	6	7
6. China	25,073,000	13	12
7. Mexico	19,810,000	9	8
8. Canada	18,825,000	7	10
9. Poland	18,820,000	22	27
10. Austria	17,352,000	5	6
11. Germany	16,511,000	8	9
12. Czech Republic	16,325,000	16	16
13. Russia	15,810,000	18	17
14. Hungary	15,000,000	11	5
15. Portugal	12,000,000	15	14
16. Greece	11,077,000	14	13
17. Switzerland	11,025,000	10	11
18. Hong Kong	9,575,000	19	19
19. Netherlands	9,102,000	20	20
20. Turkey	8,960,000	28	24
21. Thailand	7,720,000	25	21
22. Belgium	6,218,000	17	22
23. Ukraine	6,208,000	N.A.	N.A.
24. Ireland	6,073,000	24	26
25. South Africa	5,981,000	56	55
26. Singapore	5,630,000	23	23
27. Malaysia	5,551,000	21	15
28. Indonesia	4,900,000	55	38
29. Argentina	4,860,000	39	32
30. Brazil	4,818,000	35	53
World Total	**635,134,000**	**N.A.**	**N.A.**

1. Excludes same-day visitors but includes people who pass through a country for one or more nights en route to another country.   **Source:** World Tourism Organization, *Tourism Market Trends, 1999 Edition.*

Tourists in the U.S., by Country of Origin, 1996–98

1998 Rank/ Country	Arrivals in U.S.		
	1996	1997	1998
1. Canada	15,301,000	15,127,000	13,421,832
2. Mexico	8,530,000	8,431,000	9,276,000
3. Japan	5,182,555	5,367,578	4,885,369
4. United Kingdom	3,246,237	3,720,979	3,974,976
5. Germany	1,996,824	1,994,296	1,901,938
6. France	987,126	978,327	1,013,222
7. Brazil	848,453	940,698	909,477
8. Italy	545,246	580,261	610,796
9. Venezuela	447,276	487,981	540,685
10. Argentina	412,581	503,393	523,909
11. Netherlands	440,243	473,420	490,198
12. Australia	463,177	500,615	460,705
13. Switzerland	417,064	410,209	410,900
14. Taiwan	414,541	442,780	386,413
15. Colombia	249,851	317,736	367,968
16. South Korea	749,474	746,550	364,061
17. Spain	324,822	328,024	326,339
18. Sweden	268,975	292,424	300,925
19. Israel	231,347	260,052	269,752
20. Bahamas	316,687	319,240	251,929

Source: World Tourism Organization, *Tourism Market Trends, 1999 Edition.*

Top 20 Destinations for U.S. Tourists, 1987–97

1997 Rank/ Destination	U.S. tourist arrivals		
	1987	1995	1997
1. Mexico	13,044,000	19,220,523	18,193,715
2. Canada	12,719,800	13,005,200	13,401,300
3. United Kingdom	2,800,000	3,146,000	3,432,000
4. Italy	1,956,153	2,570,704	3,074,000
5. France	1,802,000	2,184,000	2,660,000
6. Puerto Rico	1,550,250	2,246,778	2,444,918
7. Germany	2,071,647	1,548,618	1,760,099
8. Bahamas	1,299,215	1,328,925	1,310,420
9. Spain	865,592	877,467	1,020,000
10. Jamaica	545,476	760,304	804,315
11. China[1]	793,341	748,911	800,539
12. Switzerland	N.A.	783,069	786,359
13. Japan	550,261	539,899	621,737
14. Colombia	N.A.	451,176	533,473
15. Philippines	N.A.	514,850	427,431
16. South Korea	326,330	358,872	424,258
17. Singapore	211,369	345,611	376,418
18. India	134,876	203,343	244,239
19. Egypt	102,603	154,851	176,346
20. South Africa	37,750	103,466	142,781

1. Includes Hong Kong.   **Source:** World Tourism Organization, *Tourism Market Trends, 1999 Edition.*

▶THE DAWN OF CIVILIZATION
(c. 3000–1500 B.C.)

The transition from pre-historic Neolithic culture to civilization seems to have involved in every case two things combined: the establishment of settled agricultural communities instead of nomadic food-gathering communities and, in those settled communities, the development of urban centers with literate religious and social hierarchies in control of irrigation projects. The first condition is found (independently, so far as is now known) in at least four centers: Mexico and Central America; the great bend of the Niger River in Africa; the Yellow River valley in China; and in Mesopotamia (the "land between the waters" of the Tigris and Euphrates Rivers). Priority in time belongs to Mesopotamia. And there also the second condition of civilization, the urban center, first emerged.

Mesopotamia

The 600-mile-long plain of the Tigris and Euphrates valleys stretching to the Persian Gulf is the site of earliest civilization. The city-state of Sumer gives its name to this first flowering which blossomed about 3000 B.C. Each of the cities was a sacred temple city, the realm of a god whose regent on earth was the priest-king. To the Sumerians we owe: the calendar, the invention of writing (cuneiform), the plow, the potter's wheel and wheeled carts, boats using sails, and a host of other "firsts."

The separate and frequently warring city-states such as Lagash, Nippur, and Ur fell under the control of the more northerly *Empire of Akkad* whose greatest king was Sargon (c. 2250 B.C.) which in turn fell under the sway of the *Babylonian Empire* whose king Hammurabi (c. 1750 B.C.) conquered all of Mesopotamia and who is credited with the first known Code of Laws. Shortly before 1500 B.C. this empire fell under the domination of the more barbarous *Kassites* whose advantage lay in the use of horse-and-chariot manned by bowmen.

Egypt

The great valley of the Nile, a thin stream traversing the eastern Sahara desert, had given birth by about 3000 B.C. to no urban centers but to a network of farming villages whose population was of urban density. The legendary founder of Egypt was Menes, whose conquest of Lower (i.e., northern) Egypt established the *Old Kingdom* (c. 3000–2200 B.C.). Political unification, quite different from the pattern of Sumer, permitted a rapid assimilation of Sumerian technology while the desert meant relative freedom from invasion. The pharaohs did not rule by permission of the gods, but were divine beings themselves; the building of their colossal tombs, the pyramids, were great religious works directed by the unitary state. The most famous is the Great Pyramid of Cheops at Gizeh (c. 2500 B.C.).

The older diversity of the valley reasserted itself during a century of dissolution and division called the *First Intermediate Period*, after which the traditions of Menes asserted themselves in the *Middle Kingdom* (c. 2100–1800 B.C.). Architecture and sculpture were consciously restorationist, modeled after the Old Kingdom, though temple architecture testifies to the importance of various priesthoods. In literature, it was Egypt's "classical age."

But this age ended with the invasion from Syria-Palestine of the barbarian charioteers known as Hyksos who ruled during the *Second Intermediate Period* (c. 1800–1600 B.C.). But the Eighteenth Dynasty, with its capital at Thebes, at last managed to drive out the Hyksos and re-establish royal authority throughout the valley, thereby initiating the *New Kingdom* (c. 1600–1100 B.C.).

Other Significant Centers

The *Indus Valley*, stretching from Tibet to the Arabian Sea, had become by about 3000 B.C. another locus of settled agriculture with obvious Sumerian influence. Innumerable small villages but only two cities have been excavated and the ancient Indian script remains a mystery to scholars. This Indian civilization flourished from about 2500 to about 1500 B.C. until it was conquered by Aryan tribesmen also utilizing chariots and arrows.

About the year 2000 B.C. three centers of civilization influenced by Mesopotamia and Egypt began to develop: the *Canaanites* in Syria and Palestine, the *Hittites* in Asia Minor, and the *Minoan civilization* on the island of Crete. It is not clear whether Minos was a name or, like "pharaoh" a title, but it was his palace, the Labyrinth, which dominated the trading city of Knossos, center of an elegant "sea empire" whose ships were in contact with Italy, Egypt, Asia Minor and mainland Greece. Yet by about 1500 B.C. Minoan trade was in decline and not long after a Greek prince was ruling at Knossos.

In China around 1875 B.C., the millet-based agricultural villages of the North China Plain gave rise to the semi-legendary Xia Dynasty, which ushered in the Bronze Age in East Asia. The Xia were overthrown around 1550 B.C. by Tang the Victorious, who established the Shang Dynasty, which endured for five hundred years. The Shang Dynasty is noted for its sophisticated bronze vessels, used in worship of the royal ancestors, and for oracle bones inscribed with an early form of Chinese script asking questions of the gods. Shang culture was enriched after around 1350 B.C. by new technologies from western Eurasia, including the chariot, the cultivation of wheat, and sheep-raising.

▶THE SPREAD OF CIVILIZATION
(c. 1500–500 B.C.)

The impact of the chariot warriors from the steppes of Eurasia, a huge stretch of grassland stretching from the Black Sea almost to the Pacific Ocean, altered the earliest civilizations in different ways and to different degrees—least in the Near East, most in India. In the millennium from about 1500 to about 500 B.C., the area of civilized life continued to spread as the civilizations took on their classic form in the "heroic age" of the ancient world.

Egypt

Almost immediately after the hated Hyksos had been expelled from Egypt proper, the pharaohs of the *New Kingdom* (1570–1065 B.C.)—preeminently Thutmose III (c. 1500–1447 B.C.) and his regent queen Hatshepsut (d. 1468 B.C.)—created an empire in Palestine and Syria in which local princes ruled their peoples while Egyptian bureaucrats and garrison commanders oversaw imperial interests, especially the tribute payments. Egyptian control southward along the Nile into the Sudan and Nubia was also reestablished. The empire functioned well until ruled by a pharaoh whose interests lay elsewhere.

The pharaoh Amenhotep IV (ruled c. 1372–1354 B.C.) changed his name to Akhenaton and led a movement after 1370 B.C. to obliterate the name and memory of all the Egyptian gods save for the sun-god Aton (and his incarnation on earth, the pharaoh). This almost-monotheistic revolution absorbed the attention of the monarchy to such an extent that it helped the empire to crumble and the dynasty to be overthrown. A rigid traditionalism accompanied the painful recovery of the empire. Tutankhamen (whose famous tomb was discovered in 1922) was Akhenaton's son-in-law; his name shows the return of the god Amon and the eclipse of Aton. But by 1200 B.C. a series of invasions brought the Egyptians to withdraw from the empire to defend the Nile Valley, a withdrawal complete by about 1100.

The *Post-Empire Period* (1065-525 B.C.) saw Egypt's survival in a cultural and religious sense; but the state grew disunified and finally fell victim to conquests by the Assyrians (671 B.C.) and the Persians (525 B.C.).

Mesopotamia and Persia

The Kassite conquest of the First Babylonian Empire led to no great revolution since the conquerors adopted the culture and political structure of the conquered. To the north, the Assyrians were left under native rulers, then took advantage of a series of barbarian incursions against the Kassites to gain their independence in the *First Assyrian Empire* (c. 1150–728 B.C.). The Assyrians were fierce warriors, and they fell upon the south of Mesopotamia, upon Syria and Palestine, and even, briefly, Egypt, and they established the *Second Assyrian Empire* (728–612 B.C.).

The destruction of the great Assyrian capital of Nineveh (612 B.C.) was the work of the mobile strike force of the cavalry of the Medes who proceeded to conquer the Assyrian territory east of the Tigris as well as Armenia and eastern Iran, forming the short-lived *Median Empire* (625–559 B.C.). Assyria's fall permitted the *Second Babylonian Empire* (625–538 B.C.) to arise in Mesopotamia.

Both fell victim to the *Persian Empire* (559–331 B.C.). Cyrus the Great (550–533 B.C.) overturned his Median overlord (559 B.C.), conquered King Croesus of Lydia in Asia Minor (546 B.C.) and overthrew King Nebuchadnezzar III of Babylon (538 B.C.). It was his son who conquered Egypt and his grandson Darius I (521–485 B.C.)who brought the empire to its greatest extent, expanding eastward beyond the Indus by 519 B.C. Dividing his empire into 20 "satrapies" (administrative offices), Darius improved communications by building good roads and was farsighted enough to commence the construction of a Mediterranean war fleet.

Under this Persian dynasty's patronage, the religious doctrines of Zoroaster (c. 628–c. 551 B.C.) spread through its immense empire. Zoroaster taught a dualist doctrine of a cosmic struggle between the god Ahuramazda, the good god of light, truth and peace, and Ahriman, the evil god of darkness, lies, and discord. It was to prove one of the most profoundly influential teachings in the history of the world.

Israel and Judah

Amidst the ebb and flow of empire emerged the people of Israel. Tracing their origin to the ancient city of Ur in Mesopotamia and the covenant between their patriarch Abraham and their god Yahweh, they migrated to Canaan sometime after 1900 B.C. Entering Egypt, probably in the Hyksos period, they dwelt in the Egyptian delta until about 1280 B.C. when, against strong resistance from the pharaoh, Moses led the Hebrews out of Egypt into the desert of Sinai where, according to the Old Testament, they became Yahweh's chosen people in the Sinai covenant. Shortly before 1200 B.C. they occupied Canaan during the decline of Egyptian power there.

The religious league of clans was transformed into the *Kingdom of Israel* (c. 1020–922 B.C.) which flourished under the kings Saul (1028–1013 B.C.), David (1013–973 B.C.), and Solomon (973–933 B.C.) in the interstices of the great powers. But after the death of Solomon, the kingdom divided into Israel in the north and Judah in the south. The northern kingdom fell to the Assyrians under Sargon II (722–705 B.C.) in 721 B.C. Judah held on until the Second Babylonian Empire under Nebuchadnezzar II (c. 605–562 B.C.)destroyed the capital Jerusalem in 587 B.C.

While ethnic Israel fell, the spiritual Israel was preserved through the work of *the prophets*, especially Isaiah (c. 700 B.C.), Jeremiah (c. 600 B.C.) and the second Isaiah (c. 540) who taught an uncompromising monotheism: Yahweh not the god of the Jews alone, but the one God of mankind.

With the establishment of the Persian Empire, the Jews were permitted (538 B.C.) to return to Palestine and to build the second Temple, there to live under the great code of law, the *Torah*.

Greece

The Minoan culture of Crete had been in contact with the Greek mainland before 1650 B.C. The people of Greece (called Achaeans) had arranged themselves in small principalities of which Mycenae, located on the Greek mainland of the Peleponnesian peninsula, had pre-eminence. Adopting the courtly style of the life of Minoans and the war chariots of the Hyksos, the Achaeans expanded their settlements and with Cretan decline became heirs of Minoan trade with Egypt and Syria. This is the culture pictured for us in the epics of Homer's (c. 800 B.C.), *The Odyssey* and *The Iliad*.

About 1100 B.C., a second wave of Greek-speaking Dorians invaded from the north and the Achaeans were forced to migrate to the islands and the coast of Asia Minor. In defeat they performed their greatest work: the preservation of Mycenaean (and therefore also Minoan) traditions both socially and in the Homeric epics. Through these great poems the enterprise against Troy became the living symbol of the unity of the Greeks, the mythology of Mycenae provided a common religious background for local cults, and the language of the Achaeans became the norm for the whole Greek world.

By about 750 B.C. the Greek world had recovered. Colonies spread westward to Italy and Sicily and eastward to the northern Aegean and the

Black Seas. The lyric poetry of Archilochus (c. 700 B.C.) and Sappho (c. 600 B.C.) flourished. The first philosophers (Thales, Heraclitus, Parmenides), later called the pre-Socratics, commenced their speculations on nature and the order of the universe; to this philosophy, the Pythagoreans added mathematical genius. And the characteristic unit of the city-state, the *polis* was created.

The greatest of these city-states were Athens and Sparta. *Sparta* emerged in 716 B.C. as conqueror of about 3,200 square miles of territory; by about 610 B.C. Sparta already had the formidable military organization based on strict education for citizenship to inculcate the "savage valor" that Spartans so esteemed. And by 540 B.C. Sparta had formed the Peloponnesian League, uniting all but two of the city-states of the peninsula.

The polis of *Athens* was, like other Greek cities, dominated by its aristocratic families. The grievous problem of increasing slavery for debt led the Athenian leaders to turn over power to Solon, a wealthy merchant and poet, descended from the old kings. Taking office in 594, he cancelled all debts, abolished debt-slavery, encouraged both agriculture and industry, and opened the assembly to all free men. But Athens remained divided among its landed wealth, its trading class and the poor peasants, the latter led by the nobleman Peisistratus who established a dictatorship in the name of the poor (546–528 B.C.). But its democratic constitution was not in place until it was imposed, in 508 B.C., by the aristocrat Cleisthenes.

India

The charioteers who invaded the civilization of the Indus valley called themselves Aryans, a word meaning "noble" in their Sanskrit language. Those they conquered were called Sudras, "slaves." The Aryans settled in villages along the Indus, organized in tribal principalities about which almost nothing is known. Over the half-millennium from about 800 B.C. to about 300 B.C. they moved south along the coast and east across the peninsula to the delta of the Ganges River. There, once the lush jungle vegetation was cleared (using the new tools of the iron age), rice could be cultivated in the rich soil, a food supply sufficient for a very dense and stable population.

Religiously, this is the classic age of Hinduism. The ancient *Vedas*, hymns to the gods, date back to about 1000 B.C.—though not written down until much later. The *Brahmanas* are a body of instructions for rituals, evidence of the rise of an important priestly body, composed over the years 800–600 B.C. Lastly, about 600 B.C. appeared the *Upanishads* with their stress on asceticism and mysticism.

Embodied in this classic religious literature are the germs of the later "caste" system, for they envision four *varnas* or castes: priests (brahmans), warriors (kshatriyas), peasants and artisans (vaisyas), and slaves (sudras).

China

The late Shang period, known for the extravagance of its royal burials, declined into misrule; the dynasty was overthrown around 1055 B.C. by the ruler of the state of Zhou, which controlled the Wei River Valley in northwestern China. The Duke of Zhou, regent for the third Zhou king, established a sort of feudal system in which the territory of China was parcelled out in small states governed by Zhou clansmen and supporters. These states gradually grew larger at the expense of the Zhou royal domain. The Zhou capital was forcibly moved eastwards from Chang'an (now Xi'an) to Luoyang around 770 B.C. but the Zhou kings continued to lose both territory and political authority. Zhou rule broke down altogether during the Warring States Period (c. 480–221 B.C.), when a handful of large feudal states swallowed up their smaller neighbors.

The principal states of northern China were known collectively as *zhongguo*, the "middle kingdoms"; the Chinese, isolated from the high cultures of western Eurasia and India, imagined their culture to be at the center of the world, surrounded by zones of ever-increasing barbarism. In this view, the Chinese ruler governed "all under heaven" by authority of the Mandate of Heaven (*tian ming*). This theory held that a dynastic founder, because of his own virtue, attracted the cosmic force of heaven itself in his support, bequeathing heaven's mandate to his descendants so long as they cherished the principle of virtuous rule. This poltical theory, which assumed that exhausted and corrupt dynasties would eventually be overthrown by righteous rebellions, was a force for renewal and long-term stability throughout Chinese history.

Confucius (c. 551–479 B.C.), China's first philosopher, sought a remedy for the political turmoil of his time in an attempted revival of the golden age of the Duke of Zhou. Thwarted in his search for a ruler who would put his ideas into practice, Confucius became a teacher whose disciples perpetuated his prescription for good government. Confucius looked to a natural aristocracy of virtue, rather than an hereditary elite, for social leadership; this led centuries later to the Chinese innovation of government by means of a professional civil service recruited through competitive examination. The Taoists, rivals of the Confucian school (and supposedly founded by Laozi, of whose life nothing is known) rejected government altogether in favor of individual self-cultivation.

The Warring States Period was an era of cultural brilliance in philosophy, technology, and the arts, a prelude to China's first great imperial age.

▶ THE GROWTH OF WORLD EMPIRES (c. 500 B.C.–A.D. 500)

The millennium after 500 B.C. had as its most characteristic development the conquest of the earliest centers of civilization by certain small nations or tribes—Persians, Macedonians, Romans, Mauryans—on their peripheries. Territories of immense extent (the whole world as they knew it) were organized by these smaller nations, although without any attempt to integrate the conquered peoples into their own cultures. Rarely constructed according to any deliberate plan, these world empires grew up haphazardly.

Significant too was the extraordinary clustering in one generation (at about 500 B.C.) of Pythagoras and Heraclitus, the second Isaiah, Confucius, and the Buddha. And yet more so was the fourth century B.C. eruption of philosophic thought with Plato and Aristotle. Finally, at the middle of the millennium, appeared Jesus Christ.

The Persian Empire and the Greeks

The Persian Wars (499–479 B.C.) began with a failed revolt of the Greek cities of coastal Asia Minor against the Persian Empire (of which they had become a part in 546 B.C.). To punish the mainland Greek allies of the rebels, the city-states of

Athens and Eretria, the Persian Empire made war on Greece, but unsuccessfully. From a Persian point of view the Athenian and Spartan victories were only a border issue of minor import; but to the Greeks, the battles of Marathon, Salamis, Plataea and Mycale were inspiring symbols of the superiority of their ideals of liberty and free citizenship over the servitude of Eastern despotism, with the unity of Athens and Sparta embodying what had been prefigured in the united Greek enterprise against Troy. The historian Herodotus first told this story.

Under the leadership of Pericles' (d. 429 B.C.) Athens transformed its naval league into an Athenian Empire, thus allowing Sparta to appear the defender of Greek liberties. The former allies, with their leagues, entered their death-struggle, the *Peloponnesian War* (431–404 B.C.) in which the Spartans won a crushing victory. The saga was told by the second great Greek historian, Thucydides (c. 460–400 B.C.) Spartan hegemony in Greece lasted only until 387 B.C. when a league of Greek cities with Persian assistance imposed a settlement which made all Greek poleis autonomous (and therefore weak) except for those in Asia under Persian rule. It was all but the end of the golden age of Greece.

But in just over a century the Greeks had created tragedy (Aeschylus, Sophocles, Euripides), philosophy (Socrates, Plato, Aristotle), history (Herodotus, Thucydides), and the imperishable glory of their monumental architecture (the Parthenon, the Acropolis) and the sculpture of Myron and Phidias.

The Macedonian Empire
Brooding above the disunited Greek city-states lay the small but militarily powerful kingdom of Macedon, militaristic but greatly influenced by Greek civilization. King Philip (356–330 B.C.), having conquered Illyria and Thrace on the northern Aegean, intervened in Greece and forced the formation of a Hellenic League which with Macedon began war against Persia (336 B.C.). No sooner had war begun than Philip was assassinated, a death which occasioned the revolt of the Greek cities he dominated. But his son and successor, Alexander the Great (336–323 B.C.) ruthlessly crushed the revolt and plunged on into Asia; after his great victory in the battle of Issus (333 B.C.) over Darius III of Persia, Alexander declared himself successor to the last Persian emperor under the title King of Asia, continuing rule through the satrapies after the final defeat of the Persians in 330 B.C. In the meantime he added Egypt to his conquests (331 B.C.) and founded the great city of Alexandria. He pushed on into Bactria (modern Uzbekistan) and then to the Indus Valley beyond which his soldiers would not go. When he died of a fever in Babylon in 323 B.C. he had assembled in but a dozen years the largest empire the world had known; but his premature death meant the division of the empire among the *Diadochi* (Alexander's generals who claimed the succession) who battled for half a century before stabilizing into fragments, each a formidable military monarchy: descendants of Antigonus ruled Macedonia, those of Ptolemy Egypt, those of Seleucus most of Asia. The fringes, the western Mediterranean and India, were left to their own development.

Rome: From Republic to Empire
About the midpoint of the western side of the 650-mile long peninsula of Italy the primitive, devout, peasant community of Rome overturned their Etruscan rulers and established a republic shortly before the year 500 B.C. as the Greek golden age was just beginning. A century of patient expansion against neighboring tribes in central Italy was undone in 390 B.C. when Celts (or Gauls) from the Po Valley plundered and burnt the city. But the Romans commenced anew and within three generations had brought under their sway all of the peninsula except the Greek cities (Magna Graecia) in the south; and these they added by 272 B.C., just at the time the Diodochi were stabilizing their sectors of Alexander's empire.

The move into southern Italy involved Rome in a struggle with Carthage. Originally a Canaanite colony, the city of Carthage in north Africa had established a necklace of commercial colonies along the Mediterranean coast from Sicily across North Africa and Spain to the mouth of the valley of the Rhone, commanding the western seas. In a prodigious struggle called the *Punic Wars* (264–146 B.C.), during which Rome itself was almost brought to ruin by Hannibal (247–183 B.C.), the Romans utterly vanquished Carthage.

After the Second Punic War (218–201 B.C.) Rome became embroiled in the east as Pergamum, Rhodes and Athens appealed for help against the Diodochi. With the war against Macedon (100–196 B.C.) Rome's eastward expansions began. One by one, Greece, Macedonia, Asia Minor, Syria, Palestine, Egypt, and the whole north African coast came under Roman rule by 62 B.C. making the Mediterranean Sea truly what the Romans called *mare nostrum:* our sea.

But Asia did not beckon; rather the Romans embarked on that extraordinary experiment in the west, the conquest of Gaul by Julius Caesar (100–44 B.C.) in which almost 100 small Celtic principalities were brought into the civilization of the Roman Mediterranean. In time Gaul would lead to Britain (A.D. 43–84), while eastern defense considerations would lead to the annexation of Armenia, Mesopotamia and Assyria (A.D. 114–16). At its greatest extent, the Roman Empire stretched from the North Sea to the Sahara Desert, from the highlands of Scotland to the Persian Gulf.

But in winning their empire, the Romans lost their republic, with its freely elected assemblies and magistrates and its famous "council of elders," the Senate. The tremendous population losses in the Second Punic War, the increase in the slave population with every conquest, the transformation from a peasant agriculture to huge *latifundia* (plantations), the rise of a class of financiers (the *equites*), the rivalry of military commanders, the involvement of the military in politics—all conspired to strangle the old republican institutions. In the century from 298 B.C. to 133 B.C., the rivalry for power among demagogues and generals—the Gracchi brothers, Marius, Sulla, the triumvirate of Pompey, Caesar and Crassus, the dictatorship of Caesar, the second triumvirate of Lepidus, Octavian, and Antony—meant endless civil war leading to the final victory of the revolutionary adventurer Octavian who, renamed Augustus, initiated imperial rule in Rome itself and the *Pax Romana*, 200 years of peace in the Roman imperial orbit (27 B.C.–A.D. 180).

Christianity and the Roman Empire
More impressive than the military aspect of the work of Rome was the spread of the Mediterranean civic tradition into continental Europe: colonies of veterans such as Cologne, legionary

headquarters such as York, imitated the old Italian, Greek, Phoenician and Syrian cities as well as the numerous foundations of Alexander. The empire became a network of administrative departments centered on cities with central power at Rome; with the external forms of civic life came economic prosperity and the intellectual culture of the Hellenized Roman civilization.

It was in this world that Christ and Christianity were born. In the reign of Augustus Jesus of Nazareth was born (c. 4 B.C.) and in the reign of Tiberius he died, crucified as a criminal (c. A.D. 30). His closest followers affirmed to his resurrection from the dead and his ascent to the one he always called "My Father" and they eagerly preached the "good news" (gospel) that God himself had become man and died for man's sins. This preaching and their communion in their liturgies were the focal points of the early Christians, as the Romans called them. Considering themselves the "second Israel" they nonetheless broke with the synagogue and through missionaries like Paul, Barnabas, and Timothy preached to the Gentiles. While numerically few, they spread through the cities of the Roman world: from Palestine to Syria, Anatolia and Greece, to Africa and Italy; in the second century to Gaul, Germany, Yugoslavia and Spain.

Because they met in secret societies and because they reused to worship the Roman imperial gods, the Christians were persecuted by Roman magistrates; after A.D. 110, adherence to Christianity became a capital offense. Yet the church continued to spread, not only among the poor and outcast but among the nobles and the philosophers (like Justin the Martyr who perished in A.D. 165). These Christians viewed the Pax Romana as providential.

When after the death of the Stoic emperor Marcus Aurelius (A.D. 180) the empire fell into civil war, economic decline, the exhaustion of civic life through excessive taxation and centralized government control, the frontiers became unsafe as well: for after A.D. 226 a revived Persian Empire grew aggressive in the east while great confederations of tribes (Goths, Vandals, Allemani, Franks) arose on the Rhine and Danube Rivers. The emperor Diocletian (284–305) attempted to stem the decline with a political and military reorganization; but it was the emperor Constantine (312–37) who saw that much more was needed.

He attempted to provide a new internal principal of spiritual unity to the Roman Empire through Christianity. His "new Rome" of Constantinople was a Christian city from the start; from persecution to toleration to favored position to state religion—such was the changed estate of the Catholic Church in less than one century. But it had become the religion of a state far gone in decline. Visigothic troops sacked Rome in 410 (for the first time in 800 years) then carved out a realm in southern Gaul and Spain by 450. Vandals tore north Africa away from Rome (429–39). Franks reached the Loire by 486. Saxons, Angles and Jutes ended the Roman province of Britain. Disintegration in the west seemed complete, under the impact of the so-called *Barbarian Invasions*.

Meanwhile in the Roman east, imperial control remained intact but the subject peoples asserted their nationality in religious, not political, forms, adopting one or another of the heresies that flourished after the formal definition of Christian orthodoxy at the Council of Chalcedon (450); that Christ was truly God and truly man.

India and Southeast Asia

The India that the armies of Alexander entered was a complex welter of tribal principalities and republics, of which a certain primacy attached to the kingdom of Magadha in the Ganges valley ruled by the Nanda dynasty. Resistance to the Macedonians was strongest among the Brahman caste: the Kshatriya princes proved more practical and accommodating. After the last Macedonian satrap left India in 317 B.C. Chandragupta Maurya, who has met Alexander, attacked and conquered Magadha with the aid of northwestern tribes, exterminating the house of Nanda and commencing the *Mauryan Empire* (317–184 B.C.). Married to a Macedonian princess, Chandragupta subdued the Indus valley as well and gained recognition from the Diadochus, Seleucus Nicator. By the reign of his grandson Asoka (269–232 B.C.), central and most of southern India had been added to the empire which extended north to the foothills of the Himalayas and west to the eastern reaches of Afghanistan.

Asoka was known as *the Buddhist Emperor*, personally devout and publicly the protector and propagator of the religion of the *Buddha*. Like Asoka, prince Siddhartha Gautama (563–483 B.C.) was not Brahman but Kshatriya; enlightenment came when he realized that desire is the source of all suffering and that salvation therefore means escape from existence into *nirvana* (or nothingness) through rightful living. (Buddha, in Sanskrit, is a title meaning "the enlightened one.") He founded no church but disciples lived in communities following his "eightfold path" to holiness. It was these communities that Asoka fostered and patronized. The more sternly ascetical *Jainism*, founded by Mahavira (probably a contemporary of the Buddha) had spread without political support amongst an elite; its characteristic doctrines were the eternity of everything that is, even matter, and the attainment of nirvana after nine reincarnations.

After the death of Asoka (233 B.C.) the Mauryan Empire began to crumble into its constituent parts, the last emperor being assassinated by one of his generals in 184 B.C. One of the successor states was the Graeco-Indian kingdom in the north and north-west founded by a general of the Diodoch king of Bactria; another was the Kushan Empire of the first and second centuries A.D., which proved to be the route by which Buddhism expanded into central Asia.

A second Chandragupta was the founder of the last great Indian imperial regime, the *Gupta Empire* (320–535 A.D.) which at its greatest extent stretched across the subcontinent from the mouth of the Indus to the mouth of the Ganges. The source of its unity was a revived Hinduism whose brahmans provided advisors to the emperors and drew up the great codes of Hindu law which articulated the structures of the caste system. It was the age also of the revival of the Sanskrit language both in the drama of Kalidasa (c. 400–55) and in the final composition of the epic poems Mahabharata and Ramayana. The Gupta period was the golden age of Indian science, especially astronomy, and mathematics, to which we owe the decimal system and the invention of the number zero. The sway of the classic Indian civilization was spread far beyond the political borders of the Gupta realm by traders and missionaries to Burma, Thailand, and Indo-China, to the Malay peninsula and beyond into Indonesia. The shores of the Bay of Bengal and of the South China Sea thus became a kind of "greater India", as the Diodoch kingdoms had become a "greater Greece."

The Chinese Empire

In 246 B.C. the cavalry troops of the far western state of Qin, hardened by years of warfare with the barbarian nomads of the steppe, hurtled eastward to conquer and subjugate, one by one, all of the other feudal principalities in a quarter century of war that brought the period of the "warring states" to an abrupt halt. On this territorial basis arose the first *Chinese Empire* under the *Qin Dynasty* (221–206 B.C.) Qin Shihuangdi ("The First Emperor of Qin") proved more than just a conqueror: he oversaw the completion of the Great Wall along the edge of Inner Mongolia and provided a structure of government for the empire by dividing the land into regions of administration and war, governed by deputies responsible to himself alone. The old nobility he destroyed by land confiscations; the Confucian schools he closed, executing many prominent scholars, cowing the rest into submission. And while a weakling successor proved unable to stem rebellion and met his death by assassination (206 B.C.) the structure of imperial rule inaugurated by the Qin would endure for over two thousand years.

A rebel leader named Liu Bang emerged victorious in the confused and bloody uprisings that brought the Qin Dynasty to an end. Liu proclaimed himself emperor of the Han Dynasty, which was to endure (with a brief interregnum under the usurper Wang Mang) for four centuries, from 206 B.C. to A.D. 220. The Han founder retained the imperial structure of Qin rule, while moderating its punitive harshness; he opened the way for renewed Confucian participation in government. The greatest Han ruler, Emperor Wu (r. 140–87 B.C.) instituted the practice of choosing officials on the basis of learning and merit. He brought the rich ricelands of the Yangtze River Valley firmly under imperial control, and also greatly extended the boundaries of the empire, conquering south to the South China Sea, southwest to the borders of Burma and Tibet, northeast to northern Korea, and westward to the deserts of Central Asia. He pacified the northern frontier, defeating the Xiongnu tribes whose descendants the Huns would later invade Europe. In an early arms race, the powerful laminated compound bow and cavalry tactics of the northern nomads were countered by Chinese infantry armed with mass-produced crossbows—a refinement of a weapon of Southeast Asian origin. At this time trade increased along the Silk Route, a network of caravan trails that, through many intermediaries, brought Chinese silk to the Roman Empire and warhorses from Central Asia to China.

The "dynastic cycle" completed its course in the last decades of the Han period, when court corruption, peasant uprisings, and military insurrections led to the overthrow of the last Han emperor in A.D. 220. There followed the Three Kingdoms Period (220–265), when rival states tries without success to reunite the empire, and the period of the Northern and Southern Dynasties (265–589), when northern China was frequently ruled by short-lived dynasties of invaders from the steppes, and southern China was fragmented into equally short-lived and ineffectual kingdoms. During this period of disunion Buddhism, which had entered China via Central Asia in late Han times, began to establish itself as one of China's major religions. Especially successful were sects of Mahayana ("Greater Vehicle") Buddhism, which promised salvation to the faithful through the mediation of saints called *bodhisattvas*.

Japan and Korea

Around 300 B.C., invaders from northeastern Asia had invaded Japan via the Korean Peninsula. These invaders, equipped with horses, bronze weapons, and the wealth produced by rice agriculture, displaced the ancient Jomon culture of the original inhabitants of Japan. This bronze-age Yayoi civilization, which also shows evidence of influence from Austronesian culture via Taiwan and Okinawa, laid the foundations for the subsequent Japanese empire. But for several centuries Japan was fragmented into small states ruled by military clans (uji), with those associated with the Shinto shrines at Izumo and Ise claiming some degree of primacy.

In Korea, the decline of the Chinese colony at Lolang led to the establishment of indigenous kingdoms; three of these—Silla, Paekche, and Koguryo—predominated during the period 313-668 A.D. Chinese cultural influence, via Korea, helped to transform the Japanese petty states into a centralized kingdom by the 5th century A.D.

▶ EUROPE'S "DARK AGE" AND THE IMPACT OF ISLAM (A.D. 500–1000)

The seventh-century eruption of Islam with its compact secular-religious civilization and its characteristic institution of the *jihad* (holy war), both rooted in the sacred writings of the Koran, created an empire stretching from the Iberian Peninsula to the Indus Valley but influencing events in far-off Ghana as well. It also provoked in response the formation of eastern and western Christendom.

Untouched by these developments, China underwent another dynastic cycle—one in which Chinese civilization spread to Korea and Japan. And in utter isolation, without iron or even the wheel, civilizations in Central American began.

The Roman Empire and Europe's "Dark Age"

The lapse of direct Roman rule in the west did not imply "the fall of the Roman Empire", for the Germanic barbarians lived in a "greater Rome" whose heir and representative was the Catholic Church while in the east Roman rule continued with enough vigor to experience a great revival under the emperor Justinian (527–65). Maintaining a rough alliance with the Christian Franks in Gaul under their *Merovingian* dynasty, Justinian's armies recovered the western provinces: Vandal Africa, Ostrogothic Italy and the Mediterranean sector of Visigothic Spain. Meanwhile his jurists codified and preserved the whole body of *Roman law* since the days of the republic. And under imperial patronage there grew up a magnificent cluster of churches whose pinnacle was the Hagia Sophia in Constantinople, constructed in 537.

But the cost was very great: the treasury was beggared and the eastern frontiers neglected so that the west might be rewon. After Justinian's death the empire had neither treasure nor troops enough to save Italy from new invaders, the Lombards. The city of Ravenna on its marshes kept its link with Constantinople and Rome itself was saved, principally through the work of the pope, Gregory the Great. In the 14 years of his papacy (590–604) he not only organized the defense of the city but oversaw the work of converting Visigothic Spain and began the restoration of Christianity in faraway Britain through the mission of St. Augustine to Kent. In this evangelizing effort Gregory relied upon the monks who followed the *Rule* of St. Benedict (480–547) who brought moderation and a Roman sense of order to the *monasticism* of the west. In a chaotic world, Benedict's *Rule* provided a uniform way of life for monks living as a community, including vows of poverty, chastity, and obedience, regular and frequent hours of prayer, study of the Bible, and manual work.

The empire, which barely held on in the east against Persia, met catastrophe at the hands of the armies of Islam (see next section). In half a dozen years (636–42) Syria, Egypt and Libya fell away; in a second wave of invasions (696–711) the rest of north Africa and Spain were lost as well; Frankish Gaul was only just saved by the cavalry of Charles Martel in the battle of Tours (732). The Mediterranean seemed on its way toward becoming a Moslem lake.

Two successor states to the old Roman empire emerged. In the east lay the empire proper, but now usually called the *Byzantine Empire* (610–1453). Its wealth and power were based in Asia Minor, its unity dependent upon three factors: Orthodox Christianity (slowly drifting away from Roman Catholicism until the final break with Rome in 1054); Hellenistic culture and the Greek language; and Roman law and administration. Missionary ventures carried Christianity and Byzantine influence to the Serbs and Croats in the Balkans, to the Moravians and Slovaks north of the Danube, and even as far as Kievian Rus, all in the ninth and tenth centuries.

In the west there arose the *Carolingian Empire* (751–888). The son of Charles Martel, Pepin III, cooperated with St. Boniface to reform the Frankish Church in close relation with Rome, deposed (with papal approval) the last Merovingian shadow-king, and was himself anointed king in 751. Before his death in 768 Pepin had made Frankish sovereignty felt southward to the Pyrenees and the Mediterranean. His son Charlemagne (768–814) conquered Lombardy, absorbed Bavaria, expanded into Saxony and beyond the Pyrenees, bringing under his sway an area equal in size to the old Roman Empire in the west. At the same time, to foster missionary endeavors, he ordered the creation of cathedral and monastic schools, drawing heavily for his scholars on Northumbria, the small English kingdom where Celtic and Roman monastic traditions had intermingled. The pinnacle of his work came on Christmas Day in the year 800 when in the city of Rome he was acclaimed and crowned as Roman Emperor, by the pope.

But with his death disintegration began. By 843 his grandsons divided his realm in three parts with a middle kingdom of the empcror Lothair separating the kingdoms of the East and West Franks (the nuclei of Germany and France yet to be). These realms faced deadly peril on all sides: Viking corsairs from the north (who also ravaged the British Isles and established commercial bases between the Baltic and Byzantium), Moslem pirates attacking from the south, and, just as these threats had abated, the fierce horsemen of the Hungarians, about the year 900. The family of the Carolingians proved unable to lead any effective resistance; that arose among the nobles of the empire who, inspired by the example of King Alfred the Great of Wessex (849–901) against the Danes in England, defended their people but demanded in return their obedience and support. This was the origin of that pattern of decentralized authority and allegiance known as *feudalism*. Not that monarchy died, but the medieval kings became "firsts amongst equals": Henry the Fowler (919–36) began the *Saxon Dynasty* of German kings while his son Otto I also assumed (962) the title of Emperor; and Hugh Capet in 987 began the *Capetian Dynasty* of France which ruled into the 19th century.

The aftermath of this terrible dark age was the creation of the new Christian monarchies on the fringe of the older Carolingian world: the restoration of the Empire in 962, replacing Charlemagne's empire, which barbarian tribes had destroyed; the consolidation and conversion of the Scandinavian monarchies about 990; the establishment of an independent and Catholic Poland (966) the already mentioned conversion of Kievian Rus (988) under St. Vladimir; and the founding in 1001 of a Catholic Hungarian kingdom under St. Stephen (997–1038).

The Islamic World

To the Roman Empire, the Arabs were a frontier annoyance, no menace as was Sassanid Persia; yet it was out of the Arabian Desert that the whirlwind of Islam arose. Its founder, Mohammed (or Muhammad) (570–632) was a religious prophet whose revelations came from God; these revelations form the heart of the Moslem sacred book, the *Koran*. Utter simplicity of doctrine (a stern monotheism and a focus on the world to come) and of moral code ("hard against the infidels, merciful among themselves") combine with an elaborate ceremonial (the strict fast of Ramadan, prayer five times daily, the Meccan pilgrimage). Driven out of Mecca to Yathrib (now Medina), Mohammed and his followers formed a religious and political community which, after eight years of desert warfare, returned to capture Mecca (630).

Within two years of Mohammed's death the armies of Islam were marching. From the Romans they wrested Syria, Mesopotamia, Egypt and Libya (636–46); the Persians they conquered outright (637–49). Not until 661 was the vexed question of the succession settled when the old tribal aristocracy triumphed over the family of the prophet and established *Umayyad Dynasty* (661–750) of caliphs ("successors") ruling not from Medina but from Damascus and utilizing the old Persian and Roman bureaucracies. For almost half a century Islam lay quiescent; then, with the conversion of the Berbers, Byzantine Africa was swept away (696) as was Visigothic Spain (711). In the same year a Moslem commander established himself in the lower Indus Valley.

A series of revolts protesting the purely Arabic dominance of the Umayyads led to the establish-ment of a new dynasty of caliphs, the *Abbasid Dynasty* (750–1258), descended from a cousin of Mohammed. Arab by descent, the Abbasids nonetheless moved the capital to the new city of Baghdad in Mesopotamia where Persian influence came to predominate in politics as in literature while the Islamic scientific and mathematical flowering owed as much to Gupta India and ancient Greece as to archaic Babylonian astral speculations, especially the decimal system of numeration and the use of the zero.

The Umayyads had not been totally overturned; Spain followed their rule when the rest of the empire turned to the house of Abbas; after about 800 there were independent Moslem states in Morocco, Tunis, and eastern Persia; and by about 875 in Egypt and Turkestan. Before the year 1000 the caliphs had lost almost all their political power, becoming largely a focus of religious unity, relying even then on the *ulema*, adepts of Islamic law and lore. To this day, ultimate authority in many Islamic states has remained with the religious leaders.

India and Africa on the Fringe of Islam

After the fall of the Gupta Dynasty in 535, India reverted to its older pattern of a large number of tribal principalities. The White Huns, whose incursion had overturned Gupta power, coexisted with the Hindu princes who knew them as *Rajputs* and established a feudal state across north India east of the Indus valley, the kingdom of Rajputana. The Sind (or lower Indus) was already in Moslem hands after 711. By the ninth century Buddhism had all but disappeared from India, absorbed into Hinduism; one exception was in the state of the Pala kings who ruled Bengal and Magadha into the 12th century. Buddhism remained influential in "greater India": in the small kingdoms of Burma, in the kingdom of Dvaravati in Siam, in Sri Lanka, and in the Sumatran state of Srivishaya under its Sailendra dynasty.

At the other extremity of the caliphate, Moslem traders from Morocco were in contact with the *Kingdom of Ancient Ghana* by about the year 800. Camel caravans crossed the Sahara to the grasslands between the upper Niger and Senegal rivers bearing salt and goods from the Mediterranean basin. There the king of Ghana supplied gold and ivory brought north from the southern reaches of the "shoulder" of Africa. Extracting import and export taxes and monopolizing the gold supply, the kings of Ghana exercised a kind of imperial control over the trading cities of the region, growing wealthy and powerful. Yet by 1076 the caliphs in Morocco were able to conquer the region.

At the opposite side of Africa, Moslem Arabs crossed the Red Sea and annexed the Somali coast (c. 1050) from the ancient Christian kingdom of Ethiopia.

China: Tang and Song Dynasties

Three centuries of disunion in China came to an end with the establishment of the *Sui Dynasty* in 589. Like the Qin, the Sui was a short-lived dynasty that paved the way for a long-enduring one. Extravagant expenditures on construction of the Grand Canal linking Hangzhou and Chang'an (a distance of over 1000 miles), a disastrous attempt to conquer Korea, and a Turkish invasion of northwestern China doomed the Sui. It was replaced in 618 by the *Tang Dynasty*, one of the most glorious eras in all of Chinese history. Buddhism flourished, as did poetry and the fine arts; Tang Chang'an was the largest and most cosmopolitan city in the world by around 700. But in 751 Chinese troops on the westernmost frontier were defeated by an Arab army in the Battle of Talas, and the Tang abandoned much of Central Asia; in 755, China's greatest general, An Lushan, rebelled against the throne. The rebellion was defeated, but the empire never recovered fully. An imperial persecution of Buddhism in the 840s, during which the wealth of many temples was confiscated, signaled the rise of Neo-Confucianism, reinvigorating China's oldest philosophical tradition. But with the imperial house in disarray, the Tang collapsed in 907.

After five decades of inconclusive attempts to restore central rule, the *Song Dynasty* was founded in 960, and endured until 1279. But the Song never had firm control of northern China. The northeast was controlled by the *Liao Dynasty* in the hands of the non-Chinese Khitan people (whose name gives us the world Cathay). They were replaced in the early 12th century by the *Jurchen Jin Dynasty*, which in 1127 conquered all of northern China, sending the Song emperors south to a new capital at Hangzhou. Although the Song were politically weak this was nevertheless a time of cultural brilliance, when Chinese landscape painting was perfected, poetry flourished, and urban life (rich with the wealth of overseas trade) attained new heights of sophistication. With the old northern aristocratic clans destroyed by the downfall of Tang and subsequent centuries of barbarian rule, the Song state was run by a surprisingly modern bureaucratic government recruited from a prosperous and well educated rural gentry.

Japan and Korea

In Korea, the state of Silla in 562 put an and to Japanese attempts to carve out colonial enclaves on the peninsula, and then, with Tang support, turned its attention to defeating its rivals Paekche and Koguryo. This process was completed by 670, and Silla grew prosperous with Tang support and cultural influence. But Silla in turn was defeated in 935 by the small western state of Koryo, which established a dynasty ruling all of Korea until 1392. Relatively isolated from Song influence by the intervening states of Liao, and later Jin, the Koryo state became culturally more independent of China.

In Japan, *the Yamato clan*, which had gradually pressed its claim to recognition as an imperial dynasty on the Chinese model, was firmly established on the throne by the fifth century A.D. Buddhism came to Japan in the following century, along with such continental innovations as the use of Chinese script to write (phonetically) the very different Japanese language. In 589 Prince Shotoku issued a 17-article "constitution" establishing imperial support for Buddhism and enjoining all aristocrats to respect the imperial throne. The throne thereupon came under the influence of the powerful *Soga clan* until 645; a restoration movement emphasized emulation of the Chinese model of government. But the principle of appointment to office on the basis of merit never caught on in Japan, which continued to be ruled by an hereditary aristocracy.

Japan's first permanent capital city was founded at Nara in 710; by 750 the city was wholly dominated by its rich and powerful Buddhist temples. In response the emperors moved the capital to the new city of Heian-kyo (now Kyoto) in 794; the emperors remained there for over a thousand years. Both Nara and Heian-kyo were built on a grid plan, modeled after Tang Chang'an; Heian-kyo especially boasted a glittering cultural life, supported by agrarian wealth from the provinces. The powerful *Fujiwara clan* gained control of the country's political life through the expedient of making sure that every emperor married a Fujiwara daughter, and abdicated the throne for a life of monastic retirement shortly after producing an heir; the head of the Fujiwara clan thus was always the father-in-law of one emperor and the legal guardian of the heir-apparent.

The Classic Age of Mayan Culture

Splendid archaeological remains wrapped in chronological obscurity give tantalizing hints of culture in central America before the year 1000. Sometime around 2500 B.C. (but perhaps a millennium earlier) the hybrid maize (or Indian corn) was developed on present-day Mexico's Gulf coast. Permanent agricultural settlements, stretching from Mexico's central plateau to the Guatemalan highlands, seem to date from about 1500 B.C. But it was not until the period A.D. 300–900 that Central America attained approximately to the cultural level of ancient Mesopotamia. From Guatemala to the Yucatan the Mayans developed temples, ritual calendars and a system of writing as yet not deciphered. Similarly, in the Mexican Plateau, there grew up a culture associated with the great city of Teotihuacan. Both seem to have been "empires" of city-states, but except for Teotihuacan itself the sites were not really cities, rather religious centers surrounded by agricultural hamlets. The Mexican development seems to have been cut short by invasions about A.D. 900, probably by the Toltecs. The abandonment about the same time of the Mayan temple sites may have been the result of drought, deforestation, and other environmental factors.

▶ THE MOSLEMS, THE TURKS, AND THE RISE OF THE CHRISTIAN WEST (A.D. 1000–1500)

The four major centers of civilization that had been established by the year 1000—European Christendom, the Islamic world, India and China—all underwent tremendous challenges from confederations of warlike Turkish and Mongol tribes in the next 500 years. Of all the developments the most significant for world history proved to be the maturation of western Christendom which had already commenced, before the period closed, its expansion to the Americas, to Africa and to southern Asia as well.

Expansion of the Moslem World: Asia and Africa

The *Abbasid* dynasty of caliphs of Baghdad had long employed Turkish auxiliaries (rather as the Romans had used German tribes) in their Near Eastern armies; one such army, under their chieftain Mohammed of Ghazni, moved out of Afghanistan into the Punjab about the year 1000 and by 1030 established a Moslem dynasty there. Over the next 200 years they spread their conquests over the Rajputs eastward into the plain of the Ganges, establishing their capital at Delhi about the year 1200. The rich Hindu temples were plundered and, as "heathen," destroyed by these Moslem Turks. Under the sultan (="ruler") Ala-ud-din (1296–1316) most of the subcontinent was brought under one rule for the first time since Asoka.

Unable to break the caste tradition, the ruling Turks became yet another caste, a minority of warrior-aristocrats extracting heavy taxes but relying upon the Hindu princes for administration. Though the Hindu temples had been destroyed, the Turks had to permit a practical tolerance for a now less sacerdotal Hinduism. After the death of Ala-ud-din his empire dissolved into a medley of warring kingdoms ruled by Moslem generals or Hindu princes over whom the sultans at Delhi exercised greater or lesser control.

In the "greater India" of Southeast Asia, Islamic influence expanded through trade and Chinese influence through trade and warfare. In Burma, the Buddhist kingdom founded by Anawrata in 1044 was destroyed by the Mongol armies of Kublai Khan in 1287 and the land was divided into a number of small principalities. Dvaravati Siam (briefly annexed to Cambodia in the 11th century) was overrun by Thai tribesmen from China in the 13th century; by 1350 a Thai kingdom of Siam had established its capital at Ayutthaya, which was to remain its capital until the end of the 18th century. Over the next century, Siam subdued the independent kingdom of Cambodia to the east and expanded against Burma as well. In the archipelago of Indonesia and curving north into the Philippines, Moslem traders and missionaries had established 20 Islamic states by the year 1500. The Hindu aristocracy of Java took refuge on the island of Bali, which still preserves elements of pre-Islamic Indonesian culture.

Moslem expansion occurred in western Africa as well. The conquest of ancient Ghana by Moslem Berbers in 1076 (who had conquered Morocco as well 20 years earlier) led to no new empire but a series of successor states. One of these, Kangaba, had by the 13th century established another trading state of immense size, the *Kingdom of Mali* which stretched, in the 14th century, from the Atlantic coast eastward beyond Gao on the Niger. Under king Mansa Musa (c. 1312–37) Islam spread through the western savanna, the king himself making a pilgrimage to Mecca in 1324. Further east, the king of the Songhay people on the great bend of the Niger had already converted to Islam in the 11th century; thus, when the dominance of Mali was replaced in the 15th century by the *Kingdom of Songhay*, Islam dominated not only the northern coast of Africa but almost the entire belt of savanna south of the Sahara as well.

It was also in this period, but obscurely and beyond the range of Islam, that African tribes (speaking various languages of the Bantu family) continued their long migrations. In the previous period (c. 600-900) they had moved out of the Cameroon highlands east to the Great Lakes; from there they migrated in two streams: southwest to the Congo basin, and south to the savanna of modern Zambia. Now in the period from about 1000 to about 1500, they occupied Kenya and Tanzania on the east and the lands south to the edge of the Kalahari desert.

Transformation of the Moslem World: The Turks

No sooner had Mohammed of Ghazni established Turkish rule in the Punjab than two brothers of the Seljuk clan revolted and took Afghanistan (1037), then expanded into Persia and Mesopotamia (by 1055). After the battle of Manzikert (1071) they took most of Asia Minor from Byzantium. When Syria was added (1084) the *Seljuk Empire* (1037–1243) stretched from Egypt to India. During the 12th century, in the aftermath of the

First Crusade (1096–99), their empire became a jumble of small emirates ruled by Seljuk princes or their generals. What brought the Seljuks low was the sudden appearance in the 1240s of the Mongols in the Near East; though menacing to both Moslems and Christians, Mongols power proved ephemeral and the true heirs of the Seljuks proved to be another clan of Turks, the Ottomans. In 1326 they drove Byzantine forces entirely out of Asia Minor, thus beginning the *Ottoman Empire* (1326–1920). By century's end they controlled all of Asia Minor and the Balkans as far north as Bosnia. Half a century later (1453) they took Constantinople, turning Hagia Sophia into a mosque in their re-named capital of Istanbul.

Eastern Christendom Submerged: Mongols and Turks

The 11th century was the apogee of the *Eastern Roman Empire* (Byzantium) as it conquered the Christian kingdom of Bulgaria (1018) and made Serbia a client state in the west, while to the east Armenia and the Crimea were annexed (1022). But by mid-century the Normans, descendants of Vikings who settled in the French province of Normandy, were establishing themselves in Byzantine Italy (and Moslem Sicily), and the battle of Manzikert (1071) proved a catastrophe from which the Empire never recovered, losing both its granary and its military recruiting ground to the Turks in a single blow. Although the first three crusades (1096–1192) were initially successful in wresting the Holy Land from Islam, the subsequent organization of the territory in the French pattern of small squabbling and isolated feudal statelets rendered them impotent and hence of only marginal help to Byzantium. The Fourth Crusade (1202-1204) was a disaster, for the crusaders took Constantinople, establishing what is called the *Latin Empire* (1204–61). In 1261, Michael Palaeologus (1261–82) restored a rump Byzantium along the shores of the Aegean and it was against this state that the Ottoman Turks expanded. The doom of Constantinople brought Turkish power right to the borders of Hungary, with the Balkans absorbed into the Ottoman Empire for 450 years.

In the northeast it was not the Turks but the Mongols whose arrival transformed Christendom. Hungary, Poland and Kievian Rus were weakened by dynastic struggles from the 11th century on, yet maintained their independence of the Holy Roman Empire to the west and the Turkish Cumans in the east. But the uniting of the Mongol federation under Genghis Khan (1206-27) created a power great enough to strike at China, the Near East, and Europe at the same time; by his death his realm extended from Korea to the borders of Persia and Rus. A decade later Mongol armies under Genghis Khan's grandson Batu (d. 1255) fell upon Europe (1237–40) attacking beyond Russia into Poland and Hungary and the lands of the German knights on the Baltic; but with the death of the Khan, the Mongols retreated. Still the "Golden Horde," an independent Mongol Khanate organized by Batu on the lower Volga River, ruled all of south Russia and reduced the north Russian principalities to vassal status.

Not until the late 15th century was the prince of Moscow sufficiently established to refuse tribute money to the Empire. His marriage to the niece of the last Byzantine emperor established the claim of Ivan III to imperial succession as he took the title "czar" (= Caesar or emperor) and his conquest of the principality of Novgorod (1478) established a large Russian state northeast of Poland. Poland had attained its status as the largest state in Christendom with the marriage (1386) of its queen Jadwiga (1384–99) to the Grand Duke Jagiello of Lithuania; in the 15th century the Jagellon Dynasty (1386–1572) controlled the entire region between the Baltic and Black Seas. But thereby it was exposed to a four-fold danger: from Ottomans to the south, Germans to the west, Swedes to the north and Russians to the northeast.

The Rise of Western Christendom

For 600 years out of the ruins of the western Roman Empire and the anarchy of barbarian invasions, Western Christendom slowly emerged, the process essentially completed with the conversion to Christianity of the Scandinavians, the Poles and the Magyars (950–1050). It was not a society associated with a great empire (for the Carolingian Empire had fallen in the ninth century) but with the feudal states of France and the tribal duchies of Germany. Its unity, such as it was, was religious and cultural as well as political.

Whether the leadership of this society should fall to the Popes or the Holy Roman Emperors was settled in the 11th century in the *Investiture Struggle* in which the papacy emerged victorious. From Pope Gregory VII (1073–85) to Boniface VIII (1294–1303) the papacy gave the lead to western Christendom often in alliance with reforming monastic leaders. In the 12th and 13th centuries the characteristic architecture and sculpture of medieval Europe (*Romanesque* and *Gothic*) spread across Europe under Church patronage while the Leagues of the Peace and the Crusades attempted to limit and channel to constructive use the warrior ethos of the feudal nobles.

Beginning in 11th century Italy and 12th century Netherlands, the commune movement, in which all the inhabitants of a town bound themselves by oath to obey their magistrates, keep the peace, and defend their liberties, revived town life and created the medieval city as a confederation of self-governing guilds. *Guilds* were associations of craftsmen of one trade or merchants bound together for mutual aid. In the west the fairs of Champagne and Burgundy provided ground for the re-establishment of trade while in the Mediterranean, the Italian cities (especially Venice and Genoa) linked the west with Byzantium and the Moslem Near East.

In these towns arose the great universities (Paris, Bologna, Salerno, Oxford) where Greek and Arab learning met with the Christian traditions of the Carolingian schools; the insights of Aristotle re-thought in Christian terms issued into the legal, philosophic, theological and scientific work of *scholasticism*, the work of men like Albertus Magnus, Thomas Aquinas, Bonaventure, Roger Bacon, and Duns Scotus—all members also of the new religious orders, Franciscans (St. Francis, 1182–1226) and Dominicans (St. Dominic, 1170–1221), which arose in the towns of the 13th century. Committed to evangelical poverty and combating heresy, they played a role in university life as well.

Late in the 12th century in Spain and Italy, in the 13th in Germany, England and France, in the 14th and 15th in Hungary, Poland and Scandinavia, the custom arose for monarchs to call the elected representatives of the towns to meet with prelates and nobles to render advice; such was the origin of *parliaments*.

The development of these social and cultural and religious institutions was accompanied by the expansion of western Christendom. One aspect was internal with the clearing of forests and the cultivation of new farmland able to support an increased population. The other was external, not so much the ephemeral Kingdom of Jerusalem (1099-1162) or Latin Empire of Constantinople (1204–61) as the reconquest of Spain from the Moslems (1085–1492), the conquest of Prussia and Livonia by the Teutonic Knights (1229–1466) and the conversion of Lithuania (1386 and after.)

The most significant check to population growth was the *Black Death*, an outbreak of bubonic plague that swept over Europe (1347–51), wiping out perhaps 25 million, a third of the population. The loose unity of western Christendom began to alter in the 14th century in significant ways. First of all, the universality of the papacy seemed compromised when seven popes in succession (1305–78) preferred to reside at Avignon rather than Rome, in too close an association with the kings of France; then, after the return to Rome arose that series of disputed elections to the papacy which is called the *Great Schism* (1378–1417); and third, with the end of the schism, the popes became more and more involved in the politics of Renaissance Italy.

Meanwhile, while theories of sovereignty derived from the study of Roman law exalted the authorities of kings, royal powers disastrously declined due to chronic feudal violence: the "age of princes" in Germany (1273-1493), the Hundred Years' War in England and France (1337–1453), and the dynastic Wars of the Roses in England (1455–85). Out of the turmoil arose the "new monarchies" of more unified states: the Tudors in England (1485), the Valois in France (1328–1529), and in Spain the Spanish branch of the Habsburgs (1504–1700).

In the Italy of the 14th and 15th centuries, increasingly the plaything of the new monarchies, there began that great cultural transformation known as the *Renaissance*. Humanists like Petrarch (1304–74), and Boccaccio (1313–75) sought a revival of Latin antiquity, both pagan (Cicero, Virgil, Tacitus) and Christian (Augustine and the other Church fathers), in an educational movement that sought to unite the values of Hellenism with Christianity. At the same time artists, studying Roman architecture and Hellenistic sculpture on the one hand and the new sciences of anatomy and perspective on the other, created a new world of beauty. In painting, Botticelli and da Vinci, in architecture Brunelleschi (1377–1446), in sculpture Ghiberti (1378–1455) and Donatello (1386–1466)—these represent the output of the city of Florence alone.

Building on medieval foundations and new navigational discoveries (magnetic compasses, the astolabe, the quadrant), the Portuguese monarchy pioneered the exploration of the African coast; the Gulf of Guinea was reached by 1470, the Cape of Good Hope by 1487, and India itself by 1498. The Spanish monarchs sponsored the western route of Columbus whose four voyages (1492–1504) brought Europeans to the shores of the Caribbean (which he mistook for Japan and the Malay Peninsula). Finally, before the period closed, the new Tudor monarchy of England financed the more northerly westward explorations of the Cabots who reached Newfoundland and New England in 1497 and 1498. Like the humanists, by seeking a very old world, the explorers found something very new as well.

The Americas

The New World which Columbus discovered was dominated by two great empires. In Mexico, the Toltecs established an empire with its capital in the magnificent temple city of Tula; it included most of the old Mayan realm (c. 900–1200). But the 12th and 13th centuries saw a series of incursions of barbarian nomadic hunters from the south known collectively as Chichimecs whose armed might destroyed the Toltec civilization. In time, one of these tribes, the Aztecs, established a capital at Tenochtitlan and over the century from about 1360 to about 1470 conquered neighboring peoples and constructed the sanguinary *Aztec Empire* (c. 1360–1520). The king Montezuma I (died c. 1470) was a ruthless conqueror but a great builder as well, transforming the capital into a magnificent city of stone. By 1500 the Aztecs had reached Guatemala. For the subject peoples war and subjections were evil enough; worse was the Aztec worship of the sun god who required for his nourishment human blood.

Stretching thousands of miles along the west coast of South America lay the empire of the Incas with their capital at Cuzco. Unlike the military Aztec empire of subject states paying tribute including the blood tax, the *Inca Empire* was a centralized bureaucratic state which engaged in social engineering as well as road and bridge building and irrigation projects. Begun about 1200, the empire attained its greatest size under Huayna Capac (c. 1493–1527).

China and East Asia (1200–1500)

Genghis Khan (b. 1162–1227), leader of the Mongol federation, wished to unite all of the nomadic peoples of the Asian steppes under his rule. The Mongol conquest of northern China, ruled by Jurchen tribesmen from Manchuria, was completed by Genghis Khan's successors in 1234. The Mongols then turned their attention to Korea, which they conquered in 1231–36, and to the Chinese Song Dynasty in the Yangtze River Valley. The Song defended their territory vigorously, while the Mongols were slowed down as their horsemen learned to cope with wet ricefields and rivers defended by heavily armed ships; but in 1271 Kubilai Khan (b. 1215–94) proclaimed himself emperor of the *Yuan Dynasty* of China, and in 1279 the last Song emperor capitulated. During his reign Kubilai Khan tried twice to invade Japan; his fleets were stopped by *kamikaze*, "divine winds," i.e. typhoons. An attempt to conquer Java also met with only limited and temporary success.

In China the Mongols were seen as an alien occupying power; their habit of using foreign, Persian-speaking tax-collectors made them especially hated. The successors to Kubilai Khan were mediocre rulers; in 1368 a Chinese nativist rebellion led by a charismatic ex-Buddhist monk named Zhu Yuanzhang succeeded in overthrowing the Mongols and establishing the *Ming Dynasty* (1368–1644). The early Ming emperors were vigorous and forward-looking; they rebuilt the Great Wall, re-routed the Grand Canal to terminate near Beijing, built a new southern capital at Nanjing, and sent maritime expeditions on missions of exploration and diplomacy throughout the South China Sea and the Indian Ocean to the east coast of Africa. These expeditions, under Admiral Zheng He, were however abruptly terminated in 1433, criticized by the conservative Confucian bureaucracy as a waste of money and resources. Thus the Chinese missed by only three decades the chance to confront the Portuguese as rival maritime powers in the Indian Ocean.

In Korea, the *Koryo Dynasty* did not long outlast the rule of their Mongol patrons. The last Koryo king in 1388 sent his best general, Yi Songgye (famous for his victories over Japanese pirates), to invade China to try to overthrow the Ming Dynasty on behalf of the Mongols. General Yi instead turned back at the border, overthrew the Koryo king, and established his own dynasty, the *Kingdom of Choson*, which soon proclaimed its support for the Ming emperors. The third Choson (or Yi Dynasty) ruler, King Sejong (r. 1418–1450) was Korea's greatest sovereign, a patron of art, science and technology during whose reign Korean scholars and craftsmen perfected printing with moveable metal type, invented a syllabic script to write vernacular Korean, and equipped Seoul with what was, for a time, the best astronomical observatory in the world. The Choson monarchs tolerated Buddhism, promoted Confucianism, ruled through a very conservative aristocracy, and remained on the throne until 1910.

In Japan, the Fujiwara-dominated aristocrats of Heian-kyo ignored the rise of a provincial warrior aristocracy in the provinces until it was too late. The Fujiwaras were ousted by the western Taira clan in 1160; they in turn were defeated by Minamoto no Yoritomo at the naval battle of Danno-Ura in 1185. Yoritomo then took the hereditary title of *shogun* ("generalissimo"), and established a military capital at Kamakura, leaving the emperors to reign but not rule in Heian-kyo. The Minamoto were shunted aside by their own hereditary retainers, the *Hojo Clan*, in 1229. A crisis was precipitated in 1331 by Emperor Daigo II, who refused to abdicate on command of the shogun, and attempted to institute direct imperial rule. In 1333 another general, Ashikaga Takauji, helped Daigo II overthrow the Hojo, but Ashikaga then promptly proclaimed himself shogun, moved the military capital to the Muromachi district of Kyoto, and put the emperors firmly in their place once again. The *Muromachi* shogunate endured until 1568, though with little military power; the shoguns were better known as patrons of Zen Buddhism, Noh theater, and the tea ceremony. With the waning of central authority, Japanese merchants were more free to establish domestic and overseas trade routes (and to engage in piracy on the China coast), leading to economic prosperity amidst political instability.

▶ THE EXPANSION OF THE WEST AND THE ENDURANCE OF THE EAST (1500–1650)

During this period, the great empires of Asia—Ottoman Turkey, Safavid Persia, Mogul India and Ming China—remained intact and even expanded, but the dynamic power and movement of this extraordinary age were driven by the emerging nation-states of Europe. Despite severe internal divisions both religious (the Reformation) and national, which led to incessant warfare among all of them, the major powers managed to dominate the sea lanes of the globe and control the coasts and islands of Africa, southern Asia, and the Americas.

The Near East: Ottoman Empire and Safavid Persia

Under their sultans Selim I the Grim (1512–20) and Suleiman I the Magnificent (1520–66) the Ottoman Turks added Syria and Egypt to their domains, then from their fortress at Belgrade launched an invasion of Hungary which climaxed at the battle of Mohacs (1526), where over 20,000 Christian soldiers were slain and three-quarters of the realm fell under Turkish rule either directly or through Ottoman client princes of Transylvania. The Turks moved on to besiege Vienna (1529), halting the campaign because of troubles with Persia. On the seas Turkish fleets added Yemen and Aden on the Persian Gulf and Tripoli, Algeria, and Tunis on the southern shores of the Mediterranean.

But Suleiman's successor was Selim II (the Sot), the first in a series of weak sultans who came to the throne between 1566–1718 as a result of that perennial weakness of Moslem dynasties, harem intrigues of wives and eunuchs, and of the specifically Ottoman problem, the "praetorian guard" of Janissaries. In 1571, the Holy League (the Papacy, Venice, Tuscany and Spain) triumphed over the Turkish navy in the battle of Lepanto, though dissolution of the League after the victory meant that the Ottoman fleet could still raid almost at will through the Mediterranean.

Persia saw the revival of a native Iranian dynasty under the *Safavid Dynasty* (1501–1736). Its founder Shah Ismail seized power from the White Sheep Turks in 1501 and successfully defended Persia from Ottoman expansion into Mesopotamia, a work continued under his son and successor (1514–55). After the reign of the dynasty's greatest representative, Abbas I the Great (1587–1629), there began a period of harem intrigues which greatly weakened the dynasty. The Turks succeeded in taking Baghdad (1638).

Christian trading presence in Persia began with the Portuguese establishment at Hormuz in 1507; by 1622 the Portuguese were turned out by Abbas, English merchants supplanting them.

Mogul India and the Portuguese Spice Trade

In 1526, a descendent of Genghis Khan attacked the sultan at Delhi and established his dominance east of the Indus. Though a Turk, because of the long association of his family with the Mongols, his empire came to be called the *Mogul Empire* (1526–1857). Babur (b. 1483–1530), the founder then expanded east to the borders of Bengal. Although his son lost almost all Babur had conquered, his grandson Akbar (1556–1605), contemporary of Philip II of Spain and Elizabeth of England, restored Babur's realm and expanded it further until it included all of India north of the Deccan Plateau. Vigorous in warfare, gracious in victory, wise in administration, tolerant in religion, Akbar's empire knew peace and prosperity. Most of the Deccan was added in the reign of his grandson Shah Jahan (1628–58), who also built the Taj Mahal.

It seems almost miraculous that Portugal, a tiny state on the edge of the Atlantic, should create a seaborne empire dominating the Indian Ocean, but that is what Portugal did in the 16th century. In 1497, Vasco da Gama (c. 1469–1524) began a journey that took him around Africa's Cape of Good Hope and across the Indian Ocean to Calicut where he encountered the great riches of India's spice trade. After da Gama's second voyage (1502), the Moslem state of Gujerat, allied with Mameluke Egypt, declared a *jihad* against the Portuguese, but at Diu, the Portuguese won a complete victory (1508). The Portuguese viceroy organized the building of a "rosary" of over a dozen forts stretching form Hormuz on the Persian Gulf through Goa to Malacca on the Malay Peninsula. Thus the Portuguese could monopolize the carrying trade in the Indian Ocean as well as divert the spice trade around Africa. And from Malacca they established trading posts in the Spice Islands (Moluccas), China and Japan. This network provided the route for Christian missionaries as well.

But it proved all too much for Portugal. The English and the Dutch had established their East India Companies in 1600 and 1602 and in the 17th century the Dutch, piecemeal, took the place of the Portuguese by war and diplomacy. One portent for the future: by 1639 the English were at Madras.

East Asia: China, Korea, Japan

The late Ming emperors were great patrons of culture, but mediocre rulers. The former Chinese protectorate of Annam, while maintaining its mandarin culture, became independent, the first true monarchy of Vietnam. In 1557 the Portuguese established a trading colony at Macao (due to revert to Chinese rule in 1999). The danger to China from Mongolia, from where Altan Khan (1543–83) raided almost annually across the Great Wall, was kept in check by adroit Ming diplomacy, and further allayed by the Mongol acceptance of Tibetan religious authority; with the spread of Lamaism, monasteries absorbed surplus sons who might otherwise have become warriors. But danger lurked in the lands north of Korea, where descendants of the 12th-century Jurched rulers of the *Jin Dynasty* were forming a new tribal confederation of people who would become known as *Manchus*. Their chieftain Nurhachi took the title of emperor; his son brought all of Mongolia under his rule, overran Korea in 1627, and took the Ming northeastern outpost of Mukden in 1636.

Domestically in China, a combination of rising imperial expenditures and increasing land tax evasion by the rural gentry eventually destabilized even so rich an empire as the Ming. Factionalism and eunuch intrigues in the capital weakened the dynasty further; popular rebellions broke out and were not thoroughly suppressed. In desperation, the last Ming emperor invited a Manchu army to Beijing to expell a rebel band that had seized the city. Having expelled the rebels, the Manchus refused to leave. The Ming emperor hanged himself, and the Manchus proclaimed the founding of the *Qing Dynasty* (1644–1911). Ming resistance in southern China was quashed by 1661; all Chinese men were required to braid their hair in a queue as a sign of submission.

During the last decades of the Ming, China began to feel the first effects of European influence. The Jesuit missionary Matteo Ricci reached Macao in 1582 and Beijing in 1601. Adapting himself to local custom, he became an accomplished Confucian scholar and used that guise as a means of introducing to China such things as the astrolabe, the weight-driven clock, prisms, and the Mercator map of the world. For a brief time Christianity became a vogue among some members of the mandarin class, but imperial disapproval (exacerbated by factional disputes among the Christian missionary orders) discouraged conversions. Under Qing the Jesuits were prohibited from preaching, but allowed to remain in China for their technical skills in astronomy, mathematics, painting, and cannon-founding.

In Korea, the *Choson Dynasty* was badly shaken by a destructive invasion (1592–98) from Japan under the leadership of the shogun Toyotomi Hideyoshi. The invasion was finally repelled with Chinese aid, but Korea suffered long-term economic and social damage. Conquered by the Manchus in 1627, the Koreans had no difficulty in transferring their loyalty from the Ming to the Qing; Choson remained a loyal vassal of China, and isolated from the rest of the world, until the late 19th century.

Japan borrowed the old Chinese term "Warring States Period" to describe the century from 1467 to 1568, when Muromachi rule dissolved in a welter of mutually hostile feudal domains. Order was gradually restored after 1568 by three remarkable generals: Oda Nobunaga, who was the first Japanese general to use firearms extensively in battle; Toyotomi Hideyoshi, a peasant who rose to rule Japan, only to squander his resources in a fruitless invasion of Korea; and Tokugawa Ieyasu, who defeated Hideyoshi's army at the Battle of Sekigahara in 1600 and established the Tokugawa shogunate, military rulers of Japan until 1868. The Tokugawa period is sometimes known as the *Edo Period*, after its capital (now Tokyo).

Japan readily absorbed European influence in the sixteenth century. The Portuguese arrived as traders in 1543; another Jesuit, Francis Xavier (1506–52) began his mission to the Japanese in 1549. Within three decades the number of Catholic converts, including some members of the high military aristocracy, reached 150,000. Thereafter Hideyoshi began to suppress Christianity as a foreign threat, banishing Portuguese missionaries in 1587. The Tokugawa shoguns persecuted Christianity even more fiercely, executing thousands after 1612 and driving the church underground after the Christian Shimabara Uprising of 1637–38 ended in an appalling slaughter. Thereafter no foreigners were allowed in Japan except for a small number of Dutch traders, who were rigorously confined to an island in Nagasaki harbor.

Africa's Time of Troubles 1500–1650

The Portuguese sea route to the east diverted attention from the earlier trading contacts with Africa where Portuguese traders brought cotton goods and metal manufactures to exchange for ivory and gold as far as the delta of the Niger river, and where, further south, at the mouth of the Congo, a Bantu-speaking Christian state developed after 1483. And the new world of the Americas, the Spanish Caribbean and Portuguese Brazil, provided a large market for traffic in human beings: the *slave trade* which the Portuguese monopolized until the Dutch drove them out of the Gold Coast in 1642. African slavery, once the result of tribal warfare, now became its cause. First the Portuguese, then the Dutch and, after 1562, the English encouraged tributary states along the west coast to provide them with workers for new world plantations.

The trading *Kingdom of Songhay* which had reached its greatest extent under Askia Mohammed and Askia Dawud in the 16th century was smashed by a Moroccan invasion in 1591. The fall of Songhay brought decline further east to the *Kingdom of Kanem (Bornu)* in the savanna surrounding Lake Chad after 1617. The paradoxical result was the decline of Islamic influence for with the destruction of the Moslem towns the old caravan routes across the Sahara dwindled to a trickle. Further south, the Portuguese established themselves on the west and east coasts in *Angola* (1574) and Mozambique (1508) and after 1628 reduced to vassal status the *Kingdom of the Makaranga* which stretched from the Zambesi to the Limpopo with its capital at Great Zimbabwe. At Africa's southern tip the Dutch established themselves, founding Capetown in 1652.

The Americas: Europe's New Provinces

The Treaty of Tordesillas (1494) between Spain and Portugal divided the world by a line 370 leagues west of the Azores, establishing monopolies for Spain westward and Portugal eastward of the line, approximately 45 degrees west longitude. Thus Brazil, not discovered until 1500, accidentally, by Pedro Cabral (c. 1467–c. 1520) on a voyage to India, became Portuguese territory. But the new world seemed a dead end: the shores of the Caribbean were clearly not the islands and coasts of Asia, the Spanish westward route to the Indies bumped up against an apparently interminable barrier, the Americas.

What altered the picture entirely were the events of 1519–22. In 1520, Ferdinand Magellan (c. 1480-1521) sailed around the southern tip of South America, bringing the Spanish to the Philippines and the Moluccas across the Pacific. Then in 1521, the *conquistador* (conqueror) Hernando Cortez's (1485–1547) brutally subdued the Aztec Empire in 1521. When Francisco Pizarro (1476–1541) toppled the Inca Empire in 1534, Spain acquired a stupendous world empire the wealth of whose silver mines dwarfed the riches of the Indies.

Organized into two vice-royalties, the *Spanish Empire* granted *encomiendas* or plantations to the conquerors; although enslavement of the Indians was forbidden, the Spanish reduced them to serflike status and forced them to work for their new lords. Christian missions were immediately established with such success that over 20 bishoprics had been created by the mid-16th century. Five universities were flourishing by the middle of the 17th century.

France also sent exploratory ventures to America led by Giovanni da Verrazano (1524) and Jacques Cartier (1534); but it was not until the 17th century that a permanent settlement was established by Samuel de Champlain (1567–1635) who founded New France (1608) with a capital at Quebec. Missions began in 1615 but the process of christianing the Indians met with no such success as did the Spanish endeavor although Jesuits were involved here. Jean de Brébeuf's conversion of the Huron tribe only exposed them the more to the Iroquois savagery who undid his work and that of Isaac Jogues among the Mohawks. The establishment of Montreal made that more westward site the focus of the fur trade on which the economy of New France was based. Earlier the French began colonizing the Lesser Antilles, right

on the fringe of the Spanish Empire and by 1656 had colonized a dozen.

England's Queen Elizabeth (1558–1603) limited herself to encouraging courtiers like Sir Humphrey Gilbert and Sir Walter Raleigh in their ill-fated attempts at early settlement (Roanoke I., 1585) and pirates and slave traders like Sir Francis Drake and Sir John Hawkins in their plundering Spanish ships. Not until the Stuart Dynasty (1603–49) did English settlement begin in earnest. Through grants to commercial companies and individual proprietors, the English established colonies from the Chesapeake to Maine broken only by the Swedes on the lower Delaware River and the Dutch in the Hudson Valley. The Chesapeake became the center of a thriving agricultural region based upon tobacco, while New England flourished as a haven for the English Calvinists known as Puritans.

Europe in the Age of the Reformation

The Europe whose sea-borne enterprise established the first truly world-wide empires was a civilization menaced from without by the Ottoman Turks and divided within both by dynastic-national rivalries and the sundering of Christian unity by the *Reformation*. For many years, leading members of the church had cried out for reform of the clergy, who often led scandalous lives amidst great wealth and who sold God's forgiveness (indulgences) for cash. But not even the powerful voices of the Dutch humanist Desiderius Erasmus (1466–1536) or the English statesman Sir Thomas More (1478–1535) had any impact.

In 1517, the call of the Augustinian monk Martin Luther (1483-1546) for a cleansing of the Church on the basis of his doctrine of "salvation by faith alone" (with its implication of the worthlessness of the priesthood and the sacramental system) swept across northern Germany from the Rhine to the Memel; the adherence of the Scandinavian monarchies to the new faith made the Baltic almost a Lutheran lake. The English king Henry VIII (1509–47), while anti-Lutheran, severed his realm from the Catholic Church after 1532. But what secured Protestantism's hold in Europe was the work of John Calvin (1509–64) who, from 1541 until his death, made Geneva a theocratic state and directed the spread of Calvinism to France, the Low Countries and the British Isles.

The attempts of the Holy Roman Emperor Charles V (1519–56) to halt the spread of Lutheranism were hampered by his need to defend the West against the Ottoman Turks (and thus not offend the Lutheran princes) and to maintain his dynastic territories against the kings of France who allied with the Turks against him. For he ruled the Netherlands and Spain in addition to holding the office of Emperor. At his abdication he willed the Empire to his brother Ferdinand along with Habsburg holdings in central Europe; Spain with its empire, both in the new world and Europe (Netherlands, Burgundy, Milan and Naples), he willed to his son Philip II (1556–98).

Philip faced rebellion in the Netherlands where by the end of his reign the northern provinces had all but won their independence while the southern provinces were held. His Armada (1588) against England met disaster, thereby confirming Queen Elizabeth's rule and the triumph of Protestantism in both England and Scotland. France was given over to the Wars of Religion (1562–98) in which Philip ineffectively intervened on the Catholic side against the Calvinists; the upshot was victory for the Calvinist claimant Henry IV (1589–1610) who, however, turned Catholic but issued the Edict of Nantes (1598) granting French Calvinists ("Huguenots") equal rights, even to the extent of maintaining their own armies.

Philip II considered himself the Catholic champion and it was during his reign that the Catholic *Counter-Reformation* made its greatest strides, not politically but ecclesiastically. Spanish religious leadership came from the new Jesuit Order founded in 1540 by Ignatius Loyola (1491–1556), a fertile source of missionaries, preachers, scholars and schoolmasters, and from the great mystic theologians Theresa of Avila and John of the Cross. Institutionally the *Council of Trent* (1545–63), while not healing the breach with the Protestants, managed to reform the most gratuitous abuses in the Church and provide a clear and authoritative expression of Catholic belief that would last for two centuries.

The uneasy balance between the opposing forces at the start of the 17th century broke down, provoking a time of great crisis. Germany and the Empire were devastated by the Thirty Years' War (1618–48) in which the triumph of the Catholic Habsburgs was prevented by the interventions of Lutheran Sweden and Catholic France personified by King Gustavus Adolphus of Lutheran Sweden and Cardinal Richelieu of France. Britain was shaken by the struggle between Anglicans and Puritans religiously, between the Stuart kings and Parliament politically, the climax coming in the English Civil Wars (1642–49) where the Puritan victory entailed the beheading of King Charles I and the establishment of a military dictatorship under Oliver Cromwell (1649–58).

In eastern Europe there was instability as well. After the long reign of Ivan IV the Terrible (1533–84) in which the entire Volga came under Russian rule and expansion began beyond the Ural Mountains, Russia underwent its "time of troubles." The nobles ("boyars") whose power he thought he had broken rose again to prominence under his weaker son Theodore and confusion as to the succession permitted Polish penetration deep into Russia until the national assembly in 1613 elected Michael Romanov, founder of the *Romanov Dynasty* (1613–1917). In Poland, under Sigismund II (1548–72), the spread of the Reformation was checked and Lithuania was united with Poland into a single state (1569). But Sigismund was the last of the Jagellonian dynasty and at his death the monarchy became in fact what it had always been in theory, elective and thus increasingly the plaything of other great powers. From 1587 to 1648 two members of the Catholic branch of Sweden's royal family, the Vasas, ruled in Poland. Their interventions in Swedish affairs and in Russia during the time of trouble made significant enemies for Poland.

It was a Polish priest, Copernicus (1473–1543) who stands at the beginning of the *Scientific Revolution*, overturning the ancient cosmology of Ptolemy for the heliocentric theory. Expanded by the work of the Dane Tycho Brahe (1546–1601) and his scientific heir, the German Johannes Kepler (1571–1630), the movement reached its first climax in the system of the Italian Galileo (1564–1642), the greatest scientist of the age.

It was also the age of the great flowering of the vernacular literatures of Europe, especially in epic poetry and the drama: in England, Spenser and Shakespeare; in Italy, Ariosto and Tasso; in Spain, Cervantes, Lope de Vega, and Calderon; in Portugal, Camoens. Ironically, this turbulent age also saw the magnificent flowering of painting and sculpture from the universal genius of Michelangelo (1475–1564), the sculptor Bernini (1598–1680), and the painters Raphael, Titian (c. 1490–1576), El Greco (c. 1541–1614), Velasquez (1599–1660), Rubens (1577–1640), and Rembrandt (1606–69).

▶ EXPANSION OF THE EUROPEAN WORLD HEGEMONY (1650–1815)

The period in Europe was characterized by the predominance of France, absolutist at the start, revolutionary at the close—a dominance that was as much cultural as it was political. In the western hemisphere, the age saw the maturing of the colonial extensions of western civilization, with the British dominating the north and the Spanish the south. In Africa and the Middle East, western influence grew primarily through trade, principally British controlled. And in the great land mass of Eurasia, two huge empires grew, those of Russia and China.

Europe in Enlightenment and Revolution

The religious wars of the previous period had a double effect: the boundaries of religious division between Catholic and Protestant Europe solidified and there grew up, especially in northwest Europe, men whom the French called *politiques*, seeking peace beyond the reach of religious controversy and division. Parallel with the rise of the politique mentality there had arisen the philosophical movement known as *rationalism* which sought to reconstruct philosophy on the basis of "clear and distinct ideas" (Rene Descartes, 1596–1650). Then came the climax of the scientific revolution in the achievement of Isaac Newton (1642–1727), whose *Principia Mathematica* (1687) united the key ideas of inertia, gravitation, and centrifugal force.

These three streams flowed together in the movement known as the *Enlightenment* whose publicists, called "philosophes," skeptical of all things except reason (and reason understood as the application to all matters of the method of Newton), called all authority into question save their own and subjected all traditional institutions, including the Church, to the corrosive solvents of their argument and mockery.

The man who gave his name to the *Age of Louis XIV* (1661–1715) was no philosopher but an absolute monarch whose court at Versailles became the model for sovereigns across Europe, establishing a French cultural dominance more significant than her political power. Not that the latter was insignificant: in a series of four wars the "Sun King" expanded France's frontiers to the Rhine and his Bourbon dynasty to the throne of Spain. It took alliances of almost all Europe to limit him even to this, alliances organized principally by the Dutch stadtholder William of Orange who conspired as well with the Protestant English aristocracy to overturn their Catholic king James II, the second of the Stuarts restored after the Cromwellian dictatorship, and install him as William III of England. This event is known as the "Glorious

Revolution" and it turned England essentially into an aristocratic republic dominated by Parliament.

Louis XIV's revocation of the Edict of Nantes (1685) forced the Protestant Huguenots to leave France for Holland, Britain, and Prussia where they became industrious businessmen and artisans; through their dominance of publishing, they laid the basis for the spread of the Enlightenment.

In eastern Europe the age of Louis XIV was principally the story of the decline of Polish and Ottoman power and the rise to dominance of Prussia and Russia in the Baltic region and the new *Habsburg Empire* in the southeast. With the Spanish Habsburgs sliding toward extinction and the Holy Roman Empire rendered ghostly by the Thirty Years' War, the Austrian Habsburgs drove the Ottomans out of Croatia and Hungary (1699) and added Galicia from helpless Poland (1772). Meanwhile, the War of the Spanish Succession (1702–13) which established the Bourbons on the throne of Spain also detached from Spain its holdings in the Netherlands (roughly modern Belgium) and Italy (Milan and Tuscany), awarding both to the Austrian Habsburgs. This unwieldy dynastic empire, so diverse as to lack even a name, is usually called the *Austrian Empire*, though that title was not taken until 1804. The heart of Catholic Baroque culture in art and architecture and music, Austria became in the reign of Joseph II (1765–80) the seat of an enlightened despotism as well.

More an army than a state, Brandenburg excelled in switching alliances: Frederick William the Great Elector gained sovereignty in the Duchy of Prussia from Poland (1660), and his son a royal title there from the Emperor (1701); thus the *Hohenzollern* dynasty's holdings are usually called *Prussia*. Under Frederick II the Great (1740–86), friend and patron of Voltaire, Prussia snatched Silesia from the Habsburgs (1748). Participating in the partitions of Poland (1772,1793,1795) the Hohenzollerns again doubled the size of their dynastic holdings.

Fought on three continents, the Seven Years' War (1756–63) was the first truly world war. In the European theater the alliances (Great Britain and Prussia against France, Austria and Russia) fought to a draw; the war was won overseas: in North America and in India the British drove out the French and established their hegemony. But in attempting to organize her new and gigantic North American holdings (the "new imperial system") Great Britain provoked into rebellion her old coastal colonies whose independence as the United States of America was recognized in the Peace of Paris (1783). (For North American developments afterward, see Part II: U.S. History.)

The French Revolution

A war for independence rather than, as its common name implies, a revolution, the American experience was an odd model for the tumultuous upheaval known as the *French Revolution*. France was the most prosperous state in Europe, but the long series of wars since 1660 combined with the clergy's and the aristocracy's exemption from taxation impoverished the monarchy. As a way out of the impasse, Louis XVI resurrected the old medieval Estates General (1789) but the representatives transformed themselves into a constitutional convention called the National Assembly. After abolishing serfdom, setting the peasants free, they remodeled the French state into a constitutional monarchy. But they also confiscated Church lands, dissolved the monasteries, and attempted to make the Church a department of the state, complete with elected bishops. This tore many devout Catholics away from the revolutionary cause.

The universal appeal of the French Revolution to so many people across Europe frightened the monarchs and encouraged the National Assembly to declare war on them all. The new mass armies of the French, fired by ideology and national pride, were a juggernaut against the old-fangled monarchical armies. At home, the war emergency and a revolt in a pro-royalist area (Vendee) against the newly declared republic were used to justify a Committee of Public Safety led by George Danton (1759–94) and Maximilien Robespierre (1758–94) and its *Reign of Terror* (1793–94); it's first victims were the royal family, including Louis XVI and his wife Marie Antoinette. The rule of the Directory (1795–99) that followed was overturned by its general, the Corsican adventurer and military genius Napoleon Bonaparte (1769–1821), who established a popular and military dictatorship (1799) first disguised as a republic, then under the name *French Empire* (1804–15).

Several coalitions of nations were formed to stop Napoleon, but he defeated all of them. Coalition after coalition broke up in defeat. At its peak, the Empire dominated all of Europe from the English Channel to the Ottoman Empire by incorporation into the Empire, or as satellites, or as allies. But a popular uprising in Spain, supported by Britain, and the failure of Napoleon's invasion of Russia (1812) began the breakup of his Empire. By 1814 the anti-French nationalisms that conquest had evoked and the recovery of the monarchs' courage brought Napoleon down and, when he returned in 1815, produced his final defeat at Waterloo (1815) at the hands of the first Duke of Wellington (1769–1852).

Scarcely noticed, another and perhaps more powerful revolution was already under way before the period ended. Enlightened British landowners were enclosing the commons (the village lands tenant farmers used to graze cattle) and developing new crops while inventors were creating the machinery (the spinning jenny, the waterframe, and the steam engine) which would provide the basis in the following period for the *Industrial Revolution*.

Europe Overseas: The Americas and Africa

Between the crises of the Cromwellian period (1643–60) and the Glorious Revolution (1688) the Stuart kings of England fostered new proprietary grants in the Hudson Valley, in Pennsylvania, and in the Carolinas. Thereafter the North American colonies became habituated to self-government under their elected assemblies in a period of "salutary neglect" by the home government. Legally colonies, they were in fact mature provinces of Britain overseas. When after the Seven Years' War the government attempted to limit settlement beyond the Appalachians, to tax the colonists for the costs of the enlarged British holdings, and to extend toleration to Catholics in Canada, the colonial resistance led to war and to independence.

The Spanish new world colonies, with new viceroyalties of New Granada (1717) (roughly modern Venezuela, Colombia, and Ecuador) and

La Plata (1776) (Bolivia, Paraguay, Uruguay, and Argentina) remained essentially Indian states governed paternalistically by *Yo, el rey*—the king, in whose name all regulations were sent to the viceroys. After about 1650 Indian population grew rapidly. While rule remained in the hands of "peninsulares" from the home country and, to a lesser degree, in those of the "creoles," colonists of Spanish descent, in the towns, the Indians' chief contact with Spanish culture was in the Church whose missionaries and bishops provided a spiritual elite. Of special note were the Jesuit "reductions" on the upper Parana: self-governing, communistic Catholic Indian republics which fell victim to European politics and Brazilian incursions. Brazil by 1800 had a population larger than Portugal's.

To the viceroyalty of New Spain (Mexico) was attached the Philippines. No one was sure where in the Pacific lay the treaty line of 1494 so that while the Philippines were in fact on the Portuguese side, it was Spain which claimed them in 1565, founding Manila in 1571 which became the western terminus for the famous Manila galleons bearing Mexican silver. Through the whole period coasting voyages of English, Dutch and Spanish mariners discovered the islands of the South Pacific: the Carolines, the Marshalls, Tasmania, New Zealand and Australia; but no settlements disturbed the hunting and gathering culture of the Stone Age people who inhabited them.

It was otherwise in Africa where the slave trade continued until the end of the period, peaking in the 1780s but with demand dropping decade by decade thereafter. And in the early years of the 19th century Britain, Denmark and the United States abolished the trade, Britain actively but not always effectively blocking the trade along the African coast. In west Africa, there was an Islamic revival in the savanna as the *Fulbe people*, over the century after 1670, spread eastward toward Lake Chad in a series of *jihads* against *Hausa* cities. In south Africa, the *Zulu* nation, utilizing trained infantry units armed with spears established a small empire in the late 1700s over their neighbors who still relied on the hurling of javelins; while the Dutch at the southern tip, with its Mediterranean climate and its few Khoikhoi (Hottentots), built a Dutch-speaking, Calvinist, multi-racial colony which by 1815 had a population of about 80,000. The pioneering "trekboers" beyond the Cape found their expansion limited by the Xhosa people and when the colony passed from the Dutch to the British (1814), British governors attempted to halt the expansion in the name of peace. Finally, on the east coast trade reached inland as far as Lake Victoria, initiated by the Nyamwezi people of Tanzania but falling after 1800 into the hands of the trade network of Oman, an ally of Britain.

Two Eurasian Empires: Russian and Ottoman

In one aspect the development of the Russian Empire was an eastward expansion of Europe, in another it was the creation of a stupendous Oriental state menacing Europe. Russian pioneers had already reached the Pacific by 1637; expansion into Central Asia brought the Russians up against Chinese expansion westward into the same region, peace being established in 1689 by the Treaty of Nerchinsk which set the common boundary along the peaks of the Stanovoi Mountains, the Russians evacuating a fort they had constructed on the Amur. This shifted Russian interests to the northeast, leading eventually to Russian settlements in Canada and California (1805-1912).

A certain important but superficial "westernizing" of Russia took place under Peter the Great (1689-1725) who in a "revolution from above" autocratically imposed upon his land western modes in manufacturing, in political administration, in military techniques, in court manners and even in dress. Russia had already taken the eastern Ukraine including Kiev from Poland (1667), then the portion (1681) that their allies the Ottomans had won in that war. Peter's attempts to gain Azov—the warm-water port on the Black Sea that would provide access to the Mediterranean—from the Ottoman Empire proved ineffectual. But in the Great Northern War (1700-21) he proved more successful against Sweden, establishing Russia on the Baltic and founding a new capital at St. Petersburg.

Under Catherine II the Great (1762-96), another "enlightened despot" favored by Voltaire, Russia fought a war with the Ottoman Empire. The Treaty of Kuchuk Kainarji (1774) established Russia in the Crimea along the north of the Black Sea, granted navigation rights to Russia in Turkish waters, including the Straits into the Mediterranean, and provided a legal basis for Russia to intervene to protect Orthodox Christians in the provinces of Moldavia and Walachia—i.e. most of what Peter the Great wanted. Catherine also participated in the partitions of Poland (1772, 1793, 1795) which obliterated that ancient Christian state.

In a third stage of expansion Russia took Finland (1809) from Sweden and Bessarabia (1812) from the Ottomans during the Napoleonic Wars. After the invasion of Russia (1812) the czar Alexander I participated in the great coalition that at last brought Napoleon down. In 1815 Russian troops were participating in the occupation of Paris and the Polish Kingdom that emerged from the post-war settlement had Alexander as its king.

The Russian ascendancy was paralleled by Ottoman decline. Of the dozen sultans who ruled between 1648 and 1839 only Selim III (1789-1807) was a man of intelligence and vigor. The period began with misleading signs of strength, as the Turks took Podolia from Poland (1672) and advanced against the Habsburgs, climaxing in the siege of Vienna (1683). The failure of the siege proved a real turning point, the beginning of a long slow sag in Ottoman fortunes that made it by the 19th century "the sick man of Europe." Facing war after war against Austria and Russia (often in tandem) in the west and Persia in the east, the Empire yielded territory, strained its already chaotic finances, and developed a defensive mentality. Its domestic power waned as well as frontier garrisons meant for defense had to be used to suppress rebellions and endemic banditry.

The year after the siege of Vienna was lifted, the Austrians were victorious in the second Battle of Mohacs (1684) which reversed that of 1526, a victory confirmed by the Battle of Zenta (1697): Hungary and Croatia fell away. After the Treaty of Kuchuk Kainarji (1774), the Black Sea was no longer a Turkish lake and Russian ships sailed freely through Ottoman waters. Egypt, temporarily independent in 1769, gained its autonomy in 1805 while Serbia became the first Christian Balkan state to gain autonomy. Even Arabia, the original homeland of Islam, slipped from Ottoman rule as the Saud clan provided the political and economic support necessary for *Wahhabism* which sought a return to the primitive theocracy of the Prophet himself.

The Growth of British Influence in the Middle East and India

With the Portuguese control of the spice route in disarray and the Dutch diverted toward the Spice Islands, British commercial interests grew ascendant in India. Bombay became the headquarters of the *East Indian Company* (1661) from which Calcutta was founded (1690). But not uncontested: the French founded their East India Company in 1664 and established a trading post at Pondichery in 1674.

The Safavid Persian Empire with which the British East India Company had established trade in 1616 entered after 1664 a decline like that which had earlier begun in the Ottoman realm.

In the long reign of Mogul emperor Aurangzeb (1659–1707) the empire had reached its greatest territorial extent, principally through conquests in the Deccan plateau in south-central India. But within the empire his rule was weak as local governors grew increasingly independent. The Maratha people, under their raja Sivadi, established an independent Hindu state against which the emperor waged inconclusive war until his death, and the religious order of Sikhs (blending Hindu and Moslem beliefs) became under Govind Singh a military order.

After Aurangzeb's death Mogul decline became precipitous. Afghanistan became independent in 1709 then invaded Persia (1722) its leader, Mir Mohammed, becoming shah in 1725. With the death of the last Safavid in 1736 the general Nadir Shah reestablished rule over Afghanistan and even invaded India (1738). But all proved ephemeral. With his death Persia came under the rule of the *Zand Dynasty* (1750–94), then the *Kajar Dynasty* (1794–1925) under whom Great Britain gained the right by treaty (1814) to negate any Persian treaty contrary to her interests. The Afghans (1809) became British allies, bound to assist Britain were Persia or France to attack India.

In India during the 18th century the Maratha state became the dominant Indian body, collecting taxes (1720) in Southern India. Nadir Shah's invasion (1738) wrested the north and west from the Moguls. In the turmoil, the European companies began forming private armies of Indian troops ("sepoys") under European officers. After the War of the Austrian Succession (1746–48) French forces ruled virtually the entire south. But in the Indian theater of the Seven Years' War (1756–63) Robert Clive (1725–74) roundly defeated the French; the Treaty of Paris left but a few holdings to the French. In the aftermath, the East India Company gained from the *nawab* (viceroy) of Bengal landowner status over Calcutta, then pensioned off the *nawab* and ruled Bengal directly (1764).

During this struggle the Afghans invaded from the northeast establishing their rule over the Maratha and Sikhs (1761–62). Faced with the two foreign powers most Indian princes gravitated towards the British, a movement not halted by Parliament's India Act (1784) which brought the Company under government control and prohibited it from interfering in Indian affairs or from engaging in war. Still, between 1786 and 1813, the Company's governors-general began a judicial system, gained control over the foreign affairs of most southern principalities in return for British protection, and entered into the treaties with Persia and Afghanistan already mentioned.

In reality, there was no British empire. The Company ruled directly only certain territories whose princes could not secure peace and order and established treaty obligations with other princes. There were no missionaries, no conversions—not even British law: an odd combination of feelings of superiority with respect for Indian culture led to a hands-off policy. And to the Hindus, the British were but another caste.

Chinese Expansion, Japanese Isolation (1650–1800)

The Manchu emperors of China adapted themselves rapidly to the ancient system of empire government, maintaining the examination system for the bureaucracy (though sometimes doubling officials, one Manchu, one Chinese). So serene and sensible (and non-theological) did the Manchu state appear to the European mind that it almost rivaled England in their fantasies.

Taiwan was annexed in 1683, Tibet gradually brought under Chinese control (1705-51) the emperor controlling succession of the Dalai Lamas. But the great expansion was into central Asia, settled diplomatically with the Russians in 1689 to China's advantage. All this was the work of Kang Xi, the contemporary of Louis XIV.

Under Qian Long, who ruled from 1736-95, Burma had to recognize Chinese overlordship (1769) as did Nepal (1792). Burma had only recently been re-united (1753) and that with British assistance to Alaungpaya, so the relationships became an avenue of British influence. At the same time Annam, largely Chinese in culture and recognizing its overlordship, nonetheless permitted Catholic missions which met with surprising success especially after Gia Long emerged as emperor in 1802.

The whole period was for China one of expansion, not only territorially. In agriculture new crops from the Americas (maize and yams) provided a larger and more diversified food supply, though by the end of the period population was pressing up against its limits. Trade with Europe and with Japan, carried in Portuguese ships, was based upon Chinese exports of tea, silk and porcelain, the latter increasingly produced on a mass basis in imperial and private kilns. But China showed little interest in the outside world. The late 19th-century mission of the British diplomat Lord George MacCartney was met with total indifference. China would soon suffer badly from this imperial self-satisfaction. The papacy's finding (1715) that reverence shown toward Confucius or toward one's ancestors was incompatible with Catholic belief led to the ban of Catholic missionaries in 1720.

In Japan the splendid isolation of the Tokugawa period continued. But the internal peace that they enforced left the samurai warriors functionless, increasingly dissolute and in debt to the thriving merchant class. The heyday of the latter in the *Genroku Period* (1688-1704) led to a flourishing of Japanese literature free of Chinese influence: the development of haiku poetry, especially under the master Matsui Basho (1644-94) and of the Kabuki drama. Late in the period there were signs of restiveness against the Tokugawa not only from the great clans excluded from power but from the imperial family as well, both merging patriotic feeling and imperial loyalty with the increasing vogue of the Shinto religion, both worried about the danger of the Westerners to Japan's isolated development.

▶ TRIUMPH AND TRAGEDY OF WESTERN CIVILIZATION (1815–1945)

With the defeat of Napoleon in 1815, Europe entered 100 years of peace, the ending of serfdom, the extraordinary development of industrial capitalism, the spread of liberal and democratic institutions, and the apogee of her world-wide imperial influence. But then ensued 30 years of tumultuous upheaval: two world wars, waged with new weapons of mass destruction, flanking the subjection of most of Europe to grim totalitarian domination. At the end Europe lay broken and prostrate, its fate and the fate of the world in the hands of the two atomic superpowers, liberal-democratic America and Communist Russia.

Europe: The Rise of Nationalism

After a quarter-century of exhausting warfare the conservative monarchs and statesmen of Britain, Austria, Prussia and Russia made a generous peace with France, restoring the Bourbon dynasty but hedging her borders with an enlarged Netherlands to the north, the Prussians on the Rhine and the Habsburgs in northern Italy. To maintain the peace they established the Concert of Europe, a series of international conferences (to which France was soon admitted) to regulate European affairs, initiating the longest sustained general European peace since Rome's Antonine emperors in the second century A.D. Fearing revolution as the source of war and so a threat to themselves, they suppressed liberal and nationalist organizations and sent troops into Italy and Spain to prop up their tottering monarchies; but Britain, supporting the "Monroe Doctrine," prevented any intervention against the revolts in Latin America. With the devolution of the Ottoman Empire in the Balkans, the powers supported an independent Greece (1829) and autonomy for Serbia, Moldavia and Walachia. Similarly, liberal revolts in Belgium and France (1830) led not to suppression but to independence for the first and a change of dynasty for the second; in the same year, however, Russia crushed a Polish revolt and absorbed that state into her empire. Britain herself, without revolution, carried out a liberal reform of her constitution (1832) abolishing "rotten" or underpopulated boroughs and expanding the electorate by 50 percent, especially in the new manufacturing centers.

The year 1848 saw a remarkable series of liberal and nationalist revolts in virtually all the capitals of the German and Italian principalities and of the Habsburg realms. Yet all proved stillborn, and the armies remained loyal to their sovereigns. Still they had lasting effects, as serfdom was abolished throughout central Europe. The liberal route to national unity, which combined political goals (representative government) with nationalist ones seemed discredited; and the 1848 revolt in Paris led to the establishment of a brief Second Republic, then, in a revival of Bonapartism, a *Second Empire* (1852–70) under Napoleon III (Louis Napoleon Bonaparte, 1808–73).

His assistance was essential in aiding Pied-

mont's conquests of all the Italian states save Venice and Rome; the *Kingdom of Italy* was proclaimed in 1861 and by 1870 it included Venice and Rome as well. The latter two it gained as an ally of Otto von Bismarck's (1815–98) Prussia, which in a series of three brief wars incorporated all of non-Habsburg Germany into the *German Empire*, proclaimed in 1871. The third of those wars (the Franco-Prussian war), took Alsace and Lorraine from France, toppled Napoleon III, and led to the formation of France's *Third Republic* (1871–1940). The second, which had excluded Austria from German affairs, led that empire to its own reform, the establishment in 1867 of the "Dual Monarchy" of *Austria-Hungary*.

In one decade the map of Europe had been transformed, its most powerful state the new Germany which, with rapid industrialization, became stronger still in the years which led up to the World War I.

Europe: Two World Wars, 1914–45

Bismarck attempted to keep France isolated. He encouraged her colonial expansion to compensate for her diminished status in Europe and in the hope that imperial rivalry with Britain would keep those western states apart. He hoped for similar results from Russian and British rivalry in Persia and Afghanistan. And he formed the Triple Alliance of Germany, Austria-Hungary, and Italy.

But France and Russia allied in 1894 and a decade later, after settling colonial issues that had nearly brought them to war, France and Britain came too a "friendly understanding." The triangle was completed in 1907 when Britain and Russia established spheres of influence in Persia. Bismarck's diplomacy was undone by Kaiser Wilhelm II's (r. 1888–1918) aggressive foreign policy and a naval arms race with Britain.

Not in the colonies but in the Balkans events moved beyond any statesman's ability. In the disintegration of Ottoman power there, Serbia, Romania and Montenegro became independent in 1878 and Bulgaria in 1908. The powers consistently checked Russian advances there while the influence of Austria-Hungary grew. Struggling for territory from the Ottomans and from each other, the Balkan states fought a series of three wars in 1912, 1913 and 1914. It was the third one, which began with the assassination of the Archduke Francis Ferdinand in Sarajevo by a Serbian nationalist that expanded into the catastrophe of World War I.

Outside Europe fighting was slight: German holdings in the Pacific and Africa were taken by British and French imperial forces; Russian and British forces engaged the Ottomans in Mesopotamia and Armenia; and western-backed Arab revolts further weakened Ottoman strength. But in Belgium and northern France developed the horror of four years of trench warfare and on the gigantic eastern front immense armies clashed but without resolution until 1917 when the Bolsheviks, led by Vladimir I. Lenin (1870–1924), took Russia out of the war after their revolution (Nov. 6, 1917) toppled the Provisional Government that had succeeded the czarist collapse. But Russia's withdrawal in the east was balanced in the west by the American entry that same year, provoked by Germany's resumption of unrestricted submarine warfare in a futile attempt to escape the noose of Britain's naval blockade. The fighting at last ended November 11, 1918.

Besides its immense cost in blood (over eight

million died in battle and six million civilians perished) and treasure, the war overturned the old European state system as four empires collapsed and were partitioned. Germany, under the Versailles Treaty (1919) emerged as the Weimar Republic with small territorial losses to France and to a resurrected Poland but burdened with the war guilt clauses and the immense financial reparations they were meant to justify. Russia lost all her western gains since Peter the Great, retreating eastward into the cruel experiment of Communist Revolution. Austria-Hungary disappeared utterly, two little republics maintaining the names at least of those once great states. And by 1923 in Asia Minor a one-party Turkish Republic emerged under Mustafa Kemal Ataturk (1818–1938).

The successor states in eastern Europe, whether republican or monarchical inform, readily adopted the parliamentary government of the victorious western Allies which, in the years after 1848, had steadily democratized the franchise. But most contained substantial ethnic minorities whose rivalries poisoned parliamentary life; tariff barriers which arose everywhere fragmented the old common markets of the empires they replaced, protecting inefficient, penalizing efficient industry; in agriculture depression was chronic.

To the east brooded the reduced but still vast Soviet Union where with the death of Lenin in 1924 the dictatorship of the party turned increasingly into the dictatorship of Joseph Stalin (1879-1953)who oversaw the murderous collectivization of agriculture and the forced industrialization of the Five Year Plans, then purged the party and the army and the secret police of all but his own men. Millions died.

Western and central Europe seemed sheltered from these grim developments by the "cordon sanitaire" of the new states of east-central Europe. After a period of post-war adjustment, prosperity returned to the western democracies, especially in Germany whose adherence to the Locarno Treaties (1925) presaged enduring peace. Yet in Italy whose wartime sacrifices seemed unrewarded by territorial gains and whose economy did not recover but rather seemed to dissolve into the chaos of socialist and anarchist and capitalist violence there arose in 1922 the second (after Lenin) of the dictators, Benito Mussolini (1883-1945). His fascist movement promised a halfway house between liberal individualism and communist class war, stressing a belligerent nationalism with a corporative economy. In fact it was little more than bombast.

But with the collapse of the world economy after 1929, the social and ethnic divisions of the successor states, their boundary grievances, and the real or imagined fear of communist revolution, most of Europe outside the monarchies of the north and west turned to right-wing authoritarian regimes which, though often called "fascist," resembled Italy less than they did Latin America. The very different and very grievous case was Germany where after 1933 Adolf Hitler (1889-1945) established the Nazi dictatorship in the heart of Europe.

The western democracies dithered, deluded themselves, and sought peace through appeasement (not that they had much alternative, unprepared as they were for military action) as Hitler, bent on overturning the Versailles settlement, successfully re-militarized the Rhineland (1936) and absorbed Austria (the Anschluss) and the ethnically German parts of Czechoslovakia (1938)

then turned the remainder of Czechoslovakia into a satellite, took the city of Memel from Lithuania, and began demands on Poland (1939). In August 1939, Germany and Russia agreed to partition Poland yet again and with Hitler's invasion in September began World War II.

It was, until 1941, a European war with non-stop totalitarian triumphs; by June of 1940, when France fell, all of Europe outside Britain was neutral or an ally or a satellite of Germany. But in June of 1941 Hitler invaded Russia and in December Hitler's ally, Japan, attacked the U.S. in Hawaii. Japanese dominion reached as far as Burma in 1942, while German armies penetrated as far east as Stalingrad. Nevertheless, the grand alliance of Britain and the U.S. with the USSR caused Nazi Germany to fight a two-front war, which ultimately spelled utter defeat in May of 1945—but not before Germany killed six million Jews during the Holocaust. Three months later, atomic bomb attacks on Hiroshima and Nagasaki, major Japanese cities, hastened Japan's surrender and World War II came to its end. The United States and the Soviet Union, with Great Britain a very junior partner, bestrode the globe. The European Age in world history was at an end.

The Troubled Independence of Latin America

The impact of the Napoleonic wars upon Europe's trans-Atlantic provinces (and the newly independent United States as well) was profound. For one thing, Haiti's success in maintaining its independence, gained in 1794, against Napoleon's attempt to reconquer it led to his abandonment of any scheme for a New World empire: Louisiana was therefore sold to the United States. For another, placing his brother Joseph on the throne of Spain (1808) threw South America into confusion: which king to obey? Juntas loyal to the Bourbon king Ferdinand VII, led by creoles such as Simon Bolivar (1783–1830) and Jose San Martin (1778–1850), resisted French rule at first, then turned against the absolutism of the restored Ferdinand in whose name they had first risen up. In colony after colony the juntas' armies fought for and won their independence: La Plata (1810), Chile (1818), New Granada (1819), Peru (1821). In separate and more complicated developments, Mexico and Brazil followed in 1822.

The *Monroe Doctrine* (1823) of the United States, instigated and given force by Great Britain, shielded the new states from Spanish repression. But nothing could shield them from the effects of their own inexperience in politics (an effect of Spanish imperial centralization) or from boundary disputes (for New World boundaries too were purely Spanish creations) or from the internal struggles of local leader (*caudillos*) seeking autonomy within the new republics. Thus independence was followed by a long period of wars, civil wars, insurrections and coups.

When the trade links with Spain were cut, the new states found a welcome from Great Britain for their products. British investment fostered mining and industrial development; American investment entered late in the 19th century. The development in the 1880s of adequate methods of refrigeration on steamships meant that beef could join wheat and sugar and coffee as exports. The needs of the Allies in World War I for massive increases in raw materials brought a great increase in trade; large-scale post-war investment from the United States both in industry and in plantation agriculture helped continue economic growth but with serious decline after 1929 in the rate of growth.

This expansion brought social tension through the growth of both a middle class and agricultural and industrial working classes, adding new elements to the older political instability. In the 1930s governments in Mexico and Argentina respectively followed the "popular front" or "corporate state" models of Europe but these were usually but trappings for a new breed of *caudillo*. In the Caribbean, the interests of the United States predominated whether as "policeman" or, as after 1934, "good neighbor."

European Empires in Africa

For 60 years after the Napoleonic wars, Europeans evinced only small interest in Africa. Liberal economic thought supported free trade rather than empire. Trading forts dotted the west African coasts while steamboats penetrated only somewhat further inland and missionaries began evangelization on a small scale. "Cash crop" agriculture was no European imposition: the profits from nuts and palm products, especially oil for lighting and machine lubrication, were enough to encouragement to African kings and chiefs, especially with the drying up of the trade in slaves. In the south, the expansion of the Zulu nation after 1818 led to disruptions lasting into the 1850s while amongst the Boers in the south, the British ban on slavery provoked the Great Trek of some 10,000 settlers into the high veld, (or grassy plateau) depopulating the old Cape Colony except for some new British settlers. On the east coast the sultan of Oman moved his capital to Zanzibar the better to control his network of trade in cloves and slaves; the latter brought increasing British estrangement from their protege. Along the Mediterranean coast, the Ottoman Empire was nominally sovereign though rule in fact was exercised by local beys and sultans who gladly countenanced piracy; this provoked the French in 1830 to occupy Algiers and a few coastal cities.

About 1880 a group of French projects—a railways scheme at Dakar, new trading posts on the Ivory Coast and north of the Congo river—alarmed the other powers into the witless "scramble for Africa" which brought Britain and Portugal and eventually even Germany into a contest to annex territory, principally to prevent the others from doing the same and gaining some unknown and unpredictable benefit. The Congress of Berlin (1885) sought to put some order into the competition and in 15 years the entire continent had been divided up, save for the colony of freed American slaves in Liberia and the ancient Christian empire of Ethiopia. Colonial theorists gained the ear of western governments for grand schemes of great belts of territory, the French to stretch from Dakar to the Red Sea, the British from Capetown to Cairo—all just after the construction of the Suez Canal (1859–69) had rendered such imaginings nugatory. One specific and concrete interest was the discovery of deposits of gold and diamonds in the republic of Transvaal which led to Britain's conquest of the Boer republics in the Boer War (1889–1901) and her formation (1910) of the Union of South Africa, which through elections Boers soon governed.

There was something illusory about it all: tiny armies setting up the national flag, treaties signed with hundreds of tribal chiefs who lacked authority, boundary lines drawn on maps in European capitals. But European administration did bring some measure of peace, some road and rail construction, some support for missionaries, some schools and hospitals, some westernizing of tribal leaders. The last would provide a certain leadership class in the independence movements after World War II which dismantled the empires even faster than they had been thrown together before World War I.

Europe's Asian Domination and the Rise of Japan

If Africa experienced European claims of sovereignty with only hints of the reality, Asia underwent the reverse as British rule was established in India, Burma and Malaya, Holland's in Indonesia, America's in the islands of the South Pacific (Hawaii, Samoa, and later the Philippines) and France's in Indochina. Two new provinces of western civilization grew in Australia and New Zealand. China underwent yet another cycle of imperial decline but with the new element of the presence of the "southern barbarians" (the Europeans) and the aggressive designs of a suddenly modernized Japan.

Three 19th century wars mark the decline of China's power and prestige. Her attempts to maintain Canton as the sole port for western trade and to end Britain's sale of opium led to the Opium War (1841–42) and a thorough British victory. The Treaty of Nanking opened four further cities to trade and ended the "tribute system," Westerners now accepted as China's equals, with a uniform tariff of 5 percent on trade; in addition Hong Kong was ceded to the United Kingdom. In the aftermath of the war, in 1844 and 1845, the United States gained the right of "extraterritoriality" (exemption from Chinese law) for its citizens, soon extended to all the western states, and the French gained toleration for Catholic Christianity, soon extended to Protestant Christians as well.

The social and economic dislocations caused by the Opium War in south China culminated in the *Taiping Rebellion* (1851-64), led by Hong Xiuquan, a failed examination candidate who, having read some Christian missionary pamphlets, imagined himself to be the younger brother of Jesus Christ. A charismatic figure, he raised a huge army and seized much of southern and central China, including the city of Nanjing. To put down the rebellion the Qing emperor resorted to the very dangerous expedient of allowing provincial governors-general to raise their own military units; these were effective but would prove destabilizing in the future. Some western military assistance helped keep the Taipings away from the trading port of Shanghai.

At the same time China experienced three other major rebellions: Moslem uprisings in the northwest and in Yunnan Province in the southwest, and the millenarian Nian Rebellion in the north-central plains. Total loss of life from these rebellions exceeded 20 million; the dynasty itself barely survived. In 1858, in the midst of this turmoil, the British provoked a small affray called the Arrow War, settled by the Treaty of Tientsin in 1860. The cost was the opening of yet another 11 ports, the legalization of the opium trade, and the collection of China's customs by Great Britain. Sir Robert Hart became, equivalently, China's finance minister through the years 1863–1908.

Japan's attempt to gain concessions like those of the western powers and to challenge Chinese control over the Manchu tributary state of Korea led to the Sino-Japanese War (1894-95): China had to cede Taiwan and certain mainland territories to Japan and recognize the independence of Korea, a prelude to that kingdom's incorporation into Japan in 1910.

Meanwhile in Indochina the French ignored Manchu protests and established protectorates over Annam (1883) and, right on China's border, Tonkin (1893).

After an unsuccessful attempt in 1898 to reform the imperial government, followed by the abortive, anti-western Boxer Rebellion (1900) discontent with the feebleness of the Manchu government led to the *Chinese Revolution* (1911). The new Chinese Republic's president, General Yuan Shih-k'ai, might have established yet another new dynasty but his death in 1916 permitted the republic to continue, at least in form. But in reality it was the return of feudal anarchy, this time with modern weapons and mass political organizations. Dr. Sun Yat-sen's party, the Kuo Min Tang (KMT), came after his death under the control of his brother-in-law, Chiang Kai-shek, the war lord who controlled south China and whose armies conquered the north in 1927. But the expelling of the Communists from the KMT in 1927 led to a failed series of Communist uprisings and their retreat to the northwest in *The Long March* In their new stronghold of Yan'an, Mao Zedong (1893–1976) emerged as the party leader and Chiang's chief rival. Their struggle was submerged in the 1930s by the need to oppose Japanese dominance; Japan in 1931–32 occupied Manchuria as a protectorate and invaded China in 1937. The great powers, especially America, kept up the illusion that China was a great power with Chiang its ruler, an illusion blown to pieces within four years after the end of World War II.

Japan's rise to great power status was rooted in an extraordinary adaptability. After the American Commodore Matthew Perry forced the opening of Japan to western trade in 1853 and 1854 patriotic sentiment, anti-foreign and pro-imperial, grew until in 1867, young patriots at the court of the emperor Mutsuhito felt strong enough to end the shogunate and restore imperial control. From his reigning name, Meiji, we speak of the *Meiji Restoration*. During his long rule until 1912, Japan embarked on a course of furious imitation of western ways, as earlier they had imitated the Chinese; western science, technology, industry and arms became the basis for attaining the goal of "wealthy land, strong army." The imitation reached the extent of inventing (1884) a Japanese peerage so that there might be an upper house on the British model when the Meiji Constitution (1889) established a Diet.

But it was the military (and industrial) aspects, not the political, that showed most rapid advance, providing the basis for triumphs over China (1895) and much more surprisingly Russia (1905), the take-over of some German holdings in the Pacific during World War I, and the incursions against China in the 1930s. The parliamentarianism of the west was repudiated in the reign of Mutsuhito's grandson Hirohito after 1926 as military cliques and gangs came to control government after government and political violence became the order of the day. The attack on Hawaii in December 1941 was designed to cripple the American Pacific fleet, protection for the invasion of southeast Asia which brought Japanese forces by mid-1942 to occupy the American Philippines, the Dutch East Indies, British Hong Kong, Malaya, Singapore and Burma while French Indochina and independent Thailand collaborated. By August 1945 however this whole proud bubble had burst and Japan itself was occupied by American forces.

In India the British kept up the fiction of Mogul rule but proceeded to act more and more like a sovereign power: commencing the repair of the Mogul system of canals (1818) and later building roads and irrigation projects; replacing Persian as the language of law courts with English in the higher courts and local tongues in local courts; founding schools whose curriculum was European and whose language of instruction was English; suppressing, in the 1830s, the funerary suicide of widows, banditry, and murder.

In the 1840s warfare in Afghanistan, in the Sind and against the Sikhs made Britain a true imperial power, the ruling authority in India, protecting Indian princes from subversion and aggression, annexing territory when princely families died out. After the *Great Mutiny* (1857–58) of the sepoys, Britain banished the last of the Moguls. Twenty years later came the symbolic climax, the proclamation (1877) of Queen Victoria as *Empress of India*.

But at the same time the British were establishing executive and legislative councils with Indians represented and courts with Indian justices sitting on the bench. And between the world wars, in which Indian troops fought loyally and with valor on the British side, the Indian National Congress, first established in 1885, came increasingly under the influence of Mahatma Gandhi. His campaigns of civil disobedience in 1921 and in 1930, which only a very liberal empire would have tolerated, presaged the post-war demands that would signal the end of British rule.

More enduring than British India or British rule in Singapore (1819) or Burma (1886) as vehicles of European influence were Australia, a convict colony founded in 1788 which was gradually transformed by generous land grants into the Commonwealth of Australia (1901) and New Zealand where assisted immigration after 1840 and land grants brought dominion status by 1907, both loyally supporting Britain in both of the world wars.

▶THE COLD WAR (1945–PRESENT)

The wartime alliance of Great Britain, France, the United States, and the Soviet Union was one of expediency rather than long-term mutual interest; suspicion and misunderstandings characterized the alliance even during the war. Soon after the war, hostility and divergent interests between the United States and its Western allies, on the one hand, and the Soviet Union, on the other, led to the Cold War, a period of international danger, distrust, and nuclear standoff, during which direct armed conflict was avoided, but wars fought indirectly by proxy nations and movements were endemic.

As the only major power to emerge from World War II with its population, infrastructure, and economy largely intact, the United States saw itself as the leader of the entire postwar world. Its goals, backed by a monopoly on nuclear weapons, included the rapid reconstruction of Western Europe, the fostering of independent and democratic countries in

Eastern Europe, rendering Japan harmless in East Asia, encouraging democratic reform in Nationalist China, and promoting peaceful decolonization in Asia and Africa. The United Nations, organized under American leadership in 1945, was to be the vehicle for a postwar *pax Americana*.

The Soviet Union, devastated by the war, its industrial base and agricultural economy in a shambles, reeling from military and civilian casualties that probably exceeded 20 million persons dead, sought on the other hand to insulate itself behind a band of friendly and submissive neighbors, vowing never again to suffer the kind of invasion that Germany had mounted against the USSR during the war. The Soviet Union also determined to make a concerted effort to match the United States in production of nuclear weapons and delivery systems; the resulting arms race eventually resulted in the production of enough nuclear weapons by the two powers to obliterate the entire population of the world. (Beginning in the 1960s, a series of agreements between the US and the USSR succeeded in limiting the testing and production of nuclear weapons, and greatly reducing their numbers.)

Sharply differing visions of a desirable postwar world thus set the stage for a prolonged conflict between America and the Soviet Union.

In Europe, the Soviet Union's interpretation of the wartime Yalta agreements enabled it to move rapidly to depose fledgling democratic governments in the Eastern European countries under Soviet Occupation; as early as 1946 Winston Churchill warned that an "Iron Curtain" was being drawn around a Soviet zone in Eastern Europe. Soviet power was made credible with the rapid development of atomic weapons, using both Russian research and atomic secrets stolen from America during the war. Pro-USSR communist governments were in place in Poland, Czechoslovakia, Hungary, Yugoslavia, Bulgaria, and Romania by 1947. Austria and Finland accepted a neutral status highly deferential to the Soviet Union; communist movements in Italy, Greece and Turkey were defeated with American and British support.

The United States moved rapidly, especially after the development of the Marshall Plan aid program in 1948, to rebuild the economic and political stability of Western Europe in part to counter Soviet expansionism. A Soviet attempt to blockade the Western occupied zone of Berlin was met with the Berlin Airlift, which preserved a Western presence in the city; thereafter West and East Germany became for the balance of the Cold War in effect two separate and mutually hostile states. The Berlin Wall was built in 1961 to stem a tide of illegal migration from East to West Germany; its fall in 1989 marked the end of the Cold War. Meanwhile the North Atlantic Treaty Organization (NATO) was founded under American leadership in 1949 as a Soviet-containment strategy; it was countered by the organization of the Eastern-bloc Warsaw Pact in 1955. Later popular anti-Soviet uprisings in Hungary (1956), Czechoslovakia (1968), and Poland (1981) were ruthlessly suppressed.

Part of the European price for bowing to American leadership was American acquiescence in the postwar reconstitution of the old colonial empires of Britain, France, the Netherlands, and others. These colonial empires were gradually relinquished during the course of the Cold War, sometimes peacefully, as with the British African colonies, sometimes after bloody nationalist uprisings, as in Portuguese Africa and the French colonies of Algeria and Vietnam. The United States tended to step into the power-vacuum of the post-colonial world, in large part to forestall Soviet influence. The hysteria of McCarthyism in the early 1950s ushered in a long period of reflexive anti-communism that led America to support a series of corrupt, unpopular and repressive—but anti-communist—regimes in various parts of the Third World.

In *Asia*, the simmering conflict between Communist and Nationalist forces in China broke into open civil war by 1946, despite American efforts at mediation. With only grudging material support from the USSR, Chinese Communists under the leadership of Mao Zedong (1893-1976) defeated the far larger and better equipped Nationalists, whose corruption, ineptitude, and bourgeois orientation proved no match for the simple Communist slogan, 'Land to the tiller.' The Nationalists retreated to Taiwan in 1948–49, and Mao proclaimed the founding of the People's Republic of China in Beijing on October 1, 1949. A break between the USSR and the People's Republic of China in the late 1950s, over both geopolitical and ideological issues, did not alter American policy assumptions of a monolithic international communism until the U.S.-Chinese rapprochement of 1973 under the leadership of Pres. Richard M. Nixon.

In Korea, divided after the war into separate occupation zones, a Soviet-backed government led by the veteran communist Kim Il-sung rapidly took control in the north, whereas in the south an inept and ill-prepared American occupation squandered the opportunity for democratic development, and eventually backed the corrupt right-wing movement of Singman Rhee. When North Korean troops invaded the south on June 25, 1950, the United States successfully obtained United Nations backing to rescue the south; the Korean War ensued, fought to a bloody standoff over the next three years.

The "loss" of China and the Korean war transformed American policy in Japan, which was suddenly seen as the anchor of a democratic and capitalist pro-American security zone surrounding communist Asia. India and Pakistan were similarly wooed by Britain and America. Elsewhere in Asia, communist-inspired uprisings in Malaysia and the Philippines were defeated, while an indigenous anti-communist backlash led to the slaughter of tens of thousands of people in Indonesia in 1965. But it was Vietnam that would prove to be the Asian battleground of the Cold War. After the French withdrawal in 1954, America felt impelled to step in to halt what seemed to be a clear case of international communist subversion of a friendly country; the results were devastating to all concerned, and in retrospect the Vietnamese communist movement seems certainly not to have been merely a cat's-paw for the Soviet Union and Communist China. The Soviet Union found its own "Vietnam" in Afghanistan, where its long attempt to install a communist government met with utter failure.

In *Latin America*, the 1959 triumph of Fidel Castro's Cuban revolution struck the American government as an unacceptable provocation on its own doorstep. The failed Bay of Pigs invasion of anti-Castro partisans trained by the CIA was a humiliation for American policy (1961). In 1954 the

Russians had exploded a hydrogen bomb, and in 1957 Sputnik proclaimed the success of Soviet rocketry; the 1960 U.S. presidential election was held in an atmosphere of fear of Russian nuclear missiles. In 1962 the Cuban Missile Crisis was the most potentially deadly confrontation of the entire Cold War. Emboldened by success in that face-off, America intervened militarily to counter what it regarded as communist subversion in Guatemala, El Salvador, Nicaragua, Grenada, and elsewhere in Latin America.

In *Africa*, both the US and the USSR supported client states in the post-colonial period; America had some success in preserving the unity of the Congo (Zaire) and Nigeria, though at the cost of supporting kleptocratic regimes; the Soviet Union maintained an African presence in Angola and Mozambique (both garrisoned with Cuban troops), among other places.

The *Middle East* was an area of strong Soviet initiatives throughout the Cold War. With Israel seen as a creature of the United States, its Arab neighbors readily accepted Soviet aid and advice. Britain's inept and humiliating loss of the Suez Canal to Egypt in 1956 bolstered Nasser's socialist regime there, already friendly to Russia for aid in building the Aswan High Dam. Iraq, Syria, and Libya became anti-Israeli Soviet clients, while the U.S. sought support among the more conservative Arab monarchies. Further east, the CIA-sponsored overthrow of the democratic Mossadegh regime in 1953 led to the return to power of the shah; in 1979 his unpopular and autocratic government fell to a fundamentalist Islamic revolution. The subsequent Iran-Iraq war led the U.S. into the anomalous position of supporting the former Soviet client, Iraq's Saddam Hussein.

America's strategy throughout the Cold War had been to use its economic power to intimidate the Soviet bloc militarily and tempt the uncommitted nations of the world commercially. In this sense, the dramatic images of Neil Armstrong walking on the moon on July 20, 1969 were a key element in American Cold War propaganda. Conversely, the image of Americans hastily evacuating Saigon at the end of the Vietnam War were devastating to American interests because it seemed to show American impotence in the face of communist-inspired nationalism, even if the reality of the situation was, of course, much more complicated.

The anti-Soviet rhetoric of Pres. Ronald Reagan in the 1980s seemed like a throwback to the Cold War paranoia of the 1950s, but it seems to have hastened the Cold War's end. With a restless population and a crumbling economy, Russia found itself unable to sustain the military expenditures needed to keep pace with the U.S. in Cold War competition around the world. With the domestic softening of policy of Mikahil Gorbachev's *glasnost* and *perestroika* in the mid-80s, people in Poland, East Germany, Czechoslovakia, and elsewhere in Eastern Europe, and also in the Baltic states, rapidly overthrew their governments and threw out Soviet troops. The fall of the Berlin Wall meant in effect the fall of international communism, and the end of the Cold War.

There was fallout, to be sure, in the Persian Gulf War (1990-91), in the turmoil of the ex-Soviet republics, in the struggle of Africa to emerge from the era of Cold War patronage and great-power rivalry. But in the end the Cold War did not seem to amount to much. For all its espionage and paranoia, all the arms races and space races, all the proxy wars in unhappy countries throughout the world, the Cold War passed away with only a whimper, an historical episode that had outlived its day. The U.S. emerged as the only superpower both militarily and economically. The challenges for the future were how to maintain peace around the world, helping poorer nations find prosperity, and still remaining faithful to its ideal of self-determination for all peoples of the world.

In the ensuing years, the U.S. response to these critical problems has centered on efforts to strengthen the world economy and to do so on its own terms by maintaining an overwhelming military dominance. Despite the absence of any serious threat from a large power or a coalition of smaller ones, American military budgets continued to exceed $250 billion a year, sufficient to maintain an advanced weaponry program and to keep 1.5 million men and women on active duty. Russia has nuclear weapons but its military is in disarray and its economy keeps hovering on the edge of collapse. Only China has a larger military force than the U.S., but it lacks anything like America's air and nuclear power.

Since 1990, China has been the focal point of U.S. foreign policy and economic strategy. Despite the Chinese government's overt acts of repression and manifest evidence of serious human rights abuses, Presidents Bush and Clinton have both aggressively pursued an economic alliance that has benefited both countries. Tens of billions of dollars have been invested in China in the last decade and, not surprisingly, China has become the chief supplier of low-cost consumer goods and other items to the U.S. In 1997, China sent exports worth $62 billion to the U.S. but imported only $13 billion.

During the 1990s, the U.S. and its allies have promulgated the idea that democracy and economic freedom are inseparable ideals that only market economy rules can bring to fruition. A central element in this creed is free trade, and the U.S. has led the fight to end tariffs and other barriers by helping to establish the 139-member World Trade Organization to develop international rules and policies for trade. In 1994, the North American Free Trade Agreement ended all trade barriers for Canada, Mexico, and the U.S. In Europe, the European Union moved nations closer to economic integration by regulating trade and establishing a single currency—the euro—that could rival the dollar in the not-too-distant future.

Rulers of the World

EMPERORS OF ROME 27 B.C.–A.D. 491

Augustus   27 B.C.–14 A.D.
Tiberius   14–37
Caligula   37–41
Claudius   41–54
Nero   54–68
Galba   68–69
Otho   69
Vitellius   69
Vespasian   69–79
Titus   79–81
Domitian   81–96
Nerva   96–98
Trajan   98–117
Hadrian   117–38
Antoninus Pius   138–61
Marcus Aurelius (co-emperor with Lucius Verus)   161–69
Marcus Aurelius alone   169–77
Marcus Aurelius (co-emperor with Commodus)   177–80
Comodus alone   180–92
Pertinax   193
Didius Julianus   193

Septimius Severus   193–98
Carcalla (co-emperor with Geta)   211–12
Caracalla alone   212–17
Macrinus   217–18
Heliogabalus   218–22
Severus Alexander   222–35
Maximinus   235–38
Gordian I (co-emperor with Gordian II)   238
Pupienus Maximus (co-emperor with Balbinus)   238
Gordian III   238–44
Philip ("The Arab")   244–49
Decius   249–51
Hostilianus   251
Gallus   251–53
Aemilianus   253
Valerian (co-emperor with Gallienus)   253–60
Gallienus alone   253–68
Claudius II ("Gothicus")   268–70
Aurelian   270–75
Tacitus   275–76
Florianus   276
Probus   276–82
Carus   282–83
Carinus (co-emperor with Numerianus)   283–84
Carinus alone   284–85

Between 270 and 283, there were seven emperors, all chosen by the army. Carus was killed in battle, and Numerianus died on the march. The other five were murderd by their soldiers. In an attempt to end the chaos of the "barracks emperors," Diocletian attempted to establish an orderly succession in the East and West halves of the Empire, the emperor in the East being the senior emperor. Dicocletian and Maximian both abdicated in 305,

although Maximian was recalled in 306. Subsequently, the succession became disputed in both East and West, and between 305 and 474 there were 39 claimants to the imperial title, five of whom ruled both the East and the West, most notably Constantine (324–37). With the demise of the last emperor in the West (476), the eastern emperor, Zeno, reunited the imperial office in one person.

East	Constantine I 312–37	West
Diocletian 284–305		Maximian 286–308
Galerius 305–11		Constantius I 305–306
Licinius 311–24		Severus 306–307
		Maximin 307–13
Constantius II 337–61		
		Constantine II 337–40
		Constans 340–50
	Constantius II 350–61	
	Julian 361–63	
	Jovian 363–64	
Valens 364–78		Valentinian I 364–75
Theodosius I 378–92		Gratian 375–83
		Valentinian II 375–92
	Theodosius I 392–95	
Arcadius 395–408		Honorius[1] 395–423
Theodosius II 408–50		Valentinian III 425–55
Marcian 450–57		Petronius Maximus 455
Leo I 457–74		Avitus 455–56
Leo II 474		Marjorian 457–61
Zeno 474–91		Libius Severus 461–65
		Anthemius 467–72
		Olybrius 472–73
		Glycerius 473–74
		Julius Nepos 474–75
		Romulus Augustus 475–76

Note: Names in **bold italics** ruled in both the East and the West. These lists are designed to make history neater than it was, so they do not reflect the turmoil of the fourth and fifth centuries, when usurpers and pretenders were numerous.
1. Stilicho was regent until 408.

DYNASTIES OF EUROPE

▶THE CAROLINGIANS (751–887)

The first Carolingian king of the Franks was Pepin the Short who usurped the title from the Merovingian line in 751. Taking their dynastic name from Pepin's father, Charles (Carolus) Martel, the Carolingians divided their realm among surviving sons. It was in this family that the papacy revived the Roman imperial title in the year 800. The lists below cover only the major figures and ignore brief reigns and minor claimants.

    Pepin the Short, King   751–68
    Charlemagne and Carloman   768–71
    Charlemagne, King   771–814
    Charlemagne, Emperor   800–814
    Louis the Pious, Emperor   814–40

West Franks
    Charles the Bald   843–77 (Emperor 875–77)
    Louis II, the Stammerer   877–879
    Louis III   879–82
    Carloman   879–84

Lotharingia
    Lothair, Emperor   840–55
    Louis II, Emperor   855–75
    Charles, King of Provence   855–63
    Lothair II, King of Lorraine   855–69

East Franks
    Louis the German   843–76
    Carloman   876–80
    Louis   876–82
    Charles the Fat   882–887, Emperor (881–87)

▶HOLY ROMAN EMPIRE (962–1806)

The Holy Roman Empire refers to the second medieval "revival" of the Roman Empire in the West, in the year 962. Though drained of most of its power after 1250 and virtually all of its power after 1648, the Empire endured until 1806 when it was abolished by the Emperor Francis II (though he had no power to do so) who thereafter ruled as Francis I of the Austrian Empire which had been founded in 1804. Whatever the power of the Emperor, the title was the most prestigious in all of Europe. Normally the king of Germany was emperor once he was crowned by the pope; in 1356 the Golden Bull established a seven-member electoral college to choose the Emperor but from the fifteenth century on it was traditional for the electors to choose the Habsburg candidate.

Saxon Dynasty
The dukes of Saxony were most able in combatting the Hungarian menace in the 10th century and thus were chosen kings of Germany. The first was Henry the Fowler (919–936). His son Otto was the first Holy Roman Emperor.

    Otto I, King   936, Emperor   962–73
    Otto II   973–83
    Otto III   983–1002
    Henry II   1002–24

Franconian (or Salian) Dynasty
When Henry II died without heirs, Conrad of Franconia (a great-great grandson of Otto I) secured the succession. The dynasty intervened in Rome to reform the papacy, perhaps too successfully, for the popes contended with the emperors for the leadership of the Christian world in the Investiture Controversy (1076–1122). Both the imperial office and the kingship of Germany were greatly weakened by the papal victory.

    Conrad II   1024–39
    Henry III   1039–56
    Henry IV   1056–1106
    Henry V   1106–25
    Lothair II   1125–37

Hohenstaufen Dynasty
The Hohenstaufen of Swabia were nephews of Henry V but the Church tended to support candidates of the Guelph (also known as Welf) family of Saxony and Bavaria. The struggle of these families and the involvement of the papacy fatally weakened the empire ushering in the "Age of the Princes" in Germany and the "Great Interregnum" in the Empire.

    Conrad III   1138–52
    Frederick I "Barbarossa"   1152–90
    Henry VI   1190–97
    Philip of Swabia   1198–1208
    Otto IV (Guelph) (anti-king)   1198–1208
    Otto IV   1208–12
    Frederick II   1212–50
    Conrad IV   1250–54
    Interregnum   1254–73

When kingship and the imperial office were restored in 1273 the princes refused to establish any one dynasty; for a century and a half candidates from four families were elected.

    Rudolf I (Habsburg)   1273–91
    Adolf (Nassau)   1292–98
    Albert I (Habsburg)   1298–1308
    Henry VII (Luxemburg)   1308–13
    Louis IV (Wittelsbach)   1314–46
    Charles IV (Luxemburg)   1346–78
    Wenceslas (Luxemburg)   1378–1400
    Rupert (Wittelsbach)   1400–1410
    Sigismund (Luxemburg)   1410–37

The Habsburgs
The House of Habsburg (the name is a contraction of the name of their castle, Habichtsburg, in Switzerland) was the most illustrious of the European dynasties. From the 15th century they became hereditary rulers of the Empire and through a series of brilliant marriages gained, by inheritance, the Netherlands, the Spanish kingdoms and Spain's empire in the New World, and Hungary and Bohemia. (From the reign of Francis I, the official family name is Habsburg-Lorraine.)

    Albert II   1440–93
    Frederick III   1440–93
    Maximilian I   1493–1519
    Charles V   1519–56
    Ferdinand I   1556–64
    Maximilian II   1564–76
    Rudolf II   1576–1612
    Matthias   1612–19
    Ferdinand II   1619–37
    Ferdinand III   1637–57
    Leopold I   1658–1705
    Joseph I   1705–11
    Charles VI   1711–40
    Interregnum   1740–42
    Charles VII   1742–45
    Francis I   1745–65
    Joseph II   1765–90
    Leopold II   1790–92
    Francis II   1792–1806

►DYNASTIES OF FRANCE (987–1848)

In 987 the West Frankish nobles elected as their king Hugh Capet. His descendants ruled France continuously until the French Revolution and again from 1814 until 1848. The direct line died out in 1328, and the collateral *Valois* branch of the Capetian family succeeded. The Valois ruled with difficulty, as the Hundred Years' War (1337–1453) blighted the beginning and the Wars of Religion (1562–98) the end of their rule. The last three Valois produced no male heirs so the throne passed to the victor in the Wars of Religion, Henry of Navarre (a distant cousin in the male line of Louis IX), who began the reign of the *Bourbon* branch of the Capetians. (After 1700, the Bourbon family became, with many interruptions, kings of Spain.)

Direct Capetians
Hugh Capet 987–96
Robert II the Pious 996–1031
Henry I 1031–60
Philip I 1060–1108
Louis VI 1108–37
Louis VII 1137–80
Philip II Augustus 1180–1223
Louis VIII 1223–26
Louis IX 1226–70
Philip III 1270–85
Philip IV 1285–1314
Louis X 1314–16
John I the Posthumous 1316
Philip V 1316–22
Charles IV 1322–28

Valois Branch
Philip VI 1328–50
John 1350–64
Charles V 1364–80
Charles VI 1380–1422
Charles VII 1422–61
Louis XI 1461–83
Charles VIII 1483–98
Louis XII (Valois-Orléans) 1498–1515
Francis I (Valois-Angoulême) 1515–47
Henry II 1547–59
Francis II 1559–60
Charles IX 1560–74
Henry III 1574–89

Bourbon Branch
Henry IV 1589–1610
Louis XIII 1610–43
Louis XIV 1643–1715
Louis XV 1715–74
Louis XVI 1774–92
French Revolution and Napoleon
1792–1814

Restored Bourbons
Louis XVIII 1814–24
Charles X 1824–30
Louis Philippe (Bourbon-Orléans) 1830–48

►DYNASTIES OF ENGLAND (871–PRESENT)

Saxons
With the end of Roman rule, seven Germanic kingdoms emerged in England. The leader of the resistance to the Vikings was Alfred the Great of Wessex (871–99) who began a reconquest of the island and is considered the first true king of England; his dynasty, with interruptions, continued until the Norman Conquest in 1066.

Alfred the Great 871–99
Edward the Elder 899–924
Aethelstan 924–39
Edmund 939–46
Eadred 946–55
Eadwig 955–59
Edgar 959–75
Edward 975–78
Aethelred "the Unready" 978–1016
Edmund Ironside 1016
Canute (of Denmark, by conquest) 1016–35
Harold Harefoot 1035–40
Hardicanute (of Denmark) 1040–42
Edward the Confessor 1042–66
Harold Godwinson 1066

Normans
Duke William of Normandy, a cousin of Edward the Confessor, made good his claim to the throne by conquest, bringing with him highly organized Continental feudalism and the French tongue which so enriched the English language.

William the Conqueror 1066–87
William II 1087–1100
Henry I 1100–1135
Stephen 1135–54

Angevins (Plantagenets)
The grandson of Henry I was Henry of Anjou who, by marrying the heiress Eleanor of Aquitaine, assembled for his family the greatest feudal state in 12th century Europe. In 1154 he established his family on the throne of England as well; the direct line continued until 1399 when Richard II was deposed and killed by his first cousin who then ruled as Henry IV and established the *Lancastrian Dynasty*. Another branch of the family, with a stronger claim than the usurping Lancastrians, contested the succession in the War of the Roses and after 1461 ruled briefly as the *Yorkist Dynasty*.

Henry II 1154–89
Richard I 1189–99
John I 1199–1216
Henry III 1216–72
Edward I 1272–1307
Edward II 1307–27
Edward III 1327–77
Richard II 1377–99

Lancastrian Kings
Henry IV 1399–1413
Henry V 1413–22
Henry VI 1422–61

Yorkist Kings
Edward IV 1461–83
Edward V 1483
Richard III 1483–85

Tudors
An obscure Welsh family and adherents of the Lancastrian line, the Tudors became champions of the faction supporting them. Richard III died in battle at Bosworth Field against Henry Tudor, who usurped the throne, ruling as Henry VII and founding the dynasty that brought the Reformation to England.

Henry VII   1485–1509
Henry VIII   1509–47
Edward VI   1547–53
Mary I   1553–58
Elizabeth I   1558–1603

Stuarts

Elizabeth never married and had no heirs, so the Tudor line died with her. Rule passed to Elizabeth's cousin, James VI of Scotland who ruled in England as James I. Serious troubles with the Puritans and Parliament twice turned the Stuarts from the throne: Charles I was beheaded and James II was betrayed by his daughters and the husband of one, William of Orange.

James I   1603–25
Charles I   1625–49
*Interregnum—Oliver Cromwell   1649–58
        Richard Cromwell   1658–59*
Charles II   1660–85
James II   1685–88
William III and Mary II   1689–94
William III alone   1694–1702
Anne   1702–14

Hanoverians and Windsors

Queen Anne had 17 children but died without leaving an heir. Geneological and religious considerations (Anne's brother "James III," the Catholic pretender, was still alive) brought to the throne the German House of Hanover. After the reign of Victoria, the family is Saxe-Coburg-Gotha but in 1917, for political reasons, George V changed the name to Windsor.

George I   1714–27
George II   1727–60
George III   1760–1820
George IV   1820–30
William IV   1830–37
Victoria   1837–1901
Edward VII   1901–10
George V   1910–36
Edward VIII   1936
George VI   1936–52
Elizabeth II   1952–present

▶ DYNASTIES OF SPAIN (1506–PRESENT)

Until 1808 there was no kingdom called Spain but a number of separate kingdoms of which Castile and Aragon were only the principal ones. With the deaths of Isabella, then Ferdinand, the crowns passed to their grandson, the Habsburg Charles of Ghent; in the Empire he was Charles V, in the Spanish kingdoms Charles I. His *Habsburg Dynasty* ruled until 1700 when the line died out and was replaced by the *Bourbon Dynasty* which has ruled with numerous interruptions until the present day.

Habsburgs

Charles I (Holy Roman Emperor as
    Charles V)   1506–56
Philip II   1556–98
Philip III   1598–1621
Philip IV   1621–65
Charles II   1665–1700

Bourbons

Philip V   1700–1746
Ferdinand VI   1746–59
Charles III   1759–88
Charles IV   1788–1808

Joseph Bonaparte   1808–13
Ferdinand VII   1814–33
Isabella II   1833–68
Interregnum   1868–70
Amadeo   1870–73
Republic   1873–75
Alphonso XII   1875–85
Alphonso XIII   1886–1931
Republic   1931–36
Civil War   1936–39
Franco regime   1939–75
Juan Carlos   1975–present

▶ AUSTRIAN HABSBURGS

When Charls V retired, his world-wide empire was divided into two parts, one Spanish, one Austrian. The Austrian branch always supplied the Holy Roman Emperors except during the reign of Maria Theresa (1740–80) when Charles Albert of Bavaria, then her husband and son held the imperial title. In 1804 Emperor Francis II proclaimed an Austrian Empire which he ruled as Francis I; two years later he abolished the Holy Roman Empire.

Francis II & I   1792–1835
Ferdinand I   1835–48
Francis Joseph   1848–1916
Charles I   1916–18

▶ HOHENZOLLERN DYNASTY

For centuries the Hohenzollern were electors of Brandenburg in northeastern Germany. In 1701, with permission of the emperor, they took the royal titles King in Prussia. (Prussia was a duchy of Poland which the family inherited in 1618.) In 1871 they added the title German Emperor. Both titles disappeared with Germany's loss in World War I.

Frederick William, the Great Elector
    1640–88
Frederick III, Elector of Brandenburg
    1688–1701
Frederick I, King of Prussia   1701–13
Frederick William I   1713–40
Frederick II   1740–86
Frederick William II   1786–97
Frederick William III   1797–1840
Frederick William IV   1840–61
William I (German Emperor after 1871)
    1861–88
Frederick III   1888
William II   1888–1918

▶ ROMANOV DYNASTY (RUSSIA)

At the end of Russia's "time of troubles" early in the 17th century, the national assembly elected Michael Romanov as czar in 1613. The dynasty died out in 1762 when at the death of czarina Elizabeth, her nephew Peter III briefly succeeded. His family ruled until the Russian Revolution. Their name was Holstein-Gottorp but ruled under the name Romanov.

Michael   1613–45
Alexius   1645–76
Theodore III   1676–82
Ivan IV and Peter I   1682–89
Peter I, the Great, alone   1689–1725
Catherine I   1725–27
Peter II   1727–30
Anna   1730–40
Ivan VI   1740–41
Elizabeth   1741–62
Peter III   1762
Catherine II the Great   1762–96

Paul 1796–1801
Alexander I 1801–25
Nicholas I 1825–55
Alexander II 1855–81
Alexander III 1881–94
Nicholas II 1894–1917

▶**HOUSE OF SAVOY-CARIGNANO**
The dukes of Savoy ruled in a personal union Piedmont, Nice, and Sardinia until 1831, when the line died out and a distant cousin, Charles Albert came to the throne. It was his son, Victor Emmanuel II of Savoy whose armies conquered the rest of Italy over the years 1858–71 and who was proclaimed King of Italy in 1861. The dynasty fell with the end of the Second World War.

Victor Emmanuel II 1861–78
Humbert I 1878–1900
Victor Emmanuel III 1900–46
Humbert II 1946

THE DYNASTIES AND EMPERORS OF CHINA

Dates for the Xia and Shang Dynasties, and for the beginning of the Zhou Dynasty, are uncertain. Rulers of these three dynasties were known as kings (*wang*); only a few notable individuals are listed below. The title "emperor" (*huangdi*) was instituted with the Qin Dynasty. As is customary, names of emperors prior to A.D. 1368 are given in the form of their posthumous "temple names" (*miaohao*); names of emperors for the Ming and Qing Dynasties are given as their reign-title names (*nianhao*).

Xia Dynasty c. 1875–1550 B.C.
Yü the Great (legendary?) c. 1875–1850 B.C.
King Jie c. 1560–1550 B.C.

Shang Dynasty c. 1550–1055 B.C.
Tang the Victorious c. 1550–1500 B.C.
King Zhou c. 1070–1055 B.C.

Zhou Dynasty c. 1055–256 B.C.
Western Zhou Period c. 1055–771 B.C.
King Wen (pre-conquest) c. 1060–1055 B.C.
King Wu c. 1055–1048 B.C.
Duke of Zhou, regent for
King Cheng c. 1048–1011 B.C.
Era of the Spring and Autumn Annals 722–481 B.C.
Warring States Period 481–256 B.C.

Qin Dynasty 221–206 B.C.
Shihuangdi 221–209 B.C.
Erhuangdi 209–207 B.C.

Han Dynasty 206 B.C.–A.D. 220
Western or Former Han 206 B.C.–A.D. 9
Gaozu 206–195 B.C.
Huidi 195–188 B.C.
Gaohou (Empress Lü) 188–180 B.C.
Wendi 180–157 B.C.
Jingdi 157–141 B.C.
Wudi 141–87 B.C.

Zhaodi 87–74 B.C.
Xuandi 74–48 B.C.
Yuandi 48–33 B.C.
Chengdi 33–7 B.C.
Aidi 7–1 B.C.
Pingdi 1 B.C.–A.D. 6
Wang Mang (usurper) A.D. 9–23
Eastern or Latter Han A.D. 23–220
Guangwudi 25–57
Mingdi 57–75
Zhangdi 75–88
Hedi 88–105
Shangdi 105
Andi 106–25
Shaodi 125
Shundi 125–44
Chongdi 144–45
Zhidi 145–46
Huandi 146–68
Lingdi 168–89
Shaodi 189
Xiandi 189–220

Period of Disunion
The fall of the Han Dynasty ushered in a period of 369 years of disunion during which no dynasty succeeded in bringing all of China under its control This period is divided into the brief Three Kingdoms Period and the longer Period of Northern and Southern Dynasties, of which only the three most important dynasties are listed below.

Three Kingdoms 220–65
Kingdom of Shu Han 220–64
Kingdom of Wei 220–65
Kingdom of Wu 220–65

Period of Northern and Southern Dynasties 265–589
Western Jin Dynasty 265–317
Eastern Jin Dynasty 317–419
Northern Wei Dynasty 424–535

Sui Dynasty 589–618
Wendi 589–604
Yangdi 604–17
Gongdi 617–18

Tang Dynasty 618–907
Gaozu 618–26
Taizong 626–49
Gaozong 649–83
Zhongzong 683–84
Ruizong 684–90
Wuhou 690–705
Zhongzong 705–10
Ruizong 710–12
Xuanzong 712–56
Suzong 756–62
Taizong 762–79
Dezong 779–805
Shunzong 805
Xianzong 805–20
Muzong 820–24
Jingzong 824–26
Wenzong 826–40
Wuzong 840–46
Xuanzong 846–59
Yizong 859–73
Xizong 873–88
Zhaozong 888–904
Jingzong 904–7

Five Dynasties   907–60

Song Dynasty   960–1279
Northern Song   960–1127
Taizu   960–76
Taizong   976–97
Zhenzong   997–1022
Renzong   1022–63
Yingzong   1063–67
Shenzong   1067–85
Zhezong   1085–1100
Huizong   1100–1125
Qinzong   1125–27
Southern Song   1127–1279
Gaozong   1127–62
Xiaozong   1162–89
Guangzong   1189–94
Ningzong   1194–1224
Lizong   1224–64
Duzong   1264–74
Gongzong   1274–76
Duanzong   1276–79

Yuan (Mongol) Dynasty   1279–1368
Shizu (Kubilai Khan)   1260–94
Chengzong (Temür)   1294–1307
Wuzong (Khaishan)   1307–11
Renzong (Buyantu)   1311–20
Yingzong (Sudhipela)   1320–23
Taiding (Yesen-Temür)   1323–28
Mingzong (Asikipa)   1328
Wenzong (Tog-Temür)   1328–33
Xunzong (Toghon-Temür)   1333–68

Ming Dynasty   1368–1644
Hongwu   1368–98
Jianwen   1398–1402
Yongle   1402–24
Hongxi   1424–25
Xuande   1425–35
Zhengtong   1435–49
Jingtai   1449–57
Tianshun   1457–64
Chenghua   1464–87
Hongzhi   1487–1505
Zhengde   1505–21
Jiaqing   1521–66
Wanli   1572–1620
Taichang   1620
Tianzhi   1620–27
Chongzhen   1627–44

Qing Dynasty   1644–1911
Shunzhi   1644–61
Kangxi   1661–1722
Yongzheng   1722–35
Qianlong   1735–96
Jiaqing   1796–1820
Daoguang   1820–50
Xianfeng   1850–61
Tongzhi   1861–75
Guangxu   1875–1908
Puyi   1908–11

CHRONOLOGICAL LISTING OF THE POPES

Peter, Apostle   d. c. 64
Linus   c.66–c.78
Anacletus   c.79–c.91
Clement I   c.91–c.101
Evaristus   c.100–c.109
Alexander I   c.109–c.116
Sixtus I   c.116–c.125
Telesphorus   c.125–c.136
Hyginus   c.138–c.142
Pius I   c.142–c.155
Anicetus   c.155–c.166
Soter   c.166–c.174
Eleutherius, or Eleutherus   c.174–89
Victor I   189–98
Zephyrinus   198/9–217
Callistus I (often Calixtus)   217–22
Hippolytus (antipope)   217–35
Urban I   222–30
Pontian   230–35
Anterus   235–36
Fabian   236–50
Cornelius   251–53
Novatian (antipope)   251–58
Lucius I   253–54
Stephen I   254–57
Sixtus II   257–58
Dionysius   260–68
Felix I   269–74
Eutychian   275–83
Gaius, or Caius   283–96
Marcellinus   296–304?
Marcellus I   306–8
Eusebius   310
Miltiades, or Melchiades   311–31

Silvester I   314–35
Mark   336
Julius I   337–52
Liberius   352–66
Felix II (antipope)[1]   355–65
Damasus I   366–84
Ursinus (antipope)   366–67
Siricius   384–99
Anastasius I   399–401
Innocent I   401–17
Zosimus   417–18
Eulalius (antipope)   418–19
Boniface I   418–22
Celestine I   422–32
Sixtus (Xystus) III   432–40
Leo I   440–61
Hilarus   461–68
Simplicius   468–83
Felix III[1]   483–92
Gelasius I   492–96
Anastasius II   496–98
Symmachus   498–514
Lawrence (antipope)   498–99, 501–6
Hormisdas   514–23
John I   523–26
Felix III[1]   526–30
Dioscorus (antipope)   530
Boniface II   530–32
John II   533–35
Agapitus I   535–36
Silverius   536–37
Vigilius   537–55
Pelagius I   556–61
John III   561–74
Benedict I   575–79
Pelagius II   579–90

Gregory I   590–604
Sabinian   604–6
Boniface III   607
Boniface IV   608–15
Deusdedit (later Adeodatus I)   615–18
Boniface V   619–25
Honorius I   625–38
Severinus   640
John IV   640–42
Theodore I   642–49
Martin I   649–53
Eugene I   654–57
Vitalian   657–72
Adeodatus II   672–76
Donus   676–78
Agatho   678–81
Leo II   682–83
Benedict II   684–85
John V   685–86
Conon   686–87
Theodore (antipope)   687
Paschal (antipope)   687
Sergius I   687–701
John VI   701–5
John VII   705–7
Sisinnius   708
Gregory II   715–31
Gregory III   731–41
Zacharias   741–52
Stephen (II)[2]   752
Stephen II (III)[2]   752–57
Paul I   757–67
Constantine (antipope)   767–68
Philip (antipope)   768
Stephen III (IV)[2]   768–72
Hadrian I   772–95

Leo III   795–816
Stephen IV (V)[2]   816–17
Paschal I   817–24
Eugene II   824–27
Valentine   827
Gregory IV   827–44
John (antipope)   844
Sergius II   844–47
Leo IV   847–55
Benedict III   855–58
*Anastasius Bibliothecarius
   (antipope)*   855
Nicholas I   858–67
Hadrian II   867–72
John VIII   872–82
Marinus I   882–84
Hadrian III   884–85
Stephen V (VI)[2]   885–91
Formosus   891–96
Boniface VI   896
Stephen VI (VII)[2]   896–97
Romanus   897
Theodore II   897
John IX   898–900
Benedict IV   900–903
Leo V   903
Christopher (antipope)   903–4
Sergius III   904–11
Anastasius III   911–13
Lando   913–14
John X   914–28
Leo VI   928
Stephen VII (VIII)[2]   928–31
John XI   931–36?
Leo VII   936–39
Stephen VIII (IX)[2]   939–42
Marinus II   942–46
Agapitus II   946–55
John XII   955–64
Leo VIII   963–65
Benedict V   964
John XIII   965–72
Benedict VI   973–74
Boniface VII (antipope)   974,
   984–85
Benedict VII   974–83
John XIV   983–84
John XV   985–96
Gregory V   996–99
John XVI (antipope)   997–98
Silvester II   999–1003
John XVII   1003
John XVIII   1003–1009
Sergius IV   1009–12
Benedict VIII   1012–24
Gregory (VI) (antipope)   1012
John XIX   1024–32
Benedict IX   1032–44, 1045,
   1047–48
Silvester III   1045
Gregory VI   1045–46
Clement II   1046–47
Damasus II   1048
Leo IX   1049–54
Victor II   1055–57
Stephen IX (X)[2]   1057–58
Benedict X (antipope)
   1058–59
Nicholas II   1058–61

Alexander II   1061–73
Honorius (II) (antipope)   1061–64
Gregory VII   1073–85
Clement III (antipope)   1080,
   1084–1100
Victor III   1086–87
Urban II   1088–99
Paschal II   1099–1118
Theoderic (antipope)   1100–1101
Albert or Adalbert (antipope)
   1101
Silvester IV (antipope)   1105–11
Gelasius II   1118–19
Gregory (VIII) (antipope)
   1118–21
Callistus II   1119–24
Celestine (II)   1124
Honorius II   1124–30
Innocent II   1130–43
Anacletus II (antipope)   1130–38
Victor IV (antipope)   1138
Celestine II   1143–44
Lucius II   1144–45
Eugene III   1145–53
Anastasius IV   1153–54
Hadrian IV   1154–59
Alexander III   1159–81
Victor IV (antipope) [3]   1159–64
Paschal III (antipope)   1164–68
Callistus (III) (antipope)   1168–78
Innocent (III) (antipope)   1179–80
Lucius III   1181–85
Urban III   1185–87
Gregory VIII   1187
Clement III   1187–91
Celestine III   1191–98
Innocent III   1198–1216
Honorius III   1216–27
Gregory IX   1227–41
Celestine IV   1241
Innocent IV   1243–54
Alexander IV   1254–61
Urban IV   1261–64
Clement IV   1265–68
Gregory X   1271–76
Innocent V   1276
Hadrian V   1276
John XXI   1276–77
Nicholas III   1277–80
Martin IV   1281–85
Honorius IV   1285–87
Nicholas IV   1288–92
Celestine V   1294
Boniface VIII   1294–1303
Benedict XI   1303–4
Clement V   1305–14
John XXII   1316–34
Nicholas (V) (antipope)
   1328–30
Benedict XII   1334–42
Clement VI   1342–52
Innocent VI   1352–62
Urban V   1362–70
Gregory XI   1370–78
Urban VI   1378–89
Clement (VII) (antipope)   1378–94
Boniface IX   1389–1404
Benedict (XIII) (antipope)
   1394–1417

Innocent VII   1404–6
Gregory XII   1406–15
Alexander V (antipope)
   1409–10
John (XXIII) (antipope)
   1410–15
Martin V   1417–31
Clement (VIII) (antipope)
   1423–29
Benedict (XIV) (antipope)   1425–?
Eugene IV   1431–47
Felix V (antipope)   1439–49
Nicholas V   1447–55
Callistus III   1455–58
Pius II   1458–64
Paul II   1464–71
Sixtus IV   1471–84
Innocent VIII   1484–92
Alexander VI   1492–1503
Pius III   1503
Julius II   1503–13
Leo X   1513–21
Hadrian VI   1522–23
Clement VII   1523–34
Paul III   1534–49
Julius III   1550–55
Marcellus II   1555
Paul IV   1555–59
Pius IV   1559–65
Pius V   1566–72
Gregory XIII   1572–85
Sixtus V   1585–90
Urban VII   1590
Gregory XIV   1590–91
Innocent IX   1591
Clement VIII   1592–1605
Leo XI   1605
Paul V   1605–21
Gregory XV   1621–23
Urban VIII   1623–44
Innocent X   1644–55
Alexander VII   1655–67
Clement IX   1667–69
Clement X   1670–76
Innocent XI   1676–89
Alexander VIII   1689–91
Innocent XII   1691–1700
Clement XI   1700–21
Innocent XIII   1721–24
Benedict XIII   1724–30
Clement XII   1730–40
Benedict XIV   1740–58
Clement XIII   1758–69
Clement XIV   1769–74
Pius VI   1775–99
Pius VII   1800–23
Leo XII   1823–29
Pius VIII   1829–30
Gregory XVI   1831–46
Pius IX   1846–78
Leo XIII   1878–1903
Pius X   1903–14
Benedict XV   1914–22
Pius XI   1922–39
Pius XII   1939–58
John XXIII   1958–63
Paul VI   1963–78
John Paul I   1978
John Paul II   1978–

Note: Antipopes, *listed in italics*, were appointed in opposition to the one canonically chosen by the college of cardinals, usually by a prince, king, or emperor. 1. Because Felix II was an antipope, subsequent Felixes were sometime misnumbered. 2. Although elected and installed as Pope, Stephen (II) died before his consecration. Though the Vatican's *Annuario Pontifico* has excluded him from the official list of Popes since 1961, subsequent Stephens have a dual numbering. 3. He should have been Victor V, but he used Victor IV because the previous Victor IV's tenure (1138) as antipope was largely ignored.

World Geography

▶GLOSSARY OF GEOGRAPHICAL WORDS AND TERMS

(Note: See also Part IV: Science and Technology, Composition of the Earth)

Altitude   How high a place or a thing is, usually measured from sea level or the surface of the land.

Archipelago   A cluster of islands.

Arctic Circle   An imaginary line drawn along approximately latitude 66° 30'N. The climate north of the Arctic Circle is very cold, and relatively few people live there.

Atmosphere   The mass of air that extends outward from the surface of the earth into space. The atmosphere is divided into four layers: the troposphere, in which temperature decreases as altitude increases; the stratosphere, in which temperature is constant, then increases; the mesosphere, in which it decreases; and the thermosphere, in which it increases again.

Atoll   A coral reef that partially or completely surrounds a lagoon.

Basin   A portion of land that is lower than the surrounding area. Basins are created when vertical movement causes the earth's crust to warp. Also, the area drained by a river and its tributaries.

Bay   Part of an ocean, sea, or other body of water which extends inland. Bays are generally smaller than gulfs.

Bight   A bay formed by a bend in the coastline.

Caldera   A huge crater formed when the top of a volcano collapses or is exploded away.

Canyon   A narrow, deep valley with steep sides. Many canyons have a river on their floor.

Climate   General weather conditions over a long period. (See "Climates of the World.")

Continent   A large unbroken land mass, distinguished from an island or peninsula. The seven continents are North America, South America, Europe, Asia, Africa, Australia, and Antarctica, though Europe and Asia are a continuous land mass divided along the spine of the Ural Mountains running south from the Arctic Ocean.

Continental drift theory   The theory, proposed in 1915 by Alfred Wegener, that all of the continents used to be joined in one supercontinent, Pangaea. Some 200 million years ago Pangaea began to break up, and the continents "drifted" through the oceans to their present locations. The continental drift theory has now largely been replaced by the *plate tectonics theory*. (See the section "Earth Sciences.")

Continental shelf   The edge of a continent covered by shallow ocean water, up to about 100 fathoms (600 feet), beyond which is the continental slope, which decends to the deep-sea plain, about 13,000-20,000 feet (4,000-6,000 m).

Cove   A small and sheltered bay or inlet. Also, a small valley in a mountain.

Crater   The bowl-shaped depression at the top of a volcano. Also, the depression made when a meteorite hits the earth. (See also *caldera*.)

Delta   A triangular-shaped piece of land formed by sediment at the mouth of a river.

Desert   (See "The Great Deserts" later in this section).

Dune   A hill or ridge of sand that has been deposited by wind.

Equator   An imaginary line circling earth halfway between the Poles. The equator is at latitude 0°.

Equinox   The two times during the year (on or about March 21 and September 23) when the sun's rays strike the equator vertically. At equinox, day and night are the same length everywhere in the world. (See also *Solstice*.)

Erosion   The gradual wearing away of the surface of the land. For example, soil is eroded by wind and water; rock is eroded by freezing and thawing.

Estuary   A valley at the mouth of a river where fresh water and sea water mix. Estuaries are created either when the land sinks or when the sea level rises, and are generally shaped like a funnel.

Fjord   A long, narrow inlet of the ocean with steeply sloping sides.

Floodplain   Flat, low-lying land along either side of a river that is subject to flooding.

Geyser   A jet of hot water or steam periodically thrown up by a hot spring.

Glacier   A large mass of slowly moving ice. Glaciers are formed on land when snow is compacted and recrystallizes.

Gorge   An especially narrow and steep-walled canyon.

Gulf   Part of an ocean or sea that extends inland. Gulfs are generally larger than bays.

Hemisphere   One half of the earth's surface, however it is divided. For example, the northern hemisphere lies north of the equator; the southern hemisphere, south of the equator. By convention, the eastern hemisphere consists of the continents of Europe, Asia, and Africa; the western hemisphere, of North America and South America.

Inlet   An indentation in the shore of a sea or an ocean or in the bank of a river. Also, a narrow waterway which connects a lagoon to a larger body of water or which passes between two peninsulas.

Island   A land mass completely surrounded by water.

Isthmus   A narrow strip of land which connects two larger land masses.

Lagoon   A shallow pool or pond completely or almost completely separated from the sea.

Lake   A body of water, often of considerable size, surrounded by land.

Latitude and Longitude   Latitude is the angle (measured in degrees, minutes, and seconds) between a point on the earth's surface north or south of the equator, the center of the earth, and the equator (0°0'0" latitude). Longitude is the angle between a point on the earth's surface, the center of the earth, and the prime meridian (0°0'0" longitude). There are 90° of latitude between the equator and each of the poles (shown on a globe as parallel horizontal lines). There are 360° of longitude (shown as vertical lines) divided into 180° east and west of the prime meridian (180°E and 180°W are the same). Since 1884, Greenwich, England (near London), has been universally recognized as the point through which the prime meridian passes. A degree (°) is 1/360 of a circle, a minute (') 1/60 of a degree, and a second (") 1/60 of a minute.

Lava   Magma which reaches the surface of the earth and from which most of the gases have escaped. (See *Magma, Volcano*.)

Leeward   The direction or side sheltered from the wind. (See *Windward*.)

Magma   Molten rock that lies deep within the earth. In a volcanic eruption, magma bursts through the outer surface of the earth's crust. (See *Lava, Volcano*.)

Mountain   Land that rises above its surroundings. Mountains are higher than hills. Older mountain ranges, like the Appalachians, are rounded because they are old and worn down; younger ranges, like the Andes or the Himalayas, have jagged peaks because they are still rising.

North Pole   The northernmost point of the Earth's axis, at latitude 90°N. From this point, the only direction is south. It is entirely surrounded by water, and usually covered by ice. The first successful expedition to the North Pole—there is some doubt as to whether they actually reached the pole—was led by by Adm. Robert E. Peary, Apr. 6, 1909.

Ocean   (See "Oceans of the World," later in this section).

Peninsula   A portion of land surrounded by water on three sides.

Plain   A large portion of level or rolling land which is treeless.

Plate tectonics theory   The theory, first proposed in 1968, that Earth's crust is made up of 20 sections or "plates," each of which consists of continental and ocean crust. The plates shift, moving continents, changing the size and shape of oceans, causing earthquakes, and creating volcanos and mountains. The plate tectonics theory has largely replaced the *continental drift theory*.

Plateau   A portion of land, generally large and with a level surface, which is sharply elevated above the surrounding land. Plateaus are created when vertical movement causes the earth's crust to warp.

Pond   A small body of water surrounded by land.

Prairie   Level or rolling land generally covered with grasses, with few trees.

Rain shadow   An area on the leeward side of a mountain range which receives little rainfall.

River   A large stream.

Sahel   The Arabic word for "shore," the Sahel is a dry region separating the Sahara desert from tropical and West Central Africa running from Senegal to Sudan. The meager rainfall (4-8 inches per year) supports limited crops and grazing.

Savanna   A portion of land in the tropics or subtropics with only scattered trees but whose grasses can survive with scant rainfall.

Sea   A large body of saltwater, generally considered smaller than an ocean.

Solstice   The time when the sun's rays strike vertically the Tropic of Cancer or the Tropic of Capricorn. At solstice, the daylight hours reach their maximum or minimum. In the Northern Hemisphere, for example, summer solstice occurs on or about June 22; that is the "longest day of the year" and signals the beginning of summer. The winter solstice occurs on or about December 22; that is the "shortest day of the year" and signals the beginning of winter. In the southern hemisphere, the longest and shortest days of the year occur on December 22 and June 22, respectively. (See also *Equinox*.)

Sound   A body of water which separates an island from the mainland; or which connects two oceans, seas, or other bodies of water. Sounds are generally long and narrow.

South Pole   The southernmost point of the Earth's axis, at 90°S. First reached by Norwegian explorer Roald Admundsen in 1911, the South Pole lies in the South Polar region.

Steppe   A portion of land with little rainfall, extreme temperature variations, and drought-resistant vegetation.

Strait   A narrow body of water that connects two large bodies of water.

Stream   Any body of running water that flows on or under the surface of the earth. Brooks and creeks are small streams; rivers are large streams.

Swamp   A portion of wet, waterlogged, or flooded land.

Tide   The rise and fall of the surface of the ocean and of bays, gulfs, and other bodies of water connected to the ocean. Tides are caused by the gravitational pull of the moon, which passes over the same meridian of the Earth about once every 24 hours and 50 minutes. The length of time between successive high (or low) tides is about 12 hours and 25 minutes.

Tributary   A stream or river that flows into a larger stream or river.

Tropic of Cancer   Latitude 23½°N, which marks the northernmost limit of the sun's vertical rays. The area between the Tropic of Cancer and the Tropic of Capricorn is known as the "tropics."

Tropic of Capricorn   Latitude 23½°S, the southernmost limit of the sun's vertical rays.

Tundra   An area of treeless plain near or above the Arctic Circle. Tundra subsoil is permanently frozen, but the soil thaws enough to support the growth of mosses, lichens, and some small flowering shrubs.

Valley   A long and sometimes narrow depression on the surface of the earth, usually between two mountain ridges or ranges.

Volcano   A mountain formed by lava and/or other materials which have burst forth from deep within the earth. (See *Caldera, Lava, Magma*.)

Windward   The direction or side facing the wind.

World Land Area and Population by Selected Region, 1995

Region	Land Area			Population			
	Square miles	Square kilometers	Percent of world total	Total ('000s)	Percent of total	Per square mile	Per square kilometer
World total[1]	57,308,738	148,429,000	100.0%	5,702,000	100.0%	99.5	38.4
Africa	11,608,156	30,065,000	20.3	719,785	12.6	62.0	23.9
Antarctica	5,100,021	13,209,000	8.9	(2)	(2)	(2)	(2)
Asia	17,212,041	44,579,000	30.0	3,493,585	61.3	203.0	78.4
Australia	2,967,966	7,687,000	5.2	18,031	0.3	6.1	2.3
Europe	3,837,082	9,938,000	6.7	686,364	12.0	178.9	69.1
North America	9,365,290	24,256,000	16.3	455,100	8.0	48.6	18.8
South America	6,879,952	17,819,000	8.9	318,611	5.6	46.3	17.9

1. Land only. Includes small islands not shown separately. 2. Antarctica has no indigenous population.
Source: *National Geographic Atlas of the World* (1995).

The Continents: Highest And Lowest Elevations

Continent	Highest point	Location	Feet above sea level	Meters above sea level
Africa	Mt. Kilimanjaro	Tanzania	19,340	5,895
Antarctica	Vinson Massif	Ellsworth Mts.	16,066	4,897
Asia	Mt. Everest	Nepal-China	29,028	8,848
Australia	Mt. Kosciusko	New South Wales	7,310	2,228
Europe	Mt. Elbrus	Russia	18,510	5,642
North America	Mt. McKinley	US (Alaska)	20,320	6,194
South America	Mt. Aconcagua	Argentina	22,834	6,960

Continent	Lowest point	Location	Feet below sea level	Meters below sea level
Africa	Lake Assal	Djibouti	512	156
Antarctica	ice covered	—	8,327	2,538
Asia	Dead Sea	Israel-Jordan	1,339	408
Australia	Lake Eyre	South Australia	52	16
Europe	Caspian Sea	Russia, Kazakhstan	92	28
North America	Death Valley	US (California)	282	86
South America	Valdes Peninsula	Argentina	131	40

Source: *National Geographic Atlas of the World* (1995).

The Oceans Of The World

Name	Area ('000s)		Maximum depth	
	Sq. km.	Sq. mi.	Meters	Feet
Atlantic Ocean:	**311,830**	**82,440**	**9,219**	**30,246**
with marginal seas	106,460	41,100	—	—
Arctic Ocean	14,090	5,400	5,450	17,881
Caribbean Sea	2,754	1,063	7,680	25,197
Mediterranean Sea	2,505	967	5,020	16,470
Norwegian Sea	1,547	597	4,020	13,189
Gulf of Mexico	1,544	596	4,380	14,370
Hudson Bay	1,230	475	259	850
Greenland Sea	1,205	465	4,846	15,899
North Sea	575	222	659	2,170
Black Sea	461	178	2,237	7,360
Baltic Sea	422	163	437	1,440
Pacific Ocean:	**165,250**	**63,800**	**11,034**	**36,200**
with marginal seas	179,680	69,370	—	—
South China Sea	3,447	1,331	5,560	18,241
Sea of Okhotsk	1,580	610	3,372	11,063
Bering Sea	2,270	876	4,191	13,750
East China Sea	1,248	482	9,840	29,840
Yellow Sea	1,243	480	91	300
Sea of Japan	1,007	389	3,733	12,280
Indian Ocean:	**73,440**	**28,360**	**7,450**	**24,442**
with marginal seas	74,920	28,930	—	—
Arabian Sea	3,863	1,492	5,800	19,029
Bay of Bengal	2,172	839	5,258	17,251
Red Sea	438	169	2,240	7,370

Source: International Hydrographic Organization.

▶THE OCEANS OF THE WORLD

The water of the world's oceans covers more than 70 percent of the world's surface. While for many years the so-called World Ocean was divided into five parts—the Pacific, Atlantic, Indian, Arctic and Antarctic—scientists today commonly recognize only the first three as separate and distinct oceans. The Arctic and Antarctic, as well as other large bodies of water such as the Caribbean Sea, the Gulf of Mexico, Hudson Bay, the Mediterranean and Black seas, and the South China Sea are termed marginal seas. The International Hydrographic Organization identifies 66 seas, gulfs, bays, bights, straits, channels, and passages, many of which are further subdivided. For instance, the Mediterranean Sea is divided into western and eastern basins, and the western basin is subdivided into the Strait of Gibraltar, Aboran Sea, Balearic Sea, Ligurian Sea, Tyrrhenian Sea, Ionian Sea, Adriatic Sea, and Aegean Sea. The table (above) gives the area and maximum depths of the world's three major oceans and selected marginal seas.

Great Deserts of the World

Desert	Location	Approximate size	
		Sq. mi.	Sq. km.
An Nafud[1]	N Saudi Arabia	40,000	103,600
Atacama	N Chile	70,000	181,300
Black Rock	NW Nevada	1,000	2,600
Chihuahuan	Texas, New Mexico, Arizona; Mexico	140,000	362,600
Dasht-e-Kavir	Central Iran	30,000	77,600
Dasht-e-Lut	E Iran	20,000	51,800
Death Valley	E California, SW Nevada	3,000	7,800
Gibson[2]	W Australia	120,000	310,800
Gobi	Mongolia; China	500,000	1,295,000
Great Sandy[2]	NW Australia	150,000	338,500
Great Victoria[2]	SW Australia	150,000	338,500
Kalahari	S Africa	225,000	582,800
Kara Kum (Turkestan)	Turkmenistan	120,000	310,800
Kyzyl Kum	Uzbekistan	100,000	259,000
Libyan[3]	Libya; SW Egypt; Sudan	450,000	1,165,500
Mojave	S California, W Arizona	15,000	38,900
Namib	Namibia	800[4]	1,290[4]
Negev[3]	S Israel	4,700	12,200
Nubian[3]	NE Sudan	100,000	259,000
Painted Desert	N Arizona	200[5]	320[5]
Rub al-Khali ("Empty Quarter")[1]	S Saudi Arabia	250,000	647,500
Sahara	N Africa	3,500,000	9,065,000
Simpson[2]	Central Australia	40,000	103,600
Sonoran	SW Arizona; SE California; NW Mexico	70,000	181,300
Syrian[1]	N Saudi Arabia; E Jordan; S Syria; W Iraq	100,000	259,000
Taklimakan	Xinjiang Uygur Autonomous Region, China	140,000	362,600
Thar (Great Indian)	NW India; Pakistan	100,000	259,000

1. Part of Great Arabian Desert. 2. Part of Great Australian Desert. 3. Part of Sahara Desert. 4. Length; width varies from 30-100 mi. (48-160 km). 5. Length; width varies from 15-30 mi. (24-48 km).

▶THE GREAT DESERTS OF THE WORLD

To many people, the word *desert* brings to mind images of shifting sand dunes, scorching sun, and occasional lush oases. But there are actually many kinds of deserts, because a desert is simply an area which receives little precipitation and has little plant cover. Thus polar areas can be considered deserts, for their precipitation is locked into ice and snow. So are places like the Taklimakan in China, which lies in a rain shadow on the leeward side of mountain ranges, and the Atacama, which is near cold ocean currents that cool the air and prevent the formation of rain clouds. But most deserts are found in the tropics, where giant high-pressure cells keep rain from forming. Some deserts are indeed flat and sandy, but others are solid rock, loose pebbles, or even mountain plateaus. One of the many fascinating characteristics of deserts is their strangely shaped rock formations, created by wind-whipped sand.

Altogether, arid lands cover about a fifth of the Earth's total land surface—a third if semi-arid areas are also included. About a billion people live in arid and semiarid areas, and more than 100 countries are facing problems associated with expanding deserts.

Uses of the desert   Even the hot, sandy tropical deserts are not necessarily, as their name implies, deserted. Traders, herders, and farmers have called the desert home for thousands of years. Settlements have grown up around oases or in irrigated areas, from ancient times to the present. Deserts are important to historians, archaeologists, paleontologists, and other scientists, for the relics of the past that are preserved there. Dinosaur eggs have been found in the Gobi Desert, for instance, and whole cities are said to lie buried beneath the Taklimakan Desert.

Deserts are also important for extractive industries. The Negev was the site of the fabled King Solomon's mines. In the 19th century, borax was mined in Death Valley. Petroleum is found in the Sahara and in the deserts of the Arabian Peninsula. The Atacama is famed for its deposits of nitrate and copper. The Rub al-Khali, or "Empty Quarter" of Saudi Arabia, is thought to contain deposits of limestone and gravel—but no one is certain because it has never been fully explored.

Desert extremes
- The Sahara is the largest desert, with an area greater than the continental United States.
- The driest place on earth is in the Atacama Desert of Chile, where no rainfall at all was recorded between 1570 and 1971.
- The highest temperature ever recorded—136° F (58° C)—was at Al-Aziziya, in the Libyan Desert, but the Dalol, Denakil Depression in Ethiopia is consistently the hottest place on earth, with an annual average temperature of 93°F (34 °C)
- The lowest point in the world—1,312 feet (400m) below sea level—is on the shores of the Dead Sea in the Negev Desert.
- The lowest point in the Western Hemisphere—282 feet (86 meters) below sea level—is in Death Valley, California.

The World's Highest Mountain Peaks

Mountain peak	Range	Location	Height Feet	Meters
Everest	Himalayas	Nepal-China	29,028	8,848
K2 (Godwin Austen)	Karakoram	Kashmir	28,250	8,611
Kanchenjunga	Himalayas	Nepal-India	28,208	8,598
Lhotse I	Himalayas	Nepal-China	27,923	8,511
Makalu I	Himalayas	Nepal-China	27,824	8,481
Lhotse II	Himalayas	Nepal-China	27,560	8,400
Dhaulagiri	Himalayas	Nepal	26,810	8,172
Manaslu I	Himalayas	Nepal	26,760	8,156
Cho Oyu	Himalayas	Nepal-China	26,750	8,153
Nanga Parbat	Himalayas	Kashmir	26,660	8,126
Annapurna	Himalayas	Nepal	26,504	8,078
Gasherbrum	Karakoram	Kashmir	26,470	8,068
Broad	Karakoram	Kashmir	26,400	8,047
Gosainthan	Himalayas	China	26,287	8,012
Annapurna II	Himalayas	Nepal	26,041	7,937
Gyachung Kang	Himalayas	Nepal-China	25,910	7,897
Disteghil Sar	Himalayas	Kashmir	25,858	7,882
Himalchuli	Himalayas	Nepal	25,801	7,864
Nuptse	Himalayas	Nepal-China	25,726	7,841
Masherbrum	Karakoram	Kashmir	25,660	7,821
Nanda Devi	Himalayas	India	25,645	7,817
Rakaposhi	Karakoram	Kashmir	25,550	7,788
Kanjut Sar	Karakoram	Kashmir	25,461	7,761
Kamet	Himalayas	India-China	25,447	7,756
Namcha Barwa	Himalayas	China	25,445	7,756
Kua-la-man-ta-t`a (Gurla Mandhata)	Himalayas	China	25,355	7,728
Wu-lu-k'o-mu-shih (Ulugh Muztagh)	Kunlun	China	25,340	7,724
Kung-ko-erh (Kungur)	Mu-ssu-t'a-ko-a-t'e (Muztagh Ata)	China	25,325	7,719
Tirich Mir	Hindu Kush	Pakistan	25,230	7,690
Saser Kangri	Karakoram	Kashmir	25,172	7,672
Makalu II	Himalayas	Nepal-China	25,120	7,657
Minya Konka (Gonggashan)	Daxue Shan	China	24,900	7,590
Kula Kangri	Himalayas	Bhutan-China	24,784	7,554
Chang-tzu	Himalayas	Nepal-China	24,780	7,553
Mu-ssu-t'a-ko-a-t'e (Muztagh Ata)	Mu-ssu-t'a-ko-a-t'e (Muztagh Ata)	China	24,757	7,546
Skyang Kangri	Himalayas	Kashmir	24,750	7,544
Communism Peak	Pamirs	Tajikistan	24,590	7,495
Jongsong Peak	Himalayas	Nepal-India	24,472	7,459
Pobeda Peak	Tien Shan	Kyrgyzstan-China	24,406	7,439
Sia Kangri	Himalayas	Kashmir	24,350	7,422
Haramosh Peak	Karakoram	Kashmir	24,270	7,397
Istoro Nal	Hindu Kush	Pakistan	24,240	7,388
Tent Peak	Himalayas	Nepal-India	24,165	7,365
Chomo Lhari	Himalayas	Bhutan-China	24,040	7,327
Chamlang	Himalayas	Nepal	24,012	7,319
Kabru	Himalayas	Nepal-India	24,002	7,316
Alung Gangri	Himalayas	China	24,000	7,315
Baltoro Kangri	Himalayas	Kashmir	23,990	7,312
Muztagh Ata	Kunlun	China	23,890	7,282
Mana	Himalayas	India	23,860	7,273
Baruntse	Himalayas	Nepal	23,688	7,220
Nepal Peak	Himalayas	Nepal-India	23,500	7,163
Amne Machin	Kunlun	China	23,490	7,160
Gauri Sankar	Himalayas	Nepal-China	23,440	7,145
Badrinath	Himalayas	India	23,420	7,138
Nunkun	Himalayas	Kashmir	23,410	7,135
Lenin Peak	Pamirs	Tajikistan	23,405	7,134
Pyramid	Himalayas	Nepal-India	23,400	7,132
Api	Himalayas	Nepal	23,399	7,132
Pauhunri	Himalayas	India-China	23,385	7,128
Trisul	Himalayas	India	23,360	7,120
Korzhenevski Peak	Pamirs	Tajikistan	23,310	7,105
Kangto	Himalayas	India-China	23,260	7,090

Mountain peak	Range	Location	Height	
			Feet	Meters
Nyainqentanglha	Nyainqentanglha Shan	China	23,255	7,088
Trisuli	Himalayas	India	23,210	7,074
Dunagiri	Himalayas	India	23,184	7,066
Revolution Peak	Pamirs	Tajikistan	22,880	6,974
Aconcagua	Andes	Argentina	22,834	6,960
Ojos del Salado	Andes	Argentina-Chile	22,572	6,880
Bonete	Andes	Argentina	22,546	6,872
Tupungato	Andes	Argentina-Chile	22,310	6,800
Moscow Peak	Pamirs	Tajikistan	22,260	6,785
Pissis	Andes	Argentina	22,241	6,779
Mercedario	Andes	Argentina	22,211	6,770
Huascaran	Andes	Peru	22,205	6,768
Llullaillaco	Andes	Argentina-Chile	22,057	6,723
El Libertador	Andes	Argentina	22,047	6,720
Cachi	Andes	Argentina	22,047	6,720
Kailas	Himalayas	China	22,027	6,714
Incahuasi	Andes	Argentina-Chile	21,720	6,620
Yerupaja	Andes	Peru	21,709	6,617
Kurumda	Pamirs	Tajikistan	21,686	6,610
Galan	Andes	Argentina	21,654	6,600
El Muerto	Andes	Argentina-Chile	21,457	6,540
Sajama	Andes	Bolivia	21,391	6,520
Nacimiento	Andes	Argentina	21,302	6,493
Illimani	Andes	Bolivia	21,201	6,462
Coropuna	Andes	Peru	21,083	6,426
Laudo	Andes	Argentina	20,997	6,400
Ancohuma	Andes	Bolivia	20,958	6,388
Ausangate	Andes	Peru	20,945	6,384
Toro	Andes	Argentina-Chile	20,932	6,380
Illampu	Andes	Bolivia	20,873	6,362
Tres Cruces	Andes	Argentina-Chile	20,853	6,356
Huandoy	Andes	Peru	20,852	6,356
Parinacota	Andes	Bolivia-Chile	20,768	6,330
Tortolas	Andes	Argentina-Chile	20,745	6,323
Ampato	Andes	Peru	20,702	6,310
El Condor	Andes	Argentina	20,669	6,300
Salcantay	Andes	Peru	20,574	6,271
Chimborazo	Andes	Ecuador	20,561	6,267
Huancarhuas	Andes	Peru	20,531	6,258
Famatina[1]	Andes	Argentina	20,505	6,250
Pumasillo	Andes	Peru	20,492	6,246
Solo	Andes	Argentina	20,492	6,246
Polleras	Andes	Argentina	20,456	6,235
Pular	Andes	Chile	20,423	6,225
Chani	Andes	Argentina	20,341	6,200
McKinley	Alaska	US (Alaska)	20,320	6,194
Aucanquilcha	Andes	Chile	20,295	6,186
Juncal	Andes	Argentina-Chile	20,276	6,180
Negro	Andes	Argentina	20,184	6,152
Quela	Andes	Argentina	20,128	6,135
Condoriri	Andes	Bolivia	20,095	6,125
Palermo	Andes	Argentina	20,079	6,120
Solimana	Andes	Peru	20,068	6,117
San Juan	Andes	Argentina-Chile	20,049	6,111
(Sierra) Nevada	Andes	Argentina-Chile	20,023	6,103
Antofalla	Andes	Argentina	20,013	6,100
Marmolejo	Andes	Argentina-Chile	20,013	6,100

1. Formerly General Manuel Belgrano.

Major Natural Lakes Of The World

Lake	Surface area		Location	Maximum depth		Elevation	
	Sq. mi.	Sq. km.		Feet	Meters	Feet	Meters
Caspian Sea[1]	143,240	370,992	Russia, Kazakhstan, Azerbaijan, Turkmenistan, Iran	3,363	1,025	- 92	- 28
Superior	31,700	82,103	Ontario, Canada; Mich., Wis., Minn.	1,333	406	600	183
Victoria	26,820	69,464	Uganda, Kenya, Tanzania	279	85	3,720	1,134
Aral Sea[1]	24,904	64,501	Uzbekistan, Kazakhstan	220	67	174	53
Huron	23,000	59,570	Ontario, Can.; Mich.	750	229	576	176
Michigan	22,300	57,757	Mich., Ind., Ill., Wis.	923	281	579	176
Tanganyika	12,350	31,987	Burundi, Tanzania, Zambia, Zaire	4,800	1,463	2,543	775
Baikal	12,160	31,494	Russia	5,315	1,620	1,493	455
Great Bear	12,028	31,153	Northwest Terr., Canada	1,356	413	512	156
Nyasa (Malawi)	11,150	28,879	Tanzania, Mozambique, Malawi	2,280	695	1,550	472
Great Slave	11,030	28,568	Northwest Terr., Canada	2,015	614	513	156
Erie	9,910	25,667	Ontario, Canada; N.Y., Pa., Ohio, Mich.	210	64	570	174
Winnipeg	9,417	24,390	Manitoba, Canada	92	28	713	217
Ontario	7,540	19,529	Ontario, Canada; N.Y.	802	244	245	75
Balkhash[1]	7,115[2]	18,428[2]	Kazakhstan	87	27	1,115	340
Ladoga	6,835	17,703	Russia	755	230	13	4
Chad	6,300	16,317	Chad, Nigeria, Niger	24	7	787	240
Maracaibo[3]	5,200	13,468	Venezuela	197	60	sea level	
Patos[3]	3,920	10,153	Brazil	15	5	([4])	([4])
Onega	3,720	9,635	Russia	394	120	108	33
Titicaca	3,200	8,288	Bolivia, Peru	990	302	12,500	3,810
Nicaragua	3,150	8,159	Nicaragua	230	70	102	31
Mai-Ndombe	3,100	8,029[2]	Zaire	36	11	1,116	340
Athabasca	3,064	7,936	Saskatchewan, Alberta, Canada	407	124	700	213
Eyre[1]	2,970[2]	7,692[2]	Australia	4	1	- 52	- 16
Reindeer	2,568	6,651	Saskatchewan, Manitoba, Canada	720	219	1,106	337
Tonle Sap	2,500[2]	6,475[2]	Cambodia	39	12	([4])	([4])
Rudolf[1]	2,473	6,405	Kenya, Ethiopia	720	219	1,230	375
Issyk-Kul[1]	2,355	6,099	Kyrghyzstan	2,303	702	5,279	1,609
Torrens[1]	2,230[2]	5,776[2]	Australia	0.5	0.2	92	28
Albert	2,160	5,594	Uganda, Zaire	168	51	2,030	619
Vanern	2,156	5,54	Sweden	325	99	144	44
Nettilling	2,140	5,543	Baffin Island, Canada	([4])	([4])	95	29
Winnipegosis	2,075	5,374	Manitoba, Canada	39	12	830	253
Bangweulu	1,930	4,999	Zambia	5	2	3,500	1,067
Nipigon	1,872	4,848	Ontario, Canada	541	165	1,050	320
Gairdner[1]	1,840[2]	4,763[2]	Australia	0.5	0.2	112	34
Urmia[1]	1,815[2]	4,701[2]	Iran	49	15	4,180	1,274
Manitoba	1,800	4,662	Manitoba, Canada	92	28	813	248
Kyoga	1,710	4,429	Uganda	26	8	4	4
Khanka	1,700	4,403	China, Russia	33	10	4	4
Lake of the Woods	1,695	4,390	Ontario, Manitoba, Canada; Minn.	55	17	1,060	323
Great Salt[1]	1,680	4,351	Utah	48	15	4,200	1,280
Mweru	1,680	4,351	Zambia, Zaire	10	3	3,008	917
Peipus	1,660	4,299	Estonia, Russia	41	12	98	30
Koko Nor (Tsing Hai)	1,650	4,274	China	125	38	10,515	3,205
Dubawnt	1,600	4,144	Northwest Terr., Canada	([4])	([4])	774	236
Tung-t'ing Hu	1,430[2]	3,704[2]	China	([4])	([4])	36	11
Van Golu[1]	1,420	3,678	Turkey	82	25	5,643	1,720
Tana	1,390	3,600	Ethiopia	30	9	6,003	1,830

1. Saltwater. A lake is a body of water surrounded by land. The Caspian Sea is thus a lake. It was called a "sea" by the Romans because of its salty water. 2. Subject to large seasonal variation in surface area. 3. Lagoon. 4 . No information available.   **Source:** U.S. Department of Commerce, National Oceanic and Atmospheric Administration, *Principal Rivers and Lakes of the World* (1982).

Major Rivers Of The World, By Length

River	Length Miles	km	Source	Outflow
Nile	4,145	6,673	Tributaries of LakeVictoria, E. Africa	Mediterranean Sea
Amazon	4,000	6,440	Andes Mts., Peru	Atlantic Ocean
Mississippi-Missouri	3,740[1]	6,021[1]	Confluence of Jefferson, Madison, and Galatin R., Montana	Gulf of Mexico
Changjiang (Yangtze)	3,720	5,989	Kunlun Mts., China	China Sea
Yenisei-Angara	3,650[2]	5,877[2]	Lake Baikal, Russia	Kara Sea (Arctic Ocean)
Amur-Argun	3,590[2]	5,780[2]	Khingan Mts., China	Tatar Strait
Ob-Irtysh	3,360[2]	5,410[2]	Altai Mts., China	Gulf of Ob (Arctic Ocean)
Plata-Parana	3,030[2]	4,878[2]	Confluence of the Paranaiba and Grande rivers, Brazil	Atlantic Ocean
Huang He (Yellow)	2,903	4,674	Kunlun Mts., China	Gulf of Chihli (Yellow Sea)
Congo (Zaire)	2,900	4,669	Confluence of the Luapula and Lualaba rivers, Zaire	Atlantic Ocean
Lena	2,730	4,395	Baikal Mts., Russia	Laptev Sea (Arctic Ocean)
MacKenzie	2,635[2]	4,242[2]	Headwaters of Finlay Rivers, British Columbia, Canada	Beaufort Sea (Arctic Ocean)
Mekong	2,600	4,186	T'ang-ku-la Mts., Tibet	South China Sea
Niger	2,600	4,186	Guinea	Gulf of Guinea
Missouri	2,533	4,078	Confluence of Jefferson, Madison, and Montana Galatin rivers, Montana	Mississippi River
Mississippi	2,348[3]	3,780[3]	Lake Itasca, northwestern Minnesota	Gulf of Mexico
Murray-Darling	2,330	3,751	Great Dividing Range, Australia	Indian Ocean
Volga	2,290	3,687	Valdai Hills, Russia	Caspian Sea
Madeira	2,013	3,241	Confluence of the Mamore and Beni rivers, Bolivia/Brazil	Amazon River
Sao Francisco	1,988	3,201	Minas Gerais State, Brazil	Atlantic Ocean
Yukon	1,979	3,186	Confluence of Lewes and Pelly rivers, Yukon Territory, Canada	Bering Sea
Rio Grande	1,885	3,035	San Juan Mts., southwestern Colorado	Gulf of Mexico
Purus	1,860	2,995	Andes Mts., Peru	Amazon River
Tunguska, Lower	1,860	2,995	North of Lake Baikal, Russia	Yenesei River
Indus	1,800	2,898	Himalayas, Tibet	Arabian Sea
Danube	1,776	2,859	Confluence of Breg and Brigach rivers, Germany	Black Sea
Brahmaputra	1,770	2,850	Himalayas, Tibet	Ganges River
Salween	1,750	2,818	Tibetan Plateau, Tibet	Bay of Bengal
Para-Tocantins	1,710[2]	2,753[2]	Goias State, Brazil	Atlantic Ocean
Zambezi	1,700	2,737	Northwestern Zambia	Mozambique Channel
Paraguay	1,610	2,592	Mato Grosso State, Brazil	Parana River
Kolyma	1,320	2,130	Kolyma Mts., Russia	Arctic Ocean
Nelson-Saskatchewan	1,600	2,576	Rocky Mts., Canada	Hudson Bay
Orinoco	1,600	2,576	Sierra Parima Mts., Venezuela	Atlantic Ocean
Amu Darya	1,578	2,541	Pamir Mts., Uzbekistan/ Turkmenistan	Aral Sea
Ural	1,575	2,536	Ural Mountains, Russia	Caspian Sea
Ganges	1,560	2,512	Himalayas, India	Bay of Bengal
Euphrates	1,510	2,431	Confluence of the Murat Nehri and Kara Su rivers, Turkey	Shatt-al-Arab
Arkansas	1,450	2,335	Central Colorado	Mississippi River
Colorado	1,450	2,335	Northern Colorado	Gulf of California
Dneiper	1,420	2,286	Valdai Hills, Russia	Black Sea
Atchafalaya-Red	1,400	2,254	Eastern New Mexico	Gulf of Mexico
Syr Darya	1,370	2,206	Tien Shan, China/Kyrghyzstan	Aral Sea
Kasai	1,338	2,154	Central Angola	Congo (Zaire) River
Irrawaddy	1,300	2,093	Confluence of Mali and Nmai rivers, Myanmar	Bay of Bengal
Ohio-Allegheny	1,300	2,093	Pennsylvania	Mississippi River
Orange	1,300	2,093	Lesotho	Atlantic Ocean
Columbia	1,243	2,001	Columbia Lake, British Columbia, Canada	Pacific Ocean
Tigris	1,180	1,900	Eastern Turkey	Shatt-al-Arab
Rhine	820	1,320	Confluence of Hinterrhein and Vorderrhein rivers, Switzerland	North Sea
St. Lawrence	800	1,288	Lake Ontario	Gulf of St. Lawrence

1. From the mouth of the Mississippi, up the Missouri to the Red Rock River in Montana. 2. Includes the length of tributaries that are part of the main trunk stream. 3. From the mouth of the Mississippi, up to its source in Minnesota. **Source**: U.S. Dept. of Commerce, National Oceanic and Atmospheric Administration, *Principal Rivers and Lakes of the World* (1982).

The World's Largest Islands

Island	Location	Flags	Area	
			Sq. mi.	Sq. km.
Greenland	N. Atlantic Ocean	Denmark	840,000	2,175,600
New Guinea	S. Pacific Ocean	Indonesia, Papua New Guinea	306,000	792,540
Borneo	Pacific Ocean	Indonesia, Malaysia, Brunei	280,100	725,459
Madagascar	Indian Ocean	Madagascar	226,658	587,044
Baffin	Arctic Ocean	Canada	195,928	507,454
Sumatra	Indian Ocean, S. Pacific Ocean	Indonesia	165,000	427,350
Honshu	N. Pacific Ocean	Japan	87,805	227,415
Great Britain	N. Atlantic Ocean	United Kingdom	84,200	218,078
Victoria	Arctic Ocean	Canada	83,896	217,291
Ellesmere	Arctic Ocean	Canada	75,767	196,237
Celebes	Pacific Ocean	Indonesia	69,000	178,710
South Island	S. Pacific Ocean	New Zealand	58,305	151,010
Java	Indian Ocean, S. Pacific Ocean	Indonesia	48,900	126,651
Cuba	Caribbean Sea	Cuba	44,218	114,525
North Island	S. Pacific Ocean	New Zealand	44,035	114,051
Newfoundland	N. Atlantic Ocean	Canada	42,030	108,858
Luzon	N. Pacific Ocean	Philippines	40,880	105,879
Iceland	N. Atlantic Ocean	Iceland	39,769	103,002
Mindanao	N. Pacific Ocean	Philippines	36,775	95,247
Novaya Zemlya	Arctic Ocean	Russia	35,000	90,650
Ireland	N. Atlantic Ocean	Irish Republic, United Kingdom	32,599	84,431
Hokkaido	S. Pacific Ocean	Japan	30,144	78,073
Hispaniola	Caribbean Sea	Haiti, Dominican Republic	29,530	76,483
Sakhalin	N. Pacific Ocean	Russia	29,500	76,405
Banks	Arctic Ocean	Canada	27,033	70,015
Tasmania	S. Pacific Ocean	Australia	26,178	67,801
Sri Lanka	Indian Ocean	Sri Lanka	25,332	65,610
Devon	Arctic Ocean	Canada	21,331	55,247

▶ THE POLAR REGIONS
Antarctica

● **GEOGRAPHY   Location:** continent mostly south of Antarctic Circle at 90°S. **Boundaries:** None. Bordered by South Atlantic, Indian and South Pacific oceans. **Total land area:** about 5,404,000 sq. mi. (14,000,000 sq. km.). **Coastline:** 11,165 mi. (17,968 km). **Comparative area:** twice the size of Australia. **Land use:** 98% continental ice sheet; 2% barren rock. **Natural Resources:** None presently exploited. Iron ore, chromium, copper, gold, nickel, platinum, and other minerals, as well as coal and hydrocarbons have been found in small uncommercial qualities. **Temperature:** Varies with location and altitude. East Antarctica is coldest; Antarctic Peninsula in the west is mildest; mean annual temperature of the interior regions is -57°C (-71°F); mean temperatures at the coastal McMurdo station range from -28°C (-18°F) in August to -3°C (27°F) in January. **Major cities:** none.

● **THE LAND**   Some 200 million years ago Antarctica was joined to South America, Africa, India and Australia as one large continent. Geological changes caused the breakup into separate continents. Studies indicate that Antarctica once had a tropical environment, but that its present ice form is at least 20 million years old. Approximately 98 percent of the continent is covered by ice; contains about 90 percent of the world's ice and 70 percent of the fresh water. Elevations average from 6,600 ft. to 13,200 ft. (2,000-4,000 m); mountain ranges up to 16,500 ft. (5,500 m) high. Ice-free coastal areas include parts of southern Victoria Land, Wilkes Land and Ross Island. The Antarctic ice sheet averages 7,090 ft. (2,160 m) in depth and is 15,670 ft. (4,776 m) deep at its thickest point. Altitude at the South Pole is about 9,800 ft. (3,000 m)

● **LAND/SEA LIFE:** Land life includes bacteria, lichens, mosses, two kinds of flowering plants in the ice-free areas, penguins and some flying birds. Sea life includes several types of seals and whales many of which were hunted to near extinction but are now protected by international conventions.

● **EXPLORATION:**   British Captain James Cook circumnavigated the continent without sighting land in 1772-75. U.S. Capt. John Davis made the first known landing on the continent on Feb. 7, 1821. In 1908 the UK became the first nation to claim a "slice" of the continent, subsequently followed by claims from New Zealand (1923), France (1924), Australia (1933), Norway (1939), Chile (1940) and Argentina (1943). The U.S. and Russia have never claimed any Antarctica territory. Claims made by other nations are not recognized by other countries nor the UN.

In 1911 Capt. Robert F. Scott and Roald Amundsen of Norway began a "race to the pole." Amundsen's party arrived at the South Pole on 14 December 1911 while Scott located the pole on 18 January 1912.

● **SCIENTIFIC RESEARCH:**   The greatest scientific study ever conducted in Antarctica occurred in 1957-58 when 67 nations participated in the International Geophysical Year (IGY). Twelve countries established more than 50 stations to study the effects of the continent's huge ice mass on global weather, the oceans, the aurora australis

World's 25 Largest Capacity Reservoirs

	Capacity (mil.)			
Reservoir	Cubic yards[1]	Cubic meters[1]	River or basin and location	Year completed
1. Owen Falls[2]	3,537,000	2,700,000	Lake Victoria/Nile, Uganda	1954
2. Kakhovskaya	238,420	182,000	Dnieper, Ukraine	1955
3. Kariba	236,586	180,600	Zambezi, Zimbabwe/Zambia	1959
4. Bratsk	221,744	169,270	Angara, Russia	1964
5. Aswan High	221,259	168,900	Nile, Egypt	1970
6. Akosombo	200,430	153,000	Volta, Ghana	1965
7. Daniel Johnson	185,826	141,852	Manicouagan, Quebec	1968
8. Guri	180,780	138,000	Caroni, Venezuela	1986
9. Krasnoyarsk	96,023	73,300	Yenesei, Russia	1967
10. W.A.C. Bennett	92,105	70,309	Peace, British Columbia	1967
11. Zeya	89,604	68,400	Zeya, Russia	1978
12. Cabora Bassa	82,530	63,000	Zambezi, Mozambique	1974
13. La Grande 2	80,847	61,715	La Grande, Quebec	1978
14. La Grande 3	78,626	60,020	La Grande, Quebec	1981
15. Ust-Ilim	77,683	59,300	Angara, Russia	1977
16. Boguchany	76,242	58,200	Russia	1989
17. Volga-V.I. Lenin (Kuibyshev)	75,980	58,000	Volga, Russia	1955
18. Caniapiscau	70,478	53,800	Caniapiscau, Quebec, Canada	1981
19. Bukhtarma	65,238	49,800	Irtysh, Russia	1960
20. Atatürk	63,797	48,700	Euphrates, Turkey	1990
21. Irkutsk	60,260	46,000	Angara, Russia	1956
22. Tucurui	56,330	45,800	Tocantins, Brazil	1984
23. Lower Kama	58,858	45,000	Kama, Russia	1987
24. Vilyui	47,029	35,900	Vilyui, Russia	1967
25. Sanmenxia	46,374	35,400	Huanghe (Yellow), China	1960

Note: Uncompleted reservoirs are not officially ranked. 1. One cubic yard equals 0.765 cubic meters. 2. Includes a natural lake.
Source: *International Water Power & Dam Construction Handbook 1993.*

World's 25 Largest Volume Dams

	Volume ('000s)			
Reservoir	Cubic yards[1]	Cubic meters[1]	River or basin and location	Year completed
1. New Cornelia Tailings	274,445	209,500	Ten Mile Wash, Arizona	1973
2. Tarbela	138,297	106,000	Indus, Pakistan	1976
3. Fort Peck	125,825	96,050	Missouri, Montana	1937
4. Lower Usuma	121,830	93,000	Usuma, Nigeria	1990
5. Tucurui	111,612	85,200	Tocantins, Brazil	1984
6. Atatürk	111,350	84,500	Euphrates, Turkey	1990
7. Guri (Raul Leoni)	102,142	77,971	Caroni, Venezuela	1986
8. Oahe	87,137	66,517	Missouri, South Dakota	1958
9. Gardiner	85,726	65,400	South Saskatchewan, Saskatchewan	1968
10. Mangla	85,646	65,379	Jhelum, Pakistan	1967
11. Afsluitdijk	83,093	63,430	Zuider Zee, Netherlands	1932
12. Oroville	80,125	61,164	Feather, California	1968
13. San Luis	78,022	59,559	San Luis, California	1967
14. Nurek	75,980	58,000	Vakhsh, Tajikistan	1980
15. Garrison	66,607	50,845	Missouri, North Dakota	1956
16. Cochiti	65,801	50,230	Grande, New Mexico	1975
17. Oosterschelde	65,500	50,000	Vense Gat Oosterschelde, Netherlands	1986
18. Tabqua (Thawra)	60,260	46,000	Euphrates, Syria	1976
19. Aswan, High	58,033	44,300	Nile, Egypt	1970
20. W.A.C. Bennett	57,290	43,733	Peace, Canada	1967
21. Kiev	55,544	42,400	Dnieper, Ukraine	1964
22. Dantiwada	53,762	41,040	Banas, India	1965
23. Saratov	52,924	40,400	Volga, Russia	1967
24. Earthquake Lake	50,079	38,228	Madison, Montana	1959
25. Fort Randall	50,042	38,200	Missouri, South Dakota	1952

Note: Volume refers to amount of material (earth, concrete, etc.) used in construction of dam. UC=Under Construction. Tailings dams are formed from waste ore (tailings) from mining. Uncompleted reservoirs are not officially ranked. 1. One cubic meter equals 1.31 cubic yards. Source: *International Water Power & Dam Construction Handbook 1993.*

and the ionosphere. During the late 1980s research was focused on the study of the ozone depletion in the stratosphere—called the "ozone hole"—which allows high levels of potentially harmful ultraviolet radiation to reach the earth's surface.

In 1998, 18 different countries maintained 42 research stations year-round. Argentina and the former Soviet Union each had six, the U.K. maintained five, Australia, Chile, South Africa and the U.S. kept three, China and Japan each had two, and Brazil, Finland, France, Germany, India, South Korea, New Zealand, Poland, and Uruguay each had one.

● **PEOPLE   Population:** No indigenous inhabitants. Staffing of research stations varies seasonally; Summer (January) popuation: approximately 4,415; Winter (July) population: approximately 1,046

● **GOVERNMENT   Antarctica Treaty:** Signed in 1959 by the 12 IGY nations (in force as of June 23, 1961), it establishes a legal framework for the management of Antarctica. The treaty was renewed in 1991 in Madrid, where 24 countries, including the United States, signed a protocol to ban mineral and oil exploration for 50 years and to provide wildlife protection. The treaty states that the area is to be used for peaceful purposes only and military activity such as weapons testing is prohibited; calls for freedom of scientific investigation and cooperation and a free exchange of information and personnel; nuclear explosions or disposal of radioactive wastes is forbidden; and, treaty-state observers have free access, including aerial observation, to any area and may inspect all stations, installations and equipment.

At the Treaty's 17th meeting in November, 1992, there were 26 consultative (voting) members and 15 acceding (non-voting) members. The 26 consultative members include the seven countries that claim part of Antarctica as national territory (Argentina, Australia, Chile, France, New Zealand, Norway, and the U.K.) as well as 15 nonclaimant nations. The claimant nations all signed the Antarctica Treaty in 1959; the 15 non-claimant nations (followed by the year they signed the treaty) are Belgium (1959), Brazil (1983), China (1985), Ecuador (1990), Finland (1989), Germany (1981), India (1983), Italy (1987), Japan (1959), South Korea (1989), Netherlands (1990), Peru (1989), Poland (1977), South Africa (1959), Spain (1988), Sweden (1988), Uruguay (1985), the U.S. (1959), and Russia (1959). The nonvoting members (and their year of accession) are Austria (1987), Bulgaria (1978), Canada (1988), Colombia (1988), Cuba (1984), Czechoslovakia (1962), Denmark (1965), Greece (1987), Guatemala (1991), Hungary (1984), North Korea (1987), Papua New Guinea (1981), Romania (1971), Slovakia (1993), Switzerland (1990), and Ukraine (1992).

The Arctic

● **GEOGRAPHY   Location:** The Arctic Regions comprise all the lands north of the Arctic Circle—66°30′N—including the northern reaches of Asia, Europe, and North America, the Arctic Ocean, and its islands. In terms of climate, geography, and culture this demarcation is relatively insignificant, but within the Arctic Circle there is at least one 24-hour period during which the sun never sets (summer solstice), and one in which it never rises (winter solstice). The Arctic Ocean is the fourth largest after the Pacific, Atlantic and Indian; its primary marginal seas are Baffin Bay, the Barents Sea, the Beaufort Sea, the Chukchi Sea,

the East Siberian Sea, the Greenland Sea, Hudson Bay, Hudson Strait, the Kara Sea, and the Laptev Sea. **Boundaries:** None. **Total area:** The Arctic Ocean is 5,430,505 sq. mi. (14,056,000 sq km). The main island groups are the Canadian Arctic Archipelago (550,000 sq. mi.; 1,424,483 sq km), Greenland (840,000 sq. mi.; 2,175,590 sq km), Novaya Zemlya (31,000 sq. mi.; 80,290 sq km), and Svalbard (24,000 sq. mi.; 62,160 sq km). **Coastline:** 17,525 sq. mi. (45,389 km). **Comparative area:** The Arctic Ocean is about 1.5 times the size of the United States. **Land use:** The central surface is covered by a perennial drifting polar ice cap which averages about 3 meters thick, although pressure ridges may be three times that size. It drifts in a clockwise pattern in the Beaufort Gyral Stream, but exhibits nearly straight-line movement from the New Siberian Islands (Russia) to the Denmark Strait (between Greenland and Iceland). The ice pack is surrounded by open seas during the summer, but more than doubles in size during the winter and extends to the encircling land masses; the ocean floor is about 50% continental shelf (the highest percentage of any ocean) with the remainder a central basin interrupted by three submarine ridges (the Alpha Cordillera, Nansen Cordillera, and Lomonsov Ridge). The maximum depth is 15,305 ft. (4,665 m) in the Fram Basin. **Natural resources:** In the Arctic Ocean there are sand and gravel aggregates, placer deposits, polymetallic nodules, oil and gas fields, fish, and marine mammals (seals and whales). **Climate:** The dominant fact of life is the frigid conditions: persistent cold and relatively modest annual temperature ranges; winters characterized by continuous darkness, cold and stable weather conditions and clear skies; summers characterized by continuous daylight, damp and foggy weather, and weak cyclones with rain or snow. Between 60°N and 75°N there is seasonal freezing, while north of 75°N there is permanent ice. In North America, temperatures during the colder months average -25°F (-31°C), while Siberia is somewhat colder at -35°F (-37°C). **Environment:** Endangered marine species include walruses and whales; ice islands occasionally break away from northern Ellesmere Island; icebergs calved from western Greenland and extreme northeastern Canada; maximum snow cover in March or April is about 20-50 cm over the frozen ocean and lasts about 10 months; permafrost in islands; virtually ice-locked from October to June; fragile ecosystem slow to change and slow to recover from disruptions or damage.

● **PEOPLE   Population** Ethnologists distinguish three native cultural areas—the Western Arctic, including Eskimo peoples (from the east coast of Greenland to Alaska), and Aleuts; Paleo-Siberian, including the Chukchi and Eskimos of Eastern Asia; and Eurasian Arctic, including some Chukchi, Yakut, Nenets, and Lapps. Today, however, the vast majority of the people living and working within the Arctic Circle are non-native peoples in industry or scientific enterprises.

● **GOVERNMENT** Governments with territory north of the Arctic Circle are Canada, the United States, Russia, Finland, Sweden, Norway, and Denmark (Greenland). Svalbard is the focus of a maritime boundary dispute between Norway and Russia.

● **ECONOMY** While there is a fair amount of economic activity in the continental portions of the Arctic—principally extractive industries in Siberia, northern Canada, and Alaska's North Slope—conditions in the numerous Arctic islands all but prevent significant development there. Norwegian and Russian miners extract about 1 million tons of coal per year from mines on Svalbard, and in Greenland there are large deposits of cryolite, lead, and other minerals, but only lead can be mined economically. Economic activity in the Arctic Ocean is limited to the exploitation of natural resources including crude oil, natural gas, fishing and sealing.

• **COMMUNICATIONS Ports:** Churchill (Canada), Murmansk (Russia), Prudhoe Bay (U.S.). **Telecommunications:** No submarine cables. **Transportation:** There is a sparse network of air, ocean, river, and land routes. The Arctic provides the shortest marine link between the extremes of eastern and western Russia. The two major waterways are the Northwest Passage, in North America, and the Northern Sea Route, in Asia, but ships are subject to superstructure icing from October to May. The U.S. and Russia operate floating research stations. Access to the Arctic Ocean from the Pacific Ocean is through the Bering Strait; from the Atlantic, through the Davis Strait (between Canada and Greenland), the Denmark Strait (between Greenland and Iceland), or the Norwegian Sea (between Iceland and Norway).

The 50 Tallest Buildings in the World

Rank/Building	City	Year	Stories	Height Meters	Feet
1. Petronas Tower 1	Kuala Lumpur	1998	88	452	1,483
2. Petronas Tower 2	Kuala Lumpur	1998	88	452	1,483
3. Sears Tower	Chicago	1974	110	442	1,450
4. Jin Mao Building	Shanghai	1999	88	421	1,380
5. World Trade Center, North	New York	1972	110	417	1,368
6. World Trade Center, South	New York	1973	110	415	1,362
7. Empire State Building	New York	1931	102	381	1,250
8. Central Plaza	Hong Kong	1992	78	374	1,227
9. Bank of China Tower	Hong Kong	1989	70	369	1,209
10. T&C Tower	Kaoshiung	1997	85	348	1,140
11. Amoco	Chicago	1973	80	346	1,136
12. The Center	Hong Kong	1998	79	346	1,135
13. John Hancock Center	Chicago	1969	100	344	1,127
14. Shun Hing Square	Shenzen	1996	69	325	1,066
15. Sky Central Plaza	Guangzhou	1997	80	322	1,056
16. Chicago Beach Tower Hotel	Dubai	UC 1999	60	321	1,053
17. Baiyoke Tower II	Bangkok	1997	90	320	1,050
18. Chrysler Building	New York	1930	77	319	1,046
19. NationsBank Plaza	Atlanta	1993	55	312	1,023
20. Library Tower	Los Angeles	1990	75	310	1,018
21. AT&T Corporate Center	Chicago	1989	60	307	1,007
22. Texas Commerce Tower	Houston	1982	75	305	1,000
23. Two Prudential Plaza	Chicago	1990	64	303	995
24. Ryugyong Hotel	Pyongyang	1995	105	300	984
25. Commerzbank Tower	Frankfurt	1997	56	299	981
26. First Interstate Bank Plaza	Houston	1983	71	296	972
27. Landmark Tower	Yokohama	1993	70	296	971
28. 311 South Wacker Drive	Chicago	1990	65	293	961
29. American International Building	New York	1932	67	290	952
30. First Canadian Place	Toronto	1975	72	290	951
31. Society Tower	Cleveland	1991	57	290	950
32. One Liberty Place	Philadelphia	1987	61	287	945
33. Columbia Seafirst Center	Seattle	1984	76	287	943
34. 40 Wall Street	New York	1930	72	283	927
35. NationsBank Plaza	Dallas	1985	72	281	921
36. Overseas Union Bank Plaza	Singapore	1986	66	280	919
37. United Overseas Bank Plaza	Singapore	1992	66	280	919
38. Republic Plaza	Singapore	1995	66	280	919
39. Citicorp Center	New York	1977	59	279	915
40. Scotia Plaza	Toronto	1989	68	275	902
41. Transco Tower	Houston	1983	64	275	901
42. Renaissance Tower	Dallas	1975	56	270	886
43. 900 North Michigan	Chicago	1989	66	265	871
44. NationsBank Corporate Center	Charlotte	1992	60	265	871
45. SunTrust Plaza	Atlanta	1992	60	265	871
46. Water Tower Place	Chicago	1976	74	262	859
47. First Interstate Tower	Los Angeles	1974	62	262	858
48. Canada Trust Tower	Toronto	1990	51	261	856
49. Transamerica Pyramid	San Francisco	1972	48	260	853
50. GE Building	New York	1933	70	259	850

Note: Height is measured from sidewalk level of main entrance to structural top of building. Television and radio antennas and flag poles are not included. UC=Under Construction, followed by expected completion date.
Source: Council on High Buildings and Urban Habitat, Lehigh University (1999).

Time Zones and Area Codes for Selected Nations and Territories

Country	Hours from EST	Country Code	City Codes
Afghanistan	+9.5	Direct dialing not available	
Albania	+6	355	Durres 52, Elbassan 545, Tirana 42
Algeria	+6	213	Adrar 7, Ain Defla 3, Bejala 5, Guerrar 9
American Samoa	-6	684	Not required
Andorra	+6	376	Not required
Angola	+6	244	Not required
Argentina	+2	54	Buenos Aires 1, Cordoba 51, Rosario 41, Santa Fe 42
Armenia	+8	374	Not required
Aruba	+1	297	All points 8
Ascension Island	+5	247	Not required
Australia[1]	+15	61	Brisbane 73, Canberra 6, Melbourne 39, Perth 9, Sydney 29
Austria	+6	43	Graz 316, Innsbruck 512, Linz 70, Salzburg 662, Vienna 1
Azerbaijan	+8	994	Baku 12, Dashkasan 216, Sumgayit 164
Bahrain	+8	973	Not required
Bangladesh	+11	880	Chittagong 31, Dhaka 2, Khulna 41
Belarus	+8	375	Loev 2347, Minsk 172, Mogilev 22
Belgium	+6	32	Antwerp 3, Brussels 2, Ghent 9, Liege 4
Belize	-1	501	Belize City 2, Belmopan 8, Orange Walk 3
Benin	+6	229	Not required
Bhutan	+10.5	975	Not required
Bolivia	+1	591	Cochabamba 42, La Paz 2, Santa Cruz 3, Sucre 64
Bosnia/ Herzegovina	+6	387	Mostar 88, Sarajevo 71, Zenica 72
Botswana	+7	267	Jwaneng 380, Molepolole 320, Serowe 430
Brazil[2]	+2	55	Belo Horizonte 31, Brasília 61, Porto Alegre 51, Recife 81, Rio de Janeiro 21, Salvador 71, São Paulo 11
Brunei	+13	673	Bandar Seri Begawan 2, Kuala Belait 3, Tutong 4
Bulgaria	+7	359	Plovdiv 32, Sofia 2, Varna 52
Burkina Faso	+5	226	Not required
Burundi	+7	257	Bujumbura 2, Gitega 40, Muyinga 30
Cambodia	+12	855	Phnom Penh 23
Cameroon	+6	237	Not required
Canada	Similar to U.S. (See "Area Codes of the U.S., Canada, and the Caribbean")		
Cape Verde Islands	+4	238	Not required
Central African Rep.	+6	236	Not required
Chad	+6	235	Not required
Chile	+1	56	Concepcion 41, La Serena 51, Santiago 2, Valparaíso 32
China (PRC)	+12	86	Beijing 10, Fuzhou 591, Ghuangzhou (Canton) 20, Shanghai 21
Colombia	0	57	Barranquilla 5, Bogotá 1, Cali 2, Cartagena 5, Medellín 4
Comoros	+9	269	Not required
Congo, Dem. Rep.[3]	+6	243	Kinshasa 12, Lubumbashi 2
Congo Republic	+6	242	Not required
Cook Islands	-5	682	Not required
Costa Rica	-1	506	Not required
Croatia	+6	385	Dubrovnik 20, Rijeka 51, Split 21 Zagreb 41
Cuba	0	53	Havana 7, Santiago de Cuba 226
Cyprus	+7	357	Kyrenia 357, Larnaca 4, Limassol 5, Nicosia 2
Czech Republic	+6	420	Brno 5, Ostrava 69, Prague 2
Denmark	+6	45	Not required
Djibouti	+8	253	Not required
Ecuador	0	593	Cuenca 7, Guayaquil 4, Machala 7, Quito 2
Egypt	+7	20	Alexandria 3, Aswan 97, Cairo 2, Port Said 66
El Salvador	-1	503	Not required
Equatorial Guinea	+6	240	Bata 8, Malabo 9
Eritrea	+8	291	All locations 1
Estonia	+7	372	Rakvere 32, Tallinn 2, Tartu 7
Ethiopia	+8	251	Addis Ababa 1, Dire Dawa 5, Nazareth 2
Faeroe Islands	+5	298	Not required
Fiji	+17	679	Not required
Finland	+7	358	Helsinki 9, Tampere 3, Turku 2
France[4]	+6	33	Bordeaux 556, Marseille 491, Nice 493, Paris 1, Toulouse 5
French Antilles	+1	596	Not required
French Guiana	+2	594	Not required
French Polynesia[5]	-5	689	Not required
Gabon	+6	241	Not required
Gambia	+5	220	Not required
Georgia	+8	995	Sukhumi 881, Tblisi 32
Germany	+6	49	Berlin 30, Cologne 221, Frankfurt (west) 69, Frankfurt (east) 335, Hamburg 40, Leipzig 341, Munich 89
Ghana	+5	233	Accra 21, Koforidua 81, Kumasi 51, Takoradi 31
Gibraltar	+6	350	Not required

Country	Hours from EST	Country Code	City Codes
Greece	+7	30	Athens 1, Corfu 661, Thessaloniki 031
Greenland	+2	299	Not required
Guadeloupe	+1	590	Base Terre 81, Jarry 26, Point a Pitre 8 or 9
Guam	+15	671	Not required
Guatemala	-1	502	Not required
Guinea	+5	224	Conakry 4, Faranah 81, Kindia 61, Labe 51, Mamou 68
Guinea-Bissau	+5	245	Not required
Guyana	+2	592	Georgetown 2, New Amsterdam 3
Haiti	0	509	Not required
Honduras	-1	504	Not required
Hong Kong	+13	852	Not required
Hungary	+6	36	Budapest 1, Miskolc 46
Iceland	+5	354	Not required
India	+10.5	91	Bombay 22, Calcutta 33, Hyderabad 40, Madras 44, New Delhi 11
Indonesia[6]	+12	62	Bandung 22, Jakarta 21, Medan 61, Surabaya 31
Iran	+8.5	98	Isfahan 31, Mashad 51, Tehran 21
Iraq	+8	964	Baghdad 1, Basra 40, Mosul 60
Ireland	+5	353	Cork 21, Dublin 1, Galway 91, Limerick 61
Israel	+7	972	Haifa 4, Jerusalem 2, Tel Aviv 3
Italy	+6	39	Florence 55, Genoa 10, Milan 2, Naples 81, Rome 6, Venice 41
Ivory Coast	+5	225	Not required
Japan	+14	81	Kobe 78, Kyoto 75, Okinawa 98, Osaka 6, Sapporo 11, Tokyo 3
Jordan	+7	962	Amman 6, Irbid 2, Zarqa 9
Kazakhstan	+11	7	Chimkent 325, Guryev 312, Petropavlovsk 3152
Kenya	+8	254	Mombasa 11, Nairobi 2, Nakuru 37
Kiribati	+17	686	Not required
Korea, North	+14	850	Pyongyang 2
Korea, South	+14	82	Inchon 32, Kwangju 62, Pusan 51, Seoul 2, Taegu 53
Kuwait	+8	965	Not required
Kyrgyzstan	+11	7	Osh 332
Laos	+12	856	Not required
Latvia	+7	371	Daugav'pils 54, Riga 34
Lebanon	+7	961	Beirut 1, Tripoli 6, Zahleh 8
Lesotho	+7	266	Not required
Liberia	+5	231	Not required
Libya	+6	218	Benghazi 61, Misurata 51, Tripoli 21
Liechtenstein	+6	41	Not required
Lithuania	+7	370	Kaunas 7, Klaipeda 6, Vilnius 2
Luxembourg	+6	352	Not required
Macau	+13	853	Not required
Macedonia	+6	389	Bitola 97, Skopje 91
Madagascar	+8	261	Antananarivo 2, Finanrantsoa 7, Moramanga 4
Malawi	+7	265	Domasi 531, Likuni 766, Thornwood 486
Malaysia[7]	+13	60	Ipoh 5, Johor Bahru 7, Kuala Lumpur 3
Maldives	+10	960	Not required
Mali Republic	+5	223	Not required
Malta	+6	356	Not required
Marshall Islands	+17	692	Ebeye 329, Majuro 625
Mauritania	+5	222	Not required
Mauritius	+9	230	Not required
Mayotte Island	+8	269	Not required
Mexico[8]	-1	52	Acapulco 74, Cancun 98, Guadalajara 3, Mexico City 5, Monterrey 8, Puebla 22, Tampico 12, Tijuana 66
Micronesia	+16	691	Kosrae 370, Truk 330, Yap 350
Moldova	+8	373	Benderi 32, Kishinev 2
Monaco	+6	377	Not required
Mongolia	+13	976	Ulan Bator 1
Morocco	+4	212	Casablanca 2, Fes 5, Marrakech 4, Rabat 7, Tangiers 9
Mozambique	+7	258	Maputo 1 Matola 4, Nampula 6
Myanmar	+11.5	95	Bassein 42, Mandalay 2, Yangon (Rangoon) 1
Namibia	+7	264	Swakopmund 64, Windhoek 61
Nauru	+17	674	Not required
Nepal	+10.5	977	Gorkha 64, Kathmandu 1
Netherlands	+6	31	Amsterdam 20, Rotterdam 10, The Hague 70, Utrecht 30
Netherlands Antilles	+1	599	Bonaire 7, Curaçao 9, St. Maarten 5
New Caledonia	+16	687	Not required
New Zealand	+17	64	Auckland 9, Christchurch 3, Rotorua 7, Wellington 4
Nicaragua	-1	505	Granada 552, León 311, Managua 2
Niger Republic	+6	227	Not required
Nigeria	+6	234	Kaduna 62, Lagos 1, Port Harcourt 84
Niue	-6	683	Not required
Norfolk Island	+16.5	672	Not required

Country	Hours from EST	Country Code	City Codes
Norway	+6	47	Not required
Oman	+9	968	Not required
Pakistan	+10	92	Islamabad 51, Karachi 21, Lahore 42
Palau	+14	680	Not required
Panama	0	507	Not required
Papua New Guinea	+15	675	Not required
Paraguay	+2	595	Asunción 21, Concepción 31, Pedro Juan Caballero 36
Peru	0	51	Arequipa 54, Callao 14, Cuzco 84, Lima 14, Trujillo 44
Philippines	+13	63	Cebu 32, Davao 82, Iloilo 33, Manila 2
Poland	+6	48	Gdansk 58, Krakow 12, Lodz 42, Warsaw 22
Portugal	+5	351	Coimbra 39, Lisbon 1, Porto 2, Setubal 65
Qatar	+8	974	Not required
Reunion Island	+9	262	Not required
Romania	+7	40	Brasov 68, Bucharest 1, Iasi 32, Timisoara 561
Russia[9]	+8	7	Moscow 095, St. Petersburg 812
Rwanda	+7	250	Not required
St. Helena	+5	290	Not required
St. Pierre/ Miquelon	+2	508	Not required
San Marino	+6	378	All points 549
São Tomé	+5	239	Not required
Saudi Arabia	+8	966	Al-Madinah 4, Jeddah 2, Makkah (Mecca) 2, Riyadh 1
Senegal	+5	221	Not required
Seychelles	+9	248	Not required
Sierra Leone	+5	232	Not required
Singapore	+13	65	Not required
Slovakia	+6	421	Bratislava 7, Presov 91
Slovenia	+6	386	Llubljana 61, Maribor 62
Solomon Islands	+16	677	Not required
Somalia	+8	252	Not required
South Africa	+7	27	Cape Town 21, Durban 31, Johannesburg 11, Pretoria 12
Spain	+6	34	Barcelona 3, Bilbao 4, Madrid 1, Seville 5, Valencia 6
Sri Lanka	+10.5	94	Colombo 1, Kandy 8
Sudan	+7	249	Not required
Suriname	+2	597	Not required
Swaziland	+7	268	Not required
Sweden	+6	46	Göteburg 31, Malmö 40, Stockholm 8
Switzerland	+6	41	Basel 61, Berne 31, Geneva 22, St. Moritz 81, Zurich 1
Syria	+8	963	Aleppo 21, Damascus 11, Hama 33
Taiwan	+13	886	Kaohsiung 7, Taichung 4, Taipei 2
Tajikistan	+11	7	Dushanbe 3772
Tanzania	+8	255	Dar Es Salaam 51, Mwanza 68, Tanga 53
Thailand	+12	66	Bangkok 2, Chiang Mai 53, Chon Buri 39
Togo	+5	228	Not required
Tonga	+18	676	Not required
Tunisia	+6	216	Bizeria 2, Kef 8, Tunis 1
Turkey	+7	90	Adana 322, Ankara 312, Istanbul 212, Izmir 232
Turkmenistan	+10	993	Chardzou 422
Tuvalu	+17	688	Not required
Uganda	+8	256	Entebbe 42, Jinja 43, Kampala 41
Ukraine	+8	380	Kharkov 57, Kiev 44
UnitedArab Emir.	+9	971	Abu Dhabi 2, Dubai 4, Sharjah 6
United Kingdom	+5	44	Belfast 1232, Birmingham 121, Glasgow 141, London: inner 171, outer 181, Manchester 161, Sheffield 1944
Uruguay	+2	598	Montevideo 2, Paysandu 722, Punta del Este 42
Uzbekistan	+11	7	Karish 375, Samarkand 3662, Tashkent 3712
Vanuatu	+16	678	Not required
Vatican City	+6	39	All points 6
Venezuela	+1	58	Caracas 2, Maracaibo 61, Valencia 41
Vietnam	+12	84	Hanoi 4, Ho Chi Minh City 8
Wallis & Futuna Isl.	+17	681	Not required
Western Samoa	-6	685	Not required
Yemen	+8	967	Aden 2, San'a 1, Taiz 4
Yugoslavia	+6	381	Belgrade 11, Novi Sad 21
Zambia	+7	260	Kitwe 2, Lusaka 1, Ndola 2
Zimbabwe	+7	263	Bulawayo 9, Harare 4, Mutare 20

1. More than one time zone; difference based on Sydney. 2. More than one time zone; difference based on Rio de Janeiro. 3. Formerly known as Zaire. 4. All codes in Paris are 1 + 8 digits beginning with 3, 4, or 6. 5. More than one time zone; difference based on Tahiti. 6. More than one time zone; difference based on Jakarta. 7. More than one time zone; difference based on Kuala Lumpur. 8. More than one time zone; difference based on Mexico City. International code applies for calls made from international direct dial areas. From other areas, to call Mexico City dial 90 + 5; consult operator for other calls. 9. More than one time zone; difference based on Moscow.
Source: *The AT&T Guide to Calling the World* (1999). **www.att.com/traveler/tools/codes.html**

Climate and Weather

►CLIMATES OF THE WORLD

Knowing the similarities and differences between climates in various parts of the world helps us understand many things about our planet: why people live where they do; how they make their living; the problems and potentials of their land. Climates are very complex, however, and no climatic classification is ideal. The most commonly used classification was developed more than 50 years ago by a German climatologist, Wladimir Koppen. The Koppen system uses temperature and precipitation as the major criteria for grouping climates. Boundaries between climatic zones are determined by the limits of where certain plants grow. The five major climatic zones are known by the capital letters **A**, **B**, **C**, **D**, and **E**; each major zone has subzones. High-altitude areas are sometimes shown with the letter **H** because their climates are so complex that small maps cannot show all the detail.

(Note: In the following chart, **R** stands for the annual rainfall in centimeters; **T** is the average annual temperature in degrees Celsius.)

A Humid tropical climates. The average temperature of every month is 64° F (18° C) or higher. There is no winter.

Af *Rain forest.* The driest month has at least 2.4 inches (6 cm) of rain. The Amazon Basin is an example of an **Af** climate.

Am *Monsoon.* Similar to **Af** but with a short dry season. The amount of rainfall in the driest month is less than 2.4 inches (6 cm) but equal to or greater than 10 - (R/25). The southwestern coast of India is an example of an **Am** climate.

Aw *Savanna.* There is a well-defined dry season in the winter. The amount of rainfall in the driest month is less than 10 - (R/25). The Brazilian Highlands are a large area with an **Aw** climate.

As (Rare) There is a well-defined dry season in the summer.

B Dry climates. Annual rainfall is less than annual potential evaporation. The boundary between dry areas and humid areas is R < 2T + 28 when at least 70% of the rainfall occurs in the warmer six months; R < 2T when at least 70% of the rainfall occurs in the cooler six months; or R < 2T + 14 when neither half of the year receives at least 70% of the total annual rainfall.

BS *Steppe.* The boundary between steppe and desert is half of the dry/humid boundary. Steppes border many of the world's large deserts.

BSh *Low-latitude steppe.* The average annual temperature is at least 64° F (18° C).

BSk *Mid-latitude steppe.* The average annual temperature is less than 64° F (18° C).

BW *Desert.* The boundary between desert and steppe is half of the dry/humid boundary. The Sahara Desert is the largest area with a **BW** climate.

BWh *Low-latitude desert.* The average annual temperature is at least 64° F (18° C).

BWk *Mid-latitude desert.* The average annual temperature is less than 64° F (18° C).

C Subtropical climates. The average temperature of the coldest month is between 64° F (18° C) and 27° F (-3° C). These are mainly humid mid-latitude areas with mild winters. The principal natural vegetation is broad-leafed forest.

Cw (Rare) The wettest month occurs in summer and has at least ten times as much rainfall as the driest month in winter. **Cw** zones are mainly areas of evergreen forest in mountainous **Aw** zones.

Cs *Dry summer.* The wettest month occurs in winter and has at least three times as much rainfall as the driest month in summer. Less than 1.5 inches (4 cm) of rain falls during the driest summer month.

Csa *Warm, dry summer.* The average temperature of the warmest month is more than 72° F (22° C), and for at least four months the average temperature is more than 50° F (10° C). Italy and other Mediterranean countries have a **Csa** climate.

Csb *Cool, dry summer.* In no month is the average temperature more than 72° F (22° C), but for at least four months the average temperature is more than 50° F (10° C). **Csb** climates are found near San Francisco, California; on the coast near Santiago, Chile; and in Portugal.

Cf *Humid summer.* Areas that cannot meet the criteria for **Cw** and **Cs**.

Cfa *Humid, warm summer.* The average temperature of the warmest month is more than 72° F (22° C), and for at least four months the average temperature is more than 50° F (10° C). Much of the eastern United States is in a **Cfa** zone.

Cfb *Marine west coast.* In no month is the average temperature more than 72° F (22° C), but for at least four months the average temperature is more than 50° F (10° C). Great Britain, New Zealand, and the west coast of Alaska are all examples of **Cfb** climates.

D Continental climates. The average temperature of the warmest month is more than 50° F (10° C), and the average temperature of the coldest month is 27° F (-3° C) or below. Forests are the principal natural vegetation.

Dfa *Humid, warm summer.* All seasons have some precipitation. The average temperature of the warmest month is more than 72° F (22° C), and for at least four months the average temperature is more than 50° F (10° C). The northern Great Plains of the United States have a **Dfa** climate.

Dwa *Humid, warm summer.* The wettest month occurs in summer and has at least ten times as much rainfall as the driest month in winter. The average temperature of the warmest month is more than 72° F (22° C), and for at least four months the average temperature is more than 50° F (10° C). The land around the northern part of the Yellow Sea has a **Dwa** climate.

Dfb *Humid, cool summer.* All seasons have some precipitation. In no month is the average temperature more than 72° F (22° C), but for at least four months the average temperature is more than 50° F (10° C). A large **Dfb** area stretches from eastern Europe into Asia.

Dwb *Humid, cool summer.* The wettest month occurs in summer and has at least ten times as much rainfall as the driest month in winter. In no month is the average temperature more than 72° F (22° C), but for at least four months the average temperature is more than 50° F (10° C). Much of the area between Manchuria and the Sea of Okhotsk has a **Dwb** climate.

Dfc *Subpolar.* All seasons have some precipitation. For one to three months, the average temperature is 50° (10° C) or more. A huge **Dfc** area is in Siberia and adjacent parts of the Soviet Union.

E Polar climates. The average temperature of the warmest month is less than 50° F (10° C). There is no summer, and no trees grow.

ET *Tundra.* The average temperature of the warmest month is less than 50° F (10° C) but more than 32° F (0° C). Vast areas of northern North America, Europe, and Asia lie in the **ET** climate zone.

EF *Ice cap.* The average temperature of the warmest 8 month is 32° F (0° C) or less. The **EF** climate is found at the North and South poles and in interior Greenland.

▶WEATHER EXTREMES

Hottest: Dalol Danakil Depression, Ethiopia. Average annual temperature: 35°C/95°F.
Coldest: Plateau Station, Antarctica. Average annual temperature: -56.7°C/-71.7°F.
Wettest: Mawsynram, Assam, India. Average annual rainfall: 11.873 m/38.925 ft.
Driest: Atacama Desert, Chile. Average annual rainfall: too small to measure

▶GLOSSARY OF WEATHER WORDS

Air mass   A large body of air that, at a given elevation, has about the same temperature and humidity throughout.
Barometric pressure   The weight of a column of air at a particular place is determined by mea-

suring the height of a column of mercury under a vacuum. The instrument for making such a measurement is called a barometer. At sea level, the standard barometric pressure is 29.92 inches (76 cm). In the International System, air pressure is measured in bars or in kiloPascals. A bar is slightly less than the standard air pressure at sea level, and a kiloPascal is one-hundredth of a bar. At any location, however, barometric pressure is affected by changes in temperature, humidity, or elevation. When the barometric pressure is falling, the air pressure is decreasing, usually a sign of a storm. When the barometer is rising, fairer weather is on its way.
Climate   General weather conditions over a long period of time.
Cold front   The place where cold air that is advancing meets warm air that is retreating before it. This kind of weather not only lowers temperature as it passes but also causes high winds and may cause thunderstorms.
Cyclone   A region of low atmospheric pressure (see "Depression"). Severe cyclones are known as hurricanes, tropical cyclones, and typhoons.
Degree-days   A degree-day is one degree of devi-

Costliest Hurricanes in U.S. History

Measuring the cost of hurricanes is an imperfect science, primarily because of the difficulty in determining whether different kinds of damages are directly attributable to a particular storm. The following table ranks hurricanes by the amount of insured losses they cause (in constant 1996 dollars, to discount the effects of inflation). Insured losses are the amount claimed by property owners against their insurance policies. It is impossible to calcu-

late the costs incurred by those without insurance. Note that even after discounting inflation, most of the costliest hurricanes have come within the past 30 years, as more and more people have built homes closer to shore, and harm's way. Improved meteorology, however, has insured that while the financial cost of hurricanes has increased, the loss of human life has declined. The 25 deadliest hurricanes in U.S. history all occurred before 1975.

Rank, Hurricane, Year	Location of primary damage	Insured losses[1]	Deaths
1. Andrew (1992)	Florida, Louisiana	$30,475,000,000	26
2. Hugo (1989)	South Carolina	8,491,561,181	(2)
3. Agnes (1972)	Northeastern states	7,500,000,000	122
4. Betsy (1965)	Florida, Louisiana	7,425,340,909	75
5. Camille (1969)	Mississippi, Alabama	6,096,287,313	256
6. Diane (1955)	Northeastern states	4,830,580,808	184
7. Frederic (1979)	Alabama, Mississippi	4,328,968,903	31
8. New England (1938)	Northeastern states	4,140,000,000	600
9. Fran (1996)	North Carolina	3,200,000,000	34
10. Opal (1995)	Florida, Alabama	3,069,395,018	59

1. In constant (1996) dollars. 2. Under 30. Exact figure not available.
Source: National Oceanic and Atmospheric Administration, National Hurricane Center. **www.nhc.noaa.gov.**

Tornadoes, Floods, Tropical Storms and Lightning in the U.S., 1987–97

Item	1987	1990	1995	1996	1997
Tornadoes	**656**	**1,133**	**1,235**	**1,170**	**1,148**
Lives lost, total	59	53	30	25	67
Most in a single tornado	30	29	6	5	27
Floods: lives lost	70	142	80	131	117
North Atlantic tropical storms and hurricanes	**7**	**14**	**19**	**13**	**7**
Number reaching U.S. mainland	1	0	2	2	1
Direct deaths, total	3	123	121	138	4
Deaths on mainland U.S.	0	10	29	33	4
Property loss (millions)[1]	$8	$57	$3,729	$3,600	$100
Lightning					
Deaths	86	74	85	52	42
Injuries	364	252	510	309	306

Note: A tornado is a violent, rotating column of air descending from a cumulonimbus cloud in the form of a tubular or funnel-shaped cloud, usually characterized by movements along a narrow path and wind speeds from 100 to 300 miles per hour also known as a twister or waterspout. Tropical cyclones have maximum winds of 39 to 73 miles per hour; hurricanes have maximum winds of 74 miles per hour or higher. The increase in number of tornadoes is due in large part to improved detection and documentation. N.A.= not available. 1. In constant (1990) dollars. **Source:** U.S. Bureau of the Census, *Statistical Abstract of the United States* (annual).

ation of the daily mean temperature from a given norm, usually 65°F. Cooling degree-days are the number of degrees Fahrenheit by which the mean temperature exceeds 65°F, while heating degree-days are the number of degrees the mean temperature is below 65°F. During a year, keeping track of the total number of degree days for each day is used to keep track of cooling or heating needs. For example, oil companies use heating degree-days to estimate how much oil their customers have used and when they might need a refill.

Depression Any region of low air pressure. In temperate regions over land, the typical depression is a *low*. The often more powerful depression occurring over tropical waters is called a *tropical depression*. If the air pressure in a tropical depression continues to fall, it becomes a tropical storm, or, lower still, a *hurricane*.

Dew point The temperature at which dew (drops of water) begins to form as air cools. Air can hold only a certain amount of water vapor at a given temperature. When the temperature falls, excess water vapor must turn into a liquid.

El Niño A change in the circulation and temperature of the waters off the west coast of South American that occurs every few years. Water that is normally cold is replace by warmer water, disrupting the local environment in many ways (e.g. moving fish away from the surface, which results in less food for water fowl, and causing rain in normally dry regions). Because El Niño is linked to other weather systems, a strong El Niño can affect weather worldwide.

Front The boundary between two different air masses.

High An air mass characterized by higher-than-normal air pressure; usually this is a fair-weather system. Some highs are typically found in the same place each year, such as the one that occurs over Bermuda in most summers.

Hurricane A huge tropical rainstorm with winds that swirl rapidly around a calm, dry central "eye." To be classified a hurricane, a tropical storm must have wind speeds of more than 74 mph (119 km/hr). The average hurricane is 375 miles (600 km) in diameter and extends up 40,000 feet (12,000 m) above the surface of the ocean. The eye averages 12.5 miles (20 km) in diameter. When a hurricane hits land, its fierce winds and floods can do great damage. On average five hurricanes each year threaten the eastern and southern United States.

Jet stream A strong river or two of high winds in the upper atmosphere (but below the stratosphere) that travels from west to east at between 75 and 150 mph (120-240 km/hr), most often in the middle latitudes. Discovered by American bomber pilots in World War II, it is now known to have significant effects on weather.

Low An air mass characterized by lower-than-normal air pressure; usually this is the heart of a storm system. Some lows are found in the same region most of the year, such as the low in the Pacific just off the coast of Alaska.

Mean temperature Technically, this should be the average of all temperatures during the day. Sometimes it is the average of 24 temperatures taken once each hour, but most often the mean temperature is simply the average of the high and low for the day.

Monsoon A wind system in which the prevailing direction of the wind reverses itself from season to season. Southeast Asia is the most typical monsoon region. The summer (southwest) monsoon, characterized by hot, moist air and heavy rains lasts from April to September. The winter (northeast) monsoon lasts from October to March and is characterized by cool, dry air.

Occluded front When a cold front overtakes a warm front, the denser cold air flows under the less dense warm air.

Prevailing winds Throughout the world, winds follow regular patterns. In some places winds are so light and infrequent as to scarcely exist, such as in the doldrums along the equator and in the horse latitudes near latitude 30° north and south. In other places the winds tend to come from a

Determining the Wind-Chill Factor

Sometimes called a wind-chill index, this is a measure of the cooling power of air movement and low temperature on the human body. Because heat passes directly from a warm body to the cooler air surrounding it—a process known as convection—wind produces a continuing source of cooler air and a chilling effect that is equivalent to a lower temperature. The effect on a warm day is pleasant, but as temperatures approach freezing, wind chill is not only unpleasant, but can be dangerous. As the table below shows, a temperature of 5°F combined with a breeze of 10 mph produces a wind-chill temperature of -15°F—a temperature at which frostbite occurs much sooner than at 5°F. Wind speeds above 45 mph have little additional cooling effect.

Actual Temperature	Wind speed								
	5 mph	10 mph	15 mph	20 mph	25 mph	30 mph	35 mph	40 mph	45 mph
35°F	33°F	22°F	16°F	12°F	8°F	6°F	4°F	3°F	2°F
30°F	27	16	9	4	1	-2	-4	-5	-6
25°F	21	10	2	-3	-4	-10	-12	-13	-14
20°F	16	3	-5	-10	-15	-18	-20	-21	-22
15°F	12	-3	-11	-17	-22	-25	-27	-29	-30
10°F	7	-9	-18	-24	-29	-33	-35	-37	-38
5°F	0	-15	-25	-31	-36	-41	-43	-45	-46
0°F	-5	-22	-31	-39	-44	49	52	-53	-54
-5°F	-10	-27	-38	-46	-51	-56	-58	-60	-62
-10°F	-15	-34	-45	-53	-59	-64	-67	-69	-70
-15°F	-21	-40	-51	-60	-66	-71	-74	-76	-78
-20°F	-26	-46	-58	-67	-74	-79	-82	-84	-85
-25°F	-31	-52	-65	-74	-81	-86	-89	-92	-93
-30°F	-36	-58	-72	-81	-88	-93	-97	-100	-102
-35°F	-42	-64	-78	-88	-96	-101	-105	-107	-109
-40°F	-47	-71	-85	-95	-103	-109	-113	-115	-117
-45°F	-52	-77	-92	-102	-110	-116	-120	-123	-125

particular direction and are called prevailing winds.

Rain shadow An area on the leeward side of a mountain range that receives little rainfall.

Relative humidity The amount of moisture (water vapor) in the air compared with the total amount it can hold expressed as a percent. Warm air can hold more water vapor than cold air, so a relative humidity of 75 percent on a warm summer day is moister than a relative humidity of 75 percent on a cool winter day. However, because evaporation is greater on warm days, the relative humidity is generally higher in summer than in winter.

Secondary cold front A cold front that sometimes forms behind another cold front and that is often even colder than the first front.

Secondary depression A low that forms to the south or east of a low that is a storm center.

Squall line A line of instability that often precedes a cold front, marked by wind gusts and often by heavy rain.

Stationary front A front that stays in the same place.

Storm surge The rise in water levels in the ocean or a large lake that comes from a combination of wind and low pressure during a storm, especially pronounced during a hurricane.

Temperature-humidity index A number derived from a formula relating temperature and humidity to discomfort. When it is 75, many are uncomfortable, while at 80 or above, almost everybody is uncomfortable. Temperatures are less comfortable at high humidities because cooling by sweating is less efficient (see also "The Heat Index," later in this section).

Temperature inversion A layer of warm air on top of a layer of cooler surface air. Such layering, usually occurring at night, can prevent air pollutants near the surface from rising into the upper air. A long-lasting inversion, especially in industrial areas, can cause an excessive concentration of pollutants to accumulate in the surrounding air.

Tornado A small and short-lived but very severe windstorm. Tornadoes are whirling columns of air that reach down from a cloud, and they often accompany thunderstorms, rain, and hail. With wind speeds up to 300 mph (480 km/hr), tornadoes can do tremendous damage. The diameter of the average tornado is between 500 and 2,000 feet (150-600 m). The average tornado moves along the ground at 28 mph (45 km/hr) and has a "path" that is 16 miles (26 km) long. In the United States, some 750 tornadoes are reported every year, most frequently between April and June.

Tropical storm A storm that forms over the ocean in the tropics and often moves onto land, where it loses strength. Technically, a storm is designated a tropical storm only when winds are between 39 and 73 miles per hour. If winds become greater, a tropical storm becomes a hurricane.

Trough A low that is long, rather than nearly circular.

Typhoon A hurricane formed in the western Pacific Ocean.

Warm front The boundary of a moving warm air mass.

Weather The condition of the atmosphere—temperature, rain, and wind, for example—in a particular place. A climate is defined by weather conditions over a long period of time.

Wind Any current of air, measured on land in miles per hour, and at sea in knots. The direction of a given wind is determined from the point of the compass from which it blows (e.g., northeast, south). In various regions of the world, names are given to seasonal winds of particular quality. Among these are the *bora*, a cold usually dry north/northeast wind along the eastern Adriatic; *brickfielder*, a hot north wind of southeastern Australia; *buran*, a cold, violent north/northeast wind of Siberia and Central Asia, common in

The Heat Index

Just as in cold weather, wind can harm the human body by causing it to cool at a faster rate than it would in stationary air, in hot weather, humidity can harm the body by preventing it from cooling. Relative humidity is the amount of water vapor in the air expressed as a percentage of the maximum amount of water the air could hold at the same temperature. When relative humidity is high, the body's ability to perspire—one of the body's principal cooling processes—is hampered, resulting in high internal body temperature and leading to heat cramps, heat exhaustion (or prostration), or heat stroke. These conditions become more common above temperatures of 105°F. The heat index measures what the temperature feels like in degrees Fahrenheit for a given temperature and relative humidity.

Air Temperature	Relative humidity										
	0%	10%	20%	30%	40%	50%	60%	70%	80%	90%	100%
70°F	64°	65°	66°	67°	68°	69°	70°	70°	71°	71°	72°
75°F	69	70	72	73	74	75	76	77	78	79	80
80°F	73	75	77	78	79	81	82	85	86	88	91
85°F	78	80	82	84	86	88	90	93	97	102	108
90°F	83	85	87	90	93	96	100	106	113	122	—
95°F	87	90	93	96	101	107	114	124	136	—	—
100°F	91	95	99	104	110	120	132	144	—	—	—
105°F	95	100	105	113	123	135	149	—	—	—	—
110°F	99	105	112	123	137	150	—	—	—	—	—
115°F	103	111	120	135	151	—	—	—	—	—	—
120°F	107	116	130	148	—	—	—	—	—	—	—

Source: U.S. National Oceanic and Atmospheric Administration.

Beaufort Wind Scale

In 1806 Adm. Francis Beaufort devised a scale for recording wind force at sea based on the effect of the wind on a full-rigged ship. In 1838, this scale was adopted by the British Admiralty, and in 1874 it was adopted for international use. It is now the chief scale for specifying the force of the wind and is used in all parts of the world, both on land and at sea. Originally, there were no specific wind speeds corresponding to various force numbers on the Beaufort Wind Scale. Since 1946, wind speed has been determined according to measurements made by an anemometer (a device for measuring wind) at 10m (30 ft) above the ground.

Force	Description of wind	Mean wind speed in knots[1]	Specification for use on land and at sea
Force 0	Calm	Less than 1	Calm, smoke rises vertically. Sea like a mirror.
Force 1	Light air	1-3	Direction of wind shown by smoke drift, but not by wind vanes. Ripples with appearance of scales are formed, but without foam crests.
Force 2	Light breeze	4-6	Wind felt on face; leaves rustle; ordinary vane moved by wind. Small wavelets, still short but more pronounced; crests have a glassy appearance and do not break.
Force 3	Gentle breeze	7-10	Leaves and small twigs in constant motion; wind extends light flag. Large wavelets; crests begin to break; foam of glassy appearance; perhaps scattered white horses.
Force 4	Moderate breeze	11-16	Raises dust and loose paper; small branches are moved. Small waves becoming longer; fairly frequent white horses.
Force 5	Fresh breeze	17-21	Small trees in leaf begin to sway; crested wavelets form on inland waters. Moderate waves, taking a more pronounced long form; many white horses are formed (chance of some spray).
Force 6	Strong breeze	22-27	Large branches in motion; whistling heard in telegraph wires; umbrellas used with difficulty. Large waves begin to form; the white foam crests are more extensive everywhere (probably some spray).
Force 7	Moderate gale, near gale	28-33	Whole trees in motion; inconvenience felt when walking against wind. Sea heaps up and white foam from breaking waves begins to be blown in streaks along the direction of the wind.
Force 8	Fresh gale, gale	34-40	Breaks twigs off trees; generally impedes progress. Moderately high waves of greater length; edges of crests begin to break into spindrift; foam is blown in well-marked streaks.
Force 9	Strong gale	41-47	Slight structural damage occurs (chimney pots and slate removed). High waves; dense streaks of foam; crests of waves begin to topple, tumble and roll over.
Force 10	Whole gale, storm	48-55	Seldom experienced inland; trees uprooted; considerable structural damage occurs. Very high waves with long overhanging crests; the resulting foam, in great patches, is blown in dense white streaks; the sea takes a white appearance; the tumbling of the sea becomes heavy and shock like; visibility affected.
Force 11	Storm, violent storm	56-63	Very rarely experienced; accompanied by widespread damage. Exceptionally high waves at sea (medium-sized ships might be lost to view behind the waves); the sea is completely covered with white patches of foam; visibility affected.
Force 12+	Hurricane[2]	64 and above	The air is filled with foam and spray; sea completely white with driving spray; visibility very seriously affected.

1. Nautical miles-per-hour; 1 nautical mile = 1.151 statute miles. 2. Force 13: 72-80 knots; force 14: 81-89; force 15: 90-99; force 16: 100-108; force 17: 109-118. **Source**: Smithsonian Institution, *Smithsonian Meteorological Tables* (1966); Hydrographer of the Navy (UK), *Ocean Passages for the World* (1977).

winter; *chinook*, a dry winter or spring wind which blows down the eastern slopes of the Rocky Mountains often warm enough to melt the snow; *harmattan*, a hot, dry north wind in West Africa which cools as it evaporates the moist air of the coast; *mistral*, a cold, strong north/northwest wind of the western Mediterranean with a surface strength of 60 km/hour, frequent in winter; *pampero*, a sudden, cold south or west wind in Argentina and Uruguay frequent in summer; *Santa Ana* a hot, dry wind that blows from the north or east in Southern California; *sirocco*, a hot south wind of North Africa and southern Italy; *southerly burster*, a cold, violent south wind of southeastern Australia; *williwaw*, a violent squall that blows in the Strait of Magellan (South America); and *zonda*, a hot, dry north wind of Argentina and Uruguay.

Climate of Selected U.S. Cities

The first line following each city lists the normal daily high temperatures for each month (in degrees Fahrenheit); the second line lists the normal monthly precipitation (rain, snow, and melted ice).

	Jan.	Feb.	Mar.	Apr.	May	June	July	Aug.	Sept.	Oct.	Nov.	Dec.
Atlanta,	50°	55°	64°	73°	80°	86°	88°	87°	82°	73°	63°	54°
Georgia	4.8″	4.8″	5.8″	4.3″	4.3″	3.6″	5.0″	3.7″	3.4″	3.1″	3.9″	4.3
Baltimore,	40°	44°	54°	64°	74°	83°	87°	85°	79°	67°	57°	45°
Maryland	3.1″	3.1″	3.4″	3.1″	3.7″	3.7″	3.7″	3.9″	3.4″	3.0″	3.3″	3.4″
Boston,	36°	38°	46°	56°	67°	76°	82°	80°	73°	63°	52°	40°
Massachusetts	3.6″	3.6″	3.7″	3.6″	3.3″	3.1″	2.8″	3.2″	3.1″	3.3″	4.2″	4.0″
Cincinnati,	37°	41°	53°	64°	74°	82°	86°	84°	78°	66°	53°	42°
Ohio	2.6″	2.7″	4.2″	3.8″	4.3″	3.8″	4.2″	3.4″	2.9″	2.9″	3.5″	3.2″
Charlotte,	49°	53°	62°	71°	78°	86°	89°	88°	82°	72°	63°	52°
North Carolina	3.7″	3.8″	4.4″	2.7″	3.8″	3.4″	3.9″	3.7″	3.5″	3.4″	3.2″	3.5″
Chicago,	29°	34°	46°	59°	70°	80°	84°	82°	75°	63°	48°	34°
Illinois	1.5″	1.4″	2.7″	3.6″	3.3″	3.8″	3.7″	4.2″	3.9″	2.4″	2.9″	2.5″
Cleveland,	32°	35°	46°	58°	69°	78°	82°	81°	74°	62°	50°	37°
Ohio	2.0″	2.2″	2.9″	3.1″	3.5″	3.7″	3.5″	3.4″	3.4″	2.5″	3.2″	3.1″
Columbus,	34°	38°	51°	62°	72°	80°	84°	82°	76°	65°	51°	39°
Ohio	2.2″	2.2″	3.3″	3.2″	3.9″	4.0″	4.3″	3.7″	3.0″	2.2″	3.2″	2.9″
Dallas-Fort Worth,	54°	59°	68°	76°	83°	92°	97°	96°	88°	79°	67°	58°
Texas	1.8″	2.2″	2.8″	3.5″	4.9″	2.9″	2.3″	2.2″	3.4″	3.5″	2.3″	1.8″
Denver,	43°	47°	52°	62°	71°	81°	88°	86°	77°	66°	53°	45°
Colorado	0.5″	0.6″	1.3″	1.7″	2.4″	1.8″	1.9″	1.5″	1.2″	0.9″	0.9″	0.6″
Detroit,	30°	33°	44°	58°	70°	79°	83°	81°	74°	62°	48°	35°
Michigan	1.8″	1.7″	2.6″	3.0″	2.9″	3.6″	3.2″	3.4″	2.9″	2.1″	2.7″	2.8″
El Paso,	56°	62°	70°	79°	87°	97°	96°	94°	87°	78°	66°	58°
Texas	0.4″	0.4″	0.3″	0.2″	0.3″	0.7″	1.5″	1.6″	1.7″	0.8″	0.4″	0.6″
Honolulu,	80°	81°	82°	83°	85°	87°	88°	89°	89°	87°	84°	81°
Hawaii	3.6″	2.2″	2.2″	1.5″	1.1″	0.5″	0.6″	0.4″	0.8″	2.3″	3.0″	3.8″
Houston,	61°	65°	71°	78°	85°	90°	93°	93°	88°	82°	72°	65°
Texas	3.3″	3.0″	2.9″	3.2″	5.2″	5.0″	3.6″	3.5″	4.9″	4.3″	3.8″	3.5″
Indianapolis,	34°	38°	51°	63°	74°	83°	86°	84°	78°	66°	52°	39°
Indiana	2.3″	2.5″	3.8″	3.7″	4.0″	3.5″	4.5″	3.6″	2.9″	2.6″	3.2″	3.3″
Jacksonville,	64°	67°	73°	79°	85°	89°	91°	91°	87°	80°	74°	67°
Florida	3.3″	4.0″	3.7″	2.8″	3.6″	5.7″	5.6″	7.9″	7.1″	2.9″	2.2″	2.7″
Kansas City,	35°	41°	53°	65°	74°	83°	89°	86°	78°	68°	53°	39°
Missouri	1.1″	1.1″	2.5″	3.1″	5.0″	4.7″	4.4″	4.0″	4.9″	3.3″	1.9″	1.6″
Las Vegas,	57°	63°	69°	78°	88°	100°	106°	103°	95°	82°	67°	58°
Nevada	0.5″	0.5″	0.4″	0.2″	0.3″	0.1″	0.4″	0.5″	0.3″	0.2″	0.4″	0.4″
Los Angeles,	68°	69°	69°	72°	74°	78°	84°	84°	83°	79°	72°	68°
California	2.9″	3.1″	2.6″	1.0″	0.2″	0.0″	0.0″	0.1″	0.5″	0.3″	2.0″	2.0″
Memphis,	49°	54°	63°	73°	81°	89°	92°	91°	84°	74°	62°	53°
Tennessee	3.7″	4.4″	5.4″	5.5″	4.9″	3.6″	3.8″	3.4″	3.5″	3.0″	5.1″	5.7″
Miami,	75°	77°	79°	82°	85°	88°	89°	89°	88°	85°	80°	77°
Florida	2.0″	2.1″	2.4″	2.9″	6.2″	9.3″	5.7″	7.6″	7.6″	5.6″	2.7″	1.8″
Milwaukee,	26°	30°	40°	53°	64°	75°	80°	78°	71°	59°	45°	31°
Wisconsin	1.6″	1.5″	2.7″	3.5″	2.8″	3.2″	3.5″	3.5″	3.4″	2.4″	2.5″	2.3″
Minneapolis-St. Paul,	21°	27°	39°	57°	69°	79°	84°	81°	71°	59°	41°	26°
Wisconsin	1.0″	0.9″	1.9″	2.4″	3.4″	4.1″	3.5″	3.6″	2.7″	2.2″	1.6″	1.1″
New Orleans,	61°	64°	72°	79°	84°	89°	91°	91°	87°	79°	71°	64°
Louisiana	5.1″	6.0″	5.0″	4.5″	4.6″	5.9″	6.1″	6.2″	5.5″	3.1″	4.4″	5.8″
New York City,	38°	40°	50°	61°	72°	80°	85°	84°	76°	65°	54°	43°
New York	3.4″	3.3″	4.1″	4.2″	4.4″	3.7″	4.4″	4.0″	3.9″	3.6″	4.5″	3.9″
Oklahoma City,	47°	52°	62°	72°	79°	87°	93°	93°	84°	74°	60°	50°
Oklahoma	1.1″	1.6″	2.7″	2.8″	5.2″	4.3″	2.6″	2.6″	3.8″	3.2″	1.9″	1.4″
Philadelphia,	38°	41°	52°	63°	73°	82°	86°	85°	78°	66°	55°	43°
Pennsylvania	3.2″	2.8″	3.5″	3.6″	3.8″	3.7″	4.3″	3.8″	3.4″	2.7″	3.3″	3.4″
Phoenix,	66°	71°	76°	84°	94°	104°	106°	104°	98°	88°	75°	66°
Arizona	0.7″	0.7″	0.9″	0.2″	0.1″	0.1″	0.8″	1.0″	0.9″	0.7″	0.7″	1.0″
Pittsburgh,	34°	37°	49°	60°	71°	79°	83°	81°	74°	63°	50°	39°
Pennsylvania	2.5″	2.4″	3.4″	3.1″	3.6″	3.7″	3.8″	3.2″	3.0″	2.4″	2.9″	2.9″
Portland,	45°	51°	56°	61°	67°	74°	80°	80°	75°	64°	53°	46°
Oregon	5.4″	3.9″	3.6″	2.4″	2.1″	1.5″	0.7″	1.1″	1.8″	2.7″	5.3″	6.1″
St. Louis,	38°	43°	55°	67°	76°	85°	89°	87°	80°	69°	55°	42°
Missouri	1.8″	2.1″	3.6″	3.5″	4.0″	3.7″	3.9″	2.9″	3.1″	2.7″	3.3″	3.0″
Salt Lake City,	36°	44°	52°	61°	72°	83°	92°	89°	79°	66°	51°	38°
Utah	1.1″	1.2″	1.9″	2.1″	1.8″	0.9″	0.8″	0.9″	1.3″	1.4″	1.3″	1.4″
San Antonio,	61°	66°	74°	80°	85°	92°	95°	95°	89°	82°	72°	64°
Texas	1.7″	1.8″	1.5″	2.5″	4.2″	3.8″	2.2″	2.5″	3.4″	3.2″	2.6″	1.5″
San Diego,	66°	67°	66°	68°	69°	72°	76°	78°	77°	75°	70°	66°
California	1.8″	1.5″	1.8″	0.8″	0.2″	0.1″	0.0″	0.1″	0.2″	0.4″	1.5″	1.6″
San Francisco,	56°	60°	61°	62°	63°	64°	65°	66°	69°	69°	63°	56°
California	4.1″	3.0″	3.1″	1.3″	0.3″	0.2″	0.0″	0.1″	0.3″	1.3″	3.2″	3.1″
Seattle,	46°	51°	54°	58°	64°	70°	74°	74°	69°	60°	52°	46°
Washington	5.4″	4.0″	3.8″	2.5″	1.8″	1.6″	0.9″	1.2″	1.9″	3.3″	5.7″	6.0″
Washington,	42°	46°	57°	67°	76°	85°	89°	87°	80°	69°	58°	47°
D.C.	2.7″	2.7″	3.2″	2.7″	3.7″	3.4″	3.8″	3.9″	3.3″	3.0″	3.1″	3.1″

Note:—= no precipitation; T = trace. **Source** U.S. Department of Commerce, National Oceanic and Atmospheric Administration, *Climatic Averages and Extremes for U.S. Cities* (June, 1995).

Climate of Selected World Cities

Average low and high temperatures for selected months in degrees Fahrenheit. Precipitation is the average monthly amount in inches of rainfall equivalent.

City	January Temp. Max.	Min.	Avg. precip.	April Temp. Max.	Min.	Avg. precip.	July Temp. Max.	Min.	Avg. precip.	October Temp. Max.	Min.	Avg. precip.
Accra, Ghana	87°	73°	0.6"	88°	76°	3.2"	81°	73°	1.8"	85°	74°	2.5"
Amsterdam, Netherlands	40	34	2.0	52	43	4.6	69	59	2.6	56	48	2.8
Athens, Greece	54	42	2.2	67	52	0.8	90	72	0.2	74	60	1.7
Auckland, New Zealand	73	60	3.1	67	56	3.8	56	46	5.7	63	52	4.0
Baghdad, Iraq	60	39	0.9	85	57	0.5	110	76	t	92	61	0.1
Bangkok, Thailand	89	67	0.2	95	78	2.3	90	76	6.9	88	76	9.9
Beirut, Lebanon	62	51	7.5	72	58	2.2	87	73	t	81	69	2.0
Berlin, Germany	35	26	1.9	55	38	1.7	74	55	3.1	55	41	1.7
Bogotá, Colombia	67	48	2.3	67	51	5.8	64	50	2.0	66	50	6.3
Bombay, India	88	62	0.1	93	74	t	88	75	24.3	93	73	2.5
Budapest, Hungary	35	26	1.5	62	44	2.0	82	61	2.0	61	45	2.1
Buenos Aires, Argentina	85	63	3.1	72	53	3.5	57	42	2.2	69	50	3.4
Cairo, Egypt	65	47	0.2	83	57	0.1	96	70	0.0	86	65	t
Calcutta, India	80	55	0.4	97	76	1.7	90	79	12.8	89	74	4.5
Cape Town, South Africa	78	60	0.6	72	53	1.9	63	45	3.5	70	52	1.2
Caracas, Venezuela	75	56	0.9	81	60	1.3	78	61	4.3	79	61	4.3
Casablanca, Morocco	63	45	2.1	69	52	1.4	79	65	0.0	76	58	1.5
Copenhagen, Denmark	36	29	1.6	50	37	1.7	72	55	2.2	53	42	2.1
Dakha, Bangladesh	77	56	0.3	92	74	5.4	89	79	13.0	88	75	5.3
Dakar, Senegal	79	64	t	81	65	t	88	76	3.5	89	76	1.5
Dublin, Ireland	47	35	2.7	54	38	1.9	67	51	2.8	57	43	2.7
Geneva, Switzerland	39	29	1.9	58	41	2.5	77	58	2.9	58	44	3.8
Hanoi, Vietnam	68	58	0.8	80	70	3.6	92	79	11.9	84	72	3.5
Hong Kong	64	56	1.3	75	67	5.4	87	78	15.0	81	73	4.5
Istanbul, Turkey	45	36	3.7	61	45	1.9	81	65	1.7	67	54	3.8
Jakarta, Indonesia	84	74	11.8	87	75	5.8	87	73	2.5	87	74	4.4
Jerusalem, Israel	55	41	5.1	73	50	0.9	87	63	0.0	81	59	0.3
Kabul, Afghanistan	36	18	1.3	66	43	3.3	92	61	0.1	73	42	0.4
Karachi, Pakistan	77	55	0.5	90	73	0.1	91	81	3.2	91	72	0.1
Kinshasa, Congo, Dem. Rep.	87	70	5.3	89	71	7.7	81	64	0.1	88	70	4.7
Lagos, Nigeria	88	74	1.1	89	77	5.9	83	74	11.0	85	74	8.1
Lima, Peru	82	66	0.1	80	63	t	67	57	0.3	71	58	0.1
Lisbon, Portugal	56	46	3.3	64	52	2.4	79	63	0.2	69	57	3.1
London, United Kingdom	44	35	2.0	56	40	1.8	73	55	2.0	58	44	2.3
Madrid, Spain	47	33	1.1	64	44	1.7	87	62	0.4	66	48	1.9
Manila, Philippines	86	69	0.9	93	73	1.3	88	75	17.0	88	74	7.6
Melbourne, Australia	78	57	1.9	68	51	2.3	56	42	1.9	67	48	2.6
Mexico City, Mexico	66	42	0.2	78	52	0.7	74	54	4.5	70	50	1.6
Montreal, Canada	21	6	3.8	50	33	2.6	78	61	3.7	54	40	3.4
Moscow, Russia	21	9	1.5	47	31	1.9	76	55	3.0	46	34	2.7
Nairobi, Kenya	77	54	1.5	75	58	8.3	69	51	0.6	76	55	2.1
New Delhi, India	71	43	0.9	97	68	0.3	95	80	7.1	93	64	0.4
Osaka, Japan	47	32	1.7	65	47	5.2	87	73	5.9	72	55	5.1
Oslo, Norway	30	20	1.7	50	34	1.6	73	56	2.9	49	37	2.9
Paris, France	42	32	1.5	60	41	1.7	76	55	2.1	59	44	2.2
Prague, Czechoslovakia	34	25	0.9	55	40	1.5	74	58	2.6	54	44	1.2
Rio de Janeiro, Brazil	84	73	4.9	80	69	4.2	75	63	1.6	77	66	3.1
Riyadh, Saudi Arabia	70	46	0.1	89	64	0.1	107	78	0.0	94	61	0.0
Rome, Italy	54	39	3.3	68	46	2.0	88	64	0.4	73	53	4.3
Santiago, Chile	85	53	0.1	74	45	0.5	59	37	3.0	72	45	0.6
São Paulo, Brazil	77	63	8.8	73	59	2.2	66	53	1.5	68	57	4.6
Seoul, South Korea	32	15	1.2	62	41	3.0	84	70	14.8	67	45	1.6
Shanghai, China	47	32	1.9	67	49	3.6	91	75	5.8	75	56	2.9
Singapore	86	73	9.9	88	75	7.4	88	75	6.7	87	74	8.2
Stockholm, Sweden	31	23	1.5	45	32	1.5	70	55	2.8	48	39	2.1
St. Petersburg, Russia	23	12	1.0	45	31	1.0	71	57	2.5	45	37	1.8
Sydney, Australia	78	65	3.5	71	58	5.3	60	46	4.6	71	56	2.8
Tahiti, French Polynesia	89	72	13.2	89	72	6.8	86	68	2.6	87	70	3.4
Taipei, Taiwan	66	53	3.8	77	64	5.3	92	76	8.8	80	68	5.5
Tehran, Iran	45	27	1.8	71	49	1.4	99	72	0.1	76	53	0.3
Tokyo, Japan	47	29	1.9	63	46	5.3	83	70	5.6	69	55	8.2
Toronto, Canada	30	16	2.7	50	34	2.5	79	59	3.0	56	40	2.4
Vienna, Austria	34	26	1.5	57	41	2.0	75	59	3.0	55	44	2.0
Warsaw, Poland	30	21	1.2	54	38	1.5	75	56	3.0	54	41	1.7

t= trace.   **Source:** U.S. Department of Commerce, National Oceanic and Atmospheric Administration, *Climates of the World* (1991).

World Population

World population topped 6 billion in 1999; the United Nations Population Fund (UNFPA) chose October 12 as the symbolic date for this milestone. The world's population has been growing exponentially in the 20th century. Total world population stood at 2 billion in 1927; it is expected to reach 8 billion by 2026 and 9.3 billion by 2050.

In 1990, 85 million people were added to the world's population, although that number was down to 79 million in 1998. Even so, global fertility is still above replacement level (i.e. the number of children needed to replace people who die) despite an increasing number of countries with below-average fertility rates. In 1998, 90 percent of the world's births, but only 77 percent of its deaths, took place in developing countries. This means that 96 percent of the natural increase (births minus deaths) occurred in the developing regions of Africa, Asia, and Latin America

Of the 79 million people who will be added to world population in 1999, over 16 million will live in India, about 11 million in China, and 34 million more in the rest of Asia and Oceania. Over 15 million will be added in Sub-Saharan Africa, nearly eight million in Latin America and the Caribbean, and seven million in the Near East and North Africa.

Four countries in Sub-Saharan Africa contribute 20 percent of total world population increase: Nigeria, Congo, Ethiopia, Sudan. The Near East and North Africa contributes nine percent of total world population increase with Egypt, Turkey, and Iraq having the largest numbers. Asia and Oceania contributes 56.8 percent of total world population increase. India contributed 37 percent of Asia and Oceania's total and China provided 23.8 percent. Latin America and the Caribbean provide 9.9 percent of total world population increase with Brazil and Mexico having the largest numbers.

The world's two largest nations accounted for over half of all population growth in Asia and Oceania in 1998. Over a third of this growth took place in India; about a fourth in China. Despite China's larger population, its rate of natural increase is 0.9 percent which is about half that of India (1.7 percent).

The more developed nations contributed 2.9 million of the 79 million people added this year, or 3.7 percent of total world population increase.

During the coming 25 years, crude birth rates and death rates will continue to decrease in the less developed countries. However, in these years 131 to 136 million babies will be born each year, even though women will be having fewer children over their reproductive lifetime. Despite falling fertility in every major region, the number of births has remained roughly the same because the number of women of childbearing age (15 to 49) has been growing.

Distribution of the World's Population, 1970–2020

Area	1970	1998	2020
Developed countries	27.1%	19.8%	16.4%
Developing countries	72.9	80.2	83.6
Sub-Saharan Africa	7.8	10.5	13.5
Near East and North Africa	3.9	5.2	6.4
China (Mainland and Taiwan)	22.5	(¹)	18.9
Other Asia	29.7	56.7[1]	35.0
Latin America and the Caribbean	7.7	8.6	8.5
Eastern Europe and New Independent States	9.5	7.0	5.8
Rest of the World	18.9	12.0	12.0

Note: Other Asia excludes China and Japan. Rest of the World includes Western Europe, North America, Japan, and Oceania. 1. China included in Other Asia category in 1998. **Source:** U. S. Bureau of the Census, *World Population Profile: 1996* (1996) and *International Data Base* (1999).

Countries with Declining Population Estimates, 1996–2025

Country	1996	2025	Decrease
Russia	147,200,000	131,400,000	15,800,000
Italy	57,200,000	51,700,000	5,500,000
Ukraine	51,200,000	46,000,000	5,200,000
Spain	39,800,000	37,500,000	2,300,000
Romania	22,600,000	21,100,000	1,500,000
Germany	82,400,000	80,900,000	1,500,000
Hungary	9,900,000	8,700,000	1,200,000
Bulgaria	8,400,000	7,500,000	900,000
Belarus	10,300,000	9,600,000	700,000
Czech Republic	10,200,000	9,600,000	600,000
Greece	10,600,000	10,100,000	500,000
Portugal	9,800,000	9,400,000	400,000
Latvia	2,400,000	2,100,000	300,000
Croatia	4,500,000	4,200,000	300,000
Lithuania	3,700,000	3,500,000	200,000
Slovenia	1,900,000	1,700,000	200,000
Estonia	1,400,000	1,300,000	100,000

Source: United Nations Population Fund (UNFPA), *The State of World Population 1998* (1998).

World Births, Deaths, and Population Growth, 1996

Characteristic	World	Developed	Developing
Population	5,926,830,000	1,175,581,000	4,751,248,000
Births	132,779,000	13,216,000	119,563,000
Deaths	54,146,000	12,248,000	41,898,000
Natural increase	78,633,000	968,000	77,665,000
Births per 1,000 population	22	11	25
Deaths per 1,000 population	9	10	9
Growth rate (percent)	1.3%	0.1%	1.6%

Source: U.S. Bureau of the Census, *International Data Base* (1996).

▶ WORLD POPULATION TRENDS

A century ago, most people died before the age of 50. By 1996 average life expectancy globally reached 65 and in many countries it is now well over 70 years; in several nations, life expectancy is approaching 80. The UN estimates that there were 380 million people aged 65 or more in 1997, a 14 percent global increase from 1990. By 2020, that number is expected to be more than 690 million.

In 1996, the child and adolescent population grew by about 0.7 percent, the adult population by 1.8 percent, and that of the elderly by 2.4 percent.

Over the next 30 years, almost 98 percent of population growth is projected to take place in developing countries. And Europe, home to many of the world's more developed countries, is projected to lose population. There are currently 498 million people in Europe. That number is expected to decline to 486 million in 2050 and to continue to decline even further thereafter. North America is projected to increase from 276 million persons in 1990 to 360 million in 2025 before its population starts to decline.

Africa has been and will continue to be the fastest-growing region. In 1950 Africa had 222 million people, 8.8 percent of the world total. By 1990 the population was 642 million, 12.1 percent of the world total, and it is projected to reach 867 million in 2000, 1.582 billion in 2025, and 2.265 billion in 2050. By 2050 Africa will contain 23 percent of the world's people.

Years to Reach Population Milestones

Population Milestone	Year Reached	Years to Reach
1 billion	1804	N.A.
2 billion	1927	123
3 billion	1960	33
4 billion	1974	14
5 billion	1987	13
6 billion	1999	12
7 billion	2012	13
8 billion	2026	14
9 billion	2043	17

Source: U.S. Census Bureau, *World Population Profile: 1998* (1999).

World Vital Events per Time Unit, 1999

Time unit	Births	Deaths	Natural Increase
Year	131,468,233	54,147,021	77,321,212
Month	10,955,686	4,512,252	6,443,434
Day	360,187	148,744	211,839
Hour	15,008	6,181	8,827
Minute	250	103	147
Second	4.2	1.7	2.5

Source: U.S Bureau of the Census, *International Data Base* (1999).

Population Under 15 and Over 65, 1996

Area/Region	Population	
	Under 15	Over 65
World	32%	7%
More Developed Countries	19	14
Less Developed Countries	35	5
Least Developed Countries	45	3
Africa	46	3
Asia	32	5
Europe	19	14
Latin America and the Caribbean	33	5
Northern American	22	13
Oceania	26	10

Source: United Nations Department for Economic and Social Information and Policy Analysis, Population Division, *World Population 1996* (chart) (1996).

World's Largest Countries, Ranked by Population, 1998, 2025, and 2050

	1998		2025		2050
Rank, Country	Population	Rank	Population	Rank	Population
1. China	1,255,100,000	1	1,480,400,000	2	1,517,000,000
2. India	975,800,000	2	1,330,200,000	1	1,533,000,000
3. United States	273,800,000	3	332,500,000	4	348,000,000
4. Indonesia	206,500,000	4	275,200,000	6	318,000,000
5. Brazil	165,200,000	7	216,600,000	7	243,000,000
6. Russia	147,200,000	10	131,400,000	16	114,000,000
7. Pakistan	147,800,000	5	268,900,000	3	357,000,000
8. Japan	125,900,000	13	121,300,000	17	110,000,000
9. Bangladesh	124,000,000	8	180,000,000	8	218,000,000
10. Nigeria	121,800,000	6	238,400,000	5	339,000,000
11. Mexico	95,800,000	11	130,200,000	12	154,000,000
12. Germany	82,400,000	19	80,900,000	N.A.	N.A.
13. Vietnam	77,900,000	14	110,100,000	14	130,000,000
14. Iran	73,100,000	12	128,300,000	10	170,000,000
15. Philippines	72,200,000	16	105,200,000	13	131,000,000
16. Egypt	65,700,000	17	95,800,000	15	115,000,000
17. Turkey	63,800,000	18	85,800,000	18	98,000,000
18. Ethiopia	62,100,000	9	136,300,000	9	213,000,000
19. Thailand	59,600,000	N.A.	N.A.	N.A.	N.A.
20. France	58,700,000	N.A.	N.A.	N.A.	N.A.

Source: United Nations Population Fund, *The State of World Population 1998* (1998).

Population Indicators by Region and Nation

Region/Country	Population estimate ('000s) 1998	Population estimate ('000s) 2025	Birth rate per 1,000 1998	Death rate per 1,000 1998	Life expectancy, 1995	Percent urban, 1995	Fertility rate per woman, 1995
World Total	5,929,800	8,039,100	24	9	64	45%	2.8
More Developed Regions	1,181,500	1,220,300	12	10	74	75	1.6
Less Developed Regions	4,748,300	6,818,900	27	9	62	38	3.1
Least Developed Countries	626,900	1,159,300	40	15	50	22	5.2
Africa	778,500	1,453,900	41	14	52	34	5.3
Asia	3,588,900	4,784,800	24	8	65	35	2.7
Europe	729,400	701,100	11	11	73	74	1.5
Latin America and the Caribbean	499,500	689,600	25	7	68	74	2.7
Northern America	304,100	369,000	15	9	76	76	1.9
Oceania	29,500	40,700	19	8	73	70	2.5
Afghanistan	23,400	45,300	50	22	43	20	6.9
Albania	3,400	4,300	24	6	71	37	2.6
Algeria	30,200	47,300	31	6	67	56	3.8
Angola	12,000	25,500	51	19	46	32	6.7
Argentina	36,100	47,200	21	8	72	88	2.6
Armenia	3,600	4,200	18	7	71	69	1.7
Australia	18,400	23,900	15	7	78	85	1.9
Austria	8,200	8,300	11	11	76	56	1.4
Azerbaijan	7,700	9,700	23	6	71	56	2.3
Bahrain	594	863	26	4	72	90	3.0
Bangladesh	124,000	180,000	27	11	56	18	3.1
Belarus	10,300	9,600	12	12	70	71	1.4
Belgium	10,200	10,300	12	11	76	97	1.6
Belize	200	400	34	5	74	47	3.7
Benin	5,900	12,300	45	14	54	31	5.8
Bhutan	1,900	3,600	42	15	51	6	5.9
Bolivia	8,000	13,100	36	10	59	61	4.4
Bosnia and Herzegovina	4,000	4,300	13	7	72	49	1.4
Botswana	1,600	2,600	37	11	54	28	4.4
Brazil	165,200	216,600	22	7	66	78	2.2
Brunei Darussalam	N.A.	N.A.	26	3	75	N.A.	N.A.
Bulgaria	8,400	7,500	11	13	71	71	1.5
Burkina Faso	11,400	23,500	48	18	46	27	6.6
Burundi	6,600	12,300	46	20	45	8	6.3
Cambodia	10,800	17,000	38	14	52	21	4.5
Cameroon	14,300	28,500	41	13	56	55	5.3
Canada	30,200	36,400	14	7	78	77	1.6
Central African Republic	3,500	6,000	39	17	50	48	5.0
Chad	6,900	12,600	44	18	47	21	5.5
Chile	14,800	19,500	22	6	75	84	2.4
China	1,255,100	1,480,400	18	7	68	30	1.8
Colombia	37,700	52,700	26	6	70	73	2.7
Congo, Democratic Republic of	49,200	105,900	48	15	52	2	6.2
Congo, Republic of	2,800	5,700	45	15	51	59	5.9
Costa Rica	3,700	5,600	26	4	76	50	3.0
Croatia	4,500	4,200	11	12	71	64	1.6
Cuba	11,100	11,800	15	7	75	76	1.6
Czech Republic	10,200	9,600	12	13	72	65	1.4
Denmark	5,300	5,300	13	12	75	85	1.8
Djibouti	652	1,134	39	16	48	83	5.4
Dominican Republic	8,200	11,200	27	6	70	65	2.8
Ecuador	12,200	17,800	28	6	69	58	3.1
Egypt	65,700	95,800	29	8	64	45	3.4
El Salvador	6,100	9,200	30	6	68	45	3.1
Eritrea	3,500	6,500	43	16	50	17	5.3
Estonia	1,400	1,300	11	13	69	73	1.3
Ethiopia	62,100	136,300	49	18	47	13	7.0
Finland	5,200	5,300	13	10	76	63	1.8
France	58,700	60,400	13	9	78	73	1.6
Gabon	1,200	2,100	35	15	54	50	5.4
Gambia	1,194	1,984	43	19	45	26	5.2
Georgia	5,400	5,800	16	9	73	58	1.9
Germany	82,400	80,900	10	12	76	87	1.3
Ghana	18,900	36,300	40	12	56	36	5.3
Greece	10,600	10,100	10	10	78	65	1.4

Region/Country	Population estimate ('000s)		Birth rate per 1,000 1998	Death rate per 1,000 1998	Life expec- tancy, 1995	Percent urban, 1995	Fertility rate per woman, 1995
	1998	2025					
Guatemala	11,600	21,700	39	8	65	41%	4.9
Guinea	7,700	15,300	51	20	44	30	6.6
Guinea-Bissau	1,100	1,900	42	22	43	22	5.4
Haiti	7,500	12,500	35	13	54	32	4.6
Honduras	6,100	10,700	37	6	68	44	4.3
Hong Kong	6,300	6,500	12	6	78	95	1.3
Hungary	9,900	8,700	11	15	69	65	1.4
Iceland	277	336	17	7	79	92	2.2
India	975,800	1,330,200	27	10	60	27	3.1
Indonesia	206,500	275,200	25	8	63	35	2.6
Iran	73,100	128,300	38	7	67	59	4.8
Iraq	21,800	41,600	38	10	59	75	5.3
Ireland	3,600	3,700	14	9	76	58	1.8
Israel	5,900	8,000	21	7	77	91	2.8
Italy	57,200	51,700	10	10	77	67	1.2
Ivory Coast	14,600	24,400	39	13	52	44	5.1
Jamaica	2,500	3,400	24	6	74	54	2.4
Japan	125,900	121,300	10	7	79	78	1.5
Jordan	6,000	11,900	39	5	68	71	5.1
Kazakhstan	16,900	20,000	20	8	68	60	2.3
Kenya	29,000	50,200	38	12	54	28	4.9
Korea, North	23,200	30,000	22	5	71	61	2.1
Korea, South	46,100	52,500	16	6	71	81	1.7
Kuwait	1,800	2,900	24	2	75	97	2.8
Kyrgyzstan	4,500	6,000	28	7	68	39	3.2
Laos	5,400	10,200	45	15	51	22	6.7
Latvia	2,400	2,100	11	14	68	73	1.4
Lebanon	3,200	4,400	27	7	69	87	2.8
Lesotho	2,200	4,000	37	11	58	23	4.9
Liberia	2,700	6,600	49	28	39	45	6.3
Libya	6,000	12,900	42	8	63	86	5.9
Lithuania	3,700	3,500	13	11	70	72	1.5
Luxembourg	422	466	13	11	76	89	1.8
Macedonia	2,200	2,500	16	7	71	60	1.9
Madagascar	16,300	34,500	44	11	56	27	5.7
Malawi	10,400	20,400	51	22	42	14	6.7
Malaysia	21,500	31,600	29	5	71	54	3.2
Mali	11,800	24,600	51	19	46	27	6.6
Malta	374	424	15	8	76	89	2.1
Mauritania	2,500	4,400	40	14	51	54	5.0
Mauritius	1,200	1,500	21	7	70	41	2.3
Melanesia	6,200	10,200	32	9	59	21	4.3
Mexico	95,800	130,200	27	5	71	75	2.8
Moldova	4,500	4,900	16	10	68	52	1.8
Mongolia	2,600	4,100	29	8	64	61	3.3
Morocco	28,000	39,900	29	8	64	48	3.1
Mozambique	18,700	35,400	45	19	46	34	6.1
Myanmar	47,600	67,600	29	11	58	26	3.3
Namibia	1,700	3,000	38	12	56	37	4.9
Nepal	23,200	40,600	40	13	55	14	5.0
Netherlands	15,700	16,100	13	9	77	89	1.6
New Zealand	3,700	4,900	17	8	76	86	2.0
Nicaragua	4,500	7,600	36	6	66	63	3.9
Niger	10,100	22,400	53	19	47	17	7.1
Nigeria	121,800	238,400	45	15	50	39	6.0
Norway	4,400	4,700	14	11	77	73	1.9
Oman	2,500	6,500	44	5	70	13	7.2
Pakistan	147,800	268,900	39	9	62	35	5.0
Panama	2,800	3,800	25	5	73	53	2.6
Papua New Guinea	4,600	7,500	33	11	56	16	4.7
Paraguay	5,200	9,400	34	6	69	53	4.2
Peru	24,800	35,500	27	7	67	72	3.0
Philippines	72,200	105,200	31	6	66	54	3.6
Poland	38,700	40,000	13	10	71	65	1.7
Portugal	9,800	9,400	11	11	74	36	1.5
Puerto Rico	3,800	4,700	18	7	75	73	2.1
Qatar	579	782	20	3	71	91	3.8
Romania	22,600	21,100	11	11	70	55	1.4

Region/Country	Population estimate ('000s) 1998	Population estimate ('000s) 2025	Birth rate per 1,000 1998	Death rate per 1,000 1998	Life expectancy, 1995	Percent urban, 1995	Fertility rate per woman, 1995
Russia	147,200	131,400	11	13	66	76%	1.4
Rwanda	6,500	13,000	44	45	23	6	6.0
Saudi Arabia	20,200	42,400	35	5	70	80	5.9
Senegal	9,000	16,900	43	16	49	42	5.6
Sierra Leone	4,600	8,200	49	30	34	36	6.1
Singapore	3,500	4,200	18	5	76	100	1.8
Slovakia	5,400	5,500	14	11	71	59	1.5
Slovenia	1,900	1,700	10	11	73	64	1.3
Somalia	10,700	23,700	50	18	47	26	7.0
South Africa	44,300	71,600	31	9	63	51	3.8
Spain	39,800	37,500	10	9	77	76	1.2
Sri Lanka	18,500	23,900	19	6	72	22	2.1
Sudan	28,500	46,900	35	14	51	25	4.6
Suriname	442	605	25	6	70	50	2.4
Swaziland	906	1,675	39	11	58	31	4.4
Sweden	8,900	9,500	14	11	78	83	1.8
Switzerland	7,300	7,600	12	9	78	61	1.5
Syria	15,300	26,300	33	6	67	52	4.0
Tajikistan	6,200	9,700	33	7	67	32	3.9
Tanzania	32,200	62,400	43	14	50	24	5.5
Thailand	59,600	69,100	18	6	69	20	1.7
Tinidad & Tobago	1,300	1,700	18	6	73	72	2.1
Togo	4,400	8,800	44	15	51	31	6.1
Tunisia	9,500	13,500	26	6	68	57	2.9
Turkey	63,800	85,800	23	7	67	69	2.5
Turkmenistan	4,300	6,500	32	8	65	45	3.6
Uganda	21,300	45,000	51	22	41	13	7.1
Ukraine	51,200	46,000	11	13	69	70	1.4
United Arab Emirates	2,400	3,300	21	3	74	84	3.5
United Kingdom	58,200	59,500	13	11	76	90	1.7
United States	273,800	332,500	16	9	76	76	2.0
Uruguay	3,200	3,700	17	10	72	90	2.3
Uzbekistan	24,100	36,500	31	7	68	41	3.5
Venezuela	23,200	34,800	27	5	72	93	3.0
Vietnam	77,900	110,100	29	8	65	21	3.0
Yemen	16,900	39,600	49	12	55	34	7.6
Yugoslavia	10,400	10,700	14	10	72	57	1.8
Zaire	48,000	105,900	48	15	52	29	6.2
Zambia	8,700	16,200	44	18	49	44	5.5
Zimbabwe	11,700	19,300	40	14	51	32	4.7

Note: Totals may not add because of rounding numbers. Data for small countries or areas, generally those with population of 200,000 or less in 1990, are not given in this table.   Sources: United Nations Population Fund (UNFPA), *The State of World Population 1998* (1998) and United Nations Department for Economic and Social Information and Policy Analysis, Population Division, "World Population 1996" chart.

▶ GLOSSARY OF DEMOGRAPHIC TERMS

Birth rate   The average annual number of births during a year per 1,000 population at midyear; also known as the crude birth rate.

Contraception   Deliberate use of methods to prevent conception or pregnancy; also known as family planning.

Death rate   The average annual number of deaths during a year per 1,000 population at midyear; also known as the crude death rate.

Growth rate   The average annual percent change in the population, resulting from a surplus (or deficit) of births over deaths and the balance of migrants entering and leaving a country The rate may be positive or negative; also known as population growth rate or average annual rate of growth.

Infant mortality rate   The number of deaths to infants under one year of age in a given year per 1,000 live births occurring in the same year.

Least developed countries   Defined by the United Nations as the countries with the poorest living standards. In 1995, the UN counted 48 countries, most of them landlocked, among the least developed.

Less developed countries   Defined by the U.N. as countries with poorer people than in a more developed country, with economies based on agricultural production, with low GNPs, and lacking in advanced technologies. Approximately 77 countries, including those in Africa, Latin America, and the Caribbean, Asia (except Japan), and regions of Melanesia, Micronesia, and Polynesia are considered less developed.

More developed countries   The United Nations defines developed countries as industrialized nations with a high gross national product (GNP), high per capita GNP, and advanced science and technology. Approximately 45 countries including those in Europe, North America, Japan, Australia and New Zealand are considered developed.

Projections   Data on population and vital rates derived for future years based on statistics from population censuses, vital registration system or sample surveys pertaining to the recent past, and on assumptions about future trends.

Vital events   Births and deaths

Vital rates   Birth rates and death rates.

▶URBANIZATION

According to the United Nations, in 1996, 45 percent of the world's population resided in urban areas. Seventy-five percent of the people in developed countries live in urban areas and 37 percent of the people in developing regions live in cities. One-third of the people in Africa and Asia live in urban areas, while in Europe, Latin America and the Caribbean, and Northern America seven out of 10 people are urban residents.

The UN estimates that in 1996, 2.5 billion people lived in urban areas of the world, of which 1.7 billion resided in less developed regions. By 2005, half of the world's population will live in urban areas and by 2025, over three-fifths of the world population will be urban. Nearly all the urban population growth is in developing countries. Two out of three urban dwellers currently live in developing nations; by 2015 more than three out of four people will be urban residents in developing countries.

The world's largest cities have been changing dramatically over the last 45 years. In 1950 only New York had a population over 10 million people. Eleven of the 15 largest cities were in developed regions. Berlin, the 15th largest city had a population of 3.3 million.

By 1994, 14 of the top 15 cities had populations over 10 million and six of these had over 14 million residents: Tokyo, 26.5 million; New York, 16.3 million; São Paulo, 16.1 million; Mexico City, 15.5 million; Shanghai 14.7 million; Bombay, 14.5 million. Only four of the 15 cities were in developed

Nations with Highest and Lowest Fertility Rates, 1995-2000[1]

Highest fertility rates		Lowest fertility rates	
Country	Fertility rate per woman	Country	Fertility rate per woman
Yemen	7.6	Italy	1.2
Oman	7.2	Spain	1.2
Niger	7.1	Estonia	1.3
Uganda	7.1	Hong Kong	1.3
Ethiopia	7.0	Germany	1.3
Somalia	7.0	Slovenia	1.3
Afghanistan	6.4	Austria	1.4
Angola	6.7	Belarus	1.4
Laos	6.7	Bosnia and Herzegovina	1.4
Malawi	6.7	Czech Republic	1.4
Burkina Faso	6.6	Greece	1.4
Guinea	6.6	Hungary	1.4
Mali	6.6	Latvia	1.4
Burundi	6.3	Romania	1.4
Liberia	6.3	Russia	1.4
Zaire (Congo, Democratic Republic of)	6.2	Ukraine	1.4
		Bulgaria	1.5
		Lithuania	1.5
Mozambique	6.1	Japan	1.5
Togo	6.1	Portugal	1.5
Nigeria	6.0	Slovakia	1.5
Rwanda	6.0	Switzerland	1.5

1. Estimated. **Source:** United Nations Population Fund (UNFPA), *The State of World Population 1998* (1998).

The World's 30 Largest Urban Areas, Ranked by 2000 Population[1]

2000 Rank, Urban area	Population (millions)					Rank	
	1950	1970	1990	2000[1]	2015[1]	1950	2015
1. Tokyo, Japan	6.9	16.5	25.0	27.9	28.7	3	1
2. Bombay, India	2.9	5.8	12.2	18.1	27.4	15	2
3. São Paulo, Brazil	2.4	8.1	14.8	17.8	20.8	18	6
4. Shanghai, China	5.3	11.2	13.5	17.2	23.4	6	4
5. New York, U.S.	12.3	16.2	16.1	16.6	17.6	1	11
6. Mexico City, Mexico	3.1	9.1	15.1	16.4	18.8	13	10
7. Beijing, China	3.9	8.1	10.9	14.2	19.4	12	8
8. Jakarta, Indonesia	N.A.	3.9	9.3	14.1	21.2	N.A.	5
9. Lagos, Nigeria	N.A.	N.A.	7.7	13.5	24.4	N.A.	3
10. Los Angeles, U.S.	4.0	8.4	11.5	13.1	14.3	11	17
11. Calcutta, India	4.4	6.9	10.7	12.7	17.6	9	12
12. Tianjin, China	2.4	5.2	9.3	12.4	17.0	17	14
13. Seoul, South Korea	N.A.	5.3	10.6	12.3	13.1	N.A.	18
14. Karachi, Pakistan	N.A.	N.A.	8.0	12.1	20.6	N.A.	7
15. Delhi, India	N.A.	3.5	8.2	11.7	17.6	N.A.	13
16. Buenos Aires, Argentina	5.0	8.4	10.6	11.4	12.4	7	19
17. Metro Manila, Philippines	N.A.	3.5	8.0	10.8	14.7	N.A.	15
18. Cairo, Egypt	2.4	5.3	8.6	10.7	14.5	16	16
19. Osaka, Japan	4.1	9.4	10.5	10.6	10.6	10	23
20. Rio de Janeiro, Brazil	2.9	7.0	9.5	10.2	11.6	14	21
21. Dhaka, Bangladesh	N.A.	N.A.	5.9	10.2	19.0	N.A.	9
22. Paris, France	5.4	8.5	9.3	9.6	9.6	5	27
23. Istanbul, Turkey	N.A.	N.A.	6.5	9.3	12.3	N.A.	20
24. Moscow, Russia	5.4	7.1	9.0	9.3	N.A.	4	N.A.
25. Lima, Peru	N.A.	N.A.	6.5	8.4	10.5	N.A.	25
26. Teheran, Iran	N.A.	N.A.	6.4	7.3	10.2	N.A.	26
27. London, U.K.	8.7	8.6	7.3	7.3	N.A.	2	N.A.
28. Bangkok, Thailand	N.A.	N.A.	5.9	7.3	10.6	N.A.	24
29. Chicago, U.S.	4.9	6.7	6.8	7.0	N.A.	8	N.A.
30. Hyderabad, India	N.A.	N.A.	N.A.	6.7	10.7	N.A.	22

Note: An urban area is a central city or central cities, and the surrounding urbanized areas, also called a metropolitan area. 1. Projected. **Source:** United Nations Department for Economic and Social Information and Policy Analysis, Population Division, *World Urbanization Prospects: The 1994 Revision* (1995).

regions: Tokyo, New York, Los Angeles, and Osaka. Eleven of the world's largest urban areas were in developing regions.

By 2015, seven cities will exceed 20 million people. Tokyo will still be the largest with 28.7 million followed by Bombay, Lagos, Shanghai, Jakarta, São Paulo and Karachi. Thirteen of the top 15 cities will be in developing regions; only Tokyo and New York will be in developed nations. The 15th largest city, Metro Manila, will have a population of 14.7 million.

Between now and 2010, Asia's share of the world's 15 largest cities will grow from nine to 11, with Tokyo, Bombay and Shanghai comprising the three largest urban areas in the world. Africa will increase from zero to one, Lagos. Latin America will go from having four of the 15 largest cities to two: São Paulo and Mexico City. And New York will be the only remaining North American city in the top 15.

▶ FERTILITY

Across the world, women are having fewer children now than 20 years ago. The United Nations estimates world fertility per woman at 2.79 births from 1995-2000. In developed regions fertility rates dropped from an average of 2.6 per woman in 1970 to 1.59 births in 1995-2000. Births in less developed regions dropped to an average of 3.08 births per woman and to 5.25 in the least developed countries in this same time period.

Replacement level fertility represents the point at which each couple has only the number of births required to replace themselves in the population. The replacement level fertility rate is usually 2.1 births per woman. Most countries in Europe and North America have fertility rates at or below that level. For the period 1995-2000, some 22 countries will have average fertility levels of 1.5 or less children per woman, with Italy (1.2) and Spain (1.2) having the lowest rates. Hong Kong and Japan are the only non-European countries with fertility levels of 1.5 or less.

The United Nations reports that fertility rates are declining in Sub-Saharan Africa and South-central Asia, where fertility levels have been very high for decades. From 1980-85 to 1995-2000 Tanzania's fertility rate dropped from 6.7 to 5.48 births per woman and Namibia's declined from 5.8 to 4.9. Bangladesh declined from 6.2 births per woman to 3.1, India from 4.5 to 3.1, and Nepal from 6.3 to 5.

China, Thailand and Mexico made the greatest fertility rate reductions from 1970 to 1995-2000. China's fertility rate went from 6.0 to 1.8, Thailand's from 6.1 to 1.7, and Mexico's from 6.7 to 2.8.

These reductions in family size are largely due to contraceptive use. The UN estimates that 18 million couples reach their childbearing years each year during the 1990s. Almost all research studies indicate that couples the world over want fewer children. Thirty years ago, less than 10 percent of couples in the developing world had access to family planning. Today 60 percent of those couples have access, causing family size to drop from an average of six children during the 1960s to less than three today.

Nevertheless, there are still close to 150 million women who want to limit or space their pregnancies, but cannot do so effectively. Some 350 million couples continue to lack information about contraception and access to a range of contraceptive services.

World Health

The World Health Organization (WHO), a specialized agency of the United Nations, is the global intergovernmental directing and coordinating authority for international health work. It was created in 1948 and since 1977 WHO's priority has been "Health for All by the Year 2000." This global health campaign focuses on improving education on current health problems, proper food supply and nutrition, safe water and sanitation, maternal and child health, immunization against major infectious diseases, prevention and control of local diseases, and provision of essential pharmaceuticals. Headquartered in Geneva, Switzerland, WHO gathers health statistics, sets international health standards, provides assistance to individual countries when invited, and issues publications. Most of the information here is from the World Health Organization (WHO).

(For information on the United States, see the section "Health and Medicine" in Part II.)

▶ THE GLOBAL SITUATION

The World Health Organization estimates that of the 54 million deaths that occurred in 1998, over 40 percent, or 16.7 million deaths, were due to cardiovascular diseases (heart attacks and strokes), 18 percent, or 9.8 million were due to infectious and parasitic diseases (tuberculosis, sexually transmitted diseases, childhood diseases, etc.), almost 14 percent, or 7.2 million, were due to cancers, and 10.7 percent, or 5.8 million were due to injuries. Acute lower respiratory infections caused 3,452,000 deaths, or 6.4 percent of the world total, while respiratory diseases (including chronic obstructive pulmonary disease and asthma) accounted for nearly 3 million deaths (5.6 percent). HIV/AIDS caused 2.3 million deaths, or 4.2 percent of the total.

Diseases are categorized as communicable (such as tuberculosis, malaria, HIV/AIDS, and hepatitis B) and noncommunicable (such as heart attacks, stroke, and cancer). As humanity is winning the battle against communicable diseases, the number of noncommunicable diseases is growing, largely due to lifestyle (smoking, obesity, and lack of exercise), high-fat diet, and aging populations. Communicable diseases caused 16.5 million deaths (30.5 percent of the total) in 1998, while noncommunicable diseases caused 31.7 million deaths (58.8 percent). WHO estimates that noncommunicable diseases will increase to 73 percent by 2020.

Aging Populations Globally

WHO estimates that the number of people over 65 will rise from 390 million in 1998 to 800 million by 2025, when the elderly will make up 10 percent of the global population. In the next 25 years, the population aged 65 and above is likely to grow by 88 percent—almost one million people a month. Two-thirds of this growth will be in developing countries.

In 1996, life expectancy worldwide reached 65

Nations with Highest and Lowest Infant Mortality Rates, 1995-2000

Country	Infant mortality rate[1]	Country	Infant mortality rate[1]
Highest infant mortality		**Lowest infant mortality**	
Sierra Leone	169	Japan	4
Afghanistan	154	Finland	5
Liberia	153	Hong Kong	5
Mali	149	Norway	5
Malawi	142	Singapore	5
Guinea-Bissau	132	Sweden	5
Rwanda	125	Switzerland	5
Angola	124	Australia	6
Guinea	124	Austria	6
Chad	115	Canada	6
Burundi	114	Germany	6
Niger	114	Ireland	6
Uganda	113	Netherlands	6
Somalia	112	United Kingdom	6
Mozambique	110	Belgium	7
Ethiopia	107	Denmark	7
Bhutan	104	France	7
Zambia	103	Israel	7
Cambodia	102	Italy	7
		New Zealand	7
		Slovenia	7
		Spain	7
		U.S.	7

1. Rate per 1,000 live births.   **Source:** United Nations Population Fund, *The State of World Population 1998* (1998).

Estimated Infant Mortality Rates by Region, 1995-2000

Region	Infant mortality rate (per 1,000 live births)
World	**57**
Developed regions	9
Less developed regions	62
Least developed regions	100
Africa	86
Asia	56
Europe	12
Latin America and Caribbean	35
Northern America	7
Oceania	24

Source: United Nations Population Fund, *The State of World Population 1998* (1998).

for the first time in human history. As people live longer, noncommunicable diseases become more common. Most deaths among the elderly will be due to cancers, and lung and heart diseases. Over 80 percent of circulatory diseases occur in people over 65. Worldwide, circulatory disease is the leading cause of death and disability in people over 65.

Resurgence of Old Diseases

Worldwide, infectious and parasitic diseases kill nearly 10 million people a year, or 18.2 percent of all deaths. Most of the victims of parasitic diseases are young children. In recent years, there have been widespread outbreaks of infectious diseases once thought to be under control.

Tuberculosis By the late 1970s, public health experts were predicting that this chronic bacterial disease would be almost completely eliminated in the United States by the end of the century. Beginning in 1988, however, the number of cases increased annually, reaching 26,673 new cases in 1992. According to WHO, tuberculosis is the "world's most neglected health crisis." An estimated 2 billion people are infected with tuberculosis worldwide, and the disease kills 1.5 million people annually. A tuberculosis vaccine, known as BCG, has been injected in an estimated 3 billion people worldwide but is used infrequently in the United States.

Malaria is caused by a parasite transmitted by the anopheles mosquito. The number of infected people has risen steadily during the 1980s and 1990s, in part because developing equatorial countries have encouraged development in swampy, anopheles-infected regions. Worldwide, an estimated 300 to 500 million cases occur annually, and 1.1 million people — mostly in sub-Saharan Africa — die from the disease. Almost all of the approximately 1,000 Americans who contract malaria each year get the disease while traveling abroad.

Cholera is caused by a bacterium that is spread principally through food and drinking water contaminated with human feces. The disease is associated with poverty and is most prevalent in places that lack clean water supplies and hygienic sewage-disposal systems. In 1991 a cholera epidemic broke out in Peru —the first major outbreak of cholera in the Western Hemisphere in the 20th century. By September 1994 a total of 1,041,422 cases and 9,643 deaths had been reported throughout Central and South America. Meanwhile, a new strain of cholera was spreading across south Asia; attacks from older strains do not produce lasting immunity to this new strain. Cholera epidemics also occur regularly in crowded refugee camps. In 1994, for example, an estimated 20,000 to 30,000 Rwandan refugees in Zaire died from cholera.

Dengue fever, another disease once thought to be nearly eliminated in the Western Hemisphere, has also made a comeback, reaching epidemic proportions in Latin America. There were 86 confirmed cases in the United States in 1995, almost twice the average number reported annually between 1987 and 1994. According to the World Health Organization, there are some 20 million cases a year worldwide. Caused by a virus, dengue fever is transmitted by mosquitoes. Though painful, recovery usually is complete within 10 days of the onset of symptoms. However, people who have been exposed to one strain of the virus and then infected with a second strain may develop hemorrhagic dengue, which is fatal about 10 percent of the time.

▶ TOBACCO USE: A GLOBAL HEALTH PROBLEM

The World Health Organization estimates that with current smoking patterns, 500 million people alive today will eventually be killed by tobacco. Worldwide, tobacco kills over four million people a year and will rise to 10 million deaths per year by 2030, with 70 percent of the deaths occurring in developing countries.

There are about 1.15 billion smokers in the world today, consuming an average of 14 cigarettes each per day. About 82 percent of these smokers live in low- and middle-income countries. In recent years, tobacco consumption in high-income countries has been falling. In 1997, an estimated 23 percent of Americans smoked; in the United Kingdom, the estimate was 28 percent. By contrast, smoking is increasing in developing

Current World Health Indicators, by Nation

Country	Life expectancy at birth (years) 1970	Life expectancy at birth (years) 1994	Daily calorie supply, 1992	Infant mortality per 1,000 births[1] 1995-2000	Population with access to: Health services 1990–95	Population with access to: Safe water 1990–96	Population with access to: Sanitation 1990–96
Afghanistan	37	44	1,523	154	29%	12%	—
Albania	67	71	—	32	—	97	100%
Algeria	53	68	2,897	44	98	78	91
Angola	37	47	1,840	124	—	32	16
Argentina	67	72	2,880	22	71	71	68
Armenia	—	71	—	25	—	—	—
Australia	71	78	3,216	6	100	—	—
Austria	70	77	3,495	6	—	100	100
Azerbaijan	—	71	—	33	—	—	—
Bahamas	65	73	—	13	—	—	—
Bahrain	62	72	—	20	—	—	—
Bangladesh	45	56	2,019	78	45	97	34
Barbados	69	76	3,223	8	—	—	—
Belarus	—	70	—	15	—	—	—
Belgium	71	77	—	7	—	100	100
Belize	—	74	2,670	30	—	—	—
Benin	44	54	2,532	84	18	50	20
Bhutan	42	52	—	104	65	58	70
Bolivia	46	60	2,100	66	67	66	55
Bosnia & Herzegovina	—	—	—	13	—	—	—
Botswana	50	52	2,288	56	—	93	55
Brazil	59	67	2,824	42	—	73	44
Brunei Darussalam	—	75	2,745	9	—	—	—
Bulgaria	70	71	—	16	—	99	100
Burkina Faso	40	46	2,387	97	90	78	18
Burundi	45	44	1,941	114	80	59	51
Cambodia	42	52	2,021	102	53	36	14
Cameroon	49	55	1,981	58	80	50	50
Canada	73	79	3,482	6	207	100	—
Cape Verde	56	65	—	48	—	—	—
Central African Republic	42	48	1,691	96	52	38	52
Chad	38	47	1,989	115	30	24	21
Chile	62	75	2,583	13	97	—	—
China	59	69	2,729	38	88	67	24
Colombia	59	70	2,678	24	81	85	85
Comoros	48	56	1,897	88	—	—	—
Congo	51	51	2,297	90	83	34	69
Costa Rica	67	77	2,889	12	—	96	84
Croatia	—	71	—	10	—	—	—
Cuba	70	76	2,833	9	100	89	92
Cyprus	71	76	3,782	8	95	100	100
Czech Republic	69	72	—	9	—	—	—
Denmark	73	75	3,628	7	—	100	99
Djibouti	40	49	—	113	—	—	—
Dominican Republic	59	70	—	34	78	65	78
Ecuador	58	69	2,587	46	—	68	76
Egypt	51	64	3,336	54	99	79	32
El Salvador	58	69	2,663	39	40	69	81
Equatorial Guinea	40	48	—	114	—	—	—
Eritrea	—	50	—	98	—	—	—
Estonia	—	69	—	12	—	—	—
Ethiopia	43	48	1,610	107	46	25	19
Fiji	64	72	3,092	22	—	—	—
Finland	70	76	3,253	5	—	95	100
France	72	79	3,465	7	—	100	100
Gabon	44	54	2,511	85	—	68	—
Gambia	36	46	2,360	79	93	48	37
Georgia	—	73	—	23	—	—	—
Germany	71	76	3,443	6	—	100	93
Ghana	49	57	2,206	73	60	65	55
Greece	72	78	3,825	8	—	98	98
Guatemala	53	66	2,255	40	57	64	59
Guinea	36	45	2,390	124	80	55	21
Guinea-Bissau	36	43	2,556	132	40	59	30
Guyana	65	63	2,385	47	—	—	—
Haiti	48	54	1,707	82	60	28	24
Honduras	53	68	2,306	35	69	87	87

Country	Life expectancy at birth (years)		Daily calorie supply, 1992	Infant mortality per 1,000 births[1] 1995-2000	Population with access to:		
	1970	1994			Health services 1990–95	Safe water 1990–96	Sanitation 1990–96
Hong Kong	—	79	3,144	5	—	100%	—
Hungary	70	69	3,644	14	—	98	100%
Iceland	74	79	—	5	—	100	100
India	48	61	2,395	72	85%	81	29
Indonesia	47	64	2,755	48	93	62	51
Iran	55	68	2,861	39	88	90	81
Iraq	55	57	2,122	95	93	78	70
Ireland	71	76	3,778	6	—	100	100
Israel	71	78	—	7	—	100	99
Italy	72	78	3,504	7	—	100	100
Ivory Coast	—	52	2,491	86	—	75	43
Jamaica	67	74	2,607	12	90	86	89
Japan	72	80	2,956	4	—	—	—
Jordan	55	69	3,031	30	97	98	77
Kazakhstan	—	68	—	34	—	—	—
Kenya	50	54	2,075	65	77	53	77
Kiribati	—	56	—	60	—	—	—
Korea, South	60	72	3,298	9	100	93	100
Korea, North	—	71	2,834	22	—	—	—
Kuwait	66	75	2,535	14	100	—	—
Kyrgzstan	—	68	—	39	—	—	—
Laos	40	52	2,259	86	67	52	28
Latvia	—	68	—	16	—	—	—
Lebanon	—	69	3,319	29	95	94	63
Lesotho	49	58	2,201	72	80	56	28
Liberia	47	56	1,640	153	39	46	30
Libya	52	64	3,310	56	95	97	98
Lithuania	—	70	—	13	—	—	—
Luxembourg	70	76	—	9	—	100	100
Macedonia	—	72	—	23	—	—	—
Madagascar	45	57	2,135	77	38	29	3
Malawi	40	41	1,827	142	35	37	6
Malaysia	62	71	2,884	11	—	78	94
Mali	40	47	2,279	149	40	45	31
Malta	70	76	—	10	—	100	100
Mauritania	39	52	2,685	92	63	66	—
Mauritius	62	71	2,696	15	100	99	99
Mexico	62	72	3,181	31	93	83	72
Micronesia	—	71	—	25	—	—	—
Moldova				26			
Monaco	—	63	2,985	58	70	55	41
Mongolia	60	64	1,899	53	95	80	74
Morocco	52	65	2,985	51	70	55	41
Mozambique	41	46	1,680	110	39	63	54
Myanmar	51	58	2,598	78	60	60	43
Namibia	48	56	2,120	60	59	57	34
Nepal	42	55	1,957	82	—	63	18
Netherlands	74	78	3,151	6	—	100	100
New Zealand	72	76	3,362	7	100	—	—
Nicaragua	54	67	2,296	44	83	53	60
Niger	38	47	2,257	114	99	54	15
Nigeria	44	51	2,125	77	51	51	58
Norway	74	78	3,326	5	—	100	100
Oman	45	70	—	25	96	82	78
Pakistan	48	62	2,316	74	55	74	47
Panama	66	73	2,239	21	70	93	83
Papua New Guinea	47	56	2,615	61	96	28	22
Paraguay	65	69	2,670	39	63	42	41
Peru	54	67	1,883	45	44	72	57
Philippines	57	67	2,258	35	71	86	77
Poland	70	71	—	13	—	89	100
Portugal	—	75	—	8	—	92	96
Qatar	61	71	—	19	—	—	—
Romania	69	70	3,155	24	—	95	98
Russia	—	66	—	19	—	—	—
Rwanda	48	23[3]	1,821	125	80	—	—
Samoa	—	68	—	64	—	—	—
Saudi Arabia	52	70	2,751	23	97	95	86
Senegal	43	50	2,265	62	90	52	58
Sierra Leone	34	34	1,695	169	38	34	11

Country[1]	Life expectancy at birth (years) 1970	Life expectancy at birth (years) 1994	Daily calorie supply, 1992	Infant mortality per 1,000 births[1] 1995-2000	Population with access to: Health services 1990-95	Population with access to: Safe water 1990-96	Population with access to: Sanitation 1990-96
Singapore	68	77	—	5	—	100%	—
Slovakia	—	71	—	12	—	—	—
Slovenia	—	73	—	7	—	—	—
Solomon Islands	40	70	2,222	25	—	—	—
Somalia	—	47	1,505	112	27%	37	18%
South Africa	53	64	2,705	48	—	99	53
Spain	72	78	3,572	7	—	100	100
Sri Lanka	64	72	2,275	15	—	57	63
St. Lucia	62	71	—	—	—	—	—
St. Vincent and The Grenadines	63	72	—	20	—	—	—
Sudan	—	51	2,202	71	70	60	22
Suriname	64	71	2,548	26	—	—	—
Swaziland	46	58	2,706	72	—	—	—
Sweden	75	78	2,960	5	—	100	100
Switzerland	73	78	3,562	5	—	100	100
Syria	56	68	3,175	33	90	85	83
Taijikstan	—	67	—	56	—	—	—
Tanzania	45	51	2,021	80	42	38	86
Thailand	58	70	2,443	30	90	89	96
Togo	45	51	2,243	86	—	63	23
Tonga	—	68	—	21	—	—	—
Trinidad and Tobago	66	73	2,589	14	100	97	79
Tunisia	54	68	3,333	37	—	98	80
Turkey	57	68	3,429	44	—	80	—
Turkmenistan	—	65	—	57	—	—	—
Uganda	47	40	2,162	113	49	38	64
United Arab Emirates	61	74	—	15	99	95	77
United Kingdom	72	77	3,149	6	—	100	100
United States	71	76	3,671	7	100	100	—
Uruguay	—	73	2,750	17	82	75	61
Uzbekistan	—	68	—	43	—	—	—
Vanuatu	—	66	2,744	38	—	—	—
Venezuela	65	72	2,622	21	—	79	59
Vietnam	—	66	2,250	37	90	43	22
Yemen	42	56	2,203	80	38	61	24
Yugoslavia	68	72	3,634	19	—	83	63
Zaire	45	52	2,060	94	26	42	18
Zambia	47	43	1,931	103	—	27	64
Zimbabwe	51	49	1,989	68	85	77	66

Note: Not every nation reports in all categories, and some do not report any information at all. Nonreporting nations do not appear in the table. 1. Rate for children under 5 per 1,000 live births. 2. For all countries in Europe, columns Health Services is dated 1987-90, Safe Water is 1988-90, and Sanitation is 1988-90. **Sources:** United Nations Population Fund, *The State of World Population 1998* (1998); United Nations Department for Economic and Social Information and Policy Analysis, chart: *World Population 1996;* United Nations Development Programme, *Human Development Report 1997* (1997); World Health Organization, World Health Statistics Annual 1991 (1992).

Leading Worldwide Causes of Death, 1998

Cause	Estimated deaths (millions)	Percent of total
World total	**54.0**	**100.0%**
Communicable diseases, maternal and perinatal conditions, and nutritional deficiencies	16.5	30.5
Infectious and parasitic diseases	9.8	18.2
Respiratory infections	3.5	6.5
Noncommunicable conditions	31.7	58.8
Cardiovascular diseases	16.7	30.9
Cancers	7.2	13.4
Injuries	5.8	10.4
Respiratory diseases	3.0	5.6
Digestive diseases	2.0	3.3

Note: Total includes causes not shown here.
Source: World Health Organization, *The World Health Report, 1999: Making a Difference* (1999).

nations by 3.4 percent each year. About 48 percent of men (and 7 percent of women) in developing countries are smokers. From 1994 to 1997, there was a 26 percent increase in cigarette production worldwide.

Deaths and illnesses due to tobacco use vary from country to country. In developed nations, cardiovascular disease, mainly ischaemic heart disease, is the most common smoking-related cause of death. In China, which has the world's highest number of tobacco deaths, smoking causes far more deaths from chronic respiratory diseases than from chronic cardiovascular disease. Smoking also causes about 12 percent of all tuberculosis deaths. By 2020, smoking will cause about one of every three adult deaths. (See also "Health and Medicine" in Part II.)

▶ **CIRCULATORY DISEASES**
According to the World Health Organization, diseases of the heart and circulation—cardiovascular and cerebrovascular—such as heart attacks and stroke—kill over 13 million people worldwide and

Killer Diseases, 1998

Cause	Estimated deaths	Percent of total
Cardiovascular Disease	16,690,000	30.9%
Ischaemic heart disease	7,375,000	13.7
Cerebrovascular disease	5,106,000	9.5
Cancer	7,228,000	13.4
Trachea, bronchus, lung	1,244,000	2.3
Stomach	822,000	1.5
Liver	609,000	1.1
Colon and rectum	556,000	1.0
Esophagus	436,000	0.8
Breast	412,000	0.8
Mouth/oropharynx	352,000	0.7
Acute lower respiratory infection	3,452,000	6.4
Respiratory disease[1]	2,995,000	5.6
HIV/AIDS	2,285,000	4.2
Diarrhea (including dysentery)	2,219,000	4.1
Perinatal conditions	2,155,000	4.0
Childhood diseases	1,650,000	3.1
Tuberculosis	1,498,000	2.8
Malaria	1,110,000	2.1

1. Includes chronic obstructive pulmonary disease and asthma.
Source: World Health Organization, *The World Health Report, 1999: Making a Difference* (1998).

account for 23.2 percent of the total number of deaths each year. Additional millions are disabled, frequently in their prime years. Worldwide, heart disease accounts for 7.4 million deaths and strokes kill another 5.1 million, but in developing countries, strokes kill twice as many people as heart disease

Coronary heart disease became an epidemic in North America, Europe, and Australasia in the early 1900s, peaked in the 1960s and early 1970s, and has since declined dramatically—by over 50 percent in some countries. The world's highest rates are now in eastern and central Europe.

In developed countries, almost half of all deaths—5 out of 12 million each year—are due to circulatory diseases. As the developing nations adopt Western lifestyles, these diseases are increasing rapidly; they now account for about 25 percent of all deaths.

Decades of research show that lifestyle, beginning in childhood, is the main cause of coronary heart disease. The major risk factors are high blood pressure, cigarette-smoking, poor dietary habits, especially the intake of saturated fat, elevated blood cholesterol, lack of physical activity, obesity, and diabetes. Lack of physical activity is the most common risk factor in industrialized countries than can be changed.

▶CANCER

The World Health Organization estimates that in 1998 more than 10 million people developed cancer and another 7.2 million died from it. Eight types of cancer caused 60 percent of all cancer deaths: lung, stomach, breast, colon/rectum, mouth, liver, cervix and esophagus. Several risk factors are linked to cancer: diet, tobacco, infections, alcohol and hormones.

In 1996 there were an estimated 17.9 million people with cancer surviving up to five years after diagnosis. Of these, 10.5 million women, 5.3 million of whom had cancer of the breast, cervix or colon-rectum. Among men, prostate, colorectal and lung cancers were the most prevalent.

Lung cancer is the biggest cancer killer, causing almost one million deaths a year and over 1.3 million new cases. Globally, about 85 percent of lung cancers in men and 46 percent in women are tobacco-related. In developed countries, the ratios are 91 percent for men and 62 percent in women. While there is no effective treatment for lung cancer, most cases can be prevented through diet and exercise. Only 7-12 percent of patients survive five years after diagnosis. Rates of lung cancer are increasing in most countries; however, in countries where smoking is declining—Finland, United Kingdom and the United States—lung cancer is also now declining.

▶MATERNAL DEATHS WORLDWIDE

Approximately 585,000 women—one every minute—die around the world each year from pregnancy-related causes, according to the World Health Organization. In parts of some developing countries, the chance of a woman dying this way is 100 times greater than in the industrialized countries.

The five major causes of maternal death are: hemorrhage (25 percent), indirect causes (19 percent), sepsis or postpartum infection (15 percent), hypertensive disorders of pregnancy and eclampsia (13 percent), and unsafe abortion (13 percent). About 70,000 women die each year from unsafe abortion—600 in developed countries and 69,000 in less developed countries—and an unknown but much larger number suffer infection, injury and trauma. There are an estimated 20 million unsafe abortions each year, 90 percent of them in developing countries.

Women who do not have adequate family planning materials and services have unwanted pregnancies and bear too many children, or they have children when they are too young or too old, or have children too close together. Virtually all studies report that most women would prefer using contraceptives and resort to abortion as a last resort.

▶DEATHS OF CHILDREN

In 1991 UNICEF and the World Health Organization certified that 80 percent of all the world's one-year-olds were immunized against the six deadly childhood diseases: diphtheria, whooping cough, measles, tuberculosis, polio and tetanus, thereby effectively stopping the spread of these diseases. An estimated 3.2 million infants in the developing world are now saved from measles, neonatal tetanus and pertussis, and 445,000 infants will not be paralyzed by polio. WHO announced the eradication of smallpox from all peoples on Earth in 1980 and expect to have polio eradicated from all countries by the year 2000.

In recent years UNICEF and WHO have turned their attention to promoting 80 percent ORT (oral rehydration therapy) use, as part of controlling diarrheal disease, eliminating vitamin A deficiency, promoting universal iodization of salt in countries with iodine deficiency disorders, and eliminating guinea worm disease (also called river blindness).

Recent conflicts and wars have had tragic effects on children. It is estimated that in the past decade, wars have killed two million children, disabled 1-5 million, left 12 million homeless, and separated another million from their parents. That's not counting the thousands of children under the age of 16 who have fought in wars in more than 25 countries. UNICEF estimates that in 1988 alone, child soldiers numbered as many as 200,000.

▶ GLOBAL SEX FACTS

According to the World Health Organization, sexual intercourse occurs more than 100 million times a day around the world. As a result, approximately 910,000 conceptions take place, as well as 350,000 cases of sexually transmitted diseases.

WHO estimates that 1,440 women die each day (an average of one a minute) because of complications during pregnancy or childbirth. About 150,000 unwanted pregnancies end each day in abortion.

The number of people using contraception in Third World countries has increased sharply in recent years, rising from 31 million in the 1960–65 period to 381 million during 1985–90. Women in developing countries had, on average, 6.1 children in the years 1965–70, but the figure declined to 3.9 in 1985–90.

Source: World Health Organization, *The World Health Report* (1998).

▶ SEXUALLY TRANSMITTED DISEASES (STDS)

One million people die each year from reproductive tract infections, including sexually transmitted diseases other than HIV/AIDS. There are an estimated 333 million new cases of STDs each year. STDs are most frequent in young people aged 15 to 24. Women contract STDs five times more often than men. Almost two-thirds of all cases of infertility are due to STDs. WHO estimates that in 1995, there were 150 million cases of STDs in adults in southern/southeastern Asia, 65 million cases in sub-Saharan Africa, 36 million in Latin America and the Caribbean, and 14 million in North America.

▶ AIDS WORLDWIDE

The Joint United Nations Programme on HIV/AIDS and the World Health Organization reported that at the end of 1998, some 13.9 million people had died of AIDS since the beginning of the epidemic 20 years ago. Of this number, 4.7 million were women and 3.2 million were children. In 1998, 2.5 million people died of AIDS, the most ever in any single year; 900,000 were women and 590,000 were children.

According to UNAIDS, in 1998, 5.8 million people (2.1 million women, 590,000 children) were newly infected with HIV, the human immunodeficiency virus that causes AIDS. More than 33.4 million people are currently living with HIV/AIDS. Of this number 13.8 million are women and 1.2 million are children under 15.

Since the beginning of the epidemic about 20 years ago, 47 million people have been infected with HIV. More than 95 percent of all these infections are in developing nations with Africa being the hardest-hit region.

Since HIV began spreading, an estimated 34 million people living in sub-Saharan Africa have been infected with the virus. A total of 11.5 million people have died in the region, a quarter of them children. In 1998, 70 percent of the world's newly HIV-infected people were in sub-Saharan Africa, and four-fifths of the 1998 deaths occurred in this region. Some 21.5 million African adults and one million children are living with HIV.

Countries in eastern and southern Africa have suffered the most. Current estimates show that 20-26 percent of people aged 15 to 49 are living with HIV or AIDS in Botswana, Namibia, Swaziland, and Zimbabwe. At least one in 10 adults are HIV-infected in Central African Republic, Djibouti, Ivory Coast, and Kenya.

The HIV/AIDS epidemic is so severe across

AIDS Facts Worldwide, 1998

- 33.4 million people are living with HIV/AIDS (13.8 million are women, 1.2 million are children under 15)
- 95 percent of all HIV-infected people now live in the developing world.
- 5.8 million people acquired HIV in 1998 (2.1 million were women, 590,000 were children).
- 2.5 million people died of AIDS in 1998 (900,000 were women, 510,000 were children).
- Since the beginning of the epidemic about 20 years ago, 47 million people have been infected with HIV.
- 11.5 million AIDS deaths, a quarter of them children, occurred in sub-Saharan Africa.
- About 7,000 young people aged 10-24 contract HIV every day.
- Women represent 43 percent of all people over 15 living with HIV/AIDS
- In Botswana, Namibia, Swaziland, and Zimbabwe, 20-26 percent of people aged 15-49 are living with HIV or AIDS.
- 95 percent of the world's orphaned children are in sub-Saharan Africa.

Source: United Nations AIDS and World Health Organization, *AIDS Epidemic Update: December 1998* (1998).

HIV/AIDS Estimates By Region, 1998

Region	Epidemic started	Adults and children living with HIV/AIDS		Percent women	New infections
		Number	Percent		
Sub-Saharan Africa	late 1970s/ early 1980s	22,500,000	8.0%	50%	4,000,000
North Africa and Middle East	late 1980s	210,000	0.13	20	19,000
South and Southeast Asia	late 1980s	6,700,000	0.69	25	1,200,000
East Asia and the Pacific	late 1980s	560,000	0.68	15	200,000
Latin America	late 1970s/ early 1980s	1,400,000	0.57	20	160,000
Caribbean	late 1970s/ early 1980s	330,000	1.96	35	45,000
Eastern Europe and Central Asia	early 1990s	270,000	0.14	20	80,000
Western Europe	late 1970s	500,000	0.25	20	30,000
North America	late 1970s/ early 1980s	890,000	0.56	20	44,000
Australia/New Zealand	late 1970s/ early 1980s	12,000	0.1	5	600
WORLD TOTAL		33,400,000	1.1%	43%	5,800,000

Source: United Nations AIDS and World Health Organization, *AIDS Epidemic Update: December 1998* (1998).

**HIV/AIDS Worldwide:
1998 (numbers in millions)**

	Total	Adult males	Adult females	Children under 15
New infections in 1998	5.8	3.1	2.1	0.6
People living with HIV/AIDS	33.4	18.4	13.8	1.2
AIDS deaths in 1998	2.5	1.1	0.9	0.5
Cumulative AIDS deaths	13.9	6.2	4.7	3.2

Source: United Nations AIDS and World Health Organization, *AIDS Epidemic Update: December 1998* (1998).

Africa that it is now reducing life expectancy rates. In the nine countries with an adult HIV prevalence of 10 percent or more (Botswana, Kenya, Malawi, Mozambique, Namibia, Rwanda, South Africa, Zambia, and Zimbabwe) calculations show that AIDS will reduce life expectancy by an average of 17 years by 2010. In 1998, life expectancy in Malawi was 36.3 years, Zambia 37.1 years, Zimbabwe 39.2 years.

HIV is also spreading through the Asian continent, especially in South Asia and East Asia; seven million Asians are already infected. In Thailand and Myanmar, 2 percent of the population is now HIV positive. Nearly 5 percent of the population in Cambodia is HIV positive. More than one percent of pregnant women are infected in at least five states in India.

In Eastern Europe, HIV-infections are concentrated in homosexual and drug-injecting communities. Ukraine has the most cases; an estimated 270,000 people are infected with HIV. In North America and Western Europe, new combinations of anti-HIV drugs continue to reduce AIDS deaths, while monogamous behavior, abstinence, and condom use are holding the rate of new infections steady. During 1998, nearly 75,000 people became infected in this region to bring the total number of people living with HIV to almost 1.4 million in North America and Western Europe. *(For more detailed information on AIDS in the United States, see "Health and Medicine: in Part II.)*

World Religions

In 1996, 4.7 billion, or an estimated 80 percent of the world's population, identified themselves as adherents of one religion or another. Four religions—Christianity, Islam, Hinduism and Buddhism—claim 4.2 billion adherents, or 72 percent of the world's population, Approximately 19 percent of the world's people are atheist or nonreligious.

This section describes the major religions of the world, their basic tenets, scriptures, schools and sects, and their history. (Additional details may be found in the section "Religion in America.")

▶ **JUDAISM**

Origins Judaism is the oldest of the world's three major monotheistic religions and a forerunner of Christianity and Islam. The Hebrew Bible recounts the story of the world and mankind from the creation, through the flood, and the work of the patriarch Abraham who brought his people from Mesopotamia to Canaan—the Promised Land. His descendants were enslaved in Egypt until Moses led them out of captivity. During the exodus, Moses received from God the Ten Commandments that form the bedrock of Jewish law. Jewish custom and law further evolved from the 10th century B.C. and the conquest of Canaan to the destruction of Jerusalem by the Romans in 70 A.D.

Scripture The sacred scripture of the Hebrew Bible, or Masorah, consists of 24 books. (The Christian Old Testament divides the same text into 39 books.) The *Torah*, or Law, was composed between the 10th and 5th centuries B.C. These five books—Genesis, Exodus, Leviticus, Numbers, and Deuteronomy—are also known by their Greek name, *Pentateuch*. The later history of Israel and the divided kingdom is told in two separate but overlapping traditions known as the Prophets (13th-6th centuries B.C.) and the Writings (11th-2nd centuries B.C.). The Hebrew Bible is also known by the Greek name *Septuagint* ("seventy"), a reference to the number of authors engaged in its translation from Hebrew to Greek in the 3rd century B.C. In addition to scripture, there is a rich ancient tradition of rabbinical commentary called the *Talmud*, a huge compilation of the Oral Law and the accepted authority for Orthodox Jews. First codified around 200 A.D., the Talmudic tradition continued through the centuries and constitutes not only commentary on the law (*Halakah*), but also stories from the bible and parables, legends, etc. (*Haggadah*) illustrating religious principles.

Beliefs Central to Jewish belief is the idea of a single God—Yahweh—who made a covenant (i.e. an agreement or contract) with His chosen people that He would protect them and provide for them if they swore Him love and obedience. Yahweh shapes history (the end of which is the kingdom of God) and imposes His will upon mankind; He saves, and He judges. The people of *Israel* have a unique relationship with God affirmed on the one hand by His covenant, and on the other, by His law. While Yahweh the creator guides human destiny, the humanity of mankind is defined by the ability of individuals to make ethical choices in keeping with His law. The failure to act according to His law—that is, to know God—is sin, and a basic tenet of Jewish faith is that sin is a willful act; so, too, is turning, or returning, to God.

The book of Isaiah (8th century B.C.) brings to the fore a messianic tradition identifying a future Israel under a divine ruler descended from the house of David as a restoration of paradise and the attainment of salvation.

Practice Jews worship in synagogues in congregations led by a rabbi—a teacher or master. The Sabbath is observed from sunset Friday to sunset Saturday; worship consists of readings from scripture, prayer, and singing. The most important holidays in the Jewish calendar are Rosh Hashanah (New Year), Yom Kippur (Day of Atonement), Hanukah (Festival of Lights), and Pesach (Passover). (See Part I: " Holidays and Holy Days").

Schools and sects There are three main branches of modern Judaism. Orthodox Jews rigorously observe Jewish law, ritual and custom. Reform Judaism professes a more liberal interpretation of Jewish doctrine and ritual, and is especially prevalent in the United States. Conservative Judaism combines elements of doctrinal reform with more traditional observance. Hasidism is today a branch of Orthodox Judaism with origins in a mystical movement in 18th century Poland that stressed prayer over studying the Torah. Hasidim are very strict observers of the Jewish religious laws.

History The Bible recounts the history of the Jewish people from the creation, through the flood and the covenant of the rainbow, the patriarchs Abraham, Isaac and Jacob, and the story of the tribe of Israel in Egypt. The foundation of Jewish faith began with the exodus from Egypt, and the transmission of the Ten Commandments (the Decalogue) from God to his people through Moses, probably sometime between 1450 and 1290 B.C. The people of Israel conquered and settled in Canaan—the promised land—and were ruled by a succession of judges. The monarchical period under Samuel and David dates to the 11th and 10th centuries B.C. Israel and Judah continued under separate rulers until the fall of Israel in 722 B.C. Judah was conquered by Babylonians, and the Temple of David in Jerusalem was destroyed in 586 B.C. at the start of the Babylonian captivity, which also marks the start of the Jewish Diaspora, or dispersal. Exile lasted until 538 B.C., and the Second Temple was dedicated in 516 B.C. Under Seleucid rule the Maccabees successfully resisted efforts to suppress Judaism (168-142 B.C.). Under Roman rule (63 B.C.-135 A.D.), there were several revolts, the first of which resulted in the destruction of the Second Temple (70 A.D.). It was at around this time that Christianity began to diverge sharply from its Jewish sectarian origins.

The early Middle Ages saw the rise of the Talmudic tradition. Following the rise of Islam, Judaism evolved into two distinct strains, the Sephardim, centered in Spain, and the Ashkenazim, found mainly in France and Germany. Organized persecution of European Jewry began with their expulsion from France (1306) and Spain (1492), and culminated in the Nazi regime in Germany's attempt to eradicate all Jews during the Holocaust (1933-45). The Jewish enlightenment (*Haskala*) in 18th-century Germany gave rise to Reform Judaism and Conservative Judaism (1845). The nationalistic Zionist movement, a reaction to extreme anti-Semitism, led eventually to the birth of the State of Israel in 1948. Though Israel is a secular republic, religious parties play an active role in politics.

Geography and numbers There are an estimated 14 million Jews in 134 countries, the overwhelming majority of whom live in the United States (5.8 million) and Israel (4.3 million). There are an estimated 2.4 million Jews in Europe.

▶ **CHRISTIANITY**

Origins Christianity is based on the acts and sayings of Jesus of Nazareth as related by his followers and apostles. Jesus was born a Jew in Bethlehem in about 4 B.C., but details of his life before about 26-28 A.D. are obscure. In his early 30s, Jesus was baptized by John the Baptist, whose ministry prophesied the coming judgment of God, and who recognized Jesus as the Messiah (Greek for the Christ, or anointed one). Jesus' ministry, chiefly among the poor and dispossessed, lasted only a few years before he was crucified by Roman authorities. According to Christian belief, Jesus rose from the dead three days after his crucifixion, and 40 days later he ascended to heaven to sit at the right hand of God.

Scripture The Bible consists of the Old Testament (the Hebrew Bible), originally written in Hebrew and Aramaic, and the New Testament (first written in Greek in the first century), which relates the life and teachings of Jesus and his early followers. A 3rd-century translation of the Bible into Latin is called the Vulgate. The central portion of the New Testament consists of the Four Gospels (each attributed to one of Christ's earliest followers: Matthew, Mark, Luke, and John). While each tells the story of Jesus' life and death, they differ in details, with Luke and John providing more stories and greater emphasis on Christ's divinity. The story of the spread of Christianity in the first century is told in the Acts of the Apostles and the epistles (letters) of St. Paul. The Roman Catholic canon also includes 15 books found in the Greek Septuagint but not in the Hebrew Bible. The Orthodox Church accepts four of these Apocryphal books; Protestants accept none.

Beliefs Christian belief is rooted in three basic ideas: incarnation—Christ was the human embodiment of God; atonement—mankind was reconciled to God through the agency of Christ; and the Trinity—the belief that the one God has three natures, God the Father, God the Son (Jesus), and God the Holy Spirit.

Practice Central to the practice of most Christians are the seven sacraments: baptism, confirmation, holy matrimony, holy orders, sacrament of the sick, reconciliation (confession), and the Eucharist, (or communion), the sacramental offering and consumption of bread and wine representing the body and blood of Christ. Christians are organized into congregations and worship in churches led by priests or ministers who administer the sacraments. Most denominations designate Sunday as the sabbath and the day for special observance and worship.

Schools and sects Christianity has three major branches: Eastern Orthodoxy, Roman Catholicism, and Protestantism. The division between Eastern Orthodoxy and Roman Catholicism came in 1054. In the sixteenth century, reform-minded priests broke with Rome and there emerged a number of distinct denominations known collectively as Protestantism.

The hierarchical authority of the Catholic Church starts with the Pope, and includes cardinals, bishops, and priests, all celibate men. In addition there are a number of Catholic lay and priestly orders for men and/or women.

The Eastern Orthodox Church embraces a number of national or regional churches. The laity are invested with more authority than are Catholics, and the bishop of Constantinople, titular head of the eastern church, is regarded as "first among equals."

Protestant denominations number in the hundreds. There is no single governing authority for all of them. (See Part II: "Religion in America" for a summary of the major sects.)

History At the time of his death, Jesus had a small handful of followers among Jews. His teachings were not widely accepted among the larger Jewish community, however, and his disciples preached to non-Jewish gentiles throughout the Roman Empire. Jesus' teachings were gathered in a collection of books known as the Gospel, or New Testament. Christians were widely persecuted until the Emperor Constantine legalized the religion in 313; in 380 Christianity became the official religion of the Roman Empire. Christianity also reached northern Ethiopia.

Disputes over theological issues such as the nature of the Trinity and the person of Christ were resolved at a series of ecumenical councils. In 1054 the eastern and western churches split over differences of theology, politics, geography and language. The papacy in Rome acquired the nature of a civil authority and within the Western church ascetic, spiritual traditions competed with secular ones. In the sixteenth century, papal authority was challenged by such reform-minded priests as Martin Luther and John Calvin, abetted by England's King Henry VIII, who transferred authority over the church in England from the Pope to himself. Sectarian wars engulfed Europe for more than a century as Catholics and Protestants vied for temporal and spiritual power.

European explorers and colonists spread Christianity to the Americas, Asia and Africa. The Spanish and Portuguese brought Catholicism to Latin America, while North America became a haven for Protestant denominations from northern Europe. Since the mid-1800s, Protestant and Catholic evangelists have carried out energetic missionary programs to Africa and East Asia.

Geography and numbers Christianity is the most populous and most widespread religion in the world, with almost 2 billion adherents in 260 countries. Europe is home to more than 555 million Christians (76 percent of the region's population), but Latin America has proportionally the highest number of Christian adherents—93 percent of the population. There are more Christians in Africa (360 million, or 48 percent of the population) and Asia (303 million) than in North America (255 million).

▶ **ISLAM**

Origins The precepts of Islam were revealed through Mohammed, the last of a line of prophets including Abraham, Moses and Jesus. Mohammed was born about 570 at Mecca (in western Saudi Arabia) and died in 632 in the nearby city of Medina.

Scripture The Koran ("recitation") consists of 114 chapters. The text is the infallible word of God as revealed to Mohammed and transcribed by his followers over the course of 23 years.

Beliefs Islam is a monotheistic religion with explicit links to Judaism and Christianity. The Koran's narrative includes stories of Abraham and Isaac, and Moses and the Ten Commandments. Unlike Jews, who trace their descent from Abraham through Isaac, the son of Sarah, Muslims trace their decent through Ishmael, Abraham's son by Hagar. The Koran recounts the virgin birth of Jesus, but does not accept his divinity.

The word Islam comes from the Arabic root "s-l-m," meaning "peace" and "submission," and a hallmark of Islam is obedience to God.

Practice A Muslim's relations with God are regulated by the Five Pillars of Islam: the Shahadah, or profession of faith—"There is no God but God, and Mohammed is his prophet;" public and collective prayer five times daily; charity to the poor; fasting during the holy month of Ramadan; and pilgrimage to Mecca, the most holy place in the Muslim world, at least once in one's lifetime.

Islam has strict dietary laws and prohibitions against promiscuity, theft, gambling and lying. Muslims worship in mosques led by imams. The principal weekly worship is on Friday at midday.

Schools and sects The overwhelming majority of Muslims are Sunnites, or "traditionalists" (83 percent, or 934 million people). Shi'ites, or "partisans," represent another 16 percent (180 million) and smaller sects make up the rest. The Shi'ite/Sunnite schism reflects differences about who should have succeeded Mohammed. Shi'ites follow somewhat different rites than Sunnites, and recognize additional holy days and places.

History Mohammed was born in Arabia in about 570 A.D. Raised by his uncle, at the age of 25 he became a trader, and later married his employer, the widow Khadija. In 610, an angel descended on Mohammed and ordered him to proclaim the word of God. Rebuked in Mecca, in 622 he was invited to Medina to help bring order to the city. He accepted on the condition that the citizens worship Allah—the one God—and accept the precepts of Islam. This move—the *hegira*—is the year from which the Muslim calendar dates. Eight years later Mohammed returned to Mecca, and by the time of his death in 632, most Arabs were Muslims.

Under a succession of secular and theocratic caliphates, Islam swept east and west from Arabia. Muslims reached the Indus River in 713, and their advance in France was only stopped in 733 at the Battle of Tours; Muslims remained in Spain until 1492. Islamic armies captured the Byzantine capital of Constantinople in 1453, and controlled much of southeastern Europe until the 19th century. In the east, Muslims swept through India at the end of the 10th century and reached the East Indies in the 15th century.

The arts, architecture and technology flourished in the golden age of Islam and Islamic learning and culture was responsible for the transmission of much of classical philosophy and science to the West.

From the 18th to 20th centuries, traditionally Islamic countries came under Western cultural and political influence. In the 20th century, some traditionally Islamic countries such as Turkey opted for a secular state; others such as Saudi Arabia and Iran came under strict fundamentalist rule.

Geography and numbers With 1.1 billion adherents in 184 countries, Islam is the second largest religion in the world. It is the dominant religion throughout the Middle East, North Africa, Central Asia, Afghanistan, Pakistan, and Indonesia, the country with the largest number of adherents (172 million people). There are 104 million Muslims in India—11 percent of that country's population.

▶ **HINDUISM**

Origins Hinduism is a complex of polytheistic religion and philosophy that evolved from Vedism, an ancient Indian religion of Indo-European origin dating from the 2nd millennium B.C.

Scripture Different Hindu sects rely on different holy texts, but common to the majority are the Vedic texts called the *Upanishads*. The *Svetasvatara Upanishad* describes Siva, the creator, preserver and destroyer of the universe. Sources for Hindu mythology include the *Mahabharata*, *Ramayana* (concerning Rama, the incarnation of the great god Vishnu), and the *Puaranas*. The *Bhagavad Gita* ("Lord's song," a part of the *Ramayana*), is a dialogue between Krishna (another incarnation of the god Vishnu) and Prince Arjuna in which are described the three paths to union with God.

Beliefs Hinduism is rooted in the belief that individuals should connect their selves (Atman) with Brahman, or Godhead, the spiritual source of the tangible universe. Hindus also believe in reincarnation—*samsara*—one's subsequent status being dependent on one's actions (*karma*) and duties (*dharma*) in this life. The cycle of reincarnation is broken when one attains liberation (moksha) from the finite world through self-discovery—the union of self with the Godhead, or *Atman-Brahman*. There are four paths to union with Brahman: *jnana yoga*, based on knowledge; *bhakti yoga*, based on service to God; *karma yoga*, based on work for God (as opposed to oneself); and *raja yoga*, based on psychophysical exercise.

Hinduism has three primary theistic traditions revolving around the cults of anthropomorphic gods. Vishnu is a loving god incarnated as Krishna; Siva is a god at once protective and destructive; and Brahma is creator. Saktism is a form of worship dedicated to the female consorts of Vishnu and Siva.

Hindus have a deep respect for all living things; the most revered animal is the cow.

Practice Hindu worship is largely an individual and family matter. Hindu temples are devoted to a particular god or group of gods. Worship in temples or before domestic shrines includes prayers and offerings to an image of the god. Such rituals are intended to bring the worshipper and the god closer together.

Hindu pilgrimage sites include seven sacred cities, among others, where thousands or even millions of Hindus worship at annual festivals. Some of the most famous temples are on the banks of the Ganges River, which is sacred to Hindus, in northern India. Important festival days include Dipavali, "festival of lights," sacred to Lakshmi, goddess of prosperity; holi, a spring festival; and Dashara, a harvest festival.

Individuals follow a code of moral and religious conduct called *dharma*. Traditional Hinduism observes complex societal divisions into four primary (and thousands of subsidiary) castes defined by occupation and social standing: *brahmins:* leaders, philosophers, artists and their families; *kshatriyas:* princes, soldiers and administrators; *vaishyas:* merchants and landowners; and *shudras*, or laborers. Beyond the caste system are untouchables, or outcasts. India's modern constitution outlawed the caste system.

Schools and sects Hinduism is comprised of myriad religious cults and various schools of philosophy. The principle of religious toleration is reflected in the Hindu belief that Christianity, Islam and other religions offer alternate paths to the same goal. Among the more prominent modes of belief are *yoga* and *tantrism*, both of which evolved in both Hinduism and Buddhism, and *bhakti*. Tantrism emphasizes meditation and ritual involving mystical diagrams (mandalas) and chants (mantras) as a means to enlightenment. *Yoga* emphasizes an eightfold path to enlightenment through physical and mental training. *Bhakti* focuses on the primacy of love for a deity.

History Hinduism is the oldest of the world's great religions. Originating in India, it spread to Nepal and southeast Asia. The oldest Hindu writings are actually Vedic texts brought by Aryan invaders in the second millennium B.C. To the Vedic concept of future life, Hinduism attached the ideas of karma, reincarnation and ultimately release from the cycle of life, death and rebirth. Following the rise of rival religions such as Buddhism and Jainism in the 6th century B.C., ritual sacrifice to Vedic deities overseen by priests gave way to polytheistic worship intended to unite the worshipper with the god worshipped.

The classical period of Hinduism dates from the 6th century B.C. to the 10th century A.D., when the major theistic sects emerged and many of the classic works of Hinduism were composed, including the epic *Mahabharata* and *Ramayana* and a variety of works that discuss the duties of caste, advice to rulers, the attainment of pleasure and the attainment of liberation, or moksha. Hindu princes successfully resisted Muslim encroachment from the West until the 10th century. The Muslim ascendancy was coupled with the rise of *bhakti*, a devotional Hinduism that stresses love for the deity, and the adoption of vernacular languages for worship rather than Sanskrit.

Since the 18th century there have been several movements to strip Hinduism of its polytheistic practices, and in this century, great emphasis has been laid on Hindu prescriptions for non-violence and social equality, especially as practiced by the founder of modern India, Mahatma Gandhi.

Geography and numbers Hinduism has an estimated 793 million adherents worldwide. With deep roots in India, and lacking a missionary tradition, it is found almost nowhere outside of India and neighboring countries except in expatriate Indian communities.

▶ BUDDHISM

Origins Buddhism was established by the followers of Siddhartha Gautama (ca. 563-483 B.C.), who was born into a kshatriya caste Hindu family in present-day Nepal. At the age of 29, he left his wife and young son in search of enlightenment. This he attained, according to tradition, while sitting under a bodhi tree near Patna. After 49 days of rapture, and withstanding the temptations of the devil Mara, Buddha—the enlightened one—inspired an order of monks and went forth to preach his philosophy of enlightenment for 45 years before passing into nirvana, in which "ideas and consciousness cease to be."

Scripture Of primary importance to all Buddhists is the *Tipitaka* ("Three baskets"), a record of the Buddha's teachings set down set down by Buddha's early followers after his death. These tell the story of his life (Buddha), his laws (Dharma) for personal conduct, and the guidelines for the monastic order (Sangha). There is a large body of other writings peculiar to individual sects and schools. The Buddhist canon continued to evolve over many centuries.

Beliefs Buddhists share with Hinduism a belief in the cycle of reincarnation and that this cycle could be broken. Buddha's teachings are predicated on the Four Noble Truths. Life is impermanent and fundamentally produces suffering, or *dukkha*, perpetuated due to the endless cycle of life, death, and rebirth. This suffering results from the pursuit of mortal desires. Desire can be overcome by attaining *nirvana*. Nirvana can be reached by adhering to the Eightfold Path. This path, or Middle Way, consists of right belief, thought, speech, action, livelihood, effort, mindfulness and concentration. These are the backbone of Buddhist ethics.

Practice A hallmark of Buddhist practice is the monastic order, to which monks withdraw from the everyday world and live austere lives of meditation either for a few years or for a lifetime. Mendicants also live on alms contributed by lay Buddhists. In certain sects, adolescents spend time in a monastery as part of a rite of passage into adulthood.

Buddhist temples are primarily for individual meditation, and collective rituals play a smaller part in the life of a Buddhist than in the lives of Jews, Christians and Muslims, or even of Hindus.

Schools and sects   There are three main sects in Buddhism. Theravada (or Hinayana) Buddhism, which predominates today in Sri Lanka, Myanmar and Thailand, adheres most closely to the tenets of the early Buddhist sects. In this tradition, attainment of nirvana for oneself is the goal. Mahayana Buddhism, which became the larger sect, spread along the Silk Road from India to China and East Asia. This includes the worship of Buddha and Buddhist saints (*bodhisattvas*). Stressing compassion for others, *boddhisatvas*—literally "wisdom beings"—withhold themselves from attaining nirvana in order to help others attain enlightenment. In Zen Buddhism, a sect of Mahayana, adherents strive for enlightenment through mental conditioning and meditation. The third sect of Tantric Buddhism (Vajrayana), most common in Tibet and Mongolia, attempts to identify the initiate with a visualized deity. The Tantric canon includes esoteric texts, and meditation engages both the mind and the senses with the use of *mantras* (chants), *mudras* (hand gestures) and *mandalas* (visible icons of the universe). The spiritual and temporal leader of Tibetan Buddhists is the Dalai Lama.

History   Following Buddha's death, his *sutras* (sermons) and *vinaya* (regulations) were written down by his disciples. Originally, Buddhist mendicants taught for nine months and held retreats during the monsoon. These retreats led to the establishment of monasteries and the rise of differing interpretations of Buddha's teaching. The Mahayana school more easily absorbs (and is absorbed by) different cultures. It received its greatest impetus in India from the Buddhist emperor Ashoka (272-232 B.C.), who sent missionaries to Ceylon, Southeast Asia and China, from where it was carried to Korea and Japan in the 6th century A.D.

The 7th century saw the rise of Zen Buddhism in China and Japan, and of Tantric Buddhism in Tibet. Chinese Buddhism reached its height in the 9th century during the T'ang Dynasty, when it was partially suppressed. Buddhism flourished in Japan until the 19th century, when Shintoism gained imperial favor.

Buddhism lost its influence in India beginning in the 8th century, partly through absorption of its ideas into Hinduism, and partly because of the rise of Islam. By the 13th century, Buddhism was all but extinct there.

Geography and numbers   There are an estimated 300 million people in 92 countries who adhere to Buddhist beliefs and practices. Mahayana Buddhists account for about 56 percent (168 million) of all Buddhists, mostly in Japan, Korea and China; Theravada Buddhists account for 38 percent (114 million), in Southeast Asia and Sri Lanka. Lamaist Buddhists account for the remaining 6 percent (18 million) in Tibet and Mongolia. Buddhist practice in Tibet is under threat from the Chinese government.

▶**OTHER ORGANIZED RELIGIONS**

Baha'i   Founded by Baha'Ullah ("glory of God") in Iran in 1844, Baha'i teaches that the revealed religions of the world are in agreement and that the respective prophet-founders of each revealed the will of God for a particular time and place in history. There are approximately 6 million members of the Baha'i faith; the center of the Baha'i faith is

in Haifa, Israel. A major temple in Wilmette, Illinois, attracts many visitors.

Chinese folk religions   Chinese folk religions consist of a blend of ancient ancestor worship with elements of Buddhism, Confucianism, and Taoism. Taoism is a philosophy or religion based on the teachings of Lao-tzu, another great teacher of Confucian times. The vast majority of the world's 215 to 220 million adherents of Chinese folk religions live in China; the remainder live in scattered Chinese settlements around the world.

Confucianism   As much a code of ethical conduct as a religion, Confucianism takes its name from the 6th-century B.C. scholar and civil servant Kung Fu-Tzu (Confucius), whose *Analects* prescribe the proper conduct for life. His impact on China has been enormous, and at times his cult has attained the status of a quasi-official religion. There are about 5 million Confucianists in the world; most of them live in South Korea.

Jainism   Jainism is a polytheistic religion established in India by Vardhamana in the 6th century B.C. Its primary features are a belief in the perfection of the soul and in non-injury to living creatures. Almost all of the world's 5 million Jainists live in India.

New Religion   This term applies to a variety of more or less organized religious systems that have grown up, primarily in East Asia, since the turn of the century. These religions are characterized by a synthesis of indigenous folk religion with various major Asian traditions (Hinduism, Buddhism, Confucianism and/or Taoism) overlaid with modern Western philosophy. There are more than 100 million people professing adherence to these religions, the majority of them in the Philippines, Indonesia, and Japan.

Parsiism   This religion has its roots in Zoroastrianism, an ancient Iranian religion whose central focus is the struggle between good and evil. Its monotheistic tendencies are thought to have influenced the development of Judaism and Christianity. Parsis emigrated to India between the 10th and 15th centuries, and prospered as merchants, especially in Bombay.

Shintoism   Evolved from ancient Japanese religious traditions, Shintoism became a state religion under the Meijis in the 19th century. Although some sacred Shinto (literally "way of the gods") texts date from the 8th century, none is considered authoritative. There are three strains of Shinto practice: State Shinto, Shrine Shinto, and Folk Shinto.

Sikhism   The Sikh religion was founded by Guru Nanak in the early 16th century. A hybrid of Hindu and Islamic beliefs, it advocates a search for eternal truth and, while believing in reincarnation, rejects the notion of divine incarnation. It was led by a succession of ten gurus, the last of whom declared himself the last human guru. Sikhs now follow the sacred text known as Guru Granth Singh, or Collection of Sacred Wisdom. There are more than 19 million Sikhs in the world; almost all of them live in the Punjab region of India.

▶**NONRELIGIOUS AND ATHEISTS**

An estimated 887 million people (15 percent of the world's population) profess no religion, are agnostic or are indifferent to religion. Another 222 million people (4 percent) are declared atheists who do not believe in God. More than three-quarters (852 million) of these nonreligious and atheists live in China, where religious observance is sharply curtailed by the government. An estimated 12 percent of people in Europe are nonreligious, compared with 9.8 percent in Oceania, 7.2 percent in North America, and 3.3 percent in Latin America.

►CHRONOLOGY OF WORLD RELIGION

B.C.

3000 Earliest elements of Hinduism develop in India.

c. 2500 Egyptian pyramids at Giza completed.

c. 1500 Aryan peoples invade India; bring additional elements of Hinduism.

c. 1290 Moses leads Israelites out of Egypt.

1010-922 Reigns of Hebrew kings David and Solomon. A great temple built at Jerusalem.

740 Hebrew prophet Isaiah flourishes.

628 Traditional birth date of Zoroaster, religious teacher in Persia. Followers today are Parsees in India.

587 Babylonians destroy Hebrew temple at Jerusalem and take many Hebrews as slaves. Fifty years later, Hebrews are freed and begin to rebuild temple.

560 Birth of Siddartha Gautama in northern India; later known as Buddha. Dies c. 480. His teachings, on which Buddhism is based, gain many followers in India, later spread to Southeast Asia.

551 Birth of Chinese teacher Confucius. Dies c. 479.

200 Mahayana Buddhism begins to spread in China and Japan.

4 Birth of Jesus Christ. The Western calendar dates from the supposed year of his birth.

A.D. 30 Death and resurrection of Jesus Christ.

66-70 Jewish revolt against Romans ends in destruction of second temple and scattering of Jews (a.k.a. The First Diaspora).

175 Apostles' Creed, a brief statement of Christian beliefs, formulated.

303-12 In final organized program of persecution, Romans kill estimated 500,000 Christians.

313 The emperor Constantine decrees toleration for Christianity in Roman Empire. In 325, he calls synod of Nicaea, which formulates Nicene

Adherents Of World Religions, 1996

Group	Adherents ('000s)	Percentage of world population
Atheism	222,195,000	3.8%
Baha'i	6,404,000	0.1
Buddhism	325,275,000	5.6
Chinese folk religions	220,971,000	3.8
Christianity	1,955,229,000	33.7
Confucianism	5,086,000	0.1
Ethnic religions	102,945,000	1.8
Hinduism	793,075,000	13.7
Jainism	4,920,000	0.1
Judaism	13,866,000	0.2
Mandeanism	45,000	z
Moslem	1,126,325,000	19.4
New-Religions	106,015,000	1.8
Nonreligious	886,928,000	15.3
Parseeism	190,000	z
Sikhism	19,508,000	0.3
Shintoism	2,897,000	z
Spiritism	10,292,000	0.2
Other religions	1,952,000	z
World population	**5,804,120,000**	**100.0%**

Note: z = less than 0.1 percent. **Source:** *1997 Britannica Book of the Year.*

Creed. By end of 300s, Christianity is official religion of empire.

354 Birth of St. Augustine, influential Christian teacher, in North Africa. Dies 430.

451 Council of Chalcedon (fourth ecumenical council) formulates long-held Christian understanding of Christ, the union in one person of two distinct natures, human and divine.

570 Muhammad, founder of Islam, born in Mecca (now in Saudi Arabia). Dies in 632 in nearby city of Medina.

600+ Tantrism, a Hindu school, grows up, emphasizing special rituals as means of enlightenment; uses mystical diagrams (mandalas) and chants (mantras).

650+ Islam sweeps into India and gains many converts.

700+ Development in China of Zen, a school of Buddhism, which later attracted particular attention in the modern Western world.

711-715 Muslim Arabs settle in Spain.

800 Roman Empire revived in the West with the coronation of Charlemagne as emperor on Christmas Day, in St. Peter's in Rome.

988 Christianity reaches Russia through missionaries from eastern churches.

1054 Eastern (or Orthodox) and Western (or Roman) churches go separate ways after disputes about doctrine and authority.

1096 Christians in Europe go on first Crusade to take Holy Land from Muslims. Seven other major Crusades pursued between 1100 and 1300. Christian warriors temporarily occupy Jerusalem and other cities, but soon lose them again to Muslims.

1216 Pope Innocent III approves formation of Franciscans and Dominicans.

1227 Thomas Aquinas, great Christian theologian, born in Italy.

1300+ Bhakti, a Hindu sect, develops emphasizing primacy of love for a deity and using love between humans as illustration; rejects caste, ritual, and creeds, and emphasizes need for sincerity.

1309 The papacy moves from Rome to Avignon, France, where it remains until 1377 ("The Babylonian Captivity of the Church").

1377 English theologian and religious reformer John Wycliffe accused of heresy by Pope Gregory XI for attacks on worldliness of the church.

1378-1417 The Great Western Schism, during which first two, then three, claimants sought recognition as pope.

1415 Excommunication and execution of Czech religious leader Jan Hus, who protested sale of indulgences and other papal excesses, sets off Hussite Wars, which end with Compactata of Prague.

1453 Ottoman Turks (Muslims) conquer capital of Eastern Roman Empire, Constantinople. Turks push westward into Europe.

1454 Johannes Gutenberg prints first Bible with moveable type.

1469 Birth of Nanak, founder of Sikhism, in Punjab region of India.

1492 Muslims overthrown in Spain; Spanish Inquisition begins.

1517 Martin Luther, a German priest, posts 95 theses on cathedral door, questioning church teachings. Luther refuses to recant; is excommunicated from Catholic church. With cooperation of north German princes, he forms new Protestant churches. This begins Reformation, which ultimately divides European Christianity into two warring camps.

1534 King Henry VIII of England denies power of pope over church in England and establishes

Church of England responsible to monarch. New church gradually adopts Protestant beliefs but maintains many practices of earlier Catholic era.

1536 John Calvin, a young French scholar, publishes *Institutes of the Christian Religion*, and becomes second major leader of Protestant Christianity; helping to create Presbyterian and other Reformed churches.

1540 Ignatius Loyola, a Spaniard, establishes the Jesuits (Society of Jesus) with papal approval. This order becomes powerful instrument of Catholic church in disputes with Protestants, in missionary efforts around world, and in education.

1545-63 Council of Trent makes major reforms in Catholic church and defines disagreements with Protestants. Its work begins Catholic Reformation, or Counter-Reformation.

1598 In the Edict of Nantes, Henry IV proclaims "peaceful coexistence" of Catholics and Calvinists in France. Revoked in 1685 by Louis XIV.

1618-48 Thirty Years War, caused in part by Protestant-Catholic hatreds, decimates central Europe. Calvinist leaders in England overthrow monarchy and execute king in civil war (1642-49). Monarchy is restored in 1660.

1620 Pilgrims, a small group of English Calvinists, establish colony at Plymouth in North America to escape persecution in England.

1683 Muslim Turks defeated near Vienna, Austria, in their last attempt to establish foothold in western Europe.

1734 The Great Awakening, a religious revival, sweeps New England, begun by prominent Massachusetts preacher Jonathan Edwards. English evangelist George Whitefield tours American colonies beginning in 1738, preaching to outdoor gatherings.

1738 Christian conversion experienced by brothers John and Charles Wesley in England. They begin evangelical activities, leading to development of independent Methodist church.

1789 U.S. Constitution guarantees separation of church and state.

1792 Second Awakening sweeps new United States, lasting more than 20 years. Revivals in Kentucky in 1800 result in formation of new denominations, ancestors of Disciples of Christ, Churches of Christ, and Christian churches.

1830 American Joseph Smith has religious visions that lead him to organize the Church of Jesus Christ of the Latter-Day Saints (Mormons).

1844 Baha'i established in Iran.

1869-79 Vatican Council I, convened by Pope Pius IX, declares that teachings of pope in matters of faith and morals are infallible.

1875 Mary Baker Eddy publishes *Science and Health with Key to the Scriptures* in Boston; it becomes basis of Church of Christ, Scientist.

1900 First documented modern Pentecostal experience—worshipers speak in unknown tongues during prayer meeting in Kansas. Within 20 years, Pentecostal churches form major new Christian denomination.

1935-45 Nazi government in Germany carries out destruction of estimated six million European Jews. This event known as the Holocaust.

1945-46 Compulsory adherence to Shintoism ended in Japan; Emperor Hirohito disavows his divinity to Japanese people.

1947 UN approves creation of the new state of Israel in Middle East for settlement by Jews.

1948 World Council of Churches established at huge assembly in Amsterdam. This ecumenical organization supported by many Protestant, Anglican, and Orthodox denominations. Headquarters are in Geneva, Switzerland.

1962-65 Vatican Council II, convened by Pope John XXIII, announces many liberalizing changes in Roman Catholic liturgy and practice; supports cautious involvement in ecumenical discussions with other Christians.

1978 Karol Josef Wojtyla, archbishop of Krakow, Poland, elected to papacy as John Paul II, the first non-Italian pope since Hadrian VI in 1523.

1988 For the first time, a woman is elected to a bishopric in U.S. Episcopal church

1991 Religious freedom granted in USSR.

The Ten Commandments

Significant differences exist among the Protestant, Catholic, and Jewish versions of the Ten Commandments, both in wording and in numbering. Even within the King James Bible, the Commandments are presented twice, first in Exodus and later in Deuteronomy. The Exodus version (Exodus 20: 2-17) is the most familiar, and is reprinted here. Numbers refer to commandment numbers, not Biblical verses.

1 I am the Lord thy God, which have brought thee out of the land of Egypt, out of the house of bondage.

2 Thou shalt have no other gods before me.

Thou shalt not make unto thee any graven image, or any likeness of any thing that is in heaven above, or that is in the earth beneath, or that is in the water under the earth:

Thou shalt not bow down thyself to them, nor serve them: for I the Lord thy God am a jealous God, visiting the iniquity of the fathers upon the children unto the third and fourth generation of them that hate me;

And showing mercy unto thousands of them that love me and keep my commandments.

3 Thou shalt not take the name of the Lord thy God in vain; for the Lord will not hold him guiltless that taketh his name in vain.

4 Remember the sabbath day, to keep it holy.

Six days shalt thou labor, and do all thy work:

But the seventh day is the sabbath of the Lord thy God: in it thou shalt not do any work, thou, nor thy son, nor thy daughter, thy manservant, nor thy maidservant, nor thy cattle, nor thy stranger that is within thy gates:

For in six days the Lord made heaven and earth, the sea, and all that in them is, and rested the seventh day: wherefore the Lord blessed the sabbath day, and hallowed it.

5 Honor thy father and thy mother: that thy days may be long upon the land which the Lord thy God giveth thee.

6 Thou shalt not kill.

7 Thou shalt not commit adultery.

8 Thou shalt not steal.

9 Thou shalt not bear false witness against thy neighbor.

10 Thou shalt not covet thy neighbor's house, thou shalt not covet thy neighbor's wife, nor his manservant, nor his maidservant, nor his ox, nor his ass, nor any thing that is thy neighbor's.

The Books of the Bible

The first five books of the Bible are known as the Torah ("to teach" in Hebrew) in the Jewish faith. Roman Catholic canon recognizes additional "deuterocanonical" books, as well as additional parts of other books. Together, they are known as the Apocrypha. They are listed in *italics* following the Old Testament.

Old Testament		**New Testament**
Genesis	Amos	Matthew
Exodus	Obadiah	Mark
Leviticus	Jonah	Luke
Numbers	Micah	John
Deuteronomy	Nahum	Acts
Joshua	Habakuk	Romans
Judges	Zephaniah	First Corinthians
Ruth	Haggai	Second Corinthians
First Samuel	Zechariah	Galatians
Second Samuel	Malachi	Ephesians
First Kings	*The Apocrypha*	Philippians
Second Kings	*Tobit*	Colossians
First Chronicles	*Judith*	First Thessalonians
Second Chronicles	*Additions to Esther*	Second Thessalonians
Ezra	*Wisdom of Solomon*	First Timothy
Nehemiah	*Ecclesisasticus (Sirach)*	Second Timothy
Esther	*Baruch*	Titus
Job	*The Letter of Jeremiah*	Philemon
Psalms	*The Prayer of Azariah and the*	Hebrews
Proverbs	*Song of the Three Young Men*	James
Ecclesiastes	*Susanna*	First Peter
Song of Solomon	*Bel and the Dragon*	Second Peter
Isaiah	*First Maccabees*	First John
Jeremiah	*Second Maccabees*	Second John
Lamentations	*First Esdras*	Third John
Ezekiel	*The Prayer of Manasseh*	Jude
Daniel	*Psalm 151*	Revelation
Hosea	*Third Maccabees*	
Joel	*Second Esdras*	
	Fourth Maccabees	

The Seven Deadly Sins

1 Pride
2 Envy
3 Anger
4 Sloth
5 Greed
6 Gluttony
7 Lust

The Koran

The sacred book of Islam was revealed by God to the prophet Mohammed over his life at Mecca and Medina. Its various versions were reconciled in the seventh century by Uthman, the third Caliph. It is divided into 114 chapters of verses, with chapters appearing in size order from longest to shortest, rather than in chronological order.

Major Languages of the World

There are approximately 100 languages designated as "official" by national governments around the world. These run the gamut from Chinese and English—with hundreds of millions of speakers worldwide—to local languages whose speakers may number only in the tens of thousands.

Chinese This is the mother tongue of more than one billion people. Although spoken dialects of Chinese are not mutually intelligible, they share the same writing system—Chinese characters, or *hanzi*—and two people can speak different dialects and still be able to read each other's writing. This is possible because *hanzi* characters represent words independently of their pronunciation (just as Arabic numerals can represent the words for numbers in any language), and also because written Chinese has diverged less from a common standard than have the various spoken dialects.

Based on the dialect spoken in northern China around Beijing, Mandarin is an official language in China, Taiwan, and Singapore, where it is the primary language of more than 800 million people. The other principal dialects are Cantonese (or *Yue*), spoken in southern China and Hong Kong; *Wu*, spoken in Shanghai and nearby provinces in eastern China; *Min*, found in southeastern China, Taiwan and Malaysia; and *Xiang, Kan*, and *Hakka*, all spoken in southeastern China and Taiwan. Chinese is also an official language of the UN.

English Although there are fewer native speakers of English than of Chinese, English is by far the most commonly found language outside of China. Some estimates suggest that as many as one-third of the world's people can speak English—which means four billion people can't. From the island kingdom in northwest Europe, the language spread throughout the British Empire to the Americas, Africa, India and Oceania. Today, 58 countries and the UN designate English as an official language, and these countries account for more than 460 million speakers. The main concentrations of English speakers are the United States (258 million), United Kingdom (57 million), Philippines (37 million), India (31 million), Canada (18 million), Australia (17 million) and Nigeria (16 million).

Hindi Spoken by an estimated 430 million people in India alone, Hindi is one of that country's two official languages, the other being English. There are significant numbers (relative to the local population) of Hindi speakers in Trinidad, Guyana, South Africa, Mauritius and other countries with large Indian expatriate communities.

Spanish Carried by Spanish conquistadors from Europe to the Americas and Asia, Spanish is now an official language of 21 nations, territories and colonies in which it is the mother tongue of more than 300 million people. By far the greatest number of Spanish speakers live in Mexico (85 million), followed by Colombia (35 million), Argentina (34 million), Spain (29 million) and Venezuela (21 million). Although the United States does not recognize an official language per se, the U.S. ranks sixth in the number of people who consider Spanish a first language with 20 million. Spanish is also an official language of the UN.

Arabic Twenty-five countries around the world have adopted Arabic as an official language, more than any other language but English and French. These 25 countries alone represent nearly 200 million Arabic speakers. Arabic is also the language of the Koran—and thus, for many Muslims, of God. For this reason, it is the second language of many Indians, Indonesians, Iranians and other inhabitants of largely Muslim countries. Arabic is also an official language of the UN.

Portuguese The transmission of Portuguese paralleled that of Spanish, but today it is used as an official language in only seven countries outside of Portugal (where there are a scant 10 million speakers): five in Africa, one in Latin America, and the tiny Asian colony of Macao. Of the 168 million native Portuguese speakers worldwide, the vast majority of them live in Brazil (154 million). In Angola, there are just over 4 million.

Russian There are an estimated 130 million people who claim Russian as their mother tongue in the two countries where it is an official language, Russia (127 million) and Belarus (3 mil-

lion). There are still significant numbers of people claiming Russian as a first language in the former republics of the Soviet Union, especially Ukraine (17 million) and Kazakhstan (8 million), Uzbekistan (2.5 million), and Kyrgyzstan and Moldova (1 million each). Russian is an official language of the UN.

Japanese The official language of only one country, Japanese is spoken by more than 125 million. The most significant Japanese-speaking minorities outside of Japan are found in Brazil (600,000 people) and the United States (490,000). Modern Japanese employs four writing systems: *kanji* (adapted from the Chinese *hanzi*), *hiragana*, *katakana* and *romaji*.

Bengali The official language of Bangladesh, where it is the mother tongue of more than 120 million people, Bengali is also the first language of an estimated 72 million Indians, chiefly the state of West Bengal.

German An official language of six European countries (Germany, Austria, Switzerland, Luxembourg, Liechtenstein, and Belgium), German is spoken by more than 117 million in those countries. There are also significant German-speaking minorities in Eastern Europe (500,000 in Poland and 350,000 in Russia), Brazil (870,000) and the United States (1.8 million).

French Although there are fewer speakers of French than of other languages—fewer than 100 million people claim it is as a first language worldwide—its significance stems from the fact that it is an official language of 32 countries—more than any other language except English—and of the UN. (These countries account for 88 million native speakers of French.) The most important in terms of numbers are France (55 million), Canada (7 million), Ivory Coast (Côte d'Ivoire) (5 million). Democratic Republic of the Congo, Belgium, Cameroon, Niger, Madagascar and Switzerland also have more than 1 million each claiming French as a first language.

Malay Variants and dialects of Malay are used as an official language in Indonesia (where it is known as *Bahasa Indonesia*), Malaysia (*Bahasa Nalaysia*), and Singapore and Brunei (*Bahasa Melayu*). Although these four countries have a combined population of more than 220 million people, Malay is not the mother tongue of the majority in any of them. A mere 33 million people claim Malay as their first language. In Indonesia, Malay runs a distant third to Javanese (78 million speakers) and Sundanese (31 million).

World Energy

The world's primary energy sources in 1997 were crude oil and natural gas liquids, natural gas, coal, and electricity from hydroelectric and nuclear power. In order to compare the energy produced by different sources, energy is measured in British thermal units (Btu) . Energy production and consumption worldwide increased drastically during the 1980s, but their growth has slowed somewhat in the 1990s. Petroleum production and consumption continues to increase, but whereas petroleum once constituted almost half the world's energy, it now accounts for less than 40 percent. Natural gas and nuclear power have made up most of the difference.

Petroleum World production of petroleum (which includes crude oil and natural gas plant liquids) reached an all-time high of 74 million barrels per day in 1997. The United States, Russia, and Saudi Arabia together accounted for 32.8 percent of world petroleum production, or more than 23 million barrels of oil per day. Venezuela and Iran accounted for an additional 10.0 percent of petroleum production.

Consumption of petroleum has kept pace with the increase in production. But the United States is by far the biggest consumer. The U.S. consumed 18.6 million barrels of petroleum per day, more than one-fourth the world's total. That's more than double the 8.3 million barrels the U.S. produces each day, forcing America to import 10.3 million barrels of petroleum each day. No other country consumes even half as much oil as the United States. Japan was second in world consumption with 5.7 million barrels (most of which it imported), followed by China (3.8 million barrels), Germany (2.9 million), and Russia (2.8 million). Saudi Arabia, the world's largest petroleum producer, consumed a mere 1.2 million barrels per day, or 1.7 percent of the world total.

Dry natural gas World production of dry natural gas increased 11 percent between 1990 and 1997, when it reached an all-time high of 82 trillion cubic feet. Russia is the world's largest producer of natural gas (20.17 trillion cubic feet, or 25 percent of the world total in 1997), followed by the United States (18.90 trillion cubic feet, or 23 percent of world production in 1997. The United States was responsible for 27 percent of world consumption, while Russia accounted for 16 percent.

Coal World coal production increased for the fourth straight year in 1997, to 5.2 billion short tons. China continues to lead the world in production, with more than 1.6 billion short tons per year. The United States, which had been the world leader until 1987, produced just under 1.2 billion short tons. Together, the U.S. and China account for close to half the world's coal production. They also accounted for the bulk of coal consumption in 1997. China consumed 1.5 billion short tons (29 percent of world consumption) and the U.S. consumed 1.0 million short tons (20 percent).

Hydroelectric power Generation of hydroelectric power worldwide rose 17 percent between 1990 and 1997 to an all-time high of 2.5 trillion kilowatthours (kWh). Canada (348 billion kWh), the U.S. (356 billion kWh), and Brazil (276 billion kWh) produced 39 percent of the worldwide total. They were also the three biggest users of hydroelectric power, making up 39 percent of world consumption.

Nuclear electric power World generation of nuclear electric power more than tripled between 1980, when all nations combined to produce 684.4 billion kWh, and 1997, when the U.S. alone produced nearly this much nuclear power (674.7 kWh). Between 1990 and 1997, worldwide nuclear power generation increased 19 percent. France (374.3 kWh) and Japan (306.1 kWh) followed the

World Primary Energy Production By Source, 1980-97 (quadrillion Btu)

Source	1980	1985	1990	1995	1996	1997[1]
Petroelum[2]	133.22	121.21	136.35	141.46	145.69	150.62
Natural gas	52.65	61.38	72.53	77.77	81.90	84.26
Coal	74.48	85.77	92.38	92.41	93.33	92.20
Hydroelectric power	18.05	20.56	22.61	25.83	26.28	26.35
Nuclear electric power	7.58	15.37	20.37	23.31	24.10	23.97
Geothermal, solar, and wind electric power	0.40	0.60	2.79	3.18	3.35	1.81
Total, all sources	286.38	304.89	347.03	363.96	374.65	381.34

Note: Totals may not add up due to independent rounding. 1. Preliminary. 2. Includes natural gas plant liquids. **Source:** Energy Information Administration, *International Energy Annual, 1997* (1999).

World Crude Oil Production, 1960-97 (million barrels per day)

Country	1960	1970	1980	1990	1995	1996	1997[1]
Organization of Petroleum Exporting Countries (OPEC)[2]	**8.70**	**23.30**	**26.61**	**23.20**	**26.09**	**26.77**	**28.36**
Iran	1.07	3.83	1.66	3.09	3.64	3.69	3.66
Iraq	0.97	1.55	2.51	2.04	0.56	0.58	1.19
Kuwait[3]	1.69	2.99	1.66	1.18	2.06	2.06	2.08
Nigeria	0.02	1.08	2.06	1.81	1.99	2.19	2.32
Saudi Arabia	1.31	3.80	9.90	6.41	8.23	8.22	8.56
United Arab Emirates	0.00	0.78	1.71	2.12	2.28	2.28	2.32
Venezuela	2.85	3.71	2.17	2.14	2.75	3.05	3.31
Total OPEC[3]							
Non-OPEC countries[2]	**12.29**	**22.59**	**32.99**	**37.37**	**36.36**	**37.23**	**37.91**
Canada	0.52	1.26	1.44	1.55	1.81	1.82	1.89
China	0.10	0.60	2.11	2.77	2.99	3.13	3.20
Mexico	0.27	0.49	1.94	2.55	2.62	2.86	3.03
Norway	0.00	0.00	0.53	1.70	2.77	3.10	3.15
Russia[5]	2.91	6.99	11.71	10.98	6.00	5.77	5.88
United Kingdom	(4)	(4)	1.62	1.82	2.49	2.57	2.52
United States	7.04	9.64	8.60	7.36	6.56	6.46	6.41
Total world	**20.99**	**45.89**	**59.60**	**60.57**	**62.45**	**63.97**	**66.27**

1. Preliminary. 2. Includes other countries not shown separately. In addition to those listed separately, current OPEC members are: Algeria, Indonesia, Libya, and Qatar. 3. Includes about one-half of the production in the Neutral Zone between Kuwait and Saudi Arabia. 4. Fewer than 5,000 barrels per day. 5. Figures for Russia before 1995 refer to the former Soviet Union. **Source:** U.S. Dept. of Energy, *Annual Energy Review 1997* (1998).

U.S. in total nuclear production in 1997, as well as in the total number of reactors (see the accompanying table).

The Strategic Petroleum Reserve In an attempt to minimize the wild fluctuations in prices caused by the Arab oil embargoes of the 1970s, the U.S. in 1977 created the Strategic Petroleum Reserve, which permitted the storage of 580 million barrels of oil. The Reserve proved useful in preventing additional oil price hikes during the Iraqi invasion of Kuwait in 1990.

The reserve can also be used as an emergency supply of oil in case of a complete oil embargo. In 1985, the reserve held enough oil to provide a normal level of petroleum to the U.S. for 115 days in the absence of any other petroleum imports. Since then, the measure has declined to 63 days, because U.S. energy consumption as well as its reliance on foreign imports have both increased.

Leading Suppliers of U.S. Oil

The United States imports about half of the oil it consumes, or close to 10 million barrels a day. In 1997 the U.S. imported more of its oil from non-OPEC (5.4 million barrels) countries than from OPEC (4.5 million barrles) countries.

Country	U.S. imports, 1997[1] (barrels/day)
Venezuela	1,648,000
Saudi Arabia	1,473,000
Canada	1,391,000
Mexico	1,366,000
Nigeria	678,000
United Kingdom	316,000
Virgin Islands/Puerto Rico	224,000
Total OPEC countries	4,487,000
Total, all imports	**9,907,000**

1. Preliminary figures. **Source:** Energy Information Administration, *Annual Energy Review, 1997* (1998).

World Energy Consumption by Type and Region, 1986–97

Energy Type and Region	Consumption (quadrillion Btu)					
	1986	1990	1993	1995	1996	1997[1]
Petroleum	**126.70**	**134.89**	**136.59**	**142.44**	**145.36**	**148.71**
North America	38.35	40.39	40.62	41.60	42.96	43.81
Central & South America	7.02	7.35	7.92	8.69	9.13	9.45
Western Europe	26.54	27.42	28.37	29.61	29.97	30.33
Eastern Europe & Former USSR	21.99	20.32	14.11	11.96	10.87	11.41
Middle East	6.25	7.09	7.84	8.54	8.57	8.78
Africa	3.67	4.17	4.56	4.83	4.91	5.11
Far East & Oceania	22.88	28.15	33.17	37.22	38.94	39.83
Dry Natural Gas	**62.37**	**75.10**	**78.47**	**80.20**	**84.13**	**83.86**
North America	19.80	22.74	24.61	26.19	26.85	26.88
Central & South America	1.86	2.21	2.55	2.86	3.06	3.24
Western Europe	9.08	10.34	11.71	12.74	14.04	14.05
Eastern Europe & Former USSR	23.22	28.50	26.20	23.22	23.61	22.17
Middle East	2.65	3.77	4.47	4.96	5.52	5.93
Africa	1.21	1.52	1.71	1.88	1.95	2.02
Far East & Oceania	4.55	6.02	7.21	8.37	9.10	9.57
Coal	**86.39**	**90.45**	**88.15**	**89.83**	**91.78**	**92.76**
North America	18.57	20.52	21.26	21.64	22.51	22.98
Central & South America	0.63	0.61	0.59	0.57	0.75	0.64
Western Europe	14.40	14.00	10.92	10.05	9.50	9.82
Eastern Europe & Former USSR	20.74	19.88	15.25	12.77	13.07	12.77
Middle East	0.13	0.15	0.22	0.24	0.26	0.28
Africa	4.01	2.98	3.27	3.41	3.47	3.54
Far East & Oceania	27.91	32.32	36.64	41.15	42.23	42.73
Hydroelectric power	**21.34**	**22.69**	**24.60**	**26.12**	**26.43**	**26.57**
North America	6.85	6.38	6.71	7.18	7.87	7.80
Central & South America	3.21	3.80	4.43	4.97	5.08	5.27
Western Europe	4.57	4.74	5.17	5.24	5.06	5.17
Eastern Europe & Former USSR	2.47	2.64	2.79	2.84	2.62	2.58
Middle East	0.09	0.13	0.19	0.16	0.17	0.17
Africa	0.51	0.57	0.57	0.59	0.60	0.62
Far East & Oceania	3.63	4.42	4.75	5.14	5.04	4.98
Nuclear electric power	**16.34**	**20.37**	**22.07**	**23.35**	**24.17**	**23.97**
North America	5.25	6.99	7.59	8.31	8.24	7.67
Central & South America	0.06	0.10	0.09	0.11	0.11	0.12
Western Europe	6.47	7.43	8.18	8.33	8.72	8.83
Eastern Europe & Former USSR	2.17	2.89	2.73	2.47	2.76	2.77
Middle East	N.A.	N.A.	N.A.	N.A.	N.A.	N.A.
Africa	0.09	0.09	0.07	0.11	0.12	0.13
Far East & Oceania	2.29	2.87	3.41	4.02	4.23	4.45
Geothermal, solar, and wind electric power	**0.37**	**1.31**	**1.55**	**1.60**	**1.68**	**1.81**
Total energy consumption	**313.48**	**346.85**	**353.36**	**365.49**	**375.56**	**379.53**

1.Preliminary. **Source:** Energy Information Administration, *International Energy Annual, 1997* (1999).

Top 10 Producers of Primary Energy, by Source, 1997

Crude oil[1]	(thousand barrels per day)	Natural gas plant liquids[2]	(thousand barrels per day)	Dry natural gas	(trillion cubic feet)
1. Saudi Arabia	8,562	1. United States	1,817	1. Russia	20.17
2. United States	6,452	2. Saudi Arabia	712	2. United States	18.90
3. Russia	5,920	3. Canada	636	3. Canada	5.85
4. Iran	3,664	4. Mexico	388	4. United Kingdom	3.24
5. Venezuela	3,315	5. United Kingdom	233	5. Netherlands	2.99
6. China	3,200	6. Russia	195	6. Algeria	2.47
7. Norway	3,143	7. Venezuela	162	7. Indonesia	2.37
8. Mexico	3,023	8. United Arab Emirates	160	8. Uzbekistan	1.74
9. United Kingdom	2,518	9. Algeria	160	9. Norway	1.60
10. Nigeria	2,332	10. Norway	139	10. Saudi Arabia	1.53

Coal[3]	(million short tons)	Hydroelectric power[4,5]	(billion kWh)	Nuclear electric power[5]	(billion kWh)
1. China	1,553	1. United States	355.9	1. United States	629.4
2. United States	1,090	2. Canada	348.4	2. France	374.3
3. India	329	3. Brazil	276.3	3. Japan	306.1
4. Australia	293	4. China	175.0	4. Germany	161.9
5. Russia	288	5. Russia	150.5	5. Russia	104.5
6. Germany	252	6. Norway	108.7	6. United Kingdom	89.3
7. South Africa	243	7. Japan	85.9	7. Canada	77.9
8. Poland	220	8. Sweden	67.9	8. Ukraine	75.4
9. Canada	87	9. India	65.0	9. South Korea	73.2
10. Uzbekistan	87	10. France	61.3	10. Sweden	66.7

Note: Preliminary. 1. Includes lease condensate. 2. Does not include China, for which data are unavailable. 3. Includes anthracite, subanthracite, bituminous, subbituminous, lignite, and brown coal. 4. Net generation; data consist of both utility and non-utility sources. Excludes generation from pumped storage. 5. Net generation; excludes energy consumed by the generating unit.
Source: U.S. Dept. of Energy, *International Energy Annual, 1997* (1999).

World Energy Production by Region, 1980–97

Region	1980	1985	1990	1995	1996	1997[1]
Crude oil *(thousand barrels/day)*	**59,599**	**53,981**	**60,566**	**62,335**	**63,711**	**66,420**
North America	11,968	13,187	11,461	10,982	11,156	11,396
Central & South America	3,647	3,602	4,318	5,481	5,848	6,367
Western Europe	2,531	3,847	4,125	5,878	6,299	6,300
Eastern Europe & Former USSR	12,038	11,909	11,216	7,017	6,917	7,067
Middle East	18,442	10,307	16,545	18,979	19,174	20,320
Africa	6,125	5,371	6,432	6,954	7,112	7,584
Far East & Oceania	4,848	5,758	6,468	7,043	7,205	7,385
Dry Natural Gas *(trillon cubic ft)*	**53.19**	**62.17**	**73.61**	**77.92**	**81.66**	**81.71**
North America	23.17	20.45	22.60	25.18	25.67	25.94
Central & South America	1.20	1.76	2.01	2.58	2.76	2.93
Western Europe	7.32	7.22	7.24	8.75	10.08	9.90
Eastern Europe & Former USSR	17.04	24.50	30.13	25.93	26.28	24.75
Middle East	1.33	2.38	3.72	4.99	5.53	6.03
Africa	0.69	1.86	2.46	3.01	3.23	3.59
Far East & Oceania	2.44	4.00	5.44	7.49	8.11	8.57
Coal *(million short tons)*	**4,196.13**	**4,869.40**	**5,353.14**	**5,133.61**	**5,207.69**	**5,218.35**
North America	877.37	955.77	1,113.01	1,125.48	1,157.52	1,186.79
Central & South America	16.66	21.31	32.93	39.72	42.85	48.56
Western Europe	845.33	928.34	873.15	554.28	547.53	526.68
Eastern Europe & Former USSR	1,282.36	1,331.37	1,336.04	891.74	875.75	840.92
Middle East	0.99	1.38	1.21	1.25	1.25	1.32
Africa	137.91	197.48	201.76	236.09	235.78	251.11
Far East & Oceania	1,035.51	1,433.75	1,795.02	2,285.06	2,347.01	2,362.78
Hydroelectric power *(bil. kWh)*	**1,735.2**	**1,973.1**	**2,170.2**	**2,488.7**	**2,512.7**	**2,536.3**
North America	546.9	611.1	605.1	667.6	727.9	730.4
Central & South America	199.3	285.7	365.2	477.4	488.8	506.4
Western Europe	431.7	453.2	453.4	503.7	486.5	496.7
Eastern Europe & Former USSR	211.3	230.7	253.6	273.1	251.6	247.7
Middle East	9.6	9.5	12.5	15.7	15.9	16.1
Africa	60.2	46.7	55.2	56.7	57.8	59.6
Far East & Oceania	276.2	336.4	425.1	494.5	484.3	479.3
Nuclear power *(billion kWh)*	**684.4**	**1,425.7**	**1905.1**	**2,206.0**	**2,286.4**	**2,267.8**
North America	287.0	440.8	649.0	774.4	770.3	717.2
Central & South America	2.2	8.4	9.0	9.5	9.2	10.5
Western Europe	219.2	572.5	707.5	793.0	830.3	840.0
Eastern Europe & Former USSR	83.2	200.3	251.3	224.3	249.8	251.1
Middle East	0.0	0.0	0.0	0.0	0.0	0.0
Africa	0.0	5.5	8.4	11.3	11.8	12.6
Far East & Oceania	92.7	198.2	279.9	393.6	415.0	436.4

1. Preliminary. **Source:** Energy Information Administration, *International Energy Annual, 1997* (1999).

World Nuclear Power Generation, by Region and Country, 1980–97

Region and country	Generation (billion killowatthours)						Operable reactors
	1980	1985	1990	1995	1996	1997[1]	1997[2]
North America	**287.0**	**440.8**	**649.0**	**774.4**	**770.3**	**717.2**	**131**
Canada	35.9	57.1	69.2	93.0	88.1	77.9	21
Mexico	—	—	2.8	8.0	7.5	9.9	2
United States	251.1	383.7	577.0	673.4	674.7	629.4	110
Central and South America	**2.2**	**8.4**	**9.0**	**9.5**	**9.2**	**10.5**	**3**
Argentina	2.2	5.4	7.0	7.1	6.9	7.5	2
Brazil	0.0	2.9	1.9	2.4	2.3	3.0	1
Western Europe	**207.4**	**572.5**	**707.5**	**793.0**	**830.3**	**840.0**	**152**
Belgium	11.9	32.7	40.6	39.3	41.2	45.0	7
Finland	6.6	18.0	18.3	18.3	18.5	19.0	4
France	63.4	211.2	298.4	358.4	377.5	374.3	57
Germany[3]	55.0	138.6	145.1	145.4	152.0	161.9	20
Italy	2.1	6.6	0.0	0.0	0.0	0.0	0
Netherlands	4.0	3.7	3.3	3.8	4.0	2.3	2
Slovenia[4]	0.0	4.0	4.4	4.5	4.4	4.8	1
Spain	5.2	28.0	51.6	52.7	53.5	52.5	9
Sweden	25.3	55.8	64.8	66.4	69.6	66.7	12
Switzerland	12.9	20.1	22.4	23.7	23.9	24.0	5
United Kingdom	32.3	53.8	58.7	80.6	85.8	89.3	35
Eastern Europe	**90.7**	**200.3**	**251.3**	**224.3**	**249.8**	**251.1**	**68**
Bulgaria	5.9	12.4	13.5	16.4	17.8	16.4	6
Former Czechoslovakia	4.3	11.9	23.4	N.A.	N.A.	N.A.	N.A.
Czech Republic	N.A.	N.A.	N.A.	11.6	12.2	12.5	4
Slovakia	N.A.	N.A.	N.A.	10.9	11.3	11.2	4
Hungary	0.0	6.1	13.0	13.3	13.5	13.3	4
Former USSR	69.3	170.0	201.3	N.A.	N.A.	N.A.	N.A.
Armenia	N.A.	N.A.	N.A.	0.0	2.1	1.4	2
Kazakhstan	N.A.	N.A.	N.A.	0.1	0.1	0.9	1
Lithuania	N.A.	N.A.	N.A.	10.6	12.7	10.9	2
Russia	N.A.	N.A.	N.A.	94.3	103.3	104.5	29
Ukraine	N.A.	N.A.	N.A.	67.0	76.0	75.4	16
Middle East	**0.0**	**0.0**	**0.0**	**0.0**	**0.0**	**0.0**	**0**
Africa	**0.0**	**5.5**	**8.4**	**11.3**	**11.8**	**12.6**	**2**
South Africa	0.0	5.5	8.4	11.3	11.8	12.6	2
Far East and Oceania	**92.6**	**198.2**	**279.9**	**393.6**	**415.0**	**436.4**	**78**
China	N.A.	N.A.	N.A.	12.4	13.6	11.4	3
India	2.7	4.7	5.6	6.5	7.4	10.5	10
Japan	78.7	149.7	192.2	276.7	287.1	306.1	53
Korea, South	3.3	15.8	50.2	63.7	70.2	73.2	11
Pakistan	0.1	0.3	0.4	0.5	0.3	0.4	1
Taiwan	7.8	27.8	31.6	33.9	36.3	34.8	6
World total	**684.4**	**1,425.7**	**1,905.1**	**2,206.0**	**2,286.4**	**2267.8**	**444**

Note: Net generation; does not include energy consumed by the generating unit. Sum of components may not equal total due to independent rounding. 1. Preliminary. 2. Totals include other countries not shown separately. 3. Includes both the former East Germany and West Germany. 4. Data before 1991 refers to the former Yugoslavia. **Source:** Energy Information Administration, *International Energy Annual, 1997* (1999) and *Nuclear Power Generation and Fuel Cycle Report 1998.*

The Global Military Situation

Following the trend of the post-Cold War period, the world has continued to demilitarize in the last years of the century. According to the London-based International Institute for Strategic Studies, global defense spending has declined steadily since the mid-1980's. In 1997, according to the IISS, defense expenditures worldwide totaled approximately $803.7 billion, a decline of 4.7% from $843.4 billion in 1996 and a drop of 33% from $1.21 trillion in 1985. Armed forces personnel totals have also declined precipitously from mid-1980s levels. At the end of 1997, according to the IISS, active-duty military personnel totaled approximately 22.3 million world-wide, down nearly 5 million (17.8%) from 1985.

Global aggregates, however, do conceal telling regional differences and shifts in military priorities on the part of major powers. Strategic interventions on the part of the United States and NATO allies, concern over the spread of chemical, biological, and nuclear weapons development, anti-terrorist initiatives, and local conflicts all have yielded a redistribution of military resources.

In the United States, largely due to cutbacks in nuclear-weapons development, the defense budget of $273 billion in 1997 represented a decrease of more than 25% ($95 billion) from 1985 levels; U.S. active-duty military personnel declined by nearly 33%, or about 704,000 over the same period. Underlying the figures has been a shift in policy toward the so-called "Bottom Up Review" study of 1993, which said that the nation should maintain the capacity to fight conventional wars in two major theaters (such as the Persian Gulf and Korean peninsula) simultaneously. U.S. naval strength remains the foundation of its military superiority. The U.S. force of 380,600 Navy personnel and fleet of 138 "principal surface combatants" (surface ships with 1,000 tons of displacement and non-defensive weapons systems) far exceed those of any other nation.

The European NATO nations have undergone similar cutbacks in military spending and personnel. Corresponding figures are difficult to derive for Russia and the former Soviet Union, but the cutbacks have been, if anything, even more drastic.

In other regions of the world, however, political developments and ongoing security issues have given rise to military expansion. In the Middle East and North Africa, where the Arab-Israeli peace process has proceeded in fits and starts and where Iraq has continued to test U.S. and NATO resolve, aggregate defense spending reached $56.4 billion in 1997, up 4.6% ($2.5 billion) from the previous year; military personnel reached 2.82 million, an increase of 11.4% (290,000) from 1985 levels.

In Central and South Asia, nuclear testing by India and Pakistan have altered the strategic landscape, while insurgencies in Sri Lanka, Bangladesh, Tajikistan, and other nations have increased political instability. In 1997, defense spending in the region climbed to $19.3 billion, 48% more than in 1985. Armed forces personnel climbed to nearly 2.6 million in 1997, up 34% from 1985.

In East Asia and Australasia, where regional strategic and defense policies are defined by the ongoing tensions between North and South Korea and between China and Taiwan, estimated military expenditures rose 32% from 1985 ($107.7 billion) to 1997 ($141.6 billion).

In Central and Latin America, several countries—notably Colombia and Mexico—have faced a proliferation of armed opposition and organized crime throughout the 1990s. Regional defense spending continued to rise in real terms in 1997, reaching $32.8 billion—a nearly 69% rise from 1985.

▶NUCLEAR WEAPONS

The end of the Cold War and compliance with disarmament agreements have yielded large-scale reductions in the size of nuclear arsenals. While the facts regarding nuclear stockpiles and the locations of storage and deployment sites remain official secrets, various sources provide similar estimates and tracking information. As of the beginning of 1998, according to the Natural Resources Defense Council (NRDC) in Washington, D.C., the five nuclear powers—the United States, Russia, China, France, and Great Britain—had approximately 36,000 nuclear warheads in their arsenals. That compares with an estimated 70,000 nuclear weapons among the five powers in the mid-1980s. The reduction in the world's nuclear arsenals has resulted in major shifts in storage and deployment sites. In less than a decade, through the end of 1997, there was a five-fold decrease in the number of nuclear weapons sites worldwide. The United States is now the only nation with nuclear weapons deployed outside its borders.

The U.S. nuclear arsenal totaled just over 12,000 warheads as 1998 began, with 8,425 of them operational and the rest awaiting dismantlement. The majority were located in 14 states, especially New Mexico, Georgia, Washington, Nevada, and North Dakota. A total of 150 nuclear weapons were deployed at air bases in seven Western European nations.

At the same time, Russia deployed some 22,500 nuclear warheads—10,240 operational—at 90 domestic sites. In the course of less than a decade, the nuclear arsenal of the former USSR was moved from hundreds of far-flung sites throughout the constituent republics and Eastern Europe to locations inside Russia.

The British nuclear stockpile totaled 260 operational warheads as 1998 began, but that figure fell to 160 in March, when the nation's arsenal was reduced to only a single weapon type—the Trident II missile on Vanguard-class submarines. The French stockpile, meanwhile, totaled 450 operational warheads of three types at four locations, down from a dozen bases at the beginning of the 1990's. China's arsenal, though harder to corroborate, was estimated at about 400 operational warheads, located at some 20 storage sites.

During 1998 progress stalled on two major treaties designed to reduce the dangers of nuclear weapons. The U.N. Comprehensive Nuclear Test Ban Treaty, which would end underground weapons testing, encountered major opposition in the U.S. Senate. And START II, which would limit deployed U.S. and Russian nuclear warheads to no more than 3,500 each, stalled in the Duma (the Russian parliament) in December 1998. A vote on the treaty was rescheduled for the fall of 1999, but U.S. officials expressed doubt that the body would vote to ratify.

Nuclear Stockpiles and Storage Locations Worldwide, Major Nuclear Powers, 1998[1]

Country	Warheads Total[2]	Warheads Operational	Storage Sites	Operational Silos	Missile Submarines
United States	12,070	8,425	24	550	18
Russia	22,500	10,240	90	350	23
China	450	400	20	7	1
France	500	450	4	0	5
Great Britain	380	260	2	0	2
Total	36,000	19,775	142	907	49

1. As of January 1, 1998. 2. A portion awaiting final dismantling. In the case of the U.S., another portion is part of reserve/hedge.
Source: *Taking Stock: Worldwide Nuclear Deployments 1998.* Copyright © 1998 Natural Resources Defense Council (Washington, D.C.). Reprinted by permission.

Defense Expenditures and Military Personnel, by Country, 1997

Country	Defense Expenditures			Military Personnel	
	Total (millions)[2]	Per Capita	Percent of GDP	Active ('000s)	Reserve ('000s)[1]
Canada	$7,757	$270	1.3%	61.6	28.7
United States	272,955	1,018	3.4	1,447.6	1,711.7
NATO Europe					
Belgium	3,769	373	1.6%	44.5	144.2
Denmark	2,826	538	1.7	32.9	70.5
France	41,545	708	3.0	380.8	292.5
Germany	33,416	412	1.6	347.1	315.0
Greece	5,552	526	4.6	162.3	291.0
Italy	21,837	377	1.9	325.2	484.0
Netherlands	6,888	442	1.9	57.2	75.0
Norway	3,336	760	2.3	33.6	234.0
Portugal	2,559	259	2.6	59.3	210.9
Spain	7,671	196	1.4	197.5	431.9
Turkey	8,110	131	4.2	639.0	378.7
United Kingdom	35,736	611	2.8	213.8	320.8
Non-NATO Europe					
Albania	$94	$26	6.7%	54.0	155.0
Armenia	138	37	8.9	60.0	300.0
Austria	1,786	222	0.8	45.5	100.7
Azerbaijan	146	19	4.0	66.7	560.0
Belarus	381	37	2.9	81.8	289.5
Bosnia-Herzegovina	327	74	5.0	40.0	100.0
Bulgaria	339	41	3.4	101.5	303.0
Croatia	1,147	244	5.7	58.0	220.0
Cyprus	505	594	5.8	10.0	88.0
Czech Republic	987	96	2.2	61.7	240.0
Finland	1,956	381	1.7	31.0	500.0
Hungary	666	66	1.4	49.1	186.4
Ireland	767	210	1.0	12.7	15.6
Poland	3,073	79	2.3	241.8	406.0
Romania	793	35	2.3	227.0	427.0
Russia	64,000	435	5.8	1,240.0	2,400.0
Serbia-Montenegro	1,489	140	7.8	114.2	400.0
Slovakia	414	77	2.1	41.2	20.0
Sweden	5,481	619	2.4	54.3	570.0
Switzerland	3,837	544	1.5	26.3	390.0
Ukraine	1,324	26	2.7	387.4	1,000.0
Middle East and North Africa					
Algeria	$2,114	$73	4.6%	124.0	150.0
Bahrain	364	608	6.5	11.0	N.A.
Egypt	2,743	45	4.3	450.0	254.0
Iran	4,695	68	6.6	518.0	350.0
Iraq	1,250	56	7.4	387.5	650.0
Israel	11,143	1,917	11.5	175.0	430.0
Jordan	496	105	6.4	104.1	35.0
Kuwait	3,618	1,681	11.4	15.3	23.7
Lebanon	676	163	4.5	55.1	N.A.
Libya	1,250	215	4.7	65.0	40.0
Morocco	1,386	48	4.2	196.3	150.0
Oman	1,815	887	10.9	43.5	N.A.
Qatar	1,346	2,380	13.7	11.8	N.A.
Saudi Arabia	18,151	1,071	12.4	162.5	N.A.
Syria	2,217	145	6.3	320.0	500.0
UAE	2,424	978	5.5	64.5	N.A.
Central and Southern Asia					
Afghanistan	$209	$10	12.5%	429.0	N.A.
Bangladesh	593	5	1.9	121.0	N.A.
India	12,805	13	3.3	1,145.0	528.4
Pakistan	3,503	26	5.8	587.0	513.0
Sri Lanka	898	49	6.1	117.0	4.2
Uzbekistan	447	19	3.9	70.0	N.A.

Country	Defense Expenditures			Military Personnel	
	Total (millions)[2]	Per Capita	Percent of GDP	Active ('000s)	Reserve ('000s)[1]
East Asia and Australasia					
Australia	$8,501	$456	2.2%	57.4	33.7
Cambodia	254	25	7.3	140.5	N.A.
China	36,551	30	5.7	2,840.0	1,200.0
Indonesia	4,812	24	2.2	284.0	400.0
Japan	40,891	325	1.0	235.6	46.7
Korea, North	5,409	246	27.0	1,055.0	4,700.0
Korea, South	14,732	320	3.3	672.0	4,500.0
Malaysia	3,377	157	3.7	111.5	37.8
Myanmar	2,167	45	7.7	429.0	N.A.
New Zealand	901	251	1.6	9.6	7.0
Philippines	1,422	20	1.7	110.5	131.0
Singapore	4,122	1,360	4.3	70.0	263.8
Taiwan	13,657	634	4.7	376.0	1,657.5
Thailand	3,248	52	2.1	266.0	200.0
Vietnam	990	13	4.1	492.0	3,000.0
Caribbean and Central America					
Cuba	$2,275	$65	5.2%	60.0	39.0
El Salvador	176	30	1.9	28.4	15.0
Guatemala	182	16	1.5	40.7	35.0
Haiti	99	14	5.2	N.A.	N.A.
Honduras	101	16	2.1	18.8	60.0
Mexico	3,664	39	1.0	175.0	300.0
Panama	114	41	1.3	N.A.	N.A.
South America					
Argentina	$4,687	$134	1.7%	73.0	375.0
Brazil	13,944	84	2.3	314.7	1,115.0
Chile	2,148	147	2.8	94.3	50.0
Colombia	3,068	85	4.0	146.3	60.7
Ecuador	692	57	3.5	57.1	100.0
Peru	1,276	52	2.2	125.0	188.0
Uruguay	307	96	2.3	25.6	N.A.
Venezuela	962	42	1.1	56.0	8.0
Sub-Saharan Africa					
Angola	$658	$58	8.8%	110.5	N.A.
Botswana	241	153	6.5	7.5	N.A.
Cameroon	240	17	2.9	13.1	N.A.
Congo	74	26	2.5	10.0	N.A.
Dem. Rep. of Congo	308	7	5.3	40.0	N.A.
Ethiopia	139	3	2.1	120.0	N.A.
Ghana	134	7	1.5	7.0	N.A.
Kenya	235	8	2.4	24.2	N.A.
Nigeria	1,965	18	4.0	77.0	N.A.
Rwanda	103	13	5.5	55.0	N.A.
South Africa	2,326	60	1.8	79.4	386.0
Sudan	418	14	5.6	79.7	N.A.
Tanzania	123	4	3.4	34.6	80.0
Uganda	166	8	2.4	55.0	N.A.
Zimbabwe	304	26	4.7	39.0	N.A.

1. U.S. dollars, 1997 constant prices.
Source: *The Military Balance, 1998/99,* The International Institute for Strategic Studies. Reprinted by permission.

▶U.S. LEADS WORLD IN ARMS SALES

According to an authoritative Government report, the United States negotiated new agreements to sell $7.1 billion worth of weapons in 1998, nearly 31 percent of the $23 billion in sales worldwide. The U.S. easily passed Germany, which sold $5.5 billion, and France, which had $3 billion in sales.

The United States also led the world in delivering arms ordered in previous years, making $7.8 billion worth of deliveries in 1998.

Russia reached agreements to sell only $1.7 billion worth of arms, compared with $3.3 billion in 1997 and $5.3 billion in 1996.

The $23 billion in worldwide arms sales showed a slight increase over 1997, when the worst of the Asian economic crisis hit, but it was far below the levels in the early 1990s, when the collapse of the Soviet Union and the Persian Gulf war led to an arms-buying spree. In 1993, arms sales worldwide reached $37 billion.

Arms sales to the developing world—defined as those countries outside Europe and excluding Russia, Japan, Australia, and New Zealand—dropped sharply overall. But the United States increased its sales to those countries to $4.6 billion, from $2.6 billion the year before.

The Global Economy

(Note: for definitions of GDP, GNP, etc. see Part II, "The U.S. Economy")

The 1990s have been a time of strong economic growth throughout much of the world. The efficient and rapid movement of capital around the globe and a surging increase in world trade have led many economists to believe that an integrated global economy could be a reality in the not-too-distant future. A severe financial crisis in Asia in 1997-98 pushed the horizon back somewhat, but experts remain optimistic.

Between 1990 and 1995, world output grew steadily at about 3 percent. In 1997, however, it rose to 4.2 percent, driven in large part by rapid growth in developing nations such as China (10 percent growth), Singapore and Malaysia (7-8 percent), and Chile (6 percent). The advanced economies (U.S., Japan, and Germany) grew at only 2 to 3 percent, but it was capital from these wealthy nations that fueled the rapid growth of the poorer ones, especially in Asia. When institutional instability, corruption, and many bad loans weakened the currencies first of Thailand, and then Malaysia, South Korea and others, investors and currency speculators withdrew rapidly. The International Monetary Fund was forced to make enormous loans to keep these economies from collapse.

Growth slowed to 2.5 percent in 1998, and the I.M.F. predicted an even greater contraction for 1999 before a slow recovery beginning with 3.4 percent growth in 2000.

►THE HIERARCHY OF NATIONS

Most contemporary analyses of the global economy begin with the assumption that the nations of the world are divided into two basic categories, developed and developing. The developed ones are those with the highest GNP figures, and are characterized by high per capita income, low rates of population growth and illiteracy, as well as having a low proportion of their labor force in agriculture and/or mining.

The wealthiest nations are at the center of the global economy and are responsible for promoting international trade, for helping to finance development in the poorer countries, and for maintaining a stable economic world. They attempt to do this through several organizations including:

Group of Seven (G-7): a loosely knit group of the largest economic powers who meet once a year to discuss policy in what has become a well-publicized media event. In 1997 Russia was invited to join despite its serious economic problems, so the G-7 is now the **G-8. Members:** Canada, France, Germany, Italy, Japan, Russia, U.K., U.S.

Organization of Economic Cooperation and Development (OECD) HQ: 2 rue André Pascal, F-75775 Paris Cedex 16, France. OECD Washington Center, 2001 L St. NW, Washington D.C. 20036. **www.oecdwash.org. Estab.** 1961, ". . . to help member countries promote economic growth, employment, and improved standards of living through the coordination of policy (and) . . . to help promote the sound and harmonious development of the world economy and improve the lot of the developing countries, particularly the

Countries With Highest and Lowest GNP per Capita, 1997 (in U.S. dollars)

Country	Highest GNP per capita	Country	Lowest GNP per capita
Switzerland	$43,060	Congo, Dem. Republic	$110
Japan	38,160	Ethiopia	110
Norway	36,100	Burundi	140
Denmark	34,890	Mozambique	140
Singapore	32,810	Sierra Leone	160
United States	29,080	Niger	200
Germany	28,280	Malawi	210
Austria	27,920	Rwanda	210
Belgium	26,730	Tanzania[1]	210
France	26,300	Nepal	220
Sweden	26,210	Chad	230
Netherlands	25,830	Eritrea	230
Hong Kong	25,200	Guinea-Bissau	230
Finland	24,790	Burkina Faso	250
United Kingdom	20,870	Madagascar	250
Australia	20,650	Angola	260
Italy	20,170	Mali	260
Canada	19,640	Yemen	270
Ireland	17,790	Nigeria	280
Israel	16,180	São Tomé and Principe	290
New Zealand	15,830	Sudan	290
Spain	14,490	Cambodia	300
Greece	11,640	Vietnam	310
Portugal	11,010	Central African Republic	320
Korea, South	10,550	Tajikistan	330

Note: Rankings based on countries reporting GNP per capita to The World Bank. Does not include countries for which GNP per capita has been estimated. 1. Mainland only.
Source: The World Bank, *The World Bank Atlas 1999.*

Change in World Economic Output, 1997-2000

Category	Annual percent change			
	1997	1998	1999[1]	2000[1]
World Total	4.2%	2.5%	2.3%	3.4%
Advanced Economies	3.2%	2.2%	2.0%	2.3%
United States	3.9	3.9	3.3	2.2
Japan	1.4	-2.8	-1.4	0.3
Germany	2.2	2.8	1.5	2.8
France	2.3	3.1	2.2	2.9
Italy	1.5	1.4	1.5	2.4
United Kingdom	3.5	2.1	0.7	2.1
Canada	3.8	3.0	2.6	2.5
Developing Countries	5.7%	3.3%	3.1%	4.9%
Africa	3.1	3.4	3.2	5.1
Asia	6.6	3.8	4.7	5.7
Middle East and Europe	4.4	2.9	2.0	3.3
Western Hemisphere	5.2	2.3	-0.5	3.5
Countries in Transition	2.2%	-0.2%	-0.9%	2.5%
Central and Eastern Europe	3.1	2.4	2.0	3.7
Russia	0.8	-4.8	-7.0	—
Transcaucasus and Central Asia	2.4	2.0	1.8	3.1

Note: Output is the value of production minus the cost of inputs by all businesses. 1. Projection. **Source:** International Monetary Fund, *World Economic Outlook*, May, 1999.

World GNP per Capita, by Type of Economy, 1997

Nearly 75 percent of the world's 5.8 billion people live in areas where per capita GNP is less than $1,740 according to these World Bank statistics, while only 16 percent live in economies whose GNP per capita is over $9,656.

Type of Economy (Number of Economies)	Population	GNP per Capita
High-income (54)	927,000,000	$25,890
Upper-middle (36)	574,000,000	4,540
Lower-middle (49)	2,283,000,000	1,230
Low-income (61)	2,036,000,000	350
Total (210)	**5,820,000,000**	**5,180**

Source: The World Bank, *The World Bank Atlas 1999.*

GNP per Capita, by World Regions, 1997

Region	GNP per Capita
South Asia	$380
Sub-Saharan Africa	510
East Asia and the Pacific	970
Middle East and North Africa	2,070
Eastern Europe and Central Asia	2,310
Latin America and the Caribbean	3,940
Western Europe, U.S. Japan, and other high-income areas	25,890

Source: The World Bank, *The World Bank Atlas 1999.*

Net Foreign Direct Investment in Developing Countries, 1990-98 (billions of U.S. dollars)

Region and country	1990	1992	1995	1996	1997	1998[1]
All developing countries[2]	**$24.5**	**$46.1**	**$105.4**	**$126.4**	**$163.4**	**$155.0**
By region						
East Asia and the Pacific[2]	$11.1	$22.2	$52.0	$59.8	$64.3	$61.0
Latin America and the Caribbean	8.2	14.6	30.7	42.3	61.6	57.9
Europe and Central Asia	1.1	4.6	17.0	16.0	22.3	20.9
Sub-Saharan Africa	0.8	1.5	3.5	4.3	5.2	4.8
Middle East and North Africa	2.8	2.4	-0.7	0.4	5.4	5.9
South Asia	0.5	0.8	2.9	3.5	4.7	4.4
Top 10 recipients						
China	$3.5	$11.2	$35.8	$40.2	$44.2	$45.0
Brazil	1.0	2.1	4.9	11.2	19.7	24.0
Mexico	2.6	4.4	9.5	9.2	12.5	10.2
Thailand	2.4	2.1	2.1	2.3	3.7	6.8
Argentina	1.8	4.0	4.8	5.1	6.6	5.7
Poland	0.1	0.7	3.7	4.5	4.9	5.5
Malaysia	2.3	5.2	4.1	5.1	5.1	5.0
Chile	0.6	0.9	3.0	4.7	5.4	4.8
Colombia	0.5	0.7	2.3	3.3	6.0	3.0[3]
Indonesia	1.1	1.8	4.3	6.2	4.7	-0.4[3]

Note: Developing countries includes countries in transition. 1. Preliminary. 2.Includes Republic of Korea. 3. Colombia and Indonesia were not among the top 10 recipients in 1998. They were replaced on the list by Republic of Korea, with $5.1 billion, and Venezuela, with $3.8 billion.   **Source:** The World Bank, *Global Development Finance* (1999) and unpublished data.

Net Private Capital Flows to Developing Nations by Region and Nation, 1990-97 (billions of U.S. dollars)

Region and country	1990	1992	1994	1995	1996	1997
All developing countries[1]	**$43.9**	**$98.3**	**$178.1**	**$201.5**	**$275.9**	**$299.0**
By Region						
East Asia and the Pacific[1]	$19.4	$45.0	$87.4	$93.8	$121.5	$104.3
Latin America and the Caribbean	12.6	30.9	59.8	63.9	100.9	118.9
Europe and Central Asia	7.7	17.2	10.8	26.3	38.0	49.9
South Asia	2.2	3.3	9.2	6.8	9.0	11.1
Middle East and North Africa	0.7	0.7	6.1	1.2	1.9	8.1
Sub-Saharan Africa	1.3	1.0	4.9	9.5	4.5	6.7
12 Leading nations						
China	$8.1	$21.3	$44.4	$43.7	$50.1	$60.8
Brazil	0.6	9.7	12.3	20.0	29.7	43.4
Mexico	8.3	9.2	20.7	16.0	25.2	20.5
Argentina	-0.2	5.6	10.1	9.7	16.1	19.8
Korea, Republic of	1.1	7.5	17.7	11.1	21.1	13.1
Russia	5.6	9.3	0.4	1.3	7.5	12.5
Turkey	1.8	4.4	1.6	2.3	8.0	12.2
Indonesia	3.2	4.6	7.7	11.5	16.2	10.9
Chile	2.1	1.8	5.1	5.5	7.4	9.6
Malaysia	0.8	6.1	8.5	10.1	12.8	9.3
India	1.9	2.1	7.1	4.9	6.7	8.3
Thailand	4.4	4.3	4.4	10.0	13.6	3.4
Top 12 countries as percentage of total	**85.3%**	**87.4%**	**78.7%**	**72.5%**	**77.7%**	**74.9%**

Note: Developing countries includes countries in transtition. 1. Includes Republic of Korea.
Source: The World Bank, *Global Development Finance* (1998) and unpublished data.

poorest." **Members (29):** Australia, Austria, Belgium, Canada, Czech Republic, Denmark, Finland, France, Germany, Greece, Hungary, Iceland, Ireland, Italy, Japan, Luxembourg, Mexico, Netherlands, New Zealand, Norway, Poland, Portugal, South Korea, Spain, Sweden, Switzerland, Turkey, UK, U.S.

The International Monetary Fund (I.M.F.) and The World Bank
Both of these organizations are specialized agencies of the United Nations (see the separate section on the UN below) charged with making loans to nations having trouble with debt (I.M.F.) or for long-term growth and development among poorer nations (World Bank).

I.M.F. Classification of Countries

Advanced economies (28): These include the seven largest countries by GDP, all the other members of the EU, the four "tigers" of Asia (Singapore, South Korea, Hong Kong, and Taiwan), and Australia, New Zealand, and Israel.

Countries in transition (28): These are almost all industrialized countries that are moving from a centrally planned economy to one based on free market principles. All of the former republics of the Soviet Union (Kazakhstan, Ukraine) the nations of central and eastern Europe (including Poland, the Czech Republic, and Estonia) and Mongolia are included.

Developing countries (127): These include the burgeoning economies of China, India, Brazil, and Chile as well as the poorest nations of sub-Saharan Africa (Mozambique, Ethiopia, Niger, for example) and Asia (Bangladesh, Cambodia, Vietnam).

U.S. Merchandise Trade Partners, 1997 (millions of dollars)

Country	U.S. exports to	U.S. imports from	U.S. net balance of trade
Belgium and Luxembourg	$13,894	$10,849	$3,045
France	15,804	20,607	-4,803
Germany	24,202	43,018	18,816
Italy	8,927	19,382	-10,455
Netherlands	19,671	7,601	12,070
United Kingdom	35,912	32,496	3,416
Canada	152,047	171,024	-18,977
Japan	64,600	121,658	-57,058
Australia	11,913	4,881	7,032
Brazil	15,806	9,625	6,181
Mexico	71,152	86,661	-15,509
Venezuela	6,583	13,476	6,893
China	12,723	62,555	-49,832
Hong Kong	15,065	10,285	4,780
South Korea	24,602	23,145	1,457
Singapore	17,550	20,077	-2,527
Taiwan	19,159	32,691	-13,532
TOTAL[1]	$679,325	$877,279	$-197,954

1. Includes other countries not shown separately.   **Source:** U.S. Dept. of Commerce, *Survey of Current Business*, July, 1998.

World's Leading Exporters and Importers in Merchandise Trade, 1998

Rank and country	Value (billions)	Share of world trade	Change in value, 1997–98	Rank and country	Value (billions)	Share of world trade	Change in value, 1997–98
EXPORTERS				**IMPORTERS**			
1. European Union	$813.8	20.3%	0%	1. United States	$944.6	22.5%	5%
2. United States	683.0	17.0	-1	2. European Union	801.4	19.1	6
3. Japan	388.0	9.7	-8	3. Japan	280.5	6.7	-17
4. Canada	214.3	5.3	-1	4. Canada	205.0	4.9	2
5. China	183.8	4.6	1	5. Hong Kong	188.7	4.5	-12
6. Hong Kong	174.1	4.3	-7	6. China	140.2	3.3	-26
7. Korea, South	133.2	3.3	-2	7. Mexico	128.9	3.1	14
8. Mexico	117.5	2.9	6	8. Chinese Taipei	104.2	2.5	-9
9. Chinese Taipei	109.9	2.7	-9	9. Singapore	101.5	2.4	-23
10. Singapore	109.8	2.7	-12	10. Korea, South	93.3	2.2	-35
11. Switzerland	78.7	2.0	3	11. Switzerland	80.0	1.9	5
12. Malaysia	73.3	1.8	-7	12. Australia	64.7	1.5	-2
13. Russian Federation[1]	56.2	1.4	-16	13. Brazil	61.0	1.5	-6
14. Australia	55.9	1.4	-11	14. Malaysia	58.5	1.4	-26
15. Thailand	53.6	1.3	-7	15. Poland	48.0	1.1	13
16. Brazil	51.0	1.3	-3	16. Turkey	46.4	1.1	-4
17. Indonesia	48.8	1.2	-9	17. Russian Federation[1]	44.7	1.1	-18
18. Norway	39.6	1.0	-18	18. India	42.9	1.0	4
19. Saudi Arabia	38.8	1.0	-35	19. Thailand	41.8	1.0	-33
20. India	33.2	0.8	-3	20. Norway	36.2	0.9	1
21. Philippines	29.3	0.7	17	21. Philippines	32.0	0.8	-17
22. Czech Republic	26.4	0.7	16	22. Argentina	31.4	0.7	3
23. South Africa	26.3	0.7	-15	23. South Africa	29.3	0.7	-11
24. Poland	26.3	0.7	2	24. Israel	29.1	0.7	-5
25. Turkey	26.1	0.7	0	25. Czech Republic	28.8	0.7	6
26. Argentina	25.2	0.6	-1	26. Indonesia	27.4	0.7	34
27. United Arab Emirates	24.2	0.6	-16	27. United Arab Emirates	27.0	0.6	-10
28. Israel	23.3	0.6	3	28. Hungary	25.8	0.6	22
29. Hungary	22.9	0.6	20	29. Saudi Arabia	23.7	0.6	-13
30. Venezuela	17.2	0.4	-25	30. Chile	18.8	0.4	-4
World Total[2]	**$4,018.0**	**100.0%**	**-4%**	**World Total**	**$4,200.0**	**100.0%**	**-3%**

1. Data exclude trade with the Baltic States and the CIS. Including trade with these States would lift Russian exports and imports to $73.9 billion and $59.5 billion, respectively.   2. Includes other countries not shown separately.   **Source:** World Trade Organization.

10 Largest U.S. Merchandise Imports and Exports, 1987-98

Product Group	Volume (millions)			
	1987	1990	1997	1998
EXPORTS				
1. Electric machinery and parts	$16,670	$31,554	$78,302	$76,872
2. Road vehicles	21,370	30,524	57,429	56,469
3. Transportation equipment	17,917	32,346	43,212	55,724
4. Office and ADP machines	19,945	27,766	51,641	47,759
5. Miscellaneous manufactured articles	10,303	20,903	31,781	31,798
6. General industrial machinery and parts	8,573	16,032	31,440	30,999
7. Power generating machinery	10,311	15,885	28,135	29,963
8. Special industrial machinery	9,676	15,737	30,375	28,688
9. Telecom & sound reproduction equipment	5,656	9,901	26,056	25,978
10. Professional/scientific/control instruments	8,381	12,601	25,042	25,386
TOTAL TOP TEN EXPORTS	**$130,940**	**$213,249**	**$403,413**	**$409,636**
IMPORTS				
1. Road vehicles	$72,585	$73,017	$112,767	$121,310
2. Electric machinery and parts	23,747	33,601	80,317	79,366
3. Office and ADP machines	18,318	26,917	75,001	76,846
4. Appparel/clothing/accessories	20,495	25,533	48,407	53,743
5. Miscellaneous manufactured articles	19,467	25,028	43,547	47,470
6. Telecom & sound reproduction equipment	20,797	22,288	36,685	42,462
7. General industrial machinery and parts	11,403	14,484	26,307	28,802
8. Power generating machinery	10,650	14,591	24,504	28,132
9. Special industrial machinery	11,233	12,945	21,192	22,970
10. Nonmetallic minerals	N.A.	9,890	17,827	19,519
TOTAL TOP TEN IMPORTS	**$217,548**	**$258,293**	**$486,554**	**$520,621**

Note: In current U.S. dollars.   Source: U.S. Dept. of Commerce, International Trade Administration, *U.S. Foreign Trade Highlights 1998* (1999). **www.ita.doc.gov/industry/otea/usfth/aggregate/H198t22.txt**

U.S. Exports and Imports in Services, by Type, 1986-96 (millions)

Category	1986	1987	1990	1995	1996
EXPORTS, TOTAL	**$77,167**	**$86,921**	**$137,224**	**$204,165**	**$221,224**
Travel	20,385	23,563	43,007	63,395	69,908
Passenger fares	5,582	7,003	15,298	19,125	20,557
Other transportation	15,784	17,471	22,745	27,412	27,216
Royalties and license fees	8,113	10,183	16,634	27,383	29,974
Other private services[1]	27,303	28,701	39,540	66,850	73,569
Education	3,495	3,821	5,126	7,512	7,807
Financial services	3,301	3,731	4,417	7,029	8,034
Insurance, net	1,385	1,573	230	1,390	2,121
Telecommunications	1,827	2,111	2,735	3,183	3,405
Business, professional, and technical services	4,428	4,280	6,951	17,765	19,247
IMPORTS, TOTAL	**$66,421**	**$75,506**	**$100,570**	**$134,523**	**$143,086**
Travel	25,913	29,310	37,349	46,053	48,739
Passenger fares	6,505	7,283	10,531	14,433	15,776
Other transportation	17,817	19,057	25,168	28,249	28,453
Royalties and license fees	1,401	1,857	3,135	6,503	7,322
Other private services[1]	14,785	17,999	24,387	39,285	42,796
Education	433	452	658	949	1,041
Financial services	1,769	2,077	2,475	2,472	3,184
Insurance, net	2,201	3,241	1,910	5,383	4,387
Telecommunications	3,253	3,736	5,583	7,773	8,385
Business, professional, and technical services	1,253	1,319	1,891	4,691	5,253

1. Includes other services not shown separately.   **Source:** U.S. Bureau of Economic Analysis. *Survey of Current Business,* Oct. 1997.

Hourly Compensation Costs in U.S. Dollars For Production Workers, Selected Countries, 1975-97

Country	1975	1980	1985	1990	1995	1996	1997
Australia	$5.62	$8.47	$8.20	$13.07	$15.05	$16.55	$16.00
Austria	4.51	8.88	7.58	17.75	25.21	24.66	21.92
Belgium	6.41	13.11	8.97	19.17	26.65	25.89	22.82
Canada	5.96	8.67	10.94	15.84	16.04	16.66	16.55
Denmark	6.28	10.83	8.13	18.04	24.07	24.11	22.02
Finland	4.61	8.24	8.16	21.03	24.14	23.56	21.44
France	4.52	8.94	7.52	15.49	20.01	19.92	17.97
Germany[1]	6.31	12.25	9.53	21.88	32.22	31.79	28.28
Greece	1.69	3.73	3.66	6.76	9.17	9.59	N.A.
Hong Kong	0.76	1.51	1.73	3.20	4.82	5.14	5.42
Ireland	3.03	5.95	5.92	11.66	13.57	13.85	13.57
Israel	2.25	3.79	4.06	8.55	10.54	10.99	12.05
Italy	4.67	8.15	7.63	17.45	16.21	17.73	16.74
Japan	3.00	5.52	6.34	12.80	23.82	20.91	19.37
Korea, South	0.32	0.96	1.23	3.71	7.29	8.09	7.22
Luxembourg	6.50	12.03	7.81	16.74	23.35	22.55	N.A.
Mexico	1.47	2.21	1.59	1.58	1.51	1.54	1.75
Netherlands	6.58	12.06	8.75	18.06	24.02	23.08	20.61
New Zealand	3.21	5.33	4.47	8.33	10.11	11.03	11.02
Norway	6.77	11.59	10.37	21.47	24.38	25.05	23.72
Portugal	1.58	2.06	1.53	3.77	5.37	5.58	5.29
Singapore	0.84	1.49	2.47	3.78	7.33	8.32	8.24
Spain	2.53	5.89	4.66	11.38	12.88	13.51	12.16
Sri Lanka	0.28	0.22	0.28	0.35	0.48	0.48	N.A.
Sweden	7.18	12.51	9.66	20.93	21.44	24.37	22.24
Switzerland	6.09	11.09	9.66	20.86	29.30	28.34	24.19
Taiwan	0.40	1.00	1.50	3.93	5.92	5.93	5.89
United Kingdom	3.37	7.56	6.27	12.70	13.67	14.13	15.47
United States	$6.36	$9.87	$13.01	$14.91	$17.19	$17.70	$18.24

Note: Hourly compensation includes wages, premiums, bonuses, vacation, holidays and other leave, insurance, and benefit plans. N.A.= Not Available. 1. Prior to 1991, data for Germany were for West Germany. **Source:** U.S. Bureau of Labor Statistics, *International Comparisons of Hourly Compensation Costs for Production Workers in Manufacturing*, September, 1998. **http://stats.bls.gov/flshome.htm.**

▶ INTERNATIONAL FINANCE—BASIC CONCEPTS

Exchange Rates Because countries have their own currencies, trade between them also involves exchanging or trading currencies. The *exchange rate* between currencies represents the ratio at which they can be exchanged or the price of one currency in terms of the other. For example, if the exchange rate between the British pound and the U.S. dollar is $1.50, then one British pound can be purchased at that price.

The exchange rate for almost all world currencies is now determined by the market. The exchange rate of a currency rises or appreciates when the demand for it rises and/or the supply falls. This may happen because foreign buyers want to buy more of a nation's goods or because consumers within the country decide to buy fewer imports. It may also happen because the country reduces its money supply. Finally, the central banks of countries can manipulate their exchange rates slightly by buying and selling their own and other currencies (see also Part II: "The Federal Reserve").

The gold standard Before World War I, exchange rates for world currencies were fixed, artificially, by tying them to a certain amount of gold—$32, for example, might equal one ounce of gold. Central banks would then buy and sell gold in order to equalize supply and demand for the currencies and maintain the fixed exchange rates. For this reason, the central banks maintained enormous gold stockpiles, like the U.S. had at Fort Knox. People therefore referred to currencies as being "backed by gold." Long-term changes in

trading relationships and in the demand for various currencies eventually made the fixed exchange rates of the gold standard impossible to support. In 1944, the Bretton Woods agreement established the U.S. dollar as the world standard, but the U.S. still backed its dollars with gold and used gold to settle its debts. After 1973, the U.S. abandoned that role, and most of the world's exchange rates were set by the market.

Balance of payments The balance of payments account is the list of transactions between a country and the rest of the world. This account has three parts: *the current account:* a record of exports and imports of goods (e.g. oil, clothing) and services (e.g. tourism); *the capital account:* a record of exports and imports of assets such as bank loans and corporate stock purchases; and *the official-reserves account:* a record of a country's sales and purchases of official reserve assets at the central bank.

The Balance of Trade When a country imports goods from another country worth more than the value of its exports to it, there is said to be a deficit in the balance of trade between the countries. Changes in exchange rates tend to equalize the supply and demand for currencies and the balance of trade; in the above case, the exchange rate for the first country's currency should fall relative to the second country's, reducing imports by making them more expensive and encouraging exports by making them cheaper. But this equalization may take a long time to occur since consumers and producers in the two countries must change their behavior. And central banks may

U.S. International Trade Balance (millions of U.S. dollars) 1965–98

Year	Exports Goods[1]	Exports Services[2]	Imports Goods[1]	Imports Services[2]	Balance Goods[1]	Balance Services[2]	Total
1965	$ 26,461	$ 8,824	$ 21,510	$ 9,111	$ 4,951	$ -287	$ 4,664
1970	42,469	14,171	39,866	14,520	2,603	-349	2,254
1975	107,088	25,497	98,185	21,996	8,903	3,501	12,404
1979	184,439	39,692	212,007	36,689	-27,568	3,003	-24,565
1980	224,250	47,584	249,750	41,491	-25,500	6,093	-19,407
1985	215,915	73,155	338,088	72,862	-122,173	294	-121,880
1990	389,307	147,922	498,337	120,021	-109,030	27,901	-81,129
1995	575,845	219,802	749,574	145,964	-173,729	73,838	-99,891
1996	611,983	238,792	803,320	156,029	-191,337	82,763	-108,574
1997	679,715	258,828	876,366	166,907	-196,652	91,921	-104,731
1998	670,246	263,661	917,178	181,011	-246,932	82,650	-164,282

Note: The balance is equal to exports minus imports. 1. Adjusted, excluding military. 2. Includes some military goods.
Source: U.S. Bureau of Economic Analysis, Foreign Trade Division, 1999. www.bea.doc.gov.

want to slow the pace at which exchange rates adjust to slow the effects on trading sectors within their economies.

The balance of trade is an important issue because it indicates something about how a nation's economy is changing and, ultimately, about its competitiveness vis-à-vis other countries. A rising balance of trade deficit indicates that an economy is not able to sell its goods abroad and that consumers are favoring imports over domestically produced goods.

Over the last five years, as the economy has grown increasingly robust, the U.S. *trade deficit* has continued to widen, climbing from $19.4 billion in 1990 to $164 billion in 1998. The entire U.S. trade deficit is in the manufactured goods sector; the U.S. runs a small surplus in the services sector. U.S. exports of goods have not kept up with imports in part because the strength of the dollar makes American goods more expensive for foreign nations to buy, while people in the U.S. have more money to spend on cheaper imports.

▶ GLOBAL CAPITAL MOVEMENT

The current dynamic interaction among these very disparate economies—aided greatly by the technological revolution—has set in motion an unprecedented global movement of capital from the wealthiest nations to developing ones. Since holders of capital always seek greater returns on their investments they will put their money in economies that show potential growth; if they own or run corporations they will look for ways to reduce the costs of manufacturing, especially labor costs, so they realize a greater profit. By investing in foreign companies or by establishing their businesses in foreign nations the power of capital can rapidly transform the economies of poorer nations while rearranging the patterns of daily life for millions.

The increase in the total amount of private capital going overseas (*net private capital flows*) from the U.S., Japan, and the EU nations to developing countries has exploded from $43.9 billion in 1990 to $201.5 billion in 1995, and an estimated $299 billion in 1997. Over 80 percent of it came in two categories: foreign direct investment and portfolio investment.

Foreign Direct Investment (FDI) is simply

investment by private companies of one nation in the territory of another nation. The invest-

ment can be in an existing enterprise of the host nation or the building of new facilities for the investing foreign company (which would then be known as a *multinational enterprise*). The amount of money flowing from the wealthy nations to the developing ones in this way increased from $24.5 billion in 1990 to $155 billion in 1998. East Asian nations received almost half of the total ($61 billion). China alone received $45 billion.

According to the World Bank, foreign direct investment "provides an important channel for global integration" while bringing technological knowledge and equipment to the host countries, and infrastructure that has been sorely lacking.

Portfolio Investment is investing in the stocks and bonds of foreign nations. In 1990 only $5.5 billion was invested in the markets of developing nations, about 12 percent of total private capital flows. By 1996, $91.8 billion (38 percent) was so invested. In the U.S. alone the number of mutual funds investing in stocks and bonds of emerging nations grew from 3 in 1990 to over 70 in 1997. The Asian financial collapse of 1997-98 curtailed this growth quickly, as stock markets in Asia plunged by as much as 50 percent, followed by strong declines in Latin American markets.

▶ INTERNATIONAL TRADE

After rising by more than 10 percent in 1997, global trade fell back to 3.5 percent growth in 1998, according to the World Trade Organization. The continuing economic slump in Asia was responsible for most of the contraction. Exports of merchandise and commercial services amounted to $6.5 trillion in 1998, down about 2 percent from 1997 levels, but still up from the numbers recorded in 1996.

The U.S. is by far the world's leading importer and exporter, accounting for over 12 percent in each category. Trade has become a crucial factor in the U.S. economy. The U.S. Dept. of Commerce estimates that trade as a percentage of GDP has grown to 23 percent and should rise to about 30 percent by the year 2000, up from 11 percent in 1990. By then, over 16 million jobs in the U.S. will be based on exports.

International trade takes place because some nations have an advantage in producing certain kinds of products either because they have a comparative wealth of resources (capital, labor, natural resources) or more efficient production techniques. Even an economy with the most efficient technology has a limit on its resources, and rather than using them to produce all variety of products, it concentrates its resources on what it makes most efficiently. It then trades that good for other commodities, importing those that it produces least efficiently. As a result, all countries are better off because specialization results in the expansion of the total supply of goods, and the cost of acquiring them then falls.

Just which commodities a country will export and import depends on the relative prices of the factors used in production. A country like India has abundant labor and low wages. It therefore exports labor-intensive products such as garments. A country like Canada, which has abundant natural resources, specializes in agriculture and raw materials. Countries such as Canada and India then import goods for which the factors of production are in relatively short supply.

Of course, there are political reasons why countries do not completely specialize their production. No country, for example, wants to import all of its military equipment for fear that supplies would be cut off in the event of international conflict. Similarly, even inefficient producers, such as farmers in Japan, where land is scarce and expensive, may have political power that forces their governments to subsidize them.

Tariffs and Quotas

One way to protect a country's own producers, especially where they are inefficient compared with the international competition, is with import tariffs—taxes on goods that are produced abroad. Import tariffs raise the price of imports relative to domestic alternatives and discourage demand for the former. If one country is the sole importer or even the main importer of another's exports, it is possible that an import tariff will simply force the exporter to cut its selling price (in order to keep the price to consumers—including the tariff—from rising sharply and cutting off demand). In this case, the exporter pays virtually the whole cost of the tariff. If, on the other hand, the importer badly needs the import and there are few substitutes, raising the tariff simply raises the costs to one's own consumers. Critics of U.S. trade policy have pointed out that because Japan has become virtually the sole supplier of many consumer electronic products in the U.S., any tariffs against those products would simply raise their prices and fuel U.S. inflation.

Import quotas attempt to achieve a restriction on imports without the price rises associated with tariffs by setting direct limits on the number of items imported. So-called trade wars start when one country imposes a tariff on imports from a second country, and the latter responds with tariffs of its own against the first country. The arguments presented above about the benefits of trade have led to efforts to restrict the use of tariffs and maintain free trade, i.e. trade without any restrictions. Economists argue that unrestricted trade will always promote economic growth by forcing domestic prices to reflect world prices, thereby encouraging the efficient allocation of resources. Over the last 50 years, i.e. since the end of World War II, many of the leading nations have made a strong and continuous effort to lower or eliminate tariffs, first regionally, then around the world. The most successful regional organization has been the European Union, which has encouraged the formation of many other such alliances in all parts of the world.

Global trade has grown rapidly over the last decade, in large part because of the General Agreement on Tariffs and Trade (GATT) and its successor organization, the World Trade Organization (WTO).

GATT The General Agreement on Tariffs and Trade was first established in 1948. In an attempt to regulate the world's trade, the representatives of 23 leading nations agreed to find ways to lower tariffs, lower quotas, and to make free trade, i.e. trade without restrictions of any kind, their final goal. The United Nations provided headquarters for the group in Geneva, Switzerland. Over a period of almost 50 years the most important trading nations met regularly to discuss specific trade matters and to continue to remove restrictions from trade. Each series of negotiations called "rounds" lasted several years. By 1975 tariffs on manufactured goods had been reduced from 40 percent to 10 percent and world trade more than tripled. By the 1980s, however, the nature of world trade had changed. In 1986 the so-called Uruguay Round of GATT (now with 92 nations represented) addressed these and other issues over a period of eight years. The results—lowering of tariffs of all kind, banning quotas, and protecting copyrights and patents—have been projected to add $500 billion annually to the global economy; the EU nations were projected to receive $164 billion of this total, the U.S. $122 billion, Japan $275 billion. Nations at the next level of development including the former Communist-ruled ones in Eastern Europe should realize $116 billion.

World Trade Organization Potentially the most important accomplishment of the 1994 GATT Agreement, the World Trade Organization (WTO), established a permanent institution with real power to oversee trade agreements, enforce trade rules, and settle disputes. When it was approved by the U.S. Congress (Jan. 1, 1995), the organization became a reality, with 110 members. In 1997, there were 129 nations with China the only major economic power not included. The basic principles of the WTO, derived from the GATT negotiations, are the encouragement of fair competition and increased access to markets as well as the development of trade without discrimination (MFN, "most favored nation" status, i.e. no nation will be given preferential trading terms). **HQ:** Centre William Rappard, 154 rue de Lausanne, CH-1211 Geneva 21, Switzerland. **Internet Address: www.wto.org Membership:** (139) Algeria, Angola, Antigua and Barbuda, Argentina, Australia, Austria, Bahrain, Bangladesh, Barbados, Belgium, Belize, Benin, Bolivia, Botswana, Brazil, Brunei, Bulgaria, Burkina Faso, Burma, Burundi, Cameroon, Canada, Central African Republic, Chad, Chile, Colombia, Congo, Congo Republic Costa Rica, Cote d'Ivoire, Cuba, Cyprus, Czech Republic, Denmark, Djibouti, Dominica, Dominican Republic, Ecuador, Egypt, El Salvador, Equatorial Guinea, Eritrea, Ethiopia, EU, Fiji, Finland, France, Gabon, The Gambia, Germany, Ghana, Greece, Grenada, Guatemala, Guinea, Guinea-Bissau, Guyana, Haiti, Honduras, Hong Kong, Hungary, Iceland, India, Indonesia, Ireland, Israel, Italy, Jamaica, Japan, Kenya, South Korea, Kuwait, Lesotho, Libya, Liechtenstein, Luxembourg, Macau, Madagascar, Malawi, Malaysia, Maldives, Mali, Malta, Mauritania, Mauritius, Mexico, Mongolia, Morocco, Mozambique, Namibia, Netherlands, New Zealand, Nicaragua, Niger, Nigeria, Norway, Pakistan, Papua New Guinea, Paraguay,

Peru, Philippines, Poland, Portugal, Qatar, Roma-
nia, Rwanda, Saint Kitts and Nevis, Saint Lucia,
Saint Vincent and the Grenadines, São Tome and
Principe, Senegal, Seychelles, Sierra Leone, Singa-
pore, Slovakia, Slovenia, Solomon Islands, South
Africa, Spain, Sri Lanka, Sudan, Suriname, Swazi-
land, Sweden, Switzerland, Tanzania, Thailand,
Togo, Tonga, Trinidad and Tobago, Tunisia,
Turkey, Uganda, United Arab Emirates, United
Kingdom, United States, Uruguay, Venezuela,
Zambia, Zimbabwe. **Observers:** (5) Azerbaijan,
Laos, Somalia, Tajikistan, Turkmenistan. **Appli-
cants:** (31, as of 1998) Albania, Armenia, The Ba-
hamas, Belarus, Cambodia, Cape Verde, China,
Comoros, Croatia, Estonia, Georgia, Jordan, Kaza-
khstan, Kiribati, Kyrgyzstan, Latvia, Lithuania,
The Former Yugoslav Republic of Macedonia,
Moldova, Nepal, Oman, Panama, Russia, Saudi
Arabia, Tuvalu, Ukraine, Uzbekistan, Vanuatu,
Vietnam, Yemen, Taiwan.

▶ EUROPEAN UNION

In 1997, the 40th year since its founding, the European Union appeared successful beyond the
dreams of its founders: the world's largest economic superpower, a gigantic market of over 370
million people in 15 nations with ever more countries aspiring to join. Yet, at the same time, it faced
two daunting major projects: the introduction of a
common currency and the inclusion of many of the
countries of post-Communist east-central Europe.

Many people in government have expressed
great caution, if not skepticism, about both ideas.
The very notion of replacing the traditional
drachma, escudo, franc, guilder, krone, lire, mark,
peseta, pound, and schilling with a new single currency (the "euro") has aroused emotional opposition; and more serious difficulties surround the
schedule of its introduction, agreed to in the 1991
Maastricht Treaty. And while enthusiasm for
membership seems high in east-central Europe,
the task of integrating their relatively backward
economies with those of the highly developed
West still appears almost Herculean.

Origins   Out of the wreckage of World War II,
with generous American Marshall Plan aid after
1948, western Europe commenced reconstruction; by 1954, several "economic miracles" occurred. Yet without economic integration, the
recoveries of the separate nations involved dupli-
cations, inefficiencies, diminished competition,
and the threats of local gluts and shortages. A
small sign of what might be achieved was
Benelux, the customs union between Belgium,
the Netherlands, and Luxembourg, constructed
even before war's end in 1944 and a going concern
by 1948 despite the very unequal status of the
three economies.

On May 9, 1950, France's foreign minister,
Robert Schuman proposed that German and
French coal and steel production (the sinews of
war) be placed under a supra-national, not intergovernmental, "high authority"; the West German
chancellor, Konrad Adenauer, responded positively that very evening. By May 1952, ratification
of the six-nation European Coal and Steel Community was complete, with Italy and the Benelux
countries joining the French and Germans. The
dramatic successes of the ECSC led the six toward
broader integration, with negotiations culminating in the March 1957 Treaties of Rome which established the European Economic Community
(EEC) and the European Atomic Energy Commission (Euratom).

The EEC was designed to reduce and eventually
abolish all tariffs among the six; to establish a single external tariff for the Community; and to foster the free movement of not only goods but of
labor and capital as well. Euratom was intended
for the common peaceful development of nuclear
power, though common action proved subsequently difficult to agree on. In 1958 the United
Kingdom, which had refused to join the original
negotiations, proposed that the EEC be expanded
into an Atlantic free-trade area, but France, under
her new president Charles de Gaulle, exercised
the veto. The rebuff led Britain with Portugal, Austria, Switzerland and the Scandinavian kingdoms
to form in 1959 the European Free Trade Association. The EFTA's successes were real but no match
for the burgeoning EEC. So in 1961 Britain sought
EEC membership. But de Gaulle, fearing American influence and objecting to the special terms
that Britain sought for Commonwealth countries,
again exercised the veto.

At the same time, de Gaulle was pushing for
agricultural integration to match the EEC's industrial unity: the huge German market beckoned for
France's chronic farm surpluses, yet Germany
hesitated to sacrifice her own farmers in return for
cheaper food. In fact, a serious crisis impended
since each of the Six had its own system of protectionist duties, farm subsidies, and crop controls. But the Dutch ("Mansholt") proposals met
with relatively easy and rapid agreement. The
Common Agricultural Policy of 1962 eventually
established a highly bureaucratized, centrally financed common market with managed prices,
common duties upon imports, and subsidies for
exports.

The European Community (EC)   With agri-
cultural integration, the stage was set for the Brus-
sels treaty of 1965 (often called the "The Second
Treaty of Rome") which founded the European
Community. The earlier three communities
(ECSC, EEC and Euratom) were merged into one
and were provided with a four-part structure of
Commission, Council, Parliament, and Court.

It was this "refounded" EC that the United Kingdom was at last permitted to join in 1973 (after another Gaullist veto in 1967). As in its earlier attempts,
it was accompanied by Ireland, Denmark and
Norway (though Norwegian voters subsequently
rejected admission in a referendum). The Nine
subsequently became the Twelve with the admission of Greece (1981), Spain, and Portugal (1986).

Twenty years after the Brussels Treaty, with the
accession of Jacques Delors as president of the
European Commission, the EC received new impetus toward what the Treaty of Rome had envisioned: a single market free of all barriers to the
free movement of goods, services, capital, and labor. The first result was the Single European Act of
1987, an unwieldy compendium of almost 300
rules and directives to bring about by 1992 a "Europe without frontiers." Even a decade later, its full
meaning remains unclear, although both families
and giant corporations have been able to hunt for
bargains across national borders, tax and interest
rates have been leveled, and trans-national regional ties have developed. The abolition of capital controls in 1990 has proven decisive in the
movement toward monetary union, the second
result of the Delors presidency (and of the strong
support given by Helmut Kohl's Germany).

The European Union (EU)   In December
1991, the EC approved its third foundational treaty,

The European Union

Year admitted	Member countries
1957	Belgium, France, Germany, Italy, Luxembourg, Netherlands
1973	Denmark, Ireland, United Kingdom
1981	Greece
1986	Portugal, Spain
1995	Austria, Finland, Sweden
Current Applicants	Bulgaria, Cyprus, Czech Republic, Estonia, Hungary, Latvia, Lithuania, Poland, Romania, Slovakia, Slovenia

the Treaty of Maastricht. Its three "pillars" were: monetary union, common foreign and security policies, and cooperation in justice and "home affairs." The latter two "pillars" are intergovernmental, not supranational affairs, and have not been dealt with since 1991, as the EU's clumsy responses to the Bosnian and Albanian crises attest.

Following the simple idea that a single market requires a single currency, the Maastricht Treaty established a three-stage (1991, 1994, 1997) creation of the *European Monetary Union* (EMU). During the first two stages, the EU members were to converge according to five criteria: inflation rates, interest rates, currency exchange, rate stability (variation within 2.25 percent), budget deficits (less than 3 percent of GDP), and public indebtedness (a debt-to-GDP ratio of less than 60 percent). During the second stage would occur the transition from central bank financing of government spending to creation of the European Central Bank. With the third stage, the European Central Bank would propose and carry out the EU's monetary policies and the "euro" would circulate as "bank money"—all preparatory to the actual introduction of the monetary union on September 1, 1999.

A tone of unreality attended attempts to establish the EMU. When Danish voters rejected Maastricht in a June 1992 referendum (the treaty taking force only with unanimous approval of the Twelve), the EU, at the time still called the EC, permitted Denmark a sort of *à la carte* membership: Denmark could ratify while opting out of the single currency (and other treaty matters); Danish voters in May 1993 thereupon reversed themselves and approved the treaty. German ratification in November of that year brought the treaty into effect. But between those two votes, the exchange rate variation was altered from 2.25 percent to 15 percent lest the French withdraw from the pact.

It was this oddly flexible EU that Austria, Finland, and Sweden joined on January 1, 1995. The Norwegian government had sought membership and been approved, but Norwegian voters, as they had in 1973, said no. Since the Twelve became the Fifteen, little has caught the attention of EU members beyond the "euro." The five criteria, especially the two "fiscal position" rules about deficits and debt, drove every government toward cuts in social spending (in part leading to the fall of the Juppe government in France) and led even Kohl's Germany, strongest and most unyielding backer of the "euro," to attempt financial trickery like its June 1997 proposed revaluation of its gold reserves.

The European Monetary Union   The EMU
had a strong domestic political impact in the member states. The European Commission forecast, April 23, 1997, of 1997 member deficits, claimed that only Italy and Greece would top the permitted 3 percent; but the very same day, the I.M.F. predicted that four others would as well:

Spain, Britain, France, and (embarrassingly) Germany.

What permitted the EU finance ministers to insist (in September, 1997) that they would hold to the Maastricht timetable was an informal agreement to scrap four of the five criteria and retain only the 3 percent deficit-to-GDP ratio. On this score, Greece was the only applicant of 12 to fall short. In March 1998, the European Commission recommended, and in May the Brusssels summit formally endorsed, participation in the EMU by the following countries: Austria, Belgium, Finland, France, Germany, Ireland, Italy, Luxembourg, Netherlands, Portugal, and Spain. (Of the 11, only Finland, France, and Luxembourg could meet the 60 percent indebtedness-to-GDP limit; Belgium and Italy had ratios in excess of 120 percent.

In the other important matter, that of the EU's expansion eastward, the December 1997 Luxembourg summit extended formal invitations to six of 12 applicants: Cyprus, the Czech Republic, Estonia, Hungary, Poland, and Slovenia. Official negotiations with those countries began in March, 1998. Five other countries (known as the "second wave")—Bulgaria, Latvia, Lithuania, Romania, and Slovakia—were encouraged to continue to apply. The EU's explicit refusal to Turkey, which has been applying for admission since 1967, infuriated the Turks and thereby complicated the issue of the reunification of Cyprus, as well as Cyprus' own bid for admission to the EU.

On January 1, 1999, the EU introduced the euro. Initially well-received in world financial markets, the euro sagged over the next six months, losing almost 20 percent of its value against the dollar. One reason for the flop seems to have been the EU's decision to permit Italy's budget deficit to substantially exceed the target 2 percent of GDP; one member's excessive spending was dragging the whole currency down. A second reason may have been the insecurity engendered by the resignation (in March) of the entire 20-member European Commission, the EU's executive body, following a European Parliament report accusing the Commission of mismanagement and corruption. Italy's former Prime Minister Romano Prodi became the new president of the Commission. Prodi and the member nations were able to put together a new Commission by July—subject to Parliament's approval. By September, the euro was making a strong comeback against the dollar as many European economies began to drag themselves out of recession.

A third significant development of 1999, unrelated to the other two, was the decision of the Council of Foreign ministers, at their June 3 summit, to develop a common defense policy, and by implication a common armed force, distinct from, if not independent of, the NATO alliance.

Additional information about the European Union (in 10 languages) can be found at the EU Web server. The address is **http://europa.eu.int.**

Foreign Exchange Rates: Currency Units Per Dollar

Country/currency	1975	1985	1990	1995	1997	1998	1999[1]
Australia/dollar	0.77	1.43	1.28	1.35	1.35	1.59	1.52
Austria/schilling	17.44	20.68	11.33	10.08	12.21	12.38	N.A.
Belgium/franc	36.80	59.34	33.42	29.47	35.81	36.31	N.A.
Canada/dollar	1.02	1.37	1.17	1.37	1.38	1.48	1.47
China/yuan	N.A.	2.94	4.79	8.37	8.32	8.30	8.28
Denmark/krone	5.75	10.60	6.19	5.60	6.61	6.70	7.16
European Community/ecu	N.A.	N.A.	N.A.	0.78	0.90	0.89	0.96
Finland/markka	3.67	6.20	3.83	4.38	5.20	5.35	N.A.
France/franc	4.29	8.98	5.45	4.99	5.84	5.90	N.A.
Germany/deutsche mark	2.46	2.94	1.62	1.43	1.73	1.76	N.A.
Greece/drachma	32.30	138.41	158.59	231.68	273.28	295.70	312.49
Hong Kong/dollar	4.94	7.79	7.79	7.74	7.74	7.75	7.76
India/rupee	8.40	12.33	17.49	32.412	36.37	41.36	43.21
Ireland/pound	0.45	0.94	0.60	0.62	0.67	1.42	N.A.
Italy/lira	653.10	1,908.88	1,198.27	1,629.45	1,703.81	1,736.85	N.A.
Japan/yen	296.79	238.47	145.00	93.96	121.06	130.99	120.72
Malaysia/ringgit	2.40	2.48	2.70	2.51	2.82	3.93	3.80
Mexico/peso	12.64	256.90	2,813.00	6.45	7.92	9.15	9.52
Netherlands/guilder	2.53	3.32	1.82	1.60	1.95	1.98	N.A.
New Zealand/dollar	0.82	2.01	1.68	1.52	1.52	1.85	1.82
Norway/krone	5.23	8.59	6.26	6.34	7.09	7.55	7.87
Portugal/escudo	25.51	172.07	142.70	149.88	175.44	180.25	N.A.
Singapore/dollar	2.37	2.20	1.81	1.42	1.49	1.67	1.71
South Africa/rand	0.74	2.23	2.59	3.63	4.61	5.54	6.09
South Korea/won	484.00	872.45	710.64	772.69	950.77	1,400.40	1,168.91
Spain/peseta	57.43	170.09	101.96	124.64	146.53	149.41	N.A.
Sri Lanka/rupee	6.98	27.19	40.08	51.05	59.03	65.00	71.21
Sweden/krona	4.15	8.60	5.92	7.14	7.64	7.95	8.51
Switzerland/franc	2.58	2.46	1.39	1.18	1.45	1.45	1.54
Taiwan/dollar	38.00	39.89	26.92	26.50	28.78	33.55	32.52
United Kingdom/pound	0.45	0.77	0.56	0.64	0.61	0.60	0.62

Note: Averages of certified noon buying rates in New York for cable transfers. 1. Figures are for June, 1999.
Source: *Federal Reserve Bulletin*, monthly.

Structure of the EU

The Commission is composed of 20 commissioners appointed by member governments. The five largest countries, France, Germany, Italy, Spain, and the United Kingdom, appoint two commissioners each. The remaining five countries each appoint one commissioner. The treaties direct Commission members to act independently of their governments and represent the entire community's interests. The Commission supervises implementation of EU treaties, initiates and implements EU policy, transacts negotiations with non-member states, and manages EU funds. The Commission can be forced to resign by two-thirds majority vote of the European Parliament. The Commission headquarters are in Brussels. The president, who is appointed by the Council, serves a two-year term.

The Council of Ministers consists of the foreign ministers of the 15 member governments and is the chief decision-making body of the EU, passing legislation on the major issues affecting all members. Each country takes the presidency for six months, and votes are by majority, though each country's vote is weighted differently. Germany, France, Italy, and the United Kingdom each have 10 votes; Spain has 8; Belgium, Greece, the Netherlands and Portugal have five votes; Austria and Sweden have four votes; Ireland, Denmark, and Finland have three votes; and Luxembourg has two. The Council meets in Brussels.

The European Parliament The 626 deputies of the European Parliament are elected directly by the citizens of the individual countries. The Parliament oversees the EU budget and passes on Commission proposals to the Council of Ministers. The Parliament also passes on new applications to the EU. Deputies are elected to five-year terms and meet monthly in Strasbourg.

The Court of Justice is the court of last resort for the EU, interpreting EU treaties and legislation and hearing complaints about member-government violations. The Court also resolves differences between EU legislation and national laws. The l3 justices are appointed by the member governments and serve six-year terms.

The Economic and Social Committee is composed of 222 members representing labor, farmers, and consumer groups. Through consultation, the Committee presents its views to the Council of Ministers and the EU Commission.

▶ MAJOR REGIONAL TRADING GROUPS

Africa
Common Market for Eastern and Southern Africa (COMESA) HQ: Lotti Hous, Cairo Rd. Box 30051, 10101 Lusaka, Zambia. **Founded:** 1994. **Purpose:** To create an environment for foreign and domestic investment by developing rational production and marketing structures. Help to maintain peace and stability among member states. **Members:** (20) Angola, Burundi, Comoros, Democratic Republic of the Congo, Eritrea, Ethiopia, Kenya, Lesotho, Madagascar, Malawi, Mauritius, Mozambique, Namibia, Rwanda, Sudan, Swaziland, Tanzania, Uganda, Zambia, Zimbabwe.

Economic Community of West African States (ECOWAS) HQ: 6 King George V Rd.

The *Fortune* 100 World's Largest Industrial Corporations, 1998

1998 Rank	Company, Country (1997 rank)	Sales (millions)	1998 Rank	Company, Country (1997 rank)	Sales (millions)
1.	General Motors, U.S. (1)	$161,315.0	51.	Fujitsu, Japan (52)	41,017.8
2.	DaimlerChrysler, Germany (17)	154,615.0	52.	Tokyo Electric Power, Japan (46)	39,808.4
3.	Ford Motor Company, U.S. (2)	144,416.0	53.	Deutsche Telekom, Germany (56)	39,710.5
4.	Wal-Mart Stores, U.S. (8)	139,208.0	54.	Sumitomo Life Insurance, Japan (48)	39,535.4
5.	Mitsui, Japan (3)	109,372.9	55.	E.I. Du Pont De Nemours, U.S. (49)	39,130.0
6.	Itochu, Japan (6)	108,749.1	56.	Zurich Financial Services, Switzerland (116)	39,115.0
7.	Mitsubishi, Japan (4)	107,184.4	57.	Philips Electronics, Netherlands (55)	38,455.6
8.	Exxon, U.S. (7)	100,697.0	58.	CGU, U.K. (189)	37,588.5
9.	General Electric, U.S. (12)	100,469.0	59.	Peugeot, France (78)	37,539.8
10.	Toyota Motor, Japan (11)	99,740.1	60.	NEC, Japan (54)	37,234.6
11.	Royal Dutch/Shell Group, Netherlands (5)	93,692.0	61.	Procter & Gamble, U.S. (64)	37,154.0
12.	Marubeni, Japan (9)	93,568.6	62.	Électricité de France, France[1](62)	36,672.9
13.	Sumitomo, Japan (10)	89,020.7	63.	RWE Group, Germany (53)	36,603.1
14.	International Business Machines, U.S. (14)	81,667.0	64.	TIAA-CREF, U.S. (94)	35,889.1
15.	AXA, France (16)	78,729.3	65.	BMW, Germany (69)	35,886.7
16.	Citigroup, U.S. (68)	76,431.0	66.	Elf Aquitaine, France (44)	35,864.0
17.	Volkswagen, Germany (22)	76,306.6	67.	Merrill Lynch & Co., Inc., U.S. (81)	35,853.0
18.	Nippon Telegraph & Telephone, Japan (15)	76,118.7	68.	Munich Re Group, Germany (131)	35,464.5
19.	BP Amoco, Britain (20)	68,304.0	69.	Vivendi, France (100)	35,292.3
20.	Nissho Iwai, Japan (13)	67,741.7	70.	Suez Lyonnaise des Eaux, France (75)	34,873.5
21.	Nippon Life Insurance, Japan (19)	66,299.6	71.	Prudential Insurance, U.S. (60)	34,427.0
22.	Siemens, Germany (24)	66,037.8	72.	ABN-AMRO Holding, Netherlands (97)	34,235.0
23.	Allianz Holding, Germany (28)	64,874.7	73.	Sinopec, China (N.A.)	34,025.2
24.	Hitachi, Japan (21)	62,409.9	74.	Prudential, U.K. (104)	33,676.8
25.	U.S. Postal Service[1] (27)	60,072.0	75.	KMart, U.S. (76)	33,674.0
26.	Matsushita Electric Industrial, Japan (23)	59,771.4	76.	American International Group, U.S. (88)	33,296.0
27.	Philip Morris, U.S. (29)	57,813.0	77.	Crédit Agricole, France (70)	33,022.4
28.	ING Group, Netherlands (57)	56,468.7	78.	ENI[1], Italy (61)	32,389.3
29.	Boeing, U.S. (39)	56,154.0	79.	Chase Manhattan Corp., U.S. (90)	32,379.0
30.	AT&T, U.S. (32)	53,588.0	80.	HypoVereinsbank, Germany (227)	31,816.2
31.	Sony, Japan (30)	53,156.7	81.	Texaco, U.S. (40)	31,707.0
32.	Metro Holding, Switzerland (73)	52,126.4	82.	Bell Atlantic Corporation, U.S.(91)	31,565.9
33.	Nissan Motor, Japan (31)	51,477.7	83.	Fannie Mae, U.S. (106)	31,498.8
34.	Fiat, Italy (33)	50,998.9	84.	Fortis, U.S. (143)	31,325.3
35.	Bank of America (N.A.)	50,777.0	85.	Enron, U.S. (179)	31,260.0
36.	Nestlé, Switzerland (36)	49,504.1	86.	Bayer, Germany (80)	31,197.2
37.	Credit Suisse Group, Switzerland (37)	49,143.3	87.	Compaq Computer, U.S. (132)	31,169.0
			88.	Morgan Stanley Dean Witter, U.S. (108)	31,131.0
38.	Honda Motor, Japan (34)	48,747.7	89.	Dayton Hudson, U.S. (107)	30,951.0
39.	Assicurazioni Generali, Italy (86)	48,478.1	90.	Tomen Corporation, Japan (45)	30,934.9
40.	Mobil, U.S. (26)	47,678.0	91.	Bank of Tokyo-Mitsubishi, Japan (67)	30,928.8
41.	Hewlett-Packard, U.S. (47)	47,061.0	92.	ABB Asea Brown Boveri, Switzerland (83)	30,872.0
42.	Deutsche Bank, Germany (51)	45,165.0	93.	BASF, Germany (77)	30,731.6
43.	Unilever, Britain/Netherlands (35)	44,908.0	94.	J.C. Penney Company, Inc., U.S. (87)	30,678.0
44.	State Farm Group, U.S. (42)	44,620.9	95.	Carrefour, France (96)	30,479.0
45.	Dai-Ichi Mutual Life Insurance, Japan (38)	44,485.6	96.	Home Depot, U.S. (136)	30,219.0
46.	Veba Group, Germany (43)	43,407.5	97.	Lucent Technologies, U.S. (117)	30,147.0
47.	HSBC Holdings, U.K. (59)	43,338.3	98.	Societe Generale, France (99)	29,762.1
48.	Toshiba, Japan (41)	41,470.9	99.	Mitsubishi Electric, Japan (85)	29,682.3
49.	Renault[1], France (65)	41,353.3	100.	Motorola, Inc., U.S. (93)	29,398.0
50.	Sears Roebuck, U.S. (50)	41,322.0			

Note: 1. Government-owned.   **Source:** *Fortune,* July, 1999. Reprinted by permission.

PMB 12745, Lagos, Nigeria. **Founded:** 1975. **Purpose:** to promote the regional economic cooperation; in recent years it has also created joint military force to deal with the civil war in Liberia. **Members:** (16) Benin, Burkina Faso, Cape Verde, The Gambia, Ghana, Guinea, Guinea-Bissau, Ivory Coast, Liberia, Mali, Mauritania, Niger, Nigeria, Senegal, Sierra Leone, Togo.

Southern African Development Community (SADC) HQ:

Private Bag 0095, Gaborone, Botswana. **Founded:** 1992. **Purpose:** To promote regional economic development and integration. **Members:** (12) Angola, Botswana, Lesotho, Malawi, Mauritius, Mozambique, Namibia, South Africa, Swaziland, Tanzania, Zambia, Zimbabwe.

Asia
Asia Pacific Economic Cooperation (APEC)
HQ: 438 Alexandra Rd., Alexandra Point Building, Singapore 119958, Singapore. **Founded:** 1989. **Purpose:** an alliance of nations from east and west seeking to promote trade and investment in the Pacific Basin. **Members:** (19) Australia, Brunei,

Canada, Indonesia, Chile, China, Hong Kong, Japan, Malaysia, Mexico, New Guinea, New Zealand, Philippines, Singapore, South Korea, Taiwan, Thailand, Vietnam.

Association of South East Asian Nations (ASEAN) HQ:
P.O. Box 2072, 70 A Jalan Sisingamangaraja, Jakarta, Indonesia. **Founded:** 1967. **Purpose:** to promote political and economic cooperation among states in region by coordinating policies in trade, transportation, communications, agriculture, science, finance, and culture. **Members:** (9) Brunei, Indonesia, Laos, Malaysia, Myanmar, Philippines, Singapore, Thailand, Vietnam.

Latin America
Mercado Comun del Cono Sur (MERCOSUR) HQ:
Rincon 575 P12, 11000 Montivideo, Uruguay. **Founded:** 1991 (established 1995). **Purpose:** to establish a free trade area and a customs union, and to negotiate free trade agreements with other Latin American countries that will eventually produce a Latin American Free Trade Area (LAFTA). **Members:** (4) Argentina, Brazil, Paraguay, Uruguay. **Associate Member:** Chile

Central American Common Market (CACM) HQ:
c/o SIECA, Apart Postal 1237, 4a Avenida 10-25, Zona 14, Guatemala 01901, Guatemala. **Founded:** 1961. **Purpose:** to promote the establishment of a Central American Common Market and to liberalize trade with other nations including the U.S. **Members:** Costa Rica, El Salvador, Guatemala, Honduras, Nicaragua.

Caribbean Community and Common Market (CARICOM) HQ:
Bank of Guyana Building, P.O. Box 10827, 1 Avenue of the Republic, Georgetown, Guyana. **Founded:** 1973. **Purpose:** to create greater unity in Caribbean, and to formulate policies and cooperation in services such as education, health, labor matters, and foreign policy. **Members:** (14) Antigua and Barbuda, Bahamas, Barbados, Belize, Dominica, Granada, Guyana, Jamaica, Montserrat, Saint Kitts and Nevis, Saint Lucia, Saint Vincent and the Grenadines, Suriname, Trinidad and Tobago.

North America
North American Free Trade Agreement (NAFTA) Founded:
1994. **Purpose:** to remove all barriers to trade among the three nations. **Members:** (3) Canada, Mexico, U.S.

World's 50 Largest Banks, by Assets, 1998

In August, 1999, three of Japan's largest banks announced a megamerger that will create the world's largest bank. The alliance among Dai-ichi Kangyo Bank, Fuji Bank, and Industrial Bank of Japan, respectively the world's 12th, 20th, and 23rd largest banks, will result in a single institution with more than $1.3 trillion in assets, or nearly twice as much as the next largest bank. Yet bankers and analysts around the world said the merger would pose little competitive threat to U.S. or European banking interests, primarily because the three banks had been losing money in Japan and were reducing, not expanding, their international presence.

Rank, Company, Country	Assets (millions)
1. Deutsche Bank AG, Frankfurt, Germany	$735,171.0
2. UBS Group, Zurich, Switzerland	687,379.7
3. Citigroup, New York	668,641.0
4. Bank of America Corp., Charlotte, N.C.	617,679.0
5. Bank of Tokyo-Mitsubishi Ltd., Tokyo, Japan	579,791.7
6. HypoVereinsbank AG, Munich, Germany	540,851.1
7. ABN-AMRO Bank NV, Amsterdam, Netherlands	507,216.7
8. HSBC Holdings PLC, London, United Kingdom	482,920.9
9. Credit Suisse Group, Zurich, Switzerland	475,017.8
10. ING Group, Amsterdam, Netherlands	463,597.6
11. Credit Agricole Group, Paris, France	457,037.0
12. Dai-ichi Kangyo Bank Ltd., Tokyo, Japan	455,900.7
13. Societe Generale, Paris, France	450,224.8
14. Dresdner Bank AG, Frankfurt, Germany	429,027.3
15. Sumitomo Bank Ltd., Osaka, Japan	428,000.8
16. Sanwa Bank Ltd., Osaka, Japan	418,373.0
17. Westdeutsche Landesbank Girozentrale, Dusseldorf, Germany	415,954.0
18. Norinchukin Bank, Tokyo, Japan	407,624.0
19. Sakura Bank Ltd., Tokyo, Japan	392,098.9
20. Fuji Bank Ltd., Tokyo, Japan	385,252.8
21. Commerzbank AG, Frankfurt, Germany	382,935.6
22. Banque Nationale de Paris, France	381,316.5
23. Industrial Bank of Japan Ltd., Tokyo, Japan	370,394.0
24. Chase Manhattan Corp., New York	365,875.0
25. Barclays PLC, London, United Kingdom	365,128.3
26. Fortis Bank, Brussels, Belgium	$323,567.0
27. Paribas, Paris, France	309,364.0
28. NatWest Group, London, United Kingdom	309,266.7
29. Abbey National PLC, London, United Kingdom	295,608.6
30. Rabobank Group, Utrecht, Netherlands	293,141.5
31. Bayerische Landesbank Girozentrale, Munich, Germany	285,237.9
32. Lloyds TSB Group, London, United Kingdom	279,343.2
33. Tokai Bank Ltd., Nagoya, Japan	264,449.4
34. DG Bank, Frankfurt, Germany	261,722.1
35. Bank One Corp., Chicago	261,496.0
36. JP Morgan & Co. Inc., New York	261,067.0
37. Credit Lyonnais, Paris, France	245,199.4
38. Halifax PLC, Leeds, United Kingdom	240,395.7
39. Asahi Bank Ltd., Tokyo, Japan	237,851.9
40. First Union Corp., Charlotte, N.C.	237,363.0
41. Dexia Group, Brussels, Belgium	234,001.7
42. Bankgesellschaft Berlin AG, Berlin, Germany	221,558.3
43. Wells Fargo & Co., San Francisco	202,475.0
44. Instituto Bancario San Paolo IMI, Turin, Italy	185,403.0
45. Canadian Imperial Bank of Commerce, Toronto, Canada	183,043.9
46. Grupo Santander, Santander, Spain	182,014.9
47. Banca Intesa SPA Group, Milan, Italy	179,654.2
48. Royal Bank of Canada, Montreal, Canada	178,470.9
49. Norddeutsche Landesbank Girozentrale, Hanover, Germany	178,337.4
50. KBC Bank and Insurance, Brussels, Belgium	173,413.1

Note: Consolidated data, including affiliates in which ownership exceeds 50%, are used whenever possible.
Source: *American Banker,* August 5, 1999.

World Economic Indicators, 1997

Country	GNP (millions of U.S. dollars) 1997	GNP per capita (in U.S. dollars) 1997	Real growth rate 1980–91	Real growth rate 1990–97	Average inflation rate 1990–97	Agriculture's share in GDP 1970	Agriculture's share in GDP 1997	Net private capital flows (millions) 1997[1]	Foreign direct investment as percent of GDP 1997
Albania	$2,540	$760	—	2.2%	58.1%	—	63%	$47	2.0%
Algeria	43,927	1,500	-0.8%	-1.6	23.8	10%	11	-543	0.0
Angola	3,012	260	—	-10.0	1,091.4	45	9	-24	4.6
Antigua and Barbuda	489	7,380	3.8	1.8	2.6	—	4	—	5.0
Argentina	319,293	8,950	-1.5	4.2	12.2	13	7	19,835	2.0
Armenia	2,112	560	2.1	-10.7	482.8	N.A.	41	51	3.1
Aruba	—	(2)	N.A.	-0.6	4.5	N.A.	—	—	—
Australia	382,705	20,650	1.2	2.4	1.7	6	3	—	2.3
Austria	225,373	27,920	2.1	1.1	2.6	7	1	—	1.2
Azerbaijan	3,886	510	0.4	-16.0	447.8	N.A.	22	658	14.8
Bahamas	—	(2)	1.3	-2.0	2.9	—	—	—	2.3
Bahrain	—	(3)	-3.8	2.6	1.2	—	1	—	0.2
Bangladesh	44,090	360	1.9	3.3	3.6	55	24	118	0.3
Barbados	—	(3)	1.3	-0.9	0.8	11	N.A	78	0.7
Belarus	22,082	2,150	3.3	-5.6	561.4	N.A.	14	169	0.9
Belgium	272,583	26,730	2.1	1.3	2.6	4	1	—	—
Belize	614	2,670	2.5	0.3	3.7	—	23	10	2.6
Benin	2,227	380	-1.1	1.7	10.6	49	38	3	0.1
Bhutan	315	430	6.8	2.0	9.7	—	38	-2	0.0
Bolivia	7,564	970	-2.0	2.0	10.4	17	16	812	7.5
Botswana	5,070	3,310	5.8	1.3	10.2	33	3	95	2.0
Brazil	784,044	4,790	0.4	1.9	475.7	12	8	43,377	2.4
Brunei	—	—	—	-2.1	1.6	—	3	—	—
Bulgaria	9,750	1,170	1.7	-2.0	109.5	—	23	569	4.9
Burkina Faso	2,579	250	1.3	0.8	6.9	44	35	0	0.0
Burundi	924	140	1.4	-5.9	10.7	71	53	1	0.1
Cambodia	3,162	300	—	2.7	37.8	—	51	200	6.7
Cameroon	8,610	620	-0.9	-3.3	6.4	31	41	16	0.5
Canada	594,976	19,640	2.1	0.8	1.4	—	<6[4]	—	1.2
Cape Verde	436	1,090	2.2	1.0	5.3	—	9	14	3.1
Central African Republic	1,104	320	-1.5	-1.0	5.9	35	54	6	0.5
Chad	1,629	230	3.8	1.0	7.3	43	39	15	0.9
Chile	70,510	4,820	1.7	6.4	10.2	7	7	9,637	7.0
China	1,055,372	860	7.8	10.0	11.2	35	19	60,828	4.9
Colombia	87,125	2,180	1.2	2.6	22.4	25	11	10,151	6.2
Comoros	209	400	-1.0	-3.1	3.9	—	39	2	1.0
Congo, Dem. Republic	5,201	110	-0.2	-9.6	2,012.8	18	58	1	0.0
Congo, Rep.	1,827	670	-1.6	-2.9	8.9	16	10	9	0.4
Costa Rica	9,275	2,680	1.0	2.3	18.0	23	15	104	0.6
Croatia	19,343	4,060	N.A.	2.7	218.1	N.A.	12	2,397	2.8
Cyprus	—	(2)	4.9	2.6	4.2	—	<6[4]	—	1.4
Czech Republic[5]	53,952	5,240	0.4	-0.3	17.1	—	6-9[4]	1,818	2.5
Denmark	184,347	34,890	2.1	2.5	1.9	—	4	—	1.7
Djibouti	—	(6)	—	—	4.6	—	4	5	1.0
Dominica	225	3,040	4.7	0.7	3.7	—	20	20	8.2
Dominican Republic	14,148	1,750	-0.2	3.5	11.5	20	12	401	2.7
Ecuador	18,785	1,570	-0.3	0.9	33.3	24	12	829	2.9
Egypt	72,164	1,200	2.0	2.8	10.5	29	18	2,595	1.2
El Salvador	10,704	1,810	-0.3	3.5	9.8	28	13	61	0.1
Equatorial Guinea	444	1,060	3.4	12.1	14.7	—	23	20	4.1
Eritrea	852	230	—	2.9	12.7	—	9	0	0.0
Estonia	4,899	3,360	2.1	-2.8	92.2	N.A.	7	347	5.7
Ethiopia	6,507	110	-1.6	2.2	8.9	56	55	28	0.1
Fiji	2,007	2,460	0.0	0.4	3.5	29	18	1	0.6
Finland	127,398	24,790	2.5	0.9	1.8	—	4	—	1.8
France	1,541,630	26,300	1.8	1.0	1.8	—	2	—	1.7
Gabon	4,752	4,120	-4.2	-0.1	8.5	17	7	-105	-1.9
Gambia	407	340	-0.1	-0.6	4.7	33	30	12	2.9
Georgia	4,656	860	2.2	-14.9	1,033.2	N.A.	32	50	1.0
Germany[8]	2,320,985	28,280	2.2	0.7	2.5	3	1	—	0.0
Ghana	6,982	390	-0.3	1.4	29.2	47	36	203	1.9
Greece	122,430	11,640	1.2	1.0	12.2	18	11	—	0.9
Grenada	300	3,140	5.3	1.3	3.2	—	10	21	6.8
Guatemala	16,582	1,580	-1.8	1.5	12.2	—	24	166	0.5
Guinea	3,830	550	—	2.7	6.2	—	23	-23	0.0
Guinea-Bissau	264	230	1.3	1.0	45.3	47	54	2	0.8
Guyana	677	800	-4.2	12.9	26.7	19	>30[4]	85	11.5
Haiti	2,864	380	-2.4	-4.4	25.3	—	30	3	0.1
Honduras	4,426	740	-0.7	1.0	20.4	32	20	124	2.7
Hong Kong[9]	163,834	25,200	—	3.3	6.7	0	0	—	—
Hungary	45,760	4,510	0.7	0.2	22.8	18	6	2,605	4.5
Iceland	—	(2)	1.3	0.4	3.1	—	11	—	0.8

Country	GNP (millions of U.S. dollars) 1997	GNP per capita (in U.S. dollars) 1997	GNP per capita Real growth rate 1980-91	GNP per capita Real growth rate 1990-97	Average inflation rate 1990-97	Agriculture's share in GDP 1970	Agriculture's share in GDP 1997	Net private capital flows (millions) 1997[1]	Foreign direct investment as percent of GDP 1997
India	$357,391	$370	3.3%	4.3%	8.8%	47%	25%	$8,307	0.9%
Indonesia	221,533	1,110	3.9	5.9	8.6	45	16	10,863	2.2
Iran	108,614	1,780	-1.1	1.9	32.5	19	25	-303	0.0
Iraq	—	(6)	—	—	—	17	—	—	—
Ireland	65,137	17,790	2.2	5.6	1.8	—	6	—	3.6
Israel	94,402	16,180	1.8	2.6	11.4	—	—	—	2.8
Italy	1,160,444	20,170	2.1	1.0	4.6	8	3	—	0.3
Ivory Coast	10,152	710	-3.4	0.9	9.3	40	27	-91	3.2
Jamaica	3,956	1,550	-0.3	0.8	32.8	7	8	377	3.3
Japan	4,812,103	38,160	3.7	1.4	0.5	6	2	—	0.1
Jordan	6,755	1,520	-3.3	2.8	3.3	10	3	61	0.3
Kazakhstan	21,317	1,350	0.9	-7.4	440.4	N.A.	12	2,158	6.0
Kenya	9,654	340	0.3	-0.3	16.0	33	29	-87	0.2
Kiribati	76	910	0.5	-0.6	7.0	—	<6[4]	—	1.8
Korea, South	485,209	10,550	8.8	6.0	5.3	26	6	13,069	0.6
Kuwait	—	(2)	—	17.5	—	0	0	—	0.1
Kyrgyzstan	2,211	480	2.1	-9.7	199.1	N.A.	45	50	2.8
Laos	1,924	400	1.2	3.9	12.2	—	52	90	5.1
Latvia	5,995	2,430	2.8	-7.3	87.7	N.A.	7	559	9.4
Lebanon	13,900	3,350	—	4.9	27.7	9	12	1,070	1.0
Lesotho	1,368	680	0.0	2.5	8.0	35	11	42	3.1
Liberia	—	(7)	—	—	—	24	—	15	—
Libya	—	(3)	—	—	—	2	—	—	—
Lithuania	8,360	2,260	2.5	-7.1	140.3	N.A.	13	637	3.7
Luxembourg	—	(7)	3.8	0.2	2.3	4	1	—	—
Macedonia, FYR	2,187	1,100	N.A.	-2.1	60.5	N.A.	12	8	0.7
Madagascar	3,575	250	-2.4	-1.6	23.6	30	32	13	0.4
Malawi	2,129	210	0.1	0.8	33.8	44	36	1	0.1
Malaysia	98,195	4,530	2.9	5.8	4.5	29	12	9,312	5.2
Maldives	301	1,180	6.7	4.3	9.1	—	—	15	2.9
Mali	2,656	260	0.1	0.3	10.0	61	49	15	0.6
Malta	3,498	9,330	3.8	3.0	3.6	7	N.A.	221	3.9
Marshall Islands	97	1,610	—	—	7.0	N.A.	N.A.	—	—
Mauritania	1,093	440	-1.8	1.5	6.0	29	25	2	0.3
Mauritius	4,444	3,870	6.1	3.7	6.4	16	9	771	1.2
Mexico	348,627	3,700	-0.5	0.2	19.3	12	5	20,533	3.1
Micronesia	213	1,920	N.A.	-1.8	3.4	N.A.	—	—	—
Moldova	1,974	460	1.8	-10.8	222.5	N.A.	31	257	3.2
Mongolia	998	390	—	-1.4	89.3	—	37	16	0.8
Morocco	34,380	1,260	1.6	0.2	3.8	20	15	1,303	3.6
Mozambique	2,405	140	-3.6	2.6	45.9	—	31	37	1.3
Myanmar	—	—	—	—	24.2	38	59	180	—
Namibia	3,428	2,110	-1.5	1.1	9.4	—	11	—	4.3
Nepal	4,863	220	2.1	2.2	9.7	67	41	12	0.5
Netherlands	403,057	25,830	1.5	1.9	2.0	6	3	—	2.4
New Zealand	59,539	15,830	0.2	1.2	1.7	—	10-19[4]	—	1.4
Nicaragua	1,907	410	-4.6	1.6	67.7	25	34	157	4.9
Niger	1,962	200	-4.1	-1.9	7.2	65	38	-12	0.1
Nigeria	33,393	280	-1.7	0.7	42.6	40	33	1,285	3.9
Norway	158,973	36,100	2.2	3.8	1.9	6	2	—	2.3
Oman	—	(3)	4.5	-0.4	-2.9	16	<6[4]	118	0.4
Pakistan	64,638	500	3.2	2.0	11.3	37	25	2,097	1.2
Panama	8,373	3,080	-1.8	3.0	2.8	15	8	1,443	2.9
Papua New Guinea	4,185	930	-0.7	2.5	6.7	37	28	143	4.3
Paraguay	10,183	2,000	-0.8	0.0	16.1	32	23	273	2.5
Peru	63,672	2,610	-2.6	4.6	40.1	19	7	3,094	3.2
Philippines	88,372	1,200	-1.2	1.6	8.6	30	19	4,164	1.5
Poland	138,909	3,590	0.5	4.2	29.5	—	6	6,787	3.6
Portugal	109,472	11,010	2.7	2.0	6.3	—	4	—	1.7
Qatar	—	(2)	-10.9	-5.3	—	—	—	—	—
Romania	31,787	1,410	-0.1	-0.1	124.0	—	20	2,274	3.5
Russian Federation	394,861	2,680	1.3	-7.9	298.8	N.A.	8	12,453	1.4
Rwanda	1,680	210	-2.6	-5.7	19.3	62	37	1	0.1
Samoa	199	1,140	5.1	0.7	2.9	—	<6[4]	4	2.1
Saint Kitts and Nevis	256	6,260	5.8	4.0	4.0	—	6	24	6.9
Saint Lucia	558	3,510	2.9	2.8	2.9	—	11	45	6.5
Saint Vincent and the Grenadines	272	2,420	5.2	1.8	3.0	—	13	40	6.9
São Tomé and Principe	40	290	-3.5	-1.7	56.9	37	23	0	0.0
Saudi Arabia	143,430	7,150	-4.2	-2.5	1.8	6	6	—	-0.8
Senegal	4,777	540	0.0	0.0	6.5	24	18	44	0.7
Seychelles	537	6,910	2.5	1.7	1.4	—	4	46	9.1
Sierra Leone	762	160	-1.3	-5.7	34.5	28	50	4	0.5
Singapore	101,834	32,810	4.9	6.7	2.9	2	0	—	9.0
Slovak Republic	19,801	3,680	N.A.	0.3	12.6	N.A.	5	1,074	0.8

Country	GNP (millions of U.S. dollars) 1997	GNP per capita (in U.S. dollars) 1997	Real growth rate 1980–91	Real growth rate 1990–97	Average inflation rate 1990–97	Agriculture's share in GDP 1970	Agriculture's share in GDP 1997	Net private capital flows (millions) 1997[1]	Foreign direct investment as percent of GDP 1997
Slovenia	$19,550	$9,840	N.A.	4.2%	32.3%	N.A.	5%	—	1.8%
Solomon Islands	350	870	3.5%	1.0	9.9	—	—	$18	5.9
Somalia	—	(7)	—	—	—	59%	—	0	—
South Africa	130,151	3,210	0.9	-0.2	10.1	8	5	3,610	1.3
Spain	569,637	14,490	2.9	1.3	4.6	—	3	—	1.0
Sri Lanka	14,781	800	2.5	4.0	9.8	28	22	575	2.8
Sudan	7,917	290	-2.4	3.7	81.6	43	—	0	0.0
Suriname	544	1,320	-4.5	-0.5	138.0	7	20-294	—	-6.4
Swaziland	1,458	1,520	3.1	-0.6	12.7	33	19	75	5.7
Sweden	231,905	26,210	1.7	0.2	2.6	—	<64	—	4.3
Switzerland	305,238	43,060	1.6	-0.5	1.9	—	—	—	1.2
Syria	16,643	1,120	-2.1	3.3	8.9	20	20-294	69	0.4
Tajikistan	2,010	330	-0.1	-16.1	394.3	N.A.	>304	20	0.8
Tanzania10	6,632	210	-1.1	0.9	25.2	41	47	143	2.3
Thailand	165,759	2,740	5.9	5.9	4.8	26	11	3,444	2.4
Togo	1,485	340	-1.7	-1.2	8.9	34	42	-6	0.0
Tonga	177	1,810	1.5	1.4	3.8	—	37	1	1.6
Trinidad and Tobago	5,553	4,250	-5.2	0.5	7.2	5	2	96	5.8
Tunisia	19,433	2,110	1.2	2.0	5.0	20	13	903	1.7
Turkey	199,307	3,130	2.9	2.3	79.3	30	15	12,221	0.4
Turkmenistan	2,987	640	0.7	-14.6	1,074.2	N.A.	>304	847	2.5
Uganda	6,608	330	3.3	4.4	17.5	54	44	179	2.7
Ukraine	52,625	1,040	2.3	-12.6	591.0	—	12	1,419	1.3
United Arab Emirates	—	(2)	-5.8	-3.8	—	—	<64	—	—
United Kingdom	1,231,269	20,870	2.6	1.9	3.2	—	2	—	3.0
United States	7,783,092	29,080	2.1	1.7	2.1	3	2	—	1.2
Uruguay	20,035	6,130	-0.4	3.5	45.4	13	8	632	0.8
Uzbekistan	24,236	1,020	0.8	-5.6	442.5	N.A.	31	435	1.1
Vanuatu	238	1,340	-0.2	-3.5	4.8	—	25	30	11.9
Venezuela	79,317	3,480	-1.5	-0.2	50.0	6	4	6,282	5.8
Vietnam	24,008	310	—	6.1	19.7	—	26	1,994	7.2
Yemen	4405	270	—	-1.5	26.7	52	18	-138	-2.4
Yugoslavia11	—	(6)	-1.4	—	—	—	18	—	0	—
Zambia	3,536	370	-2.9	-0.9	72.4	11	16	79	1.8
Zimbabwe	8,208	720	0.2	-0.7	22.4	15	19	32	0.8

Note: Figures in italics are for years other than those specified. FYR = Former Yugoslav Republic. 1. Data are shown for low and middle income countries only. 2. Estimated to be high-income ($9,656 or more). 3. Estimated to be upper-middle-income ($3,126 to $9,655). 4. Exact figures not available; estimated range given. 5. Data for years before 1990 refer to Czechoslovakia. 6. Estimated to be lower-middle-income ($786 to $3,125). 7. Estimated to be low-income ($785 or less). 8. Date for years before 1990 refer to West Germany. 9. Data for GNP are GDP. 10. Data refers to mainland Tanzania only. 11. Former Yugoslav Republics of Serbia and Montenegro.
Source: The World Bank, *The 1999 World Bank Atlas.*

Unemployment Rates in Leading Developed Nations, 1975-99

Year	1975	1980	1985	1990	1995	1997	1998	1999[1]
Australia	4.9%	6.1%	8.3%	6.9%	8.5%	8.6%	8.0%	7.4%
Canada	6.9	7.5	10.5	8.1	9.5	9.2	8.3	7.8
France	4.2	6.5	10.5	9.1	11.8	12.4	11.8[2]	11.4
Germany	3.4	2.8	7.2	5.0	6.5[2]	7.8[2]	7.5[2]	7.2
Italy	3.4	4.4	6.0	7.0	12.0	12.3	12.3	12.3
Japan	1.9	2.0	2.6	2.1	3.2	3.4	4.1	4.7
Sweden	1.6	2.0	2.8	1.8	9.1	10.1	8.4	7.4
United Kingdom	4.6	7.0	11.2	6.9	8.7	7.0	6.3[1]	6.3
United States	8.5	7.1	7.2	5.6	5.6	4.9	4.5	4.3

Note: Seasonally adjusted. 1. First quarter only. 2. Estimate.
Source: U.S. Bureau of Labor Statistics. ftp://ftp.bls.gov/pub/special.requests/ForeignLabor/flsjec.txt

NATIONS OF THE WORLD

The following section presents major facts about all the nations of the world, including statistics on each nation's geography, people, government, economy, and written text describing highlights of the country's history.

The commonly used name for each country is listed first, followed by the formal name. A list of colonial and other former names is found in the following section, "Territories of the World." Geographical descriptions are listed in both miles and kilometers, and the latitude and longitude of most islands are given.

Sources of information include the Central Intelligence Agency of the United States, the United Nations, the U.S. Bureau of the Census, and the U.S. Department of State. Names of heads of government are from the United Nations official protocol office and are valid as of Sept. 1999.

▶ AFGHANISTAN
Islamic State of Afghanistan
● **GEOGRAPHY Location:** landlocked country in southwestern Asia. **Boundaries:** Turkmenistan to NW, Tajikistan to N, China to NE, Pakistan to E and S, Iran to W. **Total area:** 250,000 sq. mi. (647,500 sq km). **Coastline:** none. **Comparative area:** slightly smaller than Texas. **Land use:** 12% arable land; negl. % permanent crops; 46% meadows and pastures; 3% forest and woodland; 39% other; includes negl. % irrigated. **Major cities:** (1982 est.) Kabul (capital) 1,036,407; Qandahar 191,345; Herat 150,497; Mazar-i-Sharif 110,367; Jalalabad 57,824.
● **PEOPLE Population:** 25,824,882 (1999 est.). **Nationality:** noun—Afghan(s); adjective—Afghan. **Ethnic groups:** 38% Pashtun, 25% Tajik, 19% Hazara, 6% Uzbek. **Languages:** 50% Afghan Persian (Dari), 35% Pashtu, 11% Turkic langs. (primarily Uzbek and Turkmen), 4% minor langs. (30, primarily Balochi and Pashai); much bilingualism. **Religions:** 84% Sunni Muslim, 15% Shi'a Muslim, 1% other.
● **GOVERNMENT Type:** transitional government. **Independence:** Aug. 1919 (from UK). **Constitution:** none. **National holiday:** Apr. 28. **Heads of government:** Since 1995 country ruled by Taliban military leaders; a civil war was ongoing as of September 1999.
● **ECONOMY Monetary unit:** afghani. **Budget:** *income:* N.A.; *expend.:* N.A. **GDP:** (1998 est.) $20 bil., $800 per capita. **Chief crops:** wheat, fruits, nuts, karakul pelts; wool, mutton. **Natural resources:** natural gas, crude oil, coal, copper, talc. **Major industries:** small-scale production of textiles, soap, furniture, shoes, fertilizer, and cement; hand-woven carpets; natural gas, oil, coal, and copper. **Labor force:** 7.1 mil.; 67.8% agriculture and animal husbandry, 10.7% services and other, 10.2% industry (1980 est.). **Exports:** $80 mil. (f.o.b., 1996); fruits and nuts, hand-woven carpets, wool, and cotton. **Imports:** $150 mil. (c.i.f., 1996); food supplies, petroleum products. **Major trading partners:** former USSR, Pakistan, Iran.

Mountainous and landlocked, Afghanistan has been a crossroads of trans-Asian trade and conquest since antiquity. A part of the Persian Empire, Bactria was conquered by Alexander the Great, and became independent in the third century b.c. before falling to the Parthians in the next century. In the seventh century a.d., a flourishing Buddhist civilization there fell to Islamic con-

quests. Genghis Khan overthrew the 11th-century empire of Mahmud of Gazni in the early 13th century, and Afghanistan was the center of Tamerlane's empire in the late 14th century. Thereafter, the region was divided among various tribes and petty kingdoms.

Modern Afghan history began with the establishment of a united emirate by Ahmed Shah Durrani in 1747. In the 19th century, Russia and Great Britain contested domination of Afghanistan. The British Afghan Wars of 1838-42 and 1878-80 left Afghanistan unconquered but within Britain's sphere of influence. Afghanistan achieved full independence from Britain in 1919 under Amanullah Khan, who proclaimed himself king in 1926. Modern reforms were instituted by Amanullah and his successors Mohammed Nadir Shah (1929-33) and Mohammed Zahir Shah (1933-73).

The monarchy fell to a military coup in 1973, and Mohammed Daud Khan established a republic. In 1978 pro-Soviet leftists took power in a coup, and, ostensibly at the government's invitation, Soviet troops invaded Afghanistan in December 1979 to put down widespread popular revolts against Communist rule. In the ensuing civil war, the government's forces and their Soviet allies (with an eventual troop strength of more than 100,000) controlled the cities and main transportation routes, but guerrilla forces contested the countryside. In 1988 the Soviet Union began a withdrawal of its troops, completed by February 1989. The rebel factions failed to achieve a united front and the pro-Soviet government confounded predictions that it would fall soon after the Soviet departure.

The government finally fell on Apr. 15, 1992, and rebel troops entered Kabul. A respected religious leader, Sibghatullah Mujaddidi, was named interim president, with the backing of a coalition of forces dominated by rebel commanders Abdul Rashid Dostam and Ahmad Shah Masoud. However, Gulbaddin Hekmatyar, leader of the fundamentalist Hizbe Islami faction, declined to join the ruling coalition. Fighting broke out in and around Kabul between coalition forces and Hekmatyar's troops.

On June 28 Mujaddidi turned over his power to the Leadership Council, which then elected Burhanuddin Rabbani as president. Fighting for control of Kabul continued between forces loyal to the Rabbani government and those backing Hekmatyar. Other factions later joined the fighting, and Kabul was subjected to continual rocket attacks in late 1992 and into the spring of 1993. Hekmatyar was named prime minister in an attempt to make peace. Fighting broke out again in early 1994 with Rabbani's followers getting the upper hand after fierce battles in Kabul.

By early 1995, the UN had brokered a scheme uniting the nine major factions in a council to which Rabbani would turn over power. But it was no sooner arranged than it was undone by the emergence of a new force: a fundamentalist Islamic militia called the Taliban, 20,000 strong and composed of students from the Islamic schools. Since 1995 Taliban forces have overrun most of the country and established a fundamentalist regime based on Islamic law. In Oct. 1996, three remaining groups of opposition forces formed a loose Northern Alliance and kept up sporadic fighting; but by August 1998, the Taliban controlled about 90 percent of Afghanistan's territory. Russia and Iran took alarm, the latter massing 200,000 troops at the border as its president, Mohammed Khatami sought the U.N. General Assembly's mediation. Secret UN-backed talks in Turkmenistan brought an agreement in March 1999 for a coalition government "in principle" but no cease-fire, and the civil war continued with the Taliban getting the upper hand by the summer of 1999.

▶ ALBANIA
Republic of Albania
● **Geography Location:** southeastern Europe. **Boundaries**: Yugoslavia to N, Macedonia to E, Greece to S, and Adriatic and Ionian Seas (parts of Mediterranean Sea) to W. **Total area**: 11,100 sq. mi. (28,750 sq km). **Coastline:** 225 mi. (362 km). **Comparative area**: slightly smaller than Maryland. **Land use:** 21% arable land; 5% permanent crops; 15% meadows and pastures; 38% forest and woodland; 21% other; includes 1% irrigated. **Major cities**: (1990 est.) Tiranë (Tirana; capital) 244,200; Durrës (Durazzo) 85,400; Elbasan 83,300; Shkodër (Scutari) 81,900; Vlorë (Vlonë or Valona) 73,800.
● **People Population:** 3,364,571 (1998 est.). **Nationality:** noun—Albanian(s); adjective—Albanian. **Ethnic groups:** 95% Albanian, 3% Greek, 2% Vlach, Gypsy, Serb, and Bulgarian (1989 est.). **Languages:** Albanian (Tosk is official dialect), Greek. **Religions:** 70% Muslim, 20% Albanian Orthodox, 10% Roman Catholic (all churches and mosques were closed in 1967 and religious observances prohibited; in November 1990, Albania began allowing private religious practice).
● **Government Type:** emerging democracy. **Independence:** Nov. 28, 1912 (from Turkey). **Constitution:** Nov. 28, 1998. **National holiday:** Independence Day, Nov. 28. **Heads of Government:** Rexhep Mejdani, president (since July 1997); Pandeli Majko, prime minister (since Oct. 1998). **Structure:** executive—president, prime minister, Council of Ministers; legislative—unicameral People's Assembly; judicial—Supreme Court.
● **Economy Monetary unit:** lek. **Budget:** (1997 est.) *income:* $624 mil.; *expend.:* $996 mil. **GDP:** (1998 est.) $5 bil., $1,490 per capita. **Chief crops:** vegetables, wheat, potatoes, tobacco, sugar beets, cotton, corn. **Natural resources:** crude oil, natural gas, coal, chromium, copper. **Major industries:** food processing, textiles and clothing, lumber. **Labor force:** 1.7 mil. (1994 est.); 49.5% agriculture, 28.3% state sector, 22.2% private sector. **Exports:** $212 mil. (f.o.b., 1998 est.); asphalt, metals and metallic ores, electricity, crude oil, vegetables, fruits, tobacco. **Imports:** $791 mil. (f.o.b., 1998 est.); machinery, consumer goods, grains. **Major trading partners:** *exports:* Italy, Greece, Germany. *imports:* Italy, Greece, Bulgaria, Turkey.

The city of Epidamnus (Durrës) was colonized by Greeks from Corinth and Corcyra in 625 b.c. Later the Roman province of Illyricum, Albania was a much-coveted area after the fall of Rome and was in turn ruled by Byzantines, Normans, Venetians, Slavs, and the kings of Naples. Under the leadership of Skanderbeg (1405-68), Albania repelled repeated Turkish invasions. But Albania was part of the Ottoman Empire from 1478 until 1912. Ottoman rule succeeded in converting most of the populace to Islam (with Catholic minorities in the north and Greek Orthodox in the south) but did not destroy the Albanian sense of national identity, based on ties of tribe, clan, and family.

Independence came in 1912 as a result of the First Balkan War, when Austria-Hungary and Italy fostered the creation of an Albanian state. Occupied by its sponsors during World War I, Albania emerged from the war in a state of near-anarchy. With Yugoslav support, a tribal chief, Ahmed Zogu, became president of the republic in 1924; he proclaimed himself King Zog I in 1928.

In 1939 Italy invaded and annexed Albania. During World War II, partisan resistance was dominated by Communist forces under the leadership of Enver Hoxha. In 1944 Hoxha seized control of the government. A socialist republic was established in 1946: foreigners were expelled and their assets nationalized; churches were closed; agriculture and industry were collectivized. Albania under Hoxha became one of the world's most thoroughly totalitarian states.

A doctrinaire Stalinist, Hoxha broke with Nikita Khruschev's Soviet Union in 1961 and became a client state of China. But with liberalization in China after 1977, Hoxha broke that link as well. Albania became almost totally isolated from world affairs.

Hoxha died in April 1985 and was succeeded as president and first secretary of the Albanian Communist party by Ramiz Alia. In 1990, Alia eased restrictions on religion, tourism, and foreign investment, expanded trade, and allowed the formation of an opposition Democratic party. But he scheduled elections to the National Assembly for 1991, before awareness had spread of the old regime's faltering power. The Communists carried the rural districts and formed a coalition government with the Democrats, who carried the cities.

A year later, the Democrats completed the rout of the Communists, winning 92 of the 140 seats in the Assembly, and replacing Alia with Sali Berisha, a heart surgeon. But by the end of the year, factions within the Democratic party were already complaining about Pres. Berisha's "autocratic rule." Meanwhile, anarchy plagued much of the country, with food riots in the cities and armed brigandage in the countryside. EC and UN grants helped pay for needed imports and Italy provided invaluable assistance to the Albanian police forces. By 1993, zones of law and order were being established, churches were reopening, and 90 percent of farming had been privatized. But in November 1994, voters rejected (54-42) a new constitution proposed by Pres. Berisha.

In 1996 Berisha's Democratic Party won a major electoral victory amidst widespread complaints of fraud, but he and his followers were driven from office in 1997 after a series of pryamid schemes collapsed ruining the finances of tens of thousands of families who had participated in them. Violence and looting occured in many areas and a multi-national force of 7,000 was sent in to help restore order. The Socialists (formerly Communists) returned to power under Fatos Nana. In the spring of 1998 NATO advisors began to train Albania's tiny army as ethnic Albanians in the Kosovo province of Yugoslavia began a violent rebellion. Yugoslavia's suppression of the rebellion drove thousands of ethnic Albanians out of Kosovo into Albania. Amidst this further tumult, internal struggled continued between supports of the Democratic Party and the Socialists, erupting into serious violence in September 1998. At the end of the month, prime minister Nano resigned and was replaced by Pandeli Majko.

▶ ALGERIA
Democratic and Popular Republic of Algeria

● **GEOGRAPHY Location:** northern coast of Africa. **Boundaries:** Mediterranean Sea to N, Tunisia and Libya to E, Mali and Niger to S, Morocco, Western Sahara, Mauritania to W. **Total area:** 919,591 sq. mi. (2,381,740 sq km). **Coastline:** 620 mi. (998 km). **Comparative area:** slightly less than 3.5 times size of Texas. **Land use:** 3% arable land; negl. % permanent crops; 13% meadows and pastures; 2% forest and woodland; 82% other; includes negl. % irrigated. **Major cities:** (1984 est.) Algiers (capital) 1,721,607; Oran 663,504; Constantine 448,578; Annaba 348,322; Blida 191,314.

● **PEOPLE Population:** 31,133,486 (1999 est.). **Nationality:** noun—Algerian(s); adjective—Algerian. **Ethnic groups:** 99% Arab-Berber, less than 1% European. **Languages:** Arabic (official), French, Berber dialects. **Religions:** 99% Sunni Muslim (state religion), 1% Christian and Jewish.

● **GOVERNMENT Type:** republic. **Independence:** July 5, 1962 (from France). **Constitution:** Nov. 19, 1976, effective Nov. 22, 1976. **National holiday:** Anniversary of the Revolution, Nov. 1. **Heads of Government:** Abdelaziz Bouteflika, head of state (since Apr. 1999), Smail Hamdani, prime minister (since Apr. 1999). **Structure:** executive; bicameral legislature; judicial—Supreme Court.

● **ECONOMY Monetary unit:** Algerian dinar. **Budget:** (1998 est.) *income:* $14.4 bil.; *expend.:* $15.7 bil. **GDP:** $140.2 bil., $4,600 per capita. **Chief crops:** wheat, barley, oats, grapes, olives. **Natural resources:** crude oil, natural gas, iron ore, phosphates, uranium. **Major industries:** petroleum, light industries, natural gas, mining. **Labor force:** 7.8 mil. (1996 est.); 29.5% government, 22% agriculture, 16.2% construction and public works, 13.6% industry, 13.5% commerce and services, 5.2% transportation and communication (1989). **Exports:** $14 bil. (f.o.b., 1997 est.); 97% petroleum and natural gas. **Imports:** $8.5 bil. (f.o.b., 1997 est.); capital goods, food, beverages, consumer goods. **Major trading partners:** *exports:* 18.8% Italy, 14.8% U.S., 11.8% France. *imports:* 29% France, 10.5% Spain, 8.2% Italy.

From around 3000 B.C. nomadic ancestors of the Berbers inhabited Algeria, as the expanding Sahara desert displaced prehistoric grasslands and forests. The Phoenicians established trading centers in the Mediterranean coastal plain around 1200 b.c. Those centers were taken over by the Romans beginning around 200 b.c. With Roman support the Berber chief Masinissa formed the kingdom of Numidia in what is now northern Algeria. From 46 b.c. to about a.d. 640, the area was controlled successively by the Romans, Germanic Vandal tribes, and the Byzantine Empire.

In the eighth century A.D., the Islamic conquests spread Arab culture to Numidia. Most of the Berbers converted to Islam. The blend of Berber and Arab culture in Algeria gave rise to a flourishing and rich Islamic civilization in the coastal plain, while Tuareg and other nomadic peoples controlled the sparsely inhabited interior.

Around 1500 the Christian kingdom of Spain captured Algiers and other coastal cities. In 1518 Barbarossa, a Turkish sea captain, captured Algiers and drove the Spanish out. In so doing, he joined Algeria to the expanding Turkish Ottoman Empire. Piracy became a key source of income for the Ottoman cities of Algeria. In the early 1800s, France, along with England and the United States, began military operations to suppress piracy in the Mediterranean. In 1830 France invaded Algeria, putting an end to Ottoman rule and establishing their own administration. Algeria was ruled as part of France itself. Many French settlers (colons) migrated to Algeria. Both they and the native Algerians were considered citizens of France, but the colons were granted substantial political and economic advantages over the indigenous population.

In 1847 a rebellion led by Abd-al-Qadir, a powerful Muslim leader, was suppressed by the French. In 1848, in the wake of the rebellion, all of Algeria was conquered by the French and legally confirmed as an integral part of France. During World War II, many Algerians joined the Free French, hoping that their display of loyalty would be rewarded with greater self-rule after the war. Those hopes were disappointed, as French administration was resumed in 1945.

In 1954 the Front de Liberation Nationale (FLN) began a guerrilla war against the French in Algeria. They were opposed by French police and military forces and by the Secret Army Organization (OAS), an underground movement of colons who favored continued French rule. As the FLN gained strength, by 1958 French premier Charles de Gaulle established a policy designed to prepare Algeria for self-rule.

Algerian independence was proclaimed on July 3, 1962; a million colons fled to France. A power struggle within the new Algerian government was resolved when Ahmed Ben Bella became the country's first premier in 1963. In 1965 Ben Bella was deposed by Col. Houari Boumidienne, who ruled as the head of a military government. In 1967 Algeria declared war on Israel, broke with the West, and established close relations with the USSR. Since the early 1970s, relations with the West, and particularly with France, have improved (mainly because of oil).

The first free, multiparty elections were held on June 12, 1990. The Islamic Salvation Front, which advocates turning Algeria into an Islamic Republic, won overwhelming control of local assemblies. In 1991 it won 188 seats in Parliament out of 231 up for election and seemed poised to win control of the government when the army interceded to keep the old power structure in place. On June 19, 1992, Pres. Mohammed Boudiaf was assassinated, presumably by Islamic fundamentalists.

Since 1992 the military's High Security Council, knowing the Islamic parties would win any free election, has repeatedly postponed a return to democracy. In January 1994 the High Security Council replaced the collective presidency of the High State Council with Gen. Liamine Zeroual. November 1995 saw the first contested presidential election since 1962, with Gen. Zeroual winning over 60 percent of the vote as major opposition groups boycotted the election. Elections in June 1997 produced Algeria's first mutliparty parliament since 1962, but the ruling military council still remained in control and in August Islamic fundamentalists killed over 300 in one night of terror. These vicious assasinations continued into 1998 with hundreds more having their throats cut in over several nights. Civil strife and assassinations have claimed the lives of over 40,000 since 1992. In Sept. 1998 Gen. Zeroual announced that elections would be held in Feb. 1999 and he would not be a candidate.

By the time the election were held in April, all candidates had withdrawn from the race save one, the army-backed Abdelaziz Bouteflika. His new government reached an accord with the rebel

Islamic Salvation Front: in return for the end of the uprising, Pres. Bouteflika pledged to release thousands of militant Islamic prisoners on July 5, Algeria's national holiday, and to submit the peace agreement to a referendum. In Sept. 98 percent of voters favored the agreement that gave amnesty to militants who surrendered.

►ANDORRA
Principality of Andorra
● **GEOGRAPHY Location:** Pyrenees Mountains, southwestern Europe. **Boundaries**: France to N and E, Spain to S and W. **Total area:** 174 sq. mi. (450 sq km). **Coastline:** none. **Comparative area:** 2.5 times size of Washington, D.C. **Land use:** 2% arable land; 0% permanent crops; 56% meadows and pastures; 22% forest and woodland; 20% other. **Major cities:** (1989) Andorra la Vella (capital) 19,566.
● **PEOPLE Population:** 65,939 (1999 est.). **Nationality:** noun—Andorran(s); adjective—Andorran. **Ethnic groups:** 61% Spanish, 30% Andorran, 6% French, 3% other. **Languages:** Catalan (official); many also speak some French and Castilian. **Religions:** virtually all Roman Catholic.
● **GOVERNMENT Type:** parliamentary democracy (since March 1993) that retains as head of state a co-principality; the two princes are the president of France and Spanish bishop of Seo de Urgel, who are represented locally by officials called veguers. **Independence:** 1278. **Constitution:** March 1993. **National holiday:** Mare de Deu de Meritxell, Sept. 8. **Heads of Government:** French co-prince Jacques Chirac, president of France (since 1995) and Spanish Episcopal co-prince Msgr. Joan Marti Alanís, bishop of Seo de Urgel, Spain (since 1971); Don Marc Forne Molne, prime minister (since Dec. 1994). **Structure:** executive—co-princes, executive council; unicameral legislature; judiciary—Supreme Court at Perpignan, France.
● **ECONOMY Monetary unit:** French franc and Spanish peseta. **Budget:** (1993) *income:* 138 mil.; *expend.:* 177 mil. **GDP:** $1.2 bil., $18,000 per capita (1995 est.). **Chief crops:** sheep raising; small quantities of tobacco, rye, wheat, barley, oats, and vegetables. **Natural resources:** hydropower, mineral water, timber, iron ore, lead. **Major industries:** tourism (particularly skiing), sheep, timber, tobacco, banking. **Labor force:** N.A. **Exports:** $47 mil. (f.o.b., 1995); electricity, tobacco products, furniture. **Imports:** $1 bil. (1995). **Major trading partners:** *exports:* 49% France, 47% Spain; *imports:* France, Spain, 4.2% U.S.

Set high in the Pyrenees, the tiny state of Andorra has been both a medieval relic and a modern capitalist land. Since 1278 Andorra has owed feudal allegiance to two co-rulers, the bishop of Seo de Urgel in Spain and, now, the president of France. Until 1993, Andorra had no constitution, so the exact rights of the corulers remained vague. Foreign affairs were handled by France.

Andorra's traditional economic mainstay had been the "transshipment of goods" (i.e., smuggling) between France and Spain. Andorra attracts tourists drawn by bargain shopping, and it is a banking center. Spain's 1986 entry into the EU led Andorra to seek a customs union with the EU. The March 1990 treaty was Andorra's first in over 700 years. In the same year, the co-princes introduced Andorra's first penal code and a sales tax, soon followed by the adoption of the EU's external tariff. In March 1993 voters—of whom there are only 9,123—adopted a modern constitution that will reduce the power of the co-princes and establish

a government of three branches that will have authority to tax and to make foreign policy. In 1997 Premier Molne's party won a majority of seats in the General Council ending the coalition government.

►ANGOLA
Republic of Angola
● **GEOGRAPHY Location:** southwestern Africa. **Boundaries**: Zaire to N and NE, Zambia to E, Namibia to S, South Atlantic Ocean to W; Cabinda district separated from rest of country by Congo to N, Zaire to S. **Total area:** 481,352 sq. mi. (1,246,700 sq km). **Coastline:** 994 mi. (1,600 km). **Comparative area**: slightly less than twice size of Texas. **Land use:** 2% arable land; negl. % permanent crops; 23% meadows and pastures; 43% forest and woodland; 32% other. **Major cities**: Luanda (capital) 1,200,000 (1982 est.); Huambo (Nova Lisboa) 61,885; Lobito 59,258; Benguela 40,996; Lubango (São da Bandeira) 31,674 (1970 census).
● **PEOPLE Population:** 11,177,537 (1999 est.). **Nationality:** noun—Angolan(s); adjective—Angolan. **Ethnic groups:** 37% Ovimbundu, 25% Kimbundu, 13% Bakongo, 2% Mestiço, 1% European, 22% other. **Languages:** Portuguese (official), Bantu and other African languages. **Religions:** 47% indigenous beliefs, 38% Roman Catholic, 15% Protestant.
● **GOVERNMENT Type:** multiparty democracy (transitional). **Independence:** Nov. 11, 1975 (from Portugal). **Constitution:** Nov. 11, 1975 (last revised Aug. 26, 1992). **National holiday:** Independence Day, Nov. 11. **Heads of Government:** José Eduardo dos Santos, president (since Sept. 1979); Fernando van Dunem, prime minister (since June 1996). **Structure:** executive; unicameral legislature; judiciary.
● **ECONOMY Monetary unit:** new kwanza. **Budget:** (1992 est.) *income:* $928 mil.; *expend.:* $2.5 bil. **GDP:** $11 bil. (1998 est.), $1,000 per capita. **Chief crops:** bananas, sugarcane, coffee, sisal, corn, cotton, manioc (tapioca), vegetables. **Natural resources:** petroleum, diamonds, iron ore, phosphates, copper. **Major industries:** petroleum, mining (diamonds, iron ore, phosphates), food processing. **Labor force:** 5 mil. (1997 est.); 85% agriculture, 15% industry. **Exports:** $3.4 bil. (f.o.b., 1998 est.); 90% oil, diamonds, refined petroleum products, gas, coffee. **Imports:** $2.2 bil. (f.o.b., 1998 est.); machinery, electrical equipment, vehicles and spare parts, medicines, food, textiles and clothing; substantial military deliveries. **Major trading partners:** *exports:* 65% U.S., E.U.; *imports:* 21% Portugal, 15% U.S, 14% France.

Bantu peoples have occupied Angola for at least 2,000 years. Portuguese explorers searching for a sea route to India founded Luanda (1575) and Benguela (1617). Portugal, at first in alliance with the north Angolan kingdom of Bakongo, engaged in an extensive trade of slaves to Brazil—3 million in 300 years.

In the late 19th century, Angola was organized as a Portuguese colony, sometimes called Portuguese West Africa. Portuguese settlers dominated local government, and trade, organized plantation-style cultivation of cotton, palm oil, bananas, and coffee. A railroad was built to transport exports of metal from the Katanga region of the Belgian Congo (now Zaire) to the coast.

By the 1950s non-Portuguese Angolans began to agitate for independence. The National Front spearheaded the liberation movement. Guerrilla warfare began in 1961, with several feuding factions fighting the Portuguese. Following the Portuguese revolution of 1974, factional warfare intensified and most Portuguese settlers fled the country. Independence came on Nov. 11, 1975.

Civil war between the National Front, the Popular Movement for the Liberation of Angola (MPLA), and the National Union for the Total Independence of Angola (UNITA) led, in 1976, to the victory of the MPLA, which organized a Marxist state with Soviet backing and Cuban technical support including 37,000 soldiers. Large portions of the country remained in the hands of UNITA, which continued the civil war with Chinese and American support through the 1980s.

Direct clashes between Angolan and South African troops occurred during the 1980s, as Angola gave shelter to SWAPO guerrilla forces seeking independence for Namibia. Cuban troops withdrew from Angola between January 1989 and May 1991, and a cease-fire between the government and UNITA was also concluded in May 1991. While agreeing to recognize the dos Santos government in the interim, UNITA called for elections to be held by September 1992, Angola's first since 1975.

In the elections, MPLA's candidate, José Eduardo dos Santos, decisively defeated UNITA's leader, Jonas Savimbi, but Savimbi's refusal to honor the results, in which 90 percent of the electorate voted, led to renewed fighting. A dramatic-sounding but completely ineffectual peace late in 1994 and the presence of thousands of U.N. peacekeepers from Feb. 1994 until Feb. 1998 have made little dent in the continuing struggle which has by now claimed perhaps 100,000 lives.

▶ANTIGUA AND BARBUDA
• **GEOGRAPHY** **Location:** eastern Caribbean Sea approximately 300 mi. (480 km) SE of Puerto Rico. Antigua 17°06'N, 61°50'W; Barbuda 17°38'N, 61°48'W. **Boundaries:** Atlantic Ocean to N and E, Caribbean Sea to S and W. **Total area:** 170 sq. mi. (440 sq km). **Coastline:** 95 mi. (153 km). **Comparative area:** 2.5 times size of Washington, D.C. **Land use:** 18% arable land; 0% permanent crops; 9% meadows and pastures; 11% forest and woodland; 62% other. **Major cities:** (1986 est.) St. John's (capital) 36,000.
• **PEOPLE** **Population:** 64,246 (1999 est.). **Nationality:** noun—Antiguan(s), Barbudan(s); adjective—Antiguan, Barbudan. **Ethnic groups:** almost entirely of black African origin; some of British, Portuguese, Lebanese, and Syrian origin. **Languages:** English (official), local dialects. **Religions:** Anglican (predominant), other Protestant sects, some Roman Catholic.
• **GOVERNMENT** **Type:** parliamentary democracy. **Independence:** Nov. 1, 1981 (from UK). **Constitution:** Nov. 1, 1981. **National holiday:** Independence Day, Nov. 1. **Heads of Government:** Dr. James B. Carlisle, governor-general (since June 1993); Lester B. Bird, prime minister (since Mar. 1994). **Structure:** executive—governor general, prime minister, and cabinet; bicameral legislature; judiciary—East Caribbean Supreme Court.
• **ECONOMY** **Monetary unit:** East Caribbean (EC) dollar. **Budget:** (1997) *income:* $122.6 mil.; *expend.:* $141.2 mil. **GDP:** $503 mil., $7,900 per capita (1998 est.). **Chief crops:** cotton, fruits and vegetables, sugar. **Natural resources:** negl.; pleasant climate fosters tourism. **Major industries:** tourism, construction, light manufacturing

(clothing, alcohol, household appliances). **Labor force:** 30,000 (1983); 82% commerce and services, 11% agriculture, 7% industry; 5%-10% unemployment (1995 est.). **Exports:** $37.8 mil. (f.o.b., 1997 est.); 48% petroleum products, 23% manufactures, 17% machinery and transportation equipment, 4% food and live animals. **Imports:** $325.5 mil. (1997 est.); food and live animals, machinery and transport equipment, manufactures, chemicals, oil. **Major trading partners:** *exports:* 26% OECS, 15% Barbados, 4% Guyana, 2% Trinidad and Tobago; *imports:* 27% U.S., 16% UK, 4% Canada.

Columbus visited and claimed Antigua for Spain in 1493. It was settled by the British in 1632, who grew tobacco, and later sugar. The island's economy was hobbled by abolition of slavery in 1834, a succession of natural disasters in the 1840s, and the closing of the Royal Dockyard in 1854. Today, tourism is a mainstay of the economy, fostered by the ruling Antigua Labor Party, which won its sixth consecutive parliamentary victory in March 1999. But its second economic mainstay, offshore banking, has been shaken by a U.S. Treasury warning in April 1999 that lax standards make it susceptible to criminal money-laundering.

▶ARGENTINA
Argentine Republic
• **GEOGRAPHY** **Location:** southern South America. **Boundaries:** Bolivia, Paraguay, Brazil to N.; Uruguay, South Atlantic Ocean to E.; Chile to W. **Total area:** 1,068,298 sq. mi. (2,766,890 sq km) (figures exclude Falkland Islands and Antarctic territory claimed by Argentina). **Coastline:** 3,099 mi. (4,989 km). **Comparative area:** slightly less than three-tenths the size of the United States. **Land use:** 9% arable land; 1% permanent crops; 52% meadows and pastures; 19% forest and woodland; 19% other. **Major cities:** (1991 census) Buenos Aires (capital) 12,960,976; Córdoba 1,148,305; La Matanza 1,111,811; Rosario 894,645; Morón 641,541.
• **PEOPLE** **Population:** 36,737,664 (1999 est.). **Nationality:** noun—Argentine(s); adjective—Argentine. **Ethnic groups:** 85% white, 15% mestizo, Indian, and other nonwhite groups. **Languages:** Spanish (official), English, Italian, German, French. **Religions:** 90% nominally Roman Catholic (less than 20% practicing), 2% Protestant, 2% Jewish, 6% other.
• **GOVERNMENT** **Type:** republic. **Independence:** July 9, 1816 (from Spain). **Constitution:** May 1, 1853 (revised Aug. 1994). **National holiday:** Revolution Day, May 25. **Head of Government:** Carlos Saúl Menem, president (since July 1989). **Structure:** executive; bicameral legislature; judiciary.
• **ECONOMY** **Monetary unit:** nuevo peso argentino. **Budget:** (1998 est.) *income:* $56 bil.; *expend.:* $60 bil. **GDP:** (1998 est.) $374 bil., $10,300 per capita. **Chief crops:** wheat, corn, sorghum, soybeans, sugar beets. **Natural resources:** fertile plains of the pampas, lead, zinc, tin, copper, iron ore, petroleum. **Major industries:** food processing (especially meat packing), motor vehicles, consumer durables. **Labor force:** 14 mil. (1997 est.); 57% services, 31% industry, 12% agriculture; 12% unemployment (1998 est.). **Exports:** $26 bil. (f.o.b., 1998); cereals, feed, motor vehicles, crude petroleum, steel manufactures. **Imports:** $32 bil. (c.i.f., 1998); motor vehicles and parts, organic chemicals, telecommunications equipment, plastics. **Major trading partners:** *exports:* 31% Brazil,

8% U.S., 7.0% Chile; *imports:* 23% Brazil, 20% U.S., 6% Italy.

The indigenous nomads of the area around the river La Plata resisted Spanish intrusion, which began with the first founding of Buenos Aires by Pedro de Mendoza in 1536. Argentina was part of Spain's Viceroyalty of Peru until reforms in the Bourbon dynasty and a need to defend against Portuguese encroachment from Brazil led to the formation of the Viceroyalty of La Plata, including Argentina, Bolivia, Paraguay, and Uruguay, in 1776. Following the relaxation of trade restrictions two years later, Buenos Aires grew from a small town to a city of 50,000 by 1800. A provisional junta of the Provinces of Río de la Plata was established in 1810 after the Napoleonic occupation of Spain, and in 1816 the United Provinces of the Río de la Plata declared their independence.

After independence the question of political relations among the United Provinces was settled by a federalist solution in which the provinces dissolved into a number of practically independent republics. In 1824, a constituent assembly created the office of president, first held by Bernardino Rivadavia. However, the failure to ratify a workable constitution caused Rivadavia to resign.

Juan Manuel de Rosas became governor of Buenos Aires in 1829 and presided over the construction of a federal agreement between the provinces in 1831. Rosas governed Buenos Aires with an iron hand until his expulsion in 1852. The other provinces formed the Argentine Federation, based on a federal constitution of 1853, but Buenos Aires refused to join. Buenos Aires and the Argentine Federation entered into war between 1859 and 1861; they reached an agreement on the inclusion of Buenos Aires in the Argentine Republic in 1862.

Argentina joined Brazil and Uruguay in a war (1865-70) against Paraguay. During the latter part of the 1870s, the government took the initiative against the indigenous populations of Patagonia and Tierra del Fuego, which were partitioned with Chile. Immigration from Europe, especially Spain and Italy, resulted in enormous growth from the mid-19th century. In 1869, there were 2 million inhabitants; by 1914, 8 million; by 1955, 19 million; and by 1990, 32 million. Prior to World War II, Argentina was acutely Eurocentric, with an eye to British finance and French culture; this has changed since.

The Argentine military, led by Lt. Gen. José F. Uriburu, ousted the civilian government of the Radical party in 1930 with the intention of following the European model of politics. In 1946 Juan Domingo Perón won the presidential election and constructed a populist political alliance that included workers, industrialists, and the armed forces. The Perón-inspired populist ideology of justicialismo included extension of the franchise to women and redistribution of income to workers and the poor. The activities of Perón's charismatic wife, Eva, bolstered justicialismo through her effort to distribute goods to the poor through the Social Aid Foundation.

Tied in with Perón's populist strategy was his policy of nationalist economic development, whereby state-led development was financed through extraction of capital from the old export-agricultural elite and politically supported through populism. The Perón government incurred great expense to gain control over foreign-owned economic infrastructure, including railway systems, telephone companies, and dock facilities. A number of events led to Perón's downfall in 1955. The market for Argentine goods deteriorated after World War II. As Perón shifted his strategy to encourage foreign investment and impose economic austerity, repression against the political opposition grew. The death of Eva Perón in 1952 robbed Perón of an important political resource, and when the government challenged the Catholic church on a number of issues, the military ousted Perón.

After a brief period of military rule, in which an attempt was made to roll back "Perónismo," Arturo Frondizi of the "Intransigent" faction of the Radical party won the presidency and assumed office in 1958. In the following years, the military repeatedly attempted to keep the Perónistas from returning to power. In 1962 the military forced Frondizi to annul Perónist victories in provincial elections and removed him from office. Pres. Arturo Illia was ousted from office in 1966 for the same reason: his failure to tame Perón's followers.

A military bureaucratic authoritarian regime led by a series of Argentine officers was established during 1966-73. Extreme violence by factions on the Left and Right led the military to accept Perón's return to the presidency in 1973. Perón died the following year, and his third wife, Isabel, replaced him in office; she was unable to retain power, and the military removed her in 1976 in the midst of economic and political upheaval.

Determined to deal with what they saw as a leftist threat, the military again opted for a bureaucratic authoritarian solution. As part of this "solution," the armed forces launched what was later called the "dirty war" against leftists, during which up to 20,000 people disappeared and were never heard from again. The authoritarian government collapsed after the ill-starred 1982 Falkland/Malvinas Islands War against Britain led to the resignation of the junta and the holding of elections. Raúl Alfonsín, of the Radical Union party, was elected president in the wake of these events in 1983. In 1989, he was succeeded by Carlos Saúl Menem, who agreed to take office early, in the midst of a severe economic crisis during which inflation reached 3,000 percent and foreign debt $58 billion.

Menem encouraged free enterprise and good relations with the U.S. Government controls on foreign investment and trade were relaxed, and the government sold off many state enterprises. In 1993 Argentina's 11-year debt crisis officially ended, and by 1995 inflation was down to 4 percent. Economic hardships caused by Menem's reforms probably led to the Perónists' relatively poor showing (38%) in parliamentary elections (Apr. 1994).

In 1995 the government introduced an austerity plan to fight the budget deficit and to cushion the shocks of Mexico's devaluation. As Argentina's economy began to flourish, Menem was reelected, and his party won majorities in both houses of the legislature and control of more than half of Argentina's provincial governments. But in May 1997, violent protests erupted in several major cities, as unemployment rose to nearly 20 percent. In October, the Peronistas lost control of the Chamber of Deputies, for the first time since 1983, to a left-wing coalition known as The Alliance. The mayor of Buenos Aires, Fernando de la Rua, was the Alliance candidate running for president in October 1999 against the Peronista candidate, Eduardo Duhalde, governor of Buenos Aires province.

ARMENIA
Republic of Armenia
● **GEOGRAPHY Location:** southwest Transcaucasia between Europe and Asia. **Boundaries:** Georgia to N, Azerbaijan to E, Iran to S, Turkey to W. Nakhichevan Autonomous Republic, an Azerbaijan territory, is an enclave within Armenian territory. **Total area:** 11,506 sq. mi. (29,800 sq km). **Coastline:** none. **Comparative area:** slightly smaller than Maryland. **Land use:** 17% arable land; 3% permanent crops; 24% meadows and pastures; 15% forest and woodlands; 41% other. **Major cities:** (1990 est.) Yerevan (capital) 1,202,000; Kumayri (formerly Leninakan) 123,000; Kirovakan 76,000.
● **PEOPLE Population:** 3,409,234 (1999 est.). **Nationality:** noun—Armenian(s); adjective—Armenian. **Ethnic groups:** 93% Armenian, 3% Azeri, 2% Russian. **Languages:** 96% Armenian, 2% Russian, 2% other. **Religions:** 94% Armenian Orthodox.
● **GOVERNMENT Type:** republic. **Independence:** Sept. 23, 1991 (from USSR). **Constitution:** July 5, 1995. **National holiday:** Referendum Day, Sept. 21. **Heads of Government:** Robert Kocharian, president (since April 1998); Vazgen Sargissian, prime minister (since June 1999). **Structure:** executive; unicameral legislatiure; judiciary.
● **ECONOMY Monetary unit:** dram. **Budget:** (1998 est.) *income:* $322 mil.; *expend.:* $424 mil. **GDP:** $9.2 bil., $2,700 per capita (1998 est.). **Chief crops:** fruit (especially wine grapes), vegetables, livestock. **Natural resources:** small deposits of gold and copper. **Major industries:** nonferrous metallurgy, electrical equipment, tires, textiles (much of industry). **Labor force:** 1.6 mil. (1997). **Exports:** $230 mil. (f.o.b., 1998); gold and jewelry, aluminum, transport equipment. **Imports:** $840 mil. (c.i.f., 1998); grain, other foods, fuel, other energy. **Major trading partners:** Iran, Russia, Turkmenistan, Georgia.

Armenia, a small landlocked country just south of the great Caucasus mountain range, is but a fragment of ancient Armenia, one of the world's oldest civilizations dating back to the sixth century b.c. In about a.d. 300, Armenia adopted Christianity, which today is still an important component of Armenian national identity. Because Armenia forms part of a land bridge between the Black and the Caspian Seas, and between Turks and Slavs, it has long been overrun and controlled by the Byzantine, Arab, Ottoman, Mongol, and Russian Empires. In 1236 the Tatar and Mongol invasion spelled the end of Armenia as a separate state. In 1639, after the conclusion of a major war between Turkey and Iran, the territory of Armenia was partitioned. By the end of the 17th century, czarist Russia was also involved in Armenia, and in 1828 eastern Armenia was ceded to the Russian empire by the Treaty of Turkmenchai.

During the First World War, those Armenians living in the western part of the country under Ottoman rule were increasingly subjected to persecution by the Turks. In April 1915, the Turks forcibly removed the Armenians from the border area, during which more than a million of them either starved or were killed. In 1918, an Armenian republic emerged as the Russian empire collapsed, but this entity was short-lived, as Turkey, Russia, and later Britain fought for control. Finally, the Soviet Red Army moved into the territory and on Nov. 29, 1920, declared it a Soviet republic. Armenia was made part of the Transcaucasian Soviet Federal Socialist Republic of the USSR in 1922, and in 1936, it became one of the Soviet Union's constituent union republics.

Armenian Christians have been subjected to many years of persecution by various invaders, causing a great diaspora of Armenians, especially to the United States and Europe. This large expatriate community has helped Armenia from abroad through difficult times.

Since 1988, Armenia's most pressing issue has been the war over Nagorno-Karabakh, the Armenian Christian enclave of Muslim Azerbaijan. Fighting broke out when 180,000 ethnic Armenians in Azerbaijan demanded that their homeland become part of Armenia. That same year, Armenia was rocked by severe earthquakes that killed thousands of people and blocked supplies from the West and the Soviet Union from getting through.

The war continued even as both nations declared their independence from the Soviet Union (Armenia on Sept. 23, 1991; Azerbaijan a month later). In October 1991, Levon Ter-Petrossian was elected president of independent Armenia, and in December, Armenia was one of 11 former Soviet republics to sign the Alma-Ata Declaration, creating the Commonwealth of Independent States. Since independence, Armenia has remained committed to the war over Nagorno-Karabakh, even though it has hindered the functioning of the stagnant Armenian economy.

On July 5, 1995, a new "strong president" constitution was approved by 68 percent in a referendum and Pres. Ter-Petrossian's six-party Republic Coalition carried a majority of seats in the first elections for the 190-seat National Assembly. He was reelected in 1996 but resigned in February 1998 in a dispute over policy toward Nagorno-Karabakh with his hard-line premier Robert Kocharian. In March, Kocharian easily won the presidential election over Soviet-era ruler Karen Demirchyan.

▶ AUSTRALIA
Commonwealth of Australia
● **GEOGRAPHY Location:** continent of Australia, between Indian and Pacific Oceans. **Boundaries:** nearest neighbor is Papua New Guinea, to N. **Total area:** 2,967,897 sq. mi. (7,686,850 sq km). **Coastline:** 16,010 mi. (25,760 km). **Comparative area:** slightly smaller than U.S. **Land use:** 6% arable land; negl. % permanent crops; 54% meadows and pastures; 19% forest and woodland; 21% other; includes negl. % irrigated. **Major cities:** (1993 est.) Canberra (capital) 325,400; Sydney 3,719,000; Melbourne 3,187,500; Brisbane 1,421,700; Perth 1,221,300.
● **PEOPLE Population:** 18,783,551 (1999 est.). **Nationality:** noun—Australian(s); adjective—Australian. **Ethnic groups:** 92% Caucasian, 7% Asian, 1% aboriginal and other. **Languages:** English, native langs. **Religions:** 26.1% Anglican, 26% Roman Catholic, 24.3% other Christian, 11% non-Christian.
● **GOVERNMENT Type:** democratic, federal-state system. **Independence:** Jan. 1, 1901 (from federation of UK colonies). **Constitution:** July 9, 1900; effective Jan. 1, 1901. **National holiday:** Australia Day, Jan. 26. **Heads of Government:** Sir William Deane, governor general (since Feb. 1996); John Howard, prime minister (since Mar. 1996). **Structure:** executive—governor general (appointed by the Queen), prime minister, and cabinet; bicameral legislature; independent judiciary.

• **ECONOMY Monetary unit:** Australian dollar. **Budget:** (FY98/99 est.) *income:* $90.73 bil.; *expend.:* $89.04 bil. **GDP:** (1998 est.) $393.9 bil.; $21,200 per capita. **Chief crops:** wheat, barley, sugarcane, fruits; poultry. **Natural resources:** bauxite, coal, iron ore, copper, tin. **Major industries:** mining, industrial and transportation equipment, food processing. **Labor force:** 9.2 mil. (1997); 73% services, 22% industry, 5% agriculture, 8.1% unemployment (1995). **Exports:** $56 bil. (f.o.b., 1998); coal, gold, meat, wool. **Imports:** $61 bil. (f.o.b., 1998); machinery and transport equipment, computers and office machines, telecommunication equipment and parts. **Major trading partners:** *exports:* 20% Japan, 16% ASEAN, 10% EU; *imports:* 25% EU, 23% U.S., 13% Japan.

The continent-nation of Australia is distinguished by its geographical isolation and by the unique flora and fauna which that isolation has fostered. The ancestors of today's aborigines arrived from Southeast Asia as much as 40,000 years ago. Thereafter, aborigine culture evolved in isolation except for some contact between the peoples of the northern coast and New Guinea. Australia was first sighted by Europeans at the beginning of the 17th century. In the 18th century, it was visited by the Dutch, who named it New Holland. The eastern coast was systematically explored in 1770 by Capt. James Cook, who claimed it for Great Britain.

British settlement began in 1788, with the landing of about 700 convicts near Sydney. Australia remained a penal colony during the first half of the 19th century, during which time the continent was explored and separate colonies were established. Aboriginal populations were displaced and in some areas (most notably the island Tasmania) they were totally exterminated. Discovery of gold in Victoria in 1851 created a gold rush that greatly accelerated immigration. By the end of the 19th century, the three mainstays of the Australian economy—livestock (beef and sheep), mining, and wheat growing—were firmly established.

In 1901, a commonwealth was established consisting of a confederation of the various states except for the Northern Territory, which was added in 1911. The British Crown is represented by an appointed governor-general; the national government is a parliamentary system, but much local authority resides in the separate states. Comprehensive social welfare legislation was passed by the state and national governments soon after the commonwealth's formation. The population is highly educated and enjoys a generally high standard of living, but most aborigines are detribalized and live in considerable poverty.

Australian troops fought with distinction in both world wars. A Japanese threat to Australia in 1942 was averted by Allied victory in the Battle of the Coral Sea. Australia and the United States are firm allies, and Australian troops joined U.S. forces in Korea, Vietnam, and the Persian Gulf War. Australia administers several external island groups and claims territory in Antarctica. (See "Territories of the World.")

The abandonment of discriminatory immigration practices in 1973 led to a new wave of immigration, particularly from Asia. In the process Australian economic ties to Asia and the Pacific Rim have expanded considerably. New exploitation of mineral resources has in many cases been accomplished with Japanese investment or with long-term export contracts to Japan. Australia has undergone considerable industrial development in the past two decades.

After 10 years in office, Prime Minister Bob Hawke was ousted by his own Labour party in 1991 and replaced by Paul Keating. Keating's government was convincingly reelected in March 1993 elections, despite a persistent economic slump. But continued high spending and taxes took their toll, and in March 1996, 13 years of Labour rule ended. A coalition of the more conservative Liberal and Nationalist parties captured 94 of 148 seats in the House of Representatives, with Labour falling to 47. The popular Liberal party leader John Howard became the new prime minister.

In Oct. 1998 elections, the Liberal-Nationalist coalition maintained its control of the House of Representatives, though by a diminished margin, with 79 of the 148 seats. In the interim, Australia's Constitutional Convention voted (in Feb. 1998) to proclaim Australia a republic, severing its residual ties to the British Crown. The Howard government promised a referendum on the matter before 2000. With respect to aboriginal claims to Australian land, the government carried a Native Title Bill in July 1998, giving Australia's state governments authority to rule on the issue, and requiring claimants to prove an actual connection to the land claimed.

▶ **AUSTRIA**
Republic of Austria

• **GEOGRAPHY Location:** landlocked country in central Europe. **Boundaries:** Germany and Czech Republic to N, Hungary and Slovak Republic to E, Slovenia and Italy to S, Switzerland and Liechtenstein to W. **Total area:** 32,377 sq. mi. (83,858 sq km). **Coastline:** none. **Comparative area:** slightly smaller than Maine. **Land use:** 17% arable land; 1% permanent crops; 23% meadows and pastures; 39% forest and woodland; 20% other; includes negl. % irrigated. **Major cities:** (1991 census) Vienna (capital) 1,533,176; Graz 232,155; Linz 202,855; Salzburg 143,971; Innsbruck 114,996.

• **PEOPLE Population:** 8,139,299 (1999 est.). **Nationality:** noun—Austrian(s); adjective—Austrian. **Ethnic groups:** 99.4% German, 0.3% Croatian, 0.2% Slovene, 0.1% other. **Languages:** German. **Religions:** 78% Roman Catholic, 5% Protestant, 17% none or other.

• **GOVERNMENT Type:** federal republic. **Constitution:** 1920; revised 1929; reinstated Dec. 1945. **National holiday:** National Day, Oct. 26. **Heads of Government:** Thomas Klestil, president (since July 1992); Viktor Klima, chancellor (since Jan. 1997). **Structure:** executive; bicameral legislature; directly elected president whose functions are largely representational; independent federal judiciary.

• **ECONOMY Monetary unit:** Austrian schilling. **Budget:** (1998 est.) *income:* $50.4 bil.; *expend.:* $55.9 bil. **GDP:** (1998 est.) $184.5 bil., $22,700 per capita. **Chief crops:** grain, fruits, potatoes, sugar beets. **Natural resources:** iron ore, crude oil, timber, magnesite, lead. **Major industries:** foods, iron, steel, machinery. **Labor force:** 3.7 mil. (1998); foreign laborers number 298,000; 67.7% services, 29% industry and crafts, 0.7% agriculture and forestry; 7% unemployment (1999 est.); estimated 150,000 Austrians are employed in other European countries. **Exports:** (1998) $62.5 bil.; vehicles, machinery and equipment, paper and cardboard, metal goods.. **Imports**: (1998) $65.8 bil.; vehicles, machinery and equipment, apparel, metal goods. **Major trading partners:** (1997) *exports:* 62% EU, 17.6% Eastern Europe, 3.7% U.S.; *imports:* 68.9% EU, 11% Eastern Europe, 7.1% Asia, 5.4% U.S.

The Celtic tribes in what is now Austria were conquered by Rome under Emperor Augustus. After the fall of Rome, it was overrun by Huns, Lombards, Ostrogoths, and Bavarians. In 788 it was incorporated into the empire of Charlemagne. From the 9th to the 13th century, its territory was divided among a variety of feudal domains. In the late 13th century, Austria was reunited under Rudolph I of Habsburg, whose dynasty became synonymous with Austrian history for the next seven centuries. Rudolph's successors steadily enlarged their domain by conquest and marital diplomacy until, by the reign of Charles V (1500-58), they ruled not only the Holy Roman Empire (encompassing most of central Europe) but also the Netherlands, Spain, and all of its colonies.

After the reign of Charles V, the Habsburg Empire was split into two branches, one governing Spain, the other the Holy Roman Empire. Habsburg power in Germany declined after the Thirty Years' War (1618-48) but was affirmed in the Danube valley after the defeat of the Turkish siege of Vienna in 1683 and the subsequent reconquest of Hungary from the Turks. The marriage of Maria Teresa to Francis of Lorraine gave rise to the House of Habsburg-Lorraine in 1745. In 1804 the Austrian empire was founded, and two years later, the defunct Holy Roman Empire was abolished. The Ausgleich ("compromise") of 1867 transformed the empire into the Dual Monarchy of Austria-Hungary.

In 1914 the assassination of Archduke Franz Ferdinand, the heir to the Austrian throne, led to the outbreak of World War I, which resulted in a wholesale redrawing of national boundaries in Central Europe. Austria emerged as a small Alpine republic, with about 12 percent of the territory of the old Dual Monarchy. The new republic faced a severe postwar economic crisis, as well as a political stalemate between the Christian Social party and the Social Democratic party, each with the support of about half of the electorate, and each with its own paramilitary organization.

In 1933, as Hitler's National Socialists rose to power in Germany, Austrian Chancellor Engelbert Dollfuss, leader of the Christian Social party, instituted rule by decree and began building a corporate state modeled on Italian fascism. His attempt to disarm the Social Democratic militia led to civil war. The government triumphed, but Dollfuss was assassinated in an attempted coup by Austrian Nazis in July 1934. Hitler finally forced Austrian union with Germany (the Anschluss) in 1938, after which Austria was considered a part of Greater Germany.

Conquered by American and Soviet troops early in 1945, Austria was divided into French, British, American, and Russian zones of occupation after World War II. But the occupying powers permitted the formation of a unified national government, formed in November 1945 and recognized by the Western powers in 1946. The occupation ended in 1955 with the signing of the Austrian State Treaty. The four powers withdrew their forces, and Austria pledged itself to a policy of permanent neutrality, with no foreign military alliances or military bases on Austrian territory.

The coalition government continued to 1966, when the People's party under Josef Klaus gained a parliamentary majority. In 1970 the Socialist party under Bruno Kreisky came to power. Socialist dominance continued until 1983, when the Socialists had to form a coalition with the right-wing Freedom party in order to stay in power. Kreisky resigned and was succeeded by Fred Sinowatz.

From 1986 to 1997, a "Grand Coalition" of the Socialist and People's Parties governed Austria under Socialist Chancellor Franz Vranitzky. In ten years, the government cautiously privatized state-owned enterprises of the already mild Austrian form of socialism, while tourism, a highly developed manufacturing sector, and substantial petroleum reserves continued to contribute to the country's prosperity. The government dramatically cut both personal and corporate taxes and began an active role in promoting regional trade with the newly-independent states of East-Central Europe. On Jan. 1, 1995, Austria entered the European Union.

Tensions arising from increasing unemployment and growing immigration of "economic refugees" from Asia and Africa as well as from Eastern Europe led to some worrisome results: amending Austria's asylum law, consideration of immigration quotas, and the growing strength of the right-wing Freedom Party. The desire to meet the EU's single currency standards led to welfare spending cuts which provoked further voter dissatisfaction. In Oct. 1996 Austrian voters (participating for the first time in European Parliament elections), gave Freedom Party candidates, who are opposed to Austria's participation in EMU, 27.6% of their votes, while Socialists garnered only 29.1% and the People's Party took 29.6%.

Denying any connection with these voting results, Chancellor Vranitzky resigned in January 1997 and was succeeded by Socialist Finance Minister Viktor Klima. In Oct. 1999 the Freedom Party again made a strong showing in national elections, making European political leaders very apprehensive.

▶ **AZERBAIJAN**
Azerbaijani Republic

● **GEOGRAPHY   Location:** southern Transcaucasia between Europe and Asia. **Boundaries:** Georgia to NW, Russian Federation to N, Caspian Sea to E, Iran to S, Armenia to SW. Nakhichevan Autonomous Republic (ASSR) is part of Azerbaijan although it is inside Armenian territory. **Total land area:** 33,436 sq. mi. (86,600 sq km). **Coastline:** Caspian Sea. **Comparative area**: about the size of Maine. **Land use:** 18% arable land, 5% permanent crops, 25% meadows and pastures, 52% other. **Major cities:** (1990 est.) Baku (capital) 1,149,000; Gyanja (formerly Kirovabad) 281,000; Sumgait 235,000.

● **PEOPLE   Population:** 7,908,224 (1999 est.). **Nationality:** noun—Azerbaijani(s) or Azeri(s); adjective—Azerbaijani. **Ethnic groups:** 90% Azeri, 3.2% Dagestani Peoples, 2.5% Russian. **Languages:** 89% Azeri, 3% Russian, 2% Armenian, 6% other (1995 est.). **Religions:** 93.4% Muslim, 2.5% Russian Orthodox, 2.3% Armenian Orthodox, 1.8% other (1995 est.).

● **GOVERNMENT   Type:** republic. **Independence:** Aug. 30, 1991 (from USSR). **Constitution:** Nov. 12, 1995. **National holiday:** Independence Day, May 28. **Heads of Government:** Heydar Aliyev, president (since Oct. 1993); Suret Husseinov, prime minister (since Aug. 1993). **Structure:** executive; unicameral legislatiure; judiciary.

• **ECONOMY Monetary unit:** manat. **Budget:** (1996 est.) *income:* $565 mil.; *expend.:* $682 mil. **GDP:** $12.9 bil., $1,640 per capita (1998 est.). **Chief crops:** cotton, tea, tobacco, wheat, fruit. **Natural resources:** petroleum, natural gas, iron ore. **Major industries:** petroleum and natural gas, construction materials, chemicals. **Labor force:** 2.9 mil. (1997). **Exports:** $781 mil. (f.o.b., 1997); oil, gas, chemicals, oil field equipment, textiles, cotton. **Imports:** $794 mil. (c.i.f., 1997); machinery and parts, consumer durables, foodstuffs, textiles. **Major trading partners:** mostly CIS and European countries.

The territory of present-day Azerbaijan has been inhabited since Paleolithic times. The name Azerbaijan is derived (via Arabic and Turkish) from Atropates (a vassal of Alexander III of Macedonia), who founded an independent state here in the fourth century b.c. The population of Azerbaijan is approximately seven million, but nearly seven million additional Azeris with the same language and faith live across the border in Iran.

For much of its history, the territory of Azerbaijan, home to an indigenous nomadic people, has been occupied by Persians, Muslim Arabs, Turkic tribes from Mongolia, Ottoman Turks, Mongols, and in the 18th century, Russians. The capital city of Baku was an important outlet on the Volga River-Caspian Sea route; under Peter the Great, the Russians occupied Baku and Derbent, and for a while controlled the Caspian Sea. Command of this territory shifted between Ottomans, Persians, and Russians in the 18th and 19th centuries, with the Russians ultimately establishing military rule by 1828 with the Treaty of Turkmenchai. This treaty ceded the southern half of the country to Persia and the northern half to Russia.

Under the Russians, Azerbaijan became an industrial center and eventually a major oil producer. In 1883 the Russians finished building the Transcaucasian Railway, which linked Baku with the Black Sea coast and central Russia and made Baku one of the most important industrial hubs in the Russian empire. Baku became a revolutionary center around the turn of the century. In 1918 an independent republic was formed, but in 1920 it was overthrown by the Soviet Red Army, and in April 1920 the Azerbaijan Soviet Socialist Republic (SSR) was proclaimed. Two years later, it was joined with the Armenian and Georgian SSRs to form the Transcaucasian Soviet Federal Socialist Republic; in 1936, however, the three again became separate union republics.

While a Soviet republic, Azerbaijan was industrialized, its agriculture collectivized, and religious persecution was severe. It also entered into a war in 1988 with neighboring Armenia over the Nagorno-Karabakh region, which is largely populated with ethnic Armenians but lies within Azerbaijani territory. The local council of Nagorno-Karabakh petitioned the Armenian and Azerbaijani Supreme Soviets to transfer the region to Armenia in February 1988, but Azerbaijan refused, spurring a war that lasts to this day and has resulted in thousands of casualties on both sides.

In January 1990, a series of attacks on Communist party buildings and against Armenians in Azerbaijan precipitated a brutal Soviet Army intervention to restore order. A state of emergency was declared, and the first secretary of the Communist party was fired and replaced by Ayaz Mutalibov. He was elected president in September 1991, and on Oct. 18, 1991, Azerbaijan's Supreme Soviet declared the country's independence. On Dec. 21, 1991, Azerbaijan joined 10 other former Soviet republics in forming the Commonwealth of Independent States.

After the dissolution of the USSR, Soviet power was diminished, but Azerbaijan had problems consolidating its own political future. In early 1992, Pres. Mutalibov was forced from office. His successor, Abulfaz Elchibey, was in turn driven out of office by armed rebels after the fighting in Nagorno-Karabakh turned decisively in Armenia's favor. He was replaced by Heydar Aliyev, a former Communist party boss, in 1993. Aliyev survived two coup attempts and the country's flagging fortunes in Nagorno-Karabakh to complete a $7.4 billion deal with western companies to develop oil fields in the Caspian Sea in September 1994. In parliamentary elections in 1995, Aliyev's New Azerbaijan party won 70 percent of the vote, despite charges of vote-rigging. And in January 1996, the Aliyev government negotiated an agreement to transport the oil from the Caspian Sea via pipeline (through Chechnya) to the Russian port of Novorossiysk for export to the world market. The pipeline opened Nov. 12, 1997 only three months after Aliyev met with Pres. Clinton in Washington to sign a treaty allowing unrestricted transfer of profits and capital between U.S. and Azerbaijan.

In Oct. 1998, Aliyev held presidential elections which were boycotted by opposition parties and which European monitors declared to be seriously irregular. Aliyev took 76 percent of the vote.

▶ **BAHAMAS**
Commonwealth of The Bahamas
• **GEOGRAPHY Location:** nearly 700 islands in an archipelago that extends 590 mi. (950 km) SE-NW between Florida and Haiti. Nassau 25°05'N, 77°20'W. **Boundaries:** western Atlantic Ocean to N, E, S, and W. **Total land area:** 5,382 sq. mi. (13,940 sq km). **Coastline:** 2,200 mi. (3,542 km). **Comparative area:** slightly larger than Connecticut. **Land use:** 1% arable land; negl. % permanent crops; negl. % meadows and pastures; 32% forest and woodland; 67% other. **Major cities:** (1990) Nassau (capital) 191,542.
• **PEOPLE Population:** 283,705 (1999 est.). **Nationality:** noun—Bahamian(s); adjective—Bahamian. **Ethnic groups:** 85% black, 15% white. **Languages:** English, some Creole among Haitian immigrants. **Religions:** 32% Baptist, 20% Anglican, 19% Roman Catholic; smaller groups of other Protestants, Greek Orthodox, and Jews.
• **GOVERNMENT Type:** independent commonwealth recognizing Elizabeth II as chief of state. **Independence:** July 10, 1973 (from UK). **Constitution:** July 10, 1973. **National holiday:** National Day, July 10. **Heads of Government:** Sir Orville Turnquest, governor-general (since Jan. 1995); Hubert A. Ingraham, prime minister (since Aug. 1992). **Structure:** executive—governor general (appointed by queen); bicameral legislature; judiciary.
• **ECONOMY Monetary unit:** Bahamian dollar. **Budget:** (FY97/98) *income:* $766 mil.; *expend.:* $845 mil. **GDP:** (1998 est.) $5.63 bil., $20,100 per capita. **Chief crops:** citrus fruits, vegetables; poultry. **Natural resources:** salt, aragonite, timber. **Major industries:** tourism, banking, cement. **Labor force:** 148,000 (1996); 40% tourism, 30% government, 10% business services; 9% unemployment (1998 est.). **Exports:** $300 mil. (f.o.b., 1998); pharmaceuticals, cement, rum, crawfish. **Imports:** $1.37 bil. (c.i.f., 1998 est.); foodstuffs, manufac-

tured goods, crude oil. **Major trading partners: exports:** 24.5% U.S., 23.9% EU (excluding UK), 12.6% UK, 5.6% Singapore. **imports:** 34.9% U.S., 24.3% EU, 15.5% Japan, 6.3% Russia.

Christopher Columbus made his first landfall in the Americas in the Bahamas Oct. 12, 1492. Though the Spanish never settled the islands, they enslaved and removed to Hispaniola 40,000 of the indigenous Arawaks by 1508. Their shallow seas (baja mar) made the islands a haven for pirates in the 17th century—as well as during the Civil War, Prohibition, and for drug smugglers today. British colonization of the Bahamas began in 1629 and continued slowly over the next two centuries.

Tourism has been the mainstay of the economy in this century, but high unemployment is a continuing problem. Parliament relaxed restrictions on offshore banking to stem the flight of international capital prompted by allegations of government corruption and involvement in drug trafficking. In 1992 the government of Prime Minister Lynden Pindling was defeated after 25 years in office, largely because of corruption charges. In recent years the economy has grown and diversified but rising crime related to gangs of unemployed young men worries the electorate.

▶ BAHRAIN
State of Bahrain
• **GEOGRAPHY Location:** group of 35 islands in western Persian Gulf. Manama 26°17'N, 50°33'E. **Boundaries:** Saudi Arabia about 15 mi. (24 km) to W and Qatar about 17 mi. (28 km) to SE. **Total land area:** 239 sq. mi. (620 sq km). **Coastline:** 161 mi. (259 km). **Comparative area:** slightly less than 3.5 times size of Washington, D.C. **Land use:** 2% arable land; 2% permanent crops; 6% meadows and pastures; 0% forest and woodland; 90% other; includes negl. % irrigated. **Major cities:** (1990 est.) Manama (capital) 138,784; Muharraq Town 75,906.
• **PEOPLE Population:** 629,090 (1999 est.). **Nationality:** noun—Bahraini(s); adjective—Bahraini. **Ethnic groups:** 63% Bahraini, 13% Asian, 10% other Arab, 8% Iranian, 6% other. **Languages:** Arabic, English, Farsi, Urdu. **Religions:** 75% Shi'a Muslim, 25% Sunni Muslim.
• **GOVERNMENT Type:** traditional monarchy. **Independence:** Aug. 15, 1971 (from UK). **Constitution:** May 26, 1973 (effective Dec. 1973). **National holiday:** Dec. 16. **Heads of Government:** Hamad Bin Isa Al-Khalifa, amir (since March 1999); Khalifa bin Sulman al-Khalifa, prime minister (since Jan. 1970). **Structure:** executive—amir is traditional arab monarch, appoints cabinet led by prime minister; legislative—amir dissolved National Assembly (Aug. 1975), appointed Advisory Council Dec. 1992; independent judiciary.
• **ECONOMY Monetary unit:** Bahraini dinar. **Budget:** (1999 est.) **income:** $1.5 bil.; **expend.:** $1.9 bil. **GDP:** (1998 est.) $8.2 bil., $13,100 per capita. **Chief crops:** not self-sufficient in food production; produces some fruits and vegetables; engages in shrimping and fishing. **Natural resources:** oil, associated and nonassociated natural gas, fish. **Major industries:** petroleum processing and refining, aluminum smelting, offshore banking. **Labor force:** 150,000 (1997 est.); 79% industry, commerce and service (note: 42% of labor force is Bahraini). **Exports:** $4.7 bil. (f.o.b. 1997 est.); 61% petroleum, 7% aluminum. **Imports:** $4.4 bil. (f.o.b., 1997 est.); 59% nonoil, 41% crude oil. **Major trading partners:** (1994) **exports:** India, Japan, Saudi Arabia; **imports:** Saudi Arabia, U.S., UK.

Bahrain has been an entrepôt of trade between Arabia and India since the second millenium b.c. The Portuguese fortified Bahrain in the 16th century but were driven out by the Persian shah Abbas I early in the 17th century. At the end of the 18th century, it became an Arab sheikhdom within the Ottoman Empire. Bahrain entered into treaty relations with Great Britain in 1820 and became a British protectorate in 1861. After British forces withdrew from the gulf, the nation became an independent emirate, in August 1971, under Amir Isa bin Sulman al-Khalifa, who came to the throne in 1961. Today the U.S. maintains a large military base here that served as naval headquarters during the Persian Gulf War.

Oil reserves—first discovered in 1932—were largely depleted by the mid-1970s. The economy now has diversified to include oil refining, aluminum smelting, international banking, and shipping services. Bahrain has close relations with Saudi Arabia; a causeway permits directroad communication between the two countries.

In June 1995 social and political unrest caused by uneven distribution of wealth, high unemployment, and a repressive government erupted into serious rioting. Protests by the Shiite majority began again in early 1996; a government crackdown led to the arrest of over 600 dissidents. Bahrain's family-run, Sunni Moslem government continued with the March 1999 death of its founding emir and his replacement with his son, Hamad bin Isa al-Khalifa.

▶ BANGLADESH
People's Republic of Bangladesh
• **GEOGRAPHY Location:** southern Asia. **Boundaries:** India to N, E, and W; Myanmar to E, Bay of Bengal to S. **Total land area:** 55,598 sq. mi. (144,000 sq km). **Coastline:** 360 mi. (580 km). **Comparative area:** between Arkansas and Wisconsin. **Land use:** 67% arable land; 2% permanent crops; 4% meadows and pastures; 16% forest and woodland; 11% other; includes 14% irrigated. **Major cities:** (1991 census) Dhaka (formerly Dacca) (capital) 3,637,892; Chittagong 1,566,070; Khulna 601,051; Rajshahi 324,532; Barisal 180,014.
• **PEOPLE Population:** 127,117,967 (1999 est.). **Nationality:** noun—Bangladeshi(s); adjective—Bangladesh. **Ethnic groups:** 98% Bengali, 250,000 Biharis, less than 1 mil. tribals. **Languages:** Bangla (official); English widely used. **Religions:** 88.3% Muslim, 10.5% Hindu, 1.2% Buddhist, Christian, and other.
• **GOVERNMENT Type:** republic. **Independence:** Dec. 16, 1971 (from Pakistan). **Constitution:** Nov. 4, 1972, effective Dec. 16, 1972, suspended following coup of Mar. 24, 1982, restored Nov. 10, 1986; amended many times. **National holiday:** March 26, Independence Day. **Heads of Government:** Shahabuddin Ahmed, president (since Oct. 1996); Ms. Sheik Hasina Wazed, prime minister (since June 1996). **Structure:** executive—president appoints prime minister and Advisory Council; unicameral legislature dissolved by president following elections on Feb. 15, 1996 and named caretaker prime minister; judiciary.
• **ECONOMY Monetary unit:** taka. **Budget:** (1997 est.) **income:** $3.8 bil.; **expend.:** $5.5 bil. **GDP:** (1998 est.) $175.5 bil., $1,380 per capita. **Chief crops:** large-scale subsistence farming, heavily dependent on monsoon rain; main crops are jute, rice, wheat, tea, sugarcane, and potatoes. **Natural**

resources: natural gas, arable land, timber. **Major industries:** jute manufactures, cotton textiles, food processing. **Labor force:** 56 mil. (1996); extensive export of labor to Saudi Arabia, UAE, and Oman; 65% agriculture, 25% services, 10% industry and mining. **Exports:** $4.4 bil. (1997 est.); garments, jute, leather, seafood. **Imports:** $7.1 bil. (1997 est.); capital foods, textiles, food, petroleum products. **Major trading partners:** (FY95/96 est.) *exports:* 42% Western Europe, 30% U.S., 4% Hong Kong, 3% Japan; *imports:* 21% India, 10% China, 8% Western Europe, 7% Hong Kong., 6% Singapore.

Located on the alluvial plain of the Ganges River northeast of India, Bengal was ruled by Buddhist kings from the eighth to 12th centuries. Conquered by Muslim invaders around 1200, many inhabitants converted to Islam and Bengal became part of the Moghul Empire in the 16th century. The British East India Company established a settlement in 1642, and by 1750 all of Bengal was under British rule. The formerly diverse agricultural economy became dominated by export crops of opium and jute, while rice continued to be grown in the fertile delta. The region's trade flowed through the British-built city of Calcutta.

With Indian independence in 1947, Bengal was partitioned along religious lines, Hindu West Bengal (including Calcutta) remaining with India and Muslim East Bengal becoming the eastern province of Pakistan. In the elections of 1971, the Bengali Awami League gained control of Pakistan's National Assembly. Seating of the new National Assembly was postponed, and riots broke out in East Pakistan. Troops from West Pakistan were sent to quell the riots on May 25; the following day East Pakistan declared its independence as Bangladesh. Civil war followed; 10 million refugees fled to India. Following Indian intervention, Pakistan acknowledged Bangladesh's independence on Dec. 15.

Since independence, Bangladesh has consistently been one of the world's poorest countries, plagued by violent political instability, military coups, overpopulation, a flagging economy, and frequent catastrophic floods (including one in 1975 that killed half a million people). The first president, Sheik Mujibur Rahman, was assassinated in 1975. Lt. Gen. Hossain Mohammad Ershad, who seized power in a coup in March 1982, was elected president in 1986, but resigned in 1990 in the face of opposition unrest.

In 1991, the Bangladesh Nationalist party (BNP) of Begum Khaleda Zia (widow of former president Ziaur Rahman, who was assassinated in 1981) won 138 of 330 parliamentary seats running on a platform of free enterprise, privatization, and an Islamic state. In September 1991, the constitution was amended to put the prime minister in charge of the government and make the presidency a largely ceremonial post.

In 1994, nearly 150 opposition members of Parliament resigned en masse, eliciting a promise from Prime Minister Zia to hold general elections in June 1996. In those elections, the Awami League, led by Sheik Hasina Wazed, returned to power for the first time since 1975, when the military massacred most of her family, including her father, Pres. Sheik Mujibur Rahman. In 1998, fifteen were convicted and sentenced to death for their role in the assassinations. Zia's call for nation-wide protest strike went unanswered, but her BNP (in Jan. 1999) was one of three parties,

with General Ershad's Jatiya and the Moslem Jamaat-e-Islami, to form a bloc seeking to force early elections upon prime minister Wazed.

▶BARBADOS
● **GEOGRAPHY Location:** easternmost of Caribbean islands, about 200 mi. (320 km) NE of Trinidad. Bridgetown 13°06'N, 59°36'W. **Boundaries:** Atlantic Ocean. **Total land area:** 166 sq. mi. (430 sq km). **Coastline:** 60 mi. (97 km). **Comparative area:** slightly less than 2.5 times size of Washington, D.C. **Land use:** 77% arable land; 9% meadows and pastures; 14% other. **Major cities:** (1990 census) Bridgetown (capital) 6,070.

● **PEOPLE Population:** 259,191 (1999 est.). **Nationality:** noun—Barbadian(s); adjective—Barbadian. **Ethnic groups:** 80% black, 16% other, 4% white. **Languages:** English. **Religions:** 67% Protestant, 4% Roman Catholic, 29% none or other.

● **GOVERNMENT Type:** parliamentary democracy recognizing Queen Elizabeth II as chief of state. **Independence:** Nov. 30, 1966 (from UK). **Constitution:** Nov. 30, 1966. **National holiday:** Independence Day, Nov. 30. **Heads of Government:** Sir Clifford Husbands, governor general (since June 1996); Owen Arthur, prime minister (since Sept. 1994). **Structure:** executive—governor general (appointed by the queen) prime minister; bicameral legislature; judiciary.

● **ECONOMY Monetary unit:** Barbadian dollar. **Budget:** (FY97/98 est.) *income:* $725.5 mil.; *expend.:* $750.6 mil. **GDP:** (1998 est.) $2.9 bil., $11,200 per capita. **Chief crops:** sugarcane, vegetables, cotton. **Natural resources:** crude oil, fish, natural gas. **Major industries:** tourism, sugar, light manufacturing. **Labor force:** 136,000 (1998 est.); 75% services, 15% industry, 10% agriculture (1996 est.). **Exports:** $280 mil. (f.o.b., 1997 est.); sugar and molasses, rum, other foods and beverages, chemicals. **Imports:** $982 mil. (c.i.f., 1997 est.); consumer goods, machinery, foodstuffs. **Major trading partners:** *exports:* 34.8% Caricom, 18.4% U.S., 16.6% UK, 4.4% Canada. *imports:* 40.5% U.S., 14.7% Caricom, 8.4% UK, 5% Canada.

Barbados is the only Caribbean island not to have changed hands prior to independence. Although the Spanish removed virtually all the indigenous Arawaks of Barbados by the mid1500s, the island was not claimed until the British arrived in the 1620s. Tobacco, cotton, and sugarcane—harvested with slave labor until 1833—were mainstays of the economy. The 1966 constitution mandates the promotion of economic equality among Barbadians, and the country was fairly prosperous relative to other Caribbean states until recently, when declining tourism and record-low sugar production have had serious adverse effects. Still, the Barbados Labor Party retains its popularity, winning 26 of the parliament's 28 seats in Jan. 1999 elections.

▶BELARUS
Republic of Belarus
● **GEOGRAPHY Location:** northeastern Europe. **Boundaries:** Lithuania and Latvia to N, Russian Federation to NE and E, Ukraine to S, Poland to W, Lithuania and Latvia to NW. **Total land area:** 80,154 sq. mi. (207,600 sq km). **Coastline:** none. **Comparative area:** slightly smaller than Kansas. **Land use:** 29% arable land; 1% permanent crops; 15% meadows and pastures; 55% other. **Major cities:** (1990 est.) Minsk (capital) 1,613,000; Gomel (Homel) 506,000; Mahilou (Mogilev) 363,000; Vitebsk 356,000; Grodno 277,000.

●**PEOPLE Population:** 10,401,784 (1999 est.). **Nationality:** noun—Belarusian(s); adjective—Belarusian. **Ethnic groups:** 77.9% Byelorussian, 13.2% Russian, 4.1% Polish, 2.9% Ukrainian, 1.9% other. **Languages:** Byelorusian (official), Russian. **Religions:** 80% Eastern Orthodox.
●**GOVERNMENT Type:** republic. **Independence:** Aug. 25, 1991 (from USSR). **Constitution:** Adopted Nov. 1996. **National holiday:** Independence Day, July 27. **Heads of Government:** Aleksander Lukashenko, president (since July 1994); Mikhail Chygir, prime minister (since July 1994). **Structure:** executive—president, prime minister, Council of Ministers; bicameral legislature—most members appointed by the president; judiciary.
●**ECONOMY Monetary unit:** Belarusian rubel. **Budget:** (1997 est.) *income:* 4 bil.; *expend.:* 4.1 bil. **GDP:** (1998 est.) $53.7 bil., $5,200 per capita. **Chief crops:** grain, potatoes, vegetables. **Natural resources:** forest, peat, oil, and natural gas. **Major industries:** tractors, metalworking, heavy-duty vehicles. **Labor force:** 4.3 mil. (1998). **Exports:** $7 bil. (f.o.b., 1998); machinery, transport equipment, chemicals, foodstuffs. **Imports:** $8.5 bil. (c.i.f., 1998); fuel, natural gas, industrial raw materials, textiles. **Major trading partners:** Russia, Ukraine, Poland, Germany.

Belarus, also known as White Russia or Byelorussia, has been inhabited since the seventh century. In the 13th and 14th centuries, present-day Belarus became part of the Grand Duchy of Lithuania, which then became part of Poland in the 16th century. Between 1772 and 1795, Poland was partitioned, which resulted in Belarus becoming part of the Russian empire. After the Bolshevik revolution in 1917, Soviet troops came to Minsk, but they were forced to withdraw in the face of approaching German troops. The Treaty of Brest-Litovsk in March 1918 ceded to Germany most of the territory of Belarus. The same year, an independent Belarusian Democratic Republic was founded, but it had little real power. Once the Germans left, the Soviets easily retook Belarus, and on Jan. 1, 1919, the Belarusian Soviet Socialist Republic (SSR) was proclaimed.

This did not end the divisions of the traditional Belarusian lands. In February 1919 they were merged within the Soviet Union with Lithuania, but the Poles launched an attack in April of the same year and took both Lithuania and Belarus. In 1920 the Belarusian SSR was re-formed, but it included only the eastern portion of historical Belarusian lands. The Treaty of Riga in March 1921 granted the western territories of Belarus to Poland and the eastern portion to the Russian Federation. In 1924 and 1925 the eastern regions were returned to the Belarusian SSR.

After the Soviets invaded Poland in 1939, the lands that Belarus had lost in 1921 were returned to it. Between 1941 and 1945, the Germans occupied the Belarusian lands, and more than a million lost their lives, including most of the large Jewish population. After the war, the Belarusian SSR was restored with all of its historic lands, and Belarus was finally unified. However, when Stalin redrew the Soviet Union's internal borders, he included Belarus's traditional capital of Vilnius in Lithuania.

Under Soviet rule, Belarus turned from a mainly agricultural to an industrial land. Large numbers of Belarusians fiercely fought Stalin's collectivization plan in the 1930s, and thousands were killed or deported. Both Stalin's purges of the 1930s and World War II, which devastated both its agri-

culture and industry, inflicted great losses on Belarus. After the war, Soviet policy in Belarus concentrated on rebuilding its economy and encouraging Russian immigration into the republic (Russian replaced Belarusian as the official language).

The Belarusian SSR was one of the more prosperous and stable of the union republics, so Mikhail Gorbachev's policy of glasnost, or openness, in the 1980s was relatively slow to have an impact. In 1987, however, two issues had come to the fore in the Belarusian SSR: the status of the Belarusian language and the ecological dangers of Chernobyl, the famous nuclear reactor that had exploded in nearby Ukraine in 1986, but which dropped almost three-quarters of its fallout on southeastern Belarus. In voicing these concerns, the Belarusians formed several new, non-Communist parties that challenged the traditional authority of the ruling Communist party. In Jan. 1990, largely due to these new forces, Belarusian became the official language over Russian, and on July 27, 1990, Belarus declared its sovereignty from the USSR.

After the fall of the Soviet government, Belarus was one of the strongest supporters of maintaining a union of republics. On Dec. 8, 1991, Belarus, Ukraine, and Russia hosted the talks leading to the Minsk Agreement, which created the Commonwealth of Independent States (CIS). On Dec. 21, 11 other former Soviet republics joined the commonwealth by signing the Alma-Ata Declaration.

While Belarus at first seemed to view the CIS as a temporary expedient, President Aleaksander Lukashenko has strongly fostered closer ties with Russia. A 1995 customs union was expanded by the 1996 Union Treaty (reinforced by a second Union Treaty in 1997) to include a common currency, joint tax and legal systems, shared energy and transport networks, and common defense and foreign policies. And meanwhile, Lukashenko tightened his dictatorial hold on Belarus with a new constitution (Nov. 1996) which permits presidential rule by decree and gives Lukashenko power to appoint half the members of the Constitutional Court and 20 of the 64 members of the Council of the Republic, the newly-created upper house of the legislature. In 1997, the U.S. announced it was cutting off $4 mil. in aid to protest the new authoritarian government.

▶**BELGIUM**
Kingdom of Belgium
●**GEOGRAPHY Location:** northwestern Europe. **Boundaries:** Netherlands to N, Luxembourg and Germany to E, France to S, and North Sea to W. **Total land area:** 11,780 sq. mi. (30,510 sq km). **Coastline:** 40 mi. (64 km). **Comparative area:** slightly larger than Maryland. **Land use:** 24% arable land; 1% permanent crops; 20% meadows and pastures; 21% forest and woodland; 34% other; includes negl. % irrigated. **Major cities:** (1993) Bruxelles (Brussels—capital) 949,070; Antwerpen (Anvers, Antwerp) 462,880; Gent (Gand, Ghent) 228,490; Charleroi 206,898; Liège (Luik) 195,389.
●**PEOPLE Population:** 10,182,034 (1999 est.). **Nationality:** noun—Belgian(s); adjective—Belgian. **Ethnic groups:** 55% Fleming, 33% Walloon, 12% mixed or other. **Languages:** 56% Flemish (Dutch), 32% French, 1% German; 11% legally bilingual (divided along ethnic lines). **Religions:** 75% Roman Catholic, remainder Protestant or other.

● **GOVERNMENT Type:** federal parliamentary democracy under a constitutional monarch. **Independence:** Oct. 4, 1830 (from Netherlands). **Constitution:** Feb. 7, 1831; last revised July 14, 1993. **National holiday:** National Day, July 21. **Heads of Government:** Albert II, king (since Aug. 1993); Guy Verhofstadt, prime minister (since July 1999). **Structure:** executive—king, prime minister, and cabinet; bicameral legislature; independent judiciary.

● **ECONOMY Monetary unit:** Belgian franc. **Budget:** *income:* $NA; *expend.:* $NA. **GDP:** (1998 est.) $236 bil., $23,400 per capita. **Chief crops:** sugar beets, vegetables, fruit, grain. **Natural resources:** coal, natural gas. **Major industries:** engineering, metal products, motor vehicle assembly, processed food, beverages, chemicals. **Labor force:** 4.283 mil. (1997); 69.7% services, 27.7% industry; 2.6% agriculture (1992 est.). **Exports:** (Belgium-Luxembourg Economic Union) $145.1 bil. (f.o.b., 1998); iron, steel, transportation equipment, tractors, diamonds. **Imports:** (Belgium-Luxembourg Economic Union) $137.1 bil. (f.o.b., 1998); fuels, grains, chemicals, foodstuffs. **Major trading partners:** (Belgium-Luxembourg Economic Union, 1994) *exports:* 67.2% EU, 5.8% U.S.; *imports:* 75% EU, 5% U.S.

The country now known as Belgium was, during the Middle Ages, part of the powerful duchy of Burgundy. By marriage and diplomacy, the "Low Countries" became part of the Habsburg Empire in 1482 (see "Austria"). In a struggle lasting from the late 16th century to the Treaty of Westphalia in 1648, the northern part of that region (Netherlands) became independent, but the southern portion remained part of the Habsburg Empire—under the Spanish branch until 1715, then under the Austrian branch until the French Revolution. The Congress of Vienna attached the lands to an enlarged Kingdom of the Netherlands in 1815.

In 1830 the Belgians revolted against the Dutch, and in 1831 the Treaty of London recognized an independent Kingdom of Belgium. Throughout the 19th century, its unity was precarious, as the country was bitterly divided politically between Catholic and Liberal parties, and ethnically between Dutch-speaking Flemings and French-speaking Walloons. In 1885 Belgium became a colonial power in Africa with Leopold II's establishment of the Congo Free State (later the Belgian Congo), which gained independence in 1960 as Zaire.

Belgium was a major battleground during World War I, but its boundaries were reestablished in 1919 by the Treaty of Versailles. When German troops of Hitler's Third Reich overran Belgium in May 1940, King Leopold III quickly signed an armistice, hoping to placate Hitler and avert further fighting. But the Belgian government fled to England, repudiated the armistice, and joined the Allies. The Germans controlled Belgium until the liberation of Brussels in September 1944.

Belgium made a swift postwar recovery. But the political atmosphere was poisoned by the issue of what to do about wartime collaborators up to and including the king. A referendum in 1950 narrowly approved Leopold III's return to the throne, but he was persuaded to abdicate in 1951 in favor of his son, Baudouin I.

Belgium has a flourishing economy with a highly modernized industrial sector complemented by tourism and agriculture. The issue of language dominates politics; since the 1960s, Belgium has devolved into a de facto confederation of Flemish-, French-, and German-speaking regions, with Brussels a multilingual region unto itself.

In the May 1995 election, the first under the new decentralized constitution of 1993, the Christian Democrat-Socialist coalition government retained a majority in the Chamber of Representatives. Since August 1996, the government has been shaken by massive demonstrations against inept police and legal handling of a widespread child prostitution and pornography ring with possible links to prominent politicians. But it was the additional "poultry scandal" of early 1999 (the government's tardy reaction to the discovery of dioxin in certain Belgian meat, eggs and dairy products) that toppled the coalition of Prime Minister Jean-Luc Dehaene. In June 1999 elections, the free-market Liberals won a plurality of seats (41) in parliament and the Greens rose from 11 to 20 seats; the coalition partners took 32 (Christian Democrats) and 33 (Socialists) seats.

▶ BELIZE

● **GEOGRAPHY Location:** northeastern coast of Central America. **Boundaries:** Mexico to N, Caribbean Sea to E, Guatemala to S and W. **Total land area:** 8,865 sq. mi. (22,960 sq km). **Coastline:** 240 mi. (386 km). **Comparative area:** between Massachusetts and New Hampshire. **Land use:** 2% arable land; 2% meadows and pastures; 44% forest and woodland; 52% other; includes negl. % irrigated. **Major cities:** (1993 est.) Belmopan (capital) 3,852; Belize City 47,723; Orange Walk 11,922; San Ignacio 9,702; Corozal 7,644.

● **PEOPLE Population:** 235,789 (1999 est.). **Nationality:** noun—Belizean(s); adjective—Belizean. **Ethnic groups:** 44% mestizo, 30% Creole, 11% Maya, 7% Garifuna. **Languages:** English (official), Spanish, Mayan, Garifuna (Carib). **Religions:** 62% Roman Catholic, 30% Protestant.

● **GOVERNMENT Type:** parliamentary democracy. **Independence:** Sept. 21, 1981 (from UK). **Constitution:** Sept. 21, 1981. **National holiday:** Independence Day, Sept. 21. **Heads of Government:** Sir Colville Norbert Young, governor general (since Nov. 1993); Said Musa, prime minister (since Aug. 1998). **Structure:** executive—governor general (appointed by Queen Elizabeth II, who is recognized as the head of state), prime minister, cabinet; bicameral legislature; judiciary.

● **ECONOMY Monetary unit:** Belizean dollar. **Budget:** (FY97/98 est.) *income:* $140 mil.; *expend.:* $142 mil. **GDP:** $700 mil., $3,000 per capita (1998 est.). **Chief crops:** bananas, coca, citrus, sugarcane; cultured shrimp; illegal producer of cannabis for international drug trade. **Natural resources:** arable land potential, timber, fish. **Major industries:** garments, food processing, tourism. **Labor force:** 71,000 (1997 est.); 30% agriculture, 16% services, 15.4% government, 11.2% commerce; shortage of skilled labor and all types of technical personnel; 13% unemployment (1997 est.). **Exports:** $95.3 mil. (f.o.b., 1998); sugar, citrus, bananas, clothing. **Imports:** $149.7 mil. (c.i.f., 1998 est.); machinery and transportation equipment, manufactured goods, food, fuels, chemicals. **Major trading partners:** (1994) *exports:* 45% U.S., 30% U.K., 3% Mexico, Canada; *imports:* 52% U.S., 13% Mexico, 5% U.K..

During the 1700s, Spain held sovereignty over Belize but never attempted to settle it. The British gradually did settle there, however, and in 1862, British Honduras, as it was called, became a Crown colony. Although Britain granted Belize independence in 1981, Guatemala claimed sovereignty over the area until 1992, when it finally recognized Belize's independence. But as British defense forces withdrew in 1994, Guatemala reasserted its old claims but without consequence.

▶BENIN
Republic of Benin
• **GEOGRAPHY Location:** western coast of Africa. **Boundaries:** Burkina Faso and Niger to N, Nigeria to E, Gulf of Guinea to S, Togo to W. **Total land area:** 43,483 sq. mi. (112,620 sq km). **Coastline:** 75 mi. (121 km). **Comparative area:** between Tennessee and Pennsylvania. **Land use:** 12% arable land; 4% permanent crops; 4% meadows and pastures; 35% forest and woodland; 45% other; includes negl. % irrigated. **Major cities:** (1985 est.) Porto-Novo (capital) 208,258; Cotonou 402,290.
• **PEOPLE Population:** 6,305,567 (1999 est.). **Nationality:** noun—Beninese (sing., pl.); adjective— Beninese. **Ethnic groups:** 99% African (predominantly Fon, Adja, Yoruba, Bariba); 5,500 Europeans. **Languages:** French (official); Fon and Yoruba in south; at least six major tribal languages in north. **Religions:** 70% indigenous beliefs, 15% Muslim, 15% Christian.
• **GOVERNMENT Type:** Multiparty democratic republic since Apr. 4, 1991. **Independence:** Aug. 1, 1960 (from France). **Constitution:** Dec. 2, 1990. **National holiday:** National Day, Aug. 1. **Head of Government:** Mathieu Kérékou, head of state, Maitre A. Houngbedji, prime minister (since Apr. 1996). **Structure:** executive—president, executive council; unicameral legislature; judiciary.
• **ECONOMY Monetary unit:** Communauté Financiere Africaine franc. **Budget:** (1995 est.) **income:** $299 mil.; **expend.:** $445 mil. **GDP:** (1998 est.) $7.6 bil., $1,300 per capita. **Chief crops:** corn, sorghum, cassava, yams. **Natural resources:** small offshore oil deposits, limestone, marble, timber. **Major industries:** textiles, cigarettes, beverages. **Labor force:** 1.9 mil. (1987); 60% agriculture, 2% industrial sector, remainder employed in transport, commerce, and public services. **Exports:** $250 mil. (f.o.b., 1998 est.); cotton, crude oil, palm products, cocoa. **Imports:** $314 mil. (f.o.b., 1998 est.); foodstuffs, beverages, tobacco, petroleum products. **Major trading partners:** *exports:* Brazil, Portugal, Morocco, Libya, France; *imports:* France, UK, Thailand, Hong Kong, China.

Although the early history of Benin is sketchy, a number of kingdoms had appeared in the region by the 11th century, and it was a center of wealth and power by the 1300s. In the 16th century, the Allada kingdom was founded in the south. In 1625, three brothers divided their power between Allada, Adjatché (Porto Novo), and Abomey. Under Ouegbadja (r. 1645-85) the latter, known as Dahomey, predominated. Much of its wealth derived from contact with Europeans, and especially the slave trade, which continued until 1885.

European contact began with the arrival of the Portuguese in 1485. Although traders and missionaries were established at Ouidah and Porto Novo in the 1500s, European influence remained slight. Dahomey expansion continued well into the 19th century. A commercial treaty with the French was signed in 1842, but relations between Dahomeyans and Europeans soon worsened. Outright hostilities began under Behanzin (r. 1858-89), who was defeated by the French, and in 1893 the French assimilated Abomey, Allada, and Porto Novo into the colony of Dahomey.

Independence from French rule came in 1960,

followed by more than a decade of coups until Mathieu Kerekou came to power in 1972. Kerekou established a Marxist regime, nationalizing large private businesses and abolishing opposition parties.

By December 1989, with the economy in a shambles and most trade conducted on the black market, there were demonstrations calling for Kerekou's resignation. A new constitution was approved in a November 1990 referendum, and Nicéphore Soglo, a former World Bank official, was named prime minister. Soglo defeated the Marxist Kerekou in the 1991 presidential election, and appealed to western nations for a "Marshall Plan" for Africa. But in a rematch four years later, Kerekou regained the presidency with 53 percent of the vote. Yet, only three years later, in April elections for the National Assembly, it was Soglo's Renaissance of Benin Party that carried the majority.

▶BHUTAN
Kingdom of Bhutan
• **GEOGRAPHY Location:** Himalaya Mountains in southern Asia. **Boundaries:** China to N and W, India to S and E. **Total land area:** 18,147 sq. mi. (47,000 sq km). **Coastline:** none. **Comparative area:** between Maryland and West Virginia. **Land use:** 2% arable land, 5% meadows and pastures, 70% forest and woodland, 23% other. **Major cities:** (1990 est.) Timphu (capital) 27,000.
• **PEOPLE Population:** 1,951,965 (1999 est.). **Nationality:** noun—Bhutanese (sing., pl.); adjective— Bhutanese. **Ethnic groups:** 50% Bhote, 35% ethnic Nepalese, 15% indigenous or migrant tribes. **Languages:** Dzongkha (official), various Tibetan dialects, various Nepalese dialects. **Religions:** 75% Lamaistic Buddhism, 25% Indian- and Nepalese-influenced Hinduism.
• **GOVERNMENT Type:** monarchy; special treaty relationship with India. **Independence:** Aug. 8, 1949 (from India). **Constitution:** no written constitution or bill of rights. **National holiday:** Dec. 17. **Head of Government:** Jigme Singye Wangchuk, king (since July 1972). **Structure:** executive—king, Royal Advisory Council, Council of Ministers; indirectly elected unicameral National Assembly consisting of 105 village elders, 12 monastic representatives, and 33 designated by the king; judicial—Supreme Court is the king.
• **ECONOMY Monetary unit:** ngultrums and Indian rupees are legal tender. **Budget:** (FY95/96) **income:** $146 mil.; **expend.:** $152 mil. **GDP:** (1998 est.) $1.9 bil., $1,000 per capita. **Chief crops:** rice, corn, barley, wheat, potatoes. **Livestock:** cattle, poultry, pigs, sheep, yaks. **Natural resources:** timber, hydropower, gypsum, calcium carbide. **Major industries:** cement, wood products, fruits. **Labor force:** N.A.; (1983) 93% agriculture, 5% services, 2% industry and commerce. **Exports:** $99 mil. (f.o.b., 1997 est.); cardamom, gypsum, timber, handicrafts. **Imports:** $131 mil. (c.i.f., 1997 est.); fuels and lubricants, grain, machinery and parts, vehicles. **Major trading partner:** India (94% of exports, 77% of imports).

A Tibetan-style Lamaistic Buddhist theocracy was established in this Himalayan enclave in the 16th century. The region came under the domination of the British raj in India in 1865, and Britain established a protectorate in 1910. A 1949 treaty with India granted independence to Bhutan. The present Druk Gyalpo, or Precious Ruler of the Dragon People, is the fourth in a dynasty dating from 1907. During the early years of his reign, he introduced reforms into this feudal, medieval country by broadening educational opportunities and compelling Buddhist monks to take up social work outside their monasteries.

Since 1988, however, King Wangchuk, who rules through a rubber-stamp National Assembly, has introduced a series of laws aimed at driving out Nepalese and Indian settlers even if their families have resided in Bhutan for decades. More than 70,000 refugees have been registered by the UN high commissioner for refugees since 1991, and the numbers continue to grow. A "Gorkha Liberation Movement" has carried out raids in Bhutan from sanctuaries in India and Nepal.

▶ BOLIVIA
Republic of Bolivia

● **GEOGRAPHY Location:** landlocked country in central South America. **Boundaries:** Brazil to N and E, Paraguay and Argentina to S, Chile and Peru to W. **Total land area:** 424,162 sq. mi. (1,098,580 sq km). **Coastline:** none. **Comparative area:** between Texas and Alaska. **Land use:** 3% arable land; negl. % permanent crops; 25% meadows and pastures; 52% forest and woodland; 20% other; includes negl. % irrigated. **Major cities:** (1992 est.) La Paz (administrative capital) 1,115,403; Sucre (legal capital and seat of judiciary) 130,952; Santa Cruz de la Sierra 694,616; Cochabamba 404,102; Oruro 183,194.

● **PEOPLE Population:** 7,982,850 (1999 est.). **Nationality:** noun—Bolivian(s); adjective—Bolivian. **Ethnic groups:** 30% Quechua, 25% Aymara, 30% mixed, 15% white. **Languages:** Spanish, Quechua, and Aymara (all official). **Religions:** 95% Roman Catholic; active Protestant minority, especially Methodist.

● **GOVERNMENT Type:** republic. **Independence:** Aug, 6, 1825 (from Spain). **Constitution:** Feb. 2, 1967. **National holiday:** Independence Day, Aug. 6. **Head of Government:** Gonzalo Sanchez de Lozada, president (since Aug. 1993). **Structure:** executive; bicameral legislature; judiciary.

● **ECONOMY Monetary unit:** boliviano. **Budget:** (1998 est.) *income:* $2.7 bil.; *expend.:* $2.7 bil. **GDP:** (1998 est.) $23.4 bil., $3,000 per capita. **Chief crops:** coffee, coca, cotton, corn, sugarcane, rice, potatoes. **Natural resources:** tin, natural gas, crude oil, zinc, tungsten. **Major industries:** mining, smelting, petroleum. **Labor force:** 2.5 mil.; NA% agriculture, NA% services and utilities, NA% manufacturing, mining, and construction. **Exports:** $1.1 bil. (f.o.b., 1998 est.); 34% metals, 9.4% natural gas, 8.4% soybeans. **Imports:** $1.7 bil. (c.i.f., 1998 est.); 48% capital goods, 11% chemicals, 5% petroleum. **Major trading partners:** (1996 est.) *exports:* 22% U.S., 9.3% U.K., 8.7% Colombia, 7.4% Peru, 7.2% Argentina. *imports:* 20% U.S., 13% Japan, 12% Brazil, 7.5% Chile.

The Incan Empire conquered the region that is now Bolivia in the 13th century. The Spanish discovered the fabulous silver deposits of the region and established their presence in the area in the cities of Sucre (1538) and Potosí (1545). From the early colonial period on, Bolivia—then called Upper Peru and part of the Viceroyalty of Peru—depended heavily on the export of minerals. The exploitation of tin and later oil and natural gas has had an important economic and political impact on the country's development.

In 1776, Upper Peru was transferred to the new Viceroyalty of La Plata centered in Buenos Aires. Upper Peru began agitating for independence in 1809, but it was not until liberation by Símon Bolívar (for whom the country was renamed) in 1825

that Bolivia became the last Spanish possession in South America to achieve independence. During 1836-39, Peru formed a brief union with Bolivia, until Chile broke up the confederation.

Bolivia has lost much of its original territory to its neighbors. The dictator Mariano Melgarejo sold large chunks of territory from 1865 to 1871. After the War of the Pacific (1879-84), Bolivia lost its access to the sea. And in the 1932-35 Chaco War with Paraguay, Bolivia lost more territory in the east.

Bolivia has suffered from Indian/non-Indian racial and cultural divisions, and political rivalry between the elites from the Potosí region and those from La Paz and Santa Cruz. Conservatives of the silver-mining southern region of Potosí controlled the government until their ouster in 1898 by the Liberal tin interests of the La Paz region, who presided over a period of stable republican politics that lasted until the Great Depression and the Chaco War.

One of the results of the Chaco War was the fragmentation of the Bolivian military into competing factions as the factions took sides in the struggle for power between conservative landowners and middle-class reformers; this caused political instability until the Bolivian National Revolution in 1952. In 1941 the National Revolutionary Movement (MNR) was formed with the aim of transferring control of the country from conservative landowning elites to the middle sectors. The leadership of the movement found itself outpaced by revolts sponsored by workers and peasants; the MNR incorporated these elements into its program. When the 1952 revolution brought the MNR to power, its leadership, which included the future four-time president Victor Paz Estenssoro, embarked on a reformist political program. The military overthrew the MNR in 1964, and civilian rule was not restored until 1982. Paz Estenssoro was again elected to the presidency in 1985. Jaime Paz Zamora, leader of the Movement of the Revolutionary Left, gained the presidency in 1989.

In elections held in June 1993, MNR candidate Gonzalo Sanchez de Lozada won the presidential election. An advocate of free-market economic reform, as planning minister (1986-88) he reduced the country's hyperinflation rate from 25,000 percent to 15 percent. In January 1995, Bolivia sought membership in the newly-formed Southern Common Market (of Argentina, Brazil, Paraguay, and Uruguay). But opposition to free-market reforms brought a general strike by the leftist Bolivian Workers' Confederation. The government declared a state of siege in April 1995, and suspended civil liberties. Further privatization plans led to another general strike in 1996, with 50,000 demonstrators in the streets of La Paz. Faced with widespread rioting and looting, the government agreed to a 13 percent raise for teachers and a 9 percent raise for other government employees.

▶ BOSNIA AND HERZEGOVINA
Republic of Bosnia and Herzegovina

● **GEOGRAPHY Location:** southeastern Europe. **Boundaries:** Croatia to N, W, Yugoslavia to S, E, and SE, Adriatic Sea to SW. **Total land area:** 19,776 sq. mi. (51,233 sq km). **Coastline:** 13 mi. (20 km). **Comparative area:** Slightly larger than Tennessee. **Land use:** 36% forest and woodland, 25% meadows and pastures, 20% arable land, 2% permanent crops, 17% other. **Major cities:** Bosnia: (1991) Sarajevo (capital) 525,980, Banja Luka 195,139. Herzegovina: (1991) Mostar 126,067.

● **PEOPLE Population:** 3,482,495 (1999 est.) Note: all population data is subject to considerable error due to dislocations caused by military actions and ethnic cleansing. **Nationality:** noun—Bosnian(s); adjective—Bosnian; noun—Herzegovine(s) or Herzegovinian(s); adjective—Herzegovine or Herzegovinian. **Ethnic groups:** 40% Serb, 38% Muslim, 22% Croat. Note: Croats claim they now make up only 17% of the population. **Languages:** Croatian, Serbian, Bosnian. **Religions:** 40% Muslim, 31% Orthodox, 15% Catholic, 4% Protestant, 10% other.

● **GOVERNMENT Type:** emerging democracy. **Independence:** Apr. 1, 1992. **Constitution:** Apr. 1, 1994; under Dayton agreement Nov. 1995, agreed to accept new basic principles. **National holiday:** N.A. **Heads of Government:** Dr. Alija Izetbegovic, president (since Dec. 1990); Hasan Muratovic, prime minister (since Jan. 1996). **Structure:** executive—3-member rotating presidency, prime minister, cabinet; bicameral legislature; judiciary.

● **ECONOMY Monetary unit:** convertible marka. **Budget:** N.A. **GDP:** (1998 est.) $5.8 bil.; $1,720 per capita. **Chief crops:** corn, wheat, fruits, vegetables; livestock. **Natural resources:** coal, iron, bauxite, manganese, timber. **Major industries:** steel production, mining, manufacturing, armaments. **Labor force:** 1,026,254 (1991 est.). **Exports:** $152 mil. (1995 est.). **Imports:** $1.1 bil. (1995 est.). **Major trading partners:** N.A.

Bosnia-Herzegovina has been in the middle of European power struggles since the 14th century. Its constantly changing boundaries have meant that its population has always been a hodgepodge of races and ethnicities. The name Bosnia comes from the region's geographic location on the Bosna River; Herzegovina was originally an Austrian border duchy (Herzog means "duke" in German). The two lands were conquered by the Ottoman Empire in the 15th century, Bosnia in 1463, Herzegovina 20 years later. The conquered peoples, united into one administrative district by the Turks, were Roman Catholic Croatians and Orthodox Serbs. Over the centuries, a number of Slavic families, Croatians more than Serbs, gave up their Christianity and adopted the religion of their conquerors: Islam.

A peasant uprising (1875) over Turkish refusal to institute reforms ultimately led to the Russo-Turkish War of 1877-78. In 1878, the Congress of Berlin put Bosnia-Herzegovina under the control of Austria-Hungary. Sarajevo, the capital city, was the birthplace of World War I, where a Serbian nationalist assassinated the Austro-Hungarian archduke Francis Ferdinand in 1914. By 1918, Serbia had annexed Bosnia-Herzegovina and held it until World War II, when Germany incorporated it into the state of Croatia. In 1946, Bosnia-Herzegovina was made one of Yugoslavia's six constituent republics, along with Serbia, Croatia, Slovenia, Montenegro, and Macedonia.

The constant redrawing of Bosnia-Herzegovina's borders has also meant that ethnicity in the region came to be based on religion, rather than a national origin. Thus a Serb who converted to Roman Catholic Christianity was considered a Croatian, while a Croatian who converted to Eastern Orthodoxy was considered a Serb. And to both groups, converts to Islam appeared to be collaborators with the Ottoman Turks.

Nevertheless, the three ethnic groups coexisted peacefully under the iron hand of president-for-life Marshall Tito (Josip Broz). And even after Tito's death in 1980, his rotating presidency scheme, in which the leaders of each republic took turns serving as "president of the presidency," worked smoothly, as long as Yugoslavia was dominated by communism. At times, the president was a Muslim, the prime minister was a Croatian, and the president of the Assembly was a Serb. But when communism fell in 1989, only Serbia and Montenegro returned Communist governments to power; the other four republics established non- and even anti-Communist governments, and quickly sought to establish political independence from the ultra-Marxist regime of Serbian president Slobodan Milosevic.

Milosevic rigged elections in the provinces of Kosovo and Vojvodina to keep them under Serbian control, but he was unsuccessful in extending Serbia's borders to ethnically Serbian areas of Slovenia, Croatia, and Bosnia-Herzegovina. Croatia and Slovenia declared their independence in 1991, forcing Bosnia to choose between independence or a diminished role in a Serb-dominated Yugoslavia.

Bosnia-Herzegovina voted for independence in March 1992. But the mostly Serbian military of the former Yugoslavian army (which was heavily concentrated in Bosnia-Herzegovina) refused to go along with the vote. Led by Radovan Karadzic, they quickly gained control of the region's heavy and light artillery and proclaimed the existence of the "Serbian Republic of Bosnia-Herzegovina." The siege of Sarajevo began a month after the vote for independence, with Serbia waging a ferocious war of "ethnic cleansing," in which they sought to rid Bosnia of Muslims and Croats. By July 1993, the Serbs surrounded the city completely, cutting off international delivery of arms and supplies to Bosnian forces. Despite growing evidence that the Serbs were raping and torturing Muslims, the Bosnian Parliament in September 1993 rejected a UN-sponsored peace plan that would have ended the war.

Several other cease-fire agreements were brokered throughout 1993 and 1994, but none led to a lasting peace in the Balkans until a 1995 pact brokered by U.S. negotiator Richard Holbrooke, in which the Bosnian Serbs agreed to follow the decisions of Yugoslavia's president Slobodan Milosevic in all peace talks. And on Nov. 21, 1995, the presidents of Bosnia-Herzegovina, Croatia, and Serbia met in Dayton, Ohio, to sign a peace accord ending the civil war and dividing Bosnia-Herzegovina into two entities: a Serb republic and a Muslim-Croat federation. The two statelets would be governed by the same legislature and president.

The UN sent 60,000 peacekeeping troops (including 20,000 Americans) in December 1995 to supervise the transition. Elections in Sept. 1996 selected a three-member collective presidency, chaired by Muslim Alijia Izethegovic, and a legislature whose 42 members were selected in two separate elections, 28 from the Federation and 14 from the Srpska Republic. In Jan. 1997, parliament approved a cabinet with joint (Serb and Muslim) premiers.

Yugoslavia and Bosnia established diplomatic relation in Oct. 1996, with Yugoslavia agreeing to respect Bosnia's boundaries while Bosnia dropped charges of genocide. A new crisis arose when on the same day (March 5, 1999), the West's "high authority" (under the Dayton Accords) deposed the President of the Serb Republic, who had just been elected in September, while a Western "arbitrator" awarded the strategic Sava River town of Brcko to the Moslem-Croat Federation, resulting in the Serb republic's effective withdrawal from Bosnia-Herzegovnia. U.N. troops remained throughout 1999.

▶ BOTSWANA
Republic of Botswana

● **GEOGRAPHY Location:** landlocked country in southern Africa. **Boundaries:** Namibia to N and W, Zimbabwe to NE, South Africa to SE and S. **Total land area:** 231,803 sq. mi. (600,370 sq km). **Coastline:** none. **Comparative area:** about size of Texas. **Land use:** 2% arable land; 75% meadows and pastures; 2% forest and woodland; 21% other. **Major cities:** (1989 est.) Gaborone (capital) 110,973; Francistown 49,396; Selebi-Phikwe 46,490; Molepolole 29,212; Serowe 28,267.
● **PEOPLE Population:** 1,464,167 (1999 est.). **Nationality:** noun and adjective—Motswana (sing.), Batswana (pl.). **Ethnic groups:** 95% Batswana; 4% Kalanga, Basarwa, and Kgalagadi; 1% white. **Languages:** English (official), Setswana. **Religions:** 50% Christian, 50% indigenous beliefs.
● **GOVERNMENT Type:** parliamentary republic. **Independence:** Sept. 30, 1966 (from UK). **Constitution:** Mar. 1965, effective Sept. 30, 1966. **National holiday:** Independence Day, Sept. 30. **Head of Government:** Festus G. Mogae, MP, head of state (since April 1998). **Structure:** executive; bicameral legislature; judiciary.
● **ECONOMY Monetary unit:** pula. **Budget:** (FY96/97) *income:* $1.6 bil.; *expend.:* $1.8 bil. **GDP:** $5.25 bil., $3,600 per capita (1998 est.). **Chief crops:** sorghum, maize, millet, pulses, peanuts. **Natural resources:** diamonds, copper, nickel, salt, soda ash. **Major industries:** diamonds, copper, nickel, coal, salt, soda ash, potash; livestock processing. **Labor force:** (1992) 428,000; 235,000 formal-sector employees; 14,300 employed in mines in South Africa; most others engaged in cattle raising and subsistence agriculture; 20-40% unemployment (1997 est.). **Exports:** $2.25 bil. (f.o.b., 1998); 76% diamonds, 4% copper and nickel, meat. **Imports:** $2.43 bil. (f.o.b., 1998); foodstuffs, vehicles, textiles, petroleum products. **Major trading partners:** (1996) *exports:* 74% EU, 21% South African Customs Union (SACU), 3% Zimbabwe; *imports:* 78% SACU, 8% Europe, 6% Zimbabwe.

Botswana, occupying a high and relatively arid tableland in southern Africa, was traditionally occupied by diverse groups of farmers, pastoralists, and hunter-gatherers. European missionaries arrived from South Africa in the early 19th century. In the late 19th century, native peoples resisted the encroachment of Afrikaners from the Transvaal; in response the British government established a protectorate in what was then called Bechuanaland in 1886. The southern part of the protectorate was organized as a Crown Colony and ultimately passed under the control of South Africa. During the 20th century, the territory remaining in the protectorate saw a steady evolution of local rule.

In 1920 two advisory councils were established to represent the interests of native and European inhabitants. In 1934 British authorities promulgated regulations establishing the powers and jurisdictions of native chiefs and the functions of native councils and courts. Local fiscal powers were established soon thereafter. In 1951 a joint (native-European) advisory council was set up, and 10 years later an elected legislature met under the provisions of a constitution promulgated on May 2, 1961.

In 1963-64 the British government accepted Botswanan proposals for self-government. A new capital was established at Gaborone in February 1965; a new constitution came into effect in the following month, and Botswana became fully independent on Sept. 30, 1966. Since independence, Botswana has been a multiparty, multiracial democracy that has remained untouched by the political turmoil affecting most of its neighbors.

Botswana is also one of the most prosperous countries in Africa. It is the world's largest producer of diamonds; revenues from diamond exports have been wisely managed, leading to significant budgetary surpluses in recent years. Gold and soda ash are also mined. Tourism, bolstered by Botswana's large herds of big game, is the country's major nonmining industry. About 75 percent of the population is engaged in agriculture and herding; Botswana is one of Africa's largest exporters of meat and animal products.

▶ BRAZIL
Federative Republic of Brazil

● **GEOGRAPHY Location:** central and northeastern South America. **Boundaries:** Colombia, Venezuela, Guyana, Suriname, French Guiana to N; Atlantic Ocean to E; Uruguay, Argentina, Paraguay to S; Peru, Bolivia to W. **Total land area:** 3,286,475 sq. mi. (8,511,965 sq km). **Coastline:** 4,652 mi. (7,491 km). **Comparative area:** slightly smaller than U.S. **Land use:** 7% arable land; 1% permanent crops; 19% meadows and pastures; 67% forest and woodland; 6% other. **Major cities:** (1991 est.) Brasília (capital) 1,841,028; São Paulo 9,700,111; Rio de Janeiro 6,011,181; Belo Horizonte 2,339,039; Salvador 2,075,392.
● **PEOPLE Population:** 171,853,126 (1999 est.). **Nationality:** noun—Brazilian(s); adjective—Brazilian. **Ethnic groups:** Portuguese, Italian, German, Japanese, black, Amerindian; 55% white, 38% mixed, 6% black, 1% other. **Languages:** Portuguese (official), Spanish, English, French. **Religions:** 70% Roman Catholic (nominal).
● **GOVERNMENT Type:** federal republic. **Independence:** Sept. 7, 1822 (from Portugal). **Constitution:** Oct. 5, 1988. **National holiday:** Independence Day, Sept. 7. **Head of Government:** Fernando Henrique Cardoso, president (since Jan. 1995). **Structure:** strong executive with broad powers; bicameral legislature with growing powers; judiciary.
● **ECONOMY Monetary unit:** real. **Budget:** (1998) *income:* $151 bil.; *expend.:* $149 bil. **GDP:** $1.0352 tril., $6,100 per capita (1998 est.). **Chief crops:** coffee, soybeans, wheat, rice; beef. **Natural resources:** bauxite, gold, iron ore, manganese, nickel. **Major industries:** textiles and other consumer goods, shoes, chemicals. **Labor force:** 57 mil. (1989 est.); 42% services, 31% agriculture, 27% industry; 8.5% unemployment (1998 est.). **Exports:** $51 bil. (f.o.b.,1998); iron ore, soybean bran, orange juice, footwear. **Imports:** $57.6 bil. (f.o.b., 1998); crude oil, capital goods, chemical products, foodstuffs, coal. **Major trading partners:** (1996) *exports:* 28% EU, 23% Latin America (excluding Argentina), 20% U.S., 12% Argentina; *imports:* 26% EU, 22% U.S., 13% Argentina, 5% Japan.

The Portuguese arrived on the coast of what would become Brazil with the expedition of Pedro Alvares Cabral in 1500 and found an indigenous population of semisedentary and nonsedentary cultures. Many of the semisedentary Indians spoke the Tupian language and shared similar cultural features. The Tupians quickly formed economic relationships with the first Europeans, who were interested in the valuable dyewood that was so abundant in Brazil.

The transition of Indian-European economic relations from barter to slavery was given momentum by the introduction of sugar export agriculture, a trend that began in the region in the 1540s. The 1560s saw epidemics of smallpox and measles in the coastal areas, which greatly reduced the indigenous population. Although the European sugar growers initially favored the use of indigenous peoples over imported African slave labor (owing to the lower price of Indian slaves), the shortage of labor resulting from the epidemics led to increasing use of African slave labor by the Portuguese.

The Portuguese vied with other European powers for control of Brazilian territory, and in 1630 the Dutch briefly seized the northeastern sugar-growing area. Brazil's southern regions were underpopulated during the early colonial period, and Portuguese activity was largely limited to cattle raising. With the discovery of gold (1690s) and diamonds (1729), European interest in and settlement of the Minas Gerais area in the southeast quickened.

In 1808, the Portuguese royal court escaped Napoleon's armies with the help of the British fleet, and the prince regent, Dom João VI, sought refuge in Brazil and made it the seat of the Portuguese empire. Dom João returned to a Portugal liberated from Napoleonic occupation in 1821, leaving his son Dom Pedro behind as prince regent. In 1822, defying orders to return to Portugal and opposed to the imminent reversion of Brazil to colonial status, Dom Pedro declared Brazil's independence and was crowned emperor. In 1825 an agreement mediated by the British led to Portuguese recognition of Brazil as a separate kingdom.

The early years of independence were rocky. Dom Pedro became increasingly estranged from his people and began losing control of the Brazilian political situation owing to a continuing series of landowner revolts and to the loss of a war with the United Provinces of Rio de la Plata over what would become Uruguay. In 1831 Dom Pedro abdicated in favor of his five-year-old son, Dom Pedro II; a regency governed Brazil until his accession to the throne in 1840.

The Brazilian empire found itself continually involved in the wars and internal politics of Uruguay, Argentina, and Paraguay in the 1850s and 1860s. The bloody five-year war with Paraguay that began in 1865 resulted in Paraguay's eventual defeat, but the process of the war had important consequences for the future of Brazil: the expansion of the military in numbers and power, the fragmentation of the political party system, and the undermining of the legitimacy of slavery. Slavery was abolished in 1888, and the following year, a military coup overthrew the emperor.

The "Old Republic," which lasted from 1889 to 1930, was a federal system in which much of the political control in Brazilian society was relegated to state-based political networks with local bosses. The presidency was assigned in a de facto rotation system called the "politics of the governors," in which the president's office was controlled by the most important state power networks. The world depression of 1929 hit the Brazilian agricultural export economy hard, and in 1930 the military overthrew the elected president; Getúlio Vargas, a politician from the state of Rio Grande do Sul, took over the presidency.

Vargas proceeded to centralize power in the presidency, diminishing states' rights dramatically. Civil unrest allowed Vargas to declare a state of siege with military backing, and in 1937 he declared the establishment of the Estado Novo, a state wherein Vargas had absolute power, in imitation of Portuguese and Italian regimes of the period. The military ousted Vargas in 1945, ushering in the period of the "Second Republic." Vargas again won re-election in 1950 but committed suicide in 1954. Juscelino Kubitschek, elected president in 1955, sought to develop the country and led the way for construction of the new capital of Brasília in the previously undeveloped interior.

His successor, Jânio da Silva Quadros, resigned in 1961 after only seven months in office, and the presidency passed to populist Vice Pres. João Goulart. The populist mobilization of peasants and workers endorsed by the Goulart government led to his overthrow by the military in 1964.

The Brazilian military governed the country until 1985. Military rule was not maintained in the form of a dictatorship; rather, the military ruled as a more or less cohesive institution. The succession of generals and their technocratic allies attempted to develop the country through a pattern of state-led growth from which civilian politics were excluded. In 1985, Tancredo Neves was elected president, but he died before taking office. José Sarney, the vice presidential candidate, became Brazil's first civilian president since 1964.

Promising to revitalize the economy with a free-market revolution, less government, and more growth, conservative Fernando Collor de Mello became president in 1990. The military's share of the budget was reduced from 6 to 2.2 percent, and some companies were privatized, but inflation and debt still strained the economy. The 1988 murder of environmental activist Chico Mendes focused world attention on the rapidly accelerating deforestation of the Amazon River basin. Pres. Collor campaigned actively to halt the destruction in Amazonia—including protecting the Stone Age Yanomami Indians—and in June 1992 Rio De Janeiro was the site of a UN-sponsored conference on development and the environment.

Pres. Collor lost the confidence of the legislature and the people as evidence mounted that he stole or misappropriated over $20 million, and he resigned in December 1992 (after a two-year investigation he was cleared of all charges). His successor, Vice Pres. Itamar Franco, worked to privatize government industries and halt rampant inflation, but a new corruption scandal involving at least 18 members of the legislature halted most government activity in 1994.

In presidential elections held in Oct. 1994, former finance minister Fernando Henrique Cardoso ran on an anti-inflation platform and won a landslide victory. The Cardoso government focused on establishing federal control over state banks and supporting land reform for peasants. The rewards were a dramatic drop in both inflation and unemployment and great popularity for Cardoso. In 1997 Congress passed a Constitutional Amendment permitting Cardoso to run for a second term.

In October 1998 Cardoso easily won re-election for a four-year term over his nearest opponent by a convincing margin and pro-Cardoso governors were elected in 21 of the 27 states. Despite an unexpected January 1999 devalutation of the *real*, the I.M.F. released the remainder of its 1998 aid package in March. In April, Brazil was able to sell $2 billion in bonds—a sign of continuing confidence by the world money markets. But Cardoso's popularity plummeted during the summer to record lows causing new fears.

▶ BRUNEI
Negara Brunei Darussalam

• **GEOGRAPHY Location:** southeastern Asia, Kalimantan (Borneo) island. Bandar Seri Begawan 4°56'N, 114°58'E. **Boundaries:** surrounded on landward side by Sarawak, state, of Malaysia; South China Sea to N. **Total land area:** 2,228 sq. mi. (5,770 sq km). **Coastline:** 100 mi. (161 km). **Comparative area:** slightly larger than Delaware. **Land use:** 1% arable land; 1% permanent crops; 1% meadows and pastures; 79% forest and woodland; 18% other. **Major cities:** Bandar Seri Begawan (formerly Brunei Town) (capital) 50,500 (1986 est.); Seria, Kuala Belait, Tutong.
• **PEOPLE Population:** 322,982 (1999 est.). **Nationality:** noun—Bruneian(s); adjective—Bruneian. **Ethnic groups:** 64% Malay, 20% Chinese, 16% other. **Languages:** Malay (official), English, Chinese. **Religions:** 63% Muslim (official), 14% Buddhist, 8% Christian, 15% indigenous and other.
• **GOVERNMENT Type:** constitutional sultanate. **Independence:** Jan. 1, 1984 (from UK). **Constitution:** Sept. 29, 1959 (some provisions suspended since Dec. 1962, others since independence). **National holiday:** National Day, Feb. 23. **Head of Government:** Sir Hassanal Bolkiah, sultan and prime minister (since Aug. 1968). **Structure:** chief of state is sultan; unicameral legislature; judiciary.
• **ECONOMY Monetary unit:** bruneian dollar. **Budget:** (1995) *income:* $2.5 bil.; *expend.:* $2.6 bil. **GDP:** $5.4 bil., $17,000 per capita (1998 est.). **Chief crops:** rice, cassava, bananas. **Natural resources:** petroleum, natural gas, timber. **Major industries:** petroleum, petroleum refining, liquefied natural gas, construction. **Labor force:** 144,000 (1995 est.); 48% government, 42% oil, natural gas, services, and construction. **Exports:** $2.62 bil. (f.o.b., 1996 est.); crude oil, liquefied natural gas, petroleum products. **Imports:** $2.65 bil. (c.i.f., 1996 est.); machinery and transport equipment, manufactured goods, foodstuffs, chemicals. **Major trading partners:** *exports:* 31% ASEAN, 27% Japan, 26% South Korea, UK, Taiwan (1996 est.); *imports:* 29% Singapore, 19% UK, 13% U.S., 9% Malaysia, 5% Japan (1994 est.).

The Islamic sultanate of Brunei became dominant in northern Borneo in the 16th century but declined in power after the 17th century under pressure from the Dutch and other foreign powers. An Anglo-Dutch agreement of 1824 assigned North Borneo to Great Britain's sphere of influence in Asia. In 1841 a British adventurer, James Brooke, aided the sultan of Brunei in putting down a rebellion and was rewarded by being given the province of Sarawak, comprising more than half of the sultanate's area. Britain established a protectorate over Sabah, the eastern portion of Brunei, in 1881. That left the sultan with a tiny realm on the Brunei River, which was ultimately placed under British protection in 1888. The discovery of Southeast Asia's richest oilfield in Brunei and its offshore waters made the sultanate an enclave of tremendous wealth from the late 1920s onward.

Following Japanese occupation during World War II, British rule resumed in North Borneo. Sarawak and Sabah became part of Malaysia in 1963. Brunei was granted independence from Great Britain on Dec. 1, 1984. The sultan of Brunei, an absolute monarch, rules from the world's largest royal palace in Bandar Seri Begawan, the nation's capital. The economy is centered almost entirely on petroleum and international banking and investments.

▶ BULGARIA
Republic of Bulgaria

• **GEOGRAPHY Location:** southeastern Europe. **Boundaries:** Romania to N, Black Sea to E, Turkey and Greece to S, Macedonia and Yugoslavia to W. **Total land area:** 42,822 sq. mi. (110,910 sq km). **Coastline:** 220 mi. (354 km). **Comparative area:** between Tennessee and Pennsylvania. **Land use:** 34% arable land; 3% permanent crops; 18% meadows and pastures; 35% forest and woodland; 10% other. **Major cities:** (1992 est.) Sofia (capital) 1,114,476; Plovdiv 341,374; Varna 308,601; Burges 195,986; Ruse 170,203.
• **PEOPLE Population:** 8,194,772 (1999 est.). **Nationality:** noun—Bulgarian(s); adjective—Bulgarian. **Ethnic groups:** 85% Bulgarian, 9% Turk, 6% other. **Languages:** Bulgarian; secondary languages closely correspond to ethnic breakdown. **Religions:** 85% Bulgarian Orthodox, 13% Muslim, 0.8% Jewish, 0.5% Roman Catholic, 0.5% Protestant, Gregorian-Armenian, and other.
• **GOVERNMENT Type:** republic. **Independence:** Sept. 22, 1908 (from Ottoman Empire). **Constitution:** July 12, 1991. **National holiday:** Independence Day, Mar. 3. **Heads of Government:** Petar Stoyanov, president (since Nov. 1996); Zhan Videnov, prime minister (since Jan. 1995). **Structure:** executive; unicameral legislature; judiciary.
• **ECONOMY Monetary unit:** lev. **Budget:** (1998) *income:* $4.1 bil.; *expend:* $3.8 bil. **GDP:** $33.6 bil., $4,100 per capita (1998 est.). **Chief crops:** grain, oilseed, vegetables, fruits, tobacco; livestock. **Natural resources:** bauxite, copper, lead, zinc, coal. **Major industries:** machine building and metal working, food processing, chemicals. **Labor force:** 3.57 mil. (1996); 41% industry, 18% agriculture; 12.2% unemployment (1998 est.). **Exports:** $4.5 bil. (f.o.b., 1998); machinery and equipment, metals and ores, chemicals and plastics, food, textiles. **Imports:** $4.6 bil. (f.o.b., 1998); fuels, minerals, and raw materials; machinery and equipment; food; textiles and apparel. **Major trading partners:** *exports:* 12% Italy, 10% Germany, Turkey, Greece, Russia; *imports:* 28% Russia, 11% Germany, Italy, Greece, U.S.

Turkic Bulgars arrived at the west shore of the Black Sea in the seventh century, mingling with the indigenous Slavic population. The Bulgars accepted Eastern Orthodox Christianity in the ninth century and were conquered and incorporated into the Byzantine Empire by Basil II in the late 10th century. With the decline of Byzantium, Bulgaria became an independent kingdom, but it was conquered by the Ottoman Turks in 1396 and remained part of the Ottoman Empire for the next 500 years.

In the Treaty of San Stefano, ending the Russo-Turkish War in 1878, a Bulgarian state was promised that was to stretch from the Adriatic to the Black Sea. But the Great Powers would not permit so large a Russian client state, and instead the Berlin Conference of 1878 sanctioned a much smaller Bulgarian state, under a German dynasty with the Ottoman sultan as nominal overlord. Bulgaria gained full independence in 1908.

The Balkan Wars of 1912 and 1913 led to a reduction of Bulgarian territory, and after World War I, Bulgaria, which had been allied with the Central Powers, lost its Aegean Coastline to Greece. A series of weak parliamentary governments under King Boris III (r. 1918-43) ended when the king established a personal dictatorship in 1935. Bulgaria joined the Axis powers in 1941 and declared war against the Western powers but not against Russia. Under occupation by its German allies, Bulgaria once again expanded to the Aegean during the war.

Russian troops entered Bulgaria in 1944 and organized a Communist government. The boy-king Simeon II remained on the throne until 1946, when the monarchy was abolished by a popular referendum. The People's Republic of Bulgaria was established in 1947.

Until the end of World War II, Bulgaria was a peasant society, with 80 percent of the population engaged in agriculture; industrial development was rudimentary. The People's Republic established a planned economy on the Soviet model; Russian credits and trade agreements permitted a rapid industrialization focused on machinery and equipment for export.

In 1954 Todor Zhivkov became first secretary of the Bulgarian Communist party. He served as premier in the 1960s and president from 1971 to 1990. In the 1960s Zhivkov promoted decentralization and responsiveness to market forces, but with the 1968 Russian invasion of Czechoslovakia, he returned the economy to central planning, collective farming, and giant state-industrial enterprises. In October 1985 Zhivkov met with Gorbachev and reforms based on Gorbachev's "self-management" policies were instituted.

Democratic reform began with Zhivkov's sudden resignation in November 1989. There followed a year of popular unrest and political turmoil with a succession of changes in the ruling hierarchy, culminating in the election of Zheliu Zhelev of the reform Union of Democratic Forces as president (Bulgaria's first non-Communist leader in 40 years), and the appointment in 1990 of political independent Dimitar Popov as premier of a coalition government dominated by the Socialist (formerly Communist) party.

Elections in October 1991 ended the Socialist grip on power, as the Union of Democratic Forces formed a government under Philip Dimitrov. But within a year the government was bankrupt, inflation at 30 percent and unemployment 40 percent, and Dimitrov's government was ousted by Parliament. Lyuben Berov, an economic adviser to Zhelev, came to power for two years and then he was ousted in elections (Dec. 1994) by the Socialists, led by Zhan Videnov.

Under the Videnov-Zhelev "gridlock," matters only grew worse, with a food crisis developing atop growing unemployment and 300% inflation in 1996. Protests and riots marked the latter half of 1996, and in the Nov. presidential elections, the UDF candidate, Peter Stoyanov (who defeated Zhelev in a party primary) won easily. And in the April 1997 elections to parliament, the UDF coalition took 137 seats to the Socialists 58. With the promise of economic reform, the IMF and the EU provided large new grants.

▶ BURKINA FASO
● GEOGRAPHY Location: landlocked country in western Africa. Boundaries: Mali to N and W,

Niger to E, Benin, Togo, Ghana, Ivory Coast to S. Total land area: 105,869 sq. mi. (274,200 sq km). Coastline: none. Comparative area: between Colorado and Nevada. Land use: 10% arable land; 37% meadows and pastures; 26% forest and woodland; 27% other. Major cities: (1985 census) Ouagadougou (capital) 441,514; Bobo-Dioulasso 228,668; Koudougou 51,926; Ouahigouya 38,902; Banfora 35,319.
● PEOPLE Population: 11,575,898 (1999 est.). Nationality: noun—Burkinabe (sing., pl.); adjective—Burkinabe. Ethnic groups: 24% Mossi, Gurunsi, Senufo, Lobi, Bobo, Mande, Fulani. Languages: French (official); tribal languages spoken by 90% of population. Religions: 50% Muslim, 40% indigenous beliefs, 10% Christian (mainly Roman Catholic).
● GOVERNMENT Type: parliamentary. Independence: Aug. 5, 1960 (from France). Constitution: June 2, 1991. National holiday: Anniversary of the Revolution, Aug. 4. Heads of Government: Blaise Compaore, president (since Dec. 1991); M. Kadré Desiré Ouédraogo, prime minister (since Feb. 1996). Structure: executive; bicameral legislature; judiciary.
● ECONOMY Monetary unit: Communauté Financière Africaine (CFA) franc. Budget: (1995) income: $277 mil.; expend.: $492 mil. GDP: $11.6 bil., $1,000 per capita (1998 est.). Chief crops: peanuts, shea nuts, sesame, cotton. Natural resources: manganese, limestone, marble; small deposits of gold, antimony, copper, nickel, bauxite. Major industries: cotton, beverages, agricultural processing. Labor force: 4.679 mil. (1991); 85% agriculture, industry, commerce, services, government; a large part of male labor force migrates annually to neighboring countries for seasonal employment. Exports: $400 mil. (f.o.b., 1997); cotton, gold, animal products. Imports: $700 mil. (f.o.b., 1997); machinery, food products, petroleum. Major trading partners: (1985) exports: Ivory Coast, France, Italy, Mali; imports: Ivory Coast, France, Togo, Nigeria.

The Mossi empire dominated the area of what is now Burkina Faso, a landlocked nation in western Africa with few natural resources and poor agricultural conditions, from as early as the 11th century. They ruled the region, often resisting Muslim invaders, until modern times.

The region was hardly visited by Europeans before the 1880s, but by 1896 the French had captured the Mossi capital city of Ouagadougou and established a protectorate over the area. The French created Upper Volta in 1919, naming it for the upper basin of the Volta River. Upper Volta became a self-governing state with the French Overseas Community in 1958 and gained independence Aug. 5, 1960.

After a brief period of military rule, the nation ratified a new constitution on June 14, 1970, and made a peaceful transition to civilian rule based on the French model. In 1980 the constitution was overthrown and a military government was set up. There was another coup on Aug. 4, 1983, and a government was established patterned after the Libyan government of Muammar al-Qaddafi. On Aug. 14, 1984, Upper Volta officially changed its name to Burkina Faso.

Two attempted coups against the government of Capt. Blaise Compaore, in September and December 1989, were put down and the leaders executed. In 1992, as president, Compaore convened a National Reconciliation Forum followed by legislative elections that resulted in a new prime minister. In 1994 the World Bank reported significant economic progress in this desperately poor country.

▶BURUNDI
Republic of Burundi
● **GEOGRAPHY Location:** landlocked country on northeastern shore of Lake Tanganyika in central Africa. **Boundaries**: Rwanda to N, Tanzania to E and S, Zaire to W. **Total land area**: 10,745 sq. mi. (27,830 sq km). **Coastline**: none. **Comparative area**: slightly larger than Maryland. **Land use:** 43% arable land; 8% permanent crops; 35% meadows and pastures; 2% forest and woodland; 12% other. **Major cities**: Bujumbura (capital) 215,243 (1987 est.); Gitega 15,943 (1978).
● **PEOPLE Population:** 5,735,937 (1999 est.). **Nationality:** noun—Burundian(s); adjective—Burundi. **Ethnic groups:** 85% Hutu (Bantu), 14% Tutsi (Hamitic), 1% Twa (Pygmy), 3,000 Europeans, 2,000 South Asians. **Languages:** Kirundi and French (both official), Swahili (along Lake Tanganyika and in Bujumbura area). **Religions:** 67% Christian (62% Roman Catholic, 5% Protestant), 32% indigenous beliefs, 1% Muslim.
● **GOVERNMENT Type:** republic. **Independence:** July 1, 1962 (from UN trusteeship under Belgian administration). **Constitution:** Mar. 13, 1992. **National holiday:** Independence Day, July 1. **Heads of Government:** Pierre Buyoya, president (since Sept. 1996); **Structure:** executive; unicameral legislature; judiciary. (Note: a miltary government took office during a 1996 coup, but the new leadership has not been officially recognized.)
● **ECONOMY Monetary unit:** Burundi franc. **Budget:** (1992 est.) *income:* $NA; *expend.:* $165 mil. **GDP:** $4.1 bil., $740 per capita (1998 est.). **Chief crops:** coffee, cotton, tea, corn, sorghum. **Natural resources:** nickel, uranium, rare earth oxide, peat, cobalt. **Major industries:** light consumer goods such as blankets, shoes, soap; assembly of imported components; public works construction. **Labor force:** (1983 est.) 1.9 mil.; 93% agriculture, 7% other. **Exports:** $49 mil. (f.o.b., 1998); coffee, tea, cotton, hides. **Imports:** $102 mil. (f.o.b., 1998); capital goods, petroleum products, foodstuffs. **Major trading partners:** *exports:* U.K., Germany, Benelux, Switzerland; *imports:* Benelux, France, Germany, Japan.

Burundi's population is divided between two ethnic groups, the majority Hutu and the minority, but politically powerful, Tutsi. The Hutu were the original settlers of the country and practiced agriculture; the cattle-herding Tutsi arrived several hundred years ago and established a form of feudal overlordship over the Hutu. The traditional government was monarchical, with a king (mwami) chosen from among a group of aristocratic families (ganwa).

European exploration of Burundi began in 1858, and the territory was incorporated into German East Africa in 1899. Following World War I, the League of Nations (1923) awarded Burundi, along with neighboring Rwanda, to Belgium as a mandated territory. Belgian rule over the Territory of Ruanda-Urundi, as it was then called, continued under a UN trusteeship after World War II.

Burundi became independent on July 1, 1962, as a constitutional monarchy under the traditional mwami. The country rapidly lapsed into political chaos. In 1966, with the backing of the army, Capt. Michel Micombero overthrew the monarchy and proclaimed a republic. A Hutu rebellion in 1972 against Tutsi political domination left 10,000 Tutsi dead; Tutsi reprisals in 1972-73 resulted in the slaughter of 150,000 Hutu. The Micombero government was overthrown in a bloodless coup, and on Nov. 1, 1976, Lt. Col. Jean-Baptiste Bagaza took control of the government.

Bagaza was overthrown in September 1987, and his successor, Maj. Pierre Buyoya, proclaimed a policy of nonalignment in foreign affairs, seeking closer links with the West, while maintaining relations with Libya and the eastern bloc. Domestically, the government pledged to eradicate Bagaza's record of persecution of the Catholic church (62% of Burundians are Catholic) and to seek ethnic reconciliation between Hutu and Tutsi. The latter policy was threatened, however, by renewed outbreaks of ethnic violence in 1988. Buyoya led the country to its first free presidential elections in June 1993. Melchior Ndadaye, a Hutu, defeated Buyoya by a wide margin.

But almost immediately (in October 1993) Ndadaye was assassinated, as was his Hutu successor (April 1994). The succeeding regime of Hutu president Ntibantunganya, unsuccesful in forming a stable, ethically balanced goverment, was overturned in a military coup (July 1996) which dissolved parliament, outlawed all political parties, and named Pierre Buyoya to return as president. Vowing yet another return to democracy after the end of civil war, Buyoya faced economic sanctions by the Organization of African Unity. Meanwhile, the complicated civil war was only worsened by Zaire's attempt to expel almost half a million Tutsi (the Banyamulenge people, settled south on Lake Kivi since the 18th century) in October 1996. The Tutsi succesful self defense had the paradoxical effect of driving yet more Hutu (50,000) into Burundi—and almost half a million more into neighboring Rwanda.

▶CAMBODIA
Kingdom of Cambodia
● **GEOGRAPHY Location:** on Indochinese peninsula in Southeast Asia. **Boundaries:** Thailand to W and N, Laos to N, Gulf of Thailand to S, Vietnam to E. **Total land area:** 69,900 sq. mi. (181,040 sq km). **Coastline:** 275 mi. (443 km). **Comparative area:** between Missouri and Oklahoma. **Land use:** 16% arable land; 1% permanent crops; 3% meadows and pastures; 76% forest and woodland; 4% other; includes 1% irrigated. **Major cities:** (1991 est.) Phnom Penh (capital) 900,000.
● **PEOPLE Population:** 11,626,520 (1999 est.). **Nationality:** noun—Cambodian(s); adjective—Cambodian. **Ethnic groups:** 90% Khmer (Cambodian), 5% Vietnamese, 1% Chinese, 5% other minorities. **Languages:** Khmer (official), French. **Religions:** 95% Theravada Buddhism.
● **GOVERNMENT Type:** multiparty liberal democracy under a constitutional monarchy. **Independence:** November 9, 1953 (from France). **Constitution:** promulgated Sept. 21, 1993. **National holiday:** Independence Day, November 9. **Heads of Government:** Norodom Sihanouk, king (reinstated Sept. 1993); Hun Sen, prime minister (since Nov. 1998). **Structure:** executive; unicameral legislature; judiciary.
● **ECONOMY Monetary unit:** new riel. **Budget:** (1995 est.) *income:* $261 mil.; *expend.:* $496 mil. **GDP:** $7.8 bil., $700 per capita (1998 est.). **Chief crops:** rice, rubber, corn, vegetables. **Natural resources:** timber, gemstones, some iron ore, manganese, phosphates, hydropower potential. **Major industries:** rice milling, fishing, wood and wood products. **Labor force:** 2.5-3 mil.; 80% agriculture (1997 est.). **Exports:** $736 mil. (f.o.b., 1997 est.); timber, garments, rubber, soybeans, sesame. **Im-**

ports: $1.1 bil. (f.o.b., 1997 est.); cigarettes, gold, construction materials, petroleum products. **Major trading partners**: Singapore, Japan.

The dominant power in Indochina from the Eighth through the 13th centuries, the Khmer Empire encompassed present-day Cambodia and much of western Thailand, southern Laos, and central and southern Vietnam. It built magnificent Buddhist temple cities at Angkor Wat and Angkor Thon. From the 14th century onward, the Khmer Empire came under increasing pressure from the expansionist Vietnamese state of Annam, which absorbed the territories east of the Mekong River. In the 18th century, the kingdom of Siam (Thailand) annexed three western provinces of the Khmer Empire. The remaining Khmer territory became the French protectorate of Cambodia in 1863, and a French colony as part of the Union of Indochina in 1887. In 1907 France forced Siam to return some territory to Cambodia.

During World War II, Cambodia was occupied by Japan from 1942 to 1945, when French control was restored. After the French defeat in Indochina, Cambodia became independent in 1953 under Prince Norodom Sihanouk, who had ascended the throne in 1941. In 1960 Sihanouk was named head of state under a constitutional monarchy. Shaken by the Vietnam War in the 1960s, Cambodia broke relations with the United States in 1965 because of South Vietnamese incursions across the border. In 1969 relations were restored when Sihanouk charged North Vietnam with arming the Khmer Rouge Cambodian Communist rebels. In the same year, American planes began secret bombing raids in Cambodia. In 1970 Sihanouk was ousted by a coup led by pro-U.S. Gen. Lon Nol; the monarchy was abolished, and Prince Sihanouk went into exile.

In April 1975 the Khmer Rouge, led by Pol Pot, captured the capital, Phnom Penh, and established a new government, the Kampuchean People's Republic. In an ensuing reign of terror, an estimated 3 million people died and hundreds of thousands more fled to refugee camps in Thailand. In 1978, Vietnamese troops invaded, capturing Phnom Penh on Jan. 7, 1979, and installing a new government led by Heng Samrin. The Kampuchean People's Republic continued to be recognized as the legal government of Cambodia in the United Nations and by most non-Soviet-bloc nations. A coalition dominated by the Khmer Rouge resisted the Vietnamese takeover, but by 1985 almost all of the country was under Vietnamese control with the Communist Party's Hun Sen as Prime Minister.

Most Vietnamese troops withdrew in 1989, and Prince Sihanouk emerged as the leader of a coalition of antigovernment forces. Starting in late 1988 conferences including representatives from all Cambodian factions were held to forge a political settlement to end the 20-year-old civil war. A peace agreement was signed on Oct. 23, 1991, providing for a cease-fire under UN supervision, the disarmament of all military factions, the formation of a coalition government, and the scheduling of a national election.

Despite bloody efforts by Khmer Rouge forces to disrupt the planned election, Cambodians went to the polls in large numbers on May 23, 1993. The Royalist party emerged with about 42 percent of the vote, ousting Hun Sen's Cambodian People's party. Hun Sen agreed to take part in a coalition cabinet as "second premier," with Sihanouk's son, Prince Ranariddh, as "first premier."

Sihanouk took the title "king." In Jan. 1994, the united government went on the offensive and captured the Khmer Rouge stronghold of Pailin, driving 3,000 troops and 20,000 civilians into Thailand. Sihanouk succesfully negotiated international loans for rebuilding the country.

The coaltion government proved ineffective due to the inherent rivalry between the prince and Hun Sen, both of whom built up their security forces. When the Khmer Rouge leadership split in mid-1997, with Pol Pot either assasinated or imprisoned, Hun Sen seized the moment and his forces attacked those of his co-ruler's and drove the prince into exile. New elections were held in July 1998 and Hun Sen emerged victorious but agreed to form a coalition government. Hun Sen became "sole premier" with 12 cabinet posts while Ranariddh became President of the Assembly with 11 cabinet posts. In December, the last Khmer Rouge troops surrendered. And by March 1999, all of the remaining Khmer Rouge leaders had surrendered or were captured. Now the question of trials for the mass murderers must be faced, a question that may seriously endanger the fragile peace.

▶ CAMEROON
Republic of Cameroon

● GEOGRAPHY **Location**: western coast of central Africa. **Boundaries**: Nigeria to NW, Chad to NE, Central African Republic to E, Congo to SE, Gabon, Equatorial Guinea to S, Gulf of Guinea to W. **Total land area**: 183,568 sq. mi. (475,440 sq km). **Coastline**: 250 mi. (402 km). **Comparative area**: slightly larger than California. **Land use**: 13% arable land; 2% permanent crops; 18% meadows and pastures; 54% forest and woodland; 13% other. **Major cities**: (1986 est.) Yaoundé (capital) 653,670; Douala 1,029,731; Nkongsamba (and environs) 123,149; Maroua (and environs) 103,653.

● PEOPLE **Population**: 15,456,092 (1999 est.). **Nationality**: noun—Cameroonian(s); adjective—Cameroonian. **Ethnic groups**: 31% Cameroon Highlanders, 19% Equatorial Bantu, 11% Kirdi, 10% Fulani, 8% Northwestern Bantu, 7% Eastern Nigritic, 13% other African; less than 1% non-African. **Languages**: English and French (both official); 24 major African language groups. **Religions**: 51% indigenous beliefs, 33% Christian, 16% Muslim.

● GOVERNMENT **Type**: unitary republic; multiparty presidential regime. **Independence**: Jan. 1, 1960 (from UN trusteeship under French administration). **Constitution**: May 20, 1972. **National holiday**: National Day, May 20. **Heads of Government**: Paul Biya, president (since Nov. 1982); Peter Mafany Musonga, prime minister (since Sept. 1996). **Structure**: executive; unicameral legislature; judiciary.

● ECONOMY **Monetary unit**: Communauté Financière Africaine franc. **Budget**: (FY96/97 est.) *income*: $2.23 bil.; *expend.*: $2.23 bil. **GDP**: $29.6 bil., $2,000 per capita (1998 est.). **Chief crops**: coffee, cocoa, cotton, rubber. **Natural resources**: crude oil, bauxite, iron ore, timber, hydropower potential. **Major industries**: crude oil production and refining, food processing. **Labor force**: (1983) 74.4% agriculture, 11.4% industry and transport, 14.2% other services. **Exports**: $1.6 bil. (f.o.b., 1998); crude oil and petroleum products, lumber, cocoa beans, aluminum. **Imports**: $1.3 bil. (f.o.b., 1998); machines and electrical equipment, transport equipment, fuel, food. **Major**

trading partners: *exports:* 25% Italy, 20% Spain, 16% France, 7% Netherlands; *imports:* 25% France, 8% Nigeria, 8% U.S., 6% Germany.

Cameroon was settled by the Sao people about 1,000 years ago. In later times others, including the Bamileke, Bassa, Douala, and Fulani, migrated into the region. Portuguese trading stations were established along the coast beginning in the 15th century, and between 1500 and the early 19th century, the population was severely depleted by the slave trade in the hands of various European nations. European rivalries for domination in Cameroon were settled temporarily in 1884 when Germany established a protectorate.

British and French troops invaded German Cameroon during World War I, and following the war the League of Nations divided the protectorate into two mandated territories—French in the eastern sector and British in the west. French Cameroon rejected the Vichy government in World War II and became an important African base for Charles de Gaulle's Free French. In 1946 British and French rule in western and eastern Cameroon was reaffirmed under UN trusteeships.

In 1958 the French trusteeship was abolished, and the Republic of Cameroon became independent on Jan. 1, 1960. In February 1961 a UN-supervised plebiscite was held in British Cameroon, allowing the people of that region to choose between union with Nigeria and union with the Republic of Cameroon. The northern two-thirds of the British territory elected union with Nigeria; the southern portion joined the Republic of Cameroon on Oct. 1, 1961, to form the Federal Republic of Cameroon. In 1972 the federal structure was abolished by a national referendum, and the United Republic of Cameroon was established. In 1984 the nation's name reverted to the Republic of Cameroon.

During the federal period, Cameroon had a multiparty political system, with party divisions coinciding with the old distinctions between west and east Cameroon. In 1966 all political parties were amalgamated to form the Cameroon National Union, which, with various changes in name, has dominated the political life of Cameroon ever since. In 1980 Pres. Ahidjo, the long-time political leader of Cameroon, was elected without opposition to a fifth five-year term in office. He resigned in 1982 and was replaced by Prime Minister Paul Biya, who was reelected in his own right in 1984. He instituted political reforms whereby multiple candidates ran for office within the structure of the country's single-party system. In 1992 he was elected president in the nation's first multiparty elections. His closest rival was put under house arrest.

The economy of Cameroon is based primarily on agriculture. The country is self-sufficient in food and exports coffee, cocoa, rubber, cotton, palm oil, and timber. Oil is the principal export, however, accounting for 60 percent of export earnings.

▶ **CANADA**
● **GEOGRAPHY Location:** northern North America (excluding Alaska and Greenland); second largest country in the world. **Boundaries:** Arctic Ocean to N, Greenland to NE across Baffin Bay, Atlantic Ocean to E, United States to S, Pacific Ocean and Alaska to W. **Total land area:** 3,851,794 sq. mi. (9,976,140 sq km). **Coastline:** 151,492 mi. (243,791 km). **Comparative area:** slightly larger than U.S. **Land use:** 9% arable land, 3% meadows

and pastures, 45% forest and woodland, 43% other. **Major cities:** (1991 census) Ottawa (capital) 912,100; Toronto 3,863,105; Montréal 3,091,115; Vancouver 1,584,115; Edmonton 832,155.
● **PEOPLE Population:** 31,006,347 (1999 est.). **Nationality:** noun—Canadian(s); adjective—Canadian. **Ethnic groups:** 40% British Isles origin, 27% French origin, 20% other European, 1.5% Amerindian, 11.5% other, mostly Asian. **Languages:** English, French (both official). **Religions:** 45% Roman Catholic, 12% United Church, 8% Anglican.
● **GOVERNMENT Type:** federation with parliamentary democracy. **Independence:** July 1, 1867 (from UK). **Constitution:** amended British North America Act of 1867 transferred power and rights to Canada, Apr. 17, 1982; charter of rights and unwritten customs. **National holiday:** Canada Day, July 1. **Heads of Government:** Jean Chrétien, prime minister (since Nov. 1993); Roméo LeBlanc, governor-general (since Feb. 1995). **Structure:** executive—cabinet collectively responsible to House of Commons and headed by prime minister; legislative—282-seat bicameral Parliament with queen represented by governor general, Senate, and House of Commons; judiciary—judges appointed by governor general with Supreme Court as highest tribunal.
● **ECONOMY Monetary unit:** Canadian dollar. **Budget:** (1998 est.) *income:* $121.3 bil.; *expend.:* $112.6 bil. **GDP:** $688.3 bil., $22,400 per capita (1998 est.). **Chief crops:** grain (principally wheat), oilseeds, tobacco. **Natural resources:** nickel, zinc, copper, gold, lead. **Major industries:** processed and unprocessed minerals, food products, wood and paper products. **Labor force:** 15.8 mil.; 75% services, 16% manufacturing; 7.8% unemployment (1998 est.). **Exports:** $210.7 bil. (f.o.b., 1998 est.); motor vehicles and parts, newsprint, wood pulp, timber, petroleum. **Imports:** $202.7 bil. (f.o.b., 1998); machinery and equipment, petroleum, chemicals, motor vehicles. **Major trading partners:** U.S., Japan, UK, Germany.

Canada is geographically the second-largest country in the world, but most of its territory is very sparsely settled. The vast majority of the country's 26 million people live in a narrow band along the border with the U.S. Despite a long tradition of national independence, Canada's history has been dominated by relations with Great Britain, the U.S., and, to a lesser extent, France.

Canada's earliest inhabitants arrived via the Bering land bridge from Asia around 15,000 years ago and diversified to form the various Inuit (Eskimo), Northwest Indian, Plains Indian, and forest Indian cultures that still contribute significantly to Canada's national identity. The earliest-known European settlers of Canada were Vikings, who established a short-lived colony in Newfoundland around a.d. 1000. British, French, and other European explorers made numerous voyages to Canada during the 16th century, stimulated by Canada's rich resources of fish, forest products, and furs.

The first permanent European settlement in Canada was the French trading station at Quebec, founded by Samuel de Champlain in 1608. Fur traders rapidly spread into the interior along the St. Lawrence River and the Great Lakes; European diseases, particularly smallpox, decimated Native American populations as the explorers advanced. In 1663 New France was organized as a French Crown Colony, and royal governors replaced private commercial interests in governing Quebec.

The Hudson Bay Company was chartered by the British Crown in 1670, inaugurating a long period of commercial and territorial rivalry in Canada between Britain and France. In general, France sought to expand New France northward and westward, while Britain sought to expand its domination southward and westward from Hudson Bay. French and British interests clashed directly along the Atlantic coast, where both British and French settlements were established. Local and regional wars between the French and the British were endemic in Canada throughout the 17th and 18th centuries; each side enlisted Native American allies. These wars were often inconclusive, but in Queen Anne's War (1702-13), Britain gained a significant advantage by winning control of Acadia and Newfoundland, and by driving the French from Hudson Bay.

The French and Indian Wars of 1756-63, a North American extension of Europe's Seven Years' War, proved to be the decisive turning point in the Anglo-French rivalry in Canada. Prior to the outbreak of full-scale war, in 1755 the British deported some 7,000-10,000 French settlers from Acadia, in Nova Scotia, to the West Indies; many later settled in Louisiana. When war broke out in Europe in 1756, Britain employed its superior sea power to cut New France off from Europe and captured Quebec in the Battle of the Plains of Abraham in 1759. Montreal capitulated in 1760, leaving Britain in control of New France.

Faced with the problem of governing New France's large and rapidly growing French population (which far outnumbered Canada's English-speaking population), the British in 1774 passed the Quebec Act, which recognized the territory's legal code and manorial system of land tenure, and granted legal status to the Roman Catholic church. The act also extended Canadian territory south to the Ohio River, enraging the inhabitants of the 13 American colonies and helping to fuel the American Revolution.

During the American Revolution, nearly 40,000 loyalists fled to Canada from the rebellious colonies, establishing English-speaking settlements in New Brunswick and western Quebec. Friction between English- and French-speaking Canadians led the British in 1791 to divide Canada (west of the Atlantic maritime provinces) into two provinces, Upper Canada and Lower Canada. Each was granted a legislature; Upper Canada's was based on British institutions, Lower Canada's retained the French forms established by the Quebec Act of 1774.

During the War of 1812 between Great Britain and the U.S., Canada became a battleground; Toronto was captured and pillaged by the Americans in 1813. Many Americans hoped to expand the territory of the U.S. at the expense of Canada, or even to entice Canada into a continental American union, but Canadians, whether English- or French-speaking, showed no enthusiasm for joining the U.S. A small British garrison, with the support of Native American irregular forces, kept the Americans at bay. The Convention of 1818 established the border between Canada and the U.S. at latitude 49° north, as far west as the Rocky Mountains, and provided for joint U.S.-British control of Oregon (i.e., the entire Columbia River basin).

Following the War of 1812, British authorities actively encouraged British immigration to Canada, and between 1815 and 1855, one million Britons answered the call. This immigration radically altered Canada's ethnic balance, making French-speaking Canadians a minority population for the first time. The francophones of Lower Canada, hemmed in on all sides by English speakers, rose in rebellion under the leadership of the Parti Patriote in 1837-38. Lord Durham recommended in 1839 that Canada be united under a single government, and the Union of Canada was enacted in 1841. This move did not, however, quell the growing nationalism of French Canadians.

War with the U.S. threatened in 1844, as the U.S. claimed the entire Columbia River basin north to 54°40' ("fifty-four forty or fight"). But diplomacy triumphed in the end: In 1846 the boundary at 49° was extended westward to the Pacific Ocean. Meanwhile, gold was discovered in British Columbia in 1856, leading to a gold rush and a substantial increase in the population of western Canada.

Growing trade between Canada and the U.S. from the 1840s onward, and the development of a continental system of railroads in both Canada and the U.S. in the 1850s, led to a relative decline in British influence in Canada. The American Civil War had the indirect effect of prompting Canadians to seek self-government in a federal union. Previously, there had been little contact between the Canadas (Upper and Lower) and the maritime provinces, while the vast territories of the west were still privately administered by the Hudson Bay Company. A federal union was forged in a series of conferences beginning in 1864, and the federation of Quebec, Ontario, Nova Scotia, and New Brunswick was recognized by the British North America Act of July 1, 1867.

The Dominion of Canada thus established in 1867 became a self-governing entity within the British Empire; Sir J.A. Macdonald became Canada's first prime minister (1867-73). The dominion rapidly expanded. In 1869 it purchased the western territories of the Hudson Bay Company, and in 1870, in response to a rebellion of French-speaking Métis in Manitoba, Manitoba was granted provincial status within the federation. In 1871 the union of British Columbia with Canada was secured with the promise of a transcontinental railway within 10 years; the Canadian Pacific Railway was completed in 1885. Prince Edward Island joined the federation in 1873, but neighboring Newfoundland remained a British colony outside the Canadian federation until 1949.

A second francophone rebellion broke out in Saskatchewan in 1885. Its leader, Louis Riel, was executed and became a symbol of French Canadian grievances against the English-speaking majority. Wilfred Laurier became Canada's first francophone prime minister in 1896, but he was unable to solve the problem of the rights of Catholics and French-speakers outside Quebec. Legislation restricting those rights had already been enacted in Manitoba in 1890.

The Klondike Gold Rush of 1897-98 brought Canada to worldwide attention and indirectly helped promote the settlement of rich agricultural lands in the Canadian west. Immigrants to the prairie region came not only from eastern Canada, but also from Europe, notably Germany, Scandinavia, and the Ukraine. Japanese farmers and Chinese railroad and mining workers settled west of the Rockies, further increasing Canada's ethnic diversity, though Asian immigrants were denied citizenship through discriminatory legislation. Alberta and Saskatchewan were granted provincial status in 1905; the Yukon Territory and the Northwest Territories continued to be governed by controllers appointed by the federal government and patrolled by the famous Royal Canadian Mounted Police.

Urbanization and industrialization were stimulated in the early 20th century by the exploitation of extensive mineral resources in western Canada and in northern Quebec, and by the development of hydroelectric projects and transportation facilities throughout the country. The long-lived Laurier government fell in 1911, when his proposal for free trade with the U.S. evoked widespread fears that Canada's nascent industries would suffer without protective tariffs.

Laurier's Conservative successor, Robert Borden, sent Canadian volunteer troops to fight in World War I in 1914 and, over the objections of most French Canadian leaders, bolstered Canada's war efforts in Europe through national conscription in 1917. The distinguished performance of Canada's armed forces in the war bought the country renewed international respect and appreciation.

Borden's wartime English-speaking Conservative-Liberal coalition collapsed in 1921. He was succeeded by the Liberal leader William L. Mackenzie King, who was to be Canada's prime minister for over 20 years (1921-30, 1935-48). He skillfully managed the economic prosperity of the 1920s, which saw the establishment in Canada of branch plants of many American industrial firms.

The Statute of Westminster, which created the British Commonwealth in 1931, had the effect of granting full self-government to Canada within the Commonwealth.

Canada's federal structure was ill-equipped to manage the economic collapse of the 1930s, which brought both industrial depression and a drought-induced agricultural crisis. Efforts to deal with unemployment, land foreclosures, and other economic ills fell almost entirely to the provincial governments, which were not up to the task. The growth of private cooperative movements brought some relief to the maritime provinces and the plains provinces, while interest grew in constitutional reform to strengthen the federal government.

Canada's recovery from the Great Depression was stimulated primarily by the advent of World War II, which Canada entered in 1939. Although the war years brought price controls, rationing, and other emergency measures, the overall effect of the war was to strengthen all sectors of Canada's economy and to enhance Canada's international status as a leading military and industrial power. A Liberal electoral victory of 1945 gave Mackenzie King a renewed mandate for the postwar era.

The two decades following the war saw the gradual expansion of federal financial responsibility for national welfare measures, including pensions, unemployment insurance, and comprehensive medical care, though the administration of such programs remained a provincial matter. These developments coincided with an increase in urbanization and industrialization in the major centers of Vancouver, Toronto, and Montreal. Formal "equalization payments" were enacted in the 1950s to reduce economic disparities between rich and poor provinces. The early stages of these developments played a part in persuading Newfoundland to join the federation as Canada's 10th province in 1949.

A landslide Conservative victory in 1958 brought John Diefenbaker to the prime ministership, but the Conservatives proved unable to offer a coherent political program and were ousted in the elections of 1963, which returned the Liberals to power. Canadian politics since the 1960s have been marked by increasing regionalization; the Liberal party is based largely in the east, while the New Democratic party, organized in 1961, has little support east of Ontario. The Conservatives offer a broad but insecure national alternative.

The language issue continues to divide Canada politically and ideologically. The rise of an aggressive Quebecois nationalism in the 1960s led directly to the Liberal prime ministership of Pierre Trudeau, a Quebecois known as a supporter of a strong federal constitution. Trudeau's efforts toward conciliation and for constitutional guarantees for Quebec within a strong federal structure proved unavailing, however. In 1970 he invoked the War Measures Act to send troops to Quebec to put down a wave of separatist terrorism, leaving the province subdued but sullen.

The 1976 electoral victory in Quebec of the Parti Québécois under René Lévesque provoked fears that Quebec would secede from Canada. Lévesque's plan for a separate "sovereignty-association" status for Quebec was rejected by a popular referendum in 1980, but only because of Trudeau's pledge to seek full autonomy for Canada in order to secure constitutional protection for Quebec's special interests.

In November 1981, Canada's provincial governments reached agreement on proposals for constitutional change. The result was the passage by the British Parliament of the Canada Act, which came into effect on Apr. 17, 1982, granting full independence and constitutional autonomy to Canada and severing its last colonial ties to the British government. Canada's new 1982 Constitution more clearly delineated the powers of the federal and provincial governments, provided for Supreme Court review of legislation, and included a Charter of Rights to protect civil liberties.

A nationwide recession led to the fall of Trudeau's Liberal government and to the election of the Conservative party leader Brian Mulroney (also a native of Quebec) as prime minister in 1984. The Mulroney government encouraged foreign investment and privatization as a means of revitalizing Canada's economy. But its most significant achievement was the negotiation and passage, in 1988-89, of a free-trade agreement with the U.S. (that also came to include Mexico).

The Meech Lake Agreement, containing a number of articles clarifying the 1982 Constitution, was worked out between Mulroney and Quebec's Liberal premier Robert Bourassa, along with the leaders of Canada's nine other provinces, and signed on June 23, 1987. Its provisions enhanced the power of the provinces; a key provision gave constitutional protection to Quebec's efforts to remain a "distinct society," linguistically and culturally French. But the aggressive measures of the Quebec government to eradicate the use of English in the public affairs of the province provoked a backlash against bilingualism. The Meech Lake Agreement failed to become law when the legislatures of Newfoundland and Manitoba declined to ratify it by the June 23, 1990, deadline. Canada plunged into the most serious constitutional crisis in its history.

An alternative agreement to restructure the federal government and give more power to the 10 provincial governments met initial opposition in

Quebec, and was decisively defeated in a national referendum, leaving the nation to deal once again with the awkward status quo.

Faced with a drastic decline in his popularity, Prime Minister Mulroney resigned in Feb. 1991. In June the Progressive Conservative party convention chose Kim Campbell to lead the government, the first woman to do so in the country's history. In the 1993 general election, however, the Conservatives were routed by Jean Chrétien and the Liberals, who gained nearly 100 additional seats in the House of Commons. The new government announced plans in early 1995 to cut the budget deficit through higher taxes and spending cuts on health care and social programs. Although they accomplished this goal, many Canadians were disconcerted because of high unemployment (9 percent in 1996) and a decrease in benefits. Chretien was also vulnerable on the problem of Quebec because he and the Liberal Party seemed to favor giving special status to the French province, where in 1995 a separatist referendum was only narrowly defeated. In July 1997 elections, the Liberals lost 19 seats, but still held a slim majority. Since the other major parties (Reform, Bloc Quebecois) are not united in any meaningful way, the Liberals have been able to govern. But this could change in the near future as the economy remains sluggish despite reforms, and another separatist referendum is in the offing. The issue of separatism rose to prominence again in Aug. 1998 when the Supreme Court ruled that a referendum on Quebec secession would be invalid without negotiations on the terms with both the provinces and the federation as a whole. In the November 1998 elections in Quebec, the Parti Quebecois lost but one seat, retaining an absolute majority of 76 of the 125 seats despite the overall Liberal vote being greater.

▶ CAPE VERDE
Republic of Cape Verde

• **GEOGRAPHY   Location:** archipelago of 15 islands in Atlantic Ocean, off northern Africa. **Boundaries:** Senegal about 300 mi. (500 km) to E. **Total land area:** 1,556 sq. mi. (4,030 sq km). **Coastline:** 600 mi. (965 km). **Comparative area:** slightly larger than Rhode Island. **Land use:** 9% arable land; negl. % permanent crops; 6% meadows and pastures; negl. % forest and woodland; 85% other; includes 1% irrigated. **Major cities:** (1990 census) Cidade de Praia (capital) 62,000.

• **PEOPLE   Population:** 405,748 (1999 est.). **Nationality:** noun—Cape Verdean(s); adjective—Cape Verdean. **Ethnic groups:** 71% Creole (mulatto), 28% African, 1% European. **Languages:** Portuguese and Crioulo (blend of Portuguese and West African). **Religions:** Roman Catholicism fused with indigenous beliefs.

• **GOVERNMENT   Type:** republic. **Independence:** July 5, 1975 (from Portugal). **Constitution:** Sept. 25, 1992. **National holiday:** Independence Day, July 5. **Heads of Government:** Antonio M. Monteiro, president (since Feb. 1991); Dr. Carlos Alberto de Carvalho Veiga, prime minister (since Feb. 1991). **Structure:** executive; unicameral legislature; judiciary.

• **ECONOMY   Monetary unit:** Cape Verdean escudo. **Budget:** (1996 est.) *income:* $188 mil.; *expend.:* $228 mil. **GDP:** $581 mil., $1,450 per capita (1998 est.). **Chief crops:** bananas, corn, beans. **Natural resources:** salt, basalt rock, pozzolana, limestone, kaolin, fish. **Major industries:** fish processing, salt mining. **Labor force:** 102,000 (1985 est.); 57% agriculture, 29% services, 14% industry

(1981); 35% unemployment (1994 est.). **Exports:** $43 mil. (f.o.b., 1997 est.); shoes, garments, fish, bananas. **Imports:** $215 mil. (f.o.b., 1997 est.); foodstuffs, consumer goods, industrial products. **Major trading partners:** *exports:* Portugal, Germany, Spain; *imports:* Portugal, Netherlands, France, U.K.

In 1462 the Portuguese founded the first European city in the tropics at Ribeira Grande on Santiago, one of the 15 islands that compose the Republic of Cape Verde. Located 385 miles off the west coast of Africa, the Cape Verde Islands prospered during the slave trade in the 16th century and later served as supply stations on sea routes and trading lanes. The rise of whaling in the 19th century led to contact with the U.S., as American ships recruited crews from the islands. The United States set up an American consulate, headquarters for the U.S. Navy African Squadron, and a transatlantic cable station in the islands.

Portugal changed the status of the archipelago from colony to overseas province in 1951; five years later, citizens of Cape Verde and Portuguese Guinea organized the African Party for the Independence of Guinea-Bissau and Cape Verde (PAIGC) to petition Portugal to improve living conditions. Beginning as a clandestine organization, the PAIGC became an overt political movement on the islands after the 1974 revolution in Portugal. An agreement between the PAIGC and Portugal, providing for a transitional government in Cape Verde, paved the way for full independence in 1975.

In 1980 the PAIGC became the PAICV, which remained the "supreme expression" of Cape Verdeans' political will until the opposition party, Movement for Democracy, won a parliamentary majority in the nation's first multiparty elections in Jan. 1991. The new government instituted free market reforms, including privatization of industries. Voters approved of the reforms, giving the Movement for Democracy 50 of the 72 seats in Parliament in Dec. 1995 elections.

▶ CENTRAL AFRICAN REPUBLIC

• **GEOGRAPHY   Location:** landlocked country in central Africa. **Boundaries:** Chad to N, Sudan to E, Zaire, Congo to S, Cameroon to W. **Total land area:** 240,533 sq. mi. (622,980 sq km). **Coastline:** none. **Comparative area:** slightly smaller than Texas. **Land use:** 3% arable land; 5% meadows and pastures; 64% forest and woodland; 28% other. **Major cities:** (1988) Bangui (capital) 451,690; Berbérati 41,891; Bouar 39,676.

• **PEOPLE   Population:** 3,444,951 (1999 est.). **Nationality:** noun—Central African(s); adjective—Central African. **Ethnic groups:** 34% Baya, 27% Banda, 21% Mandija, 10% Sara, 4% Mboum, 4% M'Baka; 6,500 Europeans, of which 3,600 are French. **Languages:** French (official), Sangho (lingua franca and national language), Arabic, Hunsa, Swahili. **Religions:** 25% Protestant, 25% Roman Catholic, 24% indigenous beliefs, 15% Muslim, 11% other; indigenous beliefs and practices strongly influence Christian majority.

• **GOVERNMENT   Type:** republic. **Independence:** Aug. 13, 1960 (from France). **Constitution:** Dec. 29, 1994. **National holiday:** National Day, Dec. 1. **Heads of Government:** Ange Félix Patassé, head of state (since Oct. 1993); Michel Gbezzera-Bria, prime minister (since Jan. 1997). **Structure:** executive; unicameral legislature; judiciary.

• **ECONOMY   Monetary unit:** Communauté Financière Africaine (CFA) franc. **Budget:** (1994 est.) *income:* $638 mil.; *expend.:* $1.9 bil. **GDP:** $5.5

bil., $1,640 per capita (1998 est.). **Chief crops:** cotton, coffee, tobacco. **Natural resources:** diamonds, uranium, timber, gold, oil. **Major industries:** sawmills, breweries, diamond mining. **Labor force:** 775,413 (1986 est.); 85% agriculture, 9% commerce and services. **Exports:** $182 mil. (f.o.b., 1998 est.); diamonds, timber, cotton, coffee, tobacco. **Imports:** $155 mil. (f.o.b., 1998 est.); food, textiles, petroleum products, machinery, electrical equipment, motor vehicles. **Major trading partners:** *exports:* 36% Belgium-Luxembourg, 5% Ivory Coast, 4% Spain; *imports:* 30% France, 18% Ivory Coast, 11% Cameroon, 4% Germany.

A landlocked country in Africa's central region, the Central African Republic is one of the least-developed countries in the world. Most of its people are farmers, and the nation has little manufacturing, few reliable roads, and no railroad. Europeans first came to the area in the early 1800s in their search for slaves, but it was not until 1889 that the French established an outpost as the current capital city of Bangui. The region was organized as the territory of Ubangi-Shari five years later. In 1910 UbangiShari was incorporated into French Equitorial Africa along with what are now the countries of Chad, the Congo, and Gabon.

The country was granted internal selfgovernment by the French under its present name in 1958 and became a member of the French Overseas Community. Independence was achieved on Aug. 13, 1960. The first prime minister, Barthelemy Boganda, was killed in an airplane crash in 1959 and was succeeded by his nephew, David Dacko. Dacko was elected to a seven-year term in January 1964, but an army coup in 1966 overthrew his government. The head of the army, Jean-Bedel Bokassa, was installed as president. Named president for life in 1972, in 1976 Bokassa declared himself emperor and changed the name of the country to the Central African Empire.

Dacko returned to power in 1979, however, and Bokassa went into exile in France. The name of the country was changed back to the Central African Republic. A multiparty political system was reinstated in March 1981, but army officers threw Dacko out of office once again six months later and banned all political parties. Opposition parties were legalized in 1991, and Bokassa was released shortly before elections in 1993, elections that made Ange Félix Patassé president. He has tried to reduce the power of the army but has been met with several rebellions requiring the intervention of peacekeepers from neighboring states. France intervened on his behalf twice in 1996.

► **CHAD**
Republic of Chad
● **GEOGRAPHY   Location:** landlocked country in north central Africa. **Boundaries:** Libya to N, Sudan to E, Central African Republic to S, Cameroon, Nigeria to SE, Niger to W. **Total land area:** 495,753 sq. mi. (1,284,000 sq km). **Coastline:** none. **Comparative area:** between Texas and Alaska. **Land use:** 2% arable land; negl. % permanent crops; 36% meadows and pastures; 11% forest and woodland; 51% other; includes negl. % irrigated. **Major cities:** (1988 est.) N'Djamena (capital) 594,000; Sarh 113,400; Moundou 102,000; Abéché 83,000.
● **PEOPLE   Population:** 7,557,436 (1999 est.). **Nationality:** noun—Chadian(s); adjective—Chadian. **Ethnic groups:** 200 distinct ethnic groups, most of whom are Muslims (Arabs, Toubou,

Fulbe, Kotoko, Hausa, Kanembou, Baguirmi, Boulala, and Maba) in north and center and non-Muslims (Sara, Ngambaye, Mbake, Goulaye, Moudang, Moussei, Massa) in south. **Languages:** French and Arabic (both official); Sara and Sango in south; more than 100 different languages and dialects. **Religions:** 50% Muslim, 25% Christian, 25% indigenous beliefs (mostly animism).
● **GOVERNMENT   Type:** republic. **Independence:** Aug. 11, 1960 (from France). **Constitution:** Mar. 31, 1995. **National holiday:** Independence Day, Aug. 11. **Heads of Government:** Idriss Deby, president (since Dec. 1990); Koibla Djimasta, prime minister (since Apr. 1995). **Structure:** executive; unicameral legislature; judiciary.
● **ECONOMY   Monetary unit:** Communauté Financière Africaine (CFA) franc. **Budget:** (1998 est.) *income:* $198 mil.; *expend.:* $218 mil., **GDP:** $7.5 bil., $1,000 per capita (1998 est.). **Chief crops:** cotton, sorghum, millet, peanuts. **Natural resources:** small quantities of crude oil (unexploited but exploitation beginning), uranium, natron (sodium carbonate), kaolin, fish (Lake Chad). **Major industries:** cotton textile mills, slaughterhouses, brewery, natron. **Labor force:** 85% agriculture—unpaid subsistence farming, herding and fishing, 15% other. **Exports:** $220 mil. (f.o.b., 1998); cotton, cattle, textiles. **Imports:** $252 mil. (f.o.b., 1998 est.); machinery and transport equipment, industrial goods, petroleum products, foodstuffs. **Major trading partners:** *exports:* 30% Portugal, 14% Germany, Thailand; *imports:* 41% France, 10% Nigeria, 7% Cameroon, 6% India.

The Sao and other ancient peoples built centers of civilization near Lake Chad that flourished for many centuries until they were displaced by the medieval kingdoms of Kanem-Bornu, Baguirmi, and Ouaddai. From about 1400 onward, Chad became a meeting ground between the Muslim cultures of the Sahara and the Sahel and the black African societies of the tropics. Between 1500 and 1800, Arab slave raiders were active around Lake Chad, supplying slaves for European traders on Africa's west coast.

French military forces reached Chad from West Africa in 1891 and fought a series of battles over the next two decades with the Arab rulers of the region. A French governorship of Chad was established in 1905 (based in Brazzaville, the Congo), but the country was not brought entirely under French control until 1914. Chad was incorporated into the federation of French Equatorial Africa in 1910 and was organized as a colony within the federation in 1920.

French Equatorial Africa was dissolved in 1959, and Chad became an autonomous member of the French Community. Full independence followed on Aug. 11, 1960; François Tombalbage became Chad's first president. In 1965 the Muslim northern and eastern parts of the country rebelled against the southern-led government; despite the aid of French troops, the government was unable to suppress the rebellion, and a long civil war ensued.

Tombalbage was overthrown in 1975 in a military coup led by Gen. Felix Malloum. Efforts to broaden the composition of the national government broke down, and in 1979 Prime Minister Hissein Habre broke with the government and led northern forces against the national army. A cease-fire was negotiated under international auspices, and a National Unity Transitional Government (GUNT) was installed in 1979, but civil war broke out again in 1980. Pres. Goukouni Oueddei sought Libyan aid in restoring order; a contingent of 7,000 Libyan troops occupied the country until 1981. They were replaced by an international peacekeeping force organized by the Organization of African Unity.

Civil war broke out again in 1982, and northern forces occupied the capital. A new republican government under the presidency of Hissein Habre was proclaimed on June 7. OAU forces withdrew, and Habre's government soon controlled all of the country except for a few northern areas held by GUNT. In 1983 GUNT launched a counterattack and regained some territory with the aid of Libyan forces. French and Zairian troops were sent to aid Habre's forces. In Sept. 1984 France and Libya agreed to the withdrawal of all foreign forces from Chad, but Libyan forces remained. GUNT forces controlled the country north of the 16th parallel; Libyan forces occupied the Aozou Strip, along the border, with the apparent intention of annexing it to Libya.

Between 1984 and 1986 Habre persuaded most Chadean dissident forces to rejoin the national government, and in Nov. 1986 he launched a campaign to recapture the north. The Chadean forces won a series of victories, and in May 1988 Libya's Col. Qaddafi declared an end to the 20-year war with Chad.

In Nov. 1990, forces led by renegade Gen. Idriss Deby launched attacks from Sudan and ousted Pres. Habre. Deby, who favors multiparty democracy, proclaimed a provisional government and suspended the constitution. A national charter calling for a new constitution and elections to be held within 30 months came into force in March 1991. Deby functioned as president after that, suppressing two attempted coups in 1992, and legalizing opposition parties. Deby's "Higher Transitional Council" remained in command until presidential elections were held in June 1996, which Deby won.

Chad, largely arid and lacking natural resources, is overwhelmingly an agricultural and pastoral country; the national economy remains at the subsistence level with only rudimentary industrial development.

▶ CHILE
Republic of Chile

● **GEOGRAPHY Location:** South Pacific coast of South America. **Boundaries:** Peru, Bolivia to N, Argentina to E, Pacific Ocean to W. **Total land area:** 292,259 sq. mi. (756,950 sq km). **Coastline:** 3,999 mi. (6,435 km). **Comparative area:** slightly larger than Texas. **Land use:** 7% arable land; negl. % permanent crops; 16% meadows and pastures; 21% forest and woodland; 56% other; includes 2% irrigated. **Major cities:** (1995) Gran Santiago (capital) 5,076,808; Viña del Mar 322,220; Concepción 350,268; Valparaíso 282,168; Temuco 239,340.

● **PEOPLE Population:** 14,973,843 (1999 est.). **Nationality:** noun—Chilean(s); adjective—Chilean. **Ethnic groups:** 95% white and white Amerindian, 3% Amerindian, 2% other. **Languages:** Spanish. **Religions:** 89% Roman Catholic, 11% Protestant, small Jewish population.

● **GOVERNMENT Type:** republic. **Independence:** Sept. 18, 1810 (from Spain). **Constitution:** Sept. 11, 1980, effective Mar. 11, 1981; modified by public referendum on July 31, 1989. **National holiday:** Independence Day, Sept. 18. **Head of Government:** Eduardo Frei Ruiz-Tagle, president (since Mar. 1994). **Structure:** executive; bicameral legislature; judiciary.

● **ECONOMY Monetary unit:** Chilean peso. **Budget:** (1996 est.) *income:* $17 bil.; *expend.:* $17 bil.

GDP: $184.6 bil., $12,500 per capita (1998 est.). **Chief crops:** wheat, corn, grapes, beans, sugar beets. **Natural resources:** copper, timber, iron ore, nitrates, precious metals. **Major industries:** copper, other minerals, foodstuffs, fish processing. **Labor force:** 5.8 mil. (1998); 38.3% services (including 12% government), 33.8% industry and commerce, 19.2% agriculture, forestry, fishing; 6.4% unemployment (1998 est.). **Exports:** $14.9 bil. (f.o.b., 1998 est.); 37% copper, 9.8% fish and fishmeal, 8.2% other metals and minerals. **Imports:** $17.5 bil. (f.o.b., 1998 est.); 25.2% capital goods, 24.8% spare parts, 15.4% raw materials. **Major trading partners:** *exports:* 25% EU, 15% U.S., 34% Asia, 20% Latin America; *imports:* 18% EU, 25% U.S., 16% Asia, 26% Latin America.

Before the arrival of Europeans in the mid 1530s, indigenous habitation of the territory that would become Chile included the Araucanian population in the south and peoples under the influence of the Inca Empire in the north.

The Spanish founded the cities of Valparaíso in 1536, Santiago in 1541, and Concepción in 1550. Chile was under the authority of the Viceroyalty of Peru, established in 1544. Between 1810 and 1818, fortunes of the Chilean independence movement ebbed and flowed, culminating in the victory of Bernardo O'Higgins and the separatist forces in 1817. Independence was finally achieved in 1818.

From 1818 to 1833, Chile underwent a period of political instability due to power struggles among elite Chilean families. In 1833 a strong presidential-dominant constitution was written under the influence of leading political figure Diego Portales that set the form of government in Chile until 1891. Chile expanded its territory at the expense of Peru and Bolivia, first in a war with the Peruvian-Bolivian Confederation (1836-39) and later as a result of the War of the Pacific (1879-83).

A civil war was fought in 1890-91 between forces of the president, José Balmaceda, and the Chilean Congress over the issue of the limits of presidential authority. The defeat of the presidential forces led to the establishment of a congressional-dominant parliamentary system. The checks on policy initiative resulting from the parliamentary system left government deadlocked in the face of mounting social and political problems arising at the turn of the century. The occurrence of a number of bloody strike actions crystallized political debate around social issues such as better wages and working conditions. The immobilized parliamentary system was unable to respond to these problems. In 1925, when Congress failed to allocate funds for military pay, the forces overthrew the parliamentary government.

A new constitution was drawn up that same year that moved governmental structure toward presidential dominance. Nevertheless, political instability continued until 1933, when the new constitution was implemented. The Chilean balance of political power from 1958 until 1973 remained almost equally divided among parties representing the right, the center, and the left of the political spectrum. In order to prevent an electoral victory for the leftist parties, forces on the right allied themselves with the centrist Christian Democrats in the 1964 election, and this resulted in the victory of Christian Democratic presidential candidate Eduardo Frei Montalva.

The program of the Christian Democrats included ambitious agrarian reform and attempts to organize Chile's urban poor. It was believed that these stances would benefit the Christian Democrats at the polls in the 1970 presidential election. As in 1958, the 1970 election fielded three presidential candidates who represented the political right, center, and left. The leftist Popular Unity coalition candidate, Dr. Salvador Allende Gossens, won with 36.3 percent of the vote, but only after bitter debate did Congress recognize Allende's victory.

The Allende government nationalized the foreign-owned copper industry, but an international boycott of Chilean copper imposed in retaliation for this action seriously hurt the country's economy. The government also nationalized the coal and steel industries as well as 60 percent of private banking. The Popular Unity government found itself unable to control peasant seizures of land and factory takeovers by workers. The copper embargo, land and factory seizures, government subsidies to the poor for basic goods, and runaway inflation resulted in a deterioration of the national economy that particularly affected the middle classes. Members of congress from the center and right had hoped to gain enough seats in the 1973 elections to impeach Allende, but instead the Popular Unity made impressive electoral gains. In order to bolster the legitimacy of the Popular Unity administration in the eyes of political opponents, Allende resorted to inclusion of military officers in the government.

On Sept. 11, 1973, segments of the military led by commanders of three of Chile's four armed forces took control of the government, killing Allende in the process. Gen. Augusto Pinochet Ugarte emerged from the junta as the new president. The junta announced the arrest of some 13,000 persons, many of whom then lost their lives in a wave of brutal repression. (Mass graves were discovered in the desert in 1990, and in 1991 a commission reported that between 1973 and 1990, more than 2,000 people were killed by the government.) In March 1974 the dictatorship published its Declaration of Principles, which included a laissez-faire economic orientation, anti-Marxism, and nationalism.

A new constitution was approved by plebiscite in 1980. The two-phase evolution of Chile's political structure included an authoritarian "transitional period" between 1980 and 1989 and implementation of a new political structure thereafter. The constitution created a presidential system with very extensive executive powers and a "guardian" role for the military.

In an Oct. 1988 plebiscite, Chileans rejected continuation of Pinochet rule and called for an end to the dictatorship. On Dec. 14, 1989, Patricio Aylwin Azocar of the Christian Democratic party (one of a 17-party alliance) was elected president with over 55 percent of the vote; he took office in March 1990, ending 17 years of military dictatorship. He was succeeded by Eduardo Frei Ruiz-Tagle in March 1994.

In recent years, Chile's economy has expanded, exports have increased, and it has succeeded in lowering its large external debt. Although exports are still dominated by copper, other minerals and manufactures have gained in importance. In 1996, Chile joined Mercosur, a free trade agreement among six of the largest South American nations. In 1997 the U.S. agreed to sell Chile advanced fighter jets, ending a 20-year ban.

In March 1998 Gen. Pinochet resigned as head of the armed forces after 25 years and was sworn in as senator-for-life. In October, while in Britain, Pinochet was arrested after Spain sought his extradition for the murder of Spanish citizens. A long legal minuet ended in April 1999 when Britain's Home Secretary decided the extradition case could proceed. Chile had already withdrawn its ambassador in December, in protest, and was backed by the other Mercosur nations. As 1999 drew to a close a trial seemed certain.

▶ **CHINA**
People's Republic of China
● **GEOGRAPHY Location:** covers vast area of eastern Asia. **Boundaries:** Russia, Mongolia to N; N. Korea to NE; Pacific Ocean to E; India, Nepal, Bhutan, Myanmar, Laos, and Vietnam to S; Afghanistan and Pakistan to W., Kazakhstan, Kyrgyzstan, and Tajikistan to NW. **Total land area:** 3,705,392 sq. mi. (9,596,960 sq km). **Coastline:** 9,112 mi. (14,500 km). **Comparative area:** between U.S. and Canada. **Land use:** 10% arable land; 31% meadows and pastures; 14% forest and woodland; 45% other; includes 5% irrigated. **Major cities:** (1994 est.) Beijing (capital) 11,250,000; Shanghai 13,560,000; Tianjin 9,350,000; (1990 est.) Shenyang 4,540,000; Wuhan 3,750,000.
● **PEOPLE Population:** 1,246,871,951 (1999 est.). **Nationality:** noun—Chinese (sing., pl.); adjective—Chinese. **Ethnic groups:** 91.9% Han Chinese; 8.1% Zhuang, Uygur, Hui, Yi, Tibetan, Miao, Manchu, Mongol, Buyi, Korean, and numerous others. **Languages:** Standard Chinese or Mandarin (Putonghua based on the Beijing dialect); Yue (Cantonese), Wu (Shanghainese), Minbei (Fuzhou), Minnan (Hokkien-Taiwanese), Xiang, Gan, Hakka dialects, and minority langs. (see "Ethnic groups" above). **Religions:** officially atheist, but traditionally pragmatic and eclectic; Taoism, Buddhism, 2-3% Muslim, 1% Christian.
● **GOVERNMENT Type:** Communist state. **Constitution:** Dec. 4, 1982. **National holiday:** National Day, Oct. 1, (1949) **Heads of Government:** Jiang Zemin, president (since Mar. 1993); Zhu Rongji, prime minister (since 1988). **Structure:** executive; unicameral legislature; judiciary.
● **ECONOMY Monetary unit:** yuan. **Budget:** $NA. **GDP:** $4.42 trillion, $3,600 per capita (1998 est.). **Chief crops:** rice, potatoes, sorghum, peanuts. **Natural resources:** coal, iron ore, crude oil, mercury, tin; world's largest hydropower potential. **Major industries:** iron, steel, coal. **Labor force:** 696 mil. (1997 est.); 50% agriculture and forestry, 24% industry and commerce. **Exports:** $183.8 bil. (f.o.b., 1998); electrical machinery and equipment, machinery and mechanical appliances, plastics, iron and steel. **Imports:** $140.17 bil. (c.i.f., 1998); electrical machinery and equipment, machinery and mechanical appliances, plastics, iron and steel. **Major trading partners:** (1997) *exports:* Hong Kong, U.S., Japan, Germany, South Korea; *imports:* Japan, U.S., Taiwan, South Korea, Germany.

China is one of the world's oldest civilizations. Dynastic rule in the North China Plain began around 2000 b.c. The unifying Qin (221 b.c.) and Han (206 b.c.) dynasties greatly expanded the territory of the empire and established the basic pattern of imperial bureaucratic government that would endure until the beginning of the 20th century. Major dynasties during that period include the Han (206 b.c.—a.d. 220), Tang (618-907), Song (960-1279), Yuan or Mongol (1279-1368), Ming (1368- 1644), and Qing (1644-1911).

By the late 18th century, the Qing dynasty faced increasingly dangerous problems of explosive population growth, bureaucratic stagnation, and trade pressure from the West. Opium— introduced by Great Britain to balance its trade in tea, silk, porcelain, and other goods—created severe social problems. Western demands for free trade resulted in the Opium War (1839-42), in which China was humiliatingly defeated by the British. The treaties of Nanjing (1842) and Tianjin (1858) opened China to Western merchants and missionaries and created foreign-ruled enclaves on Chinese soil. At the same time, the Taiping Rebellion and other popular uprisings led to the deaths of at least 20 million Chinese between 1850 and 1870.

Such reform efforts as the Self-Strengthening Movement (1870s) and the 1898 Reform Movement proved inadequate to the task of strengthening and modernizing China's dynastic government. Japan, modernizing rapidly after the Meiji Restoration of 1868, joined the race for commercial access to China, decisively winning the Sino-Japanese War of 1894-95. The antiforeign Boxer Uprising of 1900 was put down by a joint foreign military force, dealing a mortal blow to Qing rule. On Oct. 10, 1911, the dynasty fell to a coalition of forces led by the veteran revolutionary nationalist Sun Yat-sen.

China's first attempt at republican government, under Pres. Yuan Shikai and subsequent presidents, quickly degenerated into factionalism and warlord control in the provinces. In 1915 Japan successfully demanded further concessions, provoking public outcries. When news reached China on May 4, 1919, that the Treaty of Versailles granted Japan all of Germany's former concessions in China, students rioted throughout the country, demanding reforms and modernization (the May Fourth Movement). Sun Yat-sen's Nationalist party (Kuomintang, or KMT) and the Chinese Communist party (CCP, founded in 1921 by Mao Zedong) joined forces in 1922 in an attempt to create a second republican revolution.

Sun Yat-sen died in 1925. His successor, Chiang Kai-shek, consolidated KMT forces in Guangzhou and mounted the Northern Expedition (1927-29) to defeat or co-opt the various provincial warlords and reunify the country. In the course of this successful effort, Chiang turned on his Communist allies. A series of failed Communist uprisings and KMT anti-Communist extermination campaigns between 1927 and 1934 nearly wiped out the CCP. Remnants of the party broke out of encirclement in Jiangxi Province in 1934 and undertook the 6,000-mile Long March to a secure base in Yan'an, Shanxi Province. There, under Mao, Zhou Enlai, and Zhu De, the CCP recovered its strength. In the Xi'an Incident of December 1936, Chiang was kidnapped by mutinous KMT allies and forced at gunpoint to agree to forming a United Front with the CCP against Japan.

Meanwhile Japan continued its penetration of China, with the assassination of Manchurian warlord and KMT ally Jiang Zuolin in 1928, the invasion of Manchuria on Sept. 18, 1931, and the establishment of the puppet state of Manchuguo in 1934. On July 7, 1937, fighting erupted between Japanese and Chinese troops near Beijing. The Japanese rapidly moved south to the Yangtse Valley, bombing and capturing Shanghai. The Nationalist capital at Nanjing fell in November 1937, amid widespread atrocities against civilians. The KMT army and government retreated to a wartime capital at Chongqing. The remainder of World War II in China was largely a stalemate, with Japan occupying most of the country. KMT-held areas opposed the Japanese with conventional forces (supported, after 1941, by the Americans), while the Communists harassed the Japanese with guerrilla tactics.

At the end of World War II, American forces ensured that the KMT would receive Japan's surrender throughout most of China, giving the Nationalists a commanding position while U.S. general George Marshall attempted to mediate the creation of a KMT-CCP coalition government. That effort failed, and civil war broke out. The KMT advantage was dissipated by ruinous inflation, corruption, mismanagement, and military ineffectiveness. At the end of 1947, with the Communist forces making continual advances, the United States pulled out of China. After losing several major battles throughout 1948-49, KMT forces retreated to Taiwan; in Beijing, Mao Zedong proclaimed the establishment of the People's Republic of China (PRC) on Oct. 1, 1949.

With American backing, the Republic of China established a temporary capital at Taipei (see "Taiwan") and continued to claim sovereignty over all of China, retaining China's seat in the United Nations. The PRC was quickly granted diplomatic recognition by Soviet bloc nations and some Western nations, notably Great Britain, but was effectively isolated in most international affairs by American support for Nationalist China. Chinese troops entered the Korean War in November 1950, as UN forces approached the Sino-Korean border at the Yalu River. This direct confrontation between China and the United States forestalled any possibility of normal contacts for more than two decades thereafter, as U.S.-Chinese relations were held in the grip of the Cold War.

Within China the CCP rapidly consolidated its control of the country and began the task of rebuilding the nation after decades of internal and external warfare. Priority was given to land reform. Land was confiscated from landlords and returned to peasant ownership; landlords and other "class enemies" were tried and condemned by People's Courts set up under party auspices. Under the first five-year plan, announced in 1953, peasants were urged to set up rural cooperatives, while industrial recovery began with Soviet assistance. Artists, writers, and intellectuals were ordered to devote themselves to the service of the party and the nation. In 1956 Mao announced a policy of "let a hundred flowers bloom, let a hundred schools of thought contend," inviting criticism of the party and government. He was shocked by the vigor of the criticism thus produced; many critics were sent to labor camps in the ensuing Anti-Rightist Campaign of 1957.

Angered by the arrogance of Soviet advisers and by Soviet refusal to share nuclear weapons technology with China, Mao broke with the Soviet Union and expelled all Soviet personnel in 1958. At the same time, he announced the policy of the Great Leap Forward, under which China was to make rapid progress on all fronts without outside aid. Huge rural communes took the place of peasant smallholdings and cooperatives, and agriculture was placed under the direction of centralized planning. In industry, labor and enthusiasm were expected to make up for a shortage of capital and technical expertise. The Great Leap was a catastrophic failure, causing widespread famine and social dislocation, as Mao admitted in a forced self-criticism in 1960. Mao temporarily withdrew into the background as a group of party pragmatists led by Liu Shaoqi assumed power in the early 1960s.

In foreign affairs Chinese shelling of the Nationalist-held offshore islands of Quemoy and Matsu in 1958 led to a crisis in the Taiwan Straits, patrolled by the U.S. Seventh Fleet to prevent a recurrence of China's civil war. A rebellion in Tibet in 1959 was suppressed with much bloodshed, and the dalai lama fled to India. Chinese troop movements into Tibet contributed to the outbreak in 1960 of a border war with India. Throughout the 1960s China worried about being drawn into the Vietnam War.

In late 1965 Mao made a bid to return to full power. His vehicle was the Great Proletarian Cultural Revolution, formally launched in 1966. Shock troops of teenage Red Guards were used to attack the entrenched party bureaucracy; Liu Shaoqi was placed under house arrest, and other prominent officials, including Deng Xiaoping, were exiled to rural areas. By 1968 internal disorder was so great that the military intervened to restore control in many areas. Most established organs of power were replaced under the Cultural Revolution by Revolutionary Committees; intellectuals, technical workers, and bureaucrats were severely persecuted. In 1971 Mao's second-in-command, Marshal Lin Biao, staged an abortive coup and died while attempting to flee the country. With Mao increasingly old and ill, most of his power was exercised by his wife, Jiang Qing, and her associates. Her rival, Premier Zhou Enlai, attempted to maintain orderly government functions in the face of this turmoil.

The 1968 Soviet invasion of Czechoslovakia convinced Mao that the USSR was potentially a greater threat to China than America, and he quietly encouraged the growth of better relations with the United States. With tacit American approval, the PRC replaced the Republic of China (Taiwan) in the UN on Oct. 25, 1971. During Feb. 21-28, 1972, U.S. president Richard Nixon visited China. The Shanghai Communiqué, issued at the end of that visit, clarified the positions of both sides and paved the way for the resumption of U.S.-China relations short of formal diplomatic recognition.

Zhou Enlai died in January 1976, and Deng Xiaoping became acting premier. In April 1976 a rally in Beijing commemorating Zhou's birthday was dispersed by police on orders from Jiang Qing, and a riot ensued. Deng was dismissed from office. But when Mao died on Sept. 9, 1976, Deng reemerged as China's paramount leader, behind the new acting premier and acting party chairman, figurehead Hua Guofeng. Jiang Qing and three associates were arrested along with many of their allies. Labeled the Gang of Four, Jiang Qing's clique was blamed for all the ills of the Cultural Revolution; they were tried and convicted for crimes against the state in 1981.

China's post-Mao transformation took a decisive turn in 1978, with the announcement of the policy of the Four Modernizations (agriculture, industry, science and technology, and defense). Foreign investment and technology transfer were encouraged, and thousands of students were sent to study abroad. For a few months in the winter of 1978-79, the authorities tolerated the public posting of written critiques of the government ("Democracy Wall"). Deng consolidated power in his own hands, still acting behind the scenes; Hua Guofeng was dismissed from office, while Deng's allies Hu Yaobang and Zhao Ziyang were promoted to leadership of the party and government in 1982.

On Jan. 1, 1979, China and the United States entered into formal diplomatic relations; the United States rescinded its recognition of the Republic of China as China's legal government but maintained separate nongovernmental relations with the ROC under the Taiwan Relations Act. China's relations with Vietnam deteriorated in 1978 following Vietnam's invasion of Cambodia. In February 1979, China attempted, with little success, to "teach Vietnam a lesson" in a brief but violent border war. A conflict with Great Britain was resolved in 1984 as both sides agreed that Hong Kong would be returned to Chinese sovereignty, but with considerable local autonomy, in 1997. Relations with the Soviet Union remained strained, China insisting that no improvement could come before the USSR reduced its troop concentrations on the Sino-Soviet border, withdrew from Afghanistan, and pressured Vietnam into withdrawing from Cambodia. China's overall foreign-policy stance in the post-Mao era has been low-key and nonconfrontational.

In the 1980s, China achieved spectacular improvements in agricultural production through dismantling rural communes and returning land to individual peasant holdings under long-term leases. Small-scale private enterprise has been encouraged in both rural and urban areas. Reform in industry and in the centrally controlled price structure has been harder to achieve and has led to such side effects as inflation and increased corruption. Within the overall context of reform, factions of relatively more conservative and reformist leaders have coexisted uneasily. A conservative drive against "spiritual pollution" in 1986 was quickly blunted by Deng, but in January 1987, the reformist party-secretary Hu Yaobang was ousted after student demonstrations calling for more democracy. The CCP 12th Party Congress in October 1987 forced the retirement of some older conservatives, named the reformist Zhao Ziyang as party secretary, and elevated the conservative pragmatist Li Peng as premier.

In April 1989 student demonstrators in Beijing mourning the death of Hu Yaobang launched a general movement for greater democracy. Demonstrators began a hunger strike and disrupted a summit visit by Soviet president Gorbachev. Martial law was proclaimed in May as demonstrations spread to other cities. Troops opened fire in Tienanmen Square on June 3-4, killing hundreds of demonstrators. In the aftermath, Zhao Ziyang was replaced as party secretary by Jiang Zemin, thousands of protesters and suspected dissidents were arrested (and an unknown number executed), and hard-liners in the government took firm control of the country.

World opinion was outraged by the Tienanmen incident; the United States and many other countries instituted sanctions against China, tourism plummeted, and the economy went into general decline. International trade resumed during 1989-90, and the U.S. renewed China's most-favored-nation status in June 1990 after several hundred dissidents were released from prison.

China strove to put Tienanmen Square behind it by holding speedy trials of those charged in connection with demonstrations. The government also made overtures to the former USSR, and from its permanent seat on the UN Security Council supported coalition efforts against Iraq in the Persian Gulf conflict.

Economic sanctions were lifted by Western governments in 1991. China continued to pursue its economic reform policies while repressing all signs of political dissent. While national politics, dominated by an aging leadership, seemed torpid and adrift, the private-sector economy continued to grow vigorously.

In 1992-93 runaway growth made China's economy the world's fourth-largest by some standards of measurement. This resulted in higher wages and increased consumer spending, but also widening income disparities, increased corruption, smuggling, theft, etc. Official government figures put 1994 growth at 12 percent, inflation at 24 percent.

Deng's long-expected death, in 1997, produced little immediate effect on the Chinese leadership, except for a new crackdown as leaders competed to seem tough on dissent. But the transition of power to Jiang Zemin, 71, went smoothly.

Domestic affairs in general were overshadowed by national jubilation over the return of Hong Kong to Chinese sovreignty on July 1. In June 1997, America's Congress voted to renew China's most-favored-nation trade status despite misgivings about its dismal human-rights record. Pres. Clinton made a long state visit in mid-1998 and appeared on Chinese TV criticizing China for human rights abuses and urged Mr. Jiang to open Chinese society. Undismayed, the Chinese government proceeded to crush the fledgling China Democracy Party, sentencing (in December) three of its leaders to long prison terms for subversion. In Feb. 1999, new missiles menaced Taiwan and tensions grew worse in July when Taiwan's president said publicly that his country was a separate nation, not part of China. When the U.S. revealed long-term Chinese nuclear spying in the U.S., China's response was: "typical racial prejudice". (See Part I, "Major News Stories of the Year.")

▶**COLOMBIA**
Republic of Colombia
● **GEOGRAPHY Location:** northwestern coast of South America. **Boundaries:** Caribbean Sea to N, Venezuela, Brazil to E, Peru, Ecuador to S, Panama, Pacific Ocean to W. **Total land area:** 439,734 sq. mi. (1,138,910 sq km). **Coastline:** 1,992 mi. (3,208 km). **Comparative area:** between Texas and Alaska. **Land use:** 4% arable land; 2% permanent crops; 29% meadows and pastures; 49% forest and woodland; 16% other; includes negl. % irrigated. **Major cities:** (1995 est.) Bogotá (capital) 5,237,635; Cali 1,718,871; Medellín 1,621,356; Cartagena 745,689.
● **PEOPLE Population:** 39,309,422 (1999 est.). **Nationality:** noun—Colombian(s); adjective—Colombian. **Ethnic groups:** 58% mestizo, 20% white, 14% mulatto, 4% black, 4% other. **Languages:** Spanish. **Religions:** 95% Roman Catholic. ● **GOVERNMENT Type:** republic; executive branch dominates government structure. **Independence:** July 20, 1810 (from Spain). **Constitution:** July 5, 1991. **National holiday:** Independence Day, July 20. **Head of Government:** Andrés Pastrana Arango, president (since Aug. 1998). **Structure:** executive; bicameral legislature; judiciary.
● **ECONOMY Monetary unit:** Colombian peso. **Budget:** (1996 est.) *income:* $26 bil.; *expend.:* $30 bil. **GDP:** $254.7 bil., $6,600 per capita (1998 est.). **Chief crops:** coffee, flowers, bananas, rice; illegal producer of coca and cannabis for international drug trade. **Natural resources:** crude oil, natural gas, coal, iron ore, nickel. **Major industries:** textiles, food processing, oil. **Labor force:** 16.8 mil. (1997 est.); 46% services, 30% agriculture, 24% industry (1990); 15.7% unemployment (1998 est.). **Exports:** $11.3 bil. (f.o.b., 1998); petroleum, cof-

fee, coal, bananas, flowers. **Imports:** $14.4 bil. (f.o.b., 1998); industrial equipment, transportation equipment, consumer goods, chemicals. **Major trading partners:** *exports:* 38% U.S., 23% EU; *imports:* 42% U.S., 23% EU.

The territory that is now Colombia was home to various sedentary and semisedentary cultures prior to the arrival of Europeans. The Chibcha population of the Andean region might have numbered about one million prior to European contact. Portions of the area that make up modern Colombia fell under the authority of the Inca Empire.

In 1538 the colony of New Granada was established with its capital at Bogotá, and for most of the period up until 1740, the area was within the jurisdiction of the Viceroyalty of Peru. In that year a new viceroyalty was established that included modern-day Colombia, Ecuador, Panama, and Venezuela. During the wars of independence against Spain, forces under Simón Bolívar were victorious over the royalists at the Battle of Boyacá in 1819, and the region gained its independence in 1821.

Colombian territory was a part of the federation of Gran Colombia until the collapse of the federal arrangement in 1830. Thereafter, the country—called New Granada—remained a separate political entity (which included the area of Panama). By the 1850s a federal system had been adopted for the country. But this arrangement rapidly disintegrated, and the practically semisovereign states were involved in a constant struggle with the central government for autonomy. The effort to define the political structure was largely resolved with the constitution of 1886, which ended federalist regional autonomy and made Colombia a unitary republic.

Colombian political struggle since the 1850s had been characterized by a rivalry between two groups that coalesced into the Liberal and Conservative parties. During much of the 19th century, the Liberal-Conservative ideological battle was influenced to a great extent by the definition of the role of the Roman Catholic church in political and social life. The 1887-88 Concordat gave the church "official protection," while the state was given authority over public education. The settlement left a central position for the church in Colombian society that was not substantially altered by the Concordat of 1942.

The Liberal-Conservative struggle led to at least six civil wars, which often ended in interparty compromise. A struggle in 1854 involved the issue of the future direction of the country's economic development and was followed by a settlement among elites. The Liberal-Conservative war of 1860-63 led to a Liberal victory and a period of Liberal political hegemony that lasted until 1886. The period of Conservative rule from 1886 until 1930 was punctuated by the "War of a Thousand Days" (1899-1902), in which the Conservatives defeated the Liberals. In 1903 the Colombian government rejected a U.S. offer for construction of a canal in Panama. Panama (backed by the U.S.) revolted against the Colombian government, ending in the separation of Panama from Colombia.

The world depression of 1929 seriously disrupted both the economy and the politics of Colombia. The loss of popularity of the ruling Conservatives due to both the overall economic collapse and their increasingly brutal repression of the labor movement led to a Liberal victory in 1930. A new civil war between peasants loyal to the two parties also broke out that year. By 1934 Liberal president Alfonso López Pumarejo had inaugurated his "Revolution on the March" program of socioeconomic reform.

During the 1946 presidential election, Conservatives won the presidency with a minority of the overall vote, defeating a split Liberal party. Armed conflict originally instigated by the two party elites erupted. This marked the beginning of La Violencia (1948-57) during which more than 200,000 people died. In the summer of 1957, leaders of the Liberal and Conservative parties reached an agreement on constitutional reform in an attempt to end the violence. The agreement, known as the National Front, was to be in force for 16 years and included provisions for regular alternation of the presidency between the parties, as well as an accord on equal staffing of all political positions by both parties. The Liberal and Conservative parties agreed they alone would monopolize the arena of legitimate political competition for the 16-year period. The agreement held up until 1968 constitutional revisions allowed for other political groups to be officially recognized.

The emergence of terrorist and paramilitary groups on both the right and left—some with ties to the drug trade—in the 1960s and 1970s weakened the two-party power-sharing monopoly. In March 1990, one of the most notorious left-wing groups, M-19, elected to lay down its arms and enter the political mainstream and immediately captured 19 of 70 seats in a constitutional convention called to 'rewrite the constitution. Other groups followed suit in 1991.

Colombia has also had to cope with a burgeoning narcotics trade. Throughout the 1980s, narco-terrorists murdered government officials, journalists, and innocent bystanders with impunity. Despite the assassination of four presidential candidates prior to the May 1990 election, the Liberal party's César Gaviria Trujillo won the election campaigning vigorously against the drug traffickers. In 1994 another Liberal party president (Ernesto Samper Pizano) took office pledging to continue the fight against drug traffickers. Samper also promised to invest billions of dollars to improve the infrastructure with money from the newly discovered Cusiana oil field scheduled to be operational in 1996.

In the summer of 1995, the Samper government arrested three of the top seven members of the Cali drug cartel; by September 1996, all seven had been apprehended, though the ten-year sentences meted out to the Rodriguez brothers in Jan. 1997 seemed unduly light. Meanwhile, Samper faced accusations by the treasurer and campaign manager of his own race for the presidency that he knew of $6 million contributed by the Cali cartel. Formal charges instituted by Prosecutor General Valdivieso in Feb. 1996 were found groundless in May by the legislature's Accusations Committee. Still, the United States, which had decertified Colombia as a drug-war partner in March, revoked Samper's visa in May even as Colombian farmers protested government anti-coca and -poppy programs. In 1997 radical leftist terrorist groups began a wave of murders, kidnappings, and other violence against local government officials, and in 1998 attacked and defeated an army battalion. The election of Conservative Andres Pastrana in June 1998 held out promise of victory in the drug war despite violent outbursts during the remainder of 1998 and early 1999. Government meetings with FARC, the principal rebel group, and National Peace Council meetings with ELN, the second major insurgent group, continued into mid-1999. (See Part I, "Major News Stories of the Year.")

▶ **COMOROS**
Federal Islamic Republic of the Comoros
● **GEOGRAPHY Location:** part of archipelago in Mozambique Channel; three main islands, Njazidja, Nzwami, and Mwali (formerly Grande-Comore, Anjouan, and Mohéli). Moroni, Njazidja Is., 11°40'S, 43°16'E. **Boundaries:** between Madagascar and southeast Africa. **Total land area:** 838 sq. mi. (2,170 sq km). **Coastline:** 211 mi. (340 km). **Comparative area:** slightly more than 12 times size of Washington, D.C. **Land use:** 35% arable land; 8% permanent crops; 7% meadows and pastures; 16% forest and woodland; 34% other. **Major cities:** (1980 census) Moroni (capital) 17,267; Mutsamudu 13,000; Fomboni 5,400.
● **PEOPLE Population:** 562,723 (1999 est.). **Nationality:** noun—Comoran(s); adjective—Comoran. **Ethnic groups:** Antalote, Cafre, Makoa, Oimatsaha, Sakalava. **Languages:** Arabic and French (both official), Comoran (a blend of Swahili and Arabic). **Religions:** 86% Sunni Muslim, 14% Roman Catholic.
● **GOVERNEMNT Type:** independent republic. **Independence:** July 6, 1975 (from France). **Constitution:** June 1992. **National holiday:** Independence Day, July 6. **Heads of Government:** Mohamed Taki Abdoulkarim, head of state; Tadjidine Ben Said Massounde, prime minister (since Mar. 1996). **Structure:** executive; bicameral legislature; judiciary.
● **ECONOMY Monetary unit:** Comoran franc. **Budget:** (1997) *income:* $48 mil.; *expend.:* $53 mil. **GDP:** $400 mil., $700 per capita (1997 est.). **Chief crops:** vanilla, cloves, perfume essences. **Natural resources:** negligible. **Major industries:** tourism, perfume distillation. **Labor force:** 144,500 (1986); 80% agriculture, 3% government; 20% unemployment (1996). **Exports:** $11.4 mil. (f.o.b., 1996 est.); vanilla, ylang-ylang, cloves, perfume oils. **Imports:** $70 mil. (f.o.b., 1996 est.); rice and other foodstuffs, consumer goods, petroleum products, cement. **Major trading partners:** *exports:* 43% France, 43% U.S., 7% Germany; *imports:* 59% France, 15% South Africa, 6% Kenya.

The Federal Islamic Republic of Comoros is part of an archipelago composed of four prominent islands (the fourth, Mayotte, is a French dependency) and several smaller islands. Numerous groups from Africa, Europe, and Asia invaded the islands over the centuries. Shirazi Arabs introduced Islam to Comoros around the turn of the 16th century, and the French established colonial rule over the archipelago between 1841 and 1912 and developed a plantation-based economy. The islands remained a French territory until 1961 when political autonomy was granted. Comoros gained independence in 1975. Overthrown by foreign mercenaries in 1975, Pres. Ahmed Abdallah Abderemane returned to power in 1978 and helped establish the country's first constitution. In November 1989 he was assassinated by a small group of rebels who quickly dispersed under pressure from the French government. A new constitution was approved in 1992, and the country's first democratic elections were held in November 1992.

Much of the nation's soil is laden with lava, making it unsuitable for farming, especially on the island of Njazidja (Grand Comore), which is dominated by Mount Kartala, an active volcano. This obstacle to agriculture hinders the growth of Comoros, one of the poorest and least developed nations in the world. Poor transportation links between the islands and a harsh cyclone season add further to the country's problems. But Comoros has invested heavily in its tourism industry.

▶ CONGO
Democratic Republic of the Congo
(formerly Zaire)

● **GEOGRAPHY** **Location:** equatorial country in central Africa. **Boundaries:** Central African Republic, Sudan to N, Uganda, Rwanda, Burundi, Tanzania to E, Zambia to S, Angola to SW, Atlantic Ocean, Cabinda district of Angola, Congo to W. **Total land area:** 905,564 sq. mi. (2,345,410 sq km). **Coastline:** 23 mi. (37 km). **Comparative area:** about 1.5 times size of Alaska. **Land use:** 3% arable land; negl. % permanent crops; 4% meadows and pastures; 78% forest and woodland; 15% other; includes negl. % irrigated. **Major cities:** (1984 census) Kinshasa (capital) 2,653,558; Lubumbashi (Elizabethville) 543,268; Mbuji-Mayi (Bakwanga) 423,363; Kananga (Luluabourg) 290,898; Kisangani (Stanleyville) 282,650.

● **PEOPLE** **Population:** 50,481,305 (1999 est.). **Nationality:** noun—Zairian(s); adjective—Zairian. **Ethnic groups:** 45% of the people belong to one of four largest groups—Mongo, Luba, Kongo (all Bantu), and Mangbetu-Azande; over 200 other ethnic groups. **Languages:** French (official), Lingala, Kingwana, Kikongo, Tshiluba. **Religions:** 50% Roman Catholic, 20% Protestant, 10% Kimbanguist, 10% Muslim, 10% other syncretic sects and traditional beliefs.

● **GOVERNMENT** **Type:** dictatorship; presumably undergoing a transition to representative government. **Independence:** June 30, 1960 (from Belgium). **Constitution:** Apr. 1990; new transitional constitution promulgated Apr. 1994. **National holiday:** Independence Day, Nov. 24. **Heads of Government:** Laurent Kabila, president (since May, 1997). **Structure:** executive—president elected originally for seven-year term; legislative—legislative activity has been suspended pending the establishment of Kabila's reforms; judiciary.

● **ECONOMY** **Monetary unit:** zaire. **Budget:** (1996 est.) *income:* $269 mil. *expend.:* $244 mil. **GDP:** $34.9 bil., $710 per capita (1998 est.). **Chief crops:** coffee, sugar, palm oil, rubber, tea. **Natural resources:** cobalt, copper, cadmium, crude oil, industrial and gem diamonds. **Major industries:** mining, mineral processing, consumer products (including textiles, footwear, cigarettes). **Labor force:** 14.5 mil (1993 est.); 65% agriculture, 16% industry, 19% services. **Exports:** $1.6 bil. (f.o.b., 1998 est.); diamonds, copper, coffee, cobalt, crude oil. **Imports:** $819 mil. (f.o.b., 1998 est.); consumer goods, foodstuffs, mining and other machinery, transport equipment, fuels. **Major trading partners:** *exports:* 43% Benelux, 22% U.S., 8% South Africa; *imports:* 21% South Africa, 14% Benelux, 8% China..

Pygmies were probably the earliest inhabitants of the Congo region, followed much later by Bantu and Nilotic peoples. By the eighth century a.d., a number of well-established kingdoms and empires occupied the lower reaches of the Congo (now Zaire) River and the coastal plain; these included Kongo (Bakongo), Kuba, Luba, and Lunda.

Portuguese explorers and merchants arrived along the coast in the 1480s and initially traded with these kingdoms on a basis of relative equality; an indigenous Catholic church became established. Soon, however, the Portuguese established a slave trade that brought turmoil and decline to the native states. Europeans did not penetrate the interior of Zaire until the 19th century, but the slave trade (partly in Arab hands, in inland regions) had repercussions everywhere.

Henry Stanley descended the Congo River from east to west in 1876, opening the area for further exploration. In 1878 Stanley was engaged by King Leopold II of Belgium to establish Belgian trading stations along the river. King Leopold established the Congo Free State in 1885, not as a Belgian colony but as a personal possession of which he was king as well as chief stockholder.

The management corporation that ran the Free State abolished slavery but instituted a harsh and exploitative regime that reduced native peoples to a condition of involuntary servitude. Forced labor and harsh suppression of rebellion resulted in the deaths of unnumbered thousands of people. Protests against these conditions, led by Great Britain and the United States, led to the transformation of the Free State into the colony of the Belgian Congo in 1908 with promises of reforms.

By the 1920s the Belgian Congo had become a major world producer of copper, diamonds, gold, rubber, palm oil, and other commodities. Railroads were developed to bring these goods to market, notably the line from Elizabethville (now Lubumbashi) in the Katanga region through Angola to the Atlantic coast. River navigation on the Congo was also developed. All mining, plantation agriculture, industry, and administration was in Belgian hands with no native participation in government except at the most local level.

In the 1950s agitation for increased native participation in government led, in 1957, to elections for local councils. In 1959 rioting against Belgian rule broke out. Elections were held on May 31 in anticipation of independence. Joseph Kasavubu became president, and Patrice Lumumba, head of the Congolese National Movement, became prime minister. On June 30, 1960, Belgium granted independence to the Congo; many Europeans fled the country. On July 4 the army mutinied, and on July 11 the southern province of Katanga (now Shaba), under the leadership of Moise Tshombe, seceded from the Congo and declared its independence. Belgium sent troops to quell the disorder.

On Aug. 9 the United Nations called on Belgium to withdraw its troops. Kasavubu removed Lumumba as prime minister. Lumumba, with the backing of Ghana, fought for control. He fled to Stanleyville (now Kisangani) but was kidnapped in January 1961 and taken to Katanga, where he was murdered, apparently with American and Belgian complicity. Fighting continued in Katanga, where Tshombe's regime was supported by European mercenaries and opposed by UN peacekeeping forces. The Katangan rebellion ended in late 1963; rebels fled to Angola, and UN forces were withdrawn in June 1964. In a surprising political settlement, Tshombe became president of the Congo on June 30. On Sept. 7 leftist rebels attempted to establish a "people's republic" based in Stanleyville. Tshombe again resorted to the use of mercenaries to put down the rebellion. Many white settlers, as well as Congolese, were killed in fighting and terrorist atrocities. The rebellion ended in July 1965. In November 1965 Tshombe was deposed in a military coup led by

Joseph Mobutu, whose government took immediate steps to consolidate its control and reduce European influence.

In 1971 Mobutu changed the country's name to Zaire and also changed the name of Leopoldville to Kinshasa. In 1972 he ordered all Zairians with European names to change them to African names; he became Mobutu Sese Seko. Attempts in 1974 to force foreign investors to sell their holdings to Zairians brought economic disruption, and foreign investors were invited back in 1977.

In 1977 another rebellion broke out in Katanga (now Shaba) Province; the government put down the rebellion with the aid of France, Egypt, and Morocco. The rebels fled to Angola, but the province's rich mining economy was again disrupted; many European technical workers fled, and production plummeted.

Although Zaire is rich with minerals, forest products, hydroelectric potential, and agriculture, most of these natural resources remain undeveloped and the country was impoverished by the nearly unprecedented corruption of the Mobutu regime. The president is estimated to have amassed a fortune of $3 billion. Rival leaders attempted to organize opposition to the Mobutu government in late 1987 and 1988, but most were arrested or driven into exile.

In June 1991, Mobutu agreed to draft a new constitution and end a 20-year ban on multiparty elections. Étiene Tshisekedi was elected prime minister by a national conference in 1992, but Mobutu fired him in 1993. France and Belgium dispatched troops to protect their nationals and together with the United States demanded that Mobutu transfer power to Tshisekedi. Mobutu did not comply, and as his nation's economy sank, he continued to live in luxury, protected by the army and police. In May, 1997, Mobutu was driven from office by the army of Laurent Kabila, who immediately changed the name of the country to Congo and began the huge task of rebuilding the nation. Unfortunately he failed in his first year and in the summer of 1998 a new military rebellion began—a rebellion joined by Uganda and Rwanda. By June 1999, a cease-fire seemed near, one that would involve the U.N. and the Organization of African Unity as peacemakers with a mandate to disarm the rebels. (See Part I, "Major News Stories of the Year.")

▶ **CONGO, REPUBLIC OF THE**
● **GEOGRAPHY Location:** equatorial country on western coast of Africa. **Boundaries**: Cameroon to NW, Central African Republic to NE, Zaire to E and S, Angolan district of Cabinda to S, Gulf of Guinea to SW, Gabon to W. **Total land area**: 132,046 sq. mi. (342,000 sq km). **Coastline**: 105 mi. (169 km). **Comparative area**: between New Mexico and Montana. **Land use:** 2% arable land; 29% meadows and pastures; 62% forest and woodland; 7% other. **Major cities**: (1984 census) Brazzaville (capital) 596,200; Pointe-Noire 298,014; Pool 219,329; (1974) Bouenza 135,999; Cuvette 127,558.
● **PEOPLE Population:** 2,716,814 (1999 est.). **Nationality:** noun—Congolese (sing., pl.); adjective—Congolese or Congo. **Ethnic groups:** 48% Kongo, 20% Sangha, 17% Teke, 12% M'Bochi; about 8,500 Europeans (may be half that number following 1997 civil war). **Languages:** French (official); many African languages with Lingala and Kikongo most widely used. **Religions:** 50% Christian, 48% indigenous beliefs, 2% Muslim.

● **GOVERNMENT Type:** republic. **Independence:** Aug. 15, 1960 (from France). **Constitution:** Mar. 1992. **National holiday:** National Day, Aug. 15. **Heads of Government:** Denis Sassou Nguesso, president (since 1997). **Structure:** executive; bicameral legislature; judiciary.
● **ECONOMY Monetary unit:** Communauté Financière Africaine (CFA) franc. **Budget:** (1997 est.) *income:* $870 mil.; *expend.:* $970 mil. **GDP:** $3.9 bil., $1,500 per capita (1998 est.). **Chief crops:** cassava, sugar, rice. **Natural resources:** petroleum, timber, potash, lead, zinc. **Major industries:** crude oil, cement, sawmills. **Labor force:** 79,100 (1985); 75% agriculture, 25% commerce, industry, government. **Exports:** $1.7 bil. (f.o.b., 1997); 50% petroleum, lumber, plywood. **Imports:** $803 mil. (f.o.b., 1997); intermediate manufactures, capital equipment, construction materials. **Major trading partners:** *exports:* 37% U.S., 34% Belgium-Luxembourg, Taiwan, China; *imports:* 22% France, 16% Italy, 9% U.S., 6% U.K.

About 1,500 years ago, the lower reaches of the Congo River formed the focus of a number of well-organized states. The Kongo and Ndonga flourished south of the river; north of the river, in what is now the Congo, the Loango, Teke, and Bobangi were dominant. Some of these states were weakened beginning in the 16th century by the Portuguese slave trade, although the Loango benefited from the trade through the 19th century.

With the weakening of Portuguese power, the French became the dominant European power in western Africa. In 1883 they established a protectorate over the Teke kingdom, which they renamed Middle Congo. The treaty with the Teke king was concluded by Pierre Savorgnan de Brazza, for whom the capital was—and is—named.

In 1910 the French confederated their protectorates of Gabon, Middle Congo, Ubangi-Shari (later the Central African Republic), and Chad to form French Equatorial Africa. The territory became an important base of Free French activity during World War II, in acknowledgment of which Gen. Charles de Gaulle granted French citizenship to the territory's inhabitants in 1946, and local power was devolved upon advisory assemblies. The Republic of the Congo attained full autonomy upon the dissolution of the confederation of French Equatorial Africa in 1959, and the nation gained full independence on Apr. 15, 1960.

In 1963 Pres. Fulbert Youlou was driven from office by violent labor unrest; the military took control and then installed a provisional civilian government led by Alphonse Massamba-Debat, who was subsequently elected president for a five-year term.

In 1968 Massamba-Debat was overthrown in a military coup and replaced by Capt. Marien Ngouabi, who in 1969 reorganized the Congo as a People's Republic. Despite its Marxist-Leninist stance, Congo remained strongly linked to France, its main source of trade, aid, and foreign investment. Ngouabi was assassinated in 1977 and replaced by a military committee of the Congolese Labor party led by Gen. Joachim Yhomby-Opango, who resigned and was arrested for treason in 1979. He was succeeded by Denis Sassou-Nguesso, who was reelected to a third five-year term in 1989.

In 1990, Congo began a relatively smooth transition to multiparty democracy. Following mounting calls for liberalization and labor strikes, opposition parties were legalized as of Jan. 1, 1991. Pascal Lissouba was elected president in Aug. 1992. In June 1997, however, heavy fighting erupted in Brazzaville when Lissouba tried to have his rival, Sassou-Nguesso, arrested just weeks before a new election on the grounds that Sassou-Nguesso was planning a coup.

▶COSTA RICA
Republic of Costa Rica

• **GEOGRAPHY** **Location:** Central American isthmus. **Boundaries:** Nicaragua to N, Caribbean Sea to E, Panama to S, and Pacific Ocean to W. **Total land area:** 19,730 sq. mi. (51,100 sq km). **Coastline:** 801 mi. (1,290 km). **Comparative area:** slightly smaller than West Virginia. **Land use:** 6% arable land; 7% permanent crops; 45% meadows and pastures; 34% forest and woodland; 8% other; includes 1% irrigated. **Major cities:** (1995 est.) San José (capital) 318,765; Alajuela 171,840; Cartago 118,205; Puntarenas 100,266; Heredia 73,268.

• **PEOPLE** **Population:** 3,674,490 (1999 est.). **Nationality:** noun—Costa Rican(s); adjective—Costa Rican. **Ethnic groups:** 96% white, 2% black, 1% Indian, 1% Chinese. **Languages:** Spanish (official), Jamaican dialect of English spoken around Puerto Limón. **Religions:** 95% Roman Catholic.

• **GOVERNMENT** **Type:** democratic republic. **Independence:** Sept. 15, 1821 (from Spain). **Constitution:** Nov. 9, 1949. **National holiday:** Independence Day, Sept. 18. **Head of Government:** Miguel Ángel Rodríguez Echeverría, president (since May 1998). **Structure:** executive; unicameral legislature; judiciary.

• **ECONOMY** **Monetary unit:** Costa Rican colón. **Budget:** (1991 est.) *income:* $1.1 bil.; *expend.:* $1.34 bil. **GDP:** $24 bil., $6,700 per capita (1998 est.). **Chief crops:** coffee, bananas, sugarcane, corn, rice, cocoa. **Natural resources:** hydropower potential. **Major industries:** food processing, textiles, clothing, construction materials. **Labor force:** 868,300 (1985 est.); 35.1% industry and commerce, 33% government and services, 27% agriculture; 5.2% unemployment (1995 est.). **Exports:** $3.9 bil. (f.o.b., 1998 est.); manufactured products, coffee, bananas, textiles, sugar. **Imports:** $4.5 bil. (c.i.f., 1998 est.); raw materials, consumer goods, capital equipment. **Major trading partners:** *exports:* U.S., Benelux, Germany, Italy, Guatemala; *imports:* U.S., Japan, Mexico, Venezuela.

Costa Rica was under the jurisdiction of the Spanish colonial kingdom of Guatemala until it broke with Spain in 1821, along with other parts of Central America. With the collapse of the United Provinces of Central America in 1838, Costa Rica became an independent republic, and the country held its first democratic elections in 1889.

An attempt at electoral fraud in 1948 led to a brief civil war, which was won by the National Liberation forces under "Don Pepé" Jose Figueres Ferrer. The Costa Rican army was subsequently abolished.

In the 1980s, under Pres. Oscar Arias Sánchez, Costa Rica vigorously promoted the settlement of civil strife in Nicaragua and El Salvador and he was awarded the 1987 Nobel Peace Prize for his Central American peace plan.

Subsequent governments focused on economic matters. In February 1994 Jose Maria Figueres Olsen, son of the legendary "Don Pepé," was elected president of Costa Rica, besting free-market and austerity-minded Miguel Angel Rodriguez. By March 1995, government spending was out of control, threatening World Bank loan

cancelations. As a result, the president's National Liberal party and the opposition Christian Social Unity party agreed in June on a deficit-cutting program.

▶COTE D'IVOIRE
(see Ivory Coast)

▶CROATIA
Republic of Croatia

• **GEOGRAPHY** **Location:** southeastern Europe. **Boundaries:** Slovenia and Hungary to N, Yugoslavia and Bosnia and Herzegovina to E, Adriatic Sea to S, Slovenia to W. **Total land area:** 21,824 sq. mi. (56,538 sq km). **Coastline:** 1,105 mi. (1,778 km). **Comparative area:** Slightly smaller than West Virginia. **Land use:** 36% arable land, 20% permanent crops, 18% meadows and pastures, 15% forest and woodland, 10% other. **Major cities:** (1991 census) Zagreb (capital) 708,770; Split 189,388; Rijeka 167,064; Osijek 104,761; Zadar 76,343.

• **PEOPLE** **Population:** 4,676,865 (1999 est.). **Nationality:** noun—Croat(s); adjective—Croatian. **Ethnic groups:** 78% Croat, 12% Serb, 0.9% Muslim. **Languages:** Serbo-Croatian. **Religions:** 76.5% Catholic, 11.1% Orthodox, 1.2% Slavic Muslim.

• **GOVERNMENT** **Type:** presidential/parliamentary democracy. **Independence:** June 25, 1991. **Constitution:** Dec. 22, 1990. **National holiday:** Statehood Day, May 30. **Heads of Government:** Dr. Franjo Tudjman, president (since May 1990); Zlatko Matesa, prime minister (since Nov. 1995). **Structure:** executive; bicameral legislature; judiciary.

• **ECONOMY** **Monetary unit:** Croatian kuna. **Budget:** (1997 est.) *income:* $5.3 bil. *expend.:* $6.3 bil. **GDP:** $23.6 bil.; $5,100 per capita (1998 est.). **Chief crops:** wheat, corn, sugar beets, sunflowers, alfalfa. **Natural resources:** oil, coal, bauxite, low-grade iron ore, calcium. **Major industries:** chemicals and plastics, machine tools, fabricated metal, electronics, pig iron and rolled steel products. **Labor force:** 1.63 mil. (1998); 31.1% industry and mining, 19.1% government, 4.3% agriculture. **Exports:** $4.5 bil. (f.o.b., 1998); 27.6% manufactures, 14.2% chemicals, 13.6% machinery and transport equipment. **Imports:** $8.4 bil. (c.i.f., 1998); 23.1% machinery and transport equipment, 14.2% chemicals, 9% food and live animals, 8.8% fuels and lubricants. **Major trading partners:** Germany, Italy, Slovenia.

Croatia is one of Europe's most ancient states, King Tomaslav having created an independent Catholic realm in 924. In the sixth century the Croats, led by their eponymous chieftain Chrovatos, had migrated to the old Roman province of Illyricum, south of the Danube, where they dwelt in practical independence of the Byzantine Empire. Pope Gregory VII sent a papal crown, and therewith international recognition, to King Zvonimir (1076-89), but the king's death spelt the demise of the native dynasty. In 1102 Hungary's king Kalman was recognized as king of Croatia as well, in a dynastic union in which Croatia retained its own nobility and institutions. From the 14th century, Croatia (along with Hungary and Serbia) formed Europe's bulwark against the Ottoman Empire. After the Turkish victory at Mohacs (1526), the Hungarian and Croatian crowns were added to the Habsburg dynasty. Escaping Turkish sway, Croatia became controlled by Austrian military authorities as the frontier district against the Ottomans.

With the proclamation of the Austrian Empire in 1804, amalgamating the Habsburg possessions into one unified state, the estates of Croatia resisted the royal absolutism, stressing their autonomous status and ties to the Hungarian kingdom, but to slight avail, even after the Croat army of Baron Josip Jellacid proved essential in suppressing the Hungarian revolt of 1848. However, after the 1867 Ausleich ("compromise"), which established a practically independent Hungary within the Dual Monarchy, a further compromise (Nagoda) in the following year recognized Croatian autonomy within the Hungarian realm.

When the Habsburg monarchy collapsed during World War I, Croatia joined the new Yugoslavia, but since that state proved to be no federation but rather a greater Serbia, Croatia resisted Serbian dominance. And after the ferocious ethnic hostility provoked a royal dictatorship in 1929, Ante Pavelic formed the Ustase, a terrorist organization similar to and having ties with the Macedonian IMRO, with the aim of attaining Croatian independence. Just a week before the outbreak of World War II, Croatia was again granted autonomy, but it was too late. With Hitler's 1941 conquest and dismemberment of Yugoslavia, an "Independent Croat State" was established under Italian protection. While Aimone, Duke of Spoleto was proclaimed king of Croatia under the preposterous name of Tomaslov II, he had the good sense never to enter "his" kingdom, whose governance was left to Pavelic and the Ustase. An "ethnic cleansing" of Croatia commenced, in which perhaps 100,000 Serbs and Jews lost their lives. Since the "chetniks" of Gen. Mihajlovic were Serbs and royalists, anti-Ustase Croats had nowhere to turn but to the Communist "partisans" of Tito (himself a Croat). Postwar vengeance against Tito's enemies, especially the Ustase, was severe but short-lived and Croatia in 1946 became one of the "republics" of the reconstituted Yugoslavia.

With Croatia's June 1991 secession from Yugoslavia, Sebian militias backed by the army of Yugoslavia siezed about one-third of Croatian territory but by mid-1995 Croat forces had regained almost all of its land. President Franjo Tudjman also fostered the Muslim-Croat Federation in Bosnia that managed to preserve a sort of Bosnian independence. The Yugoslav-Croat war came to a formal end in September 1996 with the establishment of diplomatic relations in which Yugoslavia recognized Croatia's boundaries, leaving ethnic Serbs in the lurch. In June 1997 Tudjman was elected president for a third term, despite dissatisfaction with his authoritarian ways and rumors that he was dying.

▶ **CUBA**
Republic of Cuba
● **GEOGRAPHY Location:**   largest island in Caribbean Sea, about 100 mi. (160 km) S of Florida. **Boundaries:** North Atlantic Ocean to N, Windward Passage to E, Caribbean Sea to S, Yucatan Channel to W. **Total land area:** 42,803 sq. ml. (110,860 sq km). **Coastline:** 2,319 mi. (3,735 km). **Comparative area:** between Tennessee and Pennsylvania. **Land use:** 23% arable land; 6% permanent crops; 23% meadows and pastures; 17% forest and woodland; 31% other; includes 10% irrigated. **Major cities:** (1993 est.) Havana (capital) 2,175,995; Santiago de Cuba 440,084; Camagüey 293,961; Holguín 242,085; Guantánamo 207,796.
● **PEOPLE Population:** 11,096,395 (1999 est.). **Nationality:** noun—Cuban(s); adjective—Cuban.

Ethnic groups: 51% mulatto, 37% white, 11% black, 1% Chinese. **Languages:** Spanish. **Religions:** at least 85% nominally Roman Catholic before Castro assumed power.
● **GOVERNMENT Type:** Communist state. **Independence:** May 20, 1902 (from Spain). **Constitution:** Feb. 24, 1976. **National holiday:** Liberation Day, Jan. 1; Rebellion Day, July 26. **Head of Government:** Fidel Castro Ruz, prime minister from February 1959; president (since Dec. 1976). **Structure:** executive; unicameral legislature; controlled judiciary.
● **ECONOMY Monetary unit:** Cuban peso. **Budget:** (1998 est.) *income:* $12.3 bil.; *expend.:* $13 bil. **GDP:** $17.3 bil., $1,560 per capita (1998 est.). **Chief crops:** sugar cane, tobacco, citrus, coffee, rice. **Natural resources:** cobalt, nickel, iron ore, copper, manganese. **Major industries:** sugar, petroleum, food and tobacco processing. **Labor force:** 4.5 mil. (1996); 30% services and government, 22% industry, 20% agriculture, 11% commerce. **Exports:** $1.4 bil. (f.o.b., 1998 est.); sugar, nickel, shellfish, tobacco. **Imports:** $3 bil. (c.i.f., 1998 est.); petroleum, food, machinery, chemicals. **Major trading partners:** *exports:* 27% Russia, 18% Canada, 8% Spain; *imports:* 17% Spain, 9% France, 9% Canada.

At the time of Christopher Columbus's arrival in 1492, Cuba was home to Arawak, Ciboney, and Guanahatabey Indian people. Cuba served as a launching point for Spanish imperial conquests in the Americas, and the early- 19th-century wars of independence that swept the rest of Spanish America did not overthrow the imposing Spanish garrison there. Slavery was abolished in 1886, but Spanish colonialism lingered in Cuba until the 1890s.

Spanish control of the island began to deteriorate in the late 1860s with the beginning of the "Ten Years War" (1868-78). Under the terms of the 1898 Treaty of Paris, which ended the Cuban-U.S.-Spanish War, Cuba became a U.S. protectorate. The U.S.-sponsored Platt Amendment (1901) to the new Cuban constitution gave the United States the right to intervene in Cuban affairs.

Corruption and political repression plagued Cuban politics during the first half of the 20th century. Gerardo Machado won election to the presidency in 1925, but quickly turned his administration into a dictatorship that lasted until his ouster by a progressive coalition of students and labor in 1933. The "revolution" of 1933 installed Ramón Grau San Martín as the new head of the government, but the U.S. supported Grau's ouster, and army sergeant Fulgencio Batista replaced him. Batista ruled the country either directly or indirectly for the next quarter century.

In 1953 Fidel Castro Ruz led a failed attack on the Moncada army barracks in Santiago. In Dec. 1956 Fidel and Raúl Castro, Argentine physician Ernesto "Che" Guevara, and 79 others returned to Cuba and waged a guerrilla campaign against the government. Batista's military failed to defeat the guerrillas, and in the wake of increasing demonstrations of public antipathy for his government, the dictator fled the country. The Communist Fidelistas took control Jan. 1, 1959.

By mid-1959, revolutionary tribunals had tried and executed more than 500 political "enemies." The leaders announced an agrarian reform, and by 1960 the nationalization of the economy was in full swing. In 1961 U.S.-Cuban diplomatic relations were severed, and the U.S.-sponsored Bay of Pigs invasion by Cuban exiles failed. In 1962 the Cuban missile crisis brought the world to the brink of nuclear war when U.S. spy planes uncovered Soviet intentions to place nuclear weapons on the island. The Soviets agreed to the withdrawal of missiles in exchange for a U.S. pledge not to invade Cuba.

In its active foreign policy, Cuba provided assistance to a number of left-wing regimes in Africa and Latin America, most notably its military presence in Angola from 1975 to 1991. With the collapse of the Soviet Union in 1991, Cuba lost huge subsidies, forcing its economy into a downward spiral. In 1994, the worsening economy and a growing dissatisfaction with the Castro govenment fueled migration of Cubans to U.S. shores. With thousands of refugees arriving in Florida each day—aboard boats, homemade rafts, ferries—the U.S. and Cuba negotiated an agreement in which the United States would increase acceptance levels of Cuban immigrants to 20,000 annually in return for Cuba's promise to curb illegal migration.

Tensions flared between the U.S. and Cuba on Feb. 24, 1996, when Cuban MiGs shot down two private jets operating out of Miami. The U.S. responded by tightening economic sanctions, with penalties for foreigners investing in Cuba (the Helms-Burton Act). Castro and his party called for a renewed commitment to Marxism and shortly thereafter Castro met with Pope John Paul II who visited Cuba in 1999 and publicly confronted Castro on issues of freedom and religious liberty.

▶ CYPRUS
Republic of Cyprus
● **GEOGRAPHY** **Location:** eastern Mediterranean Sea. Nicosia 35°11'N, 33°23'E. **Boundaries:** 62 mi. (100 km) S of Turkey, Syria to E. **Total land area:** 3,571 sq. mi. (9,250 sq km). **Coastline:** 403 mi. (648 km). **Comparative area:** between Delaware and Connecticut. **Land use:** 40% arable land; 7% permanent crops; 10% meadows and pastures; 18% forest and woodland; 25% other; includes 10% irrigated. **Major cities:** Nicosia (capital) 149,100 (excludes Turkish-occupied portion); Limassol 107,200; Larnaca 48,300 (1982); Famagusta (Gazi Magusa) 39,500 (mid-1974); Phaphos 20,800 (1982).
● **PEOPLE** **Population:** 754,064 (1999 est.). **Nationality:** noun—Cypriot(s); adjective—Cypriot. **Ethnic groups:** 78% Greek, 18% Turkish. **Languages:** Greek, Turkish, English. **Religions:** 78% Greek Orthodox, 18% Muslim.
● **GOVERNMENT** **Type:** republic. **Independence:** Aug. 16, 1960 (from UK). **Constitution:** Aug. 16, 1960; negotiations have been held intermittently to create basis for new or revised constitution to govern the island and relations between Greek and Turkish Cypriots. **National holiday:** Independence Day, Oct. 1. **Heads of Government:** Glafcos Clerides, president (since Feb. 1993); Turkish sector—Rauf Denktash, president (since 1975). **Structure:** currently, government of Cyprus has effective authority over only Greek Cypriot community; headed by president of republic and comprising Council of Ministers, House of Representatives, and Supreme Court; Turkish Cypriots declared their own constitution and governing bodies within Turkish Federated State of Cyprus in 1975; state renamed Turkish Republic of Northern Cyprus in 1983.
● **ECONOMY** **Monetary unit:** Cypriot pound; Turkish lira. **Budget:** (1997 est.) *income:* $2.9 bil., Greek area; $171 mil., Turkish area; *expend.:* $3.4 bil., Greek area; $306 mil., Turkish area. **GDP:**

(1997 est.) $10 bil., $13,000 per capita. **Chief crops:** potatoes, vegetables, barley, grapes. **Natural resources:** copper, pyrites, asbestos, gypsum, timber. **Major industries:** food, beverages, textiles, chemicals. **Labor force:** (1996) Greek area—299,700; 62% services, 25% industry, 13% agriculture; 3.3% unemployment; Turkish area—76,500; 66% services, 11% industry, 23% agriculture. **Exports:** Greek area (f.o.b., 1998)—$1.2 bil.; citrus, potatoes, grapes; Turkish area (f.o.b., 1996)—$70.5 mil.; citrus, potatoes, textiles. **Imports:** Greek area (f.o.b., 1998)—$3.8 bil.; consumer goods, petroleum and lubricants, foodstuffs; Turkish area (f.o.b., 1996)—$318.4 mil.; food, minerals, chemicals. **Major trading partners:** *exports:* Greek area—Russia, Bulgaria, UK, Greece; Turkish area—Turkey, UK, other EU; *imports:* Greek area—U.S., UK., Italy; Turkish area—Turkey, UK, other EU.

Recent excavations on Cyprus indicate a human presence at least 10,000 years ago. Mycenean (Greek) culture flourished in the second millenium b.c. Phoenicians colonized the island in the 10th century b.c., and it remained a major entrepôt for eastern Mediterranean trade. Annexed to Rome in 58 b.c. it was later part of the Byzantine Empire until the English Richard I (Lion Hearted) established a crusader state in a.d. 1191. The Lusignan dynasty ruled until 1489, when Cyprus was annexed by Venice. It was subsequently conquered by the Ottoman Empire in 1571.

In 1878 the Congress of Berlin placed Cyprus under British administration. In 1914 it was annexed outright by Great Britain and was made a British colony in 1925. From 1945 to 1948, the British used Cyprus as a detention area for "illegal" Jewish immigrants to Palestine.

After 1947 the Greek Cypriot community continued its long-standing agitation for union (enosis) with Greece, a policy strongly opposed by the Turkish Cypriot community. Communal violence broke out in 1954-55. In 1960 Cyprus was granted full independence under an agreement that forbade either enosis or partition and included guarantees of the rights of both Greeks and Turks. Attempts by the president, Archbishop Makarios, to alter the constitution to favor the Greek majority provoked further communal clashes in 1964, when a UN peacekeeping force was sent to the island. On July 15, 1974, a military coup by officers favoring union with Greece deposed the Makarios government. On July 20 Turkey invaded Cyprus and, after the collapse of cease-fire talks in August, occupied the northern two-fifths of the island. In 1975 the Turkish government announced a de facto partition of Cyprus; the northern territory was proclaimed the Turkish Federated State of Cyprus, under Pres. Rauf Denktash.

Makarios returned as president of the Republic of Cyprus, which was thus reduced in size, and remained in office until his death in 1977. He was succeeded by Spyros Kyprianou. Some 200,000 Greek Cypriots were expelled from the Turkish sector to the Republic; many Turks fled from the Republic to the Turkish sector. With a return of political stability, renewed foreign investment, and a customs union negotiated with the EEC, the Republic's economy has prospered, led by agriculture, light manufacturing, and tourism.

In the Turkish sector, the economy remains stagnant, hampered by the loss of population, wartime damage, and stringent economic controls. The Turkish sector proclaimed its independence as the Turkish Republic of Northern Cyprus in 1983, but the new republic has not gained international recognition.

The decision of the EU to invite Cyprus to apply for membership and to deny Turkey's application (July and December, 1998) heightened tensions. In June 1999, both Greece and Turkey sent aircraft to Cyprus and the newly-reelected government of President Clerides sought anti-aircraft missiles from Russia. But by December Cyprus had cancelled plans for deployment, at the urging of Greek Premier Simitis. A precarious balance was re-established.

▶ CZECH REPUBLIC

• **GEOGRAPHY Location:** Central Europe. **Boundaries:** Poland to N, Slovakia to E, Austria to S, Germany to W. **Total land area:** 30,387 sq. mi. (78,703 sq. km). **Coastline:** none. **Comparative area:** about the size of South Carolina. **Land use:** N.A. **Major cities:** (1994 est.) Prague (capital) 1,213,299; Brno 389,576; Ostrava 325,827; Pilsen (Plzen) 171,908; Olomouc 106,278.

• **PEOPLE Population:** 10,280,513 (1999 est.). **Nationality:** noun—Czech; adjective—Czech. **Ethnic groups:** 94.4% Czech, 3% Slovak. **Languages:** Czech, Slovak. **Religions:** 39.8% atheist, 39.2% Roman Catholic, 4.6% Protestant.

• **GOVERNMENT Type:** parliamentary democracy. **Independence:** Oct. 29, 1918 (from Austro-Hungarian Empire); Jan. 2, 1993 (from Czechoslovakia). **Constitution:** Jan. 1, 1993. **National holiday:** Founding of the Republic, Oct. 28. **Heads of Government:** Václav Havel, president (since Jan. 1993), Miloš Zeman, prime minister (since July 1998). **Structure:** executive; bicameral legislature; judiciary.

• **ECONOMY Monetary unit:** koruna. **Budget:** (1997 est.) *income:* $16.1 bil., *expend.:* $16.6 bil. **GDP:** $116.7 bil., $11,300 per capita (1998 est.). **Chief crops:** wheat, rye, barley, oats, corn, potatoes. **Natural resources:** coal, kaolin, clay, graphite. **Major industries:** fuels, metallurgy, machines. **Labor force:** (1998) 3.655 mil.; 32.1% industry, 43.7% services, 9.1% construction, 7.2% transport and communications, 6.9% agriculture. **Exports:** $23.8 bil., (f.o.b., 1998 est.); manufactured goods, machinery and equipment, chemicals, raw materials and fuels. **Imports:** $26.8 bil. (f.o.b., 1998 est.); machinery and equipment, manufactured goods, chemicals. **Major trading partners:** (1997) Germany, Slovakia, Austria, Poland.

A Moravian empire, Christianized by Cyril and Methodius, existed in the ninth century until destroyed by the Magyars. From the 10th through the 14th century, Bohemia and Moravia, "lands of the crown of St. Vaclav," formed an independent kingdom within the Holy Roman Empire under the Czech Premsylid dynasty. In 1526 the crown lands came under Habsburg rule, a rule that lasted until World War I.

They were the richest crown lands of the Austro-Hungarian Empire. Prosperous agriculture in the central plains and mineral wealth in the hill country were supplemented in the 19th century by industrial development led by urban middle classes, who were largely German and Jewish.

With the crumbling of the Habsburg monarchy during the war, a new multinational state of Czechoslovakia emerged, founded by Eduard Beneš and Thomas Masaryk, in which the Czechs (only 45% of the population) ruled over Germans, Slovaks, Magyars, Poles, and Ukranians. Yet it was the most democratic state in Central Europe between the wars.

Following the Munich Pact of September 1938, Hitler annexed the German-speaking regions of the "Sudetenland," and in 1939 he established a "protectorate" over the Czech lands, while Slovakia became a self-governing satellite republic. With the collapse of Hitler's Reich, Czechoslovakia was reestablished (except for the Carpatho-Ukraine, which it was compelled to cede to the USSR) with Beneš again as president and a socialist government, independent but pro-Soviet. Three million Germans were expelled, with tens of thousands killed either in mob violence or after hasty trials before "Special People's Courts." In 1948 a Communist coup forced Beneš to resign; he was replaced by the Communist leader Klement Gottwald. Jan Masaryk, the foreign minister, committed suicide or was murdered. Purges and persecutions followed.

With Stalin's death in 1953, Gottwald was replaced as party first secretary by Stalinist hardliner Antonin Novotny, who also became president in 1957. In 1968 Novotny was replaced as first secretary by a Slovak liberal, Alexander Dubcek. Czechoslovakia suddenly was in the vanguard of communist reform. The new regime abolished censorship, denounced Stalin, decentralized economic decision-making, and granted real power to the National Assembly.

The brief "Prague Spring" ended in August 1968, when Warsaw Pact troops invaded. In 1969 Dubcek was replaced by Gustáv Husak. The party was purged, censorship restored, dissent repressed, and the centralized economy restored.

The 1970s brought inflation and economic stagnation but produced no change in policy. The rise of the Solidarity movement in Poland in the early 1980s provoked a backlash of preventive repression in Czechoslovakia, aimed especially at Charter 77, a human-rights organization, and at the Catholic church.

The pro-democracy movement began in earnest in October 1989, inspired by a lack of confidence in Communist rule and by reform movements throughout Eastern Europe. The resignation of Communist leaders throughout December culminated in the parliamentary election of Václav Havel, a dissident playwright and head of a loose coalition of opposition groups called Civic Forum, as president, and the vindicated Alexander Dubcek as chairman of Parliament.

Despite severe economic difficulties, revelations of state security abuses, environmental pollution, and other problems inherited from the Communist era, Czechoslovakia's "Velvet Revolution" seemed a resounding political and popular success. Soviet troops left by March; and in June Civic Forum and its Slovakian ally, Public Against Violence, won 47% of the vote in parliamentary elections, against 14% for the Communists and 12% for the Christian Democrats. Vaclav Havel was elected president, and Marian Calfa became prime minister.

But Slovak-Czech resentments and Slovakia's economic distress led to a separation of the two republics, effective Jan. 1, 1993. In June 1996, the first elections in the new Czech Republic gave 99 (out of 200) seats to the three-party center-right coalition (led by Prime Minister Vaclav Klaus and President Vaclav Havel) which had guided the Czech Republic's successful transition to a market economy. After several years of prosperity, the Czech Republic suddenly fell on hard times in 1997. The economic growth that had been the envy of other East European nations had failed to be sustained, and Klaus was forced to introduce austerity measures. Revelations of campaign finance irregularities brought Klaus' resignation in November 1997. In the subsequent June 1998 elections, the Social Democrats won a plurality of seats and, with the Civic Democrats' agreement, formed not a coalition but a minority government for the next four years. (In return, the CDs were to appoint the speakers of both houses and to chair the budget and secret service committees of the legislature.) The budget adopted in January 1999 included the republic's first planned deficit as the nagging recession continued, with little economic growth forecast and unemployment rising to 9.5 percent.

▶ DENMARK
Kingdom of Denmark
● **GEOGRAPHY Location:** northern Europe. **Boundaries:** Skagerrak channel to N, Baltic Sea to E, Germany to S, North Sea to W. **Total land area:** 16,629 sq. mi. (43,070 sq km). **Coastline:** 2,100 mi. (3,379 km). **Comparative area:** between Maryland and West Virginia. **Land use:** 61% arable land; negl. % permanent crops; 6% meadows and pastures; 12% forest and woodland; 21% other; includes 9% irrigated. **Major cities:** (1995) København (Copenhagen—capital) 1,353,333; Århus (Aarhus) 277,477; Odense 182,617; Alborg (Aalborg) 159,056; Esbjerg 82,579.
● **PEOPLE Population:** 5,356,845 (1999 est.). **Nationality:** noun—Dane(s); adjective—Danish. **Ethnic groups:** Scandinavian, Eskimo, Faeroese, German. **Languages:** Danish, Faroese, Greenlandic (Eskimo dialect); small German-speaking minority. **Religions:** 91% Evangelical Lutheran, 2% other Protestant and Roman Catholic, 7% other.
● **GOVERNMENT Type:** constitutional monarchy. **Constitution:** June 5, 1953. **National holiday:** Birthday of the Queen, Apr. 16. **Heads of Government:** Margrethe II, queen (since Jan. 1972); Poul Nyrup Rasmussen, prime minister (since Jan. 1993). **Structure:** executive power vested in Crown but exercised by cabinet responsible to Parliament; unicameral legislature; Supreme Court.
● **ECONOMY Monetary unit:** Danish krone. **Budget:** (1996 est.) *income:* $62.1 bil.; *expend.:* $66.4 bil. **GDP:** $124.4 bil., $23,300 per capita (1998 est.). **Chief crops:** grain, potatoes; meat, dairy; fish. **Natural resources:** crude oil, natural gas, fish, salt, limestone. **Major industries:** food processing, machinery and equipment, textiles, clothing. **Labor force:** 2,895,950; 40% private services, 30% government services, 19% manufacturing and mining; 6.5% unemployment (1998). **Exports:** $48.8 bil. (f.o.b., 1998); machinery and instruments, meat and meat products, fuels, dairy products. **Imports:** $46.1 bil. (f.o.b., 1998 est.); machinery and equipment, petroleum, chemicals, grain and foodstuffs. **Major trading partners:** (1994) *exports:* 21.4% Germany, 11.6% Sweden, 9.6% UK, 6.2% Norway; *imports:* 21.7% Germany, 12.7% Sweden, 7.8% Netherlands, 7.6% UK, 5.6% France.

Scandinavian by history, not geography, Denmark in the 11th century, under its second Christian king, Canute, ruled a great northern empire including Greenland, Iceland, the Faeroe Islands, Great Britain, and Norway. By 1387 Britain was long independent, but Denmark added Sweden and Finland to its domain. Yet it was never a great power. At home its kings never really controlled the nobility, while in foreign affairs it was dominated by the Hansa, the great league of German trading cities.

In the 16th century Denmark had to recognize the independence of Sweden and Finland. In the 19th century it lost Norway (to Sweden in 1814) and Schleswig-Holstein (to Prussia in 1864). In the 20th century Denmark sold the Virgin Islands to the United States in 1914 and had to recognize Iceland's independence in 1944.

In the 19th century, Denmark was transformed from a poor peasant society to one of Europe's richest agricultural nations by means of reforms that established agricultural cooperatives and emphasized intensive specialization in the production of dairy products and pork. These products remain a mainstay of the Danish economy.

Denmark remained neutral during World War I. In 1939 Denmark signed a 10-year nonaggression pact with Germany, but Germany nevertheless invaded Denmark in April 1940; the country surrendered without a fight. In

1941 Denmark's ambassador in Washington transferred defense of Greenland to the United States, and much of Denmark's merchant fleet joined the Allied war effort. Denmark was placed under German martial law in August 1943 and was treated as an enemy nation. Danish resistance succeeded in evacuating 7,000 Jews to neutral Sweden. Denmark was liberated by British troops in May 1945.

Although Denmark was not technically a participant on the Allied side in World War II, it became a UN member in 1946 and a founding member of NATO in 1949. By the latter year, the postwar recovery was complete, with industrial levels exceeding those of the prewar period. High taxes, unemployment, and inflation remained problems, but the economy was aided by the growth of trade with West Germany, which was just beginning its "economic miracle."

In 1953 the king assented to a constitutional reform that abolished the upper house of the legislature, leaving the Folketing as the sole legislative body. Proportional representation meant that it was virtually impossible for any political party to gain a parliamentary majority; Denmark is always governed by coalition regimes. In the postwar period, these normally have been led by the Social Democrats.

In the 1950s Denmark adopted a characteristically Scandinavian program of free enterprise, high taxes, and extensive social welfare systems. A high rate of economic growth, spurred by agricultural exports, continued throughout the 1960s. Denmark joined the EC in 1972. The 1970s brought economic difficulties, as Danish oil exploration in the North Sea yielded disappointing results, and inflation reached double digits annually.

The elections of 1982 installed Denmark's first Conservative government since 1905. A Conservative four-party coalition formed in 1984 remained in office until January 1993 when Prime Minister Schlüter resigned over charges of misleading the Folketing about restrictions on the immigration of Tamil refugees. Social Democrat Poul Nyrup Rasmussen formed a coalition government with only a one-seat majority.

The general revival of the world economy in the 1980s coupled with government austerity measures has led to renewed growth and lowered inflation. Although as recently as 1986 Danish voters renewed their commitment to the EC, in the June 1992 referendum on the Maastricht Treaty—providing for common defense and foreign policy as well as a common currency and central bank—Denmark said "no." The EU quickly made concessions that guaranteed Denmark's right to opt out of any common EU citizenship, police force, defense policy, or judicial arrangement. In May 1993 Danish voters approved this radically different version of the treaty.

▶ DJIBOUTI
Republic of Djibouti
● **GEOGRAPHY Location:** northeastern Africa. **Boundaries:** Red Sea to N, Gulf of Aden to E, Somalia to SE, Ethiopia to S, W, and NW. **Total land area:** 8,494 sq. mi. (22,000 sq km). **Coastline:** 195 mi. (314 km). **Comparative area:** between Massachusetts and New Hampshire. **Land use:** 9% meadows and pastures; 91% other. **Major cities:** Djibouti (capital) 200,000 (1981); Dikhil, Ali-Sabieh, Tadjourah, Obock.
● **PEOPLE Population:** 447,439 (1999 est.). **Nationality:** noun—Djiboutian(s); adjective—Djiboutian. **Ethnic groups:** 60% Somali, 35% Afar, 5% French, Arab, Ethiopian, and Italian. **Languages:** French and Arabic (official); Somali and Afar widely used. **Religions:** 94% Muslim, 6% Christian.
● **GOVERNMENT Type:** republic. **Independence:** June 27, 1977 (from France). **Constitution:** Sep. 4, 1992. **National holiday:** Independence Day, June 27. **Heads of Government:** Ismail Omar Guelleh, president (since May 1999); Barkat Gourad Hamadou, prime minister (since Sept. 1978). **Structure:** executive; unicameral legislature; judiciary.
● **ECONOMY Monetary unit:** Djiboutian franc. **Budget:** (1997 est.) *income:* $156 mil., *expend.:* $175 mil. **GDP:** $530 mil., $1,200 per capita (1998 est.). **Chief crops:** limited fruits and vegetables; goats, sheep, camels. **Natural resources:** geothermal areas. **Major industries:** limited to a few small-scale enterprises, such as dairy products and mineral-water boiling. **Labor force:** 282,000 (1991 est.); 75% agriculture, 14% services, 11% industry; over 30% unemployment (1994 est.). **Exports:** $39.6 mil. (f.o.b., 1996 est.); hides and skins and transit of coffee. **Imports:** $200.5 mil. (f.o.b., 1996 est.); foods, beverages, transport equipment, chemicals, petroleum. **Major trading partners:** *exports:* 45% Ethiopia, Somalia, Yemen, Saudi Arabia; *imports:* France, Ethiopia, Italy, Saudi Arabia, Thailand.

This small, arid region on the Horn of Africa near the southern mouth of the Red Sea became the object of British-French rivalry with the opening of the Suez Canal in 1869. The French sphere of influence, called French Somaliland, was affirmed by agreements with Ethiopia in 1897, 1945, and 1954. In the early 20th century, the French constructed a railroad from Addis Ababa to Djibouti, adding to the colony's strategic value.

French and Italian forces clashed at the border of Ethiopia and French Somaliland with the Italian invasion of Ethiopia in the 1930s. During World War II, the territorial administration at first sided with the Vichy government but in December 1942 established ties with the Free French and the Allies.

The colony was reorganized in 1957 and in 1958 became, by referendum, a French Overseas Territory. In July 1967 its name was changed to the Territory of the Afars and Issas. Growing nationalist sentiment led to a referendum in favor of complete independence. The Republic of Djibouti became independent on June 27, 1977. A new constitution was approved in 1992 and multiparty elections in December resulted in a clean sweep for Popular Rally for Democracy.

▶ DOMINICA
Commonwealth of Dominica
● **GEOGRAPHY Location:** eastern Caribbean Sea, between Guadeloupe to N and Martinique to S. Roseau 15°18'N, 61°23'W. **Boundaries:** Dominica Passage to N, Atlantic Ocean to E, Martinique Passage to S, Caribbean Sea to W. **Total land area:** 290 sq. mi. (750 sq km). **Coastline:** 92 mi. (148 km). **Comparative area:** slightly more than four times size of Washington, D.C. **Land use:** 9% arable land; 13% permanent crops; 3% meadows and pastures; 41% forest and woodland; 34% other. **Major cities:** (1991 census) Roseau (capital) 20,755.
● **PEOPLE Population:** 64,881 (1999 est.). **Nationality:** noun—Dominican(s); adjective—Dominican. **Ethnic groups:** black, Carib Amerindians. **Languages:** English (official), French patois. **Religions:** 77% Roman Catholic, 15% Protestant.
● **GOVERNMENT Type:** parliamentary democracy. **Independence:** Nov. 3, 1978 (from UK). **Constitution:** Nov. 3, 1978. **National holiday:** Independence Day, Nov. 3. **Heads of Government:** Vernon Lorden Shaw, president (since Oct. 1998); Edison C. James, prime minister (since Oct. 1998). **Structure:** executive; unicameral legislature; judiciary—East Caribbean Supreme Court.
● **ECONOMY Monetary unit:** East Caribbean (EC) dollar. **Budget:** (FY97/98 est.). *income:* $72 mil.; *expend.:* $79.9 mil. **GDP:** $216 mil., $3,300 per capita (1997 est.). **Chief crops:** bananas, citrus, mangoes; forestry and fisheries. **Natural resources:** timber. **Major industries:** soap, coconut oil, tourism. **Labor force:** 25,000 (1984); 40% agriculture, 32% industry and commerce, 28% services; 15% unemployment (1992 est.). **Exports:** $50.4 mil. (1997 est.); 50% bananas, soap, bay oil. **Imports:** $104.2 mil. (1997 est.); manufactured goods, machinery and equipment, foodstuffs. **Major trading partners:** *exports:* 47% Caricom countries, 36% UK, 7% U.S.; *imports:* 41% U.S., 25% Caricom, 13% UK.

Pre-Columbian Dominica was a stronghold of Carib Indians, who had expelled the Arawaks in the 14th century, and today it is the only island in the Caribbean with a native Carib population. Dominica was visited by Columbus on his second American voyage; but though frequented by Spanish ships, it was not settled until French missionaries arrived in the 1630s. Carib resistance was so strong that the French and British agreed to consider the island neutral territory, until it passed under British control in 1763.

Later it was administratively joined to the Leeward and then the Windward Islands, and then became part of the West Indies Federation. It entered into political association with the United Kingdom in 1967. In 1978 Dominica gained independence from Britain. Prime Minister Mary Eugenia Charles's Freedom party has held power since 1980 on a program of economic reconstruction. Hurricanes in 1979-80 largely destroyed the island's agriculture. The government of Prime Minister Mary Eugenia Charles's Freedom party implemented a program of economic reconstruction and diversification after the disaster. In 1992 it began a controversial policy of granting citizenship to businessmen, Asians in particular, in exchange for investment in Dominica's economy. In 1995, Charles resigned after 15 years in office. The United Workers party took 11 of 21 seats in parliamentary elections and named its leader, Edison James, the new prime minister.

▶DOMINICAN REPUBLIC

● **GEOGRAPHY** **Location:** eastern Hispaniola, in Caribbean Sea. Santo Domingo 19°30'N, 70°42'W. **Boundaries:** North Atlantic to N, Mona Passage to E, Caribbean Sea to S, Haiti to W. **Total land area:** 18,815 sq. mi. (48,730 sq km). **Coastline:** 800 mi. (1,288 km). **Comparative area:** slightly more than four times size of Washington, D.C. **Land use:** 23% arable land; 7% permanent crops; 43% meadows and pastures; 13% forest and woodland; 14% other; includes 4% irrigated. **Major cities:** (1981) Santo Domingo (capital) 1,313,172; Santiago de los Caballeros 278,638; La Romana 91,571; San Pedro de Macorís 78,562; San Francisco de Macorís 64,906.

● **PEOPLE** **Population:** 8,129,734 (1999 est.). **Nationality:** noun—Dominican(s); adjective—Dominican. **Ethnic groups:** 73% mixed, 16% white, 11% black. **Languages:** Spanish. **Religions:** 95% Roman Catholic.

● **GOVERNMENT** **Type:** republic. **Independence:** Feb. 27, 1844 (from Haiti). **Constitution:** Nov. 28, 1966. **National holiday:** Independence Day, Feb. 27. **Head of Government:** Leonel Fernández Reyna, president (since July 1996). **Structure:** executive; bicameral legislature; judiciary.

● **ECONOMY** **Monetary unit:** Dominican peso. **Budget:** (1999 est.) *income:* $2.3 bil.; *expend.:* $2.9 bil. **GDP:** $39.8 bil., $5,000 per capita (1998 est.). **Chief crops:** sugarcane, coffee, cotton, cocoa, tobacco; cattle, pigs. **Natural resources:** nickel, bauxite, gold, silver. **Major industries:** tourism, sugar processing, ferronickel and gold mining. **Labor force:** 2.3-2.6 mil. (1991 est.); 50% agriculture, 32% services, 18% industry. **Exports:** $997 mil. (1997 est.); ferronickel, sugar, gold, coffee. **Imports:** $3.6 bil. (1998); foodstuffs, petroleum, cotton and fabrics, chemicals and pharmaceuticals. **Major trading partners:** *exports:* 45% U.S., 19.9% EU, 3.6% Canada (1996); *imports:* 44% U.S., 16% EU, 11% Venezuela (1995).

The Dominican Republic takes up the eastern two-thirds of the island of Hispaniola, which it shares with Haiti. Christopher Columbus visited the island in 1492, and Santo Domingo is the oldest continually inhabited European settlement in the Americas, with the oldest cathedral, hospital, and monastery in the Western Hemisphere.

Western Hispaniola (Haiti) was ceded to France in 1697, and the eastern part of the island in 1795. Liberated with the Haitian slave revolts of 1801, it fell under Haitian rule from 1804 to 1808 (when it reverted to Spanish rule), and again from 1822 to 1844. It was again occupied by Spain from 1861 to 1865. Under Ulises Heureux (1882-99), the Dominican Republic enjoyed a period of independence and prosperity. The U.S. occupied the Dominican Republic between 1916 and 1924. In 1930 Rafael Trujillo set up a dictatorship lasting 31 years. Dominican political strife triggered another U.S. invasion (1965-66) to end the revolution. Reformist party candidate Joaquín Balaguer, president from 1966 to 1978, regained the presidency in 1986, was reelected in 1990, and again (at age 87) in 1994, but only for two years, a compromise arranged in the face of charges of election fraud.

The 1996 elections resulted in a runoff between Haitian-born Jose Pena Gomez and Leonel Fernandez—both center-left in politics, both committed to economic privatization. Fernandez was the winner. But even the small and halting steps towards economic reform provoked strikes by labor unions and students over low wages, chronic water and electric outages. The death in May 1998 of Pena one week before legislative elections added a sentimental boost to real opposition. His Dominican Revolutionary Party captured large majorities in both the Senate and Chamber of Deputies. In 1998 Hurricane Mitch caused extensive damage to part of the island causing massive displacement of people and requiring international aid.

▶ECUADOR
Republic of Ecuador

● **GEOGRAPHY** **Location:** northwestern South America. **Boundaries:** Colombia to N, Peru to E and S, Pacific Ocean to W. **Total land area:** 109,483 sq. mi. (283,560 sq km); incl. Galapagos Islands, 0°45'S, 90°19'W. **Coastline:** 1,389 mi. (2,237 km). **Comparative area:** between Colorado and Nevada. **Land use:** 6% arable land; 3% permanent crops; 17% meadows and pastures; 51% forest and woodland; 23% other; includes 2% irrigated. **Major cities:** (1990 census) Quito (capital) 1,401,389; Guayaquil 1,877,031; Cuenca 239,896; Machala 184,588; Portoviejo 159,566.

● **PEOPLE** **Population:** 12,562,496 (1999 est.). **Nationality:** noun—Ecuadorian(s); adjective—Ecuadorian. **Ethnic groups:** 55% mestizo, 25% Indian, 10% Spanish, 10% black. **Languages:** Spanish (official), Amerindian languages, especially Quechua. **Religions:** 95% Roman Catholic.

● **GOVERNMENT** **Type:** republic. **Independence:** May 24, 1822 (from Spain). **Constitution:** Aug. 10, 1979. **National holiday:** Independence Day, Aug. 10. **Head of Government:** Dr. Jamil Mahuad Witt, president (since Aug. 1998). **Structure:** executive; unicameral legislature; independent judiciary.

● **ECONOMY** **Monetary unit:** sucre. **Budget:** (1999) *income:* planned 5.1 bil.; *expend.:* $5.1 bil. **GDP:** $58.7 bil., $4,800 per capita (1998 est.). **Chief crops:** bananas, coffee, cocoa, rice; cattle, sheep, pigs. **Natural resources:** petroleum, fish, timber. **Major industries:** petroleum, food processing, textiles. **Labor force:** 4.2 mil. (1990); 29% agriculture, 38% services and other activities, 18% manufacturing; 12% unemployment (1998 est.). **Exports:** $3.4 bil. (f.o.b., 1997); 30% petroleum, 26% bananas, 16% shrimp. **Imports:** $2.9 bil. (c.i.f., 1997); transport equipment, consumer goods, vehicles, machinery. **Major trading partners:** *exports:* 39% U.S., 25% Latin America, 22% EU countries; *imports:* 35% Latin America, 32% U.S., 19% EU, 11% Asia.

The Inca Empire maintained control over the territory that is now Ecuador until the arrival of Spanish conqueror Francisco Pizarro in 1532. The Spanish conquistadores quickly dismantled the indigenous political structure, which had been weakened by a series of wars between the Inca chief Atahualpa and his half brother Huáscar. The Spaniards arrived in the Quito region in 1533 and established the city of Guayaquil shortly thereafter. The administrative center of Spanish rule was originally established through the viceroyalty of Peru in 1544, and an audiencia (a regional high court under the nominal authority of the viceroy) was established at Quito in 1563. Administrative control of the region was transferred to Bogotá and the viceroyalty of New Granada in 1718.

The local junta of Quito ousted the audiencia

in 1809, but they did not achieve independence for the region until after the military victory of the rebel forces over the royalists at the battle of Pichincha in 1822. Ecuador formed a part of the Confederation of Gran Colombia until the confederation's collapse in 1830. The leader of the forces for independence, Gen. Juan José Flores, removed the country from the Gran Colombian confederation and ruled as dictator until his ouster in 1845. A political rivalry existed between the Liberals of Guayaquil and the Conservatives of Quito, but Conservative dominance of the government lasted until 1895.

During the rule of Conservative president Gabriel García Moreno (1861-75), the Roman Catholic church gained a central place in the political and cultural life of the country. García Moreno tied citizenship requirements to Catholic religious affiliation, brought in the Jesuits to "purify" the country through education, and dedicated the country to the Sacred Heart of Jesus. He was assassinated in 1875.

In 1895 the Radical Liberal (anticlerical) party seized power and held it until 1944. José María Velasco Ibarra, in and out of power until 1972, dominated the political scene. Political stability within the country had much to do with the state of the economy. The traditional reliance on cacao production was superseded in the 1950s by a "banana boom," and the discovery of large oil deposits by U.S. corporations in the 1960s led to a shift toward reliance on oil revenues by the 70s.

In 1988 Rodrigo Borja, of the Democratic Left party (ID), was elected to the presidency. In 1992 conservative Sixto Durán Ballén, an advocate of free market reforms, won the presidency and immediately moved to eliminate government subsidies and encourage foreign investment.

Duran's successor in 1996 was the bizarre Abdala Bucaram Ortiz, who was removed by Congress in Feb. 1997 for "mental incapacity." Not until July of 1998 was normality restored with the election of Quito mayor Jamil Mahuad Witt. While his austerity measures provoked widespread discontent, Congress passed most of the measures and the 50-year-long border dispute with Peru was peaceably settled in October 1998. Still, in Sept. 1999, Equador defaulted on part of its international debt.

▶ EGYPT
Arab Republic of Egypt

● **GEOGRAPHY Location:** northeastern Africa and Asia (Sinai peninsula). **Boundaries:** Mediterranean Sea to N, Israel to NE, Red Sea to E, Sudan to S, and Libya to W. **Total land area:** 386,660 sq. mi. (1,001,450 sq km). **Coastline:** 1,523 mi. (2,450 km). **Comparative area:** slightly more than three times the size of New Mexico. **Land use:** 2% arable land; 98% other. **Major cities:** (1992 est.) Cairo (capital) 6,800,000; El-Iskandriyah (Alexandria) 3,380,000; Giza 3,700,100; Shoubra el-kheima 834,000; Port Said 460,000.

● **PEOPLE Population:** 67,273,906 (1999 est.). **Nationality:** noun: Egyptian(s); adjective: Egyptian. **Ethnic groups:** 99% Eastern Hamitic stock. **Languages:** Arabic (official), English and French widely understood by educated classes. **Religions:** 94% Muslim (mostly Sunni), 6% Coptic Christian and other.

● **GOVERNMENT Type:** republic. **Independence:** Feb. 28, 1922 (from UK). **Constitution:** Sept. 11, 1971. **National holiday:** Anniversary of the Revolution, July 23. **Heads of Government:** Mohammed Hosni Mubarak, president (since 1981); Dr. Kamal el Ganzoury, prime minister (since Jan. 1996). **Structure:** executive—president nominated by parliament which is validated by popular referendum; bicameral legislature; judiciary.

● **ECONOMY Monetary unit:** Egyptian pound. **Budget:** (FY97/98 est.) *income:* $20 bil.; *expend.:* $20.8 bil. **GDP:** $188 bil., $2,850 per capita (1998 est.). **Chief crops:** cotton, rice, corn, wheat, beans, fruit, vegetables; cattle, water buffalo, sheep, goats; fish. **Natural resources:** crude oil, natural gas, iron ore, phosphates, manganese. **Major industries:** textiles, food processing, tourism. **Labor force:** about 17.4 mil. (1998 est.); 40% agriculture, 38% services, including government, 22% industry (1990); 10% unemployment (1998 est.). **Exports:** $5.5 bil. (f.o.b., FY97/98 est.); crude oil and petroleum products, cotton yarn, raw cotton, textiles, metal products, chemicals. **Imports:** $16.7 bil. (c.i.f., FY97/98 est.); machinery and equipment, foods, fertilizers, wood products, durable consumer goods, capital goods. **Major trading partners:** EU, U.S., Japan.

Civilization began in the fertile valley of the Nile River around 5000 b.c. In about 3200 b.c., King Menes established the first of many dynasties of pharaohs that unified the country from the Nile Delta to Upper Egypt, creating a distinctive ancient civilization of great wealth and cultural brilliance.

The last pharaonic dynasty was overthrown by the Persians in 341 b.c. The Persians in turn were replaced by the Alexandrian and Ptolemaic Greek dynasties and then by the rule of the Roman Empire. Egypt was part of the Byzantine Empire from the third to the seventh centuries a.d., when it was conquered by the Arab Islamic expansion. Arab rule was ended around 1250 when the Mameluke dynasty, of Caucasian origin, established control. The Mamelukes were defeated by the Turks in 1517, and Egypt was incorporated into the Ottoman Empire.

The Suez Canal was built by a French corporation during 1859-69 but was taken over by the British in 1875. This, together with the expansion of the British Empire in East Africa and the Sudan, led to the establishment of de facto British rule in Egypt in 1882, although Egypt remained nominally part of the Ottoman Empire until 1914. A British protectorate in Egypt was established in that year, replaced by a League of Nations Mandate in 1922. The autonomy of the Egyptian monarchy was strengthened in an Anglo-Egyptian treaty of 1936, but Great Britain continued to maintain military forces in Egypt and controlled the Sudan as an Anglo-Egyptian condominium.

Egypt saw heavy fighting between British and Axis forces during World War II. After the war, a nationalist movement gained strength. The 1936 treaty was abrogated by Egypt in 1951. An uprising of the Society of Free Officers on July 23, 1952, forced King Farouk to abdicate. A republic was proclaimed on June 18, 1953. Lt. Col. Gamal Abdel Nasser became premier in 1954 and president in 1956.

British troops were withdrawn from the Suez Canal zone in June 1956. On July 26, 1956, Egypt announced the nationalization of the canal. Israel invaded the Sinai Peninsula at the end of October 1956. France and Great Britain landed forces and bombed Egyptian positions; a cease-fire went into effect under UN supervision on Nov. 17. A UN peacekeeping force patrolled the border between Egypt and Israel from 1957 to 1967.

Increasing Soviet involvement in Egypt was confirmed with its aid to Egypt in the construction of the Aswan High Dam. The dam, completed in 1971, provides both irrigation and hydropower but at the cost of extensive environmental damage.

Egypt and Syria joined together as the United Arab Republic in 1958. Later joined by Yemen, the union was dissolved in 1961.

Egyptian incursions into the Gaza Strip and the Sharm el Sheikh in early June 1967 led to the outbreak of full-scale war with Israel on June 5. The Six-Day War ended on June 10 with Israel in full control of Gaza and the Sinai peninsula to the banks of the Suez Canal. Sporadic fighting between Egyptian and Israeli forces continued throughout 1969-70. The Suez Canal remained closed to shipping until 1975.

Nasser died in 1970 and was succeeded by Vice Pres. Anwar Sadat, who concluded a treaty of friendship with the USSR, but expelled all Soviet troops and advisers in 1972.

On Oct. 6, 1973, Egyptian forces crossed the Suez Canal and attacked Israeli positions in the Sinai (Syrian forces also attacked Israeli positions in the Golan Heights). Israel drove back the attackers, and the Yom Kippur War ended in a cease-fire on Oct. 24.

In 1974 Sadat's government became increasingly friendly to the West, welcoming foreign investment and American aid. In 1974 and 1975 disengagement accords were signed with Israel, providing for the return of the Sinai to Egypt in stages. In November 1977 Sadat visited Jerusalem as a gesture of peace, and a peace treaty between Israel and Egypt was signed (after a series of talks mediated by Pres. Jimmy Carter at Camp David, Maryland) on Mar. 26, 1979. Formal diplomatic relations were established in 1982. As a result of the peace treaty with Israel, Egypt was suspended from the Arab League—it was readmitted in 1989—and attacked by Libyan forces on several occasions along the Egyptian-Libyan border.

Popular unrest fomented by the Muslim Brotherhood in September 1981 led to a military crackdown. Pres. Sadat was assassinated by members of a military conspiracy on Oct. 6, 1981, and was succeeded by Vice Pres. Mohammed Hosni Mubarak. The government has remained on friendly terms with Israel and the United States and has gradually improved relations with the rest of the Arab world. During the Persian Gulf War, it was a staunch member of the anti-Iraq coalition, in return for which the United States forgave $7 billion in debt.

In recent years several Muslim extremist groups such as the Jamaat Islamiya have carried out bombings and assassinations aimed at secular intellectuals, Coptic Christians, and foreigners. But despite a crackdown on Islamic activists (including a celebrated arrest of 700 in November 1995), Egypt's vital tourist industry has been crippled by the terrorism.

▶ EL SALVADOR
Republic of El Salvador
● GEOGRAPHY   Location: Pacific coast of Central America. Boundaries: Honduras to N and E, Pacific Ocean to S, Guatemala to W. Total land area: 8,124 sq. mi. (21,040 sq km). Coastline: 191 mi. (307 km). Comparative area: about size of Massachusetts. Land use: 27% arable land; 8% permanent crops; 29% meadows and pastures; 6% forest and woodland; 30% other; includes 5% irrigated.

Major cities: (1992 census) San Salvador (capital) 422,570; Soyapango 251,811; Santa Ana 202,337; San Miguel 182,817; Mejicanos 145,000.
● PEOPLE   Population: 5,839,079 (1999 est.). Nationality: noun—Salvadoran(s); adjective—Salvadoran. Ethnic groups: 94% mestizo, 5% Amerindian, 1% white. Languages: Spanish, Nahua (among some Amerindians). Religions: 75% Roman Catholic; extensive activity by Protestant groups throughout country.
● GOVERNMENT   Type: republic. Independence: Sept. 15, 1821 (from Spain). Constitution: Dec. 20, 1983. National holiday: Independence Day, Sept. 15. Head of Government: Francisco Guillermo Flores Pérez (since June 1999). Structure: executive; unicameral legislature; judiciary.
● ECONOMY   Monetary unit: Salvadoran colón. Budget: (1997 est.) income: $1.75 bil.; expend.: $1.82 bil. GDP: $17.5 bil., $3,000 per capita (1998 est.). Chief crops: coffee, sugarcane, corn; beef, dairy; shrimp. Natural resources: hydropower and geothermal power, crude oil. Major industries: food processing, beverages, petroleum. Labor force: 2.26 mil. (1997 est.); 40% agriculture, 16% commerce, 15% manufacturing, 13% government. Exports: $1.96 bil. (f.o.b., 1997 est.); coffee, sugarcane, shrimp. Imports: $3.5 bil. (c.i.f., 1997 est.); raw materials, consumer goods, foodstuffs, capital goods. Major trading partners: exports: U.S., Guatemala, Germany, Costa Rica; imports: U.S., Guatemala, Mexico, Panama, Venezuela.

A number of Indian tribes, of which the Pipil were dominant, originally inhabited the area now called El Salvador. The native population resisted the first attempt at Spanish colonization, begun in 1524, for almost 15 years. In 1821 El Salvador gained its independence from Spain, first as a jurisdiction under the Mexican empire and two years later as a member of the United Provinces of Central America. The Central American Federation collapsed in 1838, and in 1840 El Salvador emerged from a bloody two-year struggle as an independent republic.

The Salvadoran economy was dominated by coffee production from the 1860s onward, and a series of laws in the 1880s allowed for concentration of both land ownership and political power in the hands of a coffee oligarchy. In 1931 a reformist president won election, but the military subsequently dismissed him. A revolt ensued (1932) in which 10,000 to 20,000 Salvadorans—mostly peasants—were killed. The result of the massacre, which was called La Matanza, was a period of relative political stability that lasted until the 1970s.

In 1979 a political coup led by a group of junior military officers overthrew Pres. Gen. Carlos Humberto Romero. Owing to the polarization between conservative and reformist political groups, the first two civilian-military juntas resigned as a result of their failure to have their programs implemented by the military. A third government, which included Christian Democrat José Napoleón Duarte, took over on Mar. 5, 1980, on the basis of an armed forces' pledge to carry out an agrarian reform program. In 1980 the coalition of opposition political organizations became the Democratic Revolutionary Front (FDR), and five revolutionary military organizations consolidated under the banner of the Farabundo Marti Front for National Liberation (FMLN). Six social-democratic political leaders were assassinated in November 1980, further cementing the political opposition around the FMLN-FDR coalition.

A three-part agrarian reform program was initiated in 1980 in El Salvador, but the central part of the program—to redistribute most of the land involved in export agriculture—was dropped as a result of opposition from the agricultural elite.

In March 1982 elections for a constituent assembly, a majority of seats went to the rightist ARENA coalition. In December 1983 a new constitution went into effect, and in 1984 Christian Democrat José Napoleón Duarte assumed the presidency.

In 1989, Alfredo Cristiani of the conservative Alliance for National Renovation was elected president. On Nov. 11, 1989, FMLN guerrillas launched a new offensive that lasted for several weeks before fading away. The government's failure to prosecute military officers implicated in the murder of six Jesuit priests shortly thereafter jeopardized U.S. military aid, which totaled $6 billion between 1979 and 1992.

In January 1992, the government signed a peace treaty with the FMLN and the 12-year civil war, in which 70,000 people died, officially ended on December 15. The treaty called for the military to cut its forces by almost half (to 31,000 soldiers), and for the FMLN to lay down its arms and become a political party. A UN-sponsored Truth Commission found that 85 percent of all human-rights violations during the war were attributable to the Salvadoran army, security forces, or intelligence-unit death squads. Although the legislature narrowly passed a general amnesty for public officials, military officers, and political party leaders linked to human rights violations in March of 1993, the United States tried to link further military aid to the dismissal of the worst offenders in the military.

In the March 1994 elections, ARENA's candidate Armando Calderon Sol was elected president. ARENA also carried half the seats in the National Assembly. In the 1997 mid-term election, FMLN made a vary strong showing running virtually even with ARENA on the national level. In the March 1999 elections, ARENA and the FMLN carried almost the same number of seats in the National Assembly, but in the presidential election, ARENA easily won for the third straight time, their candidate (Francisco Flores Perez) gaining 51 percent of the vote, with the FMLN candidate winning only 29 percent.

▶ EQUATORIAL GUINEA
Republic of Equatorial Guinea
● **GEOGRAPHY Location:** mainland territory of Río Muni in western Africa and five inhabited islands: Bioko (3°45'N, 8°50'E), Corisco, Great Elobey, Small Elobey, and Pagalu (Annabon). **Boundaries:** Cameroon to N, Gabon to E and S, Gulf of Guinea to W. **Total land area:** 10,830 sq. mi. (28,050 sq km). **Coastline:** 184 mi. (296 km). **Comparative area:** slightly larger than Maryland. **Land use:** 8% arable land; 4% permanent crops; 4% meadows and pastures; 51% forest and woodland; 33% other. **Major cities:** (1983 census) Malabo (capital) 15,323; Bata 24,100.
● **PEOPLE Population:** 465,746 (1999 est.). **Nationality:** noun—Equatorial Guinean(s); adjective— Equatorial Guinean. **Ethnic groups:** Bioko (primarily Bubi, some Fernandinos); Río Muni (primarily Fang), less than 1,000 Europeans, mostly Spanish. **Languages:** Spanish (official), pidgin English, Fang. **Religions:** nominally Christian, predominantly Roman Catholic; indigenous practices.
● **GOVERNMENT Type:** republic in transition to multiparty democracy (the transition appears to

have halted). **Independence:** Oct. 12, 1968 (from Spain). **Constitution:** Nov. 17, 1991. **National holiday:** Independence Day, Oct. 12. **Heads of Government:** Col. Teodoro Obiang Nguema Mbasogo, president (since Aug. 1979); Don Angel-Serafin Seriche Dougan, prime minister (since Apr. 1996). **Structure:** executive; unicameral legislature; judiciary.
● **ECONOMY Monetary unit:** Communauté Financière Africaine (CFA) franc. **Budget:** (1996 est.) *income:* $47 mil.; *expend.:* $43 mil. **GDP:** $660 mil., $1,500 per capita (1997 est.). **Chief crops:** coffee, cocoa, rice, yams; livestock; timber. **Natural resources:** timber, crude oil, small unexploited deposits of gold, manganese, uranium. **Major industries:** fishing, sawmilling. **Labor force:** NA. **Exports:** $197 mil. (f.o.b., 1996); petroleum, timber, cocoa. **Imports:** $248 mil. (c.i.f., 1996); petroleum, foodstuffs, beverages, clothing, machinery. **Major trading partners:** *exports:* 34% U.S., 17% Japan, 13% Spain, 13% China; *imports:* 40% Cameroon, 18% Spain, 14% France, 8% U.S.

Equatorial Guinea consists of the Mbini River basin on the West African coast, and a number of offshore islands, chiefly Bioko and Pagalu (Annobón). Indigenous Pygmies were displaced beginning in the 17th century by migrations of various peoples that now inhabit the coastal region and by the Fang, who comprise 80 percent of the present population.

Bioko was discovered in 1473 by the Portuguese explorer Fernando Po, and until modern times the island bore his name. Portugal controlled the islands and adjacent mainland, exploiting them for the slave trade, until 1778 when the territory was ceded to Spain. Equatorial Guinea remained underdeveloped because of conflicting territorial claims and a lack of Spanish investment. Eventually, however, a plantation system was developed for the cultivation of cocoa, particularly on Bioko, using workers imported from Nigeria.

In 1959 the Spanish territories in the Gulf of Guinea were given status equivalent to a province of Spain. Investment in education, health care facilities, and other social programs, combined with the flourishing plantation economy, made the territory one of the most prosperous and best educated in West Africa. Local autonomy came in 1963, full independence in 1968.

Francisco Macias Nguema was elected Equatorial Guinea's first president in 1968. In 1970 he dissolved all opposition parties and declared a one-party state, and in 1972 proclaimed himself president for life and commenced rule by decree. During the next seven years, a reign of terror resulted in the death or exile of one-third of the country's people. Nigerian workers, along with other foreigners, were expelled from the country in 1976; without their labor and technical skills, the economy was quickly ruined.

Macias Nguema was overthrown in August 1979 in a military coup led by his nephew, Lt. Col. Teodoro Obiang Nguema Mbasogo. Macias Nguema was tried and executed a month later. The Spanish-educated Obiang moved to reduce Soviet influence and to improve relations with Spain. A new constitution was approved in a referendum in August 1982 and again in 1991, the latter calling for a multiparty political system. Obiang, however, retains firm control. Economic prospects have improved with the discovery of oil reserves estimated at over 65 million barrels a year.

▶ ERITREA
State of Eritrea

● **GEOGRAPHY** **Location:** Horn of Africa (central-eastern Africa). **Boundaries:** Sudan to N and W, Red Sea to E, Djibouti and Ethiopia to S. **Total land area:** 46,842 sq. mi. (121,320 sq km). **Coastline:** 680 mi. (1,094 km) on Red Sea. **Comparative area:** about the size of New York. **Land use:** 3% arable land, 2% permanent crops (coffee), 40% meadows and pastures, 5% forest and woodland, 50% other. **Major cities:** (1993 est.) Asmara (capital) 400,000; Asseb, Massawa, Keren.

● **PEOPLE** **Population:** 3,984,723 (1999 est.). **Nationality:** noun—Eritrean(s); adjective—Eritrean. **Ethnic groups:** 50% Tigrinya, 40% Tigre and Kunama, 4% Afar, 3% Saho. **Languages:** Afar, Amharic, Arabic, Tigre and Kunama, Tigrinya, minor ethnic group languages. **Religions:** Muslim, Coptic Christian, Roman Catholic, Protestant.

● **GOVERNMENT** **Type:** transitional government. **Independence:** May 27, 1993 (from Ethiopia). **Constitution:** promulgated May 1997. **National holiday:** Independence Day, May 24. **Head of Government:** Isaias Afwerki, president (since May 1993). **Structure:** executive; unicameral legislature; judiciary.

● **ECONOMY** **Monetary unit:** birr. **Budget: :** (1996 est.) *income:* $226 mil.; *expend.:* $453 mil. **GDP:** $2.5 bil.; $660 per capita (1998 est.). **Chief crops:** sorghum, lentils, vegetables; livestock; fish. **Natural resources:** gold, potash, zinc, copper. **Major industries:** food processing, beverages, clothing and textiles. **Labor force:** N.A. **Exports:** $95 mil. (1996 est.); livestock, sorghum, textiles. **Imports:** $514 mil. (1996 est.); processed goods, machinery, petroleum products. **Major trading partners:** Ethiopia, Italy, Saudi Arabia.

In May 1993, after 30 years of fighting, leaders of the Eritrean People's Liberation Front (EPLF) formally declared this small area of north and northeast Ethiopia to be an independent state. Ethiopia, along with the United States, the Sudan, and several other states, quickly recognized the authority of the new transitional government led by Issaias Afwerki, former head of the liberation movement.

During the early 20th century, the region of Eritrea was an outpost of the Italian empire, but it came under British rule during World War II. The British made Eritrea part of Ethiopia when independence was granted in 1952. The secessionist movement began immediately, first against Haile Selassie, then in the 1970s and '80s against the Marxist Mengistu Haile Mariam, who was finally driven from office by other forces in 1991. The new government quickly made peace with the Eritrean rebels, who promised continued access to the sea after independence became a fact. Late in 1995 Eritrea began to contest with Yemen control of Greater Hanish Island at the mouth of the Red Sea, a struggle serious enough to elicit UN mediation. Further troubles broke out in May 1998 when a small skirmish over the border with Ethiopia escalated into major military clashes in June. The U.S. was attempting to mediate. The bloody and incomprehensible border war continued, with much loss of life on both sides, into 1999.

▶ ESTONIA
Republic of Estonia

● **GEOGRAPHY** **Location:** northeastern Europe. **Boundaries:** Gulf of Finland to N and NE, Russian Federation to SE, Latvia to SW, Baltic Sea to NW. **Total land area:** 17,413 sq. mi. (45,100 sq km). **Coastline:** Gulf of Finland. **Comparative area:** about twice the size of New Hampshire. **Land use:** 25% arable land; 11% meadows and pastures; 44% forest and woodland; 20% other (mostly urban and swampland). **Major cities:** (1994 est.) Tallinn (capital) 442,700; Tartu 105,800; Narva 79,100; Kohtla-Järve 56,600; Pärnu 52,000.

● **PEOPLE** **Population:** 1,408,523 (1999 est.). **Nationality:** noun—Estonian(s); adjective—Estonian. **Ethnic groups:** 65.1% Estonian, 28.1% Russian, 2.5% Ukrainian. **Languages:** Estonian (official), Russian, Ukrainian, English, Finnish, other. **Religions:** Lutheran, Orthodox Christian, others.

● **GOVERNMENT** **Type:** parliamentary democracy. **Independence:** Sep. 6, 1991. **Constitution:** June 28, 1992. **National holiday:** Independence Day, Feb. 24. **Heads of Government:** Lennart Meri, president (since Oct. 1992); Mart Laar, prime minister (since March 1999). **Structure:** executive; unicameral legislature; judiciary.

● **ECONOMY** **Monetary unit:** Estonian kroon. **Budget:** (1997) *income:* $1.37 bil.; *expend.:* $1.37 bil. **GDP:** $7.8 bil., $5,500 per capita (1998 est.). **Chief crops:** potatoes, vegetables, fruit; livestock and dairy products; fish. **Natural resources:** oil shale (world's number two producer), peat, phosphorites. **Major industries:** oil shale processing, shipbuilding, phosphates. **Labor force:** 717,000 (1997 est.). **Exports:** $2.6 bil. (f.o.b., 1998); 17% machinery and equipment, 16% textiles, 8% food products. **Imports:** $3.9 bil. (c.i.f., 1998); 21% machinery and equipment, 12% transport equipment, 10% foodstuffs. **Major trading partners:** Finland, Russia, Germany, Sweden.

Ethnic and linguistic "cousins" of the Finns, the Ests acquired their own independent state only in the 20th century. Previously they had been "colonized" by the Danes (who founded the capital, Tallinn), then in the 13th century by the Teutonic Knights, in the 16th century by the Swedes (who brought the Lutheran Reformation), in the 17th century by the Poles, and in the 18th century by the Russians. Through all these regimes the German element predominated, the "Baltic barons" forming a territorial aristocracy with German burghers ruling the towns. The Ests were restricted to farming, normally as serfs, with serfdom not abolished until 1819.

With that abolition there began a cultural revival with the study of folklore, the collecting of folk songs, the compilation of the national epic, Kalevipoeg, published between 1857 and 1861, and the circulation of newspapers in the Estonian language. Political expression of this revived national spirit came with the 1918 Treaty of Brest-Litovsk in which the new Soviet Union recognized the independence of Estonia. By 1920 Estonia was fully independent, under its own constitution adopted on June 15 of that year.

A radical land reform dispossessed German landowners of large estates, which were distributed to peasant owners and tenants. Dangers from extremists of Left (Communists) and Right ("liberators") were averted by the strong presidency of Constantice Päts, but the Hitler-Stalin Pact of 1939 spelled the end of Estonian independence. Allotted to Stalin's sphere of influence, Estonia was forced to accept Soviet garrisons larger than its national army in 1939, and 65,000 Germans were "repatriated" (after 700 years) to the Third Reich. Rigged elections in 1940 led to a government that "requested" incorporation into the

USSR, an annexation never recognized by the United States.

There followed nationalization of private property, amalgamation of Estonia's national forces into the Red Army, and a reign of terror against former political leaders and religious and cultural organizations. During and after the war the Estonian people suffered enormous losses through death in battle, murder, flight, and deportation.

Estonia's return to freedom began Mar. 30, 1990, when a freely elected government declared its intention to secede after an unspecified transition period. Violence provoked by Russian "black berets," mass demonstrations, defiance of Gorbachev's economic sanctions and his January 1991 military crackdown, all marked stages toward the Kremlin's recognition in September 1991 of Estonian independence. Estonia, like the other Baltic states, declined to sign the December 1991 Alma-Ata Declaration that created the Commonwealth of Independent States.

Elections in Sept. 1992 produced a divided Parliament, with the majority a center-right coalition led by the Fatherland Alliance. Parliament in October chose as president Lennart Meri, a nationalist and devotee of free markets. The effective disenfranchisement of 40% of the population, mostly Russians, through laws requiring citizenship since 1940, provoked Russian ire. But by July 1994 the law was modified and Russian troops left by the end of August.

In March 1995, parliamentary elections brought into power a far-left alliance of parties led by the Coalition Party (the Communists' new name). Still, in 1998 the EU invited Estonia to apply for membership. In the March 1999 parliamentary elections, a coalition of three center-right parties regained control of the legislature, winning 53 of its 101 seats. Free-marketeer Mart Laar became Prime Minister for the second time.

▶ ETHIOPIA
Federal Democratic Republic of Ethiopia

• **GEOGRAPHY   Location:** Horn of Africa (central eastern Africa). **Boundaries:** Eritrea to N, Djibouti and Somalia to E, Kenya to S, Sudan to W. **Total land area:** 435,184 sq. mi. (1,127,127 sq km). **Coastline:** none. **Comparative area:** somewhat smaller than Alaska. **Land use:** 12% arable land; 1% permanent crops; 41% meadows and pastures; 24% forest and woodland; 22% other; includes negl. % irrigated. **Major cities:** (1993 est.) Addis Ababa (New Flower) 2,200,186; Dire Dawa 173,588; Harar 162,645; Gondar 146,777; Nazret 131,585.

• **PEOPLE   Population:** 59,680,383 (1999 est.). **Nationality:** noun—Ethiopian(s); adjective— Ethiopian. **Ethnic groups:** 40% Oromo, 32% Amhara and Tigrean, 9% Sidamo, 6% Shankella. **Languages:** Amharic, Tigrinya, Orominga, Guaraginga, Somali, Arabic, English (major foreign language taught in schools). **Religions:** 45-50% Muslim, 35-40% Ethiopian Orthodox, 12% animist.

• **GOVERNMENT   Type:** federal republic. **Independence:** oldest independent country in Africa and one of oldest in the world—at least 2,000 years. **Constitution:** Dec. 1994. **National holiday:** May 28. **Heads of Government:** Negasso Gidada, president (since Aug. 1995); Meles Zenawi, prime minister (since Aug. 1995). **Structure:** executive; bicameral legislature; judiciary.

• **ECONOMY   Monetary unit:** birr. **Budget:** (FY96/97 est.) **income:** $1 bil.; **expend.:** $1.48 bil.

GDP: $32.9 bil., $560 per capita (1998 est.). **Chief crops:** cereals, pulses, coffee, oilseed; hides, cattle. **Natural resources:** small reserves of gold, platinum, copper, potash. **Major industries:** food processing, beverages, textiles. **Labor force:** 80% agriculture and animal husbandry, 12% government and services. **Exports:** $550 mil. (f.o.b., 1998 est.); coffee, leather products, gold, oilseeds. **Imports:** $1.3 bil. (f.o.b., 1998 est) food and live animals, petroleum, chemicals, machinery (1994). **Major trading partners:** *exports:* 26% Germany, 11% Japan, 10% Italy, 8% UK; *imports:* 11% Italy, 11% U.S., 7% Germany, 4% Saudi Arabia.

Ethiopia played an important role in the Red Sea trade of the classical world and was mentioned by the Greek historian Herodotus in the fifth century b.c. According to legend, the Ethiopian monarchy was founded by Melelik I, son of Israel's King Solomon and the Queen of Sheba (Sab'a, i.e., North Yemen). Coptic Christianity became Ethiopia's dominant religion in the fourth century a.d. Ethiopia successfully resisted Islamic invasions in the seventh century except in areas along the Red Sea coast but was cut off from the rest of the Christian world by the Islamic states of North Africa and the Middle East.

Portugal established forts and trading stations on the Red Sea coast beginning in 1493, strengthening their domination of trade in the Indian Ocean. The Portuguese also sponsored Roman Catholic missionaries but with little success. A century of religious strife ended with the expulsion of all foreign missionaries in the 1630s. Ethiopia successfully resisted an attempted Italian invasion in 1880.

Ethiopia began to emerge into the modern world under Melelik II (r. 1889-1913). A period of instability after his death ended with the accession in 1930 of Haile Selassie. Italy invaded again in 1936 and soon conquered the entire country. Protests by the League of Nations had no effect; Haile Selassie fled to exile in England. The Italians were driven out during World War II by British and Ethiopian forces, and Haile Selassie returned to his throne.

Civil unrest broke out in February 1974, and Haile Selassie was deposed on Sept. 13, 1974. A coalition of urban elites and the armed forces took over, abolishing the monarchy in 1975 and curbing the power of the Coptic church. Land reform was instituted, and a socialist state proclaimed. In 1977-78 a period of "red terror" resulted in the arrest and execution of thousands of the new regime's opponents. A provisional military council, the Dergue, was confirmed in power under the leadership of Col. Mengistu Haile-Mariam.

A military assistance agreement in 1976 between Ethiopia and the USSR ended an earlier military relationship with the United States; American military advisers were expelled. In 1977 Somalia, taking advantage of Ethiopia's shifting military situation, attacked across the Ogaden desert, aiming to restore certain disputed areas of Ethiopia to Somalia. A massive infusion of Soviet arms and Cuban troops expelled the Somalis in March 1978, but border clashes continued thereafter.

After the expulsion of the Italians during World War II, the province of Eritrea, under a UN plan, was to have become autonomous in a federation with Ethiopia. Instead, Eritrea was made a province of the Ethiopian Empire in 1962. A coalition of Marxist and non-Marxist liberation forces—most prominent among them the Eritrean People's Liberation Front (EPLF)— resisted the annexation from the beginning. By the spring of 1991, Eritrean forces had gained control of all of Eritrea, including Ethiopia's only outlets to the sea.

Another rebel group, the Ethiopian People's Revolutionary Democratic Front (EPRDF), sought autonomy for Tigre, a northern region between Ethiopia and Eritrea. In February 1991, the EPRDF launched a major offensive, forcing Mengistu Haile Mariam's flight, a week before scheduled cease-fire talks were to start in London. The talks proceeded quickly under the auspices of the United States, and rebel forces under the leadership of the EPRDF entered Addis Ababa virtually unopposed at the end of May.

Nevertheless, years of civil war and devastating famines have left Ethiopia in shambles. A transition government was installed to draft a constitution in July 1991, and acknowledged Eritrean independence without incident. But the country's first multiparty elections in June 1992 were so badly handled that the powerful OLF withdrew from the government.

In June 1994, the EPRDF won 484 of the 547 seats in the Constituent Assembly, which by November had drawn up a constitution for a parliamentary government over nine partially autonomous regions. But most opposition parties boycotted the country's first multiparty elections under the new constitution, resulting in decisive victories by the EPRDF, and its leader Meles Zenawi, who became premier. A small border war with Eritrea in May-June 1998 threatened the fragile political structure. By early 1999, the small war had ballooned into a major conflict with thousands of soldiers on each side struggling for control of some barren borderland near the outpost of Badme.

▶ **FIJI**
Republic of Fiji
• **GEOGRAPHY** **Location:** more than 300 islands (100 inhabited), in South Pacific Ocean. Suva 18°08'S, 178°25'E. **Boundaries:** South Pacific Ocean to N, S, and W; Koro Sea to E; nearest neighbor is Vanuatu, about 600 mi. (1,000 km) to W. **Total area:** 7,054 sq. mi. (18,270 sq km). **Coastline:** 702 mi. (1,129 km). **Comparative area:** slightly smaller than New Jersey. **Land use:** 10% arable land; 4% permanent crops; 10% meadows and pastures; 65% forest and woodland; 11% other; includes negl. % irrigated. **Major cities:** (1986 census) Suva (capital) 69,665; Lautoka, 29,000.
• **PEOPLE** **Population:** 812,918 (1999 est.). **Nationality:** noun—Fijian(s); adjective—Fijian. **Ethnic groups:** 51% Fijian, 44% Indian. **Languages:** English (official), Fijian, Hindustani. **Religions:** 52% Christian, 38% Hindu, 8% Muslim; Fijians are mainly Christian, Indians are Hindu with Muslim minority.
• **GOVERNMENT** **Type:** republic. **Independence:** Oct. 10, 1970 (from UK). **Constitution:** new constitution to allow a non-ethnic Fijian to become prime minister was signed by the president on July 25, 1997 and came into force July 28, 1998. **National holiday:** Independence Day, Oct. 10. **Heads of Government:** Sir Kamisese Mara, head of state (since Jan. 1994); Mahendra Pal Chaudhry, prime minister (since May 1999). **Structure:** executive; bicameral legislature; judiciary.

• **ECONOMY** **Monetary unit:** Fijian dollar. **Budget:** (1997 est.) *income:* $540.65 mil.; *expend.:* $742.65 mil. **GDP:** $5.4 bil., $6,700 per capita (1998 est.). **Chief crops:** sugar cane, coconuts, cassava; cattle, pigs, horses; fish. **Natural resources:** timber, fish, gold, copper, offshore oil potential. **Major industries:** sugar, tourism, copra. **Labor force:** 235,000 (1987); 33% paid employees; remainder involved in subsistence agriculture. **Exports:** $655 mil. (f.o.b., 1996); 32% sugar, clothing, gold, processed fish. **Imports:** $838 mil. (f.o.b., 1996); machinery and transport equipment, petroleum products, food, chemicals. **Major trading partners:** *exports:* 27% Australia, 14% UK, 12% NZ, 8% U.S.; *imports:* 44% Australia, 15% New Zealand, 9% U.S.

First reported to the West by the Dutch navigator Abel Tasman in 1643, the Fiji Islands were annexed as a British Crown Colony in 1874. Between 1879 and 1916, large numbers of Indian indentured laborers were imported to work on sugar plantations; eventually the original Melanesian inhabitants were outnumbered by persons of Indian descent. Fiji became an independent parliamentary democracy on Oct. 10, 1970, with most land ownership and political power vested in the Fijian minority. A parliamentary election in 1987 brought the Indian party to power; the elected government was ousted in a military coup, and Lt. Col. Sitiveni Rabuka assumed control of the government on May 21, 1987. On June 2, 1992, he was sworn in as prime minister under a new constitution that guarantees a majority of seats for ethnic Fijians in the national legislature. He was re-elected as the head of a coalition government in Feb. 1994.

Fiji's economy is based largely on agriculture. Rice, vegetables, and livestock are produced for local consumption; sugar, copra, and ginger are important export crops. Gold and silver mining and limestone quarrying are economically important, as is tourism.

▶ **FINLAND**
Republic of Finland
• **GEOGRAPHY** **Location:** northern Europe. **Boundaries:** Norway to N, Russian Federation to E, Baltic Sea to S, Gulf of Bothnia, Sweden to W. **Total area:** 130,127 sq. mi. (337,030 sq km). **Coastline:** 700 mi. (1,126 km) excluding islands and coastal indentations. **Comparative area:** slightly smaller than Montana. **Land use:** 8% arable land; 76% forest and woodland; 16% other; includes negl. % irrigated. **Major cities:** (1995) Helsinki (capital) 525,031; Espoo 191,247; Tampere 182,742; Vantaa 166,480; Turku 164,370.
• **PEOPLE** **Population:** 5,158,372 (1999 est.). **Nationality:** noun—Finn(s); adjective—Finnish. **Ethnic groups:** 93% Finn, 6% Swede, Lapp, Gypsy. **Languages:** 93.5% Finnish, 6.3% Swedish (both official); small Lapp- and Russian-speaking minorities. **Religions:** 89% Evangelical Lutheran, 1% Greek Orthodox.
• **GOVERNMENT** **Type:** republic. **Independence:** Dec. 6, 1917 (from Russia). **Constitution:** July 17, 1919. **National holiday:** Independence Day, Dec. 6. **Heads of Government:** Martti Ahtisaari, president (since Mar. 1994); Paavo Tapio Lipponen, prime minister (since Mar. 1995). **Structure:** executive; unicameral legislature; judiciary.
• **ECONOMY** **Monetary unit:** markka. **Budget:** (1996 est.) *income:* $33 bil.; *expend.:* $40 bil. **GDP:** $103.6 bil., $20,100 per capita (1998 est.). **Chief**

crops: cereals, sugar beets, potatoes; dairy, cattle; fish. **Natural resources:** timber, copper, zinc, iron ore, silver. **Major industries:** metal manufacturing, shipbuilding, forestry and wood processing (pulp, paper), copper refining. **Labor force:** 2.533 mil. (1993 est.); 30.4% public services, 20.9% industry, 15% commerce; 12% unemployment (1998). **Exports:** $43 bil. (f.o.b., 1998); machinery, chemicals, paper and pulp. **Imports:** $30.7 bil. (f.o.b., 1998); foodstuffs, petroleum and petroleum products, chemicals, transport equipment. **Major trading partners:** *exports:* 11% Germany, 10% UK, 10% Sweden, 7% US; *imports:* 15% Germany, 12% Sweden, 8% UK, 8% Russia, 7% US.

The Finns originated in the Ural Mountains, and their language is akin to Hungarian and closely similar to Estonian. Migrating from western Siberia to what is now Finland in the eighth century, they drove the indigenous Lapps to northernmost Scandinavia. Finland was conquered and Christianized by the Swedes in the 12th century and in the 16th century became a Swedish grand duchy. Ethnic Swedes make up about 7 percent of the present population. Finland was frequently a battleground in wars between Sweden and Russia; about one-third of the population perished in a war-induced famine in 1696. In 1721 Sweden ceded the province of Viborg to Russia, and all of Finland was taken over by Russia in 1809.

Under the Russians the czars became simultaneously grand dukes of Finland and ruled it as a semiautonomous province. Attempts to "Russify" Finland in the later 19th century provoked great popular resistance. When the Russian empire and then the Russian Republic fell in the 1917 Revolution, Finland lapsed into a fierce civil war between Communists and non-Communists. The "whites" under Baron Gustaf Mannerheim were the victors, and Finland became an independent country for the first time in its history.

In 1939 the USSR attacked the Finnish Republic; Finland's resistance in the "Winter War" was heroic but unavailing. Defeated, it was forced to cede Western Keralia to the USSR. After the German invasion of Russia in 1941, fighting between Finland and Russia resumed; England, but not America, declared war on Finland as a cocombatant with Germany. Russia again defeated Finland in 1944 and obliged the Finns to wage war against the German occupying army in northern Finland; much of the country was devastated.

The terms of the 1944 armistice between Finland and the USSR were very harsh: Finland ceded the Petsamo region to the Soviet Union, and thus was cut off from the Barents Sea; the Porkkala peninsula was leased to the Soviets for 50 years, and reparations amounting to 80 percent of Finland's exports were paid in kind. Soviet pressure forced Finland to reject Marshall Plan aid after World War II, but Finland benefited indirectly from the rapid postwar recovery of the Scandinavian region. The gross national product returned to prewar levels by 1947.

Finland's economy had traditionally been centered on timber and other forest products, including pulp and paper, and on small-scale, highly productive agriculture. In the postwar period, industrial development was emphasized; the production of heavy machinery became the country's leading industry.

In 1948 the Finns signed a mutual defense pact with the USSR, renewed in 1955, 1970, and 1983.

Finland's presidents, Juho Paasikivi (1946-56), Urho Kekkonen (1956-81), and Mauno Koivisto (1982-94), although conservative and nationalistic, realized that the country's independence required the avoidance of any appearance of anti-Soviet moves in foreign policy.

With the establishment of good Soviet-Finnish relations, the Porkkala peninsula was returned to Finland in 1956. Finland joined the Nordic Council and the United Nations in 1955. It became an associate member of the European Free Trade Association in 1961 and a full member in 1985.

With a strong presidency providing stability despite revolving-door coalition governments in the Eduskunta (parliament), and a prudent foreign policy in the shadow of the USSR, Finland preserved its free economy and civil liberties.

The USSR's collapse struck a heavy blow to Finland's economy; through the 1980s 15-25 percent of Finland's exports had gone to the Soviet Union. Unemployment, recession, and currency devaluation have been constant reminders of these dramatic changes.

In politics the USSR's demise brought a rightward shift, with the first nonsocialist coalition government in 25 years being elected in April 1991 under 37-year-old Esko Aho of the Center party as prime minister. February 1994 saw Finland's first direct election of a president with Social Democrat Martti Ahtisaari carrying 54 percent of the vote. In March, the EU voted to accept Finland as a member in 1995. Prime Minister Aho announced that Finland would join NATO's "partnership for peace" but not as a step to full membership, preferring to maintain Finland's neutrality.

The Finnish electorate and Parliament approved membership in the EU by plebiscite and ratification in late 1994. But years of recession and high unemployment led to the toppling of the Center party government in March 1995 as the Social Democrats emerged as Finland's largest party, with Paavo Lipponen as prime minister. Elections in March 1999 to the Eduskunta returned the same parties of the coalition, with small adjustments, to power.

▶ FRANCE
French Republic
● **GEOGRAPHY Location:** western Europe. **Boundaries:** English Channel to N, Belgium, Luxembourg, Germany, Switzerland, Italy to E, Mediterranean Sea, Spain to S, Atlantic Ocean to W. **Total area:** 176,460 sq. mi. (547,030 sq km). **Coastline:** 2,130 mi. (3,427 km). **Comparative area:** slightly less than twice the size of Colorado. **Land use:** 33% arable land; 2% permanent crops; 20% meadows and pastures; 27% forest and woodland; 18% other; includes 2% irrigated. **Major cities:** (1990 census) Paris (capital) 2,152,423; Marseille (Marseilles) 800,000; Lyon (Lyons) 415,487; Toulouse 358,688; Nice 342,439.
● **PEOPLE Population:** 58,978,172 (1999 est.). **Nationality:** noun—Frenchman (men), Frenchwoman (women); adjective—French. **Ethnic groups:** Celtic and Latin with Teutonic, Slavic, North African, Indochinese, and Basque minorities. **Languages:** French (100% of population); rapidly declining regional dialects (Provençal, Breton, Alsatian, Corsican, Catalan, Basque, Flemish). **Religions:** 90% Roman Catholic, 2% Protestant, 1% Jewish, 1% Muslim (North African workers), 6% unaffiliated.

● **GOVERNMENT Type:** republic. **Constitution:** Sept. 28, 1958, amended concerning election of president in 1962. **National holiday:** Bastille Day, July 14. **Heads of Government:** Jacques Chirac, president (since May 1995); Lionel Jospin, prime minister (since June 1997). **Structure:** executive; bicameral legislature; judiciary.
● **ECONOMY Monetary unit:** French franc. **Budget:** (1998) *income:* $222 bil.; *expend.:* $265 bil. **GDP:** $1.32 trillion, $22,600 per capita (1998 est.). **Chief crops:** cereals, sugarbeets, potatoes, wine grapes (western Europe's foremost producer); beef, dairy products; fish. **Natural resources:** coal, iron ore, bauxite, fish, timber. **Major industries:** steel, machinery, chemicals, automobiles. **Labor force:** 25.4 mil. (1995); 69% services, 26% industry, 5% agriculture; 11.5% unemployment (1998). **Exports:** $289 bil. (f.o.b., 1998); machinery and transport equipment, chemicals, foodstuffs, agricultural products, iron and steel products. **Imports:** $255 bil. (f.o.b., 1998); crude petroleum, machinery and equipment, agricultural products, chemicals, iron and steel products. **Major trading partners:** *exports:* 16% Germany, 10% UK, 9% Italy, 8% Spain; *imports:* 17% Germany, 10% Italy, 9% US, 8% Belgium-Luxembourg.

Pre-Roman France, known as Gaul, was populated by Celtic tribes. The Mediterranean coast, colonized by Phoenician and Greek traders, was conquered by Rome in the second century b.c. The Roman conquest of all of Gaul was carried out by Julius Caesar between 58 and 51 b.c. Gaul became a prosperous and thoroughly Latinized province of the Roman Empire and Christianity was introduced in the first century a.d.

Barbarian invaders including Visigoths, Franks, and Burgundii swept through France in the fifth century. In 486 Clovis, chief of the Franks, unified the country, accepted Christianity, and established the Merovingian dynasty. France was invaded by Muslim Saracens in the seventh century, but in 732 Charles Martel defeated the Saracens. His son, Pepin the Short, overthrew the last Merovingian ruler in 751 and proclaimed himself king. Pepin's son, Charlemagne, greatly expanded his kingdom and was crowned emperor of the West by the pope in 800.

Ninth-century Viking invasions greatly weakened the power of the Carolingians and France broke up into estates, some of them effectively independent countries, ruled by great aristocrats. Among the most important were the duke- doms of Aquitaine and Burgundy and the counties of Flanders, Blois, and Anjou. In 911 the Vikings, who had repeatedly raided the Atlantic coast of France, established the duchy of Normandy.

In 987 the Carolingian dynasty died out in France (although it survived in the Holy Roman Empire) and was replaced by a new line, the Capetians. Steadily expanding in both territory and power from their base in Paris, the Capetians solidified the foundations of the French monarchy. Paris became a great monastic and university city as well as a center of trade and manufacturing. Under the crusader-king Louis IX (St. Louis), France also became an international power.

During the 14th century, the Black Death, peasant rebellions, and the beginning of the Hundred Years' War (1337-1453) with England further weakened the French monarchy. The Norman conquest of England in 1066 had entwined the fortunes of the French and English monarchies, and with the Capetian line in decline, England pursued its claims in France. Henry V of England

defeated the French at Agincourt in 1415, and in 1420 Charles IV made Henry heir to the throne of France. Henry's forces were defeated by French armies inspired by Joan of Arc, and in 1429 his claim to the French throne was overturned. In 1435 Burgundy allied itself with France, and in 1453 the English were driven out of France, except for an enclave at Calais.

Louis XI completed the consolidation of France under the French monarchy. France prospered as a center of commerce, industry, agriculture, learning, and culture throughout the 16th century but was disrupted by religious civil wars stemming from the Reformation. The Protestant Henry of Navarre, heir to the throne, was obliged to accept Catholicism before being crowned in 1594; he became founder of the Bourbon monarchy.

The consolidation of power under a highly centralized monarchy continued under Henry's heirs. With a foreign policy shaped by the powerful prime ministers Cardinal Richelieu and Cardinal Mazarin, France under Louis XIII and Louis XIV enhanced its stature in Europe by defeating the Habsburgs in the Thirty Years' War (1618-48). Louis XIV—the Sun King—moved the court from Paris to his new palace at Versailles and presided over the wealthiest and most powerful monarchy in Europe.

Louis XIV's persecution of the Huguenots resulted in a great emigration of Protestants from France. A grand alliance of European states thwarted France's expansionist aims on the continent, but France became a major colonial power in North America, controlling Canada and Louisiana (including most of the Mississippi-Missouri valley), and pursued overseas ventures in Africa and Asia as well.

In the mid-18th century, France was weakened internationally by the expensive and fruitless Wars of the Austrian Succession and the Seven Years' War. Under the Treaty of Paris (1763), France ceded control of Canada to Great Britain. The Enlightenment made France a world center of intellectual activity but also led to the questioning of the political and social bases of the French monarchy. An increasingly wealthy but powerless bourgeoisie chafed under the restrictions of an archaic socioeconomic order.

France under Louis XVI supported the American colonies in the Revolutionary War, incurring a large public debt in the process. Combined with unrestrained extravagance on the part of the court and the aristocracy, poverty increased among the rural peasantry and the urban working class, while the bourgeoisie demanded a greater voice in government. These trends came to a head with the storming of the Bastille on July 14, 1789; soon thereafter, the Estates-General took control of the country, and France was in the throes of revolution.

Revolutionary leaders at first allowed Louis XVI to remain on the throne in a limited monarchy, but the king and Marie Antoinette were subsequently tried for treason and executed in 1793. Thousands died during the Reign of Terror which continued until July 1794, ending with the execution of its primary architects, Augustin Robespierre and Georges Danton. The Directory, with five heads of each division of government (1795-99), failed to maintain public order and suffered military reverses in foreign wars in which successive revolutionary governments had been embroiled since 1792. On Nov. 9, 1799, the Directory was overthrown by the Consulate, with Napoleon Bonaparte named first consul.

Napoleon proclaimed himself emperor of France in 1804. He transformed French law through the Code Napoleon and initially expanded the French empire in Europe and the Middle East. Suffering repeated reverses against British naval forces and disastrous losses in his 1812 invasion of Russia, Napoleon was defeated by the British under Wellington at Waterloo in 1815, and the French empire collapsed.

France restored its monarchy in 1815 but not its monarchical absolutism. Charles X, successor to Louis XVIII, was ousted in a coup d'état in 1830 and replaced by the liberal Louis Philippe. The monarchy came to an end in the wave of popular revolt that swept France, along with most of Europe, in 1848; Louis Napoleon (nephew of Bonaparte) became president of the Second Republic. In 1852 he created the Second Empire, ruling as Napoleon III and presiding over a court that set the standards of fashion for the wealthy bourgeois society of 19th-century Europe.

During the 19th century, France again became a major colonial power, acquiring important possessions in North and West Africa and Indochina. It also became a world leader in art, science, and literature and began its slow transformation into a major industrial power. Politically, however, France suffered from endemic weakness. The Second Empire ended disastrously with defeat in the Franco-Prussian War of 1870-71; the Paris Commune, formed during that war, was overthrown with great bloodshed. The Third Republic (1871-1914), despite the glittering pleasures of the Belle Epoque and France's considerable prestige as a world power, was shaken by the Dreyfus Affair of 1894-1906 and ill-served by both its political and military leaders.

France joined with Great Britain and Russia in forming the Triple Entente of 1907, a defensive agreement against the Triple Alliance of Germany, Italy, and the Austro-Hungarian empire. During World War I—in effect a war between these two alliances—France suffered millions of casualties and severe damage in the north. Although its role as a leader of the victorious alliance was confirmed at the Versailles Conference of 1919, France was seriously weakened by the war and played a diminished role as a world power in the postwar era.

France suffered badly in the world depression of the 1930s and could muster neither political nor military energy to offer effective opposition to the rise of Nazi Germany and fascist Italy. France was a participant in the Munich Agreement of 1938, which sealed the fate of central Europe. When World War II broke out in 1939, Hitler initially held off his attack on France, but when it came in May-June 1940, France was swiftly and igominiously defeated.

During World War II, northern France was under German occupation, while in the south a collaborationist, semifascistic state was organized, with its capital at Vichy. Meanwhile, in London, Gen. Charles de Gaulle rallied the Free French forces, which fought on the Allied side in various campaigns. After the liberation of Paris a "provisional government" of various Resistance groups combined with de Gaulle's supporters drew up a constitution for the Fourth French Republic.

Although it suffered from inherent political weaknesses and often failed to provide stable cabinets, the Fourth Republic presided over postwar recovery, aided by the Marshall Plan; it promoted a mixed socialist-free enterprise economy and instituted social reforms such as women's suffrage and social security. It also led the way toward a united Europe, playing a leading role in the organization of the EEC in 1957. France became a founding member of NATO in 1949.

The Fourth Republic was unable, however, to withstand the strains of the dismantling of France's empire during the postwar wave of decolonization. France's recovery of Indochina in 1945 set off a war of national liberation there that lasted until France withdrew from the colony in 1954. Morocco and Tunisia won their independence in 1956; in Algeria, regarded as part of France itself, France fought on against Front de Liberation Nationale (FLN) rebels.

The Algerian War seriously polarized French public opinion, and, threatened with an army coup, the National Assembly voted in 1958 to grant Pres. Charles de Gaulle emergency powers for six months. De Gaulle outmaneuvered his army backers and negotiated to turn Algeria over to the FLN, a process completed in 1962. Meanwhile he also restored order at home and presided over the drafting of a new constitution that created the Fifth Republic in 1958.

The new constitution created a strong presidency, with powers to name the premier and the Council of Ministers and to preside over their meetings. The legislature was required to give priority to government initiatives and lacked authority over national defense, education, labor, and local government. Under the governments of premiers Michel Debré and Georges Pompidou, the Gaullist regime further advanced modernization of French industry and greatly benefited French agriculture by expanding the Common Market to include agricultural as well as industrial goods.

De Gaulle followed an independent foreign policy, pursuing European integration as well as closer relations with the Communist bloc and the Third World. He blocked British entry into the Common Market; developed an independent nuclear force, refusing to sign nuclear test-ban and nonproliferation treaties; pursued a historic rapprochement with Germany; recognized the People's Republic of China; established a leading French role in the former French colonies of Africa; and withdrew French forces from the NATO military command.

Reelected president in 1965, after a runoff election against the Socialist-Communist alliance candidate François Mitterrand, de Gaulle continued his independent policy until student riots in early 1968 provoked police repression, which led to further popular support for the students, especially in Paris. De Gaulle dissolved the National Assembly and, in an emotional campaign on behalf of national stability, won a large electoral majority. In 1969, however, following minor political reverses, de Gaulle resigned as president.

The elections of June 1969 gave the presidency to former premier Georges Pompidou, who died in office in April 1974. He was succeeded by the Independent Republican Valery Giscard d'Estaing, who served until May 1981. During these years the Gaullist heritage was developed and consolidated. In foreign policy the movement toward European unity continued with the development of the European Parliament and, in a reversal of policy in 1973, French support for British membership in the EEC. The economic shock of the OPEC price rises of 1973-74 led to a decision to stress new industrial ventures in high-technology fields, symbolized by the Anglo-French Concorde supersonic transport.

The 1970s were years of social ferment, with a relaxation of divorce laws and the legalization of contraception advertisements and abortion, and a decline in church membership and attendance. In 1978 disillusionment stemming from inflation and social difficulties under Giscard d'Estaing brought about a leftist electoral victory for the first time under the Fifth Republic.

The Gaullist era came to an end in 1981, when Socialist François Mitterrand defeated Giscard in a presidential election. He immediately dissolved the National Assembly and led his party to an absolute majority. Socialist premier Pierre Mauroy formed a government with four Communist members participating, a government which pursued an aggressive program of nationalization of banks and major industries and reform of local government. Continued economic difficulties led to a loss of popular support for Mitterrand's policies. In the elections of 1986, Jacques Chirac's coalition of Gaullists and Giscardists won an almost absolute majority in the National Assembly, and Chirac became premier—the first time since 1958 that the president and the premier were of opposing parties. An accommodation was worked out in which Mitterrand concentrated on foreign affairs, and Chirac on domestic matters. Mitterrand oversaw a restoration of French military cooperation with NATO and a continuation of Franco-German cooperation.

At home Chirac and his party reversed Mitterrand's policy of nationalization of banking and industry, cut taxes, and brought about a significant reduction in the inflation rate. Chirac ran for president against Mitterrand in 1988 but was defeated. Mitterrand's reelection with over 54 percent of the vote carried his Socialist party to a near majority in the assembly, where they constructed a coalition government of the non-Communist Left under Premier Michel Rocard, whose policies were difficult to distinguish from those of the Chirac government. Persistent 9 percent unemployment and the growing appeal of Jean-Marie Le Pen's anti-immigrant National Front brought a cabinet shake-up in May 1991 and the designation of France's first female premier, Edith Cresson.

But the shake-up did nothing to stem voter dissatisfaction with the governing Socialists. Elections to regional councils in March 1992 saw the Socialist vote drop to 18 percent, but not to the benefit of the center-right coalition Union for France, which gained only one-third of the vote. Instead, it was the National Front and the two rival "green" parties that together gained 28 percent of the vote.

Mitterand strongly supported UN intervention in the Balkans and France's participation in the Maastricht Treaty (which voters approved by a very narrow margin). But not even the formidable Mitterand could prevent the Socialist rout in the March 1993 assembly elections. The Rally for France won the most lopsided victory in the republic's history, carrying 460 (of 577) seats while the left took only 93. Rejecting calls for his resignation, Mitterand reasserted his constitutional prerogatives in defense and foreign policy, vowing to stay on until 1995. In May of that year, his unprecedented 14-year presidency came to an end as Jacques Chirac won the second round of voting over Lionel Jospin.

Pledged to tax and spending cuts and continued dismantling of state enterprises, Chirac and his followers met with surprisingly limited success as unemployment reached its highest level ever. A giant truckers' strike blocked French highways without government action, and cutting social welfare spending (to meet the EU's Euro conditions) proved elusive. So, seeking a public mandate for France's participation in the Euro, President Chirac dissolved the Assembly a year early. But the result was yet another French "cohabitation:" the left coalition took 319 seats and Lionel Jospin became prime minister. In 1998 an upturn in the French economy and an upset victory over Brazil in the World Cup buoyed French spirits.

▶ GABON
Gabonese Republic

● **GEOGRAPHY Location:** western coast of Africa. **Boundaries:** Equatorial Guinea to NW, Cameroon to N, Congo to E and S, Atlantic Ocean to W. **Total area:** 103,348 sq. mi. (267,670 sq km). **Coastline:** 550 mi. (885 km). **Comparative area:** slightly smaller than Colorado. **Land use:** 1% arable land; 1% permanent crops; 18% meadows and pastures; 73% forest and woodland; 3% other. **Major cities:** (1993 census) Libreville (capital) 419,596; Port-Gentil 78,225; Masuku 75,000 (1988).

● **PEOPLE Population:** 1,225,853 (1999 est.). **Nationality:** noun—Gabonese (sing., pl.); adjective—Gabonese. **Ethnic groups:** Bantu tribes, including four major tribal groupings (Fang, Eshira, Bapounou, Bateke); 154,000 other Africans and Europeans, including 6,000 French and 11,000 of dual nationality. **Languages:** French (official), Fang, Myene, Bateke, Bapounou/Eschira, Bandjabi. **Religions:** 55-75% Christian, less than 1% Muslim, remainder indigenous beliefs.

● **GOVERNMENT Type:** republic; multi-party presidential regime since 1990. **Independence:** Aug. 17, 1960 (from France). **Constitution:** Mar. 14, 1991 **National holidays:** Independence Day, Aug. 17. **Heads of Government:** El Hadj Omar Bongo, president (since Dec. 1967); Jean-Francois Ntoutoume-Emane, prime minister (since Jan. 1999). **Structure:** executive; bicameral legislature; independent judiciary.

● **ECONOMY Monetary unit:** Communauté Financière Africaine (CFA) franc. **Budget:** (1996 est.) *income:* $1.5 bil.; *expend.:* $1.3 bil. **GDP:** $7.7 bil., $6,400 per capita (1998 est.). **Chief crops:** coffee, cocoa, sugar; rubber; wood; cattle; fishing. **Natural resources:** crude oil, manganese, uranium, gold, timber, iron ore. **Major industries:** food, beverages; textiles, wood. **Labor force:** N.A.; 65% agriculture, industry and commerce, services. **Exports:** $2.1 bil. (f.o.b., 1998 est.); 81% crude oil, 12% wood, 5% manganese. **Imports:** $890 mil. (f.o.b., 1998 est.); machinery and equipment, foodstuffs, chemicals, petroleum products, construction materials. **Major trading partners:** *exports:* 67% US, 9% China, 8% France; *imports:* 38% France, 8% US, 5% Cameroon.

Gabon, an equatorial nation largely covered by dense rain forest, is inhabited by a highly diverse mixture of people who migrated into the region over the course of the past 700 years; the now-dominant Fang arrived during the 19th century. The first Europeans to reach the area were the Portuguese in the 15th century; they were followed by Dutch, French, and British traders in the 16th century. All engaged in the slave trade.

France established an informal protectorate in 1839-41 and set about suppressing the slave trade.

In 1849 a group of freed slaves settled near the American mission station at Baraka and renamed the town Libreville. France established a colonial administration in 1903 and in 1910 made it part of French Equatorial Africa. The territory became an important base of Free French activity during World War II, and in 1946 Gen. Charles de Gaulle granted French citizenship to the territory's inhabitants, and local power was devolved upon advisory assemblies. Gabon became fully independent on Aug. 17, 1960.

Gabon has remained politically stable under its 1961 constitution. Gabon's first president, Leon M'Ba, was briefly deposed by a military coup in 1964 but quickly reinstated with the aid of French troops. He died in 1967 and was succeeded by the vice president, Omar Bongo who combined all political parties into the Gabonese Democratic party in 1968; he was elected president in his own right in 1975, was reelected in 1979 and 1986. Despite initial resistance from the government, Gabon has recently made the transition to multiparty democracy, thereby attracting more foreign investment. Bongo's Gabonese Democratic party remains in power.

Although its per capita income is much higher than almost every African nation, there is substantial income inequality and a good deal of poverty in Gabon.

▶ THE GAMBIA
Republic of The Gambia
● **GEOGRAPHY Location**: narrow territory around Gambia River on northwestern coast of Africa. **Boundaries**: Senegal to N, E, and S, Atlantic Ocean to W. **Total area**: 4,363 sq. mi. (11,300 sq km). **Coastline**: 50 mi. (80 km). **Comparative area**: slightly less than twice the size of Delaware. **Land use**: 18% arable land; 0% permanent crops; 9% meadows and pastures; 28% forest and woodland; 45% other; includes 3% irrigated. **Major cities**: (1993 census) Banjul (capital) 43,326; Kombo St. Mary (surrounding urban area) 228,214.
● **PEOPLE Population**: 1,336,320 (1999 est.). **Nationality**: noun—Gambian(s); adjective—Gambian. **Ethnic groups**: 42% Mandinka, 18% Fula, 16% Wolof, 10% Jola, 9% Serahuli, 1% non-African. **Languages**: English (official), Mandinka, Wolof, Fula, and others. **Religions**: 90% Muslim, 9% Christian, 1% indigenous beliefs.
● **GOVERNMENT Type**: republic under multiparty democratic rule. **Independence**: Feb. 18, 1965 (from UK). **Constitution**: Apr. 24, 1970, (suspended July 1994); rewritten, approved and reestablished in Jan. 1997. **National holiday**: Independence Day, Feb. 18. **Head of Government**: Colonel Yahya Jammeh, president (since July 1994). **Structure**: following the coup on July 22, 1994 all elective officers were dissolved; military leaders have promised to return control to a democratically-elected government.
● **ECONOMY Monetary unit**: dalasi. **Budget**: (FY96/97 est.) **income**: $88.6 mil.; **expend.**: $98.2 mil. **GDP**: $1.3 bil., $1,000 per capita (1998 est.). **Chief crops**: peanuts, millet, sorghum, rice, maize; cattle, goats, sheep. **Natural resources**: fish. **Major industries**: agricultural processing, tourism, beverages. **Labor force**: N.A.; 75% agriculture, 19% industry, commerce, and services, 6.1% government. **Exports**: $120 mil. (f.o.b., 1997 est.); peanuts and peanut products, fish, cotton. **Imports**: $207 mil. (f.o.b., 1997 est.); foodstuffs, manufacturing, raw materials. **Major trading partners**: **exports**: Belgium, Japan, Senegal, Hong Kong; **imports**: Ivory Coast, Hong Kong, UK, Germany.

Thirty miles across at its widest point, and 295 miles long, the serpentine republic of The Gambia was gerrymandered into being out of competing French and British colonial interests. Once the westernmost part of the kingdom of Mali, The Gambia was visited by the Portuguese in 1455. In 1588, they sold British traders exclusive rights to the Gambia River, and in 1660 British merchants established a trading fort. England and France struggled for 200 years to gain political and economic control over the territory, but in 1783 the French ceded to Great Britain possession of The Gambia. Its present boundaries were established in 1889 when it became a British Crown Colony. Between 1901 and 1906, legislative councils were established to encourage self-government, and slavery was abolished.

After World War II the country moved quickly toward constitutional government, achieving independence as a constitutional monarchy within the British Commonwealth of Nations in 1965. The Gambia became a republic on Apr. 24, 1970, and it had the same president, Sir Dawda K. Jawara, until 1994.

In 1994, Yahya Jammeh, a 29-year-old lieutenant fresh from a military police training course in the United States, led a bloodless coup deposing the government of Pres. Jawara. Jammeh pledged to restore civilian government "as soon as we have set things right." Later that year the United Kingdom, the United States, and the European Union cut off all economic and military aid pending a return to democracy.

▶ GEORGIA
● **GEOGRAPHY Location**: west and central Transcaucasia between Asia and Europe. **Boundaries**: Russian Federation to N and E, Azerbaijan, Armenia to S, Turkey to SW, Black Sea to W. **Total area**: 26,911 sq. mi. (69,700 sq km). **Coastline**: Black Sea. **Comparative area**: slightly smaller than South Carolina. **Land use**: 9% arable land; 4% permanent crops; 25% meadows and pastures; 34% forest and woodland; 28% other. **Major cities**: (1994 est.) Tbilisi (capital) 1.3 mil.; Kutaisi 235,000; Rustavi 159,000; Batumi 136,000; Sukhumi 121,000.
● **PEOPLE Population**: 5,066,499 (1999 est.). **Nationality**: noun—Georgian(s); adjective—Georgian. **Ethnic groups**: 70.1% Georgian, 8.1% Armenian, 6.3% Russian, 5.7% Azeri, 3% Ossetian, 1.8% Abkhazian. **Languages**: 71% Georgian (official), 9% Russian, 7% Armenian, 6% Azeri. **Religions**: 75% Christian Orthodox, 11% Muslim, 8% Armenian Apostolic.
● **GOVERNMENT Type**: republic. **Independence**: Apr. 9, 1991 (from Soviet Union). **Constitution**: Oct. 17, 1995. **National holiday**: Independence Day, May 26. **Heads of Government**: Eduard A. Shevardnadze, president (since 1992); Otar Patsatsia, prime minister. **Structure**: executive; unicameral legislature; judiciary.
● **ECONOMY Monetary unit**: lari. **Budget**: (1998 est.) **income**: $364 mil; **expend.**: $568 mil. **GDP**: $11.2 bil., $2,200 per capita (1998 est.). **Chief crops**: citrus, grapes, tea, vegetables. **Natural resources**: forests, hydropower, manganese. **Major industries**: steel, aircraft, machine tools. **Labor force**: 3.08 mil. (1997); 31% industry and construction, 25% agriculture and forestry, 44% other. **Exports**: $230 mil. (f.o.b., 1997); citrus fruits, tea,

wine. **Imports**: $931 mil. (c.i.f., 1997 est.); fuel, grain and other foods, machinery and parts. **Major trading partners**: Russia, Turkey, Azerbaijan.

Georgia is a land of rugged natural beauty, renowned for its famous war heroes and its hospitality. Georgia's most famous son, Iosif Djugashvili, known as Josef Stalin, was born in the mountain village of Gori in 1879. The name of Georgia derives from the Persian name for the native people, Gorj.

Georgian culture is ancient, for an independent state was first founded in the fourth century b.c. following the conquest of the Persian empire by Alexander III. Christianity became the state religion in the 4th century a.d. Both the Georgian language and the capital city of Tbilisi date from the fifth century a.d. The Georgian people, whose main occupation was cattle raising and agriculture, began to develop feudal states in the sixth century.

Georgia's subsequent history, however, is one of almost continuous foreign domination. In the 12th century, Georgia gained independence from the Persian empire, but this was short-lived, as it came under the Mongol yoke in 1236. For centuries Georgia was a battleground between Turks and Persians, and the territory was ultimately divided into principalities, some under the control of Persia and some under Turkey. In 1801, the Persian principalities were absorbed into the Russian empire, and by the end of the century the remaining Georgian state under Turkish domination was also annexed to Russia.

Once the Russian empire collapsed in 1917 with the Bolshevik revolution, independent Georgia was once again proclaimed in May 1918. It was dominated by Mensheviks (from the Russian word "minority," as opposed to Bolshevik, meaning "majority"), whose hold on power was short-lived. Although the Soviet Union and Georgia signed a treaty in May 1920 agreeing on their respective borders, the Soviet Red Army came into Georgia and forcibly incorporated it into the Soviet Union as a Socialist republic in early 1921. In 1922 it was made part of the Transcaucasian Soviet Federal Socialist Republic with Armenia and Azerbaijan, and in 1936 it became one of the USSR's union republics.

The Georgians always have been fiercely nationalistic, even in the face of the USSR's "one Soviet people" policy. Georgian pride was evident from the first demonstrations against "russification" in 1956, and again in 1978 when the rewritten USSR constitution attempted to weaken the status of Georgian language. In November 1988, during Mikhail Gorbachev's policy of "glasnost," or openness, great numbers of Georgians began to call for Georgian sovereignty and secession from the USSR.

Even as Georgia fought for its independence from the USSR, the autonomous provinces of Abkhazia, Adzharia, and South Ossetia began fighting for independence from Georgia. Tensions continue to run high in Adzharia, where allegiances to Islam frighten many in Christian Georgia, and in South Ossetia, which is struggling to end its association with Georgia and to unite with North Ossetia in the Russian Federation.

But the greatest conflict raged in Abkhazia, the home region of Zviad Gamsakhurdia, who was elected the country's first president in May 1991, but ousted from office seven months later. Fighting between the Georgian army and troops loyal to Gamsakhurdia continued from 1991 to 1993,

resulting in more than 2,000 casualties, including Gamsakhurdia, until Pres. Eduard Shevardnadze persuaded Parliament to give him emergency powers to quell the insurgency.

His political power consolidated, Shevardnadze began to renew ties to Russia. He agreed to a cooperation pact to increase Russia's military influence in his country in February 1994. On March 2, over the objections of the opposition National Radical party, Parliament ratified Georgia's membership in the Commonwealth of Independent States.

In August 1995 Parliament overwhelmingly approved a new "strong president" constitution. And in November 1995 Shevardnadze easily won election to a new five-year term, while his two-party coalition captured close to 80 percent of the seats in Parliament. But continued instability in Abkhazia, the presence of Russian troops, and several assasinion attempts on Shevardnadze have left future development in doubt.

▶ GERMANY
Federal Republic of Germany

● **GEOGRAPHY** **Location:** central Europe. **Boundaries:** Denmark, Baltic Sea to N, Poland, Czech Republic to E, Austria, Switzerland to S, France, Luxembourg, Belgium, Netherlands to W, North Sea to NW. **Total area:** 137,803 sq. mi. (356,910 sq km). **Coastline:** 1,385 mi. (2,389 km). **Comparative area:** slightly smaller than Montana. **Land use:** 33% arable land; 1% permanent crops; 15% meadows and pastures; 31% forest and woodland; 20% other; includes 1% irrigated. **Major cities:** (1994) Berlin (capital) 3,477,900, Hamburg 1,703,800; München (Munich) 1,251,100; Köln (Cologne) 963,300; Frankfurt 656,200.

● **PEOPLE** **Population:** 82,087,361 (1999 est.). **Nationality:** noun—German(s); adjective—German. **Ethnic groups:** 91.5% German, 2.4% Turkish. **Languages:** German. **Religions:** 38% Protestant, 34% Roman Catholic, 1.7% Muslim, 26.3% unaffiliated or other.

● **GOVERNMENT** **Type:** federal republic. **Constitution:** May 23, 1949; provisional constitution known as Basic Law became constitution of reunited German state Oct. 3, 1990. **National holiday:** German Unity Day, Oct. 3. **Heads of Government:** Johannes Rau, president (since July 1999); Gerhard Schröder, chancellor (since Oct. 1988). **Structure:** president (titular head of state); bicameral parliament—Bundesrat (Federal Council, upper house), Bundestag (National Assembly, lower house); independent judiciary.

● **ECONOMY** **Monetary unit:** deutsche mark. **Budget:** (1998) *income:* $977 bil.; *expend.:* $1.024 tril. **GDP:** $1.813 trillion, $22,100 per capita (1998 est.). **Chief crops:** wheat, barley, rye, potatoes, sugar beets, fruit; cattle, pigs, poultry. **Natural resources:** iron ore, coal, potash, timber. **Major industries:** among world's largest producers of iron, steel, coal, cement, chemicals, machinery, vehicles, machine tools, electronics, food and beverages, metal fabrications, brown coal, shipbuilding, machine building, textiles, petroleum refining, and hides and skins. **Labor force:** 38.2 mil. (1998); 33.7% industry, 2.7% agriculture, 63.6% services. **Exports:** $510 bil. (f.o.b., 1998); 31% machinery, 17% vehicles, 13% chemicals. **Imports:** $426 bil. (f.o.b., 1998); 22% machinery, 10% vehicles, 9% chemicals, 8% foodstuffs. **Major trading partners:** *exports:* 55.5% EU, 8.6% US, 2.3% Japan; *imports:* 54.3% EU, 7.7% US, 4.9% Japan.

The ancient tribes of Germany resisted Roman conquest with mixed success. German federated troops served in the Roman legions, and Germanic invasions contributed to the fall of Rome. Most of Germany was united within the empire of Charlemagne. Divided among his three sons in 843, the empire's eastern regions became the heart of the Germanies. The Holy Roman Empire, founded in 962, gave some unity to the politically fragmented German territories, but its boundaries included more than Germany, and some Germans remained outside it. But that unity was fragile; the Holy Roman emperor was a feudal overlord rather than a ruler, and hundreds of separate political bodies coexisted within the imperial domain. Along the North Sea and Baltic coasts, the Hanseatic League controlled much of the commerce of northern Europe.

With the Reformation in the 16th century, religious divisions added to Germany's existing political fragmentation and local allegiances. The Thirty Years War (1618-48) resulted in the virtual extinction of the Holy Roman Empire and left Germany without even a shadow of unity.

After the Napoleonic Wars, in which much of Germany was conquered by France, the Congress of Vienna (1814-15) sanctioned the creation of a German League to succeed the Holy Roman Empire. The league consisted of 39 states, including five substantial kingdoms and the German parts of the Austrian empire. Prussia, one of the five kingdoms, had already risen to prominence under Frederick the Great in the 18th century. In a series of wars in the mid-19th century, Prussia conquered the other German states; after defeating France in the Franco-Prussian War of 1870-71, Prussia declared the establishment of the German empire. Under its chancellor, Otto von Bismarck, Germany became a major European power in the late 19th century, with a booming industrial economy, flourishing agriculture, a small colonial empire, and growing military might.

The German empire reached its height under Kaiser Wilhelm II on the eve of World War I. Germany's disastrous defeat in that war was compounded by the harsh terms of the Treaty of Versailles (1919), which stripped Germany of its colonial empire, and returned part of Schleswig to Denmark, Alsace-Lorraine to France, and part of Prussia to Poland.

The Weimar Republic, established in 1919, gradually overcame economic difficulties, including ruinous inflation, to achieve a measure of recovery in the 1920s. The republic was disrupted by labor strife, political fragmentation, and the rise of armed extremist political movements on both left and right. After the onset of the world economic depression in 1929, Adolf Hitler's National Socialist movement gained increasing power, both at the polls and through open thuggery against its opponents. Hitler's appointment as chancellor in 1933 effectively put an end to the Weimar Republic as a functioning democracy.

The onset of World War II in Europe was presaged by Hitler's annexation of Austria and Czechoslovakia in 1938 and precipitated by the German invasion of Poland in 1939. Early military successes gave Germany control of most of Europe, but the eventual victory of the Allied powers in 1945 left the country exhausted and in ruins. Much of the Jewish population of Germany, and of other territories under German control, had been killed during the Holocaust. German cities were reduced to rubble, and a quarter of the country's homes were uninhabitable. Famine and fuel shortages added to the general misery.

Politically, Germany had essentially ceased to exist in 1945. The Allies divided the country into four zones of occupation, with a similar four-part division of Berlin. As the Cold War rift between the Western powers and the USSR intensified during the late 1940s, so too the division of Germany hardened. In 1948 the USSR imposed a blockade on West Berlin; the city was supplied by a massive airlift from the West for several months. In 1949 two Germanies were created: the German Democratic Republic in the Russian zone in the east, and the Federal Republic of Germany in the Allied zone in the west.

The Federal Republic was largely the creation of one man, Konrad Adenauer. A veteran pre-Hitler politician, he founded the Federation of Christian Democratic Parties (CDU-CSU) in 1945, and as president of the Parliamentary Council formed during the occupation, he virtually wrote the new constitution for West Germany. In the first elections held in the Federal Republic (August 1949), the "bourgeois coalition" led by the CDU-CSU won a parliamentary majority in the Bundestag, and Adenauer became chancellor, a post he held for 14 years. In 1951 the Western powers granted the new state autonomy in foreign affairs, and recognized its full sovereignty in 1954.

Even before the fighting in Germany subsided in 1945, the Soviet Air Force brought Walter Ulbricht, the exiled leader of the German Communist party, back to the USSR's zone of occupation in Germany. Backed by 20 Soviet divisions, Ulbricht and the party commenced the communization of the eastern zone.

After local and state elections embarrassed the Communists, Stalin and Ulbricht forced all other parties into the National Front. With no other electoral lists permitted, voters gave a 99.7 percent approval to the National Front in the first elections to East Germany's "People's Chamber" in 1950.

While Ulbricht attempted to collectivize agriculture and plan industrial development in the eastern zone, the Soviet Union extracted heavy reparations payments, bringing on an acute economic crisis. In June 1953, shortly after Stalin's death, strikes and riots erupted. The USSR renounced further reparation payments and declared East Germany a sovereign state.

In foreign affairs Adenauer relied heavily on friendship with the United States and reconciliation with France. He also supported European integration: In 1951 West Germany joined both the Council of Europe and the Coal and Steel Community. West Germany was admitted to NATO in 1955 and in 1957 became one of the six founding members of the EEC.

In domestic affairs the political alliance between Adenauer and Ludwig Erhard led to political stability and the creation of a marketdriven economy. With a currency reform program and Marshall Plan aid in place by 1948 under occupation administration, the stage was set for Germany's "economic miracle" of the 1950s. Between 1949 and 1964, industrial production increased by 60 percent and gross national product tripled, while unemployment fell to 1 percent, even as millions of refugees from East Germany were integrated into the West German economy. In the same period, over 8 million houses and apartments were constructed.

In 1963 Erhard succeeded Adenauer as chancellor. Economic growth slowed to an annual 3 percent rate, but West Germany was already one of Europe's strongest economic powers, even providing jobs for hundreds of thousands of "guest workers" from southern Europe and Turkey.

By 1963 East Germany had become the second-largest industrial power in Eastern Europe, and in 1968 it surpassed Czechoslovakia in output. A significant shift of labor to industry reduced the farm population to under 20 percent of total population by 1960. Though farming became mechanized, it remained relatively inefficient.

Although East Germany enjoyed prestige within the Eastern bloc as an industrial power, the steady stream of emigrants to West Germany told a different story. After a renewed collectivization policy was implemented in 1960, the stream became a flood, and East Germany responded by building the Berlin Wall. The wall was a visible sign of political failure, but it did slow the stream of emigration to a trickle.

Erhard resigned in 1966 when his coalition fell apart over the issue of a planned tax increase. He was succeeded by Kurt Kiesinger, who presided over a historic "great coalition" of Christian Democrats and Social Democrats. Under Willi Brandt (who served as deputy chancellor and foreign minister), the Social Democrats had shifted their orientation from a Marxist party to a reformist, market-oriented stance.

Elections in 1969 produced a majority for the coalition headed by the Social Democrats, a coalition that governed until 1982. Brandt succeeded Kiesinger and pursued an Ostpolitik ("opening to the east"), regularizing relations with East Germany, signing a nonagression pact with the USSR, and recognizing the border between East Germany and Poland. But domestically, West Germany suffered serious dislocations from the OPEC oil price increases of the early 1970s; inflation reached almost 8 percent. Revelations that a Brandt aide was an East German spy led to his replacement as chancellor by Helmut Schmidt in 1974.

Schmidt continued Brandt's eastern policy but also pursued improved relations with the West. Economic difficulties persisted, however, and Schmidt's government fell in 1982. The Christian Democrats returned to power under chancellor Helmut Kohl. The improvement of the world economy in the 1980s led to economic recovery in Germany, boosting Kohl's popularity. Meanwhile, in East Germany an aging Ulbricht was replaced in May 1971 as party first secretary by Erich Honecker, who also became head of state in 1976. Honecker completed state ownership of all industry in 1972. Industries were grouped into 133 giant monopolies, each covering one industrial sector and vertically integrated from research to sales.

After Brandt's Ostpolitik, the two Germanies grew closer, at least economically. East Germany's trade with West Germany gave it access to the EC. However, East Germany resisted Mikhail Gorbachev's reform policies in the 1980s, trying to establish itself as a model of old-style communism in Eastern Europe.

In the fall of 1989 tens of thousands of East Germans fled to West Germany through Hungary and Czechoslovakia, triggering a series of dramatic demonstrations and the dismantling of the Berlin Wall in October. Honecker's government collapsed, as did that of his successor, as the momentum for unification became unstoppable. In March 1990 Christian Democrat Lothar de Maizière was elected prime minister on a unification platform.

In July an economic and fiscal union of the Germanies was completed, and in September the victorious wartime allies (the U.S., USSR, UK, and France) agreed to a peace treaty that paved the way for political unification. On October 3, six regions of the former East Germany entered the Federal Republic as member states; eleven days later the Christian Democrats won elections in five of them, the Social Democrats winning one.

In December 1990 all-German elections to the Bundestag were held for the first time in 58 years. The CDU-CSU and the Free Democrats won 398 seats, the Social Democrats 239. Helmut Kohl was sworn in as chancellor Jan. 17, 1991. In June Parliament voted to move the capital back to Berlin.

In the years following unification, euphoria gave way to sober realism; economic restructuring would take many years, since the economy of East Germany proved to be in even worse shape than anyone imagined, West Germans have had to pay a higher sales tax and an income tax surcharge as the cost of unification.

Related to these economic woes was the wave of violent attacks by radical nationalists and neo-Nazi gangs upon immigrants and asylum seekers (who number over 2 million). In 1993 the government banned several violent groups and amended Germany's liberal asylum law to prevent refugees seeking economic betterment from entering the country.

In the Bundestag elections of October 1994, the Kohl coalition (CDU, CSU, and FD) took 341 seats, maintaining its majority over the opposition, led by the Social Democrats. Kohl was reelected chancellor, for a fourth time, as the economy remained strong (3 percent growth in 1994). By 1996, however, unemployment was at an all-time postwar high and the Kohl government announced that the budget deficit required sweeping spending cuts, especially in social welfare programs. The economy worsened in 1997 and rebounded in 1998 but not enough to give Kohl another electoral victory as he lost to the Social Democrats and their leader, Gerhard Schröder.

On Oct. 27, the Bundestag approved new Chancellor Schröder's "red-green" cabinet whose personnel and program appeared further left than Schröder. By March 1999, finance minister La-Fontaine, an old-style SD, had been replaced by "moderate" Hans Eichel, financial markets responding positively. Already, in the previous month, the government coalition lost control of the state government of Hesse, thereby losing its majority in the Bundesrat, the upper house whose members are elected by the states, apparently dooming the government's plan to loosen citizenship restrictions (a major and controversial plank in the "red-green" platform). Schröder's attempts to introduce an austerity budget led to further electoral setbacks in state elections in Sep. 1999.

▶ GHANA
Republic of Ghana

• **GEOGRAPHY** **Location:** western Africa. **Boundaries**: Burkina Faso to N, Togo to E, Gulf of Guinea to S, Ivory Coast to W. **Total area**: 92,100 sq. mi. (238,540 sq km). **Coastline**: 335 mi. (539 km). **Comparative area**: slightly smaller than Oregon. **Land use**: 12% arable land; 7% permanent crops; 22% meadows and pastures; 35% forest and woodland; 24% other; includes negl. % irrigated. **Major cities**: (1988 est.) Accra (capital) 949,113;

Kumasi 385,192; Tamale 151,069; Tema 109,975; Sekondi-Takoradi 103,653.
● **PEOPLE Population:** 18,887,626 (1999 est.). **Nationality:** noun—Ghanaian(s); adjective—Ghanaian. **Ethnic groups:** 99.8% black African (major groups—44% Akan, 16% Moshi-Dagomba, 13% Ewe, 8% Ga), 0.2% European and other. **Languages:** English (official), Akan, Moshi-Dagomba, Ewe, Ga. **Religions:** 38% indigenous beliefs, 30% Muslim, 24% Christian, 8% other.
● **GOVERNMENT Type:** constitutional democracy. **Independence:** Mar. 6, 1957 (from UK). **Constitution:** Apr. 28, 1992. **National holiday:** Independence Day, Mar. 6. **Head of Government:** Flt. Lt. (ret.) Jerry John Rawlings, chairman of PNDC (since Dec. 1981). **Structure:** executive; unicameral legislature; judiciary.
● **ECONOMY Monetary unit:** new cedi. **Budget:** (1996 est.) *income:* $1.39 bil.; *expend.:* $1.47 bil. **GDP:** $33.6 bil., $1,800 per capita (1998 est.). **Chief crops:** cocoa, rice, coffee, timber. **Natural resources:** gold, timber, industrial diamonds, bauxite, manganese. **Major industries:** mining, lumbering, light manufacturing. **Labor force:** N.A.; 61% agriculture and fishing, 10% industry, 29% services; 20% unemployed (1997). **Exports:** $1.5 bil. (f.o.b., 1997 est.); 39% gold, 35% cocoa, 9.4% timber, tuna. **Imports:** $2.1 bil. (f.o.b., 1997 est.); capital equipment, petroleum, consumer goods, food. **Major trading partners:** *exports:* UK, Germany, U.S.; *imports:* UK, Nigeria, U.S.

The connection between modern Ghana and the 10th century Ghana empire of southern Mali is obscure. By the 13th century the Akan around the city of Kumasi were trading gold and other commodities with the Mande to the north. The number of competing states in the region grew rapidly after European contact. The Asante empire began in the early 17th century under Osei Tutu. By 1750 it controlled the northern part of Ghana, and by 1820 it had brought the coastal Fante empire, with its access to the European trade, under its control.

The Portuguese first explored the area, on Africa's west coast, in 1471, naming it the Gold Coast because of its gold deposits and its reserves of "black gold"—slaves. In the 16th and 17th centuries, the British, Danes, and Dutch established slave trading posts there, which is where most American slaves came from. The slave trade ended in the 1850s, and the British gained control of the Gold Coast, making it a protectorate in 1871 and a colony in 1886.

Great Britain gave the colony a new constitution in 1946 under which Africans held a majority of seats in the legislature. Kwame Nkrumah became prime minister of the colony in 1952 and the first prime minister of the nation when it became independent in 1960.

At independence, Ghana boasted Africa's largest man-made deep-water port and the most productive gold mine in the world, and it was the second largest producer of industrial diamonds. Nkrumah began to court Communist bloc nations and exert absolute authority. In January 1964 all opposition parties were outlawed. A military council seized power in February 1966 and ousted Nkrumah.

Civilian governments ran the country briefly, but in 1981, Flt. Lt. Jerry Rawlings took power in a coup and has ruled ever since. Ghana suffered severe economic problems throughout the 1970s and 1980s, and many of Ghana's people left for Nigeria to find work. In 1983 Nigeria returned more than one million of these migrant workers, increasing Ghana's economic woes.

After five years of stagnation, Ghana achieved a 6 percent economic growth rate in 1989 under a World Bank restructuring program. But political unrest remained. A new constitution was approved in an April 1992 referendum, and in November Rawlings received 58 percent of the vote. His National Democratic Congress all but swept the legislative elections due to an opposition boycott. Tribal and ethnic rivalries remain a problem, however. In 1994 the northern regions of the country were proclaimed to be in a state of emergency, as struggles between the Konkomba and Manumba peoples left over 100 dead and 150,000 refugees.

▶ **GREAT BRITAIN (see United Kingdom)**

▶ **GREECE**
Hellenic Republic
● **GEOGRAPHY Location:** southeastern Europe. **Boundaries**: Albania, Macedonia, Bulgaria to N, Turkey to NE, Aegean Sea to E, Mediterranean Sea to S, Ionian Sea to W, Albania to NW; numerous islands surround mainland. **Total area:** 50,942 sq. mi. (131,940 sq km). **Coastline:** 8,500 mi. (13,676 km). **Comparative area:** slightly smaller than Alabama. **Land use:** 19% arable land; 8% permanent crops; 41% meadows and pastures; 20% forest and woodland; 12% other; includes 7% irrigated. **Major cities**: (1991 census) Athinai (Athens, capital) 772,072; Thessaloniki 383,967; Piraeus 196,389; Patras 153,344; Iraklion 116,178.
● **PEOPLE Population:** 10,707,135 (1999 est.). **Nationality:** noun—Greek(s); adjective—Greek. **Ethnic groups:** 98% Greek, 2% other (note: Greek government states there are no ethnic divisions in Greece). **Languages:** Greek (official); English and French widely understood. **Religions:** 98% Greek Orthodox, 1.3% Muslim, 0.7% other.
● **GOVERNMENT Type:** parliamentary republic; monarchy rejected by referendum Dec. 8, 1974. **Constitution:** June 11, 1975. **National holiday:** Independence Day, Mar. 25. **Heads of Government:** Constantinos Stephanopoulos, president (since Mar. 1995); Costas Simitis, prime minister (since Jan. 1996). **Structure:** executive—president elected by unicameral legislature; judiciary.
● **ECONOMY Monetary unit:** drachma. **Budget:** (1998 est.) *income:* $45 bil.; *expend.:* $47.6 bil. **GDP:** $143 bil., $13,400 per capita (1998 est.). **Chief crops:** wheat, corn, barley, sugar beets, olives; meat, dairy products. **Natural resources:** bauxite, lignite, magnesite, crude oil, marble. **Major industries:** tourism, food and tobacco processing, textiles, chemicals. **Labor force:** 4.28 mil. (1998); 59.2% services, 19% agriculture, 21% industry; 10% unemployment (1998 est.). **Exports:** $12.4 bil. (f.o.b., 1998); manufactured goods, foodstuffs, fuels. **Imports:** $27.7 bil. (c.i.f., 1998); manufactured goods, foodstuffs, fuels. **Major trading partners:** *exports:* 56% EU, 16% US; *imports:* 61% EU, 11% US.

The Bronze Age and Iron Age cultures of Greece evolved to create the most glorious civilization of the ancient world. During their high point, from the fifth to the third century b.c., the city-states of Greece led the world in art, philosophy, political culture, and science. Greece vied with the Persian Empire for control of Asia Minor and competed with the Phoenicians in maritime commerce in the Mediterranean. Alexander the Great, king of

Macedonia, spread Greek civilization widely by conquering much of the Middle East and western Asia, but his empire did not long outlast his death in 323 b.c.

Greece was absorbed into the Roman Empire during the second and first centuries b.c. In the fourth century a.d., with the division of the Roman Empire, Greece became part of the Byzantine (Eastern Roman) Empire. Seven years after the Ottoman Turks captured Constantinople in 1453, they overran Greece and ruled it as part of the Ottoman Empire for 350 years.

Under Ottoman rule, much of the administration of Greece was left in local hands, keeping alive a sense of Greek nationhood and a tradition of Greek leadership, particularly through the clergy of the Greek Orthodox church. Inspired by the French Revolution, a romanticized ideal of the classical past, and the tradition of Greek orthodoxy, in 1821 Greece rebelled against Turkish rule. With the support of England, France, and Russia, Greek independence was won in 1827, although the country included only about half of its present territory.

The Western powers sponsored a monarchical government in Greece, ruled by a German prince. Deposed in a revolt, he was succeeded by King George I, a Danish prince who ruled from 1863 until his assassination in 1913. In the three Balkan Wars of 1912, 1913, and 1914, Greece expanded its borders to reach approximately its present size.

In 1923 a Greek Republic was established, but in 1935 King George II returned to his throne, placing government control in the hands of the patriotic but authoritarian Gen. Ioannis Metaxas. In 1940 Metaxas resisted Italy's attempt to conquer Greece, defeating Mussolini's armies so badly that Hitler sent crack troops to his ally's assistance. The German occupation of Greece was complete by June 1941. The Germans pillaged the country and massacred Jews; their Bulgarian allies colonized Macedonia.

During World War II, resistance grew among both Communist and anti-Communist groups. With the German withdrawal in October 1944, resistance groups battled each other; this led to full-scale civil war by 1946. British, and then American assistance (under the Truman Doctrine), enabled the Greek government to defeat the Communist forces when Stalin refused to intervene. King George II died in 1947, succeeded by his brother, King Paul I. Political instability—16 governments during 1946-52—prevailed until, under American pressure, the Greeks adopted a new constitution designed to ensure stable government.

Until the postwar period, Greece's economy had been dominated by agriculture and livestock raising. Industry was limited largely to textiles and food processing; shipping was the major service industry. Under policies instituted in 1952 by the government of Marshall Alexandros Papagos, the industrial sector led a period of vigorous economic growth lasting into the 1960s. A market-oriented economy, tariff protection for Greek industry, tight internal security, and close ties with the West formed the mainstays of Greek policy.

Greece joined NATO in 1951, as did Turkey. Conflict over Cyprus divided the two nominal allies, however. The failure of the government of Constantine Karamanlis to resolve the Cyprus situation eroded his popularity, and he was replaced in 1964 by George Papandreou, who governed at the head of a left-center coalition. King Constantine, who succeeded his father in 1963, forced Pa-

pandreou to resign in 1964, after he and members of his government were accused of various improprieties. A military coup, led by Col. George Papadopoulos, toppled the government in 1967. A countercoup by King Constantine failed, and the king fled the country.

A military dictatorship ruled from 1967 to 1974. Its failed attempt to intervene in Cyprus in 1974 provoked a Turkish invasion of the island and led to the military regime's collapse. Karamanlis headed the government once again; his party won a large majority in parliamentary elections in November, and a republic was formally established with the promulgation of a new constitution in 1975. Karamanlis's New Democracy party received a renewed but smaller majority in parliamentary elections in 1977.

Greece, an associate member of the EC since 1961, became a full member in 1981. Full military membership in NATO was restored in 1980. In 1981 the Panhellenic Socialist Movement under Andreas Papandreou won a parliamentary majority, renewed in 1984. The left-wing Papandreou government was outspokenly anti-NATO, anti-EC, and anti-American, but its policy was more moderate than its rhetoric, extending even to modest cooperation with Turkey in the Aegean. The Papandreou government was shaken by several pro-Palestinian terrorist incidents in Greece, and by a scandal involving the married Papandreou's relationship with a younger woman.

During 1989-90 Greece struggled through three parliamentary elections in less than a year. In the first two, no major party won a clear victory, leading to weak, short-lived coalition governments. The third, in the spring of 1990, resulted in a slim majority for the New Democracy party (headed by Prime Minister Constantine Mitsotakis) and the apparent decline of Papandreou's stature as a national leader.

But Papandreou strengthened his grip on power in October 1993, leading his PASOK party to a landslide (47%) victory over the New Democrats (39%), as Greek voters expressed their displeasure with Mitsotakis's deficit-cutting "austerity" policies. Papandreou returned to office promising salary and pension increases and a halt to privatization. But serious illness forced him to resign in January 1996. His successor, Costas Simitas, promised to speed up the stalled privatization program, and his new cabinet removed most Papandreou loyalists. Elections later that year gave PASOK a smaller majority.

Greece's economy failed to meet the EU's criteria for participating in the European Monetary Union in 1998, but the door was kept open for 2002. New tensions with Turkey over Cyprus, however, threatened to erupt into serious conflict during mid-year. Domestic discontent at what appeared to be Greek assistance in the Turks's capture of Kurdish rebel leader Ocalan in Nairobi led to a shakeup in the Simitis cabinet in February 1999 but in March, government investigators were recommending trials for 18 Greek officials accused of assisting Ocalan's flight from the Turks.

▶ GRENADA

● **GEOGRAPHY   Location:** southeastern Caribbean Sea, about 100 mi. (160 km) N of Trinidad. St. George's 12°03'N, 61°45'W. **Boundaries:** Atlantic Ocean to NE, E, and SE.; Caribbean Sea to SW, W, and NW. **Total area:** 131 sq. mi. (340 sq km). **Coastline:** 75 mi. (121 km). **Comparative area:** twice size of Washington, D.C. **Land use:** 15% arable land;

18% permanent crops; 3% meadows and pastures; 9% forest and woodland; 55% other. **Major cities:** (1991 census) St. George's (capital) 4,439. • **PEOPLE   Population:** 97,008 (1999 est.). **Nationality:** noun—Grenadian(s); adjective—Grenadian. **Ethnic groups:** mainly of black African descent. **Languages:** English (official), some French patois. **Religions:** 53% Roman Catholic, 13.8% Anglican, 33.2% other Protestant sects. • **GOVERNMENT   Type:** parliamentary democracy. **Independence:** Feb. 7, 1974 (from UK). **Constitution:** Dec. 19, 1973. **National holiday:** Independence Day, Feb. 7. **Heads of Government:** Sir Daniel C. Williams, governor-general (since Aug. 1996); Dr. Keith C. Mitchell, prime minister (since Jan. 1999). **Structure:** executive (cabinet led by prime minister); bicameral legislature; judiciary (West Indies Associate States Supreme Court). • **ECONOMY   Monetary unit:** East Caribbean (EC) dollar. **Budget:** (1997 est.) *income:* $85.8 mil.; *expend.:* $102.1 mil. **GDP:** $340 mil., $3,500 per capita (1998 est.). **Chief crops:** bananas, cocoa, nutmeg, mace. **Natural resources:** timber, tropical fruit, deep-water harbors. **Major industries:** food and beverages, textiles, light assembly operations. **Labor force:** 36,000 (1985); 31% services, 24% agriculture, 8% construction, 5% manufacturing, 32% other. **Exports:** $22 mil. (1997 est.); bananas, cocoa beans, nutmeg. **Imports:** $166.5 mil. (1997 est.); 25% food, 22% manufactured goods, 20% machinery, 10% chemicals, 6% fuel (1989). **Major trading partners:** U.S., UK, Caricom countries.

Dominated in the early 1600s by the warlike Carib Indians, Grenada alternated between French and British possession between 1650 and 1783, when British rule was established.

Independence came in 1974. The leftist New Jewel Movement seized power in a 1979 coup, but its leader, Maurice Bishop, was assassinated during a military coup in 1983. Shortly thereafter, the United States invaded and returned power to the governor-general until 1984. Prime Minister Nicholas Braithwaite of the National Democratic Congress party presided over a coalition government from 1990-95, when he was succeeded by George Brizan. In June 1995 the opposition New National party gained an absolute majority in Parliament and designated its leader, Keith Mitchell, as Prime Minister. It won all 18 seats in 1999.

▶ **GUATEMALA**
Republic of Guatemala
• **GEOGRAPHY   Location:** northern part of Central American isthmus. **Boundaries:** Mexico to N and W, Honduras and Belize to E, El Salvador to S. **Total area:** 42,042 sq. mi. (108,890 sq km). **Coastline:** 248 mi. (400 km). **Comparative area:** slightly smaller than Tennessee. **Land use:** 12% arable land; 5% permanent crops; 24% meadows and pastures; 54% forest and woodland; 5% other; includes 1% irrigated. **Major cities:** (1994 est.) Guatemala City (capital) 1,150,452; Quezaltenango 100,983; Escuintla 67,958; Mazatenango 42,328; Puerto Barrios 39,267. • **PEOPLE   Population:** 12,335,580 (1999 est.). **Nationality:** noun—Guatemalan(s); adjective—Guatemalan. **Ethnic groups:** 56% Ladino (mixed Spanish and Amerindian), 44% Amerindian. **Languages:** 60% Spanish, 40% Amerindian languages (23 Amerindian dialects, including Quiche, Cakchiquel, Kekchi). **Religions:** predominantly Roman Catholic, some Protestant and traditional Mayan.

• **GOVERNMENT   Type:** republic. **Independence:** Sept. 15, 1821 (from Spain). **Constitution:** May 31, 1985, effective Jan. 1986. **National holiday:** Independence Day, Sept. 15. **Head of Government:** Álvaro Arzú Irigoyen, president (since Jan. 1996). **Structure:** executive; unicameral legislature (80 seats, elected by popular vote to four-year terms); judiciary. • **ECONOMY   Monetary unit:** quetzal. **Budget:** N.A. **GDP:** $45.7 bil., $3,800 per capita (1998 est.). **Chief crops:** sugarcane, corn, bananas; cattle, sheep, pigs. **Natural resources:** crude oil, nickel, rare woods, fish, chicle. **Major industries:** sugar, textiles and clothing, furniture. **Labor force:** 3.32 mil. (1997 est.); 58% agriculture, 14% manufacturing, 14% services, 7% commerce; 5.2% unemployment (1997 est.). **Exports:** $2.9 bil. (f.o.b., 1997 est.); coffee, sugar, bananas. **Imports:** $3.3 bil. (c.i.f., 1997 est.); fuel and petroleum products, machinery, grain, fertilizers, motor vehicles. **Major trading partners:** *exports:* 37% U.S., 13% El Salvador, 7% Honduras; *imports:* 44% U.S., 10% Mexico, 4.6% Venezuela.

Modern Guatemala was the heart of the Maya civilization that began early in the Christian era and flourished from the fourth to the 10th centuries. From the 11th century on there were two major powers, the Cakchiquel and the Quiché. They were overthrown by the Spanish who invaded from the north in 1524.

The captaincy general of Guatemala was the seat of Spanish military authority in Central America until the 19th century. After an earthquake destroyed Antiqua in 1773, the capital was moved to Guatemala City. Guatemala was the center of the United Provinces of Central America after independence was gained from Spain (1821) and Mexico (1823). The United Provinces collapsed after an uprising by Rafael Carrera, and Guatemala became a separate country in 1838.

The Liberal party held power from 1851 to 1944. There was considerable economic development under the repressive regimes of Manuel Estrada Cabrera (1898-1920) and Jorge Ubico (1931-44). Juan José Arévalo was elected president in 1945. He was succeeded, with strong Communist support, by Jacobo Arbenz, who was deposed in 1954 by a U.S.-backed coup led by Col. Carlos Castillo Armas. The military has ruled either directly or indirectly since then, although democratic rule resumed officially in 1986.

A civil war involving the army, right-wing death squads, and the antigovernment guerrilla group known as the Guatemalan National Revolutionary Union (URNG) began in 1960 and intensified through the 1980s, resulting in the deaths of more than 100,000 civilians.

In surprising developments in May 1993, Pres. Jorge Serrano Elias, backed by the military, suspended the constitution in an effort to crack down on labor and student strikes. Eight days later, in the face of overwhelming popular discontent—including the business community—and international protest, the military replaced Serrano with Atty. Gen. for Human Rights Ramiro de Leon Carpio. In March 1994, the URNG and the government reached an agreement to end the 30-year-old civil war, but talks stalled for a year until the two sides could agree on a pact amending the constitution to defend Indian rights. Meanwhile, the United States cut off military aid to Guatemala for its failure to prosecute security officers for crimes committed during the civil war.

In January 1996, URNG called a cease-fire during elections, in which Álvaro Arzú Irigoyen won a narrow but clear victory over a candidate considered a puppet of the military. The new government immediately purged the military of its most corrupt members, and made plans to privatize all aspects of the economy. The 36-year civil war seemed to end when the last 200 rebels turned in their arms in May 1997.

The April 1998 slaying of a Catholic bishop, a human rights advocate who had authored a report blaming 80 percent of the killings and kidnappings upon the military and right-wing paramilitary forces, remained unsolved a year later, as the lead prosecutor and two successive judges resigned in an atmosphere of threats. In Feb. 1999, an independent report, more comprehensive than Bishop Gerardi's, accused the army and paramilitaries of over 90 percent of the civil war abuses.

▶ GUINEA
Republic of Guinea

• **GEOGRAPHY** **Location:** western Africa. **Boundaries:** Guinea-Bissau to NW, Senegal to N, Mali to NE, Ivory Coast to SE, Liberia, Sierra Leone to S, Atlantic Ocean to W. **Total area:** 94,927 sq. mi. (245,860 sq km). **Coastline:** 199 mi. (320 km). **Comparative area:** slightly smaller than Oregon. **Land use:** 2% arable land; 22% meadows and pastures; 59% forest and woodland; 17% other; includes negl. % irrigated. **Major cities:** (1983 est.) Conakry (capital) 656,000.

• **PEOPLE** **Population:** 7,538,953 (1999 est.). **Nationality:** noun—Guinean(s); adjective—Guinean. **Ethnic groups:** 40% Peuhl, 30% Malinke, 20% Soussou, 10% smaller tribes. **Languages:** French (official), tribal languages. **Religions:** 85% Muslim, 8% Christian, 7% indigenous beliefs.

• **GOVERNMENT** **Type:** republic. **Independence:** Oct. 2, 1958 (from France). **Constitution:** Dec. 23, 1990. **National holiday:** Anniversary of the Second Republic, Apr. 3. **Head of Government:** Lamine Sidimé, prime minister (since Mar. 1999). **Structure:** executive; unicameral legislature; judiciary.

• **ECONOMY** **Monetary unit:** Guinean franc. **Budget:** (1995 est.) *income:* $553 mil.; *expend.:* $652 mil. **GDP:** $8.8 bil., $1,180 per capita (1998 est.). **Chief crops:** rice, coffee, pineapples; cattle, sheep, goats; timber. **Natural resources:** bauxite, iron ore, diamonds, gold, uranium. **Major industries:** bauxite mining, alumina, diamond mining. **Labor force:** 2.4 mil. (1983); 80% agriculture, 11% industry and commerce. **Exports:** $695 mil. (f.o.b., 1998 est.); bauxite (the world's second largest producer), alumina, diamonds, coffee, fish. **Imports:** $560 mil. (f.o.b., 1998 est.); petroleum products, metals, machinery and transport equipment, foodstuffs, textiles. **Major trading partners:** *exports:* Russia, US, Belgium, Ukraine; *imports:* France, Ivory Coast, US, Belgium.

Guinea was formed out of the remains of a series of empires that flourished in West Africa between the 10th and 15th centuries. Situated to the southwest of the Sahara desert on the west coast of Africa, Guinea was a crossroads of West African trade long before Europeans arrived.

French merchants began trading in what is now Guinea in the early 17th century. France began acquiring land in the area in the mid19th century, and in 1845 the territories were organized as a separate colony. The colony received the name French Guinea in 1893.

Most high political posts were held by Europeans until after World War II. In 1946 French

Guinea became a territory in the federation of French West Africa. In September 1958 Guinea became the only French colony to reject membership in the Fifth French Republic, resulting in the severance of political ties with France. The territorial assembly proclaimed Guinean independence on Oct. 2, 1958, and a new government headed by Sékou Touré was formed on the same day.

Touré was adamant in his rejection of French colonialism, severing ties with France (1960-63) and soliciting economic and other assistance from the USSR, China, and the United States. Touré remained in power until his death in April 1984. Within a week, a military government headed by Gen. Lansana Conti took power and by 1987 had improved relations with France while introducing market mechanisms into the command economy. Conti was elected president in 1993 and in June 1995, in Guinea's first-ever multiparty election, his Unity Progress party took 71 of the 114 legislative seats. He was succeeded by Sidia Toure a year later.

▶ GUINEA-BISSAU
Republic of Guinea-Bissau

• **GEOGRAPHY** **Location:** northwestern coast of Africa. **Boundaries:** Senegal to N, Guinea to E and S, Atlantic Ocean to W. **Total area:** 13,946 sq. mi. (36,120 sq km). **Coastline:** 217 mi. (350 km). **Comparative area:** slightly less than three times the size of Connecticut. **Land use:** 11% arable land; 1% permanent crops; 38% meadows and pastures; 38% forest and woodland; 12% other. **Major cities:** (1979 census) Bissau (capital) 109,214; Bafatá 13,429; Gabú 7,803; Mansoa 5,390; Catió 5,170.

• **PEOPLE** **Population:** 1,234,555 (1999 est.). **Nationality:** noun—Guinean(s); adjective— Guinean. **Ethnic groups:** about 99% African (30% Balanta, 20% Fula, 14% Manjaca, 13% Mandinga, 7% Papel); less than 1% European and mulatto. **Languages:** Portuguese (official), Criolo, numerous African languages. **Religions:** 50% indigenous beliefs, 45% Muslim, 5% Christian.

• **GOVERNMENT** **Type:** republic; multi-party since mid-1991. **Independence:** Sept. 24, 1973 (unilaterally declared by Guinea-Bissau); Sept. 10, 1974 (recognized by Portugal). **Constitution:** May 16, 1984, amended May 4, 1991, Dec. 4, 1991, Feb. 26, 1993, June 9, 1993, and 1996. **National holiday:** Independence Day, Sept. 24. **Heads of Government:** Gen. João Bernardo Vieira, president (since Nov. 1980); Francisco José Fadul, prime minister (since Feb. 1999). **Structure:** executive; unicameral legislature; no judiciary (Ministry of Justice).

• **ECONOMY** **Monetary unit:** Communauté Financière Africaine (CFA) franc. **Budget:** N.A. **GDP:** $1.2 bil., $1,000 per capita (1998 est.). **Chief crops:** rice, corn, beans; fishing, forestry. **Natural resources:** fish, timber, phosphates, bauxite, unexploited deposits of petroleum. **Major industries:** agricultural processing, beer, soft drinks. **Labor force:** 480,000. **Exports:** $25.8 mil. (f.o.b., 1996); 95% cashews, fish, peanuts. **Imports:** $63 mil. (f.o.b., 1996); foodstuffs, transport equipment, petroleum products. **Major trading partners:** *exports:* 35% Spain, 30% India, 10% Thailand; *imports:* 29.2% Portugal, 8.4% Thailand, 8.4% Netherlands.

The Portuguese began exploring and trading in what is now Guinea-Bissau in the 15th century and in 1630 began to exert administrative control over the territory. The area became the center of the Portuguese slave trade. When the slave trade declined in the 19th century, the coastal port of

Bissau became a major commercial center. Later in the 19th century, the Portuguese began to conquer the interior of the territory and in 1879 consolidated the region into a territory called Portuguese Guinea, which in 1952 became an overseas province of Portugal.

A nationalist movement began in 1956 under the leadership of Amilcar Cabral and the African Party for the Independence of Guinea and Cape Verde (PAIGC). Armed insurrection broke out in 1961. By 1972 the PAIGC exerted influence over much of the country. Civilian rule was established in the territory that it controlled, and elections were held for a national assembly. Cabral was assassinated in 1973, but soon after the PAIGC National Assembly declared the independence of Guinea-Bissau from Portugal. Portugal acknowledged the country's new status on Sept. 24, 1973.

The civilian government was overthrown by a military coup in 1980, and the country was run by a Revolutionary Council headed by Brig. Gen. João Bernardo Vieira until a new constitution was adopted in May 1984. Under the new constitution, a new national assembly was selected, and Vieira was elected president in 1984 and 1989. In 1991 the government legalized opposition parties, but presidential elections have been postponed.

In June 1998 a former army chief of staff, Ansumane Mane, launched a coup attempt against Vieira who was supported by loyalist troops and the Senegalese army. Hundreds of thousands fled the capital and the surrounding areas as the Senegalese shelled the city. By May 1999, General Mane had driven President-General Vieira to seek asylum with the Portuguese and had installed the leader of the National Popular Assembly, Malan Sanha, as interim president until Nov. elections.

▶ GUYANA
Co-operative Republic of Guyana
● **Geography Location:** northeastern South America. **Boundaries:** North Atlantic Ocean to N, Suriname to E, Brazil to S, Venezuela to W. **Total area:** 83,000 sq. mi. (214,970 sq km). **Coastline:** 285 mi. (459 km). **Comparative area:** slightly smaller than Idaho. **Land use:** 2% arable land; 6% meadows and pastures; 84% forest and woodland; 8% other; includes 1% irrigated. **Major cities:** (1976 est.) Georgetown (capital) 72,049.
● **People Population:** 705,156 (1999 est.). **Nationality:** noun—Guyanese (sing., pl.); adjective —Guyanese. **Ethnic groups:** 49% East Indian, 32% black, 12% mixed, 6% Amerindian, 1% European and Chinese. **Languages:** English, Amerindian dialects. **Religions:** 57% Christian, 33% Hindu, 9% Muslim, 1% other.
● **Government Type:** republic. **Independence:** May 26, 1966 (from UK). **Constitution:** Oct. 6, 1980. **National holiday:** Republic Day, Feb. 23. **Heads of Government:** Bharrat Jagdeo, executive president (since Aug. 1999); Samuel Hinds, prime minister (since Feb. 1998). **Structure:** executive—president, who appoints and heads cabinet; unicameral legislature; judiciary.
● **Economy Monetary unit:** Guyanese dollar. **Budget:** (1997 est.) *income:* $253.7 mil.; *expend.:* $304.1 mil. **GDP:** $1.8 bil., $2,500 per capita (1998 est.). **Chief crops:** sugarcane, rice, wheat; beef, pork, poultry. **Natural resources:** bauxite, gold, diamonds, hardwood timber, shrimp, fish. **Major industries:** bauxite mining, sugar, rice milling. **Labor force:** 245,492 (1992). **Exports:** $593.4 mil. (1997 est.); sugar, gold, bauxite/alumina, rice, shrimp, molasses. **Imports:** $641.6 mil. (1997 est.); manufactures, machinery, food, petroleum.

Major trading partners: (1994 est.); *exports:* 25.9% Canada, 20.4% US, 22.7% UK; *imports:* 27.6% US, 17.7% Trinidad and Tobago, 12.1% Netherlands Antilles.

Although the region was visited by Europeans in the 15th century, Guyana was only colonized in the early 1600s by the Dutch. Rule in the area was contested by the French and the British, and it became the colony of British Guiana in 1831. After slavery was abolished, indentured servants from the East Indies were brought to work the land, and their descendants are in the majority today.

The People's National Congress was in power from 1964 to 1992, and socialist policies dominated the political landscape. Most of the country's large companies were nationalized, so despite its having the purest bauxite in the world, some gold, and conditions favorable to agriculture, it remains poor, dependent on foreign aid and remittances from overseas workers for much of its revenue.

In 1992 Cheddi Jagan of the People's Progressive party won the presidency, but attempts to privatize the sugar and bauxite industries have failed. In March 1997 Jagan died and Samuel Hinds, the prime minister became president while Jagan's widow took over as prime minister. In the presidential elections in Dec. 1997, Mrs. Jagan won election in her own right, with 56 percent of the vote, but her appointment of Hinds to be Prime Minister did nothing to stop the rioting and demonstrations by followers of the opposition People's National Congress. The PNC represents, principally, black, while the PPP does the same for East Indians. In Aug. 1999, Jagan resigned for health reasons and was succeeded by Bharrat Jagdeo, a 35-year-old Moscow-educated economist.

▶ HAITI
Republic of Haiti
● **Geography Location:** western part of Hispaniola in northern Caribbean Sea. Port-au-Prince 18°33'N, 72°20'W. **Boundaries:** North Atlantic Ocean to N, Dominican Republic to E, Caribbean Sea to S, Windward Passage to W. **Total area:** 10,714 sq. mi. (27,750 sq km). **Coastline:** 1,100 mi. (1,771 km). **Comparative area:** slightly smaller than Maryland. **Land use:** 20% arable land; 13% permanent crops; 18% meadows and pastures; 5% forest and woodland; 44% other; includes 3% irrigated. **Major cities:** (1984 est.) Port-au-Prince (capital) 738,342.
● **People Population:** 6,884,264 (1999 est.). **Nationality:** noun—Haitian(s); adjective—Haitian. **Ethnic groups:** 95% black, 5% mulatto and European. **Languages:** French (official, but spoken by only 20% of population); all speak Creole. **Religions:** 80% Roman Catholic—of which majority also practice voodoo (called vodun), 16% Protestant.
● **Government Type:** republic. **Independence:** Jan. 1, 1804 (from France). **Constitution:** Mar. 1987, suspended June 1988; return to constitutional rule Oct. 1994. **National Holiday:** Independence Day, Jan. 1. **Heads of Government:** René Préval, president (since Feb. 1996); Jacques Edouard Alexis, prime minister (since Mar. 1999). **Structure:** executive; bicameral legislature; judiciary.
● **Economy Monetary unit:** gourde. **Budget:** (FY 97/98) *income:* $323 mil.; *expend.:* $363 mil. **GDP:** $8.9 bil., $1,300 per capita (1998 est.). **Chief crops:** coffee, mangoes, sugarcane, rice, corn, sorghum. **Natural resources:** none. **Major industries:** sugar

refining, textiles, flour milling. **Labor force:** 3.6 mil. (1995); 66% agriculture, 25% services, 9% industry; shortage of skilled labor, unskilled labor abundant; 60% unemployment (1996 est.). **Exports:** $110 mil. (f.o.b., 1997 est.); 80.5% light manufactures, 7.6% coffee, 7.2% other agriculture. **Imports:** $486 mil. (f.o.b., 1997 est.); 50% machines and manufactures, 39% food and beverages, 2% petroleum products. **Major trading partners:** *exports:* 76% U.S., 19% EU; *imports:* 60% U.S., 12% EU.

The Arawak island of Haiti was discovered by Christopher Columbus, who renamed it Hispaniola, in 1492. In the next century the Arawaks were worked to death, murdered, or killed by disease. The western third of the island was harassed by French pirates and was ceded to France in 1697. With a diverse slave-based agricultural economy, the colony accounted for two-thirds of French overseas investment.

A slave revolt in 1791 led to abolition in 1794, and the island came under French rule the same year. Toussaint Louverture, an ex-slave, became governor-general in 1801, but he was deposed by the French. In 1803 a black army under Jean-Jacques Dessalines (Emperor Jacques I, 1804-6) and Henry Christophe (Henry I, 1806-20) defeated the French in 1803. Independence was declared in 1804. Under Jean-Pierre Boyer (1820-43), Haiti occupied Santo Domingo (which had been restored to Spain in 1808) from 1822 to 1844.

The next century was marked by political instability and an increased U.S. business and military presence in Haitian affairs. From 1905 to 1947, the United States had direct or indirect control of Haitian finances, and from 1915 to 1934 the country was under U.S. military occupation.

François "Papa Doc" Duvalier took power in 1957 and ruled Haiti with a stern hand. In 1971, he transferred power to his son, Jean-Claude (aka "Baby Doc"), whose regime was just as authoritarian. During this period, most of Haiti's wealthy and educated population fled the country, leaving it the poorest and most illiterate nation in the Western Hemisphere.

In 1986, the military ousted Baby Doc, and imposed a succession of short-lived but brutal and incompetent governments. In 1989, Supreme Court Justice Ertha-Pascal Troillot was named interim president, and in 1990, Haiti held its first democratic national elections ever. The winner of those elections was the Rev. Jean-Bertrand Aristide, a 37-year-old Roman Catholic priest. But seven months into his five-year term, Aristide was overthrown in yet another military coup. Aristide fled to the U.S., which refused to recognize the junta and suspended $650 million worth of aid to Haiti. But succesive trade embargoes by the United States, Canada, and most of Western Europe only served to increase hardship among the poorest segments of the population. As the United States stepped up its demands, the junta leaders, propped up by Haiti's wealthy elite and by money from drug trafficking, began a campaign of violence against Aristide supporters, killing more than 3,000 of them.

After many months of threats, the U.S. finally invaded on Oct. 15, 1994, forcing the junta's resignation and reinstating Aristide as president. To gain control of the army, Aristide retired 43 senior officers then disbanded the army altogether, replacing it with a civilian police force. In mid-1995, 28 parties took part in legislative elections and Aristide's three-party coalition, Lavalas Political

Organization, won overwhelming victories; in December, the Lavalas candidate, René Préval, took 88 percent in Haiti's first peaceful presidential election since independence.

By 1997 Lavalas and Pres. Préval had split. From June of that year, Haiti was without a government until Jan. 1999 when Préval announced he would rule by decree, appointed his own prime minister and commenced replacing town mayors with his own nominees. In the summer of 1999 the U.S. announced it was withdrawing its troops.

▶ HOLY SEE
The Holy See (State of the Vatican City)

● **GEOGRAPHY   Location:** entirely within city of Rome, Italy; outside Vatican City, 13 buildings in Rome and Castel Gandolfo (the pope's summer residence) enjoy extraterritorial rights. **Total area:** 0.17 sq. mi. (0.44 sq km). **Coastline:** none. **Comparative area:** about seven-tenths size of the Mall in Washington, D.C. **Land use:** 0% arable land; 0% permanent crops; 0% meadows and pastures; 0% forest and woodland; 100% other. **Major cities:** Vatican City (capital).

● **PEOPLE   Population:** 870 (1999 est.). **Nationality:** N.A. **Ethnic groups:** Italians, Swiss, other. **Languages:** Italian, Latin, various other languages. **Religion:** Roman Catholic.

● **GOVERNMENT   Type:** monarchical-sacerdotal state. **Independence:** Feb. 11, 1929 (from Italy). **Constitution:** Apostolic Constitution of 1967 (effective Mar. 1, 1968). **National holiday:** Installation Day of Pope John Paul II, Oct. 22. **Heads of Government:** John Paul II, supreme pontiff (Karol Wojtylla, elected pope Oct. 16, 1978); Archbishop Angelo Sodano, Pro-Secretary of State of the Holy See. **Structure:** pope possesses full executive, legislative, and judicial powers; he delegates these powers to president of Pontifical Commission, who is subject to pontifical appointment and recall; Secretariat of State and Council of Public Affairs (which handles Vatican diplomacy) and Prefecture of Economic Affairs; College of Cardinals acts as chief papal adviser.

● **ECONOMY   Monetary unit:** Vatican issues its own coinage called Vatican lira, which is interchangeable with Italian lira. **Budget:** (1994 est.) *income:* $175.5 mil.; *expend.:* $175 mil., supported financially by contributions (known as Peter's Pence) from Roman Catholics throughout world; some income derived from sale of Vatican postage stamps and tourist mementos, fees for admission to museums, and sale of publications. **GDP:** N.A. **Chief crops:** N.A. **Natural resources:** N.A. **Major industries:** consists of printing and production of small amount of mosaics and staff uniforms; worldwide banking and financial activities. **Labor force:** N.A.; dignitaries, priests, nuns, guards, and 3,000 lay workers who live outside the Vatican; Vatican City employees are divided into three categories—executives, office workers, and salaried employees. **Exports:** N.A. **Imports:** N.A. **Major trading partners:** N.A.

The Holy See is the smallest sovereign state in the world both in size and in population. It is a remnant of the "Patrimony of St. Peter," the secular state donated to the popes in the eighth century by Pepin the Short, father of Charlemagne. One of the major political powers on the Italian peninsula throughout the Middle Ages and into modern times, the States of the Church were conquered in 1870 by the new kingdom of Italy, which made Rome its capital.

In 1929 Mussolini's government made peace with the papacy in the Lateran Treaty, which recognized the Holy See as an independent state. The treaty was incorporated into the Italian Constitution of 1947. Under the terms of the treaty, the pope is pledged to perpetual neutrality and may intervene in international affairs as a mediator only upon request.

The pope is the sovereign of the Holy See in his capacity as bishop of Rome, and in that capacity, he accepts the credentials of foreign ambassadors assigned to the Holy See. The United States opened diplomatic relations with the Holy See in 1984, following the repeal of an 1867 law forbidding such relations. Pope John Paul II, a native of Poland, has been a source of spiritual leadership especially for Catholics in Eastern Europe. Since the collapse of communism in Eastern Europe, many countries there have renewed diplomatic relations with the Holy See. In a historic breakthrough the Holy See established diplomatic relations with Israel on Dec. 30, 1993.

As sovereign of the Holy See, the pope is an elected absolute monarch who appoints a Pontifical Council to govern the city on his behalf. The council meets only a few times each year. The economy is based on service industries, including printing; its revenues come from museum fees, philatelic sales, and sales of publications.

▶ HONDURAS
Republic of Honduras
• **Geography** **Location:** Central America. **Boundaries:** Caribbean Sea to N, Nicaragua to E, El Salvador, Nicaragua to S, Guatemala, El Salvador to W. **Total area:** 43,278 sq. mi. (112,090 sq km). **Coastline:** 509 mi. (820 km). **Comparative area:** slightly larger than Tennessee. **Land use:** 15% arable land; 3% permanent crops; 14% meadows and pastures; 54% forest and woodland; 14% other; includes 1% irrigated. **Major cities:** (1994 est.) Tegucigalpa (capital) 775,300; San Pedro Sula 368,500; El Progreso 81,200; Danli 43,300; Choluteca 72,800.
• **People** **Population:** 5,997,327 (1999 est.). **Nationality:** noun—Honduran(s); adjective—Honduran. **Ethnic groups:** 90% mestizo, 7% Amerindian, 2% black, 1% white. **Languages:** Spanish, Amerindian dialects. **Religions:** 97% Roman Catholic, small Protestant minority.
• **Government** **Type:** republic. **Independence:** Sept. 15, 1821 (from Spain). **Constitution:** Jan. 11, 1982 (effective Jan. 20, 1982). **National holiday:** Independence Day, Sept. 15. **Head of Government:** Carlos Roberto Flores Facussé, president (since Jan. 1998). **Structure:** executive—elected president; unicameral legislature (128-seat National Congress); elected judicial branch.
• **Economy** **Monetary unit:** lempira. **Budget:** (1997 est.) *income:* $655 mil.; *expend.:* $850 mil. **GDP:** $14.4 bil., $2,400 per capita (1998 est.). **Chief crops:** bananas, coffee, citrus; beef; timber; shrimp. **Natural resources:** timber, gold, silver, copper, lead. **Major industries:** agricultural processing (sugar and coffee), textiles, clothing. **Labor force:** 1.3 mil. (1997); 37% agriculture, 39% services, 24% industry; 30% underemployment (1997). **Exports:** $1.3 bil. (f.o.b., 1996 est.); bananas, coffee, shrimp, lobster. **Imports:** $1.8 bil. (c.i.f., 1996 est.); machinery and transport equipment, chemicals, basic manufactures. **Major trading partners:** *exports:* 54% U.S., 7% Germany, 5% Belgium; *imports:* 43% U.S., 5% Guatemala, 5% Japan.

Early in the Christian era, the Mayan civilization extended south to the pre-Columbian city of Copán in what is now northwestern Honduras. The territory was also home to the Lenca Indians and the indigenous people of the Moskitia area.

A silver strike in the 1570s prompted the first major influx of Spanish. The region was also celebrated for its tropical hardwood forests. Although the British controlled the Caribbean coast in the late 1700s, Honduras was a province of the Spanish captaincy of Guatemala. It became a member of the United Provinces of Central America after independence from Spain and Mexico, and an independent republic after the 1838 collapse of the Central American Federation.

Conservatives dominated Honduran politics until the 1870s, when the Liberals came to power and adopted a new constitution that reduced the influence of the church, among other things. Economic development came especially from a number of U.S. firms whose efforts were regarded as exploitative rather than beneficial; in 1912, U.S. president William Taft sent marines to protect U.S. interests.

Political unrest continued until the presidency of Gen. Tuburcio Carías Andino (1932-49), who was followed by a succession of pro-labor presidents. In 1963, a coup led by Col. Osvaldo López Arellano deposed the civilian president, and the military ruled almost uninterrupted until 1982. In 1969, the expulsion of thousands of Salvadoran peasants who had immigrated during the 1950s and 1960s led to the Soccer War with El Salvador. An armistice was negotiated by the OAS.

During the 1980s, Honduras was threatened by civil wars in El Salvador and Nicaragua. Honduran territory was used by Nicaraguan Contras, for which Honduras received substantial U.S. military and other aid. Demobilization of the Contras alleviated tensions between Left and Right, and in Jan. 1994 the new president, Carlos Roberto Reina Idiaquez, took office with the promise of controlling and reducing the power of the military which was more easily accomplished when the U.S. made severe cuts in military aid. In late 1997 the same Liberal Party easily won reelection, maintaining their control of the National Congress, while their candidate, Carlos Roberto Flores, won election as president.

In Oct. 1999, Honduras was devastated by Hurricane Mitch: 7,000 were dead, 600,000 homeless, and 70 percent of its crops destroyed — losses which were somewhat mitigated by international aid and debt reductions. Significantly, in Jan. 1999, the legislature unanimously voted to place the previously all-but-autonomous military under civilian control, control that the military has thus far given every sign of accepting.

▶ HUNGARY
Republic of Hungary
• **Geography** **Location:** landlocked country in eastern Europe. **Boundaries:** Slovakia to N, Ukraine to NE, Romania to E, Yugoslavia to SE, Croatia to SW, Slovenia to W, Austria to NW. **Total area:** 35,919 sq. mi. (93,030 sq km). **Coastline:** none. **Comparative area:** slightly smaller than Indiana. **Land use:** 51% arable land; 2% permanent crops; 13% meadows and pastures; 19% forest and woodland; 15% other; includes 2% irrigated. **Major cities:** (1994) Budapest (capital) 1,995,696; Debrecen 217,706; Miskole 189,655; Szeged 178,878; Pécs 172,177.
• **People** **Population:** 10,186,372 (1999 est.). **Nationality:** noun—Hungarian(s); adjective—Hun-

garian. **Ethnic groups:** 89.9% Hungarian, 4% Gypsy, 2.6% German, 2% Serb, 0.8% Slovak, 0.7% Romanian. **Languages:** 98.2% Hungarian, 1.8% other. **Religions:** 67.5% Roman Catholic, 20.0% Calvinist, 5.0% Lutheran, 7.5% atheist and other.
• **GOVERNMENT Type:** republic. **Constitution:** Aug. 18, 1949; effective Aug. 20, 1949; last revised Oct. 18, 1989. **National holiday:** St. Stephen's Day, Aug. 20. **Heads of Government:** Dr. Árpád Göncz, president (since May 1990); Viktor Orban, prime minister (since July 1998). **Structure:** executive—president elected by National Assembly; unicameral legislature—National Assembly (elected by direct suffrage); judicial—elected by Parliament.
• **ECONOMY Monetary unit:** forint. **Budget:** (1998) *income:* $11.2 bil.; *expend.:* $13.2 bil. **GDP:** $75.4 bil., $7,400 per capita (1998 est.). **Chief crops:** corn, wheat, sunflower seeds, potatoes, sugar beets; chickens, pigs, cattle. **Natural resources:** bauxite, coal, natural gas, fertile soils. **Major industries:** mining, metallurgy, construction materials. **Labor force:** 4.2 mil. (1997); 65% services; 26.7% industry; 8.3% agriculture; 10.8% unemployment (1997). **Exports:** $20.7 bil. (f.o.b., 1998 est.); 51.9% machinery and equipment, 32.7% other manufactures, 10.5% agriculture and food products. **Imports:** $22.9 bil. (f.o.b., 1998 est.); 46.5% machinery and equipment, 40.2% other manufactures, 6.6% fuels and electricity, 3.7% agricultural and food products, 3.6% raw materials. **Major trading partners:** *exports:* 37.3% Germany, 11.4% Austria, 6.1% Italy; *imports:* 26.7% Germany, 10.5% Austria, 9.5% Italy.

The Magyars, a tribe of Central Asian horsemen, terrorized Europe in the ninth century a.d. and settled in the Hungarian plain where, under their chieftain Arpad, they displaced earlier Germanic and Slavic settlers and organized a kingdom in 896. The Hungarians converted to Christianity late in the 10th century, and King Stephen (later St. Stephen) received a royal crown from Pope Sylvester II in 1001.

After the Battle of Mohacs in 1526, most of Hungary fell under Ottoman rule. The Turks were driven out in a series of battles with the Habsburg Holy Roman emperors at the end of the 17th century. Thereafter Hungary was part of the Habsburg Empire until 1867, when the Dual Monarchy of Austria-Hungary was organized, making Hungary independent of Austria in all but finance, military, and foreign affairs.

During the 18th and 19th centuries, Hungary experienced extensive immigration of Romanians from the east and Slovaks from the north; by 1900 Magyars formed only a bare majority of the population. The pre-World War I economy was largely agricultural. Agriculture-related industry (beet sugar factories, breweries, tanneries, textile mills) developed in the late 19th century, along with some heavy industry.

In the dismemberment of Austria-Hungary following the defeat of the Central Powers in World War I, Hungary surrendered extensive territories to Romania, Yugoslavia, and Czechoslovakia. With the Treaty of Trianon ("Bloody Trianon") in 1920, the country lost 70 percent of its territory and 60 percent of its population; one-third of the Magyar people lived on foreign soil.

Short-lived governments—a republic under Michael Karolyi, and a Bolshevist state under Bela Kun—were replaced in 1920 by a new regime, with Adm. Miklós Horthy serving as regent. The Horthy regime was authoritarian but not fascist; its main objective was the recovery of Hungary's lost territories. Hungary established common cause with Germany in 1938 and 1940, recovering some territory from Czechoslovakia and Romania in the bargain, but at the price of participating in Hitler's war with the Soviet Union. Germany occupied Hungary in 1944 and set up a Hungarian Nazi regime. Late in 1944 the Russian army drove out the Germans and set up their own occupation.

The establishment of a full-scale Soviet-satellite regime was relatively slow. A republic was declared in February 1946, and the non-Communist Zoltan Tildy was elected president. Tildy was forced out in 1947, however, and replaced by the Stalinist dictator, Matias Rakosi. After the death of Stalin in 1953, the moderate Imre Nagy became premier and introduced some economic reforms. Nagy was forced out of office in 1955.

Nikita Khrushchev's denunciation of Stalin in 1956, combined with an atmosphere of rising expectations for further reforms in Hungary, led to a popular uprising in October 1956. Nagy, backed by the army, formed a coalition government on Oct. 23, proclaimed Hungary's neutrality, ended censorship, opened the country's borders, and withdrew from the Warsaw Pact. On Nov. 4, Soviet troops launched a massive invasion that soon crushed the rebellion. The Soviet army installed János Kádár as premier; Nagy was executed. About 200,000 Hungarians fled the country, and many more were imprisoned.

After several years of repressive rule, the Kádár regime announced, in 1963, amnesty for participants in the 1956 rebellion. Stalinists were gradually removed from the government, economic reforms emphasizing profit and productivity were introduced, and trade with the West was expanded. Hungary reluctantly took part in the suppression of Czechoslovakia's "Prague Spring" in 1968. In the same year, it announced the New Economic Mechanism (NEM) policy, ending central economic planning and introducing semifree enterprise under bureaucratic control.

After a brief return to central planning in the 1970s, the NEM was reintroduced in 1979 and expanded in 1982, when Hungary joined the World Bank and the IMF. Private ownership of subsidiaries of state-owned enterprises was permitted. In 1987 a pro-Gorbachev premier, Karoly Grosz, took office and in 1988 became head of the Communist party as well.

In 1989 the boundary with Austria was opened, making Hungary a key escape point for refugees from East Germany and Czechoslovakia. Nagy's reburial was attended by 300,000. By November the Communist party had renounced Marxism and renamed itself, but to no avail.

Free elections were held in 1990, and the Democratic Forum, led by Jozsef Antall, won a plurality and formed a coalition government with the Smallholders and Christian Democratic parties. Having already achieved substantial perestroika-style economic reforms under communism, Hungary was well-placed to make a rapid transition to free enterprise and was seeking admission to the EU. Sluggish production reduced tax revenues, resulting in serious deficits and an austerity budget.

Hungarian voters signaled just how painful they found the transition in the May 1994 parliamentary elections by giving the Communists (now renamed Socialists) an absolute majority in

Parliament. Privatization moved at a snail's pace, though the new government did appoint a committee to arrange the selling off of about 1,000 state-owned enterprises and soon foreign investment increased faster than anywhere in Central Europe. In 1997 Hungary was one of three eastern European nations invited to apply for admission to NATO and it was admitted in 1999.

Elections in May 1998 gave the Socialists only 134 seats (of 386) in Parliament; the new government was formed by Civic Party which won 148 seats of its own, in coalition with the Smallholders and other parties of the right. Hungary now aims for admission to the EU.

▶ICELAND
Republic of Iceland
• **GEOGRAPHY Location:** near Arctic Circle in North Atlantic Ocean. Reykjavík 64°09'N, 21°58'W. **Boundaries:** Greenland about 190 mi. (300 km) to NW, Norway about 620 mi. (1,000 km) to E, UK 500 mi. (800 km) to S. **Total area:** 39,768 sq. mi. (103,000 sq km). **Coastline:** 3,100 mi. (4,988 km). **Comparative area:** slightly smaller than Kentucky. **Land use:** 0% arable land; 0% permanent crops; 23% meadows and pastures; 1% forest and woodland; 76% other. **Major cities:** (1994 est.) Reykjavík (capital) 103,020.
• **PEOPLE Population:** 272,512 (1999 est.). **Nationality:** noun—Icelander(s); adjective—Icelandic. **Ethnic groups:** homogeneous mixture of descendants of Norwegians and Celts. **Languages:** Icelandic (official). **Religions:** 96% Evangelical Lutheran, 3% other Protestant and Roman Catholic, 1% no affiliation.
• **GOVERNMENT Type:** constitutional republic. **Independence:** June 17, 1944 (from Denmark). **Constitution:** June 16, 1944; effective June 17, 1944. **National holiday:** Anniversary of the Establishment of the Republic, June 17. **Heads of Government:** Ólafur Ragnar Grímsson, president (since Aug. 1996); David Oddsson, prime minister (since Apr. 1991). **Structure:** executive power vested in president but exercised by cabinet responsible to Parliament; unicameral legislature; judiciary (Supreme Court justices appointed for life by president).
• **ECONOMY Monetary unit:** Icelandic króna. **Budget:** (1996 est.) *income:* $1.9 bil.; *expend.:* $2.1 bil. **GDP:** $6.06 bil., $22,400 per capita (1998 est.). **Chief crops:** potatoes, turnips; cattle, sheep; fish. **Natural resources:** fish, hydroelectric and geothermal power, diatomite. **Major industries:** fish processing, aluminum smelting, ferrosilicon production. **Labor force:** 130,000 (1998); 12.9% manufacturing; 11.8% fishing and fish processing; 10.7% construction, 5.1% agriculture, 59.5% other services; 3% unemployment (1998). **Exports:** $1.9 bil. (f.o.b. 1998); 70% fish and fish products, animal products, aluminum, ferrosilicon, diatomite. **Imports:** $2.4 bil. (f.o.b., 1998); machinery and equipment, petroleum products, foodstuffs, textiles. **Major trading partners:** *exports:* 60% EU, 14% US; *imports:* 58% EU, 9% US.

The volcanic island of Iceland was settled in the ninth century a.d. by Vikings, who established Europe's oldest body of representative government, the Althing, in 930. Christianity was introduced around 1000. In the 13th century, Iceland acknowledged Norwegian rule. In 1380 Denmark, by then in control of all of Scandinavia, conquered Iceland as well. Iceland gained its independence in 1918 but shared a common king, Christian X, with the Danes. During World War II, first British, and then American, troops garrisoned the island; in 1944, with Denmark occupied by the Nazis, Iceland deposed its king and proclaimed itself a republic.

Iceland became a UN member in 1946 and a member of NATO in 1949. Lacking its own armed forces, it grudgingly tolerated the presence of an American air base at Keflavik. The republic developed a Scandinavian-style welfare state, with comprehensive social benefits that have produced one of the world's healthiest and best-educated peoples.

Less than 1 percent of Iceland's territory is arable; the island imports grain and vegetables but is self-sufficient in meat and dairy products. Fishing is the principal industry, accounting for 75 percent of exports, 20 percent of GDP, and engaging one-seventh of the work force.

Multiparty representation in the Althing has created a trend of government by coalitions or minority cabinets. Politically stable, the republic recently faced economic problems brought on by high taxes, chronic inflation, and a huge national debt. In 1997 and 1998, however, the economy made a strong recovery with GDP growing by 5 percent a year.

Iceland maintains close ties with Scandinavia and actively participates in the Nordic Council, but not the EU, membership in which the government views as harmful to Iceland's all-important fishing industry.

▶INDIA
Republic of India
• **GEOGRAPHY Location:** Asian subcontinent, with Himalayan mountain range to N. **Boundaries:** Pakistan to NW; China, Bhutan, Nepal to N; Myanmar to NE; Bangladesh to E (surrounded by Indian territory except for short frontier with Myanmar); Bay of Bengal to E; Sri Lanka to SE across Palk Strait; Arabian Sea to W. **Total area:** 1,269,340 sq. mi. (3,287,590 sq km). **Coastline:** 4,350 mi. (7,000 km). **Comparative area:** slightly more than one-third the size of U.S. **Land use:** 56% arable land; 1% permanent crops; 4% meadows and pastures; 23% forest and woodland; 16% other; includes 13% irrigated. **Major cities:** (1991 census) New Delhi (capital) 7,174,755; Greater Bombay 9,909,547; Calcutta 4,388,262; Madras 3,795,208; Hyderabad 3,005,496.
• **PEOPLE Population:** 1,000,848,550 (1999 est.). **Nationality:** noun—Indian(s); adjective—Indian. **Ethnic groups:** 72% Indo-Aryan, 25% Dravidian, 3% Mongoloid and other. **Languages:** Hindi, English, and 14 other official languages; 24 languages spoken by a million or more persons each; numerous other languages and dialects; Hindi is national language and primary tongue of 30% of the people; English enjoys associate status but is the most important language for national, political, and commercial communication; Hindustani, a variant of Hindi/Urdu, is spoken throughout northern India. **Religions:** 80% Hindu, 14% Muslim, 2.4% Christian, 2% Sikh.
• **GOVERNMENT Type:** federal republic. **Independence:** Aug. 15, 1947 (from UK). **Constitution:** Jan. 26, 1950. **National holiday:** Anniversary of the Proclamation of the Republic, Jan. 26. **Heads of Government:** K.R. Narayanan, president (since July 1997); A. B. Vajpayee, prime minister (since March 1998). **Structure:** executive; bicameral parliament—Council of States, 250 members, up to 12 appointed by the president, remainder chosen by regionally elected officials; judiciary.

• **Economy** Monetary unit: Indian rupee. **Budget:** (FY 98/99 est.) *income:* $42.12 bil.; *expend.:* $63.79 bil. **GDP:** $1.689 trillion, $1,720 per capita (1998 est.). **Chief crops:** rice, wheat, oilseed, cotton; cattle, water, buffalo, sheep; fish. **Natural resources:** coal (4th largest reserves in world), iron ore, manganese, mica, bauxite. **Major industries:** textiles, chemicals, food processing, steel. **Labor force:** NA; 67% agriculture, 18% services, 15% industry. **Exports:** $32.17 bil. (f.o.b., 1998 est.); clothing, gems and jewelry, engineering goods, chemicals. **Imports:** $41.34 bil. (c.i.f., 1998 est.); petroleum, machinery, gems, fertilizer. **Major trading partners:** *exports:* 19% US, 6% Hong Kong, 6% UK; *imports:* 10% US, 7% Belgium, 7% UK, 7% Germany.

Indian civilization is one of the oldest in the world. Neolithic agricultural communities had appeared in the Indus River valley by 3000 b.c. and cities at Harappa and Mohenjo-Daro were founded around 2500 b.c. Around 1500 b.c. Indo-Europeans (Aryans) from Central Asia imposed their religion and political system on the indigenous population and generated population movements toward southern India.

Indo-European civilization was characterized by caste; everyone was a member of one of four fundamental divisions of society: Brahmins, hereditary priests responsible for higher learning and rituals; Ksatrias, warriors and administrators; Vaisas, merchants; and Sudras, farmers and subjugated peoples. At the bottom were casteless people, known later as untouchables.

By the mid-first millennium b.c., Brahminism had declined into a state of religious formalism. That situation prompted two reformations around 600 b.c., the first of which produced the Jain religion; the second, Buddhism. Jainism remained confined largely to India, while Buddhism eventually influenced most of the cultures of Asia, though it died out in India itself. Buddhism was adopted as a state religion by Asoka, third and greatest emperor of the Mauryan empire (325-184 b.c) under which much of India was united for the first time. Following the collapse of the Mauryan empire, Hinduism evolved out of Buddism, Brahminism, and other local cults and became the dominant religion of India.

South India in the post-Mauryan period was divided into numerous states, the most prominent of which was Chola, a Tamil kingdom in the southeast that had extensive trade connections throughout the Indian Ocean.

The Gupta dynasty (c. a.d. 320-544), based in the Ganges River valley, established its rule over most of northern India and created what is generally regarded as a golden age of north Indian culture, with flourishing cities and significant achievements in art, literature, and science.

In the seventh century, King Sri Harsha created a short-lived feudal empire that united most of the petty states in the upper Ganges valley, while the Chalyuka dynasty dominated southern India. In the early eighth century, the Indus River valley was invaded by Arabs who introduced Islam to the region. The empire of Sri Harsha fell apart, replaced by the petty kingdoms of the Rajputs.

The 11th century saw the ascendency of Islam throughout northern India, which came under the shadow of the empire of Mamud of Ghazni, based in Afghanistan. In 1192 the Ghaznavid general Kutb ud-din Aibak defeated a coalition of Rajput states; in 1206 he founded the Sultanate of Delhi, which in the 13th century held off Mongol invasions in northwestern India and brought all of the subcontinent, except for the southernmost states, under its control. While the rulers of the sultanate were Muslims, most of their subjects remained Hindu.

Internal rebellions combined with the sacking of Delhi by Timur Leng (Tamerlane) in 1398 weakened the Sultanate of Delhi. In 1526 Babur, a descendant of Timur Leng, conquered all of northern India and established the Moghul empire. Under Akbar the Great, the empire flourished; Moghul culture gave rise to new styles of architecture, painting, and music.

In the 17th century, the Moghul emperors were threatened by the Hindu Marathas, whose kingdom on the west-central coast rapidly encompassed most of south India. By the late 18th century, Maratha power had spread to the north, and most of the petty kingdoms of the Moghul empire became part of a Maratha confederacy, owing only nominal allegiance to Delhi. By that time all of India was threatened by the expansion of the European powers.

Vasco da Gama had landed at Calicut in 1498, and in 1510 the Portuguese founded a colony at Goa. Dutch traders competed with the Portuguese during the 16th century, and British and French merchants followed in the 17th century. British trading stations were established at Surat (1612), Bombay (1661), and Calcutta (1690). In the mid-18th century, warfare broke out between British and French forces in India, and the French were confined to a few small enclaves. The growing instability of the Moghul empire in the face of Marathan and Rajput revolts and the expansion of the southern kingdom of Mysore encouraged the British to seek further control of Indian territory. Robert Clive's victory at Plassey in 1757 brought Orissa, Bihar, and Bengal under British control; British rule was extended to the upper Ganges in 1775. Victory over the maharaja of Mysore in 1792 paved the way for British control over much of the south.

British parliamentary acts of 1773 and 1784 placed these acquisitions firmly under government control, and in 1803 the Moghul emperor accepted the offer of a protectorate, and British suzerainty in India was assured. After a protracted war, 1812-23, Marathan resistance to British control was broken. The first Anglo-Afghan War, 1838-42, was inconclusive in Afghanistan but led to consolidation of British control of the Punjab.

In 1833 Parliament assumed political control of British interests in South Asia, while private merchants had unrestricted access to the economy. Plantation crops, such as opium and cotton, began to displace agriculture, which made India more dependent on imported goods.

In 1857 Indian troops in the British colonial forces staged a mutiny in north-central India that lasted 14 months. In 1858 the Moghul empire was dissolved, as was the East India Company. The government of India was made directly subject to the British Crown, which exercised control through a viceroy and through the British Colonial Office. Queen Victoria was crowned empress of India in 1877.

British sovereignty in India—the raj—was a patchwork of direct and indirect rule. In general, coastal areas, major river valleys, and strategic frontier regions were ruled by British authorities, while interior states continued as British protectorates controlled by British advisers to native princes. In 1861 Indians were appointed to advisory councils of the viceroy and provincial governors.

The Indian National Congress was organized in 1885. In the wake of popular demonstrations in 1905, elections were instituted to choose Indian members of the viceroy's legislative council. Separate electorates were created for the Muslim and Hindu communities, formalizing a divisive force in Indian politics and weakening opposition to British rule.

In 1914, with Chinese loss of control in Tibet, India's northern boundary was pushed forward to the McMahon Line, following the highest peaks in the Himalayas. This set the stage for numerous later boundary disputes between China and India, Pakistan, and Burma.

The Government of India Act of 1919 transferred some political power to elected provincial officials but left the appointed British governors firmly in control. In that year Mohandas K. Gandhi organized the first passive-resistance campaigns and was imprisoned. In 1935 the Government of India Act created elected provincial legislatures. In the first elections (1937) the Congress party under Jawaharlal Nehru won control of seven of the 11 provinces. Nehru's goal of a united Indian opposition to British rule was thwarted by Mohammed Ali Jinnah's Muslim League, which demanded the creation of a separate Muslim state.

During World War II, the British military position in South Asia was complicated by calls for Indian independence. An offer of local autonomy, with independence to follow, was spurned by Nehru, and an Indian National army under Subhas Bose fought with the Japanese. Jinnah's call for an independent Pakistan was greatly enhanced by his support of the British.

In 1947, the British raj became two independent nations, predominantly Hindu India and predominantly Muslim Pakistan. Despite its considerable stature in the international community at large, India has been troubled by a number of disputes with its neighbors and separatist movements within its own borders. Following independence hundreds of semiautonomous princely states were brought under control of the central government. The French ceded their remaining trading colonies in the 1950s, and Portugal gave up Goa in 1961. In 1962, India warred with China in a still unresolved dispute over their border along Kashmir and Assam. The state of Bhutan was granted independence in 1971, and in 1974 Sikkim was annexed and its monarchy abolished.

India's most intractable disputes have been with Pakistan. Immediately after independence, Hindus in Pakistan and Muslims in India were set upon by the majority populations; hundreds of thousands were killed, and at least 12 million refugees fled over the border in both directions. On Jan. 30, 1948, Gandhi was assassinated by a Hindu extremist who blamed him for partition.

In granting independence, Britain had divided states of Bengal and Punjab between the two countries, but fighting erupted over the status of Jammu and Kashmir, and a cease-fire line negotiated by the UN in 1949 has never been ratified as a formal national boundary. In 1989, separatists in the Indian part of Kashmir began calling for an end to Indian rule, and relations with Pakistan have worsened as India accused its neighbor of providing support for the guerrillas. In 1971, after 10 million refugees poured across its border, India intervened in the Pakistani civil war in an action

that prompted an almost immediate cease-fire and the creation of an independent Bangladesh.

India's main separatist movement involves Sikh separatists in the Punjab who seek the formation of an independent state of Khalistan, but who are thought to be supported by Pakistan. The government is also contending with separatist movements in the northeastern states of Assam and its neighbor Nagaland.

The British legacy in India included a sizable national elite, well educated and committed to principles of parliamentary democracy. The English language linked the elites of India's linguistically diverse regions, easing minorities' fears of domination by a Hindi-speaking majority. India's economy had seen some industrial development under the British, but its infrastructure was geared to integration in a colonial empire rather than to independence. Port cities, heavy industry, and plantation agriculture coexisted with widespread rural poverty in subsistence-level villages, and the years following independence saw a massive migration of the rural poor into overburdened cities.

Under Prime Minister Jawaharlal Nehru, India assumed a leadership role in the world movement of nonaligned nations and followed a policy of neutrality in international affairs. The development of good relations between the United States and Pakistan led to correspondingly difficult U.S.-India relations. In August 1971 India signed a 20-year friendship treaty with the Soviet Union.

Nehru died on May 27, 1964, and was succeeded by Lal Bahadur Shastri. Nehru's daughter, Mrs. Indira Gandhi, was named prime minister on Jan. 19, 1966. In 1967 the dominant Congress party faced electoral setbacks; in 1969 it split into "Old" and "New" wings. Mrs. Gandhi's New Congress party won control of the legislature.

Faced with protests and strikes after the New Congress party was convicted of voting irregularities in 1975, Mrs. Gandhi declared a state of emergency in June; censorship was imposed, thousands were arrested for political offenses, and various economic-control measures were adopted. An opposition coalition led by the Janata Dal party won a massive victory in parliamentary elections in 1977. Mrs. Gandhi was driven from office, and the state of emergency was annulled. Mrs. Gandhi's party was returned to power in 1980, and she resumed the prime ministership. After an army attack on the Sikhs' Golden Temple in Amritsar, Gandhi was assassinated by Sikh bodyguards in October 1984. She was succeeded in office by her son, Rajiv, who placed the Punjab under direct control of the federal government.

On Dec. 3, 1984, methyl isocyanate gas leaked from a Union Carbide plant in Bhopal, killing over 2,500 people. The accident prompted a broad inquiry into industrial safety standards in India.

Indian troops, in July 1987, intervened in the growing civil war in Sri Lanka between the government and Tamil separatists. A negotiated truce under Indian auspices broke down, and Indian troops were involved in the conflict until their withdrawal in late 1989.

In November 1989, Rajiv Gandhi's Congress party was voted out of office in general elections after people close to the government were accused of taking kickbacks in a government arms purchase scandal. Gandhi was succeeded by V.P. Singh of the Janata Dal party, whose government collapsed after 11 months over a dispute involving Hindu plans to build a temple on the site of a mosque in Ayodhya. (Hindus contend the mosque was built on the site of Rama's birthplace.) Middle-class Hindus also protested an affirmative action policy to set aside federal government jobs for members of lower castes.

Singh was followed by Chandra Shekhar, whose minority government served only with the backing of the Congress party. After a parliamentary boycott by the Congress party instigated by Rajiv Gandhi, Shekhar quit the government in March 1991, agreeing to stay on as a caretaker until the May election. The election, postponed two weeks following the assassination of Gandhi, was won by the Congress party, and P.V. Narasimha Rao became prime minister.

During 1992 the Rao government attempted to foster economic growth by relaxing the centralized planning and controls on international trade and investment that had long stifled the nation's potential. This policy produced impressive economic gains despite a concurrent rise in corruption-related scandals.

A rise in Hindu extremist feeling, however, strengthened the hand of the opposition Bharatiya Janata party. On Dec. 6, 1992, a Hindu mob demolished a mosque built several hundred years earlier on a Hindu sacred site in the city of Ayodhya; in the ensuing turmoil, riots broke out in dozens of cities, most notably Bombay, leading to the deaths of hundreds of Muslims at the hands of Hindu attackers. A series of bomb explosions killed hundreds in Bombay on Mar.12, 1993, while dozens more were killed by an explosion in Calcutta four days later. Further riots followed, amid unsubstantiated accusations that Muslims, aided by Pakistan, were responsible for the explosions.

In 1993 separatist movements in Punjab and Assam waned, but violence in Kashmir and Jammu increased dramatically; despite several attempts by India and Pakistan to institute effective talks on the issue, violence continued unabated with loss of life in the hundreds if not thousands.

The Rao government's economic policies produced good results, but as India's economy strengthened its political stability weakened. The Congress Party continued to lose power to the Hindu Baratiya Janata Party. Congress was defeated in parliamentary elections in May 1996, ushering in an era of short-lived, weak coalition governments under Pres. K. R. Narayanan. Inder Kumer Gurjal formed a government in April, 1997 that fell in November. The BJP won a plurality of seats in March 1998 elections, but, to govern (under Prime Minister Vajapyee) required a 19-party coalition. Fragile authority need not exclude vigorous policy: it was the BJP coalition that carried out underground tests of five nuclear devices in May, vigorously asserted India's claims in Kashmir, and cut food subsidies as a means of reducing the deficit. It was the latter that dislodged the coalition and in April 1999, Pres. Narayanan dissolved the Lok Sabha, preparatory to India's third election campaign in three years. Perhaps sensing weakness during the interim period, Muslim insurgents launched attacks against Indian forces in Kashmir. But India retaliated forcefully and peace was restored in July, although India continued to blame Pakistan for the violence. (See Part I, "Major News Stories of the Year.")

Despite this recent instability, India has enjoyed significant domestic and international achievements in the first 50 years after independence. The nation's territory was consolidated, and separatist movements in various provinces successfully resisted. The federal parliamentary system has proved workable, and the federal government has established its constitutional right to intervene in state affairs under some conditions. India's armed forces are large, well trained, and well equipped, with some nuclear capability. India has maintained watchful, but generally peaceful, relations with two unfriendly neighbors, Pakistan and China. The Green Revolution of the 1970s made the country self-sufficient in food for the first time since the 19th century. India has a large, well-educated middle class and a growing industrial economy.

▶ INDONESIA
Republic of Indonesia

● **GEOGRAPHY** **Location:** archipelago of about 13,700 islands stretching from Malay peninsula to New Guinea between mainland of Southeast Asia and Australia. Jakarta 6°08'S, 106°45'E. **Boundaries:** land borders with Papua New Guinea, to E of Irian Jaya, and with Malaysian states of Sarawak and Sabah in northern Borneo. **Total area:** 741,097 sq. mi. (1,919,440 sq km). **Coastline:** 34,006 mi. (54,716 km). **Comparative area:** slightly less than three times the size of Texas. **Land use:** 10% arable land; 7% permanent crops; 7% meadows and pastures; 62% forest and woodland; 14% other; includes 3% irrigated. **Major cities:** (1990 census) Jakarta (capital) 8,222,515; Surabaya 2,473,272; Bandung 2,056,915; Medan 1,730,052; Semarang 1,249,230.

● **PEOPLE** **Population:** 216,108,345 (1999 est.). **Nationality:** noun—Indonesian(s); adjective—Indonesian. **Ethnic groups:** 45% Javanese, 14% Sudanese, 7.5% Madurese, 7.5% coastal Malays. **Languages:** Bahasa Indonesian (modified form of Malay; official); English and Dutch, leading foreign languages; local dialects, most widely spoken of which is Javanese. **Religions:** 88% Muslim, 5% Protestant, 3% Roman Catholic, 2% Hindu, 1% Buddhist.

● **GOVERNMENT** **Type:** republic. **Independence:** Aug. 17, 1945 (from Netherlands). **Constitution:** Aug. 1945, abrogated by Federal Constitution of 1949 and Provisional Constitution of 1950, restored July 5, 1959. **National holiday:** Independence Day, Aug. 17. **Head of Government:** (A new president was elected in Oct. 1999, see "Part I.") **Structure:** executive—headed by president who is chief of state and head of cabinet; cabinet selected by president; unicameral legislature (DPR, or House of Representatives) of 500 members (100 appointed, 400 elected); second body (MPR, or People's Consultative Assembly) of 1,000 members includes legislature and 500 other members (chosen by several processes but not directly elected); MPR meets every five years and elects president and vice president and theoretically determines national policy; judicial—Supreme Court Judges appointed by president.

● **ECONOMY** **Monetary unit:** Indonesian rupiah. **Budget:** (FY98/99) *income:* $35 bil.; *expend.:* $35 bil. **GDP:** $602 bil., $2,830 per capita (1998 est.). **Chief crops:** rice, cassava, peanuts, rubber, cocoa; poultry, pork, beef. **Natural resources:** crude oil, tin, natural gas, nickel, timber. **Major industries:** petroleum and natural gas, textiles, mining. **Labor force:** 87 mil. (1997 est.); 41% agriculture, 19.8% trade, restaurant and hotel, 14% manufacturing; 15%-20% unemployment. **Exports:** $49 bil. (f.o.b., 1998); 15.2% textiles/garments, 6.4% gas, 5.9% electrical appliances. **Imports:** $24 bil. (f.o.b., 1998); 75.3% manufactures, 9% raw materials, 7.8% foodstuffs, 7.7% fuels. **Major trading partners:** *exports:* 18% Japan, 15% EU, 14% US, 13% Singapore; *imports:* 20% Japan, 13% US, 9% Germany, 9% Singapore.

The precolonial East Indies consisted of several Islamic and Hindu kingdoms in the western islands and tribal societies in the easterly ones. The Portuguese established trading posts in the 16th century; by the 17th century, control had largely passed to the Dutch East India Company. With the company's bankruptcy in 1799, the Dutch established direct colonial rule. Several 19th-century anticolonial uprisings, though costly to the Dutch, failed to dislodge them. Nationalist sentiment grew in the early 20th century, organized around Islamic groups, the Indonesian Communist party (PKI, founded 1920), and the Indonesian Nationalist party (PNI, founded 1927). Sukarno, founder of the PNI, achieved prominence as a nationalist leader and was jailed by the Dutch.

The Dutch East Indies fell quickly to the Japanese early in 1942. Some nationalists at first hailed the Japanese as liberators but quickly turned against their harsh occupation. On Aug. 17, 1945, Sukarno proclaimed Indonesia's independence. With British aid, the Dutch returned and tried to reestablish colonial rule; in 1949, threatened with a cutoff of American Marshall Plan aid, they withdrew and acknowledged Indonesia's independent status. Under Sukarno Indonesia took a leading role in international affairs among the nonaligned nations of the Third World.

In 1963 Indonesia gained control of the last Dutch outpost in the Indies, Irian Jaya (western New Guinea). Sukarno's politics moved steadily to the left, and Indonesia became hostile to the West and friendly with China. The influence of the PKI grew steadily. On Sept. 30, 1965, the army crushed an attempted coup by the PKI, setting off a popular reaction in which several hundred thousand people were killed as suspected Communists. Sukarno was shunted aside, and power devolved to Gen. Suharto, who became president in 1968. The PKI was banned, and Indonesian policy swung sharply in favor of the West.

The economy grew rapidly, aided by oil revenue, timber exports to Japan, and the Green Revolution in rice agriculture. Foreign investment aided industrial development, which was hampered, however, by domestic content laws and other trade restrictions. A policy of "transmigration" attempted, with mixed success, to move farmers from overcrowded Java and Bali to underdeveloped areas in Sumatra, Borneo, Sulawesi, and Irian Jaya. In 1975 Indonesia invaded the former Portuguese colony of East Timor, which was annexed in 1976. More than 100,000 East Timorese have been killed and the annexation is not recognized internationally.

In recent years declining oil revenues have been partly offset by the growth of industry and tourism. Pres. Suharto remained in power, at the head of the Golkar united-front party, and was reelected president for a fifth term in 1993. Despite the most violent campaign in Indonesia's history, the ruling Golkar Party was returned to power with nearly 75 percent of the vote in the 1997 parliamentary elections. But Suharto's regime faced serious problems, including continuing unrest in East Timor and rising public dissatisfaction with the alleged corruption of Suharto's family and close associates. The economy boomed in recent years and per capita income steadily grew but in 1998 the financial crisis that swept through Asia

revealed the hollowness of the Indonesian approach. Strikes, protests, and riots forced Suharto to resign in May and his trusted aide, Vice-Pres. Habibie took power promising reforms and new elections in 1999. Habibie dropped half of Suharto's cabinet, began reforming the banking system, initiated inquiries in Suharto family wealth, and agreed with Portugal to hold a referendum on the status of East Timor. Elections were held in June 1999 with Golkar taking about 25 percent of the votes and seats; an anti-Golkar coalition headed by Sukarno's daughter, Megawati Sukarnoputri, held a majority. Megawati was expected to be elected president in October. (See Part I, "Major News Stories of the Year.") The people of East Timor voted overwhelmingly for independence from Indonesia, leading to violent attacks by militia groups and the sending of U.N. troops to stop the violence.

▶ IRAN
Islamic Republic of Iran

● **GEOGRAPHY   Location:** western Asia. **Boundaries:** Armenia and Azerbaijan to N, Caspian Sea and Turkmenistan to NE, Pakistan and Afghanistan to E, Persian (Arabian) Gulf and Gulf of Oman to S, and Turkey and Iraq to W. **Total area:** 636,294 sq. mi. (1,648,000 sq km). **Coastline:** 1,516 mi. (2,440 km); Iran also borders the Caspian Sea (740 km). **Comparative area:** slightly larger than Alaska. **Land use:** 10% arable land; 1% permanent crops; 27% meadows and pastures; 7% forest and woodland; 55% other; includes 2% irrigated. **Major cities:** (1991 census) Tehran (Teheran, capital) 6,475,527; Mashad (Meshed) 1,759,155; Isfahan (Esfahan) 1,127,050; Tabriz 1,088,985; Shiraz 965,117.

● **PEOPLE   Population:** 65,179,752 (1999 est.). **Nationality:** noun—Iranian(s); adjective—Iranian. **Ethnic groups:** 51% Persian, 24% Azerbaijani, 8% Gilaki and Mazandarani, 7% Kurd. **Languages:** 58% Persian, 26% Turkic, 9% Kurdish. **Religions:** 89% Shi'a Muslim; 10% Sunni Muslim; 1% Zoroastrian, Jewish, Christian, and Baha'i.

● **GOVERNMENT   Type:** theocratic republic. **Constitution:** Dec. 2-3, 1979; revised 1989 to expand powers of the presidency and eliminate the prime minister. **National holiday:** Islamic Republic Day, April 1. **Head of Government:** Seyed Mohammed Khatami, president (since Aug. 1997). **Structure:** executive; unicameral legislature (Islamic Consultative Assembly); judicial.

● **ECONOMY   Monetary unit:** Iranian rial. **Budget:** *income:* $34.6 bil.; *expend.:* $34.9 bil. **GDP:** $339.7 bil., $5,000 per capita (1998 est.). **Chief crops:** wheat, rice, sugar beets; dairy, wool; caviar. **Natural resources:** petroleum, natural gas, coal, chromium. **Major industries:** petroleum, petrochemicals, textiles. **Labor force:** 15.4 mil. (1988 est.); 33% agriculture, 21% manufacturing; shortage of skilled labor; more than 30% unemployment. **Exports:** $12.2 bil. (f.o.b., 1998 est.); 80% petroleum; carpets, fruits, nuts, hides. **Imports:** $13.8 bil. (f.o.b., 1998 est.); machinery, military supplies, metal works, foodstuffs, pharmaceuticals. **Major trading partners:** *exports:* Japan, Italy, Greece; *imports:* Germany, Italy, Japan.

In 549 b.c. Cyrus the Great established the Persian empire by uniting Persia and conquered Babylonia. Alexander the Great conquered Persia in 333 b.c., but the Persians regained their independence after his death. The Persian Sassanian empire, established in a.d. 226, was the principal eastern rival of the Roman Empire. In 641 the Sassanians were defeated by invading Arabs, and Islam replaced the indigenous Zoroastrian religion. Persia reasserted its national identity—though not its political independence—under Islam and became a major center of Shia Muslim culture. In the early 13th century, Persia was conquered by the Mongols, who ruled the country until 1502.

The brilliant Safavid dynasty (1499-1736) was followed by two centuries of decline. During the 19th century, Persia lost control over Afghanistan and the Caucasus, while internal affairs came increasingly under British and Russian control. In 1907 an Anglo-Russian agreement formally divided Persia into spheres of influence. Following World War I, Persia was recognized as an independent nation, but was virtually a British protectorate. The Soviet Union renounced all claims to Persia in 1921.

In 1921 Reza Khan established a military dictatorship and had himself declared a hereditary monarch, Reza Shah Pahlavi, in 1925. In March 1935, the country's name was formally changed to Iran. In 1941 Great Britain, anxious over access to Iran's rich oil fields, charged Iran with pro-Axis activity, occupied Iran, and forced the abdication of Reza Shah in favor of his son, Mohammad Reza Shah Pahlavi. In 1945 Iran became a charter member of the United Nations, and in 1946-47, the Soviets tentatively backed the creation of the autonomous Republic of Iranian Azerbaijan (in the north) and the Kurdish Republic of Mahabad (between Lake Urmia and Iraq).

Under Mohammed Mossadegh the National Front gained power in 1951. Parliament nationalized the oil industry; Britain responded with an economic blockade. The shah was briefly driven from power, but in August 1953, monarchist elements with clandestine British and American support ousted Mossadegh and restored the shah to the throne. The shah pursued a pro-Western policy of modernization and anticommunism and was rewarded with massive military and economic aid. His combination of secular, authoritarian rule and economic and social modernization was popular with the urban business sector but deeply resented by the rural population and the urban poor. Unrestrained use of the secret police to suppress any sign of dissent led to widespread popular disaffection.

Religiously inspired protests resulted in widespread violence in late 1978. A military government was installed by the shah on Nov. 6, with Prime Minister Shahpur Bakhtiar given sweeping powers. The shah went into exile on Jan. 16, 1979. On Jan. 31 Iran's dominant religious leader, Ayatollah Ruhollah Khomeini, returned to Iran from his exile in France. Government forces were routed by Khomeini's supporters, and Bakhtiar's government fell on Feb. 11. In 1979 clashes took place between rival religious factions, between religious parties and secular leftists, and between the urban middle class and the disenfranchised poor. Thousands were arrested and executed by the religious militia forces.

On Nov. 4, 1979, militants seized the U.S. embassy in Tehran and held 62 Americans hostage, provoking a long international crisis. An American military raid in April 1980 failed in an attempt to free the hostages. The hostages were finally freed on Jan. 21, 1981, minutes after Ronald Reagan's inauguration. The following day Iran's president, Abolhassan Bani-Sadr, was dismissed and the Ayatollah Khomeini took over executive power. A new wave of executions followed, with political moderates and non-Islamic religious believers among the principal victims.

On Sept. 22, 1980, a dispute between Iran and Iraq over the Shatt al-Arab waterway flared into open warfare. The war severely crippled Iran. Estimates on casualties range from 450,000 to more than a million dead on both sides, and the war absorbed nearly all Iran's revenue from oil exports, leaving the country nearly bankrupt. The United States was also drawn into the conflict. In 1986, Reagan administration officials attempted to secure the release of hostages in Lebanon by trading arms to the Iranians; and on July 3, 1988, an American ship patrolling in the Persian Gulf accidently shot down an Iranian civilian airliner, killing all aboard.

In September 1988, a UN initiative led to a cease-fire between Iran and Iraq and to the opening of negotiations to find a permanent settlement to the war. Largely isolated from the world community, Iran's domestic priority was rebuilding the nation's economy. On June 3, 1989, Ayatollah Khomeini died, but the dire predictions that his death would cause turmoil within the Iranian political hierarchy proved wrong. Ali-Akbar Rafsanjani assumed the presidency.

In elections held Apr. 10, 1992 (the first since the death of Khomeini), supporters of Rafsanjani's moderate economic and foreign policies wrested a parliamentary majority from the radical fundamentalist Islamic factions that had controlled the Iranian Parliament for 13 years. But "moderation" proved an elusive concept, as Rafsanjani's party was subjected to strong pressure from religious extremists.

Although Iran had condemned the presence of Western troops in the Middle East during the Persian Gulf conflict, it abided by UN sanctions against Iraq and grounded Iraqi planes that sought refuge from Allied bombing raids during the war. Yet Iran urged the UN in 1995 to end sanctions against Iraq, describing them as part of a U.S. plot to divide Arabs. The U.S. then accused Iran of beginning a strategic military buildup and forbade all trade with Iran.

Iran has remained mired in economic and political stagnation with evidence of popular discontent for several years. In the 1997 elections the religious authorities gave the voters a genuine choice of presidential candidates and they shockingly chose (in a landslide) a moderate reformist, Mohammed Khatami. Since May 1997 Khatami has carefully maneuvered for moderate reforms in the face of Islamic clerical opposition, opening non-governmental dialogue with the American "great Satan", quietly replacing provincial governors with reformers, reining in secret police agents and the like. In Feb. 1999, the religious leaders permitted the first local elections in twenty years: Khatami's new party, formed only in December, swept all 15 seats in the Tehran city council, winning large victories nationwide.

In July 1999, a militant Islamic group attacked pro-democracy students in Tehran, killing several and injuring 30 or 40 more. Student demonstrations against the government erupted in many cities across the country and in Tehran the police dispersed the crowd with severe violence after students attacked buildings and burned cars. Pres. Khatami condemned the riots, leaving many questions about the future of democratic reform.

▶**IRAQ**
Republic of Iraq

• **GEOGRAPHY** **Location:** western Asia with narrow outlet to Persian (Arabian) Gulf. **Boundaries:** Turkey to N, Iran to E, Saudi Arabia and Kuwait to S, Syria and Jordan to W. **Total area:** 168,754 sq. mi. (437,072 sq km). **Coastline:** 36 mi. (58 km). **Comparative area:** slightly more than twice the size of Idaho. **Land use:** 12% arable land; 0% permanent crops; 9% meadows and pastures; 0% forest and woodland; 79% other; includes 4% irrigated. **Major cities:** Baghdad (capital) 3,236,000 (1987 census); Basra (Basia) 1,540,000; Mosul 1,220,000; Kirkuk 535,000 (1977 census).
• **PEOPLE** **Population:** 22,427,150 (1999 est.). **Nationality:** noun—Iraqi(s); adjective—Iraqi. **Ethnic groups:** 75-80% Arab, 15-20% Kurdish, 5% Turkoman, Assyrian, and other. **Languages:** Arabic (official), Kurdish (official in Kurdish areas), Assyrian, Armenian. **Religions:** 97% Muslim (60-65% Shi'a, 32-37% Sunni), 3% Christian and other.
• **GOVERNMENT** **Type:** republic. **Independence:** Oct. 3, 1932 (from League of Nations mandate under British administration). **Constitution:** Sept. 22, 1968, effective July 16, 1970 (provisional constitution); new constitution drafted in 1990 but not adopted. **National holiday:** Anniversary of the Revolution, July 17. **Heads of Government:** Saddam Hussein, president (since July 1979); Ahmed Hussein Khudair, prime minister (since 1994). **Structure:** executive; unicameral legislature (National Assembly)—Kurdish assembly elected in Kurdish areas, but unrecognized by Baghdad.
• **ECONOMY** **Monetary unit:** Iraqi dinar. **Budget:** N.A. **GDP:** $52.3 bil., $2,400 per capita (1997 est.). **Chief crops:** wheat, barley, rice, cotton; cattle, sheep. **Natural resources:** crude oil, natural gas, phosphates, sulphur. **Major industries:** petroleum, chemicals, textiles, construction materials. **Labor force:** 4.4 mil. (1989); 48% services, 30% agriculture, 22% industry. **Exports:** $5 bil. (1998 est.); crude oil. **Imports:** $3 bil. (1998 est.); food, medicine, manufactures. **Major trading partners:** Russia, France, China.

The fertile lands of Mesopotamia, between the Tigris and Euphrates rivers, were the site of one of the world's oldest civilizations. The city-states of Sumer were founded before 3000 b.c. and later became the heart of the Babylonian empire. Babylon became subject to the Assyrian empire after 1350 b.c. and was conquered by the Persians under Cyrus and Darius in the mid-sixth century b.c. Mesopotamia remained under the control of various Persian dynasties for the next 1,000 years.

In the seventh century a.d., the region was rapidly incorporated into the expanding Islamic world. The battle of Basra in 656 decisively established Arab control. In 762 the Caliphate, the center of Islamic rule, was moved from Damascus to the newly founded city of Baghdad, near the ruins of ancient Babylon. Mongol invaders sacked Baghdad in 1258 and destroyed its irrigation works; thereafter the region entered a period of long-term decline. Baghdad fell to the Ottoman Turks in 1534, and Iraq remained a province of the Ottoman Empire until the 20th century.

British troops occupied Iraq in 1915, and Great Britain governed the country under a League of Nations mandate after World War I. A Hashemite monarchy was organized under British protection in 1921. The kingdom of Iraq was granted independence in 1932 but remained closely tied to Great Britain by treaties guaranteeing British interests in petroleum and regional defense. Iraqi oil flowed through British-controlled pipelines traversing Jordan to Haifa (in Israel) and through a French-controlled pipeline traversing Syria.

After 1932 several attempted coups by anti-British factions were put down with the aid of British troops. One such coup in April 1941 sought aid from Italy and Germany; British troops landed at Basra in May and restored the pro-British monarchy. Iraq declared war against the Axis powers in 1943. In 1948 Iraq joined the Arab League and participated in the first Arab-Israeli War. Most of Iraq's 85,000 Jews emigrated to Israel after the war ended.

In 1952 a new agreement with Great Britain gave the Iraq Petroleum Company greater control over the country's oil, and a greater share of oil revenues. While remaining part of the Arab League, Iraq in 1955 broke ties with Egypt and also expelled the Soviet ambassador. Iraq signed a mutual defense treaty with Turkey.

A leftist pan-Arab revolutionary coup overthrew the monarchy in 1958 and established a republic, reversing Iraq's former pro-Western stance in international affairs. Oil resources and other industries were nationalized, and large landholdings were broken up. In 1968 a local branch of the international Ba'ath Socialist party came to power and established rule by decree within the republican framework of government. In 1972 the Soviet Union sent arms and advisers to Iraq. In the 1973 Arab-Israeli War, Iraq sent troops to aid Syrian forces on the front lines.

Iranian aid to a long-standing Kurdish rebellion in Iraq's northern mountains strained relations between the two countries. The Kurds were defeated in a bloody campaign in 1975, though the rebellion continued, leading to Iraq's bombing of Kurdish villages in 1979 and other incidents.

The execution of 21 alleged Communist conspirators in 1978 disrupted relations between Iraq and the USSR. Trade relations with the West were resumed. On July 16, 1979, Gen. Saddam Hussein at-Takriti assumed control of the government and immediately purged leftist elements in the Ba'ath movement.

Several months of fighting in 1980 between Iraq and Iran for control of the Shatt al-Arab waterway in southern Iraq led to the outbreak of open warfare on Sept. 22, when each country launched bombing attacks on the other's cities. Warfare quickly spread along the entire Iraq-Iran border. The Iran-Iraq War produced eight years of fierce but generally stalemated fighting, with reports of the use of poison gas by both sides. On June 7, 1981, Israeli war planes destroyed a nuclear reactor near Baghdad, claiming it was capable of producing nuclear weapons. The war spread to the gulf in 1984, as both Iran and Iraq attacked tankers using each other's ports.

On May 17, 1987, the USS Stark, an American frigate on station in the gulf, was struck by missiles fired by an Iraqi fighter; 37 American sailors were killed. Iraq claimed that the attack was inadvertent and apologized to the United States.

In September 1988, a UN conference led to a cease-fire in the Iran-Iraq War. In the autumn of 1988, refugees in Turkey reported that poison gas had been used against Kurdish villages in northeastern Iraq as the Kurdish rebellion there continued. During 1989-90 Iraq's repressive internal policies and continued arms buildup provoked widespread international criticism. Iraqi agents were caught attempting to smuggle several components of nuclear weapons from the United States and Great Britain.

On Aug. 2, 1990, 120,000 Iraqi troops invaded, occupied, and later annexed neighboring Kuwait. The invasion was met with almost universal disapproval, led by the UN Security Council, and U.S. troops were deployed to Saudi Arabia to defend it against a possible invasion. Coalition forces eventually totaled 500,000 troops from 13 countries.

After a six-week air war that destroyed most of Iraq's military capabilities and much of the country's infrastructure, Allied ground forces liberated Kuwait and occupied much of southern Iraq in only four days. Emboldened by the proximity of such overwhelming force, Kurdish and Sunni minorities in Iraq began a civil war that was put down with surprising speed and resulted in the displacement of hundreds of thousands of refugees to Turkey and Iran.

During 1992, while the Iraqi people continued to suffer from the war's devastation, Saddam Hussein solidified his hold on the military and remained in total control of the nation. However, UN inspectors discovered his secret plans to build nuclear weapons, and he was forced to destroy the program.

Throughout 1992-93 American warplanes provided protection for Kurdish areas in the north and Sunni Muslim areas in the southern marshlands. UN arms inspectors continued to press for access to Iraqi weapons plants and military research centers. On June 19, 1993, American missiles destroyed the Baghdad headquarters of Iraq's military intelligence service, in retaliation for a 1992 Iraq-backed plot to assassinate Pres. George Bush.

In November 1994 Iraq formally recognized the sovereignty and territorial integrity of Kuwait. Nonetheless, the UN retained sanctions against Iraq until two conditions were met: destroying its stockpiles of weapons of mass destruction and improving its treatment of minorities. Sanctions were renewed in January 1995.

In October 1995 Hussein received a triumphant 99.96 percent approval in a referendum on a second seven-year term as president. In May 1996 the UN agreed to ease sanctions on Iraq, permitting the sale of $2 billion worth of oil to purchase food and medical supplies. In late 1997 Iraq reneged on its agreement to allow UN weapons inspectors free access to all sites causing new tension in the region. Hussein's on-again, off-again cooperation with international inspection teams climaxed in the Dec. 1998 U.S./U.K. air strikes against Iraq (with no U.N. approval and scanty Arab support). Since then, with a few brief halts, U.S. and U.K. patrols in the "no fly" zones have regularly clashed with Iraqi MIGs. After the Security Council decision to review all aspects of U.N.-Iraqi relations in Jan. 1999, U.S. influence was further diminished by revelations that its intelligence agents had infiltrated the UN Special Commission and used UNSCOM to spy on Iraq. Three compromise recommendations by UN panels now met Iraqi rejection in April; nonetheless, the Security Council in May extended "oil-for-food" sales for six more months.

▶ **IRELAND**

● **GEOGRAPHY** **Location:** 26 of 32 counties comprising island of Ireland, in North Atlantic Ocean. Dublin 53°20'N, 6°15'W. **Boundaries:** Northern Ireland (UK) to N, Great Britain 50 mi (80 km) to E. **Total area:** 27,135 sq. mi. (70,280 sq km). **Coast-**line: 900 mi. (1,448 km). **Comparative area:** slightly larger than W. Virginia. **Land use:** 13% arable land; negl. % permanent crops; 68% meadows and pastures; 5% forest and woodland; 14% other. **Major cities:** (1991 census) Dublin (capital) 915,516; Cork 173,694; Limerick 75,436; Galway 50,853; Waterford 41,853.

● **PEOPLE** **Population:** 3,632,944 (1999 est.). **Nationality:** noun—Irishman (men), Irishwoman (women), Irish (collective pl.); adjective—Irish. **Ethnic groups:** Celtic, with English minority. **Languages:** Irish (Gaelic) and English (official); English widely spoken. **Religions:** 92% Roman Catholic, 3% Anglican, 4% other.

● **GOVERNMENT** **Type:** republic. **Independence:** Dec. 6, 1921 (from UK). **Constitution:** Dec. 29, 1937. **National holiday:** St. Patrick's Day, Mar. 17. **Heads of Government:** Mary McAleese, president (since Oct. 1997); Bertie Ahern, prime minister (since June 1997). **Structure:** executive; bicameral parliament (Seanad, Dail); judiciary appointed by president on advice of government.

● **ECONOMY** **Monetary unit:** Irish pound. **Budget:** (1998) *income:* $23.5 bil.; *expend.:* $20.6 bil. **GDP:** $67.1 bil.; $18,600 per capita (1998 est.). **Chief crops:** turnips, barley, potatoes, sugar beets, wheat; meat, dairy. **Natural resources:** zinc, lead, natural gas, barite, copper. **Major industries:** food products, brewing, textiles, clothing. **Labor force:** 1.52 mil. (1997); 62.1% services, 27% manufacturing and construction, 10% agriculture, forestry, fishing; 7.7% unemployment (1998 est.). **Exports:** $60.9 bil. (f.o.b., 1998); chemicals, data processing equipment, industrial machinery. **Imports:** $43.7 bil. (c.i.f., 1998); food, animal feed, data processing equipment, petroleum and petroleum products. **Major trading partners:** *exports:* 67% EU (24% UK, 12% Germany, 8% France), 11% U.S.; *imports:* 55% EU (34% UK, 6% Germany, 6% France), 15% U.S.

Ireland, a collection of warring Celtic chieftainships, was converted to Christianity by St. Patrick in the fifth century. Over the next two centuries, Ireland became a great center of monastic Christianity, sending missionaries to Scotland, England, and the Continent. While the Roman Empire decayed, Ireland was a center of peace, culture, and learning. Viking invasions in the ninth and 10th centuries caused substantial damage and overturned the rule of the great monasteries and their secular allies. By the time an Irish monarchy was reestablished by Brian Boru in 1014 and the surviving invaders were integrated into Irish society, Ireland had become an isolated, poor backwater on the periphery of Europe.

Trade gave rise to English commercial interests in Ireland and to Henry II's claim to overlordship of Ireland in the 12th century. Henry VIII declared himself king of Ireland and introduced the Reformation there. Large-scale Scottish immigration to Ulster began during the reign of Elizabeth I. Penal laws were applied, banning Catholics from public life and making the Mass an act of treason. A rebellion in 1641 was crushed by Oliver Cromwell over the course of a decade, ending with a massacre of thousands of Irish at Drogheda. After William of Orange's "Glorious Revolution" of 1688, the Irish supported James II, who was defeated at the Battle of the Boyne in 1690.

Following these events, British economic sanctions destroyed Ireland's flourishing export trade in wool. "Plantations" were established by British and Scottish Presbyterian landlords and farmers on lands seized from Irish Catholics. Much of the native aristocracy fled into exile, and the Gaelic language declined to near extinction.

A separate Irish Parliament, dominated by the Anglo-Irish establishment, was instituted in 1782, but it had little power. In 1798 a popular uprising led by Wolfe Tone, with inspiration and aid from revolutionary France, was put down with great loss of life.

In 1800 Ireland and England were joined by the Act of Union, whereby Ireland was ineffectively represented in the British Parliament. After popular agitation led by Daniel O'Connell, the Catholic Emancipation Act was enacted by Parliament in 1829, though mandatory tithes continued to support the established Anglican church until 1869.

Under absentee landlords, the Irish population had been reduced to a subsistence diet based largely on potatoes. When a potato blight struck the country in the 1840s, disaster ensued. Between 1846 and 1851, one million people starved to death, and 1.6 million emigrated, most of them to America.

In the late 19th century, a home-rule movement under Charles Stewart Parnell won wide popular support. A Home Rule Act finally was passed by Parliament in 1914, but its effect was postponed for the duration of World War I. The Land Purchase Acts of the early 20th century enabled dispossessed peasants to buy land from absentee landlords, creating a rural economic basis for an independent Ireland. The country's economy, based largely on agriculture and pasturage, began to recover. (Industry, principally shipbuilding and textiles, was largely confined to Northern Ireland.)

The postponement of home rule led to the Easter Rebellion of 1916; brutally suppressed, it was followed by the "Troubles," a period of guerrilla warfare lasting to 1920. In that year the Government of Ireland Act established six of Ulster's nine counties as Northern Ireland, an integral part of the United Kingdom but with its own home-rule Parliament. The south's refusal of similar status led to the passage on Dec. 11, 1922, of the Irish Free State Act, by which Ireland became an independent dominion within the British Commonwealth.

The Fine Gael (People of Ireland) party governed until 1932, when Eamon De Valera, as the head of the Fianna Fail (Soldiers of Destiny) party, was elected president, holding that office until 1948. In 1938 the Constitution was revised to sever all connections with the British government except for an "external association" with the British monarchy. The outlawed Irish Republican Army (IRA) pressed for forcible reunification of Ireland and carried out attacks on British interests in both Ireland and Northern Ireland.

Ireland remained neutral during World War II, and its government objected to British military activities in Northern Ireland. But it was generally sympathetic to the Allied war effort, especially after the United States entered the war in 1941.

In 1949 Ireland severed all ties to the British Crown, becoming a fully independent republic. The Fianna Fail, normally the majority party since 1932, won a majority in the republic's first elections, and De Valera became prime minister. In 1954 a coalition government under John Costello took power. De Valera was elected president of the republic in 1959, as a new generation of parliamentary leadership arose.

During the 1950s, Ireland developed a moderate welfare state with the support of both the Fianna Fail and Fine Gael. In the 1960s attention turned to industrial development: zinc and lead mining, and export-oriented production of textiles, ceramics, and machinery. Ireland was admitted to the EC in 1973.

Beginning in the late 1960s, civil rights demonstrations led frequently to civil disorders and an increase in IRA guerrilla activity in the north. While the 1970s were a boom period for the Irish Republic, sectarian violence and terrorism in the north left over 2,500 dead. The 1980s saw the establishment of an Anglo-Irish Intergovernmental Council (1981) and the Hillsborough accords (1985) between the Thatcher government and the Fine Gael-Labour coalition, which gave Ireland a consultative role in Northern Irish disputes.

The government of Charles Haughey, leader of Fianna Fail, elected in 1987, continued to face severe economic problems, including high tax rates, high inflation, and unemployment, forcing Haughey to form a coalition government in the spring of 1989. After serious losses in June 1991 local elections, and amid charges of corruption, Haughey resigned in 1992. His successor, Albert Reynolds, faced a deep recession with unemployment rates of about 20 percent. In June 1992, a national vote strongly supported the EC's Maastricht Treaty. Reynolds' coalition fell in Nov. 1992, but he created a new coalition between Fianna Fail and Labour.

In 1993, Reynolds and UK prime minister John Major announced the "Downing Street Declaration" that Sinn Fein, the political arm of the IRA, would be invited to participate in negotiations on Northern Ireland in return for the IRA's promise to halt terrorism and violence. In 1994, the IRA announced a cease-fire in its 25-year-old effort to expel British troops from Northern Ireland.

Preliminary talks began optimistically, but bogged down over the British demand that the IRA disarm and the IRA demand that Britain withdraw its forces from Ulster. In 1996, the IRA announced an end to the 17-month-old cease-fire less than an hour before setting off a powerful bomb in East London, injuring 100 people. And in June, an even stronger bomb exploded in Manchester, injuring 200 and casting serious doubt on Sinn Fein leader Gerry Adams's ability to control the more militant members of his party.

Meanwhile, Ireland's governing coalition fell in Nov. 1995, and was replaced by an odd coalition with John Bruton of Fine Gael as prime minister. The new government passed legislation permitting Irish doctors to provide information about foreign abortion providers and sponsored a referendum that overturned the constitutional ban on divorce with remarriage. The Dail elections of June 1997 turned Bruton's coalition out of office, replaced by a new coalition of Fianna Fail and the Progressive Democrats with Fianna Fail's Bertie Ahern as prime minister.

In April 1998 came the breakthrough agreement (overwhelmingly approved in referendums in Northern Ireland and the Republic in May): extensive home rule in a Northern Ireland remaining part of the U.K. with some Republic of Ireland participation and with all paramilitary groups disarmed. The last-mentioned is the key to the success of the rest of the agreement and has proven the most difficult to enforce. (See Part I, "Major News Stories of the Year.")

▶ **ISRAEL**
State of Israel
• **GEOGRAPHY   Location:** western Asia, on eastern shore of Mediterranean Sea; has outlet to Red

Sea via Gulf of Aqaba. **Boundaries**: Lebanon to N, Syria to NE, Jordan to E, Egypt to SW, Mediterranean Sea to W. **Total area**: 8,019 sq. mi. (20,770 sq km). **Coastline**: 170 mi. (273 km). **Comparative area**: slightly smaller than New Jersey. **Land use**: 17% arable land; 4% permanent crops; 7% meadows and pastures; 6% forest and woodland; 66% other; includes 11% irrigated. **Major cities**: (1993 est.) Jerusalem (capital) 567,100; Tel Aviv-Jaffa 357,400; Haifa 246,500; Holon 162,800; Petach-Tikva 151,100.

• **PEOPLE Population**: 5,749,760 (1999 est.). **Nationality**: noun—Israeli(s); adjective—Israeli. **Ethnic groups**: 80.1% Jewish, 19.9% non-Jewish (mostly Arab). **Languages**: Hebrew (official), Arab (official for Arab minority); English most widely used foreign language. **Religions**: 80.1% Judaism, 14.6% Islam (mostly Sunni Muslim), 2.1% Christian, 3.2% other.

• **GOVERNMENT Type**: republic. **Independence**: May 14, 1948 (from League of Nations Mandate under British administration). **Constitution**: no formal constitution; some functions of constitution are filled by Declaration of Establishment (1948), the basic laws of the Knesset (legislature)— relating to the Knesset, Israeli lands, the president, government—and Israeli citizenship law. **National holiday**: Israel declared independence on May 14, 1948; because Jewish calendar is lunar, however, holiday varies from year to year; all major Jewish religious holidays are also observed as national holidays. **Heads of Government**: Ezer Weizman, president (since May 1993); Ehud Barak, prime minister (since July 1999). **Structure**: executive-president has largely ceremonial functions, except for authority to decide which political leader should try to form ruling coalition following election or fall of previous government, power vested in cabinet; unicameral legislature (Knesset); judiciary-legal system based on combination of English common law, British Mandate regulations, and religious law.

• **ECONOMY Monetary unit**: new Israeli shekel. **Budget**: (1998) *income*: $55 bil.; *expend.*: $58 bil. **GDP**: $101.9 bil., $18,100 per capita (1998 est.). **Chief crops**: citrus and other fruits, vegetables, cotton; beef, poultry, dairy products. **Natural resources**: copper, phosphates, bromide, potash, clay. **Major industries**: food processing, diamond cutting and polishing, textiles and clothing. **Labor force**: 2.3 mil. (1997); 31.2% public services; 20.2% manufacturing; 13.1% finance and business, 12.8% commerce, 7.5% construction, 6.4% personal and other services, 6.2% transport, storage, and communications, 2.6% agriculture, forestry, and fishing; 7.7% unemployment (1997 est.). **Exports**: $22.1 bil. (f.o.b., 1998 est.); machinery, cut diamonds, chemicals, textiles and clothing. **Imports**: $26.1 bil. (f.o.b., 1998 est.); raw materials, military equipment, investment goods, rough diamonds, oil. **Major trading partners**: U.S., EU, Japan.

In ancient times called the Land of Canaan, the region between the Jordan River and the Mediterranean Sea was one of the earliest sites of agricultural civilization in the Middle East. Hebrew exiles from Egypt arrived c. 1200 b.c.; their kingdom, Eretz Israel, was well established by 1000 b.c., with its capital at Jerusalem. The kingdom expanded under Kings Saul and David, who extended domination over the Philistines, a local seafaring people, and established the norms of Jewish religious worship at the great temple of Jerusalem.

After the reign of King Solomon, the kingdom split into two parts, Israel and Judah. Israel was conquered by the Assyrians in 722 b.c., and Judah by the Babylonians in 586 b.c. A locally autonomous state was reestablished under the Persian empire in the fifth century b.c. And in the fourth century b.c., Alexander the Great conquered the region, beginning a period of Hellenizing influence.

A new Jewish state was established in 141 b.c. after the revolt of the Maccabees against hellenic rule, the state falling to the Roman Empire around 70 b.c. Roman rule was exerted through the puppet kings of the Herodian dynasty. Christianity, a messianic religion centering on the teachings of Jesus of Nazareth, was suppressed in Israel by both the Herodian kings and the Jewish priesthood but spread widely in the eastern Mediterranean in the early first century a.d.

A Jewish rebellion against Rome in a.d. 66 was forcibly suppressed, and the temple at Jerusalem was destroyed by the Romans in a.d. 70. Large numbers of Jews were expelled from Judea, beginning the Jewish Diaspora throughout the Roman world and beyond. A second rebellion of Jews in Israel was quelled in a.d. 132.

The territory of the kingdoms of Israel and Judah became generally known as Palestine, after the name of its ancient inhabitants, the Philistines. With the official toleration of Christianity in the Roman Empire under Constantine I (early 4th century), Palestine became a major center of Christian pilgrimage. Politically, Palestine was administered as part of the Byzantine Empire.

Expansion of Islam from Arabia brought Palestine under Islamic rule in 636. Thereafter the region was ruled by the Caliphates of Damascus (661-750) and Baghdad (762-1258). Part of Palestine was captured in 1099 by European Crusaders, who established the short-lived Latin Kingdom of Jerusalem. The region was conquered by the Mongols in 1258; defeat of the Mongols in 1260 at the battle of Ain Jalyut, near Nazareth, prevented a Mongol invasion of Egypt.

Palestine next became part of the Mamluk empire and was incorporated into the Ottoman Empire in 1516. The Ottoman period was one of administrative decline, although the holy places of Judaism, Christianity, and Islam were maintained by local religious authorities.

The emigration of Jews from Europe to the homeland of Israel began around 1870, under the influence of the Zionist movement. Zionism, traceable in part to the thought of Moses Mendelssohn (1729-86), originally emphasized the need to maintain Jewish identity and religious consciousness as well as to promote Jewish assimilation into European culture. By the time of the First World Zionist Congress, convened in Basel by Theodor Herzl in 1897, emphasis had shifted to the need for a specific Jewish homeland. After 1905, under the leadership of Chaim Weizmann, Jewish emigration to Palestine increased as Weizmann attempted to win Turkish approval for a new state of Israel.

With the collapse of the Ottoman Empire during World War I, Palestine came under British rule in 1917. In that year the British government issued the Balfour Declaration, committing Britain to aiding the establishment of a Jewish homeland in Palestine. After Britain received a League of Nations Mandate to govern Palestine (as well as Transjordan) in 1923, Jewish immigration into Palestine increased significantly. Faced with rising

Palestinian Arab opposition to a further increase in Jewish immigration, Britain reinterpreted the Balfour Declaration in restricted terms and attempted to limit the number of Jewish arrivals.

The crisis lasted until the outbreak of World War II. During the war the Palestinian Jewish community (then about 500,000) generally supported the British war effort, while some Palestinian Arab leaders translated anti-Zionist sentiments into sympathy for the Axis. Despite the horrible revelations about the Holocaust—the systematic killing of six million Jews during the War—in 1946 British authorities refused a recommendation of the Anglo-American Committee of Inquiry that they permit resettlement of 100,000 European Jews in Palestine and they limited further immigration to 2,000 per month. Jewish leaders pressed their cause at the United Nations, while in Palestine, Zionist terrorist organizations waged covert war against the British authorities.

In 1947 a UN Special Committee on Palestine, boycotted by Palestinian Arabs, recommended the partition of Palestine into Jewish and Arab sectors, with Jerusalem to be administered under international control. The United Nations adopted the recommendations on Nov. 29, 1947, and the British began to withdraw their forces, while Palestinian Jews and Arabs prepared for war.

On May 14, 1948, the independent state of Israel was established, with its capital at Tel Aviv. On the same day, troops from the Arab League nations attacked Israel. Fighting and cease-fires alternated throughout 1948; Israel lost control of the Old City of Jerusalem but retained the New City, and elsewhere consolidated its territorial control. Separate armistices between Israel and the Arab nations were concluded in 1949; Jordan retained control of the West Bank, and Egypt occupied Gaza. Large numbers of Palestinian Arab refugees departed for camps in Jordan, Lebanon, and Syria, while equally large numbers of Jews from Arab countries resettled in Israel.

Elections to the Knesset (Parliament) were held in January 1949 and resulted in a coalition government. Chaim Weizmann was elected president, and David Ben-Gurion became prime minister. Laws were enacted to ensure religious control of education and civil law and to affirm the "Right of Return" of all Jews to Israel. The role of labor (organized in the Histadrut) was protected by law, as was the establishment of agricultural collectives (kibbutzim).

Taking advantage of the Suez Crisis between Great Britain, France, and Egypt, Israel invaded Egypt's Sinai Peninsula on Oct. 29, 1956. Israeli forces withdrew under the terms of a UN cease-fire on Nov. 6 but retained control of Gaza. Thereafter an uneasy peace prevailed for 11 years under UN supervision.

Throughout this period Israel's population continued to swell with immigrants from Europe, the United States, and other Western countries, and also from the dwindling Jewish communities of the Arab world. Israel's economy, aided by foreign aid and private remittances, grew rapidly, while foreign military aid and the growth of a substantial domestic armaments industry increased its military preparedness.

On May 19, 1967, UN peacekeeping forces withdrew from the Egypt-Israel border on the insistence of Egypt's president Gamal Abdel Nasser. Egyptian forces then reoccupied Gaza and closed the Gulf of Aqaba to Israeli shipping. In the Six-Day War, June 5-10, Israel recaptured Gaza, occupied the Sinai Peninsula to the Suez Canal, and captured the West Bank and the Old City of Jerusalem from Jordan and the Golan Heights from Syria. Another UN-supervised cease-fire went into effect.

Egypt and Syria, backed by Soviet airlifts, invaded Israel on Yom Kippur, Oct. 6, 1973. Israel, with strong U.S. support, counterattacked, driving back the Syrian forces and crossing the Suez Canal from the Sinai into Egypt. Fighting ceased on Oct. 24, and a disengagement agreement was signed on Jan. 18, 1974. Israeli forces withdrew from the west bank of the Suez Canal and, in stages, from the Sinai Peninsula, completing the withdrawal in 1982.

The government of Prime Minister Golda Meir fell after the Yom Kippur War, and a new coalition took power. A period of domestic and international difficulties followed, with severe inflation in the economy and a marked rise in Palestinian and other terrorist attacks against Israeli targets. Israeli forces repeatedly attacked Palestinian bases in southern Lebanon and aided the Christian militia forces in the Lebanese civil war of 1975-76. On July 3, 1976, Israeli commandos raided the airport at Entebbe, Uganda, to rescue 103 hostages held by Arab and German hijackers.

The 1977 parliamentary elections brought a conservative coalition to power, with Menachem Begin elected prime minister. Egypt's president Anwar Sadat visited Jerusalem in November 1977, and Begin and Sadat met at a conference with U.S. president Jimmy Carter at Camp David in 1979. On Mar. 26, 1979, Egypt and Israel signed a formal peace treaty ending 30 years of war and establishing diplomatic relations between the two nations.

In July 1980 Israel affirmed the transfer of its national capital from Tel Aviv to Jerusalem and the incorporation of the (formerly Jordanian) Old City into Israeli territory. The Israeli government decided in 1980 to promote increased Jewish settlement in the West Bank, provoking protest from Palestinian leaders.

Israeli forces invaded southern Lebanon in March 1978. After a brief occupation, most Israeli forces withdrew and were replaced by a UN peacekeeping force, but Israel continued to cooperate with Lebanese Christian militia forces in anti-Palestinian operations. Israeli forces again reoccupied southern Lebanon for five days in April 1980.

Israeli and Syrian forces clashed briefly in April 1981. On June 7, 1981, Israeli jets destroyed a nuclear reactor near Baghdad, Iraq, that Israel claimed could have been used to manufacture materials for nuclear weapons. Prime Minister Begin was returned to office in a close election in 1981, and he retired in 1983.

Attacking Palestine Liberation Organization strongholds in Lebanon in May, 1982, Israel mounted a full-scale invasion of Lebanon in June. Israeli and Syrian forces fought in Lebanon's Bekaa Valley but disengaged after a few days. On June 14 Israeli forces surrounded and shelled Beirut, forcing the PLO to evacuate the city. On Sept. 14 Israeli forces occupied West Beirut, following the assassination of the newly elected Lebanese president, Bashir Gemayel. Lebanese Christian militia, with tacit Israeli permission, entered two Palestinian refugee camps at Sabra and Shatila on Sept. 16 and massacred hundreds of civilians, provoking an international outcry against Israel's occupation of Lebanon. Israeli forces withdrew from Lebanon in June 1985, except for a narrow "security zone" along the border.

Parliamentary elections in 1984 resulted in a stalemate between the conservative Likud party and the Labor party. A coalition government was formed, with power shared by Likud leader Yitzhak Shamir and Labor leader Shimon Peres.

In December 1987, Palestinian residents of Gaza and the West Bank launched a series of violent demonstrations against Israeli authorities. The *intifada*, or uprising, continued into 1991 in a cycle of protest and police reaction that led to the deaths of hundreds of demonstrators and a crisis of Israeli control in the occupied territories. Tensions were exacerbated by the immigration of hundreds of thousands of Soviet Jews to Israel.

Parliamentary elections in November 1988 continued the Likud-Labor stalemate and brought increased power to the minor religious parties. A new grand-coalition government announced in January 1989, with Yitzhak Shamir as prime minister and Shimon Peres as minister of finance, collapsed in mid-March because of disagreements over an American-backed plan for peace talks with the Palestinians. This plunged the country into a crisis, resolved in June 1990 with the formation of a coalition government of Likud and several right-wing religious parties. Shamir managed to survive several no-confidence votes, and his alliance with the religious party Agudat Israel in November solidified his party's power as the Persian Gulf crisis unfolded.

After months of diplomacy spearheaded by the U.S., direct talks between Israel and a (non-PLO) Jordanian-Palestinian joint delegation opened in Washington in December 1991. The talks broke down in stalemate as Israel refused to compromise over the key issue of new Jewish settlements on the West Bank. In the election of June 1992, the Labor party led by Rabin scored an upset victory over Shamir's Likud coalition government. Rabin disclosed that the Shamir government had pursued a deliberate policy of intransigence in the peace talks in order to allow the accelerated West Bank settlement program to continue.

The Palestinian *intifada* gained renewed momentum in Dec. 1992 when Israel deported 400 Palestinians to Lebanon on the grounds that they were responsible for acts of violence. Both the U. S. and the UN opposed the move, which impeded the Arab-Israeli peace talks. Israel launched a series of air and land attacks on suspected terrorist bases in Lebanon, resulting in many casualties.

The world was stunned only a few weeks later, when on Sept. 13, 1993, Prime Minister Yitzhak Rabin and PLO leader Yasir Arafat signed an agreement in principle for a peace settlement based on Palestinian recognition of Israel's right to exist, and Israel's acceptance of at least partial self-rule for the Palestinians. By the spring of 1994, several areas in Gaza and the West Bank were under Palestinian control, while on the regional level, many of Israel's hard-line enemies, including Egypt, Jordan, and Syria began to move toward reconciliation.

By fall of 1995, Israeli troops had begun withdrawing from Palestinian settlements on the West Bank, but a month later an Israeli extremist assassinated Rabin. His successor, Shimon Peres, vowed to continue moves toward peace and moved elections forward from October to May. In early 1996 Israel faced the worst suicide bomber attacks in 20 years: in five days 60 people were dead. Hamas, the Palestinian resistance group, took responsibility for the attacks.

In Israel's first direct election of a prime minister, Likud's hard-line Benjamin Netanyahu narrowly defeated Peres as Israelis chose "security" over "peace." By 1997 the peace process came to a virtual standstill as the Netanyahu government pushed ahead with new settlements in the West Bank and in East Jerusalem. The first sign of a break in the impasse came in June 1998 when President Weizman (re-elected in March for a second five-year term) declared that Netanyahu was undermining peace talks. Negotiations with the Palestinians began anew in July and on October 23, in Washington, Netanyahu and Arafat agreed to the Wye Memorandum by which Israel agreed to surrender about 13 percent of her West Bank holdings. In December this deal was put into limbo as the Knesset toppled Netanyahu's government and rejected the agreement. But elections in May 1999 brought Ehud Barak, former army chief of staff, to the office of prime minister and his One Israel party to dominance in a seven-party coalition formed at last in July. (See "Part I, "Major News Stories of the Year.")

▶ ITALY
Italian Republic

● **GEOGRAPHY Location:** peninsula, extending from southern Europe into Mediterranean Sea, with a number of adjacent islands, principally Sicily to SW, and Sardinia to W. **Boundaries:** Switzerland and Austria to N, Slovenia to NE, Adriatic Sea to E, Ionian Sea to SE, Mediterranean Sea to W, France to NW. **Total area:** 116,305 sq. mi. (301,230 sq km). **Coastline:** 4,723 mi. (7,600 km). **Comparative area:** slightly larger than Arizona. **Land use:** 31% arable land; 10% permanent crops; 15% meadows and pastures; 23% forest and woodland; 21% other; includes 10% irrigated. **Major cities:** (1993) Roma (Rome; capital) 2,687,881; Milano (Milan) 1,334,171; Napoli (Naples) 1,061,583; Torino (Turin) 945,551; Palermo 694,749.

● **PEOPLE Population:** 56,735,130 (1999 est.). **Nationality:** noun—Italian(s); adjective—Italian. **Ethnic groups:** primarily Italian, but includes small clusters of German-, French-, and Slovene-Italians in north and Albanian-Italians in south; Sicilians. **Languages:** Italian; parts of Trentino-Alto Adige region (e.g., Bolzano) are predominantly German-speaking; significant French-speaking minority in Valle d'Aosta region; Slovene-speaking minority in Trieste-Gorizia area. **Religions:** 98% nominally Roman Catholic.

● **GOVERNMENT Type:** republic. **Constitution:** Jan. 1, 1948. **National holiday:** Anniversary of the Republic, June 2. **Heads of Government:** Carlo Azeglio Ciampi, president (since May 1999); Massimo D'Alema, prime minister (since Oct. 1998). **Structure:** executive—president empowered to dissolve Parliament and call national election; commander of armed forces presides over Supreme Defense Council; otherwise, authority to govern invested in Council of Ministers; bicameral legislature—popularly elected Parliament (315-member Senate, 630-member Chamber of Deputies); judiciary—independent.

● **ECONOMY Monetary unit:** Italian lira. **Budget:** (1998 est.) *income:* $559 bil.; *expend.:* $589 bil. **GDP:** $1.181 tril., $20,800 per capita (1998 est.). **Chief crops:** fruits, vegetables, grapes, potatoes, sugar beets, soybeans, grain, olives; meat and dairy products. **Natural resources:** mercury, potash, marble, sulfur, dwindling natural gas and crude oil reserves. **Major industries:** tourism, machinery and transport equipment, iron, steel, chemicals. **Labor force:** 23.193 mil.; 61% services, 32% industry, 7% agriculture (1996). **Exports:** $243 bil. (f.o.b., 1998); engineering products, textiles and clothing, production machinery, motor vehicles. **Imports:** $202 bil. (f.o.b., 1998); engineering products, chemicals, transport equipment, energy products. **Major trading partners:** *exports:* 16.4% Germany, 12.2% France, 7.9% US, 7.1% UK; *imports:* 18% Germany, 13.2% France, 6.7% UK, 6.2% Netherlands.

Rome became the major power in Italy around 500 b.c., dominating the Etruscans in the north and Greek settlements in the south. The Roman Republic already dominated most of the Mediterranean and western Europe by the time imperial rule was established under Julius Caesar. The empire was divided between Rome and Byzantium in the fourth century a.d. The Roman Empire in the west was severely weakened by Germanic invasions in the fifth century and thereafter gradually dissolved, so that Italy became a disunited collection of aristocratic holdings and independent cities.

By the 10th century, the city-states, especially in the north, emerged as major powers, rivaling the Papal States of the central peninsula. Venice and Genoa emerged as major maritime powers during the medieval period, while Florence, Siena, and other cities developed into centers of agricultural and commercial wealth, impelling the successive renaissances of the 12th and 15th centuries. With the rise of the Habsburg empire, the monarchical powers of northern Europe vied for power in Italy, and the peninsula's small states became pawns of France, Spain, and Austria.

At the turn of the 19th century, Napoleon created the short-lived Kingdom of Italy as a French satellite, but after his fall, there was a general return to the old pattern, with Austria dominating the north. Metternich in 1815 called Italy a "geographic expression."

The 19th century saw a growing sense of nationalism in both politics and culture. The revolutionary military leader, Giuseppe Garibaldi, and the statesman, Conte Camillo di Cavour, brought about the establishment of the Kingdom of Italy in 1861. The kingdom wrested Venice away from Austria (1866) and absorbed the Papal States in 1870.

Although united territorially, the kingdom was divided by conflict between church and state, north and south, modern urban industry versus semifeudal rural poverty. Parliamentary politics under the constitutional monarchy created a regime that was weak and venal, inspiring little popular support.

Italy joined the Allied powers in World War I, but its minor gains in the Peace of Paris scarcely seemed to justify its wartime suffering and one million dead. Postwar economic dislocation, fear of communism, and political disillusionment abetted the rise of fascism. Benito Mussolini took over the Italian government at the invitation of the king in 1922 and soon acquired dictatorial powers. Papal secular authority in Vatican City was reestablished by the Lateran Agreement of 1929. In the late 1920s and early 1930s, Italy appeared to be a major power, defending Austria from Germany, colonizing Ethiopia, supporting Francisco Franco in the Spanish civil war, and joining in an "axis" with Hitler's Germany.

Mussolini, the senior partner in the fascist axis, soon was eclipsed by Hitler, and Italy was drawn into the disaster of World War II in 1939. Italy annexed Albania and invaded Greece, but that campaign turned into a fiasco from which German troops had to save the Italian army. In 1943 Allied attacks on Italy began; the fascist Grand Council deposed Mussolini, and the king, Victor Emmanuel III, had him arrested. Hitler intervened in September 1943 and began the war in Italy anew, rescuing Mussolini who established another fascist regime in northern Italy, while the legal Italian government in the south switched sides and welcomed Italy's liberation.

The head of the first postwar government was a Christian Democrat, Alcide de Gasperi. The monarchy was abolished by plebiscite in 1946, and the Republic of Italy was established. The north supported the republic, while monarchism retained significant support in the south.

This division reflected a roughly accurate generalization that sees Italy as a progressive commercial and industrial north and a backward agricultural/pastoral south. Despite such industrial giants of the north as Fiat and Pirelli, however, Italy's manufacturing is primarily carried on by medium-size and small firms, while agriculture is characteristic of the whole country. As late as 1956, there were more Italian workers in agriculture than in industry. Agriculture in the north is generally more prosperous than in the south, with its more arid climate and impoverished soil. Italy is a net food importer.

In the first elections under the republic, in 1948, the Christian Democrats benefited from obvious American patronage and a split in the ranks of the Left to win a clear parliamentary majority. Italy accepted Marshall Plan aid and membership in NATO; reintegration into the European mainstream found expression in membership in the Council of Europe and the Coal and Steel Community.

Domestically, reconstruction was the major task, with both industrial and agricultural output severely hampered by social and physical damage from the war; inflation was rampant and basic social services impaired. The Christian Democrats, normally in Center-Right coalitions in the 1950s and Center-Left coalitions in the 1960s, adopted a policy directed at creating a stable currency, a free market, comprehensive social welfare programs, and occasional state intervention in the economy. This created an Italian "economic miracle," with industrial production doubling between 1953 and 1961 and increasing an additional 40 percent by 1966, led by steel, automobiles, machinery, and electrical equipment.

In1970s the Christian Democrats gradually declined in political influence, normally gaining less than 40 percent of the popular vote while continuing to provide premiers in often short-lived coalition cabinets. Left-wing terrorism became a major national problem. The Christian Democratic leader and former prime minister Aldo Moro was kidnapped and murdered in 1978, and U.S. Brig. Gen./NATO officer James Dozier was kidnapped (and subsequently rescued) in 1981. The government of Bettino Craxi, Italy's first Socialist premier, was severely shaken after it refused to cooperate with the United States in apprehending and trying the hijackers of the Achille Lauro in 1985. Craxi resigned in 1987.

Lacking effective political unity, Italy's coalition governments—there have been more than 50 since the war—tended to muddle along in the face of slow economic growth, inflation, and high unemployment. But awareness of Mafia assassinations and revelations of government corruption far beyond even this tolerant people's expectations led to demands for dramatic changes. In April 1993 the electorate overwhelmingly approved reforms that changed the basic elements of Italian political life. The first elections under the reformed system were held in March 1994, and ended half a century of Christian Democrat-led coalition governments. The Christian Democrats, hastily renamed the Italian Popular Party, won only 11 percent of the vote, while the Socialists, normally the second largest party, fell to 2 percent. What replaced the old guard was not the early favorite Progressive Alliance, but rather the right-wing Alliance for Freedom which captured 43 percent of the popular vote. In May, wealthy publishing executive Silvio Berlusconi was sworn in as prime minister. but his government lasted only into December. Political disputes, union opposition to his austerity budget, and the announcement that magistrates were investigating charges he had bribed tax officials diminished his authority.

Rather than call new elections, Italy's president asked Lamberto Dini to form a new "nonparty" cabinet of businessmen, judges, and professors, a cabinet that won the requisite votes of confidence in the two chambers by Feb.1, 1995. The new government showed surprising staying power, successfully passing its budget (combining tax hikes and spending cuts) and negotiating reform of Italy's bloated pension system with leading trade unions. It even began the politically touchy process of investigating the anticrime magistrates for possible violations of civil rights.

As corruption trials continued, the Dini government survived successive votes of confidence, the last on condition that he resign with the new year, which he did. New elections were not held until April 1996. The left-wing "Olive Tree Coalition," led by the once-Communist "Democratic Party of the Left," trounced the right-wing "Freedom Alliance." Its new prime minister was Professor Romano Prodi of the Popular party. Prodi concentrated on bringing the economy into line so Italy would be eligible for participation in the EMU which, with much manevering, including a stringent austerity budget, and a sudden economic upswing, he did – formal endorsement coming in May 1998. Yet, in October, the Prodi government lost a vote of confidence by 312-313; the issue was the budget's cuts in social spending, unacceptable to the "Reconstructed Communists". Prodi endorsed Massimo D'Alema of the Democratic Party of the Left (the old Communist Party). To the EU's relief, his cabinet retained Prodi's Finance Minister and Treasury/Budget Minister. Early in 1999, Prodi himself moved on to become the new President of the European Commission.

▶IVORY COAST
Republic of Côte d'Ivoire
● **GEOGRAPHY Location:** western coast of Africa. **Boundaries**: Mali and Burkina Faso to N, Ghana to E, Gulf of Guinea to S, Liberia and Guinea to W. **Total area**: 124,502 sq. mi. (322,460 sq km). **Coastline:** 320 mi. (515 km). **Comparative area:** slightly larger than New Mexico. **Land use:** 8% arable land; 4% permanent crops; 41% meadows and pastures; 22% forest and woodland; 25% other;

includes negl. % irrigated. **Major cities**: (1988) Yamoussoukro (capital—not recognized by U.S., which recognizes Abidjan) 106,786; Abidjan 1,929,079; Bouaké 329,850.

● **PEOPLE Population:** 15,818,068 (1999 est.). **Nationality:** noun—Ivorian(s); adjective—Ivorian. **Ethnic groups:** 23% Baoule, 18% Bete, 15% Senoufou, 11% Malinke and Agni; over 60 ethnic groups; 3 million foreign Africans, mostly Burkinabe and Malians. **Languages:** French (official); over 60 African languages and dialects with Dioula most widely spoken. **Religions:** 60% Muslim, 22% Christian, 18% indigenous beliefs.

● **GOVERNMENT Type:** republic; multiparty presidential regime established 1960. **Independence:** Aug. 7, 1960 (from France). **Constitution:** Nov. 3, 1960. **National holiday:** National Day, Dec. 7. **Heads of Government:** Henri Konan Bedie, president (since Dec. 1993); Daniel Kablan Duncan, prime minister (since Dec. 1993). **Structure:** executive—president has broad powers; unicameral legislature—175-member National Assembly; judiciary.

● **ECONOMY Monetary unit:** Communauté Financière Africaine franc. **Budget:** (1997) *income:* $2.3 bil.; *expend.:* $2.6 bil. **GDP:** $24.2 bil., $1,680 per capita (1998 est.). **Chief crops:** coffee, cocoa, bananas, palm oil; cotton, rubber; timber. **Natural resources:** crude oil, diamonds, manganese, iron ore, cobalt. **Major industries:** foodstuffs, wood processing, oil refinery. **Labor force:** N.A. **Exports:** $4.3 bil. (f.o.b., 1998 est.); 36% cocoa, coffee, tropical woods. **Imports:** $2.5 bil. (f.o.b., 1998 est.); food, consumer goods, capital goods, fuel. **Major trading partners:** *exports:* 17% Netherlands, 15% France, 7% Germany, 6% U.S.; *imports:* 28% France, 20% Nigeria, 6% U.S., 5% Italy.

The peoples of the Ivory Coast belong to various tribes that had established small and mutually hostile kingdoms prior to the 18th century. The dominant Baule migrated to the Ivory Coast from Ghana about 200 years ago. European contact began with the Portuguese, who established coastal trading stations in the 15th century. They were followed in rapid succession by the Dutch, British, and finally the French, who landed at Assinie in 1637. Dense tropical forests and a lack of good harbors retarded European exploration.

France established a protectorate over the coastal zone in 1842 and during the remainder of the 19th century expanded its control, by conquest and diplomacy, into the interior. In 1893 the Ivory Coast was organized as a French colony, and in 1904 it was made part of French West Africa.

France's Vichy government controlled French West Africa during World War II and harshly suppressed the region's growing nationalist movements. In 1946 a group of West African leaders, inspired by Félix Houphouet-Boigny, formed the African Democratic Assembly, which later cooperated with the French in the implementation of reforms, including, by 1956, universal suffrage and the formation of locally autonomous assemblies. Complete independence for the Ivory Coast came on Aug. 4, 1960.

Félix Houphouet-Boigny was unanimously elected the first president of the Ivory Coast, and he played a key role in forming the Organization of African Unity in 1963. Until 1990, when his Democratic party was the only political party allowed in the country, Houphouet-Boigny easily won reelection. But even after he liberalized the political process, Houphouet-Boigny retained control, winning a new five-year term in multi-party elections held in 1990, and the Democrats captured an overwhelming majority of the seats in Parliament. Under his presidency, the Ivory Coast enjoyed both political stability and economic prosperity.

Houphouet-Boigny died in 1993, and was succeeded by his fellow Democrat Henri Konan Bedie, who was president of the National Assembly. Bedie won reelection in 1995, and has continued the policies of his predecessor. In Sept. 1999, however, hidden political tensions surfaced when Pres. Bedie ordered the arrest of several hundred members of an opposition party, Rally of the Republicans.

The Ivory Coast maintains strong commercial and cultural ties to France, and is on good terms with other Western-bloc nations.

▶ JAMAICA

● **Geography Location:** northern Caribbean Sea. Kingston 17°58'N, 76°48'W. **Boundaries:** Cuba 87 mi. (145 km) to N. **Total area:** 4,243 sq. mi. (10,990 sq km). **Coastline:** 635 mi. (1,022 km). **Comparative area:** slightly smaller than Connecticut. **Land use:** 14% arable land; 6% permanent crops; 24% meadows and pastures; 17% forest and woodland; 39% other; includes 3% irrigated. **Major cities:** (1982 census) Kingston (capital) 524,638; Spanish Town 89,097; Montego Bay 70,265.

● **People Population:** 2,652,443 (1999 est.). **Nationality:** noun—Jamaican(s); adjective—Jamaican. **Ethnic groups:** 90.4% black, 1.3% East Indian, 0.2% white, 0.2% Chinese, 7.3% mixed, 0.6% other. **Languages:** English, Creole. **Religions:** 61.3% Protestant, 4% Roman Catholic, some spiritualist cults.

● **Government Type:** parliamentary democracy. **Independence:** Aug. 6, 1962 (from UK). **Constitution:** Aug. 6, 1962. **National holiday:** Independence Day, first Monday in August. **Heads of Government:** Gov. Gen. Howard F.H. Cooke, governor-general (since Aug. 1991); Percival James Patterson, prime minister (since Apr. 1993). **Structure:** cabinet headed by prime minister; bicameral legislature; judiciary follows British tradition under chief justice.

● **Economy Monetary unit:** Jamaican dollar. **Budget:** (FY98/99 est.) *income:* $2.27 bil.; *expend.:* $3.66 bil. **GDP:** $8.8 bil., $3,300 per capita (1998 est.). **Chief crops:** sugarcane, bananas, coffee, citrus, potatoes, vegetables; poultry, goats, milk. **Natural resources:** bauxite, gypsum, limestone. **Major industries:** tourism, bauxite mining, textiles. **Labor force:** 1.14 bil. (1996); 41% services, 22.5% agriculture, 19% industry and commerce; 16.5% unemployment. **Exports:** $1.7 bil. (1997 est.); alumina, bauxite, sugar, bananas, rum. **Imports:** $2.8 bil. (1997 est.); machinery and transport equipment, construction materials, fuel; food; chemicals. **Major trading partners:** *exports:* 33.3% U.S., 17.1% EU (excluding UK and Norway), 14.1% Canada; *imports:* 47.7% U.S., 12.8% EU (excluding UK), 10.2% Caricom.

Christopher Columbus visited Jamaica in 1494, and the Spanish ruled the island—exterminating the native Arawaks in the process—until it fell to British control in 1655. A haven for buccaneers, by the 18th century Jamaica was a major sugar producer and the site of one of the busiest slave markets in the world. Emancipation of the slaves in 1833 and abolition of tariff protection in 1846 contributed strongly to the subsequent downfall of the plantation economy.

In 1962 the island gained its independence. The country has been plagued by racial and class division set within the context of an underdeveloped economy. Michael Manley of the People's National party became prime minister in 1972. He nationalized some industry and established closer ties with Cuba. Edward Seaga's Jamaica Labour party came to power in 1980 and encouraged more private-sector involvement in developing the economy. Though Manley was reelected to office in 1989, he did not reverse this general trend; in 1992 he was succeeded by Percival James Patterson, who led the People's National party to a landslide victory in violence-marred elections in March 1993. He was reelected in 1997 despite continuing economic problems.

▶ JAPAN

● **Geography Location:** chain of more than 3,000 islands extending 1,300 mi. (2,200 km) NE to SW between Sea of Japan and western Pacific Ocean; southern Japan about 93 mi. (150 km) E of S. Korea; islands of Hokkaido, Honshu, Shikoku, and Kyushu account for 98% of land area. Tokyo 35°40'N, 139°45'E. **Boundaries:** Sea of Okhotsk to N, Pacific Ocean to E, East China Sea to SW, and Sea of Japan to W. **Total area:** 145,882 sq. mi. (377,835 sq km). **Coastline:** 18,487 mi. (29,751 km). **Comparative area:** slightly smaller than California. **Land use:** 11% arable land; 1% permanent crops; 2% meadows and pastures; 67% forest and woodland; 19% other; includes 9% irrigated. **Major cities:** (1995 est.) Tokyo (capital) 7,836,665; Yokohama 3,273,609; Osaka 2,478,628; Nagoya 2,086,745; Sapporo 1,733,133.

● **People Population:** 126,182,077 (1999 est.). **Nationality:** noun—Japanese (sing., pl.); adjective—Japanese. **Ethnic groups:** 99.4% Japanese, 0.6% other (mostly Korean). **Languages:** Japanese. **Religions:** most Japanese observe both Shinto and Buddhist rites; about 16% belong to other faiths, including 0.7% Christian.

● **Government Type:** constitutional monarchy. **Constitution:** May 3, 1947. **National holiday:** Birthday of the Emperor, Dec. 23. **Heads of Government:** Akihito, emperor (since Jan. 1989); Keizo Obuchi, prime minister (since July 1998). **Structure:** executive—emperor is symbolic head of state; power is vested in cabinet appointed by prime minister; bicameral legislature; judiciary.

● **Economy Monetary unit:** yen. **Budget:** (FY99/00 est.) *income:* $407 bil.; *expend.:* $711 bil. **GDP:** $2.903 trillion, $23,100 per capita (1998 est.). **Chief crops:** rice, sugar beets, vegetables, fruits; chickens, pigs, cattle; world's largest fish catch. **Natural resources:** negl. mineral resources, fish. **Major industries:** metallurgical and engineering industries, electrical and electronic industries, motor vehicles. **Labor force:** 67.72 mil. (1998); 50% trade and services, 33% manufacturing, mining, and construction. **Exports:** $440 bil. (f.o.b., 1998); 96% manufactures (including 50% machinery, 19% motor vehicles, 3% consumer electronics). **Imports:** $319 bil. (c.i.f., 1998); 54% manufactures, 28% foodstuffs and raw materials, 16% fossil fuels. **Major trading partners:** *exports:* 30% US, 18% EU, 12% Southeast Asia; *imports:* 24% US, 14% Southeast Asia, 14% EU.

Japan's ancient Jomon civilization was displaced by proto-Japanese Yayoi migrants from mainland northeast Asia beginning in the fourth century b.c. In the early Yayoi period, a mounted military aristocracy dominated rice-growing commoners. The shamanic religion of the time was ancestral to Japan's later indigenous religion, Shinto. Yayoi society evolved into the Yamato protostate, c. a.d. 250-500. The Yamato kings were buried in large, elaborate tomb mounds together with haniwa clay sculptures. From the third century a.d., contact with the mainland increased. Korean missionaries introduced Buddhism and Chinese writing in the mid-sixth century. A centralized monarchy developed in the Yamato Plain, central Honshu Island; Prince Shotoku, a great patron of Buddhism, founded the Horyuji and other great temples in the early seventh century.

In 710 the Yamato kings established a permanent capital for the first time, at Nara; the city was modeled on the Chinese capital. In 785 the court, split by factionalism and dominated by Nara's large and wealthy Buddhist temples, abandoned the capital; in 794 the new capital at Heian (Kyoto) was completed. The ensuing Heian period was one of the most brilliant in Japanese history. A small civil aristocracy, dominated by the Fujiwara family, drew great wealth from provincial estates and created a metropolitan culture of extreme refinement. From the ninth through the 11th centuries, strong Chinese influences were incorporated into Japanese culture.

In the 12th century the power of the Heian court waned as the influence of the provincial military aristocracy (samurai) grew stronger. In 1156 the capital was seized by the Taira family; in 1185 the Taira were overthrown by their rivals, the Minamoto. The Minamoto established a military government under a shogun (generalissimo) at Kamakura; the emperor remained at Kyoto, stripped of all governmental authority. In Kamakura the Minamoto were soon displaced by their former vassals, the Hojo. During the Kamakura period, the Japanese drew away from Chinese influence in art, architecture, literature, and religion in the process of creating a more distinctively Japanese culture. In 1274 and again in 1281, attempted Mongol invasions were repulsed with the aid of timely typhoons (kamikaze, "divine winds").

In the course of a failed attempt at imperial restoration, the Kamakura shogunate was overthrown, in the 1330s, by the Ashikaga family, which in 1338 established a new shogunal government at Muromachi, a precinct of Kyoto. The Muromachi period saw the flowering of a new warrior culture, marked by such military virtues as bravery, loyalty, personal honor, and skill with weapons and by adherence to Zen Buddhism and its associated arts (tea ceremony, flower arranging, calligraphy, etc.). With the Onin Wars of the mid-15th century, the Muromachi shogunate lost most of its power, and the country fell into a century of civil war.

The civil wars were brought to an end during the second half of the 16th century by three successive unifiers, Oda Nobunaga, Hideyoshi, and Tokugawa Ieyasu. At the same time, the Jesuit Francis Xavier and his successors established a short-lived Japanese Christian community. Hideyoshi made several attempts (1592-98) to conquer and annex Korea. In 1601 Tokugawa Ieyasu defeated his rivals in the Battle of Sekigahara. He established a shogunal government at Edo (later Tokyo) in 1603; he and his successors formalized the structure of Japanese feudalism, created a rigid class structure, suppressed Christianity, and enforced the isolation of Japan from virtually all outside influence. Some trade with the mainland and a small Dutch trading station at Nagasaki provided Japan's only windows to the outside world for the next 250 years. The Edo period was marked by urbanization and the development of urban culture (Kabuki theater, wood-block prints, etc.) as the merchant class prospered from internal trade.

The Tokugawa shogun's inability to repel the 1854 visit of American commodore Matthew Perry and subsequently to avoid establishing commercial and diplomatic relations with Western nations deeply shocked the samurai class. Patriotic young samurai from Choshu, Satsuma, and other outlying feudal domains began to call for the abolition of the shogunate and the restoration of imperial rule in order to confront the threat of contact with the West. Quickly realizing that isolationism was doomed, the young radicals' program changed from "respect the emperor, expel the barbarians" to "enrich the state, strengthen the military." With the accession of the Meiji emperor in 1868, shogunal government ended.

Under direct imperial rule, feudalism was abolished and a wide-ranging program of military, industrial, commercial, and social modernization was implemented. The Meiji Constitution of 1889 created a constitutional monarchy and a parliamentary system of government. Having avoided domination by Western nations, Japan itself became an imperialist power. Defeating China in the Sino-Japanese War of 1894-95 and Russia in the Russo-Japanese War of 1904-05, Japan gained a dominant position in Manchuria and in Korea, which became a Japanese colony in 1910.

Under the ineffectual Taisho emperor (reigned 1912-26), parliamentary government flourished. Japan sided with the Allied Powers in World War I, and the Treaty of Versailles advanced Japan's international interests, particularly in China. The general prosperity of the 1920s was threatened by the Tokyo earthquake of 1923, by labor strife, and by a stagnant agricultural economy. Militant right-wing nationalism began to play an important role in domestic politics.

During the international economic depression of the early 1930s, right-wing militants gained the upper hand; they assassinated many moderate political figures. Japan invaded Manchuria in 1931 and established the puppet state of Manchuguo in 1934. An attempted military coup in 1936 failed in its immediate objectives but led to the establishment of martial law, under which the Showa emperor (Hirohito; reigned 1926-89) became a pawn of the ultranationalists. An invasion and military takeover of eastern China in 1937 was seen as the first step in the creation of a "Greater East Asian Co-prosperity Sphere," designed to unite Asia under Japanese control.

In 1940 Japan entered the Tripartite Alliance with Italy and Nazi Germany. Japan occupied French Indochina in June 1941, provoking increased Allied resistance to Japanese imperial ambitions. Gen. Hideki Tojo became prime minister in October 1941 and ordered simultaneous preemptive strikes against Pearl Harbor, the Philippines, and Malaya on Dec. 7-8. By mid 1942, Japan controlled most of Southeast Asia and the western Pacific, but American victories at the Battle of the Coral Sea in May 1942 and the Battle of Midway in June 1942 halted further Japanese expansion. Thereafter, Japanese forces were steadily pushed back in "island-hopping" campaigns in the central Pacific and along the western Pacific rim, and by Allied counterattacks in Burma. Air attacks on Japan itself culminated in the nuclear bombing of Hiroshima and Nagasaki in August 1945.

Following Japan's formal surrender on Sept. 2, 1945, an American army in Japan under Gen. Douglas MacArthur took control of the country. A new constitution was promulgated, relegating the emperor to purely symbolic status, renouncing the use of military force, and guaranteeing the civil rights of citizens. The industrial combines that had lent strength to Japan's empire were partially dismantled. An international tribunal tried many wartime leaders as war criminals in 1948. In 1949 considerable authority was returned to the conservative government of Premier Shigeru Yoshida. Japan served as a base for American forces during the Korean War, 1950-53, greatly accelerating Japan's postwar economic recovery. On Apr. 28, 1952, a peace treaty between Japan and the United States went into effect, ending the Occupation. On Mar. 8, 1954, the two nations signed a mutual defense assistance pact.

Japan was admitted to the United Nations in 1956. The success of Japan's postwar recovery was symbolized by the Tokyo Olympic Games of 1964 and Expo '70 at Osaka. Violent student-protest movements in 1968-69 had no clear political goals and no lasting effect. Politically stable under an unbroken succession of Liberal Democratic party governments, Japan emerged as a major and steadily expanding world industrial power.

In general, Japan has been reluctant to play an international political role consistent with its vast economic power. From the mid-1970s onward, the balance of trade between Japan and the U.S. has weighed heavily in Japan's favor, leading to strains in U.S.-Japan relations and American charges that Japan engages in unfair trade practices. Several times during the 1980s and 1990s, especially when the yen was appreciating rapidly against the dollar, Japan pledged to take measures to even the trade balance by improving foreign access to Japan's domestic economy.

Domestically, Japan in the 1980s enjoyed a very high standard of living, marred by the extremely high cost and relatively low quality of housing, and by underinvestment in the public infrastructure. A real estate boom led prices of commercial property in downtown Tokyo to increase as much as 200-fold in the span of a decade. This boom extended to the United States, where the rapidly declining dollar made Japanese investment in the United States especially attractive.

For most of its postwar history, Japan has been essentially a one-party state, run by political professionals of the Liberal Democratic party (LDP) according to a system of consensus. But by the end of the 1980s, the system started to crumble as the regime's widespread corruption was revealed. Prime Minister Noburu Takeshita was force to resign in May 1989 after a bribery scandal. His successor, Sousuke Uno, lasted only two months before resigning in a scandal over his sexual conduct. Public opinion turned sharply against the LDP, which lost control of the upper house of the Diet in July 1989 elections; the Socialist party, led by Takako Doi, posted significant gains.

Uno's successor, Toshiki Kaifu, expected to be a mere caretaker, emerged as an unexpectedly skillful leader who enhanced Japan's international reputation by offering aid to Eastern Europe and the former Soviet Union, and by pledging billions of dollars to support the Persian Gulf War. In October 1991, Kaifu was replaced as LDP chairman by a more experienced politician, Kiichi

Miyazawa, who succeeded in passing legislation authorizing the posting abroad of Japanese troops—for the first time since World War II—for peacekeeping missions in noncombat roles.

An economic slump and political scandals continued to buffet the LDP throughout 1992 and 1993. LDP kingmaker Shin Kanemaru and other party officials resigned after admitting ties to gangsters. The LDP was forced from office in 1993 for the first time in 38 years, and formed successive coalition governments with the Socialist Party and other parties. The weak coalition governments paved the way for a LDP return to power in 1994; the years since have brought continued economic stagnation, bank failures, scandals involving government and business ties to organized crime, and general malaise.

The city of Kobe was hit by a severe earthquake in January, 1995; the government was criticized for inneffective rescue and relief efforts. The country's confidence was further shaken in March, 1995, by a bizarre attack with poison gas in the Tokyo subway, perpetrated by a religious cult, Aum Shinrikyo. Its leader, Shoko Asahara, was eventually arrested and convicted of murder.

Several instances of violent crime involving U.S. servicemen in Okinawa led Pres. Clinton and Prime Minister Hashimoto to sign an agreement in April, 1996, reducing the number of American bases in Okinawa.

Prime Minister Ryutaro Hashimoto, first elected in January 1996, was re-elected leader of the LDP in Sept., 1997, strengthening his hold on the government. But the Asian economic crisis took a toll on Japan, still in the midst of a long-term recession. The Winter Olympics in 1998 failed to give the country a lift as the government responded to the economic crisis with belated fiscal and monetary measures. In the spring of 1998 a plunge in the value of the yen doomed the Hashimoto government; he resigned after disappointing results in the upper-house election of July 12, and was replaced by party stalwart, Keizo Obuchi.

In 1999 Japan's economy rebounded slightly and the yen made sporadic gains against the dollar as the Obuchi government tried desperately to raise the levels of spending throughout the economy.

▶ JORDAN
Hashemite Kingdom of Jordan

● **GEOGRAPHY Location:** western Asia. **Boundaries:** Syria to N, Iraq to NE, Saudi Arabia to SE, Israel to W. **Total area:** 34,445 sq. mi. (89,213 sq km). **Coastline:** 16 mi. (26 km). **Comparative area:** slightly smaller than Indiana. **Land use:** 4% arable land; 1% permanent crops; 9% meadows and pastures; 1% forest and woodland; 85% other; includes 0.5% irrigated. **Major cities:** (1991) Amman (capital) 965,000; Zarqa 359,000; Irbid 216,000; Russeita 115,500.

● **PEOPLE Population:** 4,561,147 (1999 est.). **Nationality:** noun—Jordanian(s); adjective—Jordanian. **Ethnic groups:** 98% Arab, 1% Circassian, 1% Armenian. **Languages:** Arabic (official); English widely understood among upper and middle classes. **Religions:** 96% Sunni Muslim, 4% Christian.

● **GOVERNMENT Type:** constitutional monarchy. **Independence:** May 25, 1946 (from League of Nations Mandate under British administration). **Constitution:** Jan. 8, 1952. **National holiday:** Independence Day, May 25. **Heads of Government:**

Abdullah Bin Al Hussein, king (since Feb. 1999); Abdel Raof Al Rawabdeh, prime minister (since March 1999). **Structure:** executive—king is chief of state, prime minister and cabinet are appointed by king; bicameral legislature—House of Representatives has been dissolved by the king several times since 1974; House of Notables appointed by the king; judiciary.

● **ECONOMY Monetary unit:** Jordanian dinar. **Budget:** (1999 est.) *income:* $2.8 bil.; *expend.:* $3 bil. **GDP:** $15.5 bil., $3,500 per capita (1998 est.). **Chief crops:** wheat, barley, citrus, tomatoes, melons, olives; poultry, goats, sheep. **Natural resources:** phosphates, potash, shale oil. **Major industries:** phosphate mining, petroleum refining, cement. **Labor force:** 1.15 mil plus 300,000 foreign workers (1997); 11.4% industry, 10.5% commerce, 10% construction, 8.7% transport and communications, 7.4% agriculture, 52% other services. **Exports:** $1.5 bil. (f.o.b., 1997); phosphates, fertilizers, potash, agricultural products, manufactures. **Imports:** $3.9 bil. (c.i.f., 1997); crude oil, machinery, transport equipment, food, live animals, manufactured goods. **Major trading partners:** *exports:* Iraq, Saudi Arabia, India; *imports:* EU, Iraq, US.

The present territory of the Kingdom of Jordan corresponds to the biblical lands of Edom, Gilead, and Moab. The ancient rock city of Petra was the capital of the Edomite and Nabataean kingdoms. The region was incorporated into the Roman Empire, and later the Latin Kingdom of Jerusalem; it was an important early center of Christianity.

In the 630s Jordan became one of the first areas outside Arabia to fall to the expansion of Islam. It became subject to the Caliphate, located at Damascus and later at Baghdad, and in the 11th century became part of the empire of the Seljuk Turks. The Crusades brought European invaders, but with little lasting impact. The Mongols conquered Jordan in the mid-13th century, and it later passed into the control of the Mamluk sultanate. In 1517 Jordan was incorporated into the Ottoman Empire.

Following the post-World War I breakup of the Ottoman Empire, Jordan came under British control as part of a League of Nations Mandate of Palestine. In 1921 Great Britain sponsored the establishment of a monarchy by Abdullah, son of Hussein ibn Ali, ruler of the Hejaz in Arabia. Britain recognized the independence of the Hashemite Kingdom of Transjordan in 1923; a 1928 treaty gave Britain the unrestricted right to station troops in the kingdom.

Transjordan supported the Allies in World War II and was rewarded with full independence in 1946, though, by treaty, strong military ties to Great Britain were maintained. In 1948 the kingdom joined the Arab League, changed its name to Jordan, and joined other Arab states in the first Arab-Israeli War. The war resulted in the occupation by Jordanian troops of the West Bank and the Old City of Jerusalem, which were annexed in 1950.

The present ruler, King Hussein I, came to the throne on Aug. 11, 1952. All British military forces were withdrawn from the kingdom in 1957.

Israel recaptured the West Bank and the Old City of Jerusalem in the Six-Day War of 1967, and large numbers of Palestinian refugees fled to Jordan. Jordan played no substantial role in the October 1974 Arab-Israeli War. In 1974 Jordan accepted the decision of an Arab summit conference designating the Palestine Liberation Organization the sole representative of Palestinians in the West Bank. Jordan's role as a front-line opponent of Israel has won it a large annual subvention from Arab oil states; King Hussein's reputation as an Arab moderate has led to significant American economic and military support.

King Hussein strongly opposed the 1979 Camp David Accords and the Egypt-Israeli peace treaty; Jordan broke off diplomatic relations with Egypt in March 1979 but resumed full relations in 1984.

In July 1981 King Hussein, charging the Palestine Liberation Organization with subversion, forced the withdrawal of PLO troops and political headquarters from Jordan. While some hoped that Hussein would represent the Palestinians in talks with Israel, in 1988 the king flatly rejected any such role, implied that the PLO should declare an independent state on the West Bank and in the Gaza Strip, and declared that any future settlement would require direct talks between Israel and the PLO.

The Persian Gulf War had a drastic impact on Jordan's economy. King Hussein actively backed Iraq, thus jeopardizing direct aid from Kuwait and Saudi Arabia. But the historic peace treaty signed with Israel in October 1994 restored Hussein's standing while returning some territory taken in the 1967 war. In August 1998, while in the U.S. for medical care, King Hussein made a dramatic visit to the PLO-Israeli talks to appeal for a settlement. Back in Jordan, Hussein deposed his brother Hassan as Crown Prince, swearing in his eldest son Abdullah instead. Twelve days later (Feb. 7), the king died. The new king, Abdullah, pledged to continue his father's policies, asking the current cabinet to stay on.

▶ **KAZAKHSTAN**
Republic of Kazakhstan

● **GEOGRAPHY Location:** central Asia. **Boundaries:** Russian Federation to N and NE, China to SE, Kyrgystan, Uzbekistan, and Turkmenistan to S, Caspian Sea to W. **Total area:** 1,049,151 sq. mi. (2,717,300 sq km). **Coastline:** 1,441 mi. (2,320 km) on Caspian Sea. **Comparative area:** slightly less than four times the size of Texas. **Land use:** 12% arable cropland; 11% permanent crops; 57% meadows and pastures; 4% forest and woodland; 16% other (mainly mountain and desert). **Major cities:** (1993 est.) Astana (capital) 300,000; Almaty (formerly Alma-Ata) 1,176,000; Karaganda 596,000.

● **PEOPLE Population:** 16,824,825 (1999 est.). **Nationality:** noun—Kazakhstani(s); adjective—Kazakhstani. **Ethnic groups:** 46% Kazakh, 34.7% Russian, 4.9% Ukrainian, 3.1% German. **Languages:** over 40% Kazakh (state language); 66% Russian (official, used in everyday business). **Religions:** 47% Muslim, 44% Russian Orthodox, 2% Protestant.

● **GOVERNMENT Type:** republic. **Independence:** Dec. 16, 1991 (from the Soviet Union). **Constitution:** Jan 28, 1993. **National holiday:** Republic Day, Dec. 16. **Heads of Government:** Nursultan A. Nazarbaev, president (since Dec. 1991); Nurlan Balgimbayev, prime minister (since Oct. 1997). **Structure:** executive—president, prime minister, Council of Ministers; bicameral legislature; judicial.

● **ECONOMY Monetary unit:** tenge. **Budget:** (1998 est.) *income:* $2.9 bil.; *expend.:* $4.2 bil. **GDP:** $52.9 bil., $3,100 per capita (1998 est.). **Chief crops:** grains, cotton; wool, meat. **Natural resources:** major deposits of petroleum, natural gas, coal, iron ore, manganese. **Major industries:** oil, coal, iron ore, manganese. **Labor force:** 8.8 mil. (1997); 27% industry, 23% agriculture. **Exports:** $6.3 bil. (1998); oil, ferrous and nonferrous metals, chemicals, grain, wool. **Imports:** $7.4 bil. (1998); machinery and parts, industrial materials, oil and gas. **Major trading partners:** Russia, Ukraine, Uzbekistan.

Kazakhstan, the largest nation in central Asia, is a land of deserts and plateaus stretching across the rolling tablelands of the Eurasian landmass; approximately 20 percent is mountainous. The Kazakhs are descended from Mongol and Turkic tribes who settled in the area known as Kazakhstan about the 1st century b.c. In the sixth century a.d. the area formed part of the Turkish Khaganate, a loose federation of nomadic tribes, and in the seventh to ninth centuries Islam became established among the settled population. Although the Mongols ruled the area from 1219 to 1447, the Turkish subjects of the Mongol Horde were to play a decisive role in the future of the region.

In the 15th century, the Kazakhs emerged as a distinct people, but by the 17th century, due to internecine fighting, the Kazakhs split into three nomadic federations, known as the Larger, the Middle, and the Lesser Hordes. In the mid-17th century, the Mongols began to invade the region, and the Kazakhs, not being unified enough to repel them, sought protection from the Russians. By the mid-18th century, the Kazakh lands were completely under Russian control. With the freeing of serfs in 1861 in Russia, Kazakhstan experienced its first major influx of Russian and Ukrainian peasants, who were given Kazakh lands. Resentment over this grew until the Kazakhs rebelled against Russian rule in 1916. The Russians brutally repressed the uprising, but not before thousands of Kazakhs and many Russians were killed.

After the 1917 Communist revolution in Russia, a civil war ensued in Kazakhstan, from which the Bolsheviks emerged victorious. The Kazakh territory was incorporated into Russia in 1920, granted "autonomous" status in 1925, and in 1936 it formally became one of the USSR's union republics. Kazakhstan was industrialized, but it suffered enormously from the USSR's policies. In the 1930s, the traditionally nomadic Kazakh people were forcibly settled on collectivized farms, and more than a million died of starvation. In the 1950s, Khrushchev's failed "Virgin Lands" scheme and the Soviet government's repeated nuclear tests wreaked environmental havoc on Kazakhstan. As a result of years of Soviet economic development programs, the rate of Russian and Ukrainian immigration into Kazakhstan greatly increased. By 1979, 41 percent of Kazakhstan's population was Russian; 36 percent was native Kazakhs.

Under Mikhail Gorbachev's policy of glasnost, or openness, in the 1980s, the corrupt Communist party leader of Kazakhstan and Brezhnev crony Dinmukhamed Kunayev was deposed. He was ultimately replaced by Nursultan Nazarbayev, an ethnic Kazakh, who was elected in April 1990 to the new post of president.

Kazakhstan declared its independence in March 1991 and joined the Commonwealth of Independent States in December. It has pursued closer economic but not political ties with Russia and Belarus. The May 1995 customs union among the three was expanded in March 1996 to include coordination of agricultural and industrial policies and the establishment of joint transport, energy and information systems, with Kyrgystan added as a fourth member. Kazakhstan took part (April 1996) in a five-power non-agression treaty with Russia, China, Kyrgyzstan, and Tajikistan which was extended a year later to include reduction of military forces in border areas. The last remaining Soviet-era nuclear missle was detonated underground in May 1995 and the last ballistic missle silo was torn down in September 1996. In Feb. 1997 the supposedly tame legislature refused to ratify a Russian lease of four nuclear test sites in Kazakhstan.

Independent Kazakhstan's first presidential election was held in December 1991 with Nazarbayev the only candidate. An April 1995 referendum cancelled the 1996 election and extended Nazarbayev's term to 2000 with a gratifying 95 percent "yes" vote; and in August of the year 89 percent approved a new "strong president" constitution, making the president head of the Supreme Court and permitting him to dissolve parliament at will. Nazarbayev had already dissolved parliament in March 1995, a parliament in which his supporters held two-thirds of the seats, but whose pace of economic reform displeased him. He ruled by decree until new elections late in 1995 and early in 1996.

Kazakhstan's economic future looks bright because of its enormous untapped gas and oil reserves, perhaps 25 billion barrels. Several global corporations have negotiated development rights. In April 1996, Kazakhstan, Russia and Oman established a consortium with eight oil companies to build a 900-mile pipeline linking the Tengiz fields with Russia's Black Sea port of Novorossiyak. And in July of that year, the IMF chipped in with a loan of $446 million.

In 1998 the capital was moved— ostensibly for security reasons—from Almaty to remote Akmola, which was renamed Astana, a word meaning "capital" in Kazakh. In July, Navarbayev signed a pact with Russia, settling the thorny question of dividing the northern Caspian Sea (with its petroleum riches). But with falling world oil prices, the Kazakh economy stalled, bringing Nazarbayev to call for presidential elections 18 months early, elections he not surprisingly won handily, this time with 80 percent of the votes, in January 1999.

▶ **KENYA**
Republic of Kenya
● **GEOGRAPHY Location:** eastern Africa. **Boundaries:** Sudan to NW, Ethiopia to N, Somalia to E, Indian Ocean to SE, Tanzania to SW, Lake Victoria, Uganda to W. **Total area:** 224,962 sq. mi. (582,650 sq km). **Coastline:** 333 mi. (536 km). **Comparative area:** slightly more than twice the size of Nevada. **Land use:** 7% arable land; 1% permanent crops; 37% meadows and pastures; 30% forest and woodland; 25% other; includes negl. % irrigated. **Major cities:** (1989 est.) Nairobi (capital) 1,346,000; Mombasa 465,000; Nakuru 162,800; Kisumu 185,100; Thika 57,100.
● **PEOPLE Population:** 28,808,658 (1999 est.). **Nationality:** noun—Kenyan(s); adjective—Kenyan. **Ethnic groups:** 22% Kikuyu, 14% Luhya, 13% Luo, 12% Kalenjin, 11% Kamba, 6% Kisii, 6% Meru, 15% other African, 1% non-African (Asian, European, and Arab). **Languages:** English and Swahili (both official), indigenous languages. **Religions:** 38% Protestant, 28% Roman Catholic, 26% indigenous beliefs, 7% Muslim, 2% other.

• **GOVERNMENT** Type: republic. **Independence:** Dec. 12, 1963 (from UK). **Constitution:** Dec. 12, 1963. **National holiday:** Jamhuri Day, Dec. 12. **Head of Government:** Daniel T. arap Moi, president (since Oct. 1978). **Structure:** executive—president and cabinet; unicameral legislature—first multiparty election since repeal of one-party state law in 1991; judiciary.

• **ECONOMY** Monetary unit: Kenyan shilling. **Budget:** (1997 est.) *income:* $2.6 bil.; *expend.:* $2.7 bil. **GDP:** $43.9 bil., $1,550 per capita (1998 est.). **Chief crops:** coffee, tea, corn, wheat, sugarcane; cattle, pork, poultry. **Natural resources:** gold, limestone, soda ash, salt barytes. **Major industries:** small-scale consumer goods (plastic, furniture, batteries, textiles, soap, cigarettes, flour), agricultural processing, oil refining. **Labor force:** 9.2 mil. (1998); 75-80% agriculture, 20-25% non-agriculture. **Exports:** $2 bil. (f.o.b.; 1998); 18% tea, 15% coffee, petroleum products (1995). **Imports:** $3.05 bil. (f.o.b.; 1998); 31% machinery and transport equipment, 13% consumer goods, 12% petroleum and petroleum products (1995 est.) **Major trading partners:** *exports:* 16.1% Uganda, 12.8% Tanzania, 10.4% UK; *imports:* 13.2% UK, 8.2% UAE, 7.6% South Africa.

Kenya formed part of an ancient network of trade between the Red Sea and the coast of East Africa as early as the fourth century b.c. Persian and Arab trading posts were established on the coast by the eighth century a.d. At about the same time, the indigenous Cushitic people of Kenya had been joined by Bantu and Nilotic immigrants. Swahili, a mixture of Bantu and Arabic, developed as a language of trade throughout the region.

Portuguese explorers reached Kenya in 1498. Portuguese control of the coastal area ended in 1729, when the region came under the control of the sultans of Oman. British adventurers explored Kenya in the late 19th century. In 1885 the Berlin Conference divided East Africa into European spheres of influence. The British East Africa Company established a protectorate over the coastal region in 1890 and extended its control into the interior in 1895. British settlers established farms, mission stations, and towns, and Kenya was given colonial status in 1920.

During World War II, northern Kenya was briefly occupied by troops from the Italian colony of Ethiopia. After the British reasserted control, Africans were granted the right to participate in local government in 1944.

From 1952 to 1959, a state of emergency was declared in Kenya because of the "Mau Mau" rebellion against British colonial rule. In response to local unrest, British authorities widened African participation in government and Africans were elected to the Legislative Council in 1957.

Kenya became independent on Dec. 12, 1963, and in 1964 assumed the status of a republic within the British Commonwealth. Jomo Kenyatta, a member of the dominant Kikuyu population and leader of the main political party, the Kenya African National Union (KANU), was elected Kenya's first president. A leftist party, the Kenya People's Union (KPU) was organized in 1966, led by Oginga Odinga. In 1969 it was implicated in the assassination of Tom Mboya, a prominent political leader; its leaders were imprisoned and the party dissolved. From 1969 to 1992 KANU was Kenya's sole political party.

Kenyatta died on Aug. 22, 1978, and Vice Pres. Daniel arap Moi succeeded him. In 1982 the constitution was amended to make Kenya a one-party state. Moi was reelected president in 1983 and again in 1988, the latter being the first election conducted without secret ballots. Foreign observers accused the Moi government of widespread human rights abuses. Riots broke out in several cities in 1991, and sporadic ethnic violence cost thousands of lives.

In 1991, Odinga formed the opposition Forum for the Restoration of Democracy (FORD), in direct defiance of the government. With Western aid conditioned on economic reform, political pluralism, and improved human rights, Moi allowed presidential elections to be held in Dec. of 1992. The three opposition parties split, and Moi was returned to office for a fourth time.

Kenya has traditionally been viewed as the success story of postcolonial Africa, but by the 1990s, widespread government corruption, and economic inefficiency had taken a heavy toll. Tourism has fallen due to the rise in violence, and the economy was further strained by the presence of refugees from Ethiopia, Somalia, and Sudan.

Early in 1994 the government announced reforms aimed at restoring confidence in the economy, including lifting the restrictions on foreign investment. But Pres. Moi's (April 1995) arrest of two leading opposition figures (bringing the total arrested since 1993 to more than 50) led to increased frustrations among his many political enemies. In mid-1997, large demonstrations demanding Moi reform the electoral system in time for Dec. presidential elections were broken up by police with a great amount of violence. In the face of international condemnation Moi agreed to the proposed reforms (July 15), but little progress was made in subsequent meetings between the government and the opposition leaders. In the Jan. 1998 Moi won reelection but with only 40 percent of the ballots. His KANU party won 107 of the 210 legislative seats. (In an unrelated story, the U.S. embassy was attacked by a terrorist truck-bomb August 7, with 250 deaths.)

▶ **KIRIBATI**
Republic of Kiribati

• **GEOGRAPHY** Location: 33 atolls, in three main groups (E to W: Line Is., Phoenix Is., Gilbert Is.) in mid-Pacific Ocean; about 2,400 mi. (3,870 km) E to W and 1,275 mi. (2,050 km) N to S. Tarawa (Gilberts) 1°30'N, 173°00'E. **Boundaries:** surrounded by Pacific Ocean; nearest neighbors are Nauru to W, and Tuvalu and Tokelau to S. **Total area:** 277 sq. mi. (717 sq km). **Coastline:** 710 mi. (1,143 km). **Comparative area:** four times the size of Washington, D.C. **Land use:** 0% arable land; 51% permanent crops; 0% meadows and pastures; 3% forest and woodland; 46% other. **Major cities:** (1990 census) Tarawa (capital) 25,154.

• **PEOPLE** Population: 85,501 (1999 est.). **Nationality:** noun—I-Kiribati (sing., pl.); adjective—I-Kiribati. **Ethnic groups:** Micronesian. **Languages:** English (official), Gilbertese. **Religions:** 53% Roman Catholic, 41% Protestant (Congregational), some Seventh-Day Adventist, Church of God, Mormon and Baha'i.

• **GOVERNMENT** Type: republic. **Independence:** July 12, 1979 (from UK). **Constitution:** July 12, 1979. **National holiday:** Independence Day, July 12. **Head of Government:** Teburoro Tito, president (since Oct. 1994). **Structure:** executive; unicameral legislature; judiciary—all judges appointed by the president.

• **ECONOMY** Monetary unit: Australian dollar. **Budget:** (1996 est.) *income:* $33.3 mil.; *expend.:*

$47.7 mil. **GDP:** $62 mil., $800 per capita (1996 est.). **Chief crops:** copra; taro, bread fruit, vegetables; fish. **Natural resources:** phosphate (production discontinued in 1979). **Major industries:** fishing and handicrafts. **Labor force:** 7,870 economically active (1985 est.). **Exports:** $6.7 mil. (f.o.b., 1996 est.); 62% copra, seaweed, fish. **Imports:** $37.4 mil. (c.i.f., 1996 est.); foodstuffs, machinery and quipment. **Major trading partners:** *exports:* U.S., Australia, New Zealand; *imports:* 46% Australia, Fiji, Japan.

In 1892 the British established a protectorate over the Gilbert Islands, inhabited principally by Micronesians. In 1915 Britain joined the islands administratively with the Polynesian-speaking Ellice Islands to the south to form a British colony, the Gilbert and Ellice Islands (later expanded to include other islands). The Japanese occupied the Gilberts in 1942; in 1943 the Allied forces recaptured them, and Tarawa was the scene of some of the fiercest combat in the Pacific.

In 1971 Britain granted the colony self-rule. The Ellice Islands broke away in 1975, becoming the independent nation of Tuvalu in 1978. On July 12, 1979, the Gilbert Islands became independent as Kiribati. United States claims to portions of the Line and Phoenix islands were settled by a friendship treaty in 1979.

Kiribati's economy is based on subsistence farming and on fishing. Copra exports and the sale of fishing rights (principally to Japan) are the main earners of hard currency. The islands were expected to join the United Nations in late 1999.

▶ KOREA, NORTH
Democratic People's Republic of Korea

• **Geography** **Location:** northern part of Korean peninsula in eastern Asia. **Boundaries:** China to NW, Sea of Japan to E, Republic of Korea to S, Yellow Sea to SW. **Total area:** 46,541 sq. mi. (120,540 sq km). **Coastline:** 1,551 mi. (2,495 km). **Comparative area:** slightly smaller than Mississippi. **Land use:** 14% arable land; 2% permanent crops; negl. % meadows and pastures; 61% forest and woodland; 23% other; includes 9% irrigated. **Major cities:** (1986 est.) Pyongyang (capital) 2,000,000; Hamhung 670,000; Chongjin 530,000; Sinuju 330,000; Kaesong 310,000.

• **People** **Population:** 21,386,109 (1999 est.). **Nationality:** noun—Korean(s); adjective—Korean. **Ethnic groups:** racially homogeneous. **Languages:** Korean. **Religions:** Buddhism and Confucianism; religious activities now almost nonexistent.

• **Government** **Type:** communist state; one-man dictatorship. **Constitution:** adopted 1948, revised Apr. 1992. **National holiday:** Foundation Day, Sept. 9. **Heads of Government:** Kim Jong Il, president (since Oct. 1994); Hong Song San, prime minister (since Dec. 1992). **Structure:** executive—president is dominant figure in government; Supreme People's Assembly theoretically supervises legislative and judicial functions; State Administration Council (cabinet) oversees ministerial operations.

• **Economy** **Monetary unit:** North Korean won. **Budget:** (1992) *income:* $19.3 bil.; *expend.:* $19.3 bil.; **GDP:** $21.8 bil., $1,000 per capita (1998 est.). **Chief crops:** corn, rice, vegetables; pigs, cattle. **Natural resources:** coal, lead, tungsten, zinc, graphite. **Major industries:** machine building, military products, electric power, chemicals. **Labor force:** 9.615 mil. (1987); 36% agricultural, 64% nonagricultural. **Exports:** $743 mil. (f.o.b., 1997

est.); minerals, metallurgical products, agricultural and fishery products, manufactures. **Imports:** $1.83 bil. (c.i.f., 1997 est.); petroleum, machinery and equipment, coking coal, grain. **Major trading partners:** *exports:* China, Japan, South Korea; *imports:* China, Japan, Russia.

(For pre-1945 history, see "Republic of Korea.")

The Soviet Union's declaration of war against Japan in the waning days of World War II strengthened its position in northeast Asia, and particularly in Korea. After Japan's surrender, Korea was arbitrarily divided into zones of Soviet and American occupation, north and south of latitude 38° north. The Korean Communist party (KCP), founded in 1922, had functioned in exile in the USSR during the Japanese occupation, and KCP workers were quickly moved into the Soviet zone in 1945.

U.S.-Soviet talks aimed at Korean reunification broke down, and in 1948 the establishment of separate regimes in North and South Korea formalized the postwar occupation zones. The Korean Democratic People's Republic was proclaimed on May 1, 1948, and its government was organized in September of that year. It inherited most of the industrial and hydroelectric power infrastructure built during the Japanese colonial period and enjoyed strong Soviet backing.

On June 25, 1950, North Korean troops crossed the 38th parallel in an effort to force the reunification of Korea under a communist regime. UN troops under American leadership came to the defense of the South. (For the Korean War, see "South Korea.") The war was fought to a stalemate, and a truce was signed on July 27, 1953.

Until 1994 North Korea had a single leader throughout its national history: Kim Il Sung, chairman of the KCP from 1945 and president of the DPRK from 1972. Under Kim Il Sung, North Korea was a typically Stalinist Soviet nation, concentrating its economic energies on heavy industry and imposing a strictly regimented political and social life on its citizens. Economic development was strongly supported by aid from the Soviet Union and, to a lesser degree, China. After an impressive program of postwar reconstruction in the 1950s and 1960s, the country fell into economic stagnation.

Relations between North and South Korea were implacably hostile; the North has made numerous attempts to infiltrate and sabotage the South. In 1983, 17 people, including four South Korean cabinet ministers, were killed in Rangoon, Burma, by a bomb planted by North Korean agents. North Korea agreed to cosponsor the 1988 Summer Olympics with South Korea but later boycotted the games. In 1990 the leaders of both countries held three cordial but unproductive meetings. Much of the goodwill accumulated by these gestures was greatly harmed by the continuous assertions of the U.S. and others that North Korea was planning to build nuclear weapons.

In August 1992, China, North Korea's long-term ally established diplomatic relations with South Korea, leaving North Korea completely isolated. High-level contacts between North and South Korea continued, but reconciliation talks stalled in 1993 as the issue of North Korean nuclear weapons came to the fore. North Korean leaders refused to allow international arms inspectors access to some facilities and withdrew from the Nuclear Non-Proliferation Treaty. In June 1994 former U.S. president Jimmy Carter met with Kim

Il Sung and arranged for a summit meeting with South Korea and for another with Pres. Clinton to resolve the nuclear weapons issue. Kim Il Sung's sudden death in July prevented immediate progress, but in 1995 an agreement was reached that called for North Korea to dismantle its nuclear facilities in exchange for two new reactors from which weapons-grade plutonium is hard to extract. In 1996 severe floods destroyed most of the rice crop, left half a million homeless, and forced North Korea to accept emergency grants of rice from Japan and South Korea.

Continued severe famine spurred North Korea to pursue reconciliation talks with the South, but those talks were repeatedly disrupted by strife over North Korean nuclear-weapons development programs, several incidents of clandestine landing of northern commandos in the south, and the defection of several senior communist officials. In the fall of 1997 Kim Jung Il assumed his father's old position as general secretary of the Worker's Party. U.S. suspicions, voiced in 1998, of a new underground nuclear plant were proven baseless in May of 1999, the Great Leader permitting an inspection in return for food aid. (Estimates of 2.3 million deaths from the famine must have influenced the decision). Talks with South Korea in Beijing were broken off in June 1999 after South Korea sank a North Korean torpedo boat in the Yellow Sea. (See part I, "Major News Stories of the Year.")

▶ KOREA, SOUTH
Republic of Korea

● **GEOGRAPHY Location:** southern part of Korean peninsula in eastern Asia. **Boundaries:** North Korea to N, separated by frontier roughly following 38th parallel; Sea of Japan to E, East China Sea to S, and Yellow Sea to W. **Total area:** 38,023 sq. mi. (98,480 sq km). **Coastline:** 1,500 mi. (2,413 km). **Comparative area:** slightly larger than Indiana. **Land use:** 19% arable land; 2% permanent crops; 1% meadows and pastures; 65% forest and woodland; 13% other; includes 12% irrigated. **Major cities:** (1995 est.) Seoul (capital) 10,776,201; Pusan 3,802,319; Taegu 2,228,843; Inchon 1,818,293; Kwangju 1,144,695.

● **PEOPLE Population:** 46,884,800 (1999 est.). **Nationality:** noun—Korean(s); adjective—Korean. **Ethnic groups:** homogeneous; small Chinese minority (about 20,000). **Languages:** Korean; English widely taught in high school. **Religions:** 49% Christianity, 47% Buddhism, 3% Confucianism; pervasive folk religion.

● **GOVERNMENT Type:** republic. **Constitution:** Feb. 25, 1988. **National holiday:** Liberation Day, Aug. 15. **Heads of Government:** Kim Dae Jung, president (since Feb. 1998); Lee Soo-Song, prime minister (since Mar. 1998). **Structure:** executive; unicameral legislature (National Assembly); judiciary.

● **ECONOMY Monetary unit:** South Korean won. **Budget:** (1997 est.) *income:* $100.4 bil.; *expend.:* $100.5 bil. **GDP:** $584.7 bil., $12,600 per capita (1998 est.). **Chief crops:** rice, root crops, barley, vegetables, fruit; cattle, pigs, chickens, milk, eggs; fish catch of 2.9 mil. metric tons, seventh largest in the world. **Natural resources:** coal, tungsten, graphite, molybdenum. **Major industries:** electronics, automobiles, chemicals, shipbuilding. **Labor force:** 20 mil. (1991); 52% services and other, 27% mining and manufacturing; 21% agriculture, fishing, and forestry. **Exports:** $133 bil. (f.o.b., 1998); electronic and electrical equipment,

electrical machinery, steel, automobiles. **Imports:** $94 bil. (c.i.f., 1998); machinery, electronics and electronic equipment, oil, steel, transport equipment, textiles. **Major trading partners:** U.S., Japan, EU.

From ancient times Korea has struggled successfully to preserve its national independence. To the native culture—marked by a warrior aristocracy, shamanic religion, and a subject class of rice cultivators—was added, under continuous Chinese influence, a strong adherence to Buddhism and a system of government modeled on Chinese Confucian bureaucratism. The three rival kingdoms of Silla, Paekche, and Koguryo were united, through Chinese intervention, in the seventh century a.d.; unified dynastic rule was maintained thereafter.

The Yi dynasty (1392-1910), under which Korea was known as the Kingdom of Choson, was a staunch tributary ally of China under both the Ming (1368-1644) and Qing (1644-1911) dynasties. A Japanese invasion of Korea in 1592 conquered most of the country but was finally repelled by combined Chinese and Korean forces. From the late 17th century to the 1870s, all non-Chinese foreign influence was rigorously excluded from the country.

Korea's isolation, and its status as a Chinese tributary, ended in 1874, when Japan imposed on it the Treaty of Kangwha, guaranteeing Japanese commercial access and other interests. The Sino-Japanese War of 1894-95 was fought primarily over the status of Korea; following Japan's victory in that war, Korea was made a Japanese protectorate and was annexed as a Japanese colony in 1910. A harsh colonial regime was established with the aim of eradicating Korean culture and incorporating Korea entirely into the Japanese empire.

During the colonial period, Korean resistance to the Japanese regime was violently suppressed, but resistance movements survived in exile—notably the Korean Communist party in the Soviet Union and a republican movement in China. During World War II, tens of thousands of Koreans were conscripted as forced laborers to work in Japan and in Japanese-occupied territories.

Following Japan's surrender, Korea was arbitrarily divided into zones of Soviet and American occupation, north and south of 38° north latitude. The dividing line split Korea economically as well as geographically and politically; Korea's industry and hydroelectric power was concentrated in the north, while the south was primarily agricultural. In contrast to well-laid Soviet plans for installing a Communist government in the north (see "North Korea"), American attempts to reunify the country under a republican regime were inept. By 1948 it had become clear that plans for reunification were hopeless. In May of that year, the Republic of Korea was organized in the south, with Dr. Syngman Rhee as president. The United States withdrew its occupation forces in June 1949.

On June 25, 1950, North Korean troops invaded the south in an apparent attempt to unify the country forcibly under the communist regime. An emergency session of the UN Security Council voted to send troops to Korea; the USSR, having boycotted the session, was unable to exercise its veto on North Korea's behalf. UN troops, dominated by American forces and commanded by Gen. Douglas MacArthur, launched a counterattack in September with a landing at Inchon and swept north, reaching the Chinese border by Nov.

20. On Nov. 26 the tide turned again when Chinese troops entered the war, ostensibly to defend the Chinese border but also to aid their North Korean allies in driving the UN forces south again. Seoul fell once more on Jan. 4, 1951. In February and March another UN counteroffensive drove the combined Chinese and North Korean forces back to the 38th parallel again. Thereafter, the battle lines remained generally stable, although fierce fighting continued at intervals for another two years. On Apr. 11, 1951, Gen. MacArthur was relieved of the Korean command for making unauthorized policy statements and was replaced by Gen. Matthew Ridgway.

Armistice talks began in July 1951 but broke down repeatedly. A truce was signed on July 27, 1953, creating a demilitarized zone along the 38th parallel and establishing a framework for talks on a permanent settlement of the war. Negotiations have continued fruitlessly at the Panmunjom armistice conference headquarters ever since.

Postwar reconstruction, with significant U.S. aid, was overseen by the government of Syngman Rhee. Pres. Rhee resigned in 1960 after a wave of student demonstrations charging him with corruption and undemocratic practices. On May 16, 1961, Gen. Park Chung Hee seized power in a military coup. The military government was given democratic trappings when in 1972 a referendum was passed allowing Gen. Park to run for an unlimited series of six-year presidential terms. Gen. Park was assassinated on Oct. 26, 1979, by the government's chief of intelligence. Gen. Chun Doo Hwan rose to power, continuing the military rule of Gen. Park. Gen. Chun's regime was marked by widespread violent political protests.

South Korea's economy made great strides during Gen. Chun's regime. The traditionally agrarian country was transformed into a modernized, urban, industrial nation. In 1986 South Korea for the first time achieved a favorable balance-of-payments ratio in foreign trade, and the favorable balance has increased rapidly, led by exports of automobiles, textiles and clothing, and consumer electronic goods.

After weeks of widespread demonstrations in mid-1987, Gen. Chun agreed to allow direct presidential elections to choose his successor. In the elections, the government candidate, Roh Tae Woo, achieved a plurality over the sharply divided opposition parties. Under Pres. Roh, the political situation calmed, although student demonstrations continued, calling for greater efforts for Korean reunification and protesting the presence of large numbers of American troops.

High-level talks between North and South began in 1990, and an agreement in principle was reached that reunification would take place in the near future. South Korea has grown more cautious about reunification, however, after witnessing the tremendous costs West Germany continues to bear in helping East Germany. But South Korea remains one of the strongest economic powers in Asia, and the establishment of diplomatic relations with China in 1992 was a clear signal that it would remain so.

In 1992, longtime political opposition leader Kim Young Sam won election as South Korea's first postwar civilian president. Although he was initially able to liberalize some aspects of civil rights in South Korea, the renewed threat of war with North Korea became the overriding preoccupation of the government until late 1994, when an agreement was reached calling for North Korea to dismantle its nuclear facilities in exchange for new reactors.

The Democratic Labor Party was plagued by scandals and political embarassments that hampered its effectiveness. Pres. Kim's predecessor, Pres. Roh, was arrested for bribe-taking, as was his predecessor, Gen. Chun. Several key businessmen, including Kim's own son, were jailed for corruption. In legislative elections in April 1996 the party lost its parliamentary majority but continued to govern as part of a coalition.

South Korea's economy was battered by the Asian economic crisis of 1997-98, leading to severe hardship for many workers. On Dec. 18, 1997, long-time democracy advocate and dissident Kim Dae Jung was elected to succeed Kim Young Sam. Not until September did his governing coalition have even a plurality in the National Assembly. And only in May 1999 (after promising economic figures suggested a rising GDP and falling unemployment) was he able to reshuffle the cabinet to more closely accord with his "sunshine policy" of reforming the great conglomerate business empires and of improving relations with North Korea. In June talks with the North, held in Beijing, were abbreviated after South Korea sank a North Korean torpedo boat in a fishing grounds dispute in the Yellow Sea. (See Part I, "Major News Stories of the Year.")

▶ KUWAIT
State of Kuwait

● **GEOGRAPHY** **Location:** northeastern Arabian peninsula. **Boundaries:** Iraq to N, Saudi Arabia to S, Persian Gulf to E. **Total area:** 6,880 sq. mi. (17,820 sq km). **Coastline:** 310 mi. (499 km). **Comparative area:** slightly smaller than New Jersey. **Land use:** negl. % arable land; 0% permanent crops; 8% meadows and pastures; negl. % forest and woodland; 92% other; includes negl. % irrigated. **Major cities:** (1995 census); Kuwait City (capital) 28,859; Salmiya 130,215; Hawalli 82,238; Faranawiya 53,100; Abraq Kheetan 45,120.

● **PEOPLE** **Population:** 1,991,115 (1999 est.). **Nationality:** noun—Kuwaiti(s); adjective—Kuwaiti. **Ethnic groups:** 45% Kuwaiti, 35% other Arab, 9% South Asian, 4% Iranian, 7% other. **Languages:** Arabic (official), English widely spoken. **Religions:** 85% Muslim (40% Shi'a, 45% Sunni), 15% Christian, Hindu, Parsi, and other.

● **GOVERNMENT** **Type:** nominal constitutional monarchy. **Independence:** June 19, 1961 (from UK). **Constitution:** Nov. 11, 1962 (some provisions suspended since Aug. 29, 1962). **National holiday:** National Day, Feb. 25. **Head of Government:** Jaber al-Ahmad al-Jaber al Sabah, amir (since Dec. 1977); Saad Al-Abdulla Al-Salem Al-Sabah, prime minister (since Oct. 1992). **Structure:** executive; unicameral legislature; judiciary.

● **ECONOMY** **Monetary unit:** Kuwaiti dinar. **Budget:** (FY98/99 est.) *income:* $8.1 bil.; *expend.:* $14.5 bil. **GDP:** $43.7 bil., $22,700 per capita (1998 est.). **Chief crops:** virtually none; extensive fishing; about 75% of potable water must be distilled or imported. **Natural resources:** petroleum, fish, shrimp, natural gas. **Major industries:** petroleum, petrochemicals, desalination. **Labor force:** 1.1 mil. (1996 est.); 50% government and social services, 40% services, 10% industry and agriculture; 68% of population in 15-64 age group is non-Kuwaiti. **Exports:** $14.3 bil. (f.o.b., 1997); oil and refined products, fertilizers. **Imports:** $7.8 bil. (f.o.b., 1996); food, construction materials, vehicles and parts, clothing. **Major trading partners:**

exports: 24% Japan, 16% India, 13% US; *imports:* 22% US, 15% Japan, 13% UK.

Kuwait, at the head of the Persian Gulf, was part of the Abbasid empire from the eighth century and was absorbed into the Ottoman Empire in the late 16th century. It was organized as a principality under the al-Sabah dynasty in 1756, but the Ottomans continued to assert sovereignty. Increasing British influence during the 19th century was formalized in 1899, when Kuwait became a British protectorate.

The discovery of oil, first exported from Kuwait after World War II, rapidly made the principality one of the wealthiest in the Middle East. The British protectorate ended in 1961, when Kuwait gained full independence. The great majority of oil field workers in Kuwait are non-Kuwaiti Arabs, including many Palestinians. Oil revenues have made possible a total welfare state for Kuwaiti citizens, who pay no taxes and enjoy a wide range of free social services.

Kuwait allied itself with Iraq in the Iran-Iraq War of 1980-88; Kuwaiti tankers came under heavy attack from Iranian warships in the gulf. In July 1987, Kuwaiti tankers were reflagged with the U.S. flag and placed under escort of American warships in an operation that continued into 1989. Most of Kuwait's territory is barren and sparsely inhabited but with proven crude oil reserves of 94 bil. barrels—10 percent of the world's reserves—other economic endeavors are not needed.

On Aug. 2, 1990, Kuwait was invaded, and later annexed, by Iraq. In February 1991 it was liberated by a coalition of Arab, non-Arab Muslim, and Western nations led by the United States. Much of the country was destroyed or looted by the Iraqis. After its return to power, the ruling al-Sabah family came under strong pressure to institute democratic reforms. Parliamentary elections were held in 1992, and opposition candidates won 30 of 50 seats. The sultan then announced a new cabinet with more nonroyal members than ever before.

A brief war-scare flared up in October 1994 as 20,000 Iraqi Republican Guards were moved to the Kuwaiti border, only to retreat in the face of U.S. military opposition. In November, Iraq formally recognized Kuwait's sovereignty.

▶ KYRGYZSTAN
Kyrgyz Republic
● **GEOGRAPHY Location:** eastern central Asia. **Boundaries:** Kazakhstan to N and NE, China to SE and S, Tajikistan to SW, Uzbekistan to W. **Total area:** 76,641 sq. mi. (198,500 sq km). **Coastline:** none. **Comparative area:** slightly smaller than South Dakota. **Land use:** 7% cropland; 44% permanent pasture; 4% forest and woodland; 45% other (mostly urban and mountain). **Major cities:** (1990) Bishkek (known as Frunze 1926-91) (capital) 626,900.
● **PEOPLE Population:** 4,546,055 (1999 est.). **Nationality:** noun—Kyrgyzstani(s); adjective—Kyrgyzstani. **Ethnic groups:** 52.4% Kirghiz, 18% Russian, 12.9% Uzbek, 2.5% Ukrainian, 2.4% German, 11.8% other. **Languages:** Kirghiz and Russian (both official), Kirghiz is a member of south Turkic language group written in Cyrillic since 1940. **Religions:** 75% Muslim; 20% Russian Orthodox.
● **GOVERNMENT Type:** republic. **Independence:** Aug. 31, 1991 (from Soviet Union). **Constitution:** adopted May 5, 1993. **National holiday:** Independence Day, Aug. 31. **Heads of Government:** Askar A. Akayev, president (since Oct. 1991); Amangeldy

Muraliev, prime minister (since April 1999). **Structure:** executive—president, prime ministers, Cabinet of Ministers; bicameral legislature; judiciary.
● **ECONOMY Monetary unit:** som. **Budget:** (1996 est.) *income:* $225 mil.; *expend.:* $308 mil. **GDP:** $9.8 bil., $2,200 per capita (1998 est.). **Chief crops:** wool, tobacco, cotton; sheep, goats, cattle. **Natural resources:** hydroelectric potential; gold; coal, natural gas, petroleum, lead, zinc. **Major industries:** small machinery, textiles, food processing, cement. **Labor force:** 1.7 mil. (1995); 40% agriculture and forest, 19% industry and construction. **Exports:** $630 mil. (1998 est.); cotton, wool, meat, tobacco; ferrous and nonferrous metals. **Imports:** $670 mil. (1998 est.); grain, lumber, industrial products, ferrous metals, fuel, machinery. **Major trading partners:** *exports:* China, UK, FSU; *imports:* Turkey, Cuba, U.S.

Kyrgyzstan is largely mountainous, dominated by the massive Tien Shan range in the northeast and the Pamir-Alay range in the southwest. Most of the population lives in one of three major valleys, the Fergana, the Chu, and the Talas, since much of the country is permanently ice-capped and covered with glaciers. The Kyrgyz people are mentioned in early Turkic inscriptions that date back at least to the eighth century a.d.

They were one of the great nomadic tribes of central Asia, who until the 10th century settled around the Upper Yenisei River. With the Mongol invasions of the 13th century, they migrated to the areas of the Tien Shan range in present-day Kyrgyzstan, a territory that has been controlled variously by Mongols, Kalmyks, Manchus, the large tribal empire of the Kokand khanate (or state), and the Russians. In the mid-17th century, the Kyrgyz began to be converted to Islam, but at nearly the same time, the Manchus defeated the Mongols and the Kyrgyz people became Chinese subjects. The Chinese did not interfere with their nomadic life, but in the 19th century they were attacked and came under the control of the khanate of Kokand, during which time Islam was strengthened. In 1868 the khanate became a Russian protectorate and in 1876, the area was merged into the Russian empire as Fergana region. A large Russian influx followed, and many Kyrgyz migrated to China and Afghanistan.

The period immediately following the 1917 Bolshevik revolution was one of great confusion and fighting between the Kyrgyz, the Reds, the Whites, and foreign interventionists. Soviet power was established in 1919, although fighting continued in some parts until 1922. In 1918, Kyrgyzstan was included in the Russian republic's Turkestan Autonomous Soviet Socialist Republic; then, with the National Delimitation of Central Asian Republics in 1924, its name changed to Kara-Kirghiz Autonomous Province (also within the Russian republic). On Dec. 5, 1936, it became a full Soviet Socialist Republic (SSR) of the USSR.

As a Soviet Union republic, advances were made in literacy, education, and public health, although repression of nationalist Kyrgyz was also evident. In the 1920s and 1930s, land reform and collectivization ended the traditional nomadic way of life. Kyrgyz nationalists strongly opposed the changes that Soviet rule brought, but the central government won in the end, and the nationalists were repressed. From the 1930s, ethnic Russians held most of the leading Communist party and government positions in the Kyrgyz SSR.

Mikhail Gorbachev's policy of glasnost, or openness, was responsible for the first public discussion of corruption in government, the emergence of a more liberal Kyrgyz press by 1988, and the emergence of opposition parties and ethnic conflicts. In 1990 disputes over housing and land in the Osh region of the crowded Fergana Valley led to violent confrontations between the Kyrgyz and the republic's Uzbeks. Osh had been incorporated into Kyrgyzstan in 1924, even though the majority population was Uzbek, and at various times the Uzbeks had lobbied for the establishment of an autonomous Uzbek region in Osh.

In Feb. 1990 traditional Soviet-style elections brought into office many Communist party officials, and in April the Supreme Soviet elected Absamat Masaliyev, who had been the Kyrgyz republic's Communist party First Secretary. In Oct. 1990, however, largely due to the violence in Osh, Masaliyev did not receive enough Supreme Soviet votes, and the reformer Askar Akayev was elected as president. After the failed coup in Moscow in August 1991, Communist party activities were suspended, although most leaders were still party members. In Dec. 1991 Kyrgyzstan signed the Alma-Ata Declaration that founded the Commonwealth of Independent States.

Beginning in 1992, with the help of the International Monetary Fund, Akayev embarked on a radical economic program that included lowering wages, raising prices, and abolishing customs duties and tariffs with Central Asian neighbors Kazakhstan and Uzbekistan. Although the program initially caused hardship, it proved successful. In 1995, elections, Akayev was elected to a second term with 60 percent of the vote. This came six months after international lenders, led by the World Bank, agreed in June to $680 million in aid.

In March 1996 Kyrgyzstan joined the common market among Russia, Belarus, and Kazakhstan as it expanded to include development of common energy, transport and information systems. One month later the government signed a non-agression pact with Russia, China, Kazakhstan and Tajikistan, a pact extended a year later to include mutual reductions of military forces in border areas.

► LAOS
Lao People's Democratic Republic

● **GEOGRAPHY Location:** landlocked country in Southeast Asia. **Boundaries:** Myanmar to NW, China to N, Vietnam to E, Cambodia to S, and Thailand to W. **Total area:** 91,429 sq. mi. (236,800 sq km). **Coastline:** none. **Comparative area**: slightly larger than Utah. **Land use:** 3% arable land; negl. % permanent crops; 3% meadows and pastures; 54% forest and woodland; 40% other; includes 1% irrigated. **Major cities:** (1985 census) Vientiane (capital) 377,409; (1973) Savannaket 50,690; Pakse 44,860; Luang Prabang 44,244; Saya Bury 13,775.

● **PEOPLE Population:** 5,407,453 (1999 est.). **Nationality:** noun—Lao or Laotian (sing. and pl.); adjective—Lao or Laotian. **Ethnic groups:** 68% Lao Loum, 22% Lao Theung, 9% Lao Soung including Hmong and Yao. **Languages:** Lao (official), French, English, ethnic languages. **Religions:** 60% Buddhist, 40% animist and other.

● **GOVERNMENT Type:** communist state. **Independence:** July 19, 1949 (from France). **Constitution:** Aug. 14, 1991. **National holiday:** National Day, Dec. 2. **Heads of Government:** Khamtai Siphandone, president (since Feb. 1998); Sisavath

Keobounphanh, prime minister (since Feb. 1998). **Structure:** executive—unicameral legislature; independent judiciary.

● **ECONOMY Monetary unit:** new kip. **Budget:** (1996) *income:* $230.2 mil.; *expend.:* $365.9 mil. **GDP:** $6.6 bil., $1,260 per capita (1998 est.). **Chief crops:** sweet potatoes, vegetables, coffee, sugarcane, cotton; water buffalo, pigs, cattle, poultry; tobacco. **Natural resources:** tin, timber, gypsum, hydropower potential. **Major industries:** timber, hydropower, gypsum. **Labor force:** about 1-1.5 mil.; 80% agriculture. **Exports:** $330 mil. (f.o.b., 1998); electricity, wood products, coffee, tin. **Imports:** $630 mil. (c.i.f., 1998); machinery and equipment, vehicles, fuel. **Major trading partners:** *exports:* Vietnam, Thailand, Germany; *imports:* Thailand, Japan, Vietnam.

Inhabited by the Thai-speaking Lao people in the river valleys and by Hmong and other tribal people in the highlands, Laos historically had little national cohesion and was dominated by its more powerful neighbors, Siam (Thailand) to the west and Vietnam to the east. In 1893 France forced Siam to recognize Laos as a French protectorate; the country was thereafter incorporated into the French Union of Indochina. Laos was occupied by Japan during World War II but saw little major fighting.

In 1946 Laos was united under the Luang Prabang dynasty and was granted local autonomy as a constitutional monarchy in 1949. During the final phases of the Indochina War against French colonialism in 1953-54, Vietnamese Communist (Vietminh) incursions reinforced the position of the Laotian Communist party (Pathet Lao) in Laotian politics. Following the French withdrawal in December 1954, Laos became an independent nation and was admitted to the United Nations in 1955.

The creation of a coalition government under Prince Souvana Phouma in 1962 temporarily resolved a turbulent political situation; an international agreement signed in Geneva that year guaranteed Laos's neutrality. The Pathet Lao withdrew from the coalition in 1964 and renewed its armed uprising against the government, with North Vietnamese support. American planes bombed Vietnamese supply lines along the Ho Chi Minh trail, and American agents recruited Hmong tribesmen as irregular troops to attack Pathet Lao positions. The Pathet Lao nevertheless made steady gains, especially after 1970. In 1973, Prince Souvana Phouma ordered a ceasefire, and in 1975 the Pathet Lao took control of the capital, Vientiane. The Lao People's Democratic Republic was proclaimed on Dec. 3, 1975. Large numbers of Hmong and other tribal people fled to Thailand.

Subsequently, Laos was strongly dominated by Vietnam, which stationed significant numbers of troops in the country. In 1989, in Laos's first election since the communist takeover, a Supreme People's Assembly was elected specifically to approve a new constitution, which it did in 1991; the constitution confirmed the Lao People's Revolutionary party as the sole legal political party. Single-party elections in 1992 did little to alter the country's political climate, though observers predicted changes as the Communists began to pass from the scene. In 1995 Laos signed a treaty with Cambodia, Thailand, and Vietnam to establish a Mekong Commission to regulate water use among the four nations. In 1997 Laos was admitted to the Association of Southeast Asian Nations.

▶**LATVIA**
Republic of Latvia
● **GEOGRAPHY   Location:** eastern coast of Baltic
Sea in northeastern Europe. **Boundaries:** Baltic
Sea to N, Estonia to NE, Russian Federation, Belarus to S, Lithuania to W. **Total area:** 24,749 sq.
mi. (64,100 sq km). **Coastline:** Baltic Sea. **Comparative area:** slightly larger than West Virginia.
Land use: 27% cropland; 13% permanent pasture;
46% forest and woodland; 14% other. **Major cities:**
(1994 est.) Riga (capital) 856,281; Daugav'pils
121,974; Liepāja 104,628; Jelgava 71,332; Jurmala
59,581.
● **PEOPLE   Population:** 2,353,874 (1999 est.). **Nationality:** noun—Latvian(s); adjective—Latvian.
Ethnic groups: 56.5% Latvian, 30.4% Russian,
4.3% Belarussian, 2.8% Ukrainian, 2.6% Polish.
Languages: Lettish (official), Lithuanian, Russian,
other. **Religions:** Lutheran, Roman Catholic,
Russian Orthodox.
● **GOVERNMENT   Type:** parliamentary democracy.
Independence: Sep. 6, 1991 (from Soviet Union).
Constitution: the 1991 Constitutional Law which
supplements the 1922 constitution, provides for
basic rights and freedoms. **National holiday:** Independence Day, Nov. 18. **Heads of Government:**
Vaira Freiberga, president (since July 1999); Andris Skele, prime minister (since July 1999). **Structure:** executive; unicameral legislature; judiciary.
● **ECONOMY   Monetary unit:** lat. **Budget:** *income:* $1.33 bil.; *expend:* $1.27 bil. (1998 est.)
GDP: $9.7 bil., $4,100 per capita (1998 est.). **Chief
crops:** grain, potatoes, sugar beets, vegetables;
meat, milk, eggs; fish. **Natural resources:** minimal; amber, peat, limestone, dolomite. **Major industries:** machine building, metalworking,
chemical processing. **Labor force:** 1.4 mil. (1997);
41% industry, 16% agriculture, 43% services
(1990). **Exports:** $1.9 bil. (f.o.b., 1998 est.): timber,
textiles, foodstuffs. **Imports:** $3.1 bil. (f.o.b., 1998
est.); fuels, machinery and equipment, chemicals.
Major trading partners: *exports:* 21% Russia, 14%
Germany, 14% UK; *imports:* 16% Russia, 16% Germany, 10% Finland.

Though the Letts ethnically and linguistically
are quite distinct from their northern neighbors
the Ests, Latvia's history parallels that of Estonia.
German merchants, knights, and missionaries
made Latvia a semi-ecclesiastical German colony
in the 13th century; in the 16th century Latvia
passed under first Swedish, then Lithuanian rule;
in the 18th century Peter the Great's Russian empire absorbed the land.

A 19th-century cultural revival, inspired in part
by Johann von Herder, a native of Riga, found expression in folkloric societies, archaeological research and the compilation of the epic poem,
Lacplesis. Brest-Litovsk, the Soviet Union's 1918
peace treaty with Germany, granted Latvia's political independence for the first time in its history.

The constitution of 1922 established a one-
house legislature in whose system of proportional
representation about 20 different political parties participated. To avoid violence between left
and right armed extremists, Prime Minister Karlis
Umanlis dissolved the Parliament in May 1934
and ruled as dictator until a new constitution that
provided for expanded presidential powers and a
second house of the legislature, based on the conception of a corporate state, came into existence
in 1938 just before the Hitler-Stalin Pact awarded
Latvia to the Russian sphere of interest. Stalin garrisoned troops in Latvia, rigged elections, and in-

corporated the country as a new union republic of
the USSR in 1940.

For 50 years, harsh Soviet rule continued. The
larger cities were Russianized and the highly educated middle and upper-middle classes were
deported throughout Russia. Industrialization
brought relative prosperity, but the national consciousness was never eradicated.

Mikhail Gorbachev's policy of glasnost, or
openness, led to the creation of dissident groups
who staged public demonstrations on the anniversaries of the Stalin-Hitler Pact and of the establishment of Latvian independence. After the
head of the Latvian Communist party, Boris Pugo
was transferred to Moscow, Latvia's Communist
party came under the influence of the newly created Latvian Popular Front. With the new political
influence of non-Communists, on Sept. 29, 1988,
Latvian replaced Russian as the official language.

In March 1990, following Lithuania's example,
Latvia announced its intention to secede, sur-
vived Gorbachev's January 1991 military crack-
down, and after the failed August 1991 coup in
Moscow, declared independence. Latvia, like the
other Baltic states, declined to sign the Alma-Ata
Declaration that created the Commonwealth of
Independent States.

In June 1995 Latvia gained associate status with
the EU and made formal application for membership. Summer elections revealed deep political divisions as the three major political parties took
barely half the seats. It was not until December
that Andris Skele was able to become premier,
heading a cabinet containing members of six of
Latvia's nine parties. Skele was forced to resign in
July 1997 because of corruption charges and over
disappointment that the EU would not consider
Latvia's application until the "second wave." Parliamentary elections in October 1998 resulted in
the same degree of part splintering, with no party
taking even 25 percent of the seats; but Vilis
Kristopans was able to form a government. More
significantly, in a referendum voters, by 53 percent to 45 percent, eased the citizenship laws,
making it simpler for ethnic Russians (one-third
of the population) to become citizens. In June
1999 Pres. Ulmanis' second term ended; his successor, Vaira Vike Freiberga, became the first female president of an ex-Soviet republic.

▶**LEBANON**
Lebanese Republic
● **GEOGRAPHY   Location:** western Asia. **Boundaries:** Syria to N and E, Israel to S, Mediterranean
Sea to W. **Total area:** 4,015 sq. mi. (10,400 sq km).
Coastline: 140 mi. (225 km). **Comparative area:**
about 0.7 times the size of Connecticut. **Land use:**
21% arable land; 9% permanent crops; 1% meadows and pastures; 8% forest and woodland; 61%
other; includes 7% irrigated. **Major cities:** (1975
est.) Beirut (capital) 1,500,000; Tarabulus (Tripoli)
160,000; Zahleh 45,000; Saida (Sidon) 38,000; Sur
(Tyre) 14,000.
● **PEOPLE   Population:** 3,562,699 (1999 est.). **Nationality:** noun—Lebanese (sing., pl.); adjective—
Lebanese. **Ethnic groups:** 95% Arab, 4% Armenian, 1% other. **Languages:** Arabic (official),
French, Armenian, English. **Religions:** 70% Islam,
30% Christian, negl. Judaism.
● **GOVERNMENT   Type:** republic. **Independence:**
Nov. 22, 1943 (from League of Nations Mandate
under French administration). **Constitution:** May
23, 1926 (amended). **National holiday:** Indepen-

dence Day, Nov. 22. **Heads of Government:** Emile Lahoud, president (since Nov. 1998); Salim El-Hoss, prime minister (since Dec. 1998). **Structure:** executive—by custom, president is Maronite Christian, prime minister is Sunni Muslim, and president of legislature is Shia Muslim; unicameral legislature; judiciary—three courts for civil and commercial cases, one court for civil cases.

• **ECONOMY Monetary unit:** Lebanese pound. **Budget:** (1998 est.) *income:* $4.9 bil.; *expend.:* $7.9 bil. **GDP:** $15.8 bil., $4,500 per capita (1998 est.). **Chief crops:** citrus, vegetables, potatoes, olives, tobacco, hemp (hashish); sheep, goats. **Natural resources:** limestone, iron ore, salt; water-surplus state in water-deficit region. **Major industries:** banking, food processing, textiles. **Labor force:** 1 mil. plus as many as 1 mil. foreign workers (1996 est.); 62% services, 31% industry, 7% agriculture; 18% unemployment (1997 est.). **Exports:** $711 mil. (f.o.b., 1997); 20% foodstuffs and tobacco, 12% textiles, 11% chemicals, 11% metals. **Imports:** $7.5 bil. (c.i.f., 1997); 29% foodstuffs, 28% machinery & transport equipment, 18% consumer goods. **Major trading partners:** *exports:* 14% Saudi Arabia, 9% UAE, 7% France; *imports:* 13% Italy, 9% US, 9% France, 8% Germany.

The ancient history of Lebanon is essentially coextensive with that of Syria, of which it was long a part. The port cities of Tripoli, Tyre, and Sidon were important centers of the Phoenician empire. The parallel ranges of the Lebanon and Anti-Lebanon mountains, crowned with the country's famous cedar trees, enclose the fertile Bekaa Valley. The coastal cities became strongholds of early Christianity, later fragmented into numerous sects, including Maronites (Syrian Catholic), Roman Catholic, Greek Orthodox, Syrian Orthodox, and others. The mountains of the south became the center of the Druze sect of Islam, while orthodox Sunni Islam dominated in the Bekaa Valley.

Lebanon came under French influence in the late 18th century, as France claimed the role of protector of Syria's Christian community. France intervened in Lebanon in 1841 and again in 1860 when fighting between Maronite and Druze communities led to the massacre of many Christians. Under pressure from France, the Ottoman Empire granted some local autonomy to the Maronites of greater Lebanon.

In the dismemberment of the Ottoman Empire after World War I, France was granted a League of Nations Mandate over the Levant States (Lebanon and Syria), ensuring French control of the Iraq Petroleum Company pipeline from Iraq to Tripoli. In 1926 Lebanon became a selfgoverning republic under the mandate, but internal unrest and anti-French sentiment continued.

In June 1940 the French administration in Lebanon declared its allegiance to the Vichy government. British and Free French forces occupied Lebanon in June 1941 and declared it an independent republic; but the French retained control, and full independence did not come until Jan. 1, 1944.

Under a National Covenant in 1943, political power in the Lebanese parliament was apportioned among the nation's various communities. The president was always to be a Maronite Christian, the prime minister a Sunni Muslim. This provided a workable formula for power sharing but also ensured that the national government would always be hostage to the considerable power of separate communities and clans.

The years from the end of World War II to the early 1970s were a brief golden age for Lebanon. Beirut developed into a wealthy, cosmopolitan city, the center of Middle Eastern banking and trade, while agriculture and small-scale industry flourished in the rest of the country. A Syrian-backed Muslim uprising in 1958 had no significant impact; U.S. Marines landed in May 1958 to protect American interests and remained until October. By the late 1960s, however, Lebanon's stability was threatened by PLO attacks on Israel from refugee camps in southern Lebanon and by a shift in the country's demographic balance. Muslims had become a majority in Lebanon by the late 1960s and demanded a revision of the National Covenant, while Maronite Christians continued to cling to their position of political dominance.

Throughout the 1970s, Palestinian raids from Lebanon into Israel brought Israeli retaliatory strikes in southern Lebanon. Israeli troops occupied southern Lebanon in 1978 and again in 1980. The Palestinian-Israeli conflict polarized opinion within Lebanon, inflaming nationalist and anti-Western feelings among Lebanon's Sunni Muslims.

Civil war broke out in 1975, with Palestinian and leftist Muslim militias battling militias of the Maronite community, the Christian Phalange party, and other groups. More than 60,000 died, and damage ranged into the billions of dollars. Syrian troops intervened in 1976, battling Palestinian forces in an attempt to restore the status quo. Arab League efforts to negotiate a cease-fire produced an unstable peace at the end of 1976, though Syrian troops remained in Lebanon.

Fighting broke out between Syrian forces and Christian militiamen near Zahle on Apr. 1, 1981. Other groups joined the fighting in a general war of each against all. Israel staged commando raids against Palestinian positions in Tyre and Tulin. Israeli air raids on Beirut caused extensive loss of life and property damage.

Israel invaded Lebanon in a full-scale air and sea assault on June 6, 1982, in an attempt to drive out the PLO. Israeli and Syrian forces came into direct conflict in the Bekaa Valley. Israeli forces surrounded Beirut and began a heavy bombardment of the city. On Aug. 1, Palestinian forces withdrew from Beirut under international supervision. On Sept. 14 newly elected Pres. Bashir Gemayel, a Maronite Christian, was assassinated; Israeli troops occupied the Muslim quarters of West Beirut in response. With tacit Israeli approval, Christian militiamen invaded two refugee camps and slaughtered hundreds of Palestinian civilians.

Beirut remained a battle zone in 1983, divided by the "Green Line" into Christian and Muslim sectors. Terrorist bombings were common. The United States, France, Italy, and other Western nations stationed troops in Beirut in an attempt to enforce a cease-fire. Fifty people were killed when a bomb partly destroyed the U.S. embassy on Apr. 18; separate attacks on military installations on Oct. 23 killed 241 U.S. Marines and 58 French soldiers.

Rashid Karami became premier with Syrian support on Apr. 26, 1984. The civil war continued, with fighting among various groups of Christian, Druze, Sunni, Shiite, and Palestinian militias. Kidnappings of foreign nationals at the hands of various terrorist factions became commonplace. War between Shiite and Palestinian forces broke out in May 1985. Israeli forces withdrew from most of Lebanon in June, but maintained a "security zone" in the southern part of the country. Premier Karami was assassinated on June 1, 1987, when a bomb destroyed his helicopter.

At an October 1989 Arab League-sponsored meeting, Christian and Muslim leaders agreed on a new national charter. The Taif accord was condemned by Christian militants, led by Gen. Michel Aoun, and Muslim militia leaders. Newly elected Pres. René Mowad, a Syrian-backed Christian, was assassinated on Nov. 22 and succeeded by Elias Hraoui.

In November 1990, rival Shiite militias—the Syrian-backed Amal and Iranian-backed Party of God—signed an agreement ending three years of fighting. In February 1991 Lebanese troops moved to defend the area for the first time in 13 years and called for Israel to abandon its "security zone" in southern Lebanon. In addition to leaving 150,000 dead, the civil war severely disrupted the economy, virtually wiping out the international sector and causing significant damage to the domestic sector.

The government of Christian prime minister Omar Karami collapsed in May 1992, after riots protesting widespread economic hardship. New elections were held under Syrian supervision with Hizbollah and other Islamic fundamentalist parties gaining the most seats in the new parliament, in part because the Christian parties called for an electoral boycott.

In early 1994, as Israeli-Hizbollah skirmishes continued in southern Lebanon, the government banned the Christian political party Lebanese Forces, arrested some of its leaders, and stopped all "political" broadcasts not government-controlled. In 1995, Syria-backed premier Rafic Hariri won a second term together with a 2-1 backing in Parliament. Although he sought to address economic reconstruction, he was hindered by repeated skirmishes between Israel and Hizbollah Shiite guerrillas in Israel's "security zone" in southern Lebanon. In April 1996 the fighting escalated as Israel launched 600 airraids and 24,000 artillery shells some of which hit a UN refugee camp near Tyre, killing over 100 and wounding 100 more. The UN voted 64-2 (with 65 abstaining) to condemn the attack.

By the following year order had been essentially restored but no peace agreement reached with Israel. With $3 bil. in U.S. and EU aid the government set about to rebuild this ravaged land. The U.S. officially lifted its ban on travel to Lebanon in July 1997. Deadly skirmishes still occur in the "security zone" and Israel may withdraw especially after an elite commando group was ambushed—killing 12—at the end of 1997. In May and June 1998 Lebanon held its first municipal elections in 35 years; no clear pattern emerged. In Oct., the (pro-Syrian) National Assembly unanimously elected General Emile Lahoud as president after Premier Hariri declined a fourth consecutive term. In 1999 a continuance of the Israeli-Hizballah skirmishing marred the political progress.

▶ **LESOTHO**
Kingdom of Lesotho
● **GEOGRAPHY Location:** landlocked country in southern Africa. **Boundaries:** entirely surrounded by South African territory. **Total area:** 11,718 sq. mi. (30,350 sq km). **Coastline:** none. **Comparative area:** slightly smaller than Maryland. **Land use:**

11% arable land; 0% permanent crops; 66% meadows and pastures; 0% forest and woodland; 23% other. **Major cities:** (1976) Maseru (capital) 45,000.
● **PEOPLE Population:** 2,128,950 (1999 est.). **Nationality:** noun—Mosotho (sing.), Basotho (pl.); adjective—Basotho. **Ethnic groups:** 99.7% Sotho; 1,600 Europeans, 800 Asians. **Languages:** Sesotho (southern Sotho), English (official), Zulu, Xhosa. **Religions:** 80% Christian, 20% indigenous beliefs.
● **GOVERNMENT Type:** parliamentary constitutional monarchy. **Independence:** Oct. 4, 1966 (from UK). **Constitution:** Apr. 2, 1993. **National holiday:** Independence Day, Oct. 4. **Heads of Government:** Letsie III, king (since Feb. 1996); Pakalitha Bethuel Mosisili, prime minister (since May 1998). **Structure:** executive—king is chief of state but has no power and can be deposed by College of Chiefs; legislature—bicameral legislature; judiciary.
● **ECONOMY Monetary unit:** loti. **Budget:** (FY96/97 est.) *income:* $507 mil.; *expend.:* $487 mil. **GDP:** $5.1 bil., $2,400 per capita (1997 est.). **Chief crops:** corn, wheat, pulses, sorghum, barley; livestock. **Natural resources:** some diamonds and other minerals, water, agricultural and grazing land. **Major industries:** tourism, food, beverages. **Labor force:** 689,000 economically active; 86% subsistence agriculture; 35% work in South Africa. **Exports:** $200 mil. (f.o.b., 1997 est.); 65% manufactures, 7% wool and mohair, 7% food and live animals. **Imports:** $880 mil. (f.o.b., 1997 est.); food, building materials, vehicles, machinery. **Major trading partners:** *exports:* 66% South African Customs Union, 26% North America, 4% EU; *imports:* 90% South African Customs Union, 6% Asia, 2% EU.

Lesotho, formerly Basutoland, is an independent kingdom surrounded entirely by the Republic of South Africa. The area was sparsely populated by Bushmen until the 16th century when refugees from tribal wars in surrounding areas began to move in, an influx that continued through the 19th century. These immigrants coalesced into a homogenous cultural group, the Basothos.

Under King Moshoeshoe (1823-70), several Basotho groups were consolidated, but much land was lost in a series of wars with South Africa. Moshoeshoe appealed to Queen Victoria for aid, and in 1868 the nation became a British protectorate. Between 1884 and 1959 all executive and legislative authority was in the hands of a British high commissioner. In 1903 a Basotho consultative body was established, and in 1959 a new constitution gave the council power to legislate on internal affairs.

On Oct. 4, 1966, Basutoland achieved full independence as the Kingdom of Lesotho. The first elections after independence, held in 1970, were nullified by the ruling Basutoland National party (BNP) when early returns indicated that the party might lose. A state of emergency was declared, the constitution was suspended, and parliament dissolved.

Elections in 1985 were boycotted by opposition parties, and in 1986 the BNP government was ousted in a coup. The nation was run by a military council, which in February 1990 stripped King Moshoeshoe II of his remaining powers. Military rule ended finally in April 1993 when Ntsu Mokhehle was elected prime minister and his Basotholand Congress party (BCP) gained all 243 seats in the legislature. King Moshoeshoe II was restored in January 1995 but ruled for barely a year before dying in an auto accident. The Traditional College of Chiefs named his son Letsie III as his successor.

Elections in May 1998 kept the ruling party in power with a new Prime Minister, Pakalitha Mosisili, but the opposition and some outside observers said the elections were not entirely honest. In September, pro-opposition army officers mutinied and only with the assistance of troops from South Africa was the government able to quell the uprising. The government pledged new and free elections within 18 months.

▶ LIBERIA
Republic of Liberia

• **Geography   Location:** western Africa. **Boundaries:** Sierra Leone, Guinea to N, Ivory Coast to E, Atlantic Ocean to S and W. **Total area:** 43,000 sq. mi. (111,370 sq km). **Coastline:** 360 mi. (579 km). **Comparative area:** slightly larger than Tennessee. **Land use:** 1% arable land; 3% permanent crops; 59% meadows and pastures; 18% forest and woodland; 19% other; includes negl. % irrigated. **Major cities:** (1984) Monrovia (capital) 421,058.

• **People   Population:** 2,923,725 (1999 est.). **Nationality:** noun—Liberian(s); adjective—Liberian. **Ethnic groups:** 95% indigenous peoples, including Kpelle, Bassa, Gio, Kru, Grebo, Mano, Krahn, Gola, Gbandi, Loma, Kissi, Vai, Bella; 2.5% descendants of repatriated slaves known as Americo-Liberians. **Languages:** 20% English (official); more than 20 languages of Niger-Congo language group. **Religions:** 70% indigenous beliefs, 20% Muslim, 10% Christian.

• **Government   Type:** republic. **Independence:** July 26, 1847. **Constitution:** Jan. 6, 1986. **National holiday:** Independence Day, July 26. **Head of Government:** Charles Taylor, president (since July 1997). **Structure:** executive—president, assisted by appointed cabinet; bicameral legislature; judiciary.

• **Economy   Monetary unit:** Liberian dollar. **Budget:** N.A. **GDP:** $2.8 bil., $1,000 per capita (1998 est.). **Chief crops:** rubber, coffee, cocoa, rice, cassava, palm oil, sugarcane, bananas; sheep, goats; timber. **Natural resources:** iron ore, timber, diamonds, gold. **Major industries:** rubber processing, food processing, construction materials. **Labor force:** 70% agriculture. **Exports:** $1.1 bil. (f.o.b., 1998 est.); diamonds, iron ore, rubber, timber, coffee. **Imports:** $3.65 bil. (f.o.b., 1998 est.); fuels, chemicals, machinery, transportation equipment. **Major trading partners:** *exports:* Belgium, Norway, Ukraine, Singapore; *imports:* South Korea, Japan, Italy, Singapore.

Liberia was populated by migrants from the north and east beginning in the 12th century, but it remained relatively isolated from the remainder of West Africa and was not incorporated into any of the region's premodern kingdoms and empires. Portuguese explorers first reached the Liberian coast in 1461 to be followed by other European traders. Until the 19th century, Liberia was largely ignored by the world except for a small-scale coastal trade in slaves and forest products.

In 1816 the U.S. Congress granted a charter to the American Colonization Society, ACS, a private organization dedicated to the African repatriation of freed slaves. The first settlers landed in 1822 at the town that was later to become Monrovia. In 1838 the settlers organized the Commonwealth of Liberia under a governor appointed by the ACS. The commonwealth declared its independence

as the Republic of Liberia in 1847 and adopted a constitution modeled after that of the United States. The new government, Africa's first independent republic, was granted diplomatic recognition by Great Britain in 1848, France in 1852, and the United States in 1862.

Bolstered by the moral backing of the United States, Liberia in its first 100 years of independence succeeded, with difficulty, in fending off British and French attempts to encroach on its territory from their neighboring colonies. Although descendants of freed American slaves are a minority in Liberia's ethnically diverse population, they have consistently dominated the country's political life.

William V.S. Tubman was elected president in 1944 and served until his death in 1971, successfully steering Liberia through the post-World War II age of African nationalism and decolonization. He was succeeded by William R. Tolbert, Jr. On Apr. 12, 1980, Tolbert was deposed in a military coup led by Master Sgt. Samuel K. Doe. Doe suspended the constitution and imposed martial law but pledged a new constitution by 1985.

Presidential elections were held on Oct. 15, 1985, under the terms of a provisional constitution that for the first time enacted universal suffrage. Doe was elected and his party won 80 percent of the seats in the legislature. Despite allegations of fraud that led to a violent but unsuccessful coup attempt in November 1985, the Second Republic, under the new constitution, was inaugurated on Jan. 6, 1986.

On Dec. 24, 1989, about 150 antigovernment guerrillas of the National Patriotic Forces of Liberia (NPFL), led by Charles Taylor, crossed the border from the Ivory Coast. The fighting quickly degenerated into ethnic warfare between the Krahn and Mandingo, in support of the government, and the Gio and Mano, who supported the rebels. In February Prince Johnson split from Taylor's forces and took up fighting both government troops and Taylor. A peacekeeping force of the Economic Community of West African States (ECOWAS) landed at Monrovia on Aug. 24 to mediate a cease-fire and prepare for free elections. On Sept. 10 Pres. Doe was killed by Prince Johnson, but a cease-fire was not agreed upon until Nov. 28, 1990.

From 1990 to 1992 Charles Taylor solidified his hold on the country despite the establishment of a government (under Amos Sawyer) in Monrovia by the West African States. By 1993 the government and ECOWAS forces succeeded in containing Taylor's forces. In March 1994 an interim coalition government representing the country's three major factions came into power as peace talks began. Elections were scheduled for November 1995 but extensive fighting broke out continually until in April 1996, Monrovia experienced its worst fighting of the war. Yet another cease-fire was signed April 18. Over 150,000 had died up to then.

In early 1997 some positive signs could be seen as ECOWAS, led by a Nigerian peacekeeping force, helped to restore order, disarm many of the militias, and arrange for elections in July. Charles Taylor won a landslide victory. The nation's economy has been devastated by the war and the government faces a daunting task as rebuilding begins.

Doubts arose about domestic peace when Pres. Taylor attempted to arrest opposition militia leader Roosevelt Johnson in September: 50 died in the fighting as Johnson fled to the U.S. Embassy for safety. In early 1999, Taylor faced broad international condemnation for Liberia's aid to rebels in Sierra Leone. But the U.N. agreed to Taylor's proposal to place international monitors along Liberia's border with Sierra Leone.

▶ LIBYA
Socialist People's Libyan Arab Jamahiriya
• **GEOGRAPHY Location:** along Mediterranean coast of North Africa. **Boundaries**: Mediterranean Sea to N, Egypt to E, Sudan to SE, Niger, Chad to S, Tunisia, Algeria to W. **Total area:** 679,359 sq. mi. (1,759,540 sq km). **Coastline:** 1,100 mi. (1,770 km). **Comparative area**: slightly larger than Alaska. **Land use:** 1% arable land; 0% permanent crops; 8% meadows and pastures; 0% forest and woodland; 91% other. **Major cities:** in Jan. 1987, Col. Qaddafi designated Hun, a town 404 mi. (650 km) SE of Tripoli, as administrative capital of country (population N.A.); (1985) Tripoli 858,000; Benghazi 368,000; Misurata 117,000.
• **PEOPLE Population:** 4,992,838 (1999 est.). **Nationality:** noun—Libyan(s); adjective—Libyan. **Ethnic groups:** 97% Berber and Arab; some Greeks, Maltese, Italians, Egyptians, Pakistanis, Turks, Indians, Tunisians. **Languages:** Arabic, Italian, and English widely understood in major cities. **Religions:** 97% Sunni Muslim.
• **GOVERNMENT Type:** Jamahiriya (a state of the masses) in theory, governed by populace through local councils; in fact, a military dictatorship. **Independence:** Dec. 24, 1951 (from Italy). **Constitution:** Dec. 11, 1969, amended Mar. 2, 1977. **National holiday:** Revolution Day, Sept. 1. **Head of Government:** Col. Muammar al-Qaddafi (no official title; runs country and is treated as chief of state) (since Sept. 1969); Abdulmajid Algaoud, prime minister (since Jan. 1994). **Structure:** officially, paramount political power and authority rests with General People's Congress, which theoretically functions as a parliament with a cabinet called General People's Committee; elections are indirect.
• **ECONOMY Monetary unit:** Libyan dinar. **Budget:** (1998 est.) *income:* $3.6 bil.; *expend.:* $5.1 bil. **GDP:** $38 bil., $6,700 per capita (1998 est.). **Chief crops:** wheat, barley, olives, dates, citrus fruits; meat, eggs. **Natural resources:** crude oil, natural gas, gypsum. **Major industries:** petroleum, food processing, textiles. **Labor force:** 1 mil.; 31% industry, 27% services, 24% government, 18% agriculture. **Exports:** $6.8 bil. (f.o.b., 1998 est.); petroleum. **Imports:** $6.9 bil. (c.i.f., 1998 est.) machinery and transport equipment, food. **Major trading partners:** *exports:* Italy, Germany, Spain; *imports:* Italy, Germany, UK.

The coastal cities of Libya played an important cultural and commercial role in the Mediterranean in antiquity and were prized possessions of numerous empires. The Libyan coast was successively ruled by Phoenicians, Carthaginians, Berbers, Romans, and Vandals before being incorporated into the Byzantine Empire in the fourth century a.d.; nomadic tribes in the interior were beyond the reach of any government. The Islamic conquests of the seventh and eighth centuries brought Libya into the Muslim world.

Libya was incorporated into the Ottoman Empire shortly after the Ottoman conquest of Egypt in 1517 and was ruled by local Ottoman vassals until 1835 when direct Ottoman government was established. In 1911 Libya was invaded and conquered by Italy. After World WarI, local resistance to Italian colonial rule was led by King Idris I, Emir

of Cyrenaica. British troops drove Italian and German forces from Libya in 1943. King Idris returned from exile in 1944. Following World War II, most of Libya was ruled as a British protectorate with a smaller portion under French administration.

Libya became an independent constitutional monarchy on Dec. 24, 1951. In 1959 significant oil reserves were discovered, rapidly transforming Libya from one of the poorest states in North Africa to one of the wealthiest.

A military coup on Sept. 1, 1969, led by Col. Muammar al-Qaddafi, deposed the monarchy and declared the establishment of the Libyan Arab Republic. Qaddafi moved rapidly to nationalize foreign assets, expel foreign troops, and close foreign libraries and cultural centers. He also assumed full dictatorial powers under a political system that gives equal weight to Islamic law and his own political philosophy. Popular participation in elections is mandatory, although no government organization outside Qaddafi and his circle of advisers exerts any real authority.

Libya has given strong political and financial aid to various radical Palestinian groups and other enemies of Israel and its supporters, sponsoring terrorist activities throughout Europe and the Middle East in real or putative support of the Palestinian cause. Numerous anti-Qaddafi Libyan exiles were assassinated in Europe. Libya also engaged in sporadic military campaigns against Egypt and the Sudan.

Relations between Libya and the United States were very hostile in the 1980s. On May 6, 1981, the United States closed the Libyan "People's Bureau" (embassy) in Washington, D.C. On Aug. 2, 1981, American jets shot down two attacking Libyan warplanes as U.S. naval forces conducted exercises in the Gulf of Sidra, which Libya claims as national waters. In 1986 the United States imposed economic sanctions on Libya, ordered all Americans to leave the country, and froze Libyan assets in the United States. Another clash in March 1986 ended with the loss of two Libyan ships.

On Apr. 5, 1986, Libyan-sponsored terrorists bombed a nightclub in West Berlin, killing two U.S. soldiers; in response, American bombers attacked Tripoli and Benghazi on Apr. 14 in an apparent attempt to kill Col. Qaddafi himself. In 1990, investigators announced they had linked Libyan agents to the bombing of a Pan Am Jet over Lockerbie, Scotland, in 1988.

In January 1989 an international outcry arose when a West German company admitted selling equipment to Libya for a chemical weapons plant. Qaddafi's difficulties with the Western powers continued in 1992, as they demanded he release the suspected terrorists in the Lockerbie bombing. In April the United Nations imposed sanctions on Libya, including a prohibition on sales of military equipment and a ban on all flights in and out of the country. U.S. attempts to gain a worldwide embargo on Libyan oil failed in March 1995. In September 1995 Qaddafi began the expulsion of the 30,000 Palestinians in Libya, provoking fighting between Libyan security forces and Islamic militants. Over the following year Qaddafi was relatively quiet; in early 1997 as the Vatican announced that it would establish diplomatic relations, the U.S. listed Libya as one of several nations sponsoring terrorism.

Elaborate diplomatic maneuvers in 1998 and 1999 led finally in April to President Qaddafi's handing over two Libyans for trial in the 1988

CANADA

Gulf of St. Lawrence

Houlton

International Falls
MINN.
Grand Rapids

Duluth

Lake Superior

Sault Ste. Marie

Lake Huron

MAINE

Bangor

Montpelier
Burlington

Augusta
Brunswick

Marquette

WISCONSIN MICHIGAN

Minneapolis

Green Bay

Lake Michigan

VT. N.H.

Eau Claire

St. Paul

Rochester

La Crosse

Milwaukee

Madison

Rockford

Waterloo

Dubuque

Des Moines

IOWA

Cedar Rapids

Burlington

Grand Rapids

Flint

Lansing

Chicago

Gary

Kalamazoo

South Bend

Fort Wayne

Peoria

Springfield

Decatur

Muncie

Indianapolis

INDIANA

Frankfort

Evansville

Louisville

KENTUCKY

Paducah

Bowling Green

Kansas City

Quincy

Columbia

Joplin

St. Louis

ILLINOIS

Jefferson City

MISSOURI

Springfield

Fayetteville

ARKANSAS

Fort Smith

Little Rock

Hot Springs

Pine Bluff

Texarkana

Monroe

Vicksburg

Shreveport

Jackson

LOUISIANA

Hattiesburg

Baton Rouge

Lake Charles

Lafayette

Beaumont

New Orleans

N.Y.

Syracuse

Rochester

Buffalo

L. Ontario

L. Erie

Erie

PENNSYLVANIA

Cleveland

OHIO

Akron

Columbus

Wheeling

Dayton

Cincinnati

Clarksburg

Charleston

Huntington

Lexington

W.VA.

VIRGINIA

Knoxville

Nashville

TENNESSEE

Chattanooga

Memphis

Huntsville

Decatur

Oxford

Birmingham

MISSISSIPPI

Tuscaloosa

Montgomery

ALABAMA

Meridian

Dothan

Mobile

Biloxi

Pensacola

Tallahassee

Panama City

Gainesville

FLORIDA

Daytona Beach

Orlando

Tampa

St. Petersburg

Sarasota

Fort Myers

West Palm Beach

Fort Lauderdale

Miami

Key West

Harrisburg

Pittsburgh

MASS.

CONN.

CAPE COD

R.I.

N.J.

DEL.

MD.

Hagerstown

Washington

D.C.

Richmond

Newport News

Norfolk

Roanoke

Lynchburg

NORTH CAROLINA

Greensboro

Durham

Raleigh

Winston-Salem

Asheville

Charlotte

Spartanburg

Fayetteville

Wilmington

Greenville

Columbia

SOUTH CAROLINA

Atlanta

Augusta

Charleston

Macon

GEORGIA

Savannah

Brunswick

Albany

Jacksonville

Atlantic Ocean

40° North

70°

30°

Area of detail

United States: Political

90° West

Gulf of Mexico

CUBA

MEXICO

80°

20°

VERMONT

N.H.

Portland

Glens Falls

Rutland

Concord

Portsmouth

Schenectady

Brattleboro

Manchester

Lowell

Boston

MASS.

Worcester

NEW YORK

Albany

Pittsfield

Springfield

Providence

CONN.

Kingston

Hartford

R.I.

Binghamton

Newburgh

New London

Newport

Scranton

Paterson

New Haven

Newark

New York City

Allentown

Princeton

Trenton

Philadelphia

NEW JERSEY

PA.

Camden

Atlantic City

Wilmington

Baltimore

Dover

DELAWARE

Annapolis

Salisbury

MARYLAND

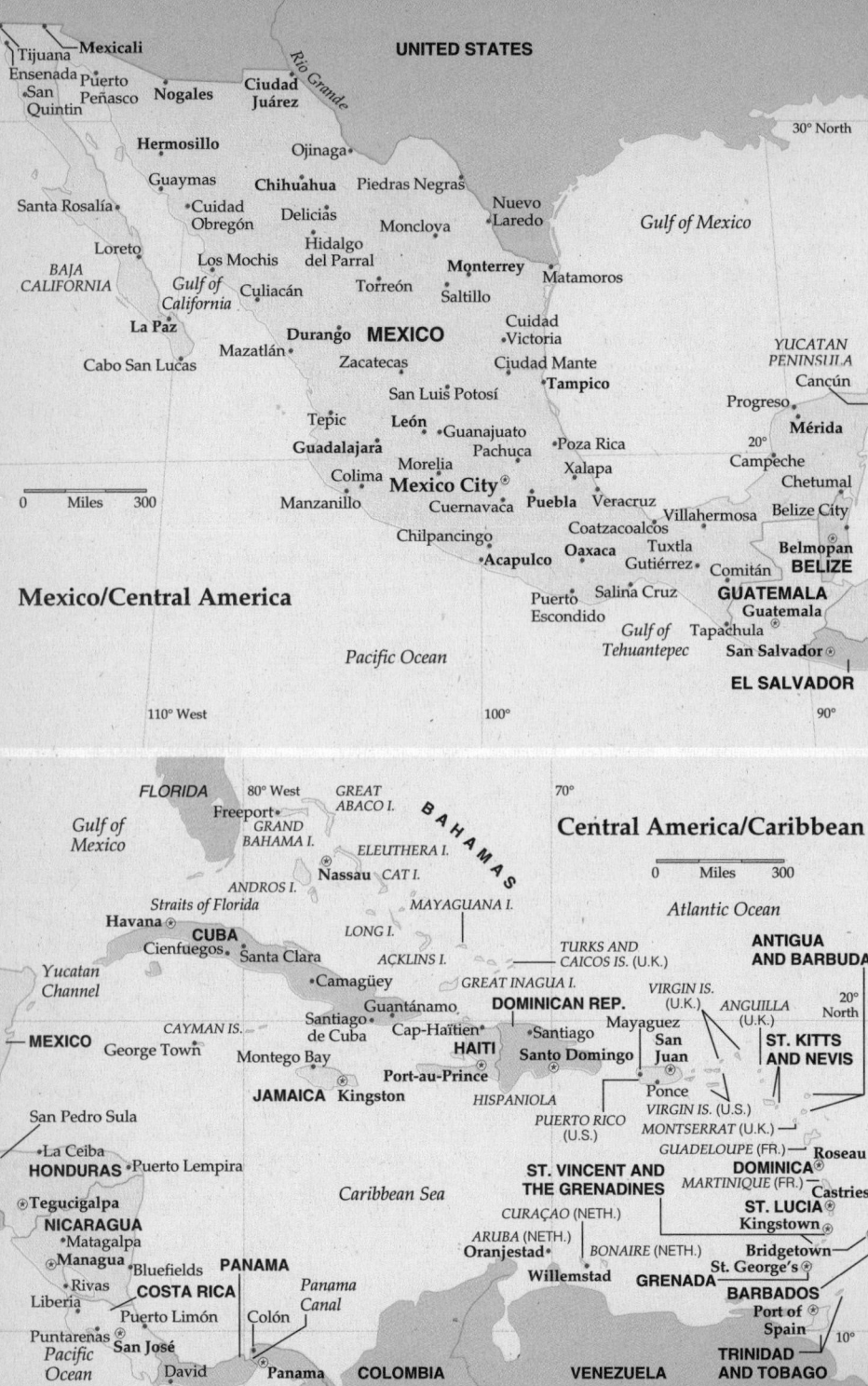

UNITED STATES

Tijuana
Mexicali
Ensenada
San Quintin
Puerto Peñasco
Nogales
Ciudad Juárez
Rio Grande
30° North

Hermosillo
Ojinaga

Guaymas
Chihuahua
Piedras Negras

Santa Rosalía
Ciudad Obregón
Delicias
Nuevo Laredo

Loreto
Hidalgo del Parral
Monclova

Gulf of Mexico

BAJA CALIFORNIA
Los Mochis
Gulf of California
Culiacán
Torreón
Monterrey
Matamoros
Saltillo

La Paz
Durango
MEXICO
Cuidad Victoria

Cabo San Lucas
Mazatlán
Zacatecas
Ciudad Mante
Tampico

YUCATAN PENINSULA

San Luis Potosí
Cancún

Tepic
León
Guanajuato
Progreso
Mérida

Guadalajara
Pachuca
Poza Rica
20°
Campeche

Morelia
Xalapa
Chetumal

0   Miles   300
Colima
Mexico City
Veracruz
Villahermosa
Belize City

Manzanillo
Cuernavaca
Puebla
Coatzacoalcos
Belmopan

Chilpancingo
Oaxaca
Tuxtla Gutiérrez
BELIZE

Mexico/Central America
Acapulco
Comitán
GUATEMALA

Puerto Escondido
Salina Cruz
Guatemala

Gulf of Tehuantepec
Tapachula

Pacific Ocean
San Salvador

EL SALVADOR

110° West
100°
90°

FLORIDA
80° West
GREAT ABACO I.
70°

Gulf of Mexico
Freeport
GRAND BAHAMA I.
Central America/Caribbean

ELEUTHERA I.
ANDROS I.
Nassau
CAT I.
MAYAGUANA I.

0   Miles   300

Straits of Florida
LONG I.
Atlantic Ocean

Havana
CUBA
ACKLINS I.
ANTIGUA AND BARBUDA

Cienfuegos
Santa Clara
TURKS AND CAICOS IS. (U.K.)

Yucatan Channel
Camagüey
GREAT INAGUA I.
VIRGIN IS. (U.K.)
ANGUILLA (U.K.)
20° North

CAYMAN IS.
Guantánamo
DOMINICAN REP.
Mayaguez
San Juan
ST. KITTS AND NEVIS

MEXICO
George Town
Santiago de Cuba
Cap-Haïtien
Santiago
Santo Domingo
Ponce

Montego Bay
HAITI
VIRGIN IS. (U.S.)
MONTSERRAT (U.K.)

JAMAICA
Kingston
Port-au-Prince
HISPANIOLA
PUERTO RICO (U.S.)
GUADELOUPE (FR.)
Roseau

San Pedro Sula
Caribbean Sea
ST. VINCENT THE GRENADINES
MARTINIQUE (FR.)
DOMINICA

La Ceiba
CURAÇAO (NETH.)
ST. LUCIA

HONDURAS
Puerto Lempira
ARUBA (NETH.)
Castries

Tegucigalpa
Oranjestad
BONAIRE (NETH.)
Kingstown

NICARAGUA
Matagalpa
PANAMA
Willemstad
St. George's
Bridgetown

Managua
Bluefields
Panama Canal
GRENADA
BARBADOS

Rivas
COSTA RICA
Port of Spain

Liberia
Puerto Limón
Colón

Puntarenas
San José
David
Panama
COLOMBIA
VENEZUELA
TRINIDAD AND TOBAGO

Pacific Ocean
10°

PANAMA

Caribbean Sea

Barranquilla
Cartagena

Valencia Caracas

TRINIDAD
AND TOBAGO

10° North

Maracaibo   Maracay

GUYANA

Cucuta   VENEZUELA   *Orinoco R.*

SURINAME

Atlantic Ocean

Medellín

Georgetown

Paramaribo

Bogotá

Puerto
Ayacucho

Cayenne

Cali

Magadalena R.

Boa Vista

Camopi

Pasto

Mitu

Serro do Navio

FRENCH
GUIANA (FR.)

Quito   COLOMBIA

Macapá

Equator

ECUADOR

Guayaquil

Negro R.

Belém   São Luis

Cuenca   PERU   Iquitos

Manaus

Santarém

Fortaleza

Talara

Tefé

Amazon R.

Imperatriz

Teresina

Chiclayo

Orellana

Jacareacanga

Trujillo

Tarauacá

Cachimbo

Recife

Huaraz

Rio Branco

Pôrto Velho

Maceió

Huanuco

Gurupi

Barreiras

Aracaju

Cerro de Pasco
Huancayo

Alvorada

BRAZIL

Salvador

Callao

Machu Picchu

Lima

Ayacucho

Cuzco

Lake
Titicaca

Cuiabá

Brasília

Canavíeiras

Ica

Puno

BOLIVIA

Goiânia

Arequipa

La Paz

Cochabamba

Belo Horizonte

20°

Arica

Santa Cruz

Campo Grande

Vitória

Sucre

Iquique

Tarija

PARAGUAY

Campinas   Rio De Janeiro

Antofagasta

Salta

Asunción

Curitiba   São Paulo

Tropic of
Capricorn

CHILE

San Miguel
De Tucumán

Florianópolis

Resistencia

Viña del Mar

Córdoba

Paraná R.

Porto Alegre

30°

Valparaíso

Tacuarembó

Santiago

Rosario

Durazno

URUGUAY

Atlantic Ocean

Concepción

Morón

Montevideo

Buenos Aires

ARGENTINA

Neuquén   Bahía Blanca

Mar Del Plata

40°

Valdivia

San Carlos
de Bariloche

Puerto Montt

Trelew

South America

Comodoro Rivadavia

0   Miles   500

Puerto Santa Cruz

50°

Río Gallegos

FALKLAND ISLANDS
(U.K.)

SOUTH
GEORGIA
ISLAND
(U.K.)

Strait of Magellan

Punta Arenas

TIERRA DEL FUEGO

Ushuaia

80° West   70°   60°   50°   40°

Pacific
Ocean

Madeira R.

Tapajos R.

Juruena R.

Araguaia R.

Tocantins R.

São Francisco R.

ANDES

Reykjavik ⊙

ICELAND

Norwegian Sea

Bodo ⊙

60° North

FAROE IS.
(DENMARK)
• Torshavn

SWEDEN

Trondheim ⊙

Alesund • Sundsvall

NORWAY

Europe

0 Miles 200

SHETLAND IS.

• Lerwick Bergen • Gavle •

Oslo ⊙ Uppsala •

ORKNEY IS. **Stockholm** — ⊙

HEBRIDES Inverness • Stavanger •

SCOTLAND *North Sea* Göteborg •

N. IRELAND Glasgow • • Edinburgh Viborg • Alborg •

Donegal • Belfast • Arhus •

IRELAND Sunderland • Vejle • **DENMARK** Copenhagen •

UNITED Alborg

Limerick • Dublin ⊙ **KINGDOM**

Cork • Waterford • Liverpool • Leeds • *ENGLAND* **NETHERLANDS** Hamburg •

15° West *WALES* • Manchester **GERMANY** Berlin • **POLAND**

Birmingham • • Leicester Amsterdam • Poznan •

Cardiff • *Ouse R.* The Hague • Essen •

Plymouth • London • Rotterdam • Cologne • Leipzig • Elbe R.

Atlantic Portsmouth • *Thames R.* Brussels • Bonn • Prague •

Ocean *English Channel* **BELGIUM** *Rhine R.* Frankfurt • **CZECH**

CHANNEL IS. (U.K.) < Le Havre • Luxembourg • Nürnberg • **REP.** Brno •

• Brest **LUX.** Paris • Stuttgart • Prague

Seine R. Strasbourg • Munich • Bratislava •

45° Nantes • *Loire R.* **FRANCE** Dijon • *Danube R.* Salzburg • Vienna •

Bern • Zurich • Vaduz **(LIECH.)** **AUSTRIA**

Bay of Biscay Clermont-Ferrand • Geneva • **SWITZERLAND** Graz •

Ljubljana •

La Coruña • Bordeaux • Lyons • *ALPS* Venice • **SLOVENIA**

Bilbao • Bayonne • *Garonne R.* Milan • *Po R.* Zagreb •

Porto • Valladolid • *Duero R.* Toulouse • Genoa • **SAN MARINO** **CROATIA**

Coimbra • Salamanca • *PYRENEES* Marseilles • Nice • *Rhone R.* Florence • *Adriatic*

PORTUGAL *Ebro R.* **ANDORRA** Monaco *Sea*

Madrid • Zaragoza • *CORSICA (FR.)* Rome • **ITALY**

Lisbon ⊙ *Tagus R.* Barcelona • **APENNINES**

Toledo • Bari •

SPAIN Valencia • *MALLORCA* Naples •

Córdoba • Palma • *SARDINIA* 15°

Seville • *Guadalquivir R.* *BALEARIC IS.* *(ITALY)* *Tyrrhenian Sea*

Málaga • *(SPAIN)*

Strait of *IBIZA* *Mediterranean Sea* Palermo •

Gibraltar — Gibraltar *SICILY* Catania •

(U.K.) 0°

MOROCCO **ALGERIA** **TUNISIA** **MALTA** Valletta •

Nations of
Former Soviet Union

Miles 0 500

—— Arctic Circle

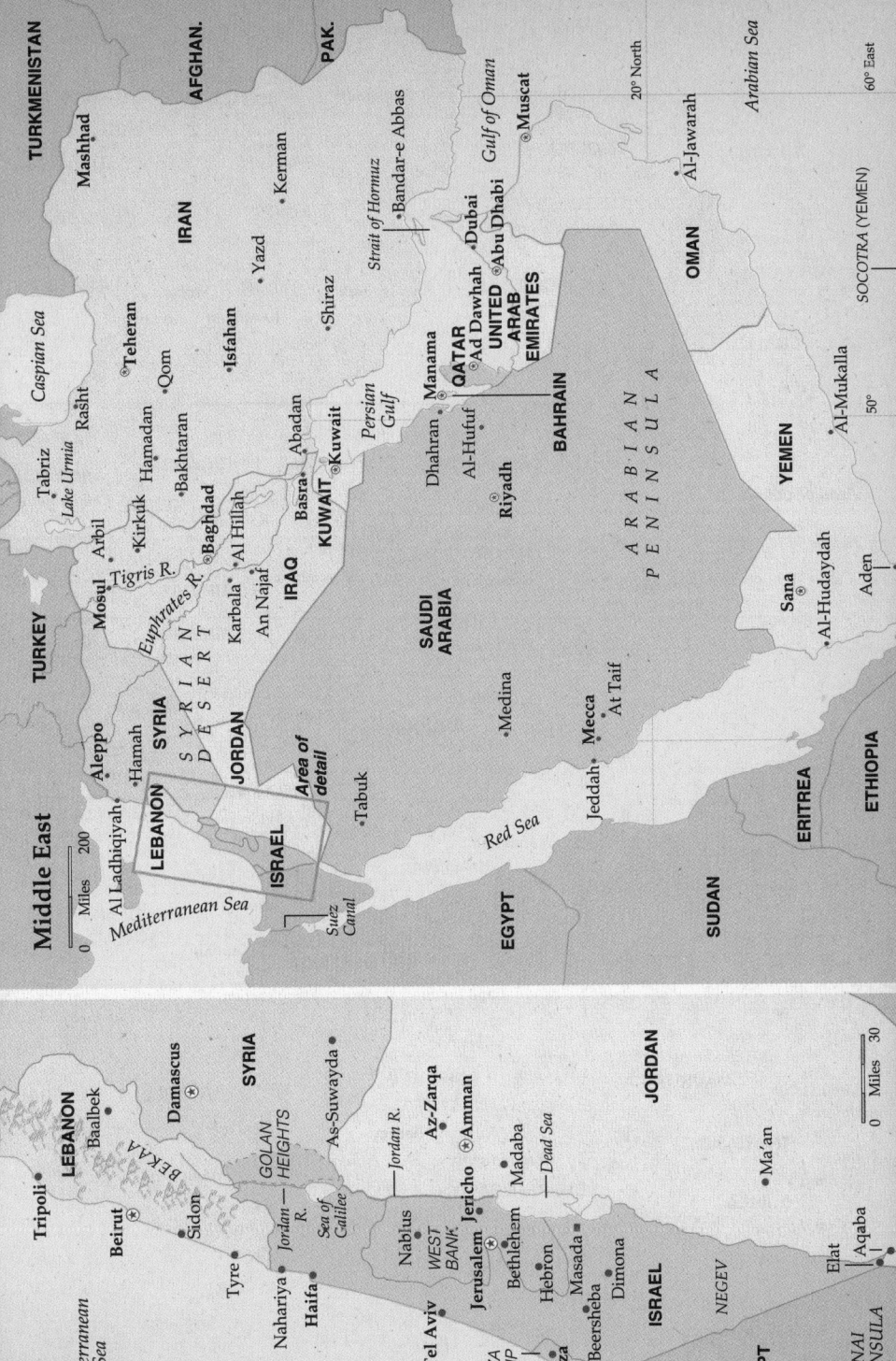

Middle East

0 — Miles — 200

Mediterranean Sea

Caspian Sea

TURKMENISTAN

Mashhad

AFGHAN.

PAK.

IRAN

Teheran

Qom

Kerman

Yazd

Isfahan

Shiraz

Bandar-e Abbas

Strait of Hormuz

Gulf of Oman

Muscat

Al-Jawarah

20° North

60° East

Arabian Sea

SOCOTRA (YEMEN)

OMAN

UNITED ARAB EMIRATES

Abu Dhabi

Dubai

Ad Dawhah

QATAR

Manama

BAHRAIN

Dhahran

Al-Hufuf

Riyadh

Persian Gulf

Kuwait

KUWAIT

Basra

Abadan

Bakhtaran

Hamadan

Kirkuk

Arbil

Mosul

Tigris R.

Euphrates R.

Baghdad

Al Hillah

Karbala

An Najaf

IRAQ

SYRIAN DESERT

Tabriz

Lake Urmia

Rasht

TURKEY

Aleppo

Hamah

SYRIA

JORDAN

LEBANON

Al Ladhiqiyah

ISRAEL

Area of detail

Tabuk

Medina

Mecca

At Taif

Jeddah

Red Sea

SAUDI ARABIA

A R A B I A N P E N I N S U L A

YEMEN

Sana

Al-Hudaydah

Aden

Al-Mukalla

Al-Mukalla

50°

ERITREA

ETHIOPIA

SUDAN

EGYPT

Suez Canal

Mediterranean Sea

Mediterranean Sea

Tripoli

LEBANON

Baalbek

Beirut

Sidon

Tyre

Nahariya

Haifa

Tel Aviv

Gaza

GAZA STRIP

Beersheba

Dimona

Hebron

Masada

Bethlehem

Jerusalem

Jericho

Nablus

WEST BANK

NEGEV

Elat

Aqaba

SINAI PENINSULA

EGYPT

ISRAEL

Sea of Galilee

Jordan R.

GOLAN HEIGHTS

BEKAA

Damascus

SYRIA

As-Suwayda

Az-Zarqa

Amman

Madaba

Dead Sea

Jordan R.

Ma'an

JORDAN

0 — Miles — 30

Tangier
Casablanca •Rabat
MOROCCO Oran Algiers
Marrakesh
30° North
CANARY ISLANDS (SPAIN)
El Aaiun
WESTERN
SAHARA
(MOROCCO)
•Atar
MAURITANIA
•Nouakchott

Annaba
Batna •Tunis
Gafsa Sfax
TUNISIA •Tripoli
Ouargla
•Sabhah

•Reggane
Timimoun
Taoudenni
•Tessalit
•Araouane

Djanet•

Marẑuq

SAHARA
DESERT

Aozou

Mediterranean Sea
Benghazi
Misratah
Alexandria
LIBYA Beni Suef
El-Minya

LEBANON SYRIA
ISRAEL IRAQ
JORDAN
Cairo
Suez KUWAIT

SAUDI ARABIA
EGYPT Aswan

MALI
GUINEA
BURKINA
FASO

NIGER Bilma•
Faya-Largeau•

CHAD

Al Jawf•

Port Sudan
SUDAN Atbara
Khartoum Asmara

Nile R.

Red
Sea ERITREA

DJIBOUTI

NIGERIA
CAMEROON

10°

Area of detail

El Fasher•
White Nile R.—
CENT.
AFRICAN
REP.
Ndele• •Wau
Bangassou•

Mekele•
Addis
Ababa• •Djibouti
•Berbera
Asela•
Goba• ETHIOPIA

Blue Nile R.

Juba• UGANDA
Congo R.
Bumba• Lake
Victoria
Gulu• KENYA SOMALIA
Mbandaka• Kisangani• Kampala•
•Eldoret Mogadishu
Kisumu•
•Nairobi Kismayu•

Equator

•Libreville
Port-Gentil GABON
CONGO
Brazzaville• (ZAIRE)
CONGO
REPUBLIC Pointe-Noire• •Kinshasa
CABINDA •Matadi
(ANGOLA) Luanda
⊛

RWANDA
Bujumbura• •Kigali
Lake BURUNDI
Tanganyika •Tabora Tanga•
Kananga• TANZANIA Dar es Salaam
Kalemie• Mbeya•
Likasi• •Kasama

SEYCHELLES
•Mombasa
ZANZIBAR
⊛
COMOROS

10°

Atlantic Ocean

Malange•
•Huambo Luena•
ANGOLA ZAMBIA
Lubango• Lusaka⊛
Mongu•

Lubumbashi•
•Lilongwe MALAWI
Antsiranana•
Nampula•
Zambezi R.

•Moroni

20°

Tsumeb• Maun•
Windhoek BOTSWANA
Walvis Bay• ⊛ Gaborone
NAMIBIA

Africa

0 Miles 500

Harare
ZIMBABWE Beira•
•Bulawayo
Pietersburg• MOZAMBIQUE
Pretoria⊛ Maputo•

Antananarivo•
MADAGASCAR
Fianarantsoa•
•Tuléar
Tolanaro•

Keetmanshoop•
Johannesburg•
Bloemfontein• Mbabane•
Kimberley• Maseru• SWAZILAND
Oudtshoorn• •Maseru Durban• LESOTHO
30°
SOUTH AFRICA •Umtata
Cape Town⊛ •Port Elizabeth East London Indian Ocean

10° 0° 10° 20° 30° 40° East

SENEGAL MAURITANIA Timbuktu• •Gao
⊛Dakar
•Kayes MALI Tahoua•
—Banjul Niger R. Niamey•
THE GAMBIA Bamako⊛ Ouagadougou•
•Bissau BURKINA FASO
GUINEA
Conakry⊛ Kankan• Tamale• BENIN
Freetown Korhogo• Porto-
⊛ Bouaké• GHANA Novo•
SIERRA Yamoussoukro• Ibadan• Lagos•
LEONE Monrovia• Man• Abidjan• Accra•
GUINEA- Lomé•
BISSAU LIBERIA IVORY COAST EQUATORIAL
GUINEA

Agadez• NIGER CHAD
Zinder• Lake Chad
Maiduguri• N'Djamena•
Katsina•
•Zaria
Kaduna•
⊛Abuja Moundou•
NIGERIA Bossangoa•
CAMEROON CENT.
Ebolowa• AFRICAN
Malabo• Yaoundé⊛ REPUBLIC
•Bangui

Pacific Islands/Australia

0 Miles 500

Pacific Ocean

15° North

Equator

Tropic of Capricorn

Philippine Sea

South China Sea

PHILIPPINES

LUZON
SAMAR
CEBU
MINDORO
PANAY
MINDANAO

Baguio
Manila
Iloilo
Cebu
Davao
Menado

BRUNEI
Bandar Seri Begawan

MALAYSIA

BORNEO

Celebes Sea
SULAWESI (CELEBES)
Ujungpandang
Banda Sea
TIMOR
SUMBA
BALI
JAVA
Surabaya
Banjarmasin
Java Sea

I N D O N E S I A

IRIAN JAYA

NORTHERN MARIANA IS. (U.S.)

GUAM (U.S.)

CAROLINE IS.

PALAU

FEDERATED STATES OF MICRONESIA

Kolonia

PAPUA NEW GUINEA

Madang
Rabaul
Port Moresby
NEW BRITAIN
BOUGAINVILLE

Arafura Sea
Timor Sea
Banda Sea
Torres Strait

WAKE I. (U.S.)

JOHNSTON ATOLL (U.S.)

MARSHALL ISLANDS

RALIK CHAIN

Majuro
Tarawa
GILBERT IS.

Yaren
NAURU

SOLOMON ISLANDS

Honiara
GUADALCANAL

KIRIBATI

PHOENIX IS.

LINE IS.

CHRISTMAS I.

15°

TUVALU
Funafuti

WALLIS AND FUTUNA (FR.)

FIJI
Suva

TOKELAU (N.Z.)

W. SAMOA
Apia
AMERICAN SAMOA (U.S.)
Pago Pago

TONGA
Nuku-alofa

NIUE (N.Z.)

COOK IS. (N.Z.)

TUAMOTU ARCHIPELAGO

SOCIETY IS.
TAHITI
BORA BORA
FRENCH POLYNESIA (FR.)
AUSTRAL IS.

Pacific Ocean

VANUATU
Port Vila

NEW CALEDONIA (FR.)
Noumea

Coral Sea

AUSTRALIA

WESTERN AUSTRALIA

Learmonth
Carnarvon
Geraldton
Perth
Kalgoorlie

Broome
Port Hedland
Derby
Fitzroy R.

Darwin
Victoria R.
NORTHERN TERRITORY
Alice Springs
Tennant Creek

Gulf of Carpentaria
Cairns
Great Barrier Reef
Mount Isa
Mackay
Rockhampton
Gladstone
Brisbane

QUEENSLAND

SOUTH AUSTRALIA
Cook
Port Lincoln
Port Augusta
Broken Hill
Adelaide

Great Australian Bight

Darling R.
NEW SOUTH WALES
Sydney
Canberra
Murray R.

VICTORIA
Melbourne

GREAT DIVIDING RANGE

Tasman Sea

TASMANIA
Hobart

NEW ZEALAND

NORTH I.
Auckland
Hamilton
Rotorua
New Plymouth
Napier
Wellington
Westport
Greymouth
Christchurch
SOUTH I.
Nelson
Timaru
Dunedin
Invercargill

Indian Ocean

120° East
130°
140°
150°
160°
170°
180°
160°
150° West

30°

Pacific Ocean

RUSSIA

KAZAKHSTAN

•Hovd

Altay

MONGOLIA

Ulaanbaatar ⊛

Aral Sea

L. Balkhash

•Karamay

Dalandzadagad •

•Urumqi

•Hami

G O B I
D E S E R T

KYRGYZSTAN

•Korla

UZBEKISTAN

Kashi *Yarkant R.*

Tarim R.

CHINA

Yumen

Yinchuan •

TAJIKISTAN

TAKLIMAKAN
DESERT

•Qiemo

•Hotan

Xining •

Lanzhou

TURKMEN.

Mazar-i-Sharif

Golmud

•Herat

Kabul

Peshawar

Islamabad ⊛

AFGHANISTAN

Kandahar

Rawalpindi

•Srinagar

Area claimed by India
JAMMU AND
KASHMIR

Xian —

Chongqing •

Mianyang •

Chengdu •

Zigong •

T I B E T

MOUNT
EVEREST

Brahmaputra R.

Mekong R.

Faisalabad •

Amritsar •

Lahore •

•Multan

Yamuna R.—

New Delhi ⊛

PAKISTAN

Indus R.

Ganges R.

NEPAL

Katmandu •

HIMALAYAS

BHUTAN

Guiyang •

Kunming •

IRAN

•Jaipur

Agra •

Kanpur •

•Patna

•Allahabad

Ganges R.

Nanning •

•Hyderabad

GREAT INDIAN
DESERT

Dhaka ⊛

•Karachi

Ahmadabad •

INDIA

Calcutta •

Chitta-
gong

MYANMAR

VIETNAM

•Surat

•Nagpur

Mandalay •

LAOS

Hanoi •

Arabian Sea

Bombay •

Godavari R.

BANGLADESH

Chang Mai •

Luang Prabang •

•Pune

Vientiane ⊛

Vinh •

Hyderabad •

Irrawaddy R.

HAINAN

15° North

Bay of Bengal

Yangon •

THAILAND

Da Nang •

•Bangalore

•Madras

Dawei •

Bangkok ⊛

CAMBODIA

Mangalore •

ANDAMAN IS.
(INDIA)

Phnom Penh •

Madurai •

•Jaffna

Andaman
Sea

Gulf of
Thailand

Ho Chi
Minh
City
(Saigon)

SRI LANKA

NICOBAR IS.
(INDIA)

Hat Yai •

Colombo ⊛ • Kotte

Kota Baharu •

Medan •

MALAYSIA

Kuala Lumpur •

⊛ Male

SINGAPORE

MALDIVES

SUMATRA

Equator

Pontianak •

Padang •

Jambi •

Palembang •

Indian Ocean

INDONESIA

Bandar Lampung •

Asia/Pacific

Jakarta ⊛

Bandung •

JAVA

0   Miles   500

70° East

90°

RUSSIA

Manzhouli

Nen R.

RUSSIA

SAKHALIN I.

Sea of Okhotsk

MONGOLIA

Qiqihar

Songhua R.

Baicheng

Harbin   Jixi

KURILE IS.
(RUSSIA)

45° North

Changchun   Jilin

Sapporo

HOKKAIDO I.

Fuxin   Shenyang   Chongjin
Benxi   Kimchaek

Beijing ⊙

Tianjin

Dalian   **NORTH KOREA**

⊙ **Pyongyang**   *Sea of Japan*   Sendai

Taiyuan

Huang
(Yellow R.)

Inchon   **SOUTH**   **JAPAN**   *HONSHU I.*
Seoul   **KOREA**

Qingdao   *Yellow Sea*   Pusan   Kyoto   Nagoya   ⊙ **Tokyo**
Hiroshima   **Ōsaka**

Kaifeng   Kwangju
Xuzhou   *SHIKOKU I.*

CHINA   Hefei   Fukuoka

Wuhan   Nagasaki   *KYUSHU I.*

Shanghai

Chang Jiang
(Yangtze R.)   Ningbo   *East China*
Sea   *Pacific Ocean*

Huangshi
Yueyang   Wenzhou

Xi R.   Fuzhou   *RYUKYU IS.*
(JAPAN)

Taipei   *OKINAWA I.*

Guangzhou
(Canton)   Xiamen   **TAIWAN**

Shantou   Kaohsiung

Hong Kong

MACAO
(PORTUGAL)

LUZON I.   **NORTHERN**
MARIANA IS. (U.S.)

15°

South
China Sea   Baguio   *Philippine Sea*

Manila   **PHILIPPINES**

MINDORO I.   *SAMAR I.*   *GUAM* (U.S.)

Iloilo
PALAWAN I.   Cebu   *CEBU I.*

PANAY I.

BRUNEI   Davao

Bandar Seri   *MINDANAO I.*   **PALAU**   *CAROLINE IS.*
Begawan   **FEDERATED STATES**
OF MICRONESIA

MALAYSIA   Manado

Equator

BORNEO   **I N D O N E S I A**   **SOLOMON IS.**

Banjarmasin   *SULAWESI I.*   Rabaul
(CELEBES)

Java Sea   *IRIAN*   Madang
Ujungpandang   *JAYA*   **PAPUA**
Banda Sea   **NEW GUINEA**   *NEW*
Surabaya   *FLORES*   *BRITAIN*

JAVA   *BALI*   Honiara
TIMOR   130°   Port Moresby ⊙   *BOUGAINVILLE*
Kupang   *Arafura Sea*   *Torres Strait*   *GUADALCANAL*

Timor Sea   *Gulf of*   *Coral Sea*
Carpentaria

AUSTRALIA   150° East

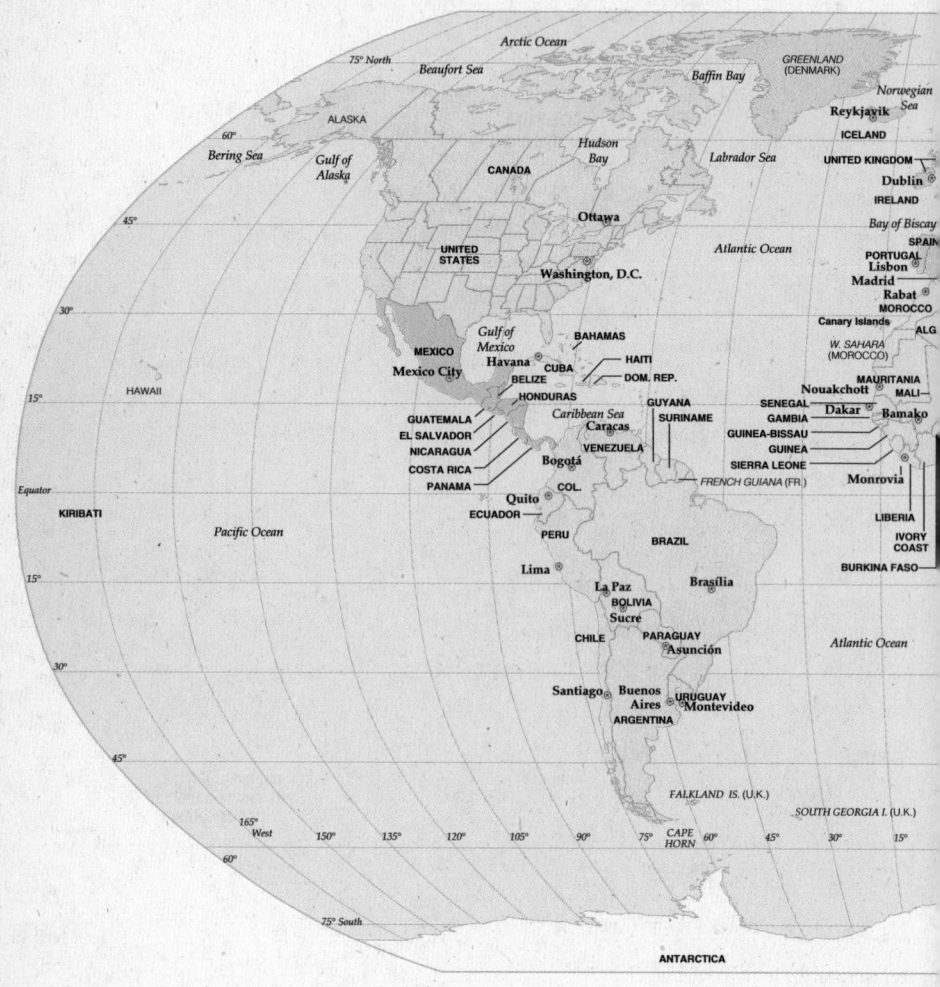

Arctic Ocean

75° North

Beaufort Sea

Baffin Bay

GREENLAND (DENMARK)

Norwegian Sea

Reykjavik

ICELAND

ALASKA

60°

Hudson Bay

Labrador Sea

UNITED KINGDOM

Bering Sea

Gulf of Alaska

CANADA

Dublin

IRELAND

45°

Ottawa

Atlantic Ocean

Bay of Biscay

SPAIN

UNITED STATES

PORTUGAL

Lisbon

Madrid

30°

Washington, D.C.

Rabat

MOROCCO

Canary Islands

ALG

Gulf of Mexico

BAHAMAS

W. SAHARA (MOROCCO)

MEXICO

Havana

CUBA

HAITI

Nouakchott

MAURITANIA

MALI

15°

HAWAII

Mexico City

BELIZE

DOM. REP.

SENEGAL

Dakar

Bamako

HONDURAS

Caribbean Sea

GUYANA

GAMBIA

GUATEMALA

SURINAME

GUINEA-BISSAU

EL SALVADOR

Caracas

GUINEA

NICARAGUA

VENEZUELA

SIERRA LEONE

Monrovia

COSTA RICA

Bogotá

FRENCH GUIANA (FR.)

Equator

PANAMA

Quito

COL.

KIRIBATI

ECUADOR

LIBERIA

PERU

BRAZIL

IVORY COAST

Pacific Ocean

15°

Lima

Brasília

BURKINA FASO

La Paz

BOLIVIA

Sucre

30°

CHILE

PARAGUAY

Asunción

Atlantic Ocean

Santiago

Buenos Aires

URUGUAY

Montevideo

ARGENTINA

45°

FALKLAND IS. (U.K.)

165° West

150°

135°

120°

105°

90°

75°

CAPE HORN

60°

SOUTH GEORGIA I. (U.K.)

45°

30°

15°

60°

75° South

ANTARCTICA

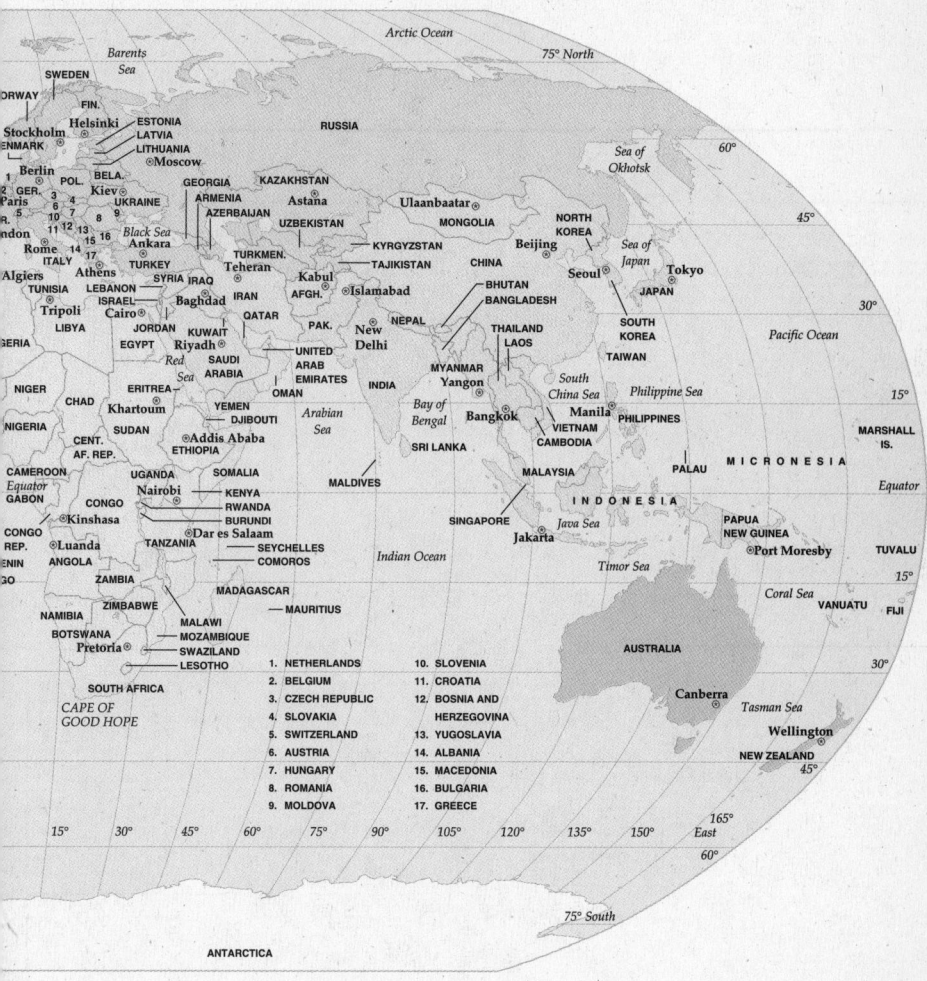

Arctic Ocean
75° North
Barents Sea
SWEDEN
NORWAY
FIN.
Stockholm
Helsinki
ESTONIA
DENMARK
LATVIA
Berlin
LITHUANIA
60°
Sea of Okhotsk
RUSSIA
Moscow
POL.
BELA.
Paris
GER.
Kiev
GEORGIA
KAZAKHSTAN
R.
UKRAINE
ARMENIA
Astana
Ulaanbaatar
45°
AZERBAIJAN
London
ITALY
Black Sea
UZBEKISTAN
MONGOLIA
NORTH
KOREA
Beijing
Seoul
Sea of Japan
Rome
Ankara
TURKMEN.
KYRGYZSTAN
Tokyo
Athens
TURKEY
Kabul
TAJIKISTAN
CHINA
JAPAN
Algiers
SYRIA
IRAQ
Teheran
AFGH.
Islamabad
BHUTAN
30°
TUNISIA
LEBANON
IRAN
SOUTH
KOREA
Pacific Ocean
Tripoli
Cairo
ISRAEL
Baghdad
PAK.
NEPAL
BANGLADESH
LIBYA
JORDAN
KUWAIT
QATAR
New
Delhi
THAILAND
TAIWAN
NIGERIA
EGYPT
Riyadh
UNITED
ARAB
EMIRATES
LAOS
15°
Red Sea
SAUDI
ARABIA
MYANMAR
South
China Sea
Philippine Sea
NIGER
CHAD
ERITREA
OMAN
INDIA
Yangon
Bangkok
MARSHALL
IS.
NIGERIA
Khartoum
YEMEN
Arabian
Sea
Bay of
Bengal
VIETNAM
PHILIPPINES
CENT.
AF. REP.
SUDAN
DJIBOUTI
CAMBODIA
MICRONESIA
CAMEROON
ETHIOPIA
Addis Ababa
SRI LANKA
PALAU
Equator
GABON
UGANDA
SOMALIA
MALDIVES
MALAYSIA
Equator
CONGO
Nairobi
KENYA
INDONESIA
PAPUA
NEW GUINEA
CONGO
REP.
Kinshasa
RWANDA
BURUNDI
SINGAPORE
Java Sea
TUVALU
BENIN
Luanda
TANZANIA
Dar es Salaam
Jakarta
Port Moresby
ANGOLA
SEYCHELLES
COMOROS
Indian Ocean
Timor Sea
15°
TOGO
ZAMBIA
Coral Sea
VANUATU
MADAGASCAR
MAURITIUS
NAMIBIA
ZIMBABWE
AUSTRALIA
FIJI
BOTSWANA
Pretoria
MALAWI
MOZAMBIQUE
Canberra
30°
SWAZILAND
LESOTHO
1. NETHERLANDS
10. SLOVENIA
Tasman Sea
SOUTH AFRICA
2. BELGIUM
11. CROATIA
Wellington
CAPE OF
GOOD HOPE
3. CZECH REPUBLIC
12. BOSNIA AND
HERZEGOVINA
NEW ZEALAND
4. SLOVAKIA
5. SWITZERLAND
13. YUGOSLAVIA
45°
6. AUSTRIA
14. ALBANIA
7. HUNGARY
15. MACEDONIA
165°
East
8. ROMANIA
16. BULGARIA
15°
30°
45°
60°
75°
90°
105°
120°
135°
150°
9. MOLDOVA
17. GREECE
60°

75° South

ANTARCTICA

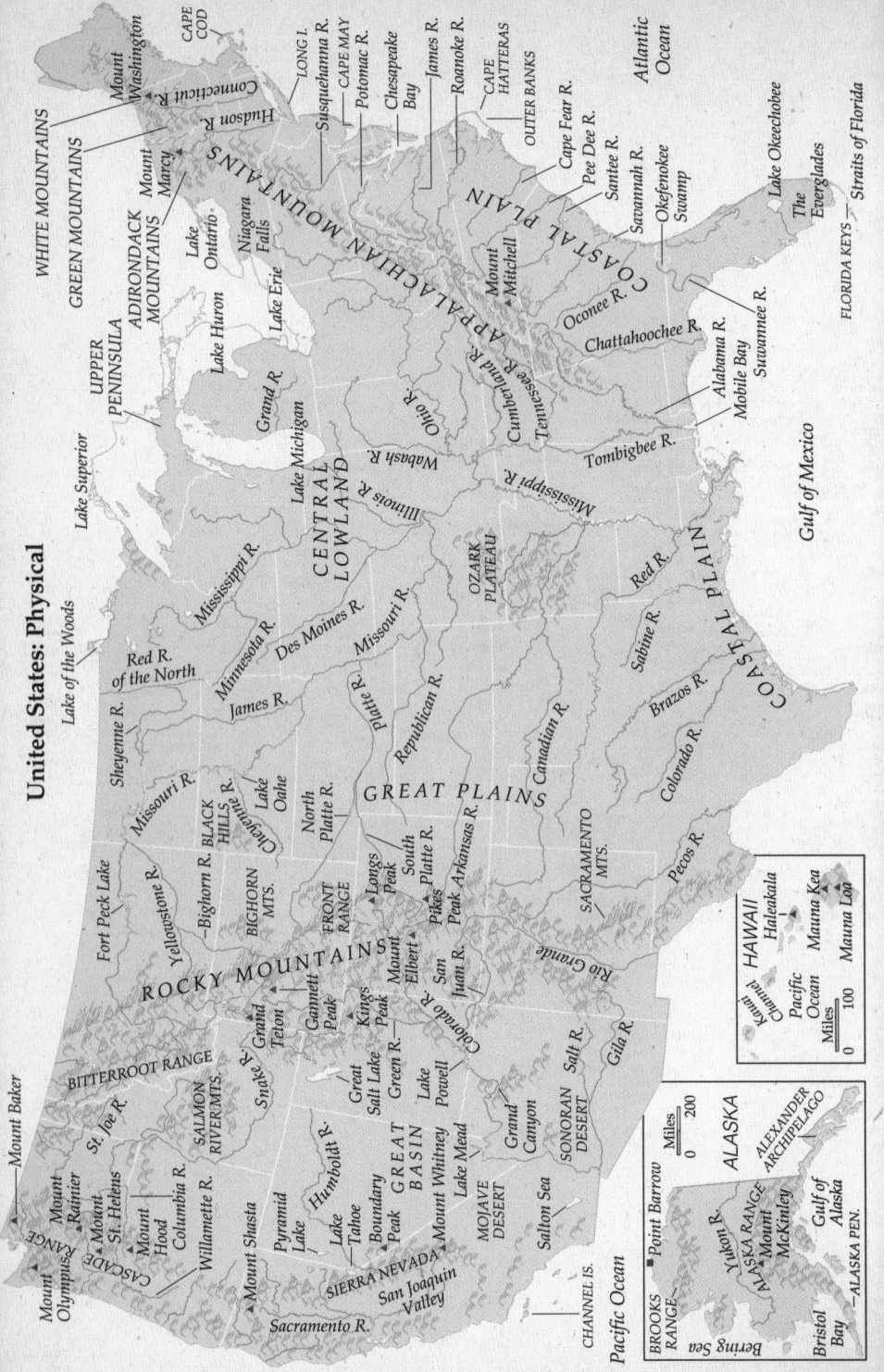

United States: Physical

Mount Olympus
CASCADE RANGE
Mount Baker
Mount Rainier
Mount St. Helens
Mount Hood
Columbia R.
Willamette R.
St. Joe R.
BITTERROOT RANGE
SALMON RIVER MTS.
Snake R.
Mount Shasta
Pyramid Lake
Lake Tahoe
Humboldt R.
GREAT BASIN
Boundary Peak
SIERRA NEVADA
Mount Whitney
San Joaquin Valley
Sacramento R.
MOJAVE DESERT
Salton Sea
Lake Mead
Grand Canyon
SONORAN DESERT
Gila R.
Salt R.
CHANNEL IS.
Pacific Ocean

ROCKY MOUNTAINS
Grand Teton
Gannett Peak
Kings Peak
Great Salt Lake
Green R.
San Juan R.
Colorado R.
Lake Powell
Mount Elbert
FRONT RANGE
Longs Peak
Pikes Peak
South Platte R.
Arkansas R.
Rio Grande
SACRAMENTO MTS.
Pecos R.
Canadian R.
Colorado R.
Brazos R.
Sabine R.
Red R.

Fort Peck Lake
Missouri R.
Yellowstone R.
Bighorn R.
BIGHORN MTS.
BLACK HILLS
Cheyenne R.
Lake Oahe
North Platte R.
Platte R.
Republican R.
GREAT PLAINS

Lake of the Woods
Red R. of the North
Sheyenne R.
Minnesota R.
James R.
Des Moines R.
Missouri R.
Mississippi R.

Lake Superior
UPPER PENINSULA
Lake Michigan
Lake Huron
Grand R.
CENTRAL LOWLAND
Illinois R.
Mississippi R.
Wabash R.
Ohio R.
OZARK PLATEAU
Red R.

WHITE MOUNTAINS
GREEN MOUNTAINS
Mount Washington
CAPE COD
ADIRONDACK MOUNTAINS
Mount Marcy
Lake Ontario
Lake Erie
Niagara Falls
LONG I.
Connecticut R.
Hudson R.
Susquehanna R.
CAPE MAY
Potomac R.
Chesapeake Bay
James R.
Roanoke R.
CAPE HATTERAS
OUTER BANKS
APPALACHIAN MOUNTAINS
Cape Fear R.
Pee Dee R.
Santee R.
Savannah R.
Okefenokee Swamp
COASTAL PLAIN
Mount Mitchell
Cumberland R.
Tennessee R.
Oconee R.
Chattahoochee R.
Alabama R.
Mobile Bay
Suwannee R.
Tombigbee R.
Lake Okeechobee
The Everglades
FLORIDA KEYS
Straits of Florida
Atlantic Ocean
Gulf of Mexico

HAWAII
Kauai Channel
Haleakala
Mauna Kea
Mauna Loa
Pacific Ocean
Miles
0   100

ALASKA
Point Barrow
BROOKS RANGE
Yukon R.
ALASKA RANGE
Mount McKinley
ALEXANDER ARCHIPELAGO
Gulf of Alaska
ALASKA PEN.
Bristol Bay
Bering Sea
Miles
0   200

bombing of Pan Am flight 103. U.N. sanctions were thereby automatically suspended but the U.S. announced that its anti-terrorism sanctions would continue. In late April, the U.S. eased food and medicine sanctions.

▶ LIECHTENSTEIN
Principality of Liechtenstein
● **GEOGRAPHY   Location:** landlocked country in central Europe. **Boundaries:** Austria to N and E, Switzerland to S and W. **Total area:** 62 sq. mi. (160 sq km). **Coastline:** none. **Comparative area:** about 0.9 times the size of Washington, D.C. **Land use:** 24% arable land; 0% permanent crops; 16% meadows and pastures; 35% forest and woodland; 25% other. **Major cities:** (1994) Väduz (capital) 5,067; Schaan 5,143; Balzers 3,917; Triesen 3,789; Eschen 3,443.

● **PEOPLE   Population:** 32,057 (1998 est.). **Nationality:** noun—Liechtensteiner(s); adjective—Liechtenstein. **Ethnic groups:** 87.5% Alemannic, 12.5% Italian, Turkish and other. **Languages:** German (official), Alemannic dialect. **Religions:** 80% Roman Catholic, 7.4% Protestant.

● **GOVERNMENT   Type:** hereditary constitutional monarchy. **Independence:** Jan 23, 1719. **Constitution:** Oct. 5, 1921. **National holiday:** Assumption Day, Aug. 15. **Heads of Government:** Hans-Adam II, prince (since Nov. 1989); Mario Frick, prime minister (since Dec. 1993). **Structure:** executive—hereditary prince; unicameral legislature; judiciary—independent.

● **ECONOMY   Monetary unit:** Swiss franc. **Budget:** (1996); *income:* $455 mil.; *expend.:* $435 mil. **GDP:** $730 mil., $23,000 per capita (1998 est.). **Chief Crops:** wheat, barley, maize, potatoes; livestock, dairy products. **Natural resources:** hydroelectric potential. **Major industries:** electronics, metal manufacturing, textiles. **Labor force:** 22,891 of which 13,847 are foreign workers (mostly from Switzerland and Austria); 53% services; 45% industry, trade, and building; 2% agriculture, fishing, forestry, and horticulture. **Exports:** $2.47 bil. (f.o.b., 1996 est.); small specialty machinery, dental products, stamps, hardware, pottery. **Imports:** $917.3 mil. (c.i.f., 1996 est.); machinery, metal goods, textiles, foodstuffs, motor vehicles. **Major trading partners:** *exports:* 60.57% EU and EFTA countries, Switzerland; *imports:* EU countries, Switzerland.

The alpine principality of Liechtenstein, bordered by Austria and Switzerland, is a remnant of the Holy Roman Empire, an ancient constitutional monarchy with a modern industrial economy. The current dynasty was established in 1699; Prince Franz Josef II came to the throne in 1938, yielding his executive powers to his heir apparent, Hans Adam, in 1984.

Liechtenstein was tied to the Austro-Hungarian monarchy until 1918. Since then it has remained in a customs union with Switzerland, which also handles its foreign affairs. The single-chamber diet, the Landtag is elected by universal suffrage, women having won the right to vote in 1984. For almost 60 years the government was a coalition of the conservative Progressive Citizens Party and the liberal Fatherland Union. Since April, 1997 Premier Mario Frick has governed with a cabinet of his own Fatherland Union with the PCP in opposition. Liechtenstein joined the United Nations in 1990.

The economy, dominated by dairy farming before 1945, has since been radically transformed by industrialization and the development of service industries. Liechtenstein is a corporate haven, with some 25,000 corporations maintaining nominal headquarters there. Foreign workers constitute about 40 percent of the work force.

▶ LITHUANIA
Republic of Lithuania
● **GEOGRAPHY   Location:** eastern coast of Baltic Sea in northeastern Europe. **Boundaries:** Latvia to N, Belarus to E and SE, Poland to SW, Russian Federation (Kaliningrad) to W, Baltic Sea to NW. **Total area:** 25,174 sq. mi. (65,200 sq km). **Coastline:** Baltic Sea. **Comparative area:** slightly larger than West Virginia. **Land use:** 35% cropland; 12% permanent crops; 7% meadows and pastures; 31% forest and woodland; 15% other. **Major cities:** (1995 est.) Vilnius (capital) 575,700; Kaunas 415,300; Klaipeda 202,800; Siauliai 147,200; Panevezys 132,000.

● **PEOPLE   Population:** 3,584,966 (1999 est.). **Nationality:** noun—Lithuanian(s); adjective—Lithuanian. **Ethnic groups:** 80.6% Lithuanian, 8.7% Russian, 7% Polish, 1.6% Belarussian. **Languages:** Lithuanian (official), Russian, Polish, ethnic languages. **Religions:** primarily Roman Catholic, also Lutheran, Russian Orthodox, Protestant, evangelical Christian Baptist, Islam, Judaism.

● **GOVERNMENT   Type:** parliamentary democracy. **Independence:** Sept. 6, 1991 (from Soviet Union). **Constitution:** Oct. 25, 1992. **National holiday:** Statehood Day, Feb. 16. **Heads of Government:** Valdas Adamkus, president (since Feb. 1998); Rolandas Paksas, premier (since June 1999). **Structure:** executive; unicameral legislature; judiciary.

● **ECONOMY   Monetary unit:** litas. **Budget:** (1997 est.). *income:* $1.5 bil.; *expend.:* $1.7 bil. **GDP:** $17.6 bil., $4,900 per capita (1998 est.). **Chief crops:** grain, potatoes, sugar beets, vegetables; meat, milk, eggs; fish; flax fiber. **Natural resources:** peat. **Major industries:** machine building, metalworking, food processing. **Labor force:** 1.8 mil. (1997); 42% industry, 20% agriculture and forestry. **Exports:** $4.2 bil. (1998); 19% machinery and equipment, 16% mineral products, 15% textiles, 8% chemicals. **Imports:** $5.9 bil. (f.o.b. 1998); 30% machinery and equipment, 18% mineral products, 9% chemicals. **Major trading partners:** *exports:* 24% Russia, 11% Germany, 10% Belarus; *imports:* 24% Russia, 19% Germany.

Lithuanians and Latvians are closely related peoples whose languages, the only two in the Baltic family of languages, are quite similar. But their histories, at least until 1795, were radically different. Fierce warriors able to stem the German tide during the Middle Ages, the Lithuanians repeatedly defeated the Teutonic knights, defending their independence and retaining their own religion.

In the 14th century, under Grand Duke Gediminas and his sons, Lithuania conquered White Russia (Belarus) and Ukraine and extended the Lithuanian dynasty from the Baltic almost to the Black Sea. The completion of Gediminas's policies came in 1386 when his grandson Jogalla was baptized, married the Polish heiress Jadwiga, and was crowned king of Poland under the title Wladislaw II, thereby creating the Poland-Lithuania Commonwealth. One condition of the union was that Lithuania had to adopt Christianity, which it did in 1387.

With the Third Partition of Poland in 1795, Lithuania was absorbed into Russia. The upper and educated classes took part in Poland's antiRussian rebellions in 1830 and 1863. After the latter, the Russians required Lithuanians to use the Russian alphabet instead of the Latin as a move to stop any national renaissance; but after 1883 literature smuggled into the czarist empire from Prussia and secret Lithuanian schools and societies kept alive a national identity based on ethnic, religious, and linguistic grounds rather than on the medieval and Renaissance traditions of political independence.

In January 1921 the victorious allies of World War I acknowledged a new Lithuanian republic in the Soviet-German Treaty of Brest-Litovsk of March 1918. Formal recognition came in 1922. The territory of Memel (Klaipeda in Lithuanian), separated from Germany in the Treaty of Versailles, was seized in January 1923 and organized as an autonomous unit of the new republic. The city itself was largely German, but its countryside was Lithuanian and in any case it was Lithuania's only possible outlet to the sea. With the historic capital Vilnius annexed by the new Polish state, the de facto capital became the university city of Kaunas.

Danger from local communists and fascists led the army to dispense with Parliament in December 1926, and an authoritarian regime under Pres. Antana Smetona followed. In 1939 Lithuania, like the other Baltic states, was doomed by the "secret protocols" of the 1939 Nazi-Soviet Pact. In June 1940 the Soviet Union invaded Lithuania and a Soviet-approved "people's government" was formed. After an election in which only pro-Soviet candidates were permitted to run, the Lithuanian Soviet Socialist Republic was proclaimed on July 21, 1940.

Thousands of Lithuanians fled westward, while other thousands disappeared into Siberia. Stalin returned Vilnius (from Poland) and Klaipeda (which Hitler had taken) to Lithuania and fostered industrialization, which elevated living standards above most of the USSR. A high Lithuanian birth rate enabled the country to resist "Russification" more easily than Latvia or Estonia.

Mikhail Gorbachev's policy of glasnost, or openness, spurred the already strong Lithuanian nationalist and dissident movement into action. It began with a public discussion of the "secret protocols" of the 1939 Nazi-Soviet Pact, which had permitted the USSR to annex Lithuania and which the Soviet government long had denied existed. In 1987 the Soviet government tolerated demonstrations in Vilnius, but by February 1988, Soviet troops prevented the Lithuanians from celebrating their 70th year of independence. The Soviet stance resulted in the founding of the new Lithuanian Movement for Reconstruction (Sajudis), which became the main political vehicle for Lithuanian independence from the USSR.

On Mar. 11, 1990, Lithuania declared its independence, and in response the Soviets began a 72-day-long economic blockade. On Jan. 13, 1991, the world watched as Soviet paratroopers and tanks attacked the radio and television centers, beginning a standoff between the Soviets and the Lithuanians that lasted until Sept. 6, 1991, when the USSR recognized Lithuanian independence.

After independence, Lithuania struggled to break a political deadlock caused by its lack of a constitution. In November 1992 free elections were held. The Democratic Labor party (the renamed Communists) gained 47 percent of the vote and 77 seats in Parliament, while Sajudis gained only 22 percent of the vote and 28 seats. In February 1993 the Democratic Labor candidate, Algirdas Brazauskas, handily won the presidential election with 61 percent of the vote.

The last Soviet troops left Lithuanian soil Aug. 31, 1993 and the government moved on a path to a free economy and worked for good relations with Russia and the other former Soviet states to the east. In 1996, however the Communists were routed and the Homeland Union party took control of the government. Over the next few years Lithuania followed strict fiscal and monetary policies thereby attracting over $1 bil. in foreign investment and strong GDP growth of 6 to 7 percent. In 1997-1998 presidential elections, Brazauskas-backed Valdas Adamkus, after being trounced in the first round, won a close victory.

▶ LUXEMBOURG
Grand Duchy of Luxembourg

● **GEOGRAPHY   Location:** landlocked country in western Europe. **Boundaries:** Belgium to N and W, Germany to E, France to S. **Total area:** 998 sq. mi. (2,586 sq km). **Coastline:** none. **Comparative area:** slightly smaller than Rhode Island. **Land use:** 24% arable land; 1% permanent crops; 20% meadows and pastures; 21% forest and woodland; 34% other. **Major cities:** (1995 est.) Luxembourg-Ville (capital) 76,446; Esch-sur-Alzette 24,255; Differdange 16,196; Dudelange 15,833; Sanem 12,170.

● **PEOPLE   Population:** 429,080 (1999 est.). **Nationality:** noun—Luxembourger(s); adjective—Luxembourg. **Ethnic groups:** Celtic base, with French and German blend; also, guest and worker residents from Portugal, Italy, and other European countries. **Languages:** Luxembourgian, German, French, English. **Religions:** 97% Roman Catholic, 3% Protestant and Jewish.

● **GOVERNMENT   Type:** constitutional monarchy. **Independence:** 1839 **Constitution:** Oct. 17, 1868, occasional revisions. **National holiday:** Grand Duke's birthday, National Day, June 23. **Heads of Government:** Jean de Luxembourg, grand duke (since Nov. 1964); Jean-Claude Juncker, prime minister (since Jan. 1995). **Structure:** executive—prime minister appointed by Grand Duke but responsible to parliament; unicameral legislature—Council of State, appointed for indefinite term, exercises some powers of an upper house; judiciary.

● **ECONOMY   Monetary unit:** Luxembourg franc. **Budget:** (1997 est.) *income:* $5.46 bil.; *expend.:* $5.44 bil. **GDP:** $13.9 bil., $32,700 per capita (1998 est.). **Chief crops:** barley, oats, potatoes, wheat, fruits, wine grapes; livestock products. **Natural resources:** iron ore (no longer exploited). **Major industries:** banking, iron and steel, food processing. **Labor force:** 226,500, one-third of which is foreign (1998); 83.2% services, 14.3% industry, 2.5% agriculture. **Exports:** $7.1 bil. (f.o.b., 1996 est.); finished steel products, chemicals, rubber products, glass, aluminum. **Imports:** $9.4 bil. (c.i.f., 1996 est.); minerals, metals, foodstuffs, machinery, quality consumer goods. **Major trading partners:** *exports:* 28% Germany, 18% France, 15% Belgium; *imports:* 38% Belgium, 25% Germany, 11% France.

One of hundreds of small principalities in the Holy Roman Empire, Luxembourg joined the German league when the empire was abolished in 1806. It shared a monarchy with the Netherlands, but the two countries remained distinct under a single sovereign. In 1831 Luxembourg lost its

French-speaking territory to Belgium. The Treaty of London granted sovereignty to Luxembourg in 1867. When King William III died in 1890, different rules of succession severed the dual monarchy; Queen Wilhelmina succeeded him in the Netherlands, while Adolf of Nassau became grand duke of Luxembourg. The nation's full independence dates from that event.

During the 19th century, Luxembourg developed a balanced modern economy, with prosperous small farms being complemented by industry, particularly mining and steel production. As late as 1970, steel accounted for over 25 percent of the nation's GDP and five-eighths of export earnings, although rising international competition has led to a decline since then.

Luxembourg was overrun by Germany during World War I and again in May 1940, in the early stages of World War II. Archduchess Charlotte fled to London and returned with the Allied armed forces in 1944. The constitutional monarchy has enjoyed political stability since the war, with the Christian Social party normally the senior partner in a three-way coalition.

Luxembourg formed a customs union with Belgium in 1921 and joined the Benelux (Belgium, Netherlands, Luxembourg) union even before World War II had ended. A founding member of the United Nations in 1945, Luxembourg abandoned its traditional neutrality in 1948 and joined NATO in 1949. It was a founding member of the EEC under the 1956 Treaty of Rome and is now home to numerous Common Market institutions, including the Secretariat of the European Parliament and the European Investment Bank; international banking accounts for over half of its gross national product. The country's chief problem is a shrinking and aging citizenry, leading to strains on social services and dependence on foreign workers.

▶ **MACEDONIA**
The Former Yugoslav Republic of Macedonia
● **GEOGRAPHY Location:** southern part of the Balkan Peninsula. **Boundaries:** Serbia to N, Bulgaria to E, Greece to S, Albania to W, Yugoslavia to NE and N. **Total area:** 9,781 sq. mi. (25,333 sq km.). **Coastline:** none. **Comparative area:** slightly larger than Vermont. **Land use:** 39% forest and woodland, 25% meadows and pastures, 24% arable land, 10% other. **Major cities:** (1994 census) Skopje (Skoplje or, in Turkish, Uskub) 440,577; Bitola 75,386; Kumanovo 66,237; Tetovo 50,376.
● **PEOPLE Population:** 2,022,604 (1999 est.). **Nationality:** noun—Macedonian(s); adj.—Macedonian. **Ethnic groups:** 66% Macedonian, 23% Albanian, 4% Turkish, 2% Serb, 7% other (includes gypsies). **Languages:** 70% Macedonian (official), 21% Albanian, 3% Turkish, 3% Serbo-Croatian, 3% other. **Religions:** 67% Eastern Orthodox, 30% Muslim, 3% other.
● **GOVERNMENT Type:** emerging democracy. **Independence:** Sept. 17, 1991 (from Yugoslavia). **Constitution:** Nov. 17, 1991. **National holiday:** Sept. 8. **Heads of Government:** Kiro Gligorov, president (since Jan. 1991); Ljubco Georgievski, prime minister (since Nov. 1998). **Structure:** executive; unicameral legislature; judiciary.
● **ECONOMY Monetary unit:** denar. **Budget:** (1996 est.) *income:* $1.06 bil.; *expend.:* $1 bil. **GDP:** $2.1 bil.; $1,050 per capita (1998 est.). **Chief crops:** rice, tobacco, wheat, corn, millet; beef, pork, poultry, mutton. **Natural resources:**

chrome, lead, marble, zinc. **Major industries:** metallurgy and metal processing, chemicals, textiles, timber. **Labor force:** 591,773 (1994); 40% industry and mining; 30% unemployed (1998 est.). **Exports:** $1.2 bil. (1997); 17% food, beverage, tobacco, 13.3% machinery and transport equipment, 58% other manufactured goods. **Imports:** $1.6 bil. (c.i.f., 1997); 19% machinery and transport equipment, 14% chemicals, 12% fuels. **Major trading partners:** Bulgaria, other former Yugoslav republics, Germany.

Located at the geographic center of the Balkan peninsula, Macedonia is an epitome of the entire region in its history and ethnic complexity as well. While there is a Macedonian language (a Slavic tongue more akin to Bulgarian than to Serbo-Croatian and codified in grammar and orthography only after World War II), the question of whether or not there is a Macedonian nation is contested: to Serbians, Macedonians are "south Serbs"; to Greeks, they are "Slavophone Greeks"; to Bulgars, they are kindred people, ethnic "cousins."

In any case, Macedonians are not related to the classical people of King Philip and Alexander the Great. Their realm had become a Roman province by 146 b.c. and remained part of the Byzantine Empire even after being invaded and settled by Slavic peoples in the sixth and seventh centuries. Contested in the Middle Ages by the Byzantine, Bulgarian, and Serbian empires, Macedonia fell at last to the Ottoman Turks in 1371. Well into the 19th century its population called itself "Christian" or "Slav," while Greek served as the language of culture and business until a literary awakening associated with scholarly collections of folk songs and heroic poetry brought a Macedonian consciousness. This found significant political expression with the formation in 1893 of the IMRO (Internal Macedonian Revolutionary Organization) that sought to unify all non-Turks—Bulgars, Greeks, Albanians, Vlacha—in an autonomous or independent state and which did not shrink from terrorism and revolution.

The peace treaties of Paris that concluded World War I divided Macedonia among three states: Greece, Bulgaria, and the newly created Yugoslavia. IMRO turned now against Serbian dominance in Yugoslavia and filled the 1930s with violent struggles against "denationalization." It was Bulgarian claims to Macedonia that led that state to ally with Hitler's Germany and to occupy Macedonia in 1941. With the victory of Tito's partisans and the reconstruction of the Yugoslav state as a federation of Communist "republics," a Macedonian People's Republic was established in 1946.

After the dictator's death in 1980, Macedonia took part in the "collegial rule" whereby the presidency of Yugoslavia and the chairmanship of the Communist party Presidium rotated annually among the republics. But as the separate republics declared independence in 1991 and civil war began, Macedonia declared its own independence in January 1992. Greece's opposition to the new nation's name and flag—as menaces to the northern Greek province of the same name—prevented international recognition until a 1995 agreement between the two countries. Under the pact, Macedonia removed an ancient Greek symbol from its flag and changed its constitution so as to remove any suggestion of a claim on Greek Macedonia. With UN recognition came both UN "peacekeeping forces" (including 300 American troops) to patrol the frontier with rump Yugoslavia and the painful need to comply with the UN embargo against Serbia, to whose economy Macedonia has been closely tied. An April 1996 treaty with Yugoslavia resolved border questions and renounced territorial claims.

Elections in 1998 saw the ruling Social Democrats ousted by the right-wing Coalition for Changes which organized a government under Ljuplo Georgievski. In April, NATO pledged to defend Macedonia from Yugoslav incursions in the latter's struggle again Albanian separatists in Kosovo. Refugees from Kosovo flooded Macedonia, straining its humanitarian capacities.

▶ MADAGASCAR
Republic of Madagascar
● **Geography   Location:** off southeast Africa in western Indian Ocean. Antananarivo: 18°52'S, 47°30'E. **Boundaries:** about 300 mi. (500 km) E of Mozambique. **Total area:** 226,656 sq. mi. (587,040 sq km). **Coastline:** 3,000 mi. (4,828 km). **Comparative area:** slightly less than twice the size of Arizona. **Land use:** 4% arable land; 1% permanent crops; 41% meadows and pastures; 40% forest and woodland; 14% other; includes 1% irrigated. **Major cities:** Antananarivo (capital) 662,585 (1985 est.); Antsirabé 78,941; Toamasina (Tamatave) 77,395; Fianarantsoa 68,054; Mahajanga (Majunga) 65,864 (1975 census).
● **People   Population:** 14,873,387 (1999 est.). **Nationality:** noun—Malagasy (sing., pl.); adjective—Malagasy. **Ethnic groups:** highlanders of predominantly Malayo-Indonesian origin (Merina and related Betsileo); coastal peoples collectively termed Cotiers, with mixed African, Malayo-Indonesian, and Arab ancestry (Betsimisaraka, Tsimihety, Antaisaka, Sakalava); French, Indian, Creole, Comoran. **Languages:** French and Malagasy (both official). **Religions:** 52% indigenous beliefs, 41% Christian, 7% Muslim.
● **Government   Type:** republic. **Independence:** June 26, 1960 (from France). **Constitution:** Aug. 19, 1992. **National holiday:** Independence Day, June 26. **Heads of Government:** Didier Ratsiraka, president (since Feb. 1997); Tantely René Gabrio Andrianarivo, premier (since May 1996). **Structure:** executive; unicameral legislature, scheduled to become bicameral —two-thirds of upper house will be filled from directly elected regional assemblies, rest by presidential appointment; judiciary.
● **Economy   Monetary unit:** Malagasy franc. **Budget:** (1996) *income:* $477 mil; *expend.:* $706 mil. **GDP:** $10.3 bil., $730 per capita (1997 est.). **Chief crops:** coffee, vanilla, cloves, sugar; livestock. **Natural resources:** graphite, chromite, coal, bauxite, salt. **Major industries:** agricultural processing (meat canneries, soap factories, brewery, tanneries, sugar refining), light consumer goods industries (textiles, glassware), cement. **Labor force:** (1995) 7 mil. **Exports:** $170 mil. (f.o.b., 1997 est.); 45% coffee, 20% vanilla, cloves, shellfish, sugar, petroleum products. **Imports:** $477 mil. (f.o.b., 1997 est.); 30% intermediate manufactures, 28% capital goods, 15% petroleum, 14% consumer goods, 13% food. **Major trading partners:** *exports:* 31.7% France, 15.8% Japan, 6.4% Germany; *imports:* 31% France, 9.1% Iran, 8.2% South Africa.

The largest island nation, and fourth largest island, in the world, Madagascar was settled by Malayo-Indonesian migrants some 2,000 years ago. Although later waves of African and Arab migrants were absorbed into the population, to a

large extent it is still ethnically and culturally Asian. A Portuguese attempt to colonize the island in the 16th century failed, and during the 18th and 19th centuries, a unified kingdom backed by the British ruled the country. Foreign interests—largely British and French—developed extensive coffee plantations, and the French made Madagascar a protectorate in 1885 and a colony in 1896.

During World War II Madagascar sided with the Free French, and French colonial rule was reestablished after the war. The Malagasy Republic was founded as an independent nation on June 26, 1960. A coup in 1972 brought a repressive anti-French and generally anti-Western government to power.

A new federal constitution was approved in 1992, and in 1993 elections, Albert Zafy, a surgeon, defeated the 17-year incumbent Didier Ratsiraka for the presidency, but the results were reversed in 1997 and Ratsiraka immediately set out to cut inflation, and renegotiate the nation's many foreign loans.

Madagascar's wildlife (a mixture of African species and others of domestic evolution) and its isolation make it of unique scientific interest. (In 1990, scientists discovered the smallest mammal known to science: the dwarf lemur.) But some 75 percent of the population live in poverty.

▶ MALAWI
Republic of Malawi
● **Geography   Location:** landlocked country in southern central Africa. **Boundaries:** Tanzania to N, Mozambique to E, S, and SW, Zambia to W; Lake Malawi forms much of eastern boundary. **Total area:** 45,745 sq. mi. (118,480 sq km). **Coastline:** none. **Comparative area:** slightly smaller than Pennsylvania. **Land use:** 18% arable land; negl. % permanent crops; 20% meadows and pastures; 39% forest and woodland; 23% other; includes negl. % irrigated. **Major cities:** (1994 est.) Lilongwe (capital) 395,500; Blantyre 446,800.
● **People   Population:** 10,000,416 (1999 est.). **Nationality:** noun—Malawian(s); adjective—Malawian. **Ethnic groups:** Chewa, Nyanja, Tumbuko, Yao, Lomwe, Sena, Tonga, Ngoni, Asian, European. **Languages:** English and Chichewa (both official); Tombuka and other regional languages. **Religions:** 55% Protestant, 20% Roman Catholic, 20% Muslim, indigenous beliefs.
● **Government   Type:** multiparty democracy. **Independence:** July 6, 1964 (from UK). **Constitution:** May 18, 1995. **National holiday:** Republic Day, July 6. **Head of Government:** Elson Bakili Muluzi, president (since May 1994). **Structure:** executive; bicameral legislature; judiciary.
● **Economy   Monetary unit:** Malawian kwacha. **Budget:** (1993 est.) *income:* $530 mil.; *expend.:* $674 mil. **GDP:** $8.9 bil., $940 per capita (1998 est.). **Chief crops:** tobacco, tea, sugar, cotton; cattle, goats. **Natural resources:** limestone; unexploited deposits of uranium, coal, bauxite. **Major industries:** agricultural processing (tea, tobacco, sugar), sawmilling, cement. **Labor force:** 3.5 mil. (1990 est.); 86% agriculture. **Exports:** $405 mil. (f.o.b., 1995 est.); tobacco, tea, sugar, coffee, wood products. **Imports:** $475 mil. (f.o.b., 1995 est.); food, petroleum products, semimanufactures, consumer goods. **Major trading partners:** *exports:* U.S., South Africa, Germany; *imports:* South Africa, Zimbabwe, Japan.

Malawi derives its name from the Maravi, a Bantu people who settled in the region in the 13th century and whose descendants, the Chewas, make up a significant segment of the current population. In the 1830s, the Ngoni, driven from what is now South Africa by the Zulus, arrived in the area around Lake Nyasa. The arrival of the Scottish missionary David Livingstone in 1859 led to the establishment of the British-controlled Nyasaland Protectorate in 1891. In 1953 Nyasaland formed a federation with Northern and Southern Rhodesia (Zambia and Zimbabwe) and began to organize an independence movement. The fight for independence was led by Dr. H. Kamuzu Banda, an expatriate who assumed the presidency of the Nyasaland African Congress, later the Malawi Congress party, upon his return in 1958. The British granted Nyasaland self-governing status in 1962, and Banda was elected prime minister the following year. Malawi achieved full independence under its present name in 1964.

Banda soon introduced one-party rule and had himself declared president for life in 1971. All dissent was crushed while corruption and nepotism strangled the economy, leaving Malawi's citizens among the poorest in the world.

By 1990 internal unrest and the decline of Banda's popularity (he was now in his 90s) rapidly led to change. In 1992 a series of violent strikes by workers in the two largest cities resulted in more than 35 deaths. The United States, Great Britain, and Germany, hoping to push the Banda government to institute democratic reforms, cut off most of the $500 million they had been giving annually in aid. In June 1993 Malawians voted 2 to 1 to institute a multiparty system and in May 1994 Banda lost his nation's only free election in 30 years to Bakili Muluzi's United Democratic Front (UDF). In December 1995, Banda was acquitted of conspiring to murder four of his political rivals in 1983.

▶ MALAYSIA

• **GEOGRAPHY Location:** 13 states in Southeast Asia; 11 are in Peninsular Malaysia and two, Sabah and Sarawak, lie about 400 mi. (640 km) across South China Sea on northern coast of island of Borneo (Kalimantan). **Boundaries:** Peninsular Malaysia—Thailand to N, South China Sea to E, Island of Singapore to S across Johor Strait, and Indonesian island of Sumatra to W across Strait of Malacca; Sabah and Sarawak—South China Sea to NW, Sulu Sea to NE, Celebes Sea to E, Indonesia to S; Brunei is enclosed within Sarawak on coast of South China Sea. **Total area:** 127,317 sq. mi. (329,750 sq km). **Coastline:** 2,905 mi. (4,675 km). **Comparative area:** slightly larger than New Mexico. **Land use:** 3% arable land; 12% permanent crops; negl. % meadows and pastures; 68% forest and woodland; 17% other; includes 1% irrigated. **Major cities:** (1991 census) Kuala Lumpur (capital) 1,145,075; Ipoh 382,633; Johor Baharu 328,646; Melaka (Malacca) 295,999; Petaling Jaya 254,849.

• **PEOPLE Population:** 21,376,066 (1999 est.). **Nationality:** noun—Malaysian(s); adjective—Malaysian. **Ethnic groups:** 58% Malay and other indigenous, 26% Chinese, 7% Indian. **Languages:** Bahasa Melayu (official); English, Chinese dialects, Tamil, Telugu, Malalalam, Panjabi, Thai; note – in addition, in East Malaysia several indigenous languages are spoken, the largest of which are Iban and Kadazan. **Religions:** Islam, Buddhism, Daoism, Hinduism, Christianity, Sikhism; note – in addition, Shamanism is practiced on East Malaysia.

• **GOVERNMENT Type:** constitutional monarchy; Peninsular Malaysian states—hereditary rulers in all but Melaka and Penang, where governors are appointed by Malaysian government, with powers of state governments limited by federal constitution; Sabah—self-governing state, holding 20 seats in House of Representatives, with foreign affairs, defense, internal security, and other powers delegated to federal government; Sarawak—self-governing state, which holds 24 seats in House of Representatives, with foreign affairs, defense, internal security, and other powers delegated to federal government. **Independence:** Aug. 31, 1957 (from UK). **Constitution:** Aug. 31, 1957, amended Sept. 16, 1963, when Federation of Malaya became Federation of Malaysia. **National holiday:** National Day, Aug. 31. **Heads of Government:** Tuanku Ja'afar, king (since Apr. 1994); Dr. Mahathir Mohamad, prime minister (since July 1981). **Structure:** executive—paramount ruler chosen by and from the nine state rulers for five-year term; bicameral legislature; judiciary.

• **ECONOMY Monetary unit:** Malaysian ringgit. **Budget:** (1996 est.) *income:* $22.6 bil. *expend.:* $22 bil. **GDP:** $215.4 bil., $10,300 per capita (1998 est.). **Chief crops:** Peninsular Malaysia—natural rubber, palm oil, rice; Sabah—mainly subsistence, main crops are rubber, timber, coconut, rice; Sarawak—rubber, timber, pepper. **Natural resources:** tin, crude oil, timber, copper, iron ore. **Major industries:** Peninsular Malaysia—rubber and oil-palm processing and manufacturing, light manufacturing industry, electronics; Sabah—logging, petroleum production; Sarawak—agriculture processing, petroleum production and refining, logging. **Labor force:** 8.398 mil. (1996); 25% manufacturing, 21% agriculture, forestry, and fisheries; 17% local trade and tourism. **Exports:** $74.3 bil. (f.o.b. 1998); electronic equipment, petroleum products, palm oil, wood products, rubber, textiles. **Imports:** $59.3 bil. (f.o.b. 1998); machinery and equipment, chemicals, food. **Major trading partners:** *exports:* 21% U.S., 20% Singapore, 12% Japan; *imports:* 27% Japan, 16% U.S., 12% Singapore.

From ancient times a group of petty principalities in the southern part of the Malay Peninsula, bordering the Strait of Malacca, maintained extensive ties of maritime commerce throughout Southeast Asia. The early Malay states were Hindu, under Indian influence; with the rise of the Kingdom of Malacca in the 15th century, conversion to Islam was widespread. European influence in the Spice Islands began in the 16th century; the Portuguese, initially dominant, gave way to the Dutch, who seized Malacca in 1641.

British influence grew during the 18th century, with the founding of a trading settlement at Penang in 1789. Singapore was founded in 1819, and the Dutch ceded Malacca to Great Britain in 1824. By a series of treaties in the late 19th century, the various Malay states became British protectorates; Britain controlled the entire southern peninsula after 1909. Under British rule, commercial tin mining and the establishment of extensive rubber plantations led to the importation of many Indian and Chinese laborers; eventually ethnic Chinese dominated most of Malaya's domestic economy.

In the 19th century, Great Britain also gained a dominant position in northern Borneo. (Borneo is divided between Brunei, Indonesia, and Malaysia.)

Japan overran Malaya by February 1942. Following World War II, the various Malay states (except Singapore) organized into a federation, which replaced the confusing prewar regime of federated and unfederated protectorates. A Communist rebellion disrupted the country throughout the early 1950s. Following the suppression of the Communist movement, elections were held in mid-1955 for a home-rule government. The elections brought the Alliance party of Tungku Abdul Rahman to power, and the Federation of Malaya became independent in 1957.

The nation expanded on Sept. 16, 1963, with the creation of Malaysia, incorporating the Federation of Malaya as well as Singapore and the former British colonies of North Borneo (thereafter called Sabah) and Sarawak. Singapore seceded from Malaysia in 1965 and became an independent nation. Malaysia is a constitutional monarchy with a parliamentary system; monarchs are chosen for five-year terms from among the hereditary rulers of the nine Malay states.

Malaysia has been ruled since 1981 by the coalition government of Mahathir Mohamad, who has transformed the country from an agriculture-based economy to one of the fastest-growing economies in Asia. The country sustained annual growth rates of 8 percent through the 1980s as it embarked on several ambitious projects, including erecting the two tallest buildings in the world and bulldozing an area 25 miles south of Kuala Lumpur that will become the new capital. In 1995 Malaysia received $5.8 bil. in foreign direct investment, the most in East Asia. The Asian financial crisis of 1997-98 hit Malaysia very hard as the currency and stockmarkets declined steeply.

Facing Malaysia's first recession in 13 years, Mahathir announced that the free market system had proven a failure and dismissed his finance minister, Anwar Ibrahim in Sept. 1998. Arrested and beaten by police, Anwar faced charges of sodomy and corruption in a nightmare trial. In April 1999 he was found guilty and sentenced to six years in prison. His wife, Azizah Ismail announced a new opposition National Justice Party.

▶MALDIVES
Republic of Maldives
● **GEOGRAPHY Location:** chain of more than 1,200 small coral islands (about 220 inhabited), 475 mi. (764 km) from N to S and 80 mi. (207 km) from W to E in Indian Ocean; northernmost atoll about 370 mi. (960 km) southwest of India. Malé 4°00'N, 73°28'E. **Boundaries:** Laccadive Sea to NE, Arabian Sea to N, Indian Ocean to S and W. **Total area:** 116 sq. mi. (300 sq km). **Coastline:** 400 mi. (644 km). **Comparative area:** about 1.7 times size of Washington, D.C. **Land use:** 10% arable land; 0% permanent crops; 3% meadows and pastures; 3% forest and woodland; 84% other. **Major cities:** (1995) Malé (capital) 62,973.
● **PEOPLE Population:** 300,220 (1999 est.). **Nationality:** noun—Maldivian(s); adjective—Maldivian. **Ethnic groups:** Sinhalese, Dravidian, Arab, and African. **Languages:** Maldivian Divehi (dialect of Sinhala; script derived from Arabic); English spoken by most government officials. **Religions:** Sunni Muslim.
● **GOVERNMENT Type:** republic. **Independence:** July 26, 1965 (from UK). **Constitution:** June 4, 1964. **National holiday:** Independence Day, July 26. **Head of Government:** Maumoon Abdul Gayoom, president (since Nov. 1978). **Structure:** executive; unicameral legislature; judiciary.
● **ECONOMY Monetary unit:** rufiyaa. **Budget:**

(1995 est.) *income:* $88 mil.; *expend.:* $141 mil. **GDP:** $500 mil., $1,840 per capita (1998 est.). **Chief crops:** coconut, corn, sweet potatoes; fishing. **Natural resources:** fish. **Major industries:** fishing, tourism, some coconut processing. **Labor force:** about 56,435 (1990 est.); 25% fishing industry and agriculture, 21% services, 21% manufacturing and construction, 16% trade, restaurants and hotels, 10% transportation and communication, 7% other. **Exports:** $59 mil. (f.o.b., 1996 est.); fish, clothing. **Imports:** $302 mil. (f.o.b., 1996 est.); intermediate and capital goods, consumer goods, petroleum products. **Major trading partners:** *exports:* Sri Lanka, U.S., Germany; *imports:* Singapore, India, Sri Lanka.

The small sultanate of the Maldive Islands, with an Islamic population of Sinhalese descent, was made a British protectorate in 1887. The islands' tiny area and poor soil limited development; fishing and fish processing are the main industries, and copra (dried coconut meat for coconut oil) is the only significant crop. The Maldives became an independent nation on July 26, 1965. In 1968 the sultanate was abolished and replaced by a republic. Since independence, tourism has become economically important and now accounts for 18 percent of the GDP. Protests over the concentration of development on the island of Malé in recent years have led to political unrest in the other islands, while attempts to address the basic needs of those islands have strained the nation's tiny economic base.

The current president, Maumoon Abdul Gayoom, was elected to office in 1978 and subsequently reelected twice. The elections of September 1988 were marked by considerable unrest and demonstrations. An attempted coup against the Gayoom government on Nov. 4, 1988, was put down with the intervention of Indian troops.

▶MALI
Republic of Mali
● **GEOGRAPHY Location:** northwestern Africa. **Boundaries:** Algeria to N, Niger to E, Burkina Faso, Ivory Coast, Guinea to S, Senegal and Mauritania to W. **Total area:** 478,765 sq. mi. (1,240,000 sq km). **Coastline:** none. **Comparative area:** slightly less than twice the size of Texas. **Land use:** 2% arable land; negl. % permanent crops; 25% meadows and pastures; 6% forest and woodland; 67% other; includes negl. % irrigated. **Major cities:** (1976 census) Bamako (capital) 404,000; Ségou 65,000; Mopti 54,000; Sikasso 47,000; Kayes 45,000.
● **PEOPLE Population:** 10,429,124 (1999 est.). **Nationality:** noun—Malian(s); adjective—Malian. **Ethnic groups:** 50% Mande (Bambara, Malinke, Sarakole), 17% Peul, 12% Voltaic, 6% Songhai, 10% Tuareg and Moor. **Languages:** French (official); Bambara spoken by 80% of population. **Religions:** 90% Muslim, 9% indigenous beliefs, 1% Christian.
● **GOVERNMENT Type:** republic. **Independence:** Sept. 22, 1960 (from France). **Constitution:** Jan. 12, 1992. **National holiday:** Anniversary of the Proclamation of the Republic, Sept. 22. **Heads of Government:** Alpha Oumar Konaré, president (since June 1992); Ihrahim Boubacar Kéita, prime minister (since Feb. 1994). **Structure:** executive; unicameral legislature; judiciary.
● **ECONOMY Monetary unit:** Communauté Financière Africaine (CFA) franc. **Budget:** (1997 est.) *income:* $730 mil.; *expend.:* $770 mil. **GDP:** $8 bil., $790 per capita (1998 est.). **Chief crops:** cotton, millet, rice, corn; goats, sheep, cattle. **Natural re-**

sources: gold, phosphates, kaolin, salt, limestone, uranium; bauxite, iron ore, manganese, tin, and copper deposits are known but not exploited. **Major industries:** small local consumer goods and food processing, construction, phosphate, gold. **Labor force:** N.A.; 80% agriculture, 19% services. **Exports:** $590 mil. (f.o.b., 1998); cotton, livestock, gold. **Imports:** $600 mil. (f.o.b., 1998); machinery and equipment, foodstuffs, construction materials, petroleum. **Major trading partners:** *exports:* 20% Thailand, 20% Italy, 9% China; *imports:* 19% Ivory Coast, 17% France., other franc zone and EU countries.

Mali has been a center of West African civilization for over 4,000 years. Iron Age civilizations flourished on the middle reaches of the Niger River from about 200 b.c. The kingdom of Ghana arose about a.d. 750 on the strength of the gold trade with North African Berbers. Ghana was overthrown by the Muslim Almoravids, who ruled only 11 years, though Islam remained a major influence from that time. From 1200 to 1400, the Kingdom of Mali was dominant in the region and was renowned throughout Islam and even in Christian Europe for its wealth and power; when Mansa Musa's retinue stopped in Cairo en route to Mecca, it carried so much gold that the price of gold fell 20 percent. By the end of the 14th century, the Mali empire had been eclipsed by the Songhai (Soyinka) empire, centered on the Niger River cities of Gao and Timbuktu.

The Songhai empire collapsed after Timbuktu was sacked by Moroccans in 1591. It fragmented into a series of smaller states, and power shifted from the desert fringe back to the Niger valley, bringing with it a further spread of Islam.

French exploration of Mali led to conquest in 1896 and the creation of the colony of French Sudan in 1898, governed from Dakar, Senegal. Timbuktu declined in importance, and Bamako became the country's principal urban center.

Malians were granted French citizenship and limited self-rule in 1946. In 1958 the territory became autonomous within the French Overseas Community. In 1959, with French support, the French Sudan and Senegal formed the Federation of Mali, which became independent on June 20, 1960. Senegal seceded from the federation almost immediately, and Mali became an independent republic on Sept. 22, 1960. Modibo Keita was elected the country's first president.

Keita's program of radical control of society and the economy by the central government provoked discontent, and he was overthrown in 1968 by military officers led by Lt. Moussa Traore. Traore's Military Committee of National Liberation ruled until 1979 when it was reorganized under a new constitution as the Malian People's Democratic Union. Traore, an autocratic military order, was ousted in a 1991 coup and a transitional government under a civilian prime minister, Soumana Sacko, set up multiparty elections for June 1992. Alpha Konaré was elected president and his Alliance for Democracy in Mali party won 76 of 116 legislative seats. In 1995, the government reached an agreement in its longstanding dispute with the ethnic Tuareg nomads in the northern part of the country.

Pres. Konaré's government has succeeded in reviving the economy (cotton and gold production rank among the top in Africa) and winning praise from the World Bank. Political opposition, though small, turned violent in 1997 and caused a cancellation of the results of elections in April. Opposition parties claimed the Government had fixed the elections and boycotted new ones held in May that gave Konare victory. He governs unopposed in the National Assembly and many fear political instability is possible.

▶ **MALTA**
Republic of Malta
● **GEOGRAPHY   Location:** archipelago (largest islands are Malta, Gozo, and Comino) in central Mediterranean. Valletta 35°54'N, 14°32'E. **Boundaries:** Sicily 58 mi. (93 km) to N, Libya 180 mi. (290 km) to S, Tunisia to W. **Total area:** 124 sq. mi. (320 sq km). **Coastline:** 87 mi. (140 km). **Comparative area:** slightly less than twice the size of Washington, D.C. **Land use:** 38% arable land; 3% permanent crops; 0% meadows and pastures; 0% forest and woodland; 59% other; includes 3% irrigated. **Major cities:** (1994 est.) Valletta 7,953, Birkirkara 21,551, Qormi 17,928, Sliema 13,823.
● **PEOPLE   Population:** 381,603 (1999 est.). **Nationality:** noun—Maltese (sing., pl.); adjective—Maltese. **Ethnic groups:** Maltese (descendants of ancient Carthaginians and Phoenicians, with strong elements of Italian and other Mediterranean stock) **Languages:** Maltese and English (both official). **Religions:** 98% Roman Catholic.
● **GOVERNMENT   Type:** parliamentary democracy. **Independence:** Sept. 21, 1964 (from UK). **Constitution:** Dec. 13, 1974. **National holiday:** Independence Day, Sept. 21. **Heads of Government:** Prof. Guido de Marco, president (since Apr. 1999); Dr. Edward Fenech Adami, prime minister (since Sept. 1998). **Structure:** executive; unicameral legislature—seats are given to largest popular party to ensure a majority, usually 65; judiciary.
● **ECONOMY   Monetary unit:** Maltese lira. **Budget:** (1998 est.) *income:* $1.32 bil.; *expend.:* $1.76 bil. **GDP:** $5 bil., $13,000 per capita (1998 est.). **Chief crops:** potatoes, cauliflower, grapes, wheat, barley; milk, pork, poultry. **Natural resources:** limestone, salt. **Major industries:** tourism, electronics, ship repair yard, construction. **Labor force:** 148,085 (1996); 34% public services, 32% other services, 22% manufacturing and construction; 5% unemployment (1997). **Exports:** $1.7 bil. (f.o.b., 1997); machinery and transport equipment, manufactures. **Imports:** $2.3 bil. (f.o.b., 1997); machinery and transport equipment, manufactured goods; food, drink and tobacco. **Major trading partners:** *exports:* 18% France, 15% US, 15% Germany; *imports:* 20% Italy, 16% France, 15% UK.

Malta, an ancient crossroads of Mediterranean trade, was ruled successively by Phoenicians, Carthaginians, Greeks, Romans, and Byzantines before being conquered by Islamic Saracens from North Africa in the ninth century. In 1090 the Norman kings of Sicily conquered it and made it a way station for the First Crusade. In 1530 Charles V gave the island to the Knights Hospitalers (the Knights of Malta). The island withstood a siege by the Ottoman Turks in 1565 and fell only to Napoleon in 1798.

The Maltese came under British rule in 1800, and it was annexed in 1814. Limited self-rule was granted under the constitutions of 1921 and 1939. During World War II, Malta suffered devastating air raids by German and Italian forces; the entire population was awarded the George Cross for bravery.

In 1964 Malta was granted independence within the British Commonwealth, with Elizabeth II as its sovereign. Abrogating its mutual defense treaty with Great Britain in 1971, the Maltese government severed all ties to the British Crown, becoming a fully independent republic. British forces withdrew from the island in 1979.

Malta was governed by the leftist, anticlerical, and neutralist Labour party from 1971 to 1987, whose leader, the ardent nationalist Dominic Mintoff, was prime minister from 1971 to 1984. He was succeeded by Mifsud Bonnici. In 1987 the Catholic and pro-Western Nationalist party won a popular electoral majority but not a majority in Parliament. Under the terms of a 1987 constitutional amendment, it was granted sufficient extra seats in Parliament to allow it to organize a government, under Prime Minister Eddie Fenech Adami.

The Nationalist party ruled for nine years until in 1996 elections the Labour party won a slim majority, but returned to power in Sept. 1998 with Adami returning as prime minister.

▶ MARSHALL ISLANDS
Republic of the Marshall Islands
● **GEOGRAPHY   Location:** two groups of islands, the Ratak and Ralik chains, comprising 31 atolls in western Pacific. Majuro 7°09′N, 171°12′E. **Boundaries**: Guam about 1,300 mi. (2,100 km) to NW, Hawaii about 2,000 mi. (3,200 km) to NE, Kiribati to S, Federated States of Micronesia to W. **Total area**: 70 sq. mi. (181 sq km). **Coastline**: 230 (370 km). **Comparative area**: about the size of Washington, D.C. **Land use:** NA% arable land; 60% permanent crops; NA% meadows and pastures; NA% forest and woodland; 40% other. **Major cities:** Majuro (capital—pop. N.A.).
● **PEOPLE   Population:** 65,507 (1999 est.). **Nationality:** noun—Marshallese; adjective—Marshallese. **Ethnic groups:** Micronesian. **Languages:** English (official), two major Marshallese dialects from Malayo-Polynesian family, Japanese. **Religions:** Christian, mostly Protestant.
● **GOVERNMENT   Type:** constitutional government in free association with U.S.; Compact of Free Association entered into force Oct. 21, 1986. **Independence:** Oct. 21, 1986 (from U.S.-administered UN trusteeship). **Constitution:** May 1, 1979. **National holiday:** Proclamation of the Republic of the Marshall Islands, May 1. **Head of Government:** Imata Kabua, president (since 1979). **Structure:** executive; unicameral legislature; judiciary.
● **ECONOMY   Monetary unit:** U.S. dollar. **Budget:** (FY95/96) *income:* $80.1 mil.; *expend:* $77.4 mil. **GDP:** $91 mil., $1,450 per capita (1998 est.). **Chief crops:** coconuts, cacao, taro, breadfruit, fruits; pigs, chickens. **Natural resources:** phosphate deposits, marine products, deep seabed minerals. **Major industries:** copra, fish, tourism. **Labor force:** NA. **Exports:** $17.5 mil. (f.o.b., 1996 est.); coconut oil, fish, trochus shells. **Imports:** $71.8 mil. (c.i.f., 1996 est.); foodstuffs, machinery and equipment, fuels, beverages and tobacco. **Major trading partners:** U.S., Japan, Australia.

The Marshall Islands, part of the geographic region known as Micronesia, are made up of 31 atolls of the Ratak (Sunrise) and Ralik (Sunset) chains located between 4° and 14°N and 160° and 173°E. Although claimed by Spain in 1592, the islands were left undisturbed by the Spanish empire for 300 years. In 1885, Germany took over the administration on the islands of Jaluit and Ebon. At that time copra (dried coconut meat) trade was the primary industry. Japan assumed control of the Marshalls at the beginning of World War I and

held them until 1944, when Allied forces occupied the islands. In 1947 the islands were included in the UN Trust Territory of the Pacific and placed under U.S. administration. In 1946 the U.S. government resettled the inhabitants of Bikini and Enewetak in order to begin nuclear tests, which continued through 1958. Residents began returning to Enewetak in 1980; but the estimated cost of a complete clean-up of Bikini is put at $100 million.

▶ MAURITANIA
Islamic Republic of Mauritania
● **GEOGRAPHY   Location:** northwestern Africa. **Boundaries**: territory of Western Sahara to N, Algeria to NE, Mali to E and S, Senegal to S, Atlantic Ocean to W. **Total area:** 397,954 sq. mi. (1,030,700 sq km). **Coastline:** 469 mi. (754 km). **Comparative area**: slightly larger than three times the size of New Mexico. **Land use:** negl. % arable land; negl. % permanent crops; 38% meadows and pastures; 4% forest and woodland; 58% other; includes negl. % irrigated. **Major cities:** Nouakchott (capital) 350,000 (1984 est.); Nouadhibou (Port Etienne) 21,961; Kaédi 20,848; Zouérate 17,474; Rosso 16,466 (1977 census).
● **PEOPLE   Population:** 2,581,738 (1999 est.). **Nationality:** noun—Mauritanian(s); adjective—Mauritanian. **Ethnic groups:** 40% mixed Maur/black, 30% Maur, 30% black. **Languages:** Hasaniya Arabic (official), Wolof (official), Pular, Soninke, French. **Religions:** 100% Muslim.
● **GOVERNMENT   Type:** republic. **Independence:** Nov. 28, 1960 (from France). **Constitution:** July 12, 1991. **National holiday:** Independence Day, Nov. 28. **Heads of Government:** Col. Maaouya Ould Sid' Ahmed Taya, president (since Dec. 1984); Cheikh El Avia Ould Mohamed Khouna, prime minister (since Nov. 1998). **Structure:** executive; bicameral legislature; judiciary.
● **ECONOMY   Monetary unit:** ouguiya. **Budget:** (1996 est.) *income:* $329 mil.; *expend.:* $265 mil. **GDP:** $4.7 bil., $1,890 per capita (1998 est.). **Chief crops:** dates, millet, sorghum; cattle, sheep; fish. **Natural resources:** iron ore, gypsum, fish, copper, phosphate. **Major industries:** fish processing, mining of iron ore and gypsum. **Labor force:** 465,000 (1981 est.); 47% agriculture, 29% services, 14% industry and commerce, 10% government; 45,000 wage earners (1980); 23% unemployment. **Exports:** $562 mil. (f.o.b., 1997 est.); fish and fish products, iron ore, gold. **Imports:** $552 mil. (f.o.b., 1997 est.); foodstuffs, consumer goods, petroleum products, capital goods. **Major trading partners:** *exports:* 22% Japan, 16% Italy, 14% France; *imports:* 30% France, 10% Algeria, 7% Spain.

The population of Mauritania is divided between an Arab and Berber majority in the north and various black African peoples in the south and southwest. From the ninth through the 15th centuries, southern Mauritania was part of the kingdoms of, successively, Ghana, Mali, and Sanghay. In the 1050s, a puritanical Muslim sect, the Almoravids, arose in the Tidra Islands, Between 1054 and 1086 they conquered Ghana, Morocco, Western Algeria, and Spain; they were eclipsed in the next century.

Portuguese trade on the Mauritania coast began in the early 15th century; the Portuguese remained dominant until about 1600 when their control was contested by the British, French, and Dutch. France established a protectorate in 1903, and the area was made a French colony in 1920.

In 1958 Mauritania became a self-governing republic within the French Overseas Community. In 1959 Mokhtar Ould Daddah was elected prime minister, and the country became fully independent on Nov. 28, 1960. A new constitution was adopted in 1961, establishing a presidential form of government. The four major political parties were combined into a single party in 1965.

Morocco claimed Mauritania as part of its sphere of influence; after talks about unifying the two countries broke down, Morocco recognized Mauritanian independence in 1970.

Spain relinquished its claim to the Spanish Sahara in 1976. The southern part of that territory was annexed by Mauritania, while the larger northern section was annexed by Morocco. Rebels of the Polisario Front proclaimed the independent state of Western Sahara, and in 1980 Mauritania relinquished its claims to its portion of the Western Sahara, signed a treaty with Polisario, and resumed relations with Algeria, Polisario's chief backer.

In 1978 Ould Daddah was removed from office in a military coup and was replaced as president by Lt. Col. Haidalla. He in turn was overthrown on Dec. 12, 1984, by Chief of Staff Maaouya Ould Sid' Ahmed Taya. Taya normalized relations with Morocco and held regional and local elections in 1986 and 1987 in a first step toward the restoration of democracy.

Border incidents erupted between Mauritania and Senegal in 1989 and Mauritania expelled 40,000 black Senegalese workers. Racial and religious strife has severely hampered the country's economy. Taya introduced multiparty elections in 1991 and a new constitution was approved; Taya and his Democratic and Social Republican party won the presidency and control of the legislature in 1992 and again in 1997

▶ MAURITIUS
Republic of Mauritius

● GEOGRAPHY Location: southwestern Indian Ocean. Port Louis 20°09'S, 57°29'E. Boundaries: nearest neighbor is Réunion to SW. Total area: 718 sq. mi. (1,860 sq km). Coastline: 110 mi. (177 km). Comparative area: almost 11 times the size of Washington D.C.. Land use: 49% arable land; 3% permanent crops; 3% meadows and pastures; 22% forest and woodland; 23% other; includes 9% irrigated. Major cities: (1994 est.) Port Louis (capital) 144,776; Beau Bassin/Rose Hill 96,621; Vacoas-Phoenix 94,042; Curepipe 76,610; Quatre Bornes 73,501.

● PEOPLE Population: 1,182,212 (1999 est.). Nationality: noun—Mauritian(s); adjective—Mauritian. Ethnic groups: 68% Indo-Mauritian, 27% Creole, 3% Sino-Mauritian, 2% Franco-Mauritian. Languages: English (official), Creole, French, Hindi, Urdu, Hakka, Bojpoori. Religions: 52% Hindu, 28.3% Christian (mostly Roman Catholic with a few Anglicans), 16.6% Muslim.

● GOVERNMENT Type: parliamentary democracy. Independence: Mar. 12, 1968 (from UK). Constitution: Mar. 12, 1968, amended Mar. 12, 1992. National holiday: Independence Day, Mar. 12. Heads of Government: Cassam Uteem, president (since July 1992); Dr. Navinchandra Ramgoolam, prime minister (since Dec. 1995). Structure: executive; unicameral legislature; judiciary.

● ECONOMY Monetary unit: Mauritian rupee. Budget: (FY95/96 est.) income: $824 mil.; expend.: $1 bil. GDP: $11.7 bil., $10,000 per capita (1998 est.). Chief crops: sugarcane, tea, corn, potatoes; cattle, goats; fish. Natural resources: arable land, fish. Major industries: food processing (largely sugar milling), textiles, and wearing apparel. Labor force: 514,000 (1995); 36% construction and industry, 24% services, 14% agriculture and fishing, 16% trade, restaurants, hotels, 7% transportation and communication, 3% finance. Exports: $1.6 bil. (f.o.b., 1997); 55% clothing and textiles, 24% sugar. Imports: $2.3 bil. (c.i.f., 1997); 37% manufactured goods, 19% capital equipment, 13% foodstuffs, 8% petroleum products, 7% chemicals. Major trading partners: exports: 34.4% UK, 19.5% France, 13% U.S.; imports: 12% South Africa, 11.1% France, 8.9% India.

The volcanic island of Mauritius and its seven smaller neighbors lie about 500 miles east of Madagascar and 2,400 miles southwest of India. They were uninhabited when discovered by the Dutch in 1507. Following sporadic Dutch settlement in the 17th century, the French took over in 1721, establishing sugarcane plantations worked by slaves imported from Africa. Mauritius was captured by the British in 1810. Following the abolition of slavery in the British Empire (1834), Indian workers were imported to labor in the cane fields. A majority of the population now is of Indian descent. On Mar. 12, 1968, Mauritius became an independent parliamentary democracy within the British Commonwealth. In 1992 it officially became a republic and the National Assembly elected Cassam Uteem as the country's first president.

In December 1995 the opposition party of Navinchandra Ramgoolam won 65.2 percent of the votes, and captured all 60 seats in Parliament defeating Anerood Jugnauth who had been PM for 13 years.

Although sugar remains an important element in the economy, textile manufacturing and tourism have helped to make Mauritius one of the strongest economies in Africa.

▶ MEXICO
United Mexican States

● GEOGRAPHY Location: southernmost state in North America. Boundaries: U.S. to N, Gulf of Mexico to E, Belize and Guatemala to S, Pacific Ocean to W. Total area: 761,603 sq. mi. (1,972,550 sq km). Coastline: 5,798 mi. (9,329 km). Comparative area: slightly less than three times the size of Texas. Land use: 12% arable land; 1% permanent crops; 39% meadows and pastures; 26% forest and woodland; 22% other; includes 3% irrigated. Major cities: (1990 census) Ciudad de México (Mexico City) (capital) 8,236,960; Guadalajara 1,628,617; Netzahualcóyotl 1,259,543; Monterrey 1,064,197; Heróica Puebla de Zaragoza (Puebla) 1,054,921.

● PEOPLE Population: 100,294036 (1999 est.). Nationality: noun—Mexican(s); adjective—Mexican. Ethnic groups: 60% mestizo, 30% Amerindian or predominantly Amerindian, 9% white or predominantly white, 1% other. Languages: Spanish, various Mayan, Nahuatl, and other regional indigenous languages. Religions: 89% nominally Roman Catholic, 6% Protestant.

● GOVERNMENT Type: federal republic operating under a centralized government. Independence: Sept. 16, 1810 (from Spain). Constitution: Feb. 5, 1917. National holiday: Independence Day, Sept. 16. Head of Government: Ernesto Zedillo Ponce de León, president (since Dec. 1994). Structure: dominant executive; bicameral legislature (National Congress—Senate, Federal Chamber of Deputies); Supreme Court.

● **ECONOMY** **Monetary unit:** peso. **Budget:** (1998 est.) *income:* $117 bil.; *expend.:* $123 bil. **GDP:** $815.3 bil., $8,300 per capita (1998 est.). **Chief crops:** corn, wheat, soybeans, rice, beans, cotton, coffee, fruit, tomatoes; beef, poultry, dairy products; wood products. **Natural resources:** crude oil, silver, copper, gold, lead. **Major industries:** food and beverages, tobacco, chemicals. **Labor force:** 37.5 mil. (1998); 28.8% services; 21.8% agriculture, forestry, hunting, fishing; 17.1% commerce; 16.1% manufacturing; 5.2% construction; 4.4% public administration and national defense; 4.1% transportation and communications; 2.6% unemployment (1998 est.), plus considerable underemployment. **Exports:** $117.5 bil. (f.o.b., 1998 est.); crude oil, oil products, coffee, silver, engines, cotton. **Imports:** $111.5 bil. (f.o.b., 1998 est.); metal manufactures, agricultural machinery, electrical equipment. **Major trading partners:** (1997 est.) *exports:* 87.5% U.S., 1.3% Canada, 0.8% Japan, Spain, Chile, Brazil; *imports:* 74.2% U.S., 3.7% Japan, 3.7% Germany.

The pre-Columbian history of indigenous Mexican cultures is very rich and includes the high civilizations of the Olmecs, Mayas, Toltecs, and Aztecs, in addition to numerous nomadic cultures. In 1519 Hernán Cortés and several hundred Spanish soldiers entered Tenochtitlán (now Mexico City). A two-year campaign against the Aztecs under Montezuma II ended with the Spanish capture of the city. The Viceroyalty of New Spain—with its center at Mexico City—was proclaimed in 1535. At its height it encompassed the lands from California to Panama, Florida, Spain's Caribbean holdings, and the Philippines.

As was the case with the rest of Spanish America, the movement for independence in New Spain coincided with the weakening of the authority of the Spanish Crown as a result of the Napoleonic takeover of Spain in 1808. In 1810 Miguel Hidalgo led a failed uprising and was executed. Following in Hidalgo's footsteps, José María Morelos led another uprising in the south, and he in turn was captured and put to death. Agustín de Iturbide, leader of the royalist forces, defected to the side of those struggling for independence in 1821. Envisioning independent Mexico as a monarchy, military groups proclaimed Iturbide emperor of Mexico in 1822.

The Mexican empire did not last long, and the Central American counties seceded after Iturbide's ouster by Antonio de Santa Anna in 1823. A republic was declared and Guadalupe Victoria was the first president (1824-29). In 1836, Texas seceded from Mexico in a revolution that cost Santa Anna the presidency. Between 1845 and 1848, Mexico fought the United States over U.S. annexation of Texas, and in 1847 U.S. troops occupied Mexico City. Under the Treaty of Guadalupe Hidalgo (1848), Mexico sold about half its territory—including California, Nevada, Utah, most of Arizona, and parts of New Mexico, Colorado, and Wyoming to the United States—for $15 million.

Santa Anna ruled again, as dictator, from 1853 to 1855, before being toppled by the liberal movement, La Reforma. A new constitution was proclaimed in 1857, but Conservatives declared it void. Following the War of Reform (1858-61), France, Britain, and Spain all claimed compensation for destruction of their nations' property, and in 1862 they landed troops at Veracruz. Britain and Spain withdrew, but Napoleon III attempted to establish a dependent empire in Mexico and installed Archduke Ferdinand Maximilian of Austria

on the Mexican throne in 1864. In the face of Mexican resistance and U.S. threats, France ended its Mexican adventure, and in 1867 Maximilian was captured and executed by Liberal forces.

Benito Juárez, who served as provisional president during the War of Reform, was a major force behind the liberal movement called La Reforma, which stressed the promotion of capitalism and the destruction of what were seen as vestiges of feudalism in Mexico. Juárez won a third presidential term in 1871 but died in office and was succeeded in office by Sebastián Lerdo de Tejada, who was in turn overthrown by Gen. Porfirio Díaz. During the stable dictatorship known as the Porfiriato (1876-1911), Mexico experienced economic growth, though wealthy landowners and the church benefited at the expense of the poor.

The Mexican Revolution began in 1910 after Porfirio Díaz had his electoral opponent, Francisco I. Madero, jailed. In response, Madero formulated his Plan of San Luis Potosí, calling for armed resistance to the dictatorship. Rebellions broke out in the northern state of Chihuahua under the leadership of Pancho Villa and in the southern state of Morelos led by Emiliano Zapata. The two states soon came under rebel control, and in 1911 Díaz left Mexico. Madero was elected president, but his failure to carry through promised reforms resulted in the continuation of the rebellion.

Backed by the U.S., Gen. Victoriano Huerta overthrew Madero in 1913. But the fighting continued, and Huerta lost the support of the U.S. and was forced from office by Zapata, Villa, and Venustiano Carranza, who became president (1914-20). Zapata and Villa continued their resistance, but by 1916 Gen. Alvaro Obregón had driven Villa back to Chihuahua and Zapata's armies had been contained. Carranza called for the election of delegates to a constitutional convention in 1916, and by the following year, the progressive Mexican Constitution of 1917 was in place.

Obregón deposed Carranza in 1920 and served as president until 1924. He was reelected to succeed Plutarco Elías Calles in 1928 but was assassinated before he could take office. In 1929 Calles founded the National Revolutionary party, which became the Institutional Revolutionary party (PRI) in 1946.

Lázaro Cárdenas won the presidency in 1934, sending Calles, the long-time power behind the scene, into exile. This, coupled with Cárdenas's decision to remove himself from politics at the end of his term, greatly stabilized the institutional structure created by the Mexican Revolution. Cárdenas was the last of the "revolutionary" leaders to make good on the promises to labor and the peasantry. He presided over extensive redistribution of land and in 1938 reorganized the ruling party into four constituencies: peasants, labor, the military, and the popular sector (middle class, professionals). Cárdenas also used the national ownership of subsoil rights enshrined in the Mexican constitution to nationalize U.S. oil companies, thus assuring his credentials as a hero of Mexican nationalism.

The political movement of Mexican presidents since Cárdenas has been away from its peasant and labor constituencies toward business and the popular sector, beginning with Miguel Alemán's election in 1946.

The PRI's stability was seriously challenged in the 1980s as a result of the economic crisis stemming from the severe decline in the price of oil.

Mexico borrowed heavily from foreign creditors during the 1970s on the expectation that oil prices would remain high. The debt problem led to cutbacks in government spending, a catastrophic drop in the value of the currency, and capital and human flight out of the country. It also nearly caused the PRI's downfall. Carlos Salinas de Gortari, the PRI's candidate in the 1988 presidential election, won by one of the narrowest margins ever in a contest that was widely believed to have been rigged.

Pres. Salinas vigorously pursued economic reform and lobbied for passage of the North American Free Trade Agreement with the United States and Canada, which promised to bring more jobs and much-needed increases in capital investment. But the very day NAFTA went into effect, Jan. 2, 1994, a guerrilla group of poor Indians calling itself the Zapata Army of National Liberation declared war against the government and began fighting government troops in the southern state of Chiapas under the leadership of "Subcomandante Marcos."

The (unrelated) assassination of the PRI presidential candidate at a campaign stop in Tiajuana led Salinas to appoint the campaign manager Ernesto Zedillo, a member of the PRI's reform-minded wing, as the PRI's presidential candidate (over the objections of the "old guard").

With just over 50 percent of the vote (the lowest majority ever for the PRI), Zedillo won an election unusually free from fraud. The immediate crisis he faced was the collapse of the peso, which declined by 40 percent in less than two months. In 1995, in exchange for austere economic measures by the Zedillo government, the IMF and US offered an enormous bail-out aid package with Mexican oil revenues as collateral. By June 1996 Mexico managed the early repayment of $4.7 billion to the US by privately refinancing the debt.

Zedillo was equally successful with the situation in Chiapas, arranging 1996 peace talks with the rebels to end the fighting and increase Indian autonomy. The appearance in June 1996 of a similar group (the Popular Revolutionary army) in the state of Guerrero began troubles which continued into 1997.

In August 1996 a political reform package (including no less than 17 constitutional amendments) passed both houses of the legislature unanimously. The result of 19 months of negotiations among the three major parties — the PRI, the right-wing PAN (National Action Party), and the left-wing PRD (Party of Democratic Revolution) — as well as the smaller Labor Party, the omnibus package attempted to guarantee fair vote counting, equal media access, caps on political spending and the like. (An unrepentant PRI later gutted the deal in November with a series of bills meant to guarantee its continued dominance.)

The July 1997 elections, almost entirely free of fraud, saw the PRI lose its majority in the Chamber of Deputies, as it carried only 39 percent of the vote, with PAN second at 27 percent, and PRD third at 26 percent. PAN additionally carried seven of the 31 state governor's races. Zedillo now had to govern with an opposition party controlling Congress who threatened to investigate PRI fraud. But the economy continued to recover and real GDP grew by 7.3 percent in 1997. A serious drought in 1998 caused over 11,000 forest fires sending smoke as far north as Oklahoma and seriously damaging agriculture and tourism.

▶ MICRONESIA
Federated States of Micronesia
● **GEOGRAPHY** **Location:** forms (with Palau) archipelago of Caroline Islands, Ponape (6°52'N, 158°15'E), Yap (9°32'N, 138°08'E), Kosrae (5°19'N, 162°59'E), and Truk (7°22'N, 151°54'E), in western Pacific Ocean. **Boundaries:** Guam to NW, Marshall Islands to E, Papua New Guinea to S, Philippines about 497 mi. (800 km) to W. **Total area:** 271 sq. mi. (702 sq km). **Coastline:** 3,798 (6,112 km). **Comparative area:** about four times size of Washington, D.C. **Land use:** N.A. **Major cities:** Kolonia (capital—population N.A.).
● **PEOPLE** **Population:** 131,500 (1999 est.). **Nationality:** noun—Micronesian(s); adjective—Micronesian, Kosrae(s), Pohnpeian(s), Trukese, Yapese. **Ethnic groups:** nine ethnic Micronesian and Polynesian groups. **Languages:** English (official and common language), Trukese, Pohnpeian, Yapese, Kosrean. **Religions:** 50% Roman Catholic, 47% Protestant.
● **GOVERNMENT** **Type:** constitutional government in free association with U.S.; the Compact of Free Association entered into force Nov. 3, 1986. **Independence:** Nov. 3, 1986 (from U.S.-administered UN Trusteeship). **Constitution:** May 10, 1979. **National holiday:** Proclamation of the Federated States of Micronesia, May 10. **Head of Government:** Leo A. Falcam, president (since May 1999). **Structure:** executive; unicameral legislature; judiciary.
● **ECONOMY** **Monetary unit:** U.S. dollar. **Budget:** (FY95/96 est.) *income:* $58 mil.; *expend.:* $52 mil. **GDP:** $220 mil., $1,760 per capita (1996 est.). **Chief crops:** black pepper, tropical fruits and vegetables, coconuts, cassava, sweet potatoes; pigs, chickens. **Natural resources:** forests, marine products, deep seabed minerals. **Major industries:** tourism, craft items from shell, wood, pearl. **Labor force:** two-thirds are government employees. **Exports:** $73 mil. (f.o.b., 1996 est.); fish, garments, bananas, black pepper. **Imports:** $168 mil. (c.i.f., 1996 est.); food, manufactured goods, machinery and equipment, beverages. **Major trading partners:** U.S., Japan, Guam, Australia.

The Federated States of Micronesia extend 1,800 miles across an archipelago of the Caroline Islands in the larger island group of Micronesia. Ethnically diverse (there are eight primary languages, not including dialects), the islands are thought to be the first in the Pacific settled by argonauts from the Philippines and Indonesia, about 1500 b.c. Ferdinand Magellan landed in the Marianas in 1521, and Spain claimed sovereignty from 1565 to 1899, when the Caroline Islands were sold to Germany. After World War I, the League of Nations mandated the islands to Japan, which developed agriculture (especially sugarcane), mining, and fishing. After World War II, the islands were included in the UN Trust Territory of the Pacific and placed under U.S. administration. A compact of free association between Micronesia and the United States was signed in 1986, and Micronesia's trust territory status with the UN trusteeship council was officially dissolved in December 1990.

▶ MOLDOVA
Republic of Moldova
● **GEOGRAPHY** **Location:** southeastern Europe. **Boundaries:** Ukraine to N, E, S, Romania to W. **Total area:** 13,012 sq. mi. (33,700 sq km). **Coastline:** none. **Comparative area:** slightly more than twice the size of Hawaii. **Land use:** 53% arable land; 14%

permanent crops; 13% meadows and pastures; 13% forest and woodland; 7% other. **Major cities**: (1992 est.) Kishinev (Chisinäu) (capital) 667,100; Tiraspol 186,200; Beltsy (Balti) 159,000.

• **PEOPLE Population:** 4,460,838 (1999 est.). **Nationality:** noun—Moldovan(s); adjective— Moldovan. **Ethnic groups:** 64.5% Moldovan, 13.8% Ukrainian, 13% Russian, 3.5% Gagauz, 1.5% Jewish, 2% Bulgarian. **Languages:** Moldovan (official), based on Romanian, but using a Cyrillic alphabet; Russian, Gagauz. **Religions:** 98.5% Eastern Orthodox, 1.5% Jewish.

• **GOVERNMENT** Type: republic. **Independence:** Aug. 27, 1991 (from Soviet Union). **Constitution:** July 28, 1994. **National holiday:** Independence Day, Aug. 27. **Heads of Government:** Petro Lucinschi, president (since Jan. 1997); Ion Sturza, prime minister (since Mar. 1999). **Structure:** executive; unicameral legislature; judiciary.

• **ECONOMY Monetary unit:** leu. **Budget:** (1997 est.) *income:* $536 mil.; *expend.:* $594 mil. **GDP:** $10 bil., $2,200 per capita (1998 est.). **Chief crops:** sugar beets, grain, vegetables, wine grapes, other fruit. **Natural resources:** lignites, phosporites, gypsum. **Major industries:** food processing, agricultural machinery, foundry equipment, textiles, chemicals. **Labor force:** 1.7 mil. (1998). 40.2% agriculture, 14.3% industry. **Exports:** $633 mil. (f.o.b., 1998); foodstuffs, wine, tobacco, textiles, footwear. **Imports:** $1.02 bil. (f.o.b., 1998); oil, gas, coal, steel, machinery, foodstuffs. **Major trading partners:** Russia, Ukraine, Kazakhstan.

Historical Moldavia, of which present-day Moldova is only a small portion, encompassed territories that are now in Romania and Ukraine (including southern Bessarabia and northern Bukovina). Moldova is a hilly, fertile land, bounded by two great rivers, the Dniester and the Prut, that flow into the Black Sea. Its climate is very favorable to agriculture.

Moldavia was part of Scythia in the first millennium b.c. and later came under the Roman Empire. Lying on the gateway to Europe, it was invaded successively, but came under the control of Kievan Rus between the 10th and 12th centuries a.d., and in the 13th century it was invaded by the Mongolian empire. In the 16th century, eastern Moldavia, or Bessarabia, came under Turkish control but in 1812 was ceded to the Russian empire. Southern Bessarabia (now in Ukraine) was controlled variously by the Russian empire and by Romania, and in 1878 it again became part of Russia. After the Bolsheviks came to power in 1917 and created the USSR, a Moldavian Autonomous Soviet Socialist Republic (ASSR) was formed on the eastern side of the Dniester River, a territory claimed by Romania but populated by Ukrainians. In June 1940, as a result of the Nazi-Soviet Pact of 1939, Romania was forced to cede Bessarabia and northern Bukovina to the Soviet Union. These lands were made part of the Ukrainian Soviet Socialist Republic (SSR) and the remaining Bessarabian sections were merged with the old Moldavian ASSR to create on Aug. 2, 1940, the Moldavian SSR. Between 1941 and 1944, while Romania and the USSR were at war, Bessarabia again became part of Romania, but in 1944 the Soviets retook the territory and reestablished it as a union republic.

While under Soviet control, Moldavians in the new republic were officially differentiated from their counterparts across the border in Romania. In 1940, the Cyrillic alphabet was imposed on the Romanian language; this official language was called "Moldavian." Contacts between the two countries were discouraged, and the USSR encouraged Russian and Ukrainian immigration to the Moldavian SSR. While a part of the USSR, Moldavia created a diversified economy, which is based on agriculture and food processing, with a small industrial base.

Mikhail Gorbachev's policy of glasnost, or openness, in the late 1980s gave vent to Moldavian complaints about "Russification" and immigration of non-Moldavians. In September 1989, Romanian, now in a Latin script, was restored as the official language. Glasnost also gave birth to new political parties, the largest of which was the Popular Front of Moldavia, which organized protest demonstrations against Soviet power. Disturbances during the 1989 celebration of Soviet Revolution Day in the capital city of Kishinev led to the dismissal of the Slavic Communist party First Secretary, and his replacement by an ethnic Romanian.

The Communist party was banned in Moldova in 1990, and laws to develop the basics of a multiparty system were adopted in September 1991. Moldova officially declared its independence from the USSR on Aug. 27, 1991, and in December, United Front-supported Mircea Snegur was elected president with 98.2% of the votes cast in the elections.

At the time Moldova declared its independence, sentiment was strong for reunification with Romania. So strong, in fact, that ethnic Russians and Ukrainians living in the Trans-Dniester region in eastern Moldova, fearing reunification with Romania, declared an independent Trans-Dniester republic, sparking ethnic violence there. But since then, most activity has focused on reestablishing ties with countries from the former USSR. In 1991, Moldova singed the Alma-Ata Declaration, joining the other former Soviet republics in the Commonwealth of Independent States. And in the country's first parlimantary elections, held in February of 1994, two nationalist parties captured a combined 15 percent of the vote, while the pro-Russian Socialist party won 25 percent, and the Agrarian Democratic Party, led by former Communists, took 45 percent. Then, in a plebiscite held Mar. 6, 1994, an overwhelming majority (90 percent) of voters rejected reunification with Romania in favor of an independent Moldova. Two-thirds of Moldova's 2.3 million eligible voters cast ballots on the plebiscite. Snegur intended to use the referendum result to entice Trans-Dniester to rejoin Moldova.

In late 1996 Snegur lost the presidency to Petro Lucinschi who quickly recognized Trans-Dniester as autonomous within a single state and began a reform program to stimulate the weak economy. A strong Communist showing in 1998 legislative elections made this agenda more difficult to establish. The slow pace of reform led Prime Minister Ion Ciubuc to resign in Feb. 1999 (replaced by Ion Sturza) and Pres. Lucinschi to propose a referendum to increase the constitutional powers of the president, a model more in accord with the other ex-Soviet states.

▶**MONACO**
Principality of Monaco
• **GEOGRAPHY Location:** tiny enclave on Mediterranean coast of France. **Boundaries:** France to N, E, and W; Mediterranean Sea to S. **Total area:** 1.21 sq. mi. (1.95 sq km). **Coastline:** 2.6 mi. (4.1 km). **Comparative area:** about three

times size of the Mall in Washington, D.C. **Land use:** 0% arable land; 0% permanent crops; 0% meadows and pastures; 0% forest and woodland; 100% other. **Major cities:** Monaco (capital).

● **PEOPLE Population:** 32,149 (1999 est.). **Nationality:** noun—Monacan(s) or Monegasque(s); adjective—Monacan or Monegasque. **Ethnic groups:** 47% French, 16% Monegasque, 16% Italian, 21% other. **Languages:** French (official), English, Italian, Monegasque. **Religions:** 95% Roman Catholic.

● **GOVERNMENT Type:** constitutional monarchy. **Constitution:** Dec. 17, 1962. **National holiday:** National Day, Nov. 19. **Head of Government:** Prince Ranier III, chief of state (since Nov. 1949); Michel Leveque, prime minister (since Feb. 1997). **Structure:** executive—prince, minister of state (senior French civil servant appointed by prince), and Council of Government as cabinet; unicameral legislature—prince and National Council of 18 members; judiciary—authority delegated by prince to Supreme Tribunal.

● **ECONOMY Monetary unit:** French franc. **Budget:** (1995 est.) *income:* $518 mil.; *expend:* $531 mil. **GDP:** $800 mil., $25,000 per capita (1996 est.). **Chief crops:** N.A. **Natural resources:** none. **Major industries:** pharmaceuticals, food processing, precision instruments. **Labor force:** (1994 est.) 30,540. **Exports:** N.A. **Imports:** N.A. **Major trading partners:** full customs integration with France, which collects and rebates Monacan trade duties; also participates in EU market system through customs union with France.

Known to Phoenicians and Greeks from the beginning of the first millennium b.c., the history of the port of Monaco is coextensive with that of southeastern France for much of its history. A western colony of the great trading city-state of Genoa in the 13th century, Monaco in 1368 became an independent principality under the rule of the Matignon-Grimaldi family. At various times a protectorate of Spain, France, and Sardinia, it was restored to independence in 1861 by the Franco-Monegasque treaty.

In 1911 Monaco became a constitutional monarchy under the Matignon-Grimaldi dynasty. In 1918 France required the principality to conform to its national interests in all respects; by an agreement of 1919, should the dynasty fail to produce a male heir, Monaco would be absorbed into France. However, the family is allowed to adopt an heir if they so choose. The marriage of Prince Ranier III to the U.S film star Grace Kelly produced an heir apparent for this generation. The constitutional monarchy under its "Most Serene Prince" is essentially a one-party state in which the National and Democratic Union won all 18 seats in the National Council in 1968, 1978, 1983, and 1988, though in competition with the Socialist party. In 1993 Monaco became the smallest member nation of the UN.

Despite the fame of the Monte Carlo casino, gambling accounts for only 4 percent of the principality's revenues. The principal industry is tourism, followed by light manufacturing. Monaco also supports a prominent institute of oceanography. Land reclamation projects, impelled by a real estate boom, have added about 20 percent to the nation's territory since World War II.

▶ **MONGOLIA**
● **GEOGRAPHY Location:** landlocked country in central Asia. **Boundaries:** Russia to N, China to E, S, and W. **Total area:** 604,247 sq. mi. (1,565,000 sq

km). **Coastline:** none. **Comparative area:** slightly larger than Alaska. **Land use:** 1% arable land; 0% permanent crops; 80% meadows and pastures; 9% forest and woodland; 10% other; includes negl. % irrigated. **Major cities:** (1994 est.) Ulan Bator (capital) 680,000; Darhan 85,800; Erdenet 63,000.

● **PEOPLE Population:** 2,617,379 (1999 est.). **Nationality:** noun—Mongolian(s) adjective—Mongolian. **Ethnic groups:** 90% Mongol, 4% Kazakh, 2% Chinese; 2% Russian, 2% other. **Languages:** Khalkha Mongol used by over 90% of population; Turkic, Russian, Chinese. **Religions:** predominantly Tibetan Buddhist, about 4% Muslim.

● **GOVERNMENT Type:** republic. **Independence:** Mar. 13, 1921 (from China). **Constitution:** Feb. 12, 1992. **National holiday:** National Day, July 11. **Heads of Government:** Natsagiin Bagabandi, president (since June 1997); Rinchinnyamyn Amarjargal, prime minister (since July 1999). **Structure:** executive; unicameral legislature; judiciary.

● **ECONOMY Monetary unit:** tughrik. **Budget:** *income:* $260 mil.; *expend.:* $330 mil. **GDP:** $5.8 bil., $2,250 per capita (1998 est.). **Chief crops:** livestock raising predominates; wheat, barley. **Natural resources:** oil, coal, copper, molybdenum, tungsten, phosphates. **Major industries:** copper, processing of animal products, building materials, foods and beverages. **Labor force:** 1.115 mil. (1993 est.); primarily agricultural; over half adult population is in labor force, including large percentage of women; shortage of skilled labor. **Exports:** $316.8 mil. (f.o.b., 1998 est.); copper, livestock, animal products, wool, hides, fluorospar, nonferrous metals. **Imports:** $472.4 mil. (f.o.b., 1998 est.); machinery and equipment, fuels, food products, industrial consumer goods, chemicals. **Major trading partners:** *exports:* 30.1% China, 21.5% Switzerland, 12.1% Russia; *imports:* 30.6% Russia, 13.3% China, 11.7% Japan.

Mongols under Genghis Khan conquered most of Eurasia in the early 13th century. The Mongol empire broke up in the mid-14th century, and Mongolia lapsed into tribal disunion and political insignificance. Chinese rule was established thereafter in Inner Mongolia (ruled directly) and, in 1691, in Outer Mongolia (a province under local rule). With the 1911 Chinese Revolution, Outer Mongolia unsuccessfully proclaimed its independence from China. The nationalist religious leader, the Bogdo Lama, sought Russian support in 1920. Under the revolutionary leaders Sukhe Bataar and Khorloin Choibalsan, a "provisional people's government" again declared independence in 1921. Sukhe Bataar died in 1923; on Nov. 26, 1924, the Mongolian People's Republic (MPR) was established with Soviet sponsorship. The early years of the republic were marked by repeated Stalinist purges of Mongol revolutionary leaders and by disastrous attempts at centralized planning.

Choibalsan emerged as party leader and was confirmed as premier in 1940. In 1939 Soviet and Mongolian armies prevented a Japanese conquest of Mongolia. In 1945 the Republic of China recognized the MPR; recognition was reaffirmed by the People's Republic of China in 1949. In 1948 the first of a series of five-year plans began to bring industrial and agricultural development to Mongolia, with extensive Soviet aid and support. Choibalsan died in 1952 and was succeeded as premier by Yumjaagiyn Tsedenbal. Following the Sino-Soviet split of 1958, heavy concentrations of

Soviet troops and missiles were stationed along the Chinese-Mongolian border. On Oct. 27, 1961, the MPR was admitted to the United Nations and diplomatic relations with various other non-Soviet bloc nations developed gradually. Tsedenbal was ousted in 1984 and replaced by Zhambyn Batmonh as party chairman and by Dumaagiin Sodnom as premier. The MPR established diplomatic relations with the United States in 1987.

Following widespread demonstrations calling for human rights, religious freedom, and an end to special privileges for Communist officials, the Communist party voted to give up its constitutional power in March 1990. After the resignation of Pres. Zhambyn Batmonh, Parliament elected Punsalmaagiin Ochirbat as president. That same year, in an attempt to strengthen economic ties with China, Ochirbat became the first Mongolian head of state to visit Beijing since 1962. But the Communists returned to power in 1992, when the ex-Communist Mongolian People's Revolutionary party, running on a platform of more moderate reform, won an overwhelming majority in Parliament. Nevertheless, the more reform-minded Ochirbat put together a coalition of opposing parties in 1993 to win reelection as president. He held office until 1997 when he was defeated by Natsagiin Bagabandi.

With a young and rapidly growing population, an obsolete industrial base, and a shrinking economy, Mongolia has endured a painful transition to democracy and free markets. Aided by new international loans, the government is pursuing a vigorous program of privatization, currency and banking reform. Trading on Mongolia's first stock exchange began in August 1995. Since 1991 over 10,000 private businesses have been created, many of them small trading companies dealing with Russia and China. In April 1997 parliament approved a decision to abolish all taxes on trade. U.S. Secretary of State Madeleine Albright visited Mongolia in 1998 and pledged continued support and friendship.

▶ **MONTENEGRO**
See "Yugoslavia"

▶ **MOROCCO**
Kingdom of Morocco
● **GEOGRAPHY Location:** northwestern Africa. **Boundaries:** North Atlantic Ocean to W and NW, Strait of Gibraltar to N, Mediterranean Sea to NE, Algeria to E and SE, Western Sahara to SW. **Total area:** 172,413 sq. mi. (446,550 sq km). **Coastline:** 1,140 mi. (1,835 km). **Comparative area:** slightly larger than California. **Land use:** 21% arable land; 1% permanent crops; 47% meadows and pastures; 20% forest and woodland; 11% other; includes 1% irrigated. **Major cities:** (1990 census) Rabat (including Sale; capital) 1,385,872; Casablanca 2,940,623; Marrakech (Marrakesh) 745,541; Fès (Fez) 774,754; Oujda 678,778.
● **PEOPLE Population:** 29,661,636 (1999 est.). **Nationality:** noun—Moroccan(s); adjective—Moroccan. **Ethnic groups:** 99.1% Arab-Berber, 0.7% non-Moroccan, 0.2% Jewish. **Languages:** Arabic (official), several Berber dialects; French is language of business, government, diplomacy, and postprimary education. **Religions:** 98.7% Muslim, 1.1% Christian, 0.2% Jewish.
● **GOVERNMENT Type:** constitutional monarchy. **Independence:** Mar. 2, 1956 (from France). **Constitution:** Mar. 10, 1972, revised Sept. 4, 1992, amended to create bicameral legislature Sept. 1996. **National holiday:** National Day, Mar. 3. **Heads of Government:** Hassan II, king (since July 1999); Abderrahman El-Youssoufi, prime minister (since Feb. 1998). **Structure:** executive—king has paramount powers; bicameral legislature—two-thirds of members are directly elected and one-third are indirectly elected; judiciary—independent of other branches.
● **ECONOMY Monetary unit:** dirham. **Budget:** (FY97/98 est.) *income:* $8.4 bil.; *expend.:* $10 bil. **GDP:** $92.9 bil., $3,200 per capita (1998 est.). **Chief crops:** cereal farming and livestock raising predominant; barley, wheat, citrus fruit, wine, vegetables; livestock. **Natural resources:** phosphates, iron ore, manganese, lead, zinc, fish, salt. **Major industries:** phosphate rock mining and processing, food processing, leather goods. **Labor force:** 11 mil. (1997); 50% agriculture, 26% services, 15% industry; 16% unemployment (1994 est.). **Exports:** $7 bil. (f.o.b., 1997); 30% food and beverages, 23% semiprocessed goods, 21% consumer goods. **Imports:** $10 bil. (c.i.f., 1997); 26% semiprocessed goods, 25% capital goods, 18% food and beverages, 15% fuel and lubricants, 4% raw materials,. **Major trading partners:** *exports:* 63% EU, 7.7% Japan, 6.6% India.; *imports:* 57% EU, 6.6% U.S., 5.3% Saudi Arabia.

Neolithic inhabitants of Morocco were displaced by Berbers around 1000 b.c. Phoenician and Carthaginian settlements were established along the Mediterranean coast. Morocco came under Roman rule around 40 a.d. and was invaded via Spain by Germanic Vandals in the fifth century. The Islamic invasions of the mid-seventh century established Arab rule in Morocco, and most of the indigenous Berbers converted to Islam. Ethnic tension between Berbers and Arabs has been a basic element of Moroccan politics and society ever since.

In the late eighth century, King Idris ibn Adballah united Berbers and Arabs in a monarchy that lasted for 200 years and made the capital city of Fez one of the major religious and cultural centers of the Islamic world. In the 11th century, the Almoravid dynasty from Mauritania conquered Morocco, western Algeria, and Spain. It was ousted by another Muslin sect, the Almohads, led by Ibn Tumart. After about 1200 the tide of Moorish expansion in the Iberian Peninsula turned; in 1492 Ferdinand and Isabella expelled the last Moors from Grenada.

Naval conflict between Morocco, Spain, and Portugal continued in the western Mediterranean and along the Atlantic coast of northwestern Africa for several centuries more. In the mid-17th century, Morocco was reunited under the present Alawid dynasty. In the early 19th century, American and British forces combatted Moroccan piracy in the Mediterranean, and Spain established colonies in Tangier in the north and along the Atlantic coast between Morocco and Mauritania.

The attempts of Sultan Hassan I (r. 1873-94) to implement reforms to strengthen Morocco's independence were thwarted by European interests. By the early 20th century, France, securely established in Algeria, began exerting increasing control in Morocco. A multipower conference at Algeciras in 1906 affirmed Moroccan independence but upheld the special rights claimed by Spain and France. The Treaty of Fez, signed in 1912 between France and Sultan Abd-al-Hafidn, ended Moroccan independence by granting the country to France and reaffirming a Spanish sphere of influence in the southwest.

Nationalist unrest and tribal uprisings disrupted French administration in Morocco throughout the 1920s and 1930s. Morocco became a battleground during World War II between the Axis-supported Vichy French government and the Free French and their Allied backers. In 1943 Churchill and Roosevelt met at Casablanca to discuss wartime strategy; in the same year, the Istiqlal (Independence) party was founded to fight for independence from the French in the postwar era.

In 1947 Moroccan liberation forces began open warfare against the French. The exiled Sultan Mohammad V was allowed to return, and France promised independence by 1955.

With the withdrawal of French forces, Morocco became independent on Mar. 2, 1956. Tangier (under international administration since 1923) was incorporated into the newly independent state in October 1956, and the Spanish enclave of Ifni was ceded to Morocco in 1969.

A period of instability ensued after 1957 as newly formed political parties vied for power. King Mohammad died in 1961 and was succeeded by his son, Hassan II. In 1962 an elected parliamentary government took power under the constitutional monarchy. Political unrest and economic difficulties led to the declaration of states of emergency in 1965 and 1970 and a new constitution in 1977.

Spain withdrew from its former territory of Spanish (now Western) Sahara, a phosphate-rich desert territory on Morocco's southern border, in February 1976. On Apr. 14, 1976, Morocco annexed the northern two-thirds of the territory, while Mauritania claimed the remainder. The Polisario Spanish Saharan liberation movement, backed by Algeria and Libya, conducted guerrilla operations against Moroccan and Mauritanian forces. In 1979 Mauritania gave up its claims, and Morocco claimed the entire region.

In April 1987, Morocco completed construction of a 2,000-mile sand wall completely enclosing Western Sahara. Polisario forces, partly cut off from Algerian aid, nevertheless control much of the Western Saharan countryside, while Morocco holds the cities and towns. In May 1987 a Moroccan-Algerian summit was held under the sponsorship of Saudi Arabia, which offered King Hassan $260 million to rebuild Morocco's war-torn economy in return for allowing a self-determination referendum in the Western Sahara. The king refused. By mid-1992 the situation was in effect resolved as Polisario's top leaders accepted an offer of amnesty, leaving the Moroccan government in undisputed possession of the territory.

The Persian Gulf crisis made an already weak economy weaker, and riots during a general strike protesting low wages, economic hardship, and poor job prospects in Fez left 100 dead and hundreds more injured in 1991. Although Morocco was an active member of the Allied coalition against Iraq, Moroccans also staged huge demonstrations in support of Saddam Hussein in Feb. at the height of the war.

In 1992, demands of Muslim fundamentalist factions for greater political power threatened the stability of King Hassan II's government. In a gesture toward political reform, parliamentary elections were held in June 1993, but the results never posed any immediate challenge to the monarchy.

In March 1998 the king appointed Morocco's first opposition-led government, a coalition of seven political parties.

▶ MOZAMBIQUE
Republic of Mozambique
● **GEOGRAPHY   Location:** eastern coast of Africa. **Boundaries:** Zambia and Malawi to NW, Tanzania to N, Indian Ocean to E and SE, South Africa and Swaziland to SW, Zimbabwe to W. **Total area:** 309,494 sq. mi. (801,590 sq km). **Coastline:** 1,535 mi. (2,470 km). **Comparative area:** slightly less than twice size of California. **Land use:** 4% arable land; negl. % permanent crops; 56% meadows and pastures; 18% forest and woodland; 22% other; includes negl. % irrigated. **Major cities:** (1987 est.) Maputo (capital) 1,006,765.

● **PEOPLE   Population:** 19,124,335 (1999 est.). **Nationality:** noun—Mozambican(s); adjective—Mozambican. **Ethnic groups:** 99.66% indigenous tribal groups (Shangaan, Chokwe, Manyika, Sena, Makua, and others). **Languages:** Portuguese (official), indigenous languages. **Religions:** 50% indigenous beliefs, 30% Christian, 20% Muslim.

● **GOVERNMENT   Type:** republic. **Independence:** June 25, 1975 (from Portugal). **Constitution:** Nov. 30, 1990. **National holiday:** Independence Day, June 25. **Heads of Government:** Joachím Alberto Chissanó, president (since Nov. 1986); Dr. Pascoal Manuel Mocumbi, prime minister (since Nov. 1994.). **Structure:** executive; unicameral legislature; judiciary.

● **ECONOMY   Monetary unit:** metical. **Budget:** (1997 est.) *income:* $402 mil.; *expend:* $799 mil. **GDP:** $16.8 bil., $900 per capita (1998 est.). **Chief crops:** cotton, cashew nuts, sugar, tea; beef, poultry. **Natural resources:** coal, natural gas, titanium. **Major industries:** food and beverages, chemicals (fertilizer, soap, paints), petroleum. **Labor force:** N.A.; 80% agriculture. **Exports:** $295 mil. (f.o.b., 1998 est.); 40% shrimp; cashews, cotton, sugar. **Imports:** $965 mil. (c.i.f., 1998 est.): food, clothing, farm equipment, petroleum. **Major trading partners:** *exports:* 17% Spain, 16% South Africa, 12% Portugal; *imports:* 55% South Africa, 7% Zimbabwe, 5% Saudi Arabia.

Mozambique has been inhabited since prehistoric times by a variety of Bantu peoples. Portuguese trading stations were established starting in 1505, and Portugal developed an extensive coastal trade in gold and ivory. Mozambique also served as a way station for Portuguese trade to East Asia.

Despite competition from other European nations, Portugal maintained control of the Mozambique coast. Settlement by sizable numbers of Portuguese immigrants began in the late 19th century. Mozambique was organized as a colony, sometimes called Portuguese East Africa, in 1885; boundaries in the interior were defined in 1891.

Economic development of Mozambique in the 20th century remained almost entirely in Portuguese hands. By the 1950s native peoples began to protest Portuguese rule; a rebellion of the Frelimo (Front for the Liberation of Mozambique) guerrilla movement began in 1961. Rebels controlled most of the northern part of the country by 1964. Fighting continued for another decade.

Following the Portuguese revolution of 1974, Portugal agreed to independence for Mozambique, and many Portuguese settlers returned to Portugal, leaving the country bereft of administrative personnel and infrastructure support.

Mozambique became fully independent on June 25, 1975. A Marxist Frelimo government took office, with Samora Michel as the country's first president. The new government formed agricultural collectives and nationalized most private land and industry as well as all social services.

In the late 1970s, fighting broke out between Mozambique and Rhodesia. When Rhodesia achieved independence (and changed its name to Zimbabwe) in 1980, relations between the two governments improved. But a rebel movement, Renamo (Mozambique National Resistance), dedicated to overthrowing the Frelimo government grew stronger during the 1980s.

In 1986, following the death of Samora Michel, Joachím Chissanó became president. The Chissano government reintroduced some private small-scale agriculture, loosened ties to the Eastern bloc, and appealed to the West for economic assistance. In 1987 a UN-led relief effort began. In 1989 Mozambique signed a cooperation agreement with South Africa, which cut off its aid to the Renamo insurgents. But fighting continued into 1990.

In November 1990, Mozambique adopted a new constitution widening individual rights and freedoms, including abolition of the death penalty, freedom of the press and speech, and an independent judiciary, as well as establishing multiparty democracy, a presidential regime, and free-market economy. On Oct. 4, 1992, Pres. Chissanó and Renamo leader Afonso Dhlakama signed a cease-fire that ended their civil war; the UN dispatched 7,500 military and civilian personnel to oversee the disarmament and organize elections.

Mozambique's first-ever multiparty elections were held in October 1994. Pres. Chissanó was elected with 53 percent of the vote while his Frelimo party took 129 of the Parliament's 250 seats. (Renamo carried all but nine of the remaining seats.)

Mozambique is rich in agricultural land and mineral resources. Nevertheless, years of communism, drought, and civil war have left the country poor and dependent on foreign aid. In 1992 the worst drought in memory brought the nation to a virtual standstill, as an estimated 1.8 million people became dependent on donations of food from outsiders for survival. In recent years the IMF has helped enormously with loans and planning advice but Mozambique remains one of the poorest nations.

▶MYANMAR
Union of Burma

● **GEOGRAPHY** **Location:** NW region of Southeast Asia. **Boundaries:** China and Laos to NE, Bangladesh, India to NW, Thailand to SE, Andaman Sea to S, and Bay of Bengal to SW. **Total area:** 261,969 sq. mi. (678,500 sq km). **Coastline:** 1,200 mi. (1,930 km). **Comparative area:** slightly smaller than Texas. **Land use:** 15% arable land; 1% permanent crops; 1% meadows and pastures; 49% forest and woodland; 34% other; includes 2% irrigated. **Major cities:** (1983 census) Yangon (formerly Rangoon) (capital) 2,458,712; Mandalay 532,895; Bassein 335,000; Moulmein 219,991; Akyab 143,000.
● **PEOPLE** **Population:** 47,305,319 (1998 est.). **Nationality:** noun—Burmese (sing., pl.); adjective—Burmese. **Ethnic groups:** 68% Burman, 9% Shan, 7% Karen, 4% Rakhine, 3% Chinese, 2% Mon, 2% Indian, 5% other. **Languages:** Burmese, minority ethnic languages. **Religions:** 89% Buddhist, 4% Muslim, 4% Christian, 1% animist beliefs.
● **GOVERNMENT** **Type:** military regime. **Independence:** Jan. 4, 1948 (from UK). **Constitution:** Jan. 3, 1974; new constitution being drafted. **National holiday:** Independence Day, Jan.4. **Head of Government:** Gen. Than Shwe, chairman State Law and Order Restoration Council (SLORC) (since Apr. 1992). **Structure:** executive—military junta controls legislature—last election held in 1990, but never convened; judiciary—not independent, no guarantees.
● **ECONOMY** **Monetary unit:** kyat. **Budget:** (FY96/97) *income:* $7.9 bil.; *expend.:* $12.2 bil. **GDP:** $55.7 bil., $1,190 per capita (1997 est.). **Chief crops:** paddy rice, corn, oilseeds; hardwood. **Natural resources:** crude oil, timber, tin, copper, tungsten. **Major industries:** agricultural processing, textiles and footwear, wood and wood products. **Labor force:** 18.8 mil. (FY95/96 est.); 65.2% agriculture, 14.3% industry, 10.1% trade, 6.3% government (FY88/89 est.); **Exports:** $693 mil. (1996); teak, rice, pulses, beans. **Imports:** $1.4 bil. (1996); machinery, transport equipment, chemicals, food products. **Major trading partners:** *exports:* China, Indonesia, Singapore; *imports:* Japan, China, Singapore.

(Until the summer of 1989 this country was known as Burma.)

Burma, an independent Buddhist monarchy from the 11th century, fell to the Mongol empire in the 13th century, and after the 14th century was a satellite state of China. Anglo-French rivalry over trade left Burma under French influence in the early 19th century, but in a series of three wars (1824-26, 1852, 1885), Great Britain succeeded in bringing all of Burma into the British raj of India. The country became self-governing under a British protectorate in 1937.

Japanese occupation of Burma in early 1942 made the country a major theater of fighting during World War II. The Burma Road, built by the Allies to connect northeastern India with southwestern China, was a key link in bringing supplies to the Chinese Nationalist army during the war.

Burma achieved independence as the Union of Burma on Jan. 4, 1948. Promises of autonomy for ethnic minority regions such as the Shan and Karen States have not been fulfilled, leading to armed separatist movements in those areas ever since. In 1962 a coup led by Gen. Ne Win overthrew the democratic government and established a one-party state under the Burmese Socialist Program party. The party's "Burmese Path to Socialism" resulted in self-imposed international isolation and economic stagnation at home despite the country's potential wealth in agriculture, timber, minerals, and gems.

In July 1988 Ne Win resigned from office in the face of mounting popular demonstrations. A series of short-lived successor governments were unable to restore public order and normal governmental functions; direct military rule was announced in September 1988 as demonstrations continued.

In the general election held on May 27, 1990 (the first multiparty free elections in three decades), the opposition National League for Democracy, led by Aung San Suu Kyi, won a decisive victory, but the results of the election were nullified by the State Law and Order Restoration Council (SLORC), and leaders of the elected government were placed under house arrest. In 1991 the continued political repression in Myanmar was brought to international attention when Aung San Suu Kyi was awarded the Nobel Peace Prize. This helped usher in a period of diminishing repression. A new leader of the ruling military junta, Gen. Than Shwe, began peace talks with the Karen rebels in early 1994, and released Aung San Suu Kyi in July 1995. In 1998, renewed pressure by NLD upon the junta (since Nov. 1997 renamed the State Peace and Development Council) to convene the 1990 parliament brought renewed repression and mass arrests; a committee of NLD delcared itself to be the legal parliament of Myanmar in September, asserting that all the junta legislation since 1990 was null and void.

▶ NAMIBIA
Republic of Namibia
• **GEOGRAPHY Location:** southwest Africa. **Boundaries:** Angola to N, Botswana to E, South Africa to S, Atlantic Ocean to W. **Total area:** 318,259 sq. mi. (824,290 sq km). **Coastline:** 976 mi. (1,572 km). **Comparative area:** slightly more than half the size of Alaska. **Land use:** 1% arable land; negl. % permanent crops; 46% meadows and pastures; 22% forest and woodland; 31% other; includes negl. % irrigated. **Major cities:** (1990) Windhoek (capital) 125,000.
• **PEOPLE Population:** 1,648,270 (1999 est.). **Nationality:** noun—Namibian(s); adjective—Namibian. **Ethnic groups:** 86% black, 6.6% white, 7.4% mixed; 50% of the population belongs to the Ovambo tribe. **Languages:** Afrikaans common language, 32% German, and 7% English (official); several indigenous languages. **Religions:** 80%-90% Christian, 10%-20% indigenous religions.
• **GOVERNMENT Type:** republic. **Independence:** Mar. 21, 1990 (from South Africa). **Constitution:** Feb. 9, 1990. **National holiday:** Independence Day, Mar. 21. **Heads of Government:** Sam Nujoma, president (since Mar. 1990); Hage G. Geingob, prime minister (since Mar. 1990). **Structure:** executive; bicameral legislature; judiciary.
• **ECONOMY Monetary unit:** Namibian dollar. **Budget:** (FY96/97) *income:* $1.1 bil.; *expend.:* $1.2 bil. **GDP:** $6.6 bil., $4,100 per capita (1998 est.). **Chief crops:** millet, sorghum, peanuts; livestock; fish. **Natural resources:** diamonds, copper, uranium, gold, lead. **Major industries:** meat packing, fish processing, dairy products, mining (copper, lead, zinc, diamonds, and uranium). **Labor force:** about 500,000 (1994); 49% agriculture, 25% industry and commerce, 18% government, 5% services, 3% mining; 30-40% unemployment (1997 est.). **Exports:** $1.44 bil. (f.o.b., 1998); diamonds, copper, gold, zinc, lead, uranium; meat, processed fish. **Imports:** $1.48 bil. (f.o.b., 1998); foodstuffs, petroleum products, machinery and equipment, chemicals. **Major trading partners:** *exports:* 38% UK, 24% South Africa, 12% Spain; *imports:* 87% South Africa, Germany, U.S.

The Kalahari desert, on the Namibian plateau, has been inhabited since ancient times by San hunter-gatherers. Various Nama and Bantu peoples migrated into the area more recently. British and Dutch explorers and traders began to penetrate Namibia in the 18th century.

In 1872 Great Britain occupied the area around Walvis Bay and in 1884 annexed it to the Cape Colony. Also in 1884 Germany claimed most of South-West Africa; negotiations between the two powers resulted in German acceptance of Britain's claim of Walvis Bay and British acceptance of Germany's claim to the rest of the coastal region with a sphere of influence in the interior.

During World War I, British troops from South Africa occupied South-West Africa in 1915. In 1920 South Africa received a League of Nations mandate to administer the area. In 1946 when the United Nations succeeded the League, the United Nations proposed that South Africa continue its administration under a UN trusteeship. South Africa refused and annexed South-West Africa.

The proposed UN trusteeship was revoked by the United Nations in 1966. At the same time, the South-West Africa People's Organization (SWAPO), operating from bases in Zambia and Angola, began guerrilla actions against South African troops in the region. In 1968 the United Nations formally renamed the territory Namibia and appointed an 11-nation council to supervise its affairs and devise a plan leading to independence.

In 1971 the International Court of Justice upheld the UN's authority over Namibia and ruled that South Africa's continued occupation of the territory was illegal. In 1975 South Africa convened the Turnhalle Conference, which proposed a plan for Namibian independence based on the racial-separation principles of apartheid. This was rejected by the United Nations, and in 1978 the UN Security Council approved Resolution 435, which called for a general cease-fire to be followed by UN-supervised elections.

In response, South Africa unilaterally held elections in Namibia, which were boycotted by SWAPO and other African organizations and rejected by the United Nations. In 1982 South Africa declared that it would enter into talks about the future of Namibia only after Cuban troops were withdrawn from Angola. In 1983 South Africa launched a major military operation against SWAPO forces in Angola.

In October 1984 Angolan president dos Santos agreed to work out a plan for withdrawal of Cuban troops as part of a settlement in Namibia. In June 1985 South Africa granted limited local authority to a Namibian government made up of a coalition of parties, excluding SWAPO. In 1987 South African troops occupied southern Angola (to aid Angolan rebels), and in early 1988, fighting between South African troops and Namibian rebels in northern Namibia and southern Angola intensified.

A new round of talks on the future of Namibia between South Africa, Cuba, and Angola, mediated by the United States, began in May 1988, and on Dec. 13, 1988, the three parties agreed on a plan for Namibian independence and a pullout of Cuban troops from Angola.

In January 1989 the Cuban withdrawal from Angola began. On Apr. 1 UN Resolution 435 went into effect in Namibia, and a UN peacekeeping force arrived to supervise the transition to independence. Elections were held in November 1989: SWAPO leader Sam Nujoma won an overwhelming victory, and opposition leaders pledged their support. A Western-style democratic constitution was adopted Feb. 16, 1990, and full independence came on Mar. 21. The first elections under the new constitution were held in December 1994 with SWAPO gaining even stronger control of Parliament.

▶ NAURU
Republic of Nauru
• **GEOGRAPHY Location:** central Pacific Ocean (0°32'S, 166°56'E), about 2,800 mi. (4,500 km) southwest of Hawaii. **Boundaries:** nearest neigh-

bor is Banaba (Ocean Island), in Kiribati, about 185 mi. (300 km) to E. **Total area**: 8 sq. mi. (21 sq km). **Coastline**: 19 mi. (30 km). **Comparative area**: about one-tenth size of Washington, D.C. **Land use**: 0% arable land; 0% permanent crops; 0% meadows and pastures; 0% forest and woodland; 100% other. **Major cities**: none as such; government offices in Yaren district.
● **PEOPLE Population**: 10,605 (1999 est.). **Nationality**: noun—Nauruan(s) adjective—Nauruan. **Ethnic groups**: 58% Nauruan, 26% other Pacific Islander, 8% Chinese, 8% European. **Languages**: Nauruan, a distinct Pacific Island language (official); English widely understood and spoken and used for most government and commercial purposes. **Religions**: Christian (two-thirds Protestant, one-third Catholic).
● **GOVERNMENT Type**: republic. **Independence**: Jan. 31, 1968 (from UN trusteeship under Australia, New Zealand, and UK). **Constitution**: Jan. 29, 1968. **National holiday**: Independence Day, Jan. 31. **Head of Government**: Bernard Dowiyogo, president (since June 1998). **Structure**: executive—president elected from and by Parliament for unfixed term; unicameral legislature; judiciary.
● **ECONOMY Monetary unit**: Australian dollar. **Budget**: (FY95/96) *income*: $23.4 mil.; *expend.*: $64.8 mil. **GDP**: $100 mil., $10,000 per capita (1993 est.). **Chief crops**: coconuts. **Natural resources**: phosphates. **Major industries**: phosphate mining (about 2 mil. tons per year), financial services, coconuts. **Labor force**: N.A. **Exports**: $25.3 mil. (f.o.b., 1991); phosphates. **Imports**: $21.1 mil. (c.i.f., 1991); food, fuel, manufactures, building materials, machinery. **Major trading partners**: Australia, New Zealand, UK.

Nauru, formerly known as Pleasant Island, is an isolated island lying west of the Gilbert Islands. It became a German protectorate in 1888. After World War I, Nauru was administered by Australia under a League of Nations mandate. It was occupied by Japan throughout World War II. In 1947 it became a UN Trust Territory administered by Australia, and on Jan. 31, 1968, an independent republic. Nauru has a parliament of 18 members, who elect a prime minister and a cabinet. Most of the island's assets are owned by the state-controlled Nauru Phosphate Corporation and by the Nauru Cooperative Society.

Much of the island is covered by phosphate deposits. Phosphate mining and exports, under leases largely controlled by Australian interests, have given Nauru one of the world's highest per-capita incomes. In 1999 Nauru was expected to join the U.N.

▶ **NEPAL**
Kingdom of Nepal
● **GEOGRAPHY Location**: central Asia, in Himalayan mountain range. **Boundaries**: China to N, India to E, S, and W. **Total area**: 54,363 sq. mi. (140,800 sq km). **Coastline**: none. **Comparative area**: slightly larger than Arkansas. **Land use**: 17% arable land; negl. % permanent crops; 15% meadows and pastures; 42% forest and woodland; 26% other; includes 2% irrigated. **Major cities**: (1991 census) Kathmandu (capital) 419,073.
● **PEOPLE Population**: 24,302,653 (1999 est.). **Nationality**: noun—Nepalese (sing. and pl.); adjective—Nepalese. **Ethnic groups**: Newars, Indians, Tibetans, Gurungs, Magars, Tamangs, Bhotias, Rais, Limbus, Sherpas. **Languages**: Nepali (offi-

cial); 20 other languages divided into numerous dialects. **Religions**: 90% Hindu, 5% Buddhist, 3% Muslim; only official Hindu kingdom in world, although no sharp distinction between many Hindu and Buddhist groups.
● **GOVERNMENT Type**: parliamentary democracy. **Constitution**: Nov. 9, 1990. **National holiday**: Birthday of His Majesty the King, Dec. 28. **Heads of Government**: Birendra Bir Bikram Shah Dev, king (since Jan. 1972); Krishna Prasad Bhattarai, prime minister (since May 1999). **Structure**: executive—prime minister appointed by king from leading party in parliament; bicameral legislature—upper house (National Assembly) consists of 60 members, 50 appointed by lower house, 10 by the king; judiciary.
● **ECONOMY Monetary unit**: Nepalese rupee. **Budget**: (FY96/97 est.) *income*: $536 mil.; *expend.*: $818 mil. **GDP**: $26.2 bil., $1,100 per capita (1998 est.). **Chief crops**: rice, corn, wheat, sugarcane; milk, water buffalo meat. **Natural resources**: quartz, water, timber, hydroelectric potential, scenic beauty. **Major industries**: small rice, jute, sugar, and oilseed mills; cigarette and brick factories; tourism. **Labor force**: 10 mil. (1996 est.); 81% agriculture, 16% services, 3% industry; severe lack of skilled labor. **Exports**: $394 mil. (f.o.b., 1997 est.) (does not include unrecorded border trade with India); clothing, carpets, leather goods, jute goods, grain. **Imports**: $1.7 bil. (c.i.f., 1997 est.); 20% petroleum products, 11% fertilizer, 10% machinery. **Major trading partners**: *exports*: India, U.S., Germany; *imports*: India, Singapore, Japan.

The birthplace of Gautama Buddha (c. 600 B.C.), Nepal was for many centuries a collection of petty principalities, inhabited by various Tibeto-Burman peoples who mostly practiced Lamaistic Buddhism. In 1769 the country's three geographical zones—floodplain, foothills, and high mountains—were united under the Gurkhas, who made Hinduism the country's official religion. Nepal established treaty relations with Great Britain in 1792 and fought a border war with British India in 1814-16, but it was never incorporated into the British Empire.

An armed revolution in 1950 overthrew a government of heridatary rulers that had overthrown the Shah dynasty in the 19th century. King Tribuhavan (a Shah) was restored and tried to introduce democratic reforms, but his son Mahendra dissolved Parliament and introduced a tiered system of town, district, and national councils. Road and air links to India, Pakistan, and Tibet were improved, and Nepal began to emerge from its customary isolation. The successful climb of Mt. Everest by Sir Edmund Hillary and Tenzing Norgay in 1953 focused international attention on Nepal.

Mahendra was succeeded in 1972 by his son Birendra. In the wake of antigovernment demonstrations in 1990 that led to the shooting deaths of 63 civilians, Birendra lifted a 30-year-old ban on political parties and ordered the constitution rewritten to establish multiparty democracy and human rights as essentials of the political system. The king retains control of the military and is still head of state.

The Nepali Congress Party formed the first government in 1991, winning 110 of the 205 legislative seats. But after 1994 a series of brief and shifting coalitions, often including the Communist Party, governed Nepal until the May 1999 elections permitted the Nepali Congress Party to again govern without coalition partners as they again carried 110 seats.

In recent years tourism, especially mountaineering and trekking, have increased the country's prosperity but also have created new ecological problems. The economy remains largely in the stage of small-scale agriculture and craft industries.

▶ NETHERLANDS
Kingdom of The Netherlands

• **GEOGRAPHY Location:** western Europe. **Boundaries:** North Sea to N and W, Germany to E, Belgium to S. **Total area:** 14,413 sq. mi. (37,330 sq km). **Coastline:** 280 mi. (451 km). **Comparative area:** slightly less than twice the size of New Jersey. **Land use:** 27% arable land; 1% permanent crops; 31% meadows and pastures; 10% forest and woodland; 31% other; includes 15% irrigated. **Major cities:** (1994) Amsterdam (capital) 724,096; Rotterdam 598,521; The Hague 445,271; Utrecht 234,106; Eindhoven 196,130. The Hague is the seat of government.

• **PEOPLE Population:** 15,807,641 (1999 est.). **Nationality:** noun—Dutchman (men), Dutchwoman (women); adjective—Dutch. **Ethnic groups:** 94% Dutch, 6% Moroccans, Turks, and other. **Languages:** Dutch (official). **Religions:** 34% Roman Catholic, 25% Protestant, 36% unaffiliated, 3% Muslim.

• **GOVERNMENT Type:** constitutional monarchy. **Independence:** 1579 (from Spain). **Constitution:** Feb. 17, 1983. **National holiday:** Queen's Day, Apr. 30. **Heads of Government:** Beatrix Wilhelmina Armgard, queen (since Apr. 1980); Wim Kok, prime minister (since Aug. 1994). **Structure:** executive—queen is constitutional monarch, prime minister is head of government; bicameral parliament; independent judiciary.

• **ECONOMY Monetary unit:** guilder, gulden, or florin. **Budget:** (1999 est.) *income:* $163 bil.; *expend.:* $170 bil. **GDP:** $348.6 bil., $22,200 per capita (1998 est.). **Chief crops:** grains, potatoes, sugar beets; livestock. **Natural recources:** natural gas, crude oil, fertile soil. **Major industries:** agroindustries, metal and engineering products, electrical machinery and equipment. **Labor force:** 7 mil. (1998 est.); 73% services, 23% manufacturing and construction, 4% agriculture; 4.1% unemployment (1998). **Exports:** $160 bil. (f.o.b., 1998); machinery and equipment, chemicals, fuels, food and tobacco. **Imports:** $142 bil. (f.o.b., 1998 est.); machinery and transport equipment, chemicals, foodstuffs, fuels, consumer goods. **Major trading partners:** (1998) *exports:* 78% EU, Central and Eastern Europe, U.S.; *imports:* 61% EU, 9% U.S., Central and Eastern Europe.

Historically, the name Netherlands referred to the low-lying areas of the Holy Roman Empire near the mouths of the Rhine, Meuse, and Scheldt rivers. The Habsburg emperor Charles V willed these territories to his son Philip II of Spain in 1555, but by the end of the 16th century, the northern provinces—the Union of Utrecht, formed in 1579 by William the Silent, of the House of Orange—won their independence in a war that was both religious (Calvinist vs. Catholic) and constitutional (aristocratic/patrician vs. foreign monarchy). The independence of the Netherlands was recognized in the Treaty of Westphalia, which ended the Thirty Years' War in 1648.

Dutch prosperity, founded on the woolen trade with England, grew tremendously through trade and seafaring under the 17th-century republic.

The Netherlands amassed a world empire, including the Indonesian archipelago, the island of Sri Lanka (then Ceylon), South Africa, Surinam, parts of the West Indies, and the Hudson valley in New Amsterdam (later New York); in addition it monopolized Western trade with Japan after 1637.

The Netherlands were incorporated into the Napoleonic empire. At the Congress of Vienna in 1815, a Dutch monarchy was established, which included Belgium until 1830. Land drainage and reclamation programs maintained the prosperity of the country's small-scale agriculture, while trade and colonial revenues were increasingly supplemented by industrial development in the 19th century. Dutch prosperity and the country's strategic position gave the Netherlands extraordinary influence and prestige in European affairs into the 20th century, despite the country's small size. It remained neutral in World War I.

Germany invaded the Netherlands in May 1940, taking control of the country after five days of fighting. Preparing to incorporate Holland into the Third Reich, Hitler installed a Nazi civilian government that ruled through totalitarian exploitation and cooperated in the persecution of Jews. But Queen Wilhelmina and the Dutch government escaped to England and maintained a government-in-exile throughout the war.

The final stages of fighting on the western front inflicted severe damage on the country, while in Asia the recovery of Indonesia from Japan led immediately to a declaration of independence under Sukarno. Marshall Plan aid was intended to support a domestic postwar recovery; an equal amount was spent by the Dutch government in an attempt to recapture control of Indonesia before that country's independence was recognized in 1949.

Devastated by World War II and the loss of its empire, the country faced a bleak future in the postwar years. Forced to turn its attention to recovery at home, the Netherlands worked through the Benelux (Belgium, Netherlands, Luxembourg) union (founded in 1944) and the Common Market to create another European "economic miracle" between the early 1950s and the 1970s. The older bases of the economy—commerce, maritime industry, dairy farming, and flower farming—were expanded and modernized; Rotterdam was rebuilt to become Europe's most important port. Newer industries, such as chemicals and oil refining, electronics, and steel, relied on the country's highly skilled and productive labor force to turn imported raw materials into finished high-value exports. A huge impoundment project turned the Zuider Zee into a new province, increasing the country's land area by 10 percent.

This postwar prosperity has been based in large part on political stability. A coalition of the Catholic State party and the Labor (formerly Social Democratic) party governed for 10 years under Premier Willem Drees. After 1958 cabinets normally were formed from coalitions headed by three Christian parties (merged in 1980 to form the United Christian Appeal) or by the Liberal party; all pursued essentially the same policies of free enterprise, comprehensive social welfare programs, high taxation, and social liberalism.

Queen Juliana was succeeded in 1980 by Queen Beatrix. From 1982 to 1989 a coalition of Christian Democrats and Liberals provided a cabinet headed by Prime Minister Ruud Lubbers; since 1989 the coalition has been of Christian Democrats and Labor. In 1994 Wim Kok, head of Labor, became prime minister, the first government to exclude the Christian Democrats since 1945.

►NEW ZEALAND

• **GEOGRAPHY   Location:**   South Pacific Ocean about 1,100 mi. (1,750 km) SE of Australia. **Boundaries**: South Pacific Ocean to N, E, and S; Tasman Sea to W. **Total area**: 103,738 sq. mi. (268,680 sq km). **Coastline:** 9,406 mi. (15,134 km). **Comparative area:** about size of Colorado. **Land use:** 9% arable land; 5% permanent crops; 50% meadows and pastures; 28% forest and woodland; 8% other; includes 1% irrigated. **Major cities**: (1993 est.) Wellington (capital) 326,900; Auckland 910,200; Christchurch 312,600; Hamilton 151,800; Napier-Hastings 111,200.

• **PEOPLE   Population:** 3,662,265 (1999 est.). **Nationality:** noun—New Zealander(s); adjective—New Zealand. **Ethnic groups:** 74.5% New Zealand European, 9.7% Maori, 4.6% other European, 3.8% Pacific Islander, 7.4% Asian and other. **Languages:** English (official) and Maori. **Religions:** 24% Anglican, 18% Presbyterian, 15% Roman Catholic, 5% Methodist, 2% Baptist, 3% other Protestant, 33% none or unspecified.

• **GOVERNMENT   Type:** parliamentary democracy. **Independence:** Sept. 26, 1907 (from UK). **Constitution:** no formal, written constitution; consists of various documents, including certain acts of UK and New Zealand Parliaments. Constitution Act 1986 was to have come into force Jan. 1, 1987, but has not been enacted. **National holiday:** Waitangi Day, Feb. 6. **Heads of Government:** Sir Michael Hardie Boys, governor-general (since March 1996); Jenny Shipley, prime minister (since Dec. 1997). **Structure:** executive—governor-general represents queen, prime minister is head of government; unicameral legislature; judiciary.

• **ECONOMY   Monetary unit:**   New Zealand dollar. **Budget:** (FY97/98) *income:* $24.9 bil.; *expend.:* $23.7 bil. **GDP:** $61.1 bil., $17,000 per capita (1998 est.). **Chief crops:** wheat, barley, potatoes, fruits; wool, meat, dairy. **Natural resources:** natural gas, iron ore, sand, coal, timber. **Major industries:** food processing, wood and paper products, textiles, aluminum smelting, tourism. **Labor force:** 1.86 mil. (1998); 65.1% services, 25.1% industry, 9.8% agriculture; 7.6% unemployment (1998). **Exports:** $12.9 bil. (1998); wool, lamb, mutton, beef, fruit, fish. **Imports:** $13 bil. (1998); machinery and equipment, vehicles and aircraft, petroleum, consumer goods, plastics. **Major trading partners:** *exports:* 20% Australia, 15% Japan, 10% US; *imports:* 27% Australia, 19% U.S., 12% Japan.

New Zealand was settled by Maori voyagers from Polynesia from about the ninth century A.D. The first European to sight it was the Dutch explorer Abel Tasman, in 1642; he named it, but did not take possession. In 1769, Capt. James Cook visited and claimed it for Britain. The first British missionaries arrived in 1814, and New Zealand became a full-fledged British colony in 1841. By the Treaty of Waitangi in 1840, the Maoris recognized Queen Victoria's protection and agreed to admit British settlers; in return, they were guaranteed possession of their lands. But in a series of bloody wars lasting until 1870, the Maoris were displaced from lands devoted to the expanding British settlements.

As a result of their defeat and of introduced diseases, the Maori population dwindled to about 40,000 by the 1890s. Their numbers have since recovered to over 400,000, and in recent decades, the Maoris have become a cohesive culture and

significant political force, directly electing several members of Parliament. In 1985, the Waitangi Tribunal was given wide power to hear Maori claims for repayment for land taken without compensation since the 1840 treaty. Large financial settlements are now being negotiated by the government.

New Zealand was one of the first nations to introduce universal adult suffrage (1893) and to establish a comprehensive welfare state. Legislation beginning in 1898 regulates labor practices, and mandates universal old-age pensions, public sector medical care, and other social services. Since 1907, the country has been an independent member of the British Commonwealth. The crown is represented by a governor-general, while government is drawn from a parliament and headed by a prime minister. Since the 1930s, government has alternated between the National and Labour parties.

New Zealand troops fought on the side of the Allies in both world wars, with UN forces in Korea, and with the United States in Vietnam. In 1951, New Zealand joined Australia and the United States in the ANZUS mutual-defense treaty, but was excluded from it in 1986 after denying port facilities to ships carrying nuclear weapons. New Zealand has also objected strenuously to French testing of nuclear weapons in the South Pacific and pressed for a comprehensive international nuclear test ban treaty.

Upon its election in 1984, the Labour government launched a profound economic restructuring program to transform the country from a protected agrarian economy to an open free-market economy. This program, continued by the National Party, which regained power in 1990, eliminated government subsidies, cut government spending, liberalized imports, deregulated financial markets, reduced tax rates, and deregulated the labor market, largely disempowering the unions. The reforms resulted in an expanding and competitive economy with low inflation, and, in 1993-94, the first budget surplus in 18 years. The government responded in 1995 by cutting taxes again, this time by a total of $1.4 billion, the largest tax cut ever in New Zealand's history. October 1996 election results, however, forced the Nationalist Party into coalition with the new populist/zenophobic New Zealand First Party. The terms commit the new government to defer tax cuts, halt sales of state-owned businesses, freeze immigration levels, and increase spending on health and education. The coalition lasted 19 months until New Zealand First left the cabinet over government plans to privatize Wellington International Airport. Yet the government did not fall as votes of confidence in September 1998 and February 1999 permitted continuance of a minority government headed by New Zealand's first female prime minister, Jenny Shipley.

►NICARAGUA
Republic of Nicaragua

• **GEOGRAPHY   Location:**   Central American isthmus. **Boundaries:** Honduras to N, Caribbean Sea to E, Costa Rica to S, Pacific Ocean to W. **Total area:** 49,998 sq. mi. (129,494 sq km). **Coastline:** 565 mi. (910 km). **Comparative area:** slightly smaller than New York State. **Land use:** 9% arable land; 1% permanent crops; 46% meadows and pastures; 27% forest and woodland; 17% other; includes 1% irrigated. **Major cities**: (1983) Managua (capital) 682,111; (1985 est.) León 100,982;

Granada 88,636; Masaya 74,946; Chinandega 67,792.

● **PEOPLE   Population:** 4,717,132 (1999 est.). **Nationality:** noun—Nicaraguan(s); adjective—Nicaraguan. **Ethnic groups:** 69% mestizo, 17% white, 9% black, 5% Amerindian. **Languages:** Spanish (official); English- and Amerindian-speaking minorities on Atlantic coast. **Religions:** 95% Roman Catholic, 5% Protestant.

● **GOVERNMENT   Type:** republic. **Independence:** Sept. 15, 1821 (from Spain). **Constitution:** Jan. 9, 1987. **National holiday:** Independence Day, Sept. 15. **Head of Government:** Arnoldo Alemán Lacayo, president (since Jan. 1997). **Structure:** executive branch; unicameral legislature; judiciary.

● **ECONOMY   Monetary unit:** córdoba. **Budget:** (1996 est.) *income:* $389 mil.; *expend.:* $551 mil. **GDP:** $11.6 bil., $2,500 per capita (1998 est.). **Chief crops:** cotton, bananas, coffee, sugarcane, rice, corn, beans. **Natural resources:** gold, silver, copper, tungsten, lead. **Major industries:** food processing, chemicals, metal products. **Labor force:** 1.5 mil. (1995); 54% services, 31% agriculture, 15% industry; 16% unemployment. **Exports:** $704 mil. (f.o.b., 1997 est.); coffee, seafood, meat, sugar, gold, bananas. **Imports:** $1.45 bil. (c.i.f., 1997 est.); consumer goods, machinery and equipment, petroleum products. **Major trading partners:** *exports:* U.S., Central America, Germany; *imports:* Central America, U.S., Venezuela.

Nicaragua gained independence from Spain in 1821 and formed a constituent part of the United Provinces of Central America in 1823. With the dissolution of the federation in 1838, Nicaragua became an independent republic. Throughout the United Provinces, an intra-elite struggle between Liberal and Conservative factions defined the political arena during the early 19th century. Nicaraguan Liberals invited the adventurer William Walker of Tennessee to take their part against their Conservative rivals in 1855. Walker took control of the country in 1856 but was driven out by a combined Central American force the following year.

The Conservatives held power in Nicaragua until 1893, when a planters' revolt brought Liberal José Santos Zelaya to the presidency. Because of Zelaya's intention to pursue an isthmian canal project, the U.S. government intervened in support of a Conservative uprising. The United States sent marines to Nicaragua in 1909, and Zelaya resigned in 1910. The marines occupied the country during 1909-25 and 1926-33.

Refusing to abide by a political settlement between the U.S. government and Nicaraguan Liberal forces in 1927, a Liberal officer, Augusto César Sandino, led a guerrilla war against U.S. occupation forces. But in 1934, Anastasio Somoza García, head of the Nicaraguan National Guard, had Sandino assassinated, and took over the presidency in 1937. Somoza and his sons Luis and Anastasio Somoza Debayle controlled Nicaragua until 1979.

A broad coalition of groups led by the Sandinista National Liberation Front (FSLN) overthrew the Somoza dictatorship in 1979. Elections were held in 1984 for the presidency, vice presidency, and a constituent assembly. The Sandinistas won the election for the presidency, captured a working majority in the National Assembly, and wrote a new constitution in 1987.

Between 1981 and 1990, the United States actively, but covertly supported Contra rebels fighting the Sandinista regime in a civil war that cost

the country dearly. In 1989, Pres. Daniel Ortega announced elections for early 1990, which he lost in a stunning upset to Violeta Barrios de Chamorro, who headed a 17-party coalition, the United Nicaragua Opposition. Since then, the transition has been relatively peaceful, highlighted by Gen. Humberto Ortega's uneventful transfer of command of the army in 1995, the first peaceful transfer in Nicaragua's history. In late 1996 presidential elections the Liberal Alliance candidate, Arnoldo Alemán, won a decisive victory over former president Daniel Ortega and voters opted for a return to free enterprise and closer ties with the U.S. Even as the Sandinistas were further weakened by Ortega's invoking of immunity (as a member of the National Assembly) against 1998 charges by his step-daughter of sexual abuse, limitations on the Aleman government's free enterprising policies were shown by 1990 student protests and transport workers' strikes which forced the government to boost university spending and abandon bus line deregulation while cutting back fuel taxes.

▶ **NIGER**
Republic of Niger

● **GEOGRAPHY   Location:** landlocked country in western Africa. **Boundaries:** Algeria and Libya to N, Chad to E, Nigeria to S, Benin, Burkina Faso to SW, Mali to W. **Total area:** 489,189 sq. mi. (1,267,000 sq km). **Coastline:** none. **Comparative area:** slighlty less than twice the size of Texas. **Land use:** 3% arable land; 0% permanent crops; 7% meadows and pastures; 2% forest and woodland; 88% other; includes negl. % irrigated. **Major cities:** (1988 census) Niamey (capital) 392,169; Zinder 119,838; Maradi 109,386; Tahoua 49,941; Agadez 49,361.

● **PEOPLE   Population:** 9,962,242 (1999 est.). **Nationality:** noun—Nigerien(s); adjective—Nigerien. **Ethnic groups:** 56% Hausa, 22% Djerma, 8.5% Fula, 8% Tuareg, 4.3% Beri Beri (Kanouri); 1.2% Arab, Toubou, and Gourmantche; about 1,200 French expatriates. **Languages:** French (official), Hausa, Djerma. **Religions:** 80% Muslim, 20% indigenous beliefs and Christians.

● **GOVERNMENT   Type:** republic. **Independence:** Aug. 3, 1960 (from France). **Constitution:** revised May 12, 1996. **National holiday:** Republic Day, Dec. 18. **Heads of Government:** Daouda Malam Wanke, president (since Apr. 1999); Ibrahim Assane Mayaki, prime minister (since Apr. 1999). **Structure:** executive; unicameral legislature—dissolved after coup of Jan. 28, 1996; judiciary.

● **ECONOMY   Monetary unit:** Communauté Financière Africaine (CFA) franc. **Budget:** (1998 est.) *income:* $370 mil.; *expend.:* $370 mil. **GDP:** $9.4 bil., $970 per capita (1998 est.). **Chief crops:** cowpeas, cotton, peanuts, millet, sorghum, cassava, rice; goats, sheep, cattle. **Natural resources:** uranium, coal, iron ore, tin, phosphates. **Major industries:** cement, brick, textiles. **Labor force:** 70,000 receive regular wages or salaries; 90% agriculture; 6% industry and commerce, 4% government. **Exports:** $269 mil. (f.o.b., 1997 est.); 50% uranium ore, 20% livestock, cowpeas, onions. **Imports:** $295 mil. (c.i.f., 1997 est.); consumer goods, primary materials, machinery, vehicles and parts, petroleum, cereals. **Major trading partners:** *exports:* 21% Greece, 18% Canada, 12% France; *imports:* 17% France, 7% Ivory Coast, 5% US.

Most of Niger's territory is dominated by the Sahara and the Sahel (the "shore" of the desert), which have spread southward since prehistoric times. Much of the population lives in the narrow fertile belt south of the Niger River. Much of Niger was incorporated during medieval times in large empires centered in neighboring Mali, Chad, and Nigeria.

In the 18th century, Tuaregs migrating from the northern desert began to form tribal confederations in Niger. They united with local Hausa peoples to wage war against the Fulani empire. In the 19th century, British and German explorers seeking the source of the Niger River explored the region. In the European rivalry that followed, the French, from bases in Mali and Chad, began to dominate Niger by 1900; Niger became a French colony in 1922, administered from Dakar, Senegal.

In 1946 the people of Niger, in common with other peoples in French Africa, were granted French citizenship, and limited self-rule began. This local autonomy was expanded in 1956, and in 1958 Niger became an autonomous state within the French Overseas Community. Full independence followed on Aug. 3, 1960; Niger maintained close ties to France.

Hamani Diori was elected Niger's first president in 1960 and was reelected in 1965 and 1970. He was overthrown in 1974 in a military coup led by Lt. Col. Seyni Kountche. In 1987, Pres. Kountche died and was succeeded by Col. Ali Saibou, who was elected president by the Supreme Military Council. The country began moving toward democracy again in 1989, and a new constitution was approved in 1992. Mahame Ousmane was elected president in 1993, but he and prime minister Hama Amadou were ousted in a violent military coup in Jan. 1996, in which five people were killed. The leader of the coup, Lt. Col. Ibrahim Barré, who criticized Ousmane's handling of the Taureg Liberation Front, became the new president. He survived an assassination attempt in Jan. 1998, but fell to another in April 1999. Junior army officers formed a junta, supported by all the civilian opposition parties,maintaining Ibrahim Mayaki in his post as prime minister. The junta has promised a "nine-month transition", including a constitutional referendum in November and a presidential election in December, 1999.

▶NIGERIA
Federal Republic of Nigeria
• **GEOGRAPHY Location:** western coast of Africa. **Boundaries:** Niger to N, Cameroon to E, Gulf of Guinea to S, Benin to W. **Total area:** 356,668 sq. mi. (923,770 sq km). **Coastline:** 530 mi. (853 km). **Comparative area:** slightly more than twice the size of California. **Land use:** 33% arable land; 3% permanent crops; 44% meadows and pastures; 12% forest and woodland; 8% other; includes negl. % irrigated. **Major cities:** (1992) Abuja (capital) 305,900; Lagos 1,347,000; Ibadan 1,295,000; Kano 699,900; Ogbomosho 660,600.
• **PEOPLE Population:** 113,828,587 (1999 est.). **Nationality:** noun—Nigerian(s); adjective— Nigerian. **Ethnic groups:** Hausa, Fulani, Yoruba, Ibo, Kanuri, Ibibio, Tiv, Ijaw. **Languages:** English (official); Hausa, Yoruba, Ibo, Fulani. **Religions:** 50% Muslim, 40% Christian, 10% indigenous beliefs.
• **GOVERNMENT Type:** republic in transition from military rule. **Independence:** Oct. 1, 1960 (from UK). **Constitution:** Oct. 1, 1979, amended Feb. 9, 1984; military government rules by decree. **National holiday:** Independence Day, Oct. 1. **Head of Government:** Olusegun Obasanjo, president

(since May 1999). **Structure:** executive; bicameral legislature; judiciary.
• **ECONOMY Monetary unit:** naira. **Budget:** (1998 est.) *income:* $13.9 bil.; *expend:* $13.9 bil. **GDP:** $106.2 bil., $960 per capita (1998 est.). **Chief crops:** peanuts, cocoa, palm oil, rubber, corn; goats, sheep, cattle, pigs; fish. **Natural resources:** crude oil, tin, columbite, iron ore, coal. **Major industries:** crude oil, natural gas, coal, tin, columbite; palm oil, peanuts, cotton, rubber; textiles, cement, building materials. **Labor force:** 42.8 mil. (1985); 54% agriculture; 19% industry, commerce, and services; 15% government; 28% unemployment (1992 est.). **Exports:** $9.7 bil. (f.o.b., 1998); 95% petroleum and petroleum products, cocoa, rubber. **Imports:** $9.8 bil. (f.o.b., 1998); machinery, chemicals, transportation equipment, manufactured goods, food and animals. **Major trading partners:** *exports:* 35% U.S., 11% Spain, 6% Italy; *imports:* 14% US, 11% UK, 10% Germany, 8% France.

The Nok culture of central Nigeria (500-200 B.C.) was one of the richest and most advanced ancient civilizations in western Africa. Around A.D. 1000, the Muslim Kanem civilization expanded into northern Nigeria; by the 14th century, the amalgamated kingdom of Kanem-Bornu took northern Nigeria as its political center, from which it dominated the Sahel and developed trade routes stretching throughout northern Africa and as far as Europe and the Middle East. During the 15th and 16th centuries, the Hausa Songhai empire rose to power. It was overthrown by the Fulani Muslim leader Uthman Dan Fodio, who created the Sokoto caliphate.

Southern Nigeria is dominated by the Yoruba, whose Oyo kingdom, centered at Ife, became a major power by A.D. 1000. Oyo gave rise to the Benin civilization, which flourished from the 15th to the 18th centuries and is famous for its brass, bronze, and ivory sculpture.

The Portuguese established trading stations on the Benin coast in the 15th century; initially, trade relations were cordial, and Benin became well-known in Europe as a powerful and advanced kingdom. With the rise of the slave trade (which began with the cooperation of the Benin kings, who brought slaves from the interior), relations became hostile, and Benin declined under European pressure. The Dutch, British, and other Europeans competed strenuously with Portugal for control of the slave trade, and by the 18th century, most of the coastal region of Nigeria was under British control. By the turn of the 19th century, Britain suppressed the slave trade; slaves captured aboard European ships were transported by the British to Freetown in Sierra Leone.

The British traded with Nigerians for agricultural and forest products and commenced exploration of the Niger River. Lagos came under British control in 1851, and in 1861 Nigeria was made a British colony. Despite native resistance the colony was expanded in 1906 to include territory east of the Niger River, which was called the Protectorate of Southern Nigeria, The two areas were administratively joined in 1914.

During the 1920s Britain began to respond to Nigerian demands for self-rule. In 1946 the colony was divided into three regions, each with an advisory assembly. In 1954 the colony was reorganized as the Nigerian Federation, and the assemblies were given more authority. Sir Akubar Tafawa Balewa became Nigeria's first prime minister.

The 1960s were marked by a struggle for political dominance among the major ethnic groups of Nigeria, including the Ibo (or Igbo), Yoruba, Hausa, and Fulani. Attempts to partition the country on tribal lines for administrative purposes provoked controversy, and charges of corruption and fraud in elections held in 1964 and 1965 led to violence and rioting.

In January 1966 civil war broke out when a group of Ibo army officers overthrew the central government and several of the regional governments. Prime Minister Balewa was killed, along with many other political leaders in the northern and western parts of the country. Gen. Johnson Aguiyi-Ironsi, leader of the Ibo forces, took control of the government.

Aguiyi-Ironsi abolished the country's federal structure and set up a strong central government, dominated by the Ibo. Anti-Ibo riots broke out in the north, and many Ibo were massacred. In July 1966 Aguiyi-Ironsi was assassinated by a group of northern army officers. Army Chief of Staff Yakubu Gowon became head of a new military government. The Eastern Region refused to acknowledge Gowon's government.

In 1967 Gowon reapportioned Nigeria into 12 states. The Eastern Region rejected this plan and seceded from Nigeria to form the independent state of Biafra, provoking a civil war that lasted until January 1970, when Biafra was rejoined with Nigeria. An estimated one million Biafrans, mostly Ibos, died in the war.

Gowon tried to rebuild the Eastern Region and create a harmonious multitribal government, but he was overthrown in a coup in 1975. His successor was assassinated in 1976 and succeeded by Lt. Gen. Olusegun Obasanjo who increased the number of states from 12 to 19 and promised a return to civilian rule. Shehu Shagari was elected president in 1979 and reelected in 1983, but in Dec. 1983 the military again intervened.

Nigeria's wealth of crude oil resources have consistently fueled the economy and made it an attractive country for foreign investment. During the 1970s, petroleum exports helped Nigeria recover economically from the Biafran War. But corruption, mismanagement, and overspending of projected petroleum revenues led to an economic crisis in the early 1980s as oil prices collapsed worldwide. Inflation, unemployment, and food shortages led to rioting in major population centers in 1986. And in March 1987, religious violence broke out between the Christian south and the Muslim north.

The government of Maj. Gen. Ibrahim Babangida responded by announcing plans for a new constitution, various economic austerity measures, and the restoration of civilian rule by 1992. Babangida also promoted a campaign to lower the birth rate and control the population—Africa's largest.

Babangida limited the number of political parties and dictated both party platforms in National Assembly elections held in 1992, and in 1993, he annulled the results of the presidential election, which international monitors said would have been won by opposition leader Moshood K. Abiola, who was taken prisoner for the "treason" of declaring himself the election winner. Babangida resigned in Aug. 1993, but his self-appointed successor was ousted in a November 1993 coup by Defense Minister Sani Abacha.

General Abacha's tyranny survived until his death (of a heart attack) in June 1998. A "transitional" military government led by Abacha's army chief of staff, Abdusalem Abubakar, freed political prisoners (Abiola dying just before his release), held local, state, and national elections (Dec.–Feb.), and turned over power, May 29, 1999 to the first popularly-elected president in 16 years, former general and once military ruler, Olusegun Obasanjo. (See "Major News Stories of the Year.")

▶ NORWAY
Kingdom of Norway

● **GEOGRAPHY** **Location:** western Scandinavian peninsula, northern Europe. **Boundaries:** Norwegian Sea to N and W, Russian Federation, Finland to NE, Sweden to E, North Sea to S and W. **Total area:** 125,182 sq. mi. (324,220 sq km). **Coastline:** 13,626 mi. (21,925 km)—2,125 mi. (3,419 km) mainland; 1,500 mi. (2,413 km) large islands; 10,002 mi. (16,093 km) long fjords, numerous small islands, and minor indentations. **Comparative area:** slightly larger than New Mexico. **Land use:** 3% arable land; negl.% permanent crops; negl. % meadows and pastures; 27% forest and woodland; 70% other; includes negl. % irrigated. **Major cities:** (1995) Oslo (capital) 483,401; Bergen 221,717; Trondheim 142,927; Stavanger 103,590; Kristiansand 68,609.

● **PEOPLE** **Population:** 4,438,547 (1999 est.). **Nationality:** noun—Norwegian(s); adjective—Norwegian. **Ethnic groups:** Germanic (Nordic, Alpine, Baltic), 20,000 Lapps (Sami). **Languages:** Norwegian (official), Lapp- and Finnish-speaking minorities. **Religions:** 87.8% Evangelical Lutheran (state church), 3.8% other Protestant and Roman Catholic, 8.4% other.

● **GOVERNMENT** **Type:** constitutional monarchy. **Independence:** Oct. 26, 1905 (from Sweden). **Constitution:** May 17, 1814, and modified in 1884. **National holiday:** Constitution Day, May 17. **Heads of Government:** Harald V, king (since Jan. 1991); Kjell Magne Bondevik, prime minister (since Oct. 1997). **Structure:** executive—prime minister heads government; unicameral legislature—for certain purposes, *Storting* divides itself into two chambers and elects 25 percent of its members to an upper house; judiciary.

● **ECONOMY** **Monetary unit:** Norwegian kroner. **Budget:** (1994 est.) *income:* $48.6 bil.; *expend.:* $53 bil. **GDP:** $109 bil.; $24,700 per capita (1998 est.). **Chief crops:** oats, feed grains; beef, milk; fish (among worlds top ten fishing nations). **Natural resources:** crude oil, copper, natural gas, pyrites, nickel. **Major industries:** petroleum and gas, food processing, shipbuilding. **Labor force:** 2.3 mil.; 71% services, 23% industry, 6% agriculture, forestry and fishing; 2.6% unemployment (1997). **Exports:** $39.8 bil. (f.o.b., 1998); 55% petroleum and petroleum products, metals, chemicals, ships, fish. **Imports:** $37.1 bil. (f.o.b., 1998); machinery and equipment, chemicals, metals, foodstuffs. **Major trading partners:** *exports:* 76% EU, 6% U.S.; *imports:* 68% EU, 6% U.S.

The Viking age began in 793 with the sack of Lindisfarne in Ireland. By the 10th century, Norse and Danish Vikings had touched in almost every navigable river of Western Europe from Germany to Spain. In addition to coastal raiding, the Norse were beginning the first open-ocean voyages from Europe, sailing direct to Iceland (800 miles) and even to Greenland (2,200 miles), which they colonized in the 10th century.

At the beginning of the 10th century, Harold I united the petty kingdoms of western Scandinavia and extended his realm as far as the Orkney and Shetland islands. Viking nobles fleeing from his conquests consolided the Norse duchy of Normandy in France. Christianity was established under Olaf II at the beginning of the 11th century.

Under Magnus VI (1263-80), medieval Norway reached the height of its power and prosperity. Norwegian independence ended with the accession in 1319 of Magnus VII, who was king of Sweden as well. Under the Kalmar Union of 1397, the three kingdoms of Scandinavia were merged under Danish control; Norway ceased to exist as a nation-state and was governed by the Danes for the following four centuries.

In 1814 Denmark, which had sided with France in the Napoleonic wars, was forced by the victorious powers to cede Norway to Sweden. Under Sweden's military control Norway attempted to establish its own monarchy. The attempt failed, but in 1815 Sweden acknowledged the independence of Norway in perpetual union with the Swedish Crown.

Relations between Norway and Sweden remained strained throughout the 19th century. In 1905 the Norwegian legislature, the Storting, declared the union void and deposed Swedish King Oscar II as king of Norway. Sweden acquiesced, and Prince Charles of Denmark was enthroned as king of Norway, ruling as Haakon VII for 52 years.

During the 19th century, large numbers of Norwegians emigrated to North America. A rising tide of cultural nationalism was expressed in the flourishing Norwegian literature and art, as well as in a tradition of Arctic exploration. In the 20th century, industrialization, aided by the development of hydroelectric power, began to supplement Norway's traditional economic mainstays of fishing and seafaring.

Norway remained neutral during World War I and was relatively unaffected by the postwar upheavals. Industrialization led to the rise of the Labor party in 1927.

Norway attempted to remain neutral in World War II as well but was invaded by German troops in April 1940; the country fell after a brief resistance aided by a Franco-British expeditionary force. The king and government fled to London and established a government-in-exile there. The Norwegian merchant marine fleet was also largely transferred to Great Britain and contributed to the Allied cause in the North Atlantic. At home, resistance grew to the collaborationist government of the Fascist leader Vidkun Quisling. As the Nazis retreated in 1945, King Haakon and his government returned home in triumph.

Elections in 1945 returned a majority Labor government in the Storting. Labor set about establishing a characteristic Scandinavian welfare state, emphasizing privately owned, free-market industry, publicly owned utilities, state planning to ensure ample housing as well as full employment through export-oriented industries, a comprehensive social welfare system, and—to pay for the latter—high taxes.

Norway was a founding member of the United Nations and provided that body with its first secretary-general, Trygve Lie. With the hardening of the Cold War, Norway's foreign policy took on a clear pro-Western stance; Norway joined the NATO alliance in 1949. In 1959 Norway became one of the original members of the European Free Trade Association. Through the 1960s industrial development and exports continued to fuel an economic boom that led to great national prosperity and stability.

The 1970s were the decade of oil and gas, with extensive development of North Sea oil and gas fields at the beginning of the decade. As international energy prices rose, the government's petroleum monopoly, Statoil, seemed to provide an endless source of funds. Because Norway's hydroelectric plants made the country self-sufficient in electric power, almost all of the oil and gas was available for export; by 1981 energy exports amounted to one-third, and by 1985 one-half, of Norway's total exports. The government expanded the welfare state and encouraged large wage increases. Public spending swelled, inflation outpaced wages, and government debt mounted; meanwhile Norway became an economic hostage to OPEC oil prices.

In the 1981 elections, the Conservative party formed a government for the first time since 1928; its austerity policy of holding down government spending while increasing taxes on consumer goods aroused popular opposition, and the government fell in 1986. The new Socialist coalition government faced even greater drops in oil revenues, combined with labor unrest and continued inflation. But in 1987 Norway negotiated the sale of gas to EU countries, and the recovery of energy prices in that year brought a partial return to economic stability and prosperity. King Olav died in Jan. 1991; his son Harald V succeeded him in June.

In 1993 the government of Prime Minister Brundtland sought admission to the EU. On Mar. 29, 1994, the EU agreed to admit Norway to membership after long and intricate negotiations limiting Spanish and Portuguese fishing rights in Norwegian waters. But Norweigian voters in a Nov. 1994 referendum rejected EU membership. Brundtland resigned in Oct. 1996 and was replaced by Thorbjoern Jagland, but he remained prime minister less than a year. After 1997 elections to the Storting, a right-wing three-party coalition, which controlled only 24 of the 165 seats, formed a government under Christian Democrat Kjell Magne Bondevik. Even Bondevik's three-week leave of absence (to treat depression) in Sept. 1998 failed to shake the stability of Norway's politics.

▶ **OMAN**
Sultanate of Oman
● **GEOGRAPHY Location:** southeastern Arabian peninsula. **Boundaries**: Gulf of Oman to N, Arabian Sea to E and S, Yemen to SW, Saudi Arabia to W, United Arab Emirates to NW; detached portion of Oman lies at tip of Musandam peninsula, on Strait of Hormuz. **Total area**: 82,031 sq. mi. (212,460 sq km). **Coastline**: 1,299 mi. (2,092 km). **Comparative area**: slightly smaller than Kansas. **Land use**: 0% arable land; negl. % permanent crops; 5% meadows and pastures; negl. % forest and woodland; 95% other; includes negl. % irrigated. **Major cities**: (1993 census) Muscat (capital) 549,150; Al-Batinah 564,677; Al-Sharquia 258,344.
● **PEOPLE Population**: 2,446,645 (1999 est.). **Nationality**: noun—Omani(s); adjective—Omani. **Ethnic groups**: Arab, Baluchi, South Asian, African. **Languages**: Arabic (official), English, Baluchi, Urdu, Indian dialects. **Religions**: 75% Ibadhi Muslim, Sunni Muslim, Shi'a Muslim, Hindu.
● **GOVERNMENT Type**: monarchy. **Constitution**: none. **National holiday**: National Day, Nov. 18. **Head of Government**: Qaboos bin Said, sultan

and prime minister (since July 1970). **Structure:** executive—sultan is hereditary monarch; unicameral legislature-advisory powers only; judiciary—traditional Islamic judges and nascent civil court system.

● **ECONOMY Monetary unit:** Omani rial. **Budget:** (1999 est.) *income:* $4 bil.; *expend.:* $5.6 bil. **GDP:** $18.6 bil., $7,900 per capita (1998 est.). **Chief crops:** dates, limes, bananas, alfalfa, vegetables, cattle, camels; annual fish catch averages 100,000 metric tons. **Natural resources:** crude oil, copper, asbestos, some marble, limestone. **Major industries:** crude oil production and refining, natural gas production, construction. **Labor force:** 850,000 (1997 est.). **Exports:** $7.6 bil. (f.o.b., 1997 est.); petroleum, reexports, fish, metals, textiles. **Imports:** $4 bil. (f.o.b., 1997); machinery, transportation equipment, manufactured goods, food, livestock, lubricants. **Major trading partners:** *exports:* 26% Japan, 19% China, 19% Thailand; *imports:* 23% UAE, 16% Japan, 14% UK.

Oman occupies the southeastern corner of Arabia. From ancient times an important center of trade in the Persian Gulf and the Indian Ocean, Oman was frequently dominated by Persia prior to the mid-18th century. The principal port, Muscat, was captured by the Portuguese in 1508 and held by them until 1659, when the Ottoman Turks took possession. They were driven out in 1741 by Ahmed ibn Said of Yemen, who consolidated the sultanate of Oman in 1744 and founded the present royal line.

In the early 19th century, Oman was the most powerful state in Arabia, controlling Zanzibar in East Africa, the southern coast of Iran, and much of Baluchistan (between Pakistan and Iran). Zanzibar was separated from Oman in 1856, and the Persian coast and much of Baluchistan was detached from Oman during the latter half of the 19th century. In 1958 Oman's sole remaining Baluchi possession, the city-state of Gwadar, was ceded to Pakistan in return for a monetary settlement.

Growing British influence was consolidated by the formation of a British protectorate in 1891, reconfirmed in 1951. In the 1950s Britain aided the sultanate in putting down rebellions in the desert interior. The British protectorate ended with Britain's withdrawal from the gulf in 1971. On July 23, 1970, Sultan Said ibn Taimur was overthrown by his son, Sultan Qaboos bin Said, who instituted a national development program and in 1975 defeated a leftist uprising in the western desert.

Petroleum makes up 95 percent of exports. Banking and shipping services are also important. The country is generally barren, with scattered flocks of sheep and camels. In April 1996 Oman joined with Russia and Kazakhstan to establish a consortium with eight oil companies to build a 900 mile pipeline to move oil to Russia's port in the Black Sea.

▶ **PAKISTAN**
Islamic Republic of Pakistan
● **GEOGRAPHY Location:** southern Asia. **Boundaries.** Afghanistan to N, China to far NE, India to E, Arabian Sea to S, and Iran to W. **Total area:** 310,402 sq. mi. (803,940 sq km). **Coastline:** 650 mi. (1,046 km). **Comparative area:** slightly less than twice the size of California. **Land use:** 27% arable land; 1% permanent crops; 6% meadows and pastures; 5% forest and woodland; 61% other; includes 19% irrigated. **Major cities:** (1991 est.) Islamabad (capital) 400,000; Karachi 7,000,000;

Lahore 3,500,000; Faisalabad (Lyallpur) 2,000,000; Rawalpindi 800,000.
● **PEOPLE Population:** 138,123,359 (1999 est.). **Nationality:** noun—Pakistani(s); adjective—Pakistani. **Ethnic groups:** Punjabi, Sindhi, Pashtun (Pathan), Baloch, Muhajir (immigrants from India and their descendants). **Languages:** 48% Punjabi, 12% Sindhi, 10% Siraiki, 8% Pashtu, 8% Urdu (official), 3% Balochi, 2% Hindko, 1% Brahui, English (official and lingua franca of Pakistani elite and most government ministries), 8% Burushaski and other. **Religions:** 97% Muslim (77% Sunni, 20% Shi'a); 3% Christian, Hindu, and other.
● **GOVERNMENT Type:** republic. **Independence:** Aug. 14, 1947 (from UK). **Constitution:** Apr. 10, 1973; suspended July 5, 1977; restored Dec. 30, 1985. **National holiday:** Pakistan Day, Mar. 23. **Heads of Government:** Mohammad Rafiq Tarar, president (since Jan. 1998); Nawaz Sharif, prime minister (since Feb. 1997). **Structure:** executive—prime minister is head of government; bicameral legislature; judiciary.
● **ECONOMY Monetary unit:** Pakistani rupee. **Budget:** (FY96/97) *income:* $10.8 bil.; *expend.:* $12 bil. **GDP:** $270 bil., $2,000 per capita (1998 est.). **Chief crops:** wheat, rice, sugarcane, cotton; beef, milk, mutton, eggs. **Natural resources:** land, extensive natural gas reserves, limited petroleum, poor quality coal, iron ore. **Major industries:** cotton textiles, food processing. **Labor force:** 37.8 mil.; 47% agriculture, 17% mining and manufacturing, 17% services; extensive export of labor, mostly to the Middle East, and use of child labor. **Exports:** $8.5 bil. (FY97/98); cotton, textiles, clothing, rice, leather, carpets. **Imports:** $10.1 bil. (FY97/98); petroleum, petroleum products, machinery, transportation equipment, cooking oils. **Major trading partners:** *exports:* EU, U.S., Hong Kong; *imports:* EU, Japan, U.S.

Pakistan occupies the heartland of ancient South Asian civilization, in the Indus River valley. Agricultural settlements in that area arose by 3000 B.C., and the great cities at Harappa and Mohenjo-Daro were founded some 500 years later. Indo-European (Aryan) invaders from Central Asia overthrew the ancient civilization around 1500 B.C. and established a new culture that spread throughout Pakistan and northern India. Brahmanism, the religious culture of the early Indo-European invaders, gave rise to Buddhism and Jainism around the sixth century B.C., and evolved into Hinduism in the early centuries A.D. The Indus valley was incorporated into the empire of Alexander the Great, c. 350 B.C., and then into the Mauryan empire of Asoka, which by the third century B.C. controlled all of South Asia except for the southernmost portion of India.

Under various rulers the Indus Valley and the areas to its northwest were a great center of Buddhist culture until the beginning of the eighth century, when the area fell to Muslim Arab invaders. Thereafter, Islam was firmly established throughout the region. But Baluchistan and the Northwest Frontier region became culturally allied to the Persian civilization of Iran and Afghanistan, while Sind and the Punjab were more closely akin to the culture of northern India.

Northern Pakistan was incorporated into the empire of Mahmud of Gazni in the 11th century, and fell to the Mongols in the 13th century. The Indus River became the boundary between the Mongol Inkhanate of Persia and the sultanate of Delhi. The region was conquered by Timur Leng at the end of the 14th century, and after the fall of the Timurid empire was divided between the kingdoms of Sind and Multan, in southern and central Pakistan, and the sultanate of Delhi, in the Punjab. All of Pakistan and northern India was reunited after 1526, when the conquests of Babur established the Mogul empire.

The expansion of British power in India during the 18th century left Pakistan largely untouched; the area was divided among various states, including Sind, the Punjab, Kashmir, and the western reaches of Rajputana. In the first half of the 19th century, British rule extended to the northwest; after the defeat of the Indian Mutiny of 1857, the entire Indus valley came under British rule. Sind and the Punjab were ruled directly by the British, while the native states were ruled as British protectorates.

From the beginning of the 20th century, various nationalist movements arose throughout British India. The Muslim League, under the leadership of Mohammad Ali Jinnah after 1916, advocated greater popular political participation, dominion status for India, and a strong Muslim voice in Indian administration. Muslims and Hindus were allied in the Non-Cooperation movement of the 1920s, but the alliance soon broke down and degenerated into communal frictions. With growing power of the Congress party in Hindu areas and Gandhi's civil disobedience movement in the 1930s, Jinnah's Muslim League charted an increasingly separate course and called for the creation of a separate Muslim state in 1940.

With the British withdrawal from India in 1947, Hindus in the Muslim majority areas of the Indus valley and in East Bengal fled to Hindu northern India, while Muslims in Hindu areas fled in the opposite direction. These massive population movements were accompanied by widespread violence leading to the loss of hundreds of thousands of lives. Jinnah, the father of modern Pakistan, died in 1948. Pakistan, encompassing Sind, the Punjab, Baluchistan, the Northwest Frontier Territories, part of Jammu and Kashmir, and adjacent areas in the west and East Bengal in the east, was granted dominion status within the British Commonwealth in 1947, becoming an independent republic in 1956.

Pakistan joined the Central Treaty Organization and became allied with the West, in contrast to the Soviet-leaning nonalignment of India. In 1958 Gen. Mohammad Ayub Khan seized power in a coup; he was elected president in 1960 and re-elected in 1965. Following border clashes with India in 1962, Pakistan entered into friendly relations with China, which also had engaged in border warfare with India. Ayub Khan resigned as president in early 1969 after failing to put down widespread demonstrations in East Pakistan. A new government was formed under Gen. Yahya Khan, and martial law was declared. A parliamentary victory by the East Pakistani Awami League in December 1970 led to civil war and the secession of East Pakistan in 1971 (see "Bangladesh").

India's intervention on behalf of East Bengal had led to war on a western front with Pakistan. On July 3, 1972, India and Pakistan agreed to a mutual withdrawal of troops and entered into negotiations designed to settle border disputes and other outstanding problems. Diplomatic relations between India and Pakistan were resumed in 1976.

The elections of 1970 that had precipitated the civil war also brought Zulfikar Ali Bhutto to the presidency. He remained in office until July 1977,

when he was overthrown in a military coup led by Gen. Mohammad Zia ul-Haq. He was convicted of complicity in a 1974 political murder and hanged in April 1979. Under Pres. Zia, Pakistan moved toward the implementation of Islamic law in parallel with the constitutional law of Pakistan's parliamentary system. In 1986 Bhutto's daughter, Benazir Bhutto, returned to Pakistan from exile in Europe to organize opposition parties against Pres. Zia; this movement led to widespread rioting in the months that followed.

On Aug. 17, 1988, Pres. Zia, several senior government officials, and the American ambassador were killed in an airplane crash. Since 1988 the position of prime minister has alternated between Benazir Bhutto as head of the Pakistan People's Party and Nawaz Sharif as leader of the Muslim League, each accusing the other in turn of tyranny and corruption, amidst apparently endless tension with India over Jammu-Kashmir. The latter struggle lay at the root of the nuclear-test rivalry in May 1998, after which the prime ministers, Vajpayee and Sharif (back as prime minister since February 1997) attempted to lower the political temperature while not appearing to "cave in" to the other. Sharif's July 1999 agreement in Washington D.C. to withdraw support for Moslems in Kashmir made it appear that he was the one who blinked first.

▶ PALAU
Republic of Palau

● **GEOGRAPHY** **Location:** more than 200 islands, in a chain about 400 mi. (650 km) long, in western central Pacific Ocean; Koror 71°21'N, 134°31'E. **Boundaries:** Guam 720 mi. (1,160 km) to NE, Federated States of Micronesia to E, island of New Guinea to S, Philippines 530 mi. (850 km) to NW. **Total area:** 177 sq. mi. (458 sq km). **Coastline:** 944 mi. (1,519 km). **Comparative area:** slightly more than 2.5 times size of Washington, D.C. **Land use:** N.A.% arable land; N.A.% permanent crops; N.A.% meadows and pastures; N.A.% forest and woodland; N.A.% other. **Major cities:** (1990 census) Koror state 10,501; Koror is the current capital; a new capital is being built at Babelthuap, 20 km northeast.

● **PEOPLE** **Population:** 18,467 (1999 est.). **Nationality:** noun—Palauan(s); adjective—Palauan. **Ethnic groups:** composite of Polynesian, Malayan, and Melanesian races. **Languages:** English (official) in all 16 states; Palauan (official) in 13 states; Sonsoralese, Angaur, Japanese, Tobi in one state each. **Religions:** Christian (Catholic, Seventh-Day Adventist, Jehovah's Witness, the Assembly of God, the Liebenzell Mission, and Latter-Day Saints), 33% Modekngei (indigenous faith).

● **GOVERNMENT** **Type:** constitutional government in free association with the U.S.; the Compact of Free Association entered into force Oct. 1, 1994. **Independence:** Oct. 1, 1994 (from U.S.-administered UN Trusteeship). **Constitution:** Jan. 1, 1981. **National holiday:** Constitution Day, July 9. **Heads of Government:** Kuniwo Nakamura, president (since Jan. 1993). **Structure:** executive—president and vice president popularly elected; legislative—bicameral legislature; judicial—Supreme Court headed by chief justice.

● **ECONOMY** **Monetary unit:** U.S. dollar. **Budget:** (1997 est.) income: $52.9 mil.; expend.: $59.9 mil. **GDP:** $160 mil., $8,800 per capita (1997 est.). **Chief crops:** coconuts, copra, cassava, sweet potatoes. **Livestock:** N.A. **Natural resources:** forests, minerals (especially gold), marine products, deep-seabed minerals. **Major industries:** tourism, craft items (shell, wood, pearl), some commercial fishing and agriculture. **Labor force:** N.A. **Exports:** $14.3 mil. (f.o.b., 1996); trochus, tuna, copra, handicrafts. **Imports:** $72.4 mil. (c.i.f., 1996). **Major trading partners:** U.S., Japan.

The first inhabitants of Palau (or Belau) probably arrived from Indonesia and the Philippines about 1500 B.C. The first European to visit the area was Ferdinand Magellan, in 1521. However, it was the British who dominated trade to Palau until 1885, when Pope Leo XIII acknowledged Spain's claims to the Carolines. Spain controlled Palau from 1885 to 1899, when it sold the territory to Germany. The Germans introduced coconut planting and phosphate mining, and introduced sanitary measures that arrested the deadly epidemics of dysentery and influenza, which over 120 years had reduced the population from 40,000 to 4,000.

Japan occupied Palau in 1914, and over the next 30 years increased the mining, agriculture, and fishing industries. In 1938, Palau became a closed military area, and it was the site of heavy fighting during World War II. On July 18, 1947, the United Nations Trusteeship Council placed the Trust Territory of the Pacific Islands, including Palau, under U.S. authority. This trusteeship ended on Oct. 1, 1994, when the Compact of Free Association with the United States (approved by the voters of Palau) went into effect, making Palau an independent country in association with the United States. The United States continues to provide for Palau's defense and to provide aid. In return, the United States has the right to dock military vessels (including nuclear-powered vessels) in the islands for 50 years, and will consult closely on economic and environmental matters.

▶ PANAMA
Republic of Panama

● **GEOGRAPHY Location:** southern Central America. **Boundaries:** Caribbean Sea to N, Colombia to E, Pacific Ocean to S, Costa Rica to W. **Total area:** 30,193 sq. mi. (78,200 sq km). **Coastline:** 1,546 mi. (2,490 km). **Comparative area:** slightly smaller than South Carolina. **Land use:** 7% arable land; 2% permanent crops; 20% meadows and pastures; 44% forest and woodland; 27% other; includes negl. % irrigated. **Major cities:** (1992 est.) Panamá (Panama City—capital) 625,150; Colón 137,825; David 99,811.
● **PEOPLE Population:** 2,778,526 (1999 est.). **Nationality:** noun—Panamanian(s); adjective—Panamanian. **Ethnic groups:** 70% mestizo, 14% Amerindian and mixed (West Indian), 10% white, 6% Amerindian. **Languages:** Spanish (official), 14% speak English as native tongue; many Panamanians are bilingual. **Religions:** 85% Roman Catholic, 15% Protestant.
● **GOVERNMENT Type:** constitutional republic. **Independence:** Nov. 3, 1903 (from Colombia); became independent from Spain Nov. 28, 1821. **Constitution:** Oct. 11, 1972, with major reforms adopted in Apr. 1983. **National holiday:** Independence Day, Nov. 3. **Head of Government:** Mireya Elisa Moscoso Rodríguez, president (since Sept. 1999). **Structure:** executive—president, two vice presidents, cabinet; unicameral legislature; judiciary.
● **ECONOMY Monetary unit:** balboa. **Budget:** (1997) *income:* $2.4 bil.; *expend.:* $2.4 bil. **GDP:** $19.9 bil., $7,300 per capita (1998 est.). **Chief crops:** bananas, rice, sugarcane, coffee, corn;

livestock, fishing. **Natural resources:** copper, mahogany forests, shrimp. **Major industries:** manufacturing and construction, petroleum refining, brewing, cement and other construction material. **Labor force:** 1.044 mil. (1997 est.); 31.8% government and community services, 26.8% agriculture, hunting, and fishing, 16.4% commerce, restaurants, and hotels, 9.4% manufacturing and mining. **Exports:** $6.68 bil. (f.o.b., 1997); 43% bananas, 11% shrimp, 5% clothing, 4% sugar, 2% coffee. **Imports:** $7.38 bil. (f.o.b., 1997); 21% capital goods, 11% crude oil, 9% foodstuffs. **Major trading partners:** *exports:* 37% U.S., EU, Central America; *imports:* 48% U.S., EU, Central America and Caribbean.

The Spanish first arrived in what is now Panama in 1501. Vasco Nuñez de Balboa returned in 1510, and Pedro Arias Dávila founded the City of Panama in 1519. Panama became attached to the viceroyalty of New Granada after 1739 and left the Spanish empire with the rest of New Granada in 1821, becoming a part of Gran Colombia. The first canal company proposing the construction of a transisthmian passageway was formed in 1825-26. The completion of a U.S.-financed railway from Colón to Panama City by 1855 enhanced Panama's importance as a transoceanic passage.

Panamanian nationalists waged a "War of a Thousand Days" against the Bogotá government between 1899 and 1902. In 1903 Panama gained independence from Colombia with U.S. complicity. Within a month Panamanian officials accepted an agreement with the United States that created a canal zone under the control of the U.S. government "in perpetuity," and the Panama Canal was completed and opened in 1914.

Panama experienced protectorate status under U.S. control after independence insofar as the United States "guaranteed the independence" of Panama. The United States explicitly upheld its right of unilateral military intervention in Panama when in 1918 it sent troops there without the permission of the Panamanian government. The 1936 Hull-Alvaro Treaty eliminated protectorate status, and the United States dropped its claim to a right of intervention in the cities of Panama and Colón.

In 1968 a power struggle between Pres. Arnulfo Arias and the Panamanian National Guard led to the ouster of the president. A National Guard junta took control of the government, and Col. (later Gen.) Omar Torrijos Herrera became the ruler of the country the following year. In 1972 a new assembly under Torrijos's control offered him the title of Jefe Maximo (chief executive) in addition to drafting a new constitution for the country. Torrijos constructed a populist following through the creation of housing projects, a new labor code, an agrarian reform, and an increase in tax rates imposed on foreign banana-interests.

The Panamanian government and the United States concluded a new canal treaty in 1977, the key provisions of which included integration of the Canal Zone with the rest of Panamanian territory and full Panamanian control of the canal in the year 2000. In 1981 Omar Torrijos died in an air accident.

In 1988 the head of the military and de facto ruler of the country, Gen. Mañuel Noriega, was indicted in the U.S. on narcotics charges. But Noriega refused to submit to demands by the U.S. and by Panamanian president Eric Arturo Delvalle for his resignation. Delvalle was forced to go into hiding, and Manuel Solis Palma replaced him in the presidency. The United States responded by freezing Panamanian assets in the United States.

In May 1989 Gen. Noriega annulled election results that showed him losing to Guillermo Endara and assumed the role of dictator. After an unsuccessful coup attempt, the United States invaded Panama on December 20, captured Noriega, and brought him to Miami, where he was convicted on narcotics charges. Endara was restored to the presidency and in December 1990 U.S. forces helped put down a rebellion led by Noriega's former chief of the national police.

Endara's government was often accused of corruption but he left power peacefully in 1994. He helped to arrange honest elections that saw U.S.-educated businessman Ernesto Perez Balladares come to power with promises of improving the economy as Panama prepares to take over control of the canal. His free market reforms and a loosening of trade barriers (Panama joined WTO in 1998) have brought strong growth in GDP. An August 1998 referendum turned down (by 64 percent) Perez' seeking a second term. Voters in May 1999 chose Mireya Moscoso de Grubar, widow of three-time president Arnulfo Arias, over Martin Torrijos, son of the dictator who negotiated the 1977 Canal Treaty with the U.S., as Panama's new president.

▶PAPUA NEW GUINEA
Independent State of Papua New Guinea
● **GEOGRAPHY Location:** eastern section of island of New Guinea and about 600 smaller islands in Bismarck Archipelago (New Britain, New Ireland, and Manus) and northern part of Solomon Islands. Port Moresby 9°30'S, 147°07'E. **Boundaries**: Bismarck Sea to N, Solomon Sea to E, Australia to S, and Indonesia to W. **Total area:** 178,259 sq. mi. (461,690 sq km). **Coastline:** 3,202 mi. (5,152 km). **Comparative area:** slightly larger than California. **Land use:** 0.1% arable land; 1% permanent crops; 0% meadows and pastures; 92.9% forest and woodland; 6% other. **Major cities** (1990 est.) Port Moresby (administrative capital) 173,500.
● **PEOPLE Population:** 4,705,126 (1999 est.). **Nationality:** noun—Papua New Guinean(s); adjective—Papua New Guinean. **Ethnic groups:** predominantly Melanesian and Papuan; some Negrito, Micronesian, and Polynesian. **Languages:** 715 indigenous languages; English spoken by 1%-2%, pidgin English widespread, Motu spoken in Papua region. **Religions:** 22% Roman Catholic, 16% Lutheran, 28% other Christian, 34% indigenous beliefs.
● **GOVERNMENT Type:** parliamentary democracy. **Independence:** Sept. 16, 1975 (from UN trusteeship under Australian administration). **Constitution:** Sept. 16, 1975. **National holiday:** Independence Day, Sept. 16. **Heads of Government:** Silas Atopare, governor-general (since Nov. 1997); Sir Mekere Morauta, prime minister (since July 1999). **Structure:** executive—British monarch (represented by governor general), chief of state, prime minister; unicameral legislature; judiciary.
● **ECONOMY Monetary unit:** kina. **Budget:** (1997 est.) *income:* $1.5 bil.; *expend.:* $1.35 bil. **GDP:** $11.1 bil., $2,400 per capita (1998 est.). **Chief crops:** cocoa, coffee, coconuts, rubber, palm kernels; pigs, chickens. **Natural resources:** gold, copper, silver, natural gas, timber. **Major industries:** copra crushing, palmoil processing, plywood processing. **Labor force:** 1.941 mil., 64% agriculture. **Exports:** $2.2 bil. (f.o.b., 1997 est.); gold, copper ore, oil, logs, coffee, palm oil, cocoa, lobster. **Imports:** $1.5 bil. (c.i.f., 1997 est.); machinery and transport equipment, manufactured goods, food, fuels, chemicals. **Major trading partners:** *exports:* Australia, Japan, Germany; *imports:* Australia, Singapore, Japan.

The island of New Guinea, the world's second-largest, was settled many thousands of years ago by waves of Papuan and Melanesian migrants who developed large numbers of linguistically diverse and mutually hostile tribes of hunters and small cultivators. In the 19th century, the island was divided between the Dutch (to the west, in what is now the Indonesian province of Irian Jaya), Germany, and the British. The German sector was occupied by Australia in 1914 and administered under a League of Nations mandate after World War I.

Japanese attempts to occupy New Guinea in 1942 met with only partial success. In a series of counteroffensives, the Allies regained control over the entire island by mid-1944.

Beginning in 1949 the former German and British colonies were administered jointly by Australia under a UN mandate. The territories were made self-governing in 1973 and achieved full independence as Papua New Guinea on Sept. 16, 1975. The nation maintains close ties with Australia. Relations are strained with Indonesia, which accuses Papua New Guinea of aiding an Irian Jaya liberation movement.

Most of the population is still engaged in small-scale agriculture. Mining is a major source of foreign investment and export earnings. An ongoing rebellion on the island of Bougainville since 1989 has closed a large Australian-run copper mine, led to the deaths of many people (including, in 1996, Bougainville's chief minister, Theodore Miriung), and frightened away many potential foreign investors. An inexplicable decision to recognize Taiwan rather than mainland China, made July 5, 1999 by politically shaky and personally unstable prime minister Bill Skate, brought domestic (as well as Chinese) opposition, Skate's resignation, and the designation of Sir Mekere Morauta as the new prime minister.

▶PARAGUAY
Republic of Paraguay
● **GEOGRAPHY Location:** landlocked country in central South America. **Boundaries:** Bolivia to N, Brazil to E, Argentina to S and W. **Total area:** 157,046 sq. mi. (406,750 sq km). **Coastline:** none. **Comparative area:** slightly smaller than California. **Land use:** 6% arable land; 0% permanent crops; 55% meadows and pastures; 32% forest and woodland; 7% other; includes negl. % irrigated. **Major cities:** (1992 census) Asunción (capital) 637,737; Ciudad del Este (formerly Presidente Stroessner) 133,893; Pedro Juan Caballero (1982) 37,331; Encarnación (1982) 27,632; Villarrica (1982) 21,203.
● **PEOPLE Population:** 5,434,095 (1999 est.). **Nationality:** noun—Paraguayan(s); adjective—Paraguayan. **Ethnic groups:** 95% mestizo, 5% white and Amerindian. **Languages:** Spanish (official), Guaraní. **Religions:** 90% Roman Catholic, Mennonite and other Protestant denominations.
● **GOVERNMENT Type:** republic. **Independence:** May 14, 1811 (from Spain). **Constitution:** June 20, 1992. **National holiday:** Independence Days, May 14-15. **Head of Government:** Luis Ángel González Macchi, president (since Mar. 1999). **Structure:** president heads executive; bicameral legislature (Senate, Chamber of Deputies); judiciary.

●**Economy** **Monetary unit:** guarani. **Budget:** (1995 est.) *income:* $1.25 bil.; *expend.:* $1.66 bil. **GDP:** $19.8 bil., $3,700 per capita (1998 est.). **Chief crops:** sugarcane, soybeans, cotton, wheat; beef, pork; timber. **Natural resources:** iron ore, manganese, limestone, hydropower, timber. **Major industries:** meat packing, oilseed crushing, milling. **Labor force:** 1.8 mil. (1995 est.); 45% agriculture; 8.2% unemployment (1996 est.). **Exports:** $1.1 bil. (f.o.b., 1997); cotton, soybeans, timber, vegetable oils, coffee, tung oil. **Imports:** $2.5 bil. (c.i.f., 1996); capital goods, foodstuffs, consumer goods, raw materials, fuels. **Major trading partners:** *exports:* 48% Brazil, 22% Netherlands, 9% Argentina; *imports:* 29% Brazil, 22% U.S., 14% Argentina.

When Europeans arrived in what is now Paraguay in the early 16th century, they encountered various groups of semisedentary and nonsedentary indigenous peoples. The Spanish entered into alliances with the Tupian semisedentary Guaraní against the nomadic Guaycuru Indians in the west of the region. Asunción, founded in 1537, was little more than a Spanish defense outpost against the Portuguese and a trading stopover between the silver mines of Potosí and Buenos Aires.

From early in the 17th century, the Jesuits established an extensive network of missions in the southern portion of the colony, and a rivalry grew between the Jesuits and the elites of Asunción over who would determine the colony's social and economic structure. The isolation of the settlers from the mainstream of Spanish colonial society combined with the lack of valuable resources led to the evolution of a relatively egalitarian social structure. The political elite of Asunción deposed Spanish authority in 1811, and Paraguayan independence was declared in 1813.

Authoritarian rule marked the period from independence until 1870. José Gaspar Rodríguez de Francia was declared ruler for life in 1816 and remained in power until his death in 1840. A period of political turmoil followed but was resolved in the election of Carlos Antonio López in 1844; in 1857 he was named president for life. López chose his son Francisco Solano López to succeed him in office in 1862. He intervened in a Brazilian attempt to control the fate of Uruguay, beginning the Paraguayan War, or the War of the Triple Alliance (Brazil, Argentina, Uruguay) from 1865 to 1870. The war was catastrophic for Paraguay, reducing the population from 450,000 to 220,000; almost the entire male population was killed, and Paraguay lost 60,000 square miles of territory while being saddled with a war debt of 19 million gold pesos ($200,000,000). The Brazilian government later dropped the unrealistic payment demand.

After the war the Colorado and Liberal parties developed, although the real political distinctions were dependent more on individuals and families than political ideology. Colorado-party general Bernardino Caballero, backed by Brazil, was the power behind the scenes of frequent changes in government personnel between 1874 and 1904. The Liberals, backed by Argentina, were in power from 1904 until 1936.

After 18 years of authoritarian military rule, Gen. Alfredo Stroessner, with the backing of Colorado party factions, began his rule in 1954. Stroessner held power until 1989, when Gen. Andrés Rodríguez overthrew him. Nevertheless, the Colorados maintained their hold on the presidency in hotly contested elections in 1993, when Juan Carlos Wasmosy gained 40 percent of the vote. However, a strong showing by the opposition Authentic Radical Liberal Party (PLRA) and National Encounter prevented a Colorado majority in Congress. A complex political struggle between Pres. Wasmosy and Lino Oviedo, one of the generals who overthrew Stroessner, led to Oviedo's imprisonment. His ally, Raul Cubas Grau, won the 1998 election by vowing to have Oviedo share power even from prison. Three days after taking office in August, however, Cubas released the popular general, causing an outburst of hostility among Congressional leaders.

In the extraordinary last week of March 1999, the vice president was assassinated, Congress accusing Cubas and Oviedo. Impeached the next day, Cubas remanded Oviedo to state custody but refused to appear at his own trial in the Senate. Oviedo fled to Argentina, Cubas to Brazil. Congress named the president of the Senate, Luis Gonzalez Macchi, as president of Paraguay. No coup ensuing, Gonzalez appointed a cabinet with four opposition members among the 10, the first coalition since 1946.

▶**PERU**
Republic of Peru
●**Geography** **Location:** western coast of South America. **Boundaries:** Ecuador, Colombia to N, Brazil, Bolivia to E, Chile to S, Pacific Ocean to W. **Total area:** 496,224 sq. mi. (1,285,220 sq km). **Coastline:** 1,546 mi. (2,414 km). **Comparative area:** slightly smaller than Alaska. **Land use:** 3% arable land; negl. % permanent crops; 21% meadows and pastures; 66% forest and woodland; 10% other; includes 1% irrigated. **Major cities:** (1993 est.) Lima (capital) 5,706,127; Arequipa 619,156; Trujillo 509,312; Chiclayo 411,536; Callao 3699,768.

●**People** **Population:** 26,624,582 (1999 est.). **Nationality:** noun—Peruvian(s); adjective—Peruvian. **Ethnic groups:** 45% Amerindian, 37% mestizo, 15% white, 3% black, Japanese, Chinese, and other. **Languages:** Spanish and Quechua (official), Aymara. **Religions:** predominantly Roman Catholic.

●**Government** **Type:** republic. **Independence:** July 28, 1821 (from Spain). **Constitution:** Dec. 31, 1993. **National holiday:** Independence Day, July 28. **Heads of Government:** Alberto Fujimori, president (since July 1990); Victor Joy Way Rojas, prime minister (since Jan. 1999). **Structure:** executive; unicameral legislature; judiciary.

●**Economy** **Monetary unit:** nuevo sol. **Budget:** (1996 est.) *income:* $8.5 bil.; *expend.:* $9.3 bil. **GDP:** $111.8 bil., $4,300 per capita (1998 est.). **Chief crops:** coffee, cotton, sugarcane, rice, poultry, meat, wool; fish. **Natural resources:** copper, silver, gold, petroleum, timber. **Major industries:** mining of metals, petroleum, fishing. **Labor force:** 7.6 mil. (1996); agriculture, mining and quarrying, manufacturing, construction, transport, services; 8.2% unemployment (1996 est.). **Exports:** $6.8 bil. (f.o.b., 1997 est.); copper, zinc, fishmeal, petroleum. **Imports:** $10.8 bil. (c.i.f., 1997 est.); machinery, transport equipment, foodstuffs, petroleum. **Major trading partners:** *exports:* 20% U.S., 7% Japan, 7% UK; *imports:* 31% U.S., 7% Colombia, 6% Chile.

Peru was the site of the civilization of the Inca empire before the arrival of Europeans. The Incas had extended their control over most of the Andean region by the late 15th century. The civilization was advanced in terms of its ability to provide for the welfare of its subjects and was in possession of sophisticated knowledge in a number of fields, including medicine. By the time of the arrival of the Spanish conqueror Francisco Pizarro in 1532, the empire was already in decline, and a combination of plague and civil war in the decade prior to the appearance of Europeans no doubt made the empire more vulnerable to Spanish conquest. Inca resistance to Spanish domination was not quelled until the execution of Tupac Amarú in 1571. European-borne diseases such as smallpox and measles devastated the Indian population of the region.

Because of the great wealth of precious metals discovered by the Spanish and the adaptability of a sedentary indigenous civilization to the imposition of Spanish imperial control, Peru quickly became a major focal point of Spanish colonialism in the Americas; they founded Lima in 1535. The viceroyalty of Peru, established in 1544, originally served as the political and administrative nerve center of Spanish colonization of South America. For nearly two centuries, Lima was the seat of power and wealth for the whole region. Peru was "liberated" by Simón Bolívar and José de San Martín in 1821 when Bolívar's army defeated the royalist forces at the battles of Junín and Ayacucho.

In the 40 years after independence, the presidency changed hands 35 times, and the country generated at least 15 different constitutions. Only four of the presidents of the period were constitutionally chosen, and the vast majority of the chief executives were military figures. In 1829 Peru tried and failed to annex Ecuador; in the 1830s an attempt at political federation between Peru and Bolivia collapsed with the Chilean invasion of 1839.

A political movement in favor of civilian rule, the Civilistas, began to organize by the 1860s. Chile defeated Peru in the War of the Pacific (1879-83), and Chileans occupied Lima and its port city of Callao for two years. The Peruvian government was deeply in debt after the war, resulting in the loss of ownership of much of Peru's infrastructure and natural resources to foreigners.

Peru experienced a period of civilian leadership between 1895 and 1930. Pres. Augusto B. Leguía (1908-12, 1919-30) extended his rule in an extraconstitutional manner until 1930, when Col. Luis Sánchez Cerro seized power; he ruled until his assassination in 1933. Gen. Oscar Benavides succeeded Cerro and managed to restore confidence in the economy. In 1939 civilian banker Manuel Prado was elected to the presidency, and the military allowed him to complete his term in office, which expired in 1945. During Prado's administration, Peru went to war with Ecuador and was victorious, seizing a great deal of territory.

Víctor Raúl Haya de la Torre founded Peru's most prominent political party, the American Popular Revolutionary Alliance (APRA), in 1924. As initiated, the party put forward an "anti-imperialist" platform aiming at nationalization of land and reconstruction of society in favor of oppressed people. Haya de la Torre was apparently fraudulently deprived of a presidential electoral victory in 1931. The following year Apristas (APRA supporters) seized Trujillo and killed some military personnel. By way of revenge, the army massacred 6,000 Apristas. The result was a continuing enmity between the Peruvian armed forces and the APRA party lasting until the 1980s. Although APRA clearly had majority support from the Peruvian electorate in the intervening period, the party was not allowed to take power directly until 1985.

The Peruvian military, led by Gen. Juan Velasco Alvarado, seized power in 1968 and embarked upon a course of reform that included the nationalization of Standard Oil's International Petroleum Company holdings. The Peruvian military took steps to restructure economic and political power in the country by joining the Andean Pact and undermining the power of the traditional agricultural elite in the country by sponsoring an agrarian reform that mobilized peasant sectors of the population and changed the relations between landlord and peasant.

The presidency of Peru returned to civilian leadership under Fernando Belaúnde Terry (1980-85). In 1985, the military allowed the APRA presidential candidate, Alan García Pérez, to take office. García promised to spend no more than 10 percent of the country's export earnings on payment of Peru's huge outstanding foreign debt and he was popular during his first years in office. But his public support was undermined by a growing insurgency sponsored by the Sendero Luminoso ("Shining Path") Maoist guerrillas and by runaway inflation.

On June 10, 1990, political novice Alberto Fujimori, the son of Japanese immigrants, defeated the well-known writer Mario Vargas Llosa for the presidency.

Throughout 1991 and 1992, Shining Path's influence spread, demoralizing and almost paralyzing the government, and at a cost of 25,000 lives. But in April 1992, Fujimoro implemented a "zero tolerance" policy toward terrorism, dissolving the legislature and proclaiming martial law. The capture in September of Abimael Guzmán Reynoso, Path's founder-leader, broke the back of the insurgency. The movement lived on, but diminished in numbers to under 1000, and its last commander was captures in July 1999. Congress and constitutional government were back by 1993. Meanwhile, economically, Fujimori pursued free-market reforms, taming runaway inflation and privatizing state-run dinosaurs, with the result that by 1994 the Peruvian economy was growing at a rate of 12 percent, fastest in the world. In April of that year, Fujimoro was elected to a second term with 64 percent of the vote.

The dramatic liberation in April 1997 of 600 prisoners held for ransom in the Japanese ambassador's compound by another radical terrorist group maintained the president's repute. In Nov. 1997, Peru completed negotiations with Ecuador (the treaty being signed in Oct. of 1998) ending a 50-year old border conflict. But all these achievements were accompanied by a rather ham-handed authoritarian streak which cost Fujimori much esteem. In June 1998 he tried to amend this image by sacking premier Alberto Pandolfi, replacing him with human-rights advocate Javier Valle; but the two could not work together and Pandolfi resigned. In 1999 Fujimori dismissed five cabinet officers when one of them accused the Customs service (a Fujimori "showpiece" of reform and modernization) of fraud and corruption; and then, at month's end, having to mobilize 20,000 police against a general strike, backed by the four main opposition parties, aimed at both the widespread enduring poverty and Fujimori's apparent intention to run in 2000 for an (unconstitutional) third term.

▶ PHILIPPINES
Republic of the Philippines

• **GEOGRAPHY Location:** archipelago of some 7,100 islands about 500 mi. (800 km) off southeastern Asia; about 1,100 mi. (2,800 km) from N to S and 650 mi. (1,684 km) from W to E; Luzon in N and Mindanao in S account for 66% of land area. Manila 14°36'N, 120°59'E. **Boundaries:** Luzon Strait to N, Philippine Sea to E, Celebes Sea to S, Sulu Sea to SW, and South China Sea to W. **Total area:** 115,830 sq. mi. (300,000 sq km). **Coastline:** 22,554 mi. (36,289 km). **Comparative area:** slightly larger than Arizona. **Land use:** 19% arable land; 12% permanent crops; 4% meadows and pastures; 46% forest and woodland; 19% other; includes 5% irrigated. **Major cities:** (1990 census) Manila (capital) 1,598,918; Quezon City 1,666,766; Davao City 849,947; Caloocan City 761,011; Cebu City 610,417.

• **PEOPLE Population:** 79,345,812 (1999 est.). **Nationality:** noun—Filipino(s); adjective—Philippine. **Ethnic groups:** 91.5% Christian Malay, 4% Muslim Malay, 1.5% Chinese, 3% other. **Languages:** Pilipino (based on Tagalog) and English (both official). **Religions:** 83% Roman Catholic, 9% Protestant, 5% Muslim, 3% Buddhist and other.

• **GOVERNMENT Type:** republic. **Independence:** July 4, 1946 (from U.S.). **Constitution:** Feb. 2, 1987, effective Feb. 11, 1987. **National holiday:** Independence Day, June 12. **Head of Government:** Joseph Estrada, president (since June 1998). **Structure:** executive; bicameral legislature; judiciary.

• **ECONOMY Monetary unit:** Philippine peso. **Budget:** (1998) *income:* $14.5 bil.; *expend.:* $12.6 bil. **GDP:** $270.5 bil., $3,500 per capita (1998 est.). **Chief crops:** rice, corn, coconut, sugarcane, bananas; pork, eggs, beef; fish. **Natural resources:** timber, crude oil, nickel, cobalt, silver. **Major industries:** textiles, pharmaceuticals, chemicals. **Labor force:** 31.3 mil. (1998 est.); 39.8% agriculture, 19.4% government services, 17.7% services; 9.6% unemployment (1998). **Exports:** $25 bil. (f.o.b., 1998); 51% electronics and telecommunications, 10% machinery and transport, 9% garments. **Imports:** $29 bil. (f.o.b., 1998); 43% raw materials and intermediate goods, 36% capital goods, 9% consumer goods, 9% fuels. **Major trading partners:** *exports:* 34% U.S., 17% Japan, 17% EU; *imports:* 21% Japan, 20% U.S., 12% ASEAN.

The Philippines were anciently settled by various Malayan peoples in several waves of migration from Southeast Asia. Tribal societies coexisted with petty principalities that had trade links to China, the East Indies, and countries in the Indian Ocean. The Philippines were visited by Magellan (who was killed there) in 1521, and Spanish conquest of the islands began in 1564. The Spanish colonial capital at Manila was founded in 1571 and became a key transit point for trade between Mexico and the Far East. Under Spanish rule a majority of Filipinos became Christian except in the southwestern islands, which remained Muslim. The Spanish period as a whole was marked by a torpid colonial administration and a gradual rise in the power and wealth of the Catholic church.

In the late 19th century, a nationalist movement led by José Rizal gained a wide following. In 1896 an armed uprising began, led by Emilio Aguinaldo. The 1898 victory of Adm. George Dewey at the Battle of Manila Bay during the Spanish-American War led Spain to cede the

Philippines to the United States in return for a payment of $20 million. Expecting immediate independence with U.S. support, Aguinaldo declared the islands a republic. When this was not recognized by the United States, Aguinaldo led a new war for independence, which was bloodily suppressed by American troops in a six-year campaign, 1899-1905.

American policy in the Philippines combined military control with a desire to encourage home rule leading to independence. In 1935 the Commonwealth of the Philippines was established, with Manuel Quezon as its first president, beginning what was conceived of as a 10-year period of controlled autonomy leading to full independence on July 4, 1946. In November 1941, Quezon was reelected to the presidency. On Dec.8, 1941, Japan attacked Manila and destroyed the American bases there. American and Filipino troops, after weeks of fierce fighting, evacuated the islands in March 1942. The battle to recapture the Philippines began with the Battle of Leyte Gulf in October 1944 and was completed by July 1945.

In April 1946, Manuel Roxas was elected president of the Commonwealth. Independence came as scheduled on July 4 of that year, with the United States retaining military bases by treaty and establishing a special economic relationship with the Philippines. The leftist Hukbalahap Rebellion, originally a partisan campaign against the Japanese, caused severe difficulties for the new nation until it was finally defeated in military campaigns led by Ramon Magsaysay who was elected to the presidency in November 1953.

The early years of independence were marked by some economic development, but also great economic inequality. Most land was held by huge estates, and the economy depended primarily on plantation crops (sugar, copra), mining, and timber. Villagers fleeing the rural subsistence economy poured into the cities, leading to huge slums and a climate of urban poverty and violence. Many Filipinos emigrated to America.

In 1966 Ferdinand Marcos was elected president on a reform platform. Overwhelmed in the early 1970s by demonstrations, a new leftist guerrilla movement, and a separatist rebellion by Islamic Moros in Mindinao, Marcos declared martial law on Sept. 21, 1972. On Jan. 17, 1973, Marcos promulgated a new constitution giving unprecedented power to the presidency. His wife, Imelda, began to wield considerable influence, and the climate of unrest, poverty, and corruption worsened throughout the 1970s. Martial law was lifted, however, on Jan. 17, 1981, and Marcos was reelected to a new six-year term as president.

The airport assassination of opposition leader Benigno Aquino on his return to the Philippines on Aug. 21, 1983, led to a new phase in opposition to Marcos's rule. Marcos retained a majority in elections to the National Assembly in 1984, amid widespread reports of electoral fraud. In a bitterly contested presidential election in February 1986, Marcos was officially declared the winner over Aquino's widow, Corazon. Mrs. Aquino also declared herself the winner, and her supporters took to the streets in massive anti-Marcos demonstrations. Deserted by key supporters in the military, church, and middle class, Marcos fled the country on Feb. 25, 1986. Mrs. Aquino took office pledging land reform, a new constitution, and a commission to recover the wealth Marcos had plundered.

Under Pres. Aquino the Philippines remained unsettled. Her former ally, Vice Pres. Salvadore

Laurel, formed an opposition party. Military and political measures aimed at putting down the Communist insurrection yielded mixed results. The economy of the Philippines continued to be dependent on U.S. and international assistance, and sentiment against the continued presence of U.S. military bases (Clark Air Base, Subic Bay Naval Base, and four smaller installations) was strong. Ironically, an eruption of Mount Pinatubo in June 1991 caused massive devastations in central Luzon and destroyed Clark Air Base. In September, the national legislature voted not to renew the leases on American military bases; the United States moved to close Subic Bay Naval Base.

Aquino declined to run for reelection in 1992. Fidel Ramos won the presidency in a field of strong contenders, including Imelda Marcos, who was decisively rejected by the voters. Lifted by a coalition that gave him a controlling majority in both houses of Congress after the 1994 legislative elections, Ramos made "national reconciliation" his highest domestic priority. In 1994 he proclaimed a cease-fire and amnesty for various insurgencies, though the Moro rebellion on Mindinao has since flared up again.

The Philippines' robust economic growth was slowed but not crippled by the Asian economic crisis of 1997-98. After some hesitation, Pres. Ramos decided not to seek re-election in1998; in a crowded field of candidates, Joseph Estrada, a popular actor, won the presidential election of May 11, 1998, but the ruling LAKAS party elected the vice-president and took 115 of the 208 lower house seats. Late in 1998 the long-running dispute with China over the Spratly Islands heated up, the Philippine Navy sequestering Chinese fishing boats. And in Feb. 1999, the Maoist kidnapping of General Obillo showed that domestic peace was not at hand.

▶ **POLAND**
Republic of Poland
● **GEOGRAPHY** **Location:** eastern Europe. **Boundaries**: Baltic Sea to N, Russia and Lithuania to NE, Belarus and Ukraine to E, Czech Republic and Slovakia to S, Germany to W. **Total area**: 120,726 sq. mi. (312,680 sq km). **Coastline**: 305 mi. (491 km). **Comparative area**: slightly smaller than New Mexico. **Land use**: 47% arable land; 1% permanent crops; 13% meadows and pastures; 29% forest and woodland; 10% other; includes negl. % irrigated. **Major cities**: (1994 est.) Warszawa (Warsaw, capital) 1,640,700; Lodz 828,500; Krakow (Cracow) 746,000; Wroclaw 642,900; Poznan 582,300.
● **PEOPLE** **Population:** 38,608,929 (1999 est.). **Nationality: noun**—Pole(s); **adjective**—Polish. **Ethnic groups:** 97.6% Polish, 1.3% German, 0.6% Ukrainian, 0.5% Byelorussian. **Languages:** Polish. **Religions:** 95% Roman Catholic (about 75% practicing), 5% Eastern Orthodox, Protestant, and other.
● **GOVERNMENT** **Type:** democratic state. **Independence:** Nov. 11, 1918 (independent republic proclaimed) **Constitution:** Oct. 16, 1997; adopted by the National Assembly on Apr. 2, 1997; passed by national referendum May 23, 1997. **National holiday:** Constitution Day, May 3. **Heads of Government:** Aleksander Kwasniewski, president (since Dec. 1995); Jerzy Buzek, prime minister (since Oct. 1997). **Structure:** executive—prime minister is head of government; bicameral legislature—4 seats in lower house are constitutionally assigned to ethnic German parties; judiciary.

● **ECONOMY** **Monetary unit:** zloty. **Budget:** (1997 est.) **income:** $36.5 bil.; **expend.:** $38.3 bil. **GDP:** $263 bil., $6,800 per capita (1998 est.). **Chief crops:** potatoes, milk, cheese, fruits, vegetables, wheat; poultry and eggs; pork, beef. **Natural resources:** coal, sulfur, copper, natural gas, silver. **Major industries:** machine building, iron and steel, extractive industries. **Labor force:** 17.4 mil. (1998); 29.9% industry and construction, 26% agriculture, 44.1% services. **Exports:** $27.2 bil. (f.o.b., 1997 est.); 57% manufactured goods, chemicals; 21% machinery and equipment; 12% food and live animals. **Imports:** $38.5 bil. (f.o.b., 1997 est.); 43% manufactured goods, chemicals; 36% machinery and equipment; 9% mineral fuels. **Major trading partners:** *exports:* 32.9% Germany, 8.4% Russia, 5.9% Italy; *imports:* 24.1% Germany, 9.9% Italy, 6.3% Russia.

The Slavic people known as Polonians accepted Christianity in the second half of the 10th century, during the reign of Duke Mieszko, whose close relationship with the papacy prevented the Holy Roman Empire from absorbing Poland. A strong and united Polish kingdom existed under the Piast dynasty until 1370. With that dynasty's extinction, the Anjou king of Hungary succeeded to the throne, followed by his daughter Jadwiga, who in 1386 married the grand duke of Lithuania. Thus was formed the great Commonwealth of Poland-Lithuania.

With the extinction of the Jagellonian line in 1572, the monarchy became elective. With a large nobility, equaling about 10 percent of the population, the monarchy grew weak, and Poland increasingly was subject to foreign intervention. The rise of the expansionist powers of Sweden, Prussia, Russia, and Austria came in part at the expense of the Poles. Jan Sobieski (1624-96), who ruled Poland as John III, saved Vienna from the Turks and briefly revived the Polish monarchy, but Polish royal power ended with his death. In a series of partitions in 1772, 1793, and 1795, Poland was dismembered and finally obliterated as a state.

Napoleon revived a Polish national entity with the Grand Duchy of Warsaw; with Napoleon's fall, the Congress of Vienna re-created a Kingdom of Poland in 1815, under the rule of the czar of Russia. After 1830 Poland was subjected to systematic Russification.

The fall of Russia in World War I led to Poland's revival. The Lithuanian Socialist Jósef Pilsudski led Poland in war against the new Bolshevik government of Russia until, in the 1921 Treaty of Riga, Poland emerged with its boundaries restored to approximately those after the partition of 1793. It was ethnically about 70 percent Polish, a triumph for Polish nationalism but the end of Pilsudski's dream of a federation of northeastern Europe. Poland also had the largest Jewish population of any country in Europe.

With a strong legislature and a weak president, the new state seemed to Pilsudski too weak for its own defense. He became a virtual dictator in 1926 and ruled until his death in 1935. After his death a weak parliamentary government was controlled by military officers; the tentative revival of republicanism was halted by Hitler's and Stalin's aggression in 1939, yet another partition of Poland.

Like other countries of east-central Europe, Poland was primarily an agricultural country, with grains, sugar beets, and potatoes its principal crops. The postwar republic attempted land reform, with some success; about 750,000 new private farm holdings were created by 1938. Mining—of coal and copper—was the principal traditional industrial activity in the 20th century, supplemented by extraction of natural gas. In the mid-1930s shipbuilding and railroad construction led the way toward a modern economy.

World War II commenced in September 1939, with attacks on Poland by Germany and the Soviet Union. The war brought severe destruction to Poland and the extermination of virtually its entire Jewish population. A government-in-exile was established in London, but the Soviet Union broke relations with it in 1943 when it requested a Red Cross investigation into the murder of 14,000 Polish officers whose bodies were discovered in Katyn Forest. (The Soviet government acknowledged responsibility for the massacre in 1990.) The Soviets established a puppet government in Lublin in 1944. In August the Red Army paused in its western advance on the outskirts of Warsaw, permitting the Nazis to obliterate the Polish Home Army. On Jan. 1, 1945, the USSR recognized the Lublin regime as Poland's provisional government.

By the time of the Allied Powers Conference in Yalta in February 1945, the Red Army was only 40 miles from Berlin and had total control of Poland. The Allies agreed to Stalin's proposal concerning the eastern boundary of Poland (allowing Russia to incorporate the eastern half of the country) and agreed that the government should be constituted from an enlargement of the Lublin regime. At Potsdam in August 1945, it was further agreed that Poland should absorb the eastern portion of Germany. Poland's borders were shifted approximately 200 miles westward from the prewar configuration, becoming once again those of the 10th century. The German population was expelled remorselessly.

The free elections promised in the Yalta Agreement were postponed until 1947, by which time a Communist victory could be assured. In 1948 the Socialists were forcibly merged into the Communist party; in 1949 Premier Boleslaw Bierut requested that Soviet general Konstantin Rokossovski be appointed minister of defense and commander in chief of the Polish army. In the same year, all cultural periodicals and all writers' and artists' associations were taken over by the Communist party.

But there was little collectivization of Polish agriculture or forced industrialization on the Stalinist model. Intellectuals, bolstered by the Catholic church (which deeply resented a 1953 law requiring government approval for appointment of bishops), questioned the regime with some boldness. In 1956 both Bierut and Party Secretary Minc died, and Wladislaw Gomulka was elected party chairman in Oct. 1956. As Soviet warships sailed through the Baltic toward Poland, Nikita Khrushchev flew to Poland with a delegation of Soviet generals, where Gomulka assured them that Poland would follow the Soviet lead in foreign policy. Distracted by the crisis in Hungary, the Russians left Gomulka in power and even canceled Poland's debt and allowed the dismantling of agricultural collectives.

For a short time Gomulka permitted cultural and educational freedom, but by 1958 he had reverted to Stalinist form, imposing controls and pursuing a somewhat anti-Semitic Polish nationalism. Gomulka ruled until 1971, when he was replaced as party secretary by Edward Gierek. But moral leadership within Poland had clearly passed to Stefan Cardinal Wyszynski, leader of the increasingly vocal Catholic church; Gierek was forced to improve relations with the church in order to maintain his own credibility as a national leader.

Gierek presided over a decade of increasing unrest, with rising prices and growing discontent. Polish exports of ham and furniture to the West under liberalized terms earned some hard currency but could not curb the rising national debt. The most significant event in Poland in the 1970s was the election of Karol Wojtyla, bishop of Krakow, as Pope John Paul II in October 1978. His visit to Poland in 1979 set the stage for the extraordinary events of the 1980s.

Gierek's austerity program of February 1980 sent meat prices soaring. Strikes for wage adjustments, especially at the Lenin Shipyards in Gdansk, thrust Lech Walesa, a shipyard worker, into a position of national leadership. Walesa was elected chairman of the national coordinating committee of independent labor unions, Solidarity. Solidarity's demands went far beyond lower prices and higher wages; they included independent labor unions with the right to strike, freedom for political prisoners, and an end to censorship. In Sept. 1980 Gierek resigned as party secretary and was replaced by Stanislaw Kania.

By December, 40 independent trade unions had been formed, and a "rural Solidarity" movement was growing. In February 1981 Soviet Army general Wojciech Jaruzelski was named prime minister, and in October he replaced Kania as party secretary. When in December Solidarity announced plans to hold a referendum on the Jaruzelski regime, martial law was declared; Solidarity leaders were arrested, all its activities were banned, and the right to strike was abolished.

But the government was never able to suppress Solidarity as a popular force, and it was legalized in 1989. In 1989 elections Solidarity won 99 of 100 Senate seats and 299 of 460 seats in the lower house, although 65 percent of these had been reserved for the Communist party. Jaruzelski was elected president by Parliament and Solidarity leader Tadeusz Mazowiecki became prime minister.

The Communist party voted to disband on Jan. 28, 1990, and the Mazowiecki government announced a program of radical economic reform, winning promises of foreign aid and increased investment from Western governments. In June 1990, a commission was appointed to draft a new constitution. Jaruzelski resigned in September, and in presidential elections, Walesa, at the head of Solidarity's labor/Catholic faction, defeated Mazowiecki, representing Solidarity's political/technocrat faction.

The new prime minister, Krzysztof Bielecki, continued the reformist policies of curbing inflation and government spending, fostering foreign investment, and privatizing state enterprises. But the shock therapy, with its higher prices and unemployment (even while creating more than a million new jobs), led to disillusionment.

In the first fully free parliamentary elections, held in October 1991, only 42 percent of the voters participated, electing a fragmented 29-party Parliament. Reluctantly, Pres. Walesa named Jan Olszewski as prime minister of a coalition government that commanded only 180 votes in the 460-deputy Sejm. The Olszewski coalition collapsed in June 1992, replaced by an equally fragile seven-party coalition led by Hanna Suchocka, Poland's first female prime minister.

Despite high inflation (40 percent) and high official unemployment (13 percent), under Poland's "iron lady" the private sector expanded and even the remaining state-owned enterprises responded to market demand, pushing exports from $8 billion in 1988 to $14 billion in 1992. And in May 1993, Parliament passed a bill privatizing 600 companies.

Still, at the end of May 1993, the Suchocka government fell, by one vote, to a Solidarity-sponsored no-confidence measure, in protest against her austerity budget. In new elections held in Oct. 1993, the Communist party (now called the Democratic Left Alliance) formed a coalition with the Peasants party to forge a surprising return to power. The Communist prime minister, Josef Oleksy, was joined by his party-mate Aleksander Kwasniewski, who defeated Walesa in presidential elections held in November 1995. Kwasniewski ran especially strong with younger voters, who regarded communism as an antiquated system that posed no threat of returning to Poland. A month after the presidential election, though, Oleksy was accused of spying for Russia, and although he protested his innocence, he resigned as premier.

Poland's economy was among the fastest growing in Europe (a 7 percent rise in GDP in recent years and billions in direct foreign investment) although inflation ran high through 1997. In 1997, a new constitution (the first since 1952) and invitations to join NATO and eventually the EU gave the Poles a reason to believe that the future looked very positive. The first elections under the new constitution produced a center-right coalition government. In 1999 Poland joined NATO, finally achieving security against the Russian expansion it always feared, but the economy slowed considerably.

▶ PORTUGAL
Portuguese Republic

● **GEOGRAPHY   Location:** Iberian Peninsula in southwest Europe; also two archipelagos in Atlantic Ocean: Azores (37°29'N, 25°40'W) and Madeira Islands (32°40'N, 16°55'W). **Boundaries:** Spain to N and E, Atlantic Ocean to S and W. **Total area:** 35,552 sq. mi. (92,080 sq km). **Coastline:** 1,114 mi. (1,793 km). **Comparative area:** slightly smaller than Indiana. **Land use:** 26% arable land; 9% permanent crops; 9% meadows and pastures; 36% forest and woodland; 20% other; includes 7% irrigated. **Major cities:** (1991 census) Lisboa (Lisbon, capital) 681,063; Porto (Oporto) 309,485; Amadora 176,137; Setubal 103,241; Coimbra 147,722.

● **PEOPLE   Population:** 9,918,040 (1999 est.). **Nationality:** noun—Portuguese (sing., pl.); adjective—Portuguese. **Ethnic groups:** homogeneous Mediterranean stock on mainland, in Azores, and on Madeira Islands; citizens of African descent who immigrated during decolonization number less than 100,000. **Languages:** Portuguese. **Religions:** 97% Roman Catholic, 1% Protestant, 2% other.

● **GOVERNMENT   Type:** parliamentary democracy. **Independence:** Oct. 5, 1910. **Constitution:** Apr. 25, 1976, revised Oct. 1982 and June 1989, Nov. 1992, Sept. 1997. **National holiday:** Day of Portugal, June 10. **Heads of Government:** Jorge Sampaio, president (since Feb. 1996); Antonio Guterres, prime minister (since Oct. 1995). **Structure:** executive—president and prime minister; unicameral legislature-(popularly elected 230-seat Assembly of the Republic); judiciary.

● **ECONOMY   Monetary unit:** escudo. **Budget:** (1996) *income:* $48 bil.; *expend.:* $52 bil. **GDP:** $144.8 bil., $14,600 per capita (1998 est.). **Chief crops:** grains, potatoes, olives, grapes for wine; livestock. **Natural resources:** fish, forests (cork), tungsten, iron ore, uranium ore. **Major industries:** textiles, footwear, wood pulp, paper, cork. **Labor force:** 4.75 mil. (1998 est.); 56% services, 22% manufacturing, 12% agriculture, forestry, fisheries, 9% construction; 5% unemployment (1998 est.). **Exports:** $25 bil. (f.o.b., 1998); clothing and footwear, machinery, chemicals, cork and paper products, hides. **Imports:** $34.9 bil. (f.o.b., 1998); machinery and transport equipment, chemicals, petroleum, textiles, agricultural products. **Major trading partners:** *exports:* 81% EU, 5% U.S.; *imports:* 76% EU, 3% U.S., 2% Japan.

Portugal traces its origins back to the warlike Lusitanian tribes of Roman times. The nation-state originated as a county of the kingdom of Leon-Castile, reconquered from the Moors in the 11th century. Portugal won recognition as an independent kingdom in 1143, and conquered Lisbon four years later. In 1267 the Algarve was conquered, and by then Portugal had expanded to its modern boundaries. Except for the period 1580-1640, when it was ruled by the Spanish Habsburgs, the Portuguese dynasty maintained its independence into the 20th century.

Portuguese fishermen had probably frequented the Grand Banks from before the time of Columbus, and the nation's tradition of seafaring gave rise to a world empire in the 15th and 16th centuries. Prince Henry the Navigator (1394-1460) colonized the Azores and the Madeiras and sponsored voyages of exploration along the west coast of Africa. Under his successors, Portugal controlled the west African coast, the shores of the Indian Ocean, and large stretches of southern Asia, as well as, in the Western Hemisphere, Brazil. Yet the rise of the empires of Spain and the Netherlands quickly reduced the Portuguese to second-rank status, leaving only Macao, Goa, and Timor in Asia; Portuguese Guinea (Guinea Bissau), Mozambique, and Angola in Africa; and the great territory of Brazil in Latin America.

In the 19th century, a series of dynastic civil wars weakened the monarchy, allowing Britain to gain control of the country's foreign policy (in addition to the wine trade of Oporto, long in British hands). Brazil declared its independence in 1822.

In 1910 Portugal became the first kingdom in the 20th century to be transformed into a republic. But in the next 15 years, chaos ensued: eight presidents, 44 governments, and a nearcollapse of the economy. Finally, the military established a dictatorship, lasting until recent times. In 1928 the military installed a civilian dictator, a professor of economics, Antonio Salazar. A firm believer in law and order, he managed to control the turbulence of political life and made the escudo one of Europe's most stable currencies, yet he could do nothing to alter Portugal's fundamental poverty. Although he ruled through civilian governments, his essential support always came from the army.

Portugal has long been Western Europe's poorest country. As late as 1960, almost half of the country's work force was engaged in agriculture, forestry, and fishing. In the north, agriculture was traditionally carried on in smallholdings; the south was characterized by large estates, remnants of feudal fiefs. Exports were traditionally cork, olive oil, port wine, and fish. Industrialization came late to Portugal, and today manufacturing is mostly carried on by small firms engaged in textile and clothing production and other labor-intensive production.

World War II affected Portugal very little. Salazar deftly managed to remain Britain's ally while keeping his country out of the war as a neutral state. In the postwar period, Portugal accepted Marshall Plan aid and became a member of NATO in 1949. Portugal was a founding member of the European Free Trade Association in 1959 and negotiated a special relationship with the EC in 1972 (when its trading partner and ally, Great Britain, joined that body).

Portugal joined the United Nations in 1955 (having been vetoed until then by the Soviet Union), just in time to become embroiled in the worldwide movement for decolonization. Protesting that Portugal had, not colonies, but "overseas provinces," Salazar refused to bow to the pressure of world opinion. In 1961 India forcibly annexed Goa and other Portuguese enclaves on the subcontinent. In the same year, nationalist revolts broke out in Angola, with Guinea and Mozambique.

The colonial wars of the 1960s placed a terrible strain on Portugal's economy and resulted in severe military losses, and had the unintended effect of spreading Marxist ideas in the armed forces and the universities. And in the end, the colonies gained their independence. Salazar, gravely ill, retired in 1968 and was replaced by Marcelo Caetano. In 1974 Caetano was deposed in a bloodless coup staged by the secret Armed Forces movement. The coup's leader, Antonio de Spinola, after reaching agreements on the independence of most of Portugal's old colonies, resigned as head of government in September 1974. Costa Gomes replaced Spinola, as a Revolutionary Council was instituted. The council survived two coup attempts, one by right-wing soldiers, the other by Communists, and it promulgated a Socialist constitution in 1976. Through a series of unstable governments (16 between 1974 and 1987), the old agrarian estates were expropriated, and banking, insurance, and large industrial concerns were nationalized. The shock of this economic transformation, along with the OPEC price rises, created an economic recession in the 1970s. In addition Portugal had to absorb about a million ethnic Portuguese refugees from the former colonies.

Attempts by center-right coalitions in the 1980s to undo the nationalizations of the 1970s were thwarted by vetoes of the Constitutional Tribunal (successor to the Revolutionary Council), even when the free-market Social Democratic party held an absolute majority in the assembly. Portugal entered the EC on Jan. 1, 1986, pledging to reduce tariffs and end agricultural subsidies over a 10-year transitional period.

In 1987 the Social Democrats, running on an almost Thatcherite platform of spending cuts, privatization of state-owned firms, reversal of agricultural collectivism, and reliance on free enterprise, became the first party since 1974 to win an absolute majority in the legislative assembly. Per capita income tripled over the years 1985-92, so that Portugal was no longer the poorest country in the EU. The 1992 sale of the huge state-owned Petrogal oil company was a harbinger of a return to free enterprise. In October 1995, Antonio Guterres of the Socialist party displaced the Social Democrats. And in January 1996, Jorge Sampaio won the presidential election, giving Portugal both a Socialist president and prime minister for the first time since democracy was restored.

Portugal's economic stability was ratified in 1998 by the EU when the latter approved Portugal's membership in the Monetary Union (the euro-zone). And her international standing was affirmed by her central role in negotiating the East Timor referendum with Indonesia.

▶ QATAR
State of Qatar

● **GEOGRAPHY Location:** occupies a peninsula projecting northward from Arabian mainland into western part of Persian (Arabian) Gulf. **Boundaries:** Persian Gulf to N, E, and W; Saudi Arabia and United Arab Emirates to S. **Total area:** 4,247 sq. mi. (11,000 sq km). **Coastline:** 350 mi. (563 km). **Comparative area:** slightly smaller than Connecticut. **Land use:** 1% arable land; 0% permanent crops; 5% meadows and pastures; 0% forest and woodland; 94% other. **Major cities:** (1993) Doha (capital) 339,471; Al Rayyan 143,046; Al Wakrah 30,976.

● **PEOPLE Population:** 723,542 (1999 est.). **Nationality:** noun—Qatari(s); adjective—Qatari. **Ethnic groups:** 40% Arab, 18% Pakistani, 18% Indian, 10% Iranian, 14% other. **Languages:** Arabic (official), English commonly used as second language. **Religions:** 95% Muslim.

● **GOVERNMENT Type:** traditional monarchy. **Independence:** Sept. 3, 1971 (from UK). **Constitution:** provisional constitution enacted Apr. 19, 1972. **National holiday:** Independence Day, Sept. 3. **Head of Government:** Hamad bin Khalifa al-Thani (since June 1995). **Structure:** executive—amir is head of government and chief of state; unicameral legislature—consultative, no elections since 1970, members terms extended every four years; judiciary.

● **ECONOMY Monetary unit:** Qatari riyal. **Budget:** (FY98/99) *income:* $3.4 bil.; *expend.:* $4.3 bil. **GDP:** $12 bil., $17,100 per capita (1998 est.). **Chief crops:** fruits, vegetables; poultry, dairy products, beef; fish. **Natural resources:** crude oil, natural gas, fish. **Major industries:** crude oil production and refining, fertilizers, petrochemicals. **Labor force:** 233,000 (1993 est.). **Exports:** $5.6 bil. (f.o.b., 1997 est.); 80% petroleum products, steel, fertilizers. **Imports:** $4.4 bil. (f.o.b., 1997 est.); machinery, consumer goods, food, chemicals. **Major trading partners:** *exports:* 49% Japan, 12% Singapore, 12% South Korea; *imports:* 25% UK, 13% France, 10% Japan.

The Qatar peninsula was ruled as part of the sheikhdom of Bahrain from the late 18th century until the mid-19th century. An informal British protectorate was established in 1868; the Ottoman Empire also asserted authority over the sheikhs of Qatar from 1872 to 1916. The Ottomans ceded authority to the British in that year, and a formal British protectorate was organized. When British forces withdrew from the Persian Gulf region in 1971, Qatar entered into negotiations with the emirates of the Trucial Coast to join the federation of the United Arab Emirates. When those negotiations broke down, Qatar declared its independence on Sept. 3, 1971. For over 30 years it has been politically stable under one ruler, Sheik Hamad bin Khalifa al-Thani, although he was deposed by his son in a bloodless coup in June 1995. He has claimed he wants to move the country toward democracy and has called for a free press, limited elections, and allowing women to vote.

Qatar's economy is dominated by oil, natural

gas (Qatar has the world's third largest supply) banking, and shipping services in the port of Doha.

▶ROMANIA

- **GEOGRAPHY Location:** southeastern Europe. **Boundaries:** Ukraine to N, Moldova to NE, Black Sea to E, Bulgaria to S, Yugoslavia (Serbia) to SW, Hungary to NW. **Total area:** 91,699 sq. mi. (237,500 sq km). **Coastline:** 140 mi. (225 km). **Comparative area:** slightly smaller than Oregon. **Land use:** 41% arable land; 3% permanent crops; 21% meadows and pastures; 29% forest and woodland; 6% other; includes 11% irrigated. **Major cities:** (1993 est.) Bucharesti (Bucharest, capital) 2,066,723; Constanta 348,985; Iasi 337,643; Timisoara 325,359; Cluj-Napoca 321,850.
- **PEOPLE Population:** 22,334,312 (1999 est.). **Nationality:** noun—Romanian(s); adjective—Romanian. **Ethnic groups:** 89.1% Romanian, 8.9% Hungarian, 0.4% German, 1.6% Ukrainian, Serb, Croat, Russian, Turk, and Gypsy. **Languages:** Romanian, Hungarian, German. **Religions:** 70% Romanian Orthodox, 6% Roman Catholic, 6% Protestant.
- **GOVERNMENT Type:** republic. **Independence:** 1881 (from Turkey). **Constitution:** Dec. 8, 1991; republic proclaimed Dec. 30, 1947. **National holiday:** National Day, Dec. 1. **Heads of Government:** Emil Constantinescu, president (since Nov. 1996); Radu Vasile, prime minister (since April 1998). **Structure:** executive; bicameral legislature; judiciary.
- **ECONOMY Monetary unit:** leu. **Budget:** (1997 est.): *income:* $10 bil.; *expend.:* $11.7 bil. **GDP:** $90.6 bil., $4,050 per capita (1998 est.). **Chief crops:** corn, wheat; milk, eggs, meat. **Natural resources:** crude oil, timber, natural gas, coal, iron ore. **Major industries:** mining, timber, construction materials. **Labor force:** 10.1 mil. (1996). **Exports:** $8.2 bil. (f.o.b., 1998); 23% textiles and footwear, 18% metals and metal products, 9% machinery and equipment, 7% chemicals. **Imports:** $10.8 bil. (f.o.b., 1998); 23% machinery and equipment, 19% fuels and minerals, 8% chemicals. **Major trading partners:** (1997) *exports:* 20% Italy, 17% Germany, 6% France, 4% Turkey; *imports:* 16% Germany, 16% Italy, 12% Russia, 6% France.

The Roman province of Dacia was sufficiently Latinized to retain the name of Rome long after the legions withdrew in A.D. 27. Overrun by invading Bulgars in the eighth century, the Romanians retained their Latinate language and orthodox Christianity; Romania remained beyond the borders of the Byzantine Empire but was in close contact with it. The area was conquered by the Mongols in the 13th century and formed the independent principalities of Moldavia and Walachia after the Mongols withdrew.

By the 15th century, Moldavia and Walachia had become vassal states of the Ottoman Empire, though with some local autonomy that permitted retention of orthodox Christianity and the creation of a rich local culture. Attempts at national unity against Ottoman rule in 1601 and 1711 failed; in 1861 the provinces united as an autonomous state under the name Romania, within the Ottoman Empire, under Greek administration. Independence came in 1878.

Romania was for centuries the poorest country in Europe. Thoroughly agricultural, it was a land of unfree peasants working the great estates of landowners who were generally wealthy, usually absentee, and often Greek. The peasants not only paid taxes but also were required to perform feudal labor services for the estate owners.

After enlarging itself at Bulgaria's expense in the Second Balkan War (1913), Romania switched sides three times in World War I, joining the Allies just before the war's end. Its reward was a huge expansion, doubling its territory with lands taken from Austria, Hungary, Russia, and Bulgaria.

The interwar period was one of political turbulence, marked by violence and assassinations. Twice King Carol II went into exile, leaving his throne to his son Prince Michael; the second time was in 1940, when Russia (in accordance with the Hitler-Stalin pact) reclaimed the territories of Bessarabia and northern Bukovina it had lost to Romania in 1920; Hitler required Romania to return about half of Transylvania to Hungary.

During World War II, the pro-Hitler dictator Marshall Ion Antonescu took power, supported by a semifascist "Iron Guard," but when the latter attempted a coup, the military crushed the uprising. Romanian troops participated in Hitler's invasion of Russia in 1941, and the country paid the price in 1944 when Russian troops "liberated" the country, with devastating results.

The country was quickly transformed into a Soviet satellite through rigged elections in which the communist National Democratic Front replaced the Peasant Alliance in power; a People's Republic was proclaimed on Dec. 30, 1947, and King Michael was forced to abdicate. A peace treaty in 1947 confirmed the loss of Bessarabia to Russia but returned Transylvania to Romania.

Under Russian occupation Romania was a virtual Soviet colony. The occupying armies did not leave until after reparation payments were completed in 1958, leaving the dictator Gheorghe Gheorghiu-Dej in power. Despite Council of Mutual Economic Assistance (COMECON) plans for Romania to become a major food supplier to the Soviet bloc, Gheorghiu-Dej pursued industrialization on the Stalinist model, in the process ruining Romanian agriculture while creating large, labor-intensive, and highly inefficient factories. The result was an economic depression; politically, however, it produced a de facto independence for Romania within the Soviet bloc. Russian troops were forbidden on Romanian soil, and Romania declined to participate in COMECON policies.

With the death of Gheorghiu-Dej in 1965, power passed to Nicolae Ceauşescu. He promulgated a new constitution and instituted a series of purges, lasting to 1968; he became successively party leader in 1965, prime minister in 1967, and president of the republic in 1974. Ceauşescu continued his predecessor's economic policy, deepening the country's misery; he also pursued a policy of "independence" from the USSR, refusing to go along with Soviet policies of de-Stalinization and liberalization.

Romania's "national communism" was expressed in intense and militant nationalism, coupled with severe repression of ethnic minorities, especially Germans and Magyars in Transylvania. Hundreds of ethnically Hungarian villages were bulldozed into oblivion in the name of agricultural collectivization.

Ceauşescu's ambitions included the creation of a family dynasty in the Romanian leadership. In 1979 his wife Elena was named first deputy premier and elevated to the Council of Ministers. Her brothers were given important government positions, Ceauşescu's son, despite his reputation as a playboy, was groomed to replace his father.

Romania's transition from Communist rule was sudden and violent. On Dec. 16-18, 1989, demonstrations in Timisoara calling for Ceauşescu's ouster were put down with brute force by the Securitate (secret police), but they spread and citizens and regular army troops fought pitched battles with Securitate forces in Bucharest. Ceauşescu and his wife fled Bucharest but were captured, tried, and executed by Christmas day. The newly organized Council of National Salvation established a provisional government, consisting primarily of anti-Ceauşescu Communists in league with the Romanian army, with former Communist party official Ion Iliescu as president.

The Communist party was outlawed on Jan. 12, 1990. Despite the Council's domination by former Communists, no effective opposition movement emerged, and in hastily called and rigged elections on May 20, Iliescu was elected president in a landslide and the Council won 233 of 296 seats in the lower house.

In June 1990, many anti-Communist demonstrators were beaten and several killed by troops and armed miners brought to Bucharest by the government, an action that was condemned internationally. Calls for Iliescu's resignation and a purge of Communists from government continued into the fall. Tensions were further aggravated when the government's abrupt move to a market economy resulted in food shortages and sharp price increases.

Continued rioting in 1991 led to the replacement of ex-Communist prime minister Petre Roman by the non-Communist Theodor Stolojan at the head of a "caretaker" coalition. Local elections in Feb. 1992 brought strong gains, especially in larger cities, for a 14-party anti-Communist coalition. More or less free elections in 1992 gave the National Salvation Front 28 percent of the seats in Parliament while the opposition Democratic Convention gained 20 percent; Iliescu defeated the Democratic Convention candidate in the presidential election with 61 percent of the vote. Both Iliescu and the prime minister he named (Nicolae Vacaroiu) were pledged to slowing the transition to a market economy but by 1994 with inflation at over 250 percent (leading to a massive workers' strike in Feb.) the government agreed to IMF's demand for increased privatization and fiscal austerity in order to receive a $700 mil. loan. Iliescu's presidency ended in Nov. 1996 with a coalition government headed by Emil Constantinescu taking charge and immediately forging public links to the Romanian Orthodox Church ending decades of official atheism and taking action against corrupt banking officials, businessmen, and politicians. The economy remained in dire straits but in early 1997 loans were secured from the IMF and the World Bank.

Elections in Nov. 1997 were won by Emil Constantinescu of the Democratic Convention party who became president and Victor Ciorbea the Prime Minister. The latter was forced to resign in early 1998 because of complaints he was not carrying out necessary economic reforms. Inflation and unemployment were falling but GDP growth was lagging and, with a patchwork tax system, international default looked likely. IMF demands for restructuring as a condition of further loans produced government plans which included the closing of mines whose operation had lost $4 billion since 1990. But that in turn produced, in early 1999, widespread protest marches and violence by mine workers whose role in 1990 was not forgotten.

▶ RUSSIA
Russian Federation

● **GEOGRAPHY Location:** northeastern Europe and northern Asia. **Boundaries:** Baltic Sea, Barents Sea, Kara Sea, East Siberian Sea to N, Bering Sea, Sea of Okhotsk, Sea of Japan to E, China, North Korea, Mongolia, Kazakhstan, Caspian Sea, Azerbaijan, Georgia, Black Sea to S, Ukraine, Belarus to W, Latvia, Estonia, Finland, Norway to NW. **Total area:** 6,592,745 sq. mi. (17,075,200 sq. km). **Coastline:** 23,402 mi. (37,653 km). **Comparative area:** slightly less than 1.8 times the size of the United States. **Land use:** 8% arable land, 4% meadows and pastures, 46% forest and woodland, 42% other. **Major cities:** (1995) Moscow (capital) 8,717,000; St. Petersburg 4,838,000; Nizhnyi Novgorod 1,383,000; Novosibirsk 1,369,000.

● **PEOPLE Population:** 146,393,569 (1999 est.). **Nationality:** noun—Russian(s); adjective—Russian. **Ethnic groups:** 81.5% Russian, 3.8% Tatar, 3% Ukrainian, 1.2% Chuvash. **Languages:** Russian, other. **Religions:** Russian Orthodox, Muslim, other.

● **GOVERNMENT Type:** federation. **Independence:** Aug. 24, 1991 (from Soviet Union). **Constitution:** Dec. 12, 1993. **National holiday:** Independence Day, June 12, celebrating first presidential election. **Heads of Government:** Boris N. Yeltsin, president (since June 1991); Vladimir V. Putin, prime minister (since Aug. 1999). **Structure:** executive—president, premier, various advisory bodies; bicameral legislature; judiciary.

● **ECONOMY Monetary unit:** ruble. **Budget:** (1998 est.) *income:* $40 bil..; *expend.:* $63 bil. **GDP:** $593.4 bil., $4,000 per capita (1998 est.). **Chief crops:** grain, sugar beets, vegetables, sunflower seed; meat, milk. **Natural resources:** oil, natural gas, coal, timber. **Major industries:** extraction and processing raw materials, machine building from rolling mills to high-performance aircraft. **Labor force:** 66 mil. (1997). **Exports:** $71.8 bil. (1998 est.); petroleum and petroleum products, natural gas, wood and wood products, coal, metals, chemicals. **Imports:** $58.5 bil. (1998 est.); machinery and equipment, consumer goods, medicines, meat, grain, sugar, semifinished metal products. **Major trading partners:** Europe, North America, Japan.

Russia is the largest and most powerful of the states to emerge from the former Soviet Union. As the seat of the Soviet empire that existed for over 70 years, the Russians wielded tremendous power both within the USSR and in the international sphere. Almost from their emergence as a separate people, the Russians have extended the boundaries of their country to include a wide variety of non-Russian people. Both the Russian Czars and the Bolsheviks who came to power in 1917 have a long history of expansionist policies, which explains why, even today, an important part of the Russian national identity is that of leader of a large empire.

In the ninth century A.D., Viking traders organized a state, which they called Rus, in the river valleys between the Baltic and the Black Seas, centered on the cities of Kiev and Novgorod. In time the Vikings were absorbed into the native Slavic population; in 998 a Ruthenian prince of Kiev accepted Christianity from Constantinople. In the 13th century, Mongols under Genghis Khan and his descendants conquered most of Russia, and the Mongol Golden Horde maintained its power through the 14th century, exercising loose control over Novgorod and Moscow.

From the mid-19th century, Moscow grew to become the center of a new state that gathered in other cities and territories as Mongol power waned. Ivan III (Ivan the Great, 1440-1505) consolidated the power of Moscow; his marriage to a Byzantine princess led him to regard his empire as a third Rome, heir to the religious tradition of Constantinople. His grandson, Ivan IV (Ivan the Terrible, 1530-84), adopted the title czar (from the Latin caesar) when he came to power. He broke the power of the aristocratic boyar class and greatly extended the power of Moscow through military conquest.

Over the next two centuries, Russia carried out a steady program of expansion eastward into Siberia and across the Bering Strait to Alaska, until the empire covered one-sixth of the land surface of the globe. Peter the Great (1672-1725) made Russia a Baltic and Black Sea naval power, brought Russia into the European state system, and instituted a sweeping, if superficial, Westernization of his realm. His new capital at St. Petersburg became one of the most splendid cities in Europe. At the end of the 18th century, Catherine the Great (1729-96) participated with Prussia and Austria in the partitions of Poland, and Russia thereby became a major power in central Europe.

Catherine's grandson Alexander I (1777-1825), member of the grand coalition that defeated Napoleon, was not only czar of Russia but also king of Poland and grand duke of Finland. His troops occupied Paris in 1815. The Russian aristocracy became ardent Francophiles in the 19th century, ignoring growing problems at home. After losing the Crimean War in 1856, Russia began to develop Siberia and the southern territories near the border of Persia. Alaska was sold to the United States in 1867. In a major reform of the agricultural system, serfdom was abolished under Alexander II in 1861, though the newly independent peasantry, organized into agricultural cooperatives, only slowly derived benefits from its freedom. The late 19th century also marked the beginning of modern industrialization in Russia and of extensive development in Siberia, aided by state investment in railroads and mining.

Under the last czar, Nicholas II (1868-1918), Russia was defeated by Japan in a war over Manchuria in 1905. The defeat sparked a naval mutiny and an abortive revolution, which led to the establishment of a constitutional monarchy and other limited political reforms. Further military losses in World War I set the stage for the monarchy's downfall in the revolution of 1917.

The initial revolution of March 1917 brought a relatively moderate socialist (Menshevik) group to power. Its principal leader, Aleksandr Kerensky, organized a republican government and tried to maintain the Russian war effort but failed to gain control of the many contending revolutionary factions of the time. The Germans allowed the radical Bolshevik leader, Vladimir I. Lenin, to return to Russia, where he and his followers organized workers' soviets (councils) hostile to the Menshevik republic. Bolshevik forces occupied Petrograd (St. Petersburg was renamed in 1914) on Nov. 7, 1917 (October in the old Byzantine calendar, hence the name October Revolution), arrested the cabiinet, and put in place a Council of People's Commissars, under Lenin's chairmanship. There followed four years of civil war between Bolshevik, Menshevik, and czarist forces, in the course of which Nicholas II and his family were executed by the Bolsheviks in 1918.

Decreeing land to the peasants, worker management in industry, and repudiation of czarist debts, the Bolsheviks won the survival of their regime by withdrawing from World War I. The 1918 Treaty of Brest-Litovsk, which gained peace with Germany, granted freedom to Finland, the Baltic republics, Poland, Ukraine, and Bessarabia. At the conclusion of the civil war in 1921, the Soviet state was established, with Ukraine reabsorbed into the Soviet Union. The Bolshevik victory also resulted in the creation in 1921 of the Mongolian People's Republic as a close Soviet ally.

The early 1920s are now remembered as a "golden age" of Soviet history. Lenin's New Economic Policy (NEP) allowed some role for market forces and private ownership and led to a brief burst of economic growth. Art, literature, and science flourished in an atmosphere of revolutionary enthusiasm and little censorship.

Lenin died on Jan. 21, 1924, and after a power struggle, was succeeded by Josef Stalin. Stalin supported Communist revolutions in China and elsewhere through the Communist International (Comintern) but generally withdrew from foreign engagements in order to concentrate on domestic affairs. Under Lenin, and even more under Stalin, the Communist party established a police state, condemning millions of people to internal exile in the 1920s and consolidating all power in the hands of the state. In 1929 agriculture was forcibly collectivized, leading to the starvation or execution of millions of peasants, while forced industrialization was carried out under a series of five-year plans.

Under the guise of socialist revolution, the Russians continued in much the same manner as their czarist heirs. The Bolsheviks forcibly incorporated most of the territories of the old empire, and once in charge, insisted that Russian be the state language and that Russian Communist party officials run the republics.

On the national level, Stalin's chief rival, Leon Trotsky, was expelled from the USSR in 1929 (and assassinated by Stalinist agents in Mexico in 1940). Stalin's obsession with eliminating all possible rivals for power led to a series of purges which, at their height, saw the summary execution of an estimated seven million of presumed "enemies of the state" and the imprisonment in concentration camps of an estimated 12 million more.

Russia's reemergence as a world power was signaled by the signing in August 1939 of the Hitler-Stalin Pact, a nonaggression treaty through which Stalin aimed to recover territories lost to Russia in 1918. Poland was again partitioned, Bessarabia annexed (as the Moldavian republic), Finland conquered and partitioned, and the Baltic republics absorbed.

When in June 1941 Hitler turned against his ally and invaded Russia, unprepared Russian armies retreated. But Stalin emerged as a national leader in the "Great Patriotic War," restructuring the army and enlisting the support of the Orthodox church and relying on calls to Russian patriotism in rallying the population. In the early winter of 1942, the war changed course as Russia broke the German siege of Stalingrad, and Russian armies began their westward push that would carry them to the Elbe River by April 1945.

By the end of World War II, Stalin had reestablished the old czarist boundaries of Russia, and he had a ring of occupied states along his western boundary and a divided Germany beyond. Over the years 1945-48, he engineered a thorough communization of those occupied states, turning them into Russian satellites.

Stalin died in March 1953. He was succeeded by a collegial form of party and government leadership, from which Nikita Khrushchev, the party chairman, emerged as the paramount figure. In a secret speech to the party leadership in 1956, Khrushchev denounced Stalin for crimes against the party. He announced a set of new policies designed to bring about rapid modernization and consolidated his power when he became premier in 1958. The Khrushchev years brought a small but steady rise in living standards and a "thaw" in police state methods, the KGB (state security police) being brought under party control.

In foreign policy there was a thaw as well. In 1953 the Soviets agreed to an armistice in Korea and tolerated the formation of a more liberal government in Hungary. In 1955 Russia returned the Porkkala peninsula to Finland and agreed to the Austrian State Treaty, which created an independent and neutral Austria. But the limits of disengagement became clear in 1956 with the ruthless Soviet suppression of the Hungarian uprising. A summit conference between Khrushchev and Eisenhower in 1960 led to a propaganda victory for Russia when an American U-2 spy plane was shot down over Russian territory on May 1. And in 1962 Khrushchev tried to install Soviet missiles in Cuba, a reckless adventure from which he had to back down during the Cuban missile crisis.

While on vacation in 1964, Khrushchev was removed from office and replaced as party secretary by Leonid Brezhnev and as premier by Aleksei Kosygin. His failure to deliver on promises for domestic economic growth and his recklessness in foreign affairs seem to have been responsible for his downfall. The new leaders embarked on an ambitious program of military (especially naval) expansion and pressed ahead vigorously with a space program that had begun with the triumphant launching of Sputnik I in 1957.

Under Brezhnev and Kosygin the USSR became more aggressive in foreign policy. The severe suppression of Czechoslovakia's "Prague Spring" in 1968 occasioned development of the Brezhnev Doctrine, whereby Russia claimed the right to intervene militarily in any socialist state. Soviet involvement in the Third World grew, with Russia supporting Vietnam against China; Syria and the PLO against Israel; leftist regimes in Angola, Ethiopia, and elsewhere in Africa; and the Sandinistas in Nicaragua. Cuba emerged as the principal Soviet proxy in supplying troops for leftist causes in the Third World. In 1979 Soviet troops moved into Afghanistan, allegedly at the invitation of its Marxist government, and remained bogged down there for a decade. Under American pressure, Brezhnev permitted the emigration of about 130,000 Jews and 40,000 ethnic Germans.

Domestically, the regime grew more oppressive; censorship was tightened and dissidents sentenced to terms in penal mental institutions. Elitism and nepotism created a self-perpetuating and interlocking network of power at the top, while the nation as a whole stagnated.

Brezhnev's death in 1982 brought about a rapid series of leadership transfers. Yuri Andropov, head of the KGB, succeeded Brezhnev as party secretary but died after only 15 months. He was succeeded by Konstantin Chernenko, who died 13 months later. In March 1985 Mikhail Gorbachev became party secretary, ushering in a new era in Soviet history.

Gorbachev first instituted a cautious shake-up of state and party bureaucrats, promoting younger men who were technocrats rather than party professionals. Under the slogan *glasnost* (openness, candor), censorship was relaxed; by 1988 criticism of not only Stalin but also Brezhnev was permitted, and policy was openly debated in the press. Jamming of broadcasts from the West was ended. By the end of 1990, freedom of the press and of religion had been approved, and private citizens were given limited rights to own small businesses.

Gorbachev's other slogan, *perestroika* (restructuring), addressed his aim to boost morale and increase economic efficiency by devolving responsibility for economic decisions away from the party and government and toward industrial and agricultural managers. Perestroika raised expectations but not output; the system remained sluggish, inefficient, and burdened with the vested interests of state planners. The nuclear power plant disaster of Chernobyl in April 1986 and a gas pipeline fire that killed hundreds of passengers in passing railroad trains in June 1989 exemplified the industrial mismanagement against which Gorbachev's policies were aimed. During 1989-91 there were strikes by coal miners, and shortages of food and consumer goods worsened.

In foreign policy Gorbachev pursued arms reduction agreements with the United States and withdrew Soviet forces from Afghanistan. His international stature exceeded that of any previous Soviet leader; but his problems at home made him increasingly unpopular. Foremost among his problems at home concerned the USSR's various ethnic nationalities. The southern Muslim regions of the USSR were the scene of turmoil since the anti-Russian riots in Kazakhstan in 1986; in 1988 riots broke out in the Christian republic of Armenia over the status of ethnic Armenians in the neighboring Muslim republic of Azerbaijan. Fighting in Armenia and Azerbaijan worsened in 1989-90, leading to a breakdown of government control in some areas. Ethnic warfare between Uzbeks and Turks in Uzbekistan led to numerous deaths, and sporadic violence in other central Asian republics broke out in 1990.

In the northwest, the Baltic republics of Estonia, Latvia, and Lithuania raised their old national flags over their parliaments, enacted laws giving their native languages priority over Russian, and proclaimed the superiority of local republican law over the laws of the Soviet Union. Lithuania proclaimed its independence from the USSR in December 1989, provoking a confrontation with strong international ramifications; Lithuania finally agreed to postpone its independence in 1990 pending negotiations with the Soviet government. Within the USSR itself, the Russian republic elected maverick Boris Yeltsin as president and pressed for greater autonomy; Yeltsin resigned from the Communist party in July 1990.

The total collapse of communist governments in Eastern Europe in 1989-90 added to Gorbachev's problems and led to the dissolution of the Warsaw Pact; the Berlin Wall fell in November 1989; and the Council of Mutual Economic Assistance (COMECON) was dissolved in July 1990. Gorbachev responded by assuming the presidency of the USSR and increasing the powers of that office, and he held off challenges to his leadership in 1990-91. Yet defections from the party by both right- and left-wing groups threw the party's future role in the USSR itself in doubt. Public demonstrations against Gorbachev and the Communist party took place in Moscow and elsewhere as the economy worsened and food supplies dwindled.

In June of 1991, Boris Yeltsin was elected president of the Russian republic in the first direct elections for the post. His stature soared when he rallied opposition to an unsuccessful coup to topple Gorbachev in August. In December 1991 Gorbachev and Yeltsin agreed that the USSR would cease to exist as of Jan. 1, 1992.

In early December 1991, Ukraine, Belarus, and the Russian Federation signed the Minsk Agreement that created the Commonwealth of Independent States, and on Dec. 21, Ukraine and 11 other former union republics officially committed themselves to the union by signing the Alma-Ata Declaration. In Feb. 1992 Russian president Yeltsin agreed to begin dismantling the vast arsenal of Russian nuclear weapons, 80 percent of which were on Russia's territory, the rest being scattered across Ukraine, Belarus, and Kazkhstan. While Belarus agreed to allow Russia to control the weapons, Kazakhstan and Ukraine used their weapons as bargaining chips.

Throughout 1992, Pres. Yeltsin took center stage, first signing the historic second Strategic Arms Reduction Treaty (START II) with the United States in January, then in April rallying the people to support a referendum on government elections and to approve his policies, and finally in June calling together a Constitutional Assembly to write a new constitution. As the Russian economy continued to founder, however, Yeltsin became the target of attacks by hard-liners, mainly former Communists. In Dec. 1992, Yeltsin barely survived a series of votes in Parliament that would have severely limited his control.

This struggle came to a violent head on Sept. 21, 1993, when Yeltsin and Parliament effectively threw each other out of office: Yeltsin declared Parliament dissolved and called for new elections to be held in December; Parliament voted to impeach Yeltsin and appointed Vice Pres. Aleksandr V. Rutskoi to replace him. Anti-Yeltsin forces called for a national strike and barricaded themselves inside the Parliament building for two weeks. Anti-Yeltsin rallies escalated into serious violence when 10,000 protesters overwhelmed riot police and broke through government barricades, causing Yeltsin to summon military police. The leaders of the revolt surrendered after tanks fired directly on the Parliament building, and were immediately sent to prison. At least 100 people were killed in the exchange.

In the aftermath, Yeltsin moved quickly to parlay his victory into even greater political power, by banning several opposition parties, firing powerful opponents, and calling for new parliamentary elections. He announced he would stay in office until his term expired in 1996, and in Nov. 1993 he unveiled the country's first post-Soviet constitution, which centralized power in the executive presidency and limited the powers of the constituent regions. One of these regions, Chechnya, had long threatened secession from Russia and in 1994 its leaders took that action. In Dec. Yeltsin ordered the army to restore government control, but it took months of fighting before Grozny, the rebel capital, fell to Russian troops.

In 1996, unrest by Russia's nationalist faction eroded much of Yeltsin's support, forcing him into a runoff election against the Communist candidate Gennadi Zyuganov in May 1996. But in the runoff, Yeltsin decisively beat back the Communist challenger. In August, Yeltsin formed a cabinet of pro-business technocrats; in the Fall he chucked National Security advisor (and future rival) Lebed, and he agreed to the final withdrawl of Russia's Chechnya brigades.

Yeltsin met Pres. Clinton in Helsinki in March 1997 subsequently agreeing to NATO's eastward expansion in return for NATO's agreement neither to deploy nor to store nuclear weapons there. Economic difficulties reached serious proportions in 1998 and the IMF and the U.S. pledged huge amounts to keep the economy from crumbling. In the spring, Yeltsin replaced many of his ministers (including Prime Minister Viktor Chernomyrdin) with reform-minded bureaucrats. But in the summer, the economy turned down again, and Yeltsin was forced to devalue the ruble and rehire Chernomyrdin and others. But this time the Communists in Parliament stood fast against him and rejected Chernomyrdin. As the economy worsened day-by-day and international lenders refused more aid, Russia stood on the brink of total collapse.

Even with Mr. Yeltsin's physical illnesses, personal volatility, and political capriciousness (the August 1999 appointment of Vladimir Putin as prime minister made him the fifth in 18 months, the third in a row drawn from the secret police), Russia was able in 1999 to play a significant role in the diplomacy concerning and the occupation of Yugoslavia's Kosovo province. And the IMF and various western investment "Clubs" manage to keep rescheduling Russian debt, so Russia manages to stumble on despite essentially defaulting on loan repayments. New trouble in and around Chechnya brought military action. (See Part I, "Major News Stories of the Year.")

▶ **RWANDA**
Rwandese Republic

● **GEOGRAPHY   Location:** landlocked country in central Africa. **Boundaries:** Uganda to N, Tanzania to E, Burundi to S, Zaire to W. **Total area:** 10,170 sq. mi. (26,340 sq km). **Coastline:** none. **Comparative area:** slightly smaller than Maryland. **Land use:** 35% arable land; 13% permanent crops; 18% meadows and pastures; 22% forest and woodland; 12% other; includes negl. % irrigated. **Major cities:** (1993) Kigali (capital) 234,500; Butare (1978) 21,691; Ruhengeri (1978) 16,025; Gisenyi (1978) 12,436.

● **PEOPLE   Population:** 8,154,933 (1999 est.). **Nationality:** noun—Rwandan(s); adjective—Rwandan. **Ethnic groups:** 80% Hutu, 19% Tutsi, 1% Twa (Pygmoid). **Languages:** Kinyarwanda (official) universal Bantu vernacular, French and English (both official), Kiswahili (Swahili) used in commercial centers. **Religions:** 65% Catholic, 9% Protestant, 1% Muslim; 25% indigenous beliefs and others.

● **GOVERNMENT   Type:** republic; presidential system; multiparty system. **Independence:** July 1, 1962 (from UN trusteeship under Belgian administration). **Constitution:** May 5, 1995, the Transitional National Assembly adopted a new constitution. **National holiday:** Independence Day, July 1. **Heads of Government:** Pasteur Bizimungu, president (since July 1994); Pierre Célestin Rwigema, prime minister (since Aug.

1995). **Structure:** executive—president; unicameral legislature; judiciary.

●**ECONOMY Monetary unit:** Rwandan franc. **Budget:** (1996 est.) *income:* $231 mil.; *expend.:* $319 mil.. **GDP:** $5.5 bil., $690 per capita (1998 est.). **Chief crops:** coffee, tea, pyrethrum, bananas, beans, sorghum, potatoes; livestock. **Natural resources:** gold, cassiterite (tin ore), wolframite (tungsten ore), natural gas, hydropower. **Major industries:** mining of cassiterite and wolframite, tin, cement. **Labor force:** 3.6 mil. (1985); 90% agriculture, government and services, commerce. **Exports:** $82.1 mil. (f.o.b., 1998 est.); 55% coffee, 21% tea, hides, tin ore. **Imports:** $326 mil. (f.o.b., 1998 est.); foodstuffs, machines and equipment, petroleum products, cement and construction material. **Major trading partners:** *exports:* 49% Brazil, 16% Germany; *imports:* Italy, Kenya, Tanzania.

Tutsi cattle-breeders came to Rwanda, in the late 15th century and slowly conquered the native Hutu farmers. The Tutsi established a monarchy, forcing the Hutus into serfdom. Germans were the first Europeans to arrive in Rwanda and declared it a protectorate in 1899. After World War I Belgium was given a League of Nations mandate over the territory, which became a UN trusteeship after World War II.

Tutsi traditionalists resisted Belgian attempts in the 1950s to institute democratic political institutions. In 1959 the Hutus revolted against the monarchy in a bloody conflict which led to a mass exodus of Tutsis. Two years later the Hutus won a UN-supervised referendum and were granted internal autonomy by Belgium on Jan. 1, 1962. Full independence came on July 1, 1962. Political unrest led to the overthrow of the government in 1973. Maj. Gen. Juvénal Habyarimana dissolved the National Assembly and banned all political activity.

Tutsi refugees in Uganda fought with the army from Oct. 1990, and by 1993 as many as one million people were displaced. A cease-fire and amnesty paved the way for political reform, and a new constitution allowing for multi-party democracy, separation of powers, and presidential term limits went into effect in June 1992. Proposals to merge the armies of the government (Hutu) and the Tutsi Rwandan Patriotic Front were signed in 1993.

But in April 1994, the Hutu presidents of Rwanda and Burundi were both killed when rocket fire (perhaps launched by Hutu dissidents) shot down their plane as it returned from a peace conference in Tanzania. In renewed civil war, the Hutu dominated army of Rwanda and the Hutu militias were driven by the Tutsi-led Patriotic Front into Zaire, Tanzania, Uganda and Burundi; the Hutus reportedly slaughtered over 500,000 Tutsi and countless Hutu moderates as they went. The result was threefold: a million dead, three million refugees, and a Tutsi-dominated but multi-ethnic "government of national unity".

As the Mobutu regime collapsed in neighboring Zaire, the Zaire military attempted to expel a Tutsi community of 400,000 (the Banyamulenge people) who had been settled south of Lake Kivu since the 18th century. The Tutsi resistance gained support from the Rwandan government (Oct. 1996); thus commenced a de facto war between Rwanda and Zaire. The 500,000 Hutu militiamen and other refugees who, as a result, fled Zaire back to Rwanda joined another half million driven from Tanzania by the Tanzanian army. Yet another

wave of killings by Hutu militants had begun in Rwanda. By 1999 the Hutu rebellion was petering out in small but vicious skirmishes and the government of Rwanda was continuing its military aid to Congo (formerly Zaire) president Kabila while attacking remaining Hutu rebel bases in eastern Congo.

▶**SAINT KITTS AND NEVIS**
Federation of Saint Kitts and Nevis
●**GEOGRAPHY Location:** two islands in eastern Caribbean Sea, about 45 mi. (72 km) NW of Antigua. Nevis 17°08'N, 62°37'W; St. Kitts 17°17'N, 62°43'W. **Boundaries:** Caribbean Sea to N, E, S, and W. **Total area:** 104 sq. mi. (269 sq km). **Coastline:** 84 mi. (135 km). **Comparative area:** 1.5 times the size of Washington, D.C. **Land use:** 22% arable land; 17% permanent crops; 3% meadows and pastures; 17% forest and woodland; 41% other; includes N.A. % irrigated. **Major cities:** (1994 est.) Basseterre (capital) 12,605.

●**PEOPLE Population:** 42,838 (1999 est.). **Nationality:** noun—Kittitian(s), Nevisian(s); adjective—Kittitian, Nevisian. **Ethnic groups:** mainly of black African descent. **Languages:** English. **Religions:** Anglican, other Protestant sects, Roman Catholic.

●**GOVERNMENT Type:** constitutional monarchy. **Independence:** Sept. 19, 1983 (from UK). **Constitution:** Sept. 19, 1983. **National holiday:** Independence Day, Sept 19. **Heads of Government:** Cuthbert Sebastian, governor-general (since Jan. 1996); Denzil Douglas, prime minister (since July 1995). **Structure:** executive—cabinet headed by prime minister; unicameral legislature; judiciary—East Caribbean Supreme Court, based on Saint Lucia.

●**ECONOMY Monetary unit:** East Caribbean (EC) dollar. **Budget:** (1997 est.) *income:* $64.1 mil.; *expend.:* $73.3 mil. **GDP:** $235 mil., $6,000 per capita (1997 est.). **Chief crops:** sugarcane, rice, yams, vegetables, bananas. **Natural resources:** negl. **Major industries:** sugar processing, tourism, cotton. **Labor force:** 18,172 (1995); 69% services, 31% manufacturing. **Exports:** $43.7 mil. (f.o.b., 1997 est.); machinery, food, electronics, beverages, tobacco. **Imports:** $129.6 mil. (f.o.b., 1997 est.); machinery, manufactures, food, fuel. **Major trading partners:** (1995) *exports:* 68.5% U.S., 22.3% UK, 5.5% Caricom nations; *imports:* 42.4% U.S., 17.2% Caricom nations, 11.3% UK.

The French settled St. Kitts in 1627; the English settled Nevis in 1628. In 1783 both became British possessions, and the two islands were united in 1882. Britain granted them independence in 1983. The country's economy is almost entirely based on sugar exports, so when Hurricane Hugo devastated sugar yields in 1990, the welfare of the entire population was affected. The reign of Kennedy Alphonse Simmonds, the only prime minister St. Kitts and Nevis had ever known, ended in July 1995, when Denzil Douglas's opposition Labour party defeated Kennedy's increasingly unpopular People's Action Movement. The continued fall of world sugar prices has hurt the economy and in 1997 some leaders in Nevis started a movement to separate from St. Kitts because of high taxes. In 1998 a referendum on separation resulted in a majority yes-vote but not the two-thirds necessary.

▶**SAINT LUCIA**
●**GEOGRAPHY Location:** southeastern Caribbean Sea, between Martinique to N and St. Vincent to SW. Castries 14°01'N, 60°59'W. **Boundaries:** St.

Lucia Channel to N, Atlantic Ocean to E, St. Vincent Passage to S, Caribbean Sea to W. **Total area:** 239 sq. mi. (620 sq km). **Coastline:** 98 mi. (158 km). **Comparative area:** 3.5 times size of Washington, D.C. **Land use:** 8% arable land; 21% permanent crops; 5% meadows and pastures; 13% forest and woodland; 53% other; includes 2% irrigated. **Major cities:** (1992 est.) Castries (capital) 53,883.

● **PEOPLE   Population:** 154,020 (1999 est.). **Nationality:** noun—St. Lucian(s); adjective—St. Lucian. **Ethnic groups:** 90% black African descent, 6% mixed, 3% East Indian, 1% Caucasian. **Languages:** English (official), French patois. **Religions:** 90% Roman Catholic, 7% Protestant, 3% Anglican.

● **GOVERNMENT   Type:** parliamentary democracy. **Independence:** Feb. 22, 1979 (from UK). **Constitution:** Feb. 22, 1979. **National holiday:** Independence Day, Feb. 22. **Heads of Government:** Perlette Louisy, governor-general (since Sept. 1997); Kenny D. Anthony, prime minister (since May 1997). **Structure:** executive—cabinet headed by prime minister; bicameral legislature—Senate, House of Representatives; judiciary—East Caribbean Supreme Court.

● **ECONOMY   Monetary unit:** East Caribbean (EC) dollar. **Budget:** (FY97/98 est.) *income:* $141.2 mil.; *expend.:* $146.7 mil. **GDP:** $625 mil., $4,100 per capita (1997 est.). **Chief crops:** bananas, coconuts, vegetables, root crops, citrus, cocoa. **Natural resources:** forests, sandy beaches, minerals (pumice), mineral springs, geothermal potential. **Major industries:** clothing, assembly of electronic components, beverages. **Labor force:** 43,800 (1983 est.); 43.4% agriculture, 38.9% services, 17.7% industry and commerce; 15% unemployment (1996). **Exports:** $70.1 mil. (f.o.b., 1997); 41% bananas, clothing, cocoa, vegetables, fruits, coconut oil. **Imports:** $292.4 mil. (f.o.b., 1997); 23% food, 21% manufactured goods, 19% machinery and transport equipment, chemicals, fuels. **Major trading partners:** *exports:* 50% UK, 24% U.S., 16% Caricom countries; *imports:* 36% U.S., 22% Caricom countries, 11% UK.

In 1650 the French settled St. Lucia, which was ceded to Britain in 4. A member of the Federation of the West Indies from 1958 to 1962, St. Lucia became internally self-governing in 1967 but was still under Great Britain's protection. In 1979 St. Lucia gained full independence and now enjoys stable competitive politics. Hurricane Allen destroyed many of the country's banana plantations in 1980, and the economy took years to recover from the disaster. The government of Prime Minister John Compton of the United Workers party worked for agrarian reform and proposed legalizing gambling to stimulate tourism but after 15 years in power lost the 1997 elections to the Labour Party led by Kenny B. Anthony.

▶ SAINT VINCENT AND THE GRENADINES

● **GEOGRAPHY   Location:** large island of St. Vincent (13°12'N, 61°14'W) and about 50 smaller islands in southeastern Caribbean Sea about 21 mi. (34 km) SW of St. Lucia and 100 mi. (160 km) W of Barbados. **Boundaries:** St. Vincent Passage to N, Atlantic Ocean to E and SE, Caribbean Sea to SW and W. **Total area:** 131 sq. mi. (340 sq km). **Coastline:** 52 mi. (84 km). **Comparative area:** twice size of Washington, D.C. **Land use:** 10% arable land; 18% permanent crops; 5% meadows and pastures; 36% forest and woodland; 31% other; includes 3% irrigated. **Major cities:** (1991 census) Kingstown (capital) 15,670.

● **PEOPLE   Population:** 120,519 (1999 est.). **Nationality:** noun—St. Vincentian(s) or Vincentian(s); adjective—St. Vincentian or Vincentian. **Ethnic groups:** mainly of black African descent, remainder mixed, with some white, East Indian, and Carib Amerindian. **Languages:** English, French patois. **Religions:** Anglican, Methodist, Roman Catholic, Seventh-Day Adventist.

● **GOVERNMENT   Type:** constitutional monarchy. **Independence:** Oct. 27, 1979 (from UK). **Constitution:** Oct. 27, 1979. **National holiday:** Independence Day, Oct. 27. **Heads of Government:** Charles Antrobus, governor-general (since June 1997); James Mitchell, prime minister (since July 1984). **Structure:** executive—prime minister is head of government; bicameral legislature— 13-member elected House of Representatives and 6-member appointed Senate; judiciary—East Caribbean Supreme Court.

● **ECONOMY   Monetary unit:** East Caribbean (EC) dollar. **Budget:** (1997 est.) *income:* $85.7 mil.; *expend.:* $98.6 mil. **GDP:** $289 mil., $2,400 per capita (1998 est.). **Chief crops:** bananas, coconuts, sweet potatoes, spices; small numbers of cattle, sheep, pigs, goats; small fish catch used locally. **Natural resources:** negl. **Major industries:** food processing (sugar, flour), cement, furniture. **Labor force:** 67,000 (1984 est.); 26% agriculture, 17% industry, 57% services; 35-40% unemployed (1994). **Exports:** $47.3 mil. (f.o.b., 1997 est.); 39% bananas, eddoes and dasheen (taro), arrowroot starch, tennis racquets. **Imports:** $158.8 mil. (f.o.b., 1997 est.); foodstuffs, machinery and equipment, chemicals and fertilizers, minerals and fuels. **Major trading partners:** *exports:* 49% Caricom countries, 16% UK, 10% U.S.; *imports:* 36% U.S., 28% Caricom countries, 13% UK.

Although ceded to Britain in 1763, St. Vincent was inhabited by the fierce Carib Indians, who continued fighting for control of the island until 1796, when they had all been either killed or deported. Just prior to its independence in 1979, St. Vincent and the Grenadines was a self-governing state in association with Great Britain. It is one of the poorest countries in the West Indies. Several natural disasters have plagued the economy, including a 1979 volcanic eruption and two destructive hurricanes in 1980 and 1986. Prime Minister James Mitchell of the New Democratic party currently governs the country, winning his fourth term after June 1997 elections gave his New Democratic Party a slender one-vote majority in the 15-seat legislature.

▶ SAMOA
Formerly Western Samoa
Independent State of Samoa

● **GEOGRAPHY   Location:** two large and seven small islands (five inhabited) in South Pacific Ocean, about 1,500 mi. (2,400 km) NE of New Zealand. Apia 13°49'S, 171°45'W. **Boundaries:** surrounded by Pacific Ocean; nearest neighbor is American Samoa to E. **Total area:** 1,104 sq. mi. (2,860 sq km). **Coastline:** 250 mi. (403 km). **Comparative area:** slightly smaller than Rhode Island. **Land use:** 19% arable land; 24% permanent crops; negl. % meadows and pastures; 47% forest and woodland; 10% other. **Major cities:** (1991 census) Apia (capital) 34,260.

● **PEOPLE   Population:** 229,979 (1999 est.). **Nationality:** noun—Samoan(s); adjective—Samoan. **Ethnic groups:** 92.6% Samoan; about 7% Euronesians (persons of European and Polynesian blood), 0.4% Europeans. **Languages:** Samoan (Polynesian), English. **Religions:** 99.7% Christian (about half of population associated with London Missionary Society; includes Congregational, Roman Catholic, Methodist, Latter-Day Saints, Seventh-Day Adventist).

• **GOVERNMENT Type:** constitutional monarchy under native chief. **Independence:** Jan. 1, 1962 (from UN trusteeship administered by New Zealand). **Constitution:** Jan. 1, 1962. **National holiday:** National Day, Jan. 1. **Heads of Government:** Malietoa Tanumafili II, head of state (since 1962); Tuilaepa Sailele Malielegaoi, prime minister (since Nov. 1998). **Structure:** executive—chief of state appoints prime minister; unicameral legislature (47-member Legislative Assembly); judiciary.

• **ECONOMY Monetary unit:** tala. **Budget:** (FY96/97 est.) *income:* $52 mil.; *expend.:* $99 mil. **GDP:** $470 mil., $2,100 per capita (1997 est.). **Chief crops:** coconuts, bananas, taro, yams. **Natural resources:** hardwood forests, fish. **Major industries:** timber, tourism, food processing. **Labor force:** 82,500 (1991 est.); 65% agriculture, 30% services. **Exports:** $14.6 mil. (f.o.b., 1997); coconut oil and cream, copra, fish, beer. **Imports:** $99.7 mil. (f.o.b., 1997 est.); intermediate goods, food, capital goods. **Major trading partners:** *exports:* 82% Australia, 6% New Zealand, Slovakia, Germany; *imports:* 33% Australia, 25% New Zealand, 15% Japan, 8% Fiji.

The Polynesian island group of Samoa (Navigator's Islands) was partitioned in 1899 between the United States, which had established a naval base at Pago Pago on Tutuila in 1878, and Germany, which organized the westerly islands into a colony in 1894. In 1914 New Zealand troops occupied the German-held islands. New Zealand administered Western Samoa under a League of Nations mandate beginning in 1920 and continued to control the islands as a UN Trust Territory after 1945. In 1959 home rule was established under an elected local government. Western Samoa became an independent nation on Jan. 1, 1962. The constitution blends Western parliamentary government and traditional Samoan forms of rule. The parliamentary electorate is limited to the malai, heads of extended families; the malai are wholly responsible for local affairs. The local culture is similarly a blend of Samoan tradition with Christianity.

The economy is based on subsistence agriculture, forestry, fishing, and tourism.

In November 1998, after 16 years of stable and peaceful rule, Prime Minister Tofilau Eti Alesana resigned for health reasons and was replaced by his deputy, Tuilaepa Sailele Malielegaoi.

▶SAN MARINO
Republic of San Marino
• **GEOGRAPHY Location:** on slopes of Mt. Titano, in the Apennines, within central Italian region of Emilia-Romagna. **Boundaries:** surrounded by Italian territory. **Total area:** 23 sq. mi. (60 sq km). **Coastline:** none. **Comparative area:** about three-tenths size of Washington, D.C. **Land use:** 17% arable land; 0% permanent crops; 0% meadows and pastures; 0% forest and woodland; 83% other. **Major cities:** (1995 est.) San Marino (capital) 4,498.

• **PEOPLE Population:** 25,061 (1999 est.). **Nationality:** noun—Sammarinese (sing., pl.); adjective—Sammarinese. **Ethnic groups:** Sammarinese,

Italian. **Languages:** Italian. **Religions:** Roman Catholic.

• **GOVERNMENT Type:** republic. **Independence:** 301 A.D. **Constitution:** Oct. 8, 1600; electoral law of 1926 serves some of functions of constitution. **National holiday:** Anniversary of the Foundation of the Republic, Sept. 3. **Heads of Government:** Antonello Bacciocchi (Apr.-Sept. 1999) and Rosa Zafferani (since Sept. 1999), minister of foreign affairs. **Structure:** executive—two captain-regents with six-month terms elected by and from the legislature, actual power wielded by secretary of state for foreign affairs; unicameral legislature—Great and General Council elected by popular vote for five-year terms; judicial—Council of Twelve is supreme judicial body.

• **ECONOMY Monetary unit:** Italian lira. **Budget:** (1995 est.) *income:* $320 mil.; *expend:* $320 mil. **GDP:** $500 mil., $20,000 per capita (1997 est.). **Chief crops:** wheat, grapes, maize, olives; cattle, pigs, horses, meat, cheese, hides. **Natural resources:** building stones. **Major industries:** tourism, textiles, electronics. **Labor force:** 15,600 (1995); 55% services, 43% industry, 2% agriculture. **Exports:** trade data included with Italian statistics; commodity trade consisting primarily of exchanging building stone, lime, wood, chestnuts, wheat, and wine for a wide variety of consumer manufactures. **Imports:** see exports. **Major trading partners:** N.A.

The "Most Serene Republic" of San Marino, entirely surrounded by Italy near the city of Rimini, is the oldest republic in the world, with communitarian roots dating to the fourth century A.D. While Piedmont-Sardinia was conquering all of the rest of the Italian peninsula during the period 1860-70, it left San Marino independent; the new kingdom of Italy signed a treaty of friendship and cooperation with the republic in 1862.

Leftist coalitions governed from 1978 through 1986, giving San Marino the only Communist government west of the Soviet bloc. Since 1986 the government has been controlled by a coalition of Communists and Christian Democrats. In 1992 San Marino joined the United Nations.

The economy is balanced between small-scale agriculture (primarily wine grapes and livestock) and industry, including textiles, ceramics, and furniture. Philatelic sales and tourism are important sources of revenue. Lacking extremes of wealth and poverty and with low unemployment, the republic enjoys general prosperity.

▶SÃO TOMÉ AND PRÍNCIPE
Democratic Republic of Saõ Tomé and Príncipe
• **GEOGRAPHY Location:** two main islands, São Tomé (0°19'N, 6°43'E) and Príncipe, and Caroço, Pedras, Tinhosas (off Príncipe), and Rolas (off São Tomé), off west coast of Africa. **Boundaries:** west of Gabon in Gulf of Guinea. **Total area:** 371 sq. mi. (960 sq km). **Coastline:** 130 mi. (209 km). **Comparative area:** more than 5.5 times size of Washington, D.C. **Land use:** 2% arable land; 36% permanent crops; 1% meadows and pastures; 0% forest and woodland; 61% other. **Major cities:** (1991) São Tomé (capital) 43,420.

• **PEOPLE Population:** 154,878 (1999 est.). **Nationality:** noun—São Toméan(s); adjective—São Toméan. **Ethnic groups:** mestiço, angolares (descendants of Angolan slaves), forros (descendents of freed slaves), servicais (contract laborers from Angola, Mozambique, and Cape Verde), tongas (children of servicais born on the islands), and

Europeans (primarily Portuguese). **Languages:** Portuguese (official). **Religions:** Roman Catholic, Evangelical Protestant, Seventh-Day Adventist.

● **GOVERNMENT** **Type:** republic. **Independence:** July 12, 1975 (from Portugal). **Constitution:** Sept. 10, 1990. **National holiday:** Independence Day, July 12. **Heads of Government:** Miguel dos Anjos da Cunha Trovoada, president (since Apr. 1991); Guilherme Posser Da Costa, prime minister (since July 1999). **Structure:** executive—president assisted by cabinet of ministers; unicameral legislature; judiciary.

● **ECONOMY** **Monetary unit:** dobra. **Budget:** (1993 est.) *income:* $58 mil.; *expend.:* $114 mil. **GDP:** $164 mil., $1,100 per capita (1998 est.). **Chief crops:** cocoa, copra, coconuts, coffee, palm kernels, bananas, cinnamon, pepper, papaya, beans; poultry, fish. **Natural resources:** fish. **Major industries:** small processing factories producing shirts, soap, beer; fish and shrimp processing. **Labor force:** most of population engaged in subsistence agriculture and fishing; labor shortages of skilled workers. **Exports:** $5.3 mil. (f.o.b., 1997 est.); 90% cocoa, copra, coffee, palm oil. **Imports:** $19.2 mil. (f.o.b., 1997 est.); machinery and electrical equipment, food products, fuels. **Major trading partners:** *exports:* 51% Netherlands, 6% Germany, 6% Portugal; *imports:* 26% Portugal, 18% France, Angola, Belgium, Japan.

The islands of São Tomé and Príncipe, located in the Atlantic Ocean 275 and 125 miles, respectively, off the northern coast of Gabon, make up one of Africa's smallest nations. They were uninhabited when first discovered by the Portuguese in 1470 but by the mid-1500s became Africa's foremost exporter of sugar. As the sugar market declined, the islands became a major slave-trading center and producer of coffee and cocoa. By 1908 São Tomé was the world's largest cocoa producer.

Portugal did not abolish slavery until 1876, and abusive labor practices continued until well into the 20th century. In 1953 hundreds of workers were killed in clashes with the Portuguese. Soon after, a small number of São Toméans formed the Movement for the Liberation of São Tomé and Príncipe (MLSTP) with its base in Gabon. But the islands did not gain independence until July 12, 1975.

The MLSTP took over after independence and became the country's only official party. By 1986 the country relied on foreign aid for approximately 41 percent of its gross national product. Although in the past it received military advisers from the former Soviet Union and economic advisers from Cuba, São Tomé and Príncipe has announced a foreign policy based upon nonalignment. Multi-party democracy was introduced in 1991.

▶ SAUDI ARABIA
Kingdom of Saudi Arabia

● **GEOGRAPHY** **Location:** occupies four-fifths of Arabian peninsula in southwestern Asia. **Boundaries:** Jordan, Iraq, and Kuwait to N, Persian Gulf, Qatar, and United Arab Emirates to E, Oman to SE, Yemen to S and SE, Red Sea to W. **Total area:** 756,982 sq. mi. (1,960,582 sq km). **Coastline:** 1,641 mi. (2,640 km). **Comparative area:** slightly more than one-fifth the size of the U.S. **Land use:** 2% arable land; negl. % permanent crops; 56% meadows and pastures; 1% forest and woodland; 41% other. **Major cities:** (1991 est.) Riyadh (capital) 1,800,000; Jid'dah 1,500,000; Mecca 630,000; Taif 410,000; Medina 400,000.

● **PEOPLE** **Population:** 21,504,613 (1999 est.). **Nationality:** noun—Saudi(s); adjective—Saudi or Saudi Arabian. **Ethnic groups:** 90% Arab, 10% Afro-Asian. **Languages:** Arabic. **Religions:** 100% Muslim.

● **GOVERNMENT** **Type:** monarchy. **Constitution:** none; governed according to Shari'a or Islamic law. **National holiday:** Unification of the Kingdom, Sept. 23. **Head of Government:** Fahd bin Abdul-Aziz al-Saud, king (since June 1982). **Structure:** king rules in consultation with royal family and Council of Ministers; no elected legislature; Supreme Council of Justice.

● **ECONOMY** **Monetary unit:** Saudi riyal. **Budget:** (1999 est.) *income:* $32.3 bil.; *expend.:* $44 bil. **GDP:** $186 bil., $9,000 per capita (1998 est.). **Chief crops:** wheat, barley, tomatoes, melons, dates, citrus; mutton, chickens, eggs, milk. **Natural resources:** crude oil, natural gas, iron ore, gold, copper. **Major industries:** crude oil production, petroleum refining, basic petrochemicals. **Labor force:** 7 mil.; 40% government, 25% industry, construction, and oil, 30% services, 5% agriculture. **Exports:** $59.7 bil. (f.o.b., 1997 est.); 90% petroleum and petroleum products. **Imports:** $26.2 bil. (f.o.b., 1997 est.); machinery and equipment, foodstuffs, chemicals, motor vehicles, textiles. **Major trading partners:** 18% Japan, 15% U.S., 11% South Korea; *imports:* 23% U.S., 17% UK, 8% Japan.

In ancient times various cultures flourished in parts of the Arabian peninsula, particularly along the western rim, in cities devoted to trade between the Gulf of Aden and the eastern Mediterranean, and in such agricultural and trading centers as Yemen and Oman. Cultural and political unity was lacking, however, until the rise of Mohammed, the prophet of Islam. In A.D. 622 Mohammed fled from Mecca, the holy city of Arabian paganism, to the nearby city of Medina; the Islamic era dates from that year. Preaching from Medina, Mohammed soon gained converts to Islam throughout Arabia. His army captured Mecca in 630, converting its sacred shrine, the Kaaba, to an Islamic place of worship. By 632, when Mohammed died, all of Arabia was unified under Islamic rule.

In 661 the Caliphate, the ruling body of early Islam, moved from Medina to Damascus. Thereafter Arabia was nominally unified under Islamic rule—but in practice was usually divided among various principalities in the arable areas and trading centers, and under tribal rule in the arid interior. Mecca fell to the Ottoman Empire in 1517, but Ottoman control of Arabia was never complete. The rise of the Wahabi sect of Islam in the 18th century posed a challenge to Ottoman rule. In the 19th century, the Saud family rose to leadership in the Wahabi movement and established a kingdom in Nejd, the central region of Arabia, with a capital at Riyadh.

In 1902 Ibn Saud (1880-1953) consolidated his family's control at Riyadh and in 1912-13 led a new Wahabi revolt against the Ottoman Turks. During World War I, the British aided Ibn Saud's rebellion in the Nejd, along with that of Ibn Saud's rival Hussein ibn Ali in the Hejaz, in the mountains of western Arabia along the coast of the Red Sea. A British protectorate was established in both regions in 1915, and Great Britain maintained a dominant position in Arabia immediately after World War I.

In 1924 Ibn Saud captured Hussein ibn Ali's capital at Mecca, and he proclaimed himself king of Hejaz in 1926 and of Nejd in 1927. Ibn Saud consolidated his control over the following two years, and his kingdom was formally recognized by Great Britain in 1927. The country was renamed Saudi Arabia in 1932.

Saudi Arabia is an absolute monarchy based on Islamic law; it has no written constitution and no parliament. The king exercises sole authority and rules in consultation with a Council of Ministers. Islamic law is enforced; alcohol is prohibited and the public activities of women severely restricted. The Saudi kings have great power within the Islamic world through their control over the holy cities of Mecca and Medina and their administration of the annual Muslim pilgrimages to those cities.

The discovery of oil in eastern Arabia in the early 1930s rapidly transformed Saudi Arabia from an impoverished nation to a center of great wealth. In 1933 an exclusive concession for the exploitation of Saudi Arabian oil was granted to an American-chartered corporation, the Arabian-American Oil Company (Aramco). For many years wealth remained concentrated in the hands of the Saudi clan, and little change was felt in the desert interior, where Bedouin nomads continued to raise sheep and camels. Large numbers of Yemenis, Palestinians, Pakistanis, and other foreign workers are employed in the oil fields.

Saudi Arabia remained neutral during most of World War II but declared war on the Axis powers in March 1945; in the same year, it became a founding member of both the United Nations and the Arab League.

Ibn Saud became a leader of Arab anti-Zionism and contributed a small contingent of troops to the 1948 Arab-Israeli War. That policy was maintained by Ibn Saud's second son and successor, King Faisal, who instituted a policy of providing large annual subsidies to Egypt and other Arab League states following the 1967 Arab-Israeli War. In 1973 King Faisal sent Saudi units to fight in the Arab-Israeli War of that year. He played a leading role in organizing the 1973-74 Arab oil embargo in an effort to force the United States and its allies to take a harder line with Israel.

King Faisal was assassinated by his nephew, Prince Faisal, on Mar. 25, 1975, and was succeeded by King Khalid. Little change in policy resulted. In 1979 Saudi Arabia denounced the Camp David talks and the Egyptian-Israeli peace treaty and led the Arab League effort to ostracize Egypt within the Arab world.

Saudi Arabia has consistently opposed leftist and radical movements in the Arab world, sending troops to help put down leftist rebellions in North Yemen and Oman in the 1970s. Saudi kings have taken a moderate approach toward relations with the West. Following the transfer of Aramco assets to full Saudi Arabian ownership during 1973-76, Saudi Arabia used its leading position within the Organization of Petroleum Exporting Countries (OPEC) to argue for a policy of stable production and prices.

This moderate policy has been rewarded by the willingness of the United States, Great Britain, France, and other Western nations to sell arms—including jet fighters, tanks, and other sophisticated weapons—to Saudi Arabia despite Israeli protests. The multibillion-dollar arms trade has helped to offset the Western oil trade deficit with Saudi Arabia.

Saudi Arabia experienced repeated disturbances in the 1980s. Muslim fundamentalist ter-

rorists seized the Grand Mosque at Mecca on Nov. 20, 1979, provoking a crisis for the Saudi monarchy. On July 31, 1987, Iranian pilgrims rioted in Mecca and were fired upon by Saudi security forces; 402 persons died, including 275 Iranians. Iran's Ayatollah Khomeini denounced the Saudi government and said it was unworthy of being the guardian of Islam's sacred shrines.

A longtime supporter of the Palestine Liberation Organization, the Saudi government gave the PLO $850 million during the 1980s, but ceased when the PLO backed Saddam Hussein's invasion of Kuwait in 1990.

During the Persian Gulf War, King Fahd granted permission to station U.S. troops in Saudi Arabia to guard against a possible Iraqi attack. The Saudis promised the United States $16.8 billion and Egypt $1.5 billion to defray the costs of the war. Little ground fighting took place on Saudi soil, but massive oil spills threatened the operation of crucial desalination plants in the Persian Gulf.

Since the war, Saudi Arabia has played a prominent and pivotal role in the diplomatic efforts of the United States and its allies to reach a permanent accord in the Middle East.

Two events in 1996 raised concerns about Saudi Arabia's future stability. The first was in January, when King Fahd, ailing from a 1995 stroke, temporarily ceded power to his legal successor, Crown Prince Abdullah. The second came in June, when terrorists bombed an apartment complex in Dhahran, killing 19 American soldiers stationed there and wounding more than 300 people.

▶ SENEGAL
Republic of Senegal

● **Geography   Location:** northwestern coast of Africa. **Boundaries:** Mauritania to N, Mali to E, Guinea and Guinea-Bissau to S, Atlantic Ocean to W; The Gambia forms narrow enclave extending 200 mi. (320 km) inland from Atlantic coast. **Total area:** 75,749 sq. mi. (196,190 sq km). **Coastline:** 330 mi. (531 km). **Comparative area:** slightly smaller than South Dakota. **Land use:** 12% arable land; 0% permanent crops; 16% meadows and pastures; 54% forest and woodland; 18% other. **Major cities:** (1992 census) Dakar (capital) 1,729,823; Thies 201,350; Kaolack 179,894.

● **People   Population:** 10,051,930 (1999 est.). **Nationality:** noun—Senegalese (sing., pl.); adjective—Senegalese. **Ethnic groups:** 43.3% Wolof, 23.8% Pular, 14.7% Serer, 3.7% Diola, 3% Mandink, 1.1% Soninke, 1% European and Lebanese. **Languages:** French (official), Wolof, Pulaar, Diola, Mandingo. **Religions:** 92% Muslim, 6% indigenous beliefs, 2% Christian (mostly Roman Catholic).

● **Government   Type:** republic under multi-party democratic rule. **Independence:** Apr. 4, 1960 (from France). **Constitution:** Mar. 3, 1963, revised 1991. **National holiday:** Independence Day, Apr. 4. **Heads of Government:** Abdou Diouf, president (since Jan. 1981); Mamadou Lamine Loum, prime minister (since July 1998). **Structure:** executive—president; unicameral legislature; judiciary—Constitutional Court, Council of State, Court of Final Appeals, Court of Appeals.

● **Economy   Monetary unit:** Communauté Financière Africaine (CFA) franc. **Budget:** (1996 est.) *income:* $885 mil.; *expend.:* $885 mil. **GDP:** $15.6 bil., $1,600 per capita (1998 est.). **Chief crops:** peanuts, millet, corn, sorghum, rice, cotton, tomotoes, green vegetables; cattle, poultry, pigs;

fish. **Natural resources:** fish, phosphates, iron ore. **Major industries:** fishing, agricultural processing, phosphate mining. **Labor force:** 60% agriculture. **Exports:** $925 mil. (f.o.b., 1998); fish, peanuts, petroleum products, phosphates, cotton. **Imports:** $1.2 bil. (f.o.b., 1998); foods and beverages, consumer goods, capital goods, petroleum products. **Major trading partners:** *exports:* 20% France, other EU countries, India, Ivory Coast; *imports:* 36% France, other EU countries, Nigeria.

Inhabited since ancient times, Senegal was dominated in the 13th and 14th centuries by the Mandingo and Jolof empires. Portuguese traders and explorers arrived in Senegal in the early 15th century and later competed with the British, Dutch, and French for domination in Senegal. The French established a trading station at Saint-Louis in 1659 and maintained possession thereafter, except for the British enclave along the Gambia River.

In the early 19th century, the French began a series of campaigns to bring the entire country under their control; the last independent sultanate surrendered in 1893. Senegal became a French colony in 1920, and Dakar became the capital of French West Africa. Senegal became a major contributor of African troops to the French armed forces.

In 1946 a territorial assembly was established, with a limited electorate and advisory powers, which were gradually expanded in subsequent years. With the creation of the French Community of Nations in 1958, Senegal achieved local self-rule within the community.

In 1959, with the encouragement of France, Senegal and French Sudan (now Mali) formed the Federation of Mali, which became fully independent on June 20, 1960. Senegal seceded from the federation on Aug. 20 and declared itself the Republic of Senegal. Leopold Sedar Senghor, one of Africa's leading statesmen, became Senegal's first president.

In 1962 Prime Minister Mamdou Dia attempted a coup against the Senghor government; it failed, and Dia was imprisoned. A new constitution was subsequently adopted, strengthening the power of the presidency. Senghor retired from office in 1981 and was succeeded by Adbou Diouf. He encouraged political pluralism and has presided over a generally stable government. Diouf was elected in his own right in 1983 and reelected in 1988. Following the 1988 elections, riots broke out over charges of electoral fraud, and a state of emergency was declared.

Diouf, who has taken a lead in African affairs, was reelected for the third time in 1993, but his Socialist party's legislative majority was diminished. Since 1982, Senegal has been troubled by a separatist insurgency fought by the Movement of Democratic Forces of Casamance, a northern region. At home, Diouf consolidated his power so well that in 1998 Parliament passed a law allowing him to become President for life. His involvement in the civil war in Guinea-Bissau, however, has caused dissension in the army. His January 1999 creation of a Senate as "upper house" to the National Assembly meant little for democracy since, with all opposition parties boycotting the election, his Socialist Party carried all 45 seats up for election.

Senegal remains closely tied to France commercially, culturally, and in foreign affairs. Senegal's economy is primarily agricultural. Industries include fishing and fish processing (the principal source of export earnings), food processing, light manufacturing, and phosphate mining. Senegalese merchants are active in commercial networks throughout West Africa.

▶ SERBIA AND MONTENEGRO
See "Yugoslavia"

▶ SEYCHELLES
Republic of Seychelles

● **GEOGRAPHY Location:** more than 90 widely scattered islands in western Indian Ocean about 1,000 mi. (1,600 km) E of Kenya and Tanzania. Victoria (Mahé Is.) 4°37'S, 55°28'E. **Boundaries:** surrounded by Indian Ocean; nearest neighbor is Madagascar about 130 mi. (210 km) S of southernmost island group. **Total area:** 176 sq. mi. (455 sq km). **Coastline:** 305 mi. (491 km). **Comparative area:** 2.5 times the size of Washington, D.C. **Land use:** 2% arable land; 13% permanent crops; 0% meadows and pastures; 11% forest and woodland; 74% other. **Major cities:** (1987) Victoria (capital) 24,325 (includes suburbs).

● **PEOPLE Population:** 79,164 (1999 est.). **Nationality:** noun—Seychellois (sing., pl.); adjective—Seychelles. **Ethnic groups:** Seychellois (mixture of Asians, Africans, Europeans). **Languages:** English, French (both official); Creole. **Religions:** 90% Roman Catholic, 8% Anglican, 2% other.

● **GOVERNMENT Type:** republic. **Independence:** June 29, 1976 (from UK). **Constitution:** June 18, 1993. **National holiday:** National Day, June 18. **Head of Government:** France Albert René, president (since June 1977). **Structure:** executive—president; unicameral legislature; judiciary.

● **ECONOMY Monetary unit:** Seychelles rupee. **Budget:** (1994 est.) *income:* $220 mil.; *expend.:* $241 mil. **GDP:** $550 mil., $7,000 per capita (1997 est.). **Chief crops:** coconuts, cinnamon, vanilla, sweet potatoes, cassava, bananas; broiler chickens; tuna fishing (expansion under way). **Natural resources:** fish, copra, cinnamon trees. **Major industries:** tourism is largest industry; processing of coconut and vanilla; fishing. **Labor force:** 26,000 (1996); 19% industry, 57% services, 14% government, 10% agriculture, forestry, and fishing. **Exports:** $53 mil. (f.o.b., 1995); fish, cinnamon bark, copra, petroleum products (reexports). **Imports:** $340 mil. (c.i.f., 1997); manufactured goods, food, petroleum products, tobacco, beverages, machinery and transportation equipment. **Major trading partners:** *exports:* France, UK, China; *imports:* China, Singapore, South Africa.

The Seychelles Islands were occupied by France in the 18th century and seized by Great Britain in 1794. They were administered along with Mauritius until 1903, when the Seychelles became a separate British colony. African and Indian workers were brought in to work in coconut and spice plantations and in guano mining. The present population is of mixed African, Indian, and European descent.

In the post-World War II period, a home-rule government rejected independence as impracticable. At the urging of the Organization of African Unity and the United Nations, the Seychelles declared independence on June 29, 1976. Its first president was ousted in a socialist coup in 1977 led by Prime Minister France Albert René. A new constitution, promulgated in March 1979, formalized one-party Socialist rule. In July 1992 a commission was elected to rewrite the constitution before the end of the year, but the delegates defeated the first results.

Since independence, the economy of the Seychelles has become heavily dependent on the tourist industry, which accounts for 90 percent of the country's foreign exchange earnings. Fishing accounts for 40 percent of exports.

▶ SIERRA LEONE
Republic of Sierra Leone
● **GEOGRAPHY Location:** west central Africa. **Boundaries:** Guinea to N and E, Liberia to S, Atlantic Ocean to W. **Total area:** 27,699 sq. mi. (71,740 sq km). **Coastline:** 250 mi. (402 km). **Comparative area:** slightly smaller than South Carolina. **Land use:** 7% arable land; 1% permanent crops; 31% meadows and pastures; 28% forest and woodland; 33% other.; **Major cities:** Freetown (capital) 384,499 (1985 census); Koindu 82,474; Bo 59,768; Kenema 52,473; Makeni 49,474.
● **PEOPLE Population:** 5,296,651 (1999 est.). **Nationality:** noun—Sierra Leonean(s); adjective—Sierra Leonean. **Ethnic groups:** over 90% African (30% Temne, 30% Mende), rest European, Creole, and Asian. **Languages:** English (official); regular use limited to literate minority; principal languages are Mende in south and Temne in north; Krio is language of resettled ex-slave population of Freetown area and is lingua franca. **Religions:** 60% Muslim, 30% indigenous beliefs, 10% Christian.
● **GOVERNMENT Type:** constitutional democracy. **Independence:** Apr. 27, 1961 (from UK). **Constitution:** Oct. 1, 1991. **National holiday:** Republic Day, Apr. 27. **Heads of Government:** Alhaj Ahmad Tejan Kabbah, president (since Mar. 1996). **Structure:** executive—president; unicameral legislature-68 elected seats, 12 filled by paramount chiefs; judiciary.
● **ECONOMY Monetary unit:** leone. **Budget:** (1996 est.) *income:* $96 mil.; *expend.:* $150 mil. **GDP:** $2.7 bil., $530 per capita (1998 est.). **Chief crops:** palm kernels, coffee, cocoa, rice, palm oil, peanuts; poultry, cattle, sheep, pigs; fish. **Natural resources:** diamonds, titanium ore, bauxite, iron ore, gold. **Major industries:** mining (diamonds, iron ore, bauxite, rutile), small-scale manufacturing (beverages, textiles, cigarettes, footwear), petroleum refinery. **Labor force:** 1.369 mil. (1981); 65% agriculture, 19% industry, 16% services; only small minority, some 65,000, earn wages. **Exports:** $41 mil. (f.o.b., 1998); diamonds, rutile, cocoa, coffee, fish. **Imports:** $166 mil. (c.i.f., 1998); foodstuffs, machinery and equipment, fuels and lubricants. **Major trading partners:** *exports:* 49% Belgium, 10% Spain, 8% US; *imports:* 16% UK, 9% US, 8% Ivory Coast.

Portuguese domination of the Sierra Leone coast began in 1462. English explorers, including Francis Drake, arrived in the late 16th century. Europeans traded for slaves in Sierra Leone, but in 1787 Freetown was founded by the British Sierra Leone Co. as a haven for freed slaves. The settlement was populated by former slaves from Great Britain, North America, and the Caribbean, and later by slaves liberated from slave trading ships by the British navy.

Sierra Leone was reorganized as a British colony in 1808. The ex-slave population, from diverse tribal and national backgrounds, developed an English-speaking Creole culture unique in Africa. Freetown became the center of British colonial administration and trade in West Africa and was the focus of missionary-supported projects in health care and economic development.

The native peoples of Sierra Leone staged numerous rebellions against the British and the Creole elite; resentment focused on the tax system and on the privileges of the English-speaking descendents of ex-slaves. During the 20th century, home rule developed through an elected advisory legislature. In 1951 a constitutional framework had been developed as the basis of decolonization. Sir Milton Margei became chief minister in 1953, and prime minister in 1961. The last ties with the British Crown were cut on Apr. 27, 1961, when Sierra Leone became a republic. A referendum in 1978 created a one-party state. In 1984 and 1985 student and public employee protests against the government led to riots and the restoration of multi-party elections.

In April 1992, Momoh was ousted in a coup by Capt. Valentine Strasser. Despite the country's wealth of natural resources, Strasser's corruption and mismanagement threatened to derail the economy. Strasser was overthrown in Jan. 1996 by army officers who pledged to continue his plan for multi-party elections the following month. Those elections proceeded smoothly, with Ahmad Tejan Kabbah of the People's party capturing close to 60 percent of the votes.

Since 1991, the Revolutionary United Front (RUF) rebel army has waged a civil war against the government. An attack on the northern town of Kambia in 1994 resulted in 30,000 refugees. After the 1996 election, the RUF announced a two-month cease-fire and said it would hold talks with Kabbah, but it refused to recognize him as the president. A peace treaty was signed in Nov. 1996 giving RUF's approval to Kabbah but this held for only a few months when Fodaj Sankoh, leader of the rebel army, refused to accept government restrictions. In May 1997 regular army troops led by Major Johnny Paul Koroma overthrew the Kabbah government. Nigeria and other West African nations refused to recognize the new government and led a coalition army against the rebels that resulted in Kabbah's restoration in March 1998. The rebel troops fled to the countryside but began a campaign of terror against civilians. The RUF was strong enough to capture half of the capital in early January 1999 until driven out by Nigerian troops a week later; the death toll was about 5000. But Nigeria's President Abubakar intended to withdraw his country's troops by May 29, the end of Nigeria's "transition" period so a cease-fire of sorts was proclaimed in May with a vague deal, apparently to involve the RUF in governing Sierra Leone, perhaps with Sankoh as vice-president and some cabinet posts. RUF forces controlled about half the country.

▶ SINGAPORE
Republic of Singapore
● **GEOGRAPHY Location:** Singapore Island and some 57 islets off southern Malay peninsula (linked by a causeway). **Boundaries:** Johor Strait to N; Pacific Ocean to E; Strait of Malacca to SW, separating Singapore from Indonesian island of Sumatra; and Indian Ocean to W. **Total area:** 244 sq. mi. (633 sq km). **Coastline:** 120 mi. (193 km). **Comparative area:** slightly more than 3.5 times size of Washington, D.C. **Land use:** 2% arable land; 6% permanent crops; 0% meadows and pastures; 5% forest and woodland; 87% other. **Major cities:** Singapore (capital).
● **PEOPLE Population:** 3,531,600 (1999 est.). **Nationality:** noun—Singaporean(s); adjective—Singapore. **Ethnic groups:** 76.4% Chinese, 14.9%

Malay, 6.4% Indian, 2.3% other. **Languages:** Chinese, Malay, Tamil, and English (all official); Malay (national). **Religions:** majority of Chinese are Buddhists or atheists; Malays nearly all Muslim; minorities include Christians, Hindus, Sikhs, Taoists, Confucianists.

• **GOVERNMENT Type:** republic within Commonwealth. **Independence:** Aug. 9, 1965 (from Malaysia). **Constitution:** June 3, 1959, amended 1965; based on preindependence State of Singapore constitution. **National holiday:** Aug. 9. **Heads of Government:** Ong Teng Cheong, president (since Sept. 1993); Goh Chok Tong, prime minister (since Nov. 1990). **Structure:** executive—ceremonial president, power exercised by prime minister and cabinet; unicameral; judiciary.

• **ECONOMY Monetary unit:** Singapore dollar. **Budget:** (FY97/98 est.) *income:* $16.3 bil.; *expend.:* $13.6 bil. **GDP:** $91.7 bil., $26,300 per capita (1998 est.). **Chief crops:** rubber, copra, fruits, vegetables; poultry. **Natural resources:** fish, deep-water ports. **Major industries:** petroleum refining, electronics, oil drilling equipment. **Labor force:** 1.856 mil. (1997 est.); 33.5% financial, business, and other services, 25.6% manufacturing, 22.9% commerce, 6.6% construction. **Exports:** $128 bil. (1998 est.); computer equipment, petroleum products, rubber and rubber products, telecommunications equipment. **Imports:** $133.9 bil. (1997 est.); aircraft, petroleum, chemicals, foodstuffs. **Major trading partners:** *exports:* 19% Malaysia, 18% U.S., 9% Hong Kong; *imports:* 21% Japan, 15% Malaysia, 15% U.S.

Singapore was founded in 1819 by Sir Thomas Stamford Raffles on land ceded to the East India Company by the sultanate of Johore (see "Malaysia"). An Anglo-Dutch treaty turned Singapore over to the British Crown in 1824, and eventually it was administered as part of the Straits Settlements. With its excellent harbor, Singapore quickly eclipsed Penang and Malacca as the dominant port for trade through the Straits of Malacca.

Fortified as a bastion of British defense in Southeast Asia, Singapore was overrun by Japanese troops in February 1942. The British reoccupied the city of Singapore in September 1945 and reorganized Singapore as a British colony in 1946. On June 5, 1959, Singapore became a self-governing parliamentary democracy within the British Commonwealth. Lee Kwan Yew, head of the People's Action party, became prime minister. On Sept. 16, 1963, Singapore, along with Malaya, Sarawak, and Sabah, formed the Malaysian Federation. Singapore, ethnically Chinese, was uncomfortable within the Malay-dominated federation and seceded after two years, becoming an independent nation on Aug. 9, 1965.

Independent Singapore has enjoyed orderly, if authoritarian, government, steady economic growth, and a high standard of living. Still a major port, its economy now also encompasses international banking, finance, communications, high-technology manufacturing, and tourism. The reporting of financial and political scandals in the international press in the 1980s led to restrictions on the domestic circulation of some foreign periodicals. On Nov. 26, 1990, Lee Kuan Yew, Singapore's only prime minister since independence and the longest serving prime minister in the world, resigned. He was succeeded by Goh Chok Tong, but he remains a force in Singapore's political life.

▶ SLOVAKIA
Slovak Republic

• **GEOGRAPHY Location:** Central Europe. **Boundaries:** Czech Republic and Poland to N, Ukraine to E, Hungary to S, Austria to W. **Total area:** 18,859 sq. mi. (48,845 sq km). **Coastline:** none. **Comparative area:** about twice the size of New Hampshire. **Land use:** 31% arable, 3% permanent crops, 17% pastures, 41% forests, 8% other. **Major cities:** (1994 est.) Bratislava (capital) 450,776; Kosice 239,927; Nitra 87,127; Presov 92,013; Banská Bystrica 84,741.

• **PEOPLE Population:** 5,396,193 (1999 est.). **Nationality:** noun—Slovak(s); adjective—Slovak. **Ethnic groups:** 85.7% Slovak, 10.7% Hungarian, 1.5% Gypsy. **Languages:** Slovak (official), Hungarian. **Religions:** 60.3% Roman Catholic, 9.7% atheist, 8.4% Protestant, 4.1% Orthodox.

• **GOVERNMENT Type:** parliamentary democracy. **Independence:** Jan. 1, 1993 (from Czechoslovakia). **Constitution:** Jan. 1, 1993. **National holiday:** Slovak Constitution Day, Sept. 1. **Heads of Government:** Rudolf Schuster, president (since Jun. 1999); Mikuláš (Dzurinda, prime minister (since Oct. 1998). **Structure:** executive—president, prime minister, Council of Ministers; legislative—unicameral (National Council); judicial—Supreme Court.

• **ECONOMY Monetary unit:** koruna. **Budget:** (1997 est.) *income:* $5.4 bil.; *expend.:* $6.5 bil. **GDP:** $44.5 bil., $8,300 per capita (1998 est.). **Chief crops:** grains, potatoes, sugar beets, hops, fruit; hogs, cattle, poultry; forest products. **Natural resources:** brown coal and lignite; small amounts of iron ore, copper and manganese ore, salt. **Major industries:** metal working, food, beverages, fuels, chemicals. **Labor force:** 3.32 mil.; 29.3% industry, 8.9% agriculture, 8.0% construction, 8.2% transport and communication, 45.6% services. **Exports:** $10.7 bil. (f.o.b., 1998 est.); 37% machinery and transport equipment; 30% intermediate manufactured goods, 13% miscellaneous manufactured goods. **Imports:** $12.9 bil. (f.o.b., 1998 est.); 40% machinery and transport equipment; 18% intermediate manufactured goods, 11% fuels. **Major trading partners:** *exports:* 56% EU, 20% Czech Republic, 7% Austria; *imports:* 50% EU, 18% Czech Republic, 10% Russia.

Though the Czech and Slovak languages are similar, the two peoples have always been far apart culturally and historically (much like the Letts and Lithuanians). The ninth-century Moravian Empire has been claimed as heritage by both peoples; but with the Magyar invasion of the Pannonian Plain in the 10th century, the Slovaks passed under Hungarian rule for 1,000 years. When in the 19th century a romantic-nationalist revival occurred, the Slovaks, under the leadership of Ludovit Štúr, decided to use their own language in literature (though some of the most prominent writers in the Czech tongue were of Slovak origin, such as the poet Jan Kollár and the historian P.J. Šafarik). Unlike the Czechs, the Slovaks took no part in the revolutions of 1848. They lacked a native aristocracy; their national leadership came from wealthy peasants, small-town shopkeepers and, above all, their priests.

In the peacemaking at the end of World War I, as the Austro-Hungarian Empire collapsed, the Czech politicians Beneš and Masaryk claimed to speak for the (nonexistent) Czechoslovak nation. They carried the day despite apparent Slovak loyalty to Hungary and even the opposition of Fr.

Hlinka's Slovak Populist party to union with the Czechs. The synthetic "nation" of Czechoslovakia was created, governed by a sort of benevolent democratic dictatorship of the Czechs over the other nations. With the Munich crisis of October 1939, Hitler imposed a federal structure giving Slovakia almost complete autonomy in the renamed Czecho-Slovakia; in the following March, when Hitler obliterated Czech independence, an "independent" Slovakia was formed with Hlinka's successor, Magr Tiso, as president.

But under the circumstances independence was illusory. German protection (against Hungarian revisionism) required complete Slovak accord with Reich foreign policy, including declarations of war on Poland (1939) and on the USSR, the United States, and Great Britain (1941). Domestically, Msgr. Tiso organized a one-party state with anti-Jewish legislation, half unwilling and half unable to resist the expulsion (and eventual extermination) of 60,000 Jews.

The cement for a restored Czechoslovakia after the war was the Communist tyranny imposed in 1948. But the "Velvet Revolution" in 1989 overturned not only Yalta but also St. Germain and Trianon. While the victory over the Communists was won by an alliance of the Czech Civic Forum and the Slovak Public against Violence, the allies soon fell out. As the Czech premier Václav Klaus pushed for free-market "shock therapy," the Slovak premier Vladimír Meciar defended a slower "Slovak way" to capitalism. Economic differences inflamed by ancient Slovak resentment of the Czech majority led to a much-diminished federal government by the spring of 1992. In the summer the split became the "Velvet Divorce."

In July 1992 Slovak deputies to the federal Parliament blocked the reelection of Václav Havel to the presidency, and the Slovak National Council approved, by a vote of 113 to 24, a declaration of sovereignty. In September the two parliaments agreed to the terms. In accord with a two-to-one ratio of the republics' populations, the military and financial assets of Czechoslovakia were divided. By February even plans for a common currency had gone by the board, with only a customs union linking the two parts of the old state.

On Feb. 15, 1993, the Slovak Parliament elected its first president, Michal Kovác, with Meciar, architect of the divorce, remaining as prime minister. Spiraling inflation and high unemployment coupled with a corruption scandal toppled the Meciar government early in 1994, but a coalition government including many former Communists restored him as prime minister later that year. In Sept. 1998, a four-party opposition coalition toppled Meciar's regime. Mikuláš Dzurinda became Prime Minister, heading a government whose principal focus was NATO and EU membership, more of a possibility now that Meciar was gone. But by March 1999, parliament remained unable to agree on a successor to President Kovac who had retired, as constitutionally required, a year earlier.

▶ **SLOVENIA**
Republic of Slovenia
● **GEOGRAPHY Location:** southeastern Europe. **Boundaries:** Austria to N, Hungary to NE, Croatia to E and S, Adriatic Sea and Italy to W. **Total area:** 7,836 sq. mi. (20,296 sq km). **Coastline:** 20 mi. (32 km). **Comparative area:** Slightly smaller than New Jersey. **Land use:** 51% forest and woodland,

28% meadows and pastures, 12% arable land, 3% permanent crops, 6% other. **Major cities:** (1994 est.) Ljubljana (capital) 269,972; Maribor 103,113; Celje 39,782; Kranj 36,770.
● **PEOPLE Population:** 1,970,570 (1999 est.). **Nationality:** noun—Slovene(s); adjective—Slovenian. **Ethnic groups:** 91% Slovene, 3% Croat, 2% Serb, 1% Muslim, 3% other. **Languages:** 91% Slovenian, 6% Serbo-Croatian. **Religions:** 70.8% Catholic, 1% Lutheran, 1% Muslim, 27.2% other.
● **GOVERNMENT Type:** parliamentary democratic republic. **Independence:** June 25, 1991 (from Yugoslavia). **Constitution:** Dec. 23, 1991. **National holiday:** National Statehood Day, June 25. **Heads of Government:** Milan Kǔcan, president of the presidency (four other members) (since Apr. 1990); Janez Drnovsek, prime minister (since May 1992). **Structure:** executive—president, prime minister, cabinet; legislative—unicameral parliament-second chamber has only advisory powers; judicial—Supreme Court, Constitutional Court.
● **ECONOMY Monetary unit:** tolar (SIT). **Budget:** (1996 est.) *income:* $8.5 bil.; *expend.:* $8.5 bil. **GDP:** $20.4 bil., $10,300 per capita (1998 est.). **Chief crops:** potatoes, hops, wheat, sugar beets, corn, grapes; cattle, sheep, poultry. **Natural resources:** lignite coal, lead, zinc, mercury, uranium. **Major industries:** ferrous metallurgy and rolling mill products, aluminum reduction and rolled products, lead and zinc smelting, electronics, trucks, electric power equipment, wood products, textiles. **Labor force:** 857,400. **Exports:** $9.2 bil. (f.o.b., 1998 est.); 45% manufactured goods, 30% machinery and transport equipment, 10% chemicals. **Imports:** $9.9 bil. (f.o.b., 1998 est.); 31% machinery and transport equipment, 31% other manufactured goods, 11% chemicals. **Major trading partners:** *exports:* 29% Germany, 15% Italy, 10% Croatia; *imports:* 21% Germany, 17% Italy, 10% France.

In the sixth century, as part of the great Slavic migrations out of the Vistula and Oder basins, the Slovene people crossed the Carpathians into the Danube plain, penetrating as far as the eastern Alps. In the eighth and ninth centuries the lands they inhabited were subject to Bavarian colonization as part of the Ostmark (Eastern March) of the Carolingian Empire. It is probable, although contested, that most current Austrians are German-speaking Slovenes while the Slovenes are Slavophone Austrians. In any case, for 1,000 years, Slovene history was Austrian history. Thus, like the Croats, Christianity came in its western (Roman Catholic) form.

Lacking their own nobility and even a burgher class for most of their history, the Slovenes tended to look to their priests for leadership, regularly electing them as their representatives to the Reichstag in Vienna (as they did later to the Skupstina in Belgrade after Slovenia became part of Yugoslavia). The 19th-century rise of a national consciousness, associated with literary collections of legend and folklore, took a special turn in the Slovene case because of Napoleon's conquests. His "province of Illyria" was the first association of the Slovenes with Croats and Serbs and his minister of education there was the Slovene Franciscan Valentin Vodnik, so that Slovene "nationalism" had from a start a "Yugoslav" tinge.

In 1815 the Slovenes were again part of the Austrian Empire and were confirmed in the Ausgleich of 1867 as part of the Austrian, not Hungarian, part of the dual Monarchy. As that monarchy collapsed in World War I, it was the Slovene monsignor Anton Korosec who served as president of "The National Council of the Serbs, Croats, and Slovenes" out of which the new state of Yugoslavia emerged. Though the new Yugoslavia was a highly centralized, unitary state with no provision for Slovene autonomy, certain circumstances brought a kind of privileged position to Slovenia. Their distinct language made Serbian administration a practical impossibility and Serbian struggles against Croat separatism led them to favor the Slovenes to Croatia's north, forestalling any additional separatism there. Moreoever, as a part of the long Austrian connection, the Slovenes were better educated and more industrially advanced than any other part of Yugoslavia.

After the interlude of Hitler's break-up of Yugoslavia (in which Slovenia itself was partitioned between Germany and Italy) Slovenia became a constituent "republic" in Tito's reconstructed Yugoslavia and, despite the enduring emnity provoked by the Communist slaughter of the Slovene Domobranci (Home Guard), again assumed a kind of priviliged status in Yugoslavia. After the dictator's death in 1980, the Slovene Socialist Republic took part in the "collegial rule" of Yugoslavia, but with the end of Communist rule in 1990, Slovenia became the first of the republics to secede, in June 1991. After the Slovene militia inflicted a humiliating defeat on the Yugoslav army in July and with EU recognition in December, Slovenia became independent for the first time in its history. Forging economic ties with Austria, Hungary, and Italy, it has remained prosperously apart from the debacle to its south.

In Nov. 1996 elections, the center-right coalition calling itself Slovenian Spring captured 45 (of 90) seats in the Parliament with the Liberal Democrats and its allies controlling the other 45. After months of deadlock LD leader Janos Drnovsek was confirmed as prime minister. In 1998 the EU invited Slovenia to apply for membership, its per capita GDP already more than 90 percent of Portugal (the EU's poorest member).

▶ SOLOMON ISLANDS
● **GEOGRAPHY   Location:** archipelago in South Pacific E of Papua New Guinea. Honiara (Guadalcanal Is.) 9°28'S, 159°57'E. **Boundaries:** South Pacific Ocean to N, E, and S, Solomon Sea to W; nearest neighbor is Santa Cruz Islands to SE. **Total area:** 10,985 sq. mi. (28,450 sq km). **Coastline:** 3,302 mi. (5,313 km). **Comparative area:** slightly smaller than Maryland. **Land use:** 1% arable land; 1% permanent crops; 1% meadows and pastures; 88% forest and woodland; 9% other. **Major cities:** (1990 est.) Honiara (capital) 35,288.
● **PEOPLE   Population:** 455,429 (1999 est.). **Nationality:** noun—Solomon Islander(s); adjective—Solomon Islander. **Ethnic groups:** 93% Melanesian, 4% Polynesian, 1.5% Micronesian, 0.8% European, 0.3% Chinese. **Languages:** 120 indigenous languages; Melanesian pidgin in much of country is lingua franca; English spoken by 1-2% of population. **Religions:** 34% Anglican, 19% Roman Catholic, 17% Baptist, 11% United (Methodist/Presbyterian), 11% Seventh-Day Adventist, 5% other Protestant, 4% traditional beliefs.
● **GOVERNMENT   Type:** parliamentary democracy. **Independence:** July 7, 1978 (from UK). **Constitution:** July 7, 1978. **National holiday:** Independence Day, July 7. **Heads of Government:** Rev. John Inni Lapli, governor-general (since July 1999); Bartholomew Ulufa'alu, prime minister

(since Aug. 1997). **Structure:** executive— authority in governor-general; unicameral legislature; judiciary.
● **ECONOMY   Monetary unit:** Solomon Islands dollar. **Budget:** (1997 est.) **income:** $147 mil.; **expend.:** $168 mil. **GDP:** $1.15 bil., $2,600 per capita (1998 est.). **Chief crops:** cocoa, beans, coconuts, palm kernels, rice, potatoes, vegetables, fruits; cattle, pigs; timber; fish. **Natural resources:** fish, forests, gold, bauxite, phosphates. **Major industries:** copra, fish (tuna). **Labor force:** 26,842 (1992 est.); 41.5% services, 23.7% agriculture, forestry, and fishing, 21.7% commerce, transport, and finance, 13.1% construction, manufacturing, and mining. **Exports:** $184 mil. (f.o.b., 1996 est.); timber, fish, palm oil, cocoa, copra. **Imports:** $151 mil. (c.i.f., 1996 est.); plant and equipment, manufactured goods, food and live animals, fuel. **Major trading partners:** (1996) **exports:** 50% Japan, 16% Spain; **imports:** 42% Australia, 10% Japan, 9% Singapore.

In 1893 Great Britain established a protectorate over the South Solomon Islands, including the large islands of Guadalcanal, San Cristobal, and Malata; the protectorate was extended to the smaller easterly islands of the chain in 1898. In 1900 Germany relinquished to Great Britain its claim to the North Solomons, including Choiseul and Santa Isabel; Bougainville Island was retained by Germany (see "Papua New Guinea"). The major islands were occupied by Japan in 1942 and retaken by the Allies in a series of bloody battles in 1943.

The Solomon Islands were made self-governing in January 1976 and became an independent nation on July 7, 1978. The economy is based on subsistence agriculture and fishing. Some light manufacturing and craft industries have been established in recent years. Copra, cocoa, palm oil, and lumber are the principal exports. The sale of tuna fishing rights in the surrounding waters has given the nation a favorable balance of payments.

▶ SOMALIA
● **GEOGRAPHY   Location:** eastern coast of Africa. **Boundaries:** short frontier with Djibouti to NW, Gulf of Aden to N, long coastline on Indian Ocean to E, Kenya to SW, Ethiopia to W. **Total area:** 246,201 sq. mi. (637,660 sq km). **Coastline:** 1,880 mi. (3,025 km). **Comparative area:** slightly smaller than Texas. **Land use:** 2% arable land; negl. % permanent crops; 69% meadows and pastures; 26% forest and woodland; 3% other. **Major cities:** (1987 est.) Mogadishu (capital) 1,000,000; Hargeysa 400,000; Kismayo 200,000; Merca 100,000.
● **PEOPLE   Population:** 7,140,643 (1999 est.). **Nationality:** noun—Somali(s); adjective—Somali. **Ethnic groups:** 85% Somali, rest mainly Bantu; 30,000 Arabs. **Languages:** Somali (official), Arabic, Italian, English. **Religions:** almost entirely Sunni Muslim.
● **GOVERNMENT   Type:** none. **Independence:** July 1, 1960 (from a merger of British Somaliland, which became independent from UK June 26, 1960, and Italian Somaliland, which became independent from Italian-administered UN trusteeship July 1, 1960, to form the Somali Republic). **Constitution:** Aug. 25, 1979, presidential approval Sept. 23, 1979. **National holiday:** N.A. **Heads of Government:** No internationally recognized government.
● **ECONOMY   Monetary unit:** Somali shilling. **Budget:** N.A. **GDP:** $4 bil., $600 per capita (1998

est.). **Chief crops:** bananas, sorghum, corn, mangoes, sugarcane, sesame seeds, beans; cattle, sheep, goats; fishing potential largely unexploited. **Natural resources:** uranium, largely unexploited reserves of iron ore, tin, gypsum, bauxite. **Major industries:** a few small industries, including sugar refining, textiles, petroleum refining. **Labor force:** about 3.7 mil. (1993 est.); very few are skilled laborers; 71% agriculture (pastoral nomadism), 29% industry and services. **Exports:** $123 mil. (f.o.b., 1995); livestock, bananas, hides, fish. **Imports:** $60 mil. (f.o.b., 1995); manufactures, petroleum products, foodstuffs, construction materials. **Major trading partners:** (1996 est.) *exports:* 55% Saudi Arabia, 19% Yemen, 11% Italy; *imports:* 28% Kenya, 21% Djibouti, 6% Brazil.

Arab trading settlements in Somalia were established in the seventh century and gradually evolved into independent sultanates. Portuguese traders established settlements and forts along the coast during the 15th and 16th centuries.

In the early 19th century, Great Britain arranged through local treaties to use harbors along the Somali coast and gained control over the northern part of the country by 1840. The border between Somalia and Ethiopia was demarcated by a treaty between Great Britain and Ethiopia in 1897. In 1885 the sultan of Zanzibar granted commercial advantages to Italy, and by further agreements in 1897 and 1908 Italy gained control over southern Somalia.

During the early 20th century, an uprising against British rule was led by Mohamed Abdullah. Abdullah was defeated by the British with help from his local rivals but is now regarded as the father of Somali nationalism.

The Italian invasion of Ethiopia in 1936 gave Italy a dominant position in the Horn of Africa. In the early phases of World War II, Italian troops drove the British from British Somaliland, but a 1940 counterattack led to British occupation of all of Somalia by 1941. After World War II, as discussions of Somalia's future continued, Britain handed over the Ogaden and neighboring territories to Ethiopia.

A UN pact of 1949 created an Italian trusteeship in the former Italian Somaliland. Italy terminated its trusteeship and British Somaliland, a UK protectorate, achieved independence on June 26, 1960. On July 1 the two entities joined to become Somalia.

The new country was plagued by regional clan-based rivalries, with the Somali Youth League emerging as a unifying national force. In 1969 Maj. Gen. Mohamed Siad Barre took control, abolished the National Assembly, established a ruling Supreme Revolutionary Council, instituted a socialist regime, and established relations with the USSR.

In 1972 Somali forces began border raids into Ethiopia's Ogaden region, peopled largely by ethnic Somalis. The Somali army invaded the Ogaden in 1977. The Soviet Union switched its support to Ethiopia, and with Soviet aid and Cuban troops, Ethiopia drove back the Somali invasion. Over a million refugees fled from Ethiopia into Somalia. The United States was Somalia's principal source of military and economic aid after 1978.

In May 1988, the Somali National Movement captured a number of cities in the northwest and held them against the army. In the summer of 1990, the United Somali Congress began a peaceful antigovernment movement around Mogadishu. In Dec. 1990, this flared into a brief but bloody civil war that resulted in the ouster of Pres. Barre on Jan. 26. The Somali National Congress proclaimed a provisional government, but it was not recognized either by the United Somali Movement, which threatened secession, or the Somali Patriotic Movement, which controlled much of central and southern Somalia.

The continued unrest made it difficult to deliver humanitarian aid despite the efforts of Western governments and nongovernment organizations to do so. An estimated 50,000 people were killed between 1988-90.

Despite UN attempts to initiate peace talks, widespread clan and tribal warfare led to a complete breakdown of government authority in 1991-92. A severe drought helped to create over two million refugees, and widespread starvation gripped the nation. Relief workers were prevented by chaotic political conditions and warring armed factions from distributing emergency food supplies. An estimated 300,000 people died in 1991-92.

In Dec. 1992, the United States began Operation Restore Hope, sending 28,000 troops to secure distribution of food and humanitarian aid. But while the U.S. presence deterred the factions from further open hostilities and brought warring leaders to the peace table, once the United States transferred control of the operation to UN peacekeeping forces the fighting resumed. Led by the followers of Gen. Mohammed Farah Aidid, Somali renegades ambushed UN troops and shot down UN helicopters. The U. S. withdrew in March 1994. The last UN troops left Mogadishu a year later.

Clan warfare reignited in March 1995, and in June, Aidid declared himself president for life. However, no other country recognized any Somali government and in Aug. 1996 Aidid was shot and killed. His son, a former U.S. Marine replaced him but brutal clan violence continued. In Dec. 1997 a tentative peace agreement was reached among the major factions. Peace settled in during 1998, helped by the worst flooding in 40 years that killed 2,000 and made 200,000 homeless. Increased inter-clan fighting in Sept. 1999 threatened to cause crop shortfalls and famine yet again.

▶ SOUTH AFRICA
Republic of South Africa

● **Geography Location:** southern Africa. **Boundaries:** Namibia to NW, Botswana, Zimbabwe to N, Mozambique to NE, Swaziland, Indian Ocean to E, Atlantic Ocean to W; Lesotho entirely surrounded by South African territory. **Total area:** 471,444 sq. mi. (1,221,040 sq km). **Coastline:** 1,739 mi. (2,798 km). **Comparative area:** slighlty less than twice the size of Texas. **Land use:** 10% arable land; 1% permanent crops; 67% meadows and pastures; 7% forest and woodland; 15% other; includes 1% irrigated. **Major cities:** (1991 census) Note: Figures are for metropolitan areas: Cape Town (legislative capital) 2,350,157; Pretoria (administrative capital) 1,080,187; Johannesburg 1,916,061; Durban 1,137,378; Port Elizabeth 853,205.

● **People Population:** 43,426,386 (1999 est.). **Nationality:** noun—South African(s); adjective—South African. **Ethnic groups:** 75.2% black, 13.6% white, 2.6% Indian; 8.6% other. **Languages:** Afrikaans, English, Zulu, Xhosa, Sotho, Ndebele, Pedi, Swazi, Tsonga, Venda, Tswana (all official). **Religions:** 68% Christian (most whites and about 60% of blacks), 2% Muslim, 1.5% Hindu (60% of Indians), 28.5% traditional and animistic beliefs.

• **GOVERNMENT** Type: republic. **Independence:** May 31, 1910 (from UK). **Constitution:** Dec. 10, 1996. **National holiday:** Freedom Day, Apr. 27. **Head of Government:** Thabo Mbeki, president (since June 1999). **Structure:** executive—president is head of government and chairman of cabinet; bicameral legislature—National Assembly, National Council of Provinces; judiciary—courts maintain substantial independence from government influence.

• **ECONOMY** **Monetary unit:** South African rand. **Budget:** (FY94/95 est.) *income:* $30.5 bil.; *expend.:* $38 bil. **GDP:** $290.6 bil., $6,800 per capita (1998 est.). **Chief crops:** corn, wheat, sugarcane, fruits, vegetables; beef, poultry, mutton, wool, dairy products. **Natural resources:** gold, chromium, antimony, coal, iron ore. **Major industries:** mining (world's largest producer of platinum, gold, chromium), automobile assembly, metalworking. **Labor force:** 15 mil. economically active (1997); 35% services, 30% agriculture, 20% industry and commerce, 9% mining; 30% unemployment (1998 est.). **Exports:** $28.7 bil. (f.o.b., 1998); 20% gold, 20%-25% minerals and metals, 5% food, 3% chemicals. **Imports:** $27.2 bil. (f.o.b., 1998); machinery, chemicals, transport equipment. **Major trading partners:** *exports:* UK, Italy, Japan, US; *imports:* Germany, US, UK, Japan.

South Africa was originally inhabited by San and related peoples. Bantu peoples, including the Zulu and Xhosa, migrated to the region beginning around the 15th century and established large native kingdoms.

The Portuguese explorer Bartholomew Diaz discovered and named the Cape of Good Hope in 1488. The Dutch East India Company established a permanent settlement at Cape Town in 1652, which served as a supply and transshipment point for Dutch trade to the East Indies and which attracted Protestant settlers from throughout Western Europe. In a series of wars, the Xhosa people were expelled from the area under Dutch rule.

Great Britain began to dispute Dutch control of the Cape of Good Hope region in the late 18th century. To escape increasing British hegemony, in 1836 many Dutch farmers undertook the Great Trek, a northward migration to lands not under the control of any European power. These Afrikaner pioneers later became known as Boers (farmers). They came into conflict with the Zulu kingdom that, under King Shaka, had recently widened its dominion in the South African interior. The Zulus were defeated at the Battle of Blood River in 1838, but they retained substantial power and territory for another 40 years.

Great Britain formally took control of the Cape Colony in 1841 and annexed Natal in 1843. The other two Afrikaner provinces, the Orange Free State and the Transvaal, remained temporarily free of British control. But when diamonds were discovered in the Orange Free State in 1867 and gold in the Transvaal in 1886, an influx of British miners and entrepreneurs provoked Boer rebellions.

In 1878 the Zulu Kingdom under its last great king, Cetewayo, rebelled against British rule in Natal. British troops attacked Zululand in 1878 and crushed the rebellion in 1879.

The first Anglo-Boer War of 1881-82 led to an inconclusive British victory. A renewed uprising led to the Boer War of 1899-1902, which was fought with great ferocity between British regular troops and Afrikaner guerrilla forces. The eventual British victory led to the establishment of British rule in all of South Africa and to the formation of the Union of South Africa in 1910. The union became a self-governing state within the British Empire in 1934.

South African politics became dominated by friction between British and Afrikaner whites; no effective black participation in government was permitted. The United South African party, led by Jan C. Smuts, advocated cooperation between the two groups and led South Africa to join World War II on the Allied side, over the opposition of the pro-Afrikaner Nationalist party.

After the war the Nationalists prevailed and won control of the government in 1948. Racial politics became the country's paramount concern, and the Nationalists introduced the policy of "apartheid" (separateness), under which racial groups were rigidly defined as white, black, Asian (primarily Indian), and colored (mixed ancestry). Each group was to be kept physically separate and develop its own political institutions within defined areas of residence; mixed neighborhoods, intermarriage, and other relations were prohibited. Blacks, in particular, were restricted by "pass laws" that allowed them only temporary access to white areas for employment.

International condemnation of these policies began almost immediately, as India broke relations with South Africa in 1946 over discrimination against Asians, and South Africa became the focus of mounting protest, UN resolutions, and international sanctions beginning in the 1960s. On May 31, 1961, South Africa gave up its dominion status and became a republic; its application for membership in the British Commonwealth was withdrawn in the face of strong opposition. The African National Congress (ANC), organized in 1912, was banned by South African authorities. The imprisonment of its leader, Nelson Mandela, provided a focus for black political protest and nationalist aspirations.

Homelands were established under the Promotion of Bantu Self-Government Act of 1959 to further the policy of apartheid by creating separate, but dependent, states for South Africa's blacks. Their form of government was set up in the Black Constitution Act of 1971. The South African government intended that the homelands be regarded as separate nations, but none was ever internationally recognized. The scattered homeland territories comprised only a tiny portion of the total area of South Africa, and tended to include marginal and underdeveloped lands. Residents of the homelands were not considered citizens of South Africa, but rather citizens only of their homeland. As such, they could be considered temporary migrant workers and were therefore ineligible for unemployment and other benefits.

An uprising in Soweto in 1976 was put down by South African police and armed forces with the loss of hundreds of lives, providing a further focus of black protest. Pieter Willem Botha was elected president in 1978, pledging to uphold apartheid while seeking solutions to racial problems. In 1983, a majority of white voters approved a new constitution that provided for limited power sharing by coloreds and Asians. Blacks, however, continued to be excluded.

In the early 1980s, South African troops intervened in civil wars in Angola and Mozambique and were deployed to counteract growing proindependence rebellions in Namibia. Within South

Africa, terrorism and uprisings led by the African National Union grew in intensity in 1983-84. A state of emergency was declared in 1985, accompanied by renewed political and economic pressure from abroad. In 1986, Bishop Desmond Tutu, a leading black nationalist, addressed the United Nations and called for renewed sanctions. The Botha government announced an end to the pass laws and promised limited black participation in government. Fighting among black groups in 1986-87 further increased domestic tension.

On May 19, 1986, South African troops conducted raids against ANC bases in Zambia, Zimbabwe, and Botswana. A new national state of emergency was declared as strikes and riots marked the 10th anniversary of the Soweto uprising. The United States announced measures designed to end American investment in South Africa.

In early 1989, in anticipation of elections to be held in September, various proposals were put forward for constitutional reform. Most called for expanded power sharing but still within the context of defined racial groups. In July 1989 Pres. Botha had an unprecedented meeting with Nelson Mandela, amid strong suggestions that the white government was seeking an accommodation with the antiapartheid leadership. Botha's successor, F.W. de Klerk, continued that policy.

A series of measures in 1989-90 resulted in the partial dismantling of apartheid, against the vehement opposition of the white right wing, but violence between supporters of the ANC and the Zulu Inkatha movement in Natal led to the declaration of a state of emergency in the province.

Mandela was released from prison in the spring of 1990 and received a rapturous welcome from South Africa's blacks, and later made a triumphant tour of Western Europe and North America. His glory was short-lived, however, as the struggle for supremacy again erupted in murder and violence between Mandela's ANC and Mangosuthu Buthelezi's Inkatha Freedom party throughout the latter part of 1990 and 1991.

At the same time, Pres. de Klerk and Parliament continued to move the nation toward the ending of apartheid by repealing 60 years of segregation in hospitals, libraries, schools, and other public institutions. The government also released other political prisoners and completely repealed the legal foundations of apartheid: the Land Acts of 1913 and 1936, the Group Areas Act, and the Population Registration Act. The United States and other countries began lifting trade sanctions against South Africa in the summer of 1991.

In September 1991, de Klerk, Mandela, and Buthelezi, together with 20 smaller antiapartheid groups, signed an accord to end factional violence. De Klerk proposed a new constitution that would provide universal suffrage and create a two-chamber parliament open to all races. The new constitution abolished the black homelands, consolidating them into one large, multiracial South Africa. In March 1992 a referendum of white voters overwhelmingly approved a government proposal to dismantle all forms of apartheid and to conduct talks with black leaders designed to end white-only rule.

The new constitution was approved on Nov. 17, 1993, by all of the country's major political parties, except for Chief Mangosuthu Buthelezi's Zulu-based Inkatha Freedom party, which withheld its support until a week before the country's first-ever multiracial elections in April.

More than 22 million voters turned out to cast ballots. An overwhelming majority chose the 75-year-old Mandela to lead a coalition government that included de Klerk's National party and Buthelezi's Inkatha Freedom party.

In May 1996 South Africa completed the transition to democracy when it approved a permanent constitution to replace the transitional one implemented three years earlier. It created a strong central government, an independent judiciary, and a bill of rights with one of the broadest guarantees of liberty in the world. In addition to freedom of speech, movement, and political activity, the South African Bill of Rights protects rights to adequate food, housing, water, education, and health care. The day after the new constitution was approved, de Klerk and his colleagues in the National party quit their cabinet posts, saying that the government was strong enough to handle "robust opposition."

In 1997 there were reminders that troubles remain: in February, riots in Johannesburg suburbs by coloreds against discrimination in favor of blacks and in March, a mass rally (which turned violent) in Johannesburg by still-unsatisfied Zulus. Bitter feelings between the Inkatha Freedom Party and Mandela's ANC surfaced again when the Truth and Reconciliation Committee reported testimony linking Inkatha leaders to assasination squads during the apartheid era.

On June 2, 1999, South Africa held its second post-apartheid elections: the ANC won a gigantic victory, taking 266 seats in the 400-seat Assembly. An "alliance" with the one member of the (Indian) Minority Front gave ANC the 2/3 majority that permits it to amend the Constitution. Thabo Mbeki, who replaced Nelson Mandela as party chief in December, was elected unopposed to be his successor as South Africa's president as well.

South Africa has the continent's most highly developed economy; it is a fully-developed, capitalist industrial-commercial society with manufacturing, mining, agricultural, service, and other sectors. It remains the world's largest producer of gold, a key source of chromium and other strategic metals, and of gem-quality diamonds.

▶ SPAIN
Kingdom of Spain
● **GEOGRAPHY Location:** Iberian Peninsula in southwest Europe; Canary Is. off West Africa (28°07'N, 15°26'W). **Boundaries:** Bay of Biscay and France to N; Mediterranean Sea to E; Morocco 19 mi. (30 km) to S, across Strait of Gibraltar; Portugal to W. **Total area:** 194,884 sq. mi. (504,750 sq km). **Coastline:** 3,085 mi. (4,964 km). **Comparative area:** slightly more than twice the size of Oregon. **Land use:** 30% arable land; 9% permanent crops; 21% meadows and pastures; 32% forest and woodland; 8% other; includes 6% irrigated. **Major cities:** (1991 est.) Madrid (capital) 2,984,576; Barcelona 1,653,175; Valencia 777,427; Sevilla (Seville) 683,487; Zaragoza (Saragossa) 614,401.
● **PEOPLE Population:** 39,167,744 (1999 est.). **Nationality:** noun Spaniard(s); adjective—Spanish. **Ethnic groups:** composite of Mediterranean and Nordic types. **Languages:** 74% Castilian Spanish; 17% Catalán, 7% Galician, 2% Basque. **Religions:** 99% Roman Catholic.
● **GOVERNMENT Type:** parliamentary monarchy. **Independence:** 1492 (expulsion of Moors and unification). **Constitution:** Dec. 6, 1978, effective Dec. 29, 1978. **National holiday:** Oct. 12. **Heads of**

Government: Juan Carlos I, king (since Nov. 1975); José María Aznar, prime minister (since May 1996). **Structure:** executive—king is chief of state, prime minister is head of government; bicameral legislature; judiciary— independent.

• **ECONOMY Monetary unit:** peseta. **Budget:** (1995 est.) *income:* $113 bil.; *expend.:* $139 bil. **GDP:** $645.6 bil., $16,500 per capita (1998 est). **Chief crops:** grains, vegetables, olives, wine grapes, sugar beets, citrus; beef, pork, poultry, dairy prodcts; fish. **Natural resources:** coal, lignite, iron ore, uranium, mercury. **Major industries:** textiles, apparel (including footwear), food and beverages, metals and metal manufacturing. **Labor force:** 16.2 mil. (1997); 64% services, 28% manufacturing, mining and construction, 8% agriculture. **Exports:** $111.1 bil. (f.o.b., 1998); cars and trucks, manufactured goods, foodstuffs, other consumer goods. **Imports:** $132.3 bil. (f.o.b., 1998); machinery, transport equipment, fuels, semifinished goods, foodstuffs, consumer goods, chemicals. **Major trading partners:** *exports:* 70% EU, 7.9% other developed countries, 4.2% U.S.; *imports:* 65% EU, 11.5% other developed countries, 6% U.S., 3% Japan.

Prehistoric Spain was populated by Iberians, Basques, and Celts. Its Mediterranean ports were frequented by Phoenician traders, and part of the country was incorporated into the empire of Carthage. Spain fell under the Roman Empire around 200 B.C.; Roman rule ended when the Visigoths invaded and took control of the Iberian Peninsula in the fifth century. The Visigoths adopted Christianity but were in turn conquered by Moors from northwest Africa in A.D. 711. The Berber/Arab civilization of the Moors produced the most elegant and cultivated culture in medieval Europe, and was an important conduit for the reintroduction of Greek science into Europe in the 12th century.

The Christian reconquest of the Iberian Peninsula began almost immediately after the Moors had established themselves and proceeded slowly but steadily over a period of 750 years. The consolidation of the region's small, contentious Christian kingdoms came with the marital alliance of Ferdinand of Aragon and Isabella of Castile in 1469. Granada, the last Moorish outpost in Spain, fell to the forces of Ferdinand and Isabella in 1492, just as Columbus, with Isabella's sponsorship, was discovering the lands that were to become Spain's New World empire. Under the Inquisition, begun in 1478, Jews were expelled from Spain in 1492, and Muslims in 1502.

Under the Habsburg dynasty (1516-1700), Spain reached the zenith of its power and prestige around the year 1600 (despite the 1588 defeat of the Spanish Armada by England), controlling an empire that embraced nearly all of South America (except Brazil), Central America, Mexico, western North America, the Philippines, and smaller territories in Africa and Asia. But Spain's loss of the Netherlands, endless struggles with the French in Europe and the Turks in the Mediterranean, and relentless inflation caused by imports of New World silver—all took their toll. During the 18th century, the Bourbons ruled a declining but still powerful Spain, until Napoleon installed his brother as king in 1808.

After Napoleon's defeat, the Bourbons returned in 1814, but in the 19th century, the loss of the South American colonies, three dynastic wars, and a brief republican interlude after 1868 were all signs of progressive weakness. The crowning blow to Spanish power and prestige was the loss of the Spanish-American War to the United States in 1898, leading to the independence of Cuba and the American takeover of Puerto Rico and the Philippines.

Spain remained neutral in World War I. In 1923 Primo de Rivera established a dictatorship; he was forced out of office by King Alfonso XIII in 1930, but in 1931 the king himself was forced to abdicate. A republic replaced the monarchy. Its volatile mixture of socialism, anticlericalism, and decentralization provoked a right-wing reaction and exacerbated regional separatist tendencies. The government moved to the Right, and in 1934 a miner's strike in Asturia was put down with great bloodshed. A left-wing government was elected in 1936 and deposed in a coup, which led to the terrible Civil War of 1936-39, in which Spain became a battleground for competing world ideologies. The Nationalists, aided by Hitler and Mussolini, defeated the Republicans, aided by Stalin and by leftist volunteers from many countries. Out of the wreckage emerged the dictatorship of the apolitical and intensely patriotic and Catholic general Francisco Franco.

At the time of the Civil War, Spain was still an agricultural country, with small holdings in the north and great estates in the south. In the Basque country, the mining of iron, copper, and lead provided both exports and a domestic iron and steel industry, which had been the case since the 19th century. In the 20th century, shipbuilding and chemicals were added to the traditional textile industries of the Mediterranean coastal cities. The war largely destroyed this industrial base, which was not rebuilt until the 1950s.

Except for a contingent of troops sent to fight with the German invaders of the Soviet Union, Spain remained precariously neutral during World War II; Franco declined to repay Hitler for his support in the Civil War. But wartime Spain, despite its neutrality, could not muster the resources to undertake national reconstruction.

In postwar Europe, the Franco regime seemed like a remnant of the fascism of the 1930s; Stalin's active hostility led the United Nations to treat Spain as an international pariah. Despite foreign disapproval, however, at home Franco represented peace and stability; few Spaniards were willing to risk a return to civil strife by opposing him. Over time the military and Catholic aspects of the regime grew more pronounced, while fascist elements were downplayed. In 1947 the Law of Succession made Spain a monarchy without a king, awaiting the restoration of the throne in the post-Franco era.

The Cold War led to friendlier American relations with Spain and the establishment of American military bases there in 1953. UN membership followed in 1955. Despite some resultant growth in international trade, Spain's economy lagged, with industrialization barely beginning.

In 1958 Franco turned the direction of the economy over to a group of technocrats, mostly neoliberal members of the Opus Dei lay Catholic order. With U.S. economic and military aid, a growing tourist industry, increased foreign investment, and, especially, freer markets, the economy revived. Older industries like iron, steel, and textiles were rejuvenated, while newer ones, such as chemicals, plastics, automobile assembly, and power plants, were created. Agriculture was increasingly mechanized, and it shifted to export-oriented ranching and horticulture.

In 1967 Franco proclaimed the Organic Law, which, while confirming him as head of state, granted some independence to the Cortes (legislature) and permitted heads of families to vote for some of its delegates. This, along with a relaxation of censorship, softened the growing opposition to the regime among students, labor unions, and regional separatists. In 1969 Prince Juan Carlos was named heir apparent to the Spanish throne.

Franco died in 1975 and was duly succeeded by Juan Carlos. With the new prime minister, Adolfo Suarez, the king worked to liberalize the Franco inheritance: Political parties were legalized; the Cortes was transformed into a bicameral legislature, with both houses elected by universal suffrage; the first elections since 1936 were held; and a new constitution was promulgated—all by 1978.

In 1980, Catalonia and the Basque country were granted home rule, following overwhelming plebiscite victories. In the Basque lands, however, violent terrorist agitation for complete independence continues to this day.

Under the new monarchy, Spain became a full participant in the affairs of Europe. It joined the Council of Europe in 1977, NATO in 1982, and the EU in 1986. The Socialist Workers' party controlled both houses of the Cortes from 1982 to 1996, but the party abandoned both Marxism and the traditional labor radicalism of prewar Spain. Instead, it resembled the mainstream Social Democratic parties of Western Europe.

Under Prime Minister Felipe Gonzalez Marquéz, Spain was for a time the economic darling of Europe. GDP grew by an average of almost 5 percent between 1986 and 1990, and business investment jumped by over 10 percent a year. In 1992, the Summer Olympics in Barcelona and the Universal Exposition in Seville focused world attention on two very different parts of Spain.

But the economic growth slowed in 1992, unemployment reached 22 percent, and the conservative Popular party made strong gains in the Cortes in 1993. In 1994, Gonzalez's power eroded when several members of his government were indicted for their involvement with an antiterrorist death squad accused of assassinating 27 Basque separatists during the 1980s. In July 1998, 12 officials of the Gonzalez government were sentenced to jail for crimes in the anti-Basque "dirty war." Although Gonzalez was not implicated in the scandal, the Catalan Nationalist party withdrew from his coalition government as a result of it, costing the Socialists their absolute majority and forcing them to schedule new elections.

After 10 years of Gonzalez and the Socialists, the May 1996 elections brought the Popular Party and its leader Jose Maria Aznar to governmental power (the Popular Party being supported by, though without a formal coalition with, Basque and Catalan nationalists).

Spain's economy has quickly reversed itself and annual growth is projected at three percent, so that Spain was able to meet the criteria for membership in the European Monetary Union.

Somewhat unexpectedly the ETA declared on September 16, 1998, a "total and indefinite" ceasefire. A dramatic move by the government at the end of 1998 sought the extradition from England of General Pinochet, Chile's retired dictator, to face charges of murder of Spanish citizens.

▶ SRI LANKA
Democratic Socialist Republic of Sri Lanka

●GEOGRAPHY Location: Indian Ocean about 50 mi. (80 km) SE of India. Colombo 6°55'N, 79°52'E. Boundaries: Palk Strait to N, Bay of Bengal to E, Indian Ocean to S and SW, and Gulf of Mannar to NW. Total area: 25,332 sq. mi. (65,610 sq km). Coastline: 833 mi. (1,340 km). Comparative area: slightly larger than West Virginia. Land use: 14% arable land; 15% permanent crops; 7% meadows and pastures; 32% forest and woodland; 32% other. Major cities: (1990 est.) Colombo (capital) 615,000; Dehiwala-Mount Lavinia 196,000; Moratuwa 170,000.

●PEOPLE Population: 19,144,875 (1999 est.). Nationality: noun—Sri Lankan(s); adjective—Sri Lankan. Ethnic groups: 74% Sinhalese; 18% Tamil; 7% Moor; 1% Burgher, Malay, and Veddah. Languages: Sinhala (official); Sinhala and Tamil listed as national languages; Sinhala spoken by about 74% of population, Tamil spoken by about 18%; English commonly used in government and spoken by about 10% of population. Religions: 69% Buddhist, 15% Hindu, 8% Christian, 8% Muslim.

●GOVERNMENT Type: republic. Independence: Feb. 4, 1948 (from UK). Constitution: Aug. 16, 1978. National holiday: Independence Day, Feb. 4. Heads of Government: Chandrika Bandaranaike Kumaratunga, president (since Nov. 1994); Sirimavo R.D. Bandaranaike, prime minister (since Nov. 1994). Structure: executive—president is head of government and chief of state; unicameral legislature; judiciary.

●ECONOMY Monetary unit: Sri Lankan rupee. Budget: (1997) income: $3 bil.; expend.: $4.2 bil. GDP: $48.1 bil., $2,500 per capita (1998 est.). Chief crops: rice, sugarcane, grains, pulses, oilseed, roots, spices, coconuts, tea, rubber; milk, eggs, hides, meat. Natural resources: limestone, graphite, mineral sands, gems, phosphates. Major industries: processing of rubber, tea, coconuts, and other agricultural commodities; cement, petroleum refining. Labor force: 6.2 mil. (1997 est.); 46% services, 37% agriculture, 17% industry. Exports: $4.5 bil. (f.o.b., 1998 est.); tea, textiles and garments, petroleum products, gems, rubber. Imports: $5.3 bil. (f.o.b., 1998 est.); machinery and equipment, textiles, petroleum, building materials, sugar. Major trading partners: exports: 36% U.S., 11% UK, 6% Japan; imports: 10% India, 9% Japan, 8% South Korea.

The ancient Veddah inhabitants of Sri Lanka were conquered by Sinhalese migrants from northern India in the sixth century B.C. The island's spices and precious stones and its position on the trans-Indian Ocean trade routes made it well known in ancient times. Sri Lanka was known to the Greeks as Tabrobane and to the Arabs as Serendip. From the third century A.D., Sri Lanka became a major center of Buddhist culture. Despite numerous invasions from India, the island was usually ruled by native kingdoms, but the invasions added a Tamil community to the premodern population.

The Portuguese conquered the coastal areas after 1505 and also introduced Roman Catholicism. The Dutch displaced the Portugese in 1648; the British expelled the Dutch in 1795. Great Britain was the first foreign power to extend its rule over the entire island, with the defeat of the central kingdom of Kandy in 1833. In that year all of Sri Lanka was incorporated into the British Crown colony of Ceylon. Under British rule, tea and rubber plantations were established in the island's interior, and coconut plantations in coastal areas were consolidated under foreign control.

Ceylon became an independent member of the British Commonwealth on Feb. 4, 1948; the Republic of Sri Lanka was proclaimed on May 22, 1972.

Prime Minister W.R.D. Bandaranaike was assassinated on Sept. 25, 1959. His widow, Sirimavo Bandaranaike, leader of the Freedom party, was elected as his successor. In 1962 her government expropriated the property of foreign oil companies. The conservative United National party won a majority in Parliament in 1965 and agreed to pay compensation for the expropriated assets. In May 1970 Mrs. Bandaranaike was again elected prime minister. Leftists secured the nationalization of foreign plantations in the mid-1970s. Mrs. Bandaranaike's party was ousted by the United National party in 1977. Constitutional reform in 1978 aimed at increasing stability by establishing a presidential form of government. Pres. J.R. Jayawardene was elected on Feb. 4, 1978.

But stability has eluded Sri Lanka because of the long struggle between Tamils and the Sinhalese. The political power acquired by the Tamil (mostly Hindu) middle class under the British was deeply resented by the Sinhalese (Buddhist) majority, which after independence slowly eroded Tamil rights. In 1957 the government proposed a Tamil state in a federal union and gave Tamil the status of a national (but not official) language. The pact was not fully implemented, and in the 1970s extremists began agitating for an independent Tamil state. The Tamils' minority status was reaffirmed in the constitution of 1972, the year the oldest insurgent group, the Liberation Tigers or Tamil Tigers, was founded.

In July 1987 Pres. Jayawardene accepted an offer from India's Prime Minister Rajiv Gandhi to supervise a truce in the Jaffna region under which the government pledged to hold a referendum aimed at granting self-rule to Tamil majority areas in the north and northeast. The plan failed, however; Indian troops became bogged down in battling the rebels, while the planned referendum was disrupted by fighting between separatists who demanded total independence for Tamil areas and more moderate Tamil groups willing to accept self-rule.

At the Sri Lankan government's request, India withdrew its forces in March 1989, and the Tamil Tigers agreed to a cease-fire as the government prepared its plan for Tamil-area autonomy. But like every agreement that followed it, this cease-fire soon broke down.

The assassination of both the opposition political leader in April 1993 and Pres. Ranasinghe Pemadasa a month later left the nation in shock, although peaceful legislative elections were held later in May. In parliamentary elections held in August 1994, the People's Alliance ended the United National party's 17-year rule. Three months later, Prime Minister Chandrika Bandaranaike Kumaratunga won a landslide (62%) victory in presidential elections, and appointed her 78-year-old mother, Sirimavo Bandaranaike, as prime minister for a third time.

Hours after the new president's inauguration, the Tamil Tigers announced a cease-fire. The truce was formalized in Jan. 1995, but when the government offered a peace plan to divide Sri Lanka into autonomous regions, the Tamil rebels responded by setting off a bomb in Colombo, killing more than 20 people and instantly renewing the 12-year-old civil war that was still being waged years later. More than 45,000 people have been killed since 1983.

▶ SUDAN
Republic of the Sudan

• **GEOGRAPHY** **Location:** northeastern Africa. **Boundaries:** Egypt to N, Red Sea, Eritrea, and Ethiopia to E, Kenya, Uganda, and Zaire to S, Central African Republic, Chad and Libya to W. **Total area:** 967,495 sq. mi. (2,505,810 sq km). **Coastline:** 530 mi. (853 km). **Comparative area:** slightly more than one-quarter the size of the U.S. **Land use:** 5% arable land; negl. % permanent crops; 46% meadows and pastures; 19% forest and woodland; 30% other; includes 1% irrigated. **Major cities:** (1993 census) Khartoum (capital) 924,505; Nyala 1,267,077; Shargen-Nil 879,105; Port Sudan 305,385; Omdurman 228, 778.

• **PEOPLE** **Population:** 34,475,690 (1999 est.). **Nationality:** noun—Sudanese (sing., pl.); adjective—Sudanese. **Ethnic groups:** 52% black, 39% Arab, 6% Beja, 2% foreigners. **Languages:** Arabic (official), Nubian, Ta Bedawie, diverse dialects of Nilotic, Nilo-Hamitic, and Sudanic languages, English; program of Arabization in progress. **Religions:** 70% Sunni Muslim in north, 25% indigenous beliefs, 5% Christian (mostly in south).

• **GOVERNMENT** **Type:** transitional, previously military junta. **Independence:** Jan. 1, 1956 (from Egypt and UK). **Constitution:** Apr. 12, 1973, suspended following coup of Apr. 6, 1985; new constitution drafted. **National holiday:** Independence Day, Jan. 1. **Head of Government:** Lt. Gen. Omer Hassan Ahmed Al Bashir, president (since Jan. 1993). **Structure:** executive—president is head of government and chief of state; unicameral legislature; judiciary.

• **ECONOMY** **Monetary unit:** Sudanese pound. **Budget:** (1996 est.) *income:* $482 mil.; *expend.:* $1.5 bil. **GDP:** $31.2 bil., $930 per capita (1998 est.). **Chief crops:** cotton, peanuts, sorghum, millet, wheat, gum arabic, sesame; sheep. **Natural resources:** petroleum, modest reserves of iron oil, copper, chromium ore, zinc. **Major industries:** cotton ginning, textiles, cement. **Labor force:** 11 mil. (1996 est.); 80% agriculture, 10% industry and commerce, 6% government; labor shortages for almost all categories of skilled employment. **Exports:** $594 mil. (f.o.b., 1997); 23% cotton, 22% sesame, 13% livestock/meat. **Imports:** $1.42 bil. (f.o.b., 1997); foodstuffs, petroleum products, manufactured goods, machinery and equipment, medicines and chemicals, textiles. **Major trading partners:** *exports:* 20% Saudi Arabia, 14% UK, 11% China; *imports:* 10% Saudi Arabia, 7% South Korea, 6% Germany.

The northern Sudan, the ancient land of Nubia, was loosely controlled by Egypt in antiquity and incorporated into the Arab world by the Islamic expansion of the seventh century. The southern Sudan was part of tribal black Africa, under no external control but subject to continual raids from slave traders from the north.

Ottoman Egypt conquered the northern Sudan in 1820-21; British influence in Egypt in the 19th century extended into the Sudan as well. In 1881 Muhammed Ahmed ibn Abdalla, a religious leader known as the Mahdi, united northern and north-central Sudan and led a resistance movement against Anglo-Egyptian control. Khartoum, defended by British general Charles George Gordon, fell in 1885, but the Mahdi died soon thereafter, and his revolt came to an end. An Anglo-Egyptian force under Kitchener regained control in 1898; Anglo-Egyptian joint rule was established in the Sudan in 1899.

Great Britain and Egypt granted self-government and self-determination to the Sudan in 1953, and a Sudanese parliament was seated in 1954. Full independence came in 1956. Gen. Ibrahim Abboud took power in a bloodless coup in 1958 but was forced to resign after riots in 1964. In 1969 a new military coup installed a ruling Revolutionary Command Council and instituted a socialist regime. The council's leader, Gen. Muhammed Nimeiri, became prime minister. Disputes between Marxists and non-Marxists, and between arabized northerners and black southerners, led to continual difficulties. In 1972 Sudan's three black southern provinces were granted local autonomy. Another attempted coup in 1976 was put down by the Nimeiri government, and hundreds of prominent citizens were arrested and executed. The government accused Libya of sponsoring the coup.

In 1983 attempts by the Nimeiri government to institute Islamic law throughout the Sudan led to riots in the south and the imposition of a nationwide state of emergency in 1984. Popular unrest was exacerbated by drought and famine in 1985. On Apr. 6, 1985, Nimeiri was overthrown in a coup by Gen. Suwar El Dahab. After a brief period of rule by a transitional military council, a civilian cabinet was installed, and free parliamentary elections were held in 1986.

In June 1989 the government was overthrown in a coup led by Lt. Gen. Omar Ahmed al-Bashir. The Bashir government renewed the fight against the southern rebels, and supported the imposition of Islamic law throughout the Sudan. Within three years the civil service, the military, the judiciary, and the educational system were under the control of Muslims and their political organization, the National Islamic Front headed by Hassan al-Turabi who is also the leader of parliament and the most powerful figure in Sudan. All opposition parties, newspapers, and unions were banned and a stepped up military campaign against christian animists in the South was launched.

In Oct. 1990, the U.S. government stopped aid to the Sudan, which openly supported Iraq during the Persian Gulf War. In 1991, the UN suspended relief efforts to help the estimated 7.1 million Sudanese threatened by famine. In 1993, the United States added the Sudan to its list of states that sponsor terrorism, and in 1995, the UN endorsed an accusation that Sudan was sheltering the Islamic militants who attempted to assassinate Egyptian Pres. Hosni Mubarak. The government in 1995 announced plans to free all political prisoners and to hold national elections in 1996 but an increase in violence against the government by rebels in the south delayed them. In 1997 the government made peace with some rebel factions, promising a referendum on self determination. The main force of the Sudan People's Liberation Army (SPLA), led by John Garang, continued to fight.

Another famine in 1998 brought a ceasefire as aid workers transported huge amounts of food to over 300,000 in the south. In Aug. 1998 the U.S. launched cruise missiles at Khartoum to retaliate for the bombing of its embassies in Kenya and Tanzania and to destroy a chemical weapons plant. Since July 1998, both the SPLA and the Sudanese government have declared a series of cease-fires to permit international food relief, though no settlement seems in sight. The rebels have lost some international support as Uganda, Ethiopia and Eritrea became embroiled in wars of their own. The Sudanese government's "restora-tion" of a multi-party system at the start of 1999 has thus far been met principally with skepticism by the opposition.

▶ SURINAME
Republic of Suriname
● **GEOGRAPHY Location:** northeastern coast of South America. **Boundaries:** North Atlantic Ocean to N, French Guiana to E, Brazil to S, Guyana to W. **Total area:** 63,039 sq. mi. (163,270 sq km). **Coastline:** 240 mi. (386 km). **Comparative area:** slightly larger than Georgia. **Land use:** negl. % arable land; negl. % permanent crops; negl. % meadows and pastures; 96% forest and woodland; 4% other; includes negl. % irrigated. **Major cities:** (1993 est.) Paramaribo (capital) 200,970.

● **PEOPLE Population:** 431,156 (1999 est.). **Nationality:** noun—Surinamer(s); adjective—Surinamese. **Ethnic groups:** 37% Hindustani (East Indian), 31% Creole (black and mixed), 15.3% Javanese, 10.3% Bush black. **Languages:** Dutch (official), English widely spoken, Sranang Tongo (Surinamese, sometimes called Taki-Taki, the native language of Creoles and much of younger population and lingua franca among others), Hindustani, Javanese. **Religions:** 27.4% Hindu, 25.2% Protestant (predominantly Moravian), 22.8% Roman Catholic, 19.6% Muslim.

● **GOVERNMENT Type:** republic. **Constitution:** Sept. 30, 1987. **Independence:** Nov. 25, 1975 (from Netherlands). **National holiday:** Independence Day, Nov. 25. **Heads of Government:** Jules Wijdenbosch, president (since Sept. 1996); **Structure:** executive—president is chief of state and head of government, Commander in Chief of the National Army maintains significant power; unicameral legislature; judiciary.

● **ECONOMY Monetary unit:** Surinamese guilder. **Budget:** (1997 est.) *income:* $393 mil.; *expend.:* $403 mil. **GDP:** $1.48 bil., $3,500 per capita (1998 est.). **Chief crops:** rice, bananas, palm oil, timber. **Natural resources:** timber, hydropower potential, fish, shrimp, bauxite. **Major industries:** bauxite mining, alumina and aluminum production, lumbering. **Labor force:** agriculture, industry, services; 20% unemployment (1997). **Exports:** $548.84 mil. (1997); alumina, aluminum, crude oil, lumber, shrimp and fish, rice, bananas. **Imports:** $551.8 mil. (1997); capital equipment, petroleum, foodstuffs, cotton, consumer goods. **Major trading partners:** (1997) *exports:* 24% Norway, 22% Netherlands, 22% U.S.; *imports:* 48% U.S., 21.2% Netherlands, 5.1% UK.

In the early 17th century, the Dutch and English settled Suriname, which became a Dutch colony in 1667. Except for brief episodes of British rule, Suriname remained under Dutch control until its independence in 1975, shifting toward authoritarian military rule in 1980. The military created its own political party (the February 25 movement) and banned opposition organizations. The 1988 National Assembly election of Pres. Ramsewak Shankar ended direct military rule, but the restriction of civil liberties continued.

The Shankar government was overthrown in a bloodless coup led by Cmdr. Ivan Graanoogst in 1990, and civilian rule was restored in 1991 although the former military ruler, Col. Desi Bouterse, who led the coup and remains "Advisor of the State," is apparently still the defacto ruler. The current President, Jules Wijdenbosch, agreed in June 1999, after the National Assembly voted "no confidence," to resign—but intends to remain in office until new elections in May 2000.

▶SWAZILAND
Kingdom of Swaziland

● **GEOGRAPHY Location:** landlocked country in southern Africa. **Boundaries:** South Africa to N, SE, S, and W; Mozambique to E. **Total area:** 6,703 sq. mi. (17,360 sq km). **Coastline:** none. **Comparative area:** slightly smaller than New Jersey. **Land use:** 11% arable land; negl. % permanent crops; 62% meadows and pastures; 7% forest and woodland; 20% other. **Major cities:** (1996 census) Mbabane (capital) 38,290; Manzini 18,084.

● **PEOPLE Population:** 985,335 (1999 est.). **Nationality:** noun—Swazi(s); adjective—Swazi. **Ethnic groups:** 97% African, 3% European. **Languages:** English and siSwati (both official); government business conducted in English. **Religions:** 60% Christian, 40% indigenous beliefs.

● **GOVERNMENT Type:** monarchy; independent member of Commonwealth. **Independence:** Sept. 6, 1968 (from UK). **Constitution:** suspended Apr. 12, 1973; new constitution promulgated Oct. 13, 1978, but not yet formally presented to people. **National holiday:** Somhlolo (Independence) Day, Sept. 6. **Heads of Government:** Mswati III, king (since Apr. 1986); Sibusiso Barnabas Dlamini, prime minister (since Aug. 1996). **Structure:** executive—king is hereditary monarch, appoints prime minister; bicameral legislature (lower house-10 members appointed by king, 55 elected; upper house-10 members appointed by king, 10 elected by lower house); judiciary—judges appointed by king.

● **ECONOMY Monetary unit:** lilangeni. **Budget:** (FY96/97) *income:* $400 mil.; *expend.:* $450 mil. GDP: $4 bil., $4,200 per capita (1998 est.). **Chief crops:** maize, cotton, maize, tobacco, rice, citrus fruits; cattle, goats, sheep. **Natural resources:** asbestos, coal, clay, cassiterite, hydropower. **Major industries:** mining (coal and asbestos), wood pulp, sugar. **Labor force:** 70% private sector, 30% public sector. **Exports:** $972 mil. (f.o.b., 1998); soft drink concentrates, sugar, wood pulp, cotton yarn. **Imports:** $1.2 bil. (f.o.b., 1998); motor vehicles, machinery, transport equipment, foodstuffs, chemicals, petroleum products. **Major trading partners:** (1994) *exports:* 58% South Africa, 17% EU, Mozambique; *imports:* 96% South Africa, Japan, UK.

The Kingdom of Swaziland, a landlocked African country, is surrounded on three sides by South Africa and on the fourth by Mozambique. The Swazi are of Bantu origin. They are believed to have migrated in the late 1700s, under their chief Ngwane II, into what is now southeastern Swazi land, finding several different peoples there. Ngwane II and his successors united these tribal clans by the beginning of the 19th century.

Although British and Boer traders began exploring the area in the 1830s, it was not until gold was discovered in the 1880s that settlers began coming in large numbers. They hoodwinked the illiterate Swazi leadership into signing away their rights to the land. The British and Boer governments agreed in 1894 that the Boers would control Swaziland, but power reverted to Great Britain after they defeated the Boers in the Boer War, which ended in 1902. Not until the 1967 did they give Swaziland authority over its internal affairs. Under the Britishauthored constitution, Swaziland gained its independence in September 1968 as a constitutional monarchy led by King Sobhuza II. He set aside the constitution in 1973 and disbanded the legislature. He ruled the country with the aid of a council of conservative ministers and named a committee to write a new constitution

that was supposed to be more in keeping with Swazi traditions. A new legislature was created in 1979. The king died in 1982 and was replaced by his 18-year-old son, who took the name King Mswati III, in 1986.

In 1986 South African forces conducted raids into Swaziland, allegedly in pursuit of African National Congress activists. Swaziland maintains cooperative but cool relations with South Africa and Mozambique.

▶SWEDEN
Kingdom of Sweden

● **GEOGRAPHY Location:** Scandinavian peninsula, northwest Europe. **Boundaries:** Norway to NE and W, Finland to NE, Gulf of Bothnia to E, Baltic Sea to E and S, Skagerrak channel to SW. **Total area:** 173,731 sq. mi. (449,964 sq km). **Coastline:** 2,000 mi. (3,218 km). **Comparative area:** slightly larger than California. **Land use:** 7% arable land; 0% permanent crops; 1% meadows and pastures; 68% forest and woodland; 24% other; includes negl. % irrigated. **Major cities:** (1994 est.) Stockholm (capital) 703,627; Göteburg (Gothenburg) 444,553; Malmö 242,706; Uppsala 181,191; Linköping 130,489.

● **PEOPLE Population:** 8,911,296 (1999 est.). **Nationality:** noun—Swede(s); adjective—Swedish. **Ethnic groups:** homogeneous white population; small Lappish minority; about 12% foreign-born or first-generation immigrants (Finns, Yugoslavs, Danes, Norwegians, Greeks, Turks). **Languages:** Swedish, small Lapp- and Finnish-speaking minorities. **Religions:** 94% Evangelical Lutheran, 1.5% Roman Catholic, 1% Pentacostal, 4.5% other.

● **GOVERNMENT Type:** constitutional monarchy. **Constitution:** Jan. 1, 1975. **National holiday:** Day of the Swedish Flag, June 6. **Head of Government:** Carl XVI Gustaf, king (since Nov. 1973); Göran Persson, prime minister (since Mar. 1996). **Structure:** executive—prime minister is head of government; unicameral legislature; judiciary.

● **ECONOMY Monetary unit:** Swedish krona. **Budget:** (FY95/96) *income:* $109.4 bil.; *expend.:* $146.1 bil. GDP: $175 bil., $19,700 per capita (1998 est.). **Chief crops:** grain, sugar beets, potatoes; meat, milk. **Natural resources:** zinc, iron ore, lead, copper, silver. **Major industries:** iron and steel, precision equipment (bearings, radio and telephone parts, armaments), wood pulp. **Labor force:** 4.552 mil. (1992); 38.3% community services, 21.2% mining and manufacturing. **Exports:** $85.5 bil. (f.o.b., 1998); 35% machinery, motor vehicles, paper products, pulp and wood, iron and steel products. **Imports:** $66.6 bil. (f.o.b., 1998); machinery, petroleum and petroleum products, chemicals, motor vehicles, foodstuffs. **Major trading partners:** *exports:* 55% EU, 8% Norway; 8% U.S.; *imports:* 68% EU, 8% Norway, 6% US.

The earliest Swedes, the Svear, conquered and merged with their southern neighbors, the Gotar, by the sixth century. Organized into petty kingdoms, Swedes joined with other Norsemen in the Viking raids of the seventh through 11th centuries; in the 10th century, they began to dominate a trading empire that stretched through Russia to the Black Sea. Christianity was introduced by St. Ansgar in 829 but became fully established only in the 12th century, during the reign of Eric IX, who also conquered Finland. For centuries Sweden warred with its neighbors, Norway and Denmark, for control in the north, and it competed with the German Hanseatic League for control of the Baltic trade.

The Swedish and Norwegian monarchies were

merged in 1319 by Magnus VII, and in 1397 Queen Margaret effected the Kalmar Union, which united Sweden, Denmark, and Norway under a single monarchy. Sweden resisted Danish rule, and in 1520 King Christian II responded with the massacre of the Swedish nobility at Stockholm. Sweden then rose against the Danish throne and in 1523 enthroned Gustavus Wasa as Gustavus I, founder of the Swedish monarchy. The Wasa dynasty slowly introduced Lutheran Christianity and in 1604 banned Catholicism.

Sweden became a European champion of Protestantism in the 17th century, intervening against the Habsburgs in the Thirty Years' War. Emerging among the victors after 1648, Sweden successfully waged wars with Denmark and Poland, built a great northern empire, and made the Baltic Sea virtually a Swedish lake. But in the late 17th century and into the 18th, the Russians deprived Sweden of the Baltic's eastern shore and, in 1808, of Finland, while the Prussians drove Sweden from the southern Baltic coast.

The kings of Sweden during the 18th century pursued a pointless despotism that weakened the country politically and socially. Sweden joined the European powers against Napoleon in 1813 and was rewarded with Norway in 1814. In 1905 Norway gained its independence, and Sweden took on its modern boundaries.

Sweden's greatest natural resources are timber, iron ore, and hydroelectric power. The first two were exploited by traditional industries, which supplemented other economic activities (fishing, maritime trade). All provided the basis for industrialization in the 19th and 20th centuries, leading to an economic prosperity that was enhanced by political neutrality.

Sweden's neutrality was largely respected by Hitler during World War II. Through the war Sweden continued to be ruled, under King Gustavus V, by a national coalition government lasting until 1945. Sweden's gross national product (GNP) rose by 20 percent during the war years.

The Social Democratic party dominated the Swedish government after 1936, and again after 1945, lasting until 1976 under the leadership of Tage Erlander. Sweden, like its Scandinavian neighbors, constructed an economy based on free enterprise, public ownership of utilities, exports, social welfare, and high taxes.

A UN charter member, Sweden accepted Marshall Plan aid and joined the Council of Europe in 1948. Sweden's plan for a Nordic Defense Alliance failed when Norway and Denmark joined NATO (Sweden refused to join the North Atlantic pact), but the political and economic Nordic Council (Sweden, Norway, Denmark, Iceland, and, after 1956, Finland) was formed in 1952-53. This consultative body backed the establishment of SAS as the joint national airline of the first three members; coordination of the welfare programs of member states; and abolition of passport controls and controls on the migration of labor within Scandinavia.

Erlander retired as prime minister in 1969 and was succeeded by Olaf Palme, who pursued a more rigid socialist program than his predecessor. He advocated legislation to make incomes more equal, provoking some labor unrest. When King Gustav VI Adolf died in 1973 the Palme government passed the 1974 Instrument of Government Act, divesting the king of his role as commander in chief of the armed forces and of his right to appoint prime ministers.

Economic growth came to a virtual halt in the 1970s; lacking petroleum and gas resources, Sweden's oil import costs rose 700 percent between 1972 and 1979. Consumer prices rose sharply, and labor unrest grew. The Social Democrats were turned out of office by a conservative coalition in 1976 but returned with a minority cabinet in 1982.

Palme was assassinated in 1986, and he was succeeded by Ingvar Carlsson, whose Social Democratic program focused on a scheme whereby business profits are taxed to fund labor union purchases of sufficient stock to gain labor ownership of private enterprise.

September 1991 elections unseated Carlsson and the Social Democrats, who had ruled Sweden for 53 of the last 59 years. A coalition government of four conservative parties pledged to cut taxes and phase out some welfare programs.

But in elections held in Sept. 1994, Carlsson returned to power as voters expressed dissatisfaction with inflation, unemployment, and an enormous public debt, all of which spiraled under the conservative coalition. The Social Democrats fell 13 votes short of a majority in Parliament, however, forcing them to seek the support of the right-centrist Liberal party in a coalition government. On Jan. 1, 1995, Sweden entered the European Union. In March 1996, Finance Minister Göran Persson succeeded Carlsson, who resigned as prime minister for personal reasons. In 1998 Sweden announced it would not join the European Monetary Union, and in Sept. elections Persson's Government won enough votes to keep power by pledging more money for social welfare services. More significant for Sweden's future was the 1999 completion of the 10-mile, $2.6 billion bridge over (and under) the Baltic, linking Copenhagen with Malmoe (Sweden's third largest city). Opening to traffic in July 2000, the bridge will allow trucks, cars and trains to by-pass costly and time-consuming ferries, linking Sweden with the south in a radically new way.

▶ SWITZERLAND
Swiss Confederation

● **GEOGRAPHY   Location:** landlocked country in central Europe. **Boundaries:** Germany to N, Austria to E, Italy to S, and France to W. **Total area:** 15,942 sq. mi. (41,290 sq km). **Coastline:** none. **Comparative area:** slightly less than twice the size of New Jersey. **Land use:** 10% arable land; 2% permanent crops; 28% meadows and pastures; 32% forest and woodland; 28% other. **Major cities:** (1994 est.) Berne (Bern, capital) 128,422; Zürich 342,872; Basel 175,561; Genève (Geneva or Genf) 172,737; Lausanne 116,795.

● **PEOPLE   Population:** 7,275,467 (1999 est.). **Nationality:** noun—Swiss (sing., pl.); adjective—Swiss. **Ethnic groups:** total population—65% German, 18% French, 10% Italian, 1% Romansch, 6% other; Swiss nationals—74% German, 20% French, 4% Italian, 1% Romansch, 1% other. **Languages:** total population—63.7% German, 19.2% French, 7.6% Italian, 0.6% Romansch, 8.9% other; Swiss nationals—74% German, 20% French, 4% Italian, 1% Romansch, 1% other. **Religions:** 46.1% Catholic, 40% Protestant.

● **GOVERNMENT   Type:** federal republic. **Independence:** Aug. 1, 1291. **Constitution:** May 29, 1874. **National holiday:** Anniversary of the Founding of the Swiss Confederation, Aug. 1. **Head of Government:** Ruth Dreifuss, president (since Jan. 1999). **Structure:** executive—president is head of government and chief of state; bicameral legislature-National Council, Council of States; judiciary left chiefly to cantons.

● **ECONOMY   Monetary unit:** Swiss franc. **Budget:** (1998 est.) *income:* $32.66 bil.; *expend.:* $34.89 bil. **GDP:** $191.8 bil., $26,400 per capita (1998 est.). **Chief crops:** grains, fruits, vegetables; meat, eggs. **Natural resources:** hydropower potential, timber, salt. **Major industries:** machinery, chemicals, watches. **Labor force:** 3.8 mil.; 850,000 foreign workers, mostly Italian; 67% services, 29% manufacturing, 4% agriculture (1995). **Exports:** $94.4 bil. (f.o.b., 1998); 29% machinery, 28% chemicals, metals, watches, agricultural products. **Imports:** $95.5 bil. (f.o.b., 1998); 22% machinery, 16% chemicals, vehicles, metals, agricultural products. **Major trading partners:** (1997 est.) *exports:* 61% EU, 10% U.S., 4% Japan; *imports:* 79% EU, 7% U.S. 3% Japan.

Switzerland, the Roman province of Helvetia, began to assume its modern form in A.D. 1291, when three independent cantons formed a defensive league against the expansion of Habsburg power. The Swiss League grew to eight cantons in 1353, 13 in 1513, 22 in 1815. The league continues to evolve; it reached its present size of 20 cantons and six half-cantons with the creation of the Canton of Jura in 1979.

The Treaty of Westphalia, which ended the Thirty Years' War in 1648, gave international recognition to the independence of Switzerland from the Holy Roman Empire. Switzerland became a client state of France in the Napoleonic period; the European powers recognized and guaranteed Swiss independence and neutrality at the Congress of Vienna in 1815. Constitutional changes in 1848 and 1874 somewhat increased the power of the central government, but the individual cantons cling stubbornly to their independence within the confederation. This policy has helped ensure stability within a multilingual nation.

The Swiss government consists of an upper house, representing the cantons, and a lower house that is directly elected. No executive can veto, nor court disallow, a bill of the Swiss legislature. Executive power is vested in a seven-member committee chosen by the legislature, with a rotating presidency.

Swiss neutrality is defended by more than simply international guarantees. Switzerland is a highly militarized society; every male is required to serve in the citizen's militia until age 47, keeping an assault rifle and other equipment ready at home. The armed forces are equipped with sophisticated modern weapons, and military spending amounts to 30 percent of the Swiss federal budget.

Landlocked, with little fertile farmland and limited Alpine pastures, lacking both natural resources and a colonial empire, Switzerland was traditionally one of Europe's poorest countries. Until the 19th century, its principal export was soldiers, mercenaries who supplied military services to any European sovereign who could pay for them. (The pope's Swiss Guard is a remnant of this tradition.) With the spread in the late 18th century of the Romantic movement, Europeans learned to appreciate the glamour of Alpine scenery, and a tourist industry was born. It was much expanded in the 20th century with the development of Alpine skiing. Tourism remains a conspicuous, though relatively minor, part of the Swiss economy.

Swiss prosperity came in the 20th century with specialized manufacturing and free trade within the world economy. By 1940 half of the population was engaged in manufacturing, producing products requiring high degrees of skill: processed foods, watches, electrical machinery, engines, fine textiles, and the like.

Neutral in both world wars, Switzerland required no postwar recovery in the 1940s. It capitalized on the restructuring of European politics and economics to expand into the service sector, which now employs half of the work force (while manufacturing has declined to about 40 percent). Tourism, banking, insurance, and clerical/bureaucratic services to the many international organizations with headquarters in Switzerland help give the nation one of Europe's highest standards of living. Under pressure from the EC and the United States, Switzerland agreed to phase out its famous "Form B" (i.e., secret bank accounts).

In the postwar period, Switzerland has enjoyed both political and economic stability. A cautious approach to economic development led to annual growth rates of over 6 percent in the 1950s and early 1960s, declining to 2 percent in the 1970s; the world economic boom of the 1980s produced higher growth rates. In general the economy has avoided inflation, and the stability of the Swiss franc has been maintained.

Switzerland is a member of the European Free Trade Association and has ties to the EU, although it is not a member. Recent referenda brought overwhelming rejection of UN membership (it currently has observer status), and support for restrictive immigration legislation. The most significant political change has been the gradual extension, canton by canton, of women's right to vote. Almost as startling were the 1989 referendum in which one-third of the voters chose to abolish the Swiss army by the year 2000, and the 1993 approval of casino gambling to fund social security.

In 1996 and 1997 the Swiss government, responding to international pressures, appointed a panel to examine what funds in Swiss banks the Nazis might have stolen or that Holocaust victims (or their families) might have deposited and were unable to retrieve. A less than rigorous accounting, however, resulted in severe criticism of the Swiss as well as several lawsuits which were settled in Aug. 1998 with the Swiss banks reluctantly agreeing to pay $1.2 bil. On December 9, 1998, Social Democrat Ruth Dreifuss became Switzerland's first female and first Jewish president.

▶ **SYRIA**
Syrian Arab Republic
● **GEOGRAPHY   Location:** western Asia. **Boundaries:** Turkey to N, Iraq to E, Jordan to S, Lebanon and Israel to SW, Mediterranean Sea to W. **Total area:** 71,498 sq. mi. (185,180 sq km). **Coastline:** 193 mi. (193 km). **Comparative area:** slightly larger than North Dakota. **Land use:** 28% arable land; 4% permanent crops; 43% meadows and pastures; 3% forest and woodland; 22% other. **Major cities:** (1994 est.) Damascus (capital) 1,444,138; Aleppo 1,542,000; Homs 558,000; Latakia 303,000; Hama 273,000.
● **PEOPLE   Population:** 17,213,871 (1999 est.). **Nationality:** noun—Syrian(s); adjective—Syrian. **Ethnic groups:** 90.3% Arab, 9.7% Kurds, Armenians, and other. **Languages:** Arabic (official), Kurdish, Armenian, Aramaic, Circassian, French. **Religions:** 74% Sunni Muslim; 16% Alawite, Druze, and other Muslim sects; 10% Christian.
● **GOVERNMENT   Type:** republic under military regime since Mar. 1963. **Independence:** Apr. 17,

1946 (from League of Nations Mandate under French administration). **Constitution:** Mar. 13, 1973. **National holiday:** National Day, Apr. 17. **Heads of Government:** Lt. Gen. Hafez al-Assad, president (since Mar. 1971); Mahmoud Zoubi, prime minister (since Nov. 1987). **Structure:** executive powers vested in president and Council of Ministers; unicameral legislature (People's Council); judiciary.

• **ECONOMY   Monetary unit:** Syrian pound. **Budget:** (1997 est.) *income:* $3.5 bil.; *expend.:* $4.2 bil. **GDP:** $41.7 bil., $2,500 per capita (1998 est.). **Chief crops:** cotton, wheat, barley, lentils; beef, lamb, eggs, poultry, milk. **Natural resources:** crude oil, phosphates, chrome and manganese ores, asphalt, iron ore. **Major industries:** petroleum, textiles, food processing, beverages. **Labor force:** 4.7 mil. (1998 est.); 40% services, 40% agriculture, 20% industry. **Exports:** $4.2 bil. (f.o.b., 1998 est.); 65% petroleum, 16% textiles, 13% food and live animals. **Imports:** $5.7 bil. (c.i.f., 1997 est.); 40% machinery, 15% foodstuffs/animals, 15% metal and metal products, 10% textiles, 10% chemicals. **Major trading partners:** (1997 est.) *exports:* 18% Italy, 13% Germany, 12% France, 10% Turkey; *imports:* 14% Ukraine, 7% Italy, 6% Germany, 5% Turkey.

The home of some of the world's most ancient centers of civilization, Syria was successively part of the Hittite, Assyrian, and Persian empires. At various times it was conquered by the Babylonians and the Egyptians. From about 1250 B.C., the coastal cities came under Phoenician rule. Alexander the Great brought Syria into the Hellenic world with his conquests in 332 B.C. After the fall of the Alexandrian empire, Syria came under the domain of the Seleucid empire but was constantly threatened by the Hellenic kingdom of Egypt, based in Alexandria.

In the classical period, Syria embraced a much larger territory than that of the present Syrian nation; it included the entire Levant and parts of present-day Turkey, Iraq, Iran, and Jordan. Greater Syria was conquered by Rome in 63 B.C. Under Roman rule the oasis region of Palmyra grew into a powerful semiautonomous kingdom. With the division of the Roman Empire in the fourth century A.D., Syria became part of the Eastern Roman (Byzantine) Empire. Throughout the Roman and Byzantine periods, the country was an important center of Christianity.

Syria was one of the first areas conquered when Islam began expansion from Arabia; Islamic rule was established by 636. From 661 to 751, Damascus was the center of the Caliphate, the ruling body of the Islamic world. By the late 11th century, the Seljuk Turks had conquered Syria. The large Syrian Christian population welcomed the European Crusaders as liberators from the Turks, but both Christians and Turks were defeated by the Arab general Saladin in the late 12th century. Saladin's rule was followed by that of the Mamluk empire of Egypt. During the Mamluk period, Mongol armies twice invaded Syria, in the mid-13th century and at the turn of the 15th century.

An Ottoman army defeated the Mamluks in Syria in 1516, making Syria part of the Ottoman Empire. In the 18th century, France declared itself the protector of Syria's Christian community against Ottoman abuses. Napoleon invaded Syria in 1799 but withdrew after a brief occupation. In the 1830s Egyptian troops occupied Syria but were forced to withdraw under pressure from the European powers.

Syrian nationalist aspirations emerged as the Ottoman Empire began to crumble before World War I. During the war the British encouraged Syrians to rebel against Turkish rule. After World War I, France governed both Syria and Lebanon under a League of Nations mandate. Under French rule, the region was divided into small territorial states along communal lines; Lebanon became independent in 1926. After prolonged negotiations much of Syria was organized into a semi-autonomous state in 1930-32.

In June 1940 the French administration in Syria declared its loyalty to the Vichy government. British and Free French forces invaded in June 1941, and an independent Syrian republic was established in September 1941. Separately administered territories were consolidated with the republic over the next two years, and full independence was declared on Jan. 1, 1944; foreign troops did not withdraw, however, until April 1946.

Syria became a founding member of the Arab League and participated in the first Arab-Israeli War in 1948. An armistice with Israel was signed in July 1949. Severe political instability marked the early years of Syrian independence; the government was overthrown by military coups three times in 1949 alone.

Most of Syria's Jews emigrated to Israel before or during 1948, and much of its once-substantial Christian population has emigrated also. Syrian politics remain dominated by communal concerns, however; the Arab majority is divided into Sunni, Shiite, Alawite, and Druze communities.

Syria and Egypt merged as the United Arab Republic in February 1958; Syria seceded from the federation on Sept. 30, 1961. In Mar. 1963 a military coup established the pan-Arab Socialist Baath party in power; all other political parties were abolished. The Baath party leadership is dominated by the minority Alawite community. Pres. Hafez al-Assad took power on Feb. 22, 1971.

In the 1967 Arab-Israeli War (the Six Day War), Israel seized and held the Golan Heights region of Syria, from which Syria had long shelled Israeli communities and military installations. The Golan Heights have since been incorporated into Israeli territory.

Syrian troops aided Palestinian forces fighting government troops in Jordan in September 1970. After the expulsion of Palestinian forces from Jordan in July 1971, Syria broke off relations with Jordan; relations were restored in 1975.

On Oct. 6, 1973, Syrian and Egyptian forces attacked Israel, touching off the third Arab-Israeli War, the Yom Kippur War. A cease-fire took effect on Oct. 24; Syria failed to regain territory lost to Israel in 1967. Following the 1973 war, Syria became a major recipient of economic aid from the Arab oil states and of military equipment from the Soviet Union.

In 1976 Syrian troops entered Lebanon in an attempt to mediate a civil war there and became enmeshed in that conflict. Major fighting between Syrian troops and Lebanese Christian militiamen broke out in April 1981. On June 6, 1982, Israeli troops invaded Lebanon and engaged Syrian troops in a five-day war in the Bekaa Valley. Following serious losses of aircraft and troops, Syria agreed to a cease-fire with Israel on June 11. Syrian troops continue to occupy parts of Lebanon.

An attempted coup, in February 1982, by the Muslim Brotherhood, led to serious fighting within Syria, but the rebellion was put down; casualties topped 5,000 on both sides.

From the time of the 1973 Arab-Israeli War (the Yom Kippur War), Syria consistently adopted a radical stance in Middle Eastern politics, rejecting the 1979 Egyptian-Israeli accord and all other attempts at Arab-Israeli reconciliation. Supporting radical movements within the Palestine Liberation Organization, Syria aided Palestinian militants in driving Yasir Arafat's centrist faction of the PLO from its headquarters in Tripoli in 1983. The government has been implicated in various acts of international terrorism in support of Palestinian, Libyan, and Iranian causes.

Syria played a major role in the Lebanese peace process, backing the governments in place since the Taif peace accord and accommodating a peace settlement between rival Shiite militias. Syria also took part in the antiIraq coalition in 1990-91, sending 20,000 troops to Saudi Arabia, as well as mobilizing forces on its common border with Iraq. Syria in 1994 made serious efforts toward achieving peace in the Middle East, including an offer to normalize relations in exchange for a return of the Golan Heights. But talks between the two countries were suspended in March 1995 after several bombings by the militant Islamic group Hamas.

In Oct. 1998, Syria reached an accord with Turkey; with 10,000 Turkish troops massed on Syria's border, Syria agreed to cease supporting Kurdish rebels. The legislative elections in Dec. 1998 contained no surprises: Assad's National Progressive Front won all 167 seats that they chose to contest, leaving 83 others to independents. Then, in Feb. 1999, Assad himself won, with 99.95 percent approval in his sole candidacy, election to a fifth seven-year term as president.

▶ TAIWAN

● **GEOGRAPHY Location:** one large and several smaller islands about 100 mi. (160 km) off SE coast of mainland China. Taipei 25°03'N, 121°30'E. **Boundaries:** East China Sea to N, Pacific Ocean to E, Bashi Channel to S, and Formosa Strait to W; separated from mainland by Formosa Strait. **Total area:** 13,892 sq. mi. (35,980 sq km). **Coastline:** 900 mi. (1,448 km). **Comparative area:** slightly smaller than Maryland. **Land use:** 24% arable land; 1% permanent crops; 5% meadows and pastures; 55% forest and woodland; 15% other; includes 14% irrigated. **Major cities:** (1992 est.) Taipei (capital) 2,696,073; Kaohsiung 1,405,909; Taichung 794,960; Tainan 694,630; Panchiao 543,982.

● **PEOPLE Population:** 22,113,250 (1999 est.). **Nationality:** noun—Chinese (sing., pl.); adjective—Chinese. **Ethnic groups:** 84% Taiwanese, 14% mainland Chinese, 2% aborigine. **Languages:** Mandarin Chinese (official); Taiwanese and Hakka dialects also used. **Religions:** 93% mixture of Buddhist, Confucian, and Taoist; 4.5% Christian, 2.5% other.

● **GOVERNMENT Type:** multi-party democratic regime headed by popularly elected president. **Constitution:** Jan. 1, 1947, amended 1992, 1994, and 1997. **National holiday:** National Day, Oct. 10. **Heads of Government:** Lee Teng-hui, president (since Jan. 1988); Vincent Siew, premier (since Aug. 1997). **Structure:** executive—president appoints premier; two-chamber legislature—Legislative Yuan, National Assembly; judiciary—Judicial Yuan.

● **ECONOMY Monetary unit:** New Taiwan dollar. **Budget:** (1998 est.) *income:* $40 bil.; *expend.:* $55 bil. **GDP:** $362 bil., $16,500 per capita (1998 est.).

Chief crops: rice, wheat, corn, soybeans, vegetables, fruit, tea; pigs, poultry, beef, milk; fish. **Natural resources:** small deposits of coal, natural gas, limestone, marble, and asbestos. **Major industries:** electronics, textiles, clothing, chemicals. **Labor force:** 9.4 mil. (1997); 38% industry and commerce, 52% services, 10% agriculture. **Exports:** $122.1 bil. (f.o.b., 1997); 21.7% electrical equipment and machinery, 14.8% electronic products, 11.8% information/communications, 11.6% textile products. **Imports:** $114.4 bil. (c.i.f., 1997); 16.5% machinery and electrical equipment, 16.3% electronic products, 10.0% chemicals, 5.6% precision instrument. **Major trading partners:** (1997 est.) *exports:* 24.2% U.S., 23.5% Hong Kong, 15.1% Europe; *imports:* 25.4% Japan, 20.3% U.S., 18.9% Europe.

Nominally part of the Chinese empire since the Song dynasty (960-1279), Taiwan was inhabited only by non-Chinese aboriginals before the 17th century. Around 1600 the Portuguese established a trading station on Taiwan; they named the island Ilha Formosa. In 1620 the Dutch built Fort Zeelandia near present-day Tainan, controlling the island until they were driven out by the Chinese pirate-patriot Koxinga (Zheng Chenggong). Remnants of the overthrown Ming dynasty (1368-1644) held out on the island until 1683, when it came under the sway of the Qing dynasty (1644-1911). Thereafter, substantial numbers of farmers from Fujian Province migrated to the fertile western lowlands of the island, driving the aboriginals into the central mountains. The Qing dynasty administered Taiwan as a semiautonomous subprovince of Fujian Province.

Following China's defeat by Japan in the Sino-Japanese War of 1894-95, Taiwan was ceded to Japan as a colony. The Japanese built roads and railroads to exploit Taiwan's resources of rice, timber, and minerals. In 1945, after Japan's defeat in World War II, Taiwan was returned to Chinese sovereignty.

As the Chinese civil war turned against the Nationalist party of Chiang Kai-shek (see "China"), Nationalist troops began to prepare Taiwan as a base for a retreat from the mainland.

In 1947 Nationalist agents executed several thousand students and others suspected of favoring Taiwan's independence from China. In 1949 approximately two million Nationalist soldiers, government officials, and civilian sympathizers retreated to Taiwan. The relocated Republic of China (ROC) continued to claim to be the legitimate government of all of China, now under Communist control. In addition to Taiwan proper, the Nationalists occupied the P'eng-hu Islands in the Taiwan Straits and the small islands of Quemoy and Matsu just off the coast of Fujian. Recovery of the mainland became a cornerstone of ROC policy, but no serious attempt was made to do so. U.S. policy in the Taiwan Straits was to defend Taiwan against Communist attack but also to keep the two rival governments of China well separated from each other.

A successful program of land reform in the early 1950s led to the creation of surplus capital, which fueled the development of an industrial base on the island. Foreign investment from Japan and the United States, and American military and economic aid, also enhanced economic development. By the early 1970s, the island had developed an export-oriented economy, producing textiles, cement, plastics, assembled electronic appliances, and other manufactured goods.

Chiang Kai-shek, president of the Republic of China since 1928, died in 1975 and was succeeded by his son, Chiang Ching-kuo. Under both father and son, the Nationalist party (Kuomintang, or KMT) controlled both the ROC and the Taiwan Provincial governments; mainland refugees and their descendants (15% of the population) dominated senior government posts and the military officer corps. Native Taiwanese played the leading role in agriculture, industry, and in local and county governments.

In 1971 China's seat in the United Nations was taken away from the ROC and awarded to the People's Republic of China, leaving Taiwan in international diplomatic limbo. On Jan. 1, 1979, the United States withdrew its recognition of the ROC and inaugurated mutual diplomatic relations with the People's Republic. Under the Taiwan Relations Act of 1979, nominally nongovernmental relations were maintained between the United States and Taiwan through the American Institute in Taipei and Taiwan's Coordination Council for North American Affairs in Washington, D.C. Similar arrangements elsewhere ensured that Taiwan's trade and other interests would be secured. Taiwan's economy has continued to be one of the world's most vigorous; Taiwan enjoys a substantial favorable balance of trade with the United States and has foreign-exchange holdings in excess of $75 billion.

In 1986 Pres. Chiang Ching-kuo began a policy of liberalization; in 1987, he abolished martial law and allowed non-KMT political parties to function legally. Some barriers to travel and communication with the mainland by ROC citizens were eased, but Taiwan's government continued to rebuff all calls from the mainland for direct contacts and discussions of reunification. Chiang Ching-kuo died in Jan. 1988 and was succeeded by his vice president, Lee Teng-hui. In March 1990, Lee was overwhelmingly reelected by the National Assembly in the first election for the office.

The ruling KMT maintained its hold on power in legislative elections on Dec. 19, 1992, but the opposition Democratic Progressive party scored a stunning success, tripling its number of legislative seats and bringing the issue of Taiwanese independence to the forefront of the island's political agenda. Meanwhile, factional rivalry deepened in the KMT, with Pres. Lee's Wisdom Coalition challenged by the New Kuomintang Alliance of Prime Minister (and former general) Hau Pei-tsun. Hau reluctantly resigned on Feb. 3, 1993, to take responsibility for the electoral fiasco, but his faction, with military backing, continued to pose a threat to Pres. Lee's power.

During the campaign for Taiwan's presidential election in March, 1996, China held aggressive military exercises off the coast of Taiwan in an effort to influence the voting; the United States sent two aircraft carriers to the area. In a rebuke to Beijing, President Lee, who had campaigned for a more visible international role for Taiwan, was resoundingly re-elected; he was also re-elected as the head of the KMT in August, 1997. Since then, talks for cross-straits cooperation between Taiwan and the PRC have been inconclusive, and the ruling KMT saw its power eroded in local elections as voters protest against corruption and economic stagnation related to the Asia-wide economic crises of 1997-98. The KMT rebounded strongly in 1998 elections but tensions rose in 1999 with mainland China, when President Lee's expressed interest in Taiwan's being included in a proposed anti-missile defense of its Asian allies (the "last straw" to Beijing). Later, Lee announced that Taiwan would conduct its relations with China on a "state-to-state" basis, meaning Taiwan was an independent state—to Beijing, and "extremely dangerous step".

▶ TAJIKISTAN
Republic of Tajikistan
● **GEOGRAPHY Location:** southeast central Asia. **Boundaries:** Kyrgyzstan to NE, China to E, Afghanistan to S and SW, Uzbekistan to NW and N. **Total area:** 55,251 sq. mi. (143,100 sq km). **Coastline:** none. **Comparative area:** slightly smaller than Wisconsin. **Land use:** 6% arable land; 25% permanent pasture; 4% forest and woodland; 65% other. **Major cities:** (1990 est.) Dushanbe (Stalinabad 1929-61) (capital) 602,000; Khodzhent (formerly Leninabad), 163,000 (1989).
● **PEOPLE Population:** 6,102,854 (1999 est.). **Nationality:** noun—Tajikistani(s); adjective—Tajikistani. **Ethnic groups:** 64.9% Tajik, 25% Uzbek, 3.5% Russian, 6.6% other. **Languages:** Tajik (official) is closely related to Farsi (Persian) and was written in Cyrillic script since 1940; Russian widely used in government and business. **Religions:** 80% Sunni Muslim, 5% Shi'a Muslim.
● **GOVERNMENT Type:** republic. **Independence:** Sept. 9, 1991 (from Soviet Union). **Constitution:** Nov. 6, 1994. **National holiday:** National Day, Sept. 9. **Heads of Government:** Emomali Rakhmonov; head of state (since Nov. 1994); Yakhyo Azimov (since Feb. 1996). **Structure:** executive—popularly-elected president appoints prime minister and cabinet unicameral legislature; judiciary.
● **ECONOMY Monetary unit:** Tajikistani ruble. **Budget:** N.A. **GDP:** $6 bil., $990 per capita (1998 est.). **Chief crops:** cotton, vegetables, fruit, grain, grapes; cattle, sheep, goats. **Natural resources:** significant hydropower potential, some petroleum, uranium, mercury, brown coal. **Major industries:** mineral processing, chemicals, fertilizers, cement. **Labor force:** 1.9 mil. (1996); 52% agriculture and forestry, 17% manufacturing, mining, and construction, 31% services. **Exports:** $740 mil. (1998 est.); cotton, aluminum, fruits, vegetable oil, textiles. **Imports:** $810 mil. (1998 est.); fuel, chemicals, machinery and transport equipment, textiles, foodstuffs. **Major trading partners:** *exports:* 78% FSU, Netherlands; *imports:* 55% FSU, Switzerland, UK.

Tajikistan is a mountainous country, with over half of its territory above 10,000 feet. Its mountain ranges are the northern and southern Tian Shan and the Pamirs, where the former Soviet Union's highest points of Lenin Peak and Communism Peak are found. The dense river system and the many fertile valleys make habitation possible in such a mountainous country, although the entire territory is prone to earthquakes.

Tajikistan exemplifies the complexities of central Asia, since, unlike other ethnic groups on the region, the Tajiks were not nomadic but sedentary, and their language was Persian, not Turkic. They are a population that somehow escaped the waves of Turkish influence that swept through central Asia. As early as the eighth century A.D., the Tajiks probably formed a distinctive ethnic group, although they have never been a completely independent people. Despite the formation of several semi-independent states in their history, they have always been a small part of the larger Uzbek lands. In the mid-19th century, the Russian empire expanded southward, and the northern Tajik territories came under Russian rule. At the same time, the tribal state known as the Khanate of Bukhara controlled the southern Tajik territories.

In April 1918 northern Tajikistan came under Soviet control and was included in the Turkestan Autonomous Soviet Socialist Republic (ASSR). Three years later, the Red Army took the other regions that had been ruled by Bukhara. There was local opposition to Soviet rule, and the fighting meant that full Soviet authority over all of the area was not established until 1925. When the USSR created the National Delimitation of the Central Asian Republics in 1924, it founded the Tajik ASSR as part of the Uzbek Soviet Socialist Republic (SSR); on Oct. 16, 1929, it became the Tajik SSR.

The Tajiks were fiercely opposed to the policies of land reform and collectivization, and during the ensuing Soviet repression of the 1930s, almost all native Tajiks were replaced by Russians in leading government and party positions. There have been reports of rising Islamic influence and increasing anti-Russian sentiment and even riots during the 1970s, evidence that the animosity toward the Russians that stemmed with its forced incorporation into the USSR had not abated since the 1920s. Under Soviet rule, there was some economic and social progress.

However, living standards in Tajikistan are still among the lowest in the former union. Most people continue to live in rural qishlaqs, or settlements, consisting of 200-700 one-family houses built along an irrigation ditch or a river. The country is a major producer of cotton, and its industries are nonferrous metallurgy, cotton processing, fruit canning, and wine making.

Mikhail Gorbachev's glasnost, or openness, policy resulted in a campaign against corruption, a relaxation of censorship in the press, and increased ethnic tensions over alleged discrimination against Tajiks living in Uzbekistan. In June 1989 there were violent clashes between the two groups on the border between the two republics. There were also riots in February 1990 in Dushanbe, when the suggestion that Armenian refugees would be resettled there spurred the local Tajiks into action. Increased freedom of the press has given rise to a growing interest in Iran and Iranian culture, for even though they are closely related, contact between Iran and the Tajiks was severely limited during the Soviet period.

In large part due to the riots, opposition candidates were barred from the March 1990 elections and the Communist party won 94 percent of the seats. After the failed August 1991 coup in Moscow, the Communist party was banned, and the president was forced to resign over his support of the coup. Since then, there have been several Communist party coups, and the party has been banned and reinstated several times. In the presidential elections in November, former Communist party leader Rakhmon Nabiyev won with 58 percent of the vote. But after a relatively tranquil six months, Islamic fundamentalists, armed allegedly by Iran and Afghanistan, rose up against the Nabiyev regime. Vicious fighting for almost four months led to Nabiyev's resignation at gunpoint and the launching of a fundamentalist government.

In December 1992 the pro-Communist forces launched a successful counterattack in which thousands were killed and perhaps 300,000 displaced. Russian troops remain in Dushanbe and support the new government.

Voters in November 1994 approved by referendum a new (highly presidential) constitution with 90 percent of the vote, and elected as president Emomali Rakhmonov with 60 percent. But the civil war of the current, ex-Communist and Russian-backed government against Islamic rebels continues, despite UN-mediated cease-fires signed in September 1994 and May 1995. Two renegade military commanders mutinied in February 1996, but called off the coup when Rakhmonov dismissed several senior officials. Sporadic fighting between government troops and several rebel groups continued throughout 1997, and while the government appeared to be taking control, flareups occurred in spring 1998.

▶ TANZANIA
United Republic of Tanzania

● **GEOGRAPHY Location:** Tanganyika, on eastern coast of Africa, and islands of Zanzibar and Pemba, about 25 mi. (40 km) off Tanganyika coast in Indian Ocean. **Boundaries**: Burundi, Rwanda to NW, Uganda, Kenya to N, Indian Ocean to E, Mozambique, Malawi to S, Zambia to SW, Zaire to W. **Total area**: 364,900 sq. mi. (945,090 sq km). **Coastline:** 885 mi. (1,424 km). **Comparative area**: slightly larger than twice size of California. **Land use:** 3% arable land; 1% permanent crops; 40% meadows and pastures; 38% forest and woodland; 18% other; includes negl. % irrigated. **Major cities**: (1985 est.) Dar es Salaam (capital) 1,096,000; Mwanza 252,000; Tabora 214,000; Mbeya 194,000; Tanga 172,000.

● **PEOPLE Population:** 31,270,820 (1999 est.). **Nationality: noun**—Tanzanian(s); **adjective**—Tanzanian. **Ethnic groups:** mainland—99% native Africans of over 130 groups; 1% Asian, European, and Arab; Zanzibar—Arab, native African, mixed Arab and native African. **Languages:** Kiswahili and Swahili and English (all official); English primary language of commerce, administration, and higher education; Swahili widely understood and generally used for communication between ethnic groups; first language of most people is one of local languages; primary education generally in Swahili. **Religions:** mainland—45% Christian, 35% Muslim, 20% indigenous beliefs; Zanzibar—almost all Muslim.

● **GOVERNMENT Type:** republic. **Independence:** Tanganyika became independent Dec. 9, 1961 (from UN trusteeship under British administration); Zanzibar became independent Dec. 19, 1963 (from UK); Tanganyika united with Zanzibar Apr. 26, 1964. **Constitution:** Apr. 25, 1977, revised Oct. 1984 (Zanzibar has own constitution but remains subject to provisions of union constitution). **National holiday:** Union Day, Apr. 26. **Heads of Government:** Benjamin William Mkapa, president (since Nov. 1995); **Structure:** executive—president is head of government and chief of state; unicameral legislature; judiciary.

● **ECONOMY Monetary unit:** Tanzanian shilling. **Budget:** (FY98/99) **income:** $700 mil.; **expend.:** $1 bil. **GDP:** $22.1 bil., $730 per capita (1998 est.). **Chief crops:** cotton, coffee, sisal, vegetables, fruits, grain on mainland; cloves and coconuts on Zanzibar; cattle, sheep, goats. **Natural resources:** hydropower potential, tin, phosphates, iron ore and coal, gemstones. **Major industries:** agricultural processing (sugar, beer, cigarettes, sisal twine), diamond mine, oil refinery. **Labor force:** 13.5 mil. (1995 est.); 90% agriculture, 10% industry and commerce. **Exports:** $952 mil. (f.o.b., 1998); coffee, manufactured goods, cotton, sisal, cashew nuts, tobacco, cloves. **Imports:** $1.46 bil. (f.o.b., 1998); consumer goods, machinery and transport equipment, crude oil. **Major trading partners:** *exports:* 9.8% India, 8.9% Germany, 7.8% Japan, 6.5% Malaysia; *imports:* 12.9% South Africa, 9.6% Kenya, 8.7% UK, Saudi Arabia 6.6%.

Formerly known as Tanganyika, Tanzania's indigenous population includes people of diverse ethnic background, including San, Bantu, and Nilotic peoples. It has been the site of a number of relatively advanced and well-organized societies.

Zanzibar and the neighboring island of Pemba have been a crossroads of trade in East Africa since ancient times. Trade via Zanzibar between the Tanganyika coast and the Middle East, primarily ivory, gold, and iron, dates to the late Roman Empire. The coast was dominated by various Arab and Persian powers, usually based in Zanzibar, from about the eighth century. Zanzibar and Tanganyika were visited by Vasco da Gama in 1498, and Portugal claimed Zanzibar in 1503 and the entire Tanganyika coast in 1506. The Portuguese established coastal trading stations but did not colonize the interior.

The Portuguese were driven from Zanzibar in 1652 by the sultanate of Oman, which soon expelled them from the mainland as well. Under Omani rule, trade in gold, ivory, and gems was supplemented by a sizable slave trade, and the clove plantations of Zanzibar became commercially important. Under Sultan Seyyid Said, the capital of the sultanate of Oman was transferred to Zanzibar in 1824, and Zanzibar became independent of Oman upon his death in 1856.

Both Germany and Great Britain became active in the region in the 19th century, motivated by trade and, in the British case, by the antislavery movement. Tanganyika was organized as the colony of German East Africa in 1884, while Zanzibar became a British protectorate in 1890. Tanganyika became a secondary battlefield of World War I, with frequent clashes between German and British troops.

Britain assumed control of Tanganyika in 1920 under a League of Nations Mandate and maintained control under a UN trusteeship after 1946. The temperate southern highlands were extensively colonized by British immigrants, and railroads and mines were developed by the British administration.

Elections for a local legislature were held in Zanzibar in July 1957. The island's politics were dominated by a split between Arab and African residents. Zanzibar became independent on Dec. 19, 1963. In January 1964 an African revolt overthrew the sultan of Zanzibar and resulted in the deaths of thousands of Arab residents and the emigration of many more. Political control shifted to the African party and Abeid Karume became president.

Tanganyika became independent in 1961. Julius K. Nyerere was Tanganyika's dominant political figure. Tanzania was formed from the union of Tanganyika and Zanzibar on April 26, 1964, with Zanzibar retaining local autonomy.

The United Republic of Tanzania, under Nyerere's leadership, advocated an "African socialist" form of development and formed close ties with China. Some British settlers left the country, but relations with Great Britain remained important. The Tan-Zan Railroad between Dar es Salaam and Lusaka, Zambia, was built with Chinese aid between 1970 and 1975. The ruling parties of Tanganyika and Zanzibar were united in 1977 under Nyerere's leadership.

Political tensions eased and Tanzania adopted a more open political structure in the 1980s. Pres. Ali Hassan Mwinyi encouraged free-market economic reforms, including encouragement of foreign investment and strengthened ties with Kenya and Uganda (Tanzania invaded the latter in 1979 in an effort to depose Idi Amin). Tanzania's economy has great potential because of the country's extensive natural resources and one of Africa's best educational systems; literacy in both English and Swahili is relatively high.

Although only an estimated 20 percent of the population was found to be in favor of political pluralism, in 1992 the Revolutionary party of Tanzania voted in favor of a secular multiparty system, that is one based on neither ethnic nor regional lines. It won the country's first-ever multiparty elections in 1995, capturing 186 of 232 seats in Parliament. Benjamin Mkapa succeeded Mwinyi, who was barred by law from seeking a third term as president.

In 1994-95, a flood of more than 700,000 refugees from the civil wars in Burundi and Rwanda put an enormous strain on Tanzania's resources; the government closed its border with Burundi in 1995. In Aug. 1998, terrorists bombed the U.S. embassy in Dar es Salaam.

▶ THAILAND
Kingdom of Thailand

● **GEOGRAPHY Location:** extends southward, along isthmus of Kra, to Malay peninsula, in Southeast Asia. **Boundaries:** Myanmar to W and N, Laos to NE, Cambodia and Gulf of Thailand to E, Malaysia to S, Andaman Sea to SW. **Total area:** 198,456 sq. mi. (514,000 sq km). **Coastline:** 2,001 mi. (3,219 km). **Comparative area:** slightly more than twice the size of Wyoming. **Land use:** 34% arable land; 6% permanent crops; 2% meadows and pastures; 26% forest and woodland; 32% other; includes 7% irrigated. **Major cities:** (1990 census), Bangkok metropolis (capital) 5,876,000; Songkhla 172,604; Chon Buri 115,350; Nakhon Si Thammarat 102,123; Chiang Mai 101,594.

● **PEOPLE Population:** 60,609,046 (1999 est.). **Nationality:** noun—Thai (sing., pl.); adjective—Thai. **Ethnic groups:** 75% Thai, 14% Chinese, 11% other. **Languages:** Thai; English is secondary language of elite; ethnic and regional dialects. **Religions:** 95% Buddhist, 3.8% Muslim, 0.5% Christianity, 0.1% Hinduism.

● **GOVERNMENT Type:** constitutional monarchy. **Constitution:** new constitution signed by King Phumiphon Oct. 11, 1997. **National holiday:** Birthday of His Majesty the King, Dec. 5. **Heads of Government:** Bhumibol Adulyadej, king (since June 1946); Chuan Leekpai, prime minister (since Nov.1997). **Structure:** executive—king is head of state with nominal powers, prime minister is head of government; bicameral legislature (National Assembly—Senate appointed by king, elected House of Representatives); judiciary relatively independent except in important political subversion cases.

● **ECONOMY Monetary unit:** baht. **Budget:** (FY96/97 est.) *income:* $24 bil. *expend.:* $25 bil. **GDP:** $369 bil., $6,100 per capita (1998 est.). **Chief crops:** rice, cassava, sugar, corn, rubber, manioc, coconuts, soybean. **Natural resources:** tin, rubber, natural gas, tungsten, tantalum. **Major industries:** tourism, textiles and garments, agricultural processing, beverages; world's second-largest tungsten producer and third-largest tin producer. **Labor force:** 32.6 mil. (1997 est.); 45% agriculture,

15% industry, 31% services including government; 3.5% unemployment (1996). **Exports:** $51.6 bil. (f.o.b., 1997); 82% manufactures, 14% agricultural and fisheries. **Imports:** $73.5 bil. (c.i.f., 1996); 50% capital goods, 22% intermediate goods, 10.2% consumer goods, 8.7% fuels. **Major trading partners:** (1997) *exports:* 19.6% U.S., 14.9% Japan, 11% Singapore; *imports:* 6% Japan, 13.9% U.S., 5% Singapore.

Ethnic Thai migrating south from China after about A.D. 1000 created a number of petty states in the region, most notably the kingdom of Sukhothai. These came under the influence of Indian civilization from the adjacent states of Burma and the Khmer empire, and Buddhism became established as the dominant religion of the Thai. A unified kingdom of Siam was established c. 1350, with its capital at Ayutthaya. Portuguese and other European traders and missionaries were active in Siam after 1511.

In 1767 Ayutthaya was destroyed in a war with Burma. In 1782 the Chakkri dynasty was established at Bangkok and restored the power of the Thai monarchy. By skillfully playing off the European powers against one another, Kings Mongkut (r. 1851-68) and Chulalongkorn (r. 1868-1910) enabled Siam to be the only Southeast Asian nation to escape European colonization or political domination. In a series of treaties with Great Britain and France, however, King Chulalongkorn was forced to renounce Siam's claims to portions of Malaya, Laos, and Cambodia.

Absolute monarchy ended in 1932, when a military coup forced the granting of a constitution. Japanese troops occupied Siam in December 1941. Siam concluded a nominal alliance with Japan in 1942 and declared war on Great Britain and the United States, while at the same time the monarchy secretly supported a strong anti-Japanese resistance movement. A period of postwar political turmoil ended with the accession in 1950 of King Phumiphon, who instituted a reformist and pro-Western policy. Thai politics since World War II have been democratic but dominated by an oligarchy of military officers and civilians with strong military ties.

During the Vietnam War, Thailand was an important staging area for American forces. Since then, U.S. and other foreign investment contributed to significant industrialization and economic growth, making Thailand one of Asia's fastest-growing economies. Its prosperity attracted a large number of refugees from Laos, Vietnam, and Cambodia.

On Dec. 8, 1990, Prime Minister Chatichai Choonhavan resigned amid charges of corruption. Reappointed by the king the next day, Chatichai was overthrown on Feb. 23 by military forces, who invited former diplomat Anand Panyarachun to serve as interim prime minister.

After parliamentary elections in March 1992, Gen. Suchinda Kraprayoon, who held no parliamentary seat, was named prime minister in a government dominated by the military. Mass demonstrations against the Suchinda government, led by former Bangkok governor Chamlong Srimuang, culminated on May 17-18, when troops fired on demonstrators, causing hundreds of fatalities. The king intervened and Suchinda resigned.Chamlong agreed to call off the demonstrations and Anand Panyarachun was invited to head another transitional government, and Parliament agreed in principle to a new constitution with a provision that the prime minister must be an elected member of Parliament.

Parliamentary elections in September 1992 gained a majority for a five-party coalition headed by Chuan Leekpai that managed to govern for almost three years, liberalizing financial arrangements, spending heavily on infrastructure, and bringing Thailand to an 8 percent growth rate in 1994. In elections held in July 1995, the Thai Nation party captured the largest number of seats; its leader, Banharn Silpa-Archa, became prime minister of a coalition government but the party lost the 1996 elections and a coalition government led by General Chavalit took over. Only six months later the Thai economy began a steep decline and the currency was devalued in June 1997. The U.S. and the IMF agreed to provide loans of $4 bil. to stabilize the economy with more promised if the government took appropriate action. Chuan Leekpai returned as prime minister in Nov. 1997 but economic recovery was only slowly under way by mid-1998.

▶ TOGO
Togolese Republic

● GEOGRAPHY   **Location:** western coast of Africa. **Boundaries:** Burkina Faso to N, Benin to E, Gulf of Guinea to S, Ghana to W. **Total area:** 21,927 sq. mi. (56,790 sq km). **Coastline:** 35 mi. (56 km). **Comparative area:** slightly smaller than West Virginia. **Land use:** 38% arable land; 7% permanent crops; 4% meadows and pastures; 17% forest and woodland; 34% other. **Major cities:** (1990 est.) Lomé (capital) 450,000; Sokodé 55,000; Kpalimé 31,000; Atakpamé 30,000; Tsevie 26,000.

● PEOPLE   **Population:** 5,081,413 (1999 est.). **Nationality:** noun—Togolese (sing., pl.); adjective—Togolese. **Ethnic groups:** 37 groups; largest are Ewe, Mina, and Kabre; under 1% European and Syrian-Lebanese. **Languages:** French (both official and language of commerce); Ewe and Mina in south, Dagomba and Kabyè in north. **Religions:** about 70% indigenous beliefs, 20% Christian, 10% Muslim.

● GOVERNMENT   **Type:** republic under transition to multiparty democratic rule; **Independence:** Apr. 27, 1960 (from UN trusteeship under French administration). **Constitution:** Sept. 27, 1992. **National holiday:** Independence Day, Apr. 27. **Heads of Government:** Gen. Gnassingbé Eyadema, president (since 1992); Eugène Koffi Adoboli, prime minister (since June 1999). **Structure:** executive—president appoints prime minister; unicameral legislature—National Assembly; judiciary.

● ECONOMY   **Monetary unit:** Communauté Financière Africaine (CFA) franc. **Budget:** (1997 est.) *income:* $232 mil.; *expend.:* $252 mil. **GDP:** $8.2 bil., $1,670 per capita (1998 est.). **Chief crops:** coffee, cocoa, cotton, yams, cassava, corn, beans, rice; meat, fish. **Natural resources:** phosphates, limestone, marble. **Major industries:** phosphate mining, agricultural processing, cement, handicrafts, textiles, beverages. **Labor force:** 1.538 mil. (1993 est.); 65% agriculture, 30% services, 5% industry. **Exports:** $345 mil. (f.o.b., 1997 est.); cotton, phosphates, coffee, cocoa. **Imports:** $400 mil. (f.o.b., 1997 est.); machinery and equipment, consumer goods, petroleum products. **Major trading partners:** (1996) *exports:* 7.6% Canada, 7.1% Taiwan, 6.8% Nigeria; *imports:* 19.1% Ghana, 10.8% France, 8.2% China.

Ewe-speaking peoples began to migrate into what is now Togo, located on Africa's west coast, early in the 14th century. Portuguese explorers arrived in the late 15th century, turning the coast into a point of departure for slaves captured from nearby villages, and between the 1600s and 1800s, the region became known as the "Slave Coast." Germans started to explore and trade in the region in the mid-19th century and declared a protectorate over the area in 1884. After World War I, however, Britain and France divided the nation between them, Britain receiving the western third, France the eastern two-thirds. The League of Nations confirmed this arrangement, giving mandates to British Togoland (later a part of Ghana) and French Togoland.

In 1956 France made French Togo an autonomous republic but retained control of its foreign affairs, defense, and currency; Nicholas Grunitzky was prime minister. The United Nations rejected this plan and in elections in 1958 advocates of complete independence won control of the legislature. On Apr. 27, 1960, French Togo cut its ties with France and became the fully independent Republic of Togo. Sylvanus Olympio became the new nation's first prime minister. Grunitzsky went into exile but returned when Olympio was assassinated in January 1963. He led the new government and oversaw the writing of a new constitution allowing more political freedoms.

In 1967 army officers led by Lt. Col. Gnassingbé Eyadema overthrew Grunitzsky, suspended the constitution, and named Eyadema president.

In 1990, Eyadema was forced out by democratic reformers, and Kokou J. Koffigoh was elected prime minister by a national conference in 1991. Eyadema resumed the presidency in 1992, but his refusal to embrace multiparty democracy and Koffigoh's weak leadership led to violence and public calls for the ouster of both men. A new constitution was ratified in September 1992, and in elections held in March 1994, Edem Kodjo took over as prime minister, he was succeeded by Kwassi Klutse in 1996, and Eugène Koffi Adoboli in 1999.

▶ TONGA
Kingdom of Tonga

● GEOGRAPHY **Location:** 172 islands in South Pacific Ocean, 36 permanently inhabited. Nuku'alofa 21°09'S, 175°14'W. **Boundaries**: surrounded by South Pacific Ocean; Fiji is about 400 mi. (650 km) to NW and Western Samoa lies N. **Total area:** 289 sq. mi. (748 sq km). **Coastline:** 260 mi. (419 km). **Comparative area:** four times the size of Washington, D.C. **Land use:** 24% arable land; 43% permanent crops; 6% meadows and pastures; 11% forest and woodland; 16% other. **Major cities:** (1986 census) Nuku'alofa (capital) 28,899; Tongatapu 63,614; Vava'u 15,170; Ha'apai 8,979; Eua 4,393.

● PEOPLE **Population:** 109,082 (1999 est.). **Nationality:** noun—Tongan(s); adjective—Tongan. **Ethnic groups:** Polynesian; about 300 Europeans. **Languages:** Tongan, English. **Religions:** Christian (Free Wesleyan Church claims over 30,000 adherents).

● GOVERNMENT **Type:** hereditary constitutional monarchy. **Independence:** June 4, 1970 (from UK). **Constitution:** Nov. 4, 1875; revised Jan. 1, 1967. **National holiday:** Emancipation Day, June 4. **Heads of Government:** Taufa'ahau Tupou IV, king (since Dec. 1965); Baron Vaea, premier (since Aug. 1991). **Structure:** executive—king, prime minister, cabinet; unicameral legislature—30-seat Legislative Assembly, 9 elected by popular vote, 12 are for cabinet ministers, 9 reserved for nobles; judiciary—appointed by king.

● ECONOMY **Monetary unit:** pa'anga. **Budget:** (FY96/97) *income:* $49 mil.; *expend.:* $120 mil.

GDP: $232 mil., $2,100 per capita (FY97/98 est.). **Chief crops:** coconut, copra, bananas, vanilla beans, cocoa, coffee, ginger, black pepper, fish. **Natural resources:** fish, fertile soil. **Major industries:** tourism, fishing. **Labor force:** 36,665 (1994 est.); 65% engaged in agriculture. **Exports:** $11.9 mil. (f.o.b., FY97/98); squash, fish, vanilla, root crops, coconut oil. **Imports:** $78.9 mil. (f.o.b., FY97/98); food products, live animals, machinery and transport equipment, manufactures, fuels, chemicals. **Major trading partners:** (1996) *exports:* 43% Japan, 19% U.S., 14% Canada; *imports:* 34% New Zealand, 16% Australia, 10% U.S.

The Polynesian islands that now compose Tonga were settled some 3,000 years ago. A highly stratified society evolved; the kings of Tonga dominated much of Polynesia by the 13th century. The islands were visited in 1643 by Abel Tasman, and in 1773 by Capt. James Cook, who named them the Friendly Islands. English missionaries arrived in 1797, and the islands came under British political influence. A code of laws was promulgated in 1862, and a constitutional monarchy established in 1875. A series of treaties with Western powers recognized Tonga's independence, but the kingdom became a British protectorate in 1900.

The islands were outside the Japanese perimeter in the Pacific theater of World War II. On June 4, 1970, the British dissolved their protectorate and the Kingdom of Tonga became independent as a member of the British Commonwealth. The present king, Taufa'ahau Tupou IV, came to the throne in 1965.

The Tongan economy is based on subsistence farming and fishing, with some handicraft industries and light manufacturing. The tourist industry is developing rapidly. Tonga was expected to join the U.N. in late 1999.

▶ TRINIDAD AND TOBAGO
Republic of Trinidad and Tobago

● GEOGRAPHY **Location:** two islands (Port of Spain, Trinidad Is., 10°38'N, 61°31'W; Tobago Is., 11°11'N, 60°45'W) in southeastern Caribbean Sea, off northeastern South America. **Boundaries**: Caribbean Sea to N and W, Atlantic Ocean to E and S. **Total area:** 1,981 sq. mi. (5,130 sq km). **Coastline:** 225 mi. (362 km). **Comparative area:** slightly smaller than Delaware. **Land use:** 15% arable land; 9% permanent crops; 2% meadows and pastures; 46% forest and woodland; 28% other; includes 4% irrigated. **Major cities:** (1991) Port of Spain (capital) 51,076; San Fernando 30,115; Arima (borough) 29,483.

● PEOPLE **Population:** 1,102,096 (1999 est.). **Nationality:** noun—Trinidadian(s), Tobagonian(s); adjective—Trinidadian, Tobagonian. **Ethnic groups:** 40% black, 40.3% East Indian, 14% mixed, 1% white, 1% Chinese. **Languages:** English (official), Hindi, French, Spanish. **Religions:** 32.2% Roman Catholic, 24.3% Hindu, 14.4% Anglican, 14% other Protestant, 6% Muslim, 9.1% unknown.

● GOVERNMENT **Type:** parliamentary democracy. **Independence:** Aug. 31, 1962 (from UK). **Constitution:** Aug. 1, 1976. **National holiday:** Independence Day, Aug. 31. **Heads of Government:** Arthur Napoleon Robinson, president (since Mar. 1997); Basdeo Panday, prime minister (since Nov. 1995). **Structure:** executive—is cabinet led by prime minister; bicameral legislature (36-member elected House of Representatives and 31-member appointed Senate); judiciary headed by chief justice and includes court of appeal, high court, and lower courts.

● ECONOMY **Monetary unit:** Trinidad and Tobago dollar. **Budget:** (1997 est.) *income:* $1.59 bil.; *expend.:* $1.54 bil. **GDP:** $8.85 bil., $8,000 per capita (1998 est.). **Chief crops:** sugar, cocoa, coffee, rice, citrus, bananas; poultry. **Natural resources:** crude oil, natural gas, asphalt. **Major industries:** petroleum, chemicals, tourism. **Labor force:** 541,000 (1997 est.); 64.1% services, 14% manufacturing, mining, and quarrying, 12.4% construction and utilities, 9.5% agriculture. **Exports:** $2.4 bil. (f.o.b., 1997); petroleum and petroleum products, chemicals, steel products, fertilizer, sugar, cocoa, coffee, citrus, flowers. **Imports:** $3.3 bil. (c.i.f., 1997); machinery, transport equipment, manufactured goods, food, live animals. **Major trading partners:** *exports:* 39.7% U.S., 24.5% CARICOM countries, 10.3% Latin America; *imports:* 52.2% U.S., 16.5% Latin American, 13.8% EU.

Trinidad was a possession of Spain from 1498 to 1797, when it was surrendered to the British. England took control of Tobago in 1802. Together the two islands achieved independence from the UK in 1962. Prime Minister Arthur Robinson's National Alliance for Reconstruction currently governs the country. Civil and political rights are well respected, and political party competition tends to divide along ethnic (black, East Indian) lines. Agrarian reform designed to create tenable landholdings is a central political issue.

In 1990, militant Muslims seized Prime Minister A.N.R. Robinson and dozens of others in Parliament, paralyzing the government for five days. Peace was restored when the government promised reforms. People's National Movement candidate Carson Charles was elected prime minister in 1991, and in the interest of preserving the peace, he granted the Muslim militants amnesty in 1992. Robinson won the presidential election in 1997 in a landslide.

▶ TUNISIA
Republic of Tunisia

• **GEOGRAPHY Location:** northern coast of Africa. **Boundaries:** Mediterranean to N and E, Libya to SE, Algeria to W. **Total area:** 63,170 sq. mi. (163,610 sq km); includes land and inland waters. **Coastline:** 714 mi. (1,148 km). **Comparative area:** slightly larger than Georgia. **Land use:** 19% arable land; 13% permanent crops; 20% meadows and pastures; 4% forest and woodland; 44% other; includes 1% irrigated. **Major cities:** (1994 census) Tunis (capital) 674,100; Sfax (Safaqis) 230,900; Ariana 152,700; Ehadhamen 149,200; Sousse 125,000.

• **PEOPLE Population:** 9,513,603 (1999 est.). **Nationality:** noun—Tunisian(s); adjective—Tunisian. **Ethnic groups:** 98% Arab, 1% European, 1% Jewish and other . **Languages:** Arabic (official), Arabic and French (commerce). **Religions:** 98% Muslim, 1% Christian, 1% Jewish and other.

• **GOVERNMENT Type:** republic. **Independence:** Mar. 20, 1956 (from France). **Constitution:** June 1, 1959, amended July 12, 1988. **National holiday:** National Day, Mar. 20. **Heads of Government:** Zine el-Abidine Ben Ali, president (since Nov. 1987); Dr. Hamed Karoui, prime minister (since Sept. 1989). **Structure:** executive dominant; unicameral legislative (National Assembly) largely advisory; judiciary patterned on French and Koranic systems.

• **ECONOMY Monetary unit:** Tunisian dinar. **Budget:** (1998 est.) *income:* $5.8 bil.; *expend.:* $6.5 bil. **GDP:** $49 bil., $5,200 per capita (1998 est.). **Chief crops:** olives, dates, oranges, almonds,

grain, sugar beets, grapes; poultry, beef, dairy products. **Natural resources:** crude oil, phosphates, iron ore, lead, zinc. **Major industries:** petroleum, mining (particularly phosphates and iron ore), tourism, textiles. **Labor force:** 3.3 mil.; 55% services, 23% industry, 22% agriculture; 15.6% unemployment (1998 est.); shortage of skilled labor. **Exports:** $5.4 bil. (f.o.b., 1997 est.); hydrocarbons, textiles, agricultural products, phosphates and chemicals. **Imports:** $7.9 bil. (c.i.f., 1997 est.); 57% industrial goods, 13% hydrocarbons, 12% food. **Major trading partners:** *exports:* 80% EU, 6% North African countries, 4% Asia; *imports:* 80% EU, 5.5% North African countries, 5.5% Asia.

The Phoenicians, an ancient seafaring people from the eastern Mediterranean, founded settlements in Tunisia dating back to 1000 B.C. The most important of these was Carthage, which dominated trade in the central Mediterranean until it was conquered and destroyed by Rome in 146 B.C. Tunisia remained part of the Roman empire until it was conquered by the Vandals in the mid-fifth century A.D. The Byzantine Empire reconquered Tunisia in the sixth century.

Tunisia became part of the Arab world with the expansion of Islam in the seventh century and soon emerged as a principal center of Islamic culture in North Africa. Tunisia was incorporated into the Ottoman Empire in 1574 and was ruled from Constantinople by Turkish governors, or beys.

With the waning of Ottoman power in the 19th century, Tunisia became a French protectorate in 1881. Nationalist movements began in the early 20th century. During World War II Tunisia was under Vichy French rule and was the scene of fighting between the Axis and Allies in 1942-43. Nationalist unrest resumed when France reestablished its rule in the postwar period. Widespread popular unrest in the early 1950s led to a French grant of self-rule in 1954. Full independence was proclaimed on Mar. 20, 1956; large numbers of French settlers returned to France. The French-sponsored monarchy was abolished in 1957, and the Neo-Destour (New Constitution) party under the leadership of Habib Bourguiba took power. Bourguiba was elected president in 1959 without opposition and was named president for life. Under his rule, political parties ranging from Communist to monarchist flourished, leading to both democratic politics and political confusion.

Relations with France were strained in 1964 when Tunisia nationalized foreign assets but have since improved. The basic thrust of Tunisian government was socialist, with state ownership of principal industries and heavy subsidies of basic commodities. In foreign affairs Tunisia has been closely tied to France and has been a moderate voice within the Arab League.

Popular unrest and labor strife characterized Tunisia's internal situation in the 1980s, as political maneuvering began in anticipation of the end of the Bourguiba era, which came in 1987 when the aged leader was overthrown by Ben Ali. In 1989 the World Bank approved a loan of $130 million to Tunisia, and new elections were planned as part of a political and economic restructuring. Ben Ali has been elected president twice winning 99 percent of the vote, while his party won virtually all the seats in the National Assembly. In 1994 and 1995, however, the political stability was threatened by radical Muslim groups both from within and from Algeria. Rumors of brutal repression were rife.

Tunisia's economy, though plagued by labor difficulties, has developed rapidly, led by textiles, food processing and other light industry, tourism, phosphate mining, and other mineral processing. The large agricultural sector includes grain, olives, dates, and winter fruits and vegetables for export to Europe. In 1998 the government reached an accord with the EU to lower trade barriers.

▶TURKEY
Republic of Turkey

• **GEOGRAPHY Location:** partly in southeastern Europe and partly in western Asia. **Boundaries:** Black Sea to N; Georgia and Armenia to NE; Iran to E; Iraq, Syria, Mediterranean Sea to S; Aegean Sea, Greece to W; and Bulgaria to NW. **Total area:** 301,382 sq. mi. (780,580 sq km). **Coastline:** 4,471 mi. (7,200 km). **Comparative area:** slightly larger than Texas. **Land use:** 32% arable land; 4% permanent crops; 16% meadows and pastures; 26% forest and woodland; 22% other; includes 3% irrigated. **Major cities:** (1993 est.) Ankara (capital) 2,719,981; Istanbul 7,331,927; Izmir 1,920,807; Adana 1,010,363; Bursa 949,810.

• **PEOPLE Population:** 65,599,206 (1999 est.). **Nationality:** noun—Turk(s); adjective—Turkish. **Ethnic groups:** 80% Turkish, 20% Kurdish. **Languages:** Turkish (official), Kurdish, Arabic. **Religions:** 99.8% Muslim (mostly Sunni), 0.2% other (mostly Christian and Jewish).

• **GOVERNMENT Type:** republican parliamentary democracy. **Independence:** Oct. 29, 1923 (from Ottoman Empire). **Constitution:** Nov. 7, 1982. **National holiday:** Anniversary of the Declaration of the Republic, Oct. 29. **Heads of Government:** Suleyman Demirel, president (since Apr. 1993); Bulent Ecevit, prime minister (since Jan. 1999). **Structure:** executive—president empowered to call new elections, promulgate laws (elected for seven-year term); unicameral legislature; independent judiciary.

• **ECONOMY Monetary unit:** Turkish lira. **Budget:** (1998) *income:* $44.4 bil.; *expend.:* $58.5 bil. **GDP:** $425.4 bil., $6,600 per capita (1998 est.). **Chief crops:** cotton, tobacco, grain, olives, sugar beets, pulses, citrus; livestock. **Natural resources:** antimony, coal, chromium, mercury, copper. **Major industries:** textiles, food processing, mining (coal, chromite, copper, boron minerals). **Labor force:** 22.7 mil.; 42.5% agriculture, 34.5% services, 23% industry; about 1.5 million Turks work abroad; 10% unemployment (1998). **Exports:** $31 bil. (f.o.b., 1998 est.); 30% textiles and apparel, 15% foodstuffs, 13% iron and steel products. **Imports:** $47 bil. (f.o.b., 1998 est.); 50% machinery, fuels, minerals, foodstuffs. **Major trading partners:** *exports:* 20% Germany, 9% U.S., 5% Russia; *imports:* 16% Germany, 9% U.S., 9% Italy.

The Hittites, an Indo-European people, created an empire in Anatolia before 2000 B.C. and controlled most of what is modern-day Turkey for nearly 1,000 years. The rise of Troy and other Hellenic city-states on the coast of Asia Minor and the expansion of the Assyrian empire led to the collapse of Hittite power by around 900 B.C. Except for some Hellenic enclaves on the Aegean Coast (Ionia), all of Turkey was incorporated into the Persian empire of Cyrus and Darius in the sixth century B.C. Alexander the Great conquered Turkey, but it returned to Persian rule following the collapse of his empire, c. 300 B.C.

All of Turkey, comprising Thracia, Galatia, Cappadocia, Cilicia, and other provinces, was incorporated into the Roman Empire by the end of the first century A.D. Constantine the Great founded the city of Constantinople on the site of ancient Byzantium in 330 as the empire's eastern capital. Following the decline of the western Roman Empire in the seventh century, Constantinople became the capital of the independent Eastern Roman (Byzantine) Empire. The Byzantine Empire fought off repeated attacks by Arab Islamic forces in the seventh and eighth centuries but lost control of central Anatolia to the Seljuk Turkish rulers of Persia after 1038.

The 13th-century Mongol invasions left Turkey largely untouched but weakened both Byzantine and Seljuk power. At the end of the 13th century, the Ottomans, a small Turkish tribe, expanded from their stronghold in western Anatolia and within a century captured most of Turkey, Bulgaria, and Serbia. Constantinople fell to the Ottomans in 1453. By the middle of the 16th century, the Ottoman Empire extended from southeastern Europe into the Crimea and Iran and included most of the Middle East, Egypt, and Arabia.

At its height the Ottoman Empire was a great world power and a substantial participant in European international relations. But in the 18th century, the empire lost much of its autonomy through unequal treaties with European powers, and throughout the 19th century, parts of the empire were detached and either granted independence or placed under European protection. The Ottoman Empire became the "Sick Man of Europe." A liberal constitution was adopted in 1876 but largely ignored until the Young Turk Rebellion of 1908 forced the sultan to accept its provisions.

Siding with the Central Powers in World War I, the Ottoman Empire lost most of its non-Turkish possessions to the Allies. The Treaty of Sèvres (1920) reduced the Ottoman state to a small part of northern Anatolia. Before the treaty was ratified, however, Kemal Ataturk seized power and regained much territory in a series of campaigns with Soviet assistance. The Treaty of Lausanne (1923) established the present boundaries of Turkey, and Turkey was proclaimed a republic in October 1923. The Caliphate was renounced in 1924, ending the Ottoman claim of spiritual leadership in the Islamic world.

The Turkish Republic became officially a secular and multiethnic state. Large numbers of Armenians had been killed or driven from the country in widespread campaigns of persecution in the late 19th and early 20th centuries; after 1923 most Greek and Bulgarian residents were forcibly repatriated. The large minority of Kurds in southeastern Turkey were pressured to abandon their ethnic identity. Today more than 85 percent of the population is Turkish, ultimately of Central Asian origin. Islam is widely practiced, but the veil and other Islamic dress are prohibited, as are religious political parties. In 1928 the Latin alphabet was adopted in place of Arabic script for writing Turkish. In 1930 Constantinople was officially renamed Istanbul.

Turkey joined the League of Nations in 1932. A series of treaties in the 1930s made small adjustments to Turkey's borders and confirmed Turkey's status as a European nation. Under Ismet Inonu, who became president upon Ataturk's death in 1938, Turkey remained neutral throughout most of World War II but declared war against Germany in Jan. 1945 and became a founding member of the United Nations at the end of the war.

Following World War II, Turkish relations with the Soviet Union cooled; Turkey became a major recipient of American aid under the Truman Doctrine. Turkish troops joined UN forces in the Korean War. Continuing the Europe-oriented policy, Turkey joined both NATO and the OECD and sought membership in the European Union.

In 1974, long-standing discord with Greece erupted over the status of Cyprus, an independent nation with strong ties to Greece. On July 20, 1974, Turkish troops invaded Cyprus, occupying the northeastern 40 percent of the island. The United States cut off military aid to Turkey in 1975. Turkey forced resettlement of Greek and Turkish Cypriot residents; the Turkish sector seceded from Cyprus and became a Turkish federated state on July 8, 1975. American aid was restored in 1978.

Politically, postwar Turkey has alternated between civil and military governments. In the wake of mounting violence, martial law was imposed in 1978, and a military takeover of the government occurred on Sept. 12, 1980. Civil government was restored in 1983, and martial law lifted in 1984.

Turkey tried to remain aloof from the political turmoil of the Middle East, but it was a crucial member of the anti-Iraq coalition in the Persian Gulf War. It supported the UN trade embargo and allowed the Allies to use Turkish bases. Turkey's Kurdish problem was aggravated after the war as the country tried to offer humanitarian assistance to Kurdish refugees from Iraq without encouraging Kurdish nationalists at home. A continuing insurgency in the southeast led to sporadic but serious violence in 1992-93. In addition, Muslim fundamentalists became more active and several violent episodes resulted in deaths and destruction.

Pres. Turgut Özal died in Apr. 1993. He was succeeded as president by Prime Minister Suleyman Demirel. On June 14 the ruling True Path party elected as the new prime minister, Mrs. Tansu Ciller, Turkey's first-ever woman prime minister, and the first since 1923 to be born on the European side of the Bosporous. While the economy was her first concern (inflation hit 70 percent in 1994), military operations against the Kurdish rebels intensified greatly, culminating in March 1995 with the launching of an attack into Iraq by 50,000 Turkish troops who aimed to end guerrilla raids by the Kurds.

The Ciller government collapsed in a corruption scandal, and elections held in December 1995 gave Refah (Welfare), a pro-Islamic political party, its first national victory, winning 158 seats in the 550-seat Parliament. The other parties, committed to the long tradition of secularism, refused to form a government with the Welfare party. After several months of successive short-lived coalition governments, in June 1996 the Welfare party leader, Necmettim Erbakan, became prime minister as the head of Turkey's first openly pro-Islamic government. But almost exactly a year later, he was forced from office by pressure from Turkey's military establishment, a blow for secularism but against democratic government. In the wake of this de facto military coup, the new prime minister, Mesut Yilmaz, put together a seemingly fragile coalition government in July 1997. The new government closed some Islamic schools and banned traditional Moslem garb while the Supreme Court ruled that Erbakan could not be in politics for five years.

Violence in Cyprus flared up briefly in 1998 but the EUs rejection of Turkey's application was the most serious event of the year. In 1999 Turkey finally wrung an accord from Syria not to aid Kurd rebels (with 10,000 Turkish troops poised on Syria's border), but the Yilmaz government still lost a vote of confidence, not on foreign policy issues but corruption charges. President Demirel asked Bulent Ecevit to form a minority, interim government until the April elections. The results were splintered, the Democratic Left gaining the plurality of 136 seats (of 550), and the president asked Ecevit to stay on as head of a coalition government. Meanwhile, Kurdish leader Ocalan was apprehended in Nairobi (February) and, after trial, sentenced (June) to death by hanging. From his cell, Ocalan renounced Kurdish independence and called upon his band to stop fighting, and to disarm.

In Aug. 1999 an earthquake brought great devastation and the loss of thousands of lives. (See Part I, "Major News Stories of the Year.")

▶TURKMENISTAN

● **GEOGRAPHY Location:** southwestern central Asia. **Boundaries:** Kazakhstan to N, Uzbekistan to N and E, Iran to S, Afghanistan to SE, Caspian Sea to W. **Total area:** 188,456 sq. mi. (488,100 sq km). **Coastline:** Caspian Sea. **Comparative area:** slightly larger than California. **Land use:** 3% arable land; 63% permanent pasture; 8% forest and woodland; 26% other (mostly urban and mountain). **Major cities:** (1994 est.) Ashkhabad (capital) 517,200; Chardzou (Carzou) 164,000.

● **PEOPLE Population:** 4,366,383 (1999 est.). **Nationality:** noun—Turkmen; adjective—Turkmen. **Ethnic groups:** 77% Turkmen, 9.2% Uzbek, 6.7% Russian, 2% Kazakh. **Languages:** 72% Turkmen (official), member of southern Turkic language group written in Cyrillic script since 1940; 12% Russian, 9% Uzbek, ethnic languages. **Religions:** 89% Muslim, 9% Eastern Orthodox, 2% unknown.

● **GOVERNMENT Type:** republic. **Independence:** Oct. 27, 1991 (from Soviet Union). **Constitution:** May 18, 1992. **National holiday:** Independence Day, Oct. 27. **Head of Government:** Saparmurat A. Niyazov, president (since Dec. 1991). **Structure:** executive—president, Council of Ministers; bicameral legislature; judicial—Supreme Court.

● **ECONOMY Monetary unit:** Turkmen manat. **Budget:** (1996 est.) *income:* $521 mil; *expend.:* $548 mil. **GDP:** $7 bil., $1,630 per capita (1998 est.). **Chief crops:** cotton, grain; livestock. **Natural resources:** petroleum, natural gas, coal, sulfur, sodium chloride. **Major industries:** natural gas, oil, petroleum products, textiles. **Labor force:** 2.34 mil. (1996). **Exports:** $689 mil. (1997 est.); natural gas, cotton, petroleum products, textiles, electricity, carpets. **Imports:** $1.1 bil. (1997 est.); machinery and parts, grain and food, plastics and rubber, consumer durables, textiles. **Major trading partners:** *exports:* FSU, Hong Kong, Switzerland; *imports:* FSU, U.S., Turkey.

Turkmenistan, long a battleground for warring Asian empires, is bordered on the north by Uzbekistan and Kazakhstan, and on the west by the Caspian Sea. It also has a long international border with Iran and Afghanistan. About 90 percent of Turkmenistan is covered by the Kara Kum (Black Sand) desert, one of the largest in the world, and the southern areas are mountainous and prone to serious earthquakes.

A very remote and sparsely populated country, Turkmenistan has been inhabited since prehistoric times, first by Iranian-speaking people, then by Turkic tribes. In the 10th century A.D., Oghuz tribes (from Mongolia) arrived, bringing Islam with them. Although the Turkmen had emerged as a distinct ethnic group by the 15th century, they were ruled by the Persians in the south and the Uzbek khanates in the north for about 200 years. In the 19th century, Russian expansionism into Turkmen territory had begun, culminating in the Russian victory in the famous 1881 battle of Gok Tepe that killed an estimated 150,000 Turkmen.

In 1917 the Bolsheviks unsuccessfully attempted to seize power in Turkmen territory. By Apr. 30, 1918, the Soviets succeeded in creating the Turkestan Autonomous Soviet Socialist Republic (ASSR) as part of the Russian republic, but in July of the same year, the ASSR was overthrown by nationalist elements with the help of the British. Once the British withdrew, however, the territory of Turkmen fell to the Soviets, and in 1924 the National Delimitation of Central Asian Republics took place. This created several central Asian republics, including the Turkmen Soviet Socialist Republic, which came into being on Oct. 27, 1924.

During the Soviet period, there were advances in medicine and public health, but the nomadic Turkmen people suffered enormously under forced collectivization and the many bloody antireligious campaigns. The purges of Turkmen intelligentsia in the 1930s were widespread. The Soviets undertook a small-scale industrialization campaign in Turkmenistan, but aside from the extraction of natural gas and petroleum, the majority of the population continued to work in agriculture, mainly growing cotton and fruits.

Under Gorbachev, the main issue for Turkmenistan became the environment. Large-scale cotton planting had led to serious environmental and health hazards. The Kara Kum Canal, which carries water from the Amu-Dar'ya to Turkmenistan's arid regions, is one of the main factors leading to the desiccation of the Aral Sea. Turkmenistan's main cultural issue was the status of the Turkmen language, for until May 1990 the official language had been listed as Russian (although only 25% of Turkmen people claimed to speak Russian). Beyond this, due to its remoteness, Turkmenistan did not become involved in the democratic political changes that engaged the other former union republics in the Gorbachev years. Its Communist party dominated and still dominates Turkmen politics, although the Turkmen president, Saparmurat A. Niyazov, stood for popular election and was elected by direct ballot in October 1990 by 98.3 percent of the population. However, the Turkmen government has banned demonstrations, picketing, and strikes, and it censors its media.

Turkmenistan was one of the early supporters of Gorbachev's proposal to form a new Union Treaty. When that led to the August 1991 coup in Moscow, the Turkmen Supreme Soviet claimed independence on Oct. 27, 1991. Turkmenistan was one of the signatories of the Alma-Ata Declaration that created the Commonwealth of Independent States in December 1991. Since then, Turkmenistan has begun to develop political and economic relations with its neighbor Iran and is working on improving its relations with Turkey. With vast oil and gas reserves Turkmenistan faces a brighter future than it ever expected.

Niyazov was overwhelmingly endorsed in the most recent referendum, held Jan. 15, 1994 extending his mandate by five years, until the year 2002, thereby bypassing a constitutional requirement for the reelection of a president every five years. In April 1998 Niyazov visited the U.S., conferring with Pres. Clinton and concluding agreements with several U.S. energy firms to study the possibility of a sub-Caspian, cross-Caucasian gas pipeline to Turkey and thence to the west (thereby by-passing Iran entirely).

▶ **TUVALU**
● **GEOGRAPHY Location:** group of nine small atolls, about 350 mi. (560 km) from N to S, in South Pacific Ocean. Funafuti 8°30'S, 179°12'E. **Boundaries:** surrounded by South Pacific Ocean; Kiribati to N, Fiji to S, Solomon Islands to W. **Total area:** 10 sq. mi. (26 sq km). **Coastline:** 15 mi. (24 km). **Comparative area:** one-tenth size of Washington, D.C. **Land use:** 0% arable land; 0% permanent crops; 0% meadows and pastures; 0% forest and woodland; 100% other. **Major cities:** (by atoll; 1985 census) Funafuti (capital) 2,810; Vaitupu 1,231; Niutao 904; Nanumea 879; Nukufetau 694.
● **PEOPLE Population:** 10,588 (1999 est.). **Nationality:** noun—Tuvaluan(s); adjective—Tuvaluan. **Ethnic groups:** 96% Polynesian. **Languages:** Tuvaluan, English. **Religions:** 97% Church of Tuvalu (Congregationalist), 1.4% Seventh-Day Adventists, 1% Baha'i.
● **GOVERNMENT Type:** constitutional monarchy with a parliamentary democracy; began debating republic status in 1992. **Independence:** Oct. 1, 1978 (from UK). **Constitution:** Oct. 1, 1978. **National holiday:** Independence Day, Oct. 1. **Heads of Government:** Manuella Tulaga, governor-general (since June 1994); Bikenibeu Paeniu, prime minister (since Dec. 1996). **Structure:** executive—prime minister and cabinet; unicameral legislature—12-member House of Parliament; judicial—high court, chief justice presides over sessions twice a year.
● **ECONOMY Monetary unit:** Tuvaluan dollar or Australian dollar. **Budget:** (1989) *income:* $4.3 mil.; *expend.:* $4.3 mil. **GDP:** $7.8 mil., $800 per capita (1995 est.). **Chief crops:** coconuts; fish. **Natural resources:** fish. **Major industries:** fishing, tourism, copra. **Labor force:** N.A. **Exports:** $165,000 (f.o.b., 1989); copra. **Imports:** $4.4 mil. (c.i.f., 1989); food, animals, mineral fuels, machinery, manufactured goods. **Major trading partners:** Fiji, Australia, New Zealand.

A British protectorate was established in 1892, and the islands were incorporated into the British colony of the Gilbert and Ellice Islands in 1915. The nine principal islands that make up the Ellice group escaped Japanese occupation in World War II and were used as Allied bases in the campaign to recapture the Pacific.

The Gilbert and Ellice Islands colony was granted self-rule in 1971. In 1975 the Ellice Islands, inhabited mainly by Polynesians, seceded from the other (mainly Micronesian) islands of the colony and became independent as Tuvalu on Oct. 1, 1978. (See also "Kiribati.") In a 1979 U.S.-Tuvalu friendship treaty, the United States relinquished claims, based on 19th-century guano mining, to the four southernmost islands, in return for access to World War II military airfields and veto power over other nations' use of the islands for military purposes.

The economy is based on subsistence farming and fishing. Exports include copra and woven palm-leaf products, and hydroponic agriculture and offshore fisheries are being developed. Tuvalu remains heavily dependent on foreign aid, principally from Australia, New Zealand, and the United Kingdom.

▶ UGANDA
Republic of Uganda

● **Geography** **Location:** landlocked equatorial country in eastern Africa. **Boundaries:** Sudan to N, Kenya to E, Tanzania to S, Rwanda to SW, Zaire to W. **Total area:** 91,135 sq. mi. (236,040 sq km). **Coastline:** none. **Comparative area:** slightly smaller than Oregon. **Land use:** 25% arable land; 9% permanent crops; 9% meadows and pastures; 28% forest and woodland; 29% other; includes negl. % irrigated. **Major cities:** (1991 census) Kampala (capital) 773,463; Jinja 60,979; Mbale 53,634; Masaka 49,070; Gulu 42,841.

● **People** **Population:** 22,804,973 (1999 est.). **Nationality:** noun—Ugandan(s); adjective— Ugandan. **Ethnic groups:** 17% Baganda, 12% Karamojong, 8% Basogo, 8% Iteso, 6% Langi, 6% Rwanda, 5% Bagisu, 4% Acholi, 4% Lugbara, 3% Bunyoro. **Languages:** English (official), Luganda, Swahili, Arabic and other Niger-Congo languages. **Religions:** 33% Roman Catholic, 33% Protestant, 16% Muslim, 18% indigenous beliefs.

● **Government** **Type:** republic. **Independence:** Oct. 9, 1962 (from UK). **Constitution:** Oct. 8, 1995. **National holiday:** Independence Day, Oct. 9. **Heads of Government:** Yoweri Kaguta Museveni, president (since Jan. 1986); Prof. Apolo Nsibambi, prime minister (since Apr. 1999). **Structure:** executive—president is head of government and state; unicameral legislature; judiciary.

● **Economy** **Monetary unit:** Ugandan shilling. **Budget:** (FY95/96) *income:* $869 mil.; *expend.:* $985 mil. **GDP:** $22.7 bil., $1,020 per capita (1998 est.). **Chief crops:** coffee, cotton, tobacco, tea; beef, milk, poultry. **Natural resources:** copper, cobalt, limestone, salt. **Major industries:** sugar, brewing, tobacco. **Labor force:** 8.361 mil. (1993 est.); 86% agriculture, 10% services, 4% industry. **Exports:** $476 mil. (f.o.b., 1998); 54% coffee, gold, fish. **Imports:** $1.4 bil. (c.i.f., 1998); transportation equipment, petroleum, medical supplies, iron and steel. **Major trading partners:** *exports:* 14% Spain, 14% Germany, 10% Netherlands, 8% France; *imports:* 31% Kenya, 12% UK, 6% Japan, 6% India.

Prior to 1800 Uganda was the site of several important kingdoms, notably Buganda, centered on Kampala on the northern shore of Lake Victoria. After 1830 Arabs from the sultanate of Oman, based in Zanzibar, asserted loose control over the region and dominated its trade. British explorers, seeking the source of the Nile, reached the Lake Victoria region in the mid-19th century. Mission stations were established in 1877; a Muslim rebellion destroyed the missions and occupied Kampala in 1888.

Buganda was brought under the control of the British East Africa Company in 1890, and Britain established a protectorate in 1894 that was expanded to include neighboring territories in 1896. In 1902 some of the protectorate's territory was transferred to Kenya. British immigrants extensively developed the agricultural potential of Uganda's fertile and temperate highlands, establishing large and prosperous farms. Lake Victoria was the scene of naval battles between Great Britain and Germany (established in neighboring Tanganyika) during World War I.

In 1955 the British administration created a local parliamentary government in which both whites and Africans held ministerial office. Talks on the terms for independence began in 1961 and after some difficulty arrived at a formula for a national structure in which Buganda and other traditional kingdoms would retain local autonomy. Several political parties competed for power; the Uganda People's Congress led by Milton Obote gradually became dominant. Uganda became independent within the British Commonwealth on Oct. 9, 1962. Several constitutional changes in the early 1960s led to an end to the autonomy of the kingdoms and the effective concentration of all power in Obote's presidency. In 1967 a new constitution proclaimed Uganda an independent republic.

Obote was overthrown on Jan. 25, 1971, by Idi Amin Dada, commander of Uganda's armed forces. Amin declared himself president, dissolved the Parliament, and assumed absolute powers. In 1972 he expelled Uganda's Asians (primarily people of Indian and Pakistani descent), who controlled most of the country's small-scale commerce. The United States broke off diplomatic relations in 1973. In 1976 Amin declared himself president for life. His eight-year reign was marked by extreme violence and persecution of political and tribal opponents; as many as 300,000 Ugandans may have been killed between 1971 and 1979. The country's prosperous agricultural, mining, and commercial economy was devastated, and its infrastructure, including a good road and rail network and Makerere University, one of Africa's preeminent educational institutions, fell into ruins.

On July 3, 1976, Israeli airborne troops landed at Entebbe and rescued 103 hostages who had been captured in a skyjacking carried out by Palestinian and German terrorists.

In 1978 Amin, with the aid of Libyan troops, invaded Tanzania. In the following year, Tanzanian troops countered by invading Uganda; they captured Kampala on Apr. 11, 1979, and drove Amin into exile. Diplomatic relations with the United States resumed. After a series of interim governments, elections in 1981 returned Obote to power. Obote's new regime was marked by repression of opponents and by rebellion in the northern part of the country by the National Resistance Army (NRA) under Yoweri Museveni.

Obote fled into exile in 1985 and was succeeded by Lt. Gen. Basilio Olara-Okello, but the NRA rebellion continued. Kenyan president Daniel arap Moi mediated peace talks between Olara-Okello and the NRA in late 1985; in Jan. 1986 Olara-Okello fled into exile, and Museveni organized a new government. Despite continued insurgencies by rival military factions and a rebellion led by the charismatic religious leader Alice Lakwena, the Museveni government has generally restored order and, with aid from the World Bank and the IMF, has begun to rebuild Uganda's shattered society.

A constituent assembly was elected in 1994. In October 1995, it enacted a new constitution, which extended for five years a ban on political parties, and scheduled presidential elections for 1996, elections Museveni won with 74 percent of the vote. By 1997 Uganda had the fastest growing economy in Africa and in 1998 Pres. Clinton's visit helped to create interst among foreign investors.

▶ UKRAINE

● **Geography** **Location:** east-central Europe. **Boundaries:** Belarus to N, Russian Federation to NE and E, Sea of Azov and Black Sea to S, Moldova and Romania to SW, Hungary, Slovakia, Poland to W. **Total area:** 233,089 sq. mi. (603,700 sq km). **Coastline:** Black Sea. **Comparative area:** slightly smaller than Texas. **Land use:** 58% arable land; 2% permanent crops, 13% meadows and pastures; 18% forest and woodland; 9% other (mostly urban). **Major cities:** (1995 est.): Kiev (capital) 2,635,000; Kharkov (Kharkiv) 1,576,000; Dnepropetrovsk 1,162,000; Donetsk (Donetske) 1,102,000; Odessa (Odesa) 1,060,000.

● **PEOPLE Population:** 49,811,174 (1999 est.). **Nationality:** noun—Ukrainian(s); adjective—Ukrainian. **Ethnic groups:** 73% Ukrainian, 22% Russian, 1% Jewish. **Languages:** Ukrainian, Russian, Romanian, Polish, Hungarian. **Religions:** Ukrainian Orthodox—Moscow Patriarchate, Ukrainian Orthodox—Kiev Patriarchate, Ukrainian Autocephalous Orthodox, Ukrainian Catholic, Protestant; Jewish.

● **GOVERNMENT Type:** republic. **Independence:** Dec. 1, 1991 (from Soviet Union). **Constitution:** June 28, 1996. **National holiday:** Independence Day, Aug. 24. **Heads of Government:** Leonid Kuchma, president (since Dec. 1991); Valeriy Pustovoytenko, prime minister (since July 1997). **Structure:** executive—president, Cabinet of Ministers; legislative—Supreme Council (450 deputies); judicial—Supreme Court.

● **ECONOMY Monetary unit:** hryvnia. **Budget:** (1997) *income:* $18 bil.; *expend.:*$21 bil. **GDP:** $108.5 bil., $2,200 per capita (1998 est.). **Chief crops:** grain, sugar beets, sunflower seeds, vegetables; meat, milk. **Natural resources:** coal, iron ore, manganese, natural gas, oil. **Major industries:** coal, electric power, metals, machinery and transport, chemicals. **Labor force:** 22.8 mil. (1997); 32% industry and construction, 24% agriculture and forestry, 17% health, education and culture, 8% trade and distribution, 7% transport and communication. **Exports:** $11.3 bil. (1998); ferrous and nonferrous metals, chemicals, machinery and transport equipment, food products. **Imports:** $13.1 bil. (1998); energy, machinery and parts, transportation equipment, chemicals, plastics and rubber. **Major trading partners:** *exports:* Russia, China, Turkey; *imports:* Russia, Germany, US.

Ukraine is the center of the original Russian state, known as Kievan Rus, which came into existence in the ninth century A.D. In the 13th and 14th centuries, during the Mongol invasion, Ukraine was controlled by Lithuania and Poland, and in 1654 it first entered the Russian empire. In the latter half of the 17th century, Ukraine was divided, with the eastern regions becoming part of Russia and the western part annexed by Poland; when Poland was subsequently partitioned, the western sections were ceded to Austria.

Until 1917 eastern Ukraine was a province of Russia called "Little Russia," and for two centuries the dominant country tried to Russianize the Ukrainian clergy and upper classes, and ban the Ukrainian language. Nevertheless, secret societies for the study of Ukrainian history, language, and culture formed, and when in the 19th century the Russians exiled Ukrainians to Siberia, modern Ukrainian nationalism was born.

In 1917, when the Russian empire collapsed, Ukrainian nationalists demanded Ukraine's autonomy by establishing a Ukrainian People's Republic, but within a few months, Red Army troops had occupied Ukraine. For the next few years, however, Ukraine was in the middle of the civil war and was even ceded to Germany under the Brest-Litovsk treaty of 1918, but in December 1920 a Ukrainian Soviet Socialist Republic (SSR) was established. Ukraine again was divided under the 1921 Treaty of Riga, which gave western Ukraine to Poland, Czechoslovakia, and Romania, while eastern Ukraine formed the Ukrainian SSR. Ukraine became one of the original members of the USSR in December 1922.

As in other Soviet republics, the Ukrainians strongly opposed Stalin's policy of forced collectivization of agriculture in the 1930s, and the resulting chaos, famine, and deportation resulted in the deaths of millions of Ukrainians. Likewise, Stalin's great terror of the 1930s hit Ukraine hard, with the first victims being Ukrainian nationalists. World War II largely devastated Ukraine and killed millions of Ukrainians, but as a result of the war, Ukraine regained its old territories from Romania and Poland and was enlarged by the addition of historical Tatar lands in 1954. (The native Tatar inhabitants were forcibly deported to central Asia in the mid-1940s.)

Mikhail Gorbachev's policy of glasnost, or openness, was slow to take root in Ukraine, largely because until 1989 the head of the Communist party in Ukraine was a loyal Brezhnev crony, Vladimir Shcherbitsky. Outwardly, he appeared to agree with Gorbachev's policies, but Ukraine dissidents were still being arrested and cultural groups harassed by secret police. In 1986 a deadly nuclear power explosion at Chernobyl—and Soviet attempts at covering it up—turned international attention to Ukraine and gave rise to a number of new, powerful opposition movements. Rukh (the Ukrainian People's Movement for Restructuring), the most important of these, was founded in Kiev by a prominent group of writers and intellectuals. By 1989 branches of Rukh had been organized in most parts of Ukraine. At the same time, Ukrainian miners became active in strikes, and the Ukrainian Catholic church and the Ukrainian Orthodox church became politically active. Shcherbitsky's failure to contain these groups led to his dismissal in September 1989.

On July 16, 1990, the Ukrainian Supreme Soviet adopted a declaration of sovereignty. Also in July, Communist party Second Secretary Leonid Kravchuk became chairman of the Supreme Soviet. In March 1991 Ukraine participated in the negotiations to form a new union treaty, despite more radical demands by Rukh for complete independence. The Ukrainian Communist party's failure to denounce the attempted coup in Moscow in August 1991 led to significant changes in Ukraine's political situation. After the coup collapsed, the Communist party was banned, and on Aug. 24, 1991, Ukraine adopted a declaration of total independence. In December, Kravchuk was elected president.

That same month, Ukraine, Belarus, and the Russian Federation signed the Minsk Agreement that created the Commonwealth of Independent States, and on Dec. 21, Ukraine and 10 other former union republics officially committed themselves to the union by signing the Alma-Ata Declaration.

Potentially dangerous conflicts with Russia remained, however, including control of the powerful Black Sea fleet. Soon after the fall of the Soviet government armed conflict erupted in April 1994, when Russia removed a ship from Odessa laden with marine-research and navigational equipment valued at more than $10 million. A compromise was reached in 1995 that divided the 635-vessel fleet equally, with Russia then buying 32 percent of the ships from the Ukraine and paying rent for use of the naval base at Sevastopol.

The other conflict involved 2,000 nuclear warheads present in Ukraine. In Jan. 1994, Kravchuk, Boris Yeltsin, and Bill Clinton negotiated an agreement to dismantle Ukraine's 175 long-range missiles and more than 1,800 warheads. But Ukraine's Parliament continually refused to approve the agreement, even after Clinton made a $350 million U.S. aid package conditional on total disarmament. Parliament's intransigence was seen as an embarrassment to Kravchuk, and in July 1994 he lost the presidential election to reformer Leonid Kuchma. In Nov. Parliament overwhelmingly approved the Nuclear Nonproliferation Treaty and loans from the United States and the IMF ensued. The United States also pledged $400 million to help dismantle the remaining missiles.

In July 1996 the Rada approved a new "strong president" Constitution which guaranteed rights to own property and to engage in business, which abolished local councils ("soviets"), and which made Ukrainian the only legal language (although Russian is the language of about one-fifth of the population). The May 1997 Friendship Treaty with Russia settled the Black Sea fleet division, guaranteed Russia's right to rent part of the port facilities of Sevastopol to service the fleet, and confirmed Ukrainian sovereignty over all of Crimea. The economy remains in disarray, however, and in Aug. 1998 the IMF agreed to loans totalling $2.2 bil. to assist the government despite its inability to make necessary reforms. Although inflation has been cut to 10 percent only 50 percent of state-owned businesses have been sold. Presidential elections were held in Oct. 1999. (See Part I for results.)

▶ UNITED ARAB EMIRATES

• **Geography   Location:** eastern Arabian peninsula. **Boundaries:** Persian Gulf to N, Gulf of Oman to NE, Oman to E, Saudi Arabia to S and W, short frontier with Qatar to NW. **Total area:** 31,969 sq. mi. (82,880 sq km). **Coastline:** 819 mi. (1,318 km). **Comparative area:** slightly smaller than Maine. **Land use:** 2% meadows and pastures; 98% other. **Major cities:** (1995 est.) Abu Dhabi (capital) 928,360; Dubai 674,100; Sharjah 400,400.

• **People   Population:** 2,344,402 (1999 est.). **Nationality:** noun—Emirian(s); adjective—Emirian. **Ethnic groups:** 19% Emirian, 23% other Arab and Iranian, 50% South Asian, 8% other expatriates (includes Westerners and East Asians); less than 20% of population are UAE citizens (1982). **Languages:** Arabic (official), Persian, English, Hindi, Urdu. **Religions:** 96% Muslim (16% Shia), 4% Christian, Hindu, and other.

• **Government   Type:** federation with specified powers delegated to UAE central government and other powers reserved to member emirates. **Independence:** Dec. 2, 1971 (from UK). **Constitution::** Dec. 2, 1971. **National holiday:** National Day, Dec. 2. **Heads of Government:** Sheikh Zayed bin Sultan al-Nahyan of Abu Dhabi, president (since Dec. 1971); Maktoum al-Maktoum, prime minister (since Oct.1990). **Structure:** executive—Supreme Council of Rulers (seven members), from which president and vice president are elected; prime minister and Council of Ministers; unicameral legislature—Federal National Council; judicial—Union Supreme Court.

• **Economy   Monetary unit:** Emirian dirham. **Budget:** (1998 est.) *income:* $5.4 bil.; *expend.:* $5.8 bil. **GDP:** $40 bil., $17,400 per capita (1998 est.). **Chief crops:** dates, vegetables, watermelons; poultry, eggs, dairy products; fish. **Natural re-**sources: crude oil, natural gas. **Major industries:** petroleum, fishing, petrochemicals. **Labor force:** 1.3 mil. (1997 est.); 60% services, 32% industry and commerce, 8% agriculture; 75% of the labor force is foreign. **Exports:** $38 bil. (f.o.b., 1997 est.); 45% crude oil, natural gas, re-exports, dried fish, dates. **Imports:** $29.7 bil. (f.o.b., 1997 est.); manufactured goods, machinery and transport equipment, chemicals, food. **Major trading partners:** *exports:* 36% Japan, 9% South Korea, 5% Singapore; *imports:* 9% U.S., 9% Japan, 8% UK.

In the 1820s Great Britain established protectorates over seven small sheikhdoms along the gulf coast between Qatar and Oman—Abu Dhabi, Dubai, Sharjah, Ajmar, Fujairah, and Umm al-Qaiwain. The region, which had been known as the Pirate Coast, then was generally referred to as the Trucial Coast or Trucial Oman. Under terms of a treaty in 1892, the sheikhdoms agreed not to enter into relations with any other country.

After Great Britain announced that it would withdraw its forces from the gulf in 1971, the seven sheikhdoms formed a federation and became independent as the United Arab Emirates on Dec. 2, 1971.

Just prior to his invasion of Kuwait in August 1990, Saddam Hussein threatened both the UAE and Kuwait for overproduction of petroleum, and the UAE was an integral part of the Allied coalition against Iraq. In 1995 the government signed a defensive alliance with France, who supplies the army with most of its weapons.

The economy is almost entirely dominated by petroleum. Citizens of the UAE receive extensive social services and enjoy one of the world's highest per capita incomes.

▶ UNITED KINGDOM
United Kingdom of Great Britain and Northern Ireland

• **Geography   Location:** northwestern Europe, occupying major portion of British Isles. **Boundaries:** Atlantic Ocean to NW and W, North Sea to E; separated from France by English Channel to S; Republic of Ireland to W. **Total area:** 94,525 sq. mi. (244,820 sq km). **Coastline:** 7,723 mi. (12,429 km). **Comparative area:** slightly smaller than Oregon. **Land use:** 25% arable land; negl. % permanent crops; 46% meadows and pastures; 10% forest and woodland; 19% other; includes 1% irrigated. **Major cities:** (1994 est.) London (capital) 6,976,500; Birmingham 1,008,400; Leeds 724,400; Glasgow 680,000; Sheffield 530,100.

• **People   Population:** 59,113,439 (1999 est.). **Nationality:** noun—Briton(s), British (collective pl.); adjective—British. **Ethnic groups:** 81.5% English, 9.6% Scottish, 2.4% Irish, 1.9% Welsh, 1.8% Ulster, 2.8% West Indian, Indian, Pakistani, and other. **Languages:** English, Welsh (about 26% of population of Wales), Scottish form of Gaelic (about 60,000 in Scotland). **Religions:** 27 mil. Anglican, 9 mil. Roman Catholic, 1 mil. Muslim, 800,000 Presbyterian, 760,000 Methodist, 400,000 Sikh, 350,000 Hindu, 300,000 Jewish.

• **Government   Type:** constitutional monarchy. **Independence:** N.A. **Constitution:** unwritten; partly statutes, partly common law and practice. **National holiday:** Celebration of the Birthday of the Queen, second Saturday in June. **Heads of Government:** Elizabeth II, queen (since Feb. 1952); Tony Blair, prime minister (since May 1997). **Structure:** executive authority lies with collectively responsible cabinet led by prime minister; legislative authority rests with Parliament

(House of Lords, House of Commons); House of Lords is supreme judicial authority and highest court of appeals.

● **ECONOMY   Monetary unit:** British pound. **Budget:** (1997) *income:* $487.7 bil.; *expend.:* $492.6 bil. **GDP:** $1.252 trillion, $21,200 per capita (1998 est.). **Chief crops:** cereals, oilseed, potatoes, vegetables; cattle, sheep, poultry; fish. **Natural resources:** coal, crude oil, natural gas, tin, limestone. **Major industries:** machinery and transportation equipment, metals, food processing. **Labor force:** 28.8 mil. (1998); 68.9% services, 17.5% manufacturing and construction, 11.3% government; 1.2% energy, 1.1% agriculture, 7.5% unemployment (1998 est.). **Exports:** $271 bil. (f.o.b., 1998 est.); manufactured goods, machinery, fuels, chemicals. **Imports:** $304 bil. (f.o.b., 1998 est.); manufactured goods, machinery, fuels, foodstuffs. **Major trading partners:** *exports:* 56% EU (12% Germany, 10% France, 8% Netherlands), 12% U.S.; *imports:* 53% EU (14% Germany, 10% France, 7% Netherlands, 5% Ireland), 13% U.S.

Early megalithic and Iron Age peoples of Britain, primarily Celtic, developed tribal states that were conquered by Roman invaders in A.D. 43. After Roman legions withdrew from Britain in 410, invasions of Jutes, Angles, and Saxons conquered much of England, while Celtic peoples flourished in Wales, Scotland, and especially Ireland. Viking invaders established settlements in the eighth century. A united Saxon kingdom fell to the Norman invasion of William the Conquerer in 1066.

An aristocratic rebellion against the royal absolutism of King John in 1215 led to the royal acceptance of the Magna Carta, guaranteeing legal rights and laying the foundations of parliamentary government. From the 12th to the 15th century, the Plantagenet dynasty ruled England and claimed overlordship over Ireland; Wales was conquered in 1283. The Plantagenets also controlled sizable territories in France.

The Hundred Years' War (1337-1453) cost England its French possessions; the War of the Roses, (1455-85) ended the Plantagenet dynasty and brought Henry Tudor (Henry VII) to the throne. The Tudors gradually centralized royal control by bringing pressure against both the church and the nobility. Henry VIII broke with Rome in 1534 and established the Church of England. Under Elizabeth I, the last of the Tudors, England defeated Spain at sea and laid the foundations of later worldwide English sea power. The English Renaissance began under Elizabeth I (1533-1603) with the works of Shakespeare and continued into the 17th century with Milton and Newton.

The Stuart dynasty was founded by James I (1566-1625), uniting the crowns of England and Scotland. The English Civil War (1642-49) culminated in the execution of Charles I and the proclamation of the Commonwealth (later the Protectorate) under Oliver Cromwell. The monarchy was restored with Charles II in 1660. In the bloodless Glorious Revolution (1688), James II fled before a Protestant army under the Dutch William of Orange, who married and ruled jointly with James's daughter Mary II. The English Bill of Rights established the supremacy of Parliament and made the government a model of constitutional monarchy.

In the last gasp of the Stuart claimants to the throne, Irish supporters of James II were defeated at the Battle of the Boyne (1690), which temporarily crushed Irish resistance to annexation by En-

gland. The United Kingdom was created when Scotland was joined with England in a common Parliament by the Act of Union in 1707. A Scottish uprising led by the Young Pretender, Charles Edward Stuart, was crushed at Culloden Moor in 1745. Ireland was made part of the United Kingdom in 1801.

In the 1700s the United Kingdom became the greatest sea power in the world, controlling an empire that included much of North America and India. Agrarian "enclosures" of the 18th century ruined the peasantry but created an entrepreneurial revolution in agriculture that ultimately led to greatly increased agricultural productivity. The capital created in the process contributed to the success of the Industrial Revolution, which over the next century made England the wealthiest land on earth.

Despite the loss of the 13 colonies after the American Revolution (1775-83), England consolidated its holdings in the Indian subcontinent, Australia and New Zealand, Malaya, Hong Kong, much of eastern Africa from "Cape to Cairo," and elsewhere. Britain's prosperity and moral purpose were embodied in the person of Victoria, Queen of Great Britain and Ireland (1836-1901) and Empress of India (from 1836).

The repeal of the protectionist Corn Laws in 1846 led to an agricultural depression and hastened the migration of labor from the countryside to the industrial cities. The rise of labor activism led in 1906 to laws granting privileged status to trade unions, which organized the Labour party to promote their interests.

Britain's involvement in the Triple Entente with France and Russia ensured its participation in World War I (1914-18) against Germany, Italy, and Austria-Hungary. Victory came at the cost of an entire generation of British youth, but Britain emerged from the war with its empire at a high point, adding Tanganyika, Jordan, Palestine, and Iraq as part of the postwar division of spoils. Most of Ireland became independent in 1921, however, leaving only Northern Ireland as part of the United Kingdom.

Between the two world wars, Britain's navy and air force were the largest in the world, its army the third largest. Yet its industry was aging, the Great Depression hit especially hard in the British Isles, strikes and labor unrest weakened the social fabric, and colonial ties began to weaken in the 1930s. Economic retrenchment led to a failure to rearm in the face of the rising threat of Hitler's Germany and Mussolini's Italy.

The Munich Pact of 1938 gave Hitler a license for war; his invasion of Poland in 1939 forced Britain into the conflict. When Winston Churchill became prime minister in 1940, Britain was under daily air attack and in danger of an invasion by sea, and the country was dependent on American friendship and lend-lease war materials. But 1941 brought alliance with the United States and the Soviet Union, and a slowly turning tide of war leading to victory in 1945. Still, postwar Britain dropped to the second rank of superpowers.

The coalition between the Conservative and Labour parties that had governed Great Britain during the war seemed no longer necessary in 1945 as the war wound down. Labour won a landslide victory in the 1945 elections; Churchill was recalled in the midst of the Potsdam Conference, and Clement Atlee became prime minister. A brief Labour flirtation with the USSR quickly ended in the postwar 1940s; England became a founding member of the United Nations and also, in 1949, of NATO. As the Cold War took shape, Britain developed its own nuclear arsenal.

The Labour party nationalized the Bank of England along with railroads, public utilities, and heavy industry. A comprehensive welfare state apparatus was created, including a national health service, unemployment and retirement benefits, and free education at all levels. But Britain was in many respects too poor to afford such changes; in order to cut expenditures, the government has-tened the process of withdrawal from colonies and military bases around the world. India was granted independence in 1947, and Palestine, Burma, and Ceylon in 1948-49.

The elections of 1951 brought Churchill back to the prime ministership at the head of a Conservative majority that would last for 13 years. The Conservatives returned steel and trucking to the private sector but in general refrained from undoing the social policies of their Labour predecessors. Economic growth began in the 1950s and held steady at about 2.5 percent per year, a significantly lower rate than in contemporary continental Europe; obsolescence, excessive wage and benefit settlements with labor, and a low savings rate all took their toll. The coronation of Elizabeth II in 1953 added a much-needed element of national celebration.

Churchill retired in 1955 and was succeeded by Anthony Eden. Eden's government fell in 1956 over the failed and bungled Anglo-French invasion of Suez. Eden's fall in 1957 brought to power Harold Macmillan, who pursued close relations with the United States. Most important, he presided over the transformation of an empire to a commonwealth; in the early 1960s, Ghana, Nigeria, Malaya, Singapore, and numerous other colonies were granted independence and Commonwealth status. Immigrants from the Commonwealth promptly flocked to England, straining housing, social services, and the labor market and creating problems of assimilation that remain unsolved.

Britain under Macmillan was the moving force behind the European Free Trade Association in 1960. In 1961 Britain applied for membership in the EEC, but that application was humiliatingly vetoed by France's Charles de Gaulle in 1963. Macmillan's government fell with the Profumo Scandal of 1963, and Douglas Home became a caretaker prime minister pending new elections.

The 1964 elections brought the Labour party to power under Harold Wilson, whose moderate positions made him unpopular with his own party, especially when he sponsored legislation to ban wildcat strikes. Strikes, wage inflation, the steady growth of the public sector (including renationalization of the steel industry), and the rise of turmoil in Northern Ireland in 1968-69 combined to make public support for Labour evaporate.

The Conservative victory in the 1970 elections brought Edward Heath to the office of prime minister. Promising to cut expenditures and taxes, reward initiative, and curb union power, the Conservatives were able to accomplish none of those aims. Heath's government imposed ineffective wage controls in an attempt to slow inflation and passed the 1971 Industrial Relations Act to regulate unions. When unions defied that act, the government fell. Heath's major achievement was the United Kingdom's admission to the EC in 1973. Continued turmoil in Northern Ireland was met with the abolition of Ulster's Stormount Par-

liament in 1972 and the imposition of direct British rule—a policy that did nothing to stem the growing sectarian violence.

Wilson returned to the prime ministership in 1974 and retired in 1976, passing on the office to James Callaghan, who governed until 1979 at the head of a Labour-Liberal coalition. The continued power of trade unions was seen in the repeal of the Industrial Relations Act and the extension of union privileges. The left wing of the Labour party brought increasing pressure against defense spending, membership in NATO, and the policy of moderation in Rhodesia (now Zimbabwe), and also loudly criticized American involvement in Vietnam.

The OPEC oil price rises of 1972-74 hurt Great Britain in the short run but also encouraged development of oil and gas fields in the North Sea, which made the nation a major petroleum exporter and helped revitalize its economy. Oil exploration in the North Sea also encouraged Scottish nationalism, with some damage to national unity, although in both Scotland and Wales, proposals in 1979 for separate parliaments were soundly defeated by plebiscites.

The 1979 elections brought the Conservatives to power again, behind Margaret Thatcher, Great Britain's (and Europe's) first female prime minister. She proved to be the only British prime minister in modern times to lead her party successfully in three elections. Thatcher took office with an agenda that involved undoing much of the course of postwar British history.

The first target was inflation, attacked through a freeze on expenditures and reduction of government borrowing. The policy was a success; inflation fell from 18 percent in 1980 to 3 percent in 1989. But the austerity program had a high cost in unemployment, which remained at 14 percent in the mid-1980s.

In 1982 national attention turned abruptly to overseas concerns, as Argentina invaded the Falkland ("Malvinas") Islands (only 300 miles east of Argentina), which it had long claimed as Argentine national territory, on Apr. 2. On May 21 British forces launched a counteroffensive, and the invading Argentine forces surrendered on June 14. The nation's success in mounting an amphibious operation 6,500 miles away provoked an upsurge of patriotism that swept Thatcher's party into a second term in 1983.

After the election the government turned to denationalization of industry. Over $30 billion in state property—from industrial giants, such as Britoil and British Gas, to individual apartments in municipal housing projects—was sold to private interests. This program was followed in 1986 by tax cuts, in which the top income-tax rate dropped from 98 percent to 40 percent. In foreign affairs, Britain agreed in 1985 to return Hong Kong to Chinese sovereignty in 1997.

The 1987 elections pitted the Conservatives against a weak Labour party that opposed NATO missile deployment in Great Britain, advocating unilateral disarmament and calling for renationalization of industry and a return to higher taxes for the wealthy. The Conservatives easily won their third straight election. By 1989 the "Thatcher Revolution" had produced a decisive long-term economic recovery, but one that was unevenly distributed: the southern part of the country enjoyed an economic boom, while the older industrial cities of the north remained stagnant. In 1990 an economic slowdown and rising inflation led to a strong decline in support for Mrs. Thatcher and her government. She resigned in November 1990.

Thatcher was replaced by Chancellor of the Exchequer John Major, whose greatest challenge has been Britain's role in a united Europe, to which Britain now has a land link (for the first time in 9,000 years) via the 31-mile Channel Tunnel (Chunnel), completed in 1994.

In the April 1992 elections, the Conservatives, led by Major, won a comfortable 21-seat margin in Parliament despite a recession. Not since the Napoleonic Wars has a British political party been able to form four consecutive governments. Yet only 13 months later Major's ratings in the polls had fallen to 21 percent as the economy stalled and the Conservatives themselves split badly over some elements in the EC's Maastricht Treaty. The Conservatives were further beset in 1994 with a series of tabloid scandals and allegations of political corruption concerning arms sales to Iraq and Malaysia. Tories only 25 percent. Conservative chances in parliamentary elections, due in the spring of 1997, were looking very slim, and they looked worse in March after the government clumsily handled the news that scientists had concluded that eating English beef could cause the fatal "mad-cow" disease. After insisting that there was no cause for alarm the government was forced to deal with an EU boycott.

The parliamentary election of May 1997 ended 18 years of Tory government with Labour winning its largest majority since 1935, 419 seats to the Conservatives 165. The new Prime Minister Tony Blair, relegating the party's left wing to sub-cabinet posts, appointed a cabinet of political moderates. In 1997 Hong Kong was returned to China without incident and in April 1998 the Blair government succeeded in negotiating a settlement in Northern Ireland although problems still remained to be solved throughout 1999.

In the January 1999 speech from the throne opening Parliament, Queen Elizabeth read the Blair government proposal to strip hereditary peers of their votes in the House of Lords, to create 50 new Labour life-peers (giving Labour a majority in that House) and to establish a commission to study a replacement body for the Lords. To that revolution aborning was added in May a revolution in fact: the first elections to the Scottish Parliament and the Welsh Assembly. Labour won a plurality in both (over nationalist parties), forming a coalition with Liberals in Scotland and ruling through a minority cabinet in Wales. The two bodies have authority over education, environment, health care, housing, and law enforcement. The Scottish Parliament also possesses what the Welsh Assembly lacks: authority to tax.

▶ **UNITED STATES OF AMERICA**
● **GEOGRAPHY   Location:** 48 conterminous states in North America, between Atlantic and Pacific Oceans; Alaska in northwest North America; Hawaiian Islands in Pacific Ocean about 3,000 miles W of California. **Boundaries:** Canada to N; Atlantic Ocean to E; Gulf of Mexico, Mexico to S; Pacific Ocean to W. Alaska bounded on E by Canada, on S and W by Pacific Ocean, on W and N by Arctic Ocean. **Total area:** 3,717,797 sq. mi. (9,629,091 sq km). **Coastline:** 11,954 mi. (19,924 km). **Comparative area:** slightly larger than Brazil; fourth-largest country. **Land use:** 19% arable land; negl. % permanent crops; 25% meadows and pastures; 30% forest and woodland; 26%

other; includes 2% irrigated. **Major cities:** (1994 est.) Washington, D.C. (capital) 567,094; New York 7,333,253; Los Angeles 3,448,613; Chicago 2,731,743; Houston 1,702,086; Philadelphia 1,524,249.
● **PEOPLE   Population:** 272,639,608 (1999 est.). **Nationality:** noun—American(s); adjective—American. **Ethnic groups:** 83.4% white, 12.4% black, 3.3% Asian, 0.8% Amerindian. **Languages:** predominantly English; sizable Spanish-speaking minority. **Religions:** 56% Protestant, 28% Roman Catholic, 10% none, 2% Jewish, 4% other.
● **GOVERNMENT   Type:** federal republic; strong democratic tradition. **Independence:** July 4, 1776 (from UK). **Constitution:** Sept. 17, 1787, effective March 4,1789. **National holiday:** Independence Day, July 4. **Heads of Government:** William J. Clinton, president (since Jan. 1993); Albert Gore, Jr., vice president (since Jan. 1993). **Structure:** executive—president, vice president, cabinet; legislative—bicameral Congress (House of Representatives and Senate); judicial—Supreme Court; branches, in principle, independent and maintain balance of power.
● **ECONOMY   Monetary unit:** United States dollar **Budget:** (1998) *income:* $1.72 trillion; *expend:* $1.653 tril. **GDP:** $8.511 tril., $31,500 per capita (1998). **Chief crops:** wheat, other grains, corn, fruits, vegetables, cotton; beef, pork, poultry, dairy products; forest products; fish. **Natural resources:** coal, copper, lead, molybdenum, phosphates. **Major industries:** leading industrial power in the world, highly diversified; petroleum, steel, motor vehicles, aerospace, telecommunications, chemicals, electronics, food processing, consumer goods, fishing, lumber, mining. **Labor force:** 137.7 mil., includes unemployed (1998); 29.6% managerial and professional, 29.3% sales and administrative support, 13.6% services, 24.8% manufacturing, mining, transportation, and crafts, 2.7% farming, forestry, and fishing; 4.9% unemployment (1998). **Exports:** $663 bil. (f.o.b., 1998); capital goods, automobiles, industrial supplies and raw materials, consumer goods, agricultural products. **Imports:** $912 bil. (c.i.f., 1998); crude oil and refined petroleum, machinery, automobiles, consumer goods, industrial raw materials, food and beverages. **Major trading partners:** (1997) *exports:* 22% Canada, 21% Western Europe, 10% Japan; *imports:* 19% Canada, 18% Western Europe, 14% Japan.

(For current events and history see Part I: "Major News Stories of the Year," and Part II: "Chronology of American History.")

▶ **URUGUAY**
Oriental Republic of Uruguay
● **GEOGRAPHY   Location:** southeastern coast of South America. **Boundaries:** Brazil to N, Atlantic Ocean to E and S, Argentina to W. **Total area:** 68,039 sq. mi. (176,220 sq km). **Coastline:** 410 mi. (660 km). **Comparative area:** slightly smaller than Washington State. **Land use:** 7% arable land; negl. % permanent crops; 77% meadows and pastures; 6% forest and woodland; 10% other; includes 1% irrigated. **Major cities:** (1992 census) Montevideo (capital) 1,383,660; Salto 77,400; Paysandú 75,200; Las Piedras 61,300; Rivera 55,400.
● **PEOPLE   Population:** 3,308,523 (1999 est.). **Nationality:** noun—Uruguayan(s); adjective—Uruguayan. **Ethnic groups:** 88% white, 8% mestizo, 4% black. **Languages:** Spanish, Portunol, or Brazilero; Portuguese-Spanish mix on the Brazilian frontier. **Religions:** 66% Roman

Catholic, 2% Protestant, 2% Jewish, 30% nonprofessing or other (less than half adult population attends church regularly).

● **GOVERNMENT Type:** republic. **Independence:** Aug. 25, 1825 (from Brazil). **Constitution:** Nov. 27, 1966; effective Feb. 1967; suspended June 27, 1973; constitutional reforms approved Jan. 7, 1997. **National holiday:** Independence Day, Aug. 25. **Head of Government:** Julio María Sanguinetti, president (since Mar. 1995). **Structure:** executive—headed by president; bicameral legislature (Senate and House of Deputies); national judiciary headed by Supreme Court.

● **ECONOMY Monetary unit:** Uruguayan peso. **Budget:** (1997 est.) *income:* $4 bil.; *expend.:* $4.3 bil. **GDP:** $28.4 bil., $8,600 per capita (1998 est.). **Chief crops:** wheat, rice, corn, sorghum; livestock; fishing. **Natural resources:** fertile soil, hydropower potential, minor minerals, fisheries. **Major industries:** meat processing, wool and hides, sugar. **Labor force:** 1.38 mil. (1997 est.); 25% government; 19% manufacturing; 12% commerce; 12% utilities, construction, transport, and communications; 11% agriculture; 10.5% unemployment (1998). **Exports:** $2.7 bil. (f.o.b., 1997 est.); wool and textile manufactures, beef and other animal products, rice, fish and shellfish. **Imports:** $3.7 bil. (c.i.f., 1997 est.); machinery and equipment, vehicles, chemicals, minerals, plastics, oil. **Major trading partners:** Brazil, Argentina, U.S.

Uruguay was known as the Banda Oriental del Uruguay (Eastern Shore of the Uruguay River) during the colonial period. Although the Spanish first explored the area in 1516, they did not immediately settle there. Instead, the Portuguese founded the Colonia de Sacramento, near Buenos Aires, in 1680. They did not permanently establish the settlement of Montevideo until 1726. Under the leadership of José Gervasio Artigas, Uruguayans fought against both the Portuguese and the junta of Buenos Aires between 1811 and 1814 in an effort to establish their independence; in 1815 they proclaimed the Autonomous Government of the Eastern Provinces.

In 1817 the Portuguese again took control of the region, but Uruguayan nationals ousted them in 1828. A new constitution for the country was promulgated in 1830; however, domestic rivalry among elites soon led to civil war. The two contending factions, Liberals (Colorados) and Conservatives (Blancos), wore red and white armbands, respectively. Civil war continued through the 1840s and 1850s, until the victory of the Colorados in 1865. In the War of the Triple Alliance (1865-70), Uruguay allied itself with Argentina and Brazil against Paraguay. The consequence of the war for Uruguay was independence from the other regional powers.

The Colorado party dominated Uruguayan government from 1865 until 1958. Waves of European immigrants transformed Uruguayan society during the latter half of the 19th century, and by 1880 immigrants made up almost half of the population. The last civil war between the Blancos and the Colorados took place in 1904; the Colorados won victory under Pres. José Batlle y Ordóñez, one of Uruguay's political legends.

Batlle inaugurated a labor and social-welfare reform program that created Latin America's first eight-hour working day as well as progressive legislation on women's rights. A proposal for the extension of the franchise to women was put forward in 1917. Impressed with the Swiss plural executive Federal Council during his stay in Switzerland, Batlle believed such a structure could help Uruguay avoid the Latin American hazard of caudillismo (authoritarian rule). Batlle proposed the idea of a plural executive, and a version of the idea became part of the constitution in 1919. The new constitution provided for both a president and a collegial National Council, both of which would make up the executive structure of the government.

In 1933 a military coup by Pres. Gabriel Terra sought to dissolve both the legislature and the National Council and to reestablish the single executive presidential system. He managed this by sponsoring a constituent assembly that drew up a new constitution in 1934. In a 1951 plebiscite, Uruguayan voters approved a return to the plural executive system, and a new constitutional order reflecting this went into effect the following year. The debate over the form of the executive was not over, however; in 1966 the public voted for yet another constitution, which once again established the single president as the executive power.

Uruguay's economy began to falter during the 1950s. This, combined with the expansion of governmental bureaucracy tied to the country's social welfare programs, led to increasing popular discontent. In 1958 the Blancos won two successive victories at the polls. A candidate from the conservative wing of the Colorado party, Jorge Pacheco Areco, regained the presidency for the traditional ruling party in 1967, but neither the Blancos nor the Colorados were able to deal with Uruguay's deteriorating economy or with its growing political unrest.

Uruguay's politics became increasingly polarized during the 1960s and into the 1970s. The leftist National Liberation Movement (MLN or Tupamaros), formed in 1967 and began urban guerrilla activity that included robbery and kidnapping. The Tupamaros, many of whom were young and middle class, embarrassed government officials and the police and were largely successful in eroding the public image of the civilian government. Tupamaro activity generated violence from the military and police, and as the political situation deteriorated in the early seventies, the government granted the military ever-expanding authority to deal with the situation.

By 1973 the military was in control of the country, and they dissolved the Congress. The military allowed Pres. Juan María Bordaberry to remain in office until 1976, at which time they installed Aparicio Méndez in the presidency. It was Bordaberry, however, who proposed the dismantling of the political parties in 1976. Uruguayan military rule was brutally repressive, and the armed forces perpetrated many human rights abuses (kidnapping, torture, murder). By some estimates, the Uruguayan military regime had the world's largest number of political prisoners in proportion to the population.

In 1980, Uruguayans decisively rejected in a plebiscite the army's constitution, which would have amounted to continued de facto military control. The rejection of the plebiscite began a slow process in which the military tried to bargain with civilian political elites while promising to restore civilian rule. Finally, in 1984, Colorado party candidate Julio María Sanguinetti won a civilian presidential election.

Sanguinetti approved a general amnesty for the leaders of the military regime, but also had success in attracting foreign investment and righting the Uruguayan economy. He was unseated five years later by National party candidate Luis Alberto Lacalle, who further liberalized trade. But his austerity on social problems led voters to overturn some of his reforms by referendum. In 1994 elections, Sanguinetti won back the presidency.

▶**UZBEKISTAN**
Republic of Uzbekistan
• **GEOGRAPHY Location:** central Asia. **Boundaries:** Kazakhstan to N, NE, and NW, Kyrgyzstan to E, Tajikistan to SE, Afghanistan to S, Turkmenistan to SW and W. **Total area:** 172,741 sq. mi. (447,400 sq km). **Coastline:** Aral Sea. **Comparative area:** slightly larger than California. **Land use:** 9% arable land; 1% permanent crops; 46% permanent pasture; 3% forest and woodland; 41% other (mostly urban and mountain). **Major cities:** (1994 est.) Tashkent (capital) 2,100,000; Samarkand 370,000; Namangan 312,000; Andizhan 297,000; Bukhara 228,000.
• **PEOPLE Population:** 24,102,473 (1999 est.). **Nationality:** noun—Uzbekistani(s); adjective—Uzbekistani. **Ethnic groups:** 80% Uzbek, 5.5% Russian, 5% Tajik, 3% Kazakh, 2.5% Karakalpak, 1.5% Tatar. **Languages:** 74.3% Uzbek (official), member of Eastern Turk language group written in Cyrillic script since 1940; 14.2% Russian, 4.4% Tajik, 7.1% other languages. **Religions:** 88% Muslim (mostly Sunnis), 9% Eastern Orthodox, 3% other.
• **GOVERNMENT Type:** republic. **Independence:** Aug. 31, 1991 (from Soviet Union). **Constitution:** Dec. 8, 1992. **National holiday:** Independence Day, Sept. 1. **Heads of Government:** Islam A. Karimov, president (since Dec. 1991); Utkir T. Sultanov, prime minister (since Dec. 1995). **Structure:** executive—president, Cabinet of Ministers; legislative—Supreme Assembly; judicial—Supreme Court.
• **ECONOMY Monetary unit:** som. **Budget:** (1997 est.) *income:* $4.4 bil.; *expend:* $4.7 bil. **GDP:** $59.2 bil., $2,500 per capita (1998 est.). **Chief crops:** cotton, vegetables, fruits, grain; livestock. **Natural resources:** natural gas, coal, petroleum, gold, uranium. **Major industries:** textiles, food processing, machine building, metallurgy, natural gas. **Labor force:** 11.9 mil. (1998). **Exports:** $3.8 bil. (1998); cotton, gold, natural gas, mineral fertilizers, ferrous metals, textiles, food products, autos. **Imports:** $4.1 bil. (1998); grain, machinery and parts, consumer durables, other foods. **Major trading partners:** other former Soviet republics.

Uzbekistan, a land of deserts and steppe, lies in the heart of central Asia. Although the territory has been inhabited since prehistoric times, today's Uzbeks are actually descendants of nomadic Mongol, Iranian, and Turkic tribes who mixed with the populations there beginning in the 13th century A.D. The Uzbeks take their name from Khan Uzbek (1282-1342), the ruler responsible for converting the Mongol Golden Horde (the westernmost part of the Mongolian empire) to Islam. In the 18th and 19th centuries, the tribal states known as the Uzbek khanates of Bukhara, Samarkand, and Kokand were formed. Russian conquest of the Uzbek lands began in the 18th century and was completed in 1876 with the conquering of the khanate of Kokand. The Russian empire quickly built the Transcaucasian Railway to connect it with the region's major cities, thus sealing its hold on the area.

As with Kazakhstan, there was a large influx of Russians into Uzbekistan, mainly to its cities.

Uzbek resentment of Russian immigrants precipitated a riot in 1898 in Andidzhan and again in 1916, when a decree that drafted central Asians into the Army was promulgated. At the time of the revolution, Soviet power was established in 1917 in the largely Russian city of Tashkent, and after some fighting, the region of Uzbekistan was incorporated into the Russian republic as the Turkestan Autonomous Soviet Socialist Republic (ASSR) in April 1918. In October 1924, the Uzbek Soviet Socialist Republic (SSR) came into being.

During 1924-25, the Soviet government initiated the National Delimitation of the Central Asian Republics to create Uzbek national symbols, to develop a new literary language, and to increase literacy among Uzbeks. It also conducted a brutal campaign against Islam and its believers. The Soviets modernized agriculture and industrialized the territory, although the native Uzbek population for the most part continued to live in rural areas and worked harvesting cotton, while the Russian population worked in industry. During World War II, Uzbekistan's industrial base expanded as many major factories and plants were moved there from the Russian areas to keep them safe from enemy attack.

Mikhail Gorbachev's policy of glasnost, or openness, did not immediately result in political changes in Uzbekistan. In time, Uzbeks became politically active over many of the same issues that affected their Kazakh neighbors, such as the environmental problems causing the drying up of its rivers, the desiccation of the Aral Sea, and the salinization of the soil. They also demanded that Uzbek (and not Russian) be the official language of Uzbekistan.

In March 1990 the Supreme Soviet elected Islam Karimov as president, and in April 1991 Uzbekistan agreed to sign a new union treaty, which was derailed by the failed August 1991 coup in Moscow. On Aug. 31, 1991, Uzbekistan declared its independence, and in December signed the Alma-Ata Declaration and joined the Commonwealth of Independent States (CIS).

In December 1991 Islam Karimov won the presidential election, and he moved to reduce Uzbekistan's dependence on Russia. In 1994 he signed an economic free-trade agreement with Kazakhstan and Kyrgyzstan and he banned use of the ruble in order to strengthen the som, Uzbekistan's monetary unit. In December 1994 Karimov's supporters (calling themselves the Democratic party) won an overwhelming majority in Uzbekistan's first parliamentary elections. Since then the country has made a slow but steady economic recovery. In Feb. 1999, Uzbekistan refused to renew its collective security treaty with the CIS.

▶**VANUATU**
Republic of Vanuatu
• **GEOGRAPHY Location:** chain of 12 principal and some 60 smaller islands in Pacific Ocean, about 500 mi. (800 km) W of Fiji and 1,100 mi. (2,800 km) E of Australia. Port Vila 17°45'S, 168°18'E. **Boundaries:** surrounded by South Pacific Ocean; nearest neighbor is Santa Cruz Islands to N. **Total area:** 5,699 sq. mi. (14,760 sq km). **Coastline:** 1,571 mi. (2,528 km). **Comparative area:** slightly larger than Connecticut. **Land use:** 2% arable land; 10% permanent crops; 2% meadows and pastures; 75% forest and woodland; 11% other. **Major cities:** (1989 census) Port Vila (capital) 19,311.

● **PEOPLE** **Population:** 189,036 (1999 est.). **Nationality:** noun—Ni-Vanuatu (sing. and pl.); adjective—Ni-Vanuatu. **Ethnic groups:** 94% indigenous Melanesian, 4% French; remainder Vietnamese, Chinese, and Pacific Islanders. **Languages:** English and French (official); pidgin (known as Bislama or Bichelama). **Religions:** 36.7% Presbyterian, 15% Anglican, 15% Catholic, 7.6% indigenous beliefs, 6.2% Seventh-Day Adventist, 3.8% Church of Christ, 15.7% other.

● **GOVERNMENT** **Type:** republic. **Independence:** July 30, 1980 (from France and UK). **Constitution:** July 30, 1980. **National holiday:** Independence Day, July 30. **Heads of Government:** John Bani, president (since Mar. 1999); Donald Kalpokas, prime minister (since March 1998). **Structure:** executive—president, prime minister, council of ministers; unicameral legislature; judiciary.

● **ECONOMY** **Monetary unit:** vatu. **Budget:** (1996 est.) *income:* $94.4 mil. *expend.:* $99.8 mil. **GDP:** $240 mil., $1,300 per capita (1997 est.). **Chief crops:** copra, coconuts, çocoa, coffee, taro, yams, fruits, vegetables; fish, beef. **Natural resources:** manganese, hardwood forests, fish. **Major industries:** food and fish freezing, forestry processing, meat canning. **Labor force:** 65% agriculture, 32% services, 3% industry (1995 est.) **Exports:** $30 mil. (f.o.b., 1996); copra, beef, cocoa, timber, coffee. **Imports:** $97 mil. (f.o.b., 1996); machines and vehicles, food and beverages, basic manufactures, raw materials and fuels, chemicals. **Major trading partners:** *exports:* 28% Japan, 21% Spain,14% Germany; *imports:* 47% Japan, 23% Australia, 8% Singapore.

Formerly known as the New Hebrides, Vanuatu is a rugged, volcanic island chain with heavily forested mountains; peaks rise to over 6,000 feet (on Espiritu Santo, the largest island). The people are Melanesians. In 1887 the islands were placed under the administration of an Anglo-French naval commission, becoming a joint Anglo-French colony (condominium) in 1906. The islands escaped Japanese occupation during World War II; they sided with the Free French and were used as bases for Allied campaigns in the Pacific. The New Hebrides were granted independence as Vanuatu on July 30, 1980, with membership in the British Commonwealth. The government is a parliamentary system, complemented by a National Council of Chiefs to decide matters of tradition and customary law.

The economy is based on subsistence agriculture, cattle raising, and fishing. Tourism is developing rapidly, and the sale of long-term tuna-fishing rights, principally to Japan, Australia, and the United States, is an important earner of foreign exchange.

▶**VENEZUELA**
Republic of Venezuela

● **GEOGRAPHY** **Location:** northern coast of South America. **Boundaries:** Caribbean Sea to N, Guyana to E, Brazil to S, Colombia to W. **Total area:** 352,144 sq. mi. (912,050 sq km). **Coastline:** 1,739 mi. (2,800 km). **Comparative area:** slightly more than twice the size of California. **Land use:** 4% arable land; 1% permanent crops; 20% meadows and pastures; 34% forest and woodland; 41% other; includes negl. % irrigated. **Major cities:** (1990 est.) Caracas (capital) 3,435,795; Maracaibo 1,400,643; Valencia 1,274,354; Maracay 956,656; Barquisimeto 787,359.

● **PEOPLE** **Population:** 23,203,466 (1999 est.). **Nationality:** noun—Venezuelan(s); adjective—Venezuelan. **Ethnic groups:** Spanish, Italian, Portuguese, Arab, German, African, indigenous people. **Languages:** Spanish (official), native dialects (spoken by about 200,000 Amerindians in remote interior). **Religions:** 96% nominally Roman Catholic, 2% Protestant.

● **GOVERNMENT** **Type:** republic. **Independence:** July 5, 1811 (from Spain). **Constitution:** Jan. 23, 1961. **National holiday:** Independence Day, July 5. **Head of Government:** Hugo Chávez Frías, president (since Feb. 1999). **Structure:** executive (president); bicameral legislature (National Congress—Senate, Chamber of Deputies); judiciary.

● **ECONOMY** **Monetary unit:** bolívar. **Budget:** (1996 est.) *income:* $11.99 bil.; *expend.:* $11.48 bil. **GDP:** $194.5 bil., $8,500 per capita (1998 est.). **Chief crops:** corn, sorghum, sugarcane, rice, bananas, vegetables, coffee; beef, pork, milk, eggs; fish. **Natural resources:** crude oil, natural gas, iron ore, gold, bauxite. **Major industries:** petroleum, iron ore mining, construction materials. **Labor force:** 9.2 mil. (1997); 64% services, 23% industry, 13% agriculture; 11.5% unemployment (1997). **Exports:** $16.9 bil. (f.o.b., 1998 est.); petroleum, bauxite, aluminum, steel, chemicals, agricultural products, basic manufactures. **Imports:** $12.4 bil. (f.o.b., 1998 est.); raw materials, construction materials, machinery and transport equipment. **Major trading partners:** (1989) *exports:* 57% U.S. and Puerto Rico, Colombia, Brazil; *imports:* 53% U.S., Japan, Colombia.

At the time of European contact in the early 16th century, coastal Venezuela was home to nearly 50,000 semisedentary Indians. Although the region was "discovered" by Christopher Columbus in 1498, European settlement of the area was slow in comparison with the neighboring region of New Granada. The Spaniards explored and exploited Venezuela in the 1520s, searching for gold and pearls.

Early attempts at agriculture by the Spaniards failed until they discovered that the area around Caracas (founded in 1567) could sustain the production of both wheat and cocoa. African slave labor was an important part of the economic structure, and as markets for cocoa expanded, Caracas grew in importance. Venezuela became a captaincy general (an administrative region below the level of viceroyalty) with an audiencia (high court) established at Caracas in 1577-78.

As early as 1797, Venezuelan society was in rebellion against the Spanish empire. A major hindrance to the revolutionary leadership of Simón Bolívar was the need to accommodate both the conservative landowners of the white elite and the pardos, lower class citizens of mixed African and European ancestry.

The wars of independence were particularly destructive in Venezuela, but in 1821 the region achieved independence and became part of the federation of Gran Colombia, which also included New Granada and Ecuador. By 1830 Gran Colombia was in a state of political collapse, and Venezuela became an independent republic.

The military caudillo (leader) José Antonio Páez controlled the country for three decades. With the demise of Páez and his conservative allies in the 1860s, the forces of liberalism under Antonio Guzmán Blanco took over. The Guzmán Blanco era ended during a brief civil war in 1889, won by Gen. Cipriano Castro, who proceeded to establish his own rule. In 1908 Gen. Juan Vicente Gómez occupied the presidency, and he controlled the politics of Venezuela until his death in 1935.

The shift from dictatorship to democracy began with the Generation of 28, a student movement that organized urban workers and peasants into a viable political opposition. The Generation of 28 later became the modern Democratic Action party. In 1945 a group of young military officers overthrew the conservative dictatorship and supported the Democratic Action group in writing a new democratic constitution. Democratic Action won the elections of 1947, but conservative military elements overthrew the new government the following year. The conservative coup brought Col. Marcos Pérez Jiménez to power until his ouster in 1958.

The election of Democratic Action candidate Romulo Betancourt as president marked the beginning of multiparty democratic politics in Venezuela. The stability of the system owed much to political possibilities provided by the country's petroleum revenues.

Venezuela nationalized foreign-owned oil and iron firms in 1975 and 1976, but dependence on petroleum revenues still precipitated economic and political problems for the country in the 1980s. The downturn of the global oil market caused Venezuela's economic base to shrink, and the country's massive foreign debt hindered the expansion of populist political strategies.

The Christian Democrats defeated Democratic Action in 1968 and again in 1978. Pres. Luis Herrera Campíns's administration (1979-84) took the country in a more conservative direction but Democratic Action regained the presidency in 1983 under Jaime Lusinchi.

Venezuela's huge foreign debt in the 1980s led to tight economic controls and a reduction in social spending, which posed serious problems for the government. The administration of Pres. Carlos Andrés Perez, elected in 1989, began with antigovernment riots in which hundreds died. In Feb. 1992, Latin America's oldest civilian government thwarted an attempted coup by soldiers angered over connections between high-ranking officers and drug traffickers; a second coup in November also failed. But in early 1993, Pres. Perez was suspended after the Senate ordered impeachment proceedings against him on charges he embezzled $17 million from the government; the Congress overwhelmingly elected Sen. Ramon Jose Valasquez Mujica to serve as interim president.

In early 1994 Rafael Caldera became president and immediately faced severe economic problems as the currency depreciated by more than 80 percent in only a few months caused by the collapse of Banco Latino, the nation's second largest bank. In June Caldera took extraordinary measures, imposing price and currency controls and suspending several constitutional guarantees, including the guarantee against search and arrest without a warrant. In July 1995, he restored those rights, except along Venezuela's borders with Colombia and Brazil, where crime and economic crises were most severe. Violent anti-government demonstrations continued into 1996 but Caldera persisted in austerity plans that resulted in a $1.4 bil. loan from IMF. By early 1997 inflation seemed to be in check and the economy stabilizing although the continuing fall in worldwide oil prices added more pressure for budget cuts. By the summer of 1998 Venezuela's economy was caught in the worldwide financial crisis and spinning toward chaos as the presidential election approached.

In the December elections, the two old parties (Christian Democrats and Democratic Action) which had dominated for 40 years all but disappeared. The Patriotic Pole Coalition candidate, Hugo Chavez Frias (who had led the unsuccessful coup in 1992 against President Perez) easily triumphed over Henrique Salas Romer of Project Venezuela. Two days later stock shares rose 22 percent despite Chavez' calls for redistribution of wealth, privatization of the government oil company and abolition of Congress. Chavez called for a Constitutional Assembly to rewrite the constitution (88 percent voted their approval in April 1999). In July elections for the Assembly Chavez' supporters won all but seven of 128 seats.

▶ VIETNAM
Socialist Republic of Viet Nam
● GEOGRAPHY   Location: Southeast Asia. Boundaries: China to N, Gulf of Tonkin to NE, South China Sea to E, Laos and Cambodia to W. Total area: 127,243 sq. mi. (329,560 sq km). Coastline: 2,140 mi. (3,444 km) excluding islands. Comparative area: slightly larger than New Mexico. Land use: 17% arable land; 4% permanent crops; 1% meadows and pastures; 30% forest and woodland; 48% other; includes 5% irrigated. Major cities: (1989) Hanoi (capital) 1,088,862; Ho Chi Minh City (formerly Saigon) 3,169,135; Haiphong 456,049; Da Nang 370,670; Long Xuyen 217,171.
● PEOPLE   Population: 77,311,210 (1999 est.). Nationality: noun—Vietnamese (sing., pl.); adjective—Vietnamese. Ethnic groups: 85-90% Vietnamese, 3% Chinese; ethnic minorities include Muong, Thai, Meo, Khmer, Man, Cham. Languages: Vietnamese (official); French, Chinese, English, Khmer, ethnic langs. (Mon-Khmer and Malayo-Polynesian). Religions: Buddhist, Taoist, Roman Catholic, indigenous beliefs, Islam, Protestant, Cao Dai, Hoa Hao.
● GOVERNMENT   Type: Communist state. Independence: Sept. 2, 1945 (from France). Constitution: Apr. 15, 1992. National holiday: Independence Day, Sept. 2. Heads of Government: Tran Duc Luong, president, (since Sept. 1997); Phan Van Khai, prime minister (since Sept. 1997). Structure: executive—president, prime minister, cabinet; unicameral legislature; judiciary—elected by legislature.
● ECONOMY   Monetary unit: new dong. Budget: (1997 est.) income: $5.6 bil.; expend.: $6 bil. GDP: $134 bil., $1,770 per capita (1997 est.). Chief crops: paddy rice, corn, potatoes, rubber, soybeans, coffee, tea, bananas; poultry, pigs; fish. Natural resources: phosphates, coal, manganese, bauxite, chromate. Major industries: food processing, textiles, machine building. Labor force: 32.7 mil. (1990 est.); 65% agriculture, 35% industry and services, 25% unemployment (1995 est.). Exports: $9.4 bil. (f.o.b., 1998 est.); crude oil, marine products, rice, coffee, rubber, tea, garments, shoes. Imports: $11.4 bil. (f.o.b., 1998 est.); machinery and equipment, petroleum products, fertilizer, steel products, raw cotton, grain, cement, motorcycles. Major trading partners: exports: Japan, Germany, Singapore; imports: Singapore, South Korea, Japan.

The southward expansion of the Chinese empire in the first millennium B.C. drove the Vietnamese peoples southward into northern Vietnam (Tonkin). The area came under direct Chinese rule in 111 B.C. Chinese rule endured, with some interruptions, until A.D. 948; thereafter, Vietnam was independent under strong Chinese influence.

The Hindu-Buddhist kingdom of Annam, in central Vietnam, gradually increased in size and power at the expense of Tonkin, to the north, and the Khmer empire and Champa, to the west and south. In 1558 the kingdom of Annam split, with independent courts established at Hanoi, controlling Tonkin and the Red River valley, and Hue, in central Vietnam. A remnant of the old Champa state remained independent in the Mekong delta in the south. In 1802 the monarchy was reunited, with the court at Hue controlling all of Vietnam and exercising hegemony over Cambodia.

European penetration of the region began in the 16th century; by the early 19th century, France was the dominant foreign power in Indochina. Efforts to establish French military control began in 1858-59 with the establishment of a colony in Cochin China, in southern Vietnam. Campaigns in the Red River valley in 1873 and 1882 were complicated by Chinese intervention and the determined resistance of the Vietnamese court. In 1884 separate protectorates were established in Tonkin and Annam; in 1887 those, along with Cochin China and Cambodia, were combined into the Union of Indochina under French colonial rule. Rubber plantations were established, and rice and timber exports were under French control. A nationalist rebellion under Phan Boi Chau was suppressed in the early 20th century.

Nationalist resistance to French colonialism continued, resulting in the creation in 1939 of the Vietminh, or Independence League. In 1940 Japanese troops occupied French Indochina, with the collaboration of colonial administrators loyal to the Vichy regime. The Vietminh spearheaded anti-Japanese guerrilla resistance and in 1945 forced the abdication of King Bao Dai, head of a pro-Japanese puppet state. In 1945 France reoccupied Indochina; in 1946 the leader of the Vietminh, Ho Chi Minh, became president of a separatist government at Hanoi. France ceded local autonomy to Tonkin and Annam but sought to retain Cochin China as a colony. Fighting between the French and the Vietminh resumed. On July 1, 1949, the French reinstalled Bao Dai as king of Vietnam, and in February 1950 recognized the independence of Vietnam within the French Union. Ho Chi Minh's republican government also claimed control of all of Vietnam.

Fighting between the two rivals culminated in the French defeat at Dienbienphu on May 7, 1954. An armistice was concluded according to which the country was partitioned at a demilitarized zone at latitude 17° north, the northern part going to the Communist-controlled Vietminh government, the southern to Bao Dai. Nearly one million refugees, including many ethnic Chinese, fled from the north to the south. An international conference in Geneva agreed that elections would be held throughout Vietnam in 1956. In June 1954 Ngo Dinh Diem became premier of South Vietnam; full sovereignty in the south was transferred by France to the Vietnamese government in December 1954. In October 1955 Diem held elections in the south that resulted in the dismissal of Bao Dai as king and the proclamation of an independent Republic of Vietnam.

The scheduled elections of 1956 were never held. French troops withdrew from South Vietnam in that year. Fighting continued in the south, as the Vietminh-backed National Liberation Front (Vietcong) sought to overthrow the Diem government. On Dec. 31, 1959, the Democratic Republic of Vietnam in the north adopted a new constitution calling for the reunification of the country; northern aid to the Vietcong increased significantly, as did American aid to the south. After 1962 American military advisers increased in number and combat exposure.

In 1963 widespead demonstrations, under Buddhist leadership, led to a coup on Nov. 1-2 in which Diem was deposed and assassinated. A series of short-lived military regimes followed until September 1967, when Nguyen Van Thieu was elected president. U.S. air strikes against North Vietnam began in 1964. In the same year, the flow of troops and supplies from north to south increased. American combat troops entered the war in 1965. Despite U.S.-South Vietnamese superiority in arms and troops, and total control of the air, Vietcong control over the countryside increased. Both Operation Phoenix, in which antigovernment rural leaders were assassinated, and the establishment of fortified strategic hamlets to control the rural population, failed to reverse the tide.

The combined Vietcong-North Vietnamese Tet Offensive in early 1968 resulted in serious losses for South Vietnamese and American forces. The war spread to Laos and to Cambodia, the latter bombed in 1969. American air strikes in North Vietnam were stepped up, and U.S. troop strength reached a maximum of 543,000 in 1969. In July 1969 a series of U.S. troop withdrawals began, and secret talks were initiated in search of a negotiated settlement of the war. Following heavy U.S. bombardment of the north in 1972, a cease-fire agreement was signed in Paris by South Vietnam, North Vietnam, the Vietcong, and the United States on Jan. 27, 1973. It was never implemented, but the American withdrawal continued. In early 1975 South Vietnamese forces collapsed in the face of a series of North Vietnamese-Vietcong offensives. Remaining U.S. personnel were evacuated, and Saigon fell on Apr. 30, 1975. Hundreds of thousands of refugees ("boat people") fled the country over the next decade.

Following the fall of Saigon, the country was occupied by northern troops and administrators. Businesses were nationalized, agriculture collectivized, and tens of thousands of people sent to labor camps for "reeducation." A unified National Assembly met in 1976, and the country was officially reunified on July 2, 1976, under the existing government of the north. Saigon was renamed Ho Chi Minh City. A Soviet naval base was established at the former U.S. base at Cam Ranh Bay.

In 1978 Vietnamese troops occupied Cambodia (called Kampuchea at the time) ousting the government of Pol Pot and installing Heng Samrin as premier. In February 1979 China launched an unsuccessful attack over its border with Vietnam to display displeasure with the invasion of Cambodia and with the treatment of ethnic Chinese in Vietnam. In 1988 Vietnam pledged to withdraw its troops from Cambodia and completed the withdrawal in September 1989.

Vietnam's communist government ruled through the party's powerful Central Committee; no strong personalities emerged to replace the leaders of the wartime generation. The economy functions only at a basic level, with the infrastructure in disrepair and agriculture and small business hampered by excessive collectivization and central planning. The collapse of the Soviet Union brought about a drastic reduction of the Soviet aid that had kept the Vietnamese economy afloat.

Facing economic ruin, Vietnam's leadership eventually turned a blind eye to individual private enterprise. By 1992 the government was encouraging foreign investment.

Resumption of contacts with the United States had been precluded by American insistence that Vietnam account more fully for American prisoners of war and troops missing in action. But high-level talks on the normalization of relations and the Cambodian question opened in 1990, and the success of those negotiations helped to open diplomatic channels between Vietnam and the United States.

In 1994, Pres. Clinton, satisfied with Vietnam's efforts to account for POWs and MIAs, ended the 19-year U.S. trade embargo against Vietnam; the following day, American firms were operating in Ho Chi Minh City. In January 1995, low-level diplomatic ties were established, and in July, full diplomatic relations were granted.

In October 1995, Vietnam's National Assembly adopted its first-ever national civil code under the Communist government. The document, which took 10 years to draft, spelled out rights to land, personal property, inheritances, and raising capital. Close to 90 percent of the Assembly members voted in favor of the code, which went into effect in July 1996.

In recent years the Government has encouraged many Western companies to build factories and open businesses but poverty and the Asian financial crisis have made progress very slow in this regard. In March 1998 Pres. Clinton waived the Jackson-Vanik amendment in order to permit U.S. firms in Vietnam to borrow from the Import-Export Bank. In the same month Pope John Paul II was able to name a new Catholic archbishop of Ho Chi Minh City (though the government in July announced that it was stepping up control of religion).

▶ **WESTERN SAMOA**
see "Samoa"

▶ **YEMEN**
Republic of Yemen
● **GEOGRAPHY   Location:** southern shore of Arabian peninsula and southwest corner of Arabian peninsula. **Boundaries:** Saudi Arabia to N, Oman to E, Gulf of Aden to S, Red Sea to W. **Total area:** 203,850 sq. mi. (527,970 sq km). **Coastline:** 1,184 mi. (1,906 km). **Comparative area:** slightly larger than twice the size of Wyoming. **Land use:** 3% arable land; negl. % permanent crops; 30% meadows and pastures; 4% forest and woodland; 63% other; includes 1% irrigated. **Major cities:** (1995 est.) Sana'a (capital) 972,000; Aden 562,000; Hodeida 155,110; Mukalla 154,360; Taiz 178,043.
● **PEOPLE   Population:** 16,942,230 (1999 est.). **Nationality:** noun—Yemini(s); adjective—Yemeni. **Ethnic groups:** predominantly Arab; Afro-Arab concentrations in western coastal locations; South Asians in southern regions; small European communities in major metropolitan areas. **Languages:** Arabic. **Religions:** Muslim including Shaf'i (Sunni) and Zaydi (Shia), small numbers of Jewish, Christian, and Hindu.
● **GOVERNMENT   Type:** republic. **Independence:** May 22, 1990 (merger of North and South Yemen). **Constitution:** May 16, 1991: amended Sept. 29, 1994. **National holiday:** Proclamation of the Republic, May 22. **Heads of Government:** Ali Abdullah Saleh, president of Republic of Yemen (since May 1994); Abdul-Karim Ali al-Iryani, prime min-

ister of Republic of Yemen (since May 1998). **Structure:** executive—president and cabinet; unicameral legislature; judicial—Supreme Court and lesser courts.
● **ECONOMY   Monetary unit:** Yemeni rial. **Budget:** (1998 est.) *income:* $2.3 bil.; *expend:* $2.6 bil. **GDP:** $12.1 bil., $740 per capita (1998 est.). **Chief crops:** grain, fruits, vegetables, qat, coffee, cotton; dairy products, poultry, meat; fish. **Natural resources:** petroleum, fish, rocksalt, marble, small deposits of coal. **Major industries:** crude oil, petroleum refining, cotton textiles and leather goods, food processing, handicrafts, aluminum products, cement. **Labor force:** mostly agriculture and herding; also services, construction, industry, commerce. **Exports:** $1.6 bil. (f.o.b., 1998 est.); crude oil, cotton, coffee, dried and salted fish. **Imports:** $2.8 bil., (c.i.f., 1998 est.); food and live animals, machinery and equipment, manufactured goods. **Major trading partners:** *exports:* 31% China, 19% S. Korea, 17% Thailand; *imports:* 9% UAE, 8% Saudi Arabia, 7% US, 6% France.

Yemen—in ancient times Sheba or Saba—is strategically located in the southwestern corner of the Arabian peninsula, near the southern end of the Red Sea. In biblical times and for many centuries thereafter, Yemen dominated the caravan trade in spices, gold, and other luxury goods from India and Africa to the Middle East.

The Islamic unification of Arabia in 628 resulted in the incorporation of Yemen into Arabia as a whole, but many local uprisings broke out over the course of the following three centuries. In the 10th century, control passed to a line of Yemeni kings who were simultaneously imams of the Zaidi sect of Islam; the Zaidi imams ruled until 1962.

Aden was the most important port of the ancient kingdom of Sheba and retained that status under the Zaidi imams of Yemen. Portuguese activity around Aden began in the 15th century; from the mid-16th century, control of the port was disputed by the Portuguese, the Yemeni kings, the Ottoman Turks, and, later, the British.

In 1839, Aden was made a British Crown Colony; the Hadramaut region of southern Arabia, north and east of Aden, became the British Protectorate of Aden. The colony and protectorate were both administered as part of British India.

Yemen came under the control of the Ottoman Empire from the mid-16th to the mid-17th centuries, and again from 1849 to 1918. The Turks were expelled at the end of World War I, and Yemen became an independent kingdom in 1918. The kingdom's independence was threatened by a Saudi invasion in 1934 and by a 1954 dispute with Great Britain over the status of Aden, which was the key to British military power in the western Indian Ocean and Persian Gulf after India's independence in 1947.

Imam Ahmed came to the throne of Yemen in 1948, following the assassination of his predecessor. Most of Yemen's large Jewish population was evacuated to Israel in 1949-50. A palace coup against the imam in 1955 failed, but after his death in 1962, his successor was quickly ousted and the country was proclaimed the Yemen Arab Republic (North Yemen) under the leadership of Brig. Gen. Abdullah al-Salal.

A struggle for independence began in Aden and the protectorate in 1963, with two rival groups competing for power. The National Liberation Front (NLF) gained the upper hand over the

Egyptian-backed Front for the Liberation of Occupied South Yemen, as both groups waged guerrilla war against the British. British forces withdrew in 1967, and South Yemen became independent on Nov. 30 of that year. The nation's territory included Socotra and adjacent islands off the Horn of Africa, which had been British possessions since 1876.

In 1969 a leftist faction of the NLF seized power, nationalized key industries, and instituted a socialist regime. In the mid-1970s, South Yemeni troops aided leftist guerrillas in Oman, and fought in Ethiopia against Eritrean rebels. Subsequently Pres. Salem Robaye Ali took a more moderate stance and improved relations with Oman and Saudi Arabia. He was overthrown in a coup in June 1978 and executed. The succeeding government was overthrown in another coup on Jan. 13, 1986; on Feb. 8, Hasin Said Numan became prime minister.

In North Yemen, civil war between royalist and republican factions lasted until April 1970, when a coalition republican government was formed with the aid of Saudi mediation. Col. Ibrahim al-Hamidi came to power in a military coup on June 13, 1974; he was assassinated on Oct. 11, 1977. Pres. Ali Abdullah Saleh assumed office on July 17, 1978, following the assassination of previously elected Pres. al-Gashmi.

Border skirmishes between North Yemen and South Yemen broke out during 1972-73. After several years of uneasy peace, South Yemen launched a full-scale war against the north on Feb. 24, 1979. Arab League pressure quickly led to a mutual disengagement. Relations improved during the 1980s and North Yemen and South Yemen merged as the Republic of Yemen on May 22, 1990. Ali Abdullah Saleh, president of North Yemen, became the new country's president; Ali Salem Al-Baidh, secretary of the South Yemeni Socialist party, was elected vice president by the unified Parliament. San'a was proclaimed the capital of the United Yemen, though Aden remained its most important economic center.

The Gulf War forced the repatriation of tens of thousands of Yemeni workers from Kuwait and other Gulf states; later Saudi Arabia expelled 850,000 more to express its displeasure with Yemen's unenthusiastic stance toward the Gulf War. These repatriations deprived Yemen of a most important source of foreign exchange, and severely damaged the economy.

Yemen held its first general election since unification on Apr. 27, 1993, and a coalition government was formed in June. In Aug. 1993, Vice Pres. Baidh left San'a for Aden protesting northern centralization and dominance. Jordanian mediation seemed to bring the crisis to an end in Feb. 1994, but fighting began almost immediately, and a full-scale civil war broke out in May. But in July the capture of Aden by government troops ended the conflict and Pres. Saleh has ruled in relative peace since. The first direct presidential election was held in Sept. 1999 but the Socialist Party was not allowed to field a candidate so Saleh won easily.

Yemen's economy has remained largely agricultural until recent years. Cotton is the chief agricultural export. Oil was discovered in North Yemen in 1984 and in South Yemen in 1987; commercial deliveries of crude oil from both areas commenced in 1987. Shipping services in the port of Aden form an important part of the country's commercial economy.

► **YUGOSLAVIA**
Federal Republic of Yugoslavia
(Note: The U.S. does not formally recognize the union of Serbia and Montenegro as Yugoslavia.)
● **GEOGRAPHY Location:** Southern central Europe. **Boundaries:** Hungary to N, Romania to NE, Bulgaria to E, Macedonia and Albania to S, Adriatic Sea, Bosnia and Herzegovina to W., Croatia to NW. **Total area:** 39,517 sq. mi. (102,350 sq km). **Coastline:** 124 mi. (199 km). **Comparative area:** Slightly smaller than Kentucky. **Land use:** N.A. **Major cities:** (mid-1992 est.) Belgrade (capital) 1,500,000; Nis 300,000; Kragujevac 250,000; Novi Sad 250,000; Podoricj 80,000.
● **PEOPLE Population:** 11,206,847 (July 1999 est.). **Nationality:** noun—Serb(s) and Montenegrin(s); adjective—Serbian and Montenegrin. **Ethnic groups:** 63% Serbian, 14% Albanian, 6% Montenegrin, 4% Hungarian, 13% other. **Languages:** 95% Serbo-Croatian (official), 5% Albanian. **Religions:** 65% Orthodox, 19% Muslim, 4% Roman Catholic, 1% Protestant, 11% other.
● **GOVERNMENT Type:** republic. **Independence:** Proclaimed itself successor to former Socialist Federal Republic of Yugoslavia Apr. 11, 1992. **Constitution:** Apr. 27, 1992. **National holiday:** St. Vitus Day, June 28. **Heads of Government:** Slobodan Milosevic, president (since July 1997); Momir Bulatovic, prime minister (since May 1998); **Structure:** executive—president; bicameral legislature; judiciary—judges elected by legislature.
● **ECONOMY Monetary unit:** Yugoslav new dinar. **Budget:** N.A. **GDP:** $25.4 bil., $2,300 per capita (1998 est.). **Chief crops:** cereal, fruits, vegetables, tobacco, olives; cattle, sheep, goats. **Natural resources:** oil, gas, coal, antimony, copper. **Major industries:** machine building, metallurgy, mining, consumer goods, electronics, petroleum products, chemicals, pharmaceuticals. **Labor force:** 2.178 mil. (1994), 41% industry, 35% services, 12% trade and tourism, 7% transportation and communication, 5% agriculture. **Exports:** $2.3 billion (f.o.b., 1998 est.); manufactured goods, food and live animals, raw materials. **Imports:** $3.9 bil. (c.i.f., 1998 est.); machinery and transport equipment, fuels and lubricants, manufactured goods, chemicals, food and live animals, raw materials. **Major trading partners:** Bosnia and Herzegovnia, Italy, Germany.

The lands that composed Yugoslavia until 1991 were incorporated into the Roman Empire as the province of Illyricum in the first century A.D. Christianity became dominant by A.D. 600. Its nucleus was Serbia, settled in the seventh century by South Slav migrants from the Over and Vistula, and converted to Christianity, in its Eastern Orthodox form, in the ninth century. Twice (in 1077 and again in 1202), the Vatican sent royal crowns to Serbian kings, emphasizing their independence, despite the religious differences. Serbia's medieval zenith came during the reign of Stephen Dushan (1331-55), who subjected Albania, Macedonia, Thessaly, and Epirus to his rule, and who gained the vassalage of Bulgaria in addition. But within 30 years of his death, the Ottoman Turks had overrun his realm, a dominance sealed by the Serbian catastrophe at the Battle of Kosovo (1389). Not until 1878 did Serbia regain independence.

The complexities of Balkan politics occupied European statesmen throughout the late 19th century, and the Balkan Wars of 1912 and 1913 led directly to the outbreak of World War I. After the collapse of the Austro-Hungarian Empire during the war, the multiethnic and multinational state of Yugoslavia was patched together in 1918-19. To Serbia were annexed the old Austro-Hungarian lands of Slovenia and Croatia, as well as the ethnically Croatian and Serbian lands of Bosnia and Herzegovina in the northwest, and, in the south and southwest, Montenegro, Macedonia, and Kosovo. The last three were Serbian, Bulgarian, and Albanian in nationality, respectively.

The nationalities coexisted in a state of mutual hostility, provoking a royal dictatorship, instituted by King Alexander in 1929 and enduring after his assassination in 1934. Hitler invaded Yugoslavia in 1941; German troops were welcomed in Croatia as liberators from the Serbs. Resistance began almost immediately, split into two mutually hostile groups: Draza Mihajlovic's Serbian royalist Chetniks, and the Partisans, a group of pan-Yugoslav Communists and non-Serbian anti-German forces led by Tito (a.k.a. Josip Broz). By the end of the war, over 2 million Yugoslavs had died, and 3.5 million were homeless. As marshal, backed by both Churchill and Stalin, Tito ruled over a ruined land: the newly created Federal People's Republic of Yugoslavia.

Until World War II, Yugoslavia was primarily agricultural and pastoral, with peasants who were virtual serfs living on a subsistence level in a largely infertile land. Agriculture was more prosperous in the northern river valleys that formerly had been under Austro-Hungarian control, and there was some industrialization in those areas as well. Virtually all of these areas had to be rebuilt after the war.

Tito imposed agricultural collectivization on the Stalinist model, and pushed for the development of industry under state ownership. Politically, harsh repression fell on members of the Chetnik resistance as well as on the Slovene Home Guard and the Croatian Ustasa. But the postwar period of tyranny was short-lived.

Tito had achieved power as an independent Communist leader and refused to permit Yugoslavia to become a Soviet satellite. In March 1948 he expelled Russian military advisers, and was himself expelled from the Cominform.

In the face of economic pressure and military threats, Tito turned westward. Stalinism yielded to decentralized communism. The 1953 Agrarian Reform Law permitted private agricultural smallholdings, and over 80 percent of the land returned to private ownership; in the rest, "self-management" rather than central control was encouraged. Self-management was instituted in the industrial sector as well, with emphasis varying between capital goods and consumer goods. Economic growth averaged over 7 percent per year for three decades, lifting Yugoslavia into the ranks of the semideveloped countries.

Despite a reconciliation with Khruschev's Soviet Union in 1955-56, Tito continued to chart an independent course, taking a leading role in the Third World Non-Aligned Movement and providing a political and economic alternative model for Eastern Europe. But Yugoslavian nationalism masked the development of separate nationalisms within the Yugoslavian federation.

The country's three major ethnic groups (Serbs, Croats, and Muslims) coexisted peacefully under Tito's iron hand, and even after Tito's death in 1980, his rotating presidency scheme, in which the leaders of each republic took turns serving as "president of the presidency," worked smoothly, as long as Yugoslavia was dominated by com-

munism. But when communism fell in 1989, only Serbia and Montenegro voted for Communist governments, while the republics of Croatia, Slovenia, Macedonia, and Bosnia-Herzegovina sought independence.

A vicious civil war ensued in which Yugoslavia's Serbian president Slobodan Milosevic sought to keep all ethnically Serbian areas under Serbian control. While Serb militias captured about one-third of Croatia in 1991, the Croatian army won back most of the region in 1995. And Yugoslavia's attempt to keep Bosnia-Herzegovina within a "greater Serbia" failed as well, the failure ratified in the November 1995 "Dayton Accords," which brought NATO peacekeepers to the region. The year 1996 saw the formal end of the civil wars, as Milosevic endorsed treaties guaranteeing the boundaries of Macedonia, Croatia and Bosnia; additionally, a pact with the Albanians of Serbia's Kossovo province permitted Albanian as the language of instruction in Kossovo's schools.

Though Milosevic and his political allies won 84 of 138 seats in Yugoslavia's parliament in November 1996, the political opposition, called Zajedno ("Together"), won control of 14 large cities later in the month. The annulments of these results by Yugoslav courts and electoral commissions provoked 11 weeks of popular protests until Milosevic conceded (in Feb. 1997) and the Serbian parliament approved the Zajedno victories. In July, however, Milosevic maneuvered to take back the presidency by receiving a majority of votes in Parliament. In 1998 ethnic Albanians in the Kosovo province of Serbia launched a terrorist campaign to secede from Serbia and join Albania. The Serbs put down the rebellion with unexpected ferocity. In the winter of 1999 Serbia launched a full-scale attack against Kosovo that drove 700,000 ethnic Albanians from their homes. Despite NATO warnings, Pres. Milosevic continued his ethnic cleansing of Serbia's province and at the end of March NATO began a bombing campaign that lasted 72 days. (See Part I, "Major News Stories of the Year.")

▶ **ZAIRE (SEE CONGO, DEMOCRATIC REPUBLIC)**

▶ **ZAMBIA**
Republic of Zambia
● **GEOGRAPHY** **Location:** landlocked country in southern central Africa. **Boundaries:** Zaire to N, Tanzania to NE, Malawi to E, Mozambique to SE, Zimbabwe to S, Namibia to SW, Angola to W. **Total area:** 290,583 sq. mi. (752,610 sq km). **Coastline:** none. **Comparative area:** slightly larger than Texas. **Land use:** 7% arable land; negl. % permanent crops; 40% meadows and pastures; 39% forest and woodland; 14% other. **Major cities:** (1990 census) Lusaka (capital) 982,362; Kitwe 338,207; Ndola 376,311; Kabwe 166,519.
● **PEOPLE** **Population:** 9,663,535 (1999 est.). **Nationality:** noun—Zambian(s); adjective—Zambian. **Ethnic groups:** 98.7% African, 1.1% European, 0.2% other. **Languages:** English (official), major vernaculars—Bemba, Kaonda, Lozi, Lunda, Luvale, Nyanja, Tonga, and about 70 indigenous languages. **Religions:** 50-75% Christian, 24-49% Muslim and Hindu, 1% indigenous beliefs.
● **GOVERNMENT** **Type:** republic. **Independence:** Oct. 24, 1964 (from UK). **Constitution:** Aug. 2, 1991. **National holiday:** Independence Day, Oct. 24. .**Heads of Government:** Frederick Chiluba, president (since Nov. 1991). **Structure:** execu-

tive—modified presidential system; legislative—unicameral National Assembly; judiciary.

• **ECONOMY Monetary unit:** kwacha. **Budget:** (1995 est.) *income:* $888 mil.; *expend.:* $835 mil. **GDP:** $8.3 bil., $880 per capita (1998 est.). **Chief crops:** corn, sorghum, rice, peanuts, sunflower seed, tobacco, cotton, sugarcane, cassava; cattle, goats, pigs, poultry, beef, pork, milk, eggs, hides. **Natural resources:** copper, cobalt, zinc, lead, coal. **Major industries:** copper mining and processing, foodstuffs, construction. **Labor force:** 3.4 mil.; 85% agriculture, 9% transport and services, 6% mining, manufacturing, and construction. **Exports:** $905 mil. (f.o.b., 1998 est.); copper, cobalt, zinc, lead, tobacco. **Imports:** $1.1 bil. (f.o.b., 1998 est.); machinery, transport equipment, foodstuffs, fuels, petroleum products, electricity. **Major trading partners:** Saudi Arabia, Japan, South Africa.

Bantu peoples—including Luba, Lunda, Ngoni, and others—moved into what is now Zambia between the 15th and the 19th centuries, displacing or absorbing aboriginal populations. Occasional Portuguese explorers from Angola and Mozambique entered the region, and Angolan slave-raiders were active in the late 18th and early 19th centuries, but serious European influence did not begin until the mid-19th century. At that time British missionaries and merchants arrived, most notably David Livingstone and Cecil Rhodes.

Local rulers granted mineral concessions to Rhodes in both Northern and Southern Rhodesia (now Zambia and Zimbabwe). Rhodesia was declared a British sphere of influence in 1888; a British protectorate was established in 1891 and enlarged in 1894-95. The borders of Northern Rhodesia were established in 1911. The country was administered by the British South Africa Co. until 1924, when direct colonial rule began. Large numbers of British settlers arrived and developed farms and ranches and mined the region's substantial copper deposits. A railroad was built linking Northern Rhodesia with Elizabethville in the Belgian Congo (now Lubumbashi, Zaire).

In 1953 Northern and Southern Rhodesia (Zimbabwe) were joined with Nyasaland (now Malawi) to form the Federation of Rhodesia and Nyasaland. The country entered a period of unrest with native peoples demanding greater participation in government, while white settlers clung to their privileged positions.

As the result of an election in 1962, the federation was dissolved in 1963. A National Assembly was created on the basis of a broader, multiracial electorate. Northern Rhodesia became independent as the Republic of Zambia on Oct. 24, 1964. Relations between Zambia and white-ruled Rhodesia (formerly Southern Rhodesia) became strained in 1965 in a dispute over ownership and administration of the railway that spanned both countries. A new constitution was promulgated in 1973, creating a stronger presidency and a unicameral legislature; the United National Independence party was made the sole legal political party. Opposition parties were allowed to form again starting in December 1990.

Pres. Kenneth Kaunda, in office after Zambia's independence, led a generally moderate government that won the support of both whites and blacks. Even when there was only one legal political party, elections were, and are, freely contested, and there is substantial freedom of the press.

Zambia's economy, however, did not fare well under independence. Although the country has diverse mineral resources, copper is overwhelmingly the nation's main earner of foreign ex-

change. A steep decline in the world price of copper led to massive foreign debt and labor unrest at home. The IMF demanded reforms as a condition for future aid, and in 1987 Pres. Kaunda announced a program of economic restructuring. In 1990 his government survived an attempted coup precipitated by a doubling in the price of the staple food, maize meal.

At the end of 1991, Kaunda was defeated by Frederick Chiluba, head of the new Labor party. Chiluba's economic reforms helped Zambia repay more than $1.2 billion in outstanding debt, prompting the IMF to restore its eligibility for international loans. But political problems resurfaced when Chiluba's government found a way to block Kaunda from winning in the 1996 presidential election. Kaunda was shot and wounded by a sniper in Aug. 1997 as he continued to criticize the government. In Oct. 1997 a failed coup attempt by junior army officers was blamed on Kaunda who was arrested in Dec. and put on trial in Jan. He was freed in June and all charges dropped probably on condition that he leave politics for good.

▶ ZIMBABWE
Republic of Zimbabwe

• **GEOGRAPHY Location:** landlocked country in southern Africa. **Boundaries:** Zambia to NW, Mozambique to E, South Africa to S, Botswana to SW. **Total area:** 150,803 sq. mi. (390,580 sq km). **Coastline:** none. **Comparative area:** slightly larger than Montana. **Land use:** 7% arable land; negl. % permanent crops; 13% meadows and pastures; 23% forest and woodland; 57% other; includes negl. % irrigated. **Major cities:** (1992) Harare (capital) 1,184,169; Bulawayo 620,936; Chitungwiza 274,035; Mutare 131,808; Gweru 124,735.

• **PEOPLE Population:** 11,163,160 (1999 est.). **Nationality:** noun—Zimbabwean(s); adjective—Zimbabwean. **Ethnic groups:** 98% African (71% Shona, 16% Ndebele, 11% other), 1% white, 1% mixed and Asian. **Languages:** English (official), Shona, Sindebele. **Religions:** 50% syncretic (part Christian, part indigenous beliefs), 25% Christian, 24% indigenous beliefs, 1% Muslim.

• **GOVERNMENT Type:** parliamentary democracy. **Independence:** Apr. 18, 1980 (from UK). **Constitution:** Dec. 21, 1979. **National holiday:** Independence Day, Apr. 18. **Head of Government:** Robert Gabriel Mugabe, president (since Dec. 1987). **Structure:** executive—cabinet led by president; unicameral legislature—120 of 150 members are popularly elected, others appointed; judiciary.

• **ECONOMY Monetary unit:** Zimbabwean dollar. **Budget:** (FY96/97 est.) *income:* $2.5 bil.; *expend.:* $2.9 bil. **GDP:** $26.2 bil., $2,400 per capita (1998 est.). **Chief crops:** tobacco, corn, tea, sugarcane, cotton, wheat, coffee, peanuts; cattle, sheep, goats, pigs. **Natural resources:** coal, chromium ore, asbestos, gold, nickel. **Major industries:** mining, steel, clothing and footwear. **Labor force:** 5 mil. (1997 est.); 27% agriculture, 46% transport and services, 27% industry. **Exports:** $1.7 bil. (f.o.b., 1998 est.); tobacco, 12% gold, ferroalloys, cotton. **Imports:** $2 bil. (f.o.b., 1998 est.); 39% machinery and transport equipment, 18% manufactures, 15% chemicals, 10% fuels. **Major trading partners:** *exports:* 12% South Africa, 11% UK, 8% Germany; *imports:* 37% S. Africa, 7% UK, 6% U.S..

Massive stone structures at Great Zimbabwe give evidence of a sizable urban society that flourished from the ninth to the 13th centuries and dominated Iron Age trade in southeastern Africa. Bantu peoples migrated into the region beginning in the 15th century; the Mashona dominated until the early 19th century, when they were displaced by the Matebele.

Portuguese slave traders from Mozambique were active in Zimbabwe from the 16th to the mid-19th centuries. Mineral concessions were granted to Cecil Rhodes by local rulers in the late 19th century, and the region became a British protectorate in 1888. Salisbury (now Harare) was founded in 1890, and the territory comprising Zimbabwe and Zambia was named Rhodesia in 1895. Rhodesia was governed by the British South Africa Co. until 1923, when it was partitioned into Northern and Southern Rhodesia. Northern Rhodesia became a British colony; Southern Rhodesia, rejecting union with South Africa, became a self-governing (and whiteruled) state within the British Empire.

Southern Rhodesia had been heavily settled by whites from Great Britain, South Africa, and elsewhere, who developed extensive farms and ranches, forest products industries, and the country's rich mines. The country prospered but with little native participation in government except at the most local level.

In 1953 Northern Rhodesia, Southern Rhodesia, and Nyasaland were joined in the Federation of Rhodesia and Nyasaland. Increasing agitation for black participation in government, especially in the north and in Nyasaland, led to the dissolution of the federation in 1963; Northern Rhodesia subsequently became independent as Zambia, Nyasaland as Malawi. In 1961 Southern Rhodesia adopted a constitution that guaranteed the continuation of white rule. White resistance to black political demands led to the rise of the Rhodesian Front party, whose leader, Ian D. Smith, became prime minister of Rhodesia (formerly Southern Rhodesia). After British-led negotiations for a biracial political compromise broke down, the Smith government on Nov. 11, 1965, issued a unilateral declaration of independence, which was declared illegal and invalid by the British government.

The UN condemned the Smith government and imposed economic sanctions. In May 1968 the UN voted to impose a trade embargo on Rhodesia.

A constitution adopted in 1970 effectively barred black participation in national politics. By 1974 mounting pressure from other African countries led the Smith government to enter into more serious negotiations. Guerrilla warfare pitting black nationalist groups against white settlers and mercenaries raged sporadically throughout the country, and many white settlers emigrated. A conference in Geneva in 1976 broke down, but a 1977 British-American proposal for majority rule

provided the basis for a settlement of the crisis. An "internal settlement" was announced in April 1978 by Smith and three major nationalist leaders: Bishop Abel Muzorewa, leader of the United African National Congress, the Rev. Ndabaningi Sithole, former leader of the Zimbabwe African National Union (ZANU), and Chief Jeremiah Chirau. The settlement was rejected by the Patriotic Front that united ZANU (now led by Robert Mugabe) and Joshua Nkomo's Zimbabwe African People's Union (ZAPU).

Elections were held in April 1979 and Bishop Muzorewa assumed office on June 1 as prime minister of "Zimbabwe-Rhodesia," but the Patriotic Front continued to oppose the government. On Dec. 10 the "Zimbabwe-Rhodesia" Parliament dissolved itself, and the country reverted briefly to British colonial rule. On Dec. 21 all parties agreed to a cease-fire and to a period of transitional British rule leading to independence. International economic sanctions were lifted.

Elections held in 1980 resulted in a clear majority for Mugabe's ZANU party. Zimbabwe became independent, with Mugabe as prime minister, on April 18. As Mugabe embarked on an ambitious program of national reconstruction, Nkomo became leader of the opposition. Guerrillas linked to ZAPU, with Nkomo's tacit leadership and with alleged support from South Africa, continued to engage in sporadic warfare against Mugabe's government, and banditry disrupted the countryside.

The elections of 1985 increased ZANU's majority in Parliament. In 1987 the constitution was amended to strengthen the presidency and to end the separate role of blacks and whites in government; new elections were held for black members of Parliament to fill seats formerly reserved for whites. Guerrillas renewed attacks on white-owned farms.

In Dec. 1987 Mugabe and Nkomo agreed to merge ZANU and ZAPU (ZANU-PF), creating a de facto one-party state under Mugabe's leadership. In 1989 a new opposition party was organized by Edgar Z. Tekere, but Mugabe's rule was unchallenged. A presidential election was scheduled for 1996, but in 1995, the Rev. Ndonga Sithole, leader of the opposition Zimbabwe African National Union, was arrested and charged with plotting to kill Mugabe.

In recent years, the economy has rapidly deteriorated. By 1998 the dollar had fallen 70 percent and inflation was nearing 40 percent. Several food riots have broken out and student protests have begun. Mugabe has resisted serious reform measures and opposition to him has grown considerably.

Selected Territories Of The World

NON-SELF-GOVERNING STATES

The community of nations has long recognized the existence of territories that do not have the status of independent states and that are subordinate in some degree to another power. The United Nations refers to these as "non-self-governing territories." Except for mandates and trusteeships specified by the League of Nations and the UN, the relationships between more and less powerful

states have tended to evolve outside any rigid legal framework, and none of the following terms has an absolutely fixed meaning.

Colonies are dependent possessions whose inhabitants are not constitutionally under the dominant state's system of government but whose inhabitants are nationals of that state.

Commonwealths are autonomous states equal in status, united in their allegiance to a central power but not subordinate either to it or to one another in internal or external affairs.

Dependencies are states, provinces, or other places subject to the control of another power of which they do not form an integral part. The best known is Hong Kong, which China ceded to the United Kingdom in perpetuity in 1842, but which reverted to Chinese rule in 1997. The governor is appointed by the British monarch and foreign relations and defense are the responsibility of the UK, but Hong Kong has substantial autonomy in commercial relations.

Mandates were territories surrendered by Turkey and Germany after World War I and, according to the League of Nations, "inhabited by peoples not yet able to stand by themselves" and therefore placed under the "tutelage" of different members of the League as "mandatories on behalf of the League." The last mandate to gain independence was South West Africa, now Namibia.

Protectorates *(associated states)* are states or territories partly under the control of another state but autonomous in domestic and certain external affairs. Protectorates are established by treaties.

Territories are regions (especially of Australia, Canada, and the United States) administered by a federal government and having some degree of self-government but not organized as a province or a state.

AUSTRALIA

▶ CHRISTMAS ISLAND
Territory of Christmas Island
● **GEOGRAPHY** **Location:** eastern Indian Ocean; 10°25'S, 105°39'E. **Boundaries:** Java Head, Indonesia, 224 mi. (360 km) to N, North West Cape, Australia, 875 mi. (1,408 km) to SE. **Total area:** 52 sq. mi. (135 sq km). **Coastline:** 86 mi. (138.9 km). **Comparative area:** about seven-tenths size of Washington, D.C. **Land use:** 0% arable land; 0% permanent crops; 0% meadows and pastures; 0% forest and woodland; 100% other. **City:** The Settlement (capital).
● **PEOPLE** **Population:** 2,373 (1999 est.). **Nationality:** noun—Christmas Islander(s); adjective—Christmas Island. **Ethnic groups:** 61% Chinese, 25% Malay, 11% European, 3% other; no indigenous population. **Language:** English. **Religions:** 55% Buddhist, 15% Christian, 10% Muslim.
● **GOVERNMENT** **Type:** territory of Australia. **Constitution:** Christmas Island Act of 1958. **National Holiday:** N.A. **Head of government:** Administrator (acting) Graham Nicholls (since N.A.). **Structure:** administrator appointed by the governor general of Australia; unicameral Christmas Island Shire Council; Supreme Court.
● **ECONOMY** **Monetary unit:** Australian dollar. **Budget:** N.A. **GDP:** N.A. **Chief Crops:** N.A. **Natural resources:** phosphate. **Major industries:** phosphate extraction (near depletion). **Labor force:** N.A.; 400 people in tourism, 100 people in mining. **Exports:** phosphate. **Imports:** consumer goods. **Major trading partners:** Australia, NZ.

▶ COCOS (KEELING) ISLANDS
Territory of Cocos (Keeling) Islands
● **GEOGRAPHY** **Location:** 27 islands in eastern Indian Ocean. West Island 12°05'S, 96°53'E. **Boundaries:** island of Sumatra (part of Indonesia) about 932 mi. (1,500 km) to NE; Perth, Australia 1,720 mi. (2,768 km) to SE. **Total area:** 5.4 sq. mi. (14.0 sq km). **Coastline:** 1.6 mi. (2.6 km). **Comparative area:** about 24 times size of the Mall in Washington, D.C. **Land use:** 0% arable land; 0% perma-

nent crops; 0% meadows and pastures; 0% forest and woodland; 100% other. **City:** West Island (capital).
● **PEOPLE** **Population:** 636 (1999 est.). **Nationality:** noun—Cocos Islander(s); adjective—Cocos Islander. **Ethnic groups:** mostly Europeans on West Island and Cocos Malays on Home Island. **Languages:** English, Malay. **Religions:** 57% Sunni Muslim, 22% Christian.
● **GOVERNMENT** **Type:** territory of Australia. **Constitution:** Cocos (Keeling) Islands Act of 1995. **National Holiday:** N.A. **Head of government:** Administrator (acting) Maureen Ellis (since N.A.). **Structure:** administrator appointed by the governor general of Australia; unicameral Cocos (Keeling) Islands Shire Council; Supreme Court.
● **ECONOMY** **Monetary unit:** Australian dollar. **Budget:** N.A. **GDP:** N.A. **Chief crops:** vegetables, bananas, pawpaws, coconuts. **Natural resources:** vegetables, bananas, pawpaws, coconuts. **Major industries:** copra products. **Labor force:** N.A.; the Cocos Island Cooperative Society Ltd. employs construction workers, stevedores, and lighterage worker operations; tourism employs others. **Exports:** copra. **Imports:** foodstuffs. **Major trading partners:** Australia.

▶ NORFOLK ISLAND
Territory of Norfolk Island
● **GEOGRAPHY** **Location:** island in western Pacific Ocean; 29°04'S, 167°57'E. **Boundaries:** Vanuatu to N, New Zealand to SE, Brisbane, Australia 870 mi. (1,400 km) to W. **Total area:** 13.3 sq. mi. (34.6 sq km). **Coastline:** 20 mi. (32 km). **Comparative area:** about one-fifth size of Washington, D.C. **Land use:** 0% arable land; 0% permanent crops; 25% meadows and pastures; 0% forest and woodland; 75% other. **City:** Kingston (capital).
● **PEOPLE** **Population:** 1,905 (1999 est.). **Nationality:** noun—Norfolk Islander(s); adjective—Norfolk Islander. **Ethnic groups:** descendants of Bounty mutineers; Australian, New Zealander, Polynesians. **Languages:** English (official), Norfolk (a mixture of 18th-century English and ancient Tahitian). **Religions:** 39% Anglican, 11.7% Roman Catholic, 16.4% Uniting Church in Australia, 4.4% Seventh-Day Adventist.
● **GOVERNMENT** **Type:** territory of Australia. **Constitution:** Norfolk Island Act of 1979. **National holiday:** Pitcairners Arrival Day Anniversary, June 8. **Head of government:** Assembly President and Chief Minister George Charles Smith, (since 1997). **Structure:** administrator appointed by the governor general of Australia; unicameral nine-member elected Legislative Assembly; Supreme Court.
● **ECONOMY** **Monetary unit:** Australian dollar. **Budget:** (FY92/93) *income:* $4.6 mil.; *expend.:* $4.8 mil. **GDP:** N.A. **Chief crops:** Norfolk Island pine seed, Kentia palm seed, cereals, vegetables, fruit; cattle, poultry. **Natural resources:** fish. **Major industries:** tourism. **Labor force:** 1,395 (1991 est.) **Exports:** $1.5 mil. (f.o.b., FY91/92); postage stamps, seeds of Norfolk Island pine and Kentia Palm, small quantities of avocados. **Imports:** $17.9 mil. (c.i.f., FY91/92). **Major trading partners:** Australia, Pacific Islands, New Zealand, Asia, Europe.

▶ UNINHABITED TERRITORIES OF AUSTRALIA
Ashmore Is. (12°15'S, 123°05'E); Cartier Is. (12°30'S, 123°30'E); Coral Sea Is. (18°00'S, 158°00'E); Heard Is. (53°00'S, 73°35'E); McDonald Is. (52°29'S, 72°50'E).

DENMARK

▶ FAEROE ISLANDS

• **GEOGRAPHY   Location:** group of 18 islands (17 inhabited) in Atlantic Ocean SE of Iceland. Tórshavn 62°02'N, 6°47'W. **Boundaries:** Iceland to NW, Norwegian Sea to N, Norway to E, Shetland Islands to SE, UK to S. **Total area:** 541 sq. mi. (1,399 sq km). **Coastline:** 694 mi. (1,117 km). **Comparative area:** eight times size of Washington, D.C. **Land use:** 6% arable land; 0% permanent crops; 0% meadows and pastures; 0% forest and woodland; 94% other. **City:** (1991 est.) Tórshavn (capital) 16,223.
• **PEOPLE   Population:** 41,059 (1999 est.). **Nationality:** noun—Faroese (sing., pl.); adjective—Faroese. **Ethnic groups:** homogeneous Scandinavian population. **Languages:** Faroese (derived from Old Norse), Danish. **Religions:** Evangelical Lutheran.
• **GOVERNMENT   Type:** self-governing (since 1979) overseas administrative division of Denmark. **Constitution:** June 5, 1953 (Danish constitution). **National Holiday:** Birthday of the Queen, April 16. **Head of government:** Anfinn Kallsberg, prime minister (since Apr. 1998). **Structure:** executive—High Commissioner, Prime Minister; legislative—32-member Parliament (Lagting) islands elect 2 representatives to Danish parliament; no separate judiciary.
• **ECONOMY   Monetary unit:** Danish krone. **Budget:** (1996 est.) *income:* $467 mil.; *expend.:* $468 mil. **GDP:** $700 mil., $16,000 per capita (1996 est.). **Chief crops:** milk, potatoes, vegetables, sheep; salmon farming; fish. **Natural resources:** fish, whales. **Major industries:** fishing. **Labor force:** 20,345 (1995 est.); fishing, manufacturing, transportation, commerce. **Exports:** $362 mil. (f.o.b., 1995 est.); 92% fish and fish products, animal feedstuffs, transport equipment. **Imports:** $315.6 mil. (c.i.f., 1995 est.); 17% machinery and transport equipment, 33% consumer goods, 26.9% raw materials and semi-manufactures, 11.4% fuels, 6.7% fish and salt. **Major trading partners:** *exports:* 22.2% Denmark, 25.8% UK, 9.7% Germany; *imports:* 34.5% Denmark, 15.9% Norway, 8.4% UK.

▶ GREENLAND

• **GEOGRAPHY   Location:** North Atlantic Ocean, largely within Arctic Circle. Godthåb 64°11'N, 51°44'W. **Boundaries:** Iceland about 190 mi. (300 km) to E across Denmark Strait, Canada to SW and W across Baffin Bay and Davis Strait. **Total area:** 840,000 sq. mi. (2,175,600 sq km); land area 131,931 sq. mi. (341,700 sq km) ice free. **Coastline:** 27,400 mi. (44,087 km). **Comparative area:** slightly more than three times size of Texas. **Land use:** 0% arable land; 0% permanent crops; 1% meadows and pastures; negl. % forest and woodland; 99% other. **City:** (1992) Godthåb (Nuuk, capital), 12,233.
• **PEOPLE   Population:** 59,827 (1999 est.). **Nationality:** noun—Greenlander(s); adjective—Greenlandic. **Ethnic groups:** 87% Greenlander (Eskimos and Greenland-born whites), 13% Danish and others. **Languages:** Eskimo dialects, Danish, Greenlandic (an Inuit dialect). **Religions:** Evangelical Lutheran.
• **GOVERNMENT   Type:** self-governing overseas administrative division of Denmark. **Constitution:** June 5, 1953 (Danish constitution). **National**

Holiday: Birthday of the Queen, April 16. **Head of government:** Prime Minister Jonathan Motzfeldt (since Sept. 1997); named to post to replace Gunnar Martens, who retired ahead of scheduled election. **Structure:** prime minister is elected by the Parliament; unicameral Parliament or Landsting (31 seats); High Court or Landsrete.
• **ECONOMY   Monetary unit:** Danish krone. **Budget:** (1995 est.) *income:* $706 mil.; *expend.:* $697 mil. **GDP:** $945 mil., $16,100 per capita (1997 est.). **Chief crops:** forage crops, small garden vegetables; sheep, fish. **Natural resources:** zinc, lead, iron ore, coal, molybdenum. **Major industries:** mining, fishing. **Labor force:** 24,500 (1995 est.). **Exports:** $363.4 mil. (f.o.b., 1995 est.); fish and fish products. **Imports:** $421 mil. (c.i.f., 1995 est.); 25% machinery and transport equipment, 18% manufactured goods, 11% food and live animals, 6% petroleum products. **Major trading partners:** *exports:* 89% Denmark, 5% Japan, 5% UK; *imports:* 7.5% Denmark, 3.8% Iceland, 3.3% Japan.

FRANCE

▶ FRENCH GUIANA
Department of Guiana

• **GEOGRAPHY   Location:** NE coast of South America. **Boundaries:** North Atlantic Ocean to N, Brazil to E and S across Oyapock River, Suriname to W across Maroni River. **Total area:** 35,135 sq. mi. (91,000 sq km). **Coastline:** 235 mi. (378 km). **Comparative area:** slightly smaller than Indiana. **Land use:** negl. % arable land; negl. % permanent crops; negl. % meadows and pastures; 83% forest and woodland; 17% other. **City:** (1990) Cayenne (capital) 41,637.
• **PEOPLE   Population:** 167,982 (1999 est.). **Nationality:** noun—French Guianese (sing., pl.); adjective—French Guianese. **Ethnic groups:** 66% black or mulatto, 12% Caucasian, 12% East Indian, Chinese or Amerindian, 10% other. **Language:** French. **Religion:** predominantly Roman Catholic.
• **GOVERNMENT   Type:** overseas department of France. **Constitution:** Sept. 28, 1958 (French constitution). **National Holiday:** National Day, Taking of the Bastille, July 14. **Head of government:** President of the General Council Stephan Phinera (since March 1994); President of the Regional Council Antoine Karam (since March 1992). **Structure:** presidents of the General and Regional Councils are appointed by the members of those councils, who vote on party lines; unicameral 19-member General Council, 31-member Regional Council—both elected by popular vote to serve 6-year terms.; Court of Appeals.
• **ECONOMY   Monetary unit:** French franc. **Budget:** (1996 est.) *income:* $191 mil.; *expend.:* $332 mil. **GDP:** $1 bil., $6,000 per capita (1998 est.). **Chief crops:** rice, corn, manioc, cocoa, vegetables, bananas, sugar; cattle, pigs, poultry. **Natural resources:** bauxite, timber, gold, cinnabar, kaolin. **Major industries:** construction, shrimp processing, forestry products. **Labor force:** 58,800 (1997); 60.6% services, government and commerce, 21.2% industry, 18.2% agriculture; 25.7% unemployment (1997). **Exports:** $148 mil. (f.o.b., 1997); shrimp, timber, gold, rum, rosewood essence, clothing. **Imports:** $600 mil. (c.i.f., 1997); food

(grains, processed meat), machinery and transport equipment, fuels and chemicals. **Major trading partners:** *exports:* 60% France, 7% EU; *imports:* 62% France, 4% Germany, 4% Belgium-Luxembourg.

▶ FRENCH POLYNESIA
Territory of French Polynesia
● **GEOGRAPHY Location:** five island groups or archipelagoes—Gambier, Marquesas, Society (includes Tahiti and Bora Bora), Tuamotu, and Tubuai (Austral Islands)—in South Pacific Ocean about halfway between South America and Australia. Papeete (Society Is.) 17°32'S, 149°34'W. **Boundaries:** Kiribati to NW, Cook Islands to W. **Total area:** 2,589 sq. mi. (4,167 sq km). **Coastline:** 1,569 mi. (2,525 km). **Comparative area:** slightly less than one-third size of Connecticut. **Land use:** 1% arable land; 6% permanent crops; 5% meadows and pastures; 31% forest and woodland; 57% other. **Cities:** (1996) Papeete (capital) 25,553; Faa'a 25,888.
● **PEOPLE Population:** 242,073 (1999 est.). **Nationality:** noun—French Polynesian(s); adjective—French Polynesian. **Ethnic groups:** 78% Polynesian, 12% Chinese, 6% local French, 4% metropolitan French. **Languages:** French, Tahitian (both official). **Religions:** 54% Protestant, 30% Roman Catholic, 16% other.
● **GOVERNMENT Type:** overseas territory of France. **Constitution:** Sept. 28, 1958 (French constitution). **National Holiday:** National Day, Taking of the Bastille, July 14. **Heads of government:** President of the Territorial Government of French Polynesia Gaston Flosse (since April 4, 1991), President of the Territorial Assembly Justin Arapari (since May 13, 1996). **Structure:** presidents of the Territorial Government and Assembly are elected by the members of the assembly; unicameral Territorial Assembly (41-seats; members are elected by popular vote to serve five-year terms); Court of Appeal.
● **ECONOMY Monetary unit:** Colonial Francs Pacifique (CFP). **Budget:** (1996) *income:* $652 mil.; *expend.:* $613 mil. **GDP:** $2.6 bil., $10,800 per capita (1997 est.). **Chief crops:** coconuts, vanilla, vegetables, fruits; poultry, beef, dairy products. **Natural resources:** timber, fish, cobalt. **Major industries:** tourism, pearls, agricultural processing. **Labor force:** 70,044 employed (1988); 13% agriculture, 19% industry, 68% services. **Exports:** $212 mil. (f.o.b., 1996); 53.8% cultured pearls, coconut products, mother-of-pearl, vanilla, shark meat. **Imports:** $860 mil. (c.i.f., 1996); fuels, foodstuffs, equipment. **Major trading partners:** *exports:* 33% France, 8.5% U.S.; *imports:* 44.7% France, 13.9% U.S.

▶ GUADELOUPE
Department of Guadeloupe
● **GEOGRAPHY Location:** eastern Caribbean Sea: Guadeloupe 16°00'N, 61°42'W; St. Barthélemy 17°55'N, 63°50'W; Marie Galante 15°57'N, 61°20'W. **Boundaries:** Antigua to N, Dominica to S. **Total area:** 687 sq. mi. (1,780 sq km). **Coastline:** 190 mi. (306 km). **Comparative area:** 10 times size of Washington, D.C. **Land use:** 14% arable land; 4% permanent crops; 14% meadows and pastures; 39% forest and woodland; 29% other; includes 1% irrigated. **Cities:** (1990 census) Basse-Terre (capital) 14,107; Les Abymes 62,809; Pointe à Pitre 26,083.
● **PEOPLE Population:** 420,943 (1999 est.). **Nationality:** noun—Guadeloupian(s); adjective—Guadeloupe. **Ethnic groups:** 90% black or

mulatto, 5% white, 5% East Indian, Lebanese, Chinese. **Languages:** 99% French (official), Creole patois. **Religions:** 95% Roman Catholic, 4% Hindu and pagan African, 1% Protestant sects.
● **GOVERNMENT Type:** overseas department of France. **Constitution:** Sept. 28, 1958 (French constitution). **National Holiday:** National Day, Taking of the Bastille, July 14. **Head of government:** President of the General Council Marcellin Lubeth (since 1998), President of the Regional Council Lucette Michaux-Chevry (since March 1992). **Structure:** presidents of the General and Regional Councils are elected by the members of those councils; unicameral General Council with 42 seats, members are elected by popular vote to serve 6-year terms; unicameral Regional Council with 41 seats, members are elected by popular vote by to serve 6-year terms; Court of Appeal.
● **ECONOMY Monetary unit:** French franc. **Budget:** (1997) *income:* $200 mil.; *expend:* $350 mil. **GDP:** $3.7 bil., $9,000 per capita (1996 est.). **Chief crops:** sugarcane, bananas, tropical fruits and vegetables; cattle, pigs, goats. **Natural resources:** cultivable land, beaches and climate that foster tourism. **Major industries:** construction, cement, rum. **Labor force:** 128,000; 65% services, 20% industry, 15% agriculture; 25% unemployment. **Exports:** $133 mil. (f.o.b., 1997); bananas, sugar, rum. **Imports:** $1.7 bil. (c.i.f., 1997); foodstuffs, fuels, vehicles, clothing and consumer goods, construction materials. **Major trading partners:** (1994) *exports:* 75% France, 13% Martinique; *imports:* 64% France, 13% EU, 4% Martinique.

▶ MARTINIQUE
Department of Martinique
● **GEOGRAPHY Location:** eastern Caribbean Sea (14°36'N, 61°05'W). **Boundaries:** Dominica to N, St. Lucia to S. **Total area:** 425 sq. mi. (1,100 sq km). **Coastline:** 218 mi. (350 km). **Comparative area:** slightly more than six times size of Washington, D.C. **Land use:** 8% arable land; 8% permanent crops; 17% meadows and pastures; 44% forest and woodland; 23% other; includes 5% irrigated. **City:** (1990 census) Fort-de-France (capital) 101,540.
● **PEOPLE Population:** 411,539 (1999 est.). **Nationality:** noun—Martiniquais (sing., pl.); adjective—Martiniquais. **Ethnic groups:** 90% African and African-Caucasian-Indian mixture, 5% Caucasian, 5% East Indian, Lebanese, Chinese. **Languages:** French, Creole patois. **Religions:** 95% Roman Catholic, 5% Hindu and pagan African beliefs.
● **GOVERNMENT Type:** overseas department of France. **Constitution:** Sept. 28, 1958. **National Holiday:** National Day, Taking of the Bastille, July 14. **Head of government:** President of the General Council Claude Lise (since March 1992), President of the Regional Council Alfred Marie-Jeanne (since March 1998). **Structure:** presidents of the General and Regional Councils are elected by the members of those councils; unicameral 45-seat General Council and unicameral 41-seat Regional Assembly members are elected by popular vote to serve 6-year terms. .
● **ECONOMY Monetary unit:** French franc. **Budget:** (1996 est.) *income:* $775 mil.; *expend.:* $2.15 bil. **GDP:** $4.24 bil., $10,700 per capita (1996). **Chief crops:** bananas, pineapples, vegetables, avocados, flowers, sugarcane for rum. **Natural resources:** coastal scenery and beaches, cultivable land. **Major industries:** construction, rum, cement. **Labor force:** 160,000 (1992); 73% services, 17% industry, 10% agriculture (1997). **Ex-**

ports: $200 mil. (f.o.b., 1997); refined petroleum products, bananas, rum, pineapples. **Imports:** $1.6 bil. (c.i.f., 1997); petroleum products, crude oil, foodstuffs, construction materials, vehicles, clothing and other consumer goods. **Major trading partners:** (1991) *exports:* 57% France, 31% Guadeloupe, French Guiana; *imports:* 62% France, UK, Italy.

▶MAYOTTE
Territorial Collectivity of Mayotte
• **GEOGRAPHY Location:** Comoros archipelago in eastern Indian Ocean (12°47'S, 45°12'E). **Boundaries:** Indian Ocean to N, Madagascar 300 mi. (480 km) to SE, Mozambique Channel to S, Mozambique to W. **Total area:** 145 sq. mi. (375 sq km). **Coastline:** 115 mi. (185.2 km). **Comparative area:** slightly more than twice size of Washington, D.C. **Land use:** N.A. **Cities:** (1985 census) Dzaoudzi (capital) 5,865; Mamoudzou 12,026; Pamanzi-Labattoir 4,106.
• **PEOPLE Population:** 149,336 (1999 est.). **Nationality:** noun—Mahorais (sing., pl.); adjective—Mahoran. **Ethnic groups:** N.A. **Languages:** Mahorian (a Swahili dialect), French. **Religions:** 99% Muslim, 1% Christian (mostly Roman Catholic).
• **GOVERNMENT Type:** territorial collectivity of France. **Constitution:** Sept. 28, 1958 (French constitution). **National Holiday:** National Day, Taking of the Bastille, July 14. **Heads of government:** President of General Council Younoussa Bamana (since 1977). **Structure:** president of the General Council elected by the members of the General Council for a six-year term; unicameral 16-seat General Council members elected by popular vote to serve 3-year terms; Supreme Court.
• **ECONOMY Monetary unit:** French franc. **Budget:** (1991). *income:* N.A.; *expend.:* $73 mil. **GDP:** $85 mil., $600 per capita (1998 est.). **Chief crops:** vanilla, ylang-ylang, coffee, copra. **Natural resources:** negl. **Major industries:** newly created lobster and shrimp industry. **Labor force:** N.A. **Exports:** $3.64 mil. (f.o.b. 1996); ylang-ylang, vanilla, copra. **Imports:** $131.5 mil. (f.o.b. 1996); building materials, machinery and transportation equipment, metals, chemicals, rice, clothing, flour. **Major trading partners:** *exports:* 80% France, 15% Comoros, Reunion; *imports:* 66% France, 14% Africa, 20% Southeast Asia.

▶NEW CALEDONIA
Territory of New Caledonia and Dependencies
• **GEOGRAPHY Location:** one large and several smaller islands in western South Pacific. Nouméa 22°16'S, 166°26'E. **Boundaries:** Vanuatu to N, Australia about 930 mi. (1,500 km) to W. **Total area:** 7,359 sq. mi. (19,060 sq km). **Coastline:** 1,401 mi. (2,254 km). **Comparative area:** slightly smaller than New Jersey. **Land use:** negl. % arable land; negl. % permanent crops; 12% meadows and pastures; 39% forest and woodland; 49% other. **City:** (1989) Nouméa (capital) 65,110.
• **PEOPLE Population:** 197,361 (1999 est.). **Nationality:** noun—New Caledonian(s); adjective—New Caledonian. **Ethnic groups:** 42.5% Melanesian, 37.1% European, 8.4% Wallisian, 3.8% Polynesian, 3.6% Indonesian, 1.6% Vietnamese, 3.0% other. **Languages:** French, Melanesian-Polynesian dialects. **Religions:** 60% Roman Catholic, 30% Protestant, 10% other.
• **GOVERNMENT Type:** overseas territory of France. **Constitution:** Sept. 28, 1958 (French Con-

stitution). **National Holiday:** National Day, Taking of the Bastille, July 14. **Heads of government:** President of the Territorial Congress Simon Loueckhote (since 1998). **Structure:** president of the Territorial Congress elected by the members of the congress; unicameral 54-seat Territorial Congress members are elected by popular vote to serve 6-year terms; Court of Appeal.
• **ECONOMY Monetary unit:** Colonial Francs Pacifique (CFP). **Budget:** (1995 est.) *income:* $755.6 mil.; *expend.:* $755.6 mil. **GDP:** $2.1 bil., $11,400 per capita (1996 est.). **Chief crops:** vegetables; beef, other livestock products. **Natural resources:** nickel, chrome, iron, cobalt, manganese. **Major industries:** nickel mining. **Labor force:** 70,044 (1988 est.); 40% services, 32% agriculture, 20% industry, 8% mining. **Exports:** $500 mil. (f.o.b., 1996); ferronickels, nickel ore. **Imports:** $845 mil. (c.i.f., 1996); food, transport equipment, machinery and electrical equipment, fuels and minerals. **Major trading partners:** *exports:* 31% Japan, 29% France, 12% U.S.; *imports:* 45% France, 18% Australia, 7% Singapore.

▶RÉUNION
Department of Réunion
• **GEOGRAPHY Location:** southwestern Indian Ocean (20°15'S, 55°27'E). **Boundaries:** 500 mi. (800 km) E of Madagascar. **Total area:** 969 sq. mi. (2,510 sq km). **Coastline:** 125 mi. (201 km). **Comparative area:** slightly smaller than Rhode Island. **Land use:** 17% arable land; 2% permanent crops; 5% meadows and pastures; 35% forest and woodland; 41% other; includes 2% irrigated. **Cities:** (1990 census) Saint-Denis (capital) 121,999; Saint-Paul 71,669; Saint-Pierre 58,846.
• **PEOPLE Population:** 717,723 (1999 est.). **Nationality:** noun—Reunionese (sing., pl.); adjective—Reunionese. **Ethnic groups:** mostly intermixed French, African, Malagasy, Chinese, Pakistani, Indian ancestry. **Languages:** French (official), Creole. **Religions:** 94% Roman Catholic, Hindu, Islam, Buddhist.
• **GOVERNMENT Type:** overseas department of France. **Constitution:** Sept. 28, 1958, (French constitution). **National Holiday:** National Day, Taking of the Bastille, July 14. **Head of government:** President of the General Council Christophe Payet (since April 1994), President of the Regional Council Margarite Sudre (since June 25, 1993). **Structure:** presidents of the General and Regional Councils are elected by the members of those councils who vote on party lines; unicameral 47-seat General Council and unicameral 45-seat Regional Council members are elected by direct popular vote to serve 6-year terms.
• **ECONOMY Monetary unit:** French franc. **Budget:** (1993) *income:* $856.7 mil.; *expend.:* $2.2437 bil. **GDP:** $3.4 bil., $4,800 per capita (1998 est.). **Chief crops:** sugarcane, vanilla, tobacco, tropical fruits and vegetables. **Natural resources:** fish, arable land. **Major industries:** sugar, rum, cigarettes, handicraft items. **Labor force:** 261,000 (1995); 73% services, 19% industry, 8% agriculture; 35% unemployment (1994) **Exports:** $171.78 mil. (f.o.b., 1994); 63% sugar, 4% rum and molasses, 3% lobster, 2% perfume essences. **Imports:** $2.35 bil. (c.i.f., 1994); manufactured goods, food, beverages, tobacco, machinery and transportation equipment, raw materials, petroleum products. **Major trading partners:** *exports:* 74% France, 6% Japan, 4% Comoros; *imports:* 67% France, 4% Bahrain, 3% Italy.

▶ ST. PIERRE AND MIQUELON
Territorial Collectivity of St. Pierre and Miquelon

● **GEOGRAPHY** **Location:** North Atlantic off east coast of Canada. St. Pierre 46°46'N, 56°12'W. **Boundaries:** Newfoundland, Canada 16 mi. (25 km) to N, North Atlantic Ocean to E and S. **Total area:** 93 sq. mi. (242 sq km). **Coastline:** 75 mi. (120 km). **Comparative area:** 1.5 times size of Washington, D.C. **Land use:** 13% arable land; 0% permanent crops; 0% meadows and pastures; 4% forest and woodland; 83% other. **Cities:** (1990 census) St. Pierre (capital) 5,683; Miquelon 709.

● **PEOPLE** **Population:** 6,966 (1999 est.). **Nationality:** noun—Frenchmen; adjective—French. **Ethnic groups:** Basques and Bretons (French fishermen). **Languages:** French. **Religions:** 99% Roman Catholic.

● **GOVERNMENT** **Type:** territorial collectivity of France. **Constitution:** Sept. 28, 1958 (French constitution). **National Holiday:** National Day, Taking of the Bastille, July 14. **Heads of government:** Bernard Le Soavec, president of the General Council. **Structure:** president of the General Council is elected by members of the General Council; unicameral 19-seat General Council members are elected by popular vote to serve six-year terms; Superior Tribunal of Appeals.

● **ECONOMY** **Monetary unit:** French franc. **Budget:** (1996 est.) *income:* $70 mil.; *expend.:* $60 mil. **GDP:** $74 mil., $11,000 per capita (1996 est.). **Chief crops:** vegetables; cattle, sheep, pigs; fish. **Natural resources:** fish, deep-water ports. **Major industries:** fishing, supply base for fishing fleets, tourism. **Labor force:** 3,000 (1996). **Exports:** $1.2 mil. (f.o.b., 1996); fish and fish products, fox and mink pelts. **Imports:** $60.5 mil. (c.i.f., 1996); meat, clothing, fuel, electrical equipment, machinery, building materials. **Major trading partners:** *exports:* 58% U.S., 17% France, 11% Canada; *imports:* Canada, France, U.S.

▶ WALLIS AND FUTUNA
Territory of the Wallis and Futuna Islands

● **GEOGRAPHY** **Location:** two island groups (Wallis to NE, Hooru, incl. Futuna Is., to SW) in South Pacific. Mata-Utu (Wallis group) 13°22'S, 176°12'W. **Boundaries:** Western Samoa to E, Fiji to SW. **Total area:** 106 sq. mi. (274 sq km). **Coastline:** 80 mi. (129 km). **Comparative area:** 1.5 times the size of Washington, D.C. **Land use:** 5% arable land; 20% permanent crops; 0% meadows and pastures; 0% forest and woodland; 75% other. **City:** Mata-Utu (capital) (1983 census) 815.

● **PEOPLE** **Population:** 15,129 (1999 est.). **Nationality:** noun—Wallisian(s), Futunan(s), or Wallis and Futuna Islander(s); adjective—Wallisian, Futunan, or Wallis and Futuna Islander. **Ethnic groups:** almost entirely Polynesian. **Languages:** French (official) Wallisian (indigenous Polynesian language). **Religions:** largely Roman Catholic.

● **GOVERNMENT** **Type:** overseas territory of France. **Constitution:** Sept. 28, 1958 (French constitution). **National Holiday:** N.A. **Head of government:** President of the Territorial Assembly Victor Brial (since June 1, 1997). **Structure:** presidents of the Territorial Assembly and Government are elected by the members of the assembly; unicameral 20-seat Territorial Assembly members are elected by popular vote to serve 5-year terms; three traditional kings administer customary law and there is a magistrate in Mata-Utu.

● **ECONOMY** **Monetary unit:** Colonial Francs Pacifique (CFP). **Budget:** (1997 est.) *income:* $20 mil.; *expend.:* $20 mil. **GDP:** $28.7 mil., $2,000 per capita (1995 est.). **Chief crops:** breadfruit, yams, taro, bananas; pigs, goats. **Natural resources:** negl. **Major industries:** copra, handicrafts. **Labor force:** N.A.; 80% agriculture, livestock, and fishing, 4% government. **Exports:** $370,000. (f.o.b., 1995 est.); copra, handicrafts. **Imports:** $13.5 mil. (c.i.f., 1995 est.); foodstuffs, manufactured goods, transportation equipment, fuel, clothing. **Major trading partners:** *exports:* N.A.; *imports:* France, Australia, New Zealand.

▶ UNINHABITED TERRITORIES OF FRANCE

Bassas da India (21°25'S, 39°42'E); Clipperton Is. (10°21'N, 109°13'W); Europa Is. (22°20'S, 40°22'E); French Southern and Antarctic Lands (Kerguelen Is. 49°20'S, 69°30'E); Glorioso Is. (11°30'S, 47°20'E); Tromelin Is. (15°52'S, 54°25'E).

MOROCCO

▶ WESTERN SAHARA

● **GEOGRAPHY** **Location:** northwestern coast of Africa. **Boundaries:** Morocco to N, Algeria, Mauritania to E, Atlantic Ocean to W. **Total area:** 102,703 sq. mi. (266,000 sq km). **Coastline:** 690 mi. (1,110 km). **Comparative area:** about the size of Colorado. **Land use:** 19% arable land; 24% permanent crops; 0% meadows and pastures; 47% forest and woodland; 10% other. **City:** (1982) El Aaiun (capital) 93,785.

● **PEOPLE** **Population:** 239,333 (1999 est.). **Nationality:** noun—Sahrawi(s), Sahraoui; adjective—Sahrawian, Sahraouian. **Ethnic groups:** Arab, Berber. **Languages:** Hassaniya Arabic, Moroccan Arabic. **Religion:** Muslim.

● **GOVERNMENT** **Type:** legal status and sovereignty still unresolved. Morocco and Polisario Front have fought over this since 1976. A UN-sponsored ceasefire has been in effect since Sept., 1991. A vote is scheduled for July 2000. **Constitution:** N.A. **National Holiday:** N.A. **Head of government:** N.A. **Structure:** N.A.

● **ECONOMY** **Monetary unit:** Moroccan dirham. **Budget:** N.A. **GDP:** N.A. **Chief crops:** fruits and vegetables in the few oases; camels, sheep, goats. **Natural resources:** phosphates, iron ore. **Major industries:** phosphate, fishing, handicrafts. **Labor force:** 12,000; 50% animal husbandry and subsistence farming. **Exports:** N.A.; 62% phosphates. **Imports:** N.A.; fuel for fishing fleet, foodstuffs. **Major trading partners:** Morocco claims administrative control over Western Sahara and controls all trade with country; trade figures are included in overall Moroccan accounts.

NETHERLANDS

▶ ARUBA

● **GEOGRAPHY** **Location:** southern Caribbean Sea (12°32'N, 70°02'W), off NW Venezuela. **Boundaries:** Curaçao, Netherlands Antilles 42 mi. (68 km) to E, Venezuela 16 mi. (25 km) to S. **Total area:** 75 sq. mi. (193 sq km). **Coastline:** about 45 mi. (about 72 km). **Comparative area:** slightly larger than Washington, D.C. **Land use:** 11% arable land; 0% permanent crops; 0% meadows and pastures; 0% forest and woodland; 89% other. **City:** Oranjestad (capital).

●**PEOPLE Population:** 68,675 (1999 est.). **Nationality:** noun—Aruban(s); adjective—Aruban. **Ethnic groups:** 80% mixed European/Caribbean Indian. **Languages:** Dutch (official), Papiamento (a Spanish-Portuguese-Dutch-English dialect); English widely spoken, Spanish. **Religions:** 82% Roman Catholic, 8% Protestant; also Hindu, Muslim, Confucian, Jewish minorities.

● **GOVERNMENT** Part of the Netherlands, but full autonomy in internal affairs obtained in 1986 upon separation from Netherlands Antilles. **Type:** parliamentary. **Constitution:** Jan. 1, 1986. **National Holiday:** Flag Day, Mar. 18. **Head of government:** Prime Minister Jan. H. Eman (since July 29, 1994). **Structure:** prime minister elected by the Staten for a four-year term; unicameral 21-seat Legislature members elected by direct popular vote and serve 4-year terms; Joint High Court of Justice.

● **ECONOMY Monetary unit:** Aruban florin. **Budget:** (1997) *income:* $345.3 mil.; *expend.:* $378.5 mil. **GDP:** $1.5 bil., $22,000 per capita (1997 est.). **Chief crops:** aloes; livestock; fishing. **Natural resources:** negl.; white sandy beaches. **Major industries:** tourism, transshipment, oil refining. **Labor force:** mostly tourism. **Exports:** $1.73 bil. (f.o.b., 1997 est.); including oil re-exports; mostly petroleum products. **Imports:** $2.12 bil. (f.o.b., 1997 est.); including oil for processing and re-export, foodstuffs, consumer goods. **Major trading partners:** U.S., EU.

▶**NETHERLANDS ANTILLES**
● **GEOGRAPHY Location:** two island groups in Caribbean Sea, about 500 mi. (800 km) apart. Curaçao Is. 12°12'N, 68°56'W; St. Maarten Is. 18°03'N, 63°05'W. **Boundaries:** southern group (Curaçao and Bonaire)—Venezuela to S; northern group (St. Eustatius, Saba, and St. Maarten)— Antigua to E, Virgin Islands to W. **Total area:** 371 sq. mi. (960 sq km). **Coastline:** 226 mi. (364 km). **Comparative area:** more than 5 times size of Washington, D.C. **Land use:** 10% arable land; 0% permanent crops; 0% meadows and pastures; 0% forest and woodland; 90% other. **City:** Willemstad (capital).

● **PEOPLE Population:** 207,827 (1999 est.). **Nationality:** noun—Netherlands Antillean(s); adjective—Netherlands Antillean. **Ethnic groups:** 85% mixed African; remainder Carib Amerindian, European, East Asian. **Languages:** Dutch (official), Papiamento (a Spanish-Portuguese-Dutch-English dialect) predominates; English widely spoken; Spanish. **Religions:** predominantly Roman Catholic; Protestant, Jewish, Seventh-Day Adventist.

● **GOVERNMENT Type:** autonomous part of Netherlands; parliamentary. **Constitution:** Dec. 29, 1954. **Ethnic groups:** **National holiday:** Queen's Day, April 30. **Head of government:** Miguel Pourier, prime minister (since Feb. 1994). **Structure:** leader of the majority party is usually elected prime minister by the Staten; unicameral 22-seat Staten members are elected by popular vote to serve 4-year terms; Joint High court of Jusice, appointed by the Netherlands monarch.

● **ECONOMY Monetary unit:** Netherlands Antillean guilder. **Budget:** (1997 est.) *income:* $710.8

mil.; *expend.:* $741.6 mil. **GDP:** $2.4 bil., $11,500 per capita (1997 est.). **Chief crops:** aloes, sorghum, peanuts. **Natural resources:** phosphates (Curaçao only), salt (Bonaire only). **Major industries:** tourism on Curaçao and St. Maarten; petroleum refining on Curaçao; petroleum transshipment facilities on Curaçao and Bonaire; light manufacturing on Curaçao. **Labor force:** 89,000 (1983); 65% government, 28% industry and commerce; 13.4% unemployment (1993 est.). **Exports:** $268.2 mil. (f.o.b, 1997); 98% petroleum products. **Imports:** $1.4 bil. (c.i.f., 1997); 64% crude petroleum, food, manufactures. **Major trading partners:** *exports:* 28.6% U.S., 6.4% Honduras, 6% Belgium-Luxembourg; *imports:* 34% Venezuela, 16.4% US, 15.5% Mexico.

NEW ZEALAND

▶**COOK ISLANDS**
● **GEOGRAPHY Location:** 15 islands (13 inhabited) in South Pacific. Avarua 21°12'S, 159° 46'W. **Boundaries:** French Polynesia to E, American Samoa to W. **Total area:** 93 sq. mi. (240 sq km). **Coastline:** 75 mi. (120 km). **Comparative area:** 1.3 times size of Washington, D.C. **Land use:** 9% arable land; 13% permanent crops; 0% meadows and pastures; 0% forest and woodland; 78% other. **City:** Avarua (capital).

● **PEOPLE Population:** 20,200 (1999 est.). **Nationality:** noun—Cook Islander(s); adjective—Cook Islander. **Ethnic groups:** 81.3% Polynesian (full blood), 7.7% Polynesian and European, 7.7% Polynesian and other, 2.4% European, 0.9% other. **Languages:** English (official), Maori. **Religions:** Christian; majority of populace members of Cook Islands Christian church.

● **GOVERNMENT Type:** self-governing parliamentary democracy in free association with New Zealand; Cook Islands government is fully responsible for internal affairs and has right at any time to move to full independence by unilateral action; New Zealand responsible for external affairs, in consultation with Cook Islands government. **Constitution:** Aug. 4, 1965. **National holiday:** Constitution Day, Aug. 4. **Head of government:** Geoffrey Henry, prime minister (since Feb. 1989). **Structure:** leader of the party that wins the most seats usually becomes prime minister; unicameral 25-seat Parliament members elected by popular vote to serve 5-year terms; High Court.

● **ECONOMY Monetary unit:** New Zealand dollar. **Budget:** N.A. **GDP:** $79 mil., $4,000 per capita (1994 est.). **Chief crops:** copra, citrus fruits, pineapples, tomatoes, beans, pawpaws, bananas, yams, taro, coffee. **Labor force:** (1993) 6,601; 29% agriculture, 27% government, 25% services, 15% industry. **Natural resources:** negl. **Major industries:** fruit processing, tourism. **Exports:** $4.2 mil. (f.o.b., 1994); copra, fresh and canned citrus fruit, coffee; fish; pearls and pearl shells; clothing. **Imports:** $85 mil. (c.i.f., 1994); foodstuffs, textiles, fuels, timber, capital goods. **Major trading partners:** *exports:* 80% New Zealand, Japan, Hong Kong; *imports:* 49% New Zealand, Italy, Australia.

▶ NIUE

● **GEOGRAPHY Location:** coral island in western South Pacific (19°02'S, 169°55'W). **Boundaries:** Tonga 300 mi. (480 km) to W, southern Cook Islands 580 mi. (930 km) to E. **Total area:** 100 sq. mi. (260 sq km). **Coastline:** 40 mi. (64 km). **Comparative area:** 1.5 times size of Washington, D.C. **Land use:** 19% arable land; 8% permanent crops; 4% meadows and pastures; 19% forest and woodland; 50% other. **City:** Alofi (capital).

● **PEOPLE Population:** 2,103 (1999 est.). **Nationality:** noun—Niuean(s); adjective—Niuean. **Ethnic groups:** Polynesian, with about 200 Europeans, Samoans, Tongans. **Languages:** Polynesian dialect closely related to Tongan and Samoan; English. **Religions:** 75% Ekalesia Niue (Niuean Church)—a Christian Protestant church closely related to London Missionary Society, 10% Latter-Day Saints, 15% Roman Catholic, Jehovah's Witnesses, Seventh-Day Adventist.

● **GOVERNMENT Type:** self-governing parliamentary democracy territory in free association with New Zealand. **Constitution:** Oct. 19, 1974. **National holiday:** Waitangi Day, Feb. 6. **Heads of government:** Frank F. Lui, premier (since March 1993). **Structure:** executive—premier (elected by assembly); Legislative Assembly consists of 20 members (14 village representatives and six elected on a common roll); Supreme Court of New Zealand.

● **ECONOMY Monetary unit:** New Zealand dollar. **Budget:** (1985 est.) *income:* $5.5 mil.; *expend.:* $6.3 mil. **GDP:** $2.4 mil., $1,200 per capita (1993 est.). **Chief crops:** coconuts, passion fruit, honey, limes, taro, yams, cassava (tapioca), sweet potatoes; pigs, poultry, beef cattle. **Natural resources:** fish, arable land. **Major industries:** tourism, handicrafts. **Labor force:** 450 (1992 est.); most Niueans work on family plantations; paid work exists only in government service, small industry, and Niue Development Board. **Exports:** $117,500 (f.o.b., 1989); canned coconut cream, copra, honey, passion fruit products, pawpaw. **Imports:** $4.1 mil. (c.i.f., 1989); food, live animals, manufactured goods, machinery, fuels, lubricants, chemicals, drugs. **Major trading partners:** *exports:* 89% New Zealand, Fiji, Cook Islands; *imports:* 59% New Zealand, 20% Fiji, 13% Japan.

▶ TOKELAU

● **GEOGRAPHY Location:** three atolls (Atafu, Nukunonu, Fakaofo) in South Pacific. Atafu 8°33'S, 172°30'W. **Boundaries:** northern Cook Islands to E, Western Samoa 300 mi. (480 km) to S, Tuvalu to W. **Total area:** 4 sq. mi. (10 sq km). **Coastline:** 62 mi. (101 km). **Comparative area:** about 17 times size of the Mall in Washington, D.C. **Land use:** 0% arable land; 0% permanent crops; 0% meadows and pastures; 0% forest and woodland; 100% other. **City:** none; each atoll has own administrative center.

● **PEOPLE Population:** 1,471 (1999 est.). **Nationality:** noun—Tokelauan(s); adjective—Tokelauan. **Ethnic groups:** Polynesian. **Languages:** Tokelauan (a Polynesian language), English. **Religions:** 70% Congregational Christian church, 28% Roman Catholic; on Atafu, all Congregational Christian Church of Samoa; on Nukunonu, all Roman Catholic; on Fakaofo, both denominations.

● **GOVERNMENT Type:** territory of New Zealand. **Constitution:** administered under the Tokelau Islands Act of 1948, as amended in 1970. **National holiday:** Waitangi Day, Feb. 6. **Head of government:** Aliki Faipule Falimateao (since 1997).

Structure: head of government is chosen from the Council of Faipule and serves a one-year term; unicameral 15-seat General Fono members chosen by each atoll's Council of Elders or Taupulega to serve 3-year terms; Supreme Court.

● **ECONOMY Monetary unit:** New Zealand dollar. **Budget:** (1987) *income:* $430,830; *expend.:* $2.8 mil. **GDP:** $1.5 mil., $1,000 per capita (1993 est.). **Chief crops:** coconuts, copra, breadfruit, papaya, bananas; pigs, poultry, goats. **Natural resources:** negl. **Major industries:** small-scale enterprises for copra production, woodwork, plaited craft goods, stamps, coins. **Labor force:** N.A. **Exports:** $98,000 (f.o.b., 1983); stamps, copra, handicrafts. **Imports:** $323,400 (c.i.f., 1983); foodstuffs, building materials, fuel. **Major trading partners:** New Zealand.

NORWAY

▶ SVALBARD

● **GEOGRAPHY Location:** nine large and numerous smaller islands in Arctic Ocean. **Boundaries:** Longyearbyen (Spitsbergen Is.) 78° 13'N, 15°38'W; Bear Is. 74°30'N, 19°00'E. Norway to S, Greenland to W. **Total area:** 38,557 sq. mi. (62,049 sq km). **Coastline:** 2,229 mi.(3,587 km). **Comparative area:** slightly smaller than West Virginia. **Land use:** 0% arable land; 0% permanent crops; 0% meadows and pastures; 0% forest and woodland; 100% other; no trees; only bushes are crowberry and cloudberry. **City:** Longyearbyen (capital).

● **PEOPLE Population:** 2,503 (1999 est.). **Nationality:** N.A. **Ethnic groups:** 62% Russian and Ukrainian, 38% Norwegian. **Languages:** Russian, Norwegian. **Religions:** N.A.

● **GOVERNMENT Type:** territory of Norway. **Constitution:** N.A. **National holiday:** N.A. **Head of government:** Ann-Kristin Olsen, governor. **Structure:** governor responsible to the Polar Department of the Ministry of Justice

● **ECONOMY Monetary unit:** Norwegian krone. **Budget:** (1997 est.) *income:* $11.7 mil.; *expend.:* $11.7 mil. **GDP:** N.A. **Chief Crops:** N.A. **Natural resources:** coal, copper, iron ore, phosphate, zinc. **Major industries:** coal mining; trapping of seal, polar bear, fox, walrus. **Labor force:** N.A. **Exports:** N.A. **Imports:** N.A. **Major trading partners:** N.A.

▶ UNINHABITED TERRITORIES OF NORWAY

Bouvet Is. (54°26'S, 3°24'E); Jan Mayen Is. (71°00'N, 8°30'W).

UNITED KINGDOM

▶ ANGUILLA

● **GEOGRAPHY Location:** island in northeastern Caribbean (18°03'N, 63°04'W). **Boundaries:** St. Martin 5 mi. (8 km) to S, St. Kitts 70 mi. (113 km) to SE. **Total area:** 35 sq. mi. (91 sq km). **Coastline:** 38 mi. (61 km). **Comparative area:** about one-half size of Washington, D.C. **Land use:** N.A.; mostly

rock with sparse scrub oak, few trees, some commercial salt ponds. **City:** The Valley (capital).
• **PEOPLE Population:** 11,510 (1999 est.). **Nationality:** noun—Anguillan(s); adjective—Anguillan. **Ethnic groups:** mainly of black African descent. **Languages:** English. **Religions:** 40% Anglican, 33% Methodist, 7% Seventh-Day Adventist, 5% Baptist, 3% Roman Catholic.
• **GOVERNMENT Type:** dependent territory of UK. **Constitution:** Apr. 1, 1982. **National holiday:** Anguilla Day, May 30. **Heads of government:** Chief Minister Hubert Hughes (since Mar. 16, 1994). **Structure:** chief minister appointed by the governor from among the members of the House of Assembly; unicameral 11-seat House of Assembly members elected by direct popular vote to serve 5-year terms; High Court.
• **ECONOMY Monetary unit:** East Caribbean dollar. **Budget:** (1997) *income:* $20.4 mil.; *expend.:* $23.3 mil. **GDP:** $81 mil., $7,300 per capita (1997 est.). **Chief crops:** pigeon peas, corn, sweet potatoes; sheep, goats, cattle, poultry; fishing (including lobster). **Natural resources:** salt, fish, lobster. **Major industries:** tourism, boat building, off shore financial services. **Labor force:** 4,400 (1992); 7% unemployment (1992). **Exports:** $1.6 mil. (1997); lobsters, fish, livestock, salt. **Imports:** $54.2 mil. (1997). **Major trading partners:** N.A.

▶ **BERMUDA**
• **GEOGRAPHY Location:** archipelago of about 150 islands, in southern North Atlantic Ocean (32° 18'N, 64°47'W). **Boundaries:** Cape Hatteras 580 mi. (933 km) to W. **Total area:** 19 sq. mi. (50 sq km). **Coastline:** 64 mi. (103 km). **Comparative area:** about three-tenths size of Washington, D.C. **Land use:** 6% arable land; N.A.% permanent crops; N.A.% meadows and pastures; N.A.% forest and woodland; 55% developed and 39% rural and open space comprise 94% of Bermudian land area. **Cities:** (1990 est.) Hamilton (capital) 6,000; St. George's 3,000.
• **PEOPLE Population:** 62,472 (1999 est.). **Nationality:** noun—Bermudian(s); adjective— Bermudian. **Ethnic groups:** 61% black, 39% white and other. **Languages:** English (official), Portuguese. **Religions:** 28% Anglican, 15% Roman Catholic, 12% African Methodist Episcopal (Zion), 6% Seventh-day Adventist, 5% Methodist, 34% other.
• **GOVERNMENT Type:** British dependent territory. **Constitution:** June 8, 1968. **National holiday:** Bermuda Day, May 24. **Heads of government:** Jennifer Smith, premier (since Nov. 1998). **Structure:** premier appointed by the governor; bicameral 11-seat Parliament members appointed by the governor, 40-seat House of Assembly members are elected by popular vote to serve 5-year terms; Supreme Court.
• **ECONOMY Monetary unit:** Bermudian dollar. **Budget:** (FY97/98) *income:* $504.6 mil.; *expend.:* $537 mil. **GDP:** $1.9 bil., $30,000 per capita (1997 est.). **Chief crops:** bananas, vegetables, flowers, dairy products, citrus fruits. **Natural resources:** limestone, pleasant climate fostering tourism. **Major industries:** tourism, finance, structural concrete products. **Labor force** 35,296 (1997); 23% clerical, 22% services, 17% laborers, 17% professional and technical, 12% administrative and managerial, 7% sales, 2% agriculture and fishing. **Exports:** $57 mil. (1997); reexports of pharmaceuticals. **Imports:** $617 mil. (1997); miscellaneous manufactured articles, machinery and transport equipment, food and live animals, chemicals. **Major trading partners:** *exports:* 50% Netherlands,

13% U.S., 6% Canada; *imports:* 73% U.S., 5% UK, 4% Canada.

▶ **BRITISH VIRGIN ISLANDS**
• **GEOGRAPHY Location:** more than 40 mountainous islands (15 inhabited) in northeastern Caribbean. City of Road Town (on Tortola Is.), 18°26'N, 64°32'W. **Boundaries:** Puerto Rico about 100 mi. (161 km) to W. **Total area:** 58 sq. mi. (150 sq km). **Coastline:** 50 mi. (80 km). **Comparative area:** 0.9 times the size of Washington, D.C. **Land use:** 20% arable land; 7% permanent crops; 33% meadows and pastures; 7% forest and woodland; 33% other. **City:** (1987 est.) Road Town (capital), 2,500.
• **PEOPLE Population:** 19,156 (1998 est.). **Nationality:** noun—Virgin Islander(s); adjective— British Virgin Islander. **Ethnic groups:** over 90% black, remainder of white and Asian origin. **Languages:** English. **Religions:** 86% Protestant (45% Methodist, 21% Anglican, 7% Church of God, 5% Seventh-Day Adventist, 4% Baptist, 2% Jehovah's Witness, 2% other), 6% Roman Catholic, 2% none.
• **GOVERNMENT Type:** dependent territory of UK. **Constitution:** June 1, 1977. **National holiday:** Territory Day, July 1. **Heads of government:** Ralph T. O'Neal, chief minister (since May 1995). **Structure:** chief minister appointed by the governor from among the members of the Legislative Council; unicameral 13-seat Legislative Council members are elected by direct popular vote to serve 5-year terms; Eastern Caribbean Supreme Court.
• **ECONOMY Monetary unit:** U.S. dollar. **Budget:** (1997) *income:* $121.5 mil.; *expend.:* $115.5 mil. **GDP:** $183 mil., $10,000 per capita (1997). **Chief crops:** fruit, vegetables; livestock, poultry, fish. **Natural resources:** negl. **Major industries:** tourism, construction, rum. **Labor force:** 4,911 (1980). **Exports:** $23.9 mil. (1996); rum, fresh fish, gravel, sand, fruits, vegetables. **Imports:** $121.5 mil. (1996); building materials, automobiles, foodstuffs, machinery. **Major trading partners:** Virgin Islands (U.S.), Puerto Rico, U.S.

▶ **CAYMAN ISLANDS**
• **GEOGRAPHY Location:** three main and numerous smaller islands in western Caribbean. George Town (Grand Cayman Is.) 19°20'N, 81°23'W. **Boundaries:** Cuba to N, Jamaica 180 mi. (290 km) to SE. **Total area:** 100 sq. mi. (260 sq km). **Coastline:** 100 mi. (160 km). **Comparative area:** 1.5 times size of Washington, D.C. **Land use:** 0% arable land; 0% permanent crops; 8% meadows and pastures; 23% forest and woodland; 69% other. **Cities:** (1989 census) Georgetown (capital) 12,921; West Bay 5,632.
• **PEOPLE Population:** 39,335 (1999 est.). **Nationality:** noun—Caymanian(s); adjective—Caymanian. **Ethnic groups:** 40% mixed, 20% white, 20% black, 20% expatriates of various ethnic groups. **Languages:** English. **Religions:** United Church (Presbyterian and Congregational), Anglican, Baptist, Roman Catholic, Church of God, other Protestant denominations.
• **GOVERNMENT Type:** British dependent territory. **Constitution:** 1959, revised 1972 and 1992. **National holiday:** Constitution Day, first Monday in July. **Head of government:** John Wynne Owen, governor and president of Executive Council (since Sept. 15, 1995). **Structure:** governor is appointed by the queen; unicameral 18-seat Legislative Assembly members elected by popular vote and serve 4-year terms; Grand Court, Cayman Islands Court of Appeals.

●**ECONOMY   Monetary unit:** Caymanian dollar. **Budget:** (1997) *income:* $265.2 mil.; *expend.:* $248.9 mil. **GDP:** $930 mil., $24,500 per capita (1997 est.). **Chief crops:** fruits and vegetables; livestock, turtle farming. **Natural resources:** fish, climate and beaches that foster tourism. **Major industries:** tourism, banking, insurance, finance. **Labor force:** 19,820 (1995); 18.7% service workers, 18.6% clerical, 12.5% construction. **Exports:** $2.65 mil. (1996); turtle products, manufactured consumer goods. **Imports:** $379.4 mil. (1996); foodstuffs, manufactured goods. **Major trading partners:** *exports:* mostly U.S.; *imports:* U.S., Trinidad and Tobago, UK.

▶**FALKLAND ISLANDS**
Colony of the Falkland Islands
●**GEOGRAPHY   Location:** two large and about 2,000 smaller islands in southwestern Atlantic Ocean. Stanley (East Falkland) 51°45'S, 57° 56'W. **Boundaries:** Cape Horn, South America, about 480 mi. (770 km) to SW. **Total area:** 4,699 sq. mi. (12,173 sq km). **Coastline:** 800 mi. (1,288 km). **Comparative area:** slightly smaller than Connecticut. **Land use:** 0% arable land; 0% permanent crops; 99% meadows and pastures; 0% forest and woodland; 1% other. **City:** (1991 census) Stanley (capital) 1,557.
●**PEOPLE   Population:** 2,758 (1999 est.). **Nationality:** noun—Falkland Islander(s); adjective—Falkland Island. **Ethnic groups:** mostly British. **Languages:** English. **Religions:** predominantly Anglican, Roman Catholic, United Free Church, Evangelist Church, Jehovah's Witnesses, Lutheran, Seventh-Day Adventist.
●**GOVERNMENT   Type:** colony of UK. **Constitution:** Oct. 3, 1985. **National holiday:** Liberation Day, June 14. **Head of government:** Donald Lamont, governor (since May 1999). **Structure:** governor appointed by the queen; unicameral 10-seat Legislative Council members are elected by popular vote to serve 5-year terms; Supreme Court.
●**ECONOMY   Monetary unit:** Falkland Island pound. **Budget:** (1997/98) *income:* $66.1 mil.; *expend.:* $66.8 mil. **GDP:** N.A. **Natural resources:** fish, wildlife. **Major industries:** wool processing. **Labor force:** 1,100 (est.); 95% agriculture, mostly sheepherding. **Exports:** $7.6 mil. (1995); wool, hides, meat. **Imports:** $24.7 mil. (1995); food and drink, clothing, fuels, building materials. **Major trading partners:** UK, Netherlands, Japan.

▶**GIBRALTAR**
●**GEOGRAPHY   Location:** narrow peninsula running southward from southwest coast of Spain, to which it is connected by an isthmus. **Boundaries:** Spain to W and N, Mediterranean Sea to E, Morocco to S across Strait of Gibraltar. **Total area:** 3 sq. mi. (6.5 sq km). **Coastline:** 7.5 mi. (12 km). **Comparative area:** about 11 times size of the Mall in Washington, D.C. **Land use:** 0% arable land; 0% permanent crops; 0% meadows and pastures; 0% forest and woodland; 100% other. **City:** Gibraltar (capital).
●**PEOPLE   Population:** 29,165 (1999 est.). **Nationality:** noun—Gibraltarian(s); adjective—Gibraltar. **Ethnic groups:** Italian, English, Maltese, Portuguese, and Spanish descent. **Languages:** English and Spanish are primary languages; Italian, Portuguese, Russian also spoken; English used in schools and for official purposes. **Religions:** 74% Roman Catholic, 11% Protestant, 8% Muslim, 2% Jewish.

●**GOVERNMENT   Type:** colony of UK. **Constitution:** May 30, 1969. **National holiday:** Commonwealth Day, second Monday of March. **Heads of government:** Peter Caruana, chief minister (since May 1996). **Structure:** chief minister appointed by the governor; unicameral 18-seat House of Assembly members elected by popular votes to serve 4-year terms; Supreme Court, Court of Appeals.
●**ECONOMY   Monetary unit:** Gibraltar pound. **Budget:** (1995/96) *income:* $111.6 mil.; *expend.:* $115.6 mil. **GDP:** $500 mil., $17,500 per capita (1997 est.). **Chief crops:** N.A. **Natural resources:** negl. **Major industries:** tourism, banking and finance, construction; support to large UK naval and air bases. **Labor force:** about 14,800 (including non-Gibraltar laborers); 60% services, 40% industry. **Exports:** $83.7 mil. (f.o.b., 1995); principally re-exports—51% petroleum, 41% manufactured goods, 8% other. **Imports:** $778 mil. (c.i.f., 1995); manufactured goods, fuels, foodstuffs. **Major trading partners:** *exports:* UK, Morocco, Portugal; *imports:* UK, Spain, Japan.

▶**MONTSERRAT**
(Two years of volcanic eruptions have left the southern half of this small island covered with ash and rock. More than half of its population had fled by mid-1997)
●**GEOGRAPHY   Location:** eastern Caribbean Sea (16°44'N, 62°14'W). **Boundaries:** Guadeloupe 35 mi. (55 km) to S, Antigua 27 mi. (47 km) to NE. **Total area:** 39 sq. mi. (100 sq km). **Coastline:** 25 mi. (40 km). **Comparative area:** about three-fifths size of Washington, D.C. **Land use:** 20% arable land; 0% permanent crops; 10% meadows and pastures; 40% forest and woodland; 30% other. **City:** (1980) Plymouth (capital) 3,500.
●**PEOPLE   Population:** 12,853 (1999 est.); figures include an estimated 8,000 refugees who left the island following the resumption of volcanic activity in July 1995. **Nationality:** noun—Montserratian(s); adjective—Montserratian. **Ethnic groups:** mostly black, with a few Europeans. **Languages:** English. **Religions:** Anglican, Methodist, Roman Catholic, Pentecostal, Seventh-Day Adventist, other Christian denominations.
●**GOVERNMENT   Type:** colony of UK. **Constitution:** present constitution came into force Dec. 19, 1989. **National holiday:** Celebration of the Birthday of the Queen, second Saturday of June. **Heads of government:** Chief Minister David Brandt (since Aug. 1997). **Structure:** the leader of the majority party ususally becomes chief minister; unicameral 11-seat Legislative Council members popularly elected to serve 5-year terms; Eastern Caribbean Supreme Court.
●**ECONOMY   Monetary unit:** East Caribbean dollar. **Budget:** (1997 est.) *income:* $31.4 mil.; *expend.:* $31.6 mil. **Chief crops:** cabbages, carrots, cucumbers, tomatoes, onions, peppers; livestock products. **Natural resources:** negl. **Major industries:** tourism, rum, textiles, electronic appliances. **Labor force:** 4,521 (1992 est.); 40.5% community, social, and personal services, 13.5% construction, 12.3% trade, restaurants, and hotels, 10.5% manufacturing. **Exports:** $8.2 mil. (1997); electronic components, plastic bags, apparel, hot peppers, live plants, cattle. **Imports:** $26.1 mil. (1997); machinery and transportation equipment, foodstuffs, manufactured goods, fuels, lubricants, related materials. **Major trading partners:** U.S., Ireland.

▶ PITCAIRN ISLANDS
Pitcairn, Henderson, Ducie, and Oeno Islands

● **GEOGRAPHY Location:** group of islands (one inhabited) in South Pacific. Pitcairn 25°04'S 130°04'W. **Boundaries:** about halfway between Panama and New Zealand; French Polynesia to NW. **Total area:** 18 sq. mi. (47 sq km). **Coastline:** 32 mi. (51 km). **Comparative area:** three-tenths size of Washington, D.C. **Land use:** N.A. **City:** Adamstown (capital).

● **PEOPLE Population:** 49 (1999 est.). **Nationality:** noun—Pitcairn Islander(s); adjective—Pitcairn Islander. **Ethnic groups:** descendants of Bounty mutineers and their Tahitian wives. **Languages:** English (official), also a Tahitian/English dialect. **Religion:** 100% Seventh-Day Adventist.

● **GOVERNMENT Type:** colony of UK. **Constitution:** Local Government Ordinance of 1964. **National holiday:** Celebration of the Birthday of the Queen, second Saturday in June. **Head of government:** Island Magistrate and Chairman of the Island Council Jay Warren. **Structure:** magistrate elected by popular vote for a 3-year term; unicameral 10-seat Island Council members (6 popularly elected, 2 appointed) serve 1-year terms; Island Court.

● **ECONOMY Monetary unit:** New Zealand dollar. **Budget:** (FY94/95) *income:* $729,884; *expend.:* $878,119. **GDP:** N.A. **Chief crops:** wide variety of fruits and vegetables. **Natural resources:** miro trees (used for handicrafts), fish. **Major industries:** postage stamps, handicrafts. **Labor force:** 14 able-bodied men; no business community in usual sense; some public works; subsistence farming and fishing. **Exports:** fruits, vegetables, curios. **Imports:** fuel oil, machinery, building materials, flour, sugar, other foodstuffs. **Major trading partners:** N.A.

▶ ST. HELENA

● **GEOGRAPHY Location:** eastern South Atlantic (15°56'S, 5°43'W). Dependencies are Ascension Is. (7°56'S, 14°25'W) 700 mi. to NW, and Tristan da Cunha (37°05'S, 12°17'W) 1,500 mi to SSW. **Boundaries:** Angola about 1,200 mi. (1,930 km) to E. **Total area:** 158 sq. mi. (410 sq km). **Coastline:** 37 mi. (60 km). **Comparative area:** slightly more than two times size of Washington, D.C. **Land use:** 6% arable land; N.A.% permanent crops; 6% meadows and pastures; 6% forest and woodland; 82% other. **Cities:** (1987) Jamestown (capital) 1,413; Ascencion 1,152 (1996).

● **PEOPLE Population:** 7,145 (1999 est.). **Nationality:** noun—St. Helenian(s); adjective—St. Helenian. **Ethnic groups:** African descent, white. **Languages:** English. **Religions:** Anglican majority; also Baptist, Seventh-Day Adventist, Roman Catholic.

● **GOVERNMENT Type:** dependent territory of UK. **Constitution:** Jan. 1, 1989. **National holiday:** Celebration of the Birthday of the Queen, second Saturday in June. **Head of government:** David Leslie Smallman, governor and commander-in-chief. **Structure:** governor is appointed by the queen; unicameral 16-seat Legislative Council members

elected by popular vote to serve 4-year terms; Supreme Court.

● **ECONOMY Monetary unit:** Saint Helenian pound. **Budget:** (FY92/93) *income:* $11.2 mil.; *expend.:* $11 mil. **GDP:** $13.9 mil.; $2,000 per capita (FY94/95 est.) **Chief crops:** maize, potatoes, vegetables; timber production being developed; crawfishing on Tristan de Cunha. **Natural resources:** fish. **Major industries:** crafts (furniture, lacework, fancy woodwork), fish. **Labor force:** 2,416 (1991 est.); 8.7% professional, technical, and related; 12.8% managerial, administrative, and clerical; 8.1% sales; 5.4% farmers and fishermen; 14.7% production process workers; 50.3% other (1987). **Exports:** $704,000 (f.o.b., 1995); fish (frozen, canned, and salt-dried skipjack, tuna), handicrafts. **Imports:** $14.434 mil. (c.i.f., 1995); food, drink, tobacco, fuel oils, animal feed, building materials. **Major trading partners:** UK, South Africa.

▶ TURKS AND CAICOS ISLANDS

● **GEOGRAPHY Location:** more than 30 islands forming southeastern end of Bahamas Islands in Caribbean Sea. **Boundaries:** Haiti 90 mi (145 km) to S. **Total area:** 166 sq. mi. (430 sq km). **Coastline:** about 186 mi. (about 389 km). **Comparative area:** 2.5 times size of Washington, D.C. **Land use:** 2% arable land; 0% permanent crops; 0% meadows and pastures; 0% forest and woodland; 98% other. **Cities:** Jamestown (capital).

● **PEOPLE Population:** 16,863 (1999 est.). **Nationality:** none. **Ethnic groups:** mostly African descent. **Languages:** English. **Religions:** 41.2% Baptist, 18.9% Methodist, 18.3% Anglican, 1.7% Seventh-Day Adventist.

● **GOVERNMENT Type:** colony of UK. **Constitution:** introduced on Aug. 30, 1976, suspended in 1986, restored and revised March 5, 1988. **National holiday:** Constitution Day, Aug. 30. **Head of government:** Derek Taylor, chief minister (since Jan. 1995). **Structure:** chief minister appointed by governor; unicameral 19-seat Legislative Council members (13 of which are popularly elected) serve 4-year terms; Supreme Court.

● **ECONOMY Monetary unit:** U.S. dollar. **Budget:** (1997/98 est.) *income:* $47 mil.; *expend.:* $33.6 mil. **GDP:** $117 mil., $7,700 per capita (1997 est.). **Chief crops:** corn, beans, cassava, citrus fruis, fish. **Natural resources:** spiny lobster, conch. **Major industries:** fishing, tourism, offshore financial services. **Labor force:** 4,848 (1990 est.); 33% government, 20% agriculture and fishing; majority engaged in fishing and tourist industries. **Exports:** $4.7 mil. (1993); lobster, dried and fresh conch, conch shells. **Imports:** $46.6 mil. (1993); food and beverages, tobacco, clothing, manufactures, construction materials. **Major trading partners:** U.S., UK.

▶ UNINHABITED TERRITORIES OF THE UNITED KINGDOM

British Indian Ocean Territory (Diego Garcia 6°34'S, 72°24'E); South Georgia Is. (54°15'S, 36°45'W); South Orkney Is. (60°35'S, 45°30'W); South Sandwich Is. (56°00'S, 26°30'W); South Shetland Is. (62°00'S, 58°00'W).

The United Nations

▶STRUCTURE

Establishment Pres. Franklin D. Roosevelt coined the name "United Nations," which was first used in the "Declaration by United Nations" of Jan. 1, 1942, during World War II, when representatives of 26 countries pledged their governments to continue fighting together against the Axis Powers. From August to October 1944, representatives of China, the Soviet Union, the United Kingdom and the United States met at Dumbarton Oaks, a mansion in Washington, D.C., to discuss creating an international peacekeeping organization. Out of these meetings came a general outline for the United Nations.

At the United Nations Conference on International Organization, which met at San Francisco from Apr. 25 to June 26, 1945, representatives from 50 countries drew up the United Nations Charter and signed it on June 26, 1945. Poland, not present at the Conference, signed on October 15, 1945, and is considered one of the founding member states.

The United Nations officially came into existence on Oct. 24, 1945, when the charter was ratified by China, France, the Soviet Union, the United Kingdom, and the United States and by a majority of the other signatories.

U.N. Charter Full text of the Charter may be purchased for $3.00 from the United Nations, Sales Section, New York, NY 10017 U.S. The Preamble to the Charter sets forth the hopes for the United Nations:

WE THE PEOPLES OF THE UNITED NATIONS DETERMINED

* to save succeeding generations from the scourge of war . . .
* to reaffirm faith in fundamental human rights, in the dignity and worth of the human person, in the equal rights of men and women and of nations large and small . . .
* to establish conditions under which justice and respect for the obligations arising from treaties and other sources of international law can be maintained . . .
* to promote social progress and better standards of life in larger freedom.

AND FOR THESE ENDS

* to practice tolerance and live together in peace with one another as good neighbors
* to unite our strength to maintain international peace and security
* to ensure, by the acceptance of principles and the institution of methods, that armed force shall not be used, save in the common interest
* to employ international machinery for the promotion of the economic and social advancement of all peoples.

HAVE RESOLVED TO COMBINE OUR EFFORTS TO ACCOMPLISH THESE AIMS. Accordingly, our respective Governments, through representatives assembled in the city of San Francisco, who have exhibited their full powers found to be in good and due form, have agreed to the present Charter of the United Nations and do hereby establish an international organization to be known as the United Nations.

Purposes The purposes of the United Nations are set forth in Article 1 of the Charter. They are: 1. To maintain international peace and security. 2. To develop friendly relations among nations based on respect for the principle of equal rights and self-determination of peoples. 3. To cooperate in solving international problems of an economic, social, cultural or humanitarian character, and in promoting respect for human rights and fundamental freedoms for all. 4. To be a center for harmonizing the actions of nations in the attainment of these common ends.

Official languages Originally, there were five official languages of the United Nations: Chinese, English, French, Russian and Spanish. Arabic was added to the General Assembly in 1973, to the Security Council in 1982 and to the Economic and Social Council in 1983. Major United Nations documents and all meetings of the General Assembly, the Security Council and the Economic and Social Council are translated into the six working languages.

United Nations headquarters United Nations, New York, NY 10017 U.S. U.N. headquarters covers a 16-acre site in New York City along the East River from 42nd to 48th Streets. It consists of the interconnected General Assembly, Secretariat and Dag Hammarskjöld Library buildings. Acquisition of the site was made possible by a gift of $8.5 million from John D. Rockefeller, Jr., and one-third of that amount from New York City. In 1951, the 39-story Secretariat building was completed and began functioning as the official home of the United Nations.

Permanent observers to the U.N. at New York headquarters cannot vote and do not have diplomatic privileges or immunities unless connected to the member nation's consulate. They do have free access to the public meetings and distribution of relevant documentation.

Non-member observers are the Holy See and Switzerland.

Intergovernmental and other observer organizations: More than 25 organizations have observer status at the U.N. Following is a representative sample: Caribbean Community, Commonwealth of Independent States; Council of Europe; International Federation of Red Cross and Red Crescent Societies; League of Arab States; Organization of African Unity; Organization of American States; Organization of Islamic Conference; Palestine.

PRINCIPAL ORGANS

General Assembly

The Assembly is the world's forum for discussing major issues facing the international community including world peace and security, human rights, global environment, disarmament, health issues including AIDS, and the rights of women and children.

The Assembly consists of all 188 member states, each having one vote. On important issues a two-thirds majority of those present and voting is required; other questions require a simple majority vote. It holds its annual session from September to December, and may call for extra sessions as needed. Its agenda of more than 150 matters for discussion is first dealt with in six main committees: Its agenda of more than 150 matters for discussion is first dealt with in six main committees: First Committee: Disarmament and International Security; Second Committee: Economic and Financial; Third Committee: Social, Humanitarian and Cultural; Fourth Committee: Special Political and De-colonization; Fifth Committee: Administrative and Budgetary; Sixth Committee: Legal. After discussing issues facing the world, it adopts recommendations (called resolutions) but has no power to enforce its decisions (resolutions), except the power of world opinion.

The Assembly considers and approves U.N. budget and assesses member states according to their ability to pay.

Security Council

The Council may investigate any dispute or situation that might lead to international friction, and may recommend methods for adjusting such disputes or terms for their settlement. While other organs of the U.N. make recommendations to governments, the Security Council alone has the power to take decisions that member states are obligated under the Charter to carry out.

The Security Council has 15 members: five permanent members, and the General Assembly elects 10 other members for two-year terms. They are not eligible for immediate re-election. The Council may be called into session at any time, and a representative of each member state must be present at U.N. headquarters at all times.

The five permanent members are China, France, Russia, the United Kingdom, and the United States.

The terms of office of each current (1999) non-permanent member ends on December 31 of the year indicated in parentheses: Argentina (2000) Bahrain (1999), Brazil (1999), Canada (2000), Gabon (1999), Gambia (1999), Malaysia (2000), Namibia (2000), Netherlands (2000), and Slovenia (1999).

Decisions on matters of procedure require the approval of at least nine of the 15 members. Decisions on all other matters also require nine votes, including the concurring votes of all five permanent members. A negative vote by any permanent member on a non-procedural matter is often referred to as the "veto," which results in the rejection of the proposal. A state that is involved in a dispute may not vote.

Economic and Social Council (ECOSOC)

The Council is the principal organ to co-ordinate the economic and social work of the U.N. and its specialized agencies. It makes recommendations and initiates activities relating to world trade, industrialization, natural resources, human rights, the status of women, population, social welfare, education, health and related matters, science and technology and many other economic and social questions.

ECOSOC has 54 members elected for three-year terms by the General Assembly.

International Court of Justice (World Court)

The Court is the judicial organ of the U.N. and sits in The Hague, Netherlands. All U.N. member states are automatically members of the Court. One country that is not a member of the U.N. is party to the Court–Switzerland. The Court is not open to individuals. It issues judgments on all questions that states refer to it and all matters provided for in the U.N. Charter or in treaties or conventions in force. Both the General Assembly and the Security Council can ask the Court for an advisory opinion on any legal question as can other organs of the U.N. or specialized agencies, when authorized to do so by the Assembly.

The Court has dealt with a wide variety of subjects, including territorial rights, the delimitation of territorial waters and continental shelves, fishing jurisdiction, questions of nationality and the right of individuals to asylum, territorial sovereignty, and the right of passage through foreign territory.

The judgment of the Court is final and without appeal. However, a revision may be applied for within ten years from the date of the judgment on the ground of a new decisive factor. If a party rejects the judgment, the other party may take the issue to the Security Council.

Judges: The ICJ has 15 independent judges, of different nationalities, elected by both the General Assembly and the Security Council. Judges hold 9-year terms and may be re-elected. All questions are decided by a majority of the judges present; the president votes only in case of a tie.

Secretariat

The Secretariat services the other organs of the U.N. and administers the programs and policies they develop. Headed by the Secretary-General, it consists of an international staff of more than 25,000 men and women from over 150 countries.

Secretaries-General: The General Assembly elects the Secretary-General to terms of office of five years (they may be re-elected). The Secretary-General, by tradition, does not come from one of the permanent member States of the Security Council–China, France, Russia, UK or the U.S. Those who have served in this post are: Trygve Lie, Norway, Feb. 1, 1946, to Nov. 10, 1952; Dag Hammarskjöld, Sweden, Apr. 11, 1953, to Sept. 17, 1961; U Thant, Burma, Nov. 3, 1961, to Dec. 31, 1971; Kurt Waldheim, Austria, Jan. 1, 1972, to Dec. 31, 1981; Javier Perez de Cuellar, Peru Jan. 1, 1982 to Dec. 31, 1991; Boutros Boutros-Ghali, Egypt, Jan 1, 1992, to Dec. 31, 1996; Kofi Annan, Ghana, Jan. 1, 1997 to present.

▶ UNITED NATIONS PROGRAMS

Each U.N. program was created by the General Assembly and reports to it through the Economic and Social Council (ECOSOC). Each member of the U.N. is a member of each Program.

International Research and Training Institute for the Advancement of Women (INSTRAW) Estab.: 1979. (made U.N. program in 1985); **HQ:** Calle Cesar Nicolas Penson, 102-A, Santo Domingo, Dominican Republic. Carries out research, training and information activities worldwide to show and increase women's key role in development.

United Nations Centre for Human Settlements (Habitat) Estab.: 1978; **HQ:** P.O. Box 30030, Nairobi, Kenya. Works to provide models and tools so people can improve their housing. Major

U.S. Representatives to the UN

The U.S. representative to the UN holds the title of Ambassador Extraordinary and Plenipotentiary Permanent Representative and heads the U.S. Mission to the UN.

Year	Ambassador
1946	Edward R. Stettinius, Jr.
1946–47	Herschel V. Johnson (acting)
1947–53	Warren R. Austin
1953–60	Henry Cabot Lodge, Jr.
1960–61	James J. Wadsworth
1961–65	Adlai E. Stevenson
1965–68	Arthur J. Goldberg
1968	George W. Ball
1968–69	James Russell Wiggins
1969–71	Charles W. Yost
1971–73	George Bush
1973–75	John A. Scali
1975–76	Daniel P. Moynihan
1976–77	William W. Scranton
1977–79	Andrew Young
1979–81	Donald McHenry
1981–85	Jeane J. Kirkpatrick
1985–89	Vernon A. Walters
1989–92	Thomas J. Pickering
1992–93	Edward J. Perkins
1993–96	Madeleine K. Albright
1997–98	Bill Richardson
1999–present	Richard C. Holbrooke

concerns are planning, financing, and management of human settlements– especially in developing countries.

United Nations Children's Fund (UNICEF) Estab.: 1946; **HQ:** UNICEF House, Three United Nations Plaza, New York, NY 10017, U.S. Provides care for children in developing countries by providing low-cost community-based services in maternal and child health, immunization, breastfeeding, growth monitoring, nutrition, clean water and sanitation, and education.

United Nations Conference on Trade and Development (UNCTAD) Estab.: 1964; **HQ:** Place des Nations, 1211 Geneva 10, Switzerland. Works to bring developing countries into global trade by formulating international trade policies, mediating multilateral trade agreements and providing assistance to governments.

United Nations Development Programme (UNDP) Estab.: 1965; **HQ:** One United Nations Plaza, New York, NY 10017, U.S. Coordinates development activities within the U.N. Operates over 5,000 projects in 150 countries and territories to facilitate development in economic and social sectors, including: farming, fishing, forestry, mining, manufacturing, power, transport, communications, housing, trade, health and environmental sanitation, economic planning and public administration.

United Nations Environment Programme (UNEP) Estab.: 1972; **HQ:** P.O. Box 30552, Nairobi, Kenya. Coordinates international environment issues, including international environment conventions, monitors significant changes in environment and coordinates sound environmental practices.

United Nations Fund for Population Activities (UNFPA) Estab.: 1969; **HQ:** 220 E. 42nd Street, New York, NY 10017, U.S. Provides assistance to population programs in developing countries; promotes understanding of key population factors: population growth, fertility, mortality, spatial distribution and migration.

Office of the United Nations High Commissioner for Refugees (UNHCR) Estab.: 1950; **HQ:** Palais des Nations, CH1211 Geneva 10, Switzerland. Provides food, clothing and shelter for refugees and works with governments to establish safe conditions whereby refugees may return home and, when that is not possible, seeks to ensure that refugees receive asylum.

United Nations Institute for Training and Research (UNITAR) Estab: 1965; **HQ:** Palais des Nations, CH1211 Geneva 10, Switzerland. Provides training for members of U.N.'s permanent missions, including courses on international economics, workshops on drafting and negotiating international legal instruments, dispute settlement, and training on peace, security, human rights and humanitarian assistance.

United Nations University (UNU) Estab.: 1973; **HQ:** 53-70 Jingumae 5-chome, Shibuya-ku, Tokyo 150, Japan. UNU has no students of its own, no campus and no faculty. It is an international community of scholars engaged in research operating through worldwide networks of academic research institutions.

World Food Council (WFC) Estab.: 1974; **HQ:** Via delle Terme di Caracalla, 00100 Rome, Italy. Encourages developing countries to adopt a national food strategy whereby they assess their food situation needs, supply, potential for increasing production, storage, processing, transportation and distribution.

World Food Programme (WFP) (Joint program operated by U.N. and Food and Agriculture Organization (FAO) **Estab.:** 1963; **HQ:** Via Cristoforo Colombo, 426, 00145 Rome, Italy. Provides food to support development activities and in times of emergencies. Operates projects in forestry, soil erosion control, irrigation, land rehabilitation and rural settlements.

▶SPECIALIZED AGENCIES OF THE U.N.

The specialized agencies associated with the United Nations are self-governing, independent organizations that work with the U.N. system and each other through the coordination machinery of the Economic and Social Council (ECOSOC). Each country affiliates with each agency on an individual basis. Membership in an agency is separate from U.N. membership. Nongovernmental organizations (NGOs) having expertise in the area may affiliate with each agency on a separate basis.

Food and Agriculture Organization of the United Nations (FAO) Member States: 174; **Estab.:** Oct. 16, 1945; **HQ:** Via delle Terme di Caracalla, 00100 Rome, Italy. Works to increase output of farmlands, forests and fisheries and to raise nutritional levels. Co-sponsors World Food Programme, which uses food, cash and services donated by member states for emergency situations.

International Atomic Energy Agency (IAEA) Member States: 127; **Estab.:** July 29, 1957; **HQ:** Vienna International Centre, P.O. Box 100, A-1400 Vienna, Austria. (Not regular specialized agency in that it does not report through ECOSOC but directly to General Assembly.) Fosters and guides development of peaceful uses of atomic energy, establishes standards for nuclear safety and environmental protection, aids member countries through technical cooperation, and fosters exchange of information on nuclear energy.

International Civil Aviation Organization (ICAO) Member States: 183; **Estab.**: Apr. 4, 1947; **HQ**: 1000 Sherbrooke Street West, Suite 400, Montreal, Quebec H3A 2R2, Canada. Works for safer air travel conditions worldwide. Establishes visual and instrument flight rules for pilots and crews; develops aeronautical charts for navigation; coordinates aircraft radio frequencies and works with customs procedures.

International Fund for Agricultural Development (IFAD) Member States: 160; **Estab.**: Nov. 30, 1977; **HQ**: Via del Serafico 10, 00142 Rome, Italy. Lends money to peoples in developing countries for agricultural development projects, including livestock, fisheries, processing and storage, irrigation, research and training.

International Labor Organization (ILO) Member States: 173; **Estab.**: 1919, under the Treaty of Versailles; (became U.N. specialized agency Dec. 14, 1946);. **HQ**: 4, route des Morillons, CH-1211 Geneva 22, Switzerland. Promotes social justice for working people everywhere by formulating international policies and programs to help improve working and living conditions; creates international labor standards as guidelines for governments and assists in vocational training, management techniques, occupational safety and health.

International Maritime Organization (IMO) Member States: 152; **Estab.**: Mar. 17, 1958; **HQ**: 4 Albert Embankment, London SE1 SR, England. Works to improve international shipping procedures and encourages highest standards in maritime safety; seeks to prevent and control marine pollution from ships and sets standards for training and certification of seafarers.

International Telecommunication Union (ITU) Member States: 184; **Estab.**: 1865, it became a U.N. specialized agency in Jan. 1949; **HQ**: Place des Nations, 1211 Geneva 20, Switzerland. Coordinates use of radio frequencies, tracks positions assigned by countries to geostationary satellites; coordinates modem and Internet standards.

United Nations Educational, Scientific and Cultural Organization (UNESCO) Member States: 186; **Estab.**: Nov. 4, 1946; **HQ**: 7, Place de Fontenoy, 75007 Paris, France. Promotes literacy through teacher training, building schools, and developing textbooks. Natural science programs include Man and the Biosphere and Intergovernmental Oceanographic Commission. Undertakes study and development of cultures, and conservation of world's inheritance of books, art and monuments.

United Nations Industrial Development Organization (UNIDO) Member States: 166; **Estab.**: 1966 (became U.N. specialized agency Jan. 1, 1986); **HQ**: Wagramerstrasse 5, Vienna XXII, Austria. Promotes and accelerates industrialization of developing countries by providing technical assistance, training programs and advisory services.

Universal Postal Union (UPU) Member States: 189; **Estab.**: July 1, 1875 (became U.N. specialized agency July 1, 1948); **HQ**: Weltpoststrasse 4, Berne, Switzerland. Establishes regulations for smooth exchange of mail worldwide.

World Bank Group Group of five closely related institutions. **HQ**: 1818 H Street, N.W., Washington, D.C. 20433 *International Bank for Reconstruction and Development (IBRD)* **Member States**: 178; **Estab.**: Dec. 27, 1945, to provide loans and technical assistance to developing countries to assist in their reconstruction and development. *International Finance Corporation (IFC)* **Member States: 165** (Membership is open only to World Bank members.); **Estab.**: July 20, 1956, to stimulate flow of private capital into productive investment in member countries. While closely associated with Bank, IFC is separate legal entity and its funds are distinct from those of Bank. *International Development Association (IDA)* **Member States**: 158; **Estab.**: Sept. 24, 1960. (Affiliate of the Bank, IDA has same directors and staff as Bank.) Lends money to poor countries with interest-free credits. Financial resources are from contributions by donor governments. *International Monetary Fund (IMF)* **Member States**: 181; Estab.: Dec. 27, 1945; HQ: 700 19th Street, N.W., Washington, D.C. 20431. Makes financing available to members in balance-of-payments difficulties and provides technical assistance to improve their economic management. *Multilateral Investment Guarantee Agency (MIGA)* **Member States**: 128; Estab.: 1988. Augments capacity of other insurers through coinsurance or reinsurance, thereby insuring investment in countries restricted or excluded by policies of other insurers.

World Health Organization (WHO) Member States: 190; **Estab.**: April 7, 1948; **HQ**: 20, avenue Appia, 1211 Geneva 27, Switzerland. Coordinates programs aimed at solving health problems by working with governments, other U.N. agencies and non-governmental organizations. See "World Health" section.

World Intellectual Property Organization (WIPO) Member States: 161; **Estab.**: 1883, (became U.N. specialized agency Dec. 17, 1974); **HQ**: 34, chemin des Colombettes, 121 Geneva 20, Switzerland. Promotes protection of intellectual property and cooperation in enforcement of agreements on matters such as copyrights, trademarks, industrial designs and patents.

World Meteorological Organization (WMO) Member States: 179; **Estab.**: 1873. (became U.N. specialized agency Mar. 23, 1950); **HQ**: 41, avenue Giuseppe-Motta, 1211 Geneva 20, Switzerland. Facilitates exchange of weather reports among countries; "World Weather Watch" tracks global weather conditions.

▶ PEACEKEEPING OPERATIONS

United Nations peacekeeping is the use of multinational forces, under U.N. command, to keep disputing countries or communities from fighting while efforts are made to help them negotiate a solution. It is undertaken only with the agreement of both hostile parties. United Nations Peacekeeping Forces received the Nobel Peace Prize in 1988. As of October, 1999, the U.N. had 19 peacekeeping operations, comprising more than 15,000 men and women peacekeepers from more than 60 countries.

United Nations Truce Supervision Organization

(UNTSO) Estab.: 1948. Mandate has evolved. Currently U.N. observers (166) assist peacekeeping operations in Middle East.

United Nations Military Observer Group in India and Pakistan (UNMOGIP) Estab.: 1948. U.N. observers (44) are stationed on both sides of Line of Control agreed upon by India and Pakistan under Simla agreement of July 1972 to observe cease-fire.

United Nations Peacekeeping Force in Cyprus (UNFICYP) Estab.: 1964. U.N. uniformed personnel (1,215) control 112-mile (180-km) buffer zone between cease-fire lines agreed on by Cyprus National Guard and Turkish forces.

United Nations Disengagement Observer Force (UNDOF) Estab.: 1974. U.N. troops and observers (1,133) maintain an "area of separation" on Golan Heights between Israel and Syria and verify arms limitation on both sides.

United Nations Interim Force in Lebanon (UNIFIL) Estab.: 1978. U.N. troops (4,488) are in Southern Lebanon to confirm withdrawal of Israeli forces, restore international peace and security, and assist Lebanese government in ensuring return of its authority in area.

United Nations Iraq-Kuwait Observation Mission (UNIKOM) Estab.: 1991. U.N. troops (1,099) monitor demilitarized zone set up by Security Council along Khor Abdullah waterway. First-time observers from five permanent members of Security Council serve together.

UN Mission for the Referendum in Western Sahara (MINURSO) Estab.: Sept. 1991. Military observers (200) monitor and verify crease-fire, pending agreement between parties on criteria for eligibility to vote in referendum.

U.N. Observer Mission in Georgia (UNOMIG) Estab.: Aug. 1993. Mandated to verify compliance with crease-fire agreement of July 27, 1993, between Georgia and Abkhazia, a territory in Georgia's northwestern region on Black Sea that tried to separate. (117 observers.)

U.N. Mission of Observers in Tajikistan (UNMOT) Estab.: Dec. 1994. Observers (20) help implement crease-fire agreement between government and opposition forces.

Former Yugoslav Republic of Macedonia (UNPREDEP) U.N. Preventive Deployment Force. Estab.: Mar. 1995. Uniformed personnel (1,105) replaced UNPROFOR and maintained its mandate to monitor and maintain security of Macedonia's border.

U.N. Mission in Bosnia and Herzegovina (UNMIBH) Estab.: Dec. 1995. Civil police (1,902) monitor, observe, impart law enforcement activities, maintain peace. Work with NATO-led multinational Force (IFOR) to ensure compliance with Dayton Peace Agreement.

U.N. Mission of Observers in Prevlaka (UNMOP) Estab.: Jan. 1996. Military observers (27) monitor demilitarization of Prevlaka peninsula in Croatia.

U.N. Observer Mission in Angola (MONUA) Estab.: July 1997. Successor to UNIVEMIII, to assist Angolan parties in consolidating peace and national reconciliation to create environment conducive to democratic development and reconstruction of the country. (193 observers.) Expected to conclude its work by Feb. 1998.

U.N. Civilian Police Mission in Haiti (MIPONUH) Estab.: Dec. 1997. Continuing to support and train Haitian National Police.

U.N. Civilian Police Support Group Estab. Jan. 1998. Continuing to monitor performance of Croatian police in Danube region, especially regarding the return of displaced persons.

Central African Republic (MINURCA) Estab.: April 1998. Assists in training police; provides advice and technical support for holding legislative elections in Aug./Sept. 1998.

United Nations Mission of Observers in Sierra Leone (UNOMSIL) Estab.: July 1998. Initially 70 uniformed personnel deployed to promote stability and security by disarming and demobilizing former combatants.

United Nations Interim Administration Mission in Kosovo (UNMIK) Estab.: June 1999. First U.N. peacekeeping mission to involve other multilateral organizations as full partners under U.N. leadership.

United Nations Mission in East Timor (UNAMET) Estab.: June 1999. Mission deploys 900 international and 4,000 local staff to direct a national election. On August 30th, 78.5 percent of voters selected independence, causing pro-autonomy militias to unleash a reign of violence. UN calls on Indonesia to restore peace as agreed in May 5, 1999 Agreements. Security Council authorizes security force of 15 nations led by Australia to restore order and oversee transition of East Timor to independence.

▶ FURTHER U.N. INFORMATION

United Nations Bookstore Room GA-32, New York, NY, 10017; 212-963-7680; 1-800-553-3210; Fax: 212-963-4910. International publications issued by U.N. bodies and independent publishers.

▶ U.N. INFORMATION ON-LINE

Official Web site for U.N. System:
http://www.unsystem.org
U.N. Headquarters: http://www.un.org

▶ KEY EVENTS IN U.N. HISTORY

1946 (Jan. 10)   First session of General Assembly begins at London with delegates of 51 member states.

1947 (Nov. 29)   General Assembly passes Plan of Partition with Economic Union concerning future government of Palestine, thereby paving way for government of Tel Aviv to declare State of Israel on May 14, 1948.

1948 (Dec. 10)   Universal Declaration of Human Rights adopted by General Assembly.

U.N. pioneers concept of peacekeeping observer missions and peacekeeping forces (1956).

1949   Mediates cease-fire between India and Pakistan, ending two years of fighting over Kashmir.

1950   Security Council calls members states to help South Korea repel invasion by North Korea.

Economic and Social Council adopts Standard International Trade Classification as basis for gathering world trade statistics.

1953   U.N. coordinates first global-census effort to establish earth's population for first time in history–2.4 billion people.

1955   First of ongoing congresses of criminologists and police officials draws up international principles and standards of criminal justice.

1959   U.N. General Assembly adopts Declaration on the Rights of the Child.

1960   Under de-colonization program, 17 territories become newly independent states; 16 in Africa join U.N.

1962 Secretary-General plays key role in resolving U.S.-Soviet confrontation over issue of nuclear missiles in Cuba.

1963 Security Council calls for arms embargo against South Africa. (Made mandatory in 1972.)

1967 After war erupts in Middle East, Security Council adopts Resolution 242, calling for withdrawal of forces from occupied territories, and recognizes right of all states in area to security. Mediates settlement of Six-Day Arab-Israeli War.

1970 General Assembly adopts first international agreed-upon set of principles on seabed and ocean floor beyond national jurisdiction. Declares area "common heritage" of humanity.

1972 Security Council orders cease-fire in 17-day-old Middle East War and sends peacekeeping force to prevent further fighting between Israel and Arab states.

1975 U.N. conference at Mexico City launches Decade for Women to begin major effort toward women's equality worldwide.

1979 World Health Organization announces smallpox eradicated from all peoples on earth.

1987 First International Conference on Drug Abuse and Illicit Trafficking develops program on international coordination of illicit-drug issues.

1988 Mediates ending of Iran-Iraq War. Mediates Soviet withdrawal from Afghanistan.

1989 Mediates withdrawal of Cuban troops from Angola and South African troops from Namibia. U.N. sends peacekeeping troops and advisers to Namibia to supervise elections aimed at setting up self-government.

1990 Upon invitation, U.N. monitors demobilization of Nicaraguan rebel forces, and for first time monitors a presidential campaign and election in an independent nation.

Security Council Resolution 678 calls upon member states to restore peace and security in Kuwait by "all necessary means."

Responding to request by Haiti, U.N. supervises election of Haiti's first freely elected president.

1991 (Apr. 3) Security Council Resolution 687 sets terms of cease-fire in Gulf War and gives U.N. variety of duties to ensure peace.

Secretary-General negotiates cease-fire in 16-year-old civil war in Angola.

(Dec. 4) Secretary-General negotiates release of last six hostages held in Lebanon.

General Assembly rescinds Resolution 3379 of Nov. 10, 1975, equating Zionism with racism.

1992 Secretary-General completes peace negotiations between government of El Salvador and rebel Farabundo Marti National Liberation Front.

1993 145 nations co–sponsor Convention on Prohibition of the Development, Production, Stockpiling and Use of Chemical Weapons.

(Feb. 23) Human Rights Commission adopts Resolution 1993/8, which states that "abhorrent practice of rape and abuse of women and children in the former Yugoslavia. . . . constitutes a war crime. This is first formal statement that declares rape, conducted during war, an international war crime under Geneva Convention.

(Dec. 13) General Assembly creates post of High Commissioner for Human Rights with power to intervene wherever basic freedom are suppressed.

1994 Security Council removes South Africa from its agenda, declaring end of apartheid.

Security Council establishes International Tribunal for Rwanda to prosecute persons responsible for genocide and other violations of international humanitarian law.

1995 Secretary-General launches 50th anniversary commemoration. International Tribunal for Former Yugoslavia, established in 1993 to prosecute persons responsible for serious violations of international humanitarian law in former Yugoslavia since 1991, schedules first trials for September with 15 judges from 15 countries.

(June) Upon request of government of Haiti, U.N. supervises free elections in the country.

1996 (Feb.-Mar.) Upon request of the government, U.N. supervises free and fair elections in Sierra Leone that changes rule from military regime to democracy.

(May) Hague-based International Criminal Tribunal for the former Yugoslavia begins trial for first war crimes in 50 years. Dusan Tadic, Bosnian Serb charged with torturing and murdering Bosnian Muslims and Croats at Omarska prison camp in Prijedor, Bosnia, in 1992. He is convicted in 1997 and sentenced to 20 years in prison.

1997 U.N. launches CyberSchoolBus to reach tens of thousands of students worldwide; provides lesson plans, global trends, quizzes; on-line Model U.N. discussion is first of its kind to reach 60,000 high schools and college students.

Thirteen nations ask for and receive U.N. assistance in holding their elections, including Algeria, Cambodia, Gambia, Guyana, Haiti, Honduras, Liberia, Mali, and Yemen.

1998 (July) U.N. establishes Permanent International Criminal Court to try individuals for genocide, war crimes, and crimes against humanity.

(July) U.N. conference in Rome adopts statute to create Permanent International Criminal Court to try individuals for genocide, war crimes and crimes against humanity.

1999 (Mar.) Secretary-General issues Global Compact—enlisting businesses to advance universally agreed principles on human rights, labor, and environment.

(June) Security Council invests U.N. peacekeeping mission authority over Kosovo territory and people, including all legislative, executive, and judicial administration. First ever cooperation with non-U.N. organizations, including the EU and the Organization for Security in Europe.

(July) Economic and Social Council holds first live broadcast of its high-level meeting over the Internet allowing global viewing.

(Sept.) Security Council authorizes security force to restore peace and security in East Timor, protect and support UNAMET in carrying out its tasks, and facilitate humanitarian assistance operations. Australia assumes command of 15-nation International Force East Timor (INTERFET).

United Nations Member States (188)

Country	Joined U.N.	Country	Joined U.N.	Country	Joined U.N.
Afghanistan	1946	Ghana	1957	Pakistan	1947
Albania	1955	Greece	1945	Palau	1994
Algeria	1962	Grenada	1974	Panama	1945
Andorra	1993	Guatemala	1945	Papua New Guinea	1975
Angola	1976	Guinea	1958	Paraguay	1945
Antigua and Barbuda	1981	Guinea-Bissau	1974	Peru	1945
Argentina	1945	Guyana	1966	Philippines	1945
Armenia	1992	Haiti	1945	Poland	1945
Australia	1945	Honduras	1945	Portugal	1955
Austria	1955	Hungary	1955	Qatar	1971
Azerbaijan	1992	Iceland	1946	Moldova	1992
Bahamas	1973	India	1945	Romania	1955
Bahrain	1971	Indonesia	1950	Russian Federation	1945
Bangladesh	1974	Iran	1945	Rwanda	1962
Barbados	1966	Iraq	1945	Saint Kitts and Nevis	1983
Belarus	1945	Ireland	1955	Saint Lucia	1979
Belgium	1945	Israel	1949	Saint Vincent and the	1980
Belize	1981	Italy	1955	Grenadines	
Benin	1960	Ivory Coast	1960	Samoa	1976
Bhutan	1971	Jamaica	1962	San Marino	1992
Bolivia	1945	Japan	1956	São Tome and Principe	1975
Bosnia and Herzegovina	1992	Jordan	1955	Saudi Arabia	1945
Botswana	1966	Kazakhstan	1992	Senegal	1960
Brazil	1945	Kenya	1963	Seychelles	1976
Brunei Darussalam	1984	Kiribati	1999	Sierra Leone	1961
Bulgaria	1955	Kuwait	1963	Singapore	1965
Burkina Faso	1960	Kyrgyzstan	1992	Slovakia[2]	1993
Burundi	1962	Laos	1955	Slovenia	1992
Cambodia	1955	Latvia	1991	Solomon Islands	1978
Cameroon	1960	Lebanon	1945	Somalia	1960
Canada	1945	Lesotho	1966	South Africa	1945
Cape Verde	1975	Liberia	1945	South Korea	1991
Central African Republic	1960	Libya	1955	Spain	1955
Chad	1960	Liechtenstein	1990	Sri Lanka	1955
Chile	1945	Lithuania	1991	Sudan	1956
China	1945	Luxembourg	1945	Suriname	1975
Colombia	1945	Macedonia[3]	1993	Swaziland	1968
Comoros	1975	Madagascar	1960	Sweden	1946
Congo	1960	Malawi	1964	Syria	1945
Congo, Democratic		Malaysia	1957	Tanzania	1961
Republic of[1]	1960	Maldives	1965	Tajikistan	1992
Costa Rica	1945	Mali	1960	Thailand	1946
Croatia	1992	Malta	1964	Togo	1960
Cuba	1945	Marshall Islands	1991	Tonga	1999
Cyprus	1960	Mauritania	1961	Trinidad and Tobago	1962
Czech Republic[2]	1993	Mauritius	1968	Tunisia	1956
Denmark	1945	Mexico	1945	Turkey	1945
Djibouti	1977	Micronesia	1991	Turkmenistan	1992
Dominica	1978	Monaco	1993	Uganda	1962
Dominican Republic	1945	Mongolia	1961	Ukraine	1945
Ecuador	1945	Morocco	1956	United Arab Emirates	1971
Egypt	1945	Mozambique	1975	United Kingdom	1945
El Salvador	1945	Myanmar	1948	United States	1945
Equatorial Guinea	1968	Namibia	1990	Uruguay	1945
Eritrea	1993	Nauru	1999	Uzbekistan	1992
Estonia	1991	Nepal	1955	Vanuatu	1981
Ethiopia	1945	Netherlands	1945	Venezuela	1945
Fiji	1970	New Zealand	1945	Viet Nam	1977
Finland	1955	Nicaragua	1945	Yemen[4]	1947
France	1945	Niger	1960	Yugoslavia	1945
Gabon	1960	Nigeria	1960	Zambia	1964
Gambia	1965	North Korea	1991	Zimbabwe	1980
Georgia	1992	Norway	1945		
Germany	1973	Oman	1971		

Source: United Nations. 1. Formerly Zaire. 2. Czechoslovakia was an original member of the UN; when the nation split into separate Czech and Slovak Republics, both new republics were admitted as member states on Jan. 19, 1993. 3. Provisionally referred to for all purposes within the UN as "The former Yugoslav Republic of Macedonia" pending settlement of a difference with Greek Macedonia over the name. 4. Includes the former Democratic Yemen (admitted as a separate member in 1967), which merged with Yemen in 1990.

Major Political International Organizations

Commonwealth HQ: Marlborough House, Pall Mall, London, SW1Y 5HX, UK. **Estab.**: By some members of British Empire through evolutionary process formalized by Statute of Westminster on Dec. 31, 1931. As voluntary association of independent states, Commonwealth has no written constitution and no rigid contractual obligations. Emphasis is on consultation and exchange of views for cooperation, especially in economic affairs, drug trafficking, international terrorism and technical assistance to less developed states. Some countries that were part of British Empire are not part of Commonwealth. **Members** (52): Antigua and Barbuda, Australia, Bahamas, Bangladesh, Barbados, Belize, Botswana, Brunei, Canada, Cyprus, Dominica, Gambia, Ghana, Grenada, Guyana, India, Jamaica, Kenya, Kiribati, Lesotho, Malawi, Malaysia, Maldives, Malta, Mauritius, Mozambique, Namibia, Nauru, New Zealand, Nigeria, Pakistan, Papua New Guinea, Saint Kitts and Nevis, Saint Lucia, Saint Vincent and the Grenadines, Seychelles, Sierra Leone, Singapore, Solomon Islands, South Africa, Sri Lanka, Swaziland, Tanzania, Tong, Trinidad and Tobago, Tuvalu, Uganda, United Kingdom, Vanuatu, Western Samoa, Zambia, Zimbabwe

Commonwealth of Independent States (CIS) HQ: Uliza Kirowa 17, Minsk 220000. **Estab.**: Dec. 8, 1991, by Byelorussia (Belarus), Russia, and Ukraine, which dissolved USSR and created CIS. Members agree to broad cooperation, including to cooperate in political, economic, ecological, humanitarian, and cultural fields. **Members** (12): Armenia, Azerbaijan, Belarus, Georgia, Kazakhstan, Kyrgyzstan, Moldova, Russia, Tajikistan, Turkmenistan, Ukraine, Uzbekistan.

European Union (EU, the Common Market), See Part III: "The Global Economy."

League of Arab States (LAS, the Arab League) HQ: Tahrir Square, Cairo, Egypt. **Estab.**: By treaty signed on Mar. 22, 1945 at Cairo, Egypt, to strengthen relations among members in financial, communications, cultural, health, social, nationality and social areas. **Members** (22): Algeria, Bahrain, Comoros, Djibouti, Egypt, Iraq, Jordan, Kuwait, Lebanon, Libya, Mauritania, Morocco, Oman, Palestine Liberation Organization, Qatar, Saudi Arabia, Somalia, Sudan, Syria, Tunisia, United Arab Emirates, Yemen.

North Atlantic Treaty Organization (NATO) HQ: B-1110 Brussels, Belgium. **Estab.**: By North Atlantic Treaty on Aug. 24, 1949, to maintain security among member states. NATO attempted to maintain military balance with countries of the Warsaw Pact: Bulgaria, Czechoslovakia, East Germany, Hungary, Poland, Romania, USSR. Since 1989 security challenges have shifted to possible adverse consequences from serious economic, social, and political difficulties, including ethnic rivalries and territorial disputes, arms proliferation, and terrorism. In 1997, leaders of NATO voted to admit Czech Republic, Hungary and Poland, and their official membership received final approval in 1999. **Members** (19): Belgium, Canada, Czech Republic, Denmark, France, Germany, Greece, Hungary, Iceland, Italy, Luxembourg, Netherlands, Norway, Poland, Portugal, Spain, Turkey, United Kingdom, U.S.

Organization of African Unity (OAU) HQ: African Unity Hall, POB 3243, Addis Ababa, Ethiopia. **Estab.**: By charter on May 25, 1963 at Addis Ababa, to promote unity and solidarity among African states. OAU works to eradicate all forms of colonialism from Africa and to defend their sovereignty and independence. **Members** (53): Algeria, Angola, Benin, Botswana, Burkina Faso, Burundi, Cameroon, Cape Verde, Central African Republic, Chad, Comoros, Congo, Democratic Republic of Congo, Djibouti, Egypt, Equatorial Guinea, Eritrea, Ethiopia, Gabon, Gambia, Ghana, Guinea, Guinea-Bissau, Ivory Coast, Kenya, Lesotho, Liberia, Libya, Madagascar, Malawi, Mali, Mauritania, Mauritius, Mozambique, Namibia, Niger, Nigeria, Rwanda, São Tomé and Príncipe, Senegal, Seychelles, Sierra Leone, Somalia, South Africa, Sudan, Swaziland, Tanzania, Togo, Tunisia, Uganda, Western Sahara, Zambia, Zimbabwe.

Organization of American States (OAS) HQ: 1889 F St., NW, Washington, DC 20006-4499, U.S. **Estab.**: By charter signed at Bogotá, Columbia, effective Dec. 13, 1951, to strengthen peace and security on continent, promote cooperation in human rights, education, economic and social development and scientific exchanges, and to seek solutions to political, juridical and economic problems. **Members** (35): Antigua and Barbuda, Argentina, Bahamas, Barbados, Belize, Bolivia, Brazil, Canada, Chile, Colombia, Costa Rica, Cuba (suspended from OAS activities but not membership in 1962), Dominica, Dominican Republic, Ecuador, El Salvador, Grenada, Guatemala, Guyana, Haiti, Honduras, Jamaica, Mexico, Nicaragua, Panama, Paraguay, Peru, Saint Kitts and Nevis, Saint Lucia, Saint Vincent and the Grenadines, Suriname, Trinidad and Tobago, U.S., Uruguay, Venezuela.

Organization of the Petroleum Exporting Countries (OPEC) HQ: Obere Donaustrasse 93, A-1020 Vienna, Austria. **Estab.**: Nov. 14, 1960 by resolution adopted at Baghdad Conference, to coordinate and unify petroleum policies and to stabilize international oil prices to prevent harmful fluctuations. **Members** (12): Algeria, Gabon, Indonesia, Iran, Iraq, Kuwait, Libya, Nigeria, Qatar, Saudi Arabia, United Arab Emirates, Venezuela.

Organization for Security and Cooperation in Europe (OSCE) HQ: Kärtnerring 5-7, A-1010 Vienna, Austria. **Estab.**: by Final Act of Conference on Security and Cooperation in Europe in 1975. In 1990, CSCE members declared end of "era of confrontation and division of Europe" and beginning of "a new era of democracy, peace and unity." Serves as forum for dialogue, negotiation, cooperation, and direction in shaping new Europe. **Members** (55): Albania, Andorra, Armenia, Austria, Azerbaijan, Belarus, Belgium, Bosnia and Herzegovina, Bulgaria, Canada, Croatia, Cyprus, Czech Republic, Denmark, Estonia, Finland, France, Georgia, Germany, Greece, Holy See, Hungary, Iceland, Ireland, Italy, Kazakhstan, Kyrgyzstan, Latvia, Liechtenstein, Lithuania, Luxembourg, Macedonia, Malta, Moldova, Monaco, Netherlands, Norway, Poland, Portugal, Romania, Russia, San Marino, Slovakia, Slovenia, Spain, Sweden, Switzerland, Tajikistan, Turkmenistan, Ukraine, UK, U.S., Uzbekistan, Yugoslavia (suspended).

ASTRONOMY

Astronomy is the oldest science, but it continues to be at the forefront of scientific thought. The ancients of the Northern Hemisphere knew the skies, probably better than most of us do. They recognized that most stars appear to rise in the east at night and travel in circular paths across the sky, and that a few are wanderers—planets—that move among the other stars. They named the groups of stars that we call constellations and recognized that constellations visible in winter are different from those visible in summer (although some are visible all year). They learned how to find the extremities of the sunrise and built giant stone structures, such as Stonehenge, probably to locate certain of the positions of the Sun or other stars.

In 1609 Galileo introduced the first artificial device for exploring the universe—the astronomical telescope. Even in that first year, he saw wonders the ancients never knew. Since then, we have built larger and better telescopes, devices for detecting radio waves, microwaves, X rays, infrared waves, and gamma rays from space, and have even traveled to our own Moon. We have sent space probes to eight of the nine planets of the solar system and to comets and asteroids.

Major Events in Astronomy and Space

B.C.
585 Thales of Miletus (Greek: c. 625–c. 547) predicts solar eclipse in Asia Minor.
c. 480 Astronomer Oenopides of Chios (Greek: 5th cent.) discovers that Earth is tilted with respect to Sun.
352 Chinese report "guest star," or supernova, the earliest known sighting.
c. 340 Astronomer Kidinnu (Kidenas; Babylon: c. 379) discovers precession of equinoxes, the apparent change in position of stars caused by Earth's wobbling on its orbit.
c. 300 Chinese astronomers compile star maps.
c. 240 Chinese astronomers observe Halley's comet.
Eratosthenes of Cyrene (Greek: c.276–c.194) correctly calculates Earth's size.
165 Chinese astronomers notice sunspots.
c. 130 Astronomer Hipparchus of Nicea (Greek: 147–127) correctly determines distance to Moon and rediscovers precession of equinoxes (see 340 B.C.).

A.D.
c. 140 Almagest of Ptolemy (Greek: c. 90–168) develops astronomy of solar system in form based on Sun and planets rotating about Earth.
1543 De Revolutionibus by Nicholas Copernicus (Polish: 1473–1543) presents convincing arguments that Earth and other planets orbit Sun.
1577 Tycho Brahe (Danish: 1546–1601) proves that comets are visitors from space, not weather phenomena as previously believed.
1592 David Fabricius (German: 1564–1617) discovers star, later named Mira, that gradually disappears; in studying it in 1638, Phocyclides Holawarda recognizes that it appears and reappears on regular basis—the first-known variable star.
1609 Johannes Kepler (German: 1571–1630) discovers that the planets move in elliptical orbits.
1610 Galileo observes Jupiter's moons, phases of Venus, and (although he does not recognize what they are) rings of Saturn.
1611 Several astronomers simultaneously discover sunspots for first time in West.
1671 Giovanni Domenico Cassini (Italian-French: 1625-1712) correctly determines distances of the planets from Sun.

1682 Edmond Halley (English: 1656–1742) describes comet now known by his name and in 1705 correctly predicts its return in 1758.
1718 Halley discovers that stars move with respect to each other.
1755 Immanuel Kant (German: 1724–1804) proposes that many nebulas are actually composed of millions of stars and that solar system formed when giant cloud of dust condensed.
1781 William Herschel (German-English: 1738–1822) discovers planet Uranus.
1785 Herschel demonstrates that Milky Way is disk- or lens-shaped group of many stars, one of which is the Sun.
1801 Guiseppe Piazzi (Italian: 1746–1826) discovers first-known asteroid, Ceres.
1838 Friedrich W. Bessel (German: 1784–1846) determines distance to star other than the Sun.
1846 Johann G. Galle (German: 1812–1910) discovers planet Neptune using predictions of Urbain J.J. Leverrier (French: 1811–77) and John Couch Adams (English: 1819–92).
1924 Edwin Hubble (American: 1889–1953) shows that galaxies are "island universes"—giant aggregations of stars as large as Milky Way.
1929 Hubble finds that universe is expanding.
1930 Clyde Tombaugh (American: 1906–97) discovers planet Pluto.
1931 Karl Jansky (American: 1905–50) discovers that radio waves are coming from space, leading to founding of radio astronomy.
1948 George Gamow (Russian-American: 1904–68), Ralph Alpher (American: 1921–), and Robert Herman (American: 1914–97) develop Big Bang theory of origin of universe.
Jan Hendrik Oort (Dutch: 1900–1992) proposes that comets come from a vast cloud of material orbiting far beyond Pluto; the material is now known as the Oort Cloud.
1957 USSR launches Sputnik 1, the first manmade satellite.
1961 Soviet cosmonaut Yuri A. Gagarin (Russian: 1934-68) is first human to orbit Earth.
1962 U.S. space probe Mariner 2 is first to reach neighborhood of another planet, Venus.
1963 Maarten Schmidt (Dutch-American: 1929–) is first astronomer to recognize a quasar.

1965 Arno Penzias (German-American: 1933–) and Robert Wilson (American: 1936–) find radio waves pervading space, proving to most astronomers that Big Bang actually occurred.

1967 Jocelyn Bell-Burnell (English: 1943–) discovers first-known pulsar while working for Antony Hewish (English: 1924–); Hewish later gets Nobel Prize for discovery.

1969 Neil Armstrong (American: 1930–) and Edwin E. ("Buzz") Aldrin (American: 1930–) walk on Moon.

1971 American spacecraft, *Mariner 9,* is first to orbit another planet, Mars.

1975 Soviet space probe transmits pictures from surface of Venus.

1976 U.S. Viking space probes begin transmitting pictures of surface of Mars—unsuccessful in detecting life on planet.

1977 Rings of Uranus are discovered.

1979 U.S. space probe *Voyager 1* discovers that, like Saturn, Jupiter has rings.

1980 Alan Guth (American: 1947–) develops theory of inflationary universe, an explanation of how Big Bang occurred.

1981 U.S. introduces reusable spacecraft, the space shuttle.

1987 The explosion of Supernova 1987A, the nearest supernova that has been visible from Earth since 1604, is observed.

1989 U.S. space probe *Voyager 2* flies by Neptune, farthest planet from the Sun at that time, imaging the planet, its rings, and its moons.

1990 The Hubble Space Telescope is launched.

1992 The Magellan Venus orbiter completes mapping 95 percent of the planet's surface with radar.

Aleksander Wolszczan and Dale Frail discover planets orbiting pulsar PSR 1257+12, the first planets confirmed to orbit a body other than the Sun.

Observations from the Cosmic Background Explorer Satellite (COBE) confirm the Big Bang theory.

1993 Members of the crew of the Space Shuttle *Endeavour* successfully repair the main lens of the Hubble Space Telescope.

1994 Comet Shoemaker-Levy 9, broken into 21 fragments, some nearly half a kilometer in diameter, slams into the far side of Jupiter in July.

1995 Swiss astronomers Michel Mayer and Didier Queloz announce the first planet known to orbit an ordinary star other than the Sun.

The *Galileo* spacecraft drops a probe into the atmosphere of Jupiter and reports on its composition and weather.

1996 Andrea Dupree and Ronald Gilliland use the Hubble Space Telescope to make the first images of a star (Betelgeuse) other than the Sun that shows the star's disc.

A two-year-long analysis of data from the *Clementine* space probe reveals that Earth's moon may have water ice mixed with dust at the surface of the lunar south pole, where there is a deep, shadowy basin.

Astronomers who have analyzed a meteorite that was once a part of the planet Mars believe that it shows evidence for life having once existed on Mars, although the evidence is inconclusive.

Firm evidence is found for a massive black hole at the center of the Milky Way galaxy.

1997 A gamma-ray burst on February 28, detected by Italian-Dutch satellite *Beppo-Sax,* is the first ever to be linked with a visible object, a fuzzy patch of light that gradually disappears.

Astronomers report that data on Jupiter's moon Europa collected by the *Galileo* space probe shows that liquid water may be found below a surface of cracked ice and that it is possible that the ocean of Europa could contain life.

A study of data from the orbiting *Gamma Ray Observatory* reveals jets of positrons, a form of antimatter, interacting with electrons and streaming from the center of the Milky Way galaxy.

The space probe *Pathfinder* on July 4 becomes the first successful lander on Mars since the Viking program of the mid-1970s. *Pathfinder's* rover, *Sojourner,* leaves the craft and provides close-up observations of Martian rocks in what appears to be an ancient flood plain.

1998 Astronomers conclude that there is not enough matter in the universe to stop expansion; expansion may be accelerated by a very small anti-gravity force.

The *Voyager 1* space probe becomes the most distant artificial object, reaching some 6.5 billion miles (10.4 billion km) from Earth on Feb. 17.

Data from satellite-borne X-ray telescopes combined with optical data from the Keck II telescope reveal the largest known explosion since the Big Bang, a burst of gamma-rays as luminous for a second or two as the rest of the universe; the cause is unknown.

A burst of X-rays from the object SGR 1900+14 provides astronomers with evidence that the object is a magnetar, a type of neutron star that produces the most intense magnetic fields in the universe; magnetars were predicted by theorists in 1992, but not previously identified.

Using pictures taken by the *Galileo* spacecraft, astronomers find that Jupiter has four separate rings, each produced by one of Jupiter's smaller, inner moons (Metis, Adrastea, Amalthea, and Thebe).

1999 Two independent teams of astronomers determine that a system of at least three planets is in orbit about the star Upsilon Andromedae.

The *Mars Global Surveyor* discovers evidence in fossil magnetism that Mars had active tectonic plates some 4 billion years ago, the only planet other than Earth to experience plate tectonics. The space probe also finds more evidence that water once flowed on the Martian surface.

An automated system that detects gamma-ray bursts and immediately directs optical telescopes and other instruments to point toward the gamma-ray source allows astronomers to connect these immense outpourings of energy to the creation of black holes.

▶GLOSSARY OF PLANETARY TERMS

Rotation period The time it takes for a planet to rotate itself.

Orbital period The time it takes for a planet to orbit the Sun.

Orbital velocity The speed of a planet in its path around the Sun.

Inclination of axis The angle that the line about which a planet rotates makes with the plane defined by its path around the Sun.

Escape velocity The speed needed for an object to be propelled from the surface of a planet and not fall back. The escape velocity for Earth is 6.96 miles (11.2 km) per second, thus an object must travel at least 7 miles (12 km) per second to leave Earth's gravitational influence.

▶THE SOLAR SYSTEM

Earth is a planet. A planet is a large, fairly cool body traveling in a path, called its orbit, around a

Basic Facts About the Planets

Characteristic	Terrestrial Planets				Gas Giants				
	Mercury	Venus	Earth	Mars	Jupiter	Saturn	Uranus	Neptune	Pluto
Distance from Sun									
miles (millions)	36.0	67.2	93.0	141.6	483.7	886.6	1,784.0	2,795.1	3,670.1
km (millions)	57.9	108.2	149.6	227.9	778.4	1,426.8	2,871.0	4,498.3	5,906.4
Rotation period	59 d	243.7 d[1]	23.9 hrs	24.6 hrs	9.9 hrs	10.5 hrs	17.2 hrs	16.1 hrs	6.4 d
Orbital period (days)	88	224.7	365.256	686.98	4,332.59	10,759.22	30,865.4	60,189	90,465.0
Orbital velocity									
(miles/second)	29.74	21.76	18.51	14.99	8.12	6.00	4.24	3.41	2.95
Inclination of axis	0.10	3.39	23.45	25.19	3.12	26.73	97.86	29.56	122.46
Equatorial diameter									
miles	3,032	7,521	7,927	4,222	88,850	74,901	31,765	30,779	1,413
km	4,880	12,104	12,756	6,794	142,984	120,536	51,118	49,532	2,274
In relation to Earth:									
Diameter	38.3%	94.9%	100%	53.3%	1,121%	945%	401%	388%	17.8%
Mass	5.53%	81.5%	100%	10.7%	31,780%	9,516.2%	1,453.6%	1,714.7%	0.21%
Gravity	37.8%	90.7%	100%	37.7%	236.4%	91.6%	88.90%	112.5%	6.75%
Escape velocity									
miles/second	2.7	6.4	7.0	3.1	37.0	22.1	13.2	14.6	0.7
km/second	4.3	10.36	11.186	5.03	59.5	35.5	21.3	23.5	1.1
Average surface	332.4°F	867.0°F	58.8°F	-81.6°F	-162.6°F	-218.6°F	-323.0°F	-330.2°F	-369.8°F
temperature	166.9°C	463.9°C	14.9°C	-63.1°C	-108.1°C	-139.2°C	-197.2°C	-201.2°C	-223.2°C
Planetary satellites	0	0	1	2	16	18	18	8	1

Note: d=days.   1. Venus's rotation is retrograde, or opposite the direction of other planets.

star. All of the bodies under the gravitational influence of our local star, the Sun, together with the Sun, form the solar system. There are nine known planets in the solar system, as well as other planets around other stars, which are discussed following the solar system. Six of the nine solar-system planets were known to the ancients and astronomers found the remaining three by early in the 20th century. Often smaller, cool bodies orbit planets. These are called satellites or moons.

Cool rocky or metallic bodies smaller than planets that orbit the Sun are called asteroids. Small icy bodies are called comets. Comets often have orbits that take them from the edge of the system to locations near the Sun (some actually hit the Sun and burn up). Very small objects in space are called meteoroids. A meteoroid that burns up in Earth's atmosphere is called a meteor. One that reaches Earth's surface without burning completely is a meteorite.

It is currently believed that the solar system formed when a cloud of gas condensed to form the Sun. Parts of the cloud formed small bodies similar to today's asteroids, comets, and meteoroids. Collectively, these small bodies are called planetesimals or planetoids. Early in the history of the solar system, about 4.6 billion years ago or even before, the planetoids frequently crashed into one another. While this sometimes resulted in one or more of the planetoids breaking up, often a small planetoid would stick to a larger one, making it larger still. The end results of this process, it is proposed, are the nine solar-system planets and their moons, along with the existing asteroids, comets, and meteoroids.

The solar system is located in a large system of stars called the Milky Way galaxy. The solar system is 28,000 light-years from the center of the Milky Way and 67 light-years from the plane defined by the galactic spiral.

The Terrestrial Planets

In terms of distance from the Sun, these are the first four planets of the solar system— Mercury,

Venus, Earth, and Mars. Terrestrial planets all have a comparatively high density, a concentration of metallic elements, and hard, rocky surfaces. Earth is the largest of the terrestrial planets but is dwarfed by the enormous sizes of the outer "gas giant" planets (Jupiter, Saturn, Uranus, and Neptune). Mercury, Earth, and Mars have magnetic fields, but Venus does not. Earth and Venus have thick atmospheres, Mars has a thin atmosphere, and Mercury's atmosphere is almost nonexistent.

Mercury

Main components of atmosphere: 98% helium, 2% hydrogen. Mercury is the planet closest to the Sun and in keeping with its namesake—Mercury, the winged messenger—moves the fastest in its orbit. Usually obscured from view from the Sun's glare, it is sometimes visible on Earth's horizon just after sunset, when it is called the Evening Star, or just before dawn, when it is called the Morning Star. About 14 times every 100 years, Mercury can also be seen crossing directly in front of the Sun's disk.

Mercury was long thought to be the smallest planet, but better measurements of Pluto's size have shown that Pluto is even smaller. The U.S. *Mariner 10* space probe provided the first detailed pictures of Mercury's surface during flybys in 1974 and 1975. *Mariner 10* mapped about 35 percent of the planet's heavily cratered, moonlike surface. No space probe has visited the planet since.

Mercury is a waterless, airless world that alternately bakes and freezes as it orbits the Sun. Its tenuous atmosphere is thought to be one-trillionth the density of Earth's atmosphere and largely composed of helium. On Mercury's sunlit side temperatures reach 850°F (450°C) and plummet to -300°F (-180°C) on the dark side. These extremes are largely due to Mercury's slow rate of one single rotation is two-thirds of one Mercury year, or 59 days for a rotation compared to 88 days for a revolution. Mercury's axis is almost perpendicular to its plane of rotation, so any single place on the planet sees dawn only once every 176 days—the planet must rotate three times and go through two of its "years" before a new day dawns.

Mercury's surface is scarred with hundreds of thousands of meteor craters. Many such craters were probably formed during the planetoid showers believed to have occurred soon after the formation of the solar system. Many areas have had the craters smoothed over by ancient lava flows, however. This indicates extensive volcanic activity on Mercury during and after the time of the planetoid showers. The surface is also crisscrossed by huge cliffs, or scarps. These probably formed as Mercury's surface cooled and shrank. Some of the scarps are up to 1.2 miles (1.9 km) high and 932 miles (1,500 km) long.

Mercury is so dense for its size that astronomers think that its rocky outer crust is very thin and that the planet is mostly iron. It probably was once larger. During the early bombardment, it is conjectured that one of the larger planetoids (about a sixth of the size of the early planet) hit Mercury so hard that it blasted most of the rocky crust away.

Venus

Main components of atmosphere: 95% carbon dioxide, 3.5% nitrogen. As seen in the night sky from Earth, Venus is second only to the Moon in brightness. Venus, named for the Roman goddess of love, is the planet that passes closest to Earth (24,000,000 mi., or 39,000,000 km). Since it is between Earth and the Sun, Venus, like Mercury, is seen either as the Morning Star or the Evening Star.

Because of its proximity to Earth and its position between Earth and the Sun, Venus became (in 1962) the first planet beyond Earth to be scanned by a space probe in its neighborhood (*Mariner 2*). The pull of the Sun's gravity makes Venus and Mercury "downhill" from the Earth; one must travel against the Sun's gravity to reach other planets. Since 1962 Venus has been visited by numerous U.S. and Soviet spacecraft. Soviet space probes *Venera 13* and *Venera 14* were the first to make a soft landing and send back pictures from the Venusian surface.

The Venusian atmosphere is thick with clouds that have shrouded the planet's surface from view, making the planet somewhat mysterious. This dense atmosphere has been studied extensively by a series of U.S. and Soviet space probes. The Venusian clouds range from about 28 to 37 miles (45 to 60 km) above the planet's surface and are differentiated into three layers. Droplets of sulfuric acid and water have been identified in the clouds.

The clouds and high level of carbon dioxide in the atmosphere have combined to trap heat in the lower atmosphere of Venus. This is an extreme form of the greenhouse effect and is responsible for high temperatures in the lower atmosphere, 870°F (460°C)—hot enough to melt lead. The atmospheric pressure at the surface is 92 times that of Earth. Radiation of heat from the lower atmosphere is so inefficient that there is little variation of temperature between night and day.

One feature of the Venusian upper atmosphere is markedly different from that of Earth. The atmosphere superrotates on Venus—that is, the atmosphere above the clouds moves 60 times faster than the planet rotates—whereas the Earth and its atmosphere rotate at the same speed. So, high winds and steady upper-atmosphere winds—100 mph (160 km/hr) or faster—are a dominant factor in Venusian weather. But at ground level, winds are calmer, with an average closer to 2 mph (3.6 km/hr).

Soviet space probes that soft-landed on Venus have provided photographs of the planet's surface. Radar maps of 99 percent of the Venusian surface, completed by the U.S. Pioneer spacecraft (from 1978 to 1993), and *Magellan* (from 1989 to 1994), now give a detailed picture of features as small as 350 ft. (100 m) in diameter. More than a thousand Venusian mountains, volcanoes, rifts, basins, impact craters, and other features have been identified.

About 10 percent of the surface is highland terrain, 70 percent rolling uplands, and 20 percent lowland plains. There are two major highland areas: one about half the size of Africa and located in the equatorial region and the other, about the size of Australia, located to the north. The highest mountain on Venus—Maxwell Montes—is in the northern highlands and is higher than Earth's Mt. Everest. Volcanic activity dominates Venus; the planet is covered with volcanic domes and lava channels.

Like Earth, Venus is thought to have an internal structure. The crust, however, is much thicker than that of Earth, perhaps twice as deep on the average, making the crust of Venus about 60 mi. (100 km) thick. Below the crust is a large layer called the mantle; below the mantle is a core thought to be molten nickel-iron, similar to Earth's outer core.

Earth

Main components of atmosphere: 78% nitrogen, 21% oxygen, 1% water, 0.93% argon. Earth is the third planet from the Sun and the only one in the solar system known to harbor life. From out in space, our planet appears as a bright, blue-and-white sphere—blue because some 70 percent of the surface is covered by water, and white because clouds cover about half the planet's surface.

The tenuous outer layer of Earth's atmosphere—the thermosphere—begins about 310 miles (500 km) above Earth's surface. Between about 60 miles down to about 30 miles (100 to 50 km) is the mesosphere; below this is the stratosphere (down to about 8 mi., or 13 km); finally, there is the troposphere, the bottom layer. The atmosphere, along with Earth's magnetic field, shields us from nearly all harmful radiation coming from the Sun and from outer space.

The interior consists of three main layers. The outer crust, largely made up of granite and basalt rock, varies from 55 miles (90 km) deep under the continents to 3 miles (5 km) deep under the oceans. The second main layer, the mantle, extends down to about 1,900 miles (3,000 km) below the surface and is composed of silicate rock rich in iron. The top part of the mantle is semiliquid, down to about 150 miles (250 km). The rigid upper crust is broken into large plates that move slowly on this partially fluid layer, which is termed the asthenosphere. Beneath this lies the Earth's iron and nickel core with a lumpy outer boundary. Scientists believe the temperature at the center of the core could be 7,200°F (4,000°C). The outer core is liquid due to the great heat, while an inner core is solid as a result of the great pressure at Earth's center.

The Moon is Earth's only natural satellite. It is over one-quarter the size of Earth in diameter (2,160 mi. or 3,476 km). At a distance of 238,000 mi. (380,000 km), it is the brightest object in Earth's nighttime sky. The Moon regularly changes in appearance as seen from Earth. See the discussion of these changes, called "Phases of the Moon," in Part I.

Because the Moon is slightly egg-shaped, the same side of the satellite always faces Earth—this side being the elongated small end. As a result, the Moon rotates once during each revolution. The side we do not see is called the far side (not the dark side—all parts of the moon undergo 14 Earth days of light, followed by 14 days of darkness).

Over a decade of exploration of the Moon by U.S. and Soviet space probes was capped by the landing of two U.S. astronauts on the Moon on July 20, 1969. A total of six two-man crews of American astronauts eventually landed on the Moon between 1969 and 1972, and they brought back some 842 pounds (382 kg) of samples of Moon rocks. The world these astronauts found was airless and devoid of life. Temperatures on the Moon range from up to 273°F (134°C) on the bright side to -274°F (-170°C) on the unlighted side.

A mixture of fine powder and broken rock blankets the Moon's surface. The near side also has large regions (called maria, or seas) of solidified lava. The lunar surface is pockmarked with craters up to 56 miles (90 km) across and is broken by huge mountain ranges. Some craters at the poles may contain frozen water in their depths.

Mars

Main components of atmosphere: 95% carbon dioxide, 3% nitrogen, 2% argon. Mars is the outermost of the four terrestrial planets and has a distinctive reddish coloring, coming from iron oxide in the Martian soil. The Romans named the planet after their god of war, and the two irregularly shaped satellites of Mars have been named after the horses—Deimos (terror) and Phobos (fear)—that pulled the war god's chariot. Mars is usually visible in Earth's nighttime sky and is lined up with Earth between it and the Sun once every 780 days, though its closest approach to Earth (35,000,000 mi., or 56,000,000 km) comes at 15- or 17-year intervals; 1997 was a year of a close approach.

The so-called canals on Mars—later found to be optical illusions—were first observed by 19th-century astronomers and led to the widespread belief that there was life on Mars. (In 1900 the French Academy offered a prize to the first person to find life on any planet except Mars, presumably because everyone knew that there was life on that planet.) The planet thus became the target of numerous space probes, both U.S. and Soviet, from the early years of interplanetary exploration.

The first successful flyby of Mars was achieved by the U.S. spacecraft *Mariner 4* in 1965. The Soviets became the first to land a probe successfully on the surface of Mars in 1971, but the probe malfunctioned and stopped transmitting after only 20 seconds. It was not until 1976, when the U.S. *Viking 1* and *Viking 2* landers touched down on Mars, that extensive study of the planet from its surface became possible. In fact, the *Viking 1* lander continued to function until 1983. *Pathfinder* landed on Mars on July 4, 1997, and continued the exploration of Martian geology and weather.

The big question of whether there is (or was) life on Mars has yet to be answered with certainty. The *Viking* landers conducted three experiments on Martian soil to check for biological processes. Some of the tests yielded positive results, but these could also be explained by the soil chemistry. The lack of other evidence of organic molecules adds to the case against life on Mars.

Orbiting satellites have mapped the entire planet down to a resolution of 500-1,000 ft. (150–300 m). The planet's surface is heavily cratered, and there is extensive evidence of once-active volca-

noes. There are also such spectacular features as Olympus Mons (an extinct volcano three times as high as Earth's Mt. Everest); mammoth canyons, one of which is four times deeper than the Grand Canyon; and a gigantic basin (larger than Alaska) in the southern hemisphere that was probably created by a single, huge asteroid. The planet has ice caps at both poles (water ice with some frozen carbon dioxide), and the ice caps advance and recede with changes in the seasons.

But the most intriguing aspect of the Martian surface is that water once flowed there in great quantities. Parts of the terrain apparently have sedimentary origins, and there are many long channels, complete with smaller tributary channels and islands, that extend for hundreds of kilometers. Scientists speculate that Mars once had a much thicker atmosphere, made up of gases vented during volcanic eruptions, which would have made it possible for water in its liquid state to exist on the surface. Martian atmospheric pressure is now so low, however, that surface water would immediately vaporize. It is conjectured that the water in the past flowed through the channels to lowland areas and then sank into the Martian regolith, or upper soil layer, since there is no geologic evidence that standing bodies of water ever existed. Astronomers believe that at least some of the primordial water may still be trapped as ice in the regolith.

Mars is too small to sustain continual volcanic activity. Its atmosphere apparently thinned out after volcanic activity ceased. Atmospheric pressure is now just seven one-thousandths of that on Earth at sea level, and the predominant gas is carbon dioxide, which is relatively heavy. A small amount of water vapor in the atmosphere is enough to form some clouds, small patches of fog in some valleys, and occasionally even patches of frost. Surface temperatures vary from a high of about 70°F (20°C) during summer at the equator to a low of about -220°F (-140°C) during winter at the poles. By far the most pronounced feature of Martian weather is dust storms, which regularly engulf the entire planet for a period of several months.

The asteroids

Considered by some to be minor planets, the asteroids are very small bodies ranging from less than 1 to 600 miles in diameter. The name asteroid means "starlike" and was given to asteroids because they are so small they appear as points of light (as do stars) even in powerful telescopes. Otherwise, asteroids are not like stars at all.

The first four asteroids were discovered between 1801-07 and were believed to be small planets. Today, more than 18,000 asteroids are known, and most orbit the Sun in a region called the asteroid belt, located between Mars and Jupiter.

The Outer Planets

Beyond Mars and the asteroid belt lie the five known outer planets of our solar system. Four of these planets—Jupiter, Saturn, Uranus, and Neptune—are the so-called gas giants. Many times larger than the terrestrial planets, these planets are huge, dense balls of hydrogen and other gases. Beyond them (most of the time) lies the solar system's outermost and smallest known planet, Pluto, which may be nothing more than a tiny ball of frozen gases.

Jupiter

Main components of atmosphere: 89% hydrogen, 11% helium. Jupiter is the largest planet in the solar system. It has 2.5 times more mass than all the other planets of the solar system together and is 11 times as large as Earth in diameter. Jupiter is so large that scientists believe it almost became a star: as the gases and dust contracted to form the planet, gravitational forces created tremendous pressure and temperature inside the core—perhaps as high as tens of thousands of degrees. But there was not enough mass available to create the temperatures needed to start a fusion reaction such as that of the Sun (above 27,000,000°F, or 15,000,000°C, at the Sun's core); thus Jupiter has been slowly cooling down ever since. Even so, Jupiter still radiates about 2.5 times as much heat as it receives from the Sun.

The first object to reach Jupiter from Earth was *Pioneer 10*. It returned the first close-up pictures of the giant planet in 1973. Subsequently, the more sophisticated space probes *Voyager 1* and *Voyager 2* passed by Jupiter in 1979 and sent back images and more data on the planet. One of the most exciting discoveries by *Voyager 1* was that Jupiter has a faint but extensive ring system that extends almost 186,000 miles (300,000 km) out from the planet's surface. *Galileo* found another faint ring at 1 million miles (1.6 million km) in 1998. A probe from *Galileo* arrived at Jupiter on December 7, 1995, finding winds of 435 mph (700 km/hr) and much less water vapor than expected. Scientists later determined that the probe had arrived in what amounts to a Jovian desert.

Jupiter's thick atmosphere, which may extend downward as much as 600 miles (1,000 km), is primarily made up of hydrogen, with some helium and traces of other gases. Because the planet spins so fast (one rotation in just under 10 hours), its clouds tend to form bands that give the planet a striped appearance. Bands of clouds at higher altitudes are carried eastward by jet streams, while those at lower levels are blown westward.

There are numerous eddies and swirls in Jupiter's atmosphere, but none can compare with the Great Red Spot, apparently a massive hurricane (rotating counterclockwise) located in the southern hemisphere near the equator. The Great Red Spot was first observed some 300 years ago, and this storm continues unabated today. Since 1938 three smaller white ovals have been observed to the south of the Great Red Spot.

Jupiter's cloud tops are extremely cold (about -202°F, or -130°C), but temperatures increase deeper inside the atmosphere. Pressure also increases, and at about 600 miles (1,000 km) below the outermost atmospheric layers, great oceans of liquid hydrogen form Jupiter's surface. These may be some 12,000 miles (20,000 km) deep. Beneath them the hydrogen is so densely compacted it is thought to be in a metallic state. Within this is the core, thought to be an iron and silicate rock ball about the size of Earth.

Jupiter is now known to have 16 moons, the four largest being the Galilean moons, so called because they were first observed by Galileo. The Galilean moons are Ganymede, Callisto, Europa, and Io—after the Roman god Jupiter's cupbearer (Ganymede) and three of Jupiter's inamorata. Ganymede is the largest moon in the solar system—although previously this honor was accorded to Saturn's Titan—and is larger even than the planets Pluto and Mercury. It is a huge, cratered ball of ice and may have a core of solid silicate rock. Callisto, with an orbit outside that of Ganymede, is also covered with ice and is riddled with thousands of craters. Europa, which orbits inside Ganymede, is about the size of our Moon

and has a smooth surface marked by networks of cracks. The most interesting of Jupiter's moons are Io, which orbits closest to Jupiter, and Europa, which may have liquid water oceans beneath an icy surface. The *Voyagers* and *Galileo* photographed volcanoes erupting on Io. Orange-red patches on Io's mottled surface are apparently molten sulfur beds, but most other parts of Io's surface are seem very cold (about -229°F, or -145°C).

Saturn

Main components of atmosphere: 89% hydrogen, 11% helium. Saturn is the sixth planet of the solar system and the second largest, after Jupiter. The outermost of the planets that can be identified easily in Earth's nighttime sky with the unaided eye, Saturn has a pale yellowish color and is not nearly so bright as Mars. Saturn's spectacular ring system, which makes it one of the most interesting of the planets, is visible only through a telescope. Its rings are more extensive than those of any other planet.

Like Jupiter, Saturn is composed of densely compacted hydrogen, helium, and other gases. Liquid or metallic hydrogen probably exists underneath the planet's thick atmosphere, and scientists believe there is a solid core of rock about two times the size of Earth at its center. Saturn's high rotational speed (once every 10 hours, 12 minutes) makes it the most oblate (flattened) of all the planets; it is almost 6,800 miles (11,000 km) wider at the equator than on a line through the poles.

Though exploration of Saturn began in 1979 with the first flyby (*Pioneer 11*), the *Voyager 1* and *Voyager 2* missions in 1980 and 1981, respectively, provided the first detailed look at the planet. Scientists have spent years sifting through the data gathered, and, though there were important new findings, many questions about Saturn remain unanswered.

The *Voyagers* found a huge storm thousands of miles across on Saturn, along with a wide band of extremely high winds—up to 1,000 miles (1,600 km) per hour—at the equator. Winds in this band all travel in the direction of the planet's rotation (unlike bands of wind on Jupiter). The *Voyagers* also discovered a vast hydrogen cloud circling the planet above the equator.

The *Voyagers'* most exciting discoveries concern the planetary rings. Previously, about six different rings had been identified within the ring system, but *Voyager 1* pictures show as many as 1,000 separate rings. Narrow rings can even be seen within the Cassini Division, once thought to be an empty gap between the two major parts of the ring system. Some rings are not circular, and at least two rings are intertwined, or "braided." A strange new phenomenon was also discovered in the rings. *Voyager 1* pictures clearly show dark, radial fingers—"spokes"—moving inside the rings in the direction of rotation. Scientists speculate that they are made of ice crystals.

Voyager 2 pictures show that Saturn has far more than 1,000 rings—perhaps as many as a hundred thousand or more. One of the brightest rings is shown to be under 152 meters (500 ft.) thick. *Voyager 2* also found seasonal differences between the planet's two hemispheres and photographed a storm 4,000 miles (6,500 km) wide.

Twelve of Saturn's moons were known before the arrival of the *Voyagers*, and instruments aboard the space probe helped locate five new ones in the 1980s. In 1990 an 18th moon, later named Pan, was located in images made by *Voyager 2*. Most of Saturn's moons are relatively small and composed of rock and ice. All but one of the small moons are pockmarked by meteor craters, and in some cases the moons appear to have been cracked by collisions with especially large meteors. But *Voyager* pictures show that one moon, Enceladus, is smooth in large regions apparently unmarked by collisions with meteors. Scientists believe that Enceladus is being pulled and stretched by the combined gravities of a nearby moon and Saturn itself. Tidal forces have apparently heated the core of Enceladus and made its surface soft enough to smooth over any craters formed by meteor impacts.

Titan, Saturn's largest moon (3,000 mi., or 4,800 km in diameter) is the only moon in the solar system known to have an atmosphere of any substance. Scientists suspect that at least some precursors of life may have formed there. For this reason *Voyager 1* was guided to within about 2,500 miles (4,000 km) of Titan during the Saturn flyby. Though Titan's surface was obscured by dense clouds, Voyager's sensors nevertheless returned a considerable amount of information about the moon and its atmosphere. Titan's atmosphere is composed mostly of nitrogen, like that of Earth, with only a small percentage of methane and carbon monoxide. Atmospheric pressure is at least 1.5 times that on Earth and temperatures range around -294°F (-181°C). Titan in fact appears to be a frozen version of Earth before life evolved.

The possibility of oceans of liquid methane (or of nitrogen or methane rain) on Titan was a matter of considerable controversy for some time after *Voyager 1* investigated the moon. But Titan is "dry," at least in the regions investigated. Pools of liquid methane might still exist in other low-lying regions, but it is unlikely that either methane or nitrogen condenses to liquid form on Titan.

Uranus

Main components of atmosphere: 89% hydrogen, 11% helium. Uranus is the seventh planet in the solar system and the third of the gas giants. The planet is barely visible in Earth's nighttime sky (it looks like a faint star) and for that reason, it went undiscovered until 1781.

Nearly the same size as Neptune and only about 5 percent of Jupiter's mass, Uranus is a faintly greenish color, perhaps because its atmosphere contains methane. The planet's axis of rotation is tipped over on its side. Astronomers discovered a system of nine faint rings in 1977, and *Voyager* found two more rings in 1986. There are 18 known moons of Uranus. Caliban and Sycorax were found in 1997, and a still-unnamed moon was noticed in 1999 by a researcher studying a 1986 photograph taken by *Voyager 2*.

Uranus's atmosphere is very cold (-355°F, or -215°C). No clouds have been observed. Scientists speculate that, as on Jupiter and Saturn, temperatures and pressures increase dramatically down through the outer layer of atmosphere. At some point the hydrogen and helium would be sufficiently compressed to form a liquid or slushy surface "crust." Underneath this crust they believe is a mantle of solidified methane, ammonia, and water; and inside this mantle, a rocky core of silicon and iron about 15 times as massive as Earth. The core is thought to be hot, probably about 12,000°F (7,000°C).

Neptune

Main components of atmosphere: 89% hydrogen, 11% helium. The last of the gas giants, Neptune is the eighth planet in the solar system. It was discovered in 1846 after mathematical calculations based on irregularities in the orbit of Uranus provided astronomers with the correct location of the planet. Neptune, like Uranus, has been surrounded by considerable uncertainty because of its enormous distance from Earth. The 1989 visit by *Voyager 2* contributed greatly to improved understanding of the planet.

Neptune is a pale bluish color, but it has a clear atmosphere, and is very cold at the cloud tops (about -365°F or -220°C).

Scientists believe that Neptune has a three-layered structure similar to that of Uranus: a crust of solidified or liquid hydrogen and helium that gradually thins outward into an atmosphere; a mantle of solidified gases and water; and a hot, rocky core (about 12,000°F or 7,000°C) some 15 times as massive as Earth. But one aspect of Neptune remains a mystery. Despite similarities with Uranus, Neptune has been found to radiate 2.7 times as much heat as it receives from the Sun (at a rate of 0.03 microwatts per ton of mass). Uranus, on the other hand, does not emit as much excess heat.

Neptune has eight known moons, Triton and Nereid, discovered from Earth, and six others discovered by *Voyager 2*, and a ring system containing two bright rings and three dim ones. Triton is the largest moon and has an atmosphere. Triton is unusual in that it travels in a direction opposite that of Neptune's rotation, suggesting that it has a different origin from the planet. Triton also has volcanic activity: geysers of nitrogen rising as high as five miles (8 km).

Pluto

Main components of atmosphere: Methane and nitrogen (quantities unknown) The ninth and outermost (most of the time) known planet of the solar system is a ball of frozen gases probably only about the size of Earth's Moon. Pluto was discovered in 1930 as a result of an extensive search by Clyde Tombaugh. Because of its relatively small size and chaotic orbit (which at times crosses inside Neptune's orbit), some scientists think that Pluto is not really a planet at all. Instead, they theorize that Pluto is only one of the large comets in the Kuiper belt, discovered outside the orbit of Neptune over several years beginning in 1992.

Frozen methane and a thin atmosphere of methane and some other gases have been detected on Pluto. Pluto has one known moon, Charon, discovered in 1978. Charon is about one-half the size of Pluto. Pluto and Charon rotate and revolve synchronously like a double planet system.

In 1996, scientists discovered a far-away body that ranges three times as far from the Sun as Pluto does. The body, named 1996TL66, is over 300 miles in diameter, earning it the designation "miniplanet."

The Sun

Virtually all of the energy used by living things comes from the Sun. The Sun's light causes photosynthesis in green plants, and its heat causes winds. Fossil fuels, such as coal, oil, and natural gas, got their energy originally from photosynthesis, as did wood. Animals derive their energy from plants that photosynthesize, either directly or indirectly. The only natural nonsolar energy sources are nuclear reactions (which also produce geothermal energy), some bacteria that metabolize sulfur, and the tides, which are produced largely by the Moon, but in part by the Sun.

Because the Sun is a ball of gases, it does not rotate as a whole. The equator rotates in about 25 days, while gas near the poles rotates in about 30 days. The period of rotation at each latitude can be found by observing sunspots, which are magnetic storms. Sunspots appear and disappear in a mysterious 11-year cycle that many think influences weather on Earth, although convincing proof is lacking. Sometimes sunspots disappear for tens of years at a time, as during the period from 1645 to 1715. It may or may not be a coincidence that those years coincided with the "Little Ice Age" in Europe, when temperatures were far below average.

Like Earth, the Sun is composed of various layers. The part we see is called the photosphere. In the Sun's interior, energy is generated when hydrogen in the core fuses to become helium. Above the photosphere is a region of pinkish gases, the chromosphere. Above that is a large halo, visible only in eclipses, called the corona. Particles from the Sun, the solar wind, stream through the solar system, creating auroras on Earth. Strong increases in solar wind during solar flares can interfere with radio communication.

▶ PLANETS OUTSIDE THE SOLAR SYSTEM

Planets circling stars other than the Sun, or extrasolar planets, became accepted in the 1990s. Approximately 30 ordinary stars are generally admitted to have definite planets, at least two pulsars also have planets, and perhaps a half-dozen stars that have dusty regions surrounding them that may be planets forming. In 1998 an object first recognized by Susan Tereby and coworkers at the Extrasolar Research Corp. in Pasadena, California, was widely heralded as the first image of a planet away from any star, although many astronomers remain skeptical. Other observable features that some have touted as planets included empty lanes in some dust clouds, (supposedly swept out by planets) and regions of higher dust density (supposedly the result of gravitational attraction of the unseen planet), and a ring, similar to the rings around gas-giant planets in the solar system, about a young star (perhaps shepherded by a planet in the way that planetary rings are shepherded by moons).

Perhaps the most interesting extrasolar-planet news of 1999 was the accumulation of evidence by two separate teams of astronomers that the star Upsilon Andromedae (Ups And) has three planets in orbit, the first known planetary system around an ordinary star. The evidence for these planets consists of slight regular changes in the position of Ups And produced by the orbiting planets. All the detected planets are about the size of Jupiter or larger, but astronomy cannot now observe effects caused by a planet the size of Earth on a star that, like Ups And, is 44 light-years away, so smaller planets are possible. New space-based telescopes scheduled for launch in the next few years should make it possible to observe smaller extrasolar planets if they are indeed present.

Before 1992 the only planetary system known to exist was the solar system of 9 planets around the Sun, although astronomers suspected that planets might exist around other stars. In 1992, however, astronomers Aleksander Wolszczan and Dale Frail observed that a pulsar known as PSR 1257+12 moved slightly back and forth as if being pulled in space by several bodies in orbit. Calculations show that two of the bodies, each about three times the size of Earth, move in small, swift orbits about the pulsar, rather like Mercury around the Sun. A third is 100 times Earth in mass and orbits at a distance from the pulsar comparable to Pluto from the Sun. Since then, another pulsar was also found to have a body too small to be a star orbiting it.

In 1995, the first planet that orbits an ordinary star was established on the basis of a wobble in the position of the Sun-like star 51 Pegasi, nearly 50 light-years from the solar system. This discovery by Swiss astronomers Michel Mayer and Didier Queloz was soon followed by observations of several other ordinary stars that move back and forth in space by small amounts that could only be caused by one or more large planets in orbit about them, notably 16 Cygni B, 47 Ursae Majoria, Rho Coronae Borealis, 55 Cancri, Tau Boötis, and of course, Upsilon Andromedae. In all these cases, the stars are less than 75 light-years from the solar system and the detected planets are very large, from three-fourths the size of Jupiter to five times its size. One unexpected discovery is that the very large planets are mostly in orbit closer to their stars than the planet Mercury is to the Sun.

The earliest evidence that planets might be forming around stars other than the Sun came from infrared observations in 1983 that showed dust clouds of the kind thought to have formed the solar system around the nearby stars Vega and Fomalhaut. In 1998 and 1999, newer Earth-based telescopes were able to image these dust clouds, and also one found about the star HR4796A, with more detail, revealing that Vega has a large region of concentrated dust while both Fomalhaut and HR4796A have empty regions near the star that could be interpreted as having been cleared of dust by the formation of planets.

Characteristics of the Sun

Position in solar system	Center
Mean distance from Earth	92,960,000 mi. (149,600,000 km)
Distance from center of Milky Way galaxy	27,710 light-years
Period of rotation	25.38 days at 16° longitude
Inclination (relative to Earth's orbit)	7.25°
Equatorial diameter	865,000 mi. (1,392,000 km)
Diameter relative to Earth	109.2 times
Mass	2.192×10^{27} tons (1.9891×10^{30} kg)
Mass converted to energy each second	9,500 pounds (4,300 kg)
Surface gravity relative to Earth's	28 times
Temperature at core	28,280,000°F (15,710,000°C)
Temperature at bottom of photosphere	12,400°F (6,900°C)
Main components	Hydrogen and helium
Present age	4.6 billion years
Expected future life of hydrogen fuel supply	6.4 billion years

The Constellations

Name	Genitive	Abbr.	Translation	Remarks
Andromeda	Andromedae	And	Andromeda	Character in Greek myth
Antlia	Antliae	Ant	Air pump	Named by Nicolas Lacaille in 1750
Apus	Apodis	Aps	Swift, or Bird of Paradise	Named by Johann Bayer in 1603
Aquarius	Aquarii	Aqr	Water Bearer	In zodiac
Aquila	Aquilae	Aql	Eagle	Contains Altair
Ara	Arae	Ara	Altar	Part of the Centaurus group
Aries	Arietis	Ari	Ram	In zodiac
Auriga	Aurigae	Aur	Charioteer	Contains Capella
Boötes	Boötis	Boo	Herdsman	Contains Arcturus
Caelum	Caeli	Cae	Chisel, or graving tool	Lacaille, 1750
Camelopardalis	Camelopardalis	Cam	Giraffe	Named by Johannes Bartsch in 1661
Cancer	Cancri	Cnc	Crab	In zodiac
Canes Venatici	Canum Venaticorum	CVn	Hunting dogs	Named by Johannes Hevelius in 1687
Canis Major	Canis Majoris	CMa	Big Dog	Contains Sirius and Adhara
Canis Minor	Canis Minoris	CMi	Little Dog	Contains Procyon
Capricornus	Capricorni	Cap	Goat	In zodiac
Carina	Carinae	Car	Ship's Keel[1]	Lacaille, 1750; contains Canopus
Cassiopeia	Cassiopeiae	Cas	Cassiopeia	Character in Greek myth
Centaurus	Centauri	Cen	Centaur	Character in Greek myth; contains Rigil Kentaurus and Hadar/Agena
Cepheus	Cephei	Cep	Cepheus	Character in Greek myth
Cetus	Ceti	Cet	Whale	Sea monster slain by Perseus
Chamaeleon	Chamaeleontis	Cha	Chameleon	Bayer, 1603
Circinus	Circini	Cir	Compass	Lacaille, 1750
Columba	Columbae	Col	Dove	Bayer, 1603
Coma Berenices	Comae Berenices	Com	Berenice's Hair	Third Century B.C. Egyptian Queen
Corona Australis	Coronae Australis	CrA	Southern Crown	Also Sagittarius' crown
Corona Borealis	Coronae Borealis	CrB	Northern Crown	Also Ariadne's crown
Corvus	Corvi	Crv	Crow	Companion of Orpheus
Crater	Crateris	Crt	Cup	—
Crux[2]	Crucis	Cru	Southern Cross	Named by Augustine Royer in 1679; Contains Beta Crucis and Acrux
Cygnus	Cygni	Cyg	Swan	Contains Deneb
Delphinus	Delphini	Del	Dolphin	
Dorado	Doradus	Dor	Goldfish	Bayer, 1603
Draco	Draconis	Dra	Dragon	Dragon slain by Hercules
Equuleus	Equulei	Equ	Little Horse	
Eridanus	Eridani	Eri	River Eridanus	Contains Achernar
Fornax	Fornacis	For	Furnace	Lacaille, 1750.
Gemini	Geminorum	Gem	Twins	In zodiac; contains Pollux
Grus	Gruis	Gru	Crane	Bayer, 1603
Hercules	Herculis	Her	Hercules	Character from Greek myth
Horologium	Horologii	Hor	Clock	Lacaille, 1750.
Hydra[3]	Hydrae	Hya	Hydra	Monster from Greek myth
Hydrus	Hydri	Hyi	Sea serpent	Bayer, 1603
Indus	Indi	Ind	Indian	Bayer, 1603
Lacerta	Lacertae	Lac	Lizard	Hevelius, 1687
Leo	Leonis	Leo	Lion	In zodiac; contains Regulus
Leo Minor	Leonis Minoris	LMi	Little Lion	Hevelius, 1687
Lepus	Leporis	Lep	Hare	Prey of Orion
Libra	Librae	Lib	Scales	In zodiac
Lupus	Lupi	Lup	Wolf	Part of Centaurus group
Lynx	Lyncis	Lyn	Lynx	Hevelius, 1687
Lyra	Lyrae	Lyr	Harp	Contains Vega
Mensa	Mensae	Men	Table (mountain)	Lacaille, 1750
Microscopium	Microscopii	Mic	Microscope	Lacaille, 1750
Monoceros	Monocerotis	Mon	Unicorn	Royer, 1679
Musca	Muscae	Mus	Fly	Bayer, 1603
Norma	Normae	Nor	Carpenter's Square	Lacaille, 1750
Octans	Octantis	Oct	Octant	Lacaille, 1750
Ophiuchus	Ophiuchi	Oph	Serpent Bearer	Character in Greek myth
Orion	Orionis	Ori	The Hunter	Character in Greek myth; contains Rigel, Betelgeuse, and Bellatrix
Pavo	Pavonis	Pav	Peacock	Bayer, 1603.
Pegasus	Pegasi	Peg	Pegasus	Winged horse in Greek myth
Perseus	Persei	Per	Perseus	Character in Greek myth
Phoenix	Phoenicis	Phe	Phoenix	Bayer, 1603
Pictor	Pictoris	Pic	Easel	Lacaille, 1750
Pisces	Piscium	Psc	Fish	In zodiac

Name	Genitive	Abbr.	Translation	Remarks
Piscis Austrinus	Piscis Austrin	PsA	Southern Fish	Contains Fomalhaut
Puppis	Puppis	Pup	Ship's Stern[1]	Lacaille, 1750
Pyxis	Pyxidis	Pyx	Ship's Compass[1]	Lacaille, 1750
Reticulum	Reticuli	Ret	Net	Lacaille, 1750
Sagitta	Sagittae	Sge	Arrow	—
Sagittarius	Sagittarii	Sgr	Archer	In zodiac
Scorpius	Scorpii	Sco	Scorpion	In zodiac; contains Antares and Shaula
Sculptor	Sculptoris	Scl	Sculptor	Lacaille, 1750
Scutum	Scuti	Sct	Shield	Hevelius, 1687
Serpens	Serpentis	Ser	Serpent	Snake held by giant Ophiuchus
Sextans	Sextantis	Sex	Sextant	Hevelius, 1687
Taurus	Tauri	Tau	Bull	In zodiac; contains Aldebran and Elnath
Telescopium	Telescopii	Tel	Telescope	Lacaille, 1750
Triangulum	Trianguli	Tri	Triangle	Contains spiral galaxy M33
Triangulum Australe	Trianguli Australis	TrA	Southern Triangle	Bayer, 1603
Tucana	Tucanae	Tuc	Toucan	Bayer, 1603
Ursa Major	Ursae Majoria	UMa	Big Bear	Big Dipper
Ursa Minor	Ursae Minoris	UMi	Little Bear	Little Dipper
Vela	Velorum	Vel	Ship's Sails[1]	Lacaille, 1750
Virgo	Virginis	Vir	Virgin	In zodiac; contains Spica
Volans	Volantis	Vol	Flying Fish	Bayer, 1603
Vulpecula	Vulpeculae	Vul	Little Fox	Hevelius, 1687

1. Formerly part of the constellation Argo Navis, the Argonauts' ship. 2. Smallest constellation. 3. Largest constellation.

►STARS AND THE UNIVERSE

Astronomical Distances

The very large distances between stars and the even larger ones between the vast groups of stars called galaxies are usually expressed in terms of units of length that are peculiar to astronomy. The most familiar is the **light-year,** defined as the distance light travels through a vacuum in a year (approximately 365¼ days). Light travels through a vacuum at the rate of about 186,250 miles per second (exactly 299,792,458 m/s—exact because the meter is defined in terms of the speed of light in a vacuum). A light-year is approximately 5,880 billion miles (9,460 billion km).

Astronomers also use a measure even larger than the light-year, the parsec, equal to about 3.26 light-years, or about 19,170 billion miles (30,840 billion km).

A smaller unit, for measurements within the solar system, is the astronomical unit, which is the average distance between the Earth and the Sun, or about 93 million miles (150 million km).

The Constellations

Constellations consist of several bright stars that are treated as a group. Long ago, before recorded history, people began naming these groups. By Sumerian times (3000-2500 B.C.), stories were already being told about how particular constellations were formed. Most of our present knowledge of such stories, however, comes from the ancient Greeks.,

One group of constellations has exerted a special influence on human thought, at least since 1500 B.C. As the Sun, Moon, and planets move through the sky, they pass through a group of 12 constellations, called the constellations of the zodiac. The belief that the presence of the Sun in one of these constellations at a person's birth influences happenings on Earth is called astrology.

Today astronomers use constellations for mapping the sky. Each part of the sky is named by a particular constellation. These constellations, especially in the southern hemisphere, may not be traditional ones, but rather, groups of stars astronomers have named so that for reference purposes all of the sky is labeled.

Bright Stars

Star Names   While astronomers often use the traditional names of stars, most of which come to us from Latin or Arabic sources, they also use another system for naming objects in the sky that is based on constellations. Generally, the brightest star in a particular astronomical constellation is called alpha ($\propto$), the next brightest beta (ß), and so on through several letters of the Greek alphabet; then numbers are used. All astronomers' constellations are named in Latin. When astronomers refer to a star within its constellation, they use the genitive case, meaning "of the thing." Thus the constellation Big Dog is officially Canis Major, but Sirius is alpha Canis Majoris, or "alpha of Big Dog," usually abbreviated to $\propto$CMa. This means it is the brightest star in the constellation Big Dog (Sirius has long been known as the dog star). Since Sirius is a binary star (see "The Universe," below), the much brighter main star is officially $\propto$CMa A. Further along, numbers are used instead of Greek letters. Numbered stars in the news in the 1990s included 51 Pegasi and 71 Virginis.

Star Brightness

The brightness of a star is designated by a number called its magnitude, although the relationship between size and brightness is complicated. When the magnitude system was first developed, by the early Greek astronomers Hipparchus (c. 190–c. 120 B.C.) and Ptolemy (c. 100–c. 170), astronomers did not know the actual distances to stars, so magnitude always referred to brightness as seen from Earth. They classed the brightest stars as the first magnitude and the dimmest they could see as the sixth. These numbers were somewhat arbitrary until 1856, when George Phillips Bond (American: 1826–65) determined that photographs of stars show magnitude in a way that is directly measurable—bright stars appear as larger spots than dim stars in photographs even though all stars appear as points to the naked eye. Astronomers could use

25 Brightest Stars: Magnitudes and Distances From Earth

The stars we see in the evening sky differ in how bright they appear because of a combination of two factors: 1) their total energy output, or **luminosity** (directly related to their absolute magnitude) and 2) their distance from Earth. Astronomers refer to this combination of effects as the **apparent magnitude** of a star, a measure of how bright the star appears in the nighttime sky. To separate the two effects, astronomers define **absolute magnitude** as the brightness of a star as measured from a fixed distance. Most of the stars we see in the sky have a large absolute magnitude but are relatively far away. If all the stars were placed the same distance from Earth, Deneb would be the brightest and the Sun would be the faintest (about 250,000 times fainter than Deneb). Note that negative magnitudes are higher than positive magnitudes.

Rank/ Common name	Star name	Apparent magnitude	Absolute magnitude	Distance from Earth (light years)
1. Sirius	α CMa	-1.44	1.45	8.6
2. Canopus[1]	α Car	-0.62	-5.53	312.6
3. Rigil Kentaurus[2]	α Cen A	-0.28	4.07	4.4
4. Arcturus	α Boo	-0.05	-0.31	36.7
5. Vega	α Lyr	0.03	0.58	25.3
6. Capella	α Aur A	0.08	-0.48	42.2
7. Rigel[1]	β Ori	0.18	-6.69	772.5
8. Procyon	β CMi	0.40	2.68	11.4
9. Achernar	α Eri	0.45	-2.77	143.7
10. Betelgeuse[1]	α Ori	0.45	-5.14	427.3
11. Hadar[1]	β Cen	0.61	-5.42	525.0
12. Altair	α Aql	0.76	2.20	16.8
13. Acrux[1,3]	α Cru	0.77	(3)	320.6
14. Aldebaran	α Tau	0.87	-0.63	65.1
15. Spica	α Vir	0.98	-3.55	262.1
16. Antares[1]	α Sco	1.06	-5.28	603.7
17. Pollux	β Gem	1.16	1.09	33.7
18. Fomalhaut	α PsA	1.17	1.74	25.1
19. Mimosa	β Cru	1.25	-3.92	352.4
20. Deneb[1]	α Cyg	1.25	-8.73	3,227.7
21. Regulus	α Leo	1.36	-0.52	77.5
22. Adhara[1]	ε CMa	1.5	-4.10	430.6
23. Castor[1]	α Gem	1.58	0.59	51.5
24. Gacrux	γ Cru	1.59	-0.56	87.9
25. Shaula[1]	λ Sco	1.62	-5.05	702.6

Note: The magnitudes of many stars on this list vary slightly over time, although for most stars, the variation is quite small. Betelgeuse and Antares have the largest variations (about 1 magnitude). For consistency, median magnitudes are shown for all stars. 1. Stars more than 300 lightyears away have an uncertainty of about 20 percent or more in their distances (and therefore in their absolute magnitudes as well). The distance of Deneb, in particular, may be wrong by half (i.e. only 1,600 lightyears away). That would reduce Deneb's absolute magnitude to -7.22, still higher than any other star on this list. 2. A binary star, with both stars orbiting around each other. They appear to the naked eye to be the same star, with a combined apparent and absolute magnitude. 3. Acrux appears to the naked eye to be a single star, but in fact, it is the combined light of two stars, each at different distances from Earth. Its absolute magnitude, therefore, is impossible to define. **Source:** NASA.

accurate measures to compare two stars and thus measure magnitude with mathematical precision. Under Bond's system, stars with a magnitude of 1.00 are exactly 100 times as bright as those with a magnitude of 5.00. The very brightest stars have negative magnitudes.

Roughly, each whole number difference in magnitude corresponds to 2.5 times the brightness.

By the time this system was introduced, astronomers already were able to determine the distances of some stars from Earth. Friedrich Wilhelm Bessel was the first to make such a measurement, which he announced in 1838. A closer star appears brighter than a similar star that is farther away. To better understand the relative brightness of stars as they actually are, astronomers imagine viewing all stars from the same distance away. A star's brightness from this distance, which is 10 parsecs or 32.6 light-years, is called its absolute magnitude.

If we could see it clearly, the star Cygnus OB2 #12 would be the brightest star in the Milky Way galaxy (absolute magnitude -9.9), but it is not only far from Earth but also is obscured by dust. The brightest single object known is not a star, but a quasar (see "The Universe," below), BR 1202-07, with an absolute magnitude of about -33. The Sun has the brightest apparent magnitude of any star, -26.8, but its absolute magnitude is only 4.75.

The Universe

Most of the universe was greatly misunderstood until the 20th century. The most common notion from the time of the ancient Greek philosophers until the end of the Middle Ages was that a number of crystal spheres revolved about Earth, and that each of the planets, the Sun, and Earth's Moon occupied one of these spheres. All the stars occupied the farthest sphere. There were only about 6,000 stars known, those visible to the naked eye (and about half of these were south of the equator, so few Europeans had ever seen them).

In 1609 Galileo of Italy turned the first astronomical telescope on the heavens. Galileo's early telescopes were good enough to show that the Milky Way was not merely a whitish band across the sky but consisted of a vast number of stars, far more than the few thousand visible with the naked eye. His observations also disproved the old idea of crystal spheres. People began to speculate about astronomical entities beyond a simple sphere of stars. Not until 1924 were telescopes sufficiently powerful to show that many cloudy patches in the sky consisted of millions of stars far away from the Milky Way. This discovery led to the recognition of the enormous complexity and diversity of the universe.

Big Bang　The accepted theory of how the universe began is known as the Big Bang theory, since it proposes that the universe began as something like an explosion, which has caused all parts of the universe to rush away from one another (the expansion of the universe). Such an expansion is observed. Other evidence for the Big Bang theory is the discovery of cosmic background radiation, a radiation that seems to come equally from all directions. Cosmic background radiation has the characteristics expected if the universe resulted from a small, dense region exploding.

Binary stars　Almost half the stars in the visible universe are actually pairs of stars that orbit each other. Astronomers can sometimes see both stars, but more commonly they recognize that a star is part of a binary because of the influence of the dimmer star's gravitational pull on the other star.

Black holes

When a body becomes so massive for its size that not even light can escape the powerful gravitational pull it exerts, it is called a black hole. Black holes were predicted as early as 1784 (by John Michell) and invoked later by various astronomers and physicists to explain many strange astronomical phenomena. Black holes have been observed at the center of many galaxies, including our own Milky Way. Several smaller black holes, thought to be remains of supernova explosions, have also been located.

Brown dwarfs

are bodies too small to be stars, but too large to be planets. They glow dimly as a result of energy released by gravitational contraction. A brown dwarf must be between 10 and 80 times the size of Jupiter. The first brown dwarf to be definitely established orbits the star Gliese 229. Although about 50 times Jupiter's mass, its diameter is about the same as Jupiter's. Since then, a number of brown dwarfs have been located, including some not in orbit about other stars.

Dwarfs

All stars can be plotted on a graph where the horizontal axis is spectral class (temperature) and the vertical axis is absolute magnitude (true brightness); such a graph is called a Hertzsprung-Russell (H-R) diagram. On an H-R diagram, most stars fall along the main sequence, a slightly curvy line from the top left to the bottom right of the graph. Stars above the line are giants. White and brown dwarfs fall below the line. Dwarfs are small stars that lie on the main sequence—the brightest are blue dwarfs, the dimmest red dwarfs.

The Sun, near the middle of the main sequence, is a yellow dwarf.

Expanding universe

When Albert Einstein developed his general theory of relativity, he found it predicted that the universe would either expand as if it were exploding, or else collapse. He tried to correct this prediction by inserting a factor in his equations to counteract the prediction, but in the 1920s, Edwin Hubble discovered that the universe actually is expanding. It is easier to measure the speed of recession than the distance, so astronomers commonly use the speed something is moving away as the measure of its distance from us. Of course, it is not just moving away from us. In the expanding universe, everything is moving away from everything else.

Galaxies

are systems of very many stars separated from one another by largely empty space (sometimes galaxies are called island universes). In the 18th century, William Herschel concluded that many cloudy patches of light seen among the stars were actually giant systems of billions of stars, but so far away from Earth as to look like clouds. Better telescopes proved him right in the early 20th century, and these far-off, great masses of stars became known as galaxies, after our own Milky Way, the galaxy that includes the Sun. Observation with large telescopes in the 20th century has revealed two main types of galaxies—spiral and elliptical—although some galaxies are neither (irregular).

Milky Way

This is the galaxy to which the Sun and Earth belong; it contains about 100 billion stars. If you are in a place unafflicted with much light pollution, when you look at the night sky, you can see a faint band crossing it. The ancient Greeks named this the Milky Way (galaxy in Greek). Early in the 19th century, William Herschel determined that our Sun was a star in a vast lens-shaped star system, and that the Milky Way was the part of the star system we see from our vantage point inside it. Today, recognizing there are very many other such star systems, scientists often call it the Milky Way galaxy.

Missing mass

is matter that is apparently in the universe but that has not been observed. Astronomers note that galaxies are rotating as if they were embedded in larger, invisible bodies. Furthermore, there are theoretical reasons to believe there is even more matter in the universe than can be accounted for by the invisible matter surrounding galaxies. Ideas as to what this "missing mass" might be include everything from brown dwarfs to undiscovered subatomic particles.

Nebulae

are patches of gas and dust observable in telescopes. Before Herschel discovered that some cloudy patches seen through telescopes were vast collections of stars, all such patches were called nebulae (meaning clouds). Some "clouds" turned out to be galaxies, but many did not. The patches of gas emit light, often by the same mechanism that a fluorescent light does; energy ionizes the gas, which gives off visible light. Some patches of dust also glow, usually reflecting the light of nearby stars. Other patches of dust are opaque or nearly so, blocking out part of the sky. Some of the most striking nebulae consist of glowing gas surrounded by opaque dust or vice versa, which gives the nebula a definite shape, such as the North America Nebula (shaped like the continent of North America) or the Horsehead Nebula (which looks like a black horse's head against a glowing background). Herschel also studied a class of nebulae that looked to be giant spheres. He correctly concluded that these planetary nebulae were balls of gas produced when a star exploded.

Neutron stars

are stars that have collapsed in a violent explosion, such as a supernova, so that the force keeping electrons apart is overcome. All the neutrons and protons can touch, forming the equivalent of a giant atomic nucleus. The star is electrically neutral because of the charge of the collapsed electrons. Such a star may be only a dozen miles in diameter but may have a mass twice that of the Sun.

Novae

are stars that seem to appear out of nowhere. Later, they disappear. Early peoples were surprised from time to time by the appearance of a new (nova) star in the sky. Ancient Chinese astronomers called them guest stars. It is now clear that a truly new star does not appear; instead, a dim, existing star suddenly brightens. In early days, before the telescope, the dim stars could not be seen at all, so it looked as if a star came from nowhere. Today we know that there are two different types of "guest stars," and we reserve the name nova for one type and call the other a supernova (see below). The type referred to today as novae are less bright than supernovae and may appear more than once. It is thought that they occur when material from one star in a binary pair falls on the other star, causing it suddenly to flare up.

Pulsars are neutron stars that emit electromagnetic signals from their magnetic poles in a direction that reaches Earth. All neutron stars emit signals and rotate very rapidly (at least when they are first formed; they gradually slow down). These signals form a tight beam. If the beam intersects Earth, a radio telescope observes a fast pulsing on and off. The pulses are so regular that when they were first discovered, they were thought to be the work of extraterrestrial beings.

Quasars are distant sources of great energy. The name quasar is short for Quasi-Stellar Object, and the objects are so called because they seem to be about the size and general appearance of stars, but produce far too much energy to be stars. No one knows for sure what they are, but there is some evidence that quasars are caused by black holes in the central part of distant galaxies. The stars in the galaxies cannot be seen because of the great distance, so we see only the central part, which is the quasar.

Red giants are stars that have used their hydrogen fuel and expanded as a result. Young stars "burn" hydrogen in a nuclear fusion process that leads to helium. When a star has consumed the hydrogen in its core, new fusion reactions that start with helium begin, leading to carbon. The new reactions are hotter than the fusion of hydrogen to helium. This added energy causes the hydrogen and helium outside the core to expand. The star is red because the outer layers are relatively cool. When the Sun becomes a red giant in the distant future, it will expand almost to the orbit of Earth, completely engulfing Mercury and Venus, and charring Earth to a cinder.

Stars are bodies of gas large enough to undergo fusion reactions in their core. As a result of the energy produced by fusion, stars emit visible light, as well as electromagnetic radiation at other wavelengths. The Sun is a star. The hotter or larger a star is, the brighter it is.

Superclusters and clusters of galaxies are groups of galaxies associated in space. There may be just a few members of a cluster or as many as thousands. About two dozen galaxies near us form, with the Milky Way, our Local Group. The members of the Local Group also include the Andromeda galaxy and the Large and Small Magellanic Clouds. All are traveling through the universe together. The Local Group is a member of a supercluster of galaxies, called the Local Supercluster, that contains about 100 clusters. Clusters and superclusters are recognized because the average distance within a cluster or a supercluster from one galaxy or cluster to another is much less than the distance to other galaxies or clusters.

Supernovae are large stars that explode. A supernova explosion is much more dramatic than the brightening of a nova. A supernova reported by Chinese astronomers from A.D. 1054 was visible in the daytime. The remnants of this explosion are known today as the Crab Nebula. At its heart the Crab Nebula has a pulsar, all that is left of the star that exploded.

Variable stars Any star that periodically changes brightness is called a variable (a nova changes brightness but not at regular intervals).

Radio Telescopes

Before 1931, all telescopes were optical—i.e. they gathered and focused electromagnetic radiation in the range people can sense with their eyes. Stars, planets, and other objects in the universe also produce other wavelengths of radiation, however. A radio telescope gathers and focuses radiation at long wavelengths, the same kind of electromagnetic radiation used for transmission of radio signals.

Year	Type	Importance
1931	Ordinary antenna	Karl Jansky accidentally discovers, in trying to track down souces of static, that radio waves are coming from space
1937	Parabolic dish	Grote Reber builds first intentional radio telescope dish, Wheaton Ill.
1957	Steerable dish	Parabolic dish (250 ft. or 75 m) at Jodrell Bank in England is first major radio telescope
1962	Steerable dish	Dish (300 ft., or 90 m) at Green Bank, W.Va., first used to search for extraterrestrial life; it has been rebuilt after a mysterious collapse on Nov. 15, 1988
1963	Fixed dish	Largest fixed-dish radio telescope, 1,000 ft. (305 m) across, is built in valley at Arecibo, Puerto Rico
1970	Steerable dish	World's largest steerable dish, at Effelsberg, W. Germany, is 328 ft. (100 m) in diameter
1977	Several antennae	First Very Long Baseline Interferometry begins operating at Cal Tech's Owens Valley Radio Observatory
1980	27 antennae	Very Large Array (VLA) is built in 13-mi. (21 km) Y shape near Socorro, New Mexico
1993	10 antennae	Very Long Baseline Array (VLBA) uses techniques that produce a resolution 500 times better than the best optical telescopes
1995	30 antennae	The Giant Meterwave Radio Telescope north of Pune, India, contains 30 parabolic 45-m (148-ft) antennae arranged in a 25-km (15-mi.) Y.

The period varies with the cause of the change and the individual star. Some variables are part of a binary system in which one star periodically passes in front of the other. Other kinds of variables are called Mira variables and Cepheid variables, after the first stars known of each type. It is not clear what causes the brightness to vary.

White dwarfs are stars whose cores have collapsed until all the atoms are pressed very close together. A single teaspoonful of the matter in a white dwarf weighs about five tons. The core collapses because a red giant has used all its helium for fuel, but the star is too small to start burning carbon.

▶NASA'S FOUR GREAT OBSERVATORIES

The success of the Hubble Space Telescope has led the U.S. National Aeronautics and Space Administration (NASA) to develop a program of space-based telescopes that together will observe all of the electromagnetic spectrum with frequencies higher than radio and microwaves, which easily penetrate the atmosphere.

- The **Hubble Space Telescope** was designed to observe both infrared radiation and visible light. The original plan was to carry out 467 projects over 15 years that would help to determine the correct age of the universe, survey the universe for faint objects, find accurately the distance to stars, study black holes, and provide new views of the planets. After repair of initial flaws in 1993 and further upgrading in 1997, the Hubble continues to be a primary tool of U.S. astronomy. The Hubble can see with clarity objects 10 times as far away as can be seen with similar clarity from ground-based telescopes and has the resolving power needed to separate the lights of two fireflies 3 m (10 ft) apart at distances as far as Washington D.C. is from Tokyo.

- The **Compton Gamma-Ray Observatory** is designed to capture high-energy events, such as the bursts of gamma rays now believed to be caused by a star being sucked into a black hole or neutron stars colliding. Launched in 1991, it has recorded about one such event every day since.

- The **Chandra X-Ray Observatory** was launched in July, 1999, and will search for X-rays produced by colliding galaxies and supernovas among other tasks.

- **Space Infrared Telescope Facility**, scheduled for launch in 2001, will focus on the infrared radiation produced by disks of dust around stars, brown dwarfs, and even extrasolar planets.

Optical Telescopes

Telescopes were first developed in Holland about 400 years ago. The first telescopes used lenses to gather light and focus it. Later in the 17th century, scientists realized that curved mirrors could also gather and focus light. Since the light did not need to pass through the mirror (as light passes through a lens), mirrors proved to be more efficient than lenses for large telescopes.

Year	Type	Importance
1608	Lens	Hans Lippershey in Holland applies for first patent on a telescope
1609	Lens	Galileo builds first astronomical telescopes, eventually reaching 30 power
1611	Lens	Johannes Kepler introduces convex eyepiece, producing greater power
1663	Mirror	James Gregory is first to think that reflecting telescope can be made
1668	Mirror	Isaac Newton builds first telescope to use mirror to collect light, rather than lens
1723	Mirror	John Hadley invents reflecting telescope based on parabola, which concentrates light at a point
1789	Mirror	William Herschel builds telescope with 48-in. (122-cm) mirror, largest for many years
1897	Lens	Alvan Clark builds what is still world's largest telescope to use lens instead of mirror, 40 in. (102 cm)
1917	Mirror	Hooker Telescope at Mount Wilson in California is put into operation; at the time, it was world's largest
1930	Combi-	Bernard Schmidt makes first nation telescopes combining lenses and mirrors; they become workhorse of astronomy
1948	Mirror	Hale Telescope (200 in., or 5 m), located on Mt. Palomar in California, becomes largest and best on Earth
1962	Mirror	Largest telescope devoted to observing the Sun is erected at Kitt Peak in Arizona
1990	Mirror	Hubble Space Telescope (94 in., or 2.4 m) becomes first optical telescope in space
1993	Mirrors	Keck I Telescope in Hawaii uses world's largest mirror, 394 in. (10 m) in diameter; joined on May 8, 1996, with identical Keck II Telescope, both on Mauna Kea volcano
1999	Mirror	Japan's Subaru telescope begins operations on Mauna Kea; its 338-in (8.3 m) mirror is the world's largest made from a single piece of glass.
1999	Mirror	Gemini North is a 319-in (8.1 m) telescope on Mauna Kea, built by a seven-member consortium including the U.S. It will be joined by its twin, Gemini South, in Chile, in 2000.
1999	Mirror	The first of the four 323 in.(8.2 m) mirrors of the The Very Large Telescope (VLT) of the European Southern Observatory (ESO) in Chile begins operations in April.

Major Accomplishments of Satellites and Space Probes, 1957–99

While much attention is focused on human beings in space, most of the serious scientific progress has been made by satellites or probes— the general name for space vehicles that neither carry humans nor orbit Earth—that are directed internally or from Earth.

10/4/57 *Sputnik 1* First satellite to orbit Earth (USSR).
11/3/57 *Sputnik 2* Carries Laika, first dog in space; burns in atmosphere 4/14/58.
1/31/58 *Explorer 1* First satellite to detect Van Allen radiation belts; first U.S. satellite.

3/17/58 *Vanguard* Demonstrates Earth is pear-shaped with a bulge in Southern Hemisphere (U.S.).
1/2/59 *Mechta* First space probe to go into orbit around Sun, passing 5,000 mi. from Moon (at which it was aimed) (USSR).

3/3/59 *Pioneer 4* First American probe aimed at Moon; like Mechta it misses and goes into orbit about Sun.

9/12/59 *Lunik 2* First space probe to reach Moon, where it crash-lands (USSR).

10/4/59 *Lunik 3* First space probe to return photographs of far side of Moon (USSR).

4/1/60 *Tiros 1* First weather satellite (U.S.).

6/22/60 *Transit 1-B* First navigational satellite (U.S.).

8/12/60 *Echo 1* First communications satellite—actually a large balloon off which radio signals could be bounced (U.S.).

8/18/60 *Corona* First U.S. spy satellite.

8/19/60 *Sputnik 5* Carries dogs Belka and Streika and successfully returns them to Earth; 18 orbits.

12/12/61 *Venera 1* First space probe intended to reach another planet—Venus (USSR).

3/7/62 *OSO 1* Orbiting Solar Observatory—first major astronomical satellite (U.S.).

4/23/62 *Ranger 4* First U.S. space probe to reach Moon.

4/26/62 *Cosmos 4* First Soviet spy satellite.

7/10/62 *Telstar* First active communications satellite, allowing direct television between Europe and U.S. (U.S.).

8/27/62 *Mariner 2* First space probe to reach vicinity of another planet (Venus) and return scientific information (U.S.).

11/1/62 *Mars 1* First space probe aimed at Mars; contact lost about 66 million mi. from Earth (USSR).

6/26/63 *Syncom 2* First communications satellite to go into synchronous orbit with Earth (U.S.).

7/28/64 *Ranger 7* Returns close-up photographs of Moon, then crashes into it (U.S.).

8/28/64 *Nimbus 1* First weather satellite to be stabilized so that its cameras always point toward Earth (U.S.).

11/28/64 *Mariner 4* Flies by Mars and takes 21 pictures of its surface, successfully transmitting them back to Earth; its closest approach is, 6,118 mi. (U.S.).

4/6/65 *Early Bird* First commercial satellite (U.S.).

7/16/65 *Proton 1* At 26,896 lbs., it is largest Earth satellite to this date (USSR).

11/16/65 *Venera 3* Crash-lands on Venus; first space probe to make physical contact with another planet; radio contact lost before it reaches immediate vicinity of planet (USSR).

11/26/65 *A-1* First satellite to be launched by nation other than the USSR or U.S. (France).

12/16/65 *Pioneer 6* Launched into solar orbit; still functions today (U.S.).

1/31/66 *Luna 9* Although main vehicle crashlands, ejected capsule lands safely on Moon and transmits photographs to Earth (USSR).

5/30/66 *Surveyor 1* First soft landing of complete vehicle on Moon (U.S.).

3/31/66 *Luna 10* First space vehicle to go into orbit about Moon (USSR).

8/10/66 *Lunar Orbiter 1* First American space vehicle to go into orbit about Moon.

9/15/68 *Zond 5* First Soviet satellite to return to Earth from vicinity of Moon.

2/11/70 *Ohsumi* First satellite launched by Japan.

4/24/70 *Mao 1* First Chinese satellite; it broadcasts song "The East Is Red" once a minute, pausing at the end for other signals.

8/17/70 *Venera 7* First Venus probe to return signals from planet's surface (USSR).

9/12/70 *Luna 16* First space probe to land on Moon without humans aboard, scoop up samples, and return them to Earth (USSR).

11/10/70 *Luna 17* Carries roving vehicle to Moon's surface; vehicle roams for 2 weeks at a time (during daylight), then "sleeps"; as it roams, it returns photos and other data to Earth (USSR).

12/12/70 *Uhuru* First X-ray satellite telescope (U.S.).

5/28/71 *Mars 3* First space probe to soft-land on Mars; it quickly ceases functioning (USSR).

5/30/71 *Mariner 9* First space probe to orbit another planet (Mars); returns 7,329 photographs of planet (U.S.).

3/2/72 *Pioneer 10* First space probe to study Jupiter and, on June 13, 1983, first to leave solar system (U.S.); returns data until 3/31/97.

7/23/72 *Landsat 1* First Earth resources satellite (U.S.).

3/6/73 *Pioneer 11* First space probe to reach vicinity of Saturn (U.S.).

11/3/73 *Mariner 10* First space probe to observe 2 planets, Venus and Mercury, and only probe ever to observe Mercury (U.S.).

12/10/74 *Helios* First W. German space probe.

6/8/75 *Venera 9* Returns first photographs from surface of Venus (USSR).

8/20/75 *Viking 1* First American space probe to soft-land on Mars; continues to return data until November, 1982.

9/20/75 *Viking 2* Successfully soft-lands on Mars (U.S.).

8/20/77 *Voyager 2* After studying Jupiter and Saturn, it becomes first space probe to reach vicinities of Uranus and Neptune (U.S.).

9/5/77 *Voyager 1* After studying Jupiter, it becomes first space probe to reach vicinity of Saturn. On Feb. 17, 1998, becomes furthest space probe from Sun, more than 6 billion miles (10 billion km) from earth (U.S.).

1/26/78 *IUE* International Ultraviolet Explorer — the first astronomical satellite to be placed in geosynchronous orbit; it sends back data until 1996 (European Space Agency, or ESA, U.S., and Britain).

5/20/78 *Pioneer 12 (Venus 1)* First space probe to go into orbit about Venus. (U.S.).

6/26/78 *Seasat* Analyzes ocean currents and ice flow (U.S.).

8/12/78 *ISEE-3* Originally the third International Sun-Earth Explorer. Renamed International Cometary Explorer when it is redirected to study tail of comet Giacobini-Zinner in 1983 (U.S.).

12/13/78 *HEAO-2* High-Energy Astronomy Observatory, also known as the Einstein Observatory—it makes high-resolution X-ray images of the universe (U.S.).

2/24/79 *P78-1* Studies solar radiation until purposely shot down by U.S. Air Force 9/13/85; still working at time of its destruction (U.S.).

2/14/80 *Solar Max* Studies solar radiation; after failure in Nov. 1980, it is repaired and relaunched from space shuttle in April 1984; finally pushed to its destruction by massive solar flare, 12/2/89 (U.S.).

1/25/83 *IRAS* Infrared Astronomical Satellite studies galactic and extragalactic infrared sources and discovers new planets forming (U.S.).

12/15/84 *Vega 1* First Soviet mission to study Halley's comet; along the way it drops balloon probe into atmosphere of Venus.

12/21/84 *Vega 2* Second Soviet mission to Halley's comet; it also releases a balloon probe at Venus.

1/7/85 *Sakigake* First Japanese mission to study Halley's comet (this one from far away).

7/2/85 *Giotto* Joint European mission to Halley's comet; passes closest to the comet—375 mi. (600 km)—and later is redirected to comet Grigg-Skjellerup, which it passes 7/10/92 at a distance of 125 mi. (200 km).

8/18/85 *Suisei* Japanese mission to Halley's comet.

2/21/86 *SPOT* French satellite; photographs surface details of Earth as small as 30 ft. across.

5/4/89 *Magellan* American probe orbits Venus and maps it in detail with radar.

10/18/89 *Galileo* After passing near Venus and Earth (twice), it is now in orbit around Jupiter, reporting on Jupiter's moons; dropped probe into Jupiter's atmosphere on 12/7/95 (U.S.).

11/18/89 *Cosmic Background Explorer (COBE)* Studied cosmic background radiation in hopes of learning cause of galaxy formation.

4/24/90 *Hubble Space Telescope* Flawed optical telescope placed in orbit about Earth by U.S.; successfully repaired 12/10/93.

10/6/90 *Ulysses* Studying previously unobserved north and south poles of the Sun (U.S.-ESA).

4/5/91 *Compton Gamma Ray Observatory* A 17-ton telescope that observes the universe at very short wavelengths.

8/31/91 *Yohkoh* Japanese satellite that reports on X-rays and gamma rays from the Sun.

6/7/92 *Extreme Ultraviolet Explorer (EUVA)* American satellite studies high range of ultraviolet radiation in universe.

7/3/92 *Solar Anomalous and Magnetospheric Particle Explorer (SAMPEX)* American satellite that reports on particles in space, including space dust and the solar wind.

7/24/92 *Geotail* Japanese satellite launched by NASA to study Earth's magnetosphere.

10/6/92 *Freja* A Swedish satellite launched by a Chinese rocket from the Gobi Desert, Freja carries experiments from the U.S., Sweden, Canada, France, and Germany; The U.S. experiment measures Earth's magnetosphere.

2/9/93 *Pegasus 3* Brazilian satellite to monitor environment in Amazonia, launched by Orbital Sciences Corp. of Fairfax, Va.

2/20/93 *ASCA* Japanese X-ray telescope.

1/25/94 *Clementine* Joint U.S. military-science mission; maps the moon from lunar orbit and later visits the asteroid Geographos.

11/1/94 *WIND* Goes into a figure-8 orbit around the Earth and Moon at first, studying the solar wind; in 1996, moved to a point in Earth's orbit and orbits the Sun itself, staying in the same relation to the Earth as it revolves, about a million miles from Earth.

11/17/95 *Infrared Space Observatory (ISO)* A satellite from the European Space Agency that extends the work of the earlier IRAS. Nicknamed "Europe's Hubble" (ESA).

12/2/95 *Solar and Heliospheric Observatory (SOHO)* Studies the sun from an orbit of about 930,000 miles (1.5 million km) from Earth (ESA/U.S.).

12/30/95 *Rossi X-Ray Timing Explorer (XTE)* First U.S. X-ray telescope since 1978; studies X-ray sources in Milky Way including stars, pulsars, and possible black holes.

2/17/96 *Near Earth Asteroid Rendezvous (NEAR)* First of the new, less-expensive Discovery series of space probes. NEAR will visit and orbit asteroid 433 Eros in February 2000, approaching as close as 24 km (15 mi.); it passes close to asteroid 253 Mathilde in June 1997 (U.S.).

2/24/96 *Polar* Like WIND, Polar is reporting on the interaction of the solar wind and Earth's magnetic field, concentrating especially on the poles. It can take UV images of Earth's auroras and X-ray images of high-speed electrons in the solar wind (U.S.).

4/30/96 *BeppoSAX (Satellite per Astronimica a Raggi X)* This small orbiting observatory studies X-ray-emitting events from outer space. It scores a major triumph when it pinpoints the location of a gamma-ray burster for the first time, showing that these events are the most powerful explosions known (Itlay/Netherlands/ESA).

8/21/96 *FAST (Fast Auroral Snapshot)* Smaller, cheaper satellite of the Small-Class Explorer series studies auroras from low-Earth orbit (U.S.).

11/7/96 *Mars Global Surveyor* A probe to Mars orbits the planet and surveys it from space for one Mars year (687 Earth days) starting in March, 1999, after delays caused by a defective solar panel. (U.S.).

12/4/96 *Mars Pathfinder* This probe bounces to the surface of Mars in the Ares Vallis region on 7/4/97, where it releases a rover named *Sojourner* to travel the surface during the day and report on Martian geology. (U.S.).

12/24/96 *Bion 11* Life sciences study involving two monkeys that orbit Earth and then are returned; one monkey dies after successful return (Russia).

2/12/97 *HALKA (USOP)* A radio observatory that adds a space component to radio telescopes on Earth, creating the Very Long Baseline Space Observatory for high-resolution astronomy (Japan).

4/21/97 *Celestis 1* Burials in space; small satellite contains some ashes of 24 individuals, notably Gene Roddenberry, creator of *Star Trek*; Gerard K. O'Neill, advocate of living in space; and Timothy Leary, LSD guru of the 1960s (U.S.).

8/25/97 *Advanced Composition Explorer (ACE)* Studies solar wind and particles from interstellar space (cosmic rays) as it orbits a stable point where the gravity from the Earth and Sun are in balance (U.S.)

10/15/97 *Cassini-Huygens* Mission to orbit Saturn and study its satellites; *Cassini* is the orbiter that will reach Saturn in July 2004 while *Huygens* is a probe into Saturn's atmosphere (U.S./ESA).

11/27/97 *TRMM (Tropical Rainfall Measuring Mission)* An Earth-observing satellite that uses microwave radar, visible light, and infrared light to investigate how El Niño is affecting precipitation in tropical and subtropical latitudes (U.S./Japan).

1/6/98 *Lunar Prospector* Studies geology of the Moon from lunar orbit; confirms presence of water at poles (U.S.).

4/2/98 *TRACE* Reports on the upper layers of the Sun and solar magnetism.(U.S.)

7/4/98 *Nozomi/Planet B Neutral Mass Spectrometer (NMS)* Planned orbit about Mars begins October 1999; the satellite will study the Martian atmosphere and its interaction with the solar wind.

10/24/98 *Deep Space 1* Will test new technologies for use in space, including an ion-propulsion system. (U.S.)

12/5/98 *Submillimeter Wave Astronomy Satellite (SWAS)* Space-based radio telescopes analyses microwaves to study chemical composition of interstellar gas clouds, the homes of new star formation. (U.S.)

12/11/98 *Mars Climate Orbiter* Planned orbit of Mars begins September 23, 1999; the satellite will orbit Mars and make a detailed climate survey as well as further studies of the Martian surface. (U.S.)

1/3/99 *Mars Polar Lander* Aimed to land near the southern polar ice cap, the space probe is equipped with cameras and a robotic arm with which to study Martian soil; the probe also carries two "microprobes" that are to detach from the Lander and penetrate below the surface at landing points some 60 mi. from the main Lander. (U.S.)

2/7/99 *Stardust* The first mission to return materials from a comet, Stardust is due to reach comet Wild 2 in January 2004, gather samples there (as well as interstellar dust samples along the way), and parachute them back to Earth in 2006. (U.S.)

Spaceflights Carrying People, 1961–99

The space programs of the former Soviet Union and the United States both had dramatic flights by human pilots as an important component, although many scientists felt that most goals of the space program could be achieved without risking lives. The *Vostok, Voskhod,* and *Soyuz* missions were part of the Soviet program; *Mercury, Gemini, Apollo, Skylab,* and the shuttle are part of the U.S. program.

Proving that People Can Venture into Space

4/12/61 *Vostok 1* (1 hr. 48 min.) Yuri A. Gagarin. First spaceflight by human.
5/5/61 *Mercury 3* (15 min.) Alan B. Shepard Jr. Suborbital.
7/21/61 *Mercury 4* (16 min.) Virgil I. Grissom. Suborbital.
8/6/61 *Vostok 2* (25 hrs. 18 min.) Gherman S. Titov. First multiorbit flight; 17 orbits.
2/20/62 *Mercury 6* (5 hrs. 55 min.) John H. Glenn. First orbital flight by American; 3 orbits.
5/24/62 *Mercury 7* (4 hrs. 56 min.) M. Scott Carpenter. 3 orbits.
8/11/62 *Vostok 3* (94 hrs. 24 min.) Andrian G. Nikolayev. 64 orbits; landing by parachute.
8/12/62 *Vostok 4* (70 hrs. 57 min.) Pavel R. Popovitch. Dual launch with *Vostok 3*; 48 orbits.
10/3/62 *Mercury 8* (9 hrs. 13 min.) Walter M. Schirra. 6 orbits.
5/15/63 *Mercury 9* (34 hrs. 20 min.) L. Gordon Cooper. 22 orbits.
6/14/63 *Vostok 5* (119 hrs. 6 min.) Valery F. Bikovsky. 81 orbits.
6/16/63 *Vostok 6* (70 hrs. 50 min.) Valentina V. Tereshkova. First woman cosmonaut; 48 orbits; dual launch with *Vostok 5*.
10/12/64 *Voskhod 1* (24 hrs. 17 min.) Vladimir M. Komarov, Konstantin P. Feoktistov, Boris B. Yegorov. First multihuman crew; 3 cosmonauts make 16 orbits.

Planning for Operations in Space

3/18/65 *Voskhod 2* (26 hrs.) Aleksei A. Leonov, Pavel I. Belyayev. First extravehicular activity (EVA) by Leonov (20 min.); 17 orbits.
3/23/65 *Gemini 3* (4 hrs. 53 min.) Virgil I. Grissom, John W. Young. First American multi-person crew; 3 orbits.
6/3/65 *Gemini 4* (97 hrs. 56 min.) James A. McDivitt, Edward H. White II. 62 orbits; first American EVA; first use of personal propulsion unit.
8/21/65 *Gemini 5* (190 hrs. 56 min.) L. Gordon Cooper, Charles Conrad Jr. 120 orbits; demonstrates feasibility of lunar mission; simulated rendezvous.
12/4/65 *Gemini 7* (330 hrs. 35 min.) Frank Borman, James A. Lovell Jr. 206 orbits; extensions of testing and performance; target for first rendezvous.
12/16/65 *Gemini 6A* (25 hrs. 51 min.) Walter M. Schirra, Thomas P. Stafford. 15 orbits; rendezvous with Gemini 7.
3/16/66 *Gemini 8* (10 hrs. 42 min.) Neil A. Armstrong, David R. Scott. 6.5 orbits; first dual launch and docking; first Pacific landing.
6/3/66 *Gemini 9A* (72 hrs. 21 min.) Thomas P. Stafford, Eugene A. Cernan. 44 orbits; unable to dock with target vehicle; 2 hrs. 7 min. of EVA.
7/18/66 *Gemini 10* (70 hrs. 47 min.) John W. Young, Michael Collins. 43 orbits; first dual rendezvous; docking maneuvers, umbilical EVA.
9/12/66 *Gemini 11* (71 hrs. 17 min.) Charles Conrad Jr., Richard F. Gordon Jr. 44 orbits; rendezvous and docking.

11/11/66 *Gemini 12* (94 hrs. 34 min.) James A. Lovell Jr., Edwin E. Aldrin Jr. 59 orbits; final Gemini mission; 5 hours of EVA.

To the Moon and Beyond

4/23/67 *Soyuz 1* (26 hrs. 48 min.) Vladimir M. Komarov, 18 orbits; Komarov is killed when parachute fails; first fatality of space program.
10/11/68 *Apollo 7* (260 hrs. 8 min.) Walter M. Schirra, Donn F. Eisele, R. Walter Cunningham. 8 service propulsion firings; 7 live TV sessions with crew; rendezvous with S-IVB stage performed.
10/26/68 *Soyuz 3* (94 hrs. 51 min.) Georgi T. Beregovoi. 64 orbits; approaches unpiloted *Soyuz 2* to distance of 650 ft. (198 m).
12/21/68 *Apollo 8* (147 hrs.) Frank Borman, James A. Lovell Jr., William A. Anders. First *Saturn-V* propelled flight; first lunar orbital mission (10 orbits); returns lunar photography.
1/14/69 *Soyuz 4* (71 hrs. 14 min.) Vladimir A. Shatalov, 48 orbits; docks with *Soyuz 5* in first linkup of 2 space vehicles both carrying people.
1/15/69 *Soyuz 5* (72 hrs. 46 min.) Boris V. Volynov, Alexei S. Yeliseyev, Yevgeni V. Khrunov. 3 cosmonauts perform EVA, transferred to *Soyuz 4* in rescue rehearsal.
3/3/69 *Apollo 9* (241 hrs. 1 min.) James A. McDivitt, David R. Scott, Russell L. Schweickart. First flight of all lunar hardware in Earth orbit, incl. lunar module (LM).
5/18/69 *Apollo 10* (192 hrs. 3 min.) Eugene A. Cernan, John W. Young, Thomas P. Stafford. Lunar mission development flight to evaluate LM performance in lunar environment; descent to within 50,000 ft. of Moon.
7/16/69 *Apollo 11* (195 hrs. 18 min.) Neil A. Armstrong, Michael Collins, Edwin E. Aldrin Jr. First lunar landing; limited inspection, photography, evaluation, and sampling of lunar soil; touchdown: July 20.
10/11/69 *Soyuz 6* (118 hrs. 42 min.) Georgi S. Shonin, Valery N. Kubasov. First triple launch (with *Soyuz 7* and *8*).
10/12/69 *Soyuz 7* (118 hrs. 41 min.) Anatoly V. Filipchenko, Vladislav N. Volkov, Viktor V. Gorbatko. With *Soyuz 6* and *8*, conducts experiments in navigation and photography.
10/13/69 *Soyuz 8* (118 hrs. 59 min.) Vladimir A. Shatalov, Aleksei S. Yeliseyev. 80 orbits.
11/14/69 *Apollo 12* (244 hrs. 36 min.) Charles Conrad Jr., Richard F. Gordon Jr., Alan L. Bean. Second lunar landing; demonstrates point landing capability; samples more area.
4/11/70 *Apollo 13* (142 hrs. 55 min.) James A. Lovell Jr., Fred W. Haise Jr., John L. Swigert Jr. Third lunar landing attempt aborted owing to loss of pressure in liquid oxygen in service module and fuel cell failure.
6/2/70 *Soyuz 9* (424 hrs. 59 min. [17 days 16 hrs.]) Andrian G. Nikolayev, Vitaly I. Sevastianov. Longest spaceflight to this time.
1/31/71 *Apollo 14* (9 days 42 min.) Alan B. Shepard Jr., Stuart A. Roosa, Edgar D. Mitchell. Third lunar landing, returns 98 lbs. of material.
4/23/71 *Soyuz 10* (47 hrs. 46 min.) Vladimir A. Shatalov, Alexei S. Yeliseyev, Nikolai N. Ruka-

vishnikov. Docks with *Salyut 1*, the first space station.

6/6/71 *Soyuz 11* (23 days 18 hrs. 22 min.) Georgi T. Dobrovolsky, Viktor I. Patsayev, Vladislav N. Volkov. All 3 cosmonauts killed during reentry.

7/26/71 *Apollo 15* (12 days 7 hrs. 12 min.) David R. Scott, Alfred M. Worden, James B. Irwin. Fourth lunar landing; first to carry Lunar Roving Vehicle (LRV).

4/16/72 *Apollo 16* (11 days 14 hrs. 51 min.) John W. Young, Thomas K. Mattingly II, Charles M. Duke Jr. Fifth lunar landing; second to carry LRV. Returns 213 lbs. of material.

12/7/72 *Apollo 17* (12 days 13 hrs. 52 min.) Eugene A. Cernan, Ronald E. Evans, Harrison H. Schmitt. Last manned lunar landing; third with LRV; total EVA time: 44 hrs. 8 min.; returns 243 lbs. of material.

First Stations in Space

5/25/73 *Skylab 2* (28 days 49 min.) Charles Conrad Jr., Joseph P. Kerwin, Paul J. Weitz. First *Skylab* launch; establishes *Skylab Orbital Assembly* in earth orbit; conducts medical and other experiments.

7/29/73 *Skylab 3* (59 days 11 hrs. 9 min.) Alan L. Bean, Owen K. Garriott, Jack R. Lousma. Second *Skylab*; crew performs systems and operational tests and thermal shield deployment.

9/27/73 *Soyuz 12* (47 hrs. 16 min.) Vasily G. Lazarev, Oleg G. Makarov. First Soviet spaceflight to carry humans since *Soyuz 11* tragedy.

11/16/73 *Skylab 4* (84 days 1 hr. 7 min.) Gerald P. Carr, Edward G. Gibson, William R. Pogue. Services unmanned Saturn workshop; obtains medical data for extending spaceflights.

12/18/73 *Soyuz 13* (7 days 20 hrs. 55 min.) Pyotr I. Klimuk, Valentin Lebedev. Performs astrophysical and biological experiments.

7/3/74 *Soyuz 14* (15 days 17 hrs. 30 min.) Pavel R. Popovich, Yuri P. Artyukhin. Crew occupies *Salyut 3* space station; studies Earth resources.

8/26/74 *Soyuz 15* (48 hrs. 12 min.) Gennady Sarafanov, Lev Demin. Makes unsuccessful attempt to dock with *Salyut 3*.

12/2/74 *Soyuz 16* (5 days 22 hrs. 24 min.) Anatoly V. Filipchenko, Nikolai N. Rukavishnikov. Taken to check modifications to *Salyut* system.

1/10/75 *Soyuz 17* (29 days 13 hrs. 20 min.) Alexei A. Gubarev, Georgi M. Grechko. Docks with *Salyut 4*; sets Soviet endurance record.

4/5/75 *Soyuz 18A* (22 min.) Vasily G. Lazarev, Oleg G. Makarov. Separation from booster fails, and craft fails to reach orbit, but crew successfully lands in western Siberia.

5/24/75 *Soyuz 18B* (63 days) Pyotr I. Klimuk, Vitaly I. Sevastyanov. Docks with *Salyut 4*.

7/15/75 *ASTP* (9 days 1 hr. 30 min.) Thomas P. Stafford, Vance D. Brand, Donald K. Slayton. Apollo-Soyuz Test Project, cooperative U.S.-Soviet mission.

7/15/75 *Soyuz 19* (5 days 23 hrs. 31 min.) Alexei A. Leonov, Valery N. Kubasov, Docks with ASTP, the U.S. *Apollo* capsule.

The Soviet Study of Human Biology in Space

11/17/75 *Soyuz 20* (90 days) No crew. Biological mission; docks with *Salyut 4*.

7/6/76 *Soyuz 21* (49 days) Boris V. Volynov, Vitaly Zholobov. Docks with *Salyut 5* and performs Earth resource work.

9/15/76 *Soyuz 22* (8 days) Valery F. Bykovsky, Vladimir Aksenov. Takes Earth-resources photographs.

10/14/76 *Soyuz 23* (2 days) Vyacheslav Zudov, Valery Rozhdestvensky. Unsuccessful attempt to dock with *Salyut 5*; first landing in water for Soviet program (in Lake Tengiz; unplanned, but crew survives).

2/7/77 *Soyuz 24* (7 days) Viktor G. Gorbatko, Yuri N. Glazkov. Docks with Salyut 5 for 18 days of experiments.

10/9/77 *Soyuz 25* (2 days) Vladimir Kovalyonok, Valery Ryumin. Unsuccessful attempt to dock with *Salyut 6*.

12/10/77 *Soyuz 26* (96 days) Yuri V. Romanenko, Georgi M. Grechko. Docks with *Salyut 6*; crew sets endurance record.

1/10/78 *Soyuz 27* (6 days) Vladimir Dzhanibekov, Oleg G. Makarov. Carries second crew to dock with *Salyut 6* space station.

3/2/78 *Soyuz 28* (8 days) Vladimir Remek, Alexi A. Gubarev. Carries third crew to board *Salyut 6*; Remek first non-Russian, non-American in space (Czech).

6/15/78 *Soyuz 29* (140 days) Vladimir Kovalyonok, Aleksander S. Ivanchenkov. Docks with *Salyut 6*; crew sets new endurance record.

6/27/78 *Soyuz 30* (8 days) Pyotr I. Klimuk, Miroslav Hermaszewski. Carries second international crew to *Salyut 6*; first Polish cosmonaut, Hermaszewski.

8/25/78 *Soyuz 31* (8 days) Valery F. Bykovsky, Sigmund Jahn. Carries third international crew to *Salyut 6*; first East German, Jahn.

2/25/79 *Soyuz 32* (175 days) Vladimir Lyakhov, Valery Ryumin. Carries crew to *Salyut 6*; new endurance record set.

4/10/79 *Soyuz 33* (2 days) Nikolai N. Rukavishnikov, Georgi Ivanov. Engine failure prior to docking forces early termination; first Bulgarian, Ivanov.

6/6/79 *Soyuz 34* (74 days) No crew. Launches with no crew; returns with crew from *Salyut 6*.

4/9/80 *Soyuz 35* (185 days) Valery Ryumin, Leonid Popov. Carries 2 crew members to *Salyut 6*.

5/26/80 *Soyuz 36* (8 days) Valery N. Kubasov, Bertalan Farkas. Carries 2 crew members to *Salyut 6*; crew returns in *Soyuz 35*; first Hungarian, Farkas.

6/5/80 *Soyuz T-2* (4 days) Yuri Malyshev, Vladimir Aksenov. Test of modified *Soyuz* craft; docks with *Salyut 6*.

7/23/80 *Soyuz 37* (8 days) Viktor F. Gorbatko, Pham Tuan. Exchanges cosmonauts in *Salyut 6*; returns *Soyuz 35* crew after 185 days in orbit; first Vietnamese in space, Tuan.

9/18/80 *Soyuz 38* (8 days) Yuri V. Romanenko, Arnaldo Tamayo-Mendez. Ferries to *Salyut 6*; first Cuban in space, Tamayo-Mendez.

11/27/80 *Soyuz T-3* (13 days) Leonard Kizim, Oleg G. Makarov, Gennadi M. Strekalov. Ferries to *Salyut 6*; first 3-person crew since Soyuz 11.

3/12/81 *Soyuz T-4* (75 days) Vladimer Kovalyonok, Viktor Savinykh. Mission to *Salyut 6*.

3/22/81 *Soyuz 39* (8 days) Vladimir Dzhanibekov, Jugderdemuduyn Gurragcha. Docks with *Salyut 6*; first Mongolian, Gurragcha.

The Space Shuttle: U.S. Reentry in Space

4/12/81 *Columbia* (2 days 6 hrs.) John W. Young, Robert L. Crippen. First flight of reusable space shuttle; first landing of U.S. spacecraft on land.

5/14/81 *Soyuz 40* (8 days) Leonid Popov, Dumitru Prunariu. First Romanian (Prunariu), in space.

11/12/81 *Columbia* (2 days 6 hrs.) Joe H. Engle, Richard H. Truly. First reuse of space shuttle; ended early due to loss of fuel cell.

3/22/82 *Columbia* (8 days) Jack R. Lousma, C. Gordon Fullerton. Third shuttle flight; payload includes space science experiments.

5/13/82 *Soyuz T-5* (211 days) Anatoly Berezovoy, Valentin Lebedev. First flight to Salyut 7; space station equipped to measure body functions.

6/24/82 *Soyuz T-6* (8 days) Vladimir Dzhanibekov, Jean-Loup Chrètien, Aleksandr Ivanchenkov. Mission to *Salyut 7*; Soviet/French team; first French cosmonaut, Chrétien.

6/27/82 *Columbia* (7 days 1 hr.) Thomas K. Mattingly II, Henry W. Hartsfield Jr. Fourth shuttle mission; first landing on hard surface.

8/16/82 *Soyuz T-7* (8 days) Leonid I. Popov, Svetlana Savitskaya, Alexander Serebrov Mission to *Salyut 7*; second Soviet woman in space.

11/11/82 *Columbia* (5 days 2 hrs.) Vance D. Brand, Robert F. Overmyer, Joseph P. Allen, William B. Lenoir. First operational mission; first 4-man crew; first deployment of satellites from shuttle.

4/4/83 *Challenger* (5 days) Paul J. Weitz, Karol J. Bobko, Donald H. Peterson, F. Story Musgrave. Second shuttle joins fleet; deploys TDRS tracking satellite; first shuttle EVA.

4/20/83 *Soyuz T-8* (48 hrs.) Vladimir G. Titov, Gennadi M. Strekalov, Aleksandr A. Serebrov. Planned rendezvous with *Salyut 7* fails.

6/18/83 *Challenger* (6 days) Robert L. Crippen, Frederick H. Hauck, John M. Fabian, Sally K. Ride, Norman E. Thagard. First 5-person crew; first U.S. woman in space; first use of Remote Manipulator Structure ("Arm") to deploy and retrieve satellite.

6/27/83 *Soyuz T-9* (150 days) Vladimir Lyakhov, Aleksandr Aleksandrov. Crew spends 149 days in *Salyut 7* after *Soyuz 10* fails in relief mission.

8/30/83 *Challenger* (6 days) Richard H. Truly, Daniel C. Brandenstein, William Thornton, Guion S. Bluford Jr., Dale A. Gardner. First night launch; first black American (Bluford); launches weather/communications satellite for India.

11/28/83 *Columbia* (10 days) John W. Young, Brewster H. Shaw Jr., Robert A.R. Parker, Owen K. Garriott, Byron K. Lichtenberg, Ulf D. Merbold. Launches Spacelab; crew performs experiments in astronomy and medicine.

2/3/84 *Challenger* (8 days) Vance D. Brand, Bruce McCandless, Robert Stewart, Ronald McNair, Robert L. Gibson. Jet-propelled backpacks carry 2 astronauts on first untethered space walks; 2 satellites lost; first landing at Kennedy Space Center.

2/8/84 *Soyuz T-10B* (237 days) Leonard Kizim, Oleg Atkov, Vladimir Solovyev. Mission to *Salyut 7* to repair propulsion system; sets new duration-in-space record for crew.

4/2/84 *Soyuz T-11* (8 days) Yuri Malyshev, Gennadi M. Strekalov, Rakesh Sharma. Docks with *Salyut 7*; first Indian cosmonaut, Sharma.

4/6/84 *Challenger* (7 days) Robert L. Crippen, F. Richard Scobee, Terry Hart, George Nelson, James D. van Hoften. Deploys Long Duration Exposure Facility for experiments in space durability; snares Solar Max satellite; repairs altitude-control system.

7/18/84 *Soyuz T-12* (12 days) Svetlana Savitskaya, Vladimir Dzhanibekov, Igor Volk. Savitskaya becomes first woman to walk in space.

8/30/84 *Discovery* (7 days) Henry W. Hartsfield Jr., Michael L. Coats, Steven A. Hawley, Judith A. Resnik, Richard M. Mullane, Charles D. Walker. Third shuttle in fleet; deploys 3 satellites and tests a solar sail.

10/5/84 *Challenger* (8 days) Robert L. Crippen, Jon A. McBride, Kathryn D. Sullivan, Sally K. Ride, Marc Gameau, David C. Leestma, Paul D. Scully-Power. First Canadian astronaut, Gameau; deploys Earth Radiation Budget Satellite and uses Sir-B radar system to see beneath surface of sand.

11/8/84 *Discovery* (8 days) Frederick H. Hauck, David M. Walker, Anna L. Fisher, Joseph P. Allen, Dale A. Gardner. Salvages two inoperative satellites.

1/24/85 *Discovery* (4 days) Thomas K. Mattingly, Loren J. Schriver, James F. Buchli, Ellison S. Onizuka, Gary E. Payton. Secret military mission.

4/12/85 *Discovery* (7 days) Karol J. Bobko, Donald E. Williams, Jake Garn, Charles D. Walker, Jeffrey A. Hoffman, S. David Griggs, Margaret Rhea Seddon. First U.S. senator in space, Garn.

4/29/85 *Challenger* (7 days) Robert F. Overmyer, Frederick D. Gregory, Don L. Lind, Taylor G. Wang, Lodewijk van den Berg, Norman E. Thagard, William Thornton. Carries European Spacelab module.

6/6/85 *Soyuz T-13* (112 days) Vladimir Dzhanibekov, Viktor Savinykh. Successful mission to repair damage to *Salyut 7*, which had suffered power failure.

6/17/85 *Discovery* (7 days) John O. Creighton, Shannon W. Lucid, Steven R. Nagel, Daniel C. Brandenstein, John W. Fabian, Prince Salman al-Saud, Patrick Baudry. First Arabian in space, al-Saud; successfully launches 4 satellites.

7/29/85 *Challenger* (8 days) Roy D. Bridges Jr., Anthony W. England, Karl G. Henize, F. Story Musgrave, C. Gordon Fullerton, Loren W. Acton, John-David F. Bartoe. Carries Spacelab 2, a group of scientific experiments.

8/27/85 *Discovery* (7 days) John M. Lounge, James D. van Hoften, William F. Fisher, Joe H. Engle, Richard O. Covey. Repairs satellite Syncom 3.

9/17/85 *Soyuz T-14* (65 days) Vladimir Vasyutin, Aleksandr N. Volkov, Georgi M. Grechko. Takes supplies to *Salyut 7*.

10/3/85 *Atlantis* (4 days) Karol J. Bobko, Ronald J. Grabe, David C. Hilmers, William A. Pailes, Robert C. Stewart. Fourth shuttle.

10/30/85 *Challenger* (7 days) Henry W. Hartsfield Jr., Steven R. Nagel, Bonnie J. Dunbar, Guion S. Bluford Jr., Ernst Messerschmid, Reinhard Furrer, Wubbo J. Ockels. Carries Spacelab 1-D; scientific experiments conducted by Germans.

11/26/85 *Atlantis* (7 days) Brewster H. Shaw Jr., Bryan D. O'Conner, Charles D. Walker, Rudolfo Neri Vela, Jerry L. Ross, Sherwood C. Spring, Mary L. Cleave. First Mexican in space, Vela.

1/12/86 *Columbia* (5 days) Robert L. Gibson, Charles F. Bolden Jr., George D. Nelson, Franklin R. Chang-Diaz, Steven A. Hawley, Robert J. Cenker. First U.S. congressman in space, Nelson.

1/28/86 *Challenger* (73 seconds) F. Richard Scobee, Michael J. Smith, Robert E. McNair, Ellison S. Onizuka, Judith A. Resnik, Gregory B. Jarvis, Christa McAuliffe. Challenger disaster: O-rings in solid-fuel boosters wear through, and fuel supply explodes, killing all 6 regular astronauts and schoolteacher McAuliffe.

The First Space Station
(Note: durations of Soyuz flights not applicable)

2/20/86 *Mir* (Variable) Soviet space station, launched without crew.

3/13/86 *Soyuz T-15* Vladimir Solovyev, Leonid Kizim. First cosmonauts to board *Mir* space station.

2/6/87 *Soyuz TM-2* Yuri Romanenko, Aleksandr Laveykin. Romanenko and Laveykin begin marathon tours in space.

7/21/87 *Soyuz TM-3* Aleksandr Alexandrov, Aleksandr S. Viktorenko, Muhammad Faris. First Syrian in space, Faris.

12/21/87 *Soyuz TM-4* Vladimir G. Titov, Musa Manarov, Anatoly Levchenko. Cosmonauts set new record of a year in space, mostly in *Mir* space station: 366 days.

6/7/88 *Soyuz TM-5* Aleksandr Alexandrov, Viktor P. Savinykh, Anatoly Y. Solovyev. First Bulgarian in space, Alexandrov (unrelated to Alexandrov of *Soyuz TM-3*).

8/29/88 *Soyuz TM-6* Vladimir Lyakhov, Valery Polyakov, (Abdul) Ahad (Mohmand). Ahad first Afghan in space; on 9/6/88 Lyakhov and Ahad are stranded as they attempt to return in *Soyuz TM-5*, but land safely on 9/7/88.

9/29/88 *Discovery* (4 days) John M. Lounge, David C. Hilmers, Frederick H. Hauck, George D. Nelson, Richard O. Covey. Redesigned shuttle makes first flight since the Challenger disaster.

11/26/88 *Soyuz TM-7* Aleksandr Volkov, Sergei M. Krikalev, Jean-Loup Chrétien. *Mir* is temporarily abandoned for first time.

12/2/88 *Atlantis* (4 days) Robert L. Gibson, Jerry L. Ross, William M. Shepherd, Guy S. Gardner, Richard M. Mullane. Secret military mission known to have deployed radar spy satellite.

3/13/89 *Discovery* (5 days) Michael L. Coats, John E. Blaha, James F. Buchli, James P. Bagian, Robert C. Springer. Deploys NASA's third relay satellite and tests thermal control system for proposed U.S. space station.

5/4/89 *Atlantis* (4 days) David M. Walker, Ronald J. Grabe, Mary L. Cleave, Norman E. Thagard, Mark C. Lee. Launches space probe Magellan on its way to map Venus with radar.

8/9/89 *Columbia* (5 days) Brewster H. Shaw Jr., Richard N. Richards, David C. Leestma, James C. Adamson, Mark N. Brown. Secret military mission to launch spy satellite.

9/5/89 *Soyuz TM-8* Alexander Viktorenko, Alexander Serebrov. Reoccupies *Mir*.

10/18/89 *Atlantis* (5 days) Donald E. Williams, Michael J. McCulley, Shannon W. Lucid, Franklin R. Chang-Diaz, Ellen S. Baker. Launches *Galileo* probe.

11/22/89 *Discovery* (5 days) Frederick D. Gregory, John E. Blaha, F. Story Musgrave, Kathryn C. Thornton, Manley Lanier Carter Jr. Secret military mission.

1/9/90 *Columbia* (11 days) Daniel C. Brandenstein, Bonnie J. Dunbar, Marsha S. Ivens, G. David Low, James D. Wetherbee. Launches communication satellite Syncom IV and retrieves the Long Duration Exposure Facility (see 4/6/84).

2/11/90 *Soyuz TM-9* Anatoly Solovyev, Aleksandr Balandin. To relieve Viktorenko and Serebrov; July 18, Solovyev and Balandin briefly locked out of *Mir* by faulty hatch.

2/28/90 *Atlantis* (4 days) John O. Creighton, John H. Caspar, David C. Hilmers, Richard M. Mullane, Pierre J. Thuot. Secret military mission.

4/24/90 *Discovery* (5 days) Loren J. Shriver, Charles F. Bolden Jr., Bruce McCandless 2nd, Steven H. Hawley, Kathryn D. Sullivan. Launches Hubble Space Telescope.

8/1/90 *Soyuz TM-10* Gennadi Manakov, Gennadi Strekalov. Replace Solovyev and Balandin.

10/6/90 *Discovery* (4 days) Richard N. Richards, Robert D. Cabana, Bruce E. Melnick, William M. Shepherd, Thomas D. Akers. Launches Ulysses space probe into solar orbit.

11/15/90 *Atlantis* (5 days) Richard O. Covey, Frank L. Culbertson Jr., Charles D. Gemar, Carl J. Meade, Robert C. Springer. NASA announces this as last secret military mission.

12/2/90 *Columbia* (9 days) Vance D. Brand, Guy S. Gardner, Jeffrey A. Hoffman, John M. Lounge, Robert A.R. Parker, Samuel T. Durrance, Ronald A. Parise. Carries 3 UV and 1 X-ray telescope.

12/2/90 *Soyuz TM-11* Viktor Afansev, Musa Manarov, Toyohiro Akiyama. Journalist Akiyama, sponsored by Japanese corporations; others replace Manakov and Strekalov on *Mir*.

4/5/91 *Atlantis* (6 days) Steven R. Nagel, Kenneth D. Cameron, Linda M. Godwin, Jerry L. Ross, Jerome Apt. Launches 17-ton Gamma Ray Observatory; unscheduled spacewalk required to open satellite's antenna properly.

4/28/91 *Discovery* (8 days) Michael L. Coats, L. Blaine Hammond Jr., Gregory J. Harbaugh, Charles Lacy Veach, Guion S. Bluford Jr., Richard J. Hieb, Donald R. McMonagle. Tests detection devices and recovers Star Wars satellite.

5/18/91 *Soyuz TM-12* Sergei Krikalev, Anatoly Artsebarsky, Helen Sharman. Political problems in Soviet Union result in Krikalev's spending an unexpected 313 days in space; Sharman is first Briton in space; returns with Manarov and Afansev.

6/5/91 *Columbia* (9 days) Bryan D. O'Connor, Sidney M. Gutierrez, James P. Bagian, Margaret Rhea Seddon, Francis A. Gaffney, Millie Hughes-Fulford, Tamara E. Jernigan. Performs human and animal space-adaptation experiments.

8/21/91 *Atlantis* (9 days) John E. Blaha, Michael A. Baker, Shannon W. Lucid, G. David Low, James C. Adamson. Performs 22 experiments and launches communications satellite.

9/12/91 *Discovery* (5 days) John O. Creighton, Kenneth S. Reightler Jr., Mark N. Brown, James F. Buchlim, Charles D. Gemar. Launches upper-atmosphere research satellite.

10/2/91 *Soyuz TM-13* Aleksandr Volkov, Franz Viehboeck, Toktar O. Aubakirov. Viehboeck, first Austrian in space, returns with Artsebarsky and Aubakirov.

11/24/91 *Atlantis* (7 days) Frederick D. Gregory, Terence T. Henricks, James S. Voss, Mario Runco Jr., F. Story Musgrave, Thomas J. Hennen. First completely nonsecret military flight; studies how well military installations can be seen from space.

1/22/92 *Discovery* (8 days) Ronald J. Grabe, Stephen S. Oswald, Norman E. Thagard, William F. Readdy, David C. Hilmers, Roberta L. Bondar, Ulf D. Merbold. Performs experiments as the First International Microgravity Lab.

3/17/92 *Soyuz TM-14* Klaus-Dietrich Flade, Alexsandr S. Viktorenko, Aleksandr Kaleri. On March 25, Flade, a German, returns with Sergei Krikalev and Aleksandr Volkov.

3/24/92 *Atlantis* (9 days) Charles F. Bolden Jr., Brian Duffy, Kathryn D. Sullivan, David C. Leestma, Michael Foale, Byron K. Lichtenberg, Dirk D. Frimout. Inaugural flight of Mission to Planet Earth studies Earth's atmosphere and auroras.

5/7/92 *Endeavour* (9 days) Daniel C. Brandenstein, Kevin B. Chilton, Thomas D. Akers, Richard J. Hieb, Bruce E. Melnick, Kathryn C. Thornton, Pierre J. Thout. The first flight of the replacement for Challenger succeeds relaunching an erring communications satellite; first ever 3-person EVA.

6/25/92 *Columbia* (14 days) Richard N. Richards, Kenneth D. Bowersox, Bonnie J. Dunbar, Lawrence J. DeLucas, Ellen S. Baker, Eugene H. Trinh, Carl J. Meade. Sets record for duration of shuttle mission; carries U.S. Microgravity Laboratory.

7/27/92 *Soyuz TM-15* Anatoly Solovyev, Sergei Avdeyev, Michael Tognini. The third trip by a French astronaut, Tognini, to Mir.

7/31/92 *Atlantis* (8 days) Loren J. Schriver, Andrew M. Allen, Marsha S. Ivins, Jeffrey A. Hoffman, Franklin R. Chang-Diaz, Claude Nicollier, Franco Mallerba. Launches European Retrievable Carrier (Eureca) satellite. First Swiss astronaut (Nicollier); first Italian (Mallerba).

9/12/92 *Endeavour* (8 days) Robert L. Gibson, Curtis L. Brown Jr., Jay Apt, N. Jan Davis, Mae Carol Jemison, Mark C. Lee, Mamoru Mohri. First professional Japanese astronaut in space (Mohri); first married couple in space (Lee and Davis); first black female astronaut (Jemison). Japanese-sponsored mission to study biology in space.

10/22/92 *Columbia* (10 days) James D. Wetherbee, Michael A. Baker, Glenwood MacLean, Tamara

E. Jernigan, William M. Shepherd, Charles Lacy Veach. Launches the Italian-made satellite LAGEOS-2, designed to provide information about Earth's gravitational field.

12/2/92 *Discovery* (7 days) Daniel M. Walker, Robert D. Cabana, Guion S. Bluford Jr., James S. Voss, Michael R. Clifford. Last scheduled military flight for the space shuttle; future military flights to use disposable rockets. Launches secret military satellite.

1/13/93 *Endeavour* (6 days) John H. Caspar, Gregory J. Harbaugh, Donald R. McMonagle, Susan J. Helms, Mario Runco Jr.. Observes X-rays and launches a TDRS (Tracking and Data Relay Satellite).

1/24/93 *Soyuz TM-16* Alexander Polishchuk, Gennadi Manakov. Docks with Mir on Kristall module, using U.S.-compatible port first developed for the joint Soviet-U.S. mission in 1975; Anatoly Solovyev and Sergei Avdeyev return after six months aboard space station.

4/8/93 *Discovery* (9 days) Kenneth D. Cameron, Stephen S. Oswald, Kenneth D. Cockrell, Michael Foale, Ellen Ochoa. Launches and retrieves the Spartan Sun probe, used to study the solar corona, and observes Earth's ozone layer.

4/26/93 *Columbia* (10 days) Steven R. Nagel, Terence T. Henricks, Jerry L. Ross, Charles Precourt, Bernard A. Harris Jr., Ulrich Walter, Hans Schlegel. The European Spacelab with two German scientists (Walter and Schlegel) aboard conducts experiments on weightlessness.

6/21/93 *Endeavour* (10 days) Ronald J. Grabe, Brian Duffy, G. Donald Low, Peter J.K. Wisoff, Nancy Jane Sherlock, Janice E. Voss. Recovers Europe's Eureca satellite; and conducts experiments using a pressurized laboratory called Spacehab.

7/1/93 *Soyuz TM-17* Vasily Tsiblyev, Alexander Serebrov, Jean-Pierre Haignere. Haignere is French astronaut who returns with Anatoly Solovyev and Sergei Andreyev on July 29.

9/12/93 *Discovery* (10 days) Frank L. Culbertson Jr., William F. Readdy, James H. Newman, Daniel W. Bursch, Carl E. Walz. Tests equipment and procedures to be used in repairing Hubble Space Telescope; first night landing at Kennedy.

10/18/93 *Columbia* (14 days) John E. Blaha, Richard A. Searfoss, William S. McArthur Jr., Shannon W. Lucid, Martin J. Fettman, Margaret Rhea Seddon, David Wolf. Conducts biological experiments on humans and rats, including first dissection of animal in space.

12/2/93 *Endeavour* (11 days) Richard O. Covey, Kenneth D. Bowersox, Claude Nicollier, F. Story Musgrave, Thomas D. Akers, Kathryn C. Thornton, Jeffrey A. Hoffman. Installs corrective lenses on defective Hubble Space Telescope.

1/8/94 *Soyuz TM-18* Victor Afanasyev, Yuri Usachyov, Valery Polyakov. Trip planned to last 14 months for Polyakov, but Afanasyev and Usachyov return after six months. Previous crew aboard Mir returns to Earth.

The U.S. and Russia Work Together in Space

2/3/94 *Discovery* (8 days) Charles F. Bolden, Sergei M. Krikalev, Kenneth S. Reightler Jr., N. Jan Davis, Franklin R. Chang-Diaz, Ronald M. Sega. Krikalev first Russian on U.S. space shuttle mission.

3/4/94 *Columbia* (14 days) John H. Caspar, Andrew M. Allen, Charles D. Gemar, Marsha S. Ivins, Pierre J. Thuot. Develops techniques for use in space-station construction.

4/9/94 *Endeavour* (11 days) Sidney M. Gutierrez, Kevin P. Chilton, Michael R. Clifford, Linda M. Godwin, Jay Apt, Thomas D. Jones. Uses radar to map details of Earth in 3-D.

7/1/94 *Soyuz TM-19* Yuri Malenchenko, Talgat Musabayev. Malenchenko from Russia and Musabayev of Kazakhstan travel to Mir to relieve Afanasyev and Usachyov.

7/8/94 *Columbia* (15 days) Robert D. Cabana, Leroy Chiao, James D. Halsell Jr., Richard J. Hieb, Chiaki Naito-Mukai, Donald A. Thomas, Carl E. Walz. Sets record for shuttle duration in orbit, orbiting Earth 236 times; first Japanese woman in space (heart surgeon Naito-Mukai).

9/9/94 *Discovery* (11 days) Richard N. Richards, L. Blaine Hammond Jr., James J. Helms, Mark C. Lee, J.M. Lineger, Carl J. Meade. Conducts laser experiments to measure pollution in atmosphere and releases and recaptures satellite that collects data on solar wind; Meade and Lee use new jet pack for untethered spacewalk.

9/30/94 *Endeavour* (11 days) Michael A. Baker, Daniel W. Bursch, Thomas D. Jones, Steven L. Smith, Peter "Jeff" J.K. Wisoff, Terrence W. Wukcytt. The Space Radar Laboratory 2 mission is follow-up of nearly identical mission flown in the spring to detect seasonal changes.

10/4/94 *Soyuz TM-20* Aleksandr Viktorenko, Yelena Kondakova, Ulf Merbold. Merbold, from the European Space Agency, studies space biology aboard Mir and returns to Earth on 11/4/94 along with Malenchenko and Musabayev, leaving Viktorenko and Kondakova on Mir.

11/3/94 *Atlantis* (11 days) Curtis L. Brown, Donald R. McMonagle, Jean-François Clervoy (from ESA), Scott E. Parazynski, Joseph R. Tanner. Third shuttle flight since 1992 to carry the Atlas lab (Atmospheric Laboratory for Applications and Science).

2/3/95 *Discovery* (8 days) James D. Wetherbee, Eileen M. Collins, C. Michael Foale, Bernard A. Harris Jr., Vladimir G. Titov, Janice Voss. Carries Russian Titov to within 11 m (37 ft.) of Mir.

3/2/95 *Endeavour* (17 days) Stephen S. Oswald, Samuel T. Durrance, Tamara E. Jernigan, William G. Gregory, John M. Grunsfeld, Wendy B. Lawrence, Ronald A. Parise. Carries the lab Astro 2, used to study volcanic eruptions on Jupiter's moon Io.

3/14/95 *Soyuz TM-21* Norman E. Thagard, Vladimir Dezhurov, Gennady Strekalov. Thagard becomes the first U.S. astronaut to live aboard Mir; he studies the body's reaction to weightlessness; Polyakov, who returns on 3/22/95, with Kondakova and Viktorenko, sets new endurance record of 14.5 straight months in space.

6/27/95 *Atlantis* (10 days) Robert L. Gibson, Charles J. Precourt, Ellen S. Baker, Gregory J. Harbaugh, Bonnie J. Dunbar, Anatoly Solovyev, Nikolai M. Budarin. Docks with Mir for 5 days. Spacelab on Atlantis and Spekter module of Mir used for biomedical research. Leaves Solovyev and Budarin as crew of Mir; returns Thagard, Dezhurov, and Strekalov.

7/13/95 *Discovery* (9 days) Terence "Tom" Henricks, Kevin Kregel, Nancy Currie, Donald Thomas, Mary Ellen Weber. Launches Tracking and Data Relay Satellite (TDRS) to replace one lost when Challenger blew up.

9/3/95 *Soyuz TM-22* Thomas Reiter (Germany), Yuri P. Gidzenko, Sergei V. Avdeyev. Replaces Solovyev and Budarin, who return to Earth 9/11/88 in Soyuz TM-21 vehicle.

9/7/95 *Endeavour* (11 days) Michael L. Gernhart, David M. Walker, Kenneth D. Cockrell, James H. Newman, James S. Voss. Uses an orbiting shield to produce a vacuum in its wake 10,000 times greater than any found on Earth.

10/20/95 *Columbia* (16 days) Kenneth D. Bowersox, Kent V. Rominger, Kathryn C. Thornton, Catherine G. "Cady" Coleman, Michael E. Lopez-Alegria, Fred W. Leslie, Albert Sacco Jr. Conducts microgravity experiments in Spacelab and other medical and commercial experiments.

11/12/95 *Atlantis* (8 days) Kenneth D. Cameron, James D. Halsell Jr., Jerry L. Ross, William S. McArthur Jr., Chris A. Hadfield (Canada). Docks with and changes configuration of Mir to make docking easier in future missions.

1/11/96 *Endeavour* (9 days) Brian Duffy, Brent W. Jett Jr., Leroy Chiao, Winston E. Scott, Daniel T. Barry, Koichi Wakata (Japan). Recovers Japanese science-experiment orbiting platform, which had been launched by a Japanese H-2 rocket in March 1995.

2/21/96 *Soyuz TM-23* Yuri Ivanovich Onufrienko, Yuri Slodmirovich Usachev. Relieves *Mir* crew.

2/22/96 *Columbia* (15 days) Nobie Stone, Jeffrey A. Hoffman, Andrew M. Allen, Scot J. "Doc" Horowitz, Franklin A. Chang-Diaz, Claude Nicollier (ESA), Maurizio Cheli (ESA), Umberto Guidoni (Italian Space Agency). Tethered satellite experiment partly successful, but satellite is mysteriously lost from end of tether.

3/22/96 *Atlantis* (9 days) Kevin P. Childon, Richard A. Seafoss, Ronald M. Sega, Michael R. Clifford, Shannon W. Lucid, Linda M. Godwin. Docks with *Mir*. Lucid stays behind on the space station.

5/19/96 *Endeavour* (10 days) John H. Caspar, Curtis L. Brown Jr., Daniel W. Bursch, Mario Runco Jr., Marc Garneau (Canadian), Andrew S.W. Thomas. Deploys first inflatable antenna from Spartan satellite. Conducts rendezvous studies of the PAMS satellite, a test of a system in which a satellite stabilizes itself without expending rocket fuel.

6/20/96 *Columbia* (17 days) Tom Henricks, Kevin Kregel, Rick Linnehan, Susan Helms, Charles Brady, Jean-Jacques Favier (from Canada), Robert Thirsk. Carries the Life/Microgravity Spacelab, to study the effects of space flight on the human body, on rats, and on fish embryos; and SAREX-II

8/17/96 *Soyuz TM-24* Valery Korzun, Aleksandr Kaleri, Claudie Andre-Deshays (France), Yuri Onufrienko, Yuri Usachev. Picks up Onufrienko and Usachev, leaves Korzun and Kaleri.

9/16/96 *Atlantis* (10 days) William F. Readdy, Terrence W. Wilcutt, Tom Akers, Jay Apt, Carl Walz, John E. Blaha, Shannon W. Lucid. Docks with Mir, picks up Lucid and leaves Blaha.

11/19/96 *Columbia* (18 days) Kenneth D. Cockrell, Kent V. Rominger, Story Musgrave, Thomas D. Jones, Tamara E. Jernigan. Deploys and retrieves ORFEUS-SPAS, a satellite gathering data about matter in space between the stars and the WSF-3/Wake Shield Facility, a satellite used in testing a method of producing a high vacuum to be used in manufacturing ultra pure semiconductor devices.

1/12/97 *Atlantis* (10 days) Mike Baker, Brent Jett, Jeff Wisoff, John Grunsfeld, Marsha Ivins, Jerry M. Linenger , John Blaha. Docks with *Mir*, picks up Blaha and leaves Linenger.

2/10/97 *Soyuz TM-25* Vasily Tsbliyev, Aleksandr Lazutkin, Reinhold Ewald (Germany), Valery Korzun, Aleksandr Kaleri. Picks up Tsbliyev and Lazutkin from Mir, leaves Korzun and Kaleri.

2/11/97 *Discovery* (10 days) Ken Bowersox, Scott Horowitz, Joe Tanner, Steve Hawley, Greg Harbaugh, Mark Lee, Steve Smith. Replaces eight instruments in the Hubble Space Telescope and adds two new ones, greatly improving its abilities.

4/4/97 *Columbia* (4 days) Jim Halsell, Susan Still, Janice Voss, Mike Gernhardt, Don Thomas, Roger Crouch, Greg Linteris. Carries the Microgravity Science Lab, but 85 percent of the experiments are canceled because of a problem with the fuel cells.

5/15/97 *Atlantis* (9 days) Charlie Precourt, Eileen Collins, Jean-François Clervoy, Carlos Noriega, Ed Lu, Elena Kondakova (Russia), Mike Foale, Jerry Linenger. Docks with Mir , taking Linenger back to Earth and leaving Foale. Brings needed supplies and replacement equipment to aging *Mir,* which has had problems with fires and failures.

7/1/97 *Columbia* (16 days) James D. Halsell, Susan L. Still, Janice Voss, Michael L. Gernhardt, Donald Thomas, Roger K. Crouch, Gregory T. Linteris. Replacement for flight of 4/4/97.

8/7/97 *Discovery* (11 days) Curt Brown, Kent Rominger, Jan Davis, Robert Curbeam, Steve Robinson, Bjarni Tryggvason. In the fourth cooperative German-American scientific mission, various experiments using infrared imagining, lasers, and cryogenic devices are conducted.

9/25/97 *Atlantis* (11 days) James D. Wetherbee, Mike Bloomfield, Vladimir Titov, Scott Parazynski, Jean-Loup Chrétien, Wendy Lawrence, David Wolf, Michael Foale. Takes Wolf to *Mir,* returns with Foale.

11/19/97 *Columbia* (16 days) Kevin Kregel, Steve Lindsey, Kalpana Chawla, Winston Scott, Takao Doi, Leonid Kadenyuk (first Ukranian to fly aboard a shuttle). Conducts microgravity experiments and attempts to launch SPARTAN solar research satellite; when SPARTAN malfunctions, astronauts retrieve it for a future attempt on a later flight.

1/22/98 *Endeavour* (9 days) Terrence W. Wilcutt, Joe Frank Edwards, James F. Reilly, Michael P. Anderson, Bonnie J. Dunbar, Salizhan Shakirovich Sharipov, Andrew S. W. Thomas, David A. Wolf. Takes Thomas to *Mir* and retrieves Wolf. Also performs microgravity experiments with plants and crystals.

4/17/98 *Columbia* (16 days) Richard A. Searfoss, Scott D. Altman, Kathryn "Kay" Hire, Richard M. Linnehan, Dafydd "Dave" Rhys Williams, Jay C. Buckey, James A. Pawelczyk. Carries the Neurolab into space where the effects of space flight on the brains and reproduction of various species of animals and plants are studied.

6/2/98 *Discovery* (10 days) Charles J. Precourt, Dominic L. Gorie, Wendy B. Lawrence, Franklin Chang-Diaz, Janet Kavandi, Andrew S. W. Thomas, Valery Victorovitch Ryumin. Final U.S. astronaut mission on *Mir* completed as Thomas is returned to Earth.

11/20/98 *Discovery* (9 days) Curtis L. Brown, Jr., Steven W. Lindsey, Scott E. Parazynski, Stephen K. Robinson, Pedro Duque, Chiaki Mukai, John H. Glenn, Jr. Senator Glenn, first American to orbit the Earth in 1962, becomes oldest astronaut for study of how weightlessness affects older humans.

12/04/98 *Endeavour* (12 days) Robert D. Cabana, Frederick W. Sturckow, James H. Newman, Nancy J. Currie, Jerry L. Ross, Sergei Konstantinovich Krikalev (Russia). Crew docks with the Russian-built Functional Energy Block and adds Node-1 to begin assembly of the International Space Station.

5/27/99 *Discovery* (10 days) Kent Rominger, Rick Husband, Tamara Jernigan, Ellen Ochoa, Daniel Barry, Julie Payette (Canada), Valery Ivanovich Tokarev (Russia). Brings cargo for outfitting International Space Station including Russian cargo crane to be mounted on exterior of Functional Energy Block.

7/19/99 *Columbia* (5 days) Eileen M. Collins, Jeffrey S. Ashby, Steve A. Hawley, Catherine G. Coleman, Michael Tognini (France). Collins first female commander. Launches *Chandra X-ray Observatory.*

EARTH SCIENCES

Earth sciences include geology (the study of Earth's rocks and interior), oceanography (the study of ocean water, currents, and the ocean floor), paleontology (the study of fossils and ancient life-forms), parts of astronomy, and meteorology (the study of the atmosphere, including weather). Except for astronomy and weather, which are covered elsewhere, this section deals with all of these studies.

▶ THE EARTH'S COMPOSITION

In their study of the Earth, scientists distinguish a number of distinct layers from the inner core—the center of which is about 6,400 km (roughly 4,000 mi.) below the surface—to the farthest limit of the atmosphere, about 1,000 km (600 mi.)

Major Discoveries in Earth Sciences

B.C.
c.300 Dicaearchus (Greek: c. 320) develops map of Earth on a sphere using lines of latitude.

A.D.
132 Zhang Heng (Chinese: 78–139) develops first crude seismograph.
1600 William Gilbert (English: 1544–1603) suggests that Earth is giant magnet, which is why magnetic compasses indicate north.
1669 Nicolaus Steno (Niels Stensen; Danish: 1638–86) correctly explains origin of fossils.
1777 Nicolas Desmarest (French: 1725–1815) proposes that the rock basalt starts as lava.
1785 James Hutton (Scottish: 1726–97) explains features of Earth on basis of tiny changes taking place over long period of time (uniformitarianism).
1795 Baron Georges Cuvier (French: 1769–1832) shows that giant bones found in Meuse River are remains of extinct giant reptile.
1797 Sir James Hall (Scottish: 1761–1832) shows that melted rocks form crystals upon cooling.
1822 Gideon A. Mantell (English: 1790–1852) and his wife, Mary Ann, discover and recognize dinosaur bones as those of a giant, extinct reptile.
1830 Sir Charles Lyell (Scottish: 1797–1875) begins to publish *Principles of Geology,* the work that convinced geologists that Earth is at least several hundred million years old.
1880 John Milne (English: 1850–1913) invents modern seismograph.
1896 Svante A. Arrhenius (Swedish: 1859–1927) discovers that global temperatures rise with higher levels of carbon dioxide in atmosphere (greenhouse effect).
1902 Léon-Philippe Teisserenc de Bort (French: 1855–1913) discovers the stratosphere.
1906 Richard D. Oldham (English: 1858–1936) establishes existence of Earth's core.
1907 Bertram B. Boltwood (American: 1870–1927) shows that age of rocks containing uranium can be determined by measuring ratio of uranium to lead.
1909 Andrija Mohorovičić (Croatia: 1857–1936) discovers boundary between Earth's crust and mantle, now known as Mohorovičić discontinuity, or "Moho."
1912 Alfred L. Wegener (German: 1880–1930) proposes theory of continental drift, idea that a single continent—Pangaea—split into present-day continents, which have drifted away from each other.
1925 The German *Meteor* expedition discovers Mid-Atlantic Ridge, a giant mountain range in middle of the Atlantic Ocean.
1929 Motonori Matuyama (Japanese: 1884–1958) shows that Earth's magnetic field reverses every few hundred million years.

1958 James A. Van Allen (American: 1914–) discovers belts of radiation that surround Earth in space, now known as Van Allen belts.
1960 Harry H. Hess (American: 1906–69) develops theory of seafloor spreading—oceans become wider as new seafloor is formed at midocean ridges.
1979 American oceanographers discover hot vents in oceans, surrounded by exotic forms of life based on sulfur, not oxygen.
1980 Walter Alvarez (American: 1940–) and coworkers discover geologic layer of iridium in region identified with the demise of the dinosaurs; he attributes both iridium and extinction to a large comet or meteorite striking Earth.
1993 Ice cores from Greenland and Antarctica reveal the record of Earth's climate for the past 250,000 years.
Weather scientists discover unexpected displays of electromagnetism in Earth's upper atmosphere; the displays are named Sprites, ELVES, and blue jets.
1994 Geologists discover that Earth's core is covered with hills and valleys, some as much as 3.5 mi. (6 km) high or deep.
1996 A farmer in Liaoning Province in China discovers what at first appears to be a feathered dinosaur; although the feathers prove to be mere down, the site proves to be rich in fossils from an era that had previously been poorly represented in the fossil record.
Scientists from the Scripps Institution of Oceanography at San Diego find evidence that life on Earth existed as early as 3.85 billion years ago.
1998 South African scientists find evidence that life has existed on land for more than 2 billion years, much before the earlier estimate of 475 million years for land-dwelling animals.
Jess F. Adkins of Lamont-Doherty Earth Observatory and colleagues establish that deep currents in the ocean change much more rapidly than previously thought, which may contribute to sudden changes in global climate.
Ji Quiong, Ji Shu An, and Mark A. Norell announce the discovery of two species of dinosaurs with true feathers in the Liaoning, China fossil bed.
Frank Kyte of the University of California at Los Angeles finds in ocean sediments near Hawaii a fragment of the object that 65 million years ago crashed into Yucatán, thereby causing the mass extinction that finished off the dinosaurs.
1999 Ji Qiang locates a nearly complete fossil of the earliest known ancestor of the mammals, almost a "missing link" between mammals and reptiles from 120 million years ago. The rat-sized tricodont had forelimbs like those of a mammal and hindlegs like those of a reptile.

above the surface. This section describes these layers, from the innermost to the outermost.

Core   The core consists of two parts—one liquid, the other solid—both thought to be a mixture of iron and a lighter element, probably sulfur or oxygen. The solid inner core begins about 4,650 km (2,890 mi.) from the surface, and the liquid outer core at about 1,100 km (1,800 mi.) from the surface.

Mantle   The bulk of the Earth—roughly two-thirds of its mass—is composed of the mantle, which extends from the outer core to within about 90 km (55 mi.) of the Earth's surface below the higher mountains, and to within only 5 to 8 km (3 to 5 mi.) of the Earth's surface below some areas of the oceans. Silicon dioxide constitutes almost half of the mantle, and there is an abundance of magnesium oxide, some iron oxide, and smaller amounts of oxides of other metals. (Although silicon dioxide is known as quartz when found in the Earth's crust, under the heat and pressure of the mantle it may have very different properties from the form we know.) Part of the upper mantle is somewhat fluid and is known as the asthenosphere.

Crust   The crust is the outermost solid layer of the Earth. Under the continents, the crust varies from 30 to 90 km (19 to 55 mi.) in thickness, while under the oceans it is generally only 5 to 8 km (3 to 5 mi.) thick. Continental and oceanic crust differ from each other in thickness and composition. Continental crust consists of granite and other relatively light rocks, while oceanic crust is made up chiefly of basalt. The crust is separated from the mantle by the Mohorovičić discontinuity, or Moho. The crust that is accessible to accurate measurements contains the following principle elements:

Element	Percent	Element	Percent
Oxygen	45.6%	Magnesium	2.8%
Silicon	27.3	Sodium	2.3
Aluminum	8.4	Potassium	1.8
Iron	6.2	Hydrogen	1.5
Calcium	4.7	Titanium	0.6

Note: Adds to more than 100% due to independent rounding.

Hydrosphere   Water—virtually all of it sea water—covers about 71 percent of the Earth's surface and thereby constitutes a distinct layer of the Earth. Sea water varies in composition from place to place, but on average it is about 3.5 percent salts—that is, evaporating 100 lb. of sea water would yield 3.5 lb. of salt. Sodium chloride (ordinary table salt) constitutes 2.7 percent of sea water, or 77.8 percent of total solids in sea water. The typical composition of solids in sea water is as follows:

Compound	Percent
Sodium chloride	77.8%
Magnesium chloride	10.9
Magnesium sulfide	4.7
Calcium sulfate	3.6
Potassium sulfate	2.5
Calcium carbonate	0.3
Magnesium bromide	0.2
Other compounds	trace

Atmosphere   The atmosphere is the gaseous layer that envelopes the Earth. The lower atmosphere consists of the troposphere and the stratosphere. The *troposphere* has an average thickness of about 11 km (7 mi.), although it is only 8 km (5 mi.) at the poles and as much as 16 km (10 mi.) around the equator. Most clouds and weather phenomena occur in this region. The composition of dry air at sea level is: nitrogen, 78.08%; oxygen, 20.05%; argon, 0.93%; and carbon dioxide, 0.03%. There are also lesser amounts of neon, helium, krypton, and xenon. These proportions change with altitude, lighter gases being more common at higher altitudes, but they are approximately the same everywhere on Earth at the same altitude. There are also variable quantities of water vapor, dust particles, and other compounds whose proportions change from place to place at the same altitude—fewer dust particles being found over oceans, and less water vapor over deserts. Temperature decreases with altitude in the troposphere.

The *stratosphere* is found between 11 km and 50 km (7-30 mi.) out from the Earth's surface. Temperatures in this region rise slightly as altitude increases, to a maximum of about 0°C (32°F). Virtually coextensive with the stratosphere is the *ozonosphere*, or ozone layer, the region in which most of the atmosphere's ozone is found. Because ozone absorbs most of the sun's ultraviolet radiation, it is vital to the continued existence of life on the planet.

Beyond the stratosphere is the upper atmosphere, or *ionosphere*, so called because it is the layer in which atmospheric gases have been ionized by solar radiation. The ionosphere reflects certain wavelengths back to the surface, making it possible to transmit radio waves around the curve of the Earth. The ionosphere is further divided into the *mesosphere*, between 50 km and 80 km (30-50 mi.), in which the temperature decreases with altitude to -90°C (-130°F); and the *thermosphere*, from about 80 km to 450 km (50-280 mi.), in which the temperature increases to as much as 1475°C (2690°F). To spacecraft traveling in the atmosphere, as the space shuttle does, however, the temperature seems cold because the molecules are so widely spaced. Beyond the thermosphere is the *exosphere*, extending to about 1,000 km (600 mi.). In this layer, temperature no longer has its customary meaning. (See also "Global Warming" and "The Ozone Layer.")

▶ THE CHANGING EARTH

Despite its apparent solidity, the interior of the Earth is constantly changing.

Plate tectonics   The earth's outer crust is composed of about 20 lithospheric (or tectonic) plates that move from a few millimeters to several centimeters per year. Hundreds of millions of years ago, these plates formed a continuous landmass known as Pangaea and surrounded by ocean. Eventually the plates separated, until they reached the positions they occupy today.

As plates move away from each other, molten rock emerges from the mantle to form oceanic crust. Where they come together, one plate is usually forced under the other, forming either oceanic trenches or mountain ranges or both. In a few places, one plate slips by the other along a giant crack called a fault, such as the San Andreas Fault in California. These areas are also the site of greatest volcanic and earthquake activity.

Geologic Time Scale

The history of the planet has been divided by geologists and other earth scientists into periods of varying length based on the fossils found in rock strata. Geologists often speak of the period before 545 million years ago as Precambrian Time. The eras after 545 million years ago are grouped into the Phanerozoic Eon.

Mass extinction—brief periods when large numbers of species become extinct—often mark the boundaries between geologic time periods. In the greatest such extinction, known as the Final Per-

mian (250 million years ago), perhaps as many as 80 to 90 percent of all species became extinct in less than a million years. No one knows what causes most mass extinctions, but the Final Cretaceous of 65 million years ago (also called the K-T extinction) was almost certainly caused by the impact of an asteroid where Yucatán is now. The most recent, at the end of the last ice age (11,000 years ago), may have been caused by human hunting. Some biologists believe that human activities are causing a new mass extinction today as well.

Era or Eon, Period, Epoch	Organisms	Time before present (millions of years)
ARCHEAN EON	Monerans: bacteria and blue-green algae	**4,600**
PROTEROZOIC EON	Protists, algae, and soft-bodied creatures similar to jellyfish and worms	**2,500**
PHANEROZOIC EON		
PALEOZOIC ERA		
Cambrian period	Tiny fossils with skeletons followed by animals with shells, notably trilobites	**545**
Ordovician period	Brachiopods (shellfish similar to clams), corals, starfish, and some organisms that have no modern counterparts, called sea scorpions and conodonts	**500**
Silurian period	Snails, clams and mussels, ammonoids (similar to the nautilus), jawless fish, sea scorpions, land plants and animals (club mosses, land scorpions); modern groups of algae and fungi	**425**
Devonian period	Spiders, amphibians, jawed fish, lobe-finned fish, sharks, lungfish, and ferns	**395**
Carboniferous period	Insects, land snails, amphibians, early reptiles, sea lilies, giant club mosses, and seed ferns	**350**
Permian period	Mammal-like reptiles and fin-backed reptiles, cycads, ginkgoes, and conifers	**290**
MEZOZOIC ERA		
Triassic period	Marine reptiles (plesiosaurs and ichthyosaurs), crocodiles, frogs, turtles, early mammals, and early dinosaurs	**235**
Jurassic period	Dinosaurs (such as stegosaurs), pterosaurs (such as pterodactyl), early birds, dinoflagellates, diatoms, early flowering plants	**190**
Cretaceous period	Dinosaurs (such as tyrannosaurs, triceratops, and apatosaurs), salamanders, modern bony fishes, mosasaurs (marine lizards), flowering plants, placental and marsupial mammals	**130**
CENOZOIC ERA		
Tertiary period		
Paleocene epoch	Early primates, early horses, rodents, sycamores	**66.5**
Eocene epoch	Whales, penguins, roses, bats, camels, early elephants, dogs, cats, weasels	**57.8**
Oligocene epoch	Deer, pigs, saber-toothed cats, monkeys	**36.6**
Miocene epoch	Seals, dolphins, grasses, daisies, asters, sunflowers, lettuce, giraffes, bears, hyenas, early apes	**23.5**
Pliocene epoch	Apes, australopithecines (early hominids) *Homo habilis* (first human species), mammoths, giant sloths, and armadillos	**5.2**
Quatemary period		
Pleistocene epoch	*Homo erectus* and related human species, modern humans, and Neandertal humans; large mammals such as giant bison and beavers; many kinds of hoofed animals.	**1.6**
Holocene epoch	Modern humans and flora and fauna of today	**0.01 (11,000 years)**

Earthquakes and tsunamis Most earthquakes are caused when rock on one side of a fault (or crack) in the Earth's crust moves with respect to the rock on the other side of the fault. The motion causes vibrations in the crust that travel through the rock as shock waves. When these reach the surface, they cause it to move in various ways, which is called seismic motion. Small earthquakes that accompany volcanic eruptions are caused by the motion of liquid rock, or magma.

More than 800,000 earthquakes are registered by seismographs each year, but the overwhelming majority go unnoticed by anyone. However, large earthquakes are of great concern to many people living in regions of significant seismic activity. Although research on earthquake prediction has yielded no breakthroughs, death and destruction have been reduced somewhat by improvements in construction codes and techniques.

One common side effect of undersea earthquakes is tsunamis—or (incorrectly) tidal waves—against which there is little protection. Tsunamis are caused when an earthquake raises or lowers a section of seabed, thereby producing a wave that, while not generally noticeable at sea, can reach great heights as it approaches land. Similar to and as destructive as tsunamis, harbor waves are generated when a landslide falls into a bay, strait, or other confined body of water causing almost immediate flooding. High waves are also caused by volcanic explosions or collapses, such as the explosion and collapse of Krakatau in 1883.

Volcanoes are openings in the Earth's crust that emit molten or partially molten rock (lava), various hot gases, and ash. (A volcano is also the mountain formed by solidified lava or ash ejected from the opening.) If the opening is like a crack, it is called a vent. If it is larger and fairly circular, it is called a crater. A caldera is a basin formed by the settling of the top of a volcanic mountain, and it may have several vents or craters on its floor.

Most volcanoes are found where two tectonic plates meet, such as along the famous "Ring of Fire" around the Pacific Ocean. A few, such as the volcanoes of the Hawaiian Islands, appear to be over "hot spots" in the Earth's crust where liquid rock flows upward with sufficient force to burn through the crust.

Although volcanoes are associated with destruction, they have many positive effects. Minerals from deep within the Earth make the land around many volcanoes extremely fertile; volcanoes can create new landforms in the sea; and the study of volcanoes contributes enormously to our understanding of the Earth's interior.

Although geologists consider a volcano active if it has shown signs of activity in historic times, it is not usually clear whether a volcano is extinct or only dormant and could be active again. (Thus Tambora, which has not erupted since 1815, is considered active.) Some volcanoes once thought to be extinct have become active, and there are now about 600 volcanoes that are considered active. The accompanying list contains about a fourth of all volcanoes known to have been active in recent years, with special emphasis on volcanoes in the United States and volcanoes that have had famous eruptions.

The destruction caused by volcanoes is usually localized, but their effects can be felt around the world and take many forms. At their worst, volcanoes can blow themselves to pieces, as the island of Thera did about 1650 B.C. More often, volcanic ash blankets an area (as Mt. Vesuvius did at Pompeii), or clouds of hot gases and dust sweep down the side of the volcano poisoning the air. Lava generally moves too slowly to be a menace to people. Even more unpredictable, heat from a volcano can melt glaciers or snowcaps, triggering massive mud slides (as happened in Colombia in 1985) or releasing lakes of boiling water.

▶ MEASURING EARTHQUAKES

The size of an earthquake is generally reported in the United States using the Richter scale, a system developed by American geologist Charles Richter in 1935. The Richter scale measures the magnitude of an earthquake, that is, the size of ground waves generated by an earthquake as shown on a measuring device called a seismograph. Each whole number on the scale represents a tenfold increase (or decrease) in magnitude: a magnitude 6 earthquake produces a ground wave 10 times greater than a magnitude 5.

This does not mean, however, that a magnitude 6 earthquake has 10 times the energy as one of magnitude 5. Measuring the actual energy requires instruments placed at the site of the earthquake. Various methods have been developed for inferring energy from magnitude and these suggest that one change in magnitude corresponds to a thirty- to sixtyfold change in energy. So the energy of a magnitude 8 earthquake, a very serious event, can be as much as 1 million to 10 million times as much as that of a magnitude 4 earthquake, one that can be felt but causes almost no damage.

Major Earthquakes, 526–1999

Date	Location and remarks	Estimated deaths	Richter magnitude	Date	Location and remarks	Estimated deaths	Richter magnitude
May 20, 526	Antioch, Turkey	250,000	—	May 16, 1875	Venezuela and Colombia	16,000	—
856	Corinth, Greece	45,000	—	Aug. 31, 1886	Charleston, South Carolina	83	7.6
1036	Shanxi, China	23,000	—	Oct. 28, 1891	Central Japan	7,300	—
1057	Chihli (Hopeh), China	25,000	—	June 15, 1896	Sanriku and Kamaishi, Japan (tsunami)	26,000	—
1170	Sicily	15,000	—				
1268	Cilicia (Turkey)	60,000	—	Apr. 4, 1905	Kangra, India	20,000	—
Sept. 27, 1290	Chihli (Hopeh), China	100,000	—	Apr. 18, 1906	San Francisco, California	667	8.3
May 20, 1293	Kamakura, Japan	30,000	—	Aug. 16, 1906	Valparaiso, Chile	20,000	8.6
Jan. 26, 1531	Lisbon, Portugal	30,000	—	1907	Tajikistan	40,000	—
Jan. 24, 1556	Shanxi, China	830,000	—	Dec. 28, 1908	Messina, Sicily	75,000	7.5
Nov. 1667	Shemakha, Azerbaijan	80,000	—	Jan. 13, 1915	Avezzano, Italy	30,000	—
June 7, 1692	Port Royal, Jamaica	30,000	—	Jan. 13, 1916	Avezzano, Italy	29,980	7.5
Jan. 11, 1693	Catania province, Sicily	60,000	—	Dec. 16, 1920	Kansu, China	180,000+	8.6
1693	Naples, Italy	93,000	—	Sept. 1, 1923	Tokyo and Yokohama, Japan	143,000	7.9
1707	Tsunami hits Japan	30,000	—	Mar. 7, 1927	Kita Tango, Japan	2,935	7.3
Dec. 30, 1730	Hokkaido Island, Japan	137,000	—	May 22, 1927	Nan-Shan, China	200,000	8.3
1731	Beijing, China	100,000	—	Dec. 26, 1932	Kansu, China	70,000	7.6
Oct. 11, 1737	Calcutta, India	300,000	—	Mar. 2, 1933	Sanriku, Japan (tsunami)	3,064	8.9
June 7, 1755	Northern Persia	40,000	—	Mar. 10, 1933	Long Beach, California	120	6.3
Nov. 1, 1755	Lisbon, Portugal (earthquake tsunami)	60,000	8.7	Jan. 15, 1934	India, Bihar, and Nepal	10,700	8.4
				May 31, 1935	Quetta, India (Pakistan)	50,000	7.5
Feb. 4-5 and Mar. 28, 1783	Calabria, Italy	35,000	—	Jan. 24, 1939	Concepción, Chile	30,000	8.3
				Dec. 27, 1939	Erzincan, Turkey	30,000	7.9
Feb. 4, 1797	Quito, Ecuador, and Cuzco, Peru	41,000	—	Apr. 1, 1946	Earthquake at Unimak Island, Alaska, causes tsunami in Hawaii that strikes Hilo	173	7.2
Dec. 16, 1811	New Madrid, Missouri	<10	8.1				
Feb. 7, 1812	New Madrid, Missouri	0	8.3	Dec. 21, 1946	Nankai on Honshu Island, Japan	1,330	8.0
Sept. 5, 1822	Aleppo (Syria)	22,000	—	June 28, 1948	Fukui, Japan	3,769	7.1
Dec. 28, 1828	Echigo, Japan	30,000	—	Oct. 1948	Ashkhabad (former USSR)	20,000	—
Dec. 24, 1854	Tokai, Japan	3,000	8.4	July 10, 1949	Tajikistan	120,000	7.5
Oct. 1855	Tokyo, Japan	2,000+	—	Aug. 5, 1949	Pelileo, Ecuador	6,000	6.8
Jan. 9, 1857	Fort Tejon, California	2	8.3	Aug. 15, 1950	Assam State, India	1,500	8.7
1857	East of Naples, Italy	10,000+	—	July 21, 1952	Bakersfield, California	12	7.7
Aug. 13-15, 1868	Peru and Ecuador	40,000	—	June 10-17, 1956	Northern Afghanistan	2,000	7.7

Date	Location and remarks	Estimated deaths	Richter magnitude	Date	Location and remarks	Estimated deaths	Richter magnitude
July 2, 1957	Northern Iran	2,500	7.4	Oct. 17, 1989	Loma Prieta, California	63	7.1
Dec. 13, 1957	Western Iran	2,000	7.1		(Santa Cruz Mountains),		
Aug. 17, 1959	Hebgen Lake, Montana	28	7.1		destructive in San Francisco		
Feb. 29, 1960	Agadir, Morocco	12,000	8.8		and Oakland		
May 21–30, 1960	Southern Chile; a tsunami strikes various Pacific islands, including Hawaii, killing 61; greatest earthquake ever recorded	5,700	9.5	June 20, 1990	Caspian Sea, near Rasht, Iran	50,000	7.6
				July 16, 1990	Cabanatuan (Luzon I.), Philippines	1,700	7.7
				Oct. 20, 1991	India and Nepal	2,000+	7.1
Sept. 1, 1962	Northwestern Iran	12,403	7.1	Dec. 13, 1992	Flores Island, Indonesia (tsunami)	2,500	7.5
Mar. 27, 1964	Southern Alaska	131	8.5				
Aug. 19, 1966	Eastern Turkey	2,520	6.9	Sept. 29, 1993	Bombay, India	30,000	6.4
Aug. 31, 1968	Khurasan, Iran	12,000	7.8	Jan. 17, 1994	Northridge, California	61	6.8
July 25, 1969	Eastern China	3,000	—	Oct. 4, 1994	Kuril Islands of Japan and Russia	190	8.2
Jan. 5, 1970	Yunnan Province, China	10,000	7.7				
May 31, 1970	Yungay, Ranrahirca, and Huarás, in Peru	66,794	7.7	Jan. 17, 1995	Near Kobe, Japan	5,300	7.2
				May 27, 1995	Sakhalin Island, Russia	2,000+	7.5
Feb. 9, 1971	San Fernando Valley, California	64	6.6	Oct. 9, 1995	Pacific Ocean off Colima, Mexico	57	7.6
Apr. 10, 1972	Ghir, Iran	5,057	6.9	Nov. 22, 1995	Gulf of Aquaba, between Israel and Egypt	44	7.7
Dec. 23, 1972	Managua, Nicaragua	10,000+	5.6				
Dec. 28, 1974	North Pakistan	5,200+	6.3	Feb. 17, 1996	Tsunamis in Irian Jaya, Indonesia	107	7.9
Feb. 5, 1975	Liaoning Province, China (predicted)	300	—				
				Feb. 4, 1997	Northeastern Iran	79	6.9
Sept. 6, 1975	Lice, Turkey	2,312	6.8	Feb. 27, 1997	Western Pakistan	100+	7.3
Feb. 4, 1976	Guatemala City, Guatemala	22,778	7.5	Feb. 28, 1997	Northwestern Iran	1,000+	6.1
				May 10, 1997	Northeastern Iran	1,600	7.3
June 26, 1976	New Guinea and Irian Jaya	8,000+	7.1	July 9, 1997	Northeast coast of Venezuela	71	6.8
July 28, 1976	Tangshan, China	750,000	8.0				
Aug. 17, 1976	Philippine island of Mindanao (earthquake and tsunami)	8,000	7.3	Jan. 10, 1998	Northeastern China	70	5.7
				Feb. 4, 1998	Afghanistan	2,323	6.1
				May 22, 1998	Central Bolivia	105	6.6
Nov. 24, 1976	Eastern Turkey	4,000	7.9	May 30, 1998	Afghanistan-Tajikistan border	4,000+	6.9
Sept. 16, 1978	Northeast Iran	25,000	7.7				
Oct. 10, 1980	Northwestern Algeria	4,500	7.3	June 27, 1998	Adana, Turkey	136	6.3
Nov. 23, 1980	Southern Italy	4,800	7.2	July 9, 1998	Azores Islands	10	6.2
July 28, 1981	Kerman province, Iran	8,000	—	July 17, 1998	Tsunamis strike Papua New Guinea	1,183	7.1
Dec. 13, 1982	Yemen	2,800	6.0				
Sept. 19, 21, 1985	Mexico City	4,200	8.1	Nov. 29, 1998	Eastern Indonesia	41	7.7
				Jan. 25, 1999	Armenia, Colombia	1,885	6.2
Oct. 10, 1986	San Salvador, El Salvador	1,000+	7.5	Feb. 11, 1999	Afghanistan	70	6.0
Mar. 5-6, 1987	Ecuador	2,000	7.0	Mar. 28, 1999	Northern India	96+	6.6
Dec. 7, 1988	Armenia	28,854	6.9	Aug. 17, 1999	Northwestern Turkey	17,000+	7.4
				Sept. 21, 1999	Nantou, Taiwan	2,000+	7.6

Richter Scale and Effects Near the Epicenter

Note: The epicenter is the point on Earth's surface above the center of the quake

Below 2.5 Not felt except by a very few under specially favorable circumstances.

2.5 to 3.5 Felt only by a few persons at rest, especially on upper floors of buildings.

3.5 to 4.5 At lower levels or further from the quake, it is felt by many people, sometimes quite noticeably indoors, especially on upper floors of buildings, but many people do not recognize as an earthquake. At somewhat higher levels or nearer to the epicenter, during the day the quake is felt indoors by many; outdoors by few. Sensation is like heavy truck striking building. At the highest level, the earth movement is felt by nearly everyone; with many awakened if during the night. Disturbances of trees, telephone poles, and other tall objects sometimes can be noticed.

4.5 to 6.0 Felt by all; many frightened and run outdoors. Some heavy furniture moved; there will be a few instances of fallen plaster or damaged chimneys. Other slight local damage may occur. At higher level, however, everybody runs outdoors. At the upper level, while damage is still negligible in buildings of good design and construction, there can be moderate damage even to well-built ordinary structures; there will be considerable damage to poorly built or badly designed structures.

6.0 to 7.0 A destructive earthquake. Damage may still be slight in specially designed structures, but will be considerable in ordinary substantial buildings, often with partial collapse. Damage will be great in poorly built structures, including collapse of chimneys, factory stacks, columns, monuments, and walls. At the upper level, damage is likely to be considerable even in specially designed structures. Most ordinary buildings will be shifted off foundations. Even the ground will be cracked conspicuously.

7.0 to 8.0 A major earthquake. Worldwide, about 10 of these occur each year. Some well-built wooden structures will be destroyed. Most masonry and frame structures will be destroyed along with their foundations. Ground becomes badly cracked.

8.0 and above Great earthquakes. These occur once every five to 10 years. Few, if any masonry structures remain standing. Bridges are destroyed. Broad fissures appear in ground. At the highest levels and near the epicenter, damage total. Waves seen on solid ground. Heavy objects thrown upward into air.

Volcano Eruptions and Landslides, 1628 B.C.–1999 A.D

Date	Event	Deaths	Date	Event	Deaths
1628 or 1645 B.C.	Mediterranean volcanic island of Thera (Santorini) explodes.	N.A.	Mar. 17-21, 1963	Mt. Agung volcano in Bali, Indonesia, erupts.	1,584
Aug. 24–26, A.D. 79	Mt. Vesuvius, near Naples, Italy, erupts, destroying towns of Pompeii and Herculaneum.	2,000 +	Aug. 10, 1963	Landslide in Nepal sweeps villages into Trisuli River.	200
260	Mt. Ilopango in El Salvador erupts, apparently destroying the early Maya civilization.	N.A.	Oct. 9, 1963	Flood occurs when Valont Dam near Langarone, Italy, overflows as result of landslide into its reservoir.	2,200
Sept. 4, 1618	Landslides hit Chiavenna Valley, Italy.	2,420	1965	Taal volcano near Manila in the Philippines erupts.	150
Dec. 16, 1631	Mt. Vesuvius erupts.	4,000 +	Aug. 30, 1965	Avalanche near Saas-Fee, Switzerland, from Allalin glacier strikes workers building dam.	40-100
Mar. 25, 1669	Mt. Etna at Catania, Sicily, erupts.	20,000			
Jan. 11, 1683	Mt. Etna erupts, accompanied by earthquakes.	60,000	1968	Eruption of Arenal in Costa Rica.	78
Aug. 11–12, 1772	Mt. Papandayan on Java explodes.	3,000 +	July 22, 1970	Landslide diverts course of Alaknanda River in India, causing sudden flood.	600
1782	Eruption of Mt. Unzen in Japan causes tidal wave.	15,000	Mar. 18, 1971	Landslide into Lake Yanahuani, creates 60-foot wave that sweeps over Chungar, Peru.	200
June 1783–Feb. 1784	Laki fissure on Mt. Skaptar in Iceland erupts; poisonous gases kill crops and livestock, and thick haze interrupts fishing on oceans.	9,800	July 29, 1971	Landslide into high lake in Hindu Kush mountains of Afghanistan causes instant flood.	1,000 +
Sept. 2, 1806	Rossberg Peak collapses, causing landslides in Goldau Valley, Switzerland.	500	June 28, 1974	Landslides along Quebrada Blanca Canyon in Eastern Colombia.	200
Apr. 5, 1815	Mt. Tambora on Sumbawa in East Indies begins series of eruptions that kill about 10,000 people; another 80,000 die of famine and disease locally; eruptions also alter global weather.	162,000	Jan. 10, 1977	Fast-moving stream of lava from volcano near Goma, Zaire, overtakes fleeing residents.	70
			Feb. 21, 1979	Sinila volcano in Java, Indonesia, erupts.	175 +
Oct. 8 and 12, 1822	Mt. Galunggung on Java erupts, causing slides of mud and boiling water.	4,000	Apr. 30, 1979	Landslide covers side of Marapi volcano in Sumatra, Indonesia.	82 +
1845	Eruption of Nevada del Ruiz in northern Colombia causes mud slides from melting snow.	1,000	July 18, 1979	Landslide on Mt. Werung causes wave to strike beach areas on Lomblen Island, Indonesia.	539
July 28, 1883	Epomeo volcano on Italian Isle of Ischia erupts, causing destructive earthquakes.	2,000 +	May 18, 1980	Mt. St. Helens volcano erupts in Washington.	61
Aug. 26, 1883	Krakatau volcano in East Indies erupts, producing giant waves that strike nearby islands.	36,000	May 20, 1981	Landslides caused by eruption of Semeru in Java, Indonesia.	252
May 7, 1902	La Soufriére on St. Vincent in West Indies erupts.	1,500–2,000	Mar. 28 and Apr. 3-4, 1982	El Chichón in Chiapas, Mexico, erupts, sending cloud of volcanic ash around world.	2,000
May 8, 1902	Pelée volcano on neighboring Martinique erupts, pouring cloud of flaming gas on city of St. Pierre.	29,000	Aug. 16, 1984	Carbon dioxide emitted by Lake Monoun, Cameroon, spreads in region around lake.	37
Aug. 30, 1902	Mt. Pelée erupts.	2,000	Nov. 13, 1985	Eruption of Nevada del Ruiz in northern Colombia causes massive mud slide covering town of Armero.	25,000
Apr. 18, 1906	Mt. Vesuvius near Naples erupts.	150 +			
1911	Taal volcano, near Manila, Philippines, erupts.	1,300	Aug. 21, 1986	Carbon dioxide from Lake Nyos, Cameroon, spreads through region.	1,700 +
May 1919	Crater lake of Mt. Kelut in Indonesia, boiling from volcanic activity, breaks through side of the mountain.	5,000 +	Feb. 10, 1990	Eruption of Mt. Kelut on Java, Indonesia.	32
			July 13, 1990	Earthquake triggers landslide in Pamir Mts., Tajikistan, USSR.	40 +
1937	Eruption of Rabaul caldera on New Britain, Papua New Guinea.	500 +	Oct. 13, 1990	Geyserlike explosion in the Ahuachapán Geothermal Field, El Salvador, releases wave of carbon dioxide and water.	26
Jan. 15, 1951	Mt. Lamington on New Guinea produces cloud of hot gas and dust, similar to that at Mt. Pelée in 1902 and Mt. St. Helens in 1980.	3,000–5,000	Jan. 5, 1991	Landslide at Zunil Geothermal Field, Guatemala.	33
			June 3, 1991	Eruption of Mt. Unzen on Kyushu, Japan.	43
Dec. 4, 1951	Mt. Catarman (Hibokhibok) in Philippines releases cloud of hot gas.	500	June 9, 1991	Mount Pinatubo erupts, as predicted, in Luzon, Philippines; 358 killed by disease in evacuation camps.	754
Sept. 24, 1952	Japanese research ship investigating undersea volcano is destroyed in eruptive event.	29	Jan. 14, 1993	Galeras in Colombia erupts unexpectedly during a scientific workshop, killing six volcanologists who had been on the rim studying the volcano.	9
Dec. 25, 1953	Dam, created by 1945 eruption of Ruapehu volcano on New Zealand, gives way; avalanche of mud and snow strikes passenger train.	150	Feb. 2, 1993	An unexpected eruption of Mayon on Luzon, Philippines produces a cloud of very hot gas and dust that rolls down the slope.	70
Jan. 10, 1962	Landslide on Mt. Huascarán, Peru.	3,000	June 6, 1994	An earthquake at the Volcano Nevada de Huila in Colombia causes mud slides that destroy a dozen villages on its slopes.	650 +
Mar. 14, 1962	Two landslides near Paucartambno Hydroelectric Station in Peru.	204			

Date	Event	Deaths	Date	Event	Deaths
Nov. 22, 1994	Various flows of hot ash and gases down the slope of Merapi volcano on Java in Indonesia kill workers at a water-treatment plant and sweep through villages where superstitious villagers ignored a call to evacuate.	64	June, 1997	Flows of hot ash and gases during eruption of Karangetan volcano in Sulawesi, Indonesia force evacuation of villages.	3
			May 5-6, 1998	Mudslides caused by heavy rains pour down Mount Sarno, east of Naples, Italy.	135
Nov. 3, 1995	Mud landslide set off by eruption of Rinjani on Lombok Island, Indonesia.	30 +	Oct. 30, 1998	Hurricane Mitch causes landslide on San Cristobal volcano in Nicaragua.	1600
Feb. 18, 1997	Mudslide caused by heavy rains destroys two Peruvian villages	300	Apr. 22, 1999	Rain triggers landslides of mountains denuded of trees on Mindanao in the Philippines.	19

Major Active Volcanoes

Volcano	Location	Height (feet above sea level)	Last reported eruption	Volcano	Location	Height (feet above sea level)	Last reported eruption
Africa and the Indian Ocean				Tiatia	Kuril Islands, Russia	6,013	1973
Cameroon Mt.	Cameroon	13,435	1999	Tjarme	Indonesia	10,098	1938
Karthala	Comoros	8,000	1991	Unzen	Kyushu, Japan	4,921	1996
Ol Donyo Lengai	Tanzania	9,482	1998	Usu	Japan	2,398	1978
Nyamuragira	Zaire	10,033	1998	**Europe and the Atlantic Ocean**			
Nyirangongo	Zaire	12,381	1995	Askja	Iceland	4,594	1961
Piton de la Fournaise	Réunion Island	8,631	1992	Beerenberg	Jan Mayen Island, Norway	7,470	1985
Antarctica				Etna	Italy	10,991	1999
Big Ben	Heard Island	9,007	1993	Fogo	Cape Verde Islands	9,281	1995
Mount Erebus	Ross Island	12,447	1990	Grimsvotn	Iceland	5,658	1998
Asia				Helka	Iceland	4,892	1991
Agung	Bali, Indonesia	10,308	1964	Krafla	Iceland	2,145	1984
Akita Komagatake	Japan	5,449	1970	Leirhnukur	Iceland	2,145	1975
Alaid	Kuril Islands, Russia	7,674	1996	Stromboli	Italy	3,038	1998
Amburomrribu	Indonesia	7,051	1969	Tristan de Cunha	St. Helena	6,760	1961
Asama	Honshu, Japan	8,339	1983	Vesuvius	Italy	3,888	1944
Aso	Kyushu, Japan	5,223	1995	**North America**			
Azuma	Honshu, Japan	6,640	1977	Akutan	Alaska	4,275	1996
Batur	Bali, Indonesia	5,633	1994	Amukta	Alaska	3,490	1996
Bezymianny	Russia	9,455	1999	Augustine	Alaska	3,995	1986
Bulusan	Philippines	5,135	1995	Carlisle	Alaska	5,315	1838
Chokai	Honshu, Japan	7,300	1974	Cerberus	Alaska	2,560	1873
Dukono	Indonesia	3,566	1995	Cinder Cone	California	7,985	1851
Fuji	Honshu, Japan	12,388	1707	Cleveland	Alaska	5,675	1994
Galanggung	Java, Indonesia	7,113	1982	Colima	Mexico	12,650	1999
Gamalama	Indonesia	5,625	1994	El Chichón	Mexico	3,478	1983
Karymsky	Russia	4,875	1999	Fisher	Alaska	3,545	1826
Kelut	Java, Indonesia	5,679	1990	Gareloi	Alaska	5,370	1982
Kerinci	Sumatra, Indonesia	12,467	1998	Great Sitkin	Alaska	5,775	1974
Kliuchevskoi	Russia	15,584	1997	Iliamna	Alaska	10,140	1978
Koryaksky	Russia	11,339	1957	Kagamil	Alaska	2,945	1929
Krakatau	Indonesia	2,667	1999	Kanaga	Alaska	4,288	1994
Lewotobi Laki laki	Indonesia	5,217	1991	Katmai	Alaska	7,540	1974
Lokon-Empung	Indonesia	5,187	1992	Kiska	Alaska	4,025	1990
Mayon	Philippines	8,077	1993	Korovin	Alaska	4,885	1998
Me-akan	Japan	4,918	1996	Lassen Peak	California	10,453	1921
Merapi	Java, Indonesia	9,550	1997	Little Sitkin	Alaska	3,945	1828
Nasu	Japan	6,289	1977	Mageik	Alaska	7,295	1946
Nigata Yakeyama	Japan	8,064	1987	Makushin	Alaska	6,680	1987
On-Take	Kyushu, Japan	10,049	1979	Martin	Alaska	6,102	1960
Oshima	Japan	2,489	1990	Mt. Baker	Washington	10,778	1870
Peuet Sague	Indonesia	9,154	1998	Mt. Hood	Oregon	11,245	1801
Pinatubo	Luzon, Philippines	5,250	1991	Mt. Rainier	Washington	14,410	1882
Raung	Java, Indonesia	10,131	1997	Mt. St. Helens	Washington	8,368	1998
Rinjani	Lombok Island, Indonesia	12,224	1995	Mt. Shasta	California	14,160	1855
				Novarupta	Alaska	2,759	1912
Sakura-jima	Kyushu, Japan	3,665	1998	Okmok	Alaska	3,540	1997
Sangeang Api	Indonesia	6,351	1988	Parícutin	Mexico	1,500	1953
Sarychev	Kuril Islands, Russia	5,115	1986	Pavlof	Alaska	8,960	1997
				Pavlof Sister	Alaska	7,050	1786
Semeru	Java, Indonesia	12,060	1999	Pogromni	Alaska	7,545	1964
Shiveluch	Russia	10,779	1997	Popocatépetl	Mexico	17,930	1999
Sinila	Indonesia	7,000	1979	Redoubt	Alaska	10,265	1990
Slamet	Java, Indonesia	11,260	1989	Sarichef	Alaska	2,015	1812
Soputan	Indonesia	5,853	1996	Seguam	Alaska	3,465	1993
Suwanose-jima	Ryukyu Islands, Japan	2,621	1997	Shishaldin	Alaska	9,430	1999
				Spurr	Alaska	11,070	1992
Taal	Luzon, Philippines	1,312	1999	Tanaga	Alaska	7,015	1914
Tambora	Sumbawa, Indonesia	9,354	1815	Tobert	Alaska	11,413	1953
Tengger Caldea	Java, Indonesia	7,641	1995	Trident	Alaska	6,830	1974

Volcano	Location	Height (feet above sea level)	Last reported eruption	Volcano	Location	Height (feet above sea level)	Last reported eruption
Veniaminof	Alaska	8,225	1995	Lopevi	New Hebrides, Vanuatu	4,636	1999
Westdahl	Alaska	5,055	1992				
Yunaska	Alaska	1,980	1937	Manam	Papua New Guinea	5,928	1999
Central America and the Caribbean				Mauna Loa	Hawaii	13,678	1984
Acatenango	Guatemala	12,992	1972	Ngauruhoe	North Island, New Zealand	7,515	1977
Arenal	Costa Rica	5,436	1998				
Concepción	Ometepe Island, Nicaragua	5,106	1986	Pagan	Mariana Islands	1,870	1993
				Piton de la Fournaise	Réunion Island	8,635	1998
El Viejo (San Cristóbal)	Nicaragua	5,840	1997	Rabaul	New Britain, Papua New Guinea	2,257	1999
Fuego	Guatemala	12,346	1999				
Irazú	Costa Rica	11,260	1965	Ruapehu	New Zealand	9,177	1997
Izalco	El Salvador	7,749	1966	Ulawun	New Britain, Papua New Guinea	7,657	1994
Pacaya	Guatemala	8,346	1998				
Pelée	Martinique	4,500	1930	White Island	New Zealand	1,053	1999
Póas	Costa Rica	8,885	1994	**South America**			
Rincón de la Vieja	Costa Rica	6,286	1998	Alcedo	Galapagos Islands, Ecuador	3,707	1993
San Miguel	El Salvador	6,988	1987				
Santiaguito Dome (Santa Maria)	Guatemala	12,375	1996	Copahue	Argentina/Chile	9,800	1992
				Cotachachi	Ecuador	16,204	1955
Soufriére	St. Vincent and the Grenadines	4,048	1979	Cotopaxi	Ecuador	19,347	1975
				Galeras	Colombia	14,025	1993
Soufriére Hills	Montserrat, West Indies	3,090	1999	Guagua Pichincha	Ecuador	15,696	1999
				Guallatiri	Chile	19,918	1960
Tacaná	Guatemala	12,400	1988	Hudson	Chile	8,580	1991
Telica	Nicaragua	3,314	1994	Láscar	Chile	18,346	1995
Oceania—Australia, New Zealand, and the Pacific Islands				Llaima	Chile	10,250	1995
Ambrym	Vanuatu	4,376	1965	Lonquimay	Chile	9,400	1990
Bagana	Bougainville Island, Papua New Guinea	5,742	1991	Puracé	Colombia	15,604	1977
				Reventador	Ecuador	11,434	1976
Haleakala	Hawaii	10,025	1790	Ruiz	Colombia	17,457	1991
Hualalai	Hawaii	8,251	1801	Sangay	Ecuador	17,020	1988
Karkar	Papua New Guinea	4,920	1979	Tupungatito	Chile	18,504	1986
Kilauea	Hawaii	4,009	1999	Villarica	Chile	9,338	1996
Langila	New Britain, Papua New Guinea	4,364	1999				

CHEMISTRY

Chemistry is concerned with the way substances interact with one another. These interactions are chiefly the result of outer electrons of an atom interacting with the outer electrons of another atom. It has increasingly become clear that the shapes of the various combinations of atoms (called molecules) also affect chemical reactions, and physical chemistry is one of the most vital parts of chemistry today. Another vital branch is biochemistry, the study of the chemistry of molecules in living organisms. Organic chemistry generally deals with chemicals formed by living organisms and other chemicals containing carbon, but it treats them as chemicals outside the organism. Inorganic chemistry is concerned with chemicals that do not contain carbon.

▶ **THE PERIODIC TABLE**
In the 19th century, chemists began to determine how much one atom of an element weighed with respect to another—the atomic weight (also known as the atomic mass and measured in atomic mass units, or amu; one amu is a mass equal to one-twelfth the mass of the most common form of carbon atom). The first comprehensive list of atomic weights was prepared by Jöns Jakob Berzelius in 1828. When chemists made lists of elements in the order of atomic weights, they noticed that every seven or eight elements in the list had similar properties. In 1869 Dmitri Mendeleyev boldly interchanged some elements

in the list and left blanks for others to make sure the properties matched for every "period" of eight elements. This was the first periodic table. Mendeleyev had only 63 elements to work with, but he correctly predicted three more that would make his list more complete. Today there are 115 elements in the periodic table.

Early in the 20th century, atoms were discovered to consist of protons and electrons (in 1932 it was discovered that neutrons also are found in atoms). The number of protons is the atomic number, which is a different counting number for every element from hydrogen (atomic number 1) to the unnamed element numbered 118 (elements 113, 115, and 117 have yet to be synthesized). The periodic table was improved by arranging the elements in order of atomic number instead of atomic weight. This clearly showed where the blanks were—all but one of which have been filled in since 1945.

Each column of the periodic table includes elements with similar properties, although hydrogen in the first column is less typical in this respect. But the other elements in the first column are all soft metals that react strongly. Similarly, the last column of the table contains only the gases that react only minimally. In general, elements are metals on the left side of the table (hydrogen is a metal only under great pressure), becoming mostly nonmetals in the last six columns. These last columns include some elements that are

Major Discoveries in Chemistry

B.C.
c. 450   Leucippus of Miletus (Greek: 5th cent.) introduces concept of atom, later expanded upon by his pupil Democritus of Abdera (c. 460–c. 370).

A.D.
1662   Robert Boyle (Anglo-Irish: 1627–91) announces what becomes known as Boyle's law: For gas kept at constant temperature, pressure and volume vary inversely.
1755   Joseph Black (Scottish: 1728–99) discovers carbon dioxide.
1766   Henry Cavendish (English: 1731–1810) discovers hydrogen.
1772   Joseph Priestley (English-American: 1733–1804) notes that burning hydrogen produces water.
   Daniel Rutherford (Scottish: 1749–1819) and several other chemists discover nitrogen. Karl Wilhelm Scheele (Swedish: 174286) discovers oxygen but does not announce discovery until after independent discovery by Joseph Priestley in 1774.
1778   Antoine-Laurent Lavoisier (French: 1743–94) discovers that air is mostly mixture of nitrogen and oxygen.
1784   Cavendish announces water is compound of hydrogen and oxygen.
1789   Lavoisier explicitly states law of conservation of matter: In chemical change, matter is neither created nor destroyed.
1791   Jeremias Benjamin Richter (German: 1762–1807) shows that acids and bases always neutralize each other in same proportion.
1803   John Dalton (English: 1766–1844) establishes atomic theory of matter.
1811   Amedeo Avogadro (Italian: 1776–1856) proposes that equal volumes of gas at same temperature and pressure contain same number of molecules (Avogadro's law).
1824   Joseph-Louis Gay-Lussac (French: 1778–1850) discovers chemical isomers, chemicals with same formula but different structures.
1828   Friedrich Wöhler (German: 1800–1882) prepares organic compound from inorganic chemicals, showing that life is basically same as other matter.
1859   Gustav Robert Kirchhoff (German: 1824–87) and Robert Wilhelm Bunsen (German: 1811–99) introduce use of spectroscope to identify elements from light they give off when heated or burned.

1868   Pierre-Jules-César Janssen (French: 1824–1907) and Sir Joseph Norman Lockyer (English: 1836–1920) discover helium by observing Sun's spectrum.
1869   Dmitry Ivanovich Mendeleyev (Russian: 1834–1907) publishes his first version of periodic table of elements.
1875   Paul-Emile Lecoq de Boisbaudran (French: 1838–1912) discovers gallium, the first discovery of an element predicted by Mendeleyev.
1906   Mikhail Tsvett (Russian: 1872–1919) develops paper chromatography, the beginning of modern methods of chemical analysis.
1908   Fritz Haber (German: 1868–1934) develops cheap process for making ammonia from nitrogen in the air.
1962   Neil Bartlett (English: 1932–) creates a compound of xenon, platinum, and fluorine, showing that the noble gases can form compounds.
1984   Dany Schechtman (American) and coworkers discover first quasicrystal, a "crystal" that violates the symmetry rules of all other crystals.
1985   Richard E. Smalley (American: 1943–) and Harry Kroto (English: 1939–) discover buckminsterfullerene, a carbon molecule containing 60 carbon atoms arranged in a geodesic sphere (nicknamed "the bucky ball").
1991   Sumio Iijima of NEC Corp. discovers that carbon forms tiny hollow cylinders called nanotubes.
1998   A collaboration between Russia's Joint Institute for Nuclear Research in Dubna and the U.S. Lawrence Livermore National Laboratory in California produces just one atom of a comparatively long-lived (30 seconds) element 114.
   Research on carbon nanotubes shows that they conduct electricity with almost no resistance at room temperature (although they are not superconductors), emit light when carrying an electric current, and can behave either as semiconductors or metals depending on the alignment of atoms in the tube.
1999   Using powerful X-rays generated by synchrotrons, scientists studying ultra-pure ice show that hydrogen bonds involve sharing electrons between the bond and the molecule.
   Scientists at Lawrence Berkeley National Laboratory in California extend the periodic table to include elements 118 and 116 by creating three atoms of element 118 that decay almost instantly to 116.

---

metals, such as aluminum. (A broken, heavy line separates the metals from the nonmetals.)
   The row of rare-earth elements beginning with lanthanum and the row of actinide elements beginning with actinium do not fit neatly into the rest of the table. Elements from atomic number 57 to 71 are all similar to lanthanum, while elements from atomic number 89 to 103 are similar to actinium. The rare earths are not generally rare, nor do they resemble soil. They are moderately common metals that, because of atomic structure, are very similar chemically. The actinide elements are radioactive metals.
   The periodic table as shown here also includes the atomic mass as well as the atomic number. The atomic mass is essentially the sum of the protons and neutrons in an atom of an element. As protons and neutrons join to form an atomic nucleus, a little of their energy becomes mass, the amount of which depends on how many protons and neutrons there are. Consequently,

a particular atom is chosen upon which to base the amu. Today the atomic mass is adjusted to make the most common form of carbon have an atomic mass of exactly 12 (6 protons and 6 neutrons). Most elements occur with several different atomic masses (in addition to carbon-12, for example, there are both carbon-13 and carbon-14; carbon-14 has 6 protons and 8 neutrons and is radioactive). These different forms are called isotopes. Therefore, in the periodic table, the atomic mass given for most elements is the one that would be found by averaging the different isotopes in the amounts they naturally occur. Carbon is given an atomic mass of 12.01 because there is so much more carbon-12 than there is carbon-13 or carbon-14 in an ordinary sample of carbon. For some radioactive elements, natural abundance is meaningless, since there is no stable form. For these, the atomic mass of the most stable form is given, indicated by putting the atomic mass in parentheses.

THE PERIODIC TABLE OF THE ELEMENTS

Legend:
6 — atomic number
C — chemical symbol
12.01 — atomic mass
Carbon — name of element

alkali metals I A	alkaline earth metals II A		III B	IV B	V B	VI B	VII B	VIII			I B	II B	III A	IV A	V A	VI A	VII A	noble gases O
1 H 1.01 Hydrogen																		**2 He** 4.00 Helium
3 Li 6.94 Lithium	**4 Be** 9.01 Beryllium												**5 B** 10.81 Boron	**6 C** 12.01 Carbon	**7 N** 14.01 Nitrogen	**8 O** 16.00 Oxygen	**9 F** 19.00 Fluorine	**10 Ne** 20.18 Neon
11 Na 22.99 Sodium	**12 Mg** 24.31 Magnesium							transition metals					**13 Al** 26.98 Aluminum	**14 Si** 28.09 Silicon	**15 P** 30.97 Phosphorus	**16 S** 32.07 Sulfur	**17 Cl** 35.45 Chlorine	**18 Ar** 39.95 Argon
19 K 39.10 Potassium	**20 Ca** 40.08 Calcium	**21 Sc** 44.96 Scandium	**22 Ti** 47.88 Titanium	**23 V** 50.94 Vanadium	**24 Cr** 52.00 Chromium	**25 Mn** 54.95 Manganese	**26 Fe** 55.85 Iron	**27 Co** 58.93 Cobalt	**28 Ni** 58.70 Nickel	**29 Cu** 63.55 Copper	**30 Zn** 65.39 Zinc	**31 Ga** 69.72 Gallium	**32 Ge** 72.61 Germanium	**33 As** 74.92 Arsenic	**34 Se** 78.96 Selenium	**35 Br** 79.90 Bromine	**36 Kr** 83.80 Krypton
37 Rb 85.47 Rubidium	**38 Sr** 87.62 Strontium	**39 Y** 88.91 Yttrium	**40 Zr** 91.22 Zirconium	**41 Nb** 92.91 Niobium	**42 Mo** 95.94 Molybdenum	**43 Tc** (98) Technetium	**44 Ru** 101.07 Ruthenium	**45 Rh** 102.91 Rhodium	**46 Pd** 106.4 Palladium	**47 Ag** 107.87 Silver	**48 Cd** 112.41 Cadmium	**49 In** 114.82 Indium	**50 Sn** 118.71 Tin	**51 Sb** 121.74 Antimony	**52 Te** 127.60 Tellurium	**53 I** 126.90 Iodine	**54 Xe** 131.29 Xenon
55 Cs 132.91 Cesium	**56 Ba** 137.33 Barium	Lanthanide series (see below)	**72 Hf** 178.49 Hafnium	**73 Ta** 180.94 Tantalum	**74 W** 183.85 Tungsten	**75 Re** 186.21 Rhenium	**76 Os** 190.23 Osmium	**77 Ir** 192.22 Iridium	**78 Pt** 195.08 Platinum	**79 Au** 196.97 Gold	**80 Hg** 200.59 Mercury	**81 Tl** 204.38 Thallium	**82 Pb** 207.2 Lead	**83 Bi** 208.98 Bismuth	**84 Po** (209) Polonium	**85 At** (210) Astatine	**86 Rn** (222) Radon
87 Fr (223) Francium	**88 Ra** 226.03 Radium	Actinide series (see below)	**104 Rf** (261) Rutherfordium	**105 Db** (262) Dubnium	**106 Sg** (263) Seaborgium	**107 Bh** (262) Bohrium	**108 Hs** (265) Hassium	**109 Mt** (266) Meitnerium	**110** (269)	**111** (272)	**112** (277)		**114** (281)		**116** (289)		**118** (293)

nonmetals

rare earth elements — Lanthanide series

57 La 138.91 Lanthanum	**58 Ce** 140.12 Cerium	**59 Pr** 140.91 Praseodymium	**60 Nd** 144.24 Neodymium	**61 Pm** (145) Promethium	**62 Sm** 150.4 Samarium	**63 Eu** 151.96 Europium	**64 Gd** 157.25 Gadolinium	**65 Tb** 158.93 Terbium	**66 Dy** 162.50 Dysprosium	**67 Ho** 164.93 Holmium	**68 Er** 167.26 Erbium	**69 Tm** 168.93 Thulium	**70 Yb** 173.04 Ytterbium	**71 Lu** 174.97 Lutetium

Actinide series

89 Ac 227.03 Actinium	**90 Th** 232.04 Thorium	**91 Pa** 231.04 Protactinium	**92 U** 238.03 Uranium	**93 Np** 237.05 Neptunium	**94 Pu** (244) Plutonium	**95 Am** (243) Americium	**96 Cm** (247) Curium	**97 Bk** (247) Berkelium	**98 Cf** (251) Californium	**99 Es** (252) Einsteinium	**100 Fm** (257) Fermium	**101 Md** (258) Mendelevium	**102 No** (259) Nobelium	**103 Lr** (260) Lawrencium

Period 1, Period 2, Period 3, Period 4, Period 5, Period 6, Period 7

Properties, Abundance, and Discovery of the Elements

All ordinary matter is made from one or more substances called elements (because they cannot be changed by chemical means). Ninety elements are found in nature, and people have created others, for a current total of 115. In this table each of the elements is listed in alphabetical order along with several of its important properties. The chemical symbol and the atomic number can be used to locate other information about the elements in the periodic table reprinted below. The relative abundance of the elements is given as parts per million in the Earth's crust—83,600 parts per million for

aluminum means that of a million atoms chosen at random from the crust, 83,600 atoms, on average, would be aluminum atoms. Some elements have so few parts per million that they are simply listed as rare, whereas others are "synthetic"—artificial elements not found in the crust at all. Many elements, known from ancient times, are labeled "prehistoric." Others are given with their first discovery—many elements having been independently rediscovered by others. In the following table, elements 110–12, 114, 116 and 118, as yet unnamed, are listed as "Element 110" and so forth.

Element/Type[1]	Symbol/ Atomic number	Melting point[1]	Boiling point[1]	Derivation of name (Discoverer, Year)
Actinium	Ac	1920°F	5790°F	Greek *aktis*, a ray. (André-Louis Debierne, 1899)
Radioactive metal	89	1050°C	3200°C	
Aluminum	Al	1220°F	4473°F	Latin *alumen*, a substance with astringent taste (Hans Christian
Metal	13	660°C	2467°C	Oersted, 1825)
Americium	Am	1821°F	4725°F	Named for America (Glenn T. Seaborg & coworkers, 1944)
Radioactive metal	95	994°C	2607°C	
Antimony	Sb	1167°F	3180°F	Greek *antimonos*, opposed to solitude; symbol Sb from Latin
Metal	51	631°C	1750°C	*stibium*. (Rhazes, c. 900)
Argon	Ar	-308.6°F	-302.3°F	Greek *argus*, neutral inactive. (Sir William Ramsay, 1894)
Gas	18	-189.2°C	-185.7°C	
Arsenic	As	1503°F[2]	1135°F[2]	Latin *arsenicum*; folk etymology connects with yellow and
Nonmetal	33	817°C[2]	613°C[2]	maleness. (Albertus Magnus, 1250)
Astatine	At	576°F	639°F	Greek *astatos*, unstable. (Emilio Segrè, D.R. Corson, & K.R.
Radioactive nonmetal	85	302°C	337°C	MacKenzie, 1940)
Barium	Ba	1337°F	2980°F	Greek *baros*, heavy, because of its dense compounds. (Humphry
Metal	56	725°C	1640°C	Davy, 1808)
Berkelium	Bk	N.A.	N.A.	First made at Univ. of California. (Glenn T. Seaborg & coworkers,
Radioactive metal	97			1949)
Beryllium	Be	2332°F	5380°F	Latin *beryllus*, Greek beryllos, gem. (Louis-Nicolas Vauquelin,
Metal	4	1278°C	2970°C	1798)
Bismuth	Bi	520°F	2840°F	German *weisse masse*, white mass; changed to *bismat*. (Claude J.
Metal	83	271°C	1560°C	Geoffrey, 1753)
Bohrium	Bh	3774°F	4620°F	Named for Danish physicist Niels Bohr. (Russian scientists at
Radioactive metal	107	N.A.	N.A.	Dubna, 1977)
Boron	B	3774°F	4620°F	Arabic *borak* (borax); BORax + carbON. (Joseph-Louis Gay-Lussac
Nonmetal	5	2079°C	2550°C	& Louis-Jacques Thénard, 1808)
Bromine	Br	19°F	137.8°F	Greek *bromos*, a stench; because of odor of its vapors. (Antoine-
Liquid nonmetal	35	-7.2°C	58.8°C	Jérôme Balard, 1826)
Cadmium	Cd	609.6°F	1409°F	Greek *cadmia*, earthy. (Friedrich Strohmeyer, 1817)
Metal	48	320.9°C	765°C	
Calcium	Ca	1542°F	2703°F	Latin *calx, calcis*, lime. (Humphry Davy, 1808)
Metal	20	839°C	1484°C	
Californium	Cf	N.A.	N.A.	First made at Univ. of California. (Glenn T. Seaborg & coworkers,
Radioactive metal	98			1949)
Carbon	C	6420°F	8721°F	Latin *carbo*, coal. (Prehistoric)
Nonmetal	6	3550°C	4827°C	
Cerium	Ce	1468°F	5875°F	Named for asteroid Ceres, discovered in 1801. (Martin Klaproth,
Rare earth	58	798°C	3246°C	1803)
Cesium	Cs	83.1°F	1236.7°F	Latin *caesius*, bluish gray. (Gustav Kirchhoff & Robert Bunsen,
Metal	55	28.4°C	669.3°C	1860)
Chlorine	Cl	-150°F	-30.3°F	Greek *chloros*, grass-green; from color of gas. (Humphry Davy,
Gas	17	-101°C	-34.6°C	1810)
Chromium	Cr	3375°F	4842°F	Greek *chroma*, color; because many of its compounds are colored.
Metal	24	1857°C	2672°C	(Louis-Nicolas Vauquelin, 1797)
Cobalt	Co	2723°F	5200°F	German *Kobalt*, a goblin. (Georg Brandt, 1735)
Metal	27	1495°C	2870°C	
Copper	Cu	1981°F	4653°F	Latin *cuprum*; for island of Cyprus. (Prehistoric)
Metal	29	1083°C	2567°C	
Curium	Cm	2444°F	N.A.	Named after Pierre and Marie Curie. (Glenn T. Seaborg &
Radioactive metal	96	1340°C		coworkers, 1944)
Dubnium	Db	N.A.	N.A.	Named for the Joint Institute for Nuclear Research at Dubna,
Radioactive metal	105			Russia. (Russian scientists at Dubna, 1967)
Dysprosium	Dy	2574°F	4653°F	Greek *dysprositos*, difficult of access. (Paul-Emile Lecoq de
Rare earth	66	1412°C	2567°C	Boisbaudran, 1886)

Element/Type[1]	Symbol/ Atomic number	Melting point[1]	Boiling point[1]	Derivation of name (Discoverer, Year)
Einsteinium	Es			Named after Albert Einstein. (Albert Ghiorso & coworkers, 1952)
Radioactive metal	99	N.A.	N.A.	
Element 110	N.A.	N.A.	N.A.	(Society for Heavy Ion Research, Darmstadt, Germany, 1994)
Radioactive metal	110			
Element 111	N.A.	N.A.	N.A.	(Society for Heavy Ion Research, Darmstadt, Germany, 1994)
Radioactive metal	111			
Element 112	N.A.	N.A.	N.A.	(Society for Heavy Ion Research, Darmstadt, Germany, 1996)
Radioactive metal	112			
Element 114	N.A.	N.A.	N.A.	(Dubna and Lawrence Livermore, 1998)
Radioactive metal	114			
Element 116	N.A.	N.A.	N.A.	(Lawrence Berkeley National Laboratory, 1999)
Radioactive metal	116			
Element 118	N.A.	N.A.	N.A.	(Lawrence Berkeley National Laboratory, 1999)
Radioactive metal	118			
Erbium	Er	2784°F	4334°F	Named for Ytterby, village in Sweden. (Carl Gustav Mosander,
Rare earth	68	1529°C	2868°C	1843)
Europium	Eu	1512°F	2907°F	Named for Europe. (Eugène-Anatole Demarçay, 1896)
Rare earth	63	822°C	1597°C	
Fermium	Fm	N.A.	N.A.	Named after Italian physicist Enrico Fermi. (Albert Ghiorso &
Radioactive metal	100			coworkers, 1952)
Fluorine	F	-363.3°F	-306.7°F	Latin *fluere*, to flow. (Ferdinand-Frédéric-Henri Moissan, 1886)
Gas	9	-219.6°C	-188.1°C	
Francium	Fr	80.6°F	1256°F	Named for France. (Marguerite Perey, 1939)
Radioactive metal	87	27°C	677°C	
Gadolinium	Gd	2395°F	5923°F	Named after gadolinite, mineral named for Johan Gadolin, Finnish
Rare earth	64	1313°C	3273°C	chemist. (Jean-Charles Marignac, 1880)
Gallium	Ga	86.6°F	4357°F	Latin *Gallia*, France; also Latin *gallus*, a cock—a pun on Lecoq de
Metal	31	29.8°C	2403°C	Boisbaudran. (Paul-Emile Lecoq de Boisbaudran, 1875)
Germanium	Ge	1719°F	5126°F	Named for Germany. (Clemens Winkler, 1886)
Metal	32	937°C	2830°C	
Gold	Au	1947°F	5086°F	Anglo-Saxon *gold*; Sanskrit *juel*, to shine; symbol from Latin
Metal	79	1064°C	2808°C	*aurum*, shining down. (Prehistoric)
Hafnium	Hf	4041°F	8316°F	From *Hafnia*, ancient name of Copenhagen. (Dirk Coster & György
Metal	72	2227°C	4602°C	Hevesy, 1923)
Hassium	Hs	N.A.	N.A.	Named for the German province of Hesse, where Darmstadt is
Radioactive metal	108			located. (Society for Heavy Ion Research, Darmstadt, Germany, 1984)
Helium	He	-458°F	-452°F	Greek *helios*, the Sun; first observed in Sun's atmosphere. (Pierre-
Gas	2	-272°C	-269°C	Jules-César Janssen & Sir Joseph Norman Lockyer, 1868)
Holmium	Ho	2678°F	4928°F	From *Holmia*, Latinized form of Stockholm. (Per Teodor Cleve,
Rare earth	67	1470°C	2720°C	1879)
Hydrogen	H	-434.6°F	-423.2°F	Greek *hydor*, water, plus *gen*, forming. (Henry Cavendish, 1766)
Gas	1	-259.1°C	-252.9°C	
Indium	In	313.9°F	3776°F	Latin *indicum*, indigo. (Ferdinand Reich & Hieronymus Theodor
Metal	49	156.6°C	2080°C	Richter, 1863)
Iodine[3]	I	236.3°F	363.9°F	Greek *iodes*, violet; from color of its vapor. (Bernard Courtois,
Nonmetal	53	113.5°C	184.4°C	1811)
Iridium	Ir	4370°F	7466°F	Greek *iris*, a rainbow, from changing color of its salts. (Smithson
Metal	77	2410°C	4130°C	Tennant, 1803)
Iron	Fe	2795°F	4982°F	Anglo-Saxon *iren*; symbol from Latin *ferrum*. (Prehistoric)
Metal	26	1535°C	2750°C	
Krypton	Kr	-249.9°F	-242.1°F	Greek *kryptos*, hidden. (Alexander Ramsay & Morris William
Gas	36	-156.6°C	-152.3°C	Travers, 1898)
Lanthanum	La	1684°F	6267°F	Greek *lanthanein*, to be concealed. (Carl Gustav Mosander, 1839)
Rare earth	57	918°C	3464°C	
Lawrencium	Lr	N.A.	N.A.	Named after American physicist Ernest Lawrence. (Albert Ghiorso
Radioactive metal	103			& coworkers, 1961)
Lead	Pb	621.5°F	3164°F	Anglo-Saxon *lead*; symbol from Latin *plumbum*. (Prehistoric)
Metal	82	327.5°C	1740°C	
Lithium	Li	356.9°F	2248°F	Greek *lithos*, stony. (J.A. Arfvedson, 1817)
Metal	3	180.5°C	1342°C	
Lutetium	Lu	3025°F	6157°F	Latin *Lutetia*, ancient name for Paris. (Georges Urbain, 1907)
Rare earth	71	1663°C	3402°C	
Magnesium	Mg	1200°F	1994°F	Latin *Magnesia*, a district in Asia Minor. (Humphry Davy, 1808)
Metal	12	649°C	1090°C	
Manganese	Mn	2271°F	3564°F	Latin *magnes*, magnet; because of confusion with magnetic iron
Metal	25	1244°C	1962°C	ores. (Johann Gottlieb Gahn, 1774)
Meitnerium	Mt	N.A.	N.A.	Named for the Austrian-Swedish physicist Lise Meitner.
Radioactive metal	109			(Society for Heavy Ion Research, Darmstadt, Germany, 1982)
Mendelevium	Md	N.A.	N.A.	Named after Russian chemist Dmitri Mendeléev. (Albert Ghiorso &
Radioactive metal	101			coworkers, 1955)
Mercury	Hg	-38.0°F	673.9°F	Named for Roman god Mercurius; symbol from Latin *hydrargyrum*.
Liquid metal	80	-38.9°C	356.6°C	(Prehistoric)

Element/Type[1]	Symbol/ Atomic number	Melting point[1]	Boiling point[1]	Derivation of name (Discoverer, Year)
Molybdenum	Mo	4743°F	8334°F	Greek *molybdos*, lead. (Karl Wilhelm Scheele, 1778)
Metal	42	2617°C	4612°C	
Neodymium	Nd	1870°F	5565°F	Greek *neo*, new, plus *didymon*, twin (with the element
Rare earth	60	1021°C	3074°C	praseodymium). (Karl Auer (Baron von Welsbach), 1885)
Neon	Ne	-416.7°F	-411°F	Greek *neo*, new. (Alexander Ramsay & Morris William Travers,
Gas	10	-248.7°C	-246°C	1898)
Neptunium	Np	1184°F	7056°F	Named for planet Neptune. (Edwin McMillan & Philip Abelson,
Radioactive metal	93	640°C	3902°C	1940)
Nickel	Ni	2647°F	4950°F	German *Nickel*, Satan (Old Nick). (Axel Cronstedt, 1751)
Metal	28	1453°C	2732°C	
Niobium	Nb	4474°F	8568°F	Latin *Niobe*, daughter of Tantalus. (Charles Hachett, 1801)
Metal	41	2468°C	4742°C	
Nitrogen	N	-345.8°F	-320.4°F	Latin, forming *niter*, a compound of nitrogen. (Daniel Rutherford,
Gas	7	-209.9°C	-195.8°C	1772)
Nobelium	No	N.A.	N.A.	Named after Alfred Nobel; made at Nobel Institute. (Albert Ghiorso
Radioactive metal	102			& coworkers, 1958)
Osmium	Os	5513°F	9081°F	Greek *osme*, smell; for malodorousness. (Smithson Tennant, 1803)
Metal	76	3045°C	5027°C	
Oxygen	O	-361°F	-297°F	Greek *oxys*, sharp, plus *gen*, forming; from incorrect belief that
Gas	8	-218.4°C	-183°C	oxygen forms acids. (Joseph Priestley, 1774)
Palladium	Pd	2829°F	5684°F	Named for Greek goddess Pallas; from asteroid Pallas. (William
Metal	46	1554°C	3140°C	Hyde Wollaston, 1803)
Phosphorus	P	111.4°F	536°F	Greek *phosphoros*, light-bringer; glows because of rapid oxidation.
Nonmetal	15	44.1°C	280°C	(Hennig Brand, 1669)
Platinum	Pt	3222°F	6921°F	Diminutive of Spanish *plata*, silver, *platina*. (Antonio de Ulloa,
Metal	78	1772°C	3827°C	1735)
Plutonium	Pu	1186°F	5850°F	Named for planet Pluto. (Glenn T. Seaborg & coworkers, 1940)
Radioactive metal	94	641°C	3232°C	
Polonium	Po	489°F	1764°F	Named by Marie Curie for her native Poland. (Marie & Pierre
Radioactive metal	84	254°C	962°C	Curie, 1898)
Potassium	K	145.9°F	1399.8°F	Named for potash, a compound of potassium; symbol from Latin
Metal	19	63.3°C	759.9°C	*kalium*. (Humphry Davy, 1807)
Praseodymium	Pr	6368°F	5814°F	Greek *prasios*, green, plus *didymos*, twin (with the element
Rare earth	59	3520°C	3212°C	Neodymium). (Karl Auer (Baron von Welsbach), 1885)
Promethium	Pm	1908°F	5430°F	Named for Greek god Prometheus, who stole fire from heaven.
Radioactive rare earth	61	1042°C[4]	3000°C[4]	(J.A. Marinsky, L.E. Glendenin, & C.D.Coryell, 1945)
Protactinium	Pa	2912°F	N.A.	Latin *proto*, first, plus actinium, one of the elements. (Otto Hahn &
Radioactive metal	91	1600°C	N.A.	Lise Meitner, 1918)
Radium	Ra	1292°F	2084°F	Latin *radius*, ray. (Marie Curie & Pierre Curie, 1898)
Radioactive metal	88	1600°C	1140°C	
Radon	Rn	-96°F	-79°F	*Radium* plus *on*, as in *neon*. (Friedrich Ernst Dorn, 1900)
Radioactive gas	86	-71°C	-61.8°C	
Rhenium	Re	5756°F	10,161°F	Latin *Rhenus*, Rhine. (Walter Noddack, Ida Tacke, & Otto Berg,
Metal	75	3180°C	5627°C	1925)
Rhodium	Rh	3571°F	6741°F	Greek *rhodon*, rose; for red color of its salts. (William Hyde
Metal	45	1966°C	3727°C	Wollaston, 1803)
Rubidium	Rb	102°F	1267°F	Latin *rubidus*, red; from red lines in its spectrum. (Gustav Kirchhoff
Metal	37	38.9°C	686°C	& Robert Bunsen, 1861)
Ruthenium	Ru	4190°F	7052°F	Named for Ruthenia in Urals, where ore was first found. (Carl
Metal	44	2310°C	3900°C	Claus, 1844)
Rutherfordium	Rf	N.A.	N.A.	Named for the New Zealand-born English physicist Ernest Rutherford.
Radioactive metal	104			(Russian scientists at Dubna, 1964)
Samarium	Sm	1965°F	3261°F	Named for Scandinavian mineral samarskite. (Paul-Emile Lecoq de
Rare earth	62	1074°C	1794°C	Boisbaudran, 1879)
Scandium	Sc	2806°F	5128°F	Named for Scandinavia. (Lars Fredrik Nilson, 1879)
Metal	21	1541°C	2831°C	
Seaborgium	Sg	N.A.	N.A.	Named for American physicist Glenn T. Seaborg. (Russian scientists
Radioactive metal	106			at Dubna and U.S. team from Berkeley and Lawrence Livermore Laboratories, 1974)
Selenium	Se	423°F	1265°F	Greek *selene*, the Moon. (Jöns Jakob Berzelius, 1818)
Nonmetal	34	217°C	685°C	
Silicon	Si	2570°F	4271°F	Latin *silex*, flint. (Jöns Jakob Berzelius, 1824)
Nonmetal	14	1410°C	2355°C	
Silver	Ag	1763.4°F	4014°F	Anglo-Saxon *sealfor*; symbol is from Latin *argentum*. (Prehistoric)
Metal	47	961.9°C	2212°C	
Sodium	Na	208.0°F	1621.2°F	English *soda*, a sodium compound; symbol from Latin
Metal	11	97.8°C	882.9°C	*natrium*.(Humphry Davy, 1807)
Strontium	Sr	1416°F	2523°F	For Strontian, a town in Scotland. (Humphry Davy, 1808)
Metal	38	769°C	1384°C	
Sulfur	S	235.0°F	832.5°F	Sanskrit *solvere*, Latin *sulphur*. (Prehistoric)
Nonmetal	16	112.8°C	444.7°C	

Element/Type[1]	Symbol/Atomic number	Melting point[1]	Boiling point[1]	Derivation of name (Discoverer, Year)
Tantalum	Ta	5425°F	9797°F	For mythical king Tantalus, condemned to thirst; because of its
Metal	73	2996°C	5425°C	insolubility. (Anders Ekeberg, 1802)
Technetium	Tc	3942°F	8811°F	Greek *technetos*, artificial; first artificial element. (Emilio Segrè,
Radioactive metal	43	2172°C	4877°C	1937)
Tellurium	Te	841.1°F	1814°F	Latin *tellus*, the Earth. (Franz Joseph Müller, 1782)
Metal	52	449.5°C	990°C	
Terbium	Tb	2473°F	5846°F	For Ytterby, village in Sweden. (Carl Gustav Mosander, 1843)
Rare earth	65	1356°C	3230°C	
Thallium	Tl	578.3°F	2655°F	Greek *thallos*, a green twig; after color of its spectrum. (William
Metal	81	303.5°C	1457°C	Crookes, 1861)
Thorium	Th	3182°F	8654°F	For Norse god Thor. (Jöns Jakob Berzelius, 1829)
Radioactive metal	90	1750°C	4790°C	
Thulium	Tm	2813°F	3542°F	Greek *Thule*, Greek name for land north of Britain. (Per Teodor
Rare earth	69	1545°C	1950°C	Cleve, 1879)
Tin	Sn	450°F	4118°F	Anglo-Saxon *tin*; symbol from Latin *stannum*. (Prehistoric)
Metal	50	232°C	2270°C	
Titanium	Ti	3020°F	5949°F	For Titans of classical mythology. (William Gregor, 1791)
Metal	22	1660°C	3287°C	
Tungsten	W	6170°F	10,220°F	Swedish *tung sten*, heavy stone; symbol from German *Wolfram*.
Metal	74	3410°C	5660°C	(Fausto and Juan José d'Elhuyar, 1783)
Uranium	U	2070°F	6904°F	For planet Uranus. (Martin Klaproth, 1789)
Radioactive metal	92	1132°C	3818°C	
Vanadium	V	3434°F	6116°F	For Scandinavian goddess Vanadis. (Andrès del Rio, 1801)
Metal	23	1890°C	3380°C	
Xenon	Xe	-169.4°F	-161°F	Greek *xenon*, stranger. (Alexander Ramsay & Morris William
Gas	54	-111.9°C	-107°C	Travers, 1898)
Ytterbium	Yb	1506°F	2185°F	For Ytterby, a village in Sweden. (George Urbain, 1907)
Rare earth	70	819°C	1196°C	
Yttrium	Y	2826°F	9640°F	For Ytterby, a village in Sweden. (Carl Gustav Mosander, 1843)
Rare earth	39	1552°C	3338°C	
Zinc	Zn	787.3°F	1665°F	German *zink*. (Prehistoric)
Metal	30	419.6°C	907°C	
Zirconium	Zr	3366°F	7911°F	Arabic *zargun*, gold color. (Martin Klaproth, 1789)
Metal	40	1852°C	4377°C	

1. At a pressure of one atmosphere and, for type, at room temperature. 2. At a pressure of 28 atmospheres. 3. This element sublimes (slowly evaporates from its solid form) at room temperature and one atmosphere. 4. Estimated

PHYSICS

Physics is the basis of the other sciences because it is concerned with the fundamental interactions of matter and energy. The first physicists studied how ordinary objects and very large objects (Moon, planets, and stars) moved in response to forces. Their study was extremely successful. Near the end of the 19th century, physicists began to investigate radiation in detail, leading to the discovery of various forms of electromagnetic radiation (of which only forms of light, including infrared and ultraviolet, were known previously) and particles smaller than the atom (subatomic particles, such as the electron and proton). In the 20th century, the study of subatomic particles, called particle physics, became a major branch of the science. Many particle physicists limit their work to the particles in the nucleus of atoms and to the behavior of nuclei. Another major branch, condensed-matter physics, is concerned with the physical behavior of materials—for example, their electrical and magnetic properties. Major successes in condensed-matter physics include development of the transistor and related devices (chips) and superconductivity, a state in which electric currents can be transmitted with no resistance. Today many physicists are also cosmologists, who study how the universe began and is constructed, or astrophysicists, who study processes in stars.

Major Discoveries in Physics

1586 Simon Stevinus (Belgian-Dutch: 1548–1620) shows that two different weights dropped at same time from same height will reach ground at same time.
1604 Galileo (Italian: 1564–1642) announces his discovery that a body falling freely will increase its distance as the square of time.
1663 Blaise Pascal (French: 1623–62) proposes what becomes known as Pascal's law: pressure in fluid is transmitted equally in all directions (published year after his death).
1675 Ole Rømer (Danish: 1644–1710) becomes first to measure speed of light, although his value is somewhat too slow by today's standards.
1676 Robert Hooke (English: 1635–1703) discovers what becomes known as Hooke's law: The amount a spring stretches varies directly with its tension.

1678   Christiaan Huygens (Dutch: 1629–95) develops wave theory of light.

1687   Sir Isaac Newton's (English: 1642–1727) *Principia* is published, containing his laws of motion and theory of gravity.

1746   At least two experimenters in Leyden, the Netherlands, invent method for storing static electricity, which becomes known as Leyden jar.

1752   Benjamin Franklin (American: 1706–90) performs kite experiment, demonstrating that lightning is form of electricity.

1787   Jacques A.C. Charles (French: 1746–1823) discovers what is later known as Charles's law: All gases expand same amount with given rise in temperature; e.g., same rise in temperature that will cause hydrogen to double in volume will also cause air to double in volume.

1791   Luigi Galvani (Italian: 1737–98) announces his discovery that when two different metals touch in frog's muscle, they produce electric current.

1798   Benjamin Thompson, Count von Rumford (American-German: 1753–1814) shows that heat is form of motion.

Henry Cavendish (English: 1731–1810) determines gravitational constant and mass of Earth.

1800   William Herschel (German-English: 1738–1822) announces his discovery of infrared light.

1801   Johann W. Ritter (German: 1776–1810) discovers ultraviolet light.

1802   Thomas Young (English: 1773–1829) develops his wave theory of light.

1819   Hans Christian Oersted (Danish: 1777–1851) discovers that magnetism and electricity are two different manifestations of same force.

1820   André-Marie Ampère (French: 1775–1836) formulates first laws of electromagnetism.

1831   Michael Faraday (English: 1791–1867) in England and Joseph Henry (American: 1797–1878) in U.S. (in 1830) independently discover principle of dynamo.

1842   Julius Robert von Mayer (German: 1814–78) is first scientist to state law of conservation of energy.

1848   William Thompson, Baron Kelvin (Scottish: 1824–1907), proposes concept of absolute zero, the lowest possible temperature (-460°F, or -273°C).

1850   Rudolf J.E. Clausius (German: 1822–88) makes first clear statement of second law of thermodynamics: Energy in closed system tends to degrade into heat.

1873   James Clerk Maxwell (Scottish: 1831–79) publishes complete theory of electromagnetism.

1888   Heinrich P. Hertz (German: 1857–94) produces and detects radio waves.

1895   Wilhelm Konrad Röntgen (German: 1845–1923) discovers X rays.

1896   Henri Becquerel (French: 1852–1908) discovers natural radioactivity.

1897   Sir Joseph John Thomson (English: 1856–1940) discovers electron.

1900   Max K.E.L. Planck (German: 1858–1947) explains behavior of electromagnetic radiation by proposing that there is smallest step a physical process can take, which he names quantum.

1905   Albert Einstein (German-American: 1879–1955) shows that photoelectric effect—ejection of electrons from metal by action of light—can be explained if light has particle nature as well as wave nature.

Einstein shows that motion of small particles in liquid ("Brownian motion") can be explained by assuming that the liquid is made of molecules.

Einstein develops his special theory of relativity and the law $E = mc^2$ (energy equals mass times square of speed of light).

1911   Heike Kamerlingh Onnes (Dutch: 1853–1926) discovers superconductivity.

Ernest Rutherford (British: 1871–1937) discovers the proton.

1915   Einstein completes his general theory of relativity, a theory of gravity more accurate than that of Sir Isaac Newton, and publishes it the following year.

1924   Louis-Victor de Broglie (French: 1892–1987) publishes his theory that particles, such as electrons, also have wave nature.

1925   Wolfgang Pauli (Austrian-American: 1900–1958) discovers exclusion principal: Two electrons or protons described by same numbers (called quantum numbers) cannot exist in same atom.

Werner Karl Heisenberg (German: 1901–76) develops matrix version of quantum mechanics, a mathematical treatment that explains behavior of electrons and protons.

1926   Erwin Schrödinger (Austrian: 1887–1961) develops wave version of quantum mechanics, a different mathematical treatment producing same results as Heisenberg's matrix mechanics.

1927   Heisenberg develops his uncertainty principle: It is impossible to measure accurately position and momentum of electron or proton at same time.

1932   Sir James Chadwick (British: 1891–1974) discovers neutron, a neutral particle about same mass as proton.

Carl D. Anderson (American: 1905–91) discovers positron, a positively charged analog of electron.

Sir John G. Cockcroft (English: 1897–1967) and Ernest Walton (Irish: 1903–95) develop first particle accelerator, a device for speeding subatomic particles, which causes them to react more intensely with atoms or other particles (often still known as "atom smasher").

1937   Carl Anderson, with other physicists, performs the work that culminates in the discovery of the muon.

1938   Otto Hahn (German: 1879–1968) and Lise Meitner (Austrian-Swedish: 1878–1968) split uranium atom, opening way for nuclear bombs and nuclear power.

1945   Scientists funded by U.S. government and led by J. Robert Oppenheimer (American: 1904–67) detonate first nuclear-fission explosion (atomic bomb).

1947   Cecil Frank Powell (English: 1903–69) and co-workers discover pion, first-known meson, a subatomic particle involved in holding nucleus of atom together.

1955   Owen Chamberlain (American: 1920–) and Emilio Segrè (Italian-American: 1905–89) produce antiprotons, negatively charged analogs of proton.

Clyde Cowan Jr. (American: 1919–74) and Frederick Reines (American: 1918–98) are first to observe neutrino, a subatomic particle with no mass or charge produced in certain forms of radioactive decay.

1957   Experiments by group led by Chien-Shiung Wu (Chinese-American: 1912–97) and quickly confirmed by others show that right and left are distinguished by behavior of electrons emitted in certain forms of radioactivity.

John Bardeen (American: 1908–91), Leon Cooper (American: 1930–), and Bob Schrieffer (American: 1931–) develop a theory explaining superconductivity.

1961   Murray Gell-Mann (American: 1929–) and, independently, Yu'val Ne'eman (Israeli: 1925–) and others develop method of classifying heavy sub-atomic particles that comes to be known as "eight-fold way."

1964   Murray Gell-Mann introduces concept of quarks as components of heavy subatomic particles, such as protons and mesons.

1967   Steven Weinberg (American: 1933–), Abdus Salam (Pakistani-British: 1926–96), and Sheldon Lee Glashow (American: 1932–) independently develop theory that combines electromagnetic force with weak force.

1980   Heinrich Rohrer (Swiss: 1933–) and Gerd Binnig (German: 1947–) invent the scanning tunneling microscope, a device with which it is possible to produce images of individual atoms or crystal surfaces.

1986   Karl Alexander Müller (Swiss: 1927–) and Johannes Georg Bednorz (German: 1950–) discover first "high-temperature" superconductor.

1995   Physicists at Fermilab in Batavia, Ill., announce that they have produced evidence for the top quark. (See "Subatomic Particles" later in this chapter.)

Eric Cornell of the U.S. National Institute of Standards

and Technology and coworkers produce the first sample of the fifth state of matter, known as a Bose-Einstein Condensate (BEC), in which atoms huddle together in essentially the same place and condition.

Physicists at CERN (the European Laboratory for Particle Physics) produce the first few atoms of antihydrogen, with a positron orbiting an antiproton.

1997   Two groups of physicists, one in Austria and one in Rome, show that it is possible to entangle two particles so that measuring an exact quantum state of one of them will instantly determine the corresponding state of the other across any distance, a phenomenon known as "quantum teleportation."

1998   Scientists working with the Super-Kamiokande neutrino telescope in Japan establish indirectly that the neutrinos must have a nonzero, although small, mass. Because there are so many neutrinos, such a mass might account for all the missing mass in the universe.

Two independent teams, one at Fermi National Accel-

erator Laboratory in Batavia, Illinois, and one at the European Laboratory for Particle Physics (CERN), show that some particle reactions would happen differently if time were reversed, providing the first clear indication of a physical basis for the direction of time's arrow.

1999   Physicists at Lawrence Livermore (Calif.) National Laboratory use lasers to fuse heavy hydrogen (deuterium) into helium using, however, about 10 million times as much energy to induce nuclear fusion as the reaction produces.

Scientists at the U.S. National Institutes of Standards and Technology create the first directional atom laser.

At Harvard University a Bose-Einstein condensate is used to slow light to 38 mph (17 m/sec).

Roy Goodrich and Zachary Fisk, working at the National High Magnetic Field Laboratory in Tallahassee, Florida, create something like a Wigner crystal of electrons, electrons that move in formation through a metal maintaining their crystalline array as they move.

▶ THE BASIC LAWS OF PHYSICS

Key Terms

Mass   is a measure of the amount of matter; it is proportional to weight. Near the surface of Earth it is roughly equivalent to weight.

Velocity   measures how an object changes position with time.

Acceleration   is how an object changes velocity with time.

Momentum   is the product of mass and velocity.

Energy   is the ability to do work.

Law of Gravity

The gravitational force between any two objects is proportional to the product of their masses and inversely proportional to the square of the distance between them. If F is the force, G is the number that represents the ratio (the gravitational constant), m and M are the two masses, and r is the distance between the objects:

$$F = \frac{GmM}{r^2}$$

In metric measure, the gravitational constant is 0.00000000006672 (6.672 x 10^{-11}) newton m²/kg², so another way of writing the basic law of gravity is

$$F = \frac{0.0000000000667 mM}{r^2}$$

This law implies that objects falling near the surface of Earth will fall with the same rate of acceleration (ignoring drag caused by air). This rate is 32.174 feet per second per second (ft./sec²), or 9.8 m/sec², and is conventionally labeled g. Applying this rate to falling objects gives the velocity, v, and distance, d, after any amount of time, t, in seconds. If the object starts at rest and 32 ft./sec² is used as an approximation for g,

$$v = 32t$$
$$d = 16t^2$$

For example, after 3 seconds, a dropped object that is still falling will have a velocity of $32 \times 3 = 96$ feet per second and will have fallen a distance of $16 \times 3^2 = 144$ feet.

If the object has an initial velocity v_0 and an initial height above the ground of a, the equations describing the velocity and the distance, d, above the ground (a positive velocity is up and a negative velocity is down) become

$$v = v_0 - 32t$$

and

$$d = -16t^2 + v_0 t + a.$$

After 3 seconds, an object tossed in the air from a height of 6 feet with a velocity of 88 feet per second will reach a speed of 88 - 96 = -8 feet per second, meaning that it has begun to descend, and will have a height of (-16 x 9) + (88 x 3) + 6 = -144 + 264 + 6 = 126 feet above the ground.

The maximum height, H, reached by the object with an initial velocity v_0 and initial height a is

$$H = a + \frac{v_0^2}{64}$$

For the object tossed upward at 88 feet per second from a height of 6 feet, the maximum height reached would be 6 + 88²/64 = 6 + 121 = 127 feet. Therefore, after 3 seconds, the object has just reached its peak and has fallen back only 1 foot.

Albert Einstein's general theory of relativity introduced laws of gravity more accurate than those just given, which were discovered by Sir Isaac Newton. Newton's gravitational theory is extremely accurate for most practical situations, however. For example, Newton's theory is used to determine how to launch satellites into proper orbits.

Newton's Laws of Motion

Newton's Laws of Motion apply to objects in a vacuum and are not easily observed in the real world, where forces such as friction tend to overwhelm the natural motion of objects. To obtain realistic solutions to problems, however, physicists and engineers begin with Newton's laws and then add in the various forces that also affect motion.

1. *Any object at rest tends to stay at rest. A body in motion moves at the same velocity in a straight line unless acted upon by a force.* This is also known as the law of inertia. Note that this law implies that an object will travel in a curved path only so long as a force is acting on it. When the force is released, the object will travel in a straight line. A weight on a string swung in a circle will travel in a straight line when the string is released, for the

string was supplying the force that caused circular motion.

2. *The acceleration of an object is directly proportional to the force acting on it and inversely proportional to the mass of the object.* This law, for an acceleration a, a force F, and a mass m, is more commonly expressed in terms of finding the force when you know the mass and the acceleration. In this form it is written as

$$F = ma.$$

The implication of this law is that a constant force will produce acceleration, which is an increase in velocity. Thus, a rocket, which is propelled by a constant force as long as its fuel is burning, constantly increases in velocity. Even with an infinite supply of fuel, the rocket would eventually cease to increase in velocity, however, because Einstein's other relativity theory, the special theory of relativity, states that no object can exceed the speed of light in a vacuum (see "Conservation of mass-energy" below). Nevertheless, even a small force, constantly applied, can cause a large mass to reach velocities near the speed of light if enough time is allowed.

3. *For every action there is an equal and opposite reaction.*

Conservation Laws

Many results in physics come from various conservation laws. A conservation law is a rule that a certain entity must not change in amount during a certain class of operations. All such conservation laws treat closed systems. Anything added from outside the system could affect the amount of the entity being conserved.

Conservation of momentum

In a closed system, momentum stays the same. This law is equivalent to Newton's third law. Since momentum is the product of mass and velocity, if the mass of a system changes, then the velocity must change. For example, consider a person holding a heavy anchor in a stationary rowboat in the water. The momentum of the system is 0, since the masses have no velocity. Now the person in the rowboat tosses the anchor toward the shore. The momentum of the anchor is now a positive number if velocity toward the shore is measured as positive. To conserve momentum, the rowboat is accelerated in the opposite direction, away from the shore. The positive momentum of the anchor is balanced by the negative momentum of the rowboat and its cargo. In terms of two masses, m and M, and matching velocities v and V,

$$mv = MV$$

Conservation of angular momentum

An object moving in a circle has a special kind of momentum, called angular momentum. As noted above, motion in a circle requires some force. Angular momentum combines mass, velocity, and acceleration (produced by the force). For a body moving in a circle, the acceleration depends on both the speed of the body in its path and the square of the radius of the circle. The product of this speed, the mass, and the square of the radius is the angular momentum of the mass.

In a closed system, angular momentum is conserved. This effect is used by skaters to change their velocity of spinning. Angular momentum is partly determined by the masses of a skater's arms combined with the rate of rotation and the square

of the radius to the center of mass of each arm (the point that can represent the total mass of the arm). When skaters bring their arms close to their body, this would tend to reduce the angular momentum, because the center of mass is closer to the body. But, since angular momentum is conserved, the rate of rotation has to increase to compensate for the decreased radius. Because the rate depends on the square of the radius, the rate increases dramatically.

Conservation of mass

In a closed system, the total amount of mass appears to be conserved in all but nuclear reactions and other extreme conditions.

Conservation of energy

In a closed system, energy appears to be conserved in all but nuclear reactions and other extreme conditions. Energy comes in very many forms: mechanical, chemical, electrical, heat, and so forth. As one form is changed into another (excepting nuclear reactions and extreme conditions), this law guarantees that the total amount remains the same. Thus, when you change the chemical energy of a dry cell into electrical energy and use that to turn a motor, the total amount does not change (although some becomes heat energy—see "Laws of Thermodynamics" below).

Conservation of mass-energy

Einstein discovered that his special theory of relativity implies that energy and mass are related. Consequently, mass and energy by themselves are not conserved, since one can be converted into the other. Mass and energy appear to be conserved in ordinary situations because the effect of Einstein's discovery is very small most of the time. The more general law, then, is the law of conservation of mass-energy: *The total amount of mass and energy must be conserved.* Einstein found the following equation that links mass and energy:

$$E = mc^2$$

In this equation, E is the amount of energy, m is the mass, and c is the speed of light in a vacuum.

One instance of energy changing to mass occurs in Einstein's equation for how the mass increases with velocity. If m_0 is the mass of the object when it is not moving, v is the velocity of the object in relation to an observer who is considered to be at rest, and c is the speed of light in a vacuum, then the mass, m, is given by the equation

$$m = \frac{m_0}{\sqrt{1 - \dfrac{v^2}{c^2}}}$$

This accounts for the rule that no object can exceed the speed of light in a vacuum. As the object approaches this speed, so much of the energy is converted to mass that it cannot continue to accelerate.

In both nuclear fission (splitting of the atomic nucleus) and nuclear fusion (the joining of atomic nuclei, producing the energy of a hydrogen bomb), mass is converted into energy.

Conservation for particles

Many properties associated with atoms and subatomic particles are also conserved. Among them are charge, spin, isospin, and a combination known as CPT for *charge conjugation, parity,* and *time.*

First and Second Laws of Thermodynamics

First law   This is the same as the law of conservation of energy. It is a law of thermodynamics, or the movement of heat, because heat must be treated as a form of energy to keep the total amount of energy constant. All bodies contain heat as energy no matter how cold they are, although there is not much heat at temperatures close to absolute zero.

Second law   *Heat in a closed system can never travel from a low temperature region to one of higher temperature in a self-sustaining process.* Self-sustaining in this case means a process that does not need energy from outside the system to keep it going. In a refrigerator, heat from the cold inside of the refrigerator is transferred to a warmer room, but energy from outside is required to make the transfer happen, so the process is not self-sustaining.

The second law has many implications. One of them is that no perpetual motion machine can be constructed. Another is that all energy in a closed system eventually becomes heat that is diffused equally throughout the system, so that one can no longer obtain work from the system.

The equations that describe the behavior of heat also can be applied to order and therefore to information. The word *entropy* refers to diffuse heat, disorder, or lack of information. Another form of the second law of thermodynamics is that in a closed system, entropy always increases.

Laws of Current Electricity

Key terms   When electrons flow in a conductor, the result is electric current. The amount of current is based on an amount of electric charge called the *coulomb*, which is the charge of about 6.25 quintillion (6.25 x 10^{18}) electrons. When 1 coulomb of charge moves past a point in 1 second, it creates a current of 1 ampere. Just as a stream can carry the same amount of water swiftly through a narrow channel or slowly through a broad channel, the energy of an electric current varies depending on the difference in charge between places along the conductor. This is called *potential difference* and is measured in volts. The voltage is affected by the nature of the conductors. Some substances conduct an electric current much more easily than others. This resistance to the current is measured in ohms. *Electric power* is the rate at which electricity is used.

Ohm's law   *Electric current is directly proportional to the potential difference and inversely proportional to resistance.* If you measure current, I, in amperes, potential difference, V, in volts, and resistance, R, in ohms, then the current is equal to the potential difference divided by the resistance.

$$I = \frac{V}{R}$$

Law of electric power   If electric power, P, is measured in watts, then the power is equal to the product of the current measured in amperes and the potential difference measured in volts.

$$P = IV$$

Laws of Light and Electromagnetic Radiation

Key terms   Light is a part of a general form of radiation known as *electromagnetic waves*, or, when thought of as particles, *photons*. Here, electromagnetic radiation is considered as a wave phenomenon for the most part. The velocity of a wave is how fast the wave travels as a whole. The *wavelength* is the distance between one crest of the wave and the next crest. The *frequency* is how many crests pass a particular location in a unit of time. One crest per second is called a hertz.

Law of electromagnetic energy   The energy of an electromagnetic wave depends on a small number known as Planck's constant. Measured in joules per hertz (energy per frequency), Planck's constant is 6.67259 x 10^{-34}. *The energy is equal to the product of Planck's constant and the frequency.* Using E for energy, h for Planck's constant, and f for frequency,

$$E = hf$$

When thought of in terms of the particles called photons, the energy of a photon obeys the same law. The law of wave motion and the law of electromagnetic energy can be combined with the speed of light in a vacuum *(c)* to give

$$E = \frac{hc}{l}$$

The energy of a photon is the product of Planck's constant and the speed of light, divided by the wavelength *(l)* of the photon.

Inverse-square law   All radiation obeys an inverse-square law, which is similar to the law of gravity. *The intensity of the radiation decreases as the inverse of the square of the distance from a point source of radiation.*

Two Basic Laws of Quantum Physics

When one considers effects on very small masses and at very small distances, it is necessary to recognize that objects behave differently than at the sizes and distances one can observe directly. Since these effects occur in discrete steps based upon Planck's constant times the frequency, called the quantum—which is the size by which energy changes in steps (instead of continuously)—the science of such effects is called quantum physics. Small masses act sometimes like particles and sometimes like waves. Two laws in particular that describe the behavior of small masses are basic and easily stated.

Heisenberg's uncertainty principle   *It is impossible to specify completely the position and momentum of a particle, such as an electron.*

Pauli's exclusion principle   *Two particles of matter cannot be in the same exact state.* Particles of matter include the electron, neutron, and proton. Bosons, particles of force, do not obey Pauli's exclusion principle. (See "Subatomic Particles.")

▶SUBATOMIC PARTICLES

The idea of an atom goes back to the ancient Greek philosophers, who thought that matter was composed of tiny indivisible particles. The concept was put on a scientific basis by John Dalton (English: 1766–1844) in 1803 and became the foundation of chemistry. Nearly a hundred years later, experiments by J.J. Thomson (English: 1856–1940) in 1899 were the first to show that atoms are not indivisible after all. In the past hundred years, physics at almost all levels has been completely revolutionized by the study of the particles that make up atoms or that are smaller than atoms. Below is a list of all the most important subatomic particles given in the chronological order of their discovery.

1897 Electron   The first subatomic particle to be identified, also by J.J. Thomson, was the electron, a low-mass particle that can be found in the outer reaches of the atom. One property of the electron is charge, the response to electric or magnetic fields. The charge of a single electron is always the same, which is identified as –1 (negative one). Each atom consists of a cloud of electrons around a center of positive charge, which is called the nucleus.

1905 Photon   The photon is the particle that carries the electromagnetic force. This concept began with Albert Einstein (German-American: 1879–1955) in 1905, when he established that light acts sometimes as a particle instead of as waves. Although we usually think of the photon as the particle of light, it is also the particle form of radio waves, X-rays, or gamma rays. The mass of the photon is 0.

1911   Proton   At least one proton is always found in the nucleus of every atom. The proton has a charge that is the same in size as that of the electron, but responds in the opposite direction to an electric or magnetic field. This charge is +1 (positive one). Each proton is almost 2,000 times as heavy as an electron, or about the same as the mass of a single hydrogen atom.

1924 Bosons   While matter is made from subatomic particles, the forces that act on matter are also produced by subatomic particles. The particles that create these forces are collectively called bosons because the mathematics of the behavior of this type of particle was worked out originally by Satyendranath Bose (Indian: 1894–1974) in 1924, although put into final form by Einstein. The observed bosons are the photon, pions, gluons, W particles, and Z particles. Bosons that are predicted, but that have not been observed, include the Higgs particle and the graviton.

1925–26 Quantum Mechanics   The basic theory of subatomic particles, called quantum mechanics, was developed in two different forms, in 1925 by Werner Heisenberg (German: 1901–76) and in 1926 by Erwin Schrödinger (Austrian: 1887–1961). Although the two forms appear very different, they produce the same results.

1926 Fermions   All the particles that make up matter are called fermions, as opposed to the bosons that create forces. The fermions include all the leptons and quarks as well as the particles made from quarks (see below). Fermions are named for Enrico Fermi (Italian-American: 1901–54), who first worked out the mathematics of their interactions in 1926. Fermions all obey the

Pauli exclusion principle (see the section on *Basic Laws of Physics*, earlier in this chapter), which means that they occupy a definite space. Two fermions cannot be in the same place at the same time.

1930 Antiparticles   When Paul A.M. Dirac (English-American: 1902–84) established a mathematical version of the theory of the electron in 1930, he observed that one solution to his equations predicted a particle that would be a mirror image of the electron, exactly the same as the electron but with a positive charge instead of negative. The particle, discovered two years later in 1932, was named the positron. The same equations predicted mirror images for all subatomic particles. These particles are called the antiparticles, so another name for positron is antielectron. A vast stream of antielectrons that was found jetting from the center of the Milky Way in 1997.

1932 Neutron   The neutron is very much like a neutral proton, with just slightly more mass. Neutrons are stable when they are found in atoms, but decay into other particles when left to themselves.

1935 Muon   The muon is now recognized as a high energy analog to the electron with a mass about 200 times that of the electron.

1947 Pion   A pion carries the strong force that holds the nucleus of atoms together, but since each pion appears and disappears almost instantly, the pions are not usually counted as part of the nucleus. (Predicted in 1935) In the same year that the pion was found, theoreticians were able to work out a comprehensive theory of the electron, called quantum electrodynamics (QED).

1950 Strange particles   Starting in 1950 experimenters observed a number of previously undetected particles that did not behave as particles were expected to do. Because these particles have masses greater than that of the proton and neutron, they were called hyperons. Other unexpected particles, about the size of the pion, were classed as mesons. A classification scheme for the hyperons developed in 1961 helped physicists understand them better, but their essential difference was already labeled "strangeness."

1955 Neutrinos   Neutrinos are thought to be among the most common particles in the universe, but they interact with ordinary matter so weakly that they are very difficult to observe. Predicted in 1930, neutrinos may have no rest mass, but recent experiments suggest that they may have a very small mass. Different neutrinos are associated with electrons, muons, and tauons.

1964–95 Quarks   Murray Gell-Mann (American: 1928–) and several other physicists determined that a way to explain the properties of protons, neutrons, mesons, and hyperons, is to think of the heavy particles as made from combinations of light ones, just as the atom is made from combinations of electrons, protons, and neutrons. The smaller particles are quarks; there are six of them in all. Two quarks, known as up and down, form protons and neutrons. The top quark is the most massive—about as heavy as an atom of gold—and the last to be detected. (First version of theory in 1964, evidence for top quark in 1995)

1965–73 Gluons The eight different bosons that produce a force between quarks known as the color force are called gluons. The color force is also the basis of the strong force that holds the nucleus together. Because of the color force, the study of quarks and gluons is today called quantum chromodynamics (QCD).

1974 J/Psi particle Like the strange hyperons, the J/psi particle is a heavy particle that appears at high energies. It also is produced by a different kind of quark, the charm quark. The odd name J/Psi comes from the particle having been discovered independently by two investigators, one of whom called it J and the other of whom named it psi.

1983 W and Z particles The particles that produce the weak force are called W and Z. At high energies, however, the weak force merges with the electromagnetic force, so the W and Z are to some extent analogs to the photon, although they could not be more different, since the photon has a 0 rest mass and both W particles and the single Z particle are very massive.

1995 Antiatoms Since antiparticles have all the properties of ordinary particles except for being mirror images, it is possible to create an antiatom by combining subatomic antiparticles. This was accomplished in 1995 with the production of a few antiatoms of antihydrogen made by causing an antielectron (positron) to orbit an antiproton.

(Not yet observed) Graviton and Higgs particle A particle that produces gravitational force by its exchange between all kinds of particles is known as the graviton, but so far it is only known in theory. The Higgs particle is the main undetected particle of the standard model of subatomic particles. Physicists believe that the Higgs, named after Peter Higgs (British (1919–) who predicted it in 1964, confers mass to all other particles. The reason that it has not been detected so far is that its own mass is thought to be very great, perhaps even greater than that of the top quark.

LIFE SCIENCES

While the scientific study of living creatures seems to have begun with Aristotle, there was considerable practical experimentation with living things much earlier, going back to the domestication of a species, the dog, perhaps as early as 14,000 B.C. In the years that followed the Scientific Revolution of the 17th century, the science of biology came to include most of the then-known life sciences: zoology (the study of animals), botany (the study of plants), and taxonomy (the classification of living things). In the 19th century, biology began to fragment into other studies:

microbiology (the study of creatures visible only through the microscope), genetics (the study of how traits are inherited), biochemistry (the study of molecules in living things), and so forth. At the same time, different ways of studying living organisms were developed, among them anthropology (the study of human beings), ecology (the study of interactions between different living things and their environment), and ethology (the study of animal behavior).

▶ MAJOR GROUPS OF LIVING ORGANISMS

Biologists classify all living things (organisms) according to a system first introduced by Carolus Linnaeus in 1735. At that time Linnaeus and other scientists divided all life forms into two kingdoms—plants and animals. Since then, biologists have learned that there are fundamental differences among organisms that go beyond the differences between plants and animals and have added four kingdoms. The six kingdoms recognized today are: Monera, Archaea, Protists, Fungi, Plants, and Animals.

Following Linnaeus, all classification terms are usually given in Latin. In the following list, English terms are substituted when they are an exact translation—for example, animals instead of Animalia and birds instead of Aves. If there is no exact translation, the Latin form is kept.

Each kingdom is divided into two or more phyla (singular: phylum). Organisms within one phylum are more closely related to one another than to members of other phyla.

The phyla are also divided into parts, which are then further divided, each time on the basis of closer and closer relationships. In descending order of size, the main divisions are as follows:
Kingdom
    Phylum
        Class
            Order
                Family
                    Genus
                        Species
Many biologists add to this list by classifying groups of species with sub- or super-, as in subphylum or superfamily.

By convention, Latin names except for genus and species are given in Roman type; genus and species are italicized.

Kingdom: Monera One-celled organisms with simple cells that lack a membrane around the genetic material. Bacteria do not produce their own food; blue-green algae do.
Phylum: Bacteria (also called Eubacteria)
Phylum: Blue-green algae, also called blue-green bacteria or cyanobacteria

Kingdom: Archaea One-celled organisms, sometimes called Archaeobacteria, that are genetically more like the other kingdoms than they are like the Monera. The Archaea were first discovered as creatures living in hot springs and other high-temperature situations. They were later observed among the one-celled creatures that metabolize chemicals such as methane or sulfur instead of using oxygen. Finally, they have been found in great abundance in the oceans and deep in the Earth's crust.

Kingdom: Protists One-celled or colonial; complex cells that have a membrane around their genetic material; protozoans and slime molds do not produce their own food; all other phyla in this kingdom can.

Phylum: Ciliated protozoans, such as Paramecium

Phylum: Protozoans with flagella, such as the trypanosome that causes African sleeping sickness.

Phylum: Amoebas and similar protozoans

Phylum: Protozoans that have no means of motion during most of their life, such as the plasmodia that cause malaria.

Phylum: Euglenas

Phylum: Golden algae and diatoms

Phylum: Fire or golden brown algae

Phylum: Green algae

Phylum: Brown algae

Phylum: Red algae

Phylum: Slime molds

Kingdom: Fungi One-celled or multicelled; cells have nuclei, which stream between cells, giving the appearance that cells have many nuclei; fungi do not produce their own food.

Phylum: Zygomycetes (e.g., black bread mold)

Phylum: Ascomycetes (includes Penicillium, truffles, yeasts)

Phylum: Basidiomycetes (includes mushrooms)

Kingdom: Plants Multicellular organisms that carry out photosynthesis; cells have nuclei and cell walls.

Phylum: Mosses and liverworts

Phylum: Club mosses

Phylum: Horsetails

Phylum: Ferns

Phylum: Conifers

Phylum: Cone-bearing desert plants

Phylum: Cycads

Phylum: The ginkgo

Phylum: Flowering plants

Subphylum: Dicots (plants with two seed leaves—e.g., most fruits and vegetables, common flowers, and trees)

Subphylum: Monocots (plants with a single seed leaf—e.g., onions, lilies, and grasses)

Kingdom: Animals Multicellular organisms that get their food by ingestion; most are able to move from place to place; cells have nuclei but not cell walls.

Phylum: Porifera (sponges)

Phylum: Cnidaria (jellyfish, anemones, corals)

Phylum: Platyhelminthes (flatworms)

Phylum: Nematodes (roundworms)

Phylum: Rotifers (microscopic wormlike or spherical animals)

Phylum: Bryozoa (moss animals)

Phylum: Brachiopods (lampshells)

Phylum: Phoronida (tube worms)

Phylum: Annelids (segmented worms, such as earthworms, leeches)

Phylum: Mollusks (soft-bodied animals with a mantle and foot)

Class: Chitons

Class: Bivalves (clams, oysters, mussels)

Class: Scaphopoda (tooth or tusk shells)

Class: Gastropods (slugs and snails)

Class: Cephalopods (octopus, squid)

Phylum: Arthropods (segmented animals with an external skeleton)

Class: Horseshoe crabs

Class: Crustaceans (lobsters, crabs, shrimp)

Class: Arachnids (scorpions, spiders, mites, ticks)

Class: Insects

Class: Millipedes and centipedes

Phylum: Cycliophora (known only as a tiny species growing in the mouths of lobsters)

Phylum: Echinoderms (starfish, brittle stars)

Phylum: Hemichordata (acorn worms)

Phylum: Chordates

Subphylum: Tunicates

Subphylum: Lancelets

Subphylum: Vertebrates (animals with backbones)

Class: Agnatha (lampreys, hagfish)

Class: Sharks and rays

Class: Bony fish

Class: Amphibians

Class: Reptiles

Class: Birds

Class: Mammals

Subclass: Monotremes (egg-laying mammals)

Subclass: Marsupials

Subclass: Placentals

Order: Insectivores (shrews, moles, hedgehogs)

Order: Flying lemurs

Order: Bats

Order: Primates (lemurs, monkeys, apes, humans)

Order: Edentates (anteaters, sloths, armadillos)

Order: Pangolins

Order: Lagomorphs (rabbits, hares)

Order: Rodents (squirrels, rats, mice, porcupines)

Order: Cetaceans (whales, dolphins)

Order: Carnivores (wolves, cats, bears, raccoons, weasels, badgers, skunks, otters, hyenas)

Order: Seals

Order: The aardvark

Order: Elephants

Order: Hyraxes

Order: Sirenians (dugongs, manatees)

Order: Odd-toed ungulates (horses, tapirs, rhinoceroses)

Order: Even-toed ungulates (pigs, hippopotamuses, camels, deer, giraffes, pronghorns, cattle, goats, sheep)

▶CLASSIFYING HUMANS

KINGDOM: Animals Organisms that use other organisms for food and that sometimes move rapidly.

PHYLUM: Chordates Animals that are partially supported by a rod of cartilage or bone vertebrae and an internal skeleton.

SUBPHYLUM: Vertebrates Chordates that have vertebrae, such as fish, amphibians, reptiles, birds, and mammals.

CLASS: Mammals Vertebrates that have hair and suckle their young.

ORDER: Primates Mammals that use sight more than scent, have nails instead of claws on grasping hands and feet, are mostly active in daylight, and have relatively large brains.

SUPERFAMILY: Hominoids Primates that are tailless, generally large in size, can climb trees, and have relatively flat faces; specifically, the great apes, australopithecines, and human beings.

FAMILY: Hominids Hominoids that walk upright, have small canines, and large brains; specifically, the australopithecines and human beings.

GENUS: Homo Hominids, with especially large brains, that speak and show other signs of culture; specifically, Homo habilis, Homo erectus and related species, and Homo sapiens.

SPECIES: Homo sapiens Modern human beings.

Major Discoveries in Life Sciences

B.C.
c.9000 Agricultural Revolution starts in Near East with domestication of sheep and goats in Persia (Iran) and Afghanistan and of pigs in Anatolia (Turkey); and cultivation of wheat in Canaan (Israel and Jordan).
c.8000 Agricultural Revolution starts independently in what are now Peru, Central America, and Indochina.
c.350 Aristotle (Greek: 384–322 B.C.) classifies known animals in system that will continue to be used until 1735.

A.D.
1648 Jan Baptista van Helmont (Flemish: 1580–1644) shows that plants do not obtain large amounts of material for their growth from soil.
1665 Robert Hooke (English: 1635–1703) observes and names the cell.
1668 Francesco Redi (Italian: 1626–97) shows that maggots in meat do not arise spontaneously but are hatched from flies' eggs.
1669 Anton van Leeuwenhoek (Dutch: 1632–1723) discovers microorganisms—creatures too small to see with naked eye—and recognizes that sperm are part of reproduction.
1683 Leeuwenhoek is first to observe bacteria.
1735 Carolus Linnaeus (Carl Linné; Swedish: 1707–78) introduces system in use today for classifying plants and animals.
1779 Jan Ingenhousz (Dutch: 1730–99) discovers that plants release oxygen when exposed to sunlight and they consume carbon dioxide; this is first step in understanding photosynthesis.
1839 Theodor A.H. Schwann (German: 1810–82), building on work of Matthias Jakob Schleiden (German: 1804–81) in 1838, develops cell theory of life.
1856 First skeleton of what we now call Neandertals is found in cave in Neander Valley, near Düsseldorf (Germany).
  Louis Pasteur (French: 1822–95) discovers that fermentation is caused by microorganisms.
1858 Charles R. Darwin (English: 1809–82) and Alfred R. Wallace (English: 1823–1913) announce their theory of evolution by natural selection to the Linnean Society.
1859 Darwin publishes *On the Origin of Species*.
1865 Gregor Johann Mendel's (Austrian: 1822–84) theory of dominant and recessive genes is published in obscure local journal.
1868 Workers building road in France discover skeletons of first-known Cro-Magnons in cave.
1894 Eugène Dubois (Dutch: 1858–1940) announces discovery of "Java ape-man," now known to be first specimen of *Homo erectus*.
1898 Mosaic disease of tobacco plants is recognized as being caused by virus, the first identification of a virus.
1900 Three different biologists rediscover laws of genetics originally found by Mendel.
1924 Raymond A. Dart (Australian-South African: 1893–1988) identifies first fossil of an australopithecine, a close relative of early humans.
1953 James D. Watson (American: 1928–) and Francis Crick (English: 1916–) determine structure of DNA, the basis of heredity.
1961 Louis S.B. Leakey (English: 1903–72) and Mary D. Leakey (English: 1913–96) discover a previously unknown ancestor of humans, *Homo habilis*, in the Olduvai Gorge of northern Tanzania.
  Marshall W. Nirenberg (American: 1927–) learns to read one of "letters" of genetic code.
1973 Stanley Cohen (American: 1922–) and Herbert Boyer (American: 1936–) succeed in putting specific gene into bacterium, the first instance of true genetic engineering.
1974 Donald C. Johanson (American: 1943–) and coworkers discover Lucy in Afar region of Ethiopia, the nearly complete skeleton—but not the skull—of *Australopithecus afarensis*, an early relative of humans (more than 3 million years old).

1975 César Milstein (Argentine-English: 1927–) announces discovery of how to produce monoclonal antibodies, highly specific chemicals that can be made to react with particular proteins or other chemicals in the body.
1980 Martin Cline (American: 1934–) and coworkers succeed in transferring functioning gene from one mouse to another.
  Chinese scientists succeed in cloning a fish.
1983 Kary B. Mullis (American: 1945–) invents the use of the polymerase chain reaction to make copies of DNA sequences, a vital tool in finding specific genes.
1988 The complete developmental history of every cell in the nematode *Caenor habditis elegans* is published.
1990 Michael T. Clegg (American: 1941–), Edward M. Golenburg (American), and coworkers isolate DNA and a gene for photosynthesis from a fossilized 17-million-year-old magnolia leaf.
1992 An ancestor of modern whales that was able to walk on land is discovered in Pakistan.
1994 Gen Suwa (Japanese), discovers the first fossil of *Ardipithecus ramidus*, the oldest known hominid, in Ethiopia.
1995 Craig Venter (American) of the Institute for Genomic Research publishes the complete base sequences for all the genes of a free-living organism, the bacterium *Haemophilus influenzae*.
1997 Ian Wilmut (English: 1944–) succeeds in cloning a sheep from a cell from an adult ewe, the first mammalian clone using a differentiated cell as the source of the chromosomes; in 1998, the cloned ewe, named Dolly, bears a lamb the natural way.
  Geneticists at the Case Western Reserve School of Medicine in Cleveland create the first artificial human chromosome.
  Svante Pääbo of the University of Munich, Germany, and coworkers clone DNA from the first discovered Neandertal fossil and compare the DNA to that of modern humans. They conclude that the Neandertal is a different species from our own.
1998 Elizabeth Gould and coworkers at Princeton University demonstrate that adult monkeys continue to grow new brain cells, a feat previously thought impossible for adult primates.
  Declines in frog populations around the world and four frog species extinctions are attributed to a newly found parasitic chytrid fungus.
  Several groups of researchers locate the specific proteins in animals, plants, and blue-green algae that set and maintain circadian rhythms.
1999 A 24,500-year-old fossil excavated from a shallow grave in Portugal is the first known that appears to be a hybrid of Neandertals and modern humans.
  Heide Schulz discovers giant bacteria, about the size of the period at the end of this sentence, in ooze off the coast of Namibia. The bacteria, *Thiomargarita manibiensis*, have a volume more than 100 times that of the previous record holder.
  Researchers find active colonies of bacteria live in the ice at the bottom of glaciers.
  Scientists clone cattle and mice.
  Berhane Asfaw and co-workers announce the discovery in Ethiopia of fossils of a new hominid species, *Australopithecus garhi* ("surprising southern ape"). The same 2.5-million-year-old strata that yielded the fossils also contains evidence of stone tools being used to butcher animals, although no one can be sure that the butchery was performed by the australopithecine or by member of some unknown human species.
  Extra legs, missing limbs, and other deformities found in frogs in North America are caused by parasitic flatworms called trematodes that infect tadpoles.
  Studies in mice show that a process in cell division called "telomere shortening" produces the effects of aging, suggesting that interference with this process or finding ways to lengthen telomeres might produce more youthful cells.

The Human Family Tree

▶EVOLUTION OF THE HUMAN FAMILY

The understanding of the various relatives of modern human beings and just how they are related is undergoing great changes. Currently there is little consensus among paleoanthropologists, the people who study early humans and their relatives, about the details of who is related to whom.

Purgatorius c. 60 million years ago. Africa.
The earliest known primate, a toothy creature somewhat like a lemur of today.

Catopithecus browni c. 40 million years ago. Egypt.
The earliest known representative of the higher primates, which include the Old World Monkeys, apes, and humans.

Aegyptopithecus c. 30 million years ago. Egypt.
Monkey-like creature, size of a large house cat. May be the earliest known ancestor of the hominoids. First fossils found in 1965.

Morotopithecus c. 20 million years ago. Uganda
Thought to be the first ape that could swing through trees as modern apes do.

Proconsul three known species. c. 20 million years ago. East Africa.
Named after Consul, a chimpanzee at the London Zoo, these apes generally recognized as ancestors of all hominoids.

Afropithecus c. 17 million years ago. Kenya.
Discovered in the mid-1980s. Like *Proconsul*, a candidate for ancestor of all hominoids.

Kenyapithecus 14 to 11 million years ago. Kenya.
A large ape that was somewhat more "advanced" than either *Afropithecus* or *Proconsul*

Dryopithecus c. 12 to 10 million years ago. France, Spain, and Hungary.
A small ape identified in 1992 as the common ancestor of the great apes, australopithecines, and modern humans.

Pan troglodytes, common chimpanzee; *P. paniscus,* pygmy chimpanzee, or bonobo c. 7 million years ago to present. Sub-Saharan Africa.
Studies of proteins and DNA suggest that the chimpanzee, especially *P. paniscus,* is the closest living relative of humans.

Ardipithecus ramidus c. 4.4 million years ago. Ethiopia
Discovered in 1994 at Aramis, Ethiopia, this woodland-dweller is one candidate for the direct ancestor of the australopithecines and very close to the common ancestor great apes and humans.

Australopithecus anamensis c. 4.2 to 3.9 million years ago. Northern Kenya (Lake Turkana region).
This group is represented by 21 fossils found by Meave G. Leakey and Alan Walker in 1994 and announced late in 1995. *A. anamensis* seems to have walked on two legs like later hominids.

Australopithecus afarensis "Lucy" and "The First Family." c. 4 million years ago to 3 million years ago. Ethiopia and East Africa.
A. afarensis is thought to be on the direct line to humans. In addition to the famous skeleton of "Lucy" and the collection known as The First Family, all from Ethiopia and dating from about 3.3 million years ago, the trail of footprints, left in volcanic ash at Laetoli, Tanzania, discovered in 1978, demonstrated that *A. afarensis* walked upright, unlike any of the great apes.

Australopithecus bahrelghazalia c. 3 million years ago. Chad and Central Africa.
The first hominid remains from Central Africa indicate a new species contemporary with *A. afarensis* from Ethiopia and East Africa.

Australopithecus africanus c. 3 million years ago to 2.5 million years ago. South Africa.
First nonhuman hominid to be discovered, in 1924, although very few anthropologists accepted the species until after World War II. Walked upright and, while large brained even for a primate, had a brain that was much smaller than that of members of *Homo* of the same general size. *A. africanus* is also thought to be on the direct line to humans.

Paranthropus (Australopithecus) robustus and *boisei* c. 2.5 million years ago to 1 million years ago. Eastern and southern Africa.
These represent a separate branch of the human family that has become extinct without issue

Australopithecus garhi c. 2.5 million years ago. Ethiopia.
Another candidate for the ancestor of the *Homo* line. The tools and butchered bones of animals found at the same sites may or may not be connected with *A. garhi.*

Homo habilis "Handy Man." c. 2.5 million years ago. East Africa.
Earliest known member of our own genus, *H. habilis* gets his nickname from tools found at sites that are both physically and chronologically close to sites where fossil *H. habilis* has been found. Recently anthropologists have argued that *H. habilis* was a scavenger instead of a hunter.

Homo erectus (H. heidlebergensis; H. ergaster, H. antecessor) "Java Ape Man," "Heidelberg Man," "Peking Man." c. 1.5 million years ago to 0.2 million years ago. Africa, Asia, Europe.
Fossils from Asia continue to be labeled *H. erectus,* with African fossils from about 1.2 million years ago considered a separate species, *H. ergaster.* European representatives are either the 800,000 year-old *H. antecessor* from Spain, or the somewhat later *H. heidelbergensis,* known from Germany and other sites in Europe and Africa. Late in 1996, new dates for *H. erectus* in Java suggested that this hominid may have occupied that island as recently as between 57,000 and 23,000 years ago.

Homo Neandertalis "Neandertal Man" c. 200,000 to 35,000 years ago. Europe, the Near East, Africa.
Neandertals were a species of hominids who in some places lived side by side with archaic *H. sapiens,* but who became extinct shortly after modern *H. sapiens* arrived in Europe.

Archaic *Homo sapiens* c. 360,000 years to 40,000 years ago. Africa and the Near East at first; Asia and Australia somewhat later.
These "archaic" humans precede the well-known Cro Magnon fossils from Europe and have some primitive features. Fragmentary fossils from the southern tip of Africa appear to be from *H. sapiens* and they are dated at 120,000 years in the past. Some think archaic *H. sapiens* appeared even earlier than 360,000 years ago.

Homo sapiens "Cro Magnon Man" c. 36,000 years ago to the present. Worldwide.
Early Europeans who used stone tools were first found at a site known as Cro Magnon. These humans completely displaced the Neandertals and are continuous with modern humans.

Elements in a 150-Pound Person

Element/Weight	Use by the body	Element/Weight	Use by the body
Oxygen 97.5 lbs	Part of all major nutrients, which make up tissues of the body, but also vital to production of energy in the form of elemental oxygen obtained from air.	Chlorine 0.3 lbs	Used in form of chloride ions to transport messages from the body to cells; helps regulate electrical activity.
Carbon 27.0 lbs	Essential element for life—most compounds based on carbon are called organic, meaning "from life." An essential part of proteins, carbohydrates, and fats, the building blocks of human cells	Sodium 0.165 lbs	Required by vertebrates to control fluid pressure in cells.
		Magnesium 0.06 lbs	Required by both plants (it is in chlorophyll) and animals. In humans, works with enzymes to speed chemical reactions, is involved in transmission of messages between nerves, and has a part in bone structure.
Hydrogen 15.0 lbs	Part of each of major nutrients, and thus a building block of every cell. Unlike oxygen, has no part in respiration.		
Nitrogen 4.5 lbs	Essential part of proteins, DNA, and RNA, the compounds most active in controlling cells; most of the body's functions depend on nitrogen compounds at one stage or another.	Iron 0.006 lbs	Essential for carrying oxygen to cells and carbon dioxide waste away. Lack of iron causes anemia.
		Cobalt 0.00024 lbs	Part of vitamin B12, found in meats and dairy products; its exact role in the body is not well understood.
Calcium 3.0 lbs	Mostly locked into hard compounds that form nonliving parts of bone. One of principal messengers between cells, telling them when to act and when to stay quiet.	Copper 0.00023 lbs	Helps form red blood cells, maintain nervous system, and regulate cholesterol levels.
Phosphorus 1.8 lbs	Important element in bone building, but, like calcium, has another role: it is essential in producing energy in cell.	Manganese 0.00020 lbs	Aids in bone formation, helps regulate nervous system, and is part of sex hormones.
		Iodine 0.00006 lbs	Part of thyroid hormone that controls rate at which food is burned for energy.
Potassium 0.3 lbs	Regulates contraction of muscle cells (and some other cell functions) along with sodium. In general, potassium is involved with muscle contractions and general maintenance of pressure a cell exerts on its covering membrane.	Zinc trace	Needed for some enzymes, for proper sex development, in healing wounds, for sense of taste, and for normal sperm count.
		Fluorine trace	Strengthens teeth and bones.
		Chromium trace	Used in metabolism of sugar and the regulation of fats.
Sulfur 0.3 lbs	Essential to most forms of life. An important constituent of proteins.	Selenium trace	In small amounts, may reduce cell damage and promote growth.

In addition, the body contains trace amounts of boron, aluminum, vanadium, molybdenum, and silicon. Their roles, however, are not fully understood.

▶THE HUMAN GENOME PROJECT

Scientists have learned that every organism is almost completely described by its genes, and that the genes are encoded as triplets of bases in long molecules of deoxyribonucleic acid (DNA). The Human Genome Project is primarily an effort to uncover the complete sequence of about 3 billion bases in human DNA, to identify the genes encoded therein, and to recognize the immediate purpose for the genes. Only 2 to 5 percent of the base sequence actually encodes human genes. There are thought to be about 50,000 to 100,000 human genes in all. The average gene consists of a sequence of about 1,500 to 3,000 bases, although genes vary considerably in length. The DNA bases are usually known by the abbreviations T, G, C, and A; thus, the ultimate goal of the project is a string of the letters T, G, C, and A that would fill 510 volumes of a standard-size encyclopedia.

The Human Genome Project started formally on Jan. 3, 1989, under the aegis of the National Institutes of Health's National Center for Human Genome Research. They developed a $3 billion plan that was scheduled to complete the project by the year 2005. Scientists from the European Union and the Japanese have also joined the project. An international coordinating group was set up called the Human Genome Organization (HUGO).

After much preliminary work, determination of base sequences began systematically in 1995. Gene sequences from non-human species have been achieved, starting with a bacterium in 1995 and several others since. Yeast was the next significant advance, with a complete sequence achieved in 1996 by the combined efforts of 96 laboratories. In 1998, sequencing of the genomes of the bacteria that cause syphilis, chlamydia, and tuberculosis and the genome of the first animal, Caenorhabditis elegans, a nematode worm, were achieved. The genome of C. elegans, expected to have 6,000 genes, was found to have 20,000, suggesting that the human genome may also be more complicated than expected. Other organisms for which gene sequencing efforts are ongoing include Arabidopsis (a mustard plant), barley, the fruit fly, the malaria parasite, the mouse, the pig, the rat, rice, the tomato, and the zebrafish.

On May 9, 1998, a separate effort for humans was announced by Craig Venter, the scientist whose laboratory achieved the first complete sequences of bacteria. His group plans to sequence the human genome by 2001, earlier than the Human Genome Project. Spurred on by this competition, the U.S. National Genome Research Institute announced that they would move their goal for the complete sequence up to 2003.

The U.S. Human Genome Project set some additional goals in 1998. It wants to cover by March, 2000 at least 90 percent of the genome using a "shotgun" technique, providing an additional resource not only for their affiliated laboratories, but also for Venter's group or other privately funded laboratories working on the project. Another new goal is to add to their research the identification of certain variations from human to human, called single-nucleotide polymorphisms (SNPs). Such variations are thought to be behind susceptibility to such complex diseases as cancer, diabetes, and some types of mental illnesses.

Milestones in the History of Mathematics

B.C.

c. 30,000   People in Europe begin using scratches or notches to record numbers.

c. 3500   Egyptians develop numeration system that can record very large numbers, with different symbols for ones, tens, hundreds, etc.

c. 2400   A numeration system based on place value (similar to Hindu-Arabic system) is introduced in Mesopotamia.

c. 2000   Mesopotamian mathematicians learn how to solve quadratic equations.

c. 1900   Mesopotamian mathematicians discover what we now call the Pythagorean theorem: The sum of the squares of the legs of a right triangle equals the square of the hypotenuse.

c. 470   Mathematician Hippasus of Metapontum (Greek: c. 500) discovers dodecahedron, a regular solid with 12 faces.

c. 450   Pythagoreans show that some lengths, such as the diagonal of a 1 x 1 square ($\sqrt{2}$), cannot be measured exactly using that unit.

c. 300   Euclid's (Greek: c. 300) *Elements* shows that virtually all parts of mathematics known at the time can be proved from short list of assumptions.

c. 260   In Central America, Maya develop numeration system based on place value.

c. 250   Archimedes (Greek: c. 287–212) establishes important theorems about volumes of solids, calculates an excellent approximation of π, and develops a system for representing very large whole numbers.

c. 230   Apollonius of Perga (Greek: c. 262–190) writes *Conics*, an analysis of such curves as parabola, ellipse, and hyperbola.

A.D.

876   The first-known use of a symbol for zero occurs in India.

c. 1100   Poet, mathematician, and astronomer Omar Khayyám (Persian: 1048–c. 1131) develops geometric methods for solving cubic equations.

1321   Levi ben Gershom (Gersonides; French: 1288–1344) is first to use mathematical induction.

c. 1515   Scipione del Ferro (Italian: 1465–1526) discovers algebraic method for solving one form of cubic equations.

1536   Niccolò Tartaglia (Italian: 1499–1557) solves two types of cubic equations.

1545   Girolamo Cardano's (Italian: 1501–76) *Ars Magna* contains Lodovico Ferrari's (Italian: 1522–65) complete solution of the quartic as well as complete solution of the cubic based on Tartaglia's work.

1572   Rafael Bombelli (Italian: 1526–c. 1573) uses complex numbers to solve equations.

1614   John Napier (Scottish: 1550–1617) describes logarithms.

1637   René Descartes (French: 1596–1650) publishes first account of analytic geometry; also discovered by Pierre de Fermat (French: 1601–65).

1639   Gérard Desargues (French: 1591–1661) introduces projective geometry.

1654   Blaise Pascal (French: 1623–62) and Pierre de Fermat develop theory of probability.

1666   Sir Isaac Newton (English: 1642–1727) describes his invention of the calculus but does not have it published at this time.

1684   Gottfried Wilhelm Leibniz (German: 1646–1716) publishes first account of his independent discovery of the calculus.

1763   Gaspard Monge (French: 1746–1818) invents descriptive geometry, the mathematical techniques that are basis of mechanical drawing.

1799   Karl Friedrich Gauss (German: 1777–1855) proves fundamental theorem of algebra, which is that every polynomial equation has solution.

Paolo Ruffini (Italian: 1765–1822) offers first proof that not all polynomial equations of fifth degree can be solved by algebraic methods.

1822   Jean-Victor Poncelet (French: 1788–1867) further develops projective geometry.

1826   Nikolai Ivanovich Lobachevski (Russian: 1793–1856) gives first public address concerning non-Euclidean geometry.

1854   Georg F.B. Riemann (German: 1826–66) shows that several non-Euclidean geometries are possible.

1877   Georg F.L.P. Cantor (German: 1845–1918) shows that number of points in a line segment is same as number in interior of a square.

1881   Josiah Willard Gibbs (American: 1839–1903) introduces vector analysis.

1882   Ferdinand von Lindemann (German: 1852–1939) proves that the circle cannot be squared with straightedge and compass.

1892   Cantor proves there are at least two types of infinities—specifically, that infinity of real numbers (including all infinite decimals) is bigger than infinity of counting numbers (1, 2, 3, . . .).

1900   David Hilbert (German: 1862–1943) proposes his famous list of 23 unsolved problems.

1931   Kurt Gödel (Austrian-American: 1906–78) shows that the laws of arithmetic are either incomplete or inconsistent: *incomplete* if not all true theorems can be proved or *inconsistent* if two contradictory theorems can be proved.

1936   Independently, Alan M. Turing (English: 1912–54) and Alonzo Church (American: 1903–95) discover there is no single infallible method for proving whether a statement in mathematics is true or false.

1949   Claude E. Shannon (American: 1916–) publishes his work on information theory, a general approach to handling communications.

1976   In first major computer-assisted proof, it is shown that any map can be colored with four colors in such a way that no two regions of the same color share common border.

1980   Classification of all finite simple groups, started in 1830, is completed, perhaps longest proof in history of mathematics.

1995   Andrew Wiles (American) publishes a corrected version of his 1993 proof that the equation $x^n + y^n = z^n$ has no solution for n greater than 2 when x, y, and z are counting numbers—known as Fermat's last theorem because Pierre Fermat claimed, in a note discovered after his death in 1665, to have proved it.

1998   Thomas C. Hales of the University of Michigan uses a computer to establish that Johannes Kepler's 1611 conjecture that stacking spheres in a face-centered cubic pattern results in the densest concentration of spheres.

Two independent studies result in the same catalog of all possible knots with 16 or fewer crossings, a total of 1,701,936 different knots. Mathematical knots are loops joined at the ends, and the catalog begins with an uncrossed loop, or circle, followed by the only two knots with one crossing, known as trefoils.

Percy Deift and Jinho Baik of New York University working with Kurt Johansson of the Royal Institute in Stockholm develop the probability distribution for a simplified version of the card game solitaire. Their result is also valid for solving problems in quantum mechanics and may lead to the resolution of a famous hypothesis by Bernhard Riemann concerning the zeta function that describes how prime numbers are distributed.

MATHEMATICS

Strictly speaking, mathematics is not considered a science but a separate branch of learning on its own. Because the use of mathematics has been so important to science, however, it is generally treated along with sciences.

Mathematics consists of a set of abstract symbols and of rules for manipulating them, along with the results of that manipulation. Because of this, some have classified mathematics as a kind of language, while others view it as a kind of game. Many mathematicians believe there is a much deeper reality than those classifications, but it is one that is very difficult to explain. Even when mathematics is treated as a game, the results seem to be strongly connected to the real world.

Most people learn numbers, arithmetic, and some geometry in elementary school. In high school more mathematics is taught, perhaps including the calculus. Almost all the mathematics taught in elementary school or high school is at least 300 years old. In the past 300 years, mathematicians have developed many new branches of the subject often requiring years of special training even to understand the basic parts. This section, however, focuses on aspects of mathematics useful in daily life or that may be encountered in school by non-mathematicians.

▶ COMMONLY USED MATHEMATICAL FORMULAS

Most formulas needed in solving everyday problems are collected below, with special emphasis on formulas relating to measurements, as these are used in everything from sewing to building a house. However, some important formulas from algebra, graphing, and trigonometry are at the end. Additional formulas can also be found in "Basic Laws of Physics."

General
The **distance** d, given the rate r and the time t:

$$d = rt.$$

Length
The **perimeter (distance around)** p **of any polygon** (closed plane figure with straight sides that do not cross), given the lengths of the sides a, b, c, and so forth:

$$p = a + b + c + \ldots$$

Perimeter p **of a rectangle,** given the length l and the width w:

$$p = 2l + 2w.$$

Perimeter p **of a square**, given the length of a side s:

$$p = 4s.$$

Circumference (distance around) C **of a circle**, given the diameter d (distance across) or the radius r (distance from the center to the circle):

$$C = \pi d$$
$$\text{or } C = 2\pi r.$$

The number π is an infinite decimal that begins $3.14159\ldots$, which is often approximated as either 3.14 or as $\frac{22}{7}$.

Area
In each of the following, the area (amount of surface) is A. For three-dimensional figures, A is the total surface area.

Rectangle, given the length l and the width w:

$$A = lw.$$

Square, given the length of a side s:

$$A = s^2$$

Circle, given the radius r:

$$A = \pi r^2$$

Triangle, given the base b and the height h:

$$A = \frac{1}{2} bh$$

Right triangle, given the lengths a and b of the two sides (legs) that form the right angle:

$$A = \frac{1}{2} ab$$

Parallelogram, given the base b and the height h:

$$A = bh$$

Trapezoid, given the two bases B and b and the height h:

$$A = \frac{1}{2} h(B + b)$$

Kite, given the lengths of the two diagonals D and d:

$$A = \frac{1}{2} Dd$$

Regular polygon (polygon with all sides of equal length and all angles of equal measure), given the perimeter p and the apothem a (the distance from the center of the regular polygon to one of its sides):

$$A = \frac{1}{2} ap$$

Equilateral triangle (all sides the same length), given the length of a side s:

$$A = \frac{s^2\sqrt{3}}{4}$$

Heron's formula Any **triangle**, given half the length of the perimeter (the semiperimeter) s and the lengths of the sides a, b, and c:

$$A = \sqrt{s(s-a)(s-b)(s-c)}.$$

Right circular cylinder (a cylinder with a circular region as its base whose sides make a right angle with the base), given the radius r of the base and the height h of the cylinder:

$$A = 2\pi r(h + r)$$

Right circular cone (a cone with a circular region as its base and whose altitude makes a right angle with the base), given the radius r of the base and the slant height l of the cone (the shortest distance from the tip of the cone to the circle of the base):

$$A = \pi r(l + r).$$

Sphere, given the radius r:

$$A = 4\pi r^2$$

Volume

In each of the following, the volume (space enclosed) is V.

Cube, given the length of an edge e:

$$V = e^3$$

Right rectangular prism (box), given the length l, the width w, and the height h:

$$V = lwh$$

Prism, given the area of the base B and the height h:

$$V = Bh$$

Right circular cylinder, given the radius r of the base and the height h:

$$V = \pi r^2 h$$

Right circular cone, given the radius r of the base and the height h:

$$V = \tfrac{1}{3} \pi r^2 h$$

Pyramid, given the area of the base B and the height h:

$$V = \tfrac{1}{3} Bh$$

Sphere, given the radius r:

$$V = \tfrac{4}{3} \pi r^3$$

Algebra

If a, b, and x are any numbers or variables ("unknowns"):

$$(a + b)^2 = a^2 + 2ab + b^2$$
$$(a - b)^2 = a^2 - 2ab + b^2$$
$$x^2 - a^2 = (x + a)(x - a)$$
$$x^3 - a^3 = (x - a)(x^2 + ax + a^2)$$
$$x^3 + a^3 = (x + a)(x^2 - ax + a^2)$$

If a, b, c, and d are any numbers or variables except that neither b nor d can be zero:

$$a/b + c/d = (ad + bc)/bd$$
$$a/b - c/d = (ad - bc)/bd$$
$$a/b \times c/d = ac/bd$$
$$a/b \div c/d = ad/bc \ (c \neq 0)$$

Quadratic formula for the solutions of a second degree polynomial equation in one variable of the form $ax^2 + bx + c = 0$:

$$x = \frac{-b \pm \sqrt{b^2 - 4ac}}{2a}$$

Laws of exponents, given that a, b, x, and y are numbers or variables:

$$a^x a^y = a^{x+y}$$
$$(a^x)^y = a^{xy}$$
$$(ab)^x = a^x b^x$$
$$(a/b)^x = a^x / b^x$$
$$a^x / a^y = a^{x-y}$$
$$a^{-x} = \frac{1}{a^x}$$
$$a^0 = 1$$
$$a^1 = a.$$

Laws of logarithms, given that a, b, x, and y are positive numbers, c is any real number, and $a \neq 1$, $b \neq 1$.

$$\log_a (xy) = \log_a x + \log_a y$$
$$\log_a 1/x = -\log_a x$$
$$\log_a (x/y) = \log_a x - \log_a y$$
$$\log_a (x^c) = c \log_a x$$
$$\log_b x = (\log_a x)/(\log_a b)$$
$$\log_a 1 = 0$$
$$\log_a a = 1$$
$$a^{\log_a x} = x$$
$$\log_a (a^c) = c$$

Graphs

In a rectangular (Cartesian) coordinate plane, where the horizontal axis is x and the vertical axis is y:

Slope of a line, m, given two particular points (x_1, y_1) and (x_2, y_2) where $x_1 \neq x_2$:

$$m = (y_2 - y_1)/(x_2 - x_1).$$

Point-slope equation of a line, given the slope m and a point on the nonvertical line (x_1, y_1):

$$y - y_1 = m(x - x_1).$$

Slope-intercept equation of a line, given the slope m and the y-intercept b (the number on the y axis where the line crosses the y axis):

$$y = mx + b.$$

Distance d between any two points, (x_1, y_1) and (x_2, y_2):

$$d = \sqrt{(x_2 - x_1)^2 + (y_2 - y_1)^2}.$$

Trigonometry

In a **right triangle** whose two shorter sides (or legs) are a and b, opposite angles A and B respectively, and whose longest side (or hypotenuse, always the side opposite the right angle, C) is c:

Pythagorean theorem:

$$c^2 = a^2 + b^2.$$

Trigonometric functions:

sine: $\sin A = a/c$
cosine: $\cos A = b/c$
tangent: $\tan A = a/b$
cotangent: $\cot A = b/a$
secant: $\sec A = c/b$
cosecant: $\csc A = c/a.$

In any triangle labeled such that side a is opposite angle A, side b is opposite angle B, and side c is opposite angle C:

Angle sum:

$$A + B + C = 180°$$

Law of sines:

$$(\sin A)/a = (\sin B)/b = (\sin C)/c$$

Law of cosines:

$$c^2 = a^2 + b^2 - 2ab \cos C$$

If x is any real number or a measure of an angle in degrees, the following statements are true:

Defining trigonometric identities:

$$\tan x = \sin x / \cos x \qquad \csc x = 1/\sin x$$
$$\cot x = \cos x / \sin x \qquad \cot x = 1/\tan x$$
$$\sec x = 1/\cos x$$

Trigonometric identities of symmetry:

$$\sin (-x) = -\sin x \qquad \cos (-x) = \cos x$$
$$\tan (-x) = -\tan x \qquad \cot (-x) = -\cot x$$
$$\sec (-x) = \sec x \qquad \csc (-x) = -\csc x.$$

Pythagorean identities:

$$\sin^2 x + \cos^2 x = 1$$
$$\tan^2 x + 1 = \sec^2 x$$
$$\cot^2 x + 1 = \csc^2 x$$

Sum and difference formulas: If x and y are any two real numbers or measures of angles:

$$\sin (x + y) = \sin x \cos y + \cos x \sin y$$
$$\cos (x + y) = \cos x \cos y - \sin x \sin y$$
$$\tan (x + y) = (\tan x + \tan y)/(1 - \tan x \tan y)$$
$$\sin (x - y) = \sin x \cos y - \cos x \sin y$$
$$\cos (x - y) = \cos x \cos y + \sin x \sin y$$
$$\tan (x - y) = (\tan x - \tan y)/(1 + \tan x \tan y).$$

Fractions and Decimals

To find the equivalent of a fraction in decimal form, divide the numerator (top number) by the denominator (bottom number). To change from a decimal to a percent, multiply by 100. To change from a percent to a decimal, divide by 100.

Fraction	Decimal	Percent
1/16	0.0625	6.25%
1/8 (= 2/16)	0.125	12.5
3/16	0.1875	18.75
1/4 (= 2/8; = 4/16)	0.25	25.0
5/16	0.3125	31.25
1/3	0.3 . . .	33.3 . . .
3/8 (= 6/16)	0.375	37.5
7/16	0.4375	43.75
1/2 (= 2/4; = 4/8; = 8/16)	0.5	50.0
9/16	0.5625	56.25
5/8 (= 10/16)	0.625	62.5
2/3	0.6 . . .	66.6 . . .
11/16	0.6875	68.75
3/4 (= 6/8; = 12/16)	0.75	75.0
13/16	0.8125	81.25
7/8 (= 14/16)	0.875	87.5
15/16	0.9375	93.75
1 (=2/2;=4/4;=8/8;=16/16)	1.0	100.0

Large Numbers

There are two primary naming systems for large numbers. The United States and France (among others) use one system, while Germany and Great Britain use the other. (Googol and googolplex, invented by the nephew of mathematician and author Edward Kasner, are rarely used outside the United States.) (See also "Standard Weights and Measures.")

Number of zeroes after 1	American name	British name
6	million	million
9	billion	milliard
12	trillion	billion
15	quadrillion	1,000 billion
18	quintillion	trillion
21	sextillion	1,000 trillion
24	septillion	quadrillion
27	octillion	1,000 quadrillion
30	nonillion	quintillion
33	decillion	1,000 quintillion
100	googol	googol
googol	googolplex	googolplex

Prefixes Used in the International System of Units (SI)

Prefix	Abbreviation	Factor by which unit is multipled	Scientific Notation
Exa-	E	1,000,000,000,000,000,000	10^{18}
Peta-	P	1,000,000,000,000,000	10^{15}
Tera-	T	1,000,000,000,000	10^{12}
Giga-	G	1,000,000,000	10^{9}
Mega-	M	1,000,000	10^{6}
Kilo-	k	1,000	10^{3}
Hecto-	h	100	10^{2}
Deka-	da	10	10^{1}
Deci-	d	0.1	10^{-1}
Centi-	c	0.01	10^{-2}
Milli-	m	0.001	10^{-3}
Micro-	µ	0.000 001	10^{-6}
Nano-	n	0.000 000 001	10^{-9}
Pico-	p	0.000 000 000 001	10^{-12}
Femto-	f	0.000 000 000 000 001	10^{-15}
Atto-	a	0.000 000 000 000 000 001	10^{-18}

STANDARD WEIGHTS & MEASURES

▶SYSTEMS OF MEASUREMENT

There are two widely used measurement systems. Most of the world uses a system known as the metric system, or the International System, abbreviated SI from *Système Internationale*, its name in French. The United States continues to use a system called U.S. customary measure, which derives from (and differs from) the British imperial series of weights and measures. From time to time, our government has taken steps to change from the customary system to the International System, but these efforts have failed. Metric measure is legal in the United States, but nearly everyone continues to use the customary system in everyday use. The International System is generally used in scientific pursuits and increasingly in international trade.

The following tables show first the U.S. customary system, then the International System, and finally some important conversion factors between the two.

Simplified Conversion Table (alphabetical order)

To convert	to	multiply by:
centimeters	feet	0.0328
centimeters	inches	0.3937
cubic cm	cubic in.	0.0610
cubic ft.	cubic m	0.0283
degrees	radians	0.0175
feet	cm	30.48
feet	meters	0.3048
gallons	liters	3.785
gal. water	lb. water	8.3453
grams	ounces	0.0353
inches	cm	2.54
kilograms	pounds	2.205
kilometers	feet	3,280.8
kilometers	miles	0.6214
knots	mi./hr.	1.151
liters	gallons	0.2642
liters	pints	2.113
meters	feet	3.281
miles	km	1.609
ounces	grams	28.3495
pounds	kg	0.4536

Length or Distance
U.S. customary system
1 foot (ft)	=	12 inches
1 yard (yd.)	=	3 feet = 36 inches
1 rod (rd.)	=	5.5 yards = 16.5 feet
1 furlong (fur)	=	40 rods = 220 yards
	=	660 feet
1 mile (mi)	=	8 furlongs
	=	1,760 yards = 5,280 feet

An international nautical mile has been defined as 6,076.1155 feet.

International System
The basic unit for length is the meter, which is slightly longer than the customary yard. Other units of length are decimal subdivisions or multiples of the meter.

1 decimeter (dm)	=	10 centimeters
	=	0.1 meter
1 centimeter (cm)	=	0.01 meter
1 millimeter (mm)	=	0.1 centimeter
	=	0.001 meter
1 micrometer (μm)	=	0.001 millimeter
	=	0.0001 centimeter
	=	0.000001 meter
1 angstrom (Å)	=	0.0001 micrometers
	=	0.0000001 milimeter
1 dekameter (dam)	=	10 meters
1 hectometer (hm)	=	10 dekameters
	=	100 meters
1 kilometer	=	10 hectometers
	=	100 dekameters
	=	1,000 meters

Conversions
In 1959 the relationship between between customary and international measures of length was officially defined as follows:

0.0254 meter (exactly)	=	1 inch
0.0245 meter x 12	=	0.3048 meter
	=	1 international foot

This definition, which makes many conversions simple, defines a foot that is shorter (by about 6 parts in 10 million) than the survey foot,

which had earlier been defined as exactly 1200/3937, or 0.3048006, meter.

Following the international foot standard, the major equivalents are as listed below:
1 in.	=	2.54 cm = 0.0254 m
1 ft.	=	30.48 cm = .3048 m
1 yd.	=	91.44 cm = 0.9144 m
1 mi.	=	1,609.344 m = 1.609344 km
1 cm	=	0.3937 in.
1 m	=	1.093613 yd. = 3.28084 ft.
1 km	=	0.62137 mi.

Area
U.S. customary system
Areas are derived from lengths as follows:
1 square foot	=	144 square inches
1 square yard	=	9 sq. ft.
1 square rod (rd²)	=	30.25 square yards
	=	272.25 square feet
1 acre	=	160 square rods
	=	4,840 square yards
	=	43,560 sq. ft.
1 square mile	=	640 acres
1 section	=	1 mile square
1 township	=	6 miles square
	=	36 square miles

International System
1 sq. millimeter (mm²)	=	1,000,000 sq. micrometers
1 sq. centimeter (cm²)	=	100 mm²
1 sq. decimeter (dm²)	=	100 cm²
1 sq. meter (m²)	=	10,000 cm²
1 are (a)	=	100 m²
1 hectare (ha)	=	100 ares
	=	10,000 m²
1 sq kilometer (km²)	=	100 hectares
	=	1,000,000 m²

Conversions
1 square inch	=	6.4516 cm²
1 square foot	=	929.0304 cm²
	=	0.09290304 m²
1 square yard	=	8,361.2736 cm²
	=	0.83612736 m²
1 acre	=	4,046.8564 m²
	=	0.40468564 hectares
1 square mile	=	2,589,988.11 m²
	=	258.998811 hectares
	=	2.58998811 km²
1 cm²	=	0.1550003 sq. in.
1 m²	=	1,550.003 sq. in.
	=	10.76391 sq. ft.
	=	1.195990 sq. yds.
1 hectare	=	107,639.1 sq. ft.
	=	11,959.90 sq. yds.
	=	2.4710538 acres
1 km²	=	247.10538 acres
	=	0.3861006 sq. miles

Cubic Measure
U.S. customary system
1 cu foot (ft³)	=	1,728 cubic inches (in³)
1 cubic yard (yd³)	=	27 cubic feet (ft³)

International System
1 cubic centimeter (cm³)	=	1,000 cubic millimeters (mm³)
1 cubic decimeter (dm³)	=	1,000 cubic centimeters (cm³)
1 cubic meter (m³)	=	1,000 cubic decimeters (dm³)
	=	1,000,000 cubic centimeters (cm³)

Cubic centimeter is sometimes abbreviated cc and is used in fluid measure interchangeably with milliliter (ml).

Conversions

1 in.^{3}	=	16.387064 cm^3
1 ft.^{3}	=	28.316846592 cm^3
	=	0.028316847 cm^3
1 yd.^{3}	=	764,554.857984 cm^3
	=	0.764554858 m^3
1 cm^3	=	0.06102374 in.^{3}
1 m^3	=	61,023.74 in.^{3}
	=	35.31467 ft.^{3}
	=	1.307951 yd.^{3}

Fluid Volume
U.S. customary system

A gallon is equal to 231 cubic inches of liquid or capacity.

1 tablespoon (tbs.)	=	3 teaspoons (tsp.)
	=	0.5 fluid ounce (fl. oz.)
1 cup	=	8 fl. oz.
1 pint (pt.)	=	2 cups = 16 fl. oz.
1 quart (qt.)	=	2 pt. = 4 cups
	=	32 fl. oz.
1 gallon (gal.)	=	4 qt. = 8 pt. = 16 cups
1 bushel (bu.)	=	8 gal. = 32 qt.

International System

Fluid-volume measurements are directly tied to cubic measure. One milliliter of fluid occupies a volume of 1 cubic centimeter. A liter of fluid (slightly more than the customary quart) occupies a volume of 1 cubic decimeter, or 1,000 cubic centimeters.

1 centiliter (cL)	=	10 mililiters (mL)
1 deciliter	=	10 cl = 100 mL
1 liter (L)	=	10 dl = 1,000 mL
1 dekaliter (daL)	=	10 L
1 hectoliter (hL)	=	10 daL = 100 L
1 kiloliter (kL)	=	10 hl = 1,000 L

Conversions

1 fluid ounce	=	29.573528 mL = 0.02957 L
1 cup	=	236.588 mL = 0.236588 L
1 pint	=	473.176 mL = 0.473176 L
1 quart	=	946.3529 mL = 0.9463529 L
1 gallon	=	3,785.41 mL = 3.78541 L
1 milliliter	=	0.0338 fluid ounce
1 liter	=	33.814 fluid ounces
	=	4.2268 cups = 2.113 pints
	=	1.0567 quarts = 0.264 gallon

Dry Volume
Conversions

1 pint, dry	=	33.600 cu. in. = 0.551 L
1 quart, dry	=	67.201 cu. in. = 1.101 L

Mass & Weight

Mass and weight are often confused. Mass is a measure of the quantity of matter in an object and does not vary with changes in altitude or in gravitational force (as on the Moon or another planet). Weight, on the other hand, is a measure of the force of gravity on an object and so does change with altitude or gravitational force.

U.S. customary system

In customary measure it is more common to measure weight than mass. The most common customary system of weight is avoirdupois:

1 pound (lb.)	=	16 ounces (oz.)
1 (short) hundred-	=	100 lb.
weight (cwt.)		
1 (short) ton	=	20 hundredweights
	=	2,000 lb.
1 long hundred-	=	112 lb.
weight		
1 long ton	=	20 long hundredweights
	=	2,240 lb.

A different system called troy weight is used to weigh precious metals. In troy weight the ounce is slightly larger than in avoirdupois, but there are only 12 ounces to the troy pound.

International System

Instead of weight, the International System generally is used to measure mass. The International System's basic unit for measurement of mass is the gram, which was originally defined as the mass of 1 milliliter (= 1 cm^3) of water at 4 degrees Celsius (about 39°F). Today the official standard of measure is the kilogram (1,000 g).

1 centigram (cg)	=	10 milligrams (mg)
1 decigram (dg)	=	10 cg = 100 mg
1 gram (g)	=	10 dg = 100 cg = 1000 mg
1 kilogram (kg)	=	10 hectograms (hg)
	=	100 dekagrams (dag)
	=	1,000 g
1 metric ton (t)	=	1000 kg

Conversions

Since mass and weight are identical at standard conditions (sea level on Earth), grams and other International System units of mass are often used as measures of weight or converted into customary units of weight. Under standard conditions:

1 ounce	=	28.3495 grams
1 pound	=	453.59 grams
	=	0.45359 kilogram
1 short ton	=	907.18 kilograms
	=	0.907 metric ton
1 milligram	=	0.000035 ounce
1 gram	=	0.03527 ounce
1 kilogram	=	35.27 ounces
	=	2.2046 pounds
1 metric ton	=	2,204.6 pounds
	=	1.1023 short tons

Time
Customary and International System

The International System in 1967 adopted a second that is based on the microwaves emitted by the vibrations of hot cesium atoms. A second (abbreviated sec. in customary usage, s in SI usage) is the time it takes the atoms to vibrate exactly 9,192,631,770 times. In the customary measure of time, the day is divided into 24 hours, the hour into 60 minutes, and the minute into 60 seconds. Since the Earth's rotation is gradually slowing, scientists must periodically add a second to a day to keep the year in sequence with their clocks. The change is so small that for almost all practical purposes an International System second and a customary second are the same.

Decimal fractions of time are used to measure smaller time intervals:

millisecond (ms)	=	0.001 second (10^{-3})
microsecond (μs)	=	0.000001 second (10^{-6})
nanosecond (ns)	=	0.000000001 second (10^{-9})
picosecond (ps)	=	0.000000000001 second (10^{-12})

Temperature
U.S. customary system

In the U.S. temperature is usually measured in degrees Fahrenheit: water freezes at 32°F and boils at 212°F. The basis of the Fahrenheit scale was 0°F, the coldest temperature that its originator, G.D. Fahrenheit (1686–1736), could obtain under laboratory conditions.

International System

The Swedish astronomer Anders Celsius (1701–44) devised the temperature scale that bears his name in 1742. On the Celsius scale, water freezes at 0°C and boils at 100°C. Very low temperatures are measured on the Kelvin scale, named for William

Thomson, Baron Kelvin (1824–1907). It is also called the absolute scale because absolute zero—0°K (-273.15° C)—is the temperature at which no body can give up heat. The interval of a degree Kelvin equals the interval of a degree Celsius. At very high temperatures, differences between the Kelvin and Celsius scales are insignificant.

Conversions

Fahrenheit to Celsius: Subtract 32 from the temperature and multiply the difference by 5; then divide the product by 9. The formula is: $C = \frac{5}{9}(F-32)$

Celsius to Fahrenheit: Multiply the temperature by 1.8 (or $\frac{9}{5}$), then add 32. The formula is: $F = \frac{9}{5}C + 32$

Celsius to Kelvin: Add 273.15 to the temperature The formula is: $K = C+273.15$

Force, Work/Energy, Power
U.S. customary system

The foot/pound/second system of reckoning includes the following units:

slug = the mass to which a force of 1 poundal will give an acceleration of 1 foot per second per second (= approximately 32.17 lbs.)
poundal = fundamental unit of force
foot-pound = the work done when a force of 1 poundal produces a movement of 1 foot
foot-pound/second = the unit of power equal to 1 foot/pound per second.

Another common unit of power is horsepower, which is equal to 550 foot-pounds per second.

Thermal work or energy is often measured in British thermal units (Btu), One Btu is defined as the energy required to increase the temperature of 1 pound of water by 1 degree Fahrenheit. The Btu is equal to about 0.778 foot-pound.

International System

In physics, compound measurements of force, work or energy, and power are essential. There are two parallel systems using International System units: the centimeter/gram/second system (cgs) is used for small measurements, and the meter/kilogram/second system (mks) is used for larger measurements. The mks system is the official one for SI. They are described below.

Measurement of force

cgs unit	dyne (dy)	The force required to accelerate a mass of 1g 1 cm/s^2 (cm/s^2 means "centimeter per second per second")
mks unit	newton (N)	The force required to accelerate a mass of 1kg l m/s^2

Measurement of work or energy

cgs unit	erg	The dyne-centimeter, i.e., the work done when a force of 1 dy produces a movement of 1 cm
mks unit	joule (j)	The newton-meter, i.e., the work done when a force of 1 N produces a movement of 1 m (=10,000,000 ergs)

Heat energy is also measured using the calorie (cal), which is defined as the energy required to increase the temperature of 1 cubic centimeter (1

Fahrenheit and Celsius Temperature Conversions

Often you need to know only the approximate values to convert a weather report or temperature in a recipe from Celsius to Fahrenheit. The following table can be used to get an approximate conversion between the two Fahrenheit and Celsius temperature scales. Note that -40°F is the same temperature as -40°C.

Celsius		Fahrenheit	Fahrenheit		Celsius
-45°	=	-49°	-45°	=	-42.8°
-40°	=	-40°	-40°	=	-40.0°
-35°	=	-31°	-35°	=	-37.2°
-30°	=	-22°	-30°	=	-34.4°
-25°	=	-13°	-25°	=	-31.7°
-20°	=	-4°	-20°	=	-28.9°
-15°	=	5°	-15°	=	-26.1°
-10°	=	14°	-10°	=	-23.3°
-5°	=	23°	-5°	=	-20.6°
0°	=	32°	0°	=	-17.8°
5°	=	41°	5°	=	-15.0°
10°	=	50°	10°	=	-12.2°
15°	=	59°	15°	=	-9.4°
20°	=	68°	20°	=	-6.7°
25°	=	77°	25°	=	-3.9°
30°	=	86°	30°	=	-1.1°
35°	=	95°	32°	=	0.0°
40°	=	104°	35°	=	1.7°
45°	=	113°	40°	=	4.4°
50°	=	122°	45°	=	7.2°
55°	=	131°	50°	=	10.0°
60°	=	140°	55°	=	12.8°
65°	=	149°	60°	=	15.6°
70°	=	158°	65°	=	18.3°
75°	=	167°	70°	=	21.1°
80°	=	176°	75°	=	23.9°
85°	=	185°	80°	=	26.7°
90°	=	194°	85°	=	29.4°
95°	=	203°	90°	=	32.2°
100°	=	212°	95°	=	35.0°
125°	=	257°	100°	=	37.8°
150°	=	302°	105°	=	40.6°
175°	=	347°	110°	=	43.3°
200°	=	392°	212°	=	100.0°
225°	=	437°	225°	=	107.2°
250°	=	482°	250°	=	121.1°
275°	=	527°	275°	=	135.0°
300°	=	572°	300°	=	148.9°
325°	=	617°	325°	=	162.8°
350°	=	662°	350°	=	176.7°
375°	=	707°	375°	=	190.6°
400°	=	752°	400°	=	204.4°
425°	=	797°	425°	=	218.3°
450°	=	842°	450°	=	232.2°
475°	=	887°	475°	=	246.1°

Kelvin, Celsius, and Fahrenheit Equivalents

Characteristic	K	C°	F°
Absolute zero	0	-273.15°	-459.7°
Freezing point, water	273.15	0°	32°
Traditional human body temperature	310.15	37°	98.6°
Boiling point, water	373.15	100°	212°

ml) of water by 1 degree C. One calorie is equal to about 4.184 joules. The kilocalorie (Kcal or Cal) is equal to 1,000 calories and is the unit in which the energy values of food are measured. This more familiar unit, also commonly referred to as a Calorie, is equal to about 4,184 joules.

Measurement of power

cgs unit	erg/second	A rate of 1 erg per second
mks unit	watt (W)	The joule/second, i.e., a rate of 1 joule per second

Conversions
Measurement of force

1 poundal	=	13,889 dynes
	=	0.13889 newtons
1 dyne	=	0.000072 poundals
1 newton	=	7.2 poundals

Measurement of work or energy

1 foot-pound	=	1,356 joules
British thermal unit	=	1,055 joules
	=	252 gram calories
1 joule	=	0.0007374 ft-lbs.
1 (gram) calorie	=	0.003968 Btu
1 (kilo) Calorie	=	3.968 Btu

Measurement of power

1 foot-pound/second	=	1.3564 watts
1 horsepower	=	746 watts
	=	0.746 kilowatts
1 watt	=	0.73725 ft-lb/sec.
	=	0.00134 horsepower
1 kilowatt	=	737.25 ft.-lb./sec.
	=	1.34 horsepower

Electrical Measure

Originally, the basic unit of quantity in electricity was the coulomb. A coulomb is equal to the passage of 6.25×10^{18} electrons past a given point in an electrical system.

The unit of electrical flow is the ampere, which is equal to a coulomb/second, i.e., the flow of 1 coulomb per second. The ampere is analogous in electrical measure to a unit of flow such as gallons-per-minute in physical measure. In SI, the ampere is taken as the basic unit.

The unit for measuring electrical potential energy is the volt, which is defined as 1 joule/coulomb, i.e., 1 joule of energy per coulomb of electricity. The volt is analogous to a measure of pressure in a water system.

The unit for measuring electrical power is the watt as defined in the previous section. Power in watts (P) is the product of the electrical flow in amperes (I) and the potential electrical energy in volts (E):

$$P = IE.$$

Since the watt is such a small unit for practical applications, the kilowatt (= 1,000 watts) is often used. A kilowatt-hour is the power of 1,000 watts over an hour's time.

The unit for measuring electrical resistance is the ohm, which is the resistance offered by a circuit to the flow of 1 ampere being driven by the force of 1 volt. It is derived from Ohm's law, which defines the relationship between flow or current (amperes), potential energy (volts), and resistance (ohms). It states that the current in amperes (I) is proportional to potential energy in volts (E) and inversely proportional to resistance in ohms (R). Thus, when voltage and resistance are known, amperage can be calculated by the simple formula

$$I = \frac{E}{R}$$

Measure of Angles and Arcs

Angles are measured by systems based on arcs (portions) of circles. Arcs of a circle can be measured by length, but they are also often measured by angles. In the latter case, the measure of the arc is the same as the measure of an angle whose vertex is at the center of the circle and whose sides pass through the ends of the arc. Such an angle is said to be subtended by the arc.

The most commonly used angle measure is degree measure. One degree is the angle subtended by an arc that is 1/360 of a circle. This is an ancient system of measurement probably originally developed by Sumerian astronomers. These astronomers used a numeration system based on 60 ($60 \times 6 = 360$), as well as a 360-day year. They divided the day into 12 equal periods of 30 smaller periods each ($12 \times 30 = 360$) and used roughly the same system for dividing the circle. Even when different years and numeration systems were adopted by later societies, astronomers continued to use a variation of the Sumerian system.

1 degree (1°)	=	60 minutes (60')
	=	3,600 seconds (3,600")
1 minute	=	60 seconds

When two lines are perpendicular to each other, they form four angles of the same size, which are called right angles. Two right angles make up a line, which in this context is considered a straight angle.

1 right angle = 90°
1 straight angle = 180°

While this system is workable for most purposes, it is artificial. Mathematicians discovered that using a natural system of angle measurement produces results that make better sense in mathematical and many scientific applications. This system is called radian measure. Radian measure is considered a supplement to SI. One radian is the measure of the angle subtended by an arc of a circle that is exactly as long as the radius of the circle.

1 radian = about 57° 17' 45"

The circumference, C, of a circle is given by the formula $C = 2\pi r$, where π is a number (approximately 3.14159) and r is the radius. Therefore, a semicircle whose radius is 1 is π units long, which implies that there are π radians in a straight angle. Many of the angles commonly encountered are measured in multiples of π radians:

0° = 0 radians	90° = $\pi/2$ radians
30° = $\pi/6$ radians	180° = π radians
45° = $\pi/4$ radians	270° = $3\pi/2$ radians
60° = $\pi/3$ radians	360° = 2π radians

To convert from radians to degrees, use the formula t radians $= (180/\pi)\ t°$. To convert from degrees to radians, use the formula

$$w° = (\pi/180) w \text{ radians.}$$

The U.S. artillery uses the mil to measure angles. A mil is the angle subtended by an arc that is 1/6400 of a circle.

1 mil = 0.05625° = 3' 22.5"
1 mil = almost 0.001 radian

The Environment

The environmental movement in the United States dates from Earth Day 1970 (April 22), when the American public first began to take stock of the ecological devastation going on around them. Then there were no pollution controls on cars; people and municipalities dumped untreated sewage into the nation's rivers, some of which were so saturated with chemical waste that they actually caught fire; and industrial cities were routinely shrouded with thick acrid smoke.

Many of these problems have been effectively addressed and dramatically diminished. Today the Environmental Protection Agency (EPA), established in 1970, routinely monitors air quality at thousands of sites around the country. Toxic emissions from smokestacks at smelters, factories, and garbage incinerators have been sharply reduced. Mandatory pollution control standards on automobiles have led to an overwhelming drop in lead emissions. Recycling as a way of reducing solid waste has taken hold in cities and towns throughout the country. Many people, however, oppose strong environmental safeguards, making it difficult to improve and enforce regulations. Growing population pressures also create environmental threats, particularly to natural habitats, arable soil, and drinking water supplies.

▶ GLOBAL WARMING

Most climatologists are convinced that over the past century the Earth has begun to warm significantly—about 1°F (0.5°C)—and that at its current rate, it is likely to warm as much as 2° to 9°F (1° to 5°C) more over the next 50 to 60 years. A 1998 study based on tree rings, ice cores, growth of corals, and historical records shows that the 1990s has been the warmest decade in the past 600 years. The Earth's average surface temperature in 1997 was the highest since thermometer records were first kept in the mid-19th century, and each of the first five months of 1998 broke global temperature records for those months, as the effects of El Niño heightened the underlying warming trend. If global temperatures continue to increase, the potential devastation is staggering. Worldwide temperatures have risen only 9°F (5°C) since the end of the last ice age 12,000 years ago. Additional warming would cause melting of polar ice caps, setting off a chain of events that begins with a rise in sea level worldwide and could end with the destruction of water supplies, forests, and agriculture in many parts of the world.

Global warming occurs when certain gases in the atmosphere prevent sunlight from being reflected from the Earth. Ordinarily, sunlight that reaches the surface of the Earth is partly absorbed and partly reflected. The absorbed light heats the surface and is later emitted from the surface as infrared radiation. Gases that are not transparent to infrared radiation (carbon dioxide is one) collect this heat and keep it in the atmosphere, hence their name, greenhouse gases. The Earth's atmosphere is only 0.03 percent carbon dioxide, but combined with other gases, this is enough to trap 30 percent of the reflected heat (the rest is radiated out to space), and maintain the Earth's average temperature at about 59°F (15°C).

In a 1996 report, the Intergovernmental Panel on Climate Change, a group of 2,500 scientists commissioned by the UN, concluded that "the balance of evidence suggests that there is a discernible human influence on global climate." Since the Industrial Revolution, human activities have released an unprecedented amount of greenhouse gases into the atmosphere, particularly carbon dioxide, chlorofluorocarbons (CFCs), methane, and nitrogen oxides.

The increased presence of carbon dioxide is due primarily to the burning of carbon fuels including oil, coal, and natural gas, as well as burning trees for deforestation. CFCs, now being phased out by many countries, are used as aerosols, in air-conditioning units, and in various industrial processes. Methane is emitted by decomposing organic wastes, natural-gas leaks, and fermenting rice paddies. The primary sources of nitrogen oxides are automobile exhaust and industrial smoke stacks. At a December 1997 conference in Kyoto, Japan, representatives of more than 150 countries reached tentative agreement to reduce greenhouse gases an average of 5 percent worldwide (from 1990 levels) by the year 2010. In the United States, which accounts for nearly a quarter of global emissions, the target is a 7 percent reduction.

In the ensuing year, the U.S. has done little to meet that goal, even though emissions in America are projected to *increase* by 30 percent by 2008 if the status quo is not altered. Meanwhile, a team of NASA scientists reported in early 1999 that two cubic miles of ice per year have been melting away from Greenland since 1993 due to increased global temperatures. They warned that if the trend continued, the results could ultimately be catastrophic.

Global warming produces a domino effect that can spell environmental disaster. Some of the main steps in this chain are as follows:

Weather patterns Climatologists think that global warming is already disrupting local weather in places around the world. In the United States, according to the National Climactic Data Center in Asheville, N.C., greenhouse effects have most likely caused the unusual and extreme weather patterns of the 1980s and 1990s. For example, the expected pattern of wetter winters and occasional wetter summers in the middle of the North American continent have been a factor in the great floods in 1993 and 1997.

Changed weather patterns can have a severe impact on crops and other forms of vegetation, as well as on the animals that depend on them. Rising temperatures also enable insects and fungal pests to migrate to previously unaffected regions. Long-lived plants, however, such as trees, spread much more slowly in the face of climate change.

Warming patterns Although global warming will cause an increase in average world temperatures, this increase is not expected to be uniform. In general, climatologists expect greater warming during winter months and at high latitudes (closer to the poles than to the equator). Some places will experience more severe effects than others. For example, the number of +95°F days in Rio de Janeiro would increase tenfold, from 5 to 52 days. Rome would go from 6 to 55 days and Tokyo from 5 to 41.

Higher temperatures, especially at the poles, have an even more dire effect than increased numbers of hot days. They can also melt polar ice caps, causing:

Sea level rise Climatologists generally expect the sea level to rise at least a foot (30-40 cm) and possibly as much as 6.6 feet (200 cm) in the next century. Generally speaking, a rise in sea level would be uniform—both geographically and seasonally—because sea level is a global phenomenon. The impact of such a rise, however, would vary greatly from place to place—a three-foot (1 m) rise would inundate 7,000 square miles (18,000 km²) of dry land—an area the size of Massachusetts—in the United States, mostly in the southeast. It would also destroy a comparable area of coastal wetlands, erode recreational beaches 100 to 200 meters, exacerbate coastal flooding, and increase the salinity of aquifers and estuaries. It is likely that the people of an industrialized continental nation such as the United States could sustain the

Major Events in the History of the Environment

1775   Percival Pott observes that chimney sweeps develop cancer as a result of their contact with soot, the first recognition of environmental factors on cancer.

1864   George Perkins Marsh (American: 1801-81) publishes *Man and Nature*, the first textbook on conservation and the first detailed study of human influence on the environment.

1872   Robert Angus Smith (Scottish: 1817-84) describes acid rain.

1885   Yellowstone, world's first national park, opens.

1892   Canada establishes first national park at Banff, Alberta.

1903   John Muir (Scottish-American: 1838-1914) founds the Sierra Club.

1905   U.S. president Theodore Roosevelt opens the first national refuge, Pelican Island in Florida, to protect nesting sites of brown pelicans.

U.S. Forest Service established.

National Audubon Society founded.

1911   Canada, Japan, Russia, and the United States sign a treaty to limit the annual harvest of northern fur seals.

1916   National Park Service established.

1928   Boulder Canyon project (Hoover Dam) authorized to bring irrigation, electric power, and flood control system to western United States.

1933   Tennessee Valley Authority created to develop the Tennessee River for flood control, navigation, electric power, agriculture, and forestry.

1939   Paul Müller (Swiss: 1899-1965) discovers insecticidal properties of DDT.

1952   Smog blamed for 4,000 deaths in London.

1955   Link between exposure to asbestos and lung cancer established.

1957   Nuclear wastes stored by the Soviet Union in a remote mountain region of the Urals explode; radioactive contamination affects thousands of square miles; several villages permanently evacuated.

1961   Investigations in Scandinavia and the U.S. Adirondacks confirm that acid rain kills some species living in lakes.

1962   *Silent Spring* by Rachel Carson (American: 1907-64) attacks pesticide use and stimulates major environmental movement.

1963   Congress passes first Clean Air Act, allocating $95 million to local, state, and national air pollution control efforts.

1964   Congress passes Wilderness Act, setting up the National Wilderness Preservation System.

1965   Congress passes Highway Beautification Act, banning many highway billboards.

Congress passes Water Quality Act, giving federal government power to set water standards in absence of state action.

Congress passes the Solid Waste Disposal Act, its first major solid waste legislation.

1966   Congress passes Rare and Endangered Species Act.

1967   S. Manabe and R.T. Wetherald predict that increased amounts of carbon dioxide in the atmosphere will lead to global warming.

1968   Congress passes Wild and Scenic Rivers Act, identifying areas of scenic beauty for preservation and recreation.

1970   First Earth Day celebrated on April 22.

Environmental Protection Agency created.

1972   Congress passes Clean Water Act, forbidding discharges of pollutants into navigable waters.

Oregon passes the nation's first bottle recycling law.

The EPA bars registration and interstate sales of DDT because of its persistence in the environment and accumulation in the food chain.

1973   Representatives of 80 nations sign the Convention of International Trade in Endangered Species of Wild Fauna and Flora, which prohibits commercial trade in 375 endangered species of wild animals.

1974   F. Sherwood Rowland and Mario Molinas warn that chlorofluorocarbons (CFCs) produced by spray cans and air conditioners are destroying ozone layer.

1976   Congress passes Toxic Substances Control Act to control hazardous industrial chemicals.

1978   Community of Love Canal, near Niagara, N.Y., evacuated after hazardous waste dumps are uncovered. EPA declares site safe in 1990.

1979   Nuclear reactor at Three Mile Island, near Harrisburg, Pa., suffers partial meltdown; radiation confined to reactor dome.

1980   Congress passes Comprehensive Environmental Response, Compensation and Liability Act (the "Superfund") to clean up hazardous waste sites.

1984   More than 2,000 die and thousands more are injured by toxic gas from an accident at the U.S.-owned Union Carbide plant in Bhopal, India.

1985   British scientists discover that a "hole" in the ozone layer develops over Antarctica each winter.

The U.S. sets up a Conservation Reserve Program to remove environmentally sensitive farmland from agricultural use.

1986   A worldwide ban on whaling begins.

Chernobyl nuclear reactor number 4 explodes and burns, causing 31 deaths within days, shortening the lives of thousands, and forcing the evacuation of hundreds of square miles in Soviet Ukraine for an unknown length of time.

1987   The worst forest fire in history burns more than 3 million acres of China's timber reserve and up to 15 million acres in the Soviet Union.

1988   The U.S. Ocean Dumping Ban Act mandates an end to ocean dumping of industrial waste and sewage sludge.

1989   Exxon Valdez grounds, leaking 35,000 tons of oil into Prince William Sound, Alaska.

Thirteen industrial nations agree to halt production of CFCs by the year 2000.

1991   Iraq dumps over a million tons of oil from occupied Kuwait into Persian Gulf.

1992   Representatives from 178 countries attend the first-ever Earth Summit in Rio de Janeiro, where they sign treaties pledging to increase the diversity of animal and plant species and to halt global warming.

1994   U.S. Fish and Wildlife Service recommends that status of American bald eagle be reduced from "endangered" to "threatened" in most of United States.

1995   The United Nations Working Group I of the Intergovernmental Panel on Climate Change endorses global warming, reporting that "the balance of evidence suggests that there is a discernible human influence on global climate."

1996   The U.S. National Oceanic and Atmospheric Administration reports that measurements show that a global campaign to lower production of chemicals that damage the ozone layer has succeeded and that by 2010 the ozone layer will have begun to recover and by 2050 the Antarctic ozone "hole" will have closed.

1997   Representatives from more than 150 countries meet in Kyoto, Japan, where they agree to reduce emissions of greenhouse gases 5.2 percent worldwide by 2010.

population shifts caused by such climatic changes. However, an estimated one-third of the world's population—about 1.75 billion people, today—lives within 40 miles of the sea, mostly along low-lying floodplains and estuaries. How the low-lying Netherlands or Bangladesh or the island nations of the Pacific can or will respond to such forces is impossible to see.

▶ THE OZONE LAYER

There are two distinct problems associated with the chemical ozone (O_3): ground-level ozone, the main component of smog (discussed under "Air Pollution," below), and stratospheric ozone. The primary difference between the two problems is that at ground level there is too much ozone, while in the stratosphere there is not enough.

The problem of stratospheric ozone depletion is closely related to global warming in terms of its causes and its remedies. Stratospheric ozone (sometimes referred to as upper-atmosphere or atmospheric ozone) absorbs most of the Sun's ultraviolet radiation. A significant reduction of the ozone layer would lead to sharp increases in the incidence of skin cancer and cataracts in humans. It is also thought that there would be serious losses of small ocean algae, which produce oxygen and break down carbon dioxide, and of bacteria important to crop production.

Complex natural forces are continually at work creating and destroying ozone in the atmosphere. This involves first the breakdown of individual molecules of oxygen (O_2) into atomic oxygen (O), through the absorption of ultraviolet radiation. In turn, each atomic oxygen normally combines with an additional molecule of O_2 to form ozone (O_3). Destruction of ozone can be caused by the occasional recombination of ozone with atomic oxygen to form two molecules of O_2. As long as the Earth's sunlit atmosphere contains molecular oxygen, as it has for more than one billion years, ozone will be maintained in this dynamic balance.

In 1974, scientists saw the first suggestion that a group of chemicals known as chlorofluorocarbons (CFCs) was destroying the ozone balance by adding chlorine to the atmosphere.

Chemically inert, nontoxic, and easily liquefied, CFCs were developed in the 1930s as an ammonia substitute for use in refrigeration, but their use became widespread in air conditioning, packaging and insulation, as a solvent for cleaning electronic circuit boards, and as an aerosol propellant.

It is this very absence of chemical reactivity that makes CFCs so dangerous to the ozone layer. Unlike less inert compounds, CFCs are not destroyed or removed in the lower atmosphere by rain, oxidation, or sunlight. Instead they drift into the upper atmosphere, where their chlorine components are released into the atmosphere under the effects of ultraviolet radiation. Almost all of these freed chlorine atoms find and react with the ozone, creating chlorine monoxide. In a subsequent reaction, the chlorine monoxide releases its oxygen atom to form molecular oxygen, and the chlorine atom is freed once again to repeat the process. The atmospheric lifetimes for the most commonly used CFC compounds have been estimated to be between 75 and 110 years, so through this continuing cycle of reactions, each chlorine atom can destroy about 100,000 molecules of ozone before the chain reaction ends. Ice crystals in the Antarctic and Arctic speed up reactions, producing "ozone holes" near both poles. Such "holes" are regions of extremely low levels of atmospheric ozone during winters. In December, 1998, the World Meteorological Organization reported that the hole in the ozone layer over Antarctica had reached record proportions.

To combat ozone depletion, there have been stringent reductions in CFC use. The United States, Russia, Japan, and the nations of the European Union have agreed to eliminate CFC use and production 100 percent by 2000. Even so, adverse effects on the ozone layer from human-produced CFCs will likely continue until at least 2020.

▶ AIR POLLUTION

Although we tend to think of air pollution as a local problem, studies reported in 1995 demonstrate that there are widespread effects. Air pollution, they report, is so pervasive in industrial regions of northeastern North America, central Europe, and eastern Asia that it partly blocks sunlight, counteracting global warming with regional cooling.

The U.S. Environmental Protection Agency (EPA) monitors air quality at about 3,000 sites for six pollutants: particulate matter (soot and dust), sulfur dioxide, carbon monoxide (mostly from automobiles), nitrogen oxides, lead, and ozone. In addition to health concerns, the effects of air pollution on vegetation, materials, and visibility are monitored.

The basic federal law dealing with air pollution is the Clean Air Act of 1990, which directs the EPA to set standards for air quality. In mid-1997, the EPA issued updated standards for particulate matter and ground-level ozone, to more adequately protect public health. A federal court declared the new rules unconstitutional, however, in 1999. The Clinton Administration is appealing the decision.

Particulate matter (PM₁₀)

The EPA measures particulate matter with an aerodynamic diameter smaller than 10 micrometers down to 2.5 micrometers. This includes dust, dirt, soot, smoke, and liquid droplets directly emitted into the air from factories, power plants, cars, construction sites, fires, and natural erosion, as well as particles formed in the atmosphere by condensation or transformation of emitted gases such as sulfur dioxide and volatile organic compounds.

Particulate matter is responsible for most adverse health effects in the lower regions of the respiratory tract. People with chronic obstructive pulmonary or cardiovascular disease, individuals with influenza, asthmatics, the elderly, and children are especially sensitive.

Sulfur dioxide (SO₂)

Ambient sulfur dioxide comes mostly from stationary-source coal and oil combustion, refineries, pulp and paper mills, and nonferrous smelters. The health hazards associated with exposure to SO_2 include impaired breathing, respiratory illness, alterations in the lungs' defenses, and aggravation of existing respiratory and cardiovascular disease. Those most sensitive to SO_2 include asthmatics and people with chronic lung disease or cardiovascular disease, children, and the elderly. Sulfur dioxide also damages leaves on trees and crops and it is an agent of acid rain.

Carbon monoxide (CO)

Carbon monoxide is a colorless, odorless, and poisonous gas produced by incomplete burning of carbon in fuels. Carbon monoxide enters the bloodstream and disrupts delivery of oxygen to the body's organs and tissues. The health threat from carbon monoxide is serious for those who suffer from cardiovascular diseases. Healthy individuals are also affected, and exposure to elevated carbon monoxide levels is associated with impairment of visual perception and manual dexterity.

Nitrogen oxides (NOₓ)

These highly reactive gases play a major role, together with volatile organic compounds, in the formation of ozone. Nitrogen oxides form when fuel is burned at high temperatures. When released into the atmosphere, they are one of the major causes of smog. The two major emissions sources are cars and trucks, and stationary fuel-combustion sources such as electric-utility and industrial boilers.

Nitrogen oxides can irritate the lungs and lower resistance to respiratory infections such as influenza.

Prolonged exposure to higher than normal concentrations can cause pulmonary angina. Nitrogen dioxide (NO_2) is also an agent of acid rain and plays a key role in nitrogen loading of forests and ecosystems. Over the past decade, Los Angeles is the only urban area that has consistently recorded violations of the EPA's annual NO_2 standards. Many other urban areas violate the EPA's standards on occasional hot summer days, when the Sun cooks hydrocarbons and nitrogen oxides, thus producing smog.

Unhealthy Days in Selected Metropolitan Areas, 1980-97

To measure air quality in urban areas, the Environmental Protection Agency has developed an indicator called the Pollutant Standard Index (PSI). The PSI integrates into a single number emission levels of five major pollutants: particulate matter (PM_{10}), sulfur dioxide (SO_2), carbon monoxide (CO), ground level ozone (O_3), and nitrogen dioxide (NO_2). A PSI of 0-50 reflects good air, 51-100 denotes moderate air, and a PSI of over 100 is classified as unhealthy (200-299 signifies very unhealthy air; 300-500 is hazardous). The following chart lists the number of days in which the PSI exceeded 100 in several major urban metropolitan areas.

Metropolitan area	1980	1985	1990	1992	1993	1994	1995	1996	1997	Total, 1995-97
Atlanta	7	9	52	19	42	13	43	22	26	91
Bakersfield	N.A.	29	97	100	97	97	104	109	55	268
Baltimore	N.A.	21	29	23	48	41	36	28	30	94
Boston	8	3	7	9	6	10	8	2	8	18
Chicago	34	8	5	4	3	8	21	6	9	36
Cincinnati	N.A.	N.A.	19	3	13	19	22	11	11	44
Cleveland	N.A.	1	10	11	13	23	24	17	12	53
Dallas	19	15	24	11	11	15	36	12	15	63
Denver	35	38	11	8	3	2	2	0	0	2
Detroit	N.A.	2	11	8	5	13	14	13	12	39
El Paso	N.A.	24	22	11	9	8	5	7	3	15
Fresno, Calif.	N.A.	21	62	61	59	55	60	65	50	175
Houston	10	48	54	32	28	45	65	28	47	140
Indianapolis	N.A.	N.A.	9	7	9	22	19	13	12	44
Las Vegas	N.A.	55	22	6	9	14	4	5	0	9
Los Angeles	220	194	174	178	137	144	109	94	63	266
Miami	N.A.	5	1	3	6	1	2	1	3	6
Milwaukee	N.A.	N.A.	8	3	4	8	13	5	4	22
Minneapolis-St. Paul	N.A.	21	4	3	0	2	7	2	0	9
New York	119	61	37	11	19	21	19	15	23	57
Oakland, Calif.	N.A.	N.A.	4	3	4	3	12	11	0	23
Orange County, Calif.	N.A.	69	46	38	25	15	9	9	3	21
Philadelphia	52	25	39	24	50	26	30	22	32	84
Phoenix	N.A.	84	13	15	17	11	25	17	15	57
Pittsburgh	20	9	19	9	13	19	25	11	20	56
Riverside-San Bernardino, Calif.	N.A.	142	158	175	167	148	125	118	106	349
Sacramento, Calif.	N.A.	67	66	48	22	37	34	33	2	69
St. Louis	N.A.	10	24	16	9	32	35	20	15	70
San Diego	N.A.	54	97	66	57	45	47	31	14	92
San Francisco	2	5	0	0	0	0	2	0	0	2
Seattle	33	24	10	3	0	3	0	6	1	7
Ventura, Calif.	N.A.	19	70	55	44	64	66	62	44	172
Washington, D.C.	38	15	26	15	47	21	30	18	28	76

Note: Figures reflect data from selected EPA trend sites. Number of unhealthy days recorded by all active EPA monitoring sites may be slightly higher in some cities. N.A.= Not available. Source: Environmental Protection Agency, *National Air Quality and Emissions Trends Report, 1997* (January, 1999).

Carbon Monoxide in Metropolitan Areas

Cities in the U.S. have done an admirable job of cleaning up carbon monoxide pollution in the 1990s. In 1990, 26 metropolitan areas exceeded the National Ambient Air Quality Standards for carbon monoxide at least once. Los Angeles exceeded the standard a whopping 47 times, while Las Vegas exceeded it 17 times. But in 1997, only six metropolitan areas exceeded the standard more than once. Los Angeles and a monitoring station near California's Mexican border both exceeded the standard 12 times, while Fairbanks, Alaska exceeded it a total of nine times. The three other areas exceeded the standard only once or twice.

World Carbon Dioxide Emissions from Fossil Fuel Consumption, 1996

Rank, Country	Millions of metric tons	Rank, Country	Millions of metric tons
1. U.S.	1,469.52	6. Germany	234.16
2. China	801.26	7. United Kingdom	153.91
3. Russia	437.91	8. Canada	140.46
4. Japan	303.72	9. Italy	116.07
5. India	235.28	10. Korea	109.36

Note: 1 metric ton is equal to 2,204.62 pounds.
Source: U.S. Dept. of Energy, Energy Information Administration, *International Energy Annual, 1997.*

Ozone (O_3) Ground-level ozone is a colorless gas and the main component of smog. Unlike most other air pollutants, ozone is not emitted by factories or automobiles, but is formed by the interaction of volatile organic compounds (VOCs) and nitrous oxide. These reactions are stimulated by sunlight and temperature so that peak ozone levels occur typically during the warmer times of year. The severity of a smog problem in a given locale is directly related to the temperature and ultraviolet radiation intensity in that area. While the problems associated with ozone depletion (see "The Ozone Layer," above) and ground-level ozone are usually viewed separately, it is worth noting that as upper-atmosphere ozone is depleted, more ultraviolet radiation reaches the Earth and stimulates the production of ozone/smog.

Both VOCs and nitrous oxide are emitted by transportation and industrial sources as diverse as autos, chemical manufacturing, dry cleaners, paint shops, and other solvent-using industries. High levels of ozone affect people with impaired respiratory systems, such as asthmatics, and exposure to relatively low concentrations of ozone for only a few hours has been found to significantly reduce lung function in normal, healthy people during exercise. This is generally accompanied by symptoms including chest pain, coughing, sneezing, and pulmonary congestion. Ozone is also responsible each year for several billion dollars worth of domestic crop yield losses, and it causes noticeable damage to leaves in many crops and species of trees.

Lead (Pb)

People can be exposed to lead via air, diet, and ingestion of lead in soil and dust. Lead accumulates in the body in blood, bone, and soft tissue, and because it is not readily excreted, it also affects the kidneys, nervous system, and blood-forming organs. Excessive exposure to lead may cause seizures, mental retardation, and/or behavioral disorders. Even at low doses, lead exposure is harmful; infants and children are especially susceptible to low doses of lead and often suffer central nervous system damage.

Lead gasoline additives, nonferrous smelters, and battery plants are the most significant contributors to atmospheric lead emissions. The decline in the share of lead emissions from internal-combustion engines of all kinds is due primarily to the introduction of unleaded gasoline in 1975, for use in automobiles equipped with catalytic control devices, which reduce emissions of carbon monoxide, VOCs, and nitrogen oxides. Today more than 99.8 percent of the lead once added to gasoline in the United States has been removed.

Air pollution worldwide

The worst air pollution is undoubtedly in Asia, where wildfires burned unchecked throughout the summer of 1998, choking the air with thick toxic smoke and a haze across all of Southeast Asia that only went away with the onset of monsoon season. According to the World Health Organization, more than 1.5 million Asians die each year from the effects of air pollution alone, and another half million die from water pollution.

Anything over 100 micrograms of particles per cubic meter of air is considered dangerous, yet in cities like Taiyuan, China, and Delhi, India, the levels routinely top 500 micrograms. The threat is compounded by the fact that so many people in these areas cook indoors with coal briquettes. Particles in the air are a major cause of respiratory ailments in Asia, which in turn is the leading cause of death in China.

▶ ACID RAIN

Acid rain refers to acidic precipitation of all kinds, including rain, snow, and fog, as well as acidic dust particles. The main component of acid rain is sulfuric acid, a product of reactions of sulfur dioxide released

Ozone in Metropolitan Areas, 1992–97

The following areas have been classified by the EPA as having severe violations of ozone standards set by the Clean Air Act of 1990 (except for the Los Angeles South Coast Air Basin, Calif. area, which has been classified as an extreme violation). They are ranked by the number of days they exceeded standards in 1995–97.

Metropolitan area	Average number of days exceeding standards	
	1992–94	1995–97
Los Angeles South Coast Air Basin, Calif.	103.3	56.7
Southeast Desert, Calif.	47.5	24.3
Houston-Galveston-Brazoria, Tex.	6.5	14.9
Ventura County, Calif.	10.3	12.4
Sacramento Metro Area, Calif.	6.9	7.4
Baltimore, Md.	3.8	5.7
New York-No. New Jersey-Long Island-Conn.	4.4	4.7
Philadelphia, Pa-Wilmington, Del.-Trenton, N.J.	4.0	4.2
Chicago, Ill.-Gary, Ind.-Lake Co., Wis.	2.0	2.4
Milwaukee-Racine, Wis.	1.7	2.1

Note: The National ambient air quality standard for ozone is 0.12 parts per million (ppm) daily maximum one-hour average. Severe violations are defined as concentrations of 0.18 ppm-0.279 ppm; extreme violations are defined as concentrations of .28 ppm or more. **Source**: Environmental Protection Agency Office of Air Quality Planning and Standards, *Green Book, 1999.*

by industrial and power plants fueled by coal or oil. Another major agent of acid rain is nitrogen oxides, which form nitric acid and which are found in motor vehicle exhaust and in emissions from industrial plants that burn any fuel at high temperatures. Burning vegetation also produces nitric acid, as well as formic acid and acetic acid. Acid rain can travel great distances from its source: 10 percent to 80 percent increases in acidity have been detected as far away as 2,500 miles from a source.

Acid rain has been implicated in the destruction of lakes, the weathering of man-made structures, and the death of trees, crops, and animals. When acid rain winds up in lakes, it can increase the level of acidity to such an extent that the lake loses its ability to buffer the acidity with alkaline chemicals from the surrounding soil and rocks. How quickly this occurs is to some extent determined by the nature of the surrounding soil, which means that lakes in some regions are more vulnerable to the effects of acid rain than others. As lakes become more acidic, small invertebrates die off. This begins a reaction up the food chain: as the smallest organisms disappear, the food supply for larger vertebrates such as fish and frogs is depleted. Because lakes are not closed ecosystems, the demise of these organisms also affects land dwellers that depend on them, directly or indirectly, for survival.

A 1999 federal study revealed that regulation has succeeded in reducing harmful levels of sulfur dioxide in the air, but that the problem remains serious. At current rates, more than half of the 2,800 lakes in the Adirondacks will be too acidic to support life by the year 2040. The study also concludes that the San Gabriel Mountains near Los Angeles are already "saturated" with nitrogen, meaning that excess nitrogen is seeping into the surrounding waters.

▶ WATER POLLUTION

Although the bad effect of air pollution on health was suspected even earlier, the first proven environmental cause of illness was water pollution. In England, a famous demonstration by physician John Snow in

1854 showed that removing the handle of a pump could reduce the incidence of cholera by depriving people living near a contaminated well from using the water. Chlorine used for water purification was already known at that time, and by the 20th century most major cities in the United States provided treated water.

Problems not directly connected to health also were recognized in the 19th century. Mining in California was, in some locations, polluting the water supply so greatly that crops could not be grown; a law against using water in extracting ores was instituted in the state in 1884. Industrial water pollution was also recognized, although not stopped. Five years after Dr. Snow's famous demonstration, a new source of water pollution was introduced when the first oil well was drilled.

The 20th century brought with it additional forms of water pollution. A series of revolutions in agriculture included use of artificial fertilizers, introduction of long-lasting pesticides, and concentration of animal wastes. Each change also introduced new forms of water pollution from runoff—water from rain or snow that fails to sink into the soil. "Point sources," such as sewage pipes and factory waste ponds, were now supplemented with the "nonpoint sources" of farming.

In 1999, the EPA released its first ever national index on the quality of the nation's 2,111 watersheds. The index asserts that 21 percent of the watersheds have serious problems, including fish-consumption advisories, pollution, and loss of wetlands. Another 36 percent are of only moderate quality.

The 1972 Clean Water Act was intended to solve many of the nation's water pollution problems, but it has been only partially effective in doing so. In 1972, only about a third of the nation's rivers were safe for fishing and swimming. That number improved to more than 50 percent during the 1970s and 1980s, but by 1998, the levels of pollution had crept back up again. The primary cause was no longer industrial pollution, residue from mining, and untreated sewage; instead, nonpoint sources from runoff, both agricultural and municipal, had taken over as the older point sources were eliminated.

Drinking Water

Americans have for many years taken their drinking water for granted. But despite this complacency, there are many threats to the water supply. These include biological threats to health from contamination, dangerous chemicals in the water supply from a variety of sources, and toxic elements introduced by water treatment or defects in plumbing. A related problem is that high water levels during storms overwhelm both industrial and municipal water treatment. This last source is somewhat more easily controlled than other nonpoint pollution, and revisions of the Clean Water Act in 1987, which went into effect in 1992, attack this problem for urban runoff at the city and county levels.

The Safe Drinking Water Act Amendments of 1996 further strengthened and expanded drinking water protections. They increased standards for microbial contamination such as cryptosporidium, which has been the source of several disease outbreaks, including a 1993 instance in Milwaukee, in which more than 100 people died.

Many municipal water supply systems regularly are found to contain levels of bacterial contamination that exceed EPA standards. Most, but not all bacterial contamination stems from the use of surface waters—rivers, lakes, and reservoirs. The other major source of water is groundwater—subsurface water contained for the most part in small cavities, or pores, in rock or soil. One common way to obtain unpolluted groundwater is to dig deep wells that find "fossil" water that has been at those levels for thousands of years. Most shallow wells obtain their water from groundwater that recently was surface water and therefore subject to greater contamination.

Groundwater pollution is especially difficult to remedy. Almost all solutions are expensive and, in many cases, not feasible at any price. Such remedies include pumping detoxification agents into the ground or treating the water before use.

Groundwater can be contaminated by industrial pollutants stored or released in ways that put them in contact with the water supply; by leakage from underground storage of volatile chemicals, such as gasoline, cleaning fluid, or petroleum; and by seepage into the soil of agricultural pesticides. A privately funded review of federal and state water tests by the Environmental Working Group in 1994 that the water supplies used by 14.1 million Americans contain agricultural pesticides in amounts that would be banned if these levels were found in food.

Formerly one of the main sources of ground water contamination had been municipal landfills, but most of these are now sealed with clay liners to prevent seepage; and truly hazardous chemicals, such as mercury or lead from batteries or volatile organic compounds, are banned from landfills.

Some drinking water pollution takes place between the time the water comes from the well or from a surface source and the time it leaves faucets. For example, even though water from municipal plants is tested for lead and kept lead-free, service pipes, home plumbing, and some brass fixtures can leach lead into water, especially hot water. People who depend on private wells can have additional problems, as most of the pumps sold in recent years contain lead in brass or bronze parts that seeps into water contained in or surrounding the pump. Lead from plumbing or from pumps can be flushed from drinking or cooking water by letting the water run before use, but for water supplied by submerged pumps in deep wells, it may be necessary to run water for as long as 10 minutes to get to the lead-free supply.

Even municipal treatment of drinking water is suspected of potentially dangerous side effects. About 70 percent of all Americans drink water that has been disinfected by chlorination. But chlorine can react with organic material in water to form compounds such as chloroform that have been implicated in causing cancer in rats and mice. Except possibly for persons who have some reason for extra caution, however, the benefits of chlorination far outweigh any known danger.

Ocean Pollution

Pollution of the oceans disturbs marine ecosystems. It is thought to be the trigger for the algal growth that has all but eliminated the scallop fishery in Long Island Sound, for example. Other ocean fisheries in protected bays and sounds have also been damaged by pollution.

Ocean pollution from oil is primarily noted by the public when an oil well at sea is damaged or when an oil-carrying ship leaks large amounts of oil into the sea as a result of an accident like the 1989 Exxon *Valdez* disaster. Despite this perception, most oil pollution in the ocean actually comes from municipal and industrial runoff, cleaning of ships' bilges or tanks, and other routine events.

Ocean pollution is often in evidence on beaches. Tar balls from oil spills, plastic, and sometimes sewage wash up on beaches. Occasionally beaches have to be closed because of high bacteria counts in the water, making swimming hazardous.

Plastic, which generally does not break down in the ocean, is a hazard to larger organisms, such as endangered sea turtles. An international treaty prohibits disposal of plastic wastes that can kill or maim creatures that become entangled, but the treaty is very difficult to enforce.

Emissions Estimates for EPA-Monitored Pollutants, 1940-97 (thousand short tons)

Year	Carbon monoxide (CO)	Nitrogen oxides (NO$_x$)	Volatile organic compounds	Sulfur dioxide (SO$_2$)	Particulate matter (PM$_{10}$)	Lead (Pb)
1940	93,615	7,374	17,161	19,953	15,956	N.A.
1950	102,609	10,093	20,936	22,358	17,133	N.A.
1960	109,745	14,140	24,459	22,227	15,558	N.A.
1970	128,079	20,625	30,646	31,161	13,044[1]	219,471
1980	115,625	23,281	25,893	25,905	7,050[1]	74,956
1990	95,794	23,436	20,935	23,678	29,845	4,975
1995	89,151	23,768	20,558	19,189	26,760	3,924
1996	90,611	23,391	19,306	19,836	33,188	3,910
1997	87,451	25,582	19,214	20,371	33,581	3,915

1.Particulate matter totals before 1990 do not include estimates for fugitive dust, which arises from construction activities, mining and quarrying and paved road resuspension. It is the leading source of PM$_{10}$ emissions. **Source:** Environmental Protection Agency, *National Air Quality and Emissions Trends Report, 1997* (January, 1999).

Emissions Estimates for EPA-Monitored Pollutants By Source, 1997 (thousand short tons)

Source	Carbon monoxide (CO)	Nitrogen oxides (NO$_x$)	Volatile organic compounds	Sulfur dioxide (SO$_2$)	Particulate matter (PM$_{10}$)
Fuel combustion, Electric utility	406	6,178	51	13,082	290
Fuel combustion, Industrial	1,110	3,270	217	3,365	314
Fuel combustion, Other	3,301	1,276	593	813	497
Chemical & Allied Processing	1,287	167	458	301	70
Metals Processing	2,465	102	73	552	220
Petroleum & Related Industries	364	115	538	385	41
Other Industrial Processes	663	421	458	427	530
Solvent Utilization	6	3	6,483	1	6
Storage and Transport	26	6	1,377	2	114
Waste Disposal and Recycling	1,242	103	449	50	296
On-Road Vehicles	50,257	7,035	5,230	320	268
Non-Road Sources	16,755	4,560	2,430	1,061	466
Miscellaneous[1]	9,568	346	858	13	30,468
Total	87,451	23,582	19,214	20,371	33,581

Note: Some columns may not sum due to independent rounding. 1. Miscellaneous includes PM$_{10}$ natural sources like fugitive dust, which arises from construction activities, mining and quarrying and paved road resuspension. It is the leading source of PM$_{10}$ emissions. **Source:** Environmental Protection Agency, *National Air Quality and Emissions Trends Report, 1997* (January, 1999).

Oil Spills of 100,000 Tons or More

Date	Cause	Location	Barrels spilled
1942	German U-boats attacks on tankers after U.S. enters World War II	U.S., East Coast	590,000
1967	Tanker *Torrey Canyon* grounds	English Channel, off Land's End, UK	119,000
1970	Tanker *Othello* collides with another ship	Tralhavet Bay, Sweden	60,000-100,000
1972	Tanker *Sea Star* collides with another ship	Gulf of Oman	115,000
1976	Tanker *Urquiola* grounds	La Coruña, Spain	100,000
1978	Tanker *Amoco Cadiz* grounds	Northwest France	223,000
1979	Itox I oil well blows	Southern Gulf of Mexico	600,000
	Tankers *Atlantic Empress* and *Aegean Captain* collide	Off Trinidad and Tobago	300,000
1983	Blowout in Norwuz oil field	Persian Gulf	600,000
	Fire aboard tanker *Castillio de Beliver*	Off Cape Town, South Africa	250,000
1988	Tanker *Odyssey* founders	Off Nova Scotia, Canada	132,000
1991	Iraq begins deliberately dumping oil into Persian Gulf	Sea Island, Kuwait	1,450,000[1]
	Tanker *Haven* grounds	Genoa, Italy	140,000
	Tanker *ABT Summer* founders	700 mi. off Angola	260,000
1994	Pipeline bursts, oil enters rivers that flow into Arctic Ocean	Near Usinik, Russia	312,500

Note: One ton equals approximately 269 gallons or 6.4 barrels. For comparison, the 1989 *Exxon Valdez* grounding in Prince William Sound, Alaska, spilled 37,000 tons of oil. 1. Based on UN mission estimates. **Source:** International Tanker Owners Federation.

▶ SOLID WASTE

Many areas of the United States continue to face serious problems in safely and effectively managing the garbage they generate. As a nation, we are generating more trash than ever before, and as the generation of municipal solid waste (MSW) increases, the capacity to handle it is decreasing. Municipal solid waste is distinct from industrial wastes produced by factories, tailings from mines, construction and demolition waste, sludge from sewage treatment, and junked machinery.

Disposing of Solid Waste   The average person disposes of more than 4 pounds of garbage each day, up significantly from 1960, when per person disposal was 2.7 pounds. This garbage consists of paper (38 percent), yard trimmings (18 percent), metals (8 percent), plastic (8 percent), glass (7 percent), food waste (7 percent), and other materials (14 percent). There are four primary methods of dealing with this waste: putting it in landfills, incinerating it, recycling it, and composting. But a fifth option, source reduction, may be the most effective way of reducing the nation's volume of MSW, which totals more than 200 million tons per year.

Landfills   By far the greatest amount of MSW is sent to MSW landfills, of which there were 3,581 in 1995, a drop from 5,345 in 1992. Landfills are the cheapest method of disposing of MSW but they pose a number of environmental problems. Because most landfills are dry, they preserve garbage by cutting it off from the rotting influences of air and moisture. Even biodegradable materials do not decay; newspapers 40 years old can still be read and hot dogs thrown out years before look more or less unchanged.

EPA regulations favor dry landfills for two reasons. As biodegradation in wet landfills occurs there is a buildup of hazardous methane gas, and contaminated water leaching out of landfills (leachate) can pollute the surrounding groundwater. But wet landfills have their supporters, who argue that by enhancing decay, a landfill's biological life can be compressed from 40-to-50 years to 5-to-10 years. Since landfills can contain hundreds of hazardous chemicals, they require continuous monitoring anyway; so shortening their active life can yield significant savings. Moreover, by decreasing the volume of trash through biodegradation, landfills can be kept open longer. This is important because some estimates indicate that 80 percent of the nation's landfills will be closed within 20 years, and people are increasingly adamant about not having landfills in their communities, which makes it harder to site new landfills.

Incineration/combustion   One popular method of disposing of municipal waste used to be simply to burn it. In the 1940s there were approximately 700 municipal incinerators in the United States. Despite the efficiency with which they reduced the volume of waste, they stank, their stacks emitted sizable particles of ash, and they produced noxious gases. For these aesthetic rather than environmental reasons, their numbers declined dramatically in the 1950s. By the time of the Clean Air Act of 1970, there were only 67 incinerators still in operation—most with no energy recovery and no air pollution controls.

Incinerator use increased in the 1980s and early 1990s as space for landfills became scarce, and as the energy produced by incineration became a valuable commodity. But in May, 1994, the U.S. Supreme Court ruled that waste from incinerators had to be treated as toxic on the same basis as any other waste. This was a blow because most incinerator ash contains dioxins that are produced by combustion and heavy metals such as lead, cadmium, and mercury, which do not burn.

In that same month, the Court ruled that localities could not prevent incinerators from taking waste away from incinerators if the landfills offered better bargains. Because landfill was usually cheaper, few chose to incinerate their waste, and few municipalities could afford to subsidize the cost of incinerators. Within six months of the Court's decision, plans for 77 proposed incinerators were canceled.

Recycling/composting   In 1995, Americans generated 208 million tons of MSW—4.3 pounds per person per day. Recycling and composting recovered 27 percent of these wastes. Recovery of paper and paperboard reached 40 percent (32.6 million tons), accounting for half of the total MSW recovered. Metal recovery reached 38.9 percent (6.2 million tons), yard trimmings 30.3 percent (9 million tons), glass 24.5 percent (3.1 million tons), and plastics 5.1 percent (1 million tons). There were more than 7,000 curbside recycling programs as well as nearly 9,000 drop-off centers for recyclables.

In addition to significantly reducing the volume of wastes that winds up in landfills and incinerators, recycling and composting limit pollution and unnecessary depletion of natural resources. They also have the potential to generate revenues from the sale of secondary materials. According to the EPA, the 56 million tons of materials recovered in the United States in 1995 through recycling (including composting) had a total market value of more than $3.6 billion. Costs of recycling are still high, but these are expected to decline as recycling programs mature and become fully integrated with the total MSW management system. The EPA has set a nationwide recycling goal of 35 percent by the year 2005.

Source reduction   Many experts believe that the key to solving the municipal waste problem is source reduction—minimizing the volume of products and the toxins they contain, and extending their useful life. Removal of toxins enhances the safety of recycling, landfilling, and combustion, while volume reduction helps to extend the capacity of existing waste systems.

A broad variety of products and packaging that reduce waste and save money have been developed. By reducing the textured design on napkins, for example, the McDonald's Corporation found that it could fit 23 percent more napkins into a shipping container, saving 294,000 pounds of corrugated cardboard and 150 truckload shipments annually.

▶ HAZARDOUS WASTE

Superfund   In 1980, Congress enacted the Comprehensive Environmental Response, Compensation, and Liability Act (CERCLA), better known as the Superfund, a $1.6 billion, five-year program to clean up thousands of hazardous waste sites. The fund was renewed in 1986 and again in 1991. The EPA, which administers the Superfund, estimated in 1996 that 70 million Americans lived within 4 miles of a toxic waste site.

The EPA evaluates hazardous waste sites for their levels of soil and water contamination, the mobility of toxins, and their proximity to human food supplies. (Contamination of petroleum, however, is excluded from this evaluation.) It then ranks the sites on a numerically based system that factors in risks to groundwater, surface water, and air. The highest ranking sites are placed on the EPA's National Priorities List (NPL). CERCLA also allows states and territories to designate one top-priority site regardless of its score; there are several such sites that would not make the NPL on the basis of their numerical score alone.

Once the EPA deems a site a national priority, it can take two types of action. It can remove the hazard in an emergency action limited to one year and/or $2 million. Or it can try to compel the individual or company responsible for the problem to provide a longterm solution.

But the second option is rarely exercised. Many of the original polluters are bankrupt or cannot be found when presented with a bill for the cleanup (which averages $25–$30 million, according to the EPA). By February, 1998 the EPA had cleaned up 590 sites, but the total number of sites on the NPL has remained around 1,200 since 1990. And in 23 states, a site from the first list (issued in September, 1983), was still the state's top cleanup priority (see the accompanying table).

Nuclear Waste   Nuclear waste in the United States comes from nuclear weapons production facilities, nuclear power plants, medical equipment (primarily used in radiation treatments), industrial sources of radioactivity used as a more powerful alternative to X rays, and residues from uranium mining. Nuclear waste is often grouped into two categories, labeled "low-level" and "high-level." Low-level waste is slightly radioactive, often from exposure to a high-level source. High-level waste is often grouped as either civilian, mainly spent fuel from nuclear reactors, or military, wastes produced in the manufacture of nuclear weapons.

The problem with nuclear waste is that it is radioactive and can remain that way for years—in some cases, thousands of years. Early methods of disposal included dumping the wastes at sea and suspending them in a liquid or in cement and injecting the radioactive combination into wells. The United States was among the signatories of a 1976 international convention banning ocean dumping and stopped deep-well injection in 1984.

Current plans call for consortiums of states to develop sites for storage of low-level wastes. One such "temporary" site is in Barnwell County, S.C., which has handled low-level waste for 37 states since 1970. Meanwhile, the federal government continues to search for suitable sites for storage of high-level wastes from nuclear power plants and for very long-lived radioactive materials from weapons production. For the time being, these wastes remain on the sites where they were generated.

In 1998, the EPA certified the Department of Energy's Waste Isolation Pilot Plan in Carlsbad, N.M., the nation's first deep-underground facility for disposal of transuranic waste generated from defense activities. (Transuranic wastes consist primarily of sludges, tools, rags, glassware, and protective clothing that has been contaminated with radioactive elements from weapons production.) The facility is approximately

Top Priority Superfund Site by State, 1998

State	Site	Location	When listed
California	Stringfellow	Imperial	Sept. 1983
Colorado	Marshall Landfill	Boulder County	Sept. 1983
Connecticut	Laurel Park Inc.	Naugatuck Borough	Sept. 1983
Delaware	Tybouts Corner Landfill	New Castle County	Sept. 1983
Georgia	LCP Chemicals Georgia	Brunswick	Sept. 1995
Illinois	Outboard Marine Corp.	Waukegan	Sept. 1983
Indiana	Seymour Recycling Corp.	Seymour	Sept. 1983
Louisiana	Old Inger Oil Refinery	Darrow	Sept. 1983
Massachusetts	New Bedford Site	New Bedford	Sept. 1983
Michigan	Gratiot County Landfill	St. Louis	Sept. 1983
Minnesota	Reilly Tar & Chemical	St. Louis Park	Sept. 1983
Missouri	Ellisville Site	Ellisville	Sept. 1983
New Hampshire	Sylvester	Nashua	Sept. 1983
New Jersey	Price Landfill	Pleasantville	Sept. 1983
New Mexico	South Valley	Albuquerque	Sept. 1983
New York	Pollution Abatement Services	Oswego	Sept. 1983
Ohio	Chem-Dyne	Hamilton	Sept. 1983
Pennsylvania	McAdoo Associates	McAdoo Borough	Sept. 1983
Rhode Island	Picillo Farm	Coventry	Sept. 1983
South Carolina	SCRDI Bluff Road	Columbia	Sept. 1983
Texas	Motco, Inc.	La Marque	Sept. 1983
Utah	Rose Park Sludge Pit	Salt Lake City	Sept. 1983
Vermont	Pine Street Canal	Burlington	Sept. 1983
Washington	Boomsnub/Airco	Vancouver	Apr., 1995
West Virginia	West Virginia Ordnance (US Army)	Point Pleasant	Sept. 1983
Wisconsin	N.W. Mauthe Co., Inc.	Appleton	Mar. 1989

Note: Not every state designates a top priority.   **Source:** Environmental Protection Agency, *National Priorities List* (February, 1998).

States with the Most NPL Hazardous Waste Sites, 1998

State	Nonfederal	Federal	Total
New Jersey	102	6	108
Pennsylvania	91	6	97
California	68	23	91
New York	75	4	79
Michigan	72	0	72
Florida	47	6	53
Washington	33	14	47
Wisconsin	39	0	39
Illinois	34	4	38
Ohio	30	3	33
Oklahoma	30	3	33

Source: Environmental Protection Agency, *National Priorities List, Supplementary Materials,* (February, 1998).

Superfund Hazardous Waste Sites, 1981–99

Date	Number of sites	Date	Number of sites
Oct. 23, 1981	115[1]	Feb., 1992	1,183
Dec. 30, 1982	418[1]	May 10, 1993	1,201
Sept. 8, 1983	406	Feb. 23, 1994	1,190
Oct. 15, 1984	538	Sept. 29, 1995	1,232
June 10, 1986	703	June 17, 1996	1,227
July 22, 1987	802	April, 1997	1,208
Oct. 4, 1989	981	Feb. 1998	1,197
Feb. 21, 1990	1,081	July 22, 1999	1,226
Feb. 11, 1991	1,189		

1. Proposed sites only. Final sites not calculated until release of first National Priorities list in 1983.   **Source:** Environmental Protection Agency, *National Priorities List, Supplementary Materials.* (July, 1999).

2,100 feet (640 meters) underground in excavated, natural salt formations. The first shipment of transuranic waste was delivered to the facility in March of 1999. By 2010, shipments from 23 military waste sites from across the nation to this site will reduce the number of Americans living within 50 miles of nuclear waste from 61 million to 4 million. Of course, the 113,000 people living within 50 miles of Carlsbad (as well as many New Mexicans beyond that radius) were understandably opposed, and fought its operation since the site was first proposed in 1974.

The Nuclear Regulatory Commission is the agency charged with monitoring the disposal of waste generated by civilian-operated nuclear reactors. However, most of the nuclear waste in the United States is the by-product of the federal government's nuclear weapons programs. Disposal and monitoring of this waste—which includes millions of cubic yards of contaminated soil and other debris at more than 100 sites in 32 states and the Marshall Islands—is the responsibility of the Department of Energy, the Department of Defense, the Nuclear Waste Technical Review Board, and the Office of the Nuclear Waste Negotiator. Total cost of the cleanup could be about $300-$400 billion over 30 years.

▶ HABITATS

The place where a species lives and its surroundings, both living and non-living, is called a habitat. Broadly speaking, habitats include forests, grasslands, deserts, tundra, and wetlands. But there are many specific types of habitats within each of these categories. The habitat of a giant panda, for example, is a bamboo forest in China, not a pine forest in Canada; that of a tuna is the open ocean, not a Florida lake.

When a species' habitat is destroyed or altered, the species may suffer dramatic population declines. For example, because so much of North America's native grasslands have been replaced by farms and other developments, many songbirds have been left without homes and food, and their populations have decreased. Similarly, destruction of China's bamboo forests threaten the giant panda with extinction.

When a species becomes extinct, the Earth's biodiversity is diminished. Biodiversity is all the organisms in the world or in a particular habitat, including all their individual variations. Loss of biodiversity affects humans as well as the threatened species. For example, all major food crops depend on new genetic material from the wild to remain healthy and productive. Noted the 1992 U.N. Earth Summit report, "Our planet's essential goods and services depend on the variety and variability of genes, species, populations and ecosystems."

The major reasons for loss of biological diversity are habitat destruction and modification, overhunting and overfishing, climate change, pollution, and the introduction of so-called alien species (non-native species, such as African tulip trees in Hawaii and Amazon water hyacinths in Africa's Lake Victoria; native species often are unable to compete with the introduced species).

▶ RAIN FORESTS

Rain forests are defined as forests that grow in regions that receive more than 70 inches (1.8 meters) of rain each year. Some rain forests occur in temperate places, such as southern Chile or the northwest coast of North America, but the majority are found in the tropics. Tropical rain forests cover more than 2 billion acres (0.8 billion hectares) or about 7 percent of the Earth's land surface. They are found in Central and South America, equatorial Africa, Southeast Asia, and northeastern Australia.

It is estimated that the world may be losing more than 49 million acres (20 million hectares) of tropical forest each year. As the 1990s began, Brazil was losing 12.5-22.5 million acres (5-9 million hectares) of rain forest annually; India was losing 3.7 million acres (1.5 million hectares); and Indonesia was losing 2.2 million acres (0.9 million hectares). Other countries experiencing rapid losses included Myanmar, Costa Rica, Sri Lanka, Vietnam, Thailand, the Philippines, and Ghana.

Tropical rain forests are lush habitats, filled with a greater variety of organisms than any other type of habitat. According to a U.S. National Academy of Sciences report, a typical patch of rain forest covering four square miles (10.4 km^2) contains 750 species of trees, 750 species of other plants, 125 species of mammals, 400 species of birds, 100 species of reptiles, and 60 species of amphibians.

The dominant plants in a tropical rain forest are broad-leaved evergreens, while northern-hemisphere temperate rain forests are filled with needle-leaved conifers. In both, the tallest trees form a dense canopy high above the forest floor. Vines climb up the trees in search of sunlight. In a tropical rain forest, nonparasitic plants grow high in the canopy, using the large trees as perches. In both types of forest, the floor is in deep shade; comparatively few shrubs and grasses grow there.

The rich plant life supports food chains that include many of the world's most spectacular animals: brightly colored frogs, fierce harpy eagles, agile monkeys, powerful tigers, slow-moving sloths, and huge columns of army ants, among many others.

While the diversity of plant life in rain forests is rich, the soil generally is not. The lush plants take up so much of the nutrients in rain forests that little is left for the soil below. A study of a rain forest in Venezuela found that 75 percent of the nutrients were in living organisms like plants and trees, 17 percent were in debris, and only 8 percent were in the soil. When an organism dies and decomposes in a rain forest, the nutrients in its cells are quickly absorbed by nearby plants.

Deforestation has many sources. Individuals often cut down rain forest trees for firewood and to clear land on which to raise crops, build ranches, and raise cattle. But erosion and poor soil fertility soon make these farms and ranches worthless. Large commercial operations deforest vast areas for lumber, paper, and other products, much of which are exported to pay debts owed to foreign governments and banks. Development projects such as roads, hydroelectric dams, and mines also destroy large areas of rain forest.

▶ WETLANDS

A wetland is a location other than a river, lake, or open ocean in which the soil for at least part of the year contains as much water as it will hold (the soil is saturated with water). Saturated soil often slows decomposition of organic matter, resulting in a thin mud or muck, or in the decayed plant remains known as peat. Common names for wetlands include: **Potholes,** which are dry land most of the year, but seasonally become shallow ponds; **Tidal flats,** which are underwater at high tide but become muddy land at low tide; **Permafrost,** which is saturated soil that is frozen most of the year at the surface, and year-round below the surface; **Bogs,** which contain saturated soil and organic material all year, but have little or no standing water; **Marshes,** which contain standing shallow water and low vegetation; and **Swamps,** where trees grow on small hillocks surrounded by standing water. Often these informal categories overlap in a given wetland.

Wetlands produce numerous invaluable benefits. They provide a natural means of flood control, absorbing water from nearby rivers and lakes during periods of high runoff. This buffers the impact of storms and reduces shoreline erosion, thereby protecting against the loss of life and property. And by filtering out pollutants and trapping sediment, wetlands help maintain water quality.

Wetlands are the nurseries for many fish, almost all amphibians, and various birds and mammals. For instance, coastal wetlands are spawning grounds and nurseries for more than two-thirds of U.S. commercial fisheries, a $10 billion a year industry.

Despite all the benefits associated with wetlands, the definition of what is and is not a wetland is still a bone of contention among environmentalists (who would like to preserve the swampy areas), developers (who would like to drain them and erect housing complexes), and farmers (who would like to divert the water to their crops). In 1987, the U.S. Army Corp. of Engineers defined a wetland as "any ground that has mucky or peat-based soils, nourishes specific plant life, and is saturated with water at least seven days a year." Partisans on all sides of the issue have sought since then to modify that definition. Since colonial days, the contiguous United States has lost 53 percent of its wetlands, and now retains just under 104 million acres (42 million hectares). The rate of decline has slowed in recent years, but it is still significant: A 1997 report by the U.S. Fish and Wildlife Service estimated that the U.S. lost an average of 117,000 acres (47,000 hectares) of wetlands every year between 1985 and 1995.

The majority of the nation's wetlands are located in Alaska (170 to 200 million acres). Ohio, Indiana, Iowa, and California have lost the greatest percentage of their wetlands, but the wet states of Florida and Louisiana have lost the greatest total number of acres of wetlands.

ENDANGERED SPECIES

A species is a specific kind of organism, such as the common earthworm, the daffodil, the American opossum, or the human. All told there are about 1.4 million classified species of all kinds, including plants, microorganisms, mammals, and fish. This is thought to represent no more than about 10 percent of all species. (And if the results of some surveys of rain forest canopies in Panama are correct, there may be as many as 30 million insect species alone.) Since life developed more than 600 million years ago, innumerable species have appeared and become extinct. Today, biological diversity faces a rate of species destruction greater than any since the mass extinctions of the dinosaurs 65 million years ago.

Animal and plant species are threatened on a number of fronts. Their natural habitats face destruction through deforestation, wetlands loss, and urban sprawl, and are also affected by processes that derive from global warming such as shifting climate and vegetation zones. Another problem is the shift to "monocultures" in agriculture, producing only one strain of crop for food.

International controls

The U.S. Endangered Species Act of 1966 is the chief bulwark protecting species in the United States. The United States is also a signatory to international treaties that protect species. The Convention on International Trade in Endangered Species of Wild Fauna and Flora (CITES) has been in force since 1975. Signed by more than 120 nations, it lists species for which international trade in the live organisms, meat, lumber, or other parts of species is banned or restricted. While smugglers are thought to violate CITES restrictions regularly in what is believed to be a $5 billion annual illegal trade, CITES continues to be one of the main forces in species preservation.

Supplementing the CITES bans on international acts against species is the Convention on Biodiversity, agreed to at the 1992 Earth Summit in Rio de Janeiro. Ratified by 161 countries (though not the U.S.), this treaty commits nations to protect and preserve species and habitats within their own borders.

Other international treaties affect more limited interests. The International Whaling Commission, with 40 members currently, has been in business since

Endangered and Threatened Species, 1999

Group	Endangered		Threatened		Total
	U.S.	Foreign	U.S.	Foreign	Listed
Mammals	60	251	8	16	335
Birds	75	178	15	6	274
Reptiles	14	65	21	14	114
Amphibians	9	8	7	1	25
Fishes	70	11	40	0	121
Snails	18	1	10	0	29
Clams	61	2	8	0	71
Crustaceans	17	0	3	0	20
Insects	28	4	9	0	41
Arachnids	5	0	0	0	5
Total Animals	357	520	121	37	1,035
Flowering Plants	540	1	132	0	673
Conifers	2	0	1	2	5
Ferns and others	26	0	2	0	28
Total Plants	568	1	135	2	706
Total Species	925	521	256	39	1,741

Note: Separate populations of a species, listed both as endangered and threatened, are tallied only once, for the endangered population only. The dual status species include Steller sea lion, gray wolf, piping plover, roseate tern, green sea turtle, olive ridley sea turtle, bull trout, chinook salmon, and steelhead in the U.S., and argali, chimpanzee, leopard, and saltwater crocodile elsewhere.
Source: U.S. Fish and Wildlife Service, *Box Score of U.S. List of Endangered and Threatened Species*, March 31, 1999.

Endangered and Threatened Species, 1967–99

Year	Listings		Year	Listings	
	New[1]	Total		New[1]	Total
1967	78	78	1984	48	880
1968	0	78	1985	61	941
1969	0	78	1986	46	987
1970	323	401	1987	60	1,047
1971	0	401	1988	46	1093
1972	9	410	1989	35	1128
1973	21	431	1990	53	1181
1974	3	434	1991	86	1267
1975	10	444	1992	82	1,349
1976	194	638	1993	73	1,422
1977	20	658	1994	128	1,550
1978	36	694	1995	49	1,599
1979	69	763	1996	0	1,523
1980	23	786	1997	117	1,640
1981	4	790	1998	54	1,694
1982	13	803	1999	47	1,741
1983	29	832			

Note: As of March 31, 1999. Separate populations of a species, listed both as endangered and threatened, are tallied twice.
1. Net new listings.
Source: U.S. Fish and Wildlife Service, unpublished data.

1949. The commission has probably saved whales from extinction with its near-total ban on whaling since the late 1980s. (Despite this moratorium, however, Norway and Japan have each killed hundreds of whales annually since the early 1990s; Norway, for example, authorized the killing of 425 minke whales in 1996.) Other groups, such as the 10-nation Inter-American Tropical Tuna Commission, are modeled on the whaling group.

To reverse the trend toward species extinction, governments around the world have set aside a total of about 425 million hectares (about 16.4 million square miles) of protected lands in about 3,500 parks and preserves. In addition, many countries try to identify and improve the status of species threatened with extinction.

The efforts come none too soon. In 1997, the World Conservation Union released its first-ever comprehensive listing of threatened and endangered plants worldwide. Entitled the Red List of Threatened Plants, it found that nearly 34,000 species of the 270,000 known vascular plants, or one of every eight species, is threatened with extinction.

▶ SELECTED ENDANGERED MAMMALS OF THE WORLD

Although the list of endangered species includes plants and animals of every type, it is the growing group of endangered mammals that have been of special interest and concern to both conservationists and the general public. The World Conservation Union also maintains a Red List of Endangered Animals, which in 1996 indicated that 1,096 mammals (nearly one-fourth of all known species) are considered threatened: 612 are listed as vulnerable, 315 as endangered, and 169 as critically endangered. The "critically endangered," a term indicating that a species' numbers have declined by at least 80 percent, include:

Bandicoot, eastern barred *(Perameles gunnii)* Range: Australia
Bat, Bulmer's fruit *(Aproteles bulmera)* Range: Papua New Guinea
Bat, Pemba flying fox *(Pteropus voeltzkowi)* Range: Tanzania
Bear, Baluchistan *(Ursus thibetanus gedrosianus)* Range: Iran, Pakistan
Chinchilla, short-tailed *(Chinchilla brevicaudata)* Range: Andes of South America
Deer, Pere David's *(Elaphurus davidianus)* Range: China
Gazelle, acacia *(Gazella gazella acaciae)* Range: Israel
Gazelle, Przewalski's *(Procapra przewalskii)* Range: China
Gibbon, silvery *(Hylobates moloch)* Range: Indonesia
Goat, Chiltan *(Capra aegagrus chialtanensis)* Range: Pakistan
Hog, pygmy *(Sus salvanius)* Range: Himalayas of Asia
Hutia, large-eared *(Mesocapromys auritus)* Range: Cuba
Lemur, golden bamboo *(Hapalemur aureus)* Range: Madagascar
Leopard, North African *(Panthera pardus panthera)* Range: North Africa
Mole, Juliana's golden *(Amblysomus julianae)* Range: South Africa
Monkey, Colombian woolly *(Lagothrix lagotricha lugens)* Range: northern South America
Monkey, Northern brown howling *(Alouata fusca fusca)* Range: Brazil
Oryx, scimitar-horned *(Oryx dammah)* Range: northern Africa, Israel
Pika, Helan Shan *(Ochotona helanshanensis)* Range: China
Potoroo, Gilbert's *(Potorous gilbertii)* Range: Australia
Pronghorn, Baja California *(Antilocapra americana peninsularis)* Range: Mexico
Rabbit, Omiltemi *(Sylvilagus insonus)* Range: Mexico
Rhinoceros, black *(Diceros bicornis)* Range: Sub-saharan Africa
Rhinoceros, Javan *(Rhinoceros sondaicus)* Range: Southeast Asia
Seal, Mediterranean monk *(Monachus monachus)* Range: Mediterranean and Black seas
Shrew, Gansu *(Sorex cansulus)* Range: China
Sika, Ryukyu *(Cervus nippon keramae)* Range: China, Japan
Tamarin, black-faced *(Leontopithecus caissara)* Range: Brazil
Tamarin, golden lion *(Leontopithecus rosalia)* Range: Brazil
Tiger, Amur *(Panthera tigris altaica)* Range: Asia
Tiger, South China *(Panthera tigris amoyensis)* Range:China
Titi, northern Bahian blond *(Callicebus personatus barbarabrownae)* Brazil
Vaquita *(Phocoena sinus)* Range: eastern central Pacific
Wombat, northern hairy-nosed *(Lasiorhinus krefftii)* Range: Australia

▶ ENDANGERED ANIMALS IN THE UNITED STATES

Although the world's attention is often on large endangered mammals from Africa or the oceans, the United States is home to hundreds of endangered species and subspecies. A subspecies, sometimes called a race, is a local population of a given animal that has some distinctive trait, such as size or color, that sets it apart from the main species.

Many endangered species and subspecies, especially birds, live on islands. Of the 100 or so known species of birds that have become extinct since 1600, 85 lived on islands. Because islands have small populations, limited habitats, and allow the introduction of new species easily, they are especially vulnerable environments.

Since the Endangered and Threatened Wildlife and Plants listing was started in 1967, at least seven listed species have become extinct: the Tecopa pupfish (*Cyprinodon nevadensis calidae*, 1982), the longjaw cisco (*Coregonus alpenae*, 1983), the blue pike (*Stizostedion vitreum glaucum*, 1983), the Santa Barbara song sparrow (*Melospiza melodia graminea*, 1983), Sampson's pearly mussel (*Epioblasma (=Dysnomia) sampsoni*, 1984), the Amistad gambusia (*Gambusia amistadensis*, 1987), and the dusky seaside sparrow (*Ammodramus (=Ammospiza) maritimus nigrescens*, 1990). Three species listed as either threatened or endangered have recovered sufficiently to be removed from the list altogether: the Palau dove (*Gallicolumba canifrons*, 1985), the Palau fantail or Old World fly catcher (*Rhipidura lepida*, 1985), and the Palau owl (*Pyroglaux (=Otus) podargina*, 1985).

In the United States, species are classified as threatened or endangered by the U.S. Fish and Wildlife service in accordance with the 1973 Endangered Species Act. The list of endangered species maintained by the Department of the Interior goes back to the original Endangered Species Act of 1966. The first list of endangered species, in March 1967, included 78 species. The 957th species, the California red-legged frog (*arana aurora draytonii*), was added in 1996. Species listed are protected in various ways, most specifically by a prohibition against killing them. Also, a critical habitat can be protected against change if the change would contribute to species extinction.

Animals in the U.S. Officially Listed as Endangered, 1999

MAMMALS

Bat, gray *(Myotis grisescens)* Found in central and southeastern U.S.

Bat, Hawaiian hoary *(Lasirius cinereus semotus)* Related to hair-tailed bats found on the mainland of the Americas.

Bat, Indiana *(Myotis sodali)* Found in both East and Midwest.

Bat, lesser (=Sanborn's) long-nosed *(Leptonycteris sanborni (=yerbabuenae))* Found in New Mexico, Texas, Mexico, and Central America.

Bat, Mexican long-nosed *(Leptonycternis nivali)* Found in New Mexico, Texas, and Central America, as well as Mexico.

Bat, Ozark big-eared *(Plecotus townsendii ingen)* Lives in caves in Missouri, Oklahoma, and Arkansas.

Bat, Virginia big-eared *(Plecotus townsendii virginianus)* A subspecies of big-eared bat found in Kentucky, North Carolina, West Virginia, and Virginia.

Caribou, woodland *(Rangifer tarandus caribou)* Endangered in Washington, Idaho, and Canada.

Deer, Columbian white-tailed *(Odocoileus virginanus leucurus)* Subspecies of white-tailed deer found in Florida.

Deer, key *(Odocoileus virginanus clavium)* Subspecies of white-tailed deer found in Florida.

Ferret, black-footed *(Mustela nigripes)* Found in Western U.S.

Fox, San Joaquin, kit *(Vulpes macrotis mutica)* California subspecies of kit fox; smaller than red fox.

Jaguar *(Panthera onca)* Found in Western U.S.

Jaguarundi *(Felis jagouaroundi cacomitli)* Found in Texas and Mexico; northern subspecies of small wildcat.

Jaguarundi *(Felis jagouaroundi tolteca)* Subspecies of small wildcat found in Mexico & Arizona.

Kangaroo rat, Fresno *(Dipodomys nitratoides exilis)* Historic range: California.

Kangaroo rat, giant *(Dipodomys ingens)* Historic range: California.

Kangaroo rat, Morro Bay *(Dipodomys heermanni morroensis)* Historic range: California.

Kangaroo rat, San Bernardino Merriam's *(Dipodomys merriami parvus)* Historic range: California.

Kangaroo rat, Stephen's *(Dipodomys stephensi (incl. D. cascus)* Historic range: California.

Kangaroo rat, Tipton *(Dipodomys nitratoides nitratoides)* Historic range: California.

Manatee, West Indian (=Florida) *(Trichechus manatus)* Large plant-eating water mammal believed to have been the inspiration for the mermaid legend.

Mountain beaver, Point Arena *(Aplodontia rufa nigra)* Found in California.

Mouse, Alabama beach *(Peromyscus polionotus ammobates)* Subspecies of white-footed beach mouse found in Alabama.

Mouse, Anastasia Island beach *(Peromyscus polionotus phasma)* Subspecies of white-footed beach mouse found in Florida.

Mouse, Choctawhatchee beach *(Peromyscus polionotus allophrys)* Subspecies of white-footed beach mouse found in Florida.

Mouse, Key Largo coton *(Peromyscus gossypinus allapaticola)* Subspecies of white-footed beach mouse found in Florida.

Mouse, Pacific pocket *(Perognathus longimembris pacificus)* Found in California.

Mouse, Perdido Key beach *(Peromyscus polionotus trissyllepsis)* Subspecies of white-footed beach mouse found in Alabama and Florida.

Mouse, Saint Andrew beach *(Peromyscus polionotus peninsularis)* Found in Florida.

Mouse, salt marsh harvest *(Reithrodontomys raviventris)* A species of American harvest mouse found only in California.

Ocelot *(Felis pardalis)* This small spotted cat is found in Arizona and Texas, but is endangered throughout Central and South America as well.

Panther, Florida *(Felis concolor coryi)* Formerly found in much of the American southeast, now confined to Florida.

Pronghorn, Sonoran *(Antilocapra americana sonoriensis)* A desert subspecies of the pronghorn found in Arizona and Mexico.

Rabbit, Lower Keys *(Sylvilagus palustris hefneri)* Found in Florida Keys.

Rice rat (=silver rice rat) *(Oryzomys palustris natator (=O. argentatus))* Species found in Florida Keys west of the 7-mile Bridge.

Seal, Hawaiian monk *(Monachus schauinslandi)* Related species in Caribbean and Meditterranean also endangered.

Sheep, bighorn *(Ovis canadensis)* Found in the western United States, especially in California's mountains.

Squirrel, Carolina northern flying *(Glaucomys sabrinus coloratus)* A subspecies of flying squirrel found in North Carolina and Tennessee.

Squirrel, Delmarva Peninsula fox *(Sciurus niger cinereus)* A subspecies of fox squirrel found in eastern Pennsylvania and Delmarva Peninsula.

Squirrel, Mt. Graham red *(Tamiasciurus hudsonicus grahamensis)* Historic range: Arizona.

Squirrel, Virginia northern flying *(Glaucomys sabrinus fuscus)* A subspecies of flying squirrel found in Virginia and West Virginia.

Vole, Amargosa *(Microtus californicus scirpensis)* California subspecies of vole.

Vole, Florida salt marsh *(Microtus pennsylvanicus dukecampbelli)* Florida subspecies of vole.

Vole, Hualapai Mexican *(Microtus mexicanus hualpaiensis)* Arizona subspecies of the Mexican vole.

Whale, gray *(Eschrichtius robustus)* Found in North Pacific Ocean.

Wolf, gray *(Canis lupis)* Most common wolf; endangered throughout continental U.S., except for Minnesota, where it is threatened.

Wolf, red *(Canis rufus)* Endangered throughout the southeastern U.S.

Woodrat, Key Largo *(Neotoma floridana smalii)* Historic range: Florida.

BIRDS

'Akepa, Hawaii (honeycreeper) *(Loxops coccineus coccineus)* Subspecies of 1 of the 22 known species of Hawaiian honeycreepers, 8 species are extinct and another 8 threatened or endangered.

'Akepa, Maui (honeycreeper) *(Loxops coccineus ochraceus)* Subspecies of Akepa found on Maui.

'Akialoa, Kauai (honeycreeper) *(Hemignathus procerus)* Species of Hawaiian honeycreeper.

'Akiapolaau (honeycreeper) *(Hemignathus munroi (=wilsoni)* Species of Hawaiian honeycreeper.

Blackbird, yellow-shouldered *(Agelaius zanthomus)* Relative of common red-winged blackbird.

Bobwhite, masked (quail) *(Colinus virginianus ridgwayi)* Subspecies of the common bobwhite found in Sonora desert of Arizona and Mexico.

Condor, California *(Gymnogyps californianus)* Species now bred in captivity, but it is slowly being reintroduced into the wild.

Coot, Hawaiian (=alae keo keo) *(Fulica americana alai)* Hawaiian subspecies of the common American coot.

Crane, Mississippi sandhill *(Grus canadensis pulla)* Subspecies of the sandhill crane.

Crane, whooping *(Grus americana)* Among the most famous endangered species; making a comeback, in part due to a program in which sandhill cranes hatch and rear whooping cranes.

Creeper, Hawaii *(Oreomystis (=Loxops) mana)* Subspecies of either finch or honeycreeper found in Hawaii.

Creeper, Molokai (=kakawahie) *(Paroreomyza (=Oreomystis=Loxops) flammea)* Subspecies of either finch or honeycreeper found on Molokai.

Creeper, Oahu (=alauwahio) *(Paroreomyza (=Oreomystis =Loxops) maculata)* Subspecies of either finch or honeycreeper found on Oahu.

Crow, Hawaiian (='alala) *(Corvus hawaiiensis (=tropicus))* Species of crow found in Hawaii.

Crow, Mariana *(Corvus kubaryi)* Historic range: Guam, Western Pacific.

Curlew, Eskimo *(Numenius borealis)* One of the rarest birds on Earth; until near turn of the century, large flocks seen and hunted in eastern U.S. during migration from Alaska and Canada to Argentina.

Duck, Hawaiian (=koloa) *(Anas wyvilliana)* Closely related to the common mallard.

Duck, Laysan *Anas laysanensis)* Historic range: Hawaii.

Falcon, American peregrine *(Falco peregrinus anatum)* Subspecies of peregrine falcon endangered throughout Americas.

Falcon, northern aplomado *(Falco femoralis septentrionalis)* Found in southwest U.S., Mexico, and Guatemala.

Falcon, peregrine *(Falco peregrinus)* Although population declined severely because DDT interferes with breeding, they have been making a comeback; continued concern about use of DDT in their winter range in Latin America.

Finch, Laysan (honeycreeper) *(Telespyza (=Psittirostra) cantans)* Found on island of Laysan, in Hawaiian chain.

Finch, Nihoa (honeycreeper) *(Telespyza (=Psittirostra) ultima)* Found on the island of Nihoa, in Hawaiian chain.

Flycatcher, southwestern willow *(Empindonax trailii extimus)* Found in southwestern U.S.

Goose, Hawaiian (=nene) *(Nesochen (=Branta) sandvicensis)* Once almost extinct; captive breeding program successful in preserving the species and reintroducing it to the wild.

Hawk, Hawaiian (=io) *(Buteo solitaris)* Found in upland forests on island of Hawaii.

Hawk, Puerto Rican broad-winged *(Buteo platypterus brunnescens)* Found in Puerto Rico.

Hawk, Puerto Rican sharp-shinned *(Accipiter striatus venator)* Historic range: Puerto Rico.

Honeycreeper, crested *(='akohekohe)* *(Palmeria dolei)* Found on Maui in Hawaii; now rarely sighted or heard.

Kingfisher, Guam Micronesian *(Halcyon cinnamomina cinnamomina)* Historic range: Guam, Western Pacific.

Kite, Everglades snail *(Rostrhamus sociabilis plumbeus)* Loss of habitat in Florida has confined this bird to one small nesting population; not endangered in Cuba.

Mallard, Mariana *(Anas oustaleti)* Historic range: Guam, Western Pacific.

Millerbird, Nihoa (Old World warbler) *(Acrocephalus familaris kingi)* Found on Hawaiian island of Nihoa; one of the rarest birds on Earth.

Moorhen, (=gallinule), Hawaiian common *(Gallinula chloropus sandvicensis)* Revered by Hawaiians as bird that brought fire to the islands.

Moorhen, (=gallinule), Mariana common *(Gallinula chloropus guami)* Historic range: Western Pacific, Guam.

Nightjar (=whippoorwill), Puerto Rican *(Caprimulgus noctitherus)* Puerto-Rican relative of the American whippoorwill; once thought extinct.

Nukupu'u (honeycreeper) *(Hemignathus lucidus)* Originally found on Maui, Oahu, and Kauai; now only occasional sightings on Kauai.

'O'o, Kauai (='O'o 'A'a) (honeyeater) *(Moho braccatus)* Of 5 species of honeyeater in Hawaii, 4 have become extinct since 1859, leaving only the 'O'o, rarely seen on Kauai

'O'u (honeycreeper) *(Psittirostra psittacea)* Once common on all the Hawaiian islands of Maui, Oahu, and Kauai, it is now extinct on Oahu, Lanai, and Molokai

Palila (honeycreeper) *(Loxiodes (=Psittirostra) bailleiu)* Once common throughout the islands, now found only on the "big island" of Hawaii.

Parrot, Puerto Rican *(Amazona vittata)* Once common on Puerto Rico and nearby islands; sole remaining population is in Luquillo National Forest, P.R.

Parrotbill, Maui (honeycreeper) *(Pseudonestor xanthophrys)* Extremely rare Hawaiian honeycreeper occasionally sighted on Maui.

Pelican, brown *(Pelecanus occidentalis)* Endangered along Pacific coast and in Central and South America, but has made a comeback along coast of southeastern U.S. since ban of DDT.

Petrel, Hawaiian dark-rumped *(Pterodroma phaeopygia sandwichensis)* Subspecies of gadfly petrel; endangered because of predation by rats introduced onto Hawaiian islands where it breeds.

Pigeon, Puerto Rican plain *(Columba inomata wetmorei)* Subspecies of pigeon related to common pigeons.

Plover, piping *(Charadrius melodus)* Endangered in Great Lakes region and part of Canada.

Po'ouli (honeycreeper) *(Melanprosops phaeosoma)* One of 28 species of Hawaiian finches, of which 20 are either endangered or threatened.

Prairie chicken, Atwater's greater *(Tympanuchus cupido attwateri)* One of 4 subspecies of prairie chicken once found in U.S.; limited to Texas.

Pygmy-owl, cactus ferruginous *(Glaucidium brasilianum attwateri)* Found in Arizona and Texas, as well as northern Mexico; endangered only in Arizona.

Rail, California clapper *(Rallus longiostric obsoletus)* Historic range: California.

Rail, light-footed clapper *(Rallus longirostris levipes)* Historic range: California and Baja California.

Rail, Yuma clapper *(Rallus longirostris yumanensis)* One of a trio of clapper rail subspecies endangered in Arizona and California.

Shrike, San Clemente loggerhead *(Lanius ludovicianus mearnsi)* California subspecies of loggerhead shrike.

Sparrow, Cape Sable seaside *(Ammodramus (=Ammospiza) martimus mirabilis)* Subspecies closely related to the dusky seaside sparrow, which became extinct in 1988.

Sparrow, Florida grasshopper *(Ammodramus savammarum floridanus)* Like the Cape Sable seaside sparrow, this subspecies is actually a New World Bunting.

Stilt, Hawaiian (= Ae'o) *(Himantopus mexicanus (=himantopus) knudseni)* Subspecies of the black-winged stilt, a wading bird.

Tern, California least *(Sterna antillarum (=albifrons) browni)* Historic range: Mexico, California.

Tern, least *(Sterna antillarum)* Endangered throughout Missippi River basin.

Tern, roseate *(Sterna dougalli dougalli)* Endangered along Atlantic Coast between North Carolina and Newfoundland.

Thrush, large Kauai *(Myadestes (=Phaeornis) myadestinus)* Subspecies of this Hawaiian thrush became extinct on Oahu (1825); Lanai (1931) and Molokai (1936); there is a subspecies on Hawaii.

Thrush, Molokai (=oloma'o) *(Myadestes (=Phaeornis) lanaiensis (=obsurus) rutha)* Once believed to have become extinct in 1936, this is another species of the "Hawaiian thrush."

Thrush, small Kauai (=puaiohi) *(Myadestes (=Phaeornis) palmeri)* Found only in forests on Kauai; probably the rarest of the surviving Hawaiian thrushes.

Vireo, black-capped *(Vireo atricapillus)* Vireo found in Kansas, Oklahoma, Texas, and Mexico.

Vireo, least Bell's *(Vireo bellii pusillus)* Subspecies of Bell's vireo found in California and Mexico.

Warbler (wood), Bachman's *(Vermivora bachmanii)* Considered the rarest North American native songbird, Bachman's may already have been near extinction when first noticed by science in 1833.

Warbler (wood), golden-cheeked *(Dendroica chrysoparia)* Affected range: Texas to Nicaragua.

Warbler (wood), Kirtland's *(Dendroica kirtlandii)* Nesting only in Michigan and wintering in the Bahamas, about 1,000 of these birds survive with human help.

White-eye, bridled *(Zosterops conspicillatus conspicillatus)* Historic range: Western Pacific, Guam.

Woodpecker, ivory-billed *(Campephilus principalis)* Large American woodpecker of old-growth forests in Cuba and southeast U.S. Probably extinct, since it was last seen in Cuba in the 1980s.

Woodpecker, red-cockaded *(Picoides (=Dendrocopos) borealis)* Another woodpecker of the forests of the Southeastern U.S.; related to more common downy and hairy woodpeckers.

REPTILES

Anole, Culebra Island giant *(Anolis roosevelti)* A lizard endangered in Puerto Rico and Culebra Island.

Boa, Puerto Rican *(Epicrates inornatus)* Boa found in Puerto Rico.

Boa, Virgin Islands tree *(Epicrates monensis granti)* Subspecies of boa found in U.S. and British Virgin Islands.

Crocodile, American *(Crocodylus acutus)* Found only in Florida in the U.S., but endangered throughout the Americas.

Gecko, Monito *(Sphaerodactylus micropithecus)* Puerto-Rican lizard.

Iguana, Mona ground *(Cyclura stejnegeri)* Large lizard found on Mona Island, P.R.

Lizard, blunt-nosed leopard *(Gambellia (=Crotaphytus) silus)* California lizard.

Lizard, St. Croix ground *(Ameiva polops)* Found in U.S. Virgin Islands.

Snake, San Francisco garter *(Thamnophis sirtalis tetrataenia)* California subspecies of garter snake.

Turtle, Alabama red-bellied *(Pseudemys alabamensis)* Alabama fresh-water turtle

Turtle, green sea *(Chelonia mydas* inclu. *agastizi)* Florida breeding ground populations endangered.

Turtle, Kemp's (=Atlantic) Ridley sea *(Lepidochelys kempii)* One of its few remaining breeding grounds is on Padre Island, Texas

Turtle, leatherback sea (*Dermochelys coriacea*) Although it no longer breeds in the U.S., the leatherback is found sometimes in U.S. waters.

Turtle, Plymouth red-bellied (*Pseudemys (=Chrysemys) rubiventris bangsi*) Subspecies of fresh-water turtle found only in Massachusetts.

AMPHIBIANS

Salamander, Barton Springs (*Eurycea sosorum*) Historic range: Texas.

Salamander, desert slender (*Batrachoseps aridus*) Lungless salamander found in California.

Salamander, Santa Cruz long-toed (*Ambystoma macroadactylum croceum*) Mole salamander subspecies found in California.

Salamander, Shenandoah Plethodon shenandoah) Historic range: Virginia.

Salamander, Sonoran tiger (*Ambystoma tigrinum stebbinsi*) Historic range: Arizona.

Salamander, Texas blind (*Typhlomolge rathbuni*) Lives in caves and has external gills, vestigial eyes, and white body.

Toad, arroyo (=arroyo southwestern) (*Bufo microscaphus californicus*) Found in California and Mexico.

Toad, Houston (*Bufo houstonensis*) True toad found in Texas

Toad, Wyoming(*Bufo hemiophrys baxteri*) Subspecies of true toad found in Wyoming.

FISH

Cavefish, Alabama (*Speoplatyrhinus poulsoni*) Found in caves in Alabama.

Chub, bonytail (*Gila elegans*) Historic range: Arizona, California, Colorado, Nevada, Utah, and Wyoming.

Chub, Borax Lake (*Gila boraxobius*) Historic range: Oregon.

Chub, humpback (*Gila cypha*) Historic range: Arizona, Colorado, Utah, and Wyoming.

Chub, Mohave tui (*Gila bicolor mohavensis*) Historic range: California.

Chub, Oregon (*Oregonichthys crameri*) Affected range: Oregon.

Chub, Owens tui (*Gila bicolor snyderi*) Historic range: California.

Chub, Pahranagat roundtail (*Gila robusta jordani*) Historic range: Nevada.

Chub, Virgin River (*Gila robusta seminuda*) Southwestern subspecies.

Chub, Yaqui (*Gila purpurea*) Historic range: Arizona, Mexico.

Cui-ui (*Chasmistes cujus*) Historic range: Nevada.

Dace, Ash Meadows speckled (*Rhinicthys osculus nevadensis*) Historic range: Nevada.

Dace, Clover Valley speckled (*Rhinichthys osculus oligoporus*) Nevada subspecies.

Dace, Independence Valley speckled (*Rhinichthys osculus lethoporous*) Nevada subspecies.

Dace, Kendall Warm Springs (*Rhinichthys osculus thermalis*) Historic range: Wyoming.

Dace, Moapa (*Moapa coriacea*) Historic range: Warm springs in southern Nevada.

Darter, amber (*Percina antesella*) Historic range: Georgia, Tennessee.

Darter, bluemask (=jewel) (*Etheostoma n. sp.*) Affected range: Tennessee.

Darter, boulder (=Elk River) (*Etheostoma wapiti*) Historic range: Alabama, Tennessee.

Darter, dusky tail (*Etheostoma (Catonotus) sp.*) Historic range: Tennessee, Virginia.

Darter, Etowah (*Etheostoma etowahae*) Affected range: Georgia.

Darter, fountain (*Etheostoma fonticola*) Historic range: Texas.

Darter, Maryland (*Etheosoma sellare*) Historic range: Maryland.

Darter, Okaloosa (*Etheosoma okaloosae*) Historic range: Florida.

Darter, relict (*Etheostoma chienense*) Affected range: Kentucky.

Darter, watercress (*Etheostoma nuchale*) Historic range: Alabama.

Gambusia, Big Bend (*Gambusia gaigei*) Historic range: Two springs near Big Bend National Park in Texas; in 1957 there were only two males and one female; has recovered somewhat since.

Gambusia, Clear Creek (*Gambusia heterochir*) Historic range: Headwaters of one creek in Texas; threatened by competition from interbreeding with introduced mosquito fish.

Gambusia, Pecos (*Gambusia nobilis*) Historic range: New Mexico, Texas.

Gambusia, San Marcos (*Gambusia georgei*) Historic range: Texas.

Goby, tidewater (*Eucyclogobius newberryi*) Affected range: California.

Killifish, Pahrump (*Empetrichthys latos*) Found in only one spring in western Nevada.

Logperch, Conasauga (*Percina jenkinsi*) Historic range: Georgia, Tennessee.

Logperch, Roanoke (*Percina rex*) Historic range: Virginia.

Madtom, pygmy (*Noturus stanauli*) Historic range: Tennessee.

Madtom, Scioto (*Noturus trautmani*) Historic range: Ohio.

Madtom, Smoky (*Noturus baileyi*) Historic range: Tennessee.

Minnow, Rio Grande silvery (*Hybognathus amarus*) Found in New Mexico and Texas.

Pupfish, Ash Meadows Amargosa (*Cyprinodon nevadensis mionectes*) Historic range: Nevada.

Pupfish, Comanche Springs (*Cyprinodon elegans*) Historic range: Large springs in Pecos County, Texas; these have gone dry and now the pupfish survives only in irrigation ditches.

Pupfish, desert (*Cyprinodon macularius*) Historic range: Arizona, California, Mexico.

Pupfish, Devils Hole (*Cyprinodon diabolis*) Historic range: One spring hole in Nevada; perhaps the most restricted range of any vertebrate.

Pupfish, Leon Springs (*Cyprinodon bovinus*) Historic range: Leon Springs, near Fort Stockton, Texas.

Pupfish, Owens (*Cyprinodon radiosus*) Historic range: California.

Pupfish, Warm Springs (*Cyprinodon nevadensis pectoralis*) Historic range: Nevada.

Salmon, chinook (*Oncorhynchus tshawytscha*) Affected range: the Snake River in Pacific Northwest and the Sacramento River in California.

Salmon, sockeye (*Oncorhynchus nerka*) Found in Snake River and its tributaries in Idaho, Oregon, and Washington.

Shiner, Cahaba (*Motropis cahabae*) Affected range: Alabama.

Shiner, Cape Fear (*Notropis mekestocholas*) Minnow found in North Carolina.

Shiner, Paleozone (*Notropis sp.*) Historic range: Alabama, Kentucky, Tennessee.

Shiner, Topeka (*Notropa topeka-tristis*) Found in Great Plains states.

Spinedace, White River (*Lepidomeda albivallis*) Historic range: Nevada.

Springfish, Hiko White River (*Crenichthys baileyi grandis*) Historic range: Nevada.

Springfish, White River (*Crenichthys baileyi baileyi*) Subspecies of springfish found in Nevada.

Squawfish, Colorado (*Ptychocheilus lucius*) Historic range: Southwestern U.S. and Mexico.

Steelhead (*Onchorhynchus (=Salmo) mykiss*) Only the naturally spawned populations in southern California and in the Columbia River Basin in Washington are endangered. Threatened elsewhere.

Stickleback, unarmored threespine (*Gasterosteus aculeatus williamsoni*) Historic range: California.

Sturgeon, pallid (*Scaphirynchus albus*) Affected in broad range from Montana to Mississippi.

Sturgeon, shortnose (*Acipenser brevirostrum*) Historic Range: Atlantic coast of U.S. and Canada.

Sturgeon, white (Kootenai River pop.) (*Acipenser transmontanus*) Historic range: Idaho and Montana.

Sucker, June (*Chasmistes liorus*) Historic range: Utah Lake in Utah a spawning run up the Provo River; nearly became extinct during droughts of the 1930's.

Sucker, Lost River (*Deltistes luxatus*) Historic range: California, Oregon.

Sucker, Modoc (*Catostomus microps*) Historic range: California.

Sucker, shortnose (*Chasmistes brevirostris*) Historic range: California, Oregon.

Topminnow, Gila (incl. Yaqui) (*Poeciliopsis occidentalis*) Historic range: Lower Gila River basin of Arizona and New Mexico and northern Mexico; competition from introduced mosquitofish.

Trout, Gila *(Onchorhychus (=Salmo) gilae)* Historic range: Gila River basin of Arizona and New Mexico; suffers from competition with introduced trout and from habitat destruction.

Trout, Umpqua River cutthroat *(Oncorhynchus (=Salmo) clarki clarki)* Endangered in Oregon's Umpqua River and its tributaries, where the species naturally spawns.

Woundfin *(Plagopterus argentissimus)* Historic range: Arizona, Nevada, and New Mexico.

CLAMS, CRUSTACEANS, AND SNAILS

Acornshell, southern *(Epioblasma othcaloogensis)* Historic range: Alabama, Georgia, Tennessee.

Ambersnail, Kanab *(Oxyloma haydeni kanabensis)* Historic range: Utah.

Amphipod, Hay's Spring *(Stygobromus hayi)* Historic range: District of Columbia.

Amphipod, Illinois cave *(Gammarus acherondytes)* Historic range: Illinois.

Amphipod, Peck's cave *(Stygobromus pecki)* Historic range: Texas.

Bean, Purple *(Villosa perpurpurea)* Historic range: Tennesee, Virginia.

Clubshell *(Pelurobema clava)* Historic range: Midwestern U.S.

Clubshell, black (=Curtus' mussel) *(Pleurobema curtum)* Historic range: Alabama, Mississippi.

Clubshell, ovate *(Pleurobema perovatum)* Historic range: Alabama, Georgia, Mississippi, and Tennessee.

Clubshell, southern *(Pleurobema decisum)* Historic range: Alabama, Georgia, Mississippi, and Tennessee.

Combshell, Cumberlandian *(Epioblasma brevidens)* Historic range: Alabama, Kentucky, Tennessee, and Virginia.

Combshell, southern (=penitent mussel) *(Epioblasma (=Dysnomia) penita)* Historic range: Alabama, Mississippi.

Combshell, upland *(Epioblasma metastriata)* Historic range: Alabama, Georgia, Tennessee.

Crayfish (no common name) *(Cabarus zophonastes)* Historic range: Arkansas.

Crayfish, Nashville *(Orconectes shoupi)* Historic range: Tennessee.

Crayfish, Shasta (=Placid) *(Pacifastacus fortis)* Historic range: California.

Elktoe, Appalachian *(Alasmidonta raveneliana)* Historic range: North Carolina, Tennessee.

Elktoe, Cumberland *(Alasmidonta atropurpurea)* Historic range: Kentucky, Tennessee.

Fairy shrimp, Conservancy *(Branchinecta conservatio)* Historic range: California.

Fairy shrimp, longhorn *(Branchinecta longiantenna)* Historic range: California.

Fairy shrimp, riverside *(Streptocephaulus woottoni)* Historic range: California.

Fairy shrimp, San Diego *(Branchinecta sandiegoensis)* Historic range: California.

Fanshell *(Cyprogenia stegaria (=irrorata)* Affected along Ohio and Mississippi valleys from Pennsylvania to Alabama.

Heelsplitter, Carolina *(Lasmigona decorata)* Historic range: North and South Carolina.

Isopod, Lee County cave *(Lirceus usdagalun)* Historic range: Virginia.

Isopod, Socorro *(Thermosphaeroma (=Exosphaeroma themophilus)* Historic range: New Mexico.

Kidneyshell, triangular *(Ptychobranchus greeni)* Historic range: Alabama, Georgia, Tennessee.

Lampmussel, Alabama *(Lampsilis virescens)* Historic range: Alabama, Tennessee.

Lioplax (snail), cylindrical *(Lioplax cyclostomaformis)* Found in Alabama and Georgia.

Limpet, Banbury Springs *(Lanx)* Historic range: Idaho.

Marstonia (snail), royal (=obese) *(Pyrgulopsis (=Marstonia) ogmoraphee)* Historic range: Tennessee.

Moccasinshell, Coosa *(Medionidus parvulus)* Historic range: Alabama, Georgia, Tennessee.

Moccasinshell, Gulf *(Medionidus penicillatus)* Historic range: Alabama, Florida, Georgia.

Moccasinshell, Ochlockonee *(Medionidus simpsonianus)* Historic range: Florida, Georgia.

Mussel, dwarf wedge *(Alasmidonta heterodon)* Historic range: Mid Atlantic and New England States.

Mussel, oyster *(Epioblasma capsaeformis)* Historic range: Alabama, Kentucky, Tennessee, Virginia.

Mussel, ring pink (=golf stick pearly) *(Obovaria retusa)* Historic range: Alabama and Appalachian states

Mussel, winged mapleleaf *(Quandrula fragosa)* Historic range: Midwestern U.S.

Pearly mussel, Appalachian monkeyface *(Quadrula sparsa)* Historic range: Tennessee, Virginia.

Pearly mussel, birdwing *(Conradilla caelata)* Historic range: Tennessee, Virginia.

Pearly mussel, cracking *(Hemistena (=Lasttena) lata)* Mississippi mussel, classified as endangered in 1989.

Pearly mussel, Cumberland bean *(Villosa (=Micromya) trabalis)* Historic range: Tennessee, Virginia.

Pearly mussel, Cumberland monkeyface *(Quadrula intermedia)* Historic range: Alabama, Tennessee, Virginia.

Pearly mussel, Curtis' *(Epioblasma (=Dysnomia) florentina curtsi)* Historic range: Missouri.

Pearly mussel, dromedary *(Dromus dromas)* Historic range: Tennessee, Virginia.

Pearly mussel, green-blossom *(Epioblasma (=Dysnomia) torulosa gubermaculum)* Historic range: Tennessee, Virginia.

Pearly mussel, Higgins' eye *(Lampsilis higginsi)* Historic range: Midwestern U.S.

Pearly mussel, little wing *(Pegias fabula)* Found from Alabama to Virginia.

Pearly mussel, orange-foot pimple back *(Plethobasus cooperianus)* Historic range: Midwestern U.S.

Pearly mussel, pale lilliput *(Toxolasma (=Carunculina) cylindrellus)* Historic range: Alabama, Tennessee.

Pearly mussel, pink mucket *(Lampsilis orbiculata)* Historic range: Midwestern U.S.

Pearly mussel, purple cat's paw *(Epioblasma (=Dysnomia) obliquata (=sulcata) o.)* Affected range: Alabama, Kentucky, Tennessee.

Pearly mussel, tubercled-blossom *(Epioblasma (=Dysnomia) torulosa torulosa)* Historic range: Midwestern U.S.

Pearly mussel, turgid blossom *(Epioblasma (=Dysnomia) turgidula)* Historic range: Alabama, Tennessee.

Pearly mussel, white cat's paw *(Epioblasma (=Dysnomia) sulcata delicata)* Historic range: Indiana, Michigan, Ohio.

Pearly mussel, white wartyback *(Plethobasus cicatricosus)* Historic range: Alabama, Indiana, Tennessee.

Pearly mussel, yellow-blossom *(Epioblasma (=Dysnomia) florentina florentina)* Historic range: Alabama, Tennessee.

Pebblesnail, Flat *(Lepyrium showalteri)* Found in Alabama.

Pigtoe, Cumberland (=Cumberland pigtoe mussel) *(Pleurobema gibberum)* Historic range: Tennessee.

Pigtoe, dark *(Pleurobema furvum)* Historic range: Alabama.

Pigtoe, fine-rayed *(Fusconaia cunelous)* Clamlike mollusk found in Alabama, Tennessee, Virginia.

Pigtoe, flat (=Marshall's mussel) *(Pleurobema marshalli)* Historic range: Mid Atlantic and New England States.

Pigtoe, heavy (=Judge Tait's mussel) *(Pleurobema taitianum)* Historic range: Mid Atlantic and New England States.

Pigtoe, oval *(Pleurobema pyriforme)* Historic range: Alabama, Florida, Georgia.

Pigtoe, rough *(Pleurobema plenum)* Historic range: Indiana, Kentucky, Tennessee, Virginia.

Pigtoe, shiny *(Fusconaiaa edgariana)* Historic range: Alabama, Tennessee, Virginia.

Pigtoe, southern *(Pleurobema georgianum)* Historic range: Alabama, Georgia, Tennessee.

Pocketbook, fat *(Potamilus (=Proptera) capax)* Clamlike mollusk found in Arkansas, Indiana, Missouri, Ohio.

Pocketbook, shinyrayed *(Lampsililis subangulata)* Historic range: Alabama, Florida, Georgia.

Pocketbook, speckled *(Lampsilis streckeri)* Historic range: Arkansas.

Rabbitsfoot, rough *(Quadrula cylindrica strigilata)* Historic range: Kentucky, Tennessee, Virginia.

Riffleshell, northern *(Epioblamsa toulosa rangiana)* Historic range: Midwestern U.S.

Riffleshell, tan *(Epioblasma walkeri)* Pearly mussel found in Kentucky, Tennessee, Virginia.

Riversnail, Anthony's *(Athearnia anthonyi)* Found in Alabama, Georgia, Tennessee.

Rocksnail, plicate *(Leptoxis plicata)* Found in Alabama.

Rock-pocketbook, Ouachita (=Wheeler's pearly mussel)

(Arkansia (=Arcidens) wheeleri) Historic range: Arkansas and Oklahoma.

Shrimp, Alabama cave *(Palaemonias alabamae)* Historic range: Alabama.

Shrimp, California freshwater *Syncaris pacifica* Classified endangered in 1988.

Shrimp, Kentucky cave *(Palaemonias ganteri)* Found in Mammoth Cave system.

Snail, Iowa Pleistocene *Discus macclintocki* Historic range: Iowa.

Snail, Morro shoulderband (=Banded dune) *(Helminthoglypta walkeriana)* Historic range: California.

Snail, Oahu tree *(Achatinella (all species))* Historic range: Hawaii.

Snail, Snake River physa *(Physa natricina)* Historic range: Idaho.

Snail, tulotoma (=Alabama live-bearing) *(Tulotoma magnifica)* Historic range: Alabama.

Snail, Utah Valvata *(Valvata utahensis)* Historic range: Idaho.

Snail, Virginia fringed mountain *Polygyriscus virginianus* Historic range: Virginia.

Spinymussel, James (=Virginia) *Pleurobema (=Fusconaia=Elliptio=Canthyria) collina* Historic Range: Virginia, West Virginia.

Spinymussel, Tar River *(Elliptio (Canthyria steinstansana))* Historic range: North Carolina.

Springsnail, Alamosa *(Tryonia alamosae)* Historic range: New Mexico.

Springsnail, Bruneau Hot *(Pyrgulopsis bruneauensis)* Historic range: Idaho.

Springsnail, Idaho *(Fontelicella idahoensis)* Historic range: Idaho.

Springsnail, Socorro *(Pyrgulopsis neomexicana)* Historic range: New Mexico.

Stirrupshell *(Quadrula stapes)* Pearly mussel found in Alabama and Mississippi.

Tadpole shrimp, vernal pool *(Lepidurus packardi)* Historic range: California.

Three-ridge (mussel), fat *(amblema neislerii)* Found in Florida and Georgia.

INSECTS & ARACHNIDS

Beetle, American burying (=giant carrion) *(Nicrophorus americanus)* Historic range: Eastern U.S., South Dakota, and Texas.

Beetle, Coffin Cave mold *(Batrisodes texanus)* Historic range: Texas.

Beetle, Comal Springs riffle *(Heterelmis comalensis)* Found in Texas.

Beetle, Comal Springs dryopid *(Stygoparnus comalensis)* Historic range: Texas.

Beetle, Hungerford's crawling water *(Brychius hungerfordi)* Historic range: Michigan.

Beetle, Kretschmarr Cave Mold *(Texamaurops reddelli)* Historic range: Texas.

Beetle, Mount Hermon June *(Polyphylla barbata)* Historic range: California.

Beetle, tooth cave ground *(Rhadine persephone)* Historic range: Texas.

Butterfly, Behren's silverspot *(Speyeria zerene behrensii)* Historic range: California.

Butterfly, callippe silverspot *(Speyeria callippe callippe)* Historic range: California.

Butterfly, El Segundo blue *(Euphilotes (=Shijimiaeoides) battoides allyni)* Historic range: California.

Butterfly, Karner blue *(Lycaeides melissa samuelis)* Historic range: New England, Great Lakes states.

Butterfly, Lange's metalmark *(Apodemia mormo langei)* Historic range: California.

Butterfly, mission blue *(Icaricia icarioidos missionensis)* Historic range: California.

Butterfly, Mitchell's satyr *(Neonympha mitchellii mitchellii)* Historic range: Indiana, Michigan, New Jersey, and Ohio.

Butterfly, Myrtle's silverspot *(Speyeria zerene myrtleae)* Historic range: California.

Butterfly, Oregon silverspot *(Speyeria zerene hippolyta)* Historic range: California, Oregon, Washington.

Butterfly, Palos Verdes blue *(Glaucopsyche lygdamus palosverdensis)* Historic range: California.

Butterfly, Quino checkerspot *(Euphydras editha quino)* Historic range: California.

Butterfly, Saint Francis' satyr *(Neonympha mitchellii francisci)* Historic range: North Carolina.

Butterfly, San Bruno elfin *(Callophrys mossiiibayensis)* Historic range: California.

Butterfly, Schaus swallowtail *(Heraclides (=Papiilo) aristodemus ponceanus)* Historic range: Florida.

Butterfly, Smith's blue *(Euphilotes (=Shijimiaeoides) enoptes smithi)* Historic range: California.

Butterfly, Uncompahgre fritilary *(Boloria acrocnema)* Historic range: Colorado.

Dragonfly, Hine's (=Ohio) emerals *(Somatochlora hineana)* Found in Great Lakes states.

Fly, Delhi Sands flower-loving *(Rhaphiomidas teminatus abdominalis)* Historic range: California.

Grasshopper, Zayante band-winged *(Trimerotropis infantilis)* Historic range: California.

Harvestman, Bee Creek Cave *(Texella reddelli)* Historic range: Texas

Harvestman, Bone Cave *(Texella reyesi)* Historic range: Texas.

Pseudoscropion, Tooth Cave *(Tartarocreagris (=Micreocreagris) texana)* Historic range: Texas.

Skipper, Laguna Mountains *(Pyrgus ruralis lagunae)* Historic range: California.

Spider, spruce-fir moss *(Microhexura montivaga)* Historic range: North Carolina, Tennessee.

Spider, Tooth Cave *(Neoleptoneta (=Leptoneta) myopica)* Historic range: Texas.

Improbably, the Tiger Survives

The following article has been excerpted from an Oct., 12, 1999 feature by Natalie Angier of the New York Times.

As recently as the early 1990's, researchers were convinced that the tiger, an animal more lionized than the lion itself, was about to be wiped out. Once the tiger abounded throughout Asia. But humanity's expanding numbers, and its lust for land, tiger body parts, and the prey on which the tiger feeds, had taken such a toll that many biologists predicted the tiger would be extinct by 2000.

But the cat has come back. Far from disappearing, the tiger in some parts of its range is practically thriving. Though conservationists emphasize that the tiger is still endangered, they admit to an unusual sensation these days: optimism.

"We're all encouraged, which is very different from how we felt five or six years ago," said Ginette Hemley of the World Wildlife Fund. "We cannot ever drop our guard again, but in some areas there's been some real progress."

At a recent conference sponsored by the Wildlife Conservation Society, researchers presented data indicating that tiger populations are better off now than they were earlier this decade in eastern Siberia, Nepal, and some areas of India.

The tiger is by no means faring well everywhere, however. There were no efforts to track tiger populations until about 1972, but most conservationists agree the number a century ago was probably at least 10 times greater than today. And in the mangrove swamps of Bangladesh, where biologists had thought tiger populations were relatively healthy, new survey results indicate fewer than the predicted number of cats.

Nevertheless, that the mighty tiger is holding its own in many pockets heartens biologists. They attribute the recovery to several factors. For one, many Asian countries have begun cracking down harshly on poachers, who in the early 1990's were killing tigers willy-nilly, mostly to obtain tiger bone, popular in traditional Chinese medicine.

For another, conservationists have succeeded in gathering critical information about tiger biology, hunting practices, and reproduction rates to advise governments on how best to save the cats. That advice varies by region, but one theme predominates: the best way to save the tiger is to save the tiger's prey: the deer, wild cattle, and wild pigs that tigers eat.

Technology

Major Discoveries in the History of Technology

(See also "Chronology of Information Processing" in "Computers" and "Satellites and Space Probes" and "Spaceflights Carrying People" in "Astronomy")

B.C.

2,400,000   Ancestors of human beings begin to manufacture stone tools.

1,000,000   Ancestors of human beings learn to control fire.

90,000   People from the Katranda culture in what is now Congo make barbed bone points, probably for use in harpoons.

25,000   People in what is now the Czech Republic were weaving cloth.

23,000   Bow and arrow developed in Mediterranean regions of Europe and Africa.

10,000   The Jomon culture of Japan makes the first known pottery.

5000   Egyptians start mining and smelting copper ore.

3500   Potter's wheel and (shortly after) wheeled vehicles appear in Mesopotamia.

2900   Great Pyramid of Giza and first form of Stonehenge (a ditch and bank) are built.

2000   Interior bathrooms are built in palaces in Crete.

1500   Earliest glass vessels from Egypt.

522   Eupalinus of Megara (Greek: 6th cent.) constructs 3,600-ft. tunnel on Samos to supply water from one side of Mt. Castro to other.

290   Pharos lighthouse at Alexandria is built.

260   Archimedes (Greek: c. 287–212 b.c.) develops mathematical descriptions of the lever and other simple machines.

200   Romans develop concrete.

140   Chinese start making paper but do not use it for writing.

100   In Illyria (now Yugoslavia and Albania), water-powered mills are introduced.

A.D.

c. 1   Chinese invent centerline rudder for ships and magnetic compass; neither found in West for 1,000 years.

190   Chinese develop porcelain.

600   First windmills are built in what is now Iran.

704   Between 704 and 751, Chinese start printing with woodblocks.

1040   Chinese develop gunpowder.

1041   Between 1041 and 1048, Chinese inventor Bi Sheng develops movable type.

1190   First-known reference to a compass in Europe.

1267   Book written by Roger Bacon (English: c. 1220–92) in 1267 mentions eyeglasses to correct farsightedness.

1288   First-known gun, a small cannon, is made in China.

1310   Mechanical clocks driven by weights begin to appear in Europe.

c. 1440   Johannes Gutenberg (German: c. 1398–1468) reinvents printing with movable type.

1450   Nicholas of Cusa (German: 1401–64) develops eyeglasses for the nearsighted.

1555   Georg Bauer (Georgius Agricola; German: 1494–1555) writes *De re metallica*, a handbook of mining techniques.

c. 1590   Compound microscope (using two lenses) developed in Holland.

1608   Telescope developed in Holland, probably by Hans Lippershey (German-Dutch: c. 1570–1619).

1620   Cornelis Jacobszoon Drebbel (Dutch: 1572–1633) builds first navigable submarine.

1643   Evangelista Torricelli (Italian: 1608–47) makes first barometer, thereby producing first vacuum known to science.

1654   Christiaan Huygens (Dutch: 1629–95) develops pendulum clock.

1658   Robert Hooke (English: 1635–1703) invents balance spring for watches.

1698   Thomas Savery (English: c. 1650–1715) patents the "Miner's Friend," first practical steam engine.

1701   Jethro Tull (English: 1674–1741), possibly inspired by Chinese devices, invents device for planting seeds called a seed drill.

1709   Daniel Gabriel Fahrenheit (German-Dutch: 1686–1736) invents alcohol thermometer; 1714, mercury thermometer.

1733   John Kay (English: 1704–64) invents flying-shuttle loom, which, along with the steam engine and improvements in making iron, is a key to the start of Industrial Revolution.

1751   Benjamin Huntsman (English: 1704–76) invents crucible process for casting steel.

1762   John Harrison (English: 1693–1776) designs a marine chronometer (clock) accurate enough to enable navigators to calculate longitude at sea.

1764   James Hargreaves (English: 1720–78) introduces spinning jenny, a machine that spins from 8 to 120 threads at once.

1765   James Watt (Scottish: 1736–1819) builds model of his improved steam engine.

1769   Sir Richard Arkwright (English: 1732–92) patents the water frame, a spinning machine that complements spinning jenny.

1783   Joseph-Michel and Jacques-Etienne Montgolfier (French: 1740-1810; 1745–99) develop first hot air balloon. Jacques A.C. Charles (French: 1746–1823) builds first hydrogen balloon.

1785   Edmund Cartwright (English: 1743–1823) invents first form of the power loom.

1792   William Murdock (Scottish: 1754–1839) is first to use coal gas for lighting.

1793   Eli Whitney (American: 1765–1825) invents cotton gin, a machine for separating cotton fibers from seeds.

1800   Alessandro G.A.A. Volta (Italian: 1745–1827) invents first form of chemical battery for producing electric current.

1804   Nicolas-François Appert (French: c.1750–1841) develops canning as means of preserving food.

1807   Robert Fulton (American: 1765–1815) introduces first commercially successful steamboat.

1816   Sir David Brewster (Scottish: 1781–1868) invents kaleidoscope.

1822   Joseph N. Niepce (French: 1765–1833) produces earliest form of the photograph.

1823   Charles Macintosh (Scottish: 1766–1843) patents a waterproof fabric.

1825   George Stephenson (English: 1781–1848) develops first steam-powered locomotive to carry both passengers and freight.

1835   William Henry Fox Talbot (English: 1800–77) invents photographic negative using silver chloride, essentially how black-and-white pictures are made today.

1837   Samuel Finley Breese Morse (American: 1791–1872) patents first commercially successful version of the telegraph.

1839   Louis J.M. Daguerre (French: 1789–1851) announces his process for making photographs, which come to be called daguerreotypes.

Charles Goodyear (American: 1800–60) discovers how to make rubber resistant to heat and cold, a process called vulcanization.

1842   Sir John Bennet Lawes (English: 1814–99) patents manufacture of superphosphate, the first manufactured fertilizer.

1843   Isambard Kingdom Brunel's (English: 1806–59) *Great Britain* is first iron-hulled screw-propellor ship to cross the Atlantic.

1846   Elias Howe (American: 1819–67) patents lock-stitch sewing machine.

Richard March Hoe (American: 1812–96) invents rotary printing press.

1851   Isaac Merrit Singer (American: 1811–75) patents continuous-stitch sewing machine.

1852   Elisha Graves Otis (American: 1811–61) installs first elevator incorporating safety device that prevents cage from falling if the cable breaks.

1856   Henry Bessemer (English: 1813–98) develops way of making inexpensive steel (Bessemer process).

1859   Edwin L. Drake (American: 1819–80) drills first oil well, in Titusville, Pa.

1862   Richard Jordan Gatling (American: 1818–1903) invents first form of machine gun.

1866   Robert Whitehead (English: 1823–1905) invents naval torpedo. Georges Leclanché (French: 1839–82) develops first form of dry cell for producing electricity.

1867   Latham Sholes (American: 1819–90) and two others invent first practical typewriter.

1869   Hippolyte Mège Mouriés (French: 1817–80) patents margarine.

1866   Cyrus W. Field (U.S.: 1819–92) succeeds in laying the Trans-Atlantic Cable under the Atlantic Ocean, connecting Europe to America by telegraph wire.

1874   Joseph Farwell Glidden (American: 1813–1906) invents the kind of barbed wire used today.

1876   Alexander Graham Bell (Scottish-American: 1847–1922) invents telephone.

Karl von Linde (German: 1842–1934) invents first practical refrigerator.

1877   Nikolaus A. Otto (German: 1832–91) invents type of internal combustion engine still used in most automobiles.

Thomas Alva Edison (U.S.: 1847–1931) invents phonograph, which uses a tinfoil-covered cylinder.

1878   Louis-Marie-Hilaire Bernigaud (French: 1839–1924) develops rayon.

Carl Gustaf Patrik de Laval (Swedish: 1845–1913) invents turbine operated centrifugal cream separator.

1879   Edison and Sir Joseph W. Swan (English: 1828–1914) independently discover how to make practical electric lights.

1885   Karl Benz (German: 1844–1929) builds precursor of modern automobile.

Rover Safety Bicycle, built in England, is first bicycle with essentially modern features.

1886   George Westinghouse (American: 1846–1914) invents air brake for railroad cars.

1888   Emile Berliner (German: 1851–1929) invents phonograph disk.

John B. Dunlop (Scottish: 1840–1921) patents air-filled tire.

George Eastman (American: 1854–1932) develops first camera using roll film.

1889   Gustave Eiffel (French: 1832–1923) builds his famous tower in Paris; at 993 ft. it is tallest freestanding structure of the time.

1893   Rudolf Diesel (German: 1858–1913) describes diesel engine.

1895   First public showing of a motion picture, "Workers Leaving the Lumière Factory" by Auguste and Louis Lumière (French: 1862–1954; 1864–1948), in Paris.

Guglielmo Marconi (Italian: 1874–1937) transmits signals for a mile with his wireless telegraph (a precursor of radio) near Bologna, Italy.

1897   Karl Ferdinand Braun (German: 1850–1918) invents cathode-ray tube oscilloscope.

1898   Valdemar Poulsen (Danish: 1869–1942) invents magnetic wire recorder, the precursor to the modern tape recorder.

1902   Willis H. Carrier (American: 1876–1950) invents air conditioning.

1903   Orville and Wilbur Wright (American: 1871–1948; 1867–1912) fly the first successful airplane at Kitty Hawk, N.C.

1904   John Fleming (English: 1849–1945) develops first vacuum tube, a device for changing alternating current to direct.

1907   Lee De Forest (American: 1873–1961) patents Audion vacuum tube, a device for magnifying weak electronic signals.

1908   Henry Ford (American: 1863–1947) introduces Model T, the first affordable automobile.

1909   Leo Baekeland (Belgian-American: 1863–1944) patents Bakelite, the first truly successful plastic.

1912   Reginald Aubrey Fessenden (Canadian-American: 1866-1932) develops heterodyne circuit, an important improvement in radio reception.

1917   Clarence Birdseye (American: 1886–1956) develops freezing as a means of preserving food.

1919   Sir Arthur W. Brown (British: 1886–1948) and Sir John W. Alcock (British: 1892–1919) make first transatlantic flight, Newfoundland to Ireland.

1924   Vladimir Kosma Zworykin (Russian-American: 1889–1982) develops iconoscope, the beginning of modern television.

1929   Robert H. Goddard (American: 1882–1945) launches first instrumented, liquid-fueled rocket.

1930   Sir Frank Whittle (British: 1907–96) patents jet engine.

1931   Ernst A.F. Ruska (German: 1906–88) builds first electron microscope.

1934   Wallace Hume Carothers (American: 1896–1937) invents nylon, first marketed in 1938.

1935   Sir Robert Alexander Watson-Watt (Scottish: 1892-1973) begins work on radio detection and ranging (radar).

1937   Chester F. Carlson (American: 1906–68) invents xerography, the first method of photocopying.

1939   Paul H. Müller (Swiss: 1899–1965) discovers that DDT is potent and long-lasting insecticide.

Igor I. Sikorsky (Russian-American: 1889–1972) designs and flies first helicopter developed for mass production.

1940   Peter Carl Goldmark (Hungarian-American: 1906–77) demonstrates first successful color television system.

1941   John Rex Whinfield (British: 1901–66) invents Dacron.

1942   Enrico Fermi (Italian-American: 1901–54) builds first nuclear reactor.

1947   Dennis Gabor (Hungarian-British: 1900–79) develops holography, a method of recording and displaying a three-dimensional object.

1948   Goldmark develops the 33⅓ rpm long-playing phonograph record.

Georges de Mestral (Swiss: 1908–90) invents Velcro, patented in 1955.

John Bardeen (American: 1908–91), Walter H. Brattain (American: 1902–87), and William B. Shockley (English-American: 1910-89) invent the transistor.

1957   Gordon Gould (American: 1920–) develops basic idea for the laser, which he succeeds in patenting in 1986 after long struggle.

The Soviet spacecraft *Sputnik 1* becomes the first satellite to orbit Earth.

1958 United States opens first experimental nuclear power plant.
1959 First industrial robot is marketed.
1962 First active communications satellite, Telstar, goes into orbit.
1963 Audiocassettes introduced.
1964 Touch-tone telephones introduced.
1966 Engineers at ITT demonstrate fiber optics as a method of transmitting data.
1968 The first supersonic airliner, the Soviet Tupolev TU-144, is demonstrated on Dec. 31.
1969 ATMs and bar-code scanners introduced.
1970 Boeing 747 jets go into service.
1975 IBM introduces first laser printer.
1982 Compact disc players introduced.
1984 Motorola introduces first commercial version of cellular phone in U.S.
1989 The U.S. Defense Department launches the first satellite in the Global Positioning System.
1990 Leigh T. Canham (British) develops a method for producing light from stimulated silicon.
1991 Woo Paik and coworkers produce the first prototype of digital high-definition television.
1994 Channel Tunnel, also known as the Chunnel, connecting England and France beneath the English Channel, is officially opened.

Charles K. Rhodes of the University of Chicago develops an X-ray-emitting laser.
1995 Scientists at Los Alamos National Laboratory in New Mexico develop a flexible tape that is superconducting at the temperature of liquid nitrogen (about −325°F).

A group led by Junji Kido of Yamagata Univ. in Japan combines three different diode layers, including a blue-emitting diode that is a major advance of its own, to make white light.

Competing groups agree on standards for the Digital Video Disc (DVD), an improved compact disc that can store a complete motion picture on a disc the size of a CD.
1998 John A. Turner and Oscar Khaselev of the U.S. National Renewable Energy Laboratory in Golden, Colo. develop a solar cell that can split water into hydrogen and oxygen.

Utility Patents Issued for Inventions, 1790–1998

Period	Patents issued	Period	Patents issued
1790–1800	309	1901–10	315,193
1801–10	1,093	1911–20	383,117
1811–20	1,930	1921–30	423,089
1821–30	3,086	1931–40	439,863
1831–40	5,519	1941–50	308,436
1841–50	5,933	1951–60	430,120
1851–60	23,065	1961–70	585,115
1861–70	79,459	1971–80	687,800[1]
1871–80	125,438	1981–90	737,017
1881–90	207,514	1991–98	864,544
1891–1900	220,608		

Note: Excludes patents granted for designs and botanical plants.
1. Numbers rounded in source. Sources: U.S. Bureau of the Census, *The Statistical History of the United States* (1976) and U.S. Patent Office, *All Technologies Report* (March, 1999).

Utility Patents Granted, 1901–98

Utility patents, also known as patents for inventions, are issued for the invention of a new and useful process, machine, manufacture, or composition of matter, or a new and useful improvement. They allow their owners to prohibit others from making, using, or selling the invention for up to 17 years from the date of the grant. Utility patents represent about 90 per-cent of all patents. The other 10 percent are divided among design patents, issued for a new, original, and ornamental design for an article of manufacture, lasting 14 years; and plant patents, issued for a new and distinct, invented, or discovered asexually reproduced plant, lasting 17 years.

Year	Total patents granted	U.S. ownership Corporations	U.S. ownership Government[1]	U.S. ownership Individuals	Foreign ownership Corporations	Foreign ownership Government	Foreign ownership Individuals
1901	25,546	4,370	N.A.	20,896[2]	280	N.A.	[2]
1921	37,798	9,860	N.A.	27,098[2]	840	N.A.	[2]
1930	45,226	19,700	N.A.	23,726[2]	1,800	N.A.	[2]
1940	42,238	22,165	40	17,627[2]	2,406	N.A.	[2]
1950	43,040	21,782	622	18,960[2]	1,660	N.A.	[2]
1960	47,170	28,187	1,244	13,069[2]	4,670	N.A.	[2]
1970	64,427	36,896	1,726	13,511[2]	12,294	N.A.	[2]
1980	61,819	27,640	1,237	9,956	18,874	254	3,858
1990	90,364	36,093	983	12,542	35,548	423	4,775
1991	96,514	39,133	1,183	13,207	37,594	472	4,924
1992	97,444	40,308	1,161	12,751	38,239	463	4,522
1993	98,342	41,826	1,166	12,281	38,401	434	4,234
1994	101,676	44,036	1,258	12,805	38,788	296	4,493
1995	101,419	44,035	1,028	12,885	38,688	245	4,538
1996	109,646	48,741	923	13,729	41,476	259	4,518
1997	111,984	50,229	935	12,914	42,908	273	4,725
1998	147,520	66,062	1,018	16,407	57,668	256	6,109

1. Excludes patents issued to Alien Property Custodian until 1942. 2. Patents issued to foreign individuals before 1980 are included with U.S. individuals. **Source:** Department of Commerce, Patent and Trademark Office, *All Technologies Report*, March, 1999.

National Inventors Hall of Fame

In 1973 the U.S. National Council of Patent Law Associations (now the National Council of Intellectual Property Law) began the practice of naming inventors who hold U.S. patents to the National Inventors Hall of Fame. Although many of those honored have many patents, the committee selects one patent for each inventor (or group of inventors) as the occasion for the award, which they identify by the title of the original patent application. When an invention is the work of more than one person, the description of the invention is given only for one inventor. The date at the end of each of the following entries denotes the year of induction. The Hall is located in Akron, Ohio.

Edward Acheson (American: 1856–1931) CARBORUNDUM The hardest man-made surface, carborundum was integral to the development of interchangeable metal parts. It was cited by the Patent and Trademark Office as one of the inventions most responsible for the industrial age. (1997)

Ernst Alexanderson (Swedish-American: 1878–1975) HIGH FREQUENCY ALTERNATOR This is the basic device that makes it possible for radio (and television) to transmit voices and music, not just dots and dashes. (1983)

Andrew Alford (Russian-American: 1904–92) LOCALIZER ANTENNA SYSTEM Alford developed the radio system for navigation as well as instrument landing systems for airplanes. (1983)

Luis Walter Alvarez (American: 1911–88) RADIO DISTANCE AND DIRECTION INDICATOR Alvarez is better known for developing methods of studying subatomic particles, which brought him a Nobel Prize for Physics in 1968. (1978)

Edwin Howard Armstrong (American: 1890–1954) METHOD OF RECEIVING HIGH FREQUENCY OSCILLATIONS Armstrong's several inventions connected with radio broadcasting and reception made possible the "radio days" of the 1920s. In 1939 he invented FM broadcasting and reception, which helped lead to another revolution in radio. (1980)

George H. Babcock (American: 1832–93) WATER TUBE STEAM BOILER The boilers designed by Babcock and Stephen Wilcox Jr. were much less likely to explode than the fire tube boilers that preceded them. To this day, nearly half the electricity produced in the U.S. comes from boilers based on Babcock and Wilcox's original design. (1997)

Leo Hendrik Baekeland (Belgian-American: 1863–1944) SYNTHETIC RESINS Baekeland's plastic (synthetic resin), which he named Bakelite, was the first to make people realize the potential of plastics. (1978)

John Bardeen (American: 1908–91) TRANSISTOR The transistor is the essential semiconductor device used on microprocessors and other chips. (1974)

Arnold O. Beckman (American: 1900–) APPARATUS FOR TESTING ACIDITY Beckman developed a precise instrument to measure how acidic a substance is as well as other precision instruments. (1987)

S. Joseph Begun (Polish-American: 1905–95) MAGNETIC RECORDING. He built the first tape recorder used for broadcasting. (1998)

Alexander Graham Bell (Scottish-American: 1874–1922) TELEGRAPHY Bell's most famous of many inventions was the telephone. (1974)

Willard H. Bennett (American: 1903–87) RADIO FREQUENCY MASS SPECTROMETER Patented in 1955, this device measures the chemical composition of elements. (1991)

Emile Berliner (German-American: 1851–1929) MICROPHONE AND GRAMOPHONE. Berliner's microphone made it possible to use the telephone over long distances. Berliner also developed the gramophone, the forerunner of the record-player. (1994)

Gerd Karl Binnig (German: 1947–) SCANNING TUNNELING MICROSCOPE, which can trace details as small as 0.1 angstrom, or one-tenth the size of an atom. It opened entirely new views of the study of the structure of atoms and won Binnig and his partner Heinrich Rohrer the Nobel Prize for Physics in 1986. (1994)

Forrest Bird (American: 1921–) MEDICAL RESPIRATORS The little green box known as "The Bird" prevented thousands from dying from cardiopulmonary failure. Bird also developed the Babybird respirator for low birthweight babies, reducing mortality rates for infants with respiratory problems. (1995)

Harold Stephen Black (American: 1898–) NEGATIVE FEEDBACK AMPLIFIER The basic principle of the negative feedback amplifier has become fundamental to many other devices since Black first used it to control distortion. (1981)

Baruch S. Blumberg (American: 1925–) HEPATITIS B VACCINE This vaccine (invented with Irving Millman) has protected hundreds of millions of people worldwide against the hepatitis B virus, which is still one of the leading causes of death worldwide. (1993)

Robert A. Bower (American: 1936–) FIELD EFFECT DEVICE WITH INSULATED GATE, which gave semiconductors the speed necessary for modern microelectronic applications. It became the primary device used in almost all modern integrated circuits. (1997)

Walter H. Brattain (American: 1902–87) TRANSISTOR (see John Bardeen) (1974)

Rachel Fuller Brown (American: 1898–1980) NYSTATIN (See Elizabeth Lee Hazen) (1994)

Luther Burbank (American: 1849–1926) PEACH Burbank's work in developing more than 800 new varieties of plants contributed to the development of the Plant Patent program in 1930. Burbank holds 16 plant patents, all issued posthumously. (1986)

Joseph H. Burckhalter (American: 1912–) FITC This yellow-green compound, known to doctors as fluorescein isothiocyanate, has proved invaluable in identifying different antibodies. In addition to helping identify the causes of AIDS, FITC has been used to speed the diagnosis of leukemia and lymphoma. (1995)

William Seward Burroughs (American: 1857–98) CALCULATING MACHINE Although the calculating machine dates from the 17th century, Burroughs's was the first that could be mass produced and easily used. (1987)

William Meriam Burton (American: 1865–1954) MANUFACTURE OF GASOLINE Burton developed the first commercially successful cracking process, which yielded twice the amount of gasoline from crude oil than the previous methods. (1984)

Donald L. Campbell (American: 1904–) FLUID CATALYTIC CRACKING This process revolutionized the petroleum industry by more efficiently transforming higher boiling oils into lighter, usable products. It is still used to produce over half of the world's gasoline. (1999)

Marvin Camras (American: 1916–95) METHOD AND MEANS OF MAGNETIC RECORDING Before the tapes currently used to record sound and pictures, sound was recorded on the wire recorder that Camras invented in the 1930s. (1985)

Chester F. Carlson (American: 1906–68) ELECTROPHOTOGRAPHY Carlson invented the dry copying method called xerography. Although patented in 1940, the dry copier was not marketed until 1958, by which time Carlson had patented many improvements. (1981)

Wallace Hume Carothers (American: 1896–1937) DIAMINE-DICARBOXYLIC ACID SALTS AND PROCESS OF PREPARING SAME AND SYNTHETIC FIBER

This is better known as nylon. Carothers also developed the first successful synthetic rubber. (1984)

Willis Haviland Carrier (American: 1876–1950) APPARATUS FOR TREATING AIR Carrier invented the first successful air-conditioning system, and many of the techniques used in modern refrigerators. (1985)

George Washington Carver (American: c. 1864–1943) PRODUCTS USING PEANUTS AND SWEET POTATOES A successful scientist in Iowa who later taught at the Tuskegee Institute, Carver developed over 300 uses for the peanut and 118 sweet-potato by-products as an incentive for farmers to plant regenerative crops rather than the traditional soil-destroying cotton and tobacco. (1990)

Frank B. Colton (Polish-American: 1923–) ORAL CONTRACEPTIVES Colton not only developed the first "pill" in 1960, but he also pioneered the development of anabolic steroids. (1988)

Lloyd H. Conover (American: 1923–) TETRACYCLINE Before Conover created tetracycline, no one thought that a natural drug could be chemically modified to improve its action; tetracycline remains the drug of choice for tick-spread disease such as Rocky Mountain spotted fever and Lyme disease. (1992)

William D. Coolidge (American: 1873–1974) VACUUM TUBE The "Coolidge tube" is actually an X-ray generator. Among his many other inventions was the modern tungsten-filament electric light. (1975)

Frederick G. Cottrell (American 1877–1948) ELECTROSTATIC PRECIPITATOR Cottrell's invention uses high-voltage electricity to capture the particulates, including fly ash, dust, and droplets of acid or other chemicals, found in smoke from the burning of fossil fuels and many industrial processes; the tons of waste can then be removed from smoke instead of being spread around the countryside. (1992)

Seymour Cray (American: 1925–96) SUPERCOMPUTER Cray's supercomputer processed information much faster than other computers because of its extraordinarily high number of integrated circuits. (1997)

Raymond V. Damadian (American: 1936–) APPARATUS AND METHOD FOR DETECTING CANCER IN TISSUE Damadian was the first to realize that the nuclear magnetic resonance technique could be used on living creatures and could detect cancer cells. (1989)

Mark Dean (American: 1957–) MICROCOMPUTER WITH BUS CONTROL MEANS FOR PERIPHERAL DEVICES Dean and Dennis Moeller, two IBM scientists, developed improvements in computer architecture that permitted rapid communication between internal and external components of IBM-compatible computers. (1997)

John Deere (American: 1804–86) PLOW Deere's vastly improved plow was the start of his commercial success, and the company he founded still makes farm tools. (1989)

Lee De Forest (American: 1873–1961) AUDION AMPLIFIER De Forest's invention of the triode was the key to modern radio and later developments in the amplification of signals. (1977)

Robert H. Dennard (American: 1932–) DYNAMIC RANDOM ACCESS MEMORY (RAM) Dennard's dense, cost-effective memory system allowed computers to shrink dramatically from warehouse size to desktop size. RAM has been used as the memory system in all computers since the 1970s. (1997)

Rudolf Diesel (German: 1858–1913) INTERNAL COMBUSTION ENGINE The pressure-ignited heat engine is still called the diesel engine. (1976)

Carl Djerassi (Austrian-American: 1923–) ORAL CONTRACEPTIVES Djerassi's research into the chemistry of steroids and his synthesis of antihistamines are two of his many contributions to modern organic chemistry. (1978)

Herbert Henry Dow (Canadian-American: 1866–1930) BROMINE Besides new methods of extracting bromine and chlorine from naturally occurring salt deposits, Dow patented over 90 inventions and founded Dow Chemical. (1983)

Charles Stark Draper (American: 1901–87) GYROSCOPIC EQUIPMENT Draper's gyroscopic stabilizer helped antiaircraft guns and falling bombs hit their targets during World War II. Later he developed gyroscopic systems for air and marine navigation and for guided missiles. (1983)

Graham J. Durant (British-American: 1934–) CIMETIDINE (TAGAMET) With John C. Emmet and C. Robin Ganellin, Durant developed the major drug used to suppress acid in stomach and intestinal ulcers. (1990)

George Eastman (American: 1854–1932) METHOD AND APPARATUS FOR COATING PLATES FOR USE IN PHOTOGRAPHY Eastman developed the dry plate negative and transparent roll film for still cameras, and a motion picture film for use in the newly invented cinema. (1977)

Harold E. Edgerton (American: 1903–90) STROBOSCOPE This device produced flashes that stopped action in a photograph at regular intervals. (His photograph of the crown produced by a drop of milk falling into a bowl of milk dates from the 1930s.) (1986)

Thomas Alva Edison (American: 1847–1931) ELECTRIC LAMP In addition to the carbon-filament electric lamp, Edison patented a phonograph, the mimeograph, the fluoroscope, and motion picture cameras and projectors. (1973)

Gertrude B. Elion (American: 1918–99) DNA-BLOCKING DRUGS Elion was the first woman elected to the Hall of Fame, for her discovery of drugs crucial to cancer treatment and anti-viral research. (1991)

John C. Emmet (British: 1938–) CIMETIDINE (TAGAMET®) (See Graham J. Durant). (1990)

Douglas Engelbart (American: 1925–) COMPUTER MOUSE Officially known as the X-Y Position Indicator for a Display System, this was the only patentable part of his pioneering work in computer design. (1998)

John Ericsson (American: 1803–89) PROPELLOR Ericsson's invention offered a highly efficient, difficult to damage, and easily maintained means of propulsion that sped the transition from wind to steam power in shipping. (1993)

Federico Faggin (Italian-American 1941–) MICROPROCESSOR Faggin and Stanley Mazor refined Ted Hoff's microprocessor concept to produce the first single-chip central processing unit in 1971. All three men helped persuade Intel to make the new computers available to the general public. (1996)

Philo Taylor Farnsworth (American: 1906–71) TELEVISION SYSTEM Farnsworth patented many components of all-electronic television. He also worked on the electronic microscope, the use of ultraviolet light for seeing in the dark, and nuclear fusion. (1984)

James L. Fergason (American: 1934–) LIQUID CRYSTAL DISPLAY This invention is used annually in more than five billion products, including computers, medical devices, and consumer electronics. (1998)

Enrico Fermi (Italian-American: 1901–54) NEUTRONIC REACTOR Fermi's nuclear reactor is the basis of nuclear power today. His many contributions to modern physics include basic theoretical work and experimental physics. (1976)

Henry Ford (American: 1863–1947) TRANSMISSION MECHANISM Best remembered for his innovative business practices, Ford also invented and patented numerous mechanisms used in automobiles. (1982)

Jay W. Forrester (American: 1918–) MULTICOORDINATED DIGITAL INFORMATION STORAGE DEVICE Forrester's main invention was the magnetic storage of information. Most computers today, from giant mainframes to lightweight laptops, still use magnetic storage to store data even when the computer has been shut off. (1979)

C. Robin Ganellin (British: 1934–) CIMETIDINE (TAGAMET®) (See Graham J. Durant). (1990)

Edmund Germer (German-American: 1901–87)

FLUORESCENT LIGHT Germer's high-pressure mercury-vapor lamp vastly increased the efficiency and safety of lighting while producing less heat. (1996)

Charles P. Ginsburg (American: 1920–) VIDEOTAPE RECORDER The VCR was originally developed by an engineering team led by Ginsburg. (1990)

Robert Hutchings Goddard (American: 1882–1945) CONTROL MECHANISM FOR ROCKET APPARATUS The father of American rocketry, Goddard devised successful rocket weapons and rocket-assisted take-off mechanisms for carrier-based airplanes for the military. (1979)

Charles Goodyear (American: 1800–60) IMPROVEMENT IN INDIA-RUBBER FABRICS In 1844 Goodyear discovered vulcanization, a process to make rubber resistant to heat and cold. (1976)

Gordon Gould (American: 1920–) OPTICALLY PUMPED LASER AMPLIFIERS Gould envisioned the basic idea for the laser in 1957, but did not win his first patent until 1977. (1991)

Wilson Greatbatch (American: 1919–) MEDICAL CARDIAC PACEMAKER Greatbatch's pacemaker has helped millions of people with heart disease. He also invented batteries to keep the pacemaker running without adverse physical effects from the battery chemicals. (1986)

Leonard M. Greene (American: 1918–) AIRPLANE STALL WARNING DEVICE Patented in 1949. (1991)

Charles Martin Hall (American: 1863–1914) MANUFACTURE OF ALUMINUM In 1886, Hall developed a cheap method to make aluminum (then selling at $5 a pound). That same year, French metallurgist Paul-Louis-Toussaint Héroult discovered the same process. Patent litigation between the two was resolved amicably. (1976)

Robert N. Hall (American: 1919–) HIGH VOLTAGE HIGH POWER SEMICONDUCTOR PIN RECTIFIER This invention greatly reduced the waste of power and dangerous heat build-up that accompanies large-scale power transmission. Hall also invented the first semi-conductor laser, which is now commonly found in CD players. (1994)

W.E. "Butch" Hanford (American: 1908–) POLYURETHANE This 1942 patent (won with Donald F. Holmes) remains the basis for chemistry used in manufacture of all polyurethanes. (1991)

Elizabeth Lee Hazen (American: 1885–1975) NYSTATIN, the world's first non-toxic anti-fungal antibiotic. This medicine cures many disfiguring and disabling skin, mouth, and throat infections. Nystatin has also been used to treat Dutch elm disease and to rescue water-damaged artworks from mold. (1994)

William R. Hewlett (American 1913–) VARIABLE FREQUENCY OSCILLATION GENERATOR Hewlett's first invention was the audio oscillator in 1939, a device for generating high-quality audio frequencies that could be used for many different purposes; among the first uses was production of special sounds for the Disney movie *Fantasia*. (1992)

René Alphonse Higonnet (French: 1902–83) PHOTO COMPOSING MACHINE Along with Louis Marius Moyroud, Higonnet developed (in 1946) the first machine to set type by recording the images of letters on film. Film composition became the standard way of setting type, replacing type set from metal. (1985)

James Hillier (Canadian-American: 1915–) ELECTRON LENS CORRECTION DEVICE Although Hillier was not the first to make a microscope using electrons, his microscopes became the standard in the field. Electron microscopes can enlarge much smaller details than light microscopes because the wavelength of an electron is much smaller than the wavelength of a photon of visible light.

Marcian Edward "Ted" Hoff, Jr. (American: 1937–) MICROPROCESSOR CONCEPT AND ARCHITECTURE Hoff was the first to recognize the possibility of a single-chip CPU, thus helping to transform the computer from a machine that occupied an entire room to one that could fit onto a desk. (1996)

Herman Hollerith (American: 1869–1929) STORAGE AND PROCESSING OF NUMERICAL DATA Hollerith's punched cards and readers, developed for the 1890 U.S. Census, became the basis of modern data processing. (1990)

Donald Fletcher Holmes (American: 1910–80) POLYURETHANE (see W.E.Hanford). (1991)

Eugene J. Houdry (French: 1892–1962) CATALYTIC CRACKING OF PETROLEUM Houdry developed a process to make high-grade gasoline and airplane fuel from crude oil, as well as other catalytic processes and devices, including the basic catalytic converter used in mufflers. (1990)

Percy F. Julian (American: 1899–1975) SYNTHESIS OF CORTISONE AND OTHER HORMONES Julian discovered that soybeans could be used as the basis for synthesizing cortisone, an important hormone with many medical applications. (1990)

Donald B. Keck (American 1941–) FUSED SILICA OPTICAL WAVEGUIDE (See Robert D. Maurer). (1993)

Charles Franklin Kettering (American: 1875–1958) ENGINE STARTING DEVICES AND IGNITION SYSTEM Kettering's Delco company produced the self-starter for automobiles and a small generator for use in isolated farms. (1980)

Jack S. Kilby (American: 1923–) MINIATURIIZED ELECTRONIC CIRCUITS The monolithic integrated circuit that Kilby developed for Texas Instruments in 1959 was the beginning of the modern integrated circuit. (1982)

Willem J. Kolff (Dutch-American: 1911–) SOFT-SHELL MUSHROOM-SHAPED HEART Although the patent cited is for an early version of an artificial heart, Kolff's most important work was the development of the artificial kidney dialysis machine. (1985)

Stephanie Kwolek (American: 1923–) KEVLAR This substance is five times as strong as steel and weighs 40% less than glass, making it ideal for use in aircraft construction, golf clubs and tennis racquets, fiber optic cables, and perhaps most important, bullet-proof vests. (1995)

Edwin Herbert Land (American: 1909–91) PHOTOGRAPHIC PRODUCT COMPRISING A RUPTURABLE CONTAINER CARRYING PHOTOGRAPHIC PROCESSING LIQUID Land's first success was the development and application of substances that polarize light. He also invented the instant Polaroid camera. (1977)

Irving Langmuir (American: 1881–1957) INCANDESCENT ELECTRIC LAMP In 1913, Langmuir realized that filling the original Edison-Swan lightbulb with a nonburning gas would result in a longer-lasting light. He later won a Nobel Prize (1932) for his work on the chemistry of surfaces. (1989)

Ernest Orlando Lawrence (American: 1901–58) METHOD AND APPARATUS FOR THE ACCELERATION OF IONS Although Lawrence did not develop the very first particle accelerator (known as an "atom smasher"), his 1930 cyclotron has been the basic pattern for the most successful and powerful machines of its kind ever since. (1982)

William P. Lear (American: 1902–78) AUTOMOBILE RADIO Though he was better known for inventing the Learjet, Lear's first claim to fame was in radio technology, with a company that went on to become Motorola. His other inventions include the first navigational radio and the first radio direction finder. (1993)

Robert S. Ledley (American: 1926–) WHOLE-BODY CAT SCANNER Ledley's device for making three-dimensional images of living tissues quickly became an established medical technique for looking inside the human body. (1990)

Theodore Harold Maiman (American: 1927–) RUBY LASER SYSTEMS Although there has been much dispute about the invention of the laser, Maiman's ruby laser was the first to be recognized worldwide and to be commercially successful. (1984)

Guglielmo Marconi (Italian: 1874–1937) TRANSMITTING ELECTRICAL SIGNALS Marconi's patent for using radio waves to carry coded messages is best known as wireless telegraphy. (1975)

Homer Z. Martin (American: 1910–1993) FLUID CATALYTIC CRACKING (See Donald L. Campbell) (1999)

Robert D. Maurer (American: 1924–) FUSED SILICA OPTICAL WAVEGUIDE (With Donald B. Keck and Peter C. Schultz). This optical fiber helped launch the information age: it carries 65,000 times more information than copper wire 30-50 times farther without boosting the signal. (1993)

Stanley Mazor (American: 1941–) MICROPROCESSOR (See Federico Faggin) (1996)

Cyrus McCormick (American: 809–94) REAPER McCormick's machine for harvesting grain (patented in 1834) and other inventions revolutionized American agriculture. (1976)

Ottmar Mergenthaler (German-American: 1854–99) MACHINE FOR PRODUCING PRINTING BARS Mergenthaler's invention, known as the Linotype, was the first major improvement in printing since Gutenberg's movable type in the 15th century. This machine, which is controlled by a keyboard, casts individual lines of type from melted lead. (1982)

George de Mestral (Swiss: 1907–1990) VELCRO® The success of his "hook and loop fastener" can be measured by the fact that the trademarked name is more commonly known than the generic name.

Irving Millman (American: 1923–) HEPATITIS B VACCINE (See Baruch S. Blumberg). (1993)

Dennis Moeller (American: 1950–) MICROCOMPUTER WITH BUS CONTROL MEANS FOR PERIPHERAL DEVICES (See Mark Dean). (1997)

Bryan B. Molloy (American: 1939–) PROZAC Unlike other antidepressants, Prozac (fluoxetine hydrochloride) does not have undesirable side effects like grogginess and gastrointestinal problems. (1999)

Samuel F.B. Morse (American: 1791–1872) TELEGRAPH SIGNALS Morse developed the first commercially successful telegraph, with a dot-dash-dot code that made instantaneous long-distance communications possible. (1975)

Andrew J. Moyer (American: 1899–1959) METHOD FOR PRODUCTION OF PENICILLIN Moyer, a microbiologist for the U.S. Department of Agriculture, developed a way of producing penicillin in bulk during World War II. The basic method is still used in manufacture of antibiotics and other substances produced by micro-organisms. (1987)

Louis Marius Moyroud (French: 1914–) PHOTO COMPOSING MACHINE (see René Alphonse Higonet). (1985)

Eger V. Murphree (American: 1898–1962) FLUID CATALYTIC CRACKING (See Donald L. Campbell) (1999)

Kary Banks Mullis (American: 1944–) POLYMERASE CHAIN REACTION (PCR) This method has revolutionized the fields of microbiology, medical diagnostics, and forensics, by allowing scientists to identify a fragment of DNA genetic code and reproducing it infinitely. (1998)

Julius A. Nieuwland (Belgian-American : 1878–1936) SYNTHETIC RUBBER Known as Neoprene, Nieuwland's invention is superior to rubber because of its resistance to sunlight, abrasion, fluctuations in temperature, and corrosion by oil. (1996)

Alfred Nobel (Swedish: 1833–96) DYNAMITE Nobel's Improved Explosive Compound made explosives far safer to handle for use in mining and construction. (1998)

Robert N. Noyce (American: 1927–90) SEMICONDUCTOR DEVICE-AND-LEAD STRUCTURE Noyce was at the center of development for two important semiconductor producers, the Fairchild and Intel corporations. (1983)

Kenneth H. Olsen (American: 1926–) IMPROVED MAGNETIC CORE MEMORY Olsen founded Digital Equipment Corp. to manufacture computers based on his new memory devices. He has also contributed extensively to the development of the minicomputer. (1990)

Elisha Graves Otis (American: 1811–61) IMPROVEMENT IN HOISTING APPARATUS Otis devised the safety elevator in 1853, when his employer asked him to build a hoist to lift heavy equipment. Eight years later Otis installed the first passenger elevators. (1988)

Nikolaus August Otto (German: 1832–91) GAS MOTOR ENGINE Otto's four-stroke engine of 1876 is the basis of the modern internal combustion engine. (1981)

Louis W. Parker (Hungarian-American: 1906–) TELEVISION RECEIVER Parker invented the basic television receiver in common use today, and the type of color television transmission and reception that is most commonly used. (1988)

John T. Parsons (American: 1913–) NUMERICAL CONTROL OF MACHINE TOOLS This 1958 patent introduced automation to manufacturing and design and provided machines that can mill steel with an accuracy of one tenth the thickness of newsprint. (1993)

Louis Pasteur (French: 1822–95) BREWING OF BEER AND ALE Pasteur's work on beer and ale is generally considered unsuccessful, but his development of pasteurization, the heating process that protects food and beverages from microbe contamination, was a landmark contribution. (1978)

Charles J. Plank (American: 1915–89) CATALYTIC CRACKING OF HYDROCARBONS WITH A CRYSTALLINE ZEOLITE CATALYST COMPOSITE Along with Edward J. Rosinski, Plank discovered in the early 1960s that zeolites (various aluminum silicates, a fairly common kind of mineral) could be used to improve the production of gasoline and other petroleum products. (1979)

Roy J. Plunkett (American: 1910–94) TETRAFLUOROETHYLENE POLYMERS In 1938 Plunkett discovered the substance known as Teflon. He later developed many of the hydrofluorocarbons (freons) since found to be eroding the ozone layer. (1985)

Robert H. Rines (American: 1922–) CONTRIBUTIONS TO HIGH RESOLUTION IMAGE-SCANNING RADAR Rines's patents were the basis for almost all the high-definition radar used to provide the armed forces with early warning radar during the Persian Gulf War. (1994)

Heinrich Rohrer (Swiss: 1933–) SCANNING TUNNELING MICROSCOPE (See Gerd Karl Binnig) (1994)

Edward J. Rosinski (American: 1921–) CATALYTIC CRACKING OF HYDROCARBONS WITH A CRYSTALLINE ZEOLITE CATALYST COMPOSITE (see Charles J. Plank) (1979)

Benjamin A. Rubin (American: 1917–) BIFURCATED VACCINATION NEEDLE Rubin's needle enabled easy use of small amounts of smallpox vaccine, making it possible to stretch vaccine supplies and helping eliminate smallpox entirely as a disease by 1980. (1992)

Lewis Hastings Sarett (American: 1917–) TREATING PREGENE COMPOUNDS In 1944, Sarett found a way to produce cortisones as an artificial steroid. By 1949, he and his collaborators had learned to make cortisone from simple inorganic chemicals. Cortisone and related steroids are used for medical treatment of conditions ranging from psoriasis to arthritis. (1980)

Arthur Schawlow (American: 1921–99) MASER Schawlow's work on masers dates back to 1954, continued through his invention of the laser (patented in 1960 with Charles Townes), and culminated with a 1981 Nobel Prize in physics. (1996)

Klaus K. Schmiegel (German-American: 1939–) PROZAC (See Bryan B. Molloy). (1999)

Peter C. Schultz (American: 1942–) FUSED SILICA OPTICAL WAVEGUIDE (See Robert D. Maurer). (1993)

Robert J. Seiwald (American: 1925–) RITC (See Joseph H. Burckhalter). (1995)

Waldo Semon (American 1898–1999) PVC PLASTISOLS Semon accidentally discovered the first synthetic rubber that bounces. It went on to become the world's second best-selling plastic and a $30 billion industry. (1995)

Gerhard M. Sessler (German: 1931–) FOIL ELECTRET MICROPHONE. This small, lightweight microphone combines high performance, accuracy, and reliability at a low cost. Nearly 90% of all microphones are based on the Foil Electret principle. (1999)

John C. Sheehan (American: 1915–92) SEMI-SYNTHETIC PENICILLIN Sheehan's research developed a synthetic penicillin that could be produced more cheaply and quickly than the natural way of producing it. (1995)

William Bradford Shockley (English-American: 1910–89) TRANSISTOR (See John Bardeen). (1974)

Igor I. Sikorsky (Russian-American: 1889–1972) HELICOPTER CONTROLS Sikorsky in 1931 made a critical breakthrough in helicopter design. His continued developments led to the helicopter of today. (1987)

Percy L. Spencer (American: 1894 –1970) RADAR His contributions to radar research during World War II earned him the Distinguished Public Service Award. He also designed the first microwave oven. (1999)

Elmer A. Sperry (American: 1860–1930) SHIP'S GYROSCOPIC COMPASS Patented in 1917. (1991)

William Stanley (American: 1858–1916) ELECTRIC TRANSFORMER This invention allowed for the long-distance transmission of Alternating Current (AC), which was far less dangerous than transmitting Direct Current (DC) at very high voltages. (1995)

Charles Proteus Steinmetz (German-American: 1865–1923) SYSTEM OF ELECTRICAL DISTRIBUTION Steinmetz's most significant work was in developing the theory of alternating current that made power grids possible. Among his inventions was a machine that produced "lightning in the laboratory." (1977)

George R. Stibitz (American: 1904–95) COMPLEX COMPUTER Stibitz was one of several scientists who developed electromechanical computers in the late 1930s and during World War II. His innovations at Bell Telephone Laboratories and in the U.S. Office of Scientific Research and Development include floating decimal arithmetic and taped computer programs. (1983)

Leo Szilard (Hungarian-American: 1898–1964) NUCLEAR REACTOR As chief physicist at the Manhattan Project in 1942, Szilard actively campaigned for the opportunity to set off the first controlled nuclear reaction. (1996)

Donalee L. Tabern (American: 1900–74) THIOBARBITURIC ACID DERIVATIVE This 1936 invention is better known as Pentothal, anesthetic of choice for short surgical procedures. He later introduced therapeutic use of radioactive chemicals. (1986)

Nikola Tesla (Croatian-American: 1857–1943) ELECTRO-MAGNETIC MOTOR Tesla's induction motor was simpler than previous electric motors and was powered by alternating current (AC), which can be distributed more easily over a long distance than direct current (DC). (1975)

Henry Timken (American: 1831–1909) TAPERED ROLLER BEARING This invention, now used on nearly every mode of transportation, releases the strong side pressures exerted on wheels and their bearings when a vehicle turns. (1998)

Max Tishler (American: 1906–) RIBOFLAVIN AND SULFAQUINOXALINE In the late 1930s, Tishler developed an economical method for synthesizing riboflavin (vitamin B2). Later he and his co-workers developed a commercial way to produce sulfaquinoxaline, an antibiotic that prevents common poultry diseases. (1982)

Charles Hard Townes (American: 1915–) MASERS The maser, which preceded the better-known laser, is essentially a laser that works at microwave wavelengths instead of at the shorter wavelength of visible light. (1976)

Charles W. Tyson (American: 1900–1977) FLUID CATALYTIC CRACKING (See Donald L. Campbell) (1999)

Ernest H. Volwiler (American: 1893–1992) THIOBARBITURIC ACID DERIVATIVES (see Donalee L. Tabern) (1986)

An Wang (Chinese-American: 1920–90) MAGNETIC PULSE CONTROLLING DEVICE Although best known for his state-of-the-art word processor of the 1960s and 1970s, Wang contributed many fundamental ideas to the development of electronic computers, including the principle on which magnetic core memory is built. (1988)

James Edward West (American: 1931–) FOIL ELECTRET MICROPHONE (See Gerhard M. Sessler). (1999)

George Westinghouse (American: 1846–1914) STEAM-POWERED BRAKE DEVICES In 1869 Westinghouse patented an air brake for locomotives, his most important contribution to railroad safety. (1989)

Eli Whitney (American: 1765–1825) COTTON GIN By making it possible to remove seeds from cotton mechanically, the gin made large-scale cotton farming possible. Whitney also introduced interchangeable parts, the beginning of mass production. (1974)

Stephen Wilcox Jr. (American: 1830–93) WATER TUBE STEAM BOILER (See George H. Babcock). (1997)

Robert R. Williams (American: 1886–1965) ISOLATION OF VITAMIN B (THIAMINE) In 1935, Williams also synthesized thiamine for commercial production. (1991)

Orville Wright (American: 1871–1948) & **Wilbur Wright** (American: 1867–1912) FLYING MACHINE The Wright brothers not only invented the first airplane in 1903, they also popularized, manufactured, and sold the new machines. (1975)

Vladimir Kosma Zworykin (Russian-American: 1889–1982) CATHODE RAY TUBE The cathode ray tube that Zworykin invented in 1928 is the kinescope, the basic picture tube used in modern television. Ten years later he developed the iconoscope, the first practical television camera. (1977)

COMPUTERS

A computer is a machine for storing and processing information. It converts any information that it receives into a binary code—a string of signals, in which each signal is either 1 or 0. The basic working component of a computer is a series of switches, each of which can be set either "off" or "on" and thus represent 1 or 0 in the binary system. The history of computers is, to some extent, a history of the switching devices that have been used to represent 1 and 0. Early computers were based on mechanical switches; computers based on electronic switches proved much faster. These fall into three main categories: vacuum tubes, transistors, and integrated circuits.

The relative size and power of these three types are so disparate that it is almost impossible to compare them; there is no single scale against which they can be measured. In 1946 the ENIAC (Electronic Numerical Integrator and Calculator)—which occupied 2,000 square feet, weighed 50 tons, and used 18,000 vacuum tubes—could perform about 10,000 multiplications per second and had an internal memory capacity of 200 decimal digits, or about 20 words. The fastest computer in 1997 was about 4 billion times as fast as the ENIAC. A silicon chip measuring a quarter inch across has been developed that is capable of storing 200 million words in memory. The newest magnetic disk drives for personal computers in 1999 can store over 14 billion bits of information. Experimental disk drives store as much as 3 billion bits per square inch, as compared to the 2,000 bits per square inch when disk drives were introduced some 40 years earlier.

Chronology of Information Processing

B.C.
500 Bead-and-wire abacus in use in Egypt.

A.D.
200 Computing trays in use in China and Japan.
1340 Double-entry bookkeeping originates in Lombardy.
c. 1621 Mathematician William Oughtred (English: 1574–1660) invents slide rule.
1642 Blaise Pascal (French: 1623–62) invents "pascaline"—the first calculating machine, capable of addition and subtraction.
1679 Gottfried Wilhelm Leibniz (German: 1646–1716) perfects binary system of notation that eventually will be used by all computers; also develops improved version of pascaline, capable of multiplication and division.
1801 Joseph-Marie Jacquard (French: 1752–1834) uses punched cards to control operation of his mechanical loom—precursor of cards used in early data-storage systems.
1822 Charles Babbage (English: 1792–1871) designs and builds prototype of "Difference Engine" for calculating logarithms.
1833 Babbage designs "Analytical Engine," a computing machine featuring printed card input, memory, and printed output, and capable of being programmed to perform different tasks. Forerunner of modern computer, it never goes beyond design stage.
1847 George Boole (English: 1815–64) publishes *Mathematical Analysis of Logic*, which treats logic as a branch of mathematics (Boolean Algebra).
1853 Pehr Georg Scheutz and his son Edvard G.R. Scheutz (Swedish: 1785–1873; 1821–81) complete version of Babbage's Difference Engine.
1886 William S. Burroughs (American: 1855–98) develops first commercially successful mechanical adding machine.
1887 U.S. Census Bureau holds competition for device to speed up computation of census information; Herman Hollerith (American: 1860–1929) designs winning tabulating machine. His Tabulating Machine Co. (founded 1911) becomes IBM in 1924.
1890 Hollerith's electromechanical machine processes U.S. Census results in six weeks—one-third the time taken in 1880.
1894 Otto Steiger develops "Millionaire," the first commercially successful machine capable of direct multiplication, as opposed to multiplication by repeated addition.
1931 Vannevar Bush (American: 1890–1974) completes "differential analyser," first computing machine to use electronic components (vacuum tubes in which values could be stored as voltages).
1936 Mathematician Alan M. Turing (English: 1912–54) publishes "On Computable Numbers," which describes hypothetical computer with infinite storage capacity, capable of performing any conceivable calculation.
1937 John V. Atanasoff (American: 1903–) starts work on first electronic computer.
1938 Konrad Zuse (German: 1910–95) builds "Z1," the first computing machine to use binary, instead of decimal, method of operation. Other features include keyboard to input information and system of electric bulbs to signal results of calculations.
1939 Atanasoff and Clifford Berry complete ABC device, first digital computer.
1940 Zuse's Z2 machine introduces electromagnetic relays (as used in telephone switching gear) to store numbers.

First Generation: Vacuum Tubes
1943 British government uses first fully electronic computer to crack German military codes. Designed by Turing, "Colossus" uses 2,000 vacuum tubes to perform calculations and digest information at rate of 5,000 characters per second.
1944 Completion of "Harvard Mark I," designed by Howard H. Aiken (American: 1900–1973) and built by IBM. Vast, over 50 ft. long, it was obsolete almost immediately because it used electromagnetic relays rather than vacuum tubes.
1946 At the University of Pennsylvania, the ENIAC (Electronic Numerical Integrator and Calculator) multiplies five-digit number by itself 5,000 times in half a second. Designed by J. Presper Eckert, Jr. (American: 1919–) and John W. Mauchly (American: 1907–80) to calculate ballistic trajectories, ENIAC occupies 2,000 sq. ft., weighs 50 tons, uses 18,000 vacuum tubes, and can store about 20 words in its memory.

John von Neumann (Hungarian-American: 1903–57) publishes paper suggesting that instructions given to computer—"programs"—can themselves be stored by computer in numerical form.

First use of term *bit* to mean binary digit.
1948 "Mark I," designed by Tom Kilburn (English: 1921–) and Sir Frederic C. Williams (English: 1911–77) at Manchester University, England, is first computer to utilize von Neumann's concept of stored programs.

John Bardeen (American: 1908–91), Walter H. Brattain (American: 1902–87), and William B. Shockley (English-American: 1910–89) invent the transistor, which will eventually replace vacuum tube and make computers faster.

IBM, Bell Telephone, and Sperry-Rand each begin production of commercial computers.

First chess-playing computer built at M.I.T.
1950 Eckert and Mauchly's EDVAC (Electronic Discrete Variable Automatic Computer) is first to use magnetic disks for storage.
1951 Lyons Tea Shop Co. in England uses specially designed computer ("LEO") to perform routine administrative functions.

Eckert and Mauchly's UNIVAC (Universal Automatic Computer) is installed at U.S. Bureau of Census. UNIVAC uses magnetic tape for input and becomes first commercially successful machine, selling over 50 models.
1952 One hour after polls close, CBS television network uses UNIVAC to predict Eisenhower's landslide victory in U.S. presidential election. Prediction was based on less than 10 percent of the votes.
1953 First high-speed printer linked to a computer.

IBM introduces its first stored-program computer, the vacuum-tube-based "701."
1956 First use of term artificial intelligence.

Second Generation: Transistors
1958 Control Data Corp. introduces first fully transistorized computer, the CDC 1604, designed by Seymour Cray (American: 1925–).

Jack St.C. Kilby (American: 1923–) of Texas Instruments and Robert Noyce (American: 1927–90) of Intel Corp. independently produce first integrated circuits.
1959 First commercially marketed program.

IBM markets its first transistorized computers, the 1620 and 1790.
1960 The PDP-1, developed by Digital Equipment Corp., is the first commercial computer to use a keyboard and monitor instead of punched cards.

Introduction of removable magnetic disks for data storage.

Third Generation: Integrated Circuits

1965   IBM markets its first integrated-circuit based computer, the 360.

Digital Equipment Corp. markets the first mini-computer, the PDP-8.

1969   Graduate student Alan Kay, later to become top designer with Apple Computer Co., writes doctoral thesis describing hypothetical "personal computer."

First international conference on artificial intelligence.

ARPANET, the first part of the Internet, is set up to link Defense Department contractors.

1970   Lexitron introduces first word processor, a computer designed specifically to handle written text. It features a cathode ray tube (CRT) terminal, as used in television sets, to display information.

Floppy disk is introduced for data storage.

1971   Intel Corp. announces first microprocessor, several integrated circuits contained on one silicon chip.

First electronic pocket calculator produced by Texas Instruments; it weighs about 2½ lbs. and costs about $150.

1973   IBM introduces "Winchester" disc drive, a sealed storage module containing several rotating magnetic discs.

Introduction of "bit-mapped" monitor capable of high-resolution graphics display.

Xerox markets first hand-held "mouse," a time-saving device for giving commands to computer.

Intel introduces 8080 microprocessor, which will become the central processing unit (CPU) of several microcomputers.

1975   First personal computer, the MITS Altair 8800, is marketed in kit form, with memory of 256 bytes.

Cray Research (founded 1972) announces the Cray-1 supercomputer, capable of 100 million operations per second.

1976   Apple Computer Co. founded by Stephen Wozniak and Steven Jobs (American: 1955–) in the Wozniak family garage; first Apple "boards" (self-assembly personal computer kits) go on sale.

1977   Apple markets Apple II—the first widely accepted personal computer. Commodore and Tandy also begin to sell personal computers.

Microsoft Corp. is founded.

1978   Hayes Microcomputer Products introduces Micromodem 100, the first microcomputer-compatible modem.

1979   Micropro International releases WordStar word processing program for personal computers.

1980   Microsoft adapts the UNIX operating system for use with microcomputers; paves way for personal computers to begin performing tasks associated with larger machines.

1981   IBM introduces its first personal computer, the IBM PC. Using operating system called PC-DOS, developed by Microsoft, it almost immediately becomes the industry standard.

First fully portable computer, the Osborne 1, is introduced.

Ashton-Tate introduces dBASE II, the first popular database program for microcomputers.

1982   Microsoft introduces MS-DOS, a version of the PC-DOS operating system designed for IBM PC; allows other manufacturers to produce copies ("clones") of the IBM machine.

Compaq announces its first portable computer (IBM-compatible).

1983   Apple introduces Apple IIe and "Lisa," an important step toward development of the Macintosh.

IBM announces PC Junior, which flops.

First IBM-compatible "laptop" computer introduced by Gavilan Corp.

Lotus Development Corp. introduces 1-2-3, a best-selling program for managing business spreadsheets.

Introduction of optical (laser-readable) disks.

1984   Apple introduces Macintosh. With list price of $2,495, it includes Apple's first "Mac" software programs, MacWrite (for text) and MacPaint (for graphics). Fifty thousand are sold within three months.

IBM markets the PC AT (Advanced Technology) model.

1985   Apple's LaserWriter printer and Aldus Corp.'s PageMaker program usher in age of desktop publishing—electronic production of documents and books.

Introduction of erasable optical storage disks.

Toshiba markets first widely used laptop computer.

Cray 2 supercomputer is capable of 1.2 billion operations per second.

1986   IBM announces OS/2, a new operating system that allows personal computers to run several programs simultaneously (called multitasking).

1987   Apple introduces Macintosh SE and Macintosh II. IBM introduces Personal System/2 (PS/2), features of which include high-resolution VGA (Video Graphics Array) display.

1988   Computer security becomes an urgent issue when a "worm" program penetrates thousands of systems on Internet information network.

Motorola announces new microprocessor, the 88000, a 32-bit RISC (Reduced Instruction Set Computer) chip.

First IBM PS/2 "clones" announced.

Compaq markets SLT/286, the first laptop with VGA display.

IBM and Sears launch Prodigy, an on-line service enabling subscribers with a computer and modem to access a central information bank.

Parallel processing technique introduced that utilizes many inexpensive microprocessors to perform a large number of operations simultaneously.

1989   Intel announces the iPSC/860 chip, containing one million transistors; designed to give a microcomputer the power and speed normally associated with supercomputers.

IBM announces production of commercial quantities of four-megabyte chips.

First portable computers with color liquid crystal displays (LCDs) announced.

1990   Software writer Tim Berners-Lee writes the program for the World Wide Web to make the Internet easier to use for physicists at CERN in Geneva.

1991   The Thinking Machines Inc. CM-200 massively parallel supercomputer can perform 9.03 billion calculations per second.

1993   Intel begins shipping the Pentium chip with 3.1 million transistors on it; it operates twice as fast as the best previous Intel chip for personal computers.

Electrical engineers from the Univ. of Colorado claim the first fully optical computer that can store, transmit, and process data entirely in the form of light, with no electron intermediaries.

1994   Apple introduces the first personal computers to use the Power PC RISC Chip.

1995   Microsoft introduces its Windows 95 operating system software, featuring an improved interface and better multimedia support.

1997   In a six-game match, the IBM RS/6000 SP supercomputer (known as Deep Blue) defeats world chess champion Garry Kasparov, the first time a computer has beaten a player of this caliber.

Called the world's fastest computer, Intel's Janus supercomputer is installed at the Sandia National Laboratories in Albuquerque, N.Mex. It is the first tetraflop machine, meaning it can perform trillions of operations per second.

Intel introduces a Pentium chip with MMX technology, enhancing multimedia capabilities on a PC.

1998   Household penetration of personal computers in the United States reaches 50 percent. An estimated 50 million Americans have used the Internet.

▶A GLOSSARY OF COMPUTER TERMS

Application   A computer *program* designed for a specific task or use, like word procesing, accounting, or missile guidance.

Artificial intelligence (AI)   The underlying assumption of artificial intelligence is that machines can be programmed to perform human functions. The primary AI functions are *expert systems*, programs that contain a body of knowledge (contributed by experts) that the machine can draw on to solve specific types of problems; *natural language interfaces* that make it possible for users to access a computer's database with commands entered in ordinary written or spoken language (for example, "Give me a list of countries bordering the Atlantic Ocean"); *speech recognition, speech synthesis, and optical recognition systems* that enable computers to understand spoken commands, make speech, and interpret visible images (such as bar codes on retail goods); and *robotics*, machines whose design and systems enable them to imitate complex "eye-hand" coordination of humans.

ASCII (American Standard Code for Information Interchange)   Computers work with numbers, not letters. ASCII is the numerical code used by personal computers (*microcomputers*). While many programs also use special codes of their own, data from one computer to another are best transmitted in "pure ASCII."

Baud rate   A transmission rate used in sending data from one computer to another, with a baud approximately equal to one *bit* per second. Rates must be the same between *modems* for data to be transmitted.

Buffer   Any memory location where data can be stored temporarily while the computer is doing something else; specifically, a memory location in the computer, in a printer, or in a separate storage device (*peripheral*) that stores a file being printed so that the computer is not tied up waiting for the printing to finish.

Bug   An error in a *software* program or in the *hardware*.

Byte   A group of eight *bits* that together represent one character, whether alphabetic, numeric, or otherwise. A byte is the smallest accessible unit in a computer's memory.

Cathode ray tube (CRT)   The display device, or *monitor*, similar to a television screen, used with most desktop computers.

CD-ROM   A Compact Disc ("CD") used as a Read-Only-Memory ("ROM"). The CD, essentially the same as an audio CD, stores data in a form readable by a laser, resulting in a storage device of great capacity and quick accessibility.

Central processing unit (CPU)   The group of circuits that directs the entire computer system by (1) interpreting and executing *program* instruction and (2) coordinating the interaction of input, output, and storage devices.

Complex Instruction Set chip   See "Reduced Instruction Set Computer chip."

Computer-aided design (CAD), engineering (CAE) and manufacturing (CAM)   Systems that automate many complex tasks such as drafting, computation, or repetitive actions. CAM is closely related to *robotics* (see "Artificial intelligence").

Cursor   A marker on the computer display that shows which region of the screen is active.

Database   Either a *program* for arranging facts in the computer and retrieving them (the computer equivalent of a filing system) or a *file* set up by such a system. Often databases are central files that can be accessed by a *modem* for a fee.

Directory   An area or data structure in which information is stored regarding the location and contents of files or file structures.

Disk drive   A mechanism for retrieving information stored on a magnetic disk. The drive rotates the disk at high speed and "reads" the data with a magnetic head similar to those used in tape recorders.

DVD   Digital Versatile Disc, an improvement on the CD-ROM that is capable of storing an entire motion picture.

DOS   Acronym for Disk Operating System and shorthand for MS-DOS, the standard operating system for 16-bit and most 32-bit IBM and IBM-compatible PCs.

File   Any group of data treated as a single entity by the computer, such as a word processor document, a *program*, or a *database*.

Floppy disk   A thin, flexible magnetic disk encased in a protective jacket. On the disk's surface are a number of "tracks" on which data may be recorded in the form of magnetic spots.

Graphical user interface (GUI)   A system that uses icons (symbols) seen on the screen to represent available functions. These icons are generally manipulated by a mouse and/or a keyboard. This approach contrasts with the more traditional method of using typed commands.

Hard disk   A sealed cartridge containing magnetic storage disk(s) that holds much more memory—typically 40 *megabytes* to 2 *gigabytes*—than *floppy disks*. Usually a hard disk is built into the computer, but it can be a peripheral.

Hardware   The physical equipment, as opposed to the programs and procedures, used in data processing. It covers not only computers themselves but also *peripherals* (see "Software").

Icon   A graphic symbol on the display screen that represents a file, peripheral, or some other object or function; for example, scissors are generally used to indicate cut-and-paste editing.

Integrated circuit   An entire electronic circuit contained on one piece of material. Originally, electronic components (transistors, capacitors, etc.) were placed on a metal chassis and wired together. The first integrated circuit began with a single board (originally plastic), onto which strips of conducting material were sprayed. Electronic components could then be inserted directly onto the board (see "Silicon chip").

Laptop   A portable *microcomputer* small enough to operate in one's lap. Generally a laptop weighs less than 15 pounds and uses a *liquid crystal display* monitor rather than a *cathode ray tube*.

Liquid crystal display (LCD)   A type of flat-panel display monitor used in *portable computers*.

Local area networks (LANs)   Systems that allow users to connect PCs to one another or to *minicomputers* or *mainframes*.

Mainframe computer   Generally the largest, fastest, and most expensive kind of computer, usually costing millions of dollars and requiring special cooling. Mainframe computers can accommodate hundreds of simultaneous users and normally are run around the clock; typically they are owned by large companies (see "Microcomputer"; "Minicomputer"; "Supercomputer").

Massively parallel   A form of computer architecture that uses hundreds or thousands of inexpensive *microprocessors* to perform many operations simultaneously.

Menu-driven   A *program* that uses a number of "menus," or lists of possible activities from which the operator chooses in order to activate the appropriate commands. This is the alternative to a command-driven program, for which the operator must remember a number of commands in order to tell the computer what to do.

MHz   Megahertz, the measure of speed used for a microprocessor, typically from 50 to 300 MHz.

Microcomputer   Generally the least expensive kind of computer, and small enough to fit on a desktop. The heart of the microcomputer is the *microprocessor* (see "Mainframe computer"; "Minicomputer").

Microprocessor   A complete central processing unit assembled on one single silicon chip.

Minicomputer A small computer, usually used by medium-size or smaller businesses. Minicomputers often perform scientific or industrial tasks, cost tens or hundreds of thousands of dollars, and are housed in large cabinets (see "Mainframe computer"; "Microcomputer").

MIPS (million instructions per second) A measure of computer processing speed.

Modem (modulator-demodulator) A device capable of converting a digital (computer-compatible) signal to an analog signal, which can be transmitted via a telephone line, reconverted, and then "read" by another computer.

Monitor The display device on a computer, similar to a television screen.

Mouse A small box connected by cable to a computer and featuring one or more button-style switches. When moved around a desk, the mouse causes a symbol on the computer screen to make corresponding movements. By selecting items on the screen and pressing a button on the mouse, the user can perform certain functions much more quickly than by typing commands on the keyboard.

Network An interconnected group of computers that can exchange information or work together on different parts of the same problem.

Notebook A type of full-function *portable computer* that uses miniaturized components, weighs about 4-6 pounds, and can be carried in a briefcase.

Operating system A sequence of programming codes that instructs a computer about its various parts and peripherals and how to operate them. Operating systems deal only with the workings of the *hardware* and are separate from *software* programs.

Peripheral A device connected to the computer that provides communication or auxiliary functions. There are three types of peripherals: input devices, such as keyboards; output devices, such as *monitors* and printers; and storage devices, such as magnetic discs.

Personal computer A *microcomputer* used by an individual at home or in the office.

Platform A fundamental layer of software required to make other systems run—used interchangeably with operating system, the most common type of platform. The Internet, local networks, Web browsers, and Java are all frequently viewed as platforms.

Program As a noun, a prepared set of instructions for the computer, often with provisions for the operator to choose among various options. As a verb, to create such a set of instructions.

Random-access memory (RAM) A temporary storage space in which data may be held on a chip rather than being stored on disk or tape. The contents of RAM may be accessed or altered at any time during a session, but will be lost when the computer is turned off (see "Read-only memory").

Read-only memory (ROM) A type of *chip* memory, the contents of which have been permanently recorded in a computer by the manufacturer and cannot be altered by the user (see "Random access memory").

RISC chip Reduced Instruction Set Computer chip, such as the Apple-IBM Power PC chip, which gains speed by using fewer instructions than the more familiar Complex Instruction Set chip.

Silicon chip A special kind of *integrated circuit* in which traditional electronic components have been replaced by chemicals. Tiny wafers (chips) of silicon are covered with layers of chemicals, each of which acts as an electrical component (a *transistor*, capacitor, etc.). The first chips, made in the early 1960s, contained two transistors. By 1992 chips existed that contained 64 million transistors.

Software The *programs* and procedures, as opposed to the physical equipment, used in data processing (see "Hardware").

Spreadsheet A *program* that performs mathematical operations on numbers arranged in large arrays; used mainly for accounting and other record keeping.

Supercomputer The fastest of the *mainframe* class of computers, usually used for complex scientific calculations.

Transistor A small piece of semiconducting material (material that conducts electricity better than, say, wood but not as well as metal). Flows of electrons within the transistor can be controlled, enabling it to act as an electronic "switching" device. In other words, it can record information in the form of an "on" or an "off" signal. Early transistors were about one-hundredth the size of *vacuum tubes*, required very little energy, and generated no heat.

UNIX A multi-user, multitasking operating system designed to run on a wide variety of computers, from microcomputers to mainframes.

Vacuum tube A glass tube, shaped like a light bulb, that contains a heating element that pumps electrons through a vacuum. In the earliest computers, the status of the electrical current—"on" or "off"—was used as a means of storing information. Two major drawbacks of the vacuum tube were that it generated excessive heat and used large amounts of energy.

Virus A computer program segment or string of code that can attach itself to another program or file, reproduce itself, and spread from one computer to another. Viruses can destroy or change data and in other ways sabotage computer systems.

Window A portion of the screen display used to view simultaneously a different part of the file in use or a part of a different file than the one in use.

Workstation High-performance *microcomputers* with advanced graphics capabilities designed for use by scientists and engineers.

Bits and Bytes: Quantifying Data

Bit In the binary system, a bit (for *bi*nary dig*it*) is either of the digits 0 or 1. It is the basic unit for storing data, with "off" representing 0 and "on" representing 1.

Byte A group of eight *bits* that together represent one character, whether alphabetic, numeric, or other. A byte is the smallest accessible unit in a computer's memory.

Kilobyte (K) A unit of measure for data storage or transmission equivalent to 1,024 *bytes*, but often rounded to 1,000.

Megabyte (M) A unit of measurement for data storage or transmission equal to one million *bytes*.

Gigabyte (G) A unit of measurement for data storage or transmission equal to one billion *bytes*.

Terabyte (TB) A unit of measurement for data storage or transmission equal to one trillion *bytes*.

Personal Computer Sales, 1984–99

Year	Unit sales[1] (thousands)	Dollar sales[1] (millions)	Average unit price
1984	3,975	$2,385	$ 600
1985	3,200	2,175	700
1990	4,000	4,187	1,050
1995	8,400	12,600	1,500
1996	9,400	15,040	1,600
1997	1,000	15,950	1,450
1998	12,800	16,640	1,300
1999[2]	14,900	17,800	1,200

1. Sales to dealers. 2. Estimate.   **Source:** Consumer Electronics Manufacturers Association.

Personal Computer Households, 1995–2000

Year	Total U.S. households (millions)	Households with PCs (millions)	Percent of households with computers
1995	97.7	33.2	34.0%
1996	98.9	38.7	39.1
1997	100.0	44.0	44.0
1998	101.0	47.8	47.3
1999	101.7	51.9	51.0
2000[1]	102.4	55.1	53.8

1. Estimate.   **Sources:** U.S. Department of Commerce; Jupiter Communications.

The Year 2000 Computer Bug

In 1999, almost every American became familiar with the apocalyptic Y2K bug, a glitch caused when some older computers, programmed to recognize only the last two digits of a year, could misinterpret the year 2000 as 1900. Doomsayers predicted everything from loss of phone service to mass rioting in the streets as every computer-controlled device simply shut down, unable to fathom how time moved back 100 years.

In the years since the Y2K bug was first discovered, software specialists have worked diligently to fix the problem, giving birth to a profitable, albeit short-lived industry. By June 1999, most American corporate managers expressed confidence that their systems wouldn't go haywire on January 1, 2000, according to a poll by CIO magazine. Most American consumers (nearly 79 percent) agreed, saying they expected the Y2K problem to have "little or no impact" on their personal finances, according to a May, 1999 Gallup poll. Still, nearly two-thirds of those surveyed said the planned to take out extra cash in the days before December 31.

The greater fear was not that computer systems would crash, but that those that did, even temporarily, would engender thousands of lawsuits, many of them frivolous. To prevent that from happening, Pres. Clinton on July 20 signed a bill that gave businesses 90 days to repair a Y2K problem before a lawsuit could be filed. The law also sets a limit on punitive damages and ensures that most defendants will be held liable only for the damages they cause.

TELECOMMUNICATIONS

Over the last decade, rapid technological change has combined with the unprecedented growth of the Internet to fuel a communications explosion in Europe, North America, and the industrialized nations of Asia that is quickly spreading around the globe. The immediate and widespread acceptance of fax machines, answering machines, wireless telephones, pagers, and modems has brought accelerated growth to the entire telecommunications industry.

In 1998, the U.S. marketplace alone generated total revenues of an estimated $467.2 billion. Of this total, $352.7 billion (up 11.6 percent from the previous year) went for services, including local and long-distance calling, network access, and wireless communication, by far the fastest-growing form of service. Another $121.3 billion went for equipment and software.

The MultiMedia Telecommunications Association, an industry monitor, is projecting more than 11 percent average annual growth for the industry through the year 2002. Considering the ever-increasing demand for phone services, this may be a conservative figure. There were approximately 110 million residential phone lines in the U.S. in 1998 (up from 89 million at the beginning of the decade). This does not even count the burgeoning number of cellular phones, personal communication services (PCS), and beepers.

In 1998, Americans placed more than 500 billion local calls, generating $56.4 billion in revenues for *local*

network services, up 8.3 percent from the year before. The country's intense drive to get onto the Internet was in large part responsible for fueling this growth, as both businesses and residences added access lines. Deregulation of this segment of the market has long been promised, but until it actually becomes a reality, most consumers won't see lower prices for their local telephone service.

The *long-distance* market continued to represent the largest segment of the telecommunications industry, with over $100 billion in revenues in 1998. This represents nearly a 100 percent increase since the beginning of the decade. And growth in the international long-distance market has been even greater, stimulated by overall growth in worldwide trade. The effects of deregulation in this segment are clear. The average price of a long-distance call has fallen from 30 cents in 1988 to less than 20 cents in 1998. Internationally, the average price has gone from $7.56 to under $5.00. Meanwhile, revenues in both these segments have increased dramatically (in the international market, they have more than tripled). And more competition promises even lower rates. Long-distance service has been deregulated for nearly 20 years, but the number of companies hoping to win over customers from AT&T, Sprint, MCI, and the other big names, has increased from 325 in 1990 to more than 600.

The 800, or *toll-free* market, in which the party that receives the call pays, is one of the fastest-growing segments of the market. All toll-free services were originally assigned a phone number beginning with 800, but the demand quickly exceeded the number of 800 exchanges, prompting the creation of two additional prefixes (888 and 877) for toll-free calls. There

Ten Largest U.S. Telephone Companies, 1998

Rank, Company	Access lines ('000s)	Operating revenues (millions)
1. Bell Atlantic Corp.	41,600	$25,563
2. SBC Communications	37,252	19,677
3. BellSouth Corp.	24,025	15,772
4. GTE Corp.	23,473	14,542
5. NYNEX Corp.	23,376	13,074
6. Ameritech	20,968	12,314
7. U.S. West Inc.	16,601	10,669
8. Sprint Corp.	7,600	5,465
9. Southern New England Telephone Co.	2,334	1,483
10. ALLTEL	1,890	650

Source: U.S. Federal Communications Commission, *Statistics of Communications Common Carriers*, (annual); annual reports; SEC filings.

U.S. Telephone Systems, 1985–97

Year	1985	1990	1995	1997
Local Exchange Carriers				
Carriers	55	51	53	51
Access lines (millions)	112	130	166	193
Business (millions)	31	36	46	53
Residential (millions)	79	89	101	108
Other (millions)	2	6	19	32
Local calls (billions)	365	402	484	522
Toll calls (billions)	N.A.	63	94	101
Long-Distance Carriers				
Carriers	N.A.	325	583	621[1]
Presubscribed lines	N.A.	132	153	59[1]
Toll service revenues (billions)	$43	$52	$72	$89
International Telephone Service				
U.S.-billed calls (millions)	411	984	2,821	4,243
U.S.-billed minutes (billions)	3.4	8.0	15.9	22.7
U.S.-billed revenues (billions)	$3.5	$8.0	$14.0	$15.2

1. 1996 figures. **Source:** U.S. Federal Communications Commission, *Statistics of Communications Common Carriers*, (annual).

were 2.5 million 800 numbers in May of 1983; by October, 1998, there were three times that number, plus nearly 7 million 888 numbers and 1.3 million 877 numbers, bringing the total number of toll-free lines to more than 15.7 million. Revenues in this segment have likewise increased, from $8.48 billion in 1993 to $21.9 billion in 1998. The number of calls has also increased over the same period, from 14.5 billion to 39.1 billion.

On the other hand, the nearly $1 billion *pay-per-call* market, in which the caller pays a premium on top of the cost of the call, experienced much slower growth. The pay-per-call market is divided into 900 numbers for national services and 976 numbers for local services. The explosion in sex-related sites on the Internet seems to have led to a corresponding decrease in the size of the market for erotic 900-numbers.

Wireless communications

In recent years, more than 90 percent of revenues for providing phone service has gone to companies that hooked up their customers to systems linked by copper and fiber optic wires and cables. Over the next decade, however, the market for phones without wires—phones that can also fax and access the Internet—is expected to grow rapidly. Given the industry's recent experience with both *pagers* and simple cellular phones, most experts expect that wireless phone service could claim half the phone service market sometime in the near future.

Between 1990 and 1998, the number of subscribers to a cellular system in the U.S. rocketed from 5.2 million to nearly 70 million; revenues increased sevenfold, from $4.55 billion to $33.1 billion. Pagers, once the almost exclusive province of doctors, have become ubiquitous, with about 55 million in use in 1998, up from 5.9 million in 1987; another 16 million are expected to be sold by 2002.

New forms of wireless communications have been developed, most notably PCS (personal communications service), which transmits cellular calls digitally,

bringing superior reception. They will also allow users to download information from the Internet or a corporate data network right to wireless phone screens. Pagers too are becoming more versatile with this technology; the latest versions can collect news, headlines, stock prices, and even voice mail.

Satellites   Much of wireless technology is being developed in Europe (firms in Sweden and Finland are among the leaders), where acceptance has been swifter. But the U.S. may hold the key to future developments in part because of its superior space technology. By the year 2000, when a World Trade Organization accord ends telephone and satellite monopolies in most countries, American corporations will have launched well over 125 communications satellites into low Earth orbit; another 350 or so are scheduled for development by 2002, when instant wireless communication between any two points on the globe should be realized. By then, an estimated 600 million plus subscribers around the world should be linked to a cellular phone system.

Today, there are an estimated 3,600 satellites orbiting the Earth. Some are for scientific purposes or weather tracking, others are for military matters, and about 200 are private communications services, including transmitting data via pagers and computers, as well as providing the signal for bar code scanners and credit card swiping devices. In addition, some observers see so-called satellite TV as the successor to cable because it can provide a much greater amount of programming.

A new era in satellite communications began on November 1, 1998, with the commercial introduction of the first worldwide, mobile satellite telephone and paging system, by Iridium. The $5 billion, 66-satellite system had trouble attracting subscribers and was forced to slash the price of its phones and service to stave off failure. Yet many industry analysts foresaw a thriving future in global, handheld communication.

Sales & Penetration of Telecommunications Products in U.S. Homes, 1990–99

Product	Sales (thousands of units)				Percent of U.S. homes			
	1990	1996	1998	1999[1]	1990	1996	1998	1999
Telephone answering device	13,560	17,570	18,250	18,850	31%	60%	69%	72%
Cordless telephone	10,148	20,555	31,600	32,600	25	59	70	75
Home computer	5,500	9,400	12,800	14,900	23	38	42	45
Fax and/or fax modems	350	9,111	11,530	13,100	N.A.	24	35	42
Cellular telephone	1,888	11,565	13,850	15,540	N.A.	28	39	43

1. Estimate.   **Source:** Consumer Electronics Manufacturers Association.

U.S. Telecommunications Industry: Revenues from Selected Services, 1993–2000 (millions of dollars)

Service	1993	1995	1997	1998	1999[1]	2000[1]
Local Network Services	$41,683	$46,128	$52,040	$56,350	$60,000	$63,500
Network Access	27,280	29,612	31,976	34,320	35,700	37,000
Toll Service	75,290	83,782	98,569	106,000	113,400	122,200
800/880 Service	7,800	10,200	13,300	N.A.	N.A.	N.A.
900/976 Service	915	975	1,064	1,110	1,175	1,240
Public Pay Phones	3,764	4,120	4,500	5,000	5,400	5,800
Wireless Communications	14,939	25,454	32,479	8,245	45,479	54,031
Total Services	**$175,704**	**$205,752**	**$315,973**	**$352,733**	**$392,727**	**$439,500**
Industry Total	**$219,492**	**$268,527**	**$419,682**	**$467,213**	**$520,319**	**$579,512**

1. Projected. 2. Includes other services not shown separately. 3. Includes revenues from all services and equipment.
Source: MultiMedia Telecommunications Association (Arlington, Va.), *MultiMedia Telecommunications Market Review and Forecast (1999).* Reprinted by permission.

U.S. Consumer Telecommunications Market, 1990–2000

Product	1990	1992	1994	1996	1998	2000[1]
Unit Shipments (millions)						
Corded telephone	22.0	24.0	23.7	26.0	28.6	29.5
Cordless telephone	10.1	14.9	16.8	20.5	29.0	33.0
Answering machine	13.6	14.6	17.6	17.6	19.7	20.8
Home fax machine	1.5	1.7	2.5	2.8	3.0	3.2
Total	**47.2**	**55.2**	**60.6**	**66.9**	**80.3**	**86.5**
Dollar Sales (millions)						
Corded telephone	$765	$690	$732	$675	$700	$710
Cordless telephone	1,170	1,516	1,536	1,650	2,030	2,150
Answering machine	953	1,077	1,329	1,000	1,045	1,080
Home fax machine	1,100	990	1,155	1,005	935	895
Total	**$3,988**	**$4,237**	**$4,752**	**$4,330**	**$4,710**	**$4,835**

1. Projected.   **Source:** MultiMedia Telecommunications Association (Arlington, Va.), *MultiMedia Telecommunications Market Review and Forecast* (1999). Reprinted by permission.

Cellular Telephone Industry Growth in U.S. , 1989–98

Year	Systems	Subscribers	Cell sites[1]	Employees	Service revenue (millions)	Average monthly bill
1989	584	3,509,000	4,169	15,927	$3,240	$89.30
1990	751	5,283,000	5,616	21,382	4,548	80.90
1991	1,252	7,557,000	7,847	26,327	5,708	72.74
1992	1,506	11,033,000	10,307	34,348	7,822	68.68
1993	1,529	16,009,000	12,805	39,775	10,091	61.48
1994	1,581	24,134,000	17,920	53,902	14,229	56.21
1995	1,827	33,786,000	22,683	68,165	19,081	51.00
1996	1,740	44,043,000	30,045	84,161	23,635	47.70
1997	2,228	55,312,293	51,600	109,387	27,486	42.78
1998	N.A.	69,209,321	65,887	134,754	33,133	39.43

1. A cell site is the basic geographic unit of a cellular system. A city or county is divided into smaller cells, each of which is equipped with a low-powered radio transmitter/receiver. The cells can vary in size depending on terrain, capacity demands, etc. By controlling the transmission power, the radio frequencies assigned to one cell can be limited to the boundaries of that cell. When a cellular phone moves from one cell to another, a computer at the switching office monitors the movement and transfers the phone call to the new cell and another radio frequency.   **Source:** Cellular Telecommunications Industry Association, *State of the Cellular Industry*, (annual).

Radios, Televisions, Telephones, and Computers per Capita, by Selected Nation, (number per 1,000 people), 1997

Nation	Radio receivers[1]	Television receivers[1]	Telephone main lines	Mobil telephones	Personal computers
Algeria	239	104	50	1	4
Argentina	677	221	190	56	39
Australia	1,385	554	500	264	362
Austria	740	518	490	144	211
Belgium	792	436	470	95	235
Brazil	435	223	100	28	26
Bulgaria	531	390	320	8	30
Canada	1,078	714	610	139	271
Chile	354	215	180	28	54
China	195	319	60	10	6
Colombia	565	123	150	35	33
Cuba	351	236	30	N.A.	N.A.
Czech Republic	806	534	320	51	83
Denmark	1,148	592	630	273	380
Dominican Republic	177	94	90	16	N.A.
Ecuador	342	128	80	13	13
Egypt	316	119	60	N.A.	7
Finland	1,385	605	560	417	311
France	943	591	580	99	174
Germany	946	564	550	99	256
Ghana	238	93	N.A.	1	2
Greece	477	238	520	89	45
Guatemala	73	57	40	6	3
Honduras	409	95	40	2	N.A.
Hungary	697	439	260	69	49
India	105	61	20	1	2
Indonesia	155	67	20	5	8
Iran	237	64	110	4	33
Iraq	228	82	30	N.A.	N.A.
Ireland	703	411	410	146	241
Israel	530	291	450	283	186
Italy	874	524	450	204	113
Jamaica	482	181	140	22	5
Japan	957	684	480	304	202
Korea, South	1,037	337	440	150	151
Kuwait	688	510	230	116	83
Lebanon	892	373	150	135	32
Malaysia	432	170	190	113	46
Mexico	324	270	100	18	37
Morocco	421	111	50	9	3
Netherlands	963	514	560	110	280
New Zealand	1,027	521	490	149	264
Norway	920	460	530	381	361
Pakistan	92	21	20	1	5
Panama	299	187	120	6	N.A.
Peru	271	125	70	18	12
Philippines	159	51	30	18	14
Poland	518	337	190	22	36
Portugal	306	336	380	152	74
Puerto Rico	715	270	340	45	N.A.
Romania	317	231	140	9	9
Russia	344	405	180	3	32
Saudi Arabia	319	260	120	17	44
Singapore	739	384	450	273	400
South Africa	316	116	110	37	42
Spain	328	406	400	110	122
Sweden	907	499	680	358	350
Switzerland	969	443	660	147	395
Syria	274	69	90	N.A.	2
Taiwan	N.A.	317	500	69	N.A.
Thailand	204	189	80	33	20
Turkey	178	333	240	26	21
United Kingdom	1,445	516	520	151	242
United States	2,115	805	640	206	407
Uruguay	610	242	230	46	22
Venezuela	471	179	120	46	37

1. Numbers for 1996.   **Source:** International Telecommunications Union, *World Telecommunication Indicators* (1997)

U.S. Area Codes and Time Zones

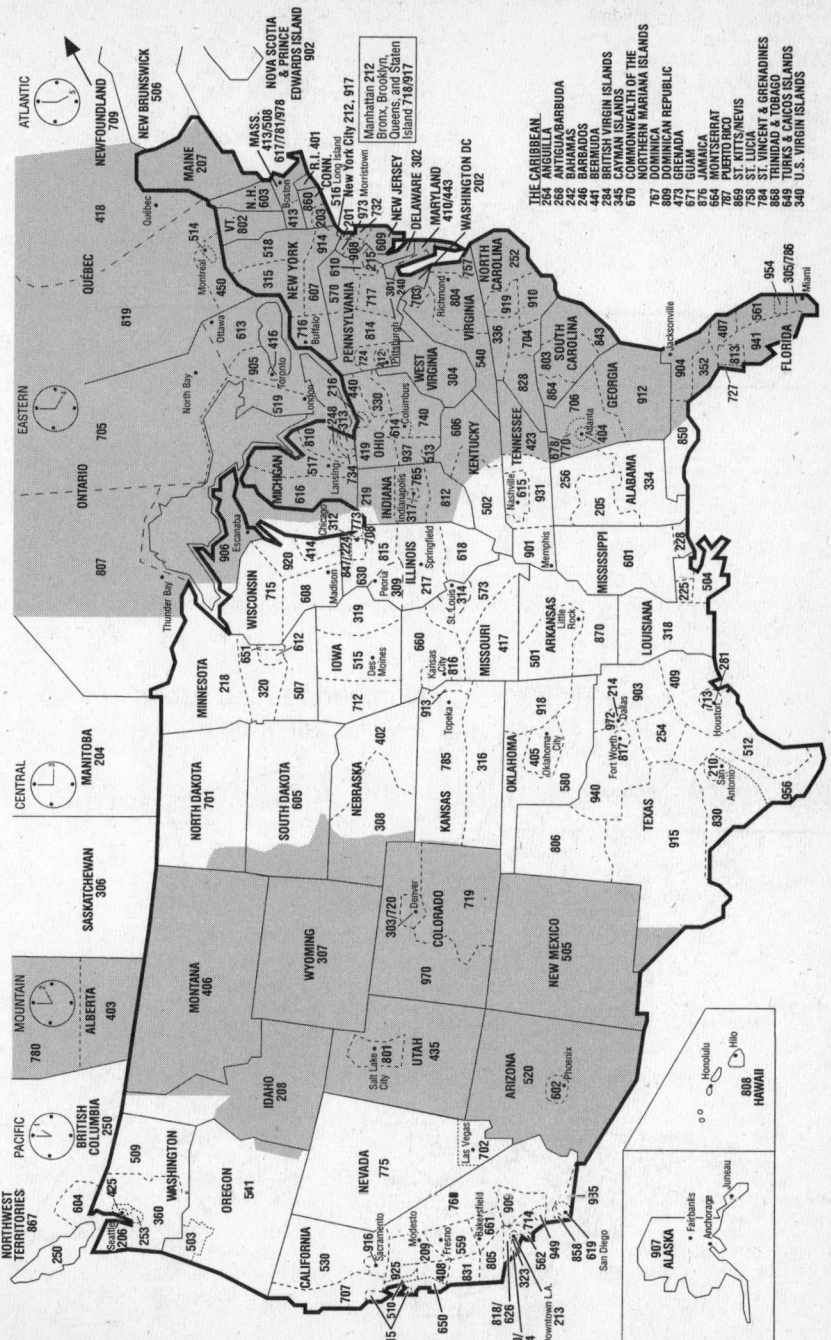

THE CARIBBEAN
ANGUILLA 264
ANTIGUA&BARBUDA 268
BAHAMAS 242
BARBADOS 246
BERMUDA 441
BRITISH VIRGIN ISLANDS 284
CAYMAN ISLANDS 345
COMMONWEALTH OF THE
NORTHERN MARIANA ISLANDS 670
DOMINICA 767
DOMINICAN REPUBLIC 809
GRENADA 473
JAMAICA 876
MONTSERRAT 664
PUERTO RICO 787
ST. KITTS/NEVIS 869
ST. LUCIA 758
ST. VINCENT & GRENADINES 784
TRINIDAD & TOBAGO 868
TURKS & CAICOS ISLANDS 649
U.S. VIRGIN ISLANDS 340

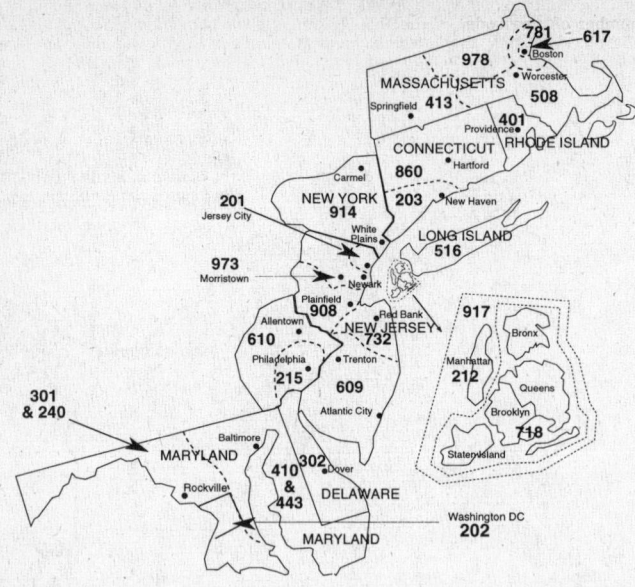

Numbering Plan Areas
Northeast U.S.

Note: Area codes have been added since the above map was drawn. See pages 815–816 for more information

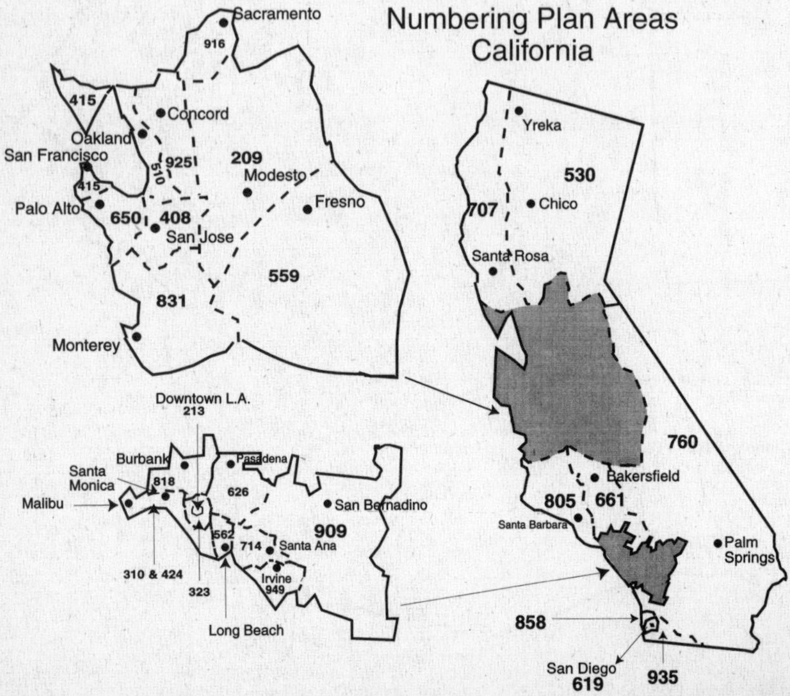

Numbering Plan Areas
California

Area Codes of the United States and Canada, by State and Province

The continuing proliferation of fax machines, modems, pagers, and cellular phones has played havoc with the number of area codes in the U.S, Canada, and the Caribbean. In 1990, there were 120 area codes, a number that increased only to 146 by 1996. But by 1999, that number had more than doubled; more than 50 area codes were added in 1999 alone. Several cities had two or more area codes in the exact same area (known as an overlay), requiring customers to dial 11 digits just to make a local call. At current growth rates, the North American area code system will run out of three-digit codes some time between 2007 and 2012. (For International Dialing codes, see Part III: "The World.")

201	New Jersey (Hoboken, Jersey City)	
202	Washington, D.C.	
203	Connecticut (Greenwich, New Haven)	
204	Manitoba, Canada	
205	Alabama (Birmingham, Tuscaloosa)	
206	Washington (Seattle)	
207	Maine	
208	Idaho	
209	California (Modesto)	
210	Texas (San Antonio)	
212	New York City (Manhattan)[1]	
213	California (dowtown Los Angeles)	
214	Texas (Dallas)[1]	
215	Pennsylvania (Philadelphia)[1]	
216	Ohio (Cleveland)	
217	Illinois (Decatur, Springfield)	
218	Minnesota (Duluth)	
219	Indiana (Gary, South Bend)	
224	Illinois (Des Plaines, Evanston)[1]	
225	Louisiana (Baton Rouge)	
228	Mississippi (Biloxi, Gulfport)	
231	Michigan (Muskegon)	
240	Maryland (Rockville, Bethesda[1])	
242	Bahamas	
246	Barbados	
248	Michigan (Pontiac)	
250	British Columbia (Vancouver, Victoria)	
252	North Carolina (Rocky Mount)	
253	Washington (Tacoma)	
254	Texas (Waco)	
256	Alabama (Huntsville)	
262	Wisconsin (Racine, Kenosha)	
264	Anguilla	
267	Pennsylvania (Philadelphia)[1]	
268	Antigua/Barbuda	
270	Kentucky (Bowling Green, Hopkinsville)	
281	Texas (Houston)[1]	
284	British Virgin Islands	
301	Maryland (Rockville, Bethesda)[1]	
302	Delaware	
303	Colorado (Denver, Englewood)[1]	
304	West Virginia	
305	Florida (Miami)[1]	
306	Saskatchewan (Regina, Saskatoon)	
307	Wyoming	
308	Nebraska (North Platte)	
309	Illinois (Moline, Peoria)	
310	California (Santa Monica)[1]	
312	Illinois (Chicago Loop)	
313	Michigan (Detroit)	
314	Missouri (downtown St. Louis)	
315	New York (Syracuse, Utica)	
316	Kansas (Emporia, Wichita)	
317	Indiana (Indianapolis)	
318	Louisiana (Shreveport)	
319	Iowa (Cedar Rapids, Dubuque)	
320	Minnesota (St. Cloud)	
321	Florida (Melbourne, Orlando)[2]	
323	California (Los Angeles, except downown)	
330	Ohio (Akron, Cuyahoga Falls)	
334	Alabama (Mobile, Montgomery)	

336	North Carolina (Greensboro)
337	Louisiana (Lafayette)[1]
340	U.S. Virgin Islands
341	California (Berkeley, Oakland)[1]
345	Cayman Islands
347	New York (Bronx, Brooklyn, Queens, Staten Island)[1]
352	Florida (Gainesville, Ocala)
360	Washington (Bellingham, Vancouver)
361	Texas (Corpus Christi)
401	Rhode Island
402	Nebraska (Lincoln, Omaha)
403	Alberta (Calgary)
404	Georgia (Atlanta)
405	Oklahoma (Oklahoma City)
406	Montana
407	Florida (Orlando, Kissimmee)[2]
408	California (San Jose)[1]
409	Texas (Galveston)
410	Maryland (Baltimore, Annapolis)[1]
412	Pennsylvania (Pittsburgh)[1]
413	Massachusetts (Springfield)
414	Wisconsin (Milwaukee)
415	California (San Francisco)
416	Ontario (Toronto)
417	Missouri (Joplin, Springfield)
418	Quebec (Quebec City)
419	Ohio (Sandusky, Toledo)
423	Tennessee (Chattanooga, Johnson City)
424	California (Santa Monica)[1]
425	Washington (Bellevue, Redmond)
435	Utah (Ogden)
440	Ohio (Cleveland suburbs)
441	Bermuda
443	Maryland (Baltimore, Annapolis)[1]
450	Quebec (Montreal suburbs)
469	Texas (Dallas)[1]
473	Grenada
480	Arizona (Mesa, Scottsdale)[1]
484	Pennsylvania (Allentown, Reading)[1]
501	Arkansas (Little Rock, Hot Springs)
502	Kentucky (Louisville)
503	Oregon (Portland, Salem)[1]
504	Louisiana (New Orleans)
505	New Mexico
506	New Brunswick, Canada
507	Minnesota (Rochester, Winona)
508	Massachusetts (Cape Cod, Plymouth, Worcester)
509	Washington (Spokane, Yakima)
510	California (Berkeley, Oakland)[1]
512	Texas (Austin)
513	Ohio (Cincinnati)
514	Quebec (downtown Montreal)
515	Iowa (Ames, Des Moines)
516	New York (Western Long Island: Nassau County)
517	Michigan (Lansing, Saginaw)
518	New York (Albany, Schenectady)
519	Ontario, Canada (London)
520	Arizona (Flagstaff, Tucson)
530	California (Chico, Redding, Yreka)

540	Virginia (Roanoke)
541	Oregon (Eugene, Medford)
559	California (Fresno)
561	Florida (Boca Raton, West Palm Beach)
562	California (Long Beach)
570	Pennsylvania (Scranton)
571	Virginia (Alexandria, Arlington)[1]
573	Missouri (Columbia, Jefferson City)
580	Oklahoma (Lawton, Stillwater)
601	Mississippi (Jackson, Natchez)
602	Arizona (Phoenix, Tempe)
603	New Hampshire
604	British Columbia (Whistler)
605	South Dakota
606	Kentucky (Covington, Lexington)
607	New York (Binghampton, Elmira)
608	Wisconsin (La Crosse, Madison)
609	New Jersey (Atlantic City, Long Branch)
610	Pennsylvania (Allentown, Reading)[1]
612	Minnesota (Minneapolis)
613	Ontario (Ottawa)
614	Ohio (Columbus)
615	Tennessee (Nashville)
616	Michigan (Grand Rapids, Kalamazoo)
617	Massachusetts (Boston)
618	Illinois (Centralia, E. St. Louis)
619	California (downtown San Diego)
623	Arizona (Glendale, Peoria)
626	California (Pasadena)
630	Illinois (Oak Brook)
636	Missouri (St. Louis suburbs)
646	New York (Manhattan)[1]
649	Turks & Caicos Islands
650	California (Los Gatos, Palo Alto)
651	Minnesota (St. Paul)
660	Missouri (Sedalia)
661	California (Bakersfield)
662	Mississippi (Yazoo City, Tupelo)
664	Montserrat
669	California (San Jose)[1]
670	Northern Mariana Islands
671	Guam
678	Georgia (Marietta, Smyrna)[1]
701	North Dakota
702	Nevada (Las Vegas)
703	Virginia (Alexandria, Arlington)[1]
704	North Carolina (Charlotte, Gastonia)
705	Ontario (North Bay)
706	Georgia (Augusta)
707	California (Santa Rosa, Eureka)
708	Illinois (Cicero, Oak Lawn)
709	Newfoundland
712	Iowa (Council Bluffs, Sioux City)
713	Texas (Houston)[1]
714	California (Santa Ana)
715	Wisconsin (Eau Claire, Wausau)
716	New York (Buffalo, Rochester)

717 Pennsylvania (Harrisburg, Scranton)	808 Hawaii	904 Florida (Jacksonville)
718 New York City (Bronx, Brooklyn, Queens, Staten Island)	809 Dominican Republic	905 Ontario (Hamilton, Niagara Falls)
	810 Michigan (Flint)	906 Michigan (Upper Peninsula)
719 Colorado (Colorado Springs, Pueblo)	812 Indiana (Evansville, Terre Haute)	907 Alaska
	813 Florida (Tampa)	908 New Jersey (Elizabeth)
720 Colorado (Denver, Englewood)[1]	814 Pennsylvania (Altoona, Erie)	909 California (San Bernardino, Pomona)
	815 Illinois (Joliet, Rockford)	910 North Carolina (Fayetteville, Wilmington)
724 Pennsylvania (Pittsburgh)	816 Missouri (Kansas City, St. Joseph)	
727 Florida (St. Petersburg)		912 Georgia (Macon, Savannah)
732 New Jersey (Middlesex)	817 Texas (Arlington, Fort Worth)	913 Kansas (Kansas City)
734 Michigan (Ann Arbor, Ypsilanti)	818 California (Burbank, Pasadena)	914 New York (White Plains, Yonkers)
	819 Quebec (Sherbrooke)	
740 Ohio (Athens)	828 North Carolina (Asheville, Morganton)	915 Texas (Abilene, El Paso)
757 Virginia (Hampton, Virginia Beach)		916 California (Sacramento)
	830 Texas (Fredericksburg)	917 New York (New York City: cell phones and pagers)
758 St. Lucia	831 California (Monterey)	
760 California (Palm Springs, Calexico)	832 Texas (Houston)[1]	918 Oklahoma (Muskogee, Tulsa)
	843 South Carolina (Charleston)	919 North Carolina (Raleigh, Durham)
765 Indiana (Kokomo, Muncie)	847 Illinois (Des Plaines, Evanston)	
767 Dominica	850 Florida (Pensacola, Tallahassee)	920 Wisconsin (Appleton, Green Bay)
770 Georgia (Marietta, Smyrna)[1]		
773 Illinois (Chicago except the Loop)	856 New Jersey (Camden, Trenton)[1]	925 California (Concord)
	858 California (Northern San Diego, La Jolla)	931 Tennessee (Murfreesboro)
775 Nevada (Carson City, Reno)		935 California (Southern San Diego, Coronado, La Mesa)
780 Alberta (Edmonton)	860 Connecticut (Hartford)	
781 Massachusetts (Arlington, Revere, Woburn)	863 Florida (Lakeland, Winter Haven)	937 Ohio (Dayton)
		940 Texas (Wichita Falls)
784 St. Vincent and the Grenadines	864 South Carolina (Greenville-Spartanburg)	941 Florida (Fort Myers, Sarasota)
785 Kansas (Topeka, Manhattan)	865 Tennessee (Knoxville)	949 California (Irvine)
786 Florida (Miami)[1]	867 Yukon and Northwest Territories	951 California (Riverside, Corona)
787 Puerto Rico		954 Florida (Ft. Lauderdale, Hollywood)
801 Utah	868 Trinidad & Tobago	
802 Vermont	869 St. Kitt's & Nevis	956 Texas (Laredo, McAllen)
803 South Carolina (Augusta, Columbia)	870 Arkansas (Jonesboro, Arkadelphia)	970 Colorado (Aspen, Grand Junction)
804 Virginia (Norfolk, Richmond)	876 Jamaica	971 Oregon (Portland, Salem)[1]
805 California (Santa Barbara)	901 Tennessee (Jackson, Memphis)	972 Texas (Dallas)[1]
806 Texas (Amarillo)	902 Nova Scotia, Prince Edward Island	973 New Jersey (Newark)
807 Ontario (Fort William, Thunder Bay)		978 Massachusetts (Andover, Salem)
	903 Texas (Paris, Texarkana)	

Note: When no cities are listed, area code is for entire state or province. 1. Area in which there is an overlay, or more than one area code for the area. 2. The 321 area code is an overlay on the 407 area code in the Orlando area only. Area codes in this area may be either 321 or 407. All area codes in the Melbourne area are 321. **Source:** Lockheed Martin, North American Numbering Plan Relief Letters, 1999. www.nanpa.com.

THE INTERNET

The Internet, an intricate web of tens of thousands computer networks linked by telephone lines, was created by the U.S. Defense Department in 1969 as a faster way for agencies to share information and as an emergency means of communications in case more traditional means were cut off. But the potential for consumer Internet use didn't occur until the 1980s, when the National Science Foundation created equipment that would allow other computer networks to connect to the government's larger network. From there, commercial services such as CompuServe, Prodigy, and America Online tapped into the ever-growing network and brought a wealth of information to anybody with a computer, a modem, and the monthly fee. In 1993 some three million people worldwide were connected to the Internet. By mid-1999, according to some estimates, the total had climbed to nearly 200 million.

Today, the Internet is the world's largest communications network. The number of names registered in the *domain name system*—Web sites of commercial enterprises, private and public institutions, and other major organizations—climbed to over 3 million in 1999. According to one study, the total number of searchable Web pages reached approximately 800 million at mid-year. The Internet carries data around the world in seconds, and links even the most remote user to a vast wealth of resources. The most popular network on the Internet is the *World Wide Web* (WWW, or simply, "the Web"), created in 1989 by CERN, the European Particle Physics Lab in Geneva and made available on the Internet in Aug. 1991. In 1993, the creation of software (Mosaic) that displayed the Internet in a format that resembled a magazine with text and graphics dramatically increased Net usage. In 1994, the Netscape *browser* came on the market, and since then, the Internet has become hugely popular as computer users found they could navigate the Web quickly and easily.

In just a few short years, the Internet and the Web have quite literally transformed the way millions of people go about their daily lives. Everything from mundane tasks such as banking or ordering tickets to the more eventful activities like searching for a job or a date, planning a vacation, or buying a house, can all be done sitting in front of a computer. The Internet also directly affects the work life of people in hundreds of occupations. Physicians, lawyers, real estate agents, and marketing specialists, among others, can all get vital public documents and statistics over the Internet, while many different kinds of businesses can quickly access lengthy government regulations. In addition, there are now thousands of sites on the Web where you can order almost any kind of consumer product. So while the Internet is often oversold and overhyped, it should not be surprising that it is accurately billed as the fastest-growing form of media in history.

▶ Who Uses the Internet

Almost unheard of before 1990, the Internet has entered the vocabulary of most Americans and the homes of a large number of them. Because Internet use is decentralized and almost completely unregulated, statistics on the number of users are not as reliable as for older media. According to a variety of sources, however, the number of regular Internet users in the United States surpassed 50 million—in 25 million households—some time during 1998. (The Internet reached the 50-million mark roughly five years after the medium became commercially viable, compared with 10 for cable TV, 13 for television, and 38 for radio.)

Based on a survey of at least 13 research studies, the organization *eMarketer* compiled the following profile of U.S. Internet users in mid-1999:

- **Gender:** 57.8 percent of Internet users were male.
- **Age:** The average age was 38 (an increase of six years from 1996).
- **Income:** The average was $58,000, with 29 percent in households earning over $75,000 and 18 percent in households over $100,000.
- **Education:** 56 percent of users were college graduates.
- **Occupation:** Education and computer-related fields account for 50 percent of Internet users, professional and managerial fields about 41 percent.

Millions of computer owners continue to access the Internet through a commercial online service such as American Online (founded in 1985). By 1999, AOL topped more than 13 million paying subscribers worldwide. More and more Internet users, however, are gaining access through Internet Service Providers (ISPs), which typically offer cheaper rates but lack some of the proprietary information sources and special features offered by commercial services. Both online services and ISPs—as well as an increasing number of Web sites—offer E-mail service, the primary method of sending messages to other Internet users. E-mail is by far the most popular activity on the Internet; well over 80 percent of U.S. online households report E-mail as a regular activity.

THE WORLD WIDE WEB

The World Wide Web is a vast network of information within the Internet, which uses a hypertext system for quickly transmitting graphics, sound, and video over phone lines. To read the information, users must have a *browser* (such as Netscape Navigator or Microsoft Internet Explorer). Because the hypertext system arranges information based on its relationship to other information rather than in linear or alphabetical order, the Web allows users to find information quickly, especially if they don't know exactly what they're looking for. Each piece of information, or *Web page*, can be connected to one or more other pages via a *link*. For example, the U.S. Census Bureau's Web site (www.census.gov) provides thousands of data tables produced by the Department of Commerce, and is also linked to data from 70 other government agencies.

The Web is divided into zones, which organize the pages according to the type of information generally contained within them. There is of course some overlap, but generally, Web pages of educational institutions end in .edu; government Web pages end in .gov; Web pages of Internet-related institutions end in .net; commercial entities end with .com; and other organizations end with .org.

Growth of the Web
It is becoming increasingly easy for companies, organizations, and even individuals to create their own Web sites. Millions of institutions, groups, and individuals have done so, resulting in such dramatic growth that researchers now estimate that 800 million pages exist on the Web. With so many sites throughout cyberspace, surfers would find it close to impossible to find what they were looking for without a *search engine*. Like a librarian who knows where in the library to find valuable information, search engines look through every Web page and create an index of what appears on each one. So if you're looking for the rules of badminton, you can ask the search engine to check every Web page for mention of the word badminton and it will return a list of Web pages that mention badminton. Yahoo!, AltaVista, Excite, Infoseek, WebCrawler, and Lycos are some of the most popular *search engines*. for an overview of the major ones and how to use then

As the Internet has emerged as a mass medium, the major online service providers, search services, and other Web companies have competed ever more vigorously for user "audience." To attract the greatest number of visitors on a regular basis, many Web sites have expanded from their core services and established broad-based portals—whole arrays of services (such as E-mail, search, special-interest forums and bulletin boards, and chat rooms), information (news, weather, stock reports, reference resources), and links to other useful sites, all accessible from one home page.

Advertising on the Web
Much as it has evolved as a communications medium, like radio and television, the Internet has also emerged as a major advertising vehicle. The ads come in the form of banners that accompany prominent Web pages, sales pitches that come on before the welcome menu when a user logs on, and E-mail offers for credit cards, discount loans, and work-at-home business opportunities.

Estimates of ad spending on the World Wide Web vary considerably, but by all accounts the outlays have skyrocketed. Conservatively estimated, Web ad spending shot from $500-$900 million in 1997 to $1.6-$2.0 billion in 1998, surpassing outdoor billboard advertising for the first time. By 2002, according to moderate forecasts, Web advertising could reach $8.0 billion.

Business on the Web
The increasing sophistication of both technology and users have made the World Wide Web a major and rapidly expanding business medium. No longer just a vehicle for publishing brochures and annual reports, the Web has emerged as a low-cost sales channel for producers of goods and services and as a highly convenient purchasing vehicle for end users. The result has been explosive growth, especially in business-to-business *e-commerce*. According to Forrester Research, Inc., companies spent $43.1 billion on Internet purchases from other companies in 1998. The total was projected to reach $109.3 billion in 1999 and $1.3 trillion by 2003. Currently, about half of the outlays are going to the computer and electronic industries.

Albeit on a much smaller scale, consumer online spending is growing almost as rapidly and bringing revolutionary change to many industries. By most accounts, Christmas 1998 represented the coming out of consumer e-commerce. America Online alone reported that its members spent $1.9 billion shopping online during the holiday season. According to Jupiter Communications, total online consumer purchases in 1998 reached $7.1 billion and were expected to surpass $12 billion in 1999. Travel, computer hardware, and books represent the three largest online consumer shopping categories, each expected to surpass $1 billion in 1999 purchases. Toys, recorded music, clothes, and health and beauty aids are seen as high-growth online commodities in the years to come.

One of the innovative and increasingly popular new forms of e-commerce is online auctioning, which enables consumers to bid from their home computers on special product offerings such as antiques and collectibles. One notable auction site, Ebay (www.ebay.com), claimed more than 6.5 million visitors per month in mid-1999. In a similar vein, Priceline.com invites travelers to name their own price for airline tickets and hotel rooms, which the airlines and hotel chains agree to honor when they have space available.

Few industries are undergoing more radical and rapid change as a consequence of online commerce than stock brokerage and financial services. Round-the-clock access, lower service fees, and push-button immediacy have made it easier, cheaper, and faster for ordinary consumers to buy stock or apply for a loan directly online.

Sex on the Internet

As is the case with almost all new media, the most profitable segment of the market is in erotic businesses. Many people who would not dream of buying an adult magazine or renting an X-rated video have taken advantage of the anonymity provided by so-called cybersex sites. Sex-related sites make up only a small portion of the total number of Web sites (there were believed to be about 40,000 of them in early 1999) but they remain both popular and profitable. According to Media Metrix, which monitors Internet traffic, about one-third of people surfing the Net drop by a sex-related site. Financial analysts report that the most successful sites generate profit margins of 30 to 40 percent.

So-called cyberporn has caused consternation among parents who worry about regulating their children's access to sexual material. In 1996, Congress passed the Communications Decency Act, which attempted to regulate explicit material on the Internet, but the Supreme Court quickly struck it down in 1997 for violating basic constitutional rights to free speech and expression.

▶ A GLOSSARY OF COMMONLY USED INTERNET TERMS

Account Permission to use a computer on a network, or an access agreement with an Internet provider.

Bandwidth The amount of data, graphics, sound, and other information that can be transmitted through cyberspace at a certain time. Bandwidth is measured in kilobits per second (kbps). Most modems have a bandwidth of 28.8 kbps (or simply 28k), though modems offering 56k bandwidth are becoming more common.

Browser A program that translates the hypertext markup language of the World Wide Web into languages humans can understand. Netscape and Microsoft Internet Explorer are the two most common Web browsers.

Cache (Pronounced "cash") The place on a hard drive where a Web browser stores images a user has downloaded off the Internet. If the user wants to see the same Web page again, the browser loads it from the cache rather than retrieve it again from the Internet.

Chat line "talk" An electronic forum in which Internet users can communicate with each other online.

Cookie A small piece of information that a Web *browser* picks up from another site and stores. Such bits of information can be read and altered by another site, thereby making it possible to identify users who have been to the site before. Another use would be to add items to your "shopping cart" as you browse several pages in a virtual shopping mall.

Cyberspace An all-encompassing term for the digital world of computer networks.

Domain The identifying portion of an Internet address (which follows the @ in an E-mail address. Domain names are followed by a period and a three-letter zone that indicates the type of organization. Commercial entities end with *.com*; Educational institutions end with *.edu*; government bodies end with *.gov*; and other organizations end with *.org*.

Download A way to transfer files, graphics, or other information from one computer to another (i.e. from the Internet into your computer). HTTP and FTP are the most common downloading methods.

Encryption A method of encoding files so that only the recipient can read the information. Encryption is necessary for transmitting secure data like credit card numbers over computer networks.

FAQs Frequently Asked Questions. This is generally the first place to stop on a newsgroup or a Web site. It has the answers to the most common questions and indicators of where to go to find the answers to less frequently asked questions.

FTP File Transfer Protocol, the easiest way to download files not on the World Wide Web.

Freeware Free software available over the Internet. This is in contrast with *shareware*, which is available freely, but usually asks the user to send payment for using the software.

Home page The first or main page of a Web site.

HTML HyperText Markup Language, the high-speed computer language used to create documents on the World Wide Web (WWW). To read documents written in HTML, one must have a browser.

HTTP HyperText Transport Protocol, the easiest way to transfer World Wide Web pages from one computer to another

HyperText A system of organizing information based on its relationship to other information, rather than linear or alphabetical orders. Hypertext allows users to *link* related Web pages and to store information in more than one place. For example, in a hypertext almanac, the winners of the National Book Awards could be accessed either through the section on books or the section on awards.

Intranet A smaller network of computers accessible only by members of the network, often members of one firm. Also known as an internal network.

25 Most Visited .com Web sites, 1999

Rank, Site	Visitors[1] (000s)
1. Yahoo.com	32,853
2. AOL.com	29,889
3. MSN.com	22,852
4. Netscape.com	19,320
5. Geocities.com	19,145
6. Go.com	19,064
7. Microsoft.com	15,932
8. Excite.com	15,425
9. Lycos.com	14,568
10. Angelfire.com	13,193
11. Hotmail.com	12,448
12. Tripod.com	11,441
13. Amazon.com	11,167
14. Bluemountainarts.com	9,860
15. Snap.com	8,999
16. Real.com	8,976
17. Ebay.com	8,655
18. Xoom.com	8,636
19. Altavista search services	8,631
20. Zdnet	7,571
21. About.com	6,816
22. Infospace.com	6,807
23. Hotbot.com	6,531
24. MSNBC.com	5,923
25. Looksmart.com	5,553

Note: As measured during the period June 1-30, 1999. 1. Unique visitors, combined at home and at work. **Source:** Media Metrix (1999).

U.S. Online Households and Internet Users, 1996–2002

Year	Total U.S. households (millions)	Online households Number (millions)	Percent	Total Internet users (millions)
1996	98.9	8.5	8.6%	12.5
1997	100.0	14.5	14.5	28.0
1998	101.0	24.4	24.2	47.0
1999	101.7	28.0	27.5	54.0
2000[1]	102.4	32.0	31.3	62.0
2001[1]	103.0	35.3	34.2	68.0
2002[1]	103.5	44.0	42.5	85.0

1. Estimate.   **Source:** U.S. Department of Commerce; eStats.

ISDN Integrated Services Digital Network, a digital type of phone service that permits higher speed transmission of data than conventional phone lines. ISDN lines operate as fast as 128 kilobytes per second (kbps), compared with 28.8 or 56 kbps for the fastest modems.

ISP Internet Service Provider, a company that provides end-user access to the Internet via its central computers and local access lines. American Online (AOL), Earthlink, and Erols are some popular ISPs.

Java A computer language developed by Sun Microsystems that produces programs that run on almost any computer or operating system. Its compatibility and ease of use make it popular for for developing *applets*, tiny applications that can be sent quickly over the World Wide Web.

Link A hypertext connection that allows a user to jump from one Internet site to another by pointing and clicking. On the World Wide Web, links are underlined or highlighted.

Newsgroups Discussion forums on the Internet, arranged by category of special interest. To read, respond to, or post information on a newsgroup, you must have a program known as a Newsreader.

Push technology Technology that pushes information onto a user's computer rather than requiring the user to navigate the Internet and "pull" the information from another computer network. E-mail and newsgroups are simple examples of push technology.

Search engine A tool used to look up Web pages. Also known as an index or a directory. Yahoo!, Excite, Lycos, and AltaVista are some of the most popular search engines.

Server The central computer in a network, providing a service or data access to client computers on that network. Frequently, a Web server is dedicated to a specific function, such as E-mail.

Shareware An honor system in which providers make their programs freely accessible over the Internet, with the understanding that those who use them will send payment to the provider after using them. See also *freeware*.

Spam (*v.*) to send thousands of copies of E-mail, usually advertising a dubious way to make extra money from the comfort of your own home. (*n.*) the junk E-mail that shows up in your E-mailbox when somebody has spammed you.

Thumbnail A tiny picture on a Web page which, when clicked, is replaced by a larger version of the same image.

URL Uniform Resource Locator, the address that identifies a Web page to a browser. Also known as a Web address.

Usenet A system of thousands of newsgroups.

Web page An HTML file, containing text, graphics, and/or mini-applications, viewed with a Web *browser*.

Web site An organized, linked collection of *Web pages* stored on an Internet *server* and read using a Web *browser*. The opening page of a site is called the *home page*.

WebTV A commercial service that accesses the World Wide Web through a television and cable TV wires rather than through a computer and phone wires.

WWW The World Wide Web, or simply the Web, a vast network of information, particularly business, commercial, and government resources, that uses a hypertext system for quickly transmitting graphics, sound, and video over phone lines and allows easy navigation among related subjects.

Zip file A file that has been compressed for simpler transmission over the Internet. To read a ZIP file, you need a program to decompress the file, such as PKUNZIP or WinZip.

▶A FIELD GUIDE TO SEARCHING THE WEB

To search the Web successfully, you need to pick the right engine and learn how to use it. Few people understand that Yahoo is fundamentally different from search engines like Hotbot, AltaVista, and Infoseek. Yahoo is really not a search engine but rather a Web directory, compiled by humans who classify Web sites under headings. The others are Web search engines, which use software agents called "crawlers" or "spiders" to index contents of individual Web pages, then follow links to other pages. Web directories like Yahoo and Web search engines may look the same, but each type of site is good for finding different types of information.

The first step in creating more effective searches is picking the right search site for the job. For a general search, Yahoo or a Yahoo-like directory like Snap or Look Smart is a good place to start. A directory-style search provides two ways to research broad topics: dive through a list of broad topics by clicking on the appropriate links or fill out a search box to find listings.

But directory searches are less effective when looking for specific information—things like the author of a book, the complete text of the Declaration of Independence or research on drug treatments for a medical condition. For this kind of information, search engines like Hotbot and Alta Vista are the way to go. Because they search an index of keywords drawn by spiders from millions of Web pages, the chances are greater that they will find obscure terms in obscure Web pages.

There's a third kind of search site, one that includes popular sites like Metacrawler, Ask Jeeves and Dogpile. These sites—also called *metasearch* tools—don't maintain any kind of index of their own but instead issue search requests to fistfuls of other Web search sites. When Yahoo, Hotbot, Alta Vista and the like return their results, the metasearch site collects them onto a single Web page for display.

Because no two search sites index exactly the same set of Web pages, metasearch tools give you a wider scope of results—but it's worth remembering that more does not necessarily equal better. What really counts is relevant results that are sorted in a relevant order. And that's the rub.

Simply picking one of two or three types of sites to search from is no guarantee of good results. Brad Hill, the author of *World Wide Web Searching for Dummies* (IDG), says most search sites deliver too much information. "Search engines do a good job on indexing," he said. "But because of that, they deliver more than you want."

So when you're faced with several hundred thousand results over dozens of pages, what should you do? "Don't go past the first page of results," Hill said. "If it doesn't have something of interest, you've probably entered the wrong search string."

Most people could get much more relevant results with a few simple tricks for constructing a search "string"—the words you enter in the search box. The most obvious is to type in several relevant words instead of just one or two. In general, the fewer words you enter, the more general your results will be.

Alta Vista (www.altavista.net) Another excellent tool for exhaustive and precise searches, Alta Vista makes it harder than Hotbot does for beginners to construct precise queries, but once you've mastered its search syntax, it's quick and easy to use. Its results, however, can include many duplicates.

Ask Jeeves (www.askjeeves.com) An excellent beginner's site that's also good for anyone's general queries, Ask Jeeves leads you through questions to help narrow your search, and also simultaneously searches six other search sites for relevant Web pages. Its ability to interpret natural language queries makes it easy to learn but also makes constructing precise queries difficult.

Dogpile (www.dogpile.com) This metasearch site can go through 13 Web search engines, more than two dozen online news services or other types of sources, and sorts the results by the search engine that found them. While this is not the most useful presentation if you just want the facts, it's a good way to check which search engine works best for you.

Excite (www.excite.com) Good for searches on broad general topics, Excite adds interesting extras like a simultaneous search of the Web, news headlines, sports scores and company information—and groups the relevant results on a single page. Some reviewers have complained that the search results aren't always relevant.

Hotbot (www.hotbot.com) This is the search site of Wired magazine, whose search engine Inktomi also powers Snap.com's and Yahoo's Web searches. It is an excellent tool for finding specific information. In addition to a thorough and up-to-date index, it provides an easy interface for constructing precise search queries—but this requires extra effort up front.

Infoseek (www.infoseek.com) When searching for Web pages, news stories and Usenet postings, Infoseek produces very accurate and relevant results. But according to Search Engine Watch (www.searchenginewatch.com), it has a much smaller index of Web pages than many others.

Internet Sleuth (www.isleuth.com) Internet Sleuth is a 3,000-strong collection of specialized online databases, which can also simultaneously search up to six other search sites for Web pages, news and other types of information. It's excellent for highly specialized searches in any subjects in its detailed directory—but the metasearch results aren't sorted intuitively.

Lycos (www.lycos.com) Lycos provides a good selection of advanced search capabilities, like the ability to search for specific media types (JPEG files, Java scripts and so on). Its advanced search, Lycos Pro, provides even more options. But general Web searches can produce checkered results. Also, Lycos's index of Web pages is small.

Metacrawler (www.metacrawler.com) This is a metasearch site, simultaneously searching Yahoo, Excite, and five other search engines, then aggregating the results. It's excellent for getting a quick hit of what's out there. But if you don't see what you want in the results, its limited search options make it difficult to issue really precise queries.

Northern Light (www.nlsearch.com) In addition to its index of Web pages, Northern Light also searches through pay-per-view articles from periodicals and books not generally available on the Web. It sorts its results into topic headings, which can prove very useful.

Yahoo (www.yahoo.com) A human-compiled directory of Web sites, Yahoo doesn't help you search for the contents of individual Web pages. It's excellent for researching broad general topics, but tends to return too many results, many of them irrelevant.

▶ Steps to Smart Searching

Pick Your Site No one site is good for every search. Search directories like Yahoo and Lycos are good for researching general topics. Search engines like Hotbot and Alta Vista are better for very specific information. Metasearch sites like Dogpile and Metacrawler use more than one search engine.

Use The Phrase That Pays Enter the two words Strawberry Fields in a search box, and you could get results as diverse as W. C. Fields and strawberry shortcake. Yahoo, Alta Vista, Hotbot and others recognize words in quotes—"Strawberry Fields"—as a phrase. Metacrawler and others provide phrase searching as an option.

Use Browser Click Tricks When checking out results, view them in a new browser window so you can quickly return to the results page without clicking the browser's Back button. In most browsers, you can open a link in a new browser window by holding down the Shift key while clicking on the link. And if a page fails to load the first time you click on a link, try clicking again.

Check Your Spelling Many Web sites are riddled with spelling errors, but for the ones that are worth finding, correct spelling helps. Ask Jeeves and Infoseek provide spelling help for the orthographically challenged. Also, vary the styling of terms, so that a search for CD-ROM, for example, will also turn up CDROM or CD ROM.

Cover All the Bases If you're looking for gardening tips, for example, you may need to account for several different words—garden, gardens, gardening, gardener and so on. Infoseek and Lycos handle plurals and word stems automatically. Alta Vista uses a different approach, the wildcard character. Enter garden* and you'll get results on all the different options. Search sites that don't recognize word stems or wildcards need you to think up variants by yourself and search for them all (e.g., garden OR gardening OR gardens).

Ask for Directions Not every search site works the same way, but all of them provide a help section and tips. A couple of minutes spent checking the help pages can pay dividends later.

Don't Stick Around If you don't find what you're looking for in the first couple of results screens, either go back and enter a different set of search terms or move on to another search site.

Take Advantage of the Operators Most search sites use code words or symbols called operators to make searches more precise. The operators vary from site to site, but the common ones are AND, OR, NOT, quotation marks and the plus and minus signs.

How Operators Work "" (quotation marks) enclose words to search for a phrase: *"Strawberry Fields Forever"*

AND connects two or more words, all of which must appear in the results: *Strawberry AND Fields AND Forever*

OR connects two or more search words, any of which may appear in the results: Strawberry Fields OR Strawberryfields

NOT excludes the word after it from the results: *Strawberry Fields NOT W.C.*

- (minus sign), like NOT, excludes the word that follows it: *Strawberry Fields -W.C.*

+ (plus sign) precedes a word that must appear: *+Strawberry +Fields*

Note that it's possible to string together several operators to construct a very precise query. To exclude certain cover versions of a certain song, for example, you could try: *"Strawberry Fields" AND "The Beatles" NOT "Sandy Farina" NOT "Nashville Superpickers"*

Source: Excerpted from *Desperately Seeking Susan OR Suzie NOT Sushi,* by Matt Lake. Reprinted from *The New York Times,* Sept. 3, 1998.

▶ A WEBSITE DIRECTORY

The Internet provides users with an ever-expanding world of information and online services in virtually every field of interest. Along with the popular *search engines* and portals described above, the sites listed below may provide the beginnings of your personal index. Explore the sites yourself and add the ones you like to the "Bookmarks" or "My Favorites" list in your *browser*.

Computer/Communication Services

eFax (www.efax.com)   A free service that provides private fax numbers. Receive faxes by E-mail; send or forward them for a fee.

ICQ (www.icq.com)   Free downloads for private chat anywhere in the world. Leave messages, alert friends to when you're online. Tens of millions of subscribers.

TalkCity (www.talkcity)   Chat, scheduled chat events, forums, member home pages, celebrity events—a Web community.

Entertainment and Learning

Broadcast.com (broadcast.com)   Live TV and radio broadcasts, CD jukebox of over 1,000 albums, movie trailers, audio books, and more. RealPlayer plug-in available.

Discovery Kids (www.discoverykids.com)   Fun, adventure, and learning from the producers at The Discovery Channel.

Disney.com (www.disney.com)   Part of the GO Network. Features games and activities for kids, content for parents, shopping for Disney merchandise.

How Stuff Works (www.howstuffworks.com)   Engaging, clear, informative explanations of common devices and instruments, digital technologies, the human body, natural phenomena.

The Internet Movie Database (www.imbd.com)   The biggest and best film resource on the Web, covering more than 200,000 movies, extensive filmographies, hundreds of thousands of biographical profiles.

NASA (www.nasa.gov)   The largest repository of space-related information on the Net. Rich in photos and the latest scoop on current and future missions, astronauts, etc.

National Geographic (www.nationalgeographic.com)   Magazine articles, virtual museum exhibits, lectures, a mini-encyclopedia, and more—for kids and adults.

Spinner (www.spinner.com)   Self-proclaimed "First and Largest Internet Music Service." Offers a RealAudio-based player, 100 music channels, and 175,000 songs.

Family and Health

Genealogy.com (www.genealogy.com)   Type in a name, begin your search. Take classes, post queries, find links to other sites. A great place to start a family tree.

Health Risk Assessment (www.youfirst.com)   Tools and information for in-depth personal health Assessment; create a confidential personal profile.

MedicineNet (www.medicinenet.com)   In-depth information, provided by physicians, on diseases, procedures, and pharmaceuticals.

SeniorNet (www.seniornet.com)   Online services and information for people over 50—classes, chat, and more. Subscription.

Finance and Investment

E*Trade (www.etrade.com)   The first and leading Internet trading/investment firm. Includes personalized portfolio management and news.

The Motley Fool (www.fool.com)   Free, easy-to-understand financial information, including timely stock updates, portfolio tracker, and investor chat boards.

MSN MoneyCentral (moneycentral.msn.com)   Portfolio management, stock screening, investment tracking and advice, financial headlines, real-time stock tracker, 401(k) planner, and more.

Quicken.com (quicken.com)   Personal finance site, featuring interactive tools to help with insurance, home-loan, tax-preparation, investment, and retirement-planning needs.

TheStreet.com (thestreet.com)   Extensive online financial information, including daily market analysis and real-time stock ticker.

Stockmaster (www.stockmaster.com)   A leading provider of on line financial information and customized investor relations services.

General Information/Reference

FreeTranslation.com   (www.freetranslation.com)   Uses the Transparent Language translation engine for free translation of documents or Web pages—English, French, German, Italian, Portuguese, and Spanish.

InfoSpace.com (infospace.com)   A rich general reference portal site: white and yellow pages, classifieds, financial information, TV listings, shopping, mapping, and many other directories.

OneLookDictionaries (www.onelook.com)   Access to over 450 general and specialized dictionaries.

Virtual Reference Desk (refdesk.com)   Vast collection of links to general and topical information sites.

Government

Capweb (www.capweb.net)   "The Internet Guide to the Congress," including The Jefferson Project, designed to stimulate electronic public discourse—forums and links.

FedStats (www.fedstats.gov)   A full range of statistics and information from more than 70 U.S. federal agencies.

Internal Revenue Service (www.irs.gov)   Tax forms and instructions, advice, online filing.

The Library of Congress (www.loc.gov)   Photos, documents, online exhibits, legislation text, and other resources make this site valuable for serious research or casual enjoyment.

Stamps.com (www.stamps.com)   Users download software that allows them to print metered postage stickers from their desktop printers and pay for the cost of postage with a credit card account.

U.S. Census Bureau (www.census.gov)   Authoritative, extensive information on U.S. population, demographics, economy, industry and agriculture, education, law enforcement, etc.

The White House (www.whitehouse.gov)   Write to the president, read documents and policy statements, take a tour, browse the archives, etc.

Jobs/Career Development

Careerpath (www.careerpath.com)   Leading career management site for job seekers and employers. Includes job classifieds from the nation's leading newspapers.

Jobs.com (www.jobs.com)   Local job search, resume posting. Extensive listings.

Monster.com (www.monster.com)   Online employment services, including job searches by location, a resume database available to recruiters, and online job application.

News

ABCNews.com (www.abcnews.com)   Headlines, online-only features, videos, instant polls, abundant links. Depth of coverage, frequent updates.

BBC Online (www.news.bbc.co.uk)   The vast international resources of BBC's news organization. World news with a unique perspective.

CNN Interactive (cnn.com)   Late-breaking news and background: multimedia galleries, in-depth analysis, polls, searchable background material, links.

Includes the CNNfn financial news network, and CNNSI, sports coverage with Sports Illustrated.

MSNBC (www.msnbc.com) The most interactive of all the news sites. Includes a personalized news page and compelling polls, chats, and discussions.

The New York Times (www.nytimes.com) Most of the daily paper is available online, as are extensive archives (now for a small fee).

Shopping/Auctions

Alibris (www.alibris.com) Locate use, rare, and hard-to-find books. Millions of titles from a worldwide network of dealers.

Amazon.com (www.amazon.com) The "granddaddy"of consumer online shopping sites, it began with books, then moved into music, video, consumer electronics, and toys. Deep discounts.

Autobytel.com (www.autoweb.com) Online car shopping, with over 2,700 participating dealers. No-haggle price quotes in 24 hours.

Bibliofind (www.bibliofind.com) Nine million used and rare books, periodicals, and ephemera offered by thousands of booksellers around the world. Search for out-of-print titles. Owned by Amazon.com

Bidder's Edge (www.biddersedge.com) Metasearch that scans eight popular online auction sites for those hard-to-find items.

eBay (www.ebay.com) The largest online auction site, with millions of items at all times.

eToys (www.toys.com) Giant online toystore, offering 100,000 items, including video games, books, and baby things.

MSN CarPoint (carpoint.msn.com) Online car shopping service, with 2,000 affiliated dealers and 100,000 used car listings. Personal Auto Pages for tracking your car's service schedule.

MySimon (www.mysimon.com) The largest comparison shopping site on the web, with over 1,000 consumer-goods merchants; includes product information, price comparison, availability.

uBid (www.ubid.com) A central (not person-to-person) online auction house. Great deals on discontinued consumer electronics and computing equipment and more typical auction items.

Sports and Games

ePLAY (www.eplay.com) Activities and games for children 8-12, with lesson plans for parents who want to get involved.

ESPN.com (espn.com) Scores, stories, stats, schedules, standings, video, sound. Up-to-the minute analyses and features. GameCast lets you follow games on your screen as they happen.

Mplayer.com (www.mplayer.com) A free multiplayer gaming service, with more than 4 million members and 80 games.

MSN Gaming Zone (www.zone.com) Backgammon, bridge, chess, spades, electronic action games—free or premium. Play alone or with other members.

The Sporting News (www.sportingnews.com) Hardcore, in-depth coverage. Analysis by 30 well-known columnists. Abundant stats and links, with customizable team/score reporting.

Sportspages.com (www.sportspages.com) Fresh links to the world's best sports pages.

Travel and Weather

BizTravel.com (www.biztravel.com) A multiple-service site for the busy business traveler, including a detailed personal profile, award-program tracking, rate-finder, booking, etc.

Expedia.com (expedia.com) Makes travel planning easy, from research to booking. Find special deals and unique vacations ideas on the Travel Network. Includes mapping features and a staff of travel agents.

Intellicast (www.intellicast.com) Instant access to local, regional, and worldwide weather; current conditions and forecasts.

National Park Service: ParkNet (www.nps.gov) Click on "Visit Your Parks" link for detailed maps and general information on the U.S. national parks.

Preview Travel (www.previewtravel.com) Geared toward business travelers and vacationers; includes *Fodor's Travel Guide* information, Farefinder, and package specials.

Travelocity.com (www.travelocity.com) Owned by Sabre Group, which mainatins the largest worldwide reservation system. Best current fares and packages, E-mail and pager bulletins.

Mapquest.com (www.mapquest.com) Interactive maps and driving directions, customized mapping, and travel information for businesses and consumers.

Part V

AWARDS AND PRIZES
Awards in the Arts and Entertainment

Academy Awards 1928–98

The "Oscars" are officially known as the Academy of Motion Picture Arts and Sciences Awards. They were inaugurated in 1928 as part of Hollywood's drive to improve its less-than-respectable image. Actress Margaret Hamilton once remarked that the statuette looked like her uncle Oscar, and the nickname has stuck ever since. Membership in the Academy (currently over 3,000) is by invitation only, with members divided into 13 branches. Each branch selects up to five nominees for awards in its own area of expertise, with the entire membership making "Best Film" nominations and then voting on all the categories. Major awards are shown in the chart. The year 1934 marked a growing number of award categories. Awards for Best Cinematography and for Best Foreign Film are shown in a separate table. Best Directors are named for films winning Best Picture except where otherwise indicated.

Year	Best picture	Best director	Best actor	Best actress	Best supporting actor	Best supporting actress
1928	Wings	Frank Borzage, Seventh Heaven Lewis Milestone, Two Arabian Knights	Emil Jannings, The Way of All Flesh, The Last Command	Janet Gaynor, Seventh Heaven, Sunrise, Street Angel	No Awards Given	No Awards Given
1929	Broadway Melody	Frank Lloyd, The Divine Lady	Warner Baxter, In Old Arizona	Mary Pickford, Coquette	No Awards Given	No Awards Given
1930	All Quiet on the Western Front	Lewis Milestone	George Arliss, Disraeli	Norma Shearer, The Divorcee	No Awards Given	No Awards Given
1931	Cimarron	Norman Taurog, Skippy	Lionel Barrymore, A Free Soul	Marie Dressler, Min and Bill	No Awards Given	No Awards Given
1932	Grand Hotel	Frank Borzage, Bad Girl	Wallace Beery, The Champ Fredric March, Dr. Jekyll and Mr. Hyde	Helen Hayes, The Sin of Madelon Claudet	No Awards Given	No Awards Given
1933	Cavalcade	Frank Lloyd	Charles Laughton, The Private Life of Henry VIII	Katharine Hepburn, Morning Glory	No Awards Given	No Awards Given
1934	It Happened One Night	Frank Capra	Clark Gable, It Happened One Night	Claudette Colbert, It Happened One Night	No Awards Given	No Awards Given
1935	Mutiny on the Bounty	John Ford, The Informer	Victor McLaglen, The Informer	Bette Davis, Dangerous	No Awards Given	No Awards Given
1936	The Great Ziegfeld	Frank Capra, Mr. Deeds Goes to Town	Paul Muni, The Story of Louis Pasteur	Luise Rainer, The Great Ziegfeld	Walter Brennan, Come and Get It	Gale Sondergaard, Anthony Adverse
1937	The Life of Emile Zola	Leo McCarey, The Awful Truth	Spencer Tracy, Captains Courageous	Luise Rainer, The Good Earth	Joseph Schildkraut, The Life of Emile Zola	Alice Brady, In Old Chicago
1938	You Can't Take It With You	Frank Capra	Spencer Tracy, Boys Town	Bette Davis, Jezebel	Walter Brennan, Kentucky	Fay Bainter, Jezebel
1939	Gone With the Wind	Victor Fleming	Robert Donat, Goodbye, Mr. Chips	Vivien Leigh, Gone With the Wind	Thomas Mitchell, Stagecoach	Hattie McDaniel, Gone With the Wind
1940	Rebecca	John Ford, The Grapes of Wrath	James Stewart, The Philadelphia Story	Ginger Rogers, Kitty Foyle	Walter Brennan, The Westerner	Jane Darwell, The Grapes of Wrath
1941	How Green Was My Valley	John Ford	Gary Cooper, Sergeant York	Joan Fontaine, Suspicion	Donald Crisp, How Green Was My Valley	Mary Astor, The Great Lie
1942	Mrs. Miniver	William Wyler	James Cagney, Yankee Doodle Dandy	Greer Garson, Mrs. Miniver	Van Heflin, Johnny Eager	Teresa Wright, Mrs. Miniver

Year	Best picture	Best director	Best actor	Best actress	Best supporting actor	Best supporting actress
1943	Casablanca	Michael Curtiz	Paul Lukas, Watch On The Rhine	Jennifer Jones, The Song of Bernadette	Charles Coburn, The More the Merrier	Katina Paxinou, For Whom the Bell Tolls
1944	Going My Way	Leo McCarey	Bing Crosby, Going My Way	Ingrid Bergman, Gaslight	Barry Fitzgerald, Going My Way	Ethel Barrymore, None But the Lonely Heart
1945	The Lost Weekend	Billy Wilder	Ray Milland, The Lost Weekend	Joan Crawford, Mildred Pierce	James Dunn, A Tree Grows in Brooklyn	Anne Revere, National Velvet
1946	The Best Years of Our Lives	William Wyler	Fredric March, The Best Years of Our Lives	Olivia De Havilland, To Each His Own	Harold Russell, The Best Years of Our Lives	Anne Baxter, The Razor's Edge
1947	Gentleman's Agreement	Elia Kazan	Ronald Colman, A Double Life	Loretta Young, The Farmer's Daughter	Edmund Gwenn, Miracle on 34th Street	Celeste Holm, Gentleman's Agreement
1948	Hamlet	John Huston, The Treasure of the Sierra Madre	Laurence Olivier, Hamlet	Jane Wyman, Johnny Belinda	Walter Huston, The Treasure of the Sierra Madre	Claire Trevor, Key Largo
1949	All the King's Men	Joseph L. Mankiewicz, A Letter to Three Wives	Broderick Crawford, All the King's Men	Olivia De Havilland, The Heiress	Dean Jagger, Twelve O'Clock High	Mercedes McCambridge, All the King's Men
1950	All About Eve	Joseph L. Mankiewicz	José Ferrer, Cyrano de Bergerac	Judy Holliday, Born Yesterday	George Sanders, All About Eve	Josephine Hull, Harvey
1951	An American in Paris	George Stevens, A Place in the Sun	Humphrey Bogart, The African Queen	Vivien Leigh, A Streetcar Named Desire	Karl Malden, A Streetcar Named Desire	Kim Hunter, A Streetcar Named Desire
1952	The Greatest Show on Earth	John Ford, The Quiet Man	Gary Cooper, High Noon	Shirley Booth, Come Back, Little Sheba	Anthony Quinn, Viva Zapata!	Gloria Grahame, The Bad and the Beautiful
1953	From Here to Eternity	Fred Zinnemann	William Holden, Stalag 17	Audrey Hepburn, Roman Holiday	Frank Sinatra, From Here to Eternity	Donna Reed, From Here to Eternity
1954	On the Waterfront	Elia Kazan	Marlon Brando, On the Waterfront	Grace Kelly, The Country Girl	Edmond O'Brien, The Barefoot Contessa	Eva Marie Saint, On the Waterfront
1955	Marty	Delbert Mann	Ernest Borgnine, Marty	Anna Magnani, The Rose Tattoo	Jack Lemmon, Mister Roberts	Jo Van Fleet, East of Eden
1956	Around the World in 80 Days	George Stevens, Giant	Yul Brynner, The King And I	Ingrid Bergman, Anastasia	Anthony Quinn, Lust for Life	Dorothy Malone, Written on the Wind
1957	The Bridge on the River Kwai	David Lean	Alec Guinness, The Bridge on the River Kwai	Joanne Woodward, The Three Faces of Eve	Red Buttons, Sayonara	Miyoshi Umeki, Sayonara
1958	Gigi	Vincente Minnelli	David Niven, Separate Tables	Susan Hayward, I Want to Live!	Burl Ives, The Big Country	Wendy Hiller, Separate Tables
1959	Ben-Hur	William Wyler	Charlton Heston, Ben-Hur	Simone Signoret, Room at the Top	Hugh Griffith, Ben-Hur	Shelley Winters, The Diary of Anne Frank
1960	The Apartment	Billy Wilder	Burt Lancaster, Elmer Gantry	Elizabeth Taylor, Butterfield 8	Peter Ustinov, Spartacus	Shirley Jones, Elmer Gantry
1961	West Side Story	Jerome Robbins, Robert Wise	Maximilian Schell, Judgment At Nuremberg	Sophia Loren, Two Women	George Chakiris, West Side Story	Rita Moreno, West Side Story
1962	Lawrence of Arabia	David Lean	Gregory Peck, To Kill a Mockingbird	Anne Bancroft, The Miracle Worker	Ed Begley, Sweet Bird of Youth	Patty Duke, The Miracle Worker
1963	Tom Jones	Tony Richardson	Sidney Poitier, Lilies of the Field	Patricia Neal, Hud	Melvyn Douglas, Hud	Margaret Rutherford, The V.I.P.s
1964	My Fair Lady	George Cukor	Rex Harrison, My Fair Lady	Julie Andrews, Mary Poppins	Peter Ustinov, Topkapi	Lila Kedrova, Zorba the Greek

Year	Best picture	Best director	Best actor	Best actress	Best supporting actor	Best supporting actress
1965	The Sound of Music	Robert Wise	Lee Marvin, Cat Ballou	Julie Christie, Darling	Martin Balsam, A Thousand Clowns	Shelley Winters, A Patch of Blue
1966	A Man for All Seasons	Fred Zinnemann	Paul Scofield, A Man for All Seasons	Elizabeth Taylor, Who's Afraid of Virginia Woolf?	Walter Matthau, The Fortune Cookie	Sandy Dennis, Who's Afraid of Virginia Woolf?
1967	In the Heat of the Night	Mike Nichols, The Graduate	Rod Steiger, In the Heat of the Night	Katharine Hepburn, Guess Who's Coming to Dinner	George Kennedy, Cool Hand Luke	Estelle Parsons, Bonnie and Clyde
1968	Oliver!	Carol Reed	Cliff Robertson, Charly	Katharine Hepburn, The Lion in Winter, Barbra Streisand, Funny Girl	Jack Albertson, The Subject Was Roses	Ruth Gordon, Rosemary's Baby
1969	Midnight Cowboy	John Schlesinger	John Wayne, True Grit	Maggie Smith, The Prime of Miss Jean Brodie	Gig Young, They Shoot Horses, Don't They?	Goldie Hawn, Cactus Flower
1970	Patton	Franklin J. Schaffner	George C. Scott, Patton	Glenda Jackson, Women in Love	John Mills, Ryan's Daughter	Helen Hayes, Airport
1971	The French Connection	William Friedkin	Gene Hackman, The French Connection	Jane Fonda, Klute	Ben Johnson, The Last Picture Show	Cloris Leachman, The Last Picture Show
1972	The Godfather	Bob Fosse, Cabaret	Marlon Brando, The Godfather	Liza Minnelli, Cabaret	Joel Grey, Cabaret	Eileen Heckart, Butterflies Are Free
1973	The Sting	George Roy Hill	Jack Lemmon, Save the Tiger	Glenda Jackson, A Touch of Class	John Houseman, The Paper Chase	Tatum O'Neal, Paper Moon
1974	The Godfather, Part II	Francis Ford Coppola	Art Carney, Harry And Tonto	Ellen Burstyn, Alice Doesn't Live Here Anymore	Robert De Niro, The Godfather, Part II	Ingrid Bergman, Murder on the Orient Express
1975	One Flew Over the Cuckoo's Nest	Milos Forman	Jack Nicholson, One Flew Over the Cuckoo's Nest	Louise Fletcher, One Flew Over the Cuckoo's Nest	George Burns, The Sunshine Boys	Lee Grant, Shampoo
1976	Rocky	John G. Avildsen	Peter Finch, Network	Faye Dunaway, Network	Jason Robards, All the President's Men	Beatrice Straight, Network
1977	Annie Hall	Woody Allen	Richard Dreyfuss, The Goodbye Girl	Diane Keaton, Annie Hall	Jason Robards, Julia	Vanessa Redgrave, Julia
1978	The Deer Hunter	Michael Cimino	Jon Voight, Coming Home	Jane Fonda, Coming Home	Christopher Walken, The Deer Hunter	Maggie Smith, California Suite
1979	Kramer vs. Kramer	Robert Benton	Dustin Hoffman, Kramer vs. Kramer	Sally Field, Norma Rae	Melvyn Douglas, Being There	Meryl Streep, Kramer vs. Kramer
1980	Ordinary People	Robert Redford	Robert De Niro, Raging Bull	Sissy Spacek, Coal Miner's Daughter	Timothy Hutton, Ordinary People	Mary Steenburgen, Melvin and Howard
1981	Chariots of Fire	Warren Beatty, Reds	Henry Fonda, On Golden Pond	Katharine Hepburn, On Golden Pond	John Gielgud, Arthur	Maureen Stapleton, Reds
1982	Gandhi	Richard Attenborough	Ben Kingsley, Gandhi	Meryl Streep, Sophie's Choice	Louis Gossett Jr., An Officer and a Gentleman	Jessica Lange, Tootsie
1983	Terms of Endearment	James L. Brooks	Robert Duvall, Tender Mercies	Shirley MacLaine, Terms of Endearment	Jack Nicholson, Terms of Endearment	Linda Hunt, The Year of Living Dangerously
1984	Amadeus	Milos Forman	F. Murray Abraham, Amadeus	Sally Field, Places in the Heart	Haing S. Ngor, The Killing Fields	Peggy Ashcroft, A Passage to India

Year	Best picture	Best director	Best actor	Best actress	Best supporting actor	Best supporting actress
1985	Out of Africa	Sydney Pollack	William Hurt, *Kiss of the Spider Woman*	Geraldine Page, *The Trip to Bountiful*	Don Ameche, *Cocoon*	Anjelica Huston, *Prizzi's Honor*
1986	Platoon	Oliver Stone	Paul Newman, *The Color of Money*	Marlee Matlin, *Children of a Lesser God*	Michael Caine, *Hannah and Her Sisters*	Dianne Wiest, *Hannah and Her Sisters*
1987	The Last Emperor	Bernardo Bertolucci	Michael Douglas, *Wall Street*	Cher, *Moonstruck*	Sean Connery, *The Untouchables*	Olympia Dukakis, *Moonstruck*
1988	Rain Man	Barry Levinson	Dustin Hoffman, *Rain Man*	Jodie Foster, *The Accused*	Kevin Kline, *A Fish Called Wanda*	Geena Davis, *The Accidental Tourist*
1989	Driving Miss Daisy	Oliver Stone, *Born on the Fourth of July*	Daniel Day-Lewis, *My Left Foot*	Jessica Tandy, *Driving Miss Daisy*	Denzel Washington, *Glory*	Brenda Fricker, *My Left Foot*
1990	Dances with Wolves	Kevin Costner	Jeremy Irons, *Reversal of Fortune*	Kathy Bates, *Misery*	Joe Pesci, *Goodfellas*	Whoopi Goldberg, *Ghost*
1991	The Silence of the Lambs	Jonathan Demme	Anthony Hopkins, *The Silence of the Lambs*	Jodie Foster, *The Silence of the Lambs*	Jack Palance, *City Slickers*	Mercedes Ruehl, *The Fisher King*
1992	Unforgiven	Clint Eastwood	Al Pacino, *Scent of a Woman*	Emma Thompson, *Howards End*	Gene Hackman, *Unforgiven*	Marisa Tomei, *My Cousin Vinny*
1993	Schindler's List	Steven Spielberg	Tom Hanks, *Philadelphia*	Holly Hunter, *The Piano*	Tommy Lee Jones, *The Fugitive*	Anna Paquin, *The Piano*
1994	Forrest Gump	Robert Zemeckis	Tom Hanks, *Forrest Gump*	Jessica Lange, *Blue Sky*	Martin Landau, *Ed Wood*	Dianne Wiest, *Bullets Over Broadway*
1995	Braveheart	Mel Gibson	Nicolas Cage *Leaving Las Vegas*	Susan Sarandon, *Dead Man Walking*	Kevin Spacey, *The Usual Suspects*	Mira Sorvino, *Mighty Aphrodite*
1996	The English Patient	Anthony Minghella	Geoffrey Rush, *Shine*	Frances McDormand, *Fargo*	Cuba Gooding Jr., *Jerry Maguire*	Juliette Binoche, *The English Patient*
1997	Titanic	James Cameron	Jack Nicholson, *As Good as it Gets*	Helen Hunt, *As Good as it Gets*	Robin Williams *Good Will Hunting*	Kim Basinger, *L.A. Confidential*
1998	Shakespeare in Love	Steven Spielberg, *Saving Private Ryan*	Roberto Benigni *Life is Beautiful*	Gwyneth Paltrow, *Shakespeare in Love*	James Coburn, *Affliction*	Judi Dench, *Shakespeare in Love*

Academy Awards for Cinematography, 1928–98

Year	Cinematographer, Film	Year	Cinematographer, Film
1928	Charles Rosher, Karl Struss, *Sunrise*	1941	Arthur Miller, *How Green Was My Valley*
1929	Clyde DeVinna, *White Shadows, In the South Seas*		Ernest Palmer, Ray Rennahan, *Blood and Sand*
1930	Joseph T. Rucker, Willard Van Der Veer, *With Byrd at the South Pole*	1942	Joseph Ruttenberg, *Mrs. Miniver*
1931	Floyd Crosby, *Tabu*		Leon Shamroy, *The Black Swan*
1932	Lee Garmes, *Shanghai Express*	1943	Arthur Miller, *The Song of Bernadette*
1933	Charles Bryant Lang Jr., *A Farewell to Arms*		Hal Mohr, W. Howard Greene, *The Phantom of the Opera*
1934	Victor Milner, *Cleopatra*	1944	Joseph LaShelle, *Laura*
1935	Hal Mohr, *A Midsummer Night's Dream*		Leon Shamroy, *Wilson*
1936	Gaetano Gaudio, *Anthony Adverse*	1945	Harry Stradling, *The Picture of Dorian Gray*
1937	Karl Freund, *The Good Earth*		Leon Shamroy, *Leave Her to Heaven*
1938	Joseph Ruttenberg, *The Great Waltz*	1946	Arthur Miller, *Anna and the King of Siam*
1939	Gregg Toland, *Wuthering Heights*		Charles Rosher, Leonard Smith, Arthur Arling, *The Yearling*
	Ernest Haller, Ray Rennahan, *Gone With the Wind*	1947	Guy Green, *Great Expectations*
1940	George Barnes, *Rebecca*	1948	William Daniels, *The Naked City*
	George Perinal, *Thief of Baghdad*		Joseph Valentine, William V. Skall, Winton Hoch, *Joan of Arc*

Year	Cinematographer, Film	Year	Cinematographer, Film
1949	Paul C. Vogel, *Battleground*	1966	Haskell Wexler, *Who's Afraid of Virginia*
	Winton Hoch, *She Wore a Yellow Ribbon*		*Woolf?* Ted Moore, *A Man for All Seasons*
1950	Robert Krasker, *The Third Man*	1967	Burnett Guffey, *Bonnie and Clyde*
	Robert Surtees, *King Solomon's Mines*	1968	Pasqualino De Santis, *Romeo and Juliet*
1951	William C. Mellor, *A Place in the Sun*	1969	Conrad Hall, *Butch Cassidy and the*
	Alfred Gilks, John Alton (ballet), *An*		*Sundance Kid*
	American in Paris	1970	Freddie Young, *Ryan's Daughter*
1952	Robert Surtees, *The Bad and the Beautiful*	1971	Oswald Morris, *Fiddler on the Roof*
	Winton Hoch, Archie Stout, *The Quiet Man*	1972	Geoffrey Unsworth, *Cabaret*
1953	Burnett Guffey, *From Here to Eternity*	1973	Sven Nykvist, *Cries and Whispers*
	Loyal Griggs, *Shane*	1974	Fred Koenekamp, Joseph Biroc,
1954	Boris Kaufman, *On the Waterfront*		*The Towering Inferno*
	Milton Krasner, *Three Coins in the Fountain*	1975	John Alcott, *Barry Lyndon*
1955	James Wong Howe, *The Rose Tattoo*	1976	Haskell Wexler, *Bound for Glory*
	Robert Burks, *To Catch a Thief*	1977	Vilmos Zsigmond, *Close Encounters of the*
1956	Joseph Ruttenberg, *Sombody Up There*		*Third Kind*
	Likes Me	1978	Nestor Almendros, *Days of Heaven*
	Lionel Lindon, *Around the World in 80 Days*	1979	Vittorio Storaro, *Apocalypse Now*
1957	Jack Hildyard, *The Bridge on the River*	1980	Geoffrey Unsworth, Ghislain Cloquet, *Tess*
	Kwai	1981	Vittorio Storaro, *Reds*
1958	Sam Leavitt, *The Defiant Ones*	1982	Billy Williams, Ronnie Taylor, *Gandhi*
	Joseph Ruttenberg, *Gigi*	1983	Sven Nykvist, *Fanny & Alexander*
1959	William C. Mellor, *The Diary of Anne Frank*	1984	Chris Menges, *The Killing Fields*
	Robert L. Surtees, *Ben-Hur*	1985	David Watkin, *Out of Africa*
1960	Freddie Francis, *Sons and Lovers*	1986	Chris Menges, *The Mission*
	Russell Metty, *Spartacus*	1987	Vittorio Storaro, *The Last Emperor*
1961	Eugene Shuftan, *The Hustler*	1988	Peter Biziou, *Mississippi Burning*
	Daniel L. Fapp, *West Side Story*	1989	Freddie Francis, *Glory*
1962	Jean Bourgoin, Walter Wottitz, *The Longest*	1990	Dean Semler, *Dances With Wolves*
	Day	1991	Robert Richardson, *JFK*
	Freddie Young, *Lawrence of Arabia*	1992	Philippe Rousselot, *A River Runs Through It*
1963	James Wong Howe, *Hud*	1993	Janusz Kaminski, *Schindler's List*
	Leon Shamroy, *Cleopatra*	1994	John Toll, *Legends of the Fall*
1964	Walter Lassally, *Zorba the Greek*	1995	John Toll, *Braveheart*
	Harry Stradling, *My Fair Lady*	1996	John Seale, *The English Patient*
1965	Ernest Laszlo, *Ship of Fools*	1997	Russell Carpenter, *Titanic*
	Freddie Young, *Dr. Zhivago*	1998	Janusz Kaminski, *Saving Private Ryan*

Academy Awards for Best Foreign Language Film, 1956–98

Year	Film, Country	Director	Year	Film, Country	Director
1956	*La Strada*, Italy	Federico Fellini	1972	*The Discreet Charm of*	Luis Buñuel
1957	*The Nights of Cabiria*, Italy	Federico Fellini		*the Bourgeoisie*, France	
1958	*Mon Oncle*, France	Jacques Tati	1973	*Day For Night*, France/Italy	François
1959	*Black Orpheus*, France/Italy/	Marcel Camus			Truffaut
	Brazil		1974	*Amarcord*, Italy/France	Federico Fellini
1960	*The Virgin Spring*, Sweden	Ingmar	1975	*Dersu Uzala*, USSR/Japan	Akira
		Bergman			Kurosawa
1961	*Through A Glass Darkly*,	Ingmar	1976	*Black and White in Color*,	Jean-Jacques
	Sweden	Bergman		France/Switzerland/Ivory	Annaud
1962	*Sundays and Cybele*,	Serge		Coast	
	France	Bourgignon	1977	*Madame Rosa*, France	Moshe Mizrahi
1963	*8½*, Italy	Federico Fellini	1978	*Get Out Your Handkerchiefs*,	Bertrand Blier
1964	*Yesterday, Today, and*	Vittorio de Sica		France	
	Tomorrow, Italy/France		1979	*The Tin Drum*, Germany	Volker
1965	*The Shop on Main Street*,	Jan Kadar			Scholondorff
	Czechoslovakia		1980	*Moscow Does Not Believe*	Vladimir
1966	*A Man and a Woman*,	Claude Lelouch		*in Tears*, USSR	Menshov
	France		1981	*Mephisto*, Austria/ Germany/	Istvan Szabo
1967	*Closely Watched Trains*,	Jiri Menzel		Hungary	
	Czechoslovakia		1982	*To Begin Again*, Spain	Jose Luis Garcia
1968	*War and Peace*, USSR	Sergei	1983	*Fanny and Alexander*,	Ingmar
		Bondarchuk		Sweden	Bergman
1969	*Z*, France/Algeria	Constantin	1984	*Dangerous Moves*, France	Richard
		Costa-Gavras			Dembo
1970	*Investigation of a Citizen*	Elio Petri	1985	*The Official Story*, Argentina	Luis Puenzo
	Above Suspicion, Italy		1986	*The Assault*, Netherlands	Fons
1971	*The Garden of the Finzi-*	Vittorio de Sica			Rademakers
	Continis, Italy		1987	*Babette's Feast*, Denmark	Gabriel Axel

Year	Film, Country	Director	Year	Film, Country	Director
1988	*Pelle the Conqueror,* Denmark	Bille August	1994	*Burnt by the Sun,* Russia	Nikita Mikhalkov
1989	*Cinema Paradiso,* Italy	Giuseppe Tornatore	1995	*Antonia's Line,* Netherlands	Marlene Gorris
1990	*Journey of Hope,* Switzerland	Xavier Koller	1996	*Kolya,* Czech Republic	Jan Sverak
1991	*Mediterraneo,* Italy	Gabriel Salvatores	1997	*Character,* Netherlands	Mike van Diem
1992	*Indochine,* France	Regis Wargnier	1998	*Life is Beautiful,* Italy	Roberto Benigni
1993	*Belle Époque,* Spain	Fernando Trueba			

Cannes Film Festival Best Film Awards, 1946–99

The Festival International du Film was scheduled to make its debut in September 1939, but was cancelled that year due to the outbreak of World War II. The first festival was held in 1946. The official name for the best film award has been, variously, Grand Prix (1949–54 and 1964–74) and the Palme d'Or (1955–63 and 1975–present).

Year	Film and director	Year	Film and director
1946	*La Bataille du Rail,* René Clément[1]	1976	*Taxi Driver,* Martin Scorsese
1949[2]	*The Third Man,* Carol Reed	1977	*Padre Padrone,* Paolo and Vittorio Taviani
1951	*Miracle in Milan,* Vittorio De Sica	1978	*The Tree of Wooden Clogs,* Ermanno Olmi
	Miss Julie, Alf Sjöberg	1979	*The Tin Drum,* Volker Schlöndorff
1952	*Two Cents Worth of Hope,* Renato Castellani	1980	*Kagemusha,* Akira Kurosawa
	Othello, Orson Welles	1981	*Man of Iron,* Andrzej Wajda
1953	*The Wages of Fear,* Georges Clouzot	1982	*Missing,* Costa-Gavras
1954	*Gate of Hell,* Teinosuke Kinugasa		*Yol,* Yilmar Güney
1955	*Marty,* Delbert Mann	1983	*The Ballad of Narayama,* Shohei Imamura
1956	*The Silent World,* Jacques Cousteau, Louis Malle	1984	*Paris, Texas,* Wim Wenders
1957	*Friendly Persuasion,* William Wyler	1985	*When Father Was Away on Business,* Emir Kusturica
1958	*The Cranes are Flying,* Mikhail Kalatozov	1986	*The Mission,* Roland Joffé
1959	*Black Orpheus,* Marcel Camus	1987	*Under Satan's Sun,* Maurice Pialat
1960	*La Dolce Vita,* Federico Fellini	1988	*Pelle the Conqueror,* Bille August
1961	*Viridiana,* Luis Buñuel	1989	*sex, lies and videotape,* Steven Soderbergh
1962	*The Given Word,* Anselmo Duarte	1990	*Wild at Heart,* David Lynch
1963	*The Leopard,* Luchino Visconti	1991	*Barton Fink,* Joel Coen
1964	*The Umbrellas of Cherbourg,* Jacques Demy	1992	*The Best Intentions,* Bille August
1965	*The Knack, and How to Get It,* Richard Lester	1993	*The Piano,* Jane Campion
1966	*A Man and a Woman,* Claude Lelouch		*Farewell My Concubine,* Chen Kaige
1967	*Blow-Up,* Michelangelo Antonioni	1994	*Pulp Fiction,* Quentin Tarantino
1969	*If . . . ,* Lindsay Anderson	1995	*Underground,* Emir Kusturica
1970	*M*A*S*H,* Robert Altman	1996	*Secrets and Lies,* Mike Leigh
1971	*The Go-Between,* Joseph Losey	1997	*Taste of Cherries,* Abbas Kiarostami
1972	*The Working Class Goes to Heaven,* Elio Petri		*Unagi (The Eel),* Shohei Imamura
	The Mattei Affair, Francesco Rosi	1998	*Eternity and a Day,* Theo Angelopoulos
1973	*Scarecrow,* Jerry Schatzberg	1999	*Rosetta,* Jean-Pierre and Luc Dardenne
	The Hireling, Alan Bridges		
1974	*The Conversation,* Francis Ford Coppola		
1975	*Chronique des Années de Braise,* M. Lakhdar Hamina		

1. Winner of the International Jury Prize. 2. In 1947, there was no "best film" award as such, but prizes were given instead to outstanding works in several categories, including "Psychological and Love Films," "Adventure and Police Films," and so on. The festival was cancelled in 1948 and 1950.

American Film Institute Life Achievement Awards, 1973–99

Awarded to individuals whose "talent has fundamentally advanced the art of American film or television . . . and whose work has withstood the test of time."

Year	Recipient	Year	Recipient	Year	Recipient	Year	Recipient
1973	John Ford	1980	James Stewart	1987	Barbara Stanwyck	1994	Jack Nicholson
1974	James Cagney	1981	Fred Astaire	1988	Jack Lemmon	1995	Steven Spielberg
1975	Orson Welles	1982	Frank Capra	1989	Gregory Peck	1996	Clint Eastwood
1976	William Wyler	1983	John Huston	1990	David Lean	1997	Martin Scorsese
1977	Henry Fonda	1984	Lillian Gish	1991	Kirk Douglas	1998	Robert Wise
1978	Bette Davis	1985	Gene Kelly	1992	Sidney Poitier	1999	Dustin Hoffman
1979	Alfred Hitchcock	1986	Billy Wilder	1993	Elizabeth Taylor		

The National Film Registry

In 1988, the Library of Congress established the National Film Preservation Board to preserve 25 films each year to add to a National Film Registry. Films selected must be culturally, historically, or aesthetically significant, and they must be at least 10 years old. Films are not limited to Hollywood movie releases; they include documentaries and other noncommercial films such as the Abraham Zapruder film of John F. Kennedy's assassination. As of 1998, the Registry contained 250 films. The 25 additions to the Registry are announced in November of each year. In the list below, years in parentheses indicate the year the film was released.

Adam's Rib (1949)
The Adventures of Robin Hood (1938)
The African Queen (1951)
All About Eve (1950)
All Quiet on the Western Front (1930)
All That Heaven Allows (1955)
American Graffiti (1973)
An American in Paris (1951)
Annie Hall (1977)
The Apartment (1960)
The Awful Truth (1937)
Badlands (1973)
The Band Wagon (1953)
The Bank Dick (1940)
The Battle of San Pietro (1945)
Ben-Hur (1926)
The Best Years of Our Lives (1946)
Big Business (1929)
The Big Parade (1925)
The Big Sleep (1946)
The Birth of a Nation (1915)
The Black Pirate (1926)
Blacksmith Scene (1893)
Blade Runner (1982)
The Blood of Jesus (1941)
Bonnie and Clyde (1967)
Bride of Frankenstein (1935)
The Bridge on the River Kwai (1957)
Bringing Up Baby (1938)
Broken Blossoms (1919)
Cabaret (1972)
Carmen Jones (1954)
Casablanca (1942)
Castro Street (1966)
Cat People (1942)
Chan Is Missing (1982)
The Cheat (1915)
Chinatown (1974)
Chulas Fronteras (1976)
Citizen Kane (1941)
The City (1939)
City Lights (1931)
The Conversation (1974)
Cops (1922)
A Corner in Wheat (1909)
The Cool World (1963)
The Crowd (1928)
Czechoslovakia 1968 (1968)
David Holzman's Diary (1968)
The Day the Earth Stood Still (1951)
Dead Birds (1964)
The Deer Hunter (1978)
Destry Rides Again (1939)
Detour (1946)
Dodsworth (1936)
Dog Star Man (1964)

Don't Look Back (1967)
Double Indemnity (1944)
Dr. Strangelove (or, How I Learned To Stop Worrying and Love the Bomb) (1964)
Duck Soup (1933)
E.T. The Extra-Terrestrial (1982)
Easy Rider (1969)
Eaux d'artifice (1953)
El Norte (1983)
The Exploits of Elaine (1914)
Fantasia (1940)
Fatty's Tintype Tangle (1915)
Flash Gordon Serial (1936)
Footlight Parade (1933)
Force of Evil (1948)
The Forgotten Frontier (1931)
42nd Street (1933)
The Four Horsemen of the Apocalypse (1921)
Frank Film (1973)
Frankenstein (1931)
Freaks (1932)
The Freshman (1925)
From the Manger to the Cross (1912)
Fury (1936)
The General (1927)
Gerald McBoing Boing (1951)
Gertie the Dinosaur (1914)
Gigi (1958)
The Godfather (1972)
The Godfather, Part II (1974)
The Gold Rush (1925)
Gone With the Wind (1939)
The Graduate (1967)
The Grapes of Wrath (1940)
Grass (1925)
The Great Dictator (1940)
The Great Train Robbery (1903)
Greed (1924)
Gun Crazy (1949)
Harlan County, U.S.A. (1976)
Harold and Maude (1972)
The Heiress (1949)
Hell's Hinges (1916)
Hindenburg disaster newsreel footage (1937)
High School (1968)
High Noon (1952)
His Girl Friday (1940)
The Hitch-hiker (1953)
Hospital (1970)
The Hospital (1971)
How Green Was My Valley (1941)
How the West Was Won (1962)
The Hustler (1961)
I Am a Fugitive From a Chain Gang (1932)
The Immigrant (1917)

Intolerance (1916)
Invasion of the Body Snatchers (1956)
It Happened One Night (1934)
It's A Wonderful Life (1946)
The Italian (1915)
Jammin' the Blues (1944)
The Jazz Singer (1927)
Killer of Sheep (1977)
King Kong (1933)
Knute Rockne, All American (1940)
The Lady Eve (1941)
Lassie Come Home (1943)
The Last of the Mohicans (1920)
The Last Picture Show (1972)
Lawrence of Arabia (1962)
The Learning Tree (1969)
Letter From an Unknown Woman (1948)
The Life and Death of 9413—a Hollywood Extra (1927)
The Life and Times of Rosie the Riveter (1980)
The Little Fugitive (1953)
Little Miss Marker (1934)
The Lost World (1925)
Louisiana Story (1948)
Love Me Tonight (1932)
M*A*S*H (1970)
Magical Maestro (1952)
The Magnificent Ambersons (1942)
The Maltese Falcon (1941)
The Manchurian Candidate (1962)
Manhatta (1921)
March of Time: Inside Nazi Germany—1938 (1938)
Marty (1955)
Mean Streets (1973)
Meet Me in St. Louis (1944)
Meshes of the Afternoon (1943)
Midnight Cowboy (1969)
Mildred Pierce (1945)
Modern Times (1936)
Modesta (1956)
Morocco (1930)
Motion Painting No. 1 (1947)
A Movie (1958)
Mr. Smith Goes to Washington (1939)
The Music Box (1932)
My Darling Clementine (1946)
The Naked Spur (1953)
Nanook of the North (1922)
Nashville (1975)
A Night at the Opera (1935)
The Night of the Hunter (1955)
Ninotchka (1939)
North by Northwest (1959)

Nothing but a Man (1964)
On the Waterfront (1954)
One Flew Over the Cuckoo's
    Nest (1975)
Out of the Past (1947)
The Ox-Bow Incident (1943)
The Outlaw Josey Wales (1976)
Pass the Gravy (1928)
Paths of Glory (1957)
Phantom of the Opera (1925)
The Philadelphia Story (1940)
Pinocchio (1940)
A Place in the Sun (1951)
Point of Order (1964)
The Poor Little Rich Girl (1917)
Powers of Ten (1978)
Primary (1960)
The Prisoner of Zenda (1937)
The Producers (1968)
Psycho (1960)
The Public Enemy (1931)
Pull My Daisy (1959)
Raging Bull (1980)
Rear Window (1954)
Rebel Without a Cause (1955)
Red River (1948)
Republic Steel Strike Riot News-
    reel Footage (1937)
Return of the Secaucus 7 (1980)
Ride the High Country (1962)
Rip van Winkle (1896)
The River (1937)
Road to Morocco (1942)

Safety Last (1923)
Salesman (1969)
Salt of the Earth (1954)
Scarface (1932)
The Searchers (1956)
Seventh Heaven (1927)
Shadow of a Doubt (1943)
Shadows (1959)
Shane (1953)
She Done Him Wrong (1933)
Sherlock, Jr. (1924)
Shock Corridor (1963)
Show Boat (1936)
Singin' in the Rain (1952)
Sky High (1922)
Snow White (1933)
Snow White and the Seven
    Dwarfs (1937)
Some Like it Hot (1959)
Stagecoach (1939)
Star Wars (1977)
Steamboat Willie (1928)
Sullivan's Travels (1941)
Sunrise (1927)
Sunset Boulevard (1950)
Sweet Smell of Success (1957
Tabu (1931)
Tacoma Narrows Bridge
    Collapse (1940)
Taxi Driver (1976)
Tevye (1939)
The Thief of Bagdad (1924)
The Thin Man (1934)

To Be or Not to Be (1942)
To Fly (1976)
To Kill a Mockingbird (1962)
Tootsie (1982)
Top Hat (1935)
Topaz (home movie footage
    taken at Japanese-American
    internment camp, the Topaz
    War Relocation Authority
    Center) (1943–45)
Touch of Evil (1958)
The Treasure of the Sierra Madre
    (1948)
Trouble in Paradise (1932)
Tulips Shall Grow (1942)
Twelve O'Clock High (1949)
2001: A Space Odyssey (1968)
Verbena Tragica (1939)
Vertigo (1958)
West Side Story (1961)
Westinghouse Works, 1904
    (1904)
What's Opera, Doc? (1957)
Where Are My Children? (1916)
The Wind (1928)
Wings (1927)
Within Our Gates (1920)
The Wizard of Oz (1939)
A Woman Under the Influence
    (1974)
Woodstock (1970)
Yankee Doodle Dandy (1942)
Zapruder film (1963)

The American Film Institute's 50 Greatest Movie Legends

After ranking the 100 greatest American films, the AFI in 1999 decided to name its top 25 men and women "screen legends," defined as "an actor or team of actors with a significant screen presence in American feature-length films whose screen debut occurred in or before 1950, or whose screen debut occurred after 1950, but whose death marked a completed body of work.

1. Humphrey Bogart
2. Cary Grant
3. James Stewart
4. Marlon Brando
5. Fred Astaire
6. Henry Fonda
7. Clark Gable
8. James Cagney
9. Spencer Tracy
10. Charlie Chaplin
11. Gary Cooper
12. Gregory Peck
13. John Wayne
14. Laurence Olivier
15. Gene Kelly
16. Orson Welles
17. Kirk Douglas
18. James Dean
19. Burt Lancaster
20. The Marx Brothers
21. Buster Keaton
22. Sidney Poitier
23. Robert Mitchum
24. Edward G. Robinson
25. William Holden

1. Katharine Hepburn
2. Bette Davis
3. Audrey Hepburn
4. Ingrid Bergman
5. Greta Garbo
6. Marilyn Monroe
7. Elizabeth Taylor
8. Judy Garland
9. Marlene Dietrich
10. Joan Crawford
11. Barbara Stanwyck
12. Claudette Colbert
13. Grace Kelly
14. Ginger Rogers
15. Mae West
16. Vivien Leigh
17. Lillian Gish
18. Shirley Temple
19. Rita Hayworth
20. Lauren Bacall
21. Sophia Loren
22. Jean Harlow
23. Carole Lombard
24. Mary Pickford
25. Ava Gardner

Source: American Film Institute. www.afionline.org.

The Emmy Awards, 1951–99

The National Academy of Television Arts and Sciences Awards, formed in 1946, presented the First Emmy Awards in 1949. The number and names of awards have changed over the years, but since 1951, the Academy has recognized an outstanding comedy and drama, as well as an actor and an actress in a comedy and in a drama.

Year	Comedy	Drama	Comedy Actor	Comedy Actress	Drama Actor	Drama Actress
1951	The Red Skelton Show (CBS)	Studio One (CBS)	Sid Caesar (NBC)	Imogene Coca (NBC)	(1)	(1)
1952	I Love Lucy (CBS)	Robert Montgomery Presents (NBC)	Thomas Mitchell	Helen Hayes	(1)	(1)
1953	I Love Lucy (CBS)	The U.S. Steel Hour (ABC)	Donald O'Connor, Colgate Comedy Hour (NBC)	Eve Arden, Our Miss Brooks (CBS)	(1)	(1)
1954	Make Room for Daddy (ABC)	The U.S. Steel Hour (ABC)	Danny Thomas, Make Room for Daddy (ABC)	Loretta Young, The Loretta Young Show (NBC)	(1)	(1)
1955	The Phil Silvers Show (CBS)	Producers' Showcase (NBC)	Phil Silvers, The Phil Silvers Show (CBS)	Lucille Ball, I Love Lucy (CBS)	(1)	(1)
1956	The Phil Silvers Show (CBS)	Requiem for a Heavyweight (CBS)	Sid Caesar, Caesar's Hour (NBC)	Nanette Fabray, Caesar's Hour (NBC)	Robert Young, Father Knows Best (NBC)	Loretta Young, The Loretta Young Show (NBC)
1957	The Phil Silvers Show (CBS)	Gunsmoke (CBS)	Robert Young, Father Knows Best (NBC)	Jane Wyatt, Father Knows Best (NBC)	(1)	(1)
1958 –59	The Jack Benny Show (CBS)	(2)	Jack Benny, The Jack Benny Show (CBS)	Jane Wyatt, Father Knows Best (NBC and CBS)	Raymond Burr, Perry Mason (CBS)	Loretta Young, The Loretta Young Show (NBC)
1959 –60	"Art Carney Special" (NBC)	Playhouse 90 (CBS)	Robert Stack, The Untouchables (ABC)	Jane Wyatt, Father Knows Best (CBS)	(1)	(1)
1960 –61	The Jack Benny Show (CBS)	"Macbeth," Hallmark Hall of Fame (NBC)	Raymond Burr, Perry Mason (CBS)	Barbara Stanwyck, The Barbara Stanwyck Show (NBC)	(1)	(1)
1960 –62	The Bob Newhart Show (CBS)	The Defenders (CBS)	E.G. Marshall, The Defenders (CBS)	Shirley Booth, Hazel (NBC)	(1)	(1)
1962 –63	The Dick Van Dyke Show (CBS)	The Defenders (CBS)	E.G. Marshall, The Defenders (CBS)	Shirley Booth, Hazel (NBC) (CBS)	(1)	(1)
1963 –64	The Dick Van Dyke Show (CBS)	The Defenders (CBS)	Dick Van Dyke, The Dick Van Dyke Show (CBS)	Mary Tyler Moore, The Dick Van Dyke Show (CBS)	(1)	(1)
1964 –65	(3)	(3)	(3)	(3)	(3)	(3)
1965 –66	The Dick Van Dyke Show (CBS)	The Fugitive (ABC) (CBS)	Dick Van Dyke, The Dick Van Dyke Show	Mary Tyler Moore, The Dick Van Dyke Show (CBS)	Bill Cosby, I Spy (NBC)	Barbara Stanwyck, The Big Valley (ABC)
1966 –67	The Monkees (NBC)	Mission: Impossible (CBS)	Don Adams, Get Smart (NBC)	Lucille Ball, The Lucy Show (CBS)	Bill Cosby, I Spy (NBC)	Barbara Bain, Mission: Impossible (CBS)
1967 –68	Get Smart (NBC)	Mission: Impossible (CBS)	Don Adams, Get Smart (NBC)	Lucille Ball, The Lucy Show (CBS)	Bill Cosby, I Spy (NBC)	Barbara Bain, Mission: Impossible (CBS)
1968 –69	Get Smart (NBC)	NET Playhouse (NET)	Don Adams, Get Smart (NBC)	Hope Lange, The Ghost and Mrs. Muir (NBC)	Carl Betz, Judd for the Defense (ABC)	Barbara Bain, Mission: Impossible (CBS)
1969 –70	My World & Welcome to It (NBC)	Marcus Welby, M.D. (ABC)	William Windom, My World & Welcome to It (NBC)	Hope Lange, The Ghost and Mrs. Muir (ABC)	Robert Young, Marcus Welby, M.D. (ABC)	Susan Hampshire The Forsyte Saga (NET)

Year	Comedy	Drama	Comedy Actor	Comedy Actress	Drama Actor	Drama Actress
1970 –71	*All in the Family* (CBS)	*The Senator* (segment), *The Bold Ones* (NBC)	Jack Klugman, *The Odd Couple* (ABC)	Jean Stapleton, *All in the Family* (CBS)	Hal Holbrook, *The Senator* (segment), *The Bold Ones* (NBC)	Susan Hampshire, *The First Churchills* (PBS)
1971 –72	*All in the Family* (CBS)	*"Elizabeth R" Masterpiece Theatre* (PBS)	Carroll O'Connor, *All in the Family* (CBS)	Jean Stapleton, *All in the Family* (CBS)	Peter Falk, *Columbo* (NBC)	Glenda Jackson, *"Elizabeth R" Masterpiece Theatre* (PBS)
1972 –73	*All in the Family* (CBS)	*The Waltons* (CBS)	Jack Klugman, *The Odd Couple* (ABC)	Mary Tyler Moore, *The Mary Tyler Moore Show* (CBS)	Richard Thomas, *The Waltons* (CBS)	Michael Learned, *The Waltons* (CBS)
1973 –74	*M*A*S*H* (CBS)	*"Upstairs, Downstairs," Masterpiece Theatre* (PBS)	Alan Alda, *M*A*S*H* (CBS)	Mary Tyler Moore, *The Mary Tyler Moore Show* (CBS)	Telly Savalas, *Kojak* (CBS)	Michael Learned, *The Waltons* (CBS)
1974 –75	*The Mary Tyler Moore Show* (CBS)	*"Upstairs, Downstairs," Masterpiece Theatre* (PBS)	Tony Randall, *The Odd Couple* (ABC)	Valerie Harper, *Rhoda* (CBS)	Robert Blake, *Baretta* (ABC)	Jean Marsh, *"Upstairs, Downstairs," Masterpiece Theater* (PBS)
1975 –76	*The Mary Tyler Moore Show* (CBS)	*Police Story* (NBC)	Jack Albertson, *Chico & the Man* (NBC)	Mary Tyler Moore, *The Mary Tyler Moore Show* (CBS)	Peter Falk, *Columbo* (NBC)	Michael Learned, *The Waltons* (CBS)
1976 –77	*The Mary Tyler Moore Show* (CBS)	*"Upstairs, Downstairs," Masterpiece Theatre* (PBS)	Carroll O'Connor, *All in the Family* (CBS)	Beatrice Arthur, *Maude* (CBS)	James Garner, *The Rockford Files* (NBC)	Lindsay Wagner, *The Bionic Woman* (ABC)
1977 –78	*All in the Family* (CBS)	*The Rockford Files* (NBC)	Carroll O'Connor, *All in the Family* (CBS)	Jean Stapleton, *All in the Family* (CBS)	Edward Asner, *Lou Grant* (CBS)	Sada Thompson, *Family* (ABC)
1978 –79	*Taxi* (ABC)	*Lou Grant* (CBS)	Carroll O'Connor, *All in the Family* (CBS)	Ruth Gordon, *Taxi* (ABC)	Ron Leibman, *Kaz* (CBS)	Mariette Hartley, *The Incredible Hulk* (CBS)
1979 –80	*Taxi* (ABC)	*Lou Grant* (CBS)	Richard Mulligan, *Soap* (ABC)	Cathryn Damon, *Soap* (ABC)	Ed Asner, *Lou Grant* (CBS)	Barbara Bel Geddes, *Dallas* (CBS)
1980 –81	*Taxi* (ABC)	*Hill Street Blues* (NBC)	Judd Hirsch, *Taxi* (ABC)	Isabel Sanford, *The Jeffersons* (CBS)	Daniel Travanti, *Hill Street Blues* (NBC)	Barbara Babcock, *Hill Street Blues* (NBC)
1981 –82	*Barney Miller* (ABC)	*Hill Street Blues* (NBC)	Alan Alda, *M*A*S*H* (CBS)	Carol Kane, *Taxi* (ABC)	Daniel Travanti, *Hill Street Blues* (NBC)	Michael Learned, *Nurse* (CBS)
1982 –83	*Cheers* (NBC)	*Hill Street Blues* (NBC)	Judd Hirsch, *Taxi* (NBC)	Shelley Long, *Cheers* (NBC)	Ed Flanders, *St. Elsewhere* (NBC)	Tyne Daly, *Cagney & Lacey* (CBS)
1983 –84	*Cheers* (NBC)	*Hill Street Blues* (NBC)	John Ritter, *Three's Company* (ABC)	Jane Curtin, *Kate & Allie* (CBS)	Tom Selleck, *Magnum P.I.* (CBS)	Tyne Daly, *Cagney & Lacey* (CBS)
1984 –85	*The Cosby Show* (NBC)	*Cagney & Lacey* (CBS)	Robert Guillaume, *Benson* (ABC)	Jane Curtin, *Kate & Allie* (CBS)	William Daniels, *St. Elsewhere* (NBC)	Tyne Daly, *Cagney & Lacey* (CBS)
1985 –86	*The Golden Girls* (NBC)	*Cagney & Lacey* (CBS)	Michael J. Fox, *Family Ties* (NBC)	Betty White, *The Golden Girls* (NBC)	William Daniels, *St. Elsewhere* (NBC)	Sharon Gless, *Cagney & Lacey* (CBS)
1986 –87	*The Golden Girls* (NBC)	*L.A. Law* (NBC)	Michael J. Fox, *Family Ties* (NBC)	Rue McClanahan, *The Golden Girls* (NBC)	Bruce Willis, *Moonlighting* (ABC)	Sharon Gless, *Cagney & Lacey* (CBS)
1987 –88	*The Wonder Years* (ABC)	*thirtysomething* (ABC)	Michael J. Fox, *Family Ties* (NBC)	Beatrice Arthur, *The Golden Girls* (NBC)	Richard Kiley, *A Year in the Life* (NBC)	Tyne Daly, *Cagney & Lacey* (CBS)
1988 –89	*Cheers* (NBC)	*L.A. Law* (NBC)	Richard Mulligan, *Empty Nest* (NBC)	Candice Bergen, *Murphy Brown* (CBS)	Carroll O'Connor, *In the Heat of the Night* (NBC)	Dana Delany, *China Beach* (ABC)

Year	Comedy	Drama	Comedy Actor	Comedy Actress	Drama Actor	Drama Actress
1989 –90	*Murphy Brown* (CBS)	*L.A. Law* (NBC)	Ted Danson, *Cheers* (NBC)	Candice Bergen, *Murphy Brown* (CBS)	Peter Falk, *Columbo* (ABC)	Patricia Wettig, *thirtysomething* (ABC)
1990 –91	*Cheers* (NBC)	*L.A. Law* (NBC)	Burt Reynolds, *Evening Shade* (CBS)	Kirstie Alley, *Cheers* (NBC)	James Earl Jones, *Gabriel's Fire* (ABC)	Patricia Wettig, *thirtysomething* (ABC)
1991 –92	*Murphy Brown* (CBS)	*Northern Exposure* (CBS)	Craig T. Nelson, *Coach* (ABC)	Candice Bergen, *Murphy Brown* (CBS)	Christopher Lloyd, *Avonlea* (Disney)	Dana Delany, *China Beach*, (ABC)
1992 –93	*Seinfeld* (NBC)	*Picket Fences* (CBS)	Ted Danson, *Cheers* (NBC)	Roseanne Arnold, *Roseanne* (ABC)	Tom Skerritt, *Picket Fences* (CBS)	Kathy Baker, *Picket Fences* (CBS)
1993 –94	*Frasier* (NBC)	*Picket Fences* (CBS)	Kelsey Grammer, *Frasier* (NBC)	Candice Bergen, *Murphy Brown* (CBS)	Dennis Franz, *NYPD Blue* (ABC)	Sela Ward, *Sisters* (NBC)
1994 –95	*Frasier* (NBC)	*NYPD Blue* (ABC)	Kelsey Grammer, *Frasier* (NBC)	Candice Bergen, *Murphy Brown* (CBS)	Mandy Patinkin, *Chicago Hope* (CBS)	Kathy Baker, *Picket Fences* (CBS)
1995 –96	*Frasier* (NBC)	*E.R.* (NBC)	John Lithgow, *Third Rock From the Sun* (NBC)	Helen Hunt, *Mad About You* (NBC)	Dennis Franz, *NYPD Blue* (ABC)	Kathy Baker, *Picket Fences* (CBS)
1996 –97	*Frasier* (NBC)	*Law & Order* (NBC)	John Lithgow, *Third Rock From the Sun* (NBC)	Helen Hunt, *Mad About You* (NBC)	Dennis Franz, *NYPD Blue* (ABC)	Gillian Anderson, *The X-Files* (FOX)
1997 –98	*Frasier* (NBC)	*The Practice* (ABC)	Kelsey Grammer, *Frasier* (NBC)	Helen Hunt, *Mad About You* (NBC)	Andre Braugher, *Homicide* (NBC)	Christine Lahti, *Chicago Hope* (CBS)
1998 –99	*Ally McBeal* (FOX)	*The Practice* (ABC)	John Lithgow, *Third Rock From the Sun* (NBC)	Helen Hunt, *Mad About You* (NBC)	Dennis Franz, *NYPD Blue* (ABC)	Edie Falco, *The Sopranos* (HBO)

Notes: 1. Before 1958, and between 1959 and 1965, the Academy did not give separate acting awards for comedy and drama. 2. *Playhouse 90* (CBS) was best drama of one hour or longer; *Alcoa-Goodyear Theatre* (NBC) was best drama of less than one hour. 3. In 1964, the Academy gave acting awards to Dick Van Dyke for *The Dick Van Dyke Show* (CBS), Lynn Fontaine and Alfred Lunt for *"The Magnificent Yankee" Hallmark Hall of Fame* (NBC), and Barbra Streisand for *My Name is Barbra* (CBS). It also gave "Achievements in Entertainment" awards to these three programs.

Emmy Awards for Variety Shows, 1951–99

Year	Show	Year	Show
1951	*Your Show of Shows* (NBC)	1975–76	*NBC's Saturday Night* (NBC)
1952	*Your Show of Shows* (NBC)	1976–77	*Van Dyke & Company* (NBC)
1953	*Omnibus* (CBS)	1977–78	*The Muppet Show* (syndicated)
1954	*Disneyland* (ABC)	1978–79	"Steve & Eydie Celebrate Irving Berlin" (NBC)
1955	*The Ed Sullivan Show* (CBS)	1979–80	"IBM Presents Baryshnikov on Broadway" (ABC)
1956	*Caesar's Hour* (NBC)	1980–81	"Lily: Sold Out "(CBS)
1957	*The Dinah Shore Show* (NBC)	1981–82	"Night of 100 Stars" (ABC)
1958–59	*The Dinah Shore Chevy Show* (NBC)	1982–83	"Motown 25: Yesterday, Today, Forever" (NBC)
1959–60	"The Fabulous '50s" (CBS)	1983–84	"The 6th Annual Kennedy Center Honors" (CBS)
1960–61	"Astaire Time" (NBC)	1984–85	"Motown Returns to the Apollo" (NBC)
1962–63	*The Andy Williams Show* (NBC)	1985–86	"The Kennedy Center Honors" (CBS)
1963–64	*The Danny Kaye Show* (CBS)	1986–87	"The 1987 Tony Awards" (CBS)
1964–65	*My Name is Barbra* (CBS).	1987–88	"Irving Berlin's 100th Birthday Celebration" (CBS)
1965–66	*The Andy Williams Show* (NBC)	1988–89	*The Tracey Ullman Show* (FOX)
1966–67	*The Andy Williams Show* (NBC)	1989–90	*In Living Color* (FOX)
1967–68	*Rowan & Martin's Laugh-In* (NBC)	1990–91	"The 63rd Annual Academy Awards" (ABC)
1968–69	*Rowan & Martin's Laugh-In* (NBC)	1991–92	*The Tonight Show Starring Johnny Carson* (NBC)
1969–70	*The David Frost Show* (syndicated)	1992–93	*Saturday Night Live* (NBC)
1970–71	*The Flip Wilson Show* (NBC)	1993–94	*Late Show with David Letterman* (CBS)
1971–72	Music: *The Carol Burnett Show* (CBS) Talk: *The Dick Cavett Show* (ABC)	1994–95	*The Tonight Show with Jay Leno* (NBC)
1972–73	*The Julie Andrews Hour* (ABC)	1995–96	*Dennis Miller Live* (HBO)
1973–74	*The Carol Burnett Show* (CBS)	1996–97	*Tracey Takes On . . .* (HBO)
1974–75	*The Carol Burnett Show* (CBS)	1997–98	*Late Show with David Letterman* (CBS)
		1998–99	*Late Show with David Letterman* (CBS)

The Tony Awards, 1947–99

The Tony Awards are presented each year by the American Theatre Wing for distinguished achievement in the Broadway theater. Named for Antoinette Perry, an actress, producer, director, and chairman of the American Theatre Wing who died in 1946, the Tonys were first presented in 1947. Awards are given to performers, authors, producers, directors, composers, and choreographers, and scenic, costume, and lighting designers. Listed here is a selection of major awards for each year: best play (author), performance by an actor in a play, performance by an actress in a play, best musical (composer and lyricist), performance by an actor in a musical, performance by an actress in a musical.

The Tony Awards, 1947–99

PLAYS

Year	Best Play	Best Actor	Best Actress
1947	no award	José Ferrer, *Cyrano de Bergerac.* Fredric March, *Years Ago* (tie)	Ingrid Bergman, *Joan of Lorraine.* Helen Hayes, *Happy Birthday.* (tie)
1948	*Mister Roberts,* Thomas Heggen and Joshua Logan	Henry Fonda, *Mister Roberts;* Paul Kelly, *Command Decision;* Basil Rathbone, *The Heiress* (tie)	Judith Anderson, *Medea;* Katharine Cornell, *Antony and Cleopatra;* Jessica Tandy, *A Streetcar Named Desire* (tie)
1949	*Death of a Salesman,* Arthur Miller	Rex Harrison, *Anne of the Thousand Days*	Martita Hunt, *The Madwoman of Chaillot*
1950	*The Cocktail Party,* T. S. Eliot	Sidney Blackmer, *Come Back, Little Sheba*	Shirley Booth, *Come Back, Little Sheba*
1951	*The Rose Tattoo,* Tennessee Williams	Claude Rains, *Darkness at Noon*	Uta Hagen, *The Country Girl*
1952	*The Fourposter,* Jan de Hartog	José Ferrer, *The Shrike*	Julie Harris, *I Am a Camera*
1953	*The Crucible,* Arthur Miller	Tom Ewell, *The Seven Year Itch*	Shirley Booth, *Time of the Cuckoo*
1954	*The Teahouse of the August Moon,* John Patrick	David Wayne, *The Teahouse of the August Moon*	Audrey Hepburn, *Ondine*
1955	*The Desperate Hours,* Joseph Hayes	Alfred Lunt, *Quadrille*	Nancy Kelly, *The Bad Seed*
1956	*The Diary of Anne Frank,* Frances Goodrich and Albert Hackett	Paul Muni, *Inherit the Wind*	Julie Harris, *The Lark*
1957	*Long Day's Journey Into Night,* Eugene O'Neill	Fredric March, *Long Day's Journey Into Night*	Margaret Leighton, *Separate Tables*
1958	*Sunrise at Campobello,* Dore Schary	Ralph Bellamy, *Sunrise at Campobello*	Helen Hayes, *Time Remembered*
1959	*J.B.,* Archibald Macleish	Jason Robards, *The Disenchanted*	Gertrude Berg, *A Majority of One*
1960	*The Miracle Worker,* William Gibson	Melvyn Douglas, *The Best Man*	Anne Bancroft, *The Miracle Worker*
1961	*Becket,* Jean Anouilh	Zero Mostel, *Rhinoceros*	Joan Plowright, *A Taste of Honey*
1962	*A Man for All Seasons,* Robert Bolt	Paul Scofield, *A Man for All Seasons*	Margaret Leighton, *Night of the Iguana*
1963	*Who's Afraid of Virginia Woolf,* Edward Albee	Arthur Hill, *Who's Afraid of Virginia Woolf*	Uta Hagen, *Who's Afraid of Virginia Woolf*
1964	*Luther,* John Osborne	Alec Guiness, *Dylan*	Sandy Dennis, *Any Wednesday*
1965	*The Subject Was Roses,* Frank Gilroy	Walter Matthau, *The Odd Couple*	Irene Worth, *Tiny Alice*
1966	*Marat/Sade,* Peter Weiss	Hal Holbrook, *Mark Twain Tonight!*	Rosemary Harris, *The Lion in Winter*
1967	*The Homecoming,* Harold Pinter	Paul Rogers, *The Homecoming*	Beryl Reid, *The Killing of Sister George*
1968	*Rosencrantz and Guildenstern Are Dead,* Tom Stoppard	Martin Balsam, *You Know I Can't Hear You When the Water's Running*	Zoe Caldwell, *The Prime of Miss Jean Brodie*
1969	*The Great White Hope,* Howard Sackler	James Earl Jones, *The Great White Hope*	Julie Harris, *Forty Carats*
1970	*Borstal Boy,* Frank McMahon	Fritz Weaver, *Child's Play*	Tammy Grimes, *Private Lives* (R)
1971	*Sleuth,* Anthony Shaffer	Brian Bedford, *The School for Wives*	Maureen Stapleton, *Gingerbread Lady*
1972	*Sticks and Bones,* David Rabe	Cliff Gorman, *Lenny*	Sada Thompson, *Twigs*
1973	*That Championship Season,* Jason Miller	Alan Bates, *Butley*	Julie Harris, *The Last of Mrs. Lincoln*
1974	*The River Niger,* Joseph A. Walker	Michael Moriarty, *Find Your Way Home*	Colleen Dewhurst, *A Moon for the Misbegotten* (R)
1975	*Equus,* Peter Shaffer	(tie) John Kani; Winston Ntshona, *Sizwe Banzi Is Dead; The Island*	Ellen Burstyn, *Same Time, Next Year*
1976	*Travesties,* Tom Stoppard	John Wood, *Travesties*	Irene Worth, *Sweet Bird of Youth* (R)
1977	*The Shadow Box,* Michael Cristofer	Al Pacino, *The Basic Training of Pavlo Hummel*	Julie Harris, *The Belle of Amherst*
1978	*Da,* Hugh Leonard	Barnard Hughes, *Da*	Jessica Tandy, *The Gin Game*
1979	*The Elephant Man,* Bernard Pomerance	Tom Conti, *Whose Life Is It Anyway?*	(tie) Constance Cummings, *Wings;* Carole Shelley, *The Elephant Man*
1980	*Children of a Lesser God,* Mark Medoff	John Rubinstein, *Children of a Lesser God*	Phyllis Frelich, *Children of a Lesser God*
1981	*Amadeus,* Peter Shaffer	Ian McKellen, *Amadeus*	Jane Lapotaire, *Piaf*
1982	*The Life and Adventures of Nicholas Nickleby,* David Edgar	Roger Rees, *The Life and Adventures of Nicholas Nickleby*	Zoe Caldwell, *Medea* (R)
1983	*Torch Song Trilogy,* Harvey Fierstein	Harvey Fierstein, *Torch Song Trilogy*	Jessica Tandy, *Foxfire*
1984	*The Real Thing,* Tom Stoppard	Jeremy Irons, *The Real Thing*	Glenn Close, *The Real Thing*
1985	*Biloxi Blues,* Neil Simon	Derek Jacobi, *Much Ado About Nothing* (R)	Stockard Channing, *Joe Egg* (R)

Year	Best Play	Best Actor	Best Actress
1986	*I'm Not Rappaport,* Herb Gardner	Judd Hirsch, *I'm Not Rappaport*	Lily Tomlin, *The Search for Signs of Intelligent Life in the Universe*
1987	*Fences,* August Wilson	James Earl Jones, *Fences*	Linda Lavin, *Broadway Bound*
1988	*M. Butterfly,* David Henry Hwang	Ron Silver, *Speed-The-Plow*	Joan Allen, *Burn This*
1989	*The Heidi Chronicles,* Wendy Wasserstein	Philip Bosco, *Lend Me a Tenor*	Pauline Collins, *Shirley Valentine*
1990	*The Grapes of Wrath,* Frank Galati	Robert Morse, *Tru*	Maggie Smith, *Lettice and Lovage*
1991	*Lost in Yonkers,* Neil Simon	Nigel Hawthorne, *Shadowlands*	Mercedes Ruhl, *Lost in Yonkers*
1992	*Dancing at Lughnasa,* Brian Friel	Judd Hirsch, *Conversations with My Father*	Glenn Close, *Death and the Maiden*
1993	*Angels in America: Millennium Approaches,* Tony Kushner	Ron Leibman, *Angels in America: Millennium Approaches*	Madeline Kahn, *The Sisters Rosensweig*
1994	*Angels in America: Perestroika,* Tony Kushner	Stephen Spinella, *Angels in America: Perestroika,*	Diana Rigg, *Medea (R)*
1995	*Love! Valour! Compassion!,* Terrence McNally	Ralph Fiennes, *Hamlet*	Cherry Jones, *The Heiress*
1996	*Master Class,* Terrence McNally	George Grizzard, *A Delicate Balance (R)*	Zoe Caldwell, *Master Class*
1997	*Last Night of Ballyhoo,* Alfred Uhry	Christopher Plummer, *Barrymore*	Janet McTeer, *A Doll's House*
1998	*Art,* Yasmina Reza	Anthony La Paglia, *A View From the Bridge*	Marie Mullen, *The Beauty Queen of Leenane*
1999	*Side Man,* Warren Leight	Brian Dennehy, *Death of a Salesman*	Judi Dench, *Amy's View*

MUSICALS

Year	Best Musical	Best Actor	Best Actress
1947	no award	no award	no award
1948	no award	Paul Hartman, *Angel in the Wings*	Grace Hartman, *Angel in the Wings*
1949	*Kiss Me Kate,* Cole Porter (M&L)	Ray Bolger, *Where's Charley?*	Nanette Fabray, *Love Life*
1950	*South Pacific,* Richard Rodgers (M), Oscar Hammerstein (L)	Ezio Pinza, *South Pacific*	Mary Martin, *South Pacific*
1951	*Guys and Dolls,* Frank Loesser (M&L)	Robert Alda, *Guys and Dolls*	Ethel Merman, *Call Me Madam*
1952	*The King and I,* Richard Rodgers (M), Oscar Hammerstein (L)	Phil Silvers, *Top Banana*	Gertrude Lawrence, *The King and I*
1953	*Wonderful Town,* Leonard Bernstein (M), Betty Comden and Adolph Green (L)	Thomas Mitchell, *Hazel Flagg*	Rosalind Russell, *Wonderful Town*
1954	*Kismet,* Alexander Borodin (M), adapted by Robert Wright and George Forrest (L)	Alfred Drake, *Kismet*	Dolores Gray, *Carnival in Flanders*
1955	*The Pajama Game,* Richard Adler and Jerry Ross (M&L)	Walter Slezak, *Fanny*	Mary Martin, *Peter Pan*
1956	*Damn Yankees,* Richard Adler and Jerry Ross (M&L)	Ray Walston, *Damn Yankees*	Gwen Verdon, *Damn Yankees*
1957	*My Fair Lady,* Frederick Loewe (M), Alan Jay Lerner (L)	Rex Harrison, *My Fair Lady*	Judy Holliday, *Bells Are Ringing*
1958	*The Music Man,* Meredith Willson (M&L)	Robert Preston, *The Music Man*	(tie) Thelma Ritter, Gwen Verdon, *New Girl in Town*
1959	*Redhead,* Albert Hague (M), Dorothy Fields (L)	Richard Kiley, *Redhead*	Gwen Verdon, *Redhead*
1960	(tie) *Fiorello,* Jerry Bock (M), Sheldon Harnick (L); *The Sound of Music,* Richard Rodgers (M), Oscar Hammerstein (L)	Jackie Gleason, *Take Me Along*	Mary Martin, *The Sound of Music*
1961	*Bye, Bye, Birdie,* Charles Strouse (M), Lee Adams (L)	Richard Burton, *Camelot*	Elizabeth Seal, *Irma la Douce*
1962	*How to Succeed in Business Without Really Trying,* Frank Loesser (M&L)	Robert Morse, *How to Succeed in Business Without Really Trying*	(tie) Anna Maria Alberghetti, *Carnival;* Diahann Carroll, *No Strings*
1963	*A Funny Thing Happened on the Way to the Forum,* Stephen Sondheim (M&L)	Zero Mostel, *A Funny Thing Happened on the Way to the Forum,*	Vivien Leigh, *Tovarich*
1964	*Hello, Dolly!* Jerry Herman (M&L)	Bert Lahr, *Foxy*	Carol Channing, *Hello, Dolly!*
1965	*Fiddler on the Roof,* Jerry Bock (M), Sheldon Harnick (L)	Zero Mostel, *Fiddler on the Roof*	Liza Minnelli, *Flora, the Red Menace*
1966	*Man of La Mancha,* Mitch Leigh (M), Joe Darion (L)	Richard Kiley, *Man of La Mancha*	Angela Lansbury, *Mame*
1967	*Cabaret,* John Kander (M), Fred Ebb (L)	Robert Preston, *I Do! I Do!*	Barbara Harris, *The Apple Tree*

Year	Best Musical	Best Actor	Best Actress
1968	*Hallelujah, Baby!* Jule Styne (M), Betty Comden & Adolph Green (L)	Robert Goulet, *The Happy Time*	Patricia Routledge, *Darling of the Day;* Leslie Uggams, *Hallelujah, Baby!* (tie)
1969	*1776,* Sherman Edwards (M&L)	Jerry Orbach, *Promises, Promises*	Angela Lansbury, *Dear World*
1970	*Applause,* Charles Strouse (M), Lee Adams (L)	Cleavon Little, *Purlie*	Lauren Bacall, *Applause*
1971	*Company,* Stephen Sondheim (M&L)	Hal Linden, *The Rothschilds*	Helen Gallagher, *No, No Nannette* (R)
1972	*Two Gentlemen of Verona* [best score: *Follies,* Stephen Sondheim (M&L)]	Phil Silvers, *A Funny Thing Happened on the Way to the Forum* (R)	Alexis Smith, *Follies*
1973	*A Little Night Music,* Stephen Sondheim (M&L)	Ben Vereen, *Pippin*	Glynis Johns, *A Little Night Music*
1974	*Raisin,* [best score: *Gigi,* Frederick Loewe (M), Alan Jay Lerner (L)]	Christopher Plummer, *Cyrano*	Virginia Capers, *Raisin*
1975	*The Wiz,* Charlie Smalls (M&L)	John Cullum, *Shenandoah*	Angela Lansbury, *Gypsy* (R)
1976	*A Chorus Line,* Marvin Hamlisch (M), Edward Kleban (L)	George Rose, *My Fair Lady* (R)	Donna McKechnie, *A Chorus Line*
1977	*Annie,* Charles Strouse (M), Martin Charnin (L)	Barry Bostwick, *The Robber Bridegroom*	Dorothy Loudon, *Annie*
1978	*Ain't Misbehavin'* [best score: *On the Twentieth Century,* Cy Coleman (M) Betty Comden and Adolph Green (L)]	John Cullum, *On the Twentieth Century*	Liza Minnelli, *The Act*
1979	*Sweeney Todd,* Stephen Sondheim	Len Cariou, *Sweeney Todd*	Angela Lansbury, *Sweeney Todd*
1980	*Evita,* Andrew Lloyd Webber (M), Tim Rice (L)	Jim Dale, *Barnum*	Patti LuPone, *Evita*
1981	*42nd Street,* [best score: *Woman of the Year,* John Kander (M), Fred Ebb (L)]	Kevin Kline, *The Pirates of Penzance*	Lauren Bacall, *Woman of the Year*
1982	*Nine,* Maury Yeston (M&L)	Ben Harney, *Dreamgirls*	Jennifer Holliday, *Dreamgirls*
1983	*Cats,* Andrew Lloyd Webber (M), T.S. Eliot (L)	Tommy Tune, *My One and Only*	Natalia Makarova, *On Your Toes*
1984	*La Cage Aux Folles,* Jerry Herman (M&L)	George Hearn, *La Cage Aux Folles*	Chita Rivera, *The Rink*
1985	*Big River,* Roger Miller (M&L)	no award	no award
1986	*The Mystery of Edwin Drood,* Rupert Holmes (M&L)	George Rose, *The Mystery of Edwin Drood*	Bernadette Peters, *Song and Dance*
1987	*Les Misérables,* Claude-Michel Schönberg (M); Herbert Kretzmer & Alain Boublil (L)	Robert Lindsay, *Me and My Girl*	Maryann Plunkett, *Me and My Girl*
1988	*The Phantom of the Opera* [best score: *Into the Woods,* Stephen Sondheim (M&L)]	Michael Crawford, *The Phantom of the Opera*	Joanna Gleason, *Into the Woods*
1989	*Jerome Robbins' Broadway* [best score: no award]	Jason Alexander, *Jerome Robbins' Broadway*	Ruth Brown, *Black and Blue*
1990	*City of Angels,* Cy Coleman (M) David Zippel (L)	James Naughton, *City of Angels*	Tyne Daly, *Gypsy* (R)
1991	*The Will Rogers Follies,* Cy Coleman (M); Betty Comden and Adolph Green (L)	Jonathan Pryce, *Miss Saigon*	Lea Salonga, *Miss Saigon*
1992	*Crazy for You,* [best score: *Falsettos,* William Finn (M&L)]	Gregory Hines, *Jelly's Last Jam*	Faith Prince, *Guys and Dolls* (R)
1993	*Kiss of the Spider Woman* [best score: (tie) *Kiss of the Spider Woman,* John Kander (M) and Fred Ebb (L)/ *Tommy,* Pete Townshend (M&L)]	Brent Carver, *Kiss of the Spider Woman*	Chita Rivera, *Kiss of the Spider Woman*
1994	*Passion,* Stephen Sondheim (M&L)	Boyd Gaines, *She Loves Me* (R)	Donna Murphy, *Passion*
1995	*Sunset Boulevard,* Andrew Lloyd Webber (M&L)	Matthew Broderick, *How to Succeed in Business Without Really Trying* (R)	Glenn Close, *Sunset Boulevard*
1996	*Rent,* Jonathan Larson (M&L)	Nathan Lane, *A Funny Thing Happened on the Way to the Forum* (R)	Donna Murphy, *The King and I* (R)
1997	*Titanic,* Maury Yeston (M&L)	James McNaughton, *Chicago* (R)	Bebe Neuwirth, *Chicago* (R)
1998	*The Lion King,* [best score: *Ragtime,* Stephen Flaherty & Lynn Ahrens (M&L)]	Alan Cumming, *Cabaret* (R)	Natasha Richardson, *Cabaret* (R)
1999	*Fosse,* [best score: *Parade,* Jason Robert Brown (M&L)]	Martin Short, *Little Me*	Bernadette Peters, *Annie Get Your Gun* (R)

M = music; L = lyrics, R = revival. **Note:** Since 1971 "Musical" and "Score" have been separate categories. However, the winner of the Tony for Best Musical usually wins the award for Best Score, except where otherwise indicated.
Source: Isabelle Stevenson, *The Tony Award* 1989; American Theatre Wing.

The Grammys, 1958–98

The "Grammys" are officially known as the National Academy of Recording Arts and Sciences Awards. Winners (in almost 70 categories) are selected yearly by the 6,000 or so voting members of the academy. The five award categories listed below have remained fairly constant over the years, although the overall "Best Vocal Performance" awards were phased out in 1968. From that year on, we list "Best Pop Vocal Performance" (male and female), except where indicated.

Year	Record of the year	Album of the year	Song of the year	Best male vocal performance	Best female vocal performance
1958	Domenico Modugno, *Nel Blu Dipinto di Blu (Volare)*	Henry Mancini, *The Music from Peter Gunn*	Domenico Modugno, "Nel Blu Dipinto di Blu *(Volare)*"	Perry Como, *Catch a Falling Star*	Ella Fitzgerald, *Ella Fitzgerald Sings the Irving Berlin Songbook*[2]
1959	Bobby Darin, *Mack the Knife*	Frank Sinatra, *Come Dance with Me*	Jimmy Driftwood, "The Battle of New Orleans"	Frank Sinatra, *Come Dance with Me*	Ella Fitzgerald, *But Not for Me*
1960	Percy Faith, *Theme from a Summer Place*	Bob Newhart, *Button-Down Mind*	Ernest Gold, "Theme from Exodus"	Ray Charles, *Georgia on My Mind*	Ella Fitzgerald, *Mack the Knife*
1961	Henry Mancini, *Moon River*	Judy Garland, *Judy at Carnegie Hall*	Henry Mancini, Johnny Mercer, "Moon River"	Jack Jones, *Lollipops and Roses*	Judy Garland, *Judy at Carnegie Hall*[2]
1962	Tony Bennett, *I Left My Heart in San Francisco*	Vaughn Meader, *The First Family*	Leslie Bricusse, Anthony Newley, "What Kind of Fool Am I?"	Tony Bennett, *I Left My Heart in San Francisco*[2]	Ella Fitzgerald, *Ella Swings Brightly with Nelson Riddle*[2]
1963	Henry Mancini, *The Days of Wine and Roses*	Barbra Streisand, *The Barbra Streisand Album*	Henry Mancini, Johnny Mercer, "The Days of Wine and Roses"	Jack Jones, *Wives and Lovers*	Barbra Streisand, *The Barbra Streisand Album*[2]
1964	Stan Getz, Astrud Gilberto, *The Girl from Ipanema*	Stan Getz, Astrud Gilberto, *Getz/Gilberto*	Jerry Herman, "Hello, Dolly!"	Louis Armstrong, *Hello, Dolly!*	Barbra Streisand, *People*
1965	Herb Alpert & the Tijuana Brass, *A Taste of Honey*	Frank Sinatra, *September of My Years*	Paul Francis Webster, Johnny Mandel, "The Shadow of Your Smile"	Frank Sinatra, *It Was a Very Good Year*	Barbra Streisand, *My Name is Barbra*[2]
1966	Frank Sinatra, *Strangers in the Night*	Frank Sinatra, *A Man and His Music*	John Lennon, Paul McCartney, "Michelle"	Frank Sinatra, *Strangers in the Night*	Eydie Gorme, *If He Walked into My Life*
1967	5th Dimension, *Up, Up and Away*	The Beatles, *Sgt. Pepper's Lonely Hearts Club Band*	Jim Webb, "Up, Up, and Away"	Glen Campbell, *By the Time I Get to Phoenix*	Bobbie Gentry, *Ode to Billie Joe*
1968	Simon & Garfunkel, *Mrs. Robinson*	Glen Campbell, *By the Time I Get to Phoenix*	Bobby Russell, "Little Green Apples"	Jose Feliciano[3], *Light My Fire*	Dionne Warwick[3], *Do You Know the Way to San Jose?*
1969	5th Dimension, *Aquarius/Let the Sunshine In*	Blood, Sweat & Tears, *Blood, Sweat & Tears*	Joe South, "Games People Play"	Harry Nilsson[4], *Everybody's Talkin'*	Peggy Lee[4], *Is That All There Is?*
1970	Simon & Garfunkel, *Mrs. Robinson*	Simon & Garfunkel, *Bridge over Troubled Water*	Paul Simon, "Bridge over Troubled Water"	Ray Stevens[4], *Everything is Beautiful*	Dionne Warwick[4], *I'll Never Fall in Love Again*[2]
1971	Carole King, *It's Too Late*	Carole King, *Tapestry*	Carole King, "You've Got a Friend"	James Taylor[5], *You've Got a Friend*	Carole King[5], *Tapestry*[2]
1972	Roberta Flack, *The First Time Ever I Saw Your Face*	George Harrison, Ravi Shankar, Bob Dylan et al, *Concert for Bangladesh*	Ewan McColl, "The First Time Ever I Saw Your Face"	Harry Nilsson, *Without You*	Helen Reddy, *I Am Woman*
1973	Roberta Flack, *Killing Me Softly with His Song*	Stevie Wonder, *Innervisions*	Norman Gimbel, Charles Fox, "Killing Me Softly with His Song"	Stevie Wonder, *You Are the Sunshine of My Life*	Roberta Flack, *Killing Me Softly with His Song*
1974	Olivia Newton-John, *I Honestly Love You*	Stevie Wonder, *Fulfillingness' First Finale*	Marilyn & Alan Bergman, Marvin Hamlisch, "The Way We Were"	Stevie Wonder, *Fulfillingness' First Finale*[2]	Olivia Newton-John, *I Honestly Love You*
1975	Captain & Tennille, *Love Will Keep Us Together*	Paul Simon, *Still Crazy After All These Years*	Stephen Sondheim, "Send in the Clowns"	Paul Simon, *Still Crazy after All These Years*[2]	Janis Ian, *At Seventeen*

Year	Record of the year	Album of the year	Song of the year	Best male vocal performance	Best female vocal performance
1976	George Benson, *This Masquerade*	Stevie Wonder, *Songs in the Key of Life*	Bruce Johnston, "I Write the Songs"	Stevie Wonder, *Songs in the Key of Life*[2]	Linda Ronstadt, *Hasten Down the Wind*[2]
1977	The Eagles, *Hotel California*	Fleetwood Mac, *Rumours*	Barbra Streisand, Paul Williams, "Evergreen"	James Taylor, *Handy Man*	Barbra Streisand, *Evergreen*
1978	Billy Joel, *Just the Way You Are*	Various Artists, *Saturday Night Fever*	Billy Joel, "Just the Way You Are"	Barry Manilow, *Copacabana (At the Copa)*	Anne Murray, *You Needed Me*
1979	The Doobie Brothers, *What a Fool Believes*	Billy Joel, *52nd Street*	Kenny Loggins, Michael McDonald, "What a Fool Believes"	Billy Joel, *52nd Street*[2]	Dionne Warwick, *I'll Never Love This Way Again*
1980	Christopher Cross, *Sailing*	Christopher Cross, *Christopher Cross*	Christopher Cross, "Sailing"	Kenny Loggins, *This Is It*	Bette Midler, *The Rose*
1981	Kim Carnes, *Bette Davis Eyes*	John Lennon/Yoko Ono, *Double Fantasy*	Donna Weiss, Jackie DeShannon, "Bette Davis Eyes"	Al Jarreau, *Breakin' Away*[2]	Lena Horne, *The Lady and Her Music Live on Broadway*[2]
1982	Toto, *Rosanna*	Toto, *Toto IV*	Johnny Christopher, Mark James, Wayne Carson, "Always on My Mind"	Lionel Richie, *Truly*	Melissa Manchester, *You Should Hear How She Talks About You*
1983	Michael Jackson, *Beat It*	Michael Jackson, *Thriller*	Sting, "Every Breath You Take"	Michael Jackson, *Thriller*[2]	Irene Cara, *Flashdance . . . What a Feeling*
1984	Tina Turner, *What's Love Got to Do with It?*	Lionel Richie, *Can't Slow Down*	Graham Lyle, Terry Britten, "What's Love Got to Do with It?"	Phil Collins, *Against All Odds (Take a Look at Me Now)*	Tina Turner, *What's Love Got to Do with It?*
1985	USA for Africa, *We Are the World*	Phil Collins, *No Jacket Required*	Michael Jackson, Lionel Richie, "We Are the World"	Phil Collins, *No Jacket Required*[2]	Whitney Houston, *Saving All My Love for You*
1986	Steve Winwood, *Higher Love*	Paul Simon, *Graceland*	Various Artists, "That's What Friends Are For"	Steve Winwood, *Higher Love*	Barbra Streisand, *The Broadway Album*[2]
1987	Paul Simon, *Graceland*	U2, *The Joshua Tree*	Linda Ronstadt, James Ingram, "Somewhere Out There"	Sting, *Bring on the Night*[2]	Whitney Houston, *I Wanna Dance with Somebody (Who Loves Me)*
1988	Bobby McFerrin, *Don't Worry, Be Happy*	George Michael, *Faith*	Bobby McFerrin, "Don't Worry, Be Happy"	Bobby McFerrin, *Don't Worry, Be Happy*	Tracy Chapman, *Fast Car*
1989	Bette Midler, *Wind Beneath My Wings*	Bonnie Rait, *Nick of Time*	Bette Midler, "Wind Beneath My Wings"	Michael Bolton, *How Am I Supposed to Live Without You*	Bonnie Raitt, *Nick of Time*
1990	Phil Collins, *Another Day in Paradise*	Quincy Jones, *Back on the Block*	Julie Gold, "From a Distance"	Roy Orbison, *Oh, Pretty Woman*	Mariah Carey, *Vision of Love*
1991	Natalie Cole, *Unforgettable*	Natalie Cole , *Unforgettable*	Irving Gordon, "Unforgettable"	Michael Bolton , *When a Man Loves a Woman*	Bonnie Raitt, *Something to Talk About*
1992	Eric Clapton, *Tears in Heaven*	Eric Clapton, *Unplugged*	Eric Clapton, "Tears in Heaven"	Eric Clapton, *Tears in Heaven*	k.d. Lang, *Constant Craving*
1993	Whitney Houston, *I Will Always Love You*	Whitney Houston, *The Bodyguard*	Alan Menken and Tim Rice, "A Whole New World (Aladdin's Theme)"	Sting, *If I Ever Lose My Faith in You*	Whitney Houston, *I Will Always Love You*
1994	Sheryl Crow, *All I Wanna Do*	Tony Bennett, *MTV Unplugged*	Bruce Springsteen, "Streets of Philadelphia"	Elton John, *Can You Feel the Love Tonight*	Sheryl Crow, *All I Wanna Do*
1995	Seal, *Kiss From a Rose*	Alanis Morissette, *Jagged Little Pill*	Seal, "Kiss From a Rose"	Seal, *Kiss From a Rose*	Annie Lennox, *No More "I Love Yous"*
1996	Eric Clapton, *Change the World*	Celine Dion, *Falling Into You*	Wayne Kirkpatrick and Tommy Sims, "Change the World"	Eric Clapton, *Change the World*	Toni Braxton, *Unbreak My Heart*

Year	Record of the year	Album of the year	Song of the year	Best male vocal performance	Best female vocal performance
1997	Shawn Colvin, *Sunny Came Home*	Bob Dylan, *Time Out of Mind*	Shawn Colvin and John Leventhal, "Sunny Came Home" 1997	Elton John, *Candle in the Wind, 1997*	Sarah McLachlan, *Building a Mystery*
1998	Celine Dion, *My Heart Will Go On*	Lauryn Hill, *The Miseducation of Lauryn Hill*	James Horner and Will Jennings, "My Heart Will Go On"	Eric Clapton, *My Father's Eyes,*	Celine Dion, *My Heart Will Go On*

1. Awarded to the composer, rather than the performer, of the song. 2. Awarded for an album, rather than an individual song. 3. Award given for "Best Contemporary Pop Vocal Performance." 4. Award given for "Best Vocal Performance Contemporary." 5. From 1971 on, all awards in these columns are for "Best Pop Vocal Performance."   **Source:** National Academy of Recording Arts and Sciences.

MTV Video Music Awards, 1984–99

Each year MTV Networks recognizes outstanding achievement in the field of video music with the MTV Video Music Awards. In addition to those listed below, there are special categories for rap, heavy metal and dance videos, as well as for technical achievement in choreography, direction and cinematography.

Year	Best video	Best male video	Best female video	Best group video	Best new artist in a video
1984	The Cars, *You Might Think*	David Bowie, *China Girl*	Cyndi Lauper, *Girls Just Want to Have Fun*	ZZ Top, *Legs*	Eurythmics, *Sweet Dreams (are Made of This)*
1985	Don Henley, *The Boys of Summer*	Bruce Springsteen, *I'm on Fire*	Tina Turner, *What's Love Got to Do With It?*	USA for Africa, *We Are the World*	til' tuesday, *Voices Carry*
1986	Dire Straits, *Money for Nothing*	Robert Palmer, *Addicted to Love*	Whitney Houston, *How Will I Know?*	Dire Straits, *Money for Nothing*	a-Ha, *Take On Me*
1987	Peter Gabriel, *Sledgehammer*	Peter Gabriel, *Sledgehammer*	Madonna, *Papa Don't Preach*	Talking Heads, *Wild Wild Life*	Crowded House, *Don't Dream it's Over*
1988	INXS, *Need You Tonight/Mediate*	Prince, *U Got the Look*	Suzanne Vega, *Luka*	INXS, *Need You Tonight/Mediate*	Guns N' Roses, *Welcome to the Jungle*
1989	Neil Young, *This Note's for You*	Elvis Costello, *Veronica*	Paula Abdul, *Straight Up*	Living Color, *Cult of Personality*	Living Color, *Cult of Personality*
1990	Sinead O'Connor, *Nothing Compares to You*	Don Henley, *End of the Innocence*	Sinead O'Connor, *Nothing Compares to You*	B-52s, *Love Shack*	Michael Penn, *No Myth*
1991	R.E.M., *Losing My Religion*	Chris Isaak, *Wicked Game*	Janet Jackson, *Love Will Never Do Without You*	R.E.M., *Losing My Religion*	Jesus Jones, *Right Here, Right Now*
1992	Van Halen, *Right Now*	Eric Clapton, *Tears in Heaven*	Annie Lennox, *Why*	U2, *Even Better Than the Real Thing*	Nirvana, *Smells Like Teen Spirit*
1993	Pearl Jam, *Jeremy*	Lenny Kravitz, *Are You Gonna Go My Way*	k.d. lang, *Constant Craving*	Pearl Jam, *Jeremy*	Stone Temple Pilots, *Plush*
1994	Aerosmith, *Cryin'*	Tom Petty and the Heartbreakers, *Mary Jane's Last Dance*	Janet Jackson, *If*	Aerosmith, *Cryin'*	Counting Crows, *Mr. Jones*
1995	TLC, *Waterfalls*	Tom Petty and the Heartbreakers, *You Don't Know How it Feels*	Madonna, *Take a Bow*	TLC, *Waterfalls*	Hootie & the Blowfish, *Hold My Hand*
1996	Smashing Pumpkins, *Tonight, Tonight*	Beck, *Where It's At*	Alanis Morissette, *Ironic*	Foo Fighters, *Big Me*	Alanis Morissette, *Ironic*
1997	Jamiroquai, *Virtual Insanity*	Beck, *Devil's Haircut*	Jewel, *You Were Meant For Me*	No Doubt, *Don't Speak*	Fiona Apple, *Sleep to Dream*
1998	Madonna, *Ray of Light*	Will Smith, *Just the Two of Us*	Madonna, *Ray of Light*	Backstreet Boys, *Everybody (Backstreet's Back)*	Natalie Imbruglia, *Torn*
1999	Lauryn Hill, *Doo-Wop (That Thing)*	Will Smith, *Miami*	Lauryn Hill, *Doo-Wop (That Thing)*	TLC, *No Secrets*	Eminem, *My Name Is*

Source: Press Department, MTV Networks.

The National Book Awards, 1950–98

The National Book Awards are given annually for outstanding literary works by American citizens. The number of prizes awarded has varied, including categories such as poetry, fiction, biography, science, philosophy, religion, and history.

FICTION

Year	Author, Title	Year	Author, Title
1950	Nelson Algren, *The Man with the Golden Arm*	1975	Robert Stone, *Dog Soldiers*
			Thomas Williams, *The Hair of Harold Roux*
1951	William Faulkner, *The Collected Stories*	1976	William Gaddis, *JR*
1952	James Jones, *From Here to Eternity*	1977	Wallace Stegner, *The Spectator Bird*
1953	Ralph Ellison, *Invisible Man*	1978	Mary Lee Settle, *Blood Ties*
1954	Saul Bellow, *The Adventures of Augie March*	1979	Tim O'Brien, *Going After Cacciato*
1955	William Faulkner, *A Fable*	1980	William Styron, *Sophie's Choice*
1956	John O'Hara, *Ten North Frederick*	1981	Wright Morris, *Plains Song*
1957	Wright Morris, *Field of Vision*	1982	John Updike, *Rabbit Is Rich*
1958	John Cheever, *The Wapshot Chronicle*	1983	Alice Walker, *The Color Purple*
1959	Bernard Malamud, *The Magic Barrel*	1984	Ellen Gilchrist, *Victory Over Japan*
1960	Philip Roth, *Goodbye, Columbus*	1985	Don DeLillo, *White Noise*
1961	Conrad Richter, *The Waters of Kronos*	1986	E. L. Doctorow, *World's Fair*
1962	Walker Percy, *The Moviegoer*	1987	Larry Heinemann, *Paco's Story*
1963	J. F. Powers, *Morte d'Urban*	1988	Pete Dexter, *Paris Trout*
1964	John Updike, *The Centaur*	1989	John Casey, *Spartina*
1965	Saul Bellow, *Herzog*	1990	Charles Johnson, *The Middle Passage*
1966	Katherine Anne Porter, *The Collected Stories*	1991	Norman Rush, *Mating*
1967	Bernard Malamud, *The Fixer*	1992	Cormac McCarthy, *All the Pretty Horses*
1968	Thornton Wilder, *The Eighth Day*	1993	E. Annie Proulx, *The Shipping News*
1969	Jerzy Kosinski, *Steps*	1994	William Gaddis, *A Frolic of His Own*
1970	Joyce Carol Oates, *Them*	1995	Philip Roth, *Sabbath's Theater*
1971	Saul Bellow, *Mr. Sammler's Planet*	1996	Andrea Barrett, *Ship Fever and Other Stories*
1972	Flannery O'Connor, *The Complete Stories*	1997	Charles Frazier, *Cold Mountain*
1973	John Barth, *Chimera*	1998	Alice McDermott, *Charming Billy*
1974	Thomas Pynchon, *Gravity's Rainbow*		
	Isaac Bashevis Singer, *A Crown of Feathers & Other Stories*		

NONFICTION

Year	Author, Title	Year	Author, Title
1950	Ralph L. Rusk, *Ralph Waldo Emerson*	1977	Bruno Bettelheim, *The Uses of Enchantment: The Meaning and Importance of Fairy Tales*
1951	Newton Arvin, *Herman Melville*		
1952	Rachel Carson, *The Sea Around Us*	1978	Walter Jackson Bate, *Samuel Johnson*
1953	Bernard De Voto, *Course of Empire*	1979	Arthur M. Schlesinger Jr., *Robert Kennedy and His Times*
1954	Bruce Catton, *A Stillness at Appomattox*		
1955	Joseph Wood Krutch, *The Measure of Man*	1980	Tom Wolfe, *The Right Stuff*
1956	Herbert Kubly, *An American in Italy*	1981	Maxine Hong Kingston, *China Men*
1957	George F. Kennan, *Russia Leaves the War*	1982	Tracy Kidder, *The Soul of a New Machine*
1958	Catherine Drinker Bowen, *The Lion and the Throne*	1983	Fox Butterfield, *China: Alive in the Bitter Sea*
1959	J. Christopher Herold, *Mistress to an Age*	1984	Robert V. Remini, *Andrew Jackson and the Course of American Democracy, 1833–45, vol. 5*
1960	Richard Ellman, *James Joyce*		
1961	William L. Shirer, *The Rise and Fall of the Third Reich*	1985	J. Anthony Lukas, *Common Ground: A Turbulent Decade in the Lives of Three American Families*
1962	Lewis Mumford, *The City in History*		
1963	Leon Edel, *Henry James, vols. 2 and 3*	1986	Barry Lopez, *Arctic Dreams*
1964	Aileen Ward, *John Keats: The Making of a Poet*	1987	Richard Rhodes, *The Making of the Atom Bomb*
1965	Louis Fisher, *The Life of Lenin*		
1966	Arthur M. Schlesinger Jr., *A Thousand Days: JFK in the White House*	1988	Neil Sheehan, *A Bright and Shining Lie: John Paul Vann and America in Vietnam*
1967	Justin Kaplan, *Mr. Clemens and Mark Twain*	1989	Thomas L. Friedman, *From Beirut to Jerusalem*
1968	Jonathan Kozol, *Death at an Early Age*	1990	Ron Chernow, *The House of Morgan*
1969	Norman Mailer, *The Armies of the Night*	1991	Orlando Patterson, *Freedom*
1970	Lillian Hellman, *An Unfinished Woman, a Memoir*	1992	Paul Monette, *Becoming a Man: Half a Life*
		1993	Gore Vidal, *United States: Essays 1952-1992*
1971	James MacGregor Burns, *Roosevelt: The Soldier of Freedom*	1994	Sherwin B. Nuland, *How We Die: Reflections on Life's Final Chapter*
1972	Joseph P. Lash, *Eleanor and Franklin*		
1973	Frances Fitzgerald, *Fire in the Lake: The Vietnamese and the Americans in Vietnam*	1995	Tina Rosenberg, *The Haunted Land: Facing Europe's Ghosts After Communism*
1974	Pauline Kael, *Deeper into the Movies*	1996	James Carroll, *An American Requiem: God, My Father and the War That Came Between Us*
1975	Richard B. Sewall, *The Life of Emily Dickinson*		
	Lewis Thomas, *The Lives of a Cell*	1997	Joseph J. Ellis, *American Sphinx: The Character of Thomas Jefferson*
1976	Paul Fussell, *The Great War and Modern Memory*	1998	Edward Ball, *Slaves in the Family*

POETRY

Year	Author, Title	Year	Author, Title
1950	William Carlos Williams, *Paterson: Book III* and *Selected Poems*	1973	A. R. Ammons, *Collected Poems: 1951–71*
1951	Wallace Stevens, *The Auroras of Autumn*	1974	Allen Ginsberg, *The Fall of America: Poems of These States, 1965–71*
1952	Marianne Moore, *Collected Poems*		Adrienne Rich, *Diving into the Wreck: Poems, 1971–72*
1953	Archibald MacLeish, *Collected Poems 1917–52*	1975	Marilyn Hacker, *Presentation Piece*
1954	Conrad Aiken, *Collected Poems*	1976	John Ashbery, *Self-Portrait in a Convex Mirror*
1955	Wallace Stevens, *The Collected Poems*	1977	Richard Eberhart, *Collected Poems, 1930–1976*
1956	W. H. Auden, *The Shield of Achilles*		
1957	Richard Wilbur, *Things of this World*	1978	Howard Nemerov, *The Collected Poems*
1958	Robert Penn Warren, *Promises: Poems, 1954–56*	1979	James Merrill, *Mirabell: Books of Number*
		1980	Philip Levine, *Ashes*
1959	Theodore Roethke, *Words for the Wind*	1981	Lisel Mueller, *The Need to Hold Still*
1960	Robert J. Lowell, *Life Studies*	1982	William Bronk, *Life Supports*
1961	Randall Jarrell, *The Woman at the Washington Zoo*	1983	Galway Kinnell, *Selected Poems*
		1984	Charles Wright, *Country Music*
1962	Alan Dugan, *Poems*	1991	Philip Levine, *What Work Is*
1963	William Stafford, *Traveling Through the Dark*	1992	Mary Oliver, *New and Selected Poems*
1964	John Crowe Ransom, *Selected Poems*	1993	A. R. Ammons, *Garbage*
1965	Theodore Roethke, *The Far Field*	1994	James Tate, *Worshipful Company of Fletchers*
1966	James Dickey, *Buckdancer's Choice*	1995	Stanley Kunitz, *Passing Through*
1967	James Merrill, *Nights and Days*	1996	Hayden Carruth, *Scrambled Eggs and Whiskey: Poems 1991–1995*
1968	Robert Bly, *The Light Around the Body*		
1969	John Berryman, *His Toy, His Dream, His Rest*	1997	William Meredith, *Effort at Speech: New and Selected Poems*
1970	Elizabeth Bishop, *The Complete Poems*		
1971	Mona Van Duyn, *To See, To Take*	1998	Gerald Stern, *This Time: New and Selected Poems*
1972	Howard Moss, *Selected Poems*		

YOUNG PEOPLE'S LITERATURE

Year	Author, Title	Year	Author, Title
1996	Victor Martinez, *Parrot in the Oven: Mi Vida*	1998	Louis Sachar, *Holes*
1997	Han Nolan, *Dancing on the Edge*		

Note: No award was given in poetry from 1985 to 1990.   **Source:** National Book Awards, Inc.

The National Book Critics Circle Award, 1975–98

Selected by a 24-member board of critics (who serve 3-year terms) from around the country, this award has been increasingly important in the last few years. Books are often recommended to the board by the more than 500 general members of the Circle.

FICTION

Year	Author, Title	Year	Author, Title
1975	E.L. Doctorow, *Ragtime*	1988	Bharati Mukherjee, *The Middleman and Other Stories*
1976	John Gardner, *October Light*		
1977	Toni Morrison, *Song of Solomon*	1989	E.L. Doctorow, *Billy Bathgate*
1978	John Cheever, *The Stories of John Cheever*	1990	John Updike, *Rabbit at Rest*
1979	Thomas Flanagan, *The Year of the French*	1991	Jane Smiley, *A Thousand Acres*
1980	Shirley Hazzard, *The Transit of Venus*	1992	Cormac McCarthy, *All the Pretty Horses*
1981	John Updike, *Rabbit is Rich*	1993	Ernest J. Gaines, *A Lesson Before Dying*
1982	Stanley Elkin, *George Mills*	1994	Carol Shields, *The Stone Diaries*
1983	William Kennedy, *Ironweed*	1995	Stanley Elkin[1], *Mrs. Ted Bliss*
1984	Louise Erdrich, *Love Medicine*	1996	Gina Berriault, *Women in Their Beds*
1985	Anne Tyler, *The Accidental Tourist*	1997	Penelope Fitzgerald, *The Blue Flower*
1986	Reynolds Price, *Kate Vaiden*	1998	Alice Munro, *The Love of a Good Woman*
1987	Phillip Roth, *The Counterlife*		

GENERAL NONFICTION

Year	Author, Title	Year	Author, Title
1975	R.W.B. Lewis, *Edith Wharton*	1988	Taylor Branch, *Parting the Waters: America in the King Years, 1954–63*
1976	Maxine Hong Kingston, *The Woman Warrior: Memoirs of a Girlhood Among Ghosts*	1989	Michael Dorris, *The Broken Cord*
1977	Walter Jackson Bate, *Samuel Johnson*	1990	Shelby Steele, *The Content of Our Character: A New Vision of Race in America*
1978	Maureen Howard, *Facts of Life*		
1979	Telford Taylor, *Munich: The Price of Peace*	1991	Susan Faludi, *Backlash*
1980	Ronald Steel, *Walter Lippmann and the American Century*	1992	Norman Maclean, *Young Men and Fire*
		1993	Alan Lomax, *The Land Where Blues Began*
1981	Stephen Jay Gould, *The Mismeasure of Man*	1994	Lynn H. Nicholas, *The Rape of Europa: The Fate of Europe's Treasures in the Third Reich and the Second World War*
1982	Robert A. Caro, *The Path of Power: The Years of Lyndon Johnson*		
1983	Seymour M. Hersh, *The Price of Power: Kissinger and the Nixon White House*	1995	Jonathan Harr, *A Civil Action*
		1996	Jonathan Raban, *Bad Land: An American Romance*
1984	Freeman Dyson, *Weapons and Hope*		
1985	J. Anthony Lukas, *Common Ground: A Turbulent Decade in the Lives of Three Americans*	1997	Anne Fadiman, *The Spirit Catches You and You Fall Down*
		1998	Philip Gourevitch, *We Wish to Inform You That Tomorrow We Will Be Killed With Our Familes*
1986	John W. Dower, *War Without Mercy: Race and Power in the Pacific War*		
1987	Richard Rhodes, *The Making of the Atomic Bomb*		

BIOGRAPHY/AUTOBIOGRAPHY

Year	Author, Title	Year	Author, Title
1983	Joyce Johnson, *Minor Characters*	1991	Philip Roth, *Patrimony*
1984	Joseph Frank, *Dostoevsky: The Years of Ordeal. 1850–1859*	1992	Carol Brightman, *Writing Dangerously: Mary McCarthy and Her World*
1985	Leon Edel, *Henry James: A Life*	1993	Edmund White, *Genet*
1986	Theodore Rosengarten, *Tombee: Portrait of a Cotton Planter*	1994	Mikal Gilmore, *Shot in the Heart*
		1995	Robert Polito, *Savage Art: A Biography of Jim Thompson*
1987	Donald R. Howard, *Chaucer: His Life, His Works, His World*		
1988	Richard Ellman, *Oscar Wilde*	1996	Frank McCourt, *Angela's Ashes*
1989	Geoffrey C. Ward, *A First-Class Temperament: The Emergence of Franklin Roosevelt*	1997	James Tobin, *Ernie Pyle's War: America's Eyewitness to World War II*
		1998	Sylvia Nasar, *A Beautiful Mind*
1990	Robert A. Caro, *Means of Ascent: The Years of Lyndon Johnson, Vol. 2*		

POETRY

Year	Author, Title	Year	Author, Title
1975	John Ashbery, *Self-Portrait in a Convex Mirror*	1985	Louise Gluck, *The Triumph of Achilles*
		1986	Edward Hirsch, *Wild Gratitude*
1976	Elizabeth Bishop, *Geography III*	1987	C.K. Williams, *Flesh and Blood*
1977	Robert Lowell, *Day by Day*	1988	Donald Hall, *The One Day*
1978	L.E. Sissman, *Hello Darkness: The Collected Poems of L.E. Sissman*	1989	Rodney Jones, *Transparent Gestures*
		1990	Amy Gerstler, *Bitter Angel*
1979	Philip Levine, *Ashes and Seven Years from Somewhere*	1991	Albert Goldbarth, *Heaven and Earth*
		1992	Hayden Carruth, *Collected Shorter Poems*
1980	Frederick Seidel, *Sunrise*	1993	Mark Doty, *My Alexandria*
1981	A.R. Ammons, *A Coast of Trees*	1994	Mark Rudman, *Rider*
1982	Katha Pollitt, *Antarctic Traveler*	1995	William Matthews, *Time & Money*
1983	James Merrill, *The Changing Light at Sandover*	1996	Robert Hass, *Sun Under Wood*
		1997	Charles Wright, *Black Zodiac*
1984	Sharon Olds, *The Dead and the Living*	1998	Marie Ponsot, *The Bird Catcher*

CRITICISM

Year	Author, Title	Year	Author, Title
1975	Paul Fussell, *The Great War and Modern Memory*	1987	Edwin Denby, *Dance Writings*
1976	Bruno Bettelheim, *The Uses of Enchantment: The Meaning and Importance of Fairy Tales*	1988	Clifford Geertz, *Works and Lives: The Anthropologist as Author*
1977	Susan Sontag, *On Photography*	1989	John Clive, *Not by Fact Alone: Essays on the Writing and Reading of History*
1978	Meyer Schapiro, *Modern Art: 19th and 20th Centuries, Selected Papers*	1990	Arthur C. Danto, *Encounters and Reflections: Art in the Historical Present*
1979	Elaine Pagels, *The Gnostic Gospels*	1991	Lawrence L. Langer, *Holocaust Testimonies*
1980	Helen Vendler, *Part of Nature, Part of Us: Modern American Poets*	1992	Garry Wills, *Lincoln At Gettysburg: The Words That Remade America*
1981	Virgil Thompson, *A Virgil Thompson Reader*	1993	John Dizikes, *Opera in America*
1982	Gore Vidal, *The Second American Revolution and Other Essays, 1976–82*	1994	Gerald Early, *The Culture of Bruising: Essays on Prizefighting, Literature and Modern American Culture*
1983	John Updike, *Hugging the Shore*	1995	Robert Darnton, *The Forbidden Best-Sellers of Pre-Revolutioary France*
1984	Robert Hass, *Twentieth Century Pleasures: Prose on Poetry*	1996	William Gass, *Finding a Form*
1985	William H. Gass, *Habitations of the Word: Essays*	1997	Mario Vargas Llosa, *Making Waves*
1986	Joseph Brodsky, *Less Than One: Selected Essays*	1998	Gary Giddons, *Visions of Jazz*

1. Awarded posthumously.   **Source:** The National Book Critics Circle.

Bollingen Prize for Poetry, 1949–99

First awarded annually, and biennially since 1965, the Bollingen Prize for Poetry is offered by Yale University to an American citizen for a distinguished book of poetry, or in recognition of a poet's entire achievement.

Year	Recipient	Year	Recipient	Year	Recipient
1949	Wallace Stevens	1961	Richard Eberhart	1981	May Swenson
1950	John Crowe Ransom		John Hall Wheelock		Howard Nemerov
1951	Marianne Moore	1962	Robert Frost	1983	Anthony E. Hecht
1952	Archibald MacLeish	1965	Horace Gregory		John Hollander
	William Carlos Williams	1967	Robert Penn Warren	1985	John Ashbery
1953	W. H. Auden	1969	John Berryman		Fred Chappel
1954	Leonie Adams		Karl Shapiro	1987	Stanley Kunitz
	Louise Bogan	1971	Richard Wilbur	1989	Edgar Bowers
1955	Conrad Aiken		Mona Van Duyn	1991	Laura Riding Jackson
1956	Allen Tate	1973	James Merrill		Donald Justice
1957	e.e. cummings	1975	A. R. Ammons	1993	Mark Strand
1958	Theodore Roethke	1977	David Ignatow	1995	Kenneth Koch
1959	Delmore Schwartz	1979	W. S. Merwin	1997	Gary Snyder
1960	Ivor Winters			1999	Robert W. Creeley

Source: Yale University.

The Newbery Medal, 1922–99

The Newbery Medal, presented by the American Library Association, is awarded annually to the author of the most distinguished contribution to American literature for children published in the United States during the previous year. The award is named in honor of John Newbery (1713–67), the first English publisher of books for children.

Year	Author, Title	Year	Author, Title
1922	Willem Van Loon, *The Story of Mankind*	1963	Madeleine L'Engle, *A Wrinkle in Time*
1923	Hugh Lofting, *The Voyages of Doctor Dolittle*	1964	Emily Cheney Neville, *It's Like This, Cat*
1924	Charles Hawes, *The Dark Frigate*	1965	Maia Wojciechowska, *Shadow of a Bull*
1925	Charles Finger, *Tales from Silver Lands*	1966	Elizabeth Borten de Trevino, *I, Juan de Pareja*
1926	Arthur Bowie Chrisman, *Shen of the Sea*	1967	Irene Hunt, *Up a Road Slowly*
1927	Will James, *Smoky, The Cowhorse*	1968	E.L. Konigsburg, *From the Mixed-up Files of Mrs. Basil E. Frankweiler*
1928	Dhan Gopal Mukerji, *Gayneck, The Story of a Pigeon*	1969	Lloyd Alexander, *The High King*
1929	Eric P. Kelly, *The Trumpeter of Krakow*	1970	William H. Armstrong, *Sounder*
1930	Rachel Field, *Hitty, Her First Hundred Years*	1971	Betsy Byars, *Summer of the Swans*
1931	Elizabeth Coatsworth, *The Cat Who Went to Heaven*	1972	Robert C. O'Brien, *Mrs. Frisby and the Rats of NIMH*
1932	Laura Adams Armer, *Waterless Mountain*	1973	Jean George, *Julie of the Wolves*
1933	Elizabeth Foreman Lewis, *Young Fu of the Upper Yangtze*	1974	Paula Fox, *The Slave Dancer*
1934	Cornelia Meigs, *Invincible Louisa*	1975	Virginia Hamilton, *M.C. Higgins the Great*
1935	Monica Shannon, *Dobry*	1976	Susan Cooper, *The Grey King*
1936	Carol Brink, *Caddie Woodlawn*	1977	Mildred D. Taylor, *Roll of Thunder, Hear My Cry*
1937	Ruth Sawyer, *Roller Skates*		
1938	Kate Seredy, *The White Stag*	1978	Katherine Paterson, *Bridge to Terabithia*
1939	Elizabeth Enright, *Thimble Summer*	1979	Ellen Raskin, *The Westing Game*
1940	James Daugherty, *Daniel Boone*	1980	Joan Blos, *A Gathering of Days: A New England Girl's Journal, 1830–32*
1941	Armstrong Sperry, *Call It Courage*	1981	Katherine Paterson, *Jacob Have I Loved*
1942	Walter D. Edmonds, *The Matchlock Gun*	1982	Nancy Willard, *A Visit to William Blake's Inn: Poems for Innocent and Experienced Travelers*
1943	Elizabeth Janet Gray, *Adam of the Road*		
1944	Esther Forbes, *Johnny Tremain*		
1945	Robert Lawson, *Rabbit Hill*	1983	Cynthia Voigt, *Dicey's Song*
1946	Lois Lenski, *Strawberry Girl*	1984	Beverly Cleary, *Dear Mr. Henshaw*
1947	Carolyn Sherwin Bailey, *Miss Hickory*	1985	Robin McKinley, *The Hero and the Crown*
1948	William Pène du Bois, *The 21 Balloons*	1986	Patricia MacLachlan, *Sarah, Plain and Tall*
1949	Marguerite Henry, *King of the Wind*	1987	Sid Fleischman, *The Whipping Boy*
1950	Marguerite de Angeli, *The Door in the Wall*	1988	Russell Freedman, *Lincoln: A Photobiography*
1951	Elizabeth Yates, *Amos Fortune, Free Man*		
1952	Eleanor Estes, *Ginger Pye*	1989	Paul Fleischman, *Joyful Noise: Poems for Two Voices*
1953	Ann Nolan Clark, *Secret of the Andes*		
1954	Joseph Krumgold, *. . . And Now Miguel*	1990	Lois Lowry, *Number the Stars*
1955	Meindert DeJong, *The Wheel on the School*	1991	Jerry Spinelli, *Maniac Magee*
1956	Jean Lee Latham, *Carry On, Mr. Bowditch*	1992	Phyllis Reynolds Naylor, *Shiloh*
1957	Virginia Sorensen, *Miracles on Maple Hill*	1993	Cynthia Rylant, *Missing May*
1958	Harold Keith, *Rifles for Watie*	1994	Lois Lowry, *The Giver*
1959	Elizabeth George Speare, *The Witch of Blackbird Pond*	1995	Sharon Creech, *Walk Two Moons*
		1996	Karen Cushman, *The Midwife's Apprentice*
1960	Joseph Krumgold, *Onion John*	1997	Elaine Konigsburg, *The View From Saturday*
1961	Scott O'Dell, *Island of the Blue Dolphins*	1998	Karen Hesse, *Out of the Dust*
1962	Elizabeth George Speare, *The Bronze Bow*	1999	Louis Sachar, *Holes*

Source: American Library Association

The Caldecott Medal, 1938–99

The Caldecott Medal, presented by the American Library Association, is awarded annually to the illustrator of the most distinguished picture book for children published in the United States during the preceding year. The award is named in honor of the English illustrator Randolph Caldecott (1846–1886). In cases where only one name is given, the book was written and illustrated by the same person.

Year	Illustrator/Author/Title	Year	Illustrator/Author/Title
1938	Dorothy Lathrop; Helen Dean Fish, Animals of the Bible	1969	Uri Shulevitz; Arthur Ransome, The Fool of the World and the Flying Ship
1939	Thomas Handforth, Mei Li	1970	William Steig, Sylvester and the Magic Pebble
1940	Ingri and Edgar Parin d'Aulaire, Abraham Lincoln	1971	Gail E. Haley, A Story—A Story
1941	Robert Lawson, They Were Strong and Good	1972	Nonny Hogrogian, One Fine Day
1942	Robert McCloskey, Make Way for Ducklings	1973	Blair Lent; retold by Arlene Mosel, The Funny Little Woman
1943	Virginia Lee Burton, The Little House		
1944	Louis Slobodkin; James Thurber, Many Moons	1974	Margot Zemach; Harve Zemach, Duffy and the Devil
1945	Elizabeth Orton Jones; Rachel Jones, Prayer for a Child	1975	Gerald McDermott, Arrow to the Sun
1946	Maude and Miska Petersham, The Rooster Crows (traditional Mother Goose)	1976	Leo and Diane Dillon; retold by Verna Aardema, Why Mosquitoes Buzz in People's Ears
1947	Leonard Weisgard; Golden MacDonald, The Little Island	1977	Leo & Diane Dillon; Margaret Musgrove, Ashanti to Zulu: African Traditions
1948	Roger Duvoisin; Alvin Tresselt, White Snow, Bright Snow	1978	Peter Spier, Noah's Ark
1949	Bert and Elmer Hader, The Big Snow	1979	Paul Goble, The Girl Who Loved Wild Horses
1950	Leo Politi, Song of the Swallows		
1951	Katherine Milhous, The Egg Tree	1980	Barbara Cooney; Donald Hall, Ox-Cart Man
1952	Nicolas Mordvinoff; Will Mordvinoff, Finders Keepers	1981	Arnold Lobel, Fables
1953	Lynd Ward, The Biggest Bear	1982	Chris Van Allsburg, Jumanji
1954	Ludwig Bemelmans, Madeline's Rescue	1983	Marcia Brown, Shadow
1955	Marcia Brown; Charles Perault, Cinderella, or the Little Glass Slipper	1984	Martin and Alice Provensen, The Glorious Flight
1956	Feodor Rojankovsky; John Langstaff, Frog Went A-Courtin'	1985	Trina Schart Hyman, Saint George and the Dragon
1957	Marc Simont; Janice May Udry, A Tree is Nice	1986	Chris Van Allsburg, The Polar Express
1958	Robert McCloskey, Time of Wonder	1987	Richard Egielski; Arthur Yorinks, Hey, Al
1959	Barbara Cooney (adapted from Geoffrey Chaucer), Chanticleer and the Fox	1988	John Schoenherr, Owl Moon
1960	Marie Hall Ets and Aurora Labastida, Nine Days to Christmas	1989	Stephen Gammell; Karen Ackerman, Song and Dance Man
1961	Nicolas Sidjakov; Ruth Robbins, Baboushka and the Three Kings	1990	Paul Fleischman, Lon Po Po: A Red-Riding Hood Story from China
1962	Marcia Brown, Once a Mouse . . .	1991	David Macaulay, Black and White
1963	Ezra Jack Keats, The Snowy Day	1992	David Wiesner, Tuesday
1964	Maurice Sendak, Where the Wild Things Are	1993	Emily Arnold McCully, Mirette on the High Wire
1965	Beni Montresor; Beatrice Schenk de Regniers, May I Bring a Friend?	1994	Allen Say, Grandfather's Journey
1966	Nonny Hogrogian; Sorche Nic Leodhas, Always Room for One More	1995	David Diaz; Eve Bunting, Smoky Night
		1996	Peggy Rathman, Officer Buckle and Gloria
1967	Evaline Ness, Sam, Bangs & Moonshine	1997	David Wisniewski, Golem
1968	Ed Emberley; Barbara Emberley, Drummer Hoff	1998	Paul O. Zelinsky, Rapunzel
		1999	Mary Azarian; Jacqueline Briggs Martin, Snowflake Bentley

Source: American Library Association.

Pritzker Prize Winners, 1979–99

Recognized as the most prestigious award in architecture, the Pritzker Prize is given annually by the Hyatt Hotel Foundation, and is named for its chairman, Jay Pritzker. The selection process is modeled after the Nobel Prizes, with secret voting by an international jury.

Year	Winner	Year	Winner	Year	Winner
1979	Philip Johnson, U.S.	1987	Kenzo Tange, Japan	1994	Christian de Portzamparc, France
1980	Luis Barragan, Mexico	1988	Gordon Bunshaft, U.S.		
1981	James Stirling, U.K.		Oscar Niemeyer, Brazil	1995	Tadao Ando, Japan
1982	Kevin Roche, U.S.	1989	Frank O. Gehry, U.S.	1996	Rafael Moneo, Spain
1983	I.M. Pei, U.S.	1990	Aldo Rossi, Italy	1997	Sverre Fehn, Norway
1984	Richard Meier, U.S.	1991	Robert Venturi, U.S.	1998	Renzo Piano, Italy
1985	Hans Hollein, Austria	1992	Alvaro Siza, Portugal	1999	Norman Foster, U.K.
1986	Gottfried Boehm, Germany	1993	Fumihiko Maki, Japan		

American Institute of Architects Gold Medalists, 1907–99

First awarded in 1907, the American Institute of Architects Gold Medal recognizes outstanding lifetime achievement by an architect. It is not given every year.

Year	Medalists
1907	Sir Aston Webb, London
1909	Charles Follen McKim, New York
1911	George B. Post, New York
1914	Jean Louis Pascal, Paris
1922	Victor Laloux, Paris
1923	Henry Bacon, New York
1925	Bertram Grosvenor Goodhue, N.Y.
1925	Sir Edwin Landseer Lutyens, London
1927	Howard Van Doren Shaw, Chicago
1929	Milton Bennett Medary, Philadelphia
1933	Ragnar Ostberg, Stockholm
1938	Paul Philippe Cret, Philadelphia
1944	Louis Henri Sullivan, Chicago
1947	Eliel Saarinen, Bloomfield Hills, Mich.
1948	Charles Donagh Maginnis, Boston
1949	Frank Lloyd Wright, Spring Green, Wis.
1950	Sir Patrick Abercrombie, London
1951	Bernard Ralph Maybeck, San Francisco
1952	Auguste Perret, Paris
1953	William Adams Delano, New York
1955	Willem Marinus Dudock, Hilversum, Netherlands
1956	Clarence S. Stein, New York
1957	Louis Skidmore, New York
1957	Ralph Walker, New York
1958	John Wellborn Root, Chicago
1959	Walter Gropius, Cambridge, Mass.
1960	Ludwig Mies van der Rohe, Chicago
1961	Le Corbusier (Charles Edouard Jeanneret-Gris), Paris

Year	Medalists
1962	Eero Saarinen, Bloomfield Hills, Mich[1]
1963	Alvar Aalto, Helsinki
1964	Pier Luigi Nervi, Rome
1966	Kenzo Tange, Tokyo
1967	Wallace K. Harrison, New York
1968	Marcel Breuer, New York
1969	William Wilson Wurster, San Francisco
1970	Richard Buckminster Fuller, Carbondale, Ill.
1971	Louis I. Kahn, Philadelphia
1972	Pietro Belluschi, Boston
1977	Richard Joseph Neutra, Los Angeles[1]
1978	Philip Johnson, New York
1979	Ieoh Ming Pei, New York
1981	Josep Lluis Sert, Cambridge, Mass.
1982	Romaldo Giurgola, New York
1983	Nathaniel A. Owings, San Francisco
1985	William Caudill, Houston[1]
1986	Arthur Erickson, Canada
1989	Joseph Esherick, San Francisco
1990	Fay Jones, Fayetteville, Arkansas
1991	Charles Willard Moore, Austin, Texas
1992	Benjamin Thompson, Boston
1993	Kevin Roche, New Haven, Conn.
	Thomas Jefferson, Virginia[1]
1994	Sir Norman Foster, London
1995	Cesar Pelli, New Haven
1997	Richard Meier, Los Angeles
1998	No Award
1999	Frank Gehry, U.S.

1. Awarded posthumously.   **Source:** American Institute of Architects.

Fields Medal Winners, 1936–98

The Fields Medal, named for Canadian mathematician J. D. Fields, is often described as the Nobel Prize for Mathematics. In agreement with Fields's wish that the awards recognize both existing work and the promise of future achievement, the medals are awarded to mathematicians no older than 40. Since 1950, medals have been awarded every four years.

Year	Winners
1936	**Lars Ahlfors,** Harvard Univ.; **Jesse Douglas,** MIT
1950	**Laurent Schwartz,** Universite de Nancy; **Atle Selberg,** Princeton/IAS
1954	**Kunihiko Kodaira,** Princeton Univ.; **Jean-Pierre Serre,** College de France
1958	**Klaus Roth,** Univ. of London; **Rene Thom,** Univ. of Strasbourg
1962	**Lars Hormander,** Univ. of Stockholm; **John Milnor,** Princeton Univ.
1966	**Michael Atiyah,** Oxford Univ.; **Paul Cohen,** Stanford Univ.; **Alex Grothendieck,** Univ. of Paris; **Stephen Smale,** Univ. of California
1970	**Alan Baker,** Cambridge Univ.; **Heisuke Hironaka,** Harvard Univ.; **Serge Novikov,** Moscow Univ.; **John Thompson,** Univ. of Chicago
1974	**Enrico Bombieri,** Univ. of Pisa; **David Mumford,** Harvard Univ.
1978	**Pierre Deligne,** IHES; **Charles Fefferman,** Princeton Univ.; **Gregori Margulis,** Moscow Univ.; **Daniel Quillen,** MIT

Year	Winners
1982	**Alain Connes,** IHES; **William Thurston,** Princeton Univ.; **Shing-Tung Yau,** IAS
1986	**Simon Donaldson,** Oxford Univ.; **Gerd Faltings,** Princeton Univ.; **Michael Freedman,** Univ. of California at San Diego
1990	**Vladimir Drinfeld,** Phys.Inst.Kharkov; **Vaughan Jones,** Univ. of California; **Shigefumi Mori,** Univ. of Kyoto; **Edward Witten,** Princeton/IAS
1994	**Pierre-Louis Lions,** Universite de Paris-Dauphine; **Jean-Chrisophe Yoccoz,** Universite de Paris-Sud; **Jean Bourgain,** Princeton/IAS; **Efim Zelmanov,** Univ. of Wisconsin
1998	**Richard E. Borcherds,** Cambridge Univ.; **William T. Gowers,** Cambridge Univ.; **Maxim Kontsevich,** IHES and Rutgers Univ.; **Curtis T. McMullen,** Harvard Univ.

Note: IAS= Institute of Advanced Study. IHES=Institut des Hautes Etudes Scientifiques.
Source: Fields Institute for Research in Mathematical Sciences. **www.fields.toronto.edu**

Templeton Prize Winners, 1973-99

Believing that religion had been unfairly excluded from consideration by the Nobel Prize committee, John Marks Templeton in 1972 established the Templeton Prize for Progress in Religion for "those who seek new and different paths in advancing the world's understanding of God and/or spirituality." Templeton, a Tennessee-born financier who became one of Wall Street's most successful fund managers, decreed that the monetary value of his prize should always exceed that of the Nobel Prize. The 1999 Prize was worth 750,000 pounds sterling, or approximately $1.24 million, making it the world's richest prize.

1973   Mother Teresa, for her "efforts to help the homeless and neglected children of Calcutta."

1974   Brother Roger, founder and director of the Taize Community in France. He harbored Jewish refugees in Nazi-occupied France, then later established the Taize Community, which aided orphaned children in France.

1975   Sir Sarvepalli Radhakrishnan, President of India (1962-67), and an Oxford Professor of Eastern Religions and Ethics, for his advocacy of "a non-aggressive, defensive military posture during India's conflicts with Pakistan." His writings made India's religious heritage accessible to both Eastern and Western audiences.

1976   Leon Joseph Cardinal Suenens, Archbishop of Malines-Brussles, for his pioneering work in the Charismatic Renewal Movement, which gained popularity in the early 1970s.

1977   Chiara Lubich, founder of Italy's Focolare Movement, for developing "an alternative to a cloistered existence for women who decided to become nuns." The movement eventually expanded to include men and married people and to communities in Europe, the U.S., and Japan.

1978   Thomas F. Torrance, former Moderator of the Church of Scotland, "one of the first religious thinkers to win the respect of both theologians and scientists for his work on the relationship between science and religion."

1979   Rev. Nikkyo Niwano, founder of Rissho Kosei-Kai in Japan and the World Conference on Religion and Peace. The Buddhist group he co-founded with Masa Naganuma literally means "establishing the teaching of the true Law in the world, mutual exchange of thought among people of faith and the perfection of the personality."

1980   Ralph Wendell Burhoe, founder and former editor of *Zygon, Journal of Religion and Science*, for providing enlightenment in understanding similarities and differences between theology and science, and for providing neutral ground for discussion.

1981   Dame Cecily Saunders, founder of the Hospice and Palliative Care Movement, which helps terminally ill patients express their physical, psycho-social and spiritual pain.

1982   The Rev. Billy Graham, televangelist, for keeping his Gospel message "pure, simple and authentic, yet tailored to address the problems and pressures of today."

1983   Aleksandr Solzhenitsyn, Soviet dissident whose "struggle to speak and think freely [gives] renewed vitality to the Orthodox tradition of spirituality and provides evidence of the strength of profound Christian faith."

1984   The Rev. Michael Bourdeaux, founder of Keston College in England, for his "long, sometimes singular struggle to reveal the systematic destruction of religion in communist countries during the Cold War."

1985   Sir Alister Hardy, founder of the Sir Alister Hardy Research Centre at Oxford, which used scientific methods to investigate religious experience.

1986   The Rev. James McCord, Chancellor of the Center of Theological Inquiry in Princeton, N.J., for his lifelong study of the relationship between science and religion through his studies of the nature of reality.

1987   The Rev. Stanley L. Jaki, professor of Astrophysics at Seton Hall University, N.J. A Benedictine monk and the author of more than two dozen books, Father Jaki carefully delineated the lines of the disciplines of science and religion, emphasizing their differences as well as similarities.

1988   Dr. Inamullah Khan, founder and Secretary-General of the Modern World Muslim Congress in Karachi, Pakistan, for his tireless work in establishing harmony among Muslims, Christians, and Jews.

1989   The very Rev. Lord MacLeod, founder of the Iona Community, a monastic island off the west coast of Scotland, for building a prayer-centered spiritual movement dedicated to peacemaking and simplicity. **Professor Carl Friedrich von Weizsacker**, for his exploration of inter-relationships of physics, cosmology, and theology.

1990   Baba Amte, a wealthy Hindu lawyer who left a comfortable life behind to help modern communities deal with India's lepers and other so-called "untouchable" social problems. Amte's community brought "employment, education, health, and other services to citizens long denied compassion." **L. Charles Birch**, professor of biology at the University of Sydney, for his "search for spiritual meaning in the realms of specialized knowledge."

1991   Lord Jakobovits, Chief Rabbi of Great Britain (1967-91), for over half a century of spiritual leadership. His steadfast principles and unwavering integrity made him a rock of unyielding ethics whose moral authority extended far beyond the Jewish community.

1992   Rev. Dr. Kyung-Chik Han, founder of Seoul's 60,000-member Young Nak Presbyterian Church, the world's largest Presbyterian congregation, with more than 500 churches worldwide. His work on behalf of refugees and the poor attracted the world's attention to the growth of Christianity in Korea.

1993   Charles W. Colson, founder of the Prison Fellowship. A former Special Counsel to U.S. President Richard M. Nixon, Colson spent time in federal prison for Watergate-related crimes before founding the largest prison outreach program in the world. It has succeeded in reducing recidivism among criminals.

1994   Michael Novak, author, journalist, professor, and diplomat, for his "revolutionary insights into the spiritual foundations of economic and political systems." A pioneer in the discipline in the theology of economics.

1995   Paul Charles William Davies, a mathematical physicist whose "inquiries into the workings of the universe have breached the barrier between science and religion." He contended that humanity's ability to calculate the physical universe evidences purpose and design to human existence.

1996   William R. "Bill" Bright, founder of Campus Crusade for Christ, which revived biblical study on the campuses of more than 1,000 colleges worldwide.

1997   Pandurang Shastri Athavale, founder of the Bhagavad Gita–based self-study known as *swadhyaya*, which encourages the recognition of God within all humans which, in turn, leads to a sense of self-esteem and respect for others. Although this interfaith movement discourages proselytizing, has no formal hierarchy, and seeks no funding whatsoever, it is credited with liberating close to 20 million people in India from poverty and other social ills.

1998   Sir Sigmund Sternberg, a Hungarian-born British philanthropist, for his tireless promotion of interfaith dialogue, especially between Catholics and Jews.

1999   Ian Barbour, professor emeritus at Carleton College in Northfield, Minn., for promoting "scrutiny of areas where science and religion might meet." An ourspoken advocate for ethics in technology, energy policy, and genetic engineering.

Source: John Marks Templeton Foundation. **www.templeton.org.**

Pulitzer Prizes

PULITZER PRIZES IN JOURNALISM

The Pulitzer Prize for Reporting is the oldest given in journalism and was first awarded in 1917 together with the Pulitzer Prizes for History and Biography. The changing nature and public perception of reporting can be seen in the various categories established over the years. Originally, the prize recognized excellence irrespective of the journalist's beat; it could be local, national or international, and it could be either reporting for a deadline or investigative reporting carried out over a longer period. In 1929 a Correspondence category was created to distinguish correspondents stationed either in Washington or abroad from local journalists. Separate categories for National and International Reporting were added in 1942, and the Correspondence category was absorbed by these categories in 1947.

Meritorious Public Service, 1918–99

Year	Paper, Distinction

1918   New York Times, Reports, documents, and speeches relating to World War I.
1919   Milwaukee Journal, Campaign for Americanism.
1920   No award
1921   Boston Post, Articles exposing operations and leading to arrest of Charles Ponzi.
1922   New York World, Articles exposing operations of Ku Klux Klan.
1923   Memphis Commercial Appeal, News and cartoons about Ku Klux Klan.
1924   New York World, Exposure of Florida peonage evil.
1925   No award
1926   Columbus (Ga.) Enquirer Sun, Articles decrying Ku Klux Klan, dishonest public officials, lynching, and a law barring the teaching of evolution.
1927   Canton (Ohio) Daily News, Articles about collusion between city government and organized crime, resulting in assassination of editor, Don R. Mellett.
1928   Indianapolis Times, Exposure of political corruption in Indiana.
1929   New York Evening World, Campaign to correct evil and corruption in administration of justice.
1930   No award
1931   Atlanta Constitution, Municipal graft exposure leading to convictions.
1932   Indianapolis News, Campaign to eliminate waste in city management and reduce tax levy.
1933   New York World-Telegram, Series of articles on veterans' relief, real estate bond evil, and articles exposing lottery schemes of fraternal organizations.
1934   Medford (Oreg.) Mail Tribune, Campaign against unscrupulous politicians in Jackson County, Oreg.
1935   Sacramento Bee, Campaign against political machine influence in appointment of two federal judges in Nevada.
1936   Cedar Rapids Gazette, Crusade against corruption and misgovernment in state of Iowa.
1937   St. Louis Post-Dispatch, Exposure of registration fraud in St. Louis, resulting in invalidation of more than 40,000 fraudulent ballots and appointment of new election board.
1938   Bismarck (N.D.) Tribune, News reports and editorials entitled "Self Help in the Dust Bowl."
1939   Miami Daily News, Campaign for recall of Miami City Commission.
1940   Waterbury (Conn.) Republican & American, Campaign exposing municipal graft.
1941   St. Louis Post-Dispatch, Campaign against city smoke nuisance.
1942   Los Angeles Times, Campaign resulting in clarification and confirmation of freedom of press rights for all American newspapers.
1943   Omaha (Nebr.) World-Herald, Campaign for collection of scrap metal for war effort.

1944   New York Times, Survey of teaching of American history.
1945   Detroit Free Press, Investigation of legislative graft and corruption at Lansing, Mich.
1946   Scranton (Pa.) Times, Fifteen-year investigation of judicial practices in U.S. District Court, resulting in removal of the district judge and indictment of many others.
1947   Baltimore Sun, Series of articles by Howard M. Norton dealing with administration of unemployment compensation in Maryland, resulting in 93 criminal convictions and/or guilty pleas.
1948   St. Louis Post-Dispatch, Coverage of Centralia, Ill. mine disaster and follow-up articles resulting in reforms in mine safety laws and regulations.
1949   Nebraska State Journal, Campaign establishing "Nebraska All-Star Primary" that called attention to issues early in presidential campaign.
1950   Chicago Daily News and St. Louis Post-Dispatch, Work of George Thiem and Roy J. Harris, respectively, in exposing presence of 37 Illinois newspapermen on an Illinois state payroll.
1951   Miami Herald and Brooklyn Eagle, Crime reporting during the year.
1952   St. Louis Post-Dispatch, Investigation and disclosures of corruption in Internal Revenue Bureau and other government departments.
1953   Whiteville (N.C.) News Reporter and Tabor City (N.C.) Tribune, Campaign against Ku Klux Klan, culminating in the conviction of more than 100 Klansman and an end to terrorism in their communities.
1954   Newsday (Garden City, N.Y.), Exposé of New York State's racetrack scandals and labor racketeering, leading to imprisonment of racketeer William C. DeKooonig Sr.
1955   Columbus (Ga.) Ledger and Sunday Ledger-Enquirer, News coverage and editorial attack on corruption in neighboring Phenix City, leading to destruction of racket-ridden city government.
1956   Watsonville (Calif.) Register-Pajaronion, Exposure of corruption in public office leading to resignation of a district attorney and conviction of one of his associates.
1957   Chicago Daily News, Exposure of $2.5 million fraud in office of Illinois state auditor, resulting in his conviction.
1958   Arkansas Gazette, Civic leadership, journalistic responsibility, and moral courage during school integration crisis.
1959   Utica Observer-Dispatch and Utica Daily Press (N.Y.), Campaign against corruption, gambling, and vice.
1960   Los Angeles Times, Attack on narcotics traffic; reporting of Gene Sherman, which led to opening of negotiations between U.S. and Mexico to halt the flow of illegal drugs into California and other border states.

1961 Amarillo (Tex.) Globe-Times, Exposure of lax law enforcement resulting in punitive action sweeping officials from their posts and creating election of reform slate.

1962 Panama City (Fla.) News-Herald, Three-year campaign against entrenched power and corruption, resulting in reforms in Panama City and Bay County.

1963 Chicago Daily News, Articles calling public attention to providing birth control services in public health programs.

1964 St. Petersburg Times, Investigation of illegal activity within Florida Turnpike Authority, resulting in major reorganization state's road construction program.

1965 Hutchinson (Kans.) News, Campaign for more equitable reapportionment of Kansas legislature.

1966 Boston Globe, Campaign to prevent confirmation of Francis X. Morrissey as federal district judge in Massachusetts.

1967 Louisville Courier Journal and Milwaukee Journal, Campaign to control Kentucky strip-mining industry; campaign to stiffen water pollution laws in Wisconsin.

1968 Riverside (Calif.) Press-Enterprise, Exposure of corruption in courts in connection with handling of property and estates of an Indian tribe in California.

1969 Los Angeles Times, Exposure of wrongdoing within Los Angeles city government commissions, resulting in criminal convictions, resignations, and sweeping reforms.

1970 Newsday (Garden City, N.Y.), Three-year investigation and exposure of secret land deals in eastern Long Island, leading to criminal convictions, resignations, and discharges among public and political officials.

1971 Winston-Salem Journal and Sentinel, Coverage of environmental problems, as exemplified by campaign to block a strip-mining operation that would have caused irreparable damage to northwest North Carolina hill country.

1972 New York Times, Publication of Pentagon Papers.

1973 Washington Post, Investigation of Watergate case.

1974 Newsday (Garden City, N.Y.), Definitive report on illicit narcotics traffic in U.S. and abroad, entitled "The Heroin Trail."

1975 Boston Globe, Coverage of Boston school desegregation crisis.

1976 Anchorage Daily News, Disclosures of impact and influence of Teamsters Union on Alaska's economy and politics.

1977 Lufkin (Tex.) News, Obituary of local men who died in Marine training camp, which grew into investigation of that death and fundamental reform in Marine Corps' recruiting and training practices.

1978 Philadelphia Inquirer, Series of articles showing abuses of power by Philadelphia police.

1979 Point Reyes (Calif.) Light, Investigation of Synanon.

1980 Gannett News Service, Series on financial contributions to Pauline Fathers.

1981 Charlotte Observer, Series called "Brown Lung: A Case of Deadly Neglect."

1982 Detroit News, Series by Sydney P. Freedberg and David Ashenfelter exposing U.S. Navy's cover-up of circumstances surrounding deaths of seamen aboard ship and leading to significant reforms in naval procedures.

1983 Jackson (Miss.) Clarion-Ledger, Campaign supporting Gov. Winter in his legislative battle for reform of Mississippi's public education system.

1984 Los Angeles Times, In-depth examination of southern California's growing Latino community.

1985 Fort Worth Star-Telegram, Reporting by Mark J. Thompson revealing that nearly 250 U.S. servicemen died because of a design problem in helicopters built by Bell Helicopter—causing the army to ground almost 600 Huey helicopters pending their modification.

1986 Denver Post, In-depth study of "missing children," revealing that most are involved in custody disputes or are runaways, and helping to mitigate national fears stirred by exaggerated statistics.

1987 Pittsburgh Press, Reporting by Andrew Schneider and Matthew Brelis, revealing inadequacy of FAA's medical screening of airline pilots, and leading to reform.

1988 Charlotte Observer, Revealing misuse of funds by the PTL television ministry, despite massive campaign by PTL to discredit the newspaper.

1989 Anchorage Daily News, For series revealing high incidence of alcoholism and suicide among Native Alaskans.

1990 Philadelphia Inquirer, For series by Gilbert M. Gaul disclosing shortcomings in federal regulation of the nation's blood banks.

Washington (N.C.) Daily News, For series by Betty Gray and Mike Voss revealing contamination of the municipal water supply in the town of 9,000 and the eight-year cover-up by elected officials.

1991 Des Moines Register, For series by Jane Schorer about a rape and its aftermath that reopened debate over whether rape victims should be identified by name.

1992 Sacramento Bee, For series by Tom Knudson about pollution, overdevelopment and overpopulation along the Sierra Nevada mountain range.

1993 Miami Herald, For helping readers cope with Hurricane Andrew's devastation and for showing "how lax zoning, inspection and building codes had contributed to the destruction."

1994 Akron Beacon Journal, For two-part examination of race relations.

1995 Virgin Islands Daily News, For 10-part series on crime that explained why crime was so prevalent on the islands, questioned the responses of police and prosecutors to crime, and ultimately led to major reforms.

1996 Raleigh News and Observer, For stories revealing how agricultural corporations, unfettered by government regulation, were elbowing out small family hog farms and polluting the environment in the process.

1997 New Orleans Times-Picayune, For series analyzing the environmental, commercial, political, and social conditions that threaten the world's fish supply. It affected changes in Federal fisheries laws.

1998 Grand Forks (N.D) Herald, For its coverage of the blizzard, flood, and fire that devastated the city and the newspaper's own plant.

1999 Washington Post, For its series that identified and analyzed patterns of reckless gunplay by city police officers who had little training or supervision.

Pulitzer Prizes for National Reporting, 1942–99

Year	Winner, Newspaper	Year	Winner, Newspaper
1942	Louis Stark, *New York Times*	1972	Jack Anderson, (Syndicated columnist)
1943	No award	1973	Robert Boyd and Clark Hoyt, Knight
1944	Dewey L. Fleming, *Baltimore Sun*		Newspapers
1945	James B. Reston, *New York Times*	1974	James R. Polk, *Washington Star-News*
1946	Edward A. Harris, *St. Louis Post-Dispatch*		Jack White, *Providence Journal and Evening*
1947	Edward T. Folliard, *Washington Post*		*Bulletin*
1948	Bert Andrews, *New York Herald Tribune*	1975	Donald L. Bartlett and James B. Steele,
	Nat S. Finney, *Minneapolis Tribune*		*Philadelphia Inquirer*
1949	C.P. Trussell, *New York Times*	1976	James Risser, *Des Moines Register*
1950	Edwin O. Guthman, *Seattle Times*	1977	Walter Mears, Associated Press
1951	No award[1]	1978	Gaylord D. Shaw, *Los Angeles Times*
1952	Anthony Leviero, *New York Times*	1979	James Risser, *Des Moines Register*
1953	Don Whitehead, Associated Press	1980	Bette Swenson Orsini and Charles Stafford, *St.*
1954	Richard Wilson, *Des Moines Register and*		*Petersburg Times*
	Tribune	1981	John M Crewdson, *New York Times*
1955	Anthony Lewis, *Washington Daily News*	1982	Rick Atkinson, *Kansas City Times*
1956	Charles L. Bartlett, *Chattanooga Times*	1983	Staff, *Boston Globe*
1957	James B. Reston, *New York Times*	1984	John Noble Wilford, *New York Times*
1958	Relman Morin, Associated Press	1985	Thomas J. Knudson, *Des Moines Register*
	Clark Mollenhoff, *Des Moines Register and*	1986	Arthur Howe, *Philadelphia Inquirer*
	Tribune		Craig Flournoy and George Rodrigues, *Dallas*
1959	Howard Van Smith, *Miami News*		*Morning News*
1960	Vance Trimble , Scripps-Howard	1987	Staff, *Miami Herald*
	Newspaper Alliance		Staff, *New York Times*
1961	Edward R. Cony, *Wall Street Journal*	1988	Tim Weiner, *Philadelphia Inquirer*
1962	Nathan G. Caldwell and Gene S. Graham,	1989	Donald L. Bartlett and James B. Steele,
	Nashville Tennessean		*Philadelphia Inquirer*
1963	Anthony Lewis, *New York Times*	1990	Ross Anderson, Bill Dietrich, Mary Ann
1964	Merriman Smith, United Press International		Gwinn, and Eric Nalder, *Seattle Times*
1965	Louis M. Kohlmeier, *Wall Street Journal*	1991	Marji Lundstrom and Rochelle Sharpe,
1966	Haynes Johnson, *Washington Evening Star*		Gannet News Service
1967	Stanley Penn and Monroe Karmin, *Wall Street*	1992	Jeff Taylor and Mike McGraw, *Kansas City Star*
	Journal	1993	David Maraniss, *Washington Post*
1968	Howard James, *Christian Science Monitor*	1994	Eileen Welsome, *Albuquerque Tribune*
	Nathan K. (Nick) Kotz, *Des Moines*	1995	Tony Horwitz, *Wall Street Journal*
	Register and *Minneapolis Tribune*	1996	Alix M. Freedman, *Wall Street Journal*
1969	Robert Cahn, *Christian Science Monitor*	1997	Staff, *Wall Street Journal*
1970	William J. Eaton, *Chicago Daily News*	1998	Russell Carollo and Jeff Nesmith, *Dayton*
1971	Lucinda Franks and Thomas Powers, United		(Ohio) *Daily News*
	Press International	1999	Staff, *New York Times*

1. The board decided that Arthur Krock of The *New York Times* deserved the prize for National Reporting, but he could not accept because he was a board member.

Pulitzer Prizes for International Reporting, 1942–99

Year	Winner, Newspaper	Year	Winner, Newspaper
1942	Lawrence Edmund Allen, Associated Press	1957	Russell Jones, United Press
1943	Ira Wolfert, North American Newspaper	1958	Staff, *New York Times*
	Alliance, Inc.	1959	Joseph Martin and Philip Santora, *New*
1944	Daniel DeLuce, Associated Press		*York Daily News*
1945	Mark S. Watson, *Baltimore Sun*	1960	A.M. Rosenthal, *New York Times*
1946	Homer William Bigart, *New York Herald*	1961	Lynn Heinzerling, Associated Press
	Tribune	1962	Walter Lippmann, *New York Herald*
1947	Eddy Gilmore, Associated Press		*Tribune Syndicate*
1948	Paul W. Ward, *Baltimore Sun*	1963	Hal Hendrix, *Miami News*
1949	Price Day, *Baltimore Sun*	1964	Malcolm W. Browne, Associated Press
1950	Edmund Stevens, *Christian Science Monitor*		David Halberstam, *New York Times*
1951	Keyes Beech, *Chicago Daily News*	1965	J. A. Livingston, *Philadelphia Bulletin*
	Homer William Bigart, *New York Herald*	1966	Peter Arnett, Associated Press
	Tribune	1967	R. John Hughes, *Christian Science Monitor*
	Marguerite Higgins, *New York Herald Tribune*	1968	Alfred Friendly, *Washington Post*
	Relman Morin, Associated Press	1969	William Tuohy, *Los Angeles Times*
	Fred Sparks, *Chicago Daily News*	1970	Seymour M. Hersh, Dispatch News Service
	Don Whitehead, Associated Press	1971	Jimmie Lee Hoagland, *Washington Post*
1952	John M. Hightower, Associated Press	1972	Peter R. Kann, *Wall Street Journal*
1953	Austin Wehrwien, *Milwaukee Journal*	1973	Max Frankel, *New York Times*
1954	Jim G. Lucas, Scripps-Howard Newspaper	1974	Hedrick Smith, *New York Times*
	Alliance	1975	William Mullen (reporter), Ovie Carter
1955	Harrison E. Salisbury, *New York Times*		(photographer), *Chicago Tribune*
1956	William Randolph Hearst Jr., Kingsbury	1976	Sydney H. Schanberg, *New York Times*
	Smith, and Frank Conniff, International	1977	No award
	News Service	1978	Henry Kamm, *New York Times*

Year	Winner, Newspaper	Year	Winner, Newspaper
1979	Richard Ben Cramer, *Philadelphia Inquirer*	1989	Glenn Frankel, *Washington Post* Bill Keller, *New York Times*
1980	Joel Brinkley (reporter), Jay Mather (photographer), *Louisville Courier-Journal*	1990	Nicholas D. Kristof and Sheryl WuDunn, *New York Times*
1981	Shirley Christian, *Miami Herald*	1991	Caryle Murphy, *Washington Post*
1982	John Darnton, *New York Times*		Serge Schmemann, *New York Times*
1983	Thomas L. Friedman, *New York Times* Loren Jenkins, *Washington Post*	1992	Patrick J. Sloyan, *Newsday* (Garden City, N.Y.)
1984	Karen Elliott House, *Wall Street Journal*	1993	John F. Burns, *New York Times*
1985	Josh Friedman and Dennis Bell (reporters) and Ozier Muhammad (photographer), *Newsday* (Garden City, N.Y.)		Roy Gutman, *Newsday* (Garden City, N.Y.)
		1994	Team of reporters, *Dallas Morning News*
		1995	Mark Fritz, Associated Press
1986	Lewis M. Simons, Pete Carey, and Katherine Ellison, *San Jose Mercury News*	1996	David Rohde, *Christian Science Monitor*
		1997	John F. Burns, *New York Times*
1987	Michael Parks, *Los Angeles Times*	1998	Staff, *New York Times*
1988	Thomas L. Friedman, *New York Times*	1999	Staff, *Wall Street Journal*

Pulitzer Prizes for Editorial Writing, 1917–99

Year	Winner, Newspaper	Year	Winner, Newspaper
1917	*Lusitania* editorial article, *New York Tribune*	1952	Louis LaCoss, *St. Louis Globe Democrat*
1918	War editorials and articles, *Louisville Courier Journal*	1953	Vermont Connecticut Royster, *Wall Street Journal*
1919	No award	1954	Don Murray, *Boston Herald*
1920	Harvey E. Newbranch, *Evening World Herald*	1955	Royce Howes, *Detroit Free Press*
1921	No award	1956	Lauren K. Soth, *Des Moines Register and Tribune*
1922	Frank M. O'Brien, *New York Herald*	1957	Buford Boone, *Tuscaloosa News*
1923	William Allen White, *Emporia (Kans.) Gazette*	1958	Harry S. Ashmore, *Arkansas Gazette*
		1959	Ralph McGill, *Atlanta Constitution*
1924[1]	Coolidge editorial, *Boston Herald*	1960	Lenoir Chambers, *Norfolk Virginian-Pilot*
1925	"Plight of the South" editorial, *Charleston (S.C.) News and Courier*	1961	William J. Dorvillier, *San Juan* (Puerto Rico) *Star*
1926	Edward M. Kingsbury, *New York Times*	1962	Thomas M. Storke, *Santa Barbara* (Calif.) *News Press*
1927	F. Lauriston Bullard, *Boston Herald*		
1928	Grover Cleveland Hall, *Montgomery Advertiser*	1963	Ira B. Harkey Jr., *Pascagoula (Miss.) U. Chronicle*
1929	Louis Isaac Jaffe, *Norfolk Virginian-Pilot*	1964	Hazel Brannon Smith, *Lexington* (Miss.) *Advertiser*
1930	No award		
1931	Charles S. Ryckman, *Fremont* (Nebr.) *Tribune*	1965	John R. Harrison, *Gainesville (Fla.) Daily Sun*
1932	No award	1966	Robert Lasch, *St. Louis Post-Dispatch*
1933	series of editorials, *Kansas City Star*	1967	Eugene Patterson, *Atlanta Constitution*
1934	E.P. Chase, *Atlantic* (Iowa) *News-Telegraph*	1968	John S. Knight, *Knight Newspapers*
1935	No award	1969	Paul Greenberg, *Pine Bluff* (Ark.) *Commercial*
1936	Felix Morley, *Washington Post* George B. Parker, Scripps-Howard Newspapers		
		1970	Philip L. Geyelin, *Washington Post*
1937	John W. Owens, *Baltimore Sun*	1971	Horance G. Davis Jr., *Gainesville* (Fla.) *Daily Sun*
1938	William Wesley Waymack, *Des Moines Register and Tribune*		
		1972	John Strohmeyer, *Bethlehem* (Pa.) *Globe-Times*
1939	Ronald G. Callvert, *Portland Oregonian*	1973	Roger B. Linscott, *Berkshire Eagle* (Pittsfield, Mass.)
1940	Bart Howard, *St. Louis Post-Dispatch*		
1941	Reuben Maury, *New York Daily News*	1974	F. Gilman Spencer, *Trentonian* (Trenton, N.J.)
1942	Geoffrey Parsons, *New York Herald Tribune*		
1943	Forrest W. Seymour, *Des Moines Register and Tribune*	1975	John D. Maurice, *Charleston* (W.V.) *Daily Mail*
1944	Henry J. Haskell, *Kansas City Star*	1976	Philip P. Kerby, *Los Angeles Times*
1945	George W. Potter, *Providence Journal-Bulletin*	1977	Warren L. Lerude, Foster Church and Norman F. Cardoza, *Reno Evening Gazette and Nevada State Journal*
1946	Hodding Carter, *Delta Democrat-Times* (Greenville, Mlss.)		
		1978	Meg Greenfield, *Washington Post*
1947	William H. Grimes, *Wall Street Journal*	1979	Edwin M. Yoder Jr., *Washington Star*
1948	Virginius Dabney, *Richmond Times-Dispatch*	1980	Robert L. Bartley, *Wall Street Journal*
		1981	No award
1949	John H. Crider, *Boston Herald* Herbert Elliston, *Washington Post*	1982	Jack Rosenthal, *New York Times*
		1983	Editorial Board, *Miami Herald*
1950	Carl M. Saunders, *Jackson* (Mich.) *Citizen Patriot*	1984	Albert Scardino, *Georgia Gazette*
		1985	Richard Aregood, *Philadelphia Daily News*
1951	William Harry Fitzpatrick, *New Orleans States*		
		1986	Jack Fuller, *Chicago Tribune*

Year	Winner, Newspaper	Year	Winner, Newspaper
1987	Jonathan Freedman, *San Diego Tribune*	1994	R. Bruce Dold, *Chicago Tribune*
1988	Jane Healy, *Orlando Sentinel*	1995	Jeffrey Good, *St. Petersburg Times*
1989	Lois Wille, *Chicago Tribune*	1996	Robert B. Semple, Jr., *New York Times*
1990	Thomas J. Hylton, *Pottstown* (Pa.) *Mercury*	1997	Michael G. Gartner, *Daily Tribune* (Ames,
1991	Ron Casey, Harold Jackson, and Joey		Iowa)
	Kennedy, *Birmingham News*	1998	Bernard L. Stein, *Riverdale* (N.Y.) *Press*
1992	Maria Henson, *Lexington Herald-Leader*	1999	Editorial Board, *N.Y. Daily News*
1993	No award		

1. A special prize was awarded to the widow of the late Frank I. Cobb of *The New York World* in recognition of his lifetime of editorial writing and service.

Pulitzer Prizes for Editorial Cartooning, 1922–99

Year	Winner, Newspaper	Year	Winner, Newspaper
1922	Rollin Kirby, *New York World*	1962	Edmund S. Valtman, *Hartford Times*
1923	No award	1963	Frank Miller, *Des Moines Register*
1924	Jay Norwood Darling, *Des Moines Register and Tribune*	1964	Paul Conrad, *Denver Post*
		1965	No award
1925	Rollin Kirby, *New York World*	1966	Don Wright, *Miami News*
1926	Daniel R. Fitzpatrick, *St. Louis Post-Dispatch*	1967	Patrick Oliphant, *Denver Post*
		1968	Eugene Gray Payne, *Charlotte Observer*
1927	Nelson Harding, *Brooklyn Daily Eagle*	1969	John Fischettii, *Chicago Daily News*
1928	Nelson Harding, *Brooklyn Daily Eagle*	1970	Thomas F. Darcy, *Newsday* (Garden City,
1929	Rollin Kirby, *New York World*		N.Y.)
1930	Charles R. Macauley, *Brooklyn Daily Eagle*	1971	Paul Conrad, *Los Angeles Times*
1931	Edmund Duffy, *Baltimore Sun*	1972	Jeffrey K. MacNelly, *Richmond News-Leader*
1932	John T. McCutcheon, *Chicago Tribune*		
1933	H.M. Talburt, *Washington Daily News*	1973	No award
1934	Edmund Duffy, *Baltimore Sun*	1974	Paul Szep, *Boston Globe*
1935	Ross A. Lewis, *Milwaukee Journal*	1975	Garry Trudeau, Universal Press Syndicate
1936	No award	1976	Tony Auth, *Philadelphia Inquirer*
1937	C.D. Batchelor, *New York Daily News*	1977	Paul Szep, *Boston Globe*
1938	Vaughn Shoemaker , *Chicago Daily News*	1978	Jeffrey K. MacNelly, *Richmond News-Leader*
1939	Charles G. Werner, *Daily Oklahoman*		
1940	Edmund Duffy, *Baltimore Sun*	1979	Herbert L. Block (Herblock), *Washington Post*
1941	Jacob Burck, *Chicago Times*		
1942	Herbert L. Block (Herblock), NEA Service	1980	Don Wright, *Miami News*
1943	Jay Norwood Darling, *Des Moines Register and Tribune*	1981	Mike Peters, *Dayton* (Ohio) *Daily News*
		1982	Ben Sargent, *Austin* (Tex.) *American-Statesman*
1944	Clifford K. Berryman, *Washington Evening Star*		
		1983	Richard Locher, *Chicago Tribune*
1945	Sergeant Bill Mauldin, United Feature Syndicate, Inc	1984	Paul Conrad, *Los Angeles Times*
		1985	Jeff MacNelly , *Chicago Tribune*
1946	Bruce Alexander Russell, *Los Angeles Times*	1986	Jules Feiffer, *Village Voice* (New York City)
1947	Vaughn Shoemaker , *Chicago Daily News*	1987	Berke Breathed, Washington Post Writers Group
1948	Reuben L. Goldberg, *New York Sun*		
1949	Lute Pease, *Newark Evening News*	1988	Doug Marlette, *Atlanta Constitution* and *Charlotte Observer*
1950	James T. Berryman, *Washington Evening Star*		
		1989	Jack Higgins, *Chicago Sun-Times*
1951	Reg Manning, *Arizona Republic*	1990	Tom Toles, *Buffalo News*
1952	Fred L. Packer, *New York Mirror*	1991	Jim Borgman, *Cincinnati Enquirer*
1953	Edward D. Kuekes, *Cleveland Plain Dealer*	1992	Signe Wilkinson, *Philadelphia Daily News*
1954	Herbert L. Block (Herblock), *Washington Post & Times Herald*	1993	Stephen R. Benson, *Arizona Republic*
		1994	Michael P. Ramirez, *Commercial Appeal* (Memphis)
1955	Daniel R. Fitzpatrick, *St. Louis Post-Dispatch*		
1956	Robert York, *Lousiville Times*	1995	Mike Luckovich, *Atlanta Constitution*
1957	Tom Little, *Nashville Tennessean*	1996	Jim Morin, *Miami Herald*
1958	Bruce M. Shanks, *Buffalo Evening News*	1997	Walt Handelsman, *New Orleans Times-Picayune*
1959	Bill Mauldin, *St. Louis Post-Dispatch*		
1960	No award	1998	Stephen P. Breen, *Asbury Park* (N.J.) *Press*
1961	Carey Orr, *Chicago Tribune*	1999	David Horsey, *Seattle Post-Intelligencer*

Pulitzer Prizes for Photography

The photography category, begun in 1942, was divided into spot news and feature photography categories in 1968.

PHOTOGRAPHY, 1942–67

Year	Winner, Newspaper	Year	Winner, Newspaper
1942	Milton Brooks, *Detroit News*	1955	John L. Gaunt Jr., *Los Angeles Times*
1943	Frank Noel, *Associated Press*	1956	Photography staff, *New York Daily News*
1944	Frank Filan, *Associated Press*	1957	Harry A. Trask, *Boston Traveler*
	Earle L. Bunker, *World-Herald* (Omaha, Nebraska)	1958	William C. Beall, *Washington Daily News*
		1959	William Seaman, *Minneapolis Star*
1945	Joe Rosenthal, *Associated Press*	1960	Andrew Lopez, United Press International
1946	No award	1961	Yasushi Nago, *Manichi* (Tokyo); photo distributed by United Press International
1947	Arnold Hardy, Amateur; photo distributed by Associated Press	1962	Paul Vathis, Associated Press
1948	Frank Cushing, *Boston Traveler*	1963	Hector Rondon, *La Republica* (Caracas, Venezuela); photo distributed by Associated Press
1949	Nathaniel Fein, *New York Herald Tribune*		
1950	Bill Crouch, *Oakland Tribune*		
1951	Max Desfor, *Associated Press*	1964	Robert H. Jackson, *Dallas Times-Herald*
1952	John Robinson and Don Ultang, *Des Moines Register and Tribune*	1965	Horst Faas, Associated Press
		1966	Kyoichi Sawada, United Press International
1953	William M. Gallagher, *Flint* (Mich.) *Journal*	1967	Jack R. Thornell, Associated Press
1954	Mrs. Walter M. Schau, Amateur; photo published by *Akron Beacon Journal*		

SPOT NEWS PHOTOGRAPHY: 1968–99

Year	Winner, Newspaper	Year	Winner, Newspaper
1968	Rocco Morabito, *Jacksonville Journal*	1984	Stan Grossfeld, *Boston Globe*
1969	Edward T. Adams, Associated Press	1985	Photography Staff, *Register* (Santa Ana, Calif.)
1970	Steve Starr, Associated Press	1986	Carol Guzy and Michael duCille, *Miami Herald*
1971	John Paul Filo, *Valley Daily News* and *Daily Dispatch,* (New Kensington, Pa.)	1987	Kim Komenich, *San Francisco Examiner*
1972	Horst Faas and Michael Laurent, Associated Press	1988	Scott Shaw, *Odessa* (Tex.) *American*
		1989	Ron Olshwanger, freelancer, *St. Louis Post-Dispatch*
1973	Hyunh Cong Ut, Associated Press		
1974	Anthony K. Roberts, freelancer , Beverly Hills, Calif.	1990	Photography Staff, *Oakland Tribune*
		1991	Greg Marinovich, Associated Press
1975	Gerald H. Gay, *Seattle Times*	1992	Photography Staff, Associated Press
1976	Stanley Forman, *Boston Herald American*	1993	William Snyder and Ken Geiger, *Dallas Morning News*
1977	Neal Ulevich, Associated Press		
	Stanley Forman, *Boston Herald American*	1994	Paul Watson, *Toronto Star*
1978	John H. Blair, United Press International	1995	Carol Guzy, *Washington Post*
1979	Thomas J. Kelly III, *Pottstown* (Pa.) *Mercury*	1996	Charles Porter 4th, freelancer, Associated Press
1980	Unnamed photographer, United Press International	1997	Annie Wells, *Press Democrat* (Santa Rosa, Calif.)
1981	Larry C. Price, *Fort Worth Star-Telegram*		
1982	Ron Edmonds, Associated Press	1998	Martha Rial, *Pittsburgh Post-Gazette*
1983	Bill Foley, Associated Press	1999	John McConnico, Associated Press

FEATURE PHOTOGRAPHY: 1968–99

Year	Winner, Newspaper	Year	Winner, Newspaper
1968	Toshio Sakai, United Press International	1985	Stan Grossfeld, *Boston Globe*
1969	Moneta Sleet Jr., *Ebony* Magazine		Larry C. Price, *Philadelphia Inquirer*
1970	Dallas Kinney, *Palm Beach Post* (West Palm Beach, Fla.)	1986	Tom Gralish, *Philadelphia Inquirer*
		1987	David Peterson, *Des Moines Register*
1971	Jack Dykinga, *Chicago Sun-Times*	1988	Michael duCille, *Miami Herald*
1972	Dave Kennerly, United Press International	1989	Manny Crisostomo, *Detroit Free Press*
1973	Brian Lanker, *Topeka Capital-Journal*	1990	David C. Turnley, *Detroit Free Press*
1974	Slava Veder, Associated Press	1991	William Snyder, *Dallas Morning News*
1975	Matthew Lewis, *Washington Post*	1992	John Kaplan, *Pittsburgh Post-Gazette,* Block Newspapers
1976	Photography Staff, *Louisville Courier Journal and Times*		
		1993	Staff, Associated Press
1977	Robin Hood, *Chattanooga News-Free Press*	1994	Kevin Carter, freelancer, *New York Times*
1978	J. Ross Baughman, Associated Press	1995	Staff, Associated Press
1979	Photography Staff, *Boston Herald American*	1996	Stephanie Welsh, freelancer, Newhouse News Service
1980	Erwin H. Hagler, *Dallas Times Herald*		
1981	Taro M. Yamasaki, *Detroit Free Press*	1997	Alexander Zemlianichenko, Associated Press
1982	John H. White, *Chicago Sun-Times*		
1983	James B. Dickman, *Dallas Times Herald*	1998	Clarence Williams, *Los Angeles Times*
1984	Anthony Suau, *Denver Post*	1999	Susan Walsh, Associated Press

Pulitzer Prizes for Commentary, 1970–99

Year	Winner, Newspaper	Year	Winner, Newspaper
1970	Marquis W. Childs, *St. Louis Post-Dispatch*	1984	Vermont Royster, *Wall Street Journal*
1971	William A. Caldwell, *The Record* (Hackensack, N.J.)	1985	Murray Kempton, *Newsday* (Garden City, N.Y.)
1972	Mike Royko, *Chicago Daily News*	1986	Jimmy Breslin, *New York Daily News*
1973	David S. Broder, *Washington Post*	1987	Charles Krauthammer, *Washington Post*
1974	Edwin A. Roberts Jr., *National Observer*	1988	Dave Barry, *Miami Herald*
1975	Mary McGrory, *Washington Star*	1989	Clarence Page, *Chicago Tribune*
1976	Walter (Red) Smith, *New York Times*	1990	Jim Murray, *Los Angeles Times*
1977	George F. Will, Washington Post Writers Group	1991	Jim Hoagland, *Washington Post*
		1992	Anna Quindlen, *New York Times*
1978	William Safire, *New York Times*	1993	Liz Balmaseda, *Miami Herald*
1979	Russell Baker, *New York Times*	1994	William Raspberry, *Washington Post*
1980	Ellen H. Goodman, *Boston Globe*	1995	Jim Dwyer, *New York Newsday*
1981	Dave Anderson, *New York Times*	1996	E.R. Shipp, *New York Daily News*
1982	Art Buchwald, *Los Angeles Times* Syndicate	1997	Eileen McNamara, *Boston Globe*
1983	Claude Sitton, *Raleigh* (N.C.) *News & Observer*	1998	Mike McAlary, *New York Daily News*
		1999	Maureen Dowd, *New York Times*

Pulitzer Prizes for Criticism, 1970–99

Year	Winner, Newspaper	Year	Winner, Newspaper
1970	Ada Louise Huxtable, *New York Times*	1986	Donal Henahan, *New York Times*
1971	Harold C. Schonberg, *New York Times*	1987	Richard Eder, *Los Angeles Times*
1972	Frank Peters, *St. Louis Post-Dispatch*	1988	Tom Shales, *Washington Post*
1973	Ronald Powers, *Chicago Sun-Times*	1989	Michael Skube, *Raleigh (N.C.) News and Observer*
1974	Emily Genauer, *Newsday* Syndicate		
1975	Roger Ebert, *Chicago Sun-Times*	1990	Allan Temko, *San Francisco Chronicle*
1976	Alan M. Kriegsman, *Washington Post*	1991	David Shaw, *Los Angeles Times*
1977	William McPherson, *Washington Post*	1992	No award
1978	Walter Kerr, *New York Times*	1993	Michael Dirda, *Washington Post*
1979	Paul Gapp, *Chicago Tribune*	1994	Lloyd Schwartz, *Boston Phoenix*
1980	William A. Henry III, *Boston Globe*	1995	Margo Jefferson, *New York Times*
1981	Jonathan Yardley, *Washington Star*	1996	Robert Campbell, *Boston Globe*
1982	Martin Bernheimer, *Los Angeles Times*	1997	Tim Page, *Washington Post*
1983	Manuela Hoelterhoff, *Wall Street Journal*	1998	Michiko Kakutani, *New York Times*
1984	Paul Goldberger, *New York Times*	1999	Blair Kamin, *Chicago Tribune*
1985	Howard Rosenberg, *Los Angeles Times*		

Pulitzer Prizes for Feature Writing, 1979–99

Year	Winner, Newspaper	Year	Winner, Newspaper
1979	Jon D. Franklin, *Baltimore Evening Sun*	1990	Dave Curtin, *Colorado Springs Gazette Telegram*
1980	Madeline Blais, *Miami Herald*		
1981	Teresa Carpenter, *Village Voice* (New York)	1991	Sheryl James, *St. Petersburg Times*
1982	Saul Pett, *Associated Press*	1992	Howell Raines, *New York Times*
1983	Nan Robertson, *New York Times*	1993	George Lardner, Jr., *Washington Post*
1984	Peter Mark Rinearson, *Seattle Times*	1994	Isabel Wilkerson, *New York Times*
1985	Alice Steinbach, *Baltimore Sun*	1995	Ron Suskind, *Wall Street Journal*
1986	John Camp, *St. Paul Pioneer Press Dispatch*	1996	Rick Bragg, *New York Times*
1987	Steve Twomey, *Philadelphia Inquirer*	1997	Lisa Pollak, *Baltimore Sun*
1988	Jacqui Banaszynski, *St. Paul Pioneer Press Dispatch*	1998	Thomas French, *St. Petersburg* (Fla.) *Times*
		1999	Angelo B. Henderson, *Wall Street Journal*
1989	David Zucchino, *Philadelphia Inquirer*		

Special Awards and Citations

Year	Winner, Newspaper	Year	Winner, Newspaper
1930	William O. Dapping, *Auburn* (N.Y.) *Citizen,* Prison reporting	1951	Cyrus L. Sulzberger, *New York Times,* Interview with Archbishop Stepinac
1938	Edmonton (Alberta) *Journal,* Freedom of the Press editorials	1952	Max Kase, *New York Journal-American,* Corruption in basketball
1941	*New York Times,* Foreign news reporting	1953	*New York Times,* Sunday *Review of the*
1944	Byron Price, Director of the Office of Censorship, Creation and administration of newspaper and radio codes.	1958	*Week* section
		1958	Walter Lippman, *New York Herald Tribune,* Lifetime achievement
1944	Mrs. William Allen White, Services to Advisory Board Graduate School of Journalism, Columbia Univ.	1964	Gannett Newspapers, "Road to Integration" program
1945	American press cartographers, Maps of war fronts	1976	Professor John Hohenberg, Administration of Pulitzer Prizes
1947	Columbia University and Graduate School of Journalism, Governing Pulitzer Prize awards	1978	Richard Lee Strout, *Christian Science Monitor,* Lifetime achievement
		1987	Joseph Pulitzer Jr., Lifetime services to Pulitzer Board
1947	*St. Louis Post Dispatch,* Adherence to ideals of journalism	1996	Herb Caen, *San Francisco Chronicle,* Lifetime achievement
1948	Dr. Frank Diehl Fackenthal, Interest and Service		

PULITZER PRIZES IN LETTERS

The Pulitzer Prize for Fiction, 1918–99

Year	Author, Title	Year	Author, Title
1918	Ernest Poole, *His Family*	1955	William Faulkner, *A Fable*
1919	Booth Tarkington, *The Magnificent Ambersons*	1956	MacKinlay Kantor, *Andersonville*
		1957	No award
1920	No award	1958	James Agee, *A Death in the Family*
1921	Edith Wharton, *The Age of Innocence*	1959	Robert Lewis Taylor, *The Travels of Jaimie McPheeters*
1922	Booth Tarkington, *Alice Adams*		
1923	Willa Cather, *One of Ours*	1960	Allen Drury, *Advise and Consent*
1924	Margaret Wilson, *The Able McLaughlins*	1961	Harper Lee, *To Kill a Mockingbird*
1925	Edna Ferber, *So Big*	1962	Edwin O'Connor, *The Edge of Sadness*
1926	Sinclair Lewis, *Arrowsmith*	1963	William Faulkner, *The Reivers*
1927	Louis Bromfield, *Early Autumn*	1964	No award
1928	Thornton Wilder, *The Bridge of San Luis Rey*	1965	Shirley Ann Grau, *The Keepers of the House*
1929	Julia Peterkin, *Scarlet Sister Mary*	1966	Katherine Anne Porter, *Collected Stories*
1930	Oliver LaFarge, *Laughing Boy*	1967	Bernard Malamud, *The Fixer*
1931	Margaret Ayer Barnes, *Years of Grace*	1968	William Styron, *The Confessions of Nat Turner*
1932	Pearl S. Buck, *The Good Earth*		
1933	T.S. Stribling, *The Store*	1969	N. Scott Momaday, *House Made of Dawn*
1934	Caroline Miller, *Lamb in His Bosom*	1970	Jean Stafford, *Collected Stories*
1935	Josephine Winslow Johnson, *Now in November*	1971	No award
		1972	Wallace Stegner, *Angle of Repose*
1936	Harold L. Davis, *Honey in the Horn*	1973	Eudora Welty, *The Optimist's Daughter*
1937	Margaret Mitchell, *Gone With the Wind*	1974	No award
1938	John Phillips Marquand, *The Late George Apley*	1975	Michael Shaara, *The Killer Angels*
		1976	Saul Bellow, *Humboldt's Gift*
1939	Marjorie Kinnan Rawlings, *The Yearling*	1977	No award
1940	John Steinbeck, *The Grapes of Wrath*	1978	James Alan McPherson, *Elbow Room*
1941	No award	1979	John Cheever, *The Stories of John Cheever*
1942	Ellen Glasgow, *In This Our Life*	1980	Norman Mailer, *The Executioner's Song*
1943	Upton Sinclair, *Dragon's Teeth*	1981	John Kennedy Toole[2], *A Confederacy of Dunces*
1944	Martin Flavin, *Journey in the Dark*		
1945	John Hersey, *A Bell for Adano*	1982	John Updike, *Rabbit Is Rich*
1946	No award	1983	Alice Walker, *The Color Purple*
1947	Robert Penn Warren, *All the King's Men*	1984	William Kennedy, *Ironweed*
1948[1]	James A. Michener, *Tales of the South Pacific*	1985	Alison Lurie, *Foreign Affairs*
		1986	Larry McMurtry, *Lonesome Dove*
1949	James Gould Cozzens, *Guard of Honor*	1987	Peter Taylor, *A Summons to Memphis*
1950	A.B. Guthrie Jr., *The Way West*	1988	Toni Morrison, *Beloved*
1951	Conrad Richter, *The Town*	1989	Anne Tyler, *Breathing Lessons*
1952	Herman Wouk, *The Caine Mutiny*	1990	Oscar Hijuelos, *The Mambo Kings Play Songs of Love*
1953	Ernest Hemingway, *The Old Man and the Sea*		
1954	No award	1992	Jane Smiley, *A Thousand Acres*

Year	Author, Title	Year	Author, Title
1991	John Updike, *Rabbit at Rest*	1996	Richard Ford, *Independence Day*
1993	Robert Olen Butler, *A Good Scent From a Strange Mountain*	1997	Steven Millhauser, *Martin Dressler: The Tale of an American Dreamer*
1994	E. Annie Proulx, *The Shipping News*	1998	Philip Roth, *American Pastoral*
1995	Carol Shields, *The Stone Diaries*	1999	Michael Cunningham, *The Hours*

1. In 1948, the name of the category was changed from "The Novel" to "Fiction." 2. Awarded posthumously.

The Pulitzer Prize for Drama, 1918–99

Year	Author, Title	Year	Author, Title
1918	Jesse Lynch Williams, *Why Marry*	1960	Jerome Weidman and George Abbott (book); Jerry Bock (music); and Sheldon Harnick (lyrics), *Fiorello!*
1919	No award		
1920	Eugene O'Neill, *Beyond the Horizon*		
1921	Zona Gale, *Miss Lulu Bett*	1961	Tad Mosel, *All the Way Home*
1922	Eugene O'Neill, *Anna Christie*	1962	Frank Loesser and Abe Burrows, *How to Succeed in Business Without Really Trying*
1923	Owen Davis, *Icebound*		
1924	Hatcher Hughes, *Hell-Bent Fer Heaven*	1963	No award
1925	Sidney Howard, *They Knew What They Wanted*	1964	No award
		1965	Frank D. Gilroy, *The Subject Was Roses*
1926	George Kelly, *Craig's Wife*	1966	No award
1927	Paul Green, *In Abraham's Bosom*	1967	Edward Albee, *A Delicate Balance*
1928	Eugene O'Neill, *Strange Interlude*	1968	No award
1929	Elmer L. Rice, *Street Scene*	1969	Howard Sackler, *The Great White Hope*
1930	Marc Connelly, *The Green Pastures*	1970	Charles Gordone, *No Place to Be Somebody*
1931	Susan Glaspell, *Alison's House*		
1932	George S. Kaufman, Morrie Ryskind, and Ira Gershwin, *Of Thee I Sing*	1971	Paul Zindel, *The Effect of Gamma Rays on Man-in-the-Moon Marigolds*
1933	Maxwell Anderson, *Both Your Houses*	1972	No award
1934	Sidney Kingsley, *Men in White*	1973	Jason Miller, *That Championship Season*
1935	Zoe Akins, *The Old Maid*	1974	No award
1936	Robert E. Sherwood, *Idiot's Delight*	1975	Edward Albee, *Seascape*
1937	Moss Hart and George S. Kaufman, *You Can't Take It With You*	1976	Michael Bennett; Nicholas Dante & James Kirkwood (book); Marvin Hamlisch (music); and Edward Kleban (lyrics), *A Chorus Line*
1938	Thornton Wilder, *Our Town*		
1939	Robert E. Sherwood, *Abe Lincoln in Illinois*	1977	Michael Cristofer, *The Shadow Box*
1940	William Saroyan, *The Time of Your Life*	1978	Donald L. Coburn, *The Gin Game*
1941	Robert E. Sherwood, *There Shall Be no Night*	1979	Sam Shepard, *Buried Child*
1942	No award	1980	Lanford Wilson, *Talley's Folly*
1943	Thornton Wilder, *The Skin of Our Teeth*	1981	Beth Henley, *Crimes of the Heart*
1944	No award	1982	Charles Fuller, *A Soldier's Play*
1945	Mary Chase, *Harvey*	1983	Marsha Norman, *'night Mother*
1946	Russel Crouse and Howard Lindsay, *State of the Union*	1984	David Mamet, *Glengarry Glen Ross*
		1985	Stephen Sondheim (music and lyrics); James Lapine (book), *Sunday in the Park With George*
1947	No award		
1948	Tennessee Williams, *A Streetcar Named Desire*	1986	No award
		1987	August Wilson, *Fences*
1949	Arthur Miller, *Death of a Salesman*	1988	Alfred Uhry, *Driving Miss Daisy*
1950	Richard Rodgers, Oscar Hammerstein II, and Joshua Logan, *South Pacific*	1989	Wendy Wasserstein, *The Heidi Chronicles*
		1990	August Wilson, *The Piano Lesson*
1951	No award	1991	Neil Simon, *Lost in Yonkers*
1952	Joseph Kramm, *The Shrike*	1992	Robert Schenkkan, *The Kentucky Cycle*
1953	William Inge, *Picnic*	1993	Tony Kushner, *Angels in America: Millennium Approaches*
1954	John Patrick, *The Teahouse of the August Moon*		
1955	Tennessee Williams, *Cat on a Hot Tin Roof*	1994	Edward Albee, *Three Tall Women*
1956	Albert Hackett and Frances Goodrich, *The Diary of Anne Frank*	1995	Horton Foote, *The Young Man From Atlanta*
		1996	Jonathan Larson, *Rent*
1957	Eugene O'Neill, *Long Day's Journey Into Night*	1997	No award
		1998	Paula Vogel, *How I Learned to Drive*
1958	Ketti Frings, *Look Homeward, Angel*	1999	Margaret Edson, *Wit*
1959	Archibald MacLeish, *J.B.*		

The Pulitzer Prize for History, 1917–99

Year	Author, Title
1917	J.J. Jusserand, *With Americans of Past and Present Days*
1918	James Ford Rhodes, *A History of the Civil War*
1919	No award
1920	Justin H. Smith, *The War with Mexico*
1921	William Sowden Sims, with Burton J. Hendrick, *The Victory at Sea*
1922	James Truslow Adams, *The Founding of New England*
1923	Charles Warren, *The Supreme Court in United States History*
1924	Charles Howard McIlwain, *The American Revolution*
1925	Frederic L. Paxson, *A History of the American Frontier*
1926	Edward Channing, *The History of the United States*
1927	Samuel Flagg Bemis, *Pinckney's Treaty*
1928	Vernon Louis Parrington, *Main Currents in American Thought*
1929	Fred Albert Shannon, *The Organization and Administration of the Union Army, 1861–1865*
1930	Claude H. Van Tyne, *The War of Independence*
1931	Bernadotte E. Schmitt, *The Coming of the War: 1914*
1932	John J. Pershing, *My Experiences in the World War*
1933	Frederick J. Turner, *The Significance of Sections in American History*
1934	Herbert Agar, *The People's Choice*
1935	Charles McLean Andrews, *The Colonial Period of American History*
1936	Andrew C. McLaughlin, *The Constitutional History of the United States*
1937	Van Wyck Brooks, *The Flowering of New England*
1938	Paul Herman Buck, *The Road to Reunion 1856–1900*
1939	Frank Luther Mott, *A History of American Magazines*
1940	Carl Sandburg, *Abraham Lincoln: The War Years*
1941	Marcus Lee Hansen, *The Atlantic Migration, 1607–1860*
1942	Margaret Leech, *Reveille in Washington*
1943	Esther Forbes, *Paul Revere and the World He Lived In*
1944	Merle Curti, *The Growth of American Thought*
1945	Stephen Bonsal, *Unfinished Business*
1946	Arthur Meier Schlesinger Jr., *The Age of Jackson*
1947	James Phinney Baxter III, *Scientists Against Time*
1948	Bernard DeVoto, *Across the Wide Missouri*
1949	Roy Franklin Nichols, *The Disruption of American Democracy*
1950	Oliver W. Larkin, *Art and Life in America*
1951	R. Carlyle Buley, *The Old Northwest*
1952	Oscar Handlin, *The Uprooted*
1953	George Dangerfield, *The Era of Good Feelings*
1954	Bruce Catton, *A Stillness at Appomattox*
1955	Paul Horgan, *Great River: The Rio Grande in North American History*
1956	Richard Hofstadter, *The Age of Reform*
1957	George F. Kennan, *Russia Leaves the War: Soviet American Relations, 1917–1920*
1958	Bray Hammond, *Banks and Politics in America*
1959	Leonard D. White, with Miss Jean Schneider, *The Republican Era: 1869–1901*
1960	Margaret Leech, *In the Days of McKinley*
1961	Herbert Feis, *Between War and Peace: The Potsdam Conference*
1962	Lawrence H. Gipson, *The Triumphant Empire: Thunder Clouds in the West*
1963	Constance McLaughlin Green, *Washington, Village and Capital, 1800–1878*
1964	Sumner Chilton Powell, *Puritan Village*
1965	Irwin Unger, *The Greenback Era*
1966	Perry Miller[1], *Life of the Mind in America*
1967	William H. Goetzmann, *Exploration and Empire*
1968	Bernard Bailyn, *The Ideological Origins of the American Revolution*
1969	Leonard W. Levy, *Origins of the Fifth Amendment*
1970	Dean Acheson, *Present at the Creation*
1971	James MacGregor Burns, *Roosevelt, The Soldier of Freedom*
1972	Carl N. Degler, *Neither Black Nor White*
1973	Michael Kammen, *People of Paradox*
1974	Daniel J. Boorstin, *The Americans: The Democratic Experience*
1975	Dumas Malone, *Jefferson and His Time*, Vols. I–V
1976	Paul Horgan, *Lamy of Santa Fe*
1977	David M. Potter[1] *The Impending Crisis*
1978	Alfred D. Chandler Jr., *The Visible Hand: The Managerial Revolution in American Business*
1979	Don E. Fehrenbacher, *The Dred Scott Case*
1980	Leon F. Litwack, *Been in the Storm So Long*
1981	Lawrence A. Cremin, *American Education*
1982	C. Vann Woodward (ed.), *Mary Chesnut's Civil War*
1983	Rhys L. Isaac, *The Transformation of Virginia, 1740–1790*
1984	No award
1985	Thomas K. McCraw, *Prophets of Regulation*
1986	Walter A. McDougall, *. . . the Heavens and the Earth*
1987	Bernard Bailyn, *Voyagers to the West*
1988	Robert V. Bruce, *The Launching of Modern American Science 1846–1876*
1989	Taylor Branch, *Parting the Waters*
	James M. McPherson, *Battle Cry of Freedom: The Civil War Era*
1990	Stanley Karnow, *In Our Image*
1991	Laurel Thatcher Ulrich, *A Midwife's Tale*
1992	Mark E. Neely Jr., *The Fate of Liberty*
1993	Gordon S. Wood, *The Radicalism of the American Revolution*
1994	No award
1995	Doris Kearns Goodwin, *No Ordinary Time: Franklin and Eleanor Roosevelt*
1996	Alan Taylor, *William Cooper's Town*
1997	Jack N. Rakove, *Original Meanings: Politics and Ideas in the Making of the Constitution*
1998	Edward J. Larson, *Summer for the Gods: The Scopes Trial and America's Continuing Debate Over Science and Religion*
1999	Edwin G. Burrows and Mike Wallace, *Gotham: A History of New York City to 1898*

1. Awarded posthumously.

The Pulitzer Prize for Biography/Autobiography, 1917–99

Year	Author, Title	Year	Author, Title
1917	Laura E. Richards and Maude Howe Elliott, with Florence Howe Hall, *Julia Ward Howe*	1954	Charles A. Lindbergh, *The Spirit of St. Louis*
1918	William Cabell Bruce, *Benjamin Franklin, Self-Revealed*	1955	William S. White, *The Taft Story*
		1956	Talbot Faulkner Hamlin, *Benjamin Henry Latrobe*
1919	Henry Adams, *The Education of Henry Adams*	1957	John F. Kennedy, *Profiles in Courage*
1920	Albert J. Beveridge, *The Life of John Marshall*	1958	Douglas Southall Freeman[1], John Alexander Carroll, Mary Wells Ashworth, *George Washington*, vols. 1–4; and vol. 7, written after Dr. Freeman's death in 1953.
1921	Edward Bok, *The Americanization of Edward Bok*	1959	Arthur Walworth, *Woodrow Wilson, American Prophet*
1922	Hamlin Garland, *A Daughter of the Middle Border*	1960	Samuel Eliot Morison, *John Paul Jones*
1923	Burton J. Hendrick, *The Life and Letters of Walter H. Page*	1961	David Donald, *Charles Sumner and the Coming of the Civil War*
1924	Michael Idvorsky Pupin, *From Immigrant to Inventor*	1962	No award
		1963	Leon Edel, *Henry James*
1925	M.A. DeWolfe Howe, *Barrett Wendell and His Letter*	1964	Walter Jackson Bate, *John Keats*
		1965	Ernest Samuels, *Henry Adams*
1926	Harvey Cushing, *The Life of Sir William Osler*	1966	Arthur M. Schlesinger Jr., *A Thousand Days*
1927	Emory Holloway, *Whitman*	1967	Justin Kaplan, *Mr. Clemens and Mark Twain*
1928	Charles Edward Russell, *The American Orchestra and Theodore Thomas*	1968	George F. Kennan, *Memoirs*
1929	Burton J. Hendrick, *The Training of an American. The Earlier Life and Letters of Walter H. Page*	1969	Benjamin Lawrence Reid, *The Man From New York: John Quinn and His Friends*
1930	Marquis James, *The Raven*	1970	T. Harry Williams, *Huey Long*
1931	Henry James, *Charles W. Eliot*	1971	Lawrance Thompson, *Robert Frost*
1932	Henry F. Pringle, *Theodore Roosevelt*	1972	Joseph P. Lash, *Eleanor and Franklin*
1933	Allan Nevins, *Grover Cleveland*	1973	W.A. Swanberg, *Luce and His Empire*
1934	Tyler Dennett, *John Hay*	1974	Louis Sheaffer, *O'Neill, Son and Artist*
1935	Douglas S. Freeman, *R.E. Lee*	1975	Robert A. Caro, *The Power Broker*
1936	Ralph Barton Perry, *The Thought and Character of William James*	1976	R.W.B. Lewis, *Edith Wharton: A Biography*
1937	Allan Nevins, *Hamilton Fish*	1977	John E. Mack, *A Prince of Our Disorder: The Life of T.E. Lawrence*
1938	Odell Shepard, *Pedlar's Progress* Marquis James, *Andrew Jackson*	1978	Walter Jackson Bate, *Samuel Johnson*
1939	Carl Van Doren, *Benjamin Franklin*	1979	Leonard Baker, *Days of Sorrow and Pain*
1940	Ray Stannard Baker, *Woodrow Wilson, Life and Letters*, vols. 7 & 8	1980	Edmund Morris, *The Rise of Theodore Roosevelt*
1941	Ola Elizabeth Winslow, *Jonathan Edwards*	1981	Robert K. Massie, *Peter the Great*
1942	Forrest Wilson, *Crusader in Crinoline*	1982	William S. McFeely, *Grant: A Biography*
1943	Samuel Eliot Morison, *Admiral of the Ocean Sea*	1983	Russell Baker, *Growing Up*
		1984	Louis R. Harlan, *Booker T. Washington*
1944	Carleton Mabee, *The American Leonardo: The Life of Samuel F.B. Morse*	1985	Kenneth Silverman, *The Life and Times of Cotton Mather*
1945	Russell Blaine Nye, *George Bancroft*	1986	Elizabeth Frank, *Louise Bogan: A Portrait*
1946	Linnie Marsh Wolfe, *Son of the Wilderness*	1987	David J. Garrow, *Bearing the Cross: Martin Luther King, Jr. and the Southern Christian Leadership Conference*
1947	William Allen White, *The Autobiography of William Allen White*	1988	David Herbert Donald, *Look Homeward: A Life of Thomas Wolfe*
1948	Margaret Clapp, *Forgotten First Citizen: John Bigelow*	1989	Richard Ellmann[1], *Oscar Wilde*
		1990	Sebastian de Grazia, *Machiavelli in Hell*
1949	Robert E. Sherwood, *Roosevelt and Hopkins*	1991	Steven Naifeh, Gregory White Smith, *Jackson Pollock*
1950	Samuel Flagg Bemis, *John Quincy Adams and the Foundations of American Foreign Policy*	1992	Lewis B. Puller Jr., *Fortunate Son*
		1993	David McCullough, *Truman*
1951	Margaret Louise Coit, *John C. Calhoun*	1994	David Levering Lewis, *W.E.B. DuBois*
1952	Merlo J. Pusey, *Charles Evan Hughes*	1995	Joan D. Hedrick, *Harriet Beecher Stowe*
1953	David J. Mays, *Edmund Pendleton 1721-1803*	1996	Jack Miles, *God: A Biography*
		1997	Frank McCourt, *Angela's Ashes*
		1998	Katharine Graham, *Personal History*
		1999	A. Scott Berg, *Lindbergh*

1. Awarded posthumously.

The Pulitzer Prize for Poetry, 1922–99

Pulitzer Prizes in poetry were first awarded in 1922. The Poetry Society awarded prizes in 1918 to Sara Teasdale for *Love Songs*, and in 1919 to Margaret Widdemer for *Old Road to Paradise* and to Carl Sandburg for *Corn Huskers*.

Year	Author, Title
1922	Edward Arlington Robinson, *Collected Poems*
1923	Edna St. Vincent Millay, *The Ballad of the Harp-Weaver; A Few Figs from Thistles; Eight Sonnets in American Poetry, 1922, A Miscellany*
1924	Robert Frost, *New Hampshire: A Poem with Notes and Grace Notes*
1925	Edward Arlington Robinson, *The Man Who Died Twice*
1926	Amy Lowell[1], *What's O'Clock*
1927	Leonora Speyer, *Fiddler's Farewell*
1928	Edward Arlington Robinson, *Tristram*
1929	Stephen Vincent Benét, *John Brown's Body*
1930	Conrad Aiken, *Selected Poems*
1931	Robert Frost, *Collected Poems*
1932	George Dillon, *The Flowering Stone*
1933	Archibald MacLeish, *Conquistador*
1934	Robert Hillyer, *Collected Verse*
1935	Audrey Wurdemann, *Bright Ambush*
1936	Robert P. Tristram Coffin, *Strange Holiness*
1937	Robert Frost, *A Further Range*
1938	Marya Zaturenska, *Cold Morning Sky*
1939	John Gould Fletcher, *Selected Poems*
1940	Mark Van Doren, *Collected Poems*
1941	Leonard Bacon, *Sunderland Capture*
1942	William Rose Benét, *The Dust Which Is God*
1943	Robert Frost, *A Witness Tree*
1944	Stephen Vincent Benét[1], *Western Star*
1945	Karl Shapiro, *V-Letter and Other Poems*
1946	No award
1947	Robert Lowell, *Lord Weary's Castle*
1948	W.H. Auden, *The Age of Anxiety*
1949	Peter Viereck, *Terror and Decorum*
1950	Gwendolyn Brooks, *Annie Allen*
1951	Carl Sandburg, *Complete Poems*
1952	Marianne Moore, *Collected Poems*
1953	Archibald MacLeish, *Collected Poems 1917–1952*
1954	Theodore Roethke, *The Waking*
1955	Wallace Stevens, *Collected Poems*
1956	Elizabeth Bishop, *Poems—North & South*
1957	Richard Wilbur, *Things of This World*
1958	Robert Penn Warren, *Promises: Poems 1954–1956*
1959	Stanley Kunitz, *Selected Poems 1928–1958*
1960	W.D. Snodgrass, *Heart's Needle*
1961	Phyllis McGinley, *Times Three: Selected Verse From Three Decades*
1962	Alan Dugan, *Poems*
1963	William Carlos Williams[1], *Pictures from Breughel*
1964	Louis Simpson, *At the End of the Open Road*
1965	John Berryman, *77 Dream Songs*
1966	Richard Eberhart, *Selected Poems*
1967	Anne Sexton, *Live or Die*
1968	Anthony Hecht, *The Hard Hours*
1969	George Oppen, *Of Being Numerous*
1970	Richard Howard, *Untitled Subjects*
1971	William S. Merwin, *The Carrier of Ladders*
1972	James Wright, *Collected Poems*
1973	Maxine Kumin, *Up Country*
1974	Robert Lowell, *The Dolphins*
1975	Gary Snyder, *Turtle Island*
1976	John Ashberry, *Self-Portrait in a Convex Mirror*
1977	James Merrill, *Divine Comedies*
1978	Howard Nemerov, *Collected Poems*
1979	Robert Penn Warren, *Now and Then*
1980	Donald Justice, *Selected Poems*
1981	James Schuyler, *The Morning of the Poem*
1982	Sylvia Plath[1], *The Collected Poems*
1983	Galway Kinnell, *Selected Poems*
1984	Mary Oliver, *American Primitive*
1985	Carolyn Kizer, *Yin*
1986	Henry Taylor, *The Flying Change*
1987	Rita Dove, *Thomas and Beulah*
1988	William Meredith, *Partial Accounts: New and Selected Poems*
1989	Richard Wilbur, *New and Collected Poems*
1990	Charles Simic, *The World Doesn't End*
1991	Mona Van Duyn, *Near Changes*
1992	James Tate, *Selected Poems*
1993	Louise Gluck, *The Wild Iris*
1994	Yusef Komunyakaa, *Neon Vernacular*
1995	Philip Levine, *Simple Truth*
1996	Jorie Graham, *The Dream of the Unified Field*
1997	Lisel Mueller, *Alive Together: New and Selected Poems*
1998	Charles Wright, *Black Zodiac*
1999	Mark Strand, *Blizzard of One*

1. Awarded posthumously.

The Pulitzer Prize for General Nonfiction, 1962–99

Year	Author, Title
1962	Theodore H. White, *The Making of the President, 1960*
1963	Barbara W. Tuchman, *The Guns of August*
1964	Richard Hofstadter, *Anti-Intellectualism in American Life*
1965	Howard Mumford Jones, *O Strange New World*
1966	Edwin Way Teal, *Wandering Through Winter*
1967	David Brion Davis, *The Problem of Slavery in Western Culture*
1968	Will and Ariel Durant, *Rousseau and Revolution*
1969	René Jules Dubos, *So Human An Animal*; Norman Mailer, *The Armies of the Night*
1970	Erik H. Erikson, *Gandhi's Truth*
1971	John Toland, *The Rising Sun*
1972	Barbara W. Tuchman, *Stilwell and the American Experience in China, 1911–45*
1973	Robert Coles, *Children of Crisis, vols.2 & 3*; Frances Fitzgerald, *Fire in the Lake*
1974	Ernest Becker[1], *The Denial of Death*

Year	Author, Title	Year	Author, Title
1975	Annie Dillard, *Pilgrim at Tinker Creek*	1988	Richard Rhodes, *The Making of the Atomic Bomb*
1976	Robert N. Butler, *Why Survive? Being Old in America*	1989	Neil Sheehan, *A Bright and Shining Lie*
1977	William N. Warner, *Beautiful Swimmers*	1990	Dale Maharidge, Michael Williamson, *And Their Children After Them*
1978	Carl Sagan, *The Dragons of Eden*	1991	Bert Holldobler, Edward O. Wilson, *The Ants*
1979	Edward O. Wilson, *On Human Nature*		
1980	Douglas R. Hofstadter, *Gödel, Escher, Bach: an Eternal Golden Braid*	1992	Daniel Yergin, *The Prize: The Epic Quest for Oil, Money and Power.*
1981	Carl E. Schorske, *Fin-de Siècle Vienna: Politics and Culture*	1993	Garry Wills, *Lincoln at Gettysburg*
1982	Tracy Kidder, *The Soul of A New Machine*	1994	David Remnick, *Lenin's Tomb: The Last Days of the Soviet Empire*
1983	Susan Sheehan, *Is There No Place on Earth for Me?*	1995	Jonathan Weiner, *The Beak of the Finch*
1984	Paul Starr, *The Social Transformation of American Medicine*	1996	Tina Rosenberg, *The Haunted Land*
		1997	¹Richard Kluger, *Ashes to Ashes*
1985	Studs Terkel, *The Good War*	1998	Jared Diamond, *Guns, Germs, and Steel: The Fates of Human Societies*
1986	Joseph Lelyveld, *Move Your Shadow* J. Anthony Lukas, *Common Ground*	1999	John McPhee, *Annals of the Former World*
1987	David K. Shipler, *Arab and Jew*		

1. Awarded posthumously.

Pulitzer Special Citations in Letters

Year	Author, Title	Year	Author, Title
1944	Richard Rodgers and Oscar Hammerstein II, *Oklahoma!*	1973	James Flexner, *George Washington,* vols. 1–4
		1977	Alex Haley, *Roots*
1957	Kenneth Roberts, for his historical novels	1978	E.B. White, Lifetime achievement
1960	Garret Mattingly, *The Armada*	1984	Theodore Seuss Geisel (Dr. Seuss), Lifetime achievement
1961	Publishers, *The American Heritage Picture History of the Civil War*	1992	Art Speigelman, *Maus*

The Pulitzer Prize for Music, 1943–99

Year	Author, Title	Year	Author, Title
1943	William Schuman, Secular Cantata No. 2, *A Free Song*	1967	Leon Kirchner, Quartet No. 3
		1968	George Crumb, *Echoes of Time and the River* orchestral suite
1944	Howard Hanson, Symphony No. 4, Opus 34		
1945	Aaron Copland, *Appalachian Spring*	1969	Karel Husa, String Quartet No. 3
1946	Leo Sowerby, *The Canticle of the Sun*	1970	Charles Wuorinen, *Time's Encomium*
1947	Charles Ives, Symphony No. 3	1971	Mario Davidovsky, Synchronisms No. 6 for Piano and Electronic Sound
1948	Walter Piston, Symphony No. 3		
1949	Virgil Thomson, Music for the film, *Louisiana Story*	1972	Jacob Druckman, *Windows*
		1973	Elliott Carter, String Quartet No. 3
1950	Gian-Carlo Menotti, Music for the *The Consul*	1974	Donald Martino, *Notturno* (chamber music piece)
1951	Douglas S. Moore, Music for the opera, *Giants in the Earth*	1975	Dominick Argento, *From the Diary of Virginia Woolf*
1952	Gail Kubik, *Symphony Concertante*	1976	Ned Rorem, *Air Music: Ten Etudes for Orchestra*
1953	No award		
1954	Quincy Porter, Concerto for Two Pianos and Orchestra	1977	Richard Wernick, *Visions of Terror and Wonder*
1955	Gian-Carlo Menotti, *The Saint of Bleecker Street* (opera)	1978	Michael Colgrass, *Deja Vu* for Percussion Quartet and Orchestra
1956	Ernest Toch, Symphony No. 3	1979	Joseph Schwantner, *Aftertones of Infinity*
1957	Norman Dello Joio, *Meditations on Ecclesiastes*	1980	David Del Tredici, *In Memory of a Summer Day*
1958	Samuel Barber, *Vanessa* (opera)	1981	No award
1959	John LaMontaine, Concerto for Piano and Orchestra	1982	Roger Sessions, Concerto for Orchestra
		1983	Ellen Taaffe Zwilich, Symphony No. 1
1960	Elliott Carter, Second String Quartet	1984	Bernard Rands, "Canti del Sole" for Tenor and Orchestra
1961	Walter Piston, Symphony No. 7		
1962	Robert Ward, *The Crucible* (opera)	1985	Stephen Albert, Symphony *RiverRun*
1963	Samuel Barber, Piano Concerto No. 1	1986	George Perle, Wind Quintet IV
1964	No award	1987	John Harbison, *The Flight Into Egypt*
1965	No award	1988	William Bolcom, 12 New Etudes for Piano
1966	Leslie Bassett, Variations for Orchestra	1989	Roger Reynolds, *Whispers Out of Time*

Year	Author, Title	Year	Author, Title
1990	Mel Powell, *Duplicates: A Concerto for Two Pianos and Orchestra*	1995	Morton Gould, *Stringmusic*
1991	Shulammit Ran, *Symphony*	1996	George Walker, *Lilacs*
1992	Wayne Peterson, *The Face of the Night, The Heart of the Dark*	1997	Wynton Marsalis, *Blood on the Fields*
1993	Christopher Rouse, *Trombone Concerto*	1998	Aaron Jay Kernis, *String Quartet No.2*
1994	Gunther Schuller, *Of Reminiscences and Reflections*	1999	Melinda Wagner, *Concerto for Flute, Strings, and Percussion*

Special Citations in Music

Year	Author, Title	Year	Author, Title
1974	Roger Sessions, Lifetime achievement	1998	George Gershwin[1], Contributions to American music
1976	Scott Joplin[1], Contributions to American music	1999	Edward "Duke" Ellington[1], Contributions to American music
1982	Milton Babbitt, Lifetime achivement		
1985	William Schuman, Lifetime achievement		

1. Awarded posthumously.   **Source:** Columbia University.

The Nobel Prizes

First awarded in 1901, the Nobel Prizes were established through a bequest of $9.2 million from Alfred Bernhard Nobel (1833–1896), a Swedish chemical engineer and the inventor of dynamite and other explosives, and by a gift from the Bank of Sweden. Nobel's will directed that the interest from the fund be divided annually among people who have made significant discoveries or inventions in the fields of chemistry, physics, and physiology or medicine, as well as to that author who has "produced in the field of literature the most outstanding work of an idealistic tendency," and to that individual or group that has "done the most or the best work for fraternity between nations, for the abolition or reduction of standing armies and for the holding and promotion of peace congresses." In 1968, the 300th anniversary of the Bank of Sweden, an additional prize for outstanding work in the economic sciences was established; it was first granted the following year. Today, all of the prizes are funded with the help of the Bank of Sweden. Final decisions are made

for physics, chemistry and economics by the Royal Swedish Academy of Sciences, Stockholm; for physiology or medicine by the Nobel Assembly at the Karolinska Institute, Stockholm; for literature by the Swedish Academy, Stockholm; and for peace by the Norwegian Nobel Committee, Oslo.

The prizes are awarded annually on December 10, the anniversary of Nobel's death. The peace prize is presented in Oslo and other awards are given in Stockholm, by the king of Sweden. The amount of each prize varies according to the interest from the fund. Each 1998 award was 7.6 million crowns (approximately $1 million), up from $489,000 in 1989 and $362,500 in 1987. Each prize includes a gold medal, a diploma and a gift of money, which is awarded at a formal ceremony. There were no prizes awarded between 1940 and 1942.

Note: For winners of the 1999 Nobel Prizes in all categories, see "Part I: The Almanac of the Year. Additional information about Nobel Prize winners can be found on the Internet at the Nobel Foundation's official web site: http://www.nobel.se/.

Nobel Peace Prize Recipients

1901 Jean-Henri Dunant (Switzerland) Founder of International Committee of the Red Cross; **Frédéric Passy** (France) Founder of first French peace society.
1902 Elie Ducommun (Switzerland) Director of Permanent International Peace Bureau; **Charles Albert Gobat** (Switzerland) Secretary-General of Inter-Parliamentary Union.
1903 Sir William R. Cremer (Great Britain) Founder of International Arbitration League.
1904 Institute of International Law Founded in 1873.
1905 Baroness Bertha S.F. von Suttner (Austria) Author of antiwar novel *Lay Down Your Arms*.
1906 Theodore Roosevelt (U.S.) President; mediated Russo-Japanese War.
1907 Ernesto T. Moneta (Italy) Founder of Lombard League of Peace; **Louis Renault** (France) Professor of International Law at Hague Peace Conference.
1908 Klas P. Arnoldson (Sweden) Founder of Swedish Peace and Arbitration League; **Fredrik Bajer**

(Denmark) Writer and peace activist, Danish parliament member.
1909 Auguste M.F. Beernaert (Belgium) Prime minister and peace activist; **Paul H.B.B. D'Estournelles de Constant** (Baron Constant de Rebecque) (France) Founder of French parliamentary group for voluntary arbitration.
1910 Permanent International Peace Bureau Founded 1891.
1911 Tobias M.C. Asser (Netherlands) A founder of Institute of International Law; **Alfred H. Fried** (Austria) Journalist and founder of many peace publications.
1912 Elihu Root (U.S.) Secretary of state and originator of several arbitration treaties.
1913 Henri Lafontaine (Belgium) President of Permanent International Peace Bureau in Bern.
1914–1916 No awards given.
1917 International Committee of the Red Cross Founded 1863.
1918 No award.

1919 Thomas Woodrow Wilson (U.S.) President; instrumental in establishing League of Nations.
1920 Léon Victor A. Bourgeois (France) Drafted framework for League of Nations.
1921 Karl H. Branting (Sweden) Prime minister and pacifist; **Christian L. Lange** (Norway) A founder of Inter-Parliamentary Union.
1922 Fridtjof Nansen (Norway) Scientist; explorer; originator of "Nansen passports" for refugees.
1923–24 No award.
1925 Sir Austen Chamberlain (Great Britain) Foreign secretary; worked for Locarno Pact; **Charles G. Dawes** (U.S.) Vice president; drafted Dawes Plan settling German reparations issue.
1926 Aristide Briand (France) and **Gustav Stresemann** (Germany) Creators of Locarno Pact.
1927 Ferdinand Buisson (France) Human rights advocate; **Ludwig Quidde** (Germany) Peace activist.
1928 No award.
1929 Frank B. Kellogg (U.S.) Secretary of state; a creator of Kellogg-Briand Pact.
1930 L.O. Nathan Söderblom (Sweden) Archbishop; leader in the ecumenical movement.
1931 Jane Addams (U.S.) President of Women's International League for Peace and Freedom; **Nicholas M. Butler** (U.S.) Promoter of Kellogg-Briand Pact.
1932 No award.
1933 Sir Norman Angell (Ralph Lane) (Great Britain) Author of antiwar book *The Great Illusion.*
1934 Arthur Henderson (Great Britain) President of League of Nations World Disarmament Conference 1932.
1935 Carol von Ossietzky (Germany) Journalist and pacifist.
1936 Carlos Saavedra Lamas (Argentina) Secretary of state; president of League of Nations and mediator in conflict between Paraguay and Bolivia.
1937 Lord Edgar Algernon R.G. Cecil (Great Britain) An architect of League of Nations.
1938 Nansen International Office for Refugees Founded 1921.
1939–1943 No awards given.
1944 International Committee of the Red Cross Founded 1863.
1945 Cordell Hull (U.S.) Secretary of state; instrumental in creating United Nations.
1946 Emily G. Balch (U.S.) Leader of international women's movement for peace; **John R. Mott** (U.S.) Leader of Christian ecumenical movement.
1947 The Friends Service Council and The American Friends Service Committee (The Quakers)
1948 No award.
1949 Lord John Boyd Orr (Great Britain) Nutritionist; worked to eliminate world hunger.
1950 Ralph Bunche (U.S.) Mediator in Middle East war.
1951 Léon Jouhaux (France) Advocate of improved working-class conditions.
1952 Albert Schweitzer (France) Missionary surgeon/founder of Lambarene Hospital in Africa.
1953 George C. Marshall (U.S.) General; originator of Marshall Plan, which provided recovery loans and technical aid to European nations after World War II.
1954 Office of the U.N. High Commissioner for Refugees for their aid work for European refugees.
1955–1956 No awards given.
1957 Lester B. Pearson (Canada) Secretary of state; worked to resolve Suez Canal Crisis of 1956.
1958 George Pire (Belgium) Dominican priest and leader of relief organization for refugees, l'Europe du Coeur au Service du Monde.
1959 Philip J. Noel-Baker (Great Britain) Lifelong worker for international peace through disarmament.
1960 Albert J. Lutuli (South Africa) President of the

African National Congress; led peaceful resistance to apartheid.
1961 Dag Hammarskjöld (Sweden) United Nations Secretary General; worked for peace in the Congo.
1962 Linus C. Pauling (U.S.) Chemist; warned against dangers of radioactive fallout in nuclear weapons testing and war.
1963 International Committee of the Red Cross and League of Nations of Red Cross Societies
1964 Martin Luther King, Jr. (U.S.) Leader of American civil rights movement.
1965 United Nations Children's Fund (UNICEF).
1966–1967 No awards given.
1968 René Cassin (France) President of European Court for Human Rights.
1969 International Labour Organization United Nations agency involved in improving worldwide working and social conditions.
1970 Norman Borlaug (U.S.) Agricultural scientist and developer of high-yield grains credited with helping to alleviate world hunger.
1971 Willy Brandt (Federal Republic of Germany) Chancellor; champion of East-West détente.
1972 No award
1973 Henry A. Kissinger (U.S.) Secretary of state and **Le Duc Tho** (Democratic Republic of Viet Nam) Foreign minister; negotiated Vietnam cease-fire agreement. Mr. Tho declined the prize.
1974 Seán MacBride (Ireland) President of International Peace Bureau and United Nations commissioner for Namibia; **Eisaku Sato** (Japan) Prime minister of Japan and campaigner against nuclear weapons.
1975 Andrei Sakharov (USSR) Nuclear physicist and human rights campaigner.
1976 Betty Williams and Mairead Corrigan (Northern Ireland) Founder of Northern Ireland Peace Movement.
1977 Amnesty International for human rights work.
1978 Anwar el-Sadat (Egypt) President, and **Menachem Begin** (Israel) Prime minister; negotiated Israeli-Egyptian peace accord.
1979 Mother Teresa (India) Worker for the poor in Calcutta.
1980 Adolfo Pérez Esquivel (Argentina) Architect, sculptor, and human rights leader.
1981 Office of the United Nations High Commissioner for Refugees for aid work with Asian refugees.
1982 Alva Myrdal (Sweden) and **Alfonso Garcia Robles** (Mexico) Campaigners for disarmament.
1983 Lech Walesa (Poland) Leader of the Solidarity trade union federation.
1984 Desmond M. Tutu (South Africa) Bishop of Johannesburg; a leader of the anti-apartheid movement.
1985 International Physicians for the Prevention of Nuclear War Organization jointly headed by a Soviet and an American doctor.
1986 Elie Wiesel (U.S.) Writer on the Holocaust and Nazi death camp survivor.
1987 Oscar Arias Sánchez (Costa Rica) President of Costa Rica; creator of a peace plan for Central America.
1988 United Nations Peacekeeping Forces
1989 Dalai Lama (Tibet) Exiled religious and political leader of Tibet for his nonviolent campaign to end China's domination of his country.
1990 Mikhail Gorbachev (USSR) President of the Soviet Union, "for his role in the peace process which today characterizes important parts of the international community."
1991 Aung San Suu Kyi (Myanmar), leader of opposition National League for Democracy (under house arrest at the time) "for her nonviolent struggle for democracy and human rights."
1992 Rigoberta Menchú (Guatemala) A Quiché Indian and an outspoken advocate of human rights during the civil war in her country.

1993 Pres. **F. W. de Klerk** of South Africa and **Nelson Mandela,** black leader of the opposition African National Congress, for negotiating an end to the apartheid policies of the state and their collaboration on the formation of a democracy not based on race.
1994 **Yitzhak Rabin** (Israel) Prime Minister, **Shimon Peres** (Israel) Foreign Minister, and **Yasir Arafat,** leader of the Palestinian Liberation Organization, for negotiating the historic peace pact allowing Palestinian self-rule in the West Bank and Gaza Strip.
1995 **Joseph Rotblat** (U.K. b. Poland), Pugwash Conferences on Science and World Affairs. A former Manhattan Project physicist who spent 40 years campaigning to eliminate nuclear weapons.
1996 Bishop **Carlos Ximenes Belo** (Australia, b.

East Timor) and **Jose Ramos-Horta** (East Timor) for "sustained and self-sacrificing contributions for a small but oppressed people" in East Timor, a former Portuguese colony invaded by Indonesia in the 1970s.
1997 **The International Campaign to Ban Landmines** and its 47-year-old coordinator, **Jody Williams** (U.S.), for their efforts to outlaw land mines worldwide. The Nobel committee admitted that it was openly trying to persuade the U.S. to sign the international treaty banning landmines.
1998 **John Hume,** 61 and **David Trimble,** 54, respectively the leaders of the largest Roman Catholic and Protestant political parties in Northern Ireland who brought about a peace agreement in April 1998.
1999 See Part I: "The Almanac of the Year"

Nobel Prizes in Physiology or Medicine

1901 **Emil A. von Behring** (Germany) Marburg Univ. "for his work on serum therapy, especially its application against diphtheria, by which he has opened a new road in the domain of medical science and thereby placed in the hands of the physician a victorious weapon against illness and deaths."
1902 **Sir Ronald Ross** (Great Britain) University College "for his work on malaria, by wheich he has shown how it enters the organism and thereby has laid the foundation for successful research on this disease and methods of combating it."
1903 **Niels R. Finsen** (Denmark) Finsen Medical Light Institute "in recognition of his contribution to the treatment of diseases, especially lupus vulgaris, with concentrated light radiation, whereby he has opened a new avenue for medical science."
1904 **Ivan P. Pavlov** (Russia) Military Medical Academy "in recognition of his work on the physiology of digestion, through which knowledge on vital aspects of the subject has been transformed and enlarged."
1905 **Robert Koch** (Germany) Institute for Infectious Diseases "for his investigations and discoveries in relation to tuberculosis."
1906 **Camillio Golgi** (Italy) Pavia Univ., and **Santiago Ramon Y Cajal** (Spain) Madrid Univ. "in recognition of their work on the structure of the nervous system."
1907 **Charles L.A. Laveran** (France) Institute Pasteur "in recognition of his work on the role played by protozoa in causing diseases."
1908 **Il'ja I. Mecnikov** (Russia) Institut Pasteur (Paris), and **Paul Ehrlich** (Germany) Goettingen Univ. and Royal Institute for Experimental Therapy "in recognition of their work on immunity."
1909 **Emil R. Kocher** (Switzerland) Berne Univ. "for his work on the physiology, pathology, and surgery for the thyroid gland."
1910 **Albrecht Kossel** (Germany) Heidelberg Univ. "in recognition of the contributions to our knowledge of cell chemistry made through his work on proteins, including the nucleic substances."
1911 **Allvar Gullstrand** (Sweden) Uppsala Univ. "for his work on the dioptrics of the eye."
1912 **Alexis Carrel** (France) Rockefeller Institute for Medical Research (New York) "in recognition of his work on vascular suture and the transplantation of blood vessels and organs."
1913 **Charles R. Richet** (France) Sorbonne Univ. "In recognition of his work on anaphylaxis."
1914 **Robert Bárány** (Austria) Vienna Univ. "for his work on the physiology and pathology of the vestibular apparatus."
1915–1918 No awards given.
1919 **Jules Bordet** (Belgium) Brussels Univ. "for his discoveries relating to immunity."

1920 **Schack A.S. Krogh** (Denmark) Copenhagen Univ. "for his discoveries of the capillary motor regulating mechanism."
1921 No award
1922 **Sir Archibald V. Hill** (Great Britain) London Univ. "for his discovery relating to the production of heat in the muscle"; **Otto F. Meyerhof** (Germany) Kiel Univ. "for his discovery of the fixed relationship between the consumption of oxygen and the metabolism of lactic acid in the muscle."
1923 **Sir Frederick G. Banting** (Canada) Toronto Univ. and **John J.R. Macleod** (Canada) Toronto Univ. "for the discovery of insulin."
1924 **Willem Einthoven** (Netherlands) Leyden Univ. "for his discovery of the mechanism of the electrocardiogram."
1925 No award
1926 **Johannes A.G. Fibiger** (Denmark) Copenhagen Univ. "for his discovery of the Spiroptera carcinoma."
1927 **Julius Wagner-Jauegg** (Austria) Vienna Univ. "for his discovery of the therapeutic value of malaria inoculation in the treatment of dementia paralytica."
1928 **Charles J.H. Nicolle** (France) Institut Pasteur "for his work on typhus."
1929 **Christiaan Eijkman** (Netherlands) Utrecht Univ. "for his discovery of the antineuritic vitamin"; **Sir Frederick G. Hopkins** (Great Britain) Cambridge Univ. "for his discovery of the growth-stimulating vitamins."
1930 **Karl Landsteiner** (Austria) Rockefeller Institute of Medical Research (New York) "for his discovery of human blood groups."
1931 **Otto H. Warburg** (Germany) Kaiser-Wilhelm Institut (Now Max-Planck-Institut) "for his discovery of the nature and mode of action of the respiratory enzyme."
1932 **Sir Charles S. Sherrington** (Great Britain) Oxford Univ. and **Lord Edgar D. Adrian** (Great Britain) Cambridge Univ. "for their discoveries regarding the functions of neurons."
1933 **Thomas H. Morgan** (U.S.) California Institute of Technology "for his discoveries concerning the role played by the chromosome in heredity."
1934 **George H. Whipple** (U.S.) Rochester Univ., **George R. Minot** (U.S.) Harvard Univ., and **William P. Murphy** (U.S.) Harvard Univ. "for their discoveries concerning liver therapy in cases of anaemia."
1935 **Hans Spemann** (German) Univ. of Freiburg "for his discovery of the organizer effect in embryonic development."
1936 **Sir Henry H. Dale** (Great Britain) National Institute for Medical Research, and **Otto Loewi** (Austria) Graz Univ. "for their discoveries relating to chemical impulses of nerve impulses."
1937 **Albert Szent-Györgyi von Nagyrapolt** (Hungary) Szeged Univ. "for his discoveries in connection

with the biological combustion processes, with special reference to vitamin C and the catalysis of fumaric acid."

1938 Corneille J.F. Heymans (Belgium) Ghent Univ. "for the discovery of the role played by the sinus and aortic mechanisms in the regulation of respiration."

1939 Gerhard Domagk (Germany) Munster Univ. for "discovery of the antibacterial effects of prontosil."

1940–1942 No awards given.

1943 Henrik C.P. Dam (Denmark) Polytechnic Institut "for his discovery of vitamin K"; **Edward A. Doisy** (U.S.) St. Louis Univ. "for his discovery of the chemical nature of vitamin K."

1944 Joseph Erlanger (U.S.) Washington Univ. and **Herbert S. Gasser** (U.S.) Rockefeller Institute for Medical Research "for their discoveries relating to the highly differentiated functions of single nerve fibers."

1945 Sir Alexander Fleming (Great Britain) London Univ., **Sir Ernst B. Chain** (Great Britain) Oxford Univ., and **Lord Howard W. Florey** (Great Britain) Oxford Univ. "for their discovery of penicillin and its curative effect in various infectious diseases."

1946 Hermann J. Muller (U.S.) Indiana Univ. "for his discovery of the production of mutations by means of X-ray irradiation."

1947 Carl F. Cori (U.S.) Washington Univ. and his wife **Gerty T. Cori** (U.S.) Washington Univ. "for their discovery of the course of the catalytic conversion of glycogen"; **Bernardo A. Houssay** (Argentina) Institute of Biology and Experimental Medicine "for his discovery of the part played by the hormone of the anterior pituitary lobe in the metabolism of sugar."

1948 Paul H. Müller (Switzerland) Laboratory of the J.R. Geigy Dye-Factory Co. "for his discovery of the high efficiency of DDT as a contact poison against several arthropods."

1949 Walter R. Hess (Switzerland) Zurich Univ. "for his discovery of the functional organization of the interbrain as a coordinator of the activities of the internal organs; **Antonio Caetano de Abreu F.E. Moniz** (Portugal) Univ. of Lisbon "for his discovery of the therapeutic value of leucotomy in certain psychoses."

1950 Edward C. Kendall (U.S.) Mayo Clinic, **Tadeus Reichstein** (Switzerland) Basel Univ., and **Philip S. Hench** (U.S.) Mayo Clinic "for their discoveries relating to the hormones of the adrenal cortex, their structure, and biological effects."

1951 Max Theiler (Union of South Africa) Laboratories Division of Medicine and Public Health, Rockefeller Foundation (New York) "for his discoveries concerning yellow fever and how to combat it."

1952 Selman A. Waksman (U.S.) Rutgers Univ. "for his discovery of streptomycin, the first antibiotic effective against tuberculosis."

1953 Sir Hans A. Krebs (Great Britain) Sheffield Univ. "for his discovery of the citric acid cycle"; **Fritz A. Lipmann** (U.S.) Harvard Medical School and Massachusetts General Hospital "for his discovery of coenzyme A and its importance for intermediary metabolism."

1954 John F. Enders (U.S.) Harvard Medical School and Research Division of Infectious Diseases, Children's Medical Center; **Thomas H. Weller** (U.S.) Research Division of Infectious Diseases, Children's Medical Center; and **Frederick C. Robbins** (U.S.) Western Reserve Univ. "for their discovery of the ability of poliomyelitis viruses to grow in cultures of various types of tissue."

1955 Axel H.T. Theorell (Sweden) Nobel Medical Institute "for his discoveries concerning the nature and mode of action of oxidation enzymes."

1956 Andre F. Cournand (U.S.) Cardio-Pulmonary Laboratory, Columbia Univ. Division. Bellevue Hospital; **Werner Forssman** (Germany) Mainz Univ. and Bad Kreuznach; and **Dickinson W. Richards** (U.S.) Columbia Univ. "for their discoveries concerning

heart catheterization and pathological changes in the circulatory system."

1957 Daniel Bovet (Italy) Chief Institute of Public Health "for his discoveries relating to synthetic compounds that inhibit the action of certain body substances, and especially their action on the vascular system and the skeletal muscles."

1958 George W. Beadle (U.S.) California Institute of Technology, and **Edward L. Tatum** (U.S.) Rockefeller Institute for Medical Research "for their discovery that genes act by regulating definite chemical events"; **Joshua Lederberg** (U.S.) Wisconsin Univ. "for his discoveries concerning genetic recombination and the organization of the genetic material of bacteria."

1959 Severo Ochoa (U.S.) New York Univ. College of Medicine, and **Arthur Kornberg** (U.S.) Stanford Univ. "for their discovery of the mechanisms in the biological synthesis of ribonucleic acid and deoxyribonucleic acid."

1960 Sir Frank M. Burnet (Australia) Walter and Eliza Hall Institute for Medical Research, and **Sir Peter B. Medawar** (Great Britain) Univ. College "for discovery of acquired immunological tolerance."

1961 Georg von Békésy (U.S.) Harvard Univ. "for his discoveries of the physical mechanism of stimulation within the cochlea."

1962 Francis H.C. Crick (Great Britain) Institute of Molecular Biology, **James D. Watson** (U.S.) Harvard Univ., and **Maurice H.F. Wilkins** (Great Britain) University of London "for their discoveries concerning the molecular structure of nuclear acids and its significance for information transfer in living material."

1963 Sir John E. Eccles (Australia) Australian National Univ. **Sir Alan L. Hodgkin** (Great Britain) Cambridge Univ., and **Sir Andrew F. Huxley** (Great Britain) University of London :for their discoveries concerning the ionic mechanisms involved in excitation and inhibition in the peripheral and central portions of the nerve cell membrane."

1964 Konrad Block (U.S.) Harvard Univ. and **Feodor Lymen** (Germany) Man-Planck-Institut fur Zellchemie "for their discoveries concerning the mechanism and regulation of the cholesterol and fatty acid metabolism."

1965 Francois Jacob (France) Institut Pasteur, **André Lwoff** (France) Institut Pasteur, and **Jacques Monod** (France) Institut Pasteur "for their discoveries concerning genetic control of enzyme and virus synthesis."

1966 Peyton Rous (U.S.) Rockefeller Univ. "for his discovery of tumor-inducing viruses"; **Charles B. Huggins** (U.S.) Ben May Laboratory for Cancer Research, Univ. of Chicago "for his discoveries concerning hormonal treatment of prostatic cancer."

1967 Ragnar Granit (Sweden) Karolinska Institutet, **Haldan K. Hartline** (U.S.) Rockefeller Univ., and **George Wald** (U.S.) Harvard Univ. "for their discoveries concerning the primary physiological and chemical visual processes in the eye."

1968 Robert W. Holley (U.S.) Cornell Univ., **Har G. Khorana** (U.S.) Univ. of Wisconsin, and **Marshall W. Nirenberg** (U.S.) National Institutes of Health "for their interpretation of the genetic code and its functions in protein synthesis."

1969 Max Delbrück (U.S.) California Institute of Technology, **Alfred D. Hershey** (U.S.) Carnegie Institution of Washington, and **Salvador Luria** (U.S.) M.I.T. for their discoveries concerning the replication mechanism and the genetic structure of viruses."

1970 Sir Bernard Katz (Great Britain) University College, **Ulf von Euler** (Sweden) Karolinska Institutet, and **Julius Axelrod** (U.S.) National Institutes of Health "for their discoveries concerning the humoral transmittors in the nerve terminals and the mechanism for their storage, release, and inactivation."

1971 Earl W. Sutherland, Jr. (U.S.) Vanderbilt Univ. "for his discoveries concerning the mechanisms of the action of hormones."

1972 **Gerald M. Edelman** (U.S.) Rockefeller Univ. and **Rodney R. Porter** (Great Britain) Oxford Univ. "for their discoveries concerning the chemical structure of antibodies."

1973 **Karl von Frisch** (W. Germany) Zoologisches Institut der Universitat Munchen; **Konrad Lorenz** (Austria) Osterreichische Akademie der Wissenschaften, Institut fur vergleichende Verhaltensforschung, and **Nikolaas Tinbergen** (Great Britain) University Museum for their discoveries concerning organization and elicitation of individual and social behavior patterns."

1974 **Albert Claude** (Belgium) Université Catholique de Louvain, **Christian de Duve** (Belgium) Rockefeller Univ. (New York), and **George E. Palade** (U.S.) Yale Univ. "for their discoveries concerning the structural and functional organization of the cell."

1975 **David Baltimore** (U.S.) M.I.T., **Renato Dulbecco** (U.S.) Imperial Cancer Research Fund Laboratory (London), and **Howard M. Temin** (U.S.) Univ. of Wisconsin "for their discoveries concerning the interaction between tumor viruses and the genetic material of the cell."

1976 **Baruch S. Blumberg** (U.S.) Institute for Cancer Research, and **D. Carleton Gajdusek** (U.S.) National Institutes of Health "for their discoveries concerning new mechanism for the origin and dissemination of infectious diseases."

1977 **Roger Guillemin** (U.S.) Salk Institute, and **Andrew V. Schally** (U.S.) Veterans Administration Hospital, New Orleans "for their discoveries concerning the peptide hormone production of the brain"; **Rosalyn Yalow** (U.S.) Veterans Administration Hospital, Bronx "for the development of radioimmunoassays of peptide hormones."

1978 **Werner Arber** (Switzerland) Biozentrum der Universitat, **Daniel Nathans** (U.S.) John Hopkins Univ., and **Hamilton O. Smith** (U.S.) John Hopkins Univ. "for the discovery of restriction enzymes and their application to problems of molecular genetics."

1979 **Alan M. Cormack** (U.S.) Tufts Univ., and **Sir Godfrey N. Hounsfield** (Great Britain) Central Research Laboratories, EMI, "for the development of computer assisted tomography."

1980 **Baruj Benacerraf** (U.S.) Harvard Medical School; **Jean Dausset** (France) Université de Paris, Laboratoire Immuno-Hemetologie; and **George D. Snell** (U.S.) Jackson Laboratory "for their discoveries concerning genetically determined structures on the cell surface that regulate immunological reactions."

1981 **Roger W. Sperry** (U.S.) California Institute of Technology "for his discoveries concerning the functional specialization of the cerebral hemispheres"; **David H. Hubel** (U.S.) Harvard Medical School, and **Torsten T. Wiesel** (Sweden) Harvard Medical School "for their discoveries concerning information processing in the visual system."

1982 **Sune K. Bergström** (Sweden) Karolinska Institute, **Bengt I. Samuelsson** (Sweden) Karolinska Institute, and **Sir John R. Vane** (Great Britain) Wellcome Research Laboratories "for their discoveries concerning prostaglandins and related biologically active substances."

1983 **Barbara McClintock** (U.S.) Cold Spring Harbor Laboratory "for her discovery of mobile genetic elements."

1984 **Niels K. Jerne** (Denmark) and **Georges J.F. Köhler** (W. Germany) of the Basel Institute for Immunology in Basel, Switzerland; and **César Milstein** (Great Britain and Argentina) Medical Research Council Laboratory of Molecular Biology (Cambridge) for theories concerning the specificity in development and controls of the immune system and the discovery of the principle for production of monoclonal antibodies."

1985 **Michael S. Brown** (U.S.) Univ. of Texas Health Science Center at Dallas, and **Joseph L.**

Goldstein (U.S.) Univ. of Texas Health Science Center at Dallas "for their discoveries concerning the regulation of cholesterol metabolism."

1986 **Stanley Cohen** (U.S.) Vanderbilt Univ., and **Rita Levi-Montalcini** (Italy and U.S.) Institute of Cell Biology of the C.N.R. (Rome) "for their discoveries of growth factors."

1987 **Susumu Tonegawa** (U.S.) M.I.T. "for discovery of the genetic principle for generation of antibody diversity."

1988 **Sir James W. Black** (UK) King's College Hospital Medical School, **Gertrude B. Elion** (U.S.) Wellcome Research Laboratories, and **George H. Hitchings** (U.S.) Wellcome Research Laboratories "for their discoveries of Important Principles for Drug Treatment."

1989 **J. Michael Bishop** and **Harold E. Varmus** (U.S.) Univ. of California, San Francisco "for their discovery of the Cellular Origin of Retroviral Oncogenes."

1990 **Joseph E. Murray** (U.S.) Brigham and Women's Hospital (Boston) who performed the first kidney transplant (1954), and **E. Donnall Thomas** (U.S.), Fred Hutchinson Cancer Research Center (Seattle), who performed the first successful bone marrow transplant between two people who were not twins (1979).

1991 **Erwin Neher** (Germany) Max-Planck Institute for Biophysical Chemistry, Göttingen, and **Bert Sakmann** (Germany) Max-Planck Institute for Medical Research, Heidelberg, for establishing existence of ion channels by developing technique that allows detection of "incredibly small electrical currents that pass through a single ion channel."

1992 **Edmond H. Fischer** (U.S.) and **Edwin G. Krebs** (U.S.), both of the Univ. of Washington for a discovery in the 1950s of a regulatory mechanism in almost all human cells linked to some cancers, to the rejection of transplanted organs, and many other processes.

1993 **Richard J. Roberts** (U.K.), New England Bio Labs, and **Phillip A. Sharp** (U.S.), MIT, for their discovery in the 1970s that the composition of genes is of several segments, which led to gene splicing and to a better understanding of hereditary diseases and cancer.

1994 **Alfred G. Gilbert** (U.S.) Univ. of Texas Southwestern Medical Center, and **Martin Rodbell** (U.S.) National Institute of Environmental Health Sciences, for their discovery of natural substances known as G-proteins and for showing how they help cells respond to external stimuli like light and odors.

1995 **Edward B. Lewis** (U.S.) California Institute of Technology, **Eric F. Wieschaus** (U.S.) Princeton Univ., and **Christiane Nüsslein-Volhard** (Germany) Max-Planck Institute in Tübingen, for their discovery of how genes control structural development of the body. Their research, performed on fruit flies, helps explain birth defects in humans.

1996 **Peter C. Doherty** (Australia) St. Jude's Medical Center in Memphis, and **Rolf Zinkernagel** (Switzerland) University of Zurich, for their discovery of how the immune system recognizes and kills virus-infected cells. Their work, performed 20 years earlier, required more than a decade of study to be proved correct.

1997 **Stanley B. Prusiner** (U.S.), for his discovery of particles called prions, which he and others claim are disease-causing proteins that can be linked to Creutzfeldt-Jakob disease (mad cow disease) and other degenerative brain diseases.

1998 **Robert F. Furchgott**, 82, (U.S.), State Univ. of New York Health Science Center; **Louis J. Ignarro**, 57, (U.S.), UCLA School of Medicine; and **Ferid Murad**, 62, (U.S.), Univ. of Texas, for their discovery of nitric oxide (NO) as a signalling molecule in the cardiovascular system.

1999 See Part I: "The Almanac of the Year"

Nobel Prizes in Economic Sciences

1969 **Ragnar Frisch** (Norway) Oslo Univ. and **Jan Tinbergen** (Netherlands) The Netherlands School of Economics "for having developed and applied dynamic models for the analysis of economic processes."

1970 **Paul A. Samuelson** (U.S.) M.I.T. "for the scientific work through which he has developed static and dynamic economic theory and actively contributed to raising the level of analysis in economic science."

1971 **Simon Kuznets** (U.S.) Harvard Univ. "for his empirically founded interpretation of economic growth which has led to new and deepened insight into the economic and social structure and process of development."

1972 **Sir John R. Hicks** (Great Britain) All Souls College, and **Kenneth J. Arrow** (U.S.) Harvard Univ. "for their pioneering contributions to general economic equilibrium theory and welfare theory."

1973 **Wassily Leontief** (U.S.) Harvard Univ. "for the development of the input-output method and for its application to important economic problems."

1974 **Gunnar Mydal** (Sweden), **Friedrich A. von Hayek** (Great Britain) "for their pioneering work in the theory of money and economic fluctuations and for their penetrating analysis of the interdependence of economic, social and institutional phenomena."

1975 **Leonid Kantorovich** (USSR) Academy of Sciences, and **Tjalling C. Koopmans** (U.S.) Yale Univ. "for their contributions to the theory of optimum allocation of resources."

1976 **Milton Friedman** (U.S.) Univ. of Chicago for "achievements in the fields of consumption analysis, monetary history and theory, and for his demonstration of the complexity of stabilization policy."

1977 **Bertil Ohlin** (Sweden) Stockholm School of Economics, and **James E. Meade** (Great Britain) Cambridge Univ. "for their pathbreaking contribution to the theory of international trade and international capital movements."

1978 **Herbert A. Simon** (U.S.) Carnegie-Mellon Univ. "for his pioneering research into the decision-making process within economic organizations."

1979 **Theodore W. Schultz** (U.S.) Univ. of Chicago, and **Sir Arthur Lewis** (Great Britain) Princeton Univ. "for their pioneering research into economic development research with particular consideration of the problems of developing countries."

1980 **Lawrence R. Klein** (U.S.) Univ. of Pennsylvania "for the creation of econometric models and their application to the analysis of economic fluctuations and economic policies."

1981 **James Tobin** (U.S.) Yale Univ. "for his analysis of financial markets and their relations to expenditure decisions, employment, production, and prices."

1982 **George J. Stigler** (U.S.) Univ. of Chicago "for his seminal studies of industrial structures, functioning markets, and causes and effects of public regulation."

1983 **Gerard Debreu** (U.S.) University of California, Berkeley "for having incorporated new analytical methods into economic theory and for his rigorous reformulation of the theory of general equilibrium."

1984 **Sir Richard Stone** (Great Britain) Cambridge Univ. "for having made fundamental contributions to the development of systems of national accounts and hence greatly improved [sic]the basis for empirical economic analysis."

1985 **Franco Modigliani** (U.S.) M.I.T. "for his pioneering analyses of saving and of financial markets.

1986 **James M Buchanan, Jr.** (U.S.) Center for Study of Public Choice "for his development of the contractual and constitutional bases for the theory of economic and political decision-making."

1987 **Robert M. Solow** (U.S.) M.I.T. "for his contributions to the theory of economic growth."

1988 **Maurice Allais** (France) Centre d'analyse économique "for his pioneering contributions to the theory of markets and efficient utilization of resources.

1989 **Trygve Haavelmo** (Norway) Univ. of Oslo "for his clarification of the probability theory foundations of econometircs and his analyses of simultaneous economic structures."

1990 **Harry Markowitz** (U.S.) Baruch College of the City Univ. of New York, for his Portfolio Theory; **William F. Sharpe** (U.S.) Stanford Univ. for his Capital Asset Pricing Model, and **Merton Miller** (U.S.) Univ. of Chicago, for his work on the Miller-Modigliani Theory. Together, their work revolutionized the financial/business industries.

1991 **Ronald H. Coase** (UK) Univ. of Chicago Law School, for his work on the role of firms in the economy and on social cost of industry, notably his articles "The Theory of the Firm" (1937) and "The Problem of Social Cost" (1960).

1992 **Gary S. Becker** (U.S.), Univ. of Chicago, for "having extended the domain of economic theory to aspects of human behavior . . ." including crime, family life, and racial bias. His book on education, *Human Capital* (1964), was cited by the Academy as his "most noteworthy contribution.

1993 **Robert W. Fogel** (U.S.), Univ. of Chicago, and **Douglass C. North** (U.S.), Washington Univ., both economic historians, for "applying economic theory and quarantine methods to historical puzzles." Fogel's work on slavery as an efficient economic system caused great controversy.

1994 **John F. Nash** (U.S.) Princeton Univ., **John C. Harsanyi** (U.S., b. Hungary) Univ. of California-Berkeley, and **Reinhard Selten** (Germany) Univ. of Bonn, for their separate contributions to the field of game theory, which is used to predict how information and competition affect economic outcomes.

1995 **Robert E. Lucas, Jr.,** (U.S.) Univ. of Chicago, "the economist who has had the greatest influence on macroeconomic research since 1970." His work challenges the Keynesian belief that the government is able to fine-tune the economy.

1996 **James A. Mirrlees** (U.K.) Cambridge, Univ. and **William Vickrey** (U.S., b. Canada), Columbia Univ. for "their fundamental contributions to the economic theory of incentives" in situations when participants have different information. Their theories have been used in designing more efficient tax codes and eliciting the highest bids at auctions. Ironically, Vickrey died three days after winning the award at the age of 82.

1997 **Robert Merton,** 53, (U.S.), Harvard University, and **Myron Scholes,** 56, (U.S.), Stanford University, for their work in creating "a pioneering formula for the valuation of stock options" and other derivatives. The Nobel committee cited their research as one of the principal reasons for the success of the derivatives markets.

1998 **Amartya Sen,** 64, (India), Cambridge Univ. and Harvard Univ., for his work on human rights, poverty, and inequality that has changed the way governments deal with famines, and for restoring "an ethical dimension to the discussion of vital economics problems".

1999 See Part I: "The Almanac of the Year"

Nobel Prizes in Chemistry

1901 Jacobus H. Van't Holt (Netherlands) Berlin Univ. (Germany) "in recognition of the extraordinary services he has rendered by the discovery of the laws of chemical dynamics and osmotic pressure in solutions."

1902 Hermann E. Fischer (Germany) "in recognition of the extraordinary services he has rendered by his work on sugar and purine synthesis."

1903 Svante A. Arrhenius (Sweden) Stockholm Univ. "in recognition of the extraordinary services he has rendered to the advancement of chemistry by his electrolytic theory of dissociation."

1904 Sir William Ramsay (Great Britain) London Univ. "in recognition of his services in the discovery of the inert gaseous elements in air; and his determination of their place in the periodic system."

1905 Johann F.W.A. von Baeyer (Germany) Munich Univ. "in recognition of his services in the advancement of organic chemistry and the chemical industry, through his work on organic dyes and hydroaromatic compounds."

1906 Henri Moissan (France) Sorbonne Univ. "in recognition of the great services rendered by him in his investigation and isolation of the element fluorine, and for the adoption in the service of science of the electric furnace called after him."

1907 Eduard Buchner (Germany) Agricultural College "for his biochemical researches and his discovery of cell-free fermentation."

1908 Lord Ernest Rutherfold (Great Britain) Victoria Univ. "for his investigation into the disintegration of the elements, and the chemistry of radioactive substances."

1909 Wilhelm Ostwald (Germany) Leipzig Univ. "in recognition of his work on catalysis, and for his investigations into the fundamental principles governing chemical equilibria and rates of reaction."

1910 Otto Wallach (Germany) Goettingen Univ. "in recognition of his services to organic chemistry and the chemical industry by his pioneer work in the field of alicyclic compounds."

1911 Marie Curie (France) Sorbonne Univ. "in recognition of her services to the advancement of chemistry by the discovery of the elements radium and polonium, by the isolation of radium and the study of the nature and compounds of this remarkable element."

1912 Victor Grignard (France) Nancy Univ. "for the discovery of the so-called Grignard reagent, which in recent years has greatly advanced the progress of organic chemistry"; **Paul Sabatier** (France) Toulouse Univ. "for his method of hydrogenating organic compounds in the presence of finely disintegrated metals whereby the progress of organic chemistry has been greatly advanced in recent years."

1913 Alfred Werner (Switzerland) Zurich Univ. "in recognition of his work on the linkage of atoms in molecules by which he has thrown new light on earlier investigations and opened up new fields of research especially in inorganic chemistry."

1914 Theodore W. Richards (U.S.) Harvard Univ. "in recognition of his accurate determinations of the atomic weight of a large number of chemical elements."

1915 Richard M. Willstätter (Germany) Munich Univ. "for his researches on plant pigments, especially chlorophyll."

1916–1917 No awards given.

1918 Fritz Haber (Germany) Kaiser-Wilhelm Institut (now Fritz-Haber-Institut) "for the synthesis of ammonia from its elements."

1919 No award

1920 Walther H. Nernst (Germany) Berlin Univ. "in recognition of his work in thermochemistry."

1921 Frederick Soddy (Great Britain) Oxford Univ. "for his contributions to our knowledge of the chemistry of radioactive substances, and his investigations into the origin and nature of isotopes."

1922 Francis W. Aston (Great Britain) Cambridge Univ. "for his discovery, by means of his mass spectrograph, of isotopes in a large number of nonradioactive elements, and for his enunciation of the whole-number rule."

1923 Fritz Pregl (Austria) Graz Univ. "for his invention of the method of microanalysis of organic substances."

1924 No award

1925 Richard A. Zsigmondy (Germany) Goettingen Univ. "for his demonstration of the heterogeneous nature of colloid solutions and for the methods he used, which have since become fundamental in modern colloid chemistry."

1926 The (Theodor) Svedberg (Sweden) Uppsala Univ. "for his work on disperse systems."

1927 Heinrich O. Wieland (Germany) Munich Univ. "for his investigations of the constitution of the bile acids and related substances."

1928 Adolf O.R. Windaus (Germany) Goettingen Univ. "for the services rendered through his research into the constitution of the sterols and their connection with the vitamins."

1929 Sir Arthur Harden (Great Britain) London Univ., **Hans K.A. von Euler-Chelpin** (Sweden) "for their investigations on the fermentation of sugar and fermentative enzymes."

1930 Hans Fischer (Germany) Institute of Technology "for his researches into the constitution of haemin and chlorophyll, and especially for his synthesis of haemin."

1931 Carl Bosch (Germany) Heidelberg Univ. I.G. Farbenindustrie A.G., and **Fredrich Bergius** (Germany) Heidelberg Univ. and I.G. Farbenindustrie A.G. "in recognition of their contributions to the invention and development of chemical high pressure methods."

1932 Irving Langmuir (U.S.) General Electric Co. "for his discoveries and investigations in surface chemistry."

1933 No award

1934 Harold C. Urey (U.S.) Columbia Univ. "for his discovery of heavy hydrogen."

1935 Frédéric Joliot (France) Institut du Radium and his wife, **Iréne Joliot-Curie,** (France) Institut du Radium "in recognition of their synthesis of new radioactive elements."

1936 Petrus (Peter) J.W. Debye (Netherlands) Berlin Univ. and Kaiser-Wilhelm-Institut (now Max-Planck-Institut) "for his contributions to our knowledge of molecular structure through his investigations on dipole moments and on the diffraction of X-rays and electrons in gases."

1937 Sir Walter N. Haworth (Great Britain) Birmingham Univ. "for his investigations on carbohydrates and vitamin C"; **Paul Karrer** (Switzerland) Zurich Univ. "for his investigations on carotenoids, flavins, and vitamins A and B-2."

1938 Richard Kuhn (Germany) Heidelberg Univ. and Kaiser-Wilhelm-Institut (now Max-Planck-Institut) "for his work on carotenoids and vitamins. (Compelled by the authorities of his country to decline the award, but later received diploma and medal.)

1939 Adolf F.J. Butenandt (Germany) Berlin Univ. and Kaiser-Wilhelm-Institut (now Max-Planck-Institut) "for his work on sex hormones. (Compelled by his country to decline the award, but later received diploma and medal); **Leopold Ruzicka** (Switzerland) Federal Institute of Technology "for his work on polymethylenes and higher terpenes."

1940–1942   No awards given.

1943   George de Hevesy (Hungary) Stockholm Univ. "for his work on the use of isotopes as tracers in the study of chemical processes."

1944   Otto Hahn (Germany) Kaiser-Wilhelm-Institut (now Max-Planck-Institut) "for his discovery of the fission of heavy nuclei."

1945   Artturi I. Virtanen (Finland) Helsinki Univ. "for his research and inventions in agricultural and nutrition chemistry, especially for his fodder preservation method."

1946   James B. Sumner (U.S.) Cornell Univ. "for his discovery that enzymes can be crystallized"; **John H. Northrop** (U.S.) Rockefeller Institute for Medical Research "for their preparation of enzymes and virus proteins in a pure form."

1947   Sir Robert Robinson (Great Britain) Oxford Univ. "for his investigations on plant products of biological importance, especially alkaloids."

1948   Arne W.K. Tiselius (Sweden) Uppsala Univ. "for his research on electrophoresis and adsorption analysis, especially for his discoveries concerning the complex nature of the serum proteins."

1949   William F. Giauque (U.S.) Univ. of California, "for his contributions in the field of chemical thermodynamics, particularly concerning the behavior of substances at extremely low temperatures."

1950   Otto P.H. Diels (Germany) Kiel Univ. and **Kurt Alder** (Germany) Cologne Univ. "for their discovery and development of the diene synthesis."

1951   Edwin M. McMillan (U.S.) and **Glenn T. Seaborg** (U.S.) both of Univ. of California, "for their discoveries in the chemistry of the transuranium elements."

1952   Archer J.P. Martin (Great Britain) Nations Institute for Medical Research, and **Richard L.M. Synge** (Great Britain) Rowett Research Institute (Scotland) "for their invention of partition chromatography."

1953   Herman Staudinger (Germany) State Research Institute for Macromolecular Chemistry "for his discoveries in the field of macromolecular chemistry."

1954   Linus C. Pauling (U.S.) California Institute of Technology "for his research into the nature of the chemical bond and its application to the elucidation of the structure of complex substances."

1955   Vincent du Vigneaud (U.S.) Cornell Univ. "for his work on biochemically important sulphur compounds, especially for the first synthesis of a polypeptide hormone."

1956   Sir Cyril N. Hinshelwood (Great Britain) Oxford Univ. and **Nikolaj N. Semenov** (USSR) Institute for Chemical Physics of the Academy of Sciences of the USSR "for their researches into the mechanism of chemical reactions."

1957   Lord Alexander R. Todd (Great Britain) Cambridge Univ. "for his work on nucleotides and nucleotide co-enzymes."

1958   Frederick Sanger (Great Britain) Cambridge Univ. "for his work on the structure of proteins, especially that of insulin."

1959   Jaroslav Heyrovsky (Czechoslovakia) Polaro-Institute of the Czechoslovakia Academy of Science for his discovery and development of the polarographic methods of analysis."

1960   Willard F. Libby (U.S.) Univ. of California, Los Angeles "for his method to use carbon-14 for age determination in archaeology, geology, geophysics, and other branches of science."

1961   Melvin Calvin (U.S.) Univ. of California, "for his research on the carbon dioxide assimilation in plants."

1962   Max F. Perutz (Great Britain) Laboratory of Molecular Biology, and **Sir John C. Kendrew** (Great Britain) Laboratory of Molecular Biology, "for their studies on the structures of globular proteins."

1963   Karl Ziegler (Germany) Max-Planck-Institute

for Carbon Research, and **Giulio Natta** (Italy) Institute of Technology "for their discoveries in the field of the chemistry and technology of high polymers."

1964   Dorothy C. Hodgkin (Great Britain) Royal Society, Oxford Univ. "for her determinations by X-ray techniques of the structures of important biochemical substances."

1965   Robert B. Woodward (U.S.) Harvard Univ. "for his outstanding achievements in the art of organic synthesis."

1966   Robert S. Mulliken (U.S.) Univ. of Chicago "for his fundamental work concerning chemical bonds and the electronic structure of molecules by the molecular orbital method."

1967   Manfred Eigen (W. Germany) Max-Planck-Institut, **Ronald G.W. Norrish** (Great Britain) Institute of Physical Chemistry, and **Sir George Porter** (Great Britain) The Royal Institution "for their studies of extremely fast chemical reactions, effected by disturbing the equilibrium by means of very short pulses of energy."

1968   Lars Onsager (U.S.) Yale Univ. "for the discovery of the reciprocal relations bearing his name, which are fundamental for the thermodynamics of irreversible processes."

1969   Sir Derek H.R. Barton (Great Britain) Imperial College of Science and Technology, and **Odd Hassel** (Norway) Kjemisk Institut "for their contributions to the development of the concept of conformation and its application in chemistry."

1970   Luis F. Leloir (Argentina) Institute for Biochemical Research for his discovery of sugar nucleotides and their role in the biosynthesis of carbohydrates."

1971   Gerhard Herzberg (Canada) National Research Council of Canada "for his contributions to the knowledge of electronic structure and geometry of molecules, particularly free radicals."

1972   Christian B. Anfinsen (U.S.) National Institutes of Health "for his work on ribonuclease, especially concerning the connection between the amino acid sequence and the biologically active conformation"; **Stanford Moore** (U.S.) Rockefeller Univ. and **William H. Stein** (U.S.) Rockefeller Univ. "for their contribution to the understanding of the connection between chemical structure and catalytic activity of the active center of the ribonuclease molecule."

1973   Ernst O. Fischer (W. Germany) Technical Univ. of Munich, and **Sir Geoffrey Wilkinson** (Great Britain) Imperial College "for their pioneering work, performed independently, on the chemistry of the organometallic, so-called sandwich compounds."

1974   Paul J. Flory (U.S.) Stanford Univ. "for his fundamental achievements, both theoretical and experimental, in the physical chemistry of the macromolecules."

1975   Sir John W. Cornforth (Australia and Great Britain) Univ. of Sussex "for his work on the stereochemistry of enzyme-catalyzed reactions"; **Vladimir Prelog** (Switzerland) Eidgenossische Technische Hochschule "for his research into the sterochemistry of organic molecules and reactions."

1976   William N. Lipscomb (U.S.) Harvard Univ. "for his studies on the structure of boranes illuminating problems of chemical bonding."

1977   Ilya Prigogine (Belgium) Université Libre de Bruxelles, (Univ. of Texas, U.S.) "for his contributions to nonequilibrium thermodynamics, particularly the theory of dissipative structures."

1978   Peter D. Mitchell (Great Britain) Glynn Research Laboratories "for his contribution to the understanding of biological energy transfer through the formulation of the chemiosmotic theory."

1979   Herbert C. Brown (U.S.) Purdue Univ., and **Georg Wittig** (Germany) Univ. of Heidelberg "for their development of the use of boron-and-phosphorus-containing compounds, respectively, into important reagents in organic synthesis."

1980   Paul Berg (U.S.) Stanford Univ. "for his fun-

damental studies of the biochemistry of nucleic acids, with particular regard to recombinant-DNA"; **Walter Gilbert** (U.S.) Biological Laboratories, and **Frederick Sanger** (Great Britain) MRC Laboratory of Molecular Biology "for their contributions concerning the determination of base sequences in nucleic acids."
1981 Kenichi Fukui (Japan) Kyoto Univ. and **Roald Hoffman** (U.S.) Cornell Univ. "for their theories, developed independently, concerning the course of chemical reactions."
1982 Aaron Klug (Great Britain) MRC Laboratory of Molecular Biology "for his development of crystallographic electron microscopy and his structural elucidation of biologically important nucleic acid-protein complexes."
1983 Henry Taube (U.S.) Stanford Univ. "for his work on the mechanisms of electron transfer reactions, especially in metal complexes."
1984 Robert B. Merrifield (U.S.) Rockefeller Univ. "for his development of methodology for chemical synthesis on solid matrix."
1985 Herbert A. Hauptman (U.S.) Medical Foundation of Buffalo, and **Jerome Karle** (U.S.) U.S. Naval Research Laboratory "for their outstanding achievements in the development of direct methods for the determination of crystal structures."
1986 Dudley R. Herschbach (U.S.) Harvard Univ., **Yuan T. Lee** (U.S.) Univ. of California, and **John C. Polanyi** (Canada) Univ. of Toronto, "for their contributions concerning the dynamics of chemical elementary processes."
1987 Donald J. Cram (U.S.) University of California, Los Angeles, **Jean-Marie Lehn** (France) Université Louis Pasteur, and **Charles J. Pedersen** (U.S.) Du Pont Laboratory "for their development and use of molecules with structure-specific interactions of high selectivity."
1988 Johann Deisenhofer (U.S.) Howard Hughes Medical Institute, Robert Huber (W. Germany) Max-Planck-Institut, and **Hartmut Michel** (W. Germany) Max-Planck-Institut, "for their determination of the three-dimensional structure of a photosynthetic reaction centre."
1989 Sidney Altman (U.S.) Yale Univ., and **Thomas Cech** (U.S.) Univ. of Colorado "for their discovery of the catalytic properties of RNA." (They worked independently.)
1990 Elias James Corey (U.S.) Harvard Univ. for developing new ways to synthesize complex molecules ordinarily found in nature, work that has contributed to "the high standard of living and health, and the longevity enjoyed at least in the Western world."
1991 Richard R. Ernst (Switzerland) Eidgenössische Technische Hochschule, Zurich, for his work in refining nuclear magnetic resonance spectroscopy for use in chemical analysis.
1992 Rudolph A. Marcus (U.S., b. Canada), Cal

Tech., for his mathematical explanation of chemical interactions involving the transfer of electrons between molecules.
1993 Kary B. Mullis (U.S.) who worked for Cetus Corp. in the 1970s when he discovered the polymerase chain reaction (PCR) that allowed scientists to make trillions of copies of DNA from very small amounts. His method has been used in the study of plant and animal fossils and in criminal investigations. **Michael Smith** (Canada), Univ. of British Columbia, for developing the technique that alters the code of genetic molecules that will facilitate new medical therapies and plants that resist disease.
1994 George A. Olah (U.S., b. Hungary) Univ. of Southern California, for his discovery of new ways of breaking apart and rebuilding carbon and hydrogen compounds. He opened a wholly new field of hydrocarbon research, leading to improved fuels based on coal, methane, and petroleum.
1995 F. Sherwood Roland (U.S.) Univ. of California-Irvine, **Mario Molina** (U.S.) M.I.T., and **Paul Crutzen** (Netherlands) Max Planck Institute for Chemistry in Mainz, Germany, for their pioneering work in explaining how production and use of refrigerants, plastic foams, aerosol propellants, and other chlorofluorocarbons deplete the ozone layer, thus increasing the risk of skin cancer, cataracts, and damage to human immune systems.
1996 Robert F. Curl, Jr., (U.S.) and **Richard E. Smalley**, (U.S.), of Rice University, and **Harold W. Kroto** (U.K.) of Univ. of Sussex, for their 1985 discovery of buckminsterfullerene, or "buckyballs": a carbon molecule containing 60 atoms arranged like a soccer ball in a geodesic sphere. Their work opened an entirely new branch of chemistry and gve scientists a greater understanding on how nature bonds carbon atoms together.
1997 Paul D. Boyer, 79, (U.S.), UCLA and **John E. Walker,** 56 (U.K.), Medical Research Council Laboratory of Molecular Biology, for demonstrating how all living things create adenosine triphosphate, a tiny molecule that stores energy and can be used to build proteins, transmit nerve impulses, and contract muscles. **Jens C. Skou,** 79, (Denmark), Aarhus Univ., for his discovery of the enzyme sodium-potassium-stimulated adenosine triphosphate, which maintains the balance of sodium and potassium ions in living cells.
1998 Walter Kohn, 75, (U.S., b. Austria), Univ. of California, Santa Barbara; **John A. Pople,** 73, (U.S., b U.K.), Northwestern Univ. Their achievements helped extend the mathematics of quantum mechanics to predicting specific chemical reactions and designing molecules for use in medicine and other applications.
1999 See Part I: "The Almanac of the Year"

Nobel Prizes in Physics

1901 Wilhelm C. Röntgen (Germany) Munich Univ. "in recognition of the extraordinary services he has rendered by the discovery of remarkable rays subsequently named after him."
1902 Hendrik A. Lorentz (Netherlands) Leyden Univ., and **Pieter Zeeman** (Netherlands) Amsterdam Univ. "in recognition of the extraordinary service they rendered by their researches into the influence of magnetism upon radiation phenomena."
1903 Antoine H. Becquerel (France) Ecole Polytechnique "in recognition of the extraordinary services he has rendered by the discovery of spontaneous radioactivity"; **Pierre Curie** (France) Municipal School of Industrial Physics and Chemistry and his wife, **Marie Curie**, (France) (born in Poland) "in recognition of the extraordinary services they have rendered by their joint researches on the

radiation phenomena discovered by Professor Henri Becquerel."
1904 Lord Rayleigh (John W. Strutt) (Great Britain) Royal Institution of Great Britain "for his investigations of the densities of the most important gases and for his discovery of argon in connection with these studies."
1905 Philipp E.A. Lenard (Germany) Kiel Univ. "for his work on cathode rays."
1906 Sir Joseph J. Thomas (Great Britain) Cambridge Univ. "in recognition of the great merits of his theoretical and experimental investigations on the conduction of electricity by gases."
1907 Albert A. Michelson (U.S.) Univ. of Chicago "for his optical precision instruments and the spectroscopic and meteorological investigations carried out with their aid."

1908   Gabriel Lippman (France) Sorbonne Univ. "for his method of reproducing colours photographically based on the phenomenon of interference."

1909   Guglielmo Marconi (Italy) Marconi Wireless Telegraph Co., Ltd., and **Carl F. Braun** (Germany) Strasbourg Univ. "in recognition of their contributions to the development of wireless telegraphy."

1910   Johannes D. van der Waals (Netherlands) Amsterdam Univ. "for his work on the equation of state for gases and liquids."

1911   Wilhelm Wien (Germany) Würzburg Univ. "for his discoveries regarding the laws governing the radiation of heat."

1912   Nils G. Dalén (Sweden) Swedish Gas-Accumulator Co. "for his invention of automatic regulators for use in conjunction with gas accumulators for illuminating lighthouses and buoys."

1913   Heike Kamerlingh-Onnes (Netherlands) Leyden Univ. "for his investigations on the properties of matter at low temperatures which led, inter alia, to the production of liquid helium."

1914   Max von Laue (Germany) Frankfurt-am-Main Univ. "for his discovery of the diffraction of X-rays by crystals."

1915   Sir William Henry Gragg (Great Britain) London Univ. and his son **Sir William Lawrence Bragg** (Great Britain) Victoria Univ. "for their services in the analysis of crystal structure by means of X-rays."

1916   No award.

1917   Charles G. Barkla (Great Britain) Edinburgh Univ. "for his discovery of the characteristic Röntgen radiation of the elements."

1918   Max K.E.L. Planck (Germany) Berlin Univ. "in recognition of the services he rendered to the advancement of Physics by his discovery of energy quanta."

1919   Johannes Stark (Germany) Greifswald Univ. "for his discovery of the Doppler effect in canal rays and the splitting of spectral lines in electric fields."

1920   Charles E. Guillaume (Switzerland) International Bureau of Weights and Measurers "in recognition of the service he has rendered to precision measurements in physics by his discovery of anomalies in nickel steel alloys."

1921   Albert Einstein (Germany) Kaiser-Wilhelm-Institut für Physik (now Max-Panck-Institut) "for his services to theoretical physics, and especially for his discovery of the law of the photoelectric effect."

1922   Niels Bohr (Denmark) Copenhagen Univ. "for his services in the investigation of the structure of atoms and of the radiation emanating from them."

1923   Robert A. Millikan (U.S.) California Institute of Technology) "for his work on the elementary charge of electricity and on the photoelectric effect."

1924   Karl M.G. Siegbahn (Sweden) Uppsala Univ. "for his discoveries and research in the field of X-ray spectroscopy."

1925   James Franck (Germany) Goettingen Univ., and **Gustav Hertz** (Germany) Halle Univ. "for their discovery of the laws of governing the impact of an electron upon an atom."

1926   Jean B. Perrin (France) Sorbonne Univ. "for his work on the discontinuous structure of matter, and especially for his discovery of sedimentation equilibrium."

1927   Arthur H. Compton (U.S.) Univ. of Chicago "for his discovery of the effect named after him;" **Charles T.R. Wilson** (Great Britain) Cambridge Univ. "for his method of making the paths of electrically charged particles visible by condensation of vapour."

1928   Sir Own W. Richardson (Great Britain) London Univ. "for his work on the thermionic phenomenon and especially for the discovery of the law named after him."

1929   Prince Louis-Victor de Broglie (France) Sorbonne Univ. "for his discovery of the wave nature of electrons."

1930   Sir Chandrasekhara V. Raman (India) Calcutta Univ. "for his work on the scattering of light and for the discovery of the effect names after him."

1931   No award.

1932   Werner Heisenberg (Germany) Leipzig Univ. "for the creation of quantum mechanics, the application of which, has, inter alia, led to the discovery of the allotropic forms of hydrogen."

1933   Edwin Schrödinger (Austria) Berlin Univ. and **Paul A.M. Dirac** (Great Britain) Cambridge Univ. "for the discovery of new productive forms of atomic theory."

1934   No award

1935   Sir James Chadwick (Great Britain) Liverpool Univ. "for his discovery of the neutron."

1936   Victor F. Hess (Austria) Innsbruck Univ. "for his discovery of cosmic radiation"; **Carl D. Anderson** (U.S.) California Institute of Technology "for his discovery of the positron."

1937   Clinton J. Davisson (U.S.) Bell Telephone Laboratories, and **Sir George P. Thomson** (Great Britain) London Univ. "for their experimental discovery of the diffraction of electrons by crystals."

1938   Enrico Fermi (Italy) Rome Univ. "for his demonstration of the existence of new radioactive elements produced by neutron irradiation, and for his related discovery of nuclear reactions brought about by slow neutrons."

1939   Ernest O. Lawrence (U.S.) Univ. of California, Berkeley "for the invention and development of the cyclotron and for results obtained with it, especially with regard to artificial radioactive elements."

1940–1942   No awards given.

1943   Otto Stern (U.S.) Carnegie Institute of Technology (now Carnegie Mellon Univ.) "for his contribution to the development of the molecular ray method and his discovery of the magnetic moment of the proton."

1944   Isidor I. Rabi (U.S.) Columbia Univ. "for his resonance method for recording the magnetic properties of atomic nuclei."

1945   Wolfgang Pauli (Austria) Princeton Univ. "for the discovery of the Exclusion Principle, also called the Pauli Principle."

1946   Percy W. Bridgman (U.S.) Harvard Univ. "for the invention of an apparatus to produce extremely high pressures, and for the discoveries he made therewith in the field of high-pressure physics."

1947   Sir Edward V. Appleton (Great Britain) Dept. of Scientific and Industrial Research "for his investigations of the physics of the upper atmosphere, especially for the discovery of the so-called Appleton layer."

1948   Lord Patrick M.S. Blackett (Great Britain) Victoria Univ. "for his development of the Wilson cloud chamber method, and his discoveries therewith in the fields of nuclear physics and cosmic radiation."

1949   Hideki Yukawa (Japan) Kyoto Imperial Univ. "for his prediction of the existence of mesons on the basis of theoretical work on nuclear forces."

1950   Cecil F. Powell (Great Britain) Bristol Univ. "for his development of the photographic method of studying nuclear processes and his discoveries regarding mesons made with this method."

1951   Sir John D. Cockcroft (Great Britain) Atomic Energy Research Establishment, and Ernest T.S. Walton (Ireland) Dublin Univ. "for their pioneer work on the transmutation of atomic nuclei by artificially accelerated atomic particles."

1952   Felix Block (U.S.) Stanford Univ., and **Edward M. Purcell** (U.S.) Harvard Univ. "for their development of new methods for nuclear magnetic precision measurements and discoveries in connection therewith."

1953   Frits (Frederik) Zernike (Netherlands) Groningern Univ. "for his demonstration of the phase contrast method, especially for his invention of the phase contrast microscope."

1954 Max Born (Great Britain) Edinburgh Univ. "for his fundamental research in quantum mechanics, especially for his statistical interpretation of the wave-function"; **Walther Bothe** (Germany) Heidelbery Univ., Max-Planck-Institut "for the coincidence method and his discoveries made therewith."

1955 Willis E. Lamb (U.S.) Stanford Univ. "for his discoveries concerning the fine structure of the hydrogen spectrum"; **Polykarp Kusch** (U.S.) Columbia Univ. "for his precision determination of the magnetic moment of the electron."

1956 William Shockley (U.S. Semiconductor Laboratory of Beckman Instruments, Inc., **John Bardeen** (U.S.) Univ. of Illinois, and **Walter H. Brattain** (U.S.) Bell Telephone Laboratories "for their researches on semiconductors and their discovery of the transistor effect."

1957 Chen N. Yang (China) Institute for Advanced Study (Princeton, NJ) and **Tsung-Dao Lee** (China) Columbia Univ. "for their penetrating investigation of the so-called parity laws which has led to important discoveries regarding the elementary particles."

1958 Pavel A. Cherenkov (USSR) Physics Institute of USSR Academy of Sciences, **Il'ja M.Frank** (USSR) Academy of Sciences, and **Igor J. Tamm** (USSR) Univ. of Moscow and Physics Institute of USSR Academy of Sciences "for their discovery and the interpretation of the Cherenkov effect."

1959 Emillio G. Sergè (U.S.) Univ. of California, Berkeley, and **Owen Chamberlain** (U.S.) Univ. of California, Berkeley "for their discovery of the antiproton."

1960 Donald A. Glaser (U.S.) Univ. of California, Berkeley "for the invention of the bubble chamber."

1961 Robert Hofstadter (U.S.) Stanford Univ. "for his pioneering studies of electron scattering in atomic nuclei and for his thereby achieved discoveries concerning the structure of the nucleons"; **Rudolf L. Mössbauer** (Germany) Technische Hochschule (Munich), and California Institute of Technology "for his researches concerning the resonance absorption of gamma radiation and his discovery in this connection of the effect which bears his name."

1962 Lev D. Landau (USSR) Academy of Sciences "for his pioneering theories for condensed matter, especially liquid helium."

1963 Eugene P. Wigner (U.S.) Princeton Univ. "for his contributions to the theory of the atomic nucleus and the elementary particles, particularly through the discovery and application of fundamental symmetry principles"; **Maria Goeppert-Mayer** (U.S.) Univ. of California, La Jolla, and **J. Hans D. Jensen** (Germany) Univ. of Heidelberg "for their discoveries concerning nuclear shell structure."

1964 Charles H. Townes (U.S.) M.I.T., **Nikolai G. Basov** (USSR) Lebedev Institute for Physics, and **Aleksandre M. Prochorov** (USSR) Lebedev Institute for Physics "for fundamental work in the field of quantum electronics, which has led to the construction of oscillators and amplifiers based on the maser-laser-principle."

1965 Schin'ichiro Tomonaga (Japan) Toyko Univ., **Julian Schwinger** (U.S.) Harvard Univ., and **Richard P. Feynman** (U.S.) California Institute of Technology "for their fundamental work in quantum electrodynamcis, with deep-ploughing consequences for the physics of elementary particles."

1966 Alfred Kastier (France) Fcole Normale Supérieure, Université de Paris "for the discovery and development of optical methods for studying hertzian resonance in atoms."

1967 Hans A. Bethe (U.S.) Cornell Univ. "for his contributions to the theory of nuclear reactions, especially his discoveries concerning the energy production in stars."

1968 Luis W. Alvarez (U.S.) Univ. of California, Berkeley "for his decisive contributions to elementary particle physics, in particular the discovery of a large number of resonance states, made possible through his development of the technique of using hydrogen bubble chamber and data analysis."

1969 Murray Gell-Mann (U.S.) California Institute of Technology "for his contributions and discoveries concerning the classification of elementary particles and their interactions."

1970 Hannes Alfvén (Sweden) Royal Institute of Technology "for fundamental work and discoveries in magneto-hydrodynamics with fruitful applications in different parts of plasma physics"; **Louis Neel** (France) Univ. of Grenoble "for fundamental work and discoveries concerning antiferromagnetism and ferrimagetism which have led to important applications in solid-state physics."

1971 Dennis Gabor (Great Britain) Imperial College of Science and Technology "for his invention and development of the holographic method."

1972 John Bardeen (U.S.) Univ. of Illinois, **Leon N. Cooper** (U.S.) Brown Univ., and **J. Robert Schrieffer** (U.S.) Univ. of Pennsylvania "for their jointly developed theory of superconductivity, usually called the BCS-theory."

1973 Leo Esaki (Japan) IBM Thomas J. Watson Research Center (New York), and **Ivar Giaever** (U.S.) General Electric Co. "for their experimental discoveries regarding tunneling phenomena in semiconductors and superconductors, respectively"; **Brian D. Josephson** (Great Britain) Cambridge Univ. "for his theoretical predictions of the properties of a supercurrent through a tunnel barrier, in particular those phenomena which are generally known as the Josephson effects."

1974 Sir Martin Ryle (Great Britain) Cambridge Univ., and **Antony Hewish** (Great Britain) Cambridge Univ. "for their pioneering research in radio astrophysics: Ryle for his observations and inventions, in particular of the aperture synthesis technique, and Hewish for his decisive role in the discovery of pulsars."

1975 Aage Bohr (Denmark) Niels Bohr Institute, **Ben Mottelson** (Denmark) Nordita, and **James Rainwater** (U.S.) Columbia Univ. "for the discovery of the connection between collective motion and particle motion in atomic nuclei and the development of the theory of the structure of the atomic nucleus based on this connection."

1976 Burton Richter (U.S.) Stanford Linear Accelerator Center, and **Samuel C.C. Ting** (U.S.) M.I.T. "for their pioneering work in the discovery of a heavy elementary particle of a new kind."

1977 Philip W. Anderson (U.S.) Bell Laboratories, **Sir Nevill F. Mott** (Great Britain) Cambridge Univ. and **John H. van Vleck** (U.S.) Harvard Univ. "for their fundamental theoretical investigations of the electronic structure of magnetic and disordered systems."

1978 Peter L. Kapitsa (USSR) Academy of Sciences "for his basic inventions and discoveries in the area of low-temperature physics, **Arno A. Penzias** (U.S.) Bell Laboratories, and **Robert W. Wilson** (U.S.) Bell Laboratories "for their discovery of cosmic microwave background radiation."

1979 Sheldon L. Glashow (U.S.) Lyman Laboratory, Harvard Univ., **Abdus Salam** (Pakistan) International Centre for Theoretical Physics (Italy) and Imperial College of Science and Technology (London), and **Steven Weinberg** (U.S.) Harvard Univ. "for their contributions to the theory of the unified weak and electromagnetic interaction between elementary particles, including, inter alia, the predictions of the weak neutral current."

1980 James W. Cronin (U.S.) Univ. of Chicago, and **Val L. Fitch** (U.S.) Princeton Univ. "for the discovery of violations of fundamental symmetry principles in the decay of neutral K-mesons."

1981 Nicolaas Bloembergen (U.S.) Harvard Univ., and **Arthur L. Schawlow** (U.S.) Stanford Univ. "for their contributions to the development of laser spec-

troscopy"; **Kai M. Siegbahn** (Sweden) Uppsala Univ. "for his contribution to the development of high-resolution electron spectroscopy."
1982 Kenneth G. Wilson (U.S.) Cornell Univ. "for his theory for critical phenomena in connection with phase transitions."
1983 Subrahmanyan Chandrasekhar (U.S.) Univ. of Chicago "for his theoretical studies of the physical processes of importance to the structure and evolution of the stars"; **William A. Fowler** (U.S.) California Institute of Technology for his "studies of the nuclear reactions of importance in the formation of the chemical elements in the universe."
1984 Carlo Rubbia (Italy) CERN (Switzerland), and **Simon van der Meer** (Netherlands) CERN (Switzerland) "for their decisive contributions to the discovery of the field particles W and Z, communicators of weak interaction."
1985 Klaus von Klitzing (W. Germany) Max-Planck-Institut for Solid State Research "for the discovery of the quantized Hall effect."
1986 Ernst Ruska (W. Germany) Fritz-Haber-Institut der Max-Planck-Gesellschaft "for his fundamental work in electron optics, and for the design of the first electron microscope"; **Gerd Binnig** (W. Germany) IBM Zurich Research Laboratory and **Heinrich Rohrer** (Switzerland) IBM Zurich Research Laboratory "for their design of the scanning tunneling microscope."
1987 Georg J. Bednorz (Switzerland) IBM Zurich research Laboratory, and **Dr. K. Alex Müller** (Switzerland) IBM Zurich Research Laboratory "for the discovery of new superconducting materials."
1988 Leon M. Lederman (U.S.) Fermi National Accelerator Laboratory, **Melvin Schwartz** (U.S.) Digital Pathways, Inc., and **Jack Steinberger** (Switzerland) "for the neutrino beam method and the demonstration of the doublet structure of the leptons through the discovery of the muon neutrino."
1989 Norman R. Ramsey (U.S.) Harvard Univ. "for the invention of the separated oscillatory fields method and its use in . . . atomic clocks"; **Hans G. Dehmelt** (U.S.) Univ. of Washington, and **Wolfgang Paul** (W. Germany) Univ. of Bonn "for the development of the ion trap technique," which allows detailed study of subatomic particles."
1990 Richard E. Taylor (Can.), Stanford U.; **Jerome I. Friedman** (U.S.) MIT; and **Henry W. Kendall** (U.S.) MIT, whose experiments between 1967 and 1973 confirmed the existence of quarks, the fundamental building blocks of matter.

1991 Pierre-Gilles de Gennes (France), Collège de France, Paris, for his discoveries about the ordering of molecules in a variety of substances but especially liquid crystals, where his work has helped in understanding superconductivity.
1992 George Charpak (France, b. Poland), affiliated with CERN, the accelerator complex, where he developed electronic detectors that traced the paths of subatomic particles with lightning speed.
1993 Joseph H. Taylor (U.S.), Princeton Univ., and **Russel A. Hulse** (U.S.), Princeton Plasma Physics Laboratory, for their discovery of a binary pulsar and their later success in measuring its pulse rate.
1994 Clifford G. Shull (U.S.) MIT, and **Bertram N. Brockhouse** (Canada) McMaster Univ., for experiments in the 1940s and '50s that exploited the penetrating power of low-energy neutron beams produced by nuclear reactors. Neutron beams are much more powerful than other forms of radiation, and are now widely used to explore the atomic structure of matter.
1995 Martin L. Perl, (U.S.) Stanford Univ. Linear Accelerator Center, and **Frederick Reines** (U.S.) Los Alamos National Laboratory, for their separate discoveries of "two of nature's most remarkable subatomic particles." Perl's discovery of the tau in the 1970s and Reines discovery of the neutrino in the 1950s are watershed events in scientists' understanding of elementary particle physics.
1996 Robert C. Richardson (U.S.) and **David M. Lee** (U.S.) of Cornell Univ., and **Douglas S. Osheroff** (U.S.) Stanford Univ., for their 1972 discovery of superfluiditiy in a rare form of helium. The superfluid helium evidences surprising magnetic properties, and may offer insights into the original formation of galaxies and the rotational behavior of neutron stars.
1997 Steven Chu, 49, (U.S.) Stanford Univ., **Claude Cohen-Tannoudji,** 64, (France), Collège de France, and **William D. Phillips,** 49, (U.S.), National Institute of Standards and Technology, for their development of a method to trap individual atoms, which allow them to be studied in greater detail.
1998 Robert B. Laughlin, 48, (U.S.), Stanford University; **Horst L. Störmer,** 49, (U.S.), Columbia University; **Daniel Tsui,** 59, (U.S.), Princeton University; for their discovery of the fractional quantum Hall effect, the culmination of studies of magnetic fields dating back to 1897.
1999 See Part I: "The Almanac of the Year"

Nobel Prizes in Literature

1901 Sully Prudhomme (pen name of René F.A. Prudhomme) (France) "in special recognition of his poetic composition."
1902 Christian M.T. Mommsen (Germany) "the greatest living master of the art of historical writing, with special reference to his monumental work, *A History of Rome.*
1903 Bjørstjerne M. Bjørnson (Norway) for "his noble, magnificent, and versatile poetry which has always been distinguished by both the freshness of its inspiration and the rare purity of its spirit."
1904 Frederic Mistral (France) "in recognition of the fresh originality and true inspiration of his poetic production, which faithfully reflects the natural scenery and native spirit of his people, and, in addition, his significant work as a Provençal philologist."
José Echegaray y Eizaguirre (Spain) "in recognition of the numerous and brilliant compositions which, in an individual and original manner, have revived the great traditions of the Spanish drama."

1905 Henryk Sienkiewicz (Poland) "because of his outstanding merits as an epic writer.
1906 Giosuè Carducci (Italy) "as a tribute to the creative energy, freshness of style, and lyrical force which characterize his poetic masterpieces."
1907 Rudyard Kipling (Great Britain) "in consideration of the power of observation, originality of imagination, virility of ideas, and remarkable talent for narration which characterize the creations of this world-famous author."
1908 Rudolf C. Eucken (Germany) "in recognition of his earnest search for truth, his penetrating power of thought, his wide range of vision, and the warmth and strength in presentation with which in his numerous works he had vindicated and developed an idealistic philosophy of life."
1909 Selma O.L. Lagerlöf (Sweden) "in appreciation of the lofty idealism, vivid imagination, and spiritual perception that characterize her writings."
1910 Paul J.L. Heyse (Germany) "as a tribute to

the consummate artistry, permeated with idealism, which he has demonstrated during his long productive career as lyric poet, dramatist, novelist, and writer of world-renowned short stories."

1911 Count Maurice (Mooris) P.M.B. Maeterlinck (Belgium) "in appreciation of his many-sided literary activities, and especially of his dramatic works, which are distinguished by a wealth of imagination and by a poetic fancy."

1912 Gerhart J.R. Hauptmann (Germany) "primarily in recognition of his fruitful, varied, and outstanding production in the realm of dramatic art."

1913 Rabindranath Tagore (India) "because of his profoundly sensitive, fresh, and beautiful verse, by which, with consummate skill, he has made his poetic thought, expressed in his own English words, a part of the literature of the West."

1914 No award

1915 Romain Rolland (France) "as a tribute to the lofty idealism of his literary production and to the sympathy and love of truth with which he has described different types of human beings."

1916 Carl G.V. von Heidenstam (Sweden) "in recognition of his significance as the leading representative of a new era in our literature."

1917 Karl A. Gjellerup (Denmark) "for his varied and rich poetry, which is inspired by lofty ideals"; **Henrik Pontoppidan** (Denmark) "for his authentic descriptions of presentday life in Denmark."

1918 No award

1919 Carl F.G. Spitteler (Switzerland) "in special appreciation of his epic, 'Olympian Spring'"

1920 Knut P. Hamsun (Norway) "for his monumental work, *Growth of the Soil.*"

1921 Antole France (pen name of Jacques A. Thibault) (France) "in recognition of his brilliant literary achievements, characterized as they are by a nobility of style, a profound human sympathy, grace, and a true Gallic temperament."

1922 Jacinto Benavent (Spain) "for the happy manner in which he has continued the illustrious traditions of the Spanish drama."

1923 William B. Yeats (Ireland) "for his always inspired poetry, which in a highly artistic form gives expression to the spirit of a whole nation."

1924 Wladyslaw S. Reymont (pen name of Reyment) (Poland) "for his great national epic, *The Peasants.*"

1925 George B. Shaw (Great Britain) "for his work which is marked by both idealism and humanity, its stimulating satire often being infused with a singular poetic beauty."

1926 Grazia Deledda (pen name of Grazia Madesani (Italy) "for her idealistically inspired writings, which picture the life on her native island and with depth and sympathy deal with human problems in general."

1927 Henri Bergson (France) "in recognition of his rich and vitalizing ideas."

1928 Sigrid Undset (Norway) "principally for her powerful descriptions of Northern life during the Middle Ages."

1929 Thomas Mann (Germany) "principally for his great novel *Buddenbrooks.*"

1930 Sinclair Lewis (U.S.) "for his vigorous and graphic art of description and his ability to create, with wit and humor, new types of characters."

1931 Erik A. Karlfeldt (Sweden) for his poetry.

1932 John Galsworthy (Great Britain) "for his distinguished art of narration which takes its highest form in *The Forsyte Saga.*"

1933 Ivan A. Bunin (stateless domicile in France) "for the strict artistry with which he has carried on the classical Russian traditions in prose writing."

1934 Luigi Pirandello (Italy) "for his bold and ingenious revival of dramatic art."

1935 No award

1936 Eugene G. O'Neill (U.S.) "for the power, hon-esty, and deep-felt emotions of his dramatic works, which embody an original concept of tragedy."

1937 Roger Martin du Gard (France) "for the artistic power and truth with which he has depicted human conflict as well as some fundamental aspects of contemporary life in his novel-cycle *Les Thibault.*"

1938 Pearl Buck (pen name of Pearl Walsh) (U.S.) "for her rich and truly epic descriptions of peasant life in China and for her biographical masterpieces."

1939 Frans E. Sillanpää (Finland) "for his deep understanding of his country's peasantry and the exquisite art with which he has portrayed their way of life and their relationship with Nature."

1940–1943 No awards given.

1944 Johannes V. Jensen (Denmark) "for the rare strength and fertility of his poetic imagination."

1945 Gabriela Mistral (pen name of Lucila Godoy y Alcayaga) (Chile) "for her lyric poetry which, has made her name a symbol of the idealistic aspirations of the entire Latin American world."

1946 Hermann Hesse (Switzerland) "for his inspired writings which exemplify the classical humanitarian ideals and high qualities of style."

1947 André P.G. Gide (France) "for his writings in which human problems and conditions have been presented with a fearless love of truth and keen psychological insight."

1948 Thomas S. Eliot (Great Britain) "for his outstanding, pioneer contribution to present-day poetry."

1949 William Faulkner (U.S.) ":for his powerful and artistically unique contribution to the modern American novel."

1950 Earl (Bertrand) Russell (Great Britain) "in recognition of his varied and significant writings in which he champions humanitarian ideals and freedom of thought."

1951 Pär G. Lägerkvist (Sweden) "for the artistic vigour and true independence of mind with which he endeavours in his poetry to find answers to the eternal questions confronting mankind."

1952 François Mauriac (France) "for the deep spiritual insight and the artistic intensity with which he has in his novels penetrated the drama of human life."

1953 Sir Winston L.S. Churchill (Great Britain) "for his mastery of historical and biographical description as well as for brilliant oratory in defending exalted human values."

1954 Ernest M. Hemingway (U.S.) "for his mastery of the art of narrative, most recently demonstrated in *The Old Man and the Sea,* and for the influence that he has exerted on contemporary style."

1955 Halldór K. Laxness (Iceland) "for his vivid epic power which has renewed the great narrative art of Iceland."

1956 Juan R. Jiménez (Spain) (domicile in Puerto Rico) "for his lyrical poetry, which in Spanish language constitutes an example of high spirit and artistic purity."

1957 Albert Camus (France) "for his important literary production, which with clearsighted earnestness illuminates the problems of the human conscience in our times."

1958 Boris L. Pasternak (USSR) "for his important achievement both in contemporary lyrical poetry and in the field of the great Russian epic tradition." (Declined the prize.)

1959 Salvatore Quasimodo (Italy) "for his lyrical poetry, which with classical fire expresses the tragic experience of life in our own times."

1960 Saint-John Perse (pen name of Alexis Léger) (France) "for the soaring flight and the evocative imagery of his poetry which in a visionary fashion reflects the conditions of our time."

1961 Ivo Andric (Yugoslavia) "for the epic force with which he has traced themes and depicted human destinies drawn from the history of his country."

1962   John Steinbeck (U.S.) "for his realistic and imaginative writings, combining as they do sympathetic humour and keen social perception."

1963   Giorgos Seferis (pen name of Giogos Seferiades) (Greece) "for his eminent lyrical writing, inspired by a deep feeling for the Hellenic world of culture."

1964   Jean-Paul Sartre (France) "for his work which, rich in ideas and filled with the spirit of freedom and the quest for truth, has exerted a far-reaching influence on our age." (Declined the prize.)

1965   Michail A. Solochov (USSR) "for the artistic power and integrity with which, in his epic of the Don, he has given expression to a historic phase in the life of the Russian people."

1966   Shmuel U. Agnon (Israel) "for his profoundly characteristic narrative art with motifs from the life of the Jewish people; **Nelly Sachs** (Germany) (domiciled in Sweden) " for her outstanding lyrical and dramatic writing, which interprets Israel's destiny with touching strength."

1967   Miguel A. Asturias (Guatemala) "for his vivid literary achievement, deep-rooted in the national traits and traditions of Indian peoples of Latin America."

1968   Yasunari Kawabata (Japan) "for his narrative mastery, which with great sensibility expresses the essence of the Japanese mind."

1969   Samuel Beckett (Ireland) "for his writing, which—in new forms for the novel and drama—in the destitution of modern man acquires its elevation."

1970   Alexander Solzhenitsyn (USSR) "for the ethical force with which he has pursued the indispensable traditions of Russian literature."

1971   Pablo Neruda (Chile) "for a poetry that brings alive a continent's destiny and dreams."

1972   Heinrich Böll (W. Germany) "for his writing which through its combination of a broad perspective on his time and a sensitive skill in characterization has contributed to a renewal of German literature."

1973   Patrick White (Australia) "for an epic and psychological narrative art which has introduced a new continent into literature."

1974   Eyvind Johnson (Sweden) "for a narrative art, far-seeing in lands and ages, in the service of freedom"; **Harry Martinson** (Sweden) "for writings that catch the dewdrop and reflect the cosmos."

1975   Eugenio Montale (Italy) "for his distinctive poetry which, with great artistic sensitivity, has interpreted human values under the sign of an outlook on life with no illusions."

1976   Saul Bellow (U.S.) "for the human understanding and subtle analysis of contemporary culture."

1977   Vincente Aleixandre (Spain) "for a creative poetic writing which illuminates man's condition in the cosmos and in present-day society, at the same time representing the great renewal of the traditions of Spanish poetry between the wars."

1978   Isaac Bashevis Singer (U.S.) "for his impassioned narrative art which, with roots in a Polish-Jewish cultural tradition, brings universal human conditions to life."

1979   Odysseus Elytis (pen name of Odysseus Alepoudhelis) (Greece) "for his poetry, which against the background of Greek tradition, depicts man's struggle for freedom and creativeness."

1980   Czeslaw Milosz (U.S. and Poland) "who with uncompromising clear-sightedness voices man's exposed condition in a world of severe conflicts."

1981   Elias Canetti (Great Britain) "for writings marked by a broad outlook, a wealth of ideas, and artistic power."

1982   Gabriel García Marquez (Colombia) "for his novels and short stories, in which the fantastic and the realistic are combined in a richly composed world of imagination, reflecting a continent's life and conflicts."

1983   William Golding (Great Britain) "for his novels, which illuminate the human condition in the world of today."

1984   Jaroslav Seifert (Czechoslovakia) "for his poetry which, endowed with freshness, sensuality, and rich inventiveness, provides a liberating image of the indomitable spirit and versatility of man."

1985   Claude Simon (France) "who in his novel combines the poet's and the painter's creativeness with a deepened awareness of time in the depiction of the human condition."

1986   Wole Soyinka (Nigeria) "who in a wide cultural perspective and with poetic overtones fashions the drama of existence."

1987   Joseph Brodsky (U.S.) "for his all-embracing authorship imbued with clarity of thought and poetic intensity."

1988   Naguib Mahfouz (Egypt) "who through works rich in nuance, has formed an Arabian narrative art that applies to all mankind."

1989   Camilo José Cela (Spain) a novelist whose "rich and inventive prose, forms a challenging vision of man's vulnerability." His most famous work is *The Family of Pascual Duarte* (1942).

1990   Octavio Paz (Mexico) poet and social essayist. Volumes include *The Labyrinth of Solitude* (1950), *Sunstone* (1957), and *Sor Juana: Or, the Traps of Faith* (1990).

1991   Nadine Gordimer (South Africa) for her "involvement on behalf of literature and free speech in a police state where censorship and persecution of books and people exist."

1992   Derek Walcott (West Indies, b. St. Lucia), poet and playwright whose works evoke the cultural diversity of the Carribean "but through them he speaks to each and every one of us."

1993   Toni Morrison (U.S.), whose novels about racial prejudice are "characterized by visionary force and poetic import."

1994   Kenzaburo Oe (Japan), best known for his accounts of the atomic bombing of Hiroshima. The poetic force of his writing "creates an imagined world where life and myth condense to form a disconcerting picture of the human predicament."

1995   Seamus Heaney (Ireland), poet and essayist, "for works of lyrical beauty and ethical depth, which exalt everyday miracles and the living past."

1996   Wislawa Szymborska (Poland), a poet whose work contemplates the oddities of daily life.

1997   Dario Fo, (Italy), a leftist playwright, best known for biting political satires (*Can't Pay, Won't Pay* and *Accidental Death of an Anarchist*), which have brought threats of censure and condemnation from the Italian government and the Roman Catholic Church.

1998   José Saramago, 75, (Portugal), for his richly imaginative works that often use the supernatural and irrational to address questions of faith. Best known novels include: *Baltasar and Blimunda* (1982), *The Year of the Death of Ricardo Reis* (1984).

1999   See Part I: "The Almanac of the Year"

THE NCAA

The NCAA acts as the governing body of intercollegiate athletics, setting the playing rules for each sport, and eligibility standards for participating athletes. Its other major functions are to conduct championships and maintain historical records.

The organization grew out of a series of meetings convened by President Theodore Roosevelt, who was concerned about the number serious injuries and deaths in college football games. In 1905 alone, 18 players died.

National Collegiate Athletic Association (NCAA)
One NCAA Place
700 W. Washington St.
Indianapolis, Ind. 46204
(317) 917–6222
www.ncaa.org

COLLEGE FOOTBALL

NCAA National Football Champions

For many years, college football selected its unofficial national champion through an arcane structure of bowl games and two press association polls, which often did not agree with each other, creating co-champions.

In 1998, however, the NCAA switched to the Bowl Alliance, in which the top two teams (as determined by the same two polls) meet on the field in a national championship game that rotates annually among the Rose, Fiesta, Orange, and Sugar Bowls. (The teams ranked 3–8 in the polls fill out the slates in the other non-championship bowl game).

The Bowl Alliance produced an undisputed national champion in 1998, when Tennessee completed an undefeated season by running over Florida State 23–16 in the Fiesta Bowl. But the system is far from foolproof. Up until the last week of the season, three teams were undefeated, leaving open the possibility that a team might finish without a loss, but not even get a chance to play in the title game. Kansas State and UCLA both lost in their final games, to prevent such a scenario, but the potential still remains. And had Florida State beaten Tennessee, five teams would have finished the season with just one loss.

Year	Team	Year	Team	Year	Team	Year	Team
1936	Minnesota	1954	Ohio State and	1969	Texas	1986	Penn State
1937	Pittsburgh		UCLA	1970	Nebraska and Texas	1987	Miami (Fla.)
1938	Texas Christian	1955	Oklahoma	1971	Nebraska	1988	Notre Dame
1939	Texas A&M	1955	Oklahoma	1972	USC	1989	Miami (Fla.)
1940	Minnesota	1957	Auburn and	1973	Notre Dame and	1990	Colorado and
1941	Minnesota		Ohio State		Alabama		Georgia Tech
1942	Ohio State	1958	Louisiana State	1974	USC	1991	Miami (Fla.) and
1943	Notre Dame	1959	Syracuse	1975	Oklahoma		Washington
1944	Army	1960	Minnesota	1976	Oklahoma	1992	Alabama
1945	Army	1961	Alabama	1977	Notre Dame	1993	Florida State
1946	Notre Dame	1962	USC	1978	Alabama and USC	1994	Nebraska
1947	Notre Dame	1963	Texas	1979	Alabama	1995	Nebraska
1948	Michigan	1964	Alabama	1980	Georgia	1996	Florida
1949	Notre Dame	1965	Alabama and	1981	Clemson	1997	Michigan and
1950	Oklahoma		Michigan State	1982	Penn State		Nebraska
1951	Tennessee	1966	Notre Dame	1983	Miami (Fla.)	1998	Tennessee
1952	Michigan State	1967	USC	1984	Brigham Young		
1953	Maryland	1968	Ohio State	1985	Oklahoma		

Source: NCAA.

NCAA Football-Major Bowl Games, 1902-99

ROSE BOWL (Pasadena, California)

1902	Michigan 49, Stanford 0	1925	Notre Dame 27, Stanford 10
1916	Washington St. 14, Brown 0	1926	Alabama 20, Washington 19
1917	Oregon 14, Pennsylvania 0	1927	Alabama 7, Stanford 7
1918	Mare Island 19, Camp Lewis 7	1928	Stanford 7, Pittsburgh 6
1919	Great Lakes 17, Mare Island 0	1929	Georgia Tech 8, California 7
1920	Harvard 7, Oregon 6	1930	USC 47, Pittsburgh 14
1921	California 28, Ohio State 0	1931	Alabama 24, Washington State 0
1922	Washington and Jefferson 0, Cal. 0	1932	USC 21, Tulane 12
1923	USC 14, Penn State 3	1933	USC 35, Pittsburgh 0
1924	Navy 14, Washington 14	1934	Columbia 7, Stanford 0
		1935	Alabama 29, Stanford 13

1936	Stanford 7, Southern Methodist 0
1937	Pittsburgh 21, Washington 0
1938	California 13, Alabama 0
1939	USC 7, Duke 0
1940	USC 14, Tennessee 0
1941	Stanford 21, Nebraska 13
1942	Oregon State 20, Duke 16 (at Durham)
1943	Georgia 9, UCLA 0
1944	USC 29, Washington 0
1945	USC 25, Tennessee 0
1946	Alabama 34, USC 14
1947	Illinois 45, UCLA 14
1948	Michigan 49, USC 0
1949	Northwestern 20, California 14
1950	Ohio State 17, California 14
1951	Michigan 14, California 6
1952	Illinois 40, Stanford 7
1953	USC 7, Wisconsin 0
1954	Michigan State 28, UCLA 20
1955	Ohio State 20, USC 7
1956	Michigan State 17, UCLA 14
1957	Iowa 35, Oregon State 19
1959	Iowa 38, California 12
1960	Washington 44, Wisconsin 8
1961	Washington 17, Minnesota 7
1962	Minnesota 21, UCLA 3
1963	USC 42, Wisconsin 37
1964	Illinois 17, Washington 7
1965	Michigan 34, Oregon State 7
1966	UCLA 14, Michigan State 12
1967	Purdue 14, USC 13
1968	USC 14, Indiana 3
1969	Ohio State 27, USC 16
1970	USC 10, Michigan 3
1971	Stanford 27, Ohio State 17
1972	Stanford 13, Michigan 12
1973	USC 42, Ohio State 17
1974	Ohio State 42, USC 21
1975	USC 18, Ohio State 17
1976	UCLA 23, Ohio State 10
1977	USC 14, Michigan 6
1978	Washington 27, Michigan 20
1979	USC 17, Michigan 10
1980	USC 17, Ohio State 16
1981	Michigan 23, Washington 6
1982	Washington 28, Iowa 0
1983	UCLA 24, Michigan 14
1984	UCLA 45, Illinois 9
1985	USC 20, Ohio State 17
1986	UCLA 45, Iowa 28
1987	Arizona State 22, Michigan 15
1988	Michigan State 20, USC 17
1989	Michigan 22, USC 14
1990	USC 17, Michigan 10
1991	Washington 46, Iowa 34
1992	Washington 34, Michigan 14
1993	Michigan 38, Washington 31
1994	Wisconsin 21, UCLA 16
1995	Penn State 38, Oregon 20
1996	USC 41, Northwestern 32
1997	Ohio State 20, Arizona State 17
1998	Michigan 21, Washington State 16
1999	Wisconsin 38, UCLA 31

COTTON BOWL (Dallas, Texas)

1937	Texas Christian 16, Marquette 6
1938	Rice 28, Colorado 14
1939	St. Mary's 20, Texas Tech 13
1940	Clemson 6, Boston College 3
1941	Texas A&M 13, Fordham 12
1942	Alabama 29, Texas A&M 21
1943	Texas 14, Georgia Tech 7
1944	Texas 7, Randolph Field 7
1945	Oklahoma A&M 34, Texas Christian 0
1946	Texas 40, Missouri 27
1947	Arkansas 0, Louisiana State 0
1948	Southern Methodist 13, Penn State 13
1949	Southern Methodist 21, Oregon 13
1950	Rice 27, North Carolina 13
1951	Tennessee 20, Texas 14
1952	Kentucky 20, Texas Christian 7
1953	Texas 16, Tennessee 0
1954	Rice 28, Alabama 0
1955	Georgia Tech 14, Arkansas 6
1956	Mississippi 14, Texas Christian 13
1957	Texas Christian 28, Syracuse 27
1958	Navy 20, Rice 7
1959	Texas Christian 0, Air Force 0
1960	Syracuse 23, Texas 14
1961	Duke 7, Arkansas 6
1962	Texas 12, Mississippi 7
1963	Louisiana State 13, Texas 0
1964	Texas 28, Navy 6
1965	Arkansas 10, Nebraska 7
1966	Louisiana State 14, Arkansas 7
1967	Georgia 24, Southern Methodist 9
1968	Texas A&M 20, Alabama 16
1969	Texas 36, Tennessee 13
1970	Texas 21, Notre Dame 17
1971	Notre Dame 24, Texas 11
1972	Penn State 30, Texas 6
1973	Texas 17, Alabama 13
1974	Nebraska 19, Texas 3
1975	Penn State 41, Baylor 20
1976	Arkansas 31, Georgia 10
1977	Houston 30, Maryland 21
1978	Notre Dame 38, Texas 10
1979	Notre Dame 35, Houston 34
1980	Houston 17, Nebraska 14
1981	Alabama 30, Baylor 2
1982	Texas 14, Alabama 12
1983	Southern Methodist 7, Pittsburgh 3
1984	Georgia 10, Texas 9
1985	Boston College 45, Houston 28
1986	Texas A&M 36, Auburn 16
1987	Ohio State 28, Texas A&M 12
1988	Texas A&M 35, Notre Dame 10
1989	UCLA 17, Arkansas 3
1990	Tennessee 31, Arkansas 27
1991	Miami (Fla.) 46, Texas 3
1992	Florida St. 10, Texas A&M 2
1993	Notre Dame 28, Texas A&M 3
1994	Notre Dame 24, Texas A&M 21
1995	USC 55, Texas Tech 14
1996	Colorado 38, Oregon 6
1997	Brigham Young 19, Kansas State 15
1998	UCLA 29, Texas A&M 23
1999	Texas 38, Mississippi State 11

ORANGE BOWL (Miami, Florida)

1935	Bucknell 26, Miami (Fla.) 0
1936	Catholic U. 20, Mississippi 19
1937	Duquesne 13, Mississippi State 12
1938	Auburn 6, Michigan State 0
1939	Tennessee 17, Oklahoma 0
1940	Georgia Tech 21, Misouri 7
1941	Mississippi State 14, Georgetown 7
1942	Georgia 40, Texas Christian 26
1943	Alabama 37, Boston College 21
1944	Louisiana State 19, Texas A&M 14
1945	Tulsa 26, Georgia Tech 12
1946	Miami (Fla.) 13, Holy Cross 6
1947	Rice 8, Tennessee 0
1948	Georgia Tech 20, Kansas 14
1949	Texas 41, Georgia 28
1950	Santa Clara 21, Kentucky 13
1951	Clemson 15, Miami (Fla.) 14
1952	Georgia Tech 20, Baylor 14

1953	Alabama 61, Syracuse 6
1954	Oklahoma 7, Maryland 0
1955	Duke 34, Nebraska 7
1956	Oklahoma 20, Maryland 6
1957	Colorado 27, Clemson 21
1958	Oklahoma 48, Duke 21
1959	Oklahoma 21, Syracuse 6
1960	Georgia 14, Missouri 0
1961	Missouri 21, Navy 14
1962	Louisiana State 25, Colorado 7
1963	Alabama 17, Oklahoma 0
1964	Nebraska 13, Auburn 7
1965	Texas 21, Alabama 17
1966	Alabama 39, Nebraska 28
1967	Florida 27, Georgia Tech 12
1968	Oklahoma 26, Tennessee 24
1969	Penn State 15, Kansas 14
1970	Penn State 10, Missouri 3
1971	Nebraska 17, Louisiana State 12
1972	Nebraska 38, Alabama 6
1973	Nebraska 40, Notre Dame 6
1974	Penn State 16, Louisiana State 9
1975	Notre Dame 13, Alabama 11
1976	Oklahoma 14, Michigan 6
1977	Ohio State 27, Colorado 10
1978	Arkansas 31, Oklahoma 6
1979	Oklahoma 31, Nebraska 21
1980	Oklahoma 24, Florida State 7
1981	Oklahoma 18, Florida State 17
1982	Clemson 22, Nebraska 15
1983	Nebraska 21, Louisiana State 20
1984	Miami (Fla.) 31, Nebraska 30
1985	Washington 28, Oklahoma 17
1986	Oklahoma 25, Penn State 10
1987	Oklahoma 42, Arkansas 8
1988	Miami (Fla.) 20, Oklahoma 14
1989	Miami (Fla.) 23, Nebraska 3
1990	Notre Dame 21, Colorado 6
1991	Colorado 10, Notre Dame 9
1992	Miami (Fla.) 22, Nebraska 0
1993	Florida State 27, Nebraska 14
1994	Florida State 18, Nebraska 16
1995	Nebraska 24, Miami 17
1996	Florida State 31, Notre Dame 26
1997	Nebraska 41, Virginia Tech 21
1998	Nebraska 42, Tennessee 17
1999	Florida 31, Syracuse 10

SUGAR BOWL (New Orleans, Louisiana)

1935	Tulane 20, Temple 14
1936	Texas Christian 3, Louisiana State 2
1937	Santa Clara 21, Louisiana State 14
1938	Santa Clara 6, Louisiana State 0
1939	Texas Christian 15, Carnegie Tech 7
1940	Texas A&M 14, Tulane 13
1941	Boston College 19, Tennessee 13
1942	Fordham 2, Missouri 0

1943	Tennessee 14, Tulsa 7
1944	Georgia Tech 20, Tulsa 18
1945	Duke 29, Alabama 26
1946	Oklahoma A&M 33, St. Mary's (Colo.) 13
1947	Georgia 20, North Carolina 10
1948	Texas 27, Alabama 7
1949	Oklahoma 14, North Carolina 6
1950	Oklahoma 35, Louisiana State 0
1951	Kentucky 13, Oklahoma 7
1952	Maryland 28, Tennessee 13
1953	Georgia Tech 24, Mississippi 7
1954	Georgia Tech 42, West Virginia 19
1955	Navy 21, Mississippi 0
1956	Georgia Tech 7, Pittsburgh 0
1957	Baylor 13, Tennessee 7
1958	Mississippi 39, Texas 7
1959	Louisiana State 7, Clemson 0
1960	Mississippi 21, Louisiana State 0
1961	Mississippi 14, Rice 6
1962	Alabama 10, Arkansas 3
1963	Mississippi 17, 13
1964	Alabama 12, Mississippi 7
1965	Louisiana State 13, Syracuse 10
1966	Missouri 20, Florida 18
1967	Alabama 34, Nebraska 7
1968	Louisiana State 20, Wyoming 13
1969	Arkansas 16, Georgia 2
1970	Mississippi 27, Arkansas 22
1971	Tennessee 34, Air Force 13
1972	Oklahoma 40, Auburn 22
1973	Notre Dame 24, Alabama 23
1974	Nebraska 13, Florida 10
1975	Alabama 13, Penn State 7
1977	Pittsburgh 27, Georgia 3
1978	Alabama 35, Ohio State 6
1979	Alabama 14, Penn State
1980	Alabama 24, Arkansas 9
1981	Georgia 17, Notre Dame 10
1982	Pittsburgh 24, Georgia 20
1983	Penn State 27, Georgia 23
1984	Auburn 9, Michigan 7
1985	Nebraska 28, Louisiana State 10
1986	Tennessee 35, Miami (Fla.) 7
1987	Nebraska 30, Louisiana State 15
1988	Syracuse 16, Auburn 16
1989	Florida State 13, Auburn 7
1990	Miami (Fla.) 33, Alabama 25
1991	Tennessee 23, Virginina 22
1992	Notre Dame 39, Florida 28
1993	Alabama 34, Miami 13
1994	Florida 41, West Virginia 7
1995	Florida State 23, Florida 17
1996	Virginia Tech 28, Texas 10
1997	Florida 52, Florida State 20
1998	Florida State 31, Ohio State 14
1999	Ohio State 24, Texas A&M 14

NCAA Football Career Leaders

CAREER POINTS (Nonkickers)				CAREER POINTS (Kickers)				
Player, Team	Years	TD	Pts.	Player, Team	Years	PAT	TD	Pts.
Ricky Williams, Texas	1995–98	75	452	Roman Anderson, Houston	1988–91	213	70	423
Anthony Thomson, Indiana	1968–69	65	394	Carlos Huerta, Miami (Fla.)	1988–91	178	73	397
Marshall Faulk, San Diego St.	1991–93	62	376	Jason Elam, Hawaii	1988–92	158	79	395
Tony Dorsett, Pittsburgh	1973–76	59	356	Derek Schmidt, Florida St.	1984–87	174	73	393
Glenn Davis, Army	1943–46	59	354	Kris Brown, Nebraska	1995–98	217	57	388
Art Luppino, Arizona	1953–56	48	337	Jeff Hall, Tennessee	1995–98	188	61	371
Troy Edwards, La. Tech.	1996–98	57	344	Luis Zendejas, Arizona St.	1981–84	134	78	368
Travis Prentice, Miami (Ohio)	1996–98	57	342	Jeff Jaeger, Washington	1983–86	118	80	358
Steve Owens, Oklahoma	1947–69	56	336	John Lee, UCLA	1982–85	116	79	353
Wilford White, Arizona St.	1947–50	48	327	Max Zendejas, Arizona	1982–85	122	77	353
Barry Sanders, Oklahoma St.	1986–88	54	324	Kevin Butler, Georgia	1981–84	122	77	353

RUSHING, Career yards				RECEIVING, Career catches			
Player, Team	Years	Carries	Yards	Player, Team	Years	Catches	Yards
Ricky Williams, Texas	1995–98	1,011	6,279	Geoff Noisy, Nevada	1995–98	295	4,249
Tony Dorsett, Pittsburgh	1973–76	1,074	6,082	Troy Edwards, Louisiana Tech.	1996–98	280	4,352
Charles White, USC	1976–79	1,023	5,598	Aaron Turner, Pacific (Calif.)	1988–91	266	4,345
Herschel Walker, Georgia	1980–82	994	5,259	Chad Mackey, Lousiana Tech.	1988–91	264	3,789
Archie Griffin, Ohio State	1972–75	845	5,177	Terance Mathis, New Mexico	1988–92	263	4,254
Darren Lewis, Texas A&M	1987–90	909	5,012	Mark Templeton, Long Beach State	1984–87	262	1,969
Anthony Thomson, Indiana	1986–89	1,089	4,965	Howard Twilley, Tulsa	1981–84	261	3,343
George Rogers, So. Carolina	1977–80	902	4,958	Marcus Harris, Wyoming	1983–86	259	4,518
Trevor Cobb, Rice	1989–92	1,091	4,948	David Williams, Illinois	1982–85	245	3,195
Paul Palmer, Temple	1983–86	948	4,895	Brandon Stokley, SW Louisiana	1995–98	241	3,702

PASSING, Career yards							
Player, Team	Years	Att.	Comp.	Int.	Pct.	Yards	TD
Ty Detmer, Brigham Young	1988–91	1,530	958	65	.626	15,031	121
Todd Santos, San Diego State	1984–87	1,484	910	57	.613	11,425	70
Peyton Manning, Tennessee	1994–87	1,381	863	33	.625	11,201	89
Eric Zeier, Georgia	1991–94	1,402	838	37	.598	11,153	67
Alex Van Pelt, Pittsburgh	1989–92	1,463	845	59	.578	10,913	64
Danny Wuerffel, Florida	1996–96	1,170	708	42	.605	10,875	114
Kevin Sweeney, Fresno State	1982–86	1,336	731	48	.547	10,623	66
Doug Flutie, Boston College	1981–84	1,270	677	54	.533	10,579	67
Steve Stenstrom, Stanford	1991–94	1,320	833	36	.631	10,531	72
Brian McClure, Bowling Green	1982–85	1,427	900	58	.631	10,280	63

Heisman Memorial Trophy

The Heisman Trophy honors the outstanding college football player in the U.S. Presented by the Downtown Athletic Club of New York, the award is named for John Heisman, former player, coach, and club director.

Year	Player	College	Pos.	Year	Player	College	Pos.
1935	Jay Berwanger	Chicago	HB	1967	Gary Beban	UCLA	QB
1936	Larry Kelley	Yale	E	1968	O.J. Simpson	USC	HB
1937	Clint Frank	Yale	HB	1969	Steve Owens	Oklahoma	HB
1938	Davey O'Brien	Texas Christian	QB	1970	Jim Plunkett	Stanford	QB
1939	Nile Kinnick	Iowa	HB	1971	Pat Sullivan	Auburn	QB
1940	Tom Harmon	Michigan	HB	1972	Johnny Rodgers	Nebraska	FL
1941	Bruce Smith	Minnesota	HB	1973	John Cappelletti	Penn State	HB
1942	Frank Sinkwich	Georgia	HB	1974	Archie Griffin	Ohio State	HB
1943	Angelo Bertelli	Notre Dame	QB	1975	Archie Griffin	Ohio State	HB
1944	Les Horvath	Ohio State	QB	1976	Tony Dorsett	Pittsburgh	HB
1945	Doc Blanchard	Army	FB	1977	Earl Campbell	Texas	HB
1946	Glenn Davis	Army	HB	1978	Billy Sims	Oklahoma	HB
1947	John Lujack	Notre Dame	QB	1979	Charles White	USC	HB
1948	Doak Walker	SMU	HB	1980	George Rogers	South Carolina	HB
1949	Leon Hart	Notre Dame	E	1981	Marcus Allen	USC	HB
1950	Vic Janowicz	Ohio State	HB	1982	Herschel Walker	Georgia	HB
1951	Dick Kazmaier	Princeton	HB	1983	Mike Rozier	Nebraska	HB
1952	Billy Vessels	Oklahoma	HB	1984	Doug Flutie	Boston College	QB
1953	John Lattner	Notre Dame	HB	1985	Bo Jackson	Auburn	HB
1954	Alan Ameche	Wisconsin	FB	1986	Vinny Testaverde	Miami (Fla.)	QB
1955	Howard Cassady	Ohio State	HB	1987	Tim Brown	Notre Dame	WR
1956	Paul Hornung	Notre Dame	QB	1988	Barry Sanders	Oklahoma State	RB
1957	John Crow	Texas A&M	HB	1989	Andre Ware	Houston	QB
1958	Pete Dawkins	Army	HB	1990	Ty Detmer	Brigham Young	QB
1959	Billy Cannon	Louisiana State	HB	1991	Desmond Howard	Michigan	WR
1960	Joe Bellino	Navy	HB	1992	Gino Toretta	Miami	QB
1961	Ernie Davis	Syracuse	HB	1993	Charlie Ward	Florida State	QB
1962	Terry Baker	Oregon State	QB	1994	Rashaan Salaam	Colorado	RB
1963	Roger Staubach	Navy	QB	1995	Eddie George	Ohio State	RB
1964	John Huarte	Notre Dame	QB	1996	Danny Wuerffel	Florida	QB
1965	Mike Garrett	USC	HB	1997	Charles Woodson	Michigan	CB
1966	Steve Spurrier	Florida	QB	1998	Ricky Williams	Texas	RB

COLLEGE BASKETBALL

NCAA Division I Men's Basketball Championship Final Four Results

Year	Champion	Score	Runner-up	Third place	Fourth place	Champion coach
1939	Oregon	46–33	Ohio State	Oklahoma[1]	Villanova[1]	Howard Hobson
1940	Indiana	60–42	Kansas	Duquesne[1]	USC [1]	Branch McCracken
1941	Wisconsin	39–34	Washington St.	Pittsburgh[1]	Arkansas[1]	Harold Foster
1942	Stanford	53–38	Dartmouth	Colorado[1]	Kentucky[1]	Everett Dean
1943	Wyoming	46–34	Georgetown	Texas[1]	DePaul[1]	Everett Shelton
1944	Utah	42–40[2]	Dartmouth	Iowa State[1]	Ohio State [1]	Vadal Peterson
1945	Oklahoma State	49–45	NYU	Arkansas[1]	Ohio State[1]	Henry Iba
1946	Oklahoma State	43–40	North Carolina	Ohio St.	California	Henry Iba
1947	Holy Cross	58–47	Oklahoma	Texas	CCNY	Alvin Julian
1948	Kentucky	58–42	Baylor	Holy Cross	Kansas State	Adolph Rupp
1949	Kentucky	46–36	Oklahoma State	Illinois	Oregon State	Adolph Rupp
1950	CCNY	71–68	Bradley	North Carolina State	Baylor	Nat Holman
1951	Kentucky	68–58	Kansas State	Illinois	Oklahoma State	Aldolph Rupp
1952	Kansas	80–63	St. John's	Illinois	Santa Clara	Forrest Allen
1953	Indiana	69–68	Kansas	Washington	Louisiana State	Branch McCracken
1954	LaSalle	92–76	Bradley	Penn State	USC	Kenneth Loeffler
1955	San Francisco	77–63	La Salle	Colorado	Iowa	Phil Woolpert
1956	San Francisco	83–71	Iowa	Temple	Southern Methodist	Phil Woolpert
1957	North Carolina	54–53[3]	Kansas	San Francisco	Michigan State	Frank McGuire
1958	Kentucky	84–72	Seattle	Temple	Kansas State	Adolph Rupp
1959	California	71–70	West Virginia	Cincinnati	Louisville	Pete Newell
1960	Ohio State	75–55	California	Cincinnati	NYU	Fred Taylor
1961	Cincinnati	70–65[2]	Ohio State	St. Joe's[4]	Utah	Edwin Jucker
1962	Cincinnati	71–59	Ohio State	Wake Forest	UCLA	Edwin Jucker
1963	Loyola (Ill.)	60–58[2]	Cincinnati	Duke	Utah	George Ireland
1964	UCLA	98–83	Duke	Michigan	Kansas State	John Wooden
1965	UCLA	91–80	Michigan	Princeton	Wichita State	John Wooden
1966	UTEP	72–65	Kentucky	Duke	Utah	Don Haskins
1967	UCLA	79–64	Dayton	Houston	North Carolina	John Wooden
1968	UCLA	78–55	North Carolina	Ohio State	Houston	John Wooden
1969	UCLA	92–72	Purdue	Drake	North Carolina	John Wooden
1970	UCLA	80–69	Jacksonville	New Mexico St.	St. Bonaventure	John Wooden
1971	UCLA	68–62	Villanova[4]	Western Kentucky[4]	Kansas	John Wooden
1972	UCLA	81–76	Florida State	North Carolina	Louisville	John Wooden
1973	UCLA	87–66	Memphis State	Indiana	Providence	John Wooden
1974	North Carolina State	76–64	Marquette	UCLA	Kansas	Norm Sloan
1975	UCLA	92–85	Kentucky	Louisville	Syracuse	John Wooden
1976	Indiana	86–68	Michigan	UCLA	Rutgers	Bob Knight
1977	Marquette	67–59	North Carolina	UNLV	UNC-Charlotte	Al McGuire
1978	Kentucky	94–88	Duke	Arkansas	Notre Dame	Joe Hall
1979	Michigan State	75–64	Indiana State	DePaul	Pennsylvania	Jud Heathcote
1980	Louisville	59–54	UCLA[4]	Purdue	Iowa	Denny Crum
1981	Indiana	63–50	North Carolina	Virginia	Louisiana State	Bob Knight
1982	North Carolina	63–62	Georgetown	Houston[1]	Louisville[1]	Dean Smith
1983	North Carolina State	54–52	Houston	Georgia[1]	Louisville[1]	Jim Valvano
1984	Georgetown	84–75	Houston	Kentucky[1]	Virginia[1]	John Thompson
1985	Villanova	66–64	Georgetown	St. John's[1]	Memphis[1,4]	Rollie Massimino
1986	Louisville	72–69	Duke	Kansas[1]	Louisiana State[1]	Denny Crum
1987	Indiana	74–73	Syracuse	UNLV[1]	Providence[1]	Bob Knight
1988	Kansas	83–79	Oklahoma	Arizona[1]	Duke[1]	Larry Brown
1989	Michigan	80–79[2]	Seton Hall	Illinois[1]	Duke[1]	Steve Fisher
1990	UNLV	103–73	Duke	Georgia Tech[1]	Arkansas[1]	Jerry Tarkanian
1991	Duke	72–65	Kansas	UNLV[1]	North Carolina[1]	Mike Krzyzewski
1992	Duke	71–51	Michigan	Cincinnati[1]	Indiana[1]	Mike Krzyzewski
1993	North Carolina	77–71	Michigan	Kansas[1]	Kentucky[1]	Dean Smith
1994	Arkansas	76–70	Duke	Arizona[1]	Florida[1]	Nolan Richardson
1995	UCLA	89–78	Arkansas	North Carolina[1]	Oklahoma State[1]	Jim Harrick
1996	Kentucky	76–67	Syracuse	Massachusetts[1,4]	Mississippi State[1]	Rick Pitino
1997	Arizona	84–79	Kentucky	Minnesota[1]	North Carolina[1]	Lute Olson
1998	Kentucky	78–69	Utah	North Carolina[1]	Stanford[1]	Tubby Smith
1999	Connecticut	77–74	Duke	Michigan State[1]	Ohio State[1]	Jim Calhoun

1. Tied for third place. 2. Overtime. 3. Triple overtime. 4. Later declared ineligible.

National Invitation Tournament Champions

Year	Champion	Year	Champion	Year	Champion	Year	Champion
1938	Temple	1954	Holy Cross	1970	Marquette	1986	Ohio State
1939	Long Island Univ.	1955	Duquesne	1971	North Carolina	1987	Southern Mississippi
1940	Colorado	1956	Louisville	1972	Maryland	1988	Connecticut
1941	Long Island Univ.	1957	Bradley	1973	Virginia Tech	1989	St. John's
1942	West Virginia	1958	Xavier (Ohio)	1974	Purdue	1990	Vanderbilt
1943	St. John's	1959	St. John's	1975	Princeton	1991	Stanford
1944	St. John's	1960	Bradley	1976	Kentucky	1992	Virginia
1945	DePaul	1961	Providence	1977	St. Bonaventure	1993	Minnesota
1946	Kentucky	1962	Dayton	1978	Texas	1994	Villanova
1947	Utah	1963	Providence	1979	Indiana	1995	Virginia Tech
1948	St. Louis	1964	Bradley	1980	Virginia	1996	Nebraska
1949	San Francisco	1965	St. John's	1981	Tulsa	1997	Michigan
1950	CCNY	1966	BYU	1982	Bradley	1998	Minnesota
1951	BYU	1967	Southern Illinois	1983	Fresno State	1999	California
1952	LaSalle	1968	Dayton	1984	Michigan		
1953	Seton Hall	1969	Temple	1985	UCLA		

NCAA Basketball Career Leaders

SCORING

Player, Team	Points
Pete Maravich, Louisiana State	3,667
Freeman Williams, Portland State	3,249
Lionel Simmons, LaSalle	3,217
Alphonzo Ford, Mississippi Valley	3,165
Harry Kelly, Texas Southern	3,066
Hersey Hawkins, Bradley	3,008
Oscar Robertson, Cincinnati	2,973
Danny Manning, Kansas	2,951
Alfredrick Hughes, Loyola (Ill.)	2,914
Elvin Hayes, Houston	2,884

ASSISTS

Player, Team	Assists
Bobby Hurley, Duke	1,076
Chris Corchiani, N.Carolina State	1,038
Keith Jennings, East Tennessee St.	983
Sherman Douglas, Syracuse	960
Tony Miller, Marquette	956
Greg Anthony, UNLV	950
Gary Payton, Oregon State	938
Orlando Smart, San Francisco	902
Andre Lafleur, Northeastern	894
Jim Les, Bradley	884

REBOUNDS

Player, team	Rebounds
Tom Gola, LaSalle	2,201
Joe Holup, George Washington	2,030
Charlie Slack, Marshall	1,916
Ed Conlin, Fordham	1,884
Dickie Hemric, Wake Forest	1,802
Paul Silas, Creighton	1,751
Art Quimby, Connecticut	1,716
Jerry Harper, Alabama	1,688
Jeff Cohen, William and Mary	1,679
Steve Hamilton, Morehead State	1,675

FIELD GOAL PERCENTAGE

Player, team	Pct.
Ricky Nedd, Appalachian State	69.0
Stephen Scheffler, Purdue	68.5
Steve Johnson, Oregon State	67.8
Murray Brown, Florida State	66.8
Lee Campbell, Southwest MO St.	66.5
Warren Kidd, Middle Tenn. State	66.4
Todd MacCulloch, Univ. of Washington	66.4
Joe Senser, West Chester	66.2
Kevin Magee, Univ. of California, Irvine	65.6
Orlando Phillips, Pepperdine	65.4

OTHER MEN'S NCAA CHAMPIONS

CROSS COUNTRY					SOCCER			
1938	Indiana	1958	Michigan State	1979	UTEP	1959	St. Louis	1977	Hartwick
1939	Michigan State	1959	Michigan State	1980	UTEP	1960	St. Louis	1978	Vacated
1940	Indiana	1960	Houston	1981	UTEP	1961	West Chester	1979	So. Illinois Univ.,
1941	Rhode Island	1961	Oregon State	1982	Wisconsin	1962	St. Louis		at Edwardsville
1942	Indiana	1962	San Jose State	1983	Vacated	1963	St. Louis	1980	San Francisco
1943	No Meet	1963	San Jose State	1984	Arkansas	1964	Navy	1981	Connecticut
1944	Drake	1964	W. Michigan	1985	Wisconsin	1965	St. Louis	1982	Indiana
1945	Drake	1965	W. Michigan	1986	Arkansas	1966	San Franciso	1983	Indiana
1946	Drake	1966	Villanova	1987	Arkansas	1967	Michigan State,	1984	Clemson
1947	Penn State	1967	Villanova	1988	Wisconsin		St. Louis	1985	UCLA
1948	Michigan State	1968	Villanova	1989	Iowa State	1968	Maryland	1986	Duke
1949	Michigan State	1969	UTEP	1990	Arkansas		Michigan State	1987	Clemson
1950	Penn State	1970	Villanova	1991	Arkansas	1969	St. Louis	1988	Indiana
1951	Syracuse	1971	Oregon	1992	Arkansas	1970	St. Louis	1989	Santa Clara,
1952	Michigan State	1972	Tennessee	1993	Arkansas	1971	Vacated		Virginia
1953	Kansas	1973	Oregon	1994	Iowa State	1972	St. Louis	1990	UCLA
1954	Oklahoma State	1974	Oregon	1995	Arkansas	1973	St. Louis	1991	Virginia
1955	Michigan State	1975	UTEP	1996	Stanford	1974	Howard	1992	Virginia
1956	Michigan State	1976	UTEP	1997	Stanford	1975	San Francisco	1993	Virginia
1957	Notre Dame	1977	Oregon	1998	Arkansas	1976	San Francisco	1994	Virginia
		1978	UTEP					1995	Wisconsin

1996	St. John's (N.Y.)
1997	UCLA
1998	Indiana

WATER POLO

1969	UCLA
1970	UC Irvine
1971	UCLA
1972	UCLA
1973	California
1974	California
1975	California
1976	Stanford
1977	California
1978	Stanford
1979	UC Santa Barbara
1980	Stanford
1981	Stanford
1982	UC Irvine
1983	California
1984	California
1985	Stanford
1986	Stanford
1987	California
1988	California
1989	California
1990	California
1991	California
1992	California
1993	Stanford
1994	Stanford
1995	UCLA
1996	UCLA
1997	Pepperdine
1998	USC

FENCING*

1941	Northwestern
1942	Ohio State
1943	No Meet
1944	No Meet
1945	No Meet
1946	No Meet
1947	NYU
1948	CCNY
1949	Army, Rutgers
1950	Navy
1951	Columbia
1952	Columbia
1953	Pennsylvania
1954	Columbia, NYU
1955	Columbia
1956	Illinois
1957	NYU
1958	Illinois
1959	Navy
1960	NYU
1961	NYU
1962	Navy
1963	Columbia
1964	Princeton
1965	Columbia
1966	NYU
1967	NYU
1968	Columbia
1969	Pennsylvania
1970	NYU
1971	NYU, Columbia
1972	Detroit
1973	NYU
1974	NYU
1975	Wayne State
1976	NYU
1977	Notre Dame
1978	Notre Dame
1979	Wayne State
1980	Wayne State
1981	Pennsylvania
1982	Wayne State
1983	Wayne State
1984	Wayne State
1985	Wayne State
1986	Notre Dame
1987	Columbia
1988	Columbia
1989	Columbia

GYMNASTICS

1938	Chicago
1939	Illinois
1940	Illinois
1941	Illinois
1942	Illinois
1943	No Meet
1944	No Meet
1945	No Meet
1946	No Meet
1947	No Meet
1948	Penn State
1949	Temple
1950	Illinois
1951	Florida State
1952	Florida State
1953	Penn State
1954	Penn State
1955	Illinois
1956	Illinois
1957	Penn State
1958	Michigan State, Illinois
1959	Penn State
1960	Penn State
1961	Penn State
1962	USC
1963	Michigan
1964	Southern Illinois
1965	Penn State
1966	Southern Illinois
1967	Southern Illinois
1968	California
1969	Iowa
1970	Michigan
1971	Iowa State
1972	Southern Illinois
1973	Iowa State
1974	Iowa State
1975	California
1976	Penn State
1977	Indiana State Oklahoma
1978	Oklahoma
1979	Nebraska
1980	Nebraska
1981	Nebraska
1982	Nebraska
1983	Nebraska
1984	UCLA
1985	Ohio State
1986	Arizona State
1987	UCLA
1988	Nebraska
1989	Illinois
1990	Nebraska
1991	Oklahoma
1992	Stanford
1993	Stanford
1994	Nebraska
1995	Stanford
1996	Ohio State
1997	California
1998	California
1999	Michigan

ICE HOCKEY

1948	Michigan
1949	Boston College
1950	Colorado College
1951	Michigan
1952	Michigan
1953	Michigan
1954	Rensselaer
1955	Michigan
1956	Michigan
1957	Colorado College
1958	Denver
1959	North Dakota
1960	Denver
1961	Denver
1962	Michigan Tech.
1963	North Dakota
1964	Michigan
1965	Michigan Tech
1966	Michigan State
1967	Cornell
1968	Denver

1969	Denver
1970	Cornell
1971	Boston University
1972	Boston University
1973	Wisconsin
1974	Minnesota
1975	Michigan Tech
1976	Minnesota
1977	Wisconsin
1978	Boston University
1979	Minnesota
1980	North Dakota
1981	Wisconsin
1982	North Dakota
1983	Wisconsin
1984	Bowling Green
1985	Rensselaer
1986	Michigan State
1987	North Dakota
1988	Lake Superior St.
1989	Harvard
1990	Wisconsin
1991	N. Michigan
1992	Lake Superior St.
1993	Maine
1994	Lake Superior St.
1995	Boston University
1996	Michigan
1997	North Dakota
1998	Michigan
1999	Maine

SWIMMING

1937	Michigan
1938	Michigan
1939	Michigan
1940	Michigan
1941	Michigan
1942	Yale
1943	Ohio State
1944	Yale
1945	Ohio State
1946	Ohio State
1947	Ohio State
1948	Michigan
1949	Ohio State
1950	Ohio State
1951	Yale
1952	Ohio State
1953	Yale
1954	Ohio State
1955	Ohio State
1956	Ohio State
1957	Michigan
1958	Michigan
1959	Michigan
1960	USC
1961	Michigan
1962	Ohio State
1963	USC
1964	USC
1965	USC
1966	USC
1967	Stanford
1968	Indiana
1969	Indiana
1970	Indiana
1971	Indiana
1972	Indiana
1973	Indiana
1974	USC
1975	USC
1976	USC
1977	USC
1978	Tennessee
1979	California
1980	California
1981	Texas
1982	UCLA
1983	Florida
1984	Florida
1985	Stanford
1986	Stanford
1987	Stanford
1988	Texas
1989	Texas
1990	Texas
1991	Texas

1992	Stanford
1993	Stanford
1994	Stanford
1995	Michigan
1996	Texas
1997	Auburn
1998	Stanford
1999	Auburn

WRESTLING

1928	Oklahoma State[1]
1929	Oklahoma State[1]
1930	Oklahoma State[1]
1931	Oklahoma State[1]
1932	Indiana
1933	Oklahoma State[1], Iowa State[1]
1934	Oklahoma State
1935	Oklahoma State
1936	Oklahoma
1937	Oklahoma State
1938	Oklahoma State
1939	Oklahoma State
1940	Oklahoma State
1941	Oklahoma State
1942	Oklahoma State
1943	No Tournament
1944	No Tournament
1945	No Tournament
1946	Oklahoma State
1947	Cornell College
1948	Oklahoma State
1949	Oklahoma State
1950	Northern Iowa
1951	Oklahoma
1952	Oklahoma
1953	Penn State
1954	Oklahoma State
1955	Oklahoma State
1956	Oklahoma State
1957	Oklahoma
1958	Oklahoma State
1959	Oklahoma State
1960	Oklahoma
1961	Oklahoma State
1962	Oklahoma State
1963	Oklahoma
1964	Oklahoma State
1965	Iowa State
1966	Oklahoma State
1967	Michigan State
1968	Oklahoma State
1969	Iowa State
1970	Iowa State
1971	Oklahoma State
1972	Iowa State
1973	Iowa State
1974	Oklahoma
1975	Iowa
1976	Iowa
1977	Iowa State
1978	Iowa
1979	Iowa
1980	Iowa
1981	Iowa
1982	Iowa
1983	Iowa
1984	Iowa
1985	Iowa
1986	Iowa
1987	Iowa State
1988	Arizona State
1989	Oklahoma State
1990	Oklahoma State
1991	Iowa
1992	Iowa
1993	Iowa
1994	Oklahoma State
1995	Iowa
1996	Iowa
1997	Iowa
1998	Iowa
1999	Iowa

1. Unofficial champions.

INDOOR TRACK

1965	Missouri
1966	Kansas
1967	USC
1968	Villanova
1969	Kansas
1970	Kansas
1971	Villanova
1972	USC
1973	Manhattan
1974	UTEP
1975	UTEP
1976	UTEP
1977	Washington St.
1978	UTEP
1979	Villanova
1980	UTEP
1981	UTEP
1982	UTEP
1983	SMU
1984	Arkansas
1985	Arkansas
1986	Arkansas
1987	Arkansas
1988	Arkansas
1989	Arkansas
1990	Arkansas
1991	Arkansas
1992	Arkansas
1993	Arkansas
1994	Arkansas
1995	Arkansas
1996	George Mason
1997	Arkansas
1998	Arkansas
1999	Arkansas

OUTDOOR TRACK

1921	Illinois
1922	California
1923	Michigan
1924	No Meet
1925	Stanford
1926	USC
1927	Illinois
1928	Stanford
1929	Ohio State
1930	USC
1931	USC
1932	Indiana
1933	Louisiana State
1934	Stanford
1935	USC
1936	USC
1937	USC
1938	USC
1939	USC
1940	USC
1941	USC
1942	USC
1943	USC
1944	Illinois
1945	Navy
1946	Illinois
1947	Illinois
1948	Minnesota
1949	USC
1950	USC
1951	USC
1952	USC
1953	USC
1954	USC
1955	USC
1956	UCLA
1957	Villanova
1958	USC
1959	Kansas
1960	Kansas
1961	USC
1962	Oregon
1963	USC
1964	Oregon
1965	Oregon, USC
1966	UCLA
1967	USC
1968	USC
1969	San Jose State
1970	BYU, Kansas

*For Fencing champions 1990–97, see "Men's and Women's Titles" on following page.

1971	UCLA
1972	UCLA
1973	UCLA
1974	Tennessee
1975	UTEP
1976	USC
1977	Arizona State
1978	UCLA, UTEP
1979	UTEP
1980	UTEP
1981	UTEP
1982	UTEP
1983	SMU
1984	Oregon
1985	Arkansas
1986	SMU
1987	UCLA
1988	UCLA
1989	Louisiana State
1990	Louisiana State
1991	Tennessee
1992	Arkansas
1993	Arkansas
1994	Arkansas
1995	Arkansas
1996	Arkansas
1997	Arkansas
1998	Arkansas
1999	Arkansas

BASEBALL

1947	California
1948	USC
1949	Texas
1950	Texas
1951	Oklahoma
1952	Holy Cross
1953	Michigan
1954	Missouri
1955	Wake Forest
1956	Minnesota
1957	California
1958	USC
1959	Oklahoma State
1960	Minnesota
1961	USC
1962	Michigan
1963	USC
1964	Minnesota
1965	Arizona State
1966	Ohio State
1967	Arizona State
1968	USC
1969	Arizona State
1970	USC
1971	USC
1972	USC
1973	USC
1974	USC
1975	Texas
1976	Arizona
1977	Arizona State
1978	USC

1979	Cal St. Fullerton
1980	Arizona
1981	Arizona State
1982	Miami (Fla.)
1983	Texas
1984	Cal St. Fullerton
1985	Miami (Fla.)
1986	Arizona
1987	Stanford
1988	Stanford
1989	Wichita State
1990	Georgia
1991	Louisiana State
1992	Pepperdine
1993	Louisiana State
1994	Oklahoma
1995	Cal St. Fullerton
1996	Louisiana State
1997	Louisiana State
1998	USC
1999	Miama (Fla.)

GOLF

1897	Yale
1898	Harvard (spring)
1898	Yale (fall)
1899	Harvard
1900	no tournament
1901	Harvard
1902	Yale (spring)
1903	Harvard
1904	Harvard
1905	Yale
1906	Yale
1907	Yale
1908	Yale
1909	Yale
1910	Yale
1911	Yale
1912	Yale
1913	Yale
1914	Princeton
1915	Yale
1916	Princeton
1917	no tournament
1918	no tournament
1919	Princeton
1920	Princeton
1921	Dartmouth
1922	Princeton
1923	Princeton
1924	Yale
1925	Yale
1926	Yale
1927	Princeton
1928	Princeton
1929	Princeton
1930	Princeton
1931	Yale
1932	Yale
1933	Yale
1934	Michigan
1935	Michigan

1936	Yale
1937	Princeton
1938	Stanford
1939	Stanford
1940	Princeton, Louisiana State
1941	Stanford
1942	Louisiana State, Stanford
1943	Yale
1944	Notre Dame
1945	Ohio State
1946	Stanford
1947	Louisiana State
1948	San Jose State
1949	North Texas
1950	North Texas
1951	North Texas
1952	North Texas
1953	Stanford
1954	SMU
1955	Louisiana State
1956	Houston
1957	Houston
1958	Houston
1959	Houston
1960	Houston
1961	Purdue
1962	Houston
1963	Oklahoma State
1964	Houston
1965	Houston
1966	Houston
1967	Houston
1968	Florida
1969	Houston
1970	Houston
1971	Texas
1972	Texas
1973	Florida
1974	Wake Forest
1975	Wake Forest
1976	Oklahoma
1977	Houston
1978	Oklahoma State
1979	Ohio State
1980	Oklahoma State
1981	Brigham Young
1982	Houston
1983	Oklahoma State
1984	Houston
1985	Houston
1986	Wake Forest
1987	Oklahoma State
1988	UCLA
1989	Oklahoma
1990	Arizona
1991	Oklahoma State
1992	Arizona
1993	Florida
1994	Stanford
1995	Oklahoma State
1996	Arizona State

1997	Pepperdine
1998	UNLV
1999	Georgia

LACROSSE

1971	Cornell
1972	Virginia
1973	Maryland
1974	Johns Hopkins
1975	Maryland
1976	Cornell
1977	Cornell
1978	Johns Hopkins
1979	Johns Hopkins
1980	Johns Hopkins
1981	North Carolina
1982	North Carolina
1983	Syracuse
1984	Johns Hopkins
1985	Johns Hopkins
1986	North Carolina
1987	Johns Hopkins
1988	Syracuse
1989	Syracuse
1990	Syracuse
1991	North Carolina
1992	Princeton
1993	Syracuse
1994	Princeton
1995	Syracuse
1996	Princeton
1997	Princeton
1998	Princeton
1999	Virginia

TENNIS

1946	USC
1947	William & Mary
1948	William & Mary
1949	San Francisco
1950	UCLA
1951	USC
1952	UCLA
1953	UCLA
1954	UCLA
1955	USC
1956	UCLA
1957	Michigan
1958	USC
1959	Notre Dame, Tulane
1960	UCLA
1961	UCLA
1962	USC
1963	USC
1964	USC
1965	UCLA
1966	USC
1967	USC
1968	USC
1969	USC
1970	UCLA
1971	UCLA

1972	Trinity (Tex.)
1973	Stanford
1974	Stanford
1975	UCLA
1976	USC, UCLA
1977	Stanford
1978	Stanford
1979	UCLA
1980	Stanford
1981	Stanford
1982	UCLA
1983	Stanford
1984	UCLA
1985	Georgia
1986	Stanford
1987	Georgia
1988	Stanford
1989	Stanford
1990	Stanford
1991	USC
1992	Stanford
1993	USC
1994	USC
1995	Stanford
1996	Stanford
1997	Stanford
1998	Stanford
1999	Georgia

VOLLEYBALL

1970	UCLA
1971	UCLA
1972	UCLA
1973	San Diego State
1974	UCLA
1975	UCLA
1976	UCLA
1977	USC
1978	Pepperdine
1979	UCLA
1980	USC
1981	UCLA
1982	UCLA
1983	UCLA
1984	UCLA
1985	Pepperdine
1986	Pepperdine
1987	UCLA
1988	USC
1989	UCLA
1990	USC
1991	Cal State Long Beach
1992	Pepperdine
1993	UCLA
1994	Penn State
1995	UCLA
1996	UCLA
1997	Stanford
1998	UCLA
1999	Brigham Young

Men's and Women's Titles

FENCING

1990	Penn State
1991	Penn State
1992	Columbia
1993	Columbia
1994	Notre Dame
1995	Penn State
1996	Penn State
1997	Penn State
1998	Penn State
1999	Penn State

RIFLE

1954	Seattle
1955	Dartmouth
1956	Dartmouth
1957	Colorado
1958	Denver
1959	Denver
1960	Denver
1961	Middlebury
1962	Colorado

1963	Colorado
1964	Dartmouth
1965	Utah
1966	W. Colorado
1967	Wyoming
1968	Denver
1969	Dartmouth
1970	Dartmouth
1971	Colorado
1972	Denver
1973	Wyoming
1974	Wyoming
1975	Vermont
1976	Colorado
1977	Wyoming
1978	Wyoming
1979	Utah
1980	Tennessee Tech
1981	Tennessee Tech
1982	Tennessee Tech
1983	West Virginia
1984	West Virginia

1985	Murray State
1986	West Virginia
1987	Murray State
1988	West Virginia
1989	West Virginia
1990	West Virginia
1991	West Virginia
1992	West Virginia
1993	West Virginia
1994	Alaska Fairbanks
1995	West Virginia
1996	West Virginia
1997	West Virginia
1998	West Virginia
1999	Alaska Fairbanks

SKIING

1954	Denver
1955	Denver
1956	Denver
1957	Denver
1958	Dartmouth

1959	Colorado
1960	Colorado
1961	Denver
1962	Denver
1963	Denver
1964	Denver
1965	Denver
1966	Denver
1967	Denver
1968	Wyoming
1969	Denver
1970	Denver
1971	Denver
1972	Colorado
1973	Colorado
1974	Colorado
1975	Colorado
1976	Dartmouth
1977	Colorado
1978	Colorado
1979	Colorado
1980	Vermont

1981	Utah
1982	Colorado
1983	Utah
1984	Utah
1985	Wyoming
1986	Utah
1987	Utah
1988	Utah
1989	Vermont
1990	Vermont
1991	Colorado
1992	Vermont
1993	Utah
1994	Vermont
1995	Colorado
1996	Utah
1997	Utah
1998	Colorado
1999	Colorado

NCAA WOMEN'S MAJOR SPORTS

Division I Women's Basketball Championship

Year	Champion	Coach	Outstanding player	Score	Runner-Up
1982	Louisiana Tech	Sonja Hogg	Janice Lawrence	76–62	Cheyney
1983	USC	Linda Sharp	Cheryl Miller	69–67	Louisiana Tech
1984	USC	Linda Sharp	Cheryl Miller	72–61	Tennessee
1985	Old Dominion	Marianne Stanley	Tracy Claxton	70–65	Georgia
1986	Texas	Jody Conradt	Clarissa Davis	97–81	USC
1987	Tennessee	Pat Summitt	Tonya Edwards	67–44	Louisiana Tech
1988	Louisiana Tech	Leon Barmore	Erica Westbrooks	56–54	Auburn
1989	Tennessee	Pat Summitt	Brigitte Gordon	76–60	Auburn
1990	Stanford	Tara VanderVeer	Jennifer Azzi	88–81	Auburn
1991	Tennessee	Pat Summitt	Dawn Staley	70–67	Virginia
1992	Stanford	Tara VanderVeer	Molly Goodenbour	78–62	Western Kentucky
1993	Texas Tech	Marcia Sharp	Sheryl Swoopes	84–82	Ohio State
1994	North Carolina	Sylvia Hatchell	Charlotte Smith	60–59	Louisiana Tech
1995	Connecticut	Geno Auriemma	Rebecca Lobo	70–64	Tennessee
1996	Tennessee	Pat Summitt	Michelle Marciniak	83–65	Georgia
1997	Tennessee	Pat Summitt	Chamique Holdsclaw	68–59	Old Dominion
1998	Tennessee	Pat Summitt	Chamique Holdsclaw	93–75	Louisiana Tech
1999	Purdue	Carolyn Peck	Ukari Figgs	62–45	Duke

Other Women's Champions

CROSS-COUNTRY
1981	Virginia
1982	Virginia
1983	Oregon
1984	Wisconsin
1985	Wisconsin
1986	Texas
1987	Oregon
1988	Kentucky
1989	Villanova
1990	Villanova
1991	Villanova
1992	Villanova
1993	Villanova
1994	Villanova
1995	Providence
1996	Stanford
1997	BYU
1998	Villanova

FIELD HOCKEY
1981	Connecticut
1982	Old Dominion
1983	Old Dominion
1984	Old Dominion
1985	Connecticut
1986	Iowa
1987	Maryland
1988	Old Dominion
1989	North Carolina
1990	Old Dominion
1991	Old Dominion
1992	Old Dominion
1993	Maryland
1994	James Madison
1995	North Carolina
1996	North Carolina
1997	North Carolina
1998	Old Dominion

SOCCER
1981	—
1982	North Carolina
1983	North Carolina
1984	North Carolina
1985	George Mason
1986	North Carolina
1987	North Carolina
1988	North Carolina
1989	North Carolina
1990	North Carolina

1991	North Carolina
1992	North Carolina
1993	North Carolina
1994	North Carolina
1995	Notre Dame
1996	North Carolina
1997	North Carolina
1998	Florida

VOLLEYBALL
1981	USC
1982	Hawaii
1983	Hawaii
1984	UCLA
1985	Pacific
1986	Pacific
1987	Hawaii
1988	Texas
1989	Cal St. Long Beach
1990	UCLA
1991	UCLA
1992	Stanford
1993	Long Beach St.
1994	Stanford
1995	Nebraska
1996	Stanford
1997	Stanford
1998	Long Beach St.

FENCING[1]
1983	Wayne State
1984	Penn State
1985	Yale
1986	Yale
1987	Pennsylvania
1988	Notre Dame
1989	Wayne St. (Mich.)
1990	Wayne St. (Mich.)

GOLF
1982	Tulsa
1983	Texas Christian
1984	Miami (Fla.)
1985	Florida
1986	Florida
1987	San Jose State
1988	Tulsa
1989	San Jose State
1990	Arizona State
1991	UCLA

1992	San Jose State
1993	Arizona State
1994	Arizona State
1995	Arizona State
1996	Arizona
1997	Arizona State
1998	Arizona State
1999	Duke

GYMNASTICS
1982	Utah
1983	Utah
1984	Utah
1985	Utah
1986	Utah
1987	Georgia
1988	Alabama
1989	Georgia
1990	Utah
1991	Alabama
1992	Utah
1993	Georgia
1994	Utah
1995	Utah
1996	Alabama
1997	UCLA
1998	Georgia
1999	Georgia

LACROSSE
1982	Massachusetts
1983	Delaware
1984	Temple
1985	New Hampshire
1986	Maryland
1987	Penn State
1988	Temple
1989	Penn State
1990	Harvard
1991	Virginia
1992	Maryland
1993	Virginia
1994	Princeton
1995	Maryland
1996	Maryland
1997	Maryland
1998	Maryland
1999	Maryland

SOFTBALL
1982	UCLA
1983	Texas A&M
1984	UCLA
1985	UCLA
1986	Cal State Fullerton
1987	Texas A&M
1988	UCLA
1989	UCLA
1990	UCLA
1991	Arizona
1992	UCLA
1993	Arizona
1994	Arizona
1995	UCLA
1996	Arizona
1997	Stanford
1998	Fresno State
1999	UCLA

SWIMMING
1982	Florida
1983	Stanford
1984	Texas
1985	Texas
1986	Texas
1987	Texas
1988	Texas
1989	Stanford
1990	Texas
1991	Texas
1992	Stanford
1993	Stanford
1994	Stanford
1995	Stanford
1996	Stanford
1997	USC
1998	Stanford
1999	Georgia

TENNIS
1982	Stanford
1983	USC
1984	Stanford
1985	USC
1986	Stanford
1987	Stanford
1988	Stanford
1989	Stanford
1990	Stanford

INDOOR TRACK
1982	—
1983	Nebraska
1984	Nebraska
1985	Florida State
1986	Texas
1987	Louisiana State
1988	Texas
1989	Louisiana State
1990	Texas
1991	Louisiana State
1992	Florida
1993	Louisiana State
1994	Louisiana State
1995	Louisiana State
1996	Louisiana State
1997	Louisiana State
1998	Texas
1999	Texas

OUTDOOR TRACK
1982	UCLA
1983	UCLA
1984	Florida State
1985	Oregon
1986	Texas
1987	Louisiana State
1988	Louisiana State
1989	Louisiana State
1990	Louisiana State
1991	Louisiana State
1992	Louisiana State
1993	Louisiana State
1994	Louisiana State
1995	Louisiana State
1996	Louisiana State
1997	Louisiana State
1998	Texas
1999	Texas

CROSS-COUNTRY (continued)
1991	North Carolina
1992	North Carolina
1993	North Carolina
1994	North Carolina
1995	Notre Dame
1996	North Carolina
1997	North Carolina
1998	Florida

1. Since 1990, the NCAA has recognized a joint fencing champion. See "Men's and Women's Titles" on previous page.

International Sports

THE WORLD CUP

From its origins in various "football" games dating back to ancient Greece and China, soccer (as it is called in the U.S.) has become the world's most popular sport. The World Cup championship, modern soccer's most spectacular event, is staged every four years by the Federation Internationale de Football Association (FIFA). The first World Cup in 1930 attracted a mere 13 nations. In 1998, 173 nations competed for a bid to the 32-team tournament. The top 16 teams among those 32 (as decided during a 48-game round-robin first round) advance to a single-elimination tournament until a single winner is crowned. Players must represent their home country, regardless of where they regularly play. Millions attend the Cup's many contests and the televised final is viewed by over a billion people worldwide.

The World Cup, 1930–98

Year	Final Score	Golden Boot Award: Leading scorer, country (goals)	Host country	Participating nations
1930	Uruguay 4, Argentina 2	Stabile, Argentina (8)	Uruguay	13
1934	Italy 2, Czechoslovakia 1 (OT)	Conen, Germany	Italy	31
		Nejedly, Czechoslovakia		
		Schiavo, Italy (4)		
1938	Italy 4, Hungary 2	Leonidas, Brazil (8)	France	36
1942	No tournament—World War II			
1946	No tournament—World War II			
1950	Uruguay 2, Brazil 1	Ademir, Brazil (7)	Brazil	33
1954	West Germany 3, Hungary 2	Kocsis, Hungary (11)	Switzerland	38
1958	Brazil 5, Sweden 2	Fontaine, France (13)	Sweden	53
1962	Brazil 3, Czechoslovakia 1	Jerkovic, Yugoslavia (5)	Chile	56
1966	England 4, West Germany 2 (OT)	Eusebio, Portugal (9)	England	71
1970	Brazil 4, Italy 1	Muller, West Germany (10)	Mexico	71
1974	West Germany 2, Netherlands 1	Lato, Poland (7)	West Germany	98
1978	Argentina 3, Netherlands 1 (OT)	Kempes, Argentina (6)	Argentina	106
1982	Italy 3, West Germany 1	Rossi, Italy (6)	Spain	109
1986	Argentina 3, West Germany 2	Lineker, England (6)	Mexico	121
1990	West Germany 1, Argentina 0	Schilacci, Italy (6)	Italy	112
1994	Brazil 0, Italy 0	Stoichkov, Bulgaria (6)	United States	144
	(Brazil won 3-2 on penalty kicks)			
1998	France 3, Brazil 0	Suker, Croatia (6)	France	173

Source: FIFA

The World Cup, 1998

When the 1998 World Cup began in June, France hardly seemed to acknowledge that it was hosting the world's largest sporting event. But the French soccer team aroused an indifferent nation and on July 12 won its first World Cup title 3–0 over Brazil, with the championship game providing the most unexpected upset in the final in nearly five decades. Zinedine Zidane, France's exquisite playmaker, scored two goals in the championship game, heading in a pair of corner kicks, to provide the home team with its first World Cup title since Argentina prevailed in 1978.

The 1998 World Cup provided a moment of sweet symmetry for the French. It was a Frenchman, Jules Rimet, who conceived of a world championship for soccer. Only seven teams have won the Cup since the tournament, held every four years, began play in 1930. France joined an exclusive club that includes four-time champion Brazil, Germany, Argentina, Italy, Uruguay and England.

France's victory over Brazil was the largest margin ever in a championship game and the biggest upset since Brazil lost 2–1 at home to Paraguay in 1950. Ronaldo, the 21-year-old Brazilian forward considered to be the best player in the world, played a listless game against France. It was later revealed that Ronaldo had suffered convulsions in the hours prior to the game.

France was the dominant squad in this 32-team tournament, allowing only two goals in seven matches. The biggest disappointments were Spain, an early favorite which did not advance beyond the first round, and the United States, which scored only one goal and lost all three of its first-round matches. Coach Steve Sampson resigned immediately after the Americans exited, and several of the team's most experienced players, including Eric Wynalda, Tab Ramos and Alexi Lalas, further shamed themselves by harshly criticizing Sampson without taking any responsibility for the total collapse.

—Jere Longman, *The New York Times*

1998 World Cup, First Round

Group A	Wins-Losses-Ties	Points
1. Brazil	2–1–0	6
2. Norway	1–0–2	5
3. Scotland	1–1–1	4
4. Morocco	0–2–1	1

Brazil 2, Scotland	1	Morocco 2, Norway	2
Scotland 1, Norway	1	Brazil 3, Morocco	0
Norway 2, Brazil	1	Morocco 3, Scotland	1

Group B	Wins-Losses-Ties	Points
1. Italy	2–0–1	7
2. Chile	0–0–3	3
3. Austria	0–1–2	2
4. Cameroon	0–1–2	2

Chile 2, Italy	2	Cameroon 1, Austria	1
Chile 1, Austria	1	Italy 3, Cameroon	0
Italy 2, Austria	1	Cameroon 1, Chile	1

Group C	Wins-Losses-Ties	Points
1. France	3–0–0	9
2. Denmark	1–1–1	4
3. South Africa	0–1–2	2
4. Saudi Arabia	0–2–1	1

Denmark 1, Saudi Arabia	0	France 3, South Africa	0
Denmark 1, South Africa	1	France 4, Saudi Arabia	0
France 2, Denmark	1	Saudi Arabia 2, S. Africa	2

Group D	Wins-Losses-Ties	Points
1. Nigeria	2–1–0	6
2. Paraguay	1–0–2	5
3. Spain	1–1–1	4
4. Bulgaria	0–2–1	1

Paraguay 0, Bulgaria	0	Nigeria 3, Spain	2
Nigeria 1, Bulgaria	0	Paraguay 0, Spain	0
Spain 6, Bulgaria	1	Paraguay 3, Nigeria	1

Group E	Wins-Losses-Ties	Points
1. Netherlands	1–0–2	5
2. Mexico	1–0–2	5
3. Belgium	0–0–3	3
4. South Korea	0–2–1	1

Mexico 3, S. Korea	1	Netherlands 0, Belgium	0
Netherlands 5, S. Korea	0	Belgium 2, Mexico	2
Netherlands 2, Mexico	2	Belgium 1, S. Korea	1

Group F	Wins-Losses-Ties	Points
1. Germany	2–0–1	7
2. Yugoslavia	2–0–1	7
3. Iran	1–2–0	3
4. United States	0–3–0	0

Yugoslavia 1, Iran	0	Germany 2, United States	0
Germany 2, Yugoslavia	2	Iran 2, United States	1
Germany 2, Iran	0	Yugoslavia 1, United States	0

Group G	Wins-Losses-Ties	Points
1. Romania	2–0–1	7
2. England	2–1–0	6
3. Colombia	1–2–0	3
4. Tunisia	0–2–1	1

England 2, Tunisia	0	Romania 1, Colombia	0
Colombia 1, Tunisia	0	Romania 2, England	1
Romania 1, Tunisia	1	England 2, Colombia	0

Group H	Wins-Losses-Ties	Points
1. Argentina	3–0–0	9
2. Croatia	2–1–0	6
3. Jamaica	1–2–0	3
4. Japan	0–3–0	0

Argentina 1, Japan	0	Croatia 3, Jamaica	1
Croatia 1, Japan	0	Argentina 5, Jamaica	0
Argentina 1, Croatia	0	Jamaica 2, Japan	1

Note: A win is worth three points and a tie is worth one point. The top two teams in each group advance to the second round.

1998 World Cup, Second Round

1. Argentina beat England 4-3 on penalty kicks. 2. France beat Italy 4-3 on penalty kicks. 3. Brazil beat the Netherlands 4-2 on penalty kicks.

The Women's World Cup, 1999

The U.S. women's soccer team won the 1999 World Cup, battling China to a 0-0 tie that wasn't decided until the penalty kick round, which the U.S. won by a narrow 5-4 margin. Goalkeeper Briana Scurry made a crucial save to give the U.S. the lead, and Brandi Chastain booted home the game-winner. More surprising than the outcome (the U.S. and China were the two favorites to win the Cup) was the popularity of the sport. Many of the early round games sold out football stadiums seating in excess of 70,000 people, and the finale, held in the cavernous Rose Bowl, drew more than 90,000 spectators. Television ratings were equally strong. The U.S.-Brazil semifinal game garnered a 3.78 Nielsen rating (or 2.9 million households), ESPN's highest rating ever for soccer, men's or women's. The rating for ABC's coverage of the championship game was an astounding 13.3, more even than 11.3 average for the five games of the NBA finals, and nearly double the 6.9 rating earned by the 1998 Men's World Cup Final between France and Brazil. Those numbers were all the more surprising coming just three years after NBC failed to air live the gold medal game at the 1996 Olympics, which the U.S. women also won on penalty kicks.

FIRST ROUND

Group A	Wins-Losses-Ties	Points
x-USA	3–0–0	9
x-Nigeria	2–1–0	6
N. Korea	1–2–0	3
Denmark	0–3–0	0

USA 3, N. Korea	1	Nigeria 2, N. Korea	1
Nigeria 2, Denmark	0	USA 7, Nigeria	1
USA 3, Denmark	0	N. Korea 3, Denmark	1

Group B	Wins-Losses-Ties	Points
x-Brazil	2–1–0	7
x-Germany	1–0–2	5
Italy	1–1–1	4
Mexico	0–3–0	0

Brazil 3, Germany	3	Germany 1, Italy	1
Italy 2, Mexico	0	Brazil 2, Italy	0
Brazil 7, Mexico	1	Germany 6, Mexico	0

Group C	Wins-Losses-Ties	Points
x-Norway	3–0–0	9
x-Russia	2–1–0	6
Japan	0–2–1	1
Canada	0–2–1	1

Canada 1, Japan	1	Norway 7, Canada	1
Norway 2, Russia	1	Russia 4, Canada	1
Russia 5, Japan	0	Norway 4, Japan	0

Group D	Wins-Losses-Ties	Points
x-China	3–0–0	9
x-Sweden	2–1–0	6
Australia	0–2–1	1
Ghana	0–2–1	1

China 2, Sweden	1	China 7, Ghana	1
Australia 1, Ghana	1	China 3, Australia	1
Sweden 3, Australia	1	Sweden 2, Ghana	0

Note: A win is worth three points, and a tie is worth one point. The top two teams in each group advance to the second round.

1999 Women's World Cup, Second Round

USA 3 · Semifinals · USA 2 · Germany 2

Semifinals · China 2 · China 5 · Russia 0

World Cup Final
USA 0 (5–4)[1]   China 0[1]

Nigeria 3 · Brazil 0 · Brazil 4 (OT)

Sweden 1 · Norway 0 · Norway 3

Third Place Game
Brazil 0 (5–4)[2]   Norway 0[2]

1. The U.S won the championship 5–4 on penalty kicks. 2. Brazil beat Norway 5–4 on penalty kicks for third place.

CHESS

World Chess Champions

Year	Name	Country	Year	Name	Country
1886–94	Wilhelm Steinitz	Austria	1960–61	Mikhail Tal	USSR
1894–1921	Emanuel Lasker	Germany	1961–63	Mikhail Botvinnik	USSR
1921–27	José R. Capablanca	Cuba	1963–69	Tigran Petrosian	USSR
1927–35	Alexander A. Alekhine	France	1969–72	Boris Spassky	USSR
1935–37	Max Euwe	Netherlands	1972–75	Bobby Fischer	USA
1937–48	Alexander A. Alekhine	France	1975–85	Anatoly Karpov	USSR
1948–57	Mikhail Botvinnik	USSR	1985–	Garry Kasparov[1]	USSR/Russia
1957–58	Vassily Smyslov	USSR	1993–	Anatoly Karpov[1]	Russia
1958–60	Mikhail Botvinnik	USSR			

1. In 1993, Kasparov started his own chess sanctioning body, the Professional Chess Association, leaving his World Chess Federation (FIDE) championship vacant, whereupon FIDE awarded the title to Karpov.   **Source:** U.S. Chess Federation

U.S. Chess Champions

Years	Name	Years	Name	Years	Name
1845–57	Charles Henry Stanley	1959–60	Bobby Fischer	1984	Lev Alburt
1857–71	Paul Morphy	1960–61	Bobby Fischer	1985	Lev Alburt
1871–90	Capt. George Mackenzie	1961–62	Larry Evans	1986	Yasser Seirawan
1890–91	Jackson Showalter	1962–63	Bobby Fischer	1987	(tie) Joel Benjamin
1891–94	Solomon Lipschutz	1963–64	Bobby Fischer		Nick deFirmian
1894	Jackson Showalter	1965	Bobby Fischer	1988	Michael Wilder
1894-95	Albert Hodges	1966	Bobby Fischer	1989	(tie) Roman
1895–97	Jackson Showalter	1968	Larry Evans		Dzindzichashvili
1897–1906	Harry Nelson Pillsbury	1969	Samuel Reshevksy		Yasser Seirawan
1906–09	Jackson Showalter	1972	Robert Byrne		Stuart Rachels
1909–36	Frank J. Marshall	1973	(tie) John Grefe	1990	Lev Alburt
1936	Samuel Reshevsky		Lubomir Kavalek	1991	Gata Kamsky
1938	Samuel Reshevsky	1974	Walter Browne	1992	Patrick Wolff
1940	Samuel Reshevsky	1975	Walter Browne	1993	(tie) Alexander Shabalov
1942	Samuel Reshevsky	1977	Walter Browne		Alex Yermolinsky
1944	Arnold Denker	1978	Lubomir Kavalek	1994	Boris Gulko
1946	Samuel Reshevsky	1980	(tie)Walter Browne	1995	(tie) Nick deFirmian,
1948	Herman Steiner		Larry Evans		Alexander Ivanov,
1951	Larry Evans		Larry Christiansen		Patrick Wolf
1952	Larry Evans	1981	(tie) Walter Browne	1996	Alex Yermolinski
1954	Arthur Bisguier		Yasser Seirawan	1997	Joel Benjamin
1957–58	Bobby Fischer	1983	(tie) Walter Browne	1998	Nick deFirmian
1958–59	Bobby Fischer		Larry Christiansen		
			Roman Dzindzichashvili		

Note: The U.S. championship is not held every year.   **Source:** U.S. Chess Federation

CYCLING

The Tour De France

Year	Champion	Year	Champion	Year	Champion	Year	Champion
1903	Maurice Garin	1929	Maurice Dewaele	1958	Charly Gaul	1979	Bernard Hinault
1904	Henri Cornet	1930	Andre Leducq	1959	Federico	1980	Joop Zoetemelk
1905	Louis Trousselier	1931	Antonin Magne		Bahamontes	1981	Bernard Hinault
1906	Rene Pottier	1932	Andre Leducq	1960	Gastone Nencini	1982	Bernard Hinault
1907	Lucien Petit-Breton	1933	Georges Speicher	1961	Jacques Anquetil	1983	Laurent Fignon
1908	LucienPetit-Breton	1934	Antonin Magne	1962	Jacques Anquetil	1984	Laurent Fignon
1909	Francois Faber	1935	Romain Maes	1963	Jacques Anquetil	1985	Bernard Hinault
1910	Octave Lapize	1936	Sylvere Maes	1964	Jacques Anquetil	1986	Greg LeMond
1911	Gustave Garrigou	1937	Roger Lapebie	1965	Felice Gimondi	1987	Stephen Roche
1912	Odile Defraye	1938	Gino Bartali	1966	Lucien Aimar	1988	Pedro Delgado
1913	Philippe Thijs	1939	Sylvere Maes	1967	Roger Pingeon	1989	Greg LeMond
1914	Philippe Thijs	1947	Jean Robic	1968	Jan Janssen	1990	Greg LeMond
1919	Firmin Lambot	1948	Gino Bartali	1969	Eddy Merckx	1991	Miguel Indurain
1920	Philippe Thijs	1949	Fausto Coppi	1970	Eddy Merckx	1992	Miguel Indurain
1921	Leon Scieur	1950	Ferdi Kubler	1971	Eddy Merckx	1993	Miguel Indurain
1922	Firmin Lambot	1951	Hugo Koblet	1972	Eddy Merckx	1994	Miguel Indurain
1923	Henri Pelissier	1952	Fausto Coppi	1973	Luis Ocana	1995	Miguel Indurain
1924	Ottavio Bottecchia	1953	Louison Bobet	1974	Eddy Merckx	1996	Bjarne Riis
1925	Ottavio Bottecchia	1954	Louison Bobet	1975	Bernard Thevenet	1997	Jan Ullrich
1926	Lucien Buysse	1955	Louison Bobet	1976	Lucien Van Impe	1998	Marco Pantini
1927	Nicolas Frantz	1956	Roger Walkowiak	1977	Bernard Thevenet	1999	Lance Armstrong
1928	Nicolas Frantz	1957	Jacques Anquetil	1978	Bernard Hinault		

FIGURE SKATING

U.S. Figure Skating Champions

Year	Men	Women	Year	Men	Women
1952	Richard Button	Tenley Albright	1976	Terry Kubicka	Dorothy Hamill
1953	Hayes Jenkins	Tenley Albright	1977	Charles Tickner	Linda Fratianne
1954	Hayes Jenkins	Tenley Albright	1978	Charles Tickner	Linda Fratianne
1955	Hayes Jenkins	Tenley Albright	1979	Charles Tickner	Linda Fratianne
1956	Hayes Jenkins	Tenley Albright	1980	Charles Tickner	Linda Fratianne
1957	Dave Jenkins	Carol Heiss	1981	Scott Hamilton	Elaine Zayak
1958	Dave Jenkins	Carol Heiss	1982	Scott Hamilton	Rosalynn Sumners
1959	Dave Jenkins	Carol Heiss	1983	Scott Hamilton	Rosalynn Sumners
1960	Dave Jenkins	Carol Heiss	1984	Scott Hamilton	Rosalynn Sumners
1961	Bradley Lord	Laurence Owen	1985	Brian Boitano	Tiffany Chin
1962	Monty Hoyt	Barbara Roles Pursley	1986	Brian Boitano	Debi Thomas
1963	Tommy Litz	Lorraine Hanlon	1987	Brian Boitano	Jill Trenary
1964	Scott Allen	Peggy Fleming	1988	Brian Boitano	Debi Thomas
1965	Gary Visconti	Peggy Fleming	1989	Christopher Bowman	Jill Trenary
1966	Scott Allen	Peggy Fleming	1990	Todd Eldredge	Jill Trenary
1967	Gary Visconti	Peggy Fleming	1991	Todd Eldredge	Tonya Harding
1968	Tim Wood	Peggy Fleming	1992	Christopher Bowman	Kristi Yamaguchi
1969	Tim Wood	Janet Lynn	1993	Scott Davis	Nancy Kerrigan
1970	Tim Wood	Janet Lynn	1994	Scott Davis	Tonya Harding[1]
1971	John Misha Petkevich	Janet Lynn	1995	Todd Eldredge	Nicole Bobek
1972	Ken Shelley	Janet Lynn	1996	Rudy Galindo	Michelle Kwan
1973	Gordon McKellen Jr.	Janet Lynn	1997	Todd Eldredge	Tara Lipinski
1974	Gordon McKellen Jr.	Dorothy Hamill	1998	Todd Eldredge	Michelle Kwan
1975	Gordon McKellen Jr.	Dorothy Hamill	1999	Michael Weiss	Michelle Kwan

1. Later stripped of title.

World Figure Skating Champions

Year	Men	Women	Year	Men	Women
1952	Richard Button, U.S.	Jacqueline du Bief, France	1973	Ondrej Nepela, Czechoslovakia	Karen Magnussen, Canada
1953	Hayes Jenkins, U.S.	Tenley Albright, U.S.	1974	Jan Hoffmann, E. Germany	Christine Errath, E. Germany
1954	Hayes Jenkins, U.S.	Gundi Busch, W. Germany	1975	Sergei Volkov, USSR	Dianne de Leeuw, Netherlands-U.S.
1955	Hayes Jenkins, U.S.	Tenley Albright, U.S.			
1956	Hayes Jenkins, U.S.	Carol Heiss, U.S.	1976	John Curry, Great Britain	Dorothy Hamill, U.S.
1957	Dave Jenkins, U.S.	Carol Heiss, U.S.	1977	Vladimir Kovalev, USSR	Linda Fratianne, U.S.
1958	Dave Jenkins, U.S.	Carol Heiss, U.S.	1978	Charles Tickner, U.S.	Anett Potzsch, E. Germany
1959	Dave Jenkins, U.S.	Carol Heiss, U.S.	1979	Vladimir Kovalev, USSR	Linda Fratianne, U.S.
1960	Alain Giletti, France	Carol Heiss, U.S.	1980	Jan Hoffmann, E. Germany	Anett Potzsch, E. Germany
1961	No champion	No champion			
1962	Don Jackson, Canada	Sjoukje Dijkstra, Netherlands	1981	Scott Hamilton, U.S.	Denise Biellmann, Switzerland
1963	Don McPherson, Canada	Sjoukje Dijkstra, Netherlands	1982	Scott Hamilton, U.S.	Elaine Zayak, U.S.
1964	Manfred Schnelldorfer, W. Germany	Sjoukje Dijkstra, Netherlands	1983	Scott Hamilton, U.S.	Rosalynn Sumners, U.S.
			1984	Scott Hamilton, U.S.	Katarina Witt, E. Germany
1965	Alain Calmat, France	Petra Burka, Canada	1985	Aleksandr Fadeev, USSR	Katarina Witt, E. Germany
1966	Emmerich Danzer, Austria	Peggy Fleming, U.S.	1986	Brian Boitano, U.S.	Debi Thomas, U.S.
			1987	Brian Orser, Canada	Katarina Witt, E. Germany
1967	Emmerich Danzer, Austria	Peggy Fleming, U.S.	1988	Brian Boitano, U.S.	Katarina Witt, E. Germany
			1989	Kurt Browning, Canada	Midori Ito, Japan
1968	Emmerich Danzer, Austria	Peggy Fleming, U.S.	1990	Kurt Browning, Canada	Jill Trenary, U.S.
1969	Tim Wood, U.S.	Gabriele Seyfert, E. Germany	1991	Kurt Browning, Canada	Kristi Yamaguchi, U.S.
			1992	Victor Petrenko, Russia	Kristi Yamaguchi, U.S.
1970	Tim Wood, U.S.	Gabriele Seyfert, E. Germany	1993	Kurt Browning, Canada	Oksana Baiul, Ukraine
			1994	Elvis Stojko, Canada	Yuka Sato, Japan
1971	Ondrej Nepela, Czechoslovakia	Beatrix Schuba, Austria	1995	Elvis Stojko, Canada	Lu Chen, China
			1996	Todd Eldredge, U.S.	Michelle Kwan, U.S.
			1997	Elvis Stojko, Canada	Tara Lipinski, U.S.
1972	Ondrej Nepela, Czechoslovakia	Beatrix Schuba, Austria	1998	Alexi Yagudin, Russia	Michelle Kwan, U.S.
			1999	Alexi Yagudin, Russia	Maria Butyrskaya, Russia

MARATHON RUNNING

Marathons are 26 miles, 385 yards long, the distance purportedly run by the Athenian messenger who announced his city-state's victory over the Persian Empire on the Plains of Marathon in 490 B.C. The oldest and best-known U.S. marathon covers a route from Hopkinton, Massachusetts to downtown Boston. For many years, the Boston Athletic Association organized the race on an amateur basis, and winners received only a laurel wreath and the traditional pot of beef stew. In 1999, the winners took home $80,000 each.

Boston Marathon

Year	Name	Time	Year	Name	Time	Year	Name	Time
	MEN		1941	Leslie Pawson	2:30:38	1986	Robert de Castella	2:07:51
1897	John J. McDermott	2:55:10	1942	Bernard Joe Smith	2:26:51	1987	Toshihiko Seko	2:11:50
1898	Ronald J. McDonald	2:42:00	1943	Gerard Cote	2:28:25	1988	Ibrahim Hussein	2:08:43
1899	Lawrence J. Brignolia	2:54:38	1944	Gerard Cote	2:31:50	1989	Abebe Mekonnen	2:09:06
1900	James J. Caffrey	2:39:44	1945	John A. Kelley	2:30:40	1990	Gelindo Bordin	2:08:20
1901	James J. Caffrey	2:29:23	1946	Stylianos Kyriakides	2:29:27	1991	Ibrahim Hussein	2:11:06
1902	Samuel A. Mellor, Yonkers	2:43:12	1947	Yun Bok Suh	2:25:39	1992	Ibrahim Hussein	2:08:14
1903	John C. Lorden	2:41:29	1948	Gerard Cote	2:31:02	1993	Cosmas N'Deti	2:09:33
1904	Michael Spring	2:38:04	1949	Karle Gosta Leandersson	2:31:50	1994	Cosmas N'Deti	2:07:15
1905	Fred Lorz	2:38:25	1950	Kee Yong Ham	2:32:39	1995	Cosmas N'Deti	2:09:22
1906	Timothy Ford	2:45:45	1951	Shigeki Tanaka	2:27:45	1996	Moses Tanui	2:09:16
1907	Thomas Longboat	2:24:24	1952	Doroteo Flores	2:31:53	1997	Lameck Aguta	2:10:34
1908	Thomas P. Morrissey	2:25:43	1953	Keizo Yamada	2:18:51	1998	Moses Tanui	2:07:34
1909	Henri Renaud	2:53:36	1954	Veikko L. Karvonen	2:20:39	1999	Joseph Chebet	2:09:52
1910	Fred L. Cameron	2:28:52	1955	Hideo Hamamura	2:18:22			
1911	Clarence H. DeMar	2:21:39	1956	Antti Viskari	2:14:14		**WOMEN**	
1912	Michael J. Ryan	2:21:18	1957	John J. Delley	2:20:05			
1913	Fritz Carlson	2:25:14	1958	Franjo Mihalic	2:25:54	1972	Nina Kuscsik	3:10:26
1914	James Duffy	2:25:01	1959	Eino Oksanen	2:22:42	1973	Jacqueline Hansen	3:05:59
1915	Edouard Fabre	2:31:41	1960	Paavo Kotila	2:20:54	1974	Miki Gorman	2:47:11
1916	Arthur V. Roth	2:27:16	1961	Eino Oksanen	2:23:39	1975	Liane Winter	2:42:24
1917	William K. Kennedy	2:28:37	1962	Eino Oksanen	2:23:48	1976	Kim Merritt	2:47:10
1918	Service team race won by Camp Devens		1963	Aurele Vandendriessche	2:18:58	1977	Miki Gorman	2:46:22
1919	Carl W. A. Linder	2:29:13	1964	Aurele Vandendriessche	2:19:59	1978	Gayle Barron	2:44:52
1920	Peter Trivoulidas	2:29:31	1965	Morio Shigematsu	2:16:33	1979	Joan Benoit	2:35:15
1921	Frank Zuna	2:18:57	1966	Kenji Kimihara	2:17:11	1980	Jacqueline Gareau	2:34:28
1922	Clarence H. DeMar	2:18:10	1967	David McKenzie	2:15:45	1981	Allison Roe	2:26:46
1923	Clarence H. DeMar	2:23:37	1968	Ambrose Burfoot	2:22:17	1982	Charlotte Teske	2:29:33
1924	Clarence H. DeMar	2:29:40	1969	Yoshiaki Unetani, Japan	2:13:49	1983	Joan Benoit	2:22:43
1925	Charles L. Mellor	2:33:00	1970	Ron Hill	2:10:30	1984	Lorraine Moller	2:29:28
1926	John C. Miles	2:25:40	1971	Alvaro Mejia	2:18:45	1985	Lisa Larsen-Weidenbach	2:34:06
1927	Clarence H. DeMar	2:40:22	1972	Olavi Suomalainen	2:15:39	1986	Ingrid Kristiansen	2:24:55
1928	Clarence H. DeMar	2:37:07	1973	Jon Anderson	2:16:03	1987	Rosa Mota	2:25:21
1929	John C. Miles	2:33:08	1974	Neil Cusack	2:13:39	1988	Rosa Mota	2:24:30
1930	Clarence H. DeMar	2:34:48	1975	Bill Rodgers	2:09:55	1989	Ingrid Kristiansen	2:24:33
1931	James P. Henigan	2:46:45	1976	Jack Fultz	2:20:19	1990	Rosa Mota	2:25:24
1932	Paul deBruyn	2:33:36	1977	Jerome Drayton	2:14:46	1991	Wanda Panfil	2:24:18
1933	Leslie Pawson	2:33:01	1978	Bill Rodgers	2:10:13	1992	Olga Markova	2:23:43
1934	Dave Komonen	2:32:53	1979	Bill Rodgers	2:09:27	1993	Olga Markova	2:25:27
1935	John A. Kelley	2:32:07	1980	Bill Rodgers	2:12:11	1994	Uta Pippig	2:21:45
1936	Ellison M. (Tarzan) Brown	2:33:40	1981	Toshihiko Seko	2:09:26	1995	Uta Pippig	2:25:11
1937	Walter Young, Verdun	2:33:20	1982	Alberto Salazar	2:08:52	1996	Uta Pippig	2:27:12
1938	Leslie Pawson	2:35:34	1983	Gregory A. Meyer	2:09:00	1997	Fatuma Roba	2:28:03
1939	Ellison M. (Tarzan) Brown	2:28:51	1984	Geoff Smith	2:10:34	1998	Fatuma Roba	2:23:21
1940	Gerard Cote	2:33:20	1985	Geoff Smith	2:14:05	1999	Fatuma Roba	2:23:25

New York Marathon

Year	Winner	Time	Year	Winner	Time	Year	Winner	Time
MEN			1990	Douglas Waikihuri	2:12:39	1980	Grete Waitz	2:25:41
1970	Gary Muhrcke	2:31:39	1991	Salvador Garcia	2:09:28	1981	Allison Roe	2:25:29
1971	Norman Higgins	2:22:55	1992	Willie Mtolo	2:09:29	1982	Grete Waitz	2:27:14
1972	Sheldon Karlin	2:27:53	1993	Andres Espinosa	2:10:04	1983	Grete Waitz	2:27:00
1973	Tom Fleming	2:21:55	1994	German Silva	2:11:21	1984	Grete Waitz	2:29:30
1974	Norbert Sander	2:26:31	1995	German Silva	2:11:00	1985	Grete Waitz	2:28:34
1975	Tom Fleming	2:19:27	1996	Giacomo Leone	2:10:09	1986	Grete Waitz	2:28:06
1976	Bill Rodgers	2:10:10	1997	John Kagwe	2:08:12	1987	Priscilla Welch	2:30:17
1977	Bill Rodgers	2:11:28	1998	John Kagwe	2:08:45	1988	Grete Waitz	2:28:07
1978	Bill Rodgers	2:12:12				1989	Ingrid Kristiansen	2:25:30
1979	Bill Rodgers	2:11:42		**WOMEN**		1990	Wanda Panfil	2:30:45
1980	Alberto Salazar	2:09:41	1970	No Finisher	—	1991	Liz McColgan	2:27:32
1981	Alberto Salazar	2:08:13	1971	Beth Bonner	2:55:22	1992	Lisa Ondieki	2:24:40
1982	Alberto Salazar	2:09:29	1972	Nina Kuscsik	3:08:42	1993	Uta Pippig	2:26:24
1983	Rod Dixon	2:08:59	1973	Nina Kuscsik	2:57:08	1994	Tegla Loroupe	2:27:37
1984	Orlando Pizzolato	2:14:53	1974	Katherine Switzer	3:07:29	1995	Tegla Loroupe	2:28:06
1985	Orlando Pizzolato	2:11:34	1975	Kim Merritt	2:46:15	1996	Anuta Catuna	2:28:18
1986	Gianni Poli	2:11:06	1976	Miki Gorman	2:39:11	1997	Franziska	
1987	Ibrahim Hussein	2:11:01	1977	Miki Gorman	2:43:10		Rochat-Moser	2:28:43
1988	Steve Jones	2:08:20	1978	Grete Waitz	2:32:30	1998	Franca Fiacconi	2:25:17
1989	Jumo Ikangaa	2:08:01	1979	Grete Waitz	2:27:33			

TRACK AND FIELD

Track and Field World Records (as of July 7, 1999)

These are the recognized records of the IAAF (International Amateur Athletic Federation). Marks pending approval by the IAAF are denoted by 'p'. All walk records must have been made on a track, and all relay records must be made by teams composed of individuals from the same country. Indoor records must be performed on tracks no larger than 200m in circumference, and the meet must be subject to drug testing.

MEN

Event	(min./sec.)	Record holder (country)	Date
100 m	9.79	Maurice Greene (U.S.)	6/16/99
200 m	19.32	Michael Johnson (U.S.)	8/1/96
400 m	43.18	Michael Johnson (U.S.)	8/26/99
800 m	1:41.11	Wilson Kipketer (Denmark)	8/24/97
1,000 m	2:12.18	Sebastian Coe (U.K.)	7/11/81
1,500 m	3:26:00	Hicham el-Guerrouj (Morocco)	7/14/98
Mile	3:43.13	Hicham el-Guerrouj (Morocco)	7/7/99
2,000 m	4:47.88	Nourredine Morceli (Algeria)	7/3/95
3,000 m	7:20.67	Daniel Komen (Kenya)	9/1/96
Steeplechase	7:55.72	Bernard Barmasai (Kenya)	8/24/97
5,000 m	12:39.36	Haile Gebrselassie (Ethiopia)	6/13/98
10,000 m	26:22.75	Haile Gebrselassie (Ethiopia)	6/1/98
Marathon	2:06:05	Ronaldo da Costa (Brazil)	9/20/98
110 m hurdles	12.91	Colin Jackson (U.K.)	8/20/93
400 m hurdles	46.78	Kevin Young (U.S.)	8/6/92
20 km walk	1:17:25.60	Bernardo Segura (Mexico)	5/7/94
50 km walk	3:40:47.90	Thierry Toutain (France)	9/29/96
4 x 100m	37.40	United States	8/8/92
		(Mike Marsh, Leroy Burrell, Dennis Mitchell, Carl Lewis)	
	37.40	United States	8/21/93
		(Jon Drummond, Andre Cason, Dennis Mitchell, Leroy Burrell)	
4x200m	1:18.68	Santa Monica Track Club (USA)	4/17/94
		(Mike Marsh, Leroy Burrell, Floyd Heard, Carl Lewis)	
4 x 400m	2:54.20	United States	7/22/98
		(Jerome Young, Antonio Pettigrew, Tyree Washington, Michael Johnson)	

WOMEN

Event	(min./sec.)	Record holder (country)	Date
100 m	10.49	Florence Griffith Joyner (U.S.)	7/16/88
200 m	21.34	Florence Griffith Joyner (U.S.)	9/29/88
400 m	47.60	Marita Koch (East Germany)	10/6/85
800 m	1:53.28	Jarmila Kratochvilova (Czech.)	7/26/83
1,000m	2:28.98	Svetlana Masterkova (Russia)	8/23/96
1,500 m	3:50.46	Yunxia Qu (China)	9/11/93
Mile	4:12.56	Svetlana Masterkova (Russia)	8/14/96
2,000 m	5:25.36	Sonia O'Sullivan (Ireland)	7/9/94
3,000 m	8:06.11	Junxia Wang (China)	9/13/93
5,000 m	14:28.09p	Bo Jiang (China)	10/23/97
10,000 m	29:31.78	Junxia Wang (China)	9/8/93
Marathon	2:20:47	Tegla Loroupe (Kenya)	4/19/98
100 m hurdles	12.21	Yordanka Donkova (Bulgaria)	8/20/88
400 m hurdles	52.61	Kim Batten (U.S.)	8/11/95
4 x 100m	41.37	East Germany	10/6/85
		(Silke Gladisch, Sabine Rieger, Ingrid Auerswald, Marlies Gohr)	
4x200m	1:28.15	East Germany	8/9/80
		(Marlies Gohr, Romy Muller, Barbel Wockel, Marita Koch)	
4 x 400m	3:15.17	Soviet Union	10/1/88
		(Tatyana Ledovskaya, Olga Nazarova, Maria Pinigina, Olga Bryzgina)	
5 km walk	20:13.26	Kerry Saxby (Australia)	2/25/96
10 km walk	41:56.23	Nadezhda Ryashkina (USSR)	7/4/90

Event	(min./sec.)		Record holder (country)	Date
High jump	2.45	8–0.5	Javier Sotomayor (Cuba)	7/27/93
Pole vault	6.14	20–1.75	Sergey Bubka (Ukraine)	7/31/94
Long jump	8.95	29–4.5	Mike Powell (U.S.)	8/30/91
Triple jump	18.29	60–0	Jonathan Edwards (Britain)	8/7/95
Shot put	23.12	75–10.25	Randy Barnes (U.S.)	5/20/90
Discus	74.08	243–0	Jurgen Schult (East Germany)	6/6/86
Hammer	86.74	284–7	Yuriy Syedikh (USSR)	8/30/86
Javelin	98.48	323–1	Jan Zelezny (Czech Republic)	5/25/96
Decathlon	8,891 points		Dan O'Brien (U.S.)	9/5/92
	(10.43, 8.08, 16.69, 2.07, 48.51, 13.98, 48.56, 5.00, 62.58, 4:42.10)			

Event	(min./sec.)		Record holder (country)	Date
High jump	2.09	6–10.25	Stefka Kostadinova (Bulgaria)	8/30/87
Pole vault	4.60p	15–1p	Emma George (Australia)	2/20/99
Long jump	7.52	24–8.25	Galina Chistyakova (USSR)	6/11/88
Triple jump	15.50	50–10.25	Inessa Kravets (Ukraine)	7/10/95
Shot put	22.63	74–3	Natalya Lisovskaya (USSR)	6/7/87
Discus	76.80	252–0	Gabriele Reinsch (East Germany)	7/9/88
Hammer	73.14	239–11.5	Michaela Melinte (Romania)	7/16/98
Javelin	80.00	262–5	Petra Felke (East Germany)	9/9/88
Heptathlon	7,291 points		Jackie Joyner-Kersee (U.S.)	9/24/88
	(12.69, 1.6, 15.80, 22.56, 7.27, 45.66, 2:08.51)			

World Indoor Records

MEN

Event	(min./sec.)	Record Holder (country)	Date
50m	5.56	Donovan Bailey (Canada)	2/6/96
60m	6.39	Maruice Green (U.S.)	2/3/98
200m	19.92	Frank Fredericks (Namibia)	2/18/96
400m	44.63	Michael Johnson (U.S.)	3/4/95
800m	1:42.67	Wilson Kipketer (Denmark)	3/9/87
1,000 m	2:15.26	Nourredine Morceli (Algeria)	2/22/92
1,500 m	3:31.18	Hicham el-Guerrouj (Morocco)	2/2/97
Mile	3:48.45	Hicham el-Guerrouj (Morocco)	2/12/97
3,000 m	7:24.90p	Daniel Komen (Kenya)	2/6/98
5,000 m	12:50.38	Haile Gebrselassie (Ethiopia)	2/14/99
50 m hurdles	6.25	Mark McKoy (Canada)	3/5/86
60 m hurdles	7.30	Colin Jackson (Great Britain)	3/6/94
5,000 m walk	18:07.08	Mikhail Shchennikov (Russia)	2/14/95
4 x 200 m	1:22.11	Great Britain	3/3/91
4 x 400 m	3:03.05	Germany	3/10/91
4 x 800 m	7:17.80	USSR	3/14/71

WOMEN

Event	(min./sec.)	Record Holder (country)	Date
50 m	5.96	Irina Privalova (Russia)	2/9/95
60 m	6.92	Irina Privalova (Russia)	2/9/95
200 m	21.87	Merlene Ottey (Jamaica)	2/13/93
400 m	49.59	Jarmila Kratochvilova (Czech.)	3/7/82
800 m	1:56.40	Christine Wachtel (E. Germany)	2/13/88
1,000 m	2:30.94	Maria Mutola (Mozambique)	2/25/99
1,500 m	4:00.27	Doina Melinte (Romania)	2/9/90
Mile	4:17.14	Doina Melinte (Romania)	2/9/90
3,000 m	8:33.82	Elly van Hulst (Holland)	3/4/89
5,000 m	14:47.35	Gabriela Szabo (Romania)	2/13/99
50 m hurdles	6.58	Cornelia Oschkenat (East Germany)	2/20/88
60 m hurdles	7.69	Lyudmila Narozhilenko (USSR)	2/4/90
3,000 m walk	11:40.33	Claudia Iovan (Romania)	1/30/99
4 x 200 m	1:32.55	SC Eintracht Hamm (West Germany)	2/20/88
4 x 400 m	3:26.84	Russia	3/9/97
4x800m	8:18.71	Russia	2/4/94

Event	Meters	Ft./In.	Record Holder (country)	Date
High jump	2.43	7–11.5	Javier Sotomayor (Cuba)	3/4/89
Pole vault	6.15	20–2	Sergey Bubka (Ukraine)	2/21/93
Long jump	8.79	28–10.25	Carl Lewis (U.S.)	1/27/84
Triple jump	17.83	58–6	Eliecer Urrutia (Cuba)	3/1/97
Shot put	22.66	74–4.25	Randy Barnes (U.S.)	1/20/89
Heptathlon		6,476 points	Dan O' Brien (U.S.)	3/14/93

Event	Meters	Ft./In.	Record Holder (country)	Date
High jump	2.07	6–9.5	Heike Henkel (Germany)	2/8/92
Pole vault	4.56	14–11.5	Nicole Rieger-Humbert (Germany)	2/25/99
Long jump	7.37	24–2.25	Heike Drechsler (East Germany)	2/13/88
Triple jump	15.16	49–8.75	Ashia Hansen (Britain)	2/28/98
Shot put	22.50	73–10	Helena Fibingerova (Czech.)	2/19/77
Pentathlon	4991 points		Irina Belova (Unified Team)	2/15/92

Source: International Amateur Athletic Federation.

Olympic Sports

The Summary Olympics

Olympiad	Year	Place	Competitors Men	Competitors Women	Nations represented	Events
I	1896	Athens, Greece	311	—	13	43
II	1900	Paris, France	1,319	11	21	85
III	1904	St. Louis, U.S.	681	6	13	96
—[1]	1906	Athens, Greece	877	7	20	—
IV	1908	London, U.K.	1,999	36	22	110
V	1912	Stockholm, Sweden	2,490	57	29	102
VI[2]	1916	Berlin, Germany	—	—	—	—
VII	1920	Antwerp, Belgium	2,543	64	29	152
VIII	1924	Paris, France	2,956	136	45	126
IX	1928	Amsterdam, Holland	2,724	290	46	109
X	1932	Los Angeles, U.S.	1,281	127	37	117
XI	1936	Berlin, Germany	3,738	328	49	129
XII[2]	1940	Tokyo, Japan	—	—	—	—
XIII[2]	1944	London, U.K.	—	—	—	—
XIV	1948	London, U.K.	3,714	385	59	136
XV	1952	Helsinki, Finland	4,407	518	69	149
XVI	1956	Melbourne, Australia	2,958	384	67	145
XVII	1960	Rome, Italy	4,738	610	84	150
XVIII	1964	Tokyo, Japan	4,457	683	94	163
XIX	1968	Mexico City, Mexico	4,750	781	113	172
XX	1972	Munich, W. Germany	6,659	1,171	122	195
XXI	1976	Montreal, Canada	4,915	1,274	93	198
XXII	1980	Moscow, USSR	4,265	1,192	81	203
XXIII	1984	Los Angeles, U.S.	5,458	1,620	140	221
XXIV	1988	Seoul, South Korea	7,105	2,438	160	237
XXV	1992	Barcelona, Spain	7,555	3,008	171	257
XXVI	1996	Atlanta, U.S.	6,562	3,684	197	271
XXVII	2000	Sydney, Australia				
XXVIII	2004	Athens, Greece				

1. Not recognized as an official Olympiad.   2. Canceled due to war.   **Source:** United States Olympic Committee.

The Winter Olympics

Olympiad	Year	Place	Competitors Men	Competitors Women	Nations represented	Events
I	1924	Chamonix, France	281	13	16	13
II	1928	St. Moritz, Switzerland	366	27	25	13
III	1932	Lake Placid, U.S.	277	30	17	14
IV	1936	Garmisch-Partenkirchen, Germany	680	76	28	17
V	1948	St. Moritz, Switzerland	636	77	28	24
VI	1952	Oslo, Norway	624	108	30	22
VII	1956	Cortina D'Ampezzo, Italy	687	132	32	24
VIII	1960	Squaw Valley, U.S.	502	146	30	27
IX	1964	Innsbruck, Austria	758	175	36	34
X	1968	Grenoble, France	1,063	230	37	35
XI	1972	Sapporo, Japan	927	218	36	35
XII	1976	Innsbruck, Austria	1,013	248	37	37
XIII	1980	Lake Placid, U.S.	1,012	271	37	39
XIV	1984	Sarajevo, Yugoslavia	1,127	283	49	40
XV	1988	Calgary, Canada	1,270	364	57	46
XVI	1992	Albertville, France	1,313	488	64	57
XVII	1994	Lillehammer, Norway	1,302	542	67	61
XVIII	1998	Nagano, Japan	2,302 (total)		72	68
XIX	2002	Salt Lake City, Utah				

SUMMER OLYMPIC CHAMPIONS

Gymnastics-Men

All-Around
1900	Gustave Sandras, France	
1904	Julius Lenhart, Austria	
1908	Alberto Braglia, Italy	
1912	Alberto Braglia, Italy	
1920	Giorgio Zampori, Italy	
1924	Leon Stukelj, Yugoslavia	
1928	Georges Miez, Switzerland	
1932	Romeo Neri, Italy	
1936	Alfred Schwarzmann, Germany	

1948	Veikko Huhtanen, Finland
1952	Viktor Chukarin, USSR
1956	Viktor Chukarin, USSR
1960	Boris Shakhlin, USSR
1964	Yukio Endo, Japan
1968	Sawao Kato, Japan
1972	Sawao Kato, Japan
1976	Nikolai Andrianov, USSR
1980	Aleksandr Dityatin, USSR
1984	Koji Gushiken, Japan

1988	Vladimir Artemov, USSR
1992	Vitali Scherbo, Unified Team
1996	Li Xiaoshuang, China

Team Combined
1908	Sweden
1912	Italy
1920	Italy
1928	Switzerland
1932	Italy

1936	Germany
1948	Finland
1952	USSR
1956	USSR
1960	Japan
1964	Japan
1968	Japan
1972	Japan
1976	Japan
1980	USSR
1984	USA
1988	USSR
1992	Unified Team
1996	Russia

Horizontal Bar

1896	Herman Weingärtner, Germany
1904	Anton Heida, U.S.
	Edward Hennig, U.S. (tie)
1924	Leon Stukelj, Yugoslavia
1928	Georges Miez
1932	Dallas Bixler, U.S.
1936	Aleksanteri Saarvala, Finland
1948	Josef Stalder, Switzerland
1952	Jack Günthard, Switzerland
1956	Takashi Ono, Japan
1960	Takashi Ono, Japan
1964	Boris Shakhlin, USSR
1968	Akinori Nakayama, Japan
1972	Mitsuo Tsukahara, Japan
1976	Mitsuo Tsukahara, Japan
1980	Stoyan Deltchev, Bulgaria
1984	Shinji Morisue, Japan
1988	Vladimir Artemov, USSR
	Valeri Lioukine, USSR (tie)
1992	Trent Dimas, U.S.
1996	Andreas Wecker, Germany

Parallel Bars

1896	Alfred Flatow, Germany
1904	George Eyser, U.S.
1924	August Güttinger, Switzerland
1928	Ladislav Vácha, Czechoslovakia
1932	Romeo Neri, Italy
1936	Konrad Frey, Germany
1948	Michael Reusch, Switzerland
1952	Hans Eugster, Switzerland

1956	Viktor Chukarin, USSR
1960	Boris Shakhlin, USSR
1964	Yukio Endo, Japan
1968	Akinori Nakayama, Japan
1972	Sawao Koto, Japan
1976	Sawao Koto, Japan
1980	Aleksandr Tkachyov, USSR
1984	Bart Conner, U.S.
1988	Vladimir Artemov, USSR
1992	Vitali Scherbo, Unified Team
1996	Rustam Sharipov, Ukraine

Long Horse Vault

1896	Karl Schumann, Germany
1904	George Eyser, U.S.
	Anton Heida, U.S. (tie)
1924	Frank Kriz, U.S.
1928	Eugen Mack, Switzerland
1932	Savino Guglielmetti, Italy
1936	Alfred Schwarzmann, Germany
1948	Paavo Aaltonen, Finland
1952	Viktor Chukarin, USSR
1956	Helmut Bantz, West Germany
1960	Takashi Ono, Japan
1964	Haruhiro Yamashita, Japan
1968	Mikhail Voronin, USSR
1972	Klaus Köste, East Germany
1976	Nikolai Andrianov, USSR
1980	Nikolai Andrianov, USSR
1984	Lou Yun, China
1988	Lou Yun, China
1992	Vitali Scherbo, Unified Team
1996	Alexei Nemov, Russia

Side (Pommel) Horse

1896	Jules Zutter, Switzerland
1904	Anton Heida, U.S.
1924	Josef Wilhelm, Switzerland
1928	Hermann Hänggi, Switzerland
1932	István Pelle, Hungary
1936	Konrad Frey, Germany
1948	Paavo Aaltonen, Finland
1952	Viktor Chukarin, USSR
1956	Boris Shakhlin, USSR
1960	Eugene Ekman, Finland
1964	Miroslav Cerar, Yugoslavia
1968	Miroslav Cerar, Yugoslavia
1972	Viktor Klimenko, USSR

1976	Zoltán Magyar, Hungary
1980	Zoltán Magyar, Hungary
1984	Li Ning, China
1988	Lyubomir Gueraskov, Bulgaria
	Dmitri Bilozertchev, USSR
	Zsolt Borkai, Hungary
1992	Vitali Scherbo, Unified Team
	Gil Su Pae, North Korea
1996	Li Donghua, Switzerland

Rings

1896	Ioannis Mitropoulos, Greece
1904	Hermann Glass, U.S.
1924	Francesco Martino, Italy
1928	Leon Stukelj, Yugoslavia
1932	George Gulack, U.S.
1936	Alois Hudec, Czechoslovakia
1948	Karl Frei, Switzerland
1952	Grant Shaginyan, USSR
1956	Albert Azaryan, USSR
1960	Albert Azaryan, USSR
1964	Takuji Haytta, Japan
1968	Akinori Nakayama, Japan
1972	Akinori Nakayama, Japan
1976	Nikolai Andrianov, USSR
1980	Aleksandr Dityatin, USSR
1984	Koji Gushiken, Japan
1988	Holger Behrendt, E. Germany
	Dmitri Bilozertchev, USSR
1992	Vitali Scherbo, Unified Team
1996	Yuri Chechi, Italy

Floor Exercises

1932	István Pelle, Hungary
1936	Georges Miez, Switzerland
1948	Ferenc Pataki, Hungary
1952	K. William Thoresson, Sweden
1956	Valentin Muratov, USSR
1960	Nobuyuki Aihara, Japan
1964	Franco Menichelli, Italy
1968	Sawao Koto, Japan
1972	Nikolai Andrianov, USSR
1976	Nikolai Andrianov, USSR
1980	Roland Brückner, E. Germany
1984	Li Ning, China
1988	Sergei Kharikov, USSR
1992	Xiaosahuang Li, China
1996	Ioannis Melissanidis, Greece

Gymnastics—Women

All-Around

1952	Maria Gorokhovskaya, USSR
1956	Larissa Latynina, USSR
1960	Larissa Latynina, USSR
1964	Vera Cáslavská, Czech.
1968	Vera Cáslavská, Czech.
1972	Lyudmila Tourischeva, USSR
1976	Nadia Comaneci, Romania
1980	Yelena Davydova, USSR
1984	Mary Lou Retton, U.S.
1988	Elena Shushunova, USSR
1992	Tatiana Goutsou, Unified Team
1996	Lilia Popkopayeva, Ukraine

Team Combined

1928	Holland
1936	West Germany
1948	Czechoslovakia
1952	Soviet Union
1956	Soviet Union
1960	Soviet Union
1964	Soviet Union
1968	Soviet Union
1972	Soviet Union
1976	Soviet Union
1980	Soviet Union
1984	Romania
1988	Soviet Union
1992	Unified Team
1996	United States

Vault

1952	Yekaterina Kalinchuk
1956	Larissa Latynina, USSR
1960	Margarita Nikolayeva, USSR
1964	Vera Cáslavská, Czech.
1968	Vera Cáslavská, Czech.
1972	Karin Janz, East Germany
1976	Nelli Kim, USSR
1980	Natalya Shaposhnikova, USSR
1984	Ecaterina Szabó, Romania
1988	Svetlana Boguinskaya, USSR
1992	Henrietta Onodi, Hungary
	Lavinia Milosovici, Romania
1996	Simona Amanar, Romania

Uneven Bars

1952	Margit Korondi, Hungary
1956	Agnes Keleti, Hungary
1960	Polina Astakhova, USSR
1964	Polina Astakhova, USSR
1968	Vera Cáslavská, Czech.
1972	Karin Janz, East Germany
1976	Nadia Comaneci, Romania
1980	Maxi Gnauck, East Germany
1984	Ma Yanhong, China
1988	Daniela Silivas, Romania
1992	Li Lu, China
1996	Svetlana Chorkina, Russia

Floor Exercises

1952	Agnes Keleti, Hungary
1956	Agnes Keleti, Hungary
1960	Larissa Latynina, USSR
1964	Larissa Latynina, USSR
1968	Vera Cáslavská, Czech.
1972	Olga Korbut, USSR
1976	Nelli Kim, USSR
1980	Nadia Comaneci, Rom.
1984	Ecaterina Szabó, Romania
1988	Daniela Silivas, Romania
1992	Lavina Milosovici, Rom.
1996	Lillia Podkopayeva, Ukraine

Balance Beam

1952	Nina Bocharova, USSR
1956	Agnes Keleti, Hungary
1960	Eva Bosáková, Czechoslovakia
1964	Vera Cáslavská, Czechoslovakia
1968	Natalya Kuchinskaya, USSR
1972	Olga Korbut, USSR
1976	Nadia Comaneci, Romania
1980	Nadia Comaneci, Romania
1984	Simona Pauca, Romania
1988	Daniela Silivas, Romania
1992	Tatiana Lyssenko, UnifiedTeam
1996	Shannon Miller, United States

Swimming and Diving, Men

50m Freestyle		Time
1904	Zoltán Halmay, Hungary	0:28.00
1988	Matt Biondi, U.S.	0:22.14
1992	Aleksandr Popov, Unified Team	0:21.91
1996	Aleksandr Popov, Russia	0:22.13

100m Freestyle		Time
1896	Alfréd Hajós, Hungary	1:22.20
1904	Zoltán Halmay, Hungary (100 yds.)	1:02.80
1908	Charles Daniels, U.S.	1:05.60
1912	Duke Paoa Kahanamoku, U.S.	1:03.40
1920	Duke Paoa Kahanamoku, U.S.	1:00.40
1924	Johnny Weissmuller, U.S.	0:59.00
1928	Johnny Weissmuller, U.S.	0:58.60
1932	Yasuji Miyazaki, Japan	0:58.20
1936	Ferenc Csík, Hungary	0:57.60
1948	Walter Ris, U.S.	0:57.30
1952	Clarke Scholes, U.S.	0:57.40
1956	Jon Henricks, Australia	0:55.40
1960	John Devitt, Australia	0:55.20
1964	Donald Schollander, U.S.	0:53.40
1968	Michael Wenden, Australia	0:52.20
1972	Mark Spitz, U.S.	0:51.22
1976	Jim Montgomery, U.S.	0:49.99
1980	Jörg Woithe, E. Germany	0:50.40
1984	Rowdy Gaines, U.S.	0:49.80
1988	Matt Biondi, U.S.	0:48.63
1992	Aleksandr Popov, Unified Team	0:49.02
1996	Aleksandr Popov, Russia	0:48.74

200m Freestyle		Time
1900	Frederick Lane, Austria	2:25.20
1904	Charles Daniels, U.S.	2:44.20
1968	Michael Wenden, Australia	1:55.20
1972	Mark Spitz, U.S.	1:52.78
1976	Bruce Furniss, U.S.	1:50.29
1980	Sergei Kopliakov, USSR	1:49.81
1984	Michael Gross, W. Germany	1:47.44
1988	Duncan Armstrong, Australia	1:47.25
1992	Evgueni Sadovyi, Unified Team	1:46.70
1996	Danyon Loader, New Zealand	1:47.63

400m Freestyle		Time
1896	Paul Neumann, Austria (500m)	8:12.60
1904	Charles Daniels, U.S. (440 yds.)	6:16.20
1908	Henry Taylor, Great Britain (440 yds.)	5:36.80
1912	George Hodgson, Canada	5:24.40
1920	Norman Ross, U.S.	5:26.80
1924	Johnny Weissmuller, U.S.	5:04.20
1928	Alberto Zorilla, Argentina	5:01.60
1932	Clarence "Buster" Crabbe, U.S.	4:48.40
1936	Jack Medica, U.S.	4:44.50
1948	William Smith, U.S.	4:41.00
1952	Jean Boiteux, France	4:30.70
1956	Murray Rose, Australia	4:27.30
1960	Murray Rose, Australia	4:18.30
1964	Donald Schollander, U.S.	4:12.20
1968	Michael Burton, U.S.	4:09.00
1972	Bradford Cooper, Australia	4:00.27
1976	Brian Goodell, U.S.	3:51.93
1980	Vladimir Salnikov, USSR	3:51.31
1984	George DiCarlo, U.S.	3:51.23
1988	Ewe Dassler, E. Germany	3:46.95
1992	Evgueni Sadovyi, Unified Team	3:45.00
1996	Danyon Loader, New Zealand	3:47.97

1,500m Freestyle		Time
1896	Alfréd Hajós, Hungary (1200m)	18:22.20
1900	John Arthur Jarvis, Great Britain (1,000 m)	13:40.20
1904	Emil Rausch, Germany (1,609 m)	27:18.20
1908	Henry Taylor, Great Britain	22:48.40
1912	George Hodgson, Canada	22:00.00
1920	Norman Ross, U.S.	22:23.20
1924	Andrew "Boy" Charlton, Australia	20:06.60
1928	Arne Borg, Sweden	19:51.80
1932	Kusuo Kitamura, Japan	19:12.40
1936	Noboru Terada, Japan	19:13.70
1948	James McLane, U.S.	19:18.50
1952	Ford Konno, U.S.	18:30.30
1956	Murray Rose, Australia	17:58.90
1960	John Konrads, Australia	17:19.60
1964	Robert Windle, Australia	17:01.7
1968	Michael Burton, U.S.	16:38.90
1972	Michael Burton, U.S.	15:52.58
1976	Brian Goodell, U.S.	15:02:40
1980	Vladimir Salnikov, USSR	14:58.27
1984	Michael O'Brien, U.S.	15:05.20
1988	Vladimir Salnikov, USSR	15:00.40
1992	Kieren Perkins, Australia	14:43.48
1996	Kieren Perkins, Australia	14:56.40

100m Backstroke		Time
1904	Walter Brack, Germany (100yds)	1:16.80
1908	Arno Bieberstein, Germany	1:24.60
1912	Harry Hebner, U.S.	1:21.20
1920	Warren Paoa Kealoha, U.S.	1:15.20
1924	Warren Paoa Kealoha, U.S.	1:13.20
1928	George Kojac, U.S.	1:08.20
1932	Masaji Kiyokawa, Japan	1:08.60
1936	Adolf Kiefer, U.S.	1:05.90
1948	Allen Stack, U.S.	1:06.40
1952	Yoshinobu Oyakawa, U.S.	1:05.40
1956	David Theile, Australia	1:02.20
1960	David Theile, Austalia	1:01.90
1964	Not held	
1968	Roland Matthes, E. Germany	0:58.70
1972	Roland Matthes, E. Germany	0:56.58
1976	John Naber, U.S.	0:55.49
1980	Bengt Baron, Sweden	0:56.33
1984	Richard Carey, U.S.	0:55.79
1988	Daichi Suzuki, Japan	0:55.05
1992	Mark Tewksbury, Canada	0:53.98
1996	Jeff Rouse, U.S.	0:54:10

200m Backstroke		Time
1900	Ernst Hoppenberg, Germany	2:47.00
1964	Jed Graef, U.S.	2:10.30
1968	Roland Matthes, E. Germany	2:09.60
1972	Roland Matthes, E. Germany	2:02.82
1976	John Naber, U.S.	1:59.19
1980	Sándor Wladár, Hungary	2:01.93
1984	Richard Carey, U.S.	2:00.23
1988	Igor Poliansky, USSR	1:59.37
1992	Martin Zubero, Spain	1:58.47
1996	Brad Bridgewater, U.S.	1:58.54

100m Breaststroke		Time
1968	Donald McKenzie, U.S.	1:07.70
1972	Nobutaka Taguchi, Japan	1:04.94
1976	John Hencken, U.S.	1:03.11
1980	Duncan Goodhew, Great Britain	1:03.44
1984	Steve Lundquist, U.S.	1:01.65
1988	Adrian Moorhouse, Great Britain	1:02.04
1992	Nelson Diebel, U.S.	1:01.50
1996	Fred Deburghgraeve, Belgium	1:00.65

200m Breaststroke		Time
1908	Frederick Holman, Great Britain	3:09.20
1912	Walter Bathe, Germany	3:01.80
1920	Haken Malmroth, Sweden	3:04.40
1924	Robert Skelton, U.S.	2:56.60
1928	Yoshiyuki Tsuruta, Japan	2:48.80
1932	Yoshiyuki Tsuruta, Japan	2:45.40
1936	Tetsuo Hamuro, Japan	2:41.50
1948	Joseph Verdeur, U.S.	2:39.30
1952	John Davies, Australia	2:34.40
1956	Masaru Furukawa, Japan	2:34.70
1960	William Mulliken, U.S.	2:37.40
1964	Ian O'Brien, Australia	2:27.80
1968	Felipe Muñoz, Mexico	2:28.70
1972	John Hencken, U.S.	2:21.55
1976	David Wilkie, Great Britain	2:15.11
1980	Robertas Zhulpa, USSR	2:15.85
1984	Victor Davis, Canada	2:13.34
1988	Jozsef Szabo, Hungary	2:13.52
1992	Mike Barrowman, U.S.	2:10.16
1996	Norbert Rozso, Hungary	2:12.57

100m Butterfly		Time
1968	Douglas Russell, U.S.	0:55.90
1972	Mark Spitz, U.S.	0:54.27
1976	Matt Vogel, U.S.	0:54.35
1980	Par Arvidsson, Sweden	0:54.92
1984	Michael Gross, W. Germany	0:53.08
1988	Anthony Nesty, Surinam	0:53.00
1992	Pablo Morales, U.S.	0:53.32
1996	Denis Pankratov, Russia	0:52.27

200m Butterfly		Time
1956	William Yorzyk, U.S.	2:19.30
1960	Michael Troy, U.S.	2:12.80
1964	Kevin Berry, Australia	2:06.60
1968	Carl Robie, U.S.	2:08.70
1972	Mark Spitz, U.S.	2:00.70
1976	Mike Bruner, U.S.	1:59.23
1980	Sergei Fesenko, USSR	1:59.76
1984	Jon Sieben, Australia	1:57.04
1988	Michael Gross, W. Germany	1:56.94
1992	Mel Stewart, U.S.	1:56.26
1996	Denis Pankratov, Russia	1:56.51

200m Individual Medley

		Time
1968	Charles Hickcox, U.S.	2:12.00
1972	Gunnar Larsson, Sweden	2:07.17
1984	Alex Baumann, Canada	2:01.42
1988	Tamas Darnyi, Hungary	2:00.17
1992	Tamas Darnyi, Hungary	2:00.76
1996	Attila Czene, Hungary	1:59.91

400m Individual Medley

		Time
1964	Richard W. Roth, U.S.	4:45.40
1968	Charles Hickcox, U.S.	4:48.40
1972	Gunnar Larsson, Sweden	4:31.98
1976	Rod Strachan, U.S.	4:23.68
1980	Aleksandr Sidorenko, USSR	4:22.89
1984	Alex Baumann, Canada	4:17.41
1988	Tamas Darnyi, Hungary	4:14.75
1992	Tamas Darnyi, Hungary	4:14.23
1996	Tom Dolan, U.S.	4:14.90

4x100m Medley Relay

					Time
1960	U.S.	4:05.40	1980	Australia	3:45.70
1964	U.S.	3:58.40	1984	U.S.	3:39.30
1968	U.S.	3:54.90	1988	U.S.	3:36.93
1972	U.S.	3:48.16	1992	U.S.	3:36.93
1976	U.S.	3:42.22	1996	U.S.	3:34.84

4x100m Freestyle Relay

					Time
1964	U.S.	3:33.20	1988	U.S.	3:16.53
1968	U.S.	3:31.70	1992	U.S.	3:16.74
1972	U.S.	3:26.42	1996	U.S.	3:15.41
1984	U.S.	3:19.03			

4x200m Freestyle Relay

					Time
1908	Great Britain	10:55.60	1960	U.S.	8:10.20
1912	Australia	10:11.60	1964	U.S.	7:52.10

1920	U.S.	10:04.40	1968	U.S.	7:52.33
1924	U.S.	9:53.40	1972	U.S.	7:35.78
1928	U.S.	9:36.20	1976	U.S.	7:23.22
1932	Japan	8:58.40	1980	USSR	7:23.50
1936	Japan	8:51.50	1984	U.S.	7:15.69
1948	U.S.	8:46.00	1988	U.S.	7:12.69
1952	U.S.	8:31.10	1992	Unified Team	7:11.95
1956	Australia	8:23.60	1996	U.S.	7:14.84

Platform Diving

1904	George E. Sheldon, U.S.	1960	Robert Webster, U.S.
1908	Hjalmar Johansson, Sweden	1964	Robert Webster, U.S.
1912	Erik Adlerz, Sweden	1968	Klaus Dibiasi, Italy
1920	Clarence Pinkston, U.S.	1972	Klaus Dibiasi, Italy
1924	Albert C. White, U.S.	1976	Klaus Dibiasi, Italy
1928	Pete DesJardins, U.S.	1980	Falk Hoffmann, E. Germany
1932	Harold Smith, U.S.	1984	Gregory Louganis, U.S.
1936	Marshall Wayne, U.S.	1988	Gregory Louganis, U.S.
1948	Dr. Samuel Lee, U.S.	1992	Sun Shuwei, China
1952	Dr. Samuel Lee, U.S.	1996	Xiong Ni, China
1956	Joaquin Capilla Perez, Mexico		

Springboard Diving

1908	Albert Zürner, Germany	1960	Gary Tobian, U.S.
1912	Paul Günther, Germany	1964	Kenneth R. Sitzberger, U.S.
1920	Louis Kuehn, U.S.	1968	Bernard Wrightson, U.S.
1924	Albert C. White, U.S.	1972	Vladimir Vasin, USSR
1928	Pete Desjardins, U.S.	1976	Philip Boggs, U.S.
1932	Michael Galitzen, U.S.	1980	Aleksandr Portnov, USSR
1936	Richard Degener, U.S.	1984	Gregory Louganis, U.S.
1948	Bruce Harlan, U.S.	1988	Gregory Louganis, U.S.
1952	David Browning, U.S.	1992	Mark Lenzi, U.S.
1956	Robert L. Clotworthy, U.S.	1996	Dmitri Saoutine, Russia

Swimming and Diving, Women

50m Freestyle

		Time
1988	Kristin Otto, E. Germany	0:25.49
1992	Yang Wenji, China	0:24.79
1996	Amy Van Dyken, U.S.	0:24.87

100m Freestyle

		Time
1912	Fanny Durack, Australia	1:22.20
1920	Ethelda Bleibtrey, U.S.	1:13.60
1924	Ethel Lackie, U.S.	1:12.40
1928	Albina Osipowich, U.S.	1:11.00
1932	Helene Madison, U.S.	1:06.80
1936	Rie Mastenbroek, Netherlands	1:05.90
1948	Greta Andersen, Denmark	1:06.30
1952	Katalin Szoke, Hungary	1:06.80
1956	Dawn Fraser, Australia	1:02.00
1960	Dawn Fraser, Australia	1:01.20
1964	Dawn Fraser, Australia	0:59.50
1968	Jan Henne, U.S.	1:00.00
1972	Sandra Neilson, U.S.	0:58.59
1976	Kornelia Ender, E. Germany	0:55.65
1980	Barbara Krause, E. Germany	0:54.79
1984	Nancy Hogshead, U.S.	0:55.92
1988	Kristin Otto, E. Germany	0:54.93
1992	Zhuang Yong, China	0:54.65
1996	Le Jingyi, China	0:54.50

200m Freestyle

		Time
1968	Deborah Meyer, U.S.	2:10.50
1972	Shane Gould, Australia	2:03.56
1976	Kornelia Ender, E. Germany	1:59.26
1980	Barbara Krause, E. Germany	1:58.33
1984	Mary Wayte, U.S.	1:59.23
1988	Heike Friederich, E. Germany	1:57.65
1992	Nicole Haislett, U.S.	1:57.90
1996	Claudia Poll, Costa Rica	1:58.16

400m Freestyle

		Time
1920	Ethelda Bleibtrey, U.S. (300 m)	4:34.00
1924	Martha Norelius, U.S.	6:02.20
1928	Martha Norelius, U.S.	5:42.80
1932	Helene Madison, U.S.	5:28.50
1936	Hendrika "Rie" Mastenbroek, Netherlands	5:26.40
1948	Ann Curtis, U.S.	5:17.80
1952	Valeria Gyenge, Hungary	5:12.10
1956	Lorraine Crapp, Australia	4:54.60
1960	S. Chris Von Saltza, U.S.	4:50.60
1964	Virginia Duenkel, U.S.	4:43.30
1968	Deborah Meyer, U.S.	4:31.80
1972	Shane Gould, Australia	4:19.44
1976	Petra Thümer, E. Germany	4:09.89
1980	Ines Diers, E. Germany	4:08.76
1984	Tiffany Cohen, U.S.	4:07.10

1988	Janet Evans, U.S.	4:03.85
1992	Dagmar Hase, Germany	4:07.18
1996	Michelle Smith, Ireland	4:07.25

800m Freestyle

		Time
1968	Deborah Meyer, U.S.	9:24.00
1972	Keena Rothhammer, U.S.	8:53.68
1976	Petra Thümer, E. Germany	8:37.14
1980	Michelle Ford, Australia	8:28.90
1984	Tiffany Cohen, U.S.	8:24.95
1988	Janet Evans, U.S.	8:20.20
1992	Janet Evans, U.S.	8:25.52
1996	Brooke Bennett, U.S.	8:27.89

100m Backstroke

		Time
1924	Sybil Bauer, U.S.	1:23.20
1928	Maria Braun, Netherlands	1:22.00
1932	Eleanor Holm, U.S.	1:19.40
1936	Nida Senff, Netherlands	1:18.90
1948	Karen Harup, Denmark	1:14.40
1952	Joan Harrison, South Africa	1:14.30
1956	Judy Grinham, Great Britain	1:12.90
1960	Lynn Burke, U.S.	1:09.30
1964	Cathy Ferguson, U.S.	1:07.70
1968	Kaye Hall, U.S.	1:06.20
1972	Melissa Belote, U.S.	1:05.78
1976	Ulrike Richter, E. Germany	1:01.83
1980	Rica Reinisch, E. Germany	1:00.86
1984	Theresa Andrews, U.S.	1:02.55
1988	Kristin Otto, E. Germany	1:00.89
1992	Krisztina Egerszegi, Hungary	1:00.68
1996	Beth Botsford, U.S.	1:01.19

200m Backstroke

		Time
1968	Lillian "Pokey" Watson, U.S.	2:24.80
1972	Melissa Belote, U.S.	2:19.19
1976	Ulrike Richter, E. Germany	2:13.43
1980	Rica Reinisch, E. Germany	2:11.77
1984	Jolanda de Rover, Netherlands	2:12.38
1988	Krisztina Egerszegi, Hungary	2:09.29
1992	Krisztina Egerszegi, Hungary	2:07.06
1996	Krisztina Egerszegi, Hungary	2:07.83

100m Breaststroke

		Time
1972	Catherine Carr, U.S.	1:13.58
1976	Hannelore Anke, E. Germany	1:11.16
1980	Ute Geweniger, E. Germany	1:10.22
1984	Petra van Staveren, Netherlands	1:09.88
1988	Tania Dangalakova, Bulgaria	1:07.95
1992	Elena Roudkovskaia, Unified Team	1:08.00
1996	Penny Heyns, South Africa	1:07.73

200m Breaststroke		Time
1924	Lucy Morton, Great Britain	3:33.20
1928	Hilde Schrader, Germany	3:12.60
1932	Clare Dennis, Australia	3:06.30
1936	Hideko Maehata, Japan	3:03.60
1948	Nelly van Vliet, Netherlands	2:57.20
1952	Eva Szekely, Hungary	2:51.70
1956	Ursula Happe, Germany	2:53.10
1960	Anita Lonsbrough, Great Britain	2:49.50
1964	Galina Prozumenshikova, USSR	2:46.40
1968	Sharon Wichman, U.S.	2:44.40
1972	Beverley Whitfield, Australia	2:41.71
1976	Marina Koshevaia, USSR	2:33.35
1980	Lina Kaciusyte, USSR	2:29.54
1984	Anne Ottenbrite, Canada	2:30.38
1988	Silke Hoerner, E. Germany	2:26.71
1992	Kyoko Iwasaki, Japan	2:26.65
1996	Penny Heyns, South Africa	2:25.41

100m Butterfly		Time
1956	Shelly Mann, U.S.	1:11.00
1960	Carolyn Schuler, U.S.	1:09.50
1964	Sharon Stouder, U.S.	1:04.70
1968	Lynnette McClements, Australia	1:05.50
1972	Mayumi Aoki, Japan	1:03.34
1976	Kornelia Ender, E. Germany	1:00.13
1980	Caren Metschuck, E. Germany	1:00.42
1984	Mary T. Meagher, U.S.	0:59.26
1988	Kristin Otto, E. Germany	0:59.00
1992	Qian Hong, China	0:58.62
1996	Amy Van Dyken, U.S.	0:59.13

200m Butterfly		Time
1968	Ada Kok, Netherlands	2:24.70
1972	Karen Moe, U.S.	2:15.57
1976	Andrea Pollack, E. Germany	2:11.41
1980	Ines Geissler, E. Germany	2:10.44
1984	Mary T. Meagher, U.S.	2:06.90
1988	Kathleen Nord, E. Germany	2:09.51
1992	Summer Sanders, U.S.	2:08.67
1996	Susan O'Neill, Australia	2:07.76

200m Individual Medley		Time
1968	Claudia Kolb, U.S.	2:24.70
1972	Shane Gould, Australia	2:23.07
1984	Tracy Caulkins, U.S.	2:12.64
1988	Daniela Hunger, E. Germany	2:12.59
1992	Lin Li, China	2:11.65
1996	Michelle Smith, Ireland	2:13.93

400m Individual Medley		Time
1964	Donna De Varona, U.S.	5:18.70
1968	Claudia Kolb, U.S.	5:08.50

4x100m Medley Relay			Time
1960	U.S.	4:41.10	
1964	U.S.	4:33.90	
1968	U.S.	4:28.30	
1972	U.S.	4:20.75	
1976	E. Germany	4:07.95	
1980	E. Germany	4:06.67	
1984	U.S.	4:08.34	
1988	E. Germany	4:03.74	
1992	U.S.	4:02.54	
1996	U.S.	4:02.88	

4x100m Freestyle Relay		Time
1912	Great Britain 5:52.80	
1920	U.S.	5:11.60
1924	U.S.	4:58.80
1928	U.S.	4:47.60
1932	U.S.	4:38.00
1938	Netherlands 4:36.00	
1948	U.S.	4:29.20
1952	Hungary 4:24.40	
1956	Australia 4:17.10	
1960	U.S.	4:08.90
1964	U.S.	4:03.80
1968	U.S.	4:02.50
1972	U.S.	3:55.19
1976	U.S.	3:44.82
1980	E. Germany	3:42.71
1984	U.S.	3:43.43
1988	E. Germany	3:40.63
1992	U.S.	3:39.46
1996	U.S.	3:39.29

4x200m Freestyle Relay		Time
1996	United States	7:59.87

Platform Diving

1912	Greta Johansson, Sweden	1960	Ingrid Krämer, E. Germany
1920	Stefani Fryland-Clausen, Denmark	1964	Lesley Bush, U.S.
		1968	Milena Duchkova, Czechoslovakia
1924	Caroline Smith, U.S.	1972	Ulrika Knape, Sweden
1928	Elizabeth Becker Pinkston, U.S.	1976	Elena Vaytsekhovskaya, USSR
1932	Dorothy Poynton, U.S.	1980	Martina Jäschke, E. Germany
1936	Dorothy Poynton Hill, U.S.	1984	Zhou Jihong, China
1948	Victoria Draves, U.S.	1988	Xu Yahmei, China
1952	Patricia McCormick, U.S.	1992	Fu Mingxia, China
1956	Patricia McCormick, U.S.	1996	Fu Mingxia, China

Springboard Diving

1920	Aileen Riggin, U.S.	1964	Ingrid Engle-Kramer, E. Germ.
1924	Elizabeth Becker, U.S.	1968	Sue Gossick, U.S.
1928	Helen Meany, U.S.	1972	Micki King, U.S.
1932	Georgia Coleman, U.S.	1976	Jennifer Chandler, U.S.
1936	Marjorie Gestring, U.S.	1980	Irina Kalinina, USSR
1948	Victoria Draves, U.S.	1984	Sylvie Bernier, Canada
1952	Patricia McCormick, U.S.	1988	Gao Min, China
1956	Patricia McCormick, U.S.	1992	Gao Min, China
1960	Ingrid Kramer, Germany	1996	Fu Mingxia, China

Track and Field, Men

100 Meter Dash		Time
1896	Thomas E. Burke, U.S.	12.00
1900	Francis W. Jarvis, U.S.	11.00
1904	Archie Hahn, U.S.	11.00
1908	Reginald E. Walker, S. Africa	10.80
1912	Ralph C. Craig, U.S.	10.80
1920	Charles W. Paddock, U.S.	10.80
1924	Harold M. Abrahams, Great Britain	10.60
1928	Percy Williams, Canada	10.80
1932	Eddie Tolan, U.S.	10.30
1936	Jesse Owens, U.S.	10.30
1948	Harrison Dillard, U.S.	10.30
1952	Lindy J. Remigino, U.S.	10.40
1956	Bobby J. Morrow, U.S.	10.50
1960	Armin Hary, Germany	10.20
1964	Robert L. Hayes, U.S.	10.00
1968	James Hines, U.S.	9.95
1972	Valery Borzov, USSR	10.14
1976	Hasely Crawford, Trinidad & Tobago	10.06
1980	Allan Wells, Great Britain	10.25
1984	Carl Lewis, U.S.	9.99
1988	Carl Lewis, U.S.	9.92
1992	Linford Christie, Great Britain	9.96
1996	Donovan Bailey, Canada	9.84

200 Meters		Time
1900	John W.B. Tewksbury, U.S.	22.20
1904	Archie Hahn, U.S.	21.60
1908	Robert Kerr, Canada	22.60
1912	Ralph C. Craig, U.S.	21.70
1920	Allen Woodring, U.S.	22.00
1924	Jackson V. Scholz, U.S.	21.60
1928	Percy Williams, Canada	21.80
1932	Eddie Tolan, U.S.	21.20
1936	Jesse Owens, U.S.	20.70
1948	Melvin Patton, U.S.	21.10
1952	Andrew W. Stanfield, U.S.	20.70
1956	Bobby J. Morrow, U.S.	20.60
1960	Livio Berruti, Italy	20.50
1964	Henry Carr, U.S.	20.30
1968	Tommie Smith, U.S.	19.83
1972	Valery Borzov, USSR	20.00
1976	Donald Quarrie, Jamaica	20.23
1980	Pietro Mennea, Italy	20.19
1984	Carl Lewis, U.S.	19.80
1988	Joe DeLoach, U.S.	19.75
1992	Mike Marsh, U.S.	20.01
1996	Michael Johnson, U.S.	19.32

400 Meters		Time
1896	Thomas E. Burke, U.S.	54.20
1900	Maxey Long, U.S.	49.40
1904	Harry I. Hillman, U.S.	49.20
1908	Wyndham Halswelle, Great Britain	50.00
1912	Charles D. Reidpath, U.S.	48.20
1920	Bevil G.D. Rudd, S. Africa	49.60
1924	Eric H. Liddel, Great Britain	47.60
1928	Ray Barbuti, U.S.	47.80
1932	William A. Carr, U.S.	46.20
1936	Archie Williams, U.S.	46.50
1948	Arthur Wint, Jamaica	46.20
1952	George Rhoden, Jamaica	45.90
1956	Charles L. Jenkins, U.S.	46.70
1960	Otis Davis, U.S.	44.90
1964	Michael D. Larrabee, U.S.	45.10
1968	Lee Evans, U.S.	43.86

1972	Vince Matthews, U.S.	44.66
1976	Alberto Juantorena, Cuba	44.26
1980	Viktor Markin, USSR	44.60
1984	Alonzo Babers, U.S.	44.27
1988	Steven Lewis, U.S.	43.87
1992	Quincy Watts, U.S.	43.50
1996	Michael Johnson, United States	43.49

800 Meters

		Time
1896	Edwin H. Flack, Australia	2:11.00
1900	Alfred E. Tysoe, Great Britain	2:01.20
1904	James D. Lightbody, U.S.	1:56.00
1908	Melvin W. Sheppard, U.S.	1:52.80
1912	Ted Meredith, U.S.	1:51.90
1920	Albert G. Hill, Great Britain	1:53.40
1924	Douglas G.A. Lowe, Great Britain	1:52.40
1928	Douglas G.A. Lowe, Great Britain	1:51.80
1932	Thomas Hampson, Great Britain	1:49.70
1936	John Woodruff, U.S.	1:52.90
1948	Malvin Whitfield, U.S.	1:49.20
1952	Malvin Whitfield, U.S.	1:49.20
1956	Thomas W. Courtney, U.S.	1:47.70
1960	Peter Snell, New Zealand	1:46.30
1964	Peter Snell, New Zealand	1:45.10
1968	Ralph Doubell, Australia	1:44.30
1972	Dave Wottle, U.S.	1:45.90
1976	Alberto Juantorena, Cuba	1:43.50
1980	Steven Ovett, Great Britain	1:45.40
1984	Joaquim Cruz, Brazil	1:43.00
1988	Paul Ereng, Kenya	1:43.45
1992	William Tanui, Kenya	1:43.66
1996	Vebjoern Rodal, Norway	1:42.59

1,500 Meters

		Time
1896	Edwin H. Flack, Australia	4:33.20
1900	Charles Bennett, Great Britain	4:06.20
1904	James D. Lightbody, U.S.	4:05.40
1908	Melvin W. Sheppard, U.S.	4:03.40
1912	Arnold N.S. Jackson, Great Britain	3:56.80
1920	Albert G. Hill, Great Britain	4:01.80
1924	Paavo Nurmi, Finland	3:53.60
1928	Harry E. Larva, Finland	3:53.20
1932	Luigi Beccali, Italy	3:51.20
1936	Jack Lovelock, New Zealand	3:47.80
1948	Henry Eriksson, Sweden	3:49.80
1952	Josy Barthel, Luxembourg	3:45.10
1956	Ronald Delany, Ireland	3:41.20
1960	Herbert Elliott, Australia	3:35.60
1964	Peter Snell, New Zealand	3:38.10
1968	Kipchoge Keino, Kenya	3:34.90
1972	Pekkha Vasala, Finland	3:36.30
1976	John Walker, New Zealand	3:39.17
1980	Sebastian Coe, Great Britain	3:38.40
1984	Sebastian Coe, Great Britain	3:32.53
1988	Peter Rono, Kenya	3:35.96
1992	Fermin Cacho Ruiz, Spain	3:40.12
1996	Noureddine Morceli, Algeria	3:35.78

5,000 Meters

		Time
1912	Johannes Kolehmainen, Finland	14:36.60
1920	Joseph Guillemot, France	14:55.60
1924	Paavo Nurmi, Finland	14:31.20
1928	Ville Ritola, Finland	14:38.00
1932	Lauri Lehtinen, Finland	14:30.00
1936	Gunnar Höckert, Finland	14:22.20
1948	Gaston Reiff, Belgium	14:17.60
1952	Emil Zátopek, Czechoslovakia	14:06.60
1956	Vladimir Kuts, USSR	13:39.60
1960	Murray Halberg, New Zealand	13:43.40
1964	Robert K. Schul, U.S.	13:48.80
1968	Mohamed Gammoudi, Tunisia	14:05.00
1972	Lasse Viren, Finland	13:26.40
1976	Lasse Viren, Finland	13:24.76
1980	Miruts Yifter, Ethiopia	13:21.00
1984	Said Aouita, Morocco	13:05.59
1988	John Ngugi, Kenya	13:11.70
1992	Dieter Baumann, Germany	13:12.52
1996	Venuste Niyongabo, Burundi	13:07.97

10,000 Meters

		Time
1912	Johannes Kolehmainen, Finland	31:20.80
1920	Paavo Nurmi, Finland	31:45.80
1924	Ville Ritola, Finland	30:23.20
1928	Paavo Nurmi, Finland	30:18.80
1932	Janusz Kusocinski, Poland	30:11.40
1936	Ilmari Salminen, Finland	30:15.40
1948	Emil Zatopek, Czechoslovakia	29:59.60
1952	Emil Zatopek, Czechoslovakia	29:17.00
1956	Vladimir Kuts, USSR	28:45.60
1960	Pyotr Bolotnikov, USSR	28:32.20

1964	William Mills, U.S.	28.24.40
1968	Naftali Temu, Kenya	29:27.40
1972	Lasse Viren, Finland	27:38.40
1976	Lasse Viren, Finland	27:40.38
1980	Miruts Yifter, Ethiopia	27:42.70
1984	Alberto Cova, Italy	27:47.54
1988	Brahim Boutaib, Morocco	27:21.46
1992	Khalid Skah, Morocco	27:46.70
1996	Haile Gebrselassie, Ethiopia	27:07.34

Marathon

		Time
1896	Spiridon Louis, Greece	2:58:50.00
1900	Michel Theato, France	2:59:45.00
1904	Thomas J. Hicks, U.S.	3:28:63.00
1908	John J. Hayes, U.S.	2:55:18.40
1912	Kenneth McArthur, S. Africa	2:36:54.80
1920	Johannes Kolehmainen, Finland	2:32:35.80
1924	Albin Stenroos, Finland	2:41:22.60
1928	Boughéra El Quafi, France	2:32:57.00
1932	Juan Carlos Zabala, Argentina	2:31:36.00
1936	Kitei Son, Japan	2:29:19.20
1948	Delfo Cabrera, Argentina	2:34:51.60
1952	Emil Zátopek, Czechoslovakia	2:23:03.20
1956	Alain Mimoun O'Kacha, France	2:25:00.00
1960	Abebe Bikila, Ethiopia	2:15:16.20
1964	Abebe Bikila, Ethiopia	2:12:11.20
1968	Mamo Wolde, Ethiopia	2:20:26.40
1972	Frank Shorter, U.S.	2:12:19.80
1976	Waldemar Cierpinski, E. Germany	2:09:55.00
1980	Waldemar Cierpinski, E. Germany	2:11:03.00
1984	Carlos Lopes, Portugal	2:09:21.00
1988	Gelindo Bordin, Italy	2:10:32.00
1992	Young-Cho Hwang, S. Korea	2:13:23.00
1996	Josia Thugwane, S. Africa	2:12:36.00

110-Meter Hurdles

		Time
1896	Thomas P. Curtis, U.S.	17.60
1900	Alvin E. Kraenzlein, U.S.	15.40
1904	Frederick N.S. Schule, U.S.	16.00
1908	Forrest Smithson, U.S.	15.00
1912	Frederick W. Kelley, U.S.	15.10
1920	Earl J. Thomson, Canada	14.80
1924	Daniel C. Kinsey, U.S.	15.00
1928	Sydney Atkinson, S. Africa	14.80
1932	George Saling, U.S.	14.60
1936	Forrest Towns, U.S.	14.20
1948	William Porter, U.S.	13.90
1952	Harrison Dillard, U.S.	13.70
1956	Lee Q. Calhoun, U.S.	13.50
1960	Lee Q. Calhoun, U.S.	13.80
1964	Hayes W. Jones, U.S.	13.60
1968	Willie Davenport, U.S.	13.30
1972	Rod Milburn, U.S.	13.24
1976	Guy Drut, France	13.30
1980	Thomas Munkelt, E. Germany	13.39
1984	Roger Kingdom, U.S.	13.20
1988	Roger Kingdom, U.S.	12.98
1992	Mark McKoy, Canada	13.12
1996	Allen Johnson, United States	12.95

400-Meter Hurdles

		Time
1900	John W. B. Tewksbury, U.S.	57.60
1904	Harry L. Hillman, U.S.	53.00
1908	Charles J. Bacon, U.S.	55.00
1920	Frank F. Loomis, U.S.	54.00
1924	F. Morgan Taylor, U.S.	52.60
1928	David Burghley, Great Britain	53.40
1932	Robert Tisdall, Ireland	51.70
1936	Glenn Hardin, U.S.	52.40
1948	Roy Cochran, U.S.	51.10
1952	Charles Moore, U.S.	50.80
1956	Glenn A. Davis, U.S.	50.10
1960	Glenn A. Davis, U.S.	49.30
1964	Warren "Rex" Cawley, U.S.	49.60
1968	David Hemery, Great Britain	48.12
1972	John Akii-Bua, Uganda	47.82
1976	Edwin Moses, U.S.	47.64
1980	Volker Beck, E. Germany	48.70
1984	Edwin Moses, U.S.	47.75
1988	Andre Phillips, U.S.	47.19
1992	Kevin Young, U.S.	46.78
1996	Derrick Adkins, United States	47.55

3,000-Meter Steeplechase

		Time
1900	George Orton, Canada/U.S.	7:34.40
1904	James Lightbody, U.S.	7:39.60
1908	Arthur Russell, Great Britain	10:47.80
1920	Percy Hodge, Great Britain	10:00.40
1924	Ville Ritola, Finland	9:33.60
1928	Toivo A. Loukola, Finland	9:21.80

1932	Volmari Iso-Hollo, Finland	
	(3,460m—extra lap by official error)	10:33.40
1936	Volmari Iso-Hollo, Finland	9:03.80
1948	Thore Sjöstrand, Sweden	9:04.60
1952	Horace Ashenfelter, U.S.	8:45.40
1956	Chris Brasher, Great Britain	8:41.20
1960	Zdzislaw Krzyszkowiak, Poland	8:34.20
1964	Gaston Roelants, Belgium	8:30.80
1968	Amos Biwott, Kenya	8:51.00
1972	Kipchoge Keino, Kenya	8:23.60
1976	Anders Gärderud, Sweden	8:08.20
1980	Bronislaw Malinowski, Poland	8:09.70
1984	Julius Korir, Kenya	8:11.80
1988	Julius Karuiki, Kenya	8:05.51
1992	Matthew Birer, Kenya	8:08.84
1996	Joseph Keter, Kenya	8:07.12

20-Kilometer Walk

		Time
1956	Leonid Spirin, USSR	1:31:27.4
1960	Vladimir Golubnichiy, USSR	1:34:07.2
1964	Kenneth Matthews, Great Britain	1:29:34.0
1968	Vladimir Golubnichiy, USSR	1:33:58.4
1972	Peter Frenkel, E. Germany	1:26:42.4
1976	Daniel Bautista Rocha, Mexico	1:24:40.6
1980	Maurizio Damilano, Italy	1:23:35.5
1984	Ernesto Canto, Mexico	1:23:13.0
1988	Josef Pribilnec, Czechoslovakia	1:19:57.0
1992	Daniel Montero, Spain	1:21:45.0
1996	Jefferson Perez, Ecuador	1:20:07.0

50-Kilometer Walk

		Time
1932	Thomas W. Green, Great Britain	4:50:10.0
1936	Harold Whitlock, Great Britain	4:30:41.4
1948	John A. Ljunggren, Sweden	4:41:52.0
1952	Guiseppe Dordoni, Italy	4:28:07.8
1956	Norman Read, New Zealand	4:30:42.8
1960	Donald Thompson, Great Britain	4:25:30.0
1964	Abdon Pamich, Italy	4:11:12.4
1968	Christoph Höhne, E. Germany	4:20:13.6
1972	Bernd Kannenberg, W. Germany	3:56:11:6
1980	Hartwig Gauder, E. Germany	3:49:24.0
1984	Raúl González, Mexico	3:47:26.0
1988	Vayachselav Ivanenko, USSR	3:38:29.0
1992	Andrei Perlov, Unified Team	3:50:13.0
1996	Robert Korveniowski, Poland	3:43:30.0

4x100-Meter Relay

						Time
1912	Great Britain	42.40	1964	U.S.		39.00
1920	U.S.	42.20	1968	U.S.		38.20
1924	U.S.	41.00	1972	U.S.		38.19
1928	U.S.	41.00	1976	U.S.		38.33
1932	U.S.	40.00	1980	U.S.		38.26
1936	U.S.	39.80	1984	U.S.		37.83
1948	U.S.	40.60	1988	USSR		38.19
1952	U.S.	40.10	1992	U.S.		37.40
1956	U.S.	39.50	1996	Canada		37.69
1960	W. Germany	39.50				

4x400-Meter Relay

						Time
1908	U.S.	3:29.40	1960	U.S.		3:02.20
1912	U.S.	3:16.60	1964	U.S.		3:00.70
1920	Great Britain	3:22.20	1968	U.S.		2:56.16
1924	U.S.	3:16.00	1972	Kenya		2:59.80
1928	U.S.	3:14.20	1976	U.S.		2:58.65
1932	U.S.	3:08.20	1980	USSR		3:01.10
1936	Great Britain	3:09.00	1984	U.S.		2:57.91
1948	U.S.	3:10.40	1988	U.S.		2:56.16
1952	Jamaica	3:03.90	1992	U.S.		2:55.74
1956	U.S.	3:04.80	1996	U.S.		2:55.99

Discus Throw

		Distance
1896	Robert Garrett, U.S.	95' 7½"
1900	Rezsö Bauer, Hungary	118'3"
1904	Martin Sheridan, U.S.	128'10½"
1908	Martin Sheridan, U.S.	134'2"
1912	Armas Taipale, Finland	148'3""
1920	Elmer Niklander, Finland	146'7"
1924	Bud Houser, U.S.	151'4"
1928	Bud Houser, U.S.	155'3"
1932	John Anderson, U.S.	162'4"
1936	W. Kenneth Carpenter, U.S.	165'7"
1948	Adolfo Consolini, Italy	173'2"
1952	Sim Iness, U.S.	180'6"
1956	Al Oerter, U.S.	184'11"
1960	Al Oerter, U.S.	194'2"
1964	Al Oerter, U.S.	200'1"
1968	Al Oerter, U.S.	212'6"
1972	Ludvik Danek, Czechoslovakia	211'3"
1976	Mac Wilkins, U.S.	221'5"
1980	Viktor Rashupkin, USSR	218'8"

1984	Rolf Danneberg, W. Germany	218'6"
1988	Jurgen Schult, E. Germany	225'9¼"
1992	Romas Ubartas, Lithuania	213'8"
1996	Lars Riedel, Germany	227' 8"

Hammer Throw

		Distance
1900	John Flanagan, U.S.	163'1"
1904	John Flanagan, U.S.	168'1"
1908	John Flanagan, U.S.	170'4"
1912	Matthew McGrath, U.S.	179'7"
1920	Patrick Ryan, U.S.	173'5"
1924	Frederick Tootell, U.S.	174'10"
1928	Patrick O'Callaghan, Ireland	168'7"
1932	Patrick O'Callaghan, Ireland	176'11"
1936	Karl Hein, Germany	185'4"
1948	Imre Nemeth, Hungary	183'11"
1952	Jozsef Csermak, Hungary	197'11"
1956	Harold V. Connolly, U.S.	207'3"
1960	Vasiliy Rudenkov, USSR	220'2"
1964	Romuald Klim, USSR	228'10"
1968	Gyula Zsivotzky, Hungary	240'8"
1972	Anatoly Bondarchuk, USSR	247'8"
1976	Yuri Sedykh, USSR	254'4"
1980	Yuri Sedykh, USSR	268'4"
1984	Juha Tiainen, Finland	256'2"
1988	Sergei Litinov, USSR	278'2½"
1992	Andrei Abduvaliyev, Unified Team	270'9"
1996	Balazs Kiss, Hungary	266' 6"

High Jump

		Height
1896	Ellery Clark, U.S.	5'11¼"
1900	Irving K. Baxter, U.S.	6'2¾"
1904	Samuel Jones, U.S.	5'11"
1908	Harry Porter, U.S.	6'3"
1912	Alma Richards, U.S.	6'4"
1920	Richmond Landon, U.S.	6'4"
1924	Harold Osborn, U.S.	6'6"
1928	Robert W. King, U.S.	6'4½"
1932	Duncan McNaughton, Canada	6'5½"
1936	Cornelius Johnson, U.S.	6'8"
1948	John Winter, Australia	6'6"
1952	Walter Davis, U.S.	6'8½"
1956	Charles E. Dumas, U.S.	6'11½"
1960	Robert Shavlakadze, USSR	7'1"
1964	Valery Brumel, USSR	7'1¾"
1968	Richard Fosbury, U.S.	7'4¼"
1972	Juri Tarmak, USSR	7'3¾"
1976	Jacek Wszola, Poland	7'4½"
1980	Gerd Wessig, E. Germany	7'8¾"
1984	Dietmar Mogenburg, W. Germany	7'8½"
1988	Guennadi Avdeenko, USSR	7'9½"
1992	Javier Sotomayor, Cuba	7'8"
1996	Charles Austin, U.S.	7' 10"

Javelin

		Distance
1908	Erik Lemming, Sweden	179'10"
1912	Erik Lemming, Sweden	198'11"
1920	Jonni Myyra, Finland	215'10"
1924	Jonni Myyra, Finland	206'7"
1928	Erik Lundquist, Sweden	218'6"
1932	Matti Jarvinen, Finland	238'6"
1936	Gerhard Stock, Germany	235'8"
1948	Kai Tapio Rautavaara, Finland	228'10"
1952	Cyrus Young, U.S.	242'1"
1956	Egil Danielson, Norway	281'2"
1960	Viktor Tsibulenko, USSR	277'8"
1964	Pauli Nevala, Finland	271'2"
1968	Janis Lusis, USSR	295'7"
1972	Klaus Wolfemann, W. Germany	296'10"
1976	Miklos Nemeth, Hungary	310'4"
1980	Dainis Kula, USSR	299'2"
1984	Arto Harkonen, Finland	284'8"
1988	Tapio Korjus, Finland	276'6"
1992	Jan Zelezny, Czechoslovakia	294'2"
1996	Jan Zelezny, Czech Republic	289' 3"

Long Jump

		Distance
1896	Ellery Clark, U.S.	20' 10"
1900	Alvin Kraenzlein, U.S.	23'6¾"
1904	Meyer Prinstein, U.S.	24'1"
1908	Frank Irons, U.S.	24'6½"
1912	Albert Gutterson, U.S.	24'11¼"
1920	William Pettersson, Sweden	23'5½"
1924	De Hart Hubbard, U.S.	24'5"
1928	Edward Hamm, U.S.	25'4"
1932	Edward Gordon, U.S.	25'¾"
1936	Jesse Owens, U.S.	26'5½"
1948	Willie Steel, U.S.	25'8"
1952	Jerome Biffle, U.S.	24'10"
1956	Gregory C. Bell, U.S.	25'8¼"

1960	Ralph H. Boston, U.S.	26'7¾"
1964	Lynn Davies, Great Britain	26'5¾"
1968	Robert Beamon, U.S.	29'2½"
1972	Randy Williams, U.S.	27'½"
1976	Arnie Robinson, U.S.	27'4¾"
1980	Lutz Bombrowski, E. Germany	28'¼"
1984	Carl Lewis, U.S.	28'¼"
1988	Carl Lewis, U.S.	28'7¼"
1992	Carl Lewis, U.S.	28'5½"
1996	Carl Lewis, U.S.	27'10¾"

Pole Vault — Height

1896	William W. Hoyt, U.S.	10'10"
1900	Irving K. Baxter, U.S.	10'10"
1904	Charles E. Dvorak, U.S.	11'5¾"
1908	Albert C. Gilbert, U.S.; Edward T. Cook Jr., U.S.	12'2"
1912	Harry S. Babcock, U.S.	12'11½"
1920	Frank K. Foss, U.S.	13'5"
1924	Lee S. Barnes, U.S.	12'11½"
1928	Sabin W. Carr, U.S.	13'9¼"
1932	William Miller, U.S.	14'1¾"
1936	Earle Meadows, U.S.	14'3¼"
1948	O. Guinn Smith, U.S.	14'1¼"
1952	Robert Richards, U.S.	14'11"
1956	Robert Richards, U.S.	14'11½"
1960	Donald Bragg, U.S.	15'5"
1964	Fred M. Hansen, U.S.	16'8¾"
1968	Robert Seagren, U.S.	17'8½"
1972	Wolfgang Nordwig, E. Germany	18'½"
1976	Tadeusz Slusarki, Poland	18'½"
1980	Wladyslaw Kozakiewicz, Poland	18'11½"
1984	Pierre Quinon, France	18'10¼"
1988	Sergei Bubka, USSR	19'9¼"
1992	Maksim Tarassov, Unified Team	19'0¼"
1996	Jean Galfiore, France	19'5¼"

Shot Put — Distance

1896	Robert Garrett, U.S.	36'9¾"
1900	Richard Sheldon, U.S.	46'3¼"
1904	Ralph Rose, U.S.	48'7"
1908	Ralph Rose, U.S.	46'7½"
1912	Patrick McDonald, U.S.	50'4"
1920	Ville Porhola, Finland	48'7¼"
1924	Bud Houser, U.S.	49'2¼"
1928	John Kuck, U.S.	52'¾"
1932	Leo Sexton, U.S.	52'6"
1936	Hans Woellke, Germany	53'1¾"
1948	Wilbur Thompson, U.S.	56'2"
1952	Parry O'Brien, Jr., U.S.	57'1½"
1956	Parry O'Brien, Jr., U.S.	60'11¼"
1960	William Nieder, U.S.	64'6¾"
1964	Dallas C. Long, U.S.	66'8½"
1968	James Randel Matson, U.S.	67'4¾"
1972	Wladyslaw Komar, Poland	69'6"

1976	Udo Beyer, E. Germany	69'6¾"
1980	Vladimir Kiselyov, USSR	70'½"
1984	Alessandro Andrei, Italy	69'9"
1988	Ulf Timmermann, E. Germany	73'8¾"
1992	Mike Stulce, U.S.	71'2½"
1996	Randy Barnes, United States	70' 11"

Triple Jump — Distance

1896	James B. Connolly, U.S.	44' 11¾"
1900	Myer Prinstein, U.S.	47'5¾"
1904	Myer Prinstein, U.S.	47'1"
1908	Timothy Ahearne, Great Britain	48'11¼"
1912	Gustaf Lindblom, Sweden	48'5¼"
1920	Vilho Tuulos, Finland	47'7"
1924	Anthony Winter, Australia	50'11¼"
1928	Mikio Oda, Japan	49'11"
1932	Chuhei Nambu, Japan	51'7"
1936	Naoto Tajima, Japan	52'6"
1948	Arne Ahman, Sweden	50'6¼"
1952	Adhemar da Silva, Brazil	53'2¾"
1956	Adhemar da Silva, Brazil	53'7¾"
1960	Jozef Schmidt, Poland	55'2"
1964	Jozef Schmidt, Poland	55'3½"
1968	Viktor Saneyev, USSR	57'¾"
1972	Viktor Saneyev, USSR	56'11¼"
1976	Viktor Saneyev, USSR	56'8¾"
1980	Jaak Uudmae, USSR	56'11¼"
1984	Al Joyner, U.S.	56'7½"
1988	Hristo Markov, Bulgaria	57'9¼"
1992	Mike Conley, U.S.	57'10¼"
1996	Kenny Harrison, United States	59'4¼"

Decathlon — Points[1]

1904	Thomas Kiely, Ireland	6,036.00
1912	Jim Thorpe, U.S.[2]	8,412.00
1920	Helge Lovland, Norway	6,803.00
1924	Harold Osborn, U.S.	7,710.77
1928	Paavo Yrjola, Finland	8,053.29
1932	James Bausch, U.S.	8,462.23
1936	Glenn Morris, U.S.	7,900.00
1948	Robert Mathias, U.S.	7,139.00
1952	Robert Mathias, U.S.	7,887.00
1956	Milton G. Campbell, U.S.	7,937.00
1960	Rafer Johnson, U.S.	8,392.00
1964	Willi Holdorf, W. Germany	7,887.00
1968	Bill Toomey, U.S.	8,193.00
1972	Nikolai Avilov, USSR	8,454.00
1976	Bruce Jenner, U.S.	8,617.00
1980	Daley Thompson, Great Britain	8,495.00
1984	Daley Thompson, Great Britain	8,798.00
1988	Christian Schenk, E. Germany	8,488.00
1992	Robert Zmelik, Czechoslovakia	8,611.00
1996	Dan O'Brien, U.S.	8,824.00

1. The scoring system was changed in 1936 and again in 1964. 2. Thorpe was disqualified and forced to return his medals in the decathlon and pentathlon (a discontinued event) because he had played professional baseball. Sweden's Hugo Wieslander was the next highest finisher, with 7,724.49 points. The International Olympic Committee posthumously restored Thorpe's medals in 1982.

Track and Field, Women

100-Meter Dash — Time

1928	Elizabeth Robinson, U.S.	12.20
1932	Stanislawa Walasiewicz, Poland	11.90
1936	Helen Stephens, U.S.	11.50
1948	Fanny Blankers-Koen, Netherlands	11.90
1952	Marjorie Jackson, Australia	11.50
1956	Betty Cuthbert, Australia	11.50
1960	Wilma Rudolph, U.S.	11.00
1964	Wyomia Tyus, U.S.	11.40
1968	Wyomia Tyus, U.S.	11.00
1972	Renate Stecher, E. Germany	11.07
1976	Annegret Richter, W. Germany	11.08
1980	Lyudmila Kondratyeva, USSR	11.06
1984	Evelyn Ashford, U.S.	10.97
1988	Florence Griffith-Joyner, U.S.	10.54
1992	Gail Devers, U.S.	10.82
1996	Gail Devers, U.S.	10.94

200 Meters — Time

1948	Fanny Blankers-Koen, Netherlands	24.40
1952	Marjorie Jackson, Australia	23.70
1956	Betty Cuthbert, Australia	23.40
1960	Wilma Rudolph, U.S.	24.00
1964	Edith McGuire, U.S.	23.00
1968	Irena Kirszenstein Szewinska, Poland	22.50

1972	Renate Stecher, E. Germany	22.40
1976	Bärbel Eckert, E. Germany	22.37
1980	Bärbel Wöckel (Eckert), E. Germany	22.03
1984	Valerie Brisco-Hooks, U.S.	21.81
1988	Florence Griffith-Joyner, U.S.	21.34
1992	Gwen Torrence, U.S.	21.81
1996	Marie-Jose Perec, France	22.12

400 Meters — Time

1964	Betty Cuthbert, Australia	52.00
1968	Colette Besson, France	52.00
1972	Monika Zehrt, E. Germany	51.08
1976	Irena Kirszenstein Szewinska, Poland	49.29
1980	Marita Koch, E. Germany	48.88
1984	Valerie Brisco-Hooks, U.S.	48.83
1988	Olga Bryzgina, USSR	48.65
1992	Marie-Jose Perec, France	48.83
1996	Marie-Jose Perec, France	48.25

800 Meters — Time

1928	Linda Radke-Batschauer, Germany	2:16.80
1960	Lyudmila Shevcova-Lysenko, USSR	2:04.30
1964	Ann Packer, Great Britain	2:01.10
1968	Madeline Manning, U.S.	2:00.90
1972	Hildegard Falck, W. Germany	1:58.55

		Time
1976	Tatyana Kazankina, USSR	1:54.94
1980	Nadezhda Olizarenko, USSR	1:53.42
1984	Doina Melinte, Romania	1:57.60
1988	Sigrun Wodars, E. Germany	1:56.10
1992	Ellen Van Langen, Netherlands	1:55.54
1996	Svetlana Masterkova, Russia	1:57.73

1,500 Meters — Time

1972	Lyudmila Bragina, USSR	4:01.40
1976	Tatyana Kazankina, USSR	4:05.48
1980	Tatyana Kazankina, USSR	3:56.60
1984	Gabrielle Dorio, Italy	4:03.25
1988	Paula Ivan, Romania	3:53.96
1992	Hassiba Boulmerka, Algeria	3:55.30
1996	Svetlana Masterkova, Russia	4:00.83

3,000 Meters — Time

1984	Maricica Puica, Romania	8:35.96
1988	Tatyana Samolenko, USSR	8:26.53
1992	Elena Romanova, Unified Team	8:46.04

5,000 Meters — Time

1996	Wang Junxia, China	14:59.88

10,000 Meters — Time

1988	Olga Boldarenko, USSR	31:44.69
1992	Derartu Tulu, Ethiopia	31:06.02
1996	Fernanda Ribeiro, Portugal	31:01.64

Marathon — Time

1984	Joan Benoit, U.S.	2:24.52
1988	Rosa Mota, Portugal	2:25.40
1992	Valentina Yegorova, Unified Team	2:32.41
1996	Fatuma Roba, Ethiopia	2:26:05

100-Meter Hurdles[1] — Time

1932	Babe Didrikson, U.S.	11.70
1936	Trebisonda Valla, Italy	11.70
1948	Fanny Blankers-Koen, Netherlands	11.20
1952	Shirley Strickland, Australia	10.90
1956	Shirley Strickland, Australia	10.70
1960	Irina Press, USSR	10.80
1964	Karin Balzer, E. Germany	10.50
1968	Maureen Caird, Australia	10.30
1972	Annelie Erhardt, E. Germany	12.59
1976	Johanna Schaller, E. Germany	12.77
1980	Vera Komisova, USSR	12.56
1984	Benita Fitzgerald-Brown	12.84
1988	Jordanka Donkova, Bulgaria	12.38
1992	Paraskevi Patoulido, Greece	12.64
1996	Ludmila Engquist, Sweden	12.58

1. 80 meters until 1972

400-Meter Hurdles — Time

1984	Nawal El Moutawakel, Morocco	54.61
1988	Debra Flintoff-King, Australia	53.17
1992	Sally Gunnell, Great Britain	53.23
1996	Deon Hemmings, Jamaica	52.82

10-Kilometer Walk — Time

1996	Yelena Nikolayeva, Russia	41:49

4x100-Meter Relay — Time

1928	Canada	48.40	1968	U.S.	42.80
1932	U.S.	46.90	1972	W. Germany	42.81
1936	U.S.	46.90	1976	E. Germany	42.55
1948	Netherlands	47.50	1980	E. Germany	41.60
1952	U.S.	45.90	1984	U.S.	41.65
1956	Australia	44.50	1988	U.S.	41.98
1960	U.S.	44.50	1992	U.S.	42.11
1964	Poland	43.60	1996	U.S.	41.95

4x400-Meter Relay — Time

1972	E. Germany	3:23.00	1988	USSR	3:15.18
1976	E. Germany	3:19.23	1992	Unified Team	3:20.20
1980	USSR	3:20.20	1996	U.S.	3:20.91
1984	U.S.	3:18.29			

Discus Throw — Distance

1928	Halina Konopacka, Poland	129'11¾"
1932	Lillian Copeland, U.S.	133'2"
1936	Gisela Mauermayer, Germany	156'3"
1948	Micheline Ostermeyer, France	137'6"
1952	Nina Romaschkova, USSR	168'8"
1956	Olga Fikotová, Czechoslovakia	176'1"
1960	Nina Ponomareva, USSR	180'9"
1964	Tamara Press, USSR	187'10"
1968	Lia Manoliu, Romania	191'2"

1972	Faina Melnik, USSR	218'7"
1976	Evelin Schlaak, E. Germany	226'4"
1980	Evelin Jahl (Schlaak), E. Germany	229'6"
1984	Ria Stalman, Netherlands	214'5"
1988	Martina Hellmann, E. Germany	237'2¼"
1992	Maritz Marten, Cuba	229'10"
1996	Ilke Wyludda, Germany	228'6"

High Jump — Height

1928	Ethel Catherwood, Canada	5'2½"
1932	Jean Shiley, U.S.	5'5¼"
1936	Ibolya Csak, Hungary	5'3"
1948	Alice Coachman, U.S.	5'6"
1952	Esther Brand, S. Africa	5'5¾"
1956	Mildred McDaniel, U.S.	5'9¼"
1960	Iolanda Balas, Romania	6'0¾"
1964	Iolanda Balas, Romania	6'2¾"
1968	Miloslava Rezkova, Czechoslovakia	5'11½"
1972	Ulrike Meyfarth, W. Germany	6'3½"
1976	Rosemarie Ackermann, E. Germany	6'4"
1980	Sara Simeoni, Italy	6'5½"
1984	Ulrike Meyfarth, W. Germany	6'7½"
1988	Louise Ritter, U.S.	6'8"
1992	Heike Henkel, Germany	6'7½"
1996	Stefka Kostadinova, Bulgaria	6'8¾"

Javelin — Distance

1932	Babe Didriksen, U.S.	143'4"
1936	Tilly Fleischer, Germany	148'3"
1948	Herma Bauma, Austria	149'6"
1952	Dana Zatopekova, Czechoslovakia	165'7"
1956	Inessa Janzeme, USSR	176'8"
1960	Elvira Ozolina, USSR	183'8"
1964	Mihaela Penes, Romania	198'7"
1968	Angela Nemeth, Hungary	198'0"
1972	Ruth Fuchs, E. Germany	209'7"
1976	Ruth Fuchs, E. Germany	216'4"
1980	Maria Colon Rueñes, Cuba	224'5"
1984	Theresa Sanderson, Great Britain	228'2"
1988	Petra Felke, E. Germany	245'0"
1992	Silke Renke, Germany	224'2"
1996	Heli Rantanen, Finland	222'11"

Long Jump — Distance

1948	Olga Gyarmati, Hungary	18'8¼"
1952	Yvette Williams, New Zealand	20'5¾"
1956	Elizbieta Krzesinska, Poland	20'10"
1960	Vyera Krepkina, USSR	20'10¾"
1964	Mary Rand, Great Britain	22'2¼"
1968	Viorica Viscopoleanu, Romania	22'4½"
1972	Heidemarie Rosendahl, W. Germany	22'3"
1976	Angela Voigt, E. Germany	22'2¾"
1980	Tatiana Kolpakova, USSR	23'0¾"
1984	Anisoara Cusmir-Stanciu. Romania	22'10"
1988	Jackie Joyner-Kersee, U.S.	24'3½"
1992	Heike Drechsler, Germany	23'5¼"
1996	Chioma Ajunwa, Nigeria	23'4½"

Shot Put — Distance

1948	Micheline Ostermeyer, France	45'1½"
1952	Galina Zybina, USSR	50'1¾"
1956	Tamara Tyshkevich, USSR	54'5"
1960	Tamara Press, USSR	56'10"
1964	Tamara Press, USSR	59'6¼"
1968	Margitta Gummel, E. Germany	64'4"
1972	Nadezhda Chizhova, USSR	69'0"
1976	Ivanka Hristova, Bulgaria	69'5¼"
1980	Ilona Slupianek, E. Germany	73'6¼"
1984	Claudia Losch, W. Germany	67'2¼"
1988	Natalya Lisovskaya, USSR	72'11½"
1992	Svetlana Krivaleva, Unified Team	69'1¼"
1996	Astrid Kumbernuss, Germany	67'5½"

Triple Jump — Distance

1996	Inessa Kravets, Ukraine	50'3½"

Pentathlon/Heptathlon[2] — Points

1964	Irina Press, USSR	5,246
1968	Ingrid Becker, W. Germany	5,098
1972	Mary Peters, Great Britain	4,801
1976	Siegrun Siegl, E. Germany	4,745
1980	Nadezhda Tkachenko, USSR	5,083
1984	Glynis Nunn, Australia	6,390
1988	Jackie Joyner-Kersee, U.S.	7,215
1992	Jackie Joyner-Kersee, U.S.	7,044
1996	Ghada Shouaa, Syria	6,780

2. In 1984, two additional events were added: the 800-meter run and the javelin throw.

Team Sports

Baseball		Basketball-Women		1964	Hungary	1980	USSR	1912	Great Britain
1988	U.S.	1976	USSR	1968	Hungary	1984	U.S.	1920	Great Britain/
1992	Cuba	1980	USSR	1972	Poland	1988	U.S.		Ireland
1996	Cuba	1984	U.S.	1976	E. Germany	1992	Brazil	1924	France
		1988	U.S.	1980	Czechoslovakia	1996	Netherlands	1928	Germany
Basketball-Men		1992	Unified Team	1984	France			1932	Hungary
1936	U.S.	1996	U.S.	1988	USSR	Volleyball-Women		1936	Hungary
1948	U.S.			1992	Spain	1964	Japan	1948	Italy
1952	U.S.	Soccer-Men		1996	Nigeria	1968	USSR	1952	Hungary
1956	U.S.	1900	Great Britain			1972	USSR	1956	Hungary
1960	U.S.	1904	Canada	Soccer-Women		1976	Japan	1960	Italy
1964	U.S.	1908	Great Britain	1996	U.S.	1980	USSR	1964	Hungary
1968	U.S.	1912	Great Britain			1984	China	1968	Yugoslavia
1972	USSR	1920	Belgium	Softball		1988	USSR	1972	USSR
1976	U.S.	1924	Uruguay	1996	U.S.	1992	Cuba	1976	Hungary
1980	Yugoslavia	1928	Uruguay			1996	Cuba	1980	USSR
1984	U.S.	1936	Italy	Volleyball-Men				1984	Yugoslavia
1988	USSR	1948	Sweden	1964	USSR	Water Polo		1988	Yugoslavia
1992	U.S.	1952	Hungary	1968	USSR	1900	Great Britain	1992	Italy
1996	U.S.	1956	USSR	1972	Japan	1904	U.S.	1996	Spain
		1960	Yugoslavia	1976	Poland	1908	Great Britain		

WINTER OLYMPIC CHAMPIONS, 1924-98

Alpine Skiing (Men)

Downhill
		Time
1948	Henri Oreiller, France	2:55.00
1952	Zeno Colo, Italy	2:30.80
1956	Anton Sailer, Austria	2:52.20
1960	Jean Vuarnet, France	2:06.00
1964	Egon Zimmerman, Austria	2:18.16
1968	Jean-Claude Killy, France	1:59.85
1972	Bernhard Russi, Switzerland	1:51.43
1976	Franz Klammer, Austria	1:45.73
1980	Leonhard Stock, Austria	1:45.50
1984	William Johnson, United States	1:45.59
1988	Pirmin Zurbriggen, Switzerland	1:59.63
1992	Patrick Ortlieb, Austria	1:50.37
1994	Tommy Moe, United States	1:45.75
1998	Jean-Luc Cretier, France	1:50.11

Slalom
		Time
1948	Edi Reinalter, Switzerland	2:10.30
1952	Othmar Schneider, Austria	2:00.00
1956	Anton Sailer, Austria	3:14.70
1960	Ernst Hinterseer, Austria	2:08.90
1964	Josef Stiegler, Austria	2:11.13
1968	Jean Claude Killy, France	1:39.73
1972	Francisco Fernandez Ochoa, Spain	1:39.73
1976	Piero Gros, Italy	2:03.29
1980	Ingemar Stenmark, Sweden	1:44.26
1984	Philip Mahre, United States	1:39.41
1988	Alberto Tomba, Italy	1:39.47
1992	Finn Christian Jagge, Norway	1:44.39
1994	Thomas Stangassinger	2:02.02
1998	Hans-Petter Buraas, Norway	1:49.31

Giant Slalom
		Time
1952	Stein Eriksen, Norway	2:25.00
1956	Anton Sailer, Austria	3:00.10
1960	Roger Staub, Switzerland	1:48.30
1964	Francois Bonlieu, France	1:46.71
1968	Jean Claude Killy, France	3:29.28
1972	Gustavo Thöni, Italy	3:09.62
1976	Heini Hemmi, Switzerland	3:26.97
1980	Ingemar Stenmark, Sweden	2:40.74
1984	Max Julen, Switzerland	2:41.18
1988	Alberto Tomba, Italy	2:06.37
1992	Alberto Tomba, Italy	2:06.98
1994	Markus Wasmeier, Germany	2:52.46
1998	Hermann Maier, Austria	2:38.51

Super Giant Slalom
		Time
1988	Frank Piccard, France	1:39.66
1992	Kjetil Andre Aamodt, Norway	1:13.04
1994	Markus Wasmeier, Germany	1:32.53
1998	Hermann Maier, Austria	1:34.82

Combined (Downhill/Slalom)
1988	Hubert Strolz, Austria
1992	Josef Polig, Italy
1994	Lasse Kjus, Norway
1998	Mario Reiter, Austria

Alpine Skiing (Women)

Downhill
		Time
1948	Hedi Schlunegger, Switzerland	2:28.30
1952	Trude Jochum-Beiser, Austria	1:47.10
1956	Madeleine Berthod, Switzerland	1:40.70
1960	Heidi Biebl, Germany	1:37.60
1964	Christl Haas, Austria	1:55.39
1968	Olga Pall, Austria	1:40.87
1972	Marie-Theres Nadig, Switzerland	1:36.68
1976	Rosi Mittermaier, West Germany	1:46.16
1980	Annemarie Moser-Pröll, Austria	1:37.52
1984	Michela Figini, Switzerland	1:13.36[1]
1988	Marina Kiehl, West Germany	1:25.86
1992	Kerrin Lee-Gartner, Canada	1:52.55
1994	Katja Seizinger, Germany	1:35.93
1998	Katja Seizinger, Germany	1:28.89

Slalom
		Time
1948	Gretchen Fraser, United States	1:57.20
1952	Andrea Mead Lawrence, United States	2:10.60
1956	Renée Colliard, Switzerland	1:52.30
1960	Anne Heggtveigt, Canada	1:49.60
1964	Christine Goitschel, France	1:29.86
1968	Marielle Goitschel, France	1:25.86
1972	Barbara Cochran, United States	1:31.24
1976	Rosi Mittermaier, West Germany	1:30.54
1980	Hanni Wenzel, Liechtenstein	1:25.09
1984	Paoletta Magoni, Italy	1:36.47
1988	Vreni Schneider, Switzerland	1:36.69
1992	Petra Kronberger, Austria	1:32.68
1994	Vreni Schneider, Switzerland	1:56.01
1998	Hilde Gerg, Germany	1:32.40

Giant Slalom
		Time
1952	Andrea Mead Lawrence, United States	2:06.80
1956	Ossi Reichert, Germany	1:56.50
1960	Yvonne Rüegg, Switzerland	1:39.90
1964	Marielle Goitschel, France	1:52.24
1968	Nancy Greene, Canada	1:51.97
1972	Marie-Theres Nadig, Switzerland	1:29.90
1976	Kathy Kreiner, Canada	1:29.13
1980	Hanni Wenzel, Liechtenstein	2:41.66
1984	Debbie Armstrong, United States	2:20.98
1988	Vreni Schneider, Switzerland	2:06.49
1992	Pernilla Wiberg, Sweden	2:12.74
1994	Deborah Compagnoni, Italy	2:30.97
1998	Deborah Compagnoni, Italy	2:50.59

Super Giant Slalom
		Time
1988	Sigrid Wolf, Austria	1:19.03
1992	Deborah Compagnoni, Italy	1:21.22
1994	Diann Roffe-Steinrotter, United States	1:22.15
1998	Picabo Street, United States	1:18.02

Combined (Downhill/Slalom)
1988	Anita Wachter, Austria
1992	Petra Kronberger, Austria
1994	Pernilla Wiberg, Sweden
1998	Katja Seizinger, Germany

1. Race shortened by weather conditions

Nordic Skiing and Jumping (Men)

10-Kilometer (6.2 Miles) Cross-Country		Time
1992	Vegard Ulvang, Norway	27:36.00
1994	Bjorn Dahlie, Norway	24:20.10
1998	Bjorn Dahlie, Norway	27:24.50

15-Kilometer (9.3 Miles) Pursuit Method[1]		Time
1924	Thorleif Haug, Norway	1:14:31.00
1928	Johan Gröttumsbraaten, Norway	1:37:01.00
1932	Sven Utterstrom, Sweden	1:23:07.00
1936	Erik-August Larsson, Sweden	1:14:38.00
1948	Martin Lundström, Sweden	1:13:50.70
1952	Hallgeir Brenden, Norway	1:01:34.00
1956	Hallgeir Brenden, Norway[1]	0:49:39.00
1960	Hakon Brusveen, Norway	0:51:55.50
1964	Eero Mäntyranta, Finland	0:50:54.10
1968	Harald Grönningen, Norway	0:47:54.20
1972	Sven-Ake Lundbäck, Sweden	0:45:28.24
1976	Nikolai Bazhukov, USSR	0:43:58.47
1980	Thomas Wassberg, Sweden	0:41:57.63
1984	Gunde Svan, Sweden	0:41:25.60
1988	Mikhail Deviatiarov, USSR	0:41:18.90
1992	Bjorn Dahlie, Norway	0:38:01.90
1994	Bjorn Dahlie, Norway	0:35:48.80
1998	Thomas Alsgaard, Norway	1:07:01.70

1. Until 1956, 18 km

30-Kilometer (18.6 Miles) Cross-Country		Time
1956	Veikko Hakulinen, Finland	1:44:06.00
1960	Sixten Jernberg, Sweden	1:51:03.90
1964	Eero Mäntyranta, Finland	1:30:50.70
1968	Franco Nones, Italy	1:35:39.20
1972	Vyacheslav Vedenin, USSR	1:36:31.15
1976	Sergei Saveliev, USSR	1:30:29.38
1980	Nikolai Zimyatov, USSR	1:27:02.80
1984	Nikolai Zimyatov, USSR	1:28:56.30
1988	Aleksei Prokourorov, USSR	1:24:26.30
1992	Vegard Ulvang, Norway	1:22:27.80
1994	Thomas Alsgaard, Norway	1:12:26.40
1998	Mika Myllylae, Finland	1:33.55.80

50-Kilometer (31.2 Miles) Cross-Country		Time
1924	Thorleif Haug, Norway	3:44:32.00
1928	Per Erik Hedlund, Sweden	4:52:03.00
1932	Veli Saarinen, Finland	4:28:00.00
1936	Elis Viklund, Sweden	3:30:11.00
1948	Nils Karlsson, Sweden	3:47:48.00
1952	Veikko Hakulinen, Finland	3:33:33.00
1956	Sixten Jernberg, Sweden	2:50:27.00
1960	Kalevi Hamalainen, Finland	2:59:06.30
1964	Sixten Jernberg, Sweden	2:43:52.60
1968	Ole Ellefsaeter, Norway	2:28:45.80
1972	Pål Tyldum, Norway	2:43:14.75
1976	Ivar Formo, Norway	2:37:30.05
1980	Nikolai Zimyatov, USSR	2:27:24.60
1984	Thomas Wassberg, Sweden	2:15:55.80
1988	Gunde Svan, Sweden	2:04:30.90
1992	Bjorn Dahlie, Norway	2:03:41.50
1994	Vladimir Smirnov, Kazakhstan	2:07:20.30
1998	Bjorn Dahlie, Norway	2:05:08.20

40-Kilometer (24.8 Miles) Cross-Country Relay (4x10)		Time
1936	Finland, Norway, Sweden	2:41:33.00
1948	Sweden, Finland, Norway	2:32:08.00
1952	Finland, Norway, Sweden	2:20:16.00
1956	USSR, Finland Sweden	2:15:30.00
1960	Finland, Norway, USSR	2:18:45.60
1964	Sweden, Finland, USSR	2:18:34.60
1968	Norway, Sweden, Finland	2:08:33.50
1972	USSR, Norway, Switzerland	2:04:47.94
1976	Finland, Norway, USSR	2:07:59.72
1980	USSR, Norway, Finland	1:57:03.46
1984	Sweden, USSR, Finland	1:55:06.30
1988	Sweden, USSR, Czechoslovakia	1:43:58.60
1992	Norway, Italy, Finland	1:39:26.00
1994	Italy, Norway, Finland	1:41:15.00
1998	Norway, Italy, Finland	1:40:55.70

Nordic Combined (15 km Cross-Country and 70-Meter Ski Jump[1])		
1924	Thorleif Haug, Norway	18.906
1928	Johan Gröttumsbraaten, Norway	17.833
1932	Johan Gröttumsbraaten, Norway	446.00
1946	Oddbjörn Hagen, Norway	430.30
1952	Simon Slåtvik, Norway	451.62
1956	Sverre Stenersen, Norway	455.00
1960	George Thoma, West Germany	457.95
1964	Tormod Knutsen, Norway	469.28
1968	Franz Keller, West Germany	449.04
1972	Ulrich Wehling, East Germany	413.34
1976	Ulrich Wehling, East Germany	423.39
1980	Ulrich Wehling, East Germany	432.20
1984	Torn Sandberg, Norway	422.59
1988	Hippolyt Kempf Switzerland	235.80
1992	Fabrice Guy, France	426.47
1994	Fred Lundberg, Norway	—
1998	Bjarte Engen Vik, Norway	—

1. Until 1956, 18 km

Nordic Combined, Team		
1988	West Germany, Switzerland, Austria	1:20:46.00
1992	Japan, Norway, Austria	1:23:36.50
1994	Japan, Norway, Switzerland	—
1998	Norway, Finland, France	—

90-Meter (293.5 ft.) Jump		Points
1964	Veikko Kankkonen, Finland	229.90
1968	Jiri Raska, Czechoslovakia	216.50
1972	Yukio Kasaya, Japan	244.20
1976	Hans-Georg Aschenbach, East Germany	252.00
1980	Anton Innauer, Austria	266.30
1984	Jens Weissflog, East Germany	215.20
1988	Matti Nykänen, Finland	229.10
1992	Ernst Vettori, Austria	222.80
1994	Espen Bredesen, Norway	282.00
1998	Jani Soininen, Finland	234.50

1. Until 1992, 70 meters

120-Meter (393.7 ft.) Jump[1]		Points
1924	Jacob Tullin Thambs, Norway	18.960
1928	Alf Andersen, Norway	19.208
1932	Birger Ruud, Norway	228.10
1936	Birger Ruud, Norway	232.00
1948	Petter Hugsted, Norway	228.10
1952	Arnfinn Bergmann, Norway	226.00
1956	Antti Hyvarinen, Finland	227.00
1960	Helmut Recknagel, Germany	227.20
1964	Toralf Engan, Norway	230.70
1968	Vladimir Beloussov, USSR	231.30
1972	Wojciech Fortuna, Poland	219.90
1976	Karl Schnabl, Austria	234.80
1980	Jouko Tormanen, Finland	271.00
1984	Matti Nykänen, Finland	231.20
1988	Matti Nykänen, Finland	224.00
1992	Toni Nieminen, Finland	239.50
1994	Jens Weissflog, Germany	274.50
1998	Kazuyoshi Funaki, Japan	272.30

1. Until 1992, 90 meters

120-Meter (393.7 ft.) Jump, Team[1]		Points
1988	Finland, Yugoslavia, Norway	634.40
1992	Finland, Austria, Czechoslovakia	644.40
1994	Germany, Japan, Austria	970.10
1998	Japan, Germany, Austria	933.00

1. Until 1992, 90 meters

Nordic Skiing (Women)

5-Kilometer (3.1 Miles) Cross-Country		Time
1964	Claudia Boyarskikh, USSR	17:50.50
1968	Toini Gustafsson, Sweden	16:45.20
1972	Galina Kulakova, USSR	17:00.50
1976	Helena Takalo, Finland	15:48.69
1980	Raisa Smetanina, USSR	15:06.92
1984	Marja-Liisa Hämäläinen, Finland	17:04.00
1988	Marjo Matikainen, Finland	15:04.00
1992	Marjut Lukkarinen, Finland	14:13.80
1994	Lyubov Egorova, Russia	14:08.80
1998	Larissa Lazutina, Russia	17:39.90

10-Kilometer (6.2 Miles) Pursuit Method		Time
1952	Lydia Wideman, Finland	41:40.00
1956	Lyubov Kosyreva, USSR	38:11.00
1960	Maria Gusakova, USSR	39:46.60
1964	Claudia Boyarskikh, USSR	40:24.30
1968	Toini Gustafsson, Sweden	36:46.50
1972	Galina Kolakova, USSR	34:17.82
1976	Raisa Smetanina, USSR	30:31.54
1980	Barbara Petzold, East Germany	30:31.54
1984	Marja-Liisa Hämäläinen, Finland	31:44.20
1988	Vida Ventsene, USSR	30:08.20
1992	Lyubov Egorova, Unified Team	40:07.70
1994	Lyubov Egorova, Russia	41:38.10
1998	Larissa Lazutina, Russia	46:06.90

15-Kilometer (9.3 Miles) Cross-Country		Time
1992	Lyubov Egorova, Unified Team	42:20.80
1994	Manuela Di Centa, Italy	39:44.50
1998	Olga Danilova, Russia	46:55.40

30-Kilometer (18.6 Miles) Cross-Country[1]		Time
1984	Marja Liisa Hämäläinen, Finland	1:01:45.0
1988	Tamara Tikhonova, USSR	55:53.6
1992	Stefania Belmondo, Italy	1:22:30.10
1994	Manuela Di Centa, Italy	1:25:41.60
1998	Yuliya Chepalova, Russia	1:22:01.50

1. 20 Km until 1992

20-Kilometer (12.4 Miles) Cross-Country Relay[1] (4x5Km)		
1956	Finland	1:09.01.00
1960	Sweden	1:04.21.00
1964	USSR	0:59:20.00
1968	Norway	0:57:30.00
1972	USSR	0:48:46.15
1976	USSR	1:07:49.75
1980	East Germany	1:02:11.10
1984	Norway	1:06:49.70
1988	USSR	0:59:51.10
1992	Unified Team	0:59:34.80
1994	Russia	0:57:12.50
1998	Russia, Norway, Italy	0:55:13.50

1. 15 Km (3 x 5 Km) until 1976

Freestyle Skiing–Men

Aerials		Points
1994	Andreas Schoenbaechler, Switzerland	234.67
1998	Eric Bergoust, United States	255.64
Moguls		**Points**
1992	Edgar Grospiron, France	25.81
1994	Jean-Luc Brassard, Canada	27.24
1998	Jonny Moseley, United States	26.93

Freestyle Skiing–Women

Aerials		Points
1994	Lina Cherjazova, Uzbekistan	166.84
1998	Nikki Stone, United States	193.00
Moguls		**Points**
1992	Donna Weinbrecht, United States	23.69
1994	Stine Lise Hattestad, Norway	25.97
1998	Tae Satoya, Japan	25.06

Biathlon–Men
(Cross-country skiing and riflery)

10-Kilometer (6.2 Miles)		Time
1980	Frank Ulrich, East Germany	32:10.69
1984	Eirik Kvalfoss, Norway	30:53.80
1988	Frank-Peter Roetsch, East Germany	25:08.10
1992	Mark Kirchner, Germany	26:02.30
1994	Sergei Tchepikov, Russia	28:07.00
1998	Ole Bjorndalen, Norway	27:16.20
20-Kilometer (12.4 Miles)		**Time**
1960	Klas Lestander, Sweden	1:33:21.60
1964	Vladimir Melanin, USSR	1:20:26.80
1968	Magnar Solberg, Norway	1:13:45.90
1972	Magnar Solberg, Norway	1:15:55.50
1976	Nikolai Kruglov, USSR	1:14:12.26
1980	Anatoli Alabyev, USSR	1:08:16.31
1984	Peter Angerer, West Germany	1:11:52.70
1988	Frank-Peter Roetsch, East Germany	0:56:33.33
1992	Evgueni Redkine, Unified Team	0:57:34.04
1994	Sergei Tarasov, Russia	0:57:25.30
1998	Halvard Hanevold, Norway	56:16.40
30-Kilometer (18.6 Miles) Relay (4x7.5 Km)[1]		**Time**
1968	USSR, Norway, Sweden	2:13:02.40
1972	USSR, Finland, East Germany	1:51:44.92
1976	USSR, Finland, East Germany	1:57:55.64
1980	USSR, East Germany, West Germany	1:34:03.27
1984	USSR, Norway, West Germany	1:38:51.70
1988	USSR, West Germany, Italy	1:22:30.00
1992	Germany, Unified Team, Sweden	1:24:43.50
1994	Germany, Russia, France	1:30:22.10
1998	Germany, Norway, Russia	1:19:43.30

1. 40 Km (4 x 10 Km) until 1980.

Biathlon–Women
(Cross-country skiing and riflery)

7.5 Kilometer (4.6 miles)		Time
1992	Anfissa Restzova, Unified Team	24:29.2
1994	Myriam Bedard, Canada	26:08.8
1998	Galina Kukleva, Russia	23:08.0
15 Kilometer (9.3 miles)		**Time**
1992	Antje Misersky	51:47.2
1994	Myriam Bedard, Canada	52:06.6
1998	Yekaterina Dafovska, Bulgaria	54:52.0
30-Kilometer (18.6 Miles) Relay (4x7.5 Km)		**Time**
1992	France, Germany, Unified Team (3x7.5)	1:15:55.6
1994	Russia, Germany, France	1:47:19.5
1998	Germany, Russia, Norway	1:40:13.6

NORDIC SKI CHAMPION

At three Winter Olympics—1956, 1960, and 1964—Sixten Jernberg of Sweden won a total of nine medals: Four gold, three silver, and two bronze. Two of his gold medals were in the 50 km, one was in the 30 km, and the last was in the 4x10 km relay.

Speed Skating

MEN, LONG TRACK

500 Meters (1,641 Ft.)		Time
1924	Charles Jewtraw, U.S	0:44.00
1928	Clas Thunberg, Finland	0:43.40
	Bernst Evensen, Norway (tie)	
1932	John A. Shea, United States	0:43.40
1936	Ivar Ballangrud, Norway	0:43.40
1948	Finn Helgesen, Norway	0:43.10
1952	Ken Henry, United States	0:43.20
1956	Yevgeny Grishin, USSR	0:40.20
1960	Yevgeny Grishin, USSR	0:40.20
1964	Terry McDermott, United States	0:40.10
1968	Erhard Keller, West Germany	0:40.30
1972	Erhard Keller, West Germany	0:39.44
1976	Yergeny Kulikov, USSR	0:39.17
1980	Eric Heiden, United States	0:38.03
1984	Sergei Fokichev, USSR	0:38.19
1988	Uwe-Jens Mey, East Germany	0:36.45
1992	Uwe-Jens Mey, Germany	0:37.14
1994	Aleksandr Golubev, Russia	0:36.33
1998	Hiroyasu Shimizu, Japan	1:11.35

1,000 Meters (3,281 Ft.)		Time
1976	Peter Mueller, United States	1:19.32
1980	Eric Heiden, United States	1:15.18
1984	Gaétan Boucher, Canada	1:15.80
1988	Nikolai Guiliaev, USSR	1:13.03
1992	Olaf Zinke, Germany	1:14.85
1994	Dan Jansen, United States	1:12.43
1998	Ids Postma, Netherlands	1:10.64

1,500 Meters (4,922 Ft.)		Time
1924	Clas Thunberg, Finland	2:20.80
1928	Clas Thunberg, Finland	2:21.10
1932	John A. Shea, United States	2:57.50
1936	Charles Mathisen, Norway	2:19.20
1948	Sverre Farstad, Norway	2:17.60
1952	Hjalmar Andersen, Norway	2:20.40
1956	Yevgeni Grishin	2:08.60
	Yuri Mikhailov, USSR (tie)	
1960	Roald Aas, Norway	2:10.40
	Yevgeni Grishin, USSR (tie)	
1964	Ants Anston, USSR	2:10.30
1968	Cornelis Verkerk, Netherlands	2:03.40
1972	Ard Schenk, Netherlands	2:02.96
1976	Jan Egil Storholt, Norway	1:59.38
1980	Eric Heiden, United States	1:55.44

1984	Gaétan Boucher, Canada	1:58.36
1988	Andre Hoffmann, East Germany	1:52.06
1992	Johann Olav Koss, Norway	1:54.81
1994	Johann Olav Koss, Norway	1:51.29
1998	Aadne Sondral, Norway	1:47.87

5,000 Meters (16,405 Ft.)		Time
1924	Clas Thunberg, Finland	8:39.00
1928	Ivar Ballangrud, Norway	8:50.50
1932	Irving Jaffee, United States	9:40.80
1936	Ivar Ballangrud, Norway	8:19.60
1948	Reidar Liaklev, Norway	8:29.40
1952	Hjalmar Andersen, Norway	8:10.60
1956	Boris Shilkov, USSR	7:48.70
1960	Viktor Kosichkin, USSR	7:51.30
1964	Knut Johannesen, Norway	7:38.40
1968	F. Anton Maier, Norway	7:22.40
1972	Ard Schenk, Netherlands	7:23.61
1976	Sten Stensen, Norway	7:24.48
1980	Eric Heiden, United States	7:02.29
1984	Sven Tomas Gustafson, Sweden	7:12.28
1988	Tomas Gustafson, Sweden	6:44.63
1992	Geir Karlstad, Sweden	6:59.97
1994	Johann Olav Koss, Norway	6:34.96
1998	Gianni Romme, Netherlands	6:22.20

10,000 Meters (32,810 Ft.)		Time
1924	Julien Skutnabb, Finland	18:04.80
1928	(ice thawed, event cancelled)	
1932	Irving Jaffee, United States	19:13.60
1936	Ivan Ballangrud, Norway	17:24.30
1948	Ake Seyffarth, Sweden	17:26.30
1952	Hjalmar Andersen, Norway	16:45.80
1956	Sigvard Ericsson, Sweden	16:35.90
1960	Knut Johannessen, Norway	15:46.60
1964	Jonny Nilsson, Sweden	15:50.10
1968	Johnny Hoeglin, Sweden	15:23.60
1972	Ard Schenk, Netherlands	15:01.35
1976	Piet Kleine, Netherlands	14:50.59
1980	Eric Heiden, United States	14:28.13
1984	Igor Malikov, USSR	14:39.90
1988	Tomas Gustafson, Sweden	13:48.20
1992	Bart Veldkamp, Netherlands	14:12.12
1994	Johann Olav Koss, Norway	13:30.55
1998	Gianni Romme, Netherlands	13:15.33

WOMEN, LONG TRACK

500 Meters (1,641 Ft.)		Time
1960	Helga Haase, Germany	0:45.90
1964	Lydia Skoblikova, USSR	0:45.00
1968	Ludmila Titova, USSR	0:46.10
1972	Anne Henning, United States	0:43.30
1976	Sheila Young, United States	0:42.76
1980	Karin Enke, East Germany	0:41.78
1984	Christa Rothenburger, East Germany	0:41.02
1988	Bonnie Blair, United States	0:39.10
1992	Bonnie Blair, United States	0:40.33
1994	Bonnie Blair, United States.	0:39.25
1998	Catriona Le May-Doan, Canada	1:16.60

1,000 Meters (3,281 Ft.)		Time
1960	Klara Guseva, USSR	1:34.10
1964	Lydia Skoblikova, USSR	1:33.20
1968	Carolina Geijssen, Netherlands	1:32.60
1972	Monka Pflug, West Germany	1:31.40
1976	Tatiana Averina, USSR	1:28.43
1980	Natalia Petruseva, USSR	1:24.10
1984	Karin Enke, East Germany	1:21.61
1988	Christa Rothenburger, East Germany	1:17.65
1992	Bonnie Blair, United States	1:21.90
1994	Bonnie Blair, United States	1:18.74
1998	Marianne Timmer, Netherlands	1:16.51

1,500 Meters (4,922 Ft.)		Time
1960	Lydia Skoblikova, USSR	2:25.20
1964	Lydia Skoblikova, USSR	2:22.60

1968	Kaija Mustonen, Finland	2:22.40
1972	Dianne Holum, United States	2:20.80
1976	Galina Stepanskaya, USSR	2:16.58
1980	Annie Borchink, Netherlands	2:10.95
1984	Karin Enke, East Germany	2:03.42
1988	Yvonne Van Gennip, Netherlands	2:00.68
1992	Jacqueline Boerner, Germany	2:05.87
1994	Emese Hunyady, Austria	2:02.19
1998	Marianne Timmer, Netherlands	1:57.58

3,000 Meters (9,843 Ft.)		Time
1960	Lydia Skoblikova, USSR	5:14.30
1964	Lydia Skoblikova, USSR	5:14.90
1968	Johanna Schut, Netherlands	4:56.20
1972	Christina Baas-Kaiser, Netherlands	4:52.14
1976	Tatiana Averina, USSR	4:45.19
1980	Bjoerg Eva Jensen, Norway	4:32.13
1984	Andrea Schöne, East Germany	4:24.79
1988	Yvonne Van Gennip, Netherlands	4:11.94
1992	Gunda Niemann, Germany	4:19.90
1994	Svetlana Bazhanova, Russia	4:17.43
1998	Gunda Niemann-Stirnemann, Germany	4:07.29

5,000 Meters (16,405 Ft.)		Time
1988	Yvonne Van Gennip, Netherlands	7:14.13
1992	Gunda Niemann, Germany	7:31.57
1994	Claudia Pechstein, Germany	7:14.37
1998	Claudia Pechstein, Germany	6:59.61

MEN, SHORT TRACK		WOMEN, SHORT TRACK	

500m (1,641 Ft.)		Time
1994	Ji-Hoon Chae, South Korea	43.45
1998	Takafumi Nishitani, Japan	42.86
1,000m (3,281 Ft.)		**Time**
1992	Kim Ki-Hoon, South Korea	1:30.76
1994	Kim Ki-Hoon, South Korea	1:34.57
1998	Kim Dong-Sung, South Korea	1:32.38
5,000m (16,405 Ft.) Relay		**Time**
1992	South Korea, Canada, Japan	7:14.02
1994	Italy, United States, Austrailia	7:11.74
1998	Canada, South Korea, China	7:06.08

500m (1,641 Ft.)		Time
1992	Cathy Turner, United States	47.04
1994	Cathy Turner, United States	45.98
1998	Annie Perreault, Canada	46.57
1,000m (3,281 Ft.)		**Time**
1994	Lee-Kyung Chun, South Korea	1:36.87
1998	Chun Lee-kyung, South Korea	1:42.78
3,000m (9,843 Ft.) Relay		**Time**
1992	Canada, United States, Unified Team	4:36.62
1994	South Korea, Canada, United States	4:26.64
1998	South Korea, China, Canada	4:16.26

Figure Skating

Men
1908	Ulrich Salchow, Sweden
1920	Gillis Grafstrom, Sweden
1924	Gillis Grafstrom Sweden
1928	Gillis Grafstrom, Sweden
1932	Karl Schafer, Austria
1936	Karl Schafer, Austria
1948	Richard Button, United States
1952	Richard Button, United States
1956	Hayes Alan Jenkins, United States
1960	David W. Jenkins, United States
1964	Manfred Schnelldorfer, Germany
1968	Wolfgang Schwartz, Austria
1972	Ondrej Nepela, Czechoslovakia
1976	John Curry, Great Britain
1980	Robin Cousins, Great Britain
1984	Scott Hamilton, United States
1988	Brian Boitano, United States
1992	Viktor Petrenko, Unified Team
1994	Aleksei Urmanov, Russia
1998	Ilya Kulik, Russia

Women
1908	Madge Syers, Great Britain
1920	Magda Julin-Mauroy, Sweden
1924	Herma von Szabo-Planck, Austria
1928	Sonja Henie, Norway
1932	Sonja Henie, Norway
1936	Sonja Henie, Norway
1948	Barbara Ann Scott, Canada
1952	Jeanette Altwegg, Great Britain
1956	Tenley Albright, United States
1960	Carol Heiss, United States
1964	Sjoukje Dijkstra, Netherlands
1968	Peggy Fleming, United States
1972	Beatrix Schuba, Austria
1976	Dorothy Hamill, United States
1980	Annett Pötzsch, East Germany
1984	Katarina Witt, East Germany
1988	Katarina Witt, East Germany
1992	Kristi Yamaguchi, United States
1994	Oksana Baiul, Ukraine
1998	Tara Lipinski, United States

Pairs
1908	Germany—Anna Hubler, Heinrich Burger
1920	Finland—Ludovika & Walter Jakobsson
1924	Austria—Helene Engelman, Alfred Berger
1928	France—Andree Joly, Pierre Brunet
1932	France—Andree & Pierre Brunet
1936	Germany—Maxie Herber, Ernst Baier
1948	Belgium—Micheline Lannoy, Pierre Baugniet
1952	Germany—Ria & Paul Falk
1956	Austria—Elisabeth Schwartz, Kurt Oppelt
1960	Canada—Barbara Wagner, Robert Paul
1964	USSR—Ludmila Beloussova, Oleg Protopopov
1968	USSR—Ludmila Beloussova, Oleg Protopopov
1972	USSR—Irina Rodnina, Alexei Ulanov
1976	USSR—Irina Rodnina, Aleksandr Zaitsev
1980	USSR—Irina Rodnina, Aleksandr Zaitsev
1984	USSR—Elena Valova, Oleg Vassiliev
1988	USSR—Ekaterina Gordeeva, Sergei Grinkov
1992	Unified Team—Natalya Mishkutienok, Artur Dmitriev
1994	Russia—Ekaterina Gordeeva, Sergei Grinkov
1998	Russia—Oksana Kazakova and Artur Dmitriev

Ice Dancing
1976	USSR—Lyudmila Pakhomova, Aleksandr Gorshkov
1980	USSR—Natalia Linichuk, Gennadi Karponosov
1984	U.K.—Jayne Torvill, Christopher Dean
1988	USSR—Natalia Bestemianova, Andrei Bukin
1992	Unified Team—Marina Kimova, Sergei Ponomarenko
1994	Russia—Pasha Grishuk and Yevgeny Platov,
1998	Russia—Pasha Grishuk and Yevgeny Platov

Ice Hockey

Year	Gold, Silver, Bronze	Year	Gold, Silver, Bronze
1920	Canada, United States Czechoslovakia	1968	USSR, Czechoslovakia, Canada
1924	Canada, United States, Great Britain	1972	USSR, United States, Czechoslovakia
1928	Canada, Sweden, Switzerland	1976	USSR, Czechoslovakia, West Germany
1932	Canada, United States, Germany	1980	U.S., USSR, Sweden
1936	Great Britain, Canada, United States	1984	USSR, Czechoslovakia, Sweden
1948	Canada, Czechoslovakia, Switzerland	1988	USSR, Finland, Sweden
1952	Canada, United States, Sweden	1992	Unified Team, Canada, Czechoslovakia
1956	USSR, United States, Canada	1994	Sweden, Canada, Finland
1960	U.S., Canada, USSR	1998	Czech Republic, Russia, Finland
1964	USSR, Sweden, Czechoslovakia		

Bobsled

Two Man		Time	Two Man		Time	Four Man		Time	Four Man		Time
1932	U.S.	8:14.74	1976	E. Germany	3:44.42	1924	Switzerland	5:45.54	1972	Switzerland	4:43.07
1936	U.S.	5:29.29	1980	Switzerland	4:09.36	1928	U.S. (5-man)	3:20.50	1976	E. Germany	3:40.43
1948	Switzerland	5:29.20	1984	E. Germany	3:25.56	1932	U.S.	7:53.68	1980	E. Germany	3:59.42
1952	Germany	5:24.54	1988	USSR	3:54.19	1936	Switzerland	5:19.85	1984	E. Germany	3:20.22
1956	Italy	5:30.14	1992	Switzerland	4:03.26	1948	U.S.	5:20.10	1988	Switzerland	3:47.51
1964	Great Britain	4:21.90	1994	Switzerland	3:30.81	1952	Germany	5:07.84	1992	Austria	3:53.90
1968	Italy	4:41.54	1998	Canada, Italy	3:37.24	1956	Switzerland	5:10.44	1994	Germany	3:27.78
1972	W. Germany	4:57.07				1964	Canada	4:14.46	1998	Germany	2:39.41
						1968	Italy (2 races)	2:17.39			

Luge

Singles (Men)		Time	1984	West Germany	1:23.62
1964	Thomas Köhler, East Germany	3:26.77	1988	E. Germany	1:31.94
1968	Manfred Schmid, Austria	2:52.48	1992	Germany	1:32.05
1972	Wolfgang Scheidel, East Germany	3:27.58	1994	Italy	1:36.72
1976	Dettlef Günther, East Germany	3:27.68	1998	Germany	1:41.10
1980	Bernhard Glass, East Germany	2:54.79	Singles (Women)		Time
1984	Paul Hildgartner, Italy	3:04.25	1964	Ortrun Enderlein, East Germany	3:24.67
1988	Jens Mueller, East Germany	3:05.54	1968	Erica Lechner, Italy	2:28.66
1992	Georg Hackl, Germany	3:02.36	1972	Anna M. Müller, East Germany	2:59.18
1994	Georg Hackl, Germany	3:21.57	1976	Margit Schumann, East Germany	2:50.62
1998	Georg Hackl, Germany	3:18.44	1980	Vera Zozulya, USSR	2:36.53
Two-seater (Men)		Time	1984	Steffi Martin, East Germany	2:46.57
1964	Austria	1:41.62	1988	Steffi Walter (Martin), East Germany	3:03.97
1968	E. Germany	1:35.85	1992	Doris Neuner, Austria	3:06.69
1972	Italy, East Germany (tie)	1:28.35	1994	Gerda Weissensteiner, Italy	3:15.52
1976	E. Germany	1:25.60	1998	Silke Kraushaar, Germany	3:23.78
1980	E. Germany	1:19.33			

The 1998 Winter Olympics at Nagano, Japan
February 7–22, 1998

Event	Gold	Silver	Bronze
ALPINE SKIING (MEN)			
Downhill	Jean-Luc Cretier, France, 1:50.11	Lasse Kjus, Norway, 1:50.51	Hannes Trinkl, Austria, 1:50.63
Slalom	Hans-Petter Buraas, Norway, 1:49.31	Ole Christian Furuseth, Norway, 1:50.64	Thomas Sykora, Austria, 1:50.68
Giant Slalom	Hermann Maier, Austria, 2:38.51	Stefan Eberharter, Austria, 2:39.36	Michael von Gruenigen, Switzerland, 2:39.69
Super Giant Slalom	Hermann Maier, Austria, 1:34.82	Didier Cuche, Switzerland, Hans Knauss, Austria, 1:35.43;	(two skiers tied for Silver)
Combined	Mario Reiter, Austria, 3:08.06	Lasse Kjus, Norway, 3:08.65	Christian Mayer, Austria, 3:10.11
ALPINE SKIING (WOMEN)			
Downhill	Katja Seizinger, Germany, 1:28.89	Pernilla Wiberg, Sweden, 1:29.18	Florence Masnada, France, 1:29.37
Slalom	Hilde Gerg, Germany, 1:32.40	Deborah Compagnoni, Italy, 1:32.46	Zali Steggall, Australia, 1:32.67
Giant Slalom	Deborah Compagnoni, Italy, 2:50.59	Alexandra Meissnitzer, Austria, 2:52.39	Katja Seizinger, Germany, 2:52.61
Super Giant Slalom	Picabo Street, United States, 1:18.02	Michaela Dorfmeister, Austria, 1:18.03	Alexandra Meissnitzer, Austria, 1:18.09
Combined	Katja Seizinger, Germany, 2:40.74	Martina Ertl, Germany, 2:40.92	Hilde Gerg, Germany, 2:41.50
BIATHLON (MEN)			
10 Kilometers	Ole Bjorndalen, Norway, 27:16.2	Frode Andresen, Norway, 28:17.8	Ville Raikkonen, Finland, 28:21.7
20 Kilometers	Halvard Hanevold, Norway, 56:16.4	Pier Alberto Carrara, Italy, 56:21.9	Aleksei Aidarov, Belarus, 56:46.5
30 Km Relay	Germany, 1:19:43.3	Norway, 1:20:03.4	Russia, 1:20:19.4
BIATHLON (WOMEN)			
7.5 Kilometers	Galina Kukleva, Russia, 23:08.0	Ursula Disl, Germany, 23:08.7	Katrin Apel, Germany, 23:32.4
15 Kilometers	Yekaterina Dafovska, Bulgaria, 54:52.0	Yelena Petrova, Ukraine, 55:09.8	Ursula Disl, Germany, 55:17.9
30 Km Relay	Germany, 1:40:13.6	Russia, 1:40:25.2	Norway, 1:40:37.3
BOBSLED			
Two-Man	Canada 1, 3:37.24; Italy 1, 3:37.24	(two teams tied for gold)	Germany 1, 3:37.89
Four-Man	Germany 2, 2:39.41	Switzerland 1, 2:40.01	Britain 1, 2:40.06; France 1, 2:40.06

Event	Gold	Silver	Bronze
CURLING			
Men	Switzerland	Canada	Norway
Women	Canada	Denmark	Sweden
FIGURE SKATING			
Men	Ilya Kulik, Russia	Elvis Stojko, Canada	Philippe Candeloro, France
Women	Tara Lipinski, United States	Michelle Kwan, United States	Lu Chen, China
Pairs	Oksana Kazakova and Artur Dmitriev, Russia	Yelena Berezhnaya and Anton Sikharulidze, Russia	Mandy Wotzel and Ingo Steuer, Germany
Ice Dancing	Pasha Grishuk and Yevgeny Platov, Russia	Angelika Krylova and Oleg Ovsyannikov, Russia	Maria Anissina and Gwendal Peizerat, France
FREESTYLE SKIING, MEN			
Aerials	Eric Bergoust, United States, 255.64	Sebastien Foucras, France, 248.79	Dmitri Daschinsky, Belarus, 240.79
Moguls	Jonny Moseley, United States, 26.93	Janne Lahtela, Finland, 26.00	Sami Mustonen, Finland, 25.76
FREESTYLE SKIING, WOMEN			
Aerials	Nikki Stone, United States, 193.00	Xu Nannan, China, 186.97	Colette Brand, Switzerland, 171.83
Moguls	Tae Satoya, Japan, 25.06	Tatjana Mittermayer, Germany, 24.62	Kari Traa, Norway, 24.09
ICE HOCKEY			
Men	Czech Republic	Russia	Finland
Women	United States	Canada	Finland
LUGE			
Men's Singles	Georg Hackl, Germany, 3:18.44	Armin Zoeggeler, Italy, 3:18.94	Jens Mueller, Germany, 3:19.09
Men's Doubles	Stefan Krausse/Jan Behrendt, Germany, 1:41.105	Chris Thorpe/Gordy Sheer, United States, 1:41.127	Mark Grimmette/Brian Martin, United States, 1:41.217
Women's Singles	Silke Kraushaar, Germany, 3:23.779	Barbara Niedernhuber, Germany, 3:23.781	Angelika Neuner, Austria, 3:24.253
NORDIC SKIING AND JUMPING (MEN)			
10 Kilometers	Bjorn Dahlie, Norway, 27:24.5	Markus Gandler, Austria, 27:32.5	Mika Myllylae, Finland, 27:40.1
15 Kilometers	Thomas Alsgaard, Norway, 1:07:01.7	Bjorn Dahlie, Norway, 1:07:02.8	Vladimir Smirnov, Kazakhstan, 1:07:31.5
30 Kilometers	Mika Myllylae, Finland, 1:33.55.8	Erling Jevne, Norway, 1:35.27.1	Silvio Fauner, Italy, 1:36.08.5
50 Kilometers	Bjorn Dahlie, Norway, 2:05:08.2	Niklas Jonsson, Sweden, 2:05:16.3	Christian Hoffmann, Austria, 2:06:01.8
40 Km (4x10 Km) Relay	Norway, 1:40:55.7	Italy, 1:40:55.9	Finland, 1:42:15.5
Nordic Combined	Bjarte Engen Vik, Norway	Samppa Lajunen, Finland	Valery Stoliarov, Russia
Nordic Combined, Team	Norway	Finland	France
90m Ski Jump	Jani Soininen, Finland, 234.5	Kazuyoshi Funaki, Japan, 233.5	Andreas Widhölzl, Austria, 232.5
120m Ski Jump	Kazuyoshi Funaki, Japan, 272.3	Jani Soininen, Finland, 260.8	Masahiko Harada, Japan, 258.3
120m Ski Jump, Team	Japan, 933.0	Germany, 897.4	Austria, 881.5
NORDIC SKIING, WOMEN			
5 Kilometers	Larissa Lazutina, Russia, 17:39.9	Katerina Neumannova, Czech Republic, 17:42.7	Bente Martinsen, Norway, 17:49.4
10 Kilometers	Larissa Lazutina, Russia, 46:06.9	Olga Danilova, Russia, 46:13.4	Katerina Neumannova, Czech Republic, 46:14.2
15 Kilometers	Olga Danilova, Russia, 46:55.4	Larissa Lazutina, Russia, 47:01.0	Anita Moen-Guidon, Norway, 47:52.6
30 Kilometers	Yuliya Chepalova, Russia, 1:22:01.5	Stefania Belmondo, Italy, 1:22:11.7	Larissa Lazutina, Russia, 1:23:15.7
20 Km (4x5 Km) Relay	Russia, 55:13.5	Norway, 55:38.0	Italy, 56:53.3
SNOWBOARDING (MEN)			
Giant Slalom	Ross Rebagliati, Canada, 2:03.96	Thomas Prugger, Italy, 2:03.98	Ueli Kestenholz, Switzerland, 2:04.08
Halfpipe	Gian Simmen, Switzerland, 85.2	Daniel Franck, Norway, 82.4	Ross Powers, United States, 82.1

Event	Gold	Silver	Bronze

SNOWBOARDING (WOMEN)

Giant Slalom	Karine Ruby, France, 2:17.34	Heidi Renoth, Germany, 2:19.17	Brigitte Koeck, Austria, 2:19.42
Halfpipe	Nicola Thost, Germany, 74.6	Stine Brun Kjeldaas, Norway, 74.2	Shannon Dunn, United States, 72.8

SPEED SKATING, MEN, LONG TRACK

500 Meters	Hiroyasu Shimizu, Japan, 1:11.35	Jeremy Wotherspoon, Canada, 1:11.84	Kevin Overland, Canada, 1:11.86
1,000 Meters	Ids Postma, Netherlands, 1:10.64	Jan Bos, Netherlands, 1:10.71	Hiroyasu Shimizu, Japan, 1:11.00
1,500 Meters	Aadne Sondral, Norway, 1:47.87	Ids Postma, Netherlands, 1:48.13	Rintje Ritsma, Netherlands, 1:48.52
5,000 Meters	Gianni Romme, Netherlands, 6:22.20	Rintje Ritsma, Netherlands, 6:28.24	Bart Veldkamp, Belgium, 6:28.31
10,000 Meters	Gianni Romme, Netherlands, 13:15.33	Bob De Jong, Netherlands, 13:25.76	Rintje Ritsma, Netherlands, 13:28.19

SPEED SKATING, WOMEN, LONG TRACK

500 Meters	Catriona Le May-Doan, Canada, 1:16.60	Susan Auch, Canada, 1:16.93	Tomomi Okazaki, Japan, 1:16.93
1,000 Meters	Marianne Timmer, Netherlands, 1:16.51	Chris Witty, United States, 1:16.79	Catriona LeMay-Doan, Canada, 1:17.37
1,500 Meters	Marianne Timmer, Netherlands, 1:57.58	Gunda Niemann-Stirnemann, Germany, 1:58.66	Chris Witty, United States, 1:58.97
3,000 Meters	Gunda Niemann-Stirnemann, Germany, 4:07.29	Claudia Pechstein, Germany, 4:08.47	Anna Friesinger, Germany, 4:09.44
5,000 Meters	Claudia Pechstein, Germany, 6:59.61	Gunda Niemann-Stirnemann, Germany, 6:59.65	Lyudmila Prokasheva, Kazakhstan, 7:11.14

SPEED SKATING, MEN, SHORT TRACK

500 Meters	Takafumi Nishitani, Japan, 42.86	An Yulong, China, 43.02	Hitoshi Uematsu, Japan, 43.71
1,000 Meters	Kim Dong-Sung, South Korea, 1:32.38	Li Jiajun, China, 1:32.43	Eric Bedard, Canada, 1:32.66
5,000 Meter relay	Canada, 7:06.08	South Korea, 7:06.78	China, 7:11.56

SPEED SKATING, WOMEN, SHORT TRACK

500 Meters	Annie Perreault, Canada, 46.57	Yang Yang, China, 46.63	Chun Lee-Kyung, Korea, 46.34
1,000 Meters	Chun Lee-kyung, South Korea, 1:42.78	Yang Yang, China, 1:43.34	Won Hye-kyung, Korea, 1:43.36
3,000 Meter relay	South Korea, 4:16.26	China, 4:16.38	Canada, 4:21.20

All-Time Olympic Medal Winners

Carl Lewis, U.S. At the age of 35, Lewis won the gold medal in the long jump at the 1996 Olympics. It was Lewis's fourth consecutive Olympic long jump gold and his ninth gold medal overall. Al Oerter, who won the discus from 1956 to 1968, is the only other track and field athlete to win an event in four straight Olympiads. In addition to his four long jump golds, Lewis won gold in the 100 meters in 1984 and 1988, the 400-meter relay in 1984 and 1992, and the 200 meters in 1984.

Mark Spitz, Swimmer, U.S. Spitz set the record for gold medals in one Olympics in 1972 with seven (100m and 200m freestyle, 100m and 200m butterfly, 400m and 800m freestyle relays, and 400m medley relay). These he added to the four medals he won at the 1968 Olympics: a bronze in the 100m freestyle, a silver in the 100m butterfly, and gold in both the 400m and 800m freestyle relays.

Paavo Nurmi, Track and Field, Finland Nurmi won the 10,000m in 1920 and 1928 and might have won in 1924 had he not been prevented by Finnish officials, who felt he had entered too many events. Nurmi had already won gold medals in the 1,500m, the 5,000m, the 3,000m team race (a discontinued event), and the individual and team cross-country races, two events he had also won in 1920 (since discontinued). Nurmi also earned three silver medals to go with his nine golds.

Larissa Latynina, Gymnastics, Soviet Union No athlete has won more Olympic medals than this Ukrainian, who won 18 between 1956 and 1964. In addition to nine gold medals in vault (1956), floor exercise (1956, 1960 and 1964), team combined (1956, 1960, and 1964), and all-around (1956 and 1960), Latynina won five silver and four bronze medals.

PROFESSIONAL SPORTS

AUTOMOBILE RACING

A number of U.S. states and cities banned automobile racing on public roads during the early 1900s, leading to the development of closed-circuit courses. The Indianapolis Motor Speedway, a 2.5 mile macadam oval, was built in 1909. It was paved with brick in 1911, when the first Indy 500 was run. The American Automobile Association, troubled by a series of fatal crashes, stopped sanctioning races in 1956, whereupon the United States Auto Club (USAC) took over the Indy 500.

Indianapolis 500 Winners, 1911–99

Year	Winner	Time	MPH	Year	Winner	Time	MPH
Under AAA Sanction				**Under USAC Sanction**			
1911	Ray Harroun	6:42.08	74.602	1956	Pat Flaherty	3:53.28	128.490
1912	Joe Dawson	6:21.06	78.719	1957	Sam Hanks	3:41.14	135.601
1913	Juses Goux	6:35:05	75.933	1958	Jim Bryan	3:44:13	133.791
1914	Rene Thomas	6:03:45	82.474	1959	Rodger Ward	3:40:49	135.857
1915	Ralph DePalma	5:33:55	89.840	1960	Jim Rathmann	3:36:11	138.767
1916	Dario Resta	3:34:17[1]	84.001	1961	A.J. Foyt, Jr.	3:35:37	139.131
1919	Howard Wilcox	5:40:42	88.050	1962	Roger Ward	3:33:50	140.293
1920	Gaston Chevrolet	5:38:32	88.618	1963	Parnelli Jones	3:29:35	143.137
1921	Tommy Milton	5:34:34	89.621	1964	A.J. Foyt, Jr.	3:23:35	147.350
1922	Jimmy Murphy	5:17:30	94.484	1965	Jim Clark	3:19:05	150.686
1923	Tommy Milton	5:29:50	90.954	1966	Graham Hill	3:27:52	144.317
1924	L.L. Corum, Joe Boyer	5:05:23	98.234	1967	A.J. Foyt, Jr.	3:18:14	151.207
1925	Peter DePaolo	4:56:39	101.127	1968	Bobby Unser	3:16:13	152.882
1926	Peter Lockhart	4:10:14[2]	95.904	1969	Mario Andretti	3:11:14	156.867
1927	George Souders	5:07:33	97.545	1970	Al Unser	3:12:37	155.749
1928	Louis Meyer	5:01:33	99.482	1971	Al Unser	3:10:11	157.735
1929	Ray Keech	5:07:25	97.585	1972	Mark Donohue	3:04:05	162.962
1930	Billy Arnold	4:58:39	100.448	1973	Gordon Johncock	2:05:26[4]	159.036
1931	Louis Schneider	5:10:27	96.629	1974	Johnny Rutherford	3:09:10	158.589
1932	Fred Frame	4:48:03	104.144	1975	Bobby Unser	2:54:55[5]	149.213
1933	Louis Meyer	4:48:00	104.162	1976	Johnny Rutherford	1:42:52[6]	148.725
1934	William Cummings	4:46:05	104.863	1977	A.J. Foyt, Jr.	3:05:57	161.331
1935	Kelly Petillo	4:42:22	106.240	1978	Al Unser	3:05:54	161.363
1936	Louis Meyer	4:35:03	109.069	1979	Rick Mears	3:08:47	158.899
1937	Wilbur Shaw	4:24:07	113.580	1980	Johnny Rutherford	3:29:59	142.862
1938	Floyd Roberts	4:15:58	117.200	1981	Bobby Unser	3:35:41	139.084
1939	Wilbur Shaw	4:20:47	115.035	1982	Gordon Johncock	3:05:09	162.029
1940	Wilbur Shaw	4:22:31	114.277	1983	Tom Sneva	3:05:03	162.117
1941	Floyd Davis, Mauri Rose	4:20:36	115.117	1984	Rick Mears	3:30:21	163.612
1946	George Robson	4:21:16	114.820	1985	Danny Sullivan	3:16:06	152.982
1947	Mauri Rose	4:17:52	116.338	1986	Bobby Rahal	2:55:43	170.722
1948	Mauri Rose	4:10:23	119.814	1987	Al Unser	3:04:59	162.175
1949	Bill Holland	4:07:15	121.327	1988	Rick Mears	3:27:10	144.809
1950	Johnnie Parsons	2:46:55[3]	124.002	1989	Emerson Fittipaldi	2:59:01	167.581
1951	Lee Wallard	3:57:38	126.244	1990	Arie Luyendyk	2:41:18	185.984[7]
1952	Troy Tuttman	3:52:41	128.922	1991	Rick Mears	2:50:01	176.457
1953	Bill Vukovich	3:53:01	128.740	1992	Al Unser, Jr.	3:43:05	134.477
1954	Bill Vukovich	3:49:17	130.840	1993	Emerson Fittipaldi	3:10:50	157.207
1955	Bob Sweikert	3:53:59	128.209	1994	Al Unser, Jr.	3:06:29	160.872
				1995	Jacques Villeneuve	3:15:18	153.616
				1996	Buddy Lazier	3:22:46	147.956
				1997	Arie Luyendyk	3:25:43	145.827
				1998	Eddie Cheever	3:26:40	145.155
				1999	Kenny Brack	3:15:51	153.176

1. 300 miles (scheduled). 2. 400 miles (rain). 3. 345 miles (rain). 4. 332.5 miles (rain). 5. 435 miles (rain). 6. 255 miles (rain). 7. Track record. **Source:** Indianapolis Motor Speedway Hall of Fame and Museum.

Winston Cup Winners 1959–98

NASCAR, The National Association for Stock Car Racing, first sponsored a Grand National championship in 1949, the 32 Winston Cup races, covering between 400 and 600 miles, are contested on 19 designated speedways around the country.

Year	Driver	Points
1959	Lee Petty	11,792
1960	Rex White	21,164
1961	Ned Jarrett	27,272
1962	Joe Weatherly	30,836
1963	Joe Weatherly	33,398
1964	Richard Petty	40,252
1965	Ned Jarrett	38,824
1966	David Pearson	35,638
1967	Richard Petty	42,472
1968	David Pearson	3,499
1969	David Pearson	4,170
1970	Bobby Isaac	3,911
1971	Richard Petty	4,435
1972	Richard Petty	8,701
1973	Benny Parsons	7,173
1974	Richard Petty	5,037
1975	Richard Petty	4,783
1976	Cale Yarborough	4,644
1977	Cale Yarborough	5,000
1978	Cale Yarborough	4,841
1979	Richard Petty	4,830
1980	Dale Earnhardt	4,661
1981	Darrell Waltrip	4,880
1982	Darrell Waltrip	4,489
1983	Bobby Allison	4,667
1984	Terry Labonte	4,508
1985	Darrell Waltrip	4,292
1986	Dale Earnhardt	4,468
1987	Dale Earnhardt	4,696
1988	Bill Elliott	4,488
1989	Rusty Wallace	4,176
1990	Dale Earnhardt	4,430
1991	Dale Earnhardt	4,287
1992	Alan Kulwicki	4,078
1993	Dale Earnhardt	4,562
1994	Dale Earnhardt	4,694
1995	Jeff Gordon	4,614
1996	Terry Labonte	4,657
1997	Jeff Gordon	4,710
1998	Jeff Gordon	5,328

Daytona 500 Winners, 1959–99

Year	Driver	Avg. speed (mph)
1959	Lee Petty	135.521
1960	Junior Johnson	124.740
1961	Marvin Panch	149.601
1962	Fireball Roberts	152.529
1963	Tiny Lund	151.566
1964	Richard Petty	154.334
1965	Fred Lorenzen	141.539
1966	Richard Petty	160.627
1967	Mario Andretti	146.926
1968	Cale Yarborough	143.251
1969	LeeRoy Yarbrough	157.950
1970	Pete Hamilton	149.601
1971	Richard Petty	144.462
1972	A.J. Foyt, Jr.	161.550
1973	Richard Petty	157.205
1974	Richard Petty	140.894
1975	Benny Parsons	153.649
1976	David Pearson	152.181
1977	Cale Yarborough	153.218
1978	Bobby Allison	159.730
1979	Richard Petty	143.977
1980	Buddy Baker	177.602
1981	Richard Petty	169.651
1982	Bobby Allison	153.991
1983	Cale Yarborough	155.979
1984	Cale Yarborough	150.994
1985	Bill Elliott	172.265
1986	Geoff Bodine	148.124
1987	Bill Elliott	176.263
1988	Bobby Allison	137.531
1989	Darrell Waltrip	148.466
1990	Derrike Cope	165.761
1991	Ernie Irvan	148.148
1992	Davey Allison	160.260
1993	Dale Jarrett	154.972
1994	Sterling Marlin	156.931
1995	Sterling Marlin	141.710
1996	Dale Jarrett	154.308
1997	Jeff Gordon	148.295
1998	Dale Earnhardt	173.712
1999	Jeff Gordon	161.551

Source: NASCAR

BOWLING

The Professional Bowlers Association was founded by 33 charter members who competed in three 1959 tournaments for prizes worth a total of $49,500. The traditional Winter Tour, which has been augmented and expanded into four separate seasonal tours, now pays more than $9 million in prize money.

PBA Leading Money Winners, 1959–98

Year	Name	Amount	Year	Name	Amount	Year	Name	Amount
1959	Dick Weber	$7,672	1974	Earl Anthony	$99,585	1988	Brian Voss	$225,485
1960	Don Carter	22,525	1975	Earl Anthony	107,585	1989	Mike Aulby	298,237
1961	Dick Weber	26,280	1976	Earl Anthony	110,833	1990	Aurelio Monacelli	204,775
1962	Don Carter	49,972	1977	Mark Roth	105,583	1991	David Ozio	225,585
1963	Dick Weber	46,333	1978	Mark Roth	134,500	1992	Marc McDowell	174,215
1964	Bob Strampe	33,592	1979	Mark Roth	124,517	1993	Walter Ray	296,370
1965	Dick Weber	47,675	1980	Wayne Webb	116,700		Williams Jr.	
1966	Wayne Zahn	54,720	1981	Earl Anthony	164,735	1994	Norm Duke	273,753
1967	Dave Davis	54,165	1982	Earl Anthony	134,760	1995	Mike Aulby	219,792
1968	Jim Stefanich	67,375	1983	Earl Anthony	135,605	1996	Walter Ray	241,330
1969	Billy Hardwick	64,160	1984	Mark Roth	158,712		Williams Jr.	
1970	Mike McGrath	52,049	1985	Mike Aulby	201,200	1997	Walter Ray	240,544
1971	Johnny Petraglia	85,065	1986	Walter Ray	145,550		Williams Jr.	
1972	Don Johnson	56,648		Williams Jr.		1998	Walter Ray	238,225
1973	Don McCune	69,000	1987	Pete Weber	179,516		Williams Jr.	

Ladies Pro Bowling Tour Leading Money Winners

1998		Career			
Rank, Bowler	Earnings	Rank, Bowler	Earnings	Rank, Bowler	Earnings
1. Carol Gianotti-Block	$150,350	1. Aleta Sill	$993,642	11. Dede Davidson	$558,932
2. Aleta Sill	122,505	2. Tish Johnson	890,963	12. Dana Miller-Mackie	554,317
3. Dede Davidson	121,600	3. Wendy Macpherson	802,430	13. Kim Adler	529,844
4. Carolyn Dorin-Ballard	118,478	4. Lisa Wagner	797,401	14. Carol Norman	518,157
5. Kim Adler	101,260	5. Anne Marie Duggan	762,231	15. Cindy Coburn-Caroll	512,268
6. Marianne DiRupo	97,955	6. Leanne Barrette	753,468	16. Carolyn Dorin-Ballard	508,526
7. Dana Miller-Mackie	90,863	7. Carol Gianotti-Block	742,784	17. Jeanne Naccarato	507,022
8. Kim Canady	81,820	8. Robin Mossontte	650,954	18. Lorrie Nichols	484,844
9. Anne Marie Duggan	77,220	9. Cheryl Daniels	633,166	19. Donna Adamek	472,244
10. Wendy Macpherson	75,625	10. Nikki Gianulias	604,300	20. Kim Canady	444,854

Note: Career figures as of May 27, 1999.   **Source:** Professional Women's Bowling Association.

BOXING

Although many governing bodies now issue and certify their own boxing championships, the three most widely accepted are the World Boxing Association (WBA), World Boxing Council (WBC), and the International Boxing Federation (IBF). Years given indicate the year the championship belt changed hands in a title bout. Champions who were awarded belts without a championship bout are not shown. Current champions (as of Sept. 20, 1999) are shown in **boldface type.**

Heavyweights (over 190 lbs.)

Years	Name	Years	Name
1885	John L. Sullivan	1970	Joe Frazier (unifies world title)
1892	James J. Corbett	1973	George Foreman
1897	Robert Fitzsimmons	1974	Muhammad Ali
1899	James J. Jeffries	1978	Leon Spinks, Larry Holmes[1], Muhammad Ali[1]
1905	Marvin Hart		(WBA)
1906	Tommy Burns	1979	John Tate (WBA)
1908	Jack Johnson	1980	Mike Weaver (WBA)
1915	Jess Willard	1982	Michael Dokes (WBA)
1919	Jack Dempsey	1983	Gerrie Coetzee (WBA)
1926	Gene Tunney[1]	1984	Tim Witherspoon (WBC), Pinklon Thomas (WBC),
1928–30	vacant		Greg Page (WBA)
1930	Max Schmeling	1985	Tony Tubbs (WBA)
1932	Jack Sharkey	1986	Tim Witherspoon (WBA), Trevor Berbick (WBC),
1933	Primo Carnera		Mike Tyson (WBC), James "Bonecrusher" Smith
1934	Max Baer		(WBA)
1935	James J. Braddock	1987	Mike Tyson (WBA), Tony Tucker (IBF)
1937	Joe Louis[1]	1990	Buster Douglas (unifies world title), Evander
1949	Ezzard Charles		Holyfield
1951	Jersey Joe Walcott	1991	Evander Holyfield
1952	Rocky Marciano[1]	1992	Riddick Bowe
1956	Floyd Patterson	1993	Evander Holyfield (WBA, IBF)
1959	Ingemar Johansson	1994	George Foreman (WBA, IBF),
1960	Floyd Patterson		Bruce Seldon (WBA),
1962	Sonny Liston		Frank Bruno[1] (WBC)
1964	Cassius Clay[1] (Muhammad Ali)	1996	Mike Tyson (WBC), Michael Moorer (IBF),
1965	Ernie Terrell (WBA)		Mike Tyson (WBA), **Evander Holyfield (WBA)**
1967	Muhammad Ali (unifies world title)	1997	**Lennox Lewis (WBC),**
1968	Jimmy Ellis (WBA)		**Evander Holyfield (IBF)**

Note: WBC = World Boxing Council. WBA = World Boxing Association. IBF= International Boxing Federation. 1. Stripped of title or abandoned belt.   **Source:** International Boxing Hall of Fame.

Light Heavyweights (169–175 lbs.)

Year	Name	Year	Name
1903	Jack Root, George Gardner	1978	Mate Parlov (WBC), Mike Rossman (WBA),
1903	Bob Fitzsimmons		Marvin Johnson (WBC)
1905	Philadelphia Jack O'Brien[1]	1979	Matthew Franklin (Matthew Saad Muhammad)
1912	Jack Dillon		(WBC),
1916	Battling Levinsky		Marvin Johnson (WBA)
1920	George Carpentier	1980	Eddie Gregory (Eddie Mustafa Muhammad) (WBA)
1922	Battling Siki	1981	Michael Spinks (WBA),
1923	Mike McTigue		Dwight Braxton (Dwight Muhammad Qawi) (WBC)
1925	Paul Berlenbach	1983	Michael Spinks (unifies world title)
1926	Jack Delaney[1]	1985	J.B. Williamson (WBC),Slobodan Kacar (IBF)
1927	Tommy Loughran[1]	1986	Marvin Johnson (WBA), Dennis Andries (WBC),
1930	Maxey Rosenbloom		Bobby Czyz (IBF)
1934	Bob Olin	1987	Thomas Hearns[1] (WBC), Leslie Stewart (WBA),
1935	John Henry Lewis[1]		Virgil Hill (WBA), Prince Charles Williams (IBF),
1939	Billy Conn[1]		Don Lalonde (WBC)
1941	Gus Lesnevich	1988	Sugar Ray Leonard (WBC)
1948	Freddie Mills	1989	Dennis Andries (WBC), Jeff Harding (WBC)
1950	Joey Maxim	1990	Dennis Andries (WBC)
1952	Archie Moore	1991	Thomas Hearns (WBA),Jeff Harding (WBC)
1960–61	vacant	1992	Iran Barkley[1] (WBA), Virgil Hill (WBA)
1962	Harold Johnson	1993	Henry Maske (IBF)
1963	Willie Pastrano	1994	Mike McCallum (WBC)
1965	Jose Torres	1995	Fabrice Tiozzo (WBC)
1966	Dick Tiger	1996	Roy Jones Jr.[1] (WBC),Virgil Hill[1] (IBF),
1968	Bob Foster	1997	William Guthrie (IBF), Dariusz Michalczewski[1]
1971	Vicente Rondon (WBA)		(WBA), Lou Del Valle (WBC)
1972	Bob Foster (unifies world title)	1998	Reggie Johnson (IBF), Graciano Rocchigiani (WBC),
1974	John Conteh (WBC), Victor		**Roy Jones Jr. (WBA, WBC)**
	Galindez (WBA)	1999	**Roy Jones Jr. (IBF)**
1977	Miguel Angel Cuello (WBC)		

Note: WBC = World Boxing Council. WBA = World Boxing Association. IBF= International Boxing Federation. 1. Stripped of title or abandoned belt. **Source:** International Boxing Hall of Fame.

Middleweights (155–160 lbs.)

Year	Name	Year	Name
1884	"Nonpareil" Jack Dempsey	1960	Paul Pender
1891	Bob Fitzsimmons[1]	1961	Terry Downes
1897	Kid McCoy[1], Tommy Ryan[1]	1962	Paul Pender
1907	Stanley Ketchel	1963	Dick Tiger
1908	Billy Papke, Stanley Ketchel[1]	1963	Joey Giardello
1911–13	vacant	1965	Dick Tiger
1913	Frank Klaus, George Chip	1966	Emile Griffith
1914	Al McCoy	1967	Nino Benvenuti, Emile Griffith
1917	Mike O'Dowd	1968	Nino Benvenuti
1920	Johnny Wilson	1970	Carlos Monzon
1921	William Bryan Downey[1]	1977	Rodrigo Valdez
1923	Harry Greb	1978	Hugo Corro
1926	Tiger Flowers, Mickey Walker	1979	Vito Antuofermo
1931	Gorilla Jones	1980	Alan Minter, Marvin Hagler[1]
1932	Marcel Thil	1987	Ray Leonard[1] (WBC), Frank Tate (IBF),
1937	Fred Apostoli		Sumbo Kalambay (WBA), Thomas Hearns (WBC)
1939	Ceferino Garcia	1988	Iran Barkley (WBC), Michael Nunn (IBF)
1940	Ken Overlin	1989	Roberto Duran[1] (WBC), Mike McCallum[1] (WBA)
1941	Billy Soose[1], Tony Zale	1990	Julian Jackson (WBC), James Toney[1] (IBF)
1947	Rocky Graziano	1991	Reggie Johnson[1] (WBA)
1948	Tony Zale, Marcel Cerdan	1993	Gerald McClellan[1] (WBC), Roy Jones[1] (IBF),
1949	Jake LaMotta		John David Jackson (WBA)
1951	Sugar Ray Robinson, Randy Turpin,	1994	Jorge Castro (WBA)
	Sugar Ray Robinson[1]	1995	Julian Jackson (WBC), **Bernard Hopkins (IBF)**,
1953	Bobo Olson		Quincy Taylor (WBC), Shinij Takehara (WBA)
1955	Sugar Ray Robinson	1996	Keith Holmes (WBC), William Joppy (WBA)
1957	Gene Fullmer (NBA), Sugar Ray	1997	Julio Cesar Green (WBA)
	Robinson, Carmen Basilio	1996	**William Joppy (WBA),** Hassine Cherifi (WBC)
1958	Sugar Ray Robinson	1999	**Keith Holmes (WBC)**

Note: WBC = World Boxing Council. WBA = World Boxing Association. IBF= International Boxing Federation. 1. Stripped of title or abandoned belt. **Source:** International Boxing Hall of Fame.

Welterweights (141–147 lbs.)

Year	Name	Year	Name
1888	Paddy Duffy	1955	Tony De Marco, Carmen Basilio
1892	Mysterious Billy Smith	1956	Johnny Saxton, Carmen Basilio
1894	Tommy Ryan[1]	1957	Carmen Basilio[1]
1896	Kid McCoy[2]	1958	Virgil Akins, Don Jordan
1898	Mysterious Billy Smith	1960	Benny Paret
1900	Matty Matthews, Eddie Connolly,	1961	Emile Griffith, Benny Paret
	Rube Ferns, Matty Matthews	1962	Emile Griffith
1901	Rube Ferns, Joe Walcott	1963	Luis Rodriguez, Emile Griffith[1]
1904	Dixie Kid[1]	1966	Curtis Cokes
1906	Honey Mellody	1969	Jose Napoles
1907	Frank Mantell	1970	Billy Backus
1908	Harry Lewis[1]	1971	Jose Napoles
1911–13	Vacant	1975	Angel Espada (WBA), John Stracey (WBC)
1914	Waldemar Holberg, Tom McCormick,	1976	Carlos Palomino (WBC), Jose Cuevas (WBA)
	Matt Wells	1979	Wilfredo Benitez (WBC),
1915	Mike Glover, Jack Britton, Ted	1980	Roberto Duran (WBC), Thomas Hearns (WBA)
	(Kid) Lewis		Sugar Ray Leonard(WBA)
1916	Jack Britton	1981	Sugar Ray Leonard[1] (unifies world title)
1917	Ted (Kid) Lewis	1983	Donald Curry (WBA), Milton McCrory (WBC)
1919	Jack Britton	1985	Donald Curry (unifies world title)
1922	Mickey Walker	1986	Lloyd Honeyghan[1]
1926	Pete Latzo	1987	Mark Breland (WBA), Marlon Starling (WBA),
1927	Joe Dundee		Jorge Vaca (WBC)
1929	Jackie Fields	1988	Simon Brown[1] (IBF), Thomas Molinares[1] (WBA)
1930	Young Jack Thompson, Tommy	1989	Marlon Starling (WBC), Mark Breland (WBA)
	Freeman	1990	Aaron Davis (WBA),
1931	Young Jack Thompson, Lou Brouillard		Maurice Blocker (WBC)
1932	Jackie Fields	1991	Meldrick Taylor (WBA), Simon Brown (WBC),
1933	Young Corbett, Jimmy McLarnin		Maurice Blocker (IBF), Buddy McGirt (WBC)
1934	Barney Ross, Jimmy McLarnin	1992	Crisanto Espana (WBA)
1935	Barney Ross	1993	Pernell Whitaker (WBC), **Felix Trinidad (IBF)**
1938	Henry Armstrong	1994	Ike Quartey[1] (WBA)
1940	Fritzie Zivic	1997	Oscar de la Hoya (WBC)
1941	Fred Cochrane	1998	**James Page (WBA)**
1946	Marty Servo[1], Ray Robinson[1]	1999	**Felix Trinidad (WBC)**
1951	Kid Gavilan J.		
1954	Johnny Saxton		

Note: WBC = World Boxing Council. WBA = World Boxing Association. IBF= International Boxing Federation. 1. Stripped of title or abandoned belt. **Source:** International Boxing Hall of Fame.

Lightweights (131–135 lbs.)

Year	Name	Year	Name
1896	Jack McAuliffe[1], Kid Lavigne	1970	Ismael Laguna, Ken Buchanan[1]
1899	Frank Erne	1971	Pedro Carrasco (WBC)
1902	Joe Gans[1]	1972	Mando Ramos (WBC), Roberto Duran[1] (WBA)
1904	Jimmy Britt		Chango Carmona (WBC), Rodolfo Gonzalez (WBC)
1905	Battling Nelson	1974	Ishimatsu Suzuki (WBC)
1906	Joe Gans	1976	Esteban De Jesus[1] (WBC)
1908	Battling Nelson	1979	Jim Watt (WBC), Ernesto España (WBA)
1910	Ad Wolgast	1980	Hilmer Kenty (WBA)
1912	Willie Ritchie	1981	Sean O'Grady (WBA), Alexis Arguello (WBC),
1914	Freddie Welsh		Claude Noel (WBA), Arturo Frias (WBA)
1917	Benny Leonard[1]	1982	Ray Mancini (WBA)
1925	Jimmy Goodrich, Rocky Kansas	1983	Edwin Rosario (WBC)
1926	Sammy Mandell	1984	Charlie (Choo Choo) Brown (IBF),
1930	Al Singer, Tony Canzoneri		Livingstone Bramble (WBA), Jose Luis Ramirez (WBC)
1933	Barney Ross[1]	1985	Jimmy Paul (IBF), Hector (Macho) Camacho[1] (WBC)
1935	Tony Canzoneri	1986	Edwin Rosario (WBA), Greg Haugen (IBF)
1936	Lou Ambers	1987	Vinny Pazienza (IBF), Jose Luis Ramirez (WBC),
1938	Henry Armstrong		Julio Cesar Chavez[1] (WBA)
1939	Lou Ambers	1988	Greg Haugen (IBF), Julio Cesar Chavez[1] (WBC)
1940	Lew Jenkins	1989	Pernell Whitaker (IBF), Edwin Rosario (WBA),
1941	Sammy Angott		Pernell Whitaker (WBC)
1942	Beau Jack	1990	Juan Nazario (WBA), Pernell Whitaker[1] (unifies world ti-
1943	Bob Montgomery, Beau Jack		tle)
1944	Bob Montgomery, Juan Zurita	1991	Vacant
1945	Ike Williams	1992	Tony Lopez (WBA)
1951	Jimmy Carter	1993	Fred Pendleton (IBF), Dingaan Thobela (WBA),
1952	Lauro Salas, Jimmy Carter		Orzubek Nazarov (WBA)
1954	Paddy De Marco, Jimmy Carter	1994	Rafael Ruelas (IBF)
1955	Bud Smith	1995	Oscar de la Hoya[1] (IBF), Phillip Holiday (IBF)
1956	Joe Brown	1996	Jean-Baptiste Mendy (WBC)
1962	Carlos Ortiz	1997	Steve Johnston (WBC), Shane Mosley (IBF)
1965	Ismael Laguna, Carlos Ortiz	1998	Jean-Baptiste Mendy (WBA), Cesar Bazan (WBC)
1968	Teo Cruz	1999	Julian Lorcy Fra (WBA), **Steve Johnston (WBC),**
1969	Mando Ramos		**Stefano Zoff (WBA), Paul Spadafora (IBF)**

Note: WBC = World Boxing Council. WBA = World Boxing Association. IBF= International Boxing Federation. 1. Stripped of title or abandoned belt. **Source:** International Boxing Hall of Fame.

Featherweights (123–126 lbs.)

Year	Name	Year	Name
1900	Terry McGovern, Young Corbett[1]	1973	Eder Jofre[1] (WBC)
1901	Abe Attell	1974	Ruben Olivares (WBA), Bobby Chacon (WBC),
1904	Tommy Sullivan[1]		Alexis Arguello[1] (WBA)
1906	Abe Attell	1975	Ruben Olivares (WBC), David Kotey (WBC)
1912	Johnny Kilbane	1976	Danny Lopez (WBC)
1923	Eugene Criqui, Johnny Dundee[1]	1977	Rafael Ortega (WBA), Cecillio Lastra (WBA)
1925	Kid Kaplan[1]	1978	Eusebio Pedrosa (WBA)
1927	Benny Bass, Ton Canzoneri	1980	Salvador Sanchez[1] (WBC)
1928	Andre Routis	1982	Juan LaPorte (WBC)
1929	Battling Battalino[1]	1984	Min Keun Oh (IBF), Wilfredo Gomez (WBC),
1932	Tommy Paul		Azumah Nelson (WBC)
1933	Freddie Miller	1985	Barry McGuigan (WBA), Ki Yung Chung[1] (IBF)
1936	Petey Sarron	1986	Steve Cruz (WBA)
1937	Henry Armstrong[1]	1987	Antonio Esparragoza (WBA)
1938	Joey Archibald	1988	Calvin Grove (IBF), Jeff Fenech[1] (WBC),
1940	Harry Jeffra, Joey Archibald		Jorge Paez (IBF)
1941	Chalky Wright	1990	Marcos Villasana (WBC)
1942	Wilie Pep	1991	Yung Kyun Park (WBA)
1948	Sandy Saddler	1992	Troy Dorsey (IBF), Manuel Medina (IBF),
1949	Willie Pep		Paul Hodkinson (WBC)
1950	Sandy Saddler[1]	1993	Tom Johnson (IBF), Goyo Vargas (WBC),
1957	Hogan (Kid) Bassey		Kevin Kelley (WBC), Eloy Rojas (WBA)
1959	Davey Moore	1995	Alejandro Gonzalez (WBC), Manuel Medina (WBC),
1963	Sugar Ramos		Luisito Espinosa (WBC)
1964	Vicente Saldivar[1]	1996	Wilfredo Vasquez[1] (WBA)
1968	Jose Legra[1] (WBA), Shojo Saijo (WBA)	1997	Naseem Hamed (IBF), Hector Lizarraga (IBF)
1969	Johnny Famechon (WBC)	1998	Fred Norwood (WBA), **Manuel Medina (IBF),**
1970	Vicente Saldivar (WBC),		Antonio Cermeño Ven (WBA)
	Kuniaki Shibata (WBC)	1999	**Cesar Soto (WBC), Fred Norwood (WBA)**
1971	Antonio Gomez (WBA)		
1972	Clemente Sanchez (WBC), Ernesto Marcel[1] (WBA), Jose Legra (WBC)		

Note: WBC = World Boxing Council. WBA = World Boxing Association. IBF= International Boxing Federation. 1. Stripped of title or abandoned belt.   **Source:** International Boxing Hall of Fame.

GOLF

No golfer has ever won the four major golf tournaments—the Masters, the U.S. Open, The British Open, and the PGA—in the same year. The player to come closest was Ben Hogan, who won the first three tounaments in 1953, but failed to capture the PGA championship. In fact, only four players have won each of golf's four major tournament at least once over their entire careers: Hogan, Jack Nicklaus (who won each at least three times), Gary Player, and Gene Sarazen. A total of ten different players have won two of the major tournaments in the same year, most recently Mark O'Meara, who captured the Masters and the British Open in 1998.

The Masters

Year	Winner	Year	Winner	Year	Winner
1934	Horton Smith	1957	Doug Ford	1979	Fuzzy Zoeller
1935	Gene Sarazen	1958	Arnold Palmer	1980	Seve Ballesteros
1936	Horton Smith	1959	Art Wall, Jr.	1981	Tom Watson
1937	Byron Nelson	1960	Arnold Palmer	1982	Craig Stadler
1938	Henry Picard	1961	Gary Player	1983	Seve Ballesteros
1939	Ralph Guldahl	1962	Arnold Palmer	1984	Ben Crenshaw
1940	Jimmy Demaret	1963	Jack Nicklaus	1985	Bernhard Langer
1941	Craig Wood	1964	Arnold Palmer	1986	Jack Nicklaus
1942	Byron Nelson	1965–66	Jack Nicklaus	1987	Larry Mize
1943–45	No tournament	1967	Gay Brewer, Jr.	1988	Sandy Lyle
1946	Herman Keiser	1968	Bob Goalby	1989	Nick Faldo
1947	Jimmy Demaret	1969	George Archer	1990	Nick Faldo
1948	Claude Harman	1970	Billy Casper	1991	Ian Woosnam
1949	Sam Snead	1971	Charles Coody	1992	Fred Couples
1950	Jimmy Demaret	1972	Jack Nicklaus	1993	Bernhard Langer
1951	Ben Hogan	1973	Tommy Aaron	1994	José María Olazábal
1952	Sam Snead	1974	Gary Player	1995	Ben Crenshaw
1953	Ben Hogan	1975	Jack Nicklaus	1996	Nick Faldo
1954	Sam Snead	1976	Ray Floyd	1997	Tiger Woods
1955	Cary Middlecoff	1977	Tom Watson	1998	Mark O'Meara
1956	Jack Burke, Jr.	1978	Gary Player	1999	José María Olazábal

Note: All Masters tournaments are held on the same course at the Augusta National Golf Club, Augusta, Ga.

U.S. Open Championship

Year	Winner	Year	Winner	Year	Winner
1895	Horace Rawlins	1929	Robert T. Jones, Jr.	1966	Billy Casper
1896	James Foulis	1930	Robert T. Jones, Jr.	1967	Jack Nicklaus
1897	Joe Lloyd	1931	Billy Burke	1968	Lee Trevino
1898	Fred Herd	1932	Gene Sarazen	1969	Orville Moody
1899	Willie Smith	1933	Johnny Goodman	1970	Tony Jacklin
1900	Harry Vardo	1934	Olin Dutra	1971	Lee Trevino
1901	Willie Anderson	1935	Sam Parks, Jr.	1972	Jack Nicklaus
1902	Laurie Auchterlonie	1936	Tony Manero	1973	Johnny Miller
1903	Willie Anderson	1937	Ralph Guldahl	1974	Hale Irwin
1904	Willie Anderson	1938	Ralph Guldahl	1975	Lou Graham
1905	Willie Anderson	1939	Byron Nelson	1976	Jerry Pate
1906	Alex Smith	1940	Lawson Little	1977	Hubert Green
1907	Alex Ross	1941	Craig Wood	1978	Andy North
1908	Fred McLeod	1942-45	No championship	1979	Hale Irwin
1909	George Sargent	1946	Lloyd Mangrum	1980	Jack Nicklaus
1910	Alex Smith	1947	Lew Worsham	1981	David Graham
1911	John McDermott	1948	Ben Hogan	1982	Tom Watson
1912	John McDermott	1949	Cary Middlecoff	1983	Larry Nelson
1913	Francis Ouimet	1950	Ben Hogan	1984	Fuzzy Zoeller
1914	Walter Hagen	1951	Ben Hogan	1985	Andy North
1915	Jerome Travers	1952	Julius Boros	1986	Ray Floyd
1916	Charles Evans, Jr.	1953	Ben Hogan	1987	Scott Simpson
1917	No championship	1954	Ed Furgol	1988	Curtis Strange
1918	No championship	1955	Jack Fleck	1989	Curtis Strange
1919	Walter Hagen	1956	Cary Middlecoff	1990	Hale Irwin
1920	Edward Ray	1957	Dick Mayer	1991	Payne Stewart
1921	James M. Barnes	1958	Tommy Bolt	1992	Tom Kite
1922	Gene Sarazen	1959	Billy Casper	1993	Lee Janzen
1923	Robert T. Jones, Jr.	1960	Arnold Palmer	1994	Ernie Els
1924	Cyril Walker	1961	Gene Littler	1995	Corey Pavin
1925	W. MacFarlane	1962	Jack Nicklaus	1996	Steve Jones
1926	Robert T. Jones, Jr.	1963	Julius Boros	1997	Ernie Els
1927	Tommy Armour	1964	Ken Venturi	1998	Lee Janzen
1928	Johnny Farrell	1965	Gary Player	1999	Payne Stewart

The British Open

Year	Winner	Year	Winner	Year	Winner
1860	Willie Park	1888	Jack Burns	1920	George Duncan
1861	Tom Morris, Sr.	1889	Willie Park, Jr.	1921	Jock Hutchison
1862	Tom Morris, Sr.	1890	John Ball	1922	Walter Hagen
1863	Willie Park	1891	Hugh Kirkaldy	1923	Arthur G. Havers
1864	Tom Morris, Sr.	1892	Harold H. Hilton[1]	1924	Walter Hagen
1865	Andrew Strath	1893	William Auchterlonie	1925	James M. Barnes
1866	Willie Park	1894	John H. Taylor	1926	Robert T. Jones, Jr.
1867	Tom Morris, Sr.	1895	John H. Taylor	1927	Robert T. Jones, Jr.
1868	Tom Morris, Jr.	1896	Harry Vardon	1928	Walter Hagen
1869	Tom Morris, Jr.	1897	Harold H. Hilton	1929	Walter Hagen
1870	Tom Morris, Jr.	1898	Harry Vardon	1930	Robert T. Jones, Jr.
1871	No championship	1899	Harry Vardon	1931	Tommy D. Armour
1872	Tom Morris, Jr.	1900	John H. Taylor	1932	Gene Sarazen
1873	Tom Kidd	1901	James Braid	1933	Denny Shute
1874	Mungo Park	1902	Alexander Herd	1934	Henry Cotton
1875	Willie Park	1903	Harry Vardon	1935	Alfred Perry
1876	Bob Martin	1904	Jack White	1936	Alfred Padgham
1877	Jamie Anderson	1905	James Braid	1937	Henry Cotton
1878	Jamie Anderson	1906	James Braid	1938	R.A. Whitcombe
1879	Jamie Anderson	1907	Arnaud Massy	1939	Richard Burton
1880	Robert Ferguson	1908	James Braid	1940-45	No championship
1881	Robert Ferguson	1909	John H. Taylor	1946	Sam Snead
1882	Robert Ferguson	1910	James Braid	1947	Fred Daly
1883	Willie Fernie	1911	Harry Vardon	1948	Henry Cotton
1884	Jack Simpson	1912	Edward (Ted) Ray	1949	Bobby Locke
1885	Bob Martin	1913	John H. Taylor	1950	Bobby Locke
1886	David Brown	1914	Harry Vardon	1951	Max Faulkner
1887	Willie Park, Jr.	1915-19	No championship	1952	Bobby Locke

Year	Winner	Year	Winner	Year	Winner
1953	Ben Hogan	1969	Tony Jacklin	1985	Sandy Lyle
1954	Peter Thomson	1970	Jack Nicklaus	1986	Greg Norman
1955	Peter Thomson	1971	Lee Trevino	1987	Nick Faldo
1956	Peter Thomson	1972	Lee Trevino	1988	Seve Ballesteros
1957	Bobby Locke	1973	Tom Weiskopf	1989	Mark Calcavecchia
1958	Peter Thomson	1974	Gary Player	1990	Nick Faldo
1959	Gary Player	1975	Tom Watson	1991	Ian Baker-Finch
1960	Kel Nagle	1976	Johnny Miller	1992	Nick Faldo
1961	Arnold Palmer	1977	Tom Watson	1993	Greg Norman
1962	Arnold Palmer	1978	Jack Nicklaus	1994	Nick Price
1963	Bob Charles	1979	Seve Ballesteros	1995	John Daly
1964	Tony Lema	1980	Tom Watson	1996	Tom Lehman
1965	Peter Thomson	1981	Bill Rogers	1997	Justin Leonard
1966	Jack Nicklaus	1982	Tom Watson	1998	Mark O'Meara
1967	Roberto DeVicenzo	1983	Tom Watson	1999	Paul Lawrie
1968	Gary Player	1984	Seve Ballesteros		

1. Championship extended from 36 to 72 Holes

PGA

Year	Winner	Year	Winner	Year	Winner
1916	James M. Barnes	1945	Byron Nelson	1973	Jack Nicklaus
1917–18	No championship	1946	Ben Hogan	1974	Lee Trevino
1919	James M. Barnes	1947	Jim Ferrier	1975	Jack Nicklaus
1920	Jock Hutchison	1948	Ben Hogan	1976	Dave Stockton
1921	Walter Hagen	1949	Sam Snead	1977	Lanny Wadkins
1922	Gene Sarazen	1950	Chandler Harper	1978	John Mahaffey
1923	Gene Sarazen	1951	Sam Snead	1979	David Graham
1924	Walter Hagen	1952	Jim Turnesa	1980	Jack Nicklaus
1925	Walter Hagen	1953	Walter Burkemo	1981	Larry Nelson
1926	Walter Hagen	1954	Chick Harbert	1982	Raymond Floyd
1927	Walter Hagen	1955	Doug Ford	1983	Hal Sutton
1928	Leo Diegel	1956	Jack Burke	1984	Lee Trevino
1929	Leo Diegel	1957	Lionel Hebert	1985	Hubert Green
1930	Tommy Armour	1958	Dow Finsterwald	1986	Bob Tway
1931	Tom Creavy	1959	Bob Rosburg	1987	Larry Nelson
1932	Olin Dutra	1960	Jay Hebert	1988	Jeff Sluman
1933	Gene Sarazen	1961	Jerry Barber	1989	Payne Stewart
1934	Paul Runyan	1962	Gary Player	1990	Wayne Grady
1935	Johnny Revolta	1963	Jack Nicklaus	1991	John Daly
1936	Denny Shute	1964	Bobby Nichols	1992	Nick Price
1937	Denny Shute	1965	Dave Marr	1993	Paul Azinger
1938	Paul Runyan	1966	Al Geiberger	1994	Nick Price
1939	Henry Picard	1967	Don January	1995	Steve Elkington
1940	Byron Nelson	1968	Julius Boros	1996	Mark Brooks
1941	Vic Ghezzi	1969	Ray Floyd	1997	Davis Love III
1942	Sam Snead	1970	Dave Stockton	1998	Vijay Singh
1943	No championship	1971	Jack Nicklaus	1999	Tiger Woods
1944	Bob Hamilton	1972	Gary Player		

PGA Leading Money Winners

1999[1]		Career[2]			
Rank, Golfer	Earnings	Rank, Golfer	Earnings	Rank, Golfer	Earnings
1. David Duval	$2,728,750	1. Greg Norman	$12,297,694	11. Mark Calcavecchia	$9,292,554
2. Jeff Maggert	1,527,889	2. Payne Stewart	11,520,444	12. Corey Pavin	8,722,959
3. Tiger Woods	1,440,198	3. Davis Love III	11,511,088	13. Paul Azinger	8,391,608
4. Davis Love III	1,374,106	4. Fred Couples	11,130,569	14. Hal Sutton	8,123,721
5. Steve Pate	1,340,909	5. Mark O'Meara	10,957,327	15. Phil Mickelson	7,964,233
6. Payne Stewart	1,216,205	6. Nick Price	10,614,344	16. Vijay Singh	7,931,046
7. Jeff Sluman	1,187,845	7. Tom Kite	10,478,502	17. Steve Elkington	7,837,388
8. John Huston	1,114,610	8. Scott Hoch	9,968,394	18. John Cook	7,698,379
9. Vijay Singh	1,113,798	9. Tom Watson	9,425,272	19. Craig Stadler	7,653,781
10. Loren Roberts	911,548	10. David Duval	9,415,526	20. Jeff Sluman	7,504,793

1. As of May 27, 1999. 2. As of June 27, 1999.   **Source:** Professional Golfers' Association (www.pga.com).

PGA Leading Money Winners, 1934–98

Year	Name	Winnings	Year	Name	Winnings	Year	Name	Winnings
1934	Paul Runyan	$6,767	1956	Ted Kroll	$72,835	1978	Tom Watson	$362,428
1935	Johnny Revolta	9,543	1957	Dick Mayer	65,835	1979	Tom Watson	462,636
1936	Horton Smith	7,682	1958	Arnold Palmer	42,607	1980	Tom Watson	530,808
1937	Harry Cooper	14,138	1959	Art Wall	53,167	1981	Tom Kite	375,698
1938	Sam Snead	19,534	1960	Arnold Palmer	75,262	1982	Craig Stadler	446,462
1939	Henry Picard	10,303	1961	Gary Player	64,540	1983	Hal Sutton	426,668
1940	Ben Hogan	10,655	1962	Arnold Palmer	81,448	1984	Tom Watson	476,260
1941	Ben Hogan	18,358	1963	Arnold Palmer	128,230	1985	Curtis Strange	542,321
1942	Ben Hogan	13,143	1964	Jack Nicklaus	113,284	1986	Greg Norman	653,296
1943	No statistics compiled		1965	Jack Nicklaus	140,752	1987	Curtis Strange	925,941
1944	Byron Nelson	37,967[1]	1966	Billy Casper	121,944	1988	Curtis Strange	1,147,644
1945	Byron Nelson	63,335[1]	1967	Jack Nicklaus	188,998	1989	Tom Kite	1,395,278
1946	Ben Hogan	42,556	1968	Billy Casper	205,168	1990	Greg Norman	1,165,477
1947	Jimmy Demaret	27,936	1969	Frank Beard	164,707	1991	Corey Pavin	979,430
1948	Ben Hogan	32,112	1970	Lee Trevino	157,037	1992	Fred Couples	1,344,188
1949	Sam Snead	31,593	1971	Jack Nicklaus	244,490	1993	Nick Price	1,478,557
1950	Sam Snead	35,758	1972	Jack Nicklaus	320,542	1994	Nick Price	1,499,927
1951	Lloyd Mangrum	26,088	1973	Jack Nicklaus	308,362	1995	Greg Norman	1,654,959
1952	Julius Boros	37,032	1974	Johnny Miller	353,021	1996	Tom Lehman	1,780,159
1953	Lew Worsham	34,002	1975	Jack Nicklaus	298,149	1997	Tiger Woods	2,066,833
1954	Bob Toski	65,819	1976	Jack Nicklaus	266,438	1998	David Duval	2,591,031
1955	Julius Boros	63,121	1977	Tom Watson	310,653			

1. Paid in War Bonds. **Source:** Professional Golfers' Association

LPGA Leading Money Winners

	1999				Career			
Rank, Golfer		Earnings	Rank, Golfer		Earnings	Rank, Golfer		Earnings
1. Juli Inkster		$952,994	1. Betsy King		$6,368,859	11. Rosie Jones		$3,960,845
2. Karrie Webb		941,198	2. Pat Bradley		5,634,559	12. Lisolotte Neumann		3,746,026
3. Meg Mallon		523,209	3. Patty Sheehan		5,479,278	13. Karrie Webb		3,635,281
4. Annika Sorenstam		412,167	4. Beth Daniel		5,468,278	14. Jane Geddes		3,564,915
5. Dottie Pepper		397,789	5. Nancy Lopez		5,229,620	15. Kelly Robbins		3,452,541
6. Lorie Kane		385,787	6. Dottie Pepper		4,915,350	16. Amy Alcott		3,339,101
7. Se Ri Pak		325,662	7. Juli Inkster		4,692,811	17. Tammie Green		3,280,954
8. Kelly Robbins		320,662	8. Annika Sorenstam		4,343,999	18. Chris Johnson		3,121,525
9. Rachel Hetherington		293,030	9. Laura Davies		4,286,484	19. JoAnne Carner		2,922,781
10. Kelli Kuehne		289,321	10. Meg Mallon		4,163,258	20. Brandie Burton		2,796,570

Note: All figures as of June 29, 1999. **Source:** Ladies' Professional Golfers' Association.

LPGA Leading Money Winners 1956–98

Year	Player	Winnings	Year	Player	Winnings	Year	Player	Winnings
1956	Marlene Hagge	$20,235	1971	Kathy Whitworth	$41,181	1986	Pat Bradley	$492,021
1957	Patty Berg	16,272	1972	Kathy Whitworth	65,063	1987	Ayako Okamoto	466,034
1958	Beverly Hanson	12,629	1973	Kathy Whitworth	82,864	1988	Sherri Turner	350,851
1959	Betsy Rawls	26,774	1974	JoAnne Carner	87,094	1989	Betsy King	654,132
1960	Louise Suggs	16,892	1975	Sandra Palmer	76,374	1990	Beth Daniel	863,578
1961	Mickey Wright	22,238	1976	Judy T. Rankin	150,734	1991	Pat Bradley	763,118
1962	Mickey Wright	21,654	1977	Judy T. Rankin	122,890	1992	Dottie Mochrie	693,335
1963	Mickey Wright	31,269	1978	Nancy Lopez	189,813	1993	Betsy King	595,992
1964	Mickey Wright	29,800	1979	Nancy Lopez	197,488	1994	Laura Davies	687,201
1965	Kathy Whitworth	28,658	1980	Beth Daniel	231,000	1995	Annika Sorenstam	666,533
1966	Kathy Whitworth	33,517	1981	Beth Daniel	206,977	1996	Karrie Webb	1,002,000
1967	Kathy Whitworth	32,937	1982	JoAnne Carner	310,399	1997	Annika Sorenstam	1,236,789
1968	Kathy Whitworth	48,379	1983	JoAnne Carner	291,404	1998	Annika Sorenstam	1,092,748
1969	Carol Mann	49,152	1984	Betsy King	266,771			
1970	Kathy Whitworth	30,235	1985	Nancy Lopez	416,472			

Source: Ladies Professional Golfers' Association

U.S. Women's Grand Slam Champions, 1972–99

In 1999, Juli Inkster became only the fourth woman to win all four major tournaments in her career, when she captured both the U.S. Women's Open and the McDonald's LPGA Classic. Inkster won both the Nabisco Dinah Shore and the du Maurier Classic as a rookie in 1984. (Note that the duMaurier was not designated a major until 1979.)

Year	U.S. Women's Open	LPGA Championship	Nabisco Dinah Shore	du Maurier Classic
1972	Susie Berning	Kathy Ahern	Jane Blalock	N.A.
1973	Susie Berning	Mary Mills	Mickey Wright	Jocelyne Bourassa
1974	Sandra Haynie	Sandra Haynie	Jo Ann Prentice	Carole Jo Callison
1975	Sandra Palmer	Kathy Whitworth	Sandra Palmer	JoAnne Carner
1976	JoAnne Carner	Betty Burfeindt	Judy Rankin	Donna Caponi
1977	Hollis Stacy	Chako Higuchi	Kathy Whitworth	Judy Rankin
1978	Hollis Stacy	Nancy Lopez	Sandra Post	JoAnne Carner
1979	Jerilyn Britz	Donna Caponi	Sandra Post	Amy Alcott
1980	Amy Alcott	Sally Little	Donna Caponi	Pat Bradley
1981	Pat Bradley	Donna Caponi	Nancy Lopez	Jan Stephenson
1982	Janet Anderson	Jan Stephenson	Sally Little	Sandra Haynie
1983	Jan Stephenson	Patty Sheehan	Amy Alcott	Hollis Stacy
1984	Hollis Stacy	Patty Sheehan	Juli Inkster	Juli Inkster
1985	Kathy Baker	Nancy Lopez	Alice Miller	Pat Bradley
1986	Jane Geddes	Pat Bradley	Pat Bradley	Pat Bradley
1987	Laura Davies	Jane Geddes	Betsy King	Jody Rosenthal
1988	Liselotte Neumann	Sherri Turner	Amy Alcott	Sally Little
1989	Betsy King	Nancy Lopez	Juli Inkster	Tammie Green
1990	Betsy King	Beth Daniel	Betsy King	Cathy Johnston
1991	Meg Mallon	Meg Mallon	Amy Alcott	Nancy Scranton
1992	Patty Sheehan	Betsy King	Dottie Mochrie	Sherri Steinhauer
1993	Lauri Merten	Patty Sheehan	Helen Alfredsson	Brandie Burton
1994	Patty Sheehan	Laura Davies	Donna Andrews	Martha Nause
1995	Annika Sorenstam	Kelly Robbins	Nanci Bowen	Jenny Lidback
1996	Annika Sorenstam	Laura Davies	Patty Sheehan	Laura Davies
1997	Alison Nicholas	Chris Johnson	Betsy King	Colleen Walker
1998	Se Ri Pak	Se Ri Pak	Pat Hurst	Brandie Burton
1999	Juli Inkster	Juli Inkster	Dottie Pepper	Karrie Webb

LPGA Champions, 1955–71

Year	Champion	Year	Champion
1955	Beverly Hanson	1964	Mary Mills
1956	Marlene Hagge	1965	Sandra Haynie
1957	Louise Suggs	1966	Gloria Ehret
1958	Mickey Wright	1967	Kathy Whitworth
1959	Betsy Rawls	1968	Sandra Post
1960	Mickey Wright	1969	Betsy Rawls
1961	Mickey Wright	1970	Shirley Englehorn
1962	Judy Kimball	1971	Kathy Whitworth
1963	Mickey Wright		

The Senior PGA Tour

The Senior Tour began with two tournaments in 1980, which offered a total of $250,000 in prize money to qualified PGA members over the age of 50. By 1984, the tour had spiralled to 24 tournaments with prize money totalling $5 million. The arrival in 1990 of Jack Nicklaus and Lee Trevino on the senior tour helped propel the 50-and-over tour to unprecedented popularity, surpassing the Ladies' Professional Tour in both prize money and television ratings. That was also the year that Trevino became the first player to win more than $1 million in prize money on the senior tour.

TENNIS

The Grand Slam Championships The four tournaments that constitute the Grand Slam are the Australian, French, Wimbledon (officially known as the All-England Club's Lawn Tennis Championships), and U.S. championships. A challenge round system, in which the defending champion automatically qualified for the following year's final, was used at Wimbledon from 1877-1921 and at the U.S. Championships from 1884-1911. Prior to 1925, entry to the French open was restricted to members of French clubs, and from 1941-45, the French tournament was closed to all foreigners. Wimbledon, the French, and U.S. Championships became open to amateurs and pros in 1968; the Australian championships joined the open era a year later. Five players have completed the Grand Slam, winning all four championships in the same year: Don Budge (1938), Maureen Connolly (with straight set victories in all four finals in 1953), Rod Laver (1962 and 1969), Margaret Court (1970) and Steffi Graf (1988). Martina Navratilova won the four tournaments consecutively, but not in the same calendar year; she won the French Open in 1984, following 1983 victories in the other three.

Men's Grand Slam Champions, 1920–99

Year	Australian Champion	French Champion	Wimbledon Champion	U.S. Champion
1920	Pat O'Hara Wood	—	Bill Tilden	Bill Tilden
1921	Rhys H. Gemmell	—	Bill Tilden	Bill Tilden
1922	Pat O'Hara Wood	—	Gerald L. Patterson	Bill Tilden
1923	Pat O'Hara Wood	—	William M. Johnston	Bill Tilden
1924	James Anderson	—	Jean Borotra	Bill Tilden
1925	James Anderson	Rene Lacoste	Rene Lacoste	Bill Tilden
1926	John Hawkes	Henri Cochet	Jean Borotra	Rene Lacoste
1927	Gerald Patterson	Rene Lacoste	Henri Cochet	Rene Lacoste
1928	Jean Borotra	Henri Cochet	Rene Lacoste	Henri Cochet
1929	John C. Gregory	Rene Lacoste	Henri Cochet	Bill Tilden
1930	Gar Moon	Henri Cochet	Bill Tilden	John H. Doeg
1931	Jack Crawford	Jean Borotra	Sidney B. Wood Jr.	H. Ellsworth Vines
1932	Jack Crawford	Henri Cochet	Ellsworth Vines	H. Ellsworth Vines
1933	Jack Crawford	John H. Crawford	Jack Crawford	Fred Perry
1934	Fred J. Perry	Gottfried von Cramm	Fred Perry	Fred Perry
1935	Jack Crawford	Fred J. Perry	Fred Perry	Wilmer L. Allison
1936	Adrian Quist	Gottfried von Cramm	Fred Perry	Fred Perry
1937	Vivian B. McGrath	Henner Henkel	Don Budge	Don Budge
1938[1]	Don Budge	Don Budge	Don Budge	Don Budge
1939	John Bromwich	W. Donald McNeill	Bobby Riggs	Bobby Riggs
1940	Adrian Quist	No competition	Not Held	Donald McNeill
1941	Foreigners excluded	Bernard Destremau	Not Held	Bobby Riggs
1942	Foreigners excluded	Bernard Destremau	Not Held	Frederick Schroeder
1943	Foreigners excluded	Yvon Petra	Not Held	Joseph R. Hunt
1944	Foreigners excluded	Yvon Petra	Not Held	Frank Parker
1945	Foreigners excluded	Yvon Petra	Not Held	Frank Parker
1946	John Bromwich	Marcel Bernard	Yvon Petra	Jack Kramer
1947	Dinny Pails	Joseph Asboth	Jack Kramer	Jack Kramer
1948	Adrian Quist	Frank Parker	Bob Falkenburg	Pancho Gonzales
1949	Frank Sedgman	Frank Parker	Ted Schroeder	Pancho Gonzales
1950	Frank Sedgman	Budge Patty	Budge Patty	Arthur Larsen
1951	Richard Savitt	Jaroslav Drobny	Dick Savitt	Frank Sedgman
1952	Ken McGregor	Jaroslav Drobny	Frank Sedgman	Frank Sedgman
1953	Ken Rosewall	Ken Rosewall	Vic Seixas	Tony Trabert
1954	Mervyn Rose	Tony Trabert	Jaroslav Drobny	E. Victor Seixas Jr.
1955	Ken Rosewall	Tony Trabert	Tony Trabert	Tony Trabert
1956	Lew Hoad	Lew Hoad	Lew Hoad	Ken Rosewall
1957	Ashley Cooper	Sven Davidson	Lew Hoad	Malcolm Anderson
1958	Ashley Cooper	Mervyn Rose	Ashley Cooper	Ashley J. Cooper
1959	Alex Olmedo	Nicola Pietrangeli	Alex Olmedo	Neale Fraser
1960	Rod Laver	Nicola Pietrangeli	Neale Fraser	Neale Fraser
1961	Roy Emerson	Manuel Santana	Rod Laver	Roy Emerson
1962[1]	Rod Laver	Rod Laver	Rod Laver	Rod Laver
1963	Roy Emerson	Roy Emerson	Chuck McKinley	Rafael Osuna
1964	Roy Emerson	Manuel Santana	Roy Emerson	Roy Emerson
1965	Roy Emerson	Fred Stolle	Roy Emerson	Manuel Santana
1966	Roy Emerson	Tony Roche	Manuel Santana	Fred Stolle
1967	Roy Emerson	Roy Emerson	John Newcombe	John Newcombe
1968	Bill Bowrey	Ken Rosewall	Rod Laver	Arthur Ashe
1969[1]	Rod Laver	Rod Laver	Rod Laver	Rod Laver
1970	Arthur Ashe	Jan Kodes	John Newcombe	Ken Rosewall
1971	Ken Rosewall	Jan Kodes	John Newcombe	Stan Smith
1972	Ken Rosewall	Andres Gimeno	Stan Smith	Ilie Nastase
1973	John Newcombe	Ilie Nastase	Jan Kodes	John Newcombe
1974	Jimmy Connors	Bjorn Borg	Jimmy Connors	Jimmy Connors
1975	John Newcombe	Bjorn Borg	Arthur Ashe	Manuel Orantes
1976	Mark Edmondson	Adriano Panatta	Bjorn Borg	Jimmy Connors
1977	Roscoe Tanner[2] Vitas Gerulaitis[2]	Guillermo Vilas	Bjorn Borg	Guillermo Vilas
1978	Guillermo Vilas	Bjorn Borg	Bjorn Borg	Jimmy Connors
1979	Guillermo Vilas	Bjorn Borg	Bjorn Borg	John McEnroe
1980	Brian Teacher	Bjorn Borg	Bjorn Borg	John McEnroe
1981	Johan Kriek	Bjorn Borg	John McEnroe	John McEnroe
1982	Johan Kriek	Mats Wilander	Jimmy Connors	Jimmy Connors
1983	Mats Wilander	Yannick Noah	John McEnroe	Jimmy Connors
1984	Mats Wilander	Ivan Lendl	John McEnroe	John McEnroe

Year	Australian Champion	French Champion	Wimbledon Champion	U.S. Champion
1985	Stefan Edberg	Mats Wilander	Boris Becker	Ivan Lendl
1986	Moved to Jan. 1987	Ivan Lendl	Boris Becker	Ivan Lendl
1987	Stefan Edberg	Ivan Lendl	Pat Cash	Ivan Lendl
1988	Mats Wilander	Mats Wilander	Stefan Edberg	Mats Wilander
1989	Ivan Lendl	Michael Chang	Boris Becker	Boris Becker
1990	Ivan Lendl	Andrés Gomez	Stefan Edberg	Pete Sampras
1991	Boris Becker	Jim Courier	Michael Stich	Stefan Edberg
1992	Jim Courier	Jim Courier	Andre Agassi	Stefan Edberg
1993	Jim Courier	Sergi Bruguera	Pete Sampras	Pete Sampras
1994	Pete Sampras	Sergi Bruguera	Pete Sampras	Andre Agassi
1995	Andre Agassi	Thomas Muster	Pete Sampras	Pete Sampras
1996	Boris Becker	Yevgeny Kafelnikov	Richard Krajicek	Pete Sampras
1997	Pete Sampras	Gustavo Kuerten	Pete Sampras	Patrick Rafter
1998	Petr Korda	Carlos Moya	Pete Sampras	Patrick Rafter
1999	Yevgeny Kafelnikov	Andre Agassi	Pete Sampras	Andre Agassi

1. Grand Slam winner. 2. Two tournaments were held in 1977, the first in January, the second in December.

Women's Grand Slam Champions, 1920–99

Year	Australian Champion	French Champion	Wimbledon Champion	U.S. Champion
1920	Not held	Suzanne Lenglen	Suzanne Lenglen	Molla Bjurstedt Mallory
1921	Not held	Suzanne Lenglen	Suzanne Lenglen	Molla Bjurstedt Mallory
1922	Margaret Molesworth	Suzanne Lenglen	Suzanne Lenglen	Molla Bjurstedt Mallory
1923	Margaret Molesworth	Suzanne Lenglen	Suzanne Lenglen	Helen Wills
1924	Sylvia Lance	Diddie Vlasto	Kathleen McKane	Helen Wills
1925	Daphne Akhurst	Suzanne Lenglen	Suzanne Lenglen	Helen Wills
1926	Daphne Akhurst	Suzanne Lenglen	Kathleen McKane Godfree	Molla Bjurstedt Mallory
1927	Edna Boyd	Kea Bouman	Helen Wills	Helen Wills
1928	Daphne Akhurst	Helen Wills	Helen Wills	Helen Wills
1929	Daphne Akhurst	Helen Wills	Helen Wills	Helen Wills
1930	Daphne Akhurst	Helen Wills Moody	Helen Wills Moody	Betty Nuthall
1931	Coral Buttsworth	Cilly Aussem	Cilly Aussem	Helen Wills Moody
1932	Coral Buttsworth	Helen Wills Moody	Helen Wills Moody	Helen Jacobs
1933	Joan Hartigan	Margaret Scriven	Helen Wills Moody	Helen Jacobs
1934	Joan Hartigan	Margaret Scriven	Dorothy Round	Helen Jacobs
1935	Dorothy Round	Hilde Sperling	Helen Wills Moody	Helen Jacobs
1936	Joan Hartigan	Hilde Sperling	Helen Jacobs	Alice Marble
1937	Nancye Wynne Bolton	Hilde Sperling	Dorothy Round	Anita Lizane
1938	Dorothy Bundy	Simone Mathieu	Helen Wills Moody	Alice Marble
1939	Emily Westacott	Simone Mathieu	Alice Marble	Alice Marble
1940	Nancye Wynne Bolton	Not Held	Not Held	Alice Marble
1941	Not Held	Not Held	Not Held	Sarah Palfrey Cooke
1942	Not Held	Not Held	Not Held	Pauline Betz
1943	Not Held	Not Held	Not Held	Pauline Betz
1944	Not Held	Not Held	Not Held	Pauline Betz
1945	Not Held	Not Held	Not Held	Sarah Palfrey Cooke
1946	Nancye Wynne Bolton	Margaret Osborne	Pauline Betz	Pauline Betz
1947	Nancye Wynne Bolton	Patricia Todd	Margaret Osborne	Louise Brough
1948	Nancye Wynne Bolton	Nelly Landry	Louise Brough	Margaret Osborne duPont
1949	Doris Hart	Margaret Osborne duPont	Louise Brough	Margaret Osborne duPont
1950	Louise Brough	Doris Hart	Louise Brough	Margaret Osborne duPont
1951	Nancye Wynne Bolton	Shirley Fry	Doris Hart	Maureen Connolly
1952	Thelma Long	Doris Hart	Maureen Connolly	Maureen Connolly
1953[1]	Maureen Connolly	Maureen Connolly	Maureen Connolly	Maureen Connolly
1954	Thelma Long	Maureen Connolly	Maureen Connolly	Doris Hart
1955	Beryl Penrose	Angela Mortimer	Louise Brough	Doris Hart
1956	Mary Carter	Althea Gibson	Shirley Fry	Shirley Fry
1957	Shirley Fry	Shirley Bloomer	Althea Gibson	Althea Gibson
1958	Angela Mortimer	Zsuzsi Kormoczy	Althea Gibson	Althea Gibson
1959	Mary Carter Reitano	Christine Truman	Maria Bueno	Maria Bueno
1960	Margaret Smith	Darlene Hard	Maria Bueno	Darlene Hard
1961	Margaret Smith	Ann Haydon	Angela Mortimer	Darlene Hard
1962	Margaret Smith	Margaret Smith	Karen Hantze Susman	Margaret Smith
1963	Margaret Smith	Lesley Turner	Margaret Smith	Maria Bueno
1964	Margaret Smith	Margaret Smith	Maria Bueno	Maria Bueno

1965	Margaret Smith	Lesley Turner	Margaret Smith	Margaret Smith
1966	Margaret Smith	Ann Jones	Billie Jean King	Maria Bueno
1967	Nancy Richey	Francoise Durr	Billie Jean King	Billie Jean King
1968	Billie Jean King	Nancy Richey	Billie Jean King	Virginia Wade
1969	Margaret Smith Court	Margaret Smith Court	Ann Jones	Margaret Smith Court
1970[1]	Margaret Smith Court	Margaret Smith Court	Margaret Smith Court	Margaret Smith Court
1971	Margaret Smith Court	Evonne Goolagong	Evonne Goolagong	Billie Jean King
1972	Virginia Wade	Billie Jean King	Billie Jean King	Billie Jean King
1973	Margaret Smith Court	Margaret Smith Court	Billie Jean King	Margaret Smith Court
1974	Evonne Goolagong	Chris Evert	Chris Evert	Billie Jean King
1975	Evonne Goolagong	Chris Evert	Billie Jean King	Chris Evert
1976	Evonne Goolagong Cawley	Sue Barker	Chris Evert	Chris Evert
1977	Kerry Melville Reid[2] Evonne Goolagong Cawley[2]	Mima Jasuovec	Virginia Wade	Chris Evert
1978	Chris O'Neil	Virginia Ruzici	Martina Navratilova	Chris Evert
1979	Barbara Jordan	Chris Evert Lloyd	Martina Navratilova	Tracy Austin
1980	Hana Mandlikova	Chris Evert Lloyd	Evonne Goolagong Cawley	Chris Evert Lloyd
1981	Martina Navratilova	Hana Mandlikova	Chris Evert Lloyd	Tracy Austin
1982	Chris Evert Lloyd	Martina Navratilova	Martina Navratilova	Chris Evert Lloyd
1983	Martina Navratilova	Chris Evert Lloyd	Martina Navratilova	Martina Navratilova
1984	Chris Evert Lloyd	Martina Navratilova	Martina Navratilova	Martina Navratilova
1985	Martina Navratilova	Chris Evert Lloyd	Martina Navratilova	Hana Mandlikova
1986	Moved to Jan. 1987	Chris Evert Lloyd	Martina Navratilova	Martina Navratilova
1987	Hana Mandlikova	Steffi Graf	Martina Navratilova	Martina Navratilova
1988[1]	Steffi Graf	Steffi Graf	Steffi Graf	Steffi Graf
1989	Steffi Graf	Arantxa Sanchez	Steffi Graf	Steffi Graf
1990	Steffi Graf	Monica Seles	Martina Navratilova	Gabriela Sabatini
1991	Monica Seles	Monica Seles	Steffi Graf	Monica Seles
1992	Monica Seles	Monica Seles	Steffi Graf	Monica Seles
1993	Monica Seles	Steffi Graf	Steffi Graf	Steffi Graf
1994	Steffi Graf	Arantxa Sánchez Vicario	Conchita Martinez	Arantxa Sánchez Vicario
1995	Mary Pierce	Steffi Graf	Steffi Graf	Steffi Graf
1996	Monica Seles	Steffi Graf	Steffi Graf	Steffi Graf
1997	Martina Hingis	Iva Majoli	Martina Hingis	Martina Hingis
1998	Martina Hingis	Arantxa Sánchez Vicario	Jana Novotna	Lindsay Davenport
1999	Martina Hingis	Steffi Graff	Lindsay Davenport	Serena Williams

1. Grand Slam winner. 2. Two tournaments were held in 1977, the first in January, the second in December.

THOROUGHBRED RACING

Thoroughbred Horse of the Year (Eclipse Award)

Year	Horse	Year	Horse	Year	Horse	Year	Horse
1936	Granville	1952	Native Dancer	1968	Dr. Fager	1984	John Henry
1937	War Admiral	1953	Tom Fool	1969	Arts and Letters	1985	Spend a Buck
1938	Seabiscuit	1954	Native Dancer	1970	Personality	1986	Lady's Secret
1939	Challedon	1955	Nashua	1971	Ack Ack	1987	Ferdinand
1940	Challedon	1956	Swaps	1972	Secretariat	1988	Alysheba
1941	Whirlaway	1957	Bold Ruler	1973	Secretariat	1989	Sunday Silence
1942	Whirlaway	1958	Round Table	1974	Forego	1990	Criminal Type
1943	Count Fleet	1959	Sword Dancer	1975	Forego	1991	Black Tie Affair
1944	Twilight Tear	1960	Kelso	1976	Forego	1992	A.P. Indy
1945	Busher	1961	Kelso	1977	Seattle Slew	1993	Kotashaan
1946	Assault	1962	Kelso	1978	Affirmed	1994	Holy Bull
1947	Armed	1963	Kelso	1979	Affirmed	1995	Cigar
1948	Citation	1964	Kelso	1980	Spectacular Bid	1996	Cigar
1949	Capot	1965	Moccasin	1981	John Henry	1997	Favorite Trick
1950	Hill Prince	1966	Buckpasser	1982	Conquistador Cielo	1998	Skip Away
1951	Counterpoint	1967	Damascus	1983	All Along		

Source: The Jockey Club

Kentucky Derby, 1875–99

The Kentucky Derby, thoroughbred racing's most celebrated single event, was first run in 1875. The distance was 1½ miles until 1896, when it was shortened to 1¼ miles. Also known as "The Run for the Roses," the Derby is the first leg of racing's Triple Crown for three-year-old horses. It is always held on the first Saturday in May.

Site: Churchill Downs, Louisville, Kentucky

Year	Horse	Jockey	Time	Year	Horse	Jockey	Time
1875	Aristides	O. Lewis	2:37¾	1937	War Admiral	C. Kurtsinger	2:03.1
1876	Vagrant	R. Swim	2:38¼	1938	Lawrin	E. Arcaro	2:04.4
1877	Baden-Baden	W. Walker	2:38.0	1939	Johnston	J. Stout	2:03.2
1878	Day Star	J. Carter	2:37¼	1940	Gallahadion	C. Bierman	2:05.0
1879	Lord Murphy	C. Shauer	2:37.0	1941	Whirlaway	E. Arcaro	2:01.2
1880	Fonso	G. Lewis	2:37½	1942	Shut Out	W. D. Write	2:04.2
1881	Hindoo	J. McLaughlin	2:40.0	1943	Count Fleet	J. Longden	2:04.0
1882	Apollo	B. Hurd	2:40¼	1944	Pensive	C. McCreary	2:04.1
1883	Leonatus	W. Donohue	2:43.0	1945	Hoop Jr.	E. Arcaro	2:07.0
1884	Buchanan	I. Murphy	2:40¼	1946	Assault	W. Mehrtens	2:06.3
1885	Joe Cotton	E. Henderson	2:37¼	1947	Jet Pilot	E. Guerin	2:06.3
1886	Ben Ali	P. Duffy	2:36½	1948	Citation	E. Arcaro	2:05.2
1887	Montrose	I. Lewis	2:39¼	1949	Ponder	S. Brooks	2:04.1
1888	MacBeth II	G. Covington	2:38¼	1950	Middleground	W. Boland	2:01.3
1889	Spokane	T. Kiley	2:34½	1951	Count Turf	C. McCreary	2:02.3
1890	Riley	I. Murphy	2:45.0	1952	Hill Gail	E. Arcaro	2:01.3
1891	Kingman	I. Murphy	2:52¼	1953	Dark Star	H. Moreno	2:02.0
1892	Azra	A. Clayton	2:41½	1954	Determine	R. York	2:03.0
1893	Lookout	E. Kunze	2:39¼	1955	Swaps	W. Shoemaker	2:01.4
1894	Chant	F. Goodale	2:41.0	1956	Needles	D. Erb	2:03.2
1895	Halma	J. Perkins	2:37½	1957	Iron Liege	W. Hartack	2:02.1
1896	Ben Brush	W. Simms	2:07¾	1958	Tim Tam	I. Valenzuela	2:05.0
1897	Typhoon II	F. Garner	2:12½	1959	Tommy Lee	W. Shoemaker	2:02.1
1898	Plaudit	W. Simms	2:09.0	1960	Venetian Way	W. Hartack	2:02.2
1899	Manuel	F. Taral	2:12.0	1961	Carry Back	J. Sellers	2:04.0
1900	Lieut.Gibson	J. Boland	2:06¼	1962	Decidedly	W. Hartack	2:00.2
1900	Lieut. Gibson	J. Boland	2:06¼	1963	Chateaugay	B. Baeza	2:01.4
1901	His Eminence	J. Winkfield	2:07¾	1964	Northern Dancer	W. Hartack	2:00.0
1902	Alan-a-Dale	J. Winkfield	2:08¼	1965	Lucky Debonair	W. Shoemaker	2:01.1
1903	Judge Himes	H. Booker	2:09.0	1966	Kauai King	D. Brumfield	2:02.0
1904	Elwood	F. Prior	2:08½	1967	Proud Clarion	R. Ussery	2:00.3
1905	Agile	J. Martin	2:10¾	1968	Forward Pass[1]	R. Ussery	2:02.1
1906	Sir Huon	R. Troxler	2:08.4	1969	Majestic Prince	W. Hartack	2:01.4
1907	Pink Star	A. Minder	2:12.3	1970	Dust Commander	M. Manganello	2:03.2
1908	Stone Street	A. Pickens	2:15.1	1971	Canonero II	G. Avila	2:03.1
1909	Wintergreen	V. Powers	2:08.1	1972	Riva Ridge	R. Turcotte	2:01.4
1910	Donau	F. Herbert	2:06.2	1973	Secretariat	R. Turcotte	1:59.2[2]
1911	Meridan	G. Archibald	2:05.0	1974	Cannonade	A. Cordero	2:04.0
1912	Worth	C. H. Shilling	2:09.2	1975	Foolish Pleasure	J. Vasquez	2:02.0
1913	Donerall	R. Goose	2:04.4	1976	Bold Forbes	A. Cordero	2:01.3
1914	Old Rosebud	J. McCabe	2:03.2	1977	Seattle Slew	J. Cruquet	2:02.1
1915	Regret	J. Notter	2:05.2	1978	Affirmed	S. Cauthen	2:01.1
1916	George Smith	J. Loftus	2:04.3	1979	Spectacular Bid	R. Franklin	2:02.2
1917	Omar Khayyam	C. Borel	2:04.0	1980	Genuine Risk	J. Vasquez	2:02.0
1918	Exterminator	W. Knapp	2:10.4	1981	Pleasant Colony	J. Velasquez	2:02.0
1919	Sir Barton	J. Loftus	2:09.4	1982	Gato Del Sol	E. Delahoussaye	2:02.2
1920	Paul Jones	T. Rice	2:09.0	1983	Sunny's Halo	E. Delahoussaye	2:02.1
1921	Behave Yourself	C. Thompson	2:04.1	1984	Swale	L. Pincay	2:02.2
1922	Morvich	A. Johnson	2:04.3	1985	Spend A Buck	A. Cordero	2:00.1
1923	Zev	E. Sande	2:05.2	1986	Ferdinand	W. Shoemaker	2:02.4
1924	Black Gold	J. D. Mooney	2:05.1	1987	Alysheba	C. McCarron	2:03.2
1925	Flying Ebony	E. Sande	2:07.3	1988	Winning Colors	G. Stevens	2:02.2
1926	Bubbling Over	A. Johnson	2:03.4	1989	Sunday Silence	P. Valenzuela	2:05.0
1927	Whiskery	L. McAtee	2:06.0	1990	Unbridled	C. Perret	2:02.0
1928	Reigh Count	C. Lang	2:10.2	1991	Strike the Gold	C. Antley	2:03.0
1929	Clyde Van Dusen	I. McAtee	2:10.4	1992	Lil E. Tee	P.Day	2:03.0
1930	Gallant Fox	E. Sande	2:07.3	1993	Sea Hero	J. Bailey	2:02.2
1931	Twenty Grand	C. Kurtsinger	2:01.4	1994	Go for Gin	C. McCarron	2:03.3
1932	Burgoo King	E. James	2:05.1	1995	Thunder Gulch	G. Stevens	2:01.1
1933	Brokers Tip	D. Meade	2:06.4	1996	Grindstone	J. Bailey	2:01.0
1934	Cavalcade	M. Garner	2:04.0	1997	Silver Charm	G. Stevens	2:02.2
1935	Omaha	W. Saunders	2:05.0	1998	Real Quiet	K. Desormeaux	2:02.1
1936	Bold Venture	I. Hanford	2:03.3	1999	Charismatic	C. Antley	2:03.2

1. In 1968, Dancer's Image finished first, but was later disqualified from the purse money, and Forward Pass was declared winner.
2. Record. **Source:** *Daily Racing Form.*

Preakness Stakes Winners 1873–1999

The Preakness was first run in 1873, and the distance varied from 1 mile 70 yards to 1½ miles until 1925, when it was standardized at 1³⁄₁₆ miles.
Site: Pimlico Racetrack, Baltimore, Maryland

Year	Horse	Jockey	Time	Year	Horse	Jockey	Time
1873	Survivor	G. Barbee	2:43.0	1937	War Admiral	C. Kurtsinger	1:58.2
1874	Culpepper	Donohue	2:56½	1938	Dauber	M. Peters	1:59.4
1875	Tom Ochiltree	L. Hughes	2:43½	1939	Challedon	G. Seabo	1:59.4
1876	Shirley	Barbee	2:44¾	1940	Bimelech	F. A. Smith	1:58.3
1877	Cloverbrook	Holloway	2:45½	1941	Whirlaway	E. Arcaro	1:58.4
1878	Duke of Magenta	Holloway	2:41¾	1942	Alsab	B. James	1:57.0
1879	Harold	Hughes	2:40½	1943	Count Fleet	J. Longden	1:57.2
1880	Grenada	L. Hughes	2:40½	1944	Pensive	C. McCreary	1:59.1
1881	Saunterer	Costello	2:40½	1945	Polynesian	W. D. Wright	1:58.4
1882	Vanguard	Costello	2:44½	1946	Assault	W. Mehrtens	2:01.2
1883	Jacobus	Barbee	2:42½	1947	Faultless	D. Dodson	1:59.0
1884	Knight of Ellerslie	Fisher	2:39½	1948	Citation	E. Arcaro	2:02.2
1885	Tecumseh	M. McLaughlin	2:49.0	1949	Capot	T. Atkinson	1:56.0
1886	The Bard	Fisher	2:45.0	1950	Hill Prince	E. Arcaro	1:59.1
1887	Dunboyne	W. Donohue	2:39½	1951	Bold	E. Arcaro	1:56.2
1888	Refund	Littlefield	2:49.0	1952	Blue Man	C. McCreary	1:57.2
1889	Buddhist	Anderson	2:17½	1953	Native Dancer	E. Guerin	1:57.4
1890	Montague	W. Martin	2:36¾	1954	Hasty Road	J. Adams	1:57.2
1891–93	Not run			1955	Nashua	E. Arcaro	1:54.3
1894	Assignee	F. Taral	1:49¼	1956	Fabius	W. Hartack	1:58.2
1895	Belmar	F. Taral	1:50½	1957	Bold Ruler	E. Arcaro	1:56.1
1896	Margrave	H. Griffin	1:51.0	1958	Tim Tam	I. Valenzuela	1:57.1
1897	Paul Kauver	Thorpe	1:51¼	1959	Royal Orbit	W. Harmatz	1:57.0
1898	Sly Fox	W. Simms	1:49¾	1960	Bally Ache	R. Ussery	1:57.3
1899	Half Time	R. Clawson	1:47.0	1961	Carry Back	J. Sellers	1:57.3
1900	Hindus	H. Spencer	1:48.2	1962	Greek Money	J. L. Rotz	1:56.1
1901	The Parader	F. Landry	1:47.1	1963	Candy Spots	W. Shoemaker	1:56.1
1902	Old England	L. Jackson	1:45.4	1964	Northern Dancer	W. Hartack	1:56.4
1903	Flocarline	W. Gannon	1:44.4	1965	Tom Rolfe	R. Turcotte	1:56.1
1904	Bryn Mawr	E. Hildebrand	1:44.1	1966	Kauai King	D. Brumfield	1:55.2
1905	Cairngorm	W. Davis	1:45.4	1967	Damascus	W. Shoemaker	1:55.1
1906	Whimsical	W. Miller	1:45.0	1968	Forward Pass	I. Valenzuela	1:56.4
1907	Don Enrique	G. Mountain	1:45.2	1969	Majestic Prince	W. Hartack	1:55.3
1908	Royal Tourist	E. Dugan	1:46.2	1970	Personality	E. Belmonte	1:56.1
1909	Effendi	W. Doyle	1:39.4	1971	Canonero II	G. Avila	1:54.0
1910	Layminister	R. Estep	1:40.3	1972	Bee Bee Bee	E. Nelson	1:55.3
1911	Watervale	E. Dugan	1:51.0	1973	Secretariat	R. Turcotte	1:54.2
1912	Colonel Holloway	C. Turner	1:56.3	1974	Little Current	M. Rivera	1:54.3
1913	Buskin	J. Butwell	1:53.2	1975	Master Derby	D. McHargue	1:56.2
1914	Holiday	A. Schuttinger	1:53.4	1976	Elocutionist	J. Lively	1:55.0
1915	Rhine Maiden	D. Hoffman	1:58.0	1977	Seattle Slew	J. Cruguet	1:54.2
1916	Damrosch	L. McAtee	1:54.4	1978	Affirmed	S. Cauthen	1:54.2
1917	Kalitan	E. Haynes	1:54.2	1979	Spectacular Bid	R. Franklin	1:54.1
1918	Jack Hare Jr.	C. Peak	1:53.2	1980	Codex	A. Cordero	1:54.1
	War Cloud	J. Loftus	1:53.3	1981	Pleasant Colony	J. Valasquez	1:54.3
1919	Sir Barton	J. Loftus	1:53.0	1982	Aloma's Ruler	J. Kaenel	1:55.2
1920	Man o' War	C. Kummer	1:51.3	1983	Deputed Testamony	D. Miller	1:55.2
1921	Broomspun	F. Coltiletti	1:54.1	1984	Gate Dancer	A. Cordero	1:53.3
1922	Pillory	L. Morris	1:51.3	1985	Tank's Prospect	P. Day	1:53.2
1923	Vigil	B. Marinelli	1:53.3	1986	Snow Chief	A. Solls	1:54.4
1924	Nellie Morse	J. Merimee	1:57.1	1987	Alysheba	C. McCarron	1:55.4
1925	Coventry	C. Kummer	1:59.0	1988	Risen Star	E. Delahoussaye	1:56.1
1926	Display	J. Maiben	1:59.4	1989	Sunday Silence	P. Valenzuela	1:53.4
1927	Bostonian	A. Abel	2:01.3	1990	Summer Squall	P. Day	1:53.3
1928	Victorian	R. Workman	2:00.1	1991	Hansel	J. Bailey	1:54.0
1929	Dr. Freeland	L. Schaefer	2:01.3	1992	Pine Bluff	C McCarron	1:55.3
1930	Gallant Fox	E. Sande	2:00.3	1993	Prairie Bayou	M. Smith	1:56.2
1931	Mate	G. Ellis	1:59.0	1994	Tabasco Cat	P. Day	1:56.2
1932	Burgoo King	E. James	1:59.4	1995	Timber Country	P. Day	1:54.2
1933	Head Play	C. Kurtsinger	2:02.0	1996	Louis Quatorze	P. Day	1:52.3
1934	High Quest	R. Jones	1:58.1	1997	Silver Charm	G. Stevens	1:54.2
1935	Omaha	W. Saunders	1:58.2	1998	Real Quiet	K. Desormeaux	1:54.4
1936	Bold Venture	G. Woolf	1:59.0	1999	Charismatic	C. Antley	1:55.1

Source: *Daily Racing Form*

Belmont Stakes Winners 1900–99

The Belmont Stakes was first run in 1867. The distance of the race varied from 1 1/16 miles to 1 5/8 miles until 1926, when it was standardized at 1 1/2 miles. **Site: Belmont Park**, New York. (The race was held at Jerome Park prior to 1890, at Morris Park from 1890 to 1904, at Aqueduct from 1963 to 1967.)

Year	Horse	Jockey	Time	Year	Horse	Jockey	Time
1900	Ildrim	N. Turner	2:21½	1951	Counterpoint	D. Gorman	2:29.0
1901	Commando	H. Spencer	2:21.0	1952	One Count	E. Arcaro	2:30.1
1902	Masterman	J. Bullman	2:22½	1953	Native Dancer	E. Guerin	2:28.3
1903	Africander	J. Bullman	2:23.1	1954	High Gun	E. Guerin	2:30.4
1904	Delhi	G. Odom	2:06.3	1955	Nashua	E. Arcaro	2:29.0
1905	Tanya	E. Hildebrand	2:08.0	1956	Needles	D. Erb	2:29.4
1906	Burgomaster	L. Lyne	2:20.0	1957	Gallant Man	W. Shoemaker	2:26.3
1907	Peter Pan	G. Mountain	No Time	1958	Cavan	P. Anderson	2:30.1
1908	Colin	J. Notter	No Time	1959	Sword Dancer	W. Shoemaker	2:28.2
1909	Joe Madden	E. Dugan	2:21.3	1960	Celtic Ash	W. Hartack	2:29.3
1910	Sweep	J. Butwell	2:22.0	1961	Sherluck	B. Baeza	2:29.1
1911–12	Not run			1962	Jaipur	W. Shoemaker	2:28.4
1913	Prince Eugene	R. Troxler	2:18.0	1963	Chateaugay	B. Baeza	2:30.1
1914	Luke McLuke	M. Buxton	2:20.0	1964	Quadrangle	M. Ycaza	2:28.2
1915	The Finn	G. Byrne	2:18.2	1965	Hail To All	J. Sellers	2:28.2
1916	Friar Rock	E. Haynes	2:22.0	1966	Amberoid	W. Boland	2:29.3
1917	Hourless	J. Butwell	2:17.4	1967	Damascus	W. Shoemaker	2:28.4
1918	Johren	F. Robinson	2:20.2	1968	Stage Door Johnny	H. Gustines	2:27.1
1919	Sir Barton	J. Loftus	2:17.2	1969	Arts and Letters	B. Baeza	2:28.4
1920	Man o'War	C. Kummer	2:14.1	1970	High Echelon	J. L. Rotz	2:34.0
1921	Grey Lag	E. Sande	2:16.4	1971	Pass Catcher	W. Blum	2:30.2
1922	Pillory	C. H. Miller	2:18.4	1972	Riva Ridge	R. Turcotte	2:28.0
1923	Zev	E. Sande	2:19.0	1973	Secretariat	R. Turcotte	2:24.0
1924	Mad Play	E. Sande	2:18.4	1974	Little Current	M. Rivera	2:29.1
1925	American Flag	A. Johnson	2:16.4	1975	Avatar	W. Shoemaker	2:28.1
1926	Crusader	A. Johnson	2:32.1	1976	Bold Forbes	A. Cordero	2:29.0
1927	Chance Shot	E. Sande	2:32.2	1977	Seattle Slew	Jean Cruguet	2:29.3
1928	Vito	C. Kummer	2:33.1	1978	Affirmed	S. Cauthen	2:26.4
1929	Blue Larkspur	M. Garner	2:32.4	1979	Coastal	R. Hernandez	2:28.3
1930	Gallant Fox	E. Sande	2:31.1	1980	Temperance Hill	E. Maple	2:29.4
1931	Twenty Grand	C. Kurtsinger	2:29.3	1981	Summing	G. Martens	2:29.0
1932	Faireno	T. Malley	2:32.4	1982	Conquistador Cielo	L. Pincay	2:28.1
1933	Hurryoff	M. Garner	2:32.3	1983	Caveat	L. Pincay	2:27.4
1934	Peace Chance	W. D. Wright	2:29.5	1984	Swale	L. Pincay	2:27.1
1935	Omaha	W. Saunders	2:30.3	1985	Creme Fraiche	E. Maple	2:27.0
1936	Granville	J. Stout	2:30.0	1986	Danzig Connection	C. McCarron	2:29.4
1937	War Admiral	C. Kurtsinger	2:28.3	1987	Bet Twice	C. Perret	2:28.1
1938	Pasteurized	J. Stout	2:29.2	1988	Risen Star	E. Delahoussaye	2:26.1
1939	Johnstown	J. Stout	2:29.2	1989	Easy Goer	P. Day	2:26.0
1940	Bimelech	F. A. Smith	2:29.3	1990	Go and Go	M. Kinane	2:27.1
1941	Whirlaway	E. Arcaro	2:31.0	1991	Hansel	J. Bailey	2:28.0
1942	Shut Out	E. Arcaro	2:29.1	1992	A.P. Indy	E. Delahoussaye	2:26.0
1943	Count Fleet	J. Longden	2:28.1	1993	Colonial Affair	J. Krone	2:29.4
1944	Bounding Home	G. L. Smith	2:32.1	1994	Tabasco Cat	P. Day	2:26.4
1945	Pavot	E. Arcaro	2:30.1	1995	Thunder Gulch	G. Stevens	2:32.0
1946	Assault	W. Mehrtens	2:30.4	1996	Editor's Note	R. Douglas	2:28.4
1947	Phalanx	R. Donoso	2:29.2	1997	Touch Gold	C. McCarron	2:28.4
1948	Citation	E. Arcaro	2:28.1	1998	Victory Gallop	G. Stevens	2:29.0
1949	Capot	T. Atkinson	2:30.1	1999	Lemon Drop Kid	J. Santos	2:27.4
1950	Middleground	W. Boland	2:28.3				

Source: *Daily Racing Form.*

The Triple Crown Winners

In more than 100 years only 11 horses have won all three jewels of the triple crown, the Kentucky Derby, the Preakness, and the Belmont Stakes.

Year	Horse	Year	Horse	Year	Horse	Year	Horse
1919	Sir Barton	1937	War Admiral	1946	Assault	1977	Seattle Slew
1930	Gallant Fox	1941	Whirlaway	1948	Citation	1978	Affirmed
1935	Omaha	1943	Count Fleet	1973	Secretariat		

The Breeders' Cup

Billed as thoroughbred racing's most glamorous and exciting day of the year, these races (one for each standard category of sex, distance, and surface) attract the finest horses in the world with unprecedented purses of $1 million to $3 million per race. The site changes from year to year.

BREEDERS' CUP JUVENILE
Purse: $1 mil.; distance: 1¹⁄₁₆ miles
(one mile in 1984, '85, '87, and '88).

Year	Winner	Jockey	Time
1984	Chief's Crown	D. MacBeth	1:36.1
1985	Tasso	L. Pincay Jr.	1:36.1
1986	Capote	L. Pincay Jr.	1:43.4
1987	Success Express	J. Santos	1:35.1
1988	Is It True	L. Pincay Jr.	1:36.3
1989	Rhythm	C. Perret	1:43.3
1990	Fly So Free	J. Santos	1:43.2
1991	Arazi	P. Valenzuela	1:44.3
1992	Gilded Time	C. McCarron	1:43.2
1993	Brocco	G. Stevens	1:42.4
1994	Timber Country	P. Day	1:44.2
1995	Unbridled's Song	M. Smith	1:41.3
1996	Boston Harbor	J. Bailey	1:43.2
1997	Favorite Trick	P. Day	1:41.2
1998	Answer Lively	J. Bailey	1:44.0

BREEDERS' CUP MILE
Purse: $1 mil.; distance: 1 mile, turf.

Year	Winner	Jockey	Time
1984	Royal Heroine	F. Toro	1:32.3
1985	Cozzene	W. Guerra	1:35.0
1986	Last Tycoon	Y. Saint-Martin	1:35.1
1987	Miesque	F. Head	1:32.4
1988	Miesque	F. Head	1:38.3
1989	Steinlen	J. Santos	1:37.1
1990	Royal Academy	L. Piggott	1:35.1
1991	Opening Verse	P. Valenzuela	1:37.2
1992	Lure	M. Smith	1:32.4
1993	Lure	M. Smith	1:33.2
1994	Barathea	F. Dettori	1:34.2
1995	Ridgewood Pearl	J. Murtagh	1:43.3
1996	Da Hoss	G. Stevens	1:35.4
1997	Spinning World	C. Asmussen	1:32.3
1998	Da Hoss	J. Velasquez	1:35.1

BREEDERS' CUP JUVENILE FILLIES
Purse: $1 mil.; distance: 1¹⁄₁₆ miles
(one mile in 1984, '85, and '87).

Year	Winner	Jockey	Time
1984	Outstandingly	W. Guerra	1:37.4
1985	Twilight Ridge	J. Velasquez	1:35.4
1986	Brave Raj	P. Valenzuela	1:43.1
1987	Epitome	P. Day	1:36.2
1988	Open Mind	A. Cordero Jr.	1:46.3
1989	Go For Wand	R. Romero	1:44.1
1990	Meadow Star	J. Santos	1:44.0
1991	Pleasant Stage	E. Delahoussaye	1:46.2
1992	Eliza	P. Valenzuela	1:42.4
1993	Phone Chatter	L. Pincay, Jr.	1:43.0
1994	Flanders	P. Day	1:45.1
1995	My Flag	J. Bailey	1:42.2
1996	Storm Song	C. Perret	1:43.3
1997	Countess Diana	S. Sellers	1:42.0
1998	Silverbulletday	G. Stevens	1:43.3

BREEDERS' CUP DISTAFF
Purse: $1 mil.; distance: 1⅛ miles (1¼ miles until 1988.).

Year	Winner	Jockey	Time
1984	Princess Rooney	E. Delahoussaye	2:02.2
1985	Life's Magic	A. Cordero Jr.	2:02.0
1986	Lady's Secret	P. Day	2:01.1
1987	Sacahuista	R. Romero	2:02.4
1988	Personal Ensign	R. Romero	1:52.0
1989	Bayakoa	L. Pincay Jr.	1:47.2
1990	Bayakoa	L. Pincay Jr.	1:49.1
1991	Dance Smartly	P. Day	1:50.4
1992	Paseana	C. McCarron	1:48.0
1993	Hollywood Wildcat	E. Delahoussaye	1:48.1
1994	One Dreamer	G. Stevens	1:50.3
1995	Inside Information	M. Smith	1:46.0
1996	Jewel Princess	C. Nakatani	1:48.2
1997	Ajina	M. Smith	1:47.1
1998	Escena	G. Stevens	1:49.4

BREEDERS' CUP SPRINT
Purse: $1 mil.; distance: 6 furlongs.

Year	Winner	Jockey	Time
1984	Eillo	C. Perret	1:10.1
1985	Precisionist	C. McCarron	1:08.2
1986	Smile	J. Vasquez	1:08.2
1987	Very Subtle	P. Valenzuela	1:08.4
1988	Gulch	A. Cordero Jr.	1:10.2
1989	Dancing Spree	A. Cordero Jr.	1:09.0
1990	Safely Kept	C. Perret	1:09.3
1991	Sheik Albadou	P. Eddery	1:09.1
1992	30 Slews	E. Delahoussaye	1:08.1
1993	Cardmania	E. Delahoussaye	1:08.3
1994	Cherokee Run	M. Smith	1:09.2
1995	Desert Stormer	K. Desormeaux	1:09.0
1996	Lit de Justice	C. Nakatani	1:08.3
1997	Elmhurst	C. Nakatani	1:08.0
1998	Reraise	C. Nakatani	1:09.0

BREEDERS' CUP TURF
Purse: $2 mil.; distance: 1½ miles, turf.

Year	Winner	Jockey	Time
1984	Lashkari	Y. Saint-Martin	2:25.1
1985	Pebbles	P. Eddery	2:27.0
1986	Manila	J. Santos	2:25.2
1987	Theatrical	P. Day	2:24.2
1988	Great Communicator	R. Sibille	2:35.1
1989	Prized	E. Delahoussaye	2:28.0
1990	In the Wings	G. Stevens	2:29.3
1991	Miss Alleged	E. Legrix	2:30.4
1992	Fraise	P. Valenzuela	2:24.0
1993	Kotashaan	K. Desormeaux	2:25.0
1994	Tikkanen	M. Smith	2:26.2
1995	Northern Spur	C. McCarron	2:42.0
1996	Pilsudski	W. Swinburn	2:25.1
1997	Chief Bearhart	J. Santos	2:23.4
1998	Buck's Boy	S. Sellers	2:28.3

CLASSIC
Purse: $3 mil.; distance: 1¼ miles.

Year	Winner	Jockey	Time	Year	Winner	Jockey	Time
1984	Wild Again	P. Day	2:03.2	1992	A.P. Indy	E. Delahoussaye	2:00.1
1985	Proud Truth	J. Velasquez	2:00.4	1993	Arcangues	J. Bailey	2:00.4
1986	Skywalker	L. Pincay Jr.	2:00.2	1994	Concern	P. Day	2:02.2
1987	Ferdinand	B. Shoemaker	2:01.2	1995	Cigar	J. Bailey	1:59.2
1988	Alysheba	C. McCarron	2:04.4	1996	Alphabet Soup	C. McCarron	2:01.0
1989	Sunday Silence	C. McCarron	2:00.1	1997	Skip Away	M. Smith	1:59.0
1990	Unbridled	P. Day	2:02.1	1998	Awesome Again	P. Day	2:02.0
1991	Black Tie Affair	J. Bailey	2:02.4				

FOOTBALL

National Football League
410 Park Avenue
New York, NY 10022
(212) 758-1500

www.nfl.com
Commissioner: Paul Tagliabue
Founded 1920.
Number of Teams: 31

1998 NFL Regular Season Final Standings

AMERICAN FOOTBALL CONFERENCE	W-L-T	PCT.	PTS.	OPP.	NATIONAL FOOTBALL CONFERENCE	W-L-T	PCT.	PTS.	OPP.
Eastern Division					**Eastern Division**				
N.Y. Jets[1]	12–4–0	.750	416	266	Dallas[1]	10–6–0	.625	381	275
Miami[2]	10–6–0	.625	321	265	Arizona[2]	9–7–0	.563	325	378
Buffalo[2]	10–6–0	.625	400	333	N.Y. Giants	8–8–0	.500	287	309
New England[2]	9–7–0	.563	337	329	Washington	6–10–0	.375	319	421
Indianapolis	3–13–0	.188	310	444	Philadelphia	3–13–0	.188	161	344
Central Division					**Central Division**				
Jacksonville[1]	11–5–0	.688	392	338	Minnesota[1]	15–1–0	.938	556	296
Tennessee	8–8–0	.500	330	320	Green Bay[2]	11–5–0	.688	408	319
Pittsburgh	7–9–0	.438	263	303	Tampa Bay	8–8–0	.500	314	295
Baltimore	6–10–0	.375	269	335	Detroit	5–11–0	.313	306	378
Cincinnati	3–13–0	.188	268	452	Chicago	4–12–0	.250	276	368
Western Division					**Western Division**				
Denver[1]	14–2–0	.875	501	309	Atlanta[1]	14–2–0	.875	442	289
Oakland	8–8–0	.500	288	356	San Francisco[2]	12–4–0	.750	479	328
Seattle	8–8–0	.500	372	310	New Orleans	6–10–0	.375	305	359
Kansas City	7–9–0	.438	327	363	Carolina	4–12–0	.250	336	413
San Diego	5–11–0	.313	241	342	St. Louis	4–12–0	.250	285	378

1. Division champion. 2. Wild Card for playoffs.

1998 NFL Post-Season Playoff Results

AFC Wild Card Playoff
JACKSONVILLE 25, New England 10
MIAMI 24, Buffalo 17

NFC Wild Card Playoff
SAN FRANCISCO 30, Green Bay 27
Arizona 20, DALLAS 7

AFC Divisional Playoff
DENVER 38, Miami 3
N.Y. JETS 34, Jacksonville 24

NFC Divisional Playoff
ATLANTA 20, San Francisco 18
MINNESOTA 41, Arizona 21

AFC Championship Game
DENVER 23, N.Y. Jets 10

NFC Championship Game
Atlanta 30, MINNESOTA 27 (OT)

Super Bowl XXXIII at Pro Player Stadium, Miami , Fla.
January 31, 1999
Denver 34, Atlanta 19

Note: Home team in CAPITAL LETTERS

NFL First Round Draft Choices, 1999

Team	Selection, Position	School	Team	Selection, Position	School
1. Cleveland	Tim Couch, QB	Kentucky	17. New England	Damien Woody, OL	Boston College
2. Philadelphia	Donovan McNabb, QB	Syracuse	18. Oakland	Matt Stinchcomb, OL	Georgia
3. Cincinnati	Akili Smith, QB	Oregon	19. N.Y. Giants	Luke Petitgout, OL	Notre Dame
4. Indianapolis	Edgerrin James, RB	Miami (Fla.)	20. Dallas	Ebenezer Ekuban, DL	North Carolina
5. New Orleans	Ricky Williams, RB	Texas	21. Arizona	Lonnie Jewel Shelton, OL	E. Michigan
6. St. Louis	Torry Holt, WR	N. Carolina St.	22. Seattle	Lamar King, DL	Saginaw Valley St. (Mich.)
7. Washington	Roland Bailey, DB	Georgia			
8. Arizona	David Boston, WR	Ohio State	23. Buffalo	Antoine Winfield, DB	Ohio State
9. Detroit	Chris Claiborne, LB	USC	24. San Francisco	Reggie McGrew, DL	Florida
10. Baltimore	Chris McAlister, DB	Arizona	25. Green Bay	Antuan Edwards, DB	Clemson
11. Minnesota	Daunte Culpepper, QB	Central Florida	26. Jacksonville	Fernando Bryant, DB	Alabama
12. Chicago	Cade McNown, QB	UCLA	27. Detroit	Aaron Gibson, OL	Wisconsin
13. Pittsburgh	Troy Edwards, WR	Louisiana Tech	28. New England	Andy Katzenmoyer, LB	Ohio State
14. Kansas City	John Tait, OL	Brigham Young	29. Minnesota	Dimitrius Underwood, DL	Michigan State
15. Tampa Bay	Anthony McFarland, DL	Louisiana State	30. Atlanta	Patrick Kerney, DL	Virginia
16. Tennessee	Jevon Kearse, LB	Florida	31. Denver	Al Wilson, LB	Tennessee

NFL Leaders, 1998

RUSHING

AFC	No.	Yds.	Avg.	TDs
Terrell Davis, Denver	392	2,008	5.1	21
Marshall Faulk, Indianapolis	324	1,319	4.1	6
Eddie George, Tennessee	348	1,294	3.7	5
Curtis Martin, N.Y. Jets	369	1,287	3.5	8
Ricky Watters, Seattle	319	1,239	3.9	9
Fred Taylor, Jacksonville	264	1,223	4.6	14
Jerome Bettis, Pittsburgh	316	1,185	3.8	3
Corey Dillon, Cincinnati	262	1,130	4.3	4
Antowain Smith, Buffalo	300	1,124	3.7	8
Robert Edwards, New England	291	1,115	3.8	9

NFC	No.	Yds.	Avg.	TDs
Jamal Anderson, Atlanta	410	1,846	4.5	14
Garrison Hearst, San Francisco	310	1,570	5.1	7
Barry Sanders, Detroit	343	1,491	4.3	4
Emmitt Smith, Dallas	319	1,332	4.2	13
Robert Smith, Minnesota	249	1,187	4.8	6
Duce Staley, Philadelphia	258	1,065	4.1	5
Gary Brown, N.Y. Giants	247	1,063	4.3	5
Adrian Murrell, Arizona	274	1,042	3.8	8
Warrick Dunn, Tampa Bay	245	1,026	4.2	2
Mike Alstott, Tampa Bay	215	846	3.9	8

RECEIVING

AFC	No.	Yds.	Avg.	TDs
O.J. McDuffie, Miami	90	1,050	11.7	7
Marshall Faulk, Indianapolis	86	908	10.6	4
Rod Smith, Denver	86	1,222	14.2	6
Keyshawn Johnson, N.Y. Jets	83	1,131	13.6	10
Carl Pickens, Cincinnati	82	1,023	12.5	5
Tim Brown, Oakland	81	1,012	12.5	9
Jimmy Smith, Jacksonville	78	1,182	15.2	8
Wayne Chrebet, N.Y. Jets	75	1,083	14.4	8
Frank Wycheck, Tennessee	70	768	11.0	2
Ben Coates, New England	67	668	10.0	6
Eric Moulds, Buffalo	67	1,368	20.4	9

NFC	No.	Yds.	Avg.	TDs
Frank Sanders, Arizona	89	1,145	12.9	3
Antonio Freeman, Green Bay	84	1,424	17.0	14
Herman Moore, Detroit	82	983	12.0	5
Jerry Rice, San Francisco	82	1,157	14.1	9
Cris Carter, Minnesota	78	1,011	13.0	12
Michael Irvin, Dallas	74	1,057	14.3	1
Larry Centers, Arizona	69	559	8.1	2
Raghib Ismail, Carolina	69	1,024	14.8	8
Johnnie Morton, Detroit	69	1,028	14.9	2
Randy Moss, Minnesota	69	1,313	19.0	17

PASSING RATING

AFC	Att.	Comp.	Pct.	Yds.	Avg.	TDs	Int.	Rating
Vinny Testaverde, N.Y. Jets	421	259	61.5	3,256	7.7	29	7	101.6
John Elway, Denver	356	210	59.0	2,806	7.9	22	10	93.0
Neil O'Donnell, Cincinnati	343	212	61.8	2,216	6.5	15	4	90.2
Mark Brunell, Jacksonville	354	208	58.8	2,601	7.4	20	9	89.9
Doug Flutie, Buffalo	354	202	57.1	2,711	7.7	20	11	87.4
Drew Bledsoe, New England	481	263	54.7	3,633	7.6	20	14	80.9
Rich Gannon, Kansas City	354	206	58.2	2,305	6.5	10	6	80.1
Steve McNair, Tennessee	492	289	58.7	3,228	6.6	15	10	80.1
Dan Marino, Miami	537	310	57.7	3,497	6.5	23	15	80.0
Warren Moon, Seattle	258	145	56.2	1,632	6.3	11	8	76.6

AFC	Att.	Comp.	Pct.	Yds.	Avg.	TDs	Int.	Rating
Randall Cunningham, Minnesota	425	259	60.9	3,704	8.7	34	10	106.0
Steve Young, San Francisco	517	322	62.3	4,170	8.1	36	12	101.1
Chris Chandler, Atlanta	327	190	58.1	3,154	9.7	25	12	100.9
Troy Aikman, Dallas	315	187	59.4	2,330	7.4	12	5	88.5
Steve Beuerlein, Carolina	343	216	63.0	2,613	7.6	17	12	88.2
Bret Favre, Green Bay	551	347	63.0	4,212	7.6	31	23	87.8
Charlie Batch, Detroit	303	173	57.1	2,178	7.2	11	6	83.5
Erik Kramer, Chicago	250	151	60.4	1,823	7.3	9	7	83.1
Trent Green, Washington	509	278	54.6	3,441	6.8	23	11	81.8
Jake Plummer, Arizona	547	324	59.2	3,737	6.8	17	20	75.0

NFL Number One Draft Picks, 1936–99

Year	Player	Team	Pos.	College
1936	Jay Berwanger	Philadelphia Eagles	RB	Chicago
1937	Sam Francis	Philadelphia Eagles	RB	Nebraska
1938	Corbett Davis	Cleveland Rams	RB	Indiana
1939	Charles Aldrich	Chicago Cardinals	OL	Texas Christian
1940	George Cafego	Chicago Cardinals	QB	Tennessee
1941	Tom Harmon	Chicago Bears	RB	Michigan
1942	Bill Dudley	Pittsburgh Steelers	RB	Virginia
1943	Frank Sinkwich	Detroit Lions	RB	Georgia
1944	Angelo Bertelli	Boston Yanks	QB	Notre Dame
1945	Charley Trippi	Chicago Cardinals	RB	Georgia
1946	Frank Dancewicz	Boston Yanks	QB	Notre Dame
1947	Bob Fenimore	Chicago Bears	RB	Oklahoma A&M
1948	Harry Gilmer	Washington Redskins	QB	Alabama
1949	Chuck Bednarik	Philadelphia Eagles	OL	Pennsylvania
1950	Leon Hart	Detroit Lions	RB	Notre Dame
1951	Kyle Rote	New York Giants	E/K	Southern Methodist
1952	Bill Wade	Los Angeles Rams	QB	Vanderbilt
1953	Harry Babcock	San Francisco 49ers	E	Georgia
1954	Bobby Garrett	Cleveland Browns	QB	Stanford
1955	George Shaw	Baltimore Colts	QB	Oregon
1956	Gary Glick	Pittsburgh Steelers	QB	Colorado State
1957	Paul Hornung	Green Bay Packers	RB	Notre Dame
1958	King Hill	St. Louis Cardinals	QB	Rice
1959	Randy Duncan	Green Bay Packers	QB	Iowa
1960	Billy Cannon	Los Angeles Rams	RB	Louisiana State
1961	Tommy Mason	Minnesota Vikings	RB	Tulane
1962	Ernie Davis	Washington Redskins	RB	Syracuse
1963	Terry Baker	Los Angeles Rams	QB	Oregon State
1964	Dave Parks	San Francisco 49ers	E	Texas Tech.
1965	Tucker Frederickson	New York Giants	RB	Auburn
1966	Tommy Nobis	Atlanta Falcons	LB	Texas
1967	Bubba Smith	Baltimore Colts	DL	Michigan State
1968	Ron Yary	Minnesota Vikings	OL	USC
1969	O.J. Simpson	Buffalo Bills	RB	USC
1970	Terry Bradshaw	Pittsburgh Steelers	QB	Louisiana Tech.
1971	Jim Plunkett	Boston Patriots	QB	Stanford
1972	Walt Patulski	Buffalo Bills	DL	Notre Dame
1973	John Matuzak	Houston Oilers	DL	Tampa
1974	Ed Jones	Dallas Cowboys	DL	Tampa
1975	Steve Bartkowski	Atlanta Falcons	QB	California
1976	Lee Roy Selmon	Tampa Bay Buccaneers	DL	Oklahoma
1977	Ricky Bell	Tampa Bay Buccaneers	RB	USC
1978	Earl Campbell	Houston Oilers	RB	Texas
1979	Tom Cousineau	Buffalo Bills	LB	Ohio State
1980	Billy Sims	Detroit Lions	RB	Oklahoma
1981	George Rogers	New Orleans Saints	RB	South Carolina
1982	Kenneth Sims	New England Patriots	DL	Texas
1983	John Elway	Baltimore Colts	QB	Stanford
1984	Irving Fryar	New England Patriots	WR	Nebraska
1985	Bruce Smith	Buffalo Bills	DL	Virginia Tech.
1986	Bo Jackson	Tampa Bay Buccaneers	RB	Auburn
1987	Vinny Testaverde	Tampa Bay Buccaneers	QB	Miami
1988	Aundray Bruce	Atlanta Falcons	LB	Auburn
1989	Troy Aikman	Dallas Cowboys	QB	UCLA
1990	Jeff George	Indianapolis Colts	QB	Illinois
1991	Russell Maryland	Dallas Cowboys	DT	Miami (Fla.)
1992	Steve Emtman	Indianapolis Colts	DT	Washington
1993	Drew Bledsoe	New England Patriots	QB	Washington State
1994	Dan Wilkinson	Cincinnati Bengals	DT	Ohio State
1995	Ki-Jana Carter	Cincinnati Bengals	RB	Penn State
1996	Keyshawn Johnson	New York Jets	WR	Southern California
1997	Orlando Pace	St. Louis Rams	OT	Ohio State
1998	Peyton Manning	Indianapolis Colts	QB	Tennessee
1999	Tim Couch	Cleveland Browns	QB	Kentucky

The Sporting News' NFL Rookie of the Year, 1955–98

Year	Player	Pos.	Team	Year	Player	Pos.	Team
1955	Alan Ameche	FB	Baltimore Colts	1977	NFC: Tony Dorsett	RB	Dallas Cowboys
1956	J.C. Caroline	HB	Chicago Bears		AFC: A.J. Duhe	DT	Miami Dolphins
1957	Jim Brown	FB	Cleveland Browns	1978	NFC: Al Baker	DE	Detroit Lions
1958	Bobby Mitchell	HB	Cleveland Browns		AFC: Earl Campbell	RB	Houston Oilers
1959	Nick Pietrosante	FB	Detroit Lions	1979	NFC: Ottis Anderson	RB	St. Louis Cardinals
1960	Gail Codgill	E	Detroit Lions		AFC: Jerry Butler	WR	Buffalo Bills
1961	Mike Ditka	E	Chicago Bears	1980	Billy Sims	RB	Detroit Lions
1962	Ronnie Bull	HB	Chicago Bears	1981	George Rogers	RB	New England Patriots
1963	Paul Flatley	WR	Minnesota Vikings	1982	Marcus Allen	RB	Los Angeles Raiders
1964	Charley Taylor	HB	Washington Redskins	1983	Dan Marino	QB	Miami Dolphins
1965	Gale Sayers	RB	Chicago Bears	1984	Louis Lipps	WR	Pittsburgh Steelers
1966	Tommy Nobis	LB	Atlanta Falcons	1985	Eddie Brown	WR	Cincinnati Bengals
1967	Mel Farr	RB	Detroit Lions	1986	Rueben Mayes	RB	New Orleans Saints
1968	Earl McCullouch	WR	Detroit Lions	1987	Robert Awalt	TE	St. Louis Cardinals
1969	Calvin Hill	RB	Dallas Cowboys	1988	Keith Jackson	TE	Philadelphia Eagles
1970	NFC: Bruce Taylor	CB	San Francisco 49ers	1989	Barry Sanders	RB	Detroit Lions
	AFC: Dennis Shaw	QB	Buffalo Bills	1990	Richmond Webb	OL	Miami Dolphins
1971	NFC: John Brockington	RB	Green Bay Packers	1991	Mike Croel	LB	Denver Broncos
	AFC: Jim Plunkett	QB	New England Patriots	1992	Santana Dotson	DE	Tampa Bay Buccaneers
1972	NFC: Chester Marcol	PK	Green Bay Packers				
	AFC: Franco Harris	RB	Pittsburgh Steelers	1993	Jerome Bettis	RB	Los Angeles Rams
1973	NFC: Chuck Foreman	RB	Minnestoa Vikings	1994	Marshall Faulk	RB	Indianapolis Colts
	AFC: Boobie Clark	RB	Cincinnati Bengals	1995	Curtis Martin	RB	New England
1974	NFC: Wilbur Jackson	RB	San Francisco 49ers	1996	Eddie George	RB	Houston Oilers
	AFC: Don Woods	RB	San Diego Chargers	1997	Warrick Dunn	RB	Tampa Bay Buccaneers
1975	NFC: Steve Bartkowski	QB	Atlanta Falcons				
	AFC: Robert Brazile	LB	Houston Oilers	1998	Randy Moss	WR	Minnesota Vikings
1976	NFC: Sammy White	WR	Minnesota Vikings				
	AFC: Mike Haynes	CB	New England Patriots				

Note: The NFL does not officially honor a rookie of the year. From 1970–79, separate players were chosen for each conference.
Source: *The Sporting News.*

NFL Player of the Year, 1954–98

Year	Player,	Pos.	Team	Year	Player,	Pos.	Team
1954	Lou Groza	OT/K	Cleveland Browns	1974	NFC: Chuck Foreman	RB	Minnesota Vikings
1955	Otto Graham	QB	Cleveland Browns		AFC: Ken Stabler	QB	Oakland Raiders
1956	Frank Gifford	HB	New York Giants	1975	NFC: Fran Tarkenton	QB	Minnesota Vikings
1957	Jim Brown	RB	Cleveland Browns		AFC: O.J. Simpson	RB	Buffalo Bills
1958	Jim Brown	RB	Cleveland Browns	1976	NFC: Walter Payton	RB	Chicago Bears
1959	Johnny Unitas	QB	Baltimore Colts		AFC: Ken Stabler	QB	Oakland Raiders
1960	Norm Van Brocklin	QB	Philadelphia Eagles	1977	NFC: Walter Payton	RB	Chicago Bears
1961	Paul Hornung	HB	Green Bay Packers		AFC: Craig Morton	QB	Denver Broncos
1962	Y.A. Tittle	QB	New York Giants	1978	NFC: Archie Manning	QB	New Orleans Saints
1963	Y.A. Tittle	QB	New York Giants		AFC: Earl Campbell	RB	Houston Oilers
1964	Johnny Unitas	QB	Baltimore Colts	1979	NFC: Ottis Anderson	RB	St. Louis Cardinals
1965	Jim Brown	RB	Cleveland Browns		AFC: Dan Fouts	QB	San Diego Chargers
1966	Bart Starr	QB	Green Bay	1980	Brian Sipe	QB	Cleveland Browns
1967	Johnny Unitas	QB	Baltimore Colts	1981	Ken Anderson	QB	Cincinnati Bengals
1968	Earl Morrall	QB	Baltimore Colts	1982	Mark Moseley	PK	Washington Redskins
1969	Roman Gabriel	QB	Los Angeles Rams	1983	Eric Dickerson	RB	Los Angeles Rams
1957	Jim Brown	RB	Cleveland Browns	1984	Dan Marino	QB	Miami Dolphins
1958	Jim Brown	RB	Cleveland Browns	1985	Marcus Allen	RB	Los Angeles Raiders
1959	Johnny Unitas	QB	Baltimore Colts	1986	Lawrence Taylor	LB	New York Giants
1960	Norm Van Brocklin	QB	Philadelphia Eagles	1987	Jerry Rice	WR	San Francisco 49ers
1961	Paul Hornung	HB	Green Bay Packers	1988	Boomer Esiason	QB	Cincinnati Bengals
1962	Y.A. Tittle	QB	New York Giants	1989	Joe Montana	QB	San Francisco 49ers
1963	Y.A. Tittle	QB	New York Giants	1990	Jerry Rice	WR	San Francisco 49ers
1964	Johnny Unitas	QB	Baltimore Colts	1991	Thurman Thomas	RB	Buffalo Bills
1965	Jim Brown	RB	Cleveland Browns	1992	Steve Young	QB	San Francisco 49ers
1966	Bart Starr	QB	Green Bay Packers	1993	Emmitt Smith	RB	Dallas Cowboys
1967	Johnny Unitas	QB	Baltimore Colts	1994	Steve Young	QB	San Francisco 49ers
1968	Earl Morrall	QB	Baltimore Colts	1995	Brett Favre	QB	Green Bay Packers
1969	Roman Gabriel	QB	Los Angeles Rams	1996	Brett Favre	QB	Green Bay Packers
1970	NFC: John Brodie	QB	San Francisco 49ers	1997	Barry Sanders	RB	Detroit Lions
	AFC: George Blanda	QB-K	Oakland Raiders	1998	Terrell Davis	RB	Denver Broncos
1971	NFC: Roger Staubach	QB	Dallas Cowboys				
	AFC: Bob Griese	QB	Miami Dolphins				
1972	NFC: Larry Brown	RB	Washington Redskins				
	AFC: Earl Morrall	QB	Miami Dolphins				
1973	NFC: John Hadl	QB	Los Angeles Rams				
	AFC: O.J. Simpson	RB	Buffalo Bills				

Note: From 1970–79, separate players were chosen for each conference.   **Source:** *The Sporting News.*

All-Time Pro Football Records

RUSHING (by yards)

Rank, Player	League	Years	Yards	Rushes	Avg.
1. Walter Payton	NFL	13	16,726	3,838	4.4
2. Barry Sanders[1]	NFL	10	15,269	3,062	5.0
3. Eric Dickerson	NFL	11	13,259	2,996	4.4
4. Tony Dorsett	NFL	12	12,739	2,936	4.3
5. Emmitt Smith	NFL	9	12,566	2,914	4.3
6. Jim Brown	NFL	9	12,312	2,359	5.2
7. Marcus Allen[1]	NFL	16	12,243	3,022	4.1
8. Franco Harris	NFL	13	12,120	2,949	4.1
9. Thurman Thomas[1]	NFL	11	11,786	2,813	4.2
10. John Riggins	NFL	14	11,352	2,916	3.9

RECEIVING (by receptions)

Rank, Player	League	Years	Receptions	Yards	Avg.
1. Jerry Rice[1]	NFL	14	1139	17,612	15.5
2. Art Monk	NFL	16	940	12,721	13.5
3. Andre Reed[1]	NFL	14	889	12,559	14.1
4. Cris Carter[1]	NFL	12	834	10,447	12.5
5. Steve Largent	NFL	14	819	13,089	16.0
6. Henry Ellard[1]	NFL	16	814	13,777	16.9
7. Irving Fryar[1]	NFL	15	784	11,983	15.3
8. James Lofton	NFL	16	764	14,004	18.3
9. Charlie Joiner	AFL-NFL	18	750	12,146	16.2
10. Michael Irvin	NFL	11	740	11,737	15.9

SCORING

Rank, Player	League	Years	Total	TDs	PATs	FGs
1. George Blanda	NFL-AFL	26	2,002	9	943	335
2. Gary Anderson[1]	NFL	17	1,845	0	585	420
3. Morten Andersen[1]	NFL	17	1,761	0	558	401
4. Nick Lowery	NFL	18	1,711	0	562	383
5. Jan Stenerud	AFL-NFL	19	1,699	0	580	373
6. Norm Johnson[1]	NFL	17	1,657	0	613	346
7. Lou Groza	AAFC-NFL	21	1,608	1	810	264
8. Eddie Murray	NFL	19	1,532	0	521	337
9. Pat Leahy	NFL	18	1,470	0	558	304
10. Jim Turner	AFL-NFL	16	1,439	1	521	304

QUARTERBACK RATING

Rank	Player	Yrs.	Att.	Comp.	Yards	TDs	Int.	Rating
1.	Steve Young[1]	14	4,065	2,622	32,678	229	103	97.6
2.	Joe Montana	15	5,391	3,409	40,551	273	139	92.3
3.	Brett Favre[1]	8	3,757	2,318	26,803	213	118	89.0
4.	Dan Marino[1]	16	7,989	4,763	58,913	408	235	87.3
5.	Mark Brunell[1]	5	1,719	1,038	12,512	72	43	86.3
6.	Jim Kelly	11	4,779	2,874	35,467	237	175	84.4
7.	Roger Staubach	11	2,958	1,685	22,700	153	109	83.4
8.	Troy Aikman[1]	10	4,011	2,479	28,346	141	115	82.8
9.	Neil Lomax	8	3,153	1,817	22,771	136	90	82.7
10.	Sonny Jurgensen	18	4,262	2,433	32,224	255	189	82.6

Passes Completed		Yards Passing		Touchdown Passes	
1. Dan Marino[1]	4,763	1. Dan Marino[1]	58,913	1. Dan Marino[1]	408
2. John Elway[1]	4,123	2. John Elway[1]	51,475	2. Fran Tarkenton	342
3. Warren Moon[1]	3,972	3. Warren Moon[1]	49,097	3. John Elway[1]	300
4. Fran Tarkenton	3,686	4. Fran Tarkenton	47,003	4. Warren Moon[1]	290
5. Joe Montana	3,409	5. Dan Fouts	43,040	4. Johnny Unitas	290
6. Dan Fouts	3,297	6. Joe Montana	40,551	6. Joe Montana	273
7. Dave Krieg[1]	3,105	7. Johnny Unitas	40,239	7. Dave Krieg[1]	261
8. Boomer Esiason	2,969	8. Dave Krieg[1]	38,147	8. Sonny Jurgensen	255
9. Steve DeBerg[1]	2,874	9. Boomer Esiason	37,920	9. Dan Fouts	254
10. Jim Kelly	2,874	10. Jim Kelly	35,467	10. Boomer Esiason	247
11. Jim Everett	2,841	11. Jim Everett	34,837	11. John Hadl	244
12. Johnny Unitas	2,830	12. Jim Hart	34,665	12. Len Dawson	239
13. Ken Anderson	2,654	13. Steve DeBerg[1]	34,241	13. Jim Kelly	237
14. Steve Young[1]	2,622	14. John Hadl	33,503	14. George Blanda	236
15. Jim Hart	2,593	15. Phil Simms	33,462	15. Steve Young[1]	229

Note: Through end of 1998 season. AAFC=All America Football Conference. AFL=American Football League. NFL=National Football League. Quarterback rating is based on a combination of performances in the following four categories: percentage of completions, percentage of touchdown passes, percentage of interceptions and average gain per pass attempts. Minimum 1,500 attempts; through end of 1998 season. 1. Player Active in 1998.   **Source:** *National Football League 1999 Record and Fact Book.*

NFL Champions, 1921–66

Year	Team (record)	Year	Team (record)	Year	Team (record)
1921	Chicago Staleys[1] (10-1-1)	1937	Washington Redskins (8-3-0)	1952	Detroit Lions (9-3-0)
1922	Canton Bulldogs (10-0-2)	1938	New York Giants (8-2-1)	1953	Detroit Lions (10-2-0)
1923	Canton Bulldogs (11-0-1)	1939	Green Bay Packers (9-2-0)	1954	Cleveland Browns (9-3-0)
1924	Cleveland Bulldogs[2] (7-1-1)	1940	Chicago Bears (8-3-0)	1955	Cleveland Browns (9-2-1)
1925	Chicago Cardinals (11-2-1)	1941	Chicago Bears (10-1-1)	1956	New York Giants (8-3-1)
1926	Frankford Yellowjackets (14-1-1)	1942	Washington Redskins (10-1-1)	1957	Detroit Lions (8-4-0)
1927	New York Giants (11-1-1)	1943	Chicago Bears (8-1-1)	1958	Baltimore Colts (9-3-0)
1928	Providence Steamrollers (8-1-2)	1944	Green Bay Packers (8-2-0)	1959	Baltimore Colts (9-3-0)
1929	Green Bay Packers (12-0-1)	1945	Cleveland Rams (9-1-0)	1960	Philadelphia Eagles (10-2-0)
1930	Green Bay Packers (10-3-1)	1946	Chicago Bears (8-2-1)	1961	Green Bay Packers (11-3-0)
1931	Green Bay Packers (12-2-0)	1947	Chicago Cardinals (9-3-0)	1962	Green Bay Packers (13-1-0)
1932	Chicago Bears (7-1-6)	1948	Philadelphia Eagles (9-2-1	1963	Chicago Bears (11-1-2)
1933	Chicago Bears (10-2-1)	1949	Philadelphia Eagles (11-1-0)	1964	Cleveland Browns (10-3-1)
1934	New York Giants (8-5-0)	1950	Cleveland Browns (10-2-0)	1965	Green Bay Packers (10-3-1)
1935	Detroit Lions (7-3-2)	1951	Los Angeles Rams (8-4-0)	1966	Green Bay Packers (12-2-0)
1936	Green Bay Packers (10-1-1)				

1. Later called the Chicago Bears. 2. Franchise moved from Canton.

Super Bowl Results

SUPER BOWL I
Jan. 15, 1967 Memorial Coliseum
Los Angeles, California
Green Bay Packers 35   Kansas City Chiefs 10
Green Bay's Max McGee was a surprise star, filling in for ailing Boyd Dowler. McGee had caught only four passes all year, but in Super Bowl I he caught seven for 138 yards and two touchdowns. Quarterback Bart Starr was the game's MVP, as he completed 16 of 23 passes for 250 yards and two touchdowns. Green Bay broke up the game with three second-half touchdowns, the first of which was set up by safety Willie Wood's 45-yard interception return.

SUPER BOWL II
Jan. 14, 1968, Orange Bowl
Miami, Florida
Green Bay Packers 33   Oakland Raiders 14
Bart Starr again dominated proceedings with 13 completions in 24 attempts, for 202 yards and a touchdown, winning his second straight MVP award. The Pack attack was in control all the way after building a 16–7 halftime lead. Don Chandler kicked four field goals and all-pro cornerback Herb Adderley capped the Green Bay scoring with a 60-yard interception return.

SUPER BOWL III
Jan. 12, 1969, Orange Bowl
Miami, Florida
New York Jets 16   Baltimore Colts 7
New York quarterback Joe Namath guaranteed victory before the game and then he and the upstart AFL Jets easily dispatched the heavily favored Colts. Namath won MVP honors by completing 17 of 28 passes for 206 yards and directing a steady attack that racked up 337 total yards. Three times in the first half, the Jet defense intercepted Colts quarterback Earl Morrall, who was playing for an injured Johnny Unitas. With the Jets ahead 13–0 in the third quarter, Unitas came off the bench and later orchestrated Baltimore's sole touchdown.

SUPER BOWL IV
Jan. 11, 1970, Tulane Stadium
New Orleans, Louisiana
Kansas City Chiefs 23   Minnesota Vikings 7
MVP quarterback Len Dawson called a nearly flawless game for Kansas City, completing 12 of 17 passes and hitting Otis Taylor on a 46-yard pass for the final Chiefs touchdown. The Kansas City defense limited Minnesota's strong rushing game to 67 yards and had three interceptions and two fumble recoveries. The second consecutive victory by an AFL team proved that AFL teams could compete with NFL franchises, and assured a smooth merger between the two leagues.

SUPER BOWL V
Jan. 17, 1971, Orange Bowl
Miami, Florida
Baltimore Colts 16   Dallas Cowboys 13
Rookie Jim O'Brien's 32-yard field goal in the closing seconds broke a 13–13 tie and gave the Colts their first Super Bowl victory. Dallas led 13–6 at halftime, but two Colt interceptions set up a Baltimore touchdown and O'Brien's crucial kick. Baltimore's first touchdown came when a Johnny Unitas pass caromed off receiver Eddie Hinton's fingertips, bounced off Dallas defensive back Mel Renfro, and finally settled into the grasp of tight end John Mackey, who went 47 yards for the score. Dallas linebacker Chuck Howley was the MVP, the only time the MVP came from the losing team.

SUPER BOWL VI
Jan. 16, 1972, Tulane Stadium
New Orleans, Louisiana
Dallas Cowboys 24   Miami Dolphins 3
The Cowboys rushed for 252 yards and their defense limited the Dolphins to 185 total yards and no touchdowns. Dallas converted Chuck Howley's recovery of Larry Csonka's first fumble of the season into a 3–0 advantage. At halftime, Dallas led 10–3. An eight-play, 71-yard march made it a 17–3 game. Cowboys' quarterback Roger Staubach was voted MVP for his 12 completions in 19 attempts, 119 yards passing and two touchdowns.

SUPER BOWL VII
Jan. 14, 1973, Memorial Coliseum
Los Angeles, California
Miami Dolphins 14   Washington Redskins 7
In a game that wasn't as close as the score, the Dolphins thoroughly dominated the Redskins to complete the NFL's only undefeated season. Quarterback Bob Griese hit Paul Warfield for 18 yards, then delivered a 28-yard strike to Howard Twilley for the Dolphins' first score. Just before the half, Dolphins linebacker Nick Buoniconti intercepted a Billy Kilmer pass and returned it to the Washington 27, setting up Miami's second touchdown. Safety Jake Scott led the Dolphin defense with two interceptions (one in the end zone killing a Redskin scoring drive) and was the MVP. The Redskins' sole touchdown resulted when Dolphin kicker Garo Yepremian tried to turn a botched field goal into a forward pass. Washington's Mike Bass picked the ball out of the air and returned it 49 yards for the score.

SUPER BOWL VIII
Jan. 13, 1974, Rice Stadium
Houston, Texas
Miami Dolphins 24   Minnesota Vikings 7
Miami scored on its first two possessions, on 62- and 56-yard marches. The initial 10-play drive was climaxed by a Larry Csonka touchdown bolt through right guard. Four plays later, Miami's Jim Kiick burst one yard through the middle for the second touchdown. By halftime Miami led 17–0. The Dolphins defense held off the Vikings on a crucial fourth-and-one play from the Miami 6-yard-line when middle linebacker Nick Buoniconti jarred the ball loose from Minnesota running back Oscar Reed and Jake Scott recovered for Miami. Csonka rushed 33 times for 145 yards, winning the MVP.

SUPER BOWL IX
Jan, 12, 1975, Tulane Stadium
New Orleans, Louisiana
Pittsburgh Steelers 16   Minnesota 6
Steeler Dwight White tackled Minnesota quarterback Fran Tarkenton in the end zone for a safety to put the Steelers on the board in the second quarter. They took advantage of another break in the second half, when Minnesota's Bill Brown fumbled the kickoff and Marv Kellum recovered for Pittsburgh on the Vikings' 30. From there, Franco Harris carried three straight times for the game's first touchdown. Minnesota blocked a Bobby Walden punt and Terry Brown recovered the ball for a touchdown to cut the lead to 9–6, but the Steelers roared back with a 66-yard march, climaxed by Terry Bradshaw's 4-yard scoring pass to Larry Brown. Pittsburgh's defense controlled the game, permitting Minnesota only 119 yards total offense. Franco Harris rushed 34 times for 158 yards to win MVP honors.

SUPER BOWL X
Jan. 18, 1976, Orange Bowl
Miami Florida
Pittsburgh Steelers 21   Dallas Cowboys 17
Steeler quarterback Terry Bradshaw hurled a 64-yard touchdown pass to Lynn Swann to win the game, while the Steel Curtain defense stopped the Cowboys' last rally with an end-zone interception in the game's final play. It was a battle of quarterbacks with Bradshaw and Cowboy Roger Staubach each hurling two touchdowns. Swann earned MVP honors with 161 yards on four receptions. The Steelers blasted out in front with a 14-point fourth quarter.

SUPER BOWL XI
Jan. 9, 1977, Rose Bowl
Pasadena, California
Oakland Raiders 32   Minnesota Vikings 14
A record 81 million TV viewers watched the Raiders gain a record-breaking 429 yards, including running back Clarence Davis' 137 yards rushing. Wide receiver Fred Biletnikoff made four key receptions, which earned him the game's MVP trophy. Oakland scored on three successive possessions in the second quarter to build a 16–0 halftime lead. Minnesota's Fran Tarkenton passed for a touchdown in the third to cut the deficit, but two fourth-quarter interceptions clinched the title for the Raiders. One set up Pete Banaszak's second touchdown run, the other resulted in cornerback Willie Brown's 75-yard interception return.

SUPER BOWL XII
Jan. 15, 1978, Louisiana Superdome
New Orleans, Louisiana
Dallas Cowboys 27   Denver Broncos 10
The TV audience climbed to 102 million, as Dallas converted two interceptions into 10 points and a 13–0 Dallas halftime lead. Butch Johnson made a spectacular diving catch in the end zone of a Roger Staubach pass to make it 20–3. Dallas clinched the victory when running back Robert Newhouse threw a 29-yard touchdown pass to Golden Richards. Co-MVP's Harvey Martin and Randy White led the Cowboys' defense, which recovered four fumbles and intercepted four passes.

SUPER BOWL XIII
Jan, 21, 1979, Orange Bowl
Miami, Florida
Pittsburgh Steelers 35   Dallas Cowboys 31
MVP Terry Bradshaw hurled four touchdown passes to lead the Steelers to victory, making them the first team to win three Super Bowls. Bradshaw completed 17 of 30 passes for 318 yards. In the fourth quarter, the Steelers broke open the contest with two touchdowns in 19 seconds. Franco Harris rambled 22 yards up the middle to put Pittsburgh in front 28–17. The Steelers got the ball right back when Randy White fumbled the kickoff and Dennis Winston recovered. On first down, Bradshaw hit Lynn Swann with an 18-yard scoring pass to boost the lead to 35–17. The Cowboys came back with a Roger Staubach touchdown pass to Billy Joe DuPree and then recovered an onside kick, which led to another Staubach touchdown pass, this time to Butch Johnson. But Rocky Bleier smothered an onside kick with 17 seconds remaining to seal the victory.

SUPER BOWL XIV
Jan. 20, 1980, Rose Bowl
Pasadena, California
Pittsburgh Steelers 31   Los Angeles Rams 19
It was all Terry Bradshaw again as he completed 14 of 21 passes for 309 records, and set two passing records as the Steelers became the first team to win four Super Bowls. Despite three interceptions by the Rams, Bradshaw brought the Steelers back from behind twice in the second half. On Pittsburgh's first possession of the final period, Bradshaw lofted a 73-yard scoring pass to John Stallworth to put the Steelers in front to stay, 24–19. Franco Harris scored on a one-yard run later to seal the verdict. Bradshaw was the MVP for the second straight Super Bowl.

SUPER BOWL XV
Jan. 25, 1981, Louisiana Superdome
New Orleans, Louisiana
Oakland Raiders 27   Philadelphia Eagles 10
Jim Plunkett threw three touchdown passes, including an 80-yarder to Kenny King, to give Oakland a decisive 14-0 advantage nine seconds before halftime. Oakland linebacker Rod Martin intercepted three passes as the Raiders completely stifled Eagle quarterback Ron Jaworski's offense. Jaworski managed an 8-yard touchdown pass in the fourth quarter, but the issue had been decided by Plunkett, who completed 13 of the 21 pass attempts for 261 yards and was named MVP.

SUPER BOWL XVI
Jan. 24, 1982, Pontiac Silverdome
Pontiac, Michigan
San Francisco 49ers 26   Cincinnati Bengals 21
This was a game of a failed comeback, as the 49ers led 20-0 at halftime, and barely hung onto their lead. Ray Wersching kicked four field goals for San Francisco and quarterback Joe Montana engineered two touchdown drives, passing for one and scoring the other himself on a one-yard dive. The Bengals rebounded in the second half as quarterback Ken Anderson ran in a touchdown and passed for another. With 16 seconds remaining, the Bengals managed to score on an Anderson-to-Dan Ross 3-yard pass, but the odds were too great. Ross set a Super Bowl record with 11 receptions for 104 yards. Montana, the MVP, completed 14 of 22 passes for 157 yards. Cincinnati compiled 356 yards to San Francisco's 275, the first time in Super Bowl history that the team that gained the most yards lost the game.

SUPER BOWL XVII
Jan. 30, 1983, Rose Bowl
Pasadena, California
Washington Redskins 27   Miami Dolphins 17
Washington fullback John Riggins carried the ball for a record 166 yards on 38 carries to lead Washington to victory, their first NFL title since 1942. Their 400 total yards offense, 276 rushing and 124 passing, was paced by Riggins, the MVP, and quarterback Joe Theismann, who passed 23 times for 15 completions, 143 yards, and two touchdowns. Miami opened the scoring with a 76-yard touchdown pass from quarterback David Woodley to wide receiver Jimmy Cefalo. But the game's main force was Riggins, who took the ball on fourth-and-one and ran 43 yards for a touchdown to put Washington in front.

SUPER BOWL XVIII
Jan, 22, 1984, Tampa Stadium
Tampa, Florida
Los Angeles Raiders 38   Washington Redskins 9
This hopelessly lopsided victory set records. Raider reserve linebacker Jack Squirek intercepted a Joe Theismann pass at the Redskins five-yard line and ran the ball in for a touchdown with seven seconds left in the first half. Raiders' Marcus Allen rushed for 191 yards on 20 carries, including two touchdowns, one on a 74-yard run. Allen was voted game MVP.

SUPER BOWL XIX
Jan. 20, 1985, Stanford Stadium
Stanford, California
San Francisco 49ers 38   Miami Dolphins 16
The Dolphins led 10-7 at the end of the first period, but 49er running back Roger Craig came back with three touchdowns. Joe Montana dominated the game with an MVP performance: 24 of 35 passes for a record 331 yards and three touchdowns. He himself rushed five times for 59 yards and a touchdown. Craig had 58 yards on 15 carries and caught seven passes for 77 yards. Wendell Tyler rushed 13 times for 65 yards, as San Francisco's running game racked

up 211 yards. As a team, San Francisco gained 537 yards, while holding the ball for 37:11.

SUPER BOWL XX
Jan 26, 1986 Louisiana Superdome
New Orleans, Louisiana
Chicago Bears 46   New England Patriots 10
The Patriots took a quick 3-0 lead when Tony Franklin kicked a 36-yard field goal with 1:19 elapsed in the first period. But the Bears rebounded by mauling the Pats. Chicago tied the record for sacks (seven), and limited the Pats to 7 yards rushing. Total yardage at intermission told the story: Chicago 236, New England -19. The Bears ran up a fat 23–3 lead in the first half. In the second, the Bears marched 96 yards in nine plays, capped by quarterback Jim McMahon's one-yard rush for a touchdown. Bears defensive end Richard Dent won the MVP after contributing 1½ sacks, and leading the ferocious Chicago defense.

SUPER BOWL XXI
Jan. 25, 1987, Rose Bowl
Pasadena, California
New York Giants 39   Denver Broncos 20
The Broncos held a 10–9 lead at halftime, backed by the passing of John Elway. He capped a 58 yard scoring drive on six plays with a four yard touchdown run. But in the second half, the Giants' defense took over, sacking Elway in his end zone for a safety. The Broncos had a first and goal, but failed to score on three plays and a field goal attempt. After that the Giants' offense rebounded, scoring 30 points in the second half. Giant quarterback Phil Simms set Super Bowl records for most consecutive completions (10), highest completion percentage (88 percent on 22 completions in 25 attempts). He passed for 268 yards and three touchdowns, and was named MVP.

SUPER BOWL XXII
Jan 31, 1988, Jack Murphy Stadium
San Diego, California
Washington Redskins 42   Denver Broncos 10
The Broncos jumped in front early as John Elway hurled a 56-yard touchdown pass to wide receiver Ricky Nattiel on the Broncos' first play from scrimmage. But the Redskins erupted for 35 points on five straight possessions. Redskins' quarterback Doug Williams led the assault, hurling a record-tying four touchdown passes, including 80- and 50-yarders to wide receiver Rick Sanders, and an 8-yarder to tight end Clint Didier. Washington scored five touchdowns in 18 plays in 5:47 of possession. MVP Williams completed 18 of 29 passes for 340 yards. Rookie running back Timmy Smith ran 22 times for 204 yards.

SUPER BOWL XXIII
January 22, 1989, Joe Robbie Stadium
Miami Florida
San Francisco 49ers 20   Cincinnati Bengals 16
San Francisco became the first NFC team to win three Super Bowls by defeating the Bengals in a rematch of Super Bowl XVI. Even though San Francisco held an advantage in total yards (453 vs. 229), they found themselves trailing when Jim Breech's field goal gave Cincinnati a 16–13 lead with 3:20 left in the game. The 49ers started their winning drive at their own 8-yard line. Over the next 11 plays, they drove 92 yards to the winning score, a 10-yard touchdown pass from Joe Montana to wide receiver John Taylor with only 34 seconds remaining. San Francisco's other wide receiver, Jerry Rice, won the MVP after catching 11 passes for 215 yards. Montana completed 23 of 36 passes for 357 yards and two touchdowns.

SUPER BOWL XXIII
Jan. 28,1990, Louisiana Superdome
New Orleans, Louisiana
San Francisco 49ers 55   Denver Broncos 10
San Francisco demolished the Broncos and became the first team to repeat as champions since the 1979–80 Steelers. Quarterback Joe Montana orchestrated the 49ers' diverse offense, completing 22 of 29 passes for 297 yards and five touchdowns, en route to winning the MVP. Montana raised his record to 122 straight Super Bowl pass attempts without an interception. His primary receiver was Jerry Rice, who hauled in seven passes for 148 yards and three touchdowns. Running backs Tom Rathman and Roger Craig ran for three more touchdowns. Meanwhile, the San Francisco defense completely dominated Denver's offense, limiting them to 167 total yards while sacking quarterback John Elway six times and intercepting two passes.

SUPER BOWL XXV
Jan. 27, 1991, Tampa Stadium
Tampa, Florida
New York Giants 20   Buffalo Bills, 19
The Giants edged the Bills in a tightly contested, nearly error-free game that was decided only when the Bills' Scott Norwood missed what would have been the winning field goal with eight seconds to play. Backup quarterback Jeff Hostetler and veteran running back Ottis Anderson directed the Giants' ball-control offense, holding the ball for a stunning 40:33. Anderson carried the ball 21 times for 102 yards and was named the MVP. After falling behind 12–3, the veteran Giants team refused to panic. Their defense slowed Buffalo's vaunted "hurry-up" offense to a crawl, surrounding Jim Kelly's receivers with extra defensive backs and linebackers. Kelly finished the day with 18 completions in 30 attempts for 205 yards, but could rarely convert on crucial third down opportunities. Hostetler, substituting for the injured Phil Simms, led the Giants on touchdown drives of 75 and 87 yards, while completing 20 of 32 passes for 214 yards and allowing no turnovers.

SUPER BOWL XXVI
Jan. 26, 1992, Hubert H. Humphrey Metrodome
Minneapolis, Minnesota
Washington Redskins 37   Buffalo Bills 24
Washington jumped out to a 17-0 lead in the first half and never looked back. MVP quarterback Mark Rypien completed 18 of 33 passes for 292 yards and two touchdowns. Meanwhile, the blitzing Redskin defense intercepted Buffalo quarterback Jim Kelly four times and sacked the Bills' signal-caller five times. Buffalo's no-huddle offense was also plagued by several dropped passes, including two that would have gone for touchdowns. In all, Kelly threw a record 58 passes, 30 of which went incomplete. Brad Edwards, Washington's free safety, had two interceptions and broke up five passes, while linebacker Wilber Marshall forced two fumbles. Bills running back Thurman Thomas, the NFL's regular season MVP, missed the first two plays of the game because he couldn't find his helmet, and was limited to 13 yards on 10 rushes.

SUPER BOWL XXVII
Jan. 31, 1993, Rose Bowl
Pasadena, California
Dallas Cowboys 52   Buffalo Bills 17
Buffalo lost its third straight Super Bowl and the second consecutive rout. Dallas capitalized on nine Bills turnovers, scoring 35 points following Buffalo miscues. The game's turning point came early in the second quarter, when Buffalo drove inside the Dallas five-yard-line twice but came away with only three points, and lost starting quarterback Jim Kelly in the process. Inspired by its defense's two goal line stands, the Cowboys' offense, which had been fairly inept up to this point, came alive for a long scoring drive. The Bills fumbled their first play from scrimmage on the ensuing drive, and one play later, the Cowboys had scored again, this time on a strike from Troy Aikman to Michael Irvin, giving Dallas a 28–10 halftime lead. Aikman passed for four touchdowns and was named MVP.

SUPER BOWL XXVIII
Jan. 30, 1994, Georgia Dome
Atlanta, Georgia
Dallas Cowboys 30   Buffalo Bills 13
Buffalo became the first team in U.S. professional sports history to lose four consecutive championship games. The Bills actually led at halftime 13–6 on the strength of Thurman Thomas's 37 yards rushing and 54- and 28-yard field goals by Steve Christie. But Thomas fumbled on the opening drive of the second half and Dallas safety James Washington returned it 46 yards for a touchdown, tying the game at 13. Dallas then drove the length of the field on its next drive, with running back Emmitt Smith grinding out 61 yards. The Cowboys added another touchdown and a field goal to secure the victory, while the Dallas defense held Buffalo scoreless in the second half. Smith, the league's regular season MVP, was named MVP of the Super Bowl as well.

SUPER BOWL XXIX
Jan. 29, 1995, Joe Robbie Stadium
Miami, Florida
San Francisco 49ers 49   San Diego Chargers 26
Favored by 20 points, (the largest margin in Super Bowl history), San Francisco scored early and often to capture a fifth Super Bowl championship. On the third play from scrimmage, quarterback Steve Young found wide receiver Jerry Rice wide open inside the San Diego 10-yard line. Young threw five more touchdowns and ran for 49 yards, making him the 49ers' leading rusher as well. Rice and running back Ricky Watters each scored three touchdowns. The outcome was never in doubt after halftime, though the Chargers did go on to score two meaningless touchdowns. On the strength of his 24-for-36 for 325 yard performance, Young was the obvious choice for MVP.

SUPER BOWL XXX
January 28, 1996, Sun Devil Stadium
Tempe, Ariz.
Dallas Cowboys 27   Pittsburgh Steelers 17
Dallas scored on its first three possessions, but failed to dominate the game, and led only 13–7 at halftime. In the second half, the Steelers threatened to close the gap, but quarterback Neil O'Donnell stunted the drive by throwing an interception to Cowboy cornerback Larry Brown. Pittsburgh rallied again in the fourth quarter to cut Dallas' lead to 20–17. But O'Donnell threw another interception to Brown, who returned it to the Steeler 6-yard line, setting up the Cowboys' final touchdown and dashing Pittsburgh's hopes for an upset. Brown was the obvious MVP choice.

SUPER BOWL XXXI
January 26, 1997, Louisiana Superdome
New Orleans, Louisiana
Green Bay Packers 35   New England Patriots 21
The Super Bowl Trophy returned to Titletown after a 29-year absence. Packer quarterback Bret Favre hit

Andre Rison for a 54-yard touchdown pass on Green Bay's second play from scrimmage, but the Patriots rallied for a 14–10 first quarter lead. The Packers recaptured the lead with a 17-point second quarter to go ahead 27–10 at halftime. In the second half, New England running back Curtis Martin scored to cut the lead to 27–21, but Desmond Howard returned the ensuing kickoff 99 yards for a touchdown that punctured the Patriots' hopes for an upset. Howard finished with 154 yards on four kickoff returns and 90 yards on six punt returns (244 total yards) to capture MVP honors.

SUPER BOWL XXXII
January 25, 1998, Qualcomm Stadium
San Diego, California
Denver Broncos 31   Green Bay Packers 24
The victory was Denver's first in five tries, and the AFC's first in 13 years. With the game tied at 24 late in the fourth quarter, Denver took over at midfield with a chance to win. A penalty and a pass moved the Broncos closer, and then running back Terrell Davis ran 17 yards to the one-yard-line. On the next play, Davis scored his third touchdown to put Denver ahead 31–24 with less than two minutes remaining. The Packers drove into Denver territory but could not convert a 4th and 6. Davis earned MVP honors for his 30 carries, 157 yards and three touchdowns.

SUPER BOWL XXXIII
Jan. 31, 1999, Pro Player Stadium
Miami, Florida
Denver Broncos 34   Atlanta Falcons 19
Denver quarterback John Elway completed 18 of 29 passes for 336 yards, as the Broncos cruised to their second straight Super Bowl victory. Broncos running back Terrell Davis added 102 yards rushing, and cornerback Darrien Gordon had interception returns of 50 and 58 yards, each setting up a Denver touchdown. Atlanta scored first on a Morten Andersen field goal to take a brief 3–0 lead. But despite driving deep into Denver territory several times, they could not crack the end zone until the fourth quarter, when the outcome was already decided. The game was a swan song for the 38-year-old Elway, who won MVP honors, and retired from pro football three months later.

Pro Football Hall of Fame Members

Alphabetical listing of the members of the Professional Football Hall of Fame. Listing includes enshrinee's name, year of enshrinement, position, and the teams he played for.

Herb Adderley (1980) CB, Packers, Cowboys.
Lance Alworth (1978) WR, Chargers, Cowboys.
Doug Atkins (1982) DE, Browns, Bears, Saints.
Morris (Red) Badgro (1981) E, Yankees, Giants, Dodgers.
Lem Barney (1992) CB, Lions.
Cliff Battles (1968) RB, QB Braves, Redskins. Coach, Dodgers.
Sammy Baugh (1963) QB, Redskins. Coach, Titans, Oilers, Lions.
Chuck Bednarik (1967) C, LB, Eagles.
Bert Bell (1963 Charter) Commissioner, NFL. Founder, Eagles. Coach Eagles, Steelers. Club president, Eagles, Steelers.
Bobby Bell (1983) LB, DE, Chiefs.
Raymond Berry (1973) E, Colts. Coach, Patriots.
Charles W. Bidwill, Sr. (1967) Owner and president, Cardinals.
Fred Biletnikoff (1988) WR, Raiders.
George Blanda (1981) QB, PK, Bears, Colts, Oilers, Raiders.
Mel Blount (1989) CB, Steelers.
Terry Bradshaw (1989) QB, Steelers.
Jim Brown (1971) FB, Browns.
Paul E. Brown (1967) Coach and GM, Browns, Bengals.
Roosevelt Brown (1975) OT, Giants.
Willie Brown (1984) CB, Broncos, Raiders.
Buck Buchanan (1990) DT, Chiefs.
Dick Butkus (1979) LB, Bears.
Earl Campbell (1991) RB, Oilers, Saints.
Tony Canadeo (1974) RB, Packers.
Joe Carr (1963) NFL President.
Guy Chamberlin (1965) E, Bulldogs, Staleys, Yellowjackets, Cardinals. Coach, Bulldogs, Yellowjackets, Cardinals.
Jack Christiansen (1970) DB, Spartans, Lions. Coach, 49ers.
Earl (Dutch) Clark (1970) DB, Spartans, Lions, Rams.
George Connor (1975) OT, DT, LB, Bears.

Jimmy Conzelman (1964) QB, Staleys, Independents, Badgers, Panthers. Owner, Steamrollers, Cardinals, Panthers.
Lou Creekmur, (1996) OL, Lions.
Larry Csonka (1987) RB, Dolphins, Giants.
Al Davis (1992) President, Owner, General Manager, Coach, Raiders. Commissioner, American Football League.
Willie Davis (1981) DE, Browns, Packers.
Len Dawson (1987) QB, Steelers, Browns, Texans, Chiefs.
Eric Dickerson, (1999) RB, Rams, Colts, Raiders, Falcons.
Dan Dierdorf, (1996) OT, Cardinals
Mike Ditka (1988) TE, Bears, Eagles, Cowboys. Coach, Bears.
Art Donovan (1968) DT, Colts, Yankees, Texans.
Tony Dorsett (1994) RB, Cowboys, Broncos.
John (Paddy) Driscoll (1965) QB, Pros, Staleys, Cardinals, Bears. Coach, Cardinals, Bears.
Bill Dudley (1966) RB, Steelers, Lions, Redskins.
Albert Glen (Turk) Edwards (1969) OT, Braves, Redskins. Coach, Redskins.
Weeb Ewbank (1978) Coach, Colts, Jets. General Manager, Jets.
Tom Fears (1970) E, Rams. Coach, Saints.
Jim Finks (1995) QB, Steelers, President, Vikings, Bears, Saints.
Ray Flaherty (1976) E, Wildcats, Yankees, Giants. Coach, Redskins, Yankees.
Len Ford (1976) DE, E, Dons, Browns, Packers.
Dan Fortmann (1965) G, Bears.
Dan Fouts (1993) QB, Chargers.
Frank Gatski (1985) C, Browns, Lions.
Bill George (1974) LB, Bears, Rams.
Joe Gibbs (1996) Coach, Chargers, Redskins.
Frank Gifford (1977) RB, Giants.
Sid Gillman (1983) Coach, Rams, Chargers, Oilers.
Otto Graham (1965) QB, Browns. Coach, Redskins.
Harold (Red) Grange (1963 Charter) RB, Bears, Yankees.

Bud Grant (1994) Coach, Vikings.
(Mean) Joe Greene (1987) DT, Steelers.
Forrest Gregg (1977) OL, Packers, Cowboys. Coach, Browns, Bengals, Packers.
Bob Griese (1990) QB, Dolphins.
Lou Groza (1974) OT, PK Browns.
Joe Guyon (1966) RB, Bulldogs, Indians, Independents, Cowboys, Giants.
George Halas (1963) Founder, Coach, player, Staleys. President, Coach, player, Bears.
Jack Ham (1988) LB, Steelers.
John Hannah (1991) G, Patriots.
Franco Harris (1990) RB, Steelers, Seahawks.
Mike Haynes (1997) CB, Patriots, Raiders.
Ed Healey (1964) OT, Independents, Bears.
Mel Hein (1963) C, Giants. Coach, Dons.
Ted Hendricks (1990) LB, Colts, Packers, Raiders
Wilbur (Pete) Henry (1963) OT, Bulldogs, Giants, Maroons. Coach, Maroons.
Arnie Herber (1966) QB, Packers, Giants.
Bill Hewitt (1971) E, Bears, Eagles.
Clarke Hinkle (1964) RB, Packers.
Elroy (Crazylegs) Hirsch (1968) HB, E, Rockets, Rams.
Paul Hornung (1986) HB, Packers.
Ken Houston (1986) S, Oilers, Redskins.
Cal Hubbard (1963) OT, Giants, Packers, Pirates.
Sam Huff (1982) LB, Giants, Redskins.
Lamar Hunt (1972) Founder, AFL; Owner Texans, Chiefs.
Don Hutson (1963) E, Packers.
Jimmy Johnson (1994) CB, 49ers.
John Henry Johnson (1987) RB, 49ers, Lions, Steelers, Oilers.
Charlie Joiner (1996), WR, Oilers, Bengals, Chargers.
David (Deacon) Jones (1980) DE, Rams, Chargers, Redskins.
Stan Jones (1991) G, DT, Bears, Redskins.
Henry Jordan (1995) DT, Packers.
Sonny Jurgensen (1983) QB, Eagles, Redskins.
Leroy Kelly (1994) RB, Browns.
Walt Kiesling (1966) G, Eskimos, Maroons, Cardinals, Bears, Packers, Pirates. Coach, Pirates, Steelers.
Frank (Bruiser) Kinard (1971) OT, Dodgers, Yankees.
Paul Krause (1998) S, Vikings, Redskins.
Early (Curly) Lambeau (1963) RB, Packers. Founder, Packers. Coach, Packers, Cardinals, Redskins.
Jack Lambert (1990) LB, Steelers.
Tom Landry (1990) Coach, Cowboys.
Dick (Night Train) Lane (1974). DB, Rams, Cardinals, Lions.
Jim Langer (1987) C, Dolphins, Vikings.
Willie Lanier (1986) LB, Chiefs.
Steve Largent (1995) WR, Seahawks.
Yale Lary (1979) DB, Lions.
Dante Lavelli (1975) E, Browns.
Bobby Layne (1967) QB, Bears, Bulldogs, Lions, Steelers.
Alphonse (Tuffy) Leemans (1978) RB, Giants.
Bob Lilly (1980) DT, Cowboys.
Larry Little (1993) G, Chargers, Dolphins.
Vince Lombardi (1971) Coach, GM, Packers, Redskins.
Sid Luckman (1965) QB, Bears.
William Roy (Link) Lyman (1964) T, Bulldogs, Yellowjackets, Bears.
Tom Mack (1999) OG, Rams.
John Mackey (1992) TE, Colts, Chargers.
Tim Mara (1963) Founder, President, Giants.
Wellington Mara (1997) Owner, Giants
Gino Marchetti (1972) DE, Texans, Colts.

George Preston Marshall (1963) Founder, President, Braves (Redskins).
Ollie Matson (1972) RB, Cardinals, Rams, Lions, Eagles.
Don Maynard (1987) WR, Giants, Titans, Jets, Cardinals.
George McAfee (1966) RB, Bears.
Mike McCormack (1984) OT, Yankees, Browns. Coach, Eagles, Colts, Seahawks.
Tommy McDonald (1988) WR, Eagles, Cowboys, Rams, Falcons, Browns.
Hugh McElhenny (1970) RB, 49ers Vikings, Giants, Lions.
Johnny (Blood) McNally (1963) RB, Badgers, Eskimos, Maroons, Packers, Pirates Packers. Coach, Pirates.
Mike Michalske (1964) G, Yankees, Packers.
Wayne Millner (1968) E, Redskins. Coach Eagles.
Bobby Mitchell (1983) WR, RB Browns, Redskins.
Ron Mix (1979) OT Chargers, Raiders.
Lenny Moore (1975) WR, RB, Colts.
Marion Motley (1968) RB, Browns, Steelers.
Anthony Muñoz (1998) T, Bengals.
George Musso (1982) OT, G, Bears.
Bronko Nagurski (1963) RB, Bears.
Joe Namath (1985) QB, Jets, Rams.
Earle (Greasy) Neale (1969) E, Bulldogs. Coach, Eagles.
Ernie Nevers (1963) RB, Eskimos, Cardinals. Coach, Eskimos, Cardinals.
Ozzie Newsome (1999) TE, Browns.
Ray Nitschke (1978) LB, Packers.
Chuck Noll (1993) Coach, Steelers.
Leo Nomellini (1969) DT, 49ers.
Merlin Olsen (1982) DT, Rams.
Jim Otto (1980) C, Raiders.
Steve Owen (1966) T, Cowboys, Giants. Coach, Giants.
Alan Page (1988) DT, Vikings, Bears.
Clarence (Ace) Parker (1972) QB, Dodgers, Yankees.
Jim Parker (1973) OL, Colts.
Walter Payton (1993) RB, Bears.
Joe Perry (1969) RB, 49ers, Colts.
Pete Pihos (1970) E, Eagles.
Hugh (Shorty) Ray Supervisor of Officials.
Dan Reeves (1967) Owner, Rams.
Mel Renfro (1996), CB, Cowboys.
John Riggins (1992) RB, Jets, Redskins.
Jim Ringo (1981) C, Packers, Eagles; Coach, Bills.
Andy Robustelli (1971) DE, Rams, Giants.
Art Rooney (1964) Founder, President, Pirates, Steelers.
Pete Rozelle (1985) Commissioner, NFL.
Bob St. Clair (1990) OT, 49ers.
Gale Sayers (1977) RB, Bears.
Joe Schmidt (1973) LB, Lions. Coach, Lions.
Tex Schramm (1991) GM, Cowboys.
Lee Roy Selmon (1995) DE, Buccaneers.
Billy Shaw (1999) OG, Bills.
Art Shell (1989) OT, Raiders. Coach, Raiders.
Don Shula (1997) Coach, Colts, Dolphins.
Mike Singletary (1998) LB, Bears.
O.J. Simpson (1985) RB, Bills, 49ers
Jackie Smith (1994) TE, Cardinals, Cowboys.
Bart Starr (1977) QB, Packers. Coach, Packers.
Roger Staubach (1985) QB, Cowboys.
Ernie Stautner (1969) DT, Steelers.
Jan Stenerud (1991) PK, Chiefs, Packers, Vikings.
Dwight Stephenson (1998) C, Dolphins.
Ken Strong (1967) RB, Stapletons, Giants, Yankees.
Joe Stydahar (1967) OT, Bears. Coach, Rams, Cardinals.
Fran Tarkenton (1986) QB, Giants, Vikings.

Charley Taylor (1984) WR, RB, Redskins.
Jim Taylor (1976) RB, Packers, Saints.
Lawrence Taylor (1999) LB, Giants.
Jim Thorpe (1963) RB, Bulldogs, Indians, Maroons, Independents, Giants, Bulldogs, Cardinals. Coach, Bulldogs, Indians.
Y.A. Tittle (1971) QB, Colts 49ers, Giants.
George Trafton (1964) C, Staleys, Bears.
Charley Trippi (1968) RB, QB, Cardinals.
Emlen Tunnell (1967) DB, Giants, Packers.
Clyde (Bulldog) Turner (1966) C, LB, Bears. Coach, Titans.
Johnny Unitas (1979) QB, Colts, Chargers.
Gene Upshaw (1987) G, Raiders.

Norm Van Brocklin (1971) QB, Rams, Eagles. Coach, Vikings, Falcons.
Steve Van Buren (1965) RB, Eagles.
Doak Walker (1986) RB, Lions.
Bill Walsh (1993) Coach, 49ers.
Paul Warfield (1983) WR, Browns, Dolphins.
Bob Waterfield (1965) QB, Coach, Rams.
Mike Webster (1997) C, Steelers.
Arnie Weinmeister, (1984) DT, Yankees, Giants.
Randy White (1994) DT, Cowboys.
Bill Willis (1977) G, MG, Browns.
Larry Wilson (1978) DB, Cardinals.
Kellen Winslow (1995) TE, Chargers.

BASKETBALL

National Basketball Association

Olympic Tower   www.nba.com
645 Fifth Avenue   Commissioner: David Stern
New York, NY 10022   Founded: 1946
(212) 826-7000   Number of teams: 29

Dr. James Naismith invented basketball in 1891, only after his indoor versions of lacrosse, rugby, and soccer proved too violent for the intended use in a YMCA fitness program. Yet even his "noncontact" amateur sport proved too rough for many YMCAs, which dropped basketball. Teams were forced to rent halls; they charged an admission fee to pay the rent, and split any leftover cash among the players.

The first pro game was played in 1896 in Trenton, N.J., and by 1898, the fledgling National Basketball League and several others were organized. The Buffalo Germans were the first powerhouse, winning 792 games against only 86 losses from 1895 to 1925. In 1914, the New York Celtics (later renamed the Original Celtics) were organized, playing a "modern" style of basketball using zone defenses, the fast break, and a pivot man.

Other "ethnic" teams dominated in the 1930s, including the Philadelphia SPHAs (South Philadelphia Hebrew Association) under Eddy Gottlieb, and the black barnstorming New York Rens. Several weak leagues continued to compete until the end of World War II. The Basketball Association of America was formed in 1946 by hockey arena managers seeking additional tenants. By 1949, it had merged with its biggest rival to form the modern NBA.

The American Basketball Association, an alternative pro league known for its three-point shots and its red, white and blue ball, lasted for nine seasons (1968–76) and featured such future NBA All-Stars as Julius Erving and Artis Gilmore. When the league folded after the 1975–76 season, four of its teams, the Denver Nuggets, Indiana Pacers, New York (now New Jersey) Nets, and San Antonio Spurs were admitted into the NBA.

The NBA expanded cautiously in the 1970s. Cleveland joined the league in 1970 along with Portland and the Buffalo Braves (now the Los Angeles Clippers); New Orleans received a franchise in 1974 but lost it to Utah in 1979; and in 1980, the NBA expanded to Dallas. Charlotte and Miami joined in 1988, followed by Orlando and Minnesota in 1989. The two Canadian expansion teams, Vancouver and Toronto, joined in 1995.

In 1998, the NBA experienced its first-ever work stoppage, when owners locked out players for the first three months of the season. The two sides reached agreement on a new collective bargaining agreement on January 7, 1999, and began a 50-game season on February 5.

Under the terms of the new agreement, which is in effect until 2003–2004, player salaries are capped at 48 percent of gross income ($30 million per team in 1998–99; $34 million per team in 1999–2000), individual salaries may not exceed $14 million per year ($9 million for players with less than 6 years experience; $11 million for players with 7–9 years service), and players in their first three years of service have severely limited contracts.

NBA Final Standings, 1998–99

EASTERN CONFERENCE	W	L	Pct.	Home	Away
Atlantic Division					
Miami Heat (1)	33	17	.660	18–7	15–10
Orlando Magic (3)	33	17	.660	21–4	12–13
Philadelphia 76ers (6)	28	22	.560	17–8	11–14
New York Knicks (8)	27	23	.540	19–6	8–17
Boston Celtics	19	31	.380	10–15	9–16
Washington Wizards	18	32	.360	13–12	5–20
New Jersey Nets	16	34	.320	12–13	4–21
Central Division					
Indiana Pacers (2)	33	17	.660	18–7	15–10
Atlanta Hawks (4)	31	19	.620	16–9	15–10
Detroit Pistons (5)	29	21	.580	17–8	12–13
Milwaukee Bucks (7)	28	22	.560	17–8	11–14
Charlotte Hornets	26	24	.520	16–9	10–15
Toronto Raptors	23	27	.460	14–11	9–16
Cleveland Cavaliers	22	28	.440	15–10	7–18
Chicago Bulls	13	37	.260	8–17	5–20

WESTERN CONFERENCE	W	L	Pct.	Home	Away
Midwest Division					
San Antonio Spurs (1)	37	13	.740	21–4	16–9
Utah Jazz (3)	37	13	.740	22–3	15–10
Houston Rockets (5)	31	19	.620	19–6	12–13
Minnesota Timberwolves (8)	25	25	.500	18–7	7–18
Dallas Mavericks	19	31	.380	15–10	4–21
Denver Nuggets	14	36	.280	12–13	2–23
Vancouver Grizzlies	8	42	.160	7–18	1–24
Pacific Division					
Portland Trailblazers (2)	35	15	.700	22–3	13–12
Los Angeles Lakers (4)	31	19	.620	18–7	13–12
Sacramento Kings (6)	27	23	.540	16–9	11–14
Phoenix Suns (7)	27	23	.540	15–10	12–13
Seattle Super Sonics	25	25	.500	17–8	8–17
Golden State Warriors	21	29	.420	13–12	8–17
Los Angeles Clippers	9	41	.180	6–19	3–22

Note: The numbers in parentheses reflect the team's seed for the playoffs.   **Source:** NBA.

NBA Playoff Results, 1998–99

FIRST ROUND

EASTERN CONFERENCE

Miami (1) v. New York (8)
New York 95, MIAMI 75
MIAMI 83, New York 73
NEW YORK 97, Miami 73
Miami 87, NEW YORK 72
New York 78, MIAMI 77
(New York wins series 3–2)

Indiana (2) v. Milwaukee (7)
INDIANA 110, Milwaukee 88
INDIANA 108, Milwaukee 107 (OT)
Indiana 99, MILWAUKEE 91
(Indiana wins series 3–0)

Orlando (3) v. Philadelphia (6)
Philadelphia 104, ORLANDO 94
ORLANDO 79, Philadelphia 68
PHILADELPHIA 87, Orlando 75
PHILADELPHIA 101, Orlando 91
(Philadelphia wins series 3–1)

Atlanta (4) vs. Detroit (5)
ATLANTA 90, Detroit 70
ATLANTA 89, Detroit 69
DETROIT 79, Atlanta 63
DETROIT 103, Atlanta 82
ATLANTA 87, Detroit 75
(Atlanta wins series 3–2)

WESTERN CONFERENCE

San Antonio (1) v. Minnesota (8)
SAN ANTONIO 99, Minnesota 86
Minnesota 80, SAN ANTONIO 71
San Antonio 85 , MINNESOTA 71
San Antonio 92, MINNESOTA 85
(San Antonio wins series 3–1)

Portland (2) v. Phoenix Suns (7)
PORTLAND 95, Phoenix 85
PORTLAND 110, Phoenix 99
Portland 103, PHOENIX 93
(Portland wins series 3–0)

Utah (3) v. Sacramento (6)
UTAH 117, Sacramento 87
Sacramento 101, UTAH 90
SACRAMENTO 84, Utah 81 (OT)
Utah 90, SACRAMENTO 89
UTAH 99, Sacramento 92 (OT)
(Utah wins series 3–2)

Los Angeles Lakers (4) vs. Houston (5)
L.A. LAKERS 101, Houston 100
L.A. LAKERS 110, Houston 98
HOUSTON 102, L.A. Lakers 88
L.A. Lakers 92, HOUSTON 85
(L.A. Lakers win series 3–1)

CONFERENCE SEMIFINALS

Atlanta v. New York
New York 100, ATLANTA 92
New York 77, ATLANTA 70
NEW YORK 90, Atlanta 78
NEW YORK 79, Atlanta 66
(New York wins series 4–0)

Indiana v. Philadelphia
INDIANA 94, Philadelphia 90
INDIANA 85, Philadelphia 82
Indiana 97, PHILADELPHIA 86
Indiana 89, PHILADELPHIA 86
(Indiana wins series 4–0)

San Antonio v. Los Angeles Lakers
SAN ANTONIO 87, L.A. Lakers 81
SAN ANTONIO 79, L.A. Lakers 76
San Antonio 103, L.A. LAKERS 91
San Antonio 118, L.A. LAKERS 107
(San Antonio wins series 4–0)

Portland v. Utah
UTAH 93, Portland 83
Portland 84, UTAH 81
PORTLAND 97, Utah 87
PORTLAND 81, Utah 75
UTAH 88, Portland 71
PORTLAND 92, Utah 80
(Portland wins series 4–2)

CONFERENCE FINALS

New York v. Indiana
New York 93, INDIANA 90
INDIANA 88, New York 86
NEW YORK 92, Indiana 91
Indiana 90, NEW YORK 78
New York 101, INDIANA 94
NEW YORK 90, Indiana 82
(New York wins series 4–2)

San Antonio v. Portland
SAN ANTONIO 80, Portland 76
SAN ANTONIO 86, Portland 85
San Antonio 85, PORTLAND 63
San Antonio 94, PORTLAND 80
(San Antonio wins series 4–0)

NBA CHAMPIONSHIP SERIES
New York v. San Antonio

SAN ANTONIO 89, New York 77
SAN ANTONIO 80, New York 67
NEW YORK 89, San Antonio 81

San Antonio 96, NEW YORK 89
San Antonio 78, NEW YORK 77

(San Antonio wins series 4–1)

Note: Home team in CAPS. Numbers in parentheses reflect team's playoff seed.

NBA Leaders, 1998–99

SCORING	G	Pts.	Avg.
Allen Iverson, Philadelphia	48	1,284	26.8
Shaquille O'Neal, L.A. Lakers	49	1,289	26.3
Karl Malone, Utah	49	1,164	23.8
Shareef Abdur-Rahim, Vancouver	50	1,152	23.0
Keith Van Horn, New Jersey	42	916	21.8
Tim Duncan, San Antonio	50	1,084	21.7
Gary Payton, Seattle	50	1,084	21.7
Stephon Marbury, Minnesota-New Jersey	49	1,044	21.3
Antnio McDyess, Denver	50	1,061	21.2
Grant Hill, Detroit	50	1,053	21.1
Kevin Garnett, Minnesota	47	977	20.8
Shawn Kemp, Cleveland	42	862	20.5
Michael Finley, Dallas	50	1,009	20.2
Alonzo Mourning, Miami	46	924	20.1
Kobe Bryant, L.A. Lakers	50	996	19.9
Mitch Richmond, Sacramento	50	983	19.7
Hakeem Olajuwon, Houston	50	945	18.9
Toni Kukoc, Chicago	44	828	18.8
Reggie Miller, Indiana	50	920	18.4
Glenn Robinson, Milwaukee	47	865	18.4

REBOUNDS	G	Reb.	Avg.
Chris Webber, Sacramento	42	545	13.0
Charles Barkley, Houston	42	516	12.3
Dikembe Mutombo, Atlanta	50	610	12.2
Danny Fortson, Denver	50	581	11.6
Tim Duncan, San Antonio	50	571	11.4
Alonzo Mourning, Miami	46	507	11.0
Antonio McDyess, Denver	50	537	10.7
Shaquille O'Neal, L.S. Lakers	49	525	10.7
Kevin Garnett, Minnesota	47	489	10.4
Vlade Divac, Sacramento	50	501	10.0
David Robinson, San Antonio	49	492	10.0

ASSISTS	G	No.	Avg.
Jason Kidd, Phoenix	50	539	10.8
Rod Strickland, Washington	44	434	9.9
Stephon Marbury, New Jersey	49	437	8.9
Gary Payton, Seattle	50	436	8.7
Terrell Brandon, Minnesota	36	309	8.6
Mark Jackson, Indiana	49	386	7.9
Brevin Knight, Cleveland	39	302	7.7
John Stockton, Utah	50	374	7.5
Avery Johnson, San Antonio	50	369	7.4
Nick Van Exel, Denver	50	368	7.4

BLOCKED SHOTS	G	No.	Avg.
Alonzo Mourning, Miami	46	180	3.91
Shawn Bradley, Dallas	49	159	3.24
Theo Ratliff, Philadelphia	50	149	2.98
Dikembe Mutombo, Atlanta	50	147	2.94
Greg Ostertag, Utah	48	131	2.73
Patrick Ewing, New York	38	100	2.63
Tim Duncan, San Antonio	50	126	2.52
Hakeem Olajuwon, Houston	50	123	2.46
David Robinson, San Antonio	49	119	2.43
Antonio McDyess, Denver	50	115	2.30

STEALS	G	No.	Avg.
Kendall Gill, New Jersey	50	134	2.68
Eddie Jones, Charlotte	50	125	2.50
Allen Iverson, Philadelphia	48	110	2.29
Jason Kidd, Phoenix	50	114	2.28
Doug Christie, Toronto	50	113	2.26
Penny Hardaway, Orlando	50	111	2.22
Gary Payton, Seattle	50	109	2.18
Darrell Armstrong, Orlando	50	108	2.16
Eric Snow, Philadelphia	48	100	2.08
Mookie Blaylock, Atlanta	48	99	2.06
Charlie Ward, New York	50	103	2.06

3-PT. FIELD GOALS	FGM	FGA	Pct.
Dell Curry, Charlotte	69	145	.476
Chris Mullin, Indiana	73	157	.465
Hubert Davis, Dallas	65	144	.451
Walt Williams, Portland	63	144	.438
Michael Dickerson, Houston	71	164	.433
Dale Ellis, Seattle	94	217	.433
Jeff Hornacek, Utah	34	81	.420
Clifford Robinson, Phoenix	58	139	.417
George McCloud, Phoenix	69	166	.416
Jud Buechler, Detroit	61	148	.412
Paul Pierce, Boston	84	204	.412

MINUTES PER GAME	G	Min.	Avg.
Allen Iverson, Philadelphia	48	1,990	41.5
Jason Kidd, Phoenix	50	2,060	41.2
Michael Finley, Dallas	50	2,051	41.0
Chris Webber, Sacramento	42	1,719	40.9
Shareef Abdur-Rahim, Vancouver	50	2,021	40.4
Gary Payton, Seattle	50	2,008	40.2
Scottie Pippen, Houston	50	2,011	40.2
Juwan Howard, Washington	36	1,430	39.7
Tim Duncan, San Antonio	50	1,963	39.3
Penny Hardaway, Orlando	50	1,944	38.9

FIELD GOAL PERCENTAGE	FGM	FGA	Pct.
Shaquille O'Neal, L.A. Lakers	510	885	.576
Otis Thorpe, Washington	240	440	.545
Hakeem Olajuwon, Houston	373	725	.514
Alonzo Mourning, Miami	324	634	.511
David Robinson, San Antonio	268	527	.509
Rasheed Wallace, Portland	242	476	.508
Bison Dele, Detroit	216	431	.501
Tim Duncan, San Antonio	418	845	.495
Danny Fortson, Denver	191	386	.495
Vitaly Potapenko, Boston	204	412	.495

FREE THROW PERCENTAGE	FTM	FTA	Pct.
Reggie Miller, Indiana	226	247	.915
Chauncey Billups, Denver	157	172	.913
Darrell Armstrong, Orlando	161	178	.904
Ray Allen, Milwaukee	176	195	.903
Hersey Hawkins, Seattle	119	132	.902
Jeff Hornacek, Utah	125	140	.893
Chris Mullin, Indiana	80	92	.870
Glenn Robinson, Milwaukee	140	161	.870
Mario Elie, San Antonio	103	119	.866
Eric Piatkowski, L.A. Clippers	88	102	.863

NBA World Championship Series

Year	Winner	Loser	Games	Year	Winner	Loser	Games
1947	Philadelphia Warriors	Chicago Stags	4-1	1974	Boston Celtics	Milwaukee Bucks	4-3
1948	Baltimore Bullets	Philadelphia Warriors	4-2	1975	Golden State Warriors	Washington Bullets	4-0
1949	Minneapolis Lakers	Washington Capitols	4-2	1976	Boston Celtics	Phoenix Suns	4-2
1950	Minneapolis Lakers	Syracuse Nationals	4-2	1977	Portland Trail Blazers	Philadelphia 76ers	4-2
1951	Rochester Royals	New York Knicks	4-3	1978	Washington Bullets	Seattle SuperSonics	4-3
1952	Minneapolis Lakers	New York Knicks	4-3	1979	Seattle SuperSonics	Washington Bullets	4-1
1953	Minneapolis Lakers	New York Knicks	4-1	1980	Los Angeles Lakers	Philadelphia 76ers	4-2
1954	Minneapolis Lakers	Syracuse Nationals	4-3	1981	Boston Celtics	Houston Rockets	4-2
1955	Syracuse Nationals	Fort Wayne Pistons	4-3	1982	Los Angeles Lakers	Philadelphia 76ers	4-2
1956	Philadelphia Warriors	Fort Wayne Pistons	4-1	1983	Philadelphia 76ers	Los Angeles Lakers	4-0
1957	Boston Celtics	St. Louis Hawks	4-3	1984	Boston Celtics	Los Angeles Lakers	4-3
1958	St. Louis Hawks	Boston Celtics	4-2	1985	Los Angeles Lakers	Boston Celtics	4-2
1959	Boston Celtics	Minneapolis Lakers	4-0	1986	Boston Celtics	Houston Rockets	4-2
1960	Boston Celtics	St. Louis Hawks	4-3	1987	Los Angeles Lakers	Boston Celtics	4-2
1961	Boston Celtics	St. Louis Hawks	4-1	1988	Los Angeles Lakers	Detroit Pistons	4-3
1962	Boston Celtics	Los Angeles Lakers	4-3	1989	Detroit Pistons	Los Angeles Lakers	4-0
1963	Boston Celtics	Los Angeles Lakers	4-2	1990	Detroit Pistons	Portland Trail Blazers	4-1
1964	Boston Celtics	San Francisco Warriors	4-1	1991	Chicago Bulls	Los Angeles Lakers	4-1
1965	Boston Celtics	Los Angeles Lakers	4-1	1992	Chicago Bulls	Portland Trail Blazers	4-2
1966	Boston Celtics	Los Angeles Lakers	4-3	1993	Chicago Bulls	Phoenix Suns	4-2
1967	Philadelphia	San Francisco Warriors	4-2	1994	Houston Rockets	New York Knicks	4-3
1968	Boston Celtics	Los Angeles Lakers	4-2	1995	Houston Rockets	Orlando Magic	4-0
1969	Boston Celtics	Los Angeles Lakers	4-3	1996	Chicago Bulls	Seattle SuperSonics	4-2
1970	New York Knicks	Los Angeles Lakers	4-3	1997	Chicago Bulls	Utah Jazz	4-2
1971	Milwaukee Bucks	Baltimore Bullets	4-0	1998	Chicago Bulls	Utah Jazz	4-2
1972	Los Angeles Lakers	New York Knicks	4-1	1999	San Antonio Spurs	New York Knicks	4-1
1973	New York Knicks	Los Angeles Lakers	4-1				

NBA Finals MVPs, 1980–99

Year	Name, Team	Year	Name, Team
1980	Magic Johnson, Los Angeles Lakers	1990	Isiah Thomas, Detroit Pistons
1981	Cedric Maxwell, Boston Celtics	1991	Michael Jordan, Chicago Bulls
1982	Magic Johnson, Los Angeles Lakers	1992	Michael Jordan, Chicago Bulls
1983	Moses Malone, Philadelphia 76ers	1993	Michael Jordan, Chicago Bulls
1984	Larry Bird, Boston Celtics	1994	Hakeem Olajuwon, Houston Rockets
1985	Kareem Abdul-Jabbar, Los Angeles Lakers	1995	Hakeem Olajuwon, Houston Rockets
1986	Larry Bird, Boston Celtics	1996	Michael Jordan, Chicago Bulls
1987	Magic Johnson, Los Angeles Lakers	1997	Michael Jordan, Chicago Bulls
1988	James Worthy, Los Angeles Lakers	1998	Michael Jordan, Chicago Bulls
1989	Joe Dumars, Detroit Pistons	1999	Tim Duncan, San Antonio Spurs

1999 NBA First Round Draft Picks

Rank, Team	Player, College	Pos.	Rank, Team	Player, College	Pos.
1. Chicago	Elton Brand, Duke	F	17. Atlanta	Cal Bowdler, Old Dominion	F
2. Vancouver	Steve Francis, Maryland	G	18. Denver	James Posey, Xavier	G
3. Charlotte	Baron Davis, UCLA	G	19. Utah	Quincy Lewis, Minnesota	F
4. L.A. Clippers	Lamar Odom, Rhode Island	F	20. Atlanta	Dion Glover, Georgia Tech	G
5. Toronto	Jonathan Bender, Picayune HS (Miss.)	F	21. Golden State[2]	Jeff Foster, SW Texas State	C
6. Minnesota	Wally Szczerbiak, Miami (Ohio)	F	22. Houston	Kenny Thomas, New Mexico	F
7. Washington	Richard Hamilton, UConn.	G	23. L.A. Lakers	Devean George, Augsburg (Minn.)	G
8. Cleveland	Andre Miller, Utah	G	24. Utah	Andrei Kirilenko, CSKA (Russia)	F
9. Phoenix	Shawn Marion, UNLV	F	25. Miami	Tim James, Miami (Fla.)	F
10. Atlanta	Jason Terry, Arizona	G	26. Indiana[2]	Vonteego Cummings, Pittsburgh	G
11. Cleveland	Trajan Langdon, Duke	G	27. Atlanta[3]	Jumaine Jones, Georgia	F
12. Toronto	Aleksandar Radojevic, Barton County CC (Kan.)	C	28. Utah	Scott Padgett, Kentucky	F
13. Seattle[1]	Corey Maggette, Duke	F	29. San Antonio[4]	Leon Smith, Martin Luther King HS (Chicago)	F
14. Minnesota	William Avery, Duke	G			
15. New York	Frederic Weis, Limoges (France)	C			
16. Chicago	Ron Artest, St. John's	G			

1. Seattle traded Maggette along with Billy Owens, Dale Ellis and Don MacLean to Orlando for Horace Grant and two second-round picks. 2. Golden State traded Foster to Indiana for Vonteego Cummings and a future first-round pick. 3. Atlanta traded Jones to Philadelphia for a future first-round pick. 4. San Antonio traded Smith to Dallas for rights to Gordan Giricek and future second-round pick.
Source: National Basketball Association.

NBA Rookies of the Year

Year	Name	Team	Year	Name	Team
1952–53	Don Meineke	Fort Wayne Pistons	1976–77	Adrian Dantley	Buffalo Braves
1953–54	Ray Felix	Baltimore Bullets	1977–78	Walter Davis	Phoenix Suns
1974–75	Keith Wilkes	Golden State Warriors	1978–79	Phil Ford	Kansas City Kings
1954–55	Bob Pettit	Milwaukee Hawks	1979–80	Larry Bird	Boston Celtics
1955–56	Maurice Stokes	Rochester Royals	1980–81	Darrell Griffith	Utah Jazz
1956–57	Tom Heinsohn	Boston Celtics	1981–82	Buck Williams	New Jersey Nets
1957–58	Woody Sauldsberry	Philadelphia Warriors	1982–83	Terry Cummings	San Diego Clippers
1958–59	Elgin Baylor	Minneapolis Lakers	1983–84	Ralph Sampson	Houston Rockets
1959–60	Wilt Chamberlain	Philadelphia Warriors	1984–85	Michael Jordan	Chicago Bulls
1960–61	Oscar Robertson	Cincinnati Royals	1985–86	Patrick Ewing	New York Knicks
1961–62	Walt Bellamy	Chicago Bulls	1986–87	Chuck Person	Indiana Pacers
1962–63	Terry Dischinger	Chicago Bulls	1987–88	Mark Jackson	New York Knicks
1963–64	Jerry Lucas	Cincinnati Royals	1988–89	Mitch Richmond	Golden State Warriors
1964–65	Willis Reed	New York Knicks	1989–90	David Robinson	San Antonio Spurs
1965–66	Rick Barry	San Francisco Warriors	1990–91	Derrick Coleman	New Jersey Nets
1966–67	Dave Bing	Detroit Pistons	1991–92	Larry Johnson	Charlotte Hornets
1967–68	Earl Monroe	Baltimore Bullets	1992–93	Shaquille O'Neal	Orlando Magic
1968–69	Wes Unseld	Baltimore Bullets	1993–94	Chris Webber	Golden State Warriors
1969–70	Kareem Abdul-Jabbar	Milwaukee Bucks	1994–95	(tie) Grant Hill	Detroit Pistons
1970–71	(tie) Dave Cowens	Boston Celtics		Jason Kidd	Dallas Mavericks
	Geoff Petrie	Portland Trail Blazers	1995–96	Damon Stoudamire	Toronto Raptors
1971–72	Sidney Wicks	Portland Trail Blazers	1996–97	Allen Iverson	Philadelphia 76ers
1972–73	Bob McAdoo	Buffalo Braves	1997–98	Tim Duncan	San Antonio Spurs
1973–74	Ernie DiGregorio	Buffalo Braves	1998–99	Vince Carter	Toronto Raptors
1975–76	Alvin Adams	Phoenix Suns			

NBA Most Valuable Players

Year	Name	Team	Year	Name	Team
1955–56	Bob Pettit	St. Louis Hawks	1977–78	Bill Walton	Portland Trail Blazers
1956–57	Bob Cousy	Boston Celtics	1978–79	Moses Malone	Houston Rockets
1957–58	Bill Russell	Boston Celtics	1979–80	Kareem Abdul-Jabbar	Los Angeles Lakers
1958–59	Bob Pettit	St. Louis Hawks	1980–81	Julius Erving	Philadelphia 76ers
1959–60	Wilt Chamberlain	Phil. Warriors	1981–82	Moses Malone	Houston Rockets
1960–61	Bill Russell	Boston Celtics	1982–83	Moses Malone	Philadelphia 76ers
1961–62	Bill Russell	Boston Celtics	1983–84	Larry Bird	Boston Celtics
1962–63	Bill Russell	Boston Celtics	1984–85	Larry Bird	Boston Celtics
1963–64	Oscar Robertson	Cincinnati Royals	1985–86	Larry Bird	Boston Celtics
1964–65	Bill Russell	Boston Celtics	1986–87	Magic Johnson	Los Angeles Lakers
1965–66	Wilt Chamberlain	Philadelphia 76ers	1987–88	Michael Jordan	Chicago Bulls
1966–67	Wilt Chamberlain	Philadelphia 76ers	1988–89	Magic Johnson	Los Angeles Lakers
1967–68	Wilt Chamberlain	Philadelphia 76ers	1989–90	Magic Johnson	Los Angeles Lakers
1968–69	Wes Unseld	Baltimore Bullets	1990–91	Michael Jordan	Chicago Bulls
1969–70	Willis Reed	New York Knicks	1991–92	Michael Jordan	Chicago Bulls
1970–71	Kareem Abdul-Jabbar	Milwaukee Bucks	1992–93	Charles Barkley	Phoenix Suns
1971–72	Kareem Abdul-Jabbar	Milwaukee Bucks	1993–94	Hakeem Olajuwon	Houston Rockets
1972–73	Dave Cowens	Boston Celtics	1994–95	David Robinson	San Antonio Spurs
1973–74	Kareem Abdul-Jabbar	Milwaukee Bucks	1995–96	Michael Jordan	Chicago Bulls
1974–75	Bob McAdoo	Buffalo Braves	1996–97	Karl Malone	Utah Jazz
1975–76	Kareem Abdul-Jabbar	Los Angeles Lakers	1997–98	Michael Jordan	Chicago Bulls
1976–77	Kareem Abdul-Jabbar	Los Angeles Lakers	1998–99	Karl Malone	Utah Jazz

WNBA Final Standings, 1999

The Houston Comets won their third straight WNBA title, defeating New York in the Championship Series. Cynthia Cooper was MVP for the third straight year as well.

East	W	L	Pct.	GB	West	W	L	Pct.	GB
New York Liberty	18	14	.563	0.0	Houston Comets	26	6	.813	0.0
Charlotte Sting	15	17	.469	3.0	Los Angeles Sparks	20	12	.625	6.0
Detroit Shock	15	17	.469	3.0	Sacramento Monarchs	19	13	.594	7.0
Orlando Miracle	15	17	.469	3.0	Phoenix Mercury	15	17	.469	11.0
Washington Mystics	12	20	.375	6.0	Minnesota Lynx	15	17	.469	11.0
Cleveland Rockers	7	25	.219	11.0	Utah Starzz	15	17	.469	11.0

PLAYOFFS

First Round (one game)
Charlotte Sting 60, Detroit Shock 54
Conference Semifinals
New York Liberty 2, Charlotte Sting 1

First Round (one game)
L.A. Sparks 71, Sacramento Monarchs 58
Conference Semifinals
Houston Comets 2, L.A. Sparks 1

WNBA CHAMPIONSHIP
Houston Comets 2, New York Liberty 1

Note: The top three teams in each division made the playoffs. **Source:** WNBA. www.wnba.com.

NBA All-Time Career Leaders

Games		Points		Scoring average (min. 400 games)	
Robert Parish	1,611	Kareem Abdul-Jabbar	38,387	Michael Jordan	31.5
Kareem Abdul-Jabbar	1,560	Wilt Chamberlain	31,419	Wilt Chamberlain	30.1
Moses Malone	1,329	Michael Jordan	29,277	Elgin Baylor	27.4
Buck Williams[1]	1,348	Karl Malone[1]	28,946	Shaquille O'Neal[1]	27.1
Elvin Hayes	1,303	Moses Malone	27,409	Jerry West	27.0
John Havlicek	1,270	Elvin Hayes	27,313	Bob Pettit	26.4
Paul Silas	1,254	Oscar Robertson	26,710	George Gervin	26.2
Eddie Johnson[1]	1,199	Dominique Wilkins[1]	26,668	Karl Malone[1]	26.1
Derek Harper[1]	1,199	John Havlicek	26,395	Oscar Robertson	25.7
Alex English	1,193	Alex English	25,613	Dominique Wilkins[1]	24.8

Assists		Rebounds		Free throw percentage (min. 400 games)	
John Stockton[1]	13,088	Wilt Chamberlain	23,924	Mark Price[1]	.901
Magic Johnson	10,141	Bill Russell	21,620	Rick Barry	.900
Oscar Robertson	9,887	Kareem Abdul-Jabbar	17,440	Calvin Murphy	.892
Isiah Thomas	9,061	Elvin Hayes	16,279	Scott Skiles	.889
Mark Jackson[1]	7,925	Moses Malone	16,212	Larry Bird	.886
Maurice Cheeks	7,392	Robert Parish	14,715	Bill Sharman	.883
Len Wilkens	7,211	Nate Thurmond	14,464	Reggie Miller[1]	.879
Bob Cousy	6,955	Walt Bellamy	14,241	Ricky Pierce[1]	.875
Guy Rodgers	6,917	Wes Unseld	13,769	Jeff Hornacek[1]	.873
Kevin Johnson[1]	6,932	Buck Williams[1]	13,201	Kiki Vandeweghe	.872

Note: At the end of 1998–99 season. 1. Player active in 1998–99. Source: NBA.

Naismith Memorial Basketball Hall of Fame

Although the Basketball Hall of Fame elected its first members in 1959, its cornerstone was not laid until 1961. The original Hall of Fame in Springfield, Mass., was opened to the public on February 17, 1968 and existed there for 17 years. On June 30, 1985 the Hall of Fame was reopened in a new, $11.5 million building, also in Springfield. Dr. James Naismith, the game's originator, was among the members elected in 1959. Note that the Basketball Hall of Fame includes players from all basketball levels, including college, women's, and foreign leagues. Admission is based on a player's total career, not just his (or her) NBA performance. Career statistics are given only for players who played some portion of their career in the NBA.

Player (Year Elected)	Games	Points	FG%	FT%	Rebs.	Assts.
Archibald, Nate (Tiny) (1991)	876	16,481	.467	.810	2,046	6,476
Averaged 18.8 ppg over 13 seasons; six-time All-Star.						
Arizin, Paul J. (1977)	713	16,266	.421	.810	6,129	1,665
NBA scoring leader in 1952 (25.4 ppg) and 1957 (25.6 ppg).						
Barry, Rick (1987)	794	18,395	.449	.900	5,168	4,017
(ABA)	226	6,884	.477	.880	1,695	935
NBA all-time free-throw percentage leader.						
Baylor, Elgin (1976)	846	23,149	.431	.780	11,463	3,650
Named to NBA All-Star First Team 10 times.						
Bellamy, Walt (1993)	1,043	20,941	.516	.632	14,241	2,544
NBA Rookie of the Year in 1962.						
Bing, Dave (1990)	901	18,327	.441	.775	3,420	5,397
NBA Rookie of the Year 1967, MVP 1976.						
Bird, Larry (1998)	897	21,791	.496	.886	8,974	5,695
NBA Rookie of the Year 1980. NBA MVP 1984, 1985, and 1986. 12-time All-star.						
Bradley, Bill (1982)	742	9,217	.448	.840	2,533	2,363
Averaged 30.2 ppg in 83 games at Princeton University.						
Chamberlain, Wilt (1978)	1045	31,419	.540	.511	23,924	4,643
Holds NBA single-game records for points (100) and rebounds (55); led league in scoring 1959-66.						
Cousy, Bob (1970)	924	16,960	.375	.803	4,786	6,955
Led NBA in assists eight consecutive seasons (1953-60)						
Cowens, Dave (1991)	766	13,516	.460	.783	10,444	2,950
Seven-time All-star; three-time All-defensive team						
Cunningham, Billy (1986)	654	13,626	.446	.720	6,638	2,625
(ABA)	116	2,684	.483	.791	1,343	680
Coached Philadelphia 76ers to 454-196 record in eight years						
Davies, Bob (1969)	462	6,594	.378	.759	980[1]	2,050
NBL MVP, 1947	(NBL)[2]	107	1177		.747	

Player (Year Elected)	Games	Points	FG%	FT%	Rebs.	Assts.
DeBusschere, Dave (1982)	875	14,053	.432	.699	2,497	2,801
NBA All-Defensive team six consecutive seasons (1969-74)						
English, Alex (1997)	1,193	25,613	.507	.832	6,538	4,351
Eight-time all-star; Averaged 21.5 points per game over 15 seasons						
Erving, Julius (Dr. J) (1993)	836	18,364	.507	.777	5,601	3,224
(ABA)	407	11,662	.504	.778	4,924	1,952
ABA MVP 1974-76; NBA MVP, 1981.						
Frazier, Walt (Clyde) (1987)	825	15,581	.490	.786	4,830	5,040
NBA All-Defensive team seven consecutive seasons (1969-75)						
Fulks, Joe (1977)	489	8,003	.302	.766	1,382[1]	587
NBA scoring leader in 1947 (23.2 ppg)						
Gallatin, Harry (1991)	682	8,843	.398	.773	6,684	1,208
Seven-time All-Star						
Gervin, George (Iceman) (1996)	791	20,708	.511	.844	3,607	2,214
(ABA)	269	5,887	.480	.831	1,995	584
All-NBA team five years in a row (1978-82).						
Gola, Tom (1975)	698	7,871	.431	.760	5,605	2,953
One of only two major-college players with over 2,000 points and 2,000 rebounds in career						
Goodrich, Gail (1996)	1,031	19,181	.456	.807	3,279	4,805
Scored 42 points in 1965 NCAA Final; averaged 18.6 points per game over 14 years in NBA						
Greer, Harold (Hal) (1981)	1,122	21,586	.452	.801	5,665	4,540
Scored 19 points in one quarter of 1968 All-Star game						
Hagan, Cliff (1977)	746	13,447	.450	.798	5,019	2,236
(ABA)	94	1,423	.496	.807	436	398
Helped St. Louis to 1958 championship with 27.7 ppg in playoffs						
Havlicek, John J. (Hondo) (1983)	1,270	26,395	.439	.815	8,007	6,114
Averaged 20.8 ppg; Member of 8 NBA championship teams						
Hawkins, Connie (1992)	499	8,233	.467	.785	3,971	2,052
(ABA)	117	3,295	.515	.765	1,479	504
Four-time All-Star; ABA MVP 1969						
Hayes, Elvin (1990)	1,303	27,313	.452	.670	16,279	2,398
Led league in scoring (1969) and rebounds per game (1970,1974)						
Heinsohn, Tom (1986)	654	12,194	.405	.790	5,749	1,318
Played for eight NBA championship teams and coached two others						
Houbregs, Robert J. (1987)	281	2,611	.404	.721	1,552	500
NCAA Player of the Year, 1953						
Issel, Dan (1993)	718	14,659	.506	.797	5,707	1,804
(ABA)	500	12,823	.488	.786	5,426	1,103
Averaged 33.7 points per game in senior year at Kentucky, 1969-70						
Jabbar, Kareem Abdul (1995)	1,560	38,387	.559	.721	17,440	5,660
Six-time NBA MVP. All-time NBA leader in scoring, games, minutes, field goals						
Jeannette, Buddy (1994) (NBL)[2]	161	1,320				
(BAA-NBA)	139	997	.341	.781	N.A.	287
Won NBL MVP three times						
Johnston, Neil (1990)	516	10,023	.444	.768	5,856	1,269
Named to four straight all-NBA First Teams (1953-56)						
Jones, K.C. (1989)	676	5,011	.387	.647	2,399	2,908
High scorer in 1955 NCAA finals (24 pts); held Tom Gola scoreless for 21 mins.						
Jones, Sam (1983)	871	15,411	.456	.803	4,305	2,209
Member of ten NBA championship teams						
Lanier, Bob (1992)	595	19,248	.514	.767	9,698	3,007
Eight-time All-Star; NBA MVP, 1974						
Lovellette, Clyde (1988)	704	11,947	.443	.756	6,663	1,165
Three-time All-American at University of Kansas (1950-52)						
Lucas, Jerry Ray (Luke) (1979)	829	14,053	.499	.783	12,942	2,730
NBA Rookie of the Year and field-goal percentage leader (.527) in 1964						
Macauley, Edward (Easy Ed) (1960)	641	11,234	.436	.761	2,079	1,667
NBA All-Star Game MVP, 1951						
Maravich, Pete (Pistol) (1987)	658	15,948	.441	.820	2,747	3,563
NCAA career record holder for points scored (3667) and scoring avg. (44.2 ppg)						
Martin, Slater (1981)	745	7,337	.364	.762	2,302[1]	3,160
Played in seven straight All-Star Games, 1953-59						
McGuire, Dick (1993)	738	5,921	.389	.644	2,784	4,205
Averaged 8.0 ppg.						
McHale, Kevin (1999)	971	17,335	.554	.798	7,122	1,670
Seven-time All-Star; won Sixth Man Award twice; won 3 NBA Championships: 1981, 1984, 1986						
Mikan, George L. (1959)	439	10,156	.404	.782	4,167[1]	1,245
(NBL)[2]	81	1,608		.756		
Three-time NBA scoring leader (1949, 1950, 1952).						
Mikkelson, Vern (1995)	699	10,063	.403	.766	5,940[1]	1,515
Six-time NBA All-Star; won 4 NBA Championships: 1950, 1952, 1953, & 1954						

Player (Year Elected)	Games	Points	FG%	FT%	Rebs.	Assts.
Monroe, Earl (The Pearl) (1990)	926	17,454	.464	.807	2,796	3,594
NBA Rookie of the Year, 1968.						
Murphy, Calvin (1993)	1,002	17,949	.482	.892	2,103	4,402
Set single-season free throw percentage record with .958 in 1980-81.						
Pettit, Bob (1970)	792	20,880	.436	.761	12,849	2,369
Led NBA in scoring (25.7 ppg) and rebounds (1164) in 1956						
Phillip, Andy (1961)	701	6,384	.368	.695	2,395[1]	3,759
Led NBA in assists, 1951 and 1952						
Pollard, Jim (1977)	438	5,762	.360	.750	2,487[1]	1,417
(NBL)[2]	59	760		.676		
Started four NBA All-Star Games						
Ramsey, Frank (1981)	623	8,378	.402	.804	3,410	1,136
Member of seven NBA championship teams						
Reed, Willis (1981)	650	12,183	.476	.747	8,414	1,186
1970 NBA Most Valuable Player, All-Star Game MVP and Playoff MVP						
Risen, Arnie (1998)	637	7,633	.381	.699	5,011	1,058
(NBL)[2]						
Three-time NBA All-star (1953, 1954, and 1955)	123	1,606		.650		
Robertson, Oscar (1979)	1,040	26,710	.485	.838	7,804	9,887
NBA MVP 1964; Member of All-NBA First team, 1961-69						
Russell, Bill (1974)	963	14,522	.440	.561	21,620	4,100
Five-time NBA Most Valuable Player; 32 rebounds in one half vs. Philadelphia, 1957						
Schayes, Adolph (Dolph) (1972)	996	18,438	.380	.849	11,256[1]	3,072
(NBL)[2]	63	811		.724		
NBA Coach of the Year (1966)						
Sharman, Bill (1974)	711	12,665	.426	.883	2,779	2,101
Led NBA in free-throw percentage seven seasons						
Thompson, David (1996)	509	11,264	.504	.778	1,921	1,631
(ABA)	83	2,158	.515	.794	525	308
NCAA player of the year 1974 and 1975; ABA Rookie of the Year, 1976.						
Thurmond, Nate (1984)	964	14,437	.421	.667	14,464	2,575
1,000+ rebounds 1964-69, 1970-73						
Twyman, Jack (1982)	23	15,840	.450	.778	5,421	1,969
Led NBA in field-goal percentage, 1958 (.452)						
Unseld, Wes (1988)	984	10,624	.509	.633	13,769	3,822
Named NBA Most Valuable Player and Rookie of the Year in same year (1969)						
Walton, Bill (1993)	468	6,215	.521	.660	4,923	1,590
MVP in 1976.						
Wanzer, Robert (1987)	502	5,891	.388	.800	1,652[1]	1,575
Free-throw percentage leader, 1952 (.904)						
West, Jerry Alan (1979)	932	25,192	.474	.814	5,376	6,238
NBA MVP in 1970; .805 free throw percentage in 13 years in the playoffs						
Wilkens, Lenny (1989)	1,077	17,772	.432	.774	5,030	7,211
600+ assists 6 consecutive seasons						
Yardley, George (1996)	472	9,063	.422	.780	4,220	815
First player in NBA history to score 2,000 points in a season						

Note: All statistics for NBA career unless otherwise noted. NBL = National Basketball League. ABA = American Basketball Association. NCAA (National Collegiate Athletic Association) 1. Does not include seasons played prior to 1950-51 when the NBA first began keeping statistics for rebounds. 2. The National Basketball League did not keep statistics for field-goal percentage, rebounds, or assists.

COACHES

Anderson, W. Harold 1984
Auerbach, Arnold J. "Red" 1968
Barry, Justin "Sam" 1978
Blood, Ernest A. 1960
Cann, Howard G. 1967
Carlson, Dr. H. Clifford 1959
Carnesecca, Lou 1992
Carnevale, Ben 1969
Carril, Pete 1997
Case, Everett 1981
Conradt, Jody 1998
Crum, Denny 1994
Daly, Chuck 1994
Dean, Everett S. 1966
Diddle, Edgar A. 1971
Drake, Bruce 1972
Gaines, Clarence 1981
Gardner, James H. "Jack" 1983
Gill, Amory T. "Slats" 1967

Hannum, Alex 1998
Harshman, Marv 1984
Haskins, Don 1997
Hickey, Edgar S. 1978
Hobson, Howard A. 1965
Holzman, William "Red" 1985-86
Iba, Henry P. "Hank" 1968
Julian, Alvin "Doggie" 1967
Keaney, Frank W. 1960
Keogan, George E. 1961
Knight, Bob 1991
Kundla, John 1995
Lambert, Ward L. 1960
Litwack, Harry 1975
Loeffler, Kenneth D. 1964
Lonborg, Arthur C. 1972
McCutchan, Arad A. 1980
McGuire, Al 1992
McGuire, Frank J. 1976

Meanwell, Dr. Walter E. 1959
Meyer, Raymond J. 1978
Miller, Ralph 1987
Moore, Billie 1999
Nikolic, Aleksandar 1998
Ramsay, Jack 1992
Rupp, Adolph F. 1968
Sachs, Leonard D. 1961
Shelton, Everett F. 1979
Smith, Dean 1982
Taylor, Fred R. 1985-86
Teague, Bertha 1984
Thompson, John 1999
Wade, L. Margaret 1984
Watts, Stanley H. 1985-86
Wilkens, Lenny 1998
Wooden, John R. 1972
Woolpert, Phil 1992

ICE HOCKEY

National Hockey League
www.nhl.com
Commissioner: Gary Bettman
Founded: 1917
Number of Teams: 27

The NHL started with six franchises, and nearly went bankrupt in the 1970s due to lack of interest and financial mismanagement. But the sport and the league are thriving in the 1990s, winning national television broadcast deals and expanding rapidly to warm-weather cities like San Jose and Tampa Bay. Franchise relocation has also become common, as teams from Minnesota, Quebec, Winnipeg, and Hartford have moved, respectively, to Dallas, Colorado, Phoenix, and North Carolina.

At the start of the 1998-99 season, the NHL expanded to Nashville. And in 1999, Atlanta took its second crack at an expansion franchise (its first, the Atlanta Flames, now plays in Calgary). In 2000, expansion teams will be added in St. Paul, Minnesota and Columbus, Ohio. The new franchises will each pay an $80 million entry fee.

NHL Standings, 1998–99

EASTERN CONFERENCE

Northeast Division	W	L	T	Pts.
Ottawa Senators	44	23	15	103
Toronto Maple Leafs	45	30	7	97
Boston Bruins	39	30	13	91
Buffalo Sabres	37	28	17	91
Montreal Canadiens	32	39	11	75

Atlantic Division	W	L	T	Pts.
New Jersey Devils	47	24	11	105
Philadelphia Flyers	37	26	19	93
Pittsburgh Penguins	38	30	14	90
N.Y. Rangers	33	38	11	77
N.Y. Islanders	24	48	10	58

Southeast Division	W	L	T	Pts.
Carolina Hurricanes	34	30	18	86
Florida Panthers	30	34	18	78
Washington Capitals	31	45	6	68
Tampa Bay Lightning	19	54	9	47

WESTERN CONFERENCE

Central Division	W	L	T	Pts.
Detroit Red Wings	43	32	7	93
St. Louis Blues	37	32	13	87
Chicago Blackhawks	29	41	12	70
Nashville Predators	28	47	7	63

Northwest Division	W	L	T	Pts.
Colorado Avalanche	44	28	10	98
Edmonton Oilers	33	37	12	78
Calgary Flames	30	40	12	72
Vancouver Canucks	23	47	12	58

Pacific Division	W	L	T	Pts.
Dallas Stars	51	19	12	114
Phoenix Coyotes	39	31	12	90
Anaheim Mighty Ducks	35	34	13	83
San Jose Sharks	31	33	18	80
Los Angeles Kings	32	45	5	69

Source: National Hockey League

Stanley Cup Playoffs 1999

(All rounds are seven-game series)

Eastern Conference				Western Conference	
ROUND 1					
Pittsburgh Penguins	4	New Jersey Devils	3	Dallas Stars	4	Edmonton Oilers	0
Buffalo Sabres	4	Ottawa Senators	0	Colorado Avalanche	4	San Jose Sharks	2
Boston Bruins	4	Carolina Hurricanes	2	Detroit Red Wings	4	Anaheim Mighty Ducks	0
Toronto Maple Leafs	4	Philadelphia Flyers	2	St. Louis Blues	4	Phoenix Coyotes	3
ROUND 2					
Toronto Maple Leafs	4	Pittsburgh Penguins	2	Colorado Avalanche	4	Detroit Red Wings	2
Buffalo Sabres	4	Boston Bruins	2	Dallas Stars	4	St. Louis Blues	2
CONFERENCE CHAMPIONSHIPS					
Buffalo Sabres	4	Toronto Maple Leafs	1	Dallas Stars	4	Colorado Avalanche	3
STANLEY CUP CHAMPIONSHIP					
		Dallas Stars 4	Buffalo Sabres 2		

The Stanley Cup

The oldest trophy competed for by professional athletes in North America, the Stanley Cup was donated by Frederick Arthur, Lord Stanley of Preston, in 1893. Lord Stanley purchased the trophy for 10 guineas (about $50) for presentation to the amateur hockey champions of Canada. Since 1910, when the National Hockey Association took possession of the Stanley Cup, the trophy has been the symbol of professional hockey supremacy. The National Hockey League took exclusive control of the cup in 1946, and now awards it annually to the team that wins the league's best-of-seven final playoff series.

Season	Champion	Finalist	GP in final	Season	Champion	Finalist	GP in final
1917–18	Toronto Arenas	Vancouver Millionaires	5	1958–59	Montreal Canadiens	Toronto Maple Leafs	5
1918–19	No decision[1]	No decision	5	1959–60	Montreal Canadiens	Toronto Maple Leafs	4
1919–20	Ottawa Senators	Seattle Millionaires	5	1960–61	Chicago Blackhawks	Detroit Red Wings	6
1920–21	Ottawa Senators	Vancouver Millionaires	5	1961–62	Toronto Maple Leafs	Chicago Blackhawks	6
1921–22	Toronto St. Pats	Vancouver Millionaires	5	1962–63	Toronto Maple Leafs	Detroit Red Wings	5
1922–23	Ottawa Senators	Edmonton	2	1963–64	Toronto Maple Leafs	Detroit Red Wings	7
1923–24	Montreal Canadiens	Calgary	2	1964–65	Montreal Canadiens	Chicago Blackhawks	7
1924–25	Victoria Cougars	Montreal Canadiens	4	1965–66	Montreal Canadiens	Detroit Red Wings	6
1925–26	Montreal Maroons	Victoria Cougars	4	1966–67	Toronto Maple Leafs	Montreal Canadiens	6
1926–27	Ottawa Senators	Boston Bruins	4	1967–68	Montreal Canadiens	St. Louis Blues	4
1927–28	New York Rangers	Montreal Canadiens	5	1968–69	Montreal Canadiens	St. Louis Blues	4
1928–29	Boston Bruins	New York Rangers	2	1969–70	Boston Bruins	St. Louis Blues	4
1929–30	Montreal Canadiens	Boston Bruins	2	1970–71	Montreal Canadiens	Chicago Blackhawks	7
1930–31	Montreal Canadiens	Chicago Blackhawks	5	1971–72	Boston Bruins	New York Rangers	6
1931–32	Toronto Maple Leafs	New York Rangers	3	1972–73	Montreal Canadiens	Chicago Blackhawks	6
1932–33	New York Rangers	Toronto Maple Leafs	3	1973–74	Philadelphia Flyers	Boston Bruins	6
1933–34	Chicago Blackhawks	Detroit Red Wings	4	1974–75	Philadelphia Flyers	Buffalo Sabres	6
1934–35	Montreal Maroons	Toronto Maple Leafs	3	1975–76	Montreal Canadiens	Philadelphia Flyers	4
1935–36	Detroit Red Wings	Toronto Maple Leafs	4	1976–77	Montreal Canadiens	Boston Bruins	4
1936–37	Detroit Red Wings	New York Rangers	5	1977–78	Montreal Canadiens	Boston Bruins	6
1937–38	Chicago Blackhawks	Toronto Maple Leafs	4	1978–79	Montreal Canadiens	New York Rangers	5
1938–39	Boston Bruins	Toronto Maple Leafs	5	1979–80	New York Islanders	Philadelphia Flyers	6
1939–40	New York Rangers	Toronto Maple Leafs	6	1980–81	New York Islanders	Minnesota North Stars	5
1940–41	Boston Bruins	Detroit Red Wings	4	1981–82	New York Islanders	Vancouver Canucks	4
1941–42	Toronto Maple Leafs	Detroit Red Wings	7	1982–83	New York Islanders	Edmonton Oilers	4
1942–43	Detroit Red Wings	Boston Bruins	4	1983–84	Edmonton Oilers	New York Islanders	5
1943–44	Montreal Canadiens	Chicago Blackhawks	4	1984–85	Edmonton Oilers	Philadelphia Flyers	5
1944–45	Toronto Maple Leafs	Detroit Red Wings	7	1985–86	Montreal Canadiens	Calgary Flames	5
1945–46	Montreal Canadiens	Boston Bruins	5	1986–87	Edmonton Oilers	Philadelphia Flyers	7
1946–47	Toronto Maple Leafs	Montreal Canadiens	6	1987–88	Edmonton Oilers	Boston Bruins	4
1947–48	Toronto Maple Leafs	Detroit Red Wings	4	1988–89	Calgary Flames	Montreal Canadiens	6
1948–49	Toronto Maple Leafs	Detroit Red Wings	4	1989–90	Edmonton Oilers	Boston Bruins	5
1949–50	Detroit Red Wings	New York Rangers	7	1990–91	Pittsburgh Penguins	Minnesota North Stars	5
1950–51	Toronto Maple Leafs	Montreal Canadiens	5	1991–92	Pittsburgh Penguins	Chicago Blackhawks	4
1951–52	Detroit Red Wings	Montreal Canadiens	4	1992–93	Montreal Canadiens	Los Angeles Kings	5
1952–53	Montreal Canadiens	Boston Bruins	5	1993–94	New York Rangers	Vancouver Canucks	7
1953–54	Detroit Red Wings	Montreal Canadiens	7	1994–95[3]	New Jersey Devils	Detroit Red Wings	4
1954–55	Detroit Red Wings	Montreal Canadiens	7	1995–96	Colorado Avalanche	Florida Panthers	4
1955–56	Montreal Canadiens	Detroit Red Wings	5	1996–97	Detroit Red Wings	Philadelphia Flyers	4
1956–57	Montreal Canadiens	Boston Bruins	5	1997–98	Detroit Red Wings	Washington Capitals	4
1957–58	Montreal Canadiens	Boston Bruins	6	1998–99	Dallas Stars	Buffalo Sabres	6

1. In the spring of 1919 the Montreal Canadiens traveled to Seattle to meet Seattle, champs of the Pacific Coast Hockey League. After five games had been played—teams were tied at 2 wins and 1 tie—the series was called off by the local Department of Health because of the influenza epidemic. 3. Strike-shortened season

Top Scorers, 1998–99

Player	Team	GP	G	A	Pts.	Player	Team	GP	G	A	Pts.
Jaromir Jagr	Pittsburgh	81	44	83	127	Martin Straka	Pittsburgh	80	35	48	83
Teemu Selanne	Anaheim	75	47	60	107	Mats Sundin	Toronto	82	31	52	83
Paul Kariya	Anaheim	82	39	62	101	Mike Modano	Dallas	77	34	47	81
Peter Forsberg	Colorado	78	30	67	97	Jason Allison	Boston	82	23	53	76
Joe Sakic	Colorado	73	41	55	96	Tony Amonte	Chicago	82	44	31	75
Alexei Yashin	Ottawa	82	44	50	94	Rod Brind'amour	Philadelphia	82	24	50	74
Theoren Fleury	Colorado	75	40	53	93	Luc Robitaille	Los Angeles	82	39	35	74
Eric Lindros	Philadelphia	71	40	53	93	Steve Yzerman	Detroit	80	29	45	74
John LeClair	Philadelphia	76	43	47	90	Steve Thomas	Toronto	78	28	45	73
Pavol Demitra	St. Louis	82	37	52	89	Jeremy Roenick	Phoenix	78	24	48	72

Source: National Hockey League

Top 10 All-Time NHL Scoring Leaders

GOALS

Player	Seasons	Games	Goals	Goals/Game
Wayne Gretzky[1]	20	1,487	894	.601
Gordie Howe	26	1,767	801	.453
Marcel Dionne	18	1,348	731	.542
Phil Esposito	18	1,282	717	.572
Mike Gartner[1]	19	1,432	708	.494
Mario Lemieux	12	745	613	.823
Bobby Hull	16	1,063	610	.574
Mark Messier[1]	20	1,413	610	.432
Dino Ciccarelli[1]	19	1,232	608	.494
Jari Kurri[1]	17	1,251	601	.480

ASSISTS

Player	Seasons	Games	Assists	Assists/Game
Wayne Gretzky[1]	20	1,487	1,963	1.320
Paul Coffey[1]	19	1,322	1,102	.834
Ray Bourque[1]	20	1,456	1,083	.745
Mark Messier[1]	20	1,413	1,050	.743

Player	Seasons	Games	Assists	Assists/Game
Gordie Howe	26	1,767	1,049	.593
Marcel Dionne	18	1,348	1,040	.771
Ron Francis[1]	18	1,329	1,037	.780
Stan Mikita	22	1,394	926	.664
Bryan Trottier	18	1,279	901	.704
Steve Yzerman[1]	16	1,178	891	.756

POINTS

Player	Seasons	Games	Goals	Assists	Points
Wayne Gretzky[1]	20	1,487	894	1,963	2,857
Gordie Howe	26	1,767	801	1,049	1,850
Marcel Dionne	18	1,348	731	1,040	1,771
Mark Messier[1]	20	1,143	610	1,050	1,660
Phil Esposito	18	1,282	717	873	1,590
Mario Lemieux	12	745	613	881	1,494
Paul Coffey[1]	19	1,322	385	1,102	1,487
Ron Francis[1]	18	1,329	449	1,037	1,486
Steve Yzerman[1]	16	1,178	592	891	1,483
Ray Bourque[1]	20	1,456	385	1083	1468

Note: As of end of 1998-99 season. 1. Player active in 1998-99. Source: NHL.

Hart Trophy Winners, 1924–99

The league's most valuable player is chosen by a poll of the Professional Hockey Writers' Association.

Season	Player	Team
1924	Frank Nighbor	Ottawa Senators
1925	Billy Burch	NY Americans
1926	Nels Stewart	Montreal Maroons
1927	Herb Gardiner	Montreal
1928	Howie Morenz	Montreal
1929	Roy Worters	New York Americans
1930	Nels Stewart	Montreal Maroons
1931	Howie Morenz	Montreal
1932	Howie Morenz	Montreal
1933	Eddie Shore	Boston
1934	Aurel Joliat	Montreal
1935	Eddie Shore	Boston
1936	Eddie Shore	Boston
1937	Babe Siebert	Montreal
1938	Eddie Shore	Boston
1939	Toe Blake	Montreal
1940	Ebbie Goodfellow	Detroit
1941	Bill Cowley	Boston
1942	Tom Anderson	New York Americans
1943	Bill Cowley	Boston
1944	Babe Pratt	Toronto
1945	Elmer Lach	Montreal
1946	Max Bentley	Toronto
1947	Maurice Richard	Montreal
1948	Buddy O'Connor	New York Rangers
1949	Sid Abel	Detroit
1950	Charlie Rayner	New York Rangers
1951	Milt Schmidt	Boston
1952	Gordie Howe	Detroit
1953	Gordie Howe	Detroit
1954	Al Rollins	Toronto
1955	Ted Kennedy	Toronto
1956	Jean Béliveau	Montreal
1957	Gordie Howe	Detroit
1958	Gordie Howe	Detroit
1959	Andy Bathgate	New York Rangers
1960	Gordie Howe	Detroit
1961	Bernie Geoffrion	Montreal

Season	Player	Team
1962	Jacques Plante	Montreal
1963	Gordie Howe	Detroit
1964	Jean Béliveau	Montreal
1965	Bobby Hull	Chicago
1966	Bobby Hull	Chicago
1967	Stan Mikita	Chicago
1968	Stan Mikita	Chicago
1969	Phil Esposito	Boston
1970	Bobby Orr	Boston
1971	Bobby Orr	Boston
1972	Bobby Orr	Boston
1973	Bobby Clarke	Philadelphia
1974	Phil Esposito	Boston
1975	Bobby Clarke	Philadelphia
1976	Bobby Clarke	Philadelphia
1977	Guy Lafleur	Montreal
1978	Guy Lafleur	Montreal
1979	Bryan Trottier	New York Islanders
1980	Wayne Gretzky	Edmonton
1981	Wayne Gretzky	Edmonton
1982	Wayne Gretzky	Edmonton
1983	Wayne Gretzky	Edmonton
1984	Wayne Gretzky	Edmonton
1985	Wayne Gretzky	Edmonton
1986	Wayne Gretzky	Edmonton
1987	Wayne Gretzky	Edmonton
1988	Mario Lemieux	Pittsburgh
1989	Wayne Gretzky	Los Angeles
1990	Mark Messier	Edmonton
1991	Bret Hull	St. Louis
1992	Mark Messier	New York Rangers
1993	Mario Lemieux	Pittsburgh
1994	Sergei Fedorov	Detroit
1995	Eric Lindros	Philadelphia
1996	Mario Lemieux	Pittsburgh
1997	Dominik Hasek	Buffalo
1998	Dominik Hasek	Buffalo
1999	Jaromir Jagr	Pittsburgh

Art Ross Trophy Winners, 1918–99

The Art Ross Trophy is given "to the player who leads the league in scoring at the end of the regular season."

Season	Player	Team	Season	Player	Team
1918	Joe Malone	Montreal	1959	Dickie Moore	Montreal
1919	Newsy Lalonde	Montreal	1960	Bobby Hull	Chicago
1920	Joe Malone	Quebec	1961	Bernie Geoffrion	Montreal
1921	Newsy Lalonde	Montreal	1962	Bobby Hull	Chicago
1922	Punch Broadbent	Ottawa	1963	Gordie Howe	Detroit
1923	Babe Dye	Toronto	1964	Stan Mikita	Chicago
1924	Cye Denneny	Ottawa	1965	Stan Mikita	Chicago
1925	Babe Dye	Toronto	1966	Bobby Hull	Chicago
1926	Nels Stewart	Montreal Maroons	1967	Stan Mikita	Chicago
1927	Bill Cook	New York Rangers	1968	Stan Mikita	Chicago
1928	Howie Morenz	Montreal	1969	Phil Esposito	Boston
1929	Ace Bailey	Toronto	1970	Bobby Orr	Boston
1930	Cooney Weiland	Boston	1971	Phil Esposito	Boston
1931	Howie Morenz	Montreal	1972	Phil Esposito	Boston
1932	Harvey Jackson	Toronto	1973	Phil Esposito	Boston
1933	Bill Cook	NY Rangers	1974	Phil Esposito	Boston
1934	Charlie Conacher	Toronto	1975	Bobby Orr	Boston
1935	Charlie Conacher	Toronto	1976	Guy Lafleur	Montreal
1936	Dave Shriner	New York Americans	1977	Guy Lafleur	Montreal
1937	Dave Shriner	New York Americans	1978	Guy Lafleur	Montreal
1938	Gordie Drillon	Toronto	1979	Bryan Trottier	New York Islanders
1939	Toe Blake	Montreal	1980	Marcel Dionne	Los Angeles
1940	Milt Schmidt	Boston	1981	Wayne Gretzky	Edmonton
1941	Bill Cowley	Boston	1982	Wayne Gretzky	Edmonton
1942	Bryan Hextall	New York Rangers	1983	Wayne Gretzky	Edmonton
1943	Doug Bentley	Chicago	1984	Wayne Gretzky	Edmonton
1944	Herbie Cain	Boston	1985	Wayne Gretzky	Edmonton
1945	Elmer Lach	Montreal	1986	Wayne Gretzky	Edmonton
1946	Max Bentley	Chicago	1987	Wayne Gretzky	Edmonton
1947	Max Bentley	Chicago	1988	Mario Lemieux	Pittsburgh
1948	Elmer Lach	Montreal	1989	Mario Lemieux	Pittsburgh
1949	Roy Conacher	Chicago	1990	Wayne Gretzky	Los Angeles
1950	Ted Lindsay	Detroit	1991	Wayne Gretzky	Los Angeles
1951	Gordie Howe	Detroit	1992	Mario Lemieux	Pittsburgh
1952	Gordie Howe	Detroit	1993	Mario Lemieux	Pittsburgh
1953	Gordie Howe	Detroit	1994	Wayne Gretzky	Los Angeles
1954	Gordie Howe	Detroit	1995	Jaromir Jagr	Pittsburgh
1955	Bernie Geoffrion	Montreal	1996	Mario Lemieux	Pittsburgh
1956	Jean Béliveau	Montreal	1997	Mario Lemieux	Pittsburgh
1957	Gordie Howe	Detroit	1998	Jaromir Jagr	Pittsburgh
1958	Dickie Moore	Montreal	1999	Jaromir Jagr	Pittsburgh

Conn Smythe Trophy Winners, 1965–99

The Conn Smythe Trophy is awarded to the most valuable player in the playoffs, as voted by the Professional Hockey Writers' Association.

Season	Player	Team	Season	Player	Team
1965	Jean Béliveau	Montreal	1983	Bill Smith	New York Islanders
1966	Roger Crozier	Detroit	1984	Mark Messier	Edmonton
1967	Dave Keon	Toronto	1985	Wayne Gretzky	Edmonton
1968	Glenn Hall	St. Louis	1986	Patrick Roy	Montreal
1969	Serge Savard	Montreal	1987	Ron Hextall	Philadelphia
1970	Bobby Orr	Boston	1988	Wayne Gretzky	Edmonton
1971	Ken Dryden	Montreal	1989	Al MacInnis	Calgary
1972	Bobby Orr	Boston	1990	Bill Ranford	Edmonton
1973	Yvan Cournoyer	Montreal	1991	Mario Lemieux	Pittsburgh
1974	Bernie Parent	Philadelphia	1992	Mario Lemieux	Pittsburgh
1975	Bernie Parent	Philadelphia	1993	Patrick Roy	Montreal
1976	Reggie Leach	Philadelphia	1994	Brian Leetch	New York Rangers
1977	Guy Lafleur	Montreal	1995	Claude Lemieux	New Jersey
1978	Larry Robinson	Montreal	1996	Joe Sakic	Colorado
1979	Bob Gainey	Montreal	1997	Mike Vernon	Detroit
1980	Bryan Trottier	New York Islanders	1998	Steve Yzerman	Detroit
1981	Butch Goring	New York Islanders	1999	Joe Nieuwendyk	Dallas
1982	Mike Bossy	New York Islanders			

James Norris Memorial Trophy, 1954–99

The James Norris Memorial Trophy for the league's best defenseman is awarded by the Professional Hockey Writers' Association. The winner receives $10,000.

Season	Player	Team	Season	Player	Team
1954	Red Kelly	Detroit	1977	Larry Robinson	Montreal
1955	Doug Harvey	Montreal	1978	Denis Potvin	New York Islanders
1956	Doug Harvey	Montreal	1979	Denis Potvin	New York Islanders
1957	Doug Harvey	Montreal	1980	Larry Robinson	Montreal
1958	Doug Harvey	Montreal	1981	Randy Carlyle	Pittsburgh
1959	Tom Johnson	Montreal	1982	Doug Wilson	Chicago
1960	Doug Harvey	Montreal	1983	Rod Langway	Washington
1961	Doug Harvey	Montreal	1984	Rod Langway	Washington
1962	Doug Harvey	New York Rangers	1985	Paul Coffey	Edmonton
1963	Pierre Pilote	Chicago	1986	Paul Coffey	Edmonton
1964	Pierre Pilote	Chicago	1987	Ray Bourque	Boston
1965	Pierre Pilote	Chicago	1988	Ray Bourque	Boston
1966	Jacques Laperrière	Montreal	1989	Chris Chelios	Montreal
1967	Harry Howell	New York Rangers	1990	Ray Bourque	Boston
1968	Bobby Orr	Boston	1991	Ray Bourque	Boston
1969	Bobby Orr	Boston	1992	Brian Leetch	New York Rangers
1970	Bobby Orr	Boston	1993	Chris Chelios	Chicago
1971	Bobby Orr	Boston	1994	Ray Bourque	Boston
1972	Bobby Orr	Boston	1995	Paul Coffey	Detroit
1973	Bobby Orr	Boston	1996	Chris Chelios	Chicago
1974	Bobby Orr	Boston	1997	Brian Leetch	New York Rangers
1975	Bobby Orr	Boston	1998	Rob Blake	Los Angeles
1976	Denis Potvin	New York Islanders	1999	Al MacInnis	St. Louis

Calder Memorial Trophy Winners, 1933–99

Hockey's rookie of the year is chosen by the Professional Hockey Writers' Association. The winner receives $10,000.

Season	Player	Team	Season	Player	Team
1933	Carl Voss	Detroit	1967	Bobby Orr	Boston
1934	Russ Blinko	Montreal Maroons	1968	Derek Sanderson	Boston
1935	Dave Schriner	New York Americans	1969	Danny Grant	Minnesota
1936	Mike Karakas	Chicago	1970	Tony Esposito	Chicago
1937	Syl Apps	Toronto	1971	Gilbert Perreault	Buffalo
1938	Cully Dahlstrom	Chicago	1972	Ken Dryden	Montreal
1939	Frank Brimsek	Boston	1973	Steve Vickers	New York Rangers
1940	Kilby MacDonald	New York Rangers	1974	Denis Potvin	New York Islanders
1941	Johnny Quilty	Montreal	1975	Eric Vail	Atlanta
1942	Grant Warwick	New York Rangers	1976	Bryan Trottier	New York Islanders
1943	Gaye Stewart	Toronto	1977	Willie Plett	Atlanta
1944	Gus Bodnar	Toronto	1978	Mike Bossy	New York Islanders
1945	Frank McCool	Toronto	1979	Bobby Smith	Minnesota
1946	Edgar Laprade	New York Rangers	1980	Ray Bourque	Boston
1947	Howie Meeker	Toronto	1981	Peter Stastny	Quebec
1948	Jim McFadden	Detroit	1982	Dale Hawerchuk	Winnipeg
1949	Pentti Lund	New York Rangers	1983	Steve Larmer	Chicago
1950	Jack Gelineau	Boston	1984	Tom Barrasso	Buffalo
1951	Terry Sawchuk	Detroit	1985	Mario Lemieux	Pittsburgh
1952	Bernie Geoffrion	Montreal	1986	Gary Suter	Calgary
1953	Lorne Worsley	New York Rangers	1987	Luc Robitaille	Los Angeles
1954	Camille Henry	New York Rangers	1988	Joe Nieuwendyk	Calgary
1955	Ed Litzenberger	Chicago	1989	Brian Leetch	New York Rangers
1956	Glenn Hall	Detroit	1990	Sergei Makarov	Calgary
1957	Larry Regan	Boston	1991	Ed Belfour	Chicago
1958	Frank Mahovlich	Toronto	1992	Pavel Bure	Vancouver
1959	Ralph Backstrom	Montreal	1993	Teemu Selanne	Winnipeg
1960	Bill Hay	Chicago	1994	Martin Brodeur	New Jersey
1961	Dave Keon	Toronto	1995	Petr Forsberg	Quebec
1962	Bobby Rousseau	Montreal	1996	Daniel Alfredsson	Ottawa
1963	Kent Douglas	Toronto	1997	Bryan Berard	New York Islanders
1964	Jacques Laperrière	Montreal	1998	Sergei Samsonov	Boston
1965	Roger Crozier	Detroit	1999	Chris Drury	Colorado
1966	Brit Selby	Toronto			

Vezina Trophy Winners, 1927–99

The Vezina Trophy is awarded to the league's best goalkeeper and is selected by a poll of the league's general managers. The winner receives $10,000

Season	Player	Team	Season	Player	Team
1927	George Hainsworth	Montreal	1968	Lorne Worsley &	Montreal
1928	George Hainsworth	Montreal		Rogie Vachon	
1929	George Hainsworth	Montreal	1969	Jacques Plante &	St. Louis
1930	Tiny Thompson	Boston		Glenn Hall	
1931	Roy Worters	New York Americans	1970	Tony Esposito	Chicago
1932	Charlie Gardiner	Chicago	1971	Ed Giacomin &	New York Rangers
1933	Tiny Thompson	Boston		Gilles Villemure	
1934	Charlie Gardiner	Chicago	1972	Tony Esposito &	Chicago
1935	Lorne Chabot	Chicago		Gary Smith	
1936	Tiny Thompson	Boston	1973	Ken Dryden	Montreal
1937	Normie Smith	Detroit	1974	Bernie Parent	Philadelphia
1938	Tiny Thompson	Boston		Tony Esposito	Chicago
1939	Frank Brimsek	Boston	1975	Bernie Parent	Philadelphia
1940	Dave Kerr	New York Rangers	1976	Ken Dryden	Montreal
1941	Turk Broda	Toronto	1977	Ken Dryden &	Montreal
1942	Frank Brimsek	Boston		Michel Larocque	
1943	Johnny Mowers	Detroit	1978	Ken Dryden &	Montreal
1944	Bill Durnan	Montreal		Michel Larocque	
1945	Bill Durnan	Montreal	1979	Ken Dryden &	Montreal
1946	Bill Durnan	Montreal		Michel Larocque	
1947	Bill Durnan	Montreal	1980	Bob Sauvé &	Buffalo
1948	Turk Broda	Toronto		Don Edwards	
1949	Bill Durnan	Montreal	1981	Richard Sevigny,	Montreal
1950	Bill Durnan	Montreal		Denis Herron &	
1951	Al Rollins	Toronto		Michel Larocque	
1952	Terry Sawchuk	Detroit	1982	Bill Smith	New York Islanders
1953	Terry Sawchuk	Detroit	1983	Pete Peeters	Boston
1954	Harry Lumley	Toronto	1984	Tom Barrasso	Buffalo
1955	Terry Sawchuk	Detroit	1985	Pele Lindbergh	Philadelphia
1956	Jacques Plante	Montreal	1986	John Vanbiesbrouck	New York Rangers
1957	Jacques Plante	Montreal	1987	Ron Hextall	Philadelphia
1958	Jacques Plante	Montreal	1988	Grant Fuhr	Edmonton
1959	Jacques Plante	Montreal	1989	Patrick Roy	Montreal
1960	Jacques Plante	Montreal	1990	Patrick Roy	Montreal
1961	Johnny Bower	Toronto	1991	Ed Belfour	Chicago
1962	Jacques Plante	Montreal	1992	Patrick Roy	Montreal
1963	Glenn Hall	Chicago	1993	Ed Belfour	Chicago
1964	Charlie Hodge	Montreal	1994	Dominik Hasek	Buffalo
1965	Terry Sawchuk &	Toronto	1995	Dominik Hasek	Buffalo
	Johnny Bower		1996	Jim Carey	Washington
1966	Lorne Worsley &	Montreal	1997	Dominik Hasek	Buffalo
	Charlie Hodge		1998	Dominik Hasek	Buffalo
1967	Glenn Hall &	Chicago	1999	Dominik Hasek	Buffalo
	Denis Dejordy				

BASEBALL

Major League Baseball,
Office of the Commissioner
350 Park Avenue
New York, NY 10022
(212) 339-7800
www.majorleaguebaseball.com
Commisioner: Allan "Bud" Sellg
Number of teams-30

The National League of
Professional Baseball Clubs
350 Park Avenue
New York, NY 10022
(212) 339-7700
www.majorleaguebaseball.com/nl
President: Leonard Coleman
Founded: 1876

The American League of
Professional Baseball Clubs
350 Park Avenue
New York, NY 10022
(212) 339-7600
www.majorleaguebaseball.com/al
President: Dr. Gene Budig
Founded: 1901

Major League Baseball All-Time Career Leaders

Average

1. Ty Cobb	.367
2. Rogers Hornsby	.358
3. Joe Jackson	.356
4. Ed Delahanty	.346
5. Ted Williams	.344
6. Tris Speaker	.344
7. Billy Hamilton	.344
8. Willie Keeler	.343
9. Dan Brouthers	.342
10. Babe Ruth	.342

(Note: minimum 4,000 at bats)

Runs Batted In

1. Hank Aaron	2,297
2. Babe Ruth	2,211
3. Lou Gehrig	1,990
4. Ty Cobb	1,961
5. Stan Musial	1,951
6. Jimmie Foxx	1,921
7. Eddie Murray	1,917
8. Willie Mays	1,903
9. Mel Ott	1,861
10. Carl Yastrzemski	1,844

Runs

1. Ty Cobb	2,245
2. Babe Ruth	2,174
3. Hank Aaron	2,174
4. Pete Rose	2,165
5. Rickey Henderson[1]	2,103
6. Willie Mays	2,062
7. Cap Anson	1,996
8. Stan Musial	1,949
9. Lou Gehrig	1,888
10. Tris Speaker	1,881

Stolen Bases

1. Rickey Henderson[1]	1,334
2. Lou Brock	938
3. Ty Cobb	892
4. Tim Raines[1]	807
5. Vince Coleman	752
6. Eddie Collins	743
7. Max Carey	738
8. Honus Wagner	703
9. Joe Morgan	689
10. Willie Wilson	688

Hits (3,000 or more)

1. Pete Rose	4,256
2. Ty Cobb	4,191
3. Hank Aaron	3,771
4. Stan Musial	3,630
5. Tris Speaker	3,515
6. Carl Yastrzemski	3,419
7. Honus Wagner	3,418
8. Paul Molitor	3,319
9. Eddie Collins	3,311
10. Willie Mays	3,283
11. Eddie Murray	3,255
12. Nap Lajoie	3,244
13. George Brett	3,154
14. Paul Waner	3,152
15. Robin Yount	3,142
16. Dave Winfield	3,110
17. Tony Gwynn[1]	3,067
18. Rod Carew	3,053
19. Cap Anson	3,041
20. Lou Brock	3,023
21. Wade Boggs[1]	3,010
22. Al Kaline	3,007
23. Roberto Clemente	3,000

Slugging Percentage

1. Babe Ruth	.690
2. Ted Williams	.634
3. Lou Gehrig	.632
4. Jimmie Foxx	.609
5. Hank Greenberg	.605
6. Mark McGwire[1]	.587
7. Joe DiMaggio	.579
8. Rogers Hornsby	.577
9. Albert Belle[1]	.573
10. Ken Griffey Jr.[1]	.569

(Note: total bases divided by at-bats. Minimum 4,000 at-bats.)

Extra Base Hits

1. Hank Aaron	1,477
2. Stan Musial	1,377
3. Babe Ruth	1,356
4. Willie Mays	1,323
5. Lou Gehrig	1,190
6. Frank Robinson	1,186
7. Carl Yastrzemski	1,157
8. Ty Cobb	1,139
9. Tris Speaker	1,132
10. George Brett	1,119

Home Runs (400 or more)

1. Hank Aaron	755
2. Babe Ruth	714
3. Willie Mays	660
4. Frank Robinson	586
5. Harmon Killebrew	573
6. Reggie Jackson	563
7. Mike Schmidt	548
8. Mickey Mantle	536
9. Jimmie Foxx	534
10. Mark McGwire[1]	522
11. Ted Williams	521
11. Willie McCovey	521
13. Eddie Mathews	512
13. Ernie Banks	512
15. Mel Ott	511
16. Eddie Murray	504
17. Lou Gehrig	493
18. Stan Musial	475
18. Willie Stargell	475
20. Dave Winfield	465
21. Carl Yastrzemski	452
22. Barry Bonds[1]	445
23. Dave Kingman	442
24. Jose Canseco[1]	431
25. Billy Williams	426
26. Darrell Evans	414
27. Joe Carter	408
27. Duke Snider	407
28. Cal Ripken[1]	402

Total Bases

1. Hank Aaron	6,856
2. Stan Musial	6,134
3. Willie Mays	6,066
4. Ty Cobb	5,863
5. Babe Ruth	5,793
6. Pete Rose	5,752
7. Carl Yastrzemski	5,539
8. Eddie Murray	5,397
9. Frank Robinson	5,373
10. Dave Winfield	5,221

Games Played

1. Pete Rose	3,562
2. Carl Yastrzemski	3,308
3. Hank Aaron	3,298
4. Ty Cobb	3,034
5. Stan Musial	3,026
5. Eddie Murray	3,026
7. Willie Mays	2,992
8. Dave Winfield	2,972
9. Rusty Staub	2,951
10. Brooks Robinson	2,896

1. Active during the 1999 season.

Career Pitching Leaders

Wins

1. Cy Young	511
2. Walter Johnson	416
3. Christy Mathewson	373
4. Grover Alexander	373
5. Warren Spahn	363
6. Pud Galvin	361
7. Kid Nichols	361
8. Tim Keefe	342
9. Steve Carlton	329
10. Eddie Plank	327
11. John Clarkson	326
12. Don Sutton	324
13. Nolan Ryan	324
14. Phil Niekro	318
15. Gaylord Perry	314
16. Charles "Old Hoss" Radbourne	311
17. Tom Seaver	311
18. Mickey Welch	308
19. Lefty Grove	300
20. Early Wynn	300

Strikeouts

1. Nolan Ryan	5,714
2. Steve Carlton	4,136
3. Bert Blyleven	3,701
4. Tom Seaver	3,640
5. Don Sutton	3,574
6. Gaylord Perry	3,534
7. Walter Johnson	3,508
8. Phil Niekro	3,342
9. Roger Clemens[1]	3,316
10 Ferguson Jenkins	3,192

Innings Pitched

1. Cy Young	7,356
2. Pud Galvin	5,941
3. Walter Johnson	5,923
4. Phil Niekro	5,403
5. Nolan Ryan	5,387
6. Gaylord Perry	5,351
7. Don Sutton	5,280
8. Warren Spahn	5,244
9. Steve Carlton	5,217
10. Grover Cleveland Alexander	5,189

Earned run average

1. Ed Walsh	1.82
2. Addie Joss	1.88
3. Mordecai "Three Finger" Brown	2.06
4. Christy Mathewson	2.13
5. Rube Waddell	2.16
6. Walter Johnson	2.17
7. Orval Overall	2.24
8. Ed Reulbach	2.28
9. Jim Scott	2.32
10. Eddie Plank	2.34

Shutouts

1. Walter Johnson	110
2. Grover Alexander	90
3. Christy Mathewson	80
4. Cy Young	76
5. Eddie Plank	69
6. Warren Spahn	63
7. Nolan Ryan	61
8. Tom Seaver	61
9. Bert Blyleven	60
10. Don Sutton	58

1. Active during the 1999 season.

Triple Crown Winners

Only 11 players have led their league in home runs, runs batted in, and batting average in one season.

Player	Club	Year	HR	RBI	AVG.
Ty Cobb	Detroit Tigers	1909	9	115	.377
Henry Zimmerman	Chicago Cubs	1912	14	98	.372
Rogers Hornsby	St. Louis Cardinals	1922	42	152	.401
Rogers Hornsby	St. Louis Cardinals	1925	39	143	.403
Chuck Klein	Philadelphia Phillies	1933	28	120	.368
Jimmie Foxx	Philadelphia A's	1933	48	163	.356
Lou Gehrig	New York Yankees	1934	49	165	.363
Joe Medwick	St. Louis Cardinals	1937	31	154	.374
Ted Williams	Boston Red Sox	1942	36	137	.356
Ted Williams	Boston Red Sox	1947	32	114	.343
Mickey Mantle	New York Yankees	1956	52	130	.353
Frank Robinson	Baltimore Orioles	1966	49	122	.316
Carl Yastrzemski	Boston Red Sox	1967	44	121	.326

Batting Champions 1876–1999

NATIONAL LEAGUE

Year	Name	Team	Avg.	Year	Name	Team	Avg.
1876	Roscoe Barnes	Chicago Cubs	.403	1889	Dan Brouthers	Boston Braves	.373
1877	James White	Boston Braves	.385	1890	Jack Glasscock	N.Y. Giants	.336
1878	Abner Dalrymple	Milwaukee Brewers	.356	1891	Billy Hamilton	Philadelphia Phillies	.338
1879	Cap Anson	Chicago Cubs	.407	1892	"Cupid" Childs	Cleveland Spiders	.335
1880	George Gore	Chicago Cubs	.365		Dan Brouthers	Brooklyn Dodgers	.335
1881	Cap Anson	Chicago Cubs	.399	1893	Hugh Duffy	Boston Braves	.378
1882	Dan Brouthers	Buffalo Bisons	.367	1894	Hugh Duffy	Boston Braves	.438
1883	Dan Brouthers	Buffalo Bisons	.371	1895	Jesse Burkett	Cleveland Spiders	.423
1884	Jim O'Rourke	Buffalo Bisons	.350	1896	Jesse Burkett	Cleveland Spiders	.410
1885	Roger Connor	N.Y. Giants	.371	1897	Willie Keeler	Baltimore Orioles	.432
1886	Mike Kelly	Chicago Cubs	.388	1898	Willie Keeler	Baltimore Orioles	.379
1887	Cap Anson	Chicago Cubs	.421	1899	Ed Delahanty	Philadelphia Phillies	.408
1888	Cap Anson	Chicago Cubs	.343	1900	Honus Wagner	Pittsburgh Pirates	.380

	NATIONAL LEAGUE				AMERICAN LEAGUE		
Year	Name	Team	Avg.		Name	Team	Avg.
1901	Jesse Burkett	St. Louis Cardinals	.382		Nap Lajoie	Philadelphia Athletics	.422
1902	C.H. Beaumont	Pittsburgh Pirates	.357		Ed Delahanty	Washington Senators	.376
1903	Honus Wagner	Pittsburgh Pirates	.355		Nap Lajoie	Cleveland Indians	.355
1904	Honus Wagner	Pittsburgh Pirates	.349		Nap Lajoie	Cleveland Indians	.381
1905	J. Bentley Seymour	Cincinnati Reds	.377		Elmer Flick	Cleveland Indians	.306
1906	Honus Wagner	Pittsburgh Pirates	.339		George Stone	St. Louis Browns	.358
1907	Honus Wagner	Pittsburgh Pirates	.350		Ty Cobb	Detroit Tigers	.350
1908	Honus Wagner	Pittsburgh Pirates	.354		Ty Cobb	Detroit Tigers	.324
1909	Honus Wagner	Pittsburgh Pirates	.339		Ty Cobb	Detroit Tigers	.377
1910	Sherwood Magee	Philadelphia Phillies	.331		Ty Cobb	Detroit Tigers	.385
1911	Honus Wagner	Pittsburgh Pirates	.334		Ty Cobb	Detroit Tigers	.420
1912	Heinie Zimmerman	Chicago Cubs	.372		Ty Cobb	Detroit Tigers	.410
1913	Jake Daubert	Brooklyn Dodgers	.350		Ty Cobb	Detroit Tigers	.390
1914	Jake Daubert	Brooklyn Dodgers	.329		Ty Cobb	Detroit Tigers	.368
1915	Larry Doyle	New York Giants	.320		Ty Cobb	Detroit Tigers	.370
1916	Hal Chase	Cincinnati Reds	.339		Tris Speaker	Cleveland Indians	.386
1917	Edd Roush	Cincinnati Reds	.341		Ty Cobb	Detroit Tigers	.383
1918	Zack Wheat	Brooklyn Dodgers	.335		Ty Cobb	Detroit Tigers	.382
1919	Edd Roush	Cincinnati Reds	.321		Ty Cobb	Detroit Tigers	.407
1920	Rogers Hornsby	St. Louis Cardinals	.370		George Sisler	St. Louis Browns	.407
1921	Rogers Hornsby	St. Louis Cardinals	.397		Harry Heilmann	Detroit Tigers	.394
1922	Rogers Hornsby	St. Louis Cardinals	.401		George Sisler	St. Louis Browns	.420
1923	Rogers Hornsby	St. Louis Cardinals	.384		Harry Heilmann	Detroit Tigers	.403
1924	Rogers Hornsby	St. Louis Cardinals	.424		Babe Ruth	New York Yankees	.378
1925	Rogers Hornsby	St. Louis Cardinals	.403		Harry Heilmann	Detroit Tigers	.393
1926	Bubbles Hargrave	Cincinnati Reds	.353		Heinie Manush	Detroit Tigers	.377
1927	Paul Waner	Pittsburgh Pirates	.380		Harry Heilmann	Detroit Tigers	.398
1928	Rogers Hornsby	Boston Braves	.387		Goose Goslin	Washington Senators	.379
1929	Lefty O'Doul	Philadelphia Phillies	.398		Lew Fonseca	Cleveland Indians	.369

| | | NATIONAL LEAGUE | | | AMERICAN LEAGUE | |
Year	Name	Team	Avg.	Name	Team	Avg.
1930	Bill Terry	New York Giants	.401	Al Simmons	Philadelphia Athletics	.381
1931	Chick Hafey[1]	St Louis Cardinals	.349	Al Simmons	Philadelphia Athletics	.390
1932	Lefty O'Doul	Brooklyn Dodgers	.368	Dale Alexander	Detroit-Boston	.367
1933	Chuck Klein	Philadelphia Phillies	.368	Jimmie Foxx	Philadelphia Athletics	.356
1934	Paul Waner	Pittsburgh Pirates	.362	Lou Gehrig	New York Yankees	.363
1935	Arky Vaughan	Pittsburgh Pirates	.385	Buddy Myer	Washington Senators	.349
1936	Paul Waner	Pittsburgh Pirates	.373	Luke Appling	Chicago White Sox	.388
1937	Joe Medwick	St. Louis Cardinals	.374	Charlie Gehringer	Detroit Tigers	.371
1938	Ernie Lombardi	Cincinnati Reds	.342	Jimmie Foxx	Boston Red Sox	.349
1939	Johnny Mize	St. Louis Cardinals	.349	Joe DiMaggio	New York Yankees	.381
1940	Debs Garms	Pittsburgh Pirates	.355	Joe DiMaggio	New York Yankees	.352
1941	Pete Reiser	Brooklyn Dodgers	.343	Ted Williams	Boston Red Sox	.406
1942	Ernie Lombardi	Boston Braves	.330	Ted Williams	Boston Red Sox	.356
1943	Stan Musial	St. Louis Cardinals	.357	Luke Appling	Chicago White Sox	.328
1944	Dixie Walker	Brooklyn Dodgers	.357	Lou Boudreau	Cleveland Indians	.327
1945	Phil Cavarretta	Chicago Cubs	.355	Snuffy Stirnweiss	New York Yankees	.309
1946	Stan Musial	St. Louis Cardinals	.365	Mickey Vernon	Washington Senators	.352
1947	Harry Walker	St. Louis-Philadelphia	.363	Ted Williams	Boston Red Sox	.343
1948	Stan Musial	St. Louis Cardinals	.376	Ted Williams	Boston Red Sox	.369
1949	Jackie Robinson	Brooklyn Dodgers	.342	George Kell	Detroit Tigers	.343
1950	Stan Musial	St. Louis Cardinals	.346	Billy Goodman	Boston Red Sox	.354
1951	Stan Musial	St. Louis Cardinals	.355	Ferris Fain	Philadelphia Athletics	.344
1952	Stan Musial	St. Louis Cardinals	.336	Ferris Fain	Philadelphia Athletics	.327
1953	Carl Furillo	Brooklyn Dodgers	.344	Mickey Vernon	Washington Senators	.337
1954	Willie Mays	New York Giants	.345	Bobby Avila	Cleveland Indians	.341
1955	Richie Ashburn	Philadelphia Phillies	.338	Al Kaline	Detroit Tigers	.340
1956	Hank Aaron	Milwaukee Braves	.328	Mickey Mantle	New York Yankees	.353
1957	Stan Musial	St. Louis Cardinals	.351	Ted Williams	Boston Red Sox	.388
1958	Richie Ashburn	Philadelphia Phillies	.350	Ted Williams	Boston Red Sox	.328
1959	Hank Aaron	Milwaukee Braves	.355	Harvey Kuenn	Detroit Tigers	.353
1960	Dick Groat	Pittsburgh Pirates	.325	Pete Runnels	Boston Red Sox	.320
1961	Roberto Clemente	Pittsburgh Pirates	.351	Norm Cash	Detroit Tigers	.361
1962	Tommy Davis	Los Angeles Dodgers	.346	Pete Runnels	Boston Red Sox	.326
1963	Tommy Davis	Los Angeles Dodgers	.326	Carl Yastrzemski	Boston Red Sox	.321
1964	Roberto Clemente	Pittsburgh Pirates	.339	Tony Oliva	Minnesota Twins	.323
1965	Roberto Clemente	Pittsburgh Pirates	.329	Tony Oliva	Minnesota Twins	.321
1966	Matty Alou	Pittsburgh Pirates	.342	Frank Robinson	Baltimore Orioles	.316
1967	Roberto Clemente	Pittsburgh Pirates	.357	Carl Yastrzemski	Boston Red Sox	.326
1968	Pete Rose	Cincinnati Reds	.335	Carl Yastrzemski	Boston Red Sox	.301
1969	Pete Rose	Cincinnati Reds	.348	Rod Carew	Minnesota Twins	.332
1970	Rico Carty	Atlanta Braves	.366	Alex Johnson	California Angels	.329
1971	Joe Torre	St. Louis Cardinals	.363	Tony Oliva	Minnesota Twins	.337
1972	Billy Williams	Chicago Cubs	.333	Rod Carew	Minnesota Twins	.318
1973	Pete Rose	Cincinnati Reds	.338	Rod Carew	Minnesota Twins	.350
1974	Ralph Garr	Atlanta Braves	.353	Rod Carew	Minnesota Twins	.364
1975	Bill Madlock	Chicago Cubs	.354	Rod Carew	Minnesota Twins	.359
1976	Bill Madlock	Chicago Cubs	.339	George Brett	Kansas City Royals	.333
1977	Dave Parker	Pittsburgh Pirates	.338	Rod Carew	Minnesota Twins	.388
1978	Dave Parker	Pittsburgh Pirates	.334	Rod Carew	Minnesota Twins	.333
1979	Keith Hernandez	St. Louis Cardinals	.344	Fred Lynn	Boston Red Sox	.333
1980	Bill Buckner	Chicago Cubs	.324	George Brett	Kansas City Royals	.390
1981[2]	Bill Madlock	Pittsburgh Pirates	.341	Carney Lansford	Boston Red Sox	.336
1982	Al Oliver	Montreal Expos	.331	Willie Wilson	Kansas City Royals	.332
1983	Bill Madlock	Pittsburgh Pirates	.323	Wade Boggs	Boston Red Sox	.361
1984	Tony Gwynn	San Diego Padres	.351	Don Mattingly	New York Yankees	.343
1985	Willie McGee	St. Louis Cardinals	.353	Wade Boggs	Boston Red Sox	.368
1986	Tim Raines	Montreal Expos	.334	Wade Boggs	Boston Red Sox	.357
1987	Tony Gwynn	San Diego Padres	.370	Wade Boggs	Boston Red Sox	.363
1988	Tony Gwynn	San Diego Padres	.313	Wade Boggs	Boston Red Sox	.366
1989	Tony Gwynn	San Diego Padres	.336	Kirby Puckett	Minnesota Twins	.339
1990	Willie McGee	St. Louis Cardinals	.335	George Brett	Kansas City Royals	.329
1991	Terry Pendleton	Atlanta Braves	.319	Julio Franco	Texas Rangers	.341
1992	Gary Sheffield	San Diego Padres	.330	Edgar Martinez	Seattle Mariners	.343
1993	Andres Galarraga	Colorado Rockies	.370	John Olerud	Toronto Blue Jays	.363
1994[2]	Tony Gwynn	San Diego Padres	.394	Paul O'Neill	New York Yankees	.359
1995[2]	Tony Gwynn	San Diego Padres	.368	Edgar Martinez	Seattle Mariners	.356
1996	Ellis Burks	Colorado Rockies	.344	Alex Rodriguez	Seattle Mariners	.358
1997	Tony Gwynn	San Diego Padres	.372	Frank Thomas	Chicago White Sox	.347
1998	Larry Walker	Colorado Rockies	.363	Bernie Williams	New York Yankees	.339
1999	Larry Walker	Colorado Rockies	.379	Nomar Garciaparra	Boston Red Sox	.357

1. Hafey led with .3489, Bill Terry, N.Y., second with .3486, Jim Bottomley, St. Louis, third with .3482. 2. Strike-shortened season.

Home Run Champions, 1938–99

Year	NATIONAL LEAGUE Name, Team	HRs	AMERICAN LEAGUE Name, Team	HRs
1938	Mel Ott, New York	36	Hank Greenberg, Detroit	58
1939	Johnny Mize, St. Louis	28	Jimmie Foxx, Boston	35
1940	Johnny Mize, St. Louis	43	Hank Greenberg, Detroit	41
1941	Dolph Camillia, Brooklyn	34	Ted Williams, Boston	37
1942	Mel Ott, New York	30	Ted Williams, Boston	36
1943	Bill Nicholson, Chicago	29	Rudy York, Detroit	34
1944	Bill Nicholson, Chicago	33	Nick Etten, New York	22
1945	Tommy Holmes, Boston	28	Vern Stephens, St. Louis	24
1946	Ralph Kiner, Pittsburgh	23	Hank Greenberg, Detroit	44
1947	Ralph Kiner, Pittsburgh; Johnny Mize, New York	51	Ted Williams, Boston	32
1948	Ralph Kiner, Pittsburgh; Johnny Mize, New York	40	Joe DiMaggio, New York	39
1949	Ralph Kiner, Pittsburgh	54	Ted Williams, Boston	43
1950	Ralph Kiner, Pittsburgh	47	Al Rosen, Cleveland	37
1951	Ralph Kiner, Pittsburgh	42	Gus Zernial, Chicago-Philadelphia	33
1952	Ralph Kiner, Pittsburgh; Hank Sauer, Chicago	37	Larry Doby, Cleveland	32
1953	Eddie Mathews, Milwaukee	47	Al Rosen, Cleveland	43
1954	Ted Kluszewski, Cincinnati	49	Larry Doby, Cleveland	32
1955	Willie Mays, New York	51	Mickey Mantle, New York	37
1956	Duke Snider, Brooklyn	43	Mickey Mantle, New York	52
1957	Hank Aaron, Milwaukee	44	Roy Sievers, Washington	42
1958	Ernie Banks, Chicago	47	Mickey Mantle, New York	42
1959	Eddie Mathews, Milwaukee	46	Rocky Colavito, Cleveland; Harmon Killebrew, Washington	42
1960	Ernie Banks, Chicago	41	Mickey Mantle, New York	40
1961	Orlando Cepeda, San Francisco	46	Roger Maris, New York	61
1962	Willie Mays, San Francisco	49	Harmon Killebrew, Minnesota	48
1963	Hank Aaron, Milwaukee; Willie McCovey, San Francisco	44	Harmon Killebrew, Minnesota	45
1964	Willie Mays, San Francisco	47	Harmon Killebrew, Minnesota	49
1965	Willie Mays, San Francisco	52	Tony Conigliaro, Boston	32
1966	Hank Aaron, Atlanta	44	Frank Robinson, Baltimore	49
1967	Hank Aaron, Atlanta	39	Harmon Killebrew, Minnesota; Carl Yastrzemski, Boston	44
1968	Willie McCovey, San Francisco	36	Frank Howard, Washington	44
1969	Willie McCovey, San Francisco	45	Harmon Killebrew, Minnesota	49
1970	Johnny Bench, Cincinnati	45	Frank Howard, Washington	44
1971	Willie Stargell, Pittsburgh	48	Bill Melton, Chicago	33
1972	Johnny Bench, Cincinnati	40	Dick Allen, Chicago	37
1973	Willie Stargell, Pittsburgh	44	Reggie Jackson, Oakland	32
1974	Mike Schmidt, Philadelphia	36	Dick Allen, Chicago	32
1975	Mike Schmidt, Philadelphia	38	Reggie Jackson, Oak.; George Scott, Milwaukee	36
1976	Mike Schmidt, Philadelphia	38	Graig Nettles, New York	32
1977	George Foster, Cincinnati	52	Jim Rice, Boston	39
1978	George Foster, Cincinnati	40	Jim Rice, Boston	46
1979	Dave Kingman, Chicago	48	Gorman Thomas, Milwaukee	45
1980	Mike Schmidt, Philadelphia	48	Reggie Jackson, New York; Ben Oglivie, Milwaukee	41
1981[1]	Mike Schmidt, Philadelphia	31	Tony Armas, Boston; Dwight Evans, Boston; Bobby Grich, California; Eddie Murray, Baltimore	22
1982	Dave Kingman, New York	37	Reggie Jackson, California; Gorman Thomas, Milwaukee	39
1983	Mike Schmidt, Philadelphia	40	Jim Rice, Boston	39
1984	Dale Murphy, Atlanta; Mike Schmidt, Philadelphia	36	Tony Armas, Boston	50
1985	Dale Murphy, Atlanta	37	Darrell Evans, Detroit	40
1986	Mike Schmidt, Philadelphia	37	Jesse Barfield, Toronto	40
1987	Andre Dawson, Chicago	49	Mark McGwire, Oakland	49
1988	Darryl Strawberry, New York	39	Jose Canseco, Oakland	42
1989	Kevin Mitchell, San Francisco	47	Fred McGriff, Toronto	36
1990	Ryne Sandberg, Chicago	40	Cecil Fielder, Detroit	51
1991	Howard Johnson, N.Y.	38	Jose Canseco, Oakland	44
1992	Fred McGriff, San Diego	35	Juan Gonzalez, Texas	43
1993	Barry Bonds, San Francisco	46	Juan Gonzalez, Texas	46
1994[1]	Matt Williams, San Francisco	43	Ken Griffey Jr., Seattle	40
1995[1]	Dante Bichette, Colorado	40	Albert Belle, Cleveland	50
1996	Andres Galarraga, Colorado	47	Mark McGwire, Oakland	52
1997	Larry Walker, Colorado[2]	49	Ken Griffey Jr., Seattle[2]	56
1998	Mark McGwire, St. Louis	70	Ken Griffey Jr., Seattle	56
1999	Mark McGwire, St. Louis	65	Ken Griffey Jr., Seattle	48

1. Strike-shortened season 2. Mark McGwire hit 34 home runs with Oakland and 24 with St. Louis for a major-league-leading total of 58. **Source:** Major League Baseball.

Rookie of the Year

	NATIONAL LEAGUE			AMERICAN LEAGUE	
Year	Name	Team	Year	Name	Team
1947[1]	Jackie Robinson	Brooklyn Dodgers			
1948[1]	Alvin Dark	Boston Braves			
1949	Don Newcombe	Brooklyn Dodgers	1949	Roy Sievers	St. Louis Browns
1950	Sam Jethroe	Boston Braves	1950	Walt Dropo	Boston Red Sox
1951	Willie Mays	New York Giants	1951	Gil McDougald	New York Yankees
1952	Joe Black	Brooklyn Dodgers	1952	Harry Byrd	Philadelphia Athletics
1953	Junior Gilliam	Brooklyn Dodgers	1953	Harvey Kuenn	Detroit Tigers
1954	Wally Moon	St. Louis Cardinals	1954	Bob Grim	New York Yankees
1955	Bill Virdon	St. Louis Cardinals	1955	Herb Score	Cleveland Indians
1956	Frank Robinson	Cincinnati Reds	1956	Luis Aparicio	Chicago White Sox
1957	Jack Sanford	Philadelphia Phillies	1957	Tony Kubek	New York Yankees
1958	Orlando Cepeda	San Francisco Giants	1958	Albie Pearson	Washington Senators
1959	Willie McCovey	San Francisco Giants	1959	Bob Allison	Washington Senators
1960	Frank Howard	Los Angeles Dodgers	1960	Ron Hansen	Baltimore Orioles
1961	Billy Williams	Chicago Cubs	1961	Don Schwall	Boston Red Sox
1962	Ken Hubbs	Chicago Cubs	1962	Tom Tresh	New York Yankees
1963	Pete Rose	Cincinnati Reds	1963	Gary Peters	Chicago White Sox
1964	Richie Allen	Philadelphia Phillies	1964	Tony Oliva	Minnesota Twins
1965	Jim Lefebvre	Los Angeles Dodgers	1965	Curt Blefary	Baltimore Orioles
1966	Tommy Helms	Cincinnati Reds	1966	Tommie Agee	Chicago White Sox
1967	Tom Seaver	New York Mets	1967	Rod Carew	Minnesota Twins
1968	Johnny Bench	Cincinnati Reds	1968	Stan Bahnsen	New York Yankees
1969	Ted Sizemore	Los Angeles Dodgers	1969	Lou Piniella	Kansas City Royals
1970	Carl Morton	Montreal Expos	1970	Thurman Munson	New York Yankees
1971	Earl Williams	Atlanta Braves	1971	Chris Chambliss	Cleveland Indians
1972	Jon Matlack	New York Mets	1972	Carlton Fisk	Boston Red Sox
1973	Gary Matthews	San Francisco Giants	1973	Al Bumbry	Baltimore Orioles
1974	Bake McBride	St. Louis Cardinals	1974	Make Hargrove	Texas Rangers
1975	John Montefusco	San Francisco Giants	1975	Fred Lynn	Boston Red Sox
1976	Pat Zachry	Cincinnati Reds	1976	Mark Fidrych	Detroit Tigers
	Butch Metzger	San Diego Padres	1977	Eddie Murray	Baltimore Orioles
1977	Andre Dawson	Montreal Expos	1978	Lou Whitaker	Detroit Tigers
1978	Bob Horner	Atlanta Braves	1979	John Castino	Minnesota Twins
1979	Rick Sutcliffe	Los Angeles Dodgers		Alfredo Griffin	Toronto Blue Jays
1980	Steve Howe	Los Angeles Dodgers	1980	Joe Charboneau	Cleveland Indians
1981	Fernando Valenzuela	Los Angeles Dodgers	1981	Dave Righetti	New York Yankees
1982	Steve Sax	Los Angeles Dodgers	1982	Cal Ripken Jr.	Baltimore Orioles
1983	Darryl Strawberry	New York Mets	1983	Ron Kittle	Chicago White Sox
1984	Dwight Gooden	New York Mets	1984	Alvin Davis	Seattle Mariners
1985	Vince Coleman	St. Louis Cardinals	1985	Ozzie Guillen	Chicago White Sox
1986	Todd Worrell	St. Louis Cardinals	1986	Jose Canseco	Oakland Athletics
1987	Benito Santiago	San Diego Padres	1987	Mark McGwire	Oakland Athletics
1988	Chris Sabo	Cincinnati Reds	1988	Walt Weiss	Oakland Athletics
1989	Jerome Walton	Chicago Cubs	1989	Greg Olson	Baltimore Orioles
1990	Dave Justice	Atlanta Braves	1990	Sandy Alomar Jr.	Cleveland Indians
1991	Jeff Bagwell	Houston Astros	1991	Chuck Knoblauch	Minnesota Twins
1992	Eric Karros	Los Angeles Dodgers	1992	Pat Listach	Milwaukee Brewers
1993	Mike Piazza	Los Angeles Dodgers	1993	Tim Salmon	California Angels
1994	Raul Mondesi	Los Angeles Dodgers	1994	Bob Hamelin	Kansas City Royals
1995	Hideo Nomo	Los Angeles Dodgers	1995	Marty Cordoba	Minnesota Twins
1996	Todd Hollandsworth	Los Angeles Dodgers	1996	Derek Jeter	New York Yankees
1997	Scott Rolen	Philadelphia Phillies	1997	Nomar Garciaparra	Boston Red Sox
1998	Kerry Wood	Chicago Cubs	1998	Ben Grieve	Oakland Athletics

1. One player selected as Major League Rookie of the Year. Policy of naming a player from each league was inaugurated in 1949.
Source: Baseball Writer's Association.

Cy Young Award Winners

BOTH LEAGUES

Year	Name, Team	W–L,	ERA	Year	Name, Team	W–L,	ERA
1956	Don Newcombe, Brooklyn Dodgers	27– 7,	3.06	1962	Don Drysdale, Los Angeles Dodgers	25– 9,	2.83
1957	Warren Spahn, Milwaukee Braves	21–11,	2.69	1963	Sandy Koufax, Los Angeles Dodgers	25– 5,	1.88
1958	Bob Turley, New York Yankees	21– 7,	2.97	1964	Dean Chance, Los Angeles Angels	20– 9,	1.65
1959	Early Wynn, Chicago White Sox	22–10,	3.17	1965	Sandy Koufax, Los Angeles Dodgers	26– 8,	2.04
1960	Vernon Law, Pittsburgh Pirates	20– 9,	3.08	1966	Sandy Koufax, Los Angeles Dodgers	27– 9,	1.73
1961	Whitey Ford, New York Yankees	25– 4,	3.21				

NATIONAL LEAGUE

Year	Name, Team	W–L,	ERA
1967	Mike McCormick, San Francisco Giants	22–10,	2.85
1968	Bob Gibson, St. Louis Cardinals	22– 9,	1.12
1969	Tom Seaver, New York Mets	25– 7,	2.21
1970	Bob Gibson, St. Louis Cardinals	23– 7,	3.12
1971	Ferguson Jenkins, Chicago Cubs	24–13,	2.77
1972	Steve Carlton, Philadelphia Phillies	27–10,	1.97
1973	Tom Seaver, New York Mets	19–10,	2.08
1974	Mike Marshall[1], Los Angeles Dodgers	15–12,	2.42
1975	Tom Seaver, New York Mets	22– 9,	2.38
1976	Randy Jones, San Diego Padres	22–14,	2.74
1977	Steve Carlton, Philadelphia Phillies	23–10,	2.64
1978	Gaylord Perry, San Diego Padres	21– 6,	2.72
1979	Bruce Sutter[2], Chicago Cubs	6– 6,	2.23
1980	Steve Carlton, Philadelphia Phillies	24– 9,	2.34
1981	Fernando Valenzuela[3], Los Angeles Dodgers	13– 7,	2.48
1982	Steve Carlton, Philadelphia Phillies	23–11,	3.10
1983	John Denny, Philadelphia Phillies	19– 6,	2.37
1984	Rick Sutcliffe, Chicago Cubs	20– 6,	3.64
1985	Dwight Gooden, New York Mets	24– 4,	1.53
1986	Mike Scott, Houston Astros	18–10,	2.22
1987	Steve Bedrosian[4], Philadelphia Phillies	5– 3,	2.83
1988	Orel Hershiser, Los Angeles Dodgers	23– 8,	2.26
1989	Mark Davis[5], San Diego Padres	4– 3,	1.85
1990	Doug Drabek, Pittsburgh Pirates	22– 6,	2.76
1991	Tom Glavine, Atlanta Braves	20–11,	2.55
1992	Greg Maddux, Chicago Cubs	20–11,	2.18
1993	Greg Maddux, Atlanta Braves	20–10,	2.36
1994	Greg Maddux[3], Atlanta Braves	16– 6,	1.56
1995	Greg Maddux[3], Atlanta Braves	19– 2,	1.53
1996	John Smoltz, Atlanta Braves	24– 8,	2.94
1997	Pedro Martinez, Montreal Expos	17– 8,	1.90
1998	Tom Glavine, Atlanta Braves	20– 6,	2.47

AMERICAN LEAGUE

Year	Name, Team	W–L,	ERA
1967	Jim Lonborg, Boston Red Sox	22– 9,	3.16
1968	Denny McLain, Detroit Tigers	31– 6,	1.96
1969	Mike Cuellar, Baltimore Orioles	23–11,	2.38
1970	Jim Perry , Minnesota Twins	24–12,	3.03
1971	Vida Blue, Oakland Athletics	24– 8,	1.82
1972	Gaylord Perry, Cleveland Indians	24–16,	1.92
1973	Jim Palmer, Baltimore Orioles	22– 9,	2.40
1974	Catfish Hunter, Oakland Athletics	25–12,	2.49
1975	Jim Palmer, Baltimore Orioles	23–11,	2.09
1976	Jim Palmer, Baltimore Orioles	22–13,	2.51
1977	Sparky Lyle[6], New York Yankees	13– 5,	2.17
1978	Ron Guidry, New York Yankees	25– 3,	1.74
1979	Mike Flanagan , Baltimore Orioles	23– 9,	3.08
1980	Steve Stone, Baltimore Orioles	25– 7,	3.23
1981	Rollie Fingers[3,7], Milwaukee Brewers	6– 3,	1.04
1982	Pete Vuckovich, Milwaukee Brewers	18– 6,	3.34
1983	LaMarr Hoyt, Chicago White Sox	24–10,	3.66
1984	Willie Henandez[8], Detroit Tigers	9– 3,	1.92
1985	Bret Saberhagen , Kansas City Royals	20– 6,	2.87
1986	Roger Clemens, Boston Red Sox	24– 4,	2.48
1987	Roger Clemens, Boston Red Sox	20– 9,	2.97
1988	Frank Viola, Minnesota Twins	24– 7,	2.64
1989	Bret Saberhagen, Kansas City Royals	23– 6,	2.16
1990	Bob Welch, Oakland Athletics	27– 6,	3.06
1991	Roger Clemens, Boston Red Sox	18–10,	3.06
1992	Dennis Eckersley[9], Oakland Athletics	7– 1,	1.91
1993	Jack McDowell, Chicago White Sox	22–10,	3.37
1994	David Cone[3], Kansas City Royals	16– 5,	2.94
1995	Randy Johnson[3], Seattle Mariners	18– 2,	2.48
1996	Pat Hentgen, Toronto Blue Jays	20–10,	3.22
1997	Roger Clemens, Toronto Blue Jays	21– 7,	2.05
1998	Roger Clemens, Toronto Blue Jays	20– 6,	2.65

1. 21 saves in 1974. 2. 37 saves in 1979. 3. Strike-shortened season. 4. 40 saves In 1987. 5. 44 saves in 1989. 6. 26 saves in 1977. 7. 28 saves in 1981. 8. 32 saves in 1984. 9. 51 saves in 1992.

Most Valuable Player Award Winners

Between 1911 and 1914 the Chalmers Award was given to the player judged to be the most valuable in each league. It was not until 1922 that the American League began to select a league MVP. The National League began to do so as well two years later. By the end of the decade, though, both leagues failed to select an MVP. In 1931 the Baseball Writers Association of America began to select the league MVP's and has continued to do so through today.

NATIONAL LEAGUE

Year	Name	Team	HRs	RBIs	Avg.
1911	Frank Schulte	Chicago Cubs	21	121	.300
1912	Larry Doyle	New York Giants	10	90	.330
1913	Jake Daubert	Brooklyn Dodgers	2	52	.350
1914	Johnny Evers	Chicago Cubs	1	40	.279
1924	Dazzy Vance (P)	Brooklyn Dodgers	28W	6L	2.16 ERA
1925	Rogers Hornsby	St. Louis Cardinals	29	143	.403
1926	Bob O'Farrell	St. Louis Cardinals	7	68	.293
1927	Paul Waner	Pittsburgh Pirates	9	131	.380
1928	Jim Bottomley	St. Louis Cardinals	31	136	.325
1929	Rogers Hornsby	St. Louis Cardinals	39	149	.380
1931	Frankie Frisch	St. Louis Cardinals	4	82	.311
1932	Chuck Klein	Philadelphia Phillies	38	137	.348
1933	Carl Hubbell (P)	New York Giants	23W	12L	1.66 ERA
1934	Dizzy Dean (P)	St. Louis Cardinals	30W	7L	2.66 ERA
1935	Gabby Hartnett	Chicago Cubs	13	91	.344
1936	Carl Hubbell (P)	New York Giants	26W	6L	2.31 ERA
1937	Joe Medwick	St. Louis Cardinals	31	154	.374
1938	Ernie Lombardi	Cincinnati Reds	19	95	.342
1939	Bucky Walters (P)	Cinncinati Reds	27W	11L	2.29 ERA
1940	Frank McCormick	Cinncinati Reds	19	127	.309
1941	Dolph Camilli	Brooklyn Dodgers	34	120	.285
1942	Mort Cooper (P)	St. Louis Cardinals	22W	7L	1.78 ERA
1943	Stan Musial	St. Louis Cardinals	13	81	.357
1944	Marty Marion	St. Louis Cardinals	6	63	.267
1945	Phil Cavarretta	Chicago Cubs	6	97	.355
1946	Stan Musial	St. Louis Cardinals	16	103	.365
1947	Bob Elliott	Boston Braves	22	113	.317
1948	Stan Musial	St. Louis Cardinals	39	131	.376
1949	Jackie Robinson	Brooklyn Dodgers	16	124	.342
1950	Jim Konstanty (P)[1]	Philadelphia Phillies	16W	7L	2.66 ERA
1951	Roy Campanella	Brooklyn Dodgers	33	108	.325
1952	Hank Sauer	Chicago Cubs	37	121	.270
1953	Roy Campanella	Brooklyn Dodgers	41	142	.312
1954	Willie Mays	New York Giants	41	110	.345
1955	Roy Campanella	Brooklyn Dodgers	32	107	.318
1956	Don Newcombe (P)	Brooklyn Dodgers	27W	7L	3.06 ERA
1957	Hank Aaron	Milwaukee Braves	44	132	.322
1958	Ernie Banks	Chicago Cubs	47	129	.313
1959	Ernie Banks	Chicago Cubs	45	143	.304
1960	Dick Groat	Pittsburgh Pirates	2	50	.325
1961	Frank Robinson	Cincinnati Reds	37	124	.323
1962	Maury Wills	Los Angeles Dodgers	6	48	.299
1963	Sandy Koufax (P)	Los Angeles Dodgers	25W	5L	1.88 ERA
1964	Ken Boyer	St. Louis Cardinals	24	119	.295
1965	Willie Mays	San Francisco Giants	52	112	.317
1966	Roberto Clemente	Pittsburgh Pirates	29	119	.317
1967	Orlando Cepeda	San Francisco Giants	25	111	.325
1968	Bob Gibson (P)	St. Louis Cardinals	22W	9L	1.12 ERA
1969	Willie McCovey	San Francisco Giants	45	126	.320
1970	Johnny Bench	Cincinnati Reds	45	148	.293
1971	Joe Torre	St. Louis Cardinals	45	137	.363
1972	Johnny Bench	Cincinnati Reds	40	125	.270
1973	Pete Rose	Cincinnati Reds	5	64	.338
1974	Steve Garvey	Los Angeles Dodgers	21	111	.312
1975	Joe Morgan	Cincinnati Reds	17	94	.327
1976	Joe Morgan	Cincinnati Reds	27	111	.320
1977	George Foster	Cincinnati Reds	52	149	.320
1978	Dave Parker	Pittsburgh Pirates	30	117	.334
1979	Keith Hernandez	St. Louis Cardinals	11	105	.344
	Willie Stargell	Pittsburgh Pirates	32	82	.281

NATIONAL LEAGUE

Year	Name	Team	HRs	RBIs	Avg.
1980	Mike Schmidt	Philadelphia Phillies	48	121	.286
1981	Mike Schmidt[2]	Philadelphia Phillies	31	91	.316
1982	Dale Murphy	Atlanta Braves	36	109	.281
1983	Dale Murphy	Atlanta Braves	36	121	.302
1984	Ryne Sandberg	Chicago Cubs	19	84	.314
1985	Willie McGee	St. Louis Cardinals	10	82	.353
1986	Mike Schmidt	Philadelphia Phillies	37	119	.290
1987	Andre Dawson	Chicago Cubs	49	137	.287
1988	Kirk Gibson	Los Angeles Dodgers	25	76	.290
1989	Kevin Mitchell	San Francisco Giants	47	125	.291
1990	Barry Bonds	Pittsburgh Pirates	33	114	.301
1991	Terry Pendleton	Atlanta Braves	22	86	.319
1992	Barry Bonds	Pittsburgh Pirates	34	103	.311
1993	Barry Bonds	San Francisco Giants	46	123	.336
1994	Jeff Bagwell[2]	Houston Astros	39	116	.368
1995	Barry Larkin[2]	Cincinnati Reds	15	66	.319
1996	Ken Caminiti	San Diego Padres	40	130	.326
1997	Larry Walker	Colorado Rockies	49	130	.366
1998	Sammy Sosa	Chicago Cubs	66	158	.308

1. 22 saves in 1950. 2. Strike-shortened season. **Source:** Baseball Writers' Association.

AMERICAN LEAGUE

Year	Player	Team	HRs	RBIs	Avg.
1911	Ty Cobb	Detroit Tigers	8	144	.420
1912	Tris Speaker	Boston Red Sox	10	98	.383
1913	Walter Johnson (P)	Washington Senators	36W	7L	1.09 ERA
1914	Eddie Collins	Philadelphia Athletics	2	85	.344
1922	George Sisler	St. Louis Browns	8	105	.420
1923	Babe Ruth	New York Yankees	41	131	.393
1924	Walter Johnson (P)	Washington Senators	23W	7L	2.72 ERA
1925	Roger Peckinpaugh	Washington Senators	4	64	.294
1926	George Burns	Cleveland Indians	4	114	.358
1927	Lou Gehrig	New York Yankees	47	175	.373
1928	Mickey Cochrane	Philadelphia Athletics	10	57	.293
1931	Lefty Grove (P)	Philadelphia Athletics	31W	4L	2.06 ERA
1932	Jimmie Foxx	Philadelphia Athletics	58	169	.364
1933	Jimmie Foxx	Philadelphia Athletics	48	163	.356
1934	Mickey Cochrane	Detroit Tigers	2	76	.320
1935	Hank Greenberg	Detroit Tigers	36	170	.328
1936	Lou Gehrig	New York Yankees	49	152	.354
1937	Charley Gehringer	Detroit Tigers	14	96	.371
1938	Jimmie Foxx	Boston Red Sox	50	175	.349
1939	Joe DiMaggio	New York Yankees	30	126	.381
1940	Hank Greenberg	Detroit Tigers	30	125	.357
1941	Joe DiMaggio	New York Yankees	30	125	.357
1942	Joe Gordon	New York Yankees	18	103	.322
1943	Spud Chandler (P)	New York Yankees	20W	4L	1.64 ERA
1944	Hal Newhouser (P)	Detroit Tigers	29W	9L	2.22 ERA
1945	Hal Newhouser (P)	Detroit Tigers	25W	9L	1.81 ERA
1946	Ted Williams	Boston Red Sox	38	123	.342
1947	Joe DiMaggio	New York Yankees	20	97	.315
1948	Lou Boudreau	Cleveland Indians	18	106	.355
1949	Ted Williams	Boston Red Sox	43	159	.343
1950	Phil Rizzuto	New York Yankees	7	66	.324
1951	Yogi Berra	New York Yankees	27	88	.294
1952	Bobby Shantz (P)	Philadelphia Athletics	24W	7L	2.48 ERA
1953	Al Rosen	Cleveland Indians	43	145	.336
1954	Yogi Berra	New York Yankees	22	125	.307
1955	Yogi Berra	New York Yankees	27	108	.272
1956	Mickey Mantle	New York Yankees	52	130	.353
1957	Mickey Mantle	New York Yankees	34	94	.365
1958	Jackie Jensen	Boston Red Sox	35	122	.286
1959	Nelson Fox	Chicago White Sox	2	70	.306
1960	Roger Maris	New York Yankees	39	112	.283
1961	Roger Maris	New York Yankees	61	142	.269
1962	Mickey Mantle	New York Yankees	30	89	.321
1963	Elston Howard	New York Yankees	28	85	.287
1964	Brooks Robinson	Baltimore Orioles	28	118	.317

Year	Player	Team	HRs	RBIs	Avg.
		AMERICAN LEAGUE			
1965	Zoilo Versalles	Minnesota Twins	19	77	.273
1966	Frank Robinson	Baltimore Orioles	49	122	.316
1967	Carl Yastrzemski	Boston Red Sox	44	121	.326
1968	Dennis McLain (P)	Detroit Tigers	31W	6L	1.96ERA
1969	Harmon Killebrew	Minnesota Twins	49	140	.276
1970	Boog Powell	Baltimore Orioles	35	114	.297
1971	Vida Blue (P)	Oakland Athletics	24W	8L	1.82ERA
1972	Dick Allen	Chicago White Sox	37	113	.308
1973	Reggie Jackson	Oakland Athletics	32	117	.293
1974	Jeff Burroughs	Texas Rangers	25	118	.301
1975	Fred Lynn	Boston Red Sox	21	105	.331
1976	Thurman Munson	New York Yankees	17	105	.302
1977	Rod Carew	Minnesota Twins	14	100	.388
1978	Jim Rice	Boston Red Sox	46	139	.315
1979	Don Baylor	California Angels	36	139	.296
1980	George Brett	Kansas City Royals	24	118	.390
1981	Rollie Fingers (P)[1,2]	Milwaukee Brewers	6W	3L	1.04 ERA
1982	Robin Yount	Milwaukee Brewers	29	114	.331
1983	Cal Ripken Jr.	Baltimore Orioles	27	102	.318
1984	Willie Hernandez (P)[3]	Detroit Tigers	9W	3L	2.48 ERA
1985	Don Mattingly	New York Yankees	35	145	.324
1986	Roger Clemens (P)	Boston Red Sox	24W	4L	2.48 ERA
1987	George Bell	Toronto Blue Jays	47	134	.308
1988	Jose Canseco	Oakland Athletics	42	124	.307
1989	Robin Yount	Milwaukee Brewers	21	103	.318
1990	Rickey Henderson	Oakland Athletics	28	61	.325
1991	Cal Ripken Jr.	Baltimore Orioles	34	114	.323
1992	Dennis Eckersley (P)[4]	Oakland Athletics	7W	1L	1.91 ERA
1993	Frank Thomas	Chicago White Sox	41	128	.317
1994	Frank Thomas[1]	Chicago White Sox	38	101	.353
1995	Mo Vaughn[1]	Boston Red Sox	39	126	.300
1996	Juan Gonzalez	Texas Rangers	47	144	.314
1997	Ken Griffey Jr.	Seattle Mariners	56	147	.304
1998	Juan Gonzalez	Texas Rangers	45	157	.318

1. Strike-shortened season. 2. 28 saves in 1981. 3. 32 saves in 1984. 4. 51 saves in 1992. **Source:** Baseball Writers' Association.

All Star Game Results, 1933–99

Year	Winner, Score	Year	Winner, Score	Year	Winner, Score	Year	Winner, Score
1933	American, 4–2	1950	National, 4–3	1964	National, 7–4	1982	National, 4–1
1934	American, 9–7	1951	National, 8–3	1965	National, 6–5	1983	American, 13–3
1935	American, 4–1	1952	National, 3–2	1966	National, 2–1	1984	National, 3–1
1936	National, 4–3	1953	National, 5–1	1967	National, 2–1	1985	National , 6–1
1937	American, 8–3	1954	American, 11–9	1968	National, 1–0	1986	American, 3–2
1938	National, 4–1	1955	National, 6–5	1969	National, 9–3	1987	National, 2–0 (10)
1939	American, 3–1	1956	National, 7–3	1970	National, 5–4	1988	American, 2–1
1940	National, 4–0	1957	American, 6–5	1971	American, 6–4	1989	American, 5–3
1941	American, 7–5	1958	American, 4–3	1972	National, 4–3	1990	American, 2–0
1942	American, 3–1	1959(1)[1]	National, 5–4	1973	National, 7–1	1991	American, 4–2
1943	American, 5–3	1959(2)	American, 5–3	1974	National , 7–2	1992	American, 13–6
1944	National, 7–1	1960(1)	National, 5–3	1975	National, 6–3	1993	American, 9–3
1945	No game due to wartime travel restrictions	1960(2)	National , 6–0	1976	National , 7–1	1994	National, 8–7 (10)
		1961(1)	National, 5–4	1977	National, 7–5	1995	National, 3–2
		1961(2)	Tie[2], 1–1	1978	National, 7–3	1996	National, 6–0
1946	American, 12–0	1962(1)	National, 3–1	1979	National, 7–6	1997	American, 3–1
1947	American, 2–1	1962(2)	American, 9–4	1980	National, 4–2	1998	American, 13–8
1948	American, 5–2	1963	National, 5–3	1981	National, 5–4	1999	American, 4–1
1949	American, 11–7						

1. Two All Star games were played 1959–62. 2. Game was called because of rain after nine innings.

The Baseball Hall of Fame

National Baseball Hall of Fame and Museum
Main Street, Cooperstown, NY 13326.
(607) 547-9988; www.baseballhalloffame.org
Hours: From May 1 to Sept. 30—9:00 a.m. to 9:00 p.m.
From Oct. 1 to April 30—9:00 a.m. to 5:00 p.m.
(Every day of the year except Thanksgiving, Christmas and New Year's.)

The Hall of Fame was established in 1936 and opened in Cooperstown, N.Y. in 1939. From the start, there were two ways to be elected: by receiving 75 percent of the votes cast by the Baseball Writers Association of America or 75 percent of the votes cast by a Committee on Old Timers. In the first year, the writers picked the top five players of the post-1900 era: Ty Cobb, Walter Johnson, Christy Mathewson, Babe Ruth, and Honus Wagner. To be elected, a player must have played at least 10 years in the major leagues and been retired for at least five years. The Committee on Old Timers, originally created to consider 19th Century players, was replaced by a Special Veterans Committee whose scope includes all players retired for a minimum of 25 years who may have been overlooked when they were first eligible. In 1971 a Special Committee on the Negro Leagues was set up to consider ballplayers who played in the old Negro Leagues.

Player/Position/Year Inducted	Games	At Bats	HRs	Avg.	Hits	RBIs
Aaron, Henry (Hank) OF 1982	3,298	12,364	755	.305	3,771	2,297
All-time leader in home runs and RBI						
Anson, Adrian (Cap) 1B 1939	2,276	9,108	96	.334	3,041	1,715
Managed 20 years, 1879-98, winning five pennants						
Aparicio, Luis SS 1984	2,599	10,230	83	.262	2,677	791
Led AL in stolen bases nine years in a row (1955–64)						
Appling, Luke SS 1964	2,422	8,857	45	.310	2,749	1,116
Batted .388 in 1936						
Ashburn, Richie OF 1995	2,189	8,365	29	.308	2,574	586
Hit .300 or more nine times						
Averill, Earl OF 1975	1,669	6,358	238	.318	2,020	1,165
232 hits in 1936						
Baker, Frank (Home Run) 3B 1955	1,575	5,985	96	.307	1,838	1,013
Batted .363 in six World Series						
Bancroft, Dave SS 1971	1,913	7,182	32	.279	2,004	591
Handled 984 chances in 1922						
Banks, Ernie SS, 1B 1977	2,528	9,421	512	.274	2,583	1,636
Consecutive MVP awards, 1958–59						
Beckley, Jake 1B 1971	2,386	9,527	88	.308	2,931	1,575
244 career triples, mostly in 19th Century						
Bench, Johnny C 1989	2,158	7,658	389	.267	2,048	1,376
Hit .529 in 1976 World Series; NL MVP 1970, 1972						
Berra, Lawrence (Yogi) C, OF 1972	2,120	7,555	358	.285	2,150	1,430
Three MVP awards, 1951, 1954, 1955						
Bottomley, Jim 1B 1974	1,991	7,471	219	.310	2,313	1,422
12 RBI in one game, 1924						
Boudreau, Lou SS 1970	1,646	6,030	68	.295	1,779	789
MVP in 1948; managed 16 years						
Bresnahan, Roger C, OF 1945	1,430	4,478	26	.279	1,251	530
212 stolen bases; first catcher elected to Hall of Fame						
Brett, George 3B, 1B 1999	2,707	10,349	317	.305	3,154	1,595
Hit .300 11 times; 13-time all-star; hit .390 in 1980.						
Brock, Lou OF 1985	2,616	10,332	149	.293	3,023	900
938 stolen bases; batted .391 in three World Series						
Brouthers, Dan 1B 1945	1,673	6,716	106	.343	2,304	1,056
Seven slugging and five batting titles during 19th Century						
Burkett, Jesse OF 1946	2,072	8,430	75	.341	2,873	952
Led NL in batting three times and in hits four times						
Campanella, Roy C 1969	1,215	4,205	242	.276	1,161	856
Three MVP awards, 1951, 1953, 1955						
Carey, Max OF 1961	2,476	9,363	69	.285	2,665	800
738 stolen bases						
Cepeda, Orlando 1B 1999	2,124	7,927	379	.297	2,351	1,365
Seven-time All-star; NL MVP 1967; .499 career slugging percentage						
Chance, Frank 1B 1946	1,286	4,295	20	.297	1,274	596
Managed Chicago (NL) to four pennants in five years, 1906–10						
Clarke, Fred OF 1945	2,245	8,588	67	.315	2,708	1,015
223 career triples, hit .300 or better 11 times						
Clemente, Roberto OF 1973	2,433	9,454	240	.317	3,000	1,305
Career average of over 18 outfield assists per season						
Cobb, Ty OF 1936	3,034	11,429	118	.367	4,191	1,961
Batted .320 or better in 23 straight years						
Cochrane, Micky C 1947	1,482	5,169	119	.320	1,652	832
Two MVP awards, 1928 and 1934						
Collins, Eddie 2B 1939	2,826	9,949	47	.333	3,311	1,299
Hit .340 or better 10 times; led AL in fielding nine times						

Player/Position/Year Inducted	Games	At Bats	HRs	Avg.	Hits	RBIs
Collins, Jimmy 3B 1945	1,728	6,796	64	.294	1,997	982
Led NL in home runs, 1898						
Combs, Earle OF 1970	1,454	5,748	58	.325	1,866	629
Averaged 127 runs scored per season						
Connor, Roger 1B 1976	1,998	7,798	136	.318	2,480	1,078
Held all-time HR record before Babe Ruth						
Crawford, Sam OF 1957	2,517	9,580	97	.309	2,964	1,525
312 triples, best ever						
Cronin, Joe SS 1956	2,124	7,579	170	.301	2,285	1,424
MVP in 1930; managed 1933-47						
Cuyler, Hazen (Kiki) OF 1968	1,879	7,161	127	.321	2,299	1,065
Led NL in runs scored twice, stolen bases four times						
Davis, George SS 1998	2,376	9,035	73	.295	2,665	1,435
Hit over .300 nine years in a row (1893–1901)						
Delahanty, Ed IF, OF 1945	1,834	7,502	100	.345	2,591	1,464
Batted .408 in 1899						
Dickey, Bill C 1954	1,789	6,300	202	.313	1,969	1,209
Catcher on eight AL-pennant-winning teams						
DiMaggio, Joe OF 1955	1,736	6,821	361	.325	2,214	1,537
56 game hitting streak in 1941						
Doby, Larry OF 1998	1,533	5,348	253	.283	1,515	969
Led AL in HR twice; seven-time all-star (1949–55); first black man to play in AL						
Doerr, Bobby 2B 1986	1,865	7,093	223	.288	2,042	1,247
Led AL in slugging 1944						
Duffy, Hugh OF 1945	1,736	7,062	103	.328	2,314	1,299
Batted .438 in 1894						
Evers, Johnny 2B 1946	1,783	6,134	12	.270	1,658	538
NL MVP in 1914						
Ewing, Buck C, IF, OF 1939	1,315	5,363	70	.303	1,625	733
Regarded as the greatest player of the 19th Century						
Ferrell, Rick C 1984	1,884	6,028	28	.281	1,692	734
Led AL catchers at times in putouts, assists, fielding average, and double plays						
Flick, Elmer OF 1963	1,484	5,603	47	.315	1,767	756
Led AL in triples 1905–07						
Fox, Nellie 2B 1997	2,367	9,232	35	.288	2,663	790
Led AL in putouts, 1951–60						
Foxx, Jimmie 1B, 3B 1951	2,317	8,134	534	.325	2,646	1,921
Slugged over .700 three seasons						
Frisch, Frank 2B, 3B 1947	2,311	9,112	105	.316	2,880	1,244
Hit .300 or better 11 years in a row (1921–31)						
Gehrig, Lou 1B 1939	2,164	8,001	493	.340	2,721	1,990
Played in 2,130 consecutive games; first player to hit 4 HRs in one game						
Gehringer, Charlie 2B 1949	2,323	8,860	184	.320	2,839	1,427
60 doubles in 1936						
Goslin, Leon (Goose) OF 1968	2,287	8,655	248	.316	2,735	1,609
100+ RBI 11 years						
Greenberg, Hank 1B 1956	1,394	5,193	331	.313	1,628	1,276
58 home runs in 1938; 63 doubles in 1934						
Hafey, Charles (Chick) OF 1971	1,283	4,625	164	.317	1,466	833
NL batting title (.349) in 1931						
Hamilton, Billy OF 1961	1,593	6284	40	.344	2,163	736
Scored 196 runs in 1894, with a .509 on-base average and 99 stolen bases						
Hartnett, Charles (Gabby) C 1955	1,990	6,432	236	.297	1,912	1,179
Played on four NL pennant winners, managed one						
Heilmann, Harry OF, 1B 1952	2,146	7,787	183	.342	2,660	1551
Batted .403 in 1923						
Herman, Billy 2B 1975	1,922	7,707	47	.304	2,345	839
57 doubles in 1935						
Hooper, Harry OF 1971	2,308	8,785	75	.281	2,466	817
375 career stolen bases						
Hornsby, Rogers 2B, IF 1942	2,259	8,173	301	.358	2,930	1584
Batted .402 in years 1921–25; nine slugging titles						
Jackson, Reggie 1993	2,820	9,864	563	.262	2,584	1,702
Played in 5 World Series and 11 divisional playoffs in 21 years; World Series MVP 1977						
Jackson, Travis SS 1982	1,656	6,086	135	.291	1,768	929
Batted over .300 six times in 1920's and 1930's						
Jennings, Hugh SS 1945	1,285	4,905	18	.312	1,531	840
Batted .398 in 1896						
Kaline, Al OF 1980	2,834	10,116	399	.297	3,007	1,583
3,007 career hits						
Keeler, Willie OF 1939	2,124	8,591	34	.345	2,962	810
Batted .432 in 1897; 495 career stolen bases						
Kell, George 3B 1983	1,795	6,702	78	.306	2,054	870
AL batting champ (.343) in 1949						
Kelley, Joe OF 1971	1,845	7,018	65	.319	2,242	1,193
Averaged 151 runs scored, 1894–96						

Player/Position/Year Inducted	Games	At Bats	HRs	Avg.	Hits	RBIs
Kelly, George 1B 1973	1,622	5,993	148	.297	1,778	1,020
Led NL in RBI, 1920 and 1925						
Kelly, Mike (King) OF, C 1945	1,463	5,923	69	.307	1,820	794
Two batting titles, 1884 and 1886; 315 career stolen bases						
Killebrew, Harmon 1B, 3B, OF 1984	2,435	8,147	573	.256	2,086	1,584
40+ home runs eight years						
Kiner, Ralph OF 1975	1,472	5,205	369	.279	1,451	1,015
Second highest home run per at bat ratio of all-time						
Klein, Chuck OF 1980	1,753	6,486	300	.320	2,076	1,201
44 outfield assists in 1930						
Lajoie, Napoleon (Larry) 2B 1937	2,475	9,589	82	.339	3,251	1,599
Batted .422 in 1901						
Lazerri, Tony IF 1991	1,740	6,297	178	.292	1,840	1,191
Batted .300 or better five times; clutch hitter in World Series						
Lindstrom, Fred 3B, OF 1976	1,438	5,611	103	.311	1,747	779
231 hits in 1928						
Lombardi, Ernie C 1986	1,853	5,855	190	.306	1,792	990
Two NL batting titles, 1938 and 1942						
Mantle, Mickey OF 1974	2,401	8,102	536	.298	2,415	1,509
52 home runs in 1956, 54 in 1961						
Manush, Heinie OF 1964	2,009	7,653	110	.330	2,524	1,173
Hit .378 in 1926						
Maranville, Rabbit SS, 2B 1954	2,670	10,078	28	.258	2,605	884
23 year career; hit .308 in two World Series						
Mathews, Eddie 3B 1978	2,388	8,537	512	.271	2,315	1,453
1,444 career walks						
Mays, Willie OF 1979	2,992	10,881	660	.302	3,283	1,903
Slugged over .600 six seasons						
McCarthy, Tommy OF 1946	1,275	5,128	44	.292	1,496	666
Averaged 122 runs scored, 1888–94						
McCovey, Willie 1B, OF 1986	2,588	8,197	521	.270	2,211	1,555
Hit 18 career grand slams						
Medwick, Joe OF 1968	1,984	7,635	205	.324	2,471	1,383
Won NL triple crown in 1937						
Mize, Johnny 1B 1981	1,884	6,443	359	.312	2,011	1,337
Four-time NL home run champ						
Morgan, Joe 2B 1990	2,649	9,277	268	.271	2,517	1,133
Won back-to-back MVP Awards (1975–76)						
Musial, Stan OF, 1B 1969	3,026	10,972	475	.331	3,630	1,951
725 doubles and 177 triples						
O'Rourke, Jim OF 1945	1,774	7,435	51	.310	2,304	830
Batted .300+ eleven times in the 19th Century						
Ott, Mel OF 1951	2,732	9,456	511	.304	2,876	1,860
Averaged 121 RBI 1929–38						
Reese, Harold (Pee Wee) SS 1984	2,166	8,058	126	.269	2,170	885
Finished in the top ten of MVP ballotting nine times						
Rice, Sam OF 1963	2,404	9,269	34	.322	2,987	1,078
Only 18 strikeouts per 154 games						
Rizzuto, Phil SS 1994	1,661	5,816	38	.273	1,588	563
AL MVP in 1950; Played in 9 World Series						
Robinson, Brooks 3B 1983	2,896	10,654	268	.267	2,848	1357
16 consecutive Gold Gloves, 1960–75						
Robinson, Frank OF 1982	2,808	10,006	586	.294	2,943	1812
MVP in both leagues; AL triple crown in 1966						
Robinson, Jackie 2B 1962	1,382	4,877	137	.311	1,518	734
First black player in MLB; Rookie of the Year 1947; MVP and batting champ 1949						
Roush, Edd OF 1962	1,967	7,363	68	.323	2,376	981
Two NL batting titles, 1917 and 1919						
Ruth, George (Babe) OF, P 1936	2,503	8,399	714	.342	2,873	2211
Slugged .847 1920–21						
Schalk, Ray C 1955	1,760	5,306	12	.253	1,345	594
176 stolen bases						
Schmidt, Mike 3B 1995	2,404	8,352	548	.267	2,234	1,595
Led NL in homers 8 times; won 10 Gold Gloves						
Schoendienst, Albert (Red) 1989	2,216	8,479	84	.289	2,449	773
Managed Cardinals to two pennants and 1967 World Series crown						
Sewell, Joe SS, 3B 1977	1,902	7,132	49	.312	2,226	1,051
Only 22 strikeouts in his last 2,500 at bats, 1929–33						
Simmons, Al OF 1953	2,215	8,761	307	.334	2,927	1,827
Drove in over 100 runs in each of his first 11 years, 1924–34						
Sisler, George 1B 1939	2,055	8,267	100	.340	2,812	1,175
Bated .400 1920–22						

Player/Position/Year Inducted	Games	At Bats	HRs	Avg.	Hits	RBIs
Slaughter, Enos OF 1985 52 doubles in 1939	2,380	7,946	169	.300	2,383	1,304
Snider, Edwin (Duke) OF 1980 Averaged 41 home runs, 1953–57	2,143	7,161	407	.295	2,116	1,333
Speaker, Tris OF 1937 Led AL in doubles eight times	2,789	10,208	117	.344	3,515	1,559
Stargell, Willie OF, 1B 1988 MVP in 1979	2,360	7,927	475	.282	2,232	1,540
Terry, Bill 1B 1954 Hit .401 in 1930	1,721	6,428	154	.341	2,193	1,078
Thompson, Sam OF 1974 166 RBI in 1887, 165 in 1895	1,410	6,005	128	.331	1,986	1,299
Tinker, Joe SS 1946 Played in four World Series with Chicago Cubs	1,805	6,441	31	.263	1,695	782
Traynor, Pie 3B 1948 100+ RBI seven years	1,941	7,559	58	.320	2,416	1,273
Vaughan, Joseph (Arky) SS 1985 .385 in 1935	1,817	6,622	96	.318	2,103	926
Wagner, Honus SS 1936 Eight batting titles, four in a row 1906–09	2786	10,427	101	.329	3,430	1,732
Wallace, Bobby SS 1953 Handled 6.1 chances per game at shortstop.	2,386	8,652	35	.267	2,314	1,121
Waner, Lloyd OF 1967 234 hits in 1929	1,992	7,772	28	.316	2,459	598
Waner, Paul OF 1952 62 doubles in 1932	2,549	9,459	112	.333	3,152	1,309
Wheat, Zack OF 1959 Batted .375 at age 36 in 1924	2,410	9,106	132	.317	2,884	1,261
Williams, Billy OF 1987 30+ home runs in five seasons	2,488	9,350	426	.290	2,711	1,475
Williams, Ted OF 1966 Last .400 hitter in majors, .406 in 1941	2,292	7,706	521	.344	2,654	1,839
Wilson, Lewis (Hack) OF 1979 56 home runs and 190 RBI in 1930	1,348	4,760	244	.307	1,461	1,062
Yastrzemski, Carl (Yaz) OF, 1B 1989 Won Triple Crown in 1967; won batting titles in 1963, 1967, and 1968	3,308	11,988	452	.285	3,419	1,844
Youngs, Ross OF 1972 Killed at age 30; .398 on-base average in four World Series, 1921–24.	1,211	4,627	42	.322	1,491	592
Yount, Robin SS, OF 1999 Won AL MVP awards at shortstop (1982) and center field (1989), the only player ever to do so.	2,856	11,008	251	.285	3,142	1,406

▶FUTURE HALL OF FAMERS

While there are no specific criteria for election in to the Hall of Fame, certain benchmark numbers almost guarantee enshrinement. For many years, those numbers were 3,000 hits or 400 home runs. Every eligible player with 3,000 hits—Pete Rose, banned for life from baseball, is ineligible—and all but two of the eligible players with 400 home runs—Dave Kingman and Darrell Evans are the exceptions—are in the Hall of Fame. (Although given the ease with which players are hitting homers these days, the bar may have to be raised to 500 homers).

Assuming the status quo, however, the following players who have retired in the past several years should start booking hotel reservations in Cooperstown: **Dave Winfield** (3,110 hits and 465 home runs), **Paul Molitor** (3,319 hits), and **Eddie Murray** (3,255 hits and 504 home runs). In addition **Wade Boggs** and **Tony Gwynn**, who both entered the 3,000 hit club on the same weekend in 1999, are first ballot locks. Injuries curtailed the 1999 season for **Cal Ripken**, leaving him just 9 hits short of 3,000, but even if he doesn't return in 2000, his 402 homers and 2,632 consecutive games will propel him to the Hall.

Some other players are the stuff of baseball arguments. **Tony Perez** was a cog in the middle of Cincinnati's Big Red Machine teams of the 1970s, but his accomplishments were often overshadowed by Joe Morgan and Johnny Bench. Perez's 1,652 RBIs are the most for a non-Hall-of-Famer and his 379 home runs are the most for a Latin players. **Gary Carter** (324 homers) and **Carlton Fisk** (376), the two premier catchers of the 1980s, both fell short of 400 home runs, but their defensive abilities will probably catapult them to Cooperstown. The career of all-time stolen base leader **Rickey Henderson** appeared to be over after a sub-par 1998 with Oakland. But the 40-year-old left fielder hit .315 in 1999 for the New York Mets, leaving him just 184 hits short of 3,000, and he pledged to play for several more years.

Lee Smith, the all-time leader in saves with 473, may join Hoyt Wilhelm as the only relief pitchers in the hall of Fame. Otherwise, the only pitchers slated for enshrinement are still active and have multiple Cy Young Awards: **Roger Clemens** with five awards, and **Greg Maddux,** with four.

Hall of Fame Pitchers

Player/Year Inducted	W	L	ERA	Games	Innings	Strikeouts
Alexander, Grover Cleveland 1938	373	208	2.56	696	5,189	2,199
Won 30 games three years; led NL in ERA five times						
Bender, Charles (Chief) 1953	210	127	2.46	459	3,017	1,711
Led AL in winning percentage three seasons						
Brown, Mordecai (Three-Finger) 1949	239	129	2.06	481	3,172	1,375
1.04 ERA in 1906						
Bunning, Jim 1996	224	184	3.27	591	3,760	2,855
Struck out 1,000 batters in each league						
Carlton, Steve (Lefty) 1994	329	244	3.22	741	5,217	4,136
Four-time Cy Young Award winner (1972, 1977, 1980, 1982)						
Chesbro, Jack 1946	198	132	2.68	392	2,897	1,265
41 wins in 1904						
Clarkson, John 1963	326	177	2.81	531	4,536	2,015
53 wins in 1885, with 623 innings pitched						
Coveleski, Stan 1969	215	142	2.88	450	3,093	981
Led AL in ERA in 1925, 2.84						
Cummings, Williams (Candy) 1939	21	22	2.78	43	372	37
Inventor of the curveball						
Dean, Jay (Dizzy) 1953	150	83	3.03	317	1,966	1,155
30 wins in 1934						
Drysdale, Don 1984	209	166	2.95	518	3,432	2,486
56 2/3 consecutive scoreless innings, 1968						
Faber, Urban (Red) 1964	254	212	3.15	669	4,088	1,471
Led AL in ERA in 1921 and 1922						
Feller, Bob 1962	266	162	3.25	570	3,827	2,581
Led AL in wins six times, in shutouts seven						
Rollie Fingers 1992	114	118	2.90	944	1,701	1,299
341 saves over 17 years; AL MVP in 1981						
Ford, Edward (Whitey) 1974	236	106	2.75	498	3,170	1,956
25–4 in 1961, 24–7 in 1963						
Galvin, James (Pud) 1965	361	310	2.87	697	5,941	1,799
46 wins in 1883 and 1884						
Gibson, Bob 1981	251	174	2.91	528	3,885	3,117
1.12 ERA in 1968, seven straight wins in World Series play						
Gomez, Vernon (Lefty) 1972	189	102	3.34	368	2,503	1,468
Led AL in shutouts three years						
Grimes, Burleigh 1964	270	212	3.53	617	4,180	1,512
Last legal spitball pitcher, he won 20+ five times						
Grove, Robert (Lefty) 1947	300	141	3.06	616	3,941	2,266
Led AL in ERA nine times, in strikeouts seven						
Haines, Jesse 1970	210	158	3.64	555	3,209	981
Twice led NL in shutouts, 1921 and 1927						
Hoyt, Waite 1969	237	182	3.59	674	3,763	1,206
1.83 in 84 World Series innings						
Hubbell, Carl 1947	253	154	2.97	535	3,589	1,678
26–6 in 1936; 1.66 ERA in 1933						
Hunter, Jim (Catfish) 1987	224	166	3.26	500	3,448	2,012
21 or more wins, 1971–75						
Jenkins, Ferguson 1991	284	226	3.34	664	4,499	3,192
Cy Young Award winner in 1971; three-time all-star						
Johnson, Walter 1936	416	279	2.17	802	5,924	3,508
36–7, 1.09 ERA in 1913						
Joss, Addie 1978	160	97	1.88	286	2,336	926
Averaged 21–11, 1.66 ERA in years 1904–08						
Keefe, Tim 1964	344	225	2.62	601	5,072	2,533
Averaged 37 wins 1883–85						
Koufax, Sandy 1972	165	87	2.76	397	2,324	2,396
95–27, 1.85 ERA for seasons 1963-66						
Lemon, Bob 1976	207	128	3.23	460	2,850	1,277
Won 20 or more seven times						
Lyons, Ted 1955	260	230	3.67	594	4,161	1,073
Pitched 27 shutouts, but never won 20 games.						
Marichal, Juan 1983	243	142	2.89	471	3,509	2,303
Only 1.8 walks per nine innings over career						
Marquard, Richard (Rube) 1971	201	177	3.08	536	3,307	1,593
73–23 in years 1911–13						
Mathewson, Christy 1936	373	188	2.13	636	4,782	2,502
80 career shutouts						
McGinnity, Joe 1946	247	144	2.64	466	3,459	1,068
35–8 in 1904, with an ERA of 1.61						

Player/Year Inducted	W	L	ERA	Games	Innings	Strikeouts
Newhouser, Hal 1992	207	150	3.06	488	2,993	1,796
Led AL in victories three years in a row (1944–46)						
Nichols, Charles (Kid) 1949	360	203	2.94	621	5,084	1,885
Won 30 or more games seven straight seasons, 1891–1897						
Niekro, Phil 1997	318	274	3.35	864	5,404	3,342
Knuckleballer pitched until age 48; five-time all-star						
Palmer, Jim 1990	268	152	2.86	558	3,948	2,212
Won Cy Young Award 1973, 1975, 1976						
Pennock, Herb 1948	240	162	3.61	617	3,558	1,227
162–90 as a New York Yankee, 1923–33						
Perry, Gaylord 1991	314	265	3.10	777	5,352	3,534
Won Cy Young Award in both leagues						
Plank, Eddie 1946	327	193	2.34	622	4,505	2,246
1.32 ERA in seven World Series games						
Radbourn, Charles (Old Hoss) 193	308	191	2.67	528	4,535	1,830
60–12 in 1884, with 679 innings pitched						
Rixey, Eppa 1963	266	251	3.15	692	4,495	1,350
Won 25 games in 1922						
Roberts, Robin 1976	286	245	3.41	676	4,689	2,357
28–7 in 1952; five-time NL leader in complete games						
Ruffing, Charles (Red) 1967	273	225	3.80	624	4,344	1,987
.645 winning percentage as a New York Yankee						
Rusie, Amos 1977	243	160	3.07	462	3,770	1,957
Won 30+ games three years						
Ryan, Nolan 1999	324	292	3.19	807	5,386	5,714
Threw seven no-hitters; struck out 300 or more six times; struck out 200 or more 15 times						
Seaver, Tom 1992	311	205	2.86	656	4,782	3,640
Won 20 or more games five times; won Cy Young Award 1969, 1973, 1975						
Spahn, Warren 1973	363	245	3.09	750	5,244	2,583
Won 20 or more games 13 times, including 23 at age 42						
Sutton, Don 1998	324	256	3.26	774	5,280	3,574
Won 15 or more games eight years in a row (1969–76)						
Vance, Clarence (Dazzy) 1955	197	140	3.24	442	2,697	2,045
60–15 over two years—1924, 1925						
Waddell, George (Rube) 1946	191	145	2.16	407	2,961	2,316
349 strikeouts in 1904						
Walsh, Ed 1946	195	126	1.82	430	2,964	1,736
40–15 in 1908 with 11 shutouts; all-time ERA leader						
Ward, Monte 1964	161	101	2.10	291	2,462	920
47 wins in 1879; 40 wins in 1880; played 1,825 games as a hitter						
Welch, Mickey 1973	311	207	2.71	564	4,802	1,850
44–11 in 1885						
Wilhelm, Hoyt 1985	143	122	2.52	1070	2,254	1,610
227 career saves; first relief pitcher elected to Hall of Fame						
Willis, Vic 1995	249	205	2.63	513	3,996	1,651
Won 20 games eight times; 45 complete games in 1902						
Wynn, Early 1972	300	244	3.54	691	4,564	2,334
Led AL in shutouts at age 40 in 1960						
Young, Cy 1937	511	313	2.63	906	7,359	2,799
All-time leader in wins, losses, complete games, and innings pitched						

Managers
Alston, Walter 1983
Durocher, Leo 1994
Hanlon, Ned 1996
Harris, Bucky 1975
Huggins, Miller 1964
Lasorda, Tommy 1997
Lopez, Al 1977
Mack, Connie 1937
McCarthy, Joe 1957
McGraw, John 1937
McKechnie, Bill 1962
Robinson, Wilbert 1945
Selee, Frank, 1999
Stengel, Casey 1966
Weaver, Earl 1996

Umpires
Barlick, Al 1989
Chylak, Nestor, 1999
Conlan, Jocko 1974
Connolly, Tom 1953
Evans, Billy 1973
Hubbard, Cal 1976

Klem, Bill 1953
McGowan, Bill 1992

Pioneers and Executives
Barrow, Ed 1953
Bulkeley, Morgan 1937
Cartwright, Alexander 1938
Chadwick, Henry 1938
Chandler, Happy 1982
Comiskey, Charles 1939
Foster, Andrew (Rube) 1981
Frick, Ford 1970
Giles, Warren 1979
Griffith, Clark 1946
Harridge, William 1972
Hulbert, William 1995
Johnson, Ban 1937
Landis, Kenesaw Mountain 1944
MacPhail, Larry 1978
MacPhail, Lee 1998
Rickey, Branch 1967
Spalding, Albert Goodwill 1939
Veeck, Bill 1991
Weiss, George 1971

Wright, George 1937
Wright, Harry 1953
Yawkey, Tom 1980

Negro Leaguers
Bell, James "Cool Papa" 1974
Charleston, Oscar 1976
Dandridge, Ray 1987
Day, Leon 1995
Dihigo, Martin 1977
Foster, Bill 1996
Gibson, Josh 1972
Irvin, Monte 1973
Johnson, Judy 1975
Leonard, William "Buck" 1972
Lloyd, Pop 1977
Paige, Satchel 1971
Rogan, "Bullet" Joe 1998
Wells, Willie 1997
Williams, "Smokey Joe", 1999

Major League Baseball League Championship Series Results

AMERICAN LEAGUE

Year	Winner	Loser	MVP
1969	Baltimore Orioles-3	Minnesota Twins-0	
1970	Baltimore Orioles-3	Minnesota Twins-0	
1971	Baltimore Orioles-3	Oakland A's-0	
1972	Oakland A's-3	Detroit Tigers-2	
1973	Oakland A's-3	Baltimore Orioles-2	
1974	Oakland A's-3	Baltimore Orioles-1	
1975	Boston Red Sox-3	Oakland A's-0	
1976	New York Yankees-3	Kansas City Royals-2	
1977	New York Yankees-3	Kansas City Royals-2	
1978	New York Yankees-3	Kansas City Royals-1	
1979	Baltimore Orioles-3	California Angels-1	
1980	Kansas City Royals-3	New York Yankees-0	Frank White, Kansas City
1981	New York Yankees-3	Oakland A's-0	Graig Nettles, New York
1982	Milwaukee Brewers-3	California Angels-2	Fred Lynn, California
1983	Baltimore Orioles-3	Chicago White Sox-1	Mike Boddicker, Baltimore
1984	Detroit Tigers-3	Kansas City Royals-0	Kirk Gibson, Detroit
1985[1]	Kansas City Royals-4	Toronto Blue Jays	George Brett, Kansas City
1986	Boston Red Sox-4	California Angels-3	Marty Barrett, Boston
1987	Minnesota Twins-4	Detroit Tigers-1	Gary Gaetti, Minnesota
1988	Oakland A's-4	Boston Red Sox-0	Dennis Eckersley, Oakland
1989	Oakland A's-4	Toronto Blue Jays-1	Rickey Henderson, Oakland
1990	Oakland A's-4	Boston Red Sox-0	Dave Stewart, Oakland
1991	Minnesota Twins-4	Toronto Blue Jays-1	Kirby Puckett, Minnesota
1992	Toronto Blue Jays-4	Oakland Athletics-2	Roberto Alomar, Toronto
1993	Toronto Blue Jays-4	Chicago White Sox-2	Dave Stewart, Toronto
1994	No League Championship Series		
1995[2]	Cleveland Indians-4	Seattle Mariners-2	Orel Hershiser, Cleveland
1996	New York Yankees-4	Baltimore Orioles-1	Bernie Williams, New York
1997	Cleveland Indians-4	Baltimore Orioles-2	Marquis Grissom, Cleveland
1998	New York Yankees-4	Cleveland Indians-2	David Wells, New York
1999	New York Yankees-4	Boston Red Sox-1	Orlando Hernandez, New York

NATIONAL LEAGUE

Year	Winner	Loser	MVP
1969	New York Mets-3	Atlanta Braves-0	
1970	Cincinnati Reds-3	Pittsburgh Pirates-0	
1971	Pittsburgh Pirates-3	San Francisco Giants-1	
1972	Cincinnati Reds-3	Pittsburgh Pirates-2	
1973	New York Mets-3	Cincinnati Reds-2	
1974	Los Angeles Dodgers-3	Pittsburgh Pirates-1	
1975	Cincinnati Reds-3	Pittsburgh Pirates-0	
1976	Cincinnati Reds-3	Philadelphia Phillies-0	
1977	Los Angeles Dodgers-3	Philadelphia Phillies-1	Dusty Baker, Los Angeles
1978	Los Angeles Dodgers-3	Philadelphia Phillies-1	Steve Garvey, Los Angeles
1979	Pittsburgh Pirates-3	Cincinnati Reds-0	Willie Stargell, Pittsburgh
1980	Philadelphia Phillies-3	Houston Astros-2	Manny Trillo, Philadelphia
1981	Los Angeles Dodgers-3	Montreal Expos-2	Burt Hooton, Los Angeles
1982	St. Louis Cardinals-3	Atlanta Braves-0	Darrell Porter, St. Louis
1983	Philadelphia Phillies-3	Los Angeles Dodgers-1	Gary Mathews, Philadelphia
1984	San Diego Padres-3	Chicago Cubs-2	Steve Garvey, San Diego
1985[1]	St. Louis Cardinals-4	Los Angeles Dodgers-2	Ozzie Smith, St. Louis
1986	New York Mets-4	Houston Astros-2	Mike Scott, Houston
1987	St. Louis Cardinals-4	San Francisco Giants-3	Jeff Leonard, San Francisco
1988	Los Angeles Dodgers-4	New York Mets-3	Orel Hershiser, Los Angeles
1989	San Francisco Giants-4	Chicago Cubs-1	Will Clark, San Francisco
1990	Cincinnati Reds-4	Pittsburgh Pirates-2	Rob Dibble, Rany Myers, Cincinnati
1991	Atlanta Braves-4	Pittsburgh Pirates-3	Steve Avery, Atlanta
1992	Atlanta Braves-4	Pittsburgh Pirates-3	John Smoltz, Atlanta
1993	Philadelphia Phillies-4	Atlanta Braves-2	Curt Schilling, Philadelphia
1994	No League Championship Series		
1995[2]	Atlanta Braves-4	Cincinnati Reds-0	Mike Devereaux, Atlanta
1996	Atlanta Braves-4	St. Louis Cardinals-3	Javier Lopez, Atlanta
1997	Florida Marlins-4	Atlanta Braves-2	Livan Hernández, Florida
1998	San Diego Padres-4	Atlanta Braves-2	Sterling Hitchcock, San Diego
1999	Atlanta Braves-4	New York Mets-2	Eddie Perez, Atlanta

Note: MVPs were not named for the championship series before 1977 in the NL or 1980 in the AL. For complete details of the 1999 League Championship Series, see page 973. 1. In 1985 the League Championship Series was switched to a best-of-seven format. 2. In 1995, an additional round of playoffs were added before the League Championship Series.

The World Series

A championship series between the winners of two leagues had been instituted in 1882 between the National League and the American Association, and was played at the end of each season until the A.A. folded in 1890. Following this, the top two N.L. clubs played each other for the "Temple Cup", but the idea never really caught on with the public. When the American League began operations in 1901, there was great animosity between the two circuits due to bidding wars for the services of star players. Peace was established before the 1903 season, and when it became clear that Pittsburgh would win the NL and Boston the AL, the owners of each club reached a private agreement to hold a "World Series" in October. Many were surprised that the newer American League won the title.

There was no agreement to play such a series every year, however, and in 1904 the New York Giants refused to meet the Boston club, probably due to John McGraw's dislike of American League President Ban Johnson. But the baseball public wanted a championship series, and by 1905 Giants owner John Brush proposed rules governing a mandatory series to be played every year. With minute changes, those rules stand to this day.

1903 Boston (A) over Pittsburgh (N), 5–3. The upstart American league emerged victorious in the first World Series, a best of nine affair. The "Pilgrims" (Red Sox) staged one of the greatest comebacks in history by sweeping the final four games. Bill Dineen won three and Cy Young won two for Boston, and held Pirate immortal Honus Wagner to a .222 average.

1904 No series. New York Giant owner John T. Brush and manager John McGraw refused to play the World Champion Boston club, dismissing them as representative of an "inferior league."

1905 New York (N) over Philadelphia (A), 4–1. Every game was a shutout, with Cristy Mathewson throwing three for the Giants. In 27 innings, he allowed 14 hits, striking out 18 and walking one. The Athletics committed five errors in Game 3, the pivotal contest.

1906 Chicago (A) over Chicago (N), 4–2. The first "subway series" was a stunning upset. The "Hitless Wonders" White Sox had batted .230 with 7 home runs during the season, while the Cubs were winning 116 games, still the all-time record. Utilityman George Rohe hit two game-winning triples for the Sox and Ed Walsh pitched two of their wins.

1907 Chicago (N) over Detroit (A), 4–0. The Cubs shut down Ty Cobb, Sam Crawford et al, behind a superb four-man pitching performance, and the hitting of Harry Steinfeldt (.471) and Johnny Evers (.350).

1908 Chicago (N) over Detroit (A), 4–1. Only a little closer this year. Johnny Evers repeated his .350 average of 1907, joining player-manager Frank Chance (.421) and outfielder Wildfire Schulte (.389) in the Cub attack. Ty Cobb led Detroit (.368), to no avail.

1909 Pittsburgh (N) over Detroit (A), 4–3. The Tigers lost their third straight series, as Honus Wagner won the Battle of the Titans with Ty Cobb. The Pirate shortstop hit .333 with six RBI and six stolen bases, and Babe Adams pitched in with three complete game victories.

1910 Philadelphia (A) over Chicago (N), 4–1. Connie Mack's infielders combined to bat .364 as the A's rolled to an easy title. Jack Coombs pitched three wins and tossed in a .385 batting average. The great Cubs pitching staff was growing old.

1911 Philadelphia (A) over New York (N), 4–2. Regarded by some as the greatest team ever, the A's wrestled down a strong New York club featuring Christy Mathewson and Rube Marquard. Frank "Home Run" Baker got his nickname from game-winning blasts in Games Two and Three.

1912 Boston (A) over New York (N), 4–3. This thrill-a-minute series featured an 11-inning tie in Game Two, and an extra-inning final game. Errors by Giants Fred Merkle and Fred Snodgrass enabled Boston to score two runs in the bottom of the tenth inning of the final contest.

1913 Philadelphia (A) over New York (N), 4–1. Home Run Baker again hammered Giant pitching, batting .450 with seven RBI. Eddie Collins also starred for the A's, hitting .421 with three stolen bases.

1914 Boston (N) over Philadelphia (A), 4–0. The red-hot "Miracle Braves" swept the heavily favored Athletics, who scored only six runs in the four games. Catcher Hank Gowdy (.545) and second baseman Johnny Evers (.438) led the Boston offense.

1915 Boston (A) over Philadelphia (N), 4–1. The famous Red Sox outfield of Speaker, Lewis, and Hooper combined to bat .364 while Rube Foster pitched two complete game wins. Foster also batted .500 driving in the winning run in Game Two.

1916 Boston (A) over Brooklyn (N), 4–1. After three one-run games, Boston took charge with 6–2 and 4–1 victories. A young lefthander named Babe Ruth twirled a 14-inning six hitter in Game Two.

1917 Chicago (A) over New York (N), 4–2. The pitching of Red Faber (3-1, 2.33) and the hitting of Eddie Collins, Buck Weaver, and Joe Jackson were too much for the Giants in a sloppy (23 errors) series.

1918 Boston (A) over Chicago (N), 4–2. Every game was a pitchers' duel. The losing Cubs posted a 1.04 ERA over the six games. The Boston staff allowed but nine runs in the series, led by Babe Ruth who extended his consecutive scoreless inning streak to 29⅔.

1919 Cincinnati (N) over Chicago (A), 5–3. The results of this surprising World Series were declared invalid after eight members of the "Black Sox," including Shoeless Joe Jackson, were accused of throwing games for money. A court later found the Chicago players not guilty (most of them never even received the money from the gamblers with whom they conspired), but commissioner Kenesaw Mountain Landis nonetheless barred them from baseball forever.

1920 Cleveland (A) over Brooklyn (N), 5–2. Game Five was surely the most freakish in series history. It featured a) the first World Series grand slam (Indians rightfielder Elmer Smith), b) the first World Series home run by a pitcher (Indians Jim Bagby), and c) the first and only unassisted triple play in series action (Indians second baseman Billy Wambsganss).

1921 New York (N) over New York (A), 5–3. Six Giants batted over .300, and their pitchers held Babe Ruth to a .500 slugging average. Giant hurler Jesse Barnes won two games and batted .444.

1922 New York (N) over New York (A), 4–0. The result was said to be final proof that "brains beat brawn." Giant pitching shut down Babe Ruth, allowing only 11 runs in the five contests (one tie).

1923 New York (A) over New York (N), 4–2. The Yankees took the last three to break the spell of their cross-river rivals, behind Babe Ruth's three homers and .368 average. Casey Stengel hit two home runs for the losers.

1924 Washington (A) over New York (N), 4–3. A 12-innning seventh game won by Walter Johnson in relief capped an exciting affair. Player-manager Bucky Harris starred for the Senators (.333, 7 RBIs), as did outfielder Goose Goslin (.344, 7 RBIs).

1925 Pittsburgh (N) over Washington (A), 4–3. Pirate centerfielder Max Carey had 11 hits and three stolen bases, as Pittsburgh became the first team since 1903 to come back from a three games to one deficit.

1926 St. Louis (N) over New York (A), 4–3. Babe Ruth hit three homers in Game 4, but in the seventh inning of the seventh contest, Grover Cleveland Alexander struck out Tony Lazzeri with the bases loaded, saving the game and the series for the Cardinals.

1927 New York (A) over Pittsburgh (N), 4–0. Generally regarded as the greatest team of all time, the "Murderers' Row" Yankees disposed of the Pirates behind two Babe Ruth homers, plus the pitching of Wilcy Moore, Herb Pennock, and George Pipgrass.

1928 New York (A) over St. Louis (N), 4–0. Another Yankee sweep. Ruth and Lou Gehrig combined to bat .593, with seven home runs and 13 RBI. Waite Hoyt pitched two complete game victories.

1929 Philadelphia (A) over Chicago (N), 4–1. Trailing 8-0 in Game 4, the A's roared back to score 10 runs in the seventh inning. In the next contest, the Mackmen took the series with a three-run ninth inning.

1930 Philadelphia (A) over St. Louis (N), 4–2. Lefty Grove and George Earnshaw pitched well, while Al Simmons, Jimmie Foxx, and Mickey Cochrane combined for 11 extra-base hits. Cardinal regulars batted only .185 in the six games.

1931 St. Louis (N) over Philadelphia (A), 4–3. Cardinal centerfielder Pepper Martin set a record that stood for 33 years with his 12 hits. Martin also stole five bases and hit a home run. Bill Hallahan and Burleigh Grimes handled the pitching, combining for a 4–0, 1.25 ERA.

1932 New York (A) over Chicago (N), 4–0. The Yankees completed a streak of 12 straight World Series victories in sweeping the Cubs. Babe Ruth and Lou Gehrig combined to bat .438, with five homers and 14 RBI.

1933 New York (N) over Washington (A), 4–1. Bill Terry's Giants defeated Joe Cronin's Senators in a battle of player-managers. Carl Hubbell won two for New York and did not allow an earned run.

1934 St. Louis (N) over Detroit (A), 4–3. Dizzy and Paul Dean hurled the Cardinals to the title, winning all four Redbird victories. A bad defensive series, with 27 errors and 13 unearned runs.

1935 Detroit (A) over Chicago (N), 4–2. The Cubs won 21 straight games in September, but came up short against Mickey Cochrane's Tigers. Charlie Gehringer and Tommy Bridges starred for Detroit, while Lou Warneke (2–0, 0.54) was superb for the losers.

1936 New York (A) over New York (N), 4–2. The Yankees hammered Giant pitching in Games 2 and 6, ending with 43 runs for the series. Tony Lazzeri and Bill Dickey each drove in five runs in the second contest, when Joe McCarthy's "Windowbreakers" scored 18 times to set a record.

1937 New York (A) over New York (N), 4–1. Lefty Gomez pitched two of the Yankee wins and drove in the winning run with a single in the final game. The Yanks scored seven runs in the sixth inning of Game 1, then coasted to an easy championship.

1938 New York (A) over Chicago (N), 4–0. In a replay of 1932, the Bronx Bombers blew out an overmatched Cub squad. Cub fans are still waiting for their team's first series victory over the Yankees.

1939 New York (A) over Cincinnati (N), 4–0. New York won its fourth straight World Championship the same way they won the first three—easily. Charlie Keller batted .438 with three homers, and scored as many runs as the entire Reds team, eight.

1940 Cincinnati (N) over Detroit (A), 4–3. The Reds repeated as NL champs, then prevailed over the

Tigers when Paul Derringer beat Bobo Newsome 2–1 in the seventh game. Derringer and Bucky Walters each won two games.

1941 New York (A) over Brooklyn (N), 4–1. With two outs in the ninth inning of Game Four, Dodger catcher Mickey Owen dropped a third strike on Tommy Henrich, allowing him to reach first base. The Yankees then scored four times to win the ballgame, and finished Brooklyn off the next day.

1942 St. Louis (N) over New York (A), 4–1. The Cardinals, winners of 106 games during the regular season, lost Game 1 with the tying run at bat. They then swept four in a row, behind the pitching of Johnny Beazley (2–0, 2.50) and Ernie White's shutout in Game 3.

1943 New York (A) over St. Louis (N), 4–1. In a turnaround from 1942, the Yanks held St. Louis to nine runs in the five games. Joe Gordon and Bill Dickey homered, while third baseman Billy Johnson drove in three runs for New York.

1944 St Louis (N) over St. Louis (A), 4–2. The Browns struggled valiantly in their only World Series appearance, but fell short against a strong Cardinal club left relatively intact by World War II. Ten Browns errors gave the Redbirds 7 unearned runs.

1945 Detroit (A) over Chicago (N), 4–3. Tiger ace Hal Newhouser was hit hard in Game 1, but he bounced back to win Games 5 and 7. Doc Cramer (.379) and Hank Greenberg (2 HR, 7 RBIs) led the Detroit offense.

1946 St. Louis (N) over Boston (A), 4–3. Enos Slaughter scored from first on a base-hit by Harry Walker in the eighth inning of Game 7, giving St. Louis its third title in five years. Harry Brecheen won three games for the Cardinals, allowing but one run.

1947 New York (A) over Brooklyn (N), 4–3. Yankee pitcher Bill Bevens had a no-hitter for 8⅔ innings in Game 4, but lost the game on a double by Cookie Lavagetto. Tommy Henrich (.323) had the game winning RBI in Games 1, 2, and 7.

1948 Cleveland (A) over Boston (N), 4–2. The series featured fine pitching on both sides, including the first game, when Boston's Johnny Sain beat Bob Feller 1–0. Cleveland's Gene Beardon did not allow a run in 10⅔ innings.

1949 New York (A) over Brooklyn (N), 4–1. Game 1 was 0–0 until Tommy Henrich led off the bottom of the ninth with a home run off Don Newcombe. Bobby Brown batted .500 with five RBIs.

1950 New York (A) over Philadelphia (N), 4–0. New York struggled to win the first three contests by scores of 1-0, 2-1, and 3–2, in a series that was closer than it looks. The "Whiz Kid" Phillies held the Yanks to a .222 batting average, but managed to hit only .203 themselves.

1951 New York (A) over New York (N), 4–2. A tired Giant pitching staff held the Yankees in check for three games, but the AL champs broke out to score 23 runs in the final three. Eddie Lopat (2–0, 0.50) starred for the winners.

1952 New York (A) over Brooklyn (N), 4–3. Allie Reynolds and Vic Raschi each won two games, combining for a 1.69 ERA. Johnny Mize hit three homers, and Mickey Mantle and Yogi Berra each hit two. Duke Snider batted .345 with four homers in a losing cause.

1953 New York (A) over Brooklyn (N), 4–2. The Yankees won their fifth straight World Championship as second baseman Billy Martin tied a record with 12 hits. Martin slugged .958 and drove in eight runs.

1954 New York (N) over Cleveland (A), 4–0. The Indians won 111 games during the season, still an AL record. But the Giants, sparked by a spectacular Willie Mays catch in Game 1, went on to defeat Cleveland easily. Pinch hitter-outfielder Dusty Rhodes drove in seven runs on two homers and two singles in six at bats.

1955 Brooklyn (N) over New York (A), 4–3. The Dodgers finally won a World Series in their eighth try, behind the pitching of series MVP Johnny Podres (2–0, 1.00). Duke Snider hit four homers in a series for the second time, and Dodger leftfielder Sandy Amoros made a game-saving catch in Game 7.

1956 New York (A) over Brooklyn (N), 4–3. Yankee righthander and series MVP Don Larsen pitched a perfect game in the fifth contest, while Mickey Mantle and Yogi Berra each hit three homers for New York.

1957 Milwaukee (N) over New York (A), 4–3. Lew Burdette won three times for the Braves, allowing but two runs in 27 innings and won the MVP. Milwaukee's hitting was led by Hank Aaron (.393, 3 HR, 7 RBIs).

1958 New York (A) over Milwaukee (N), 4–3. Yankees Hank Bauer and Moose Skowron combined for six homers and 15 RBI as the Bronx Bombers came back from a 3–1 deficit. Yankee pitcher "Bullet" Bob Turley earned MVP honors.

1959 Los Angeles (N) over Chicago (A), 4–2. Los Angeles enjoyed its first World Championship as the transplanted Dodgers prevailed, aided by the relief pitching of MVP Larry Sherry (two wins, two saves). Ted Kluszewski of the "Go-Go White Sox hit .391, with three homers and 10 RBI.

1960 Pittsburgh (N) over New York (A), 4–3. Pirate second baseman Bill Mazeroski's home run in the bottom of the ninth in Game 7 capped one of the most exciting contests in history. In the 10–9 ballgame, 10 of the runs were scored in the last two innings. Yankee second baseman Bobby Richardson, a hitting star throughout the series, was named MVP.

1961 New York (A) over Cincinnati (N), 4–1. Whitey Ford tossed two shutouts in winning the MVP, and the Yankee offense pounded out 16 extra-base hits in the five games. Bobby Richardson (.391) and John Blanchard (.400, 2 HR) starred for New York.

1962 New York (A) over San Francisco (N), 4–3. Ralph Terry's four-hit shutout won the seesaw affair for the Yanks, and earned him the MVP. Whitey Ford completed his series record 33⅔ consecutive scoreless innings in the first game, and for the Giants, Chuck Hiller hit the first National League series grand slam in Game 4.

1963 Los Angeles (N) over New York (A), 4–0. Dodger pitchers held New York to four runs, led by Sandy Koufax's two wins and 23 strikeouts, including a record-breaking 15 in the first game. Koufax was the runaway choice for MVP.

1964 St. Louis (N) over New York (A), 4–3. Ten Yankee home runs were not enough to beat the Cardinals. Bob Gibson was the series MVP, and Tim McCarver (.478) also starred. Highlights included Ken Boyer's game-winning grand slam in Game 4, and Bobby Richardson's record 13 hits.

1965 Los Angeles (N) over Minnesota (A), 4–3. As in 1963, MVP Sandy Koufax again excelled for the Dodgers, allowing only two runs in 24 innings, striking our 29. Jim "Mudcat" Grant won two games and hit a three-run homer for the Twins.

1966 Baltimore (A) over Los Angeles (N), 4–0. The Orioles made the most of their first World Series appearance, as their young pitchers did not allow a run after the third inning of the first game. Slugger Frank Robinson capped a great year with the series MVP award.

1967 St. Louis (N) over Boston (A), 4–3. Bob Gibson pitched three complete game victories, added a home run in Game Seven, and was named MVP. Lou Brock batted .414 and stole seven bases, tying Eddie Collins' record and pacing the Cards.

1968 Detroit (A) over St. Louis (N), 4–3. the Cardinals were rolling behind Bob Gibson's record 17 strikeouts in Game 1 and his record seventh straight

series win in Game 4. Again Lou Brock joined him in the record books with 13 hits and seven stolen bases. But their feats couldn't stop the Tigers, led by the MVP pitching of Mickey Lolich (3–0, 1.67).

1969 New York (N) over Baltimore (A), 4–1. The Mets stunned the baseball world by winning four in a row after dropping the opener. Their young pitchers held the Orioles to only nine runs, aided by the great outfield catches of Ron Swoboda and Tommy Agee. Series MVP Donn Clendenon (.357, 3 HR) and Al Weis (.455, 1 HR) led the Met attack.

1970 Baltimore (A) over Cincinnati, 4–1. Brooks Robinson almost singlehandedly beat the Reds with spectacular defense at third base and a .429 average with two homers and two doubles. His dominance of the series earned the MVP. Also chipping in for the O's were Paul Blair (.474), Frank Robinson, and Boog Powell (two homers each).

1971 Pittsburgh (N) over Baltimore (A), 4–3. Roberto Clemente played in 14 World Series games and hit safely in every one. Here he batted .414, slugged .759, and won MVP honors. Steve Blass, Nelson Briles, and Bruce Kison won all the Pirate victories with a combined ERA of 0.54.

1972 Oakland (A) over Cincinnati (N), 4–3. A's backup catcher Gene Tenace hit home runs in his first two series at bats, then went on to hit two more, becoming the surprise star and MVP selection. Rollie Fingers relieved in six of the contests, winning one and saving two.

1973 Oakland (A) over New York (N), 4–3. The Mets had the worst record of any pennant winner ever (82–79), but they lasted till the seventh game in a sloppy (19 errors) affair. Darold Knowles pitched in all seven games for the A's, saving two. Reggie Jackson slugged his way to the first of his two series MVP awards.

1974 Oakland (A) over Los Angeles (N), 4–1. The A's won their third straight World Championship behind the two saves and one win of MVP Rollie Fingers. Joe Rudi (.333) and Bert Campaneris (.353) starred with the bats.

1975 Cincinnati (N) over Boston (A), 4–3. Five of the seven games were decided by one run, including Game 6, a memorable 12-inning contest decided by Carlton Fisk's famous home run. Cincinnati used 23 relief pitchers. Pete Rose, the heart and soul of the Big Red Machine, hustled his way to MVP honors.

1976 Cincinnati (N) over New York (A), 4–0. The Big Red Machine drove over the Yankees, slugging .522 as a team. Seven Reds hitters batted over .300, led by MVP Johnny Bench's .533 (1.133 slugging average).

1977 New York (A) over Los Angeles (N), 4–2. Reggie Jackson hit five homers, including three in the final game, to equal records set by Babe Ruth, and win the MVP for the second time. Mike Torrez won two for the Yankees.

1978 New York (A) over Los Angeles (N), 4–2. Shortstop Bucky Dent and backup infielder Brian Doyle batted .417 and .438 respectively, pacing New York in its second straight six-game triumph. Dent was named MVP. In the last four contests, the Yankees outscored L.A. 28–8.

1979 Pittsburgh (N) over Baltimore (A), 4–3. The Pirates overcame a three games to one deficit as Earl Weaver's Orioles waited for three-run homers that never came. Led by Willie Stargell (.400, 3 HR) and Phil Garner (.500), Pittsburgh batted .323 as a team. "Pops" Stargell's on-field performance and team leadership of the Pirates' "family" was honored with the MVP.

1980 Philadelphia (N) over Kansas City (A), 4–2. The two teams batted .292 in a series decided largely by the relief pitching of Tug McGraw (1–1, 2 saves) vs. Dan Quisenberry (1–2, 1 save). Mike Schmidt took MVP honors with a .381 average and 7 RBI.

1981 Los Angeles (N) over New York (A), 4–2.
Many observers called this sloppy series a fitting end to this strike-stricken 1981 season. Even the MVP award proved impossible to settle, as Pedro Guerrero, Steve Yeager, and Ron Cey shared the honor.

1982 St. Louis (N) over Milwaukee (A), 4–3.
Joaquin Andujar won two games for the Cardinals, and Willie McGee had perhaps the greatest single series game by a rookie, with two homers and two great catches in Game 3. American League MVP Robin Yount batted .414 for the losers, but St. Louis' Darrell Porter won MVP honors for his clutch hitting and 5 RBI.

1983 Baltimore (A) over Philadelphia (N), 4–1.
The Phillies couldn't hit Orioles' pitching, scoring but nine runs in the five games. Catcher Rick Dempsey hit four doubles and a home run, held the Phils to one stolen base, and was named MVP.

1984 Detroit (A) over San Diego (N), 4–1. The Tigers belted seven homers and backed them up with the pitching of Jack Morris (2–0, 2.00). Sparky Anderson become the first manager to win World Championships in both leagues. Alan Trammell, the Tigers' sure-handed shortstop, hit two home runs to earn MVP honors.

1985 Kansas City (A) over St. Louis (N), 4–3. The Cards were one inning away from the title, but a disputed call at first base opened the door for the Royals in Game 6. They won that contest, then blew St. Louis away 11–0 in the finale. Bret Saberhagen won two for Kansas City, and the MVP.

1986 New York (N) over Boston (A), 4–3. The Red Sox were one out away from winning it all, when Bob Stanley's wild pitch let in the tying run, and Mookie Wilson's grounder slipped between Bill Buckner's legs to score the winning run in Game 6. Ray Knight hit a tie-breaking homer in Game 7 to send Boston to its fourth straight seven-game beating.

1987 Minnesota (A) over St. Louis (N), 4–3. The Twins won their first championship by taking all four games in their exotic home park, the Metrodome. Cardinal pitching held them to five runs in the three games in St. Louis, but in Minnesota the Twins could not be contained, scoring 33 times. Frank Viola (2–1,3.72) was the MVP.

1988 Los Angeles (N) over Oakland (A), 4–1. Series MVP Orel Hershiser (2–0, 17 K's) dazzled the powerful A's. Injured Dodger Kirk Gibson's dramatic two-out home run in the bottom of the ninth in Game 1 set the tone for the unexpected L.A. triumph.

1989 Oakland (A) over San Francisco (N), 4–0. The A's thoroughly dominated a weak Giants' pitching staff, pounding out 32 runs, 44 hits (including nine home runs) in only four games. Series MVP Dave Stewart and reliever Dennis Eckersley led the Oakland staff. This series will be long remembered for the major earthquake that struck the Bay area just before Game 3 and delayed the contest for 12 days.

1990 Cincinnati (N) over Oakland (A), 4–0. Cincinnati dominated the heavily favored A's in a stunning series sweep. The Reds hit .317 as a team, while their pitchers, led by MVP José Rijo, held Oakland's vaunted offense to a mere .207 series average. Billy Hatcher broke Babe Ruth's World Series record by hitting .750, with seven consecutive hits and four doubles.

1991 Minnesota (A) over Atlanta (N), 4–3. No team in baseball had ever gone from worst to first. In 1991, it happened twice, with the Twins and Braves, both of whom had finished last in their divisions, the year before met in one of the most exciting fall classics ever. Five games were decided by one run, three went into extra innings, and four were decided on the last at bat. Perhaps the best of all was Game 7, a scoreless affair until the bottom of the 10th inning, when the Twins finally scored a run. Jack Moris went the distance for Minnesota and earned MVP honors.

1992 Toronto (A) over Atlanta (N), 4–2. The Blue Jays became the first non-American team to win (or play in) the World Series. Braves closer Jeff Reardon gave up the winning hits in games 2 and 3, making Atlanta manager Bobby Cox reluctant to use him the rest of the series. Dave Winfield's first extra-base hit in World Series play broke a 2–2 tie in the 11th-inning of game 6 to send the Braves to their second straight World Series defeat. Toronto catcher Pat Borders was the MVP with a .450 average.

1993 Toronto (A) over Philadelphia (N), 4–2 The Blue Jays became the first team since the 1977–78 Yankees to repeat as World Series champions, battering the Phillies pitching staff for 45 runs (despite being shut out in Game 5). Toronto outfielder Joe Carter's home run in the bottom of the ninth in Game 6 marked only the second time the World Series had ended on a home run (Bill Mazeroski's Game 7 shot in 1960 was the other). Toronto DH Paul Molitor went 12 for 24 with six extra-base hits to win MVP honors.

1994 World Series canceled. The longest work stoppage in professional sports history, a 232-day dispute between players and owners over a cap on player salaries, forced the cancellation of the World Series and playoffs for the first time in baseball history.

1995 Atlanta (N) over Cleveland (A), 4–2 Good pitching beats good hitting as evidenced by this dramatic series. Baseball's best pitching staff (the Braves) held the game's most explosive offense (the Indians) to a .179 average, five home runs, and 19 runs. Five of the six games were decided by one run, including the clincher: a dazzling 1–0 one-hitter by the Atlanta's Tom Glavine. Glavine won two games and the MVP.

1996 New York (A) over Atlanta (N), 4–2 The Braves shellacked the Yankees 12–1 and 4–0 in the first two games in New York. But the Yankees struck back and won the next four in a row. The turning point came in Game 4, when the Yankees rallied from a 6–0 deficit to win the game 8–6 in 10 innings. Jim Leyritz provided the crushing blow: a three-run homer off Mark Wohlers to tie the game at 6–6. Yankee closer John Wetteland saved all four wins and was the MVP.

1997 Florida (N) over Cleveland (A), 4–3 This sloppy series was marked by hot bats, cold weather, porous defense, and poor relief pitching. Game 3 alone involved 17 walks and 6 errors. Cleveland was two outs away from winning it all in Game 7, when Craig Counsell's sacrifice fly tied the game at 2–2. In the bottom of the 11th, Edgar Renteria singled home the deciding run. Florida's rookie pitcher Livan Hernandez, winner of Games 1 and 5, was the MVP.

1998 New York (A) over San Diego (N), 4–0 The Yankees completed one of the greatest seasons in baseball history with a four-game sweep that gave them a combined record of 125–50 and a .714 winning percentage. Home runs from Chuck Knoblauch and Tino Martinez helped the Yankees come from behind in Game 1, while Scott Brosius's three-run blast off San Diego closer Trevor Hoffman in Game 3 broke the Padres' back. Brosius, who had hit .203 the year before, hit .471 in the series and was named MVP.

1999 See Page 974 for results and game-by-game summaries of the 1999 World Series.

World Series MVP Winners

Year	Name	Team	Year	Name	Team
1955	Johnny Podres	Brooklyn Dodgers	1978	Bucky Dent	New York Yankees
1956	Don Larsen	New York Yankees	1979	Willie Stargell	Pittsburgh Pirates
1957	Lew Burdette	Milwaukee Braves	1980	Mike Schmidt	Philadelphia Philles
1958	Bob Turley	New York Yankees	1981	Ron Cey, Pedro	Los Angeles Dodgers
1959	Larry Sherry	Los Angeles Dodgers		Guerrero, Steve Yeager	
1960	Bobby Richardson	New York Yankees	1982	Darrell Porter	St. Louis Cardinals
1961	Whitey Ford	New York Yankees	1983	Rick Dempsey	Baltimore Orioles
1962	Ralph Terry	New York Yankees	1984	Alan Trammell	Detroit Tigers
1963	Sandy Koufax	Los Angeles Dodgers	1985	Bret Saberhagen	Kansas City Royals
1964	Bob Gibson	St. Louis Cardinals	1986	Ray Knight	New York Mets
1965	Sandy Koufax	Los Angeles Dodgers	1987	Frank Viola	Minnesota Twins
1966	Frank Robinson	Baltimore Orioles	1988	Orel Hershiser	Los Angeles Dodgers
1967	Bob Gibson	St. Louis Cardinals	1989	Dave Stewart	Oakland Athletics
1968	Mickey Lolich	Detroit Tigers	1990	José Rijo	Cincinnati Reds
1969	Donn Clendenon	New York Mets	1991	Jack Morris	Minesota Twins
1970	Brooks Robinson	Baltimore Orioles	1992	Pat Borders	Toronto Blue Jays
1971	Roberto Clemente	Pittsburgh Pirates	1993	Paul Molitor	Toronto Blue Jays
1972	Gene Tenace	Oakland A's	1994	No World Series	
1973	Reggie Jackson	Oakland A's	1995	Tom Glavine	Atlanta Braves
1974	Rollie Fingers	Oakland A's	1996	John Wetteland	New York Yankees
1975	Pete Rose	Cincinnati Reds	1997	Livan Hernández	Florida Marlins
1976	Johnny Bench	Cincinnati Reds	1998	Scott Brosius	New York Yankees
1977	Reggie Jackson	New York Yankees	1999	See page 974	

World Series Records

Hits		Home runs		Runs batted in		Runs scored	
Yogi Berra	71	Mickey Mantle	18	Mickey Mantle	40	Mickey Mantle	42
Mickey Mantle	59	Babe Ruth	15	Yogi Berra	39	Yogi Berra	41
Frankie Frisch	58	Yogi Berra	12	Lou Gehrig	35	Babe Ruth	37

Most hits in one series   13
  Bobby Richardson, 1964;
  Lou Brock, 1968;
  Marty Barrett, 1986

Most home runs   5
  in one series
  Reggie Jackson, 1977

Most runs batted in   12
  in one series
  Bobby Richardson, 1960

Most Wins by Managers

Manager	Wins	Losses	Pct.
1. Connie Mack	3,776	4,025	.484
2. John McGraw	2,840	1,984	.589
3. Sparky Anderson	2,194	1,834	.545
4. Bucky Harris	2,159	2,219	.493
5. Joe McCarthy	2,126	1,335	.614
6. Walter Alston	2,040	1,613	.558
7. Leo Durocher	2,010	1,710	.540
8. Casey Stengel	1,926	1,867	.508
9. Gene Mauch	1,901	2,037	.483
10. Bill McKechnie	1,898	1,724	.524

A Most Valuable Team

Only eleven players have won the Most Valuable Player Award in consecutive seasons; oddly enough there is at least one from each fielding position.

Position	Player, Team	Years
1B	Jimmie Foxx, Philadelphia A's	1932–33
1B	Frank Thomas, Chicago White Sox	1993–94
2B	Joe Morgan, Reds	1975–76
3B	Mike Schmidt, Phillies	1980–81
SS	Ernie Banks, Cubs	1958–59
OF	Mickey Mantle, Yankees	1956–57
OF	Roger Maris, Yankees	1960–61
OF	Dale Murphy, Braves	1982–83
OF	Barry Bonds, Pirates/Giants	1992–93
C	Yogi Berra, Yankees	1954–55
P	Hal Newhouser, Tigers	1944–45

1999 Individual Leaders

AMERICAN LEAGUE

Batting average (min. 500 plate appearances)		Home runs		Runs batted in	
Nomar Garciaparra, Boston	.357	Ken Griffey, Seattle	48	Manny Ramirez, Cleveland	165
Derek Jeter, New York	.349	Rafael Palmeiro, Texas	47	Rafael Palmeiro, Texas	148
Bernie Williams, New York	.342	Manny Ramirez, Cleveland	44	Ken Griffey, Seattle	134
Edgar Martinez, Seattle	.337	Carlos Delgado, Toronto	44	Carlos Delgado, Toronto	134
Omar Vizquel, Cleveland	.333	Shawn Green, Toronto	42	Juan Gonzalez, Texas	128
Manny Ramirez, Cleveland	.333	Alex Rodriguez, Seattle	42	Shawn Green, Toronto	123
Ivan Rodriguez, Texas	.332	Juan Gonzalez, Texas	39	Jason Giambi, Oakland	123
Tony Fernandez, Toronto	.328	Dean Palmer, Detroit	38	Roberto Alomar, Cleveland	120
Juan Gonzalez, Texas	.326	Matt Stairs, Oakland	38	Jermaine Dye, Kansas City	119
Rafael Palmeiro, Texas	.324	Albert Belle, Baltimore	37	Magglio Ordonez, Chicago	117

Pitching-wins		Earned run average (min. 162 innings)		Strikeouts	
Pedro Martinez, Boston	23-4	Pedro Martinez, Boston	2.07	Pedro Martinez, Boston	313
Bartolo Colon, Cleveland	18-5	David Cone, New York	3.44	Chuck Finley, Anaheim	200
Mike Mussina, Baltimore	18-7	Mike Mussina, Baltimore	3.50	Aaron Sele, Texas	186
Aaron Sele, Texas	18-9	Brad Radke, Minnesota	3.75	David Cone, New York	177
David Wells, Toronto	17-10	Jose Rosado, Kansas City	3.85	Dave Burba, Cleveland	174
Charles Nagy, Cleveland	17-11	Jamie Moyer, Seattle	3.87	Mike Mussina, Baltimore	172
Orlando Hernandez, New York	17-9	Bartolo Colon, Cleveland	3.95	Freddy Garcia, Seattle	170
Freddy Garcia, Seattle	17-8	Mike Sirotka, Chicago	4.00	David Wells, Toronto	169
Kevin Appier, K.C-Oakland	16-14	Freddy Garcia, Seattle	4.07	Eric Milton, Minnesota	163
Omar Olivares, Ana.-Oakland	15-11	Orlando Hernandez, New York	4.12	Roger Clemens, New York	163

NATIONAL LEAGUE

Batting average (min. 500 plate appearances)		Home runs		Runs batted in	
Larry Walker, Colorado	.379	Mark McGwire, St. Louis	65	Mark McGwire, St. Louis	147
Luis Gonzalez, Arizona	.336	Sammy Sosa, Chicago	63	Matt Williams, Arizona	142
Bobby Abreu, Philadelphia	.335	Greg Vaughn, Cincinnati	45	Sammy Sosa, Chicago	141
Sean Casey, Cincinnati	.332	Chipper Jones, Atlanta	45	Dante Bichette, Colorado	133
Jeff Cirillo, Milwaukee	.326	Jeff Bagwell, Houston	42	Vladimir Guerrero, Montreal	131
Mark Grudzielanek, L. A.	.326	Vladimir Guerrero, Montreal	42	Jeff Bagwell, Houston	126
Carl Everett, Houston	.325	Mike Piazza, New York	40	Mike Piazza, New York	124
Doug Glanville, Philadelphia	.325	Brian Giles, Pittsburgh	39	Robin Ventura, New York	120
Todd Helton, Colorado	.320	Jay Bell, Arizona	38	Greg Vaughn, Cincinnati	118
Chipper Jones, Atlanta (min. 500 plate appearances)	.319	Larry Walker, Colorado	37	Brian Giles, Pittsburgh	115

Pitching-wins		Earned run average (min. 162 innings)		Strikeouts	
Mike Hampton, Houston	22-4	Randy Johnson, Arizona	2.48	Randy Johnson, Arizona	364
Jose Lima, Houston	21-10	Kevin Millwood, Atlanta	2.68	Kevin Brown, Los Angeles	221
Greg Maddux, Atlanta	19-9	Mike Hampton, Houston	2.90	Pedro Astacio, Colorado	210
Kevin Brown, Los Angeles	18-9	Kevin Brown, Los Angeles	3.00	Kevin Millwood, Atlanta	205
Kevin Millwood, Atlanta	18-7	John Smoltz, Atlanta	3.19	Shane Reynolds, Houston	197
Russ Ortiz, San Francisco	18-9	Todd Ritchie, Pittsburgh	3.49	Sterling Hitchcock, San Diego	194
Kent Bottenfield, St. Louis	18-7	Curt Schilling, Philadelphia	3.54	Jose Lima, Houston	187
Randy Johnson, Arizona	17-9	Greg Maddux, Atlanta	3.57	Jon Lieber, Chicago	186
Pedro Astacio, Colorado	17-11	Jose Lima, Houston	3.58	Mike Hampton, Houston	177
Shane Reynolds, Houston	16-14	Omar Daal, Arizona	3.65	Chan Ho Park, Los Angeles	174

Major League Baseball Final Standings, 1999

Division/Team	W	L	Pct.	GB	Division/Team	W	L	Pct.	GB
American League East					**National League East**				
New York Yankees[1]	98	64	.605	—	Atlanta[1]	103	59	.636	—
Boston[2]	94	68	.580	4	New York Mets[2]	97	66	.595	6½
Toronto	84	78	.519	14	Philadelphia	77	85	.475	26
Baltimore	78	84	.481	20	Montreal	68	94	.420	35
Tampa Bay	69	93	.426	29	Florida	64	98	.395	39
American League Central					**National League Central**				
Cleveland[1]	97	65	.599	—	Houston[1]	97	65	.599	—
Chicago White Sox	75	86	.466	21½	Cincinnati	96	67	.589	1½
Detroit	69	92	.429	27½	Pittsburgh	78	83	.484	18½
Kansas City	64	97	.398	32½	St. Louis	75	86	.466	21½
Minnesota	63	97	.394	33	Milwaukee	74	87	.460	22½
					Chicago Cubs	67	95	.414	30
American League West					**National League West**				
Texas[1]	95	67	.586	—	Arizona[1]	100	62	.617	—
Oakland	87	75	.537	8	San Francisco	86	76	.531	14
Seattle	79	83	.488	16	Los Angeles	77	85	.475	23
Anaheim	70	92	.432	25	San Diego	74	88	.457	26
					Colorado	72	90	.444	28

1. Division champion. 2. Wild card for playoffs.

The 1999 Division Series

AMERICAN LEAGUE

NEW YORK DEFEATS TEXAS, 3 GAMES TO 0
NEW YORK 8, Texas 0
Bernie Williams drove in six runs with a single, double and a three-run homer, while Orlando "El Duque" Hernández" limited the Rangers to two hits over eight innings.
NEW YORK 3, TEXAS 1
Andy Pettitte pitched his way in and out of trouble (escaping second-and-third with no outs in the fifth) for seven strong innings, while the Yankee offense scratched across single runs in the fifth, seventh, and eighth innings.
New York 3, TEXAS 0
Darryl Strawberry hit a three-run bomb in the first inning, and Roger Clemens and Mariano Rivera made it stand up, tossing a combined shutout. For the second year in a row, New York held the Rangers to a total of one run, a postseason series low.

BOSTON DEFEATS CLEVELAND, 3 GAMES TO 2
CLEVELAND 3, Boston 2
The Red Sox lost their ace in the fourth inning when Pedro Martínez left with a back injury, and they lost the game in the ninth on Travis Fryman's bases-loaded single off Rich Garces. Indians starter Bartolo Colon struck out 11 over eight innings.
CLEVELAND 11, Boston 1
The Indians shelled Red Sox starter Bret Saberhagen with a six-run third, then piled on five more in the fourth, courtesy of a Jim Thome grand slam. Charles Nagy held the Sox to five hits over seven innings.
BOSTON 9, Cleveland
The Red Sox broke open a 3-3 tie in the seventh inning by scoring six runs off a shaky Indians bullpen. Rookie Brian Daubach's three-run homer off Ricardo Rincon was the decisive blow.
BOSTON 23, Cleveland 7
The Red Sox scored early and often, setting a postseason record for runs scored. John Valentin had two homers and seven RBIs. Colon, pitching on three days' rest, lasted less than two innings.
Boston 12, CLEVELAND 8
Pedro Martínez entered an 8-8 slugfest in the fourth inning, and he no-hit the Indians for the next six innings. Troy O'Leary powered the Red Sox with a grand slam in the third and a tie-breaking three-run homer in the seventh.

NATIONAL LEAGUE

ATLANTA DEFEATS HOUSTON, 3 GAMES TO 1
Houston 6, ATLANTA 1
Astros leftfielder Daryle Ward hit a tie-breaking homer in the sixth off Greg Maddux and Ken Caminiti added a three-run shot in the ninth. It was only the second loss for the Braves in five years of Division Series play.
ATLANTA 5, Houston 1
Kevin Millwood held the Astros to just one hit, a Ken Caminiti home run. Run-scoring singles by Brian Jordan, Ryan Klesko and Andruw Jones were all the offense Atlanta needed.
Atlanta 5, HOUSTON 3 (12 innings)
Jordan provided all the Braves offense, with a three-run homer in the sixth, and a two-run double in the 12th. John Rocker escaped a bases-loaded nobody out situation in the 10th for the win, while Millwood pitched a scoreless 12th for the save.
Atlanta 7, HOUSTON 5
The Braves jumped out to a 7-0 lead behind the timely hitting of Gerald Williams and Eddie Perez. Houston rallied with four runs in the eighth, but Ken Caminiti's ninth inning blast off Rocker fell a few feet short of a game-tying homer.

NEW YORK DEFEATS ARIZONA, 3 GAMES TO 1
New York 8, ARIZONA 4
Edgardo Alfonzo hit a grand slam in the top of the ninth to break a 4-4 tie and send Randy Johnson to his sixth straight postseason loss. Alfonzo also hit a solo homer in the first.
ARIZONA 7, New York 1
Steve Finley drove in five runs with a walk, a single, and a double, while Todd Stottlemyre held the Mets' offense to a run and four hits over 6 2/3 innings.
NEW YORK 9, Arizona 2
An injured thumb sidelined Mets' star catcher Mike Piazza, but the rest of the offense rallied for six runs in the sixth; John Olerud had three RBIs. Rick Reed pitched six strong innings for New York.
NEW YORK 4, Arizona 3 (10 innings)
Piazza's backup Todd Pratt homered in the bottom of the 10th, capping a game that had it all: lead changes, ties, runners thrown out at the plate, disputed calls, ejections, odd managerial moves, and gutsy relief pitching.

New York defeats Boston, 4 games to 1

NEW YORK 4, Boston 3 (10 innings)
The Red Sox cobbled together a 3-0 lead against Orlando "El Duque" Hernandez, with two singles and a Derek Jeter throwing error in the first, and a walk, a steal, and a single in the second. Scott Brosius brought the Yanks to within a run with a two-run homer in the second, and later tripled, singled, and scored the tying run in the seventh. Hernandez and Yankee closer Mariano Rivera shut out the Red Sox the rest of the way; Bernie Williams led off the bottom of the 10th inning with a game-winning homer off Rod Beck.

NEW YORK 3, Boston 2
David Cone and Ramon Martinez hooked up in another pitching duel. Tino Martinez opened the scoring with a solo homer in the fourth, but Nomar Garciaparra answered with a two-run shot in the fifth. The Yankees rallied with two outs in the seventh to score the tying and go-ahead runs on two walks, a Chuck Knoblauch double, and a Paul O'Neill bloop single. The Red Sox loaded the bases with one out in the eighth, but Ramiro Mendoza shut the door, striking out Butch Huskey and Jose Offerman.

BOSTON 13, New York 1
This was a widely anticipated matchup between former Cy Young Award winners Pedro Martinez and Roger Clemens. But Clemens failed to live up to his end of the bargain, giving up a triple and a home run to the first two Red Sox batters, Jose Offerman and John Valentin. Clemens was gone before the end of the third inning, surrendering a total of five runs. Martinez, on the other hand, was his usual brilliant self, striking out 12 Yankees over seven innings.

New York 9, BOSTON 2
For the first seven innings, this was a tight pitcher's duel between Andy Pettitte and Bret Saberhagen. The Yankees scored first on a Daryl Strawberry solo homer, but the Red Sox rallied for the lead with single runs in the second and third innings (and had a runner thrown out at the plate). The Red Sox defense deserted them in the fourth inning, when errors by Nomar Garciaparra and Saberhagen allowed the tying and go-ahead runs to score. A blown call by second base umpire Tim Tschida helped kill a Red Sox rally in the eighth. But the Yankee batters made it academic by piling on six more runs in the ninth, the last four on a Ricky Ledee pinch-hit grand slam off Rod Beck.

New York 6, BOSTON 1
Derek Jeter hit a two-run homer in the top of the first to give the Yankees the early lead, and that was all the offense Orlando Hernandez needed. He was brilliant again, giving up one run on five hits over seven innings. The Red Sox contributed to their own demise by giving up two unearned runs in the seventh, and by going 0-for-10 with runners in scoring position. Ramiro Mendoza again extricated the Yankees from a bases-loaded one-out situation in the eighth. Hernandez, who permitted only three earned runs in 15 innings, was the series MVP.

Atlanta defeats New York, 4 games to 2

ATLANTA 4, New York 2
Greg Maddux baffled the Mets hitters for seven innings, giving up one run on five hits, and throwing just 83 pitches. The Braves scratched across single runs in the first, fifth, sixth (on an Eddie Perez homer), and eighth. Atlanta closer John Rocker gave up an unearned run in the ninth, but retired the last four batters for the save.

ATLANTA 4, New York 3
The Mets scored single runs against the stingy Kevin Millwood with a walk and two singles in the second and Melvin Mora's first career home run in the fifth. But in the sixth, Brian Jordan and Eddie Perez each hit two-run homers off Kenny Rogers, turning the 2-0 deficit into a 4-2 lead. John Rocker stranded the tying and go-ahead runs in the eighth, and John Smoltz, normally a starter, pitched a 1-2-3 ninth for the save.

Atlanta 1, NEW YORK 0
Al Leiter and Tom Glavine hooked up in a classic duel of lefties. The game's only run scored in the top of the first inning, when Mike Piazza's throwing error allowed Gerald Williams to score from second on a double steal. Glavine and relievers Mike Remlinger and John Rocker made the lone run stand up, however. Leiter gave up only three hits over seven innings, but he ended up the loser when his team couldn't score.

NEW YORK 3, Atlanta 2
The Mets seemed snakebit when Brian Jordan and Ryan Klesko each hit solo home runs in the eighth to turn a 1-0 deficit into a 2-1 lead. But New York roared back in its half of the inning with a two-out rally. John Olerud, who had homered earlier, drove in Roger Cedeño and Melvin Mora with a single to center off Mets' nemesis John Rocker. It was only the second Mets' hit off Rocker in four appearances.

NEW YORK 4, Atlanta 3 (15 innings)
This was a wild one, involving 15 pitchers, 45 players in all, and more moves than a chess game. Each team scored two runs early, but they were a distant memory by game's end. Atlanta took a 3-2 lead into the 15th, and Bobby Cox stayed with his last reliever, rookie Kevin McGlinchy, who loaded the bases with one out and then walked in the tying run. Then Robin Ventura, 1-for-18 in the series to this point, hit one over the wall for a grand slam homer. In the bedlam that ensued, however, Ventura never touched any base besides first, so he was only credited with a game-winning single. The game lasted five hours and 46 minutes, a postseason record.

ATLANTA 10, New York 9 (11 innings)
The Mets might have gone quietly after falling behind 5-0 in the first inning. But they rallied for three runs in the sixth inning and tied the game at 7-7 in the seventh on a Mike Piazza homer. New York even took the lead, briefly, with single runs in the top of the eighth and tenth innings, but each time, the Braves came back to tie. Gerald Williams led off the bottom of the 11th with a double, and scored the game-winner on a bases-loaded walk to Andruw Jones. Braves catcher Eddie Perez was the MVP.

The 1999 World Series

Game One   New York 4   Atlanta 1

For the first seven innings, this was a tight pitcher's duel between Greg Maddux and Orlando "El Duque" Hernandez, with the only run (and Atlanta's only hit) coming on Chipper Jones's solo home run in the fourth inning. But it all came apart for Atlanta in the eighth. Scott Brosius singled, and Daryl Strawberry walked, then Brian Hunter mishandled Chuck Knoblauch's bunt, loading the bases. Derek Jeter singled home the tying run, and Paul O'Neill drove in two more with a single off Atlanta's lefty closer John Rocker. The Yanks added a run on Jim Leyritz's bases-loaded walk later in the inning. Yankee closer Mariano Rivera pitched a scoreless ninth for the save.

	123	456	789	R	H	E
New York	000	000	040	4	6	0
Atlanta	000	100	000	1	2	2
W-Hernandez (3-0)		L-Maddux (1-2)		S-Rivera (5)		

Game Two   New York 7   Atlanta 2

The first three Yankees singled off Atlanta starter Kevin Millwood, and New York went on to score three runs before the Braves even came to the plate. The Yankees chased Millwood from the game in the third inning, with a single, double, and Ozzie Guillen's fielding error, then added single runs in the fourth and fifth innings off Terry Mulholland. Yankee starter David Cone didn't give up a hit until the fifth inning, and like his teammate Hernandez, held the Braves to one hit over seven innings. The Braves avoided being shut out by scoring twice in the bottom of the ninth, long after the contest had been decided.

	123	456	789	R	H	E
New York	302	110	000	7	14	1
Atlanta	000	000	002	2	5	1
W-Cone (2-0)		L-Millwood (2-1)				

Game Three New York 6 Atlanta 5 (10 innings)

Atlanta's offense exploded for five runs and 10 hits in the first four innings and chasing Yankee starter Andy Pettitte. But they also left nine runners on base (six of them in scoring position) and had two caught stealing, and never scored against the Yankee bullpen. Meanwhile, the Yankee hitters chipped away at a 5-1 deficit with solo home runs by Chad Curtis in the fifth inning and Tino Martinez in the seventh. With one on in the eighth, Chuck Knoblauch hit a ball that just barely cleared the short right field porch at Yankee Stadium to tie the game at five. Curtis led off the bottom of the 10th with his second home run of the game, off Mike Remlinger, to give the Yankees a commanding 3-0 lead in the series.

	123	456	789	10	R	H	E
Atlanta	103	100	000	0	5	14	1
New York	100	010	120	1	6	9	0
W-Rivera (2-0)		L-Remlinger (0-2)					

Game Four   New York 4   Atlanta 1

The Yankees completed their second straight World Series sweep, and won their 12th consecutive straight World Series game. Roger Clemens pitched well for 7 2/3 innings before giving way to Mariano Rivera. The Yankees pieced together two singles and two infield hits for three runs in the third off hard luck loser John Smoltz. Jim Leyritz added a solo homer in the eighth to seal the win. Rivera, who won Game 3 and saved Games 1 and 4, did not give up a run after July, won the MVP award.

	123	456	789	R	H	E
Atlanta	000	000	010	1	5	0
New York	003	010	01x	4	8	0
W-Clemens (2-1)		L-Smoltz (1-1)		S-Rivera (6)		

Note: Records are for the entire 1999 Postseason.

Composite Box Score

Yankees	G	AB	R	H	RBI	Avg.
Leyritz	2	1	1	1	2	1.000
Brosius	4	16	2	6	1	.375
Jeter	4	17	4	6	1	.353
Curtis	3	6	3	2	2	.333
Strawberry	2	3	0	1	0	.333
Knoblauch	4	16	5	5	3	.313
Girardi	2	7	1	2	0	.286
Martinez	4	15	3	4	5	.267
Posada	2	8	0	2	1	.250
Williams	4	13	2	3	0	.231
Ledee	3	10	0	2	1	.200
O'Neill	4	15	0	3	4	.200
Cone	1	4	0	0	0	.000
Davis	2	4	0	0	0	.000
Hernandez	1	1	0	0	0	.000
Mendoza	1	1	0	0	0	.000
Sojo	1	0	0	0	0	.000
Totals	**4**	**137**	**21**	**37**	**20**	**.270**

Braves	G	AB	R	H	RBI	Avg.
Boone	4	13	1	7	3	.538
Nixon	2	2	0	1	0	.500
Myers	4	6	0	2	1	.333
Hunter	2	4	0	1	0	.250
C. Jones	4	13	2	3	2	.231
Weiss	3	9	1	2	0	.222
Hernandez	2	5	0	1	2	.200
Williams	4	17	2	3	0	.176
Klesko	4	12	0	2	0	.167
Lockhart	4	7	1	1	0	.143
Perez	3	8	0	1	0	.125
A. Jones	4	13	1	1	0	.077
Jordan	4	13	1	1	1	.077
Battle	1	0	0	0	0	.000
Fabregas	1	1	0	0	0	.000
Guillen	3	5	0	0	0	.000
Maddux	1	2	0	0	0	.000
Mulholland	1	0	0	0	0	.000
Totals	**4**	**130**	**9**	**26**	**9**	**.200**

Pitching

Yankees	IP	H	R/ER	BB	K	ERA
Cone, W G2	7	1	0/0	5	4	0.00
Rivera, W G3	4.2	3	0/0	1	3	0.00
Grimsley	2.1	2	0/0	2	0	0.00
Nelson	2.2	2	0/0	1	3	0.00
Stanton	0.1	0	0/0	0	1	0.00
Clemens, W G4	7.2	4	1/1	2	4	1.17
Hernandez, W G1	7	1	1/1	2	10	1.29
Mendoza	1.2	3	2/2	1	0	10.80
Pettitte	3.2	10	5/5	1	1	12.27
Saves: Rivera, G1, G4						

Braves	IP	H	R/ER	BB	K	ERA
McGlinchy	2	2	0/0	1	2	0.00
Rocker	3	2	0/0	2	4	0.00
Springer	2.1	1	0/0	0	1	0.00
Maddux, L G1	7	5	4/2	3	5	2.57
Smoltz, L G4	7	6	3/3	3	11	3.86
Glavine	7	5	5/4	0	3	5.14
Mulholland	3.2	5	3/3	1	3	7.36
Remlinger, L G3	1	1	1/1	1	0	9.00
Millwood, L G2	2	8	5/4	2	2	18.00

INDEX